Pain
Management

Pain Management

Steven D. Waldman, MD, JD

Clinical Professor, Department of Anesthesiology
University of Missouri–Kansas City School of Medicine
Kansas City, Missouri
Medical Director, Headache and Pain Center
Leawood, Kansas

Color drawings by Joseph I. Bloch, CMI, Graphic World, and Electronic Publishing Services

Volume 1

SAUNDERS

ELSEVIER

SAUNDERS
ELSEVIER

1600 John F. Kennedy Blvd.
Ste 1800
Philadelphia, PA 19103-2899

PAIN MANAGEMENT

ISBN-13: 978-0-7216-0334-6
ISBN-10: 0-7216-0334-3
Vol 1 PN: 9997627075
Vol 2 PN: 9997627083

Notice

Knowledge and best practice in this field are constantly changing. As new research and experience broaden our knowledge, changes in practice, treatment, and drug therapy may become necessary or appropriate. Readers are advised to check the most current information provided (i) on procedures featured or (ii) by the manufacturer of each product to be administered, to verify the recommended dose or formula, the method and duration of administration, and contraindications. It is the responsibility of the practitioner, relying on his or her own experience and knowledge of the patient, to make diagnoses, to determine dosages and the best treatment for each individual patient, and to take all appropriate safety precautions. To the fullest extent of the law, neither the publisher nor the author assumes any liability for any injury and/or damage to persons or property arising out of or related to any use of the material contained in this book.

Library of Congress Cataloging-in-Publication Data
Pain management/edited by Steven D. Waldman.—1st ed.
    p. ; cm.
  Includes bibliographical references and index.
  ISBN 0-7216-0334-3
1. Pain—Treatment. I. Waldman, Steven D.
  [DNLM: 1. Pain—therapy. WL 704 P14654 2007]
RB127.P332284 2007
616'.0472—dc22
                   2006026880

Executive Publisher: Natasha Andjelkovic
Editorial Assistant: Katie Davenport
Publishing Services Manager: Tina Rebane
Project Manager: Mary Anne Folcher
Design Direction: Ellen Zanolle
Cover Designer: Ellen Zanolle

Printed in China

Last digit is the print number: 9 8 7 6 5 4 3 2 1

Working together to grow libraries in developing countries

www.elsevier.com | www.bookaid.org | www.sabre.org

ELSEVIER   BOOK AID International   Sabre Foundation

To my children: David for his caring nature and amazing work ethic, Corey for his integrity and determination, Jennifer for her intellect and compassion, and Reid for his ambition and unabashed joie de vie.

Steven D. Waldman, MD

Summer 2006

Contributors

Ahmed N. Abdelhalim, MD
Assistant Professor, Department of Radiology, State University of New York at Buffalo School of Medicine and Biomedical Sciences; Staff Neuroradiologist, Department of Diagnostic Imaging, Roswell Park Cancer Institute, Buffalo, New York

Salahadin Abdi, MD, PhD
Professor and Chief, Department of Anesthesiology, Perioperative Medicine and Pain Management, University of Miami; Chief of Pain Medicine, Jackson Memorial Hospital, Miami, Florida

Bernard M. Abrams, MD
Clinical Professor of Neurology, University of Missouri-Kansas City School of Medicine, Kansas City, Missouri; Neurologist, Menorah Medical Center, Overland Park, Kansas

Vimal Akhouri, MD, MB
Instructor, Department of Anesthesiology and Critical Care, Harvard Medical School, Beth Israel Deaconess Medical Center, Boston, Massachusetts

Ronald A. Alberico, MD
Associate Professor of Radiology and Assistant Clinical Professor of Neurosurgery, State University of New York at Buffalo School of Medicine; Director of Neuroradiology/Head and Neck Imaging, and Director of Pediatric Neuroradiology, Roswell Park Cancer Institute, Buffalo, New York

J. Antonio Aldrete, MD, MS
Professor, Department of Anesthesiology, University of Alabama at Birmingham; Aldrete Pain Care Center, Birmingham, Alabama

Frank Andrasik, PhD
Professor of Psychology, University of West Florida; Senior Research Scientist, Institute for Human and Machine Cognition, Pensacola, Florida

Sairam Atluri, MD
TriState Pain Management Institute, Loveland, Ohio

Shelley Wiechman Askay, PhD
Assistant Professor, Department of Rehabilitation Medicine, University of Washington; Attending Psychologist, Harborview Medical Center, Seattle, Washington

Zahid H. Bajwa, MD
Assistant Professor of Anesthesia and Neurology, Harvard Medical School; Director, Education and Clinical Pain Research, Beth Israel Deaconess Medical Center, Boston, Massachusetts

David P. Bankston, MD
Consultant in Pain Management, The Headache and Pain Center, Leawood, Kansas

Ralf Baron, MD
Professor of Neurology, Chair, Department of Neurological Pain Research and Therapy, Vice Chair, Neurological Clinic, Christian-Albrechts-Universität Kiel, Kiel, Germany

Jonathan Barry
Department of Anesthesiology and Pain Management, Texas Tech University Health Sciences Center, Lubbock, Texas

Andreas Binder, MD
Consultant, Department of Neurological Pain Research and Therapy, Neurological Clinic, Christian-Albrechts-Universität Kiel, Kiel, Germany

Donna Bloodworth, MD
Associate Professor, Baylor College of Medicine; Outpatient Director, Physical Medicine, Harris County Hospital District, Houston, Texas

Nikolai Bogduk, MD
Professor of Pain Medicine, Department of Clinical Research, Royal Newcastle Hospital, Newcastle, Australia

David Borenstein, MD
Clinical Professor of Medicine, The George Washington University Medical Center; Arthritis and Rheumatism Associates, Washington, DC

Mark V. Boswell, MD, PhD
Associate Professor of Anesthesiology, Chief of the
Anesthesiology Pain Service, Case Western Reserve
University School of Medicine, University Hospitals of
Cleveland, Cleveland, Ohio

Geoffrey Bove, DC, PhD
Department of Anesthesia, Critical Care, and Pain
Management, Beth Israel Deaconess Medical Center,
Boston, Massachusetts

Fadi Braiteh, MD
Medical Oncology Fellow, The University of Texas MD
Anderson Cancer Center, Houston, Texas

David L. Brown, MD
Edward Rotan Distinguished Professor and Chairman,
Department of Anesthesiology and Pain Medicine, The
University of Texas MD Anderson Cancer Center,
Houston, Texas

Eduardo Bruera, MD
Professor and Chair, Department of Palliative Care and
Rehabilitation Medicine, The University of Texas MD
Anderson Cancer Center, Houston, Texas

Allen W. Burton, MD
Associate Professor and Section Chief, Pain Management,
University of Texas MD Anderson Cancer Center,
Houston, Texas

Roger K. Cady, MD
Headache Care Center, Springfield, Missouri

Kenneth D. Candido, MD
Professor of Anesthesiology, Chief, Division of Pain
Management, Loyola University School of Medicine,
Maywood, Illinois

John A. Carrino, MD, MPH
Assistant Professor of Radiology, Harvard Medical School;
Clinical Director of Magnetic Resonance Therapy, and
Co-Director of Spine Intervention Service, Brigham
and Women's Hospital, Boston, Massachusetts; Visiting
Associate Professor of Radiology, Russell H. Morgan
Department of Radiology and Radiological Science,
and Chief, Musculoskeletal Radiology Division, Johns
Hopkins Outpatient Center, Johns Hopkins University
School of Medicine, Baltimore, Maryland

Joseph S. Chiang, MD
Professor, Department of Anesthesiology, The University of
Texas MD Anderson Cancer Center, Houston, Texas

Martin K. Childers, DO, PhD
Associate Professor, University of Missouri-Columbia,
Columbia, Missouri

Eric T. Chou, MD
Department of Radiology, Brigham and Women's Hospital,
Harvard Medical School, Boston, Massachusetts

Philip G. Conaghan, MB, BS, PhD, FRACP, FRCP
Professor, Academic Unit of Musculoskeletal Disease,
Department of Rheumatology, Faculty of Medicine and
Health, University of Leeds, Leeds, United Kingdom

Darin J. Correll, MD
Instructor of Anesthesia, Harvard Medical School; Director,
Acute Postoperative Pain Service, Department of
Anesthesiology, Perioperative and Pain Medicine,
Brigham and Women's Hospital, Boston, Massachusetts

Scott C. Cozad, DDS, MD
Therapeutic Radiologist Inc., Kansas City, Missouri

Edward V. Craig, MD
Clinical Professor of Orthopaedic Surgery, Weil Medical
College of Cornell University; Attending Orthopaedic
Surgeon, The Hospital for Special Surgery, New York,
New York

Paul Creamer, MD, FRCP
Consultant Rheumatologist, Southmead Hospital, Bristol,
United Kingdom

Miles R. Day, MD, FIPP, DABPM
Associate Professor, Department of Anesthesiology and
Pain Management, Southwestern Medical School,
McDermott Center for Pain Management, Dallas, Texas

Debra A. DeAngelo, DO
Active Staff, Hanover Hospital, Hanover, Pennsylvania

Seymour Diamond, MD
Adjunct Professor, Department of Cellular and Molecular
Pharmacology, and Clinical Professor, Department of
Family Medicine, Chicago Medical School at Rosalind
Franklin, University of Medicine and Science, North
Chicago; Director, Diamond Inpatient Headache Unit,
Saint Joseph Hospital, and Director and Founder,
Diamond Headache Clinic, Chicago, Illinois

Paul Dieppe, MB BS, MD, FRCP, FFPH
Director, Medical Research Council Health Services
Research Collaboration, Department of Social
Medicine, University of Bristol, Bristol, United
Kingdom

Charles D. Donohoe, MD
Associate Clinical Professor, University of Missouri-Kansas
City, School of Medicine, Kansas City, Missouri

James Evans, MD
Assistant Professor, Department of Neurosurgery, Medical
College of Thomas Jefferson University, Philadelphia,
Pennsylvania

Adel G. Fam, MD, FRCP, MRCP(UK), FACP
Professor Emeritus of Medicine (Rheumatology), Division of Rheumatology, University of Toronto; Staff Consultant Rheumatologist (Retired), Sunnybrook Health Sciences Centre, Toronto, Ontario, Canada

Kathleen U. Farmer, PsyD
Headache Care Center, Springfield, Missouri

Frederick G. Freitag, DO
Clinical Assistant Professor, Department of Family Medicine, The Chicago Medical School at Rosalind Franklin, University of Medicine and Science, North Chicago; Associate Director, Diamond Headache Clinic, Chicago, Illinois

M. Kay Garcia, RN, LAc, DrPH
Adjunct Associate Professor, American College of Acupuncture and Oriental Medicine; Advanced Practice Nurse/Acupuncturist, Department of Anesthesiology and Pain Medicine, MD Anderson Cancer Center, Houston, Texas

Scott Goodman, MD
Consultant in Neurology, Headache and Pain Center, Leawood, Kansas

Vitaly Gordin, DM
Associate Professor and Director, Pain Medicine Fellowship Program, Pennsylvania State University College of Medicine, Hershey, Pennsylvania

Martin Grabois, MD
Professor and Chair, Department of Physical Medicine and Rehabilitation, Baylor College of Medicine, Houston, Texas

Douglas R. Gracey, MD, FACP, FCCP
Professor of Medicine, Mayo Clinic College of Medicine; Emeritus Chair, Division of Pulmonary and Critical Care Medicine, Mayo Clinic, Rochester, Minnesota

Mark A. Greenfield, MD
Consultant in Pain Management, Headache and Pain Center, Leawood, Kansas

Rakesh Gupta, MD
Advanced Pain Consultants, Voorhees, New Jersey

Brian Hainline, MD
Clinical Associate Professor, Department of Neurology, New York University School of Medicine, New York

Howard R. Hall, PhD, PsyD
Division of Behavioral Pediatrics, Case Western Reserve University and Rainbow Babies and Children's Hospital, Cleveland, Ohio

Samuel J. Hassenbusch III, MD, PhD
Professor, Department of Neurosurgery, The University of Texas MD Anderson Cancer Center, Houston, Texas

Brian L. Hazleman, MA, MB, FRCP
Consultant Rheumatologist and Director of the Rheumatology Research Unit, Addenbrooke's Hospital; Associate Lecturer, Department of Medicine, University of Cambridge, and Fellow, Corpus Christi College, Cambridge, United Kingdom

James E. Heavner, DVM, PhD
Professor, Anesthesiology and Physiology, Texas Tech University Health Science Center, Lubbock, Texas

D. Ross Henshaw, MD
Orthopaedic Surgeon and Director of Sports Medicine, Danbury Hospital, Danbury, Connecticut

David Dai-Fu Hou, MD
Clinical Fellow, Department of Radiology, Brigham and Women's Hospital, Harvard Medical School, Boston, Massachusetts

Subhash Jain, MD
Centers for Pain Management, New York, New York

Jeffrey W. Janata, PhD
Associate Professor, Department of Psychiatry, Case Western Reserve School of Medicine; Director, Behavioral Medicine Program, University Hospitals of Cleveland, Cleveland, Ohio

Joel Katz, MD
Professor and Canada Research Chair in Health Psychology, Department of Psychology and School of Kinesiology and Health Science, York University; Director, Acute Pain Research Unit, Department of Anesthesia and Pain Management, Toronto General Hospital and Mount Sinai Hospital, Toronto, Ontario, Canada

Bruce L. Kidd, MD
Reader in Rheumatology, University of London, Bone & Joint Research Unit, Queen Mary's School of Medicine, London, United Kingdom

Matthew T. Kline, MD
Private Practice, Philadelphia, Pennsylvania

Dan J. Kopacz, MD
Staff Anesthesiologist, Southern Colorado Anesthesia Associates, Colorado Springs, Colorado

Dhanalakshmi Koyyalagunta, MD
Associate Professor, The University of Texas MD Anderson Cancer Center, Houston, Texas

Lawrence Kropp, MD
Interventional Pain Consultants of Alaska, LLC, Anchorage,
Alaska

Milton H. Landers, DO, PhD
Assistant Clinical Professor, Department of Anesthesiology,
University of Kansas School of Medicine; Pain
Management Associates, Wichita, Kansas

Mark J. Lema, MD, PhD
Professor and Chair, Department of Anesthesiology, State
University of New York at Buffalo School of Medicine
and Biomedical Sciences; Chair, Department of
Anesthesiology and Pain Medicine, Roswell Park
Cancer Institute, Buffalo, New York

Jennifer B. Levin, PhD
Assistant Professor, Department of Psychiatry, Case
Western Reserve School of Medicine; Clinical
Psychologist, University Hospitals of Cleveland,
Cleveland, Ohio

Mirjana Lovrincevic, MD
Clinical Assistant Professor of Anesthesiology, State
University of New York at Buffalo School of Medicine
and Biomedical Sciences; Staff Anesthesiologist/Pain
Physician, Roswell Park Cancer Institute, Buffalo,
New York

Z. David Luo, MD, PhD
Assistant Professor, Departments of Anesthesiology and
Pharmacology, University of California Irvine Medical
Center, Orange, California

Laxmaiah Manchikanti, MD
Pain Management Center of Paducah, Paducah, Kentucky

Chad Markert, PhD
Postdoctoral Fellow, University of Missouri-Columbia,
Columbia, Missouri

Brian McGuirk, MD
Department of Clinical Research, Royal Newcastle
Hospital, Newcastle, Australia

Ronald Melzack, PhD
Professor Emeritus, Department of Psychology, McGill
University, Montreal, Quebec, Canada

Jose L. Mendez, MD
Formerly Fellow, Pulmonary and Critical Care Medicine,
and Currently Fellow, Sleep Medicine, Mayo Clinic
and Mayo College of Medicine, Rochester,
Minnesota

Jeffrey P. Meyer
Midwest Pain Consultants, PC, Midwest City, Oklahoma

Michael Munz, MD, FACS, FRCS
Staff Neurosurgeon, Fort Wayne Neurological Center, Fort
Wayne, Indiana

David P. Myers, MD, CAP, FASAM
President, HealthCare Connection of Tampa, Inc., Tampa,
Florida

Joel A. Nielsen, DO
Private Practice, Weston, Wisconsin

George R. Nissan, DO
Clinical Assistant Professor of Medicine, The Chicago
Medical School at Rosalind Franklin University of
Medicine and Science; North Chicago; Staff Physician
and Director of Research, Diamond Headache Clinic,
Chicago, Illinois

Son Truong Nguyen, DO
Senior Anesthesiologist, St. Luke's Hospital, San Francisco,
California

Kathleen A. O'Leary, MD
Associate Professor, Department of Anesthesiology, School
of Medicine and Biomedical Sciences, State University
of New York at Buffalo; Operating Room Director,
Department of Anesthesiology and Pain Medicine,
Roswell Park Cancer Institute, Buffalo, New York

Robert H. Overbaugh, MD
Chief Fellow, Pain Medicine, Pennsylvania State University
College of Medicine, Hershey, Pennsylvania

John L. Pappas, MD
Vice Chief, Anesthesiology, and Director, Interventional
Pain Center, William Beaumont Hospital, Troy,
Michigan

Winston C. V. Parris, MD
Professor, Department of Anesthesiology, Duke University,
and Chief, Division of Pain Management, Duke
University Medical Center, Durham, North Carolina

Divya Patel, MD
Private Practice, East Hanover, New Jersey

Richard B. Patt, MD
The Patt Center for Cancer Pain and Wellness P.A.,
Houston, Texas

David R. Patterson, PhD, ABPP, ABPH
Professor, Department of Rehabilitation Medicine,
University of Washington; Attending Psychologist,
Harborview Medical Center, Seattle, Washington

Brett T. Quave, MD
Pain Management Fellow, Loma Linda University Medical
Center, Loma Linda, California

Gabor B. Racz, MD, ChB, DABPM
Grover E. Murray Professor and Chairman Emeritus, Director of Pain Services, Texas Tech University Health Sciences Center, Lubbock, Texas

P. Prithvi Raj, MD, FIPP
Professor Emeritus, Texas Tech Health Sciences Center, Lubbock, Texas

Somayaji Ramamurthy, MD
Professor, University of Texas Health Science Center; Attending Physician and Director of the Pain Clinic, University Hospital, San Antonio, Texas

K. Dean Reeves, MD, FAAPM&R
Clinical Associate Professor, Department of Physical Medicine and Rehabilitation, University of Kansas School of Medicine, Kansas City, Kansas

Lowell W. Reynolds, MD
Professor of Anesthesiology, Loma Linda University School of Medicine, and Medical Director and Fellowship Director, Loma Linda University Medical Center, Loma Linda, California

Carla Rime, BA (Psychology)
University of West Florida, Pensacola, Florida

Steven Rosen, MD
Medical Director, Fox Chase Pain Management Associates, Jenkintown, Pennsylvania

Matthew P. Rupert, MD, MS
Total Pain Care LLC, Meridian, Mississippi

Lloyd R. Saberski, MD
Medical Director, The Institute for Therapeutic Discovery, Delanson, New York

Jörn Schattschneider, MD
Consultant, Department of Neurological Pain Research and Therapy, Neurological Clinic, Christian-Albrechts-Universität Kiel, Kiel, Germany

Thomas F. Schrattenholzer, MD
Pain Management Fellow, Loma Linda University Medical Center, Loma Linda, California

Curtis P. Schreiber, MD
Headache Care Center, Springfield, Missouri

David M. Schultz, MD
Medical Director, Medical Advanced Pain Specialists, Minneapolis, Minnesota

Sam R. Sharar, MD
Professor, Department of Anesthesiology, University of Washington; Director, Harborview Anesthesiology Research Center, and Attending Anesthesiologist, Harborview Medical Center, Seattle, Washington

Shawn M. Sills
Pain Management Fellow, Loma Linda University Medical Center, Loma Linda, California

Khuram A. Sial, MD
Temecula Pain Management Center, Temecula, California

Steven Simon, MD, RPH
Assistant Clinical Professor, Department of Physical Medicine and Rehabilitation, University of Kansas Medical Center; Director, the Pain Management Institute, Overland Park, Kansas

Thomas T. Simopoulos, MD, MA
Clinical Instructor of Anesthesia and Pain Management, Harvard Medical School; Director of Acute and Interventional Pain Services, Beth Israel Deaconess Medical Center, Boston, Massachusetts

Vijay Singh, MD
Medical Director, Pain Diagnostics Associates, Niagara, Wisconsin

Kimberley Smith-Martin, MD, FAAPMR
Interventional Physiatrist, Pain Management Specialist, Premier Orthopaedics Associate, Vineland, New Jersey

Daneshvari R. Solanki, MD, FRCA
Professor of Anesthesiology, University of Texas Medical Branch, Galveston, Texas

David A. Soto-Quijano, MD
Department of Physical Medicine and Rehabilitation, Veterans Affairs Medical Center, Houston, Texas

Michael D. Stanton-Hicks, MD BS
Vice Chairman, Division of Anesthesiology, Pain Management and Research, The Cleveland Clinic Foundation, Cleveland, Ohio

M. Alan Stiles, DMD
Clinical Instructor, Department of Oral and Maxillofacial Surgery, Thomas Jefferson University and Medical School, Philadelphia, Pennsylvania

Robert B. Supernaw, PharmD
Professor and Dean, School of Pharmacy, Wingate University, Wingate, North Carolina

Rand S. Swenson, DC, MD, PhD
Assistant Professor, Section of Neurology, Dartmouth-Hitchcock Medical Center, Lebanon, New Hampshire

Gale E. Thompson, MD
Staff Anesthesiologist, Department of Anesthesiology, Virginia Mason Medical Center, Seattle, Washington

Kavin D. Treffer, DO
Associate Professor, Department of Family Medicine, and Osteopathic Manipulative Medicine Coordinator, Kansas City University of Medicine and Biosciences, College of Osteopathic Medicine; Chair, Osteopathic Principles and Utilization Committee, Kansas City, Missouri

Robert Trout, MD
Consultant in Physical Medicine and Rehabilitation, The Headache and Pain Center, Leawood, Kansas

George Urban, MD
Clinical Instructor, Department of Medicine, The Chicago Medical School at Rosalind Franklin University of Medicine and Science, North Chicago, Illinois; Associate Director, Diamond Headache Clinic, Chicago, Illinois

Luminita Vladutu, MD
Department of Anesthesiology and Pain Management, Texas Tech University Health Sciences Center, Lubbock, Texas

Howard J. Waldman, MD, DO
Consultant in Physical Medicine and Rehabilitation, The Headache and Pain Center, Leawood, Kansas; Director of Neurophysiology Laboratory, Doctors Hospital, Leawood, Kansas

Katherine A. Waldman, OTR
Headache and Pain Center, Leawood, Kansas

Steven D. Waldman, MD, JD
Clinical Professor, Department of Anesthesiology, University of Missouri–Kansas City School of Medicine, Kansas City, Missouri; Medical Director, Headache and Pain Center, Leawood, Kansas

Carol A. Warfield, MD
Lowenstein Professor of Anesthesia, Harvard Medical School; Chair, Department of Anesthesia, Critical Care, and Pain Medicine, Beth Israel Deaconess Medical Center, Boston, Massachusetts

Michael L. Whitworth, MD
President, Advanced Pain Management Surgery, Columbus, Indiana

Alon P. Winnie, MD
Professor, Department of Anesthesiology, Northwestern University Medical School, Chicago, Illinois

Gilbert Y. Wong
Assistant Professor, Department of Anesthesiology, Mayo Clinic College of Medicine; Consultant, Department of Anesthesiology, Division of Pain Medicine, Mayo Clinic, Rochester, Minnesota

Tony L. Yaksh, PhD
Professor of Anesthesiology and Pharmacology, and Vice Chair for Research in Anesthesiology, University of California, San Diego, La Jolla, California

Anthony T. Yarussi
Department of Anesthesiology and Pain Medicine, Roswell Park Cancer Institute, Buffalo, New York

Way Yin, MD
Medical Director, Interventional Medical Associates of Billingham, P.C., Billingham, Washington

Michael S. Yoon, MD
Clinical Assistant Professor, Temple University Hospital, Philadelphia; Assistant Surgeon, Abington Memorial Hospital, Abington, Pennsylvania

Preface

Pain management is a young medical specialty compared to its brethren. Its birth in the early 1950s has been attributed to Dr. John Bonica. His seminal book, *The Management of Pain,* guided the specialty though its infancy by providing those few early pain management physicians with the first comprehensive pain management text. Our specialty's toddler years were nurtured by the many excellent pain management texts edited by Dr. Prithvi Raj. Raj's *Practical Management of Pain* was the first comprehensive pain management text to truly emphasize the practical clinical aspects of the specialty. Subsequent editions of *Practical Management of Pain* have further refined this emphasis on practicality and set a high standard for pain management literature in general. As our specialty reached adolescence, it began to change as the increased subspecialization spawned a need for more topic-focused literature. Dr. Richard Patt's excellent text *Cancer Pain* and my own first attempt at textbook editing, *Interventional Pain Management,* are examples of such topic-focused literature. The teenage years of the specialty yielded a demand for more targeted how-to texts. This emphasis on how rather than why spawned the new type of book, the how-to-do-it atlas. The *Atlas of Interventional Pain Management,* first published by Saunders in 1998, was the first of this kind and its subsequent editions and many other text-atlases published since continued this practical emphasis. With early adulthood, our specialty has begun to mature. Many of us practicing the specialty of pain management have come to realize that just knowing why or just knowing how is simply not enough and this realization led me to the desire to edit this text.

This book was first conceived during my collaboration with Allan Ross, then a senior editor for anesthesiology and pain management at WB Saunders, who realized that the push toward more specialized texts and atlases had left a void in the comprehensive pain management literature. Thus, *Pain Management* was born. This two-volume text was designed to be a worthy successor to the texts that have come before it and to provide the pain management specialists with a comprehensive single-source reference for the specialty of pain management.

It should be emphasized that this treatise is the result of many dedicated pain management specialists selflessly giving up their time (often late at night or on weekends as their clinical responsibilities allowed) to contribute chapters to it. As the book's editor, I am deeply indebted to them for their contributions, encouragement, and support. All shared my desire to produce the most clinically useful text that we could to help those practitioners dedicated to the treatment of pain. I would also like to acknowledge the tireless efforts of the editorial and production staff at Elsevier led by Executive Publisher Natasha Andjelkovic and Publishing Services Manager Tina Rebane to turn the myriad chapters, revisions, and hundreds of figures, tables, and radiographs into an accurate and infinitely readable text. I can only hope that you find *Pain Management* a worthwhile addition to your reference library and enjoy reading and using it as much as I enjoyed editing and writing for it.

Steven D. Waldman, M.D.

Contents

Volume 1

Section 1 The Basic Science of Pain Management

1 A Conceptual Framework for Understanding Pain in the Human, 3
Ronald Melzack and Joel Katz

2 Anatomy of the Pain Processing System, 11
Tony L. Yaksh and Z. David Luo

3 Dynamics of the Pain Processing System, 21
Tony L. Yaksh

Section 2 The Evaluation of the Patient in Pain

4 History and Physical Examination of the Pain Patient, 35
Charles D. Donohoe

5 Patterns of Common Pain Syndromes, 49
Bernard M. Abrams

6 Rational Use of Laboratory Testing, 56
Charles D. Donohoe

7 Radiography, 74
David D. Hon and John A. Carrino

8 Nuclear Medicine Techniques, 85
David D. Hon and John A. Carrino

9 Computed Tomography, 93
Joel A. Nielsen and John A. Carrino

10 Magnetic Resonance Imaging, 106
Eric T. Chou and John A. Carrino

11 Diskography, 118
Milton H. Landers

12 Epidurography, 145
Jeffrey P. Meyer, Miles R. Day, and Gabor B. Racz

13 Neural Blockade for the Diagnosis of Pain, 149
Steven D. Waldman

14 Differential Neural Blockade for the Diagnosis of Pain, 155
Alon P. Winnie and Kenneth D. Candido

15 Spinal Canal Endoscopy, 167
Lloyd R. Saberski

16 Electromyography and Nerve Conduction Velocity, 179
Bernard M. Abrams

17 Evoked Potential Testing, 192
Howard J. Waldman

18 The Measurement of Pain: Objectifying the Subjective, 197
Darin J. Correll

19 Chronic Pain: Physiologic, Diagnostic, and Management Considerations, 212
Brian Hainline

Section 3 Generalized Pain Syndromes Encountered in Clinical Practice

Part A: Acute Pain Syndromes

20 Management of Acute and Postoperative Pain, 225
Steven D. Waldman

21 Burn Pain, 240
Sam R. Sharar, David R. Patterson, and Shelley Wiechman Askay

22 Sickle Cell Pain, 257
Kimberley Smith-Martin

23 Acute Headache, 262
Seymour Diamond and George R. Nissan

Part B: Neuropathic Pain Syndromes

24 Evaluation and Treatment of Peripheral Neuropathies, 268
Steven D. Waldman, Howard J. Waldman, and Katherine A. Waldman

25 Acute Herpes Zoster and Postherpetic Neuralgia, 279
Steven D. Waldman

26 Complex Regional Pain Syndrome Type I (Reflex Sympathetic Dystropyhy), 283
Andreas Binder, Jörn Schattschneider, and Ralf Baron

27 Complex Regional Pain Syndrome Type II (Causalgia), 302
Andreas Binder, Jörn Schattschneider, and Ralf Baron

28 Phantom Pain Syndromes, 304
Laxmaiah Manchikanti, Vijay Singh, and Mark V. Boswell

Part C: PAIN OF MALIGNANT ORIGIN

29 Identification and Treatment of Cancer Pain Syndromes, 316
Steven D. Waldman

30 Radiation Therapy in the Management of Cancer Pain, 328
Scott C. Cozad

31 Neural Blockade with Local Anesthetics and Steroids in the Management of Cancer Pain, 337
P. Prithvi Raj

32 Neural Blockade with Neurolytic Agents in the Management of Cancer Pain, 343
Subhash Jain and Rakesh Gupta

33 The Role of Spinal Opioids in the Management of Cancer Pain, 349
Steven D. Waldman

34 The Role of Neurosurgery in the Management of Intractable Pain, 353
Michael S. Yoon and Michael Munz

35 Palliative Care in the Management of Cancer Pain, 360
Fadi Braiteh and Eduardo Bruera

Part D: PAIN OF DERMATOLOGIC AND MUSCULOSKELETAL ORIGIN

36 Common Sports Injuries, 376
Steven D. Waldman

37 Fibromyalgia, 403
Steven D. Waldman

38 Painful Neuropathies Including Entrapment Syndromes, 406
Charles D. Donohoe

39 Osteoarthritis and Related Disorders, 418
Paul Dieppe, Philip Conaghan, Bruce Kidd, and Paul Creamer

40 Connective Tissue Diseases, 431
Steven D. Waldman

41 Polymyalgia Rheumatica, 449
Brian L. Hazleman

Section 4 Regional Pain Syndromes

Part A: PAIN IN THE HEAD

42 Migraine Headache, 455
Seymour Diamond

43 Tension-Type Headache, 464
Frederick G. Freitag

44 Cluster Headache, 474
Seymour Diamond and George Urban

45 Analgesic Rebound Headache, 492
Roger Cady, Curtis Schreiber, and Kathleen Farmer

46 Trigeminal Neuralgia, 502
M. Alan Stiles and James Evans

47 Glossopharyngeal Neuralgia, 511
Steven D. Waldman

48 Giant Cell Arteritis, 518
Brian L. Hazleman

49 Pain of Ocular and Periocular Origin, 523
Steven D. Waldman

50 Pain of the Ear, Nose, Sinuses, and Throat, 538
Steven D. Waldman

51 Occipital Neuralgia, 549
Steven D. Waldman

52 Reflex Sympathetic Dystrophy of the Face, 552
Kenneth D. Candido

Part B: PAIN EMANATING FROM THE NECK AND BRACHIAL PLEXUS

53 Cervical Facet Syndrome, 561
Khuram A. Sial, Thomas T. Simopoulos, Zahid H. Bajwa, and Carol A. Warfield

54 Cervical Radiculopathy, 568
Laxmaiah Manchikanti, Vijay Singh, and Mark V. Boswell

55 Brachial Plexopathy, 577
Divya Patel

56 Cervical Dystonia, 591
Martin K. Childers and Chad Markert

Part C: SHOULDER PAIN SYNDROMES

57 Degenerative Arthritis of the Shoulder, 598
Steven D. Waldman

58 Disorders of the Rotator Cuff, 603
D. Ross Henshaw and Edward V. Craig

59 Acromioclavicular Joint Pain, 615
Steven D. Waldman

60 Subdeltoid Bursitis, 619
Steven D. Waldman

61 Biceps Tendinitis, 622
Robert Trout

62 Scapulocostal Syndrome, 627
Bernard M. Abrams and Scott Goodman

Part D: ELBOW PAIN SYNDROMES

63 Tennis Elbow, 633
Steven D. Waldman

64 Golfer's Elbow, 637
Steven D. Waldman

65 Olecranon and Cubital Bursitis, 641
Steven D. Waldman

66 Entrapment Neuropathies of the Elbow and Forearm, 647
Steven D. Waldman

Part E: WRIST AND HAND PAIN SYNDROMES

67   Arthritis of the Wrist and Hand,   659
      Adel G. Fam

68   Carpal Tunnel Syndrome,   664
      Adel G. Fam

69   de Quervain's Tenosynovitis,   666
      Adel G. Fam

70   Dupuytren's Contracture,   668
      Adel G. Fam

71   Trigger Finger and Trigger Thumb,   670
      Adel G. Fam

72   Glomus Tumor of the Hand,   671
      Adel G. Fam

Part F: PAIN SYNDROMES OF THE CHEST WALL,
        THORACIC SPINE, AND RESPIRATORY SYSTEM

73   Chest Wall Pain Syndromes,   672
      Steven D. Waldman

74   Thoracic Radiculopathy,   690
      Steven D. Waldman

75   Painful Disorders of the Respiratory
      System,   693
      Jose L. Mendez and Douglas R. Gracey

76   Postmastectomy Pain,   716
      Mirjana Lovrincevic and Mark J. Lema

77   Post-thoracotomy Pain,   721
      Debra A. DeAngelo and Vitaly Gordin

78   Mononeuritis Multiplex,   724
      Steven D. Waldman

Part G: PAIN SYNDROMES OF THE ABDOMEN,
        RETROPERITONEUM, AND GROIN

79   Abdominal Wall Pain Syndromes,   727
      Steven D. Waldman

80   Evaluation and Treatment of Acute and
      Chronic Pancreatitis,   737
      Steven D. Waldman

81   Ilioinguinal, Iliohypogastric, and Genitofemoral
      Neuralgia,   742
      Steven D. Waldman

Volume 2

Part H: PAIN SYNDROMES OF THE LUMBAR SPINE AND
        SACROILIAC JOINT

82   Low Back Pain,   749
      David Borenstein

83   Lumbar Radiculopathy,   758
      Laxmaiah Manchikanti, Vijay Singh, and
      Mark V. Boswell

84   Lumbar Facet Syndrome,   769
      Nikolai Bogduk

85   Occupational Back Pain,   777
      Brian McGuirk and Nikolai Bogduk

86   Arachnoiditis and Related Conditions,   791
      J. Antonio Aldrete

87   Spondylolysis and Spondylolisthesis,   800
      Nikolai Bogduk

88   Sacroiliac Joint Pain and Related
      Disorders,   810
      Steven Simon

89   Failed Back Surgery Syndrome,   817
      J. Antonio Aldrete

Part I: PAIN SYNDROMES OF THE PELVIS AND GENITALIA

90   Osteitis Pubis,   831
      Steven D. Waldman

91   Piriformis Syndrome,   834
      Lowell W. Reynolds and Thomas F. Schrattenholzer

92   Orchialgia,   837
      Lowell W. Reynolds and Shawn M. Sills

93   Vulvodynia,   843
      Lowell W. Reynolds and Brett T. Quave

94   Coccydynia,   848
      Steven D. Waldman

95   Proctalgia Fugax,   851
      Steven D. Waldman

Part J: PAIN SYNDROMES OF THE HIP AND PROXIMAL LOWER
        EXTREMITY

96   Gluteal and Ischiogluteal Bursitis,   853
      Steven D. Waldman

97   Trochanteric Bursitis,   859
      Martin Childers

98   Iliopsoas Bursitis,   864
      Robert Trout

99   Meralgia Paresthetica,   868
      Steven D. Waldman

100   Femoral and Saphenous Neuropathies,   871
      Bernard M. Abrams

101   Obturator Neuropathy,   879
      Bernard M. Abrams

Part K: PAIN SYNDROMES OF THE KNEE AND DISTAL LOWER
        EXTREMITY

102   Painful Conditions of the Knee,   883
      Steven D. Waldman

103   Bursitis Syndromes of the Knee,   893
      Steven D. Waldman

104   Baker's Cyst of the Knee,   903
      Steven D. Waldman

105   Quadriceps Expansion Syndrome,   906
      Steven D. Waldman

Part L: PAIN SYNDROMES OF THE ANKLE AND FOOT

106   Arthritis of the Ankle and Foot,   911
      Adel G. Fam

107 Achilles Tendinitis and Bursitis and Other
Painful Conditions of the Ankle, 915
Adel G. Fam

108 Morton Interdigital Neuroma and Other Causes
of Metatarsalgia, 918
Adel G. Fam

109 Hallux Valgus, Bunion, Bunionette, and Other
Painful Conditions of the Toe, 920
Adel G. Fam

110 Heel Spur Pain, Plantar Fasciitis, and Related
Disorders, 922
Daneshvari R. Solanki

Section 5 Specific Treatment Modalities for Pain and Symptom Management

Part A: PHARMACOLOGIC MANAGEMENT OF PAIN

111 Simple Analgesics, 927
Robert B. Supernaw

112 Nonsteroidal Antiinflammatory Drugs and
COX-2 Inhibitors, 934
Steven D. Waldman

113 Opioid Analgesics, 939
Dhanalakshmi Koyyalagunta

114 Role of Antidepressants in the Management of
Pain, 965
Steven D. Waldman

115 Anticonvulsants, 972
Steven D. Waldman

116 Centrally Acting Skeletal Muscle Relaxants and
Associated Drugs, 977
*Howard J. Waldman, Steven D. Waldman, and
Katherine A. Waldman*

117 Topical and Systemic Local Anesthetics, 983
James E. Heavner

118 Alternative Pain Medicines, 989
Winston C. V. Parris and Salahadin Abdi

119 Limitations of Pharmacologic Pain
Management, 997
Richard B. Patt

Part B: PSYCHOLOGICAL AND BEHAVIORAL MODALITIES FOR
PAIN AND SYMPTOM MANAGEMENT

120 Psychological Interventions, 1003
Jennifer B. Levin and Jeffrey W. Janata

121 Biofeedback, 1010
Frank Andrasik and Carla Rime

122 Hypnosis, 1021
Howard Hall

123 Relaxation Techniques and Guided
Imagery, 1025
Carla Rime and Frank Andrasik

Part C: PHYSICAL MODALITIES IN THE MANAGEMENT OF PAIN

124 Therapeutic Heat and Cold in the Management
of Pain, 1033
*Steven D. Waldman, Katherine A. Waldman, and
Howard J. Waldman*

125 Hydrotherapy, 1043
David A. Soto-Quijano and Martin Grabois

126 Transcutaneous Electrical Nerve
Stimulation, 1052
Steven D. Waldman

127 Exercise and Physical Reconditioning, 1055
Donna Bloodworth

128 Osteopathic Manipulative Treatment of the
Chronic Pain Patient, 1069
Kevin D. Treffer

129 Nociceptors and Peripheral Sources of
Pain, 1081
Geoffrey M. Bove and Rand S. Swenson

130 Acupuncture, 1093
M. Kay Garcia and Joseph S. Chiang

131 Prolotherapy: Regenerative Injection
Therapy, 1106
K. Dean Reeves

Part D: NEURAL BLOCKADE AND NEUROLYTIC BLOCKS IN
THE MANAGEMENT OF PAIN

132 Atlanto-occipital Joint Injections, 1128
Luminita Vladutu and Gabor B. Racz

133 Atlantoaxial Injection, 1132
*Jonathan Barry, Miles R. Day, and
Gabor B. Racz*

134 Sphenopalatine Ganglion Block, 1134
*Lawrence Kropp, Miles R. Day, and
Gabor B. Racz*

135 Greater and Lesser Occipital Nerve
Block, 1140
David L. Brown and Gilbert Y. Wong

136 Gasserian Ganglion Block, 1145
Steven D. Waldman

137 Blockade of the Trigeminal Nerve and Its
Branches, 1152
Steven D. Waldman

138 Glossopharyngeal Nerve Block, 1161
Steven D. Waldman

139 Vagus Nerve Block, 1166
Steven D. Waldman

140 Phrenic Nerve Block, 1169
Mark A. Greenfield

141 Cervical Plexus Block, 1173
John L. Pappas and Carol A. Warfield

142 Stellate Ganglion Block, 1191
P. Prithvi Raj

143 Cervical Facet Block, 1199
*Laxmaiah Manchikanti, David M. Schultz, and
Vijay Singh*

144 Cervical Epidural Nerve Block, 1210
Steven D. Waldman

145 Brachial Plexus Block, 1220
Steven D. Waldman

146 Peripheral Nerve Blocks of the Upper
Extremity, 1227
Robert H. Overbaugh

147 Suprascapular Nerve Block, 1239
P. Prithvi Raj

148 Thoracic Epidural Nerve Block, 1243
Somayaji Ramamurthy

149 Intercostal Nerve Block, 1250
Dan J. Kopacz and Gale E. Thompson

150 Interpleural Catheters: Indications and
Techniques, 1259
Kathleen A. O'Leary, Anthony T. Yarussi, and
David P. Myers

151 Splanchnic and Celiac Plexus Nerve Block,
1265
Steven D. Waldman and Richard B. Patt

152 Lumbar Epidural Nerve Block, 1281
Laxmaiah Manchikanti and Sairam Atluri

153 Subarachnoid Neurolytic Block, 1294
Alon P. Winnie and Kenneth D. Candido

154 Lumbar Facet Block, 1303
Laxmaiah Manchikanti, David M. Schultz, and
Vijay Singh

155 Lumbar Sympathetic Nerve Block and
Neurolysis, 1314
Michael D. Stanton-Hicks

156 Ilioinguinal-Iliohypogastric Nerve Block, 1322
Son Truong Nguyen, Vimal Akhouri, and
Carol A. Warfield

157 Lateral Femoral Cutaneous Nerve Block, 1328
David P. Bankston

158 Obturator Nerve Block, 1331
Somayaji Ramamurthy

159 Caudal Epidural Nerve Block, 1335
Steven D. Waldman

160 Lysis of Epidural Adhesions: The Racz
Technique, 1345
Miles R. Day and Gabor B. Racz

161 Hypogastric Plexus Block and Impar Ganglion
Block, 1350
Steven D. Waldman

162 Injection of the Sacroiliac Joint, 1358
Steven D. Waldman

163 Neural Blockade of the Peripheral Nerves of the
Lower Extremity, 1362
Debra A. DeAngelo and Vitaly Gordin

Part E: NEUROAUGMENTATION AND IMPLANTABLE DRUG
DELIVERY SYSTEMS

164 Peripheral Nerve Stimulation, 1369
Matthew P. Rupert, Miles R. Day, and Gabor B.
Racz

165 Spinal Cord Stimulation, 1373
Allen W. Burton

166 Implantable Drug Delivery Systems: Practical
Considerations, 1382
Steven D. Waldman

167 Complications of Implantable Technology for
Pain Control, 1388
Richard B. Patt and Samuel J. Hassenbusch III

Part F: ADVANCED PAIN MANAGEMENT TECHNIQUES

168 Neuroadenolysis of the Pituitary, 1405
Steven D. Waldman

169 Radiofrequency Techniques, 1411
Matthew T. Kline

170 Cryoneurolysis, 1460
Lloyd R. Saberski

171 Vertebroplasty and Kyphoplasty, 1475
Ronald A. Alberico and Ahmed Nabil Abdelhalim

172 Intradiskal Electrothermal Annuloplasty, 1484
Michael L. Whitworth

173 Percutaneous Laser Diskectomy, 1489
Michael L. Whitworth

174 Percutaneous Cordotomy, 1501
Steven Rosen

Index, i

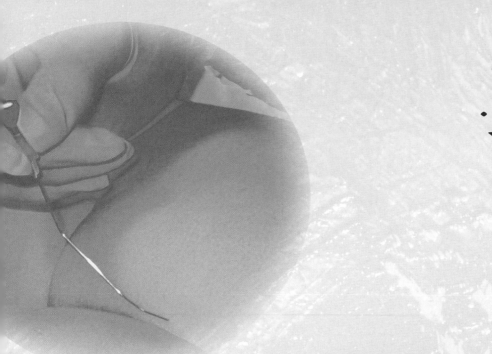

The Basic Science of Pain Management

A Conceptual Framework for Understanding Pain in the Human

Ronald Melzack and Joel Katz

Theories of pain, like all scientific theories, evolve as a result of the accumulation of new facts as well as leaps of the imagination.[1] The gate control theory's most revolutionary contribution to understanding pain was its emphasis on central neural mechanisms.[2] The theory forced the medical and biological sciences to accept the brain as an active system that filters, selects, and modulates inputs. The dorsal horns, too, are not merely passive transmission stations but also sites at which dynamic activities—inhibition, excitation, and modulation—occur. The great challenge ahead of us is to understand how the brain functions.

■ A BRIEF HISTORY OF PAIN IN THE 20TH CENTURY

The theory of pain we inherited in the 20th century was proposed by Descartes 3 centuries earlier. The impact of Descartes' specificity theory was enormous. It influenced experiments on the anatomy and physiology of pain up to the first half of the 20th century (reviewed in Melzack and Wall[3]). This body of research is marked by a search for specific pain fibers and pathways and a pain center in the brain. The result was a concept of pain as a specific, straight-through sensory projection system. This rigid anatomy of pain in the 1950s led to attempts to treat severe chronic pain by a variety of neurosurgical lesions. Descartes' specificity theory, then, determined the "facts" as they were known up to the middle of the 20th century, and even determined therapy.

Specificity theory proposed that injury activates specific pain receptors and fibers which, in turn, project pain impulses through a spinal pain pathway to a pain center in the brain. The psychological experience of pain, therefore, was virtually equated with peripheral injury. In the 1950s, there was no room for psychological contributions to pain, such as attention, past experience, anxiety, depression, and the meaning of the situation. Instead, pain experience was held to be proportional to peripheral injury or pathology. Patients who suffered back pain without presenting signs of organic disease were often labeled as psychologically disturbed and sent to psychiatrists. The concept, in short, was simple and, not surprisingly, often failed to help patients who suffered severe chronic

pain. To thoughtful clinical observers, specificity theory was clearly wrong.

There were several attempts to find a new theory. The major opponent to specificity was labeled as "pattern theory," but there were several different pattern theories and they were generally vague and inadequate (see Melzack and Wall[3]). Seen in retrospect, however, pattern theories gradually evolved (Fig. 1–1) and set the stage for the gate control theory. Goldscheider[4] proposed that central summation in the dorsal horns is one of the critical determinants of pain. Livingston's[5] theory postulated a reverberatory circuit in the dorsal horns to explain summation, referred pain, and pain that persisted long after healing was completed. The theory of Noordenbos[6] proposed that large-diameter fibers inhibited small-diameter fibers, and he even suggested that the substantia gelatinosa in the dorsal horns plays a major role in the summation and other dynamic processes described by Livingston. In none of these theories was there an explicit role for the brain other than as a passive receiver of messages. The successive theoretical concepts moved the field in the right direction: into the spinal cord and away from the periphery as the exclusive answer to pain. At least the field of pain was making its way up toward the brain.

■ THE GATE CONTROL THEORY OF PAIN

In 1965, Melzack and Wall proposed the gate control theory of pain. The final model, depicted in Figure 1–1D in the context of earlier theories of pain, is the first theory of pain that incorporated the central control processes of the brain.

The gate control theory of pain[2] proposed that the transmission of nerve impulses from afferent fibers to spinal cord transmission (T) cells is modulated by a gating mechanism in the spinal dorsal horn. This gating mechanism is influenced by the relative amount of activity in large- and small-diameter fibers, so that large fibers tend to inhibit transmission (close the gate) whereas small fibers tend to facilitate transmission (open the gate). In addition, the spinal gating mechanism is influenced by nerve impulses that descend from the brain. When the output of the spinal T cells exceeds a critical level, it activates the action system—those neural areas that

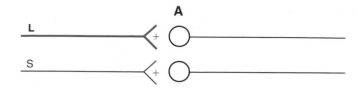

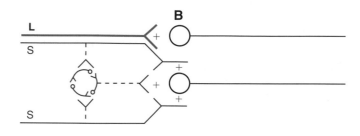

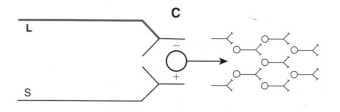

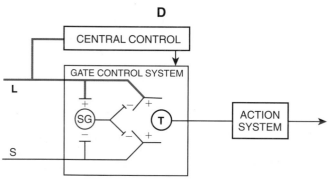

FIGURE 1–1 ■ Schematic representation of conceptual models of pain mechanisms. **A,** Specificity theory. Large (L) and small (S) fibers are assumed to transmit touch and pain impulses, respectively, in separate, specific, straight-through pathways to touch and pain centers in the brain. **B,** Goldscheider's[4] summation theory, showing convergence of small fibers onto a dorsal horn cell. The central network projecting to the central cell represents Livingston's[5] conceptual model of reverberatory circuits underlying pathologic pain states. Touch is assumed to be carried by large fibers. **C,** Sensory interaction theory, in which large (L) fibers inhibit (–) and small (S) fibers excite (+) central transmission neurons. The output projects to spinal cord neurons, which are conceived by Noordenbos[6] to comprise a multisynaptic afferent system. **D,** Gate control theory. The large (L) and small (S) fibers project to the substantia gelatinosa (SG) and first central transmission (T) cells. The central control trigger is represented by a line running from the large fiber system to central control mechanisms, which in turn project back to the gate control system. The T cells project to the entry cells of the action system. +, excitation; –, inhibition. (From Melzack R: The gate control theory 25 years later: New perspectives on phantom limb pain. In Bond MR, Charlton JE, Woolf CJ (eds): Pain Research and Therapy: Proceedings of the Sixth World Congress on Pain. Amsterdam, Elsevier, 1991, p 9.)

underlie the complex, sequential patterns of behavior and experience characteristics of pain.

The theory's emphasis on the modulation of inputs in the spinal dorsal horns and the dynamic role of the brain in pain processes had a clinical as well as a scientific impact. Psychological factors, which were previously dismissed as "reactions to pain" were now seen to be an integral part of pain processing, and new avenues for pain control by psychological therapies were opened. Similarly, cutting nerves and pathways was gradually replaced by a host of methods to modulate the input. Physical therapists and other health-care professionals who use a multitude of modulation techniques were brought into the picture, and transcutaneous electrical nerve stimulation (TENS) became an important modality for the treatment of chronic and acute pain. The current status of pain research and therapy indicates that, despite the addition of a massive amount of detail, the conceptual components of the theory remain basically intact up to the present.

■ BEYOND THE GATE

We believe the great challenge ahead of us is to understand brain function. Melzack and Casey[7] made a start by proposing that specialized systems in the brain are involved in the sensory-discriminative, motivational-affective, and cognitive-evaluative dimensions of subjective pain experience (Fig. 1–2). These names for the dimensions of subjective experience seemed strange when they were coined, but they are now used so frequently and seem so "logical" that they have become part of our language. So too, the McGill Pain Questionnaire, which taps into subjective experience—one of the functions of the brain—is widely used to measure pain.[8,9]

In 1978, Melzack and Loeser described severe pains in the phantom body of paraplegics with verified total sections of the spinal cord, and proposed a central "pattern generating mechanism" above the level of the section.[10] This concept, generally ignored for more than a decade, is now beginning to be accepted. It represents a revolutionary advance: it did not merely extend the gate; it said that pain could be generated by brain mechanisms in paraplegics in the absence of a spinal gate because the brain is completely disconnected from the cord. Psychophysical specificity, in such a concept, makes no sense; instead we must explore how patterns of nerve impulses generated in the brain can give rise to somesthetic experience.

■ PHANTOM LIMBS AND THE CONCEPT OF A NEUROMATRIX

It is evident that the gate control theory has taken us a long way. Yet, as historians of science have pointed out, good theories are instrumental in producing facts that eventually require a new theory to incorporate them. And this is what has happened. It is possible to make adjustments to the gate theory so that, for example, it includes long-lasting activity of the sort Wall has described (see Melzack and Wall[3]). But there is a set of observations on pain in paraplegics that just does not fit the theory. This does not negate the gate theory, of course. Peripheral and spinal processes are obviously an important part of pain and we need to know more about the mechanisms of peripheral inflammation, spinal modulation, midbrain

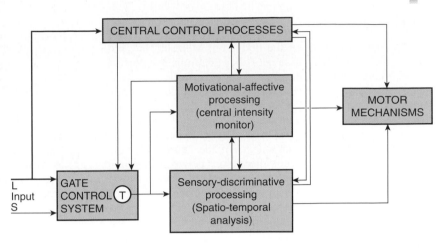

FIGURE 1–2 ■ Conceptual model of the sensory, motivational, and central control determinants of pain. The output of the T (transmission) cells of the gate control system projects to the sensory-discriminative system and the motivational-affective system. The central control trigger is represented by a line running from the large fiber system to central control processes; these, in turn, project back to the gate control system, and to the sensory-discriminative and motivational-affective systems. All three systems interact with one another and project to the motor system. (From Melzack R, Casey KL: Sensory, motivational, and central control determinants of pain. In Kenshalo D (ed): The Skin Senses. Springfield, IL, Charles C Thomas, 1968, p 423.)

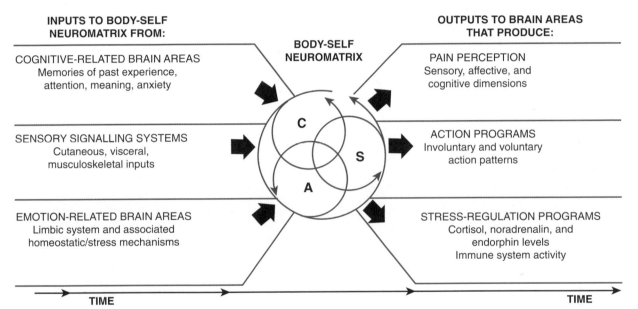

FIGURE 1–3 ■ Factors that contribute to the patterns of activity generated by the body-self neuromatrix, which is composed of sensory, affective, and cognitive neuromodules. The output patterns from the neuromatrix produce the multiple dimensions of pain experience, as well as concurrent homeostatic and behavioral responses. (From Melzack R: Pain and the neuromatrix in the brain. J Dent Educ 65:1378, 2001, with permission.)

descending control, and so forth. But the data on painful phantoms below the level of total spinal section[11,12] indicate that we need to go above the spinal cord and into the brain.

Note that we mean more than the spinal projection areas in the thalamus and cortex. These areas are important, of course, but they are only part of the neural processes that underlie perception. The cortex, Gybels and Tasker[13] made amply clear, is not the pain center and neither is the thalamus. The areas of the brain involved in pain experience and behavior must include somatosensory projections as well as the limbic system. Furthermore, cognitive processes are known to involve widespread areas of the brain. Despite this increased knowledge, we do not yet have an adequate theory of how the brain works.

Melzack's[12] analysis of phantom limb phenomena, particularly the astonishing reports of a phantom body and severe phantom limb pain in people with a total thoracic spinal cord section,[10] has led to four conclusions that point to a new conceptual model of the nervous system. First, because the phantom limb (or other body part) feels so real, it is reasonable to conclude that the body we normally feel is subserved by the same neural processes in the brain as the phantom; these brain processes are normally activated and modulated by inputs from the body but they can act in the absence of any inputs. Second, all the qualities we normally feel from the body, including pain, are also felt in the absence of inputs from the body; from this we may conclude that the origins of the patterns that underlie the qualities of experience lie in neural networks in the brain; stimuli may trigger the patterns but do not produce them. Third, the body is perceived as a unity and is identified as the "self," distinct from other people and the surrounding world. The experience of a unity of such diverse feelings, including the self as the point of orientation in the surrounding environment, is produced by central neural processes and cannot derive from the peripheral nervous system or spinal cord. Fourth, the brain processes that underlie the body-self are "built in" by genetic specification, although this built-in substrate must, of course, be modified by experience. These conclusions provide the basis of the new conceptual model[11,12,14] depicted in Figure 1–3.

Outline of the Theory

The anatomic substrate of the body-self, Melzack[11,12,14] proposed, is a large, widespread network of neurons that consists of loops between the thalamus and cortex as well as between the cortex and limbic system. He has labeled the entire network, whose spatial distribution and synaptic links are initially determined genetically and are later sculpted by sensory inputs, as a *neuromatrix*. The loops diverge to permit parallel processing in different components of the neuromatrix and converge repeatedly to permit interactions between the output products of processing. The repeated *cyclical processing and synthesis* of nerve impulses through the neuromatrix imparts a characteristic pattern: the *neurosignature*. The neurosignature of the neuromatrix is imparted on all nerve impulse patterns that flow through it; the neurosignature is produced by the patterns of synaptic connections in the entire neuromatrix. All inputs from the body undergo cyclical processing and synthesis so that characteristic patterns are impressed on them in the neuromatrix. Portions of the neuromatrix are specialized to process information related to major sensory events (such as injury, temperature change, and stimulation of erogenous tissue) and may be labeled as neuromodules that impress subsignatures on the larger neurosignature.

The neurosignature, which is a continuous output from the body-self neuromatrix, is projected to areas in the brain— the *sentient neural hub*—in which the stream of nerve impulses (the neurosignature modulated by ongoing inputs) is converted into a continually changing stream of awareness. The neurosignature patterns may also activate a neuromatrix to produce movement. That is, the signature patterns bifurcate so that a pattern proceeds to the sentient neural hub (where the pattern is transformed into the experience of movement) and a similar pattern proceeds through a neuromatrix that eventually activates spinal cord neurons to produce muscle patterns for complex actions.

The Body-Self Neuromatrix

The body is felt as a unity with different qualities at different times. Melzack[11,12,14] proposed that the brain mechanism that underlies the experience also comprises a unified system that acts as a whole and produces a neurosignature pattern of a whole body. The conceptualization of this unified brain mechanism lies at the heart of the new theory, and the word "neuromatrix" best characterizes it. The neuromatrix (not the stimulus, peripheral nerves or "brain center") is the origin of the neurosignature; the neurosignature originates and takes form in the neuromatrix. Although the neurosignature may be triggered or modulated by input, the input is only a "trigger" and does not produce the neurosignature itself. The neuromatrix "casts" its distinctive signature on all inputs (nerve impulse patterns) which flow through it. The array of neurons in a neuromatrix is genetically programmed to perform the specific function of producing the signature pattern. The final, integrated neurosignature pattern for the body-self ultimately produces awareness and action.

The neuromatrix, distributed throughout many areas of the brain, comprises a widespread network of neurons that generates patterns, processes information that flows through it, and ultimately produces the pattern that is felt as a whole body. The stream of neurosignature output with constantly varying patterns riding on the main signature pattern produces the feelings of the whole body with constantly changing qualities.

Conceptual Reasons for a Neuromatrix

It is difficult to comprehend how individual bits of information from skin, joints, or muscles can all come together to produce the experience of a coherent, articulated body. At any instant in time, millions of nerve impulses arrive at the brain from all the body's sensory systems, including the proprioceptive and vestibular systems. How can all this be integrated in a constantly changing unity of experience? Where does it all come together?

Melzack[11,12,14] conceptualized a genetically built-in neuromatrix for the whole body, producing a characteristic neurosignature for the body that carries with it patterns for the myriad qualities we feel. The neuromatrix, as Melzack conceived of it, produces a continuous message that represents the whole body in which details are differentiated within the whole as inputs come into it. We start from the top, with the experience of a unity of the body, and look for differentiation of detail within the whole. The neuromatrix, then, is a template of the whole, which provides the characteristic neural pattern for the whole body (the body's neurosignature) as well as subsets of signature patterns (from neuromodules) that relate to events at (or in) different parts of the body.

These views are in sharp contrast to the classical specificity theory in which the qualities of experience are presumed to be inherent in peripheral nerve fibers. Pain is not injury; the *quality of pain experiences* must not be confused with the physical event of breaking skin or bone. Warmth and cold are not "out there"; temperature changes occur "out there," but the *qualities of experience* must be generated by structures in the brain. There are no external equivalents to stinging, smarting, tickling, itch; the *qualities* are produced by built-in neuromodules whose neurosignatures innately produce the qualities.

We do not learn to feel qualities of experience: our brains are built to produce them. The inadequacy of the traditional peripheralist view becomes especially evident when we consider paraplegics with high-level complete spinal breaks. In spite of the absence of inputs from the body, virtually every quality of sensation and affect is experienced. It is known that the absence of input produces hyperactivity and abnormal firing patterns in spinal cells above the level of the break.[10] But how, from this jumble of activity, do we get the meaningful experience of movement, the coordination of limbs with other limbs, cramping pain in specific (nonexistent) muscle groups, and so on? This must occur in the brain, in which neurosignatures are produced by neuromatrixes that are triggered by the output of hyperactive cells.

When all sensory systems are intact, inputs modulate the continuous neuromatrix output to produce the wide variety of experiences we feel. We may feel position, warmth, and several kinds of pain and pressure all at once. It is a single unitary feeling just as an orchestra produces a single unitary sound at any moment even though the sound comprises violins, cellos, horns, and so forth. Similarly, at a particular moment in time we feel complex qualities from all of the body. In addition, our experience of the body includes visual images, affect, "knowledge" of the self (versus not-self) as well as the meaning of body parts in terms of social norms and values. It is hard to conceive of all of these bits and pieces coming together to produce a unitary body-self, but we can visualize a neuromatrix that impresses a characteristic signature on all the inputs that converge on it and thereby produces the never-ending stream of feeling from the body.

The experience of the body-self involves multiple dimensions—sensory, affective, evaluative, postural and many others. The sensory dimensions are subserved, in part at least, by portions of the neuromatrix that lie in the sensory projection areas of the brain; the affective dimensions, Melzack assumed, are subserved by areas in the brain stem and limbic system. Each major psychological dimension (or quality) of experience, Melzack[11,12,14] proposed, is subserved by a particular portion of the neuromatrix which contributes a distinct portion of the total neurosignature. To use a musical analogy once again, it is like the strings, tympani, woodwinds, and brasses of a symphony orchestra that each compose a part of the whole; each makes its unique contribution yet each is an integral part of a single symphony that varies continually from beginning to end.

The neuromatrix resembles Hebb's "cell assembly" by being a widespread network of cells that subserves a particular psychological function. Hebb[15] conceived of the cell assembly as a network developed by gradual sensory learning, whereas Melzack, proposed that the structure of the neuromatrix is predominantly determined by genetic factors, although its eventual synaptic architecture is influenced by sensory inputs. This emphasis on the genetic contribution to the brain does not diminish the importance of sensory inputs. The neuromatrix is a psychologically meaningful unit, developed by both heredity and learning, that represents an entire unified entity.[11,12,14]

Action Patterns: The Action-Neuromatrix

The output of the body neuromatrix, Melzack[11,12,14] proposed is directed at two systems: (1) the neuromatrix that produces awareness of the output, and (2) a neuromatrix involved in overt action patterns. In this discussion, it is important to keep in mind that just as there is a steady stream of awareness, there is also a steady output of behavior (including movements during sleep).

It is important to recognize that behavior occurs only after the input has been at least partially synthesized and recognized. For example, when we respond to the experience of pain or itch, it is evident that the experience has been synthesized by the body-self neuromatrix (or relevant neuromodules) sufficiently for the neuromatrix to have imparted the neurosignature patterns that underlie the quality of experience, affect, and meaning. Apart from a few reflexes (such as withdrawal of a limb, eye-blink and so on), behavior occurs only after inputs have been analyzed and synthesized sufficiently to produce meaningful experience. When we reach for an apple, the visual input has clearly been synthesized by a neuromatrix so that it has 3-dimensional shape, color, and meaning as an edible, desirable object, all of which are produced by the brain and are not in the object "out there." When we respond to pain (by withdrawal or even by telephoning for an ambulance), we respond to an experience that has sensory

qualities, affect, and meaning as a dangerous (or potentially dangerous) event to the body.

Melzack[11,12,14] proposed that after inputs from the body undergo transformation in the body-neuromatrix, the appropriate action patterns are activated concurrently (or nearly so) with the neuromatrix for experience. Thus, in the action-neuromatrix, cyclical processing and synthesis produces activation of several possible patterns and their successive elimination until one particular pattern emerges as the most appropriate for the circumstances at the moment. In this way, input and output are synthesized simultaneously, in parallel, not in series. This permits a smooth, continuous stream of action patterns.

The command, which originates in the brain, to perform a pattern such as running activates the neuromodule which then produces firing in sequences of neurons that send precise messages through ventral horn neuron pools to appropriate sets of muscles. At the same time, the output patterns from the body-neuromatrix that engage the neuromodules for particular actions are also projected to the sentient neural hub and produce experience. In this way, the brain commands may produce the experience of movement of phantom limbs even though there are no limbs to move and no proprioceptive feedback. Indeed, reports by paraplegics of terrible fatigue due to persistent bicycling movements[16] and the painful fatigue in a tightly clenched phantom fist in arm amputees[17] indicate that feelings of effort and fatigue are produced by the signature of a neuromodule rather than particular input patterns from muscles and joints.

The phenomenon of phantom limbs has allowed us to examine some fundamental assumptions in psychology. One assumption is that sensations are produced only by stimuli and that perceptions in the absence of stimuli are psychologically abnormal. Yet phantom limbs, as well as phantom seeing,[18] indicate this notion is wrong. The brain does more than detect and analyze inputs; it generates perceptual experience even when no external inputs occur.

Another entrenched assumption is that perception of one's body results from sensory inputs that leave a memory in the brain; the total of these signals becomes the body image. But the existence of phantoms in people born without a limb or who have lost a limb at an early age suggests that the neural networks for perceiving the body and its parts are built into the brain.[11,12,19,20] The absence of inputs does not stop the networks from generating messages about missing body parts; they continue to produce such messages throughout life. In short, phantom limbs are a mystery only if we assume the body sends sensory messages to a passively receiving brain. Phantoms become comprehensible once we recognize that the brain generates the experience of the body. Sensory inputs merely modulate that experience; they do not directly cause it.

■ PAIN AND NEUROPLASTICITY

There was no place in the specificity concept of the nervous system for "plasticity," in which neuronal and synaptic functions are capable of being molded or shaped so that they influence subsequent perceptual experiences. Plasticity related to pain represents persistent functional changes, or "somatic memories,"[21,22] produced in the nervous system by injuries or other pathologic events. The recognition that such changes can occur is essential to understanding the chronic pain syndromes, such as low back pain and phantom limb pain, that persist and often destroy the lives of the people who suffer them.

Denervation Hypersensitivity and Neuronal Hyperactivity

Sensory disturbances associated with nerve injury have been closely linked to alterations in CNS function. Markus and associates[23] have demonstrated that the development of hypersensitivity in a rat's hindpaw following sciatic nerve section occurs concurrently with the expansion of the saphenous nerve's somatotopic projection in the spinal cord. Nerve injury may also lead to the development of increased neuronal activity at various levels of the somatosensory system (see review by Coderre and coworkers[24]). In addition to spontaneous activity generated from the neuroma, peripheral neurectomy also leads to increased spontaneous activity in the dorsal root ganglion and spinal cord. Furthermore, after dorsal rhizotomy, there are increases in spontaneous neural activity in the dorsal horn, the spinal trigeminal nucleus, and the thalamus.

Clinical neurosurgery studies reveal a similar relationship between denervation and CNS hyperactivity. Neurons in the somatosensory thalamus of patients with neuropathic pain display high spontaneous firing rates, abnormal bursting activity, and evoked responses to stimulation of body areas that normally do not activate these neurons.[25,26] The site of abnormality in thalamic function appears to be somatotopically related to the painful region. In patients with complete spinal cord transection and dysesthesias referred below the level of the break, neuronal hyperactivity was observed in thalamic regions that had lost their normal sensory input, but not in regions with apparently normal afferent input.[25] In patients with neuropathic pain, electrical stimulation of subthalamic, thalamic and capsular regions may evoke pain[27] and in some instances even reproduce the patient's pain.[28-30] Direct electrical stimulation of spontaneously hyperactive cells evokes pain in some, but not all, pain patients—raising the possibility that in certain patients the observed changes in neuronal activity may contribute to the perception of pain.[25] Studies of patients undergoing electrical brain stimulation during brain surgery reveal that pain is rarely elicited by test stimuli unless the patient suffers from a chronic pain problem. However, brain stimulation can elicit pain responses in patients with chronic pain that does not involve extensive nerve injury or deafferentation. Lenz and colleagues[29] described the case of a woman with unstable angina who, during electrical stimulation of the thalamus, reported "heart pain like what I took nitroglycerin for" except that "it starts and stops suddenly" (p. 121). The possibility that the patient's angina was due to myocardial strain, and not the activation of a somatosensory pain memory, was ruled out by demonstrating that ECG, blood pressure, and cardiac enzymes remained unchanged over the course of stimulation.

It is possible that receptive field expansions and spontaneous activity generated in the CNS following peripheral nerve injury are, in part, mediated by alterations in normal inhibitory processes in the dorsal horn. Within 4 days of a peripheral nerve section there is a reduction in the dorsal root potential, and therefore, in the presynaptic inhibition it represents.[31] Nerve section also induces a reduction in the inhibitory effect of A-fiber stimulation on activity in dorsal horn neurons.[32] Nerve injury affects descending inhibitory controls from brain stem nuclei. In the intact nervous system, stimulation of the locus ceruleus[33] or the nucleus raphe magnus[34] produces an inhibition of dorsal horn neurons. Following dorsal rhizotomy, however, stimulation of these areas produces excitation, rather than inhibition, in one half of the cells studied.[35]

Recent advances in our understanding of the mechanisms that underlie pathologic pain have important implications for the treatment of both acute and chronic pain. Since it has been established that intense noxious stimulation produces a sensitization of CNS neurons, it is possible to direct treatments not only at the site of peripheral tissue damage, but also at the site of central changes (see review by Coderre and Katz[36]). It may be possible in some instances to prevent the development of central sensitization which contributes to pathologic pain states. The evidence that acute postoperative pain intensity and/or the amount of pain medication patients require after surgery are reduced by preoperative administration of a variety of agents *via* the epidural[37-39] or systemic route[40-42] suggests that the surgically induced afferent injury barrage arriving within the CNS, and the central sensitization it induces, can be prevented or at least obtunded significantly (see review by Katz[43]). The reduction in acute pain intensity associated with preoperative epidural anesthesia may even translate into reduced pain[44] and pain disability[45] weeks after patients have left the hospital and returned home.

The fact that amputees are more likely to develop phantom limb pain if there is pain in the limb prior to amputation[22] raises the possibility that the development of longer-term neuropathic pain also can be prevented by reducing the potential for central sensitization at the time of amputation (see Katz and Melzack[46]). Whether chronic postoperative problems such as painful scars, post-thoracotomy chest-wall pain, and phantom limb and stump pain can be reduced by blocking perioperative nociceptive inputs awaits additional well-controlled clinical trials (see Katz[47]). Furthermore, research is required to determine whether multiple-treatment approaches (involving local and epidural anesthesia, as well as pretreatment with opiates and anti-inflammatory drugs) which produce an effective blockade of afferent input may also prevent or relieve other forms of severe chronic pain, such as postherpetic neuralgia[48] and reflex sympathetic dystrophy. It is hoped that a combination of new pharmacologic developments, careful clinical trials, and an increased understanding of the contribution and mechanisms of noxious stimulus-induced neuroplasticity, will lead to improved clinical treatment and prevention of pathologic pain.

■ PAIN AND PSYCHOPATHOLOGY

Pains that do not conform to present day anatomic and neurophysiologic knowledge are often attributed to psychological dysfunction.

There are many pains whose cause is not known. If a diligent search has been made in the periphery and no cause is found, we have seen that clinicians act as though there was only one alternative. They blame faulty thinking, which for many classically thinking doctors is the same thing as saying that there is no cause and even no disease. They ignore a century's work on disorders of the spinal cord and brain stem and target the mind....These are the doctors who repeat again and again to a Second World War amputee in pain that there is nothing wrong with him and that it is all in his head.[49, p 107]

This view of the role of psychological generation in pain persists to this day—notwithstanding evidence to the contrary. Psychopathology has been proposed to underlie phantom limb pain,[17] dyspareunia,[50] orofacial pain,[51] and a host of others including pelvic pain, abdominal pain, chest pain, and headache.[52] However, the complexity of the pain transmission circuitry described in the previous sections means that many pains that defy our current understanding will ultimately be explained without having to resort to a psychopathologic etiology. Pain that is "nonanatomic" in distribution, spread of pain to noninjured territory, pain that is said to be out of proportion to the degree of injury, and pain in the absence of injury have all, at one time or another, been used as evidence to support the idea that psychological disturbance underlies the pain. Yet each of these features of supposed psychopathology can now be explained by neurophysiologic mechanisms that involve an interplay between peripheral and central neural activity.[3,51]

Recent data linking the immune and central nervous systems have provided an explanation for another heretofore medically unexplained pain problem. Mirror-image pain, or *allochira*, has puzzled clinicians and basic scientists ever since it was first documented in the late 1800s.[53] Injury to one side of the body is experienced as pain at the site of injury as well as at the contralateral, mirror-image point.[54,55] Recent animal studies show that induction of a sciatic inflammatory neuritis by perisciatic microinjection of immune system activators results in both an ipsilateral hyperalgesia and hyperalgesia at the mirror-image point on the opposite side in the territory of the contralateral healthy sciatic nerve.[56] Moreover, both the ipsilateral and contralateral hyperalgesia are prevented or reversed by intrathecal injection of a variety of proinflammatory cytokine antagonists.[57]

Mirror-image pain is likely not a unitary phenomenon and other nonimmune mechanisms may also be involved.[58] For example, recent human[59] and animal evidence[60] points to a potential combination of central and peripheral contributions to mirror-image pain because nerve injury to one side of the body has been shown to result in a 50% reduction in the innervation of the territory of the same nerve on the opposite side of the body in uninjured skin.[60] Interestingly, documented contralateral neurite loss can occur in the absence of contralateral pain or hyperalgesia, whereas pain intensity at the site of the injury correlates significantly with the extent of contralateral neurite loss.[59] This raises the intriguing possibility that the intensity of pain at the site of an injury may be facilitated by contralateral neurite loss induced by the ipsilateral injury[60]—a situation that most clinicians would never have imagined possible.

Taken together, these novel mechanisms that explain some of the most puzzling pain symptoms must keep us mindful that emotional distress and psychological disturbance in our patients are not at the root of the pain. Attributing pain to a psychological disturbance is damaging to the patient and provider alike; it poisons the patient-provider relationship by introducing an element of mutual distrust and implicit (and at times, explicit) blame. It is devastating to the patient who feels at fault, disbelieved, and alone.

■ CONCLUSION: THE MULTIPLE DETERMINANTS OF PAIN

The neuromatrix theory of pain proposes that the neurosignature for pain experience is determined by the synaptic architecture of the neuromatrix, which is produced by genetic and sensory influences. The neurosignature pattern is also modulated by sensory inputs and by cognitive events, such as psychological stress.[61] Stressors, physical as well as psychological, act on stress-regulation systems, which may produce lesions of muscle, bone, and nerve tissue, thereby contributing to the neurosignature patterns that give rise to chronic pain. In short, the neuromatrix, as a result of homeostasis-regulation patterns that have failed, may produce the destructive conditions that give rise to many of the chronic pains that so far have been resistant to treatments developed primarily to manage pains that are triggered by sensory inputs. The stress-regulation system, with its complex, delicately balanced interactions, is an integral part of the multiple contributions that give rise to chronic pain.

The neuromatrix theory guides us away from the Cartesian concept of pain as a sensation produced by injury or other tissue pathology and toward the concept of pain as a multidimensional experience produced by multiple influences. These influences range from the existing synaptic architecture of the neuromatrix to influences from within the body and from other areas in the brain. Genetic influences on synaptic architecture may determine—or predispose toward—the development of chronic pain syndromes. Figure 1–3 summarizes the factors that contribute to the output pattern from the neuromatrix that produce the sensory, affective, and cognitive dimensions of pain experience and the resultant behavior.

Multiple inputs act on the neuromatrix programs and contribute to the *output* neurosignature. They include (1) sensory inputs—cutaneous, visceral, and other somatic receptors; (2) visual and other sensory inputs that influence the cognitive interpretation of the situation; (3) phasic and tonic cognitive and emotional inputs from other areas of the brain; (4) intrinsic neural inhibitory modulation inherent in all brain function; and (5) the activity of the body's stress-regulation systems, including cytokines as well as the endocrine, autonomic, immune, and opioid systems. We have traveled a long way from the psychophysical concept that seeks a simple one-to-one relationship between injury and pain. We now have a theoretical framework in which a genetically determined template for the body-self is modulated by the powerful stress system and the cognitive functions of the brain, in addition to the traditional sensory inputs.

References

1. Kuhn TS: The Structure of Scientific Revolutions, 2nd ed. Chicago, University of Chicago Press, 1970.
2. Melzack R, Wall PD: Pain mechanisms: A new theory. Science 150:971, 1965.
3. Melzack R, Wall PD: The Challenge of Pain, 2nd ed. New York, Basic Books, 1996.

4. Goldscheider A: Uber den Schmerzes in physiologischer and klinicher Hinsicht. Berlin, Hirchwald, 1894.
5. Livingston WK: Pain Mechanisms. New York, Macmillan, 1943.
6. Noordenbos W: Pain. Amsterdam, Elsevier, 1959.
7. Melzack R, Casey KL: Sensory, motivational, and central control determinants of pain. In Kenshalo D (eds): The Skin Senses. Springfield, IL, Charles C Thomas, 1968, p 423.
8. Melzack R: The McGill Pain Questionnaire: Major properties and scoring methods. Pain 1:277, 1975.
9. Melzack R: The short-form McGill Pain Questionnaire. Pain 30:191, 1987.
10. Melzack R, Loeser JD: Phantom body pain in paraplegics: Evidence for a central "pattern generating mechanism" for pain. Pain 4:195, 1978.
11. Melzack R: Phantom limbs and the concept of neuromatrix. Trends Neurosci 13:88, 1990.
12. Melzack R: Phantom limbs, the self, and the brain (The D.O. Hebb memorial lecture). Can J Psychol 30:1, 1989.
13. Gybels JM, Tasker RR: Central neurosurgery. In Wall PD, Melzack R, (eds): Textbook of Pain. Edinburgh, Churchill Livingstone, 1999, p 1307.
14. Melzack R: Pain and the neuromatrix in the brain. J Dent Educ 65:1378, 2001.
15. Hebb DO: The Organization of Behavior. New York, Wiley, 1949.
16. Conomy JP: Disorders of body image after spinal cord injury. Neurology 23:842, 1973.
17. Katz J: Individual differences in the consciousness of phantom limbs. In Kunzendorf RG, Wallace B (eds): Individual Differences in Conscious Experience: First-Person Constraints on Theories of Consciousness, Self-Consciousness, and Subconsciousness. Amsterdam, John Benjamins, 2000, p 45.
18. Schultz G, Melzack R: The Charles Bonnet syndrome: "Phantom visual images." Perception 20:809, 1991.
19. Melzack R: Phantom limb pain and the brain. In Bromm B, Desmedt JE (eds): Pain and the brain. New York, Raven, 1995, p 73.
20. Melzack R, Israel R, Lacroix R, et al: Phantom limbs in people with congenital limb deficiency or amputation in early childhood. Brain 120:1603, 1997.
21. Salomons T, Osterman JE, Gagliese L, et al: Pain flashbacks in post-traumatic stress disorder. Clin J Pain 20:83, 2004.
22. Katz J, Melzack R: Pain "memories" in phantom limbs: Review and clinical observations. Pain 43:319, 1990.
23. Markus H, Pomeranz B, Krushelnyky D: Spread of saphenous somatotopic projection map in spinal cord and hypersensitivity of the foot after chronic sciatic denervation in adult rat. Brain Res 296:27, 1984.
24. Coderre TJ, Katz J, Vaccarino AL, et al: Contribution of central neuroplasticity to pathological pain: Review of clinical and experimental evidence. Pain 52:259, 1993.
25. Lenz FA, Tasker RR, Dostrovsky JO, et al: Abnormal single-unit activity recorded in the somatosensory thalamus of a quadriplegic patient with central pain. Pain 31:225, 1987.
26. Lenz FA, Kwan HC, Dostrovsky JO, et al: Characteristics of the bursting pattern of action potential that occurs in the thalamus of patients with central pain. Brain Res 496:357, 1989.
27. Tasker RR: Stereotactic surgery. In Wall PD, Melzack R, (eds): The Textbook of Pain. Edinburgh, Churchill Livingstone, 1989, p 840.
28. Nathan PW: Pain and nociception in the clinical context. Philos Trans R Soc Lond 308:219, 1985.
29. Lenz FA, Gracely RH, Hope EJ, et al.: The sensation of angina can be evoked by stimulation of the human thalamus. Pain 59:119, 1994.
30. Davis KD, Tasker RR, Kiss ZH, et al: Visceral pain evoked by thalamic microstimulation in humans. Neuroreport 6:369, 1995.
31. Wall PD, Devor M: The effect of peripheral nerve injury on dorsal root potentials and on transmission of afferent signals into the spinal cord. Brain Res 209:95, 1981.
32. Woolf CJ, Wall PD: Chronic peripheral nerve section diminishes the primary afferent A-fibre mediated inhibition of rat dorsal horn neurones. Brain Res 242:77, 1982.
33. Segal M, Sandberg D: Analgesia produced by electrical stimulation of catecholamine nuclei in the rat brain. Brain Res 123:369, 1977.
34. Oliveras JL, Guilbaud G, Besson JM: A map of serotoninergic structures involved in stimulation producing analgesia in unrestrained freely moving cats. Brain Res 164:317, 1979.
35. Hodge CJ, Jr., Apkarian AV, Owen MP, et al: Changes in the effects of stimulation of locus coeruleus and nucleus raphe magnus following dorsal rhizotomy. Brain Res 288:325, 1983.
36. Coderre TJ, Katz J: Peripheral and central hyperexcitability: Differential signs and symptoms in persistent pain. Behav Brain Sci 20:404, 1997.
37. Katz J, Cohen L, Schmid R, et al: Postoperative morphine use and hyperalgesia are reduced by preoperative but not intraoperative epidural analgesia: Implications for preemptive analgesia and the prevention of central sensitization. Anesthesiology 98:1449, 2003.
38. Katz J, Clairoux M, Kavanagh BP, et al: Pre-emptive lumbar epidural anaesthesia reduces postoperative pain and patient-controlled morphine consumption after lower abdominal surgery. Pain 59:395, 1994.
39. Katz J, Kavanagh BP, Sandler AN, et al: Preemptive analgesia: Clinical evidence of neuroplasticity contributing to post-operative pain. Anesthesiology 77:439, 1992.
40. Katz J, Clairoux M, Redahan C, et al: High dose alfentanil pre-empts pain after abdominal hysterectomy. Pain 68:109, 1996.
41. Katz J, Schmid R, Snijdelaar DG, et al: Pre-emptive analgesia using intravenous fentanyl plus low-dose ketamine for radical prostatectomy under general anesthesia does not produce short-term or long-term reductions in pain or analgesic use. Pain 110:707, 2004.
42. Snijdelaar DG, Cornelisse HB, Schmid RL, et al: A randomised, controlled study of peri-operative low dose s(+)-ketamine in combination with postoperative patient-controlled s(+)-ketamine and morphine after radical prostatectomy. Anaesthesia 59:222, 2004.
43. Katz J: Timing of treatment and pre-emptive analgesia. In Rowbotham DJ, Macintyre PE, (eds): Acute Pain. London, Arnold Ltd, 2003, p 113.
44. Gottschalk A, Smith DS, Jobes DR, et al: Preemptive epidural analgesia and recovery from radical prostatectomy: A randomized controlled trial. JAMA 279:1076, 1998.
45. Katz J, Cohen L: Preventive analgesia is associated with reduced pain disability three weeks but not six months after abdominal gynecological surgery by laparotomy. Anesthesiology 101:169, 2004.
46. Katz J, Melzack R: Phantom limb pain. In Grafman J, Robertson IH (eds): Handbook of Neuropsychology, 2nd ed. Oxford, Elsevier, 2003, p 205.
47. Katz J: Prevention of phantom limb pain by regional anaesthesia. Lancet 349:519, 1997.
48. Manabe H, Dan K, Hirata K, et al: Optimum pain relief with continuous epidural infusion of local anesthetics shortens the duration of zoster-associated pain. Clin J Pain 20:302, 2004.
49. Wall PD: Pain: The Science of Suffering. London, Weidenfeld & Nicolson, 1999.
50. Meana M, Binik YM: Painful coitus: A review of female dyspareunia. J Nerv Ment Dis 182:264, 1994.
51. Gagliese L, Katz J: Medically unexplained pain is not caused by psychopathology. Pain Res Manag 5:251, 2000.
52. Stoudemire A, Sandhu J: Psychogenic/idiopathic pain syndromes. Gen Hosp Psychiat 9:79, 1987.
53. Basbaum AI: A new way to lose your nerve. Sci Aging Knowledge Environ 2004. 2004: pe15.
54. Livingston WK: Pain and Suffering. Seattle, IASP Press, 1998.
55. Maleki J, LeBel AA, Bennett GJ, et al: Patterns of spread in complex regional pain syndrome, type I (reflex sympathetic dystrophy). Pain 88:259, 2000.
56. Chacur M, Milligan ED, Gazda LS, et al: A new model of sciatic inflammatory neuritis (SIN): Induction of unilateral and bilateral mechanical allodynia following acute unilateral peri-sciatic immune activation in rats. Pain 94:231, 2001.
57. Milligan ED, Twining C, Chacur M, et al: Spinal glia and proinflammatory cytokines mediate mirror-image neuropathic pain in rats. J Neurosci 23:1026, 2003.
58. Koltzenburg M, Wall PD, McMahon SB: Does the right side know what the left is doing? Trends Neurosci 22:122, 1999.
59. Oaklander AL, Romans K, Horasek S, et al: Unilateral postherpetic neuralgia is associated with bilateral sensory neuron damage. Ann Neurol 44:789, 1998.
60. Oaklander AL, Brown JM: Unilateral nerve injury produces bilateral loss of distal innervation. Ann Neurol 55:639, 2004.
61. Melzack R: From the gate to the neuromatrix. Pain Suppl 6:S121, 1999.

Anatomy of the Pain Processing System

Tony L. Yaksh and Z. David Luo

■ ANATOMIC SYSTEMS ASSOCIATED WITH PAIN PROCESSING

Extreme mechanical distortion, thermal stimuli (>42°C), or changes in the chemical milieu (plasma products, pH, K⁺) at the peripheral sensory terminal will evoke the verbal report of pain in humans and efforts to escape in animals, as well as the elicitation of activity in the adrenal-pituitary axis. This chapter provides a broad overview of the circuitry that serves in the transduction and encoding of this information. First, the stimuli already mentioned evoke activity in specific groups of small myelinated or unmyelinated primary afferents of ganglionic sensory neurons, which make their synaptic contact with several distinct populations of dorsal horn neurons. By long spinal tracts and through a variety of intersegmental systems, the information gains access to supraspinal centers that lie in the brain stem and in the thalamus. These rostrally projecting systems represent the substrate by which unconditioned, high-intensity somatic and visceral stimuli give rise to escape behavior and verbal report of pain. This circuitry constitutes the afferent limb of the pain pathway.

■ PRIMARY AFFERENTS[1-3]

Fiber Classes

Sensory neurons in dorsal root ganglia have a single process that bifurcates into peripheral and central axons. The peripheral axon collects sensory input from a receptor in the innervated tissue, whereas the central axon relays sensory input to the spinal cord or brain stem. Sensory axons are classified according to their diameter, state of myelination, and conduction velocity, as outlined in Table 2–1. In general, conduction velocity varies directly with axon diameter and presence of myelination. Thus Aß axons are large and myelinated and rapidly conducting, whereas C fibers are small and unmyelinated and slowly conducting.

Properties of Primary Afferent Function

Recording from single peripheral afferent fibers reveals three important characteristics. First, in the absence of stimulation there is minimal, if any, "spontaneous" afferent traffic. Accordingly, the system operates on a very high signal-to-noise ratio. Second, regardless of the fiber type examined, with increasing intensities of the appropriate stimulus, there will be a monotonic increase in the discharge frequency for that axon (Fig. 2–1). This reflects the fact that the more intense the stimulus, the greater is the depolarization of the terminal and the more frequently will the axon discharge. Third, different axons may respond most efficiently to a particular stimulus modality. This modality specificity reflects the nature of the terminal properties of the particular afferent axon that transduces the physical or chemical stimulus into a depolarization of the axon. These nerve endings may be morphologically specialized, as with the pacinian corpuscle that is found on the terminals of large afferents. The specialized structure translates the mechanical distortion of the structure into a transient opening of sodium channels in that axon, generating a brief burst of action potential. At the other extreme, the axon terminal may display no evident physical structure and be classified as a "free nerve ending." Such endings are commonly associated with small unmyelinated C fibers. The simplicity of the nerve ending as implied by this name is misleading. Such a terminal is often able to transduce a variety of stimuli including mechanical, thermal, and chemical. As indicated in Table 2–1, A-beta (group II) fibers are activated by low threshold mechanical stimuli (i.e., mechanoreceptors). Fibers that conduct at A-delta velocity (group III fibers) may belong to populations that are low or high threshold, and mechanical or thermal. Low-threshold afferents may begin firing at temperatures that are not noxious (30°C) and increase their firing rate monotonically—although in this range, we perceive the stimulus as warm but not noxious. Other populations of A-delta fibers may begin to show activation at temperatures that are mildly noxious and increase their firing rates up to very high temperatures (52°C to 55°C). Slowly conducting afferents constitute the largest population of afferent axons. The large majority of these afferents are activated by high-threshold thermal, mechanical, and chemical stimuli and are called *C-polymodal nociceptors* (see Fig. 2–1).

Table 2–1

Classification of Primary Afferents by Physical Characteristics, Conduction Velocity, and Effective Stimuli

Fiber Class*	Velocity Group*	Effective Stimuli
A-beta	Group II (>40-50 m/sec)	Low-threshold Specialized nerve endings (pacinian corpuscles)
A-delta	Group III (>10 and <40 m/sec)	Low-threshold mechanical or thermal High-threshold mechanical or thermal Specialized nerve endings
C	Group IV (<2 m/sec)	High-threshold thermal, mechanical, or chemical Free nerve endings

*The Erlanger-Gasser A-beta/A-delta/C classification scheme is based on anatomic characteristics. The Lloyd-Hunt group II/III/IV classification scheme is based on conduction velocity in muscle afferents.

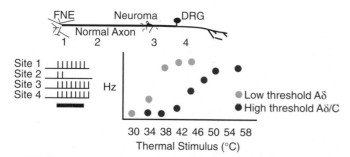

FIGURE 2–1 ■ *Top:* Schema of C fiber with peripheral free nerve ending (FNE; a region of normal axon and a local injury (neuroma) and the dorsal root ganglion (DRG). In this schema a pressure stimulus is applied to the axon at the four sites (FNE, normal axon, neuroma, and DRG), and the characteristic response is displayed in lower left cartoon. Importantly, the normal axon does not transduce the continued mechanical distortion, whereas such transduction does occur at sites 1, 3, and 4. On the *lower right*, it is indicated that low-threshold Aδ and high-threshold Aδ/C fibers typically show little if any spontaneous activity; both will show a monotonic increase in response to increasing stimulus intensities. The low-threshold axon shows a monotonic increase over a range of intensities that are not aversive. This would be a "warmth" detector. The C fiber, however, does not begin to discharge until a temperature is reached that would correspond with the behavioral report of increasing pain. This response pattern would describe that of a nociceptor.

An important characteristic of these polymodal nociceptors is that they are readily activated in a concentration-dependent fashion by specific agents released into the chemical milieu. Such agents, released from local injured cells or inflammatory cells, include a variety of amines (5HT, histamine), lipid mediators (prostaglandins), kinins (bradykinin), acidic pH, cytokines (IL-1ß) and enzymes (trypsin). Such products can evoke direct activation of the fibers and facilitate their activity. This probably represents the principal mechanism of activating afferents after the acute injury. The nature of these products is discussed later.

Afferents with High Thresholds and Pain Behavior

Electrophysiologic and correlated behavioral evidence indicate that information that can generate a pain event enters the central nervous system by the activation of small-diameter, myelinated (group III-A or A-delta) or unmyelinated (group IV or C) afferents. Thus, single-unit recording in nerve fascicles in humans reveals a close correlation between the dull pain induced by a focal high-intensity thermal stimulus (second pain) and activity in fibers conducting at velocities of less than 1 m/sec. Similarly, local anesthetics at low concentrations transiently block conduction in small, but not large, afferents—thus blocking the sensation evoked by high-threshold stimuli and leaving light touch intact. The afferent axons, particularly those derived from unmyelinated fibers, show extensive branching as they proceed distally, and the majority of the peripheral terminals of small afferents show little evidence of specialization, terminating as "free" nerve endings. Ample evidence exists to indicate that these "free" nerve endings, commonly designated as *polymodal nociceptors,* are characteristically activated only by high-intensity physical stimuli, and this property accounts for the peripheral specificity associating A-delta/C fiber activity with pain. This transduction specificity is best exemplified in tooth pulp and cornea, where "free" nerve endings predominate and local stimulation is painful.

Under certain conditions, low-intensity tactile or thermal stimuli may, in fact, generate a pain state. This anomalous linkage between noninjurious stimuli and pain is referred to as *hyperalgesia.* More specifically, when it involves light mechanical stimuli it is referred to as *tactile allodynia.* Three practical examples may be cited: (1) local tissue injury as after a local sunburn leading to increased thermal and tactile sensitivity; (2) inflammation as in rheumatoid arthritis leading to a state where normal joint movement is painful; and (3) injury to the peripheral nerve leading to states where light touch is aversive.

■ SPINAL DORSAL HORN[4-6]

Afferent Projections

In the peripheral nerve, large and small afferents are anatomically intermixed in collections of fascicles. As the nerve root approaches the spinal cord, there is a tendency for the large myelinated afferents to move medially and to displace the small, unmyelinated afferents laterally. Thus, although this pattern is not absolute, large and small afferent axons enter the dorsal horn via the medial and lateral aspects of the dorsal root entry zone (DREZ), respectively. An appreciable number of unmyelinated afferent fibers that arise from dorsal root ganglion cells also exist within the *ventral* roots, and these *ventral root afferents* likely account for the pain reports evoked by ventral root stimulation in classic clinical studies.

The sensory innervation of the body projects in a rostrocaudal distribution to the ipsilateral spinal dorsal horn. Innervation of the head and neck is mediated by a variety of cranial nerves that project into the brain stem.

Anatomy of the Dorsal Horn

In the rostrocaudal axis, the spinal cord is broadly divided into the sacral, lumbar, thoracic, and cervical segments. At each spinal level, in the transverse plane, the spinal cord is further divided on the basis of descriptive anatomy into several laminae (*Rexed laminae*) (Table 2–2 and Fig. 2–2).

On entering the spinal cord, the central processes of the primary afferents send their projections into the dorsal horn. In general, terminals from the small myelinated fibers (A-delta) terminate in the marginal zone or lamina I of Rexed, the ventral portion of lamina II (II inner), and throughout lamina V. Larger myelinated fibers (A-beta) terminate in lamina IV and deep dorsal horn (laminae V to VI). Fine-caliber, unmyelinated C fibers generally terminate throughout laminae I and II and in lamina X around the central canal.

In addition to sending their axons into the dorsal horn at the segment of entry, primary afferents also collateralize sending axons rostrally and caudally into the tract of Lissauer (small unmyelinated fibers) and into the dorsal columns (large myelinated axons). These collateralize at intervals to send projections into increasingly distal segments. This organizational property emphasizes that input from a single root may primarily activate cells in the segment of entry but can also influence the excitability of neurons in segments distal to the segment of entry (Fig. 2–3).

■ DORSAL HORN NEURONS[6-8]

Although exceedingly complex, the second-order nociresponsive elements in the dorsal horn may be considered in several principal classes on the basis of their approximate anatomic location and their response properties.

Table 2–2

Principal Aspects of Dorsal Horn Organization

Anatomic Region	Rexed Lamina(e)	Afferent Terminals	Nociceptive Cells
Marginal layer	I	A-delta/CA-beta	Marginal
Substantia gelatinosa	II	A-beta/A-delta/C	SG
Nucleus proprius	III/IV/V/VI	A-beta/A-delta	WDR
Central canal	X	A-delta/C	SG-type
Motor horn	VII/VIII/IX	A-betax	

SG, substantia gelatinosa; WDR, wide dynamic range.

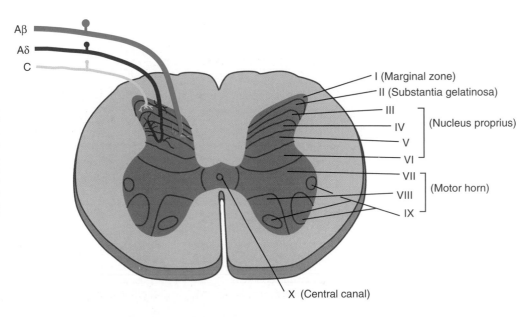

FIGURE 2–2 ■ Schematic showing the Rexed lamination *(right)* and the approximate organization of the afferents to the spinal cord *(left)* as they enter at the dorsal root entry zone and then penetrate into the dorsal horn to terminate in the laminae I and II (Aδ/C) or penetrate more deeply to loop upward and terminate as high as lamina III (Aβ). *Photo inset* shows a left dorsal horn with the root entry zone.

Aβ
Aδ
C

I (Marginal zone)
II (Substantia gelatinosa)
III
IV — (Nucleus proprius)
V
VI
VII
VIII — (Motor horn)
IX

X (Central canal)

Distribution of Afferent Terminals

A Fiber: Laminae III-V
Trifurcate: Segment of entry
    Dorsal Column

C Fiber: Laminae I-II
Trifurcate: Segment of entry
    Lissauer Tract

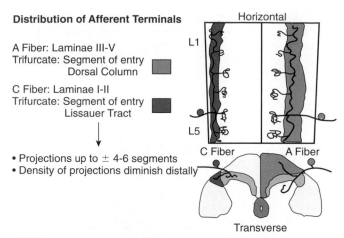

• Projections up to ± 4-6 segments
• Density of projections diminish distally

FIGURE 2–3 ■ Schematic displaying the ramification of C fibers *(left)* into the dorsal horn and collateralization into the tract of Lissauer *(stippled* area) and of A fibers *(right)* into the dorsal columns *(striped* area) and into the dorsal horn. Note that the most dense terminations are within the segment of entry and that collateralizations into the dorsal horns at the more distal spinal segments are less dense. This density of collateralization corresponds to the potency of the excitatory drive into these distal segments.

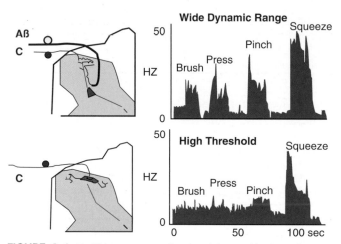

FIGURE 2–4 ■ Firing patterns of a dorsal horn wide dynamic range (WDR) neuron and a high-threshold spinothalamic neuron. Graphs present the neuronal responses to graded intensities of mechanical stimulation applied to the receptive fields.

Anatomic Localization

Marginal Zone (Lamina I)

These large neurons are oriented transversely across the cap of the dorsal gray matter (Fig. 2–4). Consistent with their locations, they receive input from mainly A-delta and C fibers and respond to intense cutaneous and muscle stimulation. Marginal neurons project to the contralateral thalamus and to the parabracheal region via the contralateral ventrolateral tracts (see later) of ascending pathways. Other marginal neurons project intrasegmentally and intersegmentally along the dorsal and dorsolateral white matter.

Substantia Gelatinosa (Lamina II)

The substantia gelatinosa contains numerous cell types. Many cells are local interneurons and likely play an important role

as inhibitory and excitatory interneurons that regulate local excitability; however, a number of these cells clearly project rostrally. A significant proportion of the substantia gelatinosa neurons receive direct input from C fibers and indirect input from A-delta fibers from lamina I and deep dorsal horn. These neurons are frequently excited by activation of thermal receptive or mechanical nociceptive afferents. Many of these cells exhibit complex response patterns with prolonged periods of excitation and inhibition following afferent activation and reflect the complicated network that regulates local excitability by local interneurons.

Nucleus Proprius (Laminae III, IV, and V)

These are magnocellular neurons that send their dendritic tree up into the overlying laminae (see Fig. 2–4). Consistent with this organization many cells in this region receive large afferent (Aß) input onto its cell body and dendrites. In addition, these neurons receive input either directly or through excitatory interneurons, from small afferents (Aα and C) which terminate in the superficial dorsal horn.

Central Canal (Lamina X)

Branches of small primary afferent fibers enter the region. This area is a peptide-rich area, and cells respond primarily to high-threshold temperature stimuli and noxious pinch with small receptive fields. Cells in this region also receive significant visceral input.

Functional Properties

Two important functional classes of neurons are frequently described: nociceptive specific and wide dynamic range (WDR).

Nociceptive Specific

Lamina I neurons tend to receive primary high-threshold input. Starting at relatively high stimulus intensities, these cells begin to show a threshold increase in discharge that is increased over the increasingly aversive range of stimulus intensities (see Fig. 2–4). In that manner, many of these cells are "nociceptive specific."

Wide Dynamic Range Neurons

Many cells in the nucleus proprius have three interesting functional characteristics:

(1) Given their connectivity, the neurons display excitation driven by low- and high-threshold afferent input. This gives the WDR neurons the property of responding with increased frequency as the stimulus intensity is elevated; they have a wide dynamic response range. Light innocuous touch evokes activity that increases as the intensity of pressure or pinch is increased (see Fig. 2–4). In addition to this property, the WDR neurons have two other characteristics.

(2) Organ convergence: Depending on the spinal level, a neuron in the nucleus proprius may be activated by both somatic stimuli and by activation of visceral afferent. This convergence results in a comingling of excitation for a visceral organ and a specific area of the body surface and leads to input from that visceral organ being referred to that area of the body surface. A given population of WDR

neurons are excited by cutaneous or deep (muscle and joint) input applied within the dermatome coinciding with the segmental location of the cell. Thus, T_1 and T_5 root stimulation activates WDR neurons that are also excited by coronary artery occlusion. These viscerosomatic and musculosomatic convergences onto dorsal horn neurons underlie the phenomenon of referred visceral or deep muscle or bone pain to particular body surfaces (Fig. 2–5).

(3) Low-frequency (above 0.33 Hz) repetitive stimulation of C fibers, but not A fibers, produces a gradual increase in the frequency discharge until the neuron is in a state of virtually continuous discharge ("wind-up"). This property will be discussed later.

▪ ASCENDING SPINAL TRACTS[6-9]

Activity evoked in the spinal cord by high-threshold stimuli reaches supraspinal sites by several long and intersegmental tract systems that travel within the ventrolateral cord and to a lesser degree in the dorsal quadrant.

Ventral Funicular Projection Systems

Within the ventrolateral quadrant of the spinal cord, several systems have been identified, on the basis of their supraspinal projections. These include spinoreticular, spinomesencephalic, and spinothalamic tracts (anterolateral system), and the recently identified spinoparabrachial tract. These systems are originated primarily from the dorsal horn neurons that are postsynaptic to primary afferents. These cells may project either ipsilaterally or contralaterally from the spinal cord. Classic studies have shown that unilateral section of the ventrolateral quadrant yields a contralateral loss in pain and temperature sense in dermatomes below the spinal level of the section, indicating that the ascending tracts may travel rostrally several segments before crossing. These findings led to the surgical ventrolateral cordotomy which was used in the early 20th century as an important method of pain control. Conversely, stimulation of the ventrolateral tracts in awake subjects undergoing percutaneous cordotomies results in reports of contralateral warmth and pain. Midline myelo-

tomies that destroy fibers crossing the midline at the levels of the cut (as well as the cells in lamina X) produce bilateral pain deficits. These observations suggest that predominantly crossed pathways are important for nociception.

Dorsal Funicular Projection Systems

The dorsal column medial lemniscal system is a major ascending pathway transmitting sensory information. This system is mainly composed of the collaterals of larger-diameter primary afferents transmitting tactile sensation and limb proprioception, Most fibers in the medial lemniscal system ascend from the spinal cord *ipsilaterally* to the medulla where they synapse on neurons in the caudal brain stem dorsal column nuclei, which send axons across the medulla to form the medial lemniscus.

Intersegmental Systems

Early studies showed that alternating hemisections poorly modify the behavioral or the autonomic responses to strong stimuli. Systems that project for short distances ipsilaterally may contribute to the rostrad transmission of nociceptive information. Several segmental pathways relevant to the rostrad transmission of nociceptive information are the lateral tract of Lissauer, the dorsolateral propriospinal system, and the dorsal intracornual tract. Selective destruction of the dorsal gray matter (e.g., in the vicinity of the DREZ), has proved to be a possible method of pain management, suggesting the relevance of nonfunicular pathways traveling in the spinal gray matter.

▪ SUPRASPINAL PROJECTIONS[10-12]

Spinofugal tracts traveling in the ventrolateral quadrant project principally into three brain stem regions: the medulla, the mesencephalon, and the diencephalon. Neurons in these regions then project further rostrally to the diencephalon and cortex or directly to cortical structures.

Spinoreticulothalamic Projections

This tract represents axons that are largely ipsilateral to the cell of origin. The tract terminates throughout the brain stem reticular formation. Spinomedullary input is believed to play an important role in initiating cardiovascular reflexes. The medullary reticular formation also performs as a 'relay' station for the rostrad transmission of nociceptive information. These medullary neurons project into the intralaminar thalamic nucleus. This forms a shell around the medial dorsal aspects of the thalamus (Fig. 2–6). The intralaminar nucleus projects diffusely to wide areas of the cerebral cortex, including the frontal, parietal, and limbic regions. This forms part of the classic ascending reticular activating system and relates to mechanisms leading to increased global cortical activation (Fig. 2–7).

Spinomesencephalic Projections

Ipsilateral projections to this region terminate in periaqueductal gray (PAG) and mesencephalic reticular formation. Stimu-

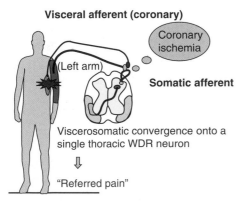

Visceral afferent (coronary)

Coronary ischemia

(Left arm)

Somatic afferent

Viscerosomatic convergence onto a single thoracic WDR neuron

⇩

"Referred pain"

FIGURE 2–5 ▪ Example of organ convergence: T_1 and T_5 root stimulation activates WDR neurons that are also excited by coronary artery occlusion. These results indicate that the phenomenon of referred visceral pain has its substrate in the viscerosomatic and musculosomatic convergence onto dorsal horn neurons.

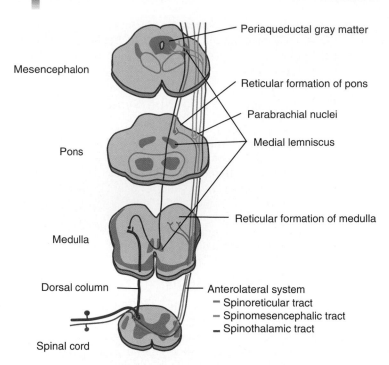

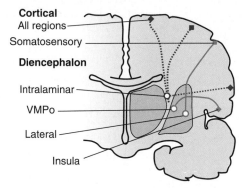

FIGURE 2–6 ■ Schematic demonstrating the brain stem projections of spinal neurons into the medulla and mesencephalon. Third-order projections arising from the medullary and mesencephalic neurons project into the intralaminar and ventrobasal thalamus.

FIGURE 2–7 ■ Schematic displaying projections from thalamic neurons to various cortical regions. See text for further discussion.

lation of the mesencephalic central gray and adjacent mesencephalic reticular formation can evoke signs of intense discomfort in animals, whereas in humans autonomic responses are elicited along with reports of dysphoria. As with more caudal medullary sites, PAG and reticular neurons project rostrally into the lateral thalamus (see Figs. 2–6 and 2–7).

Spinoparabrachial Projections

These ascending nociceptive fibers originate predominantly from neurons in contralateral laminae. Projections of these neurons terminate in a group of neurons in the parabrachial area that send out axons to the central nucleus of the amygdala and the posterior portion of the ventral medial nucleus (VMpo) in the thalamus. The VMpo projects primarily to the insula (Fig. 2–8).

Spinothalamic Projections

This predominantly crossed system displays the following three principal targets of termination (Fig. 2–9):

(1) The ventrobasal thalamus represents the classic somatosensory thalamic nucleus. Input is distributed in a strict somatotopic pattern. This region projects in a strict somatotopic organization to the somatosensory cortex (see Fig. 2–7).
(2) The VMpo then projects into the insula.
(3) The mediodorsalis nucleus receives primary input from lamina I (high-threshold nociceptive specific cells). Cells in this region then project to the anterior cingulate cortex (Fig. 2–10).

■ FUNCTIONAL OVERVIEW OF PAIN PROCESSING SYSTEMS

In the preceding text, we have considered a variety of elements that constitute linkages whereby information generated by a high-intensity stimulus activates small high-threshold afferents and activates brain stem and cortical systems. With a broad perspective, we may emphasize several salient features of this system activated by high-threshold input.

Frequency Encoding

It appears evident that stimulus intensity is encoded in terms of frequency of discharge. This holds true for any given link at the level of the primary afferent for both high- and low-threshold axons, in the spinal dorsal horn for WDR, marginal neurons, and at brain stem and cortical loci. The relation between stimulus intensity and the neuronal response is in the form of a monotonic increase in discharge frequency.

Supraspinal Projections
Spinoparabrachial
projection systems

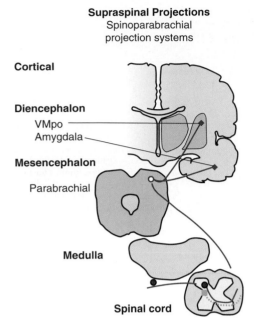

Cortical

Diencephalon
VMpo
Amygdala

Mesencephalon

Parabrachial

Medulla

Spinal cord

FIGURE 2–8 ■ Schematic demonstrating the spinal neuron projections into the parabrachial region and third-order parabrachial neurons projecting into the thalamus and amygdala.

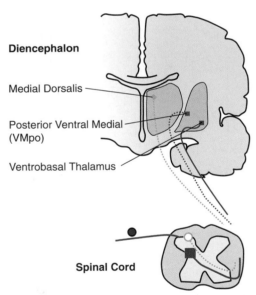

Diencephalon

Medial Dorsalis

Posterior Ventral Medial
(VMpo)

Ventrobasal Thalamus

Spinal Cord

FIGURE 2–9 ■ Schematic demonstrating spinal lamina V wide dynamic range neurons projecting into the ventrobasal thalamus and lamina I neurons (high threshold) projecting into the posterior ventral medial nucleus and medial dorsalis neurons.

Afferent Line Labeling

Although frequency of discharge covaries with intensity, it is evident that it is the nature of the connectivity that also defines the content of the afferent activity. As indicated, the biological significance of a high-frequency burst of an Aß versus a high-threshold Aδ or C fiber for pain is evident.

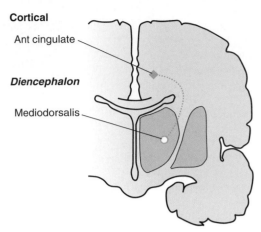

Cortical

Ant cingulate

Diencephalon

Mediodorsalis

FIGURE 2–10 ■ Schematic demonstrating mediodorsalis neurons projecting into the anterior cingulate gyrus.

Functionally Distinct Pathways

At the spinal level, it is possible to characterize two functionally distinct families of response. In one spinofugal projection system (Fig. 2–11), WDR neurons encode information over a wide range of non-noxious to severely aversive intensities consistent with the convergence of low- and high-threshold afferent neurons (either directly or through interneurons) onto their dendrites and soma. These cells project heavily into a variety of brain stem and diencephalic sites to the somatosensory cortex. At every level, the map of the body surface is precisely preserved and the broad range of intensity-frequency encoding is preserved. In the second spinofugal projection system (Fig. 2–12), populations of superficial marginal cells display a strong nociceptive-specific encoding property, as defined by the high-threshold afferent input that they receive. These marginal cells project heavily to the parabrachial nuclei, then to the amygdala, to the VMpo, the insula, the mediodorsalis, and then to the anterior cingulate cortex.

The WDR system is uniquely able to preserve spatial localization information and information regarding the stimulus over a range of intensities from modest to extreme, as initially provided by the frequency response characteristics of the WDR neurons. This type of system is able to provide the information needed for mapping the "sensory-discriminative" dimension of pain. The nociceptive-specific pathway arising from the marginal cells appears less well organized in terms of its ability to encode precise place and response intensity until it is, by definition, potentially tissue injuring. These systems project heavily through the mediodorsal region and VMpo to the anterior cingulate and the insula/amygdala, respectively. These regions are classically appreciated to be associated with emotionality and affect. Accordingly, this type of circuitry would provide an important substrate for systems underlying the affective-motivational components of the pain experience. Functional magnetic resonance imaging and positron-emission tomography have demonstrated that although non-noxious stimuli have no effect, strong somatic and visceral stimuli will initiate activation within the anterior cingulate cortex. A variety of lesions in humans and animals

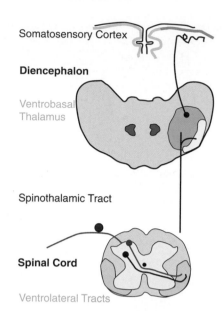

Cortical
SS cortex: **Precise map**
(place/intensity/modality)

Thalamocortical projections
VBL -> Somatosensory cortex

Ascending thalamic projections
Lam V-> Ventrobasal (VBL)
Precise anatomical mapping

Ascending axons in VLT
Spinothalamic

Spinofugal projections
Lam V: WDR-intensity encoded
High degree of localization

FIGURE 2–11 ■ Schematic of an overview of the characteristics of the projections of wide dynamic range (WDR) lamina V (Lam V) neurons in to the somatotopically mapped ventrobasal (VBL) thalamus and from there to the somatosensory (SS) cortex. As described in the text, this organization suggests the properties that would mediate the "sensory-discriminative "aspects of pain.

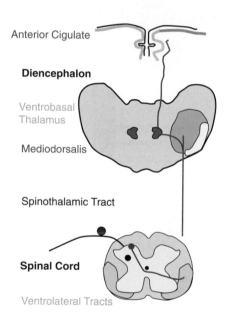

Cortical
Anterior Cingulate: **Limbic-emotion**

Thalamocortical projections
Submedius -> Anterior Cingulate

Ascending thalamic projections
Lam I -> mediodorsalis (?)

Ascending axons in VLT
Spinothalamic

Spinofugal projections
Lam I: Marginal-nociceptive specific
Poor spatial encoding

FIGURE 2–12 ■ Schematic of an overview of the characteristics of the projections of nociceptive-specific lamina I (Lam I) neurons into the mediodorsalis and from there to the anterior cingulate (Ant cingulate) cortex. As described in the text, this organization suggests the properties that would mediate the "affective motivational" aspects of pain.

have been shown to psychophysically dissociate the reported stimulus intensity from its affective component. Such disconnection syndromes are produced by prefrontal lobectomies, cingulotomies, and temporal lobe-amygdala lesions.

Plasticity of Ascending Projections

While the pathways outlined are clearly pertinent to the nature of the message generated by a high-intensity stimulus, the encoding of a pain message depends not only on the physical characteristics of the otherwise effective stimulus but also on the properties of associated systems that can modulate (either up or down) the excitability of each of these synaptic linkages. Thus, local interneurons releasing GABA and glycine at the level of the spinal dorsal horn commonly regulate the frequency of discharge of second-order neurons excited by large afferent input. Pharmacologically blocking

that local spinal inhibition can profoundly change the nature of the sensory experience to become highly aversive in character.

■ PHARMACOLOGY OF AFFERENT TRANSMITTER SYSTEMS IN NOCICEPTION[13-16]

An important question relates to the nature of the neurotransmitters and receptors that link the afferent projection systems. Such transmitter-receptor systems have several defining characteristics. First, the linkages between the primary afferent and second-order spinal neurons, the linkages between the spinofugal axon and the third-order axon, and so on, have as a common property that the interaction leads to the excitation of the approximate neurons, Thus, the neurotransmitters mediating that synaptic transmission will be excitatory in character. For example, at the spinal level there is no "monosynaptic inhibition driven by primary afferents." Although there are powerful inhibitory events that occur in the dorsal horn (and at every synaptic link), such inhibition must occur because of the excitation of a second neuron that releases an inhibitory transmitter. Second, it is increasingly evident that neurotransmission at any given synaptic link may consist not of one transmitter but of several co-contained and co-released transmitters. At the small primary afferent there is typically the release of an excitatory amino acid (glutamate) and a peptide (e.g., substance P [SP]). Third, although not discussed further here, each synaptic link is subject to modifications because of a dynamic regulation of the presynaptic transmitter content and the postsynaptic receptor and its linkages (e.g., with repetitive stimulation, the glutamate receptor undergoes phosphorylation, which serves to accentuate its excitatory response to a given amount of glutamate).

Primary Afferent Transmitters

Considerable effort has been directed at establishing the identity of the excitatory transmitters in the primary afferent transmitters. Some of these are listed in Table 2–3. Antagonists of the neurotransmitter released from polymodal C fibers would provide a direct method to intervene in the transmission of the pain message. Currently, excitatory amino acids, such as glutamate and a number of peptides, including SP, vasoactive intestinal peptide (VIP), somatostatin, a VIP homolog (phosphohexoisomerase, PHI), CGRP, bombesin, and related peptides have been observed to possess the following characteristics (Fig. 2–13):

- Peptides have been shown to exist within subpopulations of small type B dorsal root ganglion cells.
- Peptides are in the dorsal horn of the spinal cord (where the majority of primary afferent terminals are found), and these levels in the dorsal horn are reduced by rhizotomy and/or ganglionectomy or by treatment with the small afferent neurotoxin capsaicin.

- Many peptides are co-contained (e.g., SP and CGRP in the same C fiber terminal) as well as contained with excitatory amino acids (e.g., SP and glutamate).
- Release of peptides is reduced by the spinal action of agents known to be analgesic, such as opiates and α_2-agonists (see later).
- Iontophoretic application onto the dorsal horn of the several amino acids and peptides found in primary afferents has been shown to produce excitatory effects. Amino acids produce a very rapid, short-lasting depolarization. The peptides tend to produce a delayed and long-lasting discharge.
- Local spinal administration of several agents such as SP and glutamate does yield pain behavior, suggesting their possible role as transmitters in the pain process.

Receptor antagonists for some of these agents (sP, VIP, glutamate) exist, but few have significant affinity or specificity. Substance P antagonists have been shown to have some analgesic activity after spinal administration. However, given

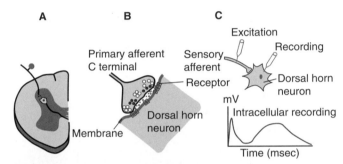

FIGURE 2–13 ■ Schematic displays the general characteristics of the primary afferent transmitters released from small, capsaicin-sensitive, primary afferents: C fibers. **A,** Small afferents terminate in laminae I and II of the dorsal horn and make synaptic contact with second-order spinal neurons. **B,** Peptides and excitatory amino acids are co-contained in small primary afferent ganglion cells (type B) and in dorsal horn terminals in dense core and clear core vesicles, respectively. **C,** On release, the excitatory amino acids are able to produce a rapid, early depolarization, whereas the peptides tend to evoke a long and prolonged depolarization of the second-order membrane. mV: transmembrane potential.

Table 2–3

Representative Putative Neurotransmitters in Small Primary Afferents

Transmitter Hyperesthesia	Small DRG	Capsaicin Depletion	k⁺Release	Neuronal Excitation
Peptides				
Substance P	+	+	Yes	Yes
CGRP	+	+	Yes	Yes
Somatostatin	+	+	Yes	Yes/No
Bombesin	+	+	Yes	Yes
Galanin	+	+	Yes	?
VIP	+	+	Yes	?
CCK	+/?	+	Yes	?
Excitatory Amino Acids				
Glutamate	+	0	Yes	+++
Aspartate	?	?	Yes	+++

Algesic behavior observed after spinal administration.
CCK, cholecystokinin; DRG, dorsal root ganglion; K, high potassium, ?, not known; VIP, vasoactive intestinal peptide.

the complexity of the transmitters which may excite a given cell, it is evident that nociceptive information is processed by a variety of excitatory transmitters.

Ascending Projection System Transmitters

Dorsal horn neurons projecting to brain-stem sites have been shown to contain a variety of peptides (including cholecystokinin, dynorphin, somatostatin, bombesin, VIPs, and SP). Glutamate has also been identified in spinothalamic projections, suggesting the probable role of that excitatory amino acid. SP-containing fibers arising from brain-stem sites have been shown to project to the parafascicular and central medial nuclei of the thalamus. In unanesthetized animals, the microinjection of glutamate in the vicinity of the terminals of ascending pathways, notably within the mesencephalic central gray area, evokes spontaneous pain-like behavior with vocalization and vigorous efforts to escape, emphasizing the presence of at least an *N*-methyl-D-aspartate (NMDA) site mediating the behavioral effects produced by NMDA in this region. Other systems will no doubt be identified as these supraspinal systems are studied in detail.

References

1. Raja SN, Meyer RA, Campbell JN: Peripheral mechanisms of somatic pain. Anesthesiology 68:571, 1988.
2. Koltzenburg M: Neural mechanisms of cutaneous nociceptive pain. Clin J Pain 16(Suppl 3):S131, 2000.
3. Wood JN: Recent advances in understanding molecular mechanisms of primary afferent activation. Gut 53(Suppl 2):9, 2004.
4. Morris R, Cheunsuang O, Stewart A, Maxwell D: Dorsal horn neurone targets for nociceptive primary afferents: Do single neurone morphological characteristics suggest how nociceptive information is processed at the spinal level. Brain Res Rev 46:173, 2004.
5. Todd AJ: Anatomy of primary afferents and projection neurones in the rat spinal dorsal horn with particular emphasis on substance P and the neurokinin 1 receptor. Exp Physiol 87:245, 2002.
6. Willis WD, Westlund KN: Neuroanatomy of the pain system and of the pathways that modulate pain. J Clin Neurophysiol 14:2, 1997.
7. Craig AD: Pain mechanisms: Labeled lines versus convergence in central processing. Annu Rev Neurosci 26:1, 2003.
8. Lu GW, Willis WD: Branching and/or collateral projections of spinal dorsal horn neurons. Brain Res Rev 29:50, 1999.
9. Willis WD, Jr, Westlund KN: The role of the dorsal column pathway in visceral nociception. Curr Pain Headache Rep 5:20, 2001.
10. Dostrovsky JO: Role of thalamus in pain. Prog Brain Res 129:245, 2000.
11. Price DD: Psychological and neural mechanisms of the affective dimension of pain. Science 288:1769, 2000.
12. Vogt BA: Pain and emotion interactions in subregions of the cingulate gyrus. Nat Rev Neurosci 6:533, 2005.
13. Mantyh PW: Neurobiology of substance P and the NK1 receptor. J Clin Psychiatry 63(Suppl 11):6, 2002.
14. Yaksh TL: Central pharmacology of nociceptive transmission. In McMahon S, Koltzenburg M (eds): Wall and Melzak's Textbook of Pain, 5th ed. Philadelphia, Churchill Livingstone, 2006, p 371.
15. Todd AJ, Spike RC: Localization of classical transmitters and neuropeptides within neurons in laminae I-III of the mammalian spinal dorsal horn. Prog Neurobiol 41:609, 1993.
16. Julius D, Basbaum AI: Molecular mechanisms of nociception. Nature 413:203, 2001.

chapter 3

Dynamics of the Pain Processing System

Tony L. Yaksh

Primary afferent input results in the activation of a number of circuits at the spinal and supraspinal levels. As reviewed in Chapter 2, there are multiple linkages in these systems. An important consequence of research in the past decade has been the appreciation that afferent input at each synaptic link is subject to modulation by a variety of specific inputs. The net result is that the response evoked by a given stimulus is subject to a variety of well-defined influences that can serve to attenuate or enhance the excitation produced by a given physical stimulus. Specifically, these interactive systems alter the encoding of the afferent message and thereby change the perceived characteristics of the stimulus.

For sake of discussion, the processing of nociceptive information may be considered in terms of the pain behavior that arises from the following three conditions: (1) the behavior evoked by an acute activation of a high-threshold, slowly conducting afferent; (2) the exaggerated pain behavior (hyperalgesia/hyperesthesia) generated following local tissue injury or inflammation; and (3) the hyperalgesia that results secondary to a local peripheral nerve injury. The pharmacology and physiology of these dynamic states will be reviewed subsequently.

ACUTE ACTIVATION OF AFFERENT PAIN PROCESSING[1]

Acute activation of small afferents by a transient, non-injurious stimulus results in a clearly defined pain behavior in humans and animals. This event is mediated by the local stimulus-evoked activation of small high-threshold afferents leading to the release of excitatory afferent transmitters outlined previously (see Chapter 2) and, consequently, the depolarization of spinal projection neurons. The organization of this acutely driven system is typically modeled in terms of a linear relationship between stimulus intensity, activity in the peripheral afferent, the magnitude of spinal transmitter release, and the activity of neurons that project out of the spinal cord to the brain (Fig. 3–1).

TISSUE INJURY-INDUCED HYPERALGESIA

Psychophysics of Tissue Injury[2,3]

With tissue injury, a triad of events is noted: (1) a dull throbbing aching sensation; (2) an exaggerated response to a moderate intense stimulus (primary hyperalgesia); and (3) an enlarged area around the injury site where a moderate stimulus applied to uninjured tissue generates an aversive sensation (secondary hyperalgesia). It is important to what initiates these pain components. It is evident that these events reflect both a peripheral and central consequence of the injury and the stimulus that it presents.

Peripheral Afferent Terminal and Tissue Injury[3]

Afferent Response Properties

Injury and inflammation in the vicinity of the receptors increases the excitability of C-polymodal nociceptors innervating the injured site. This is reflected by the appearance of spontaneous afferent activity and a left shift in the stimulus-response curve of the afferent (Fig. 3–2). These events underlie the "triple response": a red flush around the site of the stimulus (local arterial dilation); a local edema (capillary permeability); and a regional reduction in the magnitude of the stimulus required to elicit a pain response (i.e., a hyperalgesia).

Pharmacology of Peripheral Sensitization[4]

After local tissue injury and inflammation, the milieu of the peripheral terminal is altered secondary to tissue damage and the accompanying extravasation of plasma.[4] These effects result in the concurrent release of a variety of algogenic agents from damaged tissue and from the peripheral terminals of sensory afferents activated by local C-fiber axon reflexes (Table 3–1). These chemical intermediaries have two distinct effects: (1) direct excitation of afferent C fibers; and (2) facilitation of C-fiber activation, resulting in a left shift and increasing slope of the frequency response curve of the C-fiber axon. These events likely contribute to the ongoing pain and the increase in the reported magnitude of the pain response evoked by a given stimulus (hyperalgesia).

Central Sensitization and Tissue Injury[5-13]

Dorsal Horn Response Properties

As reviewed, there is a close linkage between stimulus intensity and frequency of dorsal horn discharge and pain magnitude. In the face of tissue injury, there is the onset of a persistent discharge of small afferents. It is now appreciated that this persistent discharge can lead to a facilitation of dorsal horn reactivity. In animal studies, dorsal horn wide dynamic range (WDR) in the deep dorsal horn display a stimulus-

dependent response to low-frequency (0.1 Hz) activation of afferent C fibers. Repetitive stimulation of C (but not A) fibers at a moderately faster rate (>0.5 Hz) results in a progressively facilitated discharge. This exaggerated discharge was named *wind-up* by Lorne Mendell in 1966 (Fig. 3–3). Intracellular recording has indicated that the facilitated state is represented by a progressive, long-sustained, partial depolarization of the cell, rendering the membrane increasingly susceptible to afferent input. Given the likelihood that WDR discharge frequency is part of the encoding of the intensity of a high-threshold stimulus, and that many of these WDR neurons project in the ventrolateral quadrant of the spinal cord (i.e., spinobulbar projections), this augmented response is believed to be an important component of the pain message.

Protracted pain states such as those that occur with inflamed or injured tissue would routinely result in such an augmented afferent drive of the WDR neuron and then to the ongoing facilitation. Thus, there would be an enhanced response to a given stimulus (leading to a left shift in the stimulus response curve for the dorsal horn WDR neuron). This sensitizaton also provides a probable mechanism for the otherwise puzzling change in the receptive field where a stimulus applied to an dermatome adjacent to the injury may yield a pain sensation. As reviewed in Chapter 2, primary afferents entering through a given root make synaptic contact in the spinal level of entry, but also send collaterals rostrally and caudally to more distant segments where they have the ability to activate these distant neurons (although with less security than at the segment of entry). However, as schematically defined in Figure 3–4, current thinking suggests that, in the face of a conditioning injury stimulus, the distance neuron may become sensitized by the high-frequency activity and change in local transmitter release (see later) and that now input from that moderate distant dermatome will lead to an intense activation providing a "pain signal."

The preceding observations regarding this dorsal horn system have been shown to have behavioral consequences.

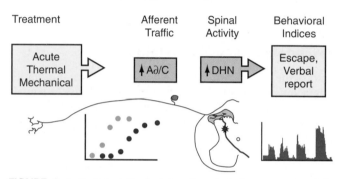

Transient High-Intensity Stimuli

FIGURE 3–1 ■ Schematic depicting the principal components of the afferent spinal cord response to an acute high-intensity afferent stimulus. There is a stimulus intensity-dependent increase in discharge frequency in specific populations of high-threshold primary afferents that initiates a stimulus intensity-dependent increase in the firing of dorsal horn neurons that projects to higher centers (here shown is a WDR neuron). The outflow of the spinal cord projects to higher centers as described in Chapter 2.

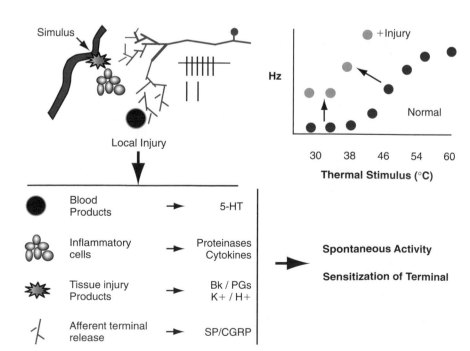

FIGURE 3–2 ■ *Left top panel,* Primary afferent terminal. Local tissue-damaging stimulus leads to firing of the fine afferents and local activation of inflammatory cells. *Right top panel,* This injury causes the response profile of a high-threshold afferent to shift up and to the left indicating the appearance of spontaneous activity at non-noxious stimulus intensities and an inflection of the stimulus response curve at a lower stimulus intensity. *Lower panel,* In response to the stimulus, afferent fibers display antidromic release of neuropeptides (SP/CGRP). Hormones, such as bradykinin, prostaglandins, and cytokines, or K^+/H^+ released from inflammatory cells and plasma extravasation products result in stimulation and sensitization of free nerve endings.

Table 3–1

Representative Classes of Agents Released by Tissue Injury—Activity and Sensitivity of Primary Afferent Fibers

1. **Amines:** Histamine (mast cells) and serotonin (platelets) are released by a variety of stimuli, including trauma, and many by chemical products of tissue damage.
2. **Kinin:** Bradykinin is synthesized by a cascade that is triggered by the activation of the clotting cascade. Bradykinin acts by specific bradykinin receptors (B1/B2) to activate free nerve endings.
3. **Lipidic acids:** Lipids such as prostanoids and leukotrienes are synthesized by cyclooxygenases and lipoxygenases. Many prostanoids, such as PGE_2, can directly activate C fibers and facilitate the excitability of C fibers through specific membrane receptors.
4. **Cytokines:** Cytokines such as the interleukins or tumor necrosis factor are formed as part of the inflammatory reaction involving macrophages and powerfully sensitize C-fiber terminals.
5. **Primary afferent peptides:** calcitonin gene-related peptide (CGRP) and substance P (SP) are found in and released from the peripheral terminals of C fibers and will produce local cutaneous vasodilation, plasma extravasation, and sensitization in the region of skin innervated by the stimulated sensory nerve.
6. **[H⁺]/[K⁺]:** Elevated H^+ (low pH) and high K^+ are found in injured tissue. These ions directly stimulate C fibers and evoke the local release of various vasodilatory peptides. A variety of receptors of triglyceride-rich lipoprotein particles (TRPV) are activated by increased hydrogen ions.
7. **Proteinases**, such as thrombin or trypsin, are released from inflammatory cells and can cleave tethered peptide ligands that exist on the surface of small primary afferents. These tethered peptides act on adjacent receptors, proteinase-activated receptors (PARs), that can depolarize the terminal.

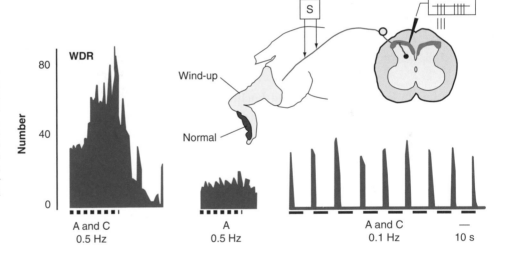

FIGURE 3–3 ■ *Right,* Single-unit recording from a wide dynamic range neuron in response to an electrical stimulus delivered at 0.1 Hz. A very reliable, stimulus-linked response is evoked at this frequency. *Left,* In contrast, when the stimulation rate is increased to 0.5 Hz, there is a progressive increase in the magnitude of the response generated by the stimulation. *Middle,* This facilitation, which results from the C-fiber input and not A-fiber input, is called "wind-up."

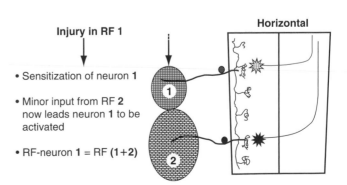

FIGURE 3–4 ■ Receptive field of dorsal horn neuron depends on its segmental input and the input from other segments that can activate it. After injury in receptive field 1 (RF1), neuron 1 becomes "sensitized." Collateral input from RF2 normally is unable to initiate sufficient excitatory activity to activate neuron 1, but after sensitization, RF2 input is sufficient. Now the RF of neuron 1 is effectively RF1 + RF2. Thus, local injury by spinal mechanisms can lead acutely to increased receptive fields such that stimuli applied to a non-injured RF can contribute to the post-tissue injury sensation.

Psychophysical studies have shown that a discrete injury to the skin of the volar surface of the arm or the direct activation of small afferents by the focal injection of a C-fiber stimulant (capsaicin) results in a small area of primary hyperesthesia surrounded by a much larger area of secondary hyperesthesia. If a local anesthetic block is placed proximal to the injection site before the insult, the onset of the secondary hyperesthesia is prevented. It is also important to note that WDR wind-up studies are frequently carried out in animals under 1 MAC (i.e., minimum alveolar concentration) anesthesia. The relevance of the observations to the performance of surgery on volatile "anesthetized" patients is clear. The implication of the afferent-evoked facilitation is that it is better to prevent small afferent input than to deal with its sequelae. This observation is believed to represent the basis for the consideration of the use of "preemptive analgesics," (e.g., agents and modalities that block small afferent input).

Pharmacology of Central Facilitation

Based on the foregoing commentary and the discussion in Chapter 2, a reduction in C-fiber-evoked excitation in the dorsal horn by blocking axon transmission, release of small afferent transmitter or the postsynaptic receptor (e.g., NK1 for SP or AMPA for glutamate) will diminish the magnitude of the afferent drive and, accordingly, diminish the facilitated processing evoked by protracted small afferent input. However, the wind-up state reflects more than the repetitive activation of a simple excitatory system. We will review systems that are part of the afferent pathway and other systems that contribute to facilitated processing at the spinal level.

Glutamate Receptors and Spinal Facilitation

The first real demonstration that spinal facilitation represented a unique pharmacology was presented by showing that the phenomenon was prevented by the spinal delivery of antagonists for the N-methyl-D-aspartate (NMDA) receptor. Importantly, these antagonists had no effect on acute evoked activity but reduced the wind-up. Subsequent behavioral work demonstrated that such drugs had no effect on acute pain thresholds but reduced the facilitated states induced after tissue injury and inflammation. As noted, the NMDA receptor does not appear to mediate acute excitation. This reflects an important property of this receptor. Under normal resting membrane potentials, the NMDA receptor is in a state referred to as a *magnesium block*. In this condition, occupancy by glutamate will not activate the ionophore. If there is a modest depolarization of the membrane (as produced during repetitive stimulation secondary to the activation of AMPA and substance P (SP) receptors, the magnesium block is removed, permitting glutamate to now activate the NMDA receptor. When this happens, the NMDA channel permits the passage of calcium (Fig. 3–5). This increase in intracellular calcium then serves to initiate the downstream components of the excitatory and facilitatory cascade. The excitation generated by small primary afferent input has been found to lead to a large number of distinct biochemical events that can serve to enhance the response of dorsal horn neurons leading to phenomena such as wind-up. Although the activation of the NMDA receptor is an important element of that facilitatory process, it is only one of many. We will consider several representative examples of cascades leading to spinal sensitization.

Lipid Mediators

In the face of repetitive afferent stimulation, increased intracellular calcium in spinal neurons leads to the activation of a cascade that leads to the release of prostaglandins. These prostanoids act on specific receptors that are pre- and postsynaptic to the primary afferent and serve to enhance primary afferent transmitter release and to facilitate the discharge of the postsynaptic dorsal horn neuron (Fig. 3–6). The

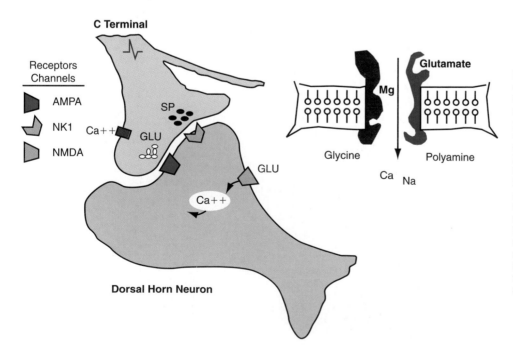

FIGURE   3–5 ■ *Left,* Schematic showing the synapse between a C fiber and a second-order dendrite I in the superficial dorsal horn. The synaptic linkage is composed of multiple excitatory transmitters acting on several receptors on the second-order neuron. *Right,* Schematic of an NMDA ionophore. As indicated in the text, the NMDA receptor is a calcium (Ca) ionophore that, when activated, results in an influx of Ca. To be activated, the receptor requires the occupancy by glutamate, the removal of the magnesium (Mg) block by a mild membrane depolarization, the occupancy of the "glycine site," and several allosterically coupled elements, including the "polyamine site." Together these events permit the ionophore to be activated.

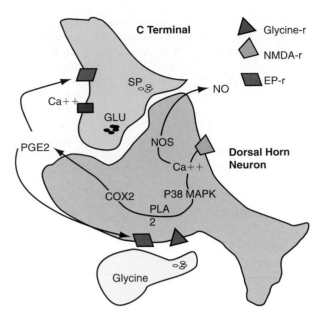

FIGURE 3–6 ■ Schematic of primary afferent synapse with second-order neuron in the superficial dorsal horn. On depolarization, multiple transmitters are released. In the face of persistent depolarization, the glutamate receptor is activated, which leads to increased intracellular calcium. This initiates a variety of cascades, including the activation of nitric oxide synthase (NOS) and the release of nitric oxide (NO). Through P38 mitogen-activated kinase (P38 MAPK), phospholipase A_2 (PLA$_2$) and cyclooxygenase (COX) lead to the formation and release of prostaglandins. Prostaglandins can act presynaptically to increase the opening of voltage-sensitive calcium channels and postsynaptically to inhibit the activation of a glycinergic inhibitory interneuron. These combined effects are believed to facilitate the activation of the second-order neuron by an afferent input.

presynaptic effect is believed to be through a facilitation of the opening of the voltage-sensitive calcium channel that is necessary for transmitter release. The postsynaptic action is mediated by the inactivation of a glycine receptor, which is otherwise acted on by glycine released from an inhibitory interneuron. This glycinergic inhibitor interneuron reflexively regulates the magnitude of the firing of the second-order neuron. Loss of the glycinergic inhibition is believed to result in an enhanced response to the afferent input. Cyclooxygenase (COX) inhibitors inhibiting the COX-2 enzyme have been shown to act spinally to block spinal prostanoid release and to diminish injury-evoked hyperalgesia. These results are consistent with the demonstration of the constitutive expression of the several synthetic enzymes, including several phospholipases (PLA$_2$) and the two COX isoforms.

Nitric Oxide (NO)

This agent is released following spinal afferent activation through several constitutively expressed NO synthases. NO has been shown to play a role in central facilitation phenomena by increasing transmitter release (see Fig. 3–6). Similarly, in the spinal cord, NO synthase inhibitors have been shown to prevent hyperalgesia.

Phosphorylating Enzymes

There are large number of enzymes found in neurons that can phosphorylate appropriate sites on various enzyme channels, receptors, and channels. Several of these protein kinases in spinal neurons have been shown to be activated by high-frequency small afferent input. Two examples of this effect

are provided by the role of protein kinase C (PKC) and P38 mitogen activated protein kinase (P38 MAPK). PKC is activated in the presence of increased intracellular calcium and has been shown to phosphorylate a number of proteins, including the NMDA receptor. This NMDA receptor phosphorylation has been shown to enhance the functionality of that channel leading to increased calcium passage when the channel is activated. This enhances the postsynaptic effect of any given amount of glutamate release. P38 MAPK is known to be one of the kinases which serve to activate phospholipase A_2. Thus, the formation of prostaglandins dependent on the freeing of arachidonic acid by this enzyme is activated by that kinase. Importantly, activation of P38 MAPK is also known to increase the transcription of specific proteins. In the case of P38 MAPK, one such protein whose expression is increased by P38 MAPK activation is COX-2. Thus, in the face of persistent afferent stimulation, activation of this isoform will initiate downstream events that change the expression of several proteins relevant to pain processing. This recitation is meant to provide an insight into the types of events that can be mediated by these kinases and is not exhaustive.

Bulbospinal Systems

It is known that afferent input particularly arising from the lamina I marginal cells (see Chapter 2) will activate ascending pathways and lead to excitatory input into the brain stem. At the medullary level, norepinephrine and serotonin-containing cells have been identified that project into the spinal dorsal horn (e.g., bulbospinal projections). Although these descending pathways have long been considered to be inhibitory in character, this inhibitory effect is likely due to the noradrenergic systems. Of particular interest, the serotoninergic systems have been shown to play an important *facilitatory* role in the wind-up observed in WDR neurons evoked by small afferent input. Thus, small afferent input activates LAM 1 projections into the medulla. These activated descending 5HT projections, which are excitatory, facilitate the discharge of WDR neurons (Fig. 3–7).

Non-neuronal Cells

At the spinal level there are large populations of astrocytes and microglia. Although these cell systems play an important trophic role, it is increasingly evident that they are also able to effectively regulate the excitability of local neuronal circuits. Thus, astrocytes can regulate extracellular glutamate levels by active reuptake and secretion. These cells also are potent releasers of a variety of active factors such as ATP, lipid mediators, and cytokines. By gap junctions, activation of one astrocyte can lead to a spread of activation that can influence cells over a spatially extended volume. Microglia are similarly interactive by their ability to be activated by a variety of products released from primary afferents, other neuronal and non-neuronal cells. Spinal agents known to block the activation of astrocytes (fluorocitrate) and microglia (minocycline) have been shown to rapidly and significantly diminish excitatory states initiated by peripheral injury and tissue injury. In addition to their ability to be influenced by local neuronal circuitry, circulating cytokines (IL-1ß/TNFα) as released by injury and inflammation can activate perivascular astrocyte/microglia. Accordingly, these cells provide an avenue

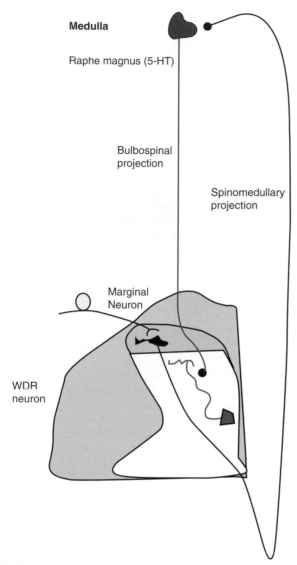

Medulla

Raphe magnus (5-HT)

Bulbospinal
projection

Spinomedullary
projection

Marginal
Neuron

WDR
neuron

FIGURE 3–7 ■ Schematic showing the linkage whereby small afferent input activates a lamina I cell that projects to the medulla. This projection has been shown to activate a raphe spinal serotonergic projection into the dorsal horn. This input, although an excitatory serotonin receptor, will augment the discharge of the WDR neuron.

whereby circulating products can influence neuraxial excitability (Fig. 3–8).

■ NERVE INJURY-INDUCED HYPERALGESIA

Psychophysics of Nerve Injury Pain

Over time, after a variety of injuries to the peripheral nerve, a constellation of pain events will appear. Frequent components of this evolving syndrome are (1) incidences of sharp, shooting sensations referred to the peripheral distribution of the injured nerve and (2) pain secondary to light tactile stimulation of the peripheral body surface (tactile allodynia).[14,15] This composite of sensory events was formally recognized by Silas Weir Mitchell in the 1860s. This pain state emphasizes the anomalous role of low-threshold mechanoreceptors (Aß

afferents). The ability of light touch evoking this anomalous pain state indicates that the injury has led to a reorganization of central processing (i.e., it is not due to a peripheral sensitization of high-threshold afferents). In addition to these behavioral changes, the neuropathic pain condition may display other contrasting anomalies, including on occasion, an ameliorating effect of sympathectomy of the afflicted limb and an attenuated responsiveness to analgesics, such as opiates. As an overview, the spontaneous pain and the miscoding of low-threshold afferent nerves are believed to reflect (1) an increase in spontaneous activity in axons in the injured afferent nerve and/or the dorsal horn neurons and (2) an exaggerated response of dorsal horn neurons to normally innocuous afferent input.

Morphologic Correlates of Nerve Injury Pain

Following peripheral nerve ligation or section, several events occur that signal long-term changes in peripheral and central processing.[16] Thus, in the periphery after an acute mechanical injury of the peripheral afferent axon, there will be an initial dying back (retrograde chromatolysis) that proceeds for some interval—at which time the axon begins to sprout, sending growth cones forward. The growth cone frequently fails to make contact with the original target and displays significant proliferation. Collections of these proliferated growth cones form structures called neuromas.

Spontaneous Pain State

Peripheral and Central Activity Generation

Under normal conditions, primary afferents show little if any spontaneous activity.[17,18] After peripheral nerve ligation or section, several events are noted to occur: (1) persistent small afferent fiber activity originating after a period from the lesioned nerve in both myelinated and unmyelinated axons; and (2) spontaneous activity develops from the dorsal root ganglia of the injured nerve. Accordingly, the spontaneous pain sensation may be related to this ongoing afferent traffic. An important question is the source of this afferent traffic. We cannot exclude the likelihood of a spinal generator. Early work indeed demonstrated that after rhizotomy, there was an increase in the activity over time observed in WDR neurons. With regard to the peripheral generator, several possible mechanisms have become likely (Fig. 3–9).

Increased Expression of Sodium Channels

After nerve injury, there is a significant up-regulation of the a variety of sodium channels in the neuroma and in the DRG of the injured axons. Consistent with a role of sodium channels is that the spontaneous activity originating from the neuromas and the DRG is blocked by intravenous lidocaine at plasma concentrations below those that block conduction in the nerve.

Changes in Afferent Terminal Sensitivity

The sprouted terminals of the injured afferent axon display a characteristic growth cone that possesses transduction properties that were not possessed by the original axon. These include significant mechanical and chemical sensitivity. Thus,

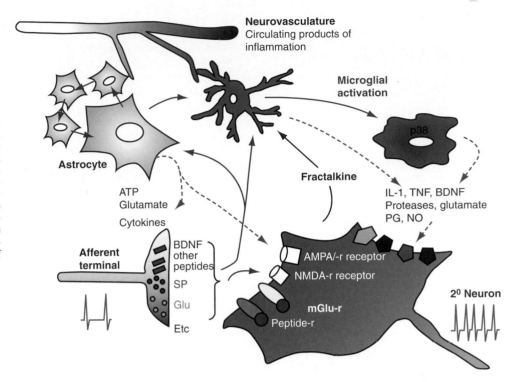

FIGURE 3–8 ■ Schematic displays the linkage between the primary afferent and the second-order neuron. The scenario also emphasizes the presence of astrocytes and microglia, which are activated by various products released from activated neurons and form the non-neuronal cells. In addition, the microglia are able to sample the content of the vasculature and these products, such as IL-1ß, can activate these cells. The net effect is that these non-neuronal cells can alter the excitability of local neuronal circuits.

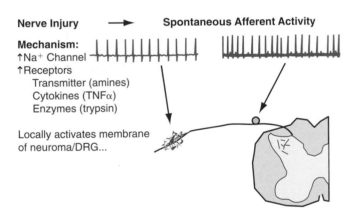

FIGURE 3–9 ■ Following nerve injury over an interval of days to weeks, the neuroma of the injured afferent and its dorsal root ganglion (DRG) cell will begin to display ectopic activity. TNFα, tumor necrosis factor alpha.

these spouted endings may have sensitivity to a number of humoral factors, such as prostanoids, catecholamines, and cytokines such as TNFα. This evolving sensitivity is of particular importance given that current data suggest that after local nerve injury there is the release of a variety of cytokines, particularly TNFα, which can directly activate the nerve and neuroma. In addition, after nerve injury, there is an important sprouting of postganglionic sympathetic efferents that can lead to the local release of catecholamines. This scenario is consistent with the observation that after nerve injury the postganglionic axons can initiate excitation in the injured axon (see later). These events are believed to contribute to the development of spontaneous afferent traffic after peripheral nerve injury.

Evoked Hyperpathia[19-22]

The observation that low-threshold tactile stimulation yields a pain state has been the subject of considerable interest. As noted, there is considerable agreement that these effects are often mediated by low-threshold afferent stimulation. Several underlying mechanisms have been proposed to account for this seemingly anomalous linkage.

Dorsal Root Ganglion Cell Cross-Talk

Following nerve injury, evidence suggests that "cross-talk" develops between afferents in the dorsal root ganglion (DRG) and in the neuroma. Here, depolarizing currents in one axon would generate a depolarizing voltage in an adjacent quiescent axon. This depolarization would permit activity arising in one axon to drive activity in a second. In this manner, it is hypothesized that a large low-threshold afferent would drive activity in an adjacent high-threshold afferent. Alternatively, DRG and that projects to higher centers cells in vitro can release a variety of transmitters and express excitatory receptors.

Afferent Sprouting

Under normal circumstances, large myelinated (Aß) afferents project into the spinal Rexed laminae III and deeper. Small afferents (C fibers) tend to project into spinal laminae II and I, a region consisting mostly of nociceptor-responsive neurons. Following peripheral nerve injury, it has been argued that the central terminals of these myelinated afferents (A fibers) sprout into lamina II of the spinal cord. With this synaptic reorganization, stimulation of low-threshold mechanoreceptors (Aß fibers) could produce excitation of these neurons and be perceived as painful. The degree to which this sprouting occurs is a point of current discussion, and although it appears to occur, it is considerably less prominent than originally proposed.

Dorsal Horn Reorganization

Following peripheral nerve injury, a variety of events occur in the dorsal horn, which suggest altered processing wherein the response to low-threshold afferent traffic can be exaggerated.

Spinal Glutamate Release

The post-nerve injury pain state is dependent on spinal glutamate release. After nerve injury, there is a significant enhancement in resting spinal glutamate secretion. This release is in accord with (1) an increased spontaneous activity in the primary afferent; and (2) the loss of intrinsic inhibition that may serve to modulate resting glutamate secretion (see later). The physiologic significance of this release is emphasized by several convergent observations: (1) Intrathecally delivered glutamate will evoke a powerful tactile allodynia and thermal hyperalgesia through the activation of spinal NMDA and non-NMDA receptors; (2) The spinal delivery of NMDA antagonists attenuates the hyperpathic states arising in animal models of nerve injury. As reviewed earlier in this chapter, NMDA receptor activation mediates neuronal excitability. In addition, the NMDA receptor is a calcium ionophore which, when activated, leads to prominent increases in intracellular calcium. This increased calcium initiates a cascade of events that includes the activation of a variety of enzymes (kinases), some of which phosphorylate membrane proteins (e.g., calcium channels and the NMDA receptors), whereas others—such as the mitogen-activated kinases (MAP kinases)—mediate intracellular signaling that leads to the altered expression of a variety of proteins and peptides (e.g., cyclooxygenase and dynorphin). This downstream nuclear action is believed to herald long-term and persistent changes in function. A variety of factors have been shown to enhance glutamate release. Two examples will be further discussed subsequently.

Non-neuronal Cells

Following nerve injury, it has been shown that there is a significant increase in activation of spinal microglia and astrocytes in the spinal segments receiving input from the injured nerves. Of particular interest is that, in the face of pathology such as bone cancer, such up-regulation has also been clearly shown. As reviewed earlier, microglia and astrocytes are activated by a variety of neurotransmitters and growth factors. Although the origin of this activation is not clear, when it occurs, it will lead to an increased spinal expression of COX/NOS/glutamate transporters/proteinases. Such biochemical components have been shown to play an important role in the facilitated state.

Loss of Intrinsic GABAergic/Glycinergic Control

In the spinal dorsal horn there are a large number of small interneurons that contain and release GABA and glycine. GABA/glycinergic terminals are frequently presynaptic to the large central afferent terminal complexes and form reciprocal synapses, whereas GABAergic axosomatic connections on spinothalamic cells have also been identified. Accordingly, these amino acids normally exert an important tonic or evoked inhibitory control over the activity of Aß primary afferent terminals and second-order neurons in the spinal dorsal horn. The relevance of this intrinsic inhibition to pain processing is provided by the observation that the simple intrathecal delivery of GABA A receptor or glycine receptor antagonists will lead to a powerful behaviorally defined tactile allodynia. Similarly, animals genetically lacking glycine-binding sites often display a high level of spinal hyperexcitability. These observations lead to consideration that following nerve injury there may be a loss of GABAergic neurons. Although there are data that do support a loss of such GABAergic neurons, the loss appears to be minimal. A second alternative is that after nerve injury, spinal neurons regress to a neonatal phenotype in which GABA-A activation becomes excitatory. This excitatory effect is secondary to reduced activity of the membrane Cl^- transporter, which changes the reversal current for the Cl^- conductance. Here increasing membrane Cl^- conductance as occurs with GABA-A receptor activation results in membrane depolarization.

Dynorphin

This peptide has been identified within the spinal cord. Following peripheral nerve injury, there is increased spinal dorsal horn expression of dynorphin. Intrathecal delivery of dynorphin can initiate the concurrent release of spinal glutamate and a potent tactile allodynia; the latter effect is reversed by NMDA antagonists.

Sympathetic Input

Following peripheral tissue injury, there is the appearance of a spontaneous discharge in otherwise silent small axons. This spontaneous activity is blocked by lidocaine, the sodium channel blocker, at concentrations that do not block the conducted potential. After peripheral nerve injury, there is an increased innervation of the peripheral neuroma by postganglionic sympathetic terminals. It has been show that an ingrowth of postganglionic sympathetic terminals occurs into the dorsal root ganglia of the injured axons. These postganglionic fibers form baskets of terminals around the ganglion cells. Several properties of this innervation are interesting: (1) They invest all sizes of ganglion cells, but particularly type A (large ganglion cells). (2) The innervation occurs principally in the DRG ipsilateral to the lesion, but in addition, there is innervation of the contralateral ganglion cell. (3) Stimulation of the ventral roots of the segments, containing the preganglionic efferents, will produce activity in the sensory axon by an interaction either at the peripheral terminal at the site of injury or by an interaction at the level of the DRG. This excitation is blocked by intravenous phentolamine, emphasizing an adrenergic effect (Fig. 3–10). The observations that sympathetic innervation increases in the ganglion after nerve injury and that afferent activity can be driven by sympathetic stimulation provide some linkage between these efferent and afferent systems and suggest that an overall increase in sympathetic activity per se is not necessary to evoke the activity. These observations also provide a mechanism for the action of α-antagonists (phentolamine) and α$_2$-agonists (clonidine) that have been reported to be effective after topical or intrathecal delivery. Thus, α$_2$-receptors may act presynaptically to reduce sympathetic terminal release. Spinally, α$_2$-agonists are known to depress preganglionic sympathetic outflow. In either case, to the extent that pain states are driven by sympathetic input, these states would be

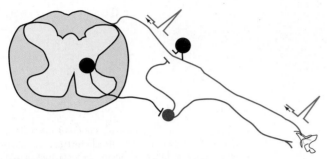

FIGURE 3–10 ■ After injury to the peripheral nerve, postganglionic sympathetic afferents will sprout into the neuroma. Similar sprouting occurs to the dorsal root ganglion (DRG) of the injured axon. Importantly, electrophysiologic studies have shown that the activation of preganglionic sympathetic outflow to the neuroma or the DRG will initiate ectopic activity.

diminished accordingly. Interestingly, this consideration provides some explanation as to why opiates do not exert a potent effect on the allodynia observed after nerve injury. As summarized earlier, neither micro-agonists nor α_2-agonists alter large afferent input, yet α_2-agonists may reduce allodynia. This differential action may result from the fact that opiates, unlike the α_2-agents, do not alter sympathetic outflow (as indicated by the lack of effect of spinal opiates on resting blood pressure).

■ OVERVIEW OF MECHANISMS OF ACTION OF SEVERAL COMMON PHARMACOLOGIC AGENTS THAT MODIFY PAIN PROCESSING

Earlier, we considered the various aspects of the pharmacology of the systems that underlie the dynamic aspects of pain processing. In the following text, we will briefly consider mechanisms whereby a number of pharmacologic modalities exert their action to produce a change in pain processing.

Opioids[23,24]

Systemic opioids have been shown to produce a powerful and selective reduction in the human and animal response to a strong and otherwise noxious stimulus. Current data emphasize that these agents may interact with one or a combination of three receptors: mu, delta, and kappa. Given the widespread use of this class of drugs, the site through which these effects are mediated and the mechanisms of those actions are a point of interest. Direct assessment of the locus of action can be addressed initially by the focal application of the agent to the various purported sites of action, and the effects of such injections on behavior and the pharmacology of those local effects (to ensure a receptor-mediated effect) can be examined.

Sites of Action

Supraspinal Sites

Microinjection mapping in animals prepared with stereotactically placed guide cannulae has revealed that opioid receptors are functionally coupled to the regulation of the animal's response to strong and otherwise noxious mechanical, thermal, and chemical stimuli, which excite small primary afferents. Of the sites that have been principally identified, the most potent is the mesencephalic periaqueductal gray matter (PAG). Here, the local action of morphine blocks nociceptive responses in a variety of species. Other sites identified to modulate pain behavior in the presence of an opiate are the mesencephalic reticular formation (MRF), medial medulla, substantia nigra, nucleus accumbens/ventral forebrain, and amygdala.

Spinal Cord

Intrathecal opiates produce a powerful effect on nociceptive thresholds in all species.

Peripheral Sites

Early studies suggested a possible action of morphine at the site of peripheral injury. It has been emphasized that the peripheral injection of opiates following the initiation of an inflammation would reduce the hyperalgesic component at doses that did not redistribute centrally.

Mechanisms of Opioid Analgesia

Given the diversity of sites, it is unlikely that all of the mechanisms whereby opiates act within the brain to alter nociceptive transmission are identical. Several mechanisms through which opiates may act to alter nociceptive transmission have been identified.

Supraspinal Action of Opioids

There are a number of specific mechanisms; two will be discussed here (Fig. 3–11).

Bulbospinal Projections

Morphine in the brain stem inhibits spinal nociceptive reflexes. Microinjection of morphine into various brain-stem sites reduces the spinal neuronal activity evoked by noxious stimuli. These effects are in accord with a variety of studies in which (1) activation of bulbospinal pathways known to contain noradrenaline or 5-HT inhibit spinal nociceptive activity; (2) pharmacologic enhancement of spinal monoamine activity (by the delivery of α-agonists) leads to an inhibition of spinal activity; (3) microinjection of morphine into the brain stem increases the spinal release noradrenaline; and (4) the spinal delivery of α_2-antagonists reverses the effects of brain-stem opiates on spinal reflexes and analgesia. These observations are in accord with the effects produced when the bulbospinal pathways are directly stimulated and emphasize that the actions of opiates in the PAG are, in fact, associated with an increase in spinofugal outflow.

Forebrain Mechanisms Modulating Afferent Input

Although there is ample evidence suggesting that opiates interact with the mesencephalon to alter input by a variety of direct and indirect systems, the behavioral sequelae of opioids possess a significant component that reflects the affective component of the organism's response to the pain state. There are significant rostral projections from the dorsal raphe nucleus (5-HT) and the locus coeruleus (noradrenaline) that connect the PAG with forebrain systems that are known to influence motivational and affective components of behavior.

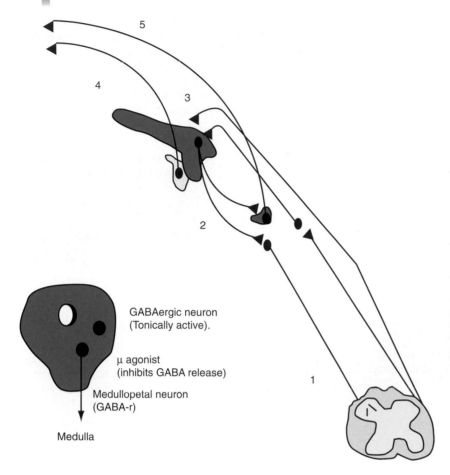

FIGURE 3–11 ■ Schematic of organization of opiate action within the periaqueductal gray matter (PAG). In this schema, μ opiate actions block the release of GABA from tonically active systems that otherwise regulate the projections to the medulla, leading to an activation of PAG outflow. The overall organization of the mechanisms whereby a PAG μ opiate agonist can alter nociceptive processing is presented in the adjacent schematic. The following mechanisms are hypothesized: (1) PAG projection to the medulla, which serves to activate bulbospinal projections releasing serotonin and/or noradrenaline at the spinal level; (2) PAG outflow to the medulla where local inhibitory interaction results in an inhibition of ascending medullary projections to higher centers; (3) Opiate binding within the PAG may be preterminal on the ascending spinofugal projection. This preterminal action would inhibit input into the medullary care and mesencephalic core; Outflow from the PAG can modulate excitability of dorsal raphe (4) and locus coeruleus (5) from which ascending serotonergic and noradrenergic projections originate to project to limbic system/forebrain.

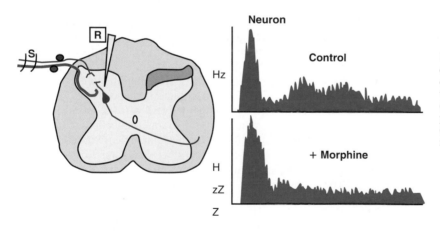

FIGURE 3–12 ■ Post-stimulus histogram showing the effects of intravenous morphine on the firing of a single dorsal horn wide dynamic range neuron after single activation of A- and C-fiber input. As indicated, there is an early (A-mediated) and late (A/C) activation of the cell. The later phase activation is preferentially sensitive to morphine (5 mg/kg intravenously) compared with the early component. These effects are readily reversed by naloxone.

Spinal Action of Opiates

At the spinal level, there are opioid receptors presynaptically on the terminals of small primary afferents and postsynaptically on the second-order neurons. The presynaptic action of morphine through the G protein-coupled receptor reduces the opening of voltage-sensitive calcium channels, thereby reducing release of small afferent transmitters. The postsynaptic action reflects a facilitating linkage to voltage-sensitive potassium channels, which then hyperpolarize the second-order neuron, rendering it resistant to depolarization. These joint effects are believed to underlie the primary regulatory effects that spinal opiates have on spinal nociceptive input (Fig. 3–12).

Peripheral Action of Opioids

Opioid binding sites are transported in the peripheral sensory axon, but there is no evidence that these sites are coupled to mechanisms governing the excitability of the membrane. High doses of agents, such as sufentanil, can block the compound action potential, but this effect is not naloxone-reversible and is thought to reflect a "local anesthetic" action of the lipid-soluble agent. It is certain that opiate receptors exist on the distant peripheral terminals. Opioid receptors have been shown to be on the distal terminals of C fibers, and agonist occupancy of these sites can block antidromic release of C-fiber transmitters (e.g., SP/CGRP [substance P/calcitonin gene-related peptide], "axon reflex"; see discussion of pharmacology of peripheral sensitization). Importantly, the models in which peripheral opiates appear to work are those that possess a significant degree of inflammation and are characterized by a hyperalgesic component. This finding raises the possibility that these peripheral actions normalize a process leading to an increased sensitivity to the local stimulus environment but do not alter normal transduction. The mechanisms of the antihyperalgesic effects of opiates applied to the inflamed regions (as in the knee joint) are, at present, unexplained. It is possible, for example, that opiates may act on inflammatory cells that are releasing cytokines and products that activate or sensitize the nerve terminal.

Interactions Between Supraspinal and Spinal Systems

As discussed earlier, opioids with an action limited to the spinal cord and to the brain stem are able to produce a powerful alteration in nociceptive processing. There is ample evidence that the effects of opiate receptor occupancy in the brain synergize with the effects produced by the concurrent occupancy of spinal receptors. A variety of studies have shown that the concurrent administration of morphine spinally and supraspinally leads to a prominent synergy (i.e., maximal effect with a minimal combination dose).

Nonsteroidal Anti-Inflammatory Drugs[25]

Nonsteroidal anti-inflammatory drugs (NSAIDs) are widely prescribed agents that have been shown to have significant utility in a variety of acute (postoperative) as well as chronic (cancer, arthritis) pain states. Although NSAIDs may differ in potency, all are believed to have the same efficacy. Importantly, human and animal studies have emphasized that these agents serve not to alter pain thresholds under normal conditions but to reduce a hyperalgesic component of the underlying pain state. NSAIDs are structurally diverse but have a common feature in their ability to function as inhibitors of the enzyme cyclooxygenase (COX), the essential enzyme in the synthesis of prostaglandins. Current thinking emphasizes both peripheral and central mechanisms of action.

Peripheral Action of NSAIDs

Prostanoids are synthesized at the site of injury and can act on the peripheral afferent terminal to facilitate afferent transduction and augment the inflammatory state. To that degree, inhibition of prostaglandin synthesis by blocking cyclooxygenase can diminish that hyperalgesic state and reduce the magnitude of inflammation. The analgesic potency of the NSAIDs, however, does not co-vary uniquely with the potency of these agents as inhibitors of inflammation.

Spinal Action of NSAIDs

Intrathecal injection of NSAIDs, at doses that are inactive with systemic administration, attenuates the behavioral response to certain types of noxious stimuli, indicating a central action of the agent. As reviewed earlier, the repetitive activation of spinal neurons or the direct excitation of dorsal horn glutamate or substance P receptors evokes a facilitated state of processing and the release of prostaglandins. The direct application of several prostanoids to the spinal cord leads to a facilitated state of processing (hyperalgesia). Accordingly, it is currently considered that COX inhibitors can, by their effect on COX-2, exert an acute action that prevents the initiation of the hyperalgesic state otherwise produced by the local spinal action of prostaglandins (see Fig. 3–6).

NMDA Receptor Antagonists[26]

Ketamine is classified as a dissociative anesthetic, but there is a clinical appreciation that ketamine can provide a significant degree of "analgesia." The current thinking is that ketamine acts as an antagonist at the glutamate receptor of the N-methyl-D-aspartate (NMDA) subtype. As reviewed earlier, the NMDA site is thought to be essential in evoking a hyperalgesic state following repetitive small afferent (C fiber) input (see Fig. 3–5). In addition, there is a belief that certain states of allodynia may be mediated by a separate spinal NMDA receptor system, and NMDA antagonists have been shown to diminish the dysesthetic component of the causalgic pain states.

Alpha₂ Adrenergic Agonists[23]

Systemic α_2-adrenoceptor agonists have been shown to produce a significant sedation and a mild analgesia. As reviewed earlier, bulbospinal noradrenergic pathways can regulate dorsal horn nociceptive processing by the release of noradrenaline and the subsequent activation of α_2-adrenergic receptors. Consequently, the spinal delivery of α_2-agonists can produce a powerful analgesia in humans and animal models. This spinal action of α_2 is mediated by a mechanism similar to that employed by spinal opiates, but the receptor is distinct, in the following three ways:

- α_2 binding is presynaptic on C fibers and postsynaptic on dorsal horn neurons.
- α_2-receptors can depress the release of C-fiber transmitters.
- α_2-agonists can hyperpolarize dorsal horn neurons through a Gi-coupled potassium channel.

There is a growing appreciation that clonidine may be useful in neuropathic pain states. The mechanism of this is not clear, but the ability of α_2-agonists to diminish sympathetic outflow, either by a direct preterminal action on the postganglionic fiber, thereby directly blocking catecholamine release, or by acting spinally on preganglionic sympathetic outflow, has been suggested.

Intravenous Local Anesthetics[27]

The systemic delivery of sodium channel blockers has been shown to have analgesic efficacy in a variety of neuropathies (diabetic), nerve injury pain states (causalgia), and late-stage cancer as well as in lowering intraoperative anesthetic requirements. Importantly, these effects occur at plasma concentrations lower than those required to produce a frank block

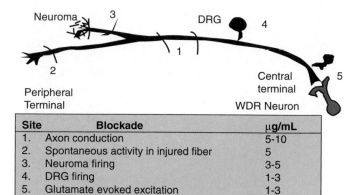

Site	Blockade	μg/mL
1.	Axon conduction	5-10
2.	Spontaneous activity in injured fiber	5
3.	Neuroma firing	3-5
4.	DRG firing	1-3
5.	Glutamate evoked excitation	1-3

FIGURE 3–13 ▮ Schematic showing sites of generation of spontaneous activity (1-5, *top*); the table (*below*) indicates the sites at which systemically administered lidocaine has been hypothesized to reduce spontaneous/evoked activity. Note that axonal and peripheral nerve terminal blockade have not been demonstrated in whole animal preparations at sublethal systemic lidocaine concentrations, whereas abnormal activity in neuromas, dorsal root ganglia (DRG), and dorsal horn is suppressed by nontoxic lidocaine plasma concentrations.

of nerve conduction; for lidocaine, effective concentrations may be on the order of 1 to 3 μg/mL. As reviewed earlier, the mechanism of this action is believed to reflect the importance of the up-regulation of the sodium channel that occurs in the injured axon and DRG. This increase is believed to underlie in part the ectopic activity arising from the injured nerve. Figure 3–13 indicates the potential sites where local anesthetics may interfere with impulse generation that leads to a pain state.

▮ CONCLUSION

The discussions of the mechanism of nociceptive processing in Chapters 2 and 3 of this textbook only touch on a complex organized substrate. The common threads connecting these comments are that the complexity emphasizes that pain is not a monolithic entity and that, as with other organ systems, such as cardiovascular regulation and hypertension, multiple etiologies lead to the pain report. Because there are many approaches to regulating elevated blood pressure, and the selection of the appropriate therapy depends on the mechanism in disorder, so too is it likely that a single approach will not be appropriate for all pain states. Our improving insight into the pharmacology and physiology of these multiple components should continue to provide new tools for the management of nociception.

References

1. Sorkin LS, Wallace MS: Acute pain mechanisms. Surg Clin North Am 79:213, 1999.

2. Frerichs JA, Janis LR: Preemptive analgesia in foot and ankle surgery. Clin Podiatr Med Surg 20:237, 2003.

3. Brennan TJ, Zahn PK, Pogatzki-Zahn EM: Mechanisms of incisional pain. Anesthesiol Clin North Am 23:1, 2005.

4. Gold MS, Flake NM: Inflammation-mediated hyperexcitability of sensory neurons. Neurosignals 14:147, 2005.

5. Dickenson AH: A cure for wind up: NMDA receptor antagonists as potential analgesics. Trends Pharmacol Sci 11:307, 1990.

6. Herrero JF, Laird JM, Lopez-Garcia JA: Wind-up of spinal cord neurones and pain sensation: Much ado about something? Prog Neurobiol 61:169, 2000.

7. Honore P, Menning PM, Rogers SD, et al: Neurochemical plasticity in persistent inflammatory pain. Prog Brain Res 129:357, 2000.

8. Koltzenburg M: Neural mechanisms of cutaneous nociceptive pain. Clin J Pain 16(Suppl):S131, 2000.

9. Salter MW: Cellular signalling pathways of spinal pain neuroplasticity as targets for analgesic development. Curr Top Med Chem 5:557, 2005.

10. Suzuki R, Rygh LJ, Dickenson AH: Bad news from the brain: Descending 5-HT pathways that control spinal pain processing. Trends Pharmacol Sci 25:613, 2004.

11. Willis WD: Long-term potentiation in spinothalamic neurons. Brain Res Rev 40:202, 2002.

12. Yaksh TL, Hua XY, Kalcheva I, et al: The spinal biology in humans and animals of pain states generated by persistent small afferent input. Proc Natl Acad Sci U S A 96:7680, 1999.

13. Yaksh TL: Central pharmacology of nociceptive transmission. In McMahon S, Koltzenburg M (eds): Wall and Melzack's Textbook of Pain, 5th ed. Philadelphia, Churchill Livingstone, 2006, p 371.

14. Gracely RH: Pain measurement. Acta Anaesthesiol Scand 43:897, 1999.

15. Singleton JR: Evaluation and treatment of painful peripheral polyneuropathy. Semin Neurol 25:185, 2005.

16. Zimmermann M: Pathobiology of neuropathic pain. Eur J Pharmacol 429:23, 2001.

17. Burchiel KJ, Ochoa JL: Pathophysiology of injured axons. Neurosurg Clin North Am 2:105, 1992.

18. Priestley T: Voltage-gated sodium channels and pain. Curr Drug Targets CNS Neurol Disord 3:441, 2004.

19. Blomqvist A, Craig AD: Is neuropathic pain caused by the activation of nociceptive-specific neurons due to anatomic sprouting in the dorsal horn? J Comp Neurol 428:1, 2000.

20. Lai J, Ossipov MH, Vanderah TW, et al: Neuropathic pain: The paradox of dynorphin. Mol Interv 1:160, 2001.

21. Tsuda M, Inoue K, Salter MW: Neuropathic pain and spinal microglia: A big problem from molecules in "small" glia. Trends Neurosci 28:101, 2005.

22. Zeilhofer HU: The glycinergic control of spinal pain processing. Cell Mol Life Sci 62:2027, 2005.

23. Yaksh TL, Jage J, Takano Y: Pharmacokinetics and pharmacodynamics of medullar agents: The spinal actions of beta-2-adrenergic agonists as analgesics. In Aitkenhead AR, Benad G, Brown BR, et al (eds): Bailliere's Clinical Anaesthesiology, vol 7, No 3. London, Bailliere Tindall, 1993, p 597.

24. Yaksh TL: The spinal actions of opioids. In Herz A (ed): Handbook of Experimental Pharmacology, vol 104/II. Berlin, Springer-Verlag, 1993, p 53.

25. Svensson CI, Yaksh TL: The spinal phospholipase-cyclooxygenase-prostanoid cascade in nociceptive processing. Annu Rev Pharmacol Toxicol 42:553, 2002.

26. Dickenson AH, Chapman V, Green GM: The pharmacology of excitatory and inhibitory amino acid-mediated events in the transmission and modulation of pain in the spinal cord. Gen Pharmacol 28:633, 1997.

27. Kalso E: Sodium channel blockers in neuropathic pain. Curr Pharm Des 11:3005, 2005.

section

2

The Evaluation of the Patient in Pain

History and Physical Examination of the Pain Patient

Charles D. Donohoe

The cornerstone of clinical success in the practice of pain management is a correct diagnosis. Yet in this era of increasing reliance on technology and constant pressure on the physician to become more efficient, the key to obtaining the correct diagnosis—namely a targeted history and physical examination—is often regarded as less critical in the care of the patient. This lack of a concise history often leads to clinical errors that not only squander our limited healthcare resources but limit the patient's opportunity to obtain pain relief.

Indeed, shortcuts taken in obtaining old records, contacting prior treating physicians, calling family members of a confused hospitalized patient, and most importantly just sitting and listening to what the patient believes to be important frequently lead to misdiagnosis and an unsatisfactory outcome for the patient and pain specialist alike.

The bond of trust that is so integral to the relationship between patient and pain specialist is often determined by the care and thoroughness with which the initial historical material is obtained. It is my experience that, when physicians are rushed for time, the intake interview becomes abbreviated, thereby setting the stage for medical errors and interpersonal dissatisfaction.

Many of the chapters that follow highlight the utility of highly sophisticated technology, invasive testing modalities, and diagnostic and therapeutic nerve blocks. Although each of these clinical interventions may be extremely important in the evaluation of a given patient, they do not replace the preeminent role of the history and physical examination in the diagnosis of the patient in pain. Most, if not all, of what a pain specialist needs to know can be gleaned from simply taking the time to take a concise history and perform a targeted physical examination. By far, the most cost-effective endeavor in the evaluation of the patient in pain is to be thorough in the initial targeted history taking and physical examination. If this initial consultation ends without a clear direction as to the underlying pathology or without insight into the predicament of the particular patient in pain, the likelihood that technology will "save the day" is very remote.

■ THE TARGETED PAIN HISTORY

Obtaining a history is a skill. Practice and repetition improve our skills, reduce the tendency to omit important material, and ultimately enable us to focus our questions to conserve time without sacrificing accuracy. As a starting point, the search should be directed to answer two questions,[1] "Where is the disease causing the pain—in the brain, spinal cord, plexus, muscle, tendon, or bone?" and "What is the nature of the disease?" It is the trademark of an experienced clinician to formulate an efficient line of questioning that deals with both of these issues simultaneously. I will highlight the critical elements in that process. The goal is to keep the process brief, simple, and workable.

The secret of becoming skilled at taking a history is being a good listener. The physician should put the patient at ease. The patient should never be given the impression that the physician is rushed or overworked and that only limited time is available to get the story across. The physician must remember that the patient in pain is usually anxious, if not overtly frightened, and may be inadequate in presenting the situation and having his or her plight properly perceived. Experience teaches us that the physician cannot force the pace of the interview without losing vital information and valuable mutual trust and insight. The following discussion describes the elements of the targeted history that not only define pain in a context useful for proper identification, localization, and source but also enable the physician to determine priorities about the urgency of care.

The Pain Litany

The *pain litany*—a formulaic exploration of the patient's pain history—enables the physician to identify the signature of the specific pain syndrome from its usual manifesting characteristics.[2,3]

The pain litany takes the following form[3]:

1. Mode of onset.
2. Location.
3. Chronicity.
4. Tempo (duration and frequency).
5. Character and severity.

6. Associated factors:
   - Premonitory symptoms and aura
   - Precipitating
   - Environmental factors (occupation)
   - Family history
   - Age at onset
   - Pregnancy and menstruation
   - Gender
   - Past medical and surgical history
   - Socioeconomic considerations
   - Psychiatric history
   - Medications, drug and alcohol use

The targeted history also allows physicians to distinguish sick patients from well ones. If it is determined that in all probability the patient is well (i.e., has no life-threatening illness), the work-up and treatment plan may proceed at a more conservative pace. From the outset, the interviewer proceeds in an orderly fashion but remains vigilant for signals of an urgent situation. Pain of uncertain origin should always be regarded as a potential emergency.

Mode of Onset and Location

The mode of onset of the pain sets the direction of the initial history and carries much weight in distinguishing sick from well. For example, the sudden, explosive presentation of a subarachnoid hemorrhage secondary to a ruptured intracranial aneurysm, manifested by severe headache, neck pain, and sense of impending doom, contrasts sharply with the chronic diffuse headache and vague neck tightness of tension-type cephalalgia.

The location of pain provides additional diagnostic information. The pain in trigeminal neuralgia, for instance, is usually limited to one or more branches of cranial nerve V and does not spread beyond the distribution of the nerve.[4] The V_2 and V_3 divisions of this nerve are much more frequently involved than V_1 (Fig. 4–1). The pain is rarely bilateral except in certain cases of multiple sclerosis, brain stem neoplasms and skull base tumors, and infections.[5]

Another example of the importance of pain location is the burning, prickling dysesthesias of meralgia paresthetica. The unilateral involvement of the lateral femoral cutaneous nerve produces painful dysesthesias in the anterior thigh, more commonly in men, who notice the disturbance when they put a hand in a trouser pocket.

The physician must find out how and where the pain started. The patient should be asked to identify the site of maximum pain.

Chronicity

The duration of awareness of a painful illness targets the initial history and heavily influences the sick from well distinction. For this reason, it often serves as a starting point. "How long have you had this pain?" is an essential question. The patient should be asked to try to date the pain in relation to other medical events, such as trauma, surgery, and other illnesses.

In general, back pain that has been present for 30 years and is not associated with any progression is strong evidence of a self-limited pain syndrome; thus, the "well" determination. Conversely, a patient with severe low back pain of

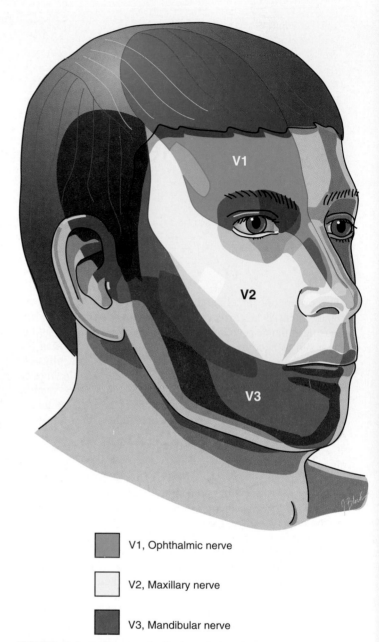

V1, Ophthalmic nerve

V2, Maxillary nerve

V3, Mandibular nerve

FIGURE 4–1 ■ Sensory distribution of the trigeminal nerve. (From Waldman SD: Atlas of Interventional Pain Management, 2nd ed. Philadelphia, Saunders, 2004, p 34, Figure 9-1, with permission.)

sudden onset or that suddenly changes in character must be assigned to the category of "sick until proved otherwise." This type of accentuated pain presentation has often been called the *first or worst syndrome.* It applies to both spinal pain and headache. Patients in this category deserve serious concern, and their pain should be viewed with medical urgency. Equating the concept of chronicity with benign disease has its pitfalls; the physician must beware of failing to:

- Identify ominous changes in a long-standing, stable pain syndrome (e.g., when a patient with chronic low back pain suddenly becomes incontinent).
- Attribute the onset of symptoms to a benign cause without adequate evaluation (e.g., dismissing a sudden increase in

low back pain in the postoperative patient as muscle spasm without considering discitis and bacterial epidural abscess).

- Recognize new symptoms superimposed on chronic complaints (e.g., attributing an increase in headache with cough to chronic cervical spondylitis disease rather than considering that because the patient has a known breast malignancy, silent metastasis may be causing increased intracranial pressure).

Indeed, the characteristics of thoroughness, experience, insight into the patient's personality, and a constant resistance to being lulled into false security prevent such diagnostic disasters. As Mark Twain observed, "Good decisions come from experience and experience comes from making bad decisions."[6]

Tempo (Duration and Frequency)

The tempo of a disorder may provide one of the best clues to the diagnosis of the pain. In facial pain, trigeminal neuralgia (tic douloureux) is described as brief electric shocks or stabbing pain. Onset and termination of attacks are abrupt, and affected patients are usually pain free between episodes. Attacks last only a few seconds. It is not unusual for a series of attacks to occur in rapid succession over several hours. In contrast, the pain of temporal (giant cell) arteritis is usually described as a dull, persistent, gnawing pain that is exacerbated by chewing.[3]

In migraine, the pain is frequently throbbing and may last hours to days. Cluster headaches, by contrast, are named for their periodicity: they occur once or more often each day, last about 30 minutes, and often appear shortly after the onset of sleep. They may occur in clusters for weeks to months with headache-free intervals. In short, the concept of pain tempo is another feature of the targeted history that is helpful in differentiating pain syndromes.

Character and Severity

Although there is considerable overlap between character and severity of pain, some generalization can be made when taking a targeted history. Vascular headaches tend to be throbbing and pulsatile and the pain intensity is often described as severe.[3] Cluster headaches may have a deeper, boring, burning, wrenching quality. This pain is reputed to be among the worst known to humans.

Trigeminal neuralgia is typically described as paroxysmal, jabbing, or shock-like, in contrast to non-neuralgic pain such as temporomandibular joint (TMJ) dysfunction, which is often described as a unilateral, dull, aching pain in the periauricular region. TMJ pain is exacerbated by bruxism, eating, and yawning but may be patternless. The characteristic pain of postherpetic neuralgia usually includes both burning and aching superimposed on paroxysms of shocks and jabs. It usually occurs in association with dysesthesias, resulting in an unpleasant sensation even with the slightest touch over the skin (allodynia).

Many of the more common pain syndromes have a distinctive character and level of severity that is helpful in properly identifying them. Clinical insight into these characteristics comes with time and through listening to many patients describe their pain. Certain patients with cluster headaches or trigeminal neuralgia have a frantic, almost desperate demeanor that is proportionate to the severity of their pain. The patient with acute lumbar disc herniation often writhes before the physician, essentially unable to sit in a chair. The body language and facial expression associated with true excruciating pain are difficult to feign, and exaggerated behaviors often immediately become suspect almost on a visceral level.

Associated Factors

Multiple associated factors round out the targeted pain history. The subtle differences between painful conditions allow us to utilize these factors to complete the various parts of the puzzle. For example, intermittent throbbing pain behind the eye would be consistent with cluster headache. If the patient is a young woman, however, the diagnosis of cluster headache is improbable because of its known male preponderance.[3] Accordingly, the combination of associated factors such as age and sex aid in the diagnosis. A dull, persistent pain over one temple in a young African American male probably is not giant cell or temporal arteritis, a disease most often seen in white women older than 50 years.

Table 4–1 describes various pain syndromes according to patient age, sex, family history, precipitating factors, and occupational issues. As Osler said, "Medicine is a science of uncertainty and an art of probability."[2] Matching our knowledge about the natural history and characteristics of the various diseases that cause pain with information derived from the patient's history is our most powerful diagnostic tool. It is through this process that the physician develops confidence in the diagnosis that often exceeds that based on information from ancillary tests. An autoworker who uses an impact wrench 10 hours a day, complains of numbness in the first three digits of his right hand, and wakes up four times a night "shaking his hand out" has carpal tunnel syndrome, regardless of the results of nerve conduction studies and electromyography.

General Aspects of the Targeted Pain History

An old clinical maxim states, "Healing begins with the history!"[2] The clinician should be able to put the patient at ease and should then ask open-ended questions that will give the patient an opportunity to describe the pain in his or her own words. "Now, tell me about your pain" is an excellent prompt. This approach allows the patient to describe what he or she believes is most important. It is therapeutic in itself. Physicians are often wary of the open-ended question, because they are afraid that the patient will ramble. Although this can occur, a far more common problem is that the physician narrows the line of questioning after jumping to a premature conclusion.

When the pain is chronic, other doctors may already have been consulted. They probably have ordered diagnostic tests and tried therapies; indeed, it is always wise to obtain previous records or, preferably, to contact the other physicians directly. If a diagnosis seems obvious but previous doctors missed it, the physician should be cautious. When nothing has worked before, there is usually a good reason for the failures. Under these circumstances, assuming that the other physicians were competent is prudent and wise. In my experience, physicians are frequent violators of the maxim, "Do unto

Table 4-1

Demographics of Some Common Pain Syndromes*

Pain Syndrome	Sex Preponderance (Ratio)	Family History	Age of Onset (yr)	Associated Features; Comments
Migraine				
Childhood (<10 yr)	M (1.5:1)	Positive	3	Abdominal pain, episodic vertigo, mood changes
Adult (>10 yr)	F (3:1)	Positive	15-20	Decrease by third month of pregnancy, increase with menstruation and oral contraceptives
Cluster headache	M (8:1)	Not positive	25-40	Common at night, precipitated by alcohol and nitrates
Multiple sclerosis	F (2:1)	Positive	20-40	Trigeminal neuralgia, tonic spasms, dysesthesia, extremity pain
Temporal arteritis	F (3:1)	Not positive	>60	Increased erythrocyte sedimentation rate (ESR), anemia, low-grade fever, jaw claudication
Trigeminal neuralgia	F (2:1)	Not positive	>55	V_2 (45%) >V_3, (35%) >V_1 (20%); triggered by jaw movement, heat, and cold
Ankylosing spondylitis	M (5:1)	Positive	20-30	Pain forces patient out of bed at night, is not relieved by lying flat
Rheumatoid arthritis	F (3:1)	Positive	35-50	Higher rate in nulliparous females not exposed to oral contraceptives
Thromboangiitis obliterans	M (8:1)	Not positive	20-40	Smoking
Carpal tunnel syndrome	F (2:1)	Not positive	30-60	Certain occupations, pregnancy, diabetes, hypothyroidism

*Data from references 1, 3, 4, 9, and 10.

others as you would have them do unto you." Frank or subtle criticism of a colleague's efforts is pointless, upsets the patient, and may even initiate litigation.

One other impulse that should be resisted is the tendency to ascribe pain to psychogenic causes. Learning to believe patients who have pain averts many awkward and potentially costly errors. Once the physician projects the belief that a patient's pain is based mainly on psychogenic mechanisms, it is an extremely difficult position to recant. At all costs, the pain specialist should remain nonjudgmental, should believe in the patient's pain, and should gain the patient's confidence. The only proven "cure" for having dismissed a patients' pain as psychogenic is to learn that serious organic disease was uncovered by another physician who saw the patient later in the course of their disease. Like everyone in medicine, pain specialists should be humble and careful with their words.

Medication History

The importance of a thorough drug history cannot be overstated, particularly in the setting of chronic benign pain. It is not unusual for a patient to relate a very involved history of pain and multiple operations, diagnostic studies, and consultations. At the end of the interview, not uncommonly as the patient is preparing to leave, he or she will casually mention needing to have a prescription renewed, adding that it is "just a pain pill." It is at this very point that an otherwise pleasant consultation can become confrontational.

I believe that there is rather widespread confusion among physicians about the differences between narcotics and opioids. Many also fail to recognize that the relative analgesic, euphoric, and anxiolytic properties of a given compound are not equivalent. For example, the analgesic strength of propoxyphene (Darvon) may be equivalent to one or two aspirins, but the magnitude of its anxiolytic effects on a given patient can be considerable. It is not only opioids that pose a problem. Carisoprodol (Soma, Rela) is a non-controlled skeletal muscle relaxant that is also available through veterinary supply catalogs.[7] Its active metabolite is meprobamate (Equanil, Miltown), an anxiolytic-sedative agent popular in the late 1950s. Patients using carisoprodol may be at risk (frequently unrecognized) for meprobamate dependency.

Triptans, ergots, aspirin, acetaminophen, nonsteroidal antiinflammatory drugs (NSAIDs), minor tranquilizers, and barbiturate-containing compounds (Fiorinal, Esgic, and Phrenilin) taken in varying doses can contribute to "rebound"-type headache. In this setting, the daily use of abortive drugs enhances and increases the frequency of daily headaches. The scope of this problem is difficult to assess, but in certain headache clinics, taking such drugs is the single most common reason for chronic refractory daily headaches.[8] Although every pharmacologic agent has some inherent risk, two practical considerations may be crucial in the targeted pain history. The first involves many individuals, particularly elderly persons, who are taking anticoagulants (warfarin, heparin) or antiplatelet agents (aspirin, clopidogrel [Plavix] and ticlopidine [Ticlid]) for any of a variety of reasons. Many disasters can occur in this setting. Inadvertent overdosing of an elderly, confused patient can cause intracerebral bleeding (headache) or back and radicular pain (secondary to retroperitoneal hemorrhage). Second, the physician evaluating headache symptoms should keep in mind that estrogen, progesterone, and nitrates can play major roles as provocative agents and that simply removing them can provide almost immediate improvement.

I believe that both the scope and frequency of problems related to chemical dependency have been underrecognized in many clinical settings. I see patients who are willing to subject themselves to expensive diagnostic studies, multiple nerve blocks, and even surgery to ensure an uninterrupted supply of specific medications (frequently opioids). The specialist in pain management is uniquely positioned to recognize these problems and to offer suggestions in a compassionate, nonjudgmental fashion that may ultimately extricate patients from both their chemical dependency and their convoluted relationship with the medical system. Until drug dependency issues are addressed, effective inroads into the management of chronic pain will be thwarted.

Certain clinicians have described a satisfactory experience administering opioids for chronic benign pain.[9,10] I believe that their positive experience (along with aggressive pharmaceutical company marketing) has promoted liberal prescribing policies in primary care physicians and specialists treating common conditions such as back pain, arthritis, and fibromyalgia. Be aware that the chronic use of opioids in these diseases is not supported by strong scientific evidence and remains controversial.[11]

In my opinion, such an ambiguous situation only accentuates the importance of obtaining a thorough drug history and assessing the true impact of drug use on the individual patient's pain problems. Table 4–2 lists the "red flag" agents that, when used by a patient in pain, should alert the physician to consider possible drug abuse or exacerbation of pain by medication. Information on dosage and duration of use is important.

Pain specialists should make it policy to insist that patients bring all their medications at the time of the consultation. If you as a physician believe that a patient has a drug dependency problem, face the problem openly and with kindness. Resist the all too common practice of writing a script for that magical minimal amount of the drug being abused, an amount that can end the consultation without a dreaded angry confrontation. For those of us in clinical practice, this all too familiar "end of consult" strategy of providing what we know to be part of the problem, prepare to assume your share of the guilt, Dr. Feelgood, in this major public health disaster.

General Aspects of the Patient Interview

The following general but significant points enhance the patient interview process:

- The surroundings are professional, comfortable, and private.

- The patient is appropriately gowned, is chaperoned if appropriate, and is sitting upright and at eye level with the interviewer, if possible.
- Old records, scans, radiographs, and consultations have been obtained and reviewed before the consultation.
- The physician listens to and does not interrupt the patient or allow outside interruptions.
- The physician remains nonjudgmental; moral, religious, and political beliefs of the physician are irrelevant to this process.
- The physician is honest and open with the patient; keeping information from the patient at the family's request is usually a bad decision.
- Both the patient and the physician can trust in the confidentiality of both the consultation and the medical records.

It is important to remember that the specialty of pain management is practiced by physicians from a number of disciplines. In particular, physicians trained in operating room anesthesia may not be as sensitive to some certain issues. In my own experience, as a neurologist for whom interviewing patients is a major component of practice, these basic rules of common etiquette are frequently ignored. First, the office should be both professional and comfortable. For reasons of economy, pain clinics are frequently placed in noisy and crowded additions to either the operating room suite or the emergency room. This atmosphere may not be conducive to dealing with patients with acute and chronic pain, who are often extremely apprehensive and easily frustrated.

It is important that patients have a private place where they undress and are examined. Although this may appear to be a small point, a chaotic examining site can inspire a patient's resentment, even if the medical care is of high quality. One other point that needs reinforcing is that physician and patient should always be properly chaperoned. It is not unusual, because of the hectic schedules of both physicians and ancillary personnel, for a patient and physician to be left alone in situations in which this arrangement is at best uncomfortable and at worst compromising and dangerous. Strict adherence to standardized protocol for chaperoning is really the best way of averting serious problems in this area. The keys to obtaining a complete and effective targeted pain history are as follows. The examiner should:

1. Build rapport with the patient by introducing self properly, taking an initial social history, and simultaneously assessing the patient's mood, anxiety level, and capability of giving a history on his or her own.
2. *Most importantly:* Establish the chief complaint at the outset of the history. Why is the patient here? Open-ended questions allow the patient to tell his or her own story.
3. Utilize the framework of the pain litany (discussed earlier) to further investigate the pain. Where is the pain? What is its nature?
4. Do not jump to conclusions. This is the most common cause of error because the interview too soon becomes too narrowly focused and important associations are not pursued

Table 4–2

"Red Flag" Drugs in the Targeted Pain History

Drug Class	Drug
Controlled Abused Substances *	
Schedule II narcotics	Morphine (Roxanol, MS Contin)
	Codeine, fentanyl (Sublimaze)
	Sufentanil (Sufenta)
	Hydromorphone (Dilaudid)
	Meperidine (Demerol)
	Methadone (Dolophine)
	Oxycodone (Percodan, Tylox, OxyContin, Roxicodone)
	Opium
	Cocaine
Non-narcotic agents	Dextroamphetamine (Dexedrine, Adderal)
	Methamphetamine (Desoxyn)
	Methylphenidate (Ritalin)
	Phenmetrazine (Preludin)
	Amobarbital (Amytal)
	Pentobarbital (Nembutal)
	Secobarbital (Seconal)
	Glutethimide (Doriden)
	Secobarbital-amobarbital (Tuinal)
Schedule III narcotics	Codeine (Tylenol w/codeine, Fiorinal w/codeine)
	Dihydrocodeine (Synalgos-DC)
	Hydrocodone (Tussionex, Hycodan, Vicodin, Lortab, Lorcet)
	Butalbital (Fiorinal, Esgic, Phrenilin, Medigesic)
Schedule IV narcotics	Propoxyphene (Darvon, Darvocet, Wygesic)
	Butorphanol (Stadol)
	Pentazocine (Talwin)
	Alprazolam (Xanax)
	Chlordiazepoxide (Librium)
	Clonazepam (Klonopin)
	Clorazepate (Tranxene)
	Diazepam (Valium)
	Flurazepam (Dalmane)
	Lorazepam (Ativan)
	Midazolam (Versed)
	Oxazepam (Serax)
	Quazepam (Doral)
	Temazepam (Restoril)
	Triazolam (Halcion)
	Zapelon (Sonata)
	Zopiclone (Lunesta)
	Zolpidem (Ambien)
Non-narcotic agents	Phenobarbital
	Mephobarbital (Mebaral)
	Chloral hydrate
	Ethchlorvynol (Placidyl)
	Meprobamate (Equanil, Equagesic)
Schedule V	Buprenorphine (Buprenex)
	Diphenoxylate (Lomotil)
	Pregabalin (Lyrica)
Noncontrolled Abused Substances	Carisoprodol (Soma, Rela)
	Ergotamine (Cafergot, Wigraine, Ergostat)
	Chlordiazepoxide (Librax)
	Tramadol (Ultram, Ultracet) ⎫ Both nonscheduled opioids
	Nalbuphine (Nubain) ⎭
	Butalbital with acetaminophen (Fioricet)
Nonabused Drugs Important in a Targeted Pain History	Oral contraceptives
	Anticoagulants (heparin, warfarin, plavix)
	Antiplatelet agents (aspirin, ticlopidine)
	Antianginals (nitrates)

*Narcotic is a nonspecific term still used by state boards to describe a drug that induces sleep or dependence: It is not interchangeable with opioid. This table lists many (but not all) drugs that may be abused by patients with pain.

From Brust JC: Neurological Aspects of Substance Abuse. Boston, Butterworth-Heinemann, 1993, and Missouri Taskforce on the Misuse, Abuse and Diversion of Prescription Drugs, 1994.

or are ignored. The examiner should ask about other doctors whom the patient has seen and their treatments.

5. Determine the impact of the pain on the patient's life—psychological fears, family issues (marriage), compensation, work record.

6. Explore past medical and family history. Using a timeline approach to establish continuity, the current pain should be placed in context with other major medical events: previous surgery, hospitalizations, cancer, medical and paramedical relationships.

7. Obtain a thorough drug history (see Table 4–2). Duration, frequency, amount, and source of medication should be asked about. The importance of this information cannot be overemphasized.

The examination should begin with the physician's introducing himself or herself to the patient and putting the patient at ease. A routine social history, such as occupation, place of employment, marital status, and number of children, should be obtained. During this interchange, the physician should be assessing the verbal and nonverbal cues that ultimately determine the caliber of the historical information. This social introduction affords the physician insight into what type of person the patient is. Over time and with the refinements of experience, this portion of the interview assumes diagnostic importance equal to that of the data-gathering portion of the consultation.

It would seem obvious that the patient's chief complaint would be the logical starting point of any history. Unfortunately, it is my experience that a great deal of time can be spent taking a history without ever addressing the chief complaint. Coming to grips with the patient's primary reason for seeking medical attention is really the crucial piece of data. Is it the pain? Is it questions about disability or worker's compensation? Is it a morbid fear of cancer? Is it that the physician who prescribed the patient's pain medications has retired and the patient is concerned about prescription renewal? Until the physician has a strong sense of the principal reason for the consultation, the history is often both misguided and aimless. Sitting in front of the patient, the physician should always ask himself or herself, "Why has this patient come to see me?" Sometimes, the patient's motives are not what they first appear to be.

Summary of the Targeted History

I cannot overstate the value of the targeted history. It affords the physician the greatest chance of understanding the nature of the pain and, more important, its effects on the patient. Diagnostic tests, laboratory reports, and other consultants' opinions often introduce error when interpreted from a perspective detached from the patient. The physician should remember that, no matter how many physicians have seen the patient earlier, historical facts critical to the diagnosis may have been overlooked or not properly sought.

Taking the targeted history is a social interaction. Courtesy, professionalism, and kindness consistently result in patient satisfaction. Issues related to compensation, returning to work, and concurrent drug use should be dealt with openly and directly, without imposing the physician's personal, political, or religious value judgments.

■ THE TARGETED PHYSICAL EXAMINATION

If after obtaining the targeted historical information, the pain specialist is lost, the chance that the situation may be suddenly illuminated by the physical examination findings is extremely remote. As a basic point, I emphasize that the physical examination should follow the history and, indeed, be specifically directed by clues obtained during the patient interview. For example, it makes little sense to concentrate on a detailed examination of the sensory function and individual muscle testing in the lower extremities for a patient who has diplopia, facial pain, and a family history of multiple sclerosis.[12] The physical examination is an extension of the history, providing objective support but performed efficiently and systematically so that important findings are not overlooked.

The examination should not consume a great deal of time. Basic aspects, such as taking blood pressure, performing a screening mental status examination, and checking visual acuity, strength, and deep tendon reflexes, however, pay multiple dividends. On occasion, certain important diseases, such as unrecognized hypertension, diabetic retinopathy, and skin cancer, can be uncovered.

The very physical aspect of examining the patient imparts a reassuring sense of personal caring to the entire consultation. The benefits of this experience are considerable. Pain patients want to be examined, expect to be examined, and ultimately derive benefit from the process. As Goethe said, "We see only what we know."[13] The facility with which we examine patients is ultimately a function of our knowledge, experience, and willingness to learn.

General Aspects

The patient's temperature, pulse, and blood pressure should always be recorded, as should height and weight. The patient should be undressed and properly gowned. It is a constant source of amazement to me how frequently patients are evaluated for painful conditions, even those involving the neck and low back, while remaining fully clothed during the entire examination. The pain specialist should examine the entire body for skin lesions such as hemangiomas, areas of hyperpigmentation, and café au lait spots (neurofibromatosis); document scars from previous operations; and inquire into other scars not mentioned in the initial history. Needle marks, skin ulcerations, and tattoos (which sometimes betray drug culture orientation) may be surprising findings.

The spine should be examined for kyphosis, lordosis, scoliosis, and focal areas of tenderness. Dimpling of the skin or excessive hair growth may suggest spina bifida or meningocele. The motility of the spine should also be evaluated in flexion, extension, and lateral rotation. During this period of the examination, an overall assessment of multiple joints can be done for deformities, arthritic change, trauma, and prior surgery. Clearly, there is much to be learned just by having the patient stand before the physician and asking the patient about abnormalities that become noticeable. No matter how inconvenient or uncomfortable it is, the physician should try never to omit this portion of the examination. Particularly in chronic pain patients, this part of the examination may yield crucial and unexpected revelations.

Table 4–3	

The "Quick and Dirty" Mental Status Examination

Orientation	Ask the following questions: What is your full name? What is today's date? What is the year? Who is the president? Who is the vice president?
Calculations	Ask the following questions: How many nickels are in a dollar? How many dollars do 60 nickles make?
Memory	Ask the following questions: What was your mother's maiden name? Who was President before George W. Bush? Give the patient three items to remember (examples, a red ball, a blue telephone, and address 66 Hill Street). After several minutes of conversation, ask the patient to repeat the list.
Speech	Have the patient repeat two simple sentences, such as: Today is a lovely day. The weather this weekend is expected to be excellent. Have the patient name several objects in the room. Ask the patient to rhyme simple words, such as ball, pat, and can.
Comprehension	Ask the patient to: Put the right hand on the left hand. Point to the ceiling with the left index finger.

This simple screening mental status examination uncovers many (but not all) cognitive deficits. It can be performed in less than 3 minutes and is useful in evaluating basic aspects of memory, language, and general intellectual capacity.

Assessment of Mental Status

Most major intellectual and psychiatric problems become apparent during the history taking. The frequency with which serious intellectual deficits are missed is, however, surprising. For example, subtle aspects of memory, comprehension, and language may not be caught unless they are specifically sought. In my experience, aphasia (a general term for all disturbances of language not the result of faulty articulation) is frequently mistaken for an organic mental syndrome or dementia. Recognition of this point not only is critical in diagnostic evaluation but also has important implications for obtaining informed consent for testing, nerve blocks, and surgical procedures.

Table 4–3 summarizes my approach to rapid assessment of the patient's mental status. Each practitioner should develop a personal set of standard questions to gain a sense of the normal versus the abnormal. Attention to these details in assessing mental status helps to avoid the embarrassment of overlooking a receptive aphasia, Alzheimer disease, or Korsakoff syndrome. Table 4–4 is the classic Folstein Mini Mental Status Examination with age-adjusted normative data. A score of 24 or above is considered normal. Although it is effective in detecting clinically significant defects in speech and cognitive function, I believe the average practitioner will find it overly tedious for use in a routine pain management evaluation. In many of these situations, patients exhibit an unusual capacity to disguise underlying deficits by reverting to evasions or generalities or by filling in gaps with stereotypical responses that they have used before to escape the embarrassment of the discovery of major problems in language, memory, and other spheres of cognitive function.[14]

One final point relates to the patient's emotional state. The examiner must remain vigilant about the patient's mood and displays of emotion. An unusually silly, euphoric, or grandiose presentation may be seen in manic states. Likewise, a discouraged, hopeless, or self-deprecating presentation may signal serious depression. As highlighted in the discussion on the targeted history, the physician must remain alert for clinical manifestations of drug use, such as slurred speech, motor hyperactivity, sweating, flushing, and distractibility. In short, the physician should get to know the patient but, in the end, should vigorously resist any early impulse to suggest that stress or anxiety alone is the principal cause of the patient's pain.

Cranial Nerves

To return to the theme of keeping the targeted physical examination simple so that important points are not missed: The evaluation of cranial nerve (CN) function often overwhelms practitioners not trained in clinical neurology. It remains an important area, particularly in the evaluation of headache and facial pain. Rapid recognition of CN dysfunction may have profound significance for localizing a cerebral lesion or identifying increased intracranial pressure, or, in combination with the history, may be a strong indicator of a specific disease (e.g., explosive headache plus CN III palsy implies a ruptured aneurysm until that is ruled out).

Table 4–5 highlights an efficient approach to the clinical evaluation of the cranial nerves. Certainly, when headache and facial pain are the basic issues, particular attention should be given to this portion of the examination. The key, once again, is developing a routine that, with practice, becomes thorough. It is far beyond the scope of this chapter to describe all the nuances of cranial nerve function.[15] Anyone evaluating patients for headache or facial pain should be able at least

Table 4–4		

Folstein Mini Mental Status Examination

Task	Instructions	Scoring	
Date Orientation	"Tell me the date?" Ask for omitted items.	One point each for year, season, date, day of week, and month	5
Place Orientation	"Where are you?" Ask for omitted items.	One point each for state, county, town, building, and floor or room	5
Register 3 Objects	Name three objects slowly and clearly. Ask the patient to repeat them.	One point for each item correctly repeated	3
Serial Sevens	Ask the patient to count backwards from 100 by 7. Stop after five answers. (Or ask them to spell "world" backwards.)	One point for each correct answer (or letter)	5
Recall 3 Objects	Ask the patient to recall the objects mentioned above.	One point for each item correctly remembered	3
Naming	Point to your watch and ask the patient "what is this?" Repeat with a pencil.	One point for each correct answer	2
Repeating a Phrase	Ask the patient to say "no ifs, ands, or buts."	One point if successful on first try	1
Verbal Commmands	Give the patient a plain piece of paper and say "Take this paper in your right hand, fold it in half, and put it on the floor."	One point for each correct action	3
Written Commands	Show the patient a piece of paper with "CLOSE YOUR EYES" printed on it.	One point if the patient's eyes close	1
Writing	Ask the patient to write a sentence.	One point if sentence has a subject, a verb, and makes sense	1
Drawing	Ask the patient to copy a pair of intersecting pentagons onto a piece of paper.	One point if the figure has ten corners and two intersecting lines	1
Scoring	A score of 24 or above is considered normal.		30

Adapted from Folstein et al: Mini Mental State. J Psych Res 12:196-198, 1975.

to recognize papilledema and abnormalities of ocular motor nerve function, be familiar with the sensory division of the trigeminal nerve, and be able to recognize isolated cranial nerve palsies. More complex problems, such as diplopia, cavernous sinus disease, and complex brainstem lesions, are best left to specialists in neuro-ophthalmology and neurology.

In general, the pain specialist, even one whose basic training has been in anesthesia or psychiatry, can, with the proper effort, become familiar with the basics of common disorders. Ultimately, the physician who does make the effort to learn this material and incorporate it into clinical pain management practice will not have to deal constantly with feeling uneasy about a weakness in clinical aptitude. Such a physician will also avoid losing precious time in developing experience with these key physical findings associated with a variety of headache and facial pain problems.

Motor Examination

Motor examination should begin with inspection of muscle volume and contour, paying particular attention to atrophy and hypertrophy. The patient should be properly gowned so that these observations can be made without invading the patient's privacy. During this examination, fasciculations, contractures, alterations in posture, and adventitious movements may be identified. Strength is measured both proximally and distally in the upper and lower extremities and is graded according to the scale shown in Table 4–6. Detailed individual muscle testing is not carried out unless a specific nerve root or plexopathy is under investigation.

Tone is best tested by passive manipulation, note being made of the resistance of muscle when voluntary control is absent. Changes in tone are more readily detected in muscles of the arms and legs than in muscles of the trunk. Relaxation is critical to proper evaluation. Hypertonicity is usually seen with lesions rostral to the anterior horn cells, including brain, brain stem, and spinal cord. Hypotonicity is associated with diseases affecting the neuroaxis below this level, involving nerve root, peripheral nerve, neuromuscular junction, and muscle. Study of the motor system should be integrated with evaluation of the sensory examination and deep tendon reflexes, to provide cumulative information

Table 4–5

Clinical Evaluations of Cranial Nerve Function

Cranial Nerve(s)

Number	Name	Evaluation Procedure(s)
I	Olfactory	Test ability to identify familiar aromatic odors, one naris at a time with eyes closed (not routinely tested)
II	Optic	Test vision with Snellen chart or Rosenbaum near-vision chart Perform ophthalmoscopic examination of fundi Be able to recognize papilledema Test fields of vision using confrontation and double simultaneous stimulation
III, IV, VI	Oculomotor, trochlear, abducens	Inspect eyelids for drooping (ptosis) Inspect pupil size for equality (direct and consensual response) Check for nystagmus Assess basic fields of gaze Note asymmetrical extraocular movements
V	Trigeminal	Palpate jaw muscles for tone and strength while patient clenches teeth Test superficial pain and touch sensation in each branch: V_1, V_2, V_3
VII	Facial	Test corneal reflex Inspect symmetry of facial features Have patient smile, frown, puff cheeks, wrinkle forehead Watch for spasmodic, jerking movements of face
VIII	Acoustic	Test sense of hearing with watch or tuning fork Compare bone and air conduction of sound
IX	Glossopharyngeal	Test gag reflex and ability to swallow
X	Vagus	Inspect palate and uvula for symmetry with gag reflex Observe for swallowing difficulty Have patient take small sip of water Watch for nasal or hoarse quality of speech
IX	Spinal accessory	Test trapezius strength (have patient shrug shoulders against resistance) Test sternocleidomastoid muscle strength (have patient turn head to each side against resistance)
XII	Hypoglossal	Inspect tongue in mouth and while protruded for symmetry, fasciculations, and atrophy Test tongue strength with index fingers when tongue is pressed against cheek

Table 4–6

Grading of Muscle Strength

Clinical Finding	Grade	Percent of Normal Response
No evidence of contractility	0	0
Slight contractility, no movement	1	10
Full range of motion, gravity eliminated	2	25
Full range of motion with gravity	3	50
Full range of motion against gravity, some resistance	4	75
Full range of motion against gravity, full resistance	5	100

From Chipps EM, Clanin NJ, Campbell VG: Neurologic Disorder. St. Louis, Mosby-Year Book, 1992.

critical to identifying "the site of lesion"—brain, brain stem, spinal cord, root, plexus, nerve, or muscle.

Sensory Examination

The sensory examination should be kept simple and should be targeted by clues obtained through the history. Certainly, time spent in defining sensory loss in the lower extremities would be justified in a patient complaining of pain, weakness, and numbness in the foot but not in one who has double vision and facial pain. Note in Figure 4–2 the difference between the skin areas innervated by dermatomes—specific segments of the cord, roots, or dorsal root ganglia—and the corresponding peripheral nerve cutaneous sensory distribution. Knowledge

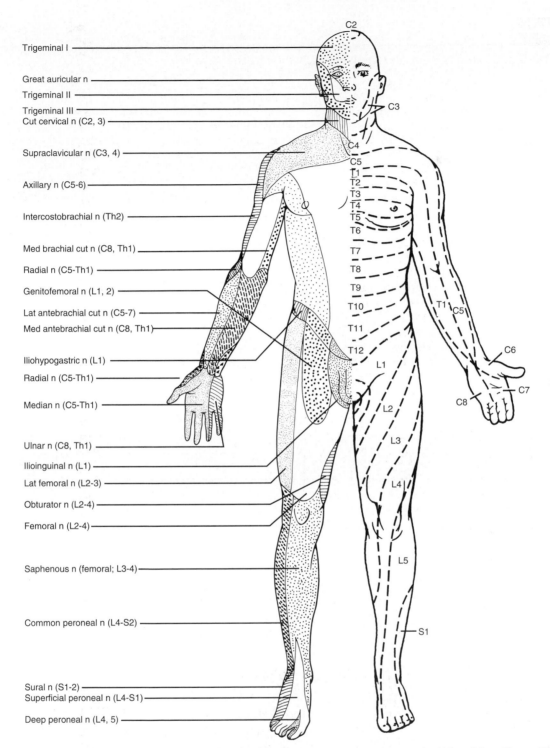

Trigeminal I
Great auricular n
Trigeminal II
Trigeminal III
Cut cervical n (C2, 3)
Supraclavicular n (C3, 4)
Axillary n (C5-6)
Intercostobrachial n (Th2)
Med brachial cut n (C8, Th1)
Radial n (C5-Th1)
Genitofemoral n (L1, 2)
Lat antebrachial cut n (C5-7)
Med antebrachial cut n (C8, Th1)
Iliohypogastric n (L1)
Radial n (C5-Th1)
Median n (C5-Th1)
Ulnar n (C8, Th1)
Ilioinguinal n (L1)
Lat femoral n (L2-3)
Obturator n (L2-4)
Femoral n (L2-4)
Saphenous n (femoral; L3-4)
Common peroneal n (L4-S2)
Sural n (S1-2)
Superficial peroneal n (L4-S1)
Deep peroneal n (L4, 5)

FIGURE 4–2 ■ Comparison of spinal segmental (dermatomal) and peripheral nerve cutaneous sensory supply. (Adapted from Haerer AF [ed]: DeJong's The Neurologic Examination, 5th ed. Philadelphia, JB Lippincott, 1992.)

of these specific differences and of changes in motor function and reflexes clinically define a nerve root from a peripheral nerve abnormality. Tables 4–7 and 4–8 highlight comparisons between specific spinal root and peripheral nerve lesions of the upper and lower extremities. With time, experience, and persistence, the pain specialist can become confident in the evaluation of peripheral nerve root lesions. So many of the common pain syndromes (cervical radiculopathies, lumbar

radiculopathies, carpal tunnel syndrome, femoral neuropathy, peroneal neuropathy) may be rapidly and accurately diagnosed without expensive and uncomfortable neurodiagnostic testing. Being persistent and resisting the fear that the task is overwhelming results in the ability to efficiently evaluate patients in pain.

For pain syndromes of the upper extremity, the examiner should be able to differentiate sensory involvement of the

Table 4–7

Clinical Manifestations of Root Versus Nerve Lesions in the Arm

Roots	C5	C6	C7	C8	T1
Sensory supply	Lateral border upper arm	Lateral forearm, including finger I	Over triceps, mid-forearm and finger III	Medial forearm to finger V	Axilla to elbow
Reflex affected	Biceps reflex	None	Triceps reflex	None	None
Motor loss	Deltoid Infraspinatus Rhomboids Supraspinatus	Biceps Brachialis Brachioradialis	Latissimus dorsi Pectoralis major Triceps Wrist extensors Wrist flexors	Finger extensors Finger flexors Flexor carpi ulnaris	Intrinsic hand muscles (in some thenar muscles through C8)
Nerves	**Axillary (C5, C6)**	**(C5, C6)**	**Radial (C5-C8)**	**Median (C6-C8, T1)**	**Ulnar (C8, T1)**
Sensory supply	Over deltoid	Lateral forearm to wrist	Lateral dorsal forearm and back of thumb and finger II	Lateral palm and lateral finger I, II, III and half of IV	Medial palm and finger V and medial half of finger IV
Reflex affected	None	Biceps reflex	Triceps reflex	None	None
Motor loss	Deltoid	Biceps Brachialis	Brachioradialis Finger extensors Forearm supinator Triceps wrist extensors	Abductor pollicis brevis Long flexors of fingers I, II, III Pronators of forearm Wrist flexors	Intrinsic hand muscles Flexor carpi ulnaris Flexors of fingers IV, V

From Patten J: Neurological Differential Diagnosis. New York, Springer-Verlag, 1977.

Table 4–8

Clinical Manifestations of Root Versus Nerve Lesions in the Leg

Roots	L2	L3	L4	L5	S1
Sensory supply	Across upper thigh	Across lower thigh	Across knee to medial malleolus	Side of leg to dorsum and sole of foot	Behind lateral malleolus to lateral foot
Reflex affected	None	None	Patellar reflex	None	Achilles reflex
Motor loss	Hip flexion	Knee extension	Inversion of foot	Dorsiflexion of toes and foot	Plantar flexion and eversion of foot
Nerves	**Obturator (L2-L4)**	**Nerve Femoral (L2-L4)**	**Peroneal Division of Sciatic Nerve (L4, L5, S1-S3)**		**Tibial Division of Sciatic Nerve (L4, L5, S1-S3)**
Sensory supply	Medial thigh	Anterior thigh to medial malleolus	Anterior leg to dorsum of foot		Posterior leg to sole and lateral aspect of foot
Reflex affected	None	Patellar reflex	None		Achilles reflex
Motor loss	Adduction of thigh	Extension of knee	Dorsiflexion, inversion, and eversion of foot		Plantar flexion and inversion of foot

From Patten J: Neurological Differential Diagnosis. New York, Springer-Verlag, 1977.

radial, median, and ulnar nerves from that of specific roots (C5-T1) (Table 4–7). For pain syndromes of the lower extremities, the examiner should be able to differentiate the peroneal and tibial nerve sensory distribution from that of the L4, L5, and S1 roots (Table 4–8). Such distinctions elucidate most of the common problems. Over time, the pain specialist can increase confidence in his examination and may develop a stronger foundation in peripheral neurology than many neurologists, neurosurgeons, and orthopedists possess.

Deep Tendon Reflexes

Deep tendon reflexes are actually muscle stretch reflexes mediated through neuromuscular spindles. They are the one

Chapter 4 History and Physical Examination of the Pain Patient ■ 47

Table 4–9

Deep Tendon Reflex Scale

Grade	Deep Tendon Reflex Response
0+	No response
1+	Sluggish
2+	Active or normal
3+	More brisk than expected, slightly hyperactive
4+	Abnormally hyperactive, with intermittent clonus

From Seidel HM, et al: Mosby's Guide to Physical Examination, 3rd ed. St. Louis, Mosby-Year Book, 1995.

facet of the clinical examination that is objective (Table 4–9). Responses to mental status testing and motor examination, performance on sensory testing, and even gait can be consciously altered by the patient for any of a variety of reasons. Guillain-Barré syndrome (acute inflammatory polyneuropathy), however, a condition that in its initial stages may be misdiagnosed as anxiety related, characteristically shows absence of all the deep tendon reflexes, which is an important early clue to the organic nature of the disorder.

A deep tendon reflex examination can be graded using the numerals 1 through 4 (Fig. 4–3). I have not found testing of the superficial reflexes, such as the abdominal or cremasteric reflexes, to be of particular value in clinical assessment. The only superficial reflex I evaluate is the plantar reflex (a superficial reflex innervated by the tibial nerve, L4-S2). The response to stroking the plantar surface of the foot is usually flexion of both the foot and the toes. In diseases of the cortical spinal system, there is dorsiflexion of the toes, especially the great toe, with separation or fanning of the others; this, Babinski sign of upper motor neuron involvement (brain, brain stem, and spinal cord), is often paired with increased deep tendon reflexes and clonus (i.e., sustained muscular contractions following a stretch stimulus noted frequently in the ankle).

Unilateral absence of a deep tendon reflex implies disease at the peripheral nerve or root level. Diffuse reduction or absence of deep tendon reflexes suggests a more generalized process affecting the peripheral nerve, seen frequently in peripheral neuropathies secondary to diabetes, alcohol abuse, or inflammation. The objective data obtained quite rapidly from testing deep tendon reflexes are correlated with motor and sensory findings to determine whether a problem lies in a specific peripheral nerve, specific nerve root, diffuse peripheral nerve, or spinal cord. It should take less than 30 seconds to complete this part of the examination.

Examination of Gait

Walking is an intricate process influenced by mechanical factors such as muscles, bones, tendons, and joints and, more importantly, dependent on nervous system integration. Just watching the patient walk during the examination is an extremely valuable exercise. I suggest that the patient be asked to walk with the eyes open and closed and to stand with the eyes open and closed (Romberg sign). Gaits associated with parkinsonism (small, short steps with a stooped posture),

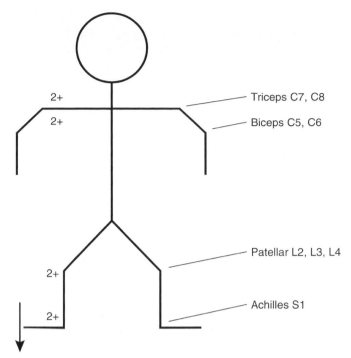

FIGURE 4–3 ■ Diagram of a deep tendon reflex examination. (From Waldman SD [ed]: Interventional Pain Management, 2nd ed. Philadelphia, Saunders, 2001, p 95, Figure 8-2, with permission.)

normal pressure hydrocephalus (magnetic gait, as if the patient were walking in magnetic shoes across a metal floor), muscular dystrophy, stroke, peripheral nerve injury, cerebellar ataxia, Huntington chorea, and hysteria (astasia-abasia) are but a few characteristic patterns of disturbed locomotion. In short, a strong measure of neuro-orthopedic well-being is implied by the patient who walks well with the eyes open and closed.

■ CONCLUSION

The basic point of this chapter is simple. A targeted, well-organized pain history is the foundation of proper diagnosis. Advances in diagnostic technology, no matter how sophisticated, cannot replace listening to the patient's story of their illness. It is through this process that we most effectively gain insight, not only into the nature of the illness but, more importantly, into the personality of the patient who is in pain. The professionalism and sensitivity with which we obtain this information does much to establish our relationship with the patient and the ultimate success of our therapies. If there is any room for shortcuts, it is not in this portion of the evaluation.

The targeted physical examination should be viewed as an extension of the insights derived from the history. It should be performed in a professional, thorough, but not laborious fashion. As the calling of pain management becomes more popular, physicians of various disciplines should avoid faddish technologic advances and opportunism made possible by inequities in reimbursement and should commit themselves to the very basics: obtaining historical data and eliciting physical findings. In my opinion, energy expended to this end will reduce costs, enhance patient satisfaction, and foster lasting credibility in the evolving field of pain management.

References

1. Rowland LP (ed): Merritt's Textbook of Neurology, ed 7. Philadelphia, Lea & Febiger, 1984.
2. Judge RD, Zuidema GD, Fitzgerald FT (eds): Clinical Diagnosis: A Physiologic Approach, ed 5. Boston, Little, Brown, 1989.
3. Diamond S, Dalessio DJ (eds): The Practicing Physician's Approach to Headache, ed 4. Baltimore, Williams & Wilkins, 1986.
4. Waldman SD: Trigeminal Neuralgia. Atlas of Common Pain Syndromes, Philadelphia. WB Saunders, 2002.
5. Patten J: Neurological Differential Diagnosis. New York, Springer-Verlag, 1977.
6. Quote attributed to Mark Twain: [1835-1910].
7. Littrell RA, Haye LR, Stillner V: Carisoprodol (Soma): A new and cautious perspective on an old agent. South Med J 86:753, 1993.
8. Waldman SD: Analgesic rebound headache. Atlas of Common Pain Syndromes, Philadelphia, WB Saunders, 2002.
9. Warfield CA (ed): Manual of Pain Management. Philadelphia, Lippincott Williams & Wilkins, 2002.
10. Trachtenberg AI: Opiates for pain: Patients' tolerance and society's intolerance (Letter to the editor). JAMA 271:427, 1994.
11. Ballantyne JC, Mao J: Opioid therapy for chronic pain. N Engl J Med 349:1943, 2003.
12. Heyman CH, Rossman HS: A multimodal approach to managing the symptoms of multiple sclerosis. Neurology 14:63:S12, 2004.
13. Goethe JW: Trilogy of Passion, 1824.
14. Chipps EM, Clanin NJ, Campbell VG: Neurologic Disorders. St. Louis, CV Mosby, 1992.
15. Goetz CG (ed): Textbook of Clinical Neurology, ed 2. Philadelphia, WB Saunders, 2002.

chapter 5

Patterns of Common Pain Syndromes

Bernard M. Abrams

Discussions of patterns of pain syndromes form a large portion of this comprehensive book. The text is divided into sections on generalized pain syndromes, including acute pain syndromes, neuropathic pain syndromes, malignant pain syndromes, pain of dermatologic origin, and pain of musculoskeletal origin, and regional pain syndromes, encompassing virtually every part of the body. This chapter does not reiterate material that is discussed in detail in appropriate chapters, but rather outlines the general features and underlying principles of patterns in pain-producing syndromes.

Pain is defined by the International Association for the Study of Pain as an unpleasant sensory and emotional experience associated with actual or potential tissue damage or described in terms of such damage. There are several types of pain.

Nociceptive pain is caused by the ongoing activation of nociceptors (pain receptors) in response to noxious or potentially noxious stimuli. It may be cutaneous, deep somatic, or visceral. It is associated with "proper functioning" of the nervous system, and generally the severity of the pain corresponds closely to the intensity of the stimulus. Although its characteristics may vary with the part of the body involved, the tissues under attack, or the intensity, acuteness, or chronicity of the process, nociceptive pain is familiar, expected, recognizable, and attributable to a source. In short, "it makes sense," or, in modern parlance, it "computes." A wide variety of pain types and patterns emerge.

Neuropathic pain is caused by aberrant signal processing in the peripheral or central nervous system and reflects nervous system damage or dysfunction. It has an unexpected aspect, detached from an obvious stimulus intensity or putative tissue damage. It is characterized by burning, tingling, or shooting sensations, which may be spontaneous or evoked, steady or intermittent. This pain may be associated with other clear-cut neurologic phenomena, such as sensory loss, allodynia (pain elicited by a non-noxious stimulus, such as clothing, air movement, touch, or an ordinarily nonpainful cold or warm stimulus), or hyperalgesia (exaggerated painful response to a mildly noxious, mechanical or thermal stimulus). Common sources of neuropathic pain include trauma, metabolic disease (e.g., diabetes mellitus), infection (e.g., herpes zoster), tumors, toxins, side effects of medications (especially chemotherapeutic and antiviral agents used to treat HIV infections), and primary neurologic diseases. Central pain may arise in the setting of stroke, tumor, spinal cord injury, or multiple sclerosis. Neuropathic pain has the characteristic of unfamiliarity, is often inexplicable, is hard to believe (even for the experienced observer), and, in short, "doesn't compute."

Another caveat concerns "what is common." This depends on the patient/physician setting (e.g., whether it is an emergency department, cancer center, or pain clinic). Physician specialty and interests also play an important role. The painful manifestations of rheumatoid arthritis or multiple sclerosis and painful peripheral neuropathies are rarely seen at an average pain clinic, which is more concerned with problems of the axial spine, complex regional pain syndrome, and postherpetic neuralgia. Conditions seen on a daily basis by podiatrists, rheumatologists, or orthopedists may be *terra incognita* to the pain physician.

There are several universals in pain patterns. Pain patterns have a temporal and spatial distribution; characteristic pain types (e.g., burning, tearing, gnawing, deep, superficial); and often associated medical diagnoses, other symptoms, and other features that offer important clues to the diagnosis and management. One of the most overlooked features of pain patterns is the occurrence of a secondary or tertiary type of pain pattern. This feature is clearly apparent in radiculopathies, which often manifest as a sharp (and sharply delineated) pain ("epicritic pain") and tend to obscure a deeper, less well-delineated gnawing-type pain ("protopathic pain"). The two types of pain originate in the same relative area of the body (e.g., cervical or lumbar region) and often at the same axial spinal level (e.g., C6-7 or L4-5), but stem from different tissues or structures (e.g., nerve root vs. vertebral body or facet joints). Careful inquiry for a secondary or tertiary type of pain (rarely volunteered by the patient) produces a much greater understanding of the pathologic process involved.

■ TEMPORAL PATTERN

It is a well-shown principle of pain management that the temporal pattern of the pain complaint is derived largely from the patient's history and sheds light on the possible etiology of the problem. A relentlessly progressive course suggests serious underlying disease and warrants further inquiry (additional comprehensive history, physical examination, appropriate associated laboratory studies, and imaging techniques) for malignancy or infection. A rapid onset and rapid relief of pain are characteristic of neuropathies or neuralgia (e.g., trigeminal neuralgia).

■ SPATIAL PATTERN

The spatial distribution of the pain in conjunction with physical examination, laboratory tests, and imaging procedures suggests the localization of the problem (e.g., cervical radiculopathy or lumbosacral plexus pathology) and tends to limit the diagnostic possibilities. All physicians with even a brief exposure to pain problems recognize the "syndromic" approach to pain management. This approach is familiar in the example of "cervical radiculopathy" with neck pain accompanied by radiation in a dermatopic nerve root distribution down into the thumb, index finger, or both. More detailed questioning may reveal a deep gnawing pain going into the root of the neck, shoulder, or intrascapular area. This approach may serve well if alternative scenarios, such as referred pain (e.g., from a distal nerve lesion such as an ulnar nerve palsy or from an internal viscus) and the possibility of a tumor rather than a cervical disk or spondylosis, are not forgotten.

■ SYMPTOMATIC/ANATOMIC/ ETIOLOGIC DIAGNOSTIC APPROACH TO PAIN PROBLEMS

It is good practice to form a *symptomatic/anatomic/etiologic diagnosis* for each pain problem. This practice eliminates jumping to a syndromic conclusion and serves as framework for an orderly approach to the problem. This approach is demonstrated by the following case scenarios.

Case 1

A 36-year-old woman developed diffuse neck pain without an antecedent history of illness or injury. The pain was deep and gnawing and accompanied by sharp pain down the radial aspect of her arm and forearm to the thumb, index, and middle fingers. It was accompanied by a deep, boring (worse at night) intrascapular pain and mild weakness of the right biceps muscle. She had mild numbness of the thumb. Examination revealed limited range of motion of the cervical spine to the right and a right Spurling sign (pain reproduced by extension and lateral rotation to the right). She had mild weakness of the right biceps and brachialis, a diminished right biceps reflex, and hyperesthesia in the right C6 distribution.

The symptomatic diagnosis in this case is pain in the neck and down the right arm with mild C6 motor and sensory signs. This diagnosis is arrived at by a combination of the history and the physical examination. Syndromically, it could be referred to as "cervical radiculopathy without evidence of a myelopathy." For reasons that become clear in the next case presentation, the syndromic diagnosis should be made cautiously. The anatomic diagnosis in this case is a C6 radicu-

lopathy as a result of physical examination findings. The anatomic diagnosis may be augmented by electromyography, which is an extension of physical examination because it is based on physiologic examination of nerve, nerve root, and muscle. It is *not* based on imaging technique at this point because imaging technique may give irrelevant information and *always* requires clinical correlation. The etiologic diagnosis is cervical radiculopathy resulting from herniated nucleus pulpous at C5-6 based on MRI of the cervical spine showing a herniated disk at C5-6 *correlated* with the history and physical examination and not *contravened* by any more plausible diagnosis.

This may seem a convoluted method of diagnosis, but its merits are better illustrated by further case scenarios.

Case 2

A 56-year-old, right-handed man developed pain in the right supraclavicular region with associated neck pain of boring quality, worse at night, with radiation of fairly sharp pain down the ulnar border of the arm. Neck turning and shoulder movements exacerbated the pain, which was particularly bad at night. Examination revealed that the right pupil was slightly smaller than the left, but fully reactive. There was some weakness of the intrinsic hand muscles and hyperesthesia along the ulnar border of the right forearm. No reflex changes were noted. MRI revealed diffuse ridging at all levels, but worst at C7-T1. No long tract signs (signs of spinal cord involvement) were noted.

Syndromic diagnosis would be lower cervical radiculopathy secondary to spondylosis. This diagnosis conceivably could lead to inappropriate therapeutic measures. The symptomatic diagnosis is neck, shoulder, and arm pain in a lower cervical distribution. The anatomic diagnosis is C8-T1 root or brachial plexus involvement (>90% of all cervical nerve root pathologies involve the C5-6 or C6-7 levels emanating from the C6 or the C7 nerve roots). The etiologic differential diagnosis includes involvement of the brachial plexus by Pancoast tumor of the lung, C8-T1 pathology or acute brachial plexitis (Parsonage-Turner syndrome), or primary tumor of the nerve roots (meningioma or neurofibroma). In this case, a chest x-ray and CT scan revealed a malignancy of the right upper lobe of the lung and MRI of the brachial plexus showed erosion by the tumor. In this case, keeping an open mind and using the symptomatic/anatomic/etiologic approach averted a significant error in diagnosis and treatment.

Case 3

A 64-year-old man presented with pain in the left shoulder blade, neck, and elbow of sharp and aching type, the sharp pain referred from the elbow into the forearm and the aching pain in the elbow (occasionally) referred to the neck and the forearm, related to exertion, although the association was unclear. There was some association (again unclear) with flexion-extension of the left elbow producing the sharp and the aching pain. There was intermittent numbness of the ulnar portion of the left hand and forearm. There also was weakness of the left abductor digiti, first dorsal interosseous muscle, and adductor pollicis brevis. There were no cranial nerve, long tract, or sphincteric signs. In this case, the symptomatic diagnosis is sharp and aching elbow pain and shoul-

Table 5–1

Partial List of Etiologic Causes of Pain

Etiology	Examples
Vascular	Claudication, hemorrhage, space-occupying vascular malformations impinging on pain-sensitive structures
Tumor	Primary (e.g., meningioma or neurofibroma) and metastatic
Osseous	Primary bone disorders (e.g., Paget's disease, fibrous dysplasia, leontiasis ossea), DISH syndrome, focal spinal overgrowth (ridging)
Degenerative	Various arthritides, degenerative spine disease (spondylosis, spinal stenosis, spondylolisthesis, degenerated intervertebral disks)
Trauma	Herniated intervertebral disks, compression fractures, microtrauma
Metabolic	Diabetes mellitus, thyroid disorders, parathyroid disorders
Infectious	HIV, viral, bacterial, fungal, rickettsial infections
Collagen-vascular disorders	Rheumatoid arthritis, systemic lupus erythematosus, polymyalgia rheumatica, temporal arteritis
Toxic	Exogenous and endogenous toxicities
Psychiatric	Substance abuse, depression, psychosis, personality disorders

DISH, disseminated idiopathic skeletal hyperostosis.

der and forearm pain potentially related to exertion or flexion-extension or both of the elbow. The anatomic diagnosis is unclear and requires further elucidation by electromyography for possible ulnar neuropathy at the elbow, brachial plexus lesion, and a cardiology work-up for atypical angina pectoris. The anatomic differential diagnosis includes such diverse possibilities as visceral (cardiac or pulmonary), musculoskeletal (scapulocostal syndrome or other chest wall syndrome), or peripheral nervous system (ulnar entrapment at the elbow with radiation to the chest wall or lower brachial plexus or cervical spine pathology) conditions. The etiologic diagnosis is in doubt at this point because there are numerous possibilities that largely depend on the anatomic location of the problem. Any attempt at syndromic diagnosis is fraught with hazard because it forces the examiner prematurely into identifying an organ system causing the pain with little or no evidence to support any one possibility. The symptomatic/anatomic/etiologic approach serves as a "holding area" while each of the diagnostic possibilities is explored without having to jump to conclusions.

The "symptomatic" diagnosis seems self-evident, although there is a tendency to try to fit it into a defined syndrome, such as cervical radiculopathy, complex regional pain syndrome, or migraine, in clear-cut circumstances. The anatomic diagnosis requires careful analysis of findings from physical examination, electromyography (when applicable), and imaging techniques. It cannot be overemphasized that the physical examination and imaging findings must be concordant (match), and in case of a discrepancy, especially in spinal imaging where abnormalities abound in asymptomatic patients, greater weight must be given to the physical examination findings, especially when they explain the clinical history. The etiologic diagnosis should include, at least preliminarily, a checklist of all possible types of pathologic processes. The author has found it useful to use the list in Table 5–1, at least giving it a brief consideration no matter how obvious the apparent cause. The putative anatomic site may be subdivided as shown in Table 5–2.

Table 5–2

Possible Generalized Sites of Anatomic Pathology Causing Pain

Skin
Subcutaneous tissues, including fat and connective tissue
Ligaments and tendons
Skeletal muscles
Nerves, nerve roots, and plexus
Central nervous system structures, including spinal cord
Vascular structures, including arteries and veins
Lymphatics
Viscera

■ REFERRED PAIN PATTERNS

Physicians become familiar with the patterns of intrathoracic and intra-abdominal pain referral from internal viscera in the earliest years of training in clinical medicine. Referral patterns are particularly well discussed and illustrated in Wiener's classic text.[1] A potential pitfall in referred pain diagnosis is the less well recognized referral of myofascial pain (e.g., referral of pain from the levator scapulae to the chest wall simulating angina or cholecystitis). So-called trigger points frequently simulate the pain of internal organs, raising the possibility of misdiagnosis and mistreatment.[2] The concept of trigger point referral is most associated with Travell and Simons, who published the classic two-volume work on pain referral patterns.[3] Volume 1 addresses referral patterns in the upper half of body (head, neck, thorax, and abdomen), and volume 2 addresses the lower extremities.

■ SPINAL PAIN PATTERNS

Vertebral Pain Syndromes

The pain tends to be deep and boring and present at rest. When associated with an aggressive process, it tends to increase stepwise and may spread to a radicular distribution, which may be "girdling" if in the abdomen or thorax. Jarring, movement, or percussion may exacerbate the pain. Although the pain characteristics may vary from condition to condition and individual to individual, the presence at rest is highly suggestive and clearly different from radiculopathies, which tend to be ameliorated by rest and recumbency.

Spinal Radiculopathies

The pain of spinal radiculopathies tends to be quite sharp and well delineated with the proviso that there often is an associated deep, gnawing pain that is usually more proximal and less well defined than the sharp pain. This pain is attributable to irritation of nonradicular structures, such as bones and tendinous attachments, and follows a sclerotogenous pattern (Fig. 5–1). Radicular pain usually follows well-understood and familiar patterns.[4,5] Pain distribution, sensory changes, motor weakness, and reflex changes in the cervical region are summarized in Table 5–3, and those corresponding to the lumbar region are summarized in Table 5–4. Clinical syndromes associated with cervical spondylosis include acute stiff neck, radiculopathy, myelopathy, myeloradiculopathy, vertebrobasilar insufficiency, cervicogenic headache, and Barre-Lieou syndrome (cervical sympathetic syndrome).

Cervical Facet Syndrome

Cervical facet syndrome is a syndrome of head, neck, shoulder, and proximal upper extremity pain largely in a nondermatomal distribution. The pain is usually dull and ill defined in character; worsened by flexion, extension, and lateral flexion of the neck (unilateral or bilateral); and unaccompanied by motor or sensory deficits. Referral patterns are presented in Table 5–5.

Table 5–3

Characteristics of Cervical Radicular Pain

Cervical Root	Pain	Sensory Changes	Weakness	Reflex Changes
C5	Neck, shoulder, antelateral arm	Numbness in deltoid area	Deltoid and biceps	Biceps reflex
C6	Neck, shoulder, lateral aspect of arm	Dorsolateral aspect of thumb and index finger	Biceps, wrist extensors, pollicis longus	Brachioradialis reflex
C7	Neck, shoulder, lateral aspect of arm, dorsal forearm	Index and middle finger, dorsum of hand	Triceps	Triceps reflex

---

Table 5–4

Characteristics of Lumbar Radicular Pain

Lumbar Root	Pain	Sensory Changes	Weakness	Reflex Changes
L4	Back, shin, thigh, leg	Shin numbness	Ankle dorsiflexors	Knee jerk
L5	Back, posterior thigh, leg	Numbness at top of foot and first web space	Extensor hallucis longus	None
S1	Back, posterior calf, leg	Numbness at lateral foot	Gastrocnemius and soleus	Ankle jerk

---

Table 5–5

Pain Referral Patterns of Cervical Facet Joints

Facet Joint	Refers Pain to
C2-3	Posterior upper cervical region and head
C3-4	Posterolateral cervical region without extension into the head or shoulder
C4-5	Posterolateral middle and lower cervical region and to the top of the shoulder
C5-6	Posterolateral middle and primarily lower cervical spine and the top and lateral parts of the shoulder and caudally to the spine of the scapula
C6-7	Top and lateral parts of the shoulder and caudally to the inferior border of the scapula

From Dwyer A, Aprill C, Bogduk N: Cervical zygapophyseal joint pain patterns: I. A study in normal volunteers. Spine 15:453, 1990.

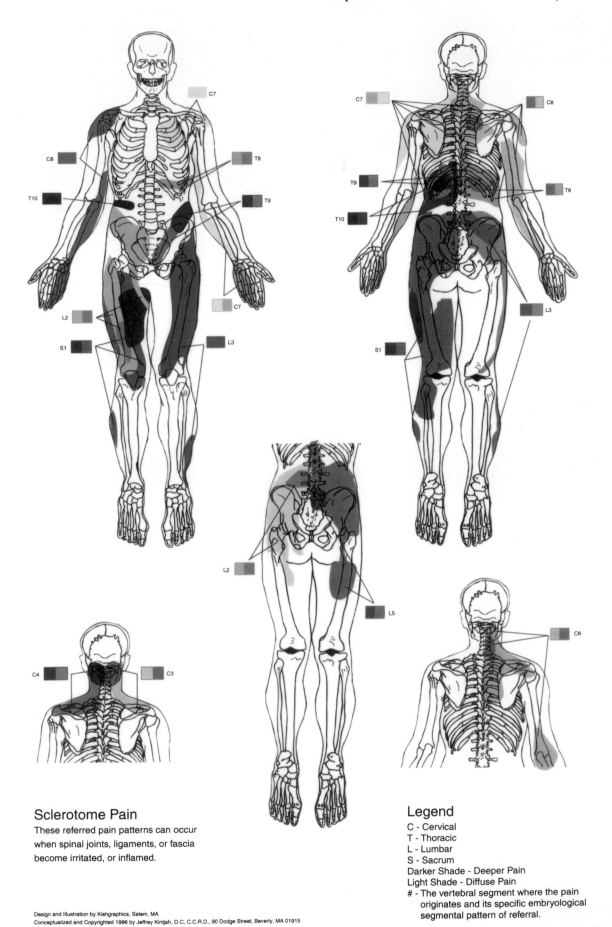

Sclerotome Pain

These referred pain patterns can occur when spinal joints, ligaments, or fascia become irritated, or inflamed.

Legend

C - Cervical
T - Thoracic
L - Lumbar
S - Sacrum
Darker Shade - Deeper Pain
Light Shade - Diffuse Pain
- The vertebral segment where the pain originates and its specific embryological segmental pattern of referral.

Design and Illustration by Kishgraphics, Salem, MA
Conceptualized and Copyrighted 1996 by Jeffrey Kintjsh, D.C, C.C.R.D., 90 Dodge Street, Beverly, MA 01915

FIGURE 5–1 ■ Illustration of sclerotogenous pain pathways, useful for pinpointing referred sclerotogenous pain from spinal levels C1 through S3. (From Clinical Charts & Supplies, Beverly, MA.)

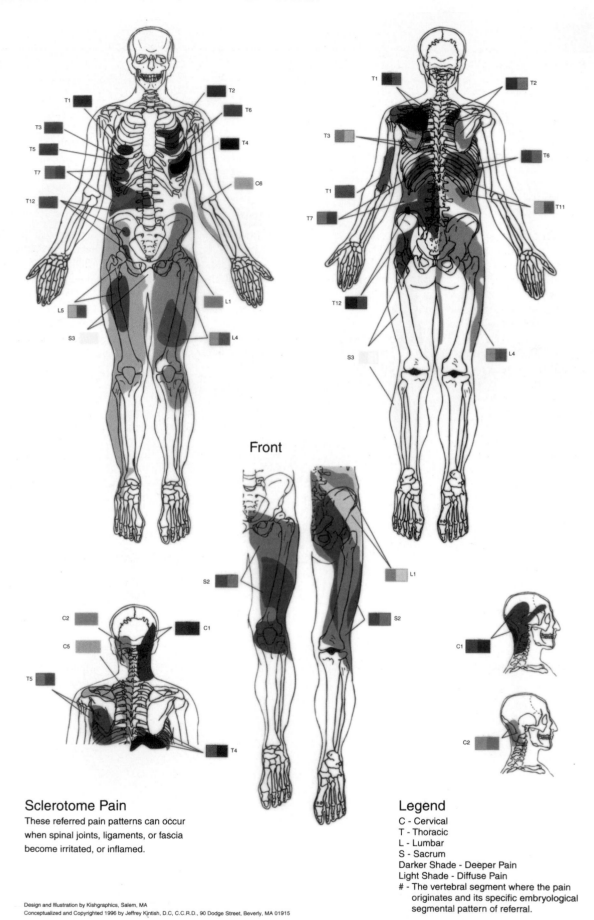

Front

Sclerotome Pain

These referred pain patterns can occur
when spinal joints, ligaments, or fascia
become irritated, or inflamed.

Legend

C - Cervical
T - Thoracic
L - Lumbar
S - Sacrum
Darker Shade - Deeper Pain
Light Shade - Diffuse Pain
- The vertebral segment where the pain
     originates and its specific embryological
     segmental pattern of referral.

Design and Illustration by Kishgraphics, Salem, MA
Conceptualized and Copyrighted 1996 by Jeffrey Kintish, D.C, C.C.R.D., 90 Dodge Street, Beverly, MA 01915

FIGURE 5–1 ■ **Cont'd.**

Table 5–6		
Spinal Stenosis Versus Disk Protrusion (Radiculopathy)		
	Spinal Stenosis	*Disc Protrusion (Radiculopathy)*
Pain pattern	Insidious, less well localized, duller Worse with walking or standing Worse with extension	Acute, sharper, better localized Worse with sitting Worse with flexion
Age at onset (yr)	Most commonly 30-50	Most commonly >60
Response to conservative therapy (%)	50	>90

Lumbar Radiculopathy

Patients complain of pain, numbness, tingling, and paresthesias in the appropriate nerve root distribution. The pain may be sharp and lancinating, but accompanied by a more vaguely, localized, proximally distributed sclerotogenous pain. Relative contributions of dorsal and ventral roots influence the character of the pain, and the ventral root pain is often duller and less well localized as a result of the predominately motor distribution. Involvement of the sinu-vertebral nerve (recurrent nerve of Luschka) ensures at least some painful involvement of the axial structures, whereas a laterally placed process may result in pain purely localized to the limb and confusing in nature because of the absence of the axial pain usually present in radiculopathies.

Lumbar Facet Syndrome

Patients usually are >65 years old, and the pain, which is less well localized than radicular pain, is deeper and duller with exacerbation by standing or lumbar extension and improved with sitting and forward flexion. Pain is not exacerbated by coughing or other Valsalva-related maneuvers, may be referred to the buttocks or ipsilateral thigh, and generally presents in a more proximal distribution than radicular pain.

Lumbar Spondylolisthesis

Dull or sharp back pain is exacerbated with lifting, twisting, or bending. Patients often complain about a "catch" in their back. Rising from a sitting to standing position often reproduces the pain.

Lumbar Spinal Stenosis

Pseudoclaudication of the lower extremities is the characteristic pattern. Multiple roots are characteristically involved. The pain may disappear with spinal flexion (e.g., riding a stationary bicycle), but results in fatigue with prolonged walking or standing (Table 5–6). Pain is characteristically in the calf, simulating vascular claudication. Pain, numbness, and weakness are seen in the affected segments. Muscle spasms and vague pains are commonly seen, including (paradoxically) the intrascapular region.

Arachnoiditis

Arachnoiditis is characterized by pain (generally duller and less well defined than radiculopathy, but may be severe and excruciating), numbness, tingling, paresthesias, and weakness, which is often in multiple nerve roots. Muscle spasm in the lumbar region with referral into the buttocks is common. Bladder and bowel symptoms are more frequent than expected with radiculopathy.

References

1. Wiener SL: Differential Diagnosis of Acute Pain by Body Regions. New York, McGraw-Hill, 1993.
2. Rachlin ES, Rachlin I (eds): Myofascial Pain and Fibromyalgia: Trigger Point Management, 2nd ed. St. Louis, Mosby, 2002.
3. Simons DG, Travell JG: Travell and Simons' Myofascial Pain and Dysfunction: The Trigger Point Manual, vols 1 and 2, 2nd ed. Baltimore, Williams & Wilkins, 1998.
4. Hoppenfeld S: Orthopedic Neurology: A Diagnostic Guide to Neurologic Levels. Philadelphia, JB Lippincott, 1977.
5. Hoppenfeld S: Physical Examination of the Spine and Extremities. Stamford, CT, Appleton & Lange, 1976.

Rational Use of Laboratory Testing

Charles D. Donohoe

The targeted history and physical examination remain the most cost effective tools aiding the clinician in the proper diagnosis of a patient's pain. The rational use of laboratory testing is often the next reasonable step to assist the clinician to confirm his or her clinical impression as well as to help the clinician implement and fine tune a treatment plan. Unfortunately, the logical use of laboratory tests is too often ignored in favor of expensive radiologic and neurophysiologic studies that, at the very least, add to the cost of a patient's care, and at the very worst, lead to an incorrect diagnosis and subsequent inappropriate therapeutic interventions.

Findings such as pyuria, profound anemia, and elevation of acute phase proteins are often crucial in identifying the cause of pain and assessing the general medical status of the patient. Although clinical laboratory medicine is a massive and rapidly evolving discipline that truly defies condensation, it is my hope that this chapter will provide the reader with a road map to the laboratory evaluation of the patient in pain.

■ PITFALLS OF CLINICAL PRACTICE

There are several areas in clinical practice where mistakes are commonly made. The first involves failure to contact family members of a confused patient who is obviously unable to give a coherent history. The second is failure to obtain old records. Third, and equally tragic, is the mistaken supposition that because the patient has seen multiple physicians in the past, basic laboratory work has been ordered.

The ability to avoid these mistakes demands a discipline that emphasizes that the clinician always consider the critical details of the targeted history and physical examination as well as assess the adequacy of the patient's earlier diagnostic work-up. This effort is extremely effective in containing costs, conserving physicians' time, and ultimately arriving at an accurate diagnosis. In difficult patients who have seen several physicians, quality control of earlier historical data and diagnostic work-up is often ignored and each additional consult simply compounds the sloppy imprecision of the preceding evaluations. Although laborious and time consuming, it almost always rewards the clinician to take time, at the beginning of the patient interaction, to get these basic steps right. Frequently the best use of technology is a telephone call to a concerned family member or a former treating physician. Yet,

often in the heat of the battle, this simple act is avoided, thereby instituting a cascade of errors.

■ THE BASICS

Table 6–1 lists a basic battery of laboratory tests commonly used to evaluate pain. The clinician can use this table as a starting point of the laboratory evaluation of the patient in pain, realizing that the selection of specific tests depends on multiple factors, including age, gender, duration and location of pain, coexisting medical problems, and results of other laboratory studies. One preliminary tenet of pain practice management is that, once a physician orders lab tests, he is responsible not only for seeing that the tests are performed but also for personally reviewing the results. Failure to do both can have serious medical-legal implications and, more importantly, can harm the patient.

■ ACUTE PHASE PROTEINS

The erythrocyte sedimentation rate (ESR) and the C-reactive protein (CRP) value are the most commonly used indicators of acute phase response. This response includes numerous protein changes, including increases in the complement system, fibrinogen, serum amyloid, and acute phase phenomena including fever, thrombocytosis, leukocytosis, and anemia. A reduction in serum albumin is characteristic of the acute phase response. These complex changes are induced by inflammation-associated cytokines, particularly interleukin-6, and are seen in response to infection, trauma, surgery, burns, cancer, inflammatory conditions, and psychological stress.[1]

The ESR, the rate at which erythrocytes fall through plasma, is actually an indirect measure of plasma acute phase protein concentration and depends mainly on the plasma concentration of fibrinogen. Unfortunately, the ESR can be influenced by other factors, including the size, shape, and number of erythrocytes, and by other plasma protein constituents such as immunoglobulins. CRP is a glycoprotein produced during acute inflammation and derives its name from its ability to react and precipitate *Pneumococcus* C polysaccharide. It has fewer associated technical problems and is resistant to the interference of anemia, pregnancy, hypercholesterolemia, or alterations of plasma protein concentrations,

Table 6-1

The Basic Pain Laboratory Battery

Complete blood count (CBC)
Acute phase proteins, erythrocyte sedimentation rate
(ESR), C-reactive protein (CRP)
Blood chemistry: Glucose, sodium, potassium,
chloride, carbon dioxide, calcium, phosphorus, urea
nitrogen, creatinine, uric acid, total protein,
albumin, globulin, bilirubin
Enzymes: Alkaline phosphatase, creatine kinase,
lactate dehydrogenase, aspartate aminotransferase,
alanine aminotransferase
Thyroid-stimulating hormone (TSH)
Vitamin B_{12}

as well as exogenous substances such as heparin that can alter the ESR. CRP is easy to perform, and its overall use has recently increased.

The ESR increases steadily with age, whereas the CRP value does not. The ESR changes relatively slowly (over several days) in response to the onset of inflammation, whereas the CRP responds rapidly (several hours). CRP has certain advantages over the ESR, and both can be used in concert.

Like the CRP, ESR determination is used to detect inflammatory disease, follow its course, and at times in a more general fashion to suggest the presence of occult organic disease in patients who have symptoms but no definitive physical or laboratory findings. The ESR is not a specific test. The Westergren ESR method is generally more resistant to the effects of anemia than the Wintrobe method. ESR values greater than 100 mm/hour generally imply infectious disease, neoplasia, inflammatory conditions, or chronic renal disease. Realizing that the ESR is affected by age, a rough index for determining the upper limits of normal can be derived by the formula:

$$\text{Age in years} + 5 \div 2$$

For an 85-year-old patient, this would place the upper range of normal of a Westergren ESR at roughly 45 mm/hour. In painful conditions affecting the elderly such as temporal arteritis, use of both the ESR and CRP is encouraged.

■ THE COMPLETE BLOOD COUNT

The complete blood count (CBC) is a good starting point for laboratory testing in that it provides a cost-effective glimpse into a person's general health. The major emphasis in hematology is placed on cellular elements, including red blood cells (RBC), white blood cells (WBC), and platelets. Several tests form the backbone of laboratory diagnosis and can be very useful in the evaluation of both acute and chronic pain. Hemoglobin is the oxygen-carrying compound contained in red cells, and, in association with red blood cell count and hematocrit, signals anemia.

Anemia is defined as hemoglobin values less than 13g/dL for men and less than 11g/dL for women. Conditions that result in pseudoanemia include overhydration, obtaining blood specimens from an intravenous line, hypoalbuminemia, and pregnancy. Heavy smoking, dehydration, and states of extreme leukocytosis may produce elevated hemoglobin and hematocrit levels.[2] The red cell indices—mean corpuscular volume (MCV), mean corpuscular hemoglobin (MCH), mean corpuscular hemoglobin concentration (MCHC), and red blood cell distribution width (RDW)—aid in the diagnosis of a variety of conditions, including anemia, hemoglobinopathies, and spherocytosis.

The peripheral blood smear examines the size, color, and other morphologic characteristics of red and white cells important in the evaluation of hematologic disease. Reticulocyte count, serum ferritin level, serum iron, and total iron-binding capacity (TIBC) enhance the evaluation of anemia. The reticulocyte can be viewed as an intermediate between a nucleated RBC in the bone marrow and a mature, non-nucleated RBC. The reticulocyte count is an index of bone marrow activity. Hemolytic anemia, acute bleeding, and the treatment of deficiency states related to vitamin B_{12}, folate, and iron result in reticulocytosis. Anemia associated with bone marrow failure is reflected in a low reticulocyte count.[3]

Because it is the major storage compound of iron, serum ferritin is a very sensitive measure for iron deficiency. Reductions in both serum iron and ferritin have been associated with restless legs syndrome. Serum TIBC is an approximation of the serum transferrin level and is elevated in iron deficiency anemia slightly before a decrease in serum iron becomes evident. Transferrin saturation (the percentage of transferrin bound to iron) declines with classic iron deficiency anemia. In hemochromatosis, a common genetic disorder of iron overload, persistent elevations of ferritin and transferrin saturation are effective screening tools in early recognition of this disorder.[4] The reduction in serum haptoglobin, a plasma glycoprotein that binds to oxyhemoglobin and delivers it to the reticuloendothelial system, is a useful test for evaluating intravascular hemolysis.

At birth, 80% of hemoglobin is fetal-type hemoglobin (HbF), which is replaced by the adult type (HbA) by age 6 months. An abnormal type of hemoglobin common in the Western Hemisphere is sickle hemoglobin (HbS). The heterozygous state, sickle trait (SA), is present in about 8% of African Americans. These persons are not anemic and are otherwise healthy. They rarely experience hematuria but may develop splenic infarcts during exposure to hypoxic conditions (e.g., nonpressurized airplanes). Homozygous sickle cell disease (SS) produces moderate to severe anemia. Crises secondary to small vessel occlusion with infarction often manifest with abdominal pain or bone pain. The disease does not manifest until after age 6 months with the disappearance of HbF, which has high affinity for oxygen.

Screening tests (sickle cell prep) rely on the tendency of hemoglobin S to become insoluble when oxygen tension is low, ultimately crystallizing and distorting the red cell into a sickle shape. A common screening method (Sickle Dex) avoids coverslip methods that utilize chemical (dithionite) deoxygenation and precipitation of hemoglobin S. This test is not useful before 6 months of age and does not distinguish between sickle cell disease and the trait. Definitive diagnosis requires hemoglobin electrophoresis. All African Americans with unexplained anemia, hematuria, arthralgias, or abdominal pain should be screened for sickle cell disease.[5]

White Blood Cells

WBC are the body's first line of defense against infection. Lymphocytes and plasma cells produce antibodies, whereas neutrophils and monocytes respond by phagocytosis. Alterations in the WBC provide a clue to a variety of diseases, both benign and malignant. Most individuals have WBC counts between 5000 and 10,000 per mm³. The mean WBC count in African Americans may be at least 500 per mm³ less than that in Europeans, with some individuals demonstrating counts as much as 3000 per mm³ lower. There are also diurnal variations in neutrophils and eosinophils. Neutrophil levels peak at about 4:00 PM at values almost 30% above those at 7:00 AM. Eosinophils more consistently parallel cortisol levels, being highest early in the morning and 40% lower later in the afternoon.

The classic picture of acute bacterial infection includes leukocytosis with an associated increased percentage of neutrophils and bands (immature forms); however, the leukocytosis and increased number of bands (shift to the left) may be absent in as many as 30% of acute bacterial infections. Overwhelming infection, particularly in debilitated elderly persons, may fail to show any leukocytosis. Heavy cigarette smoking has been associated with total WBC counts that average 1000 per mm³ higher than those for nonsmokers. Other causes of neutrophilic leukocytosis include metabolic abnormalities such as uremia, diabetic acidosis, acute gouty attacks, seizures, and pregnancy. Adrenal corticosteroids, even in low doses, can produce considerable increases in segmented neutrophils and total WBC count. Medications such as lithium carbonate (for bipolar disorder), epinephrine (for asthma), and the toxic effects of lead can result in leukocytosis.

Eosinophilia is most often associated with acute allergic reactions such as asthma, hay fever, and drug allergy. It is also seen in parasitic diseases, skin disorders such as pemphigus and psoriasis, and miscellaneous conditions such as connective tissue disorders, particularly polyarteritis nodosa, Churg-Strauss vasculitis, and sarcoidosis. Eosinophilia may also be a nonspecific indicator of occult malignancy.

Viral infection is most often manifested by lymphocytosis with an elevated (or relatively elevated) lymphocyte count in a person with a normal or decreased total WBC count. The usual lymphocytosis identified in viral infection is a relative one: granulocytes are reduced whereas the total lymphocyte number remains constant. Infectious mononucleosis is associated with absolute lymphocytosis and atypical lymphocytes. The leukemoid reaction is defined as a nonleukemic elevation in the WBC count above 50,000 per mm³. It is an exaggerated form of the non-neoplastic granulocyte reaction associated with severe bacterial infections, burns, tissue necrosis, hemolytic anemia, and juvenile rheumatoid arthritis.

Neutropenia is defined as a WBC count less than 4000 per mm³. Drug-induced agranulocytosis is a major clinical issue in pain management, particularly its association with commonly used medications, including phenytoin (Dilantin), carbamazepine (Carbatrol, Tegretol), nonsteroidal antiinflammatory drugs (NSAIDs), and many other medications used in pain management. Neutropenia should prompt an immediate review of all medications. Other conditions associated with neutropenia include aplastic anemia, aleukemic leukemia, hypersplenism, viral infections, and cyclic and chronic idiopathic neutropenia. Severe neutropenia (<1500 WBC per cubic millimeter) should be regarded as an acute emergency: careful follow-up and hematology consultation are mandatory.

In the area of hematopoietic malignancy, cells of lymphocyte origin predominate. For purposes of simplification, most lymphocytes arise from precursors in bone marrow. Of peripheral blood lymphocytes, about 75% are T cells (those lymphocytes that mature in the thymus) and 15% are B cells (those that have matured in the bone marrow, and later in the spleen or lymph nodes). All T lymphocytes develop an antigenic marker for the T cell family called CD2. The CD (cluster designation classification) applies a single CD number to all antibodies that appear to react with the same or very similar WBC antigens. Of the T cells, about 75% are of the CD4 helper-inducer type and about 25% are of the CD8 cytotoxic-suppressor type.

B cells are characterized by having a surface immunoglobulin antibody rather than the CD3 antigen receptor characteristic of mature T cells. B cells are parents of plasma cells, which can secrete specific antibodies to antigens initially recognized by the parent B lymphocyte. Initially, these antibodies are immunoglobulin M (IgM); later, the immunoglobulin changes type to IgG (or less commonly to IgA or IgE). Finally, there is a group of lymphocyte-like cells known as natural killer cells (NKCs) that possess neither a T lymphocyte marker antigen A nor B lymphocyte surface immunoglobulin. NKCs account for the remaining 10% of peripheral blood lymphocytes.[6]

Platelets and Blood Coagulation

An important aspect of any pain history is the identification of medications that influence coagulation. Heparin, aspirin, NSAIDs, warfarin (Coumadin), ticlopidine (Ticlid), and clopidogrel (Plavix) fall into this category. Any history of easy bleeding or bruising should prompt further evaluation.

Normal human platelet count generally ranges from 150,000 to 400,000 platelets per cubic millimeter. Platelet counts below 50,000 per cubic millimeter indicate severe thrombocytopenia. Platelet counts greater than 900,000 per cubic millimeter indicate thrombocytosis and a resultant hypercoagulable state. The most common causes of thrombocytopenia are immune-mediated, drug-induced, and post-blood transfusions. Many cases have no demonstrable cause. Other factors include hypersplenism, bone marrow deficiency, microangiopathic hemolytic anemia, infection, thyrotoxicosis, uremia, and preeclampsia. Drug-induced thrombocytopenia is common. Intravenous administration of heparin causes thrombocytopenia with platelet counts below 100,000 per cubic millimeter in as many as 15% of patients.[7] This effect has even been seen with heparin flushes. Other medications commonly implicated include cimetidine (Tagamet), quinine, quinidine, and furosemide (Lasix).

Thrombocytosis with platelet counts greater than 1 million are associated with myeloproliferative disorders, idiopathic thrombocythemia, and severe hemolytic anemia. Other common causes are occult malignancy, postsplenectomy, and acute and chronic infection or inflammatory disease. Both arterial and venous thrombosis can occur.

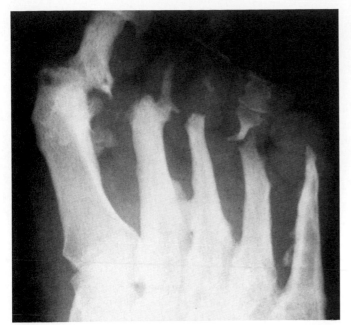

FIGURE 6–1 ■ Diabetes mellitus: metatarsophalangeal and interphalangeal joints. Neuropathic osteoarthropathy and infection in the forefoot of a diabetic patient combine to produce bizarre abnormalities consisting of osteolysis of the distal metatarsals and proximal phalanges, with tapering of the osseous contours. (From Resnick D, Kransdorf M [eds]: Bone and Joint Imaging, 3rd ed. Philadelphia, Saunders, 2005, p 1062, Figure 66–11, with permission.)

Coagulation Parameters

The prothrombin time (PT) evaluates mainly defects in the extrinsic coagulation system. It is used as a liver function test and as a general screening tool for coagulation disorders. When PT is used to monitor anticoagulation therapy with warfarin, the international normalized ratio (INR) is preferred because of its ability to standardize varied thromboplastin reagents.[8] The INR is a monitoring value for warfarin after the patient has been stabilized, but it is not useful as a general marker of coagulation or liver function. Awareness that a patient is taking warfarin or antiplatelet agents and of the patient's coagulation status is critical. We have seen several patients on warfarin with pain secondary to retroperitoneal hemorrhage who had marked elevations of PT and INR that went unrecognized for months.

■ GLUCOSE

Diabetes is a common disorder, affecting six million Americans. Approximately one million are classified as type 1 diabetics, their disease ascribed to an autoimmune process that ultimately leads to beta cell destruction. Insulin resistance, obesity, and a strong genetic predisposition characterize the more prevalent form, type 2 diabetes. The myriad painful complications to diabetes include neuropathy, foot ulceration, and Charcot joints (Fig. 6–1).

The American Diabetes Association criteria for the diagnosis of diabetes mellitus are the following (Table 6–2): (1) The classic symptoms of diabetes, including polydipsia, polyuria, and weight loss, plus a casual glucose concentration ≥ 200 mg/dL. (*Casual* is defined as a measurement taken at

Table 6–2
American Diabetes Association Criteria for the Diagnosis of Diabetes Mellitus
Symptoms of diabetes (polydipsia, polyuria, and weight loss) plus a casual glucose ≥200 mg/dL. Casual is defined as any time of the day without regard to time since last meal. Fasting glucose ≥126 mg/dL. Fasting is defined as no caloric intake for at least 8 hours. 2-hour postload glucose ≥200 mg/dL on an oral glucose tolerance test. Oral glucose tolerance test is not recommended as a first-line test because the fasting glucose is easier to perform, more acceptable to patients, and less expensive. In the absence of unequivocal hyperglycemia with acute metabolic decompensation, these criteria should be confirmed by repeat testing on a different day. For example, an abnormal casual glucose >200 mg/dL without symptoms should be confirmed on a different day with a fasting glucose determination.

any time of day, without regard for the time of the last meal.) (2) A fasting plasma glucose value ≥ 126 mg/dL (fasting defined as no caloric intake for at least 8 hours). (3) An oral glucose tolerance test value, 2 hours postload, ≥ 200 mg/dL. Note that, when the diagnosis is based purely on blood glucose measurements—either the fasting blood glucose or the oral glucose tolerance test—in the absence of clinical symptoms, abnormalities must be found on two different days rather than on a single occasion only.[9]

Hemoglobin A1C determination is a valuable tool for monitoring blood sugar, but it is not recommended for the diagnosis of diabetes. In adults, hemoglobin A constitutes about 98% of normal hemoglobin. About 7% of hemoglobin A consists of molecules that have been partially modified by the attachment of glucose. Hemoglobin A1C is the major component of this glycosylated hemoglobin. It is an effective index for monitoring diabetes therapy and patient compliance, and it generally reflects the average blood glucose level during the preceding 2 to 3 months.[10]

Clinicians must be aware that medications such as glucocorticoids, nicotinic acid, and phenytoin (Dilantin) can impair insulin activity and elevate blood glucose. Another consideration is misdiagnosis of hypoglycemia. This overused label has been sensationalized in the popular press, arbitrarily defined and applied in situations where there are vague protean symptoms but no objective abnormality of glucose metabolism. Those rather rare diseases in which hypoglycemia is actually a valid issue include insulinoma, nonpancreatic tumors such as fibrosarcoma and hepatoma, hepatic disease (including chronic alcoholism), and insulin overdose.[11]

■ ELECTROLYTES

The most frequent electrolyte abnormality involves sodium, the most important cation of the body. Hyponatremia is the most common abnormality. Symptoms related to hyponatremia, such as nausea, malaise, lethargy, psychosis, and seizures, generally do not occur until the plasma sodium value falls below 120 mEq/L. Diuretics are often implicated. Carbamazepine (Tegretol, Carbatrol) a medication commonly used in pain management, can be associated with persistent hyponatremia. The other major categories of hyponatremia include conditions of general sodium and water depletion (including gastrointestinal loss due to vomiting, diarrhea, or tube drainage), losses through skin associated with burns or sweating, endocrine loss associated with Addison disease, and sudden withdrawal of long-term steroid therapy. Dilutional hyponatremia is associated with congestive heart failure, hyperhydrosis, nephrotic syndrome, cirrhosis, hypoalbuminemia, and acute renal failure.[12]

The syndrome of inappropriate antidiuretic hormone secretion (SIADH) is characterized by hyponatremia with reduced plasma osmolality in the face of an elevated urinary sodium value but normal extracellular volume and renal, thyroid, and adrenal function. Factitious (but actually dilutional) hyponatremia can be seen when there is marked hypertriglyceridemia, marked hyperproteinemia, or severe hyperglycemia.

Hypernatremia is much less common than hyponatremia and is usually associated with severe systemic disease in a person whose impaired mental status or physical disability prevents access to water. Other associated conditions include high-protein tube feedings, severe protracted vomiting and diarrhea, and excessive water output due to diabetes insipidus (DI) or osmotic diuresis. Sodium overload can be due to administration of hypertonic sodium solutions or to endogenous causes such as primary hyperaldosteronism (Cushing syndrome).

DI is due to deficiency of antidiuretic hormone (ADH) or to renal resistance to ADH. Central DI results from hypothalamic or pituitary damage secondary to trauma, neoplasm, or intracranial surgery.[13] Nephrogenic DI can be seen with chronic renal failure, hyperglycemia, or medications such as lithium, chlorpromazine, and demeclocycline. To put hypernatremia in perspective, a serum sodium value more than 160 mEq/L that persists longer than 48 hours carries a 60% risk of death.

Abnormalities in serum potassium concentration are very common. Its laboratory determination can be spuriously increased by a hemolyzed specimen. It is also altered by acid-base abnormalities, increased extracellular osmolality, and insulin deficiency. A fall in plasma pH of 0.1 likely corresponds to an increased plasma potassium value of 0.5 mEq/L. A rise in pH causes a similar decrease in serum potassium concentration. Hypokalemia may be associated with inadequate potassium intake seen in alcoholism, malabsorption syndrome, and severe illness. Losses can be due to diarrhea, diuretic use, vomiting, trauma, cirrhosis, and to both primary (Conn syndrome) and secondary aldosteronism (cirrhosis), renal artery stenosis, and malignant hypertension.

Hyperkalemia is associated with renal failure, dehydration, thrombocythemia, tumor lysis syndrome, and multiple medications, including beta-adrenergic blockers such as propranolol, potassium-sparing diuretics (spironolactone triamterene), several NSAIDs, and cyclosporine. Overlapping clinical symptoms, including weakness, nausea, anorexia, and organic mental changes, are associated with low-sodium, low-potassium, and high-potassium states.[14]

Chloride, the most abundant extracellular anion, is affected by the same conditions that affect sodium. If the serum sodium level is low, chloride concentration is also low, with the exception of the hyperchloremic alkalosis of prolonged vomiting. When carbon dioxide is included in a serum electrolyte panel, bicarbonate accounts for most of what is actually measured. It is the opinion of many authors that neither chloride nor carbon dioxide is cost-effective as a routine assay. Most patients with abnormal serum bicarbonate values have a metabolic disturbance that would be better evaluated by blood gas determinations.

▌ CONNECTIVE TISSUE DISEASES AND VASCULITIS

The connective tissues diseases and vasculitides are immune-mediated diseases frequently marked by pain. These disorders are often difficult to diagnose in their early stages and a basic understanding of laboratory serologic studies is essential. The connective tissue diseases (Table 6–3) are multisystem disorders that share the central feature of inflammation—whether of joints, muscles, or skin. Vasculitis is a multiorgan or organ-specific disease whose central feature is blood vessel inflammation (Fig. 6–2).

Almost all patients with systemic lupus erythematosus (SLE) develop autoantibodies.[15] The immunofluorescence test for antinuclear antibodies (ANA) is the most sensitive laboratory test for detecting it. It has replaced the LE (lupus erythematosus) cell test and is positive in most patients with SLE. A negative ANA result is strong evidence against SLE. A wide variety of factors that react to either nuclear or cytoplasmic constituents have been demonstrated. Table 6–4 lists a variety of antibodies and their associated diseases. Table 6–5 lists the laboratory test abnormalities of SLE, a prototype of autoimmune disease.

The ANA is generally reported in terms of a titer and the pattern of nuclear fluorescence. Nuclear fluorescence patterns can be homogeneous (solid), peripheral (rim), speckled, nucleolar, anticentromere, or nonreactive (normal). For example, an ANA directed against nucleolar RNA suggests progressive systemic sclerosis (scleroderma), particularly when the titer is high.

Table 6–3
Common Connective Tissue Diseases and Vasculitides
Systemic lupus erythematosus
Mixed connective tissue disease
Primary Sjögren syndrome
Rheumatoid arthritis
Progressive systemic sclerosis (scleroderma)
Polymyositis and dermatomyositis
Vasculitides
Polyarteritis nodosa
Churg-Strauss angiitis
Wegener granulomatosis
Temporal arteritis
Behçet disease
Primary central nervous system vasculitis

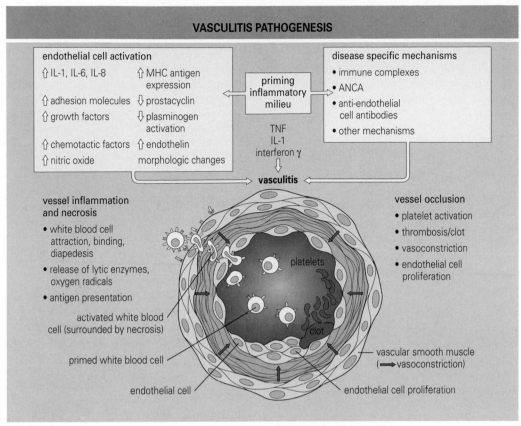

FIGURE 6–2 ■ Vasculitis syndromes. (From Klippel J, Dieppe P [eds]: Rheumatology, 2nd ed. London, Mosby, 1997, p 7.20.7, Figure 20.10, with permission.)

Table 6–4

Serologic Tests for Collagen Vascular Disorders

Rheumatoid factor: 80% sensitive in rheumatoid arthritis

Antinuclear antibodies: titer ≥1:320 have 95% specificity for systemic lupus erythematosus

Antineutrophil cytoplasmic antibody: 90% positive in Wegener granulomatosis

Anti-Ro: Antibodies to nuclear antigens extracted from human B lymphocytes present in 70% of patients with Sjögren syndrome

Antinuclear (nuclear RNA): 60%-90% positive in scleroderma

Anti-SM: Highly specific for systemic lupus erythematosus

Anti-centromere: Suggests CREST syndrome (*c*alcinosis cutis, *R*aynaud phenomenon, *e*sophageal dysmotility, *s*clerodactyly, *t*elangiectasias)

SM: Smith antigen.

Table 6–5

Laboratory Findings in Systemic Lupus Erythematosus

Hemolytic anemia
Leukopenia (<14000 leukocytes/mm³)
Thrombocytopenia (<100,000 platelets/mm³)
Antinuclear antibody positive
Lupus erythematosus cells
Antibodies to double-stranded DNA
Antibodies to SM antigen
False-positive test for syphilis

SM: Smith antigen.

ANA titers above 1:80 are considered positive, but, because the test is positive in many conditions, correlation with the history and with other clinical findings is mandatory. A positive ANA result alone is not sufficient to diagnose SLE. SLE can also be associated with a biological false-positive test for syphilis. Elevations of ANA titers can be seen in mul-

tiple conditions besides SLE, including infections (hepatitis, mononucleosis, malaria, subacute bacterial endocarditis), other connective tissue disorders (scleroderma, Sjögren syndrome, rheumatoid arthritis), and thyroid disease.[16]

The ANA can be weakly positive in almost 20% of healthy adults, but a titer of 1:320 or higher has specificity of 97% for SLE and other connective tissue diseases. Patients can demonstrate a positive ANA result because they are taking a variety of drugs, including hydralazine, isoniazid (INH), and chlorpromazine (Thorazine).

Additional testing for the specific autoantibody responsible for the positive ANA can help to identify a particular autoimmune disease. For example, antibodies to the DNA-histone complex suggest drug-induced lupus, whereas antibodies to double-stranded DNA (dsDNA) and to Smith (SM) antigen help to confirm SLE. Wegener granulomatosis is associated with a positive antineutrophilic cytoplasmic antibody (ANCA) test.[17] Antibodies directed against nuclear antigens to Ro/SS-A are found frequently in Sjögren syndrome.

Serum complement is an important component of the immune system that comprises 10% of serum globulins. Total complement (CH50) and complement fractions C3 and C4 are often reduced in SLE patients who have lupus nephritis.

Rheumatoid arthritis, a common condition in pain clinic patients, is associated with the production of immunoglobulins, including IgG, IgM, and IgA, known as *rheumatoid factors* (RF). From the laboratory standpoint, the most important of the RF is an IgM macroglobulin that combines with altered IgG antigen accompanied by complement. The average sensitivity of RF (70% to 95%) in rheumatoid arthritis is well established.

Positive RF can be found in SLE, scleroderma, dermatomyositis, and a variety of diseases associated with increased gamma globulin production—collagen vascular disorders, sarcoidosis, viral hepatitis, cirrhosis, and subacute bacterial endocarditis. As many as 20% of persons older than age 70 have a positive RF titer.

A striking example of the diagnostic crossover in autoimmune vasculitis is polyarteritis nodosa. This disease is manifested as a painful peripheral neuropathy in as many as 70% of patients. Arthritic complaints involving multiple joints have been reported in as many as 50%. These patients often exhibit various autoantibodies. The ANA test is positive in some 25% of cases, and RF in about 15%. Although sorting out the intricacies of these diseases is certainly the province of rheumatologists, pain specialists are uniquely positioned to entertain the possibility of connective tissue diseases and to initiate appropriate laboratory investigation.

■ THYROID

Thyroid dysfunction is a clinical problem often overlooked owing to its diverse manifestations. Elderly hypothyroid patients have a high incidence of gastrointestinal symptoms and atrial fibrillation, and even an apathetic, listless appearance that may be confused with dementia. After drug-induced encephalopathy, hypothyroidism ranks as the second most treatable metabolic cause of dementia.[18] The American College of Pathologists recommends thyroid evaluation for all women older than the age of 50 years who seek medical attention, all adults with newly diagnosed dyslipidemia, and all patients entering a geriatric unit, on admission and at least every 5 years thereafter.

The American Thyroid Association recommends the combination of thyroid-stimulating hormone (TSH) and free thyroxine (T_4) tests as the most efficient blood tests for the diagnosis and management of thyroid disease. The preferred method of testing for thyroid disease is a cascade starting with the TSH assay. If the TSH is normal, no further tests are performed. If TSH is abnormal, free T_4 is automatically determined. TSH usually becomes abnormal sooner than free T_4. Decreased TSH values suggest hyperthyroidism, exogenous thyroid hormone replacement, or glucocorticoid effects. Increased TSH levels usually suggest primary hypothy-

roidism—and only rarely a TSH-secreting pituitary adenoma or a state of thyroid resistance.

Testing of free T_4 should be ordered only when the TSH value is abnormal. In a large series of patients, no thyroid disease was detected in any patient who had normal TSH and low free T_4 levels. Accordingly, in persons with normal TSH and high free T_4 levels, almost all were monitored for thyroid replacement, thyroid suppression, or amiodarone therapy. None of the elevated T_4 levels led to a new diagnosis. Eliminating unnecessary testing can realize substantial savings.[19]

■ PROSTATE-SPECIFIC ANTIGEN (PSA)

Cancer of the prostate is the second most common malignancy in men and the third most common cause of cancer death in men after 55 years of age. Unfortunately, carcinoma of the prostate may remain asymptomatic even until advanced stages. Pain is a common manifesting symptom of advanced prostate cancer—dysuria, hip and back pain. Prostate-specific antigen (PSA, a glycoprotein enzyme) testing can often detect prostate cancer 3 to 5 years before clinical symptoms appear.[20]

The American Cancer Society and the American Urologic Association recommend annual screening for all men older than 50 years of age with PSA and a digital rectal examination. The PSA value is specific for prostate disease, but not necessarily for prostate cancer. Many conditions other than prostate cancer can increase the PSA level, such as benign prostatic hypertrophy, acute bacterial prostatitis, cystoscopy, and even use of exercise bicycles.

PSA is more sensitive than biochemical measurement of acid phosphatase, which was previously the accepted test. Annual PSA screening in combination with digital rectal examination has enhanced the detection of early localized cancer. Digital rectal examination and transrectal ultrasound generally do not have a significant effect on PSA measurements. Some 70% of men identified by PSA to have prostate cancer have organ-confined disease. In contrast, in the pre-PSA era, only one third of men diagnosed by digital rectal examination had organ-confined disease. PSA is one of the best tumor markers currently available.[21]

■ HUMAN IMMUNODEFICIENCY VIRUS 1

Pain is common in HIV disease, an RNA retroviral disorder that attacks T lymphocyte helper (CD4) cells. Common painful conditions associated with HIV include abdominal pain, painful neuropathies, oral cavity pain, headache, reactive arthritis, and neuropathic pain associated with herpes zoster. For multiple reasons, not the least of which is squeamishness in dealing with this disease directly, we find physicians reluctant to suggest laboratory testing for HIV. This observation is supported by the fact that many persons who are HIV positive are unaware of the disease. AIDS is a state of advanced infection marked by serologic evidence of HIV antigen plus opportunistic infections or neoplasms associated with immunodeficiency.

Enzyme immunoassay testing for HIV has been available since 1985. Specimens that are reactive in this initial screening test are subject to confirmatory Western blot analysis, an immunochromatographic technique that separates the virus into its major components by electrophoresis and exposes it to the patient's serum. Seroconversion generally occurs 6 to 10 weeks after infective exposure and persists for life. Antibody detection methods and a urine test have been developed whose sensitivity is comparable to that of serum testing.

A quantitative polymerase chain reaction (PCR) assay for HIV has been available since 1996. This test, commonly referred to as *the viral load,* is used for disease monitoring. An ultrasensitive version of this analysis can detect as few as 50 copies of viral RNA in 1 mL of plasma. The patient whose HIV viral load is greater than 100,000 copies per mL within 6 months of serum conversion is 10 times more likely to progress to AIDS within the first 5 years than one with fewer than 10,000 copies per mL. Maintaining low HIV viral loads (less than 50 copies/mL after 6 months of therapy) is currently the recommended goal of therapy.[22]

Monitoring lymphocytes is one way to assess immune system deficiency. Lymphocytes are divided into three main groups: B cells, T cells (including CD4 and CD8 cells), and natural killer cells (NKC). B cells function via antibody-mediated immunity. T cells are involved in cell-mediated immunity. HIV-1 selectively infects and reduces the number of CD4 (helper-inducer) T lymphocytes. CD8 (suppressive cytotoxic) T cell numbers remain normal or are increased.

Normal CD4 cell counts range between 600 and 1500 cells per mm³. Reduction in the CD4 cell count is a good indicator of when to start preventive therapy for numerous opportunistic HIV-associated infections. Generally, levels above 500 CD4 cells per mm³ are not associated with significant problems. Levels between 200 and 500 mm³ signal increased risk for herpes zoster, candidiasis, sinus and pulmonary infections, and tuberculosis. When cell counts fall to 50 to 200 per mm³, the risk of *Mycobacterium avium* complex or cytomegalovirus infection and of Kaposi sarcoma increases dramatically. Levels below 50 CD4 cells per mm³ indicate profound cellular immunodeficiency.

As CD4 counts decline, the possibility of opportunistic infections increases. A ubiquitous organism that can affect the central nervous system is *Toxoplasma*. Toxoplasmosis serology (IgG) is available and is usually performed when a person is found to be HIV positive. Initial positive toxoplasmosis serology would identify a potential candidate for preventive medication. Serologic tests for hepatitis should also be performed, particularly if there are abnormalities in the routine chemistry screen, such as an elevated serum transaminase level.

In summary, HIV-related disease is extremely complex. In my clinical experience, both patients and physicians consistently exhibit a tendency to ignore HIV as a possibility. Enzyme immunoassay testing for HIV antibody has been the initial screening test, followed by Western blot for confirmation. The best predictor of disease progression is not likely to be a single test but rather a combination of studies, including those for both viral load and CD4 cell count.

■ SPIROCHETAL DISEASES

Two spirochetal diseases that have distinguished themselves as "great imitators" because of their various manifestations include syphilis and Lyme disease. Syphilis is a sexually

FIGURE 6-3 ■ *Ixodes scapularis.* Larva, nymph, adult male, and adult female, on a millimeter scale. Courtesy of Pfizer Central Research, Gorton, Connecticut. (From Klippel J, Dieppe P [eds]: Rheumatology, 2nd ed. London, Mosby, 1997, page 6.5.3, Figure 5.3, with permission.)

transmitted disease caused by *Treponema pallidum,* and Lyme disease is the most common vector-borne infection in the United States, the vector being the spirochete *Borrelia burgdorferi,* which infects *Ixodes dammini* ticks (Fig. 6-3).

Serologic tests currently are the mainstay of syphilis diagnosis and management. Nontreponemal tests, including the Venereal Disease Research Laboratory (VDRL) and rapid plasma reagin (RPR), are used most often. In early primary syphilis, when antibody levels may be too low to detect, the sensitivity of nontreponemal tests ranges from 62% to 76%. As antibody levels rise in the secondary stage of syphilis, the sensitivity of nontreponemal tests approaches 100%; however, in late-stage syphilis, about one fourth of treated patients have negative VDRL results. Therefore, the combination of VDRL and RPR alone cannot be relied on for conclusive diagnosis during the very early or very late stages of syphilis.[23]

There are many false-positive nontreponemal test results. These include collagen vascular disorders, advanced malignancy, pregnancy, hepatitis, tuberculosis, Lyme disease, intravenous drug use, and multiple transfusions, among others. Because of the high frequency of false-positive results in nontreponemal serodiagnostic testing, all positive results on asymptomatic patients should be confirmed with a more specific treponemal test such as the microhemagglutination assay for *T. pallidum* and the fluorescent treponemal antibody absorption (FTA-ABS) tests. The FTA-ABS has sensitivity of 84% in primary syphilis and almost 100% for the other stages and specificity of 96%.

Titers of treponemal tests do not correlate with disease activity, whereas nontreponemal tests (VDRL and RPR) are quite useful for monitoring response to treatment. Treponemal tests should not be used for initial screening, because they are expensive and patients with previously treated infection usually remain reactive for life. Following antibiotic treatment for syphilis, VDRL and RPR should be checked once each at 6 and 12 months. Successful treatment should produce a fourfold decline in titer, although only about 60% of patients eventually become completely negative.

The other great imitator is Lyme disease, which manifests with multiple painful complaints, including headache, joint pain, cranial neuritis, unilateral or bilateral Bell's palsy, or a particularly painful syndrome of radiculitis with shooting electric pains and focal extremity weakness (Bannwarth's syndrome). Recent public awareness of Lyme disease has frequently prompted serologic testing of persons who have no clinical signs or symptoms of the disease. The pathogen, *B. burgdorferi*, is a spirochete named after Willy Burgdorfer, Ph.D., a public health researcher who identified it in 1982. A diagnosis of Lyme disease should be based primarily on the patient's symptoms and the probability of exposure to the Lyme organism (Fig. 6–4). The mainstay of clinical diagnosis of Lyme disease is based on a strong history suggesting potential exposure to the causative agent and the physical finding of erythema migrans, which is present in >60% of patients who are ultimately proved to have Lyme disease (Fig. 6–5). Laboratory evaluation is appropriate for patients who have the characteristic arthritic, neurologic, or cardiac symptoms. It is not warranted for patients who have nonspecific symptoms such as those frequently classified under the vague rubrics of *chronic fatigue syndrome* or *fibromyalgia*.

A true-positive result consists of a positive enzyme-linked immunosorbent assay (ELISA) or immunofluorescence assay (IFA) confirmed by a Western blot. It is essential to remember that positive results do not prove the diagnosis of Lyme disease and have little predictive value in the absence of clinical symptoms.[24]

False-positive Lyme results due to cross-reactive antibodies are associated with autoimmune disease or with infections secondary to other spirochetes such as *T. pallidum* and *Leptospira* species, and to bacteria such as *Helicobacter pylori*. Finally, because assays for antibody to *B. burgdorferi* should be used only for supporting a clinical diagnosis of Lyme disease, they are unsuitable as screening tools in evaluating asymptomatic persons or patients with nebulous complaints not characteristic of Lyme disease. There is evidence to suggest that many persons who do not actually have Lyme disease are receiving inappropriate treatment solely because of serology results.

■ NEUROPATHY

A frequent issue in the evaluation of pain, particularly when the cause is not obvious, involves peripheral neuropathy. Pain, sensory loss, weakness, and dysesthesias are common clinical complaints. Even after exhaustive evaluation, the cause of as many as 50% of peripheral neuropathies remains unknown. The more common causes are diabetes, alcoholism, toxins, nutritional deficits, drugs, and renal and other metabolic disorders. Less familiar disorders include the immune-mediated hereditary neuropathies. It is important to remain aware of the immune-mediated syndromes, not only to enhance diagnostic accuracy but because these patients often respond to immunomodulatory treatments with dramatic improvements in neurologic function and quality of life.[25]

It is far beyond the scope of this chapter to discuss this rapidly evolving topic in detail. We attempt to introduce the pain specialist to this aspect of neuropathy evaluation, particularly where specific laboratory tests can be critical to diagnostic accuracy. Vitamin B_{12} deficiency is characterized by macrocytic anemia, peripheral neuropathy, and ataxia, and it may be associated with cognitive deficits. B_{12} levels above

300 ng/L are normal. Levels between 200 and 300 ng/L are borderline. Measurement of methylmalonic acid, a substrate that requires cobalamin for its metabolism, is elevated (>0.4 mmol/L) in states of true vitamin B_{12} deficiency.

Levels of vitamin B_{12} below 200 ng/L are abnormal. Serum gastrin is elevated in gastric atrophy, which is usually associated with pernicious anemia. A normal serum gastrin level effectively rules out pernicious anemia, whereas intrinsic factor-blocking antibodies are detectable in only 50% of pernicious anemia patients. The expensive and time-consuming Shilling's test should be reserved for those patients with a low level of vitamin B_{12} who test negative for intrinsic factor-blocking antibodies and have an elevated serum gastrin level.

An immune-mediated neuropathy, acute or chronic, can be associated with pain and may even manifest as a life-threatening emergency. The prototype of acute inflammatory demyelinating neuropathy, Guillain-Barré syndrome, may appear after any of a number of infections, surgery, vaccinations, or immune system perturbations. Chronic inflammatory demyelinating polyneuropathy may be associated with illicit drug use, vaccination, infections, autoimmune disorders, or monoclonal gammopathy. A demyelinating neuropathy associated with anti–myelin-associated glycoprotein (anti-MAG) manifests as distal weakness and sensory loss, particularly in the legs. Measurement of IgM anti-MAG antibodies in the serum by the Western blot method detects this clinical disorder.[26]

Small myelinated and unmyelinated axons subserve pain and temperature. Diabetes and alcoholism, the most common causes of peripheral neuropathy in the United States, often manifest as a painful small-fiber neuropathy. Leprosy (Hansen disease) is the principal cause of a treatable neuropathy worldwide. Others are amyloidosis, AIDS, and ischemic lesions such as polyarteritis nodosa, SLE, and Sjögren syndrome. These small-fiber neuropathies often occur with burning, electric shock-like or lancinating pain, and uncomfortable dysesthesias. The patient may also complain of intense pain with only a minimal stimulus (allodynia), such as sheets rubbing over the feet.

Persons with a characteristic syndrome that is often dismissed as anxiety complain that "my whole body is numb and I feel tingling, painful numbness all over." In middle-aged patients, particularly those who are heavy cigarette smokers, paraneoplastic neuropathy should be considered. One indicator is serum antineuronal nuclear antibodies type I (ANNA: anti-HU). This malignant inflammatory sensory neuropathy is most often associated with small cell lung cancer, although it may associated with Hodgkin lymphoma, epidermoid cancer, or colon or breast carcinoma. As in all areas of pain diagnosis, the clinician must resist any impulse to hastily ascribe pain to psychogenic mechanisms: Once the psychogenic arrow has been fired, it is almost impossible to retrieve it gracefully.

Nonmalignant inflammatory sensory neuropathy is a disorder that commonly affects women. It can manifest as distal painful dysesthesias or ataxia. Serologic markers such as ANA, rheumatoid factor, or antineutrophil cytoplasmic antibodies (ANCA) may suggest specific connective tissue disorders, such as, respectively, SLE, rheumatoid arthritis, and Wegener granulomatosis. Certain patients with nonmalignant inflammatory neuropathy and Sjögren syndrome test positive

LYME DISEASE: US NATIONAL SURVEILLANCE CASE DEFINITION	
Definition	A systemic, tick-borne disease with protean manifestations: dermatologic, rheumatologic, neurologic and cardiac abnormalities. The initial skin lesion, erythema migrans, is the best clinical marker (occurs in 60%-80% of patients)
Case definition	1. Erythema migrans present *or* 2. At least one late manifestation and laboratory confirmation of infection
General definitions	
1. Erythema migrans (EM)	• Skin lesion typically beginning as a red macule/papule and expanding over days or weeks to form a large round lesion, often with partial central clearing • A solitary lesion must measure at least 5cm; secondary lesions may also occur • An annular erythematous lesion developing within several hours of a tick bite represents a hypersensitivity reaction and does not qualify as erythema migrans • The expanding EM lesion is usually accompanied by other acute symptoms, particularly fatigue, fever, headache, mildly stiff neck, arthralgias and myalgias, which are typically intermittent • Diagnosis of EM must be made by a physician • Laboratory confirmation is recommended for patients with no known exposure
2. Late manifestations These include any of the opposite *when an alternative explanation is not found*	Musculoskeletal system • Recurrent, brief attacks (lasting weeks or months) of objective joint swelling in one or a few joints, sometimes followed by chronic arthritis in one or a few joints • Manifestations not considered to be criteria for diagnosis include chronic progressive arthritis not preceded by brief attacks, chronic symmetric polyarthritis, or arthralgias, myalgias or fibromyalgia syndromes alone Nervous system • Lymphocytic meningitis, cranial neuritis, particularly facial palsy (may be bilateral), radiculoneuropathy or, rarely, encephalomyelitis alone or in combination • Encephalomyelitis must be confirmed by evidence of antibody production against *Borrelia burgdorferi* in cerebrospinal fluid (CSF), shown by a higher titer of antibody in the CSF than in serum • Headache, fatigue, paresthesias or mildly stiff neck alone are not accepted as criteria for neurologic involvement Cardiovascular system • Acute-onset, high-grade (2nd- or 3rd-degree) atrioventricular conduction defects that resolve in days to weeks and are sometimes associated with myocarditis • Palpitations, bradycardia, bundle-branch block or myocarditis alone are not accepted as criteria for cardiovascular involvement
3. Exposure	• Exposure to wooded, brushy or grassy areas (potential tick habitats) in an endemic county no more than 30 days before the onset of erythema migrans • A history of tick bite is not required
4. Endemic county	• A county in which at least two definite cases have been previously acquired or in which a tick vector has been shown to be infected with *B. burgdorferi*
5. Laboratory confirmation	• Isolation of the spirochete from tissue or body fluid *or* • Detection of diagnostic levels of immunoglobulin M or immunoglobulin G antibodies to the spirochete in the serum or the CSF *or* • Detection of an important change in antibody levels in paired acute and convalescent serum samples • States may separately determine the criteria for laboratory confirmation and diagnostic levels of antibody • Syphilis and other known biological causes of false-positive serologic test results should be excluded, when laboratory confirmation is based on serologic testing alone

FIGURE 6–4 ▮ Lyme disease; a summary of the US National Surveillance Case Definition. (From Klippel J, Dieppe P [eds]: Rheumatology, 2nd ed. London, Mosby, 1997, page 6.5.2, Figure 5.1, with permission.)

to extractable nuclear antigens such as ro (SS-A) and la (SS-P). Hereditary conditions, drugs, and toxins are also part of this differential diagnosis.[27]

Immune-mediated neuropathies are always worth remembering, because they can respond to immunomodulating treatments. These diagnoses are often overlooked or missed; sometimes patients suffer symptoms for years without a specific diagnosis. Frequently, pain specialists see these persons, and, not uncommonly, the patients' initial work-up was fragmented and far from thorough.

A search for serum factors associated with the immune-mediated neuropathies includes testing for monoclonal antibodies (proteins with definite antigenic targets) and for monoclonal and polyclonal antibodies that bind to specific neural components. Measurement of anti-MAG, antisulfatide, and anti-HU antibodies should be considered, as should serum and urine tests for monoclonal antibodies using immunofixation methods. Other elements of the work-up are testing serum for cryoglobulins and markers for connective tissue disorders. Table 6–6 includes a variety of specific laboratory tests that can be helpful in the evaluation of painful neuropathies. Once again, the pain specialist is in a unique position to develop expertise and knowledge, not only about the treatment of pain but in the evaluation and diagnosis of conditions that frequently escape proper identification, even by experienced subspecialists.[28]

■ SERUM PROTEINS

Laboratory tests involving the various components of serum proteins can be valuable adjuncts to the evaluation of pain. Abnormalities of the various components of serum proteins may be helpful in investigating connective tissue disorders and several malignancies. A lack of familiarity with this area of diagnosis creates a common reticence on the part of the pain specialist in ordering these studies.

Serum protein is composed of albumin and globulin. The word *globulin* is actually an old term that refers to the non-albumin portion of serum protein, a substance that has been found to contain a varied group of proteins, such as glycoproteins, lipoproteins, and immunoglobulins. The total quantity of albumin is about three times that of globulin, and albumin acts to maintain serum oncotic pressure. Globulins tend to have more varied functions, including antibodies, clotting proteins, complement, acute phase proteins, and transport systems for various substances. Serum protein electrophoresis is used to screen for serum protein abnormalities. Various bands are identified that correspond to albumin, $alpha_1$ and $alpha_2$ globulins, beta globulins, and gamma globulins (Fig. 6–6).

Acute phase proteins are seen in response to acute inflammation, trauma, necrosis, infarction, burns, and psychological stress. Increases are noted in fibrinogen, $alpha_1$-antitrypsin, haptoglobin, and complement. Albumin and transferrin are often decreased in an acute stress pattern. These changes in serum proteins during acute inflammatory responses are accompanied by polymorphonuclear leukocytosis, increased

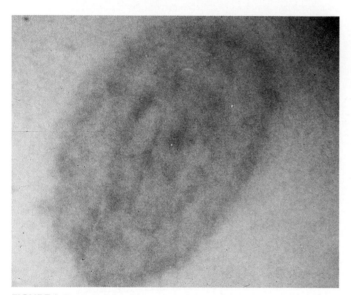

FIGURE 6–5 ■ Erythema migrans in Lyme disease. A typical annular, flat, erythematous lesion with a sharply demarcated border and partial central healing. (Courtesy of Dr Steven Luger, Olde Lyme, Connecticut. From Klippel J, Dieppe P [eds]: Rheumatology, 2nd ed. London, Mosby, 1997, page 6.5.4, Figure 5.4, with permission.)

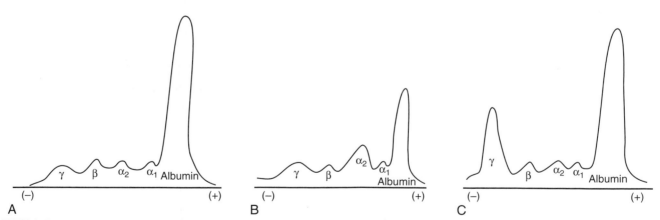

FIGURE 6–6 ■ Characteristic serum protein electrophoresis patterns. **A,** Normal pattern. **B,** Acute phase response pattern. Note decreased albumin peak and increased alpha$_2$ globulin level, which is associated with burns, rheumatoid disease, and acute stress. **C,** Monoclonal gammopathy spike. Note M protein spike in gamma area. Pattern is associated with myeloma, Waldenström macroglobulinemia, and idiopathic monoclonal gammopathy. (From Waldman SD [ed]: Interventional Pain Management, 2nd ed. Philadelphia, Saunders, 2001, p 95, Figure 9.1, with permission.)

Table 6–6

Clinical and Laboratory Features of Common Neuropathies

Neuropathic Conditions	Clinical Features	Useful Laboratory Tests (Findings)
Diabetic neuropathy	Distal symmetrical polyneuropathy Mononeuritis multiplex Diabetic amyotrophy	Fasting blood glucose HgAIC Glucose tolerance test
Alcohol neuropathy	Burning feet, ataxia Distal areflexia	Gamma-glutamyltransferase↑ Aspartate transaminase↑ Mean corpuscular volume (RBC macrocytosis)↑
Neuropathy due to renal disease	60% of dialysis patients have dysesthesias, pain, and cramps in legs	Blood urea nitrogen↑ Creatinine↑
Infectious neuropathy Leprosy Lyme disease	10 million cases worldwide Radiculoneuritis Bell's palsy	Skin biopsy+ Lyme test with Western blot confirmation+
Human immunodeficiency virus (HIV-1)	Guillain-Barré like (acute) Mononeuritis (late) Distal painful sensory neuropathy (late)	HIV test with Western blot confirmation+
Neuropathy associated with malignancy Lung cancer Myeloma	Painful sensory neuropathy Osteosclerotic myeloma	Anti-HU antibodies+ Immunoglobulins G, A, monoclonal gammopathy
Amyloidosis	Distal painful sensory neuropathy associated with plasma cell dyscrasia	Urine Bence Jones protein monoclonal gammopathy
IgM monoclonal gammopathy	Waldenström macroglobulinemia, chronic lymphocytic leukemia	Immunoglobulin M antibody to MAG, GMI, sulfatide
Vasculitic neuropathy Wegener granulomatosis Systemic lupus erythematosus Hepatitis B, C Sarcoid Sjögren syndrome Toxic neuropathy		P-ANCA+ Antinuclear antibodies+ Serology cryoglobulins+ Angiotensin-converting enzyme↑ Anti-SSA-LA Anti-SSB-Ro antibodies
Arsenic	Painful stocking and glove polyneuropathy	Urine levels >25 mg/day unless seafood was eaten recently
Lead	Abdominal pain, fatigue, wrist drop, diffuse weakness	Anemia Urine coproporphyrin↑ Urine lead level >0.2 mg/L Blood lead levels can be misleading
Vitamin B_{12} deficiency	Burning hands and feet Cognitive impairment Posterior column loss Ataxias	Low serum B_{12} Homocysteine↑ Methylmalonic acid↑

+, Positive; ↑, elevated.

ESR, and an increase in CRP that responds very rapidly after the onset of acute inflammation.

Significant changes in albumin are usually reductions rather than elevations. These can be associated with pregnancy, malnutrition, liver disease, cachexia or wasting states—such as those of tuberculosis, AIDS, or advanced cancer. Serum albumin may also be lost directly from the vascular compartment secondary to hemorrhage, burns, exudates, or protein-losing enteropathy.

Gamma globulin is composed predominantly of antibodies of the IgG, IgA, IgM, IgD, and IgE types. Marked reduction of the gamma fraction is seen in hypogammaglobulinemia and agammaglobulinemia. Secondary varieties of gamma globulin reduction may be found in patients with nephrotic syndrome, overwhelming infection, chronic lymphocytic leukemia, lymphoma, or myeloma and those on long-term corticosteroid treatment. Rheumatic and collagen vascular diseases usually demonstrate elevations in gamma globulin. Multiple myeloma and Waldenström macroglobulinemia demonstrate a homogeneous spike or peak in a localized region of the gamma area.

Immunoglobulins are a heterogeneous group of molecules. IgG constitutes about 75% of serum immunoglobulins and the majority of antibodies. IgM represents the earliest antibodies formed and accounts for about 7% of the total immunoglobulin. The IgM class includes cold agglutinins, ABO blood groups, and rheumatoid factor. IgA constitutes about 15% of immunoglobulins. IgA deficiency, the most common primary immunodeficiency, is associated with upper respiratory tract and gastrointestinal infections. Phenytoin (Dilantin) is reported to decrease IgA levels in about 50% of patients who receive long-term therapy. IgE is elevated in certain allergic and especially atopic disorders.

Multiple myeloma is a malignancy of plasma cells derived from B-type lymphocytes. The disease is most common in middle-aged males and frequently manifests as bone pain. Anemia is present in nearly 75% of patients, and RBC rouleaux formation (cells stacked like coins) can be identified in peripheral blood smears. Elevated ESR is common, and significant hypercalcemia occurs in about one third of patients. A monoclonal gammopathy spike (M protein) is seen in about 80% of myeloma patients. Of all patients who have monoclonal protein, about two thirds have myeloma. Roughly 70% have monoclonal protein characterized as IgG; most of the others, IgA.[29]

A normal immunoglobulin molecule is composed of two heavy chains and two light chains (kappa and lambda) connected by a disulfide bridge. IgM is a pentameric configuration of five complete immunoglobulin units. In addition to normal-weight serum monoclonal protein, many myeloma patients excrete a low-molecular weight protein known as *Bence Jones protein,* which is composed only of immunoglobulin light chains. Unlike normal-weight monoclonal proteins, it can pass into the urine and, generally, is not demonstrable in the serum. Other conditions associated with Bence Jones protein include Waldenström macroglobulinemia, a lymphoproliferative disorder associated with monoclonal IgM production, lymphadenopathy, hepatosplenomegaly, and hyperglobulinemia. Bence Jones proteinuria is seen in monoclonal gammopathies associated with malignancies, and significant quantities (>60 mg/L) are identified. In monoclonal gammopathies of non-neoplastic origins

such as rheumatic or collagen vascular disease, cirrhosis, and chronic infection, Bence Jones protein excretion is generally less than 60 mg/L.[30]

Cryoglobulins are immunoglobulins that precipitate reversibly in serum—or at least partially gel at cold temperatures. The most common associated symptoms are purpura, Raynaud phenomenon, and arthralgias. Cryoglobulins usually do not appear as discrete bands on serum protein electrophoresis. The conditions most often associated with cryoglobulins are rheumatoid and collagen vascular disease, leukemia, lymphomas, myeloma, and Waldenström macroglobulinemia. They are also associated with a variety of infections and hepatic disease.

■ RENAL FUNCTION TESTS

Routine urinalysis is an indispensable part of basic clinical laboratory evaluation. Dysuria is extremely common in women; 30% experience at least one episode of cystitis during their lifetime. The differential diagnosis of painful urination includes cystitis, pyelonephritis, urethritis, vaginitis, and genital herpes. The most sensitive laboratory indicator for urinary tract infection is pyuria. The basic urinalysis should include specific gravity, albumin, hemoglobin, and microscopic evaluation for casts, crystals, and red and white cells.[31]

If no vaginal contamination occurs during urine collection, vaginitis generally does not produce pyuria. The presence of WBC casts suggests pyelonephritis. A positive leukocyte esterase test is about 90% sensitive in detecting pyuria secondary to infection. Many bacteria produce an enzyme called *reductase* that converts urinary nitrates to nitrites. The nitrite test enhances the sensitivity of the leukocyte esterase test in defining urinary tract infection. A positive nitrite test is 90% specific for urinary tract infections. Its sensitivity is low but can be improved by obtaining a first voided morning urine sample.

Urinary tract infection is defined as 100,000 colony-forming units per mL on urine culture. The microscopic examination of the urine *must* proceed promptly, generally within 1 hour after voiding. Various studies report that as many as 50% of specimens that contained abnormal numbers of white cells were considered normal after standing at room temperature only several hours.[32]

Urea is a waste product of protein metabolism that is synthesized in the liver and that contains nitrogen (BUN). Creatinine is a metabolic product of creatine phosphate in muscle. Serum levels of BUN and creatinine change only with severe renal disease. Creatinine clearance rate (the amount of creatinine that can be completely eliminated into the urine in a given time) is a much more sensitive measure of mild to moderate glomerular damage. In addition to being sensitive to function, creatinine clearance is one of the more sensitive tests available to warn of impending renal failure.

Elevations of serum BUN and creatinine generally reflect severe glomerular damage, renal tubular damage, or both. An elevated BUN level (azotemia) is not specific for renal disease. Prerenal azotemia may result from decreased renal circulation secondary to shock, hemorrhage, or dehydration. It can also be caused by increased protein catabolism like that associated with overwhelming infections or toxemia. Renal azotemia usually accompanies bilateral chronic pyelonephritis, glomerular nephritis, acute tubular necrosis, and other forms of severe glomerular damage. Postrenal or obstructive azotemia can result from any external compression of the ureter, urethra, or bladder, or, in elderly men, from prostatic hypertrophy—benign or malignant. The studies that test predominantly renal tubular function include specific gravity, osmolality, and urinary excretion of electrolytes.

■ OSMOLALITY

Although the very term *osmolality* evokes an imposing and esoteric image, it has practical clinical value. Serum osmolality is an indicator of total body water and generally ranges between 280 and 300 mOsm/kg of water. The principal determinants of serum osmolality are sodium, chloride, glucose, and urea. A simplified formula with excellent clinical utility is this:

$$\text{Serum osmolality} = 2 \times \text{sodium} + \text{glucose} \div 20 + \text{BUN} \div 3$$

Urine osmolality depends on an individual's state of hydration. Under normal conditions, urine osmolality ranges from 400 to 800 mOsm/kg. Profound dehydration is associated with levels above 1100 mOsm/kg, and fluid overload demonstrates values below 100 mOsm/kg. Simultaneous measurement of urine and serum osmolality is useful in diagnosing inappropriate antidiuretic hormone secretion (SIADH), a condition that can be induced by a variety of causes, including central nervous system tumors, infections, trauma, undifferentiated small cell lung cancer, pneumonia, and various medications, among them opiates, barbiturates, and carbamazepine (Tegretol, Carbatrol). A typical patient with SIADH has a serum osmolality below 270 mOsm/kg and a urine osmolality that is higher than the serum value. In contrast, a patient with diabetes insipidus (DI) has a serum osmolality greater than 320 mOsm/kg and urine osmolality less than 100 mOsm/kg.

The osmolal gap can be used to screen for low-molecular-weight toxins. The gap is determined by subtracting the calculated osmolality (from the formula cited earlier) from the actual serum osmolality. The calculated and measured values usually fall within 10 units of each other. If the measured value exceeds the calculated value by more than 10 units, other osmotically active substances that can manifest in an emergency room setting should be considered. These include ethanol, methanol, ethylene glycol, propylene glycol, acetone, paraldehyde, and other toxins.

■ CALCIUM, PHOSPHORUS, AND MAGNESIUM

Symptoms related to hypercalcemia are varied but include vomiting, constipation, polydipsia, polyuria, and encephalopathy. Hypercalcemia is often detected on routine laboratory panels in an otherwise healthy person. Primary hyperparathyroidism accounts for about 60% of outpatient abnormalities. In hospitalized patients, malignancy-associated hypercalcemia accounts for the majority. Tumors most often associated with hypercalcemia are breast, renal, and lung cancers and myeloma. Regulation of serum calcium occurs through a negative feedback loop mediated by the secretion of parathyroid hormone (PTH). A decrease in serum calcium increases secretion of PTH, whereas an increase in serum calcium reduces it. PTH also has a direct action on bone, increasing bone resorption and the release of bone calcium and phosphorus.

Other causes of hypercalcemia include Dyazide diuretics, lithium therapy, sarcoidosis, hyperthyroidism, and vitamin D intoxication. The effects of PTH, vitamin D, and phosphate produce a reciprocal relationship between the serum calcium and phosphate levels, elevation of one ultimately leading to reduction of the other. Vitamin D deficiency results in low levels of both calcium and phosphorus but an elevated level of PTH.

Hypophosphatemia is seen in association with hypercalcemia as a manifestation of hyperparathyroidism. Severe hypophosphatemia can cause muscle weakness, bone pain, tremor, seizures, hypercalciuria, and decreased platelet function. Hyperventilation and respiratory alkalosis are major causes of hypophosphatemia in patients with pain, anxiety, sepsis, alcoholism, hepatic disease, heat stroke, or salicylate toxicity. Respiratory alkalosis causes plasma phosphate to shift into the cells. Life-threatening hypophosphatemia can occur if malnourished patients are administered carbohydrates rapidly.

Primary hyperparathyroidism reduces phosphate secondary to increased urinary excretion. Vitamin D deficiency causes hypocalcemia, secondary hyperparathyroidism, and increased urinary phosphate excretion in the face of decreased intestinal phosphate absorption.

Hypocalcemia and hyperphosphatemia are often seen in tandem. Renal failure accounts for more than 90% of hyperphosphatemia. Plasma phosphate levels rise when the glomerular filtration rate falls below 25% of normal. Rhabdomyolysis, hemolysis, and tumor lysis syndrome may produce severe hyperphosphatemia by releasing large amounts of intracellular phosphate. Hypoparathyroidism, acromegaly, and thyrotoxicosis reduce urinary phosphate excretion. Enemas with a high phosphate content can cause hyperphosphatemia, hypocalcemia, and, ultimately, tetany. The ill-advised practice of prolonged storage of blood samples can cause an artificial elevation in phosphate levels.

Routine serum calcium measures address total serum calcium, about 50% of which is bound calcium and about 50% ionized or free (dialyzable). Most of the bound calcium is complexed with albumin. The most common cause of "bound hypocalcemia" is a decrease in serum albumin. Although laboratory evidence of hypocalcemia is fairly common in hospitalized patients, true decreases of ionized calcium are less prevalent. Symptoms include neuromuscular irritability, mental status changes, and seizures. Causes of true hypocalcemia include primary hypoparathyroidism, pseudohypoparathyroidism secondary to diminished responsiveness of the kidney or skeleton to PTH, vitamin D deficiency, malabsorption, renal failure, chronic alcoholism, rhabdomyolysis, alkalosis, and certain drugs (large amounts of magnesium sulfate, anticonvulsant medication, or cimetidine).

After sodium, potassium, and calcium, magnesium is the fourth most common cation. It is often overlooked in patients with neuromuscular abnormalities. Symptoms of neuromuscular abnormalities include tremor, muscle cramping, seizures, confusion, anxiety, and hallucinations. Magnesium deficiency has been reported in as many as 10% of hospitalized patients. It is often associated with alcoholism, malabsorption, malnutrition, diarrhea, dialysis, diuretic use, and congestive heart failure. The most common cause of elevated serum magnesium is renal failure or a hemolyzed specimen.

▮ URIC ACID

Hyperuricemia is defined by a serum uric acid concentration greater than 7 mg/dL. Gout, principally a disease of middle-aged men, results from the deposition of monosodium urate crystals, typically in a joint in a lower extremity, often the first metatarsophalangeal joint (a lesion called podagra). At a physiologic pH, more than 90% of uric acid exists as monosodium urate, but at levels above 8 mg/dL, monosodium urate is likely to precipitate into tissues.

Although patients with gout generally have elevated serum uric acid levels, 10% may have levels that fall within normal range. Conversely, many patients with hyperuricemia never experience an attack of gouty arthritis, and by far the most frequent cause of hyperuricemia, particularly in hospitalized patients, is renal disease with azotemia.

Serum uric acid levels may become elevated in any disorder that results in proliferation of cells or excessive turnover of nucleoproteins. Hemolytic processes, lymphoproliferative and myeloproliferative diseases, polycythemia vera, and rhabdomyolysis may result in high uric acid levels. Obesity, alcohol abuse, and purine-rich foods such as bacon, salmon, scallops, and turkey can also result in an overproduction of urate.

About 97% of all uric acid the human body produces daily is excreted through the kidneys. In about 90% of patients with gout, the primary defect is under-excretion of uric acid. This occurs with renal insufficiency, hypertension, diabetes, and various drugs, including cyclosporine, nicotinic acid, and salicylates.

In summary, although patients with gout generally have elevated serum uric acid levels, an isolated elevation in uric acid is not diagnostic for gout, nor does a normal level conclusively rule it out. A most accurate and readily available test for gout is demonstration of uric acid crystals in the synovial fluid of an acutely inflamed joint.

▮ LIVER FUNCTION TESTS

Considerable confusion can be encountered in the interpretation of the many aspects of common liver function tests (LFTs). Many of the routine tests assess liver *injury* rather than liver function. Of the LFTs, only serum albumin, bilirubin, and prothrombin time provide useful information on how efficiently the liver is actually working. Certain of these findings may reflect problems arising outside the liver, such as an elevated bilirubin value, seen with hemolysis, or elevations in alkaline phosphatase associated with skeletal disorders. Normal LFTs do not ensure a normal liver: patients with cirrhosis or bleeding esophageal varices can have normal LFTs.[33]

The most commonly used markers of hepatic injury are the enzymes aspartate aminotransferase (AST) (formerly SGOT) and alanine aminotransferase (ALT) (formerly SGPT). AST and ALT values are higher in healthy obese patients and in males. ALT levels generally decline with weight loss. Slight elevations of the AST or ALT, within 150% of the upper range of normal, may not, in fact, indicate liver disease but rather a skewed (non–bell-shaped) distribution curve, with a higher representation on the far end of the scale (seen in blacks and Hispanic individuals).

The highest ALT levels, often more than 10,000 units/L, are found in patients with acute toxic injury such as acetaminophen overdose or acute ischemic insult to the liver. With typical viral hepatitis or toxic injury, the serum ALT rises higher than the AST value, whereas an AST/ALT ratio greater than 2:1 is more common with alcoholic hepatitis or cirrhosis. Causes of elevated ALT or AST values in asymptomatic patients include autoimmune hepatitis, hepatitis B, hepatitis C, drugs, toxins, alcohol, fatty liver, congestive heart failure, and hemochromatosis.

Lactate dehydrogenase (LDH) is a less specific marker than AST or ALT but is disproportionately elevated after ischemic hepatic injury. AST elevations greater than 500 units/L and ALT values greater than 300 units/L are unlikely to be caused by alcohol intake alone and in a heavy drinker should prompt consideration of acetaminophen toxicity. AST and ALT are found in skeletal muscle and may be elevated to several times the normal value in conditions such as severe muscular exertion, polymyositis, and hypothyroidism.

Stoppage of bile flow (cholestasis) results from blockage of the bile ducts or from a disease that impairs bile function. Alkaline phosphatase (ALP) and gamma-glutamyltransferase (GGT) levels typically rise to several times normal after bile duct obstruction or intrahepatic cholestasis. Diagnosis can be confounded during the first few hours after acute bile duct obstruction secondary to a gallstone, when AST and ALT levels rise 500 units/L or more but ALP and GGT can take several days to rise.

Serum ALP originates from both the liver and bone. Bony metastasis, Paget disease, recent fracture, placental production during the third trimester of pregnancy can all cause ALP elevations. ALP, like GGT, can be elevated in patients taking phenytoin (Dilantin), and this does not constitute an absolute indication for discontinuing the medication. ALP levels can be persistently elevated in asymptomatic women with primary biliary cirrhosis, a chronic inflammatory disease of small bile ducts associated with the presence of serum anti-mitochondrial antibodies.

The elevation of GGT alone with no other liver function abnormalities often results from enzyme induction caused by either alcohol or aromatic medications such as phenytoin or phenobarbital. The GGT level is often elevated in asymptomatic persons who take more than three alcohol-containing drinks per day. A mildly elevated GGT level in a person taking anticonvulsant medication does not indicate either liver disease or an absolute need to discontinue the medication.

Bilirubin, an indicator of liver function, is formed from the enzymatic breakdown of the hemoglobin molecule. The unconjugated bilirubin is carried to the liver, where it is rapidly transported into bile. The serum conjugated bilirubin level does not become elevated until the liver has lost half of its excretory capacity. A patient could thus have a total left or right hepatic obstruction without a rise in bilirubin.[34]

Unconjugated hyperbilirubinemia is associated with increased bilirubin production as in hemolytic anemia, resorption of a large hematoma or defective hepatic unconjugated bilirubin clearance secondary to severe liver disease, drug-induced inhibition, congestive failure, portacaval shunting, or Gilbert syndrome. Gilbert syndrome occurs in many healthy persons whose serum unconjugated bilirubin is mildly elevated (2 to 3 mg/dL). That is the only liver function abnormality: both the conjugated bilirubin value and the CBC remain normal. Gilbert syndrome has been linked to an enzymatic defect in the conjugation of bilirubin.

Visible staining of tissue with bile is called *jaundice*. The three major causes are extrahepatic and intrahepatic biliary tract obstruction and hemolysis. With hemolysis, unconjugated bilirubin increases, whereas the conjugated fraction remains normal or is only slightly elevated. In the case of extrahepatic biliary obstruction, usually in the common bile duct secondary to either a stone or carcinoma, initially there is an increase in conjugated bilirubin but no change in the unconjugated level. After several days, however, conjugated bilirubin in the blood breaks down to unconjugated bilirubin, eventually arriving at a ratio of 1:1.

Intrahepatic biliary obstruction is usually caused by liver cell injury from any of a variety of causes, including alcohol abuse, drugs, hepatitis, cirrhosis, passive congestion, or primary or metastatic tumors. Both conjugated and unconjugated fractions may increase, in varying proportions, in this type of obstruction. Hemolysis can be identified by measuring markers such as haptoglobin and reticulocyte count. A final word on jaundice relates to age. In persons younger than 30 years, viral infections account for 80% of cases. After age 60, cancer accounts for about 50% and gallstones for about 25%.

Another marker of hepatic synthetic capacity is serum albumin, which changes quite slowly in response to alterations in synthesis owing to its protracted plasma half-life of 3 weeks. Elevation of serum albumin usually implies dehydration. Patients with low serum albumin levels and no other LFT abnormalities are likely to have other, extrahepatic, causes—such as proteinuria, trauma, sepsis, active rheumatic disease, cancer, and severe malnutrition. During pregnancy, albumin levels progressively decrease until parturition and do not return to normal until about 3 months post partum.[35]

The PT is quite useful for following hepatic function during acute liver failure. The liver synthesizes clotting factors II, V, VII, IX, and X. Because factor VII has a short half-life (only 6 hours), it is sensitive to rapid changes in hepatic synthetic function. It is important to realize that PT does not become abnormal until more than 80% of hepatic function is lost. Vitamin K deficiency due to chronic cholestasis or fat malabsorption can prolong the PT. A therapeutic trial of vitamin K injections (5 mg/day subcutaneously for 3 days) is a reasonable option to exclude vitamin K deficiency.[36]

The measurement of blood ammonia provides a somewhat inexact marker for hepatic encephalopathy. Concentrations of ammonia correlate poorly with the degree of confusion. Although ammonia contributes to the encephalopathy, concentrations are often much higher in the brain than in the blood. Levels are best measured in arterial blood, because venous concentrations can be elevated as a result of muscle metabolism of amino acids. Blood ammonia determinations are most useful in evaluating encephalopathy of unknown origin rather than monitoring therapy in a person with known hepatic encephalopathic disease.[37]

The pancreas is another vital organ that, when diseased, may cause pain. Acute pancreatitis manifests with severe epigastric pain, vomiting, and abdominal distention. Two useful tests are serum amylase and lipase. Alpha-amylase is derived from both the pancreas and the salivary glands. Its sensitivity in acute pancreatitis is about 90%. Other causes of amylase elevation include biliary tract disease, peritonitis, pregnancy, peptic ulcers, diabetic ketoacidosis, and salivary gland disorders. False-normal results may be seen with lipemic serum.

The serum lipase is slightly less sensitive, but probably more specific in acute pancreatitis. The extrapancreatic disorder that most consistently elevates serum lipase is renal failure. Chronic pancreatitis is not generally a painful condition, but it reflects the end stage of acute pancreatitis, hemochromatosis, or cystic fibrosis. Diabetes, steatorrhea, and pancreatic calcification on radiographs are the signature features.

■ CREATINE KINASE

Creatine kinase (CK) is found in cardiac muscle, skeletal muscle, and brain. Total CK can be separated into three major isoenzymes: CK-BB, found predominantly in brain and lung; CK-MM, found in skeletal muscle; and CK-MB, found predominantly in heart muscle. Total CK elevation is seen in a number of conditions associated with acute muscle injury or severe muscular exertion. Total CK is also elevated after muscle trauma, myositis, muscular dystrophy, long distance running, or delirium tremens or seizures. Elevated levels can often be noted after intramuscular injections.

In evaluating chest pain, and particularly myocardial ischemia and infarction, total CK elevation is too often false-positive, owing principally to skeletal muscle injury. Troponin I is a regulatory protein that is specific for myocardial injury. It becomes elevated in about 4 to 6 hours, peaks at about 10 hours, and returns to reference range in about 4 days. Its major selling point is that it is highly specific for cardiac injury.

The CK-MB level begins to rise 3 to 4 hours after acute myocardial infarction, reaches a peak in 12 to 24 hours, and returns to normal in about 36 to 48 hours. The most rapid elevation after cardiac injury is that of serum myoglobin. Unfortunately, myoglobin is found in both cardiac and skeletal muscle. Elevations are noted as early as 90 minutes after cardiac injury. An analysis of myoglobin in conjunction with troponin I can be performed at intervals after the onset of myocardial infarction symptoms. Myoglobin may be viewed as a very early but not particularly specific marker for cardiac injury, whereas troponin is an extremely specific but not as rapidly responsive marker.

■ THERAPEUTIC DRUG MONITORING AND TESTING FOR DRUGS OF ABUSE

Particularly when the clinical information seems perplexing and contradictory, it is wise to consider the effects of prescription medications, toxic substances, and drugs of abuse. The practice of pain management inherently attracts patients prone to chemical dependency. They sometimes possess rather sophisticated pharmacologic information and present with detailed histories ultimately aimed at obtaining a specific controlled substance. It has been our experience that the treating physician often has a visceral warning about the integrity of these patients but is hampered by an overwhelming sense of social squeamishness or frank denial that ultimately misleads him to avoid drug screening and rightfully pursue a valid clinical impression.

As a practicing neurologist, I am amazed to see how many emergency room physicians faced with patients exhibiting erratic or agitated behavior fail to include toxicology screening in their evaluation. The effects of specific prescription medications or drug interactions in patients taking multiple medications should always be a primary concern.[38]

Therapeutic drug monitoring can be helpful in establishing compliance and therapeutic adequacy and avoiding toxic doses. Medications such as phenobarbital, valproic acid (Depakote), carbamazepine (Tegretol, Carbatrol), primidone (Mysoline), phenytoin (Dilantin), lithium carbonate, and the tricyclic antidepressants have readily available assays. Particularly in elderly persons, who sometimes exhibit dramatic changes in protein binding, toxicity may occur at levels normally considered therapeutic. With phenytoin, a medication that is about 90% bound to protein and that exhibits nonlinear kinetics, it is not unusual to see toxicity with a variety of symptoms, including ataxia, personality change, nystagmus, dysarthria, tremor, nausea, vomiting, and somnolence. Discovery of a toxic phenytoin level in an elderly patient with confusion and ataxia of several months' duration may not only suggest a rapid therapeutic course of action but also save several thousand dollars in unnecessary neurodiagnostic imaging studies.

Selective therapeutic drug monitoring can be very useful with phenytoin, primidone, phenobarbital, valproic acid, and carbamazepine. Valproic acid may be used for migraine prophylaxis. Carbamazepine and Dilantin are useful for trigeminal neuralgia and for neuropathic pain in general. Many of these compounds have narrow therapeutic windows, and, again particularly in the elderly, toxicity may go unnoticed and may be attributed to other causes such as cerebrovascular disease or dementia. It is not unusual to find patients with elevated medication levels who receive an incorrect diagnosis of stroke and whose drug levels consequently are allowed to remain in a protracted state of toxicity.

Lithium carbonate, used for both bipolar disorder and cluster headache management, has a distinctly narrow therapeutic window. Adverse effects include nausea, vomiting, tremor, and hypothyroidism. Lithium is excreted by the kidneys, whereas the anticonvulsant medications mentioned earlier are metabolized in the liver and interact with other drugs that are also metabolized there. Acetaminophen is a commonly used analgesic. Hepatic injury can occur with ingestion of 10 g, and 25 g has been known to be fatal. A serum level greater than 200 μg/mL is considered toxic. A pattern of acute hepatocellular injury similar to that of acute hepatitis is noted, with distinct elevations of AST and ALT.[39]

Testing for drugs of abuse is more difficult. In addition to problems with specificity and sensitivity, persistence of a drug or its metabolites in the urine varies much among individual agents and among abusers. For example, the urine can be positive for cannabinoids several days after a single casual use of marijuana. After cessation in long-term heavy users, the urine may remain positive as long as a month. All initially positive test results obtained by screening procedures should be confirmed by gas chromatography and mass spectrometry.

The different sensitivity levels of different tests must be kept in mind, as must the effect of urine concentration or dilution. It is critical to remember that detection of cannabinoids in the urine indicates that the patient has used marijuana in the past but provides no clear-cut evidence that marijuana is related to current mental impairment or a behavioral problem. Of equal importance is the concept of chain of custody, which demands strict accountability for a specimen from its collection to its ultimate analysis. A patient could be tragically stigmatized if erroneous results were obtained in a process that was flawed.[40]

Cocaine is another popular drug of abuse. Its major metabolite, benzoylecgonine, remains detectable considerably longer than cocaine and in heavy users may be detectable for several weeks. Amphetamines, usually methamphetamine, are detectable in the urine within 3 hours after a single dose. A positive result for amphetamines in the urine usually implies use within the last 24 to 48 hours.

Opioid abuse is particularly problematic in the "pain population." Morphine and codeine are made from the seeds of the opium poppy, whereas heroin is synthesized directly from morphine. Ingestion of moderate amounts of culinary poppy seeds can result in detectable concentrations of morphine in the urine that may last as long as 3 days. A speedball (a combination of cocaine and heroin) remains popular for prolonging cocaine's effects while blunting postcocaine depression. The immediate access to opioids afforded medical personnel makes this subgroup particularly susceptible to abuse. As an overview, the most common classes of drugs found when screening trauma patients, in order of frequency, are ethanol, amphetamines, opiates, and cocaine.[41]

■ TOXICOLOGY

Mercury, arsenic, bismuth, and antimony are best screened by urine sampling. Hair and nails are preferred for documenting long-term exposure to arsenic or mercury. Occupational lead exposure and lead poisoning remain serious public health problems in the United States. Most exposure is in industry—in battery manufacturing, the chemical industry, smelting, soldering, and welding. Symptoms include abdominal pain, myalgias, paresthesias, general fatigue, and, ultimately, encephalopathy and death.

Arriving at the diagnosis requires a constant high index of suspicion. At present, the blood level of lead is the single best indicator of recent absorption of a large dose of lead. The blood lead level rises rapidly within hours of an acute exposure and remains elevated for several weeks. Consecutive measurements averaging 50 μg/dL or higher indicate the necessity to remove an employee from that toxic environment. A blood lead level *and* a zinc protoporphyrin level provide sufficient information to quantitate the severity and approximate chronology of the lead exposure.

Zinc protoporphyrin reflects the toxic effects of lead on an erythrocyte enzyme system. Levels usually begin to rise when the blood lead level exceeds 40 μg/100 mL. Once elevated, zinc protoporphyrin tends to remain above background levels for several months (the 120-day life span of RBCs). The combination of an elevated blood lead level plus an elevated zinc protoporphyrin value suggests that exposure must have lasted longer than several days.[42]

Every year, the deaths of more than 100,000 Americans are associated with the use of alcohol. Intoxication is so common that physicians frequently forget that it can be fatal. Levels above 400 mg/dL are suggested lethal, but levels less than 400 mg/dL have been fatal, and levels of 800 mg/dL have been documented in alert patients. Most states define legal intoxication as a blood alcohol level of 100 mg/dL, although driving skills have been shown to become impaired at levels as low as 50 mg/dL. Alcohol is often ingested with other medications and, in combination, intoxicating levels or otherwise lethal doses may be strikingly lower. A combination of ethanol with chloral hydrate (a Mickey Finn) has a particularly devastating reputation.

Various tests have been used to screen for chronic alcoholism, including elevated GGT and AST levels, mean corpuscular volume elevation, hyperuricemia and hypomagnesemia, hyponatremia, and hypophosphatemia.[43] These indices correlate to some degree but cannot be taken as specific indicators of alcohol abuse. As in all cases with toxicology, the results should not be accepted without question. Laboratory errors do occur, and any tendency to be judgmental or punitive is strongly discouraged.

■ SUMMARY

The proper use of laboratory testing can be very valuable in evaluating pain. In this chapter, I have highlighted only the essentials. It is presented as a starting point from which readers can expand their knowledge. In my clinical experience, laboratory testing is often overlooked, with embarrassing—and sometimes tragic—consequences.

These tests, along with findings of the history and physical examination, form the foundation of clinical diagnosis. The pain specialist should embrace a primary care role in accurate diagnosis by ensuring thoroughness through methodical attention to detail. This approach is much preferred to the all too common one where patients are immediately referred for expensive procedures with a blind hope that advanced technology alone can illuminate the darkness and substitute for a careful history and physical examination.

References

1. Gabay C, Kushner I: Acute phase proteins and other responses to inflammation. N Engl J Med 340:448, 1999.
2. Brown RG: Anemia. In Taylor RB (ed): Family Medicine: Principles and Practice, ed 4. New York, Springer-Verlag, 1994, p 997.
3. Little DR: Diagnosis and management of anemia. Prim Care Rep 3:175, 1997.
4. Little DR: Hemochromatosis: Diagnosis and management. Am Fam Physician 53:2623, 1996.
5. Ranney HM: The spectrum of sickle cell disease. Hosp Pract 27(1):133, 1992.
6. Ravel R: Clinical Laboratory Medicine: Clinical Application of Laboratory Data, ed 6. St. Louis, Mosby-Year Book, 1995, p 9.
7. Schmitt BP, Adelman B: Heparin-associated thrombocytopenia. Am J Med Sci 305:208, 1993.
8. Nichols WL, et al: Standardization of the prothrombin time for monitoring orally administered anticoagulant therapy with use of the international normalized ratio system. Mayo Clin Proc 68:897, 1993.
9. The Expert Committee on the Diagnosis and Classification of Diabetes Mellitus: Report of the Expert Committee on the Diagnosis and Classification of Diabetes Mellitus. Diabetes Care 21(Suppl) 1:S5, 1998.
10. Weykamp CW, Penders TJ, Muskiet FA, van der Slik W, et al: Influence of hemoglobin variants and derivatives on glycohemoglobin determinations. Clin Chem 39:1717, 1993.
11. Service FJ: Hypoglycemia. Endocrinol Metab Clin North Am 17:601, 1988.
12. Avus JC, et al: Pathogenesis and prevention of hyponatremic encephalopathy. Endocrinol Metab Clin North Am 22:425, 1993.
13. Halevy J, et al: Severe hypophosphatemia in hospitalized patients. Arch Intern Med 148:153, 1988.
14. Vanek VW, et al: Serum potassium concentrations in trauma patients. South Med J 87:41, 1994.
15. Systemic lupus erythematosus (SLE). In Ferry JA, Harris NL (eds): Atlas of Lymphoid Hyperplasia and Lymphoma. Philadelphia, WB Saunders, 1997.
16. Tan EM, Feltkamp TEW, Smolen JS, et al: Range of antinuclear antibodies in "healthy" individuals. Arthritis Rheum 40:1601, 1997.
17. Hoffman GS, Kerr GS, Leavitt RY, et al: Wegener granulomatosis: An analysis of 158 patients. Ann Intern Med 116:488, 1992.
18. Isley WL: Thyroid dysfunction in the severely ill and elderly. Postgrad Med 94:111, 1993.
19. Helfand M, et al: Screening for thyroid dysfunction: Which test is best? JAMA 270:2297, 1993.
20. Littrup PJ, et al: Prostate cancer screening: Current trends and future implications. CA 42:198, 1992.
21. Babaian RJ, et al: The relationship of prostate-specific antigen to digital rectal examination and transrectal ultrasonography. Cancer 69:1195, 1992.
22. Saag MS, Holodniy M, Kuritzkes DR, et al: HIV viral load markers in clinical practice. Nat Med 2:625, 1996.
23. Larsen SA, Kraus SJ, Whittington WL: Diagnostic tests. In Larsen SA, Hunter EF, Kraus SJ (eds): A Manual of Tests for Syphilis. Washington, DC, American Public Health Association, 1990.
24. Centers for Disease Control and Prevention: Recommendations for test performance and interpretation from the second national conference on serologic diagnosis of Lyme disease. MMWR 44:590-591, 1995.
25. Dyck PJ, Oviatt KF, Lambert EH: Intensive evaluation of referred unclassified neuropathies yields improved diagnosis. Ann Neurol 10:222, 1981.
26. Thomas PK, Ochoa J: Symptomatology and differential diagnosis of peripheral neuropathy. In Dyck PJ, Thomas PK (eds): Peripheral Neuropathy, ed 3. Philadelphia, WB Saunders, 1993, p 749.
27. Kornberg AJ, Pestronk A: Immune-mediated neuropathies. Curr Opin Neurol Neurosurg 6:681, 1993.
28. Koski CL: Humoral mechanisms in immune neuropathies. Neurol Clin 10:629, 1992.
29. Boccadoro M, Pileri A: Diagnosis, prognosis, and standard treatment of multiple myeloma. Hematol Oncol Clin North Am 11:111, 1997.
30. Kyle RA: The monoclonal gammopathies. Clin Chem 40(11 pt 2): 2154, 1994.
31. Pappas PG: Laboratory in the diagnosis and management of urinary tract infections. Med Clin North Am 75:313, 1991.
32. Stamm WE, Hooton TM: Management of urinary tract infections in adults. N Engl J Med 329:1328, 1993.
33. Kamath PS: Clinical approach to the patient with abnormal liver function test results. Mayo Clin Proc 71:1089, 1996.
34. Westwood A: The analysis of bilirubin in serum. Ann Clin Biochem 28:119, 1991.
35. Rothschild MA, Oratz M, Schreiber SS: Serum albumin. Hepatology 8:385, 1988.
36. Kaplan MM: Laboratory tests. In Schiff L, Schiff ER (eds): Diseases of the Liver, ed 7. Philadelphia, JB Lippincott, 1993, p 108.
37. Johnston DE: Special considerations in interpreting liver function tests. Am Fam Physician 59:2223, 1999.
38. McCarron MM: The use of toxicology tests in emergency room diagnosis. J Analyt Toxicol 7:131, 1983.
39. Kaplowitz N, Tak Yee AW, Simon FR, et al: Drug-induced hepatotoxicity. Ann Intern Med 104:826, 1986.
40. Schwartz JG, Zollars PR, Okorodudu AO, et al: Accuracy of common drug screen tests. Am J Emerg Med 9:166, 1991.
41. Weisman RS, Howland MA, Flomenbaum NE: The toxicology laboratory. In Goldfrank LR, Flomenbaum NE, Lewin NA, et al (eds): Toxicologic Emergencies, ed 4. Norwalk, Conn, Appleton & Lange, 1990, p 39.
42. Staudinger KC, Roth VS: Occupational lead poisoning. Am Fam Physician 57:719, 1998.
43. Whitehead TP, Clarke CA, Whitfield AG: Biochemical and hematological markers of alcohol intake. Lancet 1(8071):978, 1978.

Radiography

David D. Hon and John A. Carrino

■ IMAGING PRINCIPLES

X-rays are produced when highly energetic electrons interact with matter and convert their kinetic energy into electromagnetic radiation. The x-ray tube contains the electron source in the form of a cathode tube filament as well as a tungsten target in a copper anode. Collimators are used to define the x-ray field. With varying voltage, current, and exposure time, x-ray beams of varying penetrability and spatial distribution can be created.

Radiography is dependent on differences in radiographic density. A radiograph is a two-dimensional image of a three-dimensional object. This is known as a projection imaging technique in contradistinction to cross-sectional modalities. The difficulty of interpreting these images is due to this superimposition of structures, and thus pathologic processes may appear less defined.

Traditional radiography systems use a film-screen combination consisting of a cassette, one or two intensifying screens, and a sheet of film. The film is simply thin plastic with a photosensitive emulsion coated onto one or both sides. The cassette is designed to protect the film from ambient light before exposing the film with x-rays. For routine radiography, double-screen, double-emulsion film-screen combinations are often used to improve sensitivity and reduce radiation exposure. Radiographic views are named by the direction of the x-ray beam from the source to the imaging recording device.

Several different systems are currently available for the acquisition of digital radiographs: the ones most commonly seen in clinical use are computed radiography (CR), charged-coupled devices (CCDs), direct detection flat panel systems, and indirect detection flat panel systems.

The workflow of CR systems is similar to that with conventional screen-film radiography. The CR imaging plate is made of barium fluorobromide or barium fluoride (barium fluorohalide). The CR imaging plate traps the x-ray beam (the electron) within the phosphor layer, and this electromagnetic energy is stored until processing. The CR plate is inserted into a reader that contains a laser that scans across the imaging plate, releasing the stored energy causing the emission of light. These light emissions are read by a photodiode scanning the imaging plate. The imaging plate is then "cleaned" with a flood of light. The prime advantage of CR over film-screen radiography is the increase in dynamic range. The system can tolerate a wider exposure range and thus result in

a smaller number of diagnostically inadequate films. However, the raw data require processing algorithms to produce clinically useful images.

Charged couple devices (CCDs) detectors form images from visible light. The surface of a CCD chip is photosensitive, and when a pixel is exposed to light, electrons are produced and built up within the pixel. This technology is used in modern video and digital cameras.

■ RADIOGRAPHY OF THE CERVICAL SPINE

Neck pain is a common human experience, although less common than that of low back pain. Neck pain may be a result of local noxious stimulation or referred from distant structures supplied by the cervical spinal nerves. Although somatic pain is typically referred distally, the acromioclavicular joint and sternoclavicular joints are two sites that may have neck pain by proximal referral. The majority of neck pain cases are self-limiting, resulting from mechanical problems; however, a small percentage of cases become chronic.

The standard cervical spinal series consists of anteroposterior, lateral, and odontoid views. If the cervicothoracic junction is not demonstrated on the lateral view, a swimmer's view, taken with one arm extended over the head, may be obtained. Plain radiographs are appropriate when there is a history of trauma likely to have produced a fracture, severe subluxation, or a concern regarding instability. In these instances, the most useful views are the lateral flexion and extension views. To assess for subluxation, four lines are traced along the lateral radiograph. Lines joining the anterior aspect of the vertebral body, the posterior aspect of the vertebral body, the laminae, and the spinous processes should appear as smooth arcs (Fig. 7–1). Oblique views of the cervical spine demonstrate the neural foramina, pedicles, articular masses, and apophyseal joints. In the setting of trauma, oblique views are particularly useful in identifying fractures and subluxations of the articular process.

Atlantoaxial instability should be specifically assessed. This is performed by evaluating the distance between the posterior aspect of the anterior arch of the atlas and the anterior aspect of the odontoid as seen on a lateral view. This measurement normally is less than 3 mm. Atlantoaxial instability can be seen in disease processes that may result in destruction of the transverse ligament complex, such as

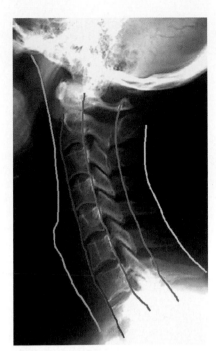

FIGURE 7–1 ▪ Lateral radiograph of a normal cervical spine. From anterior to posterior, these five parallel lines should be observed in every lateral cervical spine examination (anterior prevertebral soft tissues, anterior vertebral body line, posterior vertebral body line, spinolaminar line, spinous process line).

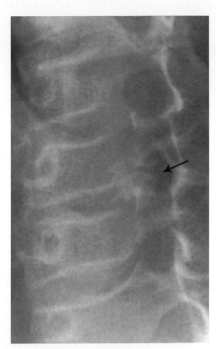

FIGURE 7–2 ▪ Neural foraminal narrowing. Left anterior oblique view of the cervical spine demonstrates small osteophytes *(arrow)* encroaching on the neural foramina.

inflammatory arthropathies (most commonly, rheumatoid arthritis).

Radiography for the evaluation of mechanical neck pain is limited and can be used to document the degree of cervical spondylosis. The term *spondylosis* is often used synonymously with *degeneration,* which includes both the nucleus pulposus and annulus fibrosus processes. Freidenburg and Miller, however, demonstrated no correlation between the presence of degenerative or spondylitic changes in the cervical spine with symptoms of neck pain.[1] Oblique views of the cervical spine allow assessment of the neural foramina and the presence of osteophytes, which may be encroaching upon the margins (Fig. 7–2).

The ligament between the vertebrae and the spinal dura is called the posterior longitudinal ligament. Ossification of the posterior longitudinal ligament (OPLL) is more common in the cervical (70%), followed by thoracic (15%) and lumbar (15%) regions. This entity was originally reported in a large number of Japanese patients with a genetic linkage. Although typically asymptomatic, patients may present with symptoms of cervical myelopathy.[2] The typical radiographic appearance is that of a linear band of ossification along the posterior margin of the vertebral body with a separating sharp, thin radiolucent line. OPLL may be apparent in as many as 50% of cases of diffuse idiopathic skeletal hyperostosis (DISH); conversely, DISH has been observed in over 20% of cases of OPLL (Fig. 7–3).[3]

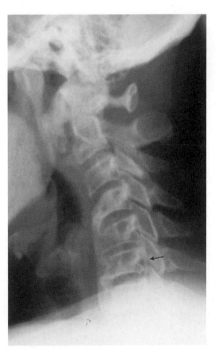

FIGURE 7–3 ▪ Ossification of the posterior longitudinal ligament (OPLL) and diffuse idiopathic skeletal hyperostosis (DISH). Lateral view of the cervical spine shows prominent flowing ossification along the anterior margin of four continuous vertebrae compatible with DISH. A dense vertical band of ossification is seen posterior to the vertebral margin *(arrow)* with a separating radiolucent line consistent with OPLL.

▪ RADIOGRAPHY OF THE THORACIC SPINE

The standard thoracic spinal series consists of anteroposterior and lateral views. Symptomatic degenerative disk disease is much less common in the thoracic spine than in the cervical and lumbar regions. Thoracic disk herniations are relatively uncommon when compared with cervical and lumbar disk disease. Commonly, thoracic disk herniations present as pain, numbness, tingling, and occasionally lower extremity weakness. If the herniation is large enough, bowel or bladder function may be affected.

Scheuermann disease is a thoracic kyphosis defined by anterior wedging of at least 5 degrees of three adjacent thoracic vertebral bodies. Secondary changes of Scheuermann kyphosis are characterized by irregularities of the vertebral end plates, disk space narrowing, and the presence of intervertebral disk herniations known as Schmorl's nodes. The thoracic spine is most commonly affected, although the lumbar spine may also be involved. This disorder of the spine is often discovered initially in adolescents and was formerly thought to be secondary to osteonecrosis but is now believed to be due to a congenital weakness in the end plates. For diagnosis, three adjacent vertebral bodies must be involved with 5 degrees or more of anterior wedging.

DISH is a common cause of regional pain syndromes in patients older than the age of 40. The peak incidence is in the sixth and seventh decades of life, and the disorder is more common in men than women. Although common in the lower thoracic spine, DISH also can be seen in the lumbar and cervical spine. Patients typically present with localized pain and stiffness with decreased range of motion of the affected area. Radiographs of the spine demonstrate the presence of flowing nonmarginal syndesmophytes along the anterolateral margins of at least four contiguous vertebrae (Fig. 7–4). A proportion of patients with DISH also have OPLL.

■ RADIOGRAPHY OF THE LUMBAR SPINE

Low back pain is the most common musculoskeletal impairment reported and the second most common complaint to primary physicians after the common cold.[4] Most instances of back pain are benign and self-limiting. Over 50% of all patients improve after 1 week, whereas more than 90% are better at 8 weeks.[5] Careful clinical evaluation is necessary to separate patients with mechanical (no primary inflammatory or neoplastic cause) from those with nonmechanical back pain.

Radiography is stated to have limited use in the evaluation of low back pain. Patients with mechanical back pain often have radiographs that are normal. Conversely and more commonly, many individuals with radiographic abnormalities are asymptomatic.[6] Evaluation of the lumbar spine includes anteroposterior and lateral views as well as flexion and extension views if instability is suspected. The anteroposterior and lateral views demonstrate alignment, disk and vertebral body height, as well as gross assessment of bone mineral density. The use of lumbar radiography should be limited because it exposes the gonads to significant ionizing radiation. The radiation exposure of oblique views is double the exposure of standard views, which alone are equivalent to female gonadal radiation or chest radiography for several years.[7]

Radiography is often used as an initial screening tool for patients with unrelenting back pain. Congenital abnormalities or developmental defects such as scoliosis, spina bifida, or anomalous lumbosacral transitional vertebral bodies may be visualized.

Spondylolysis, a break in the pars interarticularis, is the most common radiographic abnormality to result in low back pain. Spondylolysis may or may not result in spondylolisthesis. However, the combination of spondylolysis and spondylolisthesis frequently results in distortion of associated neural foramina, leading to compromise of the exiting nerve. Spondylolysis does not necessarily produce back pain. Oblique views of the lumbar spine are particularly useful for the evaluation of spondylolysis because they demonstrate the pars interarticularis in profile (Fig. 7–5).

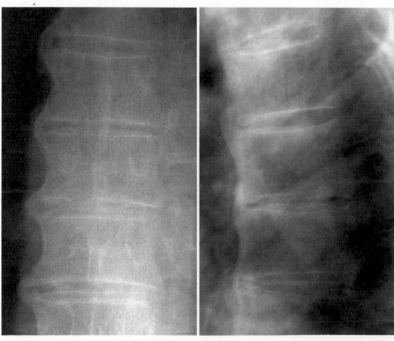

A   B

FIGURE 7–4 ■ Diffuse idiopathic skeletal hyperostosis (DISH). Anteroposterior (**A**) and lateral (**B**) views of the thoracic spine show large flowing bony excrescences along at least four vertebral bodies.

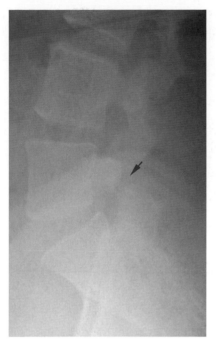

FIGURE 7–5 ■ Spondylolysis. Lateral radiograph demonstrate discontinuity of the "Scottie dog" neck compatible with a pars defect.

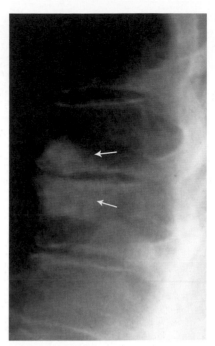

FIGURE 7–6 ■ Diskogenic vertebral sclerosis. Lateral view of the thoracic spine shows narrowing of the intervertebral disk space with associated sclerosis *(white arrows)* of the adjacent end plates primarily involving the anterior aspect of the vertebral bodies.

Disorders of the intervertebral disks and zygapophyseal joints may also result in low back pain. Lumbar radiographs may not directly demonstrate findings of disk herniation or spinal stenosis. However, it is unusual for lumbar radiographs to be absolutely normal in these conditions. Acute disk herniation may result in loss of intervertebral disk height. Normal lumbar intervertebral disk height demonstrates interval increase up to the lumbosacral junction. Plain film findings that may be associated with stenosis include narrowing of the intervertebral disk spaces with diskogenic vertebral sclerosis (Fig. 7–6), zygapophyseal joint osteoarthritis, and spondylolisthesis.[8] Congenital stenosis may occur as a result of developmentally narrow spinal canal dimensions (developmentally short pedicles) or bone dysplasias such as dwarfism. These findings are nonspecific and are common in asymptomatic older individuals, resulting in their limited predictive value.

Signs of disk degeneration include loss of disk height, sclerosis of the end plates, and osteophytic ridging. In addition, spondylolisthesis can be diagnosed and the degree of slippage visualized easily on lateral images. Spondylolisthesis as a result of degenerative changes should never be greater than 25%. Meyerding proposed a grading system for spondylolisthesis that is still used today. The degree of slippage is measured as the percentage of distance the anteriorly translated vertebral body has moved forward relative to the superior end plate of the vertebra below (Fig. 7–7). Grade 1 denotes a 1% to 25% slippage; grade 2, 26% to 50%; grade 3, 51% to 75%; grade 4, 76% to 100%; and grade 5, greater than 100% slippage.

In older individuals with low back pain, more ominous causes need to be considered. Patients with fever or weight loss may have an infection or tumor as the cause of their pain. Radiographs may be normal at the initial onset of disk

space infection but will demonstrate increasing destruction with prolonged duration. Infections are generally hematogenous in adults and begin at the vertebral end plate. Radiographic evidence of disk infection includes loss of disk height, erosions or destruction of adjacent vertebral end plates, and reactive new bone formation with sclerosis in chronic cases. If clinical suspicion persists despite normal radiographs, cross-sectional imaging with CT or MRI may be performed. Both modalities demonstrate increased sensitivity for the detection of vertebral osteomyelitis. Numerous neoplastic lesions, both benign and malignant, may be associated with the lumbar spine. Neoplastic lesions may be lytic (radiolucent), blastic (radiodense), or mixed. Thirty to 50 percent of trabecular bone must be lost before it can be visualized on a radiograph.

Osteoporotic patients are at increased risk for developing compression fractures. New or incompletely healed fractures are commonly associated with pain. Although radiographs may be able to distinguish between an acute versus chronic compression deformity via the comparison of prior radiographs, it may be impossible to assess the degree of healing. Scintigraphy and MRI are more useful in this context, demonstrating increased bone activity and bone marrow edema, respectively, of incompletely healed fractures.

Inflammatory arthropathies that affect the axial skeleton may present as low back pain. Radiographs of the sacroiliac joints are often obtained in patients suspected of having an inflammatory arthropathy of the axial skeleton. Sacroiliitis can be detected early utilizing radiography. Angled views of the sacroiliac joints by 30 degrees (Ferguson view) provide greater sensitivity than routine anteroposterior views.[9] In patients with ankylosing spondylitis, sacroiliitis begins as erosions, followed by sclerosis and eventual ankylosis. Sacroili-

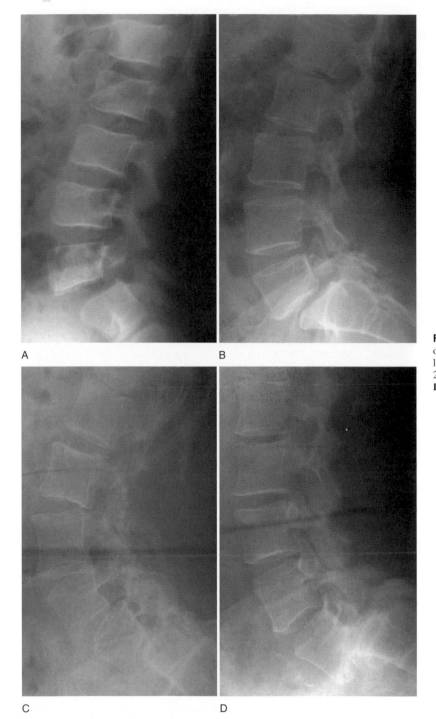

A B

C D

FIGURE 7–7 ■ Grading of spondylolisthesis. Lateral views of the lumbar spine demonstrate varying degrees of spondylolisthesis at L5/S1. **A,** Grade 1: 1% to 25% slippage. **B,** Grade 2: 26% to 50% slippage. **C,** Grade 3: 51% to 75% slippage. **D,** Grade 4: 76% to 100% slippage.

itis may be unilateral (i.e., infectious), bilaterally symmetrical (i.e., ankylosing spondylitis, enteropathic arthropathy), or bilateral and asymmetrical (i.e., seronegative spondyloarthropathies) (Fig. 7–8). CT or MRI is more sensitive and may show early involvement of the sacroiliac joint when the findings of plain radiographs are equivocal.

Kummel disease, aseptic vertebral osteonecrosis, is an entity that may present with localized pain. Although patients may be asymptomatic, local pain and progressive angular kyphotic deformity are clinical hallmarks. Radiographic diagnosis is based on vertebral body collapse or flattening with an

associated intranuclear vacuum cleft. Kummel disease is often associated with a history of trauma, severe osteoporosis, or long-term use of corticosteroids and presents most commonly at the thoracolumbar junction (Fig. 7–9).

■ RADIOGRAPHY OF THE SHOULDER

The shoulder is a complex joint with numerous bony articulations as well as multiple ligamentous and musculotendinous attachments. Shoulder pain may be a result of local trauma or

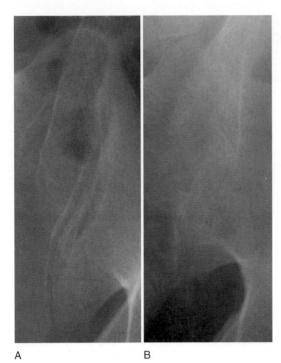

A   B

FIGURE 7–8 ■ Normal sacroiliac joint and sacroiliitis. **A,** Normal: magnified anteroposterior view of the left sacroiliac joint demonstrates sharply defined sacral and iliac sides of the joint without evidence of sclerosis or erosion. **B,** Sacroiliitis: magnified anteroposterior view demonstrates complete fusion of the left sacroiliac joint that was also evident on the right in this patient with late-stage ankylosing spondylitis.

referred pain or may be seen in association with other medical conditions.

Radiographs may demonstrate chronic rotator cuff arthropathy, as evidenced by calcific tendinitis. In these long-standing cases, cystic and sclerotic changes may been seen at the greater tuberosity insertion. Superior migration of the humeral head against the undersurface of the acromion with narrowing of the subacromial space (less than 6 mm) is another secondary sign of rotator cuff incompetence. Over time, this results in degenerative changes at the subacromial joint and eventual secondary osteoarthritis at the gleno-humeral joint.

Acromioclavicular pain is commonly a result of acute or chronic repetitious trauma. Injuries to this joint are graded according to the degree of disruption of the joint capsule and supporting ligaments. Sage and Salvatore proposed a three-grade classification that Rockwood further classified into six types.

Type I: Normal
Type II: Subluxation of acromioclavicular joint space less than 1 cm; normal coracoclavicular space
Type III: Subluxation of acromioclavicular joint space more than 1 cm; widening of the coracoclavicular space more than 50%
Types IV to VI: Subluxation of acromioclavicular joint space more than 1 cm, widening of the coracoclavicular space more than 50%; associated displacement of the clavicle

Grade I injury involves a sprain of the joint capsule without ligamentous disruption. Radiographs of both

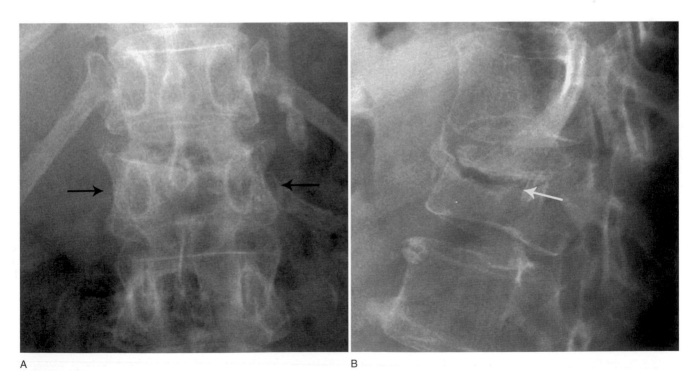

A   B

FIGURE 7–9 ■ Kummel disease. Anteroposterior (**A**) and lateral (**B**) views at the thoracolumbar junction show vertebral body collapse *(black arrows)* with associated vacuum phenomenon *(white arrow).*

shoulders may be obtained with stress views (the addition of 10-lb weights) to see if there is abnormal or asymmetrical widening of the acromioclavicular space (normal <4 mm).

Osteolysis of the distal clavicle may be seen as a result of acute injury or repetitive stress (i.e., weight lifting) to the shoulder. These changes are typically seen predominantly on the clavicular side. An inflammatory arthritis such as rheumatoid arthritis may also present with similar radiographic findings. Patients may present with aching and pain at the limits of flexion and abduction. Radiographs demonstrate resorption of the distal clavicle, often with osteophyte formation, osteoporosis, or tapering. The differential diagnosis of distal clavicular resorption includes postoperative changes, posttraumatic osteolysis, hyperparathyroidism, or changes secondary to an inflammatory arthropathy.

■ RADIOGRAPHY OF THE ELBOW

Pain at the elbow may be related to local pathology or referred pain from cervical or shoulder disease. Generally, fully extended frontal and 90-degree flexed lateral views of the elbow are adequate for evaluation of arthritis; oblique views in full extension can be helpful for further visualization of the joint margins and the radioulnar articulation. An axial view obtained with the elbow in flexion is useful to evaluate the cubital tunnel for marginal osteophytes, which can impinge on the ulnar nerve.

Local processes include both articular (arthritis, osteochondritis, loose bodies, subluxation) and periarticular (epicondylitis, olecranon bursitis, ligamentous lesions, entrapment neuropathy) disorders. Primary osteoarthritis of the elbow is unusual, but involvement frequently occurs in more generalized inflammatory arthritis. Lateral epicondylitis is the most frequent periarticular lesion, affecting 1% to 3% of the population.

Osteochondritis dissecans of the elbow usually affects adolescents and young adults. The area of the elbow most frequently affected is the anterolateral surface of the humeral capitellum. In an adolescent with elbow pain, particularly if he or she is a throwing athlete, the diagnosis of osteochondritis dissecans may be considered. Initial investigations include plain radiographs, which may demonstrate radiolucency or rarefaction of the lateral or central portion of the capitellum. In advanced stages, loose bodies, radial head hypertrophy, and osteophyte formation may be present. Radiographs may be diagnostic, but bone scan is a more sensitive diagnostic tool and MRI offers information for staging and characterization of lesions.

A second process that also involves the capitellum and should be distinguished from osteochondritis dissecans is Panner disease, which is an osteochondrosis of the capitellum. Panner disease is thought to be caused by interference in blood supply to the growing epiphysis that results in resorption and eventual repair and replacement of the ossification center. Inciting causes include repetitive trauma, congenital and hereditary factors, as well as endocrine disturbances. Initial radiographs demonstrate irregularity with areas of radiolucency involving the capitellum. Progressive radiographs will demonstrate deformity of the capitellum with eventual collapse and fragmentation.

■ RADIOGRAPHY OF THE WRIST AND HAND

Radiographs of the hands are the most informative part of any screening series for arthritis. Two views are suggested for evaluation: a posteroanterior view and a Norgaard view of both hands and wrists. Imaging of mineralization and soft tissue swelling is well evaluated by the posteroanterior view. The Norgaard view has also been described as the "ball catcher's" view and profiles the radial aspect of the base of the proximal phalanges in the hand and the triquetrum and pisiform in the wrist. This view is particularly useful for imaging early erosive changes. The hand is not rigidly positioned by the technician for the Norgaard view, and thus subtle subluxations as seen in inflammatory arthropathies and systemic lupus erythematous may be identified. Soft tissue swelling, subluxation/dislocation, mineralization, calcification, joint space narrowing, erosion, and bone production must all be examined for. Each arthropathy has its own characteristic set of changes.

The distribution of primary osteoarthritis in the hands and wrists is characteristic, affecting the scaphoid-trapezium-trapezoid, first carpometacarpal, and first metacarpophalangeal joints as well as the interphalangeal joints. The second through fifth metacarpophalangeal joints are less often involved. Large osteophytes at the interphalangeal joints can produce deformity and loss of range of motion and are referred to clinically as "Heberden's nodes" at the distal interphalangeal joints and "Bouchard's nodes" at the proximal interphalangeal joints. Secondary osteoarthritis is also common in the wrist in patients with chronic inflammatory arthropathy, especially rheumatoid arthritis, who have suffered severe cartilage damage and ligament tears as a result of their primary disease.

Positive ulnar variance, a situation in which the distal ulna projects farther than the end of the radius, can also result in wrist pain. Positive ulnar variance can cause impaction of the distal ulna or ulnar styloid on the lunate and/or triquetrum (ulnar impaction syndrome). This situation causes tearing of the triangular fibrocartilage complex, which is caught between these structures, and subsequent osteoarthritis, with pain at the ulnar aspect of the wrist, especially with activities requiring ulnar deviation.

Chondrocalcinosis, deposition of calcium pyrophosphate dihydrate (CPPD) crystal, can occur in both hyaline and fibrous cartilage. When seen in two or more joints, the radiographic diagnosis of CPPD deposition disease can be made. Idiopathic CPPD crystal deposition disease, hyperparathyroidism, and hemochromatosis are all known to cause actual deposition of CPPD crystals in cartilage. Soft tissue calcification of hydroxyapatite crystals can be seen in various systemic diseases. Classically seen in shoulder tendinitis or over the greater trochanter, CPPD deposition within the soft tissues of the hand could be related to scleroderma, dermatomyositis, and renal osteodystrophy.

De Quervain stenosing tenosynovitis most commonly is seen in women between 30 and 50 years of age as a result of occupation-related cumulative microtrauma. Secondary causes include rheumatoid arthritis, systemic lupus erythematosus, scleroderma, psoriatic arthritis, infection, microcrystalline amyloid deposition, sarcoidosis, and pigmented villonodular synovitis. Clinically, de Quervain tenosynovitis is often confused with osteoarthritis of the first carpometacarpal joint or with the intersection syndrome. Radiographs may demonstrate the changes of osteoarthritis, but MRI is necessary for identification of tenosynovitis. Typically, radiographs are unable to demonstrate changes related to tenosynovitis or ganglion, which are two common causes of wrist pain.

■ RADIOGRAPHY OF THE PELVIS AND HIP

Clinically, numerous conditions can account for the patient with hip pain. Hip pain may be related to the hip itself, peri-articular soft tissues, or adjacent bones. Referred pain from the lumbar spine may also present as hip pain. Anteroposterior (with the leg internally rotated) and frog-leg lateral (hip abducted and externally rotated) views of the hips are the only views typically required for evaluation. Joint narrowing is best assessed on the anteroposterior view; most normal hip joints are wider medially than superiorly by a ratio of approximately 2 to 1. However, it is useful to add to the protocol an anteroposterior view of the pelvis because this permits comparison with the contralateral side as well as assessment of the sacroiliac joints.

Primary hip osteoarthritis is readily diagnosed by radiography, as demonstrated by cartilage space narrowing, marginal osteophytes, and subchondral sclerosis. Normal hips should have 4 mm of cartilage space with a difference of less than 1 mm from side to side.[10] In the hips, osteoarthritis is typically associated with asymmetrical joint narrowing; usually, the cartilage loss is most noticeable at the superior weight-bearing aspect of the joint. Osteophytes form at the junction of the femoral head and neck. They are often broad and flat and form a "collar" around the head and are often seen better on the frog-leg lateral view (Fig. 7–10). Subchondral cysts can become large and can be mistaken for a lytic lesion when they occur at the acetabulum. Other cystic-appearing foci are common at the femoral neck and represent synovial herniation pits; these are often seen in asymptomatic individuals without osteoarthritis. Buttressing is seen at the medial aspect of the femoral neck and is a response to the abnormal stresses placed on the joint margins.

Pain is also a presenting complaint in many inflammatory arthritides, including seronegative spondyloarthropathies (ankylosing spondylitis, Reiter syndrome, psoriatic arthropathy, and enteropathic arthropathy), crystalline arthropathies (gout and pseudogout) and rheumatoid, viral, and septic arthritis.

Two different causes of osteonecrosis of the hip are described: traumatic and atraumatic. Traumatic osteonecrosis is secondary to direct injury to the femoral head with resultant damage to its blood supply. Fracture of the femoral head or neck and hip dislocation are the two primary mechanisms of injury. The two most common causes of atraumatic osteonecrosis are corticosteroid use and alcohol abuse. In early osteonecrosis, radiographs are typically normal. Early findings include ill-defined mottling or sclerosis of the trabecular pattern followed by a discontinuity in the subchondral bone, the "crescent sign," which represents a fracture between the subchondral line and the adjacent necrotic bone. As the disease progresses, subchondral collapse and eventual degenerative joint disease results (Fig. 7–11).

Several radiographic staging systems are used. The Ficat classification is as follows:

Stage 0: No pain, normal radiographic findings, abnormal bone scan or MRI findings
Stage I: Pain, normal radiographic findings, abnormal bone scan or MRI findings
Stage IIa: Pain, cysts, and/or sclerosis visible on radiographs, abnormal bone scan or MRI findings, without subchondral fracture
Stage III: Pain, femoral head collapse visible on radiographs, abnormal bone scan or MRI findings, crescent sign (subchondral collapse), and/or stepoff in contour of subchondral bone
Stage IV: Pain, acetabular disease with joint space narrowing and arthritis (osteoarthrosis) visible on radiographs, abnormal MRI or bone scan findings

Osteitis pubis is a syndrome characterized by pain and bony erosion of the symphysis pubis. Historically, this condition has been considered an infectious complication of pelvic infection and instrumentation or a complication of excessive pubic symphysis mobility during pregnancy. Radiographs may demonstrate symphysis widening, cystic changes, and sclerotic changes (a later finding). "Flamingo" views (i.e., anteroposterior radiographs of the pelvis with the patient standing on one leg) may reveal instability of the pubic symphysis. Bone scanning, which is more sensitive than radiography, often demonstrates increased uptake over the symphysis and pubic ramus.

Another common cause of hip pain in adults is trochanteric bursitis. This entity is much better defined by clinical examination or MRI. Radiographic findings may include calcification adjacent to the trochanter or bony irregularity. Infectious arthropathy of the hip may present radiographically as joint space narrowing and destruction. The aspiration and evaluation of the aspirate is necessary for diagnosis.

■ RADIOGRAPHY OF THE KNEE

The initial imaging studies for nontraumatic knee pain are the anteroposterior and lateral radiographs. On the lateral view with the knee flexed 20 to 35 degrees, effusion can be detected; the medial and lateral compartments can be distinguished by matching condyles to their corresponding tibial surface (medial tibial plateau concave, lateral convex). If symptoms are localized to the patellofemoral joint, a Merchant or axial (skyline) view of the patellofemoral joint is recommended.

In elderly patients, the most common cause of nontraumatic knee pain is osteoarthritis. Radiographic diagnosis includes indirect evaluation of the articular cartilage via joint space narrowing as well as the formation of osteophytes, subchondral cysts, and bony sclerosis (Fig. 7–12). Standing radiographs have been reported to more accurately demonstrate cartilage space narrowing than supine radiographs.

Although the patellofemoral joint is not a weight-bearing joint, patellofemoral joint osteoarthritis is commonly seen in older individuals in conjunction with involvement of the medial and lateral compartments ("tricompartmental

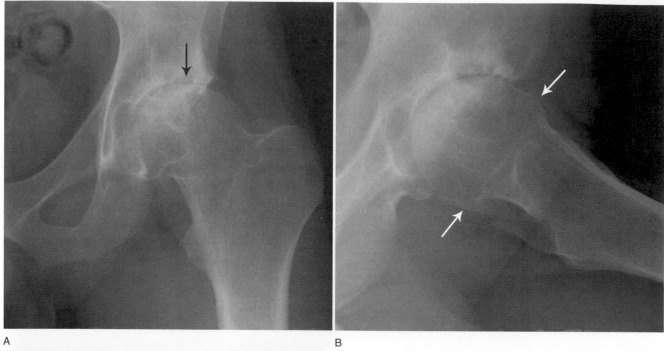

A

B

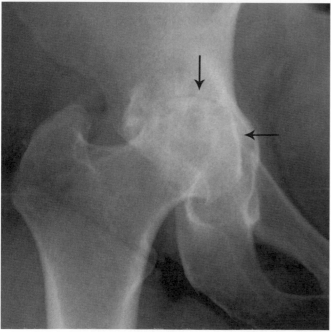

C

FIGURE 7–10 ■ Osteoarthritis of the hips. Anteroposterior (**A**) and frog-leg lateral (**B**) views of both hips show unilateral left hip joint narrowing that asymmetrically involves the superior aspect of the joint *(black arrow);* there is associated subchondral sclerosis, subchondral cystic change, and marginal osteophytes. Note improved visualization of the osteophytes *(white arrows)* on the lateral view. **C,** Anteroposterior view of a patient with chronic rheumatoid arthritis and findings of secondary osteoarthritis; note osteophyte formation and subchondral sclerosis. The diffuse joint narrowing and protrusio acetabuli *(arrows)* are more characteristic of rheumatoid arthritis.

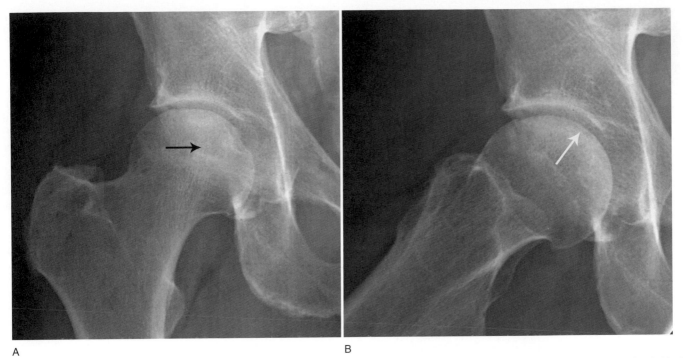

A   B

FIGURE 7–11 ■ Avascular necrosis of the hips. Anteroposterior (**A**) and lateral (**B**) views of the right hip demonstrate sclerosis of the femoral head *(black arrow)* with visualization of the "crescent sign" *(white arrow)* representing subchondral bone collapse.

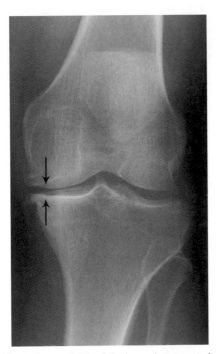

FIGURE 7–12 ■ Osteoarthritis of the knee. Anteroposterior view shows medial compartment narrowing *(arrows)*, subchondral sclerosis, cystic change at the medial tibial plateau, and large marginal osteophytes.

osteoarthritis"). Potential causes of patellofemoral joint osteoarthritis include patellar tracking abnormalities, developmentally shallow patellar sulcus, high-riding patella (patella alta), and prior patellar dislocation. CPPD arthropathy may also present as predominant patellofemoral osteoarthritis with findings of chondrocalcinosis.

Synovial osteochondromatosis is a benign condition characterized by synovial villus proliferation and metaplasia. As the synovial lining undergoes nodular proliferation, fragments may break off from the synovial surface and into the joint. Over time, these fragments may grow, calcify, or ossify. Synovial osteochondromatosis results in joint deterioration with secondary osteoarthritis. Patients are typically between the third and fifth decades, although any age group may be involved. Males are more commonly involved than females, with patients typically reporting years of monoarticular joint pain and swelling with limited range of motion. The large joints are more commonly affected, with over 50% of cases occurring within the knee, followed by the elbow. Radiographs demonstrate multiple calcified or ossified bodies within the joint or bursa (Fig. 7–13). When these fragments are not calcified, intrasynovial fragments may not be seen on radiographs.

■ RADIOGRAPHY OF THE ANKLE AND FOOT

Radiographic evaluation of the ankle includes anteroposterior, lateral, and mortise views. The mortise view is obtained by taking a frontal view with 15 degrees of lateral rotation of the foot to remove the superimposition of the distal fibula from the talar dome, or mortise. This view is best for evaluation of subtle joint narrowing, osteochondral defects, subchondral cysts, and marginal osteophytes. The anteroposterior and mortise views together provide a look at the anterior and posterior aspects of the distal tibiofibular syndesmosis, which contains a synovial recess between the syndesmotic ligaments; erosions from synovial proliferation or widening related to instability can be assessed on these views. The

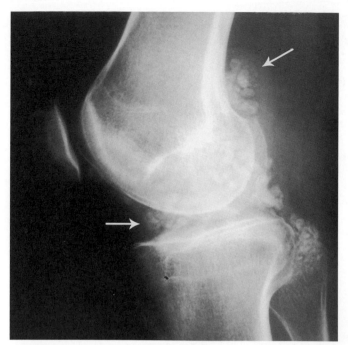

FIGURE 7–13 ■ Synovial osteochondromatosis. Lateral view of the knee shows numerous round ossific bodies *(arrows)* within the knee joint all of similar shape and size.

lateral view is not only useful for evaluation of anterior and posterior osteophytes or erosions but also provides soft tissue information such as distention of the ankle joint capsule by fluid or pannus and retrocalcaneal bursitis. Calcaneal enthesophytes at the insertion of the Achilles tendon and at the origin of the plantar fascia and long plantar ligament can be evaluated for "fuzzy" margins as seen in psoriatic arthritis and Reiter disease. The subtalar joint can also be evaluated on a well-positioned lateral film, but the beam must not be tilted or else the joint will be obliqued out of view. Evaluation of the subtalar joint can also be obtained with a Harris-Beath, or skier's, view in which the ankle is dorsiflexed and an anteriorly tilted axial view of the calcaneus is taken, a view that if properly taken will be tangential to both posterior and middle facets of the subtalar joint.

Anteroposterior and lateral images of the foot are generally all that is required for evaluation of arthritis of the foot, but it is recommended that they be obtained with weight bearing, because some deformities are only present on standing views; in addition, this aids standard positioning of the foot. Frontal views with slight obliquity are useful for detection of subtle erosions at the metatarsophalangeal joints and interphalangeal joints. They are also helpful to visualize the intertarsal and Lisfranc articulations, which have complex surfaces and various degrees of obliquity and are often obscured on the anteroposterior view.

Tarsal coalition is a congenital abnormality resulting from fibrous, cartilaginous, or osseous union of two or more tarsal bones. The two most common are calcaneonavicular and talocalcaneal coalitions. Lateral radiographs of the foot demonstrate secondary signs of talocalcaneal coalition, including talar beaking, flattening and broadening of the lateral talar process, and a positive C-sign. A Harris view may be helpful to evaluate the subtalar joint, but CT is often obtained to rule out subtalar coalition. Calcaneonavicular bony bridges can be seen on the lateral view with the classic "anteater nose" coming from the calcaneus.

References

1. Freidenburg Z, Miller W: Degenerative disc disease of the cervical spine. J Bone Joint Surg Am 45:1171, 1963.
2. Terayama K: Genetic studies on ossification of the posterior ligament of the spine. Spine 14:1184, 1989.
3. Tsuyama N: The ossification of the posterior longitudinal ligament of the spine. Clin Orthop 184:71, 1984.
4. White AA 3rd, Gordon SL: Synopsis: Workshop on idiopathic low-back pain. Spine 7:141, 1982.
5. Dixon A St J: Progress and problems in back pain research. Rheumatol Rehabil 12:165, 1973.
6. Witt I, Vestergaard A, Rosenklint A: A comparative analysis of x-ray findings of the lumbar spine in patients with and without lumbar pain. Spine 9:298, 1984.
7. Webster E, Merrill O: Radiation hazards: II. Measurements of gonadal dose in radiologic examinations. N Engl J Med 257:811, 1957.
8. Hall S, Bartleson JD, Onofrio BM, et al: Lumbar spinal stenosis: Clinical features, diagnostic procedures and results of treatment in 68 patients. Ann Intern Med 103:271, 1985.
9. Robbins SE, Morse MH: Is the acquisition of a separate view of the sacroiliac joints in the prone position justified in patients with back pain? Clin Radiol 51:637, 1996.
10. Roberts WN, Williams RB: Hip pain. Prim Care 15:783, 1988.

chapter 8

Nuclear Medicine Techniques

David D. Hou and John A. Carrino

■ BONE SCINTIGRAPHY

Nuclear scintigraphy provides both morphologic and physiologic information regarding the metabolic state of tissues. The most commonly agent used in musculoskeletal imaging is technetium-99m. Technetium emits gamma radiation at an energy level of 140 keV with a half-life of 6 hours. Chelation to various chelating agents (such as diphosphonates which are targeted to bone) can be used to achieve target organ specificity. The most commonly used diphosphonates for musculoskeletal imaging are ^{99}Tc-methylene-diphosphonate (Tc-MDP), ^{99}Tc-hydroxyethylidene-diphosphonate (Tc-HEDP), and ^{99}Tc-hydroxymethylene-diphosphonate (Tc-HMDP). There is no significant difference between these three agents, and the agent chosen is based on availability. ^{99}Tc-MDP, the most commonly used agent, is an organic analog of pyrophosphate, containing an organic P-C-P bond. This agent affixes to the bone surface by the process of chemisorption through which Tc-MDP affixes to the bone surface by attaching itself to the hydroxyapatite crystals in bone and calcium crystals in mitochondria.[1]

The adult dose of ^{99}Tc-diphosphonates is typically an intravenous dose of 15 to 20 mCi with imaging performed 2 to 4 hours after administration. The delay between injection and imaging allows clearance of the radiotracer from the soft tissues, resulting in higher target-to-background ratio and thus improved visualization of bone. For documentation of hyperemia or inflammation, dynamic blood flow and blood pool images are used in addition to standard delayed images. Typical imaging consists of anterior and posterior views as well as spot views of the area of concern with urinary bladder activity, faint renal activity, and minimal soft tissue activity present. Single-photon emission computed tomography (SPECT) can increase lesion detectability by allowing visualization in three planes. SPECT images are acquired from an arc of 180 or 360 degrees by rotating the gamma camera around the patient. Images can be reconstructed and displayed in axial, coronal, and sagittal planes.

The mechanism for increased uptake of Tc-MDP in osseous lesions is multifactorial. First, areas of new bone formation contain increased formation and mineralization of osteoid. These newly forming hydroxyapatite crystals provide for a greater surface area for binding. Second, hyperemic regions are exposed to greater tracer over any given time period and this increased flow results in an increase in bone activity compared with normal bone. Finally, interruption of the sympathetic supply can also result in increased uptake of tracer, as will be discussed later during the topic of reflex sympathetic dystrophy.[2]

■ POSITRON EMISSION TOMOGRAPHY

The most significant advancement in nuclear medicine recently is positron emission tomography (PET) and the combination of PET CT scanners with important implications for oncology, especially for soft tissue neoplasms or postoperative cancer patients. PET is a nuclear medicine technique that only recently has been widely used in clinical oncology (in part because in order to have ready availability of the agents an on-site cyclotron was required). PET uses short-lived positron-emitting radioisotopes that annihilate to form two photons that have trajectories approximately 180 degrees apart at a particular energy level (511 keV). The coincidental detection of these photons by a ring detector is reconstructed via a filtered back projection (similar to CT) to form images of tracer distribution. [^{18}F]-2-deoxy-2-fluoro-D-glucose (FDG) is a metabolic tracer most widely used in clinical PET oncology. FDG accumulation reflects the rate of glucose utilization in a tissue because FDG is transported into a tissue by the same mechanisms of glucose transport and trapped in a tissue as FDG-6-phosphate, which is a poor substrate for the further enzyme systems of glycolysis or glycogen storage. The use of FDG in evaluation of the musculoskeletal system is based on increased glycolytic rate in pathologic tissues. Thus, PET has proven to be the gold standard in metabolic imaging. FDG provides a means of quantitating the glucose metabolism, with the amount of tracer accumulation reflecting the glucose metabolism: high-grade malignancies tend to have higher rates of glycolysis than do low-grade malignancies and benign lesions; therefore, high-grade malignancies have greater uptake of FDG than that of low-grade or benign lesions. PET, as a metabolic imaging technique, demonstrates advantages over and complements structural imaging methods and also shows differences from conventional nuclear medicine, all of which have led to its growth in clinical applications in recent years. PET applications are evolving, but now it is approved for the diagnosis, staging, and restaging of many common malignancies and has shown efficacy for the detection of osseous metastasis from several malignancies, including lung carcinoma, breast carcinoma, and lymphoma. However, the significance of FDG PET in evaluations of primary bone tumors and tumor-like lesions has not been extensively elucidated. Several investigators have reported the usefulness of FDG-PET in oncologic applications for primary musculoskeletal tumors. Preliminary reports suggest a good correlation between glucose consumption measured by FDG PET and the aggressiveness of musculoskeletal tumors. However, not an insignificant overlap exists between benign and malignant groups; therefore, PET is not a solo method for differential diagnosis between benign and malignant bone lesions. Both neoplastic and inflammatory processes can cause increase in FDG activity, so tissue sampling may not be obviated but should be directed to the most metabolically active regions identified by PET. Therefore, PET has a role as a very useful adjunct to anatomic imaging techniques because it can provide an in-vivo method for quantifying functional metabolism in normal and diseased tissues.

■ BONE SCINTIGRAPHY AND SPECT IMAGING IN NEOPLASTIC DISEASE

The search for metastatic disease is one of the most common indications for bone scintigraphy, playing an integral role in tumor staging and management. Approximately 75% of patients with malignancy and pain have abnormal bone scintigraphic findings. As little as 5% to 10% change in the composition of normal bone is required to detect an abnormality on bone scan.[3] The sensitivity of bone scan in the detection of metastatic disease is between 62% and 100%.[4] However, for aggressive lytic lesions including multiple myeloma and lymphoma, metastatic lesions are detected approximately 50% of the time with nuclear scintigraphy versus 80% detection rate on skeletal survey. The specificity of bone scan in the evaluation of metastatic disease is limited, because fractures, degenerative disease, as well as a number of additional benign lesions may produce false-positive examination. SPECT imaging results in improved sensitivity in comparison to planar images, particularly in the evaluation of complex structures such as the spine. SPECT allows three-dimensional evaluation of anatomy, facilitating both localization and characterization of an abnormality.[5] Metastatic involvement should be suspected when the area of increased uptake extends from the vertebral body into the pedicle. Involvement of a vertebral body and a portion of the posterior arch, excluding the pedicle, is most often caused by benign conditions.[6] The "superscan" appearance with high axial skeletal uptake, reduced soft tissue uptake, and absent renal activity can occur with any primary tumor but is most common in prostatic and breast carcinoma (Fig. 8–1).

■ PROSTHESIS IMAGING

By 10 years after implantation, 50% of prostheses demonstrate radiographic evidence of loosening.[7] Cemented prostheses are anchored in position with polymethylmethacrylate, whereas cementless prostheses become fixed via bony ingrowth into a porous coating applied to the prosthesis surface. Mild uptake at the distal tip of a cemented prosthesis is within the variation of normal. Focal activity greater

than the intensity of the iliac crest seen on delayed images is strongly suggestive of aseptic loosening. Uptake surrounding the acetabular component that exceeds the activity of the iliac crest is also suggestive of loosening.

The introduction of porous-coated cementless prosthesis has complicated the utilization of bone scintigraphy in prosthesis evaluation. Cementless prostheses can normally demonstrate delayed activity at the distal tip, even as far as 2 years after placement. This activity may be noted to increase over time and may still be unrelated to prosthetic loosening.[8]

Differentiating aseptic loosening from infection is extremely important because the treatment of these two conditions is drastically different. Patients with aseptic loosening typically undergo single-stage revision arthroplasty, which requires one hospital admission. Septic prosthesis is a serious complication of joint replacement, which may require a lengthy hospitalization, resection arthroplasty, and a long course of antibiotics. The overall accuracy of radionuclide bone imaging in evaluation of the prosthetic joint is 50% to 70%. Nevertheless, bone imaging is useful as an initial screening test because it has a high negative predictive value.[9]

Septic prosthesis is a serious complication of joint replacement that may require a lengthy hospitalization, resection arthroplasty, and a long course of antibiotics. Postsurgical anatomic distortion as well as artifact resulting from metallic prosthesis may hinder the interpretation of high-resolution cross-sectional studies. Radionuclide imaging is not affected by the presence of metallic hardware and is therefore useful for evaluating the painful prosthesis. Bone scintigraphy is useful as a screening test because a normal result essentially excludes the presence of a prosthetic complication.[9] Joint aspiration may be performed, but large numbers of both false positive and negative results have been reported.[10]

■ BONE SCINTIGRAPHY FOR REFLEX SYMPATHETIC DYSTROPHY

Patients with reflex sympathetic dystrophy (RSD) present with pain, hyperesthesia, vasomotor disturbances, and trophic changes in the skin.[11] At bone scintigraphy, RSD typically manifests as diffuse, uniformly increased juxta-articular uptake throughout the affected region on delayed images (Fig. 8–2). This is not only the most sensitive indicator for RSD but also results in high specificity and negative predictive value.[12] Occasionally, RSD may manifest as a focal abnormality limited to a single nerve or anatomic segment.[13] Unfortunately, bone scintigraphy is only 60% sensitive[14] and does not consistently demonstrate the presence of early disease.

■ BONE SCINTIGRAPHY FOR SPONDYLOLYSIS

Bone scintigraphy is highly sensitive for detecting stress-induced changes in bone and plays an important role in the evaluation of the young athlete with low back pain. Spondylosis is a defect in the pars interarticularis of the vertebra that is believed to represent a fatigue-type fracture. This entity is an important cause of both acute and chronic pain in active young adults. Approximately 90% of pars defects occur at the

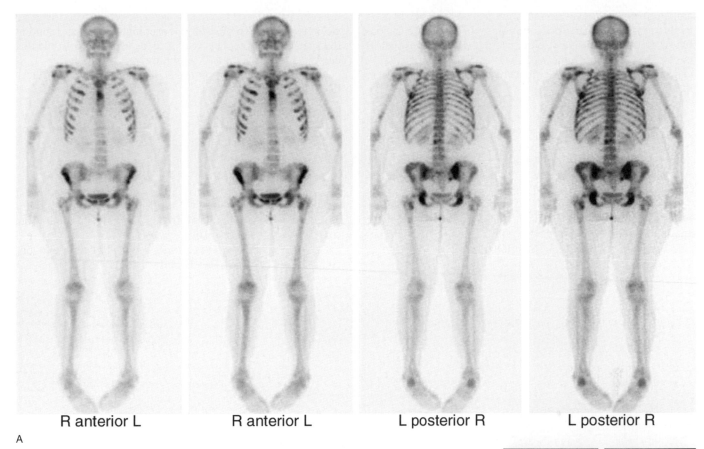

R anterior L   R anterior L   L posterior R   L posterior R

A

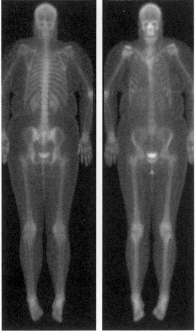

B

FIGURE 8–1 ■ **A,** Metastatic neoplasm to the bone. Whole-body anterior and posterior planar bone scans show multifocal tracer accumulation throughout the axial and proximal appendicular skeleton. This patient had widespread osseous metastasis from a primitive neuroectodermal tumor. **B,** Normal bone scan. (Courtesy of Dr. John Walter Millstine, Harvard Medical School, Brigham and Women's Hospital.)

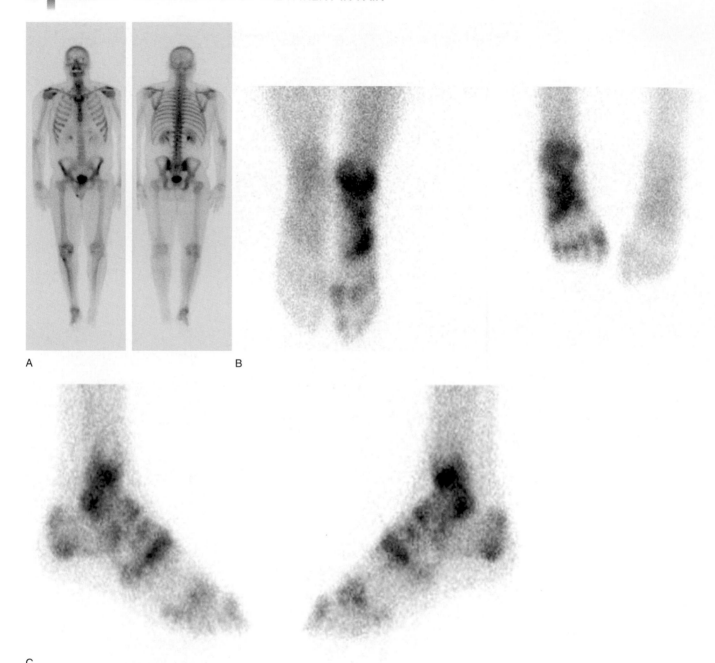

FIGURE 8–2 ■ Reflex sympathetic dystrophy (RSD). Angiographic images show increased blood flow to the right lower extremity. **A,** Whole-body anterior and posterior planar scans show increased tracer uptake in the right lower extremity, particularly the ankle and foot region. **B** and **C,** Static delayed images show diffuse, uniformly increased juxtaarticular uptake throughout the affected region.

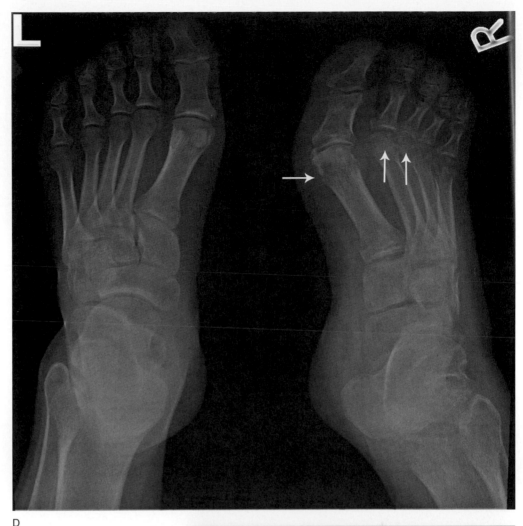

D

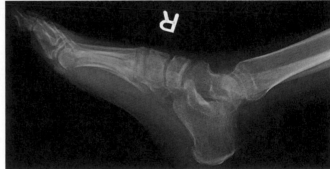

E

FIGURE 8–2—Cont'd Anteroposterior (**D**) and lateral (**E**) projection radiographs show diffuse demineralization of the right foot and ankle in an "aggressive osteoporosis" pattern with subchondral and submetaphyseal resorption *(arrows)*. (Courtesy of Dr. John Walter Millstine, Harvard Medical School, Brigham and Women's Hospital.)

L5 level. If the defect is bilateral, spondylolisthesis may occur. Initial oblique radiographs may be negative, although CT is more sensitive. Bone scintigraphy with the addition of SPECT is necessary for an adequate evaluation. On sagittal SPECT images, lesions that involve the pars interarticularis are seen in the same horizontal plane as the vertebral body.

At scintigraphy, patients with spondylolysis demonstrate increased uptake in the posterior arch (Fig. 8–3). Bone scintigraphy may also help differentiate asymptomatic spondylolysis and ongoing disease, as demonstrated by Collier and coworkers.[15] If spondylolysis is the cause of low back pain, the defect within the pars interarticularis demonstrates increased uptake. In patients with a known radiographic defect, a normal bone scan indicates that the lesion is quiescent and may represent an incidental finding.

■ BONE SCANS AND SPECT IMAGING FOR FACET OSTEOARTHRITIS

Facet joint osteoarthritis is often seen in both symptomatic and asymptomatic individuals. Patients with facetogenic pain

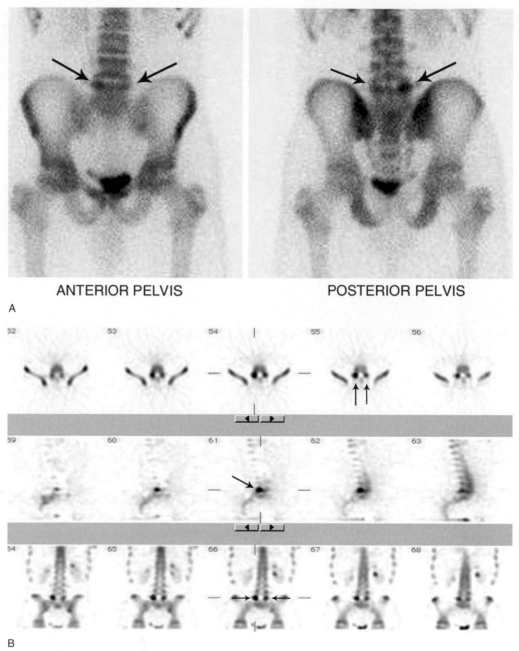

ANTERIOR PELVIS **POSTERIOR PELVIS**

A

B

FIGURE 8–3 ■ Spondylolysis. **A,** Planar images demonstrate increased uptake in the posterior arch. **B,** Transverse *(top row),* sagittal *(middle row),* and coronal *(bottom row)* SPECT images show bilateral foci of increased tracer uptake *(arrows)* localized to the posterior elements.

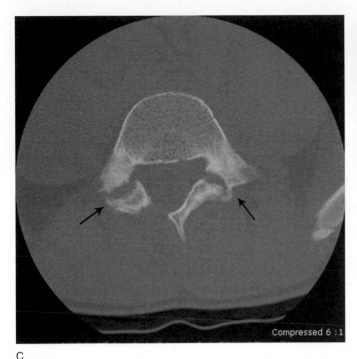

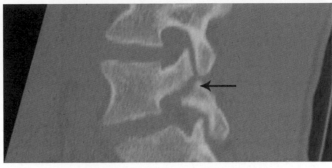

FIGURE 8–3—Cont'd Axial CT scan (**C**) and sagittal re-formation (**D**) reveal pars interarticularis defects *(arrows)*. (Courtesy of Dr. John Walter Millstine, Harvard Medical School, Brigham and Women's Hospital.)

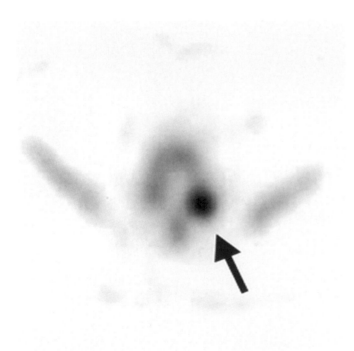

FIGURE 8–4 ■ Facet arthropathy. Transverse bone SPECT shows abnormal left facet joint *(arrow)* and a normal right facet joint at the level L5-S1. (Courtesy of Dr. Spiros G. Pneumaticos, Baylor College of Medicine, St. Luke's Episcopal Hospital.)

are referred as having painful facet syndrome. Facet joint injections are commonly used for alleviation of back pain and also used to help determine whether the facet joint is a source of pain. On sagittal SPECT images, lesions that involve the facet joints are in the same horizontal plane as the disk space.

Holder and associates[16] demonstrated that bone scanning with SPECT was useful in determining which patients are most likely to have a response to facet joint injection. This was confirmed by a recent prospective study by Pneumaticos and colleagues[17] that demonstrated that patients with positive scans (Fig. 8–4) had an excellent response to facet joint injections whereas those with negative scans are less likely to have a beneficial response.

References

1. Love C, Din AS, Tomas MB, et al: Radionuclide bone imaging: An illustrative review. Radiographics 23:341, 2003.
2. McAfee JG, Reba RC, Majd M: The musculoskeletal system. In Wagner HN Jr, Szabo Z, Buchanan JW (eds): Principles of Nuclear Medicine, 2nd ed. Philadelphia, WB Saunders, 1995, pp 986-1012.
3. Brown ML: Bone scintigraphy in benign and malignant tumors [Review]. Radiol Clin North Am 31:731, 1993.
4. Even-Sapir E: Imaging of malignant bone involvement by morphologic, scintigraphic, and hybrid modalities. J Nucl Med 46:1356, 2005.
5. Delpassand ES, Garcia JR, Bhadkamkar V, Podoloff DA: Value of SPECT imaging of the thoracolumbar spine in cancer patients. Clin Nucl Med 20:1047, 1995.
6. Even-Sapir E, Martin RH, Barnes DC, et al: Role of SPECT in differentiating malignant from benign lesions in the lower thoracic and lumbar vertebrae. Radiology 187:193, 1993.
7. Harris WH, Sledge CB: Total hip and total knee replacement. N Engl J Med 323:725, 1990.
8. Oswald SG, Van Nostrand D, Savory CG, et al: The acetabulum: A prospective study of three-phase bone and indium white blood cell scintigraphy following porous-coated hip arthroplasty. J Nucl Med 31:274, 1990.
9. Palestro CJ, Torres MA: Radionuclide imaging in orthopedic infections. Semin Nucl Med 27:334, 1997.
10. Love C, Tomas MB, Marwin SE, et al: Role of nuclear medicine in diagnosis of the infected joint replacement. Radiographics 21:1229, 2001.
11. Schweitzer ME, Mandel S, Schwartzman RJ, et al: Reflex sympathetic dystrophy revisited: MR imaging findings before and after infusion of contrast material. Radiology 195:211, 1995.

12. Holder LE, Mackinnon SE: Reflex sympathetic dystrophy in the hands: Clinical and scintigraphic criteria. Radiology 152:517, 1984.

13. Helms CA, O'Brien ET, Katzberg RW, et al: Segmental reflex sympathetic dystrophy syndrome. Radiology 135:67, 1980.

14. Kozin F, Soin JS, Ryan LM, et al: Bone scintigraphy in the reflex sympathetic dystrophy syndrome. Radiology 138:437, 1981.

15. Collier BD, Johnson RP, Carrera GF, et al: Painful spondylolysis or spondylolisthesis studied by radiography and single photon emission computer tomography. Radiology 154:207, 1985.

16. Holder LE, Machin JL, Asdourian PL, et al: Planar and high resolution SPECT bone imaging in the diagnosis of facet syndrome. J Nucl Med 36:37, 1995.

17. Pneumaticos SG, Chatziioannou SN, Hipp JA, et al: Low back pain: Prediction of short-term outcome of facet joint injection with bone scintigraphy. Radiology 238:693, 2006.

chapter 9

Computed Tomography

Joel A. Nielsen and John A. Carrino

Since introduction of the CT scanner in 1972, the technology has been continually evolving. The main advantages that CT holds over conventional radiography relate to the riddance of superimposed tissues on the images and markedly superior contrast resolution as a result of the elimination of scatter. Although early scanners were slow and had relatively poor spatial resolution, modern multi–detector row helical scanners can now achieve nearly isotropic resolution while scanning large-volume lengths in just a few seconds.

■ HISTORY

John, Paul, George, and Ringo may not have been physicians or scientists, but their contribution to medical imaging was profound all the same, albeit in a roundabout way. The massive revenues *The Beatles* generated for their record label EMI (Electric and Musical Instruments) was a fresh and considerable source of income for the company at the time. Flooded with a surge of cash from this ridiculously successful musical group and in desperate need of a tax shelter, EMI ventured into medical research by allowing one of their engineers free reign in pursing his interest in using a computer to capture x-ray data.[1] Although EMI had no previous experience producing medical imaging equipment (the company was principally concerned with the manufacture of records and electronic equipment), they were soon responsible for a *Revolution* in the field.

Godfrey Newbold Hounsfield, an engineer working for EMI, wondered whether it would be possible "to determine what was in a box by taking readings at all angles through it."[2] He soon realized that this idea had merit and practical biologic implications when one considered that in essence, the human skull was *the* box on which his theory could be tested. Hounsfield went to work on an apparatus that used the principle of acquiring quantitative measurements of the attenuation of tissues as x-rays passed through them. He did this by sending collimated x-rays through one uniformly thin slice of tissue at a time. By rescanning the subject from multiple vantage points, a matrix of intersecting *ray projections* consisting of average attenuation values could be reconstructed by the computer and displayed as a gray-scale image on a monitor.

Sir Godfrey joined forces with James Ambrose, a consulting radiologist, and with support from EMI and the Department of Health and Social Security, they were able to develop a head scanner. In 1972, this prototype EMI scanner was used successfully in the first clinical examination to reveal the presence and location of a cystic tumor in a patient with a suspected brain lesion. For the first time x-rays could be used to see what was inside "the box" without having to look at all the visual data superimposed on a single image. In fairness, Allan McLeod Cormack of Tufts University was credited with independently inventing the same process, for which he and Hounsfield shared a Nobel Prize in medicine in 1979.

■ IMAGING PRINCIPLES

Modern CT still uses this same basic principle of acquiring and reconstructing images by measurement of tissue attenuation in thin, axially oriented cross sections. Attenuation of the tissue that the x-ray beam travels through is measured from multiple angles and is related to the atomic number and density of the material being examined, as well as the energy spectrum of the x-ray beam being emitted (Fig. 9–1). Depending on the matrix size (x- and z-axis) of the scan and the thickness (z-axis) of each axial slice, the area being scanned is partitioned into a number of small boxes. Each small box-like volume of tissue, or *voxel*, is assigned a mean density number that corresponds to a scale ranging from −1024 to +3071, known as the Hounsfield scale. The actual number allotted to any given voxel is calculated from data provided by multiple measured *ray projections* and is reconstructed by the computer. The pixel itself is displayed on the screen according to the mean attenuation of the tissue in its corresponding voxel, with water having an attenuation of 0 Hounsfield units (HU) and air measuring −1000 HU. Fat is usually around −100 HU, bone typically measures +400 HU or greater, and metal implants are more than +1000. The exact CT numbers for a given tissue type varies from manufacturer to manufacturer and with changes in x-ray tube potential—with the exception of water and air.

Because radiologists were accustomed to interpreting images in which black objects were composed of less dense materials (e.g., air and fat) and white objects were more dense (e.g., bone and metal), CT was set up to display its images in similar fashion. CT images are in essence two-dimensional gray-scale representations of the relative density of the tissues imaged in a "stack" consisting of multiple axial slices. Each

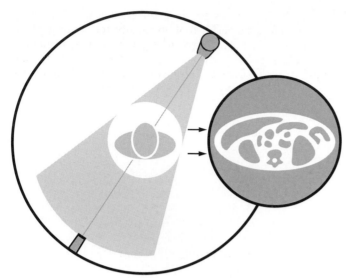

FIGURE 9–1 ■ A CT image is obtained via multiple attenuation measurements and represents a transaxial slice of the anatomy imaged. (From Haaga JR, Lanzieri CF, Gilkeson RC (eds): CT & MR Imaging of the Whole Body, 4th ed. Philadelphia, CV Mosby, 2002, p 3.)

picture element, or *pixel*, shown on the monitor represents a certain density within a pre-chosen *window* of densities—set to maximize the contrast between tissues in the area of interest. CT is able to discern a much broader range of densities than radiography is and is able to do this primarily because of elimination of scatter.

A variety of system designs have been have been used to acquire the x-ray data needed for image reconstruction. These different architectural geometries are commonly known as generations. Advancement in CT technology has come in the form of faster acquisition times, higher spatial resolution, and faster computers able to perform larger and more complex data reconstructions.

First-Generation CT Scanners

The first commercial scanner produced was the EMI Mark I. It used an x-ray beam that was collimated to a narrow beam directed through the patient to a single detector. A single projection was acquired by translating the x-ray tube and the detector in a straight line on opposite sides of the patient. The next projection was obtained by rotating the frame 1 degree and scanning in the opposite direction. This process was repeated until 180 ray projections were obtained. Such scanning was very time consuming and yielded poor spatial resolution (about 3 mm in a 25-cm field of view) and extremely poor z-axis resolution (about 13-mm thickness in each axial section obtained).[3,4]

Second-Generation CT Scanners

Scan times were improved by adding additional detectors. The extra detectors were placed at angles so that multiple projections could be obtained in each translation. Originally, this method tripled imaging speed and thereby allowed a scan to

be performed in 60 translations instead of 180. The number of detectors continued to increase until scanners were fast enough to allow acquisition during a single breath hold. This improvement opened the door for scanning of the chest and abdomen without the images being rendered useless by motion artifact.[4]

Third-Generation CT Scanners

The next advance came in the form of higher-power rotating-anode x-ray tubes. These scanners use a fan-shaped x-ray beam that passes through the patient to an arc-shaped row of detectors behind. During the scan both the x-ray source and the detectors rotate around the patient. Rotation of the x-ray tube allows a more powerful tube to be used and thereby increases the speed of scanning through thicker body parts. In addition, because the x-ray beams were no longer parallel to each other but instead divergent, new reconstruction algorithms had to be developed. This system is known as a rotate-rotate design, and nearly all modern helical scanners are versions of this geometry.[4]

Fourth-Generation CT Scanners

This design differs from third-generation scanners in that just the x-ray tube rotates within a stationary ring of detectors. Though labeled fourth generation, these scanners were developed almost at the same time as third-generation scanners and, with the exception of some special-purpose applications, are not commercially available. Fourth-generation scanners are not able to use anti-scatter collimators and are much more prone to scatter artifact than third-generation scanners are.[4]

Spiral/Helical CT

Before the late 1980s, all CT scanners acquired data in individual axial slices regardless of the generation of scanner. Every time that the x-ray tube revolved around the patient a single axial "slice" of data was obtained. The invention of slip-ring technology allowed the table to be translated through the gantry while the x-ray tube and detectors rotated continuously around the patient to create a volume of data. With new reconstruction algorithms this allowed an image to be reconstructed at any point along the path traced by the tube. This advance in technology ultimately reduced patient doses, minimized motion artifacts, and enhanced multiplanar reconstructions.[5]

Multi–Detector Row CT

What vendors call *latest-generation* CT scanners are offset from the third-generation architecture in their use of spiral CT with the addition of multiple detector row arrays. Multi–detector row CT (MDCT; also known as multislice CT) is a major improvement in helical CT technology wherein simultaneous activation of multiple detector rows positioned along the z -axis allows the acquisition of interweaving helical sections. The principal difference between MDCT and the preceding generations of CT is improved resolution in the longitudinal or z-axis (direction of the table or gantry). More of the x-rays generated by the tube are ultimately used to produce imaging data. With this design, section thickness is determined by detector size and not by the collimator itself. Rapid data acquisition times are possible because of short gantry rotation intervals combined with multiple detectors providing increased coverage along the z-axis.

Currently, configurations with up to 64-channel detectors are available (128- and 256-channel detectors are expected to be available shortly). The data from an MDCT scanner can be used to generate images of different thicknesses from the same acquisition. In MDCT, the user selects a specific beam collimation but does not need to choose a particular section thickness in advance. This parameter can be implemented after the completion of data acquisition (but cannot be changed after the original acquisition data are purged from the scanner hard drive). The minimum section thickness is reduced to approximately 0.5 mm, and images can be reconstructed at this 0.5-mm interval. Isotropic (equal dimension) voxels measuring 0.5 mm in the x, y, and z directions greatly improve spatial resolution and the quality of reconstructing algorithms and thereby allow the generation of exquisite multiplanar reformats and three-dimensional (3D) images.[4]

MDCT's increased speed of imaging allows fast imaging of large volumes of tissue without compromise in image quality. A single-pass, whole-body protocol is now easily achieved with modern scanners, which can image from the vertex of the head to below the hips in less than a minute. In the setting of hardware (joint implants), there is an improved ability to acquire high-quality images. Metal artifacts are due to photopenic defects in the back-projection and are displayed on CT images as streak artifact. With MDCT the holes in the filtered back-projection are not as pronounced, and a less severe streak artifact results. This improvement is at the expense of excess tissue radiation along the penumbra of the beam, which is then picked up by adjacent detector channels filling in these photopenic defects in the projection. This technology has forced radiologists into redefining the image-viewing process to a *volumetric* paradigm rather than a simple tile mode or section-by-section viewing.

To keep up with this paradigm shift, CT protocols had to be reformulated. Along with the recent deployment of MDCT has come a significantly expanded range of CT applications and indications. The challenges that face imagers using MDCT include selecting optimal imaging sequences, controlling patient radiation exposure, and efficiently managing the large amount of data generated. Some disadvantages of MDCT are high radiation doses to the tissue and potentially noisy images. Noise is inversely related to the number of photons per voxel, and because smaller voxels tend to have fewer photons, the result is noisier images. To keep the noise level reasonable, the exposure (and thus the radiation dose) must be increased.

Three-Dimensional Imaging

In tandem with the explosion of MDCT scanners recently placed in clinical practice, powerful new 3D applications have been fielded and have led to an increase in the interpretation

and creation of images in planes other than the traditional axial. Though a powerful tool, especially for surgical planning, it can create confusion among radiologists, technologists, and clinicians when trying to describe a particular method or type of image. Protocols need to be designed to optimize image quality and minimize patient radiation exposure. This requires an understanding of beam collimation and section collimation as they apply to MDCT while keeping in mind the time-limited nature of projection data and the need for thin axial sections to perform 3D reconstructions that will be effective in clinical practice.[6]

Multiplanar images can be thickened into slabs with projectional techniques such as average, maximum, and minimum intensity projection, raysum, and volume rendering. Volume rendering provides versatility and manipulability in the dataset for advanced imaging applications by assigning a range of colors to distinguish different tissue types and by integrating a full spectrum of opacity values within the image (Fig. 9–2). Using the data from axial CT images to reconstruct non-axial, two-dimensional images is known as multiplanar reformation (MPR). MPR images are created by transecting a set or "stack" of axial images that are only 1 voxel thick. Sagittal, oblique, or curved plane images can be generated in this way (Fig. 9–3A-D). This technique is extremely useful in musculoskeletal examinations because fractures lines and joint alignment are not always easily seen in the axial plane.[6]

■ ORTHOPEDIC TRAUMATOLOGY

One of the most recently evident benefits of MDCT imaging occurs in the setting of appendicular and axial trauma. When compared with projectional radiography, CT greatly improves the anatomic depiction of spinal injury. However, when compared with single-detector helical CT scanners, MDCT scanners have increased tube-heating capacity and run at a higher table speed, which allows an increased volume of coverage in the same amount of scanning time. This advantage makes screening examination of a portion of the spine or the entire spine feasible and may eliminate screening radiographs in certain settings. Examinations of the thorax and the lumbar spine can be extracted from a CT examination of the chest, abdomen, and pelvis. However, the routine protocols should be modified to optimize the appropriate protocol for screening both skeletal and visceral injuries. In some institutions this has been referred to as "total-body trauma CT."

For the extremities, dedicated imaging is needed. Based on information from experimental fractures imaged with MDCT, the use of a 4 × 1.25-mm mode at high speed (pitch of 1.5:1) is recommended. For routine interpretation of a cervical spine examination, bone (high spatial frequency) algorithm images are made with 2.5-mm images. In addition, standard-algorithm (soft tissue), 1.25-mm-thick images are obtained and used for MPR but are not viewed as a stack or in tile mode.

MDCT sagittal and coronal reformatted images are of sufficient quality to allow volumetric interpretation and perhaps obviate the need to review every single transverse image unless needed for clarification. However, thin transverse sections are paramount for obtaining optimal reformatted

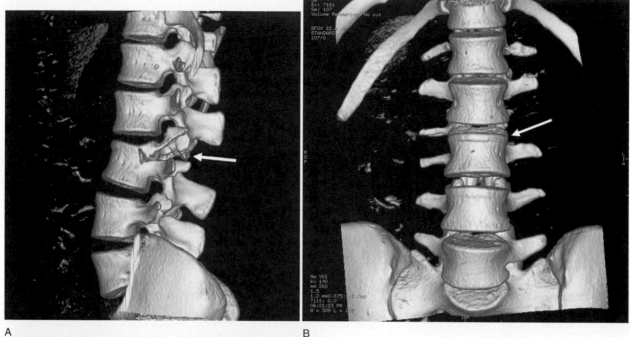

A

B

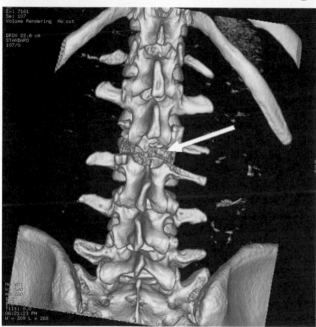

C

FIGURE 9–2 ■ Multi-detector computed tomography (MDCT) three-dimensional volume rendering of the lumbar spine demonstrates the extent of a "Chance" fracture through the posterior elements of L3 (*arrows*). **A**, Sagittal projection. **B**, Coronal projection in which only a buckle in the cortex is seen. **C**, Posterior coronal view. This three-dimensional image can be rotated in space to view the abnormality from any obliquity. (Images courtesy of Eric Chou, MD.)

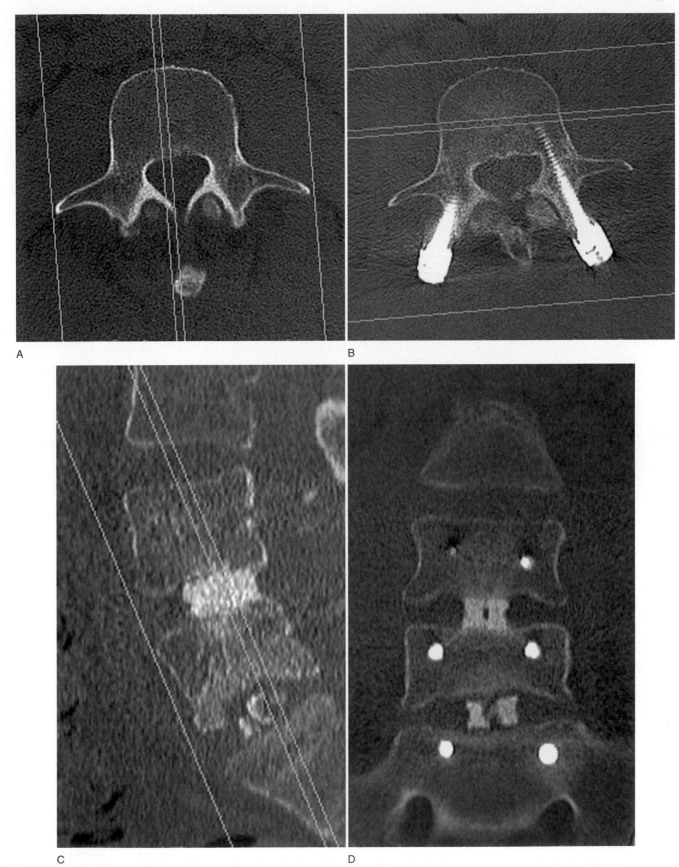

A

B

C

D

FIGURE 9–3 ■ Lumbar interbody fusion: incorporation of the graft at L4-5, with the L4 inferior end plate and the L5 superior end plate having bridging trabecula and the L5-S1 graft showing subsidence and osteolysis surrounding the cephalad portion. **A,** Prescription for a true sagittal position–compensated multiplanar reformat (MPR). **B,** Prescription for a true coronal position–compensated MPR. **C,** Sagittal position–compensated MPR. **D,** Coronal position–compensated MPR.

images. Considering the balance between obtaining optimal reformatted images, patient radiation dose, and resource utilization, the following guiding principles may be useful: use the thinnest transverse images feasible, use overlapping transverse images for the MPR images, and use standard-algorithm (soft tissue) axial images for reformatting. Bone-algorithm images have increased noise and are not useful in terms of a smooth-appearing MPR. As previously stated, this presents a new paradigm (volumetric and 3D viewing) for interpretation related to image processing and viewing software capabilities.

There are several pitfalls to be aware of, but the most important image artifacts are not unique to MDCT. Such artifacts include metal-induced streak artifact and patient motion. Because of the higher spatial resolution, the vascular channels of the vertebral bodies are better appreciated and may be mistaken for abnormal structures. MDCT has some risk, predominantly related to the radiation dose to the individual patient and to the population. The patient's radiation dose increases as the volume of coverage increases and, as always, is most weighed against the potential information needed and the clinical context of ordering the examination.

MDCT allows imaging of very thin sections quickly, much faster than previously possible, thereby allowing for effective screening of spinal injuries and evaluation of extremity injuries. Screening CT of the entire cervical spine is cost-effective if certain high-risk criteria are met, including a focal neurologic deficit referable to the cervical spine, head injury (skull fracture, intracranial hemorrhage) or unconsciousness at the time of examination, and a high-energy mechanism (motor vehicle accident at a speed greater than 35 mph, pedestrian struck by a car, or a fall greater than 10 ft).

■ SPINE IMAGING

CT imaging can detect 0.5% differences in x-ray attenuation with respect to water, the reference standard (the Hounsfield unit of water is calibrated to zero). The physical interaction is based on the linear attenuation coefficient, which is roughly proportional to density (which is why ligamentous structures such as the anulus fibrosis are hyper-attenuating and subcutaneous fat is hypo-attenuating). Therefore, for CT imaging, contrast is best between very dense structures (bone), highly compact soft tissue (tendons, ligaments, anulus fibrosus), water-containing tissue (muscle, thecal sac), low-density tissue (fat), and gas. This is an improvement over projectional radiography, which requires an approximately 10% change in full scale to detect differences in contrast. One mechanism to improve contrast resolution is to administer a "contrast" agent, which can be done through several different routes. The most commonly used routes for spine imaging are intravenous, intrathecal, and intradiskal.

Diskography

Diskography is a provocative examination performed under image guidance that is most useful for establishing a disko-

genic pain origin and confirming whether there is an anular tear or contained protrusion, often as a prelude to intradiskal therapy or fusion. There is anatomic evidence that the disk itself can be a source of pain (nociceptor) because of innervation from the ventral nerve roots, which provide branches anteriorly and posteriorly.[7] The primary purpose for diskography is to document a specific disk as a significant source of pain (nociceptor). In patients who have chronic, predominately axial and non-myelopathic and non-radicular pain, imaging may be insufficient or equivocal for determining the nature, location, and extent of symptomatic pathology.

Specific indications for diskography include persistent pain for which noninvasive imaging and other tests have not provided sufficient diagnostic information. In preoperative patients who are to undergo fusion, diskography can be used to determine whether disks within the proposed fusion segment are symptomatic and whether the adjacent disks are normal. Surgeons concerned with limiting the extent of fusion are interested in obtaining more evidence beyond MRI abnormalities to document what intervertebral disk levels are contributing to the painful syndrome. In postoperative patients who continue to experience significant pain, diskography can be used to assist in differentiating between postoperative scar and recurrent disk herniation (when MRI or CT is equivocal) or to evaluate segments adjacent to the arthrodesis. Post-diskography CT can be used to confirm a contained disk herniation as a prelude to minimally invasive intradiskal therapy. Diskography is also being used as part of the selection criteria for many clinical trials assessing lumbar interbody fusion devices or percutaneous intradiskal treatments.

Interpretation of a diskogram includes a morphologic and functional evaluation. The fundamental tenet of diskography is that injection into the disks and subsequent increased intradiskal pressure will elicit a concordant pain response (one that mimics the patient's typical pain) if that disk is a significant nociceptor. A scale of subjective pain severity from 0 (no pain) to 10 (maximal pain) can be determined during the procedure by asking the patient to relate what the level of pain is during each injection. The patient is also asked whether the pain mimics the typical pain experienced by that patient (i.e., is "concordant") or a component thereof. To evaluate the patient's pain response more "objectively," multiple vertebral levels around the suspected pain generator are injected during the procedure; the patient is not told which level is being injected or when the injection is starting. Before the procedure, patients are instructed regarding the reporting of pain and monitoring for spontaneous pain elicited during the examination. It is important to establish a "reference level," or a relatively pain-free level with injection. For diskography to be considered positive, there should be at least one reference level as defined by the absence of pain or lack of concordant symptoms on injection. An unequivocally positive diskogram consists of a single concordantly symptomatic intervertebral disk with control disks above and below that level (if it is not the lumbosacral junction).[8-10]

A morphologically normal disk demonstrates a central globule of contrast or a "hamburger bun" configuration, and degeneration is indicated by a horizontal, linear distribution of contrast. An anular tear is diagnosed if contrast extends into the periphery of the disk in the expected region of the anulus fibrosis. Transaxial CT imaging is often used as a complementary study to fluoroscopy for "spot" images or post-injection radiographs. CT imaging provides useful additional information to confirm and characterize anular pathology. The typical candidate lesion for intradiskal therapy (e.g., nucleoplasty, electrothermal anuloplasty) is an intervertebral disk level that has a contained anular fissure or a contained protrusion without substantial disk height loss and has generated a concordant pain response at the time of contrast injection (i.e., a "positive" diskogram). Anular injections can be readily differentiated from nuclear injections.

There is a method of classification of anular tears (Dallas Discogram Description) with CT imaging[11] that has undergone some modification. Grading ranges from 0 to 5, as follows: 0, contrast entirely within the nucleus pulposus; 1, contrast within the inner third of the anulus fibrosus; 2, contrast in the middle third of the anulus fibrosus; 3, contrast in the outer third of the anulus fibrosus; 4, radial dissection, which means that there are also some concentric components; and 5, full-thickness tear with contrast extravasation through the outer anulus fibrosus. Although this system of grading is a useful morphologic construct, it can be difficult to apply consistently and there are few data regarding prognostic information (Fig. 9–4A-E).

Demand for diskography is increasing[12] as a diagnostic tool to determine levels of pain generation in patients who are being considered for surgical management (e.g., interbody arthrodesis) or other type of procedure. Although the diagnostic utility of diskography is quite evident, its treatment utility based on patient outcome is paramount. Therefore, the value-added feature that diskography should provide is to identify patients amenable to available therapies and to not contribute to the management dilemma. Meanwhile, less invasive forms of intradiskal therapy are also evolving and may make diskography more relevant. Therefore, a "spine specialist" who is considering instituting disk-specific therapy most often requests diskography. This is not considered a diagnostic test used in the primary care provider setting. However, for patient-driven or other reasons it may be necessary to establish the disk as a "nociceptor" despite no change in therapeutic management.

CT Myelography

CT myelography is also predominantly used as a preoperative test to provide a "road map" to surgical planning. MRI can underestimate root compression caused by degenerative changes in the lateral recess, whereas conventional CT and CT myelography are more accurate when using surgery as the reference standard to confirm degenerative root impingement in the lateral recess as the cause of radiculopathy.[13] CT myelography continues to be requested extensively. MRI is limited not only in specificity but also in some instances in accurately depicting the pathoanatomic state. CT myelography is as accurate as MRI and can be more specific because of the ability to distinguish bone osteophytes from soft tissue. An advantage of MRI is excellent visualization of regions proximal and distal to severe

stenosis or a block. It often avoids the need for contrast, although contrast improves conspicuity. The main reasons cited for using CT myelography in conjunction with or in lieu of MRI are improved visualization of the extent of disk herniation, demonstration of focal neural compression by small herniations, and clarification of abnormalities of the facets, including synovial cysts. However, there is still an opportunity for refinement of the indications for CT myelography, given the wide range in variability of utilization (Fig. 9–5A-E).

■ CT DIAGNOSTIC STRENGTHS

Because MDCT uses x-rays to generate images, it maintains the strengths of projectional radiography with regard to exquisite bone and joint imaging and at the same time is able to supersede radiography with its improved contrast and 3D imaging. As such, MDCT can be useful in the evaluation of pain sources that might have previously been evaluated with radiographs alone, such as avascular necrosis (Fig. 9–6A and B). CT can be useful in evaluation of the appendicular skeleton for fractures, subluxations, and sclerotic and cystic bone lesions, as well as for both presurgical and postsurgical evaluation of hardware implantation. CT can be used to assess bone mineral density, which has been shown to relate to bone strength in the evaluation of osteoporosis. CT excels in evaluation of the spine for fractures, spondylolisthesis, degenerative changes, and disk disease. It can also be useful in conjunction with arthrography in the evaluation of cartilage defects, such as those commonly seen in the knee. In all cases one must weigh the increased patient exposure to radiation against the potential benefit of an accurate diagnosis.

Currently, the availability of many imaging options for evaluation of the spine has contributed to the quandary of how to best use them. Radiography is typically the first-line imaging modality of the lumbar spine and is often used as a "screening" test, in part because it is readily available, has a rapid acquisition time, and provides a reasonable global assessment. CT is used predominantly for trauma when MRI is not available or contraindicated or for a specific problem-solving application related to osseous integrity. MRI has become the mainstay for advanced imaging of the spine and offers features complementary to radiography, so most patients with chronic symptoms will undergo these two imaging modalities.

MRI and CT are more sensitive than radiography for the detection of early spinal infections, cancer, herniated disks, and spinal stenosis. The role of imaging in other situations is limited because of the poor association between low back pain symptoms and anatomic findings.[14] In isolation, an imaging finding of disk degeneration may represent part of the aging process and, in the absence of extrusion, is of only modest value in diagnosis or treatment decisions. The most common indication for the use of advanced cross-sectional imaging procedures such as MRI or CT is the clinical context of low back pain complicated by radiating pain (radiculopathy, sciatica) or cauda equina syndrome (bilateral leg weakness, urinary retention, saddle anesthesia), which is usually due to a herniated disk or canal stenosis (or both). Some believe that the use of advanced

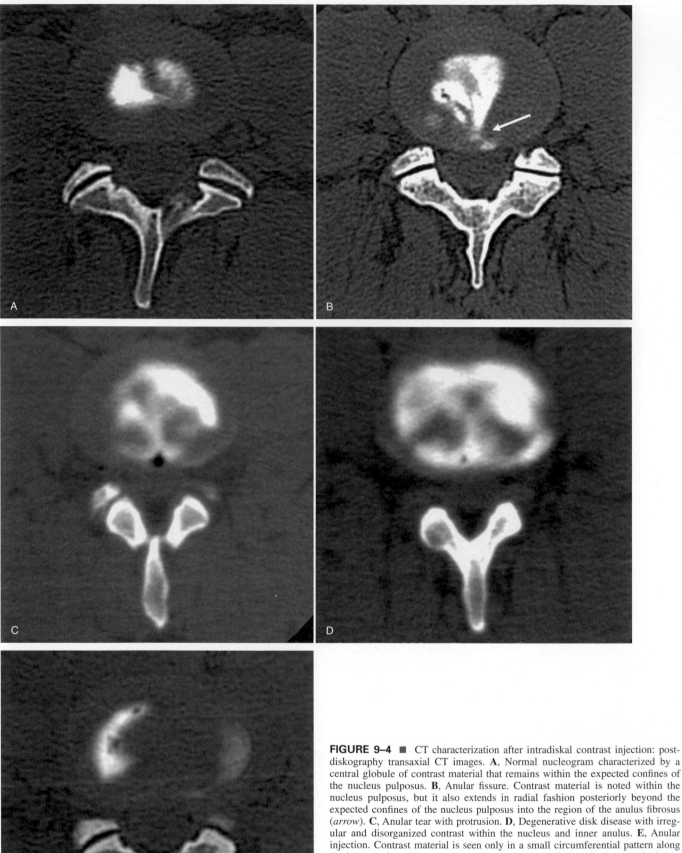

FIGURE 9–4 ■ CT characterization after intradiskal contrast injection: post-diskography transaxial CT images. **A**, Normal nucleogram characterized by a central globule of contrast material that remains within the expected confines of the nucleus pulposus. **B**, Anular fissure. Contrast material is noted within the nucleus pulposus, but it also extends in radial fashion posteriorly beyond the expected confines of the nucleus pulposus into the region of the anulus fibrosus (*arrow*). **C**, Anular tear with protrusion. **D**, Degenerative disk disease with irregular and disorganized contrast within the nucleus and inner anulus. **E**, Anular injection. Contrast material is seen only in a small circumferential pattern along the inner anulus without any central contrast accumulation. Such an anular injection could cause a false-positive pain response at provocation diskography.

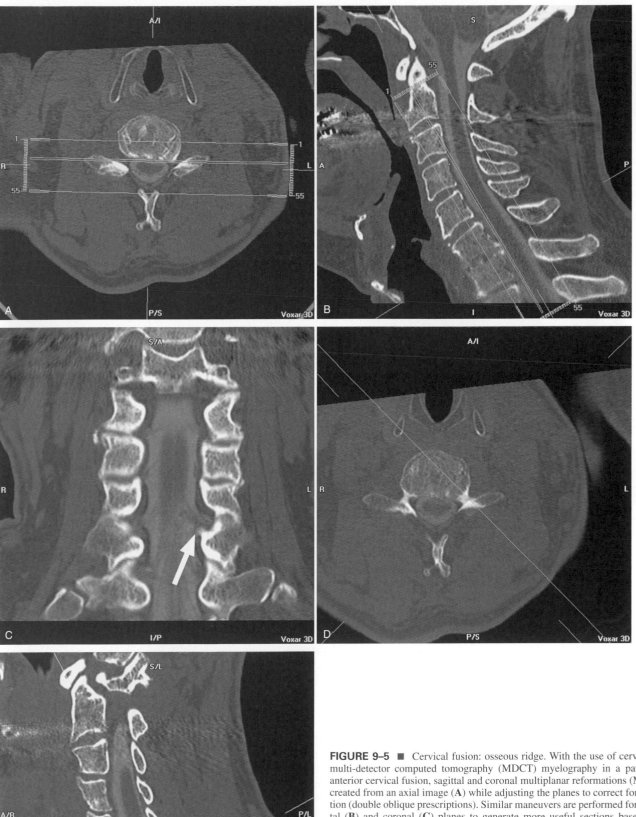

FIGURE 9–5 ■ Cervical fusion: osseous ridge. With the use of cervical spine multi-detector computed tomography (MDCT) myelography in a patient after anterior cervical fusion, sagittal and coronal multiplanar reformations (MPRs) are created from an axial image (**A**) while adjusting the planes to correct for any rotation (double oblique prescriptions). Similar maneuvers are performed for the sagittal (**B**) and coronal (**C**) planes to generate more useful sections based on true anatomic landmarks. Oblique axial images (**D**) are also used to generate sagittal oblique images (**E**) through the neural foramen at each level on each side to compensate for changes in orientation of the neural canal. Coronal and sagittal oblique MPRs show an osseous ridge compressing the nerve roots (*arrow* in **C** and **E**).

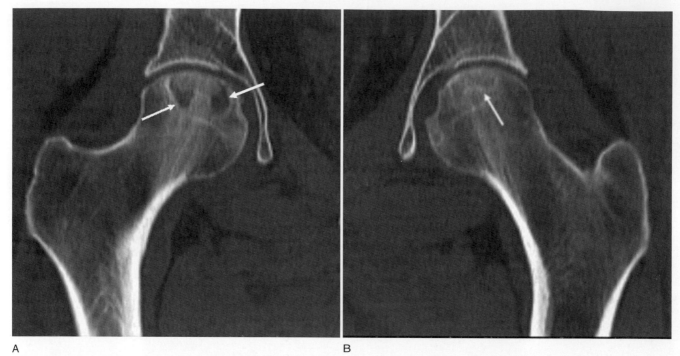

A   B

FIGURE 9–6 ■ Osteonecrosis: CT manifestations. **A,** Subchondral geographic region of demineralization with a sclerotic serpentine-shaped border (*arrows*). **B,** Cystic lesions in the subchondral bone of the femoral head.

imaging should be reserved for potential candidates for surgery.

Spinal stenosis has characteristic symptomatology, but accurate localization of the affected level requires radiologic investigation. It has been shown that degenerative structural narrowing can compress the cauda equina even in the absence of a herniated intervertebral disk. Hypertrophic articular processes, marginal vertebral body osteophytes, spondylolisthesis, and subluxation of the zygapophyseal joints with concomitant soft tissue changes can all contribute to impingement. Evaluation of these bony degenerative changes is the forte of CT.

Although MRI generally remains the first-line choice in an advanced imaging work-up of low back pain, CT is a capable investigational tool. CT has been asserted to be able to provide reliable diagnosis of intervertebral disk herniation (Figs. 9–7 and 9–8). Exacerbation of spinal stenosis from degenerative bone changes can occur in the form of hypertrophic facet capsules, thickening of the ligamentum flavum, or superimposed degenerative disk disease. Neural compression from a bulge in the anulus fibrosus is also more likely in the presence of spinal stenosis produced by bony changes. CT can be an excellent adjunct to other radiologic modalities for evaluating degenerative lumbar spinal stenosis because it directly images both bone and soft tissue. MPR provides precise 3D analysis of pathology.[15]

In spondylitic spondylolisthesis, a defect in the pars interarticularis is present (Fig. 9–9) that allows the vertebral body to slip forward while the posterior elements remain in anatomic position. This can, but rarely does, result in spinal stenosis. In spondylolisthesis caused by degenerative changes in the facet joints, the pars interarticularis remains intact. In these cases spinal stenosis commonly occurs. Degenerative spondylolisthesis can be reliably characterized by CT and distinguished from spondylolytic forms of spondylolisthesis.[15]

CT is better than MRI in demonstrating cortical bone destruction and more sensitive in identifying calcified tumor matrix to help characterize and diagnose both benign and malignant bone lesions.[16] As an example, CT is commonly considered to be the most important imaging modality for the diagnosis and localization of osteoid osteoma. Specifically, CT is more accurate than MRI in the detection of an osteoid osteoma nidus. MRI is better at showing intramedullary and soft tissue changes. However, in some cases this increased sensitivity for detection of edema can produce a misleading aggressive appearance on MRI.[17]

■ SUMMARY

The addition of CT to the clinician's diagnostic armamentarium has been an evolutionary as well as a revolutionary advance in imaging technology. CT shares many of the strengths of conventional radiography with the added advantages of elimination of superimposed tissues on the images and markedly superior contrast resolution. The ability to display both bone and soft tissue in the transaxial plane with MPR techniques allows accurate 3D examination of the spine. CT is particularly valuable in investigating bony abnormalities, including trauma, osteophytosis and other bony degenerative changes, cortically destructive lesions, spinal stenosis (with or without intrathecal contrast), and anular tears (with the introduction of intradiskal contrast).

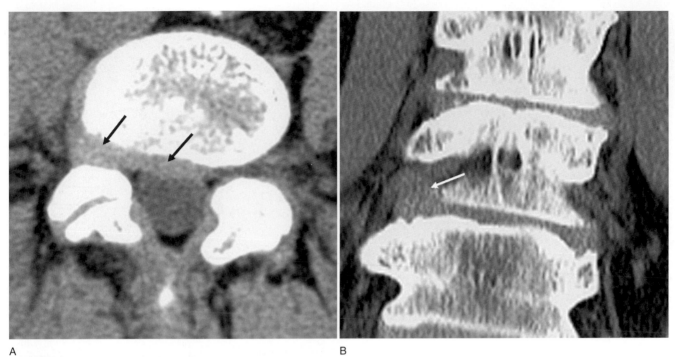

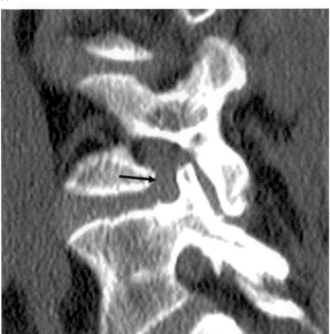

FIGURE 9–7 ■ Disk herniation. An acute disk herniation (*arrows*) is demonstrated on axial (**A**), coronal (**B**), and sagittal (**C**) multiplanar reconstructions.

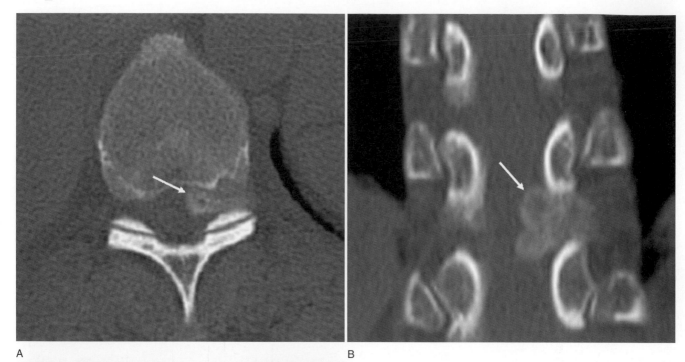

A

B

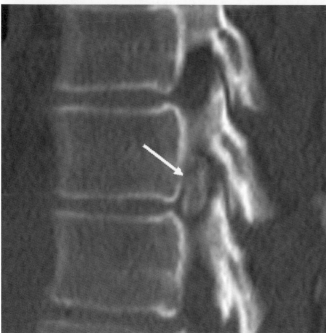

C

FIGURE 9–8 ■ Disk herniation. Chronic disk herniation denoted by a calcified disk (*arrows*) is easily identified on axial (**A**), coronal (**B**), and sagittal (**C**) multiplanar reconstructions.

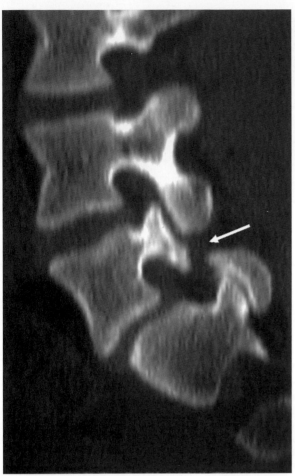

FIGURE 9–9 ■ Pars defect. A sagittal oblique multiplanar reconstruction demonstrates a pars interarticularis defect at L4 (*arrow*) with a few millimeters of spondylolisthesis of L4 on L5 (grade 1).

References

1. Isherwood CBE: In memoriam. Radiology 234:975, 2005.
2. Rodgers LF: My word, what is that?: Hounsfield and the triumph of clinical research. AJR Am J Roentgenol 180:1501, 2003.
3. Hounsfield GN: Computerized transverse axial scanning (tomography) 1. Description of a system. Br J Radiol 46:1016, 1973.
4. Mahesh M: Search for isotropic resolution in CT from conventional through multiple-row detector. Radiographics 22:949, 2002.
5. Miraldi F, Sims MS, Wiesen EJ: Imaging principles in computed tomography. In CT and MR Imaging of the Whole Body, vol 1, 4th ed. St Louis, CV Mosby, 2002, p 2.
6. Dalrymple NC, Prasad SR, Freckleton, MW, et al: Introduction to the language of three-dimensional imaging with multidetector CT. Radiographics 25:1409, 2005.
7. Bogduk N: Clinical Anatomy of the Lumbar Spine and Sacrum. New York, Churchill Livingstone, 1997.
8. Carrino JA, Morrison WB: Discography: Current concepts and techniques. Appl Radiol 31:32, 2002.
9. Aprill CN: Diagnostic disc injection. In Frymoyer JW (ed): The Adult Spine: Principles and Practice. New York, Raven Press, 1991, p 403.
10. Tehranzadeh J: Discography 2000. Radiol Clin North Am 36:463, 1998.
11. Sachs BL, Vanharanta H, Spivey MA, et al: Dallas discogram description. A new classification of CT/discography in low-back disorders. Spine 12:287, 1987.
12. Carrino JA, Morrison WB, Parker L et al: Spinal injection procedures: Utilization, provider distribution and reimbursement in the United States Medicare population from 1993 to 1999. Radiology 225:723, 2002.
13. Bartynski WS, Lin L: Lumbar root compression in the lateral recess: MR imaging, conventional myelography, and CT myelography comparison with surgical confirmation. AJNR Am J Neuroradiol 24:348, 2003.
14. Deyo RA, Weinstein JN: Low back pain. N Engl J Med 344:363, 2001.
15. McAfee PC, Ullrich CG, Levinsohn EM, et al: Computed tomography in degenerative lumbar spinal stenosis: The value of multiplanar reconstruction. Radiographics 2(4), 1982.
16. Assoun J, Richardi G, Railhac J-J: Osteoid osteoma: MR imaging versus CT. Radiology 191:217, 1994.
17. Beltran J, Noto AM, Chakeres DW, et al: Staging with MR imaging versus CT tumors of the osseous spine. Radiology 162:565, 1987.

chapter 10

Magnetic Resonance Imaging

Eric T. Chou and John A. Carrino

■ DESCRIPTION OF MODALITY

Magnetic resonance imaging (MRI) is based on the principles of nuclear magnetic resonance (NMR), a spectroscopic technique used to obtain microscopic chemical and physical information about molecules. MRI is based on the absorption and emission of energy in the radiofrequency (RF) range of the electromagnetic spectrum. It produces images based on spatial variations in the phase and frequency of the RF energy being absorbed and emitted by the imaged object. A number of biologically relevant elements, such as hydrogen, oxygen-16, oxygen-17, fluorine-19, sodium-23, and phosphorus-31 are potential candidates for producing MR images. The human body is primarily fat and water, both of which have many hydrogen atoms, making the human body approximately 63% hydrogen atoms. Hydrogen nuclei have an NMR signal, so for these reasons clinical MRI primarily images the NMR signal from the hydrogen nuclei given its abundance in the human body. Protons behave like small bar magnets, with north and south poles within the magnetic field. The magnetic moment of a single proton is extremely small and not detectable. Without an external magnetic field, a group of protons assumes a random orientation of magnetic moments. Under the influence of an applied external magnetic field, the protons assume a non-random alignment, resulting in a measurable magnetic moment in the direction of the external magnetic field. By applying RF pulses, images can then be created based on the differences in signal from hydrogen atoms in different types of tissue. A variety of systems are used in medical imaging ranging from open MRI units with magnetic field strength of 0.3 Tesla (T) to extremity MRI systems with field strengths up to 1.0 T and whole-body scanners with field strengths up to 3.0 T (in clinical use). Because of its superior soft tissue contrast resolution, MRI is best suited for evaluation of internal derangement of joints, central nervous system abnormalities, as well as other pathologic processes in the patient with pain.

The advantages of MRI over other imaging modalities include absence of ionizing radiation, superior soft tissue contrast resolution, high-resolution imaging, and multiplanar imaging capabilities. The time to acquire an MRI image has been a major weakness and continues to be so with the advent of faster CT scanners (with multislice CT). However, newer imaging techniques (e.g., parallel imaging), faster pulse sequences, and higher field strength systems are addressing this issue.

A number of pulse sequences have been invented to highlight differences in signal of various soft tissues. The most common and most basic of pulse sequences include T1-weighted and T2-weighted sequences. T1-weighted sequences have traditionally been considered good for evaluation of anatomic structures. Tissues that show a high signal (bright) and T1-weighted images include fat, blood (methemoglobin), proteinaceous fluid, some forms of calcium, melanin, and gadolinium (a contrast agent). T2-weighted sequences have generally been considered fluid-conspicuity pulse sequences, useful for identifying pathologic processes. Tissues that show a high signal on T2-weighted images include fluid-containing structures (i.e., cysts, joint fluid, cerebrospinal fluid) and pathologic states causing increased extracellular fluid (i.e., sources of infection or inflammation).

Advanced imaging techniques used in medical imaging include magnetic resonance angiography (MRA), diffusion weighted imaging, chemical shift imaging (fat suppression), functional imaging of the brain, and MR spectroscopy (MRS). Many of these techniques are especially useful in brain imaging. MRA (either time-of-flight or phase contrast) and diffusion weighted imaging are useful for the detection and characterization of ischemic insults in the brain. MRS uses the differences in chemical composition in tissues to differentiate necrosis or normal brain matter from tumor.

In musculoskeletal imaging, MR arthrography is a technique available to augment the depiction of internal derangements of joints.[1] Arthrography can be either indirect (intravenous gadolinium is administered and allowed to diffuse into the joint) or direct (a dilute gadolinium solution is percutaneously injected into the joint) to provide distention of a joint, assisting in the evaluation of ligaments, cartilage, synovial proliferation, or intraarticular bodies. MR arthrography has been most extensively used in the shoulder to outline labral-ligamentous abnormalities as well as to distinguish partial-thickness from full-thickness tears in the rotator cuff. It is also helpful in demonstrating labral tears in the hip, partial- and full-thickness tears of the collateral ligament of the elbow, and bands in the elbow. This technique is also useful in patients after meniscectomy in the knee to detect recurrent or residual meniscal tears, evaluate perforations of the ligaments and triangular fibrocartilage in the wrist, and assess the stability of osteochondral lesions in the articular surface of joints. T1-weighted images are often employed with MR arthrography to bring out the T1 shortening effects of gadolinium. Fat saturation is also added to help differentiate fat from gadolinium. A T2-weighted sequence in at least one plane is also necessary to detect cysts and edema in other soft tissues and bone marrow.

Patients in whom MRI is contraindicated include those who have the following: cardiac pacemaker, implanted cardiac defibrillator, aneurysm clips, carotid artery vascular clamp, neurostimulator, insulin or infusion pump, implanted drug infusion device, bond growth/fusion stimulator, and a cochlear or ear implant. In addition, patients who have a history of metalworking should have a pre-MRI screening radiograph of the orbits to evaluate for radiopaque foreign bodies near the ocular globe.

■ APPLICATIONS

In imaging of pain in the neurologic system, MRI is useful in cases of trauma, evaluation of the posterior fossa, and evaluation of a nonacute headache. MRI is more sensitive than CT in identifying pathologic intracranial changes. In the setting of acute trauma, CT is the modality of choice for the identification of intracranial hemorrhage. However, in the specific setting of suspected diffuse axonal injury (DAI), MRI is the preferred examination (particularly with gradient-echo sequences). Other considerations come into play, including general availability and practicality of CT versus MRI. Of patients proven eventually to have DAI, 50% to 80% demonstrate a normal CT scan on presentation. Delayed CT may be helpful in demonstrating edema or atrophy, but these are later findings. Characteristic CT findings in the acute setting are small petechial hemorrhages that are located at the gray matter/white matter junction, within the corpus callosum, and in the brain stem. The degree of confidence in CT is moderate, because the only finding may be petechial hemorrhage, and fewer than 20% of patients with DAI demonstrate this finding on CT alone. Gradient-echo sequences are particularly useful in demonstrating the paramagnetic effects of petechial hemorrhages. Gradient-echo imaging often can demonstrate signal abnormality in areas that appear normal in T1- and T2-weighted spin-echo sequences. For this reason it has become a mainstay of MRI of patients with suspected shearing-type injuries. The abnormal signal on gradient-echo images can persist for many years after the injury. The most common MRI finding is multifocal areas of abnormal signal (bright on T2-weighted images) at the white matter in the temporal or parietal corticomedullary junction or in the splenium of the corpus callosum. The degree of confidence is high, because abnormal signal in the characteristic locations in the clinical setting of recent trauma leaves little doubt about the diagnosis of DAI.

Other MRI applications in neuroimaging include the evaluation of the posterior fossa, venous sinus thrombosis, vasculitis, and further soft tissue characterization after CT has been performed. For nonacute headache and migraines, the U.S. Headache Consortium has developed evidence-based guidelines for the use of neuroimaging in patients with non-acute headache (i.e., headache occurring at least 4 weeks during a patient's lifetime).[2] Based on the studies reviewed, MRI appears to be more sensitive in finding white matter lesions and developmental venous anomalies than CT. The greater contrast resolution and discrimination of MRI, however, appears to be of little clinical importance in the evaluation of patients with nonacute headache. Therefore, the recommendation was that data were insufficient to make evidence-based recommendations regarding the relative sensitivity of MRI compared with CT in the evaluation of migraine or other nonacute headache.

Spine imaging using MRI can exquisitely provide information regarding various pathologic entities including degenerative disk disease, zygapophyseal (facet) joint disease, infection, neoplasm, and fracture (Fig. 10–1). With respect to degenerative disk disease, MRI often does not define a specific painful clinical syndrome because of the overlap of multiple nociceptors and their nonspecific appearance in painful versus painless degenerative conditions. Many findings may represent senescent changes that are the sequelae of stress applied during the course of a lifetime. Therefore, utilization of MRI within a defined clinical context is paramount.

To improve communication and consistency between providers, there is a standard nomenclature[3] for lumbar spine disk disease endorsed by the North American Spine Society (NASS), the American Society of Spine Radiologists (ASSR), and the American Society of Neuroradiologists. It is important to recognize that the definitions of diagnoses should not define or imply external etiologic events such as trauma, should not imply relationship to symptoms, and should not define or imply need for specific treatment.

Degenerative disk disease (DDD) is a term applied specifically to intervertebral disk degeneration. The term *spondylosis* is often used in general as synonymous with *degeneration* including both nucleus pulposus and anulus fibrosus processes, but such usage is confusing, so it is best that *degeneration* be the general term. *Degeneration* can be subclassified into spondylosis deformans, which is characterized by marginal osteophytosis without substantial disk height loss, reflecting predominantly anulus fibrosus disease. *Intervertebral osteochondrosis* is the term applied to the condition of mainly nucleus pulposus and vertebral body end plate disease including anular tearing (fissuring). *Osteoarthritis* is a process of synovial joints. In the spine this term is appropriately applied to the zygapophyseal (facet, Z-joint), atlantoaxial, costovertebral, and sacroiliac joints.

Herniation is defined as a localized displacement of disk material beyond the limits of the intervertebral disk space. Disk material may be nucleus, cartilage, fragmented apophyseal bone, anular tissue, or any combination thereof. Normally, the posterior disk margin tends to be concave in the upper lumbar spine and is straight or slightly convex at L4-5 and L5-S1. The normal margin is defined by the vertebral body ring apophysis exclusive of osteophytes. Hernations are either "localized" or generalized," the latter being defined as greater than 50% (180 degrees) of the periphery of the disk.

Localized displacement in the axial (horizontal) plane can be "focal," signifying less than 25% (90 degrees) of the disk circumference, or "broad-based," meaning between 25% and 50% (90 to 180 degrees) of the disk circumference. Presence of disk tissue "circumferentially" meaning 50% to 100% (180 to 360 degrees) beyond the edges of the ring apophyses may be called "bulging" and is not considered a form of herniation.

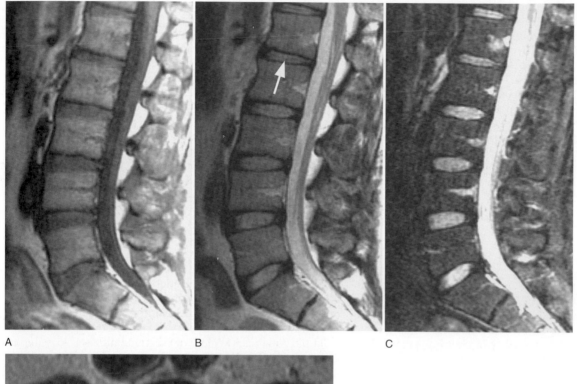

A   B   C

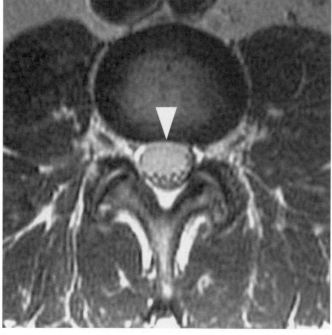

D

FIGURE 10–1 ■ Lumbar spine. Normal MRI appearance of the lumbar intervertebral disk: Sagittal T1-weighted (**A**), sagittal T2-weighted without fat suppression (**B**), sagittal T2-weighted with fat suppression (**C**), axial T2-weighted through the intervertebral disk level (**D**). Note that on T1-weighted images the disk is hypointense to the lumbar vertebral body whereas on T2-weighted images it is hyperintense, reflecting normal water content of the nucleus pulposus. Small intervertebral clefts may be present (*white arrow,* **B**). On axial imaging, the posterior margin should have a concavity (*arrowhead,* **D**), with the exception of the lumbosacral junction, which may normally have a slight convexity. The disk margins should project no more than 1 or 2 mm beyond the vertebral end plate. Note that the marrow is slightly hyperintense on the non–fat-suppressed images and dark on the fat-suppressed pulse sequences.

Beyond having descriptors of the circumferential extent of the herniation, herniated disks may take the form of protrusion, extrusion, or sequestration (free fragment) based on the shape of the displaced disk material. Protrusion is present if the greatest distance, in any plane, between the edges of the disk material beyond the disk space is less than the distance between the edges of the base in the same plane. In other words, the base against the parent disk margin is broader than any other diameter of the herniation. In the craniocaudal direction, the length of the base cannot exceed, by definition, the height of the intervertebral space. Protrusions may be broad-based or focal. Extrusion is present when, in at least one plane, any one distance between the edges of the disk material beyond the disk space is greater than the distance between the edges of the base. In other words, the base against the parent disk margin tends to be narrower than any other diameter of the herniation. Extrusion may be further specified as a "sequestration" if the displaced disk material has lost completely any continuity with the parent disk (Fig. 10–2). The term *migration* may be used to signify displacement of disk material away from the site of extrusion, regardless of whether sequestration is present. Herniated disks in the

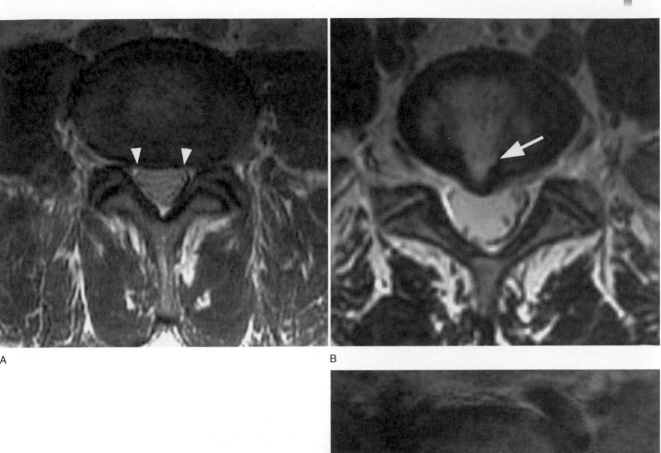

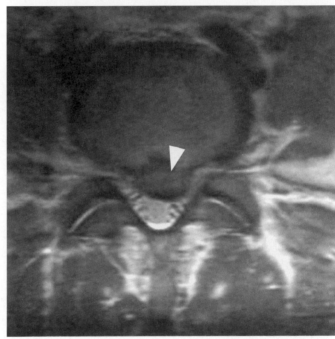

FIGURE 10–2 ■ Lumbar disk contour abnormalities: All are axial T2-weighted images at the level of the intervertebral disk. **A,** Anular bulge. There is generalized displacement of greater than 180 degrees of the disk margin beyond the normal margin of the intervertebral disk space that is the result of disk degeneration with an intact anulus *(arrowheads).* **B,** Disk protrusion. The base against the parent disk margin is broader than any other diameter of the herniation. Extension of nucleus pulposus through a partial defect in the anulus is identified *(arrow)* but the herniated disk is contained by some intact anular fibers (may or may not be distinguished at MRI). **C,** Disk extrusion: The base against the parent disk margin is narrower than any other diameter of the herniation *(arrowhead).* There may be extension of the nucleus pulposus through a complete focal defect in the anulus. Substantial mass effect is present, causing moderate central canal stenosis.

craniocaudal (vertical) direction through a break in the vertebral body end plate are referred to as intravertebral herniations (Schmorl's nodes). They often have a round or lobulated appearance and are often incidental and likely to be developmental or posttraumatic rather than purely degenerative.

Anular tear (fissure), characterized by a focal area of increased signal intensity on T2-weighted images (high intensity zone [HIZ]), implies a loss of integrity of the anulus fibrosis, such as radial, transverse, and concentric separations (Fig. 10–3). They do not imply that a significant traumatic event has occurred or that the etiology is known. Some tears may

have clinical relevance, and others may be asymptomatic and inconsequential components of the aging process. At diskography there is about an 85% concordance of imaging findings with the presence of anular tear. Correlation of the tear with responses to diskography and other clinically relevant observations may enable the clinician to make such distinctions. Another source of diskogenic pain is related to the adjacent vertebral end plate changes. Modic and associates proposed a classification of vertebral body end plate marrow changes by MRI. Modic type 1 changes appear as low signal intensity on T1-weighted images and high signal intensity on T2-weighted

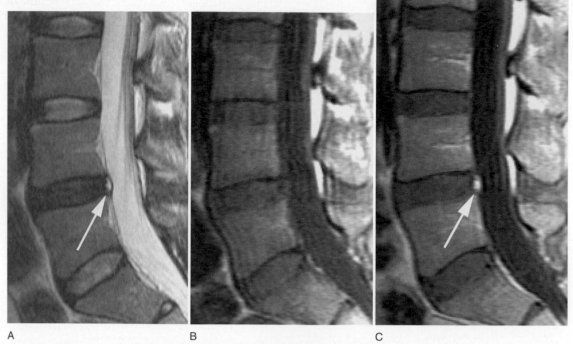

A   B   C

FIGURE 10–3 ▪ Hyperintense zone (HIZ). **A,** Sagittal T2-weighted image shows a small focus of hyperintensity *(arrow)* within the posterior anulus fibrosus that is inconspicuous on the sagittal T1-weighted image without contrast medium enhancement **(B)**. **C,** Intravenous contrast medium–enhanced sagittal T1-weighted image shows enhancement within the posterior anulus fibrosus *(arrow)* corresponding to the HIZ identified on the T2-weighted image. This phenomenon of enhancement is thought to reflect the ingrowth of fibrovascular tissue to the area.

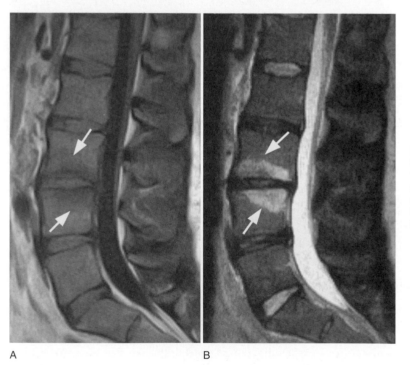

A   B

FIGURE 10–4 ▪ Vertebral marrow signal alteration (Modic type 1 change). Sagittal T1-weighted **(A)** and sagittal T2-weighted **(B)** MR images show disk height loss and desiccation at multiple levels. At the L3-4 level this is associated with rounded areas of signal alteration that abut the end plate and follow fluid-like signal with T1 hypointensity and T2 hypointensity *(arrows)*.

images (Fig. 10–4). Type 2 changes appear high signal on both T1- and T2-weighted images whereas type 3 changes appear of low signal intensity on both T1- and T2-weighted images. The type 1 changes appear edema like and may sometimes be mistaken for reactive edema from an adjacent diskitis. Type 2 changes appear similar in signal to fat and represent a reparative phase. Type 3 changes are analogous to diskogenic sclerosis seen on radiographs. Moderate and severe end plate type I and type II abnormalities on MR images may indicate painful disk derangement in patients with low back pain.[4]

A grading system for the assessment of lumbar disk degeneration using MRI was described by Pfirrmann and colleagues[5]:

Grade I: The structure of the disk is homogeneous, with a bright hyperintense white signal intensity and a normal disk height.

Grade II: The structure of the disk is inhomogeneous, with a hyperintense white signal. The distinction between nucleus and anulus is clear, and the disk height is normal, with or without horizontal gray bands.

Grade III: The structure of the disk is inhomogeneous, with an intermediate gray signal intensity. The distinction between nucleus and anulus is unclear, and the disk height is normal or slightly decreased.

Grade IV: The structure of the disk is inhomogeneous, with a hypointense dark gray signal intensity. The distinction between nucleus and anulus is lost, and the disk height is normal or moderately decreased.

Grade V: The structure of the disk is inhomogeneous, with a hypointense black signal intensity. The distinction between nucleus and anulus is lost, and the disk space is collapsed.

The following scheme is used to define the degree of canal compromise (stenosis) produced by disk displacement based on the goals of being practical, objective, reasonably precise, and clinically relevant. Canal compromise of less than one third of the canal at a given axial section is "mild," between one and two thirds is "moderate," and over two thirds is "severe" (Fig. 10–5). This same scheme may be applied to foraminal narrowing, with the sagittal images playing a primary role in determining the degree of narrowing.

■ BONE MARROW AND BONE MARROW EDEMA–LIKE (BME) LESIONS

Normal bone marrow has three constituents: osseous, myeloid elements, and adipose cells. Hematopoietic (red) marrow has approximately 40% fat content and fatty (yellow) marrow has 80% fat content. The appendicular skeleton tends to have more fatty marrow than hematopoietic marrow. However, normal variations in marrow distribution are important to recognize and not to confuse as pathologic processes. Small differences in the amount and distribution of red marrow from side to side are normal, but marked asymmetry is suggestive of a disease process. An important exception to early and complete red to yellow marrow conversion is seen in the proximal humeral and femoral epiphyses and may be seen throughout life. This epiphyseal red marrow is curvilinear and located in the subchondral regions of these bones. Heterogeneous marrow signal, where small focal islands of red marrow in predominantly yellow marrow and vice versa, can be seen. Normal marrow on T1-weighted sequences is always isointense or hyperintense to surrounding muscle or intervertebral disk. With BME lesions, they are hypointense on T1-weighted images and have high signal on fluid-sensitive sequences such as T2 weighting or STIR imaging.

BME lesions can reflect nonspecific response to injury or excess stress. The pathophysiology is related to increased extracellular fluid, which can be from hypervascularity and hyperperfusion (hyperemia, an inflammatory infiltrate causing resorption, granulation tissue, or a reactive phenomenon related to altered biomechanics). Enhancement with gadolinium occurs in BME irrespective of etiology (benign or malignant, infectious or inflammatory). Potential causes include diseases in the following categories: trauma, biomechanical, developmental, vascular, neoplastic, inflammatory, neuropathic, metabolic, degenerative, iatrogenic, and potentially idiopathic conditions (e.g., transient bone marrow edema syndromes).

One of the most common causes of BME is occult injuries. Stress fractures can be subclassified into insuffi-

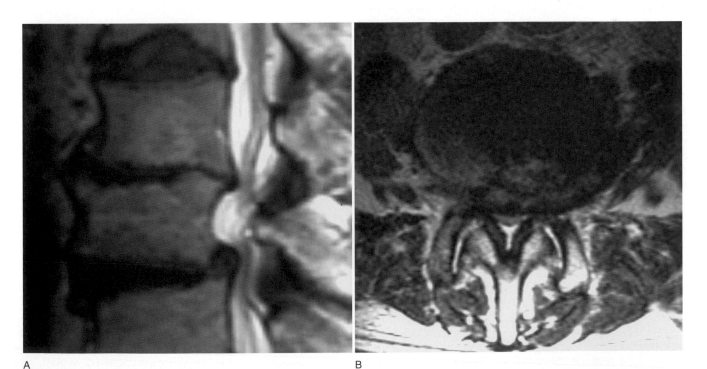

A   B

FIGURE 10–5 ■ Severe spinal stenosis. Sagittal T2-weighted (**A**) and axial T2-weighted (**B**) MR images show a broad-based disk bulge resulting in greater than two-thirds compromise of the spinal canal.

ciency or fatigue fractures. Insufficiency fractures occur with normal stresses in abnormal bone. Fatigue fractures occur in normal bone with excess or superphysiologic stress. MRI is a more sensitive technique for fracture detection and characterization than radiography. Common locations predominate in the lower extremities including the pelvis (supra-acetabular and parasymphyseal regions), femur (head and neck), tibia (proximal or distal), fibula (distal diaphysis), ankle (posterior calcaneus), and multiple regions in the foot (e.g., metatarsal shaft). Bone contusions (bruises) are considered microtrabecular fractures. On MRI there is no fracture line and the pattern of BME may be a secondary sign of associated ligament or tendon injury. These often occur in a subarticular location from osteochondral impaction injuries. Altered biomechanics can also be an important cause of BME and may reflect bone stress response without fractures and may even be asymptomatic.

Vascular causes of BME may be related to either hyperemic or ischemic causes. Of the hyperemic causes, inflammatory disorders that increase vascularity or disuse may cause subarticular BME patterns. The disuse pattern can be characteristic and parallels the radiographic pattern with multiple rounded areas of fluid-like hyperintensity in a subarticular and metaphyseal distribution. In ischemic lesions, the broad category of osteonecrosis (infarct, avascular necrosis) can have BME early that is associated with the acute painful symptomatology. Pain improvement usually parallels the resolution of the BME signal. The "double line" sign is specific and is characterized by a ring of T1-weighted hypointensity and T2-weighted hyperintensity (Fig. 10–6). MRI findings may be seen as early as 10 to 15 days and for most patients within 30 days of vascular insult. Transient osteoporosis (radiographic) or the MR correlate transient bone marrow edema syndrome may occur in numerous lower extremity locations, including the hip, knee, talus, tarsals (cuboid, navicular), and metatarsals. It is controversial whether these lesions reflect salvaged avascular necrosis or simply are biomechanical.

In the inflammatory category, infections can cause BME. Often, a difficult differential diagnosis in the clinical setting of diabetic neuropathy is distinguishing osteomyelitis from Charcot arthropathy. MRI may be helpful in differentiating the two. First, the distributions are typically different. Osteomyelitis is more common in the phalanges, distal metatarsals, and calcaneus, whereas neuropathic disease is more common in the Lisfranc and Chopart joints. Second, epicenters can be useful. Neuropathic disease has an articular epicenter. and usually multiple joints are involved. Osteomyelitis has a marrow epicenter with focal spread throughout the bone. Third, secondary soft tissue findings such as a subcutaneous ulcer, cellulitis, phlegmon, abscess, and, particularly, a sinus tract strongly support infection.[6] Noninfectious causes in the inflammatory category may also be a source of BME, such as in reflex sympathetic dystrophy (RSD). RSD is a condition characterized by localized or diffuse pain, usually with associated swelling, trophic changes, and vasomotor disturbance. Allodynia, hyperhidrosis, and nail or hair growth changes may also occur. Motor abnormalities have been reported, and contractures may occur in the later stages. Three stages are recognized, with clinical and radiologic features utilized in the staging. Stage 1 is characterized by the onset of burning type pain, with swelling and edema. Stage 2 reflects more established disease; pain diminishes with the onset of vasoconstriction and subsequent decreased skin temperature. In stage 3, pain is less prominent and the skin can be smooth and/or cyanotic with underlying muscle atrophy. MRI, because of its inherent soft tissue imaging capabilities, has been shown to be useful for the accurate diagnosis of RSD.[7] BME is a nonspecific finding in RSD, but the adjacent soft tissue changes help stage the disease in association with clinical findings. Stage 1 disease is the most accurately demonstrated stage, showing skin thickening, contrast medium enhancement, joint effusion,[8] and, less frequently, soft tissue edema (Fig. 10–7). MRI of RSD in stage 2 disease is less accurate. Findings in stage 2 disease include skin thinning and/or thickening and infrequent soft tissue enhancement. In patients with stage 3 RSD, soft tissue enhancement is not seen but muscle atrophy is a common finding (Fig. 10–8). Patients with stage 1 or 2 RSD generally do not demonstrate muscle atrophy. Skin changes seen on MRI in stage 3 RSD are variable.

Degenerative conditions can also be associated with BME, such as primary or secondary osteoarthritis. Subchondral cysts are one of the imaging hallmarks of osteoarthritis and can be identified on MRI. Early in the course there are ill-defined areas of BME, and, later, discrete cystic structures form. In the knee, marrow findings are strongly associated with the presence of pain and moderate or larger effusions and synovial thickening are more frequent among those with pain than those without pain adjusted for degree of radiographic osteoarthritis.[9] In addition, focal subchondral BME can be an indicator of focal overlying cartilage defects. A flame-shaped BME lesion in a nonarthritic joint can be a helpful secondary sign of cartilage abnormality. BME lesions can also be seen in a subtendinous location as a response to tendon abnormality from mechanical friction, hyperemia, or biomechanical reasons. This is most common in the foot and ankle.[10]

■ TENDONS

Tendons are relatively avascular structures that attach muscles to bones, consisting of dense fascicles of collagen fibers. Because normal tendons (as well as ligaments and cortical bone) have few mobile protons, they are usually of low signal intensity on all pulse sequences. There are a few instances that are exceptions to this rule. The quadriceps tendon at the knee and the distal triceps tendon at the elbow have a striated appearance with alternating areas of linear low- and intermediate-signal intensity. This striated appearance is caused by the fact that several tendons are fusing to form a single conjoined tendon. Similarly, there may be a solitary, vertical high signal intensity line in the midsubstance of many normal Achilles tendons representing the site where the soleus and gastrocnemius tendons are apposed to one another or a vascular channel in the tendon. Another exception may occur when tendons demonstrate slightly increased signal intensity near their osseous insertions. This occurs because the tendon fans out to attach to a bone and fatty material is interposed between tendon fibers. A third reason for a normal tendon to have increased signal intensity is the result of the magic angle phenomenon. The phenomenon results when the tendons are oriented at a 55-degree angle to the direction of the main magnetic field. There will be high signal intensity on short TE sequences (such as T1-weighted, proton-density, and

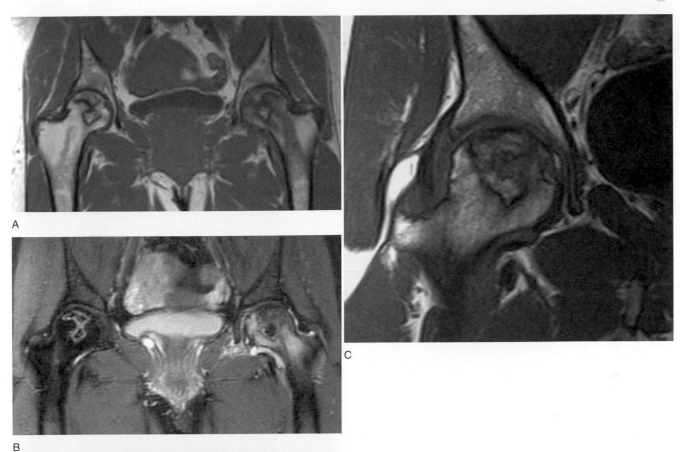

A

B

C

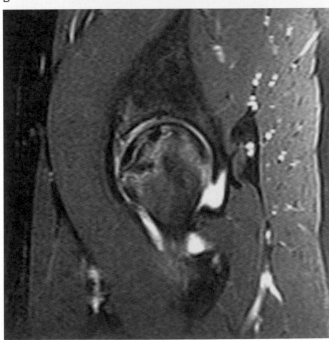

D

FIGURE 10–6 ■ Osteonecrosis. Coronal T1-weighted (**A**) and coronal STIR (**B**) images show characteristic serpentine, alternating lines of T1-weighted hypointensity and T2-weighted hyperintensity typical of osteonecrosis. Coronal T1-weighted (**C**) and sagittal T2-weighted with fat suppression (**D**) images further show a curvilinear low signal intensity line in the subarticular area of the femoral head suggesting subarticular collapse, a complication of avascular necrosis.

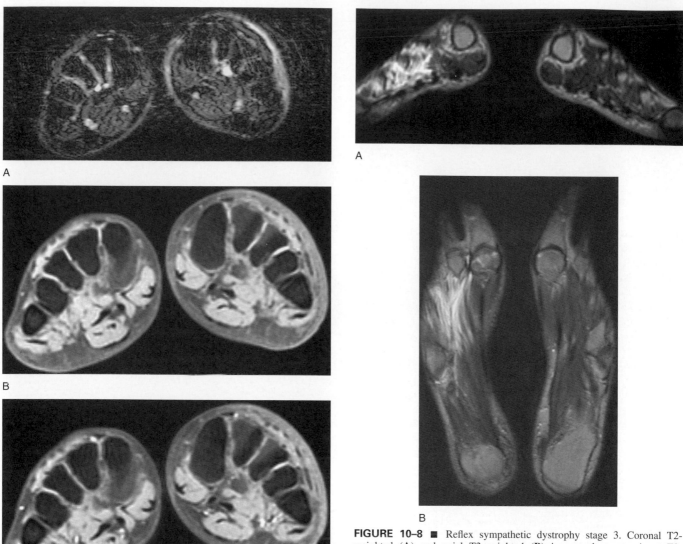

FIGURE 10–8 ■ Reflex sympathetic dystrophy stage 3. Coronal T2-weighted (**A**) and axial T2-weighted (**B**) images show prominent T2-weighted hyperintensity in the intrinsic muscles of the right foot reflecting an early stage of muscle atrophy.

FIGURE 10–7 ■ Reflex sympathetic dystrophy stage 1. **A,** Axial T2-weighted fat-suppressed image shows a prominent area of subcutaneous edema over the dorsum of the left midfoot. Axial T1-weighted fat-suppressed (**B**) and axial T1-weighted fat-suppressed post–intravenous gadolinium (**C**) images show skin thickening and enhancement in the area corresponding to subcutaneous edema. **D,** Axial T1-weighted fat-suppressed postcontrast image also shows periarticular enhancement in the left midfoot.

gradient-echo sequences). Differentiation between magic angle phenomenon and true pathology can be made by examining long TE sequences (i.e., T2-weighted sequences), where the high signal intensity will disappear if due to magic angle phenomenon.

There are a number of tendon abnormalities that may be detected by MRI. The spectrum of tendinopathy encompasses tendinosis, partial tears, compete tears, and tenosynovitis. The term *tendon degeneration* is a broad term synonymous with *tendinopathy*. Degeneration of tendons occurs with aging or from chronic overuse. This is generally painless but weakens the tendon and predisposes to partial or complete tears with minimal trauma. On MRI, a degenerated tendon demonstrates both morphologic and signal alterations. Partial tears represent incomplete disruption of tendon fibers. These can have a variable appearance on MRI. The tendon may be thickened or thinned or remain of normal caliber with abnormal signal being the only evidence of the partial tear. Partial tears can also manifest as longitudinal tears along the length of the tendon (interstitial or split tears) rather than along the transverse plane. Complete tendon tear (rupture) indicates total disruption of fibers so that there are two separate fragments. The resulting fragments may be separated (retracted) for variable distances.

Tenosynovitis is defined as inflammation of the lining of the sheath that surrounds a tendon. Tendon sheaths are present where tendons pass through fascial slings, beneath ligamentous bands, or through fibro-osseous tunnels. A thin layer of fluid exists between the tendon sheath and the tendon itself and allows for smooth gliding of the tendon. Although there are no strict criteria defining the normal amount of tendon sheath fluid, when the diameter of the tendon sheath is greater than the enclosed tendon it is probably pathologic. Tenosynovitis may occur from chronic repetitive motion, inflammatory arthritides, and infection, among other causes. Tendon sheaths that can communicate with an adjacent joint, such as the long head of the biceps tendon in the shoulder and the flexor hallucis longus tendon at the ankle, should not be considered to have tenosynovitis simply because of fluid surround the tendon. Only if this is disproportionate to the amount of joint fluid do these findings have possible clinical significance.

■ LIGAMENT ABNORMALITIES

Classification of ligamentous injuries in general is similar to that of tendon abnormalities. Ligament injuries are referred to as sprains, whereas muscle injury is correctly referred to as strain. Ligaments usually show as low signal intensity on all pulse sequences. Exceptions to this exist in which ligaments such as the anterior cruciate ligament in the knee and deep deltoid fibers in the ankle can have a striated appearance with fatty tissue interspersed between ligament fibers. Grading of ligament injuries (sprain) ranges from microscopic tearing (analogous to tendinosis of tendons) to partial and complete tears. Grade I sprain is when stretching of a ligament occurs or there is microscopic tearing. On MRI these can manifest as either fluid immediately adjacent to or surrounding the ligament or an increase in signal intensity of the ligament. The ligament may be normal or enlarged in thickness. Grade II sprain refers to a partial tear, which indicates disruption of some of the fibers of the ligament. Grade III sprain indicates a complete tear. Partial and complete ligament tears appear on MRI as discontinuity of some or all of the fibers of the ligament with interposed fluid.

■ CARTILAGE ABNORMALITIES

Over the past decade, MRI of articular cartilage has become a leading area of clinical and research interest. Development of new cartilage-specific sequences has made MRI the optimal imaging modality for the evaluation of cartilage abnormalities and also plays a significant role in determining the appropriate pharmacologic or surgical repair procedures.

Articular cartilage lesions may be categorized as degenerative or traumatic.[11] Early degenerative changes may be seen on MRI as abnormality in contour (fibrillation or surface irregularity), changes in cartilage thickness (thinning or thickening), or alterations in cartilage signal intensity. Advanced degenerative changes on MRI manifest as multiple areas of cartilage thinning of varying depth and size. Focal cartilage defects may be associated with corresponding edema-like marrow signal abnormality in the subchondral bone. Subchondral cystic change and sclerosis can also be seen. In contrast, traumatic chondral lesions usually appear on MRI as solitary focal cartilage defects with acutely angled margins. These defects are usually the results of shearing, rotational, or tangential forces and result in partial- or full-thickness cartilage defects or osteochondral injuries. Linear clefts or fissures may also be seen extending for variable depths within the articular cartilage. These may result in chondral flap lesions or delamination injuries. Associated alterations in subchondral marrow signal may also be seen and should alert the observer to the possibility of overlying articular cartilage abnormality. MRI is reliable for detection and characterization of full-thickness cartilage defects.

A number of surgical cartilage repair procedures have been developed to treat cartilage defects. These include local stimulation techniques (abrasion arthroplasty, microfracture, subchondral drilling) and autologous transplantation of cartilage: autologous osteochondral transplantation (AOT) autologous chondrocyte implantation (ACI).

■ OTHER CONSIDERATIONS

Other soft tissues that MRI is uniquely able to assess are muscles and nerves. Like other tissues, pathology in these tissues appears as increased signal intensity on T2-weighted sequences. With skeletal muscle, increased signal intensity is nonspecific, but injury, inflammation (both infectious and noninfectious), and denervation may be present.[12] With respect to denervation changes, in the acute phase, muscles appear normal. In the subacute phase, muscles appear increased in signal intensity on T2-weighted sequences. Muscles also may appear enlarged and demonstrate enhancement after intravenous administration of gadolinium. In the chronic phase, fatty infiltration and fatty atrophy occur with increased signal on T1-weighted sequences as well as decrease in muscle bulk. Muscle denervation may be multifactorial, but MRI is useful for the assessment of nerve entrapment syndromes and compressive lesions as well as nerve and nerve sheath tumors. Common nerve entrapment syndromes include suprascapular nerve entrapment in the shoulder (suprascapular nerve), carpal tunnel syndrome in the wrist (median nerve), and cubital tunnel syndrome in the elbow (ulnar nerve).

Over the past decade there have been dramatic improvements in MR scanning systems, pulse sequences, as well as high-resolution coil design. By using a technique called MR neurography, imaging of the peripheral nervous system can be performed reliably and quickly. In conjunction with electrophysiologic studies, the specific cause of peripheral nerve disorders can be anatomically localized and diagnosed. MRI has become the technique of choice for the evaluation of patients with malignancy or peripheral nerve masses (e.g., brachial and lumbosacral plexus tumors), nerve sheath tumors, and soft tissue tumors secondarily involving peripheral nerves. This technique is also used to evaluate previously mentioned nerve root compression and entrapment syndromes.

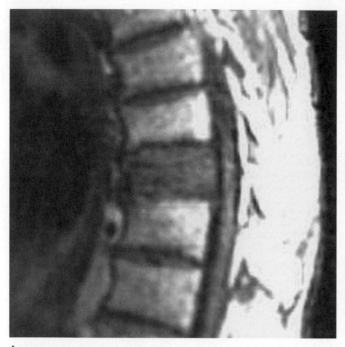
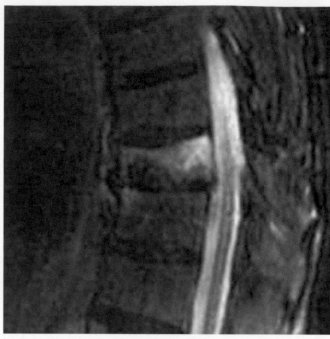

A   B

FIGURE 10–9 ■ Vertebral compression fracture. Sagittal T1-weighted (**A**) and sagittal T2-weighted with fat suppression (**B**) MR images. A vertebral wedge deformity is present in the midthoracic spine at T6. The marrow signal shows diffuse edema reflecting a subacute unhealed painful fracture.

Vertebral compression fractures (VCF) have a prevalence of 26% in women older than 50 years, and more than 84% of these injuries are associated with pain. Although many patients recover with conservative therapy, a significant number continue to have pain that is refractory to such measures. Traditional immobilization techniques, such as bed rest and bracing, may lead to a vicious cycle in which decreased activity leads to worsened bone density, with resultant fracture formation and more pain. Long-term consequences are physically and psychologically devastating and include physical deconditioning, difficulty breathing and sleeping, depression, and fear of further fracture. Imaging studies are used to guide performance of vertebral augmentation whether patients have acute or chronic fractures. Conventional radiography is helpful but not definitive, because many patients will present with multiple compression deformities. Therefore, determining appropriate level(s) to treat on the basis of conventional radiography alone can be problematic. Positive results on scintigraphy are a strong predictor of clinical outcome after vertebroplasty to treat acute fractures, but up to 59% of untreated vertebral fractures are scintigraphically negative at 12 months. One of the strengths of MRI is its high sensitivity for bone marrow edema and the greater anatomic detail it demonstrates compared with conventional radiography or scintigraphy. Therefore, MRI has become an important tool in the evaluation of patients before vertebral augmentation because of the combination of its sensitivity in detecting bone marrow edema and its multiplanar capabilities (Fig. 10–9). Acute end plate changes demonstrate increased signal on T2-weighted/STIR images and low signal on T1-weighted images. Chronic fractures are often isointense to fatty marrow on both sequences. Information obtained from MRI before vertebral augmentation also is valuable for the evaluation of canal compromise, vertebral body shape, determination of the residual height of the affected vertebral body, and identification of other vertebrae that are in the early stages of fracture or collapse.

■ CONCLUSION

MRI is the key imaging modality in diagnosis of multiple pathologic entities in the neurologic and musculoskeletal systems relating to pain. With its unparalleled soft tissue contrast, high-resolution imaging, and multiplanar capabilities, MRI is the optimal technique for evaluating structures in the brain and spine as well as evaluating internal derangement of joints. With newer technologies, including higher field strength magnets and faster pulse sequences, previous limitations of the modality will undoubtedly be overcome and further augment the utility of MRI for the healthcare provider.

References

1. Steinbach LS, Palmer WE, Schweitzer ME: Special focus session: MR arthrography. Radiographics 22:1223, 2002.
2. Neff MJ: Evidence-based guidelines for neuroimaging in patients with nonacute headache. Am Fam Physician 71(6):1219, 2005.
3. Fardon D, Milette P: Nomenclature and classification of lumbar disc pathology. Spine 26:E93, 2001.
4. Weishaupt D, Zanetti M, Hodler J, et al: Painful lumbar disk derangement: Relevance of endplate abnormalities at MR imaging. Radiology 208:420, 2001.
5. Pfirrmann CW, Metzdorf A, Zanetti M, et al: Magnetic resonance classification of lumbar intervertebral disc degeneration. Spine 26:1873, 2001.

6. Morrison WB, Schweitzer ME, Batte WG, et al: Osteomyelitis of the foot: Relative importance of primary and secondary MR imaging signs. Radiology 207:625, 1998.

7. Schweitzer ME, Mandel S, Schwartzman RJ, et al: Reflex sympathetic dystrophy revisited: MR imaging findings before and after infusion of contrast material. Radiology 195:211, 1995.

8. Graif M, Schweitzer ME, Marks B, et al: Synovial effusion in reflex sympathetic dystrophy: An additional sign for diagnosis and staging. Skeletal Radiol 27:262, 1998.

9. Felson DT, McLaughlin S, Goggins J, et al: Bone marrow edema and its relation to progression of knee osteoarthritis. Ann Intern Med 139(5 pt 1):330, 2003.

10. Morrison WB, Carrino JA, Schweitzer ME, et al: Subtendinous bone marrow edema patterns on MR images of the ankle: Association with symptoms and tendinopathy. Am J Radiol 176:1149, 2001.

11. Recht MP, Goodwin DW, Winalski CS, White LM: MRI of articular cartilage: Revisiting current status and future directions. Am J Radiol 185:899, 2005.

12. May DA, Disler DG, Jones EA, et al: Abnormal signal intensity in skeletal muscle at MR imaging: Patterns, pearls, and pitfalls. Radiographics Oct 20(spec. issue):S295, 2000.

Chapter 11

Diskography

Milton H. Landers

"The doctor enters a covenant with the patient; he penetrates his life, affecting his mode of living, often deciding his fate."[1]

The diagnostic procedure often referred to as diskography in actuality consists of two separate and distinct components. The first part, diskography (i.e., a disk picture), involves the injection of contrast medium into the nucleus pulposus of the intervertebral disk to study its internal morphology. This is a static test in which contrast is injected and radiographic images, plain film and CT, are obtained and evaluated. The second dynamic part of the procedure, the disk stimulation aspect, entails distention of the nucleus pulposus by the pressure produced by the injectate to determine whether a specific disk is involved in generating the patient's pain symptoms. In a most basic description, needles are placed within the intervertebral disks at multiple levels, and contrast material is injected into each disk to place a mechanical load on said disks. The response from the patient is then correlated with the chronic symptoms, low back, neck, or thoracic pain, as previously noted by the patient.

In the United States, low back pain is a serious individual and societal problem. Approximately 15% to 20% of the population will suffers from low back pain each year and 80% over their lifetime. This entity is the second most common cause of lost work and physician visits. Although 90% of low back pain resolves after 6 weeks and another 5% after 12 weeks, ≈5% will advance from an acute to a chronic condition. One percent of the U.S. population is chronically disabled by low back pain. Although chronic, versus acute low back pain accounts for only 5% of cases, it is responsible for >60% of the costs. There are $24 billion in medical and $50 billion in total societal costs directly attributable to this condition.

Chronic neck pain, although somewhat less common than pain of the low back region, is frequently seen in clinical practice. A history of neck pain was noted in 35% to 80% of a population, depending on the group studied.[1a-5]

Though two separate entities, axial pain of the low back or neck is often confused with radiculopathy or radicular pain. By definition, radiculopathy is a neurologic condition in which a conduction block of the motor or sensory axons is noted during physical examination. Radicular pain refers to pain originating from spinal nerves or their roots and is described as electrical, shooting, lancinating, and "band-like," with distal, rather than proximal, extremity pain.[6] In contrast, mechanical low back, or cervical, pain (i.e., referred somatic pain) is described as deep, dull, achy, and diffuse and is usually hard to localize. Lumbar radicular pain is associated with a herniated intervertebral disk about 98% of the time,[7] and cervical herniated intervertebral disks also account for cervical radicular pain in the great majority of cases.[8] However, low back pain is rarely associated with herniated disks,[9-12] although their supposed association is a common misconception.

The distinction between radicular and referred somatic pain having been made, we will now focus on the latter for the remainder of this chapter.

Chronic pain involving the cervical, thoracic, or lumbar regions is not a diagnosis; rather, it is a sign or symptom usually attributable to pathology of the spine. It has been well documented that the three structures involved in the majority of chronic low back pain are the sacroiliac joint, the zygapophyseal (facet) joints, and the intervertebral disk. Dismissing the sacroiliac joint, the cervical and thoracic segments of the spine are analogous. All these structures are known to be innervated, have been shown to cause pain, are susceptible to injury or disease known to be painful, and have been demonstrated to be the source of pain in the clinical setting. All are accompanied by deep, dull, achy low back pain often referred to the hips or buttocks, and physical examination is usually unable to differentiate between the three. The sacroiliac joint accounts for ≈15% of cases of chronic low back pain,[13,14] whereas the zygapophyseal joint is identified as the "pain generator" in ≈15% of injured workers[15] and ≈40% of the elderly.[16] Diskogenic pain is known to be highly correlated with internal disk disruption involving extension of radial anular fissures into the outer third of the anulus fibrosus.[17]

Low back pain is a common and often debilitating condition that is frequently due to pathology involving the intervertebral disk. As noted by Dr. Bogduk[18] in his classic text, *"amongst patients with chronic low back pain, the prevalence of internal disk disruption is at least 39%.*[19] This figure makes internal disk disruption the most common cause of chronic low back pain that can be objectively demonstrated,"* and provocation diskography is the only means of making the diagnosis.

■ ANATOMY OF THE INTERVERTEBRAL DISK

The juncture between adjacent vertebrae consists of a three-joint interface: two posterior synovial zygapophyseal, facet,

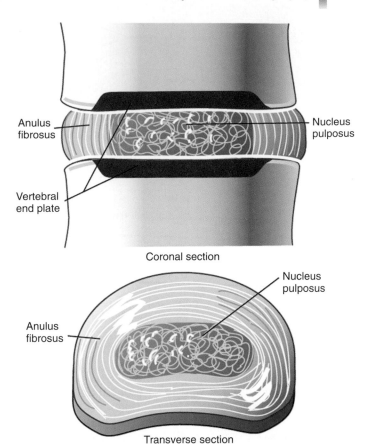

Coronal section

Transverse section

FIGURE 11–1 ■ Structure of the lumbar intervertebral disk.

joints and an anterior interbody joint. Teleologically, the intervertebral body joint requires a soft tissue spacer that allows anterior-posterior rocking and rotational movement; in addition, the spacer must be deformable and strong enough to allow movement without injury and weight bearing without collapse.

The lumbar intervertebral disk consists of three components: the outer anulus fibrosus, the inner nucleus pulposus, and two cartilaginous vertebral end plates (Fig. 11–1). The two vertebral end plates of each intervertebral disk are situated within the ring apophysis of each vertebral body and are in contact with the entire nucleus pulposus but only the inner aspect of the anulus fibrosus. This structure is 0.6 to 1 mm in thickness and consists of hyaline cartilage and fibrocartilage. The end plates derive collagen fibers from the inner anulus fibrosus. These fibers provide a strong bond between the end plates and the anulus fibrosus, whereas the attachment of the end plates to the vertebral bodies is relatively weak.[20,21] The collagen fibers shared between the anulus fibrosus and the end plates form a capsule around the entire nucleus pulposus.

The nucleus pulposus of the lumbar intervertebral disk is a viscous structure. Chemically, it is composed of 70% to 90% water, depending on age,[22-26] along with proteoglycans,[22,23] collagen,[22,27] elastic fibers, and non-collagenous proteins.[22,25,28-30] Being a viscous semi-fluid, the nucleus pulposus is freely deformable and non-compressible, with biomechanical pressure being transferred to the adjacent anulus fibrosus evenly in all directions.

The lumbar anulus fibrosus is composed of collagen fibers arranged in concentric rings of 10 to 20 lamellae (i.e.,

sheets), which results in an exceedingly strong ligamentous-type structure. Within each lamella the collagen fibers are parallel to each other, at approximately 65 degrees from the vertical, and extend between adjacent vertebral bodies. Neighboring lamellae alternate in the obliquity of the fibers between right and left. Although water is the major component of the anulus fibrosus,[22,23,25,26] with regard to dry weight, approximately 50% to 60% of the anulus fibrosus is composed of collagen,[22,25,28,31] with proteoglycans,[22] elastic fibers,[32-35] chondrocytes, and fibroblasts being represented in lesser amounts. Even though both the nucleus pulposus and anulus fibrosus are composed of the same biochemical components, water, collagen, proteoglycans, and other constituents, the proportions vary; specifically, the nucleus pulposus is proteoglycan rich, whereas the anulus fibrosus includes collagen as its major component.

The interface of the lumbar nucleus pulposus and anulus fibrosus is not a clearly delineated boundary. A transition zone, which increases with age, is present in which the inner anulus fibrosus and outer nucleus pulposus merge and take on the biochemical milieu and attributes of each other.[36]

The cervical intervertebral disk is known to be distinct from its lumbar counterpart, although there is a relative paucity of literature regarding its unique qualities. At birth, the nucleus pulposus of the cervical intervertebral disk occupies less than 25% of the disk volume, as opposed to 50% in the lumbar levels.[37] After the third decade of life, marked fibrosis of the nucleus pulposus is seen,[38] and unlike the semi-fluid nucleus pulposus of the lumbar intervertebral disk, the cervical nucleus has a semi-solid consistency resembling bar soap.

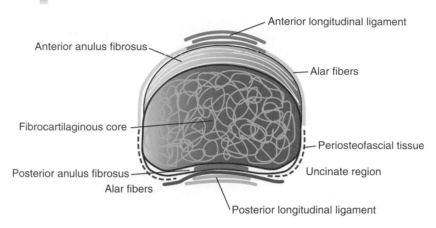

FIGURE 11–2 ■ Structure of the cervical intervertebral disk.

To allow for and in response to cervical movement, fissures are seen originating at the uncovertebral joints and progressing medially into the nucleus pulposus. These clefts have been described as joints of Luschka, or uncovertebral recesses, and should be considered normal in mature individuals.[39-41]

An excellent study by Mercer and Bogduk[42] has documented the gross and microscopic morphology of the cervical intervertebral disk. In the cervical disk, the collagen fibers of the anulus fibrosus do not circumscribe the entire structure as in the lumbar spine. Rather, the anulus fibrosus is an anterior crescent-shaped structure, thick ventrally and tapering toward each uncinate and a small, discrete paramedian posterior element. The fibers of the cervical anulus fibrosus do not form multiple distinct layers. The transitional fibers of the thin anterior superficial layer and the small posterior component are vertically oriented, whereas deeper fibers form an obliquely interwoven structure that becomes progressively embedded in the proteoglycan matrix of the nucleus pulposus. The posterior lateral aspect of the cervical intervertebral disk is unbounded by an anulus fibrosus and is contained only by fibers of the posterior longitudinal ligament (Fig. 11–2).

The thoracic intervertebral disk has been little studied. It is now known[43] that the anatomy of the thoracic disk is reminiscent of the cervical rather than lumbar model down to the T9-10 level, at which point it adopts the morphology of the lumbar disk.

The blood supply to the intervertebral disk is limited to small branches of the metaphyseal arteries, which penetrate only into the outer aspect of the anulus, and the capillary plexuses beneath the vertebral end plates.[44-47] Diffusion of nutrients through the vertebral end plates and anulus fibrosus allows a low level of metabolic activity.

Although Roofe had reported the innervation of the anulus fibrosus and posterior longitudinal ligament in 1940,[48] other histologic studies indicated that the intervertebral disk was devoid of nerve endings[49-51] and was reported to lack innervation.[52-54] It is now known that the outer third of the anulus fibrosus is not only innervated but contains a wide variety of simple and complex neural structures[55-59] derived from branches of the sinuvertebral nerves, gray rami communicantes, and lumbar ventral rami.[55,57,58,60] Histochemical studies have shown that the neural tissue present in the intervertebral disk contains peptides specific to nociceptive neural elements.[61,62] Physiologic changes are known to occur in a painful intervertebral disk, including nerve ingrowth into the usually aneural inner anulus,[63] and an increase in nerve growth factor has been demonstrated in painful versus asymptomatic intervertebral disks.[64,65]

Several possible physiologic mechanisms for the production of pain in the intervertebral disk have been postulated. Although mechanical stress across the anulus has been proposed,[60] an inflammatory mechanism appears likely.[66] The nucleus of the intervertebral disk is known to have a low pH[67] and contains a multitude of inflammatory enzymes.[55,69-70] These chemicals, when released secondary to injury or disk degradation, are thought to sensitize neural structures within and in close proximity to the disk.

Therefore, the intervertebral disk is innervated, subject to pathology, and known to contain chemicals that produce painful inflammatory responses. Can diskography pinpoint pathology and lead to a diagnosis of pain arising from a suspect intervertebral disk?

■ HISTORICAL CONSIDERATIONS

Diskography (i.e., a picture of the intervertebral disk) has a history that can be more completely appreciated by understanding its introduction and subsequent development in the context of the prevailing concept of co-evolving knowledge, techniques, and other aspects of medical science in a number of other fields, including pain anatomy and physiology of the intervertebral disk in terms of disk pathology and nociception, the development of myelographic contrast material, and the introduction of advanced imaging techniques, including CT and MRI.

During its development, diskography has achieved some notoriety as a "controversial" technique but has subsequently become a standard for the evaluation of certain conditions of the spinal intervertebral disks that cannot otherwise be diagnosed by any other present method.

Schmorl and Junghans, as referenced in their later work,[71] laid the basis for clinical diskography in their voluminous and pioneering work on the pathology of the intervertebral disk, published in monograph form in 1932. They reported their examination of 10,000 cadaveric spines in which the partially dissected spines were radiographed en bloc; they subsequently completed the dissection and noted the radiographic/pathologic correlations. In many of these specimens they injected red lead into the disk before radiographs, which allowed the first analysis of diskographic appearance. This study led to the terms protrusion and rupture of the intervertebral disk and introduced diskography as an anatomic study to evaluate the internal structure of the cadaveric disk. Their work also described the progression from radial tear to rupture.

Mixter and Barr's landmark paper in 1934 in which a surgical cure for radiculopathy secondary to a herniated nucleus pulposus was reported heralded a new era in spinal surgery and led to renewed interest in techniques for diagnosis.[72]

In the late 1930s and early 1940s, lumbar spine diagnostics consisted almost solely of plain film radiographs and myelography. During that period, myelography, which involves placement of contrast within the intrathecal space, was an extremely painful procedure that required general anesthesia. Technical limitations of myelography are many, including visualization of only the effect of a lesion (i.e., compression of the dura) rather than direct visualization and imaging limited to the central portion of the spinal canal.

Even though Lindgren reported injection of a normal disk with parabrodil[73] in 1941, fear of injuring disks in a report by Pease[74] in 1935 held up the first clinical trails in humans. It was not until Hirsch[75] showed that the disk was not damaged when injected that clinical studies of diskography became more widespread.

In an attempt to provide diagnostic clarity to the analysis of patients with back and leg pain and to directly visualize the pathology of the intervertebral disk, Dr. Kirk Lindblom[76] was influenced to develop a technique to directly visualize the lumbar intervertebral disks as a clinical examination for investigation of patients with suspected disk pathology. He published a series of papers[77-80] describing his technique and results and provided the first clinical correlation to the observations.

Among other innovations that Lindblom described was a dual-needle approach to the lower disks, albeit this was a transarachnoid (i.e., interpedicular), direct radiographic analysis of both degeneration and herniation, along with the demonstration of fissures directly communicating with the epidural and perineural spaces.[77] Even in the earliest papers, he described disk stimulation and the correlation of pain provocation during disk injection and the patient's symptomatology as a valuable aspect of diskography. This was corroborated by Hirsch,[75] who reported provocation of pain in 16 patients by injection of saline into the disk. Lindblom also advanced the concept that herniations could become asymptomatic with conservative care and the new concept that posterolateral herniations are important to the clinical syndrome of leg pain,[81] although myelography is often insensitive to this pathology.

Further work documenting that disk puncture was not damaging in animals[82] or human cadavers[83,84] was followed by the first report of diskography in the United States by Wise and Weiford in 1951.[85]

In 1952, Erlacher performed cadaveric studies to document the accuracy with which the contrast dispersal pattern defined the nuclear space and found complete agreement between the radiographic and the gross dispersal patterns in 200 disks.[86] Cloward, also in 1952, reported on the technique and indications for lumbar diskography.[87]

In his 1960 monograph,[88] Fernstrom reviewed the then current literature. He noted that back and leg pain can occur regardless of whether nerve root compression is present. He also advanced the concept that there are both neurogenic (mechanical compressive) and diskogenic (biochemical irritative) causes for the symptoms.

Early authorities embraced diskography, both lumbar and cervical, as a technique in the diagnosis of disk herniation,[86,87,89-101] including reports of enhanced surgical results when using diskography as a preoperative assessment tool.[102,103]

Hartjes et al.[104] compared diskography and myelography and concluded that indications for diskography included specific radiculopathy and a normal myelogram or symptoms with multiple myelographic defects. Some found it superior to oil-contrast myelography,[91,94,105] but others disagreed and thought that lumbar diskography should be reserved for the investigation of unusual or atypical cases.[106]

Although the development and deployment of minimally toxic contrast agents made myelography much safer,[107,108] this technique continued to have the inherent weakness of assessing the effect of lesions in the spine on the dural sac rather than direct visualization of the lesion. In addition, it did not provide the information regarding the reproduction of concordant pain as initiated by disk stimulation that diskography provides.

The development of high-quality CT scanning[109] permitted not only direct visualization of the anatomy in cross section[110] and direct diagnosis of disk herniation,[111] but also supplementary information when myelographic contrast was used.[112-115] The development of CT also enhanced the diagnostic capabilities of diskography. In 1987, Videman and colleagues[116] reported the valuable additional information gained by performing post-diskography CT in 103 cadaveric disks.

The emergence of MRI[117] in 1984 provided non-invasive characterization of a variety of disk lesions[118] and extradural[119] pathology, and it has become the primary modality for diagnosing pathology of the spine. Although MRI provides high spatial and contrast resolution, biochemical diagnostic information has led to further knowledge regarding the pathophysiology of disk disorders,[119,120] and MRI is now quite effective in the detection of disk degeneration.[122-124]

Despite this major advance in the ability to visualize anatomy and tissue characteristics, MRI was still found to be less sensitive than diskography in detecting tears and fissures,[125] although gadolinium enhancement may be of assistance.[126] There was also the problem of normal MRI and abnormal diskography findings.[127,128] Even though these new imaging technologies, i.e., CT and MRI, have helped,[129] they do not tell us whether the pathoanatomy is symptomatic.

The relationship of pain to disk rupture and nerve compression began with Mixter and Barr in 1934.[72] However, as a pathophysiologic lesion, the concept of compression of neural structures has never been sufficient to explain the majority of back pain.[130-132]

A number of authors have described lesions associated with severe pain without neural compression, including painful posterior fissures,[133] acute traumatic interosseous herniation,[134] isolated intervertebral disk resorption,[135] and painful lumbar end plate disruption.[136]

During the ensuing years, the technique used for diskography has undergone certain additional refinements, such as provocation/analgesic diskography[137] and manometry, as introduced by Derby in 1993, that have led to the acquisition of useful information.[138,139]

The use of cervical diskography for the evaluation of patients with neck, head, and shoulder pain was reported almost simultaneously in the late 1950s by George Smith and Ralph Cloward.[140,141] Both authors emphasized that stimulation of the disk was a vital aspect of the procedure and used cervical diskography to help in choosing the correct level for surgical procedures.[142,143] The similarities in their work included the basic concept that abnormal disks could exactly reproduce the patient's symptoms, that there was a high incidence of abnormal disks, and that diskography had specific value in differentiating neurogenic from somatic, diskogenic pain.[144] The literature has continued to provide evidence of the usefulness of cervical diskography for diagnosis and planning of surgical procedures.[99,100,102,145]

Analgesic diskography, in which local anesthetic is injected into the disk to relieve pain at the level thought to be positive by provocation diskography, has been shown to be of value for diagnosis and staging for cervical procedures.[146] Kofoed[147] used this technique to differentiate thoracic disk pain from thoracic outlet syndrome.

Lumbar and cervical diskography has a long history of providing accurate information about whether the intervertebral disk is a source of pain. By extrapolation it is thought that in a like manner, the thoracic disk can be a significant pain generator. Schellhas and associates described a safe technique to access the thoracic intervertebral disk,[148] as well as its role in patient evaluation.[149]

Diskography has become the "gold standard" for the diagnosis of cervical, thoracic, and lumbar diskogenic pain and has established an important position within the diagnostic armamentarium of the spine physician.

■ VALIDATION OF DISKOGRAPHY

Mechanical stimulation of the intervertebral disk has long been known to produce low back pain.[150] However, the use of diskography for detection of clinically painful disks has not been without a certain degree of controversy, which continues to the present day. The enthusiasm of certain early proponents waned,[151] and others questioned its value.[152-155]

Because all interventional procedures are associated with a certain rate of morbidity, if pain secondary to intervertebral disk pathology (i.e., diskogenic pain) could be diagnosed by physical examination or imaging studies, invasive provocation diskography would not be indicated. Physical examination has been shown to be unreliable in differentiating low back pain generated from intervertebral disks as distinct from other pain generators.[156,157] Except for a "high-intensity zone" in the area of the posterior anulus on T2-weighted MRI images, which appears to have low sensitivity (28%) but high specificity (86%),[158] there are no specific findings on imaging studies that can be used to differentiate diskogenic from other mechanical sources of pain.[159] Carragee et al.[160] have questioned the diagnostic value of the "high-intensity zone," and its prevalence in the asymptomatic population has yet to be determined with accuracy.

For any diagnostic test to be of value, the false-positive rate must be low. In that diskography is a test in which provocation of symptoms is assessed, asymptomatic volunteers should have close to zero positive responders. Unfortunately, some reports, though often based on suspect methodology, have led to questions involving the specificity of diskography in diagnosing diskogenic pain.

The most infamous opposition opinion to lumbar diskography was by Holt.[161] This 1968 study of inmates at an Illinois state prison reported a high false-positive rate in a group of asymptomatic volunteers. Multiple flaws are to be found in Holt's methods, including a suspect population of asymptomatic "volunteers," technical competence of the author, and the use of a highly irritating contrast agent. Although criticized immediately, this report was ultimately answered by Simmons et al.,[162] who provided a compelling argument why it should not be used as scientific or authoritative evidence against the use of diskography. Walsh et al.[163] reproduced Holt's experimental design, with the exception of (1) using non-suspect subjects; (2) having a single, technically skilled diskographer; (3) utilizing a lateral, "modern," extrapedicular approach; and (4) using non-irritating contrast medium. No positive painful disks were found in the asymptomatic group of volunteers, in contrast to the symptomatic group, in whom high correlation was evident between pain reproduction and pathologic disk morphology.

In an excellent series of papers,[164-166] Eugene Carragee and colleagues indicated that lumbar diskography is associated with a high false-positive rate, up to 75%. However, in a re-analysis of the data as presented by Nikolai Bogduk[167] that took into account the psychiatric history of the volunteers, manometric data, and other criteria as published by the International Association for the Study of Pain (IASP)[168] and the International Spine Intervention Society (ISIS),[1] the false-positive rate dropped to a very low, acceptable level. Because diskography is dependent on an objective patient response, it is no surprise that Minnesota Multiphasic Personality Inventory (MMPI) scores and any psychological overlay, such as somatization, hypochondriasis, hysteria, and depression, are correlated with over-reporting of pain during diskography.[169]

One measure of the validity of diskography lies in its predictive value with regard to surgical outcomes. Over the years, when stringent criteria are met, lumbar diskography has been shown to be a good predictor of surgical outcome.[139,170] Colhoun et al.[171] used very rigid criteria for evaluating clinical benefit from surgery and noted that in patients with abnormal-appearing disks, 89% of those with a positive diskogram had a positive surgical outcome whereas only 52% of those with a negative diskogram benefited in a significant manner.

In the cervical spine, pathology, as detected by imaging studies, should be considered the norm and cannot predict neck pain. Gore et al.[172] used plain film radiography and noted abnormal studies in 70% at age 60, whereas Boden et al.[173] performed MRI and reported major or minor abnormalities that could produce pain in 97% of asymptomatic individuals. Although morphologically normal disks on MRI were never painful with diskography, significant anular disruptions were often missed and MRI cannot reliably indicate the source of cervical diskogenic pain.[174] Injuries to the cervical spine were often found at autopsy when previous imaging was normal,[175] thus indicating low sensitivity with routine testing. In numerous papers going back to the late 1960s,[100,102,137,145,176-181] preoperative cervical diskography has been shown to be an excellent predictor of successful outcomes (70% to 90%), as opposed to cervical fusions performed without the benefit of this diagnostic procedure (39% to 50%).

Wood et al.[149] performed thoracic diskography on 10 symptomatic and 10 asymptomatic volunteers. In the asymptomatic group, although 3 of the 40 disks stimulated produced significant pain, this discomfort was unfamiliar and non-concordant and would be classified as a negative response during diagnostic diskography. In contrast, in the symptomatic group, 24 of the 48 disks injected produced marked concordant pain reminiscent of the patient's usual symptoms.

Although the rate of false-positive results with diskography continues to be a legitimate concern, most well-designed studies have substantiated the procedure's diagnostic credibility. International Spine Intervention Society (ISIS),[1] the North American Spine Society (NASS),[182] and Physiatric Association of Spine, Sports, and Occupational Rehabilitation (PASSOR)[183] have all indicated that diskography is an appropriate diagnostic procedure, that has value in clinical situations, if performed correctly and interpreted in the context of the totality of the patient's pertinent clinical information.

and the present indications is the concept that diskography is not an initial screening examination but must follow other conservative therapies and non-invasive diagnostic techniques before its use and that it must have a definite role in assisting in the initiation or change in the patient's treatment regimen.

The primary purpose of diskography is to examine the intervertebral disk and determine whether that disk is painful and part of the patient's clinical syndrome. All efforts in standardizing the technique and validating it as a diagnostic tool have been directed at meeting this primary purpose. The list that follows largely includes the indications that would follow from this purpose. However, with the advent of percutaneous intradiskal therapies, including intradiskal electrothermal anuloplasty, and percutaneous diskectomy, there is now a need to establish a more complete analysis of herniations, particularly with regard to their containment, to properly recommend these newer therapies. To that purpose, the initial concept of diskography (disk picture) takes on a new role and, when added to post-diskography CT, is a valuable preoperative technique. Indications and contraindications for diskography are described in Table 11–1.

■ PATIENT SELECTION

"Indications for a diagnostic disk puncture is long standing sciatica, which was not improved by conservative treatment and which was myelographed by abrodil without definite localization of the disk protrusion."[77]

Since Lindblum wrote this first indication for clinical diskography, much has changed in terms of the anatomic and physiologic knowledge of nociception with regard to back and leg pain, as well as the diagnostic tools available to the spine physician. A common theme linking this historical

■ THE TECHNIQUE OF DISKOGRAPHY

Pre- and Peri-procedure Considerations

Before disk puncture, cervical, thoracic, or lumbar, a medical history and physical examination must be performed to ensure that there are no complications and the patient is an appropriate candidate for the procedure. If intravenous sedation is to be used, *NPO* status is verified to conform to institutional guidelines. In females of childbearing age, pregnancy must be ruled out.

Table 11–1

Indications and Contraindications for Diskography

Indications	*Absolute Contraindications*	*Relative Contraindications*
1. Failed conservative treatment of spinal pain	1. Unable or unwilling to consent to the procedure	1. Allergy to contrast medium, antibiotics, or local anesthetics
2. Pain is not acute or subacute	2. Inability to assess patient response during the procedure	2. Significant psychological overlay
3. Other pain generators have been ruled out	3. Inability of the patient to cooperate	3. Beard (cervical)
4. Symptoms that may reasonably be expected to be arising from the disk	4. Known localized or systemic infection	4. Spinal canal AP diameter <11 mm (cervical)
5. Symptoms severe enough to consider surgery or percutaneous treatment	5. Pregnancy	5. Any other condition, medical, anatomic, or psychological, that would increase the risk of performance of the examination to unsafe levels
6. Surgery is planned and the surgeon desires an assessment of the adjacent disk levels regarding internal morphology or pain generation	6. Anticoagulants or bleeding diathesis	
7. Ability to understand the nature of the technique and participate appropriately during the examination	7. Spinal canal AP diameter <10 mm (cervical)	

Any allergies to non-ionic water-soluble contrast media (iohexol or iopamidol) or other drugs used must be ascertained. If allergies are present, the risks versus benefits of the procedure must be weighed and discussed with the patient. Pretreatment regimens for allergies can be considered, including the use of corticosteroids and H_1 and H_2 blockers. If the risk for an allergic reaction to contrast is significant, the use of saline for the provocation aspect of the procedure can be considered. The use of gadolinium in place of iodinated contrast has been discussed in the literature.[184,185]

Informed consent is obtained with regard to the purpose of, risks and complications inherent in, and alternatives to the procedure. A discussion with the patient concerning the nature of diskography, specifically, the pain provocation aspect, is of the utmost importance. It is imperative that the patient be made aware that the procedure is potentially painful and that during stimulation of the disk, a description of this discomfort in terms of concordance and intensity as compared with the patient's ongoing complaint will be required.

Intravenous access is obtained before the procedure. Because diskitis (i.e., intradiskal infection) is the most common, though a rare complication, prophylactic antibiotic (cefazolin, 1 g; gentamicin, 80 mg; clindamycin, 900 mg; or ciprofloxacin, 400 mg) is administered intravenously within 30 minutes of needle insertion. Aminoglycosides are not indicated for pre-procedure prophylaxis.[186] In sheep studies, Fraser et al.[187] noted antibiotic levels in the anulus 30 minutes after intravenous administration, but none was demonstrated at 60 minutes. In addition to intravenous antibiotics, it has long been advocated that antibiotics be mixed with the contrast injected into the disk.[1,188-190] Klessig et al.[190] notes that cefazolin and gentamicin, 1 mg/mL, and clindamycin, 7.5 mg/mL, exceed the minimum inhibitory concentrations for the three most common organisms implicated in diskitis, *Escherichia coli*, *Staphylococcus aureus*, and *Staphylococcus epidermidis*.

Many patients experience varying degrees of anxiety and discomfort before and during diskography. It is the author's opinion that intravenous sedation enables the patient to tolerate the procedure and allows the physician to work on a physically quiet subject. Intravenous midazolam has been shown to be quite effective in providing sedation during diskography in doses between 2.0 and 5.0 mg. In addition, this versatile medication often renders the patient amnestic of the procedure. The ultrashort-acting hypnotic propofol is used by some injectionists who have an anesthesia background. This medication enables the practitioner to render the patient unconscious during the needle insertion portion of the study but awaken the patient rapidly for the provocation part of the procedure. This author questions the safety of performing any spinal injection or unconscious, unresponsive subjects. All medications used for sedation must be titrated to effect as per patient response. The ability of the patient to tolerate the procedure, while being oriented and conversant, is mandatory. The possibility of over-sedation and respiratory depression must be considered. Adequate monitoring, in addition to competence by the physician in airway management and resuscitation, is a minimum requirement.

Although controversial, the author feels that analgesic medications should not be administered routinely before or during diskography. Provocation diskography is a study in which a mechanical load is placed on individual interverte-bral disks, and any pain produced must be analyzed by the patient with regard to whether it reproduces the patient's ongoing (i.e., familiar and accustomed) pain. In addition, the intensity of the pain produced needs to be quantified in terms of the patient's usual pain level in regard to a visual or oral analog scale. The validity of the test is based on the patient's response to disk pressurization (i.e., pain provocation). Therefore, analgesics, which by definition attenuate the pain response, are contraindicated because their use precludes accurate assessment of the provoked pain by the patient.

Diskography can be performed in any procedure room appropriate for aseptic procedures. Safety concerns require imaging equipment that provides good visualization of the relevant spinal anatomy. This aspect is critically important when performing cervical or thoracic procedures. The ability to view the spine in anteroposterior (AP), lateral, and oblique views is mandatory. Although biplane fluoroscopy can be used, the majority of spinal injectionists today use C-arm fluoroscopic units. The ability to obtain many fluoroscopic views without repositioning the patient makes the use of a quality C-arm safe and efficient. Also required is a radiolucent procedure table, without metal side rails, that can be raised and lowered as needed. Monitoring equipment should include pulse oximetry, a non-invasive blood pressure device, and electrocardiography. Oxygen, airway supplies, drugs, and suction and other resuscitation equipment and supplies should be immediately available. Adequate personnel to monitor the patient and operate the fluoroscope are required.

Sterile technique requires preparation of the skin and draping analogous to that used for surgery. Ten percent povidone-iodine (Betadine solution) or DuraPrep (0.7% iodophor and 74% isopropyl alcohol), or both, is the preparation of choice. If the patient indicates allergies to the these preparations, chlorhexidine and alcohol can be safely substituted. Standard draping is used to provide a sterile field and may include the use of sterile towels and fenestrated drapes as per the injectionist's preference. The procedure room staff should be dressed in clean clothes (scrub suits). Masks and surgical caps are mandated for anyone coming in close proximity to the sterile field. The vast majority of injectionists scrub, gown, and glove as for an open surgical procedure. The C-arm image intensifier requires a sterile cover.

Before commencing with the diskography procedure, the levels to be injected, be they lumbar, thoracic, or cervical, must be selected. This selection is based on the results of physical examination, imaging studies, and the history (pain referral pattern). At the least, the most likely level and the two adjoining levels should be included. Rarely is it necessary to inject more than four segments. When injecting, the patient should be blinded regarding the onset and level being stimulated.

Lumbar Diskography Technique

As with all spinal injections, positioning of the patient facilitates the procedure in that it allows good visualization of the target structure, thereby providing, easy, precise, and safe access. For lumbar diskography the position varies, depending on the fluoroscopic equipment used. As noted earlier, most injectionists prefer to use a C-arm because of the ability to move the C-arm to obtain various views rather than repositioning the patient. Although the following description

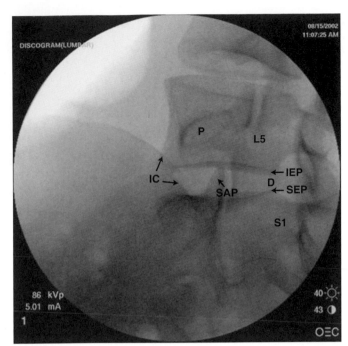

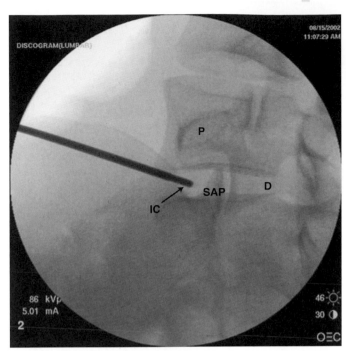

FIGURE 11–3 ■ Left oblique of the L5-S1 disk. D, intervertebral disk; IC, iliac crest; IEP, inferior end plate of L5; P, pedicle; SAP, superior articular process of SI; SEP, superior end plate of S1.

FIGURE 11–4 ■ Left oblique of the L5-S1 disk with target marked by pointer. *D*, intervertebral disk; *P*, pedicle; SAP, superior articular process of SI; IC, iliac crest.

assumes C-arm use, modifications in patient positioning can easily be made by the operator to facilitate performance of the procedure with a biplanar fluoroscope.

Historically, before the late 1960s, disk puncture was performed via a posterior (i.e., interpeduncular or transdural) approach. This technique is little used today because of the complications that are inevitable with any puncture of the dura. A lateral, or extrapedicular, approach[191,192] is now used except in rare situations.

The patient is placed in a prone position on the radiolucent procedure table with a pillow or other material under the abdomen to slightly flex the spine and decrease the normal lumbar lordotic curve. Monitoring and light sedation are initiated. The lower thoracic, lumbar, and upper sacral and gluteal regions are prepared and draped as discussed earlier.

The target disk is identified with an AP view. The image intensifier of the C-arm is then tilted in a cephalocaudad direction until the subchondral end plate of the vertebral body, caudad to the target disk, is parallel to the x-ray beam. The subchondral plate will be seen as a line rather than an oval. To ensure against the patient mistaking the discomfort from needle placement for provoked pain secondary to disk stimulation, the disk is preferentially approached from the opposite side of the patient's usual pain. In cases in which the pain is central or bilaterally equal or anatomic variation prevents disk puncture from the contralateral side of the pain, needle insertion from either side is appropriate.

After squaring of the end plate, the C-arm is rotated toward the side of needle insertion into an oblique view until the tip of the superior articular process of the level below appears to lie under the midpoint of the subchondral plate of the inferior end plate of the disk above (Figs. 11–3 and 11–4). Such positioning of the fluoroscope allows needles to be passed via "tunnel vision" (i.e., parallel to the beam of the fluoroscope when the skin puncture site is aligned with the target structure) just lateral to the superior articular process (Figs. 11–5 and 11–6). The needle will travel under the segmental nerve, (Figs. 11–5 and 11–7) which courses medial to lateral and dorsal to ventral, and will puncture the anulus fibrosus of the disk at the midpoint of the disk when seen in lateral and AP views.

Once the oblique view as just described is obtained, the skin overlying the target is marked (Figs. 11–4 and 11–6). A skin wheal is made with a 25-gauge, 1.5-inch needle containing 1% lidocaine (1 to 2 mL). A 25- or 22-gauge, 3.5-inch needle is then advanced, via "tunnel vision" (i.e., parallel to the x-ray beam), to the level of the superior articular process, and lidocaine (4 to 5 mL) is injected while withdrawing the needle to create an anesthetized tract. Care must be taken with slender individuals to ensure that local anesthetic is not placed within the foramen. If a foraminal injection were to occur, the segmental nerve might be anesthetized to such an extent that the forthcoming disk puncture needle might impale the nerve and cause lasting dysesthesia after the procedure. In addition, local anesthetic within the foramen might anesthetize the innervation of the disk (i.e., the sinu vertebral and ramus communicans nerves), which would alter the discomfort perceived during disk stimulation and create a false-negative response.

At this juncture, the injectionist can choose either a one- or two-needle technique. Before the routine administration of prophylactic antibiotics,[193] the rate of diskitis with the use of single needles without stylets was reported to be 2.7%, as opposed to 0.7% when a double-needle technique with stylets was used. In a technique involving the use of a single needle with a stylet, Aprill[189] has reported one case of diskitis in

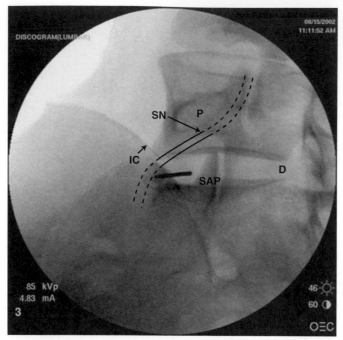

FIGURE 11–5 ■ Left oblique of the L5-S1 disk with an introducer needle in place. D, intervertebral disk; IC, iliac crest; P, pedicle; SAP, superior articular process; SN, L5 segmental nerve.

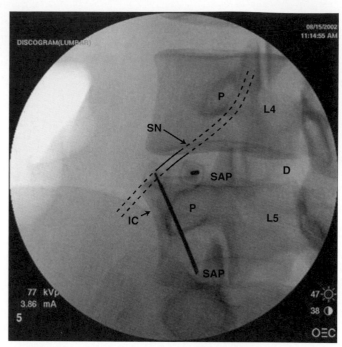

FIGURE 11–7 ■ Left oblique L4-5 with introducer needles in place at L4-5 and L5-S1. D, intervertebral disk; P, pedicles; SAP, superior articular process; IC, iliac crest; SN, L4 segmental nerve.

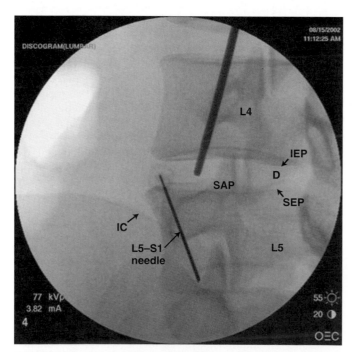

FIGURE 11–6 ■ Left oblique with L4-5 traget marked by pointer and L5-S1 introducer needle in place. D, intervertebral disk; IC, iliac crest; SAP, superior articular process; IEP, inferior end plate of L4; SEP, superior end plate of L5.

approximately 2000 patients (≈0.05% per patient). Both NASS[182] and ISIS[1] recommend a two-needle approach.

The two-needle technique involves the use of a shorter, larger-gauge introducer needle through which a longer, smaller-gauge needle is advanced past the tip of the introducer needle into the targeted intervertebral disk. The introducer needles are 18 or 22 gauge, 3.5 or 5 inches long, whereas complementary disk puncture needles are 22 or 25 gauge and 6 or 8 inches long. The body habitus of the patient dictates the combination of needles used at each level. Both the introducer and the disk puncture needles should have stylets to prevent skin from being picked up and introduced into the disk. The author advocates that a slight bend, opposite the bevel, be placed at the tip of the disk puncture needle to enable the operator to control the course of (i.e., "steer") the needle during advancement.[194-197]

The introducer needle is passed through the skin wheal at the skin puncture point via a down-the-beam, "tunnel vision" technique toward the disk entry site. Forward advancement is stopped at the approximate level of the superior articular process, although placement within, or slightly dorsal to, the foramen is acceptable. An AP view with the fluoroscope will indicate the needle tip lying at the lateral extent of the intervertebral disk (Fig. 11–8), whereas a lateral view is used to check needle depth (Fig. 11–9). The stylet is removed from the introducer, and the longer, smaller-gauge disk puncture needle is advanced slowly under active lateral fluoroscopy. The needle will be seen to traverse the intervertebral foramen, and firm resistance will be noted as the needle touches and enters the anulus fibrosus.

Because the ventral ramus crosses the posterolateral aspect of the disk in close proximity to the disk entry site, if radicular pain or dysesthesia is noted by the patient at any point during advancement of the needles, insertion of the needle is stopped, the needle is partially withdrawn, and the course is altered and redirected toward the disk. As discussed, a slight bend on the tip of the disk puncture needle facilitates this change in direction. If more aggressive direction changes are required, the introducer needle can be withdrawn and redirected as well.

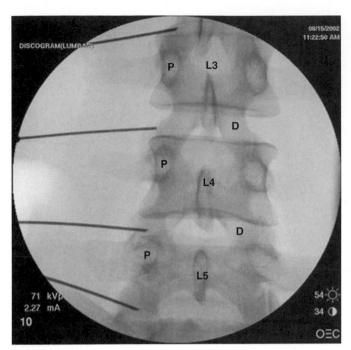

FIGURE 11–8 ■ Anteroposterior view of the lumbar spine with introducer needles in place. D, intervertebral disk; P, pedicle.

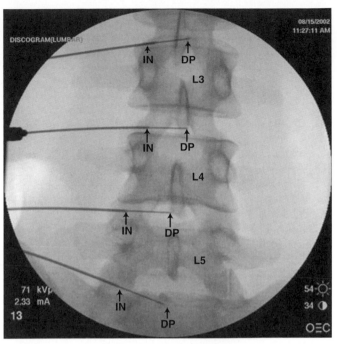

FIGURE 11–10 ■ Anteroposterior view of the lumbar spine with disk puncture needles in place. DP, disk puncture needle tips; IN, introducer needles tip.

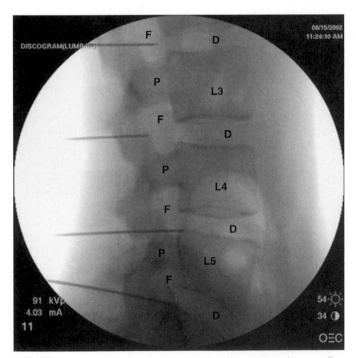

FIGURE 11–9 ■ Lateral view of the lumbar spine with introducer needles in place. D, intervertebral disks; F, intervertebral foramen; P, pedicles.

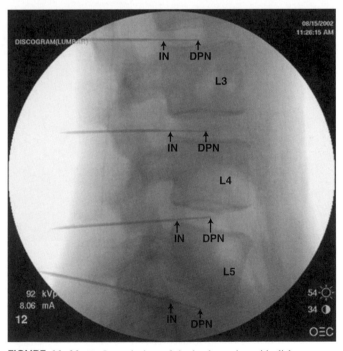

FIGURE 11–11 ■ Lateral view of the lumbar spine with disk puncture needles in place. DP, disk puncture needle tips; IN, introducer needle tips.

After contacting the anulus, the disk puncture needle should be advanced under active lateral fluoroscopy into the center of the disk (i.e., into the nucleus pulposus). Because the outer third of the anulus is abundantly supplied with nerve endings, some axial discomfort, with referral into the thigh or buttock, is often felt by the patient. AP and lateral projections are used to ensure good needle placement, with spot films saved for documentation before injection of contrast (Figs. 11–10 to 11–14).

Although the technique just presented can be used for disk puncture in >95% of lumbar disk levels, occasionally, because of anatomic variations (i.e., overriding iliac crest, osteophytes) or post-surgical changes (i.e., posterior intertransverse fusion mass or fusion hardware), variations in the

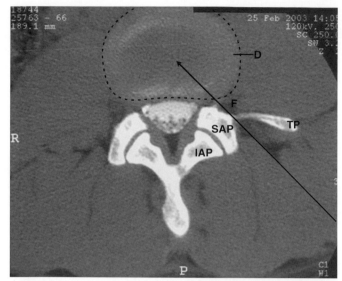

FIGURE 11–12 ■ Lumbar axial CT image at the L3-4 level with the needle path indicated. D, intervertebral disk; F, intervertebral foramen; IAP, inferior articular process; SAP, superior articular process; TP, transverse process.

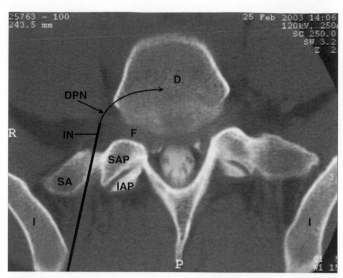

FIGURE 11–14 ■ Lumbar axial CT image at the L5-S1 level with the needle path indicated. Note that a curved disk puncture needle is required to enter the center of the disk. D, intervertebral disk; DPN, disk puncture needle; F, intervertebral foramen; I, ilium; IN, introducer needle; IP, inferior articular process; SA, sacral ala; SAP, superior articular process.

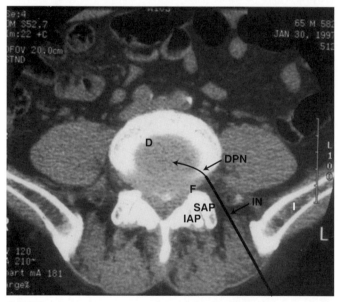

FIGURE 11–13 ■ Lumbar axial CT image at the L4-5 level with the needle path indicated. D, intervertebral disk; F, intervertebral foramen; I, ilium; IAP, inferior articular process; SAP, superior articular process; IN, introducer needle; DPN, disk puncture needle.

procedure must be implemented. A detailed description of the myriad modifications with which an injectionist might be faced is beyond the scope of this chapter; however, most involve either a more lateral or more medial needle insertion with the disk puncture needle bent or curved to varying degrees.

Rarely, the posterior interpedicular, transdural approach must be used to gain access to the disk. This approach increases the chance of morbidity because the dura is punctured twice. The risks and benefits of this technique must be weighed. At levels above the L2-3 intervertebral disk, the posterior approach should not be used because the chance of impaling the spinal cord is high.

Once all needles are positioned within the nucleus pulposus of the disks to be stimulated, injection can proceed. The patient should be blinded with regard to the disk level and initiation of the injection. At this point, the patient must be conversant in order to describe any sensations produced by stimulation of the disk.

Only non-ionic myelographic contrast agents (iohexol or iopamidol) with added antibiotic[190] should be used. Under active fluoroscopy, as the injectate is slowly instilled into the disk through a manometer-syringe (preferred) or a 3-mL syringe if a manometer cannot be obtained, the intrinsic, opening pressure of the disk is exceeded and contrast is seen to flow into the disk nucleus. As the nucleus is filled, the height of the disk space is known to increase rather than the axial cross-sectional area.[198] Pressure is applied slowly, in 0.5 aliquots, until one of four end points is noted: a 3-mL volume has been attained, significant pain is noted by the patient, an epidural or vascular pattern is evident, or a maximum pressure of 75 to 100 psi has been reached (Figs. 11–15 to 11–17).[163,199]

During pressurization of the disk, parameters of the injection are recorded on a standardized form by procedure room personnel. The disk level, volume injected, pressure generated, pain description (none, non-concordant, concordant), vocal or physical patient pain response, and pain intensity are the minimum required. Images, AP and lateral, of all disks injected must be saved for a permanent record of the study. These images should include AP and lateral both before and after contrast administration.

Although a 3-mL syringe has provided good results in the past, most experienced, well-versed diskographers now advocate the use of a manometer to accurately quantify the opening pressure and the pressure generated during disk injection. Derby et al.[139] have shown a correlation between surgical outcome and the pressure at which concordant pain is noted by the patient during disk stimulation. The opening pressure in supine patients, at levels known to be without anular dis-

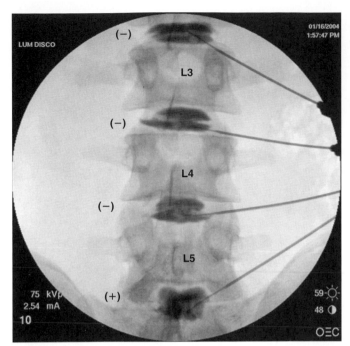

FIGURE 11–15 ■ Anteroposterior image of the lumbar spine with contrast within the intervertebral disks. (−), No provocation of concordant pain with injection; (+), positive provocation of concordant pain with injection.

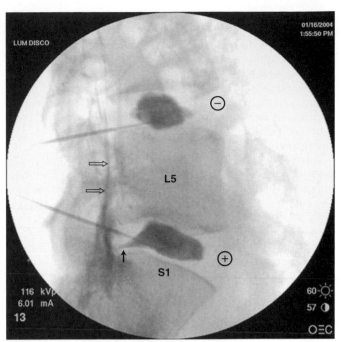

FIGURE 11–17 ■ Magnified lateral image of the lumbar spine with contrast within the intervertebral disks. (−), No provocation of concordant pain with injection; (+), positive provocation of concordant pain with injection; *open arrows*, epidural spread of contrast; *closed arrow*, anular disruption.

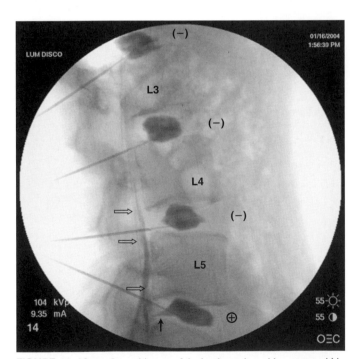

FIGURE 11–16 ■ Lateral image of the lumbar spine with contrast within the intervertebral disks. (−), No provocation of concordant pain with injection; (+), positive provocation of concordant pain with injection; *open arrows*, epidural spread of contrast; *closed arrow*, anular disruption.

ruption, is 20 to 25 psi, whereas disks with anular disruption, often have opening pressures of less than 15 psi.[138] Disks that when injected elicit positive concordant pain at <15 psi above opening pressure (30 to 40 psi end pressure) are said to be chemically sensitive and have a better prognosis after combined interbody/intertransverse fusion than after intertransverse fusion alone. Pauza et al.[200] supported this concept in

their study of intradiskal anular thermal lesioning. Patients who experience concordant pain with disk pressures between 15 and 50 psi above opening pressure (30 to 75 psi end pressure) are said to have an indeterminate response, whereas a positive response above 50 psi (65 to 75 psi) is not considered clinically significant.[1] With a 3-mL syringe it is difficult to maintain digital (thumb) pressure of greater than 60 to 75 psi.[189] Therefore, with the 3-mL syringe technique (i.e., non-manometric), pressures can be described as low or high with some degree of accuracy, and pressures that are considered "not clinically significant" are possibly excluded by the confines of the technique. Although exact quantification of pressure by manometry during provocation diskography should be considered the most appropriate technique, non-manometric studies should not automatically be assumed to be invalid especially when performed by experienced, well-trained diskographers.

Once all disks included in the study have been injected, if the stimulation part of the procedure produces concordant pain at one or more levels, a CT scan of the lumbar spine is mandated to ascertain the degree of internal architectural disruption within each level. Scout sagittal and axial views, including both bone and soft tissue windows of the levels studied, should be obtained.

Interpretation of Disk Stimulation and Imaging Studies

Diskography is based on the premise that placing a mechanical load on a symptomatic intervertebral disk will reproduce the patient's usual pain (i.e., reproduction of the pain is concordant with the ongoing complaint). The pain response must therefore be classified with respect to its location. In most cases, one of three descriptions can be used to characterize the discomfort provoked: (1) "no pain," (2) "non-concordant" (i.e., dissimilar) pain or pressure, or (3) "concordant" with the patient's familiar pain.

In addition to concordance of the pain, the severity of the response provoked must be of at least moderate to severe intensity (>6 on a 10-point visual analog, numerical rating, or other pain scale) to be considered a positive provocation. Acceptance of minimal to moderate pain or pressure as positive would increase the false-positive rate significantly.

IASP,[168] ISIS,[1] and PASSOR[183] stipulate that to be a valid study and make a diagnosis of diskogenic pain, an anatomic, internal control must be present. Therefore, provocation diskography cannot be considered valid if a single disk has been injected, even if it was shown to provoke pain. By the aforementioned criteria, the diagnosis of diskogenic pain is most ensured when a painful disk on stimulation is shown to have two adjacent asymptomatic levels.

The gross morphology of the internal disk architecture can be studied by examination of the nucleogram in lateral and AP fluoroscopic spot images. Pattern variations indicating abnormalities with regard to nuclear filling, degeneration of the disk substance, and radial fissures have been described.[10,86,201] Pain may not be associated with disk pathology. Full-thickness anular disruption, with contrast flow into the epidural space, is often encountered without a positive pain response. Because pain on injection is thought to be partially due to the mechanical load placed on the disk during pressurization, non-painful disks with large rents may not be capable of this pressurization, and therefore no painful response is forthcoming. Pathology does not equal pain.

Evaluation by axial CT imaging is integral to the diagnostic diskography study. At a minimum, CT axial images of each disk that shows evidence of concordant pain with stimulation are mandated. Axial images validate the procedure in that contrast is seen to fill the nucleus and reveals anular fissures.[202-205] Historically, post-diskography CT scans have been performed to make the diagnosis of disk herniation,[206-209] although today MRI is the "gold standard" for this diagnosis. Because CT imaging is an inherent part of diskography and not a separate imaging study per se, correlation between the two components of the test is mandatory, and separate interpretation of the CT scan by a physician not involved in the actual diskography is not appropriate.

As noted earlier, the outer third of the anulus, in contrast to the inner third, is known to have a high concentration of nerve endings.[57,58,210] One would expect a correlation between anular disruptions radiating into this area and pain. Because anular tears radiating into the outer third of the disk have been shown to be the primary indicator of diskogenic pain,[17,158,211] a grading scale of anular disruption has been developed[212] and modified.[158] The Modified Dallas Diskogram Scale is widely used in reporting findings on the axial post-diskogram CT scan images, and it describes five grades of anular fissures (Fig. 11–18).[213] Grade "0" indicates no anular disruption (Fig. 11–19). Grade I describes radial disruption into the inner third of the anulus, whereas in grade II, contrast has spread into the middle third of the anulus. Grade III and IV lesions both denote an anular fissure that has spread into the outer third of the anulus; they are differentiated by a grade IV lesion extending into a circumferential tear involving >30 degrees of the disk perimeter (Figs. 11–20 and 11–21). A grade V anular

FIGURE 11–18 ■ Grades of internal disk disruption. Grade "0," contrast confined to the nucleus pulposus, no anular disruption; grade 1, disruption involving the medial third of the anulus fibrosus; grade 2, disruption extending to the outer third of the anulus fibrosus; grade 3, disruption extending into the outer third of the anulus fibrosus with circumferential spread of contrast of <30 degrees; grade 4, disruption extending into the outer third of the anulus fibrosus with circumferential spread of contrast of >30 degrees; grade 5, disruption through the outer third of the anulus fibrosus with contrast outside the bounds of the intervertebral disk.

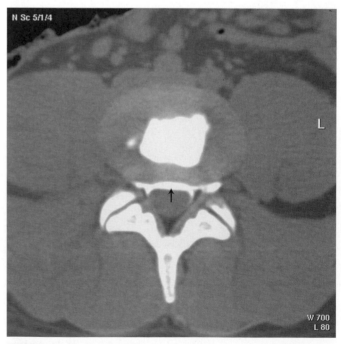

FIGURE 11–19 ■ Grade "0" anular disruption in a post-diskogram axial CT scan of the L4-5 disk from Figures 11–15 to 11–17. Contrast is confined to the nucleus pulposus. The *arrow* indicates epidural spread from a grade 5 anular disruption at the adjacent L5-S1 level.

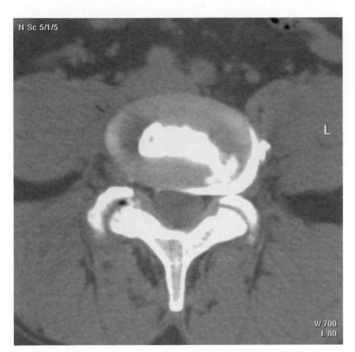

FIGURE 11–20 ■ Axial CT scan after diskography showing a grade 4 anular disruption. A fissure has extended into the outer third of the anulus with a circumferential fissure of >30 degrees.

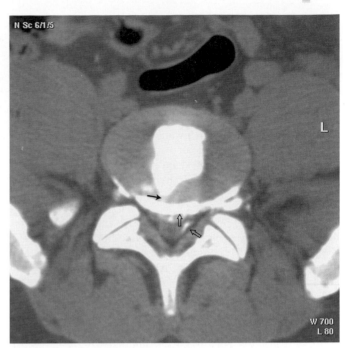

FIGURE 11–22 ■ Grade 5 anular disruption in a post-diskogram axial CT scan of the L5-S1 disk from Figures 11–15 to 11–17. A circumferential fissure of >30 degrees is noted with epidural spread of contrast. The *closed arrow* indicates posterior anular disruption; the *open arrows* indicate epidural spread (i.e., contrast outside the intervertebral disk).

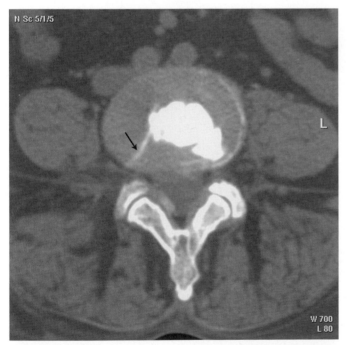

FIGURE 11–21 ■ Axial CT scan after diskography showing a grade 3 anular disruption. A fissure has extended into the outer third of the anulus with a circumferential fissure of <30 degrees. *Closed arrow,* needle tract.

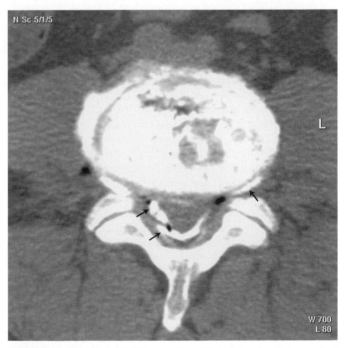

FIGURE 11–23 ■ Axial CT scan after diskography showing a marked degenerative pattern. No discrete nucleus pulposus or anulus fibrosus can be discerned. Spread of contrast throughout the intervertebral disk is an indication of complete disruption of the internal intervertebral disk anatomy. Arrows indicate contrast in epidural space and foramen.

disruption describes a full-thickness tear through the anulus with spread of contrast outside the confines of the disk (Figs. 11–22 and 11–23).

Once the procedure has been completed and all images examined, a diagnosis of diskogenic pain may be made if the following requirements are met[1]: (1) stimulation of the disk in question produces concordant pain, (2) the concordant pain is greater than 6 on a visual analog or equivalent scale, (3) the pain is produced at less than 50 psi above opening pressure when a manometer is used, and (4) an adjacent disk produces no pain when stimulated.

Though not widely used at present, a numeric scoring system in which points are awarded for the various criteria just presented has been devised[1] and, if used, should markedly decrease the frequency of false-positive studies.

Thoracic Diskography Technique

In the past, surgical procedures for the treatment of painful thoracic intervertebral disks were limited and diskography of the dorsal spine rarely indicated or requested. With newer, less invasive percutaneous disk procedures now an option—intradiskal anular thermal lesioning, percutaneous thoracic diskectomy, and others—thoracic disk stimulation is gaining in indications.

Because of the close proximity of the lung, which creates the real possibility of iatrogenic pneumothorax, and the relatively small target, thoracic disk stimulation is technically demanding and, as with cervical diskography, should be attempted only by injectionists whose skills have been well honed by significant experience in performing fluoroscopically guided procedures. The procedural technique as first described by Schellas, Pollei, and Dorwart[148] and recently codified[214] provides safe access to the thoracic intervertebral disk.

On a radiolucent procedure table, the patient is placed in the prone position. A thin pillow may be used under the chest or upper part of the abdomen to accentuate the normal kyphotic curve. The posterior thoracic and possibly the upper lumbar region is prepared and draped in a sterile manner. At each level to be studied the target disk is identified, and with a cephalocaudad tilt of the C-arm fluoroscope, the end plates are aligned so that they are parallel to the x-ray beam. The end plate will be seen as a linear rather than an ovoid structure. In most instances, needle placement will be from the side opposite the usual pain. If pain is in the midline, there is no preference with respect to the side of needle insertion. The C-arm is then rotated obliquely to the side where needle insertion will take place. The spinous processes will appear to move laterally toward the contralateral side, followed by the pedicle and rib head. When the pedicle is positioned approximately 40% of the distance across the vertebral body, rotation of the C-arm should cease. A rectangle or square hyperlucent area, or "box," will be evident and be bounded in the sagittal plane medially by the mid-interpedicular line (superior articular process and lamina) and laterally by a line connecting the medial aspect of the rib heads (costovertebral joints). In the axial plane, the rectangular hyperlucent area is delineated by the superior end plate of the vertebral body caudal to the targeted disk and the inferior end plate of the disk cephalad to the targeted disk (Fig. 11–24).

The skin is marked over the hyperlucent box (Fig. 11–25), local anesthetic is injected, and a 25- or 22-gauge, 3.5-inch needle with a slightly bent tip is inserted. Depending on target level and body habitus, a longer, 5-inch needle might be required. The needle is advanced toward the target in small increments with the frequent use of spot fluoroscopy. It is important to stay medial to the medial aspect of the rib heads (costovertebral joints) or the pleura may be penetrated. Often, as the needle is advanced, os will be contacted. By rotating the bent needle tip, continued advancement of the needle between the rib head and superior articular process

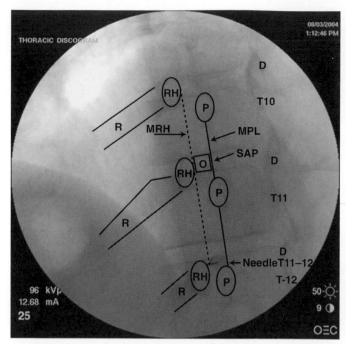

FIGURE 11–24 ■ Left oblique view of the thoracic spine at T10-11. *Closed arrow,* needle in position within the T11-12 intervertebral disk; D, intervertebral disk; MPL, projected midpedicular line; MRH, projected medial rib head line; P, pedicle; R, rib; RH, rib head; [o], target.

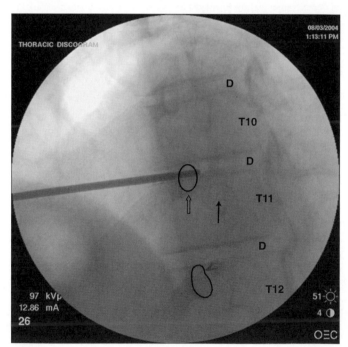

FIGURE 11–25 ■ Left oblique view of the thoracic spine. The pointer is indicating the target. *Closed arrow,* pedicle; D, intervertebral disk; *open arrow,* rib head.

should be accomplished without significant difficulty. Resistance will be met as the needle tip contacts the disk anulus (Fig. 11–26). After contacting the anulus, the disk is entered under active lateral fluoroscopic guidance and the needle positioned in the center of the disk.

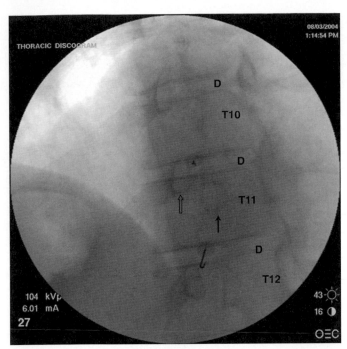

FIGURE 11–26 ■ Left oblique view of the thoracic spine. A needle in place at the T10-11 and T11-12 disks. *Closed arrow*, pedicle; D, intervertebral disk; *open arrow*, rib head.

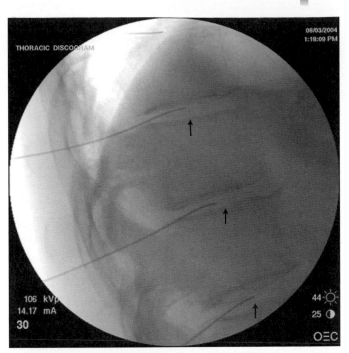

FIGURE 11–28 ■ Lateral view of the thoracic spine. Needles are in position within the intervertebral disks.

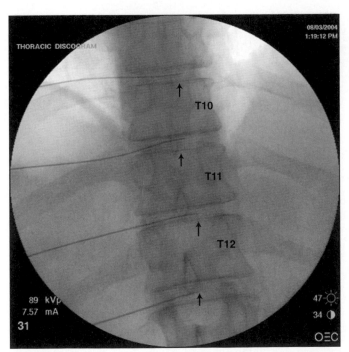

FIGURE 11–27 ■ Anteroposterior view of the thoracic spine. Needles are in position within the intervertebral disks.

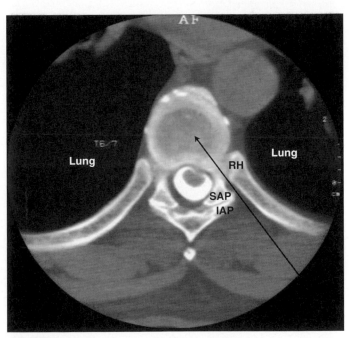

FIGURE 11–29 ■ Thoracic axial CT image at T6-7 with the needle path indicated. IAP, inferior articular process; RH, rib head; SAP, superior articular process.

Once needle position in the center of each disk is verified and documented by AP and lateral imaging (Figs. 11–27 and 11–28), contrast is injected under active lateral fluoroscopy. The capacity of injectate in a thoracic intervertebral disk with a competent anulus will range from 0.5 to 2.5 mL, depending on the level; capacity decreases as one proceeds cephalad from the lumbothoracic junction. During injection of contrast, the volume injected, the patient's pain response, the concordance of pain, the pressure generated or characteristic of the end point (none, soft, or firm), and the pattern of contrast within the disk, including anular competence, should be recorded. Spot AP and lateral films are saved (Figs. 11–30 and 11–31).

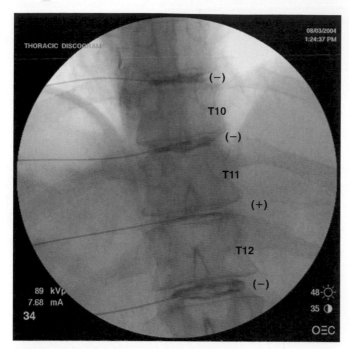

FIGURE 11–30 ■ Anteroposterior view of the thoracic spine. Contrast is seen within the intervertebral disks at T9-10 through T12-L1. (−), No provocation of concordant pain with injection; (+), positive provocation of concordant pain with injection; *arrow*, anular disruption with contrast seen outside the disk margin.

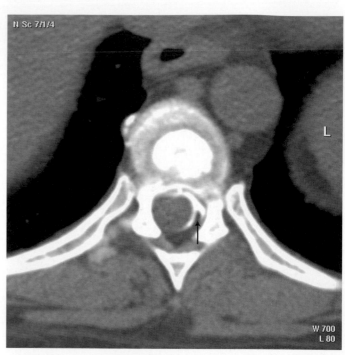

FIGURE 11–32 ■ Axial CT view of the thoracic spine through an intervertebral disk after diskography. Contrast is confined to the nucleus pulposus without anular disruption. The *arrow* indicates contrast within the epidural space from an adjacent level.

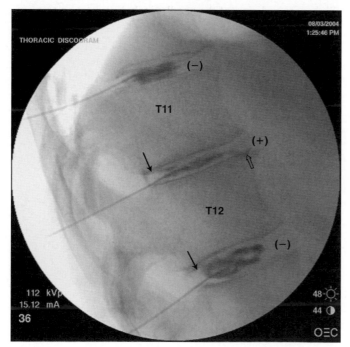

FIGURE 11–31 ■ Lateral view of the thoracic spine. Contrast is seen within the intervertebral disks at T10-11 through T12-L1. (−), No provocation of concordant pain with injection; (+), positive provocation of concordant pain with injection; *closed arrow*, posterior anular disruption; *open arrow*, anterior anular disruption.

After the procedure a CT scan will provide information on pathology involving the internal architecture of each injected intervertebral disk (Figs. 11–32 and 11–33).

Cervical Diskography Technique

The cervical region is a compact area with a high concentration of vulnerable structures; if these structures are violated, significant morbidity or mortality can occur. Cervical diskography is a technically demanding and unforgiving procedure that requires a precision gained only after much experience with fluoroscopically guided procedures. As with all diskography, the procedure should be performed only if positive results will be acted on (i.e., surgery or a percutaneous disk procedure is being contemplated).

Cervical diskography traces its history back to techniques described by Smith and Nichols[140] and Cloward.[215] Both authors discussed indications for the procedure[142,143] and surgical approaches to treatment.[215,216]

Cord compression or symptoms of myelopathy are absolute contraindications to the performance of cervical diskography. Iatrogenic disk herniation[217] and other severe untoward consequences can result from iatrogenic cord compression.[218] Therefore, before initiation of cervical diskography, high-quality CT or MRI scans, or both, must be examined by the injectionist to ensure that adequate reserve space within the spinal canal is present at the target level or levels to accommodate disk material possibly being forced into the canal during the procedure. Axial views should be examined to ensure a sagittal (i.e., AP) diameter of greater than 11 mm.[219] Patients with congenitally narrow spinal canals may not be candidates for this procedure.

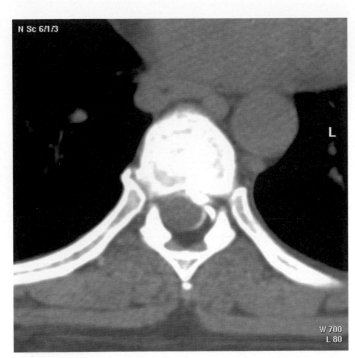

FIGURE 11–33 ■ Axial CT view of the thoracic spine at the level adjacent to that in Figure 11–32. A nucleus pulposus is seen with circumferential fissures within the anulus fibrosus and indicates marked disruption of the internal intervertebral disk anatomy. Epidural spread is noted in association with a significant disk protrusion.

A high-quality C-arm fluoroscopy unit is required. The patient is placed on a radiolucent procedure table in a supine position. A pillow or triangular sponge is positioned under the upper part of the thorax and shoulders to hyperextend the neck. Before preparation and draping of the skin, verification by pre-procedure fluoroscopic screening guarantees adequate visualization in the AP, lateral, and oblique views. Disk puncture should not be attempted at any level if all views cannot be obtained. Depending on the procedural technique used (see later discussion), the body of the C-arm will be either perpendicular to the patient on the left or at the head of the table.

The neck, including the mandible, clavicular regions, and shoulders, is prepared and draped in sterile fashion. Inclusion of the shoulders is necessary so that they may be depressed by the injectionist to improve lateral visualization of the C6-7 and C7-T1 disks. Beards prevent adequate preparation of the skin and must be removed before the procedure. Prophylactic antibiotic and light sedative medications are administered as previously discussed.

Because the esophagus lies toward the left at the lower cervical levels in most individuals, a right-sided approach is used for cervical disk access. The skin entry point will be along the medial margin of the sternocleidomastoid muscle with the needle tract running lateral to the trachea and esophagus and medial to the carotid artery. Depending on the target disk level, other structures may come into play. The hypopharynx can be distended at C2-3, and therefore a slightly more lateral approach is indicated. Thyroid cartilage is present at C5-6. A more medial approach is necessitated at C7-T1 to avoid the apex of the lung and the common carotid and thyroid arteries.

Although a double-needle technique has been described and advocated,[220] most cervical diskographers today use 25-

or 22-gauge, 3.5-inch needles with stylets.[219,221] As noted in the lumbar technique, a slight bend in the needle tip facilitates directional control. Local anesthetic, if used, should be limited to the skin because deeper infiltration may track along the cervical sympathetic chain and cause an alteration in the pain response.

Two alternative techniques are used by practitioners to gain access to the cervical disk. The traditional approach involves the use of the fluoroscope in an AP or slightly oblique view, whereas the alternative calls for a foraminal (i.e., anterior oblique) image. The actual needle insertion site and needle tract to the disk are virtually identical with both techniques, as demonstrated in cadaver studies by Dr. Charles Aprill[222] and this author.

With the traditional, more experience intensive, approach to the cervical intervertebral disk, the C-arm in an AP or slight right oblique view is used to identify the target level. Cephalocaudad tilt of the image intensifier is used to align the vertebral body end plates. Two hands are used, with the non-dominant middle and index fingers advanced toward the anterior aspect of the spine at the skin entry point. This digital pressure displaces the laryngeal structures medially, whereas the carotid artery is distracted laterally and can be palpated under the fingers. The spine is felt under the finger tips. With the dominant hand, the needle is then inserted either between, directly over, or under the fingers and, with active fluoroscopic guidance, advanced toward the right anterior-lateral aspect of the spine. Dr. Aprill[219] advocates directing the needle so that it touches the superior aspect of the vertebral body caudad to the disk in order to ascertain the depth of the disk. Slight manipulation of the needle, including rotation to make use of bevel control, is then performed to direct the needle into the disk anulus just medial to the uncinate process. With the use of a lateral view and active fluoroscopy, the needle is then advanced into the center of the disk. AP and lateral images are saved to document needle placement.

The alternative technique for cervical disk access has advantages that include ease of use, excellent visualization of the target disk, ability to use a down-the-beam (i.e., tunnel vision) approach, and minimal x-ray exposure to the hands. This approach is favored by the author. The fluoroscope is positioned at the head of the table. A right anterior oblique projection is used to visualize the intervertebral foramina at their greatest diameter (Fig. 11–34). The target disk is identified by counting down from C2-3, and the end plates are aligned by using cephalocaudad tilt of the image intensifier. A target on the disk is chosen that is approximately half the distance between the uncinate process and the anterior aspect of the disk. The skin entry site is marked with a sterile skin marker and should lie just medial to the sternocleidomastoid muscle and carotid artery (Fig. 11–35). If desired, a local anesthetic skin wheal can be made, although if 25-gauge needles are used, this is not necessary. A blunt sterile metal instrument is then pressed against the skin, over the entry point, until resistance by the underlying spine is felt. This decreases the distance between the skin and disk and distracts any vulnerable soft tissue structures away from the needle track. The position over the disk target is verified, and a 25- or 22-gauge needle is inserted at the tip of the instrument. With the assistance of active fluoroscopy the needle is quickly maneuvered toward the disk in one movement. The patient is asked to refrain from vocalization or swallowing during this

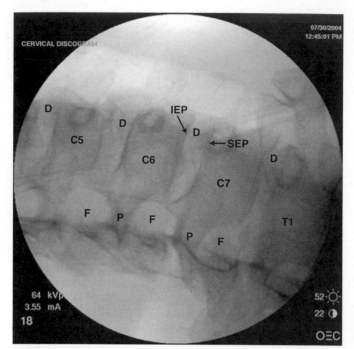

FIGURE 11–34 ■ Oblique-anterior view of the cervical spine, the "foraminal view." D, intervertebral disk; F, foramen; IEP, inferior end plate of C6; P, pedicle; SEP, superior end plate of C7.

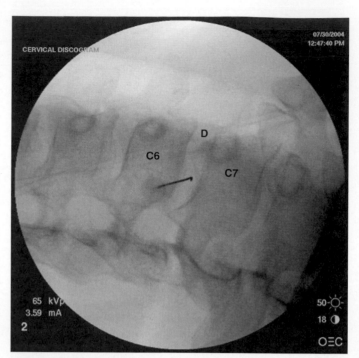

FIGURE 11–36 ■ Oblique view of the cervical spine with a needle in place in the C6-7 intervertebral disk. D, intervertebral disk.

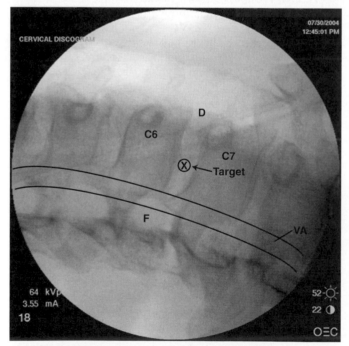

FIGURE 11–35 ■ Oblique view of the cervical spine with the target marked over C6-7 intervertebral disk. D, intervertebral disk; VA, position of the vertebral artery.

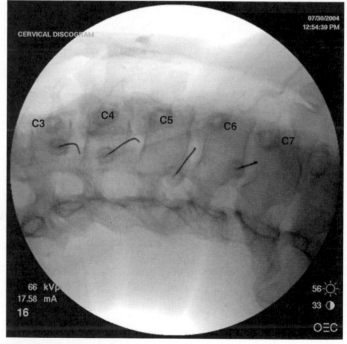

FIGURE 11–37 ■ Oblique view of the cervical spine with needles in position within the intervertebral disks C3-4 through C6-7.

portion of the procedure because movement of the soft tissue and larynx makes needle control difficult. Resistance to needle insertion is felt as the anulus is contacted and entered (Fig. 11–36). Active AP and lateral fluoroscopy is then used to advance the needle to the approximate center of the disk. Care must be taken to ensure that the needle will not be unintentionally advanced through the posterior aspect of the disk

and into the spinal canal. Once all needles are in place, AP, oblique, and lateral images are saved to document needle placement (Figs. 11–37 to 11–39).

Whether the traditional or alternative technique is used, once needle position at all disks to be studied is verified, the stylets are removed. A 3-mL Luer-Loc syringe with small-bore, minimal-volume, Luer-Loc extension tubing attached is

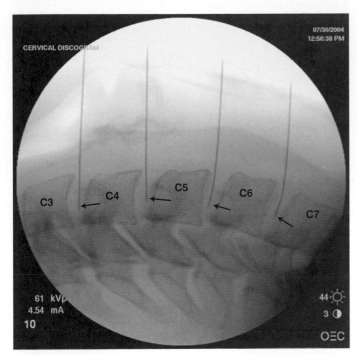

FIGURE 11–38 ■ Lateral view of the cervical spine with needles in place within the intervertebral disks C3-4 through C6-7. *Arrows* indicated needle tips in the approximate center of each disk.

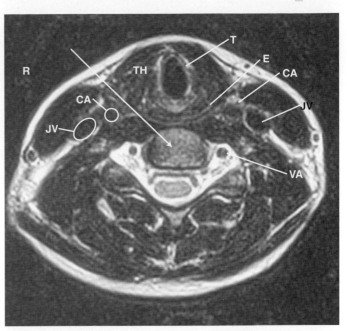

FIGURE 11–40 ■ Cervical axial CT view at C5-6 with the needle path indicated. CA, carotid artery; E, esophagus; JV, internal jugular vein; T, trachea; TH, thyroid; VA, vertebral artery.

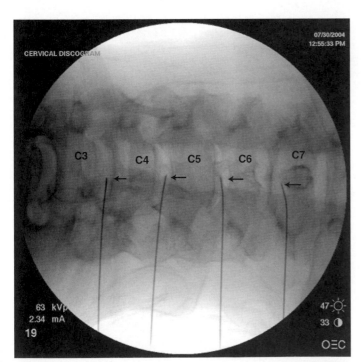

FIGURE 11–39 ■ Anteroposterior view of the cervical spine with needles in place within the intervertebral disks C3-4 through C6-7. *Arrows* indicated needle tips in the approximate center of each disk.

filled with contrast material, as described earlier, and connected to each needle. Care must be taken to ensure that the needles are not advanced or withdrawn during connection of the extension tubing. At the present time, manometry is used by few cervical diskographers because the literature on its benefit has not yet been advanced.

Active, lateral fluoroscopy is used during contrast injection (i.e., disk stimulation). The patient is blinded with respect to initiation of stimulation and the disk level. Injection into the disk proceeds by slowly increasing the pressure on the syringe until the intrinsic (i.e., opening) pressure of the disk is overcome and contrast is seen to flow into the nucleus pulposus. If injection of contrast into the disk is not forthcoming, slight rotation, advancement, or withdrawal of the needle frequently allows flow of contrast to be seen within the disk. Firm resistance is often noted with injection of as little as 0.2 mL, and separation of the disk end plates during injection is expected. Injection into a normal cervical intervertebral disk will be limited to less than 0.5 mL of solution[223] at a sustained high pressure.[224] Intervertebral disks that accept more than 0.5 mL of injectate will be seen to have evidence of abnormalities on imaging studies.

During disk stimulation, parameters of the injection are recorded on a standardized form by procedure room personnel. At a minimum, volume of injectate, the presence or absence of pain, the severity of pain, pain location and description, and concordance must be assessed at each level stimulated.[221] In addition, the pressure generated (soft versus a firm end point), and vocal or physical pain responses are often recorded. Because cervical disk stimulation is uncomfortable, even at non-pathologic levels, evaluation of the patient's response requires experience beyond that demanded by the technical aspects of the procedure. Individuals vary in their pain tolerance, and thus some degree of subjectivity is required by the diskographer.

As per the ISIS *Practice Guidelines*,[221] the injection end points include any of the following: concordant pain >6/10, neurologic symptoms reported by the patient, contrast solution escaping from the disk, displacement of the vertebral body end plates, firm resistance to injection, and the disk accepting no further volume at a reasonable pressure. To be

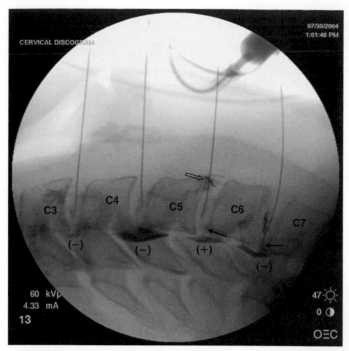

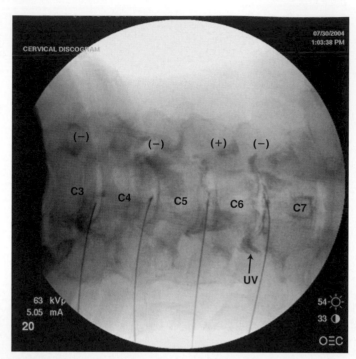

FIGURE 11–41 ■ Lateral view of the cervical spine after disk injection. (–), No provocation of concordant pain with injection; (+), positive provocation of concordant pain with injection; *closed arrow*, posterior anular disruption; *open arrow*, anterior anular disruption.

FIGURE 11–42 ■ Anteroposterior view of the cervical spine after disk injection. (–), No provocation of concordant pain with injection; (+), positive provocation of concordant pain with injection; UV, uncovertebral recess (joints of Luschka).

considered a valid study, a negative control level, without pain on stimulation, must be present.

Analgesic diskography,[146] or the injection of local anesthetic and corticosteroid into a painful, pathologic disk, has been advocated by some authors.[219,225] Although there is little consensus among diskographers concerning this practice, anecdotal experience has promoted its continued use.

AP and lateral images of all disks injected, both before and after injection of contrast, must be saved for a permanent record of the study (Figs. 11–41 and 11–42). These images confirm injection of contrast into the nucleus pulposus. However, because changes in the internal architecture of the disk are widespread in mature asymptomatic individuals, little in the way of diagnostic credibility is gained by images alone. Contrast seen to fill one or both of the uncovertebral recesses, or the joints of Luschka, is not a sign of abnormal degenerative changes but rather reflects the normal maturation of the cervical intervertebral disk.[219,226] A post-procedure CT scan may provide additional information and should be considered routine, especially if surgery is being contemplated (Figs. 11–43 and 11–44). However, with cervical diskography, because of the high frequency of internal disk disruption in non-symptomatic individuals, criteria for a diagnosis of diskogenic pain are based solely on the provocation of concordant pain rather than a combination of pain provocation and pathology by imaging studies as in the lumbar spine.

Post-procedure Considerations

After completion of the diskogram, independent of the level, sterile self-adhesive dressings are applied to the puncture wounds and the patient is taken to a recovery room with

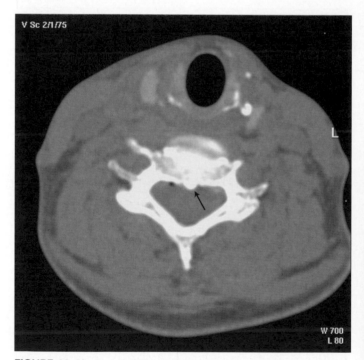

FIGURE 11–43 ■ Axial CT view of the cervical spine after diskography through the C4-5 disk from Figure 11–41. Stimulation of the disk was not painful, although significant disruption of the internal disk anatomy is present. The *arrow* indicates a small protrusion.

nurses trained to care for patients recovering from spinal injections. Periodic evaluation of the patient, including vital signs, level of comfort, level of consciousness, and visualization of the injection sites, is recommended. Analgesic medications, oral, intramuscular, or intravenous, are provided as

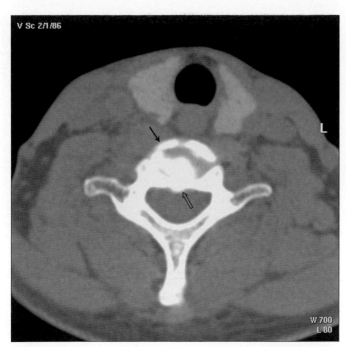

FIGURE 11–44 ■ Axial CT view of the cervical spine after diskography through the C5-6 disk from Figure 11–41. Stimulation of the disk elicited marked concordant pain. Significant anterior (*closed arrow*) and posterior (*open arrow*) disruption of the internal disk anatomy is present.

needed. Following the recovery period, once stable, the patient is taken for a post-diskogram CT to provide axial images of the injected disks if positive levels were noted.

Patients are observed for a minimum of 1 hour after the procedure and discharged home with a responsible adult. Discharge instructions include no driving the day of the procedure. The patient is told to expect some increase in discomfort for a few days after the procedure, and a limited prescription of oral analgesics is provided. Patients are encouraged to call if they feel any unusual or severe pain not relieved by the oral analgesics. Pneumothorax is discussed with all patients who have undergone diskography of the lower cervical and thoracic regions.

■ COMPLICATIONS

A myriad of complications after diskography have been well documented.[187,218,227,228] Complications can be inherent to disk penetration, the medications used, or unintentional misadventures involving needle placement. They range in severity from minor inconveniences, such as nausea and headache, to death.

Historically, diskitis is the most common complication of diskography, with a rate of less than 0.08% per disk injected.[182] Fraser, Osti, and Vernon-Roberts[229] provided evidence that all cases of diskitis are due to an infectious process, with the most common organisms being *S. aureus*, *S. epidermidis*, and *E. coli* from the skin, hypopharynx, esophagus, or bowel. The intervertebral disk is an excellent growth medium for bacteria because it is an essentially avascular structure. However, with the use of pre-procedure screening for chronic infections, strict aseptic preparation of the skin, needles with stylets, meticulous technique, and intravenous

and intradiskal antibiotics, diskitis is an exceedingly rare occurrence today.[188,219]

Whether occurring after diskography or a surgical procedure, diskitis is manifested in similar fashion.[193,230] A patient with diskitis usually has severe, intractable, debilitating pain of the cervical, thoracic, or lumbar spine days to weeks after the procedure; however, mild self-limited cases have been described.[210] Diskitis needs to be ruled out in any post-diskogram patient who notes a change in the severity or quality of the pain after the procedure. The work-up consists of obtaining laboratory and imaging studies. C-reactive protein levels will increase within days of the onset, whereas the sedimentation rate may remain in the normal range for over a month. Blood cultures and a complete blood count will be negative until the end plates are breached. MRI is the imaging study of choice,[231-233] with hyperemia of the end plates and marrow space changes noted on T2-weighted images 3 to 4 days after the onset of symptoms. Radionuclide bone scanning has been shown to be inferior to MRI in specificity and sensitivity.[234] If an adequate sample of tissue can be obtained, disk aspiration or biopsy, or both, will be positive in the acute phase of diskitis, but once the end plates are violated, a sterile environment is soon noted in response to the patient's immune system.[219]

Consultations with a spine surgeon and infectious disease specialist are appropriate. Treatment of infections within the disk and sepsis often requires antibiotic therapy. Though rare, abscess or empyema[235-237] may necessitate surgical intervention.

The cervical canal has little in the way of reserve space. Because disk herniation[217] and severe morbidity as a result of cord compression[218] have been reported after diskography, adequate reserve within the cervical spinal canal must be ensured before cervical diskography. A sagittal diameter of 11 mm or greater by CT or MRI provides an adequate margin of safety, whereas diameters of less than 11 mm at the proposed level should be viewed as a relative contraindication to proceeding with cervical disk injection. Evidence of myelopathy or cord compression is an absolute contraindication to the performance of diskography at the affected level.

The cervical region has many vulnerable structures packed in a small area. Although vascular structures are plentiful, penetration of a vein or artery will rarely cause any significant problems. Poor technique can result in penetration of the cord either during insertion of the needle or when connecting the syringe to the needle. Good visualization and verification of needle position are mandatory during all parts of the procedure.

Pneumothorax must be considered if marked shortness of breath occurs in a patient who has undergone diskography at levels between C6-7 and T12-L1.

Boswell and Wolfe[238] described a case in which intractable seizures, coma, and death developed in a woman after diskography. Their conclusion was that unintentional intrathecal administration of cefazolin (12.5 mg/mL), which had been included in the contrast agent for prophylaxis of infection, precipitated this catastrophic event.

As with any diagnostic spinal injection procedure, diskography, be it cervical, thoracic, or lumbar, can be performed in a safe manner with the appropriate training and vigilance. However, diskography is more than a technique. Analysis of data obtained from the procedure, along with knowledge of the patient's history, clinical features, and psychological condition, must be considered before a final diagnosis is determined. A highly invasive procedure may be performed on the basis on your findings, and therefore meticulous technique and awareness of the procedure's limitations are of utmost importance.

■ SUMMARY

Although the history of provocation diskography has been controversial, today it is well regarded as the only diagnostic modality that can be used to determine whether an intervertebral disk is painful to mechanical forces. In addition, it is the standard for diagnosing diskogenic pain secondary to internal disk disruption.[1,239,240] The technique has been endorsed by the majority of professional organizations whose interests lie in advancing knowledge of the spine and its myriad pathologies. In the future, although refinements in our use and interpretation of diskography are certain to occur, the procedure will continue to provide information about our patients' afflictions and guide the treatment modalities offered.

Acknowledgment

I wish to acknowledge the contribution of John D. Fisk, MD, of Precision Diagnostics, Dallas, to the section on the history of diskography.

References

1. Heschel AJ: The patient as a person. Paper presented to the American Medical Association, San Francisco, 1964.
1a. Endres S, Bogduk N: Lumbar disc stimulation (provocation discography). In Bogduk N (ed): Practice Guidelines for Spinal Diagnostic and Treatment Procedures. San Francisco, International Spine Intervention Society, 2005, pp 20-46.
2. Lawrence J: Disc degeneration. Its frequency and relationship to symptoms. Ann Rheum Dis 28:121, 1969.
3. Hult L: The Munkford investigation. Acta Orthop Scand Suppl 16:1, 1954.
4. Hult L: Cervical dorsal and lumbar spinal syndromes. Acta Orthop Scand Suppl 17:1, 1954.
5. Hult L: Frequency of symptoms for different age groups and professions. In Hirsch C, Zotterman Y (eds): Cervical Pain. New York, Pergamon Press, 1971, p 14.
6. Smyth M, Wright V: Sciatica and the intervertebral disc. An experimental study. J Bone Joint Surg Am 40:1401, 1959.
7. Bogduk N, Govind J: Acute Lumbar Radicular Pain: An Evidenced-Based Approach. Newcastle, Australia, Newcastle Bone and Joint Institute, 1999.
8. Bogduk N: Acute Cervical Radicular Pain: An Evidenced-Based Approach. Newcastle, Australia, Newcastle Bone and Joint Institute, 1999.
9. Deyo RA, Tsui-Wu YJ: Descriptive epidemiology of low back pain and its related medical care in the United States. Spine 12:264, 1987.
10. Friberg S: Lumbar disc degeneration in the problem of lumbago sciatica. Bull Hosp Jt Dis 15:1, 1954.
11. Horal J: The clinical appearance of low back pain disorders in the city of Gothenburg, Sweden. Acta Orthop Scand Suppl 118:1, 1969.
12. Mooney V: Where is the pain coming from. Spine 12:754, 1987.
13. Maigne JY, Aivaliklis A, Pfefer F: Results of sacroiliac joint double block and the value of sacroiliac pain provocation tests in 54 patients with low back pain. Spine 21:1889, 1996.
14. Schwartzer AC, Aprill CN, Bogduk N: The sacroiliac joint in chronic low back pain. Spine 20:31, 1995.
15. Schwartzer AC, Aprill, CN, Derby R, et al: Clinical features of patients with pain stemming from the lumbar zygapophysial joints. Is the lumbar facet syndrome a clinical entity? Spine 19:1132, 1994.
16. Schwartzer AC, Wang S, Bogduk N, et al: Prevalence and clinical features of lumbar zygapophysial joint pain: A study in a Australian population with chronic low back pain. Ann Rheum Dis 54:100, 1995.
17. Moneta GB, Videman T, Kaivanto K, et al: Reported pain during lumbar discography as a function of annular ruptures and disc degeneration. Spine 17:1968, 1994.
18. Bogduk N: Clinical Anatomy of the Lumbar Spine and Sacrum, 3rd ed. London, Churchill Livingstone, 1997, p 207.
19. Schwartzer AC, Aprill, CN, Derby R, et al: The prevalence and clinical features of internal disc disruption in patients with chronic low back pain. Spine 20:1878, 1995.
20. Coventry MB, Ghormley RK, Kernohan JW: The intervertebral disc: Its microscopic anatomy and pathology. J Bone Joint Surg 27:105, 1945.
21. Inoue H: Three dimensional architecture of lumbar intervertebral discs. Spine 6:1386, 1981.
22. Beard HK, Stevens RL: Biochemical changes in the intervertebral disc. In Jayson MIV (ed): The Lumbar Spine and Backache, 2nd ed. London, Pitman, 1980, p 407.
23. Gower WE, Pedrini V: Age related variation in protein polysaccharides from human nucleus pulposus, annulus fibrosus and costal cartilage. J Bone Joint Surg Am 51:1154, 1969.
24. Naylor A: Intervertebral disc prolapse and degeneration. The biochemical and biophysical approach. Spine 1:108, 1976.
25. Naylor A, Shental R: Biochemical aspects of intervertebral discs in aging and disease. In Jayson MIV (ed): The Lumbar Spine and Backache. New York, Grune & Stratton, 1976, p 317.
26. Schmorl G, Junghans H: The Human Spine in Health and Disease, 2nd Am ed. Orlando, FL, Grune & Stratton, 1971, p 18.
27. Bushell GR, Ghosh P, Taylor TKF, et al: Proteoglycan chemistry of the intervertebral disks. Clin Orthop 129:115, 1977.
28. Dickson IR, Happey F, Pearson CH, et al: Variations in the protein components of human intervertebral disk with age. Nature 215:52, 1967.
29. Melrose J, Ghosh P: The noncollagenous proteins of the intervertebral disc. In Ghosh P (ed): The Biology of the Intervertebral Disc, vol 1. Boca Raton, FL, CRC Press, 1988, p 189.
30. Taylor TKF, Little K: Intercellular matrix of the intervertebral disk in aging and in prolapse. Nature 208:384, 1965.
31. Adams P, Eyre DR, Muir H: Biochemical aspects of development and ageing of human lumbar intervertebral discs. Rheumatol Rehabil 16:22, 1977.
32. Buckwalter JA, Cooper RR, Maynard JA: Elastic fibers in human intervertebral disks. J Bone Joint Surg Am 58:73, 1976.
33. Hickey DS, Hukins DWL: Collagen fibril diameters and elastic fibers in the annulus fibrosus of human fetal intervertebral disc. J Anat 133:351, 1981.
34. Hickey DS, Hukins DWL: Aging changes in the macromolecular organization of the intervertebral disc. An X-ray diffraction and electron microscope study. Spine 7:234, 1982.
35. Johnson EF, Berryman H, Mitchell R, et al: Elastic fibres in the annulus fibrosus of the human lumbar intervertebral disc. A preliminary report. J Anat 143:57, 1985.
36. Best, BA, Guilak F, Setton LA, et al: Compressive mechanical properties of the human anulus fibrosus and their relationship to biochemical composition. Spine 19:212, 1994.
37. Taylor JR: Regional variation in the development and position of the notochordal segments of the human nucleus pulposus. J Anat 110:131, 1971.
38. Oda J, Tanaka H, Tsuzuki N: Intervertebral disc changes with aging of human cervical vertebra: From neonate to the eighties. Spine 13:1205, 1988.
39. Payne EE, Spillane JD: The cervical spine. Brain 80:571, 1957.
40. Hirsch C, Schajowicz R, Galante J: Structural changes in the cervical spine. A study on autopsy specimens in different age groups. Acta Orthop Scand Suppl 109:7, 1967.
41. Sherk H, Parke W: Developmental anatomy. In Bailey RW (ed): The Cervical Spine. Philadelphia, JB Lippincott, 1983, p 7.
42. Mercer S, Bogduk N: The ligaments and annulus fibrosus of the human adult cervical intervertebral discs. Spine 24:619, 1999.
43. Mercer S: The new anatomy of the thoracic intervertebral disc. Paper presented at the Annual Scientific Meeting of the International Spinal Injection Society, 2000, San Francisco.
44. Bogduk N: Clinical Anatomy of the Lumbar Spine and Sacrum, 3rd ed. Edinburgh, Churchill Livingston, 1999.

45. Holm S, Maroudas A, Urban J, et al: Nutrition of the intervertebral disc: Solute transport and metabolism. Connect Tissue Res 8:101, 1983.

46. Maroudas A, Nachemson A, Stockwell R, et al: Some factors involved in the nutrition of the intervertebral disc. J Anat 120:113, 1975.

47. Urban J, Holm S, Maroudas A: Diffusion of small solutes into the intervertebral disc. Biorheology 15:203, 1978.

48. Roofe PG: Innervation of the annulus fibrosus and posterior longitudinal ligament. Arch Neurol Psychiatry 44:100, 1940.

49. Wiberg G: Back pain in relation to the nerve supply of the intervertebral disc. Acta Orthop Scand 19:211, 1947.

50. Inman VT, Saunders JBCM: Anatomicrophysiological aspects of injuries to the intervertebral disc. J Bone Joint Surg 29:461-475, 1947.

51. Ikari C: A study of the mechanism of low back pain. The neurohistological examination of the disease. J Bone Joint Surg Am 36:195, 1954.

52. Lamb DW: The neurology of spinal pain. Phys Ther 59:971, 1979.

53. Anderson J: Pathogenesis of low back pain. In Grahame R, Anderson J (eds): Low Back Pain, vol 2. Eden Press, Westmount, UK (England), 1980, p 23.

54. Wyke B: The neurology of low back pain. In Jayson MIV (ed): The Lumbar Spine and Back Pain, 2nd ed. Tunbridge Wells, Pitman, England (UK), 1980, p 265.

55. Bogduk N, Tynan W, Wilson AS: The nerve supply to the human lumbar intervertebral disc. J Anat 132:39, 1981.

56. Groen GJ, Baljet B, Drukker J: Nerves and nerve plexuses of the human vertebral column. Am J Anat 188:282, 1990.

57. Yoshizawa H, O'Brian JP, Thomas-Smith W, Trumper M: The neuropathology of intervertebral discs removed for low back pain. J Pathol 132:95, 1980.

58. Malinsky J: The ontogenic development of nerve terminations in the intervertebral discs of man. Acta Anat 38:96, 1959.

59. Rabischong P, Louis R, Vignaud J, et al: The intervertebral disc. Anat Clin 1:55, 1978.

60. Groen GJ, Baljet B, Drukker J: Nerves and nerve plexuses of the human vertebral column. Am J Anat 188:282, 1990.

61. Konttinen YT, Gronblad M, Antti-Poika I, et al: Neuroimmunohistochemical analysis of peridiscal nociceptive neural elements. Spine 15:383, 1990.

62. Korkala O, Gronblad M, Liesi P, et al: Immunohistochemical demonstration of nociceptors in the ligamentous structures of the lumbar spine. Spine 10:156, 1985.

63. Coppes MH, Marani E, Thomeer RT, Groen GJ: Innervation of painful lumbar discs. Spine 22:2342, 1997.

64. Freemont AJ, Peacock TE, Goupille P, et al: Nerve ingrowth into diseased intervertebral disc in chronic back pain. Lancet 350:178, 1997.

65. Freemont AJ, Watkins A, LeMaitre C, et al: Nerve growth factor expression and innervation of the painful intervertebral disc. J Pathol 197:286, 2002.

66. Jaffray D, O'Brien JP: Isolated intervertebral disc resorption: A source of mechanical and inflammatory back pain? Spine 11:397, 1986.

67. Nachemson A: Intradiscal measurements of pH in patients with lumbar rhizopathies. Acta Orthop Scand 40:23, 1969.

68. Fanson R, Saal JS, Saal JF: Human disc phospholipase A_2 is inflammatory. Spine 17(Suppl):s190, 1992.

69. Kitano T, Zerwekh J, Usui Y, et al: Biochemical changes associated with the symptomatic human intervertebral disc. Clin Orthop 293:372, 1993.

70. Weinstein J, Claverie W, Gibson S: The pain of discography. Spine 13:1344, 1988.

71. Schmorl G, Junghans H: The Human Spine in Health and Disease. New York, Grune & Stratton, 1959.

72. Mixter WJ, Barr JS: Rupture of the intervertebral disc with involvement of the spinal canal. N Engl J Med 211:210, 1934.

73. Lindgren E: Paper read before the Swedish Radiologic Society (not printed), ref Lindblom K, 1948.

74. Pease CN: Injuries to the vertebrae and intervertebral discs following lumbar puncture. Am J Dis Child 49:849, 1935.

75. Hirsch C: An attempt to diagnose level of disc lesion clinically by disc puncture. Acta Orthop Scand 18:131, 1948.

76. Lindblom K: Protrusions of the discs and nerve compression in the lumbar region. Acta Orthop Scand 25:195, 1944.

77. Lindblom K: Diagnostic puncture of the intervertebral discs in sciatica. Acta Orthop Scand 17:231, 1948.

78. Lindblom K: Techniques and results in myelography and disc puncture. Acta Radiol Scand 34:321, 1950.

79. Lindblom K: Discography of dissecting transosseous ruptures of the intervertebral discs in the lumbar region. Acta Radiol Scand 36:12, 1951.

80. Lindblom K: Technique and results of diagnostic disc puncture and injection (discography) in the lumbar region. Acta Orthop Scand 20:315, 1951.

81. Lindblom K: Protrusions of the discs and nerve compression in the lumbar region. Acta Orthop Scand 25:195, 1944.

82. Key JA, Ford LT: Experimental intervertebral disc lesions. J Bone Joint Surg Am 30:621, 1948.

83. Frieberg S: Low back pain and sciatica by intervertebral disc herniation. Anatomical and clinical investigations. Acta Chirurg Scand (Suppl 1) 85:64, 1941.

84. Perey O: Contrast medium examination of intervertebral discs of the lumbar spine. Acta Orthop Scand 20:327, 1950.

85. Wise RE, Weiford EC: Xray visualization of the intervertebral disc. Report of a case. Cleve Clin Q 15:127, 1951.

86. Erlacher PR: Nucleography. J Bone Joint Surg Br 34:204, 1952.

87. Cloward RB, Busaid LL: Discography. Technique, indications and evaluation of normal and abnormal intervertebral discs. AJR Am J Roentgenol 68:552, 1952.

88. Fernstrom U: A discographical study of ruptured lumbar intervertebral discs. Acta Chir Scand Suppl 258:1, 1960.

89. Butt WP: Lumbar discography. J Can Assoc Radiol 14:172, 1963.

90. Collis JS, Gardner WJ: Lumbar discography. An analysis of one thousand cases. J Neurosurg 19:452, 1962.

91. Friedman J, Goldner MZ: Discography in evaluation of lumbar disk lesions. Radiology 65:653, 1955.

92. Gardner WJ, Wise R, Hughes C, et al: Xray visualization of the intervertebral disc with a consideration of the morbidity of disc puncture. Arch Surg 64:355, 1952.

93. Walk L: Clinical significance of discography. Acta Radiol 46:36, 1956.

94. Wolkin J: Comparative studies of discography and myelography. Radiology 64:704, 1955.

95. Altenstein G: Erfahrungen mit der Diskographie an Hals und Lendenwirbelsaule. Z Orthop 102:358, 1967.

96. Bettag W, Grote W: Die Bedeutung der Diskographie fur die Behandlung des Zervikalsundroms. Hippokrates 40:138, 1969.

97. Grote W, Wappenschmidt J: Uber Technik und Indication zur-zervikalen Diskographie. Rofo Fortschr Geb Rontgenstr Neuen Bildgeb Verfahr 106:721, 1967.

98. Massare C, Bard M, Tristan H: Cervical discography. Speculation on technique and indications from our experience. J Radiol 55:395, 1974.

99. Pascaud JL, Mailes F, Pascaud, E, et al: The cervical intervertebral disc: Diagnostic value of cervical discography in degenerative and post-traumatic lesions. Ann Radiol (Paris) 23:455, 1980.

100. Schaerer JP: Anterior cervical disc removal and fusion. Schweiz Neurol Neurochir Psychiatry 102:331, 1968.

101. Stuck RM: Cervical discography. AJR Am J Roentgenol 86:975, 1961.

102. Riley LH Jr, Robinson RA, Johnson KA, Walker AE: The results of anterior interbody fusion of the cervical spine. Review of 93 consecutive cases. J Neurosurg 30:127, 1969.

103. Simmons EH, Segil CM: An evaluation of discography in the localization of symptomatic levels in discogenic disease of the spine. Clin Orthop 108:57, 1975.

104. Hartjes H, Roosen K, Grote W, et al: Cervical disc syndromes: Value of metrizamide myelography and discography. AJNR Am J Neuroradiol 4:644, 1983.

105. Collis JS, Gardner WJ: Lumbar discography. An analysis of one thousand cases. J Neurosurg 19:45261, 1962.

106. Nordlander S, Salen EF, Unander-Scharin L: Discography in low back pain and sciatica; analysis of 73 operated cases. Acta Orthop Scand 28:90, 1958.

107. Vezina JL, Fontaine S, LaPerrierre J: Outpatient myelography with fine needle technique: An appraisal. AJNR Am J Neuroradiol 10:615, 1989.

108. Sackett J, Strother C: New Techniques in Myelography. Hagerstown, MD, Harper & Row, 1979.

109. Meyer GA, Haughton VM, Williams AL: Diagnosis of lumbar herniated disc with computed tomography. N Engl J Med 301:1166, 1979.

110. Williams A, Haughton V, Meyer G, Ho K: Computed topographic appearance of the bulging annulus. Radiology 142:403, 1982.

111. Williams AL, Haughton V, Daniels DL, Grogen JP: Differential CT diagnosis of extruded nucleus pulposus. Radiology 148:141, 1983.

112. Wilmink JT: CT morphology of intrathecal lumbosacral nerve-root compression. AJNR Am J Neuroradiol 10:233, 1989.

113. Badami JP, Norman D, Barbaro N: Metrizamide CT myelography in cervical myelopathy and radiculopathy: Correlation with conventional myelography and surgical findings. AJNR Am J Neuroradiol 144:675, 1985.

114. Scotti G, Scialfa G, Pieralli S, et al: Myelopathy and radiculopathy due to cervical spondylosis: Myelographic-CT correlations. AJNR Am J Neuroradiol 4:601, 1983.

115. Daniels DL, Grogan JP, Johansen JG, et al: Cervical radiculopathy: Computed tomography and myelography compared. Radiology 151:109, 1984.

116. Videman T, Malmivaara A, Mooney V: The value of axial view in assessing discograms. An experimental study with cadavers. Spine 12:299, 1987.

117. Modic MT, Pavlicek W, Weinstein M: Magnetic resonance imaging of intervertebral disc disease. Radiology 152:103, 1984.

118. Masaryk TJ, Ross JS, Modic MT, et al: High resolution MR imaging of sequestered lumbar intervertebral disc. AJR Am J Roentgenol 150:1155, 1988.

119. VanDyke C, Ross JS, Tkach J, et al: Gradient-echo MR imaging of the cervical spine: Evaluation of extradural disease. AJR Am J Roentgenol 153:393, 1989.

120. Reicher M, Gold R, Jalback V, et al: MR imaging of the lumbar spine: Anatomic correlations and the effect of technical variations. AJR Am J Roentgenol 147:891, 1986.

121. Yu SW, Sether LA, Ho PS: Tears of the annulus fibrosus: A correlation between MR and pathologic findings in cadavers. AJR Am J Roentgenol 9:367, 1988.

122. Yasuma T, Makino E, Saito S, et al : Histological development of intervertebral disc herniation. J Bone Joint Surg Am 68:1066, 1986.

123. Gibson MJ, Buckley J, Mawhinney R, et al: Magnetic resonance imaging and discography in the diagnosis of disc degeneration. A comparative study of 50 discs. J Bone Joint Surg Br 68:369, 1986.

124. Schneiderman G, Flannigan B, Kingston S, et al: Magnetic resonance imaging in the diagnosis of disc degeneration: Correlation with discography. Spine 12:276, 1987.

125. Yu SW, Haughton VM, Sether LA, Wagner M: Comparison of MR and diskography in detecting radial tears of the annulus: A postmortem study. AJNR Am J Neuroradiol 10:1077, 1989.

126. Ross JS, Modic MT, Masaryk TJ: Tears in the annulus fibrosus: Assessment with Gd-DTPA–enhanced MR imaging. AJNR Am J Neuroradiol 10:1251, 1989.

127. Zucherman J, Derby R, Hsu K, et al: Normal magnetic resonance imaging with abnormal discography. Spine 13:1355, 1988.

128. Kornberg M: Discography and magnetic resonance imaging in the diagnosis of lumbar disc disruption. Spine 14:1368, 1989.

129. Karnaze MG, Gado MH, Sartor KJ, Hodges FJ: Comparison of MR and CT myelography in imaging the cervical and thoracic spine. AJR Am J Roentgenol 150:397, 1988.

130. Hirsch C, Inglemark BE, Miller M: The anatomical basis for low back pain. Acta Orthop Scand 33:1, 1963.

131. Sherk H, Parke W: Developmental anatomy. In Bailey RW (ed): The Cervical Spine. Philadelphia, JB Lippincott, 1983, p 7.

132. Crock HV: A reappraisal of intervertebral disc lesions. Med J Aust 1:983, 1970.

133. Park WM, McCall IW, O'Brien JP, Webb JK: Fissuring of the posterior annulus fibrosus in the lumbar spine. Br J Radiol 52:382, 1979.

134. McCall IW, Park WM, O'Brien JP, Seal V: Acute traumatic intraosseous disc herniation. Spine 10:134, 1985.

135. Jaffray D, O'Brien JP: Isolated intervertebral discs: Nuclear morphology and bursting pressure. Ann Rheum Dis 32:308, 1986.

136. Hsu KY, Zucherman JF, Derby R, et al: Painful lumbar end-plate disruptions: A significant discographic finding. Spine 13:76, 1988.

137. Whitecloud TS, Seago RA: Cervical discogenic syndrome. Results of operative intervention in patients with positive discography. Spine 12:313, 1987.

138. Derby R: Lumbar discometry. International Spinal Injection Society Scientific Newsletter 1:8, 1993.

139. Derby R, Howard MW, Grant JN, et al: The ability of pressure controlled discography to predict surgical and nonsurgical outcomes. Spine 24:364, 1999.

140. Smith GW, Nichols P: The technic of cervical discography. Radiology 68:718, 1957.

141. Cloward RB: The anterior approach for removal of ruptured cervical disks. J Neurosurg 15:602, 1958.

142. Cloward RB: Cervical discography. A contribution to the etiology and mechanism of neck, shoulder and arm pain. Ann Surg 150:1052, 1959.

143. Smith GW: The normal cervical discogram with clinical observations. AJR Am J Roentgenol 81:1006, 1959.

144. Cloward RB: Cervical discography. Acta Radiol Diagn (Stockh) 11:675, 1963.

145. Kikuchi S, Macnab I, Moreau P: Localization of the level of symptomatic cervical disc degeneration. J Bone Joint Surg Br 63:272, 1981.

146. Roth DA: Cervical analgesic discography. A new test for the definitive diagnosis of painful-disk syndrome. JAMA 235:1713, 1976.

147. Kofoed H: Thoracic outlet syndrome. Clin Orthop 156:145, 1981.

148. Schellhas KP, Pollei SR, Dorwart RH: Thoracic discography: A safe reliable technique. Spine 18:2103, 1994.

149. Wood KB, Schellhas KP, Garvey TA, Aeppli D: Thoracic discography in healthy individuals. A controlled prospective study of magnetic resonance imaging and discography in asymptomatic and symptomatic individuals. Spine 24:1548, 1999.

150. Falconer MA, McGeorge M, Begg AC: Observations on the cause and mechanism of symptom production in sciatica and low back pain. J Neurol Neurosurg Psychiatry 11:13, 1948.

151. Hirsch C: Efficiency of surgery in low back disorders. J Bone Joint Surg Am 47:991, 1965.

152. Meyer RR: Cervical discography. A help or hindrance in evaluating neck, shoulder, arm pain? Am J Radiol 90:1208, 1963.

153. Sneider SE Winslow OP, Pryor TH: Cervical discography: Is it relevant? JAMA 185:163, 1963.

154. Taveras JM: Is discography a useful diagnostic procedure? J Can Assoc Radiol 18:294, 1967.

155. Klafta LA, Collis JS: An analysis of cervical discography with surgical verification. J Neurosurg 30:39, 1969.

156. Schwarzer AC, Aprill CN, Derby R, et al: The prevalence and clinical features of internal disc disruption in patients with chronic low back pain. Spine 20:1878, 1995.

157. Donelson R, Aprill C, Medcalf R, Grant W: A prospective study of centralization of lumbar and referred pain. A predictor of symptomatic discs and anular competence. Spine 22:1115, 1997.

158. Aprill C, Bogduk N: High intensity zones in the disc annulus: A sign of painful disc on magnetic resonance imaging. Br J Radiol 65:361, 1992.

159. Ito M, Incorvaia KM, Yu SF, et al: Predictive signs of lumbar discogenic pain on magnetic resonance imaging with discography correlation. Spine 23:1252, discussion 1259, 1998.

160. Carragee EJ, Paragioudakis SJ, Khurana S: Lumbar high-intensity zone and discography in subjects without low back problems. Spine 25:2987, 2000.

161. Holt EP: The question of lumbar discography. J Bone Joint Surg Am 50:720, 1968.

162. Simmons JW, Aprill CN, Dwyer A, et al: A reassessment of Holt's data on "The question of lumbar discography." Clin Orthop 237:120, 1988.

163. Walsh T, Weinstein J, Spratt K, et al: The question of lumbar discography revisited: A controlled perspective study of normal volunteers to determine the false-positive rate. J Bone Joint Surg Am 72:1081, 1990.

164. Carragee EJ, Tanner CM, Khurana S, et al: The rates of false-positive lumbar discography in select patients without low back symptoms. Spine 25:1373, 2000.

165. Carragee EJ, Chen Y, Tanner CM, et al: Provocative discography in patients after limited lumbar discectomy. Spine 25:3065, 2000.

166. Carragee EJ: Prospective controlled study of the development of low back pain in previously asymptomatic subjects undergoing experimental discography. Spine 29:1112, 2004.

167. Bogduk N: An analysis of the Carragee data on false-positive discography. ISIS Scientific Newsletter 4:3, 2002.

168. Mersky H, Bogduk N (eds): Classification of Chronic Pain. Descriptions of Chronic Pain Syndromes and Definition of Pain Terms, 2nd ed. Seattle, IASP Press, 1994, p 180.

169. Block AR, Vanharanta H, Ohnmeiss DD, Guyer RD: Discogenic pain report. Influence of psychological factors. Spine 21:334, 1996.

170. Gill E, Blumenthal S: Functional results after anterior lumbar fusion at L5-S1 in patients with normal and abnormal MRI scans. Spine 17:940, 1992.

171. Colhoun E, McCall IW, Williams L, et al: Provocation discography as a guide to planning operations on the spine. J Bone Joint Surg Br 70:267, 1988.

172. Gore DR, Septic SB, Gardner GM: Roentgenographic findings of the cervical spine in asymptomatic people. Spine 11:521, 1986.

173. Boden SD, McCowin, Davis DO, et al: Abnormal magnetic resonance scans of the cervical spine in asymptomatic subjects. A prospective investigation. J Bone Joint Surg Am 72:1178, 1990.

174. Schellhas KP, Smith MD, Grundy CR, et al: Cervical discogenic pain. Prospective correlation of magnetic resonance imaging and discography in asymptomatic subjects and pain sufferers. Spine 21:300, 1996.

175. Taylor JR, Twomy LT: Acute injuries to the cervical joints; an autopsy study of neck sprain. Spine 18:1115, 1993.

176. Gore DR, Septic SB: Anterior cervical fusion for degenerated and protruded discs: A review of one hundred and forty six patients. Spine 9:667-671, 1984.

177. Clements DH, Oleary PF: Anterior cervical discectomy and fusion. Spine 15:1023, 1990.

178. Siebenrock K, Aebi M: Cervical discography and discogenic pain syndrome and its predictive value for surgical fusion. Arch Orthop Trauma Surg 113:199, 1994.

179. Huckell CB: Clinical outcomes after cervical fusion. Orthop Clin North Am 29:787, 1998.

180. Palit M, Schofferman J, Goldthwaite N, et al: Anterior discectomy and fusion for the management of neck pain. Spine 24:2224, 1999.

181. Garvey TA, Transfeldt EE, Malcolm JR, et al: Outcome of anterior cervical discectomy and fusion as perceived by patients treated for dominant axial-mechanical cervical spine pain. Spine 27:1887, 2002.

182. Guyer RD, Ohnmeiss DD: Lumbar discography. Position statement from the North American Spine Society Diagnostic and Therapeutic Committee. Spine 20:2048, 2001.

183. Pauza K: Educational guidelines for the performance of spinal injection procedures. Paper presented at a meeting of the Physiatric Association of Spine Sports and Occupational Rehabilitation, Chicago, 2004, p 21.

184. Huang TS, Zucherman JF, Hsu KY, et al: Gadopentetate dimeglumine as an intradiscal contrast agent. Spine 27:839, 2002.

185. Falco FJ, Moran JG: Lumbar discography using gadolinium in patients with iodine contrast allergy followed by postdiscography computed tomography scan. Spine 28:E1, 2003.

186. Polk HC, Christmas AB: Prophylactic antibiotics in surgery and surgical wound infection. Am Surg 66:105, 2000.

187. Fraser RD, Osti OL, Vernon-Roberts B: Iatrogenic discitis: The role of intravenous antibiotics in prevention and treatment. An experimental study. Spine 14:1025, 1989.

188. Osti O, Fraser RD, Vernon-Roberts B: Discitis after discography. The role of prophylactic antibiotics. J Bone Joint Surg Br 72:271, 1990.

189. Aprill CN: Diagnostic disc injections: II. Diagnostic lumbar disc injection. In Frymoyer JW, (ed): The Adult Spine: Principles and Practice, 2nd ed. Philadelphia, Lippincott-Raven, 1997, p 539.

190. Klessig HT, Showsh SA, Sekorski A: The use of intradiscal antibiotics in discography: An in vitro study of gentamicin, cefazolin, and clindamycin. Spine 28:1735, 2003.

191. Day PL: Lateral approach for lumbar diskogram and chemonucleolysis. Clin Orthop 67:90, 1969.

192. Edholm P, Fernstrom I, Lindblom K: Extradural lumbar disc puncture. Acta Radiol (Diagn) Scand 6:322, 1967.

193. Fraser RD, Osti OL, Vernon-Roberts B: Discitis after discography. J Bone Joint Surg Br 69:26, 1987.

194. Drummond GB, Scott DH: Deflection of spinal needle by the bevel. Anesthesia 35:854, 1980.

195. Sitzman BT, Uncles DR: The effects of needle type, gauge, and tip bend on spinal needle deflection. Anesth Analg 82:297, 1996.

196. Dryfuss P: The power of bevel control. International Spinal Injection Society Scientific Newsletter 3:16, 1998.

197. Kumar N, Agorastides I: The curved needle technique for accessing the L5/S1 disc space. Br J Radiol 73:655, 2000.

198. Heggeness M, Doherty B: Discography causes endplate deflection. Spine 18:1050, 1993.

199. Aprill C: Personal communication, 2004.

200. Pauza K, Howwell S, Dreyfus P, et al: A randomized, placebo-controlled trial of intradiscal electrothermal therapy for the treatment of discogenic low back pain. Spine J 4:27, 2004.

201. Adams MA, Dolan P, Hutton WC: The stages of disc degeneration as revealed by discograms. J Bone Joint Surg Br 68:36, 1986.

202. Antii-Toika I, Soini J, Tallroth K, et al: Clinical relevance of discography combined with CT scanning. A study of 100 patients. J Bone Joint Surg Br 72:480, 1990.

203. Bernard T: Lumbar discography followed by computed tomography. Redefining the diagnosis of low back pain. Spine 15:690, 1990.

204. Ito S, Yamada Y, Tsuboi S: An observation of ruptured annulus fibrosus in lumbar discs. J Spinal Disord 4:462, 1991.

205. Maezawa S, Muro T: Pain provocation at lumbar discography as analyzed by computed tomography/discography. Spine 17:1309, 1992.

206. Lejeune J, Hladky J, Cotton, et al: Foraminal lumbar disc herniation. Experience with 83 patients. Spine 19:1905, 1994.

207. Marron J, Kopitnik T, Schulhof A: Diagnosis and microsurgical approach to far lateral disc herniation in the lumbar spine. J Neurosurg 72:378, 1990.

208. Milette P, Raymond J, Fontane S: Comparison of high resolution computed tomography with discography in the evaluation of lumbar disc herniations. Spine 15:525, 1990.

209. Ninomiya M, Muro T: Patho-anatomy of lumbar disc herniation as demonstrated by computed tomography, discography. Spine 17:1316, 1992.

210. Rabischong P, Louis R, Vignaud J, Massare C: The intervertebral disc. Anat Clin 1:55, 1978.

211. Vanharanta H, Sachs BL, Spivey MA, et al: The relationship of pain provocation to lumbar disc deterioration as seen by CT/discography. Spine 12:295, 1987.

212. Sachs BL, Vanharanta H, Spivey MA, et al. Dallas discogram description: A new classification of CT/discography in low back disorders. Spine 12:287, 1987.

213. Bogduk N: Clinical Anatomy of the Lumbar Spine and Sacrum, 3rd ed. New York, Churchill Livingstone, 1997, p 204.

214. Tibiletti C, Karasek M: Thoracic provocation discography. In Bogduk N (ed): Practice Guidelines for Spinal Diagnostic and Treatment Procedures. San Francisco, International Spine Intervention Society, 2005, pp 287-294.

215. Cloward RB: Cervical diskography. Technique, indications and use in the diagnosis of ruptured cervical disks. AJR Am J Roentgenol 79:563, 1958.

216. Smith GW, Robinson RA: The treatment of certain cervical-spine disorders by anterior removal of the intervertebral disc and interbody fusion. J Bone Joint Surg Am 40:607, 1958.

217. Smith M, Kim SS: Herniated cervical disc resulting from discography: An unusual complication. J Spinal Disord 3:292, 1990.

218. Laun A, Lorenz R, Agnoli AL: Complications of cervical discography. J Neurosurg Sci 25:17, 1981.

219. Aprill CN: Diagnostic disc injections: Cervical disc injection. In Frymoyer JW (ed): The Adult Spine: Principles and Practice, 2nd ed. Philadelphia, Lippincott-Raven, 1997, p 523.

220. Guyer RD, Collier R, Stith WJ, et al: Discitis after discography. Spine 13:1352, 1988.

221. Kraft M: Cervical stimulation (provocation discography). In Bogduk N (ed): Practice Guidelines for Spinal Diagnostic and Treatment Procedures. San Francisco, International Spine Intervention Society, 2005, pp 95-111.

222. Aprill C: Personal communication, 1994.

223. Saternus KS, Bornscheuer HH: [Comparative radiologic and pathologic-anatomic studies on the value of discography in the diagnosis of acute intravertebral disc injuries in the cervical spine.] Rofo Fortschr Geb Rontgenstr Neuen Bildgeb Verfahr 139:651, 1983.

224. Kambin P, Abda S, Kurpicki F: Introdiskal pressure and volume recording: Evaluation of normal and abnormal cervical disks. Clin Orthop 146:144, 1980.

225. Wilkinson HA, Schuman N: Intradiscal corticosteroids in the treatment of lumbar and cervical disc problems. Spine 5:385, 1980.

226. Payne EE, Spillane JD: The cervical spine. Brain 80:571, 1957.

227. Connor P, Darden B: Cervical discography complications and clinical efficacy. Spine 18:2035, 1993.

228. Zeidman SM, Thompson K, Ducker TB: Complications of cervical discography: Analysis of 4400 diagnostic disc injections. Neurosurgery 37:414, 1995.

229. Fraser RD, Osti OL, Vernon-Roberts B: Discitis following chemonucleolysis: An experimental study. Spine 11:679, 1986.

230. Bircher MD, Tasker T, Crashaw C, et al: Discitis following lumbar surgery. Spine 13:98, 1988.

231. Arrington JA, Murtagh FR, Silbiger ML, et al: Magnetic resonance imaging of post-discogram discitis and osteomyelitis in the lumbar spine: Case report. J Fla Med Assoc 73:192, 1986.
232. Modic MT, Feiglin D, Pirano D, et al: Vertebral osteomyelitis: Clinical assessment using MR. Radiology 157:157, 1985.
233. Ledermann H, Schweitzer M, Morrison W, et al: MR imaging findings in spinal infections: Rules or myths. Radiology 228:506, 2003.
234. Szypryt E, Hardy J, Hinton C, et al: A comparison between magnetic resonance imaging and scintigraphic bone imaging in the diagnosis of disc space infection in an animal model. Spine 13:1042, 1988.
235. Baker AS, Ojemann RG, Schwartz MN, et al: Spinal epidural abscess. N Engl J Med 293:463, 1975.
236. Ravicovitch MA, Spallone A: Spinal epidural abscess. Eur Neurol 21:347, 1982.
237. Lownie SP, Ferguson GG: Spinal subdural empyema complicating cervical discography. Spine 14:1415, 1989.
238. Boswell MV, Wolfe JR: Intrathecal cefazolin-induced seizures following attempted discography. Pain Physician 7:103, 2004.
239. Bogduk N: Diskography. Am Pain Soc J 3:149, 1994.
240. Bogduk N, Aprill C, Derby R: Discography. In White AH (ed): Spine Care, vol 1: Diagnosis and Conservative Treatment. St Louis, CV Mosby, 1995, p 298.

chapter 12

Epidurography

Jeffrey P. Meyer, Miles R. Day, and Gabor B. Racz

■ HISTORICAL CONSIDERATIONS

Epidurography is one of the most commonly performed interventional pain procedures, yet is likely taken for granted by most pain practitioners. The accurate interpretation of epidural contrast patterns is key to the success of many interventional pain procedures, and remains a vital skill in the interventional pain arena.

First described in 1921 by the accidental injection of lipiodol into the epidural space by Sicard and Forestier,[1] epidurography has been performed with many different agents including air,[2] perobrodil[3] and metrizamide.[4] The use of ionic contrast agents such as diatrizoate (Renografin, Hypaque) led to complications related to both anaphylactic and contrast-induced seizures, and the use of nonionic contrast agent has now become widely accepted. The use of radio-opaque contrast agents to identify correct needle positioning in epidural steroid injections was described by White and colleagues in 1980,[5] and has since become widespread practice.[6-8] Epidural contrast patterns and their interpretation are central to caudal neuroplasty,[7] and have been described in the management of indwelling epidural catheters.[9]

The current practice of epidurography has evolved with necessity. It is currently performed whenever confirmation of epidural localization of needle placement is desired. When performed via the caudal approach, it is useful in delineating the presence of epidural fibrosis, with concomitant nerve root entrapment. In the cervical, thoracic, and lumbar transforaminal approaches, correct needle positioning is confirmed, as well as delineating the extent of spread. Interlaminar epidurography not only confirms correct positioning but defines "safe" runoff patterns that ensure that loculation (and subsequent intrathecal space compression) is not occurring.

■ INDICATIONS

Epidurography is indicated in any instance in which correct needle positioning within the epidural space is desired. Previous reports have identified false positive rates as high as 25% in the identification of the caudal epidural space,[10] and confirmation of correct needle positioning is necessary for both therapeutic effect and safety. In the presence of failed back/neck surgery syndrome, the pattern of contrast distribution and runoff ensure that loculation is not occurring, and

that further volumes may be instilled safely. This is especially important in cervical epidural injections as there is little room within the epidural space for loculation.

In the presence of epidural fibrosis, epidurography is useful in delineating the extent and pattern of fibrosis, along with identifying the affected nerve roots. It provides a baseline from which to gauge the extent of adhesiolysis during cervical, thoracic, and caudal epidural neuroplasty, and guides therapeutic decisions as to the necessity for further interventions.

Epidurography is essential in the performance of cervical interlaminar and transforaminal epidural steroid injections. The possibility of loculation with concomitant cord compression is ever present, and only epidurography is able to adequately identify runoff. In the case of cervical transforaminal injections, the presence of radicular feeder vessels to the spinal cord necessitates that epidurography be performed to ensure that intravascular injection is not occurring.[11] There are now several reports in the literature detailing spinal cord damage following the transforaminal delivery of epidural steroids to the cervical space, and a proposed mechanism for this complication is the delivery of local anesthetic and particulate steroid into these radicular feeder vessels.[13,14]

■ CLINICALLY RELEVANT ANATOMY

The dorsal epidural space is bounded superiorly by the foramen magnum, inferiorly by the sacral notch, ventrally by the dura mater, and dorsally by the laminar periosteum and ligamentum flavum. It extends to envelop the exiting nerve roots in the foraminal sheath. The space is largest in the sacral canal, and most limited in the midcervical spine. Plica mediana dorsalis are dorsal-median bands that may separate the epidural space into left and right compartments. They are usually incomplete, but may be continuous, limiting contrast spread to the ipsilateral epidural space.[12] The ventral epidural space is bounded superiorly by the foramen magnum, inferiorly by the sacral notch, ventrally by the posterior longitudinal ligament, and dorsally by the dura mater.

The epidural space contains fat, loose connective tissue, and veins. It may also contain radicular arterial feeder vessels for the spinal cord,[11,12] which are of particular concern when performing cervical transforaminal epidural steroid injections.[14,15]

▮ MATERIALS

Epidurography may safely be performed in non-iodine-allergic patient by the injection of nonionic, water-soluble contrast material into the epidural space. Because the possibility of intrathecal administration is always present, the choice of contrast agent is based on the intrathecal application of contrast. The only agent currently approved for use is iohexol (Omnipaque). Although available in concentrations of 140 to 360 mg organic iodine per mL, only the 180, 240, and 300 mL iodine per mL are indicated for intrathecal administration. In children, only the 180 mL iodine per mL concentration is indicated. Iopamidol (Isovue) is another water-soluble, nonionic contrast agent that is available; however it is not currently approved for intrathecal injection. Gadolinium has been described as an alternative in iodine-allergic patients.[17]

The use of ionic or non-water-soluble contrast agents in epidurography is contraindicated. The possibility of inadvertent intrathecal injection is ever present, and the application of these agents to the intrathecal space may lead to life-threatening seizures. Confirmation of the agent to be injected into the epidural space is mandatory before injection because the consequences of inadvertent injection of agents not approved for epidural use may be life threatening.

▮ TECHNIQUE

Epidurography may be performed from any of the commonly used approaches to the epidural space. Following confirmation of epidural needle tip positioning by loss-of-resistance, hanging drop technique, or fluoroscopy, a syringe containing 5 mL of contrast agent is attached to the needle. Careful aspiration to assess possible intrathecal or intravascular needle positioning is carried out. The initial injection of contrast is carried out under continuous fluoroscopy to assess the flow of contrast in an epidural pattern. It is advisable to limit the volume of initial contrast injection to the smallest amount possible to ascertain distal spread of contrast in the epidural space. In the presence of suspected epidural fibrosis, loculation surrounding the access point is an ever-present possibility, and injection of even small (1 to 2 mL) volumes of contrast may compress surrounding structures. This is especially important in the cervical and thoracic epidural space.

After confirming that loculation is not occurring, additional volumes of contrast may be injected as necessary to assess the pattern of contrast spread. Contrast injection should always be carried out under continuous fluoroscopy to identify possible vascular runoff patterns, and to assess the continued runoff of contrast material. Contrast will flow to the areas of least resistance, and filling defects may be identified, indicating areas of epidural scarring. Fluoroscopy should be carried out in both the AP and lateral projections to confirm spread in an epidural pattern.

Three general patterns of contrast filling may be identified: epidural, subdural, and intrathecal. The epidural pattern is characterized by a reticular pattern limited to the midline epidural space, and flowing in a "Christmas-tree" pattern to fill the exiting nerve roots (Fig 12–1). When obtained, this

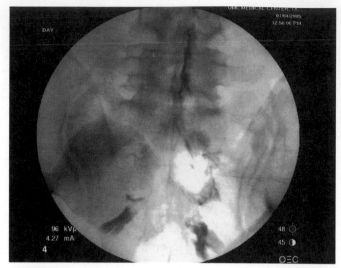

FIGURE 12–1 ▮ Normal caudal epidurogram.

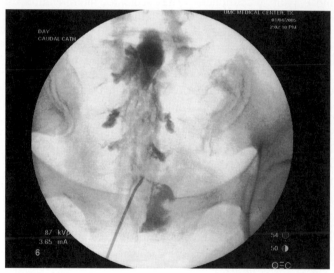

FIGURE 12–2 ▮ Normal epidurogram—note filling of S1-S3 nerve roots.

contrast pattern responds by further filling of ever higher nerve root levels with the administration of additional contrast. In the presence of plica mediana dorsalis, it is not uncommon for this pattern to fill only one half of the epidural space and exiting nerve roots. Contrast should spread both superiorly and inferiorly in a free-flowing pattern (Fig 12–2).

Subdural injection of contrast results in a patchy, fine pattern in the AP projection (Fig 12–3). Lateral fluoroscopy will reveal a solid "line" of contrast extending several levels higher than expected given the volume of contrast injected (Fig 12–4). Subdural therapeutic injections are not recommended, and repositioning of the access needle should be carried out. It is important to note that subdural contrast patterns are very difficult to identify in the AP fluoroscopic projection, emphasizing the necessity for both AP and lateral views to confirm proper needle positioning.

Intrathecal contrast injection reveals a myelographic spread, with outlining of the nerve roots/cauda equina when carried out in the lumbar spine. The injected contrast will not

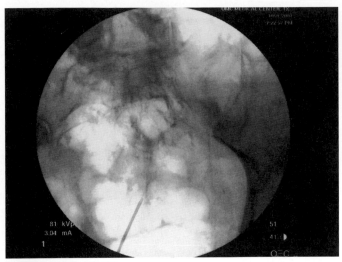

FIGURE 12–3 ■ Subdural injection of contrast—note reticular filling pattern.

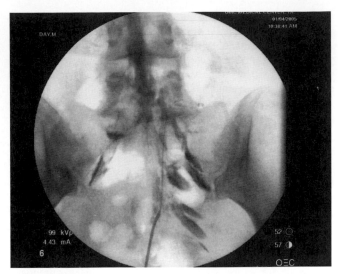

FIGURE 12–5 ■ Epidurogram—note filling defect of left S2 level.

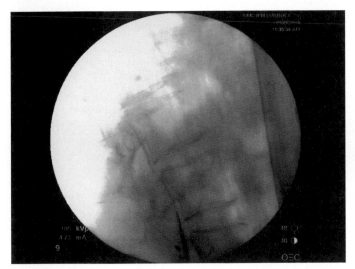

FIGURE 12–4 ■ Subdural contrast (2 mL in sacral space)—note extension to L1 level with 2 mL injection.

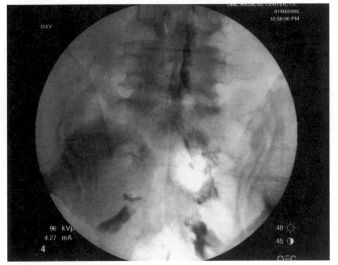

FIGURE 12–6 ■ Epidurogram—note filling defect of left S1 level.

spread to outline the exiting nerve roots, and will be limited to the midline spinal space. In the cervical and thoracic regions, intrathecal injection of contrast will flow laterally, and appear as a "double bar" outlining the spinal cord laterally within the spinal canal.

When performed in the sacral space, epidurography is very effective in identifying areas of epidural scarring that may be targeted via caudal neuroplasty. These areas appear as "filling" defects within the dye spread. It is uncommon for these filling defects to appear below the S2 level, but they are quite common above S1 (Figs. 12–5 and 12–6). Areas of filling defect may be accessed via caudal catheter and the degree of neuroplasty may be assessed by repeat epidurography following injection of hyaluronidase. When performed properly, these filling defects resolve with neuroplasty.

■ SIDE EFFECTS AND COMPLICATIONS

Epidurography can be safely performed in the cervical, thoracic, lumbar, and sacral spinal canals. Loculation with concomitant spinal cord compression and myelopathy is a real concern in the cervical and thoracic epidural spaces, and the need for visualization of distal runoff cannot be overemphasized. Injection into radicular feeder vessels of the spinal cord is a concern at all levels of the spinal cord, and careful observation for vascular patterns must be maintained.

Injection into the intrathecal space is occasionally observed. Iohexol (Omnipaque) is the only contrast agent approved for intrathecal use, and is, therefore, the only agent used at our institution. Tonic-clonic seizures with the intrathecal administration of iohexol have been reported,[16] but are a rare complication.

Anaphylactic reactions to injected contrast material may occur. Patients who are allergic to iodine or radiographic contrast material should not be subjected to epidurography until sensitivity testing by appropriate specialists has been performed. There are currently no iodine-free contrast agents approved for epidural use.

Contrast-induced nephropathy is possible with large volumes of contrast injected, but is rare in epidurography due to the slow reabsorption of contrast and limited concentrations delivered to the kidneys. Total doses of contrast should be limited to the least effective dose in patients with preexisting renal insufficiency.

■ CONCLUSION

Epidurography is a commonly performed procedure in interventional pain management. The correct interpretation of epidurograms is essential to the safe practice of epidural access procedures, and helps guide appropriate interventions in the future. All interventional pain management physicians should become proficient at the performance and interpretation of epidurograms to enhance the safety of their practice.

KEY POINTS

- Epidurography is easy to perform and it enhances the safety of epidural access procedures.
- Only nonionic, water-soluble contrast agents should be used; iohexol is the only agent approved for intrathecal delivery.
- Initial injection should be limited in volume and closely monitored for loculation and vascular runoff.
- Three patterns of spinal canal spread exist: epidural, subdural, and intrathecal. The interventional pain physician should be highly proficient in the interpretation of these patterns.
- Complications from epidurography include loculation with subsequent spinal cord compression and adverse reactions to injected contrast.

References

1. Sicard JA, Forestier J: Methode radiographique d'exploration de la cavite epidurale par le Lipiodol. Rev Neurol 28:1264, 1921.
2. Sanford H, Doub HP: Epidurography: A method of roentgenologic visualization of protruded intervertebral discs. Radiology 36:712, 1941.
3. Knutsson F: Experiences with epidural contrast investigation of the lumbosacral canal in disc prolapse. Acta Radiol 22:694, 1941.
4. Hatten HP: Lumbar epidurography with metrizamide. Radiology 137:129, 1980.
5. White AH, Derby R, Wynne G: Epidural injections in the treatment of low-back pain. Spine 5:78, 1980.
6. El-Khoury GY, Ehara S, Weinstein JN, et al: Epidural steroid injection: A procedure ideally performed under fluoroscopic control. Radiology 168:554, 1988.
7. Manchikanti L, Bakhit CE, Pampati M: Role of epidurography in caudal neuroplasty. Pain Digest 8:277, 1998.
8. Botwin K, Natalicchio J, Brown LA: Epidurography contrast patterns with fluoroscopic guided lumbar transforaminal epidural injection: A prospective evaluation. Pain Physician 7:211, 2004.
9. Du Pen SL, Du Pen A: Tunneled epidural catheters: Practical considerations and implantation techniques. In Waldman SD (ed): Interventional Pain Management, ed 2. Philadelphia, WB Saunders, 2001, p 627.
10. Stitz MY, Sommer H: Accuracy of blind versus fluoroscopically guided caudal epidural injection. Spine 24(13):1371, 1999.
11. Baker R: Cervical transforaminal injection of corticosteroids into a radicular artery: A possible mechanism for spinal cord injury. Pain 103(1-2):211, 2003.
12. Huntoon MA: The ascending and deep cervical arteries are vulnerable to injury during cervical transforaminal epidural injections: An anatomic study. Presented at the ASA Annual Meeting, October 23-27, 2004, Las Vegas, Nevada.
13. Luyendijk W: The plica mediana dorsalis of the dura mater and its relation to periurography (canclography). Neuroradiology 11:147, 1976.
14. Dietrich CL , Smith CE : Epidural granuloma and intracranial hypotension resulting from cervical epidural steroid injection . Anesthesiology 100:445, 2004.
15. Brouwers PJAM , Kottnik EJBL , Simon MAM , Prevo RL: A cervical anterior spinal artery syndrome after diagnostic blockade of the right C6-nerve root. Pain 91:397, 2001.
16. Fedutes BA: Seizure potential of concomitant medications and radiographic contrast agents. Ann Pharmacother 37(10):1506, 2003.
17. Falco JE, Rubbanni M: Visualization of spinal injection procedures using gadolinium contrast. Spine 28(23):496, 2003.

chapter 13

Neural Blockade for the Diagnosis of Pain

Steven D. Waldman

As emphasized in previous chapters, the cornerstone of successful treatment of the patient suffering from pain is a correct diagnosis. As straightforward as this statement is in theory, it may become difficult to achieve in the individual patient. The reason for this difficulty is due to four disparate, but interrelated issues (1) Pain is a subjective response that is difficult, if not impossible, to quantify; (2) Pain response in humans is made up of a variety of obvious and not so obvious factors that may modulate the patient's clinical expression of pain either upward or downward (Table 13–1); (3) Our current understanding of neurophysiologic, neuroanatomic, and behavioral components of pain is incomplete and imprecise; and (4) There is ongoing debate by the specialty of pain management of whether pain is best treated as a symptom or as a disease. The uncertainly introduced by these factors can often make accurate diagnosis problematic.

Given the difficulty in establishing a correct diagnosis of a patient's pain, the clinician often is forced to look for external means to quantify or confirm a dubious clinical impression. Laboratory and radiologic testing are often the next procedures the clinician seeks for reassurance. If such testing is inconclusive or the results are discordant with the clinical impression, diagnostic nerve block may be the next logical step. Done properly, diagnostic nerve block can provide the clinician with useful information to aid in increasing the comfort level with a tentative diagnosis. It cannot be emphasized enough, however, that over-reliance on the results of even a properly performed diagnostic nerve block can set in motion a series of events that will, at the very least, provide the patient little or no pain relief and, at the very worst, result in permanent complications from invasive surgeries or neurodestructive procedures that were justified solely on the basis of diagnostic nerve block.

■ THE HISTORICAL IMPERATIVE AND CLINICAL RATIONALE FOR USE OF DIAGNOSTIC NERVE BLOCKS

Our view of pain has changed over the centuries as our understanding of this universal condition has improved. Early humans viewed pain as a punishment from the deities for a variety of sins as exemplified by the legend of Prometheus. Prometheus was sentenced by Zeus to eternal torture for giving the fire reserved for the gods to mortals (Fig. 13–1). The 17th century scientist and philosopher, Descartes (Fig. 13–2), changed this view in a single instant by his drawing of a fire burning the foot of a man. Descartes postulated a rational basis for pain premised on the then radical notion that pain was sensed in the periphery and then carried via the nerves and spinal cord to the brain (Fig. 13–3).

It is not surprising that concurrent advances in the understanding of the anatomy of the peripheral and central nervous system led scientists and clinicians to seek new ways to stop pain. In 1774, English surgeon James Moore described the use of a "C" clamp to compress the peripheral nerves of the upper and lower extremity to induce anesthesia to decrease the pain of amputation and other surgeries of the extremities.[1] The development and refinement of the syringe and hollow needle led to the idea of injecting substances such as morphine in proximity to the peripheral nerves to relieve pain. Rynd, in 1845, postulated the utility of delivering morphine directly onto a nerve via a hollow trocar.[2] This was a radical departure from the then current practice of surgically exposing the nerve and then topically applying pain relieving agents. It is not surprising that many patients thought that the "cure was worse than the disease." However, it was the landmark clinical discovery of the utility of cocaine as a surgical anesthetic by Carl Koller in 1884 that ushered in the era of regional anesthesia.[3] Corning's first spinal anesthetic in 1885 further solidified the concept that blocking nerves could alleviate human suffering, albeit not without complications—as it was Corning himself who may have suffered the first spinal headache following induction of an anesthetic.

As the specialty of regional anesthesia matured, the technical ability to easily and consistently render nerves incapable of transmitting pain increased. The early work of Halstead and Hall, Corning, and others helped refine the "how-to-do-it" aspects of blocking a nerve. However, the relative toxicity of cocaine, which was the only local anesthetic readily available at the time, significantly limited the clinical utility of otherwise technically satisfactory nerve block techniques.

It was not until the synthesis in 1909 by Einhorn of the local anesthetic ester procaine that regional anesthesia was truly safe enough for widespread use (Fig. 13–4). Unfortunately, procaine's short duration of action made its use

Table 13–1
Factors that Influence Pain
Age
Gender
Socioeconomic status
Ethnicity
Pregnancy
Stress
Chronicity

FIGURE 13–1 ■ Artist's depiction of Prometheus.

FIGURE 13–2 ■ A portrait of Descartes.

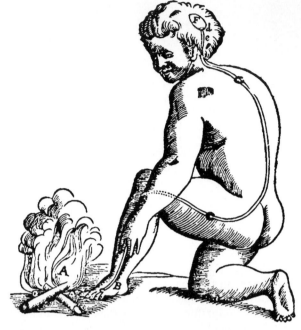

FIGURE 13–3 ■ Drawing by Descartes demonstrating the concept that pain is carried via nerves from the periphery to the brain.

Procaine

Procaine hydrochloride

FIGURE 13–4 ■ Diagram of chemical structures of procaine and procaine hydrochloride.

impractical for longer operations; this limitation led to the development of the longer-acting ester class of local anesthetics, such as tetracaine and dibucaine, albeit with increased systemic toxicity. It was the development of the safer amide class of local anesthetics, such as lidocaine by Löfgren and Lundquist in 1943, that began the most recent chapter in the quest for the ability to block human pain (Fig. 13–5).

Just as it seemed that science had finally given doctors the ability to block pain, other scientific advances began to question the construct that Descartes has given us—that pain is a simple function of a stimulus being carried over an anatomically distinct neural pathway. As clinicians were puzzled that patients who had otherwise seemingly perfect nerve blocks continued to have pain during surgical procedures, basic scientists were beginning to unravel the mystery of peripheral and central modulation of pain—as well as the

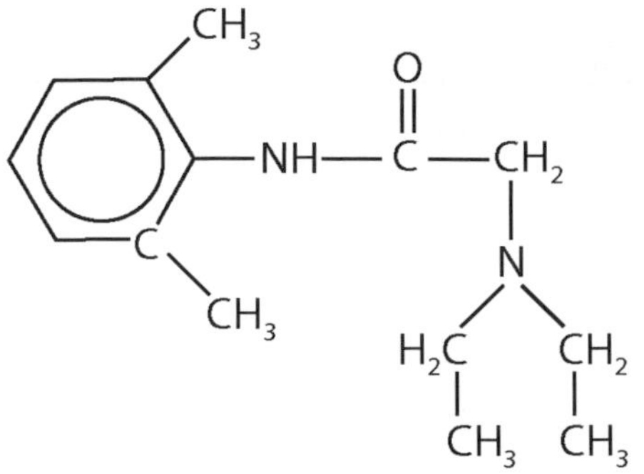

FIGURE 13–5 ■ Diagram of chemical structure of lidocaine.

Table 13–2

The Do's and Dont's of Diagnostic Nerve Blocks

Do analyze the information obtained from diagnostic nerve blocks in the context of the patient's history, physical, laboratory, neurophysiologic, and radiographic testing.

Don't over-rely on information obtained from diagnostic nerve blocks.

Do view with skepticism discordant or contradictory information obtained from diagnostic nerve blocks.

Don't rely on information obtained from diagnostic nerve block as the sole justification to proceed with invasive treatments.

Do consider the possibility of technical limitations that limit the ability to perform an accurate diagnostic nerve block.

Do consider the possibility of patient anatomic variations that may influence the results of diagnostic nerve blocks.

Do consider the presence of incidents pain when analyzing the results of diagnostic nerve blocks.

Don't perform diagnostic nerve blocks when patients are not currently having the pain you are trying to diagnose.

Do consider behavioral factors that may influence the results of diagnostic nerve blocks.

Do consider that the patient may premedicate before undergoing diagnostic nerve blocks.

---

role that the sympathetic nervous system plays in the pain response. The quest for answers as to how these disparate neuroanatomic structures affect, modulate, and subserve a patient's pain continues today. It is this quest for answers that brings us to an evaluation of the role that diagnostic nerve blocks play in contemporary pain management.

■ A ROAD MAP FOR THE APPROPRIATE USE OF DIAGNOSTIC NERVE BLOCK

It must be said at the outset of this discussion that even the perfectly performed diagnostic nerve block is not without limitations. Table 13–2 provides the reader with a list of do's and dont's when performing and interpreting diagnostic nerve blocks. First and foremost, the clinician should use with

caution the information gleaned from diagnostic nerve blocks and use it only as one piece of the overall diagnostic work-up of the patient in pain. Results of a diagnostic nerve block that contradicts the clinical impression that the pain management specialist has formed as a result of the performance of a targeted history and physical examination and consideration of confirmatory laboratory, neurophysiologic, and radiographic testing should be viewed with great skepticism. Such disparate results should never serve as the sole basis for moving ahead with neurodestructive or invasive surgical procedures that, in this setting, have little or no hope of actually helping alleviate a patient's pain.

In addition to the admonitions just mentioned, it must be recognized that the clinical utility of the diagnostic nerve block can be affected by technical limitations. In general, the reliability of data gleaned from a diagnostic nerve block is in direct proportion to the clinician's familiarity with the functional anatomy of the area in which the nerve resides and the clinician's experience in performing the block being attempted. Even in the best of hands, some nerve blocks are technically more demanding than others, which increases the likelihood of a less than perfect result. Proximity of other neural structures to the nerve, ganglion, or plexus being blocked may lead to the inadvertent and often unrecognized block of adjacent nerves, thereby invalidating the results that the clinician sees (e.g., the proximity of the lower cervical nerve roots, phrenic nerve, and brachial plexus to the stellate ganglion).

Some of these technical obstacles can be decreased, although by no means completely eliminated, by the use of fluoroscopic or computerized tomographic guidance during needle placement. The addition of small amounts of radiopaque contrast medium to the local anesthetic may also increase the accuracy of the block. However, the clinician must be aware that the over-reliance on either of these aids may lead to erroneous conclusions. It should also be remembered that the possibility of undetected anatomic abnormality always exists which may further confuse the results of the diagnostic nerve block (e.g., conjoined nerve roots, the Martin Gruber anastomosis [a median to ulnar nerve connection], and so on.)[4]

Because each pain experience is unique to the individual patient and the clinician really has no way to quantify it, special care must be taken to ensure that everybody is in agreement insofar as what pain the diagnostic block is intended to diagnose. Many patients have more than one type of pain. A patient may have both radicular pain as well as the pain of alcoholic neuropathy. A given diagnostic block may relieve one source of the patient's pain while leaving the other untouched.

If the patient is having incident pain (e.g., pain when walking or sitting), the performance of a diagnostic block in a setting other than one that will provoke the incident pain is of little or no value. This often means that the clinician must tailor the type of nerve block that is to be performed to allow the patient to be able to safely perform the activity that incites the pain. A diagnostic nerve block should never be performed if the patient is not having or is unable to provoke the pain that the pain management specialist is trying to diagnose because there is nothing to quantify.

The accuracy of diagnostic nerve block can be enhanced by assessing the duration of nerve relief relative to the expected pharmacologic duration of the agent being used to block the pain. If there is discordance between the duration of pain relief relative to duration of the local anesthetic or opioid being used, extreme caution should be exercised before relying solely on the results of that diagnostic nerve block. Such discordance can be due to technical shortcomings in the performance of the block, anatomic variations, and most commonly, behavioral components of the patient's pain.

It must be remembered that the pain and anxiety caused by the diagnostic nerve block itself may confuse the results of an otherwise technically perfect block. The clinician should be alert to the fact that many pain patients may premedicate themselves because of the fear of procedural pain. This also has the potential to confuse the observed results. Obviously, the use of sedation or anxiolytic agents before the performance of diagnostic nerve block will further cloud the very issues the nerve block is, in fact, supposed to clarify.

■ SPECIFIC DIAGNOSTIC NERVE BLOCKS

Early proponents of regional anesthesia, such as Labat and Pitkin, believed it was possible to block just about any nerve in the body.[5] Despite the many technical limitations these pioneers were faced with, these clinicians persevered. They did so not only because they believe in the clinical utility and safety of regional nerve block but because the currently available alternatives to render a patient insensible to surgical pain were much less attractive. The introduction of the muscle relaxant, curare, in 1942 by Dr. Harold Griffith changed this construct, and in a relatively short time, regional anesthesia was relegated to the history of medicine with its remaining proponents viewed as eccentric at best.[6] Just as the Egyptian embalming techniques were lost to modern man, many regional anesthesia techniques that were in common use were lost to today's pain management specialists. What we are left with today are those procedures that stood the test of time for surgical anesthesia. For the most part, these were the nerve blocks that were not overly demanding from a technical viewpoint and were reasonably safe to perform. Many of these techniques also have clinical utility as diagnostic nerve blocks. These techniques are summarized in Table 13–3. A discussion of the more commonly used diagnostic nerve blocks follows.

Neuroaxial Diagnostic Nerve Blocks

Discussed in detail in Chapter 14, differential spinal and epidural blocks have gained popularity as an aid in the diagnosis of pain. Popularized by Winnie, differential spinal and epidural blocks have as their basis the varying sensitivity of sympathetic and somatic sensory and motor fibers to blockade by local anesthetics.[7] Although sound in principle these techniques are subject to serious technical difficulties that limit the reliability of the information obtained. These difficulties include (1) inability to precisely measure the extent that each type of nerve fiber is blocked; (2) the possibility that more than one nerve fiber type is simultaneously blocked—leading the clinician to attribute the patient's pain to the wrong neuroanatomic structure; (3) the impossibility of "blinding" the patient to the sensation of warmth associ-

Table 13–3
Common Diagnostic Nerve Blocks
Neuroaxial Blocks Epidural block Subarachnoid block
Peripheral Nerve Blocks Greater and lesser occipital nerve blocks Trigeminal nerve block Brachial plexus block Median, radial, and ulnar nerve blocks Intercostal nerve block Selective nerve root block Sciatic nerve block
Intra-articular Nerve Blocks Facet block
Sympathetic Nerve Blocks Stellate ganglion block Celiac plexus block Lumbar sympathetic block Hypogastric plexus and ganglion impar blocks

ated with sympathetic blockade as well as the numbness and weakness that accompany blockade of the somatic sensory and motor fibers; (4) the construct of temporal linearity, which holds that the more "sensitive" sympathetic fibers will become blocked first—followed by the less sensitive somatic sensory fibers—and last by the more resistant motor fibers, breaks down. As a practical matter, it is not uncommon for the patient to experience some sensory block before noticing the warmth associated with block of the sympathetic fibers rendering the test results suspect. (5) Afferent nociceptive input can still be demonstrated in the brain, even in the presence of a neuroaxial block that is dense enough to allow a major surgical procedure. (6) Neurophysiologic changes associated with pain may increase or decrease the firing threshold of the nerve—suggesting that even in the present of sub-blocking concentrations, there is the possibility that the sensitized afferent nerves will stop firing. (7) Modulation of pain transmission at the spinal cord, brain stem, and higher levels is known to exist and may alter the results of even the most carefully performed differential neural blockade. And (8) significant behavioral components to a patient's pain may influence the subjective response the patient reports to the clinician who is performing differential neuroaxial blockade.

In spite of these shortcomings, neuroaxial differential block remains a clinically useful tool to aid in the diagnosis of unexplained pain. The clinician can increase the sensitivity of this technique by (1) use of reverse differential spinal or epidural block in which the patient is given a high concentration of local anesthetic that results in a dense motor, sensory, and sympathetic block and then observing the patient as the block regresses; (2) use of opioids instead of local anesthetics that remove the sensory clues that may influence patient responses; and (3) repeating the block on more than one occasion using local anesthetics or opioids of varying durations, e.g., lidocaine versus bupivacaine or morphine versus fentanyl and comparing the results for consistency. Whether or not this technique stands the test of time, Winnie's admonition to clinicians that sympathetically mediated pain is often underdiagnosed most certainly will.

Greater and Lesser Occipital Nerve Block

The greater occipital nerve arises from fibers of the dorsal primary ramus of the second cervical nerve and to a lesser extent from fibers of the third cervical nerve.[8] The greater occipital nerve pierces the fascia just below the superior nuchal ridge along with the occipital artery. It supplies the medial portion of the posterior scalp as far anterior as the vertex. The lesser occipital nerve arises from the ventral primary rami of the second and third cervical nerves. The lesser occipital nerve passes superiorly along the posterior border of the sternocleidomastoid muscle, dividing into cutaneous branches that innervate the lateral portion of the posterior scalp and the cranial surface of the pinna of the ear.

Selective blockade of greater and lesser occipital nerves can provide the pain management specialist with useful information when trying to determine the cause of cervicogenic headache. By blocking the atlantoaxial, atlanto-occipital, cervical epidural, cervical facet, and greater and lesser occipital nerves on successive visits, the pain management specialist may be able to differentiate the nerves subserving the patient's headache.

Stellate Ganglion Block

The stellate ganglion is located on the anterior surface of the longus colli muscle. This muscle lies just anterior to the transverse processes of the seventh cervical and first thoracic vertebrae.[9] The stellate ganglion is made up of the fused portion of the seventh cervical and first thoracic sympathetic ganglia. The stellate ganglion lies anteromedial to the vertebral artery and is medial to the common carotid artery and jugular vein. It is lateral to the trachea and esophagus. The proximity of the exiting cervical nerve roots and brachial plexus to the stellate ganglion make it easy to inadvertently block these structures when performing stellate ganglion block—making interpretation of the results of the block difficult.

Selective blockade of stellate ganglion can provide the pain management specialist with useful information when trying to determine the cause of upper extremity or facial pain without clear diagnosis. By blocking the brachial plexus (preferably by the axillary approach) and stellate ganglion on successive visits, the pain management specialist may be able to differentiate the nerves subserving the patient's upper extremity pain. Selective differential blockade of the stellate ganglion, trigeminal nerve, and sphenopalatine ganglion on successive visits may elucidate the nerves subserving facial pain that is often difficult to diagnose.

Cervical Facet Block

The cervical facet joints are formed by the articulations of the superior and inferior articular facets of adjacent vertebrae.[10] Except for the atlanto-occipital and atlantoaxial joints, the remaining cervical facet joints are true joints in that they are lined with synovium and possess a true joint capsule. This capsule is richly innervated and supports the notion of the facet joint as a pain generator. The cervical facet joint is susceptible to arthritic changes and trauma caused by acceleration-deceleration injuries. Such damage to the joint results in pain secondary to synovial joint inflammation and adhesions.

Each facet joint receives innervation from two spinal levels. Each joint receives fibers from the dorsal ramus at the same level as the vertebra, as well as fibers from the dorsal ramus of the vertebra above. This fact explains the ill-defined nature of facet-mediated pain and explains why the branch of the dorsal ramus arising above the offending level must often also be blocked to provide complete pain relief. At each level, the dorsal ramus provides a medial branch that wraps around the convexity of the articular pillar of its respective vertebra and provides innervation to the facet joint.

Selective blockade of cervical facet joints can provide the pain management specialist with useful information when trying to determine the cause of cervicogenic headache and/or neck pain. By blocking the atlantoaxial, atlanto-occipital, cervical epidural, and greater and lesser occipital nerve blocks on successive visits, the clinician may be able to differentiate the nerves subserving the patient's headache and/or neck pain.

Intercostal Nerve Block

The intercostal nerves arise from the anterior division of the thoracic paravertebral nerve.[11] A typical intercostal nerve has four major branches. The first branch is the unmyelinated postganglionic fibers of the gray rami communicantes, which interface with the sympathetic chain. The second branch is the posterior cutaneous branch, which innervates the muscles and skin of the paraspinal area. The third branch is the lateral cutaneous division, which arises in the anterior axillary line. The lateral cutaneous division provides the majority of the cutaneous innervation of the chest and abdominal wall. The fourth branch is the anterior cutaneous branch supplying innervation to the midline of the chest and abdominal wall. Occasionally, the terminal branches of a given intercostal nerve may actually cross the midline to provide sensory innervation to the contralateral chest and abdominal wall. This fact has specific import when utilizing intercostal block as part of a diagnostic work-up for the patient with chest wall and/or abdominal pain. The 12th thoracic nerve is called the subcostal nerve and is unique in that it gives off a branch to the first lumbar nerve, thus contributing to the lumbar plexus.

Selective blockade of intercostal and/or subcostal nerves thought to be subserving a patient's pain can provide the pain management specialist with useful information when trying to determine the cause of chest wall and/or abdominal pain. By blocking the intercostal nerves and celiac plexus on successive visits, the pain management specialist may be able to differentiate which nerves are subserving the patient's chest wall and /or abdominal pain.

Celiac Plexus Block

The sympathetic innervation of the abdominal viscera originates in the anterolateral horn of the spinal cord. Preganglionic fibers from T5-T12 exit the spinal cord in conjunction with the ventral roots to join the white communicating rami on their way to the sympathetic chain. Rather than synapsing with the sympathetic chain, these preganglionic fibers pass through it to ultimately synapse on the celiac ganglia.[12] The greater, lesser, and least splanchnic nerves provide the major preganglionic contribution to the celiac plexus. The greater splanchnic nerve has its origin from the T5-T10 spinal roots. The nerve travels along the thoracic paravertebral border through the crus of the diaphragm into the abdominal cavity, ending on the celiac ganglion of its respective side. The lesser splanchnic nerve arises from the T10-T11 roots and passes with the greater nerve to end at the celiac ganglion. The least splanchnic nerve arises from the T11-T12 spinal roots and passes through the diaphragm to the celiac ganglion.

Interpatient anatomic variability of the celiac ganglia is significant, but the following generalizations can be drawn from anatomic studies of the celiac ganglia. The number of ganglia varies from one to five and range in diameter from 0.5 to 4.5 cm. The ganglia lie anterior and anterolateral to the aorta. The ganglia located on the left are uniformly more inferior than their right-sided counterparts by as much as a vertebral level, but both groups of ganglia lie below the level of the celiac artery. The ganglia usually lie approximately at the level of the first lumbar vertebra.

Postganglionic fibers radiate from the celiac ganglia to follow the course of the blood vessels to innervate the abdominal viscera. These organs include much of the distal esophagus, stomach, duodenum, small intestine, ascending and proximal transverse colon, adrenal glands, pancreas, spleen, liver, and biliary system. It is these postganglionic fibers, the fibers arising from the preganglionic splanchnic nerves, and the celiac ganglion that make up the celiac plexus. The diaphragm separates the thorax from the abdominal cavity while still permitting the passage of the thoracoabdominal structures, including the aorta, vena cava, and splanchnic nerves. The diaphragmatic crura are bilateral structures that arise from the anterolateral surfaces of the upper two or three lumbar vertebrae and discs. The crura of the diaphragm serve as a barrier to effectively separate the splanchnic nerves from the celiac ganglia and plexus below.

The celiac plexus is anterior to the crus of the diaphragm. The plexus extends in front of and around the aorta, with the greatest concentration of fibers anterior to the aorta. With the single-needle transaortic approach to celiac plexus block, the needle is placed close to this concentration of plexus fibers. The relationship of the celiac plexus to the surrounding structures is as follows: The aorta lies anterior and slightly to the left of the anterior margin of the vertebral body. The inferior vena cava lies to the right, with the kidneys posterolateral to the great vessels. The pancreas lies anterior to the celiac plexus. All of these structures lie within the retroperitoneal space.

Selective blockade of celiac plexus can provide the pain management specialist with useful information when trying to determine the cause of chest wall, flank, and/or abdominal pain. By blocking the intercostal nerves and celiac plexus on successive visits, the pain management specialist may be able to differentiate which nerves are subserving the patient's pain.

Selective Nerve Root Block

Improvements in fluoroscopy and needle technology have led to increased interest in selective nerve root block in the diagnosis of cervical and lumbar radicular pain. Although technically demanding and not without complications, selective nerve root block is often used in conjunction with provocative discography to help identify the nidus of the patient's pain complaint. The use of selective nerve root block as a diagnostic maneuver must be approached with caution. Because of the proximity of the epidural, subdural, and subarachnoid spaces, it is easy to inadvertently place local anesthetic into these spaces when intending to block a single cervical or lumbar nerve root. This error is not always readily apparent on fluoroscopy, given the small amounts of local anesthetic and contrast medium used.

■ CONCLUSION

The use of nerve blocks as part of the evaluation of the patient in pain represents a reasonable next step if a careful targeted history and physical examination and rational radiographic, neurophysiologic, and laboratory testing fail to provide a clear diagnosis. The over-reliance on diagnostic nerve block as the sole justification to perform an invasive or neurodestructive procedure can lead to significant patient morbidity and dissatisfaction.

References

1. Moore J: A Method of Preventing or Diminishing Pain in Several Operations of Surgery. London, T. Cadell, 1784.
2. Rynd F: Neuralgia: Introduction of fluid to the nerve. Dublin Med Press 13:167, 1845.
3. Koller C: On the use of cocaine for producing anaesthesia on the eye. Lancet 2:990, 1884.
4. Dawson DM: Carpal tunnel syndrome. In Entrapment Neuropathies, 3rd ed. Philadelphia, Lippincott-Raven, 1990, p 53.
5. Pitkin G: Controllable spinal anesthesia. Am J Surg 5:537, 1928.
6. Griffith HR, Jonhson E: The use of curare in general anesthesia. Anesthesiology 3:418, 1942.
7. Winnie AP, Collins VJ: The pain clinic. I: Differential neural blockade in pain syndromes of questionable etiology. Med Clin North Am 52:123, 1968.
8. Waldman SD: Greater and lesser occipital nerve block. In Waldman SD: Atlas of Interventional Pain Management, 2nd ed. Philadelphia, Saunders, 2004, p 23.
9. Waldman SD: Stellate ganglion block. In Waldman SD: Atlas of Interventional Pain Management, 2nd ed. Philadelphia, Saunders, 2004, p 104.
10. Waldman SD: Cervical facet block. In Waldman SD: Atlas of Interventional Pain Management, 2nd ed. Philadelphia, Saunders, 2004, p 125.
11. Waldman SD: Intercostal nerve block. In Waldman SD: Atlas of Interventional Pain Management, 2nd ed. Philadelphia, Saunders, 2004, p 241.
12. Waldman SD: Celiac plexus block. In Waldman SD: Atlas of Interventional Pain Management, 2nd ed. Philadelphia, Saunders, 2004, p 265.

Differential Neural Blockade for the Diagnosis of Pain

Alon P. Winnie and Kenneth D. Candido

Clinically, differential neural blockade is the selective blockade of one type of nerve fiber without blocking other types of nerve fibers. It is an extremely useful diagnostic tool that allows the clinician to observe the effect of a sympathetic block, a sensory block, and, for that matter, a block of all nerve fibers by local anesthetic agents on a patient's pain, and to compare that effect with the effect of an injection of an inactive agent (placebo). There are two clinical approaches to the production of differential neural blockade, an *anatomic approach* and a *pharmacologic approach*. The anatomic approach is based on sufficient anatomic separation of sympathetic and somatic fibers to allow injection of local anesthetic to block one type only (see later). The pharmacologic approach is based on the presumed difference in the sensitivity of the various types of nerve fibers to local anesthetics, so that the injection of local anesthetics in different concentrations selectively blocks different types of fibers.

Because pain is a totally *subjective* phenomenon, what is needed to identify the neural pathway that subserves it is some sort of *objective* diagnostic test, and differential neural blockade is just such a test. Although differential neural blockade is not intended to replace a detailed history, a complete physical examination, and appropriate laboratory, radiographic, and psychological studies, in our practice it has been a rewarding diagnostic maneuver that has been effective in delineating the neural mechanisms subserving many puzzling pain problems, and it has been particularly useful in patients who have intractable pain with no apparent cause.

■ THE PHARMACOLOGIC APPROACH

A differential spinal is the simplest pharmacologic approach with the most discrete end points. The first clinical application of this technique[1] was based on the seminal work of Gasser and Erlanger,[2,3] and, although these investigators were wrong about the site of conduction (they believed it took place within the axoplasm), they established forever the relationship between fiber size, conduction velocity, and fiber function. Their classification of nerve fibers based on size is still used today (Table 14–1). In a simple but elegant experiment,

these researchers showed that when a nerve is stimulated and the response is recorded only a few millimeters away, the record shows a single action potential. Then they demonstrated that, as the recording electrode is moved progressively farther away from the stimulating electrode, the action potential can be shown to consist of several smaller spikes, each representing an impulse traveling at a different rate along a nerve fiber of a different size. The action potentials might be compared to runners in a race who become separated along the course as the faster contestants outstrip the slower. Thus, in a record obtained by a recording electrode 82 mm from the point of stimulation, three waves can be seen; whereas at 12 mm, the potentials are fused, and only one large wave appears (Fig. 14–1). It may be seen in Table 14–1 that the diameter of a nerve fiber is its most important physical dimension, so it is on that basis that they have been subdivided into three classes, A, B, and C fibers, A fibers being subdivided into four subclasses, alpha, beta, gamma, and delta. It may also be seen that the fiber diameter is an important determinant of conduction velocity—the conduction velocity of A fibers (in meters per second) being approximately 6 times the fiber diameter (in micrometers).[4] In addition, the diameter and myelination of a nerve fiber also determine to some degree the modality or modalities subserved by that fiber[5]: A-alpha fibers subserve motor function and proprioception; A-beta fibers subserve the transmission of touch and pressure; and A-gamma fibers subserve muscle tone. The thinnest A fibers, the A-delta group, convey pain and temperature sensation and signal nociception (tissue damage). The myelinated B fibers are thin, preganglionic, autonomic fibers, and the nonmyelinated C fibers, like the myelinated A-delta fibers, subserve pain, temperature transmission, and nociception. C fibers are thinner than the myelinated fibers and have a much slower conduction velocity than even A-delta fibers.

Although the relationship between fiber size and sensitivity to local anesthetics originally proposed by Gasser and Erlanger was challenged recently, the "bathed length principle" proposed by Fink[6,7] has restored the functional relationship between fiber size and sensitivity to local anesthetics because the larger the nerve fiber, the greater the internodal distance. It has been postulated that the density of the distribution of sodium channels at the nodes of Ranvier increases

Table 14–1

Classification of Nerve Fibers by Fiber Size and the Relation of Fiber Size to Function and Sensitivity to Local Anesthetics*

Group/Subgroup	Diameter (μm)	Conduction Velocity (m/sec)	Modalities Subserved	Sensitivity to Local Anesthetics (%)[†]
A (myelinated)				
_A-alpha	15-20	8-120	Large motor, proprioception	1.0
_A-beta	8-15	30-70	Small motor, touch, pressure	↓
_A-gamma	4-8	30-70	Muscle spindle, reflex	↓
_A-delta	3-4	10-30	Temperature, sharp pain, nociception	↓ 0.5
B (myelinated)	3-4	10-15	Preganglionic autonomic	0.25
C (unmyelinated)	1-2	1-2	Dull pain, temperature, nociception	0.5

*Subarachnoid procaine.
[†]Vertical arrows indicate intermediate values, in descending order.

Table 14–2

Preparation of Solutions for Conventional Sequential Differential Spinal Blockade

Solution	Preparation of Solution	Yield	Blockade
D	To 2 mL of 10% procaine add 2 mL of normal saline	4 mL of 5% procaine	Motor
C	To 1 mL of 5% procaine add 9 mL of normal saline	10 mL of 0.5% procaine	Sensory
B	To 5 mL of 0.5% procaine add 5 mL of normal saline	10 mL of 0.25% procaine	Sympathetic
A	Draw up 10 mL of normal saline	10 mL of normal saline	Placebo

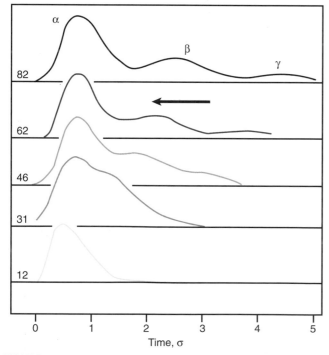

FIGURE 14–1 ■ Cathode ray oscillographs of the action current in a sciatic nerve of a bullfrog after conduction from the point of stimulation through the distances (mm) shown at the left. The delta wave is not shown. (Modified from Gasser HS, Erlanger J: Role of fiber size in establishment of nerve block by pressure or cocaine. Am J Physiol 88:587, 1929.)

with fiber size, so that the "denser channel packing at the nodes" may also result in increased minimum blocking concentration (C_m), so this may be another reason larger fibers require a higher concentration of local anesthetic for blockade than do smaller fibers.[8]

Conventional Sequential Differential Spinal Block

The conventional sequential technique of differential subarachnoid block[9,10] is a refinement of the techniques first used by Arrowood and Sarnoff[1] and later by McCollum and Stephen.[11] The technique has certain inherent shortcomings (see later), which have caused it to be replaced in our practice by the modified technique, but, because this is the prototype of differential neural blockade, understanding the technique and the problems it presents provides insight into the usefulness and the limitations of diagnostic differential spinal blockade using the pharmacologic approach.

Procedure

After detailed informed consent is obtained from the patient, an intravenous infusion is started and prehydration with crystalloid is begun, as for any spinal anesthetic. Similarly, all of the monitors routinely utilized for spinal anesthesia are applied, including blood pressure, electrocardiography (ECG), and pulse oximetry—and baseline values are recorded. Four solutions are prepared (Table 14–2), and the patient is placed in the lateral position with the painful side down, if possible. After the usual sterile preparation and draping of the back, a 25- to 27-gauge spinal needle is introduced into the lumbar subarachnoid space at the L2-L3 or L3-L4 interspace. The patient is shown the four prepared syringes, all of which appear identical, and is told that each of the solutions will be injected sequentially at 10- to 15-minute intervals. The patient is instructed to tell the physician which, if any, of the solutions relieves the pain. The solutions are referred to as *A* through *D,* so that the physicians can discuss the solutions freely in front of the patient without using the word *placebo.*

Solution A, which contains no local anesthetic, is the placebo. Solution B contains 0.25% procaine, which is the mean sympatholytic concentration of procaine in the subarachnoid space,[1] that is, the concentration that is sufficient to block B fibers but is *usually* insufficient to block A-delta and C fibers. Solution C contains 0.5% procaine, the mean sensory blocking concentration of procaine, that is, the concentration *usually* sufficient to block, in addition to B fibers, A-delta and C fibers but is insufficient to block A-alpha, A-beta, and A-gamma fibers. Solution D contains 5.0% procaine, which provides complete blockade of all fibers.

To prevent bias, it is extremely important that all of the injections be carried out in exactly the same manner, so that to the patient they are identical to and indistinguishable from one another. It is equally important that the physician make exactly the same observations after each injection (Table 14–3). The observations must be carried out in an identical manner after each injection so that the observations themselves do not influence the patient's response. Obviously, an inexperienced clinician who checks only the blood pressure after the sympatholytic injection, who checks only the response to pinprick after the sensory-blocking injection, and who checks only the motor function after the motor-blocking injection would clearly reveal the expectation that each sequential injection will produce progressively increasing effects. This would clearly compromise the validity of the information obtained from the procedure.

Interpretation

The conventional sequential differential spinal is interpreted as follows: If the patient's pain is relieved after solution A (the

Table 14–3

Observations After Each Injection

Sequence	Observation
1	Blood pressure and pulse rate
2	Patient's subjective evaluation of the pain at rest
3	Reproduction of patient's pain by movement
4	Signs of sympathetic block (temperature change, psychogalvanic reflex)
5	Signs of sensory block (no response to pinprick)
6	Signs of motor block (inability to move toes, feet, legs)

placebo), the patient's pain is classified as "psychogenic." It is well known that some 30% to 35% of all patients with true, organic pain obtain relief from an inactive agent.[12] Therefore, relief in response to the normal saline may represent a placebo reaction, but it may also indicate that an entirely psychogenic mechanism is subserving the patient's pain. Clinically, these two can usually be differentiated, because a placebo reaction is usually short-lived and self-limiting, whereas pain relief provided by a placebo to a patient suffering from true, psychogenic pain is usually long-lasting, if not permanent. If the difference between the two is not clinically evident, evaluation by a clinical psychologist or psychiatrist may be necessary.

If the patient does not obtain relief from the placebo but does obtain relief from the 0.25% procaine, the mechanism subserving the patient's pain is tentatively classified as sympathetic, provided that concurrent with the onset of pain relief, signs of sympathetic blockade are observed *without* signs of sensory block. Obviously, although 0.25% procaine is the *usual* sympatholytic concentration in most patients, in some patients (who may have a reduced C_m for A-delta and C fibers) relief may be due to the production of analgesia and/or anesthesia. The finding that a sympathetic mechanism is subserving a patient's pain is extremely fortuitous for the patient, because if the pain is truly sympathetically mediated, if treated early enough, it may be completely and permanently relieved by a series of sympathetic nerve blocks.

If 0.25% procaine does not provide pain relief but the 0.5% concentration does, this usually indicates that the patient's pain is subserved by A-delta and/or C fibers and is classified as somatic pain, *provided that* the patient did exhibit signs of sympathetic blockade after the previous injection of 0.25% procaine and that the onset of pain relief is accompanied by the onset of analgesia and/or anesthesia. This is important because if a patient has an elevated C_m for B fibers, the pain relief from 0.5% procaine could be due to sympathetic block rather than to sensory block.

If pain relief is not obtained by any of the first three injections, 5% procaine is injected to block all modalities. If the 5% concentration *does* relieve the patient's pain, the mechanism is still considered somatic, the presumption being that the patient has an elevated C_m for A-delta and C fibers. If, however, the patient obtains no relief in spite of complete sympathetic, sensory, and motor blockade, the pain is classified as "central" in origin, although this is not a specific diagnosis and may indicate any one of the four possibilities in Table 14–4.

Disadvantages

The conventional sequential differential spinal technique just described was utilized by the authors for many years and was effective in pinpointing the neural mechanisms subserving pain syndromes in a multitude of patients. It was particularly effective in establishing a diagnosis in patients with pain syndromes of questionable or unknown etiology. However, the technique has several obvious drawbacks. First of all, it is quite time consuming, because the physician must wait long enough after each injection for the response to become evident. Second, occasionally a patient is encountered whose C_m for sympathetic blockade is greater than 0.25, so when relief is produced by 0.5% procaine, one *might* erroneously conclude that this is somatic pain rather than sympathetic

Table 14–4

Diagnostic Possibilities of "Central Mechanism"

Diagnosis	Explanation/Basis of Diagnosis
Central lesion	The patient may have a lesion in the central nervous system that is above the level of the subarachnoid sensory block. For example, we have seen two patients who had a metastatic lesion in the precentral gyrus, which was the origin of the patient's peripheral pain and was clearly above the level of the block.
Psychogenic pain	The patient may have true "psychogenic pain," which obviously is not going to respond to a block at any level. This is an even more uncommon response in patients with psychogenic pain than a positive response to placebo.
Encephalization	The patient's pain may have undergone "encephalization"—that poorly understood phenomenon whereby persistent, severe, agonizing pain, originally of peripheral origin, becomes self-sustaining at a central level. This usually does not occur until severe pain has been endured for a long time, but once it has occurred, removal or blockade of the original peripheral mechanism fails to provide relief.
Malingering	The patient may be malingering. One cannot prove or disprove this with differential blocks, but if a patient is involved in litigation concerning the cause of his pain and anticipates financial benefit, it is unlikely that any therapeutic modality will relieve the pain. However, empirically, it is our belief that a previous placebo reaction from solution A followed by no relief from solution D strongly suggests that the patient whose pain ultimately appears to have a "central mechanism" is not malingering, since the placebo reaction, depending as it does on a positive motivation to obtain relief, is unlikely in a malingerer. Clearly, there is no way to document the validity of this theory, but it certainly suggests greater motivation to obtain pain relief than to obtain financial gain.

pain. Similarly, a patient may occasionally be encountered who has a lower C_m for sensory blockade than 0.5%, and when 0.25% procaine produces relief, one *might* erroneously conclude that the mechanism is sympathetic rather than somatic. Third, each successive injection with this technique deposits more procaine in the subarachnoid space, so that after the final injection, when all modalities are blocked, it takes quite a while for full function to return. Full recovery is absolutely essential, at least in our pain center, because the vast majority of the patients are outpatients and must be fully able to ambulate before they are discharged. This technique demands that the needle remain in place throughout the entire procedure, so the patient must remain in the lateral position throughout the test. Occasionally this is a serious problem, especially when the patient's pain is associated with a particular position that cannot be assumed with the needle in situ.

The "Modified Differential Spinal"

In an effort to overcome the disadvantages just described, the conventional technique has been modified in a way that simplifies it and increases its utility.[13-16] For the modified technique, only two solutions need to be prepared, as summarized in Table 14–5, namely, normal saline (solution A) and 5% procaine (solution D).

Procedure

As in the conventional technique, after informed consent has been obtained, an infusion started, and the monitors applied, the back is prepared and draped, and a small-bore spinal needle is used to enter the subarachnoid space. At this point 2 mL of normal saline is injected, and observations are made as in the conventional technique (see Table 14–3). If the patient obtains no relief or only partial relief from the placebo

Table 14–5

Preparation of Solutions for Modified Differential Spinal Blockade

Solution	Preparation and Solution	Yield
D	To 1 mL of 10% procaine add 1 mL of saline	2 mL of 5% procaine (hyperbaric)
A	Draw up 2 mL of normal saline	2 mL of normal saline

injection, 2 mL of 5% procaine is injected, the needle is removed, and the patient is returned to the supine position. Because the injected 5% procaine is hyperbaric, the position of the table may have to be adjusted to obtain the desired level of anesthesia. Once this is accomplished, the same observations are made as after the previous injection (see Table 14–3).

Interpretation

If the patient's pain is relieved after the injection of normal saline, the interpretation is the same as if it were relieved by placebo in the conventional differential spinal—that is, the pain is considered to be of psychogenic origin. Again, when the pain relief is prolonged or permanent, the pain is probably truly psychogenic, whereas if relief is transient and self-limited, the response probably represents a placebo reaction.

When the patient does not obtain pain relief after injection of 5% procaine, the diagnosis is considered to be the same as that when the patient obtains no relief after injection of all of the solutions with the conventional technique—that is, the mechanism is considered to be "central." As in the conventional technique, this diagnosis is not specific; rather, it indicates one of four possibilities (see Table 14–4).

Alternatively, when the patient does obtain complete pain relief after the injection of 5% procaine, the cause of the pain is considered to be organic. The mechanism is considered to be somatic (to be subserved by A-delta and/or C fibers) if the pain returns when the patient again perceives pinprick as sharp (recovery from analgesia); whereas it is considered sympathetic if the pain relief persists long after recovery from analgesia.

Fundamental Differences Between the Conventional Technique and the Modified Technique of Differential Spinal

The conventional sequential differential spinal sought to block specific types of nerve fibers with specific concentrations of local anesthetics. At the time when we modified the conventional technique, evidence was accumulating that the exact concentrations of local anesthetics required to block different fiber types are unpredictable, to say the least. Thus, we abandoned the practice of injecting predetermined concentrations of local anesthetics in an attempt to selectively block one fiber type at a time and adopted a technique not unlike that used to produce surgical spinal anesthesia—a technique that was much better understood. With that technique, after a placebo injection, a concentration of local anesthetic sufficient to produce surgical anesthesia is injected into the subarachnoid space to block all types of fibers, and the patient is observed as the concentration of local anesthetic in the cerebrospinal fluid decreases and the fibers recover sequentially, motor fibers first, followed by sensory fibers, and then sympathetic fibers. Whereas the conventional sequential technique attempted to correlate the *onset* of pain relief with the *onset* of blockade of the various fiber types, the modified technique attempts to correlate the *return* of pain with the *recovery* of the various blocked fibers.

It readily becomes apparent that this modified technique of differential spinal block simplifies the differentiation of sympathetic from somatic mechanisms considerably. With the conventional technique, occasionally the concentration required to produce sympathetic blockade is somewhat greater or somewhat less than the usual mean of 0.25%, and the concentration of procaine required to produce a sensory block is greater or less than the usual mean of 0.5%. Significant diagnostic confusion can result. With the modified technique, when a patient recovers sensation, the only fibers that remain blocked are the sympathetic fibers; thus, pain relief that persists beyond the recovery of sensation clearly indicates a sympathetic mechanism.

Advantages Over the Conventional Technique

The major advantage of the modified differential spinal block over the conventional technique is that it takes less time. The modified technique has consistently provided diagnostic information identical to that provided by the conventional technique, but in approximately one third of the time. The conventional differential technique requires a series of injections into the subarachnoid space of progressively increasing concentrations of local anesthetic, so that when the study is complete, the patient has a high level of anesthesia that takes

a long time to dissipate. The modified technique requires only a single injection of active drug; so in addition to the test's taking less time, the time for recovery is likewise reduced—a fact of great importance in a busy pain center. The modified technique also minimizes the extent and duration of discomfort for the patient, who does not have to lie so long in the lateral position with the needle in place. In addition, the modified technique allows a better evaluation of the subjective nature of a patient's pain. Because there is no need to keep the needle in the back throughout the procedure, the patient can lie supine, and positional changes or passive movement of the legs that may be necessary to reproduce the pain are much easier. The advantage of the modified approach over the traditional one in differentiating sympathetic from somatic pain has already been described.

Differential Epidural Block

More than 20 years ago, Raj[17] suggested using sequential differential epidural block instead of the conventional sequential differential spinal to avoid spinal headaches after the procedure. With his proposed technique, solution A was still to be the placebo, but solution B was 0.5% lidocaine, which was presumed to be the mean sympatholytic concentration of lidocaine in the epidural space; solution C was 1% lidocaine, the presumed mean sensory blocking concentration in the epidural space; and solution D was 2% lidocaine, a concentration sufficient to block all modalities. In short, the technique Raj proposed for differential epidural block was virtually identical to that used for the conventional differential spinal block, except that the local anesthetic doses were injected sequentially into the epidural space and the concentrations were modified as described earlier.

There were two problems with the technique proposed by Raj. First, because of the slower onset of blockade after each injection of local anesthetic into the epidural space, more time would be required between injections before the usual observations could be made. So a differential epidural block, as proposed by Raj, would take even longer for complete recovery than the conventional differential spinal technique. An even more serious drawback of this approach, however, relates to the fact that, if local anesthetics occasionally fail to give discrete end points when injected into the subarachnoid space, the end points are even less discrete with injections into the epidural space. For example, 0.5% lidocaine provides sympathetic blockade when injected epidurally, but it commonly causes sensory block as well. Similarly, whereas 1% lidocaine injected epidurally almost always produces sensory block, it frequently also produces paresis, if not paralysis. As a matter of fact, it was the failure of this technique to provide definitive end points that led Raj to decide not to publish it.

Nonetheless, *conceptually,* a differential epidural approach is inherently appealing because it avoids lumbar puncture and the possibility of postlumbar puncture headache in a predominantly outpatient population. The major problem with the technique Raj proposed, the lack of discrete end points, was due to the attempt to inject a different concentration of local anesthetic to block each type of nerve fiber, something we had attempted with our conventional differential spinal. Because our modified differential spinal eliminated the occasional confusing end points of the conventional technique, we decided to modify Raj's proposed differential epidural as we had modified our differential spinal. This technique as we perform it is as follows[14-16]:

Informed consent is obtained, an infusion is started, and the various monitors are applied. The patient is placed in the lateral (or sitting) position, and the back is prepared and draped in the usual manner. After a 20-gauge Husted needle has been placed in the epidural space by the modified loss-of-resistance technique, equal volumes of normal saline and 2% chloroprocaine (or lidocaine) are injected sequentially 15 to 20 minutes apart, and the needle is removed. The volume of each is that required to produce the desired level of anesthesia. After each injection, exactly the same observations are made as for a differential spinal (see Table 14–3).

The interpretation is virtually identical to that of a modified differential spinal. If the patient experiences pain relief after the injection of saline, the presumptive diagnosis is "psychogenic pain," a designation that indicates the possibility of either a placebo reaction or true psychogenic pain. If the patient does not experience pain relief after the injection of 2% chloroprocaine (or lidocaine) into the epidural space *in spite of complete anesthesia of the painful area,* the diagnosis is considered to be "central pain," that diagnosis again including the four possibilities described earlier (see Table 14–4). When the patient does experience pain relief after the injection of 2% chloroprocaine (or lidocaine), however, the pain is considered organic. It is presumed to be somatic (subserved by A-delta and C fibers) when the pain returns with the return of sensation, and sympathetic when the pain persists long after sensation has been recovered. This approach to differential epidural blockade has been used extensively at our institution and has provided the same valuable information obtained from the modified differential spinal technique without the usual risk of spinal headache. In addition, differential epidural is a useful alternative to differential spinal when a patient refuses spinal anesthesia or when spinal anesthesia is contraindicated, although both of these situations are rare. A catheter can be placed through a larger epidural needle if it is anticipated that supplemental injections may be necessary to achieve the proper level, but in our experience this has rarely been necessary.

Differential Brachial Plexus Block

Performed in a manner analogous to that of differential epidural block, a differential brachial plexus block can be extremely useful in evaluating upper extremity pain.[18] Two successive injections are made into the perivascular compartment using an approach appropriate to the site of the patient's pain, one injection consisting of normal saline and the other 2% chloroprocaine. Again, the same observations are made after each injection (see Table 14–3). If the patient is somewhat naive with respect to the injections carried out at a pain center, it may be sufficient for the placebo injection to consist of local infiltration over the anticipated site of injection of the active agent, as long as all of the appropriate observations are made after the injection. If this does not provide relief, the brachial plexus block is carried out with local anesthetic, inserting the needle through the anesthetized skin. If the patient obtains pain relief from the placebo injection, as with a differential spinal or epidural, the pain is considered psychogenic, whereas if the pain disappears after injection of chloroprocaine into the brachial plexus sheath, it is labeled organic. If the pain returns as soon as the sensory block is dissipated, the mechanism is somatic (i.e., it is subserved by A-delta and C fibers); if the relief persists long after recovery from the sensory block, the mechanism is presumed to be sympathetic. Finally, of course, if the pain does not disappear, even when the arm is fully anesthetized, the diagnosis is central pain, and the same four possibilities are again associated with that response (see Table 14–4).

It is significant to note that Durrani[19] has reported on 25 patients referred to our pain control center with a clinical diagnosis of "classic" reflex sympathetic dystrophy of the upper extremity—all of whom obtained no relief from a series of three stellate ganglion blocks, even though each patient developed Horner's syndrome after each block. The significance of this report is that, when these patients were subjected to differential brachial plexus block by one of the perivascular techniques, 16 of the 25 patients (who had not obtained relief from three stellate ganglion blocks) exhibited a typical sympathetic response to the brachial plexus block. Perhaps more importantly, 12 of the 19 patients so treated obtained complete and permanent relief from a series of therapeutic brachial plexus blocks, even though they had failed to do so after a series of stellate ganglion blocks. Thus, it would appear that perivascular brachial plexus blocks provide more complete sympathetic denervation of the upper extremity than do stellate ganglion blocks. The success of brachial plexus block and the failure of stellate ganglion blocks in this report might be explained by the fact that the local anesthetic injected at the stellate ganglion failed to reach the nerve of Kuntz, the nerve by which ascending sympathetic fibers may bypass the stellate ganglion.[20,21] Because all of the stellate ganglion blocks at our institution are carried out using a minimum of 8 mL of local anesthetic, however, this is unlikely. A more likely explanation is that stellate ganglion block interrupts only those sympathetic fibers that travel with the peripheral nerves, whereas perivascular brachial plexus block interrupts the sympathetic fibers traveling by both neural and perivascular pathways.[22]

Summary

Controversial aspects aside, the pharmacologic approach to differential neural blockade remains a simple but useful technique—whether carried out at a subarachnoid, epidural, or plexus level because it provides reproducible, objective, and definitive diagnostic information on the neural mechanisms subserving a patient's pain. Obviously, the results of this test must be interpreted in the light of other diagnostic tests (including psychological tests) and the results must be integrated with the information obtained from the patient's history and the findings on physical examination. Not infrequently, the results of a differential spinal, a differential epidural, or a differential plexus block provide the missing piece in the complex puzzle of pain.

■ THE ANATOMIC APPROACH

To obviate the problems inherent in high spinal (or epidural) anesthesia, particularly in an outpatient or a patient whose pain is in the upper part of the body, it is occasionally safer

Table 14–6

Anatomic Approach: Procedural Sequence for Differential Diagnostic Nerve Blocks

Site of Pain	Technique		
Head	Placebo block	Stellate ganglion block	Block of C_2; block of trigeminal I, II, III (or specific nerve block)
Neck	Placebo block	Stellate ganglion block	Cervical plexus block (or specific nerve block)
Arm	Placebo block	Stellate ganglion block	Brachial plexus block (or specific nerve block)
Thorax*	Placebo block	Thoracic paravertebral sympathetic block	Lumbar paravertebral somatic block
Abdomen†	Placebo block	Celiac plexus block	Paravertebral somatic or intercostal block
Pelvis†	Placebo block	Superior hypogastric plexus block	Paravertebral somatic or intercostal block
Leg	Placebo block	Lumbar paravertebral sympathetic block	Lumbosacral plexus block (or specific nerve block)

*In our opinion, thoracic paravertebral sympathetic blocks carry such a high risk of pneumothorax that a pharmacologic approach should be used.

† Because of the simplicity of intercostal blocks, as compared with celiac plexus and superior hypogastric plexus blocks, the procedural sequence is altered for abdominal pain (i.e., somatic before sympathetic).

and more appropriate to use an anatomic approach to differential neural blockade. In this approach, after the injection of a placebo, the sympathetic and then the sensory and/or motor fibers are blocked sequentially by injecting local anesthetic at points where one modality can be blocked without blocking the other. The procedural sequences by which differential nerve blocks are carried out in this approach for pain in the various parts of the body are presented in Table 14–6.

Procedure

For pain in the head, neck, and upper extremity, if a placebo injection fails to provide relief, a stellate ganglion block is carried out with any short-acting, dilute local anesthetic. If the sympathetic block cannot be carried out without spillover onto somatic nerves innervating the painful area, the sequential blocks should be carried out on two separate occasions, allowing the sympathetic block to wear off before proceeding with the somatic block. In any case, if the patient does not obtain relief from the stellate ganglion block, then a block of the somatic nerves to the painful area should be carried out.

For pain in the thorax, after a placebo injection, the safest procedure (and the one that causes the least discomfort to the patient) is a differential segmental epidural block, as described previously. It must be remembered, however, that, with thoracic pain, relief after an extensive sympathetic block, in addition to suggesting a possible sympathetic mechanism, may indicate visceral rather than somatic pain, because visceral pain is mediated by sympathetic fibers. If it is unwise to carry out a differential thoracic epidural block in a particular patient because of cachexia, hypovolemia, or dehydration, an alternative is the anatomic approach, using paravertebral or intercostal blocks of the appropriate dermatomes. Failure of these somatic blocks to provide relief implies (but does not prove) a visceral origin for the pain; however, if the blocks provide complete relief and if the pain returns immediately after recovery, a peripheral somatic mechanism is indicated. If the relief provided by the blocks persists long after recovery of sensation, this may indicate a sympathetic mechanism.

When a placebo injection fails to provide relief for abdominal pain, before a celiac block is considered, paravertebral or intercostal blocks of the appropriate dermatomes should be done to make certain that the pain is not somatic (body wall). Patients have a great deal of difficulty localizing "abdominal pain," and therefore, they usually cannot differentiate pain due to body wall extension of a lesion from that due to true visceral involvement. If the paravertebral or intercostal blocks produce complete anesthesia of the body wall overlying the patient's pain but fail to provide relief, celiac plexus block should be carried out to confirm that the pain is truly visceral in origin.

If a placebo injection fails to provide relief for pelvic pain, before a superior hypogastric plexus block is attempted, paravertebral or appropriate sacral blocks should be carried out to make certain that the pain is not somatic. If these blocks produce appropriate anesthesia but fail to provide relief, a superior hypogastric block is carried out to establish that the pain is visceral.

For pain in the lower extremities, the pharmacologic approach (differential spinal or epidural) is preferable because it is more precise and less painful than peripheral nerve blocks. Differential peripheral blocks, however, can be used if the pharmacologic approach is contraindicated or undesirable or if subsequent neurolytic blocks are anticipated. After a placebo block, lumbar paravertebral sympathetic blocks are performed at the levels L2-L4, and if these fail to provide relief, lumbosacral plexus block (or any appropriate specific peripheral nerve block) is carried out.

Interpretation

Interpretation of the results achieved with differential nerve blocks for head, neck, arm, and leg pain is self-evident. Relief after a placebo injection indicates a psychogenic mechanism, but, as with the pharmacologic approaches, it could indicate either a placebo reaction or true psychogenic pain. Relief after sympathetic blocks indicates a sympathetic mechanism, usually reflex sympathetic dystrophy (complex regional pain syndrome I [CRPS I]), and relief after blockade of somatic nerves indicates an organic, somatic mechanism. Failure to obtain relief in spite of the establishment of complete anesthesia in the appropriate area would tend to indicate a central mechanism, which could be any of the four possibilities listed in Table 14–4. Interpretation of the results of differential blocks for thoracic and abdominal pain has already been discussed.

■ DISCUSSION

In spite of the clinical success of the various techniques of differential neural blockade in many centers over the last 25 years, the validity of the results has become controversial. There are two reasons for this: (1) the changes in our understanding of the factors that determine the process of nerve conduction and blockade are believed by some to invalidate the concept of differential neural blockade; (2) the even greater changes in our understanding of the complexities of chronic pain and the physiologic, anatomic, and psychosocial factors involved are believed to limit the diagnostic utility of neural blockade. To establish both the validity and utility of differential neural blockade in the diagnosis of pain mechanisms, it is essential to understand the bases of this controversy by answering two questions.

1. Do the Factors Recently Found to Determine Nerve Conduction and Blockade Invalidate the Concept of Differential Neural Blockade?

The pharmacologic approach to differential neural blockade is based on the assumption that local anesthetic agents can selectively produce conduction block of one type of fiber in a nerve while sparing the other types in that nerve.[23] Although the concept of differential block was introduced almost 80 years ago by Gasser and Erlanger,[24] in vitro and in vivo studies carried out over the past 25 years have indicated that the basis of Gasser and Erlanger's explanation of this commonly observed clinical phenomenon was totally erroneous, as was their explanation of the process of nerve conduction itself. From the classic studies Gasser and Erlanger carried out on the peripheral nerves of dogs they concluded that, in general, small-diameter fibers were more readily blocked by cocaine than were larger-diameter fibers. At that time, however, it was believed that the site of action of conduction was the axonal protoplasm. Thus, the higher ratio of surface to volume in small-diameter fibers was supposed to make them more "sensitive" (easier to enter and render unexcitable) than large ones. Since that theory was articulated in one form or another this "size principle" has influenced the concept of differential block, has led to clinical use of differential spinal block,[1] and has provided an explanation for the persistent differential losses of function observed during subarachnoid[25] and epidural[26] anesthesia.

It was over 50 years before the concept of Gasser and Erlanger was challenged. Studies by Franz and Perry in vivo[27] and by Fink and Cairns in vitro[28] indicated that all mammalian axons require about the same blocking concentration of local anesthetic, regardless of their diameter, and the issue was rendered even more confusing when Gissen and coworkers[29]

demonstrated that the larger the diameter of an axon, the more susceptible it was to conduction block by local anesthetics, a finding diametrically opposed to Gasser and Erlanger's traditional concept. However, as de Jong pointed out,[30] a major flaw in Gissen's study was that the experiments were carried out at room temperature. Because conduction in large fibers is more affected by cold than is conduction in small fibers, relatively little anesthetic may be needed to block large fibers in conditions cooler than body temperature. Subsequently, Palmer and coworkers,[31] using a preparation maintained at body temperature, showed that C fibers were, in fact, more susceptible to conduction block by bupivacaine than were A fibers, but they were unable to demonstrate such differential effects with lidocaine.

This study introduced a new complexity: different anesthetics may affect various axon types differently. In two sequential in vitro studies, Wildsmith and colleagues[32,33] compared the differential nerve-blocking activity of a series of amide-linked local anesthetics with that of a series of ester-linked agents. These studies confirmed Gissen's finding that, in general, A fibers are the most sensitive and C fibers the least sensitive to blockade by local anesthetics but that the absolute and relative rates of development of A fiber blockade were directly related to lipid solubility and inversely related to pK_a. On the basis of the findings of these two in vitro studies, Wildsmith postulated that, in vivo, C fibers could be blocked differentially by an agent of low lipid solubility and high pK_a, because a compound with these properties (such as procaine) might produce blockade of C fibers relatively quickly, but before it could penetrate the great diffusion barriers around A fibers, it would be removed by the circulation. Ford and Raj[34] tested this hypothesis, studying several local anesthetics in a cat model in vivo and found that, regardless of the local anesthetic, A-alpha fibers were consistently less sensitive to blockade than either A-delta or C fibers, thus reaffirming the original scheme of Gasser and Erlanger.

It remained for Fink[6] to elucidate the importance of two other factors subserving differential neural blockade. First, he pointed out the importance of the nodes of Ranvier, the internodal distance, and the number of nodes bathed by a local anesthetic to differential neural blockade. It has long been known that to block conduction, an adequate concentration of local anesthetic (C_m) applied to a myelinated axon must bathe at least three consecutive nodes.[35] Because the internodal distance increases as the thickness of the axon increases, the probability of three successive nodes of Ranvier being bathed quickly by an injected local anesthetic solution decreases as the internodal distance increases, that is, as the size of the fiber increases (Fig. 14–2). In other words, the chance of a local anesthetic solution blocking a given nerve fiber decreases with increasing fiber size. For example, the internodal distance of small A-delta fibers ranges from 0.3 to 0.7 mm, so a puddle of local anesthetic solution only 2 mm long will fully cover three successive nodes. In contrast, large A-alpha fibers have an internodal distance of 0.8 to 1.4 mm, so their *critical blocking length* is at least 5 mm.[27] Thus, because the internodal distance increases with thickness of the axon, the minimal blocking length ranges from 2 to 5 mm.

Next, Fink demonstrated that the differential blockade of the sympathetic nerves observed clinically with spinal anesthesia is probably due, at least in part, to decremental block

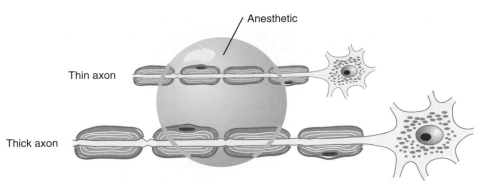

FIGURE 14–2 ■ Differential nerve block based on different internodal intervals. Two axons, one thin and one thick, are depicted lying side by side in a puddle of local anesthetic at or above the minimum blocking concentration (C_m). The internodal interval of the thick fiber is twice that of the thin one, so whereas the local anesthetic solution covers three successive nodes of the thin axon, it covers only one node of the thick one. Nerve impulses can skip easily over one node, and even over two, rendered inexcitable by the local anesthetic,[35] so conduction along the thick axon will continue uninterrupted. In the thin axon, however, because three nodes are covered by the local anesthetic solution, impulse conduction is halted. Thus, conduction appears to proceed normally in the thick (motor) fiber but is blocked in the thin (sensory) fiber. Such a differential block of thin versus thick nerve fibers occurs in spinal roots during spinal anesthesia (see text). (Modified from de Jong RH: Local Anesthetics. St. Louis, Mosby, 1994, p 89.)

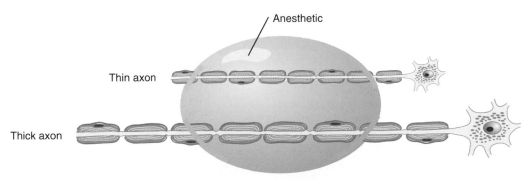

FIGURE 14–3 ■ Differential decremental nerve block and frequency-dependent block. When both thick and thin axons have more than three nodes covered by a local anesthetic solution, if the solution is at or above the minimum blocking concentration (C_m) all of the sodium channels are occupied and conduction is blocked in both fibers. However, if the concentration of local anesthetic is below C_m, a significant portion (but not all) of the sodium channels are blocked, so that at each node the action potential undergoes a progressive reduction in amplitude, with resultant decremental slowing of impulse conduction. Such decremental conduction will ultimately extinguish the impulse in the nine exposed nodes of the thin fiber (decremental block); but, although the impulse is slowed in its passage along the five incompletely blocked nodes of the thick fiber, it will resume at full speed when normally conducting membrane is reached again. The lower the concentration of the local anesthetic, the longer must be the exposure length (the number of nodes of Ranvier exposed) to yield complete impulse blockade. Conversely, the more concentrated the local anesthetic solution, the shorter is the exposure length required for complete blockade, up to the point of C_m, when the "three-node principle" again applies. In other words, below C_m, the blocking concentration of local anesthetic is inversely proportional to the length of the nerve it bathes. The greater the frequency of nerve stimulation, the shorter is the exposure length (the number of incompletely blocked nodes) required to yield complete impulse blockade. Such a frequency-dependent block superimposed on decremental block is operant clinically in the zone cephalad to the level of somatic block in a spinal anesthesia (see text). (Modified from de Jong RH: Local Anesthetics. St. Louis, Mosby, 1994, p 91.)

with a superimposed frequency-dependent effect.[36] Decremental block occurs when a nerve is bathed by a weak concentration of local anesthetic ($<C_m$): Both thick and thin axons have more than three nodes covered by local anesthetic (Fig. 14–3); because of the difference in the internodal distance, fewer nodes are bathed by local anesthetic in the thick fiber than in the thin one. Thus, when an impulse arrives at the incompletely blocked thick fiber, although there is a progressive reduction in conduction velocity and elevation of firing threshold as it traverses the incompletely blocked segment, it resumes full speed when it reaches a segment of normally conducting membrane. Put simply, too few nodes were partially blocked to completely halt conduction. However, in the thin axon, a sufficient number of nodes are partially blocked so that the progressive reduction in the action current at each node ultimately causes the impulse to be blocked. Because the action current decreases in decrements, the phenomenon is referred to as *decremental conduction block*. Because the

block is complete in the small axon and incomplete in the large one, this represents a differential (decremental) block.

In this example, decremental block of single impulses has been described, and single impulses allow enough time for membrane recovery. In reality, impulses occur in rapid sequential bursts that allow little time for recovery, and it has been demonstrated repeatedly that, as the rate of stimulation increases, so does the intensity of the block. Presumably, this phenomenon, called *frequency-dependent block*, is due to the fact that, at rapid rates of stimulation, the time between impulses is insufficient for the local anesthetic to unbind, so a fraction of the sodium channels is still blocked when the next impulse arrives. Obviously, frequency-dependent block superimposed on decremental block enhances conduction block by local anesthetics in concentrations considerably below C_m.

Because the conditions necessary for frequency-dependent block include a weak concentration of local anesthetic ($<C_m$) and a train of repetitive stimuli,[37] both conditions

are present in the zone cephalad to the level of somatic block in spinal anesthesia: The cerebrospinal fluid concentration of local anesthetic is too low to block somatic axons, but the preganglionic sympathetic fibers carry a normal tonic flow of rapid vasoconstrictor impulses. As a result, frequency-dependent block of the sympathetic fibers is superimposed on decremental block. Another observation of clinical importance is that highly lipid-soluble local anesthetics require more repetitive stimuli to reach maximal frequency-dependent blocking than less lipid-soluble agents,[38] so differential blockade of the sympathetic fibers without blockade of somatic fibers is easier to accomplish with agents of low lipid solubility such as procaine.

Applying these two concepts, Fink pointed out that the anatomy of the spinal roots in the spinal canal of an adult varies considerably at different levels because the spinal cord is substantially shorter than the dural sac that surrounds it. Thus, proceeding cephalocaudad, the length of the spinal roots from the point where they leave the cord to the point where they exit the dura increases from 0.5 cm for the C1 root to 15 cm for the S4 root. With spinal anesthesia, the densest concentration of local anesthetic is nearest the lumbar puncture site. Here the length of the lumbosacral nerve roots allows many nodes of Ranvier of all sizes of fibers to be exposed to the local anesthetic, so a solid block of the lumbosacral roots is rapidly achieved.

Progressively farther craniad, the local anesthetic solution is increasingly diluted by spinal fluid until the cephalad salient is "watered down" to C_m. At that point, fibers with a short internodal distance may still fall within the blocking zone, whereas the distal nodes of thicker fibers with a longer internodal distance may fall well outside the blocking potency range. In other words, small autonomic and nociceptive fibers are still blocked, but the thicker touch and motor fibers no longer are.[39] As fibers cephalad to the C_m zone are exposed to subthreshold local anesthetic concentrations, decremental block and/or frequency-dependent block begins to play a role. The short-to-long internode-blocking gradient still holds, but now a longer string of nodes must be bathed before an impulse is halted (see Fig. 14–3). Because of the shorter internodal intervals of thin fibers, the segment of a thin nerve that needs to be bathed to block conduction is shorter than the segment required to block thick nerves. Thus, differential spinal block is observed at threshold-blocking concentrations.[7] The other contribution of Fink, based on the same "bathed length" concept, is seen during epidural anesthesia. The length of the nerve segments from dural sac to intervertebral foramen is both shorter and less variable than that of the intrathecal roots. In fact, the few millimeters of root exposed in the cervical and thoracic epidural space barely span the three-node length of thin nerves, let alone that of thicker nerves. Differential block with epidural analgesia thus can be quite pronounced, a property used to great advantage in providing "pure" postoperative analgesia with epidural infusions of a weak local anesthetic solution.

In an editorial accompanying Fink's article, Raymond and Strichartz[40] summarized the impact of Fink's "innovative" observations on the concept of differential block as follows:

They link clinical observations to anatomical findings in both humans and animals and to measurements made in vitro on isolated nerves, thereby generating interesting predictions and possibilities. They lead the discussion of differential block away from a broad susceptibility to LA [local anesthetics] according to fiber size to focus on the number of nodes per unit length, which is correlated with fiber size. Clinically, this permits retention of familiar interpretations (based on the size principle) of phenomena consistently seen during epidural and spinal anesthesia; and it does not deny the single fiber data showing similar LA susceptibility across the fiber spectrum (for long exposed segments). The ideas are, in this sense, an extension of the size principle, not a renunciation of it.

From this summary, it is clear that differential neural blockade is a reality. Although the size principle (the thicker the fiber, the harder it is to block) has been replaced by the length principle (the fewer nodes bathed, the harder it is to block), as indicated by de Jong,[41] the clinical outcome remains functionally the same. The thicker the nerve fiber, the broader the internode and the fewer nodes per exposure length. Thus, blocking a thick nerve fiber requires a supra-C_m local anesthetic solution because there are too few nodes accessible for decremental block to come into play. In other words, for a given local anesthetic concentration, there will be an interim transition phase in which nociception (pain) conducted by thin fibers is blocked, but touch and motor function conducted by thick fibers remain virtually intact.

Although inconsistencies and contraindications about the mechanisms of differential neural blockade persist, it is conceptually valid, and in our hands, it has proved an invaluable clinical tool for identifying the mechanism subserving a patient's pain.

2. Do the Complexities of Chronic Pain and the Physiologic, Anatomic, and Psychosocial Factors Involved Limit the Diagnostic Utility of Differential Neural Blockade?

No one could deny that over the last 25 years basic research in the field of pain has produced important insights into the pathophysiology of chronic pain, the anatomic pathways involved in the processing and conduction of pain, and the important psychosocial issues that affect a patient's perception of pain. It is not readily apparent, however, why increases in our understanding of the complexities of pain should invalidate the diagnostic information provided by differential neural blockade. Better understanding of the mechanisms involved in the pain process should actually enhance our ability to interpret the information gained from diagnostic nerve blocks. Yet, just 10 years ago in a review of neural blockade for diagnosis and prognosis,[42] the authors state categorically that "complex physiologic events may confound the simple interpretation of diagnostic blocks"; that "compelling evidence with regard to placebo responses leads to the conclusion that the ambiguity created by these responses is a major impediment to the valid use of neural blockade for diagnosis"; and that "anatomic uncertainties with regard to neuroconnections and structural variability degrade the accuracy of diagnostic information obtained by neural blockade."

Furthermore, the author of an editorial supporting these views states that "several factors, such as the improper use of pain measurement scales, observer errors, problems of placebo effects, and bias introduced by patient expectations, confound the interpretation of studies on the usefulness of neural blockade in the diagnosis of chronic pain," and that "because the treatment [of pain] and prognosis often depend on accurate diagnosis, the incorrect interpretation of the results of a nerve block may result in inappropriate therapy."[43] These platitudes and attitudes do not denigrate differential neural blockade, but the intelligence, knowledge, and clinical judgment of anesthesiologists who are in the practice of pain management. There are few (if any) diagnostic techniques in all of medicine that are infallibly positive or negative or, taken by themselves, invariably indicative of a specific etiology. All such tests give false-positive and false-negative results, and knowing this, the experienced clinician integrates the result of any one test with the results of others, with the information gained from a careful history, and with the findings of the physical examination. Of course, caution must be used in interpreting any tests, but, interpreted intelligently, the results of differential neural blockade not infrequently provide the missing piece of the puzzle of pain, and the reward for the patient (and the concerned physician) is pain relief.

To abandon differential nerve blocks for the diagnosis of pain until the precise mechanisms subserving pain and its relief are understood would be as foolish as to abandon general anesthesia until the precise mechanism by which general anesthetics work is understood. Even those who decry diagnostic blocks admit that "experienced and observant clinicians have found that these procedures may, on certain occasions, provide information that is helpful in guiding subsequent therapy, so we should not be in haste to dismiss the accumulated judgement of [the] practitioner," and that "the confusion and complexity that typify the diagnosis of chronic pain may justify the selective use of diagnostic blocks that make anatomic and physiologic sense, even if their validity is incompletely proved."[42] It goes without saying that the clinician who employs diagnostic nerve blocks must exercise great care in carrying out the technique, in confirming observed effects in interpreting the results, and in applying them to clinical decisions.

■ ROLE OF DIFFERENTIAL NEURAL BLOCKADE

Many patients seeking pain relief at a pain control center present no diagnostic problem whatsoever; however, anyone experienced in the diagnosis and management of chronic pain problems has seen many apparently clear-cut diagnoses completely and unexpectedly refuted when one of the techniques of differential neural blockade was utilized to "confirm" the diagnosis. The concern in such cases is that *if this diagnostic approach had not been utilized* because the clinician felt that with his or her "experience and expertise in pain management" such supportive evidence was unnecessary, *the true diagnosis would have been missed,* and the patient's therapy, based on the clinical diagnosis, would have been unsuccessful. Human limitations being what they are and pain being the complex process that it is, no one ever develops enough experience or expertise to make the correct diagnosis 100% of the time. Differential neural blockade provides an objective means of *confirming* a diagnosis when the cause of pain

appears obvious, and, perhaps more importantly, a means of *establishing* a diagnosis when there appears to be no demonstrable cause.

Forty years ago we retrospectively reviewed a series of 100 patients referred to our pain control center "because all diagnostic attempts had failed to discover a cause for the patient's pain."[9] Reviewing these difficult cases, we were impressed by the fact that differential neural blockade was effective in identifying the mechanism as sympathetic, somatic, or central in all of these patients (Table 14–7). Even more impressive and surprising was the fact that in 74% of the patients, differential neural blockade indicated the mechanism to be sympathetic. A somatic mechanism was implicated in only 18% and a central (including psychogenic) mechanism in only 8%. These findings were important because in the vast majority of these patients, patients in whom a sympathetic mechanism was *unexpectedly* identified, the diagnosis was established early enough that complete and permanent relief could be provided by a series of sympathetic blocks.

These data provide convincing evidence that, at least in patients suffering from pain syndromes of questionable cause, sympathetically maintained pain (sympathetically maintained pain, reflex sympathetic dystrophy, complex regional pain syndrome) is not uncommon. All of these patients were referred by specialists who could find no cause for the pain, and indeed, in most of the cases the signs and symptoms were either so bizarre or so seemingly unrelated to any precipitating factor that, had differential blocks not been carried out, we (like the referring physicians) would probably have considered the pain to be psychogenic. The importance of establishing a diagnosis in this group of patients was emphasized over 60 years ago by de Takats[44] and 10 years later by Bonica,[45] both of whom pointed out that if such patients are not properly diagnosed and treated in time, they often become addicted to narcotics or become psychotic or even suicidal.

In view of the difficulty of establishing a precise diagnosis in many patients suffering intractable chronic pain and in view of the efficacy of differential neural blockade, in doing so, it has been and continues to be our practice to use differential neural blockade to confirm the diagnosis in many cases, even when the mechanism appears to be obvious on clinical grounds, and even more frequently to establish a diagnosis when the mechanism is in question or is not known.

Table 14–7

Results of Differential Neural Blockade in 100 Patients Referred Because of "No Demonstrable Cause for Pain"

Diagnosis	Incidence (%)
Psychogenic mechanism	5
Sympathetic mechanism	74
Somatic mechanism	18
Central mechanism	3

From Winnie AP, Collins VJ: The pain clinic. I: Differential neural blockade in pain syndromes of questionable etiology. Med Clin North Am 52:123, 1968.

References

1. Arrowood JG, Sarnoff SJ: Differential block. V. Use in the investigation of pain following amputations. Anesthesiology 9:614, 1948.
2. Gasser HS, Erlanger J: The compound nature of the action current of nerve as disclosed by the cathode ray oscilloscope. Am J Physiol 70:624, 1924.
3. Gasser HS, Erlanger J: The role played by the size of the constituent fibers of a nerve trunk in determining the form of its action potential wave. Am J Physiol 80:522, 1927.
4. Gasser HS, Grundfest H: Axon diameters in relation to the spike dimensions and the conduction velocity in the mammalian A fibers. Am J Physiol 127:393, 1939.
5. Collins WF, Hulsen FE, Randt CT: Relation of peripheral nerve fiber size and sensation in man. Arch Neurol 3:381, 1960.
6. Fink BR: Mechanisms of differential axial blockade in epidural and subarachnoid anesthesia. Anesthesiology 70:851, 1989.
7. Fink BR: Toward the mathematization of spinal anesthesia. Reg Anesth 17:263, 1992.
8. de Jong RH: Differential nerve block. In Local Anesthetics. St. Louis, Mosby-Year Book, 1994, p 84.
9. Winnie AP, Collins VJ: The pain clinic. I: Differential neural blockade in pain syndromes of questionable etiology. Med Clin North Am 52:123, 1968.
10. Winnie AP, Ramamurthy S, Durrani Z: Diagnostic and therapeutic nerve blocks: Recent advances in techniques. Adv Neurol 4:455, 1974.
11. McCollum DE, Stephen CR: Use of graduated spinal anesthesia in the differential diagnosis of pain of the back and lower extremities. South Med J 57:410, 1964.
12. Beecher HK: The powerful placebo. JAMA 159:1602, 1955.
13. Akkineni SR, Ramamurthy S: Simplified differential spinal block. Presented at the Annual Meeting of the American Society of Anesthesiologists, New Orleans, October 15-19, 1977.
14. Winnie AP: Differential diagnosis of pain mechanisms. ASA Refresher Courses in Anesthesiology 6:171, 1978.
15. Ramamurthy S, Winnie AP: Diagnostic maneuvers in painful syndromes. Int Anesth Clin 21:47, 1983.
16. Ramamurthy S, Winnie AP: Regional anesthetic techniques for pain relief. Semin Anesth 4:237, 1985.
17. Raj PP: Sympathetic pain mechanisms and management. Presented at the Second Annual Meeting of the American Society of Regional Anesthesia, Hollywood, Fla, March 10-11, 1977.
18. Winnie AP: Differential neural blockade for the diagnosis of pain mechanisms. In Waldman SD, Winnie AP (eds): Interventional Pain Management. Philadelphia, WB Saunders, 1996, p 129.
19. Durrani Z, Winnie AP: Role of brachial plexus block after negative response from stellate ganglion block for RSD. Anesthesiology 73:A837, 1990.
20. Kuntz A: Distribution of the sympathetic rami to the brachial plexus: Its relation to sympathectomy affecting the upper extremity. Arch Surg 15:871, 1927.
21. Kirgis HD, Kuntz A: Inconstant sympathetic neural pathways: Their relation to sympathetic denervation of the upper extremity. Arch Surg 44:95, 1942.
22. Kramer JG, Todd TW: The distribution of nerves to the arteries of the arm: With a discussion of the clinical value of results. Anat Rec 8:243, 1914.
23. Raymond SA, Gissen AJ: Mechanisms of differential nerve block. In Strichartz G (ed): Local Anesthetics. New York, Springer-Verlag, 1987, p 95.
24. Gasser HS, Erlanger J: Role of fiber size in establishment of nerve block by pressure or cocaine. Am J Physiol 88:581, 1929.
25. Greene NM: Area of differential block in spinal anesthesia with hyperbaric tetracaine. Anesthesiology 19:45, 1958.
26. Bromage PR: An evaluation of bupivacaine in epidural analgesia in obstetrics. Can Anaesth Soc J 16:46, 1969.
27. Franz DN, Perry RS: Mechanisms for differential block among single myelinated and non-myelinated axons by procaine. J Physiol (Lond) 236:193, 1974.
28. Fink BR, Cairns AM: Differential slowing and block of conduction in individual afferent myelinated and unmyelinated axons. Anesthesiology 60:111, 1984.
29. Gissen AJ, Covino BG, Gregus J: Differential sensitivities of mammalian nerve fibers to local anesthetic agents. Anesthesiology 53:467, 1980.
30. de Jong RH: Differential nerve block by local anesthetics (editorial). Anesthesiology 53:443, 1980.
31. Palmer SK, Bosnjak ZJ, Hopp FA, et al: Lidocaine and bupivacaine differential blockade of isolated canine nerves. Anesth Analg 62:754, 1983.
32. Wildsmith JAW, Gissen AJ, Gregus J, Covino BG: Differential nerve blocking activity of amino-ester local anaesthetics. Br J Anaesth 57:612, 1985.
33. Wildsmith JAW, Gissen AJ, Takman B, Covino BG: Differential nerve blockade: Esters V. Amides and the influence of pK$_a$. Br J Anaesth 59:379, 1987.
34. Ford D, Raj PP, Singh P, et al: Differential peripheral nerve block by local anesthetics in the cat. Anesthesiology 60:28, 1984.
35. Tasaki I: Nervous Transmission. Springfield, Charles C Thomas, 1953, p 164.
36. Fink BR, Cairns AM: Differential use-dependent (frequency-dependent) effects in single mammalian axons: Data and clinical considerations. Anesthesiology 67:477, 1987.
37. Scurlock JE, Meyaris E, Gregus J: The clinical character of local anesthetics: A function of frequency-dependent conduction block. Acta Anaesthesiol Scand 22:601, 1978.
38. Courtney KR, Kendig JJ, Cohen EN: Frequency-dependent conduction block. Anesthesiology 48:111, 1978.
39. Brull SJ, Green NM: Time courses of zones of differential sensory blockade during spinal anesthesia with hyperbaric tetracaine or bupivacaine. Anesth Analg 69:343, 1989.
40. Raymond SA, Strichartz GR: The long and short of differential block (editorial). Anesthesiology 70:725, 1989.
41. de Jong RH: Differential nerve blocks. In Local Anesthetics. St. Louis, Mosby-Year Book, 1994, p 96.
42. Hogan QH, Abram SE: Neural blockade for diagnosis and prognosis. Anesthesiology 86:216, 1997.
43. Raja SN: Nerve blocks in the evaluation of chronic pain: A plea for caution in their use and interpretation (editorial). Anesthesiology 86:4, 1997.
44. de Takats G: Nature of painful vasodilation in causalgic states. Arch Neurol Psychiatry 50:318, 1943.
45. Bonica JJ: Causalgia and other reflex sympathetic dystrophies. In Bonica JJ (ed): The Management of Pain. Philadelphia, Lea & Febiger, 1953, p 956.

chapter 15

Spinal Canal Endoscopy

Lloyd R. Saberski

■ HISTORICAL CONSIDERATIONS

Endoscopy plays a role in the diagnosis and treatment of many different conditions. Endoscopy platforms continue to grow into areas amenable to endoscopic visualization, particularly the epidural space, spinal cord, and contiguous structures. A review of the medical literature shows that clinicians have been working with various types of endoscopes for more than 60 years, with varying degrees of success. Today, fiberoptic technology has been integrated with computer-enhanced imaging to provide a new medium for viewing the CNS. The initial results are promising and will probably pave the way for newer, less invasive means of diagnosis and treatment of CNS pathology.

Direct visualization of the spinal canal and its contents was born in 1931 from the pioneering work of Michael Burman.[1] With each decade since then, myeloscopists and epiduroscopists have attempted to develop a means of fiberoptic visualization that would be easy and safe for application in medical practice. Burman[1] removed 11 cadaver vertebral columns and examined them with rigid arthroscopic equipment and an incandescent light source. As might be expected, the diameter of the trocar in which the lamp was mounted was greater than the average width of the spinal canal (approximately $3/8$ inch, or 9.5 mm). Thus, the viewing lens was not completely within the spinal canal. In a few locations, the spinal canal was wide enough to accommodate insertion of the endoscope, thereby permitting visualization of the spinal canal contents: the dura mater, blood vessels, and cauda equina. The endoscope's field of view was limited because of its large size to only 1 inch (2.54 cm). In 1931, Burman[1] concluded that myeloscopy was limited by the technology available. With higher-quality instrumentation, a better postmortem examination of the cauda equina could be performed in situ. He believed that visualization of the contents of cadaveric spinal canals would be especially important in establishing the diagnosis of tumor or inflammation. He did not anticipate that an improved device might allow in situ/in vivo, minimally invasive therapy. This was not to be achieved until the 1980s, when both flexible fiberoptic light sources and optics became available.[2]

In 1936, Elias Stern[3] of Columbia University's Department of Anatomy was among the first to describe a spinascope. A working model was built by American Cystoscopes Makers, Inc. The spinascope was designed for in vivo examination of the spinal canal contents in the presence of a spinal anesthetic. The instrument was never actually used, but Stern[3] did envision direct observation of the posterior roots for rhizotomies in patients with intractable pain, as well as sectioning of the anterior roots for incurable spastic conditions. He predicted that technologic improvements might allow the endoscopic platform to replace exploratory laminotomy.

In March 1937, the first anesthetized subject was examined with a myeloscope by J. Lawrence Pool[4,5] of New York (Fig. 15–1). Unfortunately, hemorrhage obscured the field of vision and permitted only a fleeting glimpse of the lumbosacral nerve roots. Subsequently, seven patients were examined without complication. The cauda equina and blood flow through epidural vessels were observed. In 1942, Pool published in the journal *Surgery* a summation of 400 cases.[6] In the era before CT and MRI he reconstructed graphics that established or confirmed the diagnosis via the myeloscope. With images in hand, he approached operations with expectation and avoided extensive explorations. He identified neuritis, herniated nucleus pulposus, hypertrophied ligamentum flavum, primary and metastatic neoplasms, varicose vessels, and arachnoid adhesions.

Despite these successes and the relative ease of performing such examinations, no further reports of similar technique are found in the literature until 1967 because of the widespread acceptance and simplicity of myelography and the need to sketch observations if performing spinal endoscopy. There was no automatic graphic capture, and photographic equipment of the era did not provide sufficient light for image formation. Dr. Pool, a talented artist, documented his observations with hand-drawn sketches.

In the late 1960s and early 1970s, Yoshio Ooi and colleagues,[7-11] working without knowledge of the American experience, developed an endoscope for intradural and extradural examination. Then available for use in the 1970s was fiberoptic light source technology, which allowed miniaturization and more lumens of light without added heat. The fiberoptic light source technology protected tissues from heat injury because fiberoptic fibers absorb infrared rays and reflect visible rays. The myeloscope could now be miniaturized because a large size was unnecessary for carrying sufficient light. The smaller size allowed the myeloscope to be inserted between lumbar spinous processes in the same manner as a needle for percutaneous lumbar puncture.[12] The

FIGURE 15–1 ■ J. Lawrence Pool (1906-2004), one of the pioneers of spinal endoscopy.

procedure was now greatly simplified and no serious complications were reported from their initial 86 patients. Postspinal cephalgia was a common, albeit temporary complication in 70% of the study patients. Dr. Ooi and colleagues[13] recorded detailed descriptions of normal and abnormal anatomy, as well as blurry black-and-white photographic images of the ligamentum flavum, epidural adipose tissue, the surface of the dural sac, and the cauda equina.

From 1967 to 1977, Ooi and colleagues[13,14] performed 208 myeloscopic procedures with various types of equipment. Their progress was reported in several publications, culminating in 1981 with their publication on myeloscopy and blood flow changes in the cauda equina during Laseøgue's test.[15] The intrathecal space was regularly entered with a 1.8-mm rigid scope. The fiberoptics used were only for the light source; fiberoptic myeloscopes with fiberoptic light sources for direct visualization were still a decade away. The authors noted changes in blood flow in vessels accompanying the cauda equina during straight-leg raising tests. During this maneuver, caudad anterior displacement of the cauda equina leading to temporary cessation of blood flow was observed. Presumably, this is clinically associated with pain in susceptible patients. Abdominal straining, coughing, and sneezing did not alter blood flow but did cause slight up-and-down movement of the cauda equina in the lateral position. Unfortunately, with the decrease in diameter of the scope, the amount of light available for good-quality pictures was reduced; a larger myeloscope (2.5 mm) was needed for visualization in the epidural space. Myeloscopy (epiduroscopy) therefore continued to be regarded as having limited value for the diagnosis of spinal stenosis but was thought to be an important aid in the diagnosis of pathology associated with spinal pain syndromes such as arachnoiditis, tumors, and vas-

cular abnormalities. Procedures such as removal of a herniated nucleus pulposus were considered, but because of limitations in flexibility of the rigid scope, insufficient light, and difficulty distinguishing normal from abnormal tissue, the surgical use of spinal endoscopic equipment remained limited. A flexible myeloscope was theorized to have many advantages, but another decade passed before arrival of the micro-myeloscope.

Blomberg[16] was the next to describe a method of epiduroscopy and spinaloscopy. It was his interest to study anatomic variation of the epidural space so that a better understanding of epidural anesthesia could be obtained. Using a fiberoptic light source with a small rigid endoscope, he determined that the contents of the epidural space varied widely, especially in regard to the amount of fat and connective tissue. In 12 of 30 postmortem examinations the epidural contents limited visibility of the epidural space. Adhesions between the dura mater and ligamentum flavum restricted opening the epidural space despite flushing with normal saline. Dr. Blomberg was able to position the epiduroscope (which was still similar to the Stern spinascope) to visualize entry of a Tuohy needle through the ligamentum flavum into the epidural space. Dural tenting was seen when an epidural catheter was threaded through the Tuohy needle into the epidural space. Once in the epidural space, the orientation of the catheter varied greatly and was ultimately determined by local anatomy. Dr. Blomberg surmised that it was "too early to decide to what extent clinical application is possible with epiduroscopy. Under all circumstances it would be necessary to improve lighting conditions, and to shorten shutter speeds in order to make the method more easily handled."[16]

In 1989, Blomberg and Olsson[17] performed 10 epiduroscopic procedures on patients scheduled for partial laminectomy for herniated lumbar disks. They believed that the conclusions drawn from previous autopsy work were not necessarily transferable to the clinical setting. Their concerns pertained to the absence of circulation in cadavers and to the possible impact of low or completely absent CSF pressure on appearance of the epidural space.[17] They determined that the epidural space was indeed only a potential space that remained open for brief periods when fluid or air was injected. Blomberg and Olsson[17] confirmed the presence of a dorsomedian connective tissue band that divided the epidural space into compartments. They determined that a midline approach to the epidural space was often associated with bleeding and that a paramedian approach was less likely to cause this complication.[18] Blomberg recorded his internal images with VCR tape. The fiberoptic light source combined with computer-assisted exposure allowed adequate video capture.

Shimoji and associates[2] were the first group to publish endoscopic experience with both a fiberoptic light source and a flexible fiberoptic catheter (instead of the traditional rigid metal endoscopes) for myeloscopy. Their experience with small (0.5- to 1.4-mm) flexible fiberoptic scopes was published in 1991. The continued availability of camcorders and VCRs made it possible to have simultaneous video images and a recording of all aspects of the internal procedure. In 10 patients with chronic, intractable spinal pain syndromes, they placed flexible fiberoptic myeloscopes/epiduroscopes into either the subarachnoid space, epidural space, or both via a lumbar paramedian approach through a

Tuohy needle. The epidural space was able to be visualized only after withdrawal of the myeloscope from the subarachnoid position because of passage of CSF into the potential epidural space, which gently distended the space, permitted tissues to be less adherent, and allowed the lens to achieve its focal length of 3 to 5 mm. (With the tissues adherent to the lens, view of the tissue bed was obliterated.) The procedures were performed without sedatives or local anesthetics to allow assessment of patient discomfort. There was an interest in seeing whether chronic pain sources could be identified with a mechanical stimulus. Accurate identification of the spinal level was determined by the simultaneous use of radiographs. In four of the study patients, subarachnoid fiberoptic scopes were advanced to the cisterna magna. In patients with a diagnosis of adhesive arachnoiditis, nerve roots were observed to be matted or clumped by filamentous tissue without evidence of other structural lesions. The excessive connective tissue made observation of the subarachnoid space difficult. Three of the five patients in whom adhesive arachnoiditis was diagnosed before the procedure had either a reduction or complete remission of their pain after the procedure. Although the myeloscopic examinations did not establish the anatomic cause of pain, the authors believed that further study was warranted. There were minimal complications consisting mainly of transient post–dural puncture headaches and fever; the few cases of dysesthesia during the procedure were rectified by slowly withdrawing the scope from the nerve root in question.

In 1991, Saberski and Kitahata began evaluation of several fiberoptic endoscopes for epiduroscopy. The technology had improved, but appropriate indications for epiduroscopy were still not clear. Uncertainty remained about whether epiduroscopy provided a diagnostic advantage over noninvasive imaging procedures—CT and MRI.[19] A number of technologic problems needed to be surmounted before clinical use of such devices could seriously be considered. The fiberoptic endoscopes could visualize tissue immediately in front of the lens when the 2-mm focal length was maintained. This focal distance was difficult to achieve in a potential space such as the epidural space. There was also difficulty getting the endoscopes into the epidural space without damage, even with simultaneous fluoroscopy. The original fiberoptic endoscopes did not have working channels for tissue sampling or delivery of medication. The ideal device needed to be maneuverable, have a working lumen, have a lens with a short focal length, and incorporate a mechanism that prevented tissue from obstructing the lens. By using the caudal approach, Saberski and Kitahata were able to steer a fiberoptic with great difficulty to specific sites and deliver steroid medication to nerve roots via the introducer after removing the fiberoptic.[20]

To achieve steering, Saberski and Kitahata curved the naked fiberoptic by wrapping it gently over a finger. When inside the epidural space, they then rotated the proximal end of the fiberoptic, which caused an exaggerated rotation inside the epidural canal. This allowed visualization of more epidural space.

These early therapeutic successes indicated that spinal canal endoscopy was not only possible but also had the advantage of placing medications directly onto structures of concern. This contrasted sharply with the widely accepted technique for epidural steroid injection in which an injection took the pathway of least resistance. Saberski and Kitahata

found that normal saline irrigation easily distended the epidural space and allowed the fiberoptic to assume its needed focal length. Once the initial 15 to 20 mL of normal saline was injected, maintenance of only slight positive pressure on the syringe was necessary to keep the epidural space distended.

Saberski and Kitahata also observed that nerves intended for visualization, on the basis of symptoms, electrodiagnostic studies, response to local anesthetic root blockade, and imaging studies, often appeared by spinal canal endoscopy to have fluffy connective tissue over them. The presence of this tissue was not appreciated before the development of spinal canal endoscopy because previous methods of entering the spine were always at the level of interest and were associated with local bleeding. The spinal canal endoscope was floated from the caudal epidural space into position to observe the lumbar epidural anatomy. Any bleeding was far removed from the sites of observation. The "cottony" tissue at times seemed to float in the saline. Some of this material could be irrigated aside to reveal denser connective tissue attached to nerves and contiguous structures. On occasion, an erythematous hue of the perineural tissue was seen after the fluffier tissues were irrigated away. These changes are probably an inflammatory reaction that represents the immune system's response to change.

Concurrent with the work done at Yale, Heavner and colleagues[21] in 1991 reported on endoscopic evaluation of the epidural and subarachnoid spaces in rabbits or dogs and in human cadavers with the aid of a flexible endoscope; the technique used flexible endoscopes with outside diameters of 2.1 and 1.4 mm, respectively. In 1992, Mollmann and associates[22] published details of spinaloscopy with a rigid 4-mm endoscope on nonfixed preparations from human cadavers. At the Seventh World Congress of Pain in 1993, Heavner and coworkers[23] reported that in anesthetized dogs, endoscopes could be passed freely from their lumbar epidural insertion sites to the cervical epidural space without producing motor or cardiovascular responses. Significant difficulty with orientation was encountered, thus suggesting that further modifications would be necessary before the vast potential of epiduroscopy could be exploited.[22] Rosenberg and colleagues[24] in 1994 performed epiduroscopy in anesthetized dogs with a thin flexible and deflectable (steerable) fiberscope. The same year, Schutze and Kurtze[25] published their experience with epiduroscopy in 12 patients with various pain syndromes. They were able to visualize normal and abnormal anatomy. Pronounced adhesions and fibrosis were observed in two patients after failed back surgery. Three permanent epidural catheters were implanted under epiduroscopic control.[25]

Though representing multiple breakthroughs in technology, these devices had limitations that needed to be addressed before further human clinical trials could begin in earnest. A channel for instrumentation and refinements in steering was necessary. An easy-to-steer system with multiple lumens for instrumentation, irrigation, and fiberoptics needed to be developed. In response to these needs, Catheter Imaging Systems, Inc., Myelotec, Inc., Clarus, K. Storz, and EBI manufactured or supplied various devices that have been used for spinal canal endoscopy throughout the 1990s.

By 1996 epidural spinal canal endoscopy was used frequently for the delivery of epidural steroid medication. Many providers throughout the world modified the Saberski/Kitahata techniques to include lysis of adhesions with blunt dissection, volumetric injection, and the use of lasers and balloons. There was a sense that these techniques provided an advantage over other percutaneous blind techniques, but there were few studies to support such use. By 1998 various versions of the technique were common. Insurance carriers began to review whether the literature supported continued reimbursement for such services despite strong advocacy from patients and physicians. Many concluded that there was insufficient peer-reviewed literature (randomized controlled studies) and stated that these technologies were experimental and denied reimbursement of services to physicians and hospital/surgery centers.

Despite considerable interest to continue research, a number of factors impeded progress. First of all, the first company to manufacturer and distribute a commercial flexible fiberoptic endoscope system for spinal canal endoscopy (Myelotec, Inc.) had limited resources for funding research. Though aware of the need to fund research, Myelotec hoped that commercial sales and widespread use of the technology would be enough to generate revenue for future research. Unfortunately, simultaneous growth within the United States of managed care slowed expansion of the endoscopy field and limited funds for research. It was also extremely difficult to develop randomized controlled studies, even with funding. Most patients were not interested in randomization, and patients opted for surgery or endoscopy, depending on patient preference and clinical circumstance. The demands of insurance review boards for randomized controlled studies seemed particularly harsh with regard to endoscopy because other surgical and minimally interventional procedures were performed in the United Sates with a dearth of outcome data. Although the platform for endoscopy was easy to use and relatively safe and made perfect sense as an option before consideration of surgical procedures involving disks, inflammation, and pain, it was a paradigm shift that required re-education of physicians, surgeons, insurance companies, and the public. Before the work of McCarron, Saberski, the Saals, and others, disk-related spine disease was usually conceptualized in terms of compression of nerves. The awareness that disk disease and spine pain could be partially or completely a medical inflammatory condition controlled by the immune system was not even a consideration. The focus was on detection of anatomic causes of pain by MRI, with the size of the herniated disk expected to determine the degree of pain. In fact, this specificity theory (size determines pain) had been debunked for more than 30 years, yet it is still subscribed to. It is now known that chemical and cell signal change at the tissue bed level in conjunction with changes in receptivity of the CNS determine the quantity of pain. Thus, a patient with a small injury can be debilitated and in pain. The pain is every bit real and organic.

The late 1990s concluded with several studies that took advantage of the spinal endoscopic platform, including examination of living anatomy by Igarissi and coworkers in Japan,[26] the risk of dural puncture during combined anesthetic techniques,[27] the effect of epidural fat on epidural catheter placement,[28] the relative effects of age on epidural fat content and local anesthetic dose requirements,[28] and changes in epidural anatomy after epidural anesthesia.[29-31] Dr. Kurtze from Germany reported on the Internet observations of the epidural space in 139 patients and placed epidural catheters and electrodes under spinal endoscopic guidance.[32] There were numerous case reports showcasing the potential of the endoscopic platform.[19,20,33-35] A distinction was made between management of acute pain and chronic pain syndromes, and it was recognized that a multitude of different pathophysiologies constitute the spinal pain syndrome. Thus, the platform was used in many different ways for many different pathologic conditions. Dr. Saberski indicated that immuno-inflammation secondary to acute disk irritation was observed regularly.[36] It appears to be independent of disk compression and may be representative of leaky disk syndromes and an autoimmune response.[36] This raises the likelihood of developing specific chemotherapies to interfere with the immunochemical events in epidural tissue beds. There is discussion but no substantiation that environmental factors (infectious disease) may influence the immune system's response to disk antigen/chemical. Animal work has begun in which cell signals and immune responses are being analyzed. When mature, this work could define many common spine afflictions as medical diseases and not surgical disorders.[36] Dr. Richardson published a review of spinal canal endoscopy in the *British Medical Journal* during autumn 1999.[37] In 2001, Richardson and colleagues also evaluated the role of spinal endoscopy in 34 patients, 17 after laminectomy. In all cases, the fibrinous material found in the epidural space and pain scales and relative disability in general improved at 1 year in this prospective study. Manchikanti and colleagues in two studies showed excellent short-term response to the endoscopic platform; the response was sustained in 22% and 7% at 12 months. Dr. Krasuski and colleagues published similar findings. Saberski retrospectively looked at the outcome of laminectomy for simple disk decompression versus spinal canal endoscopy. Seventy-two percent of the spinal endoscopy group returned to work, whereas only 28% returned to work from the surgical group. In addition, opioid use was significantly lower in the post-endoscopy group. The millennium wraps up with Dr. Saberski reporting at a conference of the World Foundation for Pain Relief and Research in New York that medical management of patients with spinal canal endoscopy is less expensive and more likely to return a patient to work than similar acute herniated disk patients treated by laminectomy/diskectomy.[38]

Terminology

The original term for endoscopic evaluation of the epidural space was *epiduroscopy*. Coining of the term is credited to Rune Blomberg. In the United States there was considerable reluctance by insurance carriers to reimburse for epiduroscopy because they were not familiar with the term (it did not appear in insurance coding books). The term *spinal canal endoscopy* was adopted because of familiarity in the American insurance market with endoscopy in other body cavities. Spinal canal endoscopy today refers to either epiduroscopy, fiberoptic evaluation in the peridural position, or myeloscopy for subarachnoid visualization.

Epiduroscopy/Spinal Canal Endoscopy Consensus

On September 17, 1998, in Iserlohn and on October 3, 1998, in Bad Durkheim, Germany, an international group of experts drew up a consensus paper titled *Standards for Epiduroscopy*.[32] The participants in the working group agreed on the following general principles governing the clinical application of spinal canal endoscopy. The scientific basis for the recommendations for the use of spinal canal endoscopy was provided from publications and the clinical experience of Drs. Groll, Heavner, Kurtze, Leu, Mollmann, Rawal, Saberski, and Schutze.

Spinal canal endoscopy (epiduroscopy) was defined as percutaneous, minimally invasive endoscopic investigation of the epidural space to enable color visualization of anatomic structures inside the spinal canal: the dura mater, blood vessels, connective tissue, nerves, fat, and pathologic structures, including adhesion (fibrosis), inflammation, and stenotic change. The general indications established for spinal canal endoscopy in the diagnosis and treatment of spinal pain syndromes included (1) observation of pathology and anatomy, (2) direct drug application, (3) direct lysis of scarring (with medication, blunt dissection, laser, and other instruments), (4) placement of catheter and electrode systems (epidural, subarachnoid), and (5) as an adjunct to minimally invasive surgery.

■ INDICATIONS FOR SPINAL CANAL ENDOSCOPY

In selecting patients for spinal canal endoscopy, the provider must realize that there are symptoms pertaining to the chief complaint and the anatomic diagnosis. Both symptom and anatomic variables need to be taken into consideration before selection of the technique. Symptoms thought to be representative of nerve irritation from a variety of causes may be responsive to directed irrigation and placement of anti-inflammatory steroid medications. The chemical mediators responsible for the immuno-inflammation may come from herniated nucleus pulposus, synovium, and other sources. Such irritants can be associated with radiculopathy, canal stenosis, fibrous adhesions, and cysts. Typical symptoms amenable to spinal canal endoscopy include those related to

lumbar and sacral radiculopathy: neuralgia and plexopathy from nerve root irritation without significant compressive lesions. The presence of a compressive lesion with signs of progressive neurologic impairment is a contraindication to further placement of fluid into the epidural space. Patient selection based on case reports suggests that better results are achieved in the subgroup of patients with an acute or subacute disk-related spinal pain syndrome who have not undergone back surgery and have no associated pain behavior.[19,20,33-35] This subgroup of patients may be more likely to be responsive to "washout" of chemical irritants and the anti-inflammatory effects of corticosteroids. In addition, changes in CNS plasticity/secondary hyperalgesia may not have developed in this subgroup and thus they may be responsive to peripheral treatment with washout alone. Spinal canal endoscopy is not indicated in patients suffering from biomechanical pain syndromes such as lumbar facet syndrome, sacroiliac joint dysfunction, or myofascial pain syndromes. Table 15–1 summarizes the indications and contraindications for spinal canal endoscopy.

■ RATIONALE FOR THE CAUDAL APPROACH

The caudal approach to the epidural space seemed to offer advantage over the paramedian approach. The straight entry into the epidural space contrasted sharply with the approximately 45-degree bend required to pass a catheter into the lumbar epidural space. Thus, there was less of a chance of fracturing the fiberoptic. The straight caudal canal placement also made it easier to add additional channels for future surgical procedures and to steer.

The previous work of Odendaal and van Aswegen[40] supported the caudal approach on an entirely different basis, the kinetics of injected fluids. They injected a radionuclide admixture into the lumbar epidural space of patients with and without previous laminectomy. By monitoring the distribution of the radioactive tracer, these researchers were able to demonstrate poor caudal spread of injectate in patients who

---

Table 15–1

Indications and Contraindications for Spinal Canal Endoscopy

Ideal Candidate	Healthy, working, no litigation, minimal medication, no dependent behavior
Indications	
Widely accepted indications	Irritative neuralgias: new-onset radiculopathy, radiculopathy associated with post-laminectomy pain syndrome
Probable indications	Adhesion related: post-laminectomy epidural adhesion, low back pain, Tarlov cyst
Contraindications	
Strong contraindications	No consent, cauda equina syndrome, urinary dynamic problem, sphincter dysfunction, footdrop, pilonidal cyst, osteomyelitis, anal fissure, raised intracranial pressure, pseudotumor cerebri, CNS tumor, coagulopathy, no sacral hiatus, unable to place a skinny needle into the sacral canal, untreated addictive behavior, unstable angina, severe COPD, meningocele/meningomyelocele, inability to lie prone (COPD, CHF, angina, back pain, etc.), inadequate facilities, allergy to proposed medications
Relative contraindications	Multiple different complaints of pain, active untreated psychiatric disorders,[39] somatoform process, unrealistic expectations, retinal disease, partial blindness

CHF, congestive heart failure; COPD, chronic obstructive pulmonary disease.

had previously undergone laminectomy. In the non-operated control group, however, there was an even spread of fluid throughout the lumbar and sacral nerve roots. Thus, an injection into the lumbar epidural space took the pathway of least resistance and would not necessarily deliver intended steroids to the sacral nerve roots. For these reasons, Cyriax[41] intuitively advocated volumetric caudal injections during the 1960s to 1980s. With such epidural injections the injectate (normal saline, local anesthetic, steroid) was more likely to go cephalad. Some injectate did escape through the sacral foramen. Using volumes of 25 to 50 mL containing local anesthetic, normal saline, and steroid, Cyriax[41] claimed lasting results in more than 40% of his patients. These results were secondary to better spread of the steroid, improved irrigation of the epidural tissue bed, and mobilization of adherent tissues via hydrostatic pressure gradients. It is presumed that the dramatic response was seen in patients with relatively acute disk inflammatory processes, not failed surgical back syndromes. The effect of Dr. Cyriax's personal choice for local anesthetic, procaine, on long-term outcome is unknown, but its role cannot be excluded.

The work of Racz and associates[42] in Lubbock, Texas, suggested that lysis of epidural adhesions was of significant benefit to many patients with refractory lumbar radiculopathy. Their pioneering work indicated that scar adhesions formed in the epidural space of patients with many chronic spine pain syndromes, after surgery or perhaps as a result of inflammation, and were responsible for pulling and tugging nerve roots and the dural sac. Their innovative technique involved placement of a catheter through the sacral hiatus into the epidural space in close approximation to the root or adhesion in question, which was indicated by an epidurogram. A total volume of 30 to 40 mL of a local anesthetic, steroid, and non-ionic contrast agent was then injected. The results showed significant variability between study groups, probably a consequence of the heterogeneous nature of persistent lumbar radiculopathy. Nonetheless, approximately 50% of the patients had marked improvement, as measured by decreased medication, enhanced function, and reduced visual analog scale scores for 1 to 6 months. Racz and associates[42,43] concluded that the overlooked epidural adhesions could cause pain, perhaps from compression and irritation of nerves. With spinal canal endoscopy, it is envisioned that a three-dimensional color view of the adhesions and adjacent anatomy will afford the operator advantage over two-dimensional, black-and-white fluoroscopic projections (epidurograms). Thus, spinal canal endoscopy will have potential as a platform for the management of chronic spinal canal–based diseases, in addition to its place in the management of acute inflammatory canal diseases.

Work by Serpell and associates[44] showed that sustained pressure applied epidurally is transmitted intrathecally and could compromise perfusion or cause barotrauma at remote locations. They noted an initial escape of fluid via leakage into the large sacral root foramina and sheaths. After capacity (around 20 mL in ewes) was achieved, there was an abrupt increase in CSF pressure with each injection. The range was variable and was reflective of each study animal and of CNS compliance. The researchers concluded that instillation of saline into the epidural space results in an eventual significant increase in CSF pressure. CNS compliance was variable and seemed to deteriorate after instrumentation (surgery). Thus,

scarring associated with surgery predisposed animals to neurologically dangerous pressure. Serpell and colleagues[44] recommend continuous monitoring of CSF pressure in humans. However, Cyriax[41] reported no major long-term complications after 50,000 volumetric caudal injections. Certainly with these injections, even if performed slowly, there were increases in CSF pressure without apparent ill effect. At higher volumes (>100 mL), Cyriax did note the potential for retinal hemorrhage with the single-shot caudal injection technique (injection completed in minutes). Dr. Cyriax indicated that the retinal hemorrhages resolved without consequence. There are other reports indicating that retinal hemorrhage can occur with routine epidural injections.[45] A few reports have now been made of retinal and macular hemorrhage with varying degrees of blindness after spinal canal endoscopy. In the cases that the author is aware of, the patients were deeply anesthetized, thus disconnecting the most sensitive monitor for elevated pressure—the patient's own complaint of pain. Patients who have a noncompliant spinal canal will have resistance to injection and will complain of significant pain, both local and remote. The pain will often begin in the lumbar region and migrate cephalad. As a precaution, all injections into the spinal canal (for both endoscopic and routine epidural injections) should be given incrementally with constant dialogue with the patient. When the patient's complaint of pain or discomfort has moved cephalad, the managing physician must take appropriate action determined by the clinical circumstance: alter the technique, infuse less volume, stop the procedure, drain/decompress the epidural space, or other measures. It is noted that the total volume that can be injected into a spinal canal with a series of injections or endoscopies often increases with each subsequent injection (presumably from stretching out the more compliant spinal canals). An injection rate of 1 mL/sec is recommended. Previous work at Yale has determined that rapid injection of fluid (>1 mL/sec) is more likely to be associated with high peak epidural pressure, measured at times in excess of 300 mm Hg. The rapidity of injection, the size of the syringe, the volume of injection, compliance of the spinal canal (epidural space), and turbulence of the injection are all determinants of peak pressure. Peak pressure falls off to pre-injection levels abruptly with disconnection of the syringe, as a rule when the total volume is less than 30 to 40 mL.[46]

■ CLINICALLY RELEVANT ANATOMY

The spinal canal extends from the foramen magnum to the sacrum. It is bounded posteriorly by the ligamentum flavum and periosteum and anteriorly by the posterior longitudinal ligament, which lies over the dorsal aspect of the vertebral bodies and disks.

The size of the canal is approximately twice the size of the cord. It is largest in the cervical and lumbar regions, corresponding to enlargements of the spinal cord. At C4 to C6, it measures 18 mm in an anteroposterior direction. The transverse diameter at C4 to C6 measures 30 mm. The thoracic canal is 17 mm in both anteroposterior and transverse measurements. The lumbar canal is 23 and 18 mm, respectively.[47] The canal in cross section appears triangular at the cervical and lumbar levels and is more cylindrical at the thoracic level.

The spinal cord is continuous with the brain and ends with the conus medullaris at the lower border of the L1 vertebra. The dural sac containing the spinal cord and conus, however, runs down to the level of S2. The cauda equina consists of the terminal fibers of the conus, which extend inside the dural sac from L1 to S2. In the fetus, the spinal cord extends down to the coccyx, but as development proceeds, it is drawn upward because of greater growth of the vertebral column; at birth, the spinal cord extends only to L3. Flexing the column draws the cord temporarily higher.[48] In nerves that are not freely movable, such as in arachnoiditis, flexion can cause lancinating pain.

The epidural space surrounds the dural sac. It is bordered posteriorly by the ligamentum flavum and periosteum and anteriorly by the posterior longitudinal ligament. Laterally, the pedicles and the 48 intervertebral foramina bound it. The epidural space extends from the foramen magnum to the end of the dural sac at S2. The sacral canal is technically not part of the epidural space because it has no dural sac.

The posterior epidural space varies greatly. It averages 2 mm at the cervical level, 3 to 5 mm at the thoracic level, and 4 to 6 mm at the lumbar level.[47] The epidural space narrows considerably at L4 through S2. The epidural space anterior to the dura is uniformly narrow (less than 1 mm) cephalad through caudad.

The epidural space is rich in content. At the midline connecting the dura to the periosteum posteriorly, there is usually a dorsal median connective tissue band, which can be complete or web-like.[49] Through the epidural space run the internal vertebral venous plexus, the spinal branches of the segmental arteries, the lymphatics, and the dura-arachnoid projections that surround the spinal nerve roots.[50] In addition, fat is abundant, but the amount present seems to bear no relationship to the patient's body fat percentage.[51]

The dura mater covering the spinal cord is a tough elastic tube that forms a loose sheath around the spinal cord. It is composed principally of longitudinal connective tissue fibers, with a proportionately small amount of circular yellow elastic tissue fibers. The spinal dura mater extends from the foramen magnum, to which it is closely adherent by its outer surface, to the S2 vertebra, where it ends in a cul-de-sac. Below this level the dura mater forms the filum terminale and descends to the coccyx, where it fuses with the periosteum.[50]

The paramedian approach for lumbar epidural injections has been advocated by anatomists (spinal endoscopists) because vessels concentrate at the midline. It is remarkable to note the success of the epidural anesthetic technique despite the plethora of fat and connective tissue. Even catheters thread better than one might predict. As demonstrated by Blomberg and Olsson,[17] the dura is fairly tough and deflects catheters away, usually cephalad or caudad, depending on the direction of the bevel of the needle and local anatomy.

▪ TECHNIQUE

Before spinal canal endoscopy, all patients must undergo a thorough and complete history and physical examination. Care should be taken to document this examination carefully with special attention to a complete neurologic examination. Imaging studies should be reviewed, as well as special testing such as electromyography and nerve conduction studies.

Lumbosacral, flexion, extension, and oblique plain x-ray views should be reviewed to assess for pathology not amenable to epidural procedures. MRI of the lumbar and sacral spine should be considered to assess the contents of the spinal canal and the presence of spinal stenosis. If a clinical decision is made to offer spinal canal endoscopy, all contraindications and relative contraindications must be addressed and documented in the medical record.

Preparation

Nonsteroidal antiinflammatory drugs, aspirin, and anticoagulants should be discontinued before spinal canal endoscopy.[52] Appropriate laboratory studies should be considered. As a rule, bleeding associated with spinal canal endoscopy is limited and occurs distally at the introducer's entrance into the sacral hiatus. The patient should use an antibacterial scrub while showering the evening before and carefully cleanse the lumbar spine and sacral areas. The patient is directed to maintain NPO status after midnight.

Equipment should be inspected, including disposables, several days in advance to ensure that all needed equipment is available. The procedure must be scheduled for a time when fluoroscopy and a post-anesthetic care unit are available. Pre-procedure discussion with the anesthesiologist should include patient positioning (prone) and the need for an awake, responsive patient. It is recommended that voice contact be maintained with the patient throughout the procedure to be able to assess the patient's response to manipulations. Informed consent must be obtained. It is preferable to obtain informed consent before the day of the procedure.

Procedure

1. Pre-procedure prophylactic antibiotic coverage is considered. The patient is placed prone with a pillow under the abdomen and the feet internally rotated (Fig. 15–2A-J). Such positioning provides better exposure of the sacral hiatus. The sacral hiatus is identified anatomically by palpating for the sacral cornua. The cornua lie on either side of the midline, just above the natal crease. In instances in which the cornua are not palpable, firm midline palpation just above the natal crease should reveal the spinal canal. A midline position is confirmed with posteroanterior (PA) fluoroscopy.

2. With a 25-gauge or smaller needle, 3 to 5 mL of local anesthetic with epinephrine is placed onto the floor of the sacral canal. The small needle is passed cephalad and should easily slide into the sacral canal.

3. A 17-gauge Tuohy needle is inserted into the sacral hiatus and advanced cephalad. The loss-of-resistance technique can be used to confirm entry into the canal. A lateral fluoroscopic projection will show the needle in the canal. If the needle is noted to be dorsal to the canal (false passageway), it should be removed and repositioned.

4. An injection of non-ionic contrast, 5 to 15 mL, followed by PA fluoroscopy will provide an epidurogram. The epidurogram will outline the nerve roots, scar adhesions, and other spinal canal structures.

5. The flexible end of the guidewire is threaded through the Tuohy needle. The guidewire should thread cephalad. This step should be followed by PA fluoroscopy. Repositioning

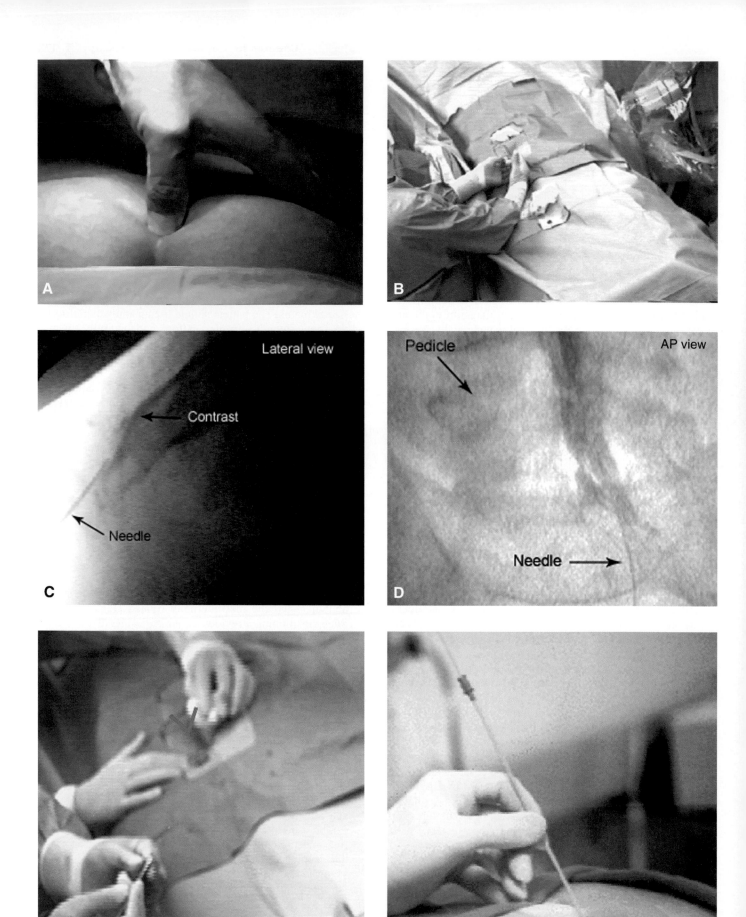

FIGURE 15–2 ■ **A-J,** Spinal endoscopy, step-by-step procedure.

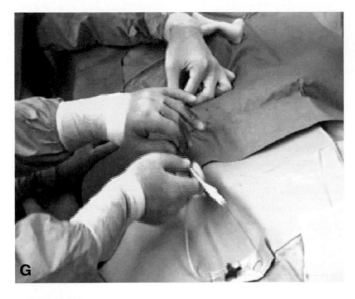

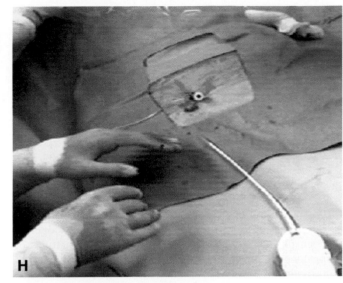

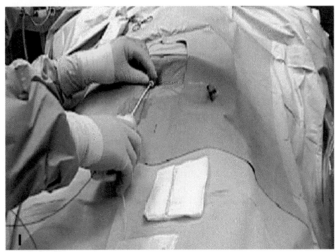

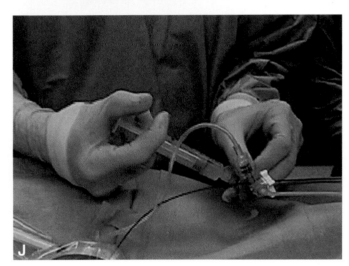

FIGURE 15–2 ■ Continued.

and flushing the Tuohy needle with normal saline might be necessary to facilitate passage of the guidewire toward the nerve root or roots in question. After confirmation of the position of the wire with PA and lateral fluoroscopy, the Tuohy needle is removed.

6. The dilator and sheath are carefully introduced over the wire. With a No. 11 scalpel, the wire's aperture is widened to allow easier passage of the introducer. (A similar technique is used for central line placement.) If significant bleeding occurs, firm pressure is applied with gauze, and additional local anesthetic with epinephrine can be given. Rotary movement as the dilator goes through the soft tissues facilitates passage. As the dilator and sheath are passed cephalad, the wire should be frequently tested to see whether it moves freely. If the guidewire cannot be moved easily, there could be a kink in the wire. PA and lateral fluoroscopy can help check whether there is a kink or loop. If a kink present, it is best to remove dilator and sheath and slide the Tuohy needle back over the guidewire so that the wire can be removed and inspected. If the wire is kinked, a new wire should be used. A kinked

wire could misdirect passage of the dilator and introducer catheter.

7. After the dilator and sheath are inserted, the dilator is removed with the introducer sheath left in place.

8. The side arm of introducer sheath is flushed with 5 to 10 mL of preservative-free normal saline. The fiberoptic cable is then placed through one of the two lumens in the steering handle. Tubing containing normal saline for irrigation of the spinal canal/epidural space is attached to the second steering handle lumen. The clinician should next orient himself to the steering direction and focus the fiberoptic on a sterile ruler or other recognizable structure.

9. The steering handle containing the fiberoptic scope and tubing for irrigation with preservative-free normal saline is inserted through the introducer. The camera and the video recorder are activated. The steering handle with the fiberoptic is advanced cephalad through the sacral canal into the epidural space. To keep the epidural space distended and achieve the correct focal length for fiberoptic visualization, gentle pressure is applied to the normal saline syringe. To complement gentle pressure on syringe,

preservative-free normal saline bags (100 mL) pressurized to less than systole for brief periods (1 to 2 minutes) can be used. This technique often frees the hands for steering. Care should always be taken to ensure that the infusion of normal saline is not excessive. For this reason, small bags of normal saline are chosen. High pressure in the epidural space may be safe for brief periods in some patients with compliant spinal canals. (The pressure generated by a bolus from a 10-mL syringe injected at 1 mL/sec can be greater than 300 mm Hg.) When using a pressurized bag, the pressure is sustained for 1 to 2 minutes and then reduced to resting pressure to prevent any compromise in perfusion. The amount of fluid injected must be accurately monitored. The amount of preservative-free normal saline used is approximately 60 mL per procedure. Most procedures last 30 to 45 minutes after the fiberoptic scope has been placed. Insertion of the introducer can at times be prolonged, depending on patient anatomy and skill of the provider.

Post-procedure Management

After the procedure is completed, a dressing is applied and the patient is taken to the recovery area. In the recovery suite a post-procedure neurologic examination is performed. Any new deficits should be detailed and monitored serially. MRI and neurosurgical consultation should be considered. Patients are instructed to not bathe for 5 days, but showers are acceptable after day 2. Hygiene instructions are important: perineal cleaning after bowel movements should be directed away from the procedural site. The patient should be discharged with a driver and should be observed by a friend or family member for the immediate post-procedure period. A 2- or 3-day supply of post-procedural short-acting opioid such as hydrocodone or oxycodone is appropriate.

❚ EPIDURAL IMAGES

To follow the internal spinal canal anatomy (epidural anatomy), it is critical to maintain one's orientation. Simultaneous use of fluoroscopy allows the operator to distinguish one level of epidural anatomy from the next. At times when confused about the location/orientation, needles can be inserted into the posterior epidural space. Blomberg's photographs of epidural catheters passing into the spinal canal (epidural space) illustrate this nicely. It is best to proceed with each spinal canal endoscopy with the objective of examining specific areas as opposed to a general exploration of the canal, epidural space, and contents. In this way the time that a spinal canal is subjected to insufflation with normal saline and potentially hazardous hydrostatic pressure is reduced.

❚ SIDE EFFECTS AND COMPLICATIONS

For spinal canal endoscopy to be performed, the epidural space must be distended with preservative-free normal saline. This allows the fiberoptic scope to achieve its required focal length and reveals intricate epidural structure that would not otherwise be possible. A possible complication of this technique is the generation of significant epidural pressure that could affect local perfusion. The epidural pressure generated can be transmitted cephalad through CSF and affect perfusion at more remote levels.[44] For these reasons it is essential that the procedure be performed on lightly sedated, well-informed, cooperative patients who can inform the provider of pain at remote areas. If such a complaint is articulated, the provider should consider adjusting the technique or terminating the procedure. An example is the spontaneous development of a headache or altered vision during endoscopy.

Complications of spinal canal endoscopy generally pertain to improper needle placement and generation of excessive epidural hydrostatic pressure.[53] Excessive pressure can potentially affect both local and distant perfusion. A new onset of scapular or neck pain during the procedure suggests elevated pressure and may portend retinal hemorrhage. Patient complaints of pain from small-volume distention of the epidural space usually signify a non-compliant epidural space and may permit transmission of pressure far from the site of fluid administration via CSF. Be very careful to keep the epidural fluid volume low and maintain contact with the patient throughout the procedure. Alert patients can inform the operator of sensations and changes inside their body as they occur. The operator uses clinical judgment during the procedure to determine whether an adjustment or termination of procedure is necessary.

Potential complications include pain at and remote from the surgical site, transient dysesthesias, paresis, paralysis, blindness, other visual changes, post–dural puncture headache, local surgical site bleeding, infection, and allergic reactions.

Pain at the surgical site is generally self-limited. Pain at sites other than the surgical site, such as severe headache, dysesthesia, and extreme back pain, require evaluation and documentation in the medical record. Such pain may be caused by epidural hematoma, cord ischemia, or elevated hydrostatic pressure. Paresis, paralysis, and pain can be complications of needle trauma, epidural hematoma, elevated hydrostatic pressure, ischemia, and nerve injury (avulsion, traction transection). Visual changes and blindness have been reported. The incidence is very low, and such complications have previously been reported with routine epidural injections. They presumably result from transmission of spinal canal pressure cephalad into the brain via CSF and cause retinal perfusion or macular hemorrhage. Local surgical site bleeding is unlikely to cause neurologic complication because the site is just above coccyx. Bleeding may predispose to infection. However, infection is rare. A soapy scrub by the patient is suggested before the procedure, prophylactic antibiotics should be administered, sterile preparation and draping should be performed, the wound should be kept dry for 3 days, and after a bowel movement the anus should be wiped away from the surgical site (posterior to anterior).

❚ CONCLUSION

The technology of spinal canal endoscopy has developed slowly over the 20th century. Contributions have been made by many innovators; however, only recently has this technique been developed and refined sufficiently to be used clinically. Further study is needed to determine whether this technique has advantages over alternative, currently used techniques of delivery of medication into the epidural space. Real-time direct visual examination of the epidural anatomy currently enables the identification of epidural pathology and localization of pain generators there. This ability to examine epidural pathology apart from operative trauma and to direct the delivery of medication is not duplicated by any other technique available at present. The future may hold the promise of minimally invasive and effective therapy for both radicular and perhaps other forms of disabling back pain. Other exciting possibilities for this technology may include removal of extradural or intradural scar tissue, cyst drainage, biopsy, study of cell biology and inflammatory mediators, and retrieval of foreign bodies. I believe that the possibility of modifying the inflammatory process by blocking mediators of inflammation holds the greatest promise. Today, the technique can be used safely and effectively to deliver medication to pathology under direct vision. It opens new doors for the diagnosis and treatment of pathology accessible through the epidural space.

References

1. Burman MS: Myeloscopy or the direct visualization of the spinal cord. J Bone Joint Surg 13:695, 1931.
2. Shimoji K, Fujioka H, Onodera M, et al: Observation of spinal canal and cisternae with the newly developed small-diameter, flexible fiberscopes. Anesthesiology 75:341, 1991.
3. Stern EL: The spinascope: A new instrument for visualizing the spinal canal and its contents. Med Rec (NY) 143:31, 1936.
4. Pool JL: Direct visualization of dorsal nerve roots of the cauda equina by means of a myeloscope. Arch Neurol Psychiatry 39:1308, 1938.
5. Pool JL: Myeloscopy: Diagnostic inspection of the cauda equina by means of an endoscope. Bull Neurol Inst N Y 7:178, 1938.
6. Pool JL: Myeloscopy: Intraspinal endoscopy. Surgery 11:169, 1942.
7. Ooi Y, Morisaki N: [Intrathecal lumbar endoscope.] Clin Orthop Surg 4:295, 1969.
8. Ooi Y, Satoh Y, Morisaki N: [Myeloscopy.] Igakuno Ayumi 81:209, 1972.
9. Ooi Y, Satoh Y, Morisaki N: [Myeloscopy.] Orthop Surg 24:181, 1973.
10. Ooi Y, Satoh Y, Morisaki N: Myeloscopy: Possibility of observing lumbar intrathecal space by use of an endoscope. Endoscopy 5:91, 1973.
11. Ooi Y, Satoh Y, Morisaki N: Myeloscopy: A preliminary report. J Jpn Orthop Assoc 47:619, 1973.
12. Ooi Y, Satoh Y, Morisaki N: Myeloscopy. Int Orthop 1:107, 1977.
13. Ooi Y, Satoh Y, Inoue K, et al: Myeloscopy. Acta Orthop Belg 44:881, 1978.
14. Satoh Y, Hirose K, Ooi Y, Mikanagi K: Myeloscopy in the diagnosis of low back pain syndrome. Paper presented at The Third Congress of International Rehabilitation Medicine Association, July 2-9, 1978, Basel.
15. Ooi Y, Satoh Y, Inoue K, et al: Myeloscopy with special reference to blood flow changes in the cauda equina during Laseøgue's test. Int Orthop 4:307, 1981.
16. Blomberg R: A method for spinal canal endoscopy and spinaloscopy: Presentation of preliminary results. Acta Anaesthesiol Scand 21:113, 1985.
17. Blomberg R, Olsson S: The lumbar epidural space in patients examined with epiduroscopy. Anesth Analg 68:157, 1989.
18. Blomberg R: Technical advantages of the paramedian approach for lumbar epidural puncture and catheter introduction. Anesthesiology 43:837, 1988.
19. Saberski LR, Kitahata LM: Direct visualization of the lumbosacral epidural space through the sacral hiatus. Anesth Analg 80:839, 1995.
20. Saberski LR, Kitahata LM: Review of the clinical basis and protocol for epidural endoscopy. Conn Med 50:71, 1995.
21. Heavner JE, Cholkhavatia S, Kizelshteyn G: Percutaneous evaluation of the epidural and subarachnoid space with the flexible fiberscope. Reg Anesth 15(Suppl 1):85, 1991.
22. Mollman M, Host D, Enk D: Spinaloskopie zur Darstellung von Problemen bei der Anwendung der kontinuierlichen Spinalanaesthesie. Anaesthesist 41:544, 1992.
23. Heavner J, Chokhavatia K, McDaniel K, et al: Diagnostic and therapeutic maneuvers in the epidural space via a flexible endoscope [abstract 1534]. In Abstracts of the Seventh World Congress on Pain, Paris, August 1993. New York, Raven Press, 1993.
24. Rosenberg P, Heavner J, Chokhavatia K, et al: Epiduroscopy with a thin flexible and deflectable fiberscope. Br J Anaesth 72(Suppl 1):74, 1994.
25. Schutze G, Kurtze H: Direct observation of the epidural space with a flexible catheter-secured epiduroscopic unit. Reg Anesth 19:85, 1994.
26. Igarashi T, Hirabayashi Y, Shimizu R, et al: Thoracic and lumbar extradural structure examined by extraduroscope. Br J Anaesth 81:121, 1998.
27. Holmstrom B, Rawal N, Axelson K, Nydahl PA: Risk of catheter migration during combined spinal epidural block: Percutaneous epiduroscopy study. Anesth Analg 80:747, 1995.
28. Igarashi T, Hirabayashi Y, Shimizu R, et al: The lumbar epidural structure changes with increasing age. Br J Anaesth 78:149, 1997.
29. Igarashi T, Hirabayashi Y, Shimizu R, et al: Inflammatory changes after extradural anaesthesia may effect the spread of local anaesthetic within the extradural space. Br J Anaesth 77:347, 1996.
30. Kitamura A, Sakamoto A, Shigemasa A, et al: Epiduroscopic changes in patients undergoing single and repeated epidural injections. Anesth Analg 82:88, 1996.
31. Wulf H, Streipling E: Postmortem findings after epidural anaesthesia. Anaesthesia 45:357, 1990.
32. SCHMERZtherapeutisches Kolloquiurn e.V., Iserlohn, Dr. med. G. Schutze, Hagenerstr. 121, 58642 Iserlohn, http://pain.de/pages/publ_02.html.
33. Saberski LR, Kitahata LM: Persistent radiculopathy diagnosed and treated with epidural endoscopy. Jpn Anesth 10:292, 1996.
34. Saberski LR, Brull SJ: Spinal and epidural endoscopy: A historical review and case report. Yale J Biol Med 68:7, 1995.
35. Saberski LR: Technical workshop: Epiduroscopy. J Back Musculoskel Rehabil 11:149, 1998.
36. Saberski LR, Fredericks R, Dunn EL, et al: Bovine model for studying nucleus pulposus related immuno-inflammation in spinal canals. Submitted for publication.
37. Richardson J: Realizing visions [editorial]. Br J Anaesth vol 83, no. 3, September 1999.
38. Saberski LR: Current application of spinal canal endoscopy: Is it a diagnostic tool or a therapeutic modality. In Syllabus: The World Foundation for Pain Relief and Research: Current Concepts in Acute, Chronic and Cancer Pain Management, Seattle, IASP Press, December 1999, p 177.
39. Holmstrom B, Raawal N: Epiduroscopic study of risk of catheter migration following dural puncture by spinal and epidural needles: A video presentation, American Society of Anesthesiology, 1992.
40. Odendaal CL, van Aswegen A: Determining the spread of epidural medication in post laminectomy patients by radionuclide admixture [abstract 1487]. In Abstracts of the Seventh World Congress on Pain, Paris, August 1993. New York, Raven Press, 1993.
41. Cyriax J: The Illustrated Manual of Orthopedic Medicine. London, Butterworth, 1983.
42. Racz GB, Holubec JT: Lysis of adhesions in the epidural space. In Racz GB (ed): Techniques of Neurolysis. Boston, Kluwer Academic, 1989.
43. Arthur J, Racz G, Heinrich R, et al: Epidural space: Identification of filling defects and lysis of adhesions in the treatment of chronic painful conditions [abstract 1485]. In Abstracts of the Seventh World Congress on Pain, Paris, August 1993. New York, Raven Press, 1993.
44. Serpell MG, Coombs DW, Colburn RW, et al: Intrathecal pressure recordings due to saline instillation in the epidural space [abstract 1535]. In Abstracts of the Seventh World Congress on Pain, Paris, August 1993. New York, Raven Press, 1993.
45. Tabandeh H: Intraocular hemorrhages associated with endoscopic spinal surgery. Am J Ophthalmol 129:688, 2000.
46. Saberski LR, Garfunkel D: Unpublished data, Yale University school of Medicine, 1991.
47. Clemente CD (ed): Gray's Anatomy of the Human Body. Philadelphia, Lea & Febiger, 1985.
48. Basmajian J: Grant's Method of Anatomy, 8th ed. Baltimore, Williams & Wilkins, 1993, p 41.

49. Shimoji K, Fujioka H, Onodera J, et al: Observation of spinal cord and cisternae with the newly developed small-diameter, flexible fiberscopes. Anesthesiology 75:341, 1991.

50. Bonica JJ: The Management of Pain. Philadelphia, Lea & Febiger, 1990, p 1411.

51. Levin SC, Stacey BR, Cantees K: Pre-operative and post-operative back pain management. In Welch WC, Jacobs GB, Jackson GP (eds): Operative Spine Surgery. Appleton & Lange, 1999.

52. Odoom JA, Sih IL: Epidural analgesia and anticoagulant therapy. Experience with 1000 cases of continuous epidurals. Anaesthesia 38:254, 1983.

53. Serpell MG, Coombs DW, Colburn RW, et al: Intrathecal pressure recordings due to saline installation in the epidural space [abstract 1535]. Paper presented at the Seventh World Congress On Pain, August 1993.

chapter 16

Electromyography and Nerve Conduction Velocity

Bernard Abrams

Electromyography (EMG) is usually performed by neurologists or physiatrists; it enters the realm of the anesthesiologist and pain specialist for several reasons (1) it can be a valuable asset in localizing the area(s) involved in peripheral pain problems; (2) it can provide evidence that the painful area(s) or mechanism is a more central one by ruling out peripheral problems; and (3) it may provide documentation as to cause, location, timing, and prognosis for nerve injuries that occur in the anesthetic and perianesthetic time frame. In addition, EMG is a procedure performed on physician referral; a working knowledge of how it is performed, the indications and reasonable expectations for information derived from the results will help the nonelectromyographer to order appropriate testing, advise the patient about the testing, and better assess the adequacy of the testing and the physician performing the test.

EMG is a useful extension of the clinical neurologic examination and, therefore, is an adjunct in the diagnosis and management of pain. Conditions in which EMG may be of use include painful peripheral neuropathies, entrapment neuropathies, traumatic nerve injuries, radicular and multiradicular problems, lumbar or cervical spinal stenosis, arachnoiditis, and painful myopathies. The problems inherent in applying electrodiagnostic techniques to pain diagnosis and management are similar to those encountered in history taking, physical examination, radiologic and other imaging procedures, and therapeutic diagnostic testing. Pain is a subjective experience, and the final diagnosis of the etiology and presumptive treatment of a pain syndrome is a clinical diagnosis that can only be supported by relevant data including EMG. There is no "litmus test" to objectify complaints of pain, and the final diagnosis of a pain syndrome is a clinical one that can be supported only by relevant data such as EMG. In this regard, EMG is no different from radiology, other forms of imaging, or laboratory tests.

■ HISTORY

The existence of electrical activity resulting from muscular contractions was first described by Galvani.[1] The first experimental work with EMG was performed by Lord Adrian in 1925. In 1928, Proebster first described the presence of "spontaneous irregular action potentials in denervated muscle."[1] In its progression to clinical application, EMG made a major step forward with the use of the cathode ray oscilloscope by Erlanger and Gasser, as well as the concentric needle electrode and loud speaker.[2] Vast numbers of nerve injuries in World War II and later conflicts added impetus to the study of nerve and muscle by electrodiagnostic techniques.

A few definitions are in order before proceeding. The term "electromyography" previously caused considerable confusion because, strictly speaking, it referred to the evaluation of muscle function (and indirectly nerve, nerve root, and anterior horn cell) by needle insertion into the muscle. In time, the term became a more inclusive one, embracing nerve conduction velocity testing and other less frequently performed tests such as the H and F reflexes, cranial nerve reflexes, and studies of the neuromuscular junction. The all-inclusive term EMG will be used here to include these tests. "Electrodiagnosis" originally referred to muscle testing in the form of chronaxie and threshold determinations but now embraces all electrical testing of the nervous system and includes evoked potentials. The national organization was originally called the American Association of Electromyography and Electrodiagnosis (AAEE) and is now known as the American Association of Neuromuscular and Electrodiagnostic Medicine (AANEM) reflecting the modernization of terminology and the vast expansion of the scope of electrodiagnostic testing.

Electromyography is a method of testing both the physiologic state and the anatomic integrity of lower motor neuron structures, their sensory components, and some spinal and brain stem reflex pathways.[3] The lower motor neuron is composed of the anterior horn cells, nerve root, plexus, peripheral nerves, neuromuscular junction, and muscles. Longmire[4] pointed out the puzzling dichotomy in the medical literature on pain and electrodiagnostic testing. In standard textbooks on electrodiagnostic testing,[5-9] there is little mention of painful syndromes. On the other hand, perusal of standard pain textbooks[1,10,11] reveals cogent attempts to correlate neurophysiologic studies in pain diagnosis and management. The reason for the paucity of references in standard textbooks appears to be, at least in part, the attitudes of some pain specialists themselves who point out "nevertheless, it should be emphasized that large caliber afferent fibers are physiologically unrelated to pain, a submodality mediated by small caliber fibers. Additionally, the test is unable to explore the bases for positive sensory phenomenon, generated by dysfunction of large caliber afferent channels."[12]

Electromyography and nerve conduction are extremely useful investigative techniques in evaluating the patient in pain because they satisfy two fundamental steps[12] in the assessment of a neuropathic pain syndrome before any attempt at therapy. First, they rigorously establish the presence or absence of a peripheral nervous system lesion, and second, they determine the relevance of an established peripheral lesion to the subjective clinical complaint. In brief, electrodiagnostic techniques may occasionally be helpful in diagnosing central nervous system disorders,[10] but are more often useful in disorders of the nerve roots, plexus lesions, neuropathies, and disorders of the peripheral nerves, and less frequently in painful myopathies. Neuromuscular junction disorders, amyotrophic lateral sclerosis, and other anterior horn cell disorders (except poliomyelitis in its acute stage) rarely produce pain. Following the discussion of test procedures and their interpretation, a full discussion of the clinical correlates of electrodiagnostic testing will be made.

■ THE ELECTRODIAGNOSTIC METHOD

There are four essential components to any electrodiagnostic measurement system (1) electrodes; (2) a stimulator; (3) a high-gain differential amplifier; and (4) a recording display or central processing device.[4] Computer-assisted analysis systems may be added.

The EMG apparatus amplifies and displays biological information derived from either surface or needle electrodes. Electrical information may be recorded from muscles, nerves, or other nervous system structures, and is generally displayed on an oscilloscope. In addition to the visual display, a permanent recording may be made, audio amplification may allow it to be heard over a loud speaker, and analog/digital signals may also be used. Electrical nerve stimulation is used to simulate nerves to measure nerve conduction and latencies of the evoked responses. Modern EMG equipment ranges from simple to complex with even "notebook" type devices coupled with electrodes and stimulators for maximum portability. A representative EMG machine is shown in Figure 16–1.

For nerve conduction studies, surface skin electrodes (Fig. 16–2) are used to record a compound muscle or nerve action potential, while in needle electromyography, needle electrodes are used with a strong trend toward use of disposable needles (Fig. 16–3). For sensory testing, ring electrodes are used for measurement (Fig. 16–4). Modern EMG equipment is manufactured by numerous companies and is generally standardized to allow reliable and reproducible testing by different laboratories,[10] but normative data should be established by each individual laboratory.[8,13,14] Extra precautions must be taken with patients on Coumadin or other anti-coagulants, patients with hemophilia or other blood dyscrasias, patients who are HIV-positive, or patients with a cardiac pacemaker, neuromodulatory implant, or transcutaneous stimulator.[3] Beyond placing a needle through an infected site, there are probably no absolute, but only relative contraindications

FIGURE 16–1 ■ A typical EMG machine.

for EMG. Extremely anxious adults and some children occasionally require sedation. After effects of EMG are negligible with rare bruising, although occasionally a highly suggestible or litigious patient may complain vehemently of increased pain or disability. Conversely, occasionally a patient may proclaim extravagant therapeutic effects from electromyography.

■ PHYSIOLOGIC MECHANISMS

Production of Muscle Potentials

When an impulse arrives at the region of the junction between nerve and muscle, the muscle fiber is thrown into an almost simultaneous contraction, assuming that the threshold for activation is exceeded. This is brought about by a wave of excitation that moves rapidly along the fiber surface and stimulates the contractile substance as it moves (excitation-

Surface electrodes

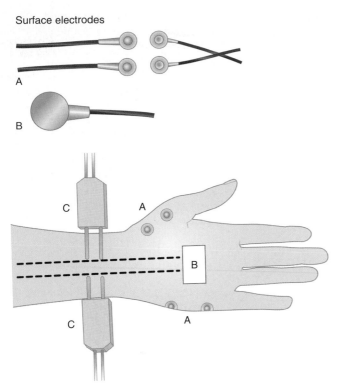

FIGURE 16-2 ■ Typical setup for nerve conduction studies with representative surface electrodes and stimulating electrodes. **A,** Surface electrodes. **B,** Ground electrodes. **C,** Stimulating electrodes.

Monopolar

Concentric

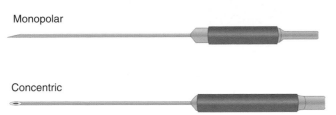

FIGURE 16-3 ■ Needle electrodes for electromyography.

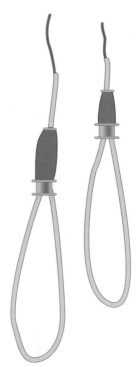

FIGURE 16-4 ■ Sensory ring electrodes.

contraction coupling). The stimulus is transmitted along the fiber by an excitable membrane that surrounds the muscle fiber. The action potential results from the breakdown of the surface membrane potential which is associated with critical changes in ionic permeability. In the resting muscle fiber the potential difference across the surface membrane is 90 μV, with a negative charge on the inside surface. During excitation, the resting potential temporarily reverses to potential of approximately 40 μV negativity on the outside surface. This action potential travels along the muscle fiber at velocities from 3.5 to 5 m/sec in different fibers. Conduction along the fine intramuscular branches of the anterior horn cell occurs so rapidly that all the muscle fibers in a motor unit are activated almost simultaneously.[15]

In extracellular recording, as in EMG, the electrode picks up the action potential as it is conducted by volume conduction through the medium surrounding the active fiber. The impedance of the external medium is small compared with the impedance of the interior of the fiber, therefore the voltage of the extracellularly recorded potential is maximally only 2%

to 10% of the intracellularly recorded potential. The functional unit for reflex or voluntary motor activity is the motor unit. The motor unit (Fig. 16-5A) is the group of muscle fibers innervated by a single anterior horn cell. The number of fibers per motor unit varies considerably from muscle to muscle. Generally, the finer the control exerted by a muscle, the fewer fibers per motor unit. Eye muscles may have as few as 5 to 7 muscle fibers per motor unit, whereas the gastrocnemius may have as many as 3500 muscle fibers per motor unit. Antigravity muscles such as the back extensors or gastrocnemius have much larger numbers of fibers per motor unit because they require less fine control and greater endurance. The motor units in various muscles cover different areas of muscle cross section (e.g, 55 mm in the biceps brachii and 8 to 9 mm in the rectus femoris, anterior tibial, and opponens pollicis muscles). The distribution of fibers is such that fibers from several different motor units are intermingled (see Fig. 16-5B), which is why four to six motor units can be identified by EMG from the same intramuscular recording point. In normal muscle, single motor unit potentials can be differentiated only during weak, voluntary contraction.[13,16] The potentials from different motor units are recognized by their frequency of discharge, amplitude, and morphology—which vary for each motor unit (some being more or less excitable). The different potentials often differ in appearance because of the differential distance of the recording electrode from the individual fibers of the activated motor units and the differential distribution of the motor end-plates in the several units within "range" of a concentric or single needle electrode in one position in the muscle. An upward deflection on the oscilloscope is considered electrically negative, whereas a downward deflection is considered electrically positive. In the immediate vicinity of a potential, there is an upward or negative deflection.

Motor Unit

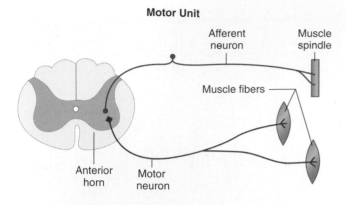

A

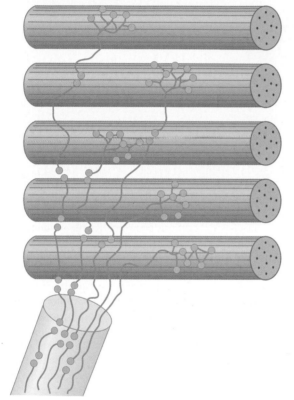

B

FIGURE 16–5 ■ **A,** Anatomy of the motor unit. **B,** Intermingling of fibers.

Nerve Conduction

The cell membrane (axolemma) of a nerve axon separates the intracellular axoplasm from the extracellular fluid.[8] The unequal distribution of ions between these fluids produces a potential difference across the cell membrane, with a resting potential of about 70 mV, negative inside with respect to the outside of the cell membrane. When a nerve fiber is stimulated, it causes a change in the membrane potential, and a rapid but brief flow of sodium ions occurs through ionic channels inward across the cell membrane, giving rise to an action potential. The way an action potential is conducted along an axon depends on whether the axon is myelinated or unmyelinated.[17] In a myelinated fiber the action potential is

regenerated only at the nodes of Ranvier, so that the resulting action potentials "jump" from node to node (salutatory conduction). The velocity of nerve conduction depends on the diameter of a myelinated fiber. Small myelinated fibers may conduct as slowly as 12 m/sec, whereas large motor and sensory fibers conduct at a rate of 50 to 70 m/sec, in humans. In an unmyelinated fiber in a human, the conduction rate is about 2 m/sec.

Several factors influence nerve conduction velocity, other than whether or not the axon is myelinated. Among them are the temperature of the limb,[18] the age of the patient (with infants having slowed conduction velocities and older adults having increasingly slowed conduction with age) as well as the height of an individual, which may increase the internodal distances of the nodes of Ranvier.[8]

■ THE BASIC EXAMINATION

EMG must be combined with the clinical examination of the patient, by the electromyographer, including a grading of muscle strength. It is of prime importance for the electromyographer to personally correlate clinical data with those data obtained by EMG. The EMG is an extension of the neurologic examination, and each examination must be planned individually. There is no "cookbook formula" to follow. Because it is an extension of the clinical examination, the patient must be evaluated fully, and the problem tentatively assigned to the portion of the affected anterior horn cell unit. The electromyographer determines the segment or segments of the peripheral nervous system suspected to be involved, and the examination is planned to either substantiate or invalidate the presumptive clinical diagnosis.

Conducting the Examination

The needle examination is designed to determine (1) the integrity of muscle and its nerve supply; (2) the location of any abnormality, and (3) any abnormalities in the muscle itself. The electrodes may be monopolar or concentric (see Fig.16–3). The examination proceeds through the following steps: (1) determination of the activity of the muscle in a relaxed state[9,13]; (2) evaluation of any insertional activity that arises; (3) assessment of the activity seen on weak voluntary effort; (4) recruitment (i.e., the more or less orderly addition of motor units as effort increases); and (5) determination of the pattern seen on maximum voluntary effort (known as the "interference pattern" (a term deriving its name from the fact that there is interference with the discernment of the initial muscle action potentials from the resting baseline).

■ NEEDLE ELECTRODE FINDINGS IN NORMAL MUSCLE

Insertional Activity

When a needle is inserted into a normal muscle, it evokes a brief burst of electrical activity that lasts no more than 2 to 3 msec, a little longer than the actual movement of the needle.[10] This activity is described as insertional activity and is generally 50 to 250 mV in amplitude (Fig. 16–6A). These inser-

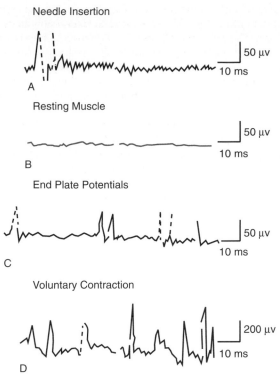

Needle Insertion

50 μv
10 ms

A

Resting Muscle

50 μv
10 ms

B

End Plate Potentials

50 μv
10 ms

C

Voluntary Contraction

200 μv
10 ms

D

FIGURE 16–6 ■ Potentials recorded from muscle. **A,** Insertion. **B,** Resting muscle. **C,** End plate potentials. **D,** Voluntary contraction.

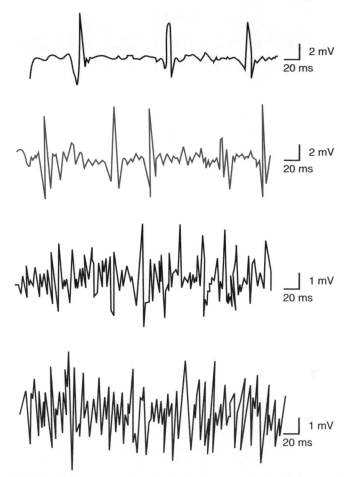

2 mV
20 ms

2 mV
20 ms

1 mV
20 ms

1 mV
20 ms

FIGURE 16–7 ■ Increasing levels of firing associated with increased muscular force.

tional potentials are believed to represent discharges from muscle fibers produced by injury, mechanical stimulation, or irritation of the muscle fibers.

Spontaneous Activity (at Rest)

When the needle is stationary and the muscle is relaxed, there should be no electrical activity present in normal muscle, except when the needle is in the area of the motor end plate (see Fig. 16–6B). Two types of end plate "noise" are normal: (1) low amplitude and undulating (see Fig. 16–6C), probably representing extracellular miniature end plate potentials (MEPP), and (2) higher amplitude intermittent spike discharges, probably representing discharges of a single muscle fiber excited by intramuscular nerve terminals irritated by the needle. Any other spontaneous activity at rest is abnormal. An increase in duration of insertional activity may be seen in loss of innervation or primary muscle fiber disease.[10] Reduction may occur in myopathies or in more advanced degeneration, in which muscle tissue has been replaced by fat or fibrous connective tissue.[19]

Voluntary Activity

Voluntary activity of the muscle is analyzed after the muscle is studied at rest. The motor unit action potential is analyzed. As previously mentioned in the discussion of physiology, the term "motor unit" refers to the number of muscle fibers supplied by one motor neuron and its axon. This varies from muscle to muscle and may be as few as 5 to 10 fibers, to more than 1000 muscle fibers. When a motor neuron discharges, it activates all the muscle fibers in the motor unit. The force of

contraction determines the number of motor units brought into play.[14,16] This begins with a single motor unit (see Fig. 16–6D) that fires and can be identified on the screen by its distinctive morphology. As the effort is increased, other motor units come into play, which still can be individually discerned and have their own individual morphology and audio representation on the loud speaker. As the contraction increases, the firing rate of each individual motor unit action potential increases and is subsequently joined by other motor unit action potentials whose firing rates also increase. In many ways, this represents an orchestra with different instruments being "recruited" to join in the musical number. This phenomenon is known as the "principle of orderly recruitment" (Fig. 16–7). In normal muscle, the strength of a voluntary muscle contraction is directly related to the number of individual motor units that have been recruited, and their firing rate.[16,20] Analysis of motor units includes their waveform, amplitude, and interference patterns.

Waveform

Most units are biphasic or triphasic. The number of phases is determined by the number of "baseline crossings" of the wave. Motor units that cross the baseline more than five times are termed "polyphasic." Although occasionally seen in healthy muscles, they do not exceed 15% of the total number

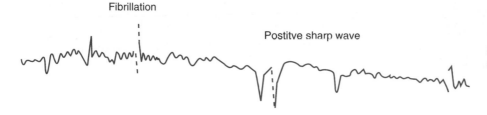

Fibrillation

Postitve sharp wave

FIGURE 16–8 ■ Fibrillations and positive sharp waves (denervation potentials).

of motor units. In some muscles, polyphasic motor units are more prevalent. Polyphasic potentials are a measure of fiber synchrony.

Amplitude

The amplitude of a motor unit depends on the number of fibers in the motor unit, and the type of EMG needle used. Monopolar needles are associated with larger amplitude normals than bipolar or coaxial needles. Normal amplitude ranges from 1 to 5 mV. Because the motor units are the sum of the action potentials of each muscle fiber of the unit, a larger motor unit has a larger amplitude, and a smaller motor unit has a smaller amplitude.

Interference Pattern

With maximum voluntary effort, a large number of motor units are brought into play and their firing rate increases. They tend to "interfere with each other," hence they cannot be recognized further as individual motor units (see Fig. 16–7). This gives rise to the interference pattern. In a normal muscle, there is a "full" interference pattern.

Various abnormalities may occur that indicate the presence of total denervation—neurogenic paresis, peripheral type, or neurogenic paresis, anterior horn cell type. In addition, myogenic paresis may be detected.

Generally, on the basis of abnormal findings with a well planned examination, the presence of a radiculopathy, generalized neuropathy, focal or mononeuropathy or plexopathy can be determined. The following are needle abnormalities in abnormal muscles: (1) insertional activity (increased or decreased); (2) spontaneous activity (fibrillations, positive sharp waves, or fasciculations) (Fig. 16–8); (3) abnormalities of voluntary motor unit activity, especially recruitment (Fig. 16–9); and (4) abnormal motor unit morphology (e.g., excessive or extreme polyphasia).

■ NERVE CONDUCTION STUDIES

Nerve conduction studies are of value in determining if a disease of nerve is present and in determining the distribution of a neuropathy (e.g., mononeuritis, polyneuropathy, or mononeuritis multiplex). This may provide valuable information in the differential diagnosis of the etiology of a neuropathy, determining at what point in a nerve there is conduction block, locating an entrapment site, and studying the progress of a disease of a peripheral nerve (e.g., is it getting better versus staying the same; is there reinnervation of a previously sectioned nerve, establishing whether conduction along the nerve is adequate or normal—which is important in diseases

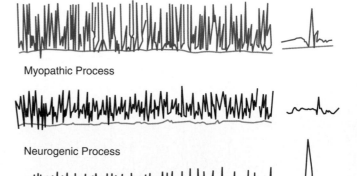

Normal

Myopathic Process

Neurogenic Process

FIGURE 16–9 ■ Patterns of abnormal motor unit recruitment.

of the neuromuscular junction such as myasthenia gravis or the myasthenic syndrome).

Motor nerve conduction velocity studies may be carried out by the insertion of a needle electrode in a muscle innervated by the nerve under study, or by the use of surface electrode over that muscle (Fig. 16–10). For example, the first dorsal interosseus muscle may be examined to determine the function of the ulnar nerve (Fig. 16–11). The nerve is stimulated (in the case of the ulnar nerve, at the elbow), and the latency (length of time for an impulse to arrive and make a "spike" on the oscilloscope screen) of the response is determined. The response is generally a spike-like large motor unit action potential. The ulnar nerve is then stimulated at the wrist and/or axillary region. The difference in latencies between the two points of stimulation, and the distance between the two points of stimulation, provide the basis for the calculation of the conduction velocity. The conduction velocity is measured by the formula:

$$\text{mcv (m/sec)} = \text{dmm (msec)} \div \text{pml (msec)} - \text{dml (msec)}$$

where dmm is the distance between the two stimulus points in mm, and pml and dml are the proximal and distal motor latencies, respectively, in msec, and mcv is the motor conduction velocity in m/sec.[3]

Textbooks of stimulation points and pick-up points are readily available.[7,8] Normal values are usually established for

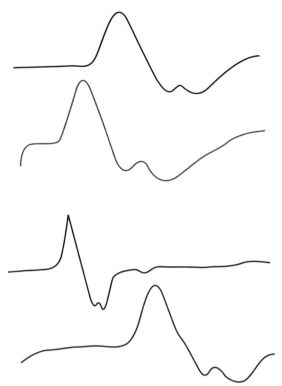

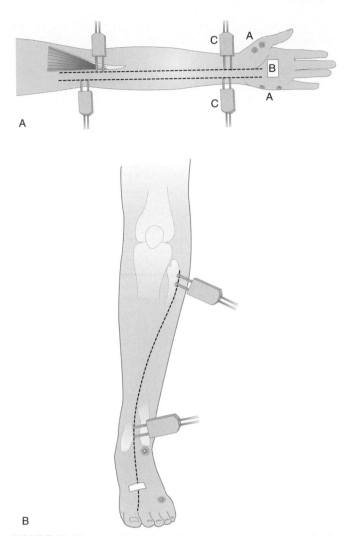

FIGURE 16–11 ■ Responses from the abductor digiti minimi from stimulation at various sites of the ulnar nerve. **A,** Below elbow. **B,** Wrist. **C,** Axilla. **D,** Above elbow.

FIGURE 16–10 ■ **A,** Set-up for typical upper extremity nerve conduction study. **B,** Set-up for typical lower extremity nerve conduction study.

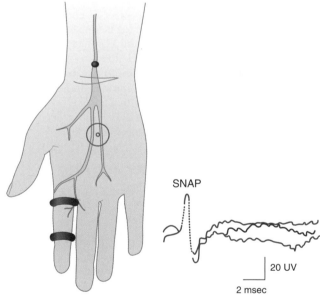

FIGURE 16–12 ■ Typical set-up for median nerve stimulation. *Inset*: Evoked sensory nerve action potential from median nerve stimulation at the wrist.

each nerve in individual laboratories, whereas normal values for commonly tested sensory and motor nerves are generally available. Median nerve stimulation is comparable to ulnar nerve stimulation (Fig. 16–12).

The F-Wave

Definition of the F-Wave

Motor conduction velocity along the whole axon, including proximal portions, can be studied by eliciting the F-wave response, a small late muscle response that occurs from back-firing of anterior horn cells.[21-23] F-waves may be obtained from almost any mixed nerve that can be stimulated, but the median, ulnar, peroneal, and posterior tibial nerves are the most commonly used. If the standard distal motor conduction velocities are normal, but the F-wave value is prolonged, then slowing must be occurring somewhere more proximal to the distal normal segment. The method used to determine F-wave latency varies from laboratory to laboratory—the F-wave value with each successive stimulus shows variability of several milliseconds, with some examiners averaging 10, 30,

or 50 responses, and some taking the shortest of 10 or 20 responses. Limb temperature and arm or leg length may influence the results. Comparison to the opposite limb may be helpful if that limb is asymptomatic.

Complications and Pitfalls

In addition to variability in F-waves and how they are obtained in different laboratories, many electromyographers overuse (or at least over-perform) the F-wave study in cases in which proximal slowing in a nerve or nerve root is not even in the differential diagnosis. The most accepted use of the study is in suspected early Guillain-Barré syndrome when usual distal nerve conduction studies are still normal, usually in the first 10 days of the illness. It is highly controversial in the work-up of radiculopathies.[24,25]

H-Reflex

Definition of the H-Reflex

The H-reflex or "Hoffmann reflex" is obtained by electrode stimulation of the posterior tibial nerve in the popliteal space—at a slow rate with long duration—submaximal electrical shock, and recorded with surface electrodes over the gastrocnemius-soleus complex. The impulse travels up the sensory fibers to the spinal cord, synapses with the alpha motor neuron and returns down the motor fibers to the calf muscle. H-reflex latencies are long, in the 40 to 45 msec range. They are mostly carried out in the S1 root distribution and cannot be recorded consistently from other muscles. To determine a delay or an asymmetry, the opposite leg should always be studied for comparison.[26-29]

The H-reflex is somewhat more useful than the F-wave, but the main reason for this study is in the work-up of a suspected S1 radiculopathy, in which the history and/or physical examination is suggestive, but the EMG is normal.[30] In most cases, when an absent H-reflex is found, suggesting a problem with S1 conduction, an absent or depressed ankle reflex has already been seen in the physical examination, so the study is, for many, redundant.

Pitfalls occur when the opposite leg is not studied to show a normal H-reflex as a contrast. If the H-reflex is bilaterally absent, it may reflect a generalized disease—for example, peripheral neuropathy. Older patients do not have good H-reflexes as a rule and this may be a normal finding. In addition, a unilaterally absent H-reflex with a normal needle EMG examination does not indicate when the injury occurred. It could be the result of a previous remote injury.

▪ QUANTITATIVE SENSORY TESTING

Quantitative Sudomotor Axon Reflex Test (QSART)

Quantitative sensory testing takes various forms, including the quantitative somatosensory thermotest, using a controlled ramp of ascending or descending temperature through a Peltier device.[31] Measurement of threshold for cold sensation reflects function of small caliber A-delta myelinated afferents. Threshold for warm sensation reflects function of warm-specific small unmyelinated afferent channels. Cold pain and heat pain thresholds test the function of unmyelinated C-fiber polymodal nociceptors, and to a lesser extent, A-delta fiber nociceptors. Certain abnormal patterns are characteristic of dysfunction of small caliber peripheral afferents.[32] To obtain maximum information from quantitative somatosensory thermotest, it is necessary to test both hot and cold sensations.[33] Quantitative sensory testing performed at different sites along an extremity in cases of polyneuropathy yields useful information about progression of the pathologic process along the

extremity, provides an estimate of the progression of the disease, and serves as a baseline for evaluation of treatment and further progression or improvement of the disease.

Quantitative sudomotor axon reflex test (Q-SART) is a quantitative thermoregulatory sweat test. It has been used to detect postganglionic sudomotor failure in neuropathies[34,35] and preganglionic neuropathies with presumed transynaptic degeneration.[36] In patients with distal small fiber neuropathy, it is the most sensitive diagnostic test.[37] Various commercial devices have been used in an attempt to differentiate axonal and demyelinating polyneuropathies.[38]

▪ CLINICAL CORRELATIONS

Clinical correlations can be based on careful history, clinical examination and electrodiagnostic studies. Electrodiagnostic studies are best for separating neuropathy from myopathy and determining if a neuropathy is generalized mixed, or focal, axonal or demyelinating—thereby giving important clues as to etiology. Nerve trauma can be followed serially to determine recovery. By careful attention to anatomic detail, the diagnosis of radiculopathy or plexopathy can often be made.

Nerve Trauma

After injury, such as a laceration, the nerve is often completely severed. At rest, denervation potentials are recorded in the muscles supplied by that nerve in the form of positive sharp waves or fibrillation potentials, and on electromyography, no motor unit action potentials are seen. However, sometimes an injury is incomplete and the type of nerve lesion and its extent are uncertain.

Neuropraxia is the mildest form of nerve injury and consists of conduction loss without associated axonal structural changes. This form of conduction block often occurs with compressive or ischemic nerve injuries, such as mild entrapment neuropathy or compression, e.g., radial nerve palsy ("Saturday night palsy"). In neuropraxic injuries, focal demyelination occurs. Serial nerve conduction determinations along the course of the nerve enable one to locate the site of the conduction block. The prognosis for complete recovery is generally good and healing occurs within days or weeks, barring further injury.

In axonotmesis, there is disruption of the axon in its myelin sheath, a more severe form of nerve injury. The neural tube consisting of the endoperineurium and the epineurium remains intact. The nerve undergoes wallerian degeneration with fragmentation of the axon distal to the site of injury. Motor and sensory loss occurs with associated atrophy of supplied muscles and loss of reflexes. After about 4 to 5 days, the distal segments of the nerve become inexcitable. In 1 to 2 weeks, positive sharp waves are seen in the EMG on needle examination. In 2 to 3 weeks, fibrillation potentials are seen in the involved muscle segments. The intact neural tube forms "lattice" for the regenerating axon and the prognosis for recovery is generally good—but not as favorable as in neuropraxia.

Neurotmesis is the most severe form of nerve injury and consists of severe disruption of or transection of the nerve. Nerve regeneration and recovery are often incomplete or nonexistent and may require surgical reanastomosis to attempt recovery of nerve integrity. Neuromas may form and are commonly associated with pain. Only serial EMG and nerve conduction studies over time can determine the difference between axonotmesis and neurotmesis in some cases, and in almost all cases, electrical signs of recovery precede clinical ones.

Nontraumatic Neuropathies

In nontraumatic neuropathies, segmental demyelination is generally associated with slowing of nerve conduction velocities and temporal dispersion of evoked responses. With axonal degeneration, however, reduction of the evoked response amplitudes with mild terminal slowing of nerve conduction velocities is typical. An EMG provides early information regarding reinnervation before clinical recovery is evident. The earliest positive evidence of reinnervation is the appearance during voluntary effort of motor units that are of low amplitude in the beginning but are highly polyphasic("nascent units"). They may be present several weeks before there is clinical evidence of functional recovery.

Polyneuropathy

EMG and nerve conduction determinations are useful in diagnosing polyneuropathy and in determining whether a pathologic process is axonal, or demyelinating, or mixed. A diagnosis of polyneuropathy is made when abnormal nerve conduction and EMG findings are bilateral and relatively symmetrical. Generalized peripheral neuropathies often associated with pain are noted in Table 16–1.[39-44]

Electrodiagnostic findings characteristic of axonal neuropathy are:

- Abnormally low or absent sensory nerve action potential amplitude
- Abnormally low or absent compound muscle action potential amplitude
- Normal distal latencies for sensory and motor potentials
- Normal or near normal sensory and motor conduction velocities

Table 16–1

Generalized Peripheral Neuropathies

Diabetes mellitus
Polyneuropathy associated with insulinoma
Polyneuropathy associated with nutritional deficiency
Alcohol-nutritional deficiency polyneuropathy
Vasculitis-associated neuropathy
Amyloidosis neuropathy
Toxic neuropathy (e.g., arsenic and thallium)
HIV-related distal symmetrical polyneuropathy
Fabry disease
Guillain-Barré syndrome (acute inflammatory demyelinating polyneuropathy)
Chronic inflammatory demyelinating polyneuropathy
Cryptogenic sensory, or (much less commonly) sensorimotor polyneuropathy
Polyneuropathy due to neoplasms, including those that are paraneoplastic

If a disease process affects the large diameter axons, some slowing of conduction velocity occurs; the velocity is seldom reduced by more than 20% to 30% of normal. However, fibrillations and positive sharp waves are present in muscles innervated by affected nerves and are generally worse distally. The feet muscles are more involved than hand muscles, and the leg muscles are more involved than the arm muscles. Motor unit potentials are decreased in number with deficient recruitment and an incomplete interference pattern. Some motor units are of increased amplitude and duration.

In contrast, diffuse demyelinating neuropathy is characterized by reduction of conduction velocities, usually more than 40% of the normal range. Distal latencies are also prolonged. The sensory nerve action potentials and compound muscle action potentials usually have low amplitudes and temporal dispersion. A needle EMG shows no fibrillations or positive sharp waves unless there is secondary axonal degeneration. In a pure demyelinating neuropathy, there is no denervation of muscle fibers. Motor units are decreased in number. Decreased recruitment is attributable to conduction block in some fibers. Usually there is no significant change in the duration, amplitude, or morphology of motor units but the number of polyphasic units may be increased if there is demyelination of terminal axons.

Once having determined electromyographically whether or not a neuropathy is primarily axonal or demyelinating, one can then consider clinically which neuropathies are diffusely axonal and which are demyelinating. Subacute and chronic diffuse axonal types include most toxic and nutritional neuropathies as from uremia, diabetes, hypothyroidism, HIV disease, paraneoplastic disease, dysproteinemias, and amyloidosis. Diabetics usually begin with slow conduction velocities, in the 32 to 38 m/sec range in the lower extremities. Fibrillations and positive waves in the intrinsic foot muscles are a later finding.

Demyelinating polyneuropathies include hereditary motor and sensory neuropathies types 1 and 3, Refsum disease, multifocal leukodystrophy, and Krabbe disease. Acute nonuniform demyelinating diseases include Guillain-Barré syndrome, diphtheria, and acute arsenic intoxication, whereas chronic demyelinating diseases include chronic inflammatory demyelinating polyneuropathy (CIDP), idiopathic disease, and neuropathies accompanying HIV disease—as well as various paraproteinemias, dysproteinemias, and osteosclerotic myeloma.[45]

Mononeuropathies, Compression Neuropathies, and Entrapment Neuropathies

A mononeuropathy is obviously one affecting only a single nerve. Its clinical implications generally are different from a polyneuropathy and a far higher percentage of affected patients have traumatic or microtraumatic etiologies. Subtypes include compression neuropathy in which acute or chronic compression of a nerve results in varying degrees of nerve impairment and entrapment neuropathy in which a nerve is subjected to an anatomic situation in which there is either inadequate space for transit of the nerve or an unyielding anatomic structure compresses the nerve.

In entrapment neuropathies and compression neuropathies, the most commonly involved nerves are the median, ulnar, radial, common peroneal and tibial. Entities such as trauma, vasculitis, diabetes mellitus, leprosy, and sarcoidosis can affect any nerve in the body. Electrophysiologic studies are of great assistance in localizing the pathologic process to the individual nerve and in differentiating mononeuropathy from diffuse polyneuropathy, plexopathy, or radiculopathy.

Median Nerve

The median nerve is most commonly entrapped at the wrist as it passes through the carpal tunnel but may also be injured at the elbow where it passes between the two heads of the pronator teres, or, less frequently, is compressed by a dense band of connective tissue (the ligament of Struthers immediately above the elbow).[46,47]

The median nerve is derived from C6 through T1 nerve roots (lateral and medial cords of the brachial plexus). The diagnosis of carpal tunnel syndrome is made by demonstrating localized slowing of sensory and motor conductions across the wrist as evidenced by prolonged sensory and motor distal latencies.[1] In addition, with advanced changes, there may be denervation in the form of fibrillations, positive sharp waves, and reduced motor units with polyphasia in median nerve-innervated hand muscles.

Pronator Teres and Anterior Interosseous Syndrome

The pronator teres and anterior interosseous syndrome are proximal compression or entrapment neuropathies of the median nerve. The pronator teres syndrome may show normal distal latency of sensory and motor determinations at the wrist and no evidence of denervation in median nerve-innervated hand and forearm muscles except for the pronator teres.[47] The anterior interosseous nerve is a motor nerve which is a branch of the median nerve with its origin just distal to the pronator teres.[47] Denervation may be seen in the flexors of the thumb and index finger.

Ulnar Nerve

The ulnar nerve is derived from the C8 and T1 cervical and thoracic nerve roots (medial cord of the brachial plexus) and is usually compressed, entrapped, or injured at the elbow but occasionally at the wrist in the canal of Guyon or deep in the palm ("silver beater's palsy"). EMG studies help to differentiate C8-T1 radiculopathy from plexopathy or more distal ulnar neuropathy.[48,49]

When the lesion is at the wrist at the canal of Guyon, usually both motor and sensory fibers are involved and the amplitude of the sensory and motor action potentials is reduced. Distal sensory and motor latencies across the wrist are prolonged and there is no focal slowing of motor conduction velocity or decrement of the compound motor action potential across the elbow. With a deep palmar branch lesion, there is no sensory abnormality and all of the changes are in a motor distribution distal to the lesion.[50] When the lesion is at the elbow, there may be slowing of nerve conduction across the elbow, often as reduced as 25% to 40% below normal. Normal values depend on the method of determination (i.e., arm straight versus arm bent). The sensory potential at the wrist may be delayed or absent and EMG may demonstrate denervation in intrinsic hand muscles as well as in the flexor

carpi ulnaris, a muscle innervated just below the elbow by the ulnar nerve in some cases.

Radial Nerve

The radial nerve is a continuation of the posterior cord of the brachial plexus and it receives fibers from the C5 through C8 cervical nerve roots. It is usually involved at the spiral groove of the humerus, often secondary to a humeral fracture. With a lesion at the spiral groove, the triceps muscle is often spared on EMG but all of the extensor muscles in the forearm are involved. An isolated superficial radial nerve lesion sometimes occurs at the wrist ("handcuff neuropathy") with the only electrophysiologic abnormality a diminution or absence of the radial sensory potential elicited over the radial aspect of the wrist.

Posterior Interosseous Syndrome

The posterior interosseous syndrome (sometimes referred to as "complicated or resistant lateral epicondylitis or tennis elbow") occurs from entrapment of the radial nerve branch in the region of the elbow at the arcade of Fröhse between the two heads of the supinator muscle. The EMG shows involvement of the extensor carpi ulnaris, extensor digitorum longus, extensor pollicis longus, and extensor indicus while sparing the more proximal supinator and extensor carpi radialis and brevis.[51] Sensation is unaffected.

Common Peroneal Nerve

The common peroneal nerve is derived from L4 through S1 lumbar and sacral nerve roots but is usually primarily from the L5 lumbar nerve root. It may be compressed at the head of the fibula. Peroneal nerve conduction studies show reduced compound motor action potentials as recorded from the extensor digitorum brevis at the ankle with stimulation above the fibular head and normal below the fibular head and at the ankle.

Posterior Tibial Nerve at the Ankle

The posterior tibial nerve is derived from the L4 through S2 lumbar and sacral nerve roots and may be compressed in the tarsal tunnel. Nerve conduction studies show prolongation of the distal motor and sensory latencies of the tibial nerve.[52-54] This syndrome is relatively uncommon.

Sciatic Nerve

The sciatic nerve arises from the L4, L5, S1, S2, and S3 lumbar and sacral nerve roots. A controversial syndrome is entrapment by the piriformis muscle as it passes through the sciatic notch. A lesion of the sciatic nerve is defined and localized by detailed needle examination of muscles in the lower extremity.

Other Uncommon Neuropathies

There are numerous potential mononeuropathies, including those involving the long thoracic nerve, dorsal scapular, suprascapular, musculocutaneous nerve, and axillary nerves in the shoulder girdle and upper extremity. In the pelvic girdle, there is potential involvement of the femoral, obturator, saphenous, and lateral femoral cutaneous nerves, as well as the genitofemoral, ilioinguinal, superior gluteal, and inferior gluteal nerves. Needle EMG reveals denervation changes in muscles supplied by the affected nerves. Cutaneous nerve conduction may reveal abnormalities in pure sensory neuropathies, such as the lateral femoral cutaneous nerve ("meralgia paresthetica"), and careful EMG will differentiate it from a high (L1, L2) radiculopathy. Nerve conduction studies are rarely of assistance in the other conditions delineated earlier.[55]

Radiculopathies

Radiculopathies are diseases of the nerve roots and must be differentiated from plexopathies as well as from complex individual nerve root and nerve lesions. Roots are commonly involved by compression, especially in the cervical and lumbar regions, but may also be involved by diseases such as diabetes mellitus, herpes zoster, carcinomatous infiltration, lymphomatous infiltration, sarcoidosis and infectious processes. Motor and sensory nerve conduction velocities are rarely useful because the lesion in a radiculopathy is proximal to the dorsal root ganglion and motor and sensory nerve conductions are usually normal, although potentials may be reduced in amplitude if the lesion is severe enough to cause axonal loss. The H-reflex is absent or delayed when the S1 nerve root is involved. Typically nerve root lesions are diagnosed by demonstrating abnormal needle examinations in the appropriate paraspinal and limb muscles.[56]

Because most limb muscles are supplied by more than one nerve root, a normal study does not exclude the diagnosis of radiculopathy; however, when the EMG is abnormal, it provides objective evidence of impairment of physiologic function in the nerve root and localizes the lesion to one or more nerve roots in addition to giving information about the severity of the involvement in the pathologic process.[1]

Plexopathies

In plexopathies, motor conduction studies are useful in excluding a peripheral nerve lesion; otherwise they are generally normal except that the amplitudes of compound muscle action potentials may be reduced. Sensory nerve conductions are usually helpful only in excluding other lesion sites such as peripheral nerves. Again, the needle examination is the most helpful element of the examination and requires knowledge of plexus anatomy and innervation of muscles by specific portions of the plexus under investigation.[57]

Anterior Horn Cell Disorders

Disorders of the anterior horn cell usually do not manifest with prominent pain except in the acute febrile stage of poliomyelitis.

Disorders of the Central Nervous System

EMG and nerve conduction studies are almost always normal in diseases of the central nervous system not complicated by peripheral nerve disease.

Primary Muscle Disorders

Many primary disorders of muscle are painless. These include the congenital muscular dystrophies. However, many

---

Table 16–2

Painful Myopathies

Dermatomyositis
Polymyositis
Toxic myopathies
Necrotizing myopathies
Cholesterol-lowering agents: cyclosporine, labetalol, propofol, alcohol
Amphilic: chloroquine, hydrochloroquine, amiodarone
Antimicrotubular: colchicine, vincristine
Mitochondrial: zidovudine and possibly other anti-HIV drugs
Inflammatory: L-tryptophan, D-penicillamine, Cimetidine, L-dopa, phenytoin, lamotrigine, interferon-alpha, hydroxyurea, imatinib
Hypokalemic: diuretics, laxatives, amphotericin, toluene abuse, licorice, corticosteroids, alcohol abuse
Unknown mechanism: critical care myopathy, corticosteroids
Nondepolarizing neuromuscular agents: sepsis (omeprazole, isotretinoin, finasteride, emetine)

---

acquired myopathies (e.g., polymyositis) are painful and metabolic muscle disorders, (e.g., glycogen and lipid storage diseases) may include pain and muscle cramps in their symptomatology. Most manifest as myalgias. Table 16–2 lists some of the painful myopathies. A large number of them are toxic in origin.[58] One of the clearest uses of EMG is in differentiating myopathies from neuropathic processes. Needle examination should clearly differentiate neuropathy from myopathy. In myopathy, the motor potentials are reduced in amplitude and may be polyphasic. In addition, the potentials show paradoxical recruitment with more potentials seen on the oscilloscope screen than would normally be seen for that degree of muscular effort. In inflammatory myopathies, such as polymyositis, there may be marked signs of muscle irritability in the form of fibrillations and positive sharp waves. In polymyositis, metabolic and congenital muscle disorders, nerve conduction studies are generally normal. EMG studies are usually normal in myofascial pain syndromes, fibromyalgia, and polymyalgia rheumatica.[59-61]

■ CONCLUSION

EMG and nerve conduction studies are useful in localizing neuromuscular disease sites and in providing information about the nature of the process (demyelinating, axonal, primary muscle disease, radiculopathy, plexopathy, and so on), but it cannot directly determine the etiology (e.g., diabetes, Guillain-Barré syndrome, polymyositis, tumor, ruptured disc, and so on). The etiology must be inferred from anatomic location, symptoms, and the examination bolstered by the EMG in certain instances. Chapter 5 (Patterns of Common Pain Management Syndromes) discusses that process in detail.

Figure 16–13 presents a summary of EMG findings in various conditions. In addition, a normal study does not mean the patient has no pain. Electrodiagnostic studies in the EMG laboratory as usually performed measure only activity related

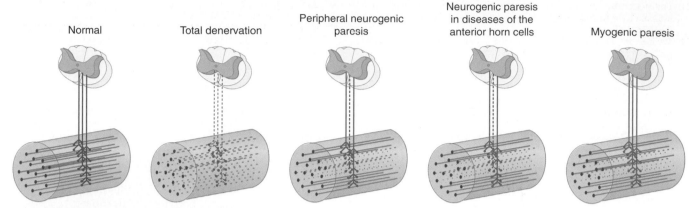

Normal   Total denervation   Peripheral neurogenic paresis   Neurogenic paresis in diseases of the anterior horn cells   Myogenic paresis

FIGURE 16–13 ■ Summary of normal and abnormal findings in needle EMG for various conditions.

to the motor fibers, the larger sensory fibers, and the muscles. Sympathetic and small unmyelinated (C) fibers are not evaluated except with quantitative sensory testing.

In addition, the timing of the EMG in relation to injury or onset of symptoms may be quite important. Early after nerve injury (0 to 14 days) the EMG may show only electrical silence, which may not be helpful. If any motor units are seen at that time, the nerve to that muscle is at least partially intact. Fibrillation potentials in denervated muscles appear only after 2 to 3 weeks. If reinnervation is occurring, small, very polyphasic recovery or "nascent" units will be noted. Serial studies after nerve injury are more helpful in determining recovery than a single study.

Cost containment issues have become extremely important and Medicare and other insurers have developed guidelines for when it is appropriate to test for various conditions. In response, the American Association of Neuromuscular and Electrodiagnostic Medicine has also issued its own practice testing guidelines.[62]

In conclusion, EMG and nerve conduction studies may find, confirm, and localize disease processes but the relevance of the findings to the patient's pain must remain a clinical determination.

References

1. Mcdermott JF, Modaff WL, Boyle RW: Electromyography. Gen Practice 27:1, 1963.
2. Norris FH: The EMG: A Guide and Atlas for Practical EMG. New York, Grune & Stratton, 1963.
3. Waldman SD, Winnie AP (eds): Interventional Pain Management. Philadelphia, Saunders, 1996.
4. Longmire D: Tutorial 10: Electrodiagnostic studies in the assessment of painful disorders. Pain Digest 3:116, 1993.
5. Aminoff MJ (ed): Electrodiagnosis in Clinical Neurology. New York, Churchill Livingstone, 1992.
6. Daube JR (ed): Clinical Neurophysiology. Philadelphia, FA Davis, 1996, p 199.
7. Dumitru D (ed): Electrodiagnostic Medicine. Philadelphia, Hanley & Belfus, 1995.
8. Oh SJ (ed): Clinical Electromyography: Nerve Conduction Studies, 2nd ed. Baltimore, Williams & Wilkins, 1993.
9. Brown WF, Bolton CF: Clinical Electromyography, 2nd ed. Boston, Butterworth-Heinemann, 1993.
10. Waldman HJ: Neurophysiologic testing in the evaluation of the patient in pain. In Waldman SD, Winnie AP (eds): Interventional Pain Management. Philadelphia, Saunders, 1996, p 104.
11. Stolov WC: Electrodiagnostic evaluation of acute and chronic pain. In Bonica JJ (ed): Management of Pain, 2nd ed. Philadelphia, Lea & Febiger, 1990.
12. Verdugo R, Ochoa JL: Use and misuse of conventional electrodiagnosis, quantitative sensory testing, thermography, and nerve blocks in the evaluation of painful neuropathic syndromes. Presented at the AAEM Symposium on Neuropathic Pain, Charleston, SC, 1992.
13. Kimura J: Electrodiagnosis in Diseases of Nerve and Muscle: Principles and Practice. Philadelphia, FA Davis, 1983.
14. Sivek M, Ochoa J, Fernandez JM: Positive manifestations of nerve fiber dysfunction: Clinical, electrophysiologic, and pathologic correlates. In Brown WF, Bolton CF (eds): Clinical Electromyography, 2nd ed. Boston, Butterworth-Heinemann, 1993.
15. Buchtal R: An Introduction to Electromyography. Copenhagen, Scandinavian University Books, 1957.
16. Wiechers DO: Normal and abnormal motor unit action potentials. In Johnson, EW (ed): Practical Electromyography, 2nd ed. Baltimore, Williams & Wilkins, 1988.
17. Waxman SG: Conduction in myelinated, unmyelinated and demyelinated fibers. Arch Neurol 34:585, 1977.
18. Bolton CF, Carter K, Koval JJ: Temperature effects on conduction studies of normal and abnormal nerve. Muscle Nerve 5S:145, 1982.
19. Ball RD: Basics of Needle Electromyography: An AAEE Workshop. Rochester, Minn, American Association of Electromyography and Electrodiagnosis, 1985.
20. Jablecki C: Physiologic basis of electromyographic activity. In AAEE Course C: Standard Needle Electromyography of Muscles. American Association of Electromyography and Electrodiagnosis, 11th Annual Continuing Education Course, San Diego, CA, 1988.
21. Kimura J: F-wave velocity in the central segment of the median and ulnar nerves: A study in normal subjects and in patients with Charcot-Marie-Tooth disease. Neurology 24:539, 1974.
22. Mayer RF, Feldman RG: Observations on the nature of the F-wave in man. Neurology 17:147, 1967.
23. Magladery JW, McDougal DB: Electrophysiological studies and reflex activity in normal man: Identification of certain reflexes in the electromyogram and conduction velocity of peripheral nerve fiber. Bull Johns Hopkins Hosp 86:265, 1950.
24. Fisher MA: F-wave studies: Clinical utility. Muscle Nerve 21:1098, 1998.
25. Rivner MH: F-wave studies: Limitations. Muscle Nerve: 21:1101, 1998.
26. Hoffmann P: Untersuchungen uber Bie Eigenreflexe (Sehnenreflexe). Nenschlicher Muskeln, Berlin, Springer, 1922.
27. Braddom RL, Johnson EW: Standardization of H-reflex and diagnostic use of S1 radiculopathy. Arch Phys Med Rehabil 55:161, 1974.
28. Braddom RL, Johnson EW: H-reflex: Review and classification with suggested clinical uses. Arch Phys Med Rehabil 55:417, 1974.
29. Schuchmann JA: H-reflex, latency and radiculopathy. Arch Phys Med Rehabil 59:185, 1978.
30. Johnson EW: Electrodiagnosis of radiculopathy. In Johnson EW (ed): Practical Electromyography, 2nd ed. Baltimore, Williams & Wilkins, 1988.

31. Fruhstorfer H, Lindblom U, Schmidt WG: Method for quantitative estimation for thermal thresholds in patients. J Neurol Neurosurg Psych 39:1071, 1971.
32. Verdugo RJ, Ochoa JL: Quantitative somatosensory thermotest: A key method for functional evaluation of small caliber afferent channels. Brain 115:893, 1992.
33. Ashbury AK, Porte D, Genuth SM, et al: Report and recommendations of the San Antonio Conference on Diabetic Neuropathy, 1988.
34. Low PA, Caskey PE, Tuck RR, et al: Quantitative sudomotor axon reflex test in normal and neuropathic subjects. Ann Neurol 14:573, 1983.
35. Low PA, Zimmerman BR, Dyck PJ: Comparison of distal sympathetic with vagal function in diabetic neuropathy. Muscle Nerve 9:592, 1986.
36. Cohen J, Low PA, Fealey R: Somatic and autonomic function in progressive autonomic failure: Multiple system atrophy. Ann Neurol 22:692, 1987.
37. Sandroni P, Ahlskog JE, Fealey RD, et al: Autonomic involvement in extrapyramidal and cerebellar disorders. Clin Auton Res 1:147, 1991.
38. Menkes DL: Quantitative sensory testing distinguishes axonal from demyelinating polyneuropathies. Presented at the 44th Annual Meeting of the AAEM, San Diego, Cal, 1997.
39. Schaumburg HH, Berger AR, Thomas PK: Disorders of Peripheral Nerve, 2nd ed. (Contemporary Neurology Series). Philadelphia, FA Davis, 1992.
40. Barohn RJ: Approach to peripheral neuropathy and neuronopathy. In Pascuzzi RM (ed): Disorders of Neuromuscular Transmission. New York, Thieme, 1998, p 7.
41. Ropper,AH, Gorson, KC: Neuropathies associated with paraproteinemia N Engl J Med, 338:1601,1998.
42. Cornblath DR, Melitts BD, Griffin JW, et al: Motor conduction studies in Guillain-Barré syndrome: Description and prognostic value. Ann Neurol 23:354, 1988.
43. Pourmand R, Maybury B: AAEM Case report #31: Paraneoplastic sensory neuropathy. AAEM, 1996.
44. Albers JW, Donofrio PD, McGonagle TK: Spectrum of patients with EMG features of polyradiculopathy without neuropathy. Muscle Nerve 13:63, 1990.
45. Bromberg MB: Comparison of electrodiagnostic criteria for primary chronic polyneuropathy. Muscle Nerve 14:968, 1991.
46. Stevens JC: AAEM Minimonograph #26: The electrodiagnosis of carpal tunnel syndrome. AAEM, 1997.
47. Rosenbaum RB, Ochoa JL: Carpal Tunnel Sndrome and other Disorders of the Median Nerve. Boston, Butterworth-Heinemann, 1993.
48. Kincaid JC, Phillips LH, Daube JR: The evaluation in suspected ulnar neuropathy at the elbow, normal conduction values. Arch Neurol 43:44, 1986.
49. Miller RG: The cubital tunnel syndrome: Diagnosis and precise localization. Ann Neurol 6:56,1979.
50. Ebling P, Gilliat RW, Thomas PK: A clinical and electrical study of ulnar nerve lesions in the hand. J Neurol Neurosurg Psychiatry 23:1, 1960.
51. Stuart JV: The radial nerve. In Stuart JD (ed): Focal Peripheral Neuropathies, 2nd ed. New York, Raven, 1993, p 231.
52. DeLisa JA, Saed MA: AAEE case report #8: The tarsal tunnel syndrome. Muscle Nerve 6:664, 1983.
53. Keck C: The tarsal tunnel syndrome. J Bone Joint Surg 44A:180, 1992.
54. Oh SJ, Sarala PK, Kuba T: Tarsal tunnel syndrome: Electrophysiological study. Ann Neurol 5:327, 1979.
55. Stuart JD: The sciatic, gluteal and pudendal nerves. In Stuart JD (ed): Focal Peripheral Neuropathies, 2nd ed. New York, Raven, 1993, p 321.
56. Tonvola RF, Ackil AA, Shahani BT, et al: Usefulness of electrophysiological studies in the diagnosis of lumbosacral root disease. Ann Neurol 9:305, 1981.
57. Ferrante MA: Brachial plexopathies: Classification, causes, and consequences. Muscle Nerve 30:547, 2004.
58. Mastaglia FL: Inflammatory myopathies: Clinical, diagnostic and therapeutic aspects. Muscle Nerve 27:407, 2003.
59. Walsh RJ, Amato AA: Toxic neuropathies. Neurol Clin 23:397, 2005.
60. Walton J: Disorders of Voluntary Muscle, 4th ed. Cambridge, Cambridge University Press, 1984.
61. Roland LP: Myopathies. In Roland LP (ed): Merritt's Textbook of Neurology, 10th ed. Philadelphia, Lippincott Williams & Wilkins, 2000, p 735.
62. American Association of Neuromuscular and Electrodiagnostic Medicine: Recommended Policy for Electrodiagnostic Medicine. AANEM, 2005. http://www.aanem.org/PracticeIssues/RecPolicy/recommended_policy_1.cfm

chapter 17

Evoked Potential Testing

Howard J. Waldman

Underutilized by many pain management specialists, evoked potentials (EP) are a useful diagnostic test to help identify abnormalities of the peripheral and central nervous system that may help explain why the patient is having pain or functional disability. EP testing is also useful in helping prove the absence of neural pathway abnormalities in the patient who complains of otherwise unexplained visual or hearing loss and/or unexplained numbness. Such information is extremely useful when there is a clinical impression of behavioral issues influencing a patient's pain response.

■ WHAT ARE EVOKED POTENTIALS?

EP are electrophysiologic responses of the nervous system to externally applied sensory stimuli. EP testing can provide information on the peripheral and the central sensory nervous system pathways that is unobtainable by electromyelography (EMG) and magnetic stimulation evaluations. EP testing provides objective and reproducible data to delineate sensory system lesions that are unsuspected or are clinically ambiguous on the basis of history and physical examination findings alone. EP testing can provide information on the anatomic location of nervous system lesions and help to monitor progression or regression.[1-4]

EP responses are of very low amplitude (0.1 to 20 µV) and are obscured by random electrical "noise" such as muscle artifact, electroencephalographic activity, and interference from surrounding electrical devices. Extraction of the EP response is accomplished by computer averaging. This technique summates the EP response, which is "time-locked" to the applied sensory stimuli, and minimizes unwanted noise interference.[1,3]

A variety of stimuli may elicit evoked potentials, but the most commonly employed are visual, auditory, and somatosensory. These three stimuli give rise to visual evoked potentials (VEPs), brain stem auditory evoked potentials (BAEPs), and somatosensory evoked potentials (SEPs), which evaluate functions of their respective sensory systems.[3,5]

EP responses consist of a sequence of peaks and waves characterized by latency, amplitude, configuration, and interval between individual peaks (interpeak latency). In this manner, EP responses are similar to conventional nerve conduction study (NCS) responses and magnetically stimulated motor EP.

There is a standardized nomenclature for the individual peaks and waves of the various EP responses.[6-9] The peaks and waves may be identified by *polarity* (positive or negative), *latency* (e.g., the positive wave occurring at 100 msec in VEP testing is designated P100), by the *anatomic site* where the response was recorded (e.g., Erb's point), or by simple numbering in sequence (e.g., waves I through V in the BAEP). Normal values for EP responses are generally established by each electrophysiology laboratory, using 2.5 or 3.0 standard deviations from mean values as the upper limits of normal.[1,3,10]

■ INSTRUMENTATION

The EP equipment, like that for EMG, is a biological amplifier. In its most basic form, EP equipment consists of recording electrodes attached to specific areas over the scalp, spine, and extremities. Input from the electrodes is routed to an amplifier, which filters, averages, displays, and records data.[3] Electrodes are placed on the scalp much as for conventional electroencephalography, following the international 10-20 system according to which electrodes are located at distances 10% or 20% of the total distance between bony landmarks of the skull.[11] The configuration of electrode placement for a specific test is referred to as a *montage*.

■ SPECIFIC EVOKED POTENTIAL TESTS

The three most commonly used EP tests are the VEP, BAEP, and SEP. For most patients who consult a pain specialist, SEPs have the most clinical utility. A fourth test, cognitive evoked potentials, will also be discussed briefly.

Visual Evoked Potentials

VEPs are utilized to evaluate pathology affecting the visual pathways. They are primarily generated in the visual cortex and, therefore, may be affected by pathology anywhere along the visual pathways, from the corneas to the visual cortex.[6,12] A reversing checkerboard pattern projected through a video monitor is most often used to stimulate the visual pathways (pattern-reversal VEP). Each eye is tested individually to localize abnormalities to the affected side. Generally, 100 pattern reversals (trials) are required to obtain a clearly defined response. The test is repeated to confirm reproducibility of responses. The resultant VEP consists of three peaks: The primary peak of interest occurs at approximately 100 msec, has positive polarity, and is thus referred to as the *P100 peak*. The remaining two peaks have negative polarities and latencies of approximately 75 and 145 msec, respectively.[1,10] The upper limits of normal for the P100 response are about 117 to 120 msec, with a differential latency between eyes of no more than 6 to 7 msec.[3]

VEP testing is useful in the diagnosis of many conditions that affect the visual pathways but is most often used in the diagnosis of MS (Fig. 17–1). The demyelination of the optic nerve that occurs in MS has the same effect as demyelination in peripheral nerves (i.e., slowing of conduction velocity), resulting in increased response latency. If axonal loss also occurs, response amplitude is also reduced.[1,13-15] These abnormalities correspond to the changes seen in demyelination and axonopathy found in conventional NCS. In MS patients, the most common abnormalities are increased P100 latency and increased interocular latencies. Reduction of P100 amplitude may also occur, although this is generally associated with compressive or ischemic lesions.[1] In patients suspected to have MS, VEP abnormality rates are approximately 63%, and they approach 85% in patients with confirmed MS.[1] VEP abnormalities may antedate typical changes of MS seen on magnetic resonance imaging.[1] MS may also produce abnormalities of BAEP and SEP; therefore, testing all three may improve the diagnostic yield over that of VEP alone.[16,17]

Ocular disorders, tumors, inflammatory conditions, and ischemia of the optic pathways may be associated with VEP abnormalities.[18-20] VEP abnormalities have also been reported in a variety of cerebral degenerative disorders and neuropathies with CNS involvement.[1-20] There are a few reports of VEP abnormalities in patients with migraine headaches.[21-25] VEP testing has been used for visual screening of infants and persons who are suspected of having visual pathway disease but are unable to respond to or comply with conventional ophthalmologic or optometric testing.[10,22]

Brain Stem Auditory Evoked Potentials

In the manner that visual stimuli are used to evaluate visual pathways, auditory stimuli are used to assess the auditory

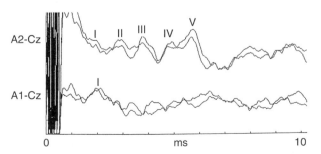

FIGURE 17–1 ■ *Upper trace,* Normal brain stem auditory evoked potential response demonstrates waves I through V. *Lower trace,* Abnormal brain stem auditory evoked potential response obtained from a patient with a left acoustic neuroma. Wave I is present, but waves II through V are absent. (From Waldman SD [ed]: Interventional Pain Management, 2nd ed. Philadelphia, Saunders, 2001, p 185, Figure 14-11, with permission.)

pathways. The auditory pathway extends from the middle ear structures through the eighth cranial nerve (CN VIII) and brain stem to the auditory cortex.[1,3,10] Auditory stimuli presented to each ear individually produce the BAEPs, which consist of a series of waves that correspond closely to these auditory pathway structures. BAEP evaluation, therefore, allows relatively specific localization of auditory pathway pathology. BAEP responses are recorded from electrodes placed on the scalp, near or on each ear. The most commonly used auditory stimulus is brief, electrical pulses, referred to as *clicks,* which are presented to each ear through audiologic earphones. (Earphones that fit *into* the auditory canal can also be used.) These click stimuli may be varied in frequency, intensity, and rate. A well-defined BAEP response generally requires 1000 to 2000 stimuli.

The typical BAEP response consists of a sequence of seven positive waves, of which the first five are used clinically. They are numbered sequentially by Roman numerals I through V and occur within the first 10 msec after presentation of auditory stimuli. Each wave closely corresponds to structures along the auditory pathway that are believed to generate it. Wave I is thought to be generated by CN VIII; wave II by CN VIII and the cochlear nucleus; wave III by the lower pons; and waves IV and V by the upper pons and lower midbrain.[1,2,10,26] Diagnosis of the anatomic site of pathology is based on which wave or waves demonstrate increased latency or are absent (see Fig. 17–1). Determination of interpeak latency is important, because disorders such as peripheral hearing loss may increase the latency of the entire BAEP response but do not change the interpeak latency relationships. Severe hearing loss may render recording of the BAEP impossible owing to degradation of the response.[1,26] BAEP response amplitudes vary considerably among normal subjects. To reduce intersubject variability, the ratio of wave I and wave V amplitudes is calculated. If the wave V amplitude is reduced in comparison to wave I, an intrinsic brain stem impairment is implied. A reduction of wave I to wave V amplitude ratio suggests possible hearing impairment.[4,27]

BAEP may aid in the diagnosis of a variety of diseases affecting the auditory pathways. The BAEP may be abnormal in 32% to 64% of persons with MS,[26,28] although it is less sensitive than either VEP or SEP testing.[15,29,30] BAEPs are particularly useful in the diagnosis of cerebellopontine angle tumors, such as acoustic neuromas (see Fig. 17–1). BAEP testing has been found to be superior to routine audiometry and computed tomography in the diagnosis of cerebellopontine angle tumors[31,32] and appears to be at least as sensitive as, and less expensive than, MRI for this diagnosis.[1] BAEPs are also useful in (1) the evaluation of strokes and tumors involving the auditory pathways[10,12,29,39]; (2) the evaluation of, and as a predictor of outcome for, comatose and head-injured persons;[34-36] and (3) the diagnosis of a variety of neurodegenerative disorders, such as Friedreich ataxia, in which the responses are abnormal.[37] BAEP abnormalities have been reported in association with Arnold-Chiari malformations, postconcussion syndrome, vertebrobasilar transient ischemic attacks, basilar migraines, and spasmodic torticollis.[38,39] These responses are utilized in audiometric screening of infants and of patients with mental deficiency who are unable to undergo routine audiometric testing.[26,40]

Somatosensory Evoked Potentials

SEPs assess the function of somatosensory pathways by stimulation of sensory nerves. SEPs may be recorded by stimulation of mixed or pure sensory nerves in the upper and lower extremities, in dermatomal areas of the skin, and from some cranial nerves with sensory function. The somatosensory pathway consists of the peripheral nerve, dorsal columns of the spinal cord, medial lemniscus, ventroposterior lateral thalamus, and primary sensory cortex.[1,10,41] SEPs appear to be related to the senses of joint position, touch, vibration, and stereognosis but are not related to pain and temperature sensation.[1,6]

Typically, SEPs are obtained through electrical stimulation of a peripheral nerve after recording electrodes are placed at sites along the somatosensory pathway. In upper and lower extremity SEPs, stimulation is generally applied at the more distal portion of major nerves, with recording sites along the extremity, over certain spinous processes, and on the scalp over regions that correspond to the somatosensory cortex. In SEP evaluation of dermatomal sensory areas, stimulation is performed over an area of skin that is innervated by a given dermatome (e.g., lateral foot for the S1 dermatome), and recording is usually limited to the scalp.[1,3,42]

SEP responses consist of a group of waveforms, each corresponding to the anatomic site of the recording electrode (Figs. 17–2 and 17–3). Abnormalities are manifested as increased latency, reduced amplitude, or absence of a given wave. The anatomic site of the lesion is determined by the point at which the abnormality is seen in a wave corresponding to recording electrode sites along the somatosensory pathway.[1,10,41] The SEP is analogous to conventional nerve conduction testing, in which the site of the NCS abnormality corresponds to the site of disease. Because peripheral nerve disorders may prolong response latencies along the entire length of the somatosensory pathway, interpeak latency determinations are important.[41,43] Additionally, conventional nerve conduction testing of the peripheral portions of the nerve can help to exclude peripheral neuropathy.

SEP are often abnormal in persons with MS. SEP testing is frequently performed in conjunction with VEP and BAEP testing to enhance diagnostic sensitivity—SEP being the most sensitive of the three modalities.[1,10,45] SEP abnormalities are more often seen in MS patients with sensory symptoms and are more common in the lower extremities.[45] Generally, conventional NCS are utilized in evaluation of sensory disturbances of the peripheral nerve, although SEP may be recordable from the scalp (owing to amplification effects of the cerebral cortex) when sensory never action potentials (SNAPs) are unrecordable. This amplification effect may be particularly useful in evaluating some entrapment neuropathies, such as meralgia paresthetica, in which recording of the response from the peripheral nerve is technically difficult or impossible.[41,46,47] SEPs are useful in the diagnosis of brachial plexus lesions and may be complementary to conventional EMG. SEP may help to confirm axonal continuity and to determine whether lesions are preganglionic or postganglionic.[25,26] Ulnar nerve SEP may be useful in the diagnosis of thoracic outlet syndrome and appear to be complementary to EMG testing.[49-53]

The use of SEPs in the diagnosis of radiculopathy has been controversial.[3,46,54-64] Many studies using SEP of peripheral nerves in the diagnosis of radiculopathy have found the test to be of limited utility. This limitation was attributed to "overshadowing" of abnormalities in a single nerve root by contributions from uninvolved nerve roots that supply the same peripheral nerve. Recording of SEP from a dermatomal area supplied by a single nerve root (e.g., the webbed space between the great and first toes innervated by the L5 nerve root) represents an attempt to circumvent this problem.[55-59] Dermatomal SEPs have been generally found to improve diagnostic yield; however, EMG testing remains the most sensitive electrodiagnostic test for radiculopathy.[1,3,46,55,58,65]

Somatosensory EPs are frequently abnormal in patients with myelopathy, and they may be abnormal in the presence of normal EMG evaluation.[50,66-69] Serial SEPs have been found useful in determining the extent of spinal cord trauma and may help to determine prognosis for recovery.[45,70]

SEPs recorded from the trigeminal nerve have been reported to be abnormal in persons with MS-related trigeminal neuralgia and with parasellar and cerebellopontine angle tumors affecting the trigeminal nerve. Alterations of trigeminal SEP also relate well to successful treatment of trigeminal neuralgia by retrogasserian injection of glycerol and thermocoagulation-induced lesions. Trigeminal SEPs generally have not been found to be useful in the diagnosis of "idiopathic" trigeminal neuralgia.[71-74]

Other uses of SEPs are evaluation of spinal cord syndromes such as transverse myelitis, syringomyelia, and spinal

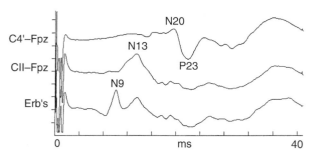

FIGURE 17–2 ■ Normal upper extremity somatosensory evoked potential response obtained by stimulating the median nerve at the wrist demonstrates responses recorded from Erb's point (N9), the second cervical vertebra (N13), and the cortex (N20-P23). (From Waldman SD [ed]: Interventional Pain Management, 2nd ed. Philadelphia, Saunders, 2001, p 186, Figure 14–12, with permission.)

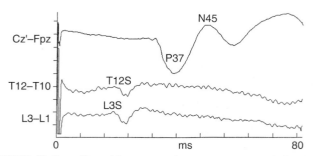

FIGURE 17–3 ■ Normal lower extremity somatosensory evoked potential response obtained by stimulating the tibial nerve at the ankle demonstrates responses recorded from the third lumbar vertebra (L3S), the twelfth thoracic vertebra (T12S), and the cortex (P37-N45). (From Waldman SD [ed]: Interventional Pain Management, 2nd ed. Philadelphia, Saunders, 2001, p 186, Figure 14–13, with permission.)

cord ischemia, and of tumors, infarctions, and hemorrhages involving the somatosensory pathways of the brain stem and cortex.[1,10,45] Some neurodegenerative disorders, such as Huntington's chorea, and some neuropathies involving the central somatosensory pathways may also be associated with SEP abnormalities.[1,10]

Cognitive Evoked Potentials

Cognitive EP, or endogenous event-related potentials, are long-latency EP related to cognitive processing. Testing consists of random presentations of infrequent stimuli (*rare* stimuli) interspersed with different, more frequently occurring stimuli (*common* stimuli). The subject is instructed to attend to the infrequent stimuli only. Normal persons produce a P300 response with a latency of approximately 300 msec and positive polarity. The P300 response latency may be abnormally prolonged or reduced in amplitude in disorders that impair cognition, such as dementias, autism, schizophrenia, and Huntington's chorea.[1,3,10,75-77]

■ SUMMARY

EMG and EP testing are essential tools in the diagnosis of neuromuscular disorders. They provide reliable and reproducible information on function of the nervous system that would not be obtainable through other means. They provide an extension of the clinical examination and are complementary to laboratory, radiologic, and other evaluations. Development of new techniques and improvements in old ones continue to expand the clinical utility of these tests. For example, the addition of transcranial magnetic stimulation has allowed evaluation of central motor pathways that had not been possible with EMG or other EP testing. Further refinements in cognitive EP testing may allow greater understanding of the nature and complexity of cognitive processing. The clinical neurophysiology laboratory is an increasingly important part of the total clinical milieu. With this thought in mind, the prudent practitioner will find greater utility and put more reliance on these tests for evaluation of patients, now and in the future.

References

1. Chiappa KH: Evoked Potentials in Clinical Medicine, ed 2. New York, Raven, 1990.
2. Nuwer MR: Evoked Potential Monitoring in the Operating Room. New York, Raven, 1986.
3. Waldman HJ: Evoked potentials. In Raj PP (ed): Practical Management of Pain, ed 2. St. Louis, Mosby-Year Book, 1992.
4. Nuwer M: Fundamentals of evoked potentials and common clinical applications today. Electroencephalog Clin Neurophysiol 106:142, 1998.
5. Starr A: Natural forms of somatosensory stimulation that can evoke cerebral, spinal, and peripheral nerve potentials in man. Presented at American Association of Electromyography and Electrodiagnosis International Symposium on Somatosensory Evoked Potentials, Rochester, Minn, 1984.
6. Braddom R: Somatosensory, brainstem, and visual evoked potentials. In Johnson EW (ed): Practical Electromyography, ed 2. Baltimore, Williams & Wilkins, 1988.
7. Celesia G: Somatosensory evoked potentials: Nomenclature. Presented at American Association of Electromyography and Electrodiagnosis International Symposium on Somatosensory Evoked Potentials, Rochester, Minn, 1984.
8. American Electroencephalography Society Clinical Evoked Potential Guidelines. J Clin Neurophysiol 1:6, 1984.
9. Guidelines for Somatosensory Evoked Potentials. Rochester, Minn, American Association of Electromyography and Electrodiagnosis, 1984.
10. Spehlmann R: Evoked Potential Primer. Boston, Butterworth, 1988.
11. Jasper HH: The ten-twenty electrode system of the International Federation: Report of the Committee on Clinical Examination in Electroencephalography. Electroencephalogr Clin Neurophysiol 10:371, 1958.
12. Chiappa K, Ropper A: Evoked potentials in clinical medicine: Part I. N Engl J Med 306:1140, 1982.
13. Halliday A: Visual evoked responses in the diagnosis of multiple sclerosis. Br Med J 4:661, 1973.
14. Halliday A: Visual evoked potentials in demyelinating disease. In Waxman S, Ritchie J (eds): Demyelinating Disease: Basic and Clinical Electrophysiology. New York, Raven, 1981.
15. Hume AL, Waxman SG: Evoked potentials in suspected multiple sclerosis: Diagnostic value and prediction of clinical course. J Neurol Sci 83:191, 1988.
16. Aminoff M: The clinical role of somatosensory evoked potential studies: A critical appraisal. AAEE Minimonograph #22. Rochester, Minn, American Association of Electromyography and Electrodiagnosis, 1984.
17. Chiappa K, Ropper A: Evoked potentials in clinical medicine: Part II. N Engl J Med 306:1205, 1982.
18. Halliday A, Mushin J: The visual evoked potential in neuro-ophthalmology. Int Ophthalmol Clin 20:155, 1980.
19. Halliday A, Halliday E, Kriss A, et al: The pattern-evoked potential in compression of the anterior visual pathways. Brain 99:357, 1976.
20. Ikeda H, Tremain K, Sanders M: Neurophysiological investigation in optic nerve disease: Combined assessment of the visual evoked response and electroretinogram. Br J Opthalmol 62:227, 1978.
21. Marsters JB, Good PA, Mortimer MJ: A diagnostic test for migraine using the visual evoked potential. Headache Sept:526, 1988.
22. Muller-Jensen A, Zschocke S: Pattern-induced visual evoked response in patients with migraine. Electroencephalogr Clin Neurophysiol 50:37, 1980.
23. Polich J, Maung A, Dalessio D: Pattern-shift visual evoked responses in cluster headache. Headache 9:446, 1987.
24. Raudino F: Visual evoked potential in patients with migraine. Headache 28:531, 1988.
25. Afra J, Cecchini P, Pasqua V, et al: Visual evoked potentials during long periods of pattern-reversal stimulation in migraine. Brain 121:233, 1998.
26. Hood L, Berlin C: Auditory Evoked Potentials. Austin, Tex, Pro-Ed, 1986.
27. Dumitru D: Electrodiagnostic Medicine. St. Louis, Mosby-Year Book, 1995.
28. Hammond S, Yiannikas C: The relevance of contralateral recordings and patient disability to assessment of brainstem auditory evoked potential abnormalities in multiple sclerosis. Arch Neurol 44:382, 1987.
29. Donohoe C: Application of the brainstem auditory evoked response in clinical neurologic practice. In Owen J, Donohoe C (eds): Clinical Atlas of Auditory Evoked Potentials. New York, Grune & Stratton, 1988.
30. Kirshner HS, Tsai SI, Runge VM, et al: Magnetic resonance imaging and other techniques in the diagnosis of multiple sclerosis. Arch Neurol 42:859, 1985.
31. Deka R, Kacker S, Tandon P: Auditory brainstem evoked responses in cerebellopontine angle tumors. Arch Otolaryngol Head Neck Surg 113:11647, 1987.
32. Musiek F, Josey A, Glasscock M: Auditory brain-stem response in patients with acoustic neuromas. Arch Otolaryngol Head Neck Surg 112:186, 1986.
33. Facco E, Behr A, Munari M, et al: Auditory and somatosensory evoked potentials in coma following spontaneous cerebral hemorrhage: Early prognosis and outcome. Electroencephalog Clin Neurophysiol 107:332, 1998.
34. Newton P, Greenberg R: Evoked potentials in severe head injury. J Trauma 24:61, 1984.
35. Stone J, Ghaly R, Hughes J: Evoked potentials in head injury and states of increased intracranial pressure. J Clin Neurophysiol 5:135, 1988.
36. Chiappa K, Hill R: Evaluation and prognostication in coma. Electroencephalogr Clin Neurophysiol 106:149, 1998.
37. Jewett D: Auditory evoked potentials: Overview of the field. In Barber C, Blum T (eds): Evoked Potentials III. Boston, Butterworth, 1987.
38. Drake M: Brainstem auditory-evoked potentials in spasmodic torticollis. Arch Neurol 45:174, 1988.

39. Yamada T, Dickins Q, Arensdorg K, et al: Basilar migraine: Polarity-dependent alteration of brainstem auditory evoked potentials. Neurology 36:1256, 1986.

40. Jerger J, Oliver T, Stack B: ABR testing strategies. In Jacobson J (ed): The Auditory Brainstem Response. San Diego, College Hill Press, 1984.

41. Aminoff M, Eisen A: Somatosensory evoked potentials. AAEM Mini-monograph 19. Muscle Nerve 21:277, 1998.

42. Assessment: Dermatomal somatosensory evoked potentials. Neurology 49:1127, 1997.

43. Jones S: Clinical applications of somatosensory evoked potentials: Peripheral nervous system. Presented at American Association of Electromyography and Electrodiagnosis International Symposium on Somatosensory Evoked Potentials, Rochester, Minn, 1984.

44. Adams RD, Victor M: Principles of Neurology, ed 5. St Louis, McGraw-Hill, 1993.

45. Oken B, Chiappa K: Somatosensory evoked potentials in neurological diagnosis. In Bodin-Wollner I, Cracco RQ (eds): Evoked Potentials: Frontiers of Clinical Neurophysiology. New York, Alan R Liss, 1986.

46. Eisen A: SEP in the evaluation of disorders of the peripheral nervous system. In Cracco R, Bodis-Wollner I (eds): Evoked Potentials. New York, Alan R Liss, 1986.

47. Aminoff M: Use of somatosensory evoked potentials to evaluate the peripheral nervous system. J Clin Neurophysiol 4:135, 1987.

48. Yiannikas C, Shahani B, Young R. The investigation of traumatic lesions of the brachial plexus by electromyography and short latency somatosensory evoked potentials evoked by stimulation of multiple peripheral nerves. J Neurol Neurosurg Psychiatry 46:1014, 1983.

49. Machleder H, Moll F, Nuwer M, et al: Somatosensory evoked potentials in the assessment of thoracic outlet compression syndrome. J Vasc Surg 6:177, 1987.

50. Oh SJ: Clinical Electromyography: Nerve Conduction Studies. Baltimore, University Park Press, 1984.

51. Synek V: Diagnostic importance of somatosensory evoked potentials in the diagnosis of thoracic outlet syndrome. Clin Electroencephalogr 17:112, 1986.

52. Yiannikas C, Walsh J: Somatosensory evoked responses in the diagnosis of thoracic outlet syndrome. J Neurol Neurosurg Psychiatry 46:234, 1983.

53. Cakmur R, Idiman F, Akalin E, et al: Dermatomal and mixed nerve somatosensory evoked potentials in the diagnosis of neurogenic thoracic outlet syndrome. Electroencephalogr Clin Neurophysiol 108:423, 1998.

54. Aminoff M, Goodin D, Parry G, et al: Electrophysiologic evaluation of lumbosacral radiculopathies: Electromyography, late responses, and somatosensory evoked potentials. Neurology 35:1514, 1985.

55. Perlik S, Fisher M, Patel D, et al: On the usefulness of somatosensory evoked responses for the evaluation of lower back pain. Arch Neurol 43:907, 1986.

56. Aminoff M, Goodin D, Barbaro N, et al: Dermatomal somatosensory evoked potentials in unilateral lumbosacral radiculopathy. Ann Neurol 17:171, 1985.

57. Katifi H, Sedgwick E: Dermatomal somatosensory evoked potentials in lumbosacral disk disease: Diagnosis and results of treatment. In Barber C, Blum T (eds): Evoked Potentials III. Boston, Butterworth, 1987.

58. Katifi H, Sedgwick E: Evaluation of the dermatomal somatosensory evoked potential in the diagnosis of lumbosacral root compression. J Neurol Neurosurg Psychiatry 50:1204, 1987.

59. Eisen A, Hoirch M, Moll A: Evaluation of radiculopathies by segmental stimulation and somatosensory evoked potentials. Can J Neurol Sci 10:178, 1983.

60. Machida M, Asai T, Sato K, et al: New approach for diagnosis in herniated lumbosacral disc. Spine 11:380, 1985.

61. Rodriguez A, Kanis L, Rodriguez AA, et al: Somatosensory evoked potentials from dermatomal stimulation as an indicator of L5 and S1 radiculopathies. Arch Phys Med Rehabil 6:366, 1987.

62. Scarff R, Dallmann D, Roleikis J: Dermatomal somatosensory evoked potentials in the diagnosis of lumbosacral root entrapment. Surg Forum 32:489, 1981.

63. Schmid U, Hess C, Ludin H: Somatosensory evoked potentials following nerve and segmental stimulation do not confirm cervical radiculopathy with sensory deficit. J Neurol Neurosurg Psychiatry 51:182, 1988.

64. Seyal M, Palma G, Sandhu L, et al: Spinal somatosensory evoked potentials following segmental sensory stimulation: A direct measure of dorsal root function. Electroencephalogr Clin Neurophysiol 69: 390, 1988.

65. Yazicioglu K, Ozgul A, Kalyon T, et al: The diagnostic value of dermatomal somatosensory evoked potentials in lumbosacral disc herniations: A critical approach. Electromyogr Clin Neurophysiol 39:175, 1999.

66. Stolov W, Slimp J: Dermatomal somatosensory evoked potentials in lumbar spinal stenosis. Presented at American Association of Electromyography and Electrodiagnosis/American Electroencephalographic Society Joint Symposium of Somatosensory Evoked Potentials and Magnetic Stimulation, Rochester, Minn, 1988.

67. Yiannikas C, Shahani B, Young R: Short-latency somatosensory evoked potentials from radial, median, ulnar, and perioneal nerve stimulation in the assessment of cervical spondylosis. Arch Neurol 43:1264, 1986.

68. Yu U, Jones S: Somatosensory evoked potentials in cervical spondylosis. Brain 108:273, 1985.

69. Noordhout A, Myressiotis S, Delvaux V, et al: Motor and somatosensory evoked potentials in cervical spondylotic myelopathy. Electroencephalogr Clin Neurophysiol 108:24, 1998.

70. Toleikis J, Sloan T: Comparison of major nerve and dermatomal somatosensory evoked potentials in the evaluation of patients with spinal cord injury. In Barber C, Blum T (eds): Evoked Potentials III. Boston, Butterworth, 1987.

71. Chiappa K: Clinical applications of short latency somatosensory evoked potentials to central nervous system disease. Presented at American Association of Electromyography and Electrodiagnosis International Symposium on Somatosensory Evoked Potentials, Rochester, Minn, 1984.

72. Buettner U, Rieble S, Altenmuller E, et al: Trigeminal somatosensory evoked potentials in patients with lesions of the mandibular branches of the trigeminal nerve. In Barber C, Blum T (eds): Evoked Potentials III. Boston, Butterworth, 1987.

73. Iraguy V, Wiederholt W, Romine J: Evoked potentials in trigeminal neuralgia associated with multiple sclerosis. Arch Neurol 43:444, 1986.

74. Leandri M, Parodi C, Favala E: Early trigeminal evoked potentials in tumors of the base of the skull and trigeminal neuralgia. Electroencephalogr Clin Neurophysiol 71:114, 1988.

75. McCallum WC: Some recent developments in ERP research related to cognitive function. In Barber C, Blum T (eds): Evoked Potentials III. Boston, Butterworth, 1987.

76. Polich J: P300 clinical utility and control of variability. J Clin Neurophysiol 15:14, 1998.

77. Keren O, Ben-Dror S, Stern M, et al: Event-related potentials as an index of cognitive function during recovery from severe closed head injury. J Head Trauma Rehabil 13:15, 1998.

The Measurement of Pain: Objectifying the Subjective

Darin J. Correll

The International Association for the Study of Pain defines pain as "an unpleasant sensory and emotional experience associated with actual or potential tissue damage, or described in terms of such damage."[1] The idea that pain is an emotion is not new. During the fifth and sixth centuries BC, Siddharta Gautama (the Buddha) taught that pain is a part of life, is due to desire, and could be ended only with the mind, and in the fourth century BC, Aristotle wrote, "pain is the passion of the soul."

It has been stated that pain is composed of three levels: sensory-discriminative (e.g., location, intensity), motivational-affective (e.g., depression, anxiety), and cognitive-evaluative (e.g., thoughts of the cause and significance).[2] Others have described pain as "a complex, subjective, perceptual phenomenon with a number of dimensions—intensity, quality, time course, impact, and personal meaning—that are uniquely experienced by each individual and, thus can only be assessed indirectly. Pain is a subjective experience and there is no way to objectively quantify it."[3] Still others have said that "emotion is not simply a consequence of pain sensation that occurs after a noxious sensory message arrives at the somatosensory cortex; rather, it is a fundamental part of the pain experience."[4]

It may seem obvious that pain is a subjective experience because people have unique, individual responses to the same stimulus (e.g., same surgery); however, this could be due to some difference in the nociceptive pathways and not be related to emotion at all. So do we know that pain is a subjective experience?

■ IS PAIN A SUBJECTIVE EXPERIENCE?

Several brain areas are activated by nociceptive stimulation, including the anterior cingulate cortex, frontal and pre-frontal cortices, primary and secondary somatosensory cortices, thalamus, basal ganglia, cerebellum, amygdala, and hippocampus.[5] The primary and secondary somatosensory cortices have a role in the location and intensity of a painful stimulus.[6] The anterior cingulate cortex is involved in the affective aspects of pain, i.e. the subjective experience of unpleasantness.[7,8] The insula seems to serve as an integrator between the two and encodes both intensity/location and affect.[9] The amygdala

appears to link sensory experiences to emotional arousal and negative emotional associations.[10]

Evidence that pain is indeed a subjective experience comes from psychophysical studies in which it was demonstrated that pain sensation and pain unpleasantness represent two distinct dimensions of pain.[11] Studies were performed on subjects who had a painful stimulus applied and then had hypnotic suggestions of either enhancing or decreasing the pain unpleasantness or intensity.[12] When the hypnotic suggestion related to unpleasantness was given, only the subjective pain rating changed, whereas when the hypnotic suggestion related to intensity was given, both the subjective rating and the pain intensity rating changed. This suggests that pain sensation is a cause of pain unpleasantness.

Humans have been equipped with the capability of negative emotion for a purpose. In terms of pain, it allows people to be aware of and adjust to tissue trauma. Therefore, pain is instrumental in guiding behavior required for self-preservation and preservation of the species.[4] Unlike the somatosensory cortex, the limbic system is complexly interconnected, and processing of the affective quality of pain may outlast the sensory processing.[4] Thus, the emotional aspect of pain may be more important for the clinical manifestation of pain and its control than the sensory component since patients do not suffer from the sensory intensity, but rather from the negative emotional quality.[4] This has been demonstrated by the fact that patients who have cingulotomies,[13] insular cortex lesions,[14] or prefrontal lobotomies[15] can appreciate the sensory characteristics of pain but do not have emotional responses to it nor properly appreciate its meaning.

Another line of evidence that pain is indeed a subjective experience and not just due to differences in nociceptive pathways comes from functional brain imaging studies. One functional magnetic resonance imaging (fMRI) study showed that as the magnitude of expected pain increased, activation increased in the thalamus, insula, prefrontal cortex, and anterior cingulate cortex; when the expected pain was manipulated, expectations of decreased pain reduced both the subjective experience of pain and activity in the primary somatosensory cortex and the affective areas of the brain (insula, prefrontal cortex, and anterior cingulate cortex).[16] Another fMRI study showed that both suggestion-induced pain and nociceptive pain activate the secondary somatosensory cortex and the anterior cingulate cortex.[17]

Another major line of evidence that pain is subjective comes from study of the placebo effect. Patients who are given a positive placebo suggestion of analgesia tolerate pain better than do those given a neutral suggestion, and those given a negative placebo suggestion tolerate pain less well than do those given a neutral suggestion.[18] A patient's understanding of the therapeutic intervention seems to be crucial to the placebo analgesic effect.[19] Verbally induced expectations affect pain, thus suggesting that placebo responses are mediated by expectation.[20] An open injection of a painkiller in full view of a patient who knows what is going on and what to expect is more effective than a hidden injection in which the patient does not know to expect any effect.[21-24] Different verbal instructions about certain and uncertain expectations of analgesia produce different placebo analgesic effects.[25] The study of placebo effects shows that "subjective" constructs such as expectation and value have physiologic bases that are powerful modulators of perceptual processes.[26] The use of fMRI has shown that placebo administration with expectation of analgesia is associated with a reduction in the activity of pain-responsive regions (anterior cingulate, insular cortex, and thalamus) during a painful experience.[27] Positron emission tomography has shown that the same regions of the brain affected by opioids are affected by placebo, specifically, the anterior cingulate cortex, orbitofrontal cortex, and anterior insula.[28] In other studies, expectations of pain relief have been shown to reduce perceived pain as much as an analgesic dose of morphine.[29]

The use of examples of placebo in this discussion is solely to demonstrate the subjective nature of pain and is not meant to endorse the use of placebo for pain management without the patient's consent and certainly never to discredit the patient's report of pain or punish the patient. The American Pain Society opposes the inadequate treatment of pain with any therapeutic modality, including the use of placebo. An analgesic effect from a placebo does not provide any useful information about the genesis or severity of the pain. The deceptive use of placebo and misinterpretation of the placebo response to discredit the patient's pain report are unethical and should be avoided.[30]

Another line of evidence that pain is a subjective experience comes from studies of the effects of emotional states on the pain experience. The relationship between reported pain intensity and the peripheral stimulus that evokes pain depends on many factors, such as the level of arousal, anxiety, depression, attention, and expectation or anticipation.[31] In general, acute pain has more associated anxiety, and chronic pain states have more associated depression.

Anxiety directed toward a painful stimulus increases attention to the stimulus, and anxiety directed away from the stimulus to an external event decreases pain sensitivity.[32] Moderate levels of fear/anxiety enhance attention to salient events such as pain, thereby augmenting its perceived intensity, whereas high levels of fear may become more salient than pain, in which case fear/anxiety would attenuate the pain.[33] Patients with higher trait anxiety (a greater disposition to experience anxiety) tend to exacerbate perceived pain stimulation.[34]

Depression has also been associated with the experience of heightened pain and emotional distress in response to pain.[35,36] The mechanism by which depression exerts its effect on pain-related emotional distress may be through response expectancy, as seen by the fact that patients who are prone to catastrophize have a heightened pain and emotional response to painful stimulation.[37]

■ CAN WE OBJECTIFY PAIN?

It is highly unlikely that we will ever be able to evaluate pain without reliance on the individual's perceptions.[3] Noninvasive functional brain imaging has allowed an objective window to the mind, but we are still a long way from objective measures of consciousness.[38] As our understanding of the brain increases, we may develop better tools, but we will also need to rely on patients to express their experience in some fashion.

In the meantime, we do need standardized measures to have some consistency and ability to communicate with patients. However, individual differences in the accuracy of pain reports are considerable.[39] It has also been shown that the reporting consistency of pain is weak within patients.[40] Therefore, the idea that patients in pain examine their consciousness to come up with a number to match a discrete internal stimulus before making a report of the sensory and affective qualities of the experience seems false. Rather, it is an attempt to construct meaning, influenced by and with reference to a range of internal and external factors and private meanings.[40] This is a function of the fact that numerous brain structures involved in not only sensation but also cognition, emotion, and memory are activated with each pain experience.

However, other studies have supported the notion that patients can capture their conscious experience and accurately report on a painful experience. The use of fMRI has shown more frequent and robust activation of the somatosensory cortex, anterior cingulate cortex, and prefrontal cortex in individuals who were highly sensitive to pain versus those who were insensitive to pain, whereas activation in the thalamic relay centers showed no difference.[41] This may point to the mechanisms involved in the central nervous system that are responsible for between-individual differences in pain sensitivity. This difference is unlikely to come from peripheral or spinal differences because the thalamic activation was the same, but rather from factors within the cognitive domain of the cortex. These findings do not, however, differentiate whether these cortical structures are the effectors or the targets of modulation of the individual pain experience. Even if unique patterns of cortical activation can be characterized in large numbers of patients for a given pain state, the subjective report will probably remain the most reliable index of the experience.[41] The most important finding was that individuals with similar patterns of activation in the primary somatosensory cortex, anterior cingulate cortex, and prefrontal cortex provide similar subjective reports of pain, thus suggesting that people can accurately capture their conscious experience via introspection.[41]

■ PAIN ASSESSMENT

The Joint Commission on Accreditation of Healthcare Organizations (JCAHO) in the United States has set standards for the assessment of pain in hospitalized patients, as outlined

Table 18–1

JCAHO Pain Assessment and Management Standards for Hospitals

Standard	Intent
Patients have the right to appropriate assessment and management of pain	Initial assessment and regular reassessment of pain Education of all relevant providers in pain assessment and management Education of patients and families when appropriate regarding their roles in managing pain, as well as the potential limitations and side effects of pain treatments After taking into account personal, cultural, spiritual, and/or ethnic beliefs, communicating to patients and families that pain management is an important part of care
Pain is assessed in all patients	The organization identifies patients with pain The assessment and a measure of pain intensity and quality (e.g., pain character, frequency, location, and duration), appropriate to the patient's age, are recorded in a way that facilitates regular reassessment and follow-up according to criteria developed by the organization
Patients are educated about pain and managing pain as part of treatment as appropriate	Patients and families are instructed about understanding pain, the risk for pain, the importance of effective pain management, the pain assessment process, and methods for pain management, when identified as part of treatment

JCAHO, Joint Commission on Accreditation of Healthcare Organizations.

in Table 18–1.[42] Pain assessment should be ongoing, individualized, and documented. Patients should be asked to describe their pain in terms of the following characteristics: location, radiation, mode of onset, character, temporal pattern, exacerbating and relieving factors, and intensity.

It has been suggested that pain be considered the "fifth vital sign."[43] Although pain cannot be considered vital, nor is it a sign, the suggestion that it be routinely measured along with temperature, pulse, blood pressure, and respiratory rate is a powerful reminder to healthcare providers to attend to their patients' suffering.[44]

It has been stated that the ideal pain measure should be sensitive, accurate, reliable, valid, and useful for both clinical and experimental conditions and able to separate the sensory aspects of pain from the emotional aspects.[45] The greatest difficulty in measuring pain is that because it is subjective, its measurement relies on patients to give an accurate assessment of their state. For a test to be valid, it needs to have a strong correlation with its underlying variable. Because this is not possible with subjective experiences such as pain, any measurement or number obtained is only an estimation of pain.[46] Medicine has always been strongly attracted to diagnostic methods that promise to objectify what is inherently subjective, such as a patient's report of pain.[47] It would be ideal if pain could be measured like other variables in medicine, such as weight, blood pressure, and electrolyte levels, but as yet it cannot, so surrogate measures of the experience are needed. The measures presently available fall into two categories, single-dimension scales and multidimensional scales. The numbers obtained from these instruments must be viewed as guides and not absolutes. Care must be taken to not rely solely on the results of the measurement but instead to wholly evaluate patients clinically so that their experience is not misinterpreted.

Single-Dimension Scales

Visual Analog Scale

The Visual Analog Scale (VAS) (Fig. 18–1) is most commonly a straight 100-mm line, without demarcation, that has the words "no pain" at the left-most end and "worst pain imaginable" (or something similar) at the right-most end.[48] Patients are instructed to place a mark on the line indicating the amount of pain that they feel at the time of the evaluation. The distance of this mark from the left end is then measured, and this number is used as a numeric representation of the severity of the patient's pain.

The benefits of the VAS are that it has been validated and shown to be sensitive to changes in a patient's pain experience.[49-51] It is quick to use and relatively easy to understand for most patients.[49,52] It avoids the imprecise use of descriptive words to describe pain and allows a meaningful comparison of measurements over time. The latter is possible because the VAS has been shown to have ratio scale properties, which means that changes in VAS measurements represent actual percent differences between the measures.[53,54]

One disadvantage of the VAS is that it attempts to assign a single value to a complex, multidimensional experience. Some patients will have trouble deciding how to choose a single number to represent their pain sensation. In addition, they often have no real concept of what "worst pain imaginable" actually means because every experience of pain is different and one can never know whether the present experience is the "worst." Thus, even though the VAS is looked at as linear, it actually has a ceiling at the upper-most end. If a patient marks the pain at the 100-mm end and then at a later time decides that it has become worse, the patient has no way to document this change.

Visual Analog Scale:

No Pain   Worst Pain
                                                           Imaginable
Numerical Rating Scale:

  0   1   2   3   4   5   6   7   8   9   10
No Pain   Worst
                                                           Pain
                                                           Imaginable
Verbal Descriptor Scales:

           None   Mild   Moderate   Severe

No Pain Mild Discomforting Distressing Horrible Excruciating

FIGURE 18–1 ▪ Single-dimension pain scales.

Another disadvantage of the VAS is that because it offers a value for the patient's pain intensity, care providers assume that this represents a specific "amount" of pain and will base treatment decisions on it. It is commonly accepted that a value of 30 mm or less represents an acceptable treatment goal. One study showed that for most patients, a VAS score greater than 30 mm (with a mean of 49 mm) represents "moderate pain" and a score greater than 54 mm (with a mean of 79 mm) represents "severe pain."[55] However, another study has shown that the number generated from the VAS is actually meaningless because the value for "moderate pain" ranged from 22 to 65 mm.[56] There is also disagreement about what amount of change in the VAS is necessary for it to be considered an acceptable improvement in pain from the patient's perspective. Some suggest a 30% reduction in the VAS,[57] whereas others claim that at least a 50% reduction is needed to be considered meaningful relief to patients.[58,59]

Numerical Rating Scale

The numerical rating scale (NRS) (see Fig. 18–1) is similar to the VAS in that it is bounded at the left-most end with "no pain" and at the right-most end with "worst pain imaginable" (or something similar). The difference is that instead of a line without marks, numbers from 0 to 10 are spaced evenly across the page. Patients are instructed to circle the number that represents the amount of pain that they are experiencing at the time of the evaluation. A variation of this scale is the *verbal numeric scale* (VNS), in which patients are asked to verbally state a number between 0 and 10 that corresponds to their present pain intensity.[60,61]

The benefits of the NRS and VNS are that they are validated,[49,60,61] as well as quick and easy to use. The VNS is especially straightforward to use clinically, particularly in the acute setting, when speed of evaluation is of importance.

Disadvantages of the NRS and VNS are similar to those of the VAS in that they attempt to assign a single number to the pain experience. They also suffer from the same ceiling effect in that if a value of "10" is chosen and the pain worsens, the patient officially has no way to express this change. In practice, at least with the VNS, patients will often rate their pain as some number higher than 10 (e.g., "15 out of 10") in an attempt to express their extreme level of pain intensity.

Also similar to studies of the VAS, attempts have been made to define what is considered a meaningful change in the NRS. At least a 30% reduction or an absolute reduction in the value of at least 2 has been suggested as representing meaningful pain relief to patients.[62,63] However, it is unlikely that these scales are actually linear; the numbers and the changes between them represent different things to different individuals.

Verbal Descriptor Scale

A verbal descriptor scale (VDS) (see Fig. 18–1) is a list of words, ordered in terms of severity from least to most, that describe the amount of pain that a patient may be experiencing. Patients are asked to either circle or state the word that best describes their pain intensity at that moment in time.

The benefits of VDS instruments are that they have been validated and are simple for patients to understand and quick to use.[49,64] The disadvantage of all single-dimensional scales—assigning a single value (in this case one adjective) to the pain experience—is also seen with the VDS. Another disadvantage is that a VDS forces patients to select words that are not of their own choosing to describe their pain. In addition, like the VAS and NRS, changes in pain over time are difficult to interpret and probably have different meanings to each individual. This may especially be a problem with the VDS when only a limited number of possible choices are offered to the patient (i.e. only four to six words).

Multidimensional Scales

McGill Pain Questionnaire

The McGill Pain Questionnaire (MPQ) (Fig. 18–2) is a form that contains three different parts to assess a patient's pain experience.[65] One part consists of line drawings of the back and front of a human body that patients use to mark where they are experiencing pain. The second part is a six-word VDS that patients use to record their present pain intensity. The third part of the form is composed of 78 adjectives divided into 20 sets that describe the sensory, affective, and evaluative qualities of the patient's pain. Within each set, the words (from two to six in number) describe a given quality of pain and are ranked in terms of intensity. Patients circle the words that best describe their present pain experience, and generation of a score is based on the rank of the words chosen within each category and the total number of words chosen. A score is generated for each of the three pain dimensions, as well as a total score.

The benefits of the MPQ are that it is valid, reliable, and consistent in its ability to assign seemingly appropriate descriptions to a given pain experience.[52,66-70] The MPQ may be able to discriminate between different types of pain syndromes.[71,72] Moreover, it has been shown to be sensitive to changes in the amount of pain experienced by patients in response to receiving various analgesic therapies in both the acute and chronic setting.[73-76]

One disadvantage of the MPQ is its length. It is claimed to take from 5 to 15 minutes to complete, which for some patients may be seen as more trouble than it is worth. In addition, this amount of time is prohibitive for use on a repeated basis over a short period (e.g., in a clinical acute pain setting). Another potential disadvantage of the MPQ is that it may not

McGill Pain Questionnaire

Patient's Name_____ Date _____ Time _____ am/pm

PRI: S _____ A _____ E _____ M _____ PRI(T) _____ PPI _____
    (1-10)   (11-15)   (16)   (17-20)   (1-20)

BRIEF ___	RHYTHMIC ___	CONTINUOUS ___
MOMENTARY ___	PERIODIC ___	STEADY ___
TRANSIENT ___	INTERMITTENT ___	CONSTANT ___

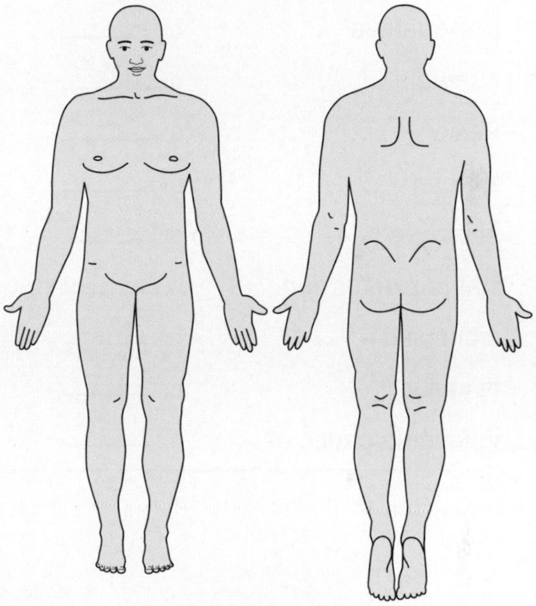

1 FLICKERING ___
  QUIVERING ___
  PULSING ___
  THROBBING ___
  BEATING ___
  POUNDING ___

2 JUMPING ___
  FLASHING ___
  SHOOTING ___

3 PRICKING ___
  BORING ___
  DRILLING ___
  STABBING ___
  LANCINATING ___

4 SHARP ___
  CUTTING ___
  LACERATING ___

5 PINCHING ___
  PRESSING ___
  GNAWING ___
  CRAMPING ___
  CRUSHING ___

6 TUGGING ___
  PULLING ___
  WRENCHING ___

7 HOT ___
  BURNING ___
  SCALDING ___
  SEARING ___

8 TINGLING ___
  ITCHY ___
  SMARTING ___
  STINGING ___

9 DULL ___
  SORE ___
  HURTING ___
  ACHING ___
  HEAVY ___

10 TENDER ___
  TAUT ___
  RASPING ___
  SPLITTING ___

11 TIRING ___
  EXHAUSTING ___

12 SICKENING ___
  SUFFOCATING ___

13 FEARFUL ___
  FRIGHTFUL ___
  TERRIFYING ___

14 PUNISHING ___
  GRUELLING ___
  CRUEL ___
  VICIOUS ___
  KILLING ___

15 WRETCHED ___
  BLINDING ___

16 ANNOYING ___
  TROUBLESOME ___
  MISERABLE ___
  INTENSE ___
  UNBEARABLE ___

17 SPREADING ___
  RADIATING ___
  PENETRATING ___
  PIERCING ___

18 TIGHT ___
  NUMB ___
  DRAWING ___
  SQUEEZING ___
  TEARING ___

19 COOL ___
  COLD ___
  FREEZING ___

20 NAGGING ___
  NAUSEATING ___
  AGONIZING ___
  DREADFUL ___
  TORTURING ___

PPI

0 NO PAIN ___
1 MILD ___
2 DISCOMFORTING ___
3 DISTRESSING ___
4 HORRIBLE ___
5 EXCRUCIATING ___

E = EXTERNAL
I = INTERNAL

COMMENTS:

FIGURE 18–2 ■ McGill Pain Questionnaire. (From Melzack R: The McGill Pain Questionnaire: Major properties and scoring methods. Pain 1:277, 1975.)

SHORT-FORM McGILL PAIN QUESTIONNAIRE
RONALD MELZACK

PATIENT'S NAME: _____   DATE: _____

	NONE	MILD	MODERATE	SEVERE
THROBBING	0) _____	1) _____	2) _____	3) _____
SHOOTING	0) _____	1) _____	2) _____	3) _____
STABBING	0) _____	1) _____	2) _____	3) _____
SHARP	0) _____	1) _____	2) _____	3) _____
CRAMPING	0) _____	1) _____	2) _____	3) _____
GNAWING	0) _____	1) _____	2) _____	3) _____
HOT-BURNING	0) _____	1) _____	2) _____	3) _____
ACHING	0) _____	1) _____	2) _____	3) _____
HEAVY	0) _____	1) _____	2) _____	3) _____
TENDER	0) _____	1) _____	2) _____	3) _____
SPLITTING	0) _____	1) _____	2) _____	3) _____
TIRING-EXHAUSTING	0) _____	1) _____	2) _____	3) _____
SICKENING	0) _____	1) _____	2) _____	3) _____
FEARFUL	0) _____	1) _____	2) _____	3) _____
PUNISHING-CRUEL	0) _____	1) _____	2) _____	3) _____

PPI

NO PAIN |————————————————————————————| WORST POSSIBLE PAIN

0 NO PAIN _____
1 MILD _____
2 DISCOMFORTING _____
3 DISTRESSING _____
4 HORRIBLE _____
5 EXCRUCIATING _____

FIGURE 18–3 ■ McGill Pain Questionnaire—Short Form. (From Melzack R: The Short-Form McGill Pain Questionnaire. Pain 30:191, 1987.)

be able to adequately assess the specific multidimensional aspects of pain (sensory, affective, and evaluative) because of a lack of validity in the scoring or the consistency of the test.[77,78]

Short-Form McGill Pain Questionnaire

The short-form McGill Pain Questionnaire (SF-MPQ) (Fig. 18–3) contains three different parts to assess a patient's pain experience.[79] There is a six-word VDS, as well as a VAS that patients use to record their present pain intensity. In addition, there are 15 adjectives that describe the sensory (11 words) and affective (4 words) qualities of the patient's pain. The

patient ranks each of the words on a categoric scale of "none, mild, moderate, severe."

The SF-MPQ has been validated and appears to correlate well with the original long-form MPQ.[80] Like the long form, the SF-MPQ may be able to discriminate between different types of pain syndromes.[79] Also like the long form, it has been shown to be sensitive to changes in pain brought about by various analgesic therapies in both the acute and chronic setting.[81-83]

Even though the SF-MPQ may take only around 5 minutes to complete, it is still too cumbersome for repeated use in an acute pain setting. The other disadvantages mentioned earlier for the long-form MPQ may also apply to the SF-MPQ.

Brief Pain Inventory

The Brief Pain Inventory (BPI) (Fig. 18–4) evaluates a patient's pain experience through a number of different scales.[84] There are line drawings of the front and back of a human body on which patients mark the location of their pain. Patients are asked to list the treatments or medications that they are using and how much relief they have provided in the past 24 hours. In addition, patients fill out 11 different NRS that ask about pain intensity (present as well as least, most, and average for the past 24 hours) and the effect of the pain on their ability to function during various activities of daily living.

The benefits of the BPI are that it has been validated and shown to be reliable in a number of different pain states.[85-88] It is an excellent tool to use for monitoring the effect of pain or treatment of pain, or both, in terms of a patient's functional ability or disability over time.[89] Its major disadvantage is that it takes 5 to 15 minutes to complete (depending on which form is used), thus making it less desirable for repeated use in an acute pain setting.

Memorial Pain Assessment Card

The Memorial Pain Assessment Card (MPAC) (Fig. 18–5) is a tool designed for use in cancer patients that contains three VAS lines to measure pain intensity, pain relief, and the mood of the patient.[90-92] In addition, it contains a set of eight adjectives that patients choose from to describe their present pain intensity.

The major benefit of the MPAC is that it is extremely quick to use, with only a few seconds needed in most cases, so repeated measures are not a burden to either the patient or the care provider. The disadvantage is that it is not an extensively used or very well studied tool and has mostly been used only in cancer patients.

Multidimensional Affect and Pain Survey

The Multidimensional Affect and Pain Survey (MAPS) (Fig. 18–6) is a form consisting of 101 descriptors of pain and emotion.[93,94] The descriptors are divided into three superclusters (somatosensory pain, emotional pain, and well-being). Each supercluster is then divided into subclusters. Each of the 30 subclusters contains from one to three descriptors. The patient answers a question related to each descriptor (e.g., "The sensation and/or pain is itchy") by using a numeric response scale from 0 to 5 ("none at all" to "very much so," respectively).

The benefits of the MAPS are that it has been validated and it seems to accurately assess the patient's pain experience in both the acute and chronic setting.[94-98] One disadvantage is that it has thus far been used only to evaluate cancer patients. Another disadvantage is its length, which makes it burdensome on patients and impracticable for repeated use in a clinical setting. A short form of the MAPS has recently been devised that contains only 30 descriptors.[99] This may make it more palatable to patients but it is still a bit too long for repeated use over a short period.

Which Scale Is Best?

In an outpatient chronic pain setting it is probably best to use one of the multidimensional scales (MPQ, SF-MPQ, BPI,

MAPS). It is important to assess all aspects of the patient's pain experience, and the length of these surveys is less prohibitive when they are used only occasionally. If the functionality of the patient is also of importance, use of the BPI will probably be best.

In the acute, inpatient setting the multidimensional forms are generally too long for repeated use. If the pain state of interest is acute postoperative pain and the patient was not in a chronic pain state previously, the somatic portion of the experience is probably a major component and use of the single-dimension scales (VAS, NRS, VDS) probably gives adequate information for treatment. However, if the patient has chronic pain or underwent surgery for an emotionally charged condition (e.g., cancer), the affective qualities of pain are probably still major determinants of the experience, so something such as the MPAC, which attempts to address a limited multidimensional aspect, may be helpful. It is also possible to use multiple NRS or VAS instruments to address the various issues that appear to be important to patients.

The exact questions to best assess patients in the acute setting are still to be determined, but one set of questions that has been suggested is to ask patients specifically about the following aspects of their experience: pain, anxiety, depression, anger, fear, and interference with physical activity.[96] These recommendations come from a study of patients in the postoperative period who were evaluated with the MAPS, which showed no correlation between a single pain intensity NRS and any of the somatosensory pain clusters. Rather, four of the descriptors from the emotional pain supercluster (depressed mood, anger, anxiety, and fear) were highly predictive of the pain NRS.[95] In another study, MAPS was administered preoperatively to patients to predict how they thought that they would feel postoperatively.[94] Here the descriptors depressed mood, anger, anxiety, and fear correlated with the amount of postoperative analgesic used and the number of demand presses on a patient-controlled analgesia (PCA) device. The post-surgery MAPS and post-surgery NRS did not correlate with PCA use. These findings also add another line of evidence that pain is indeed subjective.

Assessment of Children

Assessment of pain in children younger than 3 years can be difficult. Because children this young have a limited ability to verbalize their pain, there have been attempts to develop observational scales that incorporate biologic and behavioral measures. Some of these scales are the COMFORT, CRIES, and FLACC (Figs. 18–7 to 18–9).[31,100,101] Although these scales have been validated, they unfortunately do not measure issues that are specific to pain and may represent other causes of distress such as hunger, fear, or anxiety. These tools have generally been developed for assessment of pain in the acute setting, such as in the postoperative period or during procedures in an intensive care unit. Thus, they have not been validated for assessment of ongoing pain in children.

Once children are older than 3 years, there are a number of validated and reliable tools to use for the self-assessment of pain. One such tool is the Wong-Baker Faces Scale (Fig. 18–10), which combines a 6-point NRS with corresponding simply drawn faces ranging from smiling to crying.[102] Some have challenged this scale's use of a crying face to represent

(Text continued on p. 208)

Brief Pain Inventory (Short Form)

Study ID#_____ Hospital# _____

Do not write above this line.

Date:_____

Time:_____

Name: _____
Last   First   Middle initial

1) Throughout our lives, most of us have had pain from time to time (such as minor headaches, sprains, and toothaches). Have you had pain other than these everyday kinds of pain today?

1. yes   2. no

2) On the diagram, shade in the areas where you feel pain. Put an X on the area that hurts the most.

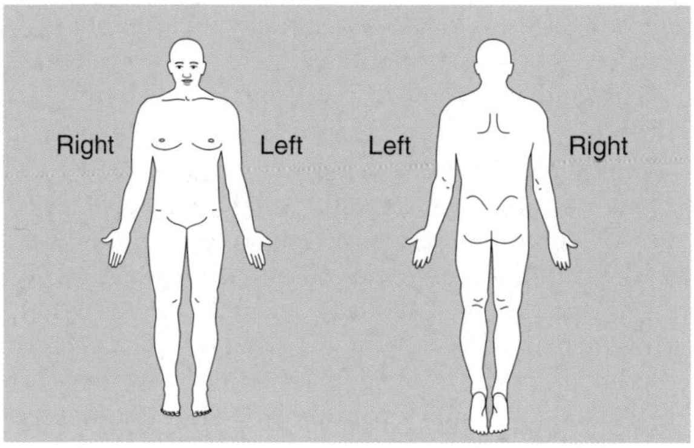

3) Please rate your pain by circling the one number that best describes your pain at its **WORST** in the past 24 hours.

0   1   2   3   4   5   6   7   8   9   10
No   Pain as bad as
Pain   you can imagine

4) Please rate your pain by circling the one number that best describes your pain at its **LEAST** in the past 24 hours.

0   1   2   3   4   5   6   7   8   9   10
No   Pain as bad as
Pain   you can imagine

5) Please rate your pain by circling the one number that best describes your pain on the **AVERAGE.**

0   1   2   3   4   5   6   7   8   9   10
No   Pain as bad as
Pain   you can imagine

6) Please rate your pain by circling the one number that tells how much pain you have **RIGHT NOW.**

0   1   2   3   4   5   6   7   8   9   10
No   Pain as bad as
Pain   you can imagine

7) What treatments or medications are you receiveing for your pain?

_____

8) In the past 24 hours, how much **RELIEF** have pain treatments or medications provided? Please circle the one percentage that most shows how much relief you have received.

0% 10% 20% 30% 40% 50% 60% 70% 80% 90% 100%
No   Complete
Relief   Relief

9) Circle the one number that describes how, during the past 24 hours **PAIN HAS INTERFERED** with your:

A. General Activity:

0   1   2   3   4   5   6   7   8   9   10
Does not   Completely
interfere   interferes

B. Mood

0   1   2   3   4   5   6   7   8   9   10
Does not   Completely
interfere   interferes

C. Walking Ability

0   1   2   3   4   5   6   7   8   9   10
Does not   Completely
interfere   interferes

D. Normal work (includes both work outside the home and housework)

0   1   2   3   4   5   6   7   8   9   10
Does not   Completely
interfere   interferes

E. Relation with other people

0   1   2   3   4   5   6   7   8   9   10
Does not   Completely
interfere   interferes

F. Sleep

0   1   2   3   4   5   6   7   8   9   10
Does not   Completely
interfere   interferes

G. Enjoyment of life

0   1   2   3   4   5   6   7   8   9   10
Does not   Completely
interfere   interferes

FIGURE 18–4 ■ Brief Pain Inventory. (From Cleeland CS, Ryan KM: Pain assessment: Global use of the Brief Pain Inventory. Ann Acad Med Singapore 23:129, 1994.)

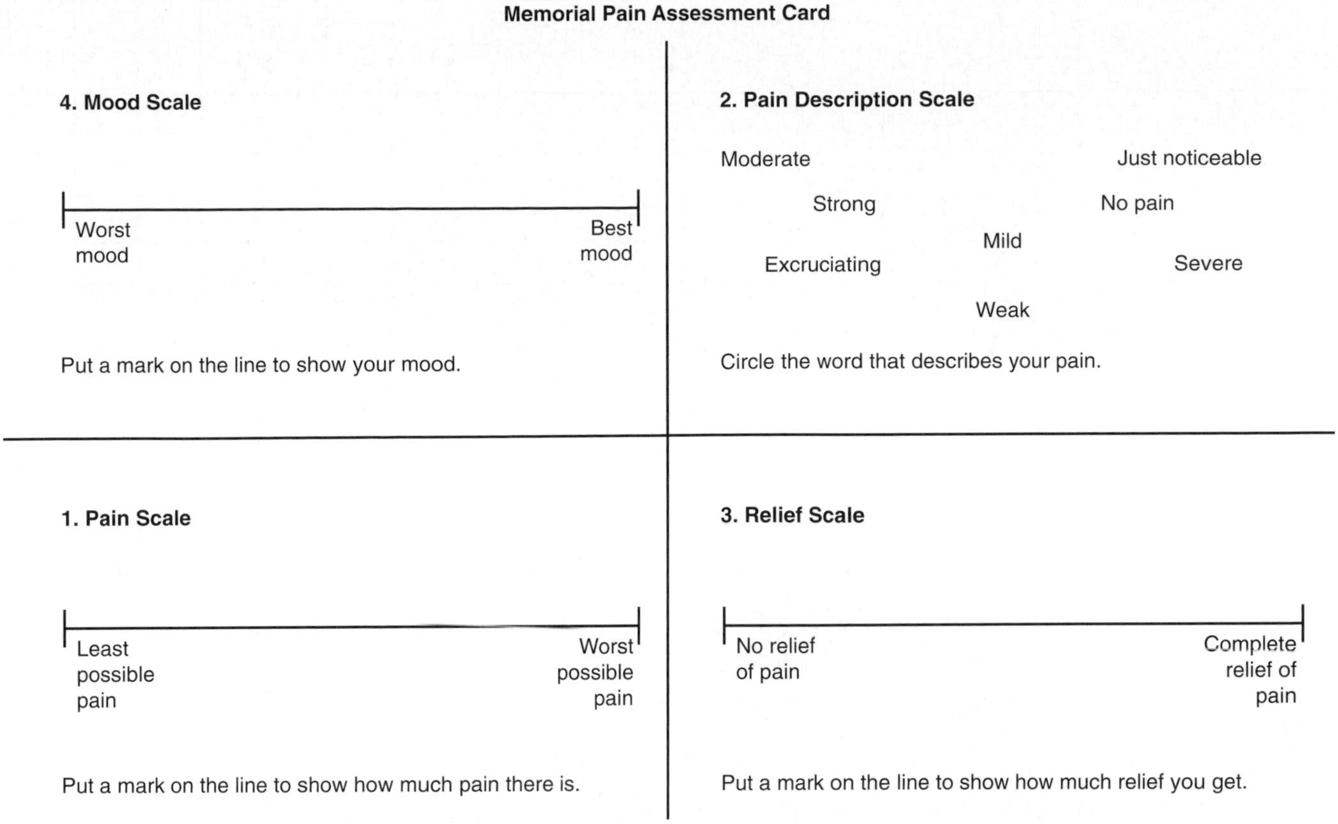

Memorial Pain Assessment Card

4. Mood Scale

Worst   Best
mood   mood

Put a mark on the line to show your mood.

2. Pain Description Scale

Moderate   Just noticeable

Strong   No pain

Mild

Excruciating   Severe

Weak

Circle the word that describes your pain.

1. Pain Scale

Least   Worst
possible   possible
pain   pain

Put a mark on the line to show how much pain there is.

3. Relief Scale

No relief   Complete
of pain   relief of
                                                                  pain

Put a mark on the line to show how much relief you get.

FIGURE 18–5 ■ Memorial Pain Assessment Card. (From Fishman B, Pasternak S, Wallenstein SL, et al: The memorial pain assessment card: A valid instrument for the evaluation of cancer pain. Cancer 60:1151, 1987.)

FIGURE 18–6 ■ Multidimensional Affect and Pain Survey descriptors. (From Yang JC, Clark WC, Tsui SL, et al: Preoperative multidimensional affect and pain survey (MAPS) scores predict post-colectomy analgesia requirement. Clin J Pain 16:314, 2000.)

I. Somatosensory Pain Super Cluster
1. Cutaneous Sensations (itchy, crawling)
2. Temporal Qualities (flickering, intermittent)
3. Faint Pain (dull-pain, mild-pain)
4. Muscle/Joint Pain (stiff, tight, aching)
5. Nausea (disgusting, nauseating)
6. Sensory Distress (disturbing, bothersome)
7. Heat (burning, hot)
8. Pain Extent (spreading, persistent)
9. Intense Pain (vicious, excruciating)
10. Intermittent Pressure (throbbing, pounding)
11. Stinging (stinging, smarting)
12. Incisive Pressure (gnawing, penetrating)
13. Traction/Abrasion (tugging, crushing)
14. Respiratory Distress (choking, suffocating)
15. Cold (cold, cool)
16. Numb
17. Circumscribed Pain (localized, restricted)

II. Emotional Pain Super Cluster
18. Response to Illness (ailing, suffering)
19. Depressed Mood (miserable, lonely)
20. Self-Blame (guilty, negligent)
21. Anger (angry, outraged, annoyed)
22. Anxiety (stressed, anxious)
23. Fear (startling, frantic, terrified)
24. Apathy (apathetic, stoical)
25. Fatigue (exhausting, sleepy)

III. Well-Being Super Cluster
26. Treatable Illness (curable, manageable)
27. Mentally Engaged (interested, involved)
28. Physically Active (active, vigorous)
29. Affiliative Feelings (loved, forgiving)
30. Positive Affect (hopeful, happy, relaxed)

		DATE/TIME						
ALERTNESS	1 - Deeply asleep 2 - Lightly asleep 3 - Drowsy 4 - Fully awake and alert 5 - Hyper alert							
CALMNESS	1 - Calm 2 - Slightly anxious 3 - Anxious 4 - Very anxious 5 - Panicky							
REPIRATORY DISTRESS	1 - No coughing and no spontaneous respiration 2 - Spontaneous repiration with little or no response to ventilation 3 - Occasional cough or resistance to ventilation 4 - Actively breathes against ventilator or coughs regularly 5 - Fights ventilator; coughing or choking							
CRYING	1 - Quiet breathing; no crying 2 - Sobbing or gasping 3 - Moaning 4 - Crying 5 - Screaming							
PHYSICAL MOVEMENT	1 - No movement 2 - Occasional, slight movement 3 - Frequent, slight movement 4 - Vigourous movement 5 - Vigorous movements including torso and head							
MUSCLE TONE	1 - Muscles totally relaxed; no muscle tone 2 - Reduced muscle tone 3 - Normal muscle tone 4 - Reduced muscle tone and flexion of fingers and toes 5 - Extreme muscle rigidity and flexion of fingers and toes							
FACIAL TENSION	1 - Facial muscles totally relaxed 2 - Facial muscle tone normal; no facial muscle tension evident 3 - Tension evident in some facial muscles 4 - Tension evident throughout facial muscles 5 - Facial muscles contorted and grimacing							
BLOOD PRESSURE (MAP) BASELINE	1 - Blood pressure below baseline 2 - Blood pressure consistently at baseline 3 - Infrequent elevations of 15% or more above baseline (1-3 during 2 minutes observation) 4 - Frequent elevations of 15% or more above baseline (>3 during 2 minutes observation) 5 - Sustained elevations of 15% or more							
HEART RATE BASELINE	1 - Heart rate below baseline 2 - Heart rate consistently at baseline 3 - Infrequent elevations of 15% or more above baseline (1-3 during 2 minutes observation) 4 - Frequent elevations of 15% or more above baseline (>3 during 2 minutes observation) 5 - Sustained elevations of 15% or more							
	TOTAL SCORE							

FIGURE 18–7 ■ The COMFORT Scale. (From Ambuel B, Hamlett KW, Marx CM, Blumer JL: Assessing distress in pediatric intensive care environments: The COMFORT Scale. J Pediatr Psychol 17:95, 1992.)

	DATE/TIME						
Crying - Charactersistic cry of pain is high pitched. 0 – No cry or cry that is not high-pitched 1 – Cry high pitched but baby is easily consolable 2 – Cry high pitched and baby is inconsolable							
Requires O₂ for SaO₂ <95% - Babies experiencing pain manifest decreased oxygenation. Consider other causes of hypoxemia, e.g., oversedation, atelectasis, pneumothorax 0 – No oxygen required 1 – <30% oxygen required 2 – >30% oxygen required							
Increased vital signs (BP* and HR*) - Take BP last as this may awaken child making other assessments difficult 0 – Both HR and BP unchanged or less than baseline 1 – HR or BP increased but increase in <20% of baseline 2 – HR or BP is increased >20% over baseline.							
Expression - The facial expression most often associated with pain is a grimace. A grimace may be characterized by brow lowering, eyes squeezed shut, deepening naso-labial furrow, or open lips and mouth. 0 – No grimace present 1 – Grimace alone is present 2 – Grimace and non-cry vocalization grunt is present							
Sleepless - Scored based upon the infant's state during the hour preceding this recorded score. 0 – Child has been continuously asleep 1 – Child has awakened at frequent intervals 2 – Child has been awake constatly							
TOTAL SCORE							

FIGURE 18–8 ■ CRIES. (From Krechel SW, Bildner J: CRIES: A new neonatal postoperative pain measurement score. Initial testing of validity and reliability. Pediatr Anesth 5:53, 1995.)

*Use baseline preoperative parameters from a non-stressed period. Multiply baseline HR by 0.2 then add to baseline HR to determine the HR that is 20% over baseline. Do the same for BP and use the mean BP.

Indications: For neonates (0–6 months)

Instructions:
Each of the five (5) categories is scored from 0-2, which results in a total score between 0 and 10. The interdisciplinary team in collaboration with the patient/family (if appropriate), can determine appropriate interventions in response to CRIES Scale scores.

	DATE/TIME						
Face 0 - No particular expression or smile 1 - Occasional grimace or frown, withdrawn, disinterested 2 - Frequent to constant quivering chin, clenched jaw							
Legs 0 - Normal position or relaxed 1 - Uneasy, restless, tense 2 - Kicking, or legs drawn up							
Activity 0 - Lying quietly, normal position, moves easily 1 - Squirming, shifting back and forth, tense 2 - Arched, rigid or jerking							
Cry 0 - No cry (awake or asleep) 1 - Moans or whimpers; occasional complaint 2 - Crying steadily, screams or sobs, frequent complaints							
Consolability 0 - Content, relaxed 1 - Reassured by occasional touching, hugging or being talked to, distractible 2 - Difficult to console or comfort							
	TOTAL SCORE						

FIGURE 18–9 ■ FLACC. (From Merkle SI, Shayevitz JR, Voepel-Lewis T, Malviya S: The FLACC: A behavioral scale for scoring postoperative pain in young children. Pediatr Nurs 23:293, 1997.)

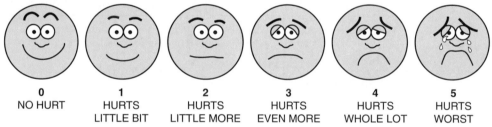

0	1	2	3	4	5
NO HURT	HURTS LITTLE BIT	HURTS LITTLE MORE	HURTS EVEN MORE	HURTS WHOLE LOT	HURTS WORST

FIGURE 18–10 ■ Wong-Baker Faces Scale. (From Wong DL, Baker CM: Pain in children: Comparison of assessment scales. Pediatr Nurs 14:9, 1988.)

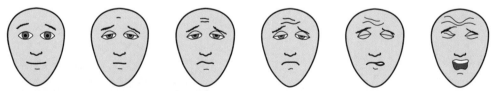

FIGURE 18–11 ■ Faces Pain Scale. (From Bieri D, Reeve R, Champion G, et al: The FACES pain scale for the self-assessment of the severity of pain experienced by children: Development, initial validation and preliminary investigation for ratio scale properties. Pain 41:139, 1990.)

the upper limit because it may make children not choose this degree of pain unless they are actually tearful. The Faces Pain Scale (Fig. 18–11) was devised with six somewhat more realistically drawn faces ranging from a content-looking smiling face to a distressed-looking face but without tears.[103] Another scale is the Oucher scale (Fig. 18–12), which incorporates a vertically oriented 11-point NRS with six faces of an actual child in various states of distress from none to extreme.[104] There are three versions of the Oucher scale, one with a Cau-

casian child, one with an African American child, and one with a Hispanic child.

Assessment of the Elderly

There is limited information on assessment of pain in the elderly. If the patient is cognitively intact, it appears that a VAS or an NRS can be used effectively. However, it has been suggested that the VAS is the least preferred method by the

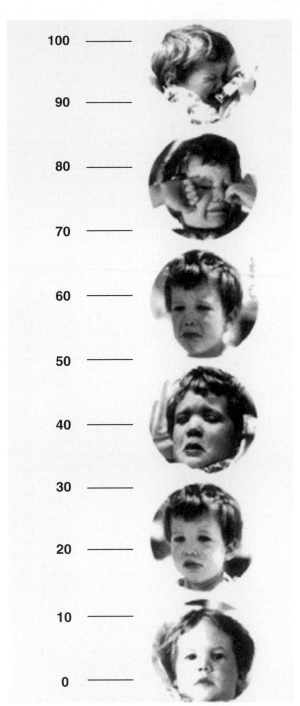

100 ——

90 ——

80 ——

70 ——

60 ——

50 ——

40 ——

30 ——

20 ——

10 ——

0 ——

FIGURE 18–12 ■ The Caucasian version of the Oucher scale. (Copyright Judith E. Beyer, PhD, RN, University of Missouri-Kansas City, 1983.)

elderly.[105] If there is any question about the cognitive abilities of the patient, it is preferable to use a VDS or the Faces Pain Scale, both of which have been shown to be easy to understand and use in this population.[106,107]

■ CONCLUSION

Multiple lines of evidence support the fact that pain is subjective. No truly objective measure of pain is available, nor might any be appropriate. There are instruments that can yield useful information, and patients can effectively relate what is needed to treat pain, even if the experience cannot be fully objectified. One just needs to understand the limitations of the measures and always listen to the patient.

References

1. Merskey H: Pain terms: A list with definitions and notes on usage. Recommended by the International Association for the Study of Pain (IASP) Subcommittee on Taxonomy. Pain 6:249, 1979.
2. Melzack R, Casey KL: Sensory, motivational, and central control determinants of pain: A new conceptual model. In Kenshalo D (ed): The Skin Senses. Springfield, IL, Charles C Thomas, 1968, p 423.
3. Turk DC: Assess the person, not just the pain. Pain: Clinical Updates vol 1, issue 3, 1993.
4. Chapman CR: Limbic processes and the affective dimension of pain. Prog Brain Res 110:63, 1996.
5. Tracey I: Nociceptive processing in the human brain. Curr Opin Neurobiol 15:478, 2005.
6. Bushnell M, Guncan G, Hofbauer R, et al: Pain perception: Is there a role for primary somatosensory cortex? Proc Natl Acad Sci USA 96:7705, 1999.
7. Talbot JD, Marrett S, Evans AC, et al: Multiple representations of pain in human cerebral cortex. Science 251:1355, 1991.
8. Rainville P, Duncan GH, Price DD, et al: Pain affect encoded in human anterior cingulated but not somatosensory cortex. Science 277:968, 1997.
9. Coghill R, Sang C, Maisog J, Iadorola M: Pain intensity processing within the human brain: A bilateral, distributed mechanism. J Neurophysiol 82:1934, 1999.
10. LeDoux JE, Farb C, Ruggiero DA: Topographic organization of neurons in the acoustic thalamus that project to the amygdala. J Neurosci 10:1043, 1990.
11. Price DD: Psychological and neural mechanisms of the affective dimension of pain. Science 288:1769, 2000.
12. Rainville P, Carrier B, Hofbauer RK, et al: Dissociation of sensory and affective dimensions of pain using hypnotic modulation. Pain 82:159, 1999.
13. Corkin S, Hebben N: Subjective estimates of chronic pain before and after psychosurgery or treatment in a pain unit. Pain 1(Suppl):150, 1981.
14. Berthier M, Starkstein S, Leiguarda R: Asymbolia for pain: A sensory-limbic disconnection syndrome. Ann Neurol 24:41, 1988.
15. Freeman W, Watts JW: Pain mechanisms and the frontal lobes: A study of prefrontal lobotomy for intractable pain. Ann Intern Med 28:747, 1948.
16. Koyama T, McHaffie JG, Laurienti PJ, Coghill RC: The subjective experience of pain: Where expectations become reality. Proc Natl Acad Sci U S A 102:12950, 2005.
17. Raij TT, Numminen J, Narvanen S, et al: Brain correlates of subjective reality of physically and psychologically induced pain. Proc Natl Acad Sci USA 102:2147, 2005.
18. Staats P, Hekmat H, Staats A: Suggestion/placebo effects on pain: Negative as well as positive. J Pain Symptom Manage 15:235, 1998.
19. Vase L, Riley JL, Price DD: A comparison of placebo effects in clinical analgesic trials versus studies of placebo analgesia. Pain 99:443, 2002.
20. Benedetti F, Pollo A, Lopiano L, et al: Conscious expectation and unconscious conditioning in analgesic, motor, and hormonal placebo/nocebo responses. J Neurosci 23:4315, 2003.
21. Colloca L, Lopiano L, Lanotte M, Benedetti F: Overt versus covert treatment for pain, anxiety and Parkinson's disease. Lancet Neurol 3:679, 2004.
22. Amanzio M, Pollo A, Maggi G, Benedetti F: Response variability to analgesics: A role for non-specific activation of endogenous opioids. Pain 90:205, 2001.
23. Levine JD, Gordon NC, Smith R, Fields HL: Analgesic responses to morphine and placebo in individuals with postoperative pain. Pain 10:379, 1984.
24. Levine JD, Gordon NC: Influence of the method of drug administration on analgesic response. Nature 312:755, 1984.
25. Pollo A, Amanzio M, Arslanian A, et al: Response expectancies in placebo analgesia and their clinical relevance. Pain 93:77, 2001.

26. Benedetti F, Mayberg HS, Wager TD, et al: Neurobiological mechanisms of the placebo effect. J Neurosci 25:10390, 2005.
27. Wager TD, Rilling JK, Smith EE, et al: Placebo-induced changes in fMRI in the anticipation and experience of pain. Science 303:1162, 2004.
28. Petrovic P, Kalso E, Petersson KM, Ingvar M: Placebo and opioid analgesia—imaging a shared neural network. Science 295:1737, 2002.
29. Price DD, Von der Gruen A, Miller J, et al: A psychophysical analysis of morphine analgesia. Pain 22:261, 1985.
30. Sullivan M, Terman GW, Peck B, et al: APS position statement on the use of placebos in pain management. J Pain 6:215, 2005.
31. Merkle SI, Shayevitz JR, Voepel-Lewis T, Malviya S: The FLACC: A behavioral scale for scoring postoperative pain in young children. Pediatr Nurs 23:293, 1997.
32. Janssen SA, Arntz A: Anxiety and pain: Attentional and endorphinergic influences. Pain 66:145, 1996.
33. Rhudy JL, Meagher MW: Negative affect: Effects on an evaluation measure of human pain. Pain 104:617, 2003.
34. Tang J, Gibson SJ: A psychophysical evaluation of the relationship between trait anxiety, pain perception, and induced state anxiety. J Pain 6:612, 2005.
35. Haythornthwaite JA, Sieber WJ, Kerns RD: Depression and the chronic pain experience. Pain 46:177, 1991.
36. Walsh TM, Smith CP, McGrath PJ: Pain correlates of depressed mood in young adults. Pain Res Manage 3:135, 1998.
37. Sullivan MJL, Rodgers WM, Kirsch I: Catastrophizing, depression and expectancies for pain and emotional distress. Pain 91:147, 2001.
38. Nakamura Y, Chapman CR: Measuring pain: An introspective look at introspection. Conscious Cogn 11:582, 2002.
39. Chapman CR, Donaldson D, Nakamura Y, et al: A psychophysical causal model of pain report validity. J Pain 3:143, 2002.
40. Williams AC de C, Davies HTO, Chadury Y: Simple pain rating scales hide complex idiosyncratic meanings. Pain 85:457, 2000.
41. Coghill RC, McHaffie JG, Yen YF: Neural correlates of interindividual differences in the subjective experience of pain. Proc Natl Acad Sci USA 100:8538, 2003.
42. Comprehensive Accreditation Manual for Hospitals (CAMH): The Official Handbook. Oakbrook Terrace, IL, Joint Commission on Accreditation of Healthcare Organizations, 2004.
43. Joel LA: The fifth vital sign: Pain. Am J Nurs 99:9, 1999.
44. Noble B, Clark D, Meldrum M, et al: The measurement of pain, 1945-2000. J Pain Symptom Manage 29:14, 2005.
45. Gracely RH, Dubner R: Pain assessment in humans—a reply to Hall. Pain 11:109, 1981.
46. Chapman CR, Syrjala KL: Measurement of Pain. In Loeser JD (ed): Bonica's Management of Pain. Philadelphia, Lippincott Williams & Wilkins, 2001, p 310.
47. Gallagher RM: Waddell signs: Objectifying pain and the limits of medical altruism. Pain Med 4:113, 2003.
48. Joyce CRB, Zutshi DW, Hrubes V, Mason RM: Comparison of fixed interval and visual analogue scales for rating chronic pain. Eur J Clin Pharmacol 8:415, 1975.
49. Jensen MP, Karoly P, Braver S: The measurement of clinical pain intensity: A comparison of six methods. Pain 27:117, 1986.
50. Carlsson AM: Assessment of chronic pain. I. Aspects of the reliability and validity of the visual analogue scale. Pain 16:87, 1983.
51. Price DD, Harkins SW, Rafii A, Price C: A simultaneous comparison of fentanyl's analgesic effects on experimental and clinical pain. Pain 24:197, 1986.
52. Chapman CR, Casey KL, Dubner R, et al: Pain measurement: An overview. Pain 22:1, 1985.
53. Price DD, Harkins SW: Combined use of experimental pain and visual analogue scales in providing standardized measurement of clinical pain. Clin J Pain 3:1, 1987.
54. Price DD, McGrath PA, Rafii A, Buckingham B: The validation of visual analogue scales as ratio scale measures for chronic and experimental pain. Pain 17:45, 1983.
55. Collins SL, Moore A, McQuay HJ: The visual analogue pain intensity scale: What is moderate pain in millimeters? Pain 72:95, 1997.
56. Lund I, Lundberg T, Sandberg L, et al: Lack of interchangeability between visual analogue and verbal rating pain scales: A cross sectional description of pain etiology groups. BMC Med Res Methodol 5:31, 2005.
57. Dworkin RH, Turk DC, Farrar JT, et al: Core outcome measures for chronic pain clinical trials: IMMPACT recommendations. Pain 113:9, 2005.
58. Moore A, McQuay H, Gavaghan D: Deriving dichotomous outcome measures from continuous data in randomized controlled trials of analgesics. Pain 66:229, 1996.
59. ten Klooster PM, Drossaers-Bakker KW, Taal E, van de Laar MAFJ: Patient-perceived satisfactory improvement (PPSI): Interpreting meaningful change in pain from the patient's perspective. Pain 121:151, 2006.
60. Berthier F, Potel G, Leconte P, et al: Comparative study of methods of measuring acute pain in an ED. Am J Emerg Med 16:132, 1998.
61. Paice JA, Cohen FL: Validity of a verbally administered numeric rating scale to measure cancer pain intensity. Cancer Nurs 20:88, 1997.
62. Farrar JT, Young JP, LaMoreaux L, et al: Clinical importance of changes in chronic pain intensity measured on an 11-point numerical rating scale. Pain 94:149, 2001.
63. Farrar JT, Berlin JA, Strom BL: Clinically important changes in acute pain outcome measures: A validation study. J Pain Symptom Manage 25:406, 2003.
64. Jensen MP, Karoly P: Self-report scales and procedures for assessing pain in adults. In Turk DC, Melzack R (eds): Handbook of Pain Assessment. New York, Guilford, 1992, p 135.
65. Melzack R: The McGill Pain Questionnaire: Major properties and scoring methods. Pain 1:277, 1975.
66. Wilkie DJ, Savedra MC, Holzemer WL, et al: Use of the McGill Pain Questionnaire to measure pain: A meta-analysis. Nurs Res 39:36, 1990.
67. Melzack R, Wall PD, Ty TC: Acute pain in an emergency clinic: Latency of onset and description patterns related to different injuries. Pain 14:33, 1982.
68. Reading AE: A comparison of the McGill Questionnaire in chronic and acute pain. Pain 13:185, 1982.
69. Graham C, Bond SS, Gerkovitch MM, Cook MR: Use of the McGill Pain Questionnaire in the assessment of cancer pain: Replicability and consistency. Pain 8:377, 1980.
70. Grushka M, Sessle BJ: Applicability of the McGill Pain Questionnaire to the differentiation of 'toothache' pain. Pain 19:49, 1984.
71. Perry F, Heller PH, Levine JD: Differing correlations between pain measures in syndromes with or without explicable organic pathology. Pain 34:185, 1988.
72. Melzack R, Terrence C, Fromm G, Amsel R: Trigeminal neuralgia and atypical facial pain: Use of the McGill Pain Questionnaire for discrimination and diagnosis. Pain 27:297, 1986.
73. Jenkinson C, Carroll D, Egerton M, et al: Comparison of the sensitivity to change of long and short form pain measures. Qual Life Res 4:353, 1995.
74. Burchiel KJ, Anderson VC, Brown FD, et al: Prospective, multicenter study of spinal cord stimulation for relief of chronic back and extremity pain. Spine 21:2786, 1996.
75. Eija K, Tiina T, Pertti NJ: Amitriptyline effectively relieves neuropathic pain following treatment of breast cancer. Pain 64:293, 1996.
76. Katz J, Clairoux M, Kavanagh BP, et al: Pre-emptive lumbar epidural anaesthesia reduces postoperative pain and patient-controlled morphine consumption after lower abdominal surgery. Pain 59:395, 1994.
77. Turk DC, Rudy TE, Salovey P: The McGill Pain Questionnaire reconsidered: Confirming the factor structure and examining appropriate uses. Pain 21:385, 1985.
78. Holroyd KA, Talbot F, Holm JE, et al: Assessing the dimensions of pain: A multitrait-multimethod evaluation of seven measures. Pain 67:259, 1996.
79. Melzack R: The short-form McGill Pain Questionnaire. Pain 30:191, 1987.
80. Dudgeon D, Ranbertas RF, Rosenthal S: The Short-Form McGill Pain Questionnaire in chronic cancer pain. J Pain Symptom Manage 8:191, 1993.
81. Lowe NK, Walker SN, McCallum RC: Confirming the theoretical structure of the McGill Pain Questionnaire in acute clinical pain. Pain 46:53, 1990.
82. Harden RN, Carter TD, Gilman CS, et al: Ketorolac in acute headache management. Headache 31:463, 1991.
83. Serrao JM, Marks RL, Morley SJ, Goodchild CS: Intrathecal midazolam for the treatment of chronic mechanical low back pain: A controlled comparison with epidural steroid in a pilot study. Pain 48:5, 1992.
84. Cleeland CS, Ryan KM: Pain assessment: Global use of the Brief Pain Inventory. Ann Acad Med Singapore 23:129, 1994.

85. Daut RL, Cleeland CS, Flanery RC: Development of the Wisconsin Brief Pain Questionnaire to assess pain in cancer and other diseases. Pain 17:197, 1983.

86. Cleeland CS: Measurement and prevalence of pain in cancer. Semin Oncol Nurs 1:87, 1985.

87. Portenoy RK, Miransky J, Thaler HT, et al: Pain in ambulatory patients with lung or colon cancer: Prevalence, characteristics, and effect. Cancer 70:1616, 1992.

88. Raichle KA, Osborne TL, Jensen MP, Cardenas D: The reliability and validity of pain interference measures in persons with spinal cord injury. J Pain 7:179, 2006.

89. Keller S, Bann CM, Dodd SL, et al: Validity of the Brief Pain Inventory for use in documenting the outcomes of patients with noncancer pain. Clin J Pain 20:309, 2004.

90. Fishman B, Pasternak S, Wallenstein SL, et al: The Memorial Pain Assessment Card. A valid instrument for the evaluation of cancer pain. Cancer 60:1151, 1987.

91. Kelsen DP, Portenoy RK, Thaler HT, et al: Pain and depression in patients with newly diagnosed pancreas cancer. J Clin Oncol 13:748, 1995.

92. Portenoy RK, Payne D, Jacobsen P: Breakthrough pain: Characteristics and impact in patients with cancer pain. Pain 81:129, 1999.

93. Clark WC, Fletcher JD, Janal MN, Carroll JD: Hierarchical clustering of 270 pain/emotion descriptors: Toward a revision of the McGill Pain questionnaire. In Bromm B, Desmedt J (eds): Pain and the Brain: From Nociception to Sensation. New York, Raven Press, 1995, p 319.

94. Yang JC, Clark WC, Tsui SL, et al: Preoperative multidimensional affect and pain survey (MAPS) scores predict post-colectomy analgesia requirement. Clin J Pain 16:314, 2000.

95. Knotkova H, Clark WC, Mokrejs P, et al: What do ratings on unidimensional pain and emotion scales really mean? A multidimensional affect and pain survey (MAPS) analysis of cancer patient responses. J Pain Symptom Manage 28:19, 2004.

96. Clark WC, Yang JC, Tsui SL, et al: Unidimensional pain rating scales: A multidimensional affect and pain survey (MAPS) analysis of what they really measure. Pain 98:241, 2002.

97. Knotkova H, Clark WC, Keohan ML, et al: Validation of the multidimensional affect and pain survey (MAPS). J Pain 7:161, 2006.

98. Clark WC, Kuhl JP, Keohan ML, et al: Factor analysis validates the cluster structure underlying the Multidimensional Affect and Pain Survey (MAPS), and challenges the a priori classification of the descriptors in the McGill Pain Questionnaire (MPQ). Pain 106:357, 2003.

99. Griswold GA, Clark WC: Item analysis of cancer patient responses to the Multidimensional Affect and Pain Survey demonstrates high inter-item consistency and discriminability and determines the content of a short form. J Pain 6:67, 2005.

100. Ambuel B, Hamlett KW, Marx CM, Blumer JL: Assessing distress in pediatric intensive care environments: The COMFORT scale. J Pediatr Psychol 17:95, 1992.

101. Krechel SW, Bildner J: CRIES: A new neonatal postoperative pain measurement score. Initial testing of validity and reliability. Pediatr Anesth 5:53, 1995.

102. Wong DL, Baker CM: Pain in children: Comparison of assessment scales. Pediatr Nurs 14:9, 1988.

103. Bieri D, Reeve R, Champion G, et al: The faces pain scale for the self-assessment of the severity of pain experienced by children: Development, initial validation and preliminary investigation for ratio scale properties. Pain 41:139, 1990.

104. Beyer JE, Denyes M, Villarruel A: The creation, validation, and continuing development of the Oucher. A measure of pain intensity in children. J Pediatr Nurs 7:335, 1992.

105. Gagliese L, Melzack R: Age differences in the quality of chronic pain: A preliminary study. Pain Res Manage 2:157, 1997.

106. Herr KA, Mobily PR, Kohout FJ, Wagenaar DMS: Evaluation of the Faces Pain Scale for use with the elderly. Clin J Pain 14:29, 1998.

107. Herr KA, Spratt K, Mobily PR, Richardson G: Pain intensity assessment in older adults: Use of experimental pain to compare psychometric properties and usability of selected pain scales with younger adults. Clin J Pain 20:207, 2004.

chapter 19

Chronic Pain: Physiologic, Diagnostic, and Management Considerations

Brian Hainline

The following descriptions of pain by patients who suffer from chronic pain syndromes suggest the complexity of the conscious experience of chronic pain:

"I feel as though someone has pulled the skin off my left leg and is then constantly rubbing salt into my leg."

"I feel as though my leg is on fire. My skin feels burnt, and it is as though someone is taking claws and tearing into my skin 24 hours a day."

"I feel as though someone has taken a hot poker knife and is jabbing it deep in my right eye. If I could pull my eye out, only to remove this sensation, I would gladly do so."

The suffering experienced by patients who have chronic pain is immense. Something distinguishes their perception of pain from the simpler sensory experience of acute pain: chronic pain is processed within the nervous system in a more complex manner than acute pain.

Acute pain is a universal experience and is biologically protective. It is generally short lived, although when there is an ongoing component of tissue injury, the pain may persist for days or weeks as the body attempts to heal from the initial insult. Acute pain is an appropriate response to an inciting event associated with actual or potential tissue damage.

Chronic pain is pain that persists for more than 1 month longer than might reasonably be expected after an inciting event and is sustained by aberrant somatosensory nervous system processing. Chronic pain can last for months, years, and even decades. It may be considered a pain sensation that arises from within the nervous system rather than from an external source.[1] This salient feature of chronic pain becomes the basis for differentiating it from acute pain and for understanding that patients who suffer from chronic pain are suffering from dysfunction of the nervous system.

■ PAIN PROCESSING AND PERCEPTION

The International Association for the Study of Pain has defined pain as "an unpleasant sensory and emotional experi-ence which we primarily associate with tissue damage or describe in terms of such damage, or both."[2] An analysis of this definition makes it clear that the experience of pain is multimodal and includes physical, sensory, emotional, and cognitive experiences, as well as a perception that may or may not be related to an actual tissue insult.[3-5] The quotations presented earlier give evidence of this experience.

Acute pain essentially arises from activation of periph-eral pain receptors called nociceptors. Activation of nocicep-tors alone is not sufficient for the experience of pain because there are CNS modifiers for the processing of nociceptive pain.[6] Illustrative of this concept are the familiar wartime stories of soldiers who are severely injured but who are also in imminent danger and experience no pain until they reach safety. Thus, pain is a subjective experience that depends on the state of the nervous system.

The normal processing of acute, nociceptive pain begins in the peripheral nervous system in primary afferent neurons. These neurons, known as nociceptors, distinguish noxious from innocuous events. The transmitting nerves may be lightly myelinated or unmyelinated and are special-ized to respond to mechanical, heat, thermal, and chemical stimuli. Threshold activation of nociceptive afferent neurons leads to afferent transmission of signals to the spinal cord. Most afferent input occurs by way of the dorsal root (Fig. 19–1), although some fibers traverse the ventral route. Noci-ceptive input can be modified within the spinal cord. Both nociceptive-specific neurons and more non-specific, wide-dynamic-range cells can be activated from these afferent sensory pathways.[7] In the most simplistic view of pain pro-cessing, nociceptive-specific cells in the spinal cord ascend to the contralateral thalamus by way of the neocorticospinal thalamic tract. From the thalamus, afferent pathways then activate both primary and secondary somatosensory cortices (Fig. 19–1).

Pain-processing pathways, however, are more complex than previously realized. Wide-dynamic-range cells, which are activated by innocuous and noxious stimuli, can amplify afferent stimuli. In addition, more widespread ascending pathways from the spinal cord to the brain activate multiple

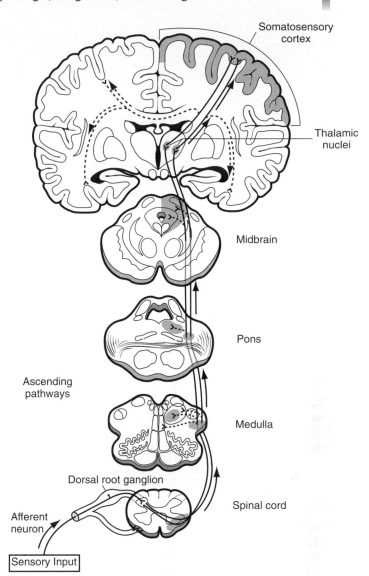

FIGURE 19–1 ■ *Ascending pain pathways. Solid lines* represent established pathways. *Broken lines* represent putative pathways.

brain stem and subcortical regions, limbic pathways, and both ipsilateral and contralateral cortical brain regions (Fig. 19–1).[6] These pathways intermingle with regions of the brain that mediate emotions, autonomic activity, attention and localization, motor planning, and cognition.[8]

Several descending pain pathways influence the perception of pain (Fig. 19–2). The best-studied descending pathway originates from the midbrain periaqueductal gray matter.[6] This brain region subserves the endogenous opiate system. The endogenous opioids consist of endorphins and enkephalins, which regulate the pain response, homeostasis, immune function, and the normal stress response. Activation of the periaqueductal gray matter leads to inhibition of dorsal horn neurons and subsequent analgesia, primarily through an excitatory connection with the dorsal raphe nucleus. The dorsal raphe nucleus (serotoninergic) and locus ceruleus (noradrenergic) are two other brain stem centers that relay key descending pain-inhibitory pathways (Fig. 19–2). These brain stem centers are modified by cortical, subcortical, and limbic pathways.

Additional brain regions are intimately involved in pain modulation through the activation of endogenous neurotransmitters, including acetylcholine, γ-aminobutyric acid (GABA), vasoactive intestinal polypeptide, oxytocin, somatostatin, cholecystokinin, vasopressin, histamine, prolactin, and cannabinoids.[9-11] Indeed, a host of endogenous neurotransmitters either inhibit or augment pain perception, but the manner in which these pathways become activated is poorly understood. These pain-modulating pathways and their neurochemical substrate are one basis for the pharmacologic management of chronic pain.

Functional brain imaging studies have furthered the understanding of pain processing. In control situations, noxious stimuli lead to somatotrophic activation of the contralateral primary and secondary somatosensory cortex. Additional activation occurs in the contralateral insular cortex, anterior cingular and prefrontal cortices, and ipsilateral secondary somatosensory and parietal cortices.[12] These diverse, but interlinked pathways demonstrate that simple physical pain processing is an outdated concept; pain perception is

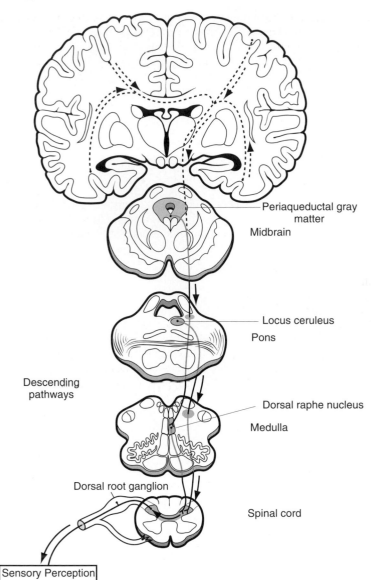

Periaqueductal gray
matter

Midbrain

Locus ceruleus

Pons

Descending
pathways

Dorsal raphe nucleus

Medulla

Dorsal root ganglion

Spinal cord

Sensory Perception

FIGURE 19–2 ■ Descending pain pathways. *Solid lines* represent established pathways. *Broken lines* represent putative pathways.

mediated by attentional, cognitive, emotional, and motor-planning brain responses.[8,12]

Neuropathic pain responses demonstrate recruitment of brain areas outside the control network. Regardless of whether an individual with neuropathic pain has a well-defined lesion, functional brain imaging studies consistently reveal abnormalities in the ipsilateral hemisphere, including the somatosensory cortex; the insular, motor, and premotor cortices; and the anterior cingulate cortex.[12] The contralateral posterior parietal cortex is activated in patients who have mechanical allodynia,[13] and dysfunction of the left temporal and anterior cingulate cortices is described in patients who experience chronic pain after thoracotomy when compared with surgical controls who heal uneventfully (H. Nemoto, M.D., personal communication, December 2004).

Such complex pain processing demonstrates that the CNS may reorganize after injury or perception of injury. Thus, plasticity, which is the ability of the CNS to adapt to or to reorganize in response to new internal or external environmental requirements, may underlie the basis of neuropathic pain.[14]

The cause of such reorganization is unclear, and the search for explanations must move beyond a simplistic lesion-oriented and single–pain pathway model to an appreciation of the conscious and non-conscious processing of pain.

There may be a genetic predisposition to the development of chronic pain that involves the *N*-methyl-D-aspartic acid (NMDA) receptors within the spinal cord and brain,[15] but such evidence is tentative. Psychological maladaptation may be a significant factor in some individuals with chronic pain. Studies have demonstrated that patients who suffer from neuropathic pain have a statistically significantly increased incidence of childhood abuse.[16-19] Such statistics, however, do not lay a foundation for a causal relationship between childhood abuse and neuropathic pain and should not lead to an assumption that patients with chronic pain have an underlying psychological or psychosomatic illness. Ultimately, the dysfunction and misprocessing that occur in individuals who suffer from neuropathic pain need to be understood in terms of biological predisposition and central processing of internal and external perception.[8]

An understanding of the complexity of the central processing of pain, coupled with the clinical observation that patients who have chronic pain are not experiencing pain as a result of simplistic processing of nociceptive input, leads to acceptance of the definition of neuropathic pain. Understanding neuropathic pain is the cornerstone of effective diagnosis and management. Investigators have argued about the definitions of chronic pain versus central pain versus neuropathic pain.[20] In this chapter, *chronic pain, central pain, and neuropathic pain* are considered interchangeable terms.

The International Association for the Study of Pain defines neuropathic pain as "initiated or caused by a primary lesion or dysfunction in the nervous system."[2] Although some argue that the term "dysfunction" makes this definition too vague, others believe that this term allows a better understanding that neuropathic pain is not simply the result of a localizable anatomic lesion.[21,22] For example, complex regional pain syndrome is a well-defined clinical entity in which patients have severe, unrelenting pain and autonomic dysfunction but no lesion that accounts for the pain. Essentially, neuropathic pain represents a dysfunction in pain processing and perception and involves multiple nervous system sites.

■ COMORBID CONDITIONS

Neuropathic pain affects every aspect of a patient's being. In many ways, the patient defines his life by pain rather than by a more soulful sense of being. In other words, the patient identifies himself primarily as one who has pain; virtually every aspect of life becomes associated with a maladaptive response. Whereas the purported initial injury or insult that leads to chronic pain may seem simplistic, the ultimate course, outcome, and cost of chronic pain are affected by a multitude of factors, including emotional, social, economic, and environmental issues.[23]

Depression is the most common comorbidity associated with chronic pain and axis I disorders in the *Diagnostic and Statistical Manual of Mental Disorders*, fourth edition. Indeed, some studies find a prevalence rate approaching 100%.[24] The relationship between depression and pain is complex. Although depression is not an independent risk factor for the development of neuropathic pain, patients suffering from depression report higher levels of pain than do patients without depression.[25,26] Depression augments the impairment associated with chronic pain, and there is a very low likelihood of successfully treating neuropathic pain if the depression is not treated as well.[23]

Anxiety similarly has a high comorbid association with chronic pain, and some postulate that chronic neuropathic pain may be an expression of chronic posttraumatic stress disorder.[27-30] Functional and metabolic similarities exist between neuropathic pain and posttraumatic stress disorder.[31,32] For example, some patients adapt to prior traumatic stress with chronic behavioral strategies, and then develop complex regional pain syndrome develops after a seemingly innocuous inciting event years later. Thus, investigation must focus both on the injury or inciting event per se that leads to chronic pain and on the meaning or perception of that event within the context of the individual's life experience.[8]

Sleep deprivation is common in chronic pain patients, and sleep deprivation alone causes a hyperexcitability state that amplifies the pain response.[23] Social support systems for patients who have chronic pain may be dysfunctional both at home and at work, and self-esteem can be diminished considerably. Some patients believe that they deserve to suffer pain and place such reasoning within a religious or metaphysical context. Patients who have chronic pain often develop several maladaptive physical responses that then predispose to perpetuating the cycle of chronic pain.

■ EXAMPLES OF NEUROPATHIC PAIN SYNDROMES

An exhaustive discussion of various chronic pain syndromes is beyond the scope of this chapter. The following is a brief discussion of some common chronic pain syndromes.

Low Back Pain

Although chronic low back pain is ubiquitous, there is no single satisfactory treatment regimen for this problem. Too often, back pain is viewed as a biomechanical problem that can be fixed by either local injections or surgical therapy. It is more useful, however, to view chronic low back pain as neuropathic pain. Chronic low back pain may comprise elements of acute biomechanical pain and active nerve root entrapment.

Patients who have chronic low back pain without active biomechanical symptomatology complain of essentially constant pain that is independent of position. Pain may be felt across the lower part of the back and may radiate into one or both legs. The pain can have a burning quality but may also be described as stabbing or cramp-like, as a deep pressure, or less often, with other pain characteristics described later. Some patients report position-dependent pain superimposed on chronic pain. For example, patients who have segmental lumbar instability complain of acute, severe pain occurring with sudden positional changes. Patients with lumbar stenosis have progressively severe low back pain, with or without leg pain, when walking more than one block. Patients with active facet syndrome complain of sudden pain with back extension. It is important to distinguish these variations when obtaining a history. Treatment may combine interventions targeted at the acute, biomechanical pain while addressing the overall chronic pain syndrome.

The multitude of failed back surgeries is a testament that low back surgery, including laminectomy/diskectomy, spinal fusion, and disk replacement, is not the answer for patients who suffer from chronic low back pain.[33] Similarly, to label all chronic low back pain as myofasciitis does not advance the scientific and clinical understanding of chronic low back pain.[34] As with all neuropathic pain syndromes, chronic low back pain represents a transformation from acute pain to a chronic somatosensory processing disorder. The clinician's management should shift so that the chronic nature of the pain becomes the guiding principle for multidisciplinary management.

Postherpetic Neuralgia

Postherpetic neuralgia is one of the better-studied chronic pain syndromes and is a clear example of how a peripheral nerve insult can lead to dysfunction of the CNS. Postherpetic neuralgia is caused by reactivation of varicella-zoster virus along a single dermatome related to either a spinal dorsal root ganglion or a brain-stem cranial nerve-ganglion. Pain develops along the same dermatome as the rash. The initial pain of postherpetic neuralgia is an appropriate nociceptive response to irritation of the peripheral nerve. In a substantial number of individuals, however, postherpetic neuralgia becomes transformed into chronic pain. Such chronic pain, like other neuropathic pain syndromes, affects multiple aspects of life, including affect, physical activities, social interactions, self-esteem, and sleep.

The transition from nociceptive pain to chronic neuropathic pain may result from deafferentation of the second-order neurons of the spinothalamic tract because of primary sensory neuronal death. This possibility has not been conclusively demonstrated, however, and pain transformation may involve other aspects of sensory processing, including an alteration in descending inhibitory signals. The key point in all neuropathic pain syndromes is that the transition from acute pain to chronic pain is probably multifactorial and differs from individual to individual. In terms of the final syndrome, it is irrelevant whether the transforming event is a lesion with subsequent deafferentation, in the classic lesion-oriented model of allopathic medicine, or the transforming event is one of processing, thus raising the possibility that the transformation is physiologically based. Ultimately, CNS expression of chronic pain involves similar pathways, and the overlap between physiologic dysfunction and physical dysfunction becomes blurred, both causally and from a management viewpoint.

Patients who suffer from postherpetic neuralgia typically describe a burning, stabbing, or lancinating pain along the affected dermatome. The pain is unremitting and hypersensitive to touch, and substantial behavioral adaptations are made to protect this region of the body. As with all neuropathic pain states, treatment directed at the peripheral nerve alone is unrewarding; successful management involves a multidisciplinary approach.

Diabetic Peripheral Neuropathy

Peripheral neuropathy develops in approximately a quarter of the 17 million diabetic Americans. A considerable number of these patients experience neuropathic pain, but there is no clear peripheral nerve feature distinguishing patients who have diabetic neuropathic pain from those who have non-painful peripheral neuropathy.[35] Diabetic peripheral neuropathy is another example of a peripheral nerve lesion transforming into a chronic, sustaining pain mediated by dysfunction of the nervous system.

Patients with painful diabetic neuropathy and other painful peripheral neuropathies typically complain of pain in a stocking distribution. The pain is often burning and may be sharp or lancinating. Frequently, the pain is worse in a recumbent position and is somewhat better with weight bearing. There may be associated allodynia, thus leading to avoidance-type behavior. Patients often have severe interruption of sleep because the pain is typically worse at nighttime. As with all neuropathic pain syndromes, other aspects of the patient's life can be affected in a cascade involving the breakdown of affect, social support, and self-esteem. Treatment directed simply at the peripheral nerves is not successful.

Complex Regional Pain Syndrome

Complex regional pain syndrome, formerly known as *reflex sympathetic dystrophy,* is a poorly understood chronic condition. Unlike low back pain, postherpetic neuralgia, and diabetic neuropathy, the initial inciting event of complex regional pain syndrome may not be evident. Often, the inciting event is a seemingly innocuous soft tissue injury, but the injury then becomes transformed into an unrelenting, debilitating pain syndrome. The term *reflex sympathetic dystrophy,* though still commonly used, was changed to *complex regional pain syndrome* because it is not clear that the pain of complex regional pain syndrome is simply related to dysfunction of the sympathetic nervous system. In addition, dystrophic changes are not universal, and the transformation from an inciting event to chronic pain is not reflexive. Complex regional pain syndrome is divided into type I (no evidence of peripheral nerve injury) and type II (documented peripheral nerve injury).

Complex regional pain syndrome illustrates the enormous complexity of neuropathic pain. Frequently, the inciting event is a seemingly trivial trauma. Indeed, the inciting event can be so trivial that patients are often led to believe that they are fabricating the pain. Additionally, because there is no clear-cut, satisfactory pathophysiologic explanation for the severe transformed pain, some authors have even doubted the neuropathic nature of this syndrome and have concluded that complex regional pain syndrome is a somatoform disorder.[36] Complex regional pain syndrome has been described as a peripheral nerve insult that results in one of the following: local peripheral nerve trauma with secondary ephaptic conduction and ectopic pacemaker activity, crosstalk between unmyelinated C-fibers and interlinked sympathetic fibers, or wide-dynamic-range neuron hypersensitivity in the spinal cord from prolonged, intense nociceptive input.[37]

The following four criteria are used to diagnose complex regional pain syndrome[38]:

1. An initiating noxious event is responsible for the patient's immobilization.
2. The patient has continuing pain, allodynia, or hyperalgesia that is disproportionate to any inciting event.
3. There is evidence at some time of edema, changes in skin blood flow, or abnormal sudomotor activity in the region of the pain.
4. The syndrome is excluded by the existence of a condition that would otherwise account for the degree of pain and dysfunction.

Thus, the diagnosis is made purely on clinical grounds, with objective, autonomic nervous system pathophysiology taken into account. The changes in the autonomic nervous system led to sympathetic blockade becoming one of the hallmarks of treatment. Although pain relief from sympathetic blockade helps support the diagnosis of complex regional pain syndrome, sympathetically independent pain may develop early in the course of this condition and is unresponsive to peripheral sympathetic blockade.[39,40]

Even though unusual autonomic activity is present early in the course of complex regional pain syndrome and this activity may be caused by dysregulation of the sympathetic nervous system, the condition quickly becomes transformed to neuropathic pain. In other words, the pain becomes sustained by dysfunction in somatosensory processing and is not simply secondary to sympathetic nervous system dysfunction. There is some controversy concerning this latter point: some authors have argued that complex regional pain syndrome has nothing to do with the sympathetic nervous system, but they are confusing the difference between transient sympathetic nervous system dysfunction and long-lasting neuropathic pain.[41,42]

The sometimes seemingly trivial inciting event of complex regional pain syndrome has led some to speculate that this condition is emotionally based. Even though there may be truth in this supposition, it is likewise true that all neuropathic pain syndromes have a component of emotional dysfunction. On the one hand, depression and anxiety coexist almost universally with neuropathic pain syndromes. On the other hand, there may be a fundamentally important emotional processing component in the transformation from simple pain to more complex, chronic pain. It would be more useful to break down the arbitrary barriers between psychiatry and neurology, mind and body, and emotionality and physicality and to consider neuropathic pain a neuropsychiatric disorder. Chronic pain syndromes should not be viewed as either emotionally based or physically based problems.

Pain Secondary to Central Nervous System Injury

A variety of chronic pain states have been described after well-documented CNS injury, including trauma, multiple sclerosis, cerebrovascular accidents, infections, spinal cord syrinx, neoplasms, and others.[43-47] All have in common a well-documented lesion of the CNS. It is not clear, however, how a transformed pain syndrome develops in some patients who have such lesions whereas others with the same lesion have a neurologic deficit without such pain. The only thing that is known with certainty is that the clinical expression of pain can become the overwhelming chronic manifestation in such patients and that the same comorbid conditions develop in these patients as in individuals with other neuropathic pain syndromes. Pain usually occurs weeks to months after the insult to the CNS, thus indicating that CNS reorganization may develop over time.[17]

■ DIAGNOSIS

History

Clinicians can make a diagnosis of neuropathic pain with confidence by taking a careful history, performing a focused physical examination, and judiciously using ancillary diagnostic studies. When taking a history, it is important to understand the characteristics of the pain. The following are the five most important characteristics:

1. Temporal qualities, including acute, recurrent, or chronic; daily variation; and onset and duration
2. Intensity, including average pain, pain at its worst, pain at its least, and pain at the time of history taking
3. Topography, including localized versus regional pain, superficial versus deep pain, and focal versus radiating pain

4. Quality, including descriptors such as burning, aching, freezing, stabbing, electric shock–like, toothache-like, cramping, or knife-like
5. Palliative and precipitating factors, including physical activities, emotional stressors, nutritional triggers, and circadian rhythms

It is beneficial for patients to use a rapid rating scale such as the Brief Pain Inventory or the Visual Analog Scale.[48] Patients rate the temporal aspects of pain from zero (no pain) to 10 (the worst imaginable pain). Such rating scales are helpful in monitoring patients and aid in understanding the relationship between the patient and pain. Some patients rate their pain as a constant "10" but seem to be in no acute distress, thus suggesting a dissociation between their perception of pain and their physical manifestations.

Clinicians should spend considerable time trying to understand the inciting event of the pain, which may provide insight into a disease state or injury that has not been diagnosed. In addition, it is critical to understand the patient's perception of the inciting event, which takes into account life experiences. Daily activities need to be considered, including physical limitations caused by pain and the amount of daily exercise. Some patients are so debilitated by pain that they are essentially homebound and perform little in the way of even sedentary activities. The support system must be explored, including the immediate family and the patient's work environment, if appropriate. Frequently, patients suffering from neuropathic pain feel alone and abandoned and essentially become imprisoned by pain. Many patients have discontinued all sexual activity as a manifestation of depression, rejection, or fear that such activity will further exacerbate the pain.

In addition to a general past medical history, careful attention must be paid to any prior psychiatric conditions or previous episodes of prolonged pain-related conditions. This investigation may provide important insight into the patient's adaptive responses over time. Childhood trauma must be considered, although probing into childhood trauma must be done in a delicate and non-invasive manner. Even though there is a high incidence of childhood trauma and abuse in chronic pain patients, one cannot suggest or assume that a patient with chronic pain has experienced such trauma. Alcohol and drug histories are critical because one facet of chronic neuropathic pain treatment may be the use of narcotic analgesics.

A careful search for comorbid medical conditions is important. The three most common comorbid conditions are depression, anxiety, and sleep deprivation. If these conditions are not managed properly, pain management is unlikely to be successful. Simple questions may suffice. For example, asking whether the patient has felt depressed or hopeless or has lost pleasure may uncover an otherwise undiagnosed depression. Pain centers often use more formal depression scales as part of the initial assessment. The family history may provide a clue to a possible genetic predisposition to psychiatric disease, pain syndromes, or both.

The patient's expectations of treatment must be assessed.[23] It is unrealistic to expect that a simple procedure or medication will completely alleviate the pain. Realistic goals must be set. Too often, patients arrive with an expectation of obtaining a simple anatomic explanation and subsequent treatment of pain. Once the clinician begins to discuss neuropathic pain, patients may fail to understand that their pain is a result of a somewhat ill-defined dysfunction of the nervous system. Patients can feel a lack of validation, which can undermine future treatments. It is frequently helpful to end a discussion by asking the patient something such as the following: "Just so I can be certain I have explained myself well, please summarize for me your understanding of your condition." Such a statement does not assume that the patient is not intelligent or was not paying attention but places the burden on the clinician for having satisfactorily explained the condition.

Once the patient understands that the pain is a chronic condition, the foundation for multidisciplinary, long-term treatment is laid. Patients need to understand that the ultimate goal of treatment is to reduce pain, increase function, and improve quality of life. The focus on complete cessation of pain alone will lead to treatment failure. Patients should feel that they are an integral component of the treatment by actively participating in their pain management.

Physical Examination

A careful physical examination should include vital signs, a focused musculoskeletal and extremity examination, and a neurologic examination. Patients with chronic pain are not generally in acute distress, and their vital signs should be stable. The musculoskeletal examination is important in many ways. First, some patients will demonstrate evidence of chronic maladaptation because of prolonged muscle spasm and avoidance-type behavior. Second, the musculoskeletal examination may reveal evidence of active mechanical signs of an entrapped nerve or an irritated spinal segment. Third, the musculoskeletal examination may reveal evidence of psychological maladaptation in which patients claim pain when they are directly confronted with a musculoskeletal maneuver, but careful observation reveals that the patient is capable of such maneuvers when they are performing other tasks.

Examination of the extremity may demonstrate altered autonomic activity, for example, an alteration in hair growth or nail bed pattern, a change in extremity color or temperature, or swelling of an extremity out of proportion to the injury. Such changes are hallmarks of complex regional pain syndrome. Diabetic patients may have a diminution in peripheral blood flow, which can aggravate peripheral neuropathic pain. Findings in the neurologic examination may be normal in patients who have neuropathic pain but often point to dermatomal, regional, spinal, or brain dysfunction that correlates with the pain syndrome.

The sensory aspect of a neurologic examination is exceedingly important. In addition to testing for the presence or absence of primary sensory modality perception (vibration, proprioception, light touch, and pin prick), the examiner should test for alterations in sensory experience that are consistent with neuropathic pain. Allodynia is pain in response to a normally non-noxious, mild stimulus. Hyperalgesia indicates an increased sensation of pain in response to a normally painful stimulus such as a pin prick. Hyperpathia is a prolonged painful experience after pin prick assessment.

Other findings of the neurologic examination may be abnormal and result from either a documented lesion or a functional aberration caused by CNS dysfunction. For example, dystonia has been well described in patients with complex regional pain syndrome or in those who have a basal ganglia lesion.[49] Tremor may develop with peripheral neuropathy or may be manifested as a physiologic aberration in patients who have chronic pain.

Ancillary Studies

Ancillary studies should be used to exclude medical conditions that can either mimic or exacerbate the patient's clinical condition and to confirm or aid in understanding the origin of the pain. For example, deep venous thrombosis is manifested as extremity swelling with abnormal temperature sensation and can either mimic complex regional pain syndrome or coexist with this condition. Chronic low back and lumbar radicular pain, rarely, can be caused by a cauda equina tumor. Chronic extremity pain can coexist with active denervation in a nerve dermatome. Ultimately, all diagnostic tests are taken in conjunction with the history and physical examination to secure a diagnosis, which then becomes the springboard for effective management.

■ MANAGEMENT

As discussed previously, treatment of neuropathic pain should be multidisciplinary. Although many pain centers focus on anesthesiology-based procedures, such procedures are but one aspect of an important component of successful pain management. The following text presents a general discussion of the principles of multidisciplinary treatment. Such principles can be applied to any neuropathic pain state. Treatment must be individualized for the physical manifestation of pain and also for the patient's psychosocial adaptation.

Psychotherapy

Because of the high prevalence of depression and anxiety with chronic neuropathic pain, psychotherapy is an important component of successful management. Even in patients who are not depressed, learning effective coping strategies for chronic pain is helpful. Although patients may be resistant to psychotherapy because they sense that the clinician views their pain as "psychosomatic," clinicians must stress the importance of psychological intervention because this intervention will help manage depression and coping skills and may uncover a previously undiagnosed, repressed trauma or other significant life event.

Cognitive behavioral therapy helps patients understand the interplay of pain perception, affect, and daily thought patterns. The focus is on developing positive expectations in patients.[1] Patients who have chronic pain are often resistant to insight-oriented therapy. It is the author's experience that many patients who have chronic pain are sufficiently disassociated from their emotions that such therapy is not possible. Insight-oriented therapy should be recommended only when there is a trusting bond between the patient and clinician and the patient expresses a desire to explore a possible relationship between previously unrecognized emotions and chronic pain. Group therapy is extremely beneficial, especially for patients who feel that they are uniquely alone in their experience of chronic pain. Family therapy becomes important in helping other family members understand that chronic neuropathic pain is a real medical condition. Patients need to be validated within the family, and they also need to understand that at times they isolate themselves from the family because of pain.

In some cases, acute psychiatric intervention becomes necessary for chronic pain management. Long-term treatment is sometimes associated with a sudden insight or flashback into previously unrecognized trauma, severe depression, or poorly managed anxiety, and a skilled psychiatrist is needed to help manage such conditions.

Pharmacologic Therapy

Several pharmacologic strategies can be used to treat chronic pain. No single drug effectively treats neuropathic pain. The following is a general discussion of various classes of drugs frequently used in chronic pain management. The best-studied conditions for using pharmacologic management are diabetic neuropathic pain and postherpetic neuralgia. The efficacy of pharmacologic therapy is less studied for other chronic neuropathic pain syndromes. Nonetheless, several generalizable treatment strategies exist.

Anticonvulsants

Anticonvulsants have become first-line treatment of neuropathic pain syndromes.[50-52] Carbamazepine, phenytoin, valproate, and clonazepam were the first anticonvulsants to be well studied in treating patients who have neuropathic pain, especially with such conditions as trigeminal neuralgia and diabetic peripheral neuropathy.[51] Many well-controlled studies have shown that gabapentin is effective in treating postherpetic neuralgia and other neuropathic pain conditions.[51-53] The list has extended to newer anticonvulsants, including progabalin, topiramate, oxcarbazepine, lamotrigine, zonisamide, and levetiracetam.[54-58] The mechanism by which such drugs work is not completely clear but generally has to do with reduction in a hyperexcitability state, either peripherally or centrally. Interaction with GABA and other neurotransmitters may also be important.

The initial choice of drugs should be based on clinician comfort and relative indications. The Food and Drug Administration (FDA) has approved gabapentin and pregabalin for restricted use in neuropathic pain (postherpetic neuralgia and diabetic neuropathy). However, it is common practice to provide these and other anticonvulsants off-label for various neuropathic pain conditions. One can take advantage of the side effect profile of some medications, for example, topiramate for weight loss and zonisamide for sedative side effects. Anticonvulsants are administered at the dosing schedules commonly used for treating epilepsy. Generally, only one anticonvulsant should be prescribed at a time, and upward titration should be based on efficacy and tolerability. Anticonvulsants may be used in conjunction with other medications described in the subsequent sections.

Antidepressants

Tricyclic antidepressants have been a front-list treatment for neuropathic pain for many years.[59-61] Low-dose amitriptyline, in particular, has been shown in many well-controlled studies to be efficacious in treating various neuropathic pain conditions, independent of depression. The sedative side effects of amitriptyline often provide a useful adjunct in treating patients who have comorbid sleep deprivation. The dosage of tricyclic antidepressants should begin at 10 mg per night, with upward weekly titration in 10-mg increments as tolerated and needed.

Several studies have also demonstrated that selective serotonin reuptake inhibitors (fluxetine, paroxetine), serotonin-norepinephrine reuptake inhibitors (venlafaxine, duloxetine), and dopaminergic-mediated antidepressants (bupropion) are efficacious in treating neuropathic pain.[57,62-66] Selective serotonin reuptake inhibitors, combined serotonin and norepinephrine reuptake inhibitors, and dopaminergic-mediated antidepressants are less well-studied as medication adjuncts in treating neuropathic pain, but several studies have demonstrated efficacy.[62-66] These agents become particularly useful when patients have comorbid depression, anxiety, or both. Antidepressants may be beneficial because of their influence on descending serotoninergic, adrenergic, and other pain-inhibitory pathways and because of interaction with common pathways in depression and pain.[67-69]

Narcotic Analgesics

Narcotic analgesics (opioids) are the most potent prescription analgesics. Although there is wide acceptance in prescribing narcotic analgesics for patients who have cancer, acceptance is not so universal in treating patients with pain from other causes. Problems arise because of lack of acceptance of long-term use of such medication in these patients, combined with fear of causing drug addiction. Narcotic analgesics take advantage of the innate opioid receptor system in the CNS. These medications mimic the action of endogenous opioids by providing powerful pain signal transmission.[70]

It is common practice in pain medicine clinics for patients to sign a narcotic agreement if they are to begin chronic narcotic analgesic treatment. Such agreements help provide clarity with regard to intent of narcotic intake and the manner in which the medications will be used. The agreement usually stipulates that patients may obtain narcotics from only one physician, may use only one pharmacy, and may take medication only in the manner prescribed. Patients must return for monthly visits and are subject to random drug screening. Although a contract may seem harsh, the medical literature supports the use of such contracts, which help minimize narcotic abuse by drug-seeking patients.[1]

Initially, short-acting narcotics should be prescribed. When a patient's daily narcotic need is discerned, clinicians should switch to a long-acting medication that allows the patient to obtain sustained pain relief and to eliminate the sometimes intrusive behavioral pattern of taking a pain medication every 3 to 4 hours. Once a long-acting medication has been prescribed, short-acting medications can be used for breakthrough pain.

Tramadol hydrochloride is a unique narcotic-like medication. It does have weak μ-opioid receptor agonism and enhances the inhibitory effect of the descending serotoninergic and adrenergic systems. Tramadol is efficacious in a variety of neuropathic pain conditions and can be used as a first-line medication before a more traditional narcotic analgesic is prescribed.[1]

Topical Analgesics

The best-studied topical analgesic is a 5% lidocaine patch.[70] This device may be especially useful in well-localized pain syndromes such as postherpetic neuralgia. Capsaicin may also be effective in relatively localized neuropathic pain conditions. It leads to a depletion of substance P, a pain-generating neuropeptide in sensory afferent neurons. Capsaicin itself, however, may lead to a disquieting, burning pain, thus limiting its efficacy.[71]

Other Adjunctive Medications

Tizanidine is a centrally acting α_2-adrenergic agonist with prominent antispasticity effects. This medication may be an important adjunct in patients with chronic muscle spasm or tension-type headache. Baclofen, a GABA agonist, may benefit patients who have chronic muscle spasm or paroxysmal pain. Mexiletine is an antiarrhythmic drug with demonstrable efficacy in treating some neuropathic pain conditions. Clonidine, another central α_2-adrenergic agonist, may be helpful in treating complex regional pain syndrome and related conditions when taken orally or transdermally.[70]

Pulse therapy with corticosteroids or nonsteroidal antiinflammatory drugs should be considered in patients with acute musculoskeletal pain superimposed on chronic neuropathic pain. For example, some patients who have chronic back pain suffer acute radicular pain with active, mechanical stretch signs on examination. In such patients, a 1- to 2-week course of nonsteroidal antiinflammatory drugs or oral corticosteroids can help break the cycle of acute or chronic pain. Long-term corticosteroid and nonsteroidal antiinflammatory drugs have little role in the treatment of chronic, neuropathic pain.[70] Neuroleptics and benzodiazepines are sometimes useful in and of themselves or in treating comorbid conditions.[70,72]

There is some evidence that NMDA receptor antagonists ameliorate chronic neuropathic pain. Ketamine infusions have been studied, but the high rate of toxicity (causing hallucinations and anorexia) limits this medication's usefulness. Smaller doses of ketamine may be useful in select circumstances.[73,74] Oral NMDA receptor antagonist drugs have demonstrated little efficacy in treating chronic, neuropathic pain.

Interventional Strategies

Several anesthesiology-based interventions are appropriate as one aspect of multidisciplinary pain management. It is a mistaken notion in some pain practices that management should be primarily intervention based. Indeed, in some practices, failure of one intervention leads to an escalation in intervention strategies, often to the detriment of the patient.[20]

Nerve blocks may be helpful for diagnostic purposes and may sometimes provide an important break in the cycle of chronic pain.[75] Once a successful nerve block is obtained, physical therapy and other strategies should be used immediately to help the patient overcome maladaptive postures. Sympathetic blockade, which by definition does not include primary sensory or somatic blockade, has been used both diagnostically and therapeutically for complex regional pain syndrome and related conditions.[76] (The lack of benefit from sympathetic blockade does not preclude the diagnosis of complex regional pain syndrome, however.) As with other nerve blocks, successful sympathetic blockade should be followed immediately by progressive physical therapy.

Epidural and transforaminal corticosteroid injections may benefit patients who suffer from back conditions that have a demonstrable mechanical component, such as lumbar disk herniation and lumbar stenosis. Similarly, facet blocks may be exceedingly useful in breaking the cycle of chronic facet locking or in providing transient relief to patients who

have segmental lumbar instability. Such relief allows the patient to begin more progressive physical therapy strategies.

Spinal cord stimulation relies on the principle that a stimulator placed in the dorsal spinal cord blocks central pain processing from a peripheral pain generator. Spinal cord stimulators should be considered only in patients who have relatively well-localized extremity pain and have exhausted all other treatment strategies.[77] Too often, spinal cord stimulators are placed as part of a rapid escalation in interventional techniques, when other multidisciplinary strategies have been neglected.

Intrathecal administration of narcotic analgesics takes advantage of a very low-dose narcotic coupled with strong binding to spinal cord receptors, in addition to having minimal systemic side effects. Such strategies are particularly useful in patients who have demonstrated a positive effect with narcotic analgesics but cannot tolerate their systemic side effects.[70,77] These medications can be combined with intrathecal clonidine, which also has independent pain-alleviating effects, and baclofen, which may be useful in alleviating spasticity.

Other surgical interventions, including spinal surgery, must be approached with caution. Other than for trigeminal neuralgia, placing a lesion in the nervous system or performing decompressive surgery in an attempt to alleviate a chronic, neuropathic pain pathway has yielded equivocal results.[20]

Physical Therapy

Most patients who have neuropathic pain—especially those who have chronic low back pain but also patients with severe extremity neuropathic pain—have developed several maladaptive physical manifestations. Physical therapy should be an important consideration in treating chronic neuropathic pain.[78]

Some physical therapy, such as craniosacral technique and myofascial release, is more intuitive and may help patients understand the link between physiology and the perception of physical pain. In these therapies, patients lie on a table while being extremely quiet, and the therapy is quite subtle. More conventional physical therapy includes the use of a transcutaneous electrical nerve stimulation unit, which may alleviate localized pain, as well as the use of other modalities. In addition, range-of-motion, strengthening, and spine stabilization exercises help overcome chronic maladaptive manifestations.

Complementary Strategies

Acupuncture is recognized by the World Health Organization as an effective treatment of pain. Several evidenced-based studies have demonstrated the efficacy of acupuncture in treating pain, although the difficulty of performing sham acupuncture leads to methodologic flaws.[79] Acupuncture is not a stand-alone treatment but should be considered as part of a multidisciplinary approach, especially in patients who wish to explore non-pharmacologic strategies.

Nutritional counseling should be considered in patients who suffer from chronic neuropathic pain. Many such patients have poor eating habits, often because of chronic nausea or depression. In addition, many patients have a diet that is shifted toward high-carbohydrate and high-fat or junk food.

Such foods have an immediate gratifying effect, and poor eating habits often become part of a cycle of self-treatment underlying anxiety and depression.[80]

Massage therapy can be used to desensitize areas of hyperalgesia and to help alleviate muscular and emotional stress. In some cases, massage therapy becomes a transition into developing greater insight into the interplay between physiology and physical pain perception.[81]

■ SUMMARY

Neuropathic pain is a neuropsychiatric condition in which pain is initiated or caused by a primary lesion or dysfunction in the nervous system. Understanding the complexity of neuropathic pain becomes the cornerstone for appropriate diagnosis and management. Diagnosis must take into account comorbid conditions. Successful management depends on realistic patient and physician expectations and an individualized, multidisciplinary approach.

References

1. Staats PS, Argoff CE, Brewer R, et al: Neuropathic pain: Incorporating new consensus guidelines into the reality of clinical practice. Adv Stud Med 4(7B):S550, 2004.
2. Merskey H, Bogduk N: Classification of Chronic Pain: Descriptions of Chronic Pain Syndromes and Definitions of Pain Terms, 2nd ed. Seattle, IASP Press, 1994.
3. Melzack R, Casey KL: Sensory, motivational, and central control determinants of pain: A new conceptual model. In Kenshalo D (ed): The Skin Senses. Springfield, IL, Charles C Thomas, 1968, p 423.
4. Treede RD, Kenshalo DR, Gracely RH, et al: The cortical representation of pain. Pain 79:105, 1999.
5. Talbot JD, Marrett S, Evans AC, et al: Multiple representations of pain in human cerebral cortex. Science 251:1355, 2001.
6. Basbaum AI, Fields HL: Endogenous pain control systems: Brainstem spinal pathways and endorphin circuitry. Annu Rev Neurosci 7:309, 1984.
7. Woolf CJ, Fitzgerald M: The properties of neurons recorded in the superficial dorsal horn of the rat spinal cord. J Comp Neurol 221:313, 1983.
8. Basbaum AI, Jessell TM: The perception of pain. In Kandel ER, Schwartz JH, Jessell TM (eds): Principles of Neural Science. New York, McGraw Hill, 2000, p 472.
9. Duggan AW, Weihe E: Central transmission of impulses in nociceptors: Events in the superficial dorsal horn. In Basbaum AI, Besson JM (eds): Toward a New Pharmacotherapy of Pain. Chichester, UK, John Wiley & Sons, 1991, p 35.
10. Hokfelt T, Johansson O, Ljungdahl A: Peptidergic neurons. Nature 284:515, 1980.
11. Meng ID, Manning BH: An analgesia circuit activated by cannabinoids. Nature 394:381, 1998.
12. Peyron R, Schneider F, Faillenot MS, et al: An fMRI study of cortical representation of mechanical allodynia in patients with neuropathic pain. Neurology 63:1838, 2004.
13. Witting N, Kupers RC, Svensson P, et al: Experimental brush-evoked allodynia activates posterior parietal cortex. Neurology 57:1817, 2001.
14. Shih JJ, Cohen LG: Cortical reorganization in the human. Neurology 63:1772, 2004.
15. Mogil JS, Sternberg WF, Marek P, et al: The genetics of pain and pain inhibition. Proc Natl Acad Sci USA 93:3048, 1996.
16. Katan W, Egan K, Miller D: Chronic pain: Lifetime psychiatric diagnoses and family history. Am J Psychiatry 142:1156, 1984.
17. Dickinson LM, de Gruy FV, Dickinson WP, et al: Health-related quality of life and symptom profiles of female survivors of sexual abuse. Arch Fam Med 8:35, 1999.
18. Fillingim RB, Wilkinson CS, Powell T: Self-reported abuse history and pain complaints among young adults. Clin J Pain 15:85, 1999.
19. Goldberg RT, Goldstein R: A comparison of chronic pain patients and controls on traumatic events in childhood. Disabil Rehabil 22:756, 2000.
20. Scadding JW: Treatment of neuropathic pain: Historical aspects. Pain Med 5:S3, 2004.
21. Dworkin RH, Backonja M, Rowbotham MC, et al: Advances in neuropathic pain; diagnosis, mechanisms, and treatment recommendations. Arch Neurol 60:1524, 2003.
22. Staats PS: Expanding the current management of neuropathic pain. Adv Stud Med 4(7B):S548, 2004.
23. Nicholson B, Verma S: Comorbidities in chronic neuropathic pain. Pain Med 5:S9, 2004.
24. Romano JM, Turner JA: Chronic pain and depression: Does the evidence support a relationship? Psychol Bull 97:18, 1985.
25. Keefe FJ, Wilkins RH, Cook WA, et al: Depression, pain, and pain behavior. J Consult Clin Psychol 54:665, 1986.
26. Krause SJ, Wiener RL, Tait RC: Depression and pain behavior in patients with chronic pain. Clin J Pain 10:122, 1994.
27. Grande LA, Loeser JD, Ashleigh OJ, et al: Complex regional pain syndrome as a stress response. Pain 110:295, 2004.
28. Frayne SM, Seaver MR, Loveland S, et al: Burden of medical illness in women with depression and posttraumatic stress disorder. Arch Intern Med 164:1306, 2004.
29. Asmundson GJ, Wright KD, Stein MB: Pain and PTSD symptoms in female veterans. Eur J Pain 8:345, 2004.
30. Otis JD, Keane TM, Kerns RD: An examination of the relationship between chronic pain and posttraumatic stress disorder. J Rehabil Res Dev 40:397, 2003.
31. Feldman JB: The neurobiology of pain, affect and hypnosis. Am J Clin Hypn 46:187, 2004.
32. Liberizon I, Phan KL: Brain-imaging studies in posttraumatic stress disorder. CNS Spectr 8:641, 2003.
33. Saberski LR: When is it time for pain management? Pain Clin 6:3, 2004.
34. Sarno JE: Healing Back Pain: The Mind-Body Connection. New York, Warner, 1991.
35. Backonja M-M, Serra J: Pharmacologic management part 1: Better-studied neuropathic pain diseases. Pain Med 5:S28, 2004.
36. Ochoa JL, Verdugo RJ: Reflex sympathetic dystrophy: A common clinical avenue for somatoform expression. Neurol Clin 13:351, 1995.
37. Hainline B: Reflex sympathetic dystrophy. In Spivak JM, DiCesare PE, Feldman DS, et al (eds): Orthopaedics: A Comprehensive Study Guide. New York, McGraw-Hill, 1999, p 943.
38. Stanton-Hicks M, Janig W, Hassenbusch S, et al: Reflex sympathetic dystrophy: Changing concepts and taxonomy. Pain 63:127, 1995.
39. Max MB, Gilron I: Sympathetically maintained pain: Has the emperor no clothes? Neurology 52:905, 1999.
40. Schwartzman RJ, Grothusen J, Kiefer TR, et al: Neuropathic central pain: Epidemiology, etiology, and treatment options. Arch Neurol 58:1547, 2001.
41. Verdugo RJ, Ochoa JL: Sympathetically maintained pain. I. Phentolamine block questions the concept. Neurology 44:1003, 1994.
42. Verdugo RJ, Campero M, Ochoa JL: Phentolamine sympathetic block in painful polyneuropathies. II. Further questioning of the concept of sympathetically maintained pain. Neurology 44:1010, 1994.
43. Deejeerine J, Roussy G: Le syndrome thalamique. Rev Neurol 12:521, 1906.
44. Boivie J, Leijon G, Johansson I: Central post-stroke pain: Study of the mechanisms through analyses of the sensory abnormalities. Pain 37:173, 1989.
45. Leijon G, Boivie J, Johansson I: Central post-stroke pain: Neurological symptoms and pain characteristics. Pain 36:13, 1989.
46. Woolsey RM: Chronic pain following spinal cord injury. J Am Paraplegia Soc 9:39, 1986.
47. Moulin DE, Foley KM, Ebers GC: Pain syndromes in multiple sclerosis. Neurology 38:1830, 1988.
48. Chang VT, Hwang SS, Feuerman M: Validation of the Edmonton symptom assessment scale. Cancer 88:2164, 2000.
49. Schwartzman RJ, Popescu A: Reflex sympathetic dystrophy. Curr Rheumatol Rep 4:165, 2002.
50. Namaka M, Gramlich CR, Ruhlen D, et al: A treatment algorithm for neuropathic pain. Clin Ther 26:951, 2004.
51. Wiffen P, Collins S, McQuay H, et al: Anticonvulsant drugs for acute and chronic pain. Cochrane Database Syst Rev 3:CD001133, 2000.

52. Tremont-Lukats IW, Megeff C, Backonja MM: Anticonvulsants for neuropathic pain syndromes: Mechanisms of action and place in therapy. Drugs 60:1029, 2000.

53. Backonja M, Glanzman RL: Gabapentin dosing for neuropathic pain: Evidence from randomized, placebo-controlled clinical trials. Clin Ther 25:81, 2003.

54. Chandramouli J: Newer anticonvulsant drugs in neuropathic pain and bipolar disorder. J Pain Palliat Care Pharmacother 16:19, 2002.

55. Vu TN: Current pharmacologic approaches to treating neuropathic pain. Curr Pain Headache Rep 8:15, 2004.

56. Guay DR: Oxcarbazepine, topiramate, zonisamide, and levetiracetam: Potential use in neuropathic pain. Am J Geriatr Pharmacother 1:18, 2003.

57. Maizels M, McCarberg B: Antidepressants and antiepileptic drugs for chronic non-cancer pain. Am Fam Phys 71:483, 2005.

58. LaRoche SM, Helmers SL: The new antiepileptic drugs: Scientific review. JAMA 291:605, 2004.

59. Max MB, Lynch SA, Muir J, et al: Effects of desipramine, amitriptyline and fluoxetine on pain in diabetic neuropathy. N Engl J Med 326:1250, 1992.

60. Kvinesdal B, Molin J, Froland A, et al: Imipramine treatment of painful diabetic neuropathy. JAMA 251:1727, 1984.

61. Max MB, Culnane M, Schafer SC, et al: Amitriptyline relieves diabetic neuropathy pain in patients with normal or depressed mood. Neurology 37:589, 1987.

62. Ansari A: The efficacy of newer antidepressants in the treatment of chronic pain: A review of current literature. Harv Rev Psychiatry 7:257, 2000.

63. Semenchuk MR, Sherman S, Davis B: Double-blind, randomized trial of bupropion SR for the treatment of neuropathic pain. Neurology 13:1583, 2001.

64. Mattia C, Paoletti F, Coluzzi F, et al: New antidepressants in the treatment of neuropathic pain. A review. Minerva Anestesiol 68:105, 2002.

65. Goldstein D, Iyengar S, Mallinckrodt C, et al: Duloxetine: A potential new treatment for depressed patients with comorbid pain. Pain Med 3:177, 2002.

66. Mattia C, Coluzzi F: Antidepressants in chronic neuropathic pain. Mini Rev Med Chem 3:773, 2003.

67. Mochizucki D: Serotonin and noradrenaline reuptake inhibitors in animal models of pain. Hum Psychopharmacol 19:S15, 2004.

68. Schreiber S, Rigai T, Katz Y, et al: The antinociceptive effect of mirtazapine in mice is mediated through serotonergic, noradrenergic and opioid mechanisms. Brain Res Bull 58:601, 2002.

69. Delgado PL: Common pathways of depression and pain. J Clin Psychiatry 65(Suppl 12):16, 2004.

70. Caraceni A, Portenoy AC: Pain. In Griggs RC, Joynt RJ (eds): Clinical Neurology, 2004 ed (CD-ROM). New York, Lippincott Williams & Wilkins, 2004.

71. Hautkappe M, Roizen MF, Toledano A, et al: Review of the effectiveness of capsaicin for painful cutaneous disorders and neural dysfunction. Clin J Pain 14:97, 1998.

72. Fishbain DA, Cutler RB, Lewis J, et al: Do the second-generation "atypical neuroleptics" have analgesic properties? A structured evidence-based review. Pain Med 5:359, 2004.

73. Goldberg ME, Domsky R, Scaring D, et al: Multi-day low dose ketamine infusion for the treatment of complex regional pain syndrome. Pain Phys 8:175, 2005.

74. Correll GE, Maleki J, Gracely EJ, et al: Subanesthetic ketamine infusion therapy: A retrospective analysis of a novel therapeutic approach to complex regional pain syndrome. Pain Med 5:263, 2004.

75. Abram SE: Neural blockade for neuropathic pain. Clin J Pain 16:S56, 2000.

76. Boas RA: Sympathetic nerve blocks: In search of a role. Reg Anesth Pain Med 23:292, 1998.

77. Hassenbusch SJ, Stanton-Hicks M, Covington EC: Spinal cord stimulation versus spinal infusion for low back and leg pain. Acta Neurochir Suppl 64:109, 1995.

78. Singh G, Willen SN, Boswell MV, et al: The value of interdisciplinary pain management in complex regional pain syndrome type I: A prospective outcome study. Pain Physician 7:203, 2004.

79. Rosman SM, Hainline B: Complementary and alternative medicine. In Hainline B, Devinsky O (eds): Neurological Complications of Pregnancy, 2nd ed. Philadelphia, Lippincott Williams & Wilkins, 2002, p 307.

80. Dallman MF, Pecoraro N: Chronic stress and obesity: A new view of "comfort food." Proc Natl Acad Sci U S A 100:11696, 2003.

81. Hasson D, Arnetz B: A randomized clinical trial of the treatment effects of massage compared to relaxation tape recordings on diffuse long-term pain. Psychother Psychosom 73:17, 2004.

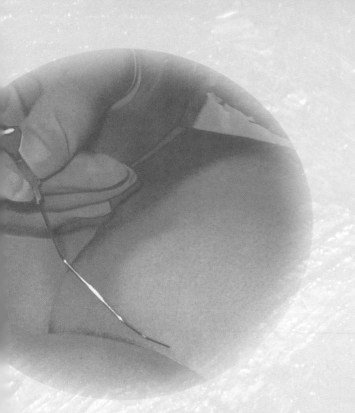

Generalized Pain Syndromes Encountered in Clinical Practice

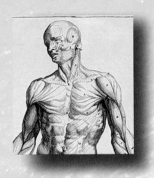

Part A

ACUTE PAIN SYNDROMES

chapter

20

Management of Acute and Postoperative Pain

Steven D. Waldman

Pain is the most common medical complaint among civilized populations. The National Pain Survey[1] estimated that more than 75 million Americans have pain that is severe enough to require medical care. In this survey, of individuals complaining of pain severe enough to seek medical attention, 25 million had acute pain as a result of surgery or trauma, with other causes of acute pain further increasing this number. Societal costs of pain in terms of medical bills, reduced productivity, and absenteeism are staggering. Although much of the medical and lay literature focuses on chronic pain, acute pain is also a major problem. About 8% of the U.S. population experience acute or postoperative pain each year; this figure is relatively constant throughout the industrialized nations of the world.

Despite the high prevalence worldwide, acute and postoperative pain is poorly managed, as studies have repeatedly shown.[2,3] The following factors are noted in discussions of the reasons for inadequate pain management:

- Appropriate adjuvant drugs, such as simple analgesics and nonsteroidal antiinflammatory drugs (NSAIDs), are often overlooked.
- Patients receive significantly fewer narcotics than are ordered by their physician.
- Nursing staff and physicians are overly concerned about drug addiction.
- Selection of analgesics is often irrational and confined to a limited number of the available options.
- Physicians' knowledge of the nature and properties of the analgesics selected is often inadequate.

Physicians can do many things to help minimize and alleviate needless suffering from acute or postoperative pain.[2] This chapter provides an overview of strategies that are useful in managing acute pain syndromes commonly encountered in clinical practice. Each approach has advantages and disadvantages. Armed with an understanding of the individual patient's needs, physicians can provide optimal pain relief that results in a high degree of patient satisfaction.

■ PROPHYLACTIC MEASURES USEFUL IN MANAGEMENT OF ACUTE AND POSTOPERATIVE PAIN

Explaining the cause and the expected course of acute or postoperative pain in detail can do much to alleviate patients' stress and anxiety. In addition, the use of relaxation techniques (e.g., breathing and body maneuvers) may help relieve pain. Intraoperatively, subsequent postoperative pain can be decreased by gentle intubation, careful positioning and transfer of the patient, adequate muscle relaxation, and minimization of surgical trauma.

■ PHARMACOLOGIC MEASURES

Nonsteroidal Antiinflammatory Drugs

NSAIDs are a chemically heterogeneous class of drugs that can reduce fever, pain, and inflammation without producing chemical dependence.[4] Regardless of their diverse structures, all NSAIDs decrease inflammation by their inhibitory effect on prostaglandin synthesis (Fig. 20–1).[5] NSAIDs also inhibit platelet function, decrease white blood cell chemotaxis, and impede production of the by-products of inflammation and the chemical messengers of pain. All of these actions may explain in part the efficacy of this class of drugs in the management of many of the acute pain syndromes frequently seen in clinical practice.

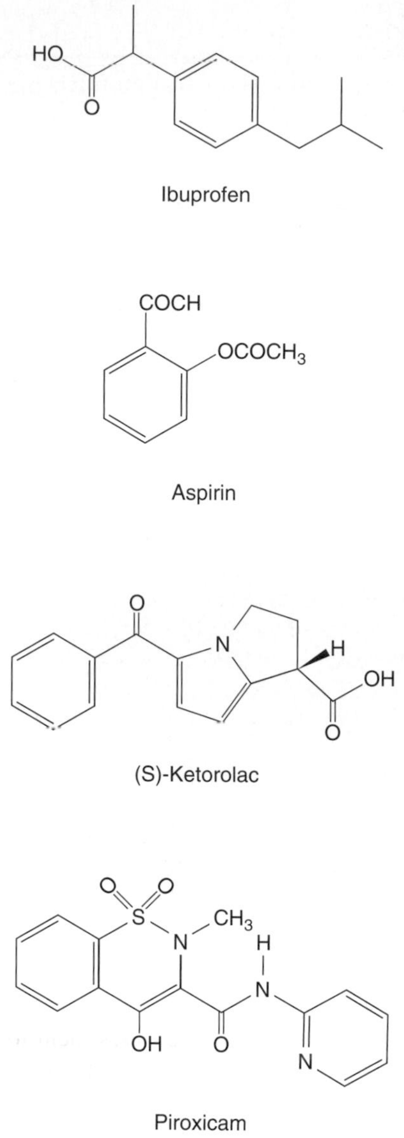

Selection of Nonsteroidal Antiinflammatory Drugs

There are many NSAIDs available. Busy clinicians need not be familiar with each drug, but they should have a working knowledge of one or two agents in each of the pharmacologic groups, as follows:

- Proprionic acid derivatives—ibuprofen and naproxen
- Salicylates—aspirin and choline salicylate
- Anthranilic acid derivatives—indomethacin and ketorolac
- Oxicams—piroxicam
- Cyclooxygenase-2 inhibitors—celecoxib

For each drug, physicians should be aware of the need for a loading dose, time from onset of activity to peak effect, routes of administration, cost, and side effect profile. Also, efficacy may be enhanced by choosing a drug that can be given by a nonoral route (e.g., rectal administration of indomethacin, intramuscular administration of ketorolac tromethamine). By capitalizing on the unique properties of each drug, physicians can tailor a treatment plan to meet each individual patient's needs. Table 20–1 lists practical suggestions for choosing an NSAID.

Because of the great variation in dosage ranges and frequency of administration of NSAIDs, physicians should review carefully the properties of the agent chosen. In general, dosing should be started at the low end of the recommended range and titrated upward as therapeutic response and side

Ibuprofen

Aspirin

(S)-Ketorolac

Piroxicam

FIGURE 20–1 ■ The heterogeneous structures of some common NSAIDs.

Table 20–1

Guidelines for Choosing a Nonsteroidal Antiinflammatory Drug

Assess patient's renal status before starting drug treatment

Determine best route of administration

Identify drugs that are appropriate for route of administration desired

Select familiar agent among the drugs whose time between onset of activity and peak effect is appropriate for pain syndrome being treated

effects dictate. A loading dose should be used if indicated, especially for abortive treatment of headache. Under no circumstances should the recommended ceiling dose be exceeded. Table 20–2 lists practical suggestions for administering NSAIDs.

Table 20–2

Guidelines for Administering Nonsteroidal Antiinflammatory Drugs

Review properties of agent selected
Start at low end of dosing range
Use loading dose when appropriate
Do not exceed ceiling dose
Ensure that equianalgesic doses are given if route of administration is changed

Side Effects of Nonsteroidal Antiinflammatory Drugs

Considering their diversity in chemical structure, NSAIDs are extremely well tolerated. In addition, compared with all of the other drugs currently used to treat acute pain, NSAIDs have among the most favorable risk-to-benefit ratios.[6] As with all medications, NSAIDs can cause side effects, however, ranging from minor annoyances (e.g., dyspepsia, diarrhea, constipation) to life-threatening conditions (e.g., gastrointestinal hemorrhage, hepatic dysfunction, renal insufficiency).[7] Consequently, physicians need to anticipate the potential for side effects and choose and use NSAIDs appropriately.

NSAIDs can cause a decline in renal functions in high-risk patients, such as patients with hypertensive or diabetic nephropathy, or with overuse or misuse. Because identifying patients with borderline renal function purely on clinical grounds is often impossible, the clinician faced with a patient who has acute or postoperative pain should strongly consider obtaining a baseline measurement of the serum creatinine level before beginning NSAID therapy. This measurement alerts physicians to preexisting renal problems that may be exacerbated by NSAID use and enables them to attribute to the drug any changes in renal function that occur during therapy in patients who had normal function at baseline.[8]

NSAIDs generally should be taken with food to minimize gastrointestinal side effects. A past history of dyspepsia and gastrointestinal upset may indicate the need for the concurrent use of gastric cytoprotective agents. A past history of gastric ulceration or hemorrhage requires that NSAIDs be used only after medications that are free of gastrointestinal side effects have failed to control the pain adequately. In this event, histamine blocking and cytoprotective agents should be given concurrently with NSAIDs, and patients should be monitored carefully for occult gastrointestinal blood loss. NSAID therapy should be discontinued at the first sign of gastrointestinal difficulties.

The concurrent use of two or more NSAIDs increases the risk of side effects, as may the concurrent use of an NSAID and a simple analgesic (e.g., acetaminophen). Patients with acute pain must be questioned carefully about their use of over-the-counter agents because patients may fail to mention such use during the initial pain evaluation.

Narcotic Analgesics

Effective use of narcotics for acute pain requires a working knowledge of their potency, narcotic class, side effects or toxicity, and duration of effect and the principles of dosing.

Regardless of the route of administration, failure to take these factors into account can result in suboptimal pain relief.

Potency

"Weak" narcotics are those typically administered orally to patients with mild to moderate pain. These include preparations containing codeine, propoxyphene, oxycodone hydrochloride, meperidine hydrochloride, pentazocine hydrochloride, or hydrocodone bitartrate. None of these drugs has a ceiling dose, but at high doses, their use may be limited by side effects or toxicity (e.g., seizures from meperidine or propoxyphene, psychotomimetic effects from pentazocine, gastrointestinal intolerance from codeine).[9] "Strong" narcotics include morphine sulfate, methadone hydrochloride, levorphanol tartrate, hydromorphone hydrochloride, and fentanyl citrate. These drugs also seem to have no ceiling dose in terms of analgesia, but side effects (e.g., respiratory and central nervous system depression) may limit upward titration of doses to obtain pain relief.

Class

Narcotics can be divided into pure agonists (i.e., morphine, hydromorphone, methadone, levorphanol, meperidine, codeine, propoxyphene, fentanyl, hydrocodone, and oxycodone) and agonist-antagonists (i.e., pentazocine, nalbuphine hydrochloride, butorphanol tartrate, buprenorphine hydrochloride, and dezocine) (Fig. 20–2).[10] The agonist-antagonist class is characterized by a balance of agonism and competitive antagonism at one or more of the opiate receptors.[9,11] All agonist-antagonist agents have a ceiling effect above which respiratory depression occurs and analgesic effect reaches its capacity. These agents have the potential to reverse such agonist effects as analgesia and a lesser propensity than pure narcotic agonists to produce physical dependence. Administering an agonist-antagonist agent to a patient who is physically dependent on an agonist agent may cause an acute narcotic abstinence syndrome, which may be confused with uncontrolled pain. Agonist-antagonists, particularly pentazocine, also have prominent psychotomimetic effects.[9,11] The lack of an oral form of most of these agents may limit their clinical utility in the acute pain setting; however, dezocine may have a special place in the management of postoperative pain and warrants further evaluation.[10]

Toxicity

Because meperidine is commonly used, special mention should be made of its potential toxicity when taken long-term or in high doses, as may occur with patient-controlled analgesia. Meperidine is metabolized to normeperidine.[11] This compound has a half-life about four times that of the parent drug, and its accumulation in plasma may result in signs of central nervous system excitation (e.g., myoclonus, tremor, seizures). The risk of toxicity precludes the long-term or high-dose use of meperidine in the management of acute or postoperative pain.

Duration of Effect and Dosing

These factors are an important consideration in narcotic selection. Narcotics with a short half-life (e.g., hydrocodone, oxycodone, morphine, hydromorphone) must be administered at least every 4 hours, whereas methadone, the narcotic with the longest half-life, usually can be given every 6 hours.[9,11] If

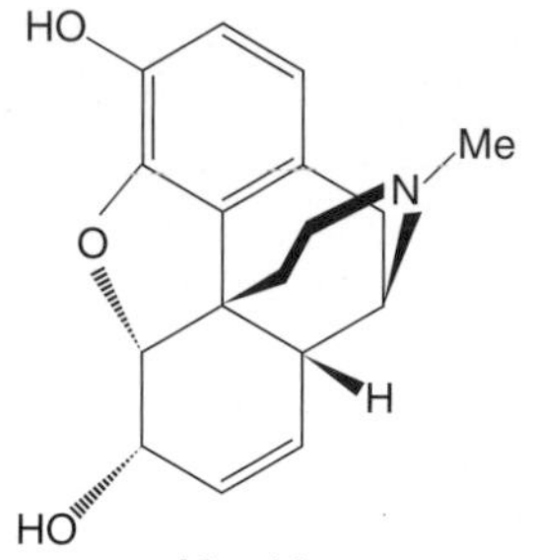

FIGURE 20–2 ■ Some common narcotic agonists.

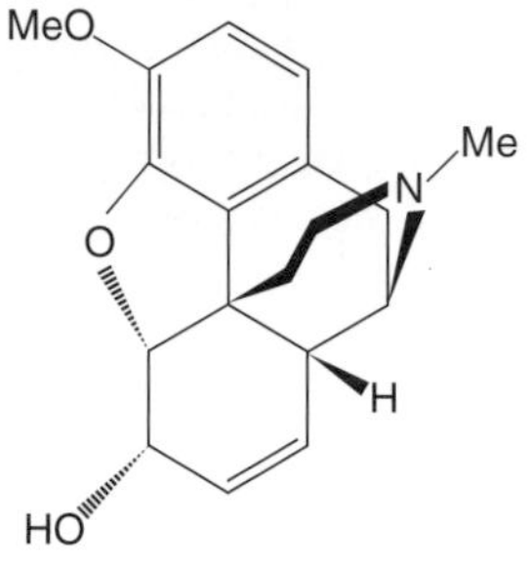

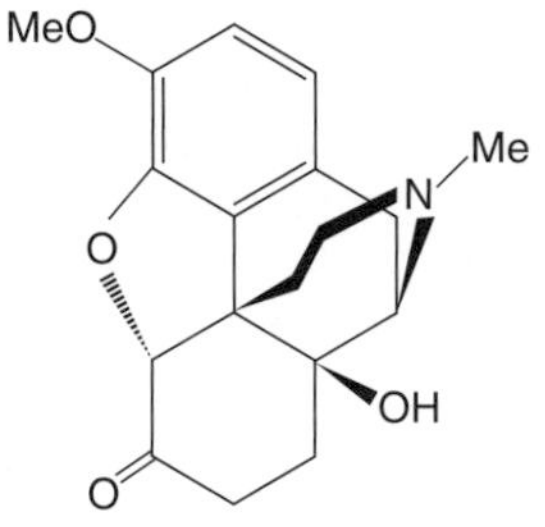

around-the-clock dosing in a frequency appropriate to the chosen narcotic is not provided, periods of inadequate pain control result.

In patients with moderate pain that is not relieved by simple analgesics and NSAIDs, a reasonable next step is the addition of a weak narcotic analgesic (e.g., 30 to 60 mg of codeine or 5 mg of oxycodone plus 325 mg of acetaminophen, aspirin, or another NSAID). The dose of the narcotic can be increased until side effects or toxicity precludes further increases. If a weak narcotic does not provide adequate pain relief, therapy with a strong narcotic alone or in combination with simple analgesics or NSAIDs is indicated. Morphine elixir, 5 to 10 mg every 4 hours, is a reasonable choice. In elderly patients and patients with compromised hepatic or renal function, the starting dose should be low to avoid side effects.

If pain remains severe after the initial dose of a strong narcotic, the dose can be doubled. If partial analgesia occurs, daily dose titration is usually appropriate. An effective approach involves the concurrent use of a fixed around-the-clock dose, usually every 4 hours, together with a "rescue

dose," which is usually equal to 5% to 10% of the total daily dose and is administered every 1 to 2 hours as needed for "breakthrough" pain. This approach provides patients with some control over analgesic dosing and can be used to estimate the amount of narcotic patients require.

Route of Administration of Narcotic Analgesics

Oral administration of narcotics is preferred whenever patients with acute pain can tolerate it. Other routes are available, however, and each has specific advantages and disadvantages.

Intramuscular Administration

In patients who are unable to take medication orally, narcotics can be administered intramuscularly.[12] Disadvantages of this route include pain on administration, variable and sometimes slow onset of effect, and peaks and valleys of analgesic effect.[12]

Intravenous Bolus

Delivery of narcotics by intravenous bolus has the advantages of a rapid onset of effect and a high level of efficacy in terms of pain relief.[9,11,12] Compared with the use of pumps and patient-controlled analgesia devices, this method of drug administration is relatively inexpensive. Disadvantages include more pronounced peaks and valleys of analgesic effect and side effects and a relatively short duration of analgesic.[12]

Continuous Infusion

Continuous infusion of narcotics achieves a high level of pain relief when the minimal effective analgesic concentration has been reached.[11,12] Peaks and valleys of effect are decreased with this route of administration, which results in fewer side effects than are seen with intravenous bolus or intramuscular administration of narcotics. Generally, the level of patient satisfaction is high.

One disadvantage of continuous infusions of narcotics is the significant delay in onset of analgesic activity if a bolus dose is not given with the infusion. Another is that the cost, in terms of infusions and the labor required during setup and monitoring, is considerable. Also, the nursing staff may express some resistance to this method because of a perceived possibility of an increased risk of respiratory depression and other side effects.[13]

Patient-Controlled Analgesia

Many of the objections to continuous infusion of narcotics have been overcome with the advent of patient-controlled analgesia devices. Instead of medical personnel determining an appropriate infusion regimen and administering it, the patient is given an element of control.[14] The drug administration rate is titrated against the desired end point—analgesia.

Advantages of patient-controlled analgesia include a high level of efficacy after the minimal effective analgesic concentration has been reached, lower rates of side effects than are seen with other methods, and high patient satisfaction.[12] These advantages have led to the rapid acceptance of patient-controlled analgesia in the treatment of acute and postoperative pain. Labor and cost savings also are positive factors. Disadvantages include the cost of the device and the drugs used with it, the significant delay in implementation in some institutions that do not use this method routinely, the need for special pumps and supplies that may not be readily available, and significant nursing staff resistance at some institutions.[13]

■ NEURAL BLOCKADE IN THE MANAGEMENT OF ACUTE AND POSTOPERATIVE PAIN

Neural blockade with a local anesthetic may be used to identify specific pain pathways and to aid in diagnosing the origin and site of the pain. Therapeutic neural blockade with a local anesthetic plus a corticosteroid, a narcotic, or, rarely, a neurolytic agent can be useful in relieving a variety of acute pain syndromes. Neural blockade should not be viewed as stand-alone therapy for most acute pain syndromes; rather, it should be intelligently integrated into a comprehensive treatment plan.[15]

Sympathetic Neural Blockade

Sphenopalatine Ganglion

Anatomy

Located in the pterygopalatine fossa, posterior to the middle turbinate, the sphenopalatine (i.e., pterygopalatine, nasal, or Meckel's) ganglion comprises the largest group of neurons in the head outside the brain. The ganglion, a triangular structure 5 mm in diameter, is covered by a layer of connective tissue and mucous membrane that is 1 to 5 mm thick. It gives rise to major branches of the trigeminal nerve, carotid plexus, facial nerve, and superior cervical ganglion.[16]

Indications

Blockade of the sphenopalatine ganglion with a local anesthetic is useful in the management of acute migraine, acute cluster headache, and a variety of facial neuralgias. It also may relieve status migrainosus and chronic cluster headache.[17-19]

Technique

Blockade of the sphenopalatine ganglion is accomplished by applying a local anesthetic to the mucous membrane overlying the ganglion.[16] With the patient in the supine position, the cervical spine is extended, and the anterior nares space is inspected for polyps, tumors, and foreign bodies. A small amount of 2% lidocaine viscous solution, 4% lidocaine hydrochloride topical solution, or 10% cocaine hydrochloride solution is instilled into each nostril. The patient is asked to inhale briskly through the nose. This inhalation draws the local anesthetic into the posterior nasal pharynx, serving the double function of lubricating the nasal mucosa and providing topical anesthesia to allow easier passage of a 35-inch cotton-tipped applicator into each nostril.

These applicators are saturated with a local anesthetic and advanced along the superior border of the middle turbinate until the tip contacts the mucosa overlying the ganglion (Fig. 20–3). Local anesthetic (1.2 mL) is placed alongside each applicator, which acts as a tampon, keeping the anesthetic in contact with the mucosa overlying the ganglion and allowing it to diffuse through the mucosa to the ganglion. The applicators are removed after 20 minutes. The patient's pulse rate, blood pressure, and respiration rate must be monitored for untoward effects secondary to blockade.

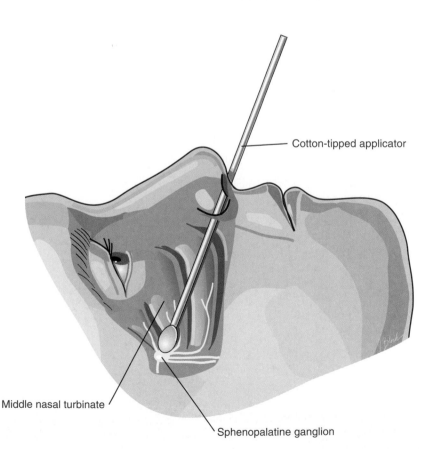

FIGURE 20–3 ■ Injection technique for sphenopalatine ganglion block. (From Waldman SD: Sphenopalatine ganglion Block. In: Atlas of Interventional Pain Management, 2nd ed. Philadelphia, WB Saunders, 2004, p 12.)

Cotton-tipped applicator

Middle nasal turbinate

Sphenopalatine ganglion

Practical Considerations

Clinical experience has shown that sphenopalatine ganglion blockade can be useful in aborting acute attacks of migraine or cluster headache.[16-20] Because of its simplicity, sphenopalatine ganglion blockade lends itself to use at the bedside, in the emergency department, and in the headache or pain clinic. For patients with acute headache, this procedure can be combined with oxygen inhalation through the mouth (by mask) while the applicators are in place.[18,19] It may be used on a once-daily basis for chronic headache and facial pain, with the end point being total pain relief. My clinical experience indicates that five successive treatments usually bring pain relief.

Complications

Epistaxis is the major complication of blockade of the sphenopalatine ganglion, and it occurs more often during winter months, when forced-air heating may cause drying of the nasal mucosa. Given the highly vascular nature of the nasal mucosa, attention must be paid to the total dose of local anesthetic used if toxic effects are to be avoided.[16] Occasionally, patients experience significant orthostatic hypotension after the procedure. For this reason, they should be moved to a sitting position after the procedure, monitored carefully, and allowed to walk only with assistance.

Stellate Ganglion Block

Anatomy

Located between the anterior lateral surface of the seventh cervical vertebral body and the neck of the first rib, the stellate ganglion lies central to the vertebral artery and the transverse process. It is separated from the transverse process by the longus colli muscle and is medial to the common carotid artery and jugular vein and lateral to the trachea and esophagus.[21]

Indications

Blockade of the stellate ganglion is used to treat acute vascular insufficiency of the upper extremities, frostbite of the face and upper extremities, and acute herpes zoster.[21-23] Other indications are early treatment of reflex sympathetic dystrophy of the face, neck, upper extremities, and upper thorax and sympathetically mediated pain caused by malignant disease. It also may provide short-term palliation of some atypical vascular headaches.

Technique

The medial edge of the sternocleidomastoid muscle is identified at the level of the cricothyroid notch (C6), and the muscle is displaced laterally with two fingers. Pulsations of the carotid artery should be identified. The skin medial to the carotid pulsation is prepared with alcohol, and a 1½-inch 22-gauge needle is advanced until contact is made with the transverse process of C6 (Fig. 20–4). The needle is withdrawn about 2 mm, careful aspiration is performed, and 7 mL of 0.5% preservative-free bupivacaine hydrochloride is injected. Pulse rate, blood pressure, and respiration rate should be carefully monitored.

Practical Considerations

Daily stellate ganglion blockade with a local anesthetic is beneficial for the previously mentioned pain syndromes. To avoid undue anxiety, the unique side effect of Horner's syndrome should be explained to patients before the block is administered. The local anesthetic should never be injected if the

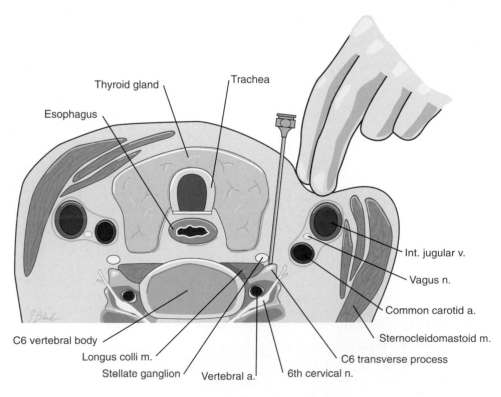

Thyroid gland
Trachea
Esophagus
Int. jugular v.
Vagus n.
Common carotid a.
Sternocleidomastoid m.
C6 vertebral body
Longus colli m.
Stellate ganglion
Vertebral a.
6th cervical n.
C6 transverse process

FIGURE 20–4 ■ Injection technique for stellate ganglion block. (From Waldman SD: Stellate ganglion block. In: Atlas of Interventional Pain Management, 2nd ed. Philadelphia, WB Saunders, 2004, p 101.)

transverse process of C6 cannot be identified with the needle because doing so leads to an unacceptably high rate of potentially life-threatening complications.

Complications

Hematoma, hoarseness caused by blockade of the laryngeal nerves, difficulty swallowing, and pneumothorax can occur.[21] Because of the proximity of the great vessels of the neck, intravascular injection—with almost immediate toxic effects from the anesthetic—is a distinct possibility unless aspiration and needle placement are carefully carried out. Epidural and subarachnoid anesthesia can occur if the needle is allowed to pass between the transverse process of C5 and C6 and impinge on the cervical root.

Celiac Plexus Block

Anatomy

Situated in the prevertebral area at the level of the T12-L1 vertebral body, the celiac plexus is composed of the right and left celiac, superior mesenteric, and aorticorenal ganglia and the dense network of connecting sympathetic nerve fibers (Fig. 20–5).[24]

Indications

Blockade of the celiac plexus with a local anesthetic is indicated to determine whether flank, retroperitoneal, or upper abdominal pain is sympathetically mediated via the celiac plexus.[24,25] Daily blockade with a local anesthetic palliates

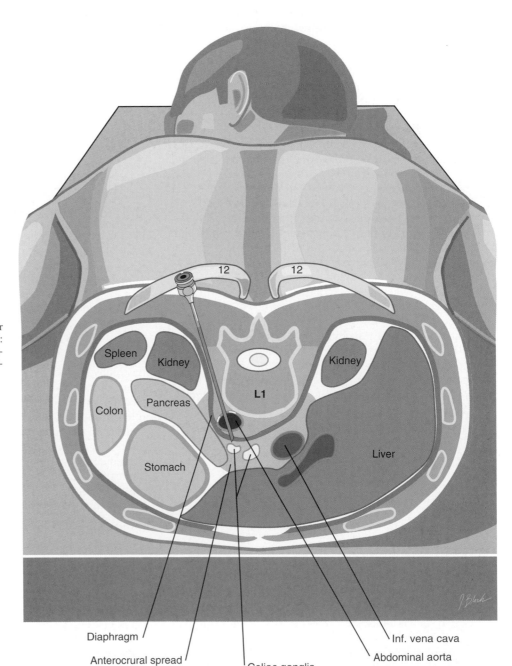

FIGURE 20–5 ■ Injection technique for celiac plexus block. (From Waldman SD: Celiac plexus block. In: Atlas of Interventional Pain Management, 2nd ed. Philadelphia, WB Saunders, 2004, p 286.)

pain secondary to acute pancreatitis.[26] According to clinical reports, celiac plexus blockade with a local anesthetic and/or corticosteroid or both carried out early in the course of acute pancreatitis may reduce markedly the associated morbidity and mortality.

Technique

Diagnostic blockade of the celiac plexus with a local anesthetic may be performed without radiographic guidance. Many pain management specialists believe, however, that neurolytic blockade can be performed most safely under the guidance of CT or fluoroscopy if CT is unavailable. Radiographic guidance should improve not only the safety, but also the efficacy of the following technique.

The patient is well hydrated with intravenous fluids and placed prone on the CT table. A scout film is obtained to identify the T12-L1 interspace. A CT scan is taken through this area and reviewed for the position of the aorta relative to the vertebral body; the position of the intra-abdominal and retroperitoneal organs; and distortion of normal anatomy caused by tumor, previous surgery, or adenopathy.

The level at which the scan was taken is marked with gentian violet on the patient's skin, which is prepared with antiseptic solution. At about 10 cm left of the midline, the skin and subcutaneous tissue are anesthetized with 1% lidocaine using a 1½-inch 22-gauge needle. A 13-cm 22-gauge styleted Hinck needle is inserted through the anesthetized area and advanced until the posterior wall of the aorta is encountered. The needle is advanced into the aorta, and the stylet is removed. Free flow of arterial blood should be present. After a well-lubricated 5-mL glass syringe filled with preservative-free saline solution is attached to the Hinck needle, the needle is advanced through the anterior wall of the aorta using the loss-of-resistance technique (see Fig. 20–5).[27] The glass syringe is removed, and a small amount of 0.5% lidocaine in solution with water-soluble contrast medium is injected through the needle. Another CT scan is taken at the same level. The scan is reviewed for needle placement and, most important, for contrast medium spread. Contrast medium should be seen in the area surrounding the aorta, but not in the retrocrural area. When satisfactory needle placement and spread of contrast medium have been confirmed, 12 to 15 mL of absolute alcohol or 6% aqueous phenol is injected through the needle. The needle is flushed with a small amount of saline solution and removed. The patient should be monitored carefully for hemodynamic changes, including hypotension and tachycardia, secondary to the profound sympathetic blockade induced.

Practical Considerations

CT-guided celiac plexus neurolysis using the loss-of-resistance technique has been shown to be safe and efficacious in the treatment of the pain syndromes mentioned.[25] This procedure may be performed with patients in the lateral position if they are unable to lie prone because of such factors as intractable abdominal pain or the presence of colostomy or ileostomy appliances.

Celiac plexus blockade avoids spread of the neurolytic substance onto the lumbar plexus. Posterior retrocrural spread of the local anesthetic and contrast medium, which are injected before the neurolytic substance, alerts the physician to the possibility of this complication and provides the opportunity to reposition the needle.

Complications

The most feared complications of celiac plexus blockade arise from inadvertent injection of neurolytic substance onto the lumbar plexus or from epidural, subarachnoid, or intravascular injection. Inappropriate needle placement can result in damage to the kidneys.[24] If the needle is placed too far anteriorly, injection into the pancreas, peritoneal cavity, or liver can occur. As mentioned, the incidence of these complications can be reduced markedly by CT guidance.

When properly performed, this technique results in profound sympathetic neural blockade. In cancer patients with compromised cardiac reserve, resultant hypotension can be life-threatening. Patients should be well hydrated before the procedure, and blood pressure should be monitored closely after the procedure. Because orthostatic hypotension may persist for several days, patients should be cautioned not to stand up without assistance until compensation has occurred.

Lumbar Sympathetic Ganglion

Anatomy

The lumbar sympathetic nerve lies along the anterolateral surface of the lumbar vertebral bodies and anteromedial to the psoas muscle. The anterior vena cava lies just anterior to the right sympathetic chain, and the aorta lies anterior and slightly medial to the right sympathetic chain (Fig. 20–6).[28] Sympathetic innervation of the lower extremities arises from preganglionic fibers originating from the cell bodies located in the T10-L2 level of the spinal cord. Nearly all postganglionic fibers leading to the lower extremities leave the sympathetic chain interval below L2. Anterior to the chain are the visceral peritoneum and the great vessels.

Indications

Blockade of the lumbar sympathetic nerve with a local anesthetic is indicated to determine if lower extremity pain is sympathetically mediated via this chain and to detect sympathetic dystrophy of the lower extremity. The lumbar sympathetic chain may be blocked with a local anesthetic to ascertain whether blood flow to the lower extremities and greater pain relief would be achieved by destroying the chain with a neurolytic substance (e.g., phenol, alcohol, radiofrequency lesioning) or surgically excising a portion of the chain. This procedure is used therapeutically for acute peripheral vascular insufficiency, ischemia secondary to frostbite, acute herpes zoster of the lower extremities, and a variety of peripheral neuropathic pains of the lower extremities.[29]

Technique

The technique used for lumbar sympathetic blockade and neurolysis is similar to that for celiac plexus neurolysis. The patient is placed in the prone position on the CT table with a pillow under the abdomen to allow flexion of the thoracolumbar spine and opening of the space between adjacent transverse processes. A scout film is taken to identify the L2 vertebral body. The skin overlying the transverse process of L2 is marked with gentian violet and prepared with povidone-iodine. The skin and subcutaneous tissue are anesthetized

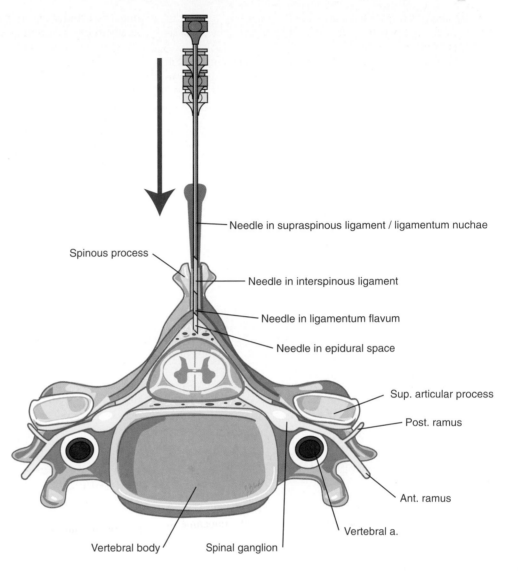

Needle in supraspinous ligament / ligamentum nuchae

Spinous process

Needle in interspinous ligament

Needle in ligamentum flavum

Needle in epidural space

Sup. articular process

Post. ramus

Ant. ramus

Vertebral a.

Vertebral body

Spinal ganglion

FIGURE 20–6 ■ Anatomy of the lumbar epidural space. (From Waldman SD: Lumbar sympathetic block. In: Atlas of Interventional Pain Management, 2nd ed. Philadelphia, WB Saunders, 2004, p 342.)

with 1% lidocaine using a 1½-inch 22-gauge needle. A 13-cm 22-gauge styleted needle is advanced through the anesthetized area until the tip rests against the vertebral body. The needle is redirected in a trajectory to pass just lateral to the vertebral body. A well-lubricated glass syringe filled with preservative-free saline solution is attached, and the loss-of-resistance technique is used to advance the needle through the body of the psoas muscle. As soon as the needle tip passes through the fascia of the muscle, a loss of resistance is felt, indicating that the needle is adjacent to the sympathetic chain (see Fig. 20–6). A small amount of local anesthetic and water-soluble contrast medium is injected to ensure appropriate spread of the contrast material in the prevertebral region, and 12 mL of 0.5% preservative-free lidocaine or absolute alcohol is injected through the needle. The needle is flushed with preservative-free saline solution and removed. The patient should be observed carefully for hypotension and tachycardia secondary to sympathetic blockade.

Practical Considerations

CT guidance during lumbar sympathetic neurolysis can decrease markedly the risk of complications. Patients should

be told that some backache is likely because of trauma to the muscles of posture by the needle. They also should be advised that after lumbar sympathetic blockade, the affected lower extremity may feel hot and be swollen as compared with the unaffected extremity. This side effect is normal and resolves with time.

Complications

Complications of lumbar sympathetic blockade are similar to those of celiac plexus neurolysis. Because the needle tip is more medial in its trajectory, damage to lumbar nerve roots at their exit from the spinal column is possible.[28]

Somatic Neural Blockade

Similar to sympathetic neural blockade, somatic neural blockade should be only one part of a comprehensive diagnostic and treatment plan for patients who have pain syndromes. The failure to use rational pharmacologic therapy as a first step or in conjunction with somatic neural blockade results in less than optimal results for patients with acute and postoperative pain.

Epidural Nerve Block

Anatomy

The epidural space extends from the foramen magnum, where the periosteal and spinal layers of dura fuse with the sacro-coccygeal membrane (Figs. 20–7 and 20–8). Its anterior portion is bounded by the posterior longitudinal ligament, which covers the posterior aspect of the vertebral body and the intravertebral disk. The epidural space is posteriorly bounded by the anterior lateral surface of the vertebral lamina and the ligamentum flavum and laterally bounded by the pedicles of the vertebra and the intravertebral foramen. From a technical viewpoint, the ligamentum flavum is the key landmark for identification of the epidural space. It is composed of dense fibroelastic tissue and is thinnest in the cervical region. In men, the epidural space is narrowest in the cervical region (anteroposterior diameter 2 to 3 mm when the neck is flexed).

Indications

Epidural nerve blockade with a local anesthetic or corticosteroid or both can be used to diagnose and treat a variety of acute pain syndromes. It relieves pain secondary to acute cervical, thoracic, and lumbar strain and radiculopathy; tension-type headache; bilateral sympathetically mediated pain (e.g., reflex sympathetic dystrophy); pain caused by peripheral vascular insufficiency; and ischemic pain secondary to frost-bite.[30-32] In addition, this procedure is valuable in the management of acute herpes zoster and postherpetic neuralgia of the extremities or trunk.[33]

Technique

Epidural nerve blockade is carried out most easily with the patient in the sitting position and the cervical spine flexed and the forehead resting on a padded bedside table. The arms should rest comfortably in the patient's lap or at his or her sides. After the skin overlying the appropriate intervertebral space is prepared with antiseptic solution, a sterile fenestrated drape is placed over the area.

The spinous process and intervertebral space are carefully palpated to identify the exact midline position. The skin and subcutaneous tissue at the midline are anesthetized with 1% preservative-free lidocaine or 0.25% preservative-free bupivacaine. An 18-gauge or 20-gauge Hustead or Tuohy needle is inserted into the anesthetized area in a midline, slightly cephalad trajectory. On removal of the stylet, a well-lubricated 5-mL glass syringe filled with preservative-free saline solution is attached to the epidural needle. With continuous pressure applied on the plunger of the syringe, the epidural needle is carefully advanced until the tip impinges on the dense ligamentum flavum. A sudden loss of resistance is felt as the tip of the needle passes through the ligamentum flavum into the epidural space; 0.5 mL of air is injected through the needle to confirm epidural placement (Fig. 20–9).

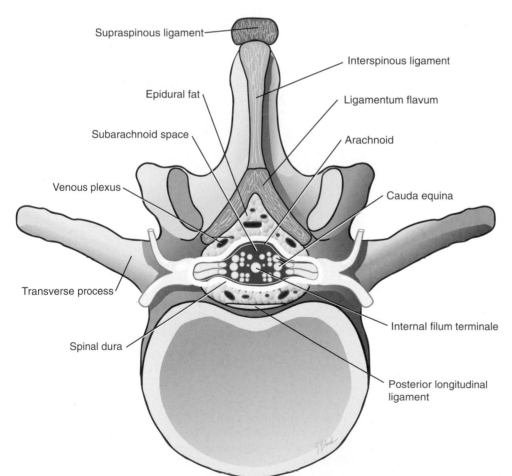

Supraspinous ligament

Interspinous ligament

Epidural fat

Ligamentum flavum

Subarachnoid space

Arachnoid

Venous plexus

Cauda equina

Transverse process

Internal filum terminale

Spinal dura

Posterior longitudinal ligament

FIGURE 20–7 ■ Injection technique for cervical epidural block. (From Waldman SD: Cervical epidural block. In: Atlas of Interventional Pain Management, 2nd ed. Philadelphia, WB Saunders, 2004, p 132.)

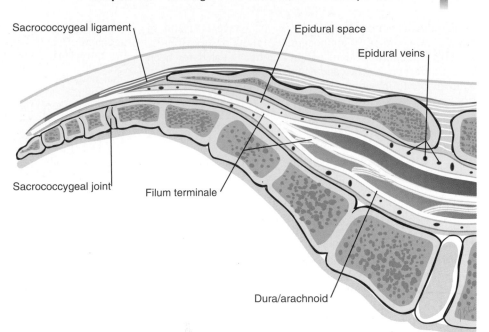

FIGURE 20–8 ■ Anatomy of the triangular sacrum. (From Waldman SD: Caudal epidural block. In: Atlas of Interventional Pain Management, 2nd ed. Philadelphia, WB Saunders, 2004, p 382.)

Sacrococcygeal ligament

Epidural space

Epidural veins

Sacrococcygeal joint

Filum terminale

Dura/arachnoid

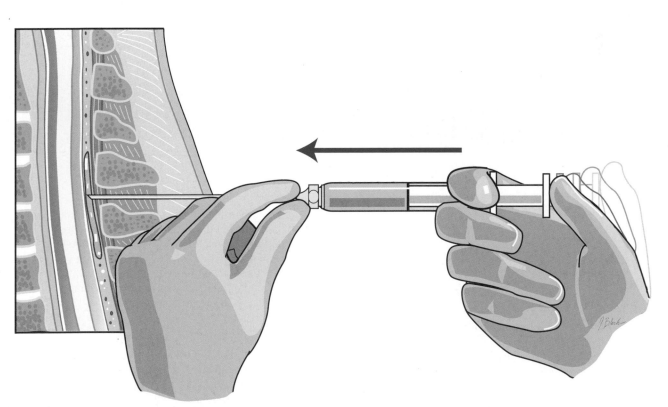

FIGURE 20–9 ■ Correct needle placement for epidural nerve block. (From Waldman SD: Cervical epidural block. In: Atlas of Interventional Pain Management, 2nd ed. Philadelphia, WB Saunders, 2004, p 134.)

After careful aspiration, 0.5% preservative-free lidocaine or 0.25% preservative-free bupivacaine combined with a depot corticosteroid preparation or preservative-free opioid, such as morphine or fentanyl, is injected, and the epidural needle is removed. A 4 × 4-inch gauze pad is placed over the injection site, and pressure is applied. The patient is returned to the supine position, and blood pressure, pulse rate, and respiration rate are monitored closely until recovery is complete.

Thoracic and lumbar epidural block can be performed in the sitting, lateral, or prone position using the loss-of-resistance technique described previously. Additionally, the caudal approach to the epidural space offers numerous theoretical advantages over the lumbar approach to the epidural space, including the markedly decreased incidence of postdural puncture headaches and the fact that caudal epidural block can be performed with a 25-gauge needle in the presence of anticoagulation. This latter advantage is useful in patients who are fully anticoagulated after lower extremity salvage procedures and in patients anticoagulated for deep venous thrombosis. The caudal approach to the epidural space is amenable to the administration of opioids by single injection or continuous infusion.

Practical Considerations

Epidural nerve blockade with a corticosteroid may be used early in the course of treatment of the pain syndromes described until other methods (e.g., use of antidepressants, physical therapy) become effective. Experience suggests that epidural neural blockade is most efficacious when it is performed in the following manner:

- The initial block is achieved with 80 mg of methylprednisolone and 7 mL of 0.25% preservative-free bupivacaine in the cervical region, 10 mL in the lower thoracic region, or 12 mL in the lumbar region or in the alternative 0.5 mg of preservative-free morphine in the cervical and upper thoracic region, 10 mg of preservative-free morphine in the lower thoracic and upper lumbar region, and 12 mg of preservative-free morphine via the caudal approach to the epidural space.
- Subsequent blocks are administered every other day with 40 mg of methylprednisolone being substituted for the initial 80-mg dose and the appropriate amount of preservative-free bupivacaine or morphine. Six blocks may be given in this manner, with the end point being complete pain relief.
- The amount of methylprednisolone should be decreased in patients who have diabetes or who have received systemic corticosteroid therapy.

Complications

Because epidural nerve blockade interrupts somatic and sympathetic nerve conduction, cardiovascular changes (e.g., hypotension, tachycardia) may occur and can produce devastating complications if they are not identified and treated promptly.[36] Respiratory compromise or failure may result from blockade of the phrenic nerve or respiratory centers of the brain stem. For this reason, epidural nerve blockade should be performed only by personnel trained in airway management and resuscitation. Appropriate monitoring of vital signs is imperative, and resuscitation equipment must be readily available.

Other major complications include damage to neural structures, epidural hematoma, and epidural abscess. These complications occur rarely, but can be life-threatening.[37] Minor untoward effects and complications of epidural nerve blockade include pain at the injection site, inadvertent dural puncture, and vasovagal syncope.

Trigeminal Nerve Block

Anatomy

The trigeminal nerve is the largest of the cranial nerves and contains sensory and motor fibers. It can be approached extraorally via the coronoid notch into the pterygopalatine fossa.[38] The fossa is a triangular space between the pterygoid process of the sphenoid bone and the maxilla of the upper part of the infratemporal fossa.

Indications

Trigeminal nerve blockade with a local anesthetic and corticosteroid is an excellent adjunct to drug treatment of trigeminal neuralgia.[38,39] This procedure affords rapid palliation of pain while doses of oral medications are being titrated to effective levels. It also may be valuable in alleviating atypical facial pain. Other indications include pain in maxillary neoplasms, cluster headache uncontrolled by sphenopalatine ganglion blockade, and acute herpes zoster in the area of the trigeminal nerve that is not controlled by stellate ganglion blockade.

Technique

Palpation of the coronoid notch is facilitated by opening and closing the patient's mouth. The notch should be encountered about 4 cm anterior to the acoustic auditory meatus. The skin is anesthetized with antiseptic solution, and a 1½-inch 22-gauge needle is directed through the middle of the coronoid notch. The tip of the needle may encounter the lateral lamina of the pterygoid process (Fig. 20–10). If blockade of the maxillary nerve is desired, the needle is withdrawn into the subcutaneous tissue, and the tip is redirected 1 cm more anterior and 1 cm more superior to the first bony contact. Paresthesias may be elicited in the area of the maxillary nerve. If blockade of the mandibular nerve is desired, the needle is withdrawn into the subcutaneous tissue, and the tip is redirected 1 cm more posterior and 1 cm more inferior to the first bony contact. Paresthesias may be elicited in the area of the mandibular nerve. After careful aspiration, 5 to 7 mL of 0.5% preservative-free bupivacaine with 80 mg of methylprednisolone is injected. Subsequent daily nerve blockade is carried out in a similar manner, with the dose of methylprednisolone lowered to 40 mg.

Practical Considerations

This procedure is an excellent emergency treatment of uncontrolled pain of trigeminal neuralgia. It can be used while doses of carbamazepine, baclofen, phenytoin sodium, or other medications are being titrated.[39] In patients with atypical facial pain secondary to temporomandibular joint dysfunction, trigeminal nerve blockade makes physical therapy and range-of-motion exercises of the joint possible.

Complications

The major complication of trigeminal nerve blockade is inadvertent vascular injection.[38] The pterygopalatine fossa is traversed by many arteries and veins. Careful and frequent aspiration should be carried out during injection of the local anesthetic. Needle damage to this vasculature can result in significant hematoma formation. Patients should be advised of the potential for this untoward effect and informed of its self-limiting nature so that they are not unduly alarmed if it occurs.

Intercostal Nerve Block

Anatomy

The thoracic spinal nerves give off the white and gray rami communicantes of the sympathetic system, which communicate with particular ganglia of the sympathetic chain. Distal

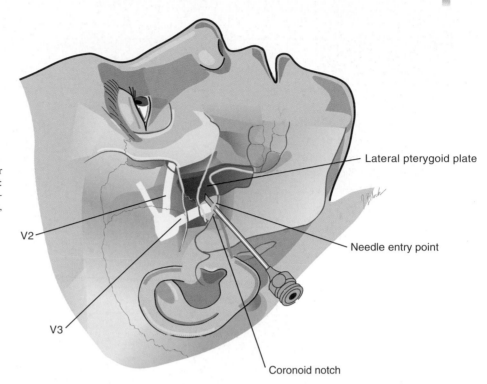

Lateral pterygoid plate

Needle entry point

V2

V3

Coronoid notch

FIGURE 20–10 ■ Injection technique for trigeminal nerve block. (From Waldman SD: Trigeminal nerve block. In: Atlas of Interventional Pain Management, 2nd ed. Philadelphia, WB Saunders, 2004, p 36.)

to the rami communicantes, the nerve trunk divides into the dorsal and ventral branches. The dorsal branch innervates the skin and muscles of the back and the periosteum of the vertebra. The ventral branch follows the rib via the costal sulcus, traveling into the dorsal thoracic region between the two laminae of the intercostal muscles and into the lateral and ventral portions of the thorax. This intercostal nerve travels in tandem with the intercostal artery and vein.[40]

Indications

Intercostal nerve blockade with a local anesthetic or corticosteroid or both can be performed at the bedside or in the outpatient setting. This procedure may palliate pain secondary to acute traumatic or pathologic rib fractures, chest wall metastasis, intercostal neuralgia, or thoracotomy and is useful for right upper quadrant pain secondary to hepatic metastasis.[41-43] Intercostal nerve blockade also may reduce pain caused by percutaneous drainage devices (e.g., chest or nephrostomy tubes). Clinically significant improvement in pulmonary function has been shown in patients treated with this procedure.

Technique

Intercostal nerve blockade can be performed with the patient in the sitting, lateral decubitus, or prone position. The rib in the anatomic region to be blocked is identified with palpation, and the skin in the posterior axillary line is prepared with antiseptic solution. A 1½-inch 22-gauge needle attached to a 5-mL syringe is advanced vertically until contact with the rib is made. The needle is withdrawn into the subcutaneous tissue and "walked off" the inferior margin of the rib (Fig. 20–11). Care must be taken not to advance the needle more than 0.5 cm. After careful aspiration, 3 to 5 mL of 0.5% or 0.75% preservative-free bupivacaine is injected, and the needle is

removed. This procedure may be repeated at each level subserving the pain.

Practical Considerations

Therapeutic intercostal nerve blockade is an excellent adjunct in the treatment of a variety of acute pain syndromes. Its simplicity allows its use in the emergency department or at the bedside, provided that appropriate resuscitation equipment and drugs are readily available. The highly vascular nature of the intercostal region mandates careful monitoring of the total amount of local anesthetic used. With the use of a long-acting protein-bound local anesthetic (e.g., 0.75% bupivacaine), intercostal nerve blockade can be performed daily to provide long-lasting relief from pain caused by trauma or surgical incision.

Complications

The major complication of intercostal nerve blockade is inadvertent and unrecognized pneumothorax. The incidence of this complication is about 0.5% to 1%.[41] If the patient is being maintained on positive-pressure ventilatory support, tension pneumothorax can occur. As mentioned, systemic toxic effects from vascular uptake of the local anesthetic may occur if dosing guidelines are not carefully observed.

Other Somatic Nerve Blocks

As can be seen from the discussion of some of the nerve blocks commonly used in the management of acute and postoperative pain, these techniques are a reasonable next step if pharmacologic modalities fail to control the patient's pain adequately. Many somatic nerve blocks are useful as anesthesia-sparing adjuncts to general anesthesia and as adjuncts to analgesia in the postoperative period. Table 20–3 provides an overview of other somatic nerve blocks that have utility in the management of acute and postoperative pain.

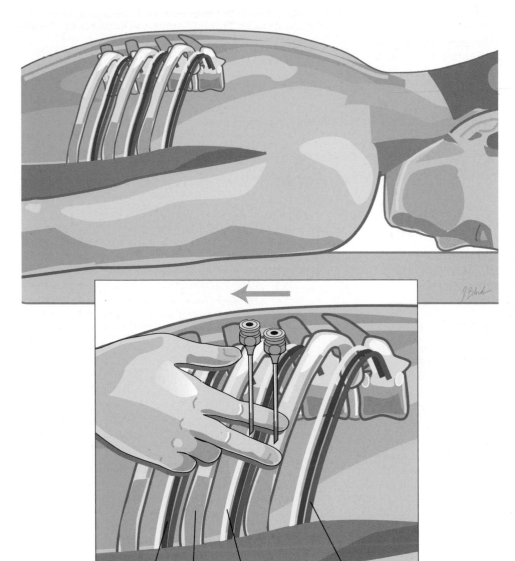

Intercostal a.

Rib

Intercostal n.

Intercostal v.

FIGURE 20–11 ■ Correct needle placement for intercostal nerve block. (From Waldman SD: Intercostal nerve block. In: Atlas of Interventional Pain Management, 2nd ed. Philadelphia, WB Saunders, 2004, p 243.)

Table 20–3

Useful Somatic Nerve Blocks in the Management of Acute and Postoperative Pain

Nerve Block	*Indication*
Occipital nerve block	Post-craniotomy pain
Auriculotemporal nerve block	Post-craniotomy pain
Glossopharyngeal nerve block	Glossopharyngeal neuralgia
Phrenic nerve block	Intractable hiccups
Cervical plexus block	Carotid artery and neck surgery
Cervical epidural block	Acute herpes zoster and upper extremity pain
Brachial plexus block	Shoulder and upper extremity surgery
Median, radial, and ulnar nerve blocks	Upper extremity and hand surgery
Intercostal nerve blocks	Fractured ribs, chest wall pain, metastatic lesions to chest wall, liver pain, postoperative pain
Thoracic epidural block	Vertebral compression fractures, postoperative pain
Ilioinguinal, iliohypogastric, and genitofemoral nerve block	Groin and pelvic pain
Obturator nerve block	Hip fracture pain
Femoral nerve block	Femoral fractures
Lumbar epidural block	Vertebral compression fractures, postoperative pain
Lumbar plexus and sciatic nerve block	Lower extremity pain
Ankle block	Foot and ankle pain

■ SUMMARY

Most pain is controllable. Patient education and careful intraoperative technique are useful prophylactic measures. Simple analgesics and NSAIDs reduce pain, fever, and inflammation and are well tolerated when dosing guidelines are followed carefully. In patients whose pain is not controlled with these measures, the addition of a weak narcotic analgesic is reasonable. If relief is still inadequate, a stronger narcotic alone or in combination with another analgesic may be needed. The advent of patient-controlled analgesia has diminished some of the objections to continuous intravenous infusion of narcotics. Various acute pain syndromes respond to blockade of the sympathetic or somatic neural pathways. Knowledge of the appropriate anatomic structures and careful technique are mandatory with this method. It should be considered only one part of a comprehensive treatment plan.

References

1. National Pain Survey. Conducted for Ortho-McNeil Pharmaceutical, 1999.
2. Bartel J, Beasley J, Berry PH, et al: Approaches to Pain Management. Oakbrook Terrace, IN, Joint Commission on the Accreditation of Healthcare Organizations, 2003.
3. Pain in America: A research report. Conducted for Merck by the Gallup Organization 2003.
4. Bruno GR, Carter WA: Nonsteroidal antiinflamatory agents. In Emergency Medicine: A Comprehensive Study Guide, 5th ed. New York, McGraw-Hill, 2000, pp 1132-1135.
5. Brooks PM, Day RO: Nonsteroidal antiinflammatory drugs—differences and similarities. N Engl J Med 324:1716, 1991.
6. Ellenhorn M: Nonsteroidal antiinflammatory drugs. In: Medical Toxicology, 2nd ed. Amsterdam, Elsevier Applied Science, 1997, p 196.
7. Amadio P Jr, Cummings DM, Amadio P: Nonsteroidal anti-inflammatory drugs: Tailoring therapy to achieve results and avoid toxicity. Postgrad Med 93:73, 1993.
8. Sandier DP, Smith JC, Weinberg CR, et al: Analgesic use and chronic renal disease. N Engl J Med 320:1238, 1989.
9. Foley KM: The practical use of narcotic analgesics. Med Clin North Am 66:1091, 1982.
10. Waldman SP: Dezocine and ketorolac. Pain Digest 1:216, 1991.
11. Mather LE: Clinical pharmacokinetics of analgesic drugs. In Raj PP (ed): Practical Management of Pain, 3rd ed. Philadelphia, WB Saunders, 2000, p 462.
12. Portenoy RK, Waldman SD: Recent advances in the management of cancer pain: I. Pharmacologic approaches. Pain Manage 4:10, 1991.
13. Dahl JL: Pain: Impediments and suggestions for solutions. Presented at NIH State-of-the-Science Conference on Symptom Management in Cancer: Pain, Depression, and Fatigue, Bethesda, MD, 2002.
14. Dawson R, Spross JA, Jablonski ES, et al: Probing the paradox of patients' satisfaction with inadequate pain management. J Symptom Pain Manage 23:211, 2002.
15. Waldman SD: The role of neural blockade in the management of headache and facial pain. Headache Q 2:286, 1991.
16. Waldman SD: Sphenopalatine ganglion Block. In: Atlas of Interventional Pain Management, 2nd ed. Philadelphia, WB Saunders, 2004, p 11.
17. Diamond S, Dalesslo D: Cluster headache. In Diamond S, Dalessio DJ (eds): The Practicing Physician's Approach to Headache, 3rd ed. Baltimore, Williams & Wilkins, 1982, p 64.
18. Waldman SD: Cluster headache. In: Common Pain Syndromes. Philadelphia, WB Saunders, 2002, p 16.
19. Waldman SD: Migraine headache. In: Common Pain Syndromes. Philadelphia, WB Saunders, 2002, p 8.
20. Waldman SD: Sphenopalatine ganglion block—eighty years later: A historical vignette. Reg Anesth 18:274, 1993.
21. Waldman SD: Stellate ganglion block. In: Atlas of Interventional Pain Management, 2nd ed. Philadelphia, WB Saunders, 2004, p 100.
22. Waldman SD: Acute herpes zoster of the first division of the trigeminal nerve. In: Common Pain Syndromes. Philadelphia, WB Saunders, 2002, p 3.
23. Waldman SD, Waldman K: Reflex sympathetic dystrophy of the face and neck: report of six patients treated with stellate ganglion block. Reg Anesth 12:15, 1987.
24. Waldman SD: Celiac plexus block. In: Atlas of Interventional Pain Management, 2nd ed. Philadelphia, WB Saunders, 2004, p 265.
25. Lieberman RP, Waldman SD: Celiac plexus neurolysis with the modified transaortic approach. Radiology 175:274, 1990.
26. Waldman SD: Acute pancreatitis. In: Common Pain Syndromes. Philadelphia, WB Saunders, 2002, p 185.
27. Feldstein GS, Waldman SD, Allen ML: Loss of resistance technique for transaortic celiac plexus block (letter). Anesth Analg 65:1092, 1986.
28. Waldman SD: Lumbar sympathetic block. In: Atlas of Interventional Pain Management, 2nd ed. Philadelphia, WB Saunders, 2004, p 308.
29. Lobstrom JB, Cousins MJ: Sympathetic neural blockade of upper and lower extremity. In Cousins MJ, Bridenbaugh PO (eds): Neural Blockade in Clinical Anesthesia and Management of Pain, 2nd ed. Philadelphia, JB Lippincott, 1988, p 479.
30. Waldman SD: Cervical epidural block. In: Atlas of Interventional Pain Management, 2nd ed. Philadelphia, WB Saunders, 2004, p 129.
31. Waldman SD: Lumbar epidural block. In: Atlas of Interventional Pain Management, 2nd ed. Philadelphia, WB Saunders, 2004, p 340.
32. Cronen MC, Waldman SD: Cervical steroid epidural nerve blocks in the palliation of pain secondary to intractable tension-type headache. J Pain Sympt Manage 5:379, 1990.
33. Waldman SD: Thoracic epidural block. In: Atlas of Interventional Pain Management, 2nd ed. Philadelphia, WB Saunders, 2004, p 210.
34. Waldman SD: Caudal epidural block. In: Atlas of Interventional Pain Management, 2nd ed. Philadelphia, WB Saunders, 2004, p 380.
35. Waldman SD: The current status of caudal epidural nerve block in contemporary practice. Pain Digest 7:187, 1997.
36. Waldman SD: Complications of cervical epidural nerve blocks with steroids: a prospective study of 790 consecutive blocks. Reg Anesth 14:149, 1989.
37. Waldman SD: Epidural abscess following cervical epidural block with local anesthetic and steroid. Anesth Analg 72:385, 1991.
38. Waldman SD: Trigeminal nerve block. In: Atlas of Interventional Pain Management, 2nd ed. Philadelphia, WB Saunders, 2004, p 33.
39. Waldman SD: Trigeminal neuralgia. In: Common Pain Syndromes. Philadelphia, WB Saunders, 2002, p 29.
40. Waldman SD: Intercostal nerve block. In: Atlas of Interventional Pain Management, 2nd ed. Philadelphia, WB Saunders, 2004, p 241.
41. Waldman SD: Fractured ribs. In: Common Pain Syndromes. Philadelphia, WB Saunders, 2002, p 161.
42. Waldman SD: Intercostal neuralgia. In: Common Pain Syndromes. Philadelphia, WB Saunders, 2002, p 149-152.
43. Waldman SD, Feldstein GS, Donohue CD, et al: The relief of body wall pain secondary to malignant hepatic metastases by intercostal nerve block with bupivacaine and methylprednisolone. J Pain Sympt Manage 3:39, 1988.

chapter

21

Burn Pain

Sam R. Sharar, David R. Patterson, and Shelley Wiechman Askay

■ HISTORICAL CONSIDERATIONS

Cutaneous burn injuries are a widespread medical hazard of human activities in the contemporary world, whether the result of occupation, recreation, or daily living. Although burn injuries conjure visions of tragic and lethal fires, such as the 1942 Cocoanut Grove nightclub fire in Boston (491 deaths), the 1981 Stardust Nightclub fire in Dublin, (48 deaths), or the 2003 Station Concert Club fire in Warwick, Rhode Island (96 deaths), the far more common hospitalized burn victim sustains survivable injuries, yet is then forced to experience recurrent and often intense pain associated with both the injury itself and its days- to months-long treatment. As death rates for burn injuries have declined (33% between 1985 and 1995[1]) due primarily to improved surgical care, more patients with large burns are surviving and posing unique physical and psychological rehabilitation challenges with issues such as scarring, contractures, amputations, pain, and psychological adjustment. In the United States, it is estimated that there are 1.25 million burn injuries annually, resulting in more than 51,000 acute hospitalizations.[2] For each of these burn survivors there are several important medical issues, including burn wound management, prevention of infectious complications, pulmonary function (in cases of smoke inhalation), nutritional demands, physical and rehabilitation therapy requirements, and particularly in the case of large or aesthetically disfiguring burns, long-term issues of psychosocial adjustment. Common to all of these issues is the pain associated not only with the burn injury itself, but also with the ongoing, painful therapeutic medical care (e.g., wound débridement, aggressive physical therapy, and occupational therapy) required for optimal burn wound and overall patient outcomes.

Historically, the occurrence of a fire tragedy has resulted in increased attention to, and improved medical care of, various aspects of patient care. This is particularly true for issues of fire-safety management, inhalation-injury management, and wound-care management, but has *not* been true for burn pain management, which until recently has not a been a medical care priority in this population. For example, a national survey of U.S. burn centers in 1982 reported that 17% of centers used no analgesics or anesthesia in hospitalized children during burn wound débridement, and 8% recommended no analgesic medications at all.[3] Furthermore,

burn pain treatment techniques have historically been applied more liberally in adults than in children, as demonstrated by Schecter in 1985,[4] who reported that in a large teaching hospital, children hospitalized for burns of up to 20% body surface area (BSA) received an average of 1.3 opioid doses per day, compared to 3.6 opioid doses per day for adults with similar BSA injuries. Over the ensuing 30 years since these reports, the active participation of clinical behavioral scientists, anesthesiologists, and some burn surgeons in improving burn pain assessment and management has led to a broader application of conventional analgesic techniques and the introduction of newer analgesic techniques in burn patients. Despite these advances, recent reports indicate that inadequate acute pain management still exists and can directly influence poor functional outcomes in the long-term, rehabilitation phase of wound care.[5] With encouragement from the Joint Commission on Accreditation of Healthcare Organizations (JCAHO) declaring that pain should be regarded as a fifth vital sign,[6] however, an increased emphasis on pain assessment and management has occurred more recently in all medical settings, including burns. Associated with this emphasis, a recent review of research presented at the American Burn Association annual meeting reported that the research category of "pain/anxiety/patient comfort" was the third most popular of 10 burn-related clinical and laboratory research areas.[7] From this encouraging observation, continued clinical improvements in the acute and long-term analgesic management of burn survivors may be expected in the years to come.

■ THE CLINICAL SYNDROME— SIGNS, SYMPTOMS, AND PHYSICAL FINDINGS

Acute cutaneous burn pain results from the combination of thermal tissue injury of the dermal sensory organs and a resulting acute inflammatory response[8] that, at least in the early post-burn period, is related to the depth of tissue injury (Figs. 21–1 and 21–2). *First-degree burns* (e.g., sunburn) are characterized by tissue injury that is limited to the epidermal skin layer and an inflammatory response in the superficial dermal layers resulting in hyperemia (manifest as erythema), an intact epidermis (no skin blistering), and sensitization of dermal sensory organelles that results in hyperalgesia and mild-to-moderate pain. *Second-degree burns* or *partial thickness* burns involve tissue injury that extends to variable depths into the dermis—*superficial second-degree* burns involve only the upper, papillary dermis and are more likely to heal spontaneously; whereas *deep second-degree* burns involve the deeper, collagen-dense reticular dermis and are more likely to require surgical treatment. Because second-degree burns consistently injure and/or inflame sensory receptors in the dermis, these burns are associated with marked hyperalgesia and produce moderate to severe pain. *Third-degree burns* are characterized by complete destruction of the dermis, includ-

ing its sensory and vascular structures, so that although pain may still be a manifesting symptom, hypalgesia to cutaneous stimulation is common, as is a leathery skin texture and lack of capillary refill. Acute pain complaints with third-degree burns are typically minimal, but can be variable, and are universally present with respect to the transition zone between burned and unburned skin. All burn injuries involving the dermis (i.e., second- and third-degree) result in sensitized and reorganized states of both peripheral mechanoheat receptors and dorsal horn neurons. Models of these cellular alterations provide a conceptual framework for understanding how such peripheral neuronal injuries that are present after a burn can cause acute and subacute pain, hyperalgesia and chronic pain, and are described elsewhere.[8]

Attempts to define burn pain have focused largely on the variable of pain intensity, with less emphasis on variables of pain quality. Perry[3] reported that burn patients typically report their pain as being severe or excruciating, despite receiving opioid analgesics. However, it is important to realize that burn pain varies greatly from patient to patient, shows substantial fluctuation over the time course of hospitalization, and can be unpredictable due to the complex interaction of anatomic, physiologic, psychosocial, and premorbid behavior issues.[9] In contrast to the approximate relationship between burn depth and pain described above for the acute post-injury period, burn pain that is reported after the initial injury is not reliably correlated with the size or depth of a burn. Specifically, a patient with a superficial (second-degree) burn may show substantially more pain than one with a full-thickness (third-degree) burn, due to both physical factors (e.g., location and mechanism of the injury, individual differences in pain threshold and tolerance, response to analgesics) and psychological

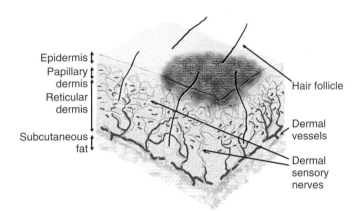

FIGURE 21–1 ■ Anatomic layers of skin. Graphic representation of skin layers including the outer epidermis, the thin papillary dermis, the collagen-dense reticular dermis, and the deep subcutaneous fat. The dermal sensory neurons of mechanoheat receptors and dermal capillaries are shown, relative to a first-degree burn injury (confined to the outer epidermal skin layer).

FIGURE 21–2 ■ Definitions and examples of partial- and full-thickness burn injuries. Superficial and deep skin burns are defined, including clinical characteristics (etiology, physical examination findings, tissue injury, and usual treatment), photographic examples, and graphic representations of tissue injury (including zones of hyperemia, stasis, and coagulation). (Images and illustrations courtesy of Nicole Gibram, MD, University of Washington Burn Center.)

First-Degree

Example: sunburn
Physical Exam: erythema, painful, + capillary refill
Injury: damaged epidermis, inflamed papillary dermis
Treatment: spontaneous healing in 3–4 days

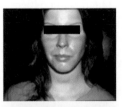
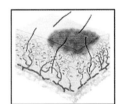

Superficial Second-Degree (partial-thickness)

Example: scald burn
Physical Exam: pink, painful, + capillary refill, blisters, moist
Injury: damaged epidermis and papillary dermis
Treatment: spontaneous healing in 7–10 days

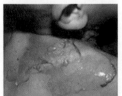
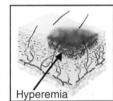
Hyperemia

Deep Second-Degree (partial-thickness)

Example: scald, grease burn
Physical Exam: mottled red/white, +/− painful, − capillary refill
Injury: damaged epidermis and papillary/reticular dermis
Treatment: spontaneous healing or excision/grafting

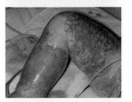
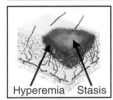
Hyperemia   Stasis

Third-Degree (full-thickness)

Example: flame, contact burn
Physical Exam: white/black, painless, dry, charred, leathery, − capillary refill
Injury: damaged epidermis, dermis, +/− subcutaneous fat
Treatment: excision/grafting

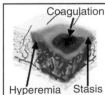
Coagulation
Hyperemia   Stasis

factors (e.g., previous pain experiences, anxiety, depression). Emotional distress, including traumatic memories, guilt or loss of loved ones or family members, anticipatory fears about treatment and recovery, and unexpected confinement in the hospital environment all may contribute to, and complicate, the post-burn pain experience.

Finally, indirect assessments of pain and nociception using measures of sympathetic nervous system activation (e.g., hypertension, tachycardia, and tachypnea) that may be of value in other acute pain settings are notoriously inaccurate in the acute burn victim. This is the result of a generalized increase in sympathetic tone that occurs, particularly in seriously injured burn patients, in response to the combination of immediate post-burn intravascular hypovolemia and as much as a 100% increase in resting metabolic rate. As a result, it is critical to realize that predicting the amount of nociception or suffering a patient will experience based on the nature of, or the physiologic response to, his or her burn injury is not possible, and the patient's pain experience can change dramatically—for better or for worse—over the course of both inpatient and outpatient care.

Because of this unpredictability, a more useful paradigm for describing acute and subacute burn pain is based on the clinical settings in which it commonly occurs. This approach is also useful because analgesic treatment decisions can also be based on such a classification. Thus, acute burn pain is generally classified into the following four clinical settings (Fig. 21–3):[10] (1) *background*—pain that is present while the patient is at rest, results from the thermal tissue injury itself, and is typically of low to moderate intensity and long duration (until the burn wound is healed); (2) *procedural*—brief but intense pain generated by wound care (e.g., débridement and dressing change) or rehabilitation activities (physical and occupational therapies); (3) *breakthrough*—unexpected spiking of pain levels that occurs when current analgesic efforts are exceeded, either at rest or during procedures; and (4) *postoperative*—a predictable and temporary (2 to 5 days) increase in pain complaints following burn excision and grafting, in large part due to the creation of new wounds in the process of skin-graft harvesting and autografting.

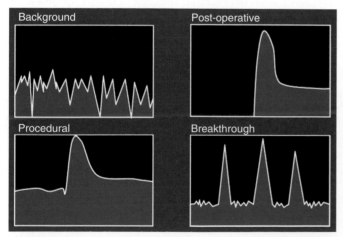

FIGURE 21–3 ■ Four clinical burn pain settings. Graphic representations of the relative pain intensity (vertical axis) and time course (horizontal axis) for the four common types of burn pain—background, postoperative, procedural, and breakthrough (see text for details).

Chronic burn pain typically lasts longer than 6 months or remains after all burn wounds and skin graft donor sites have healed, and is thus a challenge primarily in the outpatient setting. The mechanisms and treatment of chronic burn pain are inadequately studied and poorly understood. Although most acute burn pain results from tissue damage, it is important to be aware that pain from nerve damage may also be present—particularly in severe injuries associated with extremity amputations—and represents an anatomic source for chronic burn pain complaints. Acute and chronic pain arising from such nerve damage is often treated differently than conventional burn pain, and is addressed elsewhere in this text.

■ TESTING

Because of the obvious history and physical examination findings that accompany cutaneous burn injuries, no specialized testing is necessary to diagnose acute burn pain. The assessment of chronic pain conditions (e.g., complex regional pain syndromes [CRPS]) and associated psychological disorders that can accompany some burn injuries (e.g., depression due to disfigurement or functional impairment issues) is not unlike that in other pain settings, and is described in detail elsewhere in this text. However, due to the high incidence (25% to 74%) of psychiatric diagnoses in patients admitted for burn care (e.g., depression, character disorder, and substance abuse),[11] one should maintain a high index of vigilance for these diagnoses, as well as a low threshold for collaborative patient management with clinical psychologists and/or psychiatric professionals throughout the management period.

■ DIFFERENTIAL DIAGNOSIS

The obvious history and physical examination findings that accompany burn injuries usually leave little doubt as to the etiology of burn pain, whether acute or chronic. In addition, however, there may be other pain findings consistent with associated trauma (e.g., blunt trauma associated with a motor vehicle crash and subsequent car fire) or premorbid medical issues (e.g., substance abuse in a patient sustaining burns from clandestine methamphetamine production). Although these associated findings rarely affect the diagnosis of acute burn pain, they certainly may complicate its treatment.

■ TREATMENT

General Treatment Philosophy

Because burn pain is highly variable and cannot be reliably predicted by clinical assessment of either the patient or their burn wound, universally agreed upon burn pain management protocols are not available. As a result, the analgesic approaches to burn pain are variable, and often institution specific. In a recent survey of pediatric pain control practices in 82 North American burn centers,[12] for example, opioid analgesic use for procedural wound care and background pain control was ubiquitous, and a large fraction (77%) of responders also reported the adjunctive use of nonpharmacologic analgesic techniques (mostly limited to distraction). Only a limited number of responders reported the routine use of general anesthesia for exceptionally challenging wound care procedures (21%), the regular consultation of pain specialists (17%), or the use of an established protocol for the critically important first inpatient wound care procedure (33%).

To provide comprehensive and consistent analgesic care for burn patients, many burn centers advocate a structured approach to burn analgesia that incorporates both pharmacologic and nonpharmacologic therapies, targets the specific clinical pain settings unique to the burn patient (see Fig. 21–3), and yet can be individualized to meet specific patient needs and institutional capabilities. Such structured protocols help to avoid the undertreatment of burn pain that has been observed[3] when burn staff members fail to medicate patients adequately with opioid analgesics, despite education regarding the low risks for addictive and other side effects. The source of such undertreatment has been conceptualized in psychodynamic terms by Perry.[13] Specifically, some staff members required to perform repeated and painful procedures on burn patients have a subconscious need for patients to demonstrate pain as a means to create a psychological distance between themselves and the realities of burn care. Alternatively, the unfounded fear of creating psychological dependence on opioid analgesics may also explain the reluc-

tance of some burn care staff to aggressively treat burn pain. There is no evidence that opioid addiction occurs more commonly in burn patients without premorbid substance abuse issues than in other patient populations that require such analgesics for acute pain.[14]

The establishment of succinct, yet detailed institutional guidelines has been advocated to assist burn physicians and burn nurses who do not specialize in pain control, to avoid extremes of dosing by assisting with the choice of pharmacologic analgesics that target specific analgesic needs.[15,16] To maximize simplicity and utility, it is recommended that such guidelines be safe and effective over a broad range of ages, be explicit in their dosing recommendations, have a limited formulary to maximize staff familiarity, and allow the bedside nurse flexibility to respond quickly to the changing needs of the patient.[16] An example of such pharmacologic dosing guidelines from our institution is shown in Table 21–1. In addition, the regular use of a weight-based pediatric medication worksheet (placed at the bedside and in the patient record), containing all analgesic and resuscitation drugs likely to be administered for each pediatric patient, provides a supplemental safeguard against accidental overdose. This is particularly needed in the young pediatric age group in whom both analgesic risks and clinical unfamiliarity may be elevated.[17]

Table 21–1

Example of Institutional Burn Pain Medication Guidelines

	ICU (No PO Intake)	ICU (Taking PO)	Ward (Large Open Areas)	Ward (Small Open Areas/Predischage)
Background Pain	Continuous morphine sulfate (IV) drip	Scheduled methadone or MS Contin	Scheduled methadone or MS Contin	Scheduled NSAIDs/acetaminophen or scheduled oxycodone or none
Procedural Pain	Morphine sulfate (IV) or fentanyl (IV)	Oxycodone, fentanyl IV, or fentanyl Actiq	Oxycodone, fentanyl (IV), Nitrox (IH), or fentanyl Actiq	Oxycodone
Breakthrough Pain (prn dosing)	Morphine sulfate (IV) or fentanyl (IV)	Oxycodone	Oxycodone	NSAIDs/acetaminophen or oxycodone
Background Anxiolysis	Scheduled lorazepam (IV) or continuous lorazepam (IV) drip	Scheduled lorazepam	None or scheduled lorazepam	None
Procedural Anxiolysis	Lorazepam or midazolam (IV)	Lorazepam	None or lorazepam	None
Discharge or Transfer Pain Medications	N/A	For transfer to ward: wean drips; establish PO pain medication early; anticipate dose tapering as needs decrease	Oxycodone for procedural pain; methadone taper or MS Contin. Taper if applicable	Oxycodone or NSAIDs for procedural pain

IH, inhalation; IV, intravenously; NSAIDs, nonsteroidal antiinflammatory drugs; PO, by mouth; prn, as needed.
Representative pain and sedation management guideline for adult (nonpediatric, nongeriatric) burn patients from the University of Washington Burn Center. General medication recommendations are provided for specific pain and anxiolysis needs encountered in various intensive care units and ward-care settings. Medication options are intentionally limited (for simplicity) and do not include specific dose recommendations (to allow for individual patient variability). Complex or refractory cases are managed through special consultation with the burn care team and/or pain specialists.

The generalized burn pain management paradigm should involve both pharmacologic and nonpharmacologic analgesic techniques, selected on the basis of institutional availability and experience, as well as patient factors.[10,18] In general, selection of an analgesic regimen is first based on the answers to two general questions (1) what is the clinical setting for which analgesia is needed (i.e., treatment of background versus procedural versus breakthrough versus postoperative pain), and (2) what specific treatment limitations are imposed by the patient (presence of intravenous [IV] access, endotracheal intubation/mechanical ventilation, or opioid tolerance) or by clinical facilities (available monitoring capabilities, training, and skills of burn care staff). For example, the presence or absence of IV access (particularly in children, in whom IV access may be challenging to obtain) directly influences pharmacologic analgesic options. Similarly, patients who are mechanically ventilated are largely "protected" from the risk of opioid-induced respiratory depression, and thus, can be administered larger doses of opioids. Tolerance may be a relevant issue in patients requiring prolonged opioid analgesic therapy or in those with preexisting substance abuse histories. Because of the development of drug tolerance with prolonged medical use (>2 weeks) or recreational abuse of opioids (both commonly seen in burn patients), doses needed for burn analgesia may significantly exceed those recommended in standard guidelines. One clinically important consequence of drug tolerance is the potential for opioid withdrawal to occur during inpatient burn treatment. Thus, the period of inpatient burn care is not an appropriate time to institute deliberate opioid withdrawal or detoxification measures in the premorbid substance-abusing patient because such treatment ignores the very real, acute pain analgesic needs of these patients. Such practices might also lead to illegal drug seeking in hospitalized patients, with associated health risks and system problems. Similarly, when reductions in analgesic therapy are considered as burn wounds heal, reductions should occur by careful tapering to prevent acute opioid withdrawal syndrome.

Because nociception at the burn site is the predominant mechanism of pain and suffering in these patients acutely, pharmacologic treatment with potent opioids, anxiolytics, and/or other anesthetics is the first line and cornerstone of analgesic therapy. In addition, nonpharmacologic methods of treating burn pain are also extremely useful, but are best applied only after optimal pharmacologic therapy has been established. Brief descriptions of the analgesic goals and potential, and general therapeutic options for each of the four clinical settings of burn pain are discussed subsequently.

Background Pain Management

Because background pain is relatively constant and of mild-to-moderate severity, it is best treated pharmacologically with mild to moderately potent analgesics administered so that plasma drug concentrations remain relatively constant throughout the day. Examples include continuous IV opioid infusion (+/- patient-controlled analgesia [PCA]), oral administration of long-acting opioids with prolonged elimination (methadone) or prolonged enteral absorption (sustained-release morphine, sustained-release oxycodone), or oral administration on a regular schedule of short-acting opioid analgesics or nonsteroidal antiinflammatory agents (NSAIDs). Background pain decreases with time as the burn wound (and associated donor sites) heals, so that analgesics

can be slowly tapered. Nonpharmacologic techniques applicable to background pain might include approaches to enhance coping, relaxation, information provision, and participation (see later).

Procedural Pain Management

Procedural pain associated with burn wound care presents a unique and significant challenge for medical staff in that potent sedation and/or analgesia is often required on a daily basis, yet general anesthesia is too dangerous, expensive, or logistically challenging to use on an ongoing basis. Thus, the provision of *moderate sedation* (formerly *conscious sedation*) or *deep sedation* (as defined by the American Society of Anesthesiologists [ASA])[19] is frequently required, and should conform to the sedation guidelines set by the ASA[19] and adopted by the JCAHO. For example, the institutional capability to provide adequate monitoring (pulse oximetry, independent patient observer) for moderate sedation by nonanesthesiologists may also dictate which specific agents are used for procedural analgesia because some of the more potent opioids (e.g., remifentanil) or anesthetics (e.g., ketamine) may result in depths of sedation that far exceed the intended target of moderate sedation. Careful individual and institutional interpretation of sedation levels is required to ensure safety and practicality in meeting the appropriate sedation guidelines. The use of potent opioids and anxiolytics should occur only in settings with adequate monitoring, personnel, and resuscitation equipment appropriate for the degree of sedation anticipated. For most wound débridement procedures, opioid analgesia—with or without the concurrent use of anxiolytic sedatives (e.g., benzodiazepines)—will typically produce a clinical response consistent with moderate sedation.

In contrast to background pain, procedural pain is significantly more intense, but shorter in duration; therefore, pharmacologic analgesic regimens for procedural pain are best composed of moderately to highly potent opioids that have a short duration of action, often in combination with benzodiazepine anxiolytics. Intravenous access is helpful in this setting because opioids with a rapid onset of action and short duration (e.g., fentanyl, remifentanil) may be used, as can other IV anesthetic agents—such as ketamine and dexmedetomidine. In the absence of IV access, orally administered opioids are commonly used, although their relatively long durations of action (2 to 6 hours) may potentially limit postprocedure recovery for other rehabilitative or nutritional activities. Oral ketamine,[20] oral transmucosal fentanyl,[21,22] and inhaled nitrous oxide[23] are agents of particular use when IV access is not present because of their rapid onsets and short durations of action. When a particularly painful dressing change or one that requires extreme cooperation in a noncompliant patient (e.g., face débridement in a young child) is anticipated, the provision of brief general anesthesia[24,25] or regional anesthesia in the burn unit setting may be indicated.

Anticipatory anxiety is an important issue that can develop with the repeated (usually daily) performance of such wound care. When adequate analgesia is not provided for an initial painful procedure, the effectiveness of analgesia for subsequent procedures is reduced, in large part due to anticipatory anxiety and heightened arousal.[26,27] Thus, efforts to provide effective procedural burn sedation should begin as early in the hospitalization as possible, preferably with the first (and often most painful) wound care procedure. In addition, nonpharmacologic analgesic techniques are of particular value in the clinical setting of procedural pain, and include coping, imagery, distraction, hypnosis, virtual reality, information provision, and participation (see later).

Breakthrough Pain Management

Breakthrough pain occurs when the pain exceeds the comfort provided by background pain therapies; it can be the result of inadequate analgesic support (e.g., undertreatment, development of opioid tolerance) or predictable changes in the burn wound itself that may produce increased pain (e.g., proliferation of epidermal skin buds during the spontaneous burn healing process). Recognition of the correct cause of the breakthrough pain is of utmost importance, so that the appropriate change in pharmacologic and/or nonpharmacologic management can take place rapidly.

Postoperative Pain Management

Postoperative pain is an anticipated and temporary (2 to 5 days) increase in background pain that occurs following burn excision and/or grafting procedures and is most commonly the result of increased pain from newly created wounds at the skin graft harvesting site. Pharmacologic management of postoperative pain includes a temporary increase in background opioid analgesic support, but can also include the use of continuous regional block techniques in the immediate postoperative period.[28] One of the most useful nonpharmacologic analgesic techniques in this setting is information provision, so that patients may anticipate both the increase and the temporary nature of the postoperative pain.

Pharmacologic Approaches to the Management of Burn Pain

In describing pharmacologic approaches for burn analgesia, three consistent observations can be made. First, for patients with injuries extensive enough to require hospitalization, potent opioid administration forms the cornerstone of pharmacologic pain control, whereas the mild to moderate analgesia provided by NSAIDs or acetaminophen may provide some degree of opioid-sparing effect, but will have limited use as single analgesic agents until the later rehabilitative and/or outpatient phases of treatment. Second, because burn pain has well-defined components—background, procedural, breakthrough, and postoperative pain—pharmacologic choices for analgesia should target individually each of the four clinical pain settings. Third, because burn pain will vary somewhat unpredictably throughout hospitalization, analgesic regimens should be continuously evaluated and reassessed to avoid problems of under- or overmedication. Pain assessment is facilitated by the regular use of standardized, self-report scales for adults and older children, and observational scoring systems for the very young, as described elsewhere in this text. Of special note is that the reliance on nurse assessment of patients' burn pain can be problematic because it is well documented that nurses' and patients' assessments of burn pain and analgesic effects are not always comparable.[29-31] Unfortunately, nursing staff assessments typically underestimate the need for analgesic therapy in the burn setting (a problem that is likely echoed in similar evaluations of physicians and other health care professionals). Thus, whenever possible, patient reports of pain should be elicited and should be the basis for analgesic decisions, rather than observations of the staff.

Opioid Analgesics

Opioid agonists are the most commonly used analgesics in the treatment of burn pain, in part because (1) they are potent analgesics; (2) the benefits and risks of their use are familiar to the majority of care providers; and (3) they provide some dose-dependent degree of sedation that can be advantageous to both burn patients and staff, particularly during burn wound care procedures. The wide spectrum of opioids available for clinical use provides dosing flexibility (i.e., variable routes of administration, variable durations of action) that is ideal for the targeted treatment of burn pain. The pharmacokinetic action of opioids in burn patients is not consistently different from nonburn patients,[32,33] although decreased volume of distribution and clearance, and increased elimination half-life have been reported for morphine.[34] Similarly, pharmacodynamic potency of opioids has inconsistently been reported as increased[35] and decreased[34] in burn patients.

The route of opioid administration is an important issue in burn patients, with the principal choice between IV or oral administration dictated by the severity of burn (critically ill patients require IV access and may have abnormal gut function) and the high risk of burn patients for developing intravascular catheter-related sepsis (hence, physician reluctance to maintain long-term IV access).[36] Intramuscular opioid administration is avoided because of the need for repeated, painful injections, and because of variable vascular absorption due to unpredictable compartmental fluid shifts and muscle perfusion in burn patients, particularly those undergoing burn shock resuscitation immediately following the burn injury. Patient-controlled analgesia (PCA) with IV opioids offers the burn patient a safe and efficient method of achieving more flexible analgesia. PCA also offers the patient the nonpharmacologic benefit of allowing some degree of control over his or her medical care—this often being a major issue for burn patients whose waking hours are often completely scheduled with care activities ranging from wound care to physical and rehabilitation therapy, all within the foreign confines of the hospital. Studies comparing PCA opioid use to other routes of administration in the burn population have shown positive but limited benefits of PCA.[37] Oral transmucosal administration of opioids is reported in burn patients[21,22] and appears to be particularly advantageous in those patients without IV access and in children.

Non-opioid Analgesics

The list of non-opioid analgesics in widespread use for the treatment of burn pain is currently limited, although not without potential benefit. Oral NSAIDs and acetaminophen, as discussed earlier, are mild analgesics that exhibit a ceiling effect in their dose-response relationship, rendering them unsuitable for the treatment of typical, severe burn pain—except to the degree that they provide a limited opioid-sparing effect. They are of benefit, however, in treating minor burns—particularly in the outpatient setting. The opioid agonist-antagonist drugs (e.g., nalbuphine, butorphanol) produce "mixed" actions at the opiate receptor level, theoretically providing analgesia (agonist property) with lesser side effects (antagonist properties), but also exhibit ceiling effects. Although studies have shown this class of drugs to be effective in treating burn pain,[38] experience with them is both limited and suggestive of efficacy only in patients with relatively mild burn pain.

Centrally-acting α_2-agonists have been proposed as potential analgesic agents for burn pain based on their known mechanisms of action in other acute pain states. In case reports, clonidine has demonstrated analgesic efficacy in burned children,[39,40] whereas the efficacy of dexmedetomidine is limited to anecdotal reports.

Anxiolytics

Aggressive surgical treatment and débridement of burn wounds, together with the persistent and repetitive qualities of background and procedural burn pain, make burn care an experience that creates significant anxiety in most patients of all ages. The recognition that anxiety can exacerbate acute pain has led to the common practice in U.S. burn centers of using anxiolytic drugs in combination with opioid analgesics, a practice that has become more widespread in the past 2 decades.[3,12] Intuitively, this practice is particularly useful in premedicating patients for wound care, due to the anticipatory anxiety experienced by these patients prior to and during such procedures. However, benzodiazepine therapy has also been shown to improve postoperative pain scores in non-burn[41] and burn[42] settings. Specific to burns, it appears that the patients most likely to benefit from this therapy are not necessarily those with high trait (premorbid) anxiety, but rather those with either high state (at the time of the procedure) anxiety or high baseline pain scores.[42]

Anesthetics

Given the brief but intense pain associated with many burn wound procedures, the provision of a limited-duration general anesthetic may, at first glance, seem a reasonable analgesic approach. However, the repeated (often daily) need for such procedures poses economic and logistical obstacles that make general anesthesia not feasible on a regular basis. Nonetheless, the provision of deep sedation with carefully titrated inhaled or IV anesthetic agents, brief general anesthetics, and regional analgesic techniques has a large role in procedural burn pain settings.

Inhaled nitrous oxide is an anesthetic agent safe for administration by appropriately trained, nonanesthesia personnel, and provides safe and effective analgesia without loss of consciousness for moderately painful procedures in other healthcare settings. It is also used for the treatment of burn pain,[43,44] typically as a 50% mixture in 50% oxygen, and self-administered by an awake, cooperative, spontaneously breathing patient *via* a mouthpiece or mask. Although the level of sedation achieved with such inhalation is typically light ("minimal" or "moderate" by ASA definitions), the analgesic effect of the drug can be very good. The technique allows patients some degree of control in their medical care (i.e., deciding when to inhale the agent and when not to inhale it during the procedure), and can consequently benefit patients psychologically. On the negative side, nitrous oxide has also been implicated in a very small, but measurable incidence of toxicity issues (e.g., spontaneous abortion, bone marrow suppression) to patients or staff exposed for prolonged periods,[45,46] although not in the setting of burn pain treatment.

Despite the economic and logistic limitations of repeated general anesthesia, there are certain aggressive wound care procedures that are, in terms of invasiveness, on a scale well below that of surgical burn care, yet are nonetheless difficult to perform on a conscious patient (e.g., the removal of hundreds of skin staples from recently grafted wounds, meticulous wound care of recently grafted and often tenuous skin on the face or neck, or wound care procedures in variably cooperative children). For such cases, deep sedation or general anesthesia with intravenous agents may be indicated. Historically, IV or intramuscular ketamine has been used for these procedures,[47,48] and more recently oral ketamine use is described for pediatric burn patients.[20] However, ketamine use is limited by the potential risk of associated emergence delirium reactions (5% to 30% incidence), particularly in the elderly. Alternatively, propofol has been reported safe and effective when administered by appropriately trained physicians (anesthesiologists) in the burn setting,[49] and has even been suggested to be a potential drug for PCA use for less aggressive wound care procedures.[50] Propofol is particularly advantageous because it can be titrated to effect in terms of both level of consciousness and duration of action using continuous IV infusion techniques, and carries the benefit of a rapid awakening with a minimal risk of nausea.

The extension of full anesthetic care capabilities outside of the operating room and into the burn ward has been implemented in high-volume, specialized burn centers.[24,25] This has been facilitated by the introduction into clinical anesthetic practice of a variety of drugs with a rapid onset and short duration of action, a more rapid awakening/recovery, and fewer associated side effects—ideal qualities for agents to be used for procedural burn wound care. These agents include IV propofol, IV remifentanil, and inhaled sevoflurane. The provision of brief, dense analgesia/anesthesia in a comprehensively monitored setting by individuals specifically trained to provide the service appears safe and efficient, both in terms of allowing wound care to proceed rapidly under ideal conditions for patient and nursing staff, and in terms of cost-effective use of the operating room only for true surgical burn care procedures.

Various forms of regional anesthetic blockade may also be considered for inpatient burn pain management. Neuraxial administration of local anesthetics (and/or opioids) via an epidural catheter would seem to be of benefit in patients with lower extremity burns, resulting in both background and procedural analgesia, as well as autonomic sympathectomy and peripheral vasodilation (of theoretical benefit to wound healing). However, such use has been reported only anecdotally.[51] A major drawback of this technique is the use of an indwelling catheter in patients densely colonized with infectious organisms at the wound site, thus increasing the risk for the serious complication of epidural abscess formation.[52] Targeted non-neuraxial regional blockade, in contrast, is relatively easy to perform, carries minimal risks, and has been reported primarily for lower extremity analgesia following skin graft harvesting (fascia iliaca block). The technique can be used both for immediate postoperative analgesia (one-shot injection[53]) and for prolonged postoperative analgesia (continuous local anesthetic infusion via indwelling catheter[28]).

Local anesthetics are of obvious use in regional blockade for wound care procedures, but may also be considered for burn pain analgesia in the form of a topical gel. Topical local anesthetic use on the burn wound is controversial. The commonly available prilocaine-lidocaine cream (eutetic mixture of local anesthetics [EMLA]) had no effect in a study on burn pain in volunteers.[54] Topical 5% lidocaine applied at 1 mg/cm^2 offers analgesic benefit without associated side effects,[55] however enthusiasm for its use is significantly tempered by reports of local anesthetic-induced seizures due to enhanced systemic absorption at open wound sites.[56]

Nonpharmacologic Approaches to the Management of Burn Pain

Both pharmacologic and nonpharmacologic treatments are complementary in treating pain and anxiety in the burn patient. There is considerable empirical evidence for the efficacy of nonpharmacologic treatments, particularly when used as an adjunct to opioid medications. It is important to begin nonpharmacologic treatments as early as possible in the patient's hospital course to help reduce anticipatory anxiety and the subsequent anxiety-pain cycle. Before focusing on the various nonpharmacologic techniques, it is useful to understand the psychological factors that come into play that can exacerbate pain. Perhaps the most important example of such processes is the loss of control that burn patients experience and its relation to coping.

Coping with Decreased Control

Sustaining a burn injury, as well as enduring the many subsequent treatments, taxes a person's coping resources by reducing his or her sense of control. Most patients describe feelings of being out of control in the hospital setting owing to a number of factors, including high pain levels, the unfamiliar environment, the dependency patients have on their care givers, lack of input into daily schedules and routines, and the uncertainty about the future (e.g., appearance, wound status, work, or even survival). In this new environment, patients are also uncertain about their ability to cope with these new challenges, and must do so while experiencing high levels of pain, while under the influence of a variety of medications, and often with diminished physical capacity. Such uncertainty often leads to feelings of helplessness in both adults and children. It is crucial that patients and staff find effective coping strategies that maximize a patient's sense of control.[27]

To select appropriate strategies, it is useful to understand the types of coping mechanisms that patients are using, or that may be of use to them.[28] The Two-Process Model of Control is applicable to the burn care setting for both adults and children.[57] This model distinguishes between primary control, secondary control, and relinquished control strategies. Primary control is when a person manipulates the situation or environment to fit their needs and secondary control is when a person modifies oneself to fit the situation. Relinquished control describes the coping style of "giving up" and often involves a process of emoting or withdrawal and depression. Research has shown that flexible coping, using both primary and secondary control coping strategies, is most adaptable to burn care situations.[58] Selecting a coping style that suits the particular situation works better than strictly adhering to one coping style. Patients who assertively request more medication in response to pain may be demonstrating adaptive primary coping, and those who meditate or pray while having a particularly bad day may be benefiting from secondary coping strategies. On the other hand, adults and children who adopt the relinquished control style show greater psychological distress.[59,60] This type of coping often leads to learned helplessness and is characterized by negative, catastrophic thoughts, more pain behaviors, higher pain levels, and slower physical recovery.[27,61] The nonpharmacologic pain management techniques listed in the remainder of this chapter ideally will help patients regain some control over their environment through primary or secondary control coping.

Many choices are available when considering a nonpharmacologic treatment. In choosing the most effective approach, the care team should be guided by the manner in which patients typically respond to stressful medical procedures. Patient responses in these circumstances lie on a continuum ranging from giving up control to the health care professional and desiring little information, to seeking as much information as possible and participating in the procedures. Those patients who wish to give up control to the healthcare professional have a tendency toward cognitive avoidance and will likely use various types of distraction techniques to avoid the painful stimuli. These patients are said to have more of an *avoidance* coping style. Those who seek information about the procedure and want to participate as much as they can, often find distraction techniques distressing; for them, trying to ignore a procedure may seem to relinquish too much control. Such patients are thought to have more of an *approach* coping style.[62] It is important to note that both coping styles can be adaptive and it is best for the care team to support an individual's coping style rather than try to change his or her natural response. Healthcare professionals may also find that patients may change their coping style depending on the procedure. For example, a patient may find it is easier to use distraction techniques for short procedures such as receiving injections, whereas they are more comfortable attending to details of their long wound care sessions and participating when possible. Patients may also change their coping style as they become more familiar and comfortable with the environment. The *approach to avoidance* coping continuum and the interventions that can be considered along this continuum are illustrated in Figure 21–4. Although techniques such as imagery or hypnosis may fall into various categories on the continuum, depending on the outcome goals and script, the continuum is a useful heuristic guide for clinicians in choosing an appropriate technique. The remainder of this section will describe the various nonpharmacologic interventions for burn pain management in relation to where they fall on the continuum.

Avoidance

Distraction

The types of distraction techniques available are limited only by the creativity of the patient and staff. Common distraction techniques used with children include bubble blowing, singing songs, reading a story and counting. Adults may require a bit more creativity, but can engage in enjoyable conversation during the procedure, listen to music, play a video game or immerse themselves in interactive virtual reality (see later) during the procedure.

Imagery

Imagery is simply creating or recreating an image in one's mind, presumably one that patients find pleasant and engag-

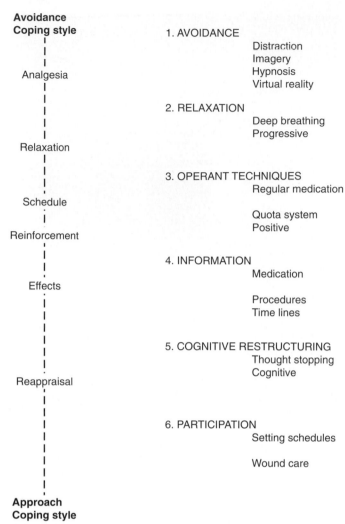

Avoidance
Coping style

Analgesia

Relaxation

Schedule

Reinforcement

Effects

Reappraisal

Approach
Coping style

1. AVOIDANCE
   Distraction
   Imagery
   Hypnosis
   Virtual reality

2. RELAXATION
   Deep breathing
   Progressive

3. OPERANT TECHNIQUES
   Regular medication

   Quota system
   Positive

4. INFORMATION
   Medication

   Procedures
   Time lines

5. COGNITIVE RESTRUCTURING
   Thought stopping
   Cognitive

6. PARTICIPATION
   Setting schedules

   Wound care

FIGURE 21–4 ▪ Control coping continuum and associated nonpharmacologic techniques. The spectrum of coping styles from *avoidance* to *approach* is depicted, including specific clinical interventions for patients whose coping styles fall on different positions along the continuum (see text for details).

ing. Types of imagery can be infinite and depend on the desired goals. For example, many people use "healing imagery" to promote this result when overcoming disease or injury. They might imagine processes such as increased blood flow to the injured area in an effort to carry away damaged tissue and rebuild new tissue or to decrease inflammation in the injured area. Although healing imagery can be an effective means of helping the burn patient feel more in control of their situation, it forces a person to focus on their injury and is, therefore, not a distraction technique when used in this way.

In contrast, *relaxation imagery* tends to work best for pain control and is another form of distraction. Before a painful procedure, we often talk with the patient about their *safe* or *favorite* place to go. This can be a place where they have been before (e.g., a favorite vacation spot) or simply a place that they imagine to be relaxing and safe. Some common examples include the beach, camping or hiking, fishing, a grandmother's kitchen, or their childhood bedroom. We then collect as many details as possible about what this

place looks like—the colors, the sounds, the smells, objects in this place—and have the patient practice the imagery. Before the procedure, patients are encouraged to relax through deep breathing, closing their eyes, and imagining this favorite place. We simply cue the patient with the details that they have provided prior to beginning relaxation. Next, we encourage them to imagine this place during their subsequent wound care, and if necessary, we are present during the wound care to facilitate "taking them" to this place. Children often enjoy more active forms of imagery that relate to fantasy, such as taking a "magic carpet ride" or jumping on a broomstick with Harry Potter and flying through the woods at Hogwarts.[63]

There are also numerous imagery scripts that have been published and can be used when a person is unable to think of a safe or favorite place. These scripts usually entail a person "flying" or "floating on a cloud" through beautiful places. It is important to note that a patient should be asked about any fears such as heights, flying, or water so that use of these images does not actually create more anxiety.

Imagery is usually most effective when all of the senses are incorporated to make the image as realistic as possible. Most people require practice to be able to create vivid images, and some people are unable to visualize these images, particularly when they are in significant pain and are too distracted. Virtual reality may be a better option for these patients (see later).

Hypnotic Analgesia

Although hypnosis involves much more than just avoidance or distraction, the end result is often similar in that this technique takes a person's focus off the painful procedure they are undergoing. Hypnosis is an altered state of consciousness characterized by an increased receptivity to suggestion, ability to alter perceptions and sensations, and an increased capacity for dissociation. Several of these features make it a unique method of pain control that differs markedly from imagery or relaxation. In fact, hypnosis may or may not lead to relaxation depending on the nature of the suggestions. In turn, it is not necessary for a patient to be relaxed or even in a deep hypnotic state in order for suggestions to be useful. It is believed that the dramatic shift in consciousness that occurs with hypnosis is the cornerstone of an individual's ability to change their awareness of pain.[64] Hypnosis involves several stages, including building clinician-patient rapport, enhancing relaxation through deep breathing, suggestions for deepening the hypnotic state and narrowing their attention, providing posthypnotic suggestions, and alerting.[65] We typically use a Rapid Induction Analgesia format described by Patterson[65] and originally published by Barber,[66] but there are numerous scripts for hypnotic analgesia that can be used directly or with improvisation. However, the technique should be used only by trained clinicians who can assess the risks and benefits of this powerful technique. As an example, patients with a history of sexual abuse may have a tendency to dissociate too easily and will not be served by hypnosis in some instances.

Hypnotic analgesia has increased in popularity with recent reports that it can reduce medical costs[67] or possibly even facilitate wound healing.[68,69] Although the mechanism for how hypnosis works is not fully understood, hypnotic analgesia has shown demonstrable brain function changes in neuroimaging studies.[70] A meta-analysis by Montgomery and colleagues[71] reported analgesic effects in the majority of studies that employed hypnosis for clinical and experimental pain. A more recent review by Patterson and Jensen[72] indicated that anecdotal reports of hypnotic pain relief have been published for decades on virtually every type of pain imaginable. They found 17 randomized controlled studies on the use of hypnosis for acute pain and concluded that the evidence for hypnotic analgesia was strong and seems to be related to the trait of hypnotizability. Several studies have demonstrated the efficacy of hypnosis for patients with burn injuries.[73-75] Patterson and colleagues[76] have proposed several reasons why patients with burn injuries may make good candidates for hypnotic analgesia. First, the intense nature of burn pain motivates patients to engage in this technique that they might normally reject. This is supported by research findings that show that patients with higher baseline pain levels have a greater drop in pain after hypnosis than patients with lower baseline pain levels.[75,77] Second, the behavioral regression that often occurs after a traumatic injury makes patients more willing to be taken care of by others. Third, patients with burn injuries often experience a dissociative response as a means of coping that may moderate hypnotizability. Although burn pain associated with procedures is the most intense, it is also the most amenable to hypnotic analgesia. These procedures are often planned in advance, so there is time to adequately prepare patients for these aversive events with hypnosis.

Despite occasional dramatic responses to hypnosis in burn patients, it is also clear that not every patient benefits from this technique, and resources for a trained clinician may not be available on every burn unit. It will be valuable to research ways of making hypnosis more available to patients and more effective for those with low hypnotizability scores.[78] These goals could be accomplished by eliminating the need for a live hypnotist by using either audio-taped or computer-assisted hypnosis, and by making hypnosis less-effortful for those with low hypnotizability scores or whose cognitive effort is compromised because of pain.

Virtual Reality

Immersive virtual reality (VR) is a technology that isolates patients from the outside world, including any threatening stimuli associated with healthcare. Immersive VR uses a helmet that blocks the user's view of the real world and gives the patient the illusion of going into the three-dimensional computer-generated environment, a condition known as "presence." This quality makes immersive VR particularly effective in capturing participants' attention.[79] In the burn pain setting, we use a virtual environment called "SnowWorld" (Fig. 21–5)[80] where patients float through an icy canyon and are able to direct snowballs at virtual snowmen and igloos as they appear. The image of snow was specifically chosen because its connotation of cooling is in direct contrast to the "hot" sensations often associated with burn pain.

The theory behind the effectiveness of VR is that attention involves the limited selection of relevant information from a variety of inputs or tasks, and each human has a finite amount of attention available.[81,82] The strength of the illusion, or *presence*, is thought to reflect the amount of attention drawn into the virtual world.[83] Because it is designed to be a highly attention-grabbing experience, VR reduces the amount of conscious attention available to process pain (Fig. 21–6). Less attention to pain can result in a reduction in perceived

FIGURE 21–5   ■   Virtual reality environment "SnowWorld". The SnowWorld virtual environment as seen by the patient/user. Snow/ice motif and blue/white colors suggest a cool temperature setting in direct contrast to the hot setting in which most burn injuries occur. Virtual igloos and snowmen on canyon walls facilitate user interaction with the virtual world through user-targeted shooting of virtual snowballs at these virtual objects.

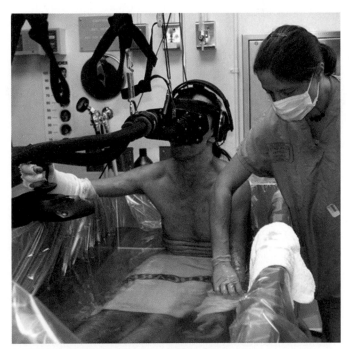

FIGURE 21–6   ■   Clinical use of virtual reality distraction during burn wound care. A burn patient undergoes burn wound débridement in the hydrotherapy tank while distracted with interactive *water-friendly* (photonic) virtual reality. Both auditory and visual stimulation is provided in a safe, shock-free setting, and user interaction with objects in the virtual environment is controlled by manual joystick.

pain intensity and unpleasantness, and can also reduce the amount of time patients spend thinking about their pain. VR has been shown to be effective in reducing pain in a number of clinical studies using it for pain distraction.[80,84-86] VR technology can also be used to administer hypnotic analgesia and is particularly effective with patients who have difficulty imagining a scene.[79]

Relaxation

Deep Breathing

Deep breathing, also known as diaphragmatic breathing, is one of the least time-consuming techniques to employ and easiest for adults and children to learn. When a person becomes anxious and/or experiences pain, breathing becomes shallow and irregular due to the increased muscle tension in the chest wall. This type of shallow breathing, known as thoracic breathing,[87] leads to an increase in muscle tension and subsequent heightened pain. Teaching patients to have an awareness of this cycle, along with deep breathing techniques that allow them to break it, will lead to a relaxation response that can alleviate some pain. Bubble blowing and blowing on a pinwheel are helpful tools to use with children to encourage deep breathing. Adults can be taught to place a hand on the stomach and to take a deep enough breath that it passes through the chest and "fills" the stomach. Their hand should rise and fall with the stomach. The exhalation is the most important part of the deep breath and should not be rushed. Diaphragmatic breathing is central to all forms of relaxation and is simple and time efficient.[87]

Progressive Muscle Relaxation

When patients are experiencing stress, such as pain, they tend to use muscles inefficiently,[87] resulting in muscle bracing that can lead to an increase in pain. Progressive muscle relaxation is a technique developed by a physician, Edmund Jacobson, after observing increased muscle tension in hospitalized patients and discovering that the more tense patients took longer to recuperate and had poorer outcomes.[88] He taught patients to systematically focus on a muscle group, tense and relax it, and then progress to a different group. This progression usually starts with the distal muscle groups and moves to the proximal groups until total body relaxation is achieved. Most patients will be able to learn this technique with practice, using a pre-written or individually tailored script, or independently using commercial audiotapes. If a person is unable to actively tense a muscle group due to pain or injury, he or she can still imagine each muscle becoming progressively "warm, heavy, and relaxed," a process known as autogenic training. Patients repeat each statement as they hear it on a tape (e.g., my right hand is heavy, my right hand is relaxed, my right hand is becoming warm . . .).

Operant Techniques

Operant techniques refer to the principles of reinforcement learning based on the specific assumption that patients will repeat behaviors that are positively reinforced and will avoid behaviors that lead to punishment. These principles can be applied in various ways to alleviate burn pain.

Regular Medication Scheduling

Many inpatient acute care settings administer medication on a "pro re nata" (prn) or "as needed" basis (i.e., waiting for patients to report that they are in pain before providing analgesic medications). From a behavioral perspective, waiting to medicate a patient until he or she complains of pain reinforces pain behaviors; this can later become a problem.[10] The reinforcing properties of this process come in the form of the euphorigenic properties of short-acting opioid analgesics, as well as the attention received from care givers and family for displaying pain behaviors. In contrast, providing opioid analgesics on a regular schedule minimizes the potential for these reinforcing properties of drugs and attention to worsen the pain problem. The superiority of regularly scheduled medications over prn dosing has been demonstrated with non-burn pain[89] and has also been confirmed in background pain management for burn-injured children.[90]

Although research has shown that there is little chance of creating a chronic drug problem when opioid analgesics are given for acute pain in patients with no previous substance abuse histories, there is a risk of exacerbating a preexisting substance abuse problem.[91] Therefore, adhering to a regular opioid schedule is even more important for patients with substance abuse histories. Patients with drug histories often demonstrate frequent pain complaints or drug-seeking behaviors, and have lower tolerance for pain. They may also approach multiple care givers for medications that create staff-splitting and care giver resentment toward the patient. Adhering to a regular medication schedule and having only one care giver responsible for discussing or changing medications/doses can help alleviate some of these problems. As noted earlier, it is critical for patients who present with premorbid opioid abuse issues, or who are on methadone maintenance programs, to receive adequate levels of opioid analgesics to manage the acute burn pain. The consequences of patients self-administering street narcotics for pain control can be extremely disruptive, if not fatal.

Quota System

The quota system is an operant technique used by burn care providers to promote a sense of mastery among patients who are undergoing painful wound care procedures and difficult physical therapies.[92] Care givers are encouraged to pace their procedural demands in a manner that is consistent with what is within the individual's level of tolerance by taking baseline measurements for each task that needs to be performed, and gradually (10% per day) increasing the demands of each task. Rest is used as the reinforcement for successfully reaching a quota or, in other words, meeting a predetermined task goal. Goals for each task are determined based on what was done the previous day and patients are expected to work until the goal is accomplished, rather than work until they feel pain or fatigue. This technique puts more control in the hands of the patient, preventing a syndrome of learned helplessness that can often develop as a result of painful therapies. It also avoids reinforcing pain behaviors. The quota system is based on the notion that, although physical therapies after a burn injury will be painful, this pain itself is not damaging and will not negatively affect the outcome. As will be discussed subsequently, patients are taught the difference between *hurt* and *harm*.

Positive Reinforcement

Another operant principle that is often successful with patients with burn injuries, particularly children, is positive reinforcement. There is no intrinsically rewarding aspect of a burn injury or of burn recovery. In fact, children often see the treatment for a burn injury as a punishment. Therefore, children need to be rewarded for participation in the recovery process and for displaying appropriate behavior. For example, it is common within a burn unit to find a sticker board and prize box in each child's room. Behavioral expectations are established in advance and define what responsibilities the child has for that day, including wound care, physical and occupational therapy, eating meals, and so on. They receive a reward (sticker) for each responsibility that is accomplished. Once they have a set amount of stickers, they are able to pick a bigger prize from the prize box. This is known as establishing a token economy. Other creative means of positive reinforcement can also be effective—such as reading stories, watching movies or television, or offering adult attention through playing a game or reading a story. When children are frequently reinforced for good behavior or after completing a therapeutic goal, it makes the hospital environment more tolerable.

Care givers should also be careful not to reward inappropriate behaviors such as tantrums or escape/avoidance behavior. For example, children will often have a tantrum during wound care to get the nurse to cease what he or she is doing. If the nurse complies and stops wound care, the child has just been reinforced for his tantrum and learns that all he needs to do is scream and cry to get what he or she wants. This tactic will then likely be tried in situations outside of wound care, as well as the next day's wound care. In contrast, once a behavioral expectation has been established, (i.e., "we need to do our wound care now") staff and parents need to commit to following through on the task, regardless of the child's response. Some of these responses can be avoided by allowing children to determine when their wound care will be, or to assist in the wound care, as well as giving them positive reinforcement throughout wound care.

Although it is often important to minimize attention to acting out in response to pain, it is important that reinforcement contingencies for children not be based on their bravery or stoic acceptance of pain. It is a subtle form of punishment to withhold rewards in wound care except when the child reacts calmly. Rather, acting out is ignored and the child is rewarded for successfully completing a therapy or wound care session.

Information

Patients differ in how much detailed information they wish to receive about their medical care. Most patients, however, find that the unknown provokes anxiety and that receiving general information is helpful in reducing some of their anxiety. It is important to ask a patient how much detail they desire to know, and/or follow their individual proclivities in providing information. There are several aspects of burn care in which patients may benefit from information. First, side effects from medication can be worrisome, particularly for patients who have no experience with potent opioids. Letting them know that their weird dreams, itching, and constipation are normal effects of narcotics, and that long-term opioid dependency or addiction is very unlikely, can help alleviate these concerns. Second, some patients may not want to know details of procedures or tests, but they should be warned that they will be occurring, why they will happen, and when they will take place. This information will then allow patients to garner their coping skills and appropriately prepare for the situation. Finally, patients will often report that not knowing the medical plan or time line for upcoming surgeries, treatments, and so on is one of the biggest stressors in burn care. The nature of wound healing is such that the medical team cannot predict whether the burn will require surgery or will heal on its own. Once this determination is made, however, it is important to sit down with patients and lay out a time line for upcoming surgeries, dressing removals, therapies, rehabilitation, estimated discharge dates, and long-term care plans.

Cognitive Restructuring

Cognitive restructuring is frequently used as a coping technique for patients with chronic pain.[93,94] There are reports in the literature of using this technique for various types of acute pain, including those from dental work and surgical procedures.[95] A handful of studies have evaluated this approach with burn pain.[27,96] These techniques are successful only with patients wanting to use more of the *approach* coping style because it forces them to be aware and tend to their thoughts of pain.

Thought Stopping

The first step in cognitive restructuring is to identify and stop negative, catastrophizing thoughts. Thoughts such as "this is really going to hurt" and "I can't handle this pain" only lead to an increase in anxiety and a subsequent increase in pain. Patients can learn to recognize these negative thoughts and stop them, perhaps by picturing a stop sign or red light in their mind. They can also distract themselves by turning their attention to another topic. Children as young as 7 years of age have been taught to use this technique successfully.[27,97]

Reappraisal

Ideally, we want patients to transform their catastrophizing thoughts into a positive statement. This is known as reappraisal or reframing. For example, they may change the thoughts in the above example to " I have been through this wound care procedure before and it did not hurt as much as I thought it would," or " I have a very high pain tolerance and can cope with whatever will happen." Patients may also benefit from being taught the difference between *hurt* and *harm* when interpreting their pain sensations.[98] Specifically, an increase in pain is often a good sign with respect to burn wound healing. As discussed early in the chapter, deep (third-degree) burns often destroy nerve endings and limit the capacity for nociception. In deep burns that begin to heal or in more shallow burns, skin buds develop that are highly innervated and sensitive to pain and temperature.[10] Explaining this healing process to patients can help them to understand the nature of their pain and to reframe negative thoughts into reassuring, positive ones.

The treatment for burn wounds, including removing bandages daily and the aggressive washing of the open wounds, is counterintuitive to what most adults and children instinctively believe should be the appropriate treatment for open wounds. Most of us are taught that we do not touch open wounds, and we certainly should not rub them aggressively. Explaining that this type of treatment and the subsequent pain is what is necessary to heal the wound can help them to reframe any negative beliefs they may have had toward wound care. Given the counterintuitive nature of the information, patients may need to be given this information repeatedly; they must have trust in the staff member (particularly children); and, in many instances, it will be useful to combine the information with relaxation or hypnosis.

Participation

Allowing patients who have more of an *approach* coping style to participate in their own burn care and recovery is one of the simplest and most effective ways to increase their sense of control and reduce anxiety. We often use the technique of "forced-choice" for children to create more of a sense of control over their environment without overwhelming them with choices. When a child needs to accomplish an unpleasant task, parents and care givers can often create a situation where the child is given two choices in how to proceed with the task. For example, a child who is having difficulty in wound care may be given the choice of having the nurse wash their arm or washing their arm themselves. Or, if a child needs to get out of bed to walk, they can be given the choice of either doing it before lunch or after lunch. They must choose one of the two options, and if they cannot decide within a certain time frame, they are told that the nurse/parent will decide for them. This method will likely fail if more than two choices are given, or if a child is presented with an option that care givers or parents have no intention of allowing. Although patient participation may not be feasible in all aspects of burn care, there are several areas that lend themselves to giving patients more control (e.g., uncomplicated wound care, physical therapy, nutritional intake).

Setting Schedules

Both adults and children may benefit from having input into when certain tasks are done, such as wound care or physical therapy. Although it is not feasible to give patients open-ended choices in this matter, a choice of two or three options may be reasonable. For example, giving them a choice of having their wound care before lunch or after lunch, or their physical therapy immediately following wound care in the morning or in the later afternoon. If this is not possible, giving a patient sufficient notice of when it will be can help patients to adequately prepare themselves.

Wound Care

There are several ways patients who use more of an *approach* coping style can participate in their own wound care. One simple way to participate is to allow them to choose if and what type of music is played during wound care. We often encourage patients to create a repeatable routine for each wound care procedure, wherein they are mentally preparing and doing certain things the same way every day in an effort to help reduce anxiety. Because patients will have different nurses from day to day, it is up to the patient to let the nurses know what works best for them, as well as the details of their routine. Patients should be encouraged to take responsibility for communicating these plans. Patients can also regulate the pace of wound care by asking for periodic breaks, or telling a nurse to wash slower or faster. One useful approach is to give children a set number of "timeout cards" (around 5) that allow them a short (30-second) break during wound care. They can use them at any time until they are gone. Often, patients will progress to the point of wanting to assist the nurses in their own wound care, particularly after they have been in the hospital for some time. Easy ways to assist are to have them unwrap their bandages or wash areas that are easily reachable and/or particularly painful. Finally, patients preparing for hospital discharge may even want to perform their entire wound care independently, if possible.

■ SIDE EFFECTS AND COMPLICATIONS

Analgesic Management Based on Valid Pain Assessment

As with any type of pain management paradigm, therapeutic burn pain decisions related to which analgesic technique(s) to use, what drugs to use, and what drug doses to use hinge dramatically on the valid assessment of the patient's pain. Pain assessment is no less challenging in burn patients, and may be further complicated by the multiple premorbid or comorbid psychological issues that frequently accompany the burn injury.[11] We have already noted that patient reports of pain are preferred because they differ from (and are typically greater than) those reported by burn care givers.[29-31] However, this is not always possible, as in cases of severely injured, noncommunicative (intubated and mechanically ventilated) adults, or young children who cannot provide meaningful pain reports. Pain assessment in burns has been extensively reviewed, with details on appropriate tools for various clinical settings described elsewhere in adults[99] and children.[18]

Although pain assessment in the clinical and research setting has traditionally relied on patient reports 0 to 10 verbal scales, 0 to 10 visual analog scales (VAS), or 0 to 10 graphic rating scales (GRS), there is increasing interest in assessing patient satisfaction with pain control as an alternative measure of analgesic success. For example, asking a patient for their "treatment or analgesic goal" using the same measurement scale as for pain intensity can be useful because this process provides a yardstick for analgesic management and may encourage more active patient participation in pain management plans. This concept has been recommended for clinical use by the JCAHO,[6] but is not in widespread use. However, in limited studies in the burn population[100] it appears that those patients who experience the least amount of pain (by standard pain ratings) have greater analgesic satisfaction than do those who report pain ratings that most closely match their stated analgesic treatment goals. Thus, the ideal choice and interpretation of pain assessment tools in burn pain settings is yet to be defined.

Complications from Excessive Analgesic Medications

The wide spectrum of untoward side effects associated with potent benzodiazepines, opioid analgesics, and anesthetics is well known, and it ranges from the relatively benign (e.g., transient nausea) to life threatening (e.g., respiratory depression). The prevention and treatment of these various analgesic side effects is detailed elsewhere in this text. However, general recommendations should include that all analgesia/sedation procedures be carried out under the guidelines published by the American Society of Anesthesiologists[19] and supported by the JCAHO.[6] These guidelines include requirements for appropriate physiologic and consciousness monitoring, and for appropriate training of all care givers who administer pharmacologic sedation. Specifically, because the desired level of sedation (e.g., moderate sedation) cannot be guaranteed in a given patient with a given pharmacologic regimen, providers must be trained and skilled at managing the next greater depth of sedation (e.g., deep sedation), including airway, respiratory, and cardiovascular support, in the event this level of sedation unexpectedly occurs.

Overlooking Anxiety

One of the biggest mistakes made in burn pain management is not recognizing anxiety and treating it accordingly. As mentioned earlier, anxiety exacerbates, and often precedes pain. Poorly managed pain, particularly early in the hospitalization, leads to anticipatory anxiety for any future procedures. An effective pain management program needs to target anxiety as well as pain, using both pharmacologic and nonpharmacologic techniques. To assess anxiety, one can ask a patient to rate both their pain and their anxiety on separate 0 to 10 scales. In both adults and children who are unable to distinguish between pain and anxiety, staff should watch for behavioral signs, such as the display of pain behaviors before a procedure even begins.

Staff Changeover

It is reasonable to assume that patients will each have many care givers during their hospitalization. Inconsistencies in the care that patients receive from various staff members can frustrate patients and make pain and anxiety harder to manage. There will also be significant variations in the familiarity and training that various staff have had in nonpharmacologic pain management techniques. It should also be noted, however, that there is often a shortage of nurses on inpatient units and their time may be stretched between multiple patients. Thus, even when care givers are well trained in nonpharmacologic techniques, they may not have adequate time to apply them effectively. Most burn centers recognize the importance of having psychologists and other specialists trained in these techniques as part of the burn team. These individuals may be available to assist in applying the techniques in many cases; however, it is not reasonable to assume that they will be available to meet every patient's daily needs. Therefore, they should continue to train nurses and patients in these techniques to the extent possible. Differences in how nurses perform wound care, and lack of training in nonpharmacologic techniques can cause patients to lose confidence in the medical team and make pain even harder to manage. This makes it even more necessary to empower patients to direct their own care by sharing with care givers their care needs and preferences.

Mismatch of Techniques and Coping Style

As mentioned earlier, it is crucial to match the various nonpharmacologic techniques to a patient's coping style. For example, one can see the problem in utilizing a distraction technique with patients who have a high need for control and need to participate in their wound care. Further, providing patients who are closer to the *avoidance* end of the control continuum with too much information on a medical procedure may actually increase their anxiety. Again, it is important to periodically assess a person's preference because patients often move from one end of the continuum to the other during a hospitalization.

Inadequate Planning—"Surprises"

Even with the most vigilant preparation, unplanned procedures, quick changes in schedules and other "surprises" are bound to occur. These unplanned procedures can cause significant anxiety for patients and may increase pain levels. Teaching patients distress tolerance and to "expect the unexpected," as well as providing them with quick strategies to use when the unexpected occurs can go a long way toward decreasing anxiety and pain. Patients may even get to the point of being able to "thrive" on the chaos often associated with acute inpatient hospitalization. Although seemingly counterintuitive to the clinician, this is an example of the patient adopting a secondary coping mechanism as described earlier.

Premorbid Psychological Problems

Patients with preexisting problems, including anxiety disorders, substance abuse problems, and chronic pain problems, make the management of acute pain and anxiety even more difficult. As noted earlier, preinjury psychological problems are common in burn patients and are much higher than in the general population.[11] A burn injury and the subsequent treatment can often exacerbate depression in patients with this premorbid diagnosis. Treatment for depression should not only continue on the burn unit, but should be pursued even more aggressively. Patients with DSM-IV revised (American Psychiatric Association) Axis II personality disorders often cause great difficulty for the staff. Care givers need to be educated about such personality disorders and understand that a person with a burn injury will not be "cured" of such disorders while in the burn unit. Psychologists or psychiatrists should be consulted to devise appropriate behavior plans and to train staff in managing these patients. Often patients with substance abuse problems will have a strong reliance on the pharmacologic management of pain. Depending on their drug of choice, they may have a lower pain tolerance or display more pain behaviors. Pain specialists and/or anesthesiologists may need to be consulted. Patients with substance abuse problems should still be offered nonpharmacologic approaches and should be encouraged to use them. Medicating sufficiently for their acute pain through a regular medication schedule (versus prn) will also help in managing pain for these patients. In the instance of premorbid anxiety and chronic pain problems, patients should be encouraged to use whatever coping techniques they have used in the past to manage these problems. Burn hospitalization and care may be an ideal time for these patients to learn new coping techniques.

Sleep Disturbance

Sleep disturbance is a common problem in the inpatient setting irrespective of medical diagnosis or condition. However, a significant proportion of burn patients, once discharged from the hospital, also suffer from sleep problems. Sleep is disrupted by pain, itching, excessive fatigue, medication effects, and changes in sleep cycles. Treatment ideally focuses first on sleep hygiene, including reestablishment of sleep cycles (avoiding daytime naps, caffeine, and late night alcohol, and teaching patients to use the bed as a stimulus for sleep [i.e., no television]). Failing such educational/behavioral techniques, the relatively short-acting benzodiazepines usually provide patients with the ability to fall asleep with minimal hangover effects. If this class of drug fails or the patient is depressed, sedating antidepressant medications may be of use, particularly in keeping the patient asleep.[101]

Wound Care Environment

Nurses can help make wound care procedures more relaxing by having the dressings and necessary supplies prepared in advance and laid out before the patient arrives in the tank room, keeping the room warm, having some relaxing music playing low in the background, dimming bright lights, reducing clutter in the tank room, keeping their voices low, and speaking in relaxed tones. If a patient comes into the tank room that is not prepared, is cold and uninviting, and encounters nurses who are rushed, this will often create an atmosphere of tension and anxiety for both the nurses and the patient. When a patient is expressing significant anxiety and pain, it is crucial that the nurses remain calm, because patients will become sensitive to the anxiety or discomfort of the staff. We should also emphasize that any painful procedure, including wound care, should be done in a location outside of the patient's room, particularly when caring for children. It is critical for a pediatric patient to feel that his or her room is a safe, relaxing place that can be viewed as a retreat after painful procedures or therapies. This will also lead to more restful sleep.

■ CONCLUSION

The control of burn pain continues to be a challenge that demands creativity and continued staff training on pain assessment, traditional pharmacologic analgesic approaches, and adjunctive nonpharmacologic techniques. Pharmacologic analgesics need to be administered by appropriately trained and experienced staff, under appropriate monitoring conditions. Likewise, it is critical to assess a patient's coping style and match nonpharmacologic techniques accordingly. Assessment is necessarily ongoing because patient's coping styles and preferences may change throughout the hospitalization.

Future directions in burn pain management include improvements in the diagnostic and prognostic assessment of burn wounds, as well as prediction of which analgesic techniques are best suited for individual patients. With regard to burn wound diagnosis, improved early and accurate definition of burns that will heal only by surgical excision and grafting will help minimize the number of patients who currently undergo days to weeks of hopeful watching of the burn wound, waiting for the wound to declare itself as self-healing or not. There is a subpopulation of these patients who undergo days to weeks of painful wound care and significant background pain, only to discover that their burn could have been treated initially with excision and grafting, thus avoiding the prolonged period of burn pain. With regard to predicting the most effective analgesic techniques in an individual burn patient, advances in both pharmacologic and nonpharmacologic techniques are anticipated. Pharmacologic analgesia potential for specific drugs may be more accurately predicted

as genetic screening for opioid metabolic enzymes or receptor genotypes comes into common clinical practice, enabling care givers to choose the most appropriate drug and dose for a given genotype.[102] Similarly, tools that predict the success of nonpharmacologic analgesic interventions will undoubtedly be developed. One such example is the assessment of hypnotizability (Stanford Hypnotic Clinical Scale[103]) that predicts the potential success of hypnotic analgesia in individual patients. With numerous such genetic and behavioral screening tools available for clinical use, one can imagine the power and clinical benefit of identifying and implementing, early in the clinical course of the burn patient, the most effective pharmacologic and nonpharmacologic analgesic techniques for a particular patient, thereby maximizing analgesic benefit and minimizing analgesic side effects.

References

1. Esselman PC, Thombs BD, Fauerbach JA, et al: Burn rehabilitation: State of the science review. Am J Phys Med Rehabil 85:383-413, 2006.
2. Brigham PA, McLoughlin E: Burn incidence and medical care use in the United States: Estimates, trends, and data sources. J Burn Care Rehabil 17:95, 1996.
3. Perry S, Heidrich G: Management of pain during débridement: A survey of U.S. burn units. Pain 13:267, 1982.
4. Schecter NL: Pain and pain control in children. Curr Probl Pediatr 15:1, 1985.
5. Ptacek JT, Patterson DR, Montgomery BK, Heimbach DM: Pain, coping, and adjustment in patients with burns: Preliminary findings from a prospective study. J Pain Symptom Manage. (6):446, 1995.
6. JCAHO: Pain Management Across the Continuum of Care: The Patient's Experience. Oakbrook Terrace, Ill, Joint Commission Resources, 2000.
7. Loor MM, Vern TZ, Latenser BA, Kowal-Vern A: Trends in burn research as reflected in American Burn Association presentations, 1998 to 2003. J Burn Care Rehabil 26:397, 2005.
8. Silbert BS, Osgood PF, Carr DB: Burn pain. In Yaksh TL, Lynch C, Zapol WM, Maze M (eds): Anesthesia: Biologic Foundations. Philadelphia, Lippincott, 1997, p 759.
9. Choiniere M, Melzack R, Rondeau J, et al: The pain of burns: Characteristics and correlates. J Trauma 29:1531, 1989.
10. Patterson DR, Sharar SR: Burn pain. In Loeser JD, et al (eds): Bonica's Management of Pain. Philadelphia, Lippincott, p 780, 2001.
11. Patterson DR, Everett JJ, Bombardier CH, et al: Psychological effects of severe burn injuries. Psychol Bull 113:362, 1993.
12. Martin-Herz SP, Patterson DR, Honari S, et al: Pediatric pain control practices of North American burn centers. J Burn Care Rehabil 24:26, 2003.
13. Perry S, Heidrich G, Ramos E: Assessment of pain by burn patients. J Burn Care Rehabil 2:322, 1981.
14. Porter J, Jick H: Addiction rare in patients treated with narcotics. N Engl J Med 302:123, 1980.
15. Cortiella J, Marvin JA. Management of the pediatric burn patient. Nurs Clin North Am 32:311, 1997.
16. Sheridan RL, Hinson M, Nackel A, et al: Development of a pediatric burn pain and anxiety management program. J Burn Care Rehabil 18:455, 1997.
17. Gibbons J, Honari SR, Sharar SR, et al: Opiate-induced respiratory depression in young pediatric burn patients. J Burn Care Rehabil 19: 225, 1998.
18. Stoddard FJ, Sheridan RL, Saxe GN, et al: Treatment of pain in acutely burned children. J Burn Care Rehabil 23:135, 2002.
19. American Society of Anesthesiologists: Practice guidelines for sedation and analgesia by non-anesthesiologists. Anesthesiology 96:1004, 2002.
20. Humphries Y, Melson M, Gore D: Superiority of oral ketamine as an analgesic and sedative for burn wound care procedures in the pediatric patient with burns. J Burn Care Rehabil 18:34, 1997.
21. Sharar SR, Bratton SL, Carrougher GJ, et al: A comparison of oral transmucosal fentanyl citrate and oral hydromorphone for inpatient pediatric burn wound care. J Burn Care Rehabil 19:516, 1998.

22. Sharar SR, Carrougher GJ, Selzer K, et al: A comparison of oral transmucosal fentanyl citrate and oral oxycodone for pediatric outpatient wound care. J Burn Care Rehabil 23:27, 2002.

23. Filkins SA, Cosgrove P, Marvin JA, et al: Self-administered anesthetic: A method of pain control. J Burn Care Rehabil 1:33, 1981.

24. Dimick P, Helvig E, Heimbach D, et al: Anesthesia-assisted procedures in a burn intensive care unit procedure room: Benefits and complications. J Burn Care Rehabil 14:446, 1993.

25. Powers PS, Cruse CW, Daniels S, Stevens BA: Safety and efficacy of débridement under anesthesia in patients with burns. J Burn Care Rehabil 14:176, 1993.

26. Weisman SJ, Bernstein B, Schechter NL: Consequences of inadequate analgesia during painful procedures in children. Arch Pediatr Adolesc Med 152:147, 1998.

27. Thurber CA, Martin-Herz SP, Patterson DR: Psychological principles of burn wound pain in children. I: Theoretical framework. J Burn Care Rehabil 21:376, 2000.

28. Cuignet O, Mbuyamba J, Pirson J: The long-term analgesic efficacy of a single-shot fascia iliaca compartment block in burn patients undergoing skin-grafting procedures. J Burn Care Rehabil 26:409, 2005.

29. Choinere M, Melzack R, Girard N, et al: Comparisons between patients' and nurses' assessment of pain and medication efficacy in severe burn injuries. Pain 40:143, 1990.

30. Iafrati NS: Pain on the burn unit: Patient vs. nurse perceptions. J Burn Care Rehabil 7:413, 1986.

31. Marvin JA: Pain assessment versus measurement. J Burn Care Rehabil 16:348, 1995.

32. Perry S, Inturrisi C: Analgesia and morphine disposition in burn patients. J Burn Care Rehabil 4:276, 1983.

33. Herman RA, Veng Pedersen P, Miotto J, et al: Pharmacokinetics of morphine sulfate in patients with burns. J Burn Care Rehabil 15:95, 1994.

34. Furman WR, Munster AM, Cone EJ: Morphine pharmacokinetics during anesthesia and surgery with burns. J Burn Care Rehabil 11:391, 1990.

35. Silbert BS, Lipkowski AW, Cepeda MS, et al: Enhanced potency of receptor-selective opioids after acute burn injury. Anesth Analg 73:427, 1991.

36. Franceschi D, Gerding RL, Phillips G, Fratianne RB: Risk factors associated with intravascular catheter infections in burned patients: A prospective, randomized study. J Trauma 29:811, 1989.

37. Rovers J, Knighton J, Neligan P, Peters W: Patient-controlled analgesia in burn patients: A critical review of the literature and case report. Hosp Pharm 29:108, 1994.

38. Lee JJ, Marvin JA, Heimbach DM: Effectiveness of nalbuphine for relief of burn débridement pain. J Burn Care Rehabil 10:241, 1989.

39. Kariya N, Shindoh M, Nishi S, et al: Oral clonidine for sedation and analgesia in a burn patient. J Clin Anesth 10:514, 1998.

40. Lyons B, Casey W, Doherty P, et al: Pain relief with low-dose intravenous clonidine in a child with severe burns. Intensive Care Med 22:249, 1996.

41. Egan KJ, Ready LB, Nessly M, Greer BE: Self-administration of midazolam for postoperative anxiety: A double blinded study. Pain 49:3, 1992.

42. Patterson, DR, Ptacek, JT, Carrougher, GJ, Sharar, SR: Lorazepam as an adjunct to opioid analgesics in the treatment of burn pain. Pain 72:367, 1997.

43. Basket PJF, Hyland J, Deane M, Wray G: Analgesia for burns dressing in children. Br J Anaesth 41:684, 1969.

44. Filkins SA, Cosgrove P, Marvin JA, et al: Self-administered anesthetic: A method of pain control. J Burn Care Rehabil 1:33, 1981.

45. American Society of Anesthesiologists: Report of an ad hoc committee on the effect of trace anesthetics on the health of operating room personnel. Occupational disease among operating room personnel: A national study. Anesthesiology 41:32, 1974.

46. Nunn JF, Chanarin I, Tanner AG: Megaloblastic bone marrow changes after repeated nitrous oxide anaesthesia. Br J Anaesth 58;1469, 1986.

47. Demling RH, Ellerbee S, Jarrett F: Ketamine anesthesia for tangential excision of burn eschar: A burn unit procedure. J Trauma 18:269, 1978.

48. Ward CM, Diamond AW: An appraisal of ketamine in the dressing of burns. Postgrad Med J 5:222, 1976.

49. Mills DC, Lord WD: Propofol for repeated burns dressings in a child: A case report. Burns 18:58, 1992.

50. Coimbra C, Choiniere M, Hemmerling TM: Patient-controlled sedation using propofol for dressing changes in burn patients: A dose-finding study. Anesth Analg 97:839, 2003.

51. Punja K, Graham M, Cartotto R. Continuous infusion of epidural morphine in frostbite. J Burn Care Rehabil 19:142, 1998.

52. Still JM, Abramson R, Law EJ: Development of an epidural abscess following staphylococcal septicemia in an acutely burned patient: Case report. J Trauma 38:958, 1995.

53. Cuignet O, Pirson J, Boughrouph J, Duville D: The efficacy of continuous fascia iliaca compartment block for pain management in burn patients undergoing skin grafting procedures. Anesth Analg (4):1077, 2004.

54. Pedersen JL, Callesen T, Moiniche S, Kehlet H: Analgesic and anti-inflammatory effects of lignocaine-prilocaine (EMLA) cream in human burn injury. Br J Anaesth 76:806, 1996.

55. Brofeldt BT, Cornwell P, Doherty D, et al: Topical lidocaine in the treatment of partial thickness burns. J Burn Care Rehabil 10:63, 1989.

56. Wehner D, Hamilton GC: Seizures following application of local anesthetics to burn patients. Ann Emerg Med 13:456, 1984.

57. Rothbaum F, Wiesz JR, Snyder S: Changing the world and changing the self: A two-process model of perceived control. J Personality Soc Psychol 42:5, 1982.

58. Schechter NL, Bernstein BA, Beck A, et al: Individual differences in children's response to pain: Role of temperament and parental characteristics. Pediatrics 87:171, 1991.

59. Thurber CA, Weisz JR: "You can try or you can just give up": The impact of perceived control and coping style on childhood homesickness. Dev Psychol 33:508, 1997.

60. Weisz JR: Development of control-related beliefs, goals, and styles in childhood and adolescence: A clinical perspective. In Schaie KW, Rodin J, Scholler C, eds: Self-directedness and Efficacy: Causes and Effects Throughout the Life Course. New York, Erlbaum, 1990, p 103.

61. Bennett-Branson SM, Craig KD: Postoperative pain in children: Developmental and family influences on spontaneous coping strategies. Canadian J Behav Science 25:355, 1993.

62. Martin-Herz SP, Thurber CA, Patterson DR: Psychological principles of burn wound pain in children, II: Treatment applications. J Burn Care Rehabil 21:458, 2000.

63. Rowling JK: Prisoner of Azkaban. New York, Arthur A. Levine Books, Scholastic Press; 1999.

64. Barber J: A brief introduction to hypnotic analgesia. In Barber J, ed: Hypnosis and suggestion in the treatment of pain. A clinical guide. New York, W.W. Norton, 1996, p 3.

65. Patterson DR: Burn Pain. In Barber J, ed: Hypnosis and Suggestion in the Treatment of Pain. New York, W.W. Norton, 1996, p 267.

66. Barber J: Rapid induction analgesia: A clinical report. Am J Clin Hypn 19:138, 1977.

67. Lang EV, Benotsch EG, Fick LJ, et al: Adjunctive non-pharmacological analgesia for invasive medical procedures: A randomised trial. Lancet 355:1486, 2000.

68. Ewin D: Hypnosis in burn therapy. In Burrows GD, Dennerstein L (eds): Hypnosis. Amsterdam, Elsevier, 1979, p 210.

69. Ewin DM: Emergency room hypnosis for the burned patient. Am J Clin Hypn 29:7, 1986.

70. Rainville P, Duncan GH, Price DD, et al: Pain affect encoded in human anterior cingulate but not somatosensory cortex. Science 277:968, 1997.

71. Montgomery GH, DuHamel KN, Redd WH: A meta-analysis of hypnotically induced analgesia: How effective is hypnosis? Int J Clin Exp Hypn 48:138, 2000.

72. Patterson DR, Jensen M: Hypnosis and clinical pain. Psychol Bull 129:495, 2003.

73. Patterson DR, Questad KA, Boltwood M: Patient reports about their health and physical functioning three months after a major burn. J Burn Care Rehabil 8:274, 1987.

74. Wakeman JR, Kaplan JZ: An experimental study of hypnosis in painful burns. Am J Clin Hypn 21:3, 1978.

75. Patterson DR, Everett JJ, Burns GL, Marvin JA: Hypnosis for the treatment of burn pain. J Consult Clin Psychol 60:713, 1992.

76. Patterson DR, Adcock RJ, Bombardier CH: Factors predicting hypnotic analgesia in clinical burn pain. Int J Clin Exp Hypn 45:377, 1997.

77. Patterson DR, Ptacek JT: Baseline pain as a moderator of hypnotic analgesia for burn injury treatment. J Consult Clin Psychol 65:60, 1997.

78. Holroyd J: Hypnosis treatment of clinical pain: Understanding why hypnosis is useful. Int J Clin Exp Hypn XLIV(1), 1996.

79. Patterson DR, Tininenko JR, Schmidt AE: Virtual reality hypnosis: A case report. Int J Clin Exp Hypn 52:27, 2004.

80. Hoffman HG, Patterson DR, Carrougher GJ, Sharar SR: Effectiveness of virtual reality-based pain control with multiple treatments. Clin J Pain 17:229, 2001.

81. Kahneman D: Attention and Effort. Englewood Cliffs, NJ, Prentice-Hall, 1973.

82. Shiffrin R, Schneider W: Controlled and automatic human information processing, II. Perceptual learning, automatic attending, and a general theory. Psych Rev 84:127, 1977.

83. Hoffman HG: Physically touching virtual objects using tactile augmentation enhances the realism of virtual environments. In IEEE Virtual Reality Annual International Symposium 1998. Atlanta, Ga, IEEE Computer Society Press, 1998, p 59.

84. Hoffman HG, Doctor JN, Patterson DR, et al: Use of virtual reality as an adjunctive treatment of adolescent burn pain during wound care: A case report. Pain 85:305, 2000.

85. Hoffman HG, Patterson DR, Carrougher GJ: Use of virtual reality for adjunctive treatment of adult burn pain during physical therapy: A controlled study. Clin J Pain 16:244, 2000.

86. Hoffman HG, Patterson DR, Carrougher GJ, et al: The effectiveness of virtual reality pain control with multiple treatments of longer durations: A case study. Int J Hum Comput Interact 13:1, 2001.

87. Greenberg JS: Comprehensive Stress Management. Dubuque, Ia, Brown & Benchmark, 1993.

88. Jacobson E: Progressive Relaxation. Chicago, University of Chicago Press, 1938.

89. Paice JA, Noskin GA, Vanagunas A, Shott S: Efficacy and safety of scheduled dosing of opioid analgesics: A quality improvement study. J Pain 6:639, 2005.

90. Patterson DR, Ptacek JT, Carrougher G, et al: The 2002 Lindberg Award. PRN vs. regularly scheduled opioid analgesics in pediatric burn patients. J Burn Care Rehabil, 23:424, 2002.

91. Melzack R: The tragedy of needless pain. Sci Am 262:27, 1990.

92. Ehde DM, Patterson DR, Fordyce WE: The quota system in burn rehabilitation. J Burn Care Rehabil 19:436, 1998.

93. Holzman AD, Turk DC: Pain Management. Oxford, Pergamon, 1986.

94. Turk DC, Meichenbaum D, Genest M: Pain and behavioral medicine: A cognitive-behavioral perspective. New York, Guilford, 1983.

95. Langer EL, Janis IL, Wolfer JA: Reduction of psychological stress in surgical patients. J Exp Soc Psychol 11:165, 1975.

96. Everett JJ, Patterson DR, Chen AC: Cognitive and behavioral treatments for burn pain. Pain Clin 3:133, 1990.

97. Zeltzer L: Pain and symptom management. In Bearson DJ, Mulhern RK (eds): Pediatric Psycho-oncology: Psychological perspectives on children with cancer. New York, Oxford University Press, 1994, p 61.

98. Fordyce WE: Behavioral Methods for Chronic Pain and Illness. St. Louis, Mosby Year Book, 1976.

99. Marvin JA: Pain assessment versus measurement. J Burn Care Rehabil 16:348, 1995.

100. Carrougher GJ, Ptacek JT, Sharar S et al: Comparison of patient satisfaction and self-reports of pain in adult burn-injured patients. J Burn Care Rehabil 24:1, 2003.

101. Jaffe SE, Patterson DR: Treating sleep problems in patients with burn injuries: Practical considerations. J Burn Care Rehabil 25:294, 2004.

102. Fishbain DA, Fishbain D, Lewis J, et al: Genetic testing for enzymes of drug metabolism: Does it have clinical utility for pain medicine at the present time? A structured review. Pain Med 5:81, 2004.

103. Morgan A, Hilgard J: The Stanford Hypnotic Clinical Scale for Children. Am J Clin Hypn 21:148, 1978.

chapter 22

Sickle Cell Pain

Kimberley Smith

■ HISTORICAL PERSPECTIVES

In 1910, sickle cell disease was discovered in the United States when sickle-shaped red blood cells were found in the blood of a medical student from Africa (Fig. 22–1).[1,2] Later, in 1923, further studies showed that its inheritance is autosomal dominant. Four years later oxygen deprivation was shown to mediate sickling. In 1949, the discovery that sickle hemoglobin had an abnormal electrophoretic mobility prompted Linus Pauling and his colleagues to proclaim sickle cell anemia a molecular disease.[3] The ensuing 5 decades produced a plethora of information—the mechanisms by which a single base substitution in gene encoding human β globin subunit with the resulting substitution of glutamic acid by valine (Fig. 22–2). Later studies showed that endothelial cells and altered erythrocytes possess surface molecules that cause intracellular adhesions, which leads to the polymerization of deoxygenated hemoglobin and vaso-occlusion.[4] Advances in clinical and basic research did not change the prognosis of sickle cell disease until the use of hydroxyurea and bone marrow transplantation. Pain management and supportive care have been paramount in the treatment of sickle cell disease since the beginning and still remain the best intervention to reduce morbidity and improve the quality of life of a majority of patients.

■ CLINICAL PRESENTATION

Sickle cell disease is a group of inherited disorders with abnormalities caused by hemoglobin S. Sickle cell anemia in which only hemoglobin S is produced (HbSS) is the most severe and most common form. Affected individuals suffer a wide range of clinical problems that result from vascular obstruction and ischemia. The most common clinical problems include: stroke, acute chest syndrome, renal dysfunction, splenic sequestration, bone infarction, multiple infections, and painful crises. The clinical severity varies considerably.

Stroke

Although it is unusual for children to have strokes, approximately 11% of patients with sickle cell anemia have strokes before they reach the age of 20 years.[5] Hemiparesis is the usual presentation. Other deficits may be found, depending on the location of the infarct.

Acute Chest Syndrome

The lung is a major target organ for acute and chronic complications of sickle disease. Acute chest syndrome is a frequent cause of death in both children and adults with sickle cell disease. It is an acute illness characterized by fever and respiratory symptoms, accompanied by a new pulmonary infiltrate on chest radiographs. Acute chest syndrome is the second most common cause of hospitalization in patients with sickle cell disease and the most common cause of complication after surgery.[6]

Renal Abnormalities

The kidney in patients with sickle cell disease exhibits lots of structural and functional abnormalities, changes that are seen along the entire length of the nephron. The environment of the renal medulla—hypoxia, acidosis, and hypertonicity—promotes hemoglobin S polymerization and red cell sickling.[7]

Splenic Sequestration

Acute splenic sequestration is caused by intrasplenic trapping of red blood cells, which causes a drop in the hemoglobin level and the potential for hypoxic shock. This is a leading cause of death in children with sickle cell disease.[8]

Bony Infarction

Musculoskeletal manifestations of sickle cell disease are common and may lead to severe morbidity. Bone and joint involvement result from three main causes (1) bone marrow hyperplasia, which causes distortion and growth disturbance—particularly in the skull, vertebrae, and long bones; (2) vaso-occlusive events that lead to infarction of metaphyseal and diaphyseal bone and to osteonecrosis of juxta-articular bone; and (3) hematogenous bacterial infection that results in osteomyelitis and septic arthritis.[9]

Infection

Infection is a major complication of sickle cell disease. Special preventive measures against infection exist in

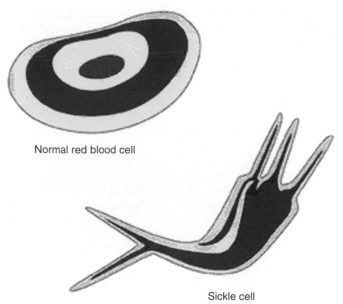

FIGURE 22–1 ■ Illustration demonstrating a sickle-shaped cell versus a normal red blood cell.

Table 22–1	
The Most Common Pain States Associated with Sickle Cell Disease	
Chronic neuropathic pain	Usually due to iron overload neuropathy
Priapism	Due to sickling in the sinusoids of the penis
Acute painful crisis	Due to vaso-occlusion and endothelial damage
Acute chest syndrome	Due to vaso-occlusion, infarcts, and infection
Dactylitis	Due to infarctions of metatarsals and metacarpals that cause occlusion of developing blood vessels
Avascular necrosis of humerus or femur	Associated with bone infarction or sickle cell arthritis

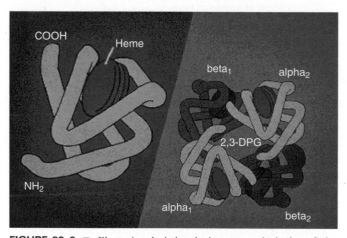

FIGURE 22–2 ■ Illustration depicting the important substitution of glutamate for valine in sickle cell disease.

addition to routine immunizations; treatment regimens are based on local formularies and antibiotic sensitivity tests.

■ PAIN

The hallmark clinical manifestation of sickle cell disease is the acute vaso-occlusive event, or painful episode. This unique type of pain can begin as early as 6 months of age and recurs throughout a patient's life. Painful events are the number one cause of hospitalizations of patients with sickle cell disease.[10]

Types and Characteristics of Pain

The most common pain states associated with sickle cell disease are summarized in Table 22–1. Sickle cell pain can be characterized as acute, chronic, or mixed.

Acute Pain

The acute painful event is the most common type of pain associated with sickle cell pain. Acute pain tends to be unpredictable and intensity can vary from a mild ache to severe debilitating pain. Acute pain tends to be more visceral than somatic. Visceral pain reflects pain from solid organs such as the kidneys, liver, or spleen. Visceral pain tends to be characterized as a dull ache, not well localized, and is referred.[10]

Chronic Pain

Chronic pain is often defined as being present for 3 to 6 months or longer. Chronic pain tends to be more somatic than visceral. Somatic pain involves pain in the deep structures of the body such as tendons, ligaments, and bones. Somatic pain is characterized as a sharp pain and tends to be more localized. Chronic pain can be debilitating—physically and psychologically. The involvement of sensation, emotion, cognition, memory, and context are difficult problems to manage.[10]

Mixed Pain

Pain is frequently mixed as to type and mechanism due to confounding factors. Acute pain can be superimposed on chronic pain, and frequent episodes of acute pain can resemble chronic pain. Neuropathic pain is often underdiagnosed in patients with sickle cell disease. Neuropathic pain in this population is often due to iron overload anemia.[11]

■ DIAGNOSIS

Screening Tests

Screening tests for sickle cell disease involve newborn hemoglobinopathy screening. Imaging studies include MRI and CT scan, which can evaluate the numerous body systems affected by sickle cell disease.

Assessment of patients with sickle cell disease is primarily subjective. In fact, there is no standard for the evaluation of the severity of pain. Pain assessment relies solely on the patient's interpretation of pain and the clinician's use of valid and reliable assessment tools. Such tools include the Visual Analog Scale, the Numeric Intensity Rating Scale, the Wong-Baker Faces Pain Rating Scale, and the Oucher Scale (Figs. 22–3, 22–4, and 22–5).[12]

There are two major kinds of assessment. A rapid assessment of an acute painful episode involves evaluating an isolated pain event and focusing on prompt treatment and relief versus a comprehensive assessment for chronic pain or follow-up of persons who have acute pain.

Differential Diagnosis

The differential diagnosis of sickle cell disease includes other hemoglobinopathies and thalassemias. Table 22–2 summarizes these diseases.

■ TREATMENT OF PAIN

Emergency Treatment of Acute Pain Episodes

The patient in acute pain in a clinician's office or the emergency department usually has tried all means of alleviating the pain. Failure of home therapy usually signals the need for

parenteral medications, which include strong opioids like morphine. If a patient is on long-term opioids, tolerance may have developed, so the new acute painful episode may require higher doses of opioid or a different opioid.

In general, medications and loading doses are selected after careful assessment of the patient, which requires patient's home medications, medications that alleviated the last painful crisis, and medications that the patient has increased during the current painful crisis. For patients with recurrent pain, the best initial dose of opioids for severe sickle pain is the dosage that provided analgesia in the last painful crisis. Some clinicians prefer a loading dose of parenteral morphine, usually equivalent to 5 to 10 mg (0.1 to 0.15 mg/kg for children), depending on pain intensity, patient's size, and prior opioid experience.[13] Intramuscular administration of medication should be avoided because absorption is unpredictable. For severe pain, intravenous administrations are the route of choice. For intractable sickle crisis, intraspinal medications—usually fentanyl and a local anesthetic—have been deemed effective in some patients.

Pharmacologic Management of Sickle Pain

Analgesics are the mainstay of treatment of sickle cell pain. Usually sedatives and anxiolytics alone should be avoided because these medications can mask the behavioral response to pain. Management of pain associated with sickle cell disease consists of the use of nonsteroidal anti-inflammatory drugs (NSAIDs), opioids, and adjuvant medications.[14]

For the management of mild pain, NSAIDS or acetaminophen is recommended. Clinicians should be aware of inducing nephritic analgesia in patients who are at an added

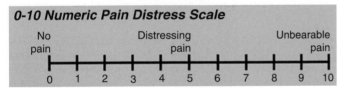

FIGURE 22–3 ■ The numeric pain scale is a linear scale in which patients can circle the level of pain they are in. This scale is intended for use with adolescents and adults.

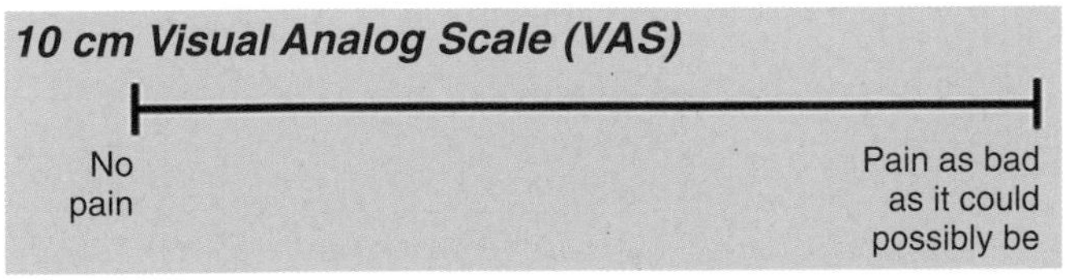

FIGURE 22–4 ■ The visual analog scale is a 10-cm horizontal line in which the patient can draw a line depicting their levels of pain. This scale is intended for adolescents and adults.

Table 22–2	
Differential Diagnosis of Sickle Cell Disease	
SCD-SS	Hemolysis and anemia by 6-12 mo
SCD-SC	Mild or no anemia by 2 yr
SCD-S β+ thal	Mild or no anemia by 2 yr
SCD-S β⁰ thal	Hemolysis and anemia by 6-12 mo
SCD-S δβ thal	Mild anemia by 2 yr
S HPFH	No hemolysis or anemia

SCD, sickle cell disease; sickle cell disease-S; sickle cell disease-SC; sickle cell disease-SS; S HPFH, ; thal, thalassemia.

FIGURE 22–5 ■ The Wong-Baker Faces Scale, used primarily with pediatric patients.

risk of developing renal failure. Many patients with sickle cell disease have varying degrees of hepatic impairment, and acetaminophen may be toxic when liver disease is present. If mild pain persists, an opioid can be added.

Treatment of persistent or moderate to severe pain requires the use of opioids. The type of opioid used depends on the characteristics and duration of pain. If a patient's pain is less than 24 hours, short-acting opioids can be tried. If the pain continues for several days, sustained-release opioid is indicated. Meperidine is the most commonly used opioid in hospitals for sickle cell disease patients with acute painful episodes. There is general consensus that oral meperidine should not be used for acute or chronic pain and the indication of parenteral meperidine use for acute sickle pain is controversial. Meperidine is excreted exclusively via the kidneys. It is relatively contraindicated with patients who have renal failure and therefore should definitely be used with caution in sickle cell patient. The active metabolite of meperidine, normeperidine, is a CNS irritant and can cause dysphoria, clonus, and seizures. The American Pain Society recommends that meperidine should not be used for more than 48 hours or at doses greater than 600 mg/24 hours.[15] For patients with several days of pain, or who need chronic opioid therapy, sustained-release or long half-life opioid preparations are used to provide consistent analgesia. Short-acting opioids can be used for rescue dosing.

Adjuvant medications are used to increase the analgesic effect of opioids, reduce the side effects of primary medications, and manage associated symptoms. No controlled studies on the use of adjuvant medications in the treatment of sickle cell pain exist; however, guidelines for their use are based on other chronic pain states. Antidepressants, anticonvulsants, and clonidine can be used for neuropathic pain. Antihistamines may counteract histamine release by mast cells secondary to opioids.

A small percentage of patients have unusually frequent and severe pain episodes. They have a poor quality of life and cannot perform daily activities. There is evidence that chronic transfusions may reduce debilitating pain.[16]

Hydroxyurea

Hydroxyurea is a chemotherapeutic agent used to increase hemoglobin F. It is relatively nontoxic and has not been proved to induce tumors. A national multicenter clinical trial of treatment with hydroxyurea for 2 years in adults with sickle cell disease showed that the drug was relatively nontoxic and was effective in reducing the frequency and severity of painful crises.[17] It has also been shown to reduce the incidence of acute chest syndrome and the need for transfusions.

Bone Marrow Transplantation

While sickle cell disease can be alleviated with allogeneic marrow transplantation, the current application of bone marrow transplantation is complex. Studies have shown there is an 84% survival rate and mortality is under 6%.[18] The guidelines for transplant are

1. Donors must be HLA compatible and full siblings
2. Candidates should be limited to patients with HbSS or HbS-beta zero thalassemia who are younger than 16 and have evidence of severe disease.

Severe disease is defined by stroke, recurrent acute chest syndrome, recurrent severe pain crisis (more than two per year), recurrent priapism, and sickle cell nephropathy.

Complications and Pitfalls

Most of the pitfalls associated with the treatment of sickle cell pain are the lack of understanding of the following key terminology: (1) tolerance; (2) physical dependence; (3) addiction; and (4) pseudoaddiction.

1. Tolerance is the physiologic response to chronic opioid use. When tolerance develops, a patient requires a larger amount of opioid to achieve their prior analgesic effect.
2. Physical dependence is a physiologic response to chronic opioid use as well. It involves the adaptation of the body to the amount of opioid to maintain the same level of analgesia.
3. Addiction is a pattern of compulsive drug use behaviors characterized by a continued craving for an opioid and the need to use the opioid for effects other than pain relief.
4. Pseudoaddiction is a pattern of compulsive drug use behaviors that occurs in a population of patients who are under-treated for pain. It is often confused with addiction.

▌ CONCLUSION

Research on sickle cell disease-related pain is sparse, but the under treatment of pain in patients with sickle cell disease is not due to lack of knowledge. Instead, barriers to implementing available knowledge are key to this shortfall. Like cancer pain, advancing knowledge through research, although clearly necessary, will not benefit the majority of patients without concurrent change in attitudes and beliefs.[19] Current healthcare systems inadequately address the need of patients with sickle-related pain. Many painful crises cannot and should not be managed at home. Although emergency departments are central to the care of patients with sickle pain who cannot manage at home, most provide neither consistent nor adequate multifaceted assessment or follow-up. One of the most important steps in adequate pain management in sickle pain is education of the patient and the healthcare provider.

References

1. Herrick JB: Peculiar elongated and sickle cell shaped corpuscles in a case of severe anemia. Arch Int Med 6:517, 1910.
2. Pauling L, Itano HA, Singer SJ, Wells IC: Sickle cell anemia, a molecular disease. Science 110: 543, 1949.
3. Nagel RL, Johnson J, Bookchin RM, et al: Beta-chain contact sites in the hemoglobin S polymer. Nature 283:832, 1980.
4. Ohene-Frempong K, Weiner SJ, Sleeper LA, et al: Cerebrovascular accidents in sickle cell disease: Rates and risk factors. Blood 91:288, 1998.
5. Castro O: The acute chest syndrome in sickle cell disease incidence and risk factors. The Cooperative Study of Sickle Cell Disease. Blood 84:643, 1995.
6. Gill FM, Sleeper LA, Weiner SJ, et al: Clinical events in the first decade in a cohort of infants with sickle cell disease. Cooperative Study of Sickle Cell Disease. Blood 86:776, 1995.
7. Brown AK, Sleeper LA: Reference values and hematologic changes from birth to 5 years in patients with sickle cell disease. Cooperative Study of Sickle Cell Disease. Arch Pediatr Adolesc Med 148:796, 1994.
8. Quinn CT, Buchanan GR: Sickle cell anemia with unusual bony changes. J Pediatr 143:350, 2003.

9. Platt OS, Throrington BD: Pain and sickle cell disease. Rates and risk factors. N Eng J Med 325:11, 1991.

10. Benjamin LJ, Swinson GI, Nagel RL: Sickle cell anemia day hospital: An approach for the management of uncomplicated sickle cell crisis. Blood 95:1130, 2000.

11. Wong DL Baker CM. Pain in children: Comparison of assessment scales. Pediatr Nurse 14:9, 1998.

12. Vichinsky EP, Johnson R: Multidisciplinary approach to pain management in sickle cell disease. Am J Pediatr Hematol Onc 4:328, 1982.

13. Ballas SK, Carlos TM: Guidelines for the Standard of Care of Acute Painful Episodes in Patients with Sickle Cell Disease. Harrisburg, PA, Pennsylvania Department of Health, 2000.

14. American Pain Society: Principles of Analgesic Use in the Treatment of Acute Pain and Cancer Pain. Evanston, Ill, The American Pain Society, 1999.

15. Francis RB: Vascular occlusion in sickle cell disease: Current concepts and unanswered questions. Blood 25:1405, 1991.

16. Charache S, Terrin ML: Effect of hydroxyurea on the frequency of painful crisis in sickle cell anemia. Investigator of the Multicenter Study of Hydroxyurea in Sickle Cell Anemia. N Engl J Med 332:1317, 1995.

17. Walters MC, Patience M, Leisenring W, et al: Bone marrow transplantation for sickle cell disease. N Engl J Med 335:369-376, 1996.

18. Fishman B, Foley KM: The Memorial Pain Assessment Card. A valid instrument for the evaluation of cancer pain. Cancer 60,1151, 1987.

19. American Pain Society: Guidelines for the Management of Acute and Chronic Sickle Cell Disease. Evanston, Ill, The American Pain Society, August 1999.

chapter 23

Acute Headache

Seymour Diamond and George R. Nissan

Acute headache is often encountered as a presenting complaint in the emergency department setting. One study noted the occurrence of headache as the chief complaint on admission to range from 0.36% to as high as 2.5% of patients.[1] The incidence of headache with significant mortal or fatal outcome is not frequent.[2] However, it is of the utmost importance to rule out organic disease in the patient presenting with a complaint of acute headache. After the appropriate diagnosis has been established, a treatment plan can be implemented.

When encountering a patient with acute headache in an emergency department setting, the physician must be familiar with the various categories of headaches. In an acute setting, it is helpful to divide headaches into three categories—organic, vascular, and tension-type headaches.[3] Multiple disease processes are included in the category of organic headaches (Table 23–1), and are only rarely seen in an emergency department setting where the physician is more likely to encounter vascular headaches in up to 20% of patients who present with a complaint of acute headache.[4] Tension-type headache is, by far, the most prevalent diagnosis among patients presenting with acute headache. Both migraine and tension-type headaches will be discussed in Chapters 42 and 43 of this textbook.

■ SIGNS AND SYMPTOMS

All patients presenting with a complaint of acute headache should be interviewed extensively regarding their headache history including location, severity, character, associated symptoms, and any precipitating factors (Table 23–2). Any recent-onset headaches or changes in headache pattern should be thoroughly investigated to rule out organic disease and possible life-threatening illness. A detailed headache history should also include risk factors for vascular disease, family history, and medication history.

It is important that patients be encouraged to describe their headache pain as accurately as possible because the clinical details may suggest the location and pathogenesis of the pain. The timing of the headache, particularly if the headache appears suddenly or on awakening in the early morning, often has diagnostic value in secondary headache disorders. A *sentinel headache*, which is a sudden onset, severe headache that disappears, may be a precursor to impending hemorrhage, and can occur days or weeks before subarachnoid hemorrhage.

The site of pain can be an important consideration in the headache history because pathologic lesions are more likely than others to produce headache.[5] Lesions in the posterior cerebral and vertebral arteries are most likely to be accompanied by headache, whereas lesions in the anterior cerebral artery are least likely. Lesions in the carotid, middle cerebral, and basilar arteries commonly produce headache. Posterior circulation strokes are more likely to cause headache than are anterior circulation strokes.

The age of the patient is important in the consideration of primary headache disorders versus secondary headache disorders, which can include intracranial masses such as abscesses and brain tumors, as well as intracranial and extracranial vascular disorders. Patients with primary headache disorders such as migraine, tension-type, and cluster headaches are likely to have onset of their symptoms before the age of 25. The typical presentation is unilateral or bilateral head pain. No associated neurologic dysfunction is usually observed, with the exception of aura preceding or associated with migraine. In contrast, patients with intracranial pathology are often older than age 45 and manifest some neurologic symptoms. Only rarely do the symptoms caused by intracranial lesions overlap with those of primary headache disorders.[6]

Physical and Neurologic Examination

Physical examination of the patient with acute headache should include the following:

- Measurement of vital signs, including blood pressure in both arms
- Palpation of the carotid and superficial temporal arteries
- Auscultation of the carotid arteries for bruits
- Evaluation of the neck for signs of meningismus
- Evaluation of the cranium for any evidence of trauma
- A thorough funduscopic examination to rule out:
  - arteriovenous nicking
  - blurring of the optic disks
  - papilledema

Table 23-1[3]

Organic Causes of Headache

Stroke
Hemorrhagic
Thrombotic
Embolic

Infection
Meningitis
Brain abscess
Encephalitis
Sinusitis

Inflammation
Temporal arteritis
Vasculitis

Brain Tumor
Primary
Metastatic

Hypertension
Hypertensive headache
Malignant (accelerated) hypertension
Hypertensive encephalopathy

From Solomon GD: Classification and mechanism of headache. In Diamond ML, Solomon GD (eds): Diamond and Dalessio's The Practicing Physician's Approach to Headache, 6th ed. Philadelphia, WB Saunders, 1999, p 8.

Table 23-2

Components of Headache History

Onset
Frequency
Location
Duration
Severity and character
Prodromata
Associated symptoms
Precipitating factors
Sleep pattern
Emotional factors
Family history
Medical, surgical, and/or obstetric history
Allergies
Current medications
Previous medications and therapies

Adapted from Diamond S: Diagnosing and Managing Headaches, 4th ed. Caddo, Oklahoma, Professional Communications, 2004.

Neurologic examination should include the following:

- Complete mental status examination
- Assessment of
  - cranial nerves
  - muscle strength and motor tone
  - upper and lower extremity reflexes
- Sensory examination
- Tests for coordination and gait

Any abnormalities uncovered during the neurologic examination should warrant an immediate further investigation.

Testing

The physical examination and headache history will usually facilitate the choice of diagnostic tests to be ordered in the evaluation of the acute headache patient. A complete blood count (CBC) should be obtained if there is suspicion of infection or anemia, which can be a precursor of a hypoxia-associated vascular headache. Evaluation of electrolytes and renal function should be undertaken in patients who have been vomiting, appear dehydrated, or have been taking excessive amounts of analgesics, either prescribed or over the counter. An erythrocyte sedimentation rate (ESR) according to the Westergen method should be obtained on all patients older than the age of 50 who present with acute headache or a change in the character of the headache to rule out temporal arteritis. If the ESR is elevated, a temporal artery biopsy should be scheduled as soon as possible, and treatment with corticosteroids should be initiated immediately to avoid irreversible blindness.

Following the complete history and physical examination, the next step in diagnosing a secondary headache disorder usually requires a computed tomography (CT) scan of the head. The CT scan is generally preferable to magnetic resonance imaging (MRI) for the evaluation of acute subarachnoid hemorrhage, acute head trauma, and bony abnormalities. In an emergency department setting, the CT scan affords easier monitoring of the patient and is less time-consuming to obtain. It will detect most, but not all, abnormalities that cause headache and is usually sufficient to exclude conditions that require immediate treatment. A CT scan is also indicated for patients presenting with hypertension and a change in sensorium with focal neurologic symptoms to rule out intracerebral bleeding or hydrocephalus. Although sensitivity of a CT scan decreases as time from onset of symptoms elapses, nearly 90% of patients with subarachnoid hemorrhage will demonstrate the abnormality on CT scan. Obstructive hydrocephalus can often be diagnosed with CT scan, and may appear as a mass obstructing the ventricular system.

When the findings on CT scan are inconclusive or if significant physical signs or symptoms are observed, an MRI is indicated to narrow the list of differential diagnoses. In contrast to CT scanning, which employs the attenuation of an x-ray beam by the body, magnetic resonance imaging measures the response of the body to a strong magnetic field. Fat, subacute blood, and highly paramagnetic substances such as gadolinium are highlighted on T1-weighted images. T2-weighted images highlight tissues with protons that remain in phase with each other for a long time after the radiofrequency pulse is turned off, and the prototypical bright signal is *water*. The addition of gadolinium to T1-weighted MR images causes enhancing structures to appear bright and is analogous to the enhancement seen on contrast-enhanced CT in which breakdown of the blood-brain barrier has occurred. Gadolinium enhancement is useful in imaging tumor, acute infarctions, infectious and inflammatory conditions, and vascular abnormalities.

An MRI of the brain usually follows the CT scan in order to further define the anatomic position of the lesion prior to surgery. MRI is more sensitive than CT for detecting posterior fossa and cervicomedullary lesions, ischemia, white matter abnormalities, cerebral venous thrombosis, subdural and epidural hematoma, neoplasms, meningeal disease, cerebritis, and brain abscess.[7]

Magnetic resonance angiography (MRA) is usually indicated when there is a suspicion of aneurysm, either by unusual headache presentation or by family history of aneurysm. Small aneurysms, less than 5 mm in size, are less reliably imaged than larger ones, and considerable debate exists surrounding the use of MRA for the detection of aneurysms.[8] When aneurysm is strongly suspected owing to symptoms and physical findings, catheter angiography remains the standard. If findings on MRI suggest vasculitis, catheter angiography is also indicated.

If subarachnoid hemorrhage, meningitis, or both are suspected in the acute headache patient, a lumbar puncture should be performed. If a focal lesion is suspected, a CT scan must be obtained prior to a lumbar puncture. In patients with subarachnoid hemorrhage, xanthochromia—a yellow-tinged supernatant caused by the enzymatic breakdown of in vivo red blood cells—is always present in the cerebrospinal fluid (CSF) within 7 to 12 hours. In bacterial meningitis, white blood cells with decreased glucose and elevated protein will be present in the spinal fluid. The CSF opening pressure should always be measured in these cases and the spinal fluid should be sent immediately for culture. For patients presenting with fever, neck stiffness, and vomiting, treatment with appropriate intravenous antibiotics should be initiated immediately.

An electroencephalogram (EEG) is usually not indicated for the acute headache patient because it has minimal diagnostic significance in these cases. If symptoms suggest possible seizure disorder, such as an atypical migrainous aura or episodic loss of consciousness, then an EEG is appropriate. If a structural lesion such as a neoplasm is suspected, CT scan or MRI of the brain is preferred.

■ DIFFERENTIAL DIAGNOSIS

As stated earlier in this chapter, we will focus on the approximately 10% of patients who present with an acute headache and are found to have a secondary cause rather than a primary headache disorder such as migraine, tension-type, and cluster headaches. Organic causes of headache are primarily divided into five categories:

- Strokes
- Infections
- Inflammatory disorders
- Tumors
- Hypertension

Stroke and Subarachnoid Hemorrhage

Cerebrovascular disorders and stroke are included in the differential diagnosis for acute headache patients older than the age of 35 and with a history of cardiac and/or peripheral vascular disease. When evaluating a patient with acute headache, it is important to consider modifiable risk factors for stroke including hypertension, coronary artery disease, diabetes mellitus, hyperlipidemia, history of stroke, cigarette smoking, and obesity. Overall, headache occurs in about one fourth of patients with acute stroke.[9] This figure includes up to 16% of patients who experience an acute headache with a transient ischemic attack (TIA). In patients with cerebellar hemor-

rhage, up to 65% to 80% experience an acute headache.[10] Headache is less likely to occur in a lacunar infarct and in a deep basal ganglia stroke, most likely due to the lack of innervation of small intracerebral arterioles.

Approximately 10% of all cerebrovascular accidents are related to the presence of a subarachnoid hemorrhage (SAH), of which there is a nearly 50% mortality rate.[11] The most common causes of subarachnoid hemorrhage are ruptured berry aneurysms, arteriovenous malformations, and trauma. These patients present with an acute headache that is usually described as "the worst ever." The headache associated with aneurysmal rupture usually is bilateral and the intensity becomes severe in a very brief interval. A transient loss of consciousness associated with the onset of bleeding is sometimes noted. Other associated symptoms include nausea, vomiting, meningismus, and focal neurologic symptoms. Up to 15% of patients will experience seizures. Papilledema and meningeal signs may not be evident for approximately 7 hours after SAH. CT scan of the head without contrast is imperative as early as possible because subarachnoid blood can be found in up to 85% of cases if the CT scan is performed immediately after the event.[12] The sensitivity of the CT scan decreases to 74% after 3 days.

Infections

Bacterial Meningitis

One of the most life-threatening conditions that can manifest as an acute headache is bacterial meningitis. Meningitis should be suspected in all patients who present with headache, fever, and stiff neck—regardless of age or season. Headache is often the first symptom and rapidly increases in severity over several minutes. Patients typically describe a generalized or frontal headache that can radiate into the occipital region and the neck and spine. Associated symptoms include severe pain, fever, photophobia, phonophobia, nausea, vomiting, altered consciousness, nuchal rigidity, and rarely, seizures. In examining the patient with suspected meningitis, an inability to completely extend the legs (*Kernig sign*) and forward flexion of the neck may result in flexion at the hips and knees (*Brudzinski sign*).

The age of the patient can often determine which bacterial organism is most likely responsible for the meningitis. In children aged 2 through 5, *Haemophilus influenzae* is the most prevalent cause of bacterial meningitis. *Neisseria meningitidis* is more frequently the causative organism in older children and adolescents, and *Streptococcus pneumoniae* is more frequent in adults older than the age of 40. Patients who are immunosuppressed or who are receiving immunosuppressive therapy are particularly susceptible to bacterial meningitis.

If there are no contraindications, including increased intracranial pressure, mass lesions, or coagulopathy, then lumbar puncture should be performed immediately without neuroimaging. The CSF should be sent for Gram stain and bacterial cultures, and determination of CSF glucose, protein, and cell counts should be performed.

Brain Abscess

The incidence of brain abscess in the United States is approximately 1 per 100,000 and is predominantly found in children and in those older than 60 years.[13] Headache is the most common initial symptom of brain abscess. Associated signs and symptoms include drowsiness, confusion, seizures, and focal neurologic deficits. The primary site of the abscess will determine the accompanying signs and symptoms. Papilledema is present in less than half of all patients at presentation.[14] Most abscesses are the result of an infection elsewhere in the body (i.e., paranasal sinuses, middle ear, mastoid, pulmonary sites, and infective endocarditis). In up to 20% of patients, no source of infection is identified.[15]

Early in the course of infection, fever and leukocytosis may occur and resolve as the abscess becomes encapsulated. Approximately 1 week after the onset of headache, nausea and vomiting usually begins and may be due to increased intracranial pressure.[15] Neuroimaging with either CT scan or MRI of the brain will confirm the diagnosis of brain abscess.

Other Infectious Disorders

Other infectious disorders that may be associated with acute headache include viral and bacterial encephalitis, HIV, Lyme disease, fungal infections, and protozoan infections.

Inflammatory Disorders

Early diagnosis and management of temporal (giant cell) arteritis is essential in an acute headache patient who is over the age of 50 and who had been asymptomatic before headache onset. Headache is the most common presenting symptom of temporal arteritis in elderly patients and can be associated with weight loss, night sweats, low-grade fever, jaw claudication, and aching of joints.[16] When this cluster of symptoms is present, the term *polymyalgia rheumatica* is used. There is a 2:1 female-to-male preponderance.

The headache associated with temporal arteritis usually is throbbing and continuous, focally worse in the temporal region and localized to the affected scalp vessels. Pain that occurs with chewing is also a characteristic symptom. On examination, many patients exhibit painful, swollen, and erythematous superficial temporal arteries. The involved arteries generally dictate which physical signs will manifest. Temporal arteritis is often associated with an elevated ESR or an elevated C-reactive protein (CRP). An ESR of greater than 40 mm/hour in the presence of correlating symptoms indicates the need for a temporal artery biopsy. Initiation of early treatment is critical due to the possibility of irreversible blindness of one or both eyes in up to 50% of untreated cases.

Other less common systemic vasculitides include *polyarteritis nodosa* and *Kawasaki syndrome,* which are both of the medium vessel vasculitis class, and several small vessel vasculitides. These include *Wegener's granulomatosis, microscopic polyarteritis,* and *Churg-Strauss syndrome,* which are all affiliated with the presence of antineutrophil cytoplasmic antibodies (ANCA). *Henoch-Schönlein purpura, cryoglobulinemic vasculitis, Goodpasture disease,* and *leukocytoclastic vasculitis* are not associated with the presence of ANCA.

Brain Neoplasms

One of the most common fears in patients presenting with an acute headache is the possibility of a brain tumor. Headache is an initial symptom in 20% of patients with brain tumor and can occur in up to 60% during the disease.[17] It is a common symptom in patients with infratentorial tumors and uncommon in patients with pituitary tumors, craniopharyngiomas, or cerebellopontine angle tumors.[18] Headache is a frequent manifestation of increased intracranial pressure (ICP), although elevation of ICP is not required for its production. The headache associated with brain tumors is usually bilateral and described as dull, aching, and rarely throbbing, similar to the presentation of a tension-type headache. The pain is usually worse on the side ipsilateral to the tumor, and increases in ICP due to Valsalva maneuvers or exertion may exacerbate the pain. Headaches that are worse in the morning occur in approximately one third of patients.

In patients with a previous history of headaches, suspicion should arise when headaches become more severe or when accompanied by neurologic signs or symptoms. Nausea and vomiting accompany the headache in up to one half of patients. Focal signs may occur depending on the area of the brain involved. Increased blood pressure may also be present. CT scanning or preferably MRI of the brain is indicated when there is suspicion of an intracranial neoplasm.

A clinical disorder that is not a neoplasm but is worth mentioning in this section is *idiopathic intracranial hypertension,* which is also called *pseudotumor cerebri* or *benign intracranial hypertension.* The disorder is one of elevated CSF pressure and occurs predominantly in women in the child-bearing years. More than 90% of patients are obese and over 90% are women. The mean age at the time of diagnosis is 32 years. The primary manifesting symptom is headache; associated signs and symptoms can include transient episodes of visual loss, diplopia secondary to sixth cranial nerve paresis, papilledema, and pulse-synchronous tinnitus.

The headache associated with idiopathic intracranial hypertension is usually a severe daily headache that is described as a pulsatile pain that increases in intensity. Most of the patients describe the headache as the most severe head pain ever (91%) and different from previous headaches (85%). Nausea and neck stiffness are commonly seen. The headache can awaken the patient from sleep in more than 60% of cases.[19] In the absence of papilledema, a lumbar puncture is indicated to confirm the diagnosis in patients with suspicious symptoms. The resting spinal pressures vary from 220 to 600 mm of water. The CSF is always clear and colorless with an unusually low protein count. The remaining cellular constituents are normal.

Hypertensive Headache

Essential hypertension is generally not a cause of acute headache. Headaches can develop when the diastolic blood pressure is greater than or equal to 110 mm Hg. The elevation in blood pressure is usually a manifestation of a secondary disorder, such as acute nephritis or acute pressor reactions. The degree of elevation of blood pressure may not necessarily correlate with the severity of the acute headache. The headache is usually bilateral, although it can occur at the occiput and can also be global. Patients will usually describe the pain as severe, "throbbing" or "bursting" in nature. The headache is usually most severe in the early morning on awakening and gradually improves throughout the day. Symptoms of catecholamine release, such as tremors or palpitations, can occur.

If intracerebral bleeding is suspected, then neuroimaging with CT or MRI of the brain should be undertaken. If a secondary cause of the hypertensive headache including acute nephritis is suspected, then a complete renal work-up and follow-up is essential after the blood pressure has been adequately controlled and palliative measures for the headache are initiated.

▪ TREATMENT

Stroke and Subarachnoid Hemorrhage

Treatment of ischemic stroke now includes thrombolytic therapy with recombinant tissue-type plasminogen activator (rt-PA) if given within 3 hours of symptom onset, which can improve long-term outcomes. There is a small but significant risk of symptomatic intracranial hemorrhage with rt-PA use. Because most patients present outside the 3-hour window period, most patients with stroke are treated with aspirin and/or antiplatelet agents to reduce the risk of recurrent stroke. Heparin and low-molecular-weight heparin sometimes are used in the treatment of ischemic stroke in patients with comorbid atrial fibrillation, basilar artery thrombosis, or progressive infarction. However, no long-term neurologic benefit is associated with the use of heparin, and the increased risks of intracranial and extracranial bleeding often negate its use in the treatment of acute ischemic stroke. During and after hospitalization, physical and occupational therapy are part of the overall treatment plan.

Subarachnoid hemorrhage treatment involves surgical obliteration of the aneurysm responsible for the SAH. Multiple aneurysms are present in up to 20% of patients, and four-vessel cerebral angiography is preferred because both ruptured and unruptured aneurysms may be revealed. Several randomized controlled trials have shown that oral nimodipine reduces the vasospasm that is associated with poor outcomes in SAH. Catheter-based deployment of detachable coils or balloons prevents rebleeding and affords the opportunity to treat complications appropriately should they arise. The most serious early complications of SAH include rebleeding, vasospasm with delayed ischemic deficit, obstructive hydrocephalus, seizures, hyponatremia and volume depletion secondary to a central salt-wasting syndrome, pulmonary edema, and cardiac arrhythmias. Despite considerable diagnostic and therapeutic advances, the mortality of SAH is still 25%.

Infections

Bacterial meningitis is a life-threatening emergency and should be treated immediately with intravenous antibiotics after lumbar puncture is performed. The antibiotics should be administered before receiving CSF Gram stain and culture results. Analgesics and antipyretics may also be given to treat the associated headache. In addition, intravenous fluid hydration should accompany the antibiotics. The choice of antibiotics should be made based on the most likely organisms involved and the age of the patient. If pneumococcal meningitis is suspected, then intravenous vancomycin and ceftriaxone should be administered until Gram stain and culture results are available, secondary to the high level of *S. pneumoniae* resistance to penicillin in the United States. If the patient is immunosuppressed, then *Listeria* meningitis is also a consideration, and treatment with intravenous ampicillin should also be included.

The treatment of a brain abscess may require needle aspiration or excision of the abscess, ideally before antibiotics are initiated. Intravenous antibiotics are administered for a minimum of 6 weeks and are used to cover the possibility of polymicrobial infection. In nontraumatic brain abscesses, anaerobic streptococci are most commonly implicated. In surgical and posttraumatic cases, staphylococci and Enterobacteriaceae are most commonly involved, which requires the addition of intravenous vancomycin in place of penicillin.[20] Steroids are indicated only when the intracranial pressure is markedly elevated because the antibiotic penetration will be compromised with concomitant steroid use. Fungal abscesses are more common in HIV and immunocompromised patients, and appropriate antifungal agents should be administered in these cases.

Temporal Arteritis

If temporal arteritis is suspected, treatment should be started immediately with steroids, and most patients require a starting dose of prednisone 40 to 60 mg daily. A temporal artery biopsy should be performed as soon as possible after steroid initiation to avoid histologic suppression or alteration of vasculitis in the biopsy specimen. Despite steroid treatment, there may be continued histologic evidence of vasculitis up to 6 weeks after initiation of treatment, even with clinical resolution of symptoms.[21] The dose of prednisone is then tapered by 2.5 mg to 5 mg decrements every 1 to 3 weeks as tolerated. The headache associated with temporal arteritis usually resolves within days following the initiation of steroid treatment. The ESR may improve within a few days and may become normal within 1 or 2 weeks.

Patients treated with long-term steroids should be instructed regarding the possible complications including diabetes mellitus, steroid myopathy, vertebral compression fractures, psychosis, and infections due to immunosuppression. Data are limited regarding the use of steroid-sparing agents, including dapsone, azathioprine, and cyclophosphamide, and the toxicity of these agents should be considered before their incorporation into the treatment regimen.

Brain Neoplasms and Pseudotumor Cerebri

The prognosis of a brain neoplasm is determined by tumor grade and anatomic location. Tumor resectability, which greatly influences prognosis, is determined by the proximity of the tumor to essential neuroanatomic structures. Resectability is also affected by the degree of demarcation between tumor and normal brain tissue. For example, astrocytomas frequently extend beyond the gross tumor margin, whereas meningiomas have a well-defined demarcation between tumor and normal tissue. Once the diagnosis of a malignant intracranial tumor is established, it is important to distinguish whether the tumor is a metastatic or a primary lesion. The presence of multiple lesions on contrast-enhanced MRI or CT of the brain favors a metastatic process, although metastases can manifest as a single lesion in up to 50% of patients.

Patients with vasogenic edema secondary to an intracranial neoplasm should be treated with steroids. Intracranial hypertension is usually accompanied by a headache and vomiting, papilledema, decreased level of consciousness, and MRI or CT evidence of significant mass effect or impending hydrocephalus. The typical loading dose of dexamethasone is 10 mg intravenously followed by a maintenance dose of 4 mg four times daily. A neurosurgeon should be consulted emergently because deterioration from intracranial hypertension can occur rapidly.

Management of *pseudotumor cerebri* includes a structured weight reduction program for all obese patients and may involve gastric surgery when medications and diet fail. The most commonly used oral agents to reduce intracranial pressure include furosemide and acetazolamide, which is usually started at a dose of 250 mg twice daily.[22] The headache associated with pseudotumor cerebri usually responds to nonsteroidal anti-inflammatory agents (NSAIDs) and non-narcotic analgesics. Chronic headaches may respond to migraine prophylactic agents including tricyclic antidepressants, beta blockers, anticonvulsants, and so on. Repeated lumbar punctures have unproven efficacy and are not currently recommended in the treatment regimen. Neurosurgical procedures, including lumboperitoneal shunting (LPS) and optic nerve sheath fenestration, should be reserved for patients with progressive visual loss on medical therapy. Optic nerve sheath fenestration rarely improves headache, so if headache accompanies visual loss, LPS should be considered the procedure of choice.

Hypertensive Headache

Control of blood pressure is most important in a patient presenting with a hypertensive headache, because end-organ damage may occur secondary to the hypertensive state. The general goal is to reduce the mean arterial pressure by approximately 20% to 25% or to reduce the diastolic blood pressure to 100 to 110 mm Hg. If central nervous system, cardiovascular, or renal damage is occurring, prompt treatment with intravenous medication is indicated. If hypertensive encephalopathy is evident, preferred intravenous agents include nitroprusside, labetalol, or diazoxide infusion. The blood pressure should return to normal levels within 24 hours of treatment. No studies are available that have proven that intravenous treatment should be initiated in patients with severe hypertension but no end-organ damage.

After treatment is initiated to control blood pressure levels, the headache may be treated with analgesics. The headache usually resolves within 2 days after the reduction of blood pressure. If hypertensive encephalopathy is present, the headache may persist for up to 7 days.

■ CONCLUSION

Although the incidence of headache with significant morbid or fatal outcome is not frequent, it is essential to recognize organic causes as part of the differential diagnosis. The headache history and physical examination provide important clues to facilitate the choice of diagnostic tests and subsequent treatment regimen. For the clinical practitioner, it is preferable to divide organic causes of headache into the five categories discussed in this chapter: stroke, infection, inflammatory disorders, tumor, and hypertension. The physician should be aggressive in diagnosing the acute headache patient to rule out life-threatening illness and should be reassured that organic causes of headache occur rarely.

References

1. Fodden DI, Peatfield RC, Milsom PL: Beware the patients with a headache in the accident and emergency department. Arch Emerg Med 6:7, 1989.
2. Leicht MJ: Non-traumatic headache in the emergency department. Ann Emerg Med 9:404, 1980.
3. Solomon GD: Classification and mechanism of headache. In Diamond ML, Solomon GD (eds): Diamond and Dalessio's The Practicing Physician's Approach to Headache, 6th ed. Philadelphia, WB Saunders, 1999, p 8.
4. Dhopesh V, Anwar R, Herring C: A retrospective assessment of emergency department patients with complaint of headache. Headache 19:37, 1979.
5. Rapaport, AM: Cerebrovascular disease and headache. In Diamond ML, Solomon GD (eds): Diamond and Dalessio's The Practicing Physician's Approach to Headache, 6th ed. Philadelphia, WB Saunders, 1999, p 151.
6. Edmeads JG: Headache as a symptom of organic disease. Curr Opin Neurol 8:233, 1995.
7. Evans RW, Rozen TD, Adelman JU: Neuroimaging and other diagnostic testing in headache. In Silberstein SD, Lipton RB, Dalessio DJ (eds): Wolff's Headache and Other Head Pain, 7th ed. New York, Oxford University Press, 2001, p 27.
8. Winn HR: Intracranial aneurysms and MR angiography: Questions and answers. Am J Neuroradiol 15:1617, 1994.
9. Vestergaard K, Andersen G, Nielsen MI, et al: Headache in stroke. Stroke 24:1621, 1993.
10. van der Hoop RG, Vermeulen M, van Gijn J: Cerebellar hemorrhage: Diagnosis and treatment. Surg Neurol 20:6, 1988.
11. Solomon RA, Rink ME: Current strategies for the management of aneurysmal subarachnoid hemorrhage. Arch Neurol 144:L769, 1987.
12. Ward TN: Headache in cerebrovascular disease. In Samuels MA, Feske S (eds): Office Practice of Neurology. New York, Churchill Livingstone, 1996, p 1141.
13. Nicolosi A, Hauser MA, Mussico, et al: Incidence and prognosis of brain abscess in a defined population: Olmsted County, Minnesota, 1935-1981. Neuroepidemiology 10:122, 1991.
14. Chun CH, Johnson JD, Hofstetter M, et al: Brain abscess: A study of 45 consecutive cases. Medicine 65:415, 1986.
15. Murphy FK, Mackowiak P, Luby J: Management of infections affecting the nervous system. In Rosenberg RN (ed): The Treatment of Neurological Diseases. New York, Spectrum, 1979, p 249.
16. Lance JW: Mechanism and Management of Headache, 5th ed. Oxford, Butterworth-Heinemann, 1993.
17. Jaeckle KA: Causes and management of headache in cancer patients. Oncology 7:27, 1993.
18. Jaeckle KA: Clinical presentations and therapy of nervous system tumors. In Bradley WG, Daroff RB, Fenichel GM, et al (eds): Neurology in Clinical Practice. Boston, Butterworth-Heinemann, 1991, p 1008.
19. Wall M: The headache profile of idiopathic intracranial hypertension. Cephalalgia 10:331, 1990.
20. Mathisen GE, Johnson JP: Brain abscess. Clin Infect Dis 25:763, 1997.
21. Achkar AA, Lie JT, Hunder, et al: How does previous corticosteroid treatment affect the biopsy findings in giant cell (temporal) arteritis? Ann Intern Med 120:987, 1994.
22. Schoeman JF: Childhood pseudotumor cerebri: Clinical and intracranial pressure response to acetazolamide and furosemide treatment in a case series. J Child Neurol 9:130, 1994.

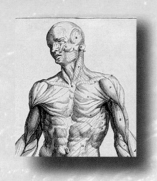

Part B

NEUROPATHIC PAIN SYNDROMES

Evaluation and Treatment of Peripheral Neuropathies

Steven D. Waldman, Howard J. Waldman, and Katherine A. Waldman

The peripheral neuropathies are one of the most common, yet most misunderstood causes of pain, numbness, and functional disability encountered in clinical practice. Although the exact incidence of peripheral neuropathy is unknown because of a lack of standardized diagnostic criteria, failure to include this heterogeneous group of diseases in the differential diagnosis of pain would lead to much frustration for the clinician and unnecessary suffering for the patient. This chapter provides the physician with a concise roadmap to aid in the diagnosis and treatment of peripheral neuropathies.

■ HISTORY AND PHYSICAL EXAMINATION

Anatomic Classification System

Although there are many causes of peripheral neuropathy, the relatively consistent signs and symptoms associated with this

group of diseases make it easy to consider in the differential diagnosis of patients with pain. Similar to the sympathetically maintained pain syndromes, a universal classification system for the peripheral neuropathies is unavailable. We have found it useful, however, to group patients suspected to have peripheral neuropathy into groups based on their clinical presentation using the anatomic distribution of their symptoms as a starting point in the evaluation process (Table 24–1). To accomplish this first step, the clinician must obtain a careful history from the patient and perform a careful physical examination with an eye to identifying neurologic findings that show the isolated or more diffuse nature of the disease process. The clinician must direct his or her efforts at determining whether the patient's complaints stem from an isolated mononeuropathy, such as carpal tunnel syndrome, or a symmetric polyneuropathy, such as diabetic polyneuropathy.[1] Such efforts are crucial if the clinician is to bring order to this myriad group of diseases that manifest in such a clinically similar manner.

Table 24–1

Classification of Common Peripheral Neuropathies Based on Anatomic Distribution

Symmetric Polyneuropathies
Diabetic polyneuropathy
Toxic neuropathies
  Alcohol induced
  Drug induced (e.g., chemotherapy, nitrofurantoins)
  Heavy metal poisoning
Inflammatory neuropathies
  Guillain-Barré syndrome
  Vasculitic neuropathy
  Chronic inflammatory demyelinating
  polyradiculopathy
Nutrition-related neuropathies
  Thiamine deficiency neuropathy
  Cobalamin deficiency neuropathy
  Vitamin E deficiency neuropathy
Cancer-related neuropathies
  Paraneoplastic syndromes
  Plexopathies secondary to tumor infiltration
  Peripheral nerve compromise secondary to tumor
    infiltration
Infectious neuropathies
  Leprosy
  HIV-related neuropathy
  Lyme disease
Organ failure–related neuropathies
  Renal failure
  Hepatic failure
  Pulmonary failure
  Organ transplant–related neuropathy

Mononeuropathies
Entrapment neuropathies (e.g., carpal tunnel
  syndrome)
Trauma to a specific nerve (e.g., post–inguinal hernia
  ilioinguinal neuropathy)

Multiple Mononeuropathies*
Leprosy
Diabetic multiple mononeuropathies
HIV-related neuropathies
Sarcoidosis-related neuropathy

---

*All multiple mononeuropathies can manifest initially as a simple mononeuropathy and progress in a nonsymmetric pattern to involve other nerves.

Verbal Descriptors of Peripheral Neuropathy

A patient with peripheral neuropathy often presents with a constellation of symptoms that may contain the complaints of pain, numbness, weakness, and lack of coordination (Table 24–2).[2] The adjectives used to describe the pain component of the neuropathy often include burning, tingling, hot, stabbing, and shocklike. The adjectives used to describe the numbness component of the neuropathy often include dead, cold, and wooden. Weakness often is described in terms of what the patient could do in the past and is now unable to do (e.g., I am unable to stand on my tiptoes, my little finger catches on the side of my pocket when I try to retrieve my

---

Table 24–2

Verbal Descriptors of Peripheral Neuropathy

Pain
Burning
Tingling
Raw
Searing
Hot
Stabbing
Shocklike

Numbness
Dead asleep
Cold
Wooden
Walking on sand
Novocaine wearing off

Weakness
I am unable to stand on my tiptoes
My little finger catches on the side of my pocket
when I try to retrieve my keys
My foot slaps the ground when I walk

Lack of Coordination
Clumsiness
Inability to button a shirt
Inability to pick up small items

---

keys, my foot slaps the ground when I walk) (Fig. 24–1). Incoordination is often described by the patient as clumsiness, an inability to button a shirt, or inability to pick up small items.

Temporal Classification of Peripheral Neuropathy

In addition to the aforementioned clinical descriptors that help point the clinician toward a diagnosis of peripheral neuropathy, it is useful for the clinician to classify the patient's clinical symptoms in terms of a timeframe. Table 24–3 provides an arbitrary but useful framework for the temporal classification of peripheral neuropathies. Acute peripheral neuropathies have presented and evolved over 4 weeks or less.[3] Subacute peripheral neuropathies have evolved over 4 to 8 weeks. Chronic peripheral neuropathies have evolved over greater than 8 weeks to years. There is much overlap to this temporal classification system, but the clinician may find this approach especially useful in classifying patients who present with more than one type of neural compromise (e.g., double-crush syndrome).

Targeted Past Medical and Surgical History

Table 24–4 provides the clinician with a framework of salient points of the past medical history when questioning a patient with suspected peripheral neuropathy.[4] As a starting point, the clinician should ascertain if the patient has a history of any systemic illness known to be associated with peripheral neuropathy. Specific questions as to the presence of diabetes,

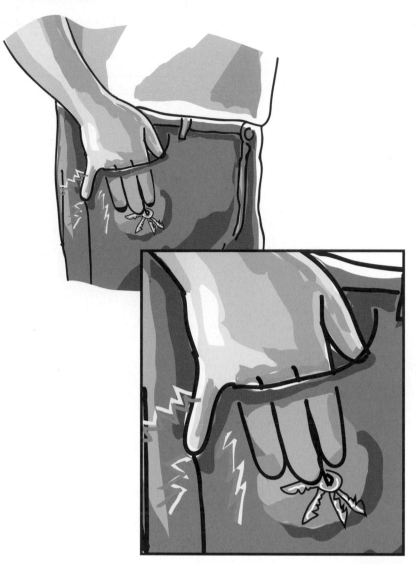

FIGURE 24–1 ■ Functional disability associated with ulnar nerve entrapment.

Table 24–3

Classification of Peripheral Neuropathies Based on Time of Onset

Acute peripheral neuropathies	Manifest and evolve over ≤4 wk
Subacute peripheral neuropathies	Manifest and evolve over 4-8 wk
Chronic peripheral neuropathies	Manifest and evolve over >8 wk to years

Table 24–4

Past Medical and Surgical History

Systemic Illnesses Associated with Peripheral Neuropathies
Diabetes
Collagen-vascular diseases
Hepatic disease
Renal disease
Thyroid disease
Other endocrine diseases
Amyloidosis
Sarcoidosis

Nutritional Status Evaluation
Vitamin deficiencies
Anorexia
Malabsorption syndrome

Hereditary Diseases
Charcot-Marie-Tooth disease
Fabry disease
Refsum disease

Surgical History
Carpal tunnel syndrome and other entrapment neuropathies
Laminectomies
Cancer surgeries

collagen-vascular disease, or hepatic, renal, or endocrine abnormalities need to be asked.[5] In addition, a careful past surgical history should be obtained with special attention to surgeries that suggest previous neurologic compromise (e.g., carpal tunnel surgery, ulnar entrapment at the elbow release, laminectomy). Perhaps most important in a patient with a suspected peripheral neuropathy is obtaining a detailed medication history. As summarized in Table 24–5, numerous drugs are implicated in peripheral neuropathy. Some of these drugs are obvious to the clinician (e.g., chemotherapeutic agents) and some less so, such as vitamin overuse, which is occurring with increasing frequency as patients become more concerned about a healthy diet.[6]

Targeted Family History

Perhaps nowhere in the specialty of pain medicine is the family history more helpful than in the diagnosis of peripheral neuropathy. Although a comprehensive discussion of the heritable diseases associated with peripheral neuropathies

is beyond the scope of this chapter, several generalizations can be made: (1) There are a significant number of heritable peripheral neuropathies (with the most common being Charcot-Marie-Tooth disease with an incidence of 1:2500 patients). (2) Failure to diagnose these disorders early on can lead to significant problems for the patient in the future. (3) It is important to ask the patient about the history of both parents, siblings, and children relative to signs and symptoms suggesting a peripheral neuropathy. (4) All family members should be asked, "Do you have any difficulty walking?" (5) All family members should be asked if they or any other family members require canes, walkers, or wheelchairs. (6) All family members should be asked if they or any family members have "funny looking feet" or have foot problems. Many patients with peripheral neuropathy have pain and functional disability that they and their physicians have attributed erroneously to "arthritis" or getting older.[7]

Social History

From a statistical perspective, with the exception of alcohol exposure, the incidence of patients with a toxic neuropathy is extremely small. Because it is possible to remove or limit the patient's ongoing exposure to nerve-damaging substances, however, careful inquiry as to high-risk occupations and behaviors is important. As summarized in Table 24–6, certain occupations and behaviors put the patient at greater risk for the development of peripheral neuropathies, some of which are reversible if the cause is identified and removed in a timely manner. As the number of patients with HIV increases and their mean survival is becoming longer, the number of patients presenting to the pain center with HIV as the underlying cause of peripheral neuropathy will increase.

Review of Systems

A targeted review of systems aids the clinician in identifying systemic diseases that are often a factor in the evolution of a patient's peripheral neuropathy. To maximize the useful information received from the review of systems, the questions asked should be tailored to ferret out underlying diseases. Polyuria and polydipsia might point the clinician toward a

---

Table 24–5

Common Drugs Associated with Peripheral Neuropathy

Chloroquine
Cisplatin
Colchicine
Dapsone
Disulfiram
Gold salts
Isoniazid
Metronidazole
Nitrous oxide
Nitrofurantoins
Paclitaxel
Phenytoin
Pyridoxine overuse
Thalidomide
Vinca alkaloids

Table 24–6

Occupations and Behaviors Associated with Peripheral Neuropathies

Occupation/Behavior	*Offending Agent*
Agriculture	Organophosphates
Alcohol overuse	Nutritional/vitamin deficiencies
Anesthesia delivery (anesthesiologists, nurse anesthetists, dentists)	Nitrous oxide
Dry cleaning	Tricholoethylene solvent
Homosexuality	HIV
Intravenous drug abuse	HIV
Painters	Hexacarbon solvents
Plastics manufacturing	Acrylamide residue
Rayon manufacturing	Carbon disulfide
Plumbers/building demolition crews	Lead
Tobacco abuse	Paraneoplastic syndromes
Tree sprayers, copper smelters/jewelers	Arsenic
Vegetarian diet	Cobalamin deficiency

diagnosis of diabetes mellitus.[8] Temperature intolerance might suggest to the clinician possible thyroid disease. Arthralgias and musculoskeletal complains might suggest a diagnosis of collagen-vascular disorders. Previous lung cancer might point the clinician toward a paraneoplastic syndrome. Although time-consuming, a carefully performed review of symptoms often helps identify the underlying cause of a previously undiagnosed peripheral neuropathy and allows the clinician to implement treatment.

Physical Examination

The targeted physical examination can often provide the clinician with important clues to aid in diagnosing peripheral neuropathy (Table 24–7). Although the patient may encourage the clinician to focus his or her examination on a numb hand or numb feet, many of the physical findings associated with peripheral neuropathy are identified in locations far removed from the anatomic region the patient is concerned about.

Foot Examination

Perhaps the best single piece of advice that can be given regarding the non-neurologic portion of the physical examination of the patient suspected to have peripheral neuropathy is "Don't forget to take the shoes off!" Many heritable peripheral neuropathies are associated with abnormal-looking feet. Often, such physical findings are overlooked because patients are embarrassed about the way their feet appear and go to great lengths to avoid exposing their feet. Often, the combination of embarrassment coupled with the functional disability the peripheral neuropathy imposes causes patients with peripheral neuropathy to avoid activities such as running or swimming. Many patients with feet affected by peripheral neuropathy relate that the first time they realized that their feet "weren't right" was when they saw their footprints in the dirt or sand when playing as a child with their shoes off. These abnormal footprints are often due to pes cavus or pes planus deformities, which are easily identified on physical examination. In addition to these structural abnormalities of the foot, patients with peripheral neuropathy often develop additional physical findings as a result of distal denervation of the joints of the phalanges and tarsal and metatarsal bones, such as claw toes, hammer toes, and the like. If the peripheral neuropathy remains undiagnosed and untreated, the clinician may observe

Charcot neuropathic joint destruction, characteristic plantar foot ulcers called mals perforans, and ultimately necrotic acropathy as repeatedly traumatized phalanges become ischemic and autoamputate (Figs. 24–2 and 24–3).

Neurologic Examination

The neurologic examination of a patient suspected to have peripheral neuropathy can yield important information to aid the clinician in diagnosis and treatment. Most peripheral neuropathies have in common the following findings on physical examination: (1) reflex changes, (2) weakness, and (3) sensory deficit (Table 24–8). In addition to this classic triad of physical findings, many patients with peripheral neuropathy have significant autonomic dysfunction, especially patients with diabetic polyneuropathy.

The order in which the neurologic examination of a patient with peripheral neuropathy is performed may seem counterintuitive at first, but experience has shown that using this stepwise approach helps the patient relax and be better able to cooperate during the examination, yielding better information. The starting point of the neurologic examination should be the deep tendon reflexes of the upper and lower extremities. Most patients with peripheral neuropathy exhibit diminished or absent deep tendon reflexes. The objective findings of diminished or absent deep tendon reflexes may be symmetric, suggesting a polyneuropathy, such as diabetic polyneuropathy, or asymmetric, suggesting a mononeuropathy, such as an entrapment neuropathy of the tibial nerve impacting the Achilles reflex. The diminution of reflexes also may be diffuse involving all extremities, as is often seen in inflammatory polyneuropathies or localized distally in the length-dependent axonopathies of the lower extremities. Electromyography (EMG) is helpful to differentiate what is actually occurring (see later). A word of caution is warranted when examining a patient with suspected polyneuropathy. If examination of the deep tendon reflexes yields normal or hyperreflexive reflexes, the examiner should look carefully for physical findings suggesting long tract signs (e.g., Babinski sign and clonus) and should strongly consider other diagnoses, including cervical myelopathy, amyotrophic lateral sclerosis, and other central nervous system processes. The clinician should proceed cautiously with the diagnosis of peripheral neuropathy in the presence of normal to hyperreflexive deep tendon reflexes or pathologic reflexes such as the Babinski sign. In the presence of proven peripheral polyneuropathy, the presence of normal or hyperreflexive reflexes is even more suggestive of a possible associated central nervous system disorder because generally deep tendon reflexes are diminished or absent.

The next step in the neurologic examination of a patient suspected to have a peripheral neuropathy is careful manual

---

Table 24–7

Components of the Physical Examination in a Patient with Suspected Peripheral Neuropathy

Examination of the feet
Neurologic examination
   Deep tendon reflexes
   Pathologic reflexes
   Manual muscle testing
   Sensory examination
Autonomic nervous system evaluation
Eye examination
Skin, hair, and nail examination
Organ system examination

Table 24–8

Triad of Physical Findings in Peripheral Neuropathy

Loss of deep tendon reflexes
Weakness
Loss of sensation

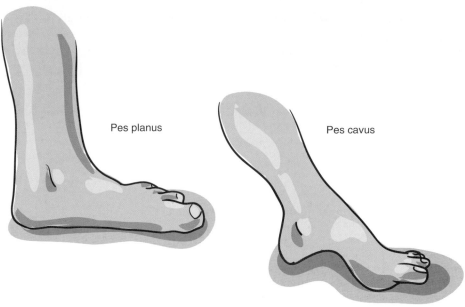

Pes planus

Pes cavus

FIGURE 24–2 ■ Physical findings in the foot associated with peripheral neuropathy.

Claw toe

Hammer toe

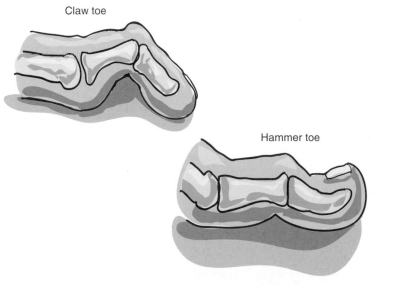

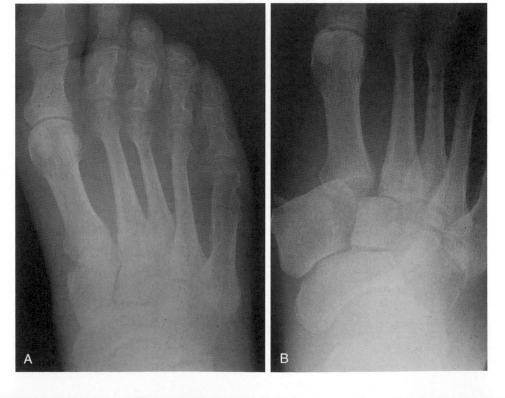

FIGURE 24–3 ■ A and B, MRI of Charcot joint. (From Resnick D: Diagnosis of Bone and Joint Disorders, 4th ed. Philadelphia, WB Saunders, 2002, p 2123.)

motor testing. Similar to deep tendon reflex evaluation, this provides more objective information than the sensory examination, which largely depends on the patient's subjective response. Similar to the deep tendon reflex evaluation, the clinician should assess not only the presence or absence of muscle weakness when testing the muscle groups, but also the pattern in which any abnormality occurs. Muscle weakness associated with the polyneuropathies tends to be symmetric, although the length-dependent polyneuropathies tend to affect the distal motor groups preferentially. Asymmetric weakness is seen most commonly in the entrapment neuropathies, such as carpal tunnel syndrome, although serious systemic diseases, such as amyloidosis, may manifest as an isolated mononeuropathy that may be misdiagnosed as a simple entrapment neuropathy. Plexopathies may present with a confusing pattern of muscle weakness and pain that may seem out of proportion to the patient's physical findings. EMG combined with MRI helps in making a correct diagnosis.

Finally, the sensory examination is performed. As mentioned earlier, obtaining clinically useful information from the sensory examination is more difficult than gleaning information from the deep tendon reflex and motor examination because the clinician must rely on the patient's subjective responses. For this reason, it is important for the clinician to confirm findings of abnormal pain sensation with side-to-side temperature sensation evaluation in the affected areas. The clinician should not ignore sensory and temperature testing of the thoracoabdominal regions, or more subtle neuropathic changes are often missed. Testing of vibration sense and proprioception also helps confirm the pattern of the neural compromise—symmetric versus asymmetric, diffuse versus localized. All of this information can be used to confirm the clinical diagnosis.

Two other points about the neurologic examination of the patient suspected to have peripheral neuropathy are in order: (1) Many patients with common peripheral neuropathies (e.g., diabetic polyneuropathy) experience significant autonomic dysfunction. For this reason, careful testing of lying and sitting blood pressures should be carried out. (2) Cranial nerve dysfunction is a common finding in patients with peripheral neuropathies. Careful attention should be given to examination of smell, pupillary response, facial weakness, and optic neuritis when caring for a patient with peripheral neuropathy.

Eye Examination

Although beyond the scope of expertise of most clinicians caring for patients in pain, eye complaints in the presence of the triad of peripheral neuropathy should raise the index of suspicion that a peripheral neuropathy exists. The complaint of dry eyes is often associated with Sjögren syndrome. Uveitis is often associated with the inflammatory systemic diseases associated with peripheral neuropathies, such as Behçet disease, inflammatory bowel disease, and sarcoidosis. Optic atrophy has long been known to be associated with Charcot-Marie-Tooth disease, and scleritis is commonly seen in patients with vasculitis and connective tissue disease. Any of these complaints warrants immediate referral to an ophthalmologist.

Skin, Hair, and Nail Examination

Similar to the ophthalmologic examination, the clinician caring for the patient in pain may not have adequate clinical

Table 24–9

Common Skin, Nail, and Hair Changes Associated with Peripheral Neuropathies

Abnormal Physical Finding	Cause
Foot ulcers	Diabetes
Angiokeratomas	Fabry disease
Pruritus	Renal and liver failure
Hair loss	Hypothyroidism, thallium poisoning
Mees' lines	Heavy metal poisoning, especially arsenic
Clubbing of digits	Pulmonary failure, lung cancer
Livedo reticularis	Cryoglobulinemia
Tight curly hair	Giant axonal neuropathy
Hypopigmentation	Leprosy, sarcoid
Hyperpigmentation	Cobalamin deficiency
Vesicles and bullae	Porphyria

expertise to diagnosis the myriad abnormalities of the skin, hair, and nails associated with peripheral neuropathies. The presence of such abnormalities should strengthen the clinical impression that peripheral neuropathy is the correct diagnosis, however, and prompt referral to a qualified dermatologist to help sort things out. Obvious findings on the skin, nail, and hair examination are summarized in Table 24–9.

Finding of Organomegaly

The finding of organomegaly, although nonspecific, is often associated with peripheral neuropathies. Hepatomegaly and splenomegaly are often seen in patients with amyloidosis, sarcoidosis, AIDS, and collagen-vascular diseases. Chronic alcohol abuse also can lead to hepatosplenomegaly, as can a variety of heritable causes of peripheral neuropathy, such as Tangier disease. An enlarged tongue is thought to be pathognomonic for amyloidosis. Whether or not ultimately found to be associated with peripheral neuropathy, the finding of organomegaly should alert the clinician to search diligently for the systemic disease responsible for this physical finding.

■ NEUROPHYSIOLOGIC TESTING

Neurophysiologic testing, including the rational use of nerve conduction testing, EMG, and in selected patients quantitative sensory testing, is invaluable in the evaluation of a patient suspected to have peripheral neuropathy.[9] Neurophysiologic testing is an extension of the targeted history and physical examination, rather than a replacement for it. In most instances, the results of neurophysiologic testing are used to confirm or fine-tune a diagnosis of peripheral neuropathy, rather than make the diagnosis. For the purposes of this chapter, the following generalizations may break down in the individual patient given the highly complex subject matter, but may serve to improve the basic understanding of the clinician faced with the presumptive diagnosis of peripheral neuropathy. Neurophysiologic testing is discussed in detail in Chapter 16.

Sensory Nerve Conduction Testing

Sensory nerve conduction testing is usually the starting point for neurophysiologic testing of a patient suspected to have peripheral neuropathy for confirming or excluding sensory nerve involvement.[10] For the purposes of this discussion, it can be assumed that normal sensory nerve action potentials mean that the cells of the dorsal root ganglion and the large myelinated axons are healthy, and that if the patient is having numbness, the pathologic process lies proximal to the dorsal root ganglion, or the patient has common small fiber or nociceptive neuropathy. This information can lead the clinician to look to diagnoses other than peripheral neuropathy to explain the patient's symptoms (e.g., myelopathy).

Sensory nerve conduction testing also has clinical utility in that in some instances the sensory nerve conduction may become abnormal earlier in the course of a disease relative to motor nerve conduction testing. In addition, sensory nerve conduction testing can be used to help localize the anatomic basis for a lesion (e.g., carpal tunnel syndrome or other entrapment neuropathies in which the motor fibers may be spared or pure sensory neuropathics, such as superficial radial nerve lesions as seen in cheiralgia paresthetica or handcuff palsy) (Fig. 24–4). Although sensory nerve conduction testing is highly specific, it is temperature dependent; reduced temperature results in slowed nerve conduction and prolongation of sensory latencies. Side-to-side comparisons of temperature and sensory conduction are important to avoid erroneous conclusions.

Motor Nerve Conduction Testing

Motor nerve conduction studies represent another piece of the neurodiagnostic puzzle in the diagnosis of peripheral neu-ropathy. The motor nerve conduction test is performed by stimulating a nerve and recording a response for the corresponding muscle. The motor nerve conduction study is useful in the identification and localization of lesions of the motor neuron, root, plexus, and peripheral nerve. As with sensory nerve conduction studies, side-by-side comparisons are useful.

Needle Electromyography

Needle EMG is most useful in helping the clinician determine if there is loss of motor unit fibers innervating the muscle.[11] EMG needle examination shows the presence of muscle denervation by (1) identifying the presence of muscle fibrillation and positive sharp waves, (2) identifying the presence of increased amplitude of motor unit potentials, (3) identifying the presence of an increased recruitment pattern, (4) identifying the presence of an increased firing rate to offset the loss of motor nerve fibers, and (5) identifying the presence of reduced recruitment of motor units as the muscle contracts. Although the information obtained from EMG needle examination is extremely useful in helping diagnose the myriad causes of muscle weakness and pain, EMG generally provides less specific information in and of itself regarding the presence of peripheral neuropathy relative to the nerve conduction testing.

Quantitative Sensory Testing

Quantitative sensory testing is gaining acceptance as a useful adjunct in the evaluation of peripheral neuropathies.[12] Although its widespread use has been limited by the lack of third-party reimbursement, quantitative sensory testing is extremely helpful in diagnosing a relatively large subset of

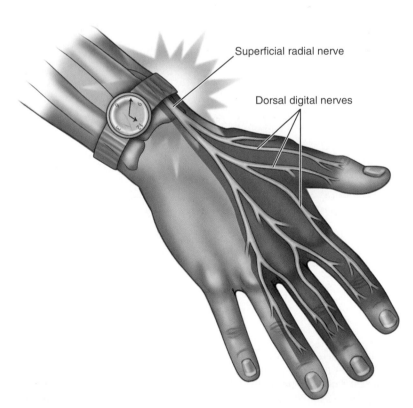

FIGURE 24–4 ■ Radial nerve or handcuff palsy. (From Waldman SD: Atlas of Uncommon Pain Syndromes. Philadelphia, WB Saunders, 2003, p 99.)

patients who clinically have peripheral neuropathy, but conventional nerve conduction testing and EMG are nondiagnostic. This subset of patients have in common damage to small nociceptive fibers that may not be identified on nerve conduction testing, which focuses primarily on large fiber function. Diseases that have a propensity to cause such damage include idiopathic distal painful neuropathy, HIV-related neuropathy, and some subsets of painful diabetic polyneuropathy. Because quantitative sensory testing still requires patient participation, it cannot be considered a true "objective" neurophysiologic test, and in patients with suspected small fiber neuropathy, a confirmatory skin biopsy for analysis of intraepidermal small nerve fibers and peripheral nerve biopsy (e.g., sural nerve) may be helpful.

Autonomic Reflex Testing

As mentioned earlier, the autonomic nervous system is often profoundly affected by peripheral neuropathies. Despite the frequency of autonomic dysfunction in patients with peripheral neuropathies, given the lack of easy and readily available testing of autonomic dysfunction, this component of the patient's disease often may go overlooked and often undertreated. If the patient is experiencing significant abnormalities of sweating, orthostatic hypotension, hypertension, tachycardia or bradycardia, gastrointestinal hypomotility, or urinary retention, referral to a center skilled in diagnosis of autonomic dysfunction is indicated.

■ MAGNETIC RESONANCE IMAGING AND COMPUTED TOMOGRAPHY

Although not a specific test for the diagnosis of peripheral neuropathy per se, MRI and CT are useful adjuncts in the evaluation of a patient thought to have peripheral neuropathy because of their ability to help diagnose accurately many of the underlying pathologies associated with peripheral neuropathy. MRI and CT are of particular clinical utility in evaluating the central nervous system, axial skeleton, brachial and lumbar plexus, and anatomic area of suspected entrapment neuropathy (e.g., the tarsal tunnel). The clinician should use these modalities early on in the diagnostic work-up of patients who present with pain, numbness, weakness, and functional disability because they often may provide a specific diagnosis without the need for more invasive testing.

■ TREATMENT OF COMMON PERIPHERAL NEUROPATHIES

As mentioned previously, the goal of the evaluation of patients suspected to have peripheral neuropathy is the identification of the specific cause of the patient's pain, numbness, weakness, and functional disability whenever possible because this would allow a treatment plan to be designed specifically to treat the underlying pathologic process. Table 24–10 provides the clinician with treatment strategies that have been shown to be useful in the treatment of specific types of peripheral neuropathy. Although using the diagnostic approach as outlined previously allows the clinician to make such a specific diagnosis in many instances, there remains a relatively large subset of patients in whom a specific cause of the neuropathy cannot be identified. Most of these patients seem to have some form of idiopathic small fiber nociceptive neuropathy. Treatment for these patients centers primarily on symptom management and restoration of function.

In general, a rational approach to the treatment of patients with peripheral neuropathy includes the following treatment strategies (Table 24–11): (1) treatment of any underlying disease or diseases thought to be contributing to the patient's problem (e.g., better control of hyperglycemia in a diabetic); (2) removal of any toxic substance that may be causing ongoing damage to the nerve (e.g., removal of thallium or lead exposure); (3) rational use of simple analgesics, nonsteroidal antiinflammatory drugs and, on an acute basis, opioids to provide symptomatic relief; (4) rational use of adjuvant analgesics, such as the tricyclic antidepressants and anticonvulsants (e.g., amitriptyline and gabapentin) (Table 24–12); (5) rational use of topical pharmacologic treatments, such as topical lidocaine patches, capsaicin, and analgesic balms; (6) rational use of somatic and sympathetic nerve blocks and neuroaugmentation techniques, such as spinal cord stimulation, in carefully selected patients; (7) appropriate use of occupational and physical therapy to instruct the patient in how to protect insensate areas and joints and to restore and maintain function; and (8) use of nonpharmacologic pain-relieving techniques (e.g., hypnosis, guided-imagery, coping strategies,

Table 24–10

Treatment Strategies for Most Common Causes of Peripheral Neuropathy

Disease	*Treatment*
Diabetes	Control of hyperglycemia
Nutritional and vitamin deficiencies	Add missing nutrients or vitamins or both
Alcohol overuse	Abstain from alcohol
HIV-induced neuropathy	Improve nutrition and symptomatic treatment
Amyloidosis	Liver transplantation (?)
Toxic substances	Removal of toxic substances
Uremia	Vigorous dialysis and renal transplantation
Cryoglobulinemias	Plasmapheresis and immunosuppression
Guillain-Barré syndrome	Plasmapheresis
Porphyria-induced neuropathy	Glucose infusions and hematin
Entrapment neuropathies	Surgery, splinting

acupuncture, and contrast baths). In our experience, the best way to implement treatment for the peripheral neuropathies is to adhere to a simple step-by-step approach to treatment.

After ensuring that all that can be done to make a specific diagnosis has been done, and any specific treatments have been implemented (e.g., better control of hyperglycemia), the clinician should determine what symptoms are causing the patient the most distress. Frequently, the numbness, functional disability, or sleep disturbance associated with the peripheral neuropathy bothers the patient more than pain. By focusing on the most troublesome aspects of the disease first, the clinician can maximize success and avoid making the cure worse than the disease by doing too much too soon. In general, it is strongly recommended that the clinician avoid the temptation to treat everything at once with polypharmacy and begin treatment with monotherapy targeted at the most problematic symptoms. For pain alone, treatment should begin with simple analgesics or nonsteroidal antiinflammatory drugs with an eye to end-organ side effects. Topical lidocaine patches or capsaicin also may be considered. If there is dysesthesia or numbness or both, a good starting point is gabapentin, which should be started slowly as outlined in Table 24–13. If sleep disturbance is a prominent feature of the patient's pain complaint, the use of amitriptyline in a starting nighttime dose of 35 to 50 mg is indicated. Given the relative resistance of neuropathic pain to treatment with opioids, and given the increasingly obvious downside to the use of long-term opioid therapy in this setting, the routine use of opioids as a primary treatment of the symptoms of peripheral neuropathy should be discouraged.

A proper treatment plan for a patient with peripheral neuropathy must include a careful assessment of the impairment of sensation. Although the symptom of numbness may not be the patient's primary complaint, the failure to identify and protect insensate joints and areas of the body can be devastating (see Fig. 24–4). Early and aggressive use of occupational and physical therapy is important if function is to be maintained.

■ SUMMARY

Peripheral neuropathies are a common problem encountered in clinical practice. Often misdiagnosed, a patient with peripheral neuropathy may present to the pain specialist

---

Table 24–11

Treatment Strategies for Painful Peripheral Neuropathies

Treat any underlying disease or diseases thought to be contributing to the patient's problem (e.g., better control of hyperglycemia in a diabetic patient)

Remove any toxic substance that may be causing ongoing damage to the nerve (e.g., removal of thallium or lead exposure)

Use simple analgesics, nonsteroidal antiinflammatory drugs, and opioids to provide acute symptomatic relief

Use adjuvant analgesics such as tricyclic antidepressants and anticonvulsants (e.g., amitriptyline and gabapentin)

Use topical pharmacologic treatments, such as topical lidocaine patches, capsaicin, and analgesic balms

Use somatic and sympathetic nerve blocks and neuroaugmentation techniques, such as spinal cord stimulation, in carefully selected patients

Use occupational and physical therapy to instruct the patient how to protect insensate areas and joints and to restore and maintain function

Use nonpharmacologic pain relief techniques (e.g., hypnosis, guided imagery, coping strategies, acupuncture, contrast baths)

Table 24–13

Use of Gabapentin for Management of Painful Peripheral Neuropathies

Start with 100 mg at bedtime for 2 nights
Increase to 100 mg twice daily for 2 days
Increase to 100 mg three times daily for 2 days
Increase to 300 mg four times daily
Increase to 400 mg at bedtime and 300 mg three times daily
Increase to 400 mg four times daily

Table 24–12

Adjuvant Analgesics in Pharmacologic Management of Painful Peripheral Neuropathies

Drug	Starting Dose	Maximum Daily Dose
Antidepressants		
Amitriptyline	25-50 mg at bedtime	200 mg
Nortriptyline	25 mg at bedtime	200 mg
Desipramine	25 mg at bedtime	200 mg
Trazodone	50 mg at bedtime	300 mg
Anticonvulsants		
Gabapentin	100 mg at bedtime	3600 mg in divided doses
Phenytoin	100 mg at bedtime	400 mg in divided doses
Topiramate	25 mg daily	300 mg twice daily
Carbamazepine	100 mg at bedtime	1200 mg in divided doses
Antiarrhythmics		
Mexiletine	150 mg at bedtime	200 mg three times daily

feeling frustrated, discouraged, sleep deprived, and often iatrogenically addicted to narcotic analgesics. The goal of evaluation of peripheral neuropathies is to identify specific types of peripheral neuropathies with an eye to implementing specific successful treatment strategies. When this is not possible, the goal is to rule out other treatable causes of the patient's symptoms and to begin a rational course of treatment that maximizes results and minimizes iatrogenic complications.

References

1. Waldman SD: Carpal tunnel syndrome. In: Common Pain Syndromes. Philadelphia, WB Saunders, 2002, p 118.
2. Poncelet AN: An algorithm for the evaluation of peripheral neuropathy. Am Fam Physician 57:1, 1998.
3. Pascuzzi RM, Fleck JD: Acute peripheral neuropathy in adults. Neurol Clin 15:529, 1997.
4. Morgenlander JC: Recognizing peripheral neuropathy: How to read the clues to underlying causes. Postgrad Med 102:71, 1997.
5. Waldman SD: Diabetic truncal neuropathy. In: Common Pain Syndromes. Philadelphia, WB Saunders, 2002, p 153.
6. Chalk CH: Acquired peripheral neuropathies. Neurol Clin 15:501, 1997.
7. Siddique N, Sufit R, Siddique T: Degenerative motor, sensory, and autonomic disorders. In Goetz CG (ed): Textbook of Clinical Neurology. Philadelphia, WB Saunders, 2003, p 759.
8. Perkins TA, Morgenlander JC: Endocrine causes of peripheral neuropathy. Postgrad Med 102:81.
9. Kimura J: Polyneuropathies. In: Electrodiagnosis in Diseases of Nerve and Muscle: Principles and Practice, 3rd ed. Oxford, Oxford University Press, 2001, p 650.
10. Kimura J: Principles and variations of nerve conduction studies. In: Electrodiagnosis in Diseases of Nerve and Muscle: Principles and Practice, 3rd ed. Oxford, Oxford Press, 2001, p 91.
11. Kimura J: Techniques to assess muscle function. In: Electrodiagnosis in Diseases of Nerve and Muscle: Principles and Practice, 3rd ed. Oxford, Oxford Press, 2001, p 307.
12. Dyck PJ: Quantitative sensory testing: A consensus report from the Peripheral Neuropathy Association. Neurology 43:1050, 1993.

Acute Herpes Zoster and Postherpetic Neuralgia

Steven D. Waldman

Herpes zoster is an infectious disease that is caused by the varicella-zoster virus (VZV), which also is the causative agent of chickenpox (varicella). Primary infection in the nonimmune host manifests itself clinically as the childhood disease chickenpox. It is postulated that during the course of primary infection with VZV, the virus migrates to the dorsal root or cranial ganglia. The virus then remains dormant in the ganglia, producing no clinically evident disease. In some individuals the virus may reactivate and travel along peripheral or cranial sensory pathways to the nerve endings, producing the pain and skin lesions characteristic of shingles. The reason that reactivation occurs in only some individuals is not fully understood, but it is theorized that a decrease in cell-mediated immunity allows the virus to multiply in the ganglia and spread to the corresponding sensory nerves, producing clinical disease.[1]

Patients who are suffering from malignancies (particularly lymphoma), receiving immunosuppressive therapy (chemotherapy, steroids, radiation), or suffering from chronic diseases are generally debilitated and much more likely than the healthy population to develop acute herpes zoster.[2] These patients all have in common a decreased cell-mediated immune response, which may be the reason for their propensity to develop shingles. This may also explain why the incidence of shingles increases dramatically in patients older than 60 years and is relatively uncommon in persons younger than age 20.

■ SIGNS AND SYMPTOMS

As viral reactivation occurs, ganglionitis and peripheral neuritis cause pain, which is generally localized to the segmental distribution of the posterior spinal or cranial ganglia affected. Approximately 52% of cases involve the thoracic dermatomes, 20% the cervical region, 17% the trigeminal nerve, and 11% the lumbosacral region.[2] Rarely, the virus may attack the geniculate ganglion, resulting in facial paralysis, hearing loss, vesicles in the ear, and pain. This combination of symptoms is called the Ramsay Hunt syndrome.[3]

Herpetic pain may be accompanied by flu-like symptoms and generally progresses from a dull, aching sensation to uni-lateral, segmental, band-like dysesthesias and hyperpathia. Because the pain of herpes zoster usually precedes the eruption of skin lesions by 5 to 7 days, erroneous diagnosis of other painful conditions (e.g., myocardial infarction, cholecystitis, appendicitis, or glaucoma) may be made. Some pain specialists believe that in some immunocompetent hosts, when reactivation of virus occurs, a rapid immune response may attenuate the natural course of the disease and the rash may not appear. This segmental pain without rash is called zoster *sine herpete* and is, by necessity, a diagnosis of exclusion. In most patients, however, clinical diagnosis of shingles is readily made when the rash appears. Like chickenpox, the rash of herpes zoster appears in crops of macular lesions, which progress to papules and then to vesicles. At this point, should the diagnosis of herpes zoster be in doubt, it can be confirmed by isolation of the virus from vesicular fluid (differentiating it from localized herpes simplex infection) or by Tzanck smear of the base of the vesicle, which will reveal multinucleated giant cells and eosinophilic intranuclear inclusions.

As the disease progresses, the vesicles coalesce and crusting occurs. The area affected by the disease can be extremely painful, and the pain tends to be exacerbated by any movement or contact (e.g., with clothing or sheets). As healing takes place, the crusts fall away, leaving pink scars in the distribution of the rash that gradually becomes hypopigmented and atrophic. As a general rule, the quicker all the vesicles in a given patient appear, the quicker the rash will heal.

The clinical severity of the skin lesions of herpes zoster varies widely from patient to patient, although the severity of skin lesions and scarring tends to increase with age as does the duration of pain (Fig. 25–1). In most patients, the hyperesthesia and pain generally resolve as the skin lesions heal; in some, however, pain may persist beyond lesion healing. This most common and feared complication of herpes zoster is called postherpetic neuralgia, and the elderly are affected at a higher rate than the general population suffering from acute herpes zoster (Fig. 25–2).

The symptoms of postherpetic neuralgia can vary from a mild self-limited problem to a debilitating, constantly burning pain that is exacerbated by light touch, movement, anxiety, and/or temperature change. This unremitting pain may be so

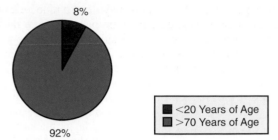

FIGURE 25–1 ■ Postherpetic neuralgia—pain 1 year after attack.

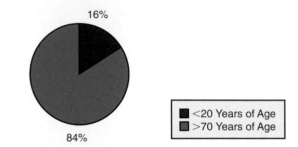

FIGURE 25–2 ■ Postherpetic neuralgia—pain beyond lesion healing.

severe that it often completely devastates the patient's life and can lead to suicide. It is the desire to avoid this disastrous sequela to a usually benign self-limited disease that dictates all therapeutic efforts for the patient suffering from acute herpes zoster.

■ TREATMENT

Basic Considerations

The therapeutic challenge of the patient presenting with acute herpes zoster is twofold—the relief of acute pain and symptoms and the prevention of complications, including postherpetic neuralgia. It is the consensus of most pain specialists that the earlier in the natural course of the disease that treatment is initiated, the less likely the patient will develop postherpetic neuralgia.[4] Because the older patient is at highest risk for developing postherpetic neuralgia, early and aggressive treatment of this group of patients is mandatory.

Careful initial evaluation, including a thorough history and physical examination, is indicated to rule out occult malignancy or systemic disease that may be responsible for the patient's immunocompromised state and to allow early recognition of changes in clinical status that may presage the development of complications, including myelitis or dissemination of the disease.

Treatment Options

There are as many therapeutic approaches to the treatment of acute herpes zoster as there are clinicians treating the disease.

Inherent problems in assessing the efficacy of a specific treatment are that the disease has many different clinical expressions and the natural history of the disease, as well as the incidence of complications—including postherpetic neuralgia—cannot be predicted reliably in any single patient. Most studies of the efficacy of a proposed treatment have failed to take these problems into account; therefore, only the most general conclusions may be reached.

Nerve Blocks

Sympathetic neural blockade appears to be the treatment of choice to relieve the symptoms of acute herpes zoster as well as to prevent the occurrence of postherpetic neuralgia.[5] Sympathetic nerve block appears to achieve these goals by blocking the profound sympathetic stimulation that is a result of the viral inflammation of the nerve and ganglion. If untreated, this sympathetic hyperactivity can cause ischemia secondary to decreased blood flow of the intraneural capillary bed. If this ischemia is allowed to persist, endoneural edema forms, increasing endoneural pressure and causing a further reduction of endoneural blood flow with irreversible nerve damage. This damage appears to preferentially destroy large myelinated nerve fibers, which are metabolically more active, and to spare small fibers.

Noordenbos was first to report this phenomenon and correlate it with the pain symptomatology of herpes zoster. He postulated that large neural fibers modulate or inhibit entry of pain impulses into the CNS, whereas small fibers enhance entry of pain impulses into the CNS. Therefore, enhanced transmission of painful stimuli, as well as misinterpretation of the non-noxious stimuli of the small fibers as pain by the CNS, would result if large fibers were preferentially destroyed. Interestingly, the theory of Noordenbos "fiber dissociation" predated Melzack and Wall's gate control theory by 6 years. His theory may also explain the clinical finding of Winnie and others that sympathetic neural blockade is more efficacious when used early in the course of the disease by presumably interrupting the neural ischemia before irreversible large fiber changes occur.[6]

For patients with acute herpes zoster involving the trigeminal nerve (Fig. 25–3) and the geniculate, cervical, and high thoracic regions, blockade of the stellate ganglion with a local anesthetic on a daily basis should be implemented immediately. For patients with acute herpes zoster involving the thoracic, lumbar, and sacral regions, daily epidural neural blockade with local anesthetic should be implemented immediately (Fig. 25–4). As vesicular crusting occurs, the addition of steroids to the local anesthetic may decrease neural scarring and further decrease the incidence of postherpetic neuralgia. These sympathetic blocks should be continued aggressively until the patient is pain free and should be reimplemented at the return of pain. Failure to use sympathetic neural blockade immediately and aggressively, especially in the elderly, may sentence the patient to a lifetime of suffering.

Drug Therapy

Narcotic analgesics may be useful in relieving the aching pain that is often present during the acute stages of herpes zoster as sympathetic nerve blocks are being implemented. They are

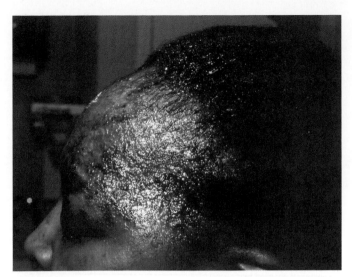

FIGURE 25–3 ■ Acute herpes zoster involving the trigeminal nerve.

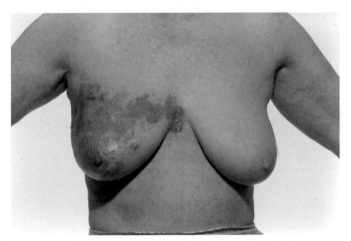

FIGURE 25–4 ■ Acute herpes zoster involving the thoracic dermatome.

less effective in the relief of the neuritic pain that is often present. Careful administration of potent, long-acting narcotic analgesics (e.g., oral morphine elixir or methadone) on a time contingent rather than on a prn basis may represent a beneficial adjunct to the pain relief provided by sympathetic neural blockade. Because many patients suffering from acute herpes zoster are elderly or may have severe multisystem disease, close monitoring for the potential side effects of potent narcotic analgesics (e.g., confusion or dizziness, which may cause a patient to fall) is warranted. Daily dietary fiber supplementation and milk of magnesia should be started along with narcotic analgesics to prevent the side effect of constipation.

Antidepressants may be useful adjuncts in the initial treatment of the patient suffering from acute herpes zoster. On an acute basis, these drugs will help alleviate the significant sleep disturbance that is commonly seen in this setting. In addition, the antidepressants may be valuable in helping ameliorate the neuritic component of the pain, which is treated less effectively with narcotic analgesics. After several weeks

of treatment, the antidepressants may exert a mood-elevating effect that may be desirable in some patients. Care must be taken to observe closely for CNS side effects in this patient population. These drugs may cause urinary retention and constipation that may be mistakenly attributed to herpes zoster myelitis.

Anticonvulsants may also be of value as an adjunct to sympathetic neural blockade in the management of pain secondary to acute herpes zoster. They may be particularly useful in relieving persistent paresthetic or dysesthetic pain. As with the narcotic analgesics and antidepressants, careful monitoring for CNS side effects is mandatory. Gabapentin at a bed-time dose of 300 mg is a reasonable starting place with the dosage of this drug being increased by 300 mg in divided doses every 48 to 72 hours as side effects allow. If carbamazepine is used, rigid monitoring for hematologic parameters, especially in patients receiving chemotherapy or radiation therapy, is indicated. Phenytoin should not be used in patients with lymphoma because the drug may induce a pseudolymphoma-like state that is difficult to distinguish from the actual disease.

Minor tranquilizers (e.g., diazepam) have a limited place in the adjunctive therapy of pain of acute herpes zoster. Although anxiety is often present in this setting, these drugs may actually increase pain perception. In addition, the addiction potential and CNS side effects limit their usefulness. Anxiety may be treated pharmacologically with hydroxyzine or, perhaps more appropriately, with behavioral interventions (e.g., monitored relaxation training and hypnosis).

A limited number of antiviral agents, including famcyclovir, acyclovir, and perhaps interferon have been shown to shorten the course of acute herpes zoster.[7] Of these drugs, famciclovir and acyclovir appear to have fewer side effects. There is a difference of opinion as to whether these drugs prevent the occurrence of postherpetic neuralgia. They are probably useful in attenuating the disease in immunosuppressed patients and may provide symptomatic relief. Careful monitoring for side effects is mandatory with the use of these relatively toxic drugs.

In the past, corticosteroids have been advocated as an adjunct in the treatment of acute herpes zoster. Proponents of this approach cite more rapid healing and a decreased incidence of postherpetic neuralgia. Other studies have been unable to confirm these findings. Local infiltration of affected skin areas with corticosteroid with or without local anesthetic may be of value as an adjunct to sympathetic neural blockade in decreasing localized areas of pain not amenable to other treatment modalities. Some authors believe that corticosteroids may increase the risk of dissemination in immunosuppressed patients if used prior to vesicular crusting. Our experience has not confirmed this to be the case.

Adjunctive Treatments

Local application of ice packs to the lesions of acute herpes zoster may provide relief in some patients. Application of heat will increase pain in most patients, presumably because of increased conduction of small fibers, but is beneficial in an occasional patient and may be worth trying if application of cold is ineffective. Transcutaneous electrical nerve stimulation and vibration may also be effective in a limited number of patients. The favorable risk-to-benefit ratio of all these modalities makes them reasonable alternatives for patients who cannot or will not undergo sympathetic neural blockade. As a last resort, spinal cord stimulation may be considered in those patient in whom no other treatment modalities have provided pain relief.

Topical application of aluminum sulfate as a tepid soak provides excellent drying of the crusting and weeping lesions of acute herpes zoster, and most patients find these soaks soothing. Zinc oxide ointment may also be used as a protective agent, especially during the healing phase when temperature sensitivity is a problem. Topical lidocaine patches provide some patients suffering from postherpetic neuralgia symptomatic relief, but this modality should not be used on broken or inflamed skin or skin with active lesions. Topical capsaicin has also been advocated as a treatment for postherpetic neuralgia; however, experience has shown that this treatment is poorly tolerated by many patients.[8] Disposable diapers can be used as an absorbent padding to protect healing lesions from contact with clothing and sheets.

■ COMPLICATIONS

In most patients, acute herpes zoster is a self-limited disease. In the elderly and the immunosuppressed, however, complications may occur.[2] Cutaneous and visceral dissemination may range from a mild rash resembling chickenpox to an overwhelming, life-threatening infection in those already suffering from severe multisystem disease. Myelitis may cause bowel, bladder, and lower-extremity paresis. Ocular compli-

cations from trigeminal-nerve involvement range from severe photophobia to keratitis with loss of vision.

■ CONCLUSION

In view of the devastating effects of inadequately treated acute herpes zoster on the patient, their family, and society in terms of cost and lost productivity, it is incumbent for all healthcare professionals to initiate immediate and aggressive treatment for all patients suffering from acute herpes zoster.

References

1. Bennet GJ: Hypothesis on the pathogenesis of herpes zoster-associated pain. Ann Neurol 35S38, 1994.
2. Waldman SD: Acute herpes zoster. In Waldman SD: Common Pain Syndromes. Philadelphia, WB Saunders, 2002, p171.
3. Waldman SD: Ramsey Hunt syndrome. In Waldman SD: Uncommon Pain Syndromes. Philadelphia, WB Saunders, 2003, p 25.
4. Dworkin RH, Portenoy RK: Pain and its persistence in herpes zoster. Pain 67:241, 1996.
5. Wu CL, Marsh A, Dworkin RH: The role of sympathetic nerve blocks in herpes zoster and postherpetic neuralgia. Pain 87:121, 2000.
6. Winne AP, Hartwell PW: Relationship between time of treatment of acute herpes zoster with sympathetic blockade and the prevention of postherpetic neuralgia. Reg Anesth 36:1089, 1993.
7. Kost RG, Staus SD: Postherpetic neuralgia pathogenesis, treatment, and prevention. N Engl J Med 335:32, 1996.
8. Kingery WS: A critical review of controlled clinical trials for peripheral neuropathic pain and complex regional pain syndromes. Pain 73:123, 1997.

Complex Regional Pain Syndrome Type I (Reflex Sympathetic Dystrophy)

Andreas Binder, Jörn Schattschneider, and Ralf Baron

Complex regional pain syndrome (CRPS) types I and II share most of the same pathophysiologic, clinical, and therapeutic features. Therefore, all main information regarding CRPS in general is included in this chapter dealing with CRPS I. Specific information on CRPS type II is added in Chapter 27.

During the past decades complex regional pain syndromes were recognized as poorly defined pain disorders that mostly confused basic researchers, clinicians, and epidemiologists rather than stimulating their scientific activities. This was mainly because diagnostic criteria were defined vaguely; underlying pathophysiologic mechanisms were unknown and therapeutic options were limited. No data on incidence, prognosis, and prevention were available, and research on mechanisms focused primarily on pain and controlled treatment studies were absent. However, the insight into pathophysiologic mechanisms has progressed dramatically during the past few years. Researchers became aware of the fact that CRPS I and II are not just neuropathic pain syndromes. In fact, CRPS I is unlikely to be a neuropathic pain syndrome because no obvious nerve lesion is present and all symptoms occur irrespective of the type of the preceding lesion. Based on this notion it has become obvious that multiple different pathophysiologic mechanisms may occur in different individual patterns.[1] These consist of somatosensory changes (including pain) that interact with changes related to the sympathetic nervous system, peripheral inflammatory changes, and changes in the somatomotor system.[2]

■ DEFINITION

The International Association for the Study of Pain (IASP) *Classification of Chronic Pain* redefined pain syndromes formerly known as reflex sympathetic dystrophy and causalgia. The term *complex regional pain syndrome* describes "a variety of painful conditions following injury which appears regionally having a distal predominance of abnormal findings, exceeding in both magnitude and duration the expected clinical course of the inciting event often resulting in significant impairment of motor function, and showing variable progression over time."[3]

These chronic pain syndromes comprise different additional clinical features including spontaneous pain, allodynia, hyperalgesia, edema, autonomic abnormalities, and trophic signs. In CRPS type I (reflex sympathetic dystrophy), minor injuries or fractures of a limb precede the onset of symptoms. CRPS type II (causalgia) develops after injury to a major peripheral nerve.

■ HISTORY

The American Civil War physician Weir Mitchell observed that about 10% of patients with traumatic partial peripheral nerve injuries in the distal extremity had a dramatic clinical syndrome that consisted of prominent, distal, spontaneous burning pain. In addition, patients reported exquisite hypersensitivity of the skin to light mechanical stimulation. Furthermore, movement, loud noises, or strong emotions could trigger their pain. The distal extremity showed considerable swelling, smoothness and mottling of the skin, and, in some cases, acute arthritis. In most cases the limb was cold and sweaty. Mitchell named this syndrome "causalgia." He was emphatic that the sensory and trophic abnormalities spread beyond the innervation territory of the injured peripheral nerve and often occurred remote from the site of injury. The nerve lesions giving rise to this syndrome were always partial; complete transection never caused it. Because of this and the peripheral signs of the disease, he concluded that, in addition to pathology in the nerve, some process in the skin or other peripheral tissue was responsible for the pain.

After World War II Leriche for the first time reported that sympathectomy dramatically relieves causalgia. This notion was supported by several large clinical series, primarily in wounded soldiers. Richards described the clinical features of causalgia and the effect of sympatholytic interventions in hundreds of cases. He repeatedly stressed the dramatic response of causalgia to sympathetic blockade: "One of the outstanding surgical lessons that was learned during World War II was that interruption of the appropriate sympathetic nerve fibres is almost invariably effective in the treatment of causalgia. When the sympathetic chain is blocked by a local

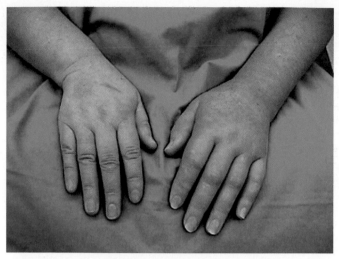

FIGURE 26–1 ■ Clinical picture of patient with CRPS type I of the upper left extremity after distortion of the left wrist. (From Baron R: Complex regional pain syndromes. In McMahon SB, Koltzenburg M [eds]: Wall and Melzack's Textbook of Pain, 5th ed. London, Elsevier, 2006, pp 1011-1027, with permission.)

anaesthetic, complete relief occurs almost immediately if the injection has been correctly placed, and the dramatic change in the patient's appearance and attitude is remarkable." The finding that sympatholysis relieves causalgic pain gave rise to the concept of sympathetically maintained pain.

In the years between World Wars I and II, the concept that sympathetic outflow can influence pain was extended to a group of patients without detectable nerve injury. These patients develop asymmetrical distal extremity pain and swelling (Fig. 26–1). The disorder had first been described by Sudeck early in the century. Precipitating events include fracture or minor soft tissue trauma, low-grade infection, frostbite, and burns, as well as stroke and myocardial infarction. The swelling and pain often develop at a site remote from the inciting injury, without any obvious local tissue-damaging process at the site of pain and swelling. This syndrome was named reflex sympathetic dystrophy (RSD) because vasomotor (altered skin color and temperature) and sudomotor abnormalities (altered sweat production) are common, the pain and swelling are often spatially remote from the inciting injury, and patients typically obtain dramatic relief with sympathetic block.

■ EPIDEMIOLOGY

Incidence and Prevalence

A population-based study on CRPS I calculated an incidence of about 5.5 per 100,000 person-years at risk and a prevalence of about 21 per 100,000.[4] Thus, CRPS I develops more often than CRPS II. Estimations suggest an incidence of CRPS I of 1% to 2% after fractures, 12% after brain lesions, and 5% after myocardial infarction. However, the latter data for brain lesions and myocardial infarctions are relatively high and have to be interpreted with some care because of the lack of uniform diagnostic criteria in the past. Females are more often affected than males, with a female-to-male ratio ranging from 2:1 to 4:1. CRPS shows a distribution over all ages, with a mean age peak of 37 to 50 years.

■ CLINICAL PRESENTATION

The most common precipitating event is a trauma affecting the distal part of an extremity (65%), especially fractures, postsurgical conditions, contusions, and strain or sprain. Less common incidents are central nervous system lesions such as spinal cord injuries and cerebrovascular accidents as well as cardiac ischemia.

CRPS I patients develop asymmetrical distal extremity pain and swelling without presenting an overt nerve lesion (Table 26–1; see also Fig. 26–1). These patients often report a burning spontaneous pain felt in the distal part of the affected extremity. Characteristically, the pain is disproportionate in intensity to the inciting event. The pain usually increases when the extremity is in a dependent position. Stimulus-evoked pains are a striking clinical feature; they include mechanical and thermal allodynia and/or hyperalgesia. These sensory abnormalities often appear early, are most pronounced distally, and have no consistent spatial relationship to individual nerve territories or to the site of the inciting lesion. Typically, pain can be elicited by movement of and pressure on the joints (deep somatic hyperalgesia), even if these are not directly affected by the inciting lesion. Autonomic abnormalities include swelling and changes of sweating and skin blood flow. In the acute stages of CRPS I the affected limb is often warmer than the contralateral limb. Sweating abnormalities—either hypohidrosis or, more frequently, hyperhidrosis—are present in nearly all CRPS I patients. The acute distal swelling of the affected limb depends very critically on aggravating stimuli. Because it may diminish after sympathetic blocks it is likely that it is maintained by sympathetic activity.

Trophic changes such as abnormal nail growth, increased or decreased hair growth, fibrosis, thin glossy skin, and osteoporosis may be present, particularly in chronic stages. Restrictions of passive movement are often present in long-standing cases and may be related to both functional motor disturbances and trophic changes of joints and tendons.

Weakness of all muscles of the affected distal extremity is often present. Small accurate movements are characteristically impaired. Nerve conduction and electromyography studies are normal, except in patients in very chronic and advanced stages. About half of the patients have a postural or action tremor representing an increased physiologic tremor. In about 10% of cases dystonia of the affected hand or foot develops.[5]

Spatial Distribution

Predominantly, CRPS occurs in one extremity. Retrospective studies in large cohorts showed a distribution in the upper and lower extremity from 1:1 to 2:1. In 113 retrospectively reviewed cases the symptoms occurred in 47% on the right, in 51% on the left side, and in 2% bilaterally. Multiple extremities were affected in up to 7%.[4,6-8]

Time Course

For therapeutic reasons, any effort should be undertaken to diagnose CRPS as early as possible. CRPS mostly starts acutely; that is, the cardinal symptoms may appear within hours or days. At the onset, the main symptoms of CRPS are spontaneous pain, generalized swelling, and difference in skin

| Table 26–1 |

Signs and Symptoms of CRPS

	Duration		
	2-6 Months	*>12 Months*	*Total from 0 to 12 Months (%)*
Pain	88	97	93
Increase of complaints after exercise	95	97	96
Neurologic			
Hyperesthesia/allodynia	75	85	76
Coordination deficits	47	61	54
Tremor	44	50	49
Muscle spasm	13	42	25
Paresis	93	97	95
Sympathetic			
Hyperhidrosis	56	40	47
Color difference	96	84	92
Temperature difference	91	91	92
Changed growth of hair	71	35	55
Changed growth of nails	60	52	60
Edema	80	55	69
Atrophy			
Skin	37	44	40
Nails	23	36	27
Muscle	50	67	55
Bone (diffuse/spotty osteoporosis on radiograph)	41	52	38

Modified from Veldman PH, Reynen HM, Arntz IE, et al: Signs and symptoms of reflex sympathetic dystrophy: Prospective study of 829 patients. Lancet 342:1012, 1993.

temperature on the symptomatic side. These early symptoms already develop in areas and tissues that are not affected by the preceding lesion. Thus, swelling and pain provide valuable information for an early diagnosis of CRPS: before the onset of CRPS, pain is felt inside the area of the preceding lesion; with the onset of CRPS, the pain becomes diffuse and deep inside the distal extremity and the swelling generalizes, yet the initial pain may already have disappeared.

To some extent the tendency of symptoms to generalize may be a physiologic phenomenon in posttraumatic states that will disappear without any treatment. An exact differentiation of these physiologic diffuse posttraumatic reactions and the development of "real" CRPS is not possible at the present time.

Stages

A sequential progression of untreated CRPS has been repeatedly described, each stage of which (usually three are proposed) differs in patterns of signs and symptoms. Nevertheless, this concept has come into question in the past few years. In 2002 the clinical validity of this concept was tested in 113 patients by Bruehl and colleagues.[7] Using a cluster analysis three subgroups were identified that could be differentiated by their symptoms and signs regardless of disease duration. The sequential concept relies on the course of untreated CRPS; however, so far all studies performed to test its clinical validity investigated patients already under treatment. Furthermore, vascular disturbances and skin temperature measurements indicated different thermoregulatory types depending on time.

In conclusion, it is questionable whether staging of CRPS is appropriate. It is much more practical with direct implication to therapy that patients with CRPS have their disease graded according to the intensity of the sensory, autonomic, motor, and trophic changes as being mild, moderate, or severe (see later).

Psychology

Most patients with CRPS exhibit significant psychologic distress, most commonly depression and anxiety. Many patients become overwhelmed by the pain and associated symptoms and, without adequate psychosocial support, may develop maladaptive coping skills. Based on these symptoms there is a tendency to ascribe the etiology of CRPS to emotional causes and it has been proposed that CRPS is a psychiatric illness. In fact, sometimes it is difficult to recognize the organic nature of the symptoms. However, when describing the clinical picture in the 1940s, Livingston was convinced: "The ultimate source of this dysfunction is not known but its organic nature is obvious and no one seems to doubt that these classical pain syndromes are real." Covington[9] drew several conclusions on psychological factors in CRPS:

1. No evidence was found to support the theory that CRPS is a psychogenic condition.
2. Because anxiety and stress increase nociception, relaxation and antidepressive treatment are helpful.
3. The pain in CRPS is the cause of psychiatric problems and not the converse.

4. Maladaptive behavior by patients, such as volitional or inadvertent actions, is mostly due to fear, regression, or misinformation and does not indicate psychopathology.
5. Some patients with conversion disorders and factitious diseases have been diagnosed incorrectly with CRPS.

In summary, Covington concluded that the widely proposed "CRPS personality" is clearly unsubstantiated. This assumption was further strengthened because no differences in psychologic patterns were found in patients with radius fracture developing CRPS I in comparison to patients who recovered without developing CRPS.[10]

According to this view, an even distribution of childhood trauma, of pain intensity, and of psychological distress was confirmed in patients with CRPS in comparison with patients with other neuropathic pain and chronic back pain.[11] Further studies demonstrated a high psychiatric comorbidity, especially depression, anxiety, and personality disorders, in CRPS patients. These findings are also present in other patients with chronic pain and are more likely a result of the long and severe pain disease.[12] Compared with patients with low back pain, CRPS patients showed a higher tendency to somatization but did not show any other psychologic differences.[13] In 145 patients 42% reported stressful life events in close relationship to the onset of CRPS and 41% had a previous history of chronic pain.[14] Thus, stressful life events could be risk factors for the development of CRPS.

Genetics of CRPS

One of the unsolved features in human pain diseases is the fact that only a minority of patients develop chronic pain after seemingly identical inciting events. Similarly, in certain nerve lesion animal models, differences in pain susceptibility were found to be due to genetic factors. The clinical importance of genetic factors in CRPS is not clear. A mendelian law does not seem to impact the incidence and prevalence. However, there is evidence for certain genotypes predisposing a risk to develop CRPS. Human leukocyte antigen (HLA) associations with different phenotypes have shown an increase in A3, B7, and DR(2) major histocompatibility complex (MHC) antigens in a small group of CRPS patients in whom resistance to

treatment was associated with positivity of DR(2). In a cohort of 52 CRPS patients class I or II MHC antigens were typed. The frequency of HLA-DQ1 was found to be significantly increased compared with control frequencies.[15] In patients with CRPS who progressed toward multifocal or generalized tonic dystonia an association with HLA-DR13 was reported.[16] Furthermore, a different locus, centromeric in HLA class I, was found to be associated with spontaneous development of CRPS, suggesting an interaction between trauma severity and genetic factors that describe CRPS susceptibility.[17]

▮ PATHOPHYSIOLOGIC MECHANISMS

Sensory Abnormalities and Pain

Based on numerous animal experimental findings, spontaneous pain and various forms of hyperalgesia at the distal extremity are thought to be generated by processes of peripheral and central sensitization. In addition to positive sensory phenomena, up to 50% of patients with chronic CRPS I develop hypoesthesia and hypoalgesia on the entire half of the body or in the upper quadrant ipsilateral to the affected extremity. Systematic quantitative sensory testing has shown that patients with these generalized hypoesthesias have increased thresholds to mechanical, cold, warmth, and heat stimuli compared with the responses generated from the corresponding contralateral healthy body side. Patients with these extended sensory deficits have a longer disease duration, greater pain intensity, a higher frequency of mechanical allodynia, and a higher tendency to develop changes in the somatomotor system than do patients with spatially restricted sensory deficits.

These changed somatosensory perceptions are likely due to changes in the central representation of somatosensory sensations in the thalamus and cortex. Accordingly, positron emission tomography (PET) studies demonstrated adaptive changes in the thalamus during the course of the disease.[18] The magnetoencephalographic (MEG) first somatosensory (SI) responses were increased on the affected side, indicating processes of central sensitization (Fig. 26–2). Psychophysical and transcranial magnetic stimulation (TMS) studies suggest

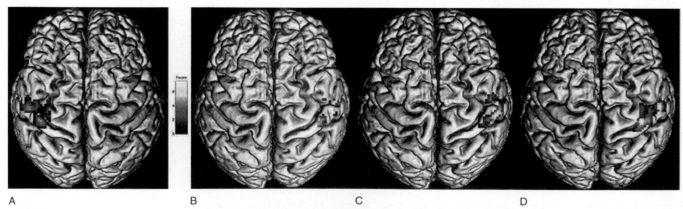

A   B   C   D

FIGURE 26–2 ▮ Central reorganization of the somatosensory cortex in a patient with CRPS I on the right hand. Functional MRI after mechanical stimulation of digits 1 and 5 on both sides. Shrinkage of the hand representation that recovers after successful treatment. **A,** Acute stage: nearly complete absence of the fMRI signal on the left hemisphere; normal representation on the contralateral side. **B** to **D,** Normalization of the representation after 3 (**B**), 6 (**C**), and 12 (**D**) months of the course. (From Pleger B, Tegenthoff M, Ragert P, et al: Sensorimotor retuning in complex regional pain syndrome parallels pain reduction. Ann Neurol 57:425, 2005, with permission.)

sensory and motor hyperexcitability within the central nervous system.[19] Furthermore, recent MEG and functional magnetic resonance imaging (fMRI) studies demonstrated a shortened distance between little finger and thumb representations in the SI cortex on the painful side.[20,21] This cortical reorganization was reversible, and correlated with pain reduction and improvement of tactile impairment.[22,23]

The dependency of these phenomena on structural or functional changes in the peripheral nerve system is not known so far. However, skin preparations from CRPS I patients showed diminished axonal density[24] and mixed decreased and increased innervation of epidermal and vascular structures as well as sweat glands.[25] The relevance of these findings to distinct pathophysiologic mechanisms remains unclear.[26]

Autonomic Abnormalities

Denervation Supersensitivity

A partial nerve lesion is the important preceding event in CRPS II. Therefore, it has generally been assumed that abnormalities in skin blood flow within the territory of the lesioned nerve are due to peripheral impairment of sympathetic function and sympathetic denervation. During the first weeks after transection of vasoconstrictor fibers, vasodilatation is present within the denervated area. Later the vasculature may develop increased sensitivity to circulating catecholamines, probably due to up-regulation of adrenoceptors.

Central Autonomic Dysregulation

Sympathetic denervation and denervation hypersensitivity cannot completely account for vasomotor and sudomotor abnormalities in CRPS. First, in CRPS I there is no overt nerve lesion and, second, in CRPS II the autonomic symptoms spread beyond the territory of the lesioned nerve. In fact, there is direct evidence for a reorganization of central autonomic control in these syndromes.[2,27]

Hyperhidrosis, for example, is found in many CRPS patients. Resting sweat output as well as thermoregulatory and axon reflex sweating are increased in CRPS I patients.[28] Increased sweat production cannot be explained by a peripheral mechanism because, unlike blood vessels, sweat glands do not develop denervation supersensitivity.

To study cutaneous sympathetic vasoconstrictor innervation in CRPS I patients, we have analyzed central sympathetic reflexes induced by thermoregulatory (whole-body warming, cooling) and respiratory stimuli.[29-31] Sympathetic effector organ function (i.e., skin temperature and skin blood flow) was measured bilaterally at the extremities by infrared thermometry and laser Doppler flowmetry. Under normal conditions these reflexes do not show interside differences. In CRPS patients three distinct vascular regulation patterns were identified related to the duration of the disorder:

1. In the warm regulation type (acute stage, <6 months) the affected limb was warmer and skin perfusion values were higher than contralaterally during the entire spectrum of sympathetic activity. Even massive body cooling failed to activate sympathetic vasoconstrictor neurons.[30] Consistently, direct measurements of norepinephrine levels from the venous effluent above the area of pain show a reduction in the affected extremity.[30,32]

2. In the intermediate type temperature and perfusion were either elevated or reduced depending on the degree of sympathetic activity.

3. In the cold type (chronic stage) temperature and perfusion were lower on the affected side during the entire spectrum of sympathetic activity. Norepinephrine levels, however, were still lower on the affected side.[31]

These data support the idea that CRPS I is associated with a pathologic unilateral inhibition of cutaneous sympathetic vasoconstrictor neurons leading to a warmer affected limb in the acute stage.[29,33] The locus of pathophysiologic changes underlying such disturbed reflex activity must be in the central nervous system. Secondary changes in neurovascular transmission may induce severe vasoconstriction and cold skin in chronic CRPS.[34,35] Accordingly, α-adrenoceptor density has been reported to be increased in skin biopsies of patients with CRPS I.[36] Furthermore, skin lactate was increased in CRPS patients, indicating an enhanced anaerobic glycolysis, probably as a result of vasoconstriction and chronic tissue hypoxia.[37,38]

The few microneurographic studies of small sympathetic nerve fascicles that have been performed so far in patients with CRPS, however, have not confirmed the presence of reflex abnormalities; the average skin sympathetic activity (i.e., a combination of vasoconstrictor and sudomotor activity) was not different on the two sides.[39]

In our study performed in patients suffering from "cold type" CRPS, iontophoresis of acetylcholine into the skin of the affected and unaffected extremity revealed a decrease of the vasodilatatory response in the CRPS extremity.[40] The pathophysiology of the hereby proven endothelial dysfunction in "cold type" CRPS is not known so far. However, it can be assumed that production of free radicals is triggered by tissue hypoxia and tissue acidosis due to peripheral vasoconstriction. Thus, the production of free radicals is responsible for the observed endothelial function. The vasoconstrictor- and nociceptor-sensitizing agent endothelin-1 seems not to be involved in the pathophysiology of CRPS.[41]

Neurogenic Inflammation

Some of the clinical features of CRPS, particularly in its early phase, could be explained by an inflammatory process.[42] Consistent with this idea, corticosteroids are often successfully used in acute CRPS.[43]

There is increasing evidence that a localized neurogenic inflammation might be involved in the generation of acute edema, vasodilatation, and increased sweating. Scintigraphic investigations with radiolabeled immunoglobulins show extensive plasma extravasation in patients with acute CRPS I.[44] Analysis of joint fluid and synovial biopsies in CRPS patients have shown an increase in protein concentration and synovial hypervascularity. Furthermore, synovial effusion is enhanced in affected joints as measured with MRI. In acute untreated CRPS I patients neurogenic inflammation was elicited by strong transcutaneous electrical stimulation via intradermal microdialysis capillaries. Protein extravasation that was simultaneously assessed by the microdialysis system was only provoked on the affected extremity as compared with the normal side. Furthermore, axon reflex vasodilatation was increased significantly. The time course of electrically induced protein extravasation in the patients resembled the one observed[45] after application of exogenous substance P or did not show differences from healthy controls. Additionally, high substance P levels may be caused by impaired substance P inactivation in acute stages of CRPS.[46] As further support of a neurogenic inflammatory process, systemic calcitonin gene–related peptide (CGRP) levels were found to be increased in acute CRPS but not in chronic stages.[47] In the fluid of artificially produced skin blisters significantly higher levels of interleukin (IL)-6 and tumor necrosis factor-α (TNFα) were observed in the involved extremity as compared with the uninvolved extremity.[48] These findings persisted although pain and signs of CRPS I improved, questioning the direct relation between clinical signs and symptoms and proinflammatory cytokines.[49] However, proinflammatory cytokine levels were also significantly elevated, first in CRPS patients complaining of mechanical hyperalgesia more than in CRPS patients without hyperalgesia[50] and, second, in the venous blood of the affected limb compared with the unaffected contralateral extremity.[51] Moreover, analysis of the cerebrospinal fluid in CRPS I and II revealed higher levels of proinflammatory IL-1β and IL-6, whereas TNF levels did not differ from levels in patients with painful conditions of other origin.[52]

As an indicator of an exogenous infection, a significantly higher seroprevalence of erythrovirus (formerly parvovirus) B19 was observed in CRPS I patients.[53] Recent studies discussed whether an exogenous *Campylobacter* infection may trigger autoimmune activation.[54,55] However, the importance of antecedent infections as well as detected autoantibodies against autonomic nervous system structures[56] in the pathophysiology of CRPS (e.g., in the generation of a facilitated chronic inflammation) is yet not known.

Thus, evidence indicates that inflammatory processes are involved in the pathogenesis of early CRPS. However, the exact mechanisms of the initiation and maintenance of these inflammatory reactions are unclear.[57] One central issue is whether the sympathetic nervous system may contribute to the early inflammatory state. De novo expression of adrenoreceptors on macrophages after an experimental nerve lesion supports this idea. However, this concept has yet to be proven in patients with CRPS. Figure 26–3 illustrates the possible interactions between sympathetic fibers, afferent fibers, blood vessels, and non-neural cells related to the immune system (e.g., macrophages) leading theoretically to the inflammatory changes observed in CRPS patients.

Motor Abnormalities

About 50% of the patients with CRPS show a decrease of active range of motion, an increased amplitude of physiologic tremor, and reduced active motor force of the affected extremity. In about 10% of cases dystonia of the affected hand or foot develops, especially in chronic cases. It is unlikely that these motor changes are related to a peripheral process (e.g., influence of the sympathetic nervous system on neuromuscular transmission and/or contractility of skeletal muscle). These somatomotor changes are more likely generated by changes of activity in the motor neurons; that is, they have a central origin. Furthermore, we used kinematic analysis of target reaching as well as grip force analysis to quantitatively assess motor deficits in CRPS patients.[58] These results pointed to

abnormalities in cerebral motor processing. A pathologic sensorimotor integration located in the parietal cortex was found that may induce abnormal central programming and processing of motor tasks. Interestingly, the motor performance is also slightly impaired on the contralateral unaffected side.[59] Furthermore, a sustained disinhibition of the motor cortex was found in CRPS patients on the contralateral as well as the ipsilateral hemisphere.[60,61] Interestingly, repetitive TMS applied to the motor cortex contralateral to the affected extremity in CRPS I showed potential to modulate, that is, decrease pain.[62]

According to this view, a neglect-like syndrome was clinically described as being responsible for the disuse of the extremity.[63] Delayed recognition of hand laterality that is related to the duration and pain intensity[64] in CRPS I and impairment of self-perception of the affected extremity that is related to pain intensity, illness duration, and extent of sensory deficits[65] may contribute to disuse, impaired motor planning, and function. A controlled study also supports an incongruence between central motor output and sensory input as an underlying mechanism in CRPS. Using the method of mirror visual feedback the visual input from a moving unaffected limb to the brain was able to reestablish the pain-free relationship between sensory feedback and motor execution. After 6 weeks of therapy, pain and function were improved as compared with the control group.[66,67] A study extension comparing the combined therapy regimen of hand laterality recognition training, imagination of movements, and mirror movements demonstrated the efficacy to reduce pain and disability.[68]

Sympathetically Maintained Pain

Definition

On the basis of experience and recent clinical studies the term *sympathetically maintained pain* was redefined. Neuropathic pain patients presenting with similar clinical signs and symptoms can clearly be divided into two groups by the negative or positive effect of selective sympathetic blockade or antagonism of α-adrenoceptor mechanisms. The pain component that is relieved by specific sympatholytic procedures is considered to be sympathetically maintained pain (SMP). Thus, SMP is now defined as a symptom or the underlying mechanism in a subset of patients with neuropathic disorders, and not a clinical entity. The positive effect of a sympathetic blockade is not essential for the diagnosis. On the other hand, the only way to differentiate between SMP and sympathetically independent pain (SIP) is the efficacy of a correctly applied sympatholytic intervention.[69]

Studies on Patients

Clinical studies in CRPS support the idea that nociceptors develop catecholamine sensitivity.[70] Intraoperative stimulation of the sympathetic chain induces an increase of spontaneous pain in patients with causalgia (CRPS II) but not in patients with hyperhidrosis. In CRPS II and posttraumatic neuralgias, intracutaneous application of norepinephrine into a symptomatic area rekindles spontaneous pain and dynamic mechanical hyperalgesia that had been relieved by sympathetic blockade, supporting the idea that noradrenergic sensitivity of human nociceptors is present after partial nerve lesion. Also, intradermal norepinephrine, in physiologically

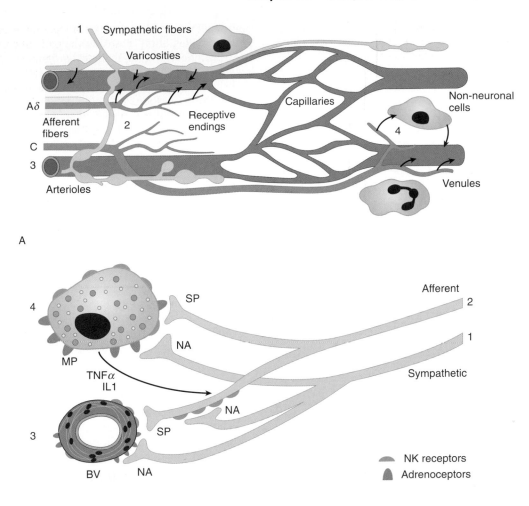

FIGURE 26–3 ■ **A,** The micromilieu of nociceptors. The microenvironment of primary afferents is thought to affect the properties of the receptive endings of myelinated (A) and unmyelinated (C) afferent fibers. This has been particularly documented for inflammatory processes, but one may speculate that pathologic changes in the direct surroundings of primary afferents may contribute to other pain states as well. The vascular bed consists of arterioles (directly innervated by sympathetic and afferent fibers), capillaries (not innervated and not influenced by nerve fibers), and venules (not directly innervated but influenced by nerve fibers). The micromilieu depends on several interacting components: neural activity in postganglionic noradrenergic fibers (1) supplying blood vessels (3, BV) causes release of norepinephrine (NA) and possibly other substances and vasoconstriction. Excitation of primary afferents (Aδ and C fibers) (2) causes vasodilatation in precapillary arterioles and plasma extravasation in postcapillary venules (C fibers only) by the release of substance P (SP) and other vasoactive compounds (e.g., calcitonin gene–related peptide [CGRP]). Some of these effects may be mediated by non-neuronal cells such as mast cells and macrophages (4). Other factors that affect the control of the microcirculation are the myogenic properties of arterioles (3) and more global environmental influences such as a change of temperature and metabolic state of the tissue. **B,** Hypothetical relation between sympathetic noradrenergic nerve fibers (1), peptidergic afferent nerve fibers (2), blood vessels (3), and macrophages (4). The activated and sensitized afferent nerve fibers activate macrophages (MP) possibly via SP release. The immune cells start to release cytokines, such as tumor necrosis factor-α (TNFα) and interleukin 1 (IL1), which further activate afferent fibers. SP (and CGRP) released from the afferent nerve fibers reacts with neurokinin 1 (NK1) receptors in the blood vessels (arteriolar vasodilatation, venular plasma extravasation, neurogenic inflammation). The sympathetic nerve fibers interact with this system on three levels: (1) via adrenoceptors (mainly α) on the blood vessels (vasoconstriction); (2) via adrenoceptors (mainly β) on macrophages (further release of cytokines), and (3) via adrenoceptors (mainly α) on afferents (further sensitization of these fibers). (**A,** Modified from Jänig W, Koltzenburg M: What is the interaction between the sympathetic terminal and the primary afferent fiber? In Basbaum AI, Besson J-M [eds]): Towards a New Pharmacotherapy of Pain. Chichester, Wiley, 1991, pp 331-352, with permission; **B,** Modified from Jänig W, Baron R: Complex regional pain syndrome: Mystery explained? Lancet Neurol 2:687-697, 2003, with permission.)

relevant doses, was demonstrated to evoke greater pain in the affected regions of patients with SMP than in the contralateral unaffected limb and in control subjects.[71]

We performed a study in patients with CRPS I using physiologic stimuli of the sympathetic nervous system.[72] Cutaneous sympathetic vasoconstrictor outflow to the painful extremity was experimentally activated to the highest possible physiologic degree by whole-body cooling. During the thermal challenge the affected extremity was clamped to 35°C to avoid thermal effects at the nociceptor level. The intensity

as well as the area of spontaneous pain and mechanical hyperalgesia (dynamic and punctate) increased significantly in patients who had been classified as having SMP by positive sympathetic blocks but not in SIP patients (Fig. 26–4). The experimental setup used in the latter study selectively alters sympathetic cutaneous vasoconstrictor activity without influencing other sympathetic systems innervating the extremities (i.e., piloerector, sudomotor, and muscle vasoconstrictor neurons). Therefore, the interaction of sympathetic and afferent neurons measured here is likely to be located within the

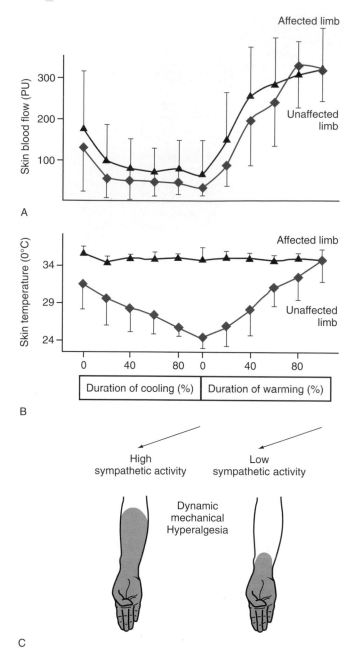

FIGURE 26–4 ■ Experimental modulation of cutaneous sympathetic vasoconstrictor neurons by physiologic thermoregulatory reflex stimuli in 13 CRPS patients. With the help of a thermal suit, whole-body cooling and warming was performed to alter sympathetic skin nerve activity. The subjects were lying in a suit supplied by tubes in which running water of 12°C and 50°C, respectively (inflow temperature) was used to cool or warm the whole body. By these means sympathetic activity can be switched on and off. **A,** High sympathetic vasoconstrictor activity during cooling induces considerable drop in skin blood flow on the affected and unaffected extremity (laser Doppler flowmetry). Measurements were taken at 5-minute intervals at the fingertips (mean + SD). **B,** On the unaffected side a secondary decrease of skin temperature was documented. On the affected side the forearm temperature was clamped at 35°C by a feedback-controlled heat lamp to exclude temperature effects on the sensory receptor level. Measurements were taken at 5-minute intervals (mean + SD). **C,** Effect of cutaneous sympathetic vasoconstrictor activity on dynamic mechanical hyperalgesia in one CRPS patient with sympathetically maintained pain. Activation of sympathetic neurons (during cooling) leads to a considerable increase of the area of dynamic mechanical hyperalgesia. (From Baron R, Schattschneider J, Binder A, et al: Relation between sympathetic vasoconstrictor activity and pain and hyperalgesia in complex regional pain syndromes: A case-control study. Lancet 359:1655, 2002, with permission.)

skin as predicted by the pain-enhancing effect of intracutaneous norepinephrine injections.[71] Interestingly, the relief of spontaneous pain after sympathetic blockade was more pronounced than changes in spontaneous pain that could be induced experimentally by sympathetic activation. One explanation for this discrepancy might be that a complete sympathetic block affects all sympathetic outflow channels projecting to the affected extremity. It is very likely that in addition to a coupling in the skin, a sympathetic-afferent interaction may also occur in other tissues, in particular in deep somatic domains such as bone, muscle, and joints. Supporting this view, these structures in particular are extremely painful in some cases with CRPS.[73] Furthermore, there may be patients who are characterized by a selective or predominant sympathetic-afferent interaction in deep somatic tissues sparing the skin.[30] Additionally, nonresponsiveness to sympathetic blockades or modulation of sympathetic activity may be explained by the observation that the sympathetic maintained pain component is not a constant phenomenon over time and decreases in the course of the disease.[74]

Summary of Pathophysiologic Mechanisms

In the light of the numerous novel studies on pathophysiologic mechanisms in CRPS we are currently at a turning point in recognizing that important parts of the CRPS pathophysiology are obviously located within the CNS and it can therefore be described as a neurologic disease (Fig. 26–5) including the autonomic, sensory, and motor systems as well as cortical areas involved in the processing of cognitive and affective information. In addition to these neural abnormalities the inflammatory component appears to be particularly important in the acute phase of the disease.

■ DIAGNOSIS

The diagnosis of CRPS I and II follows the IASP clinical criteria.[69] If two clinical signs are joined by "or" and if either sign is present or both are, the condition of the statement is satisfied. For CRPS type I (former RSD) the criteria are as follows:

1. Type I is a syndrome that develops after an initiating noxious event.
2. Spontaneous pain or allodynia/hyperalgesia occurs, is not limited to the territory of a single peripheral nerve, and is disproportionate to the inciting event.
3. There is or has been evidence of edema, skin blood flow abnormality, or abnormal sudomotor activity in the region of the pain since the inciting event.
4. This diagnosis is excluded by the existence of conditions that would otherwise account for the degree of pain and dysfunction.

Pain is essential for the diagnosis, whereby "spontaneous" indicates pain without external cause. Motor symptoms and findings are not included in this classification, although they are common and can include tremor, dystonia, and weakness.

Diagnostic Tests

For the present the diagnosis of CRPS is based on the clinical criteria described earlier. However, several tests and pro-

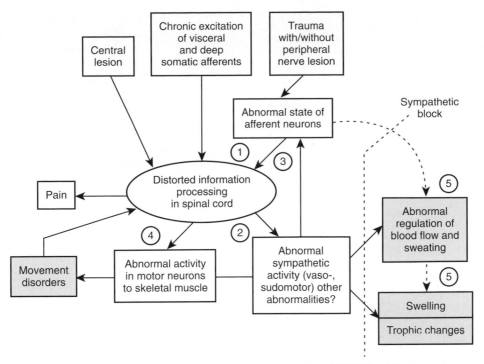

FIGURE 26–5 ■ General explanatory hypothesis about the neural mechanisms of generation of CRPS I and II after peripheral trauma with and without nerve lesions, chronic stimulation of visceral afferents (e.g. myocardial infarction) and of deep somatic afferents, and, rarely, central trauma. The clinical observations are double framed. Note the vicious circle *(solid arrows)*. An important component of this circle is the excitatory influence of postganglionic sympathetic axons on primary afferent fibers in the periphery. The numbers indicate changes of activity in peripheral neurons that have not been measured directly in CRPS patients but that have been postulated on the basis of measurements of effector responses of somatic sensations (including pain): 1, afferent traumatized neurons; 2, sympathetic neurons; 3, sympathetic-afferent coupling; 4, motor neurons; 5 *(interrupted arrow;* hypothetical mechanism), 'antidromically' conducted activity in peptidergic afferent C fibers leading to increase of blood flow (arteriolar vasodilatation) and venular plasma extravasation, both hypothetically contributing to increase in blood flow and to swelling. *Dotted line:* effect of sympathectomy or sympathetic blocks on positive vicious feedback circuit. (From Baron R: Complex regional pain syndromes. In McMahon SB, Koltzenburg M (eds): Wall and Melzack's Textbook of Pain, 5th ed. London, Elsevier, 2006, pp 1011-1027, with permission.)

cedures are valuable diagnostic tools that can add information to confirm the diagnostic impression about autonomic, sensory and motor function and dysfunction.

Osseous changes are common in CRPS. Thus, three-phase bone scintigraphy can provide valuable information. A homogeneous unilateral hyperperfusion in the perfusion (30 seconds post injection) and blood-pool phases (2 minutes post injection) is characteristic and will help to exclude differential diagnoses (e.g., osteoporosis due to inactivity). At 3 hours post injection the mineralization phase will show an increased unilateral periarticular tracer uptake (Fig. 26–6). A pathologic uptake in the metacarpophalangeal or metacarpal bones is thought to be highly sensitive and specific for CRPS. However, a gold standard to compare with is as yet unknown but it is useful to rule out pain syndromes of other origin. Bone scintigraphy only shows significant changes during the subacute period (up to 1 year).

Endosteal and intracortical excavation, subperiosteal and trabecular bone resorption, spotty and localized bone demineralization, and osteoporosis have been thought to be specific signs of CRPS, but these are only positive in chronic stages. A comparison of radiography and three-phase scintigraphy in early post-fracture CRPS showed a lower sensitivity and specificity of the radiography. MRI is suggested as being more reliable than radiographic examination and scintigraphy but has to prove its value in further studies.

Quantitative sensory testing can provide information about the sensory symptom profile (function or dysfunction of unmyelinated and myelinated afferent fibers) using psychophysical testing of thermal pain and vibratory thresholds. However, there is no sensory profile that is characteristic for CRPS.

Autonomic testing with the quantitative sudomotor axon reflex test (QSART) can provide information about the function of sudomotor reflex loops. Swelling can be quantified by measuring water displacement. Autonomic vascular function can be tested by laser Doppler flowmetry[30,31,33] and infrared thermography.

Skin temperature measurements are an easy measure of vascular function and may be particularly helpful for diagnosis of CRPS. We performed a study using controlled thermoregulation (whole-body warming, cooling) to change cutaneous sympathetic vasoconstrictor activity.[75] Skin temperature at the affected and unaffected limbs (infrared thermometry) was measured under resting conditions (before temperature challenge in the office at room temperature) and continuously monitored during controlled modulation of sympathetic activity. Only minor skin temperature asymmetries were present between both limbs under resting conditions in most patients. However, during controlled thermoregulation temperature differences between both sides increased dynamically and were most prominent at a high to medium level of

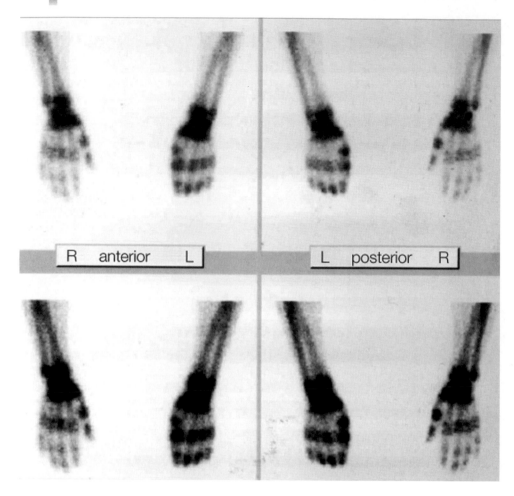

FIGURE 26–6 ■ Three-phase bone scintigraphy in a patient with CRPS type I of the upper left extremity: characteristic increased unilateral periarticular tracer uptake. (From Baron R: Complex regional pain syndromes. In McMahon SB, Koltzenburg M (eds): Wall and Melzack's Textbook of Pain, 5th ed. London, Elsevier, 2006, pp 1011-1027, with permission.)

vasoconstrictor activity. In patients suffering from painful limbs of other origin and in healthy volunteers (control groups), there were only minor side differences in temperature both at rest and during thermoregulatory changes of sympathetic activity. When comparing the diagnostic value of skin temperature asymmetries in CRPS, sensitivity was only 32% under resting conditions but increased up to 76% during controlled alteration of sympathetic activity. Specificity was 100% at rest and 93% at controlled thermoregulation (Fig. 26–7).

In conclusion, the degree of unilateral vascular disturbances in CRPS and the temperature side differences depend critically on environmental temperature and spontaneous sympathetic activity. However, the maximal skin temperature difference that occurs during the thermoregulatory cycle distinguishes CRPS from other extremity pain syndromes with high sensitivity and specificity.

Validation of Clinical Diagnostic Criteria

The definition of standardized diagnostic criteria for CRPS in 1994 was a major advance in the classification of regional pain disorders associated with vasomotor or sudomotor abnormalities.[69] Based on these criteria, clinical research on mechanisms was performed on a much more homogeneous group of patients and was therefore for the first time comparable. However, the current criteria were derived based on the consensus opinion of a small group of expert clinicians. While this was an appropriate first step it is important to continuously improve the criteria, that is, to validate and, if necessary, modify these initial consensus-based criteria based on results of systematic validation research. The current CRPS diagnostic criteria are adequately sensitive (i.e., rarely miss a case of actual CRPS). However, both internal and external validation research suggests that CRPS is currently overdiagnosed.[76,77] Possibly due to this drawback the new terminology did not replace the former denominations immediately.

The inclusion of motor and trophic signs and symptoms, for example, improves specificity to 85% without losing sensitivity.[7] The establishment of such modified diagnostic criteria will have in turn a huge impact on the quality of studies on pathophysiologic mechanisms and therapy.

Differential Diagnosis

Due to the lack of a gold standard in diagnosis of CRPS the risk of overdiagnosing has to be taken into account. To differentiate CRPS from other neuropathic and other pain syndromes, a detailed history and physical examination according to the specifications outlined earlier are mandatory.

Posttraumatic Neuralgia

It is important to recognize that many posttraumatic neuropathy patients have pain but do not have the full clinical

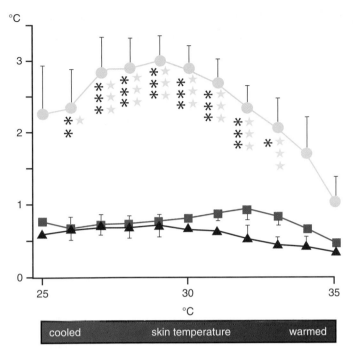

°C

cooled   skin temperature   warmed

FIGURE 26–7 ■ Average absolute side differences in skin temperature of the fingers (toes) of both hands (feet) in 25 patients with CRPS *(circle),* in 20 healthy controls *(triangle),* and in 15 control patients with extremity pain of other origin *(square)* during a controlled thermoregulatory cycle (controlled alteration in cutaneous sympathetic activity). The level of the overall cutaneous sympathetic vasoconstrictor activity was estimated indirectly by using the skin temperature on the unaffected side (or right side in healthy controls) as reference value. A skin temperature on the healthy side of 25°C indicates a high level, a temperature of 30°C, an intermediate level, and a temperature of 35°C, a complete inhibition of sympathetic vasoconstrictor activity to the skin (mean ± SEM). CRPS compared with healthy controls *(asterisk);* CRPS compared with control patients with extremity pain of other origin *(star):* one symbol, $P < .05$; two symbols, $P < .01$; three symbols, $P < .001$. (From Wasner G, Schattschneider J, Heckmann K, et al: Vascular abnormalities in reflex sympathetic dystrophy [CRPS I]: Mechanisms and diagnostic value. Brain 124:587, 2001, with permission.)

picture of causalgia (CRPS II). In these cases, in contrast to causalgia patients, the pain is located largely within the innervation territory of the injured nerve. Although these patients often describe their pain as burning, they exhibit a less complex clinical picture than patients with causalgia and do not show marked swelling or progressive spread of symptoms. The cardinal symptoms are spontaneous burning pain, hyperalgesia, and mechanical and especially cold allodynia. These sensory symptoms are confined to the territory of the affected peripheral nerve, although allodynia may extend beyond the border of nerve territories for some centimeters. Spontaneous and evoked pain are felt superficially and not deep inside the extremity, and the intensity of both is not dependent on the position of the extremity. The patients occasionally obtain relief with sympatholytic procedures, although much less often than those with CRPS.

Following the IASP classification it is possible to use the term *neuralgia* for this type of neuropathic pain (pain within the innervation territory of a lesioned nerve, e.g., post-traumatic neuralgia). However, the new definition of CRPS II includes the statement that symptoms may also be limited to the territory of a single peripheral nerve. Therefore, the term *CRPS II* provides a window to include these localized post-traumatic neuropathies. An inherent weakness of this definition of CRPS II is that different syndromes with different underlying mechanisms are obviously included.

Neuropathies (e.g., diabetic polyneuropathy) may also present as spontaneous pain, skin color changes, and motor deficits but are distinguished by their symmetrical distribution and the patient's history. Furthermore, all kinds of inflammations or infections (e.g., rheumatism, phlegmons) might induce an intense unilateral skin warming. Unilateral arterial or venous occlusive diseases can cause unilateral pain and vascular abnormalities and have to be excluded. Repetitive artificial occlusion of the blood supply to one limb (as in the psychiatric factitious disorders, artifact syndrome) might induce secondary structural changes of the blood vessels with consecutive abnormalities in perfusion and, therefore, mimic CRPS symptoms and signs.

■ TREATMENT

A lack of understanding of the underlying pathophysiologic abnormalities and a lack of objective diagnostic criteria result in inherent difficulties in conducting clinical trials with therapeutic modalities. Therefore, only few evidence-based treatment regimens for CRPS are available so far; these are summarized in Table 26–2. In fact, three literature reviews of outcome studies found discouragingly little consistent information regarding the pharmacologic agents and methods for treatment of CRPS.[78-80] Moreover, the methodology is often of low quality within the 30 studies available. In the absence of more specific information about pathophysiologic mechanisms and treatment of CRPS one has to rely on outcomes from treatment studies for other neuropathic pain syndromes. Furthermore, the still hypothetical mechanism-based treatment concept has to be transferred from ideas derived from animal experiments on peripheral nerve lesions to the situation in CRPS patients. However, functional imaging and neurophysiologic studies indicate that a reduction of pain does not reduce the burden of illness only. Moreover, it can contribute to the reversibility of cortical reorganization leading to an improvement of functional (i.e., motor function) and sensory capacity.

Pharmacologic Therapy

Nonsteroidal Anti-inflammatory Drugs (NSAIDs)

NSAIDs have not been investigated in the treatment of CRPS to date. However, from clinical experience they can control mild to moderate pain.

Opioids

Opioids are clearly effective in postoperative, inflammatory, and cancer pain. The use of opioids in CRPS has not been studied. In other neuropathic pain syndromes compounds such as tramadol, morphine, oxycodone, and levorphanol are clearly analgesic when compared with placebo. However, there are no long-term studies of oral opioid use for treatment of neuropathic pain, CRPS included. Even without solid scientific evidence, the expert opinion of pain clinicians is that opioids could be and should be used as a part of a comprehensive pain treatment program. Given that some patients with neuropathic pain may obtain considerable pain relief,

Table 26–2

Pharmacologic Treatment of Complex Regional Pain Syndromes

	Result	No. Patients	References
Anticonvulsants			
Gabapentin	Positive	85 (of 305)	Mellick and Mellick, 1995
	Weak effect on pain	58	van de Vusse et al, 2004
			Serpell 2002
Sodium Channel Blockers			
Lidocaine (IV)	Positive	16	Wallace et al, 2000
Corticosteroids			
Prednisone (oral)	Positive	23	Christensen et al, 1982
Calcium-Regulating Drugs			
Clodronate (IV)	Positive	32	Varenna et al, 2000
Alendronate (IV)	Positive	20	Adami et al, 1997
Alendronate (oral)	Positive	40	Manicourt et al, 2004
Calcitonin (intranasal)	Positive	66	Gobelet et al, 1992
Calcitonin (intranasal)	Negative	40	Bickerstaff and Kanis, 1991
Free Radical Scavengers			
DMSO (topical)	Positive	26	Geertzen et al, 1994
			Perez et al, 2003
DMSO (topical)	Negative	32	Zuurmond et al, 1996
N-Acetylcysteine (oral)	Positive	146	Perez et al, 2003

DMSO, dimethylsulfoxide.
From Baron R: Complex regional pain syndromes. In McMahon SB, Koltzenburg M (eds): Wall and Melzack's Textbook of Pain, 5th ed. London, Elsevier, 2006, pp 1011-1027.

opioids should be prescribed immediately if other agents do not achieve sufficient analgesia.

Antidepressants

Tricyclic antidepressants (TCAs) have been intensely studied in different neuropathic pain conditions but not in CRPS. There is solid evidence that reuptake blockers of serotonin and norepinephrine (e.g., amitriptyline) and selective norepinephrine blockers (e.g., desipramine) produce pain relief in diabetic or postherpetic neuropathy. The effectiveness of selective serotonin reuptake inhibitors in neuropathic pain states is still discussed. Only one of four studies performed so far showed a significant pain reduction in painful diabetic neuropathy. None has been performed on CRPS patients.

Sodium Channel Blocking Agents

Lidocaine (lignocaine) administered intravenously is effective in CRPS I and II regarding spontaneous and evoked pain.[81] Carbamazepine has not been tested in CRPS.

GABA Agonists

Intrathecally administered baclofen is effective in the treatment of dystonia in CRPS.[82] Oral baclofen has been effective in the treatment of trigeminal neuralgia. No further trials in CRPS are available, and there is no evidence for an analgesic effect of baclofen, valproic acid, vigabatrin, and benzodiazepines in CRPS or other neuropathic pain conditions.

Gabapentin

Promising preliminary evidence was revealed by two studies on patients with CRPS that showed an analgesic effect of gabapentin.[83,84] A randomized double-blind placebo-controlled trial demonstrated a mild effect of gabapentin on pain and a good effect on sensory deficit symptoms in CRPS I.[85] Gabapentin is effective in painful diabetic neuropathy and postherpetic neuralgia.

Corticosteroids

Orally administered prednisone, 10 mg three times daily, has clearly demonstrated efficacy in the improvement of the entire clinical status (up to 75%) of acute CRPS patients (<13 weeks).[43] No evidence has been obtained with other immune-modulating therapies, such as immunoglobulins or immunosuppressive drugs.

N-Methyl-D-Aspartate (NMDA) Receptor Blockers

Clinically available compounds that are demonstrated to have NMDA receptor blocking properties include ketamine, dextromethorphan, and memantine. Dextromethorphan, for example, is effective in the treatment of painful diabetic neuropathy and not effective in postherpetic neuralgia and central pain. NMDA receptor blockers may therefore offer new options in the treatment of CRPS pain, but studies that would help clinicians to fully utilize these agents are not yet available.

Calcium-Regulating Drugs

Calcitonin administered three times daily intranasally demonstrated a significant pain reduction in CRPS patients.[86] Clodronate (300 mg daily IV) and alendronate (7.5 mg daily IV or 40 mg orally daily) showed a significant improvement in pain, swelling, and movement range in acute CRPS.[87-89] The mode of action of these compounds in CRPS is unknown.

Free Radical Scavengers

Recently, a placebo-controlled trial was performed using the free radical scavengers dimethylsulfoxide (DMSO) 50% topically or *N*-acetylcysteine (NAC) orally for the treatment of CRPS I.[90] Both drugs were found to be equally effective; however, DMSO seemed more favorable for "warm" and NAC was more effective for "cold" CRPS I. The results were negatively influenced by a longer disease duration. A previous trial with DMSO failed to show a positive result in CRPS[91]; however, DMSO has been shown to be more effective than regional blocks with guanethidine in a small population of CRPS patients.[92]

Transdermal application of the α_2-adrenoceptor agonist clonidine, which is though to prevent the release of catecholamines by a presynaptic action, may be helpful when small areas of hyperalgesia are present.[93]

Interventional Therapy at the Sympathetic Nervous System Level

Currently, two therapeutic techniques to block sympathetic activity are used:

1. Injections of a local anesthetic around sympathetic paravertebral ganglia that project to the affected body part (sympathetic ganglion blocks)
2. Regional intravenous application of guanethidine, bretylium, or reserpine (which all deplete norepinephrine in the postganglionic axon) to an isolated extremity blocked with a tourniquet (intravenous regional sympatholysis [IVRS]).

There are many uncontrolled surveys in the literature reviewing the effect of sympathetic interventions in CRPS. In CRPS, about 70% of the patients report full or partial response.[94] The efficacy of these procedures is, however, still discussed controversially and has been questioned in the past.[80,95] In fact, the specificity and the long-term results as well as the techniques used have rarely been adequately evaluated.

Sympathetic Ganglion Blocks

One controlled study in patients with CRPS I has shown that sympathetic ganglion blocks with local anesthetic have the same immediate effect on pain as a control injection with saline.[96] However, after 24 hours patients in the local anesthetic group were much better, indicating that nonspecific effects are important initially and that evaluating the efficacy of sympatholytic interventions is best done after 24 hours. With these data in mind, the uncontrolled studies mentioned earlier must be interpreted cautiously. Only 10 of the 24 studies we reviewed assessed long-term effects. A meta-analysis of studies assessing the effect of local anesthetic sympathetic blockade for CRPS failed to drew conclusions concerning the effectiveness of this procedure mainly due to small sample sizes.[97]

Intravenous Regional Sympatholysis (IVRS)— Open Studies

No improvement compared with baseline was found for IVRS with reserpine and guanethidine.[98] No differences were also obtained between IVRS with guanethidine or lidocaine (lignocaine).[99] Guanethidine and pilocarpine versus placebo showed no differences after application of four blocks.[100] However, stellate blocks with bupivacaine as well as regional blocks with guanethidine demonstrated a significant improvement of pain compared with baseline but no differences between these two therapies.[101] One study demonstrated that IVRS with bretylium and lidocaine (lignocaine) produced significantly longer pain relief than lidocaine (lignocaine) alone.[102] No effect was obtained by IVRS with droperidol.[103] Hanna and Peat[104] demonstrated a significant improvement of pain due to a single IVRS bolus of ketanserin. Bounameaux and associates[105] failed to show any significant effect with the same procedure. Bier's block with methylprednisolone and lidocaine in CRPS I did not provide a short- or long-lasting benefit compared with placebo.[106]

There is a desperate need for controlled studies that assess the acute as well as the long-term effects of sympathetic blockade and IVRS on pain and other CRPS symptoms, in particular motor function. Well-performed sympathetic ganglion blocks should be performed rather than IVRS.[107]

Surgical Sympathectomy

There is only limited evidence regarding the efficacy of thoracoscopic or surgical sympathectomy. Four open studies report partly long-lasting benefits in CRPS I and II.[108-111] The most important independent factor in determining a positive outcome of sympathectomy is a time interval of less than 12 months between inciting event and sympathectomy.[108,110] The videoscopic lumbar sympathectomy is as effective as the open surgical intervention.[112]

We investigated skin blood flow, sympathetic vasoconstrictor reflexes, and pain after surgical sympathectomy in a small cohort of CRPS patients.[29] Postoperatively no vasoconstriction due to deep inspiration (vasoconstrictor reflex) could be elicited at the affected extremity, indicating complete sympathetic denervation. Additionally, the skin temperature at the affected hand increased. After 4 weeks, skin temperature decreased without signs of reinnervation. This denervation supersensitivity was associated with the recurrence of pain and is thought to rely on vascular supersensitivity to cold and circulating catecholamines. Only 2 of 12 patients experienced long-term pain relief.

The irreversible sympathectomy may be effective in selected cases. Because of the risk of development of adaptive supersensitivity even on nociceptive neurons and consecutive pain increase and prolongation, these procedures should not be recommended on a broad indication basis.

Stimulation Techniques and Spinal Drug Application

Transcutaneous electrical nerve stimulation (TENS) may be effective in some cases and has minimal side effects. Epidural spinal cord stimulation (SCS) has shown efficacy in one randomized study in selected chronic CRPS patients.[113] Interestingly, these patients had previously undergone unsuccessful surgical sympathectomy. The pain-relieving effect was not associated with peripheral vasodilatation, suggesting that central disinhibition processes are involved. Sensory detection threshold was not affected by the stimulation.[114] A meta-analysis showed that in selected patients SCS can relieve pain and allodynia and improve quality of life.[115] Other stimulation techniques (i.e., peripheral nerve stimulation with implanted electrodes, repetitive transcranial magnetic stimulation, and deep brain stimulation [sensory thalamus and medial lemniscus, motor cortex]) have been reported to be effective in selected cases of CRPS.[62,116,117]

In selected patients with severe refractory CRPS the epidural application of clonidine showed a greater pain reduction in higher dosages (700 µg) than in lower dosages (300 µg).[118] However, the drug was associated with marked side effects (e.g., sedation and hypotension). Intrathecally administered baclofen is effective in the treatment of dystonia in CRPS.[82]

Physical Therapy and Occupational Therapy

Clinical experience clearly indicates that physiotherapy is of utmost importance to achieve recovery of function and rehabilitation. Standardized physiotherapy has shown long-term relief in pain and physical dysfunction in children.[119]

Physical and, to a lesser extent, occupational therapy are able to reduce pain and improve active mobility in CRPS I.[120] Lymph drainage provides no benefit when applied together with physiotherapy in comparison with physiotherapy alone.[121] Patients with initially less pain and better motor function are predicted to benefit to a greater degree than others.[122] Physical therapy of CRPS is both more effective and less costly than either occupational therapy or control treatment.[123]

Recent studies have demonstrated the combination of hand laterality recognition training, imagination of movements, and mirror movements reduces pain and disability in CRPS patients.[68] Thus, physical and occupational therapy and attentional training have become important parts of a successful therapy in CRPS patients.

Psychological Therapy

Although there is evidence of a psychological impact on CRPS patients, only one study has addressed the efficacy of psychological treatment. A prospective, randomized, single-blind trial of cognitive-behavioral treatment was conducted together with physical therapy of different intensities in children and adults and showed a long-lasting reduction of all symptoms in both arms.[124] Fear of injury or reinjury by moving the affected limb is thought to be a possible predictor of chronic disability. Thus, in a small group of patients graded exposure therapy was successful to decrease pain-related fear, pain intensity, and disability.[125]

Treatment Guidelines

Treatment should be immediate and most importantly directed toward restoration of full function of the extremity. This objective is best attained in a comprehensive interdisciplinary setting with particular emphasis on pain management and functional restoration.[126,127] A treatment algorithm is proposed in Figure 26–8. The pain specialists should include neurologists, anesthesiologists, orthopedic surgeons, physiotherapists, psychologists, and the general practitioner.

The severity of the disease determines the therapeutic regimen. The reduction of pain is the precondition with which all other interventions have to comply. All therapeutic approaches must not hurt. At the acute stage of CRPS when the patient still suffers from severe pain at rest and during movements, it is mostly impossible to carry out intensive active therapy. Painful interventions and, in particular, aggressive physical therapy at this stage often lead to deterioration. Therefore, immobilization and careful contralateral physical therapy should be the acute treatment of choice and intense pain treatment should be initiated immediately. First-line analgesics and co-analgesics are opioids, tricyclic antidepressants, gabapentin, and carbamazepine. Additionally, corticosteroids should be considered if inflammatory signs and symptoms are predominant. Sympatholytic procedures, preferably sympathetic ganglion blocks, should identify the component of the pain that is maintained by the sympathetic nervous system.

For efficacy, a series should be perpetuated. Calcium-regulating agents should be used in cases of refractory pain. If resting pain subsides, first passive physical therapy, then later active isometric therapy followed by active isotonic training should be performed in combination with sensory desensitization programs until restitution of complete motor function. Psychological treatment has to flank the regimen to strengthen coping strategies and discover contributing factors. In refractory cases spinal cord stimulation and epidural clonidine could be considered. If refractory dystonia develops, intrathecal baclofen application is worth considering.

■ CRPS IN CHILDREN

CRPS I and II also occur in children. The diagnosis seems to be more often delayed than in adults. The incidence increases with puberty, and females are predominantly affected with a ratio of 4:1. In contrast to adults the lower limb is more often affected (5.3:1). The mean age was 12.5 years in a cohort of 396 children. Significant emotional dysfunction was demonstrated in a small number of children with CRPS. A possible association of intensive, parental forced sports and leisure activities with the occurrence of the inciting trauma was discussed. A sign of escape from parents' excessive demands was hypothesized.

Diagnostic bone scintigraphy in children seems to be of minor value compared with adults, showing a higher variability and interestingly often decreased diffuse uptake. To minimize exposure to radiation, scintigraphy should not be performed in children on a routine basis.

Limited attention has been paid to differences in therapy response in children. So far, conservative strategies, such as TENS and cognitive and behavioral pain management, as well as physical therapy are effective in treating childhood CRPS and preventing symptom prolongation. Between 50% and 90% of the children with CRPS I showed good long-term resolution of all symptoms.[124]

■ PREVENTION STUDIES

Only two reliable randomized placebo-controlled prevention studies have been conducted to date. Zollinger and colleagues[128] proved a significantly reduced incidence of CRPS after Colles' fracture under vitamin C (500 mg/day) treatment.

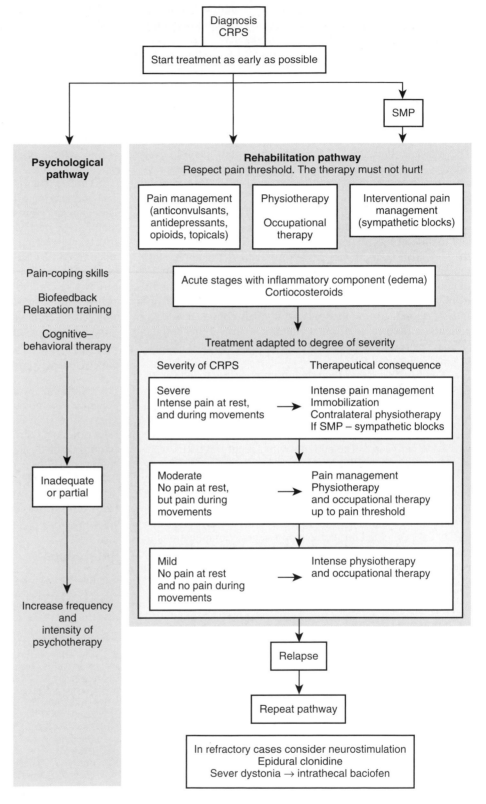

FIGURE 26–8 ▪ Treatment algorithm. 1. At the acute stage of CRPS with severe pain at rest, immobilization and careful contralateral physical therapy is the treatment of choice. Sympatholytic procedures, preferably sympathetic ganglion blocks, should identify the component of the pain that is maintained by the sympathetic nervous system. 2. If resting pain subsides, physical therapy should be performed in combination with sensory desensitization programs and pain therapy. 3. If movement-induced pain subsides, physiotherapy and occupational therapy should be intensified. (Modified from Baron R, Binder A, Ulrich W, et al: Complex regional pain syndrome: Reflex sympathetic dystrophy and causalgia. Nervenarzt 73:305, 2002; and Stanton-Hicks M, Burton A W, Bruehl SP, et al: An updated interdisciplinary clinical pathway for CRPS: Report of an expert panel. Pain Practice 2:1, 2002, with permission.)

The recurrence rate of CRPS in patients with a history of CRPS undergoing surgery of the formerly affected extremity was significantly reduced by a perioperative stellate ganglion block.[129] Preoperatively administered guanethidine did not prevent CRPS in patients undergoing fasciotomy for Dupuytren's disease.[130]

■ PROGNOSIS

The disease duration is variable and may persist over decades. In rare cases, a causal therapy (e.g., the decompression of an entrapment syndrome) may lead to complete recovery.

A 5.5-year follow-up study showed that 62% of patients were still limited in their activities of daily living, the pain and the motor impairment being the most important factors.[92] In more than 60% of patients with CRPS II the complaints remained unchanged even after 1 year of intensive therapy).[131] In contrast, a retrospective population-based study reported a resolution of symptoms in 74% of the patients with CRPS I.[4] In a 13-month follow-up study in a small cohort, nearly all patients still suffered from a functional impairment of the affected extremity although most of the other clinical features of CRPS had resolved.[132]

The severity rather than the etiology seems to determine the disease course. Age, sex, and affected side are not associated with the outcome.[4] Fractures may be associated with a higher resolution rate (91%) than sprain (78%) or other inciting event (55%).[4] In 1183 patients the incidence of recurrence was 1.8% per year.[133] The patients with a recurrent CRPS were significantly younger but did not differ in gender or primary localization. The recurrence of CRPS presents more often with few symptoms and signs and spontaneous onset. A low skin temperature at the onset of the disease may predict an unfavorable course and outcome.[8] A retrospective analysis of 1006 CRPS cases showed an incidence of severe complications in about 7%. These comprised infection, ulceration, chronic edema, dystonia, and/or myoclonus. Mostly female and younger patients with CRPS of the lower limb were affected.[134]

■ CONCLUSION

CRPS is clinically characterized by pain, abnormal regulation of blood flow and sweating, edema of skin and subcutaneous tissues, active and passive movement disorders, and trophic changes of skin, appendages of skin, and subcutaneous tissues. It is classified into type I (reflex sympathetic dystrophy) and type II (causalgia).

CRPS patients exhibit changes that occur in somatosensory systems processing noxious, tactile and thermal information, in sympathetic systems innervating skin (blood vessels, sweat glands), and in the somatomotor system. This indicates that the central representations of these systems are changed and that CRPS, in particular type I, is a systemic disease involving these neuronal systems. CRPS patients also demonstrate peripheral changes, such as edema, signs of inflammation, sympathetic-afferent coupling (as a basis for sympathetically maintained pain), and trophic changes, which cannot be explained by but also not be seen independently of the central changes. Therefore, CRPS cannot be reduced to

one system or to one mechanism only. This view is based on clinical observations, experimentation on humans, and experimentation on animals.

So far, very few evidence-based treatment regimens for CRPS are available. Treatment of the individual patient is empirical using evidence-based techniques that have been proven to be effective in other neuropathic conditions. Treatment should be immediate and most importantly directed toward restoration of full function of the extremity. This objective is best attained in a comprehensive interdisciplinary setting with particular emphasis on pain management and functional restoration.

The key future question to be asked in research is: What is the organizing principle leading to this complex syndrome? The changed view of pathophysiologic interactions we have acquired in past years will shift the focus of our research efforts, will bring about a diagnostic reclassification and redefinition of CRPS, and finally will have bearing on novel therapeutic approaches.

The key task to be addressed in therapy is to perform controlled multicenter studies that assess the acute as well as the long-term effects of drug and interventional therapies as well as physiotherapy and psychotherapy.

Acknowledgments

The authors' work was supported by the Deutsche Forschungsgemeinschaft (DFG Ba 1921/1-3) and the German Ministry of Research and Education, German Research Network on Neuropathic Pain (BMBF, 01EM01/04). The authors thank Prof. Dr. C. Maier for his support and contribution of Figure 26–2. This chapter was adapted from Baron R: Complex regional pain syndromes. In McMahon SB, Koltzenburg M (eds): Wall and Melzack's Textbook of Pain, 5th ed. London, Elsevier, 2006, pp 1011-1027, with permission.

References

1. Baron R, Fields HL, Jänig W, et al: National Institutes of Health Workshop: Reflex sympathetic dystrophy/complex regional pain syndromes—state-of-the-science. Anesth Analg 95:1812, 2002.
2. Jänig W, Baron R: Complex regional pain syndrome: Mystery explained? Lancet Neurol 2:687, 2003.
3. Merskey H, Bogduk N: Classification of Chronic Pain, 2nd ed. IASP Task Force on Taxonomy. Seattle, IASP Press, 1994.
4. Sandroni P, Benrud-Larson LM, McClelland RL, et al: Complex regional pain syndrome type I: Incidence and prevalence in Olmsted County, a population-based study. Pain 103:199, 2003.
5. Harden RN, Baron R, Jänig W: Complex Regional Pain Syndrome. Seattle, IASP Press, 2001, vol 22.
6. Allen G, Galer BS, Schwartz L: Epidemiology of complex regional pain syndrome: A retrospective chart review of 134 patients. Pain 80:539, 1999.
7. Bruehl S, Harden RN, Galer BS, et al: Complex regional pain syndrome: Are there distinct subtypes and sequential stages of the syndrome? Pain 95:119, 2002.
8. Veldman PH, Reynen HM, Arntz IE, et al: Signs and symptoms of reflex sympathetic dystrophy: Prospective study of 829 patients. Lancet 342:1012, 1993.
9. Covington EC: Psychological issues in reflex sympathetic dystrophy. In Stanton-Hicks JW, Stanton-Hicks M (eds): Reflex Sympathetic Dystrophy: A Reappraisal. Progress in Pain Research and Management, vol 6. Seattle, IASP Press, 1996, pp 192–216.
10. Puchalski P, Zyluk A: Complex regional pain syndrome type 1 after fractures of the distal radius: A prospective study of the role of psychological factors. J Hand Surg [Br] 30:574, 2005.

11. Ciccone DS, Bandilla EB, Wu W: Psychological dysfunction in patients with reflex sympathetic dystrophy. Pain 71:323, 1997.

12. Monti DA, Herring CL, Schwartzman RJ, et al: Personality assessment of patients with complex regional pain syndrome type I. Clin J Pain 14:295, 1998.

13. Bruehl S, Husfeldt B, Lubenow TR, et al: Psychological differences between reflex sympathetic dystrophy and non-RSD chronic pain patients. Pain 67:107, 1996.

14. Birklein F, Riedl B, Sieweke N, et al: Neurological findings in complex regional pain syndromes—analysis of 145 cases. Acta Neurol Scand 101:262, 2000

15. Kemler MA, van de Vusse AC, van den Berg-Loonen EM, et al: HLA-DQ1 associated with reflex sympathetic dystrophy. Neurology 53:1350, 1999.

16. van Hilten JJ, van de Beek WJ, Roep BO: Multifocal or generalized tonic dystonia of complex regional pain syndrome: A distinct clinical entity associated with HLA-DR13. Ann Neurol 48:113, 2000.

17. van de Beek WJ, Roep BO, van der Slik AR, et al: Susceptibility loci for complex regional pain syndrome. Pain 103:93, 2003.

18. Fukumoto M, Ushida T, Zinchuk VS, et al: Contralateral thalamic perfusion in patients with reflex sympathetic dystrophy syndrome. Lancet 354:1790, 1999.

19. Eisenberg E, Chistyakov AV, Yudashkin M, et al: Evidence for cortical hyperexcitability of the affected limb representation area in CRPS: A psychophysical and transcranial magnetic stimulation study. Pain 113:99, 2005.

20. Maihofner C, Handwerker HO, Neundorfer B, et al: Patterns of cortical reorganization in complex regional pain syndrome. Neurology 61:1707, 2003.

21. Pleger B, Tegenthoff M, Schwenkreis P, et al: Mean sustained pain levels are linked to hemispherical side-to-side differences of primary somatosensory cortex in the complex regional pain syndrome I. Exp Brain Res 155:115, 2004.

22. Maihofner C, Handwerker HO, Neundorfer B, et al: Cortical reorganization during recovery from complex regional pain syndrome. Neurology 24:693, 2004.

23. Pleger B, Tegenthoff M, Ragert P, et al: Sensorimotor retuning in complex regional pain syndrome parallels pain reduction. Ann Neurol 57:425, 2005.

24. Oaklander AL, Rissmiller JG, Gelman LB, et al: Evidence of focal small-fiber axonal degeneration in complex regional pain syndrome-I (reflex sympathetic dystrophy). Pain 120:235, 2006.

25. Albrecht PJ, Hines S, Eisenberg E, et al: Pathological alterations of cutaneous innervation and vasculature in affected limbs from patients with complex regional pain syndrome. Pain 120:244, 2006.

26. Jänig W, Baron R: Is CRPS I a neuropathic pain syndrome? Pain 120:227, 2006.

27. Jänig W, Baron R: Complex regional pain syndrome is a disease of the central nervous system. Clin Auton Res 12:150, 2002.

28. Birklein F, Sittle R, Spitzer A, et al: Sudomotor function in sympathetic reflex dystrophy. Pain 69:49, 1997.

29. Baron R, Maier C: Reflex sympathetic dystrophy: Skin blood flow, sympathetic vasoconstrictor reflexes and pain before and after surgical sympathectomy. Pain 67:317, 1996.

30. Wasner G, Heckmann K, Maier C, et al: Vascular abnormalities in acute reflex sympathetic dystrophy (CRPS I)—complete inhibition of sympathetic nerve activity with recovery. Arch Neurol 56:613, 1999.

31. Wasner G, Schattschneider J, Heckmann K, et al: Vascular abnormalities in reflex sympathetic dystrophy (CRPS I): Mechanisms and diagnostic value. Brain 124:587, 2001.

32. Harden RN, Duc TA, Williams TR, et al: Norepinephrine and epinephrine levels in affected versus unaffected limbs in sympathetically maintained pain. Clin J Pain 10:324, 1994.

33. Birklein F, Riedl B, Neundörfer B, et al: Sympathetic vasoconstrictor reflex pattern in patients with complex regional pain syndrome. Pain 75:93, 1998

34. Goldstein DS, Tack C, Li ST: Sympathetic innervation and function in reflex sympathetic dystrophy. Ann Neurol 48:49, 2000.

35. Haensch CA, Jorg J, Lerch H: I-123-metaiodobenzylguanidine uptake of the forearm shows dysfunction in peripheral sympathetic mediated neurovascular transmission in complex regional pain syndrome type I (CRPS I). J Neurol 249:1742, 2002.

36. Drummond PD, Skipworth S, Finch PM: Alpha 1-adrenoceptors in normal and hyperalgesic human skin. Clin Sci (Lond) 91:73, 1996.

37. Birklein F, Weber M, Neundorfer B: Increased skin lactate in complex regional pain syndrome: Evidence for tissue hypoxia? Neurology 55:1213, 2000.

38. Koban M, Leis S, Schultze-Mosgau S, et al: Tissue hypoxia in complex regional pain syndrome. Pain 104:149, 2003.

39. Casale R, Elam M: Normal sympathetic nerve activity in a reflex sympathetic dystrophy with marked skin vasoconstriction. J Auton Nerv Syst 41:215, 1992.

40. Schattschneider J, Hartung K, Stengel M, et al: Endothelial dysfunction in cold type complex regional pain syndrome. Neurology 2006, in press.

41. Eisenberg E, Erlich T, Zinder O, et al: Plasma endothelin-1 levels in patients with complex regional pain syndrome. Eur J Pain 8:533, 2004.

42. van der Laan L, Veldman PH, Goris RJ: Severe complications of reflex sympathetic dystrophy: Infection, ulcers, chronic edema, dystonia, and myoclonus. Arch Phys Med Rehabil 79:424, 1998.

43. Christensen K, Jensen EM, Noer I: The reflex dystrophy syndrome response to treatment with systemic corticosteroids. Acta Chir Scand 148:653, 1982.

44. Oyen WJ, Arntz IE, Claessens RM, et al: Reflex sympathetic dystrophy of the hand: An excessive inflammatory response? Pain 55:151, 1993.

45. Weber M, Birklein F, Neundorfer B, et al: Facilitated neurogenic inflammation in complex regional pain syndrome. Pain 91:251, 2001.

46. Leis S, Weber M, Isselmann A, et al: Substance-P–induced protein extravasation is bilaterally increased in complex regional pain syndrome. Exp Neurol 183:197, 2003.

47. Birklein F, Schmelz M, Schifter S, et al: The important role of neuropeptides in complex regional pain syndrome. Neurology 57:2179, 2001.

48. Huygen FJ, De Bruijn AG, De Bruin MT, et al: Evidence for local inflammation in complex regional pain syndrome type 1. Mediators Inflammation 11:47, 2001.

49. Munnikes RJ, Muis C, Boersma M, et al: Intermediate stage complex regional pain syndrome type I is unrelated to proinflammatory cytokines. Mediators Inflammation 6:366, 2005.

50. Maihofner C, Handwerker HO, Neundorfer B, et al: Mechanical hyperalgesia in complex regional pain syndrome: A role for TNF-alpha? Neurology 25:311, 2005.

51. Schinkel C, Gaertner A, Zaspel J, et al: Inflammatory mediators are altered in the acute phase of posttraumatic complex regional pain syndrome. Clin J Pain 22:235, 2006.

52. Alexander GM, van Rijn MA, van Hilten JJ, et al: Changes in cerebrospinal fluid levels of pro-inflammatory cytokines in CRPS. Pain 116:213, 2005.

53. van de Vusse AC, Goossens VJ, Kemler MA, et al: Screening of patients with complex regional pain syndrome for antecedent infections. Clin J Pain 17:110, 2001.

54. Gross O, Tschernatsch M, Brau ME, et al: Increased seroprevalence of parvovirus B19 IgG in complex regional pain syndrome is not associated with antiendothelial autoimmunity. Eur J Pain 2006 [Mar 16]; ePub ahead of print.

55. Goebel A, Vogel H, Caneris O, et al: Immune response to *Campylobacter* and serum autoantibodies in patients with complex regional pain syndrome. J Neuroimmunol 162:184, 2005.

56. Blaes F, Schmitz K, Tschernatsch M, et al: Autoimmune etiology of complex regional pain syndrome. Neurology 63:1743, 2004.

57. Kingery WS, Davies MF, Clark JD: A substance P receptor (NK(1)) antagonist can reverse vascular and nociceptive abnormalities in a rat model of complex regional pain syndrome type II. Pain 104:75, 2003.

58. Schattschneider J, Wenzelburger R, Deuschl G, et al: Kinematic analysis of the upper extremity in CRPS. In Harden RN, Baron R, Jänig W (eds): Complex Regional Pain Syndrome. Seattle, IASP Press, 2001, vol 22, pp 119-128.

59. Ribbers GM, Mulder T, Geurts AC: Reflex sympathetic dystrophy of the left hand and motor impairments of the unaffected right hand: Impaired central motor processing? Arch Phys Med Rehabil 83:81, 2002.

60. Juottonen K, Gockel M, Silen T, et al: Altered central sensorimotor processing in patients with complex regional pain syndrome. Pain 98:315, 2002.

61. Schwenkreis P, Janssen F, Rommel O, et al: Bilateral motor cortex disinhibition in complex regional pain syndrome (CRPS) type I of the hand. Neurology 61:515, 2003.

62. Pleger B, Janssen F, Schwenkreis P, et al: Repetitive transcranial magnetic stimulation of the motor cortex attenuates pain perception

in complex regional pain syndrome type I. Neurosci Lett 356:87, 2004.

63. Galer BS, Butler S, Jensen MP: Case reports and hypothesis: A neglect-like syndrome may be responsible for the motor disturbance in reflex sympathetic dystrophy (Complex Regional Pain Syndrome-1). J Pain Symptom Manage 10:385, 1995.

64. Moseley GL: Why do people with complex regional pain syndrome take longer to recognize their affected hand? Neurology 62:2182, 2004.

65. Forderreuther S, Sailer U, Straube A: Impaired self-perception of the hand in complex regional pain syndrome (CRPS). Pain 110:756, 2004.

66. Moseley GL: Graded motor imagery is effective for long-standing complex regional pain syndrome: A randomised controlled trial. Pain 108:192, 2004.

67. McCabe CS, Haigh RC, Ring EF, et al: A controlled pilot study of the utility of mirror visual feedback in the treatment of complex regional pain syndrome (type 1). Rheumatology (Oxford) 42:97, 2003.

68. Moseley GL: Is successful rehabilitation of complex regional pain syndrome due to sustained attention to the affected hand? A randomised clinical trial. Pain 114:54, 2005.

69. Stanton-Hicks M, Jänig W, Hassenbusch S, et al: Reflex sympathetic dystrophy: Changing concepts and taxonomy. Pain 63:127, 1995.

70. Baron R, Levine JD, Fields HL: Causalgia and reflex sympathetic dystrophy: Does the sympathetic nervous system contribute to the generation of pain? Muscle Nerve 22:678, 1999.

71. Ali Z, Raja SN, Wesselmann U, et al: Intradermal injection of norepinephrine evokes pain in patients with sympathetically maintained pain. Pain 88:161, 2000.

72. Baron R, Schattschneider J, Binder A, et al: Relation between sympathetic vasoconstrictor activity and pain and hyperalgesia in complex regional pain syndromes: A case-control study. Lancet 359:1655, 2002.

73. Baron R, Wasner G: Complex regional pain syndromes. Curr Pain Headache Rep 5:114, 2001.

74. Schattschneider J, Binder A, Siebrecht D, et al: Complex regional pain syndromes: The influence of cutaneous and deep somatic sympathetic innervation on pain. Clin J Pain 22:240, 2006.

75. Wasner G, Schattschneider J, Baron R: Skin temperature side differences—a diagnostic tool for CRPS? Pain 98:19, 2002.

76. Bruehl S, Harden RN, Galer BS, et al: External validation of IASP diagnostic criteria for complex regional pain syndrome and proposed research diagnostic criteria. Pain 81:147, 1999.

77. Harden RN, Bruehl S, Galer BS, et al: Complex regional pain syndrome: Are the IASP diagnostic criteria valid and sufficiently comprehensive? Pain 83:211, 1999.

78. Forouzanfar T, Koke AJ, van Kleef M, et al: Treatment of complex regional pain syndrome type I. Eur J Pain 6:105, 2002.

79. Kingery WS: A critical review of controlled clinical trials for peripheral neuropathic pain and complex regional pain syndromes. Pain 73:123, 1997.

80. Perez RS, Kwakkel G, Zuurmond WW, et al: Treatment of reflex sympathetic dystrophy (CRPS type 1): A research synthesis of 21 randomized clinical trials. J Pain Symptom Manage 21:511, 2001.

81. Wallace MS, Ridgeway BM, Leung AY, et al: Concentration–effect relationship of intravenous lidocaine on the allodynia of complex regional pain syndrome types I and II. Anesthesiology 92:75, 2000.

82. van Hilten BJ, van de Beek WJ, Hoff JI, et al: Intrathecal baclofen for the treatment of dystonia in patients with reflex sympathetic dystrophy. N Engl J Med 343:625, 2000.

83. Mellick GA, Mellick LB: Gabapentin in the management of reflex sympathetic dystrophy. J Pain Symptom Manage 10:265, 1995.

84. Serpell MG: Gabapentin in neuropathic pain syndromes: A randomised, double-blind, placebo-controlled trial. Pain 99:557, 2002.

85. van de Vusse AC, Stomp-van den Berg SG, Kessels AH, et al: Randomised controlled trial of gabapentin in complex regional pain syndrome type 1. BMC Neurol 4:13, 2004.

86. Gobelet C, Waldburger M, Meier JL: The effect of adding calcitonin to physical treatment on reflex sympathetic dystrophy. Pain 48:171, 1992.

87. Adami S, Fossaluzza V, Gatti D, et al: Bisphosphonate therapy of reflex sympathetic dystrophy syndrome. Ann Rheum Dis 56:201, 1997.

88. Varenna M, Zucchi F, Ghiringhelli D, et al: Intravenous clodronate in the treatment of reflex sympathetic dystrophy syndrome: A randomized, double blind, placebo controlled study. J Rheumatol 27:1477, 2000.

89. Manicourt DH, Brasseur JP, Boutsen Y, et al: Role of alendronate in therapy for posttraumatic complex regional pain syndrome type I of the lower extremity. Arthritis Rheum 50:3690, 2004.

90. Perez RS, Zuurmond WW, Bezemer PD, et al: The treatment of complex regional pain syndrome type I with free radical scavengers: A randomized controlled study. Pain 102:297, 2003.

91. Zuurmond WW, Langendijk PN, Bezemer PD, et al: Treatment of acute reflex sympathetic dystrophy with DMSO 50% in a fatty cream. Acta Anaesth Scand 40:364, 1996.

92. Geertzen JH, de Bruijn H, de Bruijn-Kofman AT, et al: Reflex sympathetic dystrophy: Early treatment and psychological aspects. Arch Phys Med Rehabil 75:442, 1994.

93. Davis KD, Treede RD, Raja SN, et al: Topical application of clonidine relieves hyperalgesia in patients with sympathetically maintained pain [see comments]. Pain 47:309, 1991.

94. Cepeda MS, Lau J, Carr DB: Defining the therapeutic role of local anesthetic sympathetic blockade in complex regional pain syndrome: A narrative and systematic review. Clin J Pain 18:216, 2002.

95. Schott GD: Interrupting the sympathetic outflow in causalgia and reflex sympathetic dystrophy [editorial]. BMJ 316:792, 1998.

96. Price DD, Long S, Wilsey B, et al: Analysis of peak magnitude and duration of analgesia produced by local anesthetics injected into sympathetic ganglia of complex regional pain syndrome patients. Clin J Pain 14:216, 1998.

97. Cepeda MS, Carr DB, Lau J: Local anesthetic sympathetic blockade for complex regional pain syndrome. Cochrane Data System Rev 19:CD004598, 2005.

98. Jadad AR, Carroll D, Glynn CJ, et al: Intravenous regional sympathetic blockade for pain relief in reflex sympathetic dystrophy: A systematic review and a randomized, double-blind crossover study. J Pain Symptom Manage 10:13, 1995.

99. Ramamurthy S, Hoffman J: Intravenous regional guanethidine in the treatment of reflex sympathetic dystrophy/causalgia: A randomized, double-blind study. Guanethidine Study Group. Anesth Analg 81:718, 1995.

100. Livingstone JA, Atkins RM: Intravenous regional guanethidine blockade in the treatment of posttraumatic complex regional pain syndrome type 1 (algodystrophy) of the hand. J Bone Joint Surg Br 84:380, 2002.

101. Bonelli S, Conoscente F, Movilia PG, et al: Regional intravenous guanethidine vs. stellate ganglion block in reflex sympathetic dystrophies: A randomized trial. Pain 16:297, 1983.

102. Hord AH, Rooks MD, Stephens BO, et al: Intravenous regional bretylium and lidocaine for treatment of reflex sympathetic dystrophy: A randomized, double-blind study. Anesth Analg 74:818, 1992.

103. Kettler RE, Abram SE: Intravenous regional droperidol in the management of reflex sympathetic dystrophy: A double-blind, placebo-controlled, crossover study. Anesthesiology 69:933, 1998.

104. Hanna MH, Peat SJ: Ketanserin in reflex sympathetic dystrophy: A double-blind placebo controlled cross-over trial. Pain 38:145, 1998.

105. Bounameaux HM, Hellemans H, Verhaeghe R: Ketanserin in chronic sympathetic dystrophy: An acute controlled trial. Clin Rheumatol 3:556, 1984.

106. Taskaynatan MA, Ozgul A, Tan AK, et al: Bier block with methylprednisolone and lidocaine in CRPS type I: A randomized, double-blinded, placebo controlled study. Region Anesth Pain Med 29:408, 2004.

107. Hord ED, Oaklander AL: Complex regional pain syndrome: A review of evidence-supported treatment options. Curr Pain Headache Rep 7:188, 2003.

108. AbuRahma AF, Robinson PA, Powell M, et al: Sympathectomy for reflex sympathetic dystrophy: Factors affecting outcome. Ann Vasc Surg 8:372, 1994.

109. Bandyk DF, Johnson BL, Kirkpatrick AF, et al: Surgical sympathectomy for reflex sympathetic dystrophy syndromes. J Vasc Surg 35:269, 2002.

110. Schwartzman RJ, Liu JE, Smullens SN, et al: Long-term outcome following sympathectomy for complex regional pain syndrome type 1 (RSD). J Neurol Sci 150:149, 1997.

111. Singh B, Moodley J, Shaik AS, et al: Sympathectomy for complex regional pain syndrome. J Vasc Surg 37:508, 2003.

112. Lacroix H, Vander Velpen G, Penninckx F, et al: Technique and early results of videoscopic lumbar sympathectomy. Acta Chir Belg 96:11, 1996.

113. Kemler MA, Barendse GA, van Kleef M, et al: Spinal cord stimulation in patients with chronic reflex sympathetic dystrophy. N Engl J Med 343:618, 2000.

114. Kemler MA, Barendse GA, van Kleef M, et al: Pain relief in complex regional pain syndrome due to spinal cord stimulation does not depend on vasodilation. Anesthesiology 92:1653, 2000.

115. Taylor RS: Spinal cord stimulation in complex regional pain syndrome and refractory neuropathic back and leg pain/failed back surgery syndrome: results of a systematic review and meta-analysis. J Pain Symptom Manage 31:S13, 2006.

116. Hassenbusch SJ, Stanton-Hicks M, Schoppa D, et al: Long-term results of peripheral nerve stimulation for reflex sympathetic dystrophy. J Neurosurg 84:415, 1996.

117. Son UC, Kim MC, Moon DE, et al: Motor cortex stimulation in a patient with intractable complex regional pain syndrome type II with hemibody involvement: Case report. J Neurosurg 98:175, 2003.

118. Rauck RL, Eisenach JC, Jackson K, et al: Epidural clonidine treatment for refractory reflex sympathetic dystrophy [see comments]. Anesthesiology 79:1163; discussion 27A, 1993.

119. Sherry DD, Wallace CA, Kelley C, et al: Short- and long-term outcomes of children with complex regional pain syndrome type I treated with exercise therapy. Clin J Pain 15:218, 1999.

120. Oerlemans HM, Oostendorp RA, de Boo T, et al: Adjuvant physical therapy versus occupational therapy in patients with reflex sympathetic dystrophy/complex regional pain syndrome type I. Arch Phys Med Rehabil 81:49, 2000.

121. Uher EM, Vacariu G, Schneider B, et al: [Comparison of manual lymph drainage with physical therapy in complex regional pain syndrome, type I. A comparative randomized controlled therapy study]. Wien Klin Wochenschr 112:133, 2000.

122. Kemler MA, Rijks CP, de Vet HC: Which patients with chronic reflex sympathetic dystrophy are most likely to benefit from physical therapy? J Manipulative Physiol Ther 24:272, 2001.

123. Severens JL, Oerlemans HM, Weegels AJ, et al: Cost-effectiveness analysis of adjuvant physical or occupational therapy for patients with reflex sympathetic dystrophy. Arch Phys Med Rehabil 80:1038, 1999.

124. Lee BH, Scharff L, Sethna NF, et al: Physical therapy and cognitive–behavioral treatment for complex regional pain syndromes. J Pediatr 141:135, 2002.

125. de Jong JR, Vlaeyen JW, Onghena P, et al: Reduction of pain-related fear in complex regional pain syndrome type I: The application of graded exposure in vivo. Pain 116:264, 2005.

126. Stanton-Hicks M, Baron R, Boas R, et al: Complex regional pain syndromes: Guidelines for therapy. Clin J Pain 14:155, 1998.

127. Stanton-Hicks M, Burton AW, Bruehl SP, et al: An updated interdisciplinary clinical pathway for CRPS: Report of an expert panel. Pain Practice 2:1, 2002.

128. Zollinger PE, Tuinebreijer WE, Kreis RW, et al: Effect of vitamin C on frequency of reflex sympathetic dystrophy in wrist fractures: A randomised trial. Lancet 354:2025, 1999.

129. Reuben SS, Rosenthal EA, Steinberg RB: Surgery on the affected upper extremity of patients with a history of complex regional pain syndrome: A retrospective study of 100 patients. J Hand Surg [Am] 25:1147, 2002.

130. Gschwind C, Fricker R, Lacher G, et al: Does perioperative guanethidine prevent reflex sympathetic dystrophy? J Hand Surg [Br] 20:773, 1995.

131. Karstetter K, Sherman RA: Use of thermography for initial detection of early reflex sympathetic dystrophy. J Am Podiatr Med Assoc 81:437, 1991.

132. Zyluk A: The natural history of post-traumatic reflex sympathetic dystrophy. J Hand Surg [Br] 23:20, 1998.

133. Veldman PH, Goris RJ: Multiple reflex sympathetic dystrophy: Which patients are at risk for developing a recurrence of reflex sympathetic dystrophy in the same or another limb [see comments]. Pain 64:463, 1996.

134. van der Laan L, Goris RJ: Reflex sympathetic dystrophy: An exaggerated regional inflammatory response? Hand Clin 13:373, 1997.

chapter 27

Complex Regional Pain Syndrome Type II (Causalgia)

Andreas Binder, Jörn Schattschneider, and Ralf Baron

■ DEFINITION

The International Association for the Study of Pain (IASP) *Classification of Chronic Pain* redefined pain syndromes formerly known as reflex sympathetic dystrophy and causalgia.[1] The term *complex regional pain syndrome* describes "a variety of painful conditions following injury which appears regionally having a distal predominance of abnormal findings, exceeding in both magnitude and duration the expected clinical course of the inciting event often resulting in significant impairment of motor function, and showing variable progression over time."

These chronic pain syndromes comprise different additional clinical features, including spontaneous pain, allodynia, hyperalgesia, edema, autonomic abnormalities, and trophic signs. In contrast to CRPS type I (reflex sympathetic dystrophy), CRPS type II (causalgia) develops after injury to a major peripheral nerve.

■ EPIDEMIOLOGY

Incidence and Prevalence

A population-based study on CRPS I calculated an incidence of about 5.5 per 100,000 person-years at risk and a prevalence of about 21 per 100,000. An incidence of 0.8 per 100,000 person-years at risk and a prevalence of about 4 per 100,000 was reported for CRPS II.[2] Thus, CRPS II develops less often than CRPS I. The incidence of CRPS II in peripheral nerve injury varies from 2% to 14% in different series, with a mean around 4%.[3]

■ CLINICAL PRESENTATION

The symptoms of CRPS II are similar to those of CRPS I, the only exception being that a lesion of peripheral nerve structures and subsequent focal deficits are mandatory for the diagnosis. The symptoms and signs spread beyond the innervation territory of the injured peripheral nerve and often occur remote from the site of injury, but a restriction to the territory is not in conflict with the current definition.

■ PATHOPHYSIOLOGIC MECHANISMS

Pathophysiologic Concepts in CRPS after Stroke and Spinal Cord Injury

CRPS may occasionally develop after lesions of the central nervous system.[4] In patients with stroke, visual deficits, neglect, paresis of the shoulder girdle, and somatosensory deficits are risk factors for recurrent initiating events (e.g., trauma of the affected extremity) that may self-perpetuate a vicious cycle of CRPS. Accordingly, affected extremities after brain injury are at higher risk of developing CRPS than unaffected extremities.

CRPS after spinal cord injury is relatively rare, ranging from 5% to 12% in selected cohorts. It develops within a few months, more often unilaterally at the upper extremity in tetraplegic patients. Medullary gunshot wounds seem to predispose to the development of CRPS. Similar to stroke patients, the association of paresis and limb trauma may initiate a vicious cycle in the pathophysiology. Additionally, CRPS may contribute to contractures in the course of spinal cord injury.

■ DIAGNOSIS

The diagnosis of CRPS I and II follows the IASP clinical criteria.[5] If two clinical signs are joined by "or," if either sign is present, or if both occur, the condition of the statement is satisfied.

CRPS Type II (Formerly Causalgia)

1. Type II is a syndrome that develops after nerve injury. Spontaneous pain or allodynia/hyperalgesia occurs and is not necessarily limited to the territory of the injured nerve.
2. There is or has been evidence of edema, skin blood flow abnormality, or abnormal sudomotor activity in the region of the pain since the inciting event.
3. This diagnosis is excluded by the existence of conditions that would otherwise account for the degree of pain and dysfunction.

Pain is essential for the diagnosis, whereby "spontaneous" indicates pain without external cause. Motor symptoms and findings are not included in this classification, although they are common and can include tremor, dystonia, and weakness.

Differential Diagnosis

Due to the lack of a gold standard in the diagnosis of CRPS the risk of overdiagnosing has to be taken into account. To differentiate CRPS from other neuropathic and other pain syndromes, a detailed history and physical examination according to the specifications just outlined are mandatory.

Post-traumatic Neuralgia

It is important to recognize that many post-traumatic neuropathy patients have pain but do not have the full clinical picture of causalgia (CRPS II). In these cases, in contrast to causalgia patients, the pain is located largely within the innervation territory of the injured nerve. Although these patients often describe their pain as burning, they exhibit a less complex clinical picture than patients with causalgia and do not show marked swelling or progressive spread of symptoms. The cardinal symptoms are spontaneous burning pain, hyperalgesia, and mechanical and especially cold allodynia. These sensory symptoms are confined to the territory of the affected peripheral nerve, although allodynia may extend beyond the border of nerve territories for some centimeters. Spontaneous and evoked pain are felt superficially and not deep inside the extremity and the intensity of both is not dependent on the position of the extremity. The patients occasionally obtain relief with sympatholytic procedures, although much less often than those with CRPS.

Following the IASP classification it is possible to use the term *neuralgia* for this type of neuropathic pain (pain within the innervation territory of a lesioned nerve, e.g., post-traumatic neuralgia). However, the new definition of CRPS II includes the statement that symptoms may also be limited to the territory of a single peripheral nerve. Therefore, the term *CRPS II* provides a window to include these localized post-traumatic neuropathies. An inherent weakness of this definition of CRPS II is that different syndromes with different underlying mechanisms are obviously included.

Neuropathies (e.g., diabetic polyneuropathy) may also present as spontaneous pain, skin color changes, and motor deficits but are distinguished by their symmetrical distribution and the patient's history. Furthermore, all kinds of inflammations or infections (e.g., rheumatism, phlegmons) might induce an intense unilateral skin warming. Unilateral arterial or venous occlusive diseases can cause unilateral pain and vascular abnormalities and have to be excluded. Repetitive artificial occlusion of the blood supply to one limb (as in the psychiatric factitious disorders, artifact syndrome) might induce secondary structural changes of the blood vessels with consecutive abnormalities in perfusion and, therefore, mimic CRPS symptoms and signs.

▪ PROGNOSIS

The disease duration is variable and may persist over decades. In rare cases, a causal therapy (e.g., the decompression of an entrapment syndrome) may lead to complete recovery.

A 5.5-year follow-up study showed that 62% of patients were still limited in their activities of daily living, the pain and the motor impairment being the most important factors.[6] In more than 60% of patients with CRPS II the complaints remained unchanged even after 1 year of intensive therapy.[7] In contrast, a retrospective population-based study reported a resolution of symptoms in 74% of the patients with CRPS I.[2] In a 13-month follow-up study in a small cohort, nearly all patients still suffered from a functional impairment of the affected extremity although most of the other clinical features of CRPS had resolved.[8]

References

1. Merskey H, Bogduk N: Classification of Chronic Pain, 2nd ed. IASP Task Force on Taxonomy. Seattle, IASP Press, 1994.
2. Sandroni P, Benrud-Larson LM, McClelland RL, et al: Complex regional pain syndrome type I: Incidence and prevalence in Olmsted County, a population-based study. Pain 103:199, 2003.
3. Veldman PH, Reynen HM, Arntz IE, et al: Signs and symptoms of reflex sympathetic dystrophy: Prospective study of 829 patients. Lancet 342:1012, 1993.
4. Wasner G, Schattschneider J, Binder A, et al: Complex regional pain syndrome—diagnostic, mechanisms, CNS involvement and therapy. Spinal Cord 41:61, 2003.
5. Stanton-Hicks M, Janig W, Hassenbusch S, et al: Reflex sympathetic dystrophy: Changing concepts and taxonomy. Pain 63:127, 1995.
6. Geertzen JH, de Bruijn H, de Bruijn-Kofman AT, et al: Reflex sympathetic dystrophy: Early treatment and psychological aspects. Arch Phys Med Rehabil 75:442, 1994.
7. Karstetter K, Sherman RA: Use of thermography for initial detection of early reflex sympathetic dystrophy. J Am Podiatr Med Assoc 81:437, 1994.
8. Zyluk A: The natural history of post-traumatic reflex sympathetic dystrophy. J Hand Surg [Br] 23:20, 1998.

Phantom Pain Syndromes

Laxmaiah Manchikanti, Vijay Singh, and Mark V. Boswell

■ HISTORICAL CONSIDERATIONS

Phantom sensation or pain is the persistent perception that a body part exists or is painful after it has been removed by amputation or trauma. The first medical description of post-amputation phenomena was reported by Ambrose Paré, a French military surgeon, in 1551 (Fig. 28–1).[1,2] He noticed that amputees complained of severe pain in the missing limb long after amputation. Civil War surgeon Silas Weir Mitchell[3] popularized the concept of phantom limb pain and coined the term *phantom limb* with publication of a long-term study on the fate of Civil War amputees in 1871 (Fig. 28–2). Herman Melville immortalized phantom limb pain in American literature, with graphic descriptions of Captain Ahab's phantom limb in *Moby Dick* (Fig. 28–3).

The three most commonly used terms are *phantom sensation, phantom pain*, and *stump pain*. Phantom sensation refers to any sensation of the missing limb or organ except pain. In contrast, phantom pain refers to painful sensations referred to the missing organ or limb. Stump pain refers to the pain in the stump.

Phantom sensations may occur in any part of the body but are most often described in the extremities. Phantom sensation of the tongue, nose, breast, bladder, uterus, rectum, penis, and other organs have been described in the literature.[4-11]

■ THE CLINICAL SYNDROME

Epidemiology

Phantom limb sensation is an almost universal occurrence at some time during the first month following surgery. Patients generally describe the limb in terms of definite volume and length and may try to reach out with or stand on the phantom limb.[4] Phantom limb sensation is strongest in amputations above the elbow and weakest in amputations below the knee,[12] and is more frequent in the dominant limb of double amputees.[13] The incidence of phantom limb sensation increases with the age of the amputee.[4] Phantom limb sensation in 85% to 98% of the amputees is seen in the first 3 weeks after amputation,[14] whereas in a small proportion of the patients (approximately 8%), phantom limb sensation may not occur until 1 to 12 months following amputation.[15] Most phantom sensations generally resolve after 2 to 3 years

without treatment, except in the cases where phantom pain develops.

The incidence of phantom limb pain has been reported to vary from 0% to 88%.[16-32] Prospective evaluations[31,37] suggested that in the year after amputation, 60% to 70% of amputees experience phantom limb pain, but it diminishes with time.[14,31] The incidence of phantom limb pain increases with more proximal amputations. The reports of phantom limb pain after hemipelvectomy ranged from 68% to 88% and following hip disarticulation 40% to 88%.[28,30] However, wide variations exist with reports of phantom limb pain after lower extremity amputation as high as 72%[21] and as low as 51% after upper limb amputation.[22] Further, 0% prevalence was reported in below-knee amputations compared to 19% in above-knee amputations.[30] Phantom limb pain has been reported to occur as early as 1 week after amputation and as late as 40 years after amputation.[4,33,34] Although phantom pain may diminish with time and eventually fade away, some prospective studies indicate that even 2 years after amputation, the incidence is almost the same as at onset.[31,37] It is reported that nearly 60% of patients continue to have phantom limb pain[24,31] after 1 year, whereas in the first month following amputation, 85% to 97% of patients experience phantom limb pain.[24,29,30] Although phantom limb pain may begin months to years after an amputation, pain starting after 1 year following amputation occurs in fewer than 10% of patients.[4]

Stump pain is reported with a prevalence of up to 50% of the amputees.[16,18,21-23,35,36] Stump pain results in disuse of the limb prosthesis in approximately 50% of the patients.[16,18,21-23,35,36] The stump pain usually coincides with the development of phantom limb pain.[37] In one study, it was shown that 88% of the patients with phantom pain also reported stump pain.[23] In another study, it was reported in only 50% of the patients.[30]

Phantom limb pain is also associated with multiple pain problems in other areas of the body, with reports indicating headache or pain in joints in 35% of the patients, sore throat in 28% of the patients, abdominal pain in 18%, and back pain in 13%.[38]

Disability and Risk Factors

Multiple risk factors identified for phantom pain include phantom sensations, stump pain, pain prior to the amputation,

FIGURE 28–1 ■ Ambrose Paré.

FIGURE 28–2 ■ Silas Weir Mitchell.

cause of amputation, prosthesis use, and years elapsed since amputation.[39] The most important risk factors for phantom pain were "bilateral amputation" and lower limb amputation." The risk for phantom pain ranged from 0.33 for a 10-year-old patient with a distal upper limb amputation to 0.99 for a subject of 80 years with a bilateral lower limb amputation, of which one side is an above-knee amputation. Van der Schans and colleagues[40] showed that amputees with phantom pain had a poorer health-related quality of life than amputees without phantom pain. Sunderland,[41] based on the frequency and severity of pain and the degree to which pain interferes with the patient's lifestyle, proposed a classification to divide patients into four groups:

- Group I patients have mild, intermittent paresthesias that do not interfere with normal activity, work, or sleep.
- Group II patients have paresthesias that are uncomfortable and annoying but do not interfere with activities or sleep.
- Group III patients may have pain that is of sufficient intensity, frequency, or duration to be distressful; however, some patients in group III have pain that is bearable, that intermittently interferes with their lifestyle, and that may respond to conservative treatment.
- Group IV patients complain of nearly constant severe pain that interferes with normal activity and sleep.

The usual course of phantom limb pain is to remain unchanged or to improve.[4,27,31] However, up to 56% of patients report improvement or complete resolution.[27]

Ehde and coworkers[21] evaluated not only the characteristics of phantom limb sensation, phantom limb pain, and residual limb pain, but also pain-related disability associated with phantom limb pain, in a retrospective, cross-sectional survey of 255 participants after lower limb amputation. Seventy-two percent of patients with phantom limb pain were classified into two low pain-related disability categories: grade I, low disability/low pain intensity—47% or grade II, low disability/high pain intensity—28%.

Etiology

Of the three issues involved, namely phantom sensations, phantom pain, and stump pain, phantom sensations are the easiest to explain. It is believed that, throughout life, an individual's body image develops from proprioceptive, tactile, and visual inputs.[42] Once a cortical representation of the body image is established, it is unchanged following limb amputation.[4,7]

The etiology and pathophysiologic mechanisms of phantom pain are not clearly defined. However, both peripheral and central neuronal mechanisms are likely to occur. In addition, psychological mechanisms have also been proposed. None of the theories independently, fully explain the clinical characteristics of this condition.

Nikolajsen and Jensen[43] described several clinical observations suggesting that mechanisms in the periphery, either in

FIGURE 28–3 ■ Herman Melville.

the stump or in the central parts of sectioned primary afferents, may play a role in the phantom limb percept.

- Phantom limb sensations can be modulated by various stump manipulations.
- Phantom limb sensations are temporarily abolished after local stump anesthesia.
- Stump revisions and removal of tender neuromas often reduce pain, at least transiently.
- Phantom pain is significantly more frequent in those amputees with long-term stump pain than in those without persistent pain.
- Although obvious stump pathology is rare, altered cutaneous sensibility in the stump is a common, if not universal, feature.
- Changes in stump blood flow alter the phantom limb perception.

There may be experimental support for these clinical observations. First, peripherally, spontaneous and abnormal evoked activity following mechanical or neurochemical stimulation is observed in nerve-end neuromas.[44,45] This increased activity is assumed to be the result of a novel expression or up-regulation of sodium channels.[46,47] Thus, the

increased sensitivity of neuroma to norepinephrine may, in part, explain the exacerbation of phantom pain by stress and other emotional states associated with increased catecholamine release from sympathetic efferent terminals that are in proximity to afferent sensory nerves and sprouts.[43] It has also been shown that cell bodies in the dorsal root ganglion show similar abnormal spontaneous activity and increased sensitivity to mechanical and neurochemical stimulation.[48] Thus, abnormal activity from neuromas and dorsal root ganglion cell bodies may contribute to the phantom limb percept, including pain.

The second mechanism is considered at spinal cord level. The increased barrage from neuromas and from dorsal root ganglia cells is thought to induce long-term changes in central projecting neurons in the dorsal horn, including spontaneous neuronal activity, induction of immediate early genes, increases in spinal cord metabolic activity, and expansion of receptive fields.[49,50] Nikolajsen and Jensen[43] described that the pharmacology of spinal sensitization involves an increased activity in N-methyl-D-aspartate (NMDA) receptor-operated systems,[51] and many aspects of the central sensitization can be reduced by NMDA receptor antagonists. This was further confirmed in human amputees with one aspect of such central sensitization, the evoked stump or phantom pain produced by repetitive stimulation of the stump by non-noxious pinprick, can be reduced by the NMDA receptor antagonist ketamine.[52] Besides the functional changes in the dorsal horn, an anatomic reorganization also has been described.[53] It has been shown that peripheral nerve transection results in a substantial degeneration of afferent C-fiber terminals in lamina II, thus reducing the number of synaptic contacts with second-order neurons in lamina II, which normally respond best to noxious stimulation. Consequently, central terminals of Aß mechanoreceptive afferents, which normally terminate in deeper laminae, sprout into lamina II and may form synaptic contacts with vacant nociceptive second-order neurons. As a result of this organization, evocation of pain is seen with simple touch, by Aß-fiber input.

The third element is the supraspinal or central mechanism. Based on peripheral and spinal cord mechanisms, it is reasonable to assume that amputation not only produces a cascade of events in the periphery and in the spinal cord, but these changes eventually sweep more centrally and alter neuronal activity in cortical and subcortical structures. It has been shown that thalamic stimulation results in phantom sensation and pain in amputees.[54] This suggests that plastic changes in the thalamus are involved in the generation of chronic pain because normally such stimulation does not evoke pain. Other studies in humans have documented a cortical reorganization after amputation using multiple cerebral imaging techniques.[55-70]

Psychological theories have been forwarded as to the cause of phantom pain; whereas a biopsychosocial mechanism may be involved in development and persistence of phantom pain, no consistent personality disorders or clinical syndromes have shown to be increased in patients with phantom limb pain. However, psychological disturbances related to the loss of a limb or feelings of dependence, as well as chronic pain and disability, may lead to a host of psychological problems in these patients.[36,71-76] Patients reporting phantom limb pain have been shown to be more rigid, compulsive, and self-reliant than their cohorts.[14]

Etiology of stump pain is often associated with definite pathologic findings that may account for the pain in the stump and/or the phantom, such as skin pathology, circulatory disturbances, infection of the skin or underlying tissue, bone spurs, or neuromas. However, stump pain and phantom pain may occur without obvious stump pathology.

Symptoms and Signs

Phantom sensations are painless. Patients generally describe the sensations in their phantom limb either as normal in character or as pleasant warmth and tingling.[4] The strongest sensations come from body parts with the highest brain cortical representation, such as fingers and toes.[4,7,77] The phantom limb may undergo "telescoping," in which the patient loses sensations from the mid-portion of the limb, with subsequent shortening of the phantom.[25] During telescoping, the last body parts to disappear are those with the highest representation in the cortex, such as the thumb, index finger, and big toe. Telescoping occurs only with painless phantoms, and it is most common in the upper extremity. Lengthening of the phantom may occur if pain returns. Figure 28–4 illustrates telescoping of the phantom limb sensation in the upper extremity.

Phantom pain is primarily localized in distal parts of the missing limb.[14,22,25-27,31,78-82] Phantom pain is usually intermittent. Only a few patients are in constant pain. Episodes of pain are reported to occur at daily or weekly intervals, with only a few reporting monthly or yearly, or rare episodes. Duration of individual attacks may last from seconds to hours, but rarely days or longer.

The pain is usually described as burning, aching, or cramping.[30,83] However, pain may also be described as crushing, twisting, grinding, tingling, drawing, stabbing with needles, knifelike, sticking, burning, squeezing, sharp, shocklike, and excruciating, and so on.[27,30,31,35,83] Phantom pain may mimic preamputation pain—not only in location, but also in character.[27,79] The frequency with which preamputation pain persists as phantom pain is highly variable from 12.5% to 80%.[14,28,31,37,79,84] Several authors have considered preamputation pain as a risk factor for phantom pain,[24,43,80,85] even though some have not agreed.[22,28,86]

Phantom pain may be modulated by multiple factors, both internal as well as external. Exacerbations of pain may be produced by trivial, physical, or emotional stimuli. Anxiety, depression, urination, cough, defecation, sexual activity, cold environment, or changes in the weather may worsen phantom limb pain.[25,26,28,30,31,42,83,87] It also has been reported that general, spinal, or regional anesthesia in amputees may cause appearance of phantom pain in otherwise pain-free subjects.[77,88-92]

In contrast to the phantom pain, stump pain is often located in the stump itself and is often described as pressing, throbbing, burning, or squeezing.[87] Other descriptions have included stabbing sensation or an electrical current. An additional variant involves complaints of spontaneous movements of the stump ranging from painful, hardly visible myoclonic jerks to severe clonic contractions lasting as long as 2 days.

Physical Examination

Physical examination is not very useful except for the trigger points in the stump to reproduce the phantom limb pain. Physical examination may reveal altered sensitivity in the stump. Neuromas are also found in only 20% of the patients. The stump may be cold and thermography may be a useful diagnostic test if symptoms consistent with reflex sympathetic dystrophy are present. Sherman and coworkers[51] demonstrated an inverse relationship between pain intensity and skin temperature in patients who described burning, throbbing, or tingling in the phantom limb or stump.

■ DIAGNOSTIC TESTING

At present, there is no proven diagnostic test in evaluation of phantom pain or stump pain except for the physical abnormalities on physical examination. However, response to sympathetic blocks may be assessed by diagnostic sympathetic blocks to assist in therapeutic management.

■ DIFFERENTIAL DIAGNOSIS

The usual course of phantom limb pain is to remain unchanged or to improve gradually. It has been shown that up to 56% of patients report improvement or even complete resolution.[27] Thus, if symptoms of phantom limb pain increase in severity or they start after long periods of time after amputation, a differential diagnosis must be entertained. Multiple causes, which may increase phantom limb pain other than the changes in the weather, autonomic stimulation, and so on, to

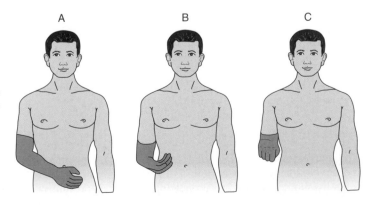

FIGURE 28–4 ■ Illustration of telescoping of the phantom limb. The highly innervated areas (hands) remain, whereas the mid-portion of the phantom limb shortens in length.

be entertained in differential diagnosis include radicular pain, angina, postherpetic neuralgia, and metastatic cancer.

- Radicular pain in the phantom limb may be associated with disc herniation.[93]
- Increased levels of pain in the phantom limb may be triggered by new onset herpes zoster or reactivation of herpes zoster by suppressed immunologic mechanisms.[94,95]
- Angina may manifest as exacerbated phantom limb pain.[96,97]
- In patients undergoing amputation secondary to malignant disease, if phantom limb pain increases significantly, metastatic disease should be evaluated.

■ TREATMENT

Treatment of phantom limb pain or stump pain is difficult and has generally not been very successful. Halbert and colleagues[98] conducted a systematic review to evaluate the evidence for the optimal management of acute and chronic phantom pain. They concluded that there is currently a gap between research and practice in the area of phantom limb pain. Nevertheless, in the past decade, clinical trials have examined treatments for phantom limb pain. Surveys suggest that although physicians believe treatments are effective,[99] fewer than 10% of patients with phantom limb pain receive lasting relief from prescribed medical treatments.[27] Even then, clinicians have been restricted by the lack of clinical trials that would aid in treatment decisions and by the absence of evidence-based treatment guidelines. In a literature review in1980, there were 43 methods for treating phantom limb pain identified; however, it was concluded that few produced relief and that placebo responses were common.[100] Multiple authors also have recommended treatment for phantom limb pain in line with the management of neuropathic pain states.[101-103] Literature review suggests, however, that trials of treatments for neuropathic pain rarely include patients with phantom limb pain.

Early trials concentrated on the reduction of established postoperative phantom limb pain, but newer approaches have used analgesic agents administered before amputation.[104] Treatment approaches continue to be based on the assumption that long-term phantom limb pain is the result of functional or structural changes in the central nervous system in response to noxious somatosensory input.[105] Thus, therapies are directed at early reduction of pain.

Halbert and associates[98] summarized that their review was limited by the poor quality of the included trials. Although they identified 186 articles, they were able to use only 12 trials. Of the 12 trials, only 3 randomized, controlled studies with parallel groups and 3 randomized cross-over trials were identified. They also mentioned the following challenges associated with examining phantom limb pain: extremely low number of amputees; high mortality rate among the amputees; and interventions designed to examine operative and perioperative treatments that were ethically unacceptable.

Prevention

The increasing knowledge about the mechanisms involved in the development and perpetuation of neuropathic pain theoretically should allow us a rational approach to its prevention.

However, initially hopeful attempts such as the use of pre- and postsurgical epidural blockade have been questioned and its utility now appears to be controversial.[106] The advance in neuroimaging techniques is just unveiling some keys to the problem. The current emphasis is put on the adaptive processes taking place in the central nervous system following a deafferentation. In this sense, it seems that our ability to prevent postamputation pain will depend on our capability to modulate the plasticity of the central nervous system. Feria[106] stated that the problem needs a broad-based approach including control of perioperative pain and inflammation, adequate information and follow-up of the patients, a correct surgical technique and a long-term rehabilitation, and the use of the pharmacologic and behavioral approaches reflecting current knowledge.

Multiple authors have attempted psychological preparation, drug therapy, epidural anesthesia, regional nerve blocks, among others to reduce occurrence of phantom limb pain and to delay or stop the process of progressing from acute to chronic pain. At least some of the postamputation pain may be prevented by appropriate psychological preparation of the patients.

Epidural Anesthesia

Gehling and Tryba[107] showed that pre-, intra-, and postoperative epidural anesthesia was associated with a significant reduction of phantom limb pain 12 months after amputation. They concluded, however, that a reduction of phantom limb pain by postoperative epidural anesthesia alone could not be confirmed on the basis of the analyzed data. They also concluded that perioperative epidural anesthesia has been shown to be an effective prophylaxis of phantom limb pain; however, it does not completely abolish phantom limb pain, but increases the number of patients with a milder form of phantom pain.

Investigators in four trials[108-111] assessed preoperative epidural pain relief and were unable to provide definitive evidence to support its routine use. The results of two studies involving a small number suggested that epidural analgesia may help but were inconsistent: one showed relief at 7 days, 6 months, and 1 year postoperatively,[109] the second study[108] showed less phantom limb pain in the intervention group at 1 week, 6 months, and 1 year, and the difference reached significance only at 6 months. The largest of the studies[110] showed no difference in phantom pain at 7 days, 3 months, 6 months, and 12 months. In a randomized prospective study by Lambert and associates,[111] 30 patients scheduled for lower limb amputation were randomly assigned epidural bupivacaine or an intraoperatively placed perineural catheter for intra- and postoperative administration of bupivacaine. All patients had general anesthesia. The results showed there was no significant difference between perioperative epidural block and perineural infusion of local anesthetic. However, phantom pain after 3 days in the epidural group was 29%, at 6 months it was 63%, and at 12 months it was 38%. Thus, it is not known whether epidural anesthesia reduces the prevalence of phantom limb pain.

Regional Anesthesia

Multiple trials assessed perineural,[111-113] and intraneural[114] bupivacaine blocks, either at the time of surgery or immediately postoperatively. Despite some early benefits, there was no difference in pain between the intervention and control groups in the postoperative period.[112,113] Perineural block was similar to infusion of local anesthetic through epidural catheter.[111] Evaluation of continuous brachial plexus analgesia showed prevention of the establishment of phantom limb pain, which did not reappear during follow-up of 1 year.[115] Nerve sheath catheter analgesia also showed reduced prevalence.[116]

Other Interventions

Other treatments assessed for prevention of phantom limb pain included administration of calcitonin, ketamine, intravenous lidocaine, and transcutaneous electrical nerve stimulation (TENS).[117-121] Intravenous calcitonin in one study[121] evaluating 8 patients showed only 2 of 8 patients developed phantom limb pain after 10 days of intravenous treatment with salmon calcitonin with prevalence of phantom limb pain remaining at 25% in systematic follow-up examinations after 3, 6, and 12 months. However, in another study,[117] intravenous calcitonin reduced phantom limb pain in the early postoperative period, but phantom limb pain on longer-term follow-up was not adequately controlled. The effectiveness of ketamine was studied in a prospective, observational study with historical controls with 14 patients in each group.[120] However, the results showed that the phantom limb pain remained high at 72%, even though only 9% of the patients after ketamine compared to 71% of the patients in the control group, complained of severe phantom limb pain. TENS was assessed in the 2-week postoperative period, with the treated group reporting less pain at 4 weeks.[118] However, by 12 months, there was no difference between the groups.

■ MANAGEMENT OF ESTABLISHED PHANTOM PAIN SYNDROME

Drug Therapy

Medical therapy is the most commonly used modality of treatment for phantom pain syndromes. The most commonly used classes of medications are antidepressants and anticonvulsants. A large number of randomized, controlled clinical trials have shown a beneficial effect of tricyclic antidepressants and sodium channel blockers under different neuropathic pain conditions. Even though no controlled trials in phantom pain have been performed, the drugs are generally considered to be effective—at least in some patients.[122-127] Tricyclic antidepressants have been thoroughly studied in other denervation syndromes, such as postherpetic neuralgia and diabetic neuropathy.[125] However, there have been no studies of their use in treatment of phantom limb pain specifically.

Canovas and colleagues[122] assessed the analgesic effectiveness and tolerance of amitriptyline versus nefazodone for the management of neuropathic pain. Of the 120 patients included in this study, fewer than 10 patients suffered with phantom limb pain. The quality of pain was burning and cutting in 62.3% of the cases, lancinating in 40%, and sharp in 25%. The results demonstrated that after 3 months of therapy, the amitriptyline group showed a pain severity of 2

± 0.9 and in nefazodone group, 3 ± 1.1. Pain relief was greater than 75% (excellent) in 42 patients treated with amitriptyline and in 36 patients treated with nefazodone; between 50% to 75% (good) in 18 patients treated with amitriptyline and in 12 patients treated with nefazodone; and below 50% (poor) in 3 patients treated with amitriptyline and 3 patients treated with nefazodone. They concluded that both drugs were effective for the management of neuropathic pain. The group treated with nefazodone showed lower incidence of side effects, except for nausea and vomiting. The amitriptyline group showed significant incidence of orthostatic hypotension, dry mouth, nausea, and vomiting.

Historically, carbamazepine is the most commonly used anticonvulsant.[126,127] Elliott and associates[126] and Patterson[127] reported cases of lancinating phantom limb pains that improved with oral carbamazepine. Logan[128] reported incomplete relief with carbamazepine but complete relief with chlorpromazine in long-standing phantom limb pain. There is no evidence that carbamazepine is effective for pains that are not of the intense, brief, lancinating type.

Currently, gabapentin is the most common anticonvulsant used for phantom limb pain. Other than sedation, side effects are rare and patients become tolerant to sedation with time. Because there is no known long-term toxicity, monitoring of blood levels, as with other anticonvulsants is not necessary. The effectiveness of gabapentin in postamputation phantom limb pain was studied in a randomized, double-blind, placebo-controlled, cross-over study by Bone and coworkers[129] They evaluated analgesic efficacy of gabapentin in phantom limb pain in patients attending a multidisciplinary pain clinic. Each treatment was 6 weeks separated by a 1-week washout. The daily dose of gabapentin was titrated in increments of 300 mg to 2400 mg of the maximum tolerated dose. Nineteen eligible patients were randomized, of whom 14 completed both arms of the study. Both placebo and gabapentin treatments resulted in reduced visual analog scale (VAS) scores compared with baseline. However, pain intensity difference was significantly greater than placebo for gabapentin therapy at the end of the treatment. They concluded that after 6 weeks, gabapentin monotherapy was better than placebo in relieving postamputation phantom limb pain. There were no significant differences in mood, sleep interference, or activities of daily living. Serpell and colleagues[130] evaluated the use of gabapentin in neuropathic pain in a randomized, double-blind, placebo-controlled trial of 305 patients in a wide range of neuropathic pain syndromes, including phantom limb pain in 2% of patients. They concluded that at an average dose of 900 mg to 2400 mg per day, the gabapentin was well tolerated and was associated with significant pain control with few secondary effects—dizziness and somnolence, most of which were transient and occurred during the titration phase.

Analgesic effects of intravenous lidocaine and morphine on postamputation pain were evaluated in a randomized double-blind, active placebo-controlled, cross-over trial by Wu and coworkers.[119] An intravenous bolus followed by an intravenous infusion of morphine, lidocaine, and the active placebo (diphenhydramine), were performed on 3 consecutive days. The results showed that 31 of 32 subjects enrolled completed the study. Eleven subjects had both stump and phantom pains, 11 and 9 subjects had stump and phantom pain alone, respectively. They concluded that stump pain was diminished by both morphine and lidocaine, whereas phantom pain was diminished only by morphine, suggesting that the mechanisms and pharmacologic sensitivity of stump and phantom pains are different.

The effect of an NMDA receptor antagonist have been examined in different studies.[51,131-134] In a double-blind, placebo-controlled study, intravenous ketamine reduced pain, hyperalgesia, and "wind-up" like pain in 11 amputees with stump and phantom pain.[52] In another controlled trial by the same authors,[132] 19 patients received memantine, an NMDA receptor antagonist available for oral use, in a blinded, placebo-controlled, cross-over fashion. Memantine failed to have any effect on spontaneous pain, allodynia, or hyperalgesia. In another randomized, double-blinded, placebo-controlled trial,[134] Memantine failed to demonstrate a significant clinical benefit of the NMDA receptor antagonist in chronic phantom limb pain.

Beta-adrenergic blockers have also been suggested for treatment of phantom limb pain based on three cases.[135] However, in a double-blind cross-over trial of propranolol up to 240 mg daily, authors were unable to show significant improvement in posttraumatic neuralgias.[136]

Salmon calcitonin has been shown to provide analgesic effect in a series of painful conditions, including phantom limb pain.[117,137-139] However, there are no controlled trials available to show the effectiveness of calcitonin in chronic phantom limb pain. Dextromethorphan was studied for attenuation of phantom pain in cancer amputees in a double-blind cross-over trial involving three patients.[140] Results showed that oral dextromethorphan effectively reduced postamputation phantom limb pain, bestowing improvement in feeling and minimizing sedation in comparison with the pretreatment or placebo conditions, with no side effects. Capsaicin also was tried in phantom limb pain.[141,142] In this study of 24 patients, which was done in a double-blind fashion, authors concluded that capsaicin may be used as an alternative treatment for the phantom limb pain. Some have reported a beneficial effect of benzodiazepines,[143] however the general impression is that benzodiazepines do not produce substantial pain relief. Mexiletine (the oral congener of lidocaine) also has been reported to be effective.[144]

Opioid analgesics with or without other drugs are considered the mainstay of treatment in modern medicine. Generally, it is quoted in the textbooks that narcotic analgesics are not effective in producing long-term pain relief in patients with phantom limb pain.[27] However, modern evidence suggests that opioids can be used safely for years with a limited risk of drug dependence.[4,27,43,66,102,145-147] Further, patients undergoing amputation related to systemic medical diseases have only a 42% 5-year survival rate; thus the risk of opioid addiction may be weighed against quality-of-life issues.[36] In a review of five patients, a 50% to 90% reduction in pain at 12 to 26 months' follow-up of patients taking methadone 10 to 20 mg daily was reported.[146] In a placebo-controlled trial,[66] morphine was shown to reduce pain significantly.

Neural Blockade

Nerve blocks are commonly used in the treatment of phantom limb pain, and although physicians performing these blocks report a high success rate, it has not been substantiated.[99]

These blocks range from trigger point injections to neurolytic sympathetic blocks with stump injections, sympathetic blocks, peripheral nerve blocks, and epidural or subarachnoid blocks. However, it has been shown that only 14% of the patients with phantom limb pain report even a significant temporary change, whereas less than 5% report a large permanent change or cure.[27] The use of neural blockade in the treatment of phantom limb pain is largely based on anecdotal reports in the literature.[148-150]

Blankenbaker[148] reported that sympathetic blocks are successful if amputees are treated soon after the onset of phantom limb pain. Halbert and colleagues,[98] in a systematic review to evaluate evidence for the optimal management of acute and chronic phantom pain, was unable to find any trials to meet the criteria for inclusion.

Lesions of the dorsal root entry zone have been reported to provide long-term pain relief in patients with phantom limb pain following avulsion of nerve roots or amputation.[83,151,152] It has been reported that 36% of patients had pain relief on follow-up at 6 months to 4 years following dorsal root entry zone lesions.[83,152] However, they reported very poor relief in patients with stump pain alone.

Neurostimulation

TENS has been used with some success in the treatment of phantom pain. However, the results are inconclusive and not encouraging. Spinal cord stimulation (SCS), deep brain stimulation (DBS) of the thalamic nucleus ventralis chordalis, and motor cortex stimulation (MCS) are all used in managing phantom limb pain with variable success.

Some authors have reported excellent relief with TENS. One author reported success in 5 of 6 patients with phantom pain following TENS treatment.[153] Another author reported a 66% reduction in pain lasting less than 10 hours.[154] Yet, other authors reported good to excellent results in only 25% of the patients treated with TENS.[155] Stimulation of the contralateral extremity with TENS also has been shown to have favorable response in some patients.[156,157]

Recent evaluations of spinal cord stimulation have shown encouraging results in neuropathic pain, including reflex sympathetic dystrophy.[158,159] Thus, stimulation of posterior columns of the spinal cord is the most common neurosurgical technique used for the treatment of phantom limb pain. Selection process is very crucial. Response to transcutaneous stimulation or percutaneous electrical stimulation may predict a response to dorsal column stimulation.[160] Even with appropriate patient selection, it has been reported that only 65% of the patients receive a greater than 25% reduction in pain immediately after surgical implantation.[161] Further, the success rate of dorsal column stimulation steadily declines over time, and greater than 50% long-term pain reduction is present in only one third of patients originally showing improvement.[162,163] Spinal cord stimulation may not show any improvement in patients with severe pain and phantom limb sensations. In one case report, it was shown that good to excellent results were observed in five patients, as judged by decreased pain and increased functional status with decrease in medication.[164] However, in another report, dorsal column stimulation provided minimal relief in patients with phantom limb pain.[165] Yet another report showed that dorsal column stimulation showed improvement in only 25% of the patients.[166] Thus, one should weigh the risk-benefit ratio with caution and diligence.

Intracranial neurostimulation demonstrated initial pain relief in 80% of the patients with sensory thalamic stimulation[167] and 86% of the patients had significant relief with deep brain stimulation.[168] Thalamic stimulation, in contrast to spinal cord stimulation, may block spontaneous neuronal activity, which has been proposed to mediate phantom sensation in some models.[54] Thus, some believe that it may be more effective than spinal cord stimulation; however, it has not thus far been proven. Percutaneous stimulation of the periosteum has been used, even though it has not been well studied.[169]

Neurosurgical Techniques

Some authors have reported multiple neurosurgical techniques apart from electrical stimulation, including intrathecal implantables, stereotactic thermocoagulation lesions, and cordotomy. Some of these treatments may have more serious complications than benefits.[26,170] Sporadic success has been reported with many physical therapy modalities—including ultrasound or vibration, heat or cold, massage therapy, and stump percussion.[99] It was noted that neither surgeons nor patients reported good success rates with currently recommended surgical procedures.[27,99]

Stump Revision

Patients with continued phantom limb pain and also issues related to the stump with vascular insufficiency, infection, or extensive neuromas may undergo stump revision, which may provide benefit in 50% of the patients.[30]

Physical Therapy

Physical therapy has been shown to be useful, especially the educational aspect with attention to stump and preparation for prosthesis because phantom limb pain is most commonly seen in patients who are unable to use a prosthesis within the 6 months following amputation.

Acupuncture

Electroacupuncture has been shown to provide relief from phantom limb pain of the arm.[171] Mostly, short-term relief has been reported with the first few acupuncture treatments; no long-term improvement in patients with a history of nerve damage, including phantom limb pain, has been reported.[172]

Electroconvulsive Therapy

A case report of electroconvulsive therapy (ECT) with study of regional cerebral blood flow[173] suggested that total resolution of the pain in this particular patient and the regional cerebral blood flow of the anterior cingulate cortex and insula were related to the analgesic effectiveness of the ECT. In another case report,[174] authors reported two patients with severe phantom limb pain refractory to multiple therapies, without concurrent psychiatric disorder, enjoying substantial

pain relief of phantom pain on long-term follow-up at 3.5 years.

Psychological Therapies

Multiple psychological modalities have been attempted in managing phantom limb pain.[68,175-181] Psychotherapy was reported to yield good results.[68] Relaxation training with or without biofeedback or hypnosis has been studied.[175-181] It has been reported that in 12 of the 14 patients with chronic phantom limb pain, significant improvement was noted with muscular relaxation training to disrupt the pain-anxiety-tension cycle.[175] In this study, patients required an average of six treatments to produce therapeutic effect, and it was also associated with decreased anxiety levels and increased pain relief. In a case report, combined EMG and thermal biofeedback was shown to be effective in a patient with extreme phantom limb pain at 12-month follow-up. Hypnotic suggestion of stocking-glove anesthesia may lead to a reduction in phantom limb pain.[177,178] It was shown that 45% of the patients were successfully hypnotized, and 35% had successful improvement in phantom limb pain.[178] Relapses occurred soon after the discontinuation of the treatment in 34% of the patients. In a case report describing two patients utilizing hypnotic imagery as a treatment for phantom limb pain,[179] the authors concluded that hypnotic procedures appear to be a useful adjunct to establish strategies for the treatment of phantom limb pain.

■ SIDE EFFECTS AND COMPLICATIONS

Most complications are related to the problems related to the stump, prosthesis, and management techniques. Improper prosthesis may cause a multitude of problems, including psychological problems, as well as local irritation, neuroma formation, and so on. Physical therapy may increase or exacerbate pain levels. Acupuncture and neural blockade therapy may cause complications related to needle insertion, drugs, and physiologic and pharmacologic effects of various drugs. Neuroablation techniques may cause serious complications ranging from minor persistent neurologic deficits to hemiplegia and incontinence. Neuroablation techniques may also increase the pain by loss of inhibitory control. Neurosurgical techniques may be associated with significant complications.

■ CONCLUSION

Phantom pain syndromes are a common consequence of removal of a limb or organ. Approximately two thirds of patients complain of phantom pain following the removal of a limb. However, in fewer than 10% of the patients, this pain manifests as a severe incapacitating condition. The understanding of phantom limb pain has improved substantially in the past 2 decades with a series of morphologic, physiologic, and biological changes resulting in hyperexcitability in the nervous system based on experimental studies. Prevention of phantom pain by various modalities has shown to be ineffective. Similarly, most treatment modalities of chronic phantom pain syndrome are in their infancy and not well studied. At present, there is no evidence-based approach to managing phantom pain syndromes.

References

1. Keynes G: The Apologie and Treatise of Ambroise Paré. Chicago, University of Chicago Press, 1952.
2. Keil G: Sogenannte Erstbeschreibung des Phantomschmerzes von Ambroise Paré. Fortschritte der Medicine 108:58, 1990.
3. Mitchell SW: Injuries of Nerves and Their Consequences. London, Smith, Elder, 1872.
4. Hord AH, Shannon C: Phantom pain. In Raj PP (ed): Practical Management of Pain, 3rd ed. Philadelphia, Mosby, 2000, p 212.
5. Hanowell ST, Kennedy SF: Phantom tongue pain and causalgia: Case presentation and treatment. Anesth Analg 58:436, 1979.
6. Jamison K, Wellisch DK, Katz Rl, et al: Phantom breast syndrome. Arch Surg 114:93, 1979.
7. Rothemund Y, Grüsser SM, Liebeskind U, et al: Phantom phenomena in mastectomized patients and their relation to chronic and acute pre-mastectomy pain. Pain 107:140, 2004.
8. Cherng CH, Wong CS, Ho ST, et al: Prevalence and clinical character-istics of phantom rectum syndrome after rectum resection in Chinese patients. Pain Clinic 13:113, 2001.
9. Biley FC: Phantom bladder sensations: A new concern for stoma care workers. Br J Nurs 10:1290, 2001.
10. Thomas CR, Brazeal BA, Rosenberg L, et al: Phantom limb pain in pediatric burn survivors. Burns 29:139, 2003.
11. Simmel ML: Phantoms in patients with leprosy and in elderly digital amputees. Am J Psychol 69:529, 1956.
12. Weiss SA, Fishman S: Extended and telescoped phantom limb in uni-lateral amputees. J Abnorm Soc Psychol 66:489, 1963.
13. Almagor M, Jaffe Y, Lomranz J: The relation between limb dominance, acceptance of disability, and the phantom limb phenomenon. J Abnorm Psychol 87:377, 1978.
14. Parkes CM: Factors determining the persistence of phantom pain in the amputee. J Psychosom Res 17:97, 1973.
15. Gillis L: The management of the painful amputation stump: A new theory for the phantom phenomena. Br J Surg 51:87, 1964.
16. Alamo Tomillero F, Rodriguez de la Torre R, Caba Barrientos F, et al: Prospective study of prevalence and risk factors for painful phantom limb in the immediate postoperative period of patients undergoing amputation for chronic arterial ischemia. Rev Esp Anestesiol Reanim 49:295, 2002.
17. Lacoux PA, Crombie IK, Macrae WA: Pain in traumatic upper limb amputees in Sierra Leone. Pain 99:309, 2002.
18. Gallagher P, Allen D, Maclachlan M: Phantom limb pain and residual limb pain following lower limb amputation: A descriptive analysis. Disabil Rehabil 23:522, 2001.
19. Fraser CM, Halligan PW, Robertson IH, et al: Characterizing phantom limb phenomena in upper limb amputees. Prosthet Orthot Int 25:235, 2001.
20. Araya E, Pernía J, Teran P, et al: Phantom limb pain following trau-matic upper limb amputation. Cirugia Plastica Ibero-Latinoamericana 27:159, 2001.
21. Ehde DM, Czerniecki JM, Smith DG, et al: Chronic phantom sensations, phantom pain, residual limb pain, and other regional pain after lower limb amputation. Arch Phys Med Rehabil 81:1039, 2000.
22. Kooijman CM, Dijkstra PU, Geertzen JH, et al: Phantom pain and phantom sensations in upper limb amputees: An epidemiological study. Pain 87:33, 2000.
23. Wilkins KL, McGrath PJ, Finley GA, et al: Phantom limb sensations and phantom limb pain in child and adolescent amputees. Pain 78:7, 1998.
24. Hagberg K, Brånemark R: Consequences of non-vascular trans-femoral amputation: A survey of quality of life, prosthetic use and problems. Prosthet Orthot Int 25:186, 2001.
25. Jensen TS, Krebs B, Nielsen J, et al: Phantom limb, phantom pain and stump pain in amputees during the first 6 months following limb ampu-tation. Pain 17:243, 1983.
26. Sherman RA, Sherman CJ: Prevalence and characteristics of chronic phantom limb pain among American veterans: Results of a trial survey. Am J Phys Med 62:227, 1983.
27. Sherman RA, Sherman CJ, Parker L: Chronic phantom and stump pain among American veterans: Results of a survey. Pain 18:83, 1984.
28. Wall R, Novotny-Joseph P, MacNamara TE: Does preamputation pain influence phantom limb pain in cancer patients? South Med J 78:34, 1985.
29. Dijkstra PU, Geertzen JH, Stewart R, et al: Phantom pain and risk factors: A multivariate analysis. J Pain Symptom Manage 24:578, 2002.
30. Bailey AA, Moersch FP: Phantom limb. Can Med Assoc J 45:37, 1941.
31. Jensen TS, Krebs B, Nielsen J, et al: Immediate and long-term phantom limb pain in amputees: Incidence, clinical characteristics and relation-ship to pre-amputation limb pain. Pain 21:267, 1985.
32. Sternbach T, Nadvorna H, Arazi D: A five-year follow-up study of phantom limb pain in post-traumatic amputees. Scand J Rehab Med 14:203, 1982.
33. Ribera H, Cano P, Dora A, et al: Phantom limb pain secondary to post-trauma stump hematoma 40 years after amputation: Description of one case. Revista de la Sociedad Espanola del Dolor 8:217, 2001.
34. Rajbhandari SM, Jarett JA, Griffiths PD, et al: Diabetic neuropathic pain in a leg amputated 44 years previously. Pain 83:627, 1999.
35. Sherman RA, Sherman CJ: A comparison of phantom sensations among amputees whose amputations were of civilian and military origins. Pain 21:91, 1985.
36. Helm P, Engel T, Holm A, et al: Function after lower limb amputation. Acta Orthop Scand 57:154, 1986.
37. Nikolajsen L, Ilkjaer S, Kroner K, et al: The influence of pre-amputation pain on postamputation stump and phantom pain. Pain 72:393, 1997.
38. Houser SA: Phantom limb pain. In Warfield CA, Fausett HJ (eds): Manual of Pain Management, 2nd ed. Philadelphia, Lippincott Williams & Wilkins, 2002, p 181.
39. Loeser JD. Pain after amputation: Phantom limb and stump pain. In Bonica JJ (ed): The Management of Pain, 2nd ed. Philadelphia, Lea & Febiger, 1990, p 244.
40. Van der Schans CP, Geertzen JH, Schoppen T, et al: Phantom pain and health-related quality of life in lower limb amputees. J Pain Symptom Manage 24:429, 2002.
41. Sunderland S: Nerves and Nerve Injuries. New York, Churchill Livingstone, 1978.
42. Frazier SH: Psychiatric aspects of causalgia, the phantom limb, and phantom pain. Dis Nerv Syst 27:441, 1966.
43. Nikolajsen L, Jensen TS: Postamputation pain. In Melzack R, Wall PD (eds): Handbook of Pain Management. Edinburgh, Churchill Livingstone, 2003, p 247.
44. Wall PD, Gutnick M: Ongoing activity in peripheral nerves: The phys-iology and pharmacology of impulses originating from a neuroma. Exp Neurol 43:580, 1974.
45. Devor M, Seltzer Z: Pathophysiology of damaged nerves in relation to chronic pain. In Wall PD, Melzack R (eds): Textbook of Pain, 4th ed. Edinburgh, Churchill Livingstone, 1999, p 129.
46. Devor M, Govrin-Lippman R, Angelides K: Na$^+$ channels immunolo-calization in peripheral mammalian axons and changes following nerve injury and neuroma formation. J Neurosci 135:1976, 1993.
47. Novakovic SD, Tzoumaka E, McGivern JG, et al: Distribution of the tetrodotoxin-resistant sodium channel PN3 in rat sensory neurons in normal and neuropathic pain conditions. J Neurosci 18:2174, 1998.
48. Kajander KC, Wakisaka S, Bennett GJ: Spontaneous discharge origi-nates in the dorsal root ganglion at the onset of a painful peripheral neu-ropathy in the rat. Neurosci Lett 138:225, 1992.
49. Price DD, Mao J, Mayer DJ: Central consequences of persistent pain states. In Jensen TS, Turner JM, Wiesenfeld-Hallin Z (eds): Proceed-ings of the 8th World Congress on Pain, Progress in Pain Research and Management, vol. 8. Seattle, IASP Press, 1997, p 155.
50. Cook AJ, Woolf CJ, Wall PD, et al: Dynamic receptive field plasticity in rat spinal cord dorsal horn following c-primary afferent input. Nature 325:151, 1987.
51. Doubell TP, Mannion RJ, Woolf CJ: The dorsal horn: State-dependent sensory processing, plasticity and the generation of pain. In Wall PD, Melzack R (eds): Textbook of Pain, 4th ed. Edinburgh, Churchill Livingstone, 1999, p 165.
52. Nikolajsen L, Hansen CL, Nielsen J, et al: The effect of ketamine on phantom pain: A central neuropathic disorder maintained by peripheral input. Pain 67:69, 1996.
53. Woolf CJ, Shortland P, Coggeshaal RE: Peripheral nerve injury triggers central sprouting of myelinated afferents. Nature 355:75, 1992.

54. Davis KD, Kiss ZH, Luo L: Phantom sensations generated by thalamic microstimulation. Nature 391:385, 1998.
55. Willoch F, Rosen G, Tolle TR, et al: Phantom limb pain in the human brain: Unraveling neural circuitries of phantom limb sensations using positron emission tomography. Ann Neurol 48:842, 2000.
56. Mackert BM, Sappok T, Grüsser S, et al: The eloquence of silent cortex: Analysis of afferent input to deafferented cortex in arm amputees. Neuroreport 14:409, 2003.
57. Dettmers C, Adler T, Rzanny R, et al: Increased excitability in the primary motor cortex and supplementary motor area in patients with phantom limb pain after upper limb amputation. Neurosci Lett 307:109, 2001.
58. Karl A, Birbaumer N, Lutzenberger W, et al: Reorganization of motor and somatosensory cortex in upper extremity amputees with phantom limb pain. J Neurosci 21:3609, 2001.
59. Wei F, Zhuo M: Potentiation of sensory responses in the anterior cingulate cortex following digit amputation in the anaesthetised rat. J Physiol 532:823, 2001.
60. Flor H: The modification of cortical reorganization and chronic pain by sensory feedback. Appl Psychophysiol Biofeedback 27:215, 2002.
61. Huse E, Larbig W, Birbaumer N, et al: Cortical reorganization and pain. Empirical findings and therapeutic implication using the example of phantom pain. Schmerz 15:131, 2001.
62. Roux FE, Ibarrola D, Lazorthes Y, et al: Chronic motor cortex stimulation for phantom limb pain: A functional magnetic resonance imaging study: Technical case. Neurosurgery 48:681, 2001.
63. Flor H, Elbert T, Knecht S: Phantom limb pain as a perceptual correlate of cortical reorganization following arm amputation. Nature 375:482, 1995.
64. Flor H, Elbert T, Mühlnickel W: Cortical reorganization and phantom phenomena in congenital and traumatic upper-extremity amputees. Exp Brain Res 119:205, 1998.
65. Birbaumer N, Lutzenberger W, Montoya P, et al: Effects of regional anesthesia on phantom limb are mirrored in changes in cortical reorganization in upper limb amputees. J Neurosci 17:5503, 1997.
66. Huse E, Larbig W, Flor H, et al: The effect of opioids on phantom limb pain and cortical reorganization. Pain 90:47, 2001.
67. Matzer O, Devor M: Contrasting thermal sensitivity of spontaneously active A- and C-fibers in experimental nerve-end neuromas. Pain 30:373, 1987.
68. Kolb LC: The Painful Phantom. Springfield, Charles C Thomas, 1954.
69. University of California: Progress Report to the Advisory Committee on Artificial Limbs, 2nd ed. Berkeley, University of California Press, 1952.
70. Ewalt JR, Randall GC, Morris H: The phantom limb. Psychosom Med 9:118, 1947.
71. Lindesay J: Validity of the general health questionnaire (GHQ) in detecting psychiatric disturbance in amputees with phantom pain. J Psychosom Res 30:277, 1986.
72. Whyte AS, Niven CA. Psychological distress in amputees with phantom limb pain. J Pain Symptom Manage 22:938, 2001.
73. Sherman RA, Sherman CJ, Bruno GM: Psychological factors influencing chronic phantom limb pain: An analysis of the literature. Pain 28:285, 1987.
74. Frazier SH, Kolb LC: Psychiatric aspects of pain and the phantom limb. Orthop Clin North Am 1:481, 1970.
75. Ewalt JR: The phantom limb. Ann Intern Med 44:668, 1956.
76. Larbig W, Montoya P, Flor H, et al: Evidence for a change in neural processing in phantom limb patients. Pain 67:275, 1996.
77. Miles JE: Phantom limb syndrome occurring during spinal anesthesia: Relationship to etiology. J Nerv Ment Dis 123:365, 1956.
78. Carlen PL, Wall PD, Nadvorna H, et al: Phantom limbs and related phenomena in recent traumatic amputations. Neurology 28:211, 1978.
79. Katz J, Melzack R: Pain 'memories' in phantom limbs: Review and clinical observations. Pain 43:319, 1990.
80. Krane EJ, Heller LB: The prevalence of phantom sensation and pain in pediatric amputees. J Pain Sympt Manage 10:21, 1995.
81. Wartan SW, Hamann W, Wedley JR, et al: Phantom pain and sensation among British veteran amputees. Br J Anaesth 78:652, 1997.
82. Montoya P, Larbig W, Grulke N: Relationship of phantom limb pain to other phantom limb phenomena in upper extremity amputees. Pain 72:87, 1997.
83. Saris SC, Iacono RP, Nashold BS Jr: Dorsal root entry zone lesions for post-amputation pain. J Neurosurg 62:72, 1985.
84. Appenzeller O, Bicknell JM: Effects of nervous system lesions on phantom experience in amputees. Neurology 19:141, 1969.
85. Houghton AD, Nicolls G, Houghton AL, et al: Phantom pain: Natural history and association with rehabilitation. Ann R Coll Surg Engl 76:22, 1994.
86. Henderson WR, Smyth GE: Phantom limbs. J Neurol Neurosurg Psych 11:88, 1948.
87. Sherman RA, Barja RH, Bruno GM: Thermographic correlates of chronic pain: Analysis of 125 patients incorporating evaluations by a blind panel. Arch Phys Med Rehabil 68:273, 1987.
88. Mackenzie N: Phantom limb pain during spinal anaesthesia. Recurrence in amputees. Anaesthesia 38:886, 1983.
89. Martin G, Grant SA, MacLeod DB, et al: Severe phantom leg pain in an amputee after lumbar plexus block. Reg Anesth Pain Med 28:475, 2003.
90. Murphy JP, Anandaciva SP: Phantom limb pain and spinal anesthesia. Anaesthesia 39:188, 1984.
91. Sellick BC: Phantom limb pain and spinal anesthesia. Anesthesiology 62:801, 1985.
92. Lee ED, Donovan K. Reactivation of phantom limb pain after combined interscalene brachial plexus block and general anesthesia: Successful treatment with intravenous lidocaine. Anesthesiology 82:295, 1995.
93. Finneson BE, Haft H, Krueger EG: Phantom limb syndrome associated with herniated nucleus pulposus. J Neurosurg 14:344, 1957.
94. Wilson PR, Person JR, Su DW, et al: Herpes zoster reactivation of phantom limb pain. Mayo Clin Proc 53:336, 1978.
95. Sugarbaker PH, Weiss CM, Davidson DD, et al: Increasing phantom limb pain as a symptom of cancer recurrence. Cancer 54:373, 1984.
96. Cohen H: Anginal pain in a phantom limb. Br Med J 2:475, 1976.
97. Mester SW, Cintron GB, Long C: Phantom angina. Am Heart J 116:1627, 1988.
98. Halbert J, Crotty M, Cameron ID: Evidence for optimal management of acute and chronic phantom pain: A systematic review. Clin J Pain 18:84, 2002.
99. Sherman RA, Sherman CJ, Gall NG: A survey of current phantom limb pain treatment in the United States. Pain 8:85, 1980.
100. Sherman R: Published treatments of phantom limb pain. Am J Phys Med 59:232, 1980.
101. McQuay H, Carroll D, Jadad AR, et al: Anticonvulsant drugs for management of pain: A systematic review. BMJ 311:1047, 1995.
102. Baron R, Wasner G, Lindner V: Optimal treatment of phantom limb pain in the elderly. Drugs Aging 12:361, 1998.
103. Esquenazi A, Meier RH: Rehabilitation in limb deficiency; IV. Limb amputation. Arch Phys Med Rehabil 77:S18, 1996.
104. Katz J: Prevention of phantom limb pain by regional anesthesia. Lancet 349:519, 1997.
105. McQuay HJ, Dickenson AH: Implications of nervous system plasticity for pain management. Anaesthesia 45:101, 1990.
106. Feria M: Can we prevent post-amputation pain. DOLOR 16:73, 2001.
107. Gehling M, Tryba M: Prophylaxis of phantom pain: Is regional analgesia ineffective? Schmerz 17:11, 2003.
108. Bach S, Noreng MF, Tjellden NU: Phantom limb pain in amputees during the first 12 months following limb amputation, after preoperative lumbar epidural blockade. Pain 33:297, 1988.
109. Jahangiri M, Jayatunga AP, Bradley JWP, et al: Prevention of phantom pain after major lower limb amputation by epidural infusion of diamorphine, clonidine, and bupivacaine. Ann R Coll Surg Engl 76:324, 1994.
110. Nikolajsen L, Ilkjær S, Christensen JH, et al: Randomised trial of epidural bupivacaine and morphine in prevention of stump and phantom pain in lower-limb amputation. Lancet 350:1353, 1997.
111. Lambert AW, Dashfield AK, Cosgrove C, et al: Randomized prospective study comparing preoperative epidural and intraoperative perineural analgesia for the prevention of postoperative stump and phantom limb pain following major amputation. Reg Anesth Pain Med 26:316, 2001.
112. Fisher A, Meller Y: Continuous postoperative regional analgesia by nerve sheath block for amputation surgery-A pilot study. Anesth Analg 72:300, 1991.
113. Pinzur M, Garla PG, Pluth T, et al: Continuous postoperative infusion of a regional anaesthetic after an amputation of the lower extremity. J Bone Joint Surg Am 79:1752, 1996.
114. Elizanga AM, Smith DG, Sharar SR, et al: Continuous regional analgesia by intraneuronal block: Effect on postoperative opioid requirements and phantom limb pain following amputation. J Rehabil Res Dev 31:179, 1994.

115. Keifer RT, Wiech K, Töpfner S, et al: Continuous brachial plexus analgesia and NMDA-receptor blockade in early phantom limb pain: A report of two cases. Pain Med 3:156, 2002.

116. Morey TE, Giannoni J, Duncan E, et al: Nerve sheath catheter analgesia after amputation. Clin Orthop 397:281, 2002.

117. Jaeger H, Maier C: Calcitonin in phantom limb pain: A double-blind study. Pain 48:21, 1992.

118. Finsen V, Persen L, Lovlien M, et al: Transcutaneous electrical nerve stimulation after major amputation. J Bone Joint Surg Br 70:109, 1988.

119. Wu CL, Tella P, Staats PS, et al: Analgesic effects of intravenous lidocaine and morphine on postamputation pain: A randomized double-blind, active placebo-controlled, crossover trial. Anesthesiology 96:841, 2002.

120. Dertwinkel R, Heinrichs C, Senne I, et al: Prevention of severe phantom limb pain by perioperative administration of ketamine—An observational study. Acute Pain 4:9, 2002.

121. Simanski C, Lempa M, Koch G, et al: Therapy of phantom pain with salmon calcitonin and effect on postoperative patient satisfaction. Chirurg 70:674, 1999.

122. Canovas L, Martinez-Salgado J, Barros C, et al: Management of neuropathic pain: Preliminary study of amitriptyline versus nefazodone. Revista de la Sociedad Espanola del Dolor 7J:425, 2000.

123. Iacono RP, Sandyk R, Baumford CR, et al: Post-amputation phantom pain and autonomous stump movements responsive to doxepin. Funct Neurol 2:343, 1987.

124. Sindrup SH, Jensen TS: Efficacy of pharmacological treatments of neuropathic pain: An update and effect related to mechanism of drug action. Pain 83:389, 1999.

125. Getto CJ, Sorkness CA, Howell T: Antidepressants and chronic nonmalignant pain: A review. J Pain Symptom Manage 2:9, 1987.

126. Elliott F, Little A, Milbrandt W: Carbamazepine for phantom limb phenomena. New Engl J Med 295:678, 1976.

127. Patterson JF: Carbamazepine in the treatment of phantom limb pain. South Med J 81:1100, 1988.

128. Logan TP: Persistent phantom limb pain: Dramatic response to chlorpromazine. South Med J 76:1585, 1983.

129. Bone M, Critchley P, Buggy DJ: Gabapentin in postamputation phantom limb pain: A randomized, double-blind, placebo-controlled, cross-over study. Reg Anesth Pain Med 27:481, 2002.

130. Serpell MG: Neuropathic Pain Study Group. Gabapentin in neuropathic pain syndromes: A randomized, double-blind, placebo-controlled trial. Pain 99:557, 2002.

131. Nikolajsen L, Hansen PO, Jensen TS: Oral ketamine therapy in the treatment of postamputation stump pain. Acta Anaesthesiol Scand 41:427, 1997.

132. Nikolajsen L, Gottrup H, Kristensen AGD, et al: Memantine (a N-methyl D-aspartate receptor antagonist) in the treatment of neuropathic pain following amputation or surgery: A randomized, double-blind, cross-over study. Anesth Analg 91:960, 2000.

133. Stannard CF, Porter GE: Ketamine hydrochloride in the treatment of phantom limb pain. Pain 54:227, 1993.

134. Maier C, Dertwinkel R, Mansourian N, et al: Efficacy of the NMDA-receptor antagonist memantine in patients with chronic phantom limb pain—Results of a randomized double-blinded, placebo-controlled trial. Pain 103:277, 2003.

135. Marsland AR, Weekes JW, Atkinson RL, et al: Phantom limb pain: A case for beta blockers? Pain 12:295, 1982.

136. Scadding JW, Wall PD, Parry CB, et al: Clinical trial of propranolol in post-traumatic neuralgia. Pain 14:283, 1982.

137. Appelboom T: Calcitonin in reflex sympathetic dystrophy syndrome and other painful conditions. Bone 30:84S, 2002.

138. Kessel C, Wörz R: Clinical note: Immediate response of phantom limb pain to calcitonin. Pain 30:79, 1987.

139. Gennari C, Francini G, Gonneli S, et al: Dolore osseo, endofine e calcitonine. In Gennari C, et al (eds): The Effects of Calcitonin in Man. Milano, Italy, Masson, 1983.

140. Ben Abraham R, Marouani N, Kollender Y, et al: Dextromethorphan for phantom pain attenuation in cancer amputees: A double-blind cross-over trial involving three patients. Clin J Pain 18:282, 2002.

141. Rayner HC, Atkins RC, Westerman RA: Relief of local stump pain by capsaicin cream. Lancet 2:1276, 1989.

142. Atesalp AS, Ozkan Y, Komurcu M, et al: The effects of capsaicin in phantom limb pain. Agri 12:30, 2000.

143. Bartusch SL, Sanders J, Dálessio JG, et al: Clonazepam for the treatment of lancinating phantom limb pain. Clin J Pain 12:59, 1996.

144. Davis RW: Successful treatment for phantom pain. Orthopedics 16:691, 1993.

145. Dellemijn P: Are opioids effective in relieving neuropathic pain? Pain 80:453, 1999.

146. Urban BJ, France RD, Steinberger EK, et al: Long-term use of narcotic/antidepressant medication in the management of phantom limb. Pain 24:191, 1986.

147. Bergmans L, Snijdelaar DG, Katz J, et al: Methadone for phantom limb pain. Clin J Pain 18:203, 2002.

148. Blankenbaker WL: The care of patients with phantom limb pain in a pain clinic. Anesth Analg 56:842, 1977.

149. Wassef MR: Phantom pain with probable reflex sympathetic dystrophy. Efficacy of fentanyl infiltration of the stellate ganglion. Reg Anesth 22:287, 1997.

150. Lierz P, Schroegendorfer K, Choi S, et al: Continuous blockade of both brachial plexus with ropivacaine in phantom pain: A case report. Pain 78:135, 1998.

151. Moossy JJ, Nashold BS Jr, Osborne D, et al: Conus medullaris nerve root avulsions. J Neurosurg 66:835, 1987.

152. Saris SC, Iacono RP, Nashold BS Jr: Successful treatment of phantom pain with dorsal root entry zone coagulation. Appl Neurophysiol 51:188, 1988.

153. Long DM: Cutaneous afferent stimulation for relief of chronic pain. Clin Neurosurg 21:257, 1974.

154. Melzack R: Prolonged relief of pain by brief, intense transcutaneous somatic stimulation. Pain 1:357, 1975.

155. Shealy CN: Transcutaneous electrical stimulation for control of pain. Clin Neurosurg 21:269, 1974.

156. Winnem MF, Amundsen T: Treatment of phantom limb pain with TENS. Pain 12:299, 1982.

157. Carabelli RA, Kellerman WC: Phantom limb pain: Relief by application of TENS to contralateral extremity. Arch Phys Med Rehabil 66:466, 1985.

158. Grabow TS, Tella PK, Raja SN: Spinal cord stimulation for complex regional pain syndrome: An evidence-based medicine review of the literature. Clin J Pain 19:371, 2003 .

159. Manchikanti L, Staats P, Singh V, et al: Evidence-based practice guidelines for interventional techniques in the management of chronic spinal pain. Pain Physician 6:3, 2003.

160. Miles J, Lipton S: Phantom limb pain treated by electrical stimulation. Pain 5:373, 1978.

161. Krainick JU, Thoden U, Riechert T: Spinal cord stimulation in post-amputation pain. Surg Neurol 4:167, 1975.

162. Krainick JU, Thoden U, Riechert T: Pain reduction in amputees by long-term spinal cord stimulation: Long-term follow-up study over 5 years. J Neurosurg 52:346, 1980.

163. Krainick JU, Thoden U: Spinal cord stimulation in post-amputation pain. In Siegfriend J, Zimmerman M (eds): Phantom and Stump Pain. New York, Springer, 1981.

164. Nielson KD, Adams JE, Hosobuchi Y: Phantom limb pain: Treatment with dorsal column stimulator. J Neurosurg 42:301, 1975.

165. Wester K: Dorsal column stimulation in pain treatment. Acta Neurol Scand 75:151, 1987.

166. Hunt WE, Goodman JH: Dorsal column stimulation for phantom limb pain. J Neurosurg 43:250, 1975.

167. Levy RM, Lamb S, Adams JE: Treatment of chronic pain by deep brain stimulation: Long-term follow-up and review of the literature. Neurosurgery 21:885, 1987.

168. Mundinger F, Nermuller H: Programmed transcutaneous (TNS) and central (DBS) stimulation for control of phantom limb pain and causalgia: A new method for treatment. In Siegfriend J, Zimmerman M (eds): Phantom and Stump Pain. New York, Springer, 1981.

169. Lawrence RM: Persistent limb pain in below-knee amputee. JAMA 236:822, 1976.

170. Steinbach TV, Nadvorna H, Arazi D: A five year follow-up study of phantom limb pain in posttraumatic amputees. Scand J Rehabil Med 14:203, 1982.

171. Monga TN, Jaksic T: Acupuncture in phantom limb pain. Arch Phys Med Rehabil 62:229, 1981.

172. Levine JD, Gormley J, Fields HL: Observations on the analgesic effects of needle puncture (acupuncture). Pain 2:149, 1976.

173. Fukui S, Shigemori S, Komoda Y, et al: Phantom pain with beneficial response to electroconvulsive therapy (ECT) and regional cerebral blood flow (rCBF) studied with xenon-CT. Pain Clinic 13:355, 2002.

174. Rasmussen KG, Rummans TA: Electroconvulsive therapy for phantom limb pain. Pain 85:297, 2000.

175. Sherman RA, Gall N, Gormley J: Treatment of phantom limb pain with muscular relaxation training to disrupt the pain-anxiety-tension cycle. Pain 6:47, 1979.

176. Dougherty J: Relief of phantom limb pain after EMG biofeedback-assisted relaxation: A case report. Behav Res Ther 18:355, 1980.

177. Seigel EF: Control of phantom limb pain by hypnosis. Am J Clin Hypnosis 21:285, 1979.

178. Cedercreutz C: Hypnotic treatment of phantom sensations in 100 amputees. Acta Chir Scand 107:158, 1954.

179. Oakley DA, Whitman LG, Halligan PW: Hypnotic imagery as a treatment for phantom limb pain: Two case reports and a review. Clin Rehabil 16:368, 2002.

180. Belleggia G, Birbaumer N: Treatment of phantom limb pain with combined EMG and thermal biofeedback: A case report. Appl Psychophysiol Biofeedback 26:141, 2001.

181. Frischenschlager O, Pucher I: Psychological management of pain. Disabil Rehabil 24:416, 2002.

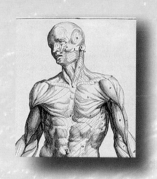

Part C

PAIN OF MALIGNANT ORIGIN

Identification and Treatment of Cancer Pain Syndromes

Steven D. Waldman

Pain is extremely prevalent in cancer patients. It is a major impediment to an adequate quality of life and may undermine efforts to assess and treat the underlying disease.[1] Pain severe enough to require treatment with opioids occurs in about one third of patients undergoing active treatment and in more than two thirds of those with advanced disease.[2] Although extensive clinical experience indicates that most cancer patients can attain acceptable pain relief, there is compelling evidence that treatment often is inadequate.[2,3] In a small portion of patients, this is due to the refractoriness of pain or to the patient's reluctance to comply with an effective therapy; far more often, however, uncontrolled cancer pain reflects a failure of clinical management. Physicians and nurses often seem unaware of the problem of cancer pain and frequently compromise treatment with inappropriate concerns about the risks of therapy (particularly addiction) and ignorance about the assessment and treatment of pain.[2,4]

A comprehensive approach to managing cancer pain can have a gratifying outcome and should be reviewed as a fundamental element in the treatment of the cancer patient. Simple pharmacologic approaches alone can provide relief in more than 70% of cancer patients with pain; and other treatment modalities, which include nerve blocks and neurodestructive procedures, can help many others.[3] This review describes the basic principles of pain evaluations and treatment in cancer patients and discusses recent advances that may further improve the results of therapy.

■ PAIN

Pain assessment in the cancer patient requires understanding of the relationships among pain, nociception, and suffering.[5] Nociception refers to the activity in the afferent nervous system induced by potentially tissue-damaging stimuli. A comprehensive assessment will identify a nociception lesion in most patients with cancer pain. Pain is the perception of nociception. It is strongly influenced by affective and cognitive processes unique to the individual. These processes may result in an intensity of pain that is either greater or less than that anticipated by the degree of tissue damage. Suffering is a construct that refers to a more global response, which is related to unrelieved symptoms (including pain) and many perceived losses—including those related to evolving physical disability, social isolation, financial concerns, loss of role in the family, and fear of death. It is important for the clinician to recognize that suffering may occur in the absence of active nociception.

Clinical interventions targeted solely at the complaint of pain—particularly at the nociceptive component—are unlikely to measurably benefit patients whose complaints are an expression of a more global degree of suffering. Indeed, such treatment plans often are perceived by patient and family as lacking in compassion.

■ ESTABLISHING A PAIN DIAGNOSIS

The goals of pain assessment in the cancer patient are to identify the underlying nociceptive lesion, clarify the various non-nociceptive contributions to the pain, and determine the degree and causes of suffering. From this information a "pain diagnosis" can be elaborated; practically, this is a problem list that can be used to target specific problems for treatment and organize a multimodal therapeutic approach.

The first step in establishing the diagnosis is to characterize the pain complaint fully. Specific inquiries should evaluate onset, duration, severity, quality, location, radiation, temporal characteristics, provocative and palliative factors, and course. A medical history should access both previous and current use of analgesic and other drugs. The physicians should elicit any history of chronic nonmalignant pain, chronic opioids use and/or substance abuse. The extent of disease at the time of evaluation and the patients' general medical condition also should be assessed. An integral part of this initial evaluation is the assessment of the affective, behavioral, and social disturbances related to the pain. Cancer pain patients commonly experience anxiety and vegetative signs, such as sleep disturbances, lassitude, and anorexia.

After taking an adequate history, the physician should perform a general medical and neurologic examination. The physical examination, like the history, should attempt to clarify the specific pain syndrome, determine the extent of the disease, clarify the nature of the specific nociceptive lesions underlying the pain, and assess the degree of physical impairment (Table 29–1).[6]

After obtaining a working clinical diagnosis from the history and physical examination, the physician should consider appropriate laboratory, or electrodiagnostic, or radiographic procedures; these evaluations further clarify the nature of the nociceptive lesion presumed to underlie the pain. The primary clinician must carefully review all test results, including radiographs, to obtain clinicopathologic correlation for the pain. It is important that the clinician avoid overreliance on past test results when there is a change in the patient's clinical status if incorrect diagnosis is to be avoided. When in doubt, this is one clinical setting where repeating tests will often yield important clinical information. Effective analgesic treatment should be provided to the patient throughout the evaluation, particularly during procedures; the psy-

Table 29–1

Cancer Pain Syndromes

Pain Syndromes Associated with Direct Tumor Involvement

Bone
Base of skull
  Orbital
  Parasellar
  Sphenoidal sinus
  Middle cranial fossa
  Clivus
  Jugular foramen
  Occipital condyle
Vertebral body
  Atlantoaxial
  C7 to T1
  L1
  Sacral
  Generalized bone pain

Nerves
Peripheral nerve syndromes
  Paraspinal tumor
  Chest wall tumor
  Retroperitoneal tumor
Leptomeningeal metastases
Painful polyneuropathy
Brachial, lumbar, sacral plexopathies
Epidural spinal cord compression

Viscera

Blood vessels

Mucous membranes

Pain Associated with Cancer Therapy

Postoperative
Thoracotomy
Mastectomy
Radical surgery of the neck
Amputation

Postchemotherapy
Painful polyneuropathy
Aseptic necrosis of bone
Pseudorheumatism caused by steroids

Postradiation
Fibrosis of brachial or lumbosacral plexus
Myelopathy
Radiation-induced peripheral nerve tumors
Mucositis

Pain Indirectly Related or Unrelated to Cancer

Myofascial pain

Postherpetic neuralgia

Chronic headache syndromes

chological impact of the evaluation will be far less averse and the quality of tests enhanced if the patient's cooperation is not compromised by pain.

The pain diagnosis can be clarified in most patients after this comprehensive assessment is completed. The problem list may include the pain itself; physical and psychological disturbances contributing to the pain; associated symptoms;

physical impairments; and psychological, social or familial problems that independently augment the patient's suffering. These problems can be prioritized according to their impact on the patient's quality of life and allow planned therapeutic interventions to be staged appropriately.

■ THERAPEUTIC APPROACHED TO CANCER PAIN MANAGEMENT

Antineoplastic therapies should be considered as a first step in the analgesic management of patients whose pain is a direct effect of the neoplasm. Radiotherapy provides adequate analgesia in more than one half of patients treated and pain is a common primary indication for this modality.[7] Although toxicity and unpredictable pain relief limit the utility of chemotherapy as an analgesic intervention, some patients obtain symptom relief from the administration of chemotherapeutic drugs.[8] The variable analgesic response and risks associated with surgical extirpation of a neoplasm limit surgery as a primary analgesic therapy. However, tumor resection performed for other indications, such as vertebral body resection for epidural spinal cord compression, may provide analgesia.[9] Although all patients with cancer pain should be considered for antineoplastic therapy, most pain management depends on the expert application of one or more primary analgesic modalities. Pharmacotherapy is the most important of these.

■ PHARMACOLOGIC APPROACHES

Three categories of analgesic medications—nonsteroidal anti-inflammatory drugs (NSAIDs), opioid analgesics, and the so-called adjuvant analgesics—are used in the pharmacotherapy of cancer pain. The Cancer Pain Relief Program of the World Health Organization has developed guidelines for the selection of drugs from these categories.[10] The approach, known as the "analgesic ladder," can be summarized as follows: For mild pain, an NSAID is administered and an adjuvant is added if a specific indication for one exists. If the regimen fails to control pain or the patient presents with moderate to serve pain, a so-called "weak" oral opioid is administered in combination with an NSAID; again, adjuvants are added if indicated. If maximal doses of this opioid do not control the pain or the patient's pain is severe, a so-called "strong" opioid is administered, with or without an NSAID or adjuvant drugs. Considerable expertise is required to appropriately select and administer specific drugs within this general framework. Guidelines are described subsequently.

Nonsteroidal Anti-inflammatory Drugs and the COX-2 Inhibitors

All NSAIDs including the COX-2 inhibitors inhibit cyclooxygenase, thereby reducing tissue levels of prostagladins.[11] This anti-inflammatory effect probably contributes to the analgesic efficacy of NSAIDs and is the basis for the traditional view that these drugs are peripherally acting—although a central mechanism may also underlie the analgesic effects of this class. Although the COX-2 inhibitors have a more favorable gastrointestinal side effect profile relative to the nonselective

NSAIDs, recent concerns about their role in causing increased cardiac side effects makes their use in cancer pain management less clear.[12] The analgesia provided by NSAIDs is characterized by a ceiling dose, beyond which additional dosage increments produce no further analgesic effect. Although there are published dosing guidelines for each NSAID, individual differences in both the ceiling dose and dose-related toxicity vary widely; consequently, the standard recommended dose my be inappropriate for any given patient. This consideration is especially salient in cancer patients, who may have altered NSAID pharmacokinetics or a predisposition to adverse effects on the basis of multisystem disease or the coadministration of other drugs. This observation suggests the value of dose titration in this population. The analgesia provided by NSAIDs also is characterized by a lack of demonstrable tolerance or physical dependence.

Drug Selection and Administration

The NSAIDs (Table 29–2) are useful alone for mild to moderate pain and, in combination with opioids, provide additive analgesia to patients with more severe pain. Anecdotally, patients with bone pain or pain associated with grossly inflammatory lesions appear most likely to benefit from NSAIDs.

NSAIDs must be used cautiously in the elderly and they should be considered relatively contraindicated in cancer patients with renal insufficiency, congestive heart failure, hypertension, or a remote history of peptic ulcer disease. In patients with mild bleeding or ulcer diatheses, including some patients with thrombocytopenia or coagulopathy, a history of peptic ulcer disease, or concurrent use of acrogenic medications such as steroid, the preferred drugs are those with the least potential to damage the gastric mucosa and to impair platelet aggregation. These drugs are acetaminophen and two salicylates, choline magnesium trisalicylate and salsalate.[13] Acetaminophen traditionally has been considered the safest drug for patients with significantly impaired renal function; however, recent evidence of renal toxicity from long-term acetaminophen use suggests caution in its use.[14] Acetaminophen should also be used cautiously in patients with significant hepatic disease. Of the various subclasses, the toxicity of the pyrazoles—of which only phenylbutazone is available in the United States—is greatest; however, the use of the drug has been supplanted by newer NSAIDs.

It is reasonable to explore the dose-response relationship when NSAIDs are administered to cancer patients. Because the clinician cannot know if the optimal NSAID dose for a given patient is higher or lower than the standard recommended dose, therapy should be initiated with a relatively low dose and the dose should then be increased to identify the ceiling dose or most efficacious dose that yields tolerable side effects. Using ibuprofen as an example, the clinician should consider that the ceiling dose has been reached if an increase in the dose from 400 mg four times daily to 600 mg four times daily produces no additional analgesia. If the 400-mg dose is effective, dosing should continue at this level; if it is inadequate, the drug should be discontinued and the trial of another begun. If the higher dose produces additional analgesia but relief is still inadequate and there are no significant side effects, the dose can be increased further.

Dose titration, however, cannot proceed without limit because of the potential for dose-related toxicity. In the absence of studies establishing the safety of very high NSAID

Table 29–2

Simple Analgesics and Nonsteroidal Anti-inflammatory Drugs

Chemical Class	Generic Name	Time Between Doses (h)	Recommended Starting Doses (mg/d) *	Maximum Recommended Doses (mg/d)
p-Aminophenol	Acetaminophen	4-6	1400	6000

Comments: Overdosage produces hepatic toxicity. Not anti-inflammatory and thus not preferred as first-line analgesic or coanalgesic in patients with bone pain or pain due to grossly inflammatory lesions. Lack of gastrointestinal (GI) or platelet toxicity may be important in some cancer patients.

Salicylates	Aspirin	4-6	1600	6000

Comments: Standard for comparison. May be tolerated as well as some of the newer NSAIDs.

	Diflunisal	12	1000 ×1, then 500 q12h	1500

Comment: Less GI toxicity than aspirin

	Salsalate	12	1500 × 1 then 1000 q12h	4000
	Choline magnesium trisalicylate	12	1500 × 1 then 1000 q12h	4000

Comments: Unlike other NSAIDs, these have minimal GI toxicity and no platelet aggregation, despite potent anti-inflammatory effects. May be particularly useful in some patients.

Propionic acids	Ibuprofen	4-8	1200	4200

Comment: Available over the counter

	Naproxen	12	500	1000
	Naproxen sodium	12	550	1100
	Fenoprofen	6	800	3200
	Ketoprofen	6-8	150	300
Acetic acids	Indomethacin	8-12	75	200

Comments: Available in sustained-release and rectal formulations. Higher incidence of side effects, particularly GI and central nervous system, than propionic acids.

	Tolmetin	6-8	600	2000
	Sulindac	12	300	400

Comment: Some reports suggest less renal toxicity than other NSAIDs.

	Diclofenac sodium	6	75	200
Oxicams	Piroxicam	24	20	40

Comment: Administration of 40 mg for more than 3 weeks is associated with high incidence of peptic ulcer, particularly in the elderly.

Fenamates	Mefenamic acid	6	500 × 1, then 250 q6h	1000

Comment: Not recommended for use longer than 1 week and, therefore, not indicated in cancer pain therapy.

	Meclofenamic	6-8	150	400
Pyrazoles	Phenylbutazone	6-8	300	400

Comments: Not a first-line drug because of risk of serious bone marrow toxicity. Not preferred for cancer pain therapy. If used, frequent monitoring of blood count is needed in early therapy—in addition to other tests.

*Starting dose should be one half to two thirds of recommended dose in the elderly, those on multiple drugs, and those with renal insufficiency. Doses must be individualized. Low initial doses should be titrated upward if tolerated and clinical effect is inadequate. Doses can be incrementally increased weekly. Studies of NSAIDs in the cancer population are meager; dosing guidelines are thus empirical.

doses in the cancer population, the physician must base selection for the maximum NSAID dose on clinical experience and customary use. A reasonable maximum is 1.5 to 2 times the standard recommended dose. If relatively high doses (higher then the standard recommended dose) are used, patients should be monitored every 1 to 2 months for occult gastrointestinal (GI) bleeding or changes in renal or hepatic function.

The administration of an NSAID must continue for a duration adequate to judge clinical effects. The efficacy of a drug can usually be determined in 2 to 3 weeks. Clinical experience suggests that 1 week is typically long enough to clarify the need for further dose titration during the initial trial of a drug.

If an NSAID proves to be ineffective, consideration should be given to a trial of another. Because patients may respond poorly to one NSAID but very well to another, switching to a different drug is reasonable if the target symptom continues to be mild pain (or mild residual pain during opioid therapy).

Opioid Analgesics

Effective administration of opioids requires a working knowledge of pharmacology and dosing principles in cancer pain. The most important points of these dosing guidelines are summarized below.[15]

Opioid Selection and Administration

Opioid selection is based on a variety of pharmacologic factors and patient variables. Important considerations include the division of opioids into "weak" and "strong" opioid class, differential toxicities, pharmacokinetic distinctions, and duration of effect (Table 29–3). The so-called "weak" opioids are those typically administered orally to patients with mild to moderate pain; they include preparations containing codeine, propoxyphene, oxycodone, hydrocodone, or dihydrocodeine. Meperidine and pentazocine are sometimes used but are not recommended for the reasons discussed subsequently.

It is important to recognize that, with the exception of pentazocine, none of these drugs has a ceiling dose, the property that would be the pharmacologic basis for their designation as "weak." Rather, their customary use at relatively low doses, which are adequate only to treat moderate pain in non-tolerant patients, is based on other consideration, such as toxicity at high doses (e.g., seizures from meperidine, psychotomimetic effects form pentazocine, and possible GI intolerance from codeine). Recognition that these drugs are not inherently weak provides added therapeutic flexibility because if the patient's pain is not controlled at the usual doses, and the drug is well tolerated, consideration can be given to increasing the dose, rather than switching to another drug.

In the United States, the reasonable "weak" opioid for the second rung of the analgesic ladder is typically a combination product containing an NSAID and an opioid, such as 30 to 60 mg of codeine or 5 mg of oxycodone combined with 325 mg of aspirin or acetaminophen. The dose of this drug can be increased until the risks associated with the NSAID become prohibitive. With an acetaminophen- or aspirin-containing product, three tablets every 4 hours is a prudent maximum dose.

Table 29–3

Agonist Opioid Analgesics

Drug	Dose (mg) Equianalgesic to Morphine Sulfate 10 mg*	Peak Effect (h)	Duration(h)	Toxicity
Morphine	10 mg IM	0.5-1	3-6	Constipation, nausea, sedation most common; respiratory depression most serious; itch and urinary retention uncommon
Controlled-release morphine	20-60 PO	3-4	8-12	Same as morphine
Hydromorphone	1.5 IM	0.5-1	3-4	Same as morphine
	7.5 PO	1-2	3-4	
	Comment: Used for multiple routes			
Oxymorphone	1 IM	0.5-1	3-6	Same as morphine
	10 rectally	1.5-3	4-6	
	Comment: No oral formulation			
Meperidine hydrochloride	75 IM	0.5-1	3-4	Same as morphine, plus CNS excitation. Contraindicated in those taking monoamine oxidase inhibitors
	Comment: Not preferred for cancer pain because of potential toxicity.			
Heroin	5 IM	0.5-1	4-5	Same as morphine
Methadone hydrochloride	10 IM	0.5-1.5	4-6	Same as morphine
	20 PO			
	Comments: Risk of delayed toxicity caused by accumulation is a significant problem; dosing should start on prn basis, with close monitoring.			
Codeine	130 IM	1.5-2	3-6	Same as morphine
	200 PO			
	Comments: Usually is combined with NSAID.			
Propoxyphene Hydrochloride	?	1.5-2	3-6	Same as propoxyphene hydrochloride
Hydrocodone bitartrate	?	0.5-1	3-4	Same as morphine

*Dose that provides analgesia equivalent to 10 mg intramuscular morphine.
IM, intramuscularly; PO, by mouth; prn, as needed,

The opioids can be divided into the pure agonist class (e.g., morphine, hydromorphone, methadone, meperidine, and oxycodone) and the agonist-antagonist class (pentazocine, nalbuphine, dezocine, butorphanol, and buprenorphine). The latter class is characterized by a balance between agonists and competitive antagonists at one or more of the opioid receptors; based on receptor interactions, these drugs can be additionally categorized into partial agonists and the mixed agonist-antagonists, which include pentazocine, nalbuphine, dezocine, and butorphanol.[16]

Agonist-antagonist drugs are characterized by a lesser propensity to produce physical dependence, and by a ceiling effect for respiratory depression and, probably, for analgesia. These drugs have the potential to reverse effects in patients receiving agonist opioids. Administration to patients physically dependent on an agonist drug may cause an abstinence syndrome. The mixed agonist-antagonist subclass, particularly pentazocine, also has prominent psychotomimetic effects. These characteristics, combined with the lack of oral formulations, justify the conclusions that agonist-antagonist drugs are not preferred for cancer pain management. The only exception to this generalization may be sublingual buprenorphine, which has achieved some acceptance due to the potential value of the route of administration and its relatively long duration of action.

Thus, the management of severe cancer pain in the tolerant patient generally relies on the pure agonist drugs—morphine, hydromorphone, and methadone. Oxycodone as a single entity is sometimes used as well. Meperidine is not preferred because it is metabolized to normeperidine, a compound with significant central nervous system toxicity, including myoclonus, tremulousness, and seizures.

In most countries, morphine is the first-line drug for cancer pain. New information about morphine metabolites may influence this use, however. Morphine is metabolized to an active compound, morphine 6-glucuronide, which is cleared by the kidney. The metabolite may contribute to the clinical effects of the parent compound, particularly in patients with relatively high concentrations due to renal insufficiency. Patients with renal failure have been reported who developed respiratory compromise during morphine treatment and were found to have high levels of the metabolite in the plasma, with no measurable morphine.[17] Given the available data, it is reasonable to administer morphine cautiously to patients with stable renal insufficiency and to consider an alternative opioid in those with unstable renal function, in whom the amount of morphine 6-glucuronide may change and unpredictably influence drug effects.

The most important pharmacokinetic parameter in drug selection is its half-life. Regardless of the drug, dose, or route of administration, four to five half-lives are required to approach steady-state plasma levels. This becomes a clinical issue only in the case of methadone, the half-life of which may be so long that drug accumulation can continue for a week or longer when dosing is instituted or the dose is increased. Failure to recognize this potential for accumulation has resulted in serious delayed toxicity. Methadone should be used as a second-line agent in patients with the potential for significantly prolonged drug metabolism and those who are at particular risk of adverse drug effects. Such patients include the elderly, those with organ failure (lungs, kidneys, liver, or brain), and those whose compliance or communication with the physician is in question.

Another important consideration in opioid selection is duration of analgesic effect. The short-half-life opioids, such as morphine and hydromorphone, must be administered at least every 4 hours, whereas methadone—the opioid with the longest half-life—can often be administered every 6 hours and sometimes even less frequently. Controlled-release formulations of morphine and other opioid agonists can be given every 8 to 12 hours.

In summary, morphine, oxycodone, and hydromorphone are the preferred first-line drugs for severe cancer pain in the elderly and in those with major organ dysfunction. However, morphine should be used cautiously, if at all, in the patient with changing renal function. In the younger, compliant patient without organ failure, therapy can begin with morphine, or any other drug on the third rung of the "analgesic ladder." A favorable previous experience with one of these drugs may be considered in this decision. Patients who may benefit from less frequent dosing should be considered for a trial of controlled-release morphine, usually after titration with an immediate-release morphine formulation.

The physician should start with the lowest dose that produces analgesia. Relatively nontolerant patients with severe pain, including those who have failed a trial with a "weak" opioid, are generally administered an opioid intramuscularly at a dose equivalent to 5 to 10 mg of morphine. Patients who are switched from a higher dose of an opioid to an alternative drug should begin at a dose that is one half to two thirds the equianalgesic dose of their current medication. This reduction is recommended in the expectation that a new drug will have relatively greater effects, due to the occurrence of incomplete cross-tolerance between opioids. To avoid side effects, elderly patients and those with compromised hepatic or renal function should receive even lower starting doses. Clinical experience also suggests that a switch to methadone should be accompanied by a greater decrement, perhaps to one third the equianalgesic dose.

Dose titration is the most important principle in opioid therapy. The dose should be gradually increased until favorable effects occur or intolerable and unmanageable side effects supervene. If pain remains severe after the initial dose, the subsequent dose can be doubled. If partial analgesia occurs, dose titration can usually follow on a daily basis. A useful approach involves concurrently administering a fixed, around-the-clock dose together with a "rescue dose," which is usually equal to 5% to 10% of the total daily dose and is offered "as needed" every 1 to 2 hours for "breakthrough" pain. This approach provides the patient with some personal control over analgesic dosing and can be used to estimate the increment in the fixed dose. For example, a patient receiving 100 mg of morphine every four hours, who required six "rescue" doses of 60 mg during the previous 24 hours, has demonstrated the need for at least an additional 360 mg/day; hence, it is reasonable to increase the fixed dose to 160 mg every 4 hours and simultaneously to increase the "rescue" dose to 90 mg, thereby maintaining it at 10% of the total daily dose.

For all agonist drugs except methadone, the "rescue" dose medication should be the same as the drug administered on a fixed basis. When methadone is administered around the clock, concurrently administering a short-half-life opioid, such as morphine or hydromorphone, will avoid unanticipated toxicity from drug accumulation.

Scheduled around-the-clock dosing should be used in all patients who endure relatively constant pain. It is important to recognize, however, that "as needed" dosing may be valuable in selected circumstances. The use of the "rescue dose" was described previously. In addition, "as needed" dosing without a concurrent fixed dosing regimen may have advantages in some settings, including (1) defining the analgesic requirement in a nontolerant patient who is beginning opioid therapy; (2) titrating methadone at less risk of drug accumulation; and (3) facilitating dose changes during rapidly changing nociception (such as that occurring with radiotherapy to a painful bony lesion).

The physician should always choose an appropriate route of administration. If the patient can swallow and absorb the drug, the oral route is always preferable. Many other routes of opioid administration are available, however, and clinicians who manage patients with cancer pain should have knowledge of those used more frequently (Table 29–4). However, the usual starting place for the implementation of opioid therapy in the management of cancer pain is with immediate-release oral formulations rather than immediately utilizing sustained-release formulations and novel routes of administration (e.g., transdermal fentanyl).

The clinician must also be aware of equianalgesic doses. As noted, awareness of equianalgesic doses is necessary to safely change drugs or routes of administration. These ratios, which were developed from controlled single-dose studies of relative potency, are available for parenteral and oral dosing.

The relative potency of drug administration by other routes (e.g., epidural or sublingual) is not known and complicates the management of patients treated with these approaches.

It is important to recognize that published equianalgesic doses should be viewed as broad guidelines. The dose of a new drug must be reduced in all patients due to anticipated incomplete cross-tolerance, and this reduction should be greater in patients predisposed to adverse effects because of advanced age or organ failure. Dose titration is almost always required after a switch to a new drug or route of administration.

Side Effects

Opioid side effects vary greatly among patients. The pattern and severity of side effects vary from drug to drug in the same patient. This observation suggests that a trial with an alternative opioid should be undertaken if tolerable side effects occur during dose titration. Early and appropriate management of side effects may enhance patient comfort and permit dose escalation to proceed.

Common side effects include constipation, sedation, and nausea. Opioid-induced constipation is so common that many practitioners believe that laxatives should always be administered concurrently with the opioid. This probably is the best course in the elderly and others with predisposing factors for constipation (e.g., use of other drugs with constipating effects or intra-abdominal neoplasm); younger patients without these factors can be observed for the development of constipation and treated only if needed. Constipation can usually be managed by an increase in fiber consumption and the use of

Table 29–4

Routes of Administration

Route	Comment
Oral	Preferred in cancer pain management
Buccal	Variable absorption limits clinical utility
Sublingual	Efficacy of morphine controversial
Rectal	Available for morphine, oxymorphone, and hydromorphone. Customarily used as if dose is equianalgesic to oral dose
Transdermal	Kinetics that mimic continuous infusion
Intranasal	May be efficacious with some drugs
Subcutaneous Repetitive bolus Continuous infusion Continuous infusion with patient-controlled analgesia (PCA)	Recent advent of ambulatory infusion pumps permits outpatient continuous infusion. Can be accomplished with any drug with a parenteral formulation
Intravenous Repetitive bolus Continuous infusion PCA (with or without infusion)	This route indicated if other routes unavailable or not tolerated. Infusion most useful in obviating bolus effect (i.e., peak concentration toxicity or pain breakthrough at the trough)
Epidural	Epidural catheter can be percutaneous portal, depending on life expectancy. Intrathecal usually administered via subcutaneous pump.
Intracerebroventricular	Rarely indicated but efficacious

one of the following therapies:[18] (1) an osmotic laxative, such as magnesium citrate, milk of magnesia, or sodium citrate, administered every 2 or 3 days; (2) chronic administration of a stool softener and a contact laxative (senna, bisacodyl, or phenolphthalein); or (3) chronic administration of lactulose, beginning at a dose of 15 to 30 mL twice daily, and titrated upward as needed. The choice of therapy should be based on the specific needs and desires of the patient.

Sedation, if not transitory, can usually be reversed with a small dose of a psychostimulant, with dextroamphetamine or methlyphenidate.[19] The starting dose is 2.5 to 5 mg once or twice daily and is gradually increased if needed. Some patients also benefit from a change in the dosing interval or opioid administered.

Nausea usually can be managed by an antiemetic,, such as metoclopramide, prochlorperazine, haloperidol, or ode-stronon. Because tolerance to this effect often develops within 1 or 2 weeks, it is often useful to administer one of these drugs on a fixcd schedule for a brief time after nausea begins, then discontinuing it to determine if treatment is still needed. If movement induced nausea or vertigo is prominent, an antivertiginous medication, such a meclizine, cyclizine, or scopolamine, may be helpful. Finally, if epigastric fullness or early satiety is a significant complaint, a trial of meto-clopramide, a drug that enhances gastric emptying, is appropriate.

Opioid drugs can cause psychotomimetic effects (ranging from nightmares to frank psychosis), dry mouth, itch, or urinary retention (usually in men with prostatism or patients with pelvic cancer). Management includes discontinuation of other nonessential drugs with additive side effects, a change to an alternative opioid, and symptomatic treatment, if available (e.g., antihistamines for those with uncomfortable itch).

Tolerance

The physician should be aware of tolerance, a poorly understood phenomenon defined as a need for increasing doses to maintain opioid effects. The need for escalating doses may not reflect the primary effect of tolerance, however, and most patients who require rapidly increasing doses have progression of painful lesions or an increase in the level of psychological distress. Indeed, if progressive disease is not clinically overt, the need for increasing opioid doses should be considered a possible indication for reevaluation of the neoplasm.

When pharmacologic tolerance does occur, it typically manifests as a reduction in the duration of analgesia after a dose. This can usually be managed by dose escalation or an increase in dosing frequency. There is no limit to tolerance and, in an effort to maintain analgesia, doses can become extremely high; for example, a dose higher than that equivalent to 35,000 mg of morphine has been reported.[20]

Tolerance to respiratory depression usually develops rapidly, and drug-induced respiratory compromise is rare in patients receiving chronic opioid therapy. Should respiratory symptoms occur, there is almost always another cause, such as pneumonia or pulmonary embolism. Patients who are receiving high opioid doses may show great sensitivity to the antagonist drugs; therefore, naloxone (0.4 mg in 10 mL of saline) should be given slowly until the respiratory rate improves. A return to consciousness, which is often accompanied by a severe narcotic abstinence syndrome and the return of pain, should not be viewed as the goal of this inter-vention. Repeated doses of naloxone are usually required due to its relatively short half-life.

Distinction Between Physical Dependence and Addiction

Physical dependence is a pharmacologic property of opioid drugs defined by an abstinence syndrome that occurs after abrupt discontinuation of the drug or administration of an antagonist. Presumably, all patients administered high enough doses for a long enough period of time will become physically dependent. This presents no difficulties in management if the opioid dose is tapered before discontinuation and antagonist drugs, including the agonist-antagonist analgesics, are avoided.

In contrast, addiction is a psychological and behavioral syndrome characterized by psychological dependence (drug craving and overwhelming concern with drug acquisition) and aberrant drug-related behaviors, including drug selling or hoarding, acquisition of drugs from nonmedical sources, and unsanctioned dose escalation. Unlike physical dependence, there is little evidence to support the conclusion that otherwise normal patients with painful medical diseases are at substantial risk of developing addiction from the administration of opioids in a medical context.[21] It is uncommon for addiction to develop in a patient with no drug abuse history who is administered opioids for the treatment of cancer pain. Concern about addiction should never inhibit the aggressive management of this symptom.

Adjuvant Analgesics

Adjuvant analgesics are drugs with other specific indications that may be effective in the management of selected types of pain. They include the tricyclic antidepressants, anticonvulsants, neuroleptics, corticosteroids, and other miscellaneous drugs.

Tricyclic Antidepressants

There is extensive literature supporting the use of tricyclic antidepressants as analgesics in a wide variety of chronic pain syndromes.[22] In cancer patients, these drugs generally are administered for neuropathic pain (usually related to nerve infiltration or compression) or pain associated with prominent sleep disturbance or depression. To reduce the risk of side effects, it is usually prudent to titrate the opioid first and then add the adjuvant.

The initial dose of a tricyclic antidepressant should be low (e.g., 10 to 25 mg of amitriptyline). If tolerated, doses should be titrated upward gradually. The analgesic dose is usually 50 to 150 mg/day, typically administered as a single nighttime dose. Higher doses should be administered if the drug is ineffective and has produced no significant side effects. Depression is a prominent component of the pain syndrome.

Anticonvulsants

Anticonvulsants can be useful in the management of paroxysmal lancinating neuropathic pains,[23] such as those accompanying nerve infiltration by tumor. Gabapentin, carbamazepine, phenytoin, clonazepam, and valproate are used for this indication. Baclofen is a non-anticonvulsant drug that also may be efficacious in managing paroxysmal lancinating neuropathic pains. These drugs can have significant hematologic or hepatic adverse effects, and cancer patients should be monitored carefully during treatment.

Oral Local Anesthetics

Mexiletine has demonstrated efficacy in painful diabetic polyneuropathy[24] and has been used to treat diverse neuropathic pain.[25] This drug is only available in parenteral formulation and has a side-effect profile, including its limited applicability to bedridden patients with advanced disease; in this setting, the sedative and anxiolytic properties of the drug can be salutary. Given the lack of evidence of analgesic effects and potential for side effects, other neuroleptics should be considered as second-line agents for continuous neuropathic pain that is refractory to other measures. These drugs remain primary therapy for pain patients with delirium or nausea.

Corticosteroids

Methylprednisolone is efficacious as an analgesic in patients with advanced cancer.[26] Clinical experience suggests that any of them may be useful in patients with pain from diffuse bony metastasis or tumor infiltration of neural structures. Dexamethasone is often chosen because of its modest mineralocorticoid effect. Dosing is empirical, and the duration of effect is undetermined.

Miscellaneous Drugs

Although hydroxyzine has been reported to be analgesic,[27] clinical responses at the usual oral doses have been disappointing. The drug may be a reasonable adjuvant in patients with pain complicated by nausea or anxiety.

In addition to corticosteroids, refractory bone pain has been treated with calcitonin, diphosphonates, and L-dopa.[28,29] Although experience with these agents is limited, trials are indicated in select patients with bone pain that is unresponsive to radiotherapy and drug treatment with opioids, NSAIDs, and corticosteroids.

■ NONPHARMACOLOGIC APPROACHES

A majority of cancer patients can achieve adequate pain relief through the expert application of pharmacologic therapies alone. Some attain a better quality of relief or balance between analgesia and side effects through the complementary use of adjunctive nonpharmacologic approaches. One or more of these approaches may become the primary analgesic therapy for the relatively small number of patients who fail to gain any meaningful relief from systemic drugs. The following review describes the most important of the nonpharmacologic therapies used in the management of cancer pain (Table 29–5).

■ ANESTHETIC APPROACHES

Neural Blockade

Neural blockade should be intelligently integrated into the multimodal approach, which includes an optimal trial of opioid therapy (see the first part of this review). For some patients, the early use of neural blockade is indicated to provide immediate relief of uncontrolled pain, thereby allow-

Table 29–5
Nonpharmacologic Approaches to Cancer Pain
Anesthetic approaches
Neural blockade
Intercostal nerve block
Interpleural catheters
Epidural nerve block
Sympathetic nerve block
Celiac plexus block
Neurostimulatory approaches
Physiatric approaches
Neurolytic anesthetic and neurodestructive approaches

ing time for opioid titration. Transient blockade also can be useful for patients with positional pain who must undergo procedures. Neural blockade of longer duration may be appropriate in patients who fail to obtain relief with routine noninvasive procedures.

Intercostal Nerve Block

Intercostal nerve block with a local anesthetic or corticosteroid can be performed at the bedside or in the outpatient setting. This procedure may palliate pain secondary to pathologic rib fractures or chest wall metastasis, post-thoracotomy pain, or right upper quadrant pain secondary to hepatic metastasis.[30] Intercostal blocks also may reduce pain caused by percutaneous drainage devices, such as chest or nephrostomy tubes. Studies have demonstrated a clinically significant improvement in pulmonary function in patients treated with this procedure.[31] The major complication is pneumothorax, which occurs in 0.5% to 1.0% of patients.

Interpleural Catheters

Recent studies have demonstrated that local anesthetic instillation into the pleural space via a catheter may be effective in the management of some acute and chronic cancer pains.[32] This simple technique may be performed at the bedside or on an outpatient basis. Although the primary indications are essentially the same as those for intercostal nerve blocks, several reports suggest that this technique also can reduce pain below the diaphragm.[33] Complications of interpleural catheters are similar to those of intercostal nerve block. If the patient has significant pleural disease or pleural effusion, the dose of local anesthetic must be decreased to avoid toxic blood levels. If long-term use is anticipated, the catheter should be tunneled to avoid the risk of subcutaneous infection and empyema.

Epidural Nerve Block

Epidural nerve block with local anesthetic infusion or repeated local anesthetic injections with or without steroid has been demonstrated to provide pain relief in a variety of cancer pain syndromes.[34] These techniques can be safely performed at the bedside or on an outpatient basis, provided appropriate monitoring and resuscitation equipment are readily available. Epidural nerve blocks can be used to gain rapid control of pain while other approaches are implemented, to facilitate lengthy diagnostic or therapeutic procedures, or to provide primary analgesic therapy for specific syndromes (e.g., steroid-induced spinal compression fractures or acute herpes zoster).

Epidural blockade interrupts both somatic and sympathetic nerve conduction; cardiovascular complications, including hypotension and tachycardia, may occur. Respiratory compromise is possible if there is inadvertent blockade of the phrenic nerve or brain stem respiratory centers. These procedures should be performed only by personnel trained in airway management and resuscitation.

Other major complications of epidural blockade include damage to neural structures, epidural hematoma, and epidural abscess. Although these complications are rare, they may occur more frequently in cancer patients who are immunocompromised and who may have a coagulopathy. In spite of these potential complications, epidural block with local anesthetic and/or steroids has a positive risk-to-benefit ratio when treating cancer pain and this technique is probably underutilized.

Sympathetic Nerve Block

Many cancer pain syndromes are mediated, at least in part, via sympathetic efferent activity (known as sympathetically maintained pain). Syndromes that may benefit from interruption of the sympathetic nervous system by stellate ganglion or lumbar sympathetic nerve block with local anesthetics include postmastectomy pain and acute herpes zoster. Complications of these procedures are uncommon and include bleeding at the injection site, infection, inadvertent dural puncture, and trauma to neural structures. Because sympathetic neural blockade may induce profound cardiovascular changes, the practitioner must be ready to treat hypotension and tachycardia during the procedure.

Celiac Plexus Block

Celiac plexus block, in which a neurolytic solution is injected into the region of the celiac plexus, is useful in the management of pain caused by upper abdominal and retroperitoneal tumors, including the pain of pancreatic malignancy. Extensive clinical experience suggests a very favorable risk-to-benefit ratio with this procedure, and it is appropriate to consider it in selected patients early in the course of pain management.[35] Complications include bleeding, infection, and damage to neural structures or intra-abdominal organs. The incidence of these serious complications is substantially decreased by performing the procedure under the guidance of computed tomography. Because the celiac plexus is a major sympathetic ganglion, profound hypotension and orthostatic changes should be expected and treated aggressively.

Spinal Opioids

Spinal opioid administration, like neural blockade, must be integrated into a comprehensive pain treatment plan. In contrast to local anesthetics, spinal opioids produce effects through activation of opioid receptors in the spinal cord; there is no compromise of sympathetic or motor function.[36]

The short-term use of spinal opioids may be appropriate in patients receiving primary antineoplastic treatments that are expected to provide long-term relief of pain, patients with

severe movement-related pain who are unable to undergo diagnostic or therapeutic procedures, and patients with very severe pain (pain emergencies) that cannot be controlled quickly by other cancer pain treatment modalities. Chronic administration of spinal opioids should not be implemented until more conservative approaches—specifically, trials of systemic opioids—have failed to control the pain without also causing intolerable side effects. Other factors to be considered before implementing a long-term trial include physiologic and behavioral abnormalities that may interfere with the ability of the patient to assess his or her pain relief, the presence of coagulopathy or infection, and the adequacy of the support system necessary to institute this therapy.[37]

Many techniques have been developed to deliver spinal opioids. An implanted pump can be used to administer drugs continuously into the subarachnoid space, and epidural administration can be implemented by using any of a variety of approaches, including a percutaneous catheter, a subcutaneous tunneled catheter connected to an implanted portal, or a tunneled catheter connected to a pump. Epidural opioids can be administered by continuous infusion or repetitive bolus. Although morphine continues to be the agent used most frequently, other opioids, such as hydromorphone, have been delivered successfully, and combinations of opioids and local anesthetics are an innovation that may improve the outcome in some patients who fail to attain adequate relief with spinal opioids alone. The selection of a specific drug, site of delivery, and technique is based on many factors, including the clinical status (e.g., life expectancy) of the patient, characteristics of the drug, and patient preference.[37-39]

Side effects of spinal opioids may or may not be systemically mediated. Because the epidural space is highly vascular; any drug administered via this route will rapidly enter the systemic circulation. If systemic redistribution is sufficiently great, the patient may experience the same side effects that would occur with oral or parenteral administration of the drug. The degree of systemic redistribution is determined by numerous factors, including the lipid solubility of the drug and the dose. The most dreaded side effect of spinal opioids—respiratory depression—is exceedingly rare in the cancer population, presumably as a result of the opioid tolerance induced by previous intake of opioid drugs. Aggressive treatment of side effects may permit continuation of the therapy at analgesic doses.

■ PHYSIATRIC APPROACHES

The use of orthotics and prostheses and the techniques applied in physical and occupational therapy are intended to prevent impairment of function. In addition, however, these approaches may have value as analgesic techniques. For example, a patient with malignant vertebral collapse may obtain considerable relief from back pain with a brace, and an arm splint may benefit a patient whose pain is caused by neoplastic infiltration of the brachial plexus. Aggressive physical therapy may prevent the development of painful contractures or joint ankylosis, and myofascial pains, which are common in the cancer population, may improve with local massage, application of heat and cold, or passive muscle stretching.

Physical and occupational therapy may also enhance the cancer patient's sense of personal control over pain and encourage the maintenance of independent function, with potentially great psychological benefits. The use of physiatric techniques in the management of patients with cancer pain should be expanded.

■ NEUROSTIMULATORY APPROACHES

It is well known that stimulation of afferent neural pathways may relieve pain. The most widely applied of such techniques is transcutaneous nerve stimulation. The safety of this approach suggests that a trial can be recommended for patients with localized pain, particularly neuropathic pain. Beneficial effects, if any, usually are transitory, and other analgesic approaches are almost always necessary. The invasive neurostimulatory procedures, including percutaneous electrical nerve stimulation, dorsal column stimulation, and deep brain stimulation, are rarely used in cancer patients and should be considered only by practitioners experienced in cancer pain therapy. These procedures require an invasive technique to implant the apparatus. Given the immunocompromised, fragile medical status, and limited experiences with these approaches in cancer patients, they have a very limited role in this setting.

■ NEUROLYTIC ANESTHETIC AND NEUROSURGICAL APPROACHES

The use of neurolytic celiac plexus block was discussed previously. Other neurolytic procedures have been developed to interrupt somatosensory transmission at various levels of the nervous system, from peripheral nerves to the cerebrum. Other neurolytic techniques are not intended to block afferent information. These include lobotomy and cingulotomy—which are now rarely performed and purportedly relieve suffering without necessarily altering pain—and chemical or surgical hypophysectomy.[40] Studies of hypophysectomy, which can be performed by injecting alcohol into the pituitary gland, indicate that the procedure can reduce pain from disseminated cancer in a majority of patients for several months. The tumor need not be hormone dependent for the procedure to be successful. The use of neurolytic procedures, most of which are intended to isolate the painful site from the central nervous system, is best limited to patients with localized nociceptive pain. These procedures should be considered only when more conservative approaches have failed to adequately control the pain.

■ PSYCHOLOGICAL APPROACHES

Some patients with cancer pain have psychiatric disorders, such as major depression or anxiety disorder and require formal psychological assessment and treatment.[41] All patients, including those with no psychiatric disease, benefit from supportive interaction with staff, during which disease-related issues can be addressed openly. Some patients also may be candidates for specific cognitive approaches to pain control, including hypnosis, relaxation training, and distraction techniques.[41] Although the latter interventions have not been studied adequately in cancer patients, experience suggests that they may be particularly useful in patients with predictable pain (e.g., pain that accompanies dressing changes) and those with pain that is associated with high levels of anxiety.

■ SUMMARY

Pain management is a compelling issue in the care of patients with cancer. Adequate pain relief allows the patient the greatest opportunity to live normally during the early stages of disease and to have an optimal quality of life if the cancer progresses. Effective symptom control also eases the burden on the family, who otherwise may experience helplessness as uncontrolled pain occurs in a loved one. Ongoing and careful assessment, a systematic approach to pharmacotherapy, and the judicious use of other approaches are fundamental elements of the successful management of cancer pain.

References

1. Levin DN, Cleeland CS, Dar R: Public attitudes toward cancer pain. Cancer 56:2337, 1985.
2. Bonica JJ: Treatment of cancer pain: Current status and future needs. In Fields HL, Dubner R, Cervero F (eds): Advances in Pain Research and Therapy. New York, Raven, Vol 9, p 589, 1985.
3. Ventafridda V, Tamburini M, DeConno F: Comprehensive treatment in cancer pain. In Fields HL, Dubner R, Cervero F (eds): Advances in Pain Research and Therapy. New York, Raven, Vol 9, p 617, 1985.
4. Charap AD: The knowledge, attitudes, and experience of medical personnel treating pain in the terminally ill. Mt Sinai J Med 45:561, 1978.
5. Loeser JD: Perspectives on pain. In Proceeding of First World Conference on Clinical Pharmacology and Therapeutics. London, Macmillan, 1980, p 313.
6. Foley KM: Pain syndromes in patients with cancer. In Bonica JJ, Ventafridda V (eds): Advances in Pain Research and Therapy. New York, Raven Press, Vol 2, pp 9-75, 1979.
7. Gilbert HA, Kagan AR, Nussbaum H, et al: Evaluation of radiation therapy for bone metastases: Pain relief and quality of life. Am J Roentgenol 129(6):1095, 1977.
8. Bonadonna G, Molinari R: Role and limits of anticancer drugs in the treatment of advanced cancer pain. In Bonica JJ, Ventafridda V (eds): Advances in Pain Research and Therapy. New York, Raven Press, Vol 9, p 582, 1985.
9. Williams MR: The place of surgery in terminal care. In Saunders C (ed): The Management of Terminal Malignant Disease. London, Edward Arnold, 1984. p 148.
10. World Health Organization: Cancer Pain Relief. Geneva, World Health Organization, 1986.
11. Goldstein JL, Correa P, Zhao WW, et al: Reduced incidence of gastroduodenal ulcers with celecoxib, a novel cyclooxygenase-2 inhibitor, compared to naproxen in patients with arthritis. Am J Gastroenterol 96:1019, 2001.
12. Mukherjee D, Nissen SE, Topol EJ: Risk of cardiovascular events associated with selective COX-2 inhibitors. JAMA 286:954, 2001.
13. Cohen A, Thomas GB, Coen EE: Serum concentration, safety and tolerance of oral doses of choline magnesium trisalicylate. Curr Ther Res 23:358, 1978.
14. Sandler DP, Smith TC, Weinbert CR, et al: Analgesic use and chronic renal disease. N Engl J Med 320:1238, 1989.
15. Foley KM: The treatment of cancer pain. N Engl J Med 313:84, 1985.
16. Houde RW: Analgesic effectiveness of the narcotic agonist-antagonists. Br J Clin Pharmacol 7:2975, 1979.
17. Osborne RF, Joel SP, Slevin ML: Morphine interactions in renal failure: The role of morphine-6-glucuronide. BMJ 292:1548, 1986.
18. Portenoy RK: Constipation in the cancer patient: Causes and management. Med Clin North Am 71:303, 1987.
19. Bruera E, Brenneis C, Paterson AH, MacDonald RN: Use of methylphenidate as an adjuvant to narcotic analgesics in patients with advanced cancer. J Pain Symptom Manage 4:3, 1989.
20. Coyle N, Adelhardt J, Foley KM, Portenoy RK: Character of terminal illness: Pain and terminal illness in the last 4 weeks of life. J Pain Symptom Manage 5:83, 1990.

21. Portenoy RK: Chronic opioid therapy for nonmalignant pain. J Pain Symptom Manage 5:546, 1990.

22. Getro CJ, Sorkness CA, Howell T: Antidepressants and chronic nonmalignant pain: A review. J Pain Symptom Manage 2:9, 1987.

23. Swerdlow M: Anticonvulsant drugs and chronic pain. Clin Neuropharmacol 7:51, 1984.

24. Dejgard A, Peterson P, Kastrup J: Mexiletine in the treatment of painful diabetic neuropathy. Lancet 1:9, 1988.

25. Beaver WT, Wallenstein SM, Houde RW, Rogers A: A comparison of the analgesic effects of methotrimeprazine and morphine in patients with cancer. Clin Pharmacol Ther 7:436, 1966.

26. Bruera E, Roca E, Cedaro L, et al: Action of oral methylprednisolone in terminal cancer patient: A prospective randomized double-blind study. Cancer Treat Rep 69:751, 1985.

27. Rumore MM, Schlichting DA: Clinical efficacy of antihistamines as analgesics. Pain 25:7, 1986.

28. Hindley AC, Hill AB, Leyland MJ, Wiles AF: A double blind controlled trial of salmon calcitonin in pain due to malignancy. Cancer Chemother Pharmacol 9:71, 1982.

29. Eloma I, Blomquist C, Grohn P, et al: Long-term controlled trial with diphosphonate in patients with osteolytic bone metastasis. Lancet 1:1460, 1983.

30. Waldman SD: Intercostal nerve block. In Waldman S (ed): Atlas of Interventional Pain Management. Philadelphia, Saunders, 2004, pp 241-243.

31. Jakobson S, Fridiksson H, Ivarsson I: Effects of intercostal nerve blocks on pulmonary mechanics in healthy men. Acta Anaesthesiol Scand 24:482, 1980.

32. Kvalheim L, Reiestad F: Interpleural catheter in the management of postoperative pain. Anesthesiology 61:A231, 1984.

33. Waldman SD: Subcutaneous tunneled interpleural catheter in the long term relief of right upper quadrant pain of malignant origin. J Pain Symptom Manage 4:86, 1989.

34. Abram SE: The role of non-neurolytic blocks. In Abram SE (ed): Cancer Pain. Boston, Kluwer, 1989, p 67.

35. Lieberman RP, Waldman SD: Celiac plexus neurolysis. Radiology 175:274, 1990.

36. Coombs DW: Spinal narcotics for intractable cancer pain. In Abram SE (ed): Cancer Pain. Boston, Kluwer; 1989, p 77.

37. Waldman SD, Feldstein GS, Allen ML: Selection of patients for implantable intraspinal narcotic delivery systems. Anesth Analg 65:883, 1986.

38. Waldman SD, Coombs DW: Selection of implantable narcotic delivery systems. Anesth Analg 68:377, 1989.

39. Rawal N: Indications for the use of intraspinal opioids. In Rawal N, Coombs DW (eds): Spinal Narcotics. Boston, Kluwer, 1990, p 43.

40. Waldman SD, Feldstein GS, Allen ML: Neuroadenolysis of the pituitary: Description of a modified technique. J Pain Symptom Manage 2:45, 1987.

41. Fishman B, Loscalzo M: Cognitive-behavioral interventions in management of cancer pain: Principles and applications. Med Clin North Am 71:271, 1987.

chapter 30

Radiation Therapy in the Management of Cancer Pain

Scott C. Cozad

■ HISTORY

Ionizing radiation was coincidentally discovered by Frederic Röntgen, while experimenting with Crooke's tubes. He presented his finding to the Physical Society at Würzburg, Germany on December 28, 1895. The discovery of radium by the Curies followed in 1898. Therapeutic applications, including palliation of pain, ensued almost immediately.[1]

In spite of almost a century of use, the mechanism of action is still unsettled. It is likely that there is some cytotoxic effect as shown by Hillman and colleagues.[2] In experimental prostate cancer cell lines grown in bone, irradiation with photon or neutron beams was evaluated, with or without interleukin-2 (IL-2). A dose-dependent inhibition of tumor growth was found. Additional delay was noted with the addition of IL-2 to photon irradiation but there was no effect of IL-2 alone. Histologic sections confirmed areas of tumor destruction with fibrosis and inflammatory changes. Compared to controls, viable tumor cells were noted in 10% to 40% of the specimens—depending on radiation dose.

The early response for radiation implies other mechanisms as well. Hoskins has found an association between urinary markers of bone resorption before and after radiation and subsequent pain relief—suggesting that bone, not tumor effects determines response.[3] Osteoclastic production of cytokines, which stimulate pain receptors, may also play a role.

This theory fits well with emerging concepts of bone metastases. Normal bone homeostasis is maintained by a balance between osteoclasts and osteoblasts. Both are necessary for the development and propagation of metastases.[4] Products of normal bone turnover such as type I collagen have been shown to attract cancer cells in vitro.[5-7] Once the non-mineralized surface is broken down by collagenase, produced by osteoblasts, bone matrix resorption by osteoclasts can proceed, with resultant release of cytokines that can further attract and promote the growth of bone cancer cells and lead to the recruitment of additional osteoclasts.[8] Once the process has proceeded sufficiently, direct destruction of bone by tumor cells can occur.[8,9] Further clarification of the relative contributions of these different mechanisms will be of importance in defining the role and timing of radiation in the treatment of osseous metastases.

■ INDICATIONS FOR RADIATION IN PAIN MANAGEMENT

Metastatic disease to bone is the most common cause of pain in oncology practice.[10] Approximately 100,000 new cases are diagnosed annually in the United States[11] with an overall incidence of twice this. Pain may be caused by several mechanisms, more than one of which could be present in any given case[10]

- Stimulation of endosteal nerve by humoral or cytokine agents
- Stretching of the periosteum by tumor mass
- Fractures with disruption of the periosteum
- Tumor growth into neural structures

Special cases of this last mechanism would include spinal cord compression with resultant myelopathy, cauda equina syndrome with bowel and bladder dysfunction and lower motor neuron leg weakness, and brachial plexopathy from tumors in the lung apex or celiac plexopathy, usually from pancreatic carcinoma. Other indications are pain secondary to CNS metastases, visceral organ involvement, and trigeminal neuralgia.

■ TESTING

Treatment with radiation depends on accurate diagnosis and precise localization of the lesion(s). Signs or symptoms of pain and neurologic deficits are helpful in generally locating the site of involvement and guiding effective use of imaging studies. Plain films are very specific but lack sensitivity, requiring more than 50% trabecular bone destruction or size of 1.0 cm for detection (Fig. 30–1).[12] Bone scans are much more sensitive with a false-negative rate of about 8% but may have a false-positive rate as high of 40% to 50% depending on the number of lesions. CT scan or MRI may be necessary to confirm the diagnosis of metastases and define the extent of the lesion and associated soft tissue mass if present. These studies are also helpful in identifying the position of normal structures in the area as the

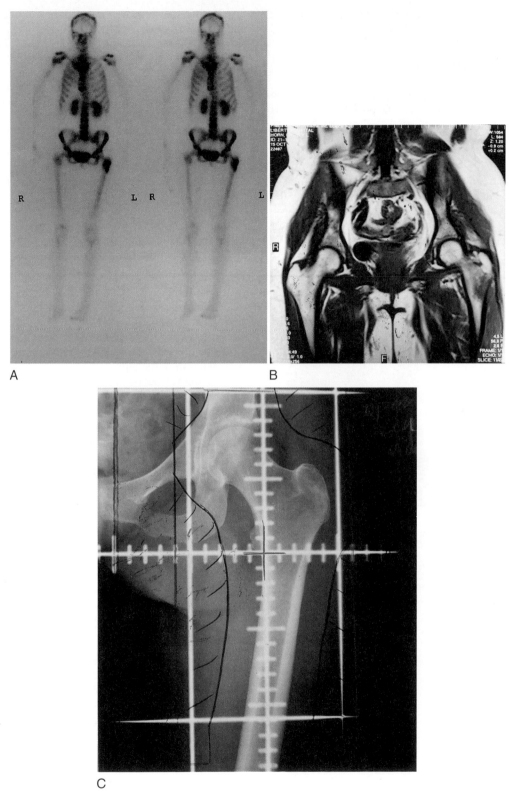

FIGURE 30–1 ■ **A,** Bone scan showing marked uptake in left greater trochanter. **B,** T1-weighted MRI showing marrow replacement. **C,** Simulation film showing treatment field for the patient in **A** and **B**. Note essentially normal appearance of bone in the trochanteric area.

radiation oncologist begins to conceptualize techniques for treatment.

■ TREATMENT TECHNIQUE

After a diagnosis is established, the process of simulation follows to localize the treatment area. Depending on the area to be treated, history of prior radiation, and presence of sensitive normal structures, the simulation-treatment planning process may be either simple or complex (Fig. 30–2). After this step is completed, a set of physical data relating to both the patient and treatment delivery system will have been generated for use in calculating "beam on" time to deliver the prescription dose.

The optimal prescription dose has been the subject of numerous randomized trials (Table 30–1).[13-27] These can be divided into those evaluating different multi-fraction schedules; multi-fraction schedules versus single fraction; and single fraction of higher versus lower dose. These trials have had various entry criteria and methodology for response of evaluation and cannot be directly compared.

In general, approximately one third of patients will have a complete pain response and an additional one third will have a partial response. With the exception of single-fraction treatment of 4.0 Gy there is little, if any, apparent difference in pain response by dose or fractionation. This conclusion is still challenged based on

- Uncontrolled or unreported use of analgesics in most of the studies
- Differences in re-treatment rates in favor of higher dose
- Improvement in remineralization rates at higher dose
- Differences in durability of response
- Lack of toxicity and quality of life data

To address these shortcomings in future trials, a consensus conference has agreed on entry criteria, treatment technique, end points, reporting of analgesic use, and statistical analysis.[28]

In light of the uncertainties, especially of various secondary end points, the specific radiation prescription requires consideration of the anticipated toxicities and life expectancy of the patient. A decision should also take into account patient preference because many patients may prefer a short multi-fraction schedule over single fraction if there is a lower risk of pathologic fracture or re-treatment.[29] The cited studies suggest more favorable responses in patients with breast or prostate cancer and in those with less intense pain at the time of treatment.

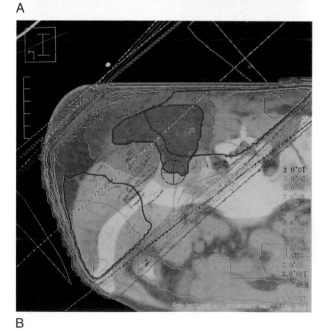

FIGURE 30–2 ■ **A,** CT scan of patient with metastatic prostate carcinoma to the left sacral iliac area with soft tissue mass. **B,** CT generated set-up and isodose lines for the patient in **A.** Note: The solid orange area is the area of soft tissue mass and gross bone involvement. The heavy orange lines are the 100% isodose line. Note the oblique field angles to avoid the bowel in this patient who had previously received radiation to the pelvic area.

■ HEMIBODY RADIATION AND RADIOPHARMACEUTICALS

In an effort to increase pain responses and avoid progression at new sites, wide-field radiation to the upper, middle, or lower body has been piloted by the Radiation Therapy Oncology Group (RTOG).[30] Doses of 6.0 to 8.0 Gy in a single fraction lead to pain relief in 73%; however, severe or life-threatening GI or hemologic toxicity was seen in 10%. A phase III fractionation trial was subsequently performed. Poor response was seen for a dose of 8.0 Gy at 4.0 Gy twice daily compared to 15.0 Gy in five fractions or 12.0 Gy at 3.0 Gy twice daily for 2 days. Overall response was 91% with 12% severe acute toxicity.[31]

An alternative approach is the use of bone-seeking radionuclides including strontium-89 (Sr-89), samarium-153, and rhenium-188. Strontium-89 is the most extensively studied. Its use requires blastic lesions with the overwhelming experience in prostate and breast cancer patients. Initial therapy with these agents requires adequate blood counts, usually a WBC greater than 3000 and platelets greater than 100,000. Repeated treatment can lead to significant cytopenias. Treatment has not consistently led to measurable tumor response, decreased bone turnover markers, or remineralization,[32] making them unsuitable for lytic lesions, bone fracture, cord compression, or neuropathic syndromes.

In a small trial from Germany no difference in pain relief was noted in those treated with Sr-89 compared to placebo.[33]

Table 30–1

Optimal Prescription Dose Trials

	Fractionation Schedule (number of patients in trial)	Pain Relief (partial complete)	Duration	Retreatment	Re-ossification	Fracture	Toxicity
Kirkbride[13]	4.0 Gy × 5	40% (p = 0.03)	—	—	—	—	—
	8.0 Gy × 1 (N = 398)	32%					
Bone Pain Trial Working Party[14]	3.0 Gy × 10 4.0 Gy × 5	78%	—	10%	—	2/378	No change 61% with symptoms
	8.0 Gy × 1 (N = 761)	78%	—	23%		7/383	
Steenland[15]	4.0 Gy × 6	71%	24 weeks	7%	—	2%	No change
	8.0 Gy × 1 (N = 1171)	71%	20 weeks (time to progression)	25%		4%	
Nielsen[16]	5.0 Gy × 4	60%	60% control (for groups as a whole at 6 months)	14/119	—	5%	35%
	8.0 Gy × 1 (N = 239)	60%		25/120		5%	35%
Gaze[17]	4.5 Gy × 5	89%	25 weeks (mean)	—	—	—	37%
	10.0 Gy × 1 (N = 265)	84%	22.5 weeks (mean)				37%
Cole[18]	4.0 Gy × 6	~80%	—	0%	—	1/13	33%/22%
	8.0 Gy × 1 N = 29	~85%		25%		0/16	77%/30% (upper/lower GI)
Price[19]	3.0 Gy × 10	~85%	57%	4/148 (3%)	—	1/148	No change
	8.0 Gy × 1 N = 288	~85%	59% (at 1 year)	15/140 (11%)		0/140	
Hartsell[20] RTOG97-14	3.0 Gy × 10	66%	10% (for group as a whole: progression 3 months)	—	—	—	17%
	8.0 Gy × 1 N = 949	65%					10% Grade 2-4 acute toxicity
Niewald[21]	3.0 Gy × 10	68%	245 days	1	20%	4%	—
	4.0 Gy × 5 N = 100	83%	247 days (mean duration)	1	28%	6%	
Rasmusson[22]	3.0 Gy × 10	69%	12 months	—	~70%	—	Minimal
	5.0 Gy × 3 N = 217	66%	12 months		~76%		Minimal
Okawa[23]	2.0 Gy × 15	76%	—	—	—	—	—
	4.5 Gy × 5	75%					
	2.0 Gy BID × 5 (900) N = 80	78%					
Madsen[24]	4.0 Gy × 6 (2 fractions/week)	47%	—	—	—	—	8/30
	10.0 Gy × 2 (over 3 weeks) (N = 57)	48%					10/27 Slight/severe nausea
Tong: RTOG[25]	Solitary mets						
	2.7 Gy × 15	85%	29 weeks			18%	
	4.0 Gy × 5 (N = 266)	82%	20 weeks			4%	
	Multiple mets						
	3.0 Gy × 10	82%	23 weeks	—	—	8%	—
	3.0 Gy × 5	85%	20 weeks			5%	
	4.0 Gy × 5	83%	17 weeks			7%	
	5.0 Gy × 5 (N = 750)	78%	15 weeks			9%	
Jeremic[26]	4.0 Gy × 1	57%	42 weeks	42%		6%	19%/13%
	6.0 Gy × 1	72%	50 weeks	44%		7%	18%/11%
	8.0 Gy × 1 (N = 327)	78%	47 weeks (mean time to progression)	38%		7%	22%/15% Grade 1-2 upper/lower GI toxicity
Hoskin[27]	8.0 Gy × 1	76%	No change at 12 weeks	20%	—	—	—
	4.0 Gy × 1 (N = 270)	53%		9%			

A similar study of only 32 patients reached a contradictory conclusion, with significant pain response in metastatic prostate carcinoma.[34] Differences in result may be explained by the higher doses of Sr-89 and control of hormonal manipulation in the latter trial.

Strontium has also been directly compared to external beam radiation or as an adjunct. Either treatment by itself led to pain relief in 61% to 65% with no significant differences. Fewer patients receiving Sr-89 required treatment to new sites, 36% versus 58%.[35]

Porter found that the addition of Sr-89 to external beam radiation did not improve pain responses but did decrease new sites of pain.[36] A similar trial from Norway found no significant benefit from Sr-89, although there was a 10% difference in the number of new sites with fewer seen in the Sr-89 arm.[37] Time to development of new sites of disease was 4 months.

The application of wide-field or systemic radiation does not improve on pain responses compared to focal radiation alone. Although there is a reduction or delay for new sites, this is at the cost of significant acute GI or hemologic toxicity, especially in pretreated patients.

■ BISPHOSPHONATES

Bisphosphonates are preferentially delivered to sites of bone resorption or formation where they are incorporated into osteoclasts on which they have an inhibitory effect. Ongoing studies suggest these agents may also cause apoptosis of tumor cell lines and inhibit adhesion of tumor cells to bone matrix elements.[38,39] Bisphosphonates have been recommended in patients with lytic disease based on their ability to limit complications such as pathologic fracture, spinal cord compression, and need for radiation.[40,41] Time to progression for metastatic complications was 10 to 13 months, which is comparatively longer than the 4 months achieved with Sr-89. Initial studies primarily focused on osseous metastases secondary to breast cancer, but new, more potent agents, have demonstrated similar outcomes for a wide range of solid tumors.[42]

Given the mechanism of action, lack of hematologic or GI side effects, and applicability to a wide range of tumor systems, combinations of bisphosphonates and radiation are an attractive therapeutic approach. Animal studies suggest administration of bisphosphonates proceeding radiation may lead to greater bone remineralization.[43] Early studies in human subjects suggest improved pain relief and remineralization as well.[44-46] Trials evaluating newer agents, timing, and duration of bisphosphonates are a promising area of research.

■ NEUROPATHIC PAIN

Neuropathic pain is caused by pressure on or direct invasion of neural structures and is characterized by symptoms in a dermatome distribution. It is often described as a burning sensation but may manifest as an area of hypoesthesia or dysesthesia. It is often thought of as being intractable to common analgesics and more resistant to relief from radiation.

The Trans-Tasman Radiation Oncology Group has specifically studied this group of patients.[47] Entry required neuropathic pain with most patients having spine involvement but without spinal cord compression. An interim analysis of the first 90 patients randomized to either a single fraction of 8.0 Gy or 5 fractions of 4.0 Gy revealed an overall pain response of 59%. This response rate is similar, albeit at the lower end of the range, to responses reported for uncomplicated bone pain.

■ SPINAL CORD COMPRESSION

Although most patients entering the Trans-Tasman trial had spine lesions, cord compression was an exclusion. In this population, radiation is also a well-established therapy. Although there are numerous studies, information on pain relief is scarce because the usual end point is neurologic function. In general, for a given functional level, radiation has been considered equivalent to surgical decompression followed by radiation.[48-51] This paradigm has recently been challenged by Patchell and coworkers.[52] In this randomized trial, patients undergoing an anterior decompression and stabilization followed by radiation had improved neurologic outcomes and ability to ambulate compared to those managed with radiation alone. Narcotic use was significantly less as well. It is important to note that the surgical approach used in this trial is more aggressive than that commonly employed, and perhaps more importantly, surgery was initiated within 24 hours.

■ PLEXOPATHY

Involvement of the brachial plexus by superior sulcus tumors or the celiac plexus by retroperitoneal tumors, most commonly pancreatic carcinoma, can cause severe pain. The natural history of these is markedly different because the former can be treated curatively, whereas the latter signifies advanced disease and is only palliated by currently available therapy.

Superior sulcus tumors often manifest with pain in the upper chest, neck, shoulder, and arm. The distribution corresponds to the trunk(s) of the brachial plexus involved and indicates the position of the tumor in the upper lung (Fig. 30-3).

Approaches to superior sulcus tumors without evidence of metastases have historically included surgery or a short course of radiation followed by surgery. This approach was extensively reported by Paulson[53] and leads to approximately 25% long-term survival. Local failure was the dominant recurrence pattern with approximately 40% of patients failing at the primary site. Many of these experience local symptoms including pain subsequent to their relapse.

Current treatment is preoperative radiation and chemotherapy. The Southwest Oncology Group (Intergroup 0160) reported the results of this approach in a phase II trial.[54] Radiation was delivered to a dose of 45.0 Gy in 25 fractions concurrent with cisplatin and VP-16. Seventy-five percent of patients entered had ECOG performance status 1 due to pain. Although no specific data on pain relief were given, 92% of patients had a complete resection. Equal proportions had a pathologic complete response, microscopic residual, or gross residual. The plateau for survival curves was 55% for all patients. The pattern of recurrence was altered as well with marked improvement in control at the primary site.

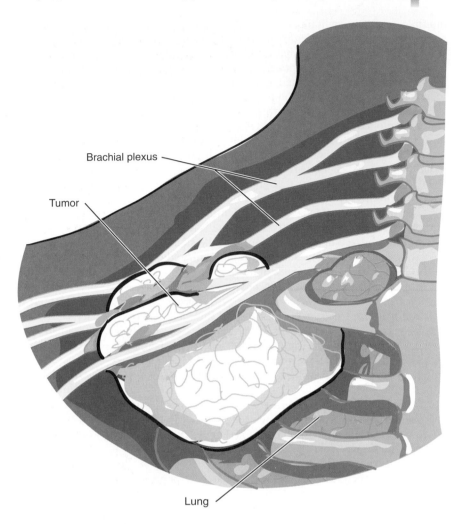

FIGURE 30–3 ■ Brachial plexus and nerve distribution in relation to the upper chest.

Brachial plexus

Tumor

Lung

In contrast, those with locally advanced pancreatic cancer treated with combined chemoradiation have 2-year survival of approximately 10%.[55-58] They can, however, have clinical regression of their disease and accompanying pain relief in 50% to 65%. This compares favorably with chemotherapy alone in which 5% treated with 5-fluorouracil (5-FU) and 24% treated with gemcitabine achieved a clinical benefit, primarily pain relief.[59]

■ VISCERAL PAIN

Neoplastic involvement of organs can lead to pain—primarily by capsular distention. Pain is usually diffuse and dull as it is transmitted via visceral nerve fibers. The liver is commonly involved in advanced metastatic disease, with accompanying pain. Although often thought of as too radiation-sensitive for treatment, numerous reports of palliative radiation exist. Karnofsky and colleagues reported complete relief in 26 of 30 patients with various primary carcinomas involving the liver treated at Memorial Sloan Kettering.[60] The RTOG has reported various fractionation schedules.[61,62] Pain relief was achieved in 55%. Mass effect, fever, and nausea were also improved in approximately one half of the patients. No cases of radiation hepatitis occurred at doses less than 30.0 Gy. Median survival overall is 3 to 4 months

and highly dependent on performance status and extent of extrahepatic disease. Because many patients will have extensive metastases and corresponding poor performance status, radiation is rarely employed in this setting.

■ BRAIN METASTASES

Involvement of the CNS by metastatic disease is usually a late event. Manifestations are dependent on the area of involvement with headache as a component of presentation in 52% to 55%.[63-65] Radiation treatment is usually delivered over 2 to 3 weeks to the whole brain although resection or stereotactic radiation for selected patients is increasingly used. Headaches improved in 85% to 95%, with one half to two thirds of patients having complete resolution. Benefits in neurologic and cognitive function, and decreased seizure activity are also common. Median survivals are highly dependent on performance or neurologic status and can be as limited as a few weeks for those presenting with severe deficits or neurologic class IV but generally are 4 to 6 months.

■ TRIGEMINAL NEURALGIA

This entity can be a debilitating disease occurring as a consequence of tumors of the gasserian ganglion, associated with multiple sclerosis, or idiopathically. The pain is lancinating and often repetitive in the distribution of one or more divisions of cranial nerve V. It may be bilateral and can have an accompanying sensory component. When conservative management fails or is not tolerated, more invasive procedures are indicated. One potential option is stereotactic radiosurgery.

The first system used in this setting was the Gamma Knife developed by Leksell in 1951.[66] Current models consist of a spherical shell housing 201 cobalt-60 sources that can be differentially unshielded to produce a highly conformal radiation dose distribution around a target. An important characteristic of this is the steep dose gradient outside of the target area allowing for sparing of normal structures.

The root of the affected nerve is identified as it exits the pons by MRI. Treatment is delivered in one fraction, with the patient immobilized in a rigid ring fixed to the skull with pins placed under local anesthesia. Pain relief with radiosurgery has been reported in 75% to 89% of those treated,[67-69] although with further follow up this may decrease to 50% to 60%.[70,71] Higher response rates are seen in those with shorter symptom duration who have not undergone surgical intervention. Toxicity primarily consists of new sensory deficits, seen in 7.3% in the University of Maryland series. Toxicity is increased with dose escalation above the standard 70.0 Gy, or longer length of nerve treated, without a concomitant improvement in pain relief.[72]

Controlled trials comparing radiosurgery to surgical approaches have not been performed. Pain relief in series of microvascular decompression tends to be in the range of 70% to 90%, although typically younger patients with better prognoses are selected for this approach.[73]

In a retrospective review of patients matched for prior surgical procedures and Barrow Neurologic Index, radiosurgery led to excellent or good outcomes (Barrow Neurologic Index 1 or 2) in 29% and 10% compared to 33% and 0% in those treated with glycerol rhizotomy. Complications, primarily facial numbness, were higher in the glycerol rhizotomy group (53%) compared to the radiosurgery group (33%).[74]

■ COST EFFECTIVENESS

In clinical practice, the cost of intervention is usually considered last, however it is an important consideration from the viewpoint of public policy. The agency for Healthcare Policy and Research from the Department of Health and Human Services has published clinical practice guidelines on pain management. As discussed in the *New England Journal of Medicine*,[75] these called for a number of measures including

- A collaborative, interdisciplinary approach
- An individualized plan agreed on by patients, families, and caregivers
- Ongoing assessment
- Both drug and nondrug therapies
- Institutional policies on pain management and monitoring

Given the prevalence of pain in cancer patients, effective management will carry a high aggregate cost. This is balanced against the cost of uncontrolled pain, which can lead to complications and hospitalizations as well as the indirect losses from decreased quality of life.

In a pilot study evaluating cost effectiveness, 66 patients treated at the Cleveland Clinic by radiation for bone metastasis were evaluated.[76] Entry required a Karnofsky performance status of 70% and estimated survival of 6 months. Radiation fractionation was chosen by the physician with the most common prescription being 30.0 Gy in 10 fractions in 75% of patients. On a ten-point scale, pain scores at rest improved by 4 points and with movement by 5 points. Cost was based on Medicare-allowable charges and ranged from $1,200.00 to $2,500.00 for radiation compared to an estimated $9,000.00 to $36,000.00 for 9 months of oral narcotics. These costs are in close agreement with other estimates of $1,000.00 to $4,000.00 monthly for oral narcotics.[77]

The radiation costs are similar to those seen in a national survey of Swedish practices. This study found the cost of a palliative course of radiation to be $2,000.00. They concluded it was underused in the palliative setting.[78]

■ CONCLUSIONS

- Radiation palliates pain in a large proportion of those with bone metastases.
- There are benefits in preservation of osseous and neural function.
- Pain from other types of metastases such as visceral and CNS can also be improved.
- A rapidly increasing indication is stereotactic radiosurgery for trigeminal neuralgia.
- Radiation is cost effective in the palliative care setting.

References

1. Levin I: The prognostic and therapeutic significance of skeletal metastases in cancer of the breast. Ann Surg 65:326, 1917.
2. Hillman G, Maughan R, Grignon D, et al: Responsiveness of experimental prostate carcinoma bone tumors to neutron or photon radiation combined with cytokine therapy. Int J Radiol Oncol Biol Phys 56:1426, 2003.
3. Hoskin PJ, Stratford MR, Folkes LK, et al: Effect of local radiotherapy for bone pain on urinary markers of osteoclast activity. Lancet 355 1428, 2000.
4. Dodwell DJ: Malignant bone resorption: Cellular and biochemical mechanisms. Ann Oncol 3:257, 1992.
5. Paterson AHG: Bone metastases in breast cancer, prostate cancer and myeloma. Bone 8 (Supplement 1):17, 1987.
6. Manishen WJ, Sivananthan K, Orr FW: Resorbing bone stimulates tumor cell growth. A Role for the host microenvironment in bone metastasis. Am J Pathol 123:39, 1986.
7. Lam WC, Delikatny EJ, Orr FW, et al: The chemotactic response of tumor cells: a model for cancer metastases. Am J Pathol 104:69, 1981.
8. Garrett IR: Bone destruction in cancer. Semin Oncol 20 (Supplement 2): 4, 1993.
9. Hulth A, Olerud S: The reaction of bone to experimental cancer. Acta Orthop Scand 36:230, 1965.
10. Nielsen OS, Munro AJ, Tannock IF: Bone Metastases: Pathophysiology and Management Policy. J Clin Oncol 9:509, 1991.
11. American Cancer Society: Cancer Facts and Figures, 1996. Atlanta. American Cancer Society. 1996.
12. Adams JE, Isherwood I: Conventional and new techniques in radiological diagnosis. In Stoll BA, Parbhoo S (eds): Bone Metastases: Monitoring and Treatment. New York, Raven, 1983, p107.
13. Kirkbride P, Warde PR, Panzarella T, et al: A randomised trial comparing the efficacy of a single radiation fraction with fractionated radiated therapy in the palliation of skeletal metastases. Int J Radiat Oncol Biol Phys 48 (Suppl):185 (Abstract 147), 2000.
14. Bone Pain Trial Working Party: 8 Gy single fraction radiotherapy for the treatment of metastatic skeletal pain: Randomised comparison with a

multi-fractionated schedule over 12 months of patient follow-up. Radiother Oncol 52:111, 1999.

15. Steenland E, Leer J, Houwelingen H, et al: The effect of a single fraction compared to multiple fractions on painful bone metastases: A global analysis of the Dutch Bone Metastasis Study. Radiother Oncol 52:101, 1999.

16. Nielsen OS, Bentzen SM, Sandberg E, et al: Randomized trial of single dose versus fractionated palliative radiotherapy of bone metastases. Radiother Oncol 47:233, 1998.

17. Gaze MN, Kelly CG, Kerr GR, et al: Pain relief and quality of life following radiotherapy for bone metastases: A randomised trial of two fractionation schedules. Radiother Oncol 45:109, 1997.

18. Cole DJ: A randomized trial of a single treatment versus conventional fractionation in the palliative radiotherapy of painful bone metastases. Clin Oncol 1:59, 1989.

19. Price P, Hoskin PJ, Easton D, et al: Prospective randomised trial of single and multi-fraction radiotherapy schedules in the treatment of bony metastases. Radiother Oncol 6:247, 1986.

20. Hartsell WF, Scott C, Bruner DW, et al: Phase III randomized trial of 8 Gy in one fraction versus 30 Gy in 10 fractions for palliation of painful bone metastases: Preliminary results of RTOG 97-14. Int J Radiat Oncol Biol Phys 57(S):S-124, (Abstract 1), 2003.

21. Niewald M, Tkocz HJ, Abel U, et al: Rapid course radiation therapy versus more standard treatment: A randomized trial for bone metastases. Int J Radiat Oncol Biol Phys 36:1085, 1996.

22. Rasmusson B, Vejborg I, Jensen AB, et al: Irradiation of bone metastases in breast cancer patients: A randomized study with 1 year follow-up. Radiother Oncol 34:179, 1995.

23. Okawa T, Kita M, Goto M, et al: Randomized prospective clinical study of small, large, and twice a day fraction radiotherapy for painful bone metastases. Radiother Oncol 13:99, 1988.

24. Madsen EL: Painful Bone Metastases: Efficacy of radiotherapy assessed by the patients: A randomized trial comparing 4 Gy ×6 versus 10 Gy ×2. Int J Radiat Oncol Biol Phys 9:1775, 1983.

25. Tong D, Gillick L, Hendrickson F: The palliation of symptomatic osseous metastases: Final results of the study by the Radiation Therapy Oncology Group. Cancer 50:893, 1982.

26. Jeremic B, Shibamoto Y, Acimovic L, et al: A randomized trial of three single dose radiation therapy regimens in the treatment of metastatic bone pain. Int J Radiat Oncol Biol Phys 42:161, 1998.

27. Hoskin PJ, Price P, Easton D, et al: A prospective randomised trial of 4 Gy or 8 Gy single doses in the treatment of metastatic bone pain. Radiother Oncol 23:74, 1992.

28. Chow E, Wu JS, Hoskin P, et al: International consensus on palliative radiotherapy endpoints for future clinical trials in bone metastases. Radiother Oncol 64:275, 2002.

29. Shakespeare TP, Lu JJ, Back MF, et al: Patient preference for radiotherapy fractionation schedule in the palliation of painful bone metastases. J Clin Oncol 21:2156, 2003.

30. Salazar OM, Rubin P, Hendrickson FR, et al: Single dose half-body irradiation for palliation of multiple bone metastases from solid tumors. Final Radiation Therapy Oncology Group Report. Cancer 58:29, 1986.

31. Salazar OM, Sandhu T, Motta NW, et al: Fractionated half-body irradiation (hbi) for the rapid palliation of widespread symptomatic, metastatic bone disease: A Randomized Phase III Trial of the International Atomic Energy Agency (IAEA). Int J Radiat Oncol Biol Phys 50:765, 2001.

32. Lewington VJ: Targeted radionuclide therapy for bone metastases. Eur J Nuclear Med 20:66, 1993.

33. Buchali K, Correns HJ, Schuerer M: Results of a double-blind study of 89-strontium therapy of skeletal metastases of prostatic carcinoma. Eur J Nuclear Med 14: 349, 1988.

34. Lewington VJ, McEwan AJ, Ackery DM, et al: A prospective, randomised double-blind crossover study to examine the efficacy of strontium-89 in pain palliation in patients with advanced prostate cancer metastatic to bone. Eur J Cancer 27:954, 1991.

35. Quilty PM, Kirk D, Bolger JJ, et al: A comparison of the palliative effects of strontium-89 and external beam radiotherapy in metastatic prostate cancer. Radiother Oncol 31:33, 1994.

36. Porter AT, McEwan AJB, Powe JE, et al: Results of a randomized phase iii trial to evaluate the efficacy of strontium-89 adjuvant to local field external beam irradiation in the management of endocrine resistant metastatic prostate cancer. Int J Radiat Oncol Biol Phys 25: 805, 1993.

37. Smelend S, Erikstein B, Aas M, et al: Role of strontium-89 as adjuvant to palliative external beam radiotherapy is questionable: Results of a double-blind randomized study. International Int J Radiat Oncol Biol Phys 56:1397, 2003.

38. Clezardin P: The Anti-tumor potential of bisphosphonates. Semin Oncol 29 (6 Suppl 21):33, 2002.

39. Pickering LM, Mansi JL, Colston KW: Adhesion of breast cancer cells to extracellular matrices is inhibited by zoledronic acid and enhanced by aberrant RAS signaling. J Clin Oncol 22 (S):863 (Abstract 3468), 2003.

40. Horbtobagyi GN, Theriault RL, Porter L, et al: Efficacy of pamidronate in reducing skeletal complications in patients with breast cancer and lytic bone metastases. N Engl J Med 335:1785, 1996.

41. Theriault RL, Lipton A, Hortobagi GN, et al: Pamidronate reduces skeletal morbidity in women with advanced breast cancer and lytic bone lesions. A randomized placebo controlled trial—protocol 18. Aredia Breast Cancer Study Group. J Clin Oncol 17: 846, 1999.

42. Rosen LS, Gordon D, Tchekmedyian S, et al: Zoledronic acid versus placebo in the treatment of skeletal metastases in patients with lung cancer and other solid tumors: A Phase III, double-blind, randomized trial. The Zoledronic Acid, Lung Cancer and Other Solid Tumor Study Group. J Clin Oncol 21:3150, 2003.

43. Krempien R, Huber PE, Harms W, et al: Combination of early bisphosphonate administration and irradiation leads to improved remineralization and re-stabilization of osteolytic bone metastases in an animal tumor model. Cancer 98:1318, 2003.

44. Micke O, Berning D, Schaefer U, et al: Combination of ibandronate and radiotherapy in metastatic bone disease—results of a randomized study. J Clin Oncol 22 (S):759 (Abstract 3052), 2003.

45. Koulloulias V, Matsopoulos G, Kouvaris J: Radiotherapy in conjunction with intravenous infusion of 180-mg of disodium pamidronate and management of osteolytic metastases from breast cancer: Clinical evaluation, biochemical markers, quality of life, and monitoring of recalcification using assessment of gray-level histogram and plain radiographs. International Int J Radiat Oncol Biol Phys 57:143, 2003.

46. Wong R, Franssen E, Danjoux C, et al: A randomized double-blind placebo controlled trial of radiotherapy (xrt) with or without single dose pamidronate (PAM) pain relief in patients with painful bone metastases. J Clin Oncol 22(S):771 (Abstract 3099), 2003.

47. Roos, DE, O'Brien PC, Smith JG, et al: A role for radiotherapy in neuropathic bone pain: Preliminary response rates from a prospective trial (Trans-Tasman Radiation Oncology Group, TROG 96.05). Int J Radiat Oncol Biol Phys 46:975, 2000.

48. Faul CM, Flickinger JC: The use of radiation in the management of spinal metastases. J Neurooncol 23:149, 1995.

49. Leviov M, Dale J, Stein M, et al: The management of metastatic spinal cord compression: A radiotherapeutic success ceiling. Int J Radiat Oncol Biol Phys 27:231, 1993.

50. Zevalos M, Chan PYM, Munov L, et al: Epidural spinal cord compression from metastatic tumor. Int J Radiat Oncol Biol Phys 13:875, 1987.

51. Payne R, Gaughan E, Chou C, et al: A randomized trial of radiation alone versus best decompressive surgery plus radiation therapy for single site spinal cord compression: Interim analysis. J Clin Oncol (Proceedings)16:79a (Abstract 275), 1997.

52. Patchell R, Tibbs PA, Regine WF, et al: A randomized trial of direct decompressive surgical resection in the treatment of spinal cord compression caused by metastases. J Clin Oncol (Proceedings) 22:1 (Abstract 2), 2003.

53. Paulson DL: Carcinomas in the superior pulmonary sulcus. J Thorac-Cardiovasc Surg 70:1095, 1975.

54. Rusch VW, Giroux DJ, Kraut MJ, et al: Induction chemoradiation and surgical resection for non-small cell lung carcinoma of the superior sulcus: Initial results of the Southwest Oncology Group Trial (Intergroup Trial 0160). J Thorac Cardiovasc Surg 121:472, 2001.

55. Moertel CG, Frytak S, Hahn HG, et al: Therapy of locally unresectable pancreatic carcinoma: A randomized comparison of high-dose (6000 rad) radiation alone, moderate dose radiation (4000 rad + 5-fluorouracil) and high dose radiation + 5-fluorouracil. The Gastrointestinal Tumor Study Group. Cancer 48:1705, 1991.

56. Douglass HO for the Gastrointestinal Study Group: Treatment of locally unresectable carcinoma of the pancreas: Comparison of combined modality therapy (chemotherapy + radiotherapy) to chemotherapy alone. J Nat Cancer Inst 80:751, 1988.

57. Flickinger JC, Jawalekar K, Deutsch M, et al: Split course radiation therapy for adenocarcinoma of the pancreas. Int J Radiat Oncol Biol Phys 15:359, 1988.

58. Whittington R, Dobelbower RR, Mohiuddin M, et al: Radiotherapy of unresectable pancreatic carcinoma: A 6-year experience with 104 patients. Int J Radiat Oncol Biol Phys 7:1639, 1981.
59. Burris HA, Moore MJ, Anderson J, et al: Improvements in survival and clinical benefit with gemcitabine as first line therapy for patients with advanced pancreas cancer: A randomized trial. J Clin Oncol 15:2403, 1997.
60. Phillips R, Karnofsky DA, Hamilton LD, et al: Roentgen therapy of hepatic metastases. Am J Roentgenol 71:826, 1954.
61. Borgelt BB, Gelber R, Brady LW, et al: The palliation of hepatic metastases: Results of the Radiation Oncology Group Pilot Study. Int J Radiat Oncol Biol Phys 7:587, 1981.
62. Russell AH, Clyde C, Wasserman TH, et al: Accelerated hyperfractionated hepatic irradiation in the management of patients with liver metastases: Results of the RTOG dose escalating protocol. Int J Radiat Oncol Biol Phys 27:117, 1993.
63. Hendrickson FR: The Optimum schedule for palliative radiotherapy for metastatic brain cancer. Int J Radiat Oncol Biol Phys 2:165, 1977.
64. Kurtz JM, Gelber R, Brady LW, et al: The palliation of brain metastases in a favorable patient population: A randomized clinical trial by The Radiation Therapy Oncology Group. Int J Radiat Oncol Biol Phys 2: 891, 1981.
65. Priestman TJ, Dunn J, Brada M, et al: Final results of the Royal College of Radiologists Trial comparing two different radiotherapy schedules in the treatment of cerebral metastases. Clin Oncol 8:308, 1996.
66. Leksell L: Stereotaxic radiosurgery and trigeminal neuralgia, Acta Chir Scandinavia 137:311, 1971.
67. Kondziolka D, Lunsford LD, Flickinger JC: Stereotactic radiosurgery for the treatment of trigeminal neuralgia. Clin J Pain 18:42, 2002.
68. Pollock BE, Phuong LK, Gorman DA, et al: Stereotactic radiosurgery for idiopathic trigeminal neuralgia. J Neurosurg 97:347, 2002.
69. Young RF, Vermeulen SS, Grimm P, et al: Gamma Knife radiosurgery for treatment of trigeminal neuralgia. Neurology 48:608, 1997.
70. Maesawa S, Salame C, Flickinger JC, et al: Clinical outcomes after sterotactic radiosurgery for idiopathic trigeminal neuralgia. J Neurosurg 94:14, 2001.
71. Petit JH, Herman JM, Nagda S, et al: Radiosurgical treatment of trigeminal neuralgia: Evaluating quality of life in treatment outcomes. Int J Radiat Oncol Biol Phys 56:1147, 2003.
72. Flickinger JC, Pollock BE, Kondziolka D, et al: Does increased nerve length within the treatment volume improve trigeminal neuralgia radiosurgery? A prospective double-blind randomized study. Int J Radiat Oncol Biol Phys 51:449, 2001.
73. Tyler-Kabara EC, Kassarn AB, Horowitz MH, et al: Predictors of outcome in surgically managed patients with typical and atypical trigeminal neuralgia: Harrison results following microvascular decompression. J Neurosurg 96:527, 2002.
74. Febles C, Werner-Wasik M, Rosenwasser RH, et al: A comparison of treatment outcomes with Gamma Knife radiosurgery versus glycerol rhizotomy in the management of trigeminal neuralgia. Int J Radiat Oncol Biol Phys. Proceedings of the 45th Annual ASTRO Meeting 57 (2S): S253 (Abstract 210), 2003.
75. Jacox A, Carr DB, Payne R: Special report: New clinical practice guidelines for the management of pain in patients with cancer. N Engl J Med 330:651, 1994.
76. Macklis RM, Cornelli H, Lasher J: Brief courses of palliative radiotherapy for metastatic bone pain: A pilot cost-minimization comparison with narcotic analgesics. Am J Clin Oncol 21:617, 1998.
77. Ferrell BR, Griffith H: Cost issues related to pain management: Report from the Cancer Pain Panel of the Agency for Healthcare Policy and Research. J Pain Sympt Manage 9:221, 1994.
78. Swedish Council on Technology Assessment and Healthcare: A prospective survey of radiotherapy in Sweden. ACTA Oncol 35 (Supplement 6): 1, 1996.

Neural Blockade with Local Anesthetics and Steroids in the Management of Cancer Pain

P. Prithvi Raj

Pain is one of the most prevalent symptoms among patients with advanced cancer. Numerous studies have shown that 30% to 50% of all cancer patients undergoing chemotherapy or other antitumor treatments and 50% to 80% of those with advanced cancer suffer severe pain.[1]

Drug therapy remains the foundation of cancer pain management. Numerous studies have demonstrated that the World Health Organization (WHO) three-step hierarchy for pain management is effective in controlling pain for 70% to 90% of patients with cancer.[2] However, for the 10% to 30% of cancer patients whose pain is not being controlled by the WHO three-step ladder or for patients who are experiencing severe side effects from the treatments, regional anesthetic techniques can be valuable. This chapter focuses on the role of regional anesthetic techniques in the treatment of cancer pain.

■ ROLE OF REGIONAL ANESTHETIC TECHNIQUES FOR THE TREATMENT OF CANCER PAIN

There is no clear consensus on when more invasive therapies should be used in cancer patients, but as a general rule of thumb, therapies should start with more conservative, low-risk procedures and progress to more invasive high-risk procedures that are justified by the presence of severe refractory pain. The United States Agency for Health Care Policy and Research (AHCPR) has published guidelines for the management of cancer pain.[3,4] Although their report focuses more on the pharmacologic management of cancer pain, they endorse the use of regional anesthetic techniques for the treatment of severe cancer pain. However, they are critical of the lack of well-controlled studies on the outcome of interventional techniques for cancer pain. In 1996, the American Society of Anesthesiologists published guidelines for the treatment of cancer pain that focused more on the regional anesthetic techniques.[5] The take-home message from these published guidelines is "first do no harm." If more conservative noninvasive measures have not been tried in the cancer pain patient, do

not forge ahead to more invasive, high-risk procedures. On the one hand, 70% to 90% of patients can be successfully treated with conservative measures outlined in the WHO three-step ladder. On the other hand, cancer patients who are suffering from severe unrelieved pain or who are experiencing debilitating side effects from systemic therapy should not be denied the benefits of regional anesthetic techniques that can turn a major pain crisis into a manageable one.[6] Table 31–1 summarizes the indications for regional anesthetic techniques in cancer pain.

■ LOCAL ANESTHETIC INJECTIONS

Although temporary, local anesthetic regional anesthesia is a valuable tool in the management of cancer pain.[7,8] Because the effects are temporary, the role of regional anesthesia must be clearly outlined to the patient, family, and health care providers. It can be distressing to the patient to experience significant pain relief with the regional anesthesia only to have the severe pain return after a few hours. Local anesthetic neural blockade regional anesthesia serves several purposes: (1) diagnosis; (2) prognosis; and (3) therapy.

Diagnosis

For diagnostic purposes, regional anesthesia can be valuable in determining the pathway or mechanism of the pain. Table 31–2 gives examples of useful diagnostic blocks. The anatomic source of the pain can be diagnosed with a variety of regional anesthesia techniques. Joint pain resulting from cancer (i.e., osteonecrosis, sacroiliac joint metastasis) can be diagnosed with intra-articular injections. Muscle spasms as a result of tumor invasion of bony structures can be diagnosed with trigger point injections, and peripheral nerve blocks can diagnose the peripheral neural pathway of the pain.

Although thoracoabdominal pain is often described as more localized and sharp as compared to thoracic and visceral pain, which is described as diffuse and dull, it can sometimes

Table 31-1

Indications for Regional Anesthesia Techniques in Cancer Pain Management

Pain unrelieved by the WHO three-step hierarchy of pain management
Unacceptable side effects with systemic therapies
Pain crisis
Patient's desire to avoid systemic therapy

From Wallace MS, Leung AY, McBeth MD: Malignant pain. In Raj PP (ed): Textbook of Regional Anesthesia. Philadelphia, Churchill Livingstone, 2002, p 562, with permission.

Table 31-2

Diagnostic Blocks in Cancer Pain Management

Anatomic Source of Pain
Intra-articular injection
Trigger point injection
Peripheral nerve block

Visceral versus Somatic Pain
Intercostal nerve block—differentiates thoracoabdominal wall pain from thoracic and abdominal visceral pain
Celiac plexus block—differentiates abdominal wall pain from abdominal visceral pain
Hypogastric plexus block—differentiates pelvic wall pain from pelvic visceral pain
Cervicothoracic ganglion (stellate-T4) block—differentiates thoracic wall pain from thoracic visceral pain

Sympathetic versus Somatic Pain
Stellate ganglion block—differentiates sympathetically mediated pain from somatic pain of the head, neck, and upper extremity
Lumbar sympathetic block—differentiates sympathetically mediated pain from somatic pain of the lower extremity
Differential spinal block—differentiates sympathetically mediated pain from somatic spinal pain

From Wallace MS, Leung AY, McBeth MD: Malignant pain. In Raj PP (ed): Textbook of Regional Anesthesia. Philadelphia, Churchill Livingstone, 2002, p 562, with permission.

be difficult to differentiate visceral pain from thoracoabdominal wall pain, especially as the pain becomes more severe. For thoracic pain, intercostal blocks can differentiate between thoracic wall and visceral pain. With the exception of the cardiac structures, most of the sensory innervation of the thoracic viscera travels through the T1-T4 sympathetic ganglion. Therefore, cervicothoracic sympathetic blocks can be used to diagnose thoracic visceral pain. For abdominal pain, intercostal, celiac plexus, and hypogastric plexus blocks can differentiate abdominal wall and visceral pain.

Sympathetic blocks can be used to diagnose sympathetically mediated pain and guide treatment. Because somatic

peripheral nerves contain both sympathetic and somatic fibers, it is necessary to block the sympathetic nervous system at locations that are free of somatic nerves. This can be accomplished at the stellate ganglion for diagnosis of head, neck, and upper extremity pain and at the lumbar ganglion for diagnosis of lower extremity pain.

The technique of differential blockade may be useful in cancer pain diagnosis. Since the description of this technique by Winnie and Collins, it has generated much controversy.[9] Both in vitro and in vivo studies have cast doubt on the existence of a differential effect of local anesthetics on varying sizes of nerve fibers. Although zones of differential sensory block after neuraxial local anesthetics have been demonstrated in humans,[10-13] both in vivo and in vitro studies have produced conflicting results.[14,15] Differential blockade can be achieved with the following different techniques: (1) spinal, (2) epidural, and (3) peripheral somatic blocks. All three techniques commonly use 2% lidocaine, which results in motor, sensory, and sympathetic block. The block is then evaluated as it regresses to determine if the pain correlates with the return of somatic sensory function or sympathetic function.

The use of placebo injections (i.e., saline) is controversial and should be used with caution in the cancer patient population. As many as one third of the patients will respond to placebo and that does not necessarily mean that they do not have pain.[16] In addition, saline injected into trigger points has been reported to be as effective as local anesthetic injection.[17]

Prognosis

Before any permanent neurolytic procedure, it is recommended that a prognostic local anesthetic block of the nerve to be ablated be performed. An exception is for the terminally ill patient who incurs an extreme inconvenience during performance of the block. An example is a patient with terminal pancreatic cancer and severe pain who may experience severe discomfort from positioning during the block. Many practitioners would proceed with the neurolytic block in this setting. If numbness and motor blockade are unlikely to result from the block (i.e., celiac plexus block), it is more acceptable to proceed with the permanent neurolytic block without a diagnostic block.

The purpose of prognostic blocks is to allow the patient to experience not only the pain relief that may result from the block but also the numbness and motor blockade that may result. The numbness and motor blockade that results may be more distressing to the patient than the pain itself.[18] Unfortunately, the prognostic value for long-term pain relief from a positive regional anesthesia is not guaranteed.[19] However, a negative regional anesthesia almost certainly will predict failure, thus supporting the use of the prognostic regional anesthesia prior to an ablative procedure.[8]

Therapy

Regional anesthesia is useful in the management of myofascial pain, sympathetically mediated pain, long-term treatments utilizing catheter techniques and continuous delivery, and in crisis management of severe pain.

Reflex muscle spasms caused by tumor invasion of deep tissues can be debilitating. Some patients will receive long-term benefit from trigger point injections of local anesthetics. If long-lasting benefit results, trigger point injections can be repeated at intervals of 1 to several weeks.[20] As tumors encroach on the nervous system, neural damage can result.[21] This neural damage can lead to complex regional pain syndromes that may be responsive to sympathetic blockade. It is known that the pain relief from such blockade can far outlast the duration of the local anesthetic.[22,23] It is in these cases that the sympathetic blockade can be repeated at intervals of 1 to several weeks. Whereas the use of sympathetic blockade in chronic benign pain is focused more to improve function, the use of this technique in cancer pain is focused more on pain control.

Continuous regional anesthesia can be achieved by placement of catheters at peripheral nerve sites, epidurally or intrathecally. The brachial and lumbar plexus are the most common sites for placement of peripheral nerve catheters. A case report on long-term continuous axillary plexus blockade demonstrated no adverse effects for up to 16 days.[24] Other sites that can be cannulated include the intercostal nerve, celiac plexus, hypogastric plexus, stellate ganglion, and lumbar sympathetic ganglion.[25] The ease and low complication rate of epidural catheters favor this technique over peripheral nerve catheters for long-term pain management of localized pain (i.e., lower extremity, sacrum, upper extremity).[26] Even the chronic delivery of cervical epidural local anesthetics is safe, and studies have shown that high concentrations of local anesthetic do not result in phrenic nerve block.[27] There are several studies on the use of intrathecal local anesthetics in combination with opioids for the treatment of cancer pain[28-32] with bupivacaine doses as high as 100 mg/day. It can be concluded from these studies that a sensory-motor block does not occur at doses below 30 to 40 mg/day. There is one case report on severe refractory cancer pain treated with daily intrathecal bupivacaine doses as high as 800 mg/day.[33]

Some cancer patients develop severe pain refractory to opioid analgesics, even in high doses. These patients can benefit from continuous techniques to give them respite from the debilitating pain and allow a drug holiday from the opioids. This technique may also provide pain control until palliative techniques such as chemotherapy, radiation therapy, and radionuclide therapy take effect.

■ STEROID INJECTIONS

Invasion or compression of nerves by growing tumors is a common source of pain. It is thought that inflammation plays a major role in the production of pain;[34,35] however, other pain mechanisms responsive to the local application of steroids that have been postulated include a weak local anesthetic action,[36] a change in the activity in dorsal horn cells[37] and reduced ectopic discharge from neuromas.[38,39] The local instillation of steroid in the compartment of the affected neural structure (i.e., brachial plexus, lumbar plexus, intercostal nerve) can result in significant and prolonged pain.[8] If the tumor invades the vertebral column and compresses nerve roots, epidural steroid injection (ESI) can be very helpful. A number of steroids may be used locally or epidurally; these include methylprednisolone, triamcinolone, betamethasone, and dexamethasone.[40,41] Although not performed routinely, the

intrathecal delivery of steroids has been used for lumbar radiculopathy. There is a concern of inducing arachnoiditis with this technique but many reports fail to show any serious adverse events.[41-43] A comprehensive review by Abram and O'Connor concluded that most cases of arachnoiditis following subarachnoid steroid injections occur with multiple injections over a prolonged time period.[44]

Pages first described his technique for accessing the epidural space via a paramedian approach in 1921.[45] The technique involved the use of "lack of resistance" to the needle as it entered the epidural space, and needle placement was confirmed by the lack of free-flowing spinal fluid. This was a technique that was obviously fraught with complications. Several modifications to this technique were proposed over the years, including the use of a fluid-filled syringe attached directly to the spinal needle as it was being introduced[46] and the "hanging drop" technique,[47] which relied on the theory that the epidural space was under negative pressure at all times. Not until 1933, when Dogliotti[48] developed the "loss of resistance" technique that used a syringe filled with air to identify the epidural space, did the technique become reasonably reliable. The introduction of the Touhy needle would later become the most significant breakthrough with regard to the clinical application of this procedure as it greatly reduced the incidence of iatrogenic dural punctures (and thus the associated morbidity), and also allowed for the placement of indwelling catheters for relatively long-term analgesia.

The list of indications is quite extensive and includes several well described conditions such as lumbar/cervical radiculopathy, spinal stenosis, postlaminectomy syndrome, failed back syndrome, postherpetic neuralgia, complex regional pain syndrome, pelvic pain syndromes, phantom limb pain, and periaxial malignancies and tumor invasion.[49] Conversely, the list of contraindications is relatively short and includes: sepsis, local infection, anticoagulation or coagulopathy, and hypovolemia (relative contraindication).[49] White and colleagues,[50] in a study of 304 patients, found that the response to ESI was most closely related to onset of symptoms, presence of nerve root compression, and the lack of any associated psychological issues. Others[51-55] have identified some of the primary positive and negative predictive factors of the response to ESI. Factors associated with the patient's history that correlate with a favorable response to the procedure include the presence of radicular pain and radicular numbness, relatively short duration of symptoms (<6 months), advanced educational background, absence of previous back surgery, and young age. Findings on the physical examination or in diagnostic studies that correlate well with a positive response to ESI include the presence of dermatomal sensory loss, motor loss correlating with the involved nerve root, positive straight leg raise test, positive findings on electromyography involving the affected nerve root, and radiographic confirmation of a herniated disk affecting the suspected nerve root. Negative predictive factors that have been identified include pain duration of greater than 6 to 24 months, occupational injuries, previous back surgery, primarily axial pain, injury-related litigation, history and examination consistent with myofascial pain syndrome, and the so-called "nonorganic" physical signs (Waddell signs).

The mechanism of action of epidural steroids also remains somewhat controversial. It is known, however, that the enzyme phospholipase A_2 is contained in relatively high concentrations within the nucleus pulposus of intervertebral disks.[56] This enzyme initiates the release of arachidonic acid from cell membranes, thus initiating an enzymatic cascade that—in the presence of annular tears or severe degenerative disk disease—can cause a chemical irritation (or radiculitis) of an adjacent nerve root. Steroids induce the synthesis of a phospholipase A_2 inhibitor that inhibits arachidonic acid metabolism one step earlier in the pathway when compared with nonsteroidal antiinflammatory drugs. In addition, steroids have been shown to have an affect on local membrane depolarization. Johansson and coworkers[57] demonstrated that local administration of methylprednisolone blocks the transmission of C fibers but not A-beta fibers. The effect was noted to be reversible, suggesting that there is a direct membrane action of the steroid.

The efficacy of ESI for back pain, neck pain, and radicular pain remains a fairly controversial issue. This is partly because most of the literature has been hindered by poor study design or inconclusive data. Kepes and Duncalf[58] concluded, in 1985, that the role of steroids in this subgroup of patients was not warranted. However, their study included patients who were treated with both epidural and systemic steroids. Benzon[59] concluded, in a study of patients with lumbosacral radiculopathy who were treated only with ESI, that epidural steroids were effective in the treatment of those with acute radiculopathy. More recently, Kocs and associates[60] concluded that epidural steroids were not effective in patients with chronic back pain without evidence of ongoing radiculopathy, but that those with ongoing radiculopathy showed a positive response in 50% of the cases. They reviewed all available randomized controlled trials published up to 1994 and determined that only four studies adhered to acceptable standards of quality, and that only two of those supported the use of epidural steroids in the treatment of radicular pain. In 1995, Watts and Silagy[61] performed a meta-analysis of the same data using odd ratios; with the goal of answering the question "Do epidural steroids work?" In it, they defined efficacy as at least 75% improvement for short-term (60 days) and long-term (1-year) outcomes. With an odds ratio of >1 suggestive of efficacy and >2 suggestive of significant efficacy, they determined that ESI had an odds ratio of 2.61 for short-term outcomes and 1.87 for long-term outcomes. This meta-analysis provided quantitative evidence of the efficacy of epidural steroids in the management of radicular pain. In 1998, McQuay and Moore[62] sought the answer to the question "How well do epidural steroids work?" They used the same data as Watts and Silagy, in addition to the work of Carette and colleagues[63] and used Number Needed to Treat (NNT) as the measure of clinical benefit. In the short-term outcomes group, the NNT was seven. In other words, to achieve a goal of 75% improvement in pain in one patient, one would have to treat seven patients with ESI. However, if a more reasonable goal of 50% improvement in pain were the standard, the NNT was just under three. In the long-term group, the NNT corresponding to 50% improvement at 12 months was 13. It was also noted that there was no difference in the functional level or the need for subsequent surgery in these patients after receiving the injections. These data seem to indicate a significant short-term improvement in the leg pain, but minimal improvement in back pain or function after ESI for radiculopathy.

There are relatively few long-term follow-up studies in the literature with regard to ESIs. Most patients report diminished effect after 120 days. However, Dilke and associates[64] reported 36% with complete relief and 55% with partial relief at 3 months. Ridley and coworkers[65] noted 65% of their patients reported sustained relief at 6 months. At 1 year, Green and colleagues[66] reported that 41% of their patients experienced sustained relief, whereas White and associates[50] reported persistent improvement after 6 months in 34% of patients with acute pain, but only 12% of patients with chronic pain. In this study, White also concluded that ESIs are most appropriately used in the presence of root compression, root irritation, or annular tears. ESIs are least effective when given for chronic degenerative disk disease, herniated disks without neurologic deficit, spinal stenosis, and functional low back pain.

The response time to epidural steroids is between 4 and 6 days in most patients (59%), but many others (37%) experience an earlier effect and a small percentage of patients (4%) respond after 6 days.[23] It is, therefore, advisable to allow at least 7 days between each injection. The decision to proceed with another ESI after the initial one is usually based on the results of the first. A positive response to the initial injection—usually measured by a subjective claim by the patient of 50% reduction in pain—is considered a good indication that the patient will receive further benefit from additional injections. Brown[67] demonstrated that there is generally no further benefit to the patient after three injections. Duration of pain or onset of symptoms has also been positively correlated with the response to ESIs.[66,68-70] Patients with symptoms less than 3 months have response rates of 83% to 100%. Symptoms for up to 6 months correspond to a response rate of 67% to 81%, and 44% to 69% in those with symptoms for more than 6 months.

The preponderance of the literature supports the use of ESIs as another treatment modality to be used in the comprehensive management of patients with chronic back and neck pain. There is some controversy over the mandatory use of fluoroscopy; the main points being less than 100% certainty of epidural steroid placement due to intravascular or other extra-epidural location of the needle or catheter tip.[71,72] The absolute efficacy depends on the diagnosis and amount of pain relief deemed "successful." ESIs are particularly beneficial in patients with signs of acute or ongoing radiculopathy. They play a vital role in the armamentarium of the pain management specialist.

Acknowledgment

Portions of this chapter were adapted from Wallace MS, Leung AY, McBeth MD: Malignant pain; and Bender JB, Lord EAR, Burton AW: Outcomes using procedures for nociceptive pain. In Raj PP (ed): Textbook of Regional Anesthesia. Philadelphia, Churchill Livingstone, 2002, with permission.

References

1. von Gunten CF (ed): Palliative Care and Rehabilitation of Cancer Patients. New York, Springer, 1999.
2. de Conno F, Ripamonti C, Sbanotto A, et al: The pharmacological management of cancer pain. Ann Oncol 4:267, 1993.
3. Jacox A, Carr DB, Payne R, et al: Management of cancer pain: Clinical practice guidelines number 9. AHCPR publication no. 94-0592.

Rockville, Md: U.S. Department of Health and Human Services, Agency for Health Care Policy and Research, 1994.

4. Jacox A, Carr DB, Payne R: New clinical practice guidelines for the management of pain in-patients and with cancer. N Engl J Med 330:651, 1994.

5. Ferrante FM, Bedder M, Caplan RA, et al: Practice guidelines for cancer pain management. A report by the American Society of Anesthesiologists Task Force on Pain Management, Cancer Pain Section. Anesthesiology 84:1243, 1996.

6. Lund PC: The role of analgesic blocking in the management of cancer pain: Current trends. A review article. J Med 13(3):161, 1982.

7. Abram SE. The role of nonneurolytic nerve blocks in the management of cancer pain. In Abram SE (ed): Cancer Pain. Boston, Kluwer Academic, 1989, p 67.

8. Raj PP: Local anesthetic blockade. In Patt RB (ed): Cancer Pain. Philadelphia, Lippincott, 1993, p 329.

9. Winnie AP, Collins VJ: Differential neural blockade in pain syndromes of questionable etiology. Med Clin North Am 52:123, 1968.

10. Brull SJ, Greene NM: Time-courses of zones of differential sensory blockade during spinal anesthesia with hyperbaric tetracaine or bupivacaine. Anesth Analg 69:342, 1989.

11. Brull SJ, Greene NM: Zones of differential sensory block during extradural anaesthesia. Brit J Anaesth 66:651, 1991.

12. Rocco AG, Raymond SA, Murray E, et al: Differential spread of blockade of touch, cold, pinprick during spinal anesthesia. Anesth Analg 64:917, 1985.

13. Greene NM: Area of differential block in spinal anesthesia with hyperbaric tetracaine. Anesthesiology 19:45, 1958.

14. Gasser HS, Erlanger J: The role of fiber size in the establishment of nerve block by pressure or cocaine. Am J Physiol 88:581, 1929.

15. Gissen AJ, Covino BG, Gregust J: Differential sensitivities of mammalian nerve fibers to local anesthetic agents. Anesthesiology 53:467, 1980.

16. Turner JA, Deyo RA, Loeser JD, et al: The importance of placebo effects in pain treatment and research. JAMA 271:1609, 1994.

17. Sola AE, Kuitert JH: Myofascial trigger point pain in the neck and shoulder girdle. Northwest Med 54:980, 1955.

18. Bonica JJ: Current role of nerve blocks in the diagnosis and therapy of pain. In Bonica JJ (ed): Advances in Neurology. New York, Raven, 1974, p 445.

19. Loeser JD: Dorsal rhizotomy for the relief of chronic pain. J Neurosurg 36:745, 1972.

20. Travell J, Simons DG: Myofascial Pain and Dysfunction: The Trigger Point Manual. Baltimore, Williams & Wilkins, 1983.

21. Patchell RA, Posner JB: Neurologic complications of systemic cancer. Neurologic Clin 3:729, 1985.

22. Bonica JJ: Causalgia and other reflex sympathetic dystrophies. In Bonica JJ, Liebeskind JC, Albe-Fessard D (eds): Advances in Pain Research and Therapy, vol 3. New York, Raven, 1979, p 141.

23. Bonica JJ: Sympathetic nerve blocks for pain diagnosis and therapy. Breon Laboratories, New York, 1984.

24. Sarma VJ: Long-term continuous axillary plexus blockade using 0.25% bupivacaine. Acta Anaesthesiol Scand 34:511, 1990.

25. Ramamurthy S, Winnie AP: Regional anesthetic techniques for pain relief. Seminars in Anesth IV:237, 1985.

26. Du Pen S, Williams AR: Management of patients receiving combined epidural morphine and bupivacaine for the treatment of cancer pain. J Pain Sympt Manage 7:125, 1992.

27. Kasaba T, Inoue T: The effects of cervical epidural anesthesia on epidural somatosensory evoked potentials and phrenic nerve activities. Masui 46:321, 1997.

28. Nitescu P, Appelgren L, Linder L-E, et al: Epidural versus intrathecal morphine-bupivacaine: Assessment of consecutive treatments in advanced cancer pain. J Pain Sympt Manage 5:8, 1990.

29. Nitescu P, Sjoberg M, Appelgren L, et al: Complications of intrathecal opioids and bupivacaine in the treatment of "refractory" cancer pain. Clin J Pain 11:45, 1995.

30. Sjoberg M, Appelgren S, Einarsson E, et al: Long-term intrathecal morphine and bupivacaine in "refractory" cancer pain. I. Results from the first series of 52 patients. Acta Anaesthesiol Scand 35:30, 1991.

31. Sjoberg M, Nitescu P, Appelgren L, et al: Long-term intrathecal morphine and bupivacaine in patients with refractory cancer pain. Anesthesiology 80:284, 1994.

32. Van Dongen RTM, Crul BJP, De Bock M: Long-term intrathecal infusion of morphine and morphine/bupivacaine mixtures in the treatment of cancer pain: A retrospective analysis of 51 cases. Pain 55:119, 1993.

33. Berde CB, Sethna NF, Conrad LS, et al: Subarachnoid bupivacaine analgesia of seven months for a patient with a spinal cord tumor. Anesthesiology 72:1094, 1990.

34. Hanks GW, Trueman T, Twycross RG: Corticosteroids in terminal cancer—a prospective analysis of current practice. Postgrad Med J 59:28, 1983.

35. Elliot KJ, Portenoy RK: Cancer pain: Pathophysiology and syndromes. In Yaksh TL, Lynch C, Zapol WM, et al (eds): Anesthesia: Biologic Foundations. Philadelphia, Lippincott, 1998, p 803.

36. Seeman PM: Membrane stabilization by drugs: Tranquilizers, steroids and anaesthetics. Int Rev Neurobiol 9:145, 1966.

37. Hall ED: Acute effects of intravenous glucocorticoids on cat spinal motor neuron electrical properties. Brain Res 240:186, 1982.

38. Devor M, Govin-Lippman R, Raber P: Corticosteroid application blocks transmission in normal nociceptive C-fibers. Acta Anaesthesiol Scand 34:335, 1990.

39. Johansson A, Bennett GJ: Effect of local methylprednisolone on pain in a nerve injury model. Reg Anesth 22:59, 1997.

40. Benzon HT: Epidural steroid injections. Pain Digest 1:271, 1992.

41. Langmayr JJ, Obwegeser AA, Schwarz AB, et al: Intrathecal steroids to reduce pain after lumbar disc surgery: A double blind, placebo-controlled prospective study. Pain 62:357, 1995.

42. Feldman S, Behar AJ: Effect of intrathecal hydrocortisone on advanced adhesive arachnoiditis and cerebrospinal fluid pleocytosis: An experimental study. Neurology 11:251, 1961.

43. Hartmann IT, Winnie AP, Ramamurthy S: Intradural and extradural corticosteroids for sciatic pain. Orthop Rev 3:21, 1974.

44. Abram SE, O'Connor TC: Complications associated with epidural steroid injections. Reg Anesth 21:149, 1996.

45. Pages E: Anestesia metamerica. Rev Sanid Mil Madr 11:351, 1921.

46. Bromage PR: Identification of the epidural space. In Bromage PR (ed): Epidural Analgesia. Philadelphia, WB Saunders, 1978, p178.

47. Gutierrez A: Valor de la aspiracion liquada en al espacio peridural en la anestesia peridural. Rev Circ 12:225, 1933.

48. Dogliotti AM: Segmental periductal anesthesia. Am J Surg 20:107, 1933.

49. Waldman SD: Epidural nerve block. In Weiner RS (ed): Innovations in Pain Management. Orlando, Fla, PMD Press, 1990, p 4.

50. White AH, Derby R, Wynne G: Epidural injections for the diagnosis and treatment of low back pain. Spine 5:78, 1980.

51. Abram S, Hopwood MB: What factors contribute to outcome with lumbar epidural steroids? In Bond MR, Charlton JE, Woolf CJ (eds): Proceedings of the Sixth World Congress on Pain. Amsterda, Elsevier, 1991, p 495.

52. Jamison RN, VadeBoncouer T, Ferrante FM: Low back pain patients unresponsive to an epidural steroid injection: Identifying predictive factors. Clin J Pain 7:311, 1991.

53. Abram SE, Anderson RA: Using a pain questionnaire to predict response to steroid epidurals. Reg Anesth 5:11, 1980.

54. Sandrock NJG, Warfield CA: Epidural steroids and facet injections. In Warfield CA (ed): Principles and Practice of Pain Management. New York, McGraw-Hill, 1993, p 401.

55. Hopwood MB, Abram SE: Factors associated with failure of lumbar epidural steroids. Reg Anesth 18:238, 1993.

56. Saal, JS, Franson RC, Dovrow R, et al: High levels of inflammatory phospholipase A2 activity in lumbar disc herniations. Spine 15:674, 1990.

57. Johansson A, Hao J, Sjolund B: Local corticosteroid application block transmission in normal nociceptive C-fibers. Acta Anaesthesiol Scand 34:335, 1990.

58. Kepes ER, Duncalf D: Treatment of backache with spinal injections of local anesthetics, spinal and systemic steroids. Pain 22:33, 1985.

59. Benzon HT: Epidural steroid injections for low back pain and lumbosacral radiculopathy. Pain 24:277, 1986.

60. Koes BW, Scholten RJPM, Mens JMA, et al: Efficacy of epidural steroid injections for low back pain and sciatica: A systemic review of randomized clinical trials. Pain 63:279, 1995.

61. Watts RW, Silagy CA: A meta-analysis on the efficacy of epidural steroids in the treatment of sciatica. Anaesth Intensive Care, 23:564, 1995.

62. McQuay HJ, Moore RA: Epidural Corticosteroids for Sciatica. An Evidence-Based Resource for Pain Relief. Oxford University Press, 1998, p 216.

63. Carette S, Leclaire R, Marcoux S, et al: Epidural corticosteroid injection for sciatica due to herniated nucleus pulposus. N Engl J Med 336:1634, 1997.

64. Dilke TFW, Burry HC, Grahame R: Extradural corticosteroid injection in management of lumbar nerve root compression. BMJ 2:635, 1973.
65. Ridley MG, Kingsley GH, Gibson T, et al: Outpatient lumbar epidural corticosteroid injection in the management of sciatica. Br J Rheumatol 27:295, 1988.
66. Green PWB, Burke AJ, Weiss CA, et al: The role of epidural cortisone injection in treatment of discogenic pain. Clin Orthop 153:121, 1980.
67. Brown FW: Protocol for management of acute low back pain with or without radiculopathy, including the use of epidural and intrathecal steroids. In Brown FW (ed): American Academy of Orthapaedic Surgeons Symposium on the Lumbar Spine, St Louis, Mosby, 1981.
68. Harley C: Extradural corticosteroid infiltration. A follow-up study of 50 cases. Ann Phys Med 9:22, 1967.
69. Brown FW: Management of discogenic pain using epidural and intrathecal steroids. Clin Orthop 129:72, 1977.
70. Warr AC, Winkinson JA, Burn JM, Langdon L: Chronic lumbosciatic syndrome treated by epidural steroid injection and manipulation. Practitioner 209:53, 1972.
71. Liu SS, Melmed AP, Klos JW, et al. Prospective experience with a 20-gauge Touhy needle for lumbar epidural steroid injections: Is confirmation with fluoroscopy necessary? Reg Anesth Pain Med 26(2):143, 2001.
72. Furman MB, O'Brien EM, Zgleszwski TM: Incidence of intravascular penetration in transforaminal lumbosacral epidural steroid injections. Spine 25(20):2628, 2000.

chapter 32

Neural Blockade with Neurolytic Agents

Subhash Jain and Rakesh Gupta

Optimal use of a neurolytic agent requires that it be administered to produce effective analgesia without devastating side effects. Careful selection of patients, thorough knowledge of the pathophysiologic mechanisms of disease, and an understanding of the physiochemical properties of neurolytic agents and their effects on various body systems are necessary before these agents are used for neurolysis.

■ GENERAL CONSIDERATIONS

Chemical agents have been used for neurolysis since the turn of the 20th century. Schloesser[1] reported using alcohol for trigeminal neuralgia in 1903 and noted the degeneration and subsequent absorption of most of the nerve. A neurolytic sympathetic block with alcohol was performed by Swetlow[2] in 1926 to relieve angina pectoris and abdominal pain. Dogliotti[3] employed alcohol for the first subarachnoid injection in 1930. Although a variety of agents have been used since then for neurolysis, only alcohol and phenol have withstood the test of time. Here we discuss all neurolytic agents used for the management of intractable pain. To understand their effects on the nerve fiber, it is important to review the anatomy and discuss the process of degeneration and regeneration of nerve fibers.

■ PHYSIOLOGIC CONSIDERATIONS IN NEUROLYTIC BLOCKADE

Peripheral nerve fibers are maintained in a specialized connective tissue called *peripheral gliocytes* or *Schwann cells,* which are responsible for myelination of these fibers. After an injury, Schwann cells help to sustain and guide the regeneration of the axon. *Epineurium,* the outer covering of the peripheral nerve, is rich in vascular supply and has an abundance of fat cells, fibroblasts, and mast cells that lend strength to the fiber and help to protect it against compression effects. Bundles or fascicles of nerve fiber are covered by a semipermeable membrane, *perineurium,* which helps to regulate the interstitial fluid exchange in and around the fascicles. *Endoneurium,* an extension of the perineurium, surrounds individual myelinated or unmyelinated nerve fibers and their Schwann cells. It also provides and maintains an environment suitable for nerve conduction. Endoneurium contains capillaries that provide a blood-nerve barrier similar to the blood-brain barrier, and the normal endoneurial fluid pressure as measured with micropipettes is between 1 and 3 cm H_2O.[4, 5] The axon is covered by an *axolemma,* which encloses the axoplasm rich in neurofilaments, neuroblasts, vesicles, and other organelles.

■ NEUROPHYSIOLOGIC ASPECTS OF NERVE CONDUCTION

The process of myelination starts during the 16th to 20th week of gestation. In the peripheral nerve, a single Schwann cell is capable of myelinating only one part of the axon, whereas in the central nervous system, one Schwann cell can myelinate as many as three dozen axons. Along the length of the axon, a chain of Schwann cells encloses the axon completely, creating a mesentery or *mesaxon.* The successive cells interdigitate at the nodes of Ranvier with a nodal gap of about 0.5 to 1 μ.[6] During impulse conduction, myelin acts as an insulating sheath, so that the underlying axoplasm is not depolarized and current travels from one node to the next (*saltatory conduction*).

The conduction velocity in peripheral nerve fibers is a function of the diameter of myelinated nerve fibers. A factor of 6 applies to fibers more than 5 μ in diameter, possibly because of longer internodal segments in thicker fibers. Although it is not necessary to have myelinated fibers for motor function in utero (as evidenced by movement at 10 weeks of intrauterine life), demyelination of adult nerve fibers seriously impairs nerve conduction. Regeneration of a nerve fiber is facilitated by the basal lamina of Schwann cells, which covers even the nodes of Ranvier and thus provides a continuous tube. When, however, a nerve is transected, the basal lamina is interrupted, making regeneration more difficult.

■ DEGENERATION AND REGENERATION

Wallerian degeneration is a process that follows an insult to the nerve fiber. Described first by Waller[7] in 1850, it starts at the distal stump almost immediately after the initial injury. The axon breaks down, and the axoplasm is enclosed within ellipsoids of myelin formed as a result of retraction of the myelin sheath. Lysosomal enzymes cause hydrolysis within these ellipsoids. Schwann cells start multiplying during the first week of injury, and macrophages continue to ingest debris. By the end of the first week, Schwann cells form a chain within the endoneurium. After about 2 weeks, macrophages disappear, leaving behind endoneurial tubes filled with Schwann cells.

Regeneration may start as early as 6 hours after a clean cut but may be delayed several weeks after a crush or tearing injury. Each axon produces several regenerating sprouts. Some of the sprouts succeed in making contact with the distal stump and begin growing distally at a rate of about 5 mm/day in the larger nerve trunks and 1 to 2 mm/day in the smaller ones. Functional recovery depends on the integrity of the endoneurium. Outcome is better with crush injuries than after a clean cut. Although sprouts of sensory fibers easily travel along motor neurons and vice versa, no functional contact is established. An accurate coaptation of the two severed ends is, therefore, essential to restore function in a clean-cut nerve.

Because the peripheral nerve lacks lymphatic innervation, any toxic, metabolic, or traumatic insult leads to an increase in endoneurial fluid pressure, probably secondary to mast cell degranulation and release of vasoactive substances, which increase the permeability of the blood-nerve barrier and thus lead to accumulation of fluid in the endoneurial space. This process peaks in 6 to 7 days and reverts to normal in about 30 days. Elevated endoneurial fluid pressure causes stretching of the perineurium and compression of perineurial vessels, thus producing ischemia of the nerve fiber.[8]

■ NEUROLYTIC BLOCKADE

Skillful performance of neurolytic blockade after very careful assessment and selection of patients has produced successful results for the last 90 years. Nevertheless, a thorough understanding of the actions, side effects, and possible complications of neurolytics, familiarity with various opioids, and knowledge of adjunctive pharmacologic agents are necessary before neurolysis is undertaken. Even among cancer patients with intractable pain, only about 30% require neurolysis as the ultimate means of producing effective analgesia.[9] Never-

theless, it remains an invaluable tool in the management of pain for certain patients with terminal cancer, certain neuralgias, vascular occlusive diseases, and hypophysectomy and when neurosurgical ablation is not an option.[10] Also, neurolytic blockade spares the basal lamina, facilitating regeneration of the axon, unlike surgical interruption, which has a higher incidence of neuroma formation. Thorough, informed patient consent must be obtained before the procedure. Although a diagnostic or prognostic block may not predict the exact outcome of the subsequent neurolysis, it can help to familiarize the patient with possible side effects. After neurolysis, the patient should be assessed for efficacy, side effects, and possible complications of the procedure. Opioid and adjuvant medications should be adjusted with necessary precautions being taken to avoid opiate withdrawal.

Neurolytic Agents

Although a wide range of neurolytic agents may be used for the purpose of neurolysis, only a few are available as commercial preparations. Commonly used agents or procedures are absolute alcohol, phenol, cryoanalgesia, and radiofrequency lesions.

Ethyl Alcohol

Absolute alcohol is commercially available in the United States as a higher-than-95% concentration in 1-mL, single-dose ampules. Alcohol is a local irritant and can cause considerable pain during injection. The pain can be avoided by preinjection of small doses of a local anesthetic drug. Since the earliest reports on alcohol neurolysis, various concentrations and mixtures of alcohol have been used, with inconsistent results. One consensus was reached: a concentration stronger than 95% results in complete paralysis. Another study also concluded that a minimum concentration of 33% alcohol was necessary to obtain satisfactory analgesia without any motor paralysis (Table 32–1).[11-16]

Histopathologic studies have shown that alcohol extracts cholesterol, phospholipids, and cerebrosides from the nerve tissue and causes precipitation of lipoproteins and mucoproteins.[17] Topical application of alcohol to peripheral nerves produces changes typical of wallerian degeneration, as described earlier. A subarachnoid injection of absolute alcohol causes similar changes in the rootlets.[18] Mild focal inflammation of meninges and patchy areas of demyelination are seen in

Table 32–1

Experimental Use of Ethanol as a Neurolytic Agent in Peripheral Nerves: Summary

Study (Year)	Concentration of Alcohol (%)	Result
Finkelberg (1907)[11]	60-80	Persistent paralysis
May (1912)[12]	76, 80, 90, 100	Motor paralysis
	50	No motor paralysis
Gordon (1914)[13]	80	Progressive motor paralysis
Nasaroff (1925)[14]	70	Incomplete and temporary paralysis
Labat (1933)[15]	48 (with 1% procaine), 95	No demonstrable difference in paralysis
Labat and Greene (1931)[16]*	33	No paresis or paralysis

*Study was undertaken for management of painful disorders.

posterior columns, Lissauer tract, and dorsal roots and rootlets. Later, wallerian degeneration is seen to extend into the dorsal horns. Injection of a larger volume can result in degeneration of the spinal cord. Owing to its hypobaric nature relative to CSF (specific gravity, 0.8:1.1, respectively), alcohol rises quickly to reach the top of the fluid level after intrathecal injection. Skillful positioning of the patient is of utmost importance to avoid undesirable side effects from nonselective neurolysis by absolute alcohol (see Chapter 52).

After injection into the CSF, alcohol diffuses rapidly from the injection site. Only 10% of the initial dose remains at the site of the injection after 10 minutes, and about 4% remains after 30 minutes.[19] When injected near the sympathetic chain, alcohol destroys the ganglion cells and thus blocks all postganglionic fibers to all effector organs.[20] A temporary and incomplete block results if the injection affects only the rami communicantes of preganglionic and postganglionic fibers. Histopathologically, wallerian degeneration is evident in the sympathetic chain fibers.

Commonly, neurolytic blocks with alcohol are performed for cranial neuralgias (trigeminal and glossopharyngeal nerves), epidural and intrathecal interruption of neuraxial transmission, and lumbar sympathetic and celiac plexus lysis. Because the volume used is quite small, none of the side effects of ingested ethanol are seen. Extreme care should be taken at the time of injection to avoid local tissue injury and cellulitis or necrosis of adjacent tissues. After the injection, the needle should be flushed with a local anesthetic or normal saline to avoid depositing residual alcohol along the needle track.

Complications of Alcohol Neurolysis

Use of alcohol for neurolysis is sometimes associated with very painful, annoying, and psychologically distressing neuralgias. Patients often complain bitterly about the neuralgia despite adequate and effective analgesia if they were not thoroughly oriented when their informed consent was obtained for the procedure. The pain is described as dull to severe, sometimes as burning, and occasionally as a sharp, shooting pain. Recovery from the pain may occur as soon as a few weeks after neurolysis or may take many months. The incidence of this complication is higher after a thoracic paravertebral sympatholytic injection, possibly because of the greater proximity of the somatic fibers to the sympathetic chain in the thoracic region, than in the lumbar region.

Hypesthesia or anesthesia of the dermatomal distribution of the nerve roots treated with neurolysis is another distressing complication. Sometimes the pain relief is overshadowed by this lack of sensation. Fortunately, this complication is rare and recovery is relatively quick.

Loss of bowel or bladder sphincter tone, leading to bowel or urinary incontinence, has also been seen with intrathecal alcohol neurolysis in the lower lumbar and sacral areas. Hypobaric alcohol should be used to advantage to avoid this complication. During sacral nerve root neurolysis, only one side should be blocked at a time. Genitofemoral neuralgia can cause severe groin pain in patients who undergo lumbar sympathetic neurolysis with alcohol. This is referred pain caused by degeneration of the rami communicantes from the L2 nerve root to the genitofemoral nerve.[21-23] Paraplegia can result if injection of alcohol causes spasm of the artery of Adamkiewicz.

Phenol

Phenol has been used extensively since the earliest published reports of its use on rabbit blood vessels (Table 32–2). It is not available commercially in the injectable form but can be prepared by the hospital pharmacy. Phenol acts as a local anesthetic in lower concentrations and as a neurolytic agent in higher concentrations and thus has the advantage of causing minimal discomfort on injection.

Phenol is available as a mixture with glycerin, in which it is highly soluble, and diffuses out slowly, resulting in pronounced localized tissue effects. This solution is hyperbaric relative to the cerebrospinal fluid and can be prepared in concentrations ranging from 4% to 10%. Another form is as an aqueous mixture, which is a far more potent neurolytic agent. Various concentrations between 3% and 10% have been studied in the past. Commonly, concentrations between 6% and 8% are used (see Table 32–2). A concentration of 20% in glycerin has been reported for treatment of certain cases of spasticity.[34] Phenol may also be dissolved in a radiopaque dye to make a hyperbaric contrast solution.

Also called *carbolic acid,* phenol has a benzene ring with one hydroxyl group substituted for a hydrogen ion. In its pure state, phenol is colorless and poorly soluble, forming a 6.7% solution in water. Exposure to air causes oxidation and gives

Table 32–2

Use of Phenol as a Neurolytic Agent: History

Study (Year)	Application
Nechaev (1933)[24]	Local anesthesia
Putnam and Hampton (1936)[25]	Gasserian ganglion neurolysis
Mandl (1947)[26]	Chemical sympathectomy
Haxton (1949)[27] and Boyd et al., (1949)[28]	Paravertebral injection for intermittent claudication
Maher (1955)[29]	Intrathecal injection for cancer pain
Kelly and Gautier-Smith (1959)[30]	Intrathecal injection for spasticity of upper motor neuron disease
Nathan (1959)[31]	Intrathecal injection for spasticity of paraplegia
Nathan and Sears (1960)[32]	Effects on nerve conduction in cat spinal nerve roots
Iggo and Walsh (1960)[33]	Blockade of fibers in cat spinal nerve roots

it a reddish tinge. Phenol is excreted by the kidneys as various conjugated derivatives.[35] As compared with alcohol, phenol produces shorter-lived and less intense blockades. Moller and associates[36] compared various concentrations of alcohol and of phenol and concluded that 5% phenol is equal to 40% alcohol in neurolytic potency.

Phenol spares posterior root ganglia while causing nonselective neurolysis by denaturing the proteins of axons and perineural blood vessels.[37] The process of degeneration takes about 14 days, and regeneration is completed in about 14 weeks. After an intrathecal injection of phenol, its concentration decreases rapidly—to 30% of the original concentration in 60 seconds and to 0.1% within 15 minutes.[38] High affinity of phenol for vascular tissues has been proposed by Wood[39] to be an important pathophysiologic factor in the observed neuropathy. This factor may raise concerns about the use of phenol for celiac plexus neurolysis, because major blood vessels lie very close to the plexus. Phenol causes concentration-dependent degeneration of the peripheral nerves as well. Given subcutaneously, however, it may cause ulceration of the overlying skin.

Glycerol

Earlier reports on the use of glycerol for relieving pain of trigeminal neuralgia[40] generated widespread interest in its use. Histopathologic examination revealed extensive myelin sheath swelling, axonolysis, and severe inflammatory response after intraneuronal injection. Electron microscopy confirmed wallerian degeneration, phagocytosis, and mast cell degranulation. The differential effects of various concentrations of glycerol have been studied in experimental models, but no histologic data are available to support these observations.

Ammonium Compounds

In 1942, Bates and Judovich[38] published their experience using ammonium salts for relief of intractable pain. They prepared an extract from a pitcher plant distillate (*Sarracenia purpurea*) and used it for various neuralgias. A selective action on the sensory fibers was noted, but motor function and cutaneous sensation were spared. Use of 6% ammonium salts (ammonium chloride and ammonium hydroxide) was reported in 5000 doses with favorable results. Subsequent clinical trials, however, have yielded unpredictable and unreliable results. Since then, a concentration of 10% has been used for intercostal blocks with acceptable analgesia and intact motor function.[41, 42] Histopathologically, injection of ammonium salts near a peripheral nerve causes acute degenerative neuropathy affecting all fibers.[43]

Hypertonic and Hypotonic Solutions

Use of hypertonic and hypotonic solutions in intrathecal injections for the treatment of pain[44] has been associated with changes of neuropathy[45-47] that have not been corroborated by histologic evidence.[48, 49] Osmotic swelling of the nerve bundle is proposed as the mechanism of nerve conduction blockade.[50] Later experiments demonstrated myelin degeneration and axonolysis after a nerve was soaked for at least 1 hour in distilled water or solutions of osmolality greater than 1000 mmol/L. Thus, earlier clinical observations were probably attributed to endoneurial edema rather than structural damage to the nerve fibers.

Hypothermia and Cryoanalgesia

Depending on the degree of hypothermia, a temporary or longer-lasting injury to nerve fibers can be produced. The effect of cold on A-delta and C fibers was studied by Denny-Brown and colleagues in 1945.[51] Physiologically, prolongation of action potential is seen when the nerve is cooled to 5° C.[43] All myelinated fibers can be blocked at a given temperature, whereas unmyelinated fibers require a lower temperature.[52,53] Cytopathologic findings suggested acceleration of Schwann cell enzyme production as the possible cause of endoneurial capillary damage.[40]

Cryoanalgesia is the freezing of a small nerve segment with a 2-mm probe cooled to −60° C by rapid expansion of pressurized nitrous oxide from its tip. The probe is left in contact with the nerve tissue for 60 to 90 seconds and then allowed to "thaw" for another 45 to 60 seconds before being removed. An ice ball 2 to 4 mm in diameter is formed that freezes the nerve and completely damages the nerve fiber.[54] Endoneurial fluid pressure is elevated to 20 mm H_2O within 90 minutes. It drops over the next 24 hours and then increases again to reach a plateau after 6 days, secondary to changes of wallerian degeneration. An acute injury is produced that lasts approximately 4 to 6 weeks. The basal lamina remains unharmed, thus acting as a conduit for the process of regeneration.

Selection of a Neurolytic Agent

Physical characteristics of the two more commonly used neurolytic agents make them suitable for two different subgroups of patients (Table 32–3). Alcohol, on the one hand, is hypobaric and can be injected with the patient prone. Thus, it is suitable for a patient who is unable to lie supine owing to pain. Hyperbaric phenol, on the other hand, can reach dorsal nerve roots of a supine patient after intrathecal injection. Jacob and Howland[55] found a higher incidence of sphincter impairment with alcohol injection than with phenol. In cases of intractable pain, however, analgesic efficacy was equal for the two agents.[56-58] Phenol in glycerin diffuses out very slowly. Therefore, its degenerative action can be well-controlled by adjusting patient position. Alcohol has a quicker onset of action, but its site of action can be controlled in the vertical neuraxis by tilting the table head to foot or to one side. Neuritis and burning pain on injection are seen with alcohol. For intrathecal use, Maher[59] advocates phenol over alcohol because of its slow release and lower complication rate.

■ CONCLUSION

The use of neurolytic agents, such as alcohol, phenol, glycerol, and ammonium compounds, in various concentrations and at various sites in the body, has proved that the ideal of achieving adequate analgesia without attendant side effects is difficult. Enough damage needs to be done to the nerve to produce the changes of wallerian degeneration. Cautious use of neurolytic agents in carefully selected patients who have given fully informed consent is, therefore, warranted.

Table 32–3

Comparison of Phenol and Alcohol as Neurolytic Agents

Property	Phenol	Alcohol
Physical properties	Clear, colorless, pungent odor Poorly soluble in water Unstable at room temperature Hyperbaric relative to cerebrospinal fluid	Clear, colorless Absorbs water on exposure to air Stable at room temperature Hypobaric relative to cerebrospinal fluid
Chemical structure	Acid	Alcohol
Concentrations (%)	6-10	50-100
Equipotent neurolytic concentration (%)	5	40
Complications of use in neurolysis	Neuritis (uncommon) Toxicity at higher doses Hepatic and cardiac complications	Neuritis (common) Toxicity at commonly used doses
Sites of use (listed in order of preference)	Epidural Paravertebral Peripheral nerve roots Intrathecal Cranial nerves	Intrathecal Celiac ganglion Lumbar sympathetic chain Cranial nerves Paravertebral Epidural (low concentrations)

References

1. Schloesser: Heilung peripherer Reizzustande sensibler und motorischer Nerven. Klin Monatsbl Augenheilkd 41:244, 1903.
2. Swetlow GI: Paravertebral alcohol block in cardiac pain. Am Heart J 1:393, 1926.
3. Dogliotti AM: A new method of block anesthesia: Segmental peridural spinal anesthesia. Am J Surg 20:107, 1933.
4. Low PA: Endoneurial fluid pressure and microenvironment of nerve. In Dyck PJ, Thomas PK, Lambert EH, Bunge R (eds): Peripheral Neuropathy. Philadelphia, WB Saunders, 1984.
5. Myers RR, Powell HC, Costello ML, et al: Endoneurial fluid pressure: Direct measurement with micropipettes. Brain Res 148:510, 1978.
6. Fitzgerald MJT: Degeneration and regeneration. In Neuroanatomy: Basic and Clinical. Philadelphia, WB Saunders, 1985, p 16.
7. Waller A: Experiments on the section of the glossopharyngeal and hypoglossal nerves of the frog and observations of the alterations produced thereby in the structure of their primitive fibres. Philos Trans R Soc 140:423, 1850.
8. Myer RR, Powell HC: Galactose neuropathy: Impact of chronic endoneurial edema on nerve blood flow. Ann Neurol 16:587, 1984.
9. Ventafridda V, Narcello T, Augusto C, et al: A validation study of the WHO method for cancer pain relief. Cancer 59:850, 1987.
10. Cousins MJ, Dwyer B, Gibb D: Chronic pain and neurolytic neural blockade. In Cousins MJ, Bridenbaugh PO (eds): Neural Blockade in Clinical Anesthesia and Management of Pain, 2nd ed. Philadelphia, JB Lippincott, 1988, p 1053.
11. Finkelburg R: Experimentelle Untersuchungen über den Einfluss von Alkoholinjektionen und peripherische Nerven. Verh Dtsch Ges Inn Med 24:75, 1907.
12. May O: Functional and histological effects of intraneural and intraganglionic injection of alcohol. BMJ 2:365, 1912.
13. Gordon A: Experimental study of intraneural injections of alcohol. J Nerv Ment Dis 41:81, 1914.
14. Nasaroff NN: Über Alkoholinjecktionen in Nervenstamine. Zentralbl Chir 52:2777, 1925.
15. Labat G: Action of alcohol on the living nerve. Curr Res Anesth Analg 12:190, 1933.
16. Labat G, Greene MB: Contribution to the modern method of diagnosis and treatment of so-called sciatic neuralgias. Am J Surg 11:435, 1931.
17. Rumbsy MG, Finean JB: The action of organic solvents on the myelin sheath of peripheral nerve tissue-II (short-chain aliphatic alcohols). J Neurochem 13:1509, 1966.
18. Gallagher HS, Yonezawa T, Hoy RC, Derrick WS: Subarachnoid alcohol block. II: Histological changes in the central nervous system. Am J Pathol 35:679, 1961.
19. Matsuki M, Kato Y, Ichiyangi L: Progressive changes in the concentrations of ethyl alcohol in the human and canine subarachnoid space. Anesthesiology 36:632, 1972.
20. Merrick RL: Degeneration and recovery of autonomic neurones following alcoholic block. Ann Surg 113:298, 1941.
21. Rocco A: Radiofrequency lumbar sympatholysis: The evolution of a technique for managing sympathetically mediated pain. Reg Anesth 20:3, 1995.
22. Bogduk N, Tynan W, Wilson SS: The nerve supply to the human lumbar intervertebral discs. J Anat 132:39, 1981.
23. Edwards EA: Operative anatomy of the lumbar sympathetic chain. Angiology 12:184, 1951.
24. Nechaev VA: Solutions of phenol in local anesthesia. Soviet Khir 5:203, 1933.
25. Putnam TJ, Hampton OJ: A technique of injection into the gasserian ganglion under roentgenographic control. Arch Neurol Psychiatry 35:92, 1936.
26. Mandl F: Paravertebral Block. New York, Grune & Stratton, 1947.
27. Haxton HA: Chemical sympathectomy. Br Med J 1:1026, 1949.
28. Boyd AM, Ratcliff AH, Jepson RP, et al: Intermittent claudication. J Bone Joint Surg 3B:325, 1949.
29. Maher RM: Phenol for pain and spasticity. In Pain-Henry Ford Hospital International Symposium. Boston, Little, Brown, 1966, p 335.
30. Kelly RE, Gautier-Smith PC: Intrathecal phenol in the treatment of reflex spasms and spasticity. Lancet 2:1102, 1959.
31. Nathan PW: Intrathecal phenol to relieve spasticity in paraplegia. Lancet 2:1099, 1959.
32. Nathan PW, Sears TA: Effects of phenol on nervous conduction. J Physiol (Lond) 150:565, 1960.
33. Iggo A, Walsh EG: Selective block of small fibres in the spinal roots by phenol. Brain 83:701, 1960.
34. Pederson E, Juul-Jensen P: Treatment of spasticity by subarachnoid phenol glycerin. Neurology (Minneap) 15:256, 1965.
35. Felsenthal G: Pharmacology of phenol in peripheral nerve blocks: A review. Arch Phys Med Rehabil 55:13, 1974.

36. Moller JE, Helweg-Larson J, Jacobson E: Histopathological lesions in the sciatic nerve of the rat following perineural application of phenol and alcohol solutions. Dan Med Bull 16:116, 1969.

37. Smith MC: Histological findings following intrathecal injection of phenol solutions for the relief of pain. Anaesthesia 36:387, 1964.

38. Bates W, Judovich BD: Intractable pain. Anesthesiology 3:363, 1942.

39. Wood KM: The use of phenol as a neurolytic agent: A review. Pain 5:205, 1978.

40. Hakanson S: Trigeminal neuralgia treated by the injection of glycerol into the trigeminal cistern. Neurosurgery 9:638, 1981.

41. Miller RD, Johnston RR, Hosbuchi Y: Treatment of intercostal neuralgia with 10% ammonium sulfate. J Thorac Cardiovasc Surg 69:476, 1975.

42. Davies JJ, Stewart PB, Fink AP: Prolonged sensory block using ammonium salts. Anesthesiology 28:244, 1967.

43. Myers RR, Katz J: Neural pathology of neurolytic and semidestructive agents. In Cousins MJ, Bridenbaugh PO (eds): Neural Blockade in Clinical Anesthesia and Management of Pain, ed 2. Philadelphia, JB Lippincott, 1988, p 1031.

44. Hitchcock E: Osmolytic neurolysis for intractable facial pain. Lancet i:434, 1969.

45. Jewett DL, King JS: Conduction block of monkey dorsal rootlets by water and hypertonic saline solutions. Exp Neurol 33:225, 1971.

46. King JS, Jewett DL, Phil D, Sundberg HR: Differential blockade of cat dorsal root C fibers by various chloride solutions. J Neurosurg 36:569, 1972.

47. Robertson JD: Structural alterations in nerve fibers produced by hypotonic and hypertonic solutions. J Biophys Biochem Cytol 4:349, 1958.

48. Nicholson MF, Roberts FW: Relief of pain by intrathecal injection of hypothermic saline. Med J Aust 1:61, 1968.

49. Ochs S: Basic properties of axoplasmic transport. In Dyck PJ, Thomas PK, Lambert EH, Bunge R (eds): Peripheral Neuropathy. Philadelphia, WB Saunders, 1984, p 453.

50. Fink BR: Mechanism of hypo-osmotic conduction block. Reg Anesth 5:7, 1980.

51. Denny-Brown D, Adams R, Brenner C, Doherty MM: The pathology of injury to nerve induced by cold. J Neuropathol Exp Neurol 4:305, 1945.

52. Paintal AS: Block of conduction in mammalian myelinated nerve fibres by low temperatures. J Physiol 180:1, 1965.

53. Douglas WW, Malcolm JL: Effect of localized cooling on conduction in cat nerves. J Physiol (Lond) 130:63, 1955.

54. Myers RR, Powell HC, Costello ML, et al: Biophysical and pathologic effects of cryogenic nerve lesions. Ann Neurol 10:478, 1981.

55. Jacob RG, Howland WS: A comparison of intrathecal alcohol and phenol. J Ky Med Assoc 64:408, 1966.

56. Evans RJ, Mackay IM: Subarachnoid phenol nerve blocks for relief of pain in advanced malignancy. Can J Surg 15:50, 1972.

57. Wood KA: The use of phenol as a neurolytic agent: A review. Pain 5:205, 1978.

58. Gentil FF, Russo RP, Monti A, et al: Pain relief in cancerous patients by the use of phenol solution. Acta Univ Int Cancer 19:982, 1963.

59. Maher RM: Neurone selection in relief of pain: Further experiences with intrathecal injections. Lancet 1:16, 1957.

chapter 33

The Role of Spinal Opioids in the Management of Cancer Pain

Steven D. Waldman

Spinal opioids were first administered in humans in the late 1970s to palliate cancer pain that was unrelieved by all traditional treatments.[1] The choice of cancer pain as a first proving ground for this exciting new treatment derived from the favorable risk-to-benefit ratio in these terminally ill patients who had intractable cancer pain, and from the frustration born of the inability to control cancer pain in such patients without the use of invasive neurodestructive procedures.

The initial positive results of these early clinical trials led to rapid and widespread acceptance of spinal opioids as a treatment for cancer pain. As a result, spinal opioids have dramatically influenced the way intractable pain of malignant origin is managed. The continued decline in the number of neurodestructive procedures performed to palliate cancer pain attests to this fact.[2]

■ ETIOLOGY OF CANCER PAIN

To evaluate and treat the cancer pain patient adequately, it is helpful to delineate the specific pathophysiologic processes responsible for the pain. Precise evaluation allows the development of a rational treatment plan.

More than two thirds of cancer pain is due to direct tumor involvement of pain-sensitive structures.[3] Bone pain, which is probably related to disruption of the sensitive periosteum, is most common, followed by neuropathic pain caused by invasion of neural structures and visceral pain caused by obstruction of hollow viscus. Pain also may result as a side effect of cancer treatment, including surgery, chemotherapy, and radiation therapy; 10% of patients have pain that is unrelated to the cancer or its treatment.[4] Failure to recognize this latter group can lead to the use of inappropriate treatment modalities.

■ DESIGNING A TREATMENT PLAN FOR CANCER PAIN

Primary Cancer Treatments

When the pathophysiologic mechanism of the patient's pain is determined, an appropriate pain treatment plan can be designed. One should first determine if any primary antineo-plastic therapies are available and are likely to provide long-lasting pain relief.[5] Hormonal treatments for prostate and breast cancer and radiation therapy for bony metastatic disease fall into this category, as would surgical decompression of a bowel obstruction or laminectomy for spinal tumor. If the possibility of primary antineoplastic therapy exists, pain treatment should be approached as in the acute pain patient. Analgesic therapy in this setting should be flexible and easily withdrawn, allowing the opportunity for rapid adjustment should the primary antineoplastic therapy prove to have analgesic consequences. If palliation of cancer pain by primary treatment modalities is impossible or these efforts are ineffective, the implementation of analgesic treatments need not be constrained by the requirement of easy reversibility.

Pharmacologic Treatments

The World Health Organization (WHO) estimates that every day at least 3.5 million people worldwide have cancer pain.[6] Numerous reports have indicated that cancer pain is inadequately treated in many of these patients.[7] In an effort to provide a systematic approach to the pharmacologic treatment of cancer pain, the WHO Cancer Pain Relief Program developed an "analgesic ladder" to guide the selection of pharmacotherapy for cancer pain (Fig. 33–1).[6]

According to this approach, cancer patients with mild pain should first be administered simple non-opioid analgesics, such as aspirin, acetaminophen, or other nonsteroidal antiinflammatory agents. Adjuvant drugs, such as tricyclic antidepressants and antiemetics, are added to provide additional analgesic effects or palliation of other symptoms. Patients who fail to achieve adequate relief with these drugs or present with moderate cancer pain should be treated with a "weak" narcotic analgesic, such as codeine and tramadol with or without adjuvant analgesics. A non-opioid analgesic also should be given, and adjuvants are added as needed. Virtually all patients require a laxative. Finally, patients who fail to attain pain relief with these drugs or who present with severe pain should be administered a "strong" narcotic agonist, such as morphine with or without adjuvant analgesics. There is no ceiling effect with these drugs, and doses should be titrated upward until analgesia occurs or intolerable and unmanageable side effects occur.[5]

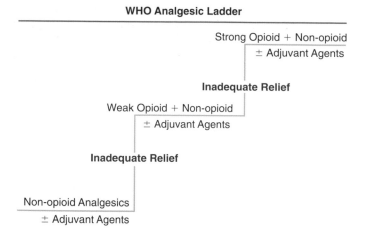

FIGURE 33–1 ■ WHO analgesic ladder.

Studies have suggested that if the first three steps of the therapeutic ladder are used appropriately, pain relief can be expected in at least 70% of cancer pain patients.[8] Pitfalls in the use of the therapeutic ladder involve failure to individualize treatment, failure to use appropriate routes of administration, failure to anticipate side effects, and failure to progress rapidly up the pain ladder to control acute pain breakthrough aggressively.

Neural Blockade

For the 30% of patients who do not obtain relief with the routine implementation of the analgesic ladder, a trial of neural blockade with local anesthetics alone or combined with long-acting steroids (corticosteroids such as methylprednisolone) may be indicated.[9] Neural blockade should not be viewed as a stand-alone treatment for cancer pain, but should be intelligently integrated into the therapeutic ladder. Patients with acute pain from a pathologic rib fracture may undergo intercostal nerve block simultaneously with implementation of opioid therapy.[10] Other acute pain problems amenable to neural blockade include acute vertebral compression fractures, post-thoracotomy or post-laparotomy pain, painful chest and nephrostomy tubes, painful biliary drainage catheters, and acute herpes zoster.[11] Neural blockade also may provide pain relief during painful procedures, such as biopsies and interventional radiology procedures.

Many cancer pain syndromes are mediated at least in part via the sympathetic nervous system.[9] Acute cancer pain syndromes that may benefit from interruption of the sympathetic nervous system by neural blockade with local anesthetics include post-mastectomy upper extremity pain, biliary and ureteral colic, pancreatitis, acute herpes zoster, and vascular insufficiency.[11,12]

Spinal Opioids

Indications

Similar to neural blockade, spinal opioid administration must be integrated into a comprehensive pain treatment plan. In contrast to local anesthetics, spinal opioids produce effects through activation of opioid receptors in the spinal cord[13] and do not compromise sympathetic or motor function. They may be useful in many situations not otherwise amenable to neural blockade.[14]

Spinal opioids may be useful acutely as a palliative measure in patients receiving primary antineoplastic treatments expected to provide long-term relief of pain. They may be used transiently to allow patients with severe movement-related pain to undergo diagnostic or therapeutic procedures.[2] Finally, acute administration of spinal opioids may be useful for aggressive treatment of "pain emergencies" that cannot be quickly controlled with other cancer pain treatment modalities.

Long-term administration of spinal opioid should not be implemented until the approach outlined in the analgesic ladder proves unable to control the pain. This recommendation recognizes that these more traditional treatments have a more favorable risk-to-benefit ratio than spinal opioids.

Patient Selection

Proper patient selection is crucial if spinal opioids are to be used successfully to treat cancer pain.[15] Factors to be considered include physiologic and behavioral abnormalities that may interfere with the patient's ability to assess pain relief; the presence of coagulopathy or infection, which may preclude the injection of spinal opioids; and the adequacy of the support system necessary to obtain, prepare, and administer spinal opioids.[2,15]

Choice of Drug

The choice of the specific opioid to be administered is based on an analysis of three variables: (1) onset of action, (2) duration of action, and (3) side effect profile. Although onset of action may be of paramount importance in the acute pain patient, it is of little importance when choosing a spinal opioid for the treatment of chronic cancer pain. In general, the onset of analgesia correlates with the lipophilicity of the opioid.[16] Duration of action has a direct bearing on the mode of administration (bolus versus continuous infusion) required to obtain around-the-clock pain relief. Factors that may determine the duration of action of spinal opioids include lipophilicity, receptor affinity, intrinsic agonist activity of the opioid, rate of disassociation from spinal cord binding sites, and removal of the opioid via the circulation of the spinal cord.[17] Although generalizations can be made regarding the side effect profile of each spinal opioid, significant patient-to-patient variability exists. To use spinal opioids successfully, the clinician must anticipate and treat side effects aggressively (see later).

Route of Administration

There are advantages and disadvantages to epidural and subarachnoid routes for administration of spinal opioids to cancer patients.[2] An important factor in selecting the route of administration is the technical expertise of the anesthesiologist in identifying the epidural space. If technical expertise is lacking, the subarachnoid route is preferred.

Subarachnoid Route

The subarachnoid route bypasses the dura, depositing the opioid in close proximity to receptors in the spinal cord.[18] This deposition results in a more rapid onset and longer duration of action, but also a higher incidence of centrally mediated side effects. Because the dura must be punctured to inject the opioid, the risk of post–dural puncture headache exists. If infection occurs, meningitis rather than epidural abscess results.

Epidural Route

The major advantage of the epidural route of administration is the ability to place the opioid at any dermatomal level.[2,15] This ability has proved especially useful in the treatment of upper body pain, such as that caused by superior sulcus lung tumors.[19] The epidural route is not associated with post–dural puncture headache, and if infection occurs, epidural abscess rather than meningitis results. Because higher doses of opioid are necessary to obtain analgesia, a slightly greater incidence of systemic side effects, such as hives and bronchospasm, may be seen with epidural administration.[2,14]

Dosage

As a general rule, the dosage of epidurally administered opioid equianalgesic to the subarachnoid dosage approximates a ratio of 10:1.[16] The initial epidural dose of morphine administered in the lumbar region is approximately 5 mg, whereas the subarachnoid dose is approximately 0.5 mg. Table 33–1 provides recommended starting dosages of commonly used spinally administered opioids for the relatively nontolerant patient. Because most patients with cancer pain have a variable degree of opioid tolerance (related to the dose and duration of prior opioid intake), these doses may be too low to initiate therapy in an individual patient. The increase in the starting dose is empirical, based on the judgment of the clinician that the patient is tolerant. The development of guidelines for the selection of the dose has been hampered by the lack of studies in which relative potency of spinal opioids compared with other routes has been determined.

Intermittent Bolus Versus Continuous Infusion

The duration of action of spinally administered opioids should be the major determinant of the mode of administration.[16] Drugs with a longer duration of action, such as morphine (18-20 hours), are more suitable for intermittent injection. Drugs with a short duration of action, such as fentanyl, must be administered via continuous infusion to provide around-the-clock pain relief.[2,15]

Side Effects

Side effects can be systemic or centrally mediated.[14,16,17] Because the epidural space is highly vascular, any drug administered via this route enters the systemic circulation.[18] If the epidural dose is high enough, the patient may experience the same systemic side effects that would occur with intravenous administration of the drug. These side effects include the release of histamine that may result in urticaria or wheezing and occasionally gastrointestinal side effects.

Centrally mediated side effects of spinal opioids include pruritus, nausea and vomiting, urinary retention, sedation, and late respiratory depression.[14,16,20] Although potentially life-threatening, the actual occurrence of late respiratory depression in a cancer pain patient is exceedingly rare, presumably because of opioid tolerance induced by prior intake of these drugs. An opioid-naive patient is at higher risk for this potentially serious problem.[20]

Treatment of the side effects of spinal opioids, with the exception of respiratory depression, should be directed at symptomatic relief.[16,21] The clinician and patient must be aware of the potential side effects to anticipate and recognize the need for treatment. For milder symptoms, reassurance often is all that is required. Adjuvant drugs to treat pruritus, nausea and vomiting, or other symptoms can be given if necessary. A standing order for bladder catheterization as needed should be considered for the first few doses of spinal opioids in nontolerant patients. If symptoms persist, or respiratory depression occurs, minute doses of narcotic antagonists, such as naloxone, or administration of small amounts of agonist/antagonist drugs, such as nalbuphine, also can be used.[16,20] These drugs should be titrated carefully to avoid reversal of the analgesic properties of systemic or spinally administered opioids because patients in this setting may experience increased sensitivity to narcotic antagonists. Table 33–2 provides an example of standing post–spinal opioid orders that have worked well in a variety of clinical settings for our cancer patients.

■ CONCLUSION

Spinal opioids represent a great advance in cancer pain management. Proper selection of patients is crucial if optimal results are to be achieved. The long-term administration of opioids and other drugs into the epidural or subarachnoid space is in its infancy. Advances in the pharmacology of spinal drugs and the development of new delivery system technology in time no doubt will expand the options available for the relief of cancer pain.

Table 33–1			
Recommended Starting Dosages of Commonly Used Spinally Administered Opioids			
Drug	*Epidural Dose (mg)*	*Volume/Diluent (mL)*	*Duration (hr)*
Meperidine	50 Lumbar	5 Lumbar	7
	5 Cervical	1 Cervical	7
Morphine	5 Lumbar	0.5 Lumbar	18
	0.5 Cervical	0.1 Cervical	18
Fentanyl	0.1 Lumbar	5 Lumbar	4
	0.01 Cervical	0.1 Cervical	4

Table 33–2

Standing Orders—Post–Spinal Opioid Injection

1. Measure vital signs every 15 min × 1 hr, every 30 min × 1 hr, then every hour × 4 hr, then every 4 hr × 24 hr
2. Check and record respiratory rate every hour × 24 hr
3. Maintain patient supine with head of bed up 30 degrees for 30 min after injection
4. Administer naloxone (Narcan) intravenous push for respirations <6/min as follows: Dilute 1 ampule of naloxone (0.4 mg) with 8 mL of normal saline, and give 3 mL every 5 min until respirations >10/min. Notify pain management physician if this is done
5. Administer diphenhydramine (Benadryl) 50 mg intramuscularly every 4-6 hr as needed for severe itching
6. Give droperidol (Inapsine) 2.5 mg intramuscularly every 4 hr as needed for nausea in the absence of any other standing antiemetic order
7. If patient develops hypotension, administer ephedrine intravenous push in 10-mg increments every 3-5 min to a total of 50 mg. Notify pain management physician if ephedrine is given. *Note:* To effect an accurate dose of ephedrine, mix 1 mL of ephedrine (50 mg/mL) with 4 mL of sterile normal saline to equal 50 mg in 5 mL or 10 mg in 1 mL
8. If not sedated, patient may be up with assistance 30 min after injection of spinal opioids
9. Document pain complaints carefully (i.e., onset, intensity, location, duration, precipitating and alleviating factors)
10. If any problems or questions arise, contact pain management physician
11. Monitor for urinary retention and insert straight catheter as needed for urinary retention. Notify pain management physician if this is done

References

1. Wang JK, Nauss LE, Thomas JE: Pain relief by intrathecally applied morphine in man. Anesthesiology 50:149, 1979.
2. Waldman SD, Coombs DW: Selection of implantable narcotic delivery systems. Anesth Analg 68:377, 1989.
3. Foley KM: The treatment of cancer pain. N Engl J Med 313:84, 1985.
4. Portenoy RK, LaSage P: Management of cancer pain. Lancet 353:1696, 1999.
5. Portenoy RK: Practical aspects of pain control in the patient with cancer. CA Cancer J Clin 38(6):327, 1988.
6. World Health Organization: Cancer Pain Relief, 2nd ed. Geneva, WHO, 1996.
7. Meuser T, Pietruck C, Radbruch L, et al: Symptoms during cancer pain treatment following the WHO guidelines: A longitudinal follow-up study of symptom prevalence, severity and etiology. Pain 93:247, 2001.
8. Ventafridda V, Tamburini M, Caraceni A, et al: A validation study for the WHO method of cancer pain relief. Cancer 59:850, 1987.
9. Abram SE: The role of nonneurolytic nerve blocks in the management of cancer pain. In Abram SE (ed): Cancer Pain. Boston, Kluwer, 1989, p 67.
10. Waldman SD: Caudal nerve block. In: Atlas of Interventional Pain Management, 2nd ed. Philadelphia, WB Saunders, 2004, p 380-383.
11. Waldman SD: Intercostal nerve block. In: Atlas of Interventional Pain Management, 2nd ed. Philadelphia, WB Saunders, 2004, p 241.
12. Waldman SD: Lumbar sympathetic ganglion block. In: Atlas of Interventional Pain Management, 2nd ed. Philadelphia, WB Saunders, 2004, p 308.
13. Yaksh TL, Noueihed R: The physiology and pharmacology of spinal opiates. Annu Rev Pharmacol Toxicol 25:433, 1985.
14. Coombs DW: Spinal narcotics for intractable cancer pain. In Abram SE (ed): Cancer Pain. Boston, Kluwer, 1989, p 77.
15. Waldman SD, Feldstein GS, Allen ML: Selection of patients for implantable intraspinal narcotic delivery systems. Anesth Analg 65:883, 1986.
16. Rawal N: Indications for the use of intraspinal opioids. In Rawal N, Coombs DW (eds): Spinal Narcotics. Boston, Kluwer, 1990, p 43.
17. Reynolds LL, Kedlaya D: Spinal administration of opioids for pain of malignant origin. In Waldman SD (ed): Interventional Pain Management, 2nd ed. Philadelphia, WB Saunders, 2001, p 605.
18. Gustafsson LL: Systemic and local distribution of opioids after spinal administration. In Rawal N, Coombs DW (eds): Spinal Narcotics. Boston, Kluwer, 1990, p 33.
19. Waldman SD, Cronen MC: Thoracic epidural morphine in the palliation of chest wall pain secondary to relapsing polychondritis. J Pain Symptom Manage 4:60-63, 1989.
20. Rawal R: Adverse effects of spinal opioids in acute pain and their management. In Rawal N, Coombs DW (eds): Spinal Narcotics. Boston, Kluwer, 1990, p 77.
21. Cousins MJ, Mather LE: Intrathecal and epidural administration of opioids. Anesthesiology 61:276, 1984.

chapter 34

The Role of Neurosurgery in the Management of Intractable Pain

Michael S. Yoon and Michael Munz

The neurosurgeon can play a vital role in the team approach to the management of chronic intractable pain. A number of procedures are available to assist the anesthesiologist or other caretaker in treating the patient when other measures have failed. This introductory chapter to the neurosurgical techniques will briefly cover a number of the more common procedures that neurosurgeons have in their armamentarium to combat pain refractory to conservative therapies.

■ TECHNIQUES FOR THE TREATMENT OF TRIGEMINAL NEURALGIA

For medically refractory trigeminal neuralgia, three basic options are now available (1) percutaneous techniques; (2) microvascular decompression; and (3) stereotactic radiosurgery. The choice of the procedure to use depends on the surgeon's preference and experience, as all have advantages and disadvantages. In general, the less invasive procedures are used for older, less healthy patients owing to life expectancy and the likelihood of medical complications.

Percutaneous techniques involve lesioning the trigeminal ganglion with glycerol, radiofrequency electrocoagulation, balloon compression, or permanent stimulating electrode placement. For a glycerol rhizotomy, the patient is given mild sedation and local anesthesia is administered. A 20-gauge spinal needle is placed through the patient's cheek under fluoroscopic guidance into the foramen ovale, where the mandibular branch of the trigeminal nerve exits (Fig. 34–1, Fig. 34–2). Cerebrospinal fluid is obtained once the dural sleeve is pierced, and intrathecal contrast medium is then injected to fill the trigeminal cistern. The appropriate divisions of the trigeminal nerve are then lesioned by injecting a controlled amount of anhydrous glycerol into the cistern.

A similar approach is used for the radiofrequency technique, except a 19-gauge needle is used. Once cerebrospinal fluid is encountered, the stylet is replaced with a radiofrequency electrode thermistor (Fig. 34–3, Fig. 34–4). The ultimate position of the needle is determined by stimulating the patient and evaluating the sensory response. When motor responses alert the surgeon to the proximity of the electrode to the motor root, the electrode should be repositioned. A lesion is made by heating the electrode tip with the generator to 75° C for 90 seconds. This is considered the procedure of choice for trigeminal neuralgia secondary to multiple sclerosis.

Percutaneous balloon compression of the trigeminal ganglion requires general anesthesia and a 14-gauge needle. A no. 4 Fr Fogarty catheter is then advanced into the needle and inflated with contrast to achieve a pear shape within the Meckel cave (Fig. 34–5). The balloon is inflated and allowed to compress the ganglion for approximately 1 minute. Reflex hypertension and bradycardia typically occur during this procedure. Alternatively, a stimulating electrode can be placed via the foramen ovale to provide neuro-augmentation of the affected division of the trigeminal nerve (Fig. 34–6).

Microvascular decompression requires general anesthesia and a lateral suboccipital craniectomy to access the posterior fossa of the skull. With the use of a microscope, a piece of teased Teflon felt is placed between the trigeminal nerve and a loop of the superior cerebellar artery, which is most often the offending lesion, as it pulsates against the nerve (Fig. 34–7). This technique has also been found to be effective in treating vascular compression of other cranial nerves in disorders such as hemifacial spasm and glossopharyngeal neuralgia.

More recently, stereotactic radiosurgery has come into use as a noninvasive procedure to treat trigeminal neuralgia. This technique requires that the patient be placed into a stereotactic head frame using local anesthesia and mild sedation. An MRI is then obtained to identify the trigeminal nerve as it exits the pons and enters the Meckel cave. A neurosurgeon, radiation oncologist, and medical physicist then plan the radiosurgery and select the proper dose. Typically, 70 to 90 Gy is focused on the target site with a Gamma Knife. A few patients with refractory cluster headaches have also been treated with radiosurgery targeted at the trigeminal nerve root entry zone, with good results.[1]

In a recent article that combined the results of a number of series, initial pain relief was found to be 98% for successfully completed procedures with both microvascular decompression and radiofrequency rhizotomy, 93% with balloon compression, and 91% with glycerol rhizotomy.[2] With

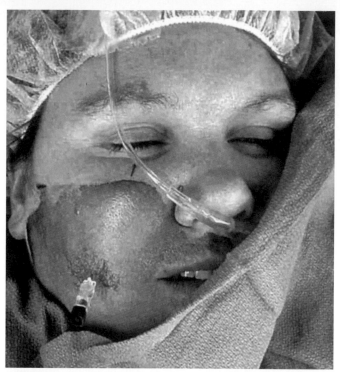

FIGURE 34–1 ■ A percutaneous glycerol rhizotomy for trigeminal neuralgia involves placing a spinal needle through the patient's cheek into the foramen ovale. (From Waldman SD [ed]: Interventional Pain Management, 2nd ed. Philadelphia, Saunders, 2001, p 672, Fig. 65–1.)

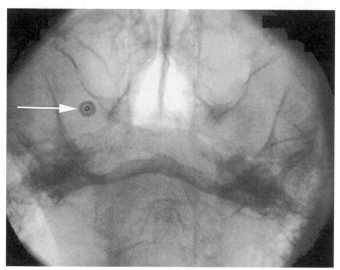

FIGURE 34–2 ■ The submental view of the face with the needle in the foramen ovale. Note the "tunnel view" of the hub of the needle. The *arrow* indicates the rim of the foramen ovale. (From Raj PP, Lou L, Erdine S, Straats P, Waldman S: Radiographic Imaging for Regional Anesthesia and Pain Management. Philadelphia, Churchill Livingstone, 2003, p 40, Fig. 6–8.)

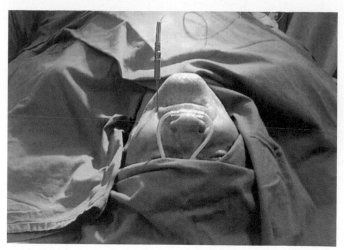

FIGURE 34–3 ■ Radiofrequency needle entering the facial skin without a catheter. Note the draping of the patient with the area of entry exposed and an O₂ cannula in place for trigeminal ganglion radiofrequency. (From Raj PP, Lou L, Erdine S, Straats P, Waldman S: Radiographic Imaging for Regional Anesthesia and Pain Management. Philadelphia, Churchill Livingstone, 2003, p 42. Fig. 6–13.)

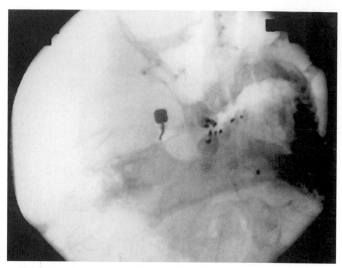

FIGURE 34–4 ■ Submental view with a fluoroscope. Note the curved-blunt Racz-Finch radiofrequency needle entering the foramen ovale in its lateral aspect. (From Raj PP, Lou L, Erdine S, Straats P, Waldman S: Radiographic Imaging for Regional Anesthesia and Pain Management. Philadelphia, Churchill Livingstone, 2003, p 43, Fig. 6–15.)

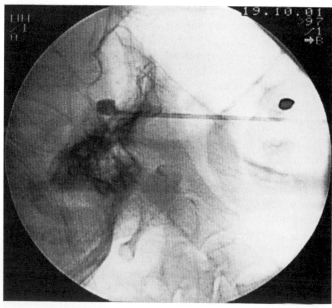

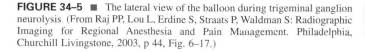

FIGURE 34–5 ■ The lateral view of the balloon during trigeminal ganglion neurolysis. (From Raj PP, Lou L, Erdine S, Straats P, Waldman S: Radiographic Imaging for Regional Anesthesia and Pain Management. Philadelphia, Churchill Livingstone, 2003, p 44, Fig. 6–17.)

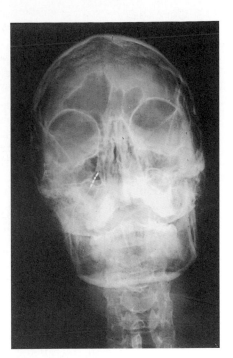

FIGURE 34–6 ■ Anteroposterior view of the electrode in place. (From Raj PP, Lou L, Erdine S, Straats P, Waldman S: Radiographic Imaging for Regional Anesthesia and Pain Management. Philadelphia, Churchill Livingstone, 2003, p 44, Fig. 6–18.)

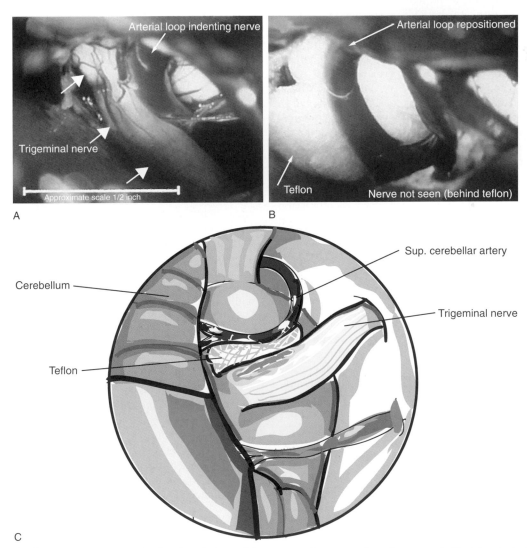

FIGURE 34–7 ■ A microvascular decompression for trigeminal neuralgia as seen under an operating microscope. **A,** The trigeminal nerve, as it exits the brain stem, is being compressed by a loop of the superior cerebellar artery. **B,** The same view after a piece of Teflon has been placed between the nerve and the artery. **C,** Drawing of view in **B**. (Courtesy of Peter J, Jannetta, MD. From: Waldman SD [ed]: Interventional Pain Management, 2nd ed. Philadelphia, Saunders, 2001, p 672, Fig. 65–2A and B.)

stereotactic radiosurgery, initial complete pain relief was reported at 60% and an additional 17% experienced significant reduction in their pain.[3] It should be noted that 15% of patients who intended to have a microvascular decompression underwent open partial rhizotomy instead because significant vascular compression was not seen or adequate decompression was not considered safe. Six percent of glycerol rhizotomies are not completed owing to failure to locate the needle site, and 1% of balloon compressions are incomplete because of failure to cannulate the foramen ovale. Radiofrequency rhizotomy was completed in all patients in the series reviewed.

Long-term pain recurrence is 54% with glycerol rhizotomy, 21% with balloon decompression, 20% with radiofrequency rhizotomy, and 15% with microvascular decompression. Stereotactic radiosurgery has a reported recurrence rate of 10% in short-term follow-up (mean 18 months) of those who initially reported complete pain relief.

Facial numbness was experienced by 98% after radiofrequency rhizotomy, 72% after balloon compression, 60% after glycerol rhizotomy, and 10% after stereotactic radiosurgery. Only 2% experienced facial numbness after microvascular decompression, but this rate should be considered in light of the fact that 15% of patients who intend to undergo microvascular decompression receive a partial rhizotomy, for the reasons mentioned earlier; 100% of patients experience facial numbness after partial rhizotomy. Nevertheless, most facial numbness is mild and limited in severity. Major dysesthesia occurs in 2% to 10% of the percutaneous procedures but in only 0.3% of patients undergoing microvascular decompression. Anesthesia dolorosa occurs in 0.1% to 1.8% after the percutaneous techniques and not at all after microvascular decompression or stereotactic radiosurgery.

The prevalence of corneal anesthesia after radiofrequency rhizotomy is 7%, after glycerol rhizotomy 3.7%, after balloon compression 1.5%, and after microvascular decompression 0.05%. The rate of trigeminal motor dysfunction after balloon compression is 66% and after radiofrequency rhizotomy 23%, but it is very low after glycerol rhizotomy (1.7%) and does not complicate microvascular decompression.

Permanent cranial nerve deficit occurs in 3% of patients who undergo posterior fossa exploration for microvascular decompression and does not occur after the percutaneous techniques. Perioperative complications such as wound infection and meningitis are highest (10%) with posterior fossa exploration for microvascular decompression and less likely in the percutaneous techniques (≤1.7%). Posterior fossa exploration is also associated with a 1% rate of major intracranial hemorrhage or infarction and a 0.6% rate of death. These complications did not occur after the percutaneous procedures in the series reviewed. There are rare reports of temporal lobe hemorrhage, seizure, stroke, and death after percutaneous techniques.[4]

∎ CORDOTOMY

Patients who suffer from intractable cancer pain can benefit significantly from a percutaneous or open cordotomy. Cordotomy is not recommended in patients with long life expectancy due to its nonpermanent effects. The percutaneous approach is performed under local anesthesia and mild seda-

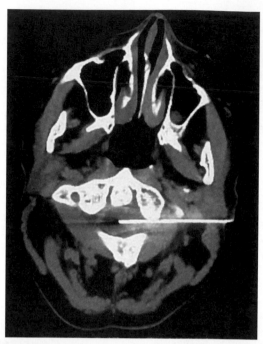

FIGURE 34–8 ∎ CT view through the level of C1 demonstrates the placement of the radiofrequency needle in a percutaneous cordotomy. The needle has entered the spinal canal and pierced the spinal cord. (From: Waldman SD [ed]: Interventional Pain Management, 2nd ed. Philadelphia, Saunders, 2001, p 673, Fig. 65–3.)

tion. Using the guidance of fluoroscopy or computed tomography, a 20-gauge spinal needle is introduced through the neck, contralateral to the affected region, into the spinal canal at the C1-C2 interspace. The contralateral approach is used because spinothalamic tract fibers cross at the level of the spinal cord, not the brainstem. Once cerebrospinal fluid is encountered, contrast medium is injected to delineate the cord and the dentate ligament. A second needle with a stylet is then introduced ventral to the ligament where the lateral spinothalamic tract is located (Fig. 34–8). After the stylet is removed, a radiofrequency electrode is introduced through the needle and, after physiologic data are gathered from the electrode within the cord and anatomic data from radiography, a thermal lesion is generated by heating the electrode to 80° C for 10 seconds. The open cordotomy requires general anesthesia and a laminectomy to gain access to the spinal cord. Using microsurgical technique, a small part of the lateral cord is exposed and then divided.

A recent study of percutaneous cordotomy performed for malignant pain found that 87% were completely relieved of pain after a unilateral procedure.[5] Complications included severe motor deficit (8.1%), urinary retention (6.5%), and mirror-image pain (6.5%). The incidence of complications was higher after bilateral cordotomy and the success rate much lower (50%). Bilateral cordotomy has been reported to cause sleep-induced apnea (Ondine curse) and severe hypotension.[6]

∎ DEEP BRAIN STIMULATION

With the proven effectiveness and more widespread use of spinal cord stimulation and intrathecal pumps, which are both discussed elsewhere in this textbook, deep brain stimulation

(DBS) certainly is not considered an early-line treatment for chronic pain, but it can be very useful in certain patients. The technique involves placing the patient in a stereotactic head frame under local anesthesia and mild sedation. Magnetic resonance or computed tomography images are then obtained to stereotactically localize the target sites, typically the periventricular and periaqueductal gray matter of the mesencephalic-diencephalic transition area, the specific sensory thalamic nuclei, the internal capsule, and the motor cortex. Once the coordinates for the target site are obtained, an electrode is placed into the brain via a burr hole under local anesthesia and sedation (Fig. 34–9). Electrophysiologic recording and

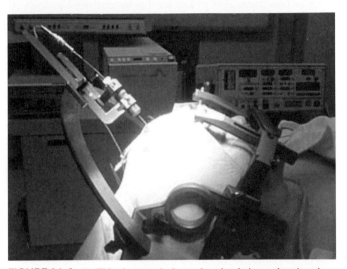

FIGURE 34–9 ■ This photograph shows the stimulating and testing phase of the placement of a deep brain stimulator. The patient's head is in a stereotactic head frame. (From Waldman SD [ed]: Interventional Pain Management, 2nd ed. Philadelphia, Saunders, 2001, p 674, Fig 65–4.)

motor and sensory responses with a stimulating electrode guide the neurosurgeon to the ultimate placement of the permanent DBS electrode. After the electrode is placed in the appropriate position, the patient is given general anesthesia and the proximal lead is tunneled in the subcutaneous space to the infraclavicular space of the chest, where it is attached to a pulse generator, much as a cardiac pacemaker is implanted (Fig. 34–10). The pulse generator can be programmed to various settings by external interrogation.

A long-term follow-up study found DBS to be most effective for failed back syndrome, trigeminal neuropathy, and peripheral neuropathy, whereas patients with thalamic pain, spinal cord injury, and postherpetic neuralgia did poorly.[7] Nociceptive pain was relieved in 71%, whereas neuropathic pain was relieved in only 44%. The majority of the patients in this study had failed back syndrome, and of these 91% had early pain relief and 74% continued to have long-term relief. Overall complications included headache pain (22%), infection (6%), fractured electrode (3%), hardware malfunction (3%), postoperative seizures (3%), blurred vision with stimulation (3%), electrical leak (1%), and intracerebral hematoma (1%). The pulse generator battery has to be replaced approximately every 3 to 5 years. A distinct advantage of DBS over ablative procedures is that it is potentially nondestructive and reversible.

■ DORSAL ROOT ENTRY ZONE LESIONING

A dorsal root entry zone (DREZ) lesion destroys nociceptive secondary neurons in the spinal cord. It is useful for refractory phantom limb, postherpetic, and reflex sympathetic pain; in the partially damaged dorsal horn associated with paraplegia, with or without syringomyelia; or in the completely

FIGURE 34–10 ■ Placement of the permanent DBS electrode.

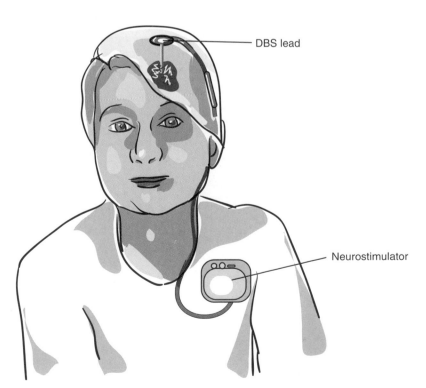

DBS lead

Neurostimulator

denervated dorsal horn of brachial plexus avulsion injuries. The technique involves laminectomy and intradural exposure of the spinal cord. With an operating microscope, the dorsal roots are identified, and then a small radiofrequency electrode is placed into the dorsal horn of the affected side (Fig 34–11). A contiguous series of lesions is made by heating the electrode tip with a generator to 75° C for 15 seconds. For avulsion injuries, the pain relief from the DREZ operation is often immediate, although in a rare patient the pain initially is worse. In a series of more than 100 patients with brachial plexus avulsion, 70% have experienced good pain relief that lasted longer than 5 years after a DREZ operation.[8] The major complication, weakness in the ipsilateral leg (5% overall rate), is due to involvement of the adjacent pyramidal tract. This complication occurs most frequently in patients with postherpetic chest or abdominal pain, for which lesions are made in

the thoracic spinal cord. Leg weakness after cervical DREZ lesioning is rare.

■ SYMPATHECTOMY

Surgical procedures to disrupt the sympathetic nervous system can be used to treat causalgia, reflex sympathetic dystrophy, Sudeck atrophy, and painful ischemic states such as Raynaud phenomenon or angina pectoris. To determine which patients might be good candidates for sympathectomy, a temporary sympathetic blockade can be performed, most commonly by injecting local anesthesia into the stellate ganglion or into the region of the lumbar sympathetic ganglia. If the patient responds favorably, an ablative sympathectomy can be performed via a posterior costotransversectomy

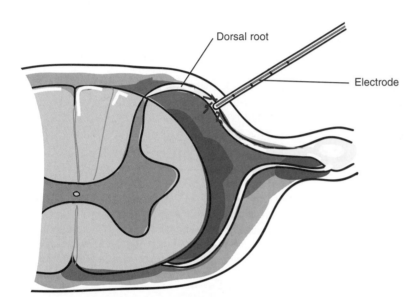

FIGURE 34–11 ■ The radiofrequency electrode is touching the dorsal root of the peripheral nerve.

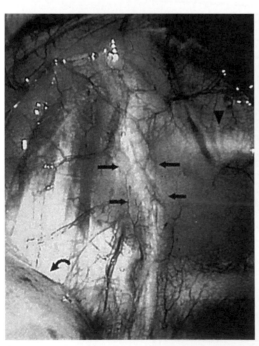

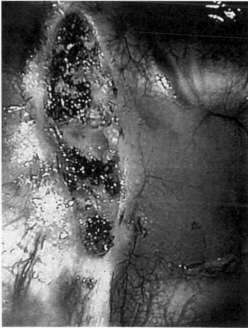

A   B

FIGURE 34–12 ■ The view from a left-sided endoscopic transthoracic sympathectomy. **A,** The *arrows* delineate the sympathetic chain indenting the pleura. The *arrowhead* points to the superior portion of the second rib, and the curved arrow points to the collapsed lung. **B,** A slightly more magnified view after the sympathetic chain has been ablated by thermal coagulation. (Courtesy of Raj K, Narayan, MD. From Waldman SD [ed]: Interventional Pain Management, 2nd ed. Philadelphia, Saunders, 2001, p 674, Fig 65–5.

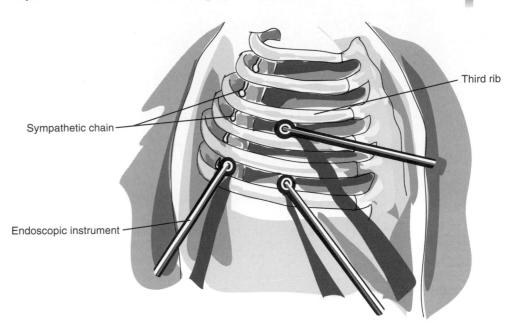

Third rib

Sympathetic chain

Endoscopic instrument

FIGURE 34–13 ■ Endoscopic instruments are entering the pleural cavity at several points between ribs.

approach, percutaneously, or endoscopically. Recently, the transthoracic endoscopic approach has gained favor for upper thoracic ganglionectomy owing to improved instrumentation and minimal invasiveness. It is actually very effective for the treatment of hyperhidrosis. This particular approach involves collapsing the lung on the affected side with a double-lumen endotracheal tube. Through small lateral chest incisions, the endoscopic instruments are introduced through the pleural cavity, and the thoracic sympathetic chain is clearly identified and thermally coagulated (see Fig. 34–5). As many as 95% of patients with causalgia obtain significant pain relief after sympathectomy[9]; however, only about 50% apparently receive lasting relief.[10] Complications from sympathectomies include Horner syndrome and tension pneumothorax. The major complication associated with lumbar sympathectomy is loss of male sexual function (when sympathectomy is bilateral).

■ CONCLUSION

Certainly, a wide range of techniques are available to the neurosurgeon to treat a variety of intractable pain entities, including the benign pain of trigeminal neuralgia and the pain of many cancers. The newly reported success of stereotactic radiosurgery in alleviating trigeminal neuralgia and cluster headaches is an encouragement, as it adds yet another tool for neurosurgeons to fight severe pain. Better equipment and instrumentation are also making procedures such as the endoscopic sympathectomy more likely to be technically success-

ful and better tolerated by patients. As the field of pain management and the specialty of neurosurgery continue to evolve, many more options should become available to treat patients who otherwise have little hope of relief.

References

1. Ford RG, Ford KT, Swaid S, Young P, Jennelle R: Gamma knife treatment of refractory cluster headache. Headache 38(1):3, 1998.
2. Taha JM, Tew JM: Comparison of surgical treatments for trigeminal neuralgia: Reevaluation of radiofrequency rhizotomy. Neurosurgery 38(5):834, 1996.
3. Kondziolka D, Perez B, Flickinger JC, Habeck M, Lunsford LD: Gamma knife radiosurgery for trigeminal neuralgia: Results and expectations. Arch Neurol 55(12):1524, 1998.
4. Sweet WH, Poletti C: Complications of percutaneous rhizotomy and microvascular decompression operations for facial pain. In Schmidek HH, Sweet WH (eds): Operative Neurosurgical Techniques: Indications, Methods, and Results, ed 3. Philadelphia, WB Saunders, 1995, p 1543.
5. Sanders M, Zuurmond W: Safety of unilateral and bilateral percutaneous cervical cordotomy in 80 terminally ill cancer patients. J Clin Oncol 13(6):1509, 1995.
6. Tranmer BI, Tucker WS, Bilbao JM: Sleep induced apnea following percutaneous cervical cordotomy. Can J Neurol Sci 14:262, 1987.
7. Kumar K, Toth C, Nath RK: Deep brain stimulation for intractable pain: A 15-year experience. Neurosurgery 40(4):736, 1997.
8. Nashold BS, Nashold JRB: The DREZ operation. In Tindall GT, Cooper PR, Barrow DL (eds): The Practice of Neurosurgery. Baltimore, Williams & Wilkins, 1996.
9. Ochoa JL: The newly recognized painful ABC syndrome: Thermographic aspects. Thermology 2:34, 1986.
10. Young RF: Sympathetic nervous system and pain. In Tindall GT, Cooper PR, Barrow DL (eds): The Practice of Neurosurgery. Baltimore, Williams & Wilkins, 1996.

chapter 35

Palliative Care in the Management of Cancer Pain

Fadi Braiteh and Eduardo Bruera

Worldwide, the majority of cancer patients still present, in 2004, with advanced-stage disease. For many, the only sensible treatment option remains pain relief and palliative care. Effective approaches to palliative care are available to improve the quality of life for cancer patients.

■ PALLIATIVE CARE

Palliative care is a discipline in medicine that changed its names frequently and encountered multiple definitions. One can find different nomenclature varying from palliative medicine, to supportive medicine, hospice care, specialist palliative care, generalist palliative care, generic palliative care, and basic palliative care.[1]

The World Health Organization (WHO) recently provided a newer, more appropriate definition of palliative medicine.[2] According to this new definition, palliative care:

- Provides relief from pain and other distressing symptoms;
- Affirms life and regards dying as a normal process;
- Intends neither to hasten nor postpone death;
- Integrates the psychological and spiritual aspects of patient care;
- Offers a support system to help patients live as actively as possible until death;
- Offers a support system to help the family cope during the patient's illness and in their own bereavement;
- Uses a team approach to address the needs of patients and their families, including bereavement counseling, if indicated;
- Will enhance quality of life, and may also positively influence the course of illness;
- Is applicable *early* in the course of illness, in conjunction with other therapies that are intended to prolong life, such as chemotherapy or radiation therapy, and includes those investigations needed to better understand and manage distressing clinical complications.

The WHO broadened its approach to palliative care. The newer definition clearly emphasizes the superior outcome of the early delivery of palliative care. It extends the spectrum of the care to the family because the health and well being of family members is important as well.[3] It stresses the relevance of palliative care to all life-threatening conditions and recognizes the preventive component of the discipline by understanding that end-of-life problems have their origins at an earlier time in the trajectory of disease. The new definition reinforces the unquestionable focus of palliative care on quality of life.[1,3]

Because traditions, cultural attitudes, health systems, and resources vary widely among countries, the framework into which palliative care service must fit varies accordingly. The WHO designed three sets of general recommendations for countries according to the level of resources available (Table 35–1).[4]

Cancer Pain Epidemiology

Three percent of the American population is living with cancer. Many of these patients have pain that is caused by the disease or by the treatment they are receiving for the disease. Annually, more than 500,000 persons have terminal cancer, and 60% to 80% of them have severe pain. Prevalence of pain complaints ranges from 20% to 50% of all cancer patients in early stages, and it may rise to between 55% and 95% in patients with advanced disease.[5] Although 75% will have moderate to severe pain, more than 80% of patients with cancer can find relief when their pain is managed with simple noninvasive procedures.

Many guidelines for the management of cancer pain have been revised,[6-8] and major efforts are being made to broaden their application worldwide[9]; however, poor assessment techniques and misconceptions of pain management remain a major barrier to adequate pain relief in cancer patients.[10]

There is considerable variability in the treatment of cancer pain. Surveyed oncologists recognized that 86% of patients with cancer pain were under-treated and 31% of the physicians waited until the patient's prognosis for death was 6 months or less before they would initiate maximal analgesia.[11] Several studies documented disparities in cancer pain treatment among cancer patients. The Eastern Cooperative Oncology Group physicians demonstrated that most cancer pain is under-treated, and particularly at risk for poor pain

Table 35–1

Priority Actions for National Cancer Control Programs According to Level of Resources

Component	All countries	Scenario A: Low Level of Resources	Scenario B: Medium Level of Resources	Scenario C: High Level of Resources
Pain relief and palliative care	Implement comprehensive palliative care that provides pain relief, other symptom control, and psychosocial and spiritual support Promote national minimum standards for management Ensure availability and accessibility of opioids Provide education and training for caregivers and public	Ensure that minimum standards for pain relief and palliative care are progressively adopted by all levels of care in targeted areas and that there is high coverage of patients through services provided mainly by home-based care	Ensure that minimum standards for pain relief and palliative care are progressively adopted by all levels of care and nationwide there is rising coverage of patients through services provided by primary healthcare clinics and home-based care	Ensure that national pain relief and palliative care guidelines are adopted by all levels of care and nationwide there is high coverage of patients through a variety of options, including home-based care

From World Health Organization National Cancer Programs: Policies and Managerial Guidelines, 2nd ed. Geneva, World Health Organization, 2002, p 164.

management, as identified in earlier studies, are women, minorities, and the elderly.[12-16]

Pain occurs within the context of complex syndromes. Some of these affect the expression of pain, such as depression, anxiety, constipation, and dyspnea. Pain treatment itself can inflict multiple different symptoms causing distress as well—varying from nausea, constipation, cognitive impairment, neurotoxicity, sedation, and hallucinations.

■ CLINICAL ASSESSMENT OF THE PALLIATIVE CARE PATIENT

Pain is one of the most feared consequences of cancer.[17] Successful control of pain in a cancer patient depends on adequate broad assessment of the patient's satellite comorbidities and symptoms. The unidimensional pain assessment can lead to pharmacologic over-treatment and toxicities.[18] A thorough history and physical examination are required. In the cancer patient, an organic process responsible for the patient's complaints of pain can usually be identified. A new onset of pain in an established patient is, by principal, due to recurrent or metastatic disease until otherwise proven.

The purposes of assessment are multiple. Assessment of symptoms for intervention in the terminally ill patient has the ultimate goal of improving the quality of life, but it also influences the course of the disease. Pain can kill.[19] Laboratory data have shown that pain can inhibit immune function and enhance tumor growth.[20,21] Therefore, appropriate cancer pain management can enhance life expectancy. Uncontrolled pain was found to be a major factor in suicidal deaths in cancer patients.[22,23] Depression can also kill. High levels of depres-

sive symptoms are an independent risk factor for mortality in community-residing older adults[24] independent of suicide incidence. Cachexia up-regulates cytokine production and enhances tumor progression.[25] Degree of interference with activity and enjoyment of life was greater when the pain was caused by cancer than when it had another cause.[26]

Assessment of Cancer Pain: The Edmonton Staging System

Pain occurred in 67% of patients with metastatic cancer; when asked about barriers to good pain management in their own practice setting, 76% of surveyed oncologists[27] cited poor assessment of pain as the major problem. This finding is consistent with the strong predictive role of the discrepancy between patients' and physicians' assessments of the patients' pain and inadequate analgesia. There are many diagnostic tools for assessment of pain intensity. The most common ones used in clinical practice are the Verbal or Visual Analog Pain Scales (VAPS) and McGill Pain Questionnaire. In addition, the Memorial Pain Assessment Card allows us to distinguish pain intensity from both pain relief and global suffering.[28]

Pain assessment scores should not be interpreted blindly by a rigid therapeutic intervention. One should carefully consider the wide spectrum of the underlying pain and suffering mechanisms. Unidimensional pain rating scales can miss the affective dimensions on pain expression and their impact. Multidimensional rating scales that include the various pain-related symptoms will identify those affective dimensions and allow optimal palliation. The affective dimensions such as delirium, catastrophizing, somatization, depression, and anxiety are components of suffering, and can have considerable impact on the expression of pain.

Besides the usual assessment tools of pain such as numeric rating scales or visual analog scales, valid tools have been developed to help in daily assessment: the Edmonton Symptom Assessment System, the Mini-Mental State Examination, and the CAGE questionnaire.[29-31]

The Edmonton Symptom Assessment System (ESAS) consists of 10 visual analog scales (0 = best, 10 = worst) for pain, fatigue, drowsiness, nausea, anxiety, depression, appetite, dyspnea, insomnia, and sense of well-being.[32] The ESAS is a simple, validated tool that is completed by the patient and allows for screening and monitoring for the most common symptoms in patients with advanced incurable illness.[33,34] The Mini-Mental State Questionnaire (MMSQ), measures the level of cognitive function in a point system from 0 to 30 (abnormal defined as lower than the score adjusted for age and level of schooling or as a score of 24 or lower). It has been shown to be an accurate objective instrument for screening cognitive impairment in patients with advanced cancer.[35] The CAGE questionnaire consists of four simple questions used to screen for alcoholism (*c*utting down, *a*nnoyance, *g*uilty feeling, and *e*ye-opener). An abnormal CAGE score (defined as a positive answer to at least 2 of the 4 questions) has been shown to be of prognostic value in the opioid management of cancer pain.[36]

Types of Pain

The key step in pain assessment is characterization of the pain complaint, which can be somatic, visceral, or neuropathic.

Somatic nociceptive pain is usually described as a well localized, sharp aching in the complaint area, with or without throbbing or pressure sensation. It is caused by the activation of nociceptors in the affected tissue secondary to damage of peripheral and deep tissues. The causes of somatic pain are usually related to bone disease and postsurgical pain.

Visceral pain is poorly localized and diffuse. It can be crampy, squeezing, colicky, or gnawing because it is usually associated with distention of a hollow viscus, stretching of the capsule of a solid organ, or invasion of an internal organ by a tumor. Sometimes, it is referred to other anatomic areas beyond the area of the pathologic process. Visceral pain is also frequently associated with autonomic activation manifested by nausea, vomiting, perspiration, and peripheral vasospasm.

Neuropathic pain is commonly described as burning, sharp, shooting, or tingling. A pain that a patient "cannot describe" is probably neuropathic pain. It can be caused either by direct injury to nervous tissue by the cancer itself (e.g., tumor infiltration of a nerve, plexus, or the spinal cord) or by antineoplastic therapy (e.g., peripheral neuropathy caused by cisplatinum, paclitaxel, vincristine, postradiation neuritis, or fibrosis). It is sometimes associated with motor neurologic deficits. Neuropathic pain is difficult to control and is associated with a high incidence of suffering.[37]

Edmonton Staging System

Pain is a subjective sensation and therefore more difficult to assess but research identified a number of features to influence its response to different treatments. The Edmonton Staging System (Fig. 35–1) provides a clinical staging system

for cancer pain and it includes known prognostic factors for the response to treatment. The system is accurate in predicting the outcome of patients with cancer pain. Three stages are identified

Stage 1: Indicates a good prognosis for pain control
Stage 2: Indicates intermediate prognosis
Stage 3: Indicates poor prognosis

Patients with visceral or bone/soft tissue pain, on low dose of opioids, intact cognitive status, and absence of severe psychological distress are classified in stage I and are more likely to respond well to analgesic treatment. Patients with features such as incidental pain, neuropathic pain, tolerance to the present opioid, a past history of alcoholism, severe psychosocial distress, and cognitive impairment will be classified in Stage 3 and have a diminished likelihood of good response to analgesic treatment. This is the case scenario in which the assessment of the complex pain will guide a multiaxial intervention to reduce suffering.

The effectiveness of a staging system in predicting the outcome of patients with cancer pain has been limited when patients with a poor prognosis were proved to be able to achieve pain control in 55% of the cases during a 3-week assessment period, but it is highly accurate in predicting patients with good prognosis.[38] This lack of specificity makes this staging system impractical in certain situations. "A new onset of pain or change in character or intensity of an established pain raises the strongest possibility of metastatic disease or a tumor growth of the original site."

Multidimensional Assessment: Pain in Palliative Care

The multidimensional nature of pain and overall expressions of patient suffering fall under the label of pain. In palliative care, a complex spectrum of various symptoms can be reported by patients: pain in 41% to 76%, depression 33% to 40%, anxiety, 57% to 68%, nausea 24% to 68%, constipation 65%, sedation/confusion 46% to 60%, dyspnea 12% to 58%, anorexia 85%, and asthenia 90%.[39-42]

Instruments for the Measurement of Multiple Symptoms

Results from palliative studies are often difficult to compare because many different evaluation tools are used. There is no consensus as to which instruments are most appropriate. Many different questionnaires are used in palliative care but no selection of questionnaires can cover all of the palliative needs of all patients: the European Organization for Research and Treatment of Cancer-Quality of Life-Core 30 (EORTC QLQ-C30), the Palliative Care Outcome Scale (POS), the McGill Quality of Life Questionnaire (MQOL).[43-45] The Functional Assessment of Chronic Illness Therapy (FACIT), the Brief Pain Inventory (BPI), the Memorial Symptom Assessment Scale (MSAS), the Hospital Anxiety and Depression Scale (HADS), the Edinburgh Depression Scale (EDS), Edmonton Pain Staging System for cancer pain (ESS), and the ESAS. Few of those tools are practical for the daily clinical setting.

To minimize the burden on patients, questionnaires should be brief and manageable, and validated.[46] The Edmon-

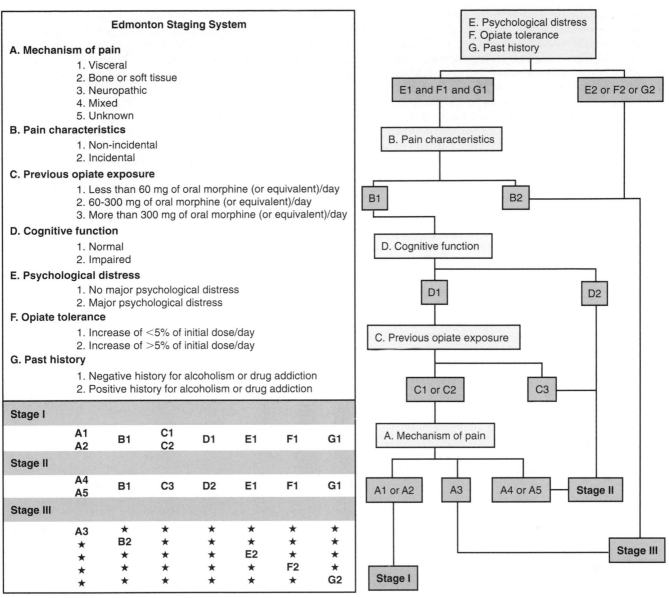

Edmonton Staging System

A. Mechanism of pain
1. Visceral
2. Bone or soft tissue
3. Neuropathic
4. Mixed
5. Unknown

B. Pain characteristics
1. Non-incidental
2. Incidental

C. Previous opiate exposure
1. Less than 60 mg of oral morphine (or equivalent)/day
2. 60-300 mg of oral morphine (or equivalent)/day
3. More than 300 mg of oral morphine (or equivalent)/day

D. Cognitive function
1. Normal
2. Impaired

E. Psychological distress
1. No major psychological distress
2. Major psychological distress

F. Opiate tolerance
1. Increase of <5% of initial dose/day
2. Increase of >5% of initial dose/day

G. Past history
1. Negative history for alcoholism or drug addiction
2. Positive history for alcoholism or drug addiction

Stage I						
A1 A2	B1	C1 C2	D1	E1	F1	G1
Stage II						
A4 A5	B1	C3	D2	E1	F1	G1
Stage III						
A3	★	★	★	★	★	★
★	B2	★	★	★	★	★
★	★	★	★	E2	★	★
★	★	★	★	★	F2	★
★	★	★	★	★	★	G2

★ Any of the other categories

FIGURE 35–1 ■ Edmonton Staging System.

ton Symptom Assessment Scale (ESAS) is a 10-item patient-rated symptom visual analog scale developed for use in symptom assessment of palliative care patients.[47] It has been validated[48] when compared with other multidimensional symptom assessment instruments—the MSAS,[49] a multidimensional quality-of-life instrument; the FACIT; and the self-administered BPI.[50]

Measurement of Specific Symptoms and Its Instruments

Fatigue

Fatigue is the most common symptom in advanced cancer, affecting 60% to 90% of the patients as identified by the diverse criteria used.[51] Cancer-related fatigue is characterized by an unusual, persistent, subjective sense of tiredness that interferes with usual functioning.[52]

The modes of expression are physical (e.g., decreased energy), cognitive (e.g., decreased concentration), and affective (e.g., decreased motivation) modes of expression.[53] Fatigue is a multidimensional syndrome with major contributing factors, including cancer cachexia, depression, pain, opioid medications, radiation therapy, and chemotherapy agents. Deconditioning and anemia are common among cancer patients as well.[54] Unlike fatigue in healthy individuals, cancer-related fatigue occurs despite adequate amounts of rest or sleep. It occurs early, often before the diagnosis of cancer, and increases during the course of cancer treatment and progression. Fatigue persists long after cancer treatment is completed and can be reported in 17% of cancer survivors more than 1 year after treatment.[55]

Several fatigue assessment tools exist and include functional capacity tests, subjective assessments during function, and objective and subjective assessments of function.

Multidimensional fatigue assessment incorporating multiple characteristics of fatigue and their impact on function such as the Functional Assessment of Cancer Therapy-Anemia Scale[56] and the Piper Fatigue Self-Report Scale[57] can be more informative but also more time-consuming to administer. Simpler unidimensional scales, such as a numerical scale (0-10) can be used, especially for screening because patients are often reluctant to discuss fatigue with their physicians, who, in turn, do not frequently assess this symptom. When screening reveals moderate (4 to 6) or severe (7 to 10) fatigue, then a more focused history and physical examination should be performed with attention to possible etiologic factors.[58] The goal of treatment can be to reduce fatigue intensity, help patients function at a stable fatigue level, or both. Fatigue management involves specific (targeting potentially reversible causes of fatigue such as anemia or hypothyroidism) and symptomatic (targeting symptoms because no obvious etiology or reversible cause for fatigue can be identified) intervention and treatment measures. Specific interventions include treating other endocrine abnormalities such as hypogonadism—evidence of opioid-induced hypothalamic hypogonadism is strong[59]—as well as managing pain, insomnia, depression, and anxiety. Treatment of anemia with red blood cell transfusion and epoetin alpha has been shown to improve quality-of-life outcomes, including fatigue[60]; symptomatic interventions such as education, counseling, and pharmacologic and nonpharmacologic measures may be used. Sleep hygiene measures can be initiated for insomnia and thyroid hormone replacement may be initiated for hypothyroidism. Patients with mood disorders should be referred for counseling and possible pharmacologic therapy. Medications that contribute to fatigue should be discontinued, if possible. Prednisone 20 to 40 mg/day for a limited period of 2 to 4 weeks has been shown to decrease fatigue, although the mechanism of action is unknown. Prolonged regimens can potentially induce myopathy and worsen fatigue.

Psychostimulants, such as methylphenidate, have been used to treat opioid-induced somnolence, reduce pain intensity, treat depression, and improve cognition.[61] Preliminary results show that patient-controlled methylphenidate administration rapidly improved fatigue and quality of life. Patients were able to appropriately titrate their methylphenidate to their symptom distress.[62] Modafinil has been studied in cancer fatigue; it is a psychostimulant with potentially fewer side effects than methylphenidate.Progestational agents, traditionally used to improve appetite, were shown to have a beneficial effect on activity levels in patients after a 10-day treatment course.[63] Thalidomide, which is thought to act through inhibiting tumor necrosis factor alpha and modulating interleukins, has been shown to improve the sensation of well-being in patients with cancer cachexia, and it may also be beneficial for cancer-related fatigue.[64] Monoclonal anti-interleukin antibodies, pentoxifylline and bradykinin antagonists, and alpha-melanocyte-stimulating hormone offer fields for future investigation in the treatment of cancer-related fatigue.[65] Donepezil appears to improve sedation and fatigue in patients receiving opioids for cancer pain.[66] Alternative approaches such as acupuncture, healing touch and massage therapy are promising.[67] Adding massage therapy and healing touch to standard care improves pain scores, mood disturbance, and fatigue in patients receiving cancer chemotherapy.

Nausea

Chronic nausea is a common symptom in patients with advanced cancer, with a frequency of 32% to 98%.[69] It is mandatory to screen for nausea in the palliative care setting and distinguish it from chemotherapy-induced nausea. Ondansetron and the newer selective 5-hydroxytryptamine (anti-5HT3) granisetron and palonosetron, along with the neurokinin NK(1) receptor antagonist aprepitant, reduce significantly chemotherapy-induced nausea, but have less promising effects on chronic nausea.[70,71] This is because of the difference in the pathophysiology of nausea. Causes of nausea and vomiting include gastrointestinal motility disorders, metabolic derangement, raised intracranial pressure, chemotherapy and radiotherapy, psychosomatic factors, and opioids (Table 35–2).

Gastroparesis due to autonomic dysfunction is one of the most frequent problems in these patients.[72] More than 80% of terminal cancer patients receive opioid analgesics for pain and dyspnea. Opioids induce nausea and vomiting by direct stimulation of the chemoreceptor trigger zone,[73] decrease gastric emptying and gastrointestinal motility, and the induction of constipation.

Table 35–2

Etiology of Nausea in the Palliative Care Setting

Preexisting comorbidities	Congestive heart failure, hypothyroidism, or neurologic disorders
Cancer	Paraneoplastic neurologic syndromes
Cancer treatment	Chemotherapy, radiotherapy, immunotherapy, or surgery
Endocrine abnormalities	Hypothyroidism or hypogonadism
Cancer/treatment complications	Anemia, sepsis, pulmonary and cardiac disorders, renal and hepatic failure, metabolic complications, dehydration, hypoxia, autonomic failure, or neuromuscular disorders
Psychologic factors	Anxiety, depression, or stress
Medications	Opioids, hypnotics, anxiolytics, antihistamines, antiemetics, or antihypertensives
Cachexia/malnutrition	
Deconditioning	
Sleep disorders	
Interrelationship with other physical symptoms	

Opioids stimulate nausea and vomiting by an action on the chemoreceptor trigger zone in the area postrema by increasing vestibular sensitivity and delaying gastric emptying.[74] In the majority of patients, nausea can be well controlled using safe and simple antiemetic regimens such as metoclopramide, haloperidol, and phenothiazines.[75] Different drugs have been proposed to treat nausea and vomiting induced by opioids. Opioid rotation and change of route of administration may widen the therapeutic window of opioids in some circumstances.

Management of nausea in the palliative care setting includes assessment for constipation: a rectal examination and abdominal radiographs to be reviewed and assessed for constipation. Appropriate management of constipation with laxatives, stool softeners, and enemas is cornerstone.

Haloperidol, a potent narrow-spectrum drug with antidopaminergic activity, is frequently used before broadspectrum drugs such as methotrimeprazine.[76] Figure 35–2 summarizes management options including metoclopramide and steroids.

Metoclopramide is a benzamide derivative with gastrointestinal motility and antiemetic activity.[77] An efficient treatment requires frequent administration around the clock of short-acting formulations of metoclopramide to ensure a sustained plasma concentration to suppress nausea, vomiting, and other gastrointestinal symptoms associated with cancer. Controlled-release metoclopramide reduces gastrointestinal symptoms in advanced cancer patients, with an easier administration regimen.[78] Metoclopramide should be maximized in the form of continuous infusion with the added steroids. In the postoperative period, it is important to discuss with the surgeon whether any procedure has been performed on the intestinal lumen because prokinetic agents run the risk of perforation or dehiscence of sutures.

Ondansetron in doses of 4 to 16 mg may be effective in preventing opioid-induced emesis when the opioids are administered via intravenous or intraspinal route.[79,80] Once the antiemetic measures are exhausted and the obstruction cannot be reversed (about 50% of the obstructions reverse spontaneously) then the approach is for palliative dessication of the secretions using octreotide or glycopyrrolate.

Dyspnea

Dyspnea, the uncomfortable awareness of breathing, is a frequent and distressing symptom in patients with advanced cancer and is often difficult to control. Studies have shown that the incidence of dyspnea in terminally ill patients with cancer ranges from 20% to 80%.[81,82] There is evidence that

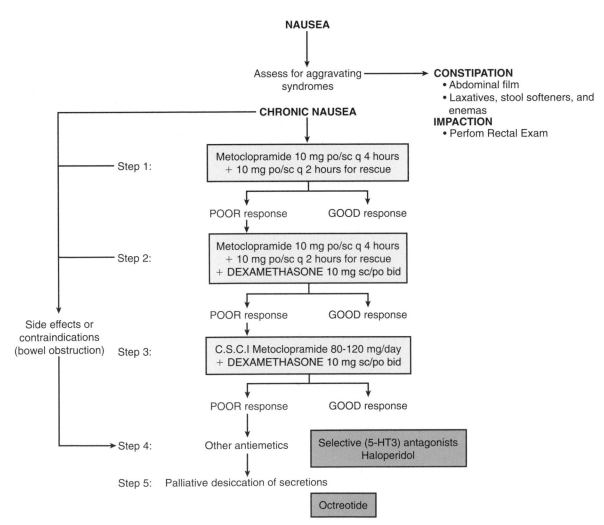

FIGURE 35–2 ■ Algorithm for management of chronic nausea.

good symptom control, even by experienced palliative care teams, is achieved less frequently for dyspnea than for other symptoms such as pain or nausea.[83] Very limited research has been conducted on the frequency and correlates of dyspnea in patients with advanced cancer.[84] Our group conducted several prospective and randomized control trials investigating the dimensions of this problem and the outcomes of oxygen supplementation. Lung involvement, anxiety, and maximum inspiratory pressure all influence the intensity of dyspnea in advanced cancer patients.[85] Supplemental oxygen is proven to be beneficial to patients with hypoxia and dyspnea at rest,[86,87] but did not improve the physical function or performance in patients with non-hypoxic dyspnea associated with cancer.[88] Intermittent injections of subcutaneous morphine are safe and effective for the management of dyspnea in terminal cancer.[89] They decrease the intensity of dyspnea without statistically modifying oxygen saturation, respiratory rate, or the end-tidal $Paco_2$.[90] There is controversy regarding the superiority of aerosolized opiates in relieving dyspnea.[91]

Drowsiness

Opioid-induced sedation is a major complication in patients with cancer pain.[92] Several approaches have been attempted for improvement of sedation—opioid dose reduction, opioid rotation, neuraxial analgesia, and the use of psychostimulants.[93]

Methylphenidate has been found to reduce opioid-induced sedation and to increase cognitive function and analgesia in patients with cancer pain, with clinical applications limited by the development of tolerance, potential aggravation of agitation or anxiety, and concerns about cardiovascular safety and addiction.[94] Donepezil is a new long-acting selective acetyl-cholinesterase inhibitor that we studied for its effectiveness in opioid-induced sedation and related symptoms in patients with cancer pain. Significant improvement of sedation, fatigue, anxiety, well-being, depression, anorexia and problems with sleep were observed.[95]

Sleep Disturbances

Sleep problems are commonly inadequately assessed in routine clinical care. Insomnia is more frequent in cancer patients than in the general population.[96] Prevalence of cancer-related sleep disturbance is estimated between 24% and 95%, and persists even years after treatment and cure of cancer.[97,98] The prevalence of sleep disturbances tends to be higher in women and in the elderly.[98] It is a heterogeneous complaint that may involve difficulties in falling asleep, trouble staying asleep, early-morning awakening, or a complaint of nonrestorative sleep with corresponding sleep efficiency less than 85%.[98] Sleep disorders may generate a further burden of distress to patients and families, and symptoms such as depression, anxiety, pain, and fatigue tend to be exacerbated. Sleep disturbance scores of cancer patients and community subjects were significantly correlated with fatigue severity.[99] Inadequate pain control can be considered a risk factor for sleep disturbances in advanced cancer patients.[100] Anxiety, falling asleep, awaking, early awakening, getting back to sleep , and nightmares were significantly associated with fewer hours slept.[101] Sleep disturbances co-existed with psychiatric conditions such as depressive and anxiety disorders, which can be consequences of this disturbance.

Depression may influence sleep, but having persistent insomnia could precipitate depression.[102] In advanced cancer patients, medications contribute to the insomnia. Insomnia is a well-known side effect of dexamethasone, and other antiemetic medications have also been found to disturb sleep.

Research suggests that stress-reduction programs tailored to the cancer setting help patients cope with the effects of treatment and improve their quality of life. Tibetan yoga, which incorporates controlled breathing and visualization, mindfulness techniques, and low-impact postures, had a positive effect on improving the subjective sleep quality, fastening the sleep latency, prolonging sleep duration, and reducing the use of sleep medications among cancer patients.[103]

Appetite Disturbances

Poor appetite in advanced cancer patients is part of both the cachexia and gastroparesis syndromes. Anorexia, early satiety, nausea, vomiting, bloating, and postprandial fullness may all be, at least partially, the result of gastroparesis due to autonomic dysfunction.[104] Our group conducted a prospective randomized, placebo-controlled trial using fish oil in patients with advanced cancer and loss of weight and appetite. Fish oil did not significantly influence appetite, tiredness, nausea, well-being, caloric intake, nutritional status, or function after 2 weeks compared with placebo.

There is limited evidence for effectiveness of cannabinoids on appetite stimulation, with minor or no overall nutritional advantages in AIDS or cancer cachexia. The remaining indications are largely supported by anecdotal case reports and small uncontrolled case series.[105] The main active compound present in marijuana was identified as tetrahydrocannabinol (THC). Nabilone, levonantradol and dronabinol are the potent synthetic cannabinoids.

The two proven indications for the use of the synthetic cannabinoid dronabinol are chemotherapy-induced nausea and vomiting and AIDS-related anorexia. It is superior to low doses of metoclopramide in patients receiving moderately emetogenic chemotherapy but inferior to high-dose metoclopramide in cisplatin-based chemotherapy.[106,107] With the newer antiemetics available, it remains a fourth-line agent for this indication after high-dose metoclopramide plus dexamethasone, 5-HT3 antagonists, and neurokinin 1 (NK-1) antagonists.[108] Other possible uses that may prove beneficial in the oncology population include analgesia, muscle relaxation, mood elevation, and relief of insomnia.

The main limitation of cannabinoids has been the high frequency of adverse effects on the central nervous system.[109] These consist mostly in perceptual abnormalities, including occasional hallucinations, dysphoria, abnormal thinking, depersonalization, and somnolence.[110]

Depression

Psychological distress of terminally ill cancer patients has major impact on their clinical care. One half of cancer patients in one study had been diagnosed with a psychiatric disorder, and most of them had an adjustment disorder and/or major depression.[111] In published data, 3% to 35% of cancer patients experience full-syndrome posttraumatic stress disorder (PTSD), but little is known about this incidence in the terminally ill advanced cancer patients.[112] Psychological distress can have a severe negative impact on patients with advanced or terminal cancer, including reducing their quality of life,[113] causing significant suffering,[114] a request for physician-assisted suicide or euthanasia,[115] and suicide,[116] as well as psychological distress in family members.[117] The incidence at baseline among terminally ill patients diagnosed with adjustment disorders, major depression, and PTSD were 16.3%, 6.7%, and 0%, respectively—those patients experienced lower performance status, concern about being a burden to others, and lower satisfaction with social support. On follow-up, only 10.6% were diagnosed with adjustment disorders and major depression rate increased to 11.8%.[118]

Depression is a significant symptom for approximately 25% of palliative care patients, but it is frequently unrecognized and untreated.[119] Multiple factors are involved from patients not disclosing complaints[120] to physicians who may attribute somatic symptoms of depression to the cancer illness.[121] Consequently, nearly 80% of the psychological and psychiatric morbidity in patients with cancer is unrecognized and untreated in the general oncologic practice.[122]

The majority of palliative medicine physicians surveyed in the United Kingdom assessed patients for depression routinely in 73% of the cases, with 27% using the Hospital Anxiety and Depression (HAD) Scale and 10% asking the patient "Are you depressed"? The most frequently prescribed medications were selective serotonin reuptake inhibitors (80%). Fewer than 6% of practitioners prescribed psychostimulants.[123]

Interestingly, a recent study illustrated that effective tools for depression do not have to be complex: the single question "Are you depressed?" proved to be the tool with the highest sensitivity, specifity, and positive predictive value when compared with HADS and the EDS. It is crucial to have a psychiatric counselor on the palliative care team or access to an oncologist-psychiatrist familiar with the common syndromes that affect the terminally ill and their families in the inpatient or outpatient setting. The counselor should be experienced with special treatment delivery framed. In the literature, there was focus on depression risk factors such as younger age, female gender, physical symptoms (pain) and functioning, cancer site (pancreatic cancer), cancer therapy (chemotherapy, radiotherapy), brain metastasis, hypercalcemia, and use of steroids, several types of concerns (existential concerns), past history of major depression, and lack of social support.[124] Systemic screening, with a low threshold for referral for professional assessment by psychiatrist or psychologist experienced in palliative care, is highly beneficial.

Anxiety

Despite a wide variability across studies, prevalence rates of anxiety and depressive disorders in cancer patients have been found to be as high as 49% and 53%, respectively.[125] Meta-analysis confirmed that relaxation training had a significant effect on the emotional adjustment variables of depression, anxiety, and hostility of cancer patients in acute medical treatment.[126]

Well-Being

Patients with advanced cancer often experience physical, psychological, social, and existential distress associated with the disease or its treatment. Subjective health-related quality of life is thought to characterize the interaction between the circumstance or experiences associated with illness and the patient's personal values and expectations.[127,128] Many tools

attempt a further evaluation and scoring of the subjective quality of life and service effectiveness in the form of patient reported outcomes (PRO) such as Self-Perception and Relationship Tool (S-PRT), the Ferrans and Powers Quality of Life Index, Functional Living Index-Cancer (FLIC) Scale , the Functional Assessment of Cancer Therapy Scale, the Short Form-36 Health Survey, and the General Well-Being Scale.[129-131] The "well-being" scoring between 0 and 10 in the ESAS could be a valid summary of subjective quality of life integrating all the symptoms of distress.

Assessment of Cognitive Impairment

The symptom of distress due to pain and delirium will further increase suffering among patients with advanced cancer. One of the main reasons for inadequate pain treatment has been poor assessment of cognitive function. Delirium occurs in 26% to 44% of cancer patients admitted to hospital or hospice. Approximately 90% of the patients experience delirium in hours to days before death. Diagnosis of delirium is defined as a disturbance of consciousness and attention with a change in cognition and/or perception (Fig. 35–3). In addition, it develops suddenly and follows a fluctuating course related to the cancer, metabolic disorders, or the effects of drugs (Table 35–3).

Frail elderly patients are at high risk for delirium. There is extreme distress for the patient and the patient's family in the presence of the delirium. The treatment proposes a clinical challenge for the physician (Fig. 35–4). Terminally ill elderly patients also have distinct needs due to the coalescence of symptoms, accumulation of debility, and increasing dependence on the care giver.

STEP 1: Team training in recognition and management of delirium in general

- Regular use of the term "delirium" and no others
- Train the team in key concepts
- Inclusion of MMSE (or other screening tests) as a routine tool in the evaluation of the patient

STEP 2: Systematic screening of risk factors for delirium and prevention of opioid-induced neurotoxicity

- Psychological distress (examination)
- Previous abuse of substances
- Renal failure or dehydration
- Pre-existing progressive cognitive failure
- Incidental or neuropathic pain
- Abundance of drugs

STEP 3: Evaluation of delirium

- Recognize changes in the mental state of the patient
- Identify cognitive decline and attention disturbances through clinical examination, MMSE or other tests
- Rule out other causes of cognitive changes: dementia, depression or psychosis
- Verification of DSM-IV criteria
- Maintain evaluation of delirium; use specific tests to follow-up the patient

FIGURE 35–3 ■ Three-step approach to detect delirium in cancer patients.

Table 35–3

Etiology of Delirium in the Palliative Care Setting

Intracranial disease	Brain neoplasm
	Leptomeningeal disease
	Postictal
Medications	Psychoactives
	Opioids
	Benzodiazepines
	Anticholinergics
	SSRIs
	Tricyclics
	Antihistamines
	Others
	Steroids
	Ciprofloxacin
	H_2-blockers
Systemic disease	Organ failure
	Cardiac
	Hepatic
	Renal
	Respiratory
	Infection
	Pulmonary
	UTI
	Decubitus ulcer
	Hematologic
	Anemia
	DIC
	Metabolic
	Dehydration
	Hypercalcemia
	Hyponatremia, hyperkalemia
	Hypoglycemia

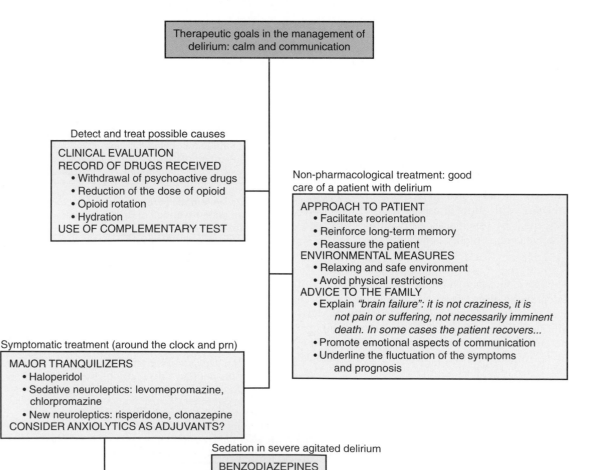

FIGURE 35–4 ■ Therapeutic approach to delirium in advanced cancer patients.

Managing delirium is of major importance in end-of-life care and frequently gives rise to controversies and to clinical and ethical dilemmas. Excluding terminal delirium, delirium is reversible in 50% of cases.[132] These dilemmas are rooted in the poor recognition or even misdiagnosis of delirium despite its frequent occurrence. Delirium generates major distress to the patient, the family, and even the health care providers, opening the field to misinterpret delirium symptomatology, and behavioral management challenges for health care professionals. The challenge is to recognize when the delirium is potentially reversible, knowing that the majority of patients will die with a nonreversible terminal episode that we can qualify as "end stage delirium."

Greater educational efforts are required to improve the recognition of delirium and lead to a better understanding of its impact in end-of-life care. Awaiting the development of low-burden instruments for assessment, communication strategies, and family education regarding the manifestations of delirium should be further integrated into the management of delirium. The challenge is to identify the reversibility components of delirium, targeting precipitating factors superimposed onto baseline vulnerability.[133]

The Mini-Mental State Examination (MMSE) is a widely used, well-validated screening tool for cognitive impairment. It briefly measures orientation to time and place, immediate recall, short-term verbal memory, calculation, language, and construct ability. Each area tested has a designated point value, with the maximum possible score on the MMSE being 30/30. Delirium is associated with changes in the circadian distribution of breakthrough analgesia, which is possibly related to reversal of the normal circadian rhythm.[134] Delirium precipitated by opioids and other psychoactive medications and dehydration is frequently reversible with change of opioid or dose reduction, discontinuation of unnecessary psychoactive medication, opioid rotation, or hydration, respectively.[135] Haloperidol is the most frequently used drug, and new neuroleptics such as risperidone or olanzapine are being tested with good results. Methylphenidate has been used for hypoactive delirium. A crucial step in the management is withdrawal of benzodiazepine compounds. They are a major contributor or precipitator of delirium and should be reserved for sedation in severe agitated delirium after failure of the above measures.

■ COMMUNITY ISSUES AND ADJUNCT TREATMENTS

Psychological Support

In order to make a positive impact on the overall quality of life, one needs to address suffering in addition to managing nociception and pain. Pain is usually only one of the components of suffering, which can be defined as a more global aversive experience. Other contributors to suffering can be depression, anxiety, fatigue, and social isolation.

The Angry Patient

When facing an angry patient, expressive supportive counseling is contraindicated. The required steps in assessing an angry patient start with ruling out an agitated delirium syndrome. Once delirium diagnosis is excluded, assess mood status, mainly for depression, because 25% of cancer patient may develop depression before death. The three diagnoses in a setting of depressed mood are (1) adjustment disorder; (2) adjustment disorder with depressed mood; and (3) major depression. Anxiety is another mood disorder that cancer patients may suffer from, as part of the delirium syndrome or a component of their depression. In fact 15% to 20 % of depressions manifest with agitation.

The third step is use of the CAGE questionnaire to identify a missed diagnosis of chemical coping mechanism; anger may be a conscious strategy that the patient uses to obtain opioids. Anger can be merely adaptive, and the possibility of a patient's anger being a personality trait should be further explored.

Communication and Family Involvement

Good communication is the foundation to create an atmosphere of sensitivity and compassion; it can elicit honesty and openness. Better communication and better interpersonal care can translate into improved patient satisfaction,[136] compliance with medical recommendations, and health outcomes.[137]

Ong and coworkers found that doctor-patient communication during oncological consultation is related to patients' quality of life and satisfaction. The affective quality of the consultation seems to be the most important factor in determining these outcomes.[138] Communication with patients and with their families is crucial. The word "family" is used in the broad spectrum designating the relatives and other close people important to the patient and involved in the patient's care. Research revealed that relatives are intensely attuned to the conditions and reactions of their loved ones. They perceive discomfort the way care givers would but have a tendency to associate more pain as a reason of discomfort in nonverbal patients.[139] Communication facilitates development of relationships, allows exchange of information, and assists in medical decision making.[140]

Medical decision-making preferences were assessed in a palliative care setting where physicians are trained in communication skills.[141] About 63% of patients chose a shared approach with physicians, when physicians predicted the shared decision making only in 38% of the cases.[142] Agreement on decision-making preferences occurs in 38%[143] to 42%.[144] Physicians, even those highly trained in communication skills, are not good at predicting the decision-making preferences. Asking the patient directly rather than assuming a prediction of the level of involvement should be the foundation of a decision-making preference.

Families may have little knowledge of the disease and its prognosis, and may have low expectations of pain relief or unrealistically high expectations of curative treatment. Patients with narrowed disparities between expectations and reality have a better quality of life. Older cancer patients, those living with others, those enrolled in managed care organizations, and those who report better than expected experience are more likely to have a higher overall health-related quality of life.[145] Communication allows empowerment of the family and the patient by involving them in decision making with regard to treatment. Explain treatment in detail so patients can give informed consent or refusal, and create an environment of their being in control.[146]

Communication strategies and educating the family regarding the manifestations of delirium are paramount in managing delirium—a major cause of distress for the family, and a risk factor for iatrogenic harm when misdiagnosed. Delirium-related symptoms can cause great distress in both patients and family members.[147] A majority of patients with delirium recall their delirium as highly distressing. Delirium is also a highly distressing experience for spouses, care givers, and nurses who are caring for delirious patients.[147]

The degree of emotional distress of family members concerning terminal delirium was studied. More than two thirds of the bereaved family members perceived all delirium-related symptoms, other than somnolence, as distressing or very distressing when they occurred frequently.[148] It is crucial to counsel families about terminal delirium and explain the potential causes, course, possible interventions, and outcomes, especially when it is terminal delirium. The key point is to prepare families for potential future delirium episodes and the high likelihood of recurrence. Communication is crucial in the setting of delirium requiring terminal sedation. In fact, the patients who were terminally sedated varied from 4% in the hospice setting to 10% in the tertiary palliative care unit. Uncontrolled delirium is only one of the indications for sedation.

Other centers reported terminal sedation indications to be dyspnea, pain, general malaise, agitation, and nausea.[149] We recommend that terminal sedation be restricted for uncontrollable symptoms such as delirium, dyspnea, suffocation, and dramatic hemorrhage.

Midazolam seems to be the agent most commonly used. Prior to its induction, a thorough assessment of the underlying reversible factors, such as medications, should be undertaken.

■ TREATMENT

Principles of Management

Besides a physician and a nurse, members of various disciplines, such as psychology, social work, nutrition, rehabilitation, pastoral care, pharmacology, speech therapy, and respiratory care, can be efficiently involved in patient care to address their complex needs.[150]

The treatment of nociceptive cancer pain, once fully assessed, is mainly achieved with pharmacological analgesics but can involve multiple treatment modalities. These include antitumor therapy, nonanalgesic adjuvant pharmacological management, psychosocial therapy, and, occasionally, invasive therapy including nerve blocks and neuroablative procedures and various nonpharmacologic treatments (Table 35–4).

Effective pain management is best achieved by a broad-based assessment platform of the pain and other symptoms, an interdisciplinary interventional approach, and extensive plan of action involving patients, their families, and health care providers. Barriers to effective pain management (Fig. 35–5) include a sense of fatalism, denial, the desire to be "the good patient," geographical barriers, and financial limitations. The physician should do the following:

- Initiate prophylactic anticonstipation intervention in every patient treated with opiates. Unlike nausea, complete tolerance to the constipation does not generally develop.
- Discuss pain and its management with the patients and their families.

Table 35–4

Cancer Pain Management Modalities

A. Systemic analgesic therapy	C. Antitumor therapy
1. Non-opioid analgesics	D. Psychosocial therapy
2. Opioid analgesics	E. Nonpharmacologic therapy
3. Adjuvant agents	1. Heat or cold application
Antidepressants	2. Exercise
Anticonvulsants	3. Counter-stimulation (TENS)
Local Anesthetics	4. Relaxation/imagery
Corticosteroids	5. Distraction/reframing
Other	6. Hypnosis
4. Side effect management	7. Peer group support
B. Invasive therapy	8. Pastoral counseling
1. Peripheral nerve blocks	9. Occupational therapy aids
2. Plexus blocks	10. Physical therapy appliances
3. Neuraxial therapy	
4. Neuroablative techniques	

- Encourage patients to report their pain and explain to them that there are many safe and effective ways to relieve pain.
- Understand that some patients may be reluctant to report pain due to "opiophobia," spiritual belief in the meaning of pain and suffering as part of the healing process.
- Explain the reality of risks of addiction and the spectrum of the side effects, their prevention, and interventions to control them.
- Consider the cost of proposed drugs and interventions.
- Communicate the pain assessment and its management with other clinicians treating the patient.
- Know the state and local regulations regarding controlled substances.

The WHO introduced a simple and effective method for cancer pain management (Fig. 35–6) based on titration of therapy,[151] which should allow adequate pain control in the majority (90%) of cancer patients[152] and most (75%) of the terminally ill patients.[153]

The WHO guides cancer pain treatment through a five-concept approach. Oral administration of medications is the preferred route of administration. Medications should be administered on an around-the-clock basis rather than on an as-needed basis. The dosages should be individualized for each patient. Vigilance and considering details and side effects when administering or prescribing the various drugs are crucial.

Interventional Procedures for Intractable Pain in Palliative Care

In the setting of failure to control a pain syndrome, consider interventional pain management such as intrathecal catheter or pump opioid infusion. It is crucial to consider a safe road map toward such an intervention with the following five safety checkpoints (Table 35–5): (1) Is the pain refractory? (2) Are there non-nociceptive components (somatization, delirium, and chemical coping)? (3) Is the pain mainly

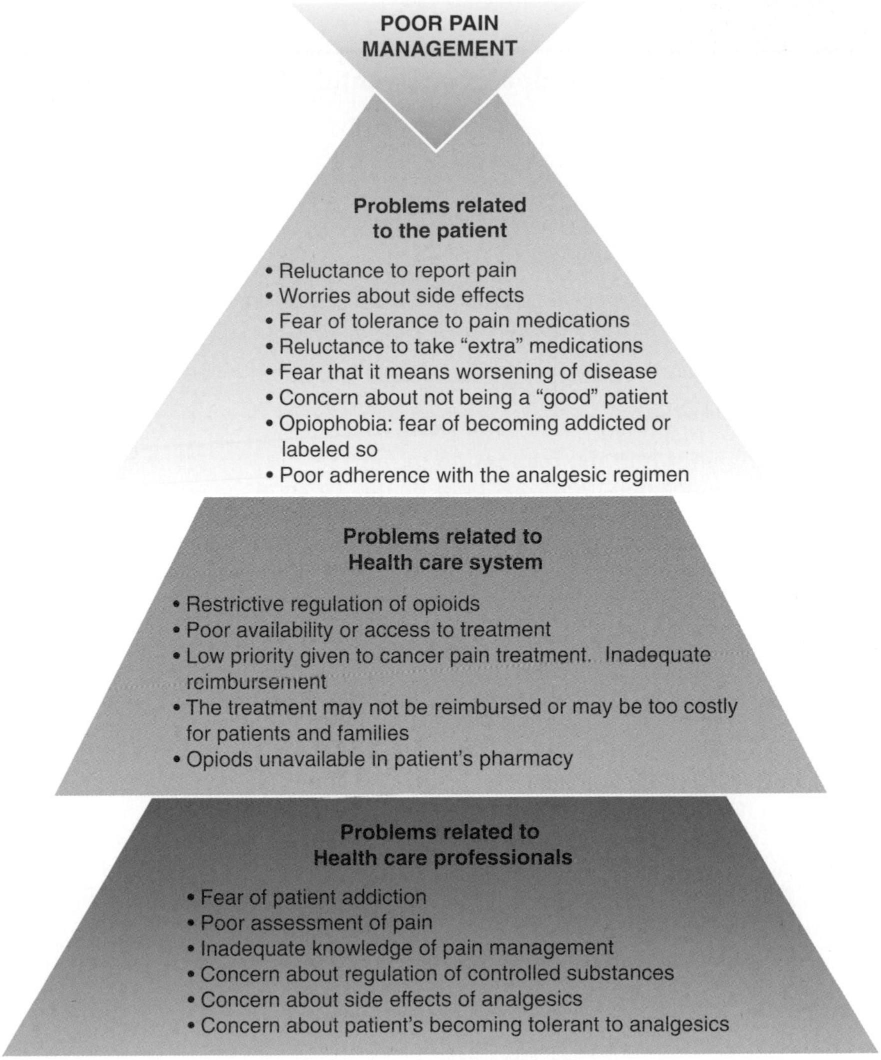

FIGURE 35–5 ■ Barriers to effective pain management.

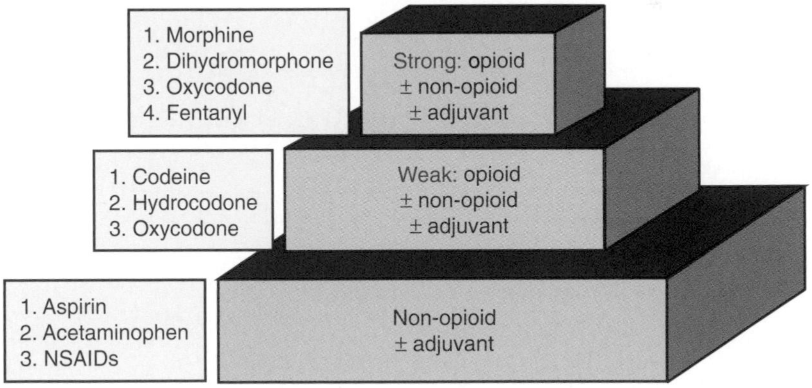

FIGURE 35–6 ■ World Health Organization pain ladder for cancer pain management.

nociceptive? (4) What is the likelihood of response to the intervention? (5) What are the logistics of postintervention pain service and their availability to the patient?

■ CONCLUSION

Multidisciplinary acute care is the most successful approach in the management of complex symptoms in patients with advanced cancer. Multidimensional approaches to cancer pain will allow a comprehensive assessment of the nonorganic components of pain, such as psychosocial distress, which will not respond to escalating doses of opioid medication. Additionally, nociceptive pain is just a component of the suffering and improving quality of life requires targeting all of the variables when possible. Not recognizing these complex interactive syndromes will lead to misdiagnosis and mismanagement, with tremendous harm to the patient, care givers, and

Table 35–5

Checklist for Administration of Interventional Opioids

Is the pain refractory?
  Are the opioids adequately titrated?
  Is rotation of opioids done?
  Are adjuvants used?
  Are other side effects treated?
Is the pain mainly nociceptive?
Have non-nociceptive components of pain expression
    been taken into consideration
  Somatization
  Delirium
  Chemical coping
Likelihood of response
  Will the pain syndrome respond to intrathecal
    opioids (consider components of deafferentation
    pain and anatomic location)
Have logistics of postintervention pain care in the
  community been considered and resolved?

family. Reducing frustration of the healthcare provider can be achieved with better management of the patient. The following five interventions are needed in the palliative care pain management setting for optimal service to the dying: (1) a digital rectal examination; (2) the CAGE score test, (3) the MMSE, (4) evaluation for supportive counseling; and (5) the DNR status determination. These interventions should be administered in appropriate early timing, sometimes even repeatedly. The patient will not benefit from palliative care service consultation unless these five protocols have been followed.

References

1. Doyle D: Proposal for a new name as well as having the new WHO definition of palliative care. Palliat Med (1):9, 2003.
2. World Health Organization National Cancer Programs: Policies and Managerial Guidelines, 2nd ed. Geneva, World Health Organization, 83, 2002.
3. Sepulveda C, Marlin A, Yoshida T, Ullrich A: Palliative Care: The World Health Organization's Global Perspective. J Pain Symptom Manage 2:91, 2002.
4. World Health Organization National Cancer Programs: Policies and Managerial Guidelines, 2nd ed. Geneva, World Health Organization,164, 2002.
5. Bonica JJ: Cancer Pain. In Bonica JJ (ed.) The Management of Pain, 2nd ed. Philadelphia, Lea & Febiger, 1990, p 400.
6. World Health Organization. Cancer Pain Relief with a Guide to Opioids Availability. Geneva, World Health Organization, 1986.
7. World Health Organization. Cancer Pain Relief and Palliative Care. Geneva, World Health Organization, 1990.
8. World Health Organization: Symptom Relief in Terminal Illness. Geneva, World Health Organization, 1998.
9. World Health Organization. National Cancer Control Programmes: Policies and Managerial Guidelines, 2nd ed. Geneva, World Health Organization, 2002.
10. Cleeland CS, Gonin R, Hatfield AK, et al. Pain and its treatment in outpatients with metastatic cancer. N Engl J Med 330:592, 1994.
11. Von Roenn JH, Cleeland CS, Gonin R, et al: Physician attitudes and practice in cancer pain management: A survey from the Eastern Cooperative Oncology Group. Ann Intern Med 119:121, 1993.
12. Cleeland CS, Gonin R, Hateld AK, et al: Pain and its treatment in outpatients with metastatic cancer. N Engl J Med 330:592, 1994.
13. Blendon RJ, Aiken LH, Freeman HE, Corey CR: Access to medical care for black and white Americans: A matter of continuing concern. JAMA 261:278, 1989.
14. Todd KH, Samaroo N, Hoffman JR: Ethnicity as a risk factor for inadequate emergency department analgesia. JAMA 269:1537, 1993.
15. Anderson KO, Richman SP, Hurley J, et al: Cancer pain management among underserved minority outpatients: Perceived needs and barriers to optimal control. Cancer 94(8):2295, 2002.
16. Greenfield S, Blanco DM, Elashoff RM, Ganz PA: Patterns of care related to age of breast cancer patients. JAMA 257:2766, 1987.
17. Foley KM: The treatment of cancer pain. N Engl J Med 313:84, 1985.
18. Bruera E, Watanabe S: New developments in the assessment of pain in cancer patients. Support Care Cancer Sep2 (5):312, 1994.
19. Liebeskind JC. Pain can kill. Pain 44(1):3, 1991.
20. Keller SE, Weiss JM, Schleifer SJ, et al: Suppression of immunity by stress: Effect of a graded series of stressors on lymphocyte stimulation in the rat. Science 213:1397, 1981.
21. Lewis JW, Shavit Y,. Terman GW, et al: Stress and morphine affect survival of rats challenged with a mammary ascites tumor (MAT 13762B). Nat Immun Cell Growth Regul 3:43, 1983/1984.
22. Cleeland CS: The impact of pain on the patient with cancer. Cancer 58 (Suppl.):2635, 1984.
23. Bolund C: Suicide and cancer. II. Medical and care factors in suicide by cancer patients in Sweden 1973-1976. J Psychosocial Oncol 3:17, 1985.
24. Schulz R, Beach SR, Ives DG, et al: Association between depression and mortality in older adults: The Cardiovascular Health Study. Arch Intern Med 160(12):1761, 2000.
25. Dunlop RJ, Campbell CW: Cytokines and advanced cancer. J Pain Symptom Manage 20(3):214, 2000
26. Daut RL, Cleeland CS. The prevalence and severity of pain in cancer. Cancer 50:1913, 1982.
27. Cleeland CS, Gonin R, Hatfield AK, et al. Pain and its treatment in outpatients with metastatic cancer. N Engl J Med 330:592, 1994.
28. Fishman B, Pasternak S, Wallenstein SL. et al: The memorial pain assessment card: A valid instrument for the evaluation of cancer pain. Cancer 60:1151, 1987.
29. Bruera E, MacDonald RN: Audit methods: The Edmonton Symptom Assessment System. In Higginson I (ed): Clinical Audit in Palliative Care. Oxford, Radcliffe Medical, 1993, p 61.
30. Folstein MF, Folstein SE, McHugh PR: Mini-mental state: A practical method for grading the cognitive state of patients for the clinician. J Psychiatr Res 12:189, 1975.
31. Bruera E, Moyano J, Seifert L, et al: The frequency of alcoholism among patients with pain due to terminal cancer. J Pain Symptom Manage 10:599, 1995.
32. Bruera E, Kuehn N, Miller MJ, et al: The Edmonton Symptom Assessment System (ESAS): A simple method for the assessment of palliative care patients. J Palliat Care 7;6, 1991.
33. Chang T, Hwang SS, Feuerman M: Validation of the Edmonton Symptom Assessment Scale. Cancer 88:2164, 2000.
34. Philip J, Smith WB, Craft P, Lickiss N: Concurrent validity of the modified Edmonton Symptom Assessment System with the Rotterdam Symptom Checklist and the Brief Pain Inventory. Support Care Cancer 6:539, 1998.
35. Pereira J, Hanson J, Bruera E: The frequency and clinical course of cognitive impairment in patients with terminal cancer. Cancer 79:835, 1997.
36. Bruera, T. Schoeller, R. Wenk, et al: A prospective multicenter assessment of the Edmonton Staging System for cancer pain. J Pain Symptom Manage 10:348, 1995.
37. Cherney NI, Portenoy RK: The management of cancer pain. CA J Cancer Pain 44:262, 1994.
38. Bruera E, Schoeller T, Wenk R, et al: A prospective multicenter assessment of the Edmonton staging system for cancer pain. J Pain Symptom Manage (5):348, 1995.
39. Cleeland CS, Gonin R, Hatfield AK, et al: Pain and its treatment in outpatients with metastatic cancer. N Engl J Med 330:592, 1994.
40. Anderson KO, Richman SP, Hurley J, et al: Cancer pain management among underserved minority outpatients: Perceived needs and barriers to optimal control. Cancer 15;94(8):2295, 2002.
41. Bruera E: Research into symptoms other than pain. In Doyle D, Hanks GW, Macdonald N: Oxford Textbook of Palliative Medicine, 3rd ed. New York, Oxford University Press, 1999.

42. Chang VT, Hwang SS, Feuerman M: Validation of the Edmonton Symptom Assessment Scale. Cancer 88(9):2164, 2000.

43. Hearn J, Higginson IJ: Outcome measures in palliative care for advanced cancer patients: A review. J Public Health Med 19:193, 1997.

44. Kaasa S, De Conno F: Palliative care research. Eur J Cancer 37: S153, 2001.

45. Ingham JM, Portenoy RK: The measurement of pain and other symptoms. In Doyle D, Hanks G, Cherny N, Calman K (eds): Oxford Textbook of Palliative Medicine. Oxford, Oxford University Press, 2003, p 163.

46. Stromgren AS, Groenvold M, Pedersen L, et al: Symptomatology of cancer patients in palliative care: Content validation of self-assessment questionnaires against medical records. Eur J Cancer 38(6):788, 2002.

47. Bruera E, Kuehn N, Miller MJ, et al: The Edmonton Symptom Assessment System (ESAS): A simple method for the assessment of palliative care patients. J Palliat Care 7:6, 1991.

48. Chang VT, Hwang SS, Feuerman M: Validation of the Edmonton Symptom Assessment Scale. Cancer 88(9):2164, 2000.

49. Portenoy RK, Thaler HT, Kornblith AB, et al: The Memorial Symptom Assessment Scale: An instrument for the evaluation of symptom prevalence, characteristics and distress. Eur J Cancer 30A(9):1326, 1994.

50. Daut RL, Cleeland CS, Flanery RC: Development of the Wisconsin Brief Pain Questionnaire to assess pain in cancer and other diseases. Pain 17(2):197, 1983.

51. Vogelzang N, Breitart W, Cella D: Patient, caregiver, and oncologist perceptions of cancer-related fatigue: Results of a tri-part assessment survey. Semin Hematol 34:4, 1997.

52. Mock V, Piper B, Sabbatini P, Escalante C: National Comprehensive Cancer Network fatigue practice guidelines. Oncology 14:151, 2000.

53. Servaes P, Verhagen C, Bleijenberg G: Fatigue in cancer patients during and after treatment: Prevalence, correlates and interventions. Eur J Cancer 38:27, 2002.

54. Barnes EA, Bruera E: Fatigue in patients with advanced cancer: A review. Int J Gynecol Cancer 12:424, 2002.

55. Cella D, Davis K, Breitbart W, Curt G, for the Fatigue Coalition: Cancer-related fatigue: Prevalence of proposed diagnostic criteria in a United States sample of cancer survivors. J Clin Oncol 19:3385, 2001.

56. Cella D: The Functional Assessment of Cancer Therapy-Anemia (FACT-An) Scale: A new tool for the assessment of outcomes of cancer anemia and fatigue. Semin Hematol 34:13, 1997.

57. Piper BF, Dibble SL, Dodd MJ, et al: The revised Piper Fatigue Scale: Psychometric evaluation in women with breast cancer. Oncol Nurs Forum 25:677, 1998.

58. Barnes EA, Bruera E: Fatigue in patients with advanced cancer: A review. Int J Gynecological Cancer 12(5):424, 2002.

59. Rajagopal A, Vassilopoulou-Sellin R, Palmer JL, et al: Symptomatic hypogonadism in male survivors of cancer with chronic exposure to opioids. Cancer 100(4):851, 2004.

60. Turner R, Anglin P, Burkes R, et al: Epoetin alfa in cancer patients: Evidence-based guidelines. J Pain Symptom Manage 22:954, 2001.

61. Rozans M, Dreisbach A, Lertora JJ, Kahn MJ. Palliative uses of methylphenidate in patients with cancer: A review. J Clin Oncol 20:335, 2002.

62. Bruera E, Driver L, Barnes EA, et al: Patient-controlled methylphenidate for the management of fatigue in patients with advanced cancer: A preliminary report. J Clin Oncol 21(23):4439, 2003.

63. Bruera E, Ersnt S, Hagen N, et al: Effectiveness of megestrol acetate in patients with advanced cancer: A randomized, double-blind, crossover study. Cancer Prev Control 2:74, 1998.

64. Bruera E, Neumann CM, Pituskin E, et al: Thalidomide in patients with cachexia due to terminal cancer: Preliminary report. Ann Oncol10:857, 1999.

65. Burks TF: New agents for the treatment of cancer-related fatigue. Cancer15 (Suppl. 6):1714, 2001

66. Bruera E, Strasser F, Shen L, et al:The effect of donepezil on sedation and other symptoms in patients receiving opioids for cancer pain: A pilot study. J Pain Symptom Manage 5:1049, 2003.

67. Vickers AJ, Straus DJ, Fearon B, Cassileth BR: Acupuncture for postchemotherapy fatigue: A phase II study. J Clin Oncol. 22(9):1731, 2004.

68. Post-White J, Kinney ME, Savik K, et al: Therapeutic massage and healing touch improve symptoms in cancer. Integr Cancer Ther (4):332, 2003.

69. E. Bruera: Update on adjuvant drugs in patients with cancer. In Bond MR, Charlton JE, Woolf CJ (eds): Proceedings World Congress on Pain. New York, Elsevier Science, 1991, p 459.

70. Dando TM, Perry CM: Aprepitant: A review of its use in the prevention of chemotherapy-induced nausea and vomiting. Drugs 64(7):777, 2004.

71. Gralla R, Lichinitser M, Van Der Vegt S, et al: Palonosetron improves prevention of chemotherapy-induced nausea and vomiting following moderately emetogenic chemotherapy: Results of a double-blind randomized phase III trial comparing single doses of palonosetron with ondansetron. Ann Oncol 10:1570, 2003.

72. Pereira J, Bruera E: Chronic nausea. In Bruera E, Higginson I, eds: Cachexia-anorexia in cancer patients, Oxford, Oxford University Press, 1996, p 23.

73. Borrison HL, Wang SC: Physiology and pharmacology of vomiting. Pharmacol Rev 5:193, 1953.

74. Chronic nausea in advanced cancer patients: A retrospective assessment of a metoclopramide-based antiemetic regimen. J Pain Symptom Manage 11(3):147, 1996.

75. Bruera E, Seifert L, Watanabe S, et al: Chronic nausea in advanced cancer patients: A retrospective assessment of a metoclopramide-based antiemetic regimen. J Pain Symptom Manage 11(3):147, 1996.

76. Bruera E, Seifert L, Watanabe S, et al: Chronic nausea in advanced cancer patients: A retrospective assessment of a metoclopramide-based antiemetic regimen. J Pain Symptom Manage 11:147, 1996.

77. Ripamonti C, Rodriguez C: Gastrointestinal motility disorders in patients with advanced cancer. In Topics in Palliative Care. New York,Oxford University Press, 1997, p 61.

78. Bruera E, Belzile M, Neumann C, et al: A double-blind, crossover study of controlled-release metoclopramide and placebo for the chronic nausea and dyspepsia of advanced cancer. J Pain Symptom Manage. (6):427, 2000.

79. Rung GW, Claybon L, Hord A, et al: Intravenous ondansetron for postsurgical opioid-induced nausea and vomiting. Anesth Analg 84:832, 1997.

80. Mercadante S, Sapio M, Serretta R: Ondansetron in nausea and vomiting induced by spinal morphine. J Pain Symptom Manage 4:259, 1998.

81. Ripamonti C, Bruera E: Dyspnea: Pathophysiology and assessment. J Pain Symptom Manage 4:220, 1997.

82. Bruera E, Schmitz B, Pither J, et al: The frequency and correlates of dyspnea in patients with advanced cancer. J Pain Symptom Manage 19:357, 2000.

83. Higginson I, McCarthy M: Measuring symptoms in terminal cancer: Are pain and dyspnoea controlled?. J R Soc Med 82:264, 1989.

84. Davis CL: The therapeutics of dyspnoea. Cancer Surveys 21:85, 1994.

85. Bruera E, Schmitz B, Pither J, et al: The frequency and correlates of dyspnea in patients with advanced cancer. J Pain Symptom Manage 5:357, 2000.

86. Bruera E, Schoeller T, Maceachern T: Symptomatic benefit of supplemental oxygen in hypoxemic patients with terminal cancer: The use of the N of 1 randomized controlled trial. J Pain Symptom Manage 7:365, 1992.

87. Bruera E, de Stoutz N, Velasco-Leiva A, et al: Effects of oxygen on dyspnea in hypoxemic terminal-cancer patients. Lancet 342:13, 1993.

88. Bruera E, Sweeney C, Willey J, et al: A randomized controlled trial of supplemental oxygen versus air in cancer patients with dyspnea. Palliat Med 8:659, 2003.

89. Bruera E, MacEachern T, Ripamonti C, Hanson J: Subcutaneous morphine for dyspnea in cancer patients. Ann Intern Med 119(9):906, 1993.

90. Bruera E, Macmillan K, Pither J, MacDonald RN: Effects of morphine on the dyspnea of terminal cancer patients. J Pain Symptom Manage 5(6):341, 1990.

91. Foral PA, Malesker MA, Huerta G, Hilleman DE: Nebulized opioids use in COPD. Chest 125(2):691, 2004.

92. Cherny N, Ripamonti C, Pereira J, et al: Expert Working Group of the European Association of Palliative Care Network. Strategies to manage the adverse effects of oral morphine: An evidence-based report. J Clin Oncol 19:2542, 2001.

93. Ripamonti C, Bruera E: CNS adverse effects of opioids in cancer patients. Guidelines for treatment. CNS Drugs 8:21, 1997.

94. Rozans M, Dreisbach A, Lertora JJ, et al: Palliative uses of methylphenidate in patients with cancer: A review. J Clin Oncol 20:335, 2002.

95. Bruera E, Strasser F, Shen L, et al: The effect of donepezil on sedation and other symptoms in patients receiving opioids for cancer pain: A pilot study. J Pain Symptom Manage 26(5):1049, 2003.

96. McCorcke R, Quintin-Benoliel J: Symptom distress, current concerns and mood disturbances after diagnosis of life-threatening disease. Soc Sci Med 17:431, 1983.

97. Davidson JR, MacLean AW, Brudage MD, Schulze K: Sleep disturbances in cancer patients. Soc Sci Med 54:1309, 2002.

98. Savard J, Morin CM: Insomnia in the context of cancer: A review of a neglected problem. J Clin Oncol 19:895, 2001.

99. Anderson K, Getto G, Mendoza T, et al: Fatigue and sleep disturbance in patients with cancer, patients with clinical depression, and community-dwelling adults. J Pain Symptom Manage 25:307, 2003.

100. Sanna P, Bruera E: Insomnia and sleep disturbances. Eur J Palliat Care 9:8, 2002.

101. Mercadante S, Girelli D, Casuccio A: Sleep disorders in advanced cancer patients: Prevalence and factors associated. Support Care Cancer 5:355, 2004.

102. Ford DE, Kamerow DB: Epidemiologic study of sleep disturbances and psychiatric disorders. An opportunity for prevention? JAMA 262:1479, 1989.

103. Cohen L, Warneke C, Fouladi RT, et al: Psychological adjustment and sleep quality in a randomized trial of the effects of a Tibetan yoga intervention in patients with lymphoma. Cancer 100(10):2253, 2004.

104. Nelson KA, Walsh DT, Sheehan FG, et al: Assessment of upper gastrointestinal motility in the cancer associated dyspepsia syndrome. J Palliat Care 9:27, 1993.

105. Bruera E, Castro M: Cannabinoids in supportive care: Are they necessary? Support Care Cancer (3):133, 2003.

106. Nelson K, Walsh D, Deeter P, Sheehan F: A phase II study of delta-9-tetrahydrocannabinol for appetite stimulation in cancer-associated anorexia. J Palliat Care 10:14, 1994.

107. Crawford SM, Buckman R: Nabilone and metoclopramide in the treatment of nausea and vomiting due to cisplatinum: A double blind study. Med Oncol Tumor Pharmacother 3:39, 1986.

108. Gralla RJ: New agents, new treatment, and antiemetic therapy. Semin Oncol 29 (Suppl. 14):119, 2002.

109. Walsh D, Nelson KA, Mahmoud FA: Established and potential therapeutic applications of cannabinoids in oncology. Support Care Cancer 11(3):137, 2003.

110. Marhin BR: Identification of the endogenous cannabinoid system through integrative pharmacological approaches. J Pharmacol Exp Ther 301:790, 2002.

111. Derogatis LR, Morrow GR, Fetting J, et al: The prevalence of psychiatric disorders among cancer patients. JAMA 249:751, 1983.

112. Gurevich M, Devins GM, Rodin GM: Stress response syndromes and cancer: Conceptual and assessment issues. Psychosomatics 43:259, 2002.

113. Grassi L, Indelli M, Marzola M, et al: Depressive symptoms and quality of life in home-care-assisted cancer patients. J Pain Symptom Manage 12:300, 1996.

114. Cherny NI, Coyle N, Foley KM: Suffering in the advanced cancer patient: A definition and taxonomy. J Palliat Care 10:57, 1994.

115. Akechi T, Okamura H, Nishiwaki Y, et al: Predictive factors for suicidal ideation in patients with unresectable lung carcinoma: A 6-month follow-up study. Cancer 95:1085, 2002.

116. Henriksson MM, Isometsa ET, Hietanen PS, et al: Mental disorders in cancer suicides. J Affect Dis 36:11, 1995.

117. Cassileth BR, Lusk EL, Strouse TB, et al: A psychological analysis of cancer patients and their next-of-kin. Cancer 55:72, 1985.

118. Akechi T, Okuyama T, Sugawara Y, et al:Major depression, adjustment disorders, and post-traumatic stress disorder in terminally ill cancer patients: Associated and predictive factors. J Clin Oncol 22(10):1957, 2004.

119. Hotopf M, Chidgey J, Addington-Hall J, Lan Ly K: Depression in advanced disease: A systematic review. Part 1: Prevalence and case finding. Palliat Med 16:81, 2002.

120. Brugha T: Depression in the terminally ill. Br J Hosp Med 50:175, 1993.

121. Tucker J: Modification of attitudes to influence survival from breast cancer. Lancet 354:1320, 1999.

122. Maguire P: Improving the detection of psychiatric problems in cancer patients. Soc Sci Med 20:819, 1985.

123. Lawrie I, Lloyd-Williams M, Taylor F: How do palliative medicine physicians assess and manage depression. Palliat Med 18(3):234, 2004.

124. Wilson KG, Chochinov HM, Faye BJD, et al: Diagnosis and management of depression in palliative care. In Chochinov HM, Breitbart W (eds): Handbook of Psychiatry in Palliative Medicine. New York, Oxford University Press, 2000, p 25.

125. Van t Spijker A, Trijsburg RW, Duivenvoorden HJ: Psychological sequelae of cancer diagnosis: A meta-analytical review of 58 studies after 1980. Psychosom Med 59:280, 1997.

126. Luebbert K, Dahme B, Hasenbring M: The effectiveness of relaxation training in reducing treatment-related symptoms and improving emotional adjustment in acute non-surgical cancer treatment: A meta-analytical review. Psychooncology 10(6):490, 2001.

127. Anderson RT, McFarlane M, Naughton MJ, Shumaker SA: Conceptual issues and considerations in cross-cultural validation of generic health-related quality of life instruments. In Spilker B (ed): Quality of Life and Pharmacoeconomics in Clinical Trials. Philadelphia, Lippincott-Raven, 1996, p 605.

128. Naughton MJ, Shumaker SA, Anderson R, Czajkowski S: Psychological aspects of health-related quality of life measurement: Tests and scales. In Spilker B (ed): Quality of Life and Pharmacoeconomics in Clinical Trials. Philadelphia, Lippincott-Raven, 1996, p 117.

129. Atkinson MJ, Wishart PM, Wasil BI, Robinson JW: The self-perception and relationships tool (S-PRT): A novel approach to the measurement of subjective health-related quality of life. Health Qual Life Outcomes 2(1):36, 2004.

130. Ferrans CE, Powers MJ: Quality of life index: Development and psychometric properties. ANS Adv Nurs Sci (1):15, 1985.

131. Finkelstein DM, Cassileth BR, Bonomi PD, et al: A pilot study of the Functional Living Index-Cancer (FLIC) Scale for the assessment of quality of life for metastatic lung cancer patients. An Eastern Cooperative Oncology Group study. Am J Clin Oncol (6):630, 1988.

132. Centeno C, Sanz A, Bruera E: Delirium in advanced cancer patients. Palliat Med 3:184, 2004.

133. Lawlor PG, Bruera ED: Delirium in patients with advanced cancer. Hematol Oncol Clin North Am (3):701, 2002.

134. Gagnon B, Lawlor PG, Mancini IL, et al: The impact of delirium on the circadian distribution of breakthrough analgesia in advanced cancer patients. J Pain Symptom Manage 22(4):826, 2001.

135. Lawlor PG, Gagnon B, Mancini IL, et al: Occurrence, causes, and outcome of delirium in patients with advanced cancer: A prospective study. Arch Intern Med 160:786, 2000.

136. Kaplan SH, Ware J: The patient's role in health care and quality assessment. In Goldfield N, Nash DB (eds): Providing Quality Care. Ann Arbor, Mich, Health Administration Press, 1995, p 25.

137. Greenfield S, Kaplan SH, Ware J: Expanding patient involvement in care: Effects on patient outcomes. Ann Intern Med 102: 520, 1985.

138. Ong LM, Visser MR, Lammes FB, de Haes JC: Doctor-patient communication and cancer patients' quality of life and satisfaction. Patient Educ Couns 1(2):145, 2000.

139. Bruera E, Sweeney C, Willey J, et al: Perception of discomfort by relatives and nurses in unresponsive terminally ill patients with cancer: A prospective study. J Pain Symptom Manage (3):818, 2003.

140. Degner LF, Kristjanson LJ, Bowman D, et al: Information needs and decisional preferences in women with breast cancer. JAMA 277:1485, 1997.

141. Onhg LM, de Haes JC, Hoos AM, Lammes FB: Doctor-patient communication: A review of the literature. Soc Sci Med 40(7):903, 1995.

142. Bruera E, Sweeney C, Calder K, et al: Patient preferences versus physician perceptions of treatment decisions in cancer care. J Clin Oncol 19(11):2883, 2001.

143. Wan GJ, Counte MA, Cella DF: The influence of personal expectations on cancer patients' reports of health-related quality of life. Psychooncology 1:1, 1997.

144. World Health Organization National Cancer Programs: Policies and Managerial Guidelines, 2nd ed. Geneva, World Health Organization, 2002, p 83.

145. Shuster J: Delirium, confusion and agitation at the end-of-life. J Palliat Med 1:177, 1998.

146. Breitbart W, Gibson C, Tremblay A: The delirium experience: Delirium recall and delirium-related distress in hospitalized patients with cancer, their spouse/caregivers, and their nurses. Psychosomatics 43:183, 2002.

147. Morita T, Hirai K, Sakaguchi Y, et al: Family-perceived distress from delirium-related symptoms of terminally ill cancer patients. Psychosomatics 45:107, 2004.

148. Fainsinger RL, De Moissac D, Mancini I, Oneschuk D: Sedation for delirium and other symptoms in terminally ill patients in Edmonton. J Palliat Care 16(2):5, 2000.

149. Morita T, Inoue S, Chihara S: Sedation for symptom control in Japan: The importance of intermittent use and communication with family members. J Pain Symptom Manage 12(1):32, 1996.

150. Bruera E, Michaud M, Vigano A, et al.: Multidisciplinary symptom control clinic in a cancer center: A retrospective study. Support Care Cancer 9:162, 2001.

151. World Health Organization: Cancer pain relief and palliative care. Report of a WHO expert committee. World Health Organization Technical Report Series, 804. Geneva: World Health Organization, 1990, p 1.

152. Ventafridda V, Caraceni A, Gamba A: Field-testing of the WHO Guidelines for Cancer Pain Relief: Summary report of demonstration projects. Adv Pain Res Ther 16:451, 1990.

153. Grond S, Zech D, Schug SA, et al. Validation of World Health Organization guidelines for cancer pain relief during the last days and hours of life. J Pain Symptom Manage 6:411, 1991.

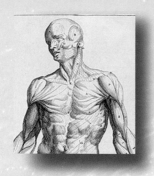

Part D

PAIN OF DERMATOLOGIC AND MUSCULOSKELETAL ORIGIN

chapter

36

Common Sports Injuries

Steven D. Waldman

Injuries following recreational sports activities are becoming increasingly common with the new emphasis in recent years on physical and cardiovascular fitness. For the purposes of this chapter, the clinician can classify sports injuries into two broad classes (1) accidental traumatic injuries and (2) overuse injuries (Table 36–1). On the one hand, accidental traumatic injuries are, for the most part, readily apparent and do not present significant diagnostic challenges. Overuse injuries, on the other hand, can manifest in a more subtle manner and may elude easy diagnosis. The following discussion will center on some of the most common sports injuries and will provide the clinician with a concise approach to diagnosis and treatment. Some of the syndromes discussed here can also result from activities not related to sports. Several of these conditions, such as carpal tunnel syndrome, DeQuervain tenosynovitis, and biceps tendinitis, are important pain syndromes that are described in greater detail in separate chapters; this chapter discusses them from the sports injury perspective.

■ SUPRASPINATUS TENDINITIS

Supraspinatus tendinitis can manifest as either an acute or chronic painful condition of the shoulder. Acute supraspinatus tendinitis will usually occur in a younger group of patients following overuse or misuse of the shoulder joint. Inciting factors may include carrying heavy loads in front and away from the body, throwing injuries, or the vigorous use of exercise equipment. Chronic supraspinatus tendinitis tends to occur in an older group of patients and manifests in a more gradual or insidious manner without a single specific event of antecedent trauma. The pain of supraspinatus tendinitis will be constant and severe with sleep disturbance often reported. The pain of supraspinatus tendinitis is felt primarily in the deltoid region.[1] It is moderate to severe in intensity and may be associated with a gradual loss of range of motion of the affected shoulder. The patient will often awaken at night when he or she rolls over onto the affected shoulder.

Signs and Symptoms

The patient suffering from supraspinatus tendinitis may attempt to splint the inflamed tendon by elevating the scapula to remove tension from the ligament giving the patient a

Table 36–1	
Types of Overuse and Traumatic Sports Injuries	
Overuse Sports Injuries	*Traumatic Sports Injuries*
Tendinitis	Torn ligaments
Bursitis	Torn and ruptured
Muscle strains	tendons
Entrapment neuropathies	Fractures
	Dislocations
	Meniscal tears
	Muscle sprains
	Lacerations

"shrugging" appearance (Fig. 36–1). There is usually point tenderness over the greater tuberosity. The patient will exhibit a painful arc of abduction and complain of a catch or sudden onset of pain in the midrange of the arc due to impingement of the humeral head onto the supraspinatus tendon. Patients with supraspinatus tendinitis will exhibit a positive Dawbarn sign, which is pain to palpation over the greater tuberosity of the humerus when the arm is hanging down that disappears when the arm is fully abducted.[2] Early in the course of the disease, passive range of motion is full and without pain. As the disease progresses, patients suffering from supraspinatus tendinitis will often experience a gradual decrease in functional ability with decreasing shoulder range of motion making simple everyday tasks such as hair combing, fastening a brassiere, or reaching overhead quite difficult. With continued disuse, muscle wasting may occur and a frozen shoulder may develop.

Testing

Plain radiographs are indicated in all patients who present with shoulder pain. Based on the patient's clinical presenta-

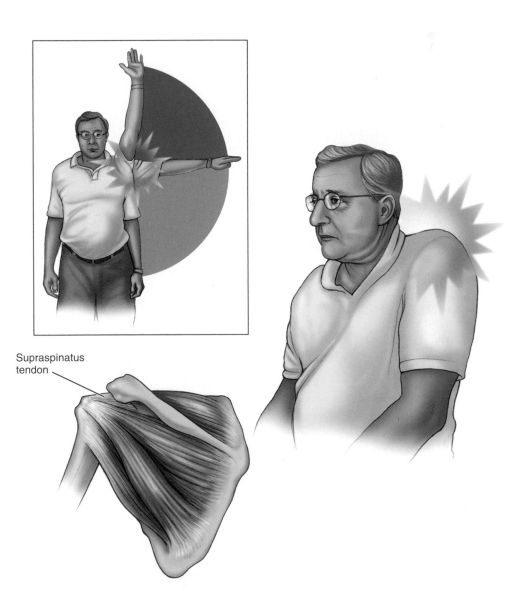

FIGURE 36–1 ■ Patients with supraspinatus tendinitis exhibit point tenderness of the greater tuberosity and a painful arc of abduction. (From Waldman SD: Atlas of Uncommon Pain Syndromes. Philadelphia, Saunders, 2003, p 68.)

Supraspinatus tendon

tion, additional testing including complete blood count, erythrocyte sedimentation rate, and antinuclear antibody testing may be indicated. MRI scan of the shoulder is indicated if rotator cuff tear is suspected. The injection technique mentioned subsequently will serve as both a diagnostic and therapeutic maneuver.

Differential Diagnosis

Because supraspinatus tendinitis may occur after seemingly minor trauma or develop gradually over time, the diagnosis will often be delayed. Tendinitis of the musculotendinous unit of the shoulder frequently coexists with bursitis of the associated bursae of the shoulder joint, creating additional pain and functional disability. This ongoing pain and functional disability can cause the patient to splint the shoulder group with resultant abnormal movement of the shoulder, which puts additional stress on the rotator cuff. This can lead to further trauma to the entire rotator cuff. It should be remembered that with rotator cuff tears, passive range of motion is normal, but active range of motion is limited in contradistinction to frozen shoulder where both passive and active range of motion is limited. Rotator cuff tear rarely occurs before the age of 40 except in cases of severe acute trauma to the shoulder. Cervical radiculopathy may rarely cause pain limited to the shoulder, although in most instances, there is associated neck and upper extremity pain and numbness.

Treatment

Initial treatment of the pain and functional disability associated with supraspinatus tendinitis should include a combination of the nonsteroidal antiinflammatory agents or COX-2 inhibitors and physical therapy. The local application of heat and cold may also be beneficial. For patients who do not respond to these treatment modalities, the following injection technique may be a reasonable next step. The use of physical therapy including gentle range-of-motion exercises should be introduced several days after the patient undergoes this injection technique for shoulder pain. Vigorous exercises should be avoided because they will exacerbate the patients symptoms.

To inject the supraspinatus tendon, the patient is placed in the supine position with the forearm medially rotated behind the back. This positioning of the upper extremity will place the lateral epicondyle of the elbow in an anterior position and make its identification easier. After identifying the lateral epicondyle of the elbow, the humerus is traced superiorly to the anterior edge of the acromion. A slight indentation just below the anterior edge of the acromion marks the point of insertion of the supraspinatus tendon into the upper facet of the greater tuberosity of the humerus. The point is marked with a sterile marker.

Proper preparation with antiseptic solution of the skin overlying the shoulder, subacromial region, and joint space is then carried out. A sterile syringe containing 1.0 mL of 0.25% preservative-free bupivacaine and 40 mg of methylprednisolone is attached to a 1½-inch 25-gauge needle using strict aseptic technique. With strict aseptic technique, the previously marked point is palpated and the indentation indicating the insertion of the supraspinatus tendon is re-identified with the gloved finger. The needle is then carefully advanced perpendicularly at this point through the skin and subcutaneous

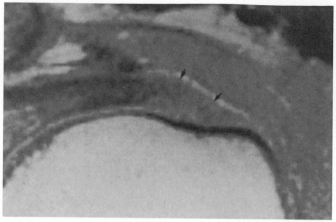

FIGURE 36–2 ■ Tendinosis of tendinopathy of the rotator cuff. A coronal oblique protein density-weighted (TR/TE, 2000/25) spin-echo magnetic resonance image reveals increased signal intensity in the distal part of the supraspinatus tendon (*arrows*). There was no further increase in signal intensity in T2-weighted spin-echo magnetic resonance images. The peribursal fat plane is intact. (From Kjellin I, Ho CP, Cervilla V, et al: Alterations in the supraspinatus tendon at MR imaging: Correlation with histopathologic findings in cadavers. Radiology 181:837, 1991.)

tissues through the joint capsule until it impinges on bone (Fig. 36–2).[3] The needle is then withdrawn 1 to 2 mm out of the periosteum of the humerus and the contents of the syringe is gently injected. There should be slight resistance to injection. If no resistance is encountered, either the needle tip is in the joint space itself or the supraspinatus tendon is ruptured. If there is significant resistance to injection, the needle tip is probably in the substance of a ligament or tendon and should be advanced or withdrawn slightly until the injection proceeds without significant resistance. The needle is then removed and a sterile pressure dressing and ice pack are placed at the injection site.

The major complication of this injection technique is infection. This complication should be exceedingly rare if strict aseptic technique is followed. The possibility of trauma to the supraspinatus tendon from the injection itself remains an ever present possibility. Tendons that are highly inflamed or previously damaged are subject to rupture if they are directly injected. This complication can be greatly decreased if the clinician uses gentle technique and stops injecting immediately if significant resistance to injection is encountered. Approximately 25% of patients will complain of a transient increase in pain following this injection technique and should be warned of this possibility.

■ ROTATOR CUFF TENDINOPATHY AND TEAR

Rotator cuff tendinopathy and tears represent a common cause of shoulder pain and dysfunction encountered in clinical practice. A rotator cuff tear will frequently occur after seemingly minor trauma to the musculotendinous unit of the shoulder. However, in most cases, the pathology responsible for the tear is usually a long time in the making and is the most often the result of ongoing tendinitis. The rotator cuff is made up of the subscapularis, supraspinatus, infraspinatus, and teres minor muscles and associated tendons (Fig. 36–3).[4] The

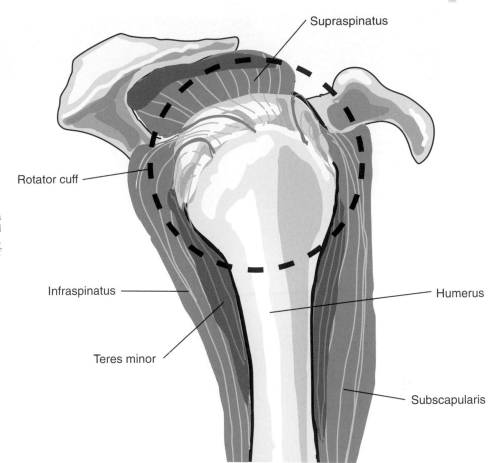

FIGURE 36–3 ■ The rotator cuff is a functional musculotendinous unit composed of four muscles, their fascia, and tendons. (From Waldman SD: Physical Diagnosis of Pain. Philadelphia, Saunders, 2006, p 86.)

function of the rotator cuff is to rotate the arm to help provide shoulder joint stability along the other muscles, tendons, and ligaments of the shoulder.

The supraspinatus and infraspinatus muscle tendons are particularly susceptible to the development of tendinitis for several reasons.[5] First, the joint is subjected to wide ranges of motion that are often repetitive in nature. Second, the space in which the musculotendinous unit functions is restricted by the coracoacromial arch, making impingement a likely possibility with extreme movements of the joint. Third, the blood supply to the musculotendinous unit is poor, making healing of microtrauma more difficult. All of these factors can contribute to tendinitis of one or more of the tendons of the shoulder joint. Calcium deposition around the tendon may occur if the inflammation continues—making subsequent treatment more difficult.

Bursitis often accompanies rotator cuff tears and may require specific treatment. In addition to the previously mentioned pain, patients suffering from rotator cuff tear will often experience a gradual decrease in functional ability with decreasing shoulder range of motion—making simple everyday tasks such as hair combing, fastening a brassiere, or reaching over head quite difficult. With continued disuse, muscle wasting may occur and a frozen shoulder may develop.

Signs and Symptoms

Patients presenting with rotator cuff tear will frequently complain that they can't lift the arm above the level of the shoul-

FIGURE 36–4 ■ Inability to elevate the arm above the level of the shoulder is the hallmark of rotator cuff disturbance. (From Waldman SD: Atlas of Common Pain Syndromes. Philadelphia, Saunders, 2002, p 89.)

der without using the other arm to lift it (Fig. 36–4). On physical examination, the patient will have weakness on external rotation if the infraspinatus is involved and weakness in abduction above the level of the shoulder if the supraspinatus is involved. Tenderness to palpation in the subacromial region

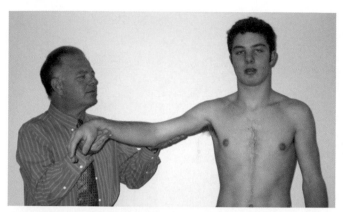

FIGURE 36–5 ■ The drop arm test for complete rotator cuff tear. (From Waldman SD: Physical Diagnosis of Pain: An Atlas of Signs and Symptoms. Philadelphia, Saunders, 2006, p 91.)

is often present. Patients with partial rotator cuff tears will exhibit loss of the ability to smoothly reach overhead. Patients with complete tears will exhibit anterior migration of the humeral head as well as a complete inability to reach above the level of the shoulder. A positive drop arm test, which is the inability to hold the arm abducted at the level of the shoulder after the supported arm is released, will often be present with complete tears of the rotator cuff (Figs. 36–5 and 36 6).[6] The Moseley test for rotator cuff tear—performed by having the patient actively abduct the arm to 80° and then adding gentle resistance, which will force the arm to drop if complete rotator cuff tear is present—will also be positive. Passive range of motion of the shoulder is normal, but active range of motion is limited.

The pain of rotator cuff tear is constant and severe and is made worse with abduction and external rotation of the shoulder. Significant sleep disturbance is often reported. The patient may attempt to splint the inflamed subscapularis tendon by limiting medial rotation of the humerus.

Testing

Plain radiographs are indicated in all patients who present with shoulder pain. Based on the patient's clinical presentation, additional testing including complete blood count, erythrocyte sedimentation rate, and antinuclear antibody testing may be indicated. MRI scan of the shoulder is indicated if rotator cuff tear is suspected.

Differential Diagnosis

Because rotator cuff tears may occur after seemingly minor trauma, the diagnosis will often be delayed. The tear may be either partial or complete, further confusing the diagnosis, although careful physical examination can help distinguish the two. Tendinitis of the musculotendinous unit of the shoulder frequently coexists with bursitis of the associated bursae of the shoulder joint, creating additional pain and functional disability. This ongoing pain and functional disability can cause the patient to splint the shoulder group with resultant abnormal movement of the shoulder, which puts additional stress on the rotator cuff. This can lead to further trauma to the rotator cuff. It should be remembered that with rotator cuff

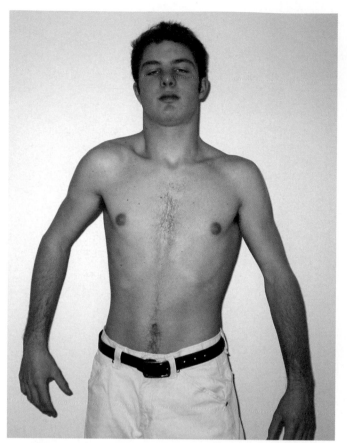

FIGURE 36–6 ■ A patient with a complete rotator cuff tear will be unable to hold the arm in the abducted position, and it will fall to the patient's side. The patient will often shrug or hitch the shoulder forward to use the intact muscles of the rotator cuff and the deltoid to keep the arm in the abducted position. (From Waldman SD: Physical Diagnosis of Pain: An Atlas of Signs and Symptoms. Philadelphia, Saunders, 2006, p 92.)

tears, passive range of motion is normal but active range of motion is limited, in contradistinction to frozen shoulder where both passive and active range of motion is limited. Rotator cuff tear rarely occurs before the age of 40 except in cases of severe acute trauma to the shoulder.

Treatment

Initial treatment of the pain and functional disability associated with rotator cuff tear should include a combination of the nonsteroidal antiinflammatory agents or COX-2 inhibitors and physical therapy. The local application of heat and cold may also be beneficial. For patients who do not respond to these treatment modalities, injection of the rotator cuff may be a reasonable next step before surgical intervention.

■ BICIPITAL TENDINITIS

The tendons of the long and short heads of the biceps, either alone or together, are particularly prone to the development of tendinitis which is known as bicipital tendinitis.[7] The etiology of this syndrome is usually, at least in part, due to impingement on the tendons of the biceps at the coracoacromial arch. The onset of bicipital tendinitis is usually acute occurring after overuse or misuse of the shoulder joint. Inciting factors may include activities such as trying to start a recalcitrant lawn mower, practicing an overhead tennis serve, or overaggressive follow-through when driving golf balls. The biceps muscle and tendons are susceptible to trauma and to wear and tear from overuse and misuse as mentioned earlier. If the damage becomes severe enough, the tendon of the long head of the biceps can rupture, leaving the patient with a telltale "Popeye" biceps (Fig. 36–7). This deformity can be accentuated by having the patient perform the Ludington maneuver, which is having the patient place his or her hands behind the head and flex the biceps muscle (Fig. 36–8).[8]

Signs and Symptoms

The pain of bicipital tendinitis is constant and severe and is localized in the anterior shoulder over the bicipital groove (Fig. 36–9). A catching sensation may also accompany the pain. Significant sleep disturbance is often reported. The patient may attempt to splint the inflamed tendons by internal rotation of the humerus, which moves the biceps tendon from beneath the coracoacromial arch. Patients with bicipital tendinitis will exhibit a positive Yergason sign, which is production of pain on active supination of the forearm against resistance with the elbow flexed at a right angle (Fig. 36–10).[9] Bursitis often accompanies bicipital tendinitis.

In addition to this pain, patients suffering from bicipital tendinitis will often experience a gradual decrease in functional ability with decreasing shoulder range of motion—making simple everyday tasks such as hair combing, fastening a brassiere, or reaching over head quite difficult. With continued disuse, muscle wasting may occur and a frozen shoulder may develop.

Testing

Plain radiographs are indicated in all patients who present with shoulder pain. Based on the patient's clinical presentation, additional testing—including complete blood count, erythrocyte sedimentation rate, and antinuclear antibody testing may be indicated. MRI scan of the shoulder is indicated if rotator cuff tear is suspected. The injection technique (described later) will serve as both a diagnostic and therapeutic maneuver.

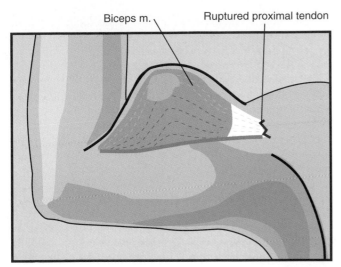

Biceps m.   Ruptured proximal tendon

FIGURE 36–7 ■ "Popeye" deformity associated with ruptured long tendon of the biceps. (From Waldman SD: Physical Diagnosis of Pain: An Atlas of Signs and Symptoms. Philadelphia, Saunders, 2006, p 83.)

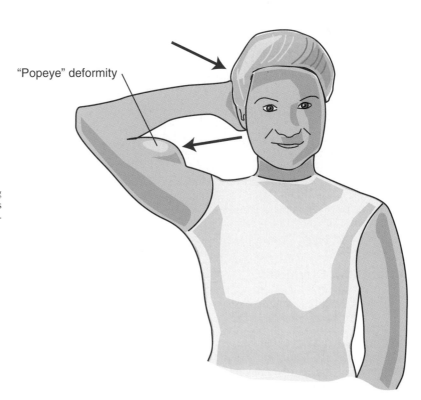

"Popeye" deformity

FIGURE 36–8 ■ The Ludington test for ruptured long tendon of the biceps. (From Waldman SD: Physical Diagnosis of Pain: An Atlas of Signs and Symptoms. Philadelphia, Saunders, 2006, p 84.)

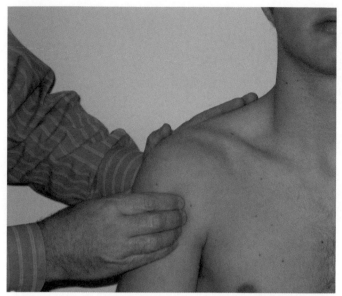

FIGURE 36–9 ■ Palpation of the long tendon of the biceps. (From Waldman SD: Physical Diagnosis of Pain: An Atlas of Signs and Symptoms. Philadelphia, Saunders, 2006, p 83.)

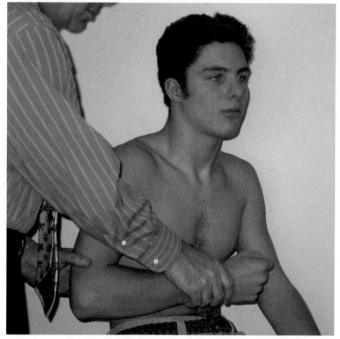

FIGURE 36–10 ■ Yergason test for bicipital tendinitis. (From Waldman SD: Physical Diagnosis of Pain: An Atlas of Signs and Symptoms. Philadelphia, Saunders, 2006, p 76.)

Differential Diagnosis

Bicipital tendinitis is usually a straightforward clinical diagnosis. However, coexisting bursitis or tendinitis of the shoulder from overuse or misuse may confuse the diagnosis. Occasionally partial rotator cuff tear can be mistaken for bicipital tendinitis. If the clinical situation dictates, consideration should be given to primary or secondary tumors involving the shoulder, superior sulcus of the lung, or proximal humerus.

The pain of acute herpes zoster, which occurs before the eruption of vesicular rash, can also mimic bicipital tendinitis.

Treatment

Initial treatment of the pain and functional disability associated with bicipital tendinitis should include a combination of the nonsteroidal antiinflammatory agents or COX-2 inhibitors and physical therapy. The local application of heat and cold may also be beneficial. For patients who do not respond to these treatment modalities, the following injection technique with local anesthetic and steroid may be a reasonable next step.

Injection for bicipital tendinitis is carried out by placing the patient in the supine position. The arm is then externally rotated approximately 45 degrees. The coracoid process is then identified anteriorly. Just lateral to the coracoid process is the lesser tuberosity. The lesser tuberosity will be more easily palpated as the arm is passively rotated. The point overlying the tuberosity is marked with a sterile marker.

Proper preparation with antiseptic solution of the skin overlying the anterior shoulder is carried out. A sterile syringe containing 1.0 mL of 0.25% preservative-free bupivacaine and 40 mg of methylprednisolone is attached to a 1½-inch 25-gauge needle using strict aseptic technique. With strict aseptic technique, the previously marked point is palpated and the insertion of the bicipital tendon is re-identified with the gloved finger. The needle is then carefully advanced at this point through the skin and subcutaneous tissues and underlying tendon until it impinges on bone (Figs. 36–11 and 36–12).[10] The needle is then withdrawn 1 to 2 mm out of the periosteum of the humerus and the contents of the syringe is gently injected. There should be slight resistance to injection. If no resistance is encountered, either the needle tip is in the joint space itself or the tendon is ruptured. If there is significant resistance to injection, the needle tip is probably in the substance of a ligament or tendon and should be advanced or withdrawn slightly until the injection proceeds without significant resistance. The needle is then removed and a sterile pressure dressing and ice pack are placed at the injection site.

The major complication of this injection technique is infection. This complication should be exceedingly rare if strict aseptic technique is followed. The possibility of trauma to the bicipital tendon from the injection itself remains an ever-present possibility. Tendons that are highly inflamed or previously damaged are subject to rupture if they are directly injected. This complication can be greatly decreased if the clinician uses gentle technique and stops injecting immediately if significant resistance to injection is encountered. Approximately 25% of patients will complain of a transient increase in pain following intra-articular injection of the shoulder joint and should be warned of this possibility.

■ LATERAL EPICONDYLITIS

Tennis elbow (also known as lateral epicondylitis) is caused by repetitive microtrauma to the extensor tendons of the forearm.[11] The pathophysiology of tennis elbow is initially caused by micro-tearing at the origin of extensor carpi

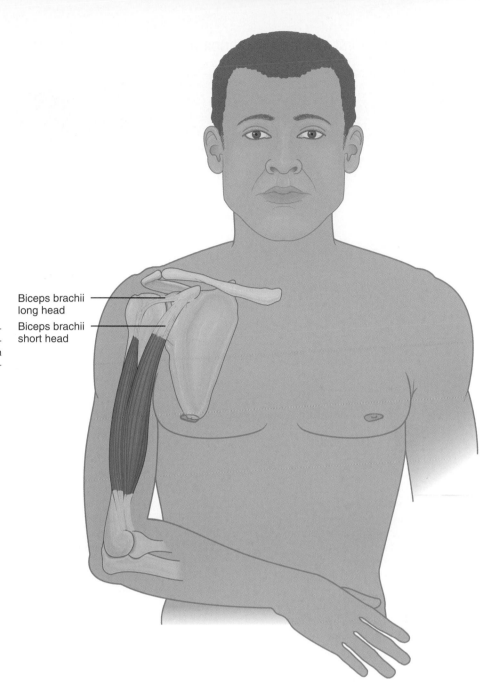

Biceps brachii
long head

Biceps brachii
short head

FIGURE 36–11 ■ Drawing of clinically relevant anatomy for injection for bicipital tendinitis. (From Waldman SD: Atlas of Pain Management Injection Techniques, Philadelphia, Saunders, 2000, pp 53.)

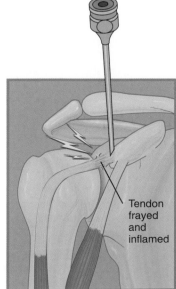

Tendon
frayed
and
inflamed

FIGURE 36–12 ■ Injection technique for bicipital tendinitis. (From Waldman SD: Atlas of Pain Management Injection Techniques, Philadelphia, Saunders, 2000, p 53.)

FIGURE 36–13 ■ Mechanism of elbow injury in tennis players. (From Waldman SD: Physical Diagnosis of Pain: An Atlas of Signs and Symptoms. Philadelphia, Saunders, 2006, p 137.)

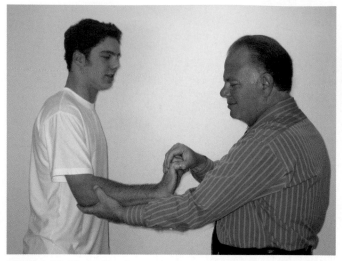

FIGURE 36–14 ■ Test for tennis elbow (From Waldman SD: Physical Diagnosis of Pain: An Atlas of Signs and Symptoms. Philadelphia, Saunders, 2006, p 138.)

radialis and extensor carpi ulnaris. Secondary inflammation, which can become chronic as the result of continued overuse or misuse of the extensors of the forearm, may occur. Coexistent bursitis, arthritis, and gout may also perpetuate the pain and disability of tennis elbow.

Tennis elbow occurs in patients engaged in repetitive activities that include hand grasping (e.g., politicians shaking hands) or high-torque wrist turning (e.g., scooping ice cream at an ice cream parlor). Tennis players develop tennis elbow by two separate mechanisms: First, increased pressure grip strain as a result of playing with too heavy a racquet; and second, making backhand shots with a leading shoulder and elbow rather than keeping the shoulder and elbow parallel to the net (Fig. 36–13). Other racquet sports players are also susceptible to the development of tennis elbow.

Signs and Symptoms

The pain of tennis elbow is localized to the region of the lateral epicondyle. It is constant and is made worse with active contraction of the wrist. Patients will note the inability to hold a coffee cup or hammer. Sleep disturbance is common. On physical examination, there will be tenderness along the extensor tendons at, or just below, the lateral epicondyle. Many patients with tennis elbow will exhibit a band-like thickening within the affected extensor tendons.[11] Elbow range of motion will be normal. Grip strength on the affected side will be diminished. Patients with tennis elbow will demonstrate a positive tennis elbow test.[12] The test is performed by stabilizing the patient's forearm and then having the patient clench his or her fist and actively extend the wrist. The examiner then attempts to force the wrist into flexion (Fig. 36–14). Sudden severe pain is highly suggestive of tennis elbow.

Testing

Electromyography will help distinguish cervical radiculopathy and radial tunnel syndrome from tennis elbow. Plain radiographs are indicated in all patients who present with tennis elbow to rule out joint mice and other occult bony pathology. Based on the patient's clinical presentation, additional testing including complete blood count, uric acid, erythrocyte sedimentation rate, and antinuclear antibody testing may be indicated. MRI scan of the elbow is indicated if joint instability is suspected. The injection technique described below will serve as both a diagnostic and therapeutic maneuver.

Differential Diagnosis

Radial tunnel syndrome and occasionally C6-C7 radiculopathy can mimic tennis elbow. Radial tunnel syndrome is an entrapment neuropathy that is the result of entrapment of the radial nerve below the elbow. Radial tunnel syndrome can be distinguished from tennis elbow in that with radial tunnel syndrome, the maximal tenderness to palpation is distal to the lateral epicondyle over the radial nerve, whereas with tennis elbow, the maximal tenderness to palpation is over the lateral epicondyle.

The most common nidus of pain from tennis elbow is the bony origin of the extensor tendon of extensor carpi radialis brevis at the anterior facet of the lateral epicondyle. Less commonly, tennis elbow pain can originate from the extensor carpi radialis longus at the supracondylar crest, or, rarely, more distally at the point where the extensor carpi radialis brevis overlies the radial head. As mentioned earlier, bursitis may accompany tennis elbow. The olecranon bursa lies in the posterior aspect of the elbow joint and may also become inflamed as a result of direct trauma or overuse of the joint. Other bursae susceptible to the development of bursitis exist between the insertion of the biceps and the head of the radius as well as in the antecubital and cubital areas.

Treatment

Initial treatment of the pain and functional disability associated with tennis elbow should include a combination of the nonsteroidal antiinflammatory agents or COX-2 inhibitors and physical therapy. The local application of heat and cold may also be beneficial. Avoidance of any repetitive activity that may exacerbate the patient's symptoms should be avoided. A Velcro band placed around the extensor tendons may also help relieve the symptoms of tennis elbow. For patients who do not respond to these treatment modalities, injection of the lateral epicondyle may be a reasonable next step.

■ CARPAL TUNNEL SYNDROME

Carpal tunnel syndrome is the most common entrapment neuropathy encountered in clinical practice. It is caused by compression of the median nerve as it passes through the carpal canal at the wrist. The more common causes of compression of the median nerve at this anatomic location include flexor tenosynovitis, rheumatoid arthritis, pregnancy, amyloidosis, and other space-occupying lesions that compromise the median nerve as it passes though this closed space.[13] This entrapment neuropathy manifests as pain, numbness, paresthesias, and associated weakness in the hand and wrist; these symptoms radiate to the thumb, index, middle, and radial half of the ring fingers (Fig. 36–15), and may also radiate proximal to the entrapment into the forearm. Untreated, progressive motor deficit and, ultimately, flexion contracture of the affected fingers can result. The onset of symptoms is usually after repetitive wrist motions or from repeated pressure on the wrist, such as resting the wrists on the edge of a computer keyboard. Direct trauma to the median nerve as it enters the carpal tunnel may also result in a similar clinical presentation.

Signs and Symptoms

Physical findings include tenderness over the median nerve at the wrist. A positive Tinel sign over the median nerve as it passes beneath the flexor retinaculum is usually present (Fig. 36–16).[14] A positive Phalen test is highly suggestive of carpal tunnel syndrome. The Phalen test is performed by having the patient place his or her wrists in complete, unforced flexion for at least 30 seconds (Fig. 36–17).[15] If the median nerve is entrapped at the wrist, this maneuver will reproduce the symptoms of carpal tunnel syndrome. Weakness of thumb opposition and wasting of the thenar eminence are often seen in advanced carpal tunnel syndrome, although because of the

FIGURE 36–15 ■ Carpal tunnel syndrome: relevant anatomy. (From Waldman SD: Physical Diagnosis of Pain: An Atlas of Signs and Symptoms. Philadelphia, Saunders, 2006, p 176.)

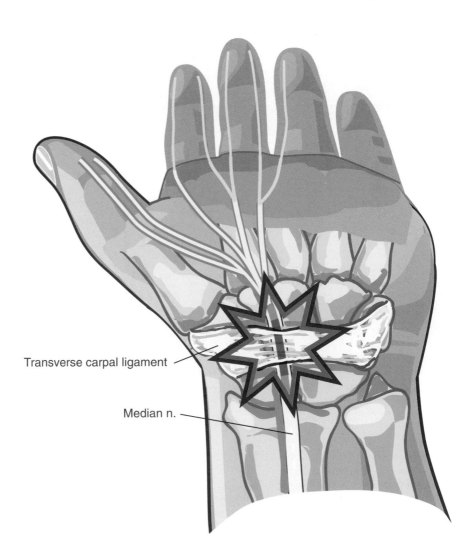

Transverse carpal ligament

Median n.

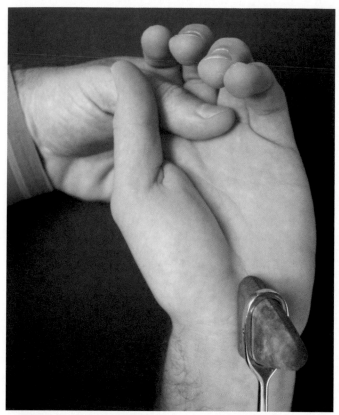

FIGURE 36–16 ■ The Tinel sign for carpal tunnel syndrome. (From Waldman SD: Physical Diagnosis of Pain: An Atlas of Signs and Symptoms. Philadelphia, Saunders, 2006, p 178.)

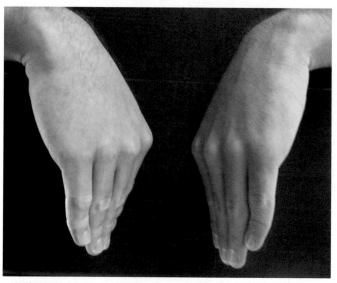

FIGURE 36–17 ■ The Phalen test for carpal tunnel syndrome. (From Waldman SD: Physical Diagnosis of Pain: An Atlas of Signs and Symptoms. Philadelphia, Saunders, 2006, p 179.)

complex motion of the thumb, subtle motor deficits may be easily missed (Fig. 36–18). Early in the course of the evolution of carpal tunnel syndrome, the only physical finding other than tenderness over the nerve may be the loss of sensation on the thumb, index, middle, and radial half of the ring fingers.

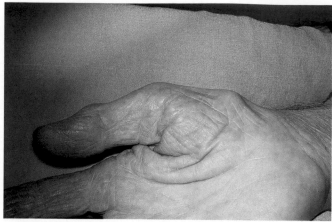

FIGURE 36–18 ■ Thenar muscle atrophy. Chronic entrapment of the median nerve in the carpal tunnel or more proximally can produce thenar atrophy as seen in this patient. (From Nathan DJ: Soft tissue. In Klippel JH, Dieppe PA (eds): Rheumatology, 2nd ed. London, Mosby, 1998, p 4.)

Testing

Electromyography will help distinguish cervical radiculopathy and diabetic polyneuropathy from carpal tunnel syndrome. Plain radiographs are indicated in all patients who present with carpal tunnel syndrome to rule out occult bony pathology. Based on the patient's clinical presentation, additional testing including complete blood count, uric acid, erythrocyte sedimentation rate, and antinuclear antibody testing may be indicated. MRI scan of the wrist is indicated if joint instability or a space-occupying lesion is suspected. The injection technique described below will serve as both a diagnostic and therapeutic maneuver.

Differential Diagnosis

Carpal tunnel syndrome is often misdiagnosed as arthritis of the carpometacarpal joint of the thumb, cervical radiculopathy, or diabetic polyneuropathy. Patients with arthritis of the carpometacarpal joint of the thumb will have a positive Watson's test and radiographic evidence of arthritis (Fig. 36–19). Most patients suffering from a cervical radiculopathy will have reflex, motor and sensory changes associated with neck pain, whereas patients with carpal tunnel syndrome will have no reflex changes and motor and sensory changes will be limited to the distal median nerve. Diabetic polyneuropathy will generally manifest as symmetrical sensory deficit involving the entire hand rather than limited to the distribution of the median nerve. It should be remembered that cervical radiculopathy and median nerve entrapment may coexist as the so-called "double crush" syndrome. Because carpal tunnel syndrome is commonly seen in patients with diabetes, it is not surprising that diabetic polyneuropathy is usually present in diabetic patients with carpal tunnel syndrome.

Treatment

Mild cases of carpal tunnel syndrome will usually respond to conservative therapy; surgery should be reserved for more severe cases. Initial treatment of carpal tunnel syndrome

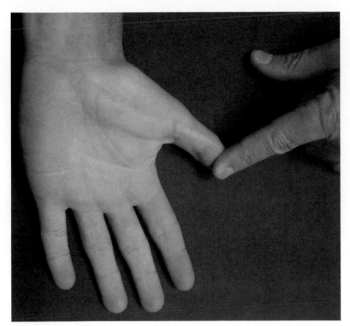

FIGURE 36–19 ■ The Watson stress test for arthritis of the carpometacarpal joint of the thumb. (From Waldman SD: Physical Diagnosis of Pain: An Atlas of Signs and Symptoms. Philadelphia, Saunders, 2006, p 172.)

should consist of treatment with simple analgesics, nonsteroidal antiinflammatory agents or COX-2 inhibitors and splinting of the wrist. At a minimum, the splint should be worn at night, but ideally it should be worn 24 hours a day. Avoidance of repetitive activities thought to be responsible for the evolution of carpal tunnel syndrome, e.g. keyboarding, hammering, and so on, will also help ameliorate the patient's symptoms. If the patient fails to respond to these conservative measures, a next reasonable step is injection of the carpal tunnel with local anesthetic and steroid.

Carpal tunnel injection is performed by placing the patient in a supine position with the arm fully abducted at the patient's side and the elbow slightly flexed, with the dorsum of the hand resting on a folded towel. A total of 3 mL of local anesthetic and 40 mg of methylprednisolone is drawn up in a 5-mL sterile syringe. The clinician then has the patient make a fist and at the same time flex his or her wrist to aid in identification of the palmaris longus tendon. After preparation of the skin with antiseptic solution, a 5/8 inch 25-gauge needle is inserted just medial to the tendon and just proximal to the crease of the wrist at a 30-degree angle (Fig. 36–20). The needle is slowly advanced until the tip is just beyond the tendon.[16] A paresthesia in the distribution of the median nerve is often elicited and the patient should be warned of this. The

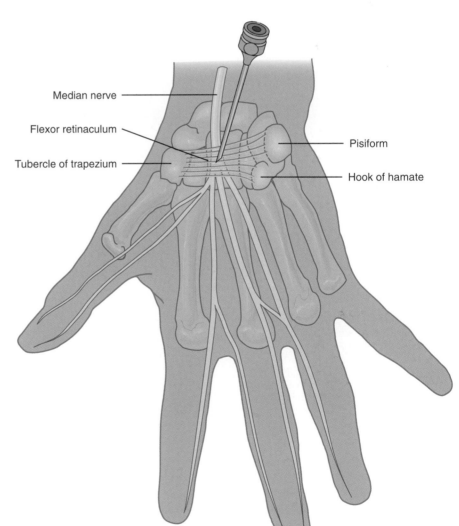

FIGURE 36–20 ■ Injection technique for carpal tunnel syndrome. (From Waldman SD: Atlas of Pain Management Injection Techniques, Philadelphia, Saunders 2000, p 145.)

Median nerve

Flexor retinaculum

Tubercle of trapezium

Pisiform

Hook of hamate

patient should be warned that should a paresthesia occur, he or she is to say "There!" as soon as the paresthesia is felt. If a paresthesia is elicited, the needle is withdrawn slightly away from the median nerve. Gentle aspiration is then carried out to identify blood. If the aspiration test is negative and no persistent paresthesia into the distribution of the median nerve remains, 3 mL of solution is slowly injected, with the patient being monitored closely for signs of local anesthetic toxicity. If no paresthesia is elicited and the needle tip hits bone, the needle is withdrawn out of the periosteum and after careful aspiration, 3 mL of solution is slowly injected.

For patients who fail these treatment modalities, surgical release of the median nerve at the carpal tunnel is indicated. Endoscopic techniques are showing promise and appear to result in less postoperative pain and dysfunction.

■ DE QUERVAIN TENOSYNOVITIS

De Quervain tenosynovitis is caused by an inflammation and swelling of the tendons of the abductor pollicis longus and extensor pollicis brevis at the level of the radial styloid process.[17] This inflammation and swelling is usually the result of trauma to the tendon from repetitive twisting motions. If the inflammation and swelling becomes chronic, a thickening of the tendon sheath occurs with a resulting constriction of

the sheath (Fig. 36–21). A triggering phenomenon may result with the tendon catching within the sheath, causing the thumb to lock or "trigger." Arthritis and gout of the first metacarpal joint may also coexist and exacerbate the pain and disability of de Quervain tenosynovitis.

De Quervain tenosynovitis occurs in patients engaged in repetitive activities that include hand grasping (e.g., politicians shaking hands) or high-torque wrist turning (e.g., scooping ice cream at an ice cream parlor). It may also develop without obvious antecedent trauma in the parturient.

The pain of de Quervain tenosynovitis is localized to the region of the radial styloid. It is constant and is made worse with active pinching activities of the thumb or ulnar deviation of the wrist. Patients will note the inability to hold a coffee cup or turn a screwdriver. Sleep disturbance is common.

Signs and Symptoms

On physical examination, there will be tenderness and swelling over the tendons and tendon sheaths along the distal radius with point tenderness over the radial styloid (Fig. 36–22). Many patients with de Quervain tenosynovitis will exhibit a creaking sensation with flexion and extension of the thumb. Range of motion of the thumb may be decreased

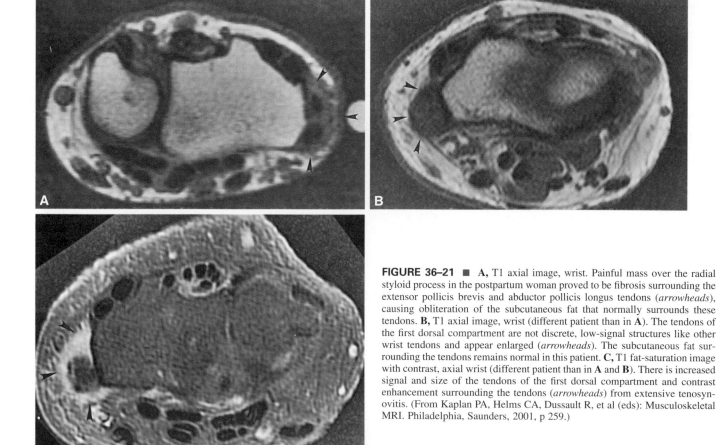

FIGURE 36–21 ■ **A,** T1 axial image, wrist. Painful mass over the radial styloid process in the postpartum woman proved to be fibrosis surrounding the extensor pollicis brevis and abductor pollicis longus tendons (*arrowheads*), causing obliteration of the subcutaneous fat that normally surrounds these tendons. **B,** T1 axial image, wrist (different patient than in **A**). The tendons of the first dorsal compartment are not discrete, low-signal structures like other wrist tendons and appear enlarged (*arrowheads*). The subcutaneous fat surrounding the tendons remains normal in this patient. **C,** T1 fat-saturation image with contrast, axial wrist (different patient than in **A** and **B**). There is increased signal and size of the tendons of the first dorsal compartment and contrast enhancement surrounding the tendons (*arrowheads*) from extensive tenosynovitis. (From Kaplan PA, Helms CA, Dussault R, et al (eds): Musculoskeletal MRI. Philadelphia, Saunders, 2001, p 259.)

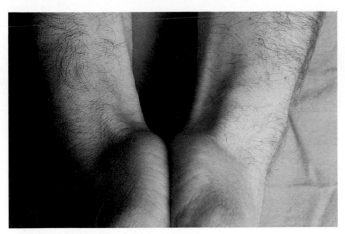

FIGURE 36–22 ■ De Quervain tenosynovitis. (From Fam AG: The wrist and hand. In Klippel JH, Dieppe PA (eds): Rheumatology, 2nd ed. London, Mosby, 1998, p 4.)

because of the pain and a trigger thumb phenomenon may be noted. Patients with de Quervain tenosynovitis will demonstrate a positive Finkelstein test (Fig. 36–23).[18] The Finkelstein test is performed by stabilizing the patient's forearm and then having the patient fully flex his or her thumb into the palm and actively force the wrist toward the ulna. Sudden, severe pain is highly suggestive of de Quervain tenosynovitis.

Testing

There is no specific test to diagnose de Quervain tenosynovitis. The diagnosis is generally made on clinical grounds. Electromyography will help distinguish de Quervain tenosynovitis from neuropathic processes such as cervical radiculopathy and cheiralgia paresthetica. Plain radiographs are indicated in all patients who present with de Quervain tenosynovitis to rule out occult bony pathology. Based on the

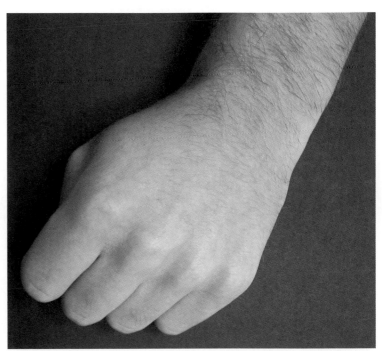

A

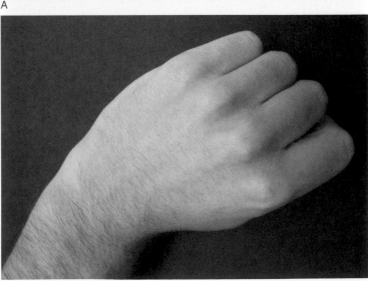

B

FIGURE 36–23 ■ **A** and **B**, the Finkelstein test for de Quervain tenosynovitis. (From Waldman SD: Physical Diagnosis of Pain: An Atlas of Signs and Symptoms. Philadelphia, Saunders, 2006, p 171.)

patient's clinical presentation, additional testing including complete blood count, uric acid, erythrocyte sedimentation rate, and antinuclear antibody testing may be indicated. MRI scan of the wrist is indicated if joint instability is suspected. The injection technique described subsequently will serve as both a diagnostic and therapeutic maneuver.

Differential Diagnosis

Entrapment of the lateral antebrachial cutaneous nerve, arthritis of the first metacarpal joint, gout, cheiralgia parethestica, and occasionally C6-C7 radiculopathy can mimic de Quervain tenosynovitis. Cheiralgia paresthetica is an entrapment neuropathy that is the result of entrapment of the superficial branch of the radial nerve at the wrist. All of these painful conditions can coexist with de Quervain tenosynovitis.

Treatment

Initial treatment of the pain and functional disability associated with de Quervain tenosynovitis should include a combination of the nonsteroidal antiinflammatory agents or COX-2 inhibitors and physical therapy. The local application of heat and cold may also be beneficial. Avoidance of any repetitive

activity that may exacerbate the patient's symptoms should be avoided. Nighttime splinting of the affected thumb may also help avoid the "trigger finger" phenomenon that can occur on awakening in many patients suffering from this condition. For patients who do not respond to these treatment modalities, injection of the inflamed tendons may be a reasonable next step.

■ TROCHANTERIC BURSITIS

Trochanteric bursitis is a commonly encountered pain complaint in clinical practice. The patient suffering from trochanteric bursitis will frequently complain of pain in the lateral hip which can radiate down the leg, thereby mimicking sciatica.[19] The pain is localized to the area over the trochanter. Often, the patient will be unable to sleep on the affected hip and may complain of a sharp, catching sensation with range of motion of the hip, especially on first arising. The patient may note that walking upstairs becomes increasingly more difficult. Trochanteric bursitis often coexists with arthritis of the hip joint, back and sacroiliac joint disease, and gait disturbance.

The trochanteric bursa lies between the greater trochanter and the tendon of the gluteus medius and the iliotibial tract (Fig. 36–24). This bursa may exist as a single bursal sac or in

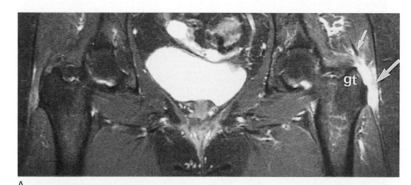

A

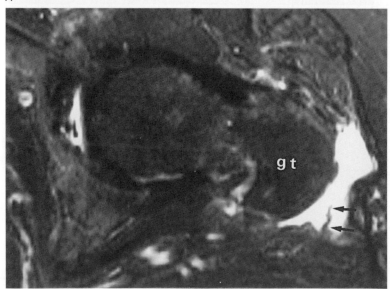

B

FIGURE 36–24 ■ Greater trochanteric bursitis and torn gluteus medius tendon. **A,** Coronal STIR image shows focal high signal around the greater trochanter (*gt; arrow*). The torn and retracted gluteus medius tendon also is seen (*small arrow*). **B,** Axial image shows the well-defined fluid collection that is compatible with greater trochanteric bursitis. The gluteus medius bursitis often is seen in association with gluteus medius tendon tears. (From Kaplan PA, Helms CA, Dussault R, et al (eds): Musculoskeletal MRI. Philadelphia, Saunders, 2001, p 351.)

some patients may exist as a multisegmented series of sacs which may be loculated in nature. The trochanteric bursa is vulnerable to injury from both acute trauma and repeated microtrauma. Acute injuries frequently take the form of direct trauma to the bursa via falls directly onto the greater trochanter or previous hip surgery as well as from overuse injuries including running on soft or uneven surfaces. If the inflammation of the trochanteric bursa becomes chronic, calcification of the bursa may occur.

Signs and Symptoms

Physical examination of the patient suffering from trochanteric bursitis will reveal point tenderness in the lateral thigh just over the greater trochanter. Passive adduction and abduction as well as active resisted abduction of the affected lower extremity will reproduce the pain. Sudden release of resistance during this maneuver will markedly increase the pain (Fig. 36–25).[20] There should be no sensory deficit in the distribution of the lateral femoral cutaneous nerve as seen with meralgia paresthetica, which is often confused with trochanteric bursitis

Testing

Plain radiographs of the hip may reveal calcification of the bursa and associated structures consistent with chronic inflammation. MRI scan is indicated if occult mass or tumor of the hip or groin is suspected. Complete blood count and erythrocyte sedimentation rate are useful if infection is suspected. Electromyography will help distinguish trochanteric bursitis from meralgia paresthetica and sciatica. The injection technique described below will serve as both a diagnostic and therapeutic maneuver.

Differential Diagnosis

Trochanteric bursitis frequently coexists with arthritis of the hip, which may require specific treatment to provide palliation of pain and return of function. Occasionally, trochanteric bursitis can be confused with meralgia paresthetica because both manifest with pain in the lateral thigh. The two syndromes can be distinguished in that patients suffering from meralgia paresthetica will not have pain on palpation over the greater trochanter. Electromyography will help sort out confusing clinical presentations. The clinician must consider the potential for primary or secondary tumors of the hip in the differential diagnosis of trochanteric bursitis.

Treatment

A short course of conservative therapy consisting of simple analgesics, nonsteroidal antiinflammatory agents or COX-2 inhibitors, is a reasonable first step in the treatment of patients suffering from trochanteric bursitis. The patient should be instructed to avoid repetitive activity that may be responsible for the development of trochanteric bursitis, e.g., running on sand. If the patient does not experience rapid

improvement, the following injection technique is a reasonable next step.

Injection of the trochanteric bursa can be carried out by placing the patient in the lateral decubitus position with the affected side up. The midpoint of the greater trochanter is identified. Proper preparation with antiseptic solution of the skin overlying this point is then carried out (Figs. 36–26 and 36–27). A syringe containing 2.0 mL of 0.25% preservative-free bupivacaine and 40 mg of methylprednisolone is attached to a 1½-inch 25-gauge needle.

Before needle placement, the patient should be advised to say "There!" immediately if they feel a paresthesia into the lower extremity—indicating that the needle has impinged on the sciatic nerve. Should a paresthesia occur, the needle should be immediately withdrawn and repositioned more laterally. The needle is then carefully advanced through the previously identified point at a right angle to the skin directly toward the center of the greater trochanter.[21] The needle is advanced very slowly to avoid trauma to the sciatic nerve until it hits the bone. The needle is then withdrawn back out of the periosteum and, after careful aspiration for blood and if no paresthesia is present, the solution is then gently injected into the bursa. There should be minimal resistance to injection.

■ ADDUCTOR TENDINITIS

The increased use of exercise equipment for lower extremity strengthening has resulted in an increased incidence of adductor tendinitis. The adductor muscles of the hip include the gracilis, adductor longus, adductor brevis, and adductor magnus muscles.[22] The adductor function of these muscles is innervated by the obturator nerve, which is susceptible to trauma from pelvic fractures and compression by tumor. The tendons of the adductor muscles of the hip have their origin along the pubis and ischial ramus and it is at this point that tendinitis frequently occurs (Fig. 36–28). These tendons and their associated muscles are susceptible to the development of tendinitis due to overuse or trauma caused by stretch injuries. Inciting factors may include the vigorous use of exercise equipment for lower extremity strengthening and acute stretching of the musculotendinous units as a result of sports injuries (e.g., sliding into bases when playing baseball).

The pain of adductor tendinitis is sharp, constant, and severe with sleep disturbance often reported. The patient may attempt to splint the inflamed tendons by adopting an adductor lurch type of gait , that is, shifting the trunk of the body over the affected extremity when walking. In addition to this pain, patients suffering from adductor tendinitis will often experience a gradual decrease in functional ability with decreasing hip range of motion, making simple everyday tasks such as getting in or out of a car quite difficult. With continued disuse, muscle wasting may occur and an adhesive capsulitis of the hip may develop.

Signs and Symptoms

On physical examination, the patient suffering from adductor tendinitis will report pain on palpation of the origins of the

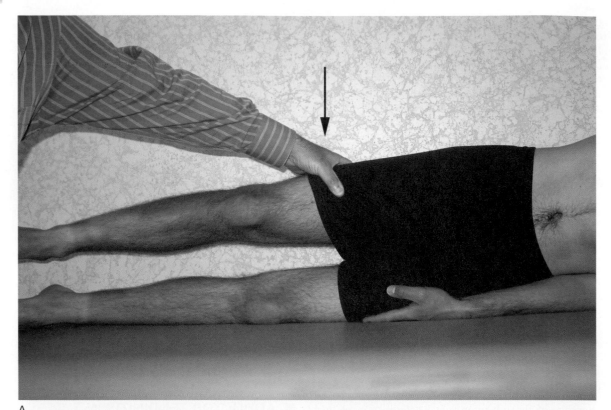

A

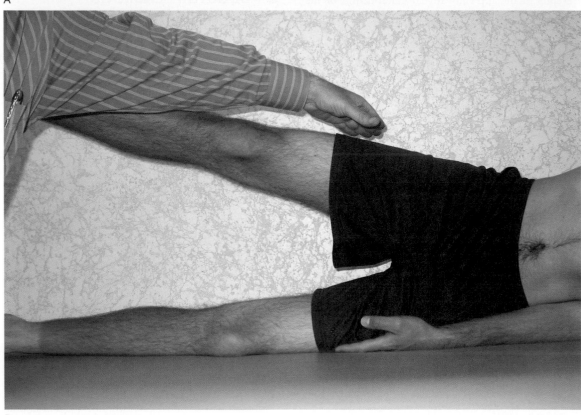

B

FIGURE 36–25 ■ **A** and **B,** The resisted abduction release test. (From Waldman SD: Physical Diagnosis of Pain: An Atlas of Signs and Symptoms. Philadelphia, Saunders, 2006, p 316.)

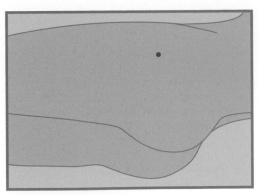

FIGURE 36–26 ■ Patient positioning for trochanteric bursa injection. (From Waldman SD: Atlas of Pain Management Injection Techniques, Philadelphia, Saunders 2000, p 221.)

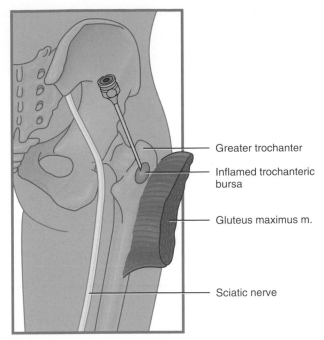

Greater trochanter

Inflamed trochanteric bursa

Gluteus maximus m.

Sciatic nerve

FIGURE 36–27 ■ Injection technique for trochanteric bursitis. (From Waldman SD: Atlas of Pain Management Injection Techniques, Philadelphia, Saunders, 2000, p 221.)

FIGURE 36–28 ■ Mechanism of injury in adductor tendinitis. (From Waldman SD: Atlas of Uncommon Pain Syndromes. Philadelphia, Saunders, 2003, p 204.)

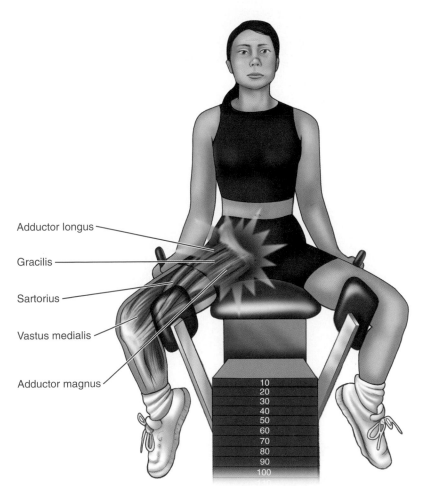

Adductor longus

Gracilis

Sartorius

Vastus medialis

Adductor magnus

10
20
30
40
50
60
70
80
90
100

adductor tendons and will exhibit a positive Waldman knee squeeze test (Fig. 36–29). Active resisted adduction will reproduce the pain as will passive abduction.[23] Tendinitis of the musculotendinous unit of the hip frequently coexists with bursitis of the associated bursae of the hip joint, creating additional pain and functional disability. Neurologic examination of the hip and lower extremity will be within normal limits unless there has been concomitant stretch injury to the plexus or obturator nerve.

Testing

Plain radiographs are indicated in all patients who present with hip, thigh, and groin pain. Based on the patient's clinical presentation, additional testing including complete blood count, erythrocyte sedimentation rate, and antinuclear antibody testing may be indicated. MRI scan of the hip is indicated if aseptic necrosis or occult mass is suspected. Radionuclide bone scanning should be considered if the possibility of occult fracture of the pelvis is being considered. Electromyography can help rule out compression neuropathy or trauma of the obturator nerve as well as plexopathy and radiculopathy. Injection of the insertion of the adductor tendons will serve as both a diagnostic and therapeutic maneuver.

Differential Diagnosis

Internal derangement of the hip may mimic the clinical presentation of adductor tendinitis. Occasionally, indirect inguinal hernia can produce pain that can be confused with adductor tendinitis. If trauma has occurred, consideration of the possibility of occult pelvic fracture, especially in those individuals with osteopenia or osteoporosis should be entertained and radionucide bone scanning should be obtained. Avascular necrosis of the hip may also produce hip pain which can mimic the clinical presentation of adductor tendinitis. Entrapment neuropathy and/or stretch injury to the ilioinguinal, genitofemoral, and obturator nerves as well as plexopathy and radiculopathy should be considered if there is the physical finding of neurologic deficit in patients thought to suffer from adductor tendinitis because all of these clinical entities may coexist.

Treatment

Initial treatment of the pain and functional disability associated with adductor tendinitis should include a combination of the nonsteroidal antiinflammatory agents or COX-2 inhibitors and physical therapy. The local application of heat and cold may also be beneficial. For patients who do not respond to these treatment modalities, the injection of the insertion of the

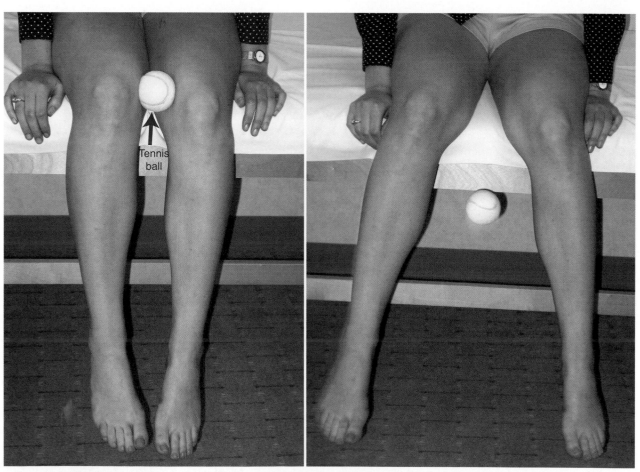

FIGURE 36–29 ■ The Waldman knee squeeze test for adductor tendinitis. (From Waldman SD: Physical Diagnosis of Pain: An Atlas of Signs and Symptoms. Philadelphia, Saunders, 2006, p 307.)

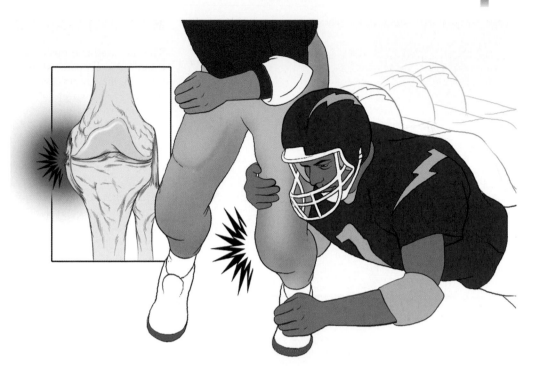

FIGURE 36–30 ■ Medial collateral ligament syndrome is characterized by medial joint pain that is made worse with flexion or external rotation of the knee. (From Waldman SD: Atlas of Common Pain Syndromes. Philadelphia, Saunders, 2002, p 253.)

adductor tendons of the hip with local anesthetic and steroid may be a reasonable next step.

■ MEDIAL COLLATERAL LIGAMENT SYNDROME

Patients with medial collateral ligament syndrome will present with pain over the medial knee joint and increased pain on passive valgus and external rotation of the knee.[24] Activity, especially involving flexion and external rotation of the knee will make the pain worse, with rest and heat providing some relief. The pain is constant and characterized as aching in nature. The patient with injury to the medial collateral ligament may complain of locking or popping with flexion of the affected knee. The pain may interfere with sleep. Coexistent bursitis, tendinitis, arthritis and/or internal derangement of the knee may confuse the clinical picture following trauma to the knee joint.

The medial collateral ligament syndrome is characterized by pain at the medial aspect of the knee joint. It is usually the result of trauma to the medial collateral ligament from falls with the leg in valgus and externally rotated, typically during snow skiing accidents or football clipping injuries (Fig. 36–30). The medial collateral ligament is a broad, flat, band-like ligament that runs from the medial condyle of the femur to the medial aspect of the shaft of the tibia where it attaches just above the groove of the semimembranosus muscle. It also attaches to the edge of the medial semilunar cartilage. The ligament is susceptible to strain at the joint line or avulsion at its origin or insertion.

Signs and Symptoms

Patients with injury of the medial collateral ligament will exhibit tenderness along the course of the ligament from the medial femoral condyle to its tibial insertion. If the ligament is avulsed from its bony insertions, tenderness may be localized to the proximal or distal ligaments, whereas patients suffering from strain of the ligament will exhibit more diffuse tenderness. Patients with severe injury to ligament may exhibit laxity of the joint when valgus and varus stress is placed on the affected knee (Fig. 36–31).[25] Because pain may produce muscle guarding, MRI scanning of the knee may be necessary to confirm the clinician's clinical impression. Joint effusion and swelling may be present with injury to the medial collateral ligament, but it is also suggestive of intra-articular damage.

Testing

Plain radiographs are indicated in all patients who present with medial collateral ligament syndrome pain. Based on the patient's clinical presentation, additional testing including complete blood count, erythrocyte sedimentation rate, and antinuclear antibody testing may be indicated. MRI scan of the knee is indicated if internal derangement or occult mass or tumor is suspected. Bone scan may be useful to identify occult stress fractures involving the joint, especially if trauma has occurred.

Treatment

Initial treatment of the pain and functional disability associated with injury to the medial collateral ligament should include a combination of the nonsteroidal antiinflammatory agents or COX-2 inhibitors and physical therapy. The local application of heat and cold may also be beneficial. Avoidance of any repetitive activity that may exacerbate the patient's symptoms should be avoided. For patients who do not respond to these treatment modalities and who do not have a lesion that will require surgical repair, injection of the medial collateral ligament may be a reasonable next step.

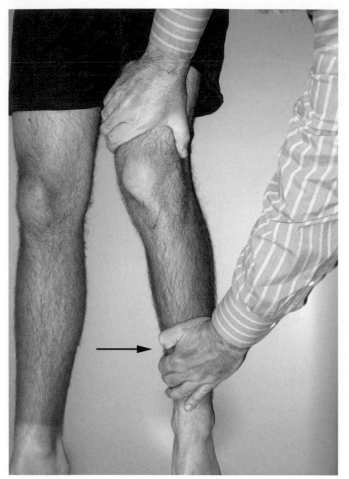

FIGURE 36–31 ■ The valgus stress test for medial collateral ligament integrity. (From Waldman SD: Physical Diagnosis of Pain. Philadelphia, Saunders, 2006, p 334.)

■ PREPATELLAR BURSITIS

The prepatellar bursa is vulnerable to injury from both acute trauma and repeated microtrauma. The prepatellar bursa lies between the subcutaneous tissues and the patella.[26] This bursa may exist as a single bursal sac or in some patients may exist as a multisegmented series of sacs that may be loculated in nature. Acute injuries frequently take the form of direct trauma to the bursa via falls onto the knee or from patellar fractures, as well as from overuse injuries including running on soft or uneven surfaces (Fig. 36–32). Prepatellar bursitis may also result from jobs requiring crawling or kneeling such as in carpet laying or scrubbing floors; hence, the other name for prepatellar bursitis is *housemaid's knee*. If the inflammation of the prepatellar bursa becomes chronic, calcification of the bursa may occur.

Signs and Symptoms

The patient suffering from prepatellar bursitis will frequently complain of pain and swelling in the anterior knee over the patella that can radiate superiorly and inferiorly into the area surrounding the knee.[27] Often, the patient will be unable to kneel or walk down stairs. The patient may also complain of a sharp, catching sensation with range of motion of the knee, especially on first arising. Prepatellar bursitis often coexists with arthritis and tendinitis of the knee joint and these other pathologic processes may confuse the clinical picture.

Testing

Plain radiographs of the knee may reveal calcification of the bursa and associated structures including the quadriceps tendon, which is consistent with chronic inflammation. MRI scan is indicated if internal derangement, occult mass, or

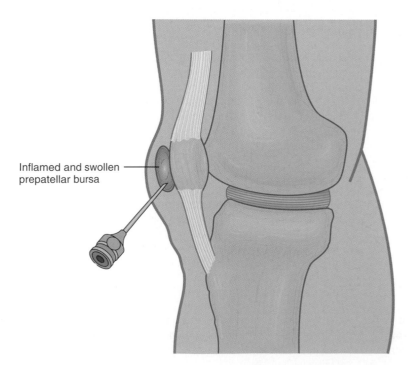

Inflamed and swollen prepatellar bursa

FIGURE 36–32 ■ Correct needle placement for injection of the prepatellar bursa. (From Waldman SD: Atlas of Pain Management Injection Techniques. Philadelphia, Saunders, 2000, p 272.)

tumor of the knee is suspected. Electromyography will help distinguish prepatellar bursitis from femoral neuropathy, lumbar radiculopathy, and plexopathy. The following injection technique will serve as a diagnostic and therapeutic maneuver. Antinuclear antibody testing is indicated if collagen vascular disease is suspected. If infection is considered, aspiration, Gram stain, and culture of bursal fluid is indicated on an emergent basis

Differential Diagnosis

Because of the unique anatomy of the region, not only the prepatellar bursa but the associated tendons and other bursae of the knee can become inflamed and confuse the diagnosis. The prepatellar bursa lies between the subcutaneous tissues and the patella. The bursa is held in place by ligamentum patellae. Both the quadriceps tendon as well as the prepatellar bursa are subject to the development of inflammation following overuse, misuse, or direct trauma. The quadriceps tendon is made up of fibers from the four muscles that compose the quadriceps muscle: the vastus lateralis, the vastus intermedius, the vastus medialis, and the rectus femoris. These muscles are the primary extensors of the lower extremity at the knee. The tendons of these muscles converge and unite to form a single, exceedingly strong tendon. The patella functions as a sesamoid bone within the quadriceps tendon with fibers of the tendon expanding around the patella thereby forming the medial and lateral patellar retinacula, which help strengthen the knee joint. These fibers are called expansions and are subject to strain, and the tendon proper is subject to the development of tendinitis. The suprapatellar, infrapatellar, and prepatellar bursae may also concurrently become inflamed with dysfunction of the quadriceps tendon. It should be remembered that anything that alters the normal biomechanics of the knee can result in inflammation of the prepatellar bursa.

Treatment

A short course of conservative therapy consisting of simple analgesics, nonsteroidal anti-inflammatory agents or COX-2 inhibitors, and a knee brace to prevent further trauma is a reasonable first step in the treatment of patients suffering from prepatellar bursitis. If the patient does not experience rapid improvement, injection of the prepatellar bursa is a reasonable next step. The use of local heat and gentle range-of-motion exercises should be introduced after the acute inflammation begins to subside.

■ DELTOID LIGAMENT STRAIN

The deltoid ligament is susceptible to strain from acute injury from sudden over-pronation of the ankle or from repetitive microtrama to the ligament from overuse or misuse—such as long distance running on soft or uneven surfaces. The deltoid ligament is exceptionally strong and is not as subject to strain as the anterior talofibular ligament.[28] The deltoid ligament has two layers (Fig. 36–33). Both attach above to the medial malleolus. A deep layer attaches below to the medial body of the talus with the superficial fibers attaching to the medial talus and the sustentaculum tali of the calcaneus and the navicular tuberosity.

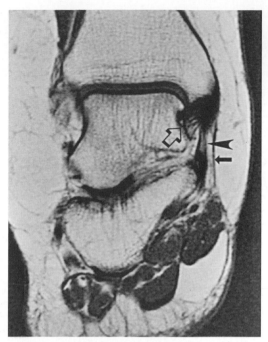

FIGURE 36–33 ■ Medial ankle ligaments: Normal. T1 coronal image, ankle. Two layers of the deltoid (medial) ligament are seen on routine MRI. The deep tibiotalar ligament is striated (*open arrow*). The more superficial tibiocalcaneal ligament (*arrowhead*) may have vertical striations also. The thin, vertical, low-signal structure superficial to the tibiocalcaneal ligament is the flexor retinaculum (*solid arrow*). (From Kaplan PA, Helms CA, Dussault R, et al (eds): Musculoskeletal MRI. Philadelphia, Saunders, 2001, p 835.)

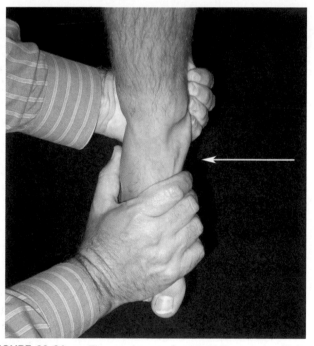

FIGURE 36–34 ■ The eversion test for deltoid ligament insufficiency. (From Waldman SD: Physical Diagnosis of Pain: An Atlas of Signs and Symptoms. Philadelphia, Saunders, 2006, p 369.)

Signs and Symptoms

Patients with strain of the deltoid ligament will complain of pain just below the medial malleolus. Plantar flexion and eversion of the ankle joint will exacerbate the pain (Fig. 36–34). Often patients with injury to the deltoid ligament will note a "pop" followed by significant swelling and inability to walk.

On physical examination, there will be point tenderness over the medial malleolus. With acute trauma, ecchymosis over the ligament may be noted. Passive eversion and plantar flexion of the ankle joint will exacerbate the pain.[29] Coexistent bursitis and arthritis of the ankle and subtalar joint may also be present and confuse the clinical picture.

Testing

Plain radiographs are indicated in all patients who present with ankle pain. Based on the patient's clinical presentation, additional testing including complete blood count, erythrocyte sedimentation rate, and antinuclear antibody testing may be indicated. MRI scan of the ankle is indicated if disruption of the deltoid ligament, joint instability, occult mass or tumor is suspected. Radionuclide bone scanning should be utilized if occult fracture is suspected.

Differential Diagnosis

Avulsion fractures of the calcaneus, talus, medial malleolus, and the base of the fifth metatarsal can mimic the pain of injury to the deltoid ligament. Bursitis and tendinitis as well as gout of the midtarsal joints may coexist with deltoid ligament strain and may confuse the diagnosis. Tarsal tunnel syndrome may occur following ankle trauma and may further confuse the clinical picture.

Treatment

Initial treatment of the pain and functional disability associated with deltoid ligament strain should include a combination of the nonsteroidal antiinflammatory agents or COX-2 inhibitors and physical therapy. The local application of heat and cold may also be beneficial. Avoidance of repetitive activities that aggravate the patient's symptoms as well as short-term immobilization of the ankle joint may also provide relief. For patients who do not respond to these treatment modalities, injection of the deltoid ligament may be a reasonable next step.

■ ACHILLES BURSITIS

Achilles bursitis is being seen with increasing frequency in clinical practice as jogging has increased in popularity. The Achilles tendon is susceptible to the development of bursitis both at its insertion on the calcaneus and at its narrowest part at a point approximately 5 cm above its insertion. Additionally, the Achilles tendon is subject to repetitive motion injury, which may result in microtrauma that heals poorly due to the tendon's avascular nature.[30] Running is often implicated as the inciting factor of acute Achilles bursitis. Bursitis of the Achilles tendon frequently coexists with Achilles tendinitis, creating additional pain and functional disability. Calcium deposition around the Achilles bursa may occur if the inflammation continues, making subsequent treatment more difficult.

Signs and Symptoms

The onset of Achilles bursitis is usually acute occurring after overuse or misuse of the ankle joint. Inciting factors may include activities such as running and sudden stopping and starting as when playing tennis. Improper stretching of the gastrocnemius and Achilles tendon before exercise has also been implicated in the development of Achilles bursitis as well as acute tendinitis and tendon rupture. The pain of Achilles bursitis is constant and severe and is localized in the posterior ankle. Significant sleep disturbance is often reported. The patient may attempt to splint the inflamed Achilles bursa by adopting a flat-footed gait to avoid plantar flexing the affected foot. Patients with Achilles bursitis will exhibit pain with resisted plantar flexion of the foot. A creaking or grating sensation may be palpated when passively plantar flexing the foot due to coexisting tendinitis.[31] As mentioned earlier, the chronically inflamed Achilles tendon may suddenly rupture with stress or during vigorous injection procedures to treat Achilles bursitis.

Testing

Plain radiographs are indicated in all patients who present with posterior ankle pain. Based on the patient's clinical presentation, additional testing including complete blood count, erythrocyte sedimentation rate, and antinuclear antibody testing may be indicated. MRI scan of the ankle is indicated if joint instability is suspected. Radionuclide bone scanning is useful to identify stress fractures of the tibia not seen of plain radiographs. The injection technique (described later) will serve as both a diagnostic and therapeutic maneuver.

Differential Diagnosis

Achilles bursitis is generally easily identified on clinical grounds. Because tendinitis frequently accompanies Achilles bursitis, the specific diagnosis may be unclear. Stress fractures of the ankle may also mimic Achilles bursitis and may be identified on plain radiographs or radionuclide bone scanning.

Treatment

Initial treatment of the pain and functional disability associated with Achilles bursitis should include a combination of the nonsteroidal antiinflammatory agents or COX-2 inhibitors and physical therapy. The local application of heat and cold may also be beneficial. Avoidance of repetitive activities responsible for the evolution of the bursitis (e.g., jogging) should be encouraged. For patients who do not respond to these treatment modalities, the following injection technique with local anesthetic and steroid may be a reasonable next step.

Injection for Achilles bursitis is carried out by placing the patient in the prone position with the affected foot hanging off the end of the table. The foot is gently dorsiflexed to facilitate identification of the margin of the tendon to aid in avoiding injection directly into the tendon.[32] The tender points at the tendinous insertion and/or at its most narrow part—approximately 5 cm above the insertion—are identified and marked with a sterile marker (Fig. 36–35).

Proper preparation with antiseptic solution of the skin overlying these points is then carried out. A sterile syringe containing the 2.0 mL of 0.25% preservative-free bupivacaine and 40 mg of methylprednisolone is attached to a 1½-inch 25-gauge needle using strict aseptic technique. With strict aseptic technique, the previously marked points are palpated. The needle is then carefully advanced at this point alongside the tendon through the skin and subcutaneous tissues with care being taken not to enter the substance of the tendon (Fig. 36–36). The contents of the syringe is then gently injected while slowly withdrawing the needle. There should be minimal resistance to injection. If there is significant resistance to injection, the needle tip is probably in the substance of the Achilles tendon and should be withdrawn slightly until the injection proceeds without significant resistance. The

needle is then removed and a sterile pressure dressing and ice pack are placed at the injection site.

■ SESAMOIDITIS

Sesamoiditis is being seen with increased frequency in clinical practice due to the increased interest in jogging and long-distance running. The sesamoid bones are small rounded structures that are embedded in the flexor tendons of the foot and are usually in close proximity to the joints.[33] These sesamoid bones decrease friction and pressure of the flexor tendon as it passes in proximity to a joint. Sesamoid bones of the first metatarsal occur in almost all patients, with sesamoid bones being present in the flexor tendons of the second and fifth metatarsals in a significant number of patients.

Although the sesamoid bone associated with the first metatarsal head is affected most commonly, the sesamoid bones of the second and fifth metatarsal heads are also subject to the development of sesamoiditis. Sesamoiditis is characterized by tenderness and pain over the metatarsal heads. The patients often feel that they are walking with a stone in their shoe. The pain of sesamoiditis worsens with prolonged standing or walking for long distances and is exacerbated by improperly fitted or padded shoes. Sesamoiditis is most often associated with pushing off injuries during football or repetitive microtrauma from running or dancing.

Signs and Symptoms

On physical examination, pain can be reproduced by pressure on the affected sesamoid bone. In contradistinction to metatarsalgia, in which the tender area remains over the metatarsal heads, with sesamoiditis, the area of maximum tenderness will move along with the flexor tendon when the patient actively flexes his or her toe (Fig. 36–37). The patient with sesamoiditis will often exhibit an antalgic gait in an effort to reduce weight bearing during walking. With acute trauma to the sesamoid, ecchymosis over the plantar surface of the foot may be present.

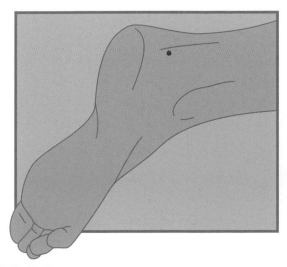

FIGURE 36–35 ■ Foot positioning for injection for Achilles bursitis. (From Waldman SD: Atlas of Pain Management Injection Techniques, Philadelphia, Saunders 2000, p 329.)

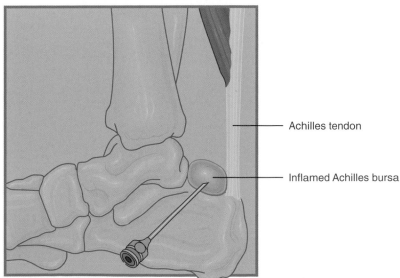

Achilles tendon

Inflamed Achilles bursa

FIGURE 36–36 ■ Injection technique for Achilles bursitis. (From Waldman SD: Atlas of Pain Management Injection Techniques, Philadelphia, Saunders 2000, p 329.)

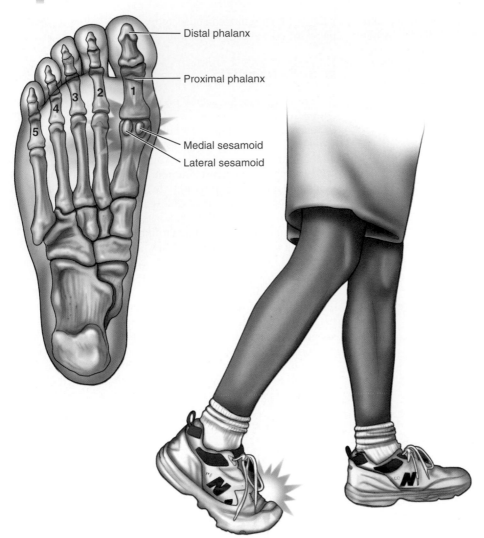

Distal phalanx

Proximal phalanx

Medial sesamoid

Lateral sesamoid

FIGURE 36–37 ■ Mechanism of injury in sesamoiditis. (From Waldman SD: Atlas of Uncommon Pain Syndromes. Philadelphia, Saunders, 2003, p 252.)

Testing

Plain radiographs are indicated in all patients who present with sesamoiditis to rule out fractures and identify sesamoid bones that may have become inflamed. Based on the patient's clinical presentation, additional testing including complete blood count, erythrocyte sedimentation rate, and antinuclear antibody testing may be indicated. MRI scan of the metatarsal bones is indicated if joint instability, occult mass or tumor is suspected. Radionuclide bone scanning may be useful in identifying stress fractures of the metatarsal bones or sesamoid bones that may be missed on plain radiographs of the foot.

Differential Diagnosis

Primary pathology of the foot including gout and occult fractures may mimic the pain and disability associated with sesamoiditis. Entrapment neuropathies such as tarsal tunnel syndrome may also confuse the diagnosis as may bursitis and plantar fasciitis of the foot—both of which may coexist with sesamoiditis. Metatarsalgia is another common cause of forefoot pain and may be distinguished from sesamoiditis by the fact that the pain of metatarsalgia is over the metatarsal heads

and does not move when the patient actively flexes his or her toes—as is the case with sesamoiditis. Primary and metastatic tumors of the foot may also manifest in a manner analogous to arthritis of the midtarsal joints.

Treatment

Initial treatment of the pain and functional disability associated with sesamoiditis should include a combination of the nonsteroidal antiinflammatory agents or COX-2 inhibitors and physical therapy. The local application of heat and cold may also be beneficial. Avoidance of repetitive activities that aggravate the patient's symptoms, as well as short-term immobilization of the midtarsal joint may also provide relief. For patients who do not respond to these treatment modalities, injection of the affected sesamoid bone with local anesthetic and steroid may be a reasonable next step.

■ PLANTAR FASCIITIS

Plantar fasciitis is characterized by pain and tenderness over the plantar surface of the calcaneus.[34] Occurring twice as commonly in women, plantar fasciitis is thought to be caused

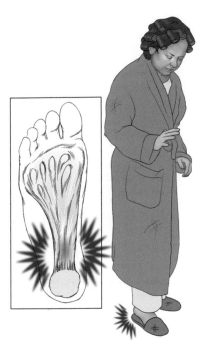

FIGURE 36–38 ▮ The pain of plantar fasciitis is often localized to the hindfoot and can cause significant functional disability. (From Waldman SD: Atlas of Common Pain Syndromes. Philadelphia, Saunders, 2002, p 309.)

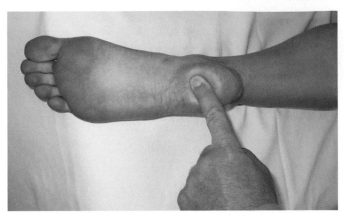

FIGURE 36–39 ▮ Eliciting the calcaneal jump sign for plantar fasciitis. (From Waldman SD: Physical Diagnosis of Pain: An Atlas of Signs and Symptoms. Philadelphia, Saunders, 2006, p 379.)

by an inflammation of the plantar fascia. This inflammation can occur alone or can be part of a systemic inflammatory condition such as rheumatoid arthritis, Reiter's syndrome, or gout. Obesity also seems to predispose to the development of plantar fasciitis as does going barefoot or wearing house slippers for prolonged periods (Fig. 36–38). High-impact aerobic exercise and jogging with excessive heel strike have also been implicated.

Signs and Symptoms

The pain of plantar fasciitis is most severe on first walking after nonweight bearing and is made worse by prolonged standing or walking. Characteristic radiographic changes are lacking in plantar fasciitis, but radionuclide bone scanning may show increased uptake at the point of attachment of the plantar fascia to the medial calcaneal tuberosity.

On physical examination, the patient will exhibit a positive calcaneal jump sign when pressure is applied over the plantar medial calcaneal tuberosity (Fig. 36–39).[35] The patient's foot may also be tender along the plantar fascia as it moves anteriorly. Pain will be increased by dorsiflexing the toes, which pulls the plantar fascia taut, and then palpating along the fascia from the heel to the forefoot.

Differential Diagnosis

The pain of plantar fasciitis can often be confused with the pain of Morton's neuroma or sesamoiditis. The characteristic pain on dorsiflexion of the toes associated with plantar fasciitis should help distinguish these painful conditions of the foot. Stress fractures of the metatarsals or sesamoid bones, bursitis, and tendinitis may also confuse the clinical picture.

Testing

Plain radiographs are indicated in all patients who present with pain thought to be emanating from plantar fasciitis to rule out occult bony pathology and tumor. Based on the patient's clinical presentation, additional testing including complete blood count, prostate specific antigen, erythrocyte sedimentation rate, and antinuclear antibody testing may be indicated. MRI scan of the foot is indicated if occult mass or tumor is suspected. Radionuclide bone scanning may be useful to rule out stress fractures not seen on plain radiographs. The following injection technique will serve as both a diagnostic and therapeutic maneuver.

Treatment

Initial treatment of the pain and functional disability associated with plantar fasciitis should include a combination of the nonsteroidal antiinflammatory agents or COX-2 inhibitors and physical therapy. The local application of heat and cold may also be beneficial. Avoidance of repetitive activities that aggravate the patient's symptoms as well as avoidance of walking barefoot or with shoes that do not provide good support—combined with short-term immobilization of the affected foot—may also provide relief. For patients who do not respond to these treatment modalities, injection technique with local anesthetic and steroid may be a reasonable next step.

▮ CONCLUSION

Painful sports injuries are a common problem confronting the clinician given today's ever-increasing interest in physical and cardiovascular fitness. Understanding the problems of misuse and overuse, as well as rapidly identifying potentially dangerous injuries, is the mainstay of the successful diagnosis and treatment of these common afflictions. Often the biggest barrier to successful treatment is the patient's unwillingness to modify his or her exercise routine. The concept of relative rest with the patient resting the affected anatomic area—while continuing to maintain the remainder of the workout routine—can go a long way to overcoming this obstacle to success. Because the areas most frequently injured during sports injuries often have poor blood supplies (e.g., tendon, cartilage, and so on) the risk of further damage if the acute injury is not aggressively treated remains ever present. The use of injectable antiinflammatory steroids is extremely effective in the treatment of many of the foregoing conditions, but it must be used with care to avoid further injury to already compromised and weakened anatomic structures.

References

1. Waldman SD: Supraspinatus tendinitis. In Waldman SD: Atlas of Uncommon Pain Syndromes. Philadelphia, Saunders, 2003, p 67.
2. Waldman SD: The Dawbarn sign for supraspinatus tendinitis. In Waldman SD: Physical Diagnosis of Pain: An Atlas of Signs and Symptoms. Philadelphia, Saunders, 2006, p 71.
3. Waldman SD: Supraspinatis tendinitis. In Waldman SD: Atlas of Pain Management Injection Techniques. Philadelphia, Saunders, 2000, p 43.
4. Waldman SD: Clinical correlates: The rotator cuff. In Waldman SD: Physical Diagnosis of Pain: An Atlas of Signs and Symptoms. Philadelphia, Saunders, 2006, p 85.
5. Waldman SD: Rotator cuff tear. In Waldman SD: Atlas of Common Pain Syndromes. Philadelphia, Saunders, 2002, p 88.
6. Waldman SD: The drop arm test for complete rotator cuff tear. In Waldman SD: Physical Diagnosis of Pain: An Atlas of Signs and Symptoms. Philadelphia, Saunders, 2006, p 91.
7. Waldman SD: Bicipital tendinitis. In Waldman SD: Atlas of Common Pain Syndromes. Philadelphia, Saunders, 2002, p 84.
8. Waldman SD: The Ludington test for ruptured long tendon of the biceps. In Waldman SD: Physical Diagnosis of Pain: An Atlas of Signs and Symptoms. Philadelphia, Saunders, 2006, p 83.
9. Waldman SD: The Yergason test for bicipital tendinitis. In Waldman SD: Physical Diagnosis of Pain: An Atlas of Signs and Symptoms. Philadelphia, Saunders, 2006, p 76.
10. Waldman SD: Bicipital tendinitis. In Waldman SD: Atlas of Pain Management Injection Techniques. Philadelphia, Saunders, 2000, p 52.
11. Waldman SD: Tennis elbow. In Waldman SD: Atlas of Common Pain Syndromes. Philadelphia, Saunders, 2002, p 98.
12. Waldman SD: The tennis elbow test. In Waldman SD: Physical Diagnosis of Pain: An Atlas of Signs and Symptoms. Philadelphia, Saunders, 2006, p 136.
13. Waldman SD: Carpal tunnel syndrome. In Waldman SD: Atlas of Common Pain Syndromes. Philadelphia, Saunders, 2002, p 118.
14. Waldman SD: The Tinel sign for carpal tunnel syndrome. In Waldman SD: Physical Diagnosis of Pain: An Atlas of Signs and Symptoms. Philadelphia, Saunders, 2006, p 178.
15. Waldman SD: The Phalen test for carpal tunnel syndrome. In Waldman SD: Physical Diagnosis of Pain: An Atlas of Signs and Symptoms. Philadelphia, Saunders, 2006, p 179.
16. Waldman SD: Carpal tunnel syndrome. In Waldman SD: Atlas of Pain Management Injection Techniques. Philadelphia, Saunders, 2000, p 144.
17. Waldman SD: de Quervain's tenosynovitis. In Waldman SD: Atlas of Common Pain Syndromes. Philadelphia, Saunders, 2002, p 122.
18. Waldman SD: The Finkelstein test for de Quervain tenosynovitis. In Waldman SD: Physical Diagnosis of Pain: An Atlas of Signs and Symptoms. Philadelphia, Saunders, 2006, p 170.
19. Waldman SD: Trochanteric bursitis. In Waldman SD: Atlas of Common Pain Syndromes. Philadelphia, Saunders, 2002, p 242.
20. Waldman SD: The resisted abduction release test for trochanteric bursitis. In Waldman SD: Physical Diagnosis of Pain: An Atlas of Signs and Symptoms. Philadelphia, Saunders, 2006, p 314.
21. Waldman SD: Trochanteric bursitis pain. In Waldman SD: Atlas of Pain Management Injection Techniques. Philadelphia, Saunders, 2000, p 219.
22. Waldman SD: Adductor tendinitis. In Waldman SD: Atlas of Uncommon Pain Syndromes. Philadelphia, Saunders, 2003, p 203.
23. Waldman SD: The Waldman knee squeeze test for adductor tendinitis. In Waldman SD: Physical Diagnosis of Pain: An Atlas of Signs and Symptoms. Philadelphia, Saunders, 2006, p 305.
24. Waldman SD: Medial collateral ligament syndrome. In Waldman SD: Atlas of Common Pain Syndromes. Philadelphia, Saunders, 2002, p 251.
25. Waldman SD: The valgus stress test for medial collateral ligament integrity. In Waldman SD: Physical Diagnosis of Pain: An Atlas of Signs and Symptoms. Philadelphia, Saunders, 2006, p 334.
26. Waldman SD: Prepatellar bursitis. In Waldman SD: Atlas of Common Pain Syndromes. Philadelphia, Saunders, 2002, p 257.
27. Waldman SD: Bursitis of the knee. In Waldman SD: Physical Diagnosis of Pain: An Atlas of Signs and Symptoms. Philadelphia, Saunders, 2006, p 350.
28. Waldman SD: Deltoid ligament strain. In Waldman SD: Atlas of Common Pain Syndromes. Philadelphia, Saunders, 2002, p 283.
29. Waldman SD: The eversion test for deltoid ligament insufficiency. In Waldman SD: Physical Diagnosis of Pain: An Atlas of Signs and Symptoms. Philadelphia, Saunders, 2006, p 369.
30. Waldman SD: Achilles bursitis. In Waldman SD: Atlas of Uncommon Pain Syndromes. Philadelphia, Saunders, 2003, p 239.
31. Waldman SD: The creak sign for Achilles tendinitis. In Waldman SD: Physical Diagnosis of Pain: An Atlas of Signs and Symptoms. Philadelphia, Saunders, 2006, p 377.
32. Waldman SD: Achilles bursitis pain. In Waldman SD: Atlas of Pain Management Injection Techniques. Philadelphia, Saunders, 2000, p 328.
33. Waldman SD: Sesamoiditis. In Waldman SD: Atlas of Uncommon Pain Syndromes. Philadelphia, Saunders, 2003, p 251.
34. Waldman SD: Plantar fasciitis. In Waldman SD: Atlas of Common Pain Syndromes. Philadelphia, Saunders, 2002, p 308.
35. Waldman SD: The calcaneal jump sign for plantar fasciitis. In Waldman SD: Physical Diagnosis of Pain: An Atlas of Signs and Symptoms. Philadelphia, Saunders, 2006, p 379.

chapter 37

Fibromyalgia

Steven D. Waldman

Fibromyalgia is one of the most common painful conditions encountered in clinical practice. It is thought to affect approximately 2% of women and 0.5% of men.[1] Fibromyalgia is a chronic pain syndrome which affects a focal or regional portion of the body. The sine qua non of fibromyalgia of the cervical spine is the finding of myofascial trigger points on physical examination. Although these trigger points manifest as localized areas of tenderness, the pain of fibromyalgia is often referred to other areas. This referred pain is often misdiagnosed or attributed to other organ systems leading to extensive evaluations and ineffective treatment. Whether fibromyalgia is a distinct clinical entity or simply a point on the spectrum of a disease called chronic musculoskeletal pain syndrome is the subject of much debate.[2]

While pain is the central symptom of fibromyalgia, it is important for the clinician to recognize that this disease affects many aspects of the patient's clinical well-being. Poor exercise tolerance and easy fatigability with routine activities are present in many patients with fibromyalgia.[3,4] Some investigators feel that chronic fatigue syndrome is simply one variation of fibromyalgia.[5] Part and parcel to fatigue is the frequent presence of sleep disturbance with nonrestorative sleep patterns predominating rather than insomnia.[6] Poor concentration and faulty short-term memory are also common, as is depressive affect.[7] Abnormalities of the hypothalamic-pituitary adrenal axis and irritable bowel syndrome are also common in patients suffering from fibromyalgia. Treatment of these somatic, psychological, and behavioral abnormalities must be an integral part of any successful treatment plan for fibromyalgia.[8] Treating just the pain without taking these other difficulties into account will yield less than optimal results.

The trigger point is the pathognomonic lesion of fibromyalgia pain and is thought to be the result of microtrauma to the affected muscles.[9] Stimulation of the myofascial trigger point will reproduce or exacerbate the patient's pain. Often, stiffness and joint pain will coexist with the pain of fibromyalgia, increasing the functional disability associated with this disease and complicating its treatment. Fibromyalgia may occur as a primary disease state or may occur in conjunction with other painful conditions including radiculopathy, the collagen vascular diseases, overuse syndromes, and chronic regional pain syndromes.[10-12]

Although the exact etiology of fibromyalgia remains unknown, tissue trauma seems to be the common denominator. Acute trauma to muscle as a result of overstretching will commonly result in the development of fibromyalgia. More subtle injury to muscle in the form of repetitive microtrauma can also result in the development of fibromyalgia as can damage to muscle fibers from exposure to extreme heat or cold. Extreme overuse or other coexistent disease processes, such as radiculopathy and the overuse syndromes may also result in the development of fibromyalgia.

In addition to tissue trauma, a variety of other factors seem to predispose the patient to develop fibromyalgia. The weekend athlete who subjects his or her body to unaccustomed physical activity may often develop fibromyalgia. Poor posture while sitting at a computer keyboard or while watching television has also been implicated as a predisposing factor to the development of fibromyalgia. Previous injuries may result in abnormal muscle function and may also predispose to the subsequent development of fibromyalgia. All of these predisposing factors may be intensified if the patient also suffers from poor nutritional status or coexisting psychological or behavioral abnormalities including depression.

Signs and Symptoms

The sine qua non of fibromyalgia is the identification of myofascial trigger points.[9] The trigger point is the pathological lesion of fibromyalgia of the cervical spine and is characterized by a local point of exquisite tenderness in affected muscle. Mechanical stimulation of the trigger point by palpation or stretching will produce not only intense local pain but referred pain as well. In addition to this local and referred pain, there will often be an involuntary withdrawal of the stimulated muscle that is called a jump sign (Fig. 37–1). This jump sign is characteristic of fibromyalgia and is associated with stiffness of the affected area, decreased pain of range of motion, and pain referred into other anatomic areas in a nondermatomal or peripheral nerve distribution or pattern.

Although the referred pain has been well studied and occurs in a characteristic pattern, it is often misdiagnosed and attributed to diseases of organ systems in the distribution of the referred pain. This often leads to extensive evaluation for nonexistent disease and ineffective treatments. Taut bands of muscle fibers are often identified when myofascial trigger points are palpated. In spite of this consistent physical finding

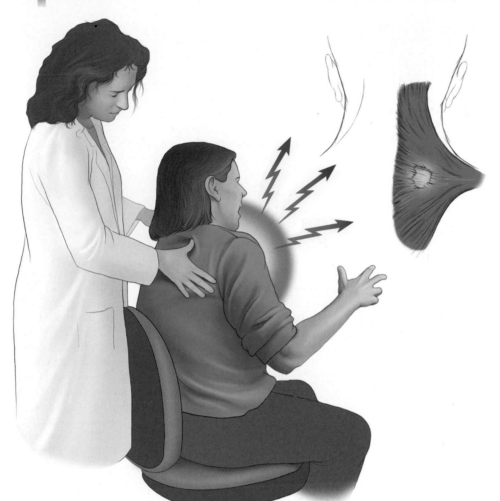

FIGURE 37–1 ▪ Palpation of a trigger point will result in a positive jump sign. (From Waldman SD: Atlas of Common Pain Syndromes. Philadelphia, Saunders, 2002, p 53, Fig 13–1.)

in patients suffering from fibromyalgia, the pathophysiology of the myofascial trigger point remains elusive, although many theories have been advanced. Common to all of these theories is the belief that trigger points are the result of microtrauma to the affected muscle. This microtrauma may occur as a single injury to the affected muscle or as the result of repetitive microtrauma or chronic deconditioning of the agonist and antagonist muscle unit.

Testing

The exact pathophysiologic processes responsible for the development of fibromyalgia remain elusive and there is no specific test that will positively diagnose the disease.[9] Biopsies of clinically identified trigger points have not revealed consistently abnormal histology. The muscle hosting the trigger points has been alternatively described as "moth eaten" or containing "waxy degeneration." Increased plasma myoglobin has been reported in some patients with fibromyalgia, but this finding has not been reproduced by other investigators. Electrodiagnostic testing of patients suffering from fibromyalgia has revealed an increase in muscle tension in some patients. Again, this finding has not been reproducible. However, whatever the pathophysiology of

fibromyalgia, there is little doubt that the clinical findings of trigger points in the affected muscles and associated jump sign exist in combination with a clinically recognizable constellation of symptoms that are consistently diagnosed as fibromyalgia.

Differential Diagnosis

The diagnosis of fibromyalgia of the cervical spine is made on the basis of clinical findings rather that specific diagnostic laboratory, electrodiagnostic, or radiographic testing. For this reason, a targeted history and physical examination with a systematic search for trigger points and identification of a positive jump sign must be carried out on every patient suspected of suffering from fibromyalgia. Because of the lack of objective diagnostic testing, the clinician must also rule out other coexisting disease processes that may mimic fibromyalgia, including primary inflammatory muscle disease and collagen vascular disease.[10,11] The judicious use of electrodiagnostic and radiographic testing will also help identify coexisting pathology such as herniated nucleus pulposus and rotator cuff tears. The clinician must also identify coexisting psychological and behavioral abnormalities that may mask or exacerbate the symptoms associated with fibromyalgia and other coexisting pathologic processes.[12]

Treatment

The treatment of fibromyalgia involves the use of techniques that will help eliminate the trigger point that may be the source of the perpetuation of this painful condition.[9,13] Hopefully, the interruption of the pain cycle by the elimination of trigger points will allow the patient to experience prolonged relief. The mechanism of action of each of the above modalities is poorly understood and trial and error in developing a treatment plan is the expected norm.[14]

Because underlying sleep disturbance, depression, and a substrate of anxiety are present in many patients suffering from fibromyalgia, the inclusion of antidepressant compounds as an integral part of most treatment plans represents a reasonable choice.[15]

In addition to these treatment modalities, a variety of additional treatments are available for the treatment of fibromyalgia. The therapeutic use of heat and cold is often combined with trigger point injections and antidepressant compounds to effect pain relief and normalize sleep. Some patients will experience decreased pain with the use of transcutaneous nerve stimulation or electrical stimulation to fatigue-affected muscles. Although not currently approved by the Food and Drug Administration, the injection of minute quantities of botulinum toxin A directly into trigger points has recently gained favor in the treatment of persistent fibromyalgia of the cervical spine that has not responded to traditional treatment modalities.[16]

Trigger point injections are an extremely safe procedure if careful attention is paid to the clinically relevant anatomy in the areas to be injected. Care must be taken to utilize sterile technique to avoid infection as well as the use of universal precautions to avoid risk to the operator. Most side effects of trigger point injection are related to needle-induced trauma to the injection site and underlying tissues. The incidence of ecchymosis and hematoma formation can be decreased if pressure is placed on the injection site immediately following trigger point injection. The avoidance of overly long needles will help decrease the incidence of trauma to underlying structures. Special care must be taken to avoid pneumothorax when injecting trigger points in proximity to the underlying pleural space

▮ CONCLUSION

Fibromyalgia is a common disorder that commonly coexists with a variety of somatic and psychological disorders. Fibromyalgia is often misdiagnosed. In patients suspected of suffering from fibromyalgia, a careful evaluation to identify underlying disease processes is mandatory.

Treatment is focused on the blocking of the myofascial trigger and achieving prolonged relaxation of the affected muscle. Conservative therapy consisting of treatment with the antidepressant compounds and trigger point injections with local anesthetics or saline is the starting point for the treatment of fibromyalgia of the cervical spine. Adjunct therapies including physical therapy, therapeutic heat and cold, transcutaneous nerve stimulation, and electrical stimulation can be used on a case-by-case basis. For patients who do not respond to these traditional measures, consideration should be given to the use of botulinum toxin A which has been shown to be a safe and effective treatment for this disorder.

References

1. Felson DT, Goldenberg DL: The natural history of fibromyalgia. Arthritis Rheum 29:1522, 1986.
2. Goldenberg DL: Fibromyalgia syndrome. An emerging but controversial condition. JAMA 257:2782, 1987.
3. Goldenberg DL: Fatigue in rheumatic disease. Bull Rheum Dis 44:4, 1995.
4. Cathey MA, Wolfe F, Kleinheksel SM, et al: Functional ability and work status in patients with fibromyalgia. Arthritis Care Res 1:85, 1988.
5. Hudson Jl, Pope HG: The concept of affective spectrum disorder: Relationship to fibromyalgia and other syndromes of chronic fatigue and chronic muscle pain. Bailliere's Clin Rheumatol 8:839, 1994.
6. Moldofsky H: Chronobiological influences on fibromyalgia syndrome: Theoretical and therapeutic implications. Bailliere's Clin Rheumatol 8:801, 1994.
7. White KR, Nielson WR: Cognitive behavioral treatment of fibromyalgia syndrome: A follow-up assessement. J Rheumatol 22:717, 1995.
8. Hawley DJ, Wolfe F, Cathey MA: Pain, functional disability, and psychological status: A 12-month study of severity in fibromyalgia. J Rheumatol 15:1551, 1988.
9. Waldman SD: Fibromyalgia of the cervical spine. In Waldman SD: Common Pain Syndromes. Philadelphia, WB Saunders, 2002, p.52.
10. Middleton GD, McFarlin JE, Lipsky PE: The prevalence and clinical impact of fibromyalgia in systemic lupus erythematosus. Arthritis Rheum 37:1181, 1994.
11. Bonafede RP, Downey DC, Bennett RM. An association of fibromyalgia with primary Sjögren's syndrome: A prospective study of 72 patients. J Rheumatol 22:133, 1995.
12. Simms RW, Goldenberg DL: Symptoms mimicking neurologic disorders in fibromyalgia syndrome. J Rheumatol 15:1271, 1988.
13. Hong C-Z: Lidocaine injection versus dry needling to myofascial trigger point. The importance of the local twitch response. Am J Phys Med Rehab 73:256, 1994.
14. Hopwood MB, Abram SE: Factors associated with failure of trigger point injections. Clin J Pain.10:227, 1994.
15. Goldenberg DL, Felson DT, Dinerman H: Randomized, controlled trial of amitriptyline and naproxen in the treatment of patients with fibromyalgia. Arthritis Rheum 29:1, 1986.
16. Cheshire WP, Abashian SW, Mann JD: Botulinum toxin in the treatment of myofascial pain syndrome. Pain 59:65, 1994.

Painful Neuropathies Including Entrapment Syndromes

Charles D. Donohoe

Pain management has evolved extremely rapidly as a distinct medical subspecialty. Its meteoric growth aptly reflects medicine's dismal record of inadequate pain treatment. To date, most pain management practitioners are trained anesthesiologists. These physicians are now evaluating patients with pain through direct referral from a primary care physician or, in many cases, as the only treating physician. In essence, they are functioning in a primary diagnostic role similar to a neurologist or rheumatologist. This could easily be a precarious situation without clinical insight into other medical disciplines, including rheumatology, radiology, infectious disease, and clinical neurology.

The cause of neuropathic pain is a vast topic. This chapter focuses on only a few painful neuropathies, including certain entrapment syndromes that highlight the many practical subtleties in clinical diagnosis (Table 38–1). The intention is to debunk the concept that any clinician with a coding book, a vial of steroids, and a 22-gauge needle can present himself or herself to patients as a pain expert. Pain is truly a common symptom, but its proper evaluation requires an uncommonly broad knowledge and experience in general medicine.

Anesthesiologists and other non-neurologists have limited experience with laboratory studies, electrodiagnosis, electromyography (EMG), nerve conduction velocity (NCV), and neuroimaging (CT and MRI). For pain specialists, these are basic tools. Using these modalities properly and realizing their intrinsic limitations will distinguish pain management physicians in their field. In the words of George Bernard Shaw, "Beware of false knowledge, it is more dangerous than ignorance."

This chapter outlines painful neuropathies frequently encountered in a neurologic practice. The chapter provides a few basic concepts on which the pain management physician can build and ultimately develop confidence in the role of a pain specialist.

■ CLINICAL EVALUATION OF PAINFUL NEUROPATHIES

The evaluation of painful neuropathies begins with the history. This is the most important part of the diagnostic process. The nature of the pain, its duration, description, provocative factors, and association with other clinical findings, such as weakness and sensory loss, constitute essential information. The history includes a detailed past medical history for prior conditions, such as cancer, diabetes, thyroid disorders, connective tissue diseases, surgeries, and constitutional symptoms such as fever or weight loss. The history sets the stage and proper focus for the physical examination and the proper selection of diagnostic studies, including blood work, CT, MRI, magnetic resonance angiography, and electrodiagnosis (NCV and EMG). If the history does not provide any clear direction as to the nature or location of the pathology, the hope that extensive laboratory work, electrodiagnosis, and neuroimaging will provide miraculous clarification is highly remote.

In my experience, laboratory work is frequently overlooked by primary care physicians and specialists alike. A basic panel includes complete blood count, erythrocyte sedimentation rate, thyroid-stimulating hormone, serum vitamin B_{12}, and complete chemical profile including lipids. The evaluation of any painful neuropathy should address the possibility of underlying diabetes. This disease is epidemic in the United States and now the type 2 variant is seen commonly in adolescents.[1] The laboratory work should be done in a fasting state. A fasting glucose below 100 mg/dL is considered normal; 100 to 125 mg/dL is considered impaired fasting glucose. A plasma glucose level above 126 mg/dL is consistent with a provisional diagnosis of diabetes. This diagnosis can be confirmed using a 75-g glucose load. If the 2-hour post-load glucose is below 140 mg/dL, it is considered normal. If glucose is 140 to 199 mg/dL, it is designated as impaired glucose tolerance. A level above 200 mg/dL is consistent with diabetes. The use of hemoglobin A_{1C} is not recommended as a screening tool for diabetes.

Impaired glucose tolerance and impaired fasting glucose represent high-risk states for the ultimate development of diabetes, cardiovascular disease, and metabolic syndrome (abdominal obesity, dyslipidemia, and hypertension). These states can be associated with several of the neuropathic conditions mentioned in this chapter before clear-cut diabetes is manifest. The practical importance of the proper identification of these prediabetic states is supported by early evidence suggesting that they may be positively affected by preventive weight loss and exercise in postponing a wide range of diabetic complications. If testing is limited to a single casual

Table 38-1		

Painful Neuropathies

Nerves	*Vascular/Inflammatory*	*Compression/Entrapment*
CN III (oculomotor)	Pupil reactive–diabetic CN III palsy	CN III palsy with pupil dilated and unreactive. Compression due to posterior communicating artery aneurysm.
CN V (trigeminal)	—	Trigeminal neuralgia—CN V compression by vascular loop at root entry zone.
Combined CNs III, V, and VI (abducens)	Tolosa-Hunt syndrome (cavernous sinus inflammation) (Fig. 38–5)	—
Upper extremity	Brachial neuritis (neuralgic amyotrophy, Parsonage-Turner syndrome) (Fig. 38–8)	Carpal tunnel syndrome (median nerve compression at the wrist) Cubital tunnel syndrome (ulnar nerve compression at the elbow)
Lower extremity	Lumbosacral plexus neuropathy (diabetic amyotrophy, Bruns-Garland syndrome, proximal diabetic neuropathy)	Meralgia paresthetica (lateral femoral cutaneous nerve compression below inguinal ligament) Tarsal tunnel syndrome (tibial nerve compression in tarsal tunnel)

glucose measurement, the opportunity to identify these pre-diabetic states may be lost. Finally with respect to laboratory studies, individuals with impaired glucose tolerance can be euglycemic (normal serum glucose), and impaired glucose tolerance and impaired fasting glucose patients may have completely normal hemoglobin A_{1C} levels. In short, diabetes is one of the most frequent and important conditions underlying painful neuropathy, and its identification can be aided by understanding the laboratory criteria.

In contrast to laboratory evaluation, in which there are objective parameters, the other cornerstones of neurologic diagnosis, electrodiagnosis (EMG and NCV) and neuroimaging (CT and MRI) require practical insight and experience into the proper use of these valuable studies. EMG and NCV are extremely helpful in identifying conditions such as carpal tunnel syndrome, brachial neuritis, and lumbosacral plexopathy. These studies depend on the technical expertise, clinical insight, and diligence of the electromyographer. The adage that a bad laboratory is worse than no laboratory at all is true. As in many branches of medicine, electrodiagnosis has its superstars, its average performers, and many players who have no business being on the field. The results of these studies cannot be viewed as truly definitive and always must be correlated with the clinical history and the physical examination. It my experience, many patients have been subjected to unnecessary surgeries, and other clinical mistakes have been made based on sloppy, inaccurate electrodiagnosis.

CT and MRI have revolutionized neurologic diagnosis. It is now more than 30 years since the introduction of CT, and it is almost impossible to consider the field of neurology without these tools. CT and MRI are extremely sensitive. This sensitivity detects pathology, such as disk protrusions, osteophytic spurring, and facet degenerations, in many individuals who are completely asymptomatic.[2] Such pathologic findings increase statistically with advancing age, and neuroimaging results always must be correlated with the history and physical examination.[3]

There is considerable interobserver variability with respect to the interpretation of MRI, and terms such as *disc*

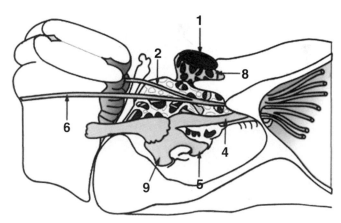

FIGURE 38–1 ■ Anatomic diagram of cavernous sinus, showing structure of cavernous sinus. 1 = carotid artery, 2 = oculomotor nerve, 3 = trochlear nerve, 4 = ophthalmic nerve, 5 = maxillary nerve, 6 = abducens nerve, 7 = pituitary gland, 8 = sympathetic nerve, 9 = mandibular nerve.

protrusion, disc extrusion, and *moderate* and *severe spinal stenosis* are subjective and observer dependent. The pain management physician should review all imaging studies and over time develop his or her own expertise with these modalities. The pain management physician has a tremendous advantage over the radiologist in that he or she has examined the patients as well as the imaging studies. That added insight is crucial in the proper use of these technologies.

■ CRANIAL NERVES

Knowledge of the anatomic relationships of the cranial nerves in essential in evaluating facial pain and localizing neurologic pathology (Fig. 38–1 and 38–2): CN III (oculomotor nerve), CN IV (trochlear nerve), CN V (trigeminal nerve), CN VI (abducens nerve), and CN VII (facial nerve). Acute and chronic cranial neuropathies may be associated with pain and present difficulty for the specialist trained predominantly as an anesthesiologist. The most commonly involved CN is the facial nerve (CN VII) (Fig. 38–3). Although there are many

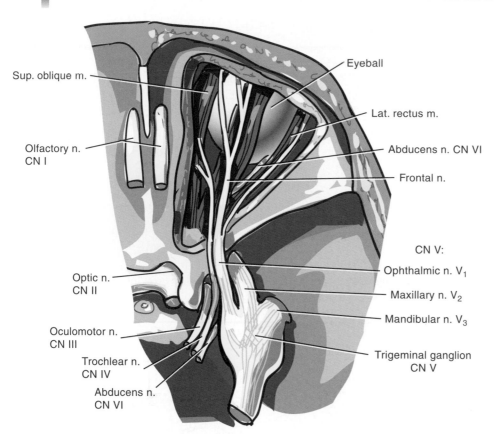

Sup. oblique m.

Olfactory n.
CN I

Optic n.
CN II

Oculomotor n.
CN III

Trochlear n.
CN IV

Abducens n.
CN VI

Eyeball

Lat. rectus m.

Abducens n. CN VI

Frontal n.

CN V:

Ophthalmic n. V₁

Maxillary n. V₂

Mandibular n. V₃

Trigeminal ganglion
CN V

FIGURE 38–2 ■ Anatomy of the cranial nerves I to VI.

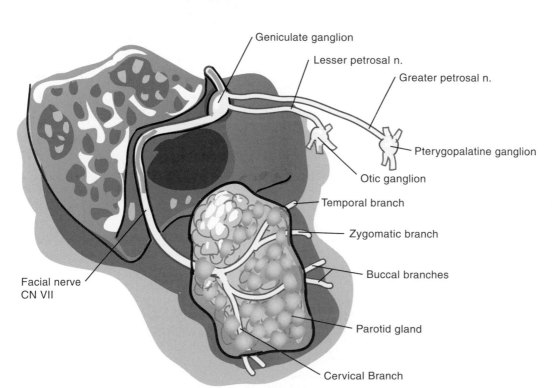

Geniculate ganglion

Lesser petrosal n.

Greater petrosal n.

Pterygopalatine ganglion

Otic ganglion

Temporal branch

Zygomatic branch

Buccal branches

Parotid gland

Cervical Branch

Facial nerve
CN VII

FIGURE 38–3 ■ Anatomy of the facial nerve (CN VII).

Table 38–2

Differential Diagnosis of Facial Paralysis (CN VII)

Idiopathic	Bell's palsy (diagnosis of exclusion)
	Melkersson-Rosenthal syndrome (recurrent swelling of face [lip] with facial paralysis)
Infectious	Herpes zoster oticus (Ramsay-Hunt syndrome)
	Acute and chronic otitis media
	Lyme disease
Neoplastic	
Extracranial	Parotid tumors
	Metastatic
	Facial nerve neurinomas
Intracranial	Cholesteatoma
	Glomus tumors
	Acoustic neuroma
	Squamous cell carcinoma
	Metastatic
Trauma and iatrogenic	Newborn paralysis
	Fractures of petrous pyramid and other temporal bone fracture
	Penetrating injuries to the parotid gland
Inflammatory	Sarcoidosis
	Wegener's granulomatosis

Table 38–3

Abducens (CN VI) Palsies Associated with Pain

Nonlocalizing	
	Diabetes/hypertension
	Increased intracranial pressure (e.g., pseudotumor cerebri)
	Lumbar puncture or spinal anesthesia
	Basal meningitis
Localizing	
Pontine (ipsilateral facial palsy, horizontal gaze weakness, and contralateral hemiparesis)	Tumor
	Demyelinating disease (multiple sclerosis)
	Infarction
Cavernous sinus (in combination with disorders of CNs III and IV and first division of CN V)	Inflammation (Tolosa-Hunt syndrome)
	Tumor
	Vascular (aneurysm, dural fistula, carotid/cavernous fistula)
Clivus and middle cranial fossa (in combination with facial numbness [CN V], facial weakness [CN VII], and hearing loss [CN VIII])	Tumor (acoustic neuroma, nasopharyngeal carcinoma, perineural spread of head and neck cancer, meningioma, chordoma)
	Infection (meningitis, petrositis, HIV, immunocompromised opportunistic infections)

causes of facial nerve involvement, the idiopathic variant (Bell's palsy) is more commonly seen (Table 38–2).

Disease states of the oculomotor nerves (CNs III, IV, and VI) manifest with diplopia and varying degrees of pain. Dysfunction of CN VI and dysfunction of CN III are the most common oculomotor neuropathies seen in clinical practice. The combination of the two, CN III and VI, is the most commonly observed multiple cranial neuropathy.

Classic oculomotor nerve (CN III) involvement includes ptosis (drooping of the eyelid) and a globe that does not move upward, downward, or medially. If CN VI is intact, lateral movement is preserved. The trochlear nerve (CN IV) is rarely involved as a painful condition, and its action (intorsion of the eye) is best seen when CN III function is interrupted.

In my experience with the oculomotor nerves, an isolated CN VI palsy and CN III palsy are the two most commonly encountered entities. CN VI palsy can be caused by myriad factors (Table 38–3), as can CN III palsy (Table 38–4). Involvement is frequently secondary to infarction of the nerve trunk associated with diabetes and hypertension (diabetic ophthalmoplegia). In CN III palsy, a droopy eye, with or without pain, that is unable to look upward, downward, or medially should prompt immediate concern. If the pupil is normal in size and reacts briskly to light, this suggests CN III

Table 38–4

Oculomotor (CN III) Palsies Associated with Pain

Aneurysm
Diabetic ophthalmoplegia
Migraine
Inflammation (orbital pseudotumor, cavernous sinus [Tolosa-Hunt syndrome])
Infection (contiguous sinusitis, mucormycosis [other fungi])
Neoplasm (lymphoma, meningioma, nasopharyngeal carcinoma)
Vascular (arteritis, carotid-cavernous fistula, cavernous sinus thrombosis)

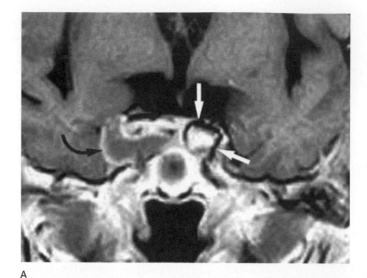

A

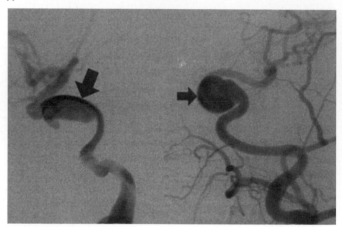

B

FIGURE 38–4 ■ Bilateral saccular aneurysms of internal carotid arteries in cavernous sinuses in a 67-year-old woman with diplopia. **A,** Axial T2-weighted image shows large signal void *(arrows)* resulting from aneurysm of internal carotid artery in both cavernous sinuses. **B,** Digital subtraction angiogram of both internal carotid arteries shows partially thrombosed aneurysms of internal carotid artery of right cavernous sinus *(large arrow)* and another aneurysm of internal carotid artery of left cavernous sinus *(small arrow).*

paresis resulting from microvascular infarction of the central core of CN III, a condition often found in diagnosed or undiagnosed diabetics. It is believed that the more peripheral fibers, those that innervate the pupil, are spared. With this variant of CN III palsy, when pupillary function is preserved, the initial periorbital pain, which may be quite intense, usually resolves in 1 to 2 weeks, and the function of the ocular muscles returns spontaneously in 3 to 4 months.

With external compression of the nerve resulting from a tumor or the pulsations of a posterior communicating artery aneurysm, the peripheral aspect of the nerve is damaged early and the pupil is found to be dilated and unreactive to light. Assigning a benign etiology to CN III palsy because pupillary function is intact, although having a statistical foundation, is not absolute. It has been found that such pupillary sparing is found in 8% to 15% of patients with isolated CN III palsy resulting from aneurysms.[4] In addition, patients with aneurysmal CN III palsy may have pupillary sparing on initial presentation, but if followed closely, the pupil becomes dilated and ultimately unreactive to light within 3 to 5 days.

Brain and orbital imaging with high-field MRI and magnetic resonance angiography of the circle of Willis is indicated (Fig. 38–4). I have seen insurance-based protocols suggesting that in a painful CN III palsy with pupillary sparing, neuroimaging is not indicated. I disagree. In the real world of clinical medicine, even delaying imaging carries too much risk. These patients exhibit a high level of concern and rightfully so. Normal imaging studies are psychologically reassuring and medically relevant to the patient and the physician.

Abnormalities of CN VI are more common than abnormalities of CN III. It is the most common CN to exhibit bilateral involvement. Its action innervating the lateral rectus muscle moves the globe laterally. Impaired function of any of the extraocular muscles is not limited to involvement of CNs III, IV, and VI. Eye movements may be impaired as a result of processes directly affecting the muscle rather than the nerve. These include myasthenia gravis, thyroid eye disease, and orbital pseudotumor and may present with pain.

In the setting of involvement of multiple cranial nerves or bilateral involvement, skull-based tumors and neoplastic or infectious meningeal infiltrates are causes where delayed diagnosis or misdiagnosis frequently occurs. With multiple CN palsies in which initial contrast-enhanced neuroimaging (CT or MRI) is normal, lumbar puncture and CSF analysis for cells, cytology, protein, glucose, and culture should be

considered. Imaging, repeat imaging, lumbar puncture, and referral to physicians in allied specialties, such as otorhinolaryngology (ENT) and neuro-ophthalmology, is an appropriate way to proceed in cases with multiple CN palsies where a specific diagnosis remains elusive (Fig. 38–5).

These cases are often difficult ones. Patients are frustrated because they can see obviously there is something wrong. The physician is frustrated because the initial laboratory studies and imaging examinations can be normal. This situation ultimately results in doctor shopping, loss of continuity, and misplaced trust in the concept that "we've done everything and it's all normal." In evaluating patients in pain with multiple CN palsies, the physician should be willing to start over from the beginning, repeat previously "normal" studies, continue to follow the patient regularly, and enlist the help of allied specialists. Although the locations and causes of multiple CN palsies are diverse, tumor is the underlying

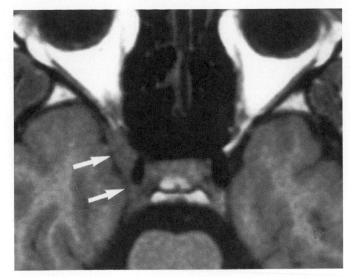

A

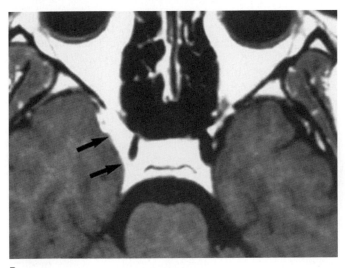

B

FIGURE 38–5 ■ Tolosa-Hunt syndrome in a 21-year-old woman with painful ophthalmoplegia. Unenhanced (**A**) and contrast-enhanced (**B**) axial T1-weighted images reveal homogeneous infiltrating lesion *(arrows)* narrowing carotid artery in orbital apex and in anterior cavernous sinus, which shows homogeneous intense enhancement.

diagnosis in more than one quarter of these cases. This fact alone places a premium on rapid and accurate diagnosis.[5]

Neuralgia and Neuropathy of the Trigeminal Nerve (Cranial Nerve V)

Although the sharp, electric, lancinating, unilateral pain of trigeminal neuralgia is quite distinctive, 90% of patients experience paroxysms of pain for over 1 year before receiving an accurate diagnosis and treatment. With an incidence of 4 cases per 100,000 in the United States, many medical practitioners and dentists see very few cases during their careers. It is a diagnosis made predominantly in a middle-aged or elderly individuals and is so characteristic that it can be made over the telephone. Despite its striking pattern, about one third of patients with trigeminal neuralgia undergo unnecessary dental extractions and a variety of expensive treatments for temporomandibular joint disorders.[6]

Most pain specialists are familiar with the sharp, shooting, electric shock–like pain that can last several seconds to minutes with pain-free intervals between attacks. Less well appreciated is when this classic form of trigeminal neuralgia, particularly if left untreated, is transformed into an aching, throbbing, or burning pain that is almost constant in nature and present at least 50% of the time. The persistence of this background pain is its most significant attribute and may signify advancing neural injury. The progression of the lancinating episodic pain into pain with a more constant nature or the combination of both should be noted when evaluating trigeminal neuralgia.

Trigeminal neuralgia should be distinguished from trigeminal neuropathy. In classic trigeminal neuralgia, the basic pathophysiologic feature has been postulated to be compression of the trigeminal nerve root by a blood vessel at or near the root entry zone. In classic trigeminal neuralgia, there is little sensory loss other than hypoesthesia that may be identified at the nasolabial fold. In trigeminal neuropathy, objective sensory loss is more apparent in any or all of the three divisions of the trigeminal nerve. In the case of the mandibular nerve, CN V₃, sensory loss is identified over the skin of the lower face, including the mandibular teeth, the mucosa of the mandibular gingiva, the floor of the mouth, and the anterior two thirds of the tongue. In addition, the mandibular nerve provides motor innervation to the muscles of mastication, the mylohyoid muscle, and the anterior belly of the digastric muscle. Facial pain associated with objective sensory loss in any or all territories of the trigeminal nerve, with or without weakness of the muscles of mastication, signifies involvement of the trigeminal nerve other than trigeminal neuralgia.

In evaluating patients with facial pain, the physician should be aware of perineural spread. Perineural spread is a mechanism whereby a benign or malignant head and neck tumor, an infectious process such as rhinocerebral mucormycosis, or a granulomatous process such as sarcoidosis can spread along the tissues of the neural sheath (Fig. 38–6). The most common signs of this process include pain and paresthesias in the second and third divisions of the trigeminal nerve and involvement of the facial nerve often misdiagnosed as Bell's palsy.

The most common malignancies associated with head and neck perineural spread are tumors of the salivary gland, particularly adenoid cystic carcinoma of the parotid, squamous cell carcinoma, and melanoma. These head and neck tumors and other skull-based tumors frequently are missed or have long delays in their proper identification. Facial pain associated with objective facial sensory loss, weakness of chewing, or facial weakness should be viewed as an ominous clinical complex. Initial CT and MRI can be normal. A high index of suspicion in these cases with a low threshold for repeat imaging and alerting the radiologist to focus on the skull base is crucial to making these difficult diagnoses. The pain management physician should be suspicious of facial pain associated with multiple cranial nerve palsies. These cases are fraught with misdiagnosis, delayed diagnosis, initial normal neuroimaging, patient dissatisfaction, and ultimately considerable liability.

The use of the term *atypical facial pain* is discouraged. This is a label and not a true medical diagnosis. It says more about the physician's lack of insight than it does about the

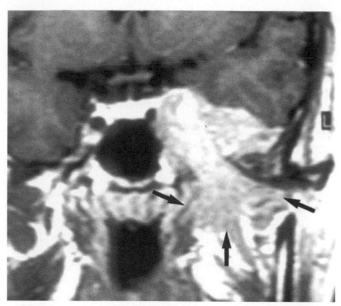

FIGURE 38–6 ■ Perineural spread of adenoid cystic carcinoma of parotid gland in a 36-year-old woman with diplopia and left-sided hemifacial pain. Coronal contrast-enhanced T1-weighted image shows strongly enhancing infiltrating mass in left parapharyngeal space *(arrows)* extending into cavernous sinus through widened foramen ovale.

nature of the facial pain. Although in certain circles *atypical facial pain* is also used as a euphemism for somatoform disorder, any premature tendency to ascribe facial pain to psychogenic mechanisms is also discouraged. Facial pain, particularly when associated with atypical features, is best viewed in a professional and nonjudgmental fashion. In cases that are not clear-cut, the best policy is frequent patient follow-up examinations, repeat neuroimaging, referral to other specialists, and resistance to suggesting stress as the primary mechanism. There already are too many amateur pain specialists competing with countless amateur psychiatrists.

Facial Neuropathy (Cranial Nerve VII)

Acute idiopathic facial neuropathy (Bell's palsy) is the most common cranial neuropathy. The main symptom is usually unilateral facial weakness that begins abruptly and can be preceded by severe pain behind the ipsilateral ear. It has an annual incidence of about 30 per 100,000. The facial weakness usually reaches a maximum within 24 hours after onset. Patients may experience altered taste and hyperacusis in the ipsilateral ear. Although patients often complain of numbness about the face, objective sensory loss is rarely found. Most medical students have seen Bell's palsy, yet it is not unusual to see misdiagnosis in the emergency department, frequently confusing its presentation with stroke. Bell's palsy can recur in 5% to 10% of patients, particularly patients with diabetes or a family history.

Bell's palsy is a diagnosis of exclusion (see Table 38–2). Most patients with Bell's palsy do not experience protracted periods of pain, and if painful facial paralysis remains unresolved after 6 to 8 weeks, the patient should undergo contrast-enhanced MRI of the head, internal auditory canals, and parotid gland with and without contrast enhancement. Neo-

plastic invasion of the facial nerve may mimic signs and symptoms of Bell's palsy. When the clinical picture does not fit, or when a patient with a previously diagnosed Bell's palsy is not experiencing improvement or is developing increasing facial pain, facial numbness, diplopia, or dysarthria, this is a red flag. The pain of Bell's palsy generally improves within 1 to 2 weeks and is usually localized behind the ipsilateral ear.

Perineural spread is a well-described phenomenon in which a head and neck tumor can migrate away from its primary site along the neural sheath.[7] This most commonly occurs in the distribution of the second and third divisions of the trigeminal nerve and the facial nerve. As expected, squamous cell carcinoma would be the most common, followed by many others, including adenoid cystic carcinoma, lymphoma, melanoma, sarcoma, and salivary gland malignancies.

Imaging, and frequently repeat imaging, is essential in these cases. CT is superior for bone detail at the skull base, whereas MRI excels in soft tissue detail. In this subgroup of patients with skull-based malignancies, incredible delays in diagnosis are common. It is not unusual for these patients to have seen several physicians. Each new physician is lulled into a false sense of security by reports of previously normal imaging studies. I have seen a patient with four normal MRI studies over an 18-month period (even when viewed in retrospect) before a parotid tumor causing protracted facial pain and paralysis (incorrectly identified as Bell's palsy) became sufficiently conspicuous on a fifth MRI study to make a diagnosis of adenoid cystic carcinoma.

■ CARPAL TUNNEL SYNDROME

Carpal tunnel is the most common focal compression neuropathy. It results from compression of the median nerve at the wrist. This syndrome effects 3% of adult Americans and is about three times more common in women than in men. It is extremely common in diabetic patients with neuropathy, where its prevalence increases to almost 40%. Other medical causes include acromegaly, rheumatoid arthritis, renal failure, hypothyroidism, and amyloidosis. The cause of carpal tunnel syndrome has been linked to work-related repetitive wrist activity, although the validity of this relationship continues to be challenged.[8]

Classic symptoms of carpal tunnel syndrome are pain, numbness, and paresthesias in the distribution of the median nerve, although numbness of the entire hand may be a more common presenting clinical complaint. Symptoms usually are worse at night and as the compression becomes more severe can awaken patients from sleep on a nightly basis. These patients often exhibit a tendency to flick their wrist as if they were shaking a thermometer in an attempt to relieve the painful paresthesias ("flick sign"). In my experience, a patient who exhibits the flick sign on a nightly basis or several times a week generally requires carpal tunnel surgical release. Although Tinel's sign and a positive Phalen maneuver are classically described with carpal tunnel syndrome, they are notoriously unreliable. Diminished sensation in a median distribution and weak thumb abduction are far more strongly correlated with abnormal NCV studies.[9]

Regarding NCV, although they are recognized as a diagnostic gold standard for carpal tunnel syndrome, 25% of patients with positive clinical histories and examinations for carpal tunnel syndrome can have normal NCV studies. These studies essentially assess demyelinization and axonal loss by determining conduction velocities, distal latencies, and response amplitude.[10] The largest diameter axons of the motor or sensory nerve disproportionately contribute to these measurements. The conduction velocity of a nerve is the conduction velocity of the fastest fibers. If in some patients with carpal tunnel syndrome the smaller diameter axons in the median nerve were preferentially compressed, but the larger diameter axons were spared, it is understandable that clinically they may complain of significant entrapment, but have normal median sensory and motor nerve conduction results. In the end, carpal tunnel syndrome remains a clinical diagnosis.

Much has been made of the double-crush syndrome (Fig. 38–7), particularly in relationship to carpal tunnel syndrome. The concept of double-crush as postulated by Upton and McComas[11] in 1973 suggests that the presence of a proximal lesion, such as a cervical root compression involving the C6 or C7 roots, renders the distal median nerve more susceptible to mild compression producing carpal tunnel symptoms. The beauty of the double-crush concept lies not in the strength of its scientific foundation, but rather in the ease with which it can be applied. Carpal tunnel syndrome whose characteristics are atypical or that does not respond to surgery can be explained by a coexistent cervical root lesion. In the lower extremity, peroneal neuropathy that appears after a total knee arthroplasty can be linked with an unsuspected lumbosacral radiculopathy from osteoarthritic involvement.

These are all common situations, and linking them together casually can provide an explanation for almost anything. It can provide an excuse for a suboptimal result or a reason to do additional surgery based on how strongly the practitioner believes in the double, triple, or quadruple sites of crush. In my opinion, there is no scientific evidence to prove that a proximal root lesion, either in the upper or in the lower extremities, results in a magnified susceptibility of a distal nerve to an insult such as compression that would have been otherwise inadequate to cause symptoms.

It is ironic that the hypothesis of Upton and McComas, who were firm advocates of conservative management of entrapment neuropathies and cervical root lesions, ultimately would gain wide acceptance as a universal impetus supporting more surgery, more nerve blocks, and more chiropractic manipulations in treating a variety of symptoms where the initial treatment had failed. The "principle" of double-crush likely has been frequently misapplied in medicolegal settings and worker's compensation cases, and its usage has only added to the vast body of pseudoscience and misinformation that so characterizes these proceedings.[12]

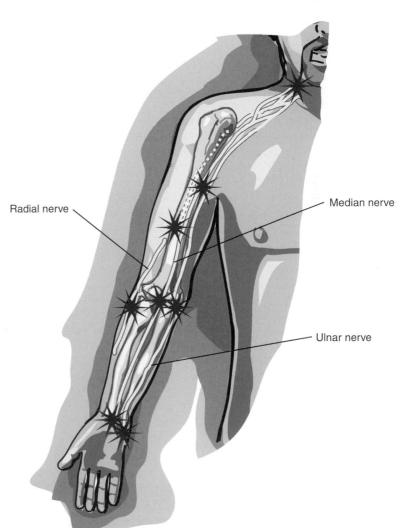

FIGURE 38–7 ■ Double-crush syndrome. A proximal nerve lesion makes the distal nerve more vulnerable to injury. It is a concept that remains unproven.

Radial nerve

Median nerve

Ulnar nerve

Carpal tunnel syndrome remains a clinical diagnosis that is frequently supported by electrodiagnostic studies. Despite reported advances in ultrasound and MRI evaluation of the carpal tunnel, these modalities remain unproven adjuncts to the clinical examination. Although recognized in some circles as the diagnostic gold standard for carpal tunnel syndrome, electrodiagnostic studies, including NCV, have distinct limitations. Many asymptomatic individuals can have abnormal NCV suggestive of median neuropathy at the wrist. Equally important to note is that surgery may be effective in patients with clinical symptoms who have normal NCV studies.

Although carpal tunnel surgery is effective, it is performed too often and often prematurely. We believe that the decision regarding surgery should be based on significant symptoms that do not respond to conservative measures, including splinting and local combined injections of a corticosteroid and anesthetic into the carpal tunnel. If these patients are followed, many improve with or without treatment. Persistent wrist pain, nocturnal awakening associated with the flick sign and thenar muscle weakness or atrophy are the best indicators of the need for surgery.

■ BRACHIAL NEURITIS

Brachial neuritis (neuralgic amyotrophy, Parsonage-Turner syndrome) is a rare, but exquisitely painful syndrome involving the shoulder girdle.[13] Its incidence is approximately 1.6 cases per 100,000 person-years; Bell's palsy has an incidence of 30 cases per 100,000 person-years. In my practice, we see one such patient about every 2 years. The first symptom is severe sharp, stabbing, throbbing, or aching pain that begins abruptly in the shoulder girdle, scapular area, or hand. The pain is of high intensity and is exacerbated by any movement of the shoulder. The pain may be bilateral in 10% to 20% of cases. There is a distinct male-to-female predominance ranging from 2:1 to 4:1.

This condition initially goes unrecognized, and the patient develops a sense of desperation as he or she travels from physician to physician hoping for a specific diagnosis. The patient typically walks with the effected arm supported by the uninvolved arm. After several weeks, the pain subsides, and the patient becomes aware of weakness followed by atrophy. This weakness usually involves the shoulder girdle muscles, but the hand or forearm also may be involved. A patchy proximal sensory loss in the arm also may be noted.

This condition is most common in young and middle-aged men. Its cause is unknown, but it has been linked to multiple antecedent events, including vaccinations, viral and bacterial infections, surgery, and trauma not involving the shoulder. Biopsy specimens of the involved plexus have shown florid inflammation, and the disorder is believed to have an immune-mediated origin. The clinical findings are predominantly that of a lower motor neuron lesion. Fasciculations and hyperreflexia are not seen. Deep tendon reflexes may be diminished. Involvement of the axillary and suprascapular nerves was the most common combination resulting in weakness and atrophy in descending order of frequency of the deltoid, serratus anterior, biceps, and triceps.

MRI or CT myelography should be considered to rule out cervical radiculopathy, particularly at C5-6, or a neoplasm. MRI neuronography with special sequences to identify the

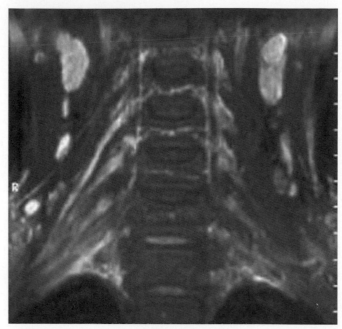

FIGURE 38–8 ■ Diffuse plexitis of unclear origin in the right branchial plexus. Note bright signal involving multiple roots of the right brachial plexus (left side of figure).

brachial plexus is an evolving technique that may help in ruling out carcinomatous infiltration of the plexus (Fig. 38–8). Nerve conductions often reveal loss of sensory or reduction in motor amplitudes with preserved conduction velocities. Needle EMG shows denervation including fibrillations and positive waves in affected muscles 2 to 3 weeks after the onset. These EMG changes may be bilateral, even when only one extremity is involved clinically.[14] Treatment is largely symptomatic, and in the face of such intense pain, opioid analgesics and corticosteroids are often necessary.

The diagnosis, although often delayed, frequently is made based on a history of the sudden onset of neuropathic pain in the shoulder girdle, followed by weakness and atrophy. The prognosis is good, although the period of improvement may be protracted. Approximately 80% of patients recover by 2 years, and almost 90% make a functional recovery by 3 years. In its initial stages, brachial neuritis can be misdiagnosed as cervical radiculopathy, rotator cuff disease, entrapment neuropathy, or drug-seeking behavior.

The diagnosis usually is made by a careful review of the history and a thorough physical examination. In the current climate of clinical medicine, the days of detailed history taking and careful neurologic examination are quickly disappearing. Brachial neuritis is such a condition that when one has seen a case, its clinical characteristics are not forgotten. The patient is in terrible pain and describes the shoulder as being "on fire." The patient typically is a young or middle-aged man whose shoulder pain does not respond to opioids. MRI of the cervical spine may be normal or show moderate age-related degenerative changes that have nothing to do with the current problem.

By keeping this diagnosis in mind, referring to an experienced electromyographer, and offering reassurance that the process is a benign one with a good outcome, the pain

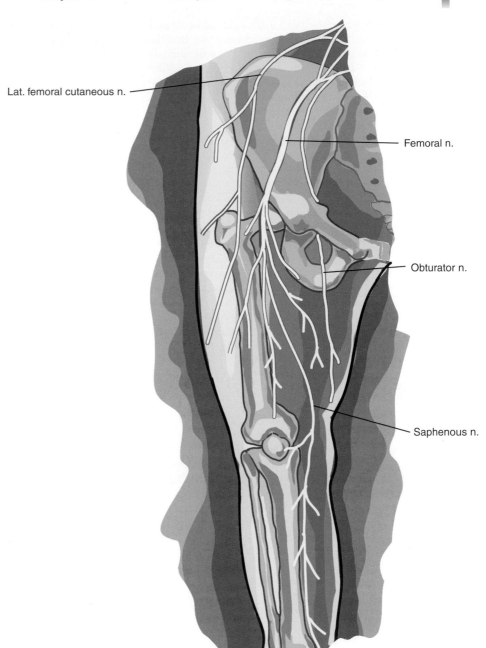

FIGURE 38–9 ■ Anatomy of lateral femoral cutaneous nerve.

■ MERALGIA PARESTHETICA

Meralgia paresthetica is a painful neuropathy caused by lateral femoral cutaneous nerve compression below the inguinal ligament (Fig. 38–9). This entrapment neuropathy was reported more than 100 years ago. The involved nerve is purely sensory, and there is no associated weakness or loss of

management physician's contribution to the patient's well-being is enormous. A pain specialist, who may actually be functioning in a primary diagnostic role, should not underestimate the healing power of face-to-face interaction with the patient. In the end, it is the essence of the physician's role.

deep tendon reflexes. The symptoms of meralgia paresthetica consist of varying degrees of pain, paresthesias, and numbness in the upper lateral thigh (see Fig. 38–9). The pain may be worsened by standing, walking, or adduction of the thigh. The most common area of hypoesthesia is frequently described in the trouser pocket area. Touch may evoke an unpleasant sensation when the hand is placed in the pocket. Physical examination reveals sensory loss along the lateral aspect of the upper thigh, but the objective loss of sensation is often in a much smaller area than the subjective area of pain and paresthesias.

This is another diagnosis made predominantly based on history and physical examination. Although electrodiagnostic studies, including NCV and evoked potentials, have been reported useful, these are extremely technically difficult and have not been reliable or helpful in my clinical practice. In situations in which the clinical findings are atypical, including a more extensive area of sensory involvement supplied by the lateral femoral cutaneous nerve, or if there is any weakness, CT or MRI of the spine and pelvis is indicated. Imaging studies are indicated for patients who are at risk of neoplastic disease, have bleeding disorders, or those on anticoagulation, who are at added risk of a retroperitoneal hematoma.

The major issue is a proper diagnosis and putting the patient at ease. Meralgia paresthetica usually improves spontaneously. The cause is usually idiopathic, although it has been reported in relation to transfemoral angiography, tight bandaging, laparoscopic repair of inguinal hernias, iliac bone crest harvesting, seatbelt injury, weight gain and weight loss, pregnancy, and gymnastic practice in which the uneven parallel bars are used. Diabetics have a higher incidence of this entrapment neuropathy.[15]

Management should be conservative including addressing the causative factors, such as losing weight, wearing looser clothing, or avoiding activities that exacerbate the discomfort. Analgesic patches, such as lidocaine (Lidoderm), and medications used in treating neuropathic pain, such as gabapentin (Neurontin) and pregabalin (Lyrica), have been found to be useful. If conservative treatments fail, local anesthetic injections lateral to the inguinal ligament with hydrocortisone and local anesthetics can provide temporary relief. Rarely, if ever, surgical decompression is necessary. This is a diagnosis that when recognized should alleviate the fears of the patient and set the proper stage for spontaneous recovery. It is another example where the history and physical examination are the primary tools.

■ LUMBOSACRAL PLEXUS NEUROPATHY

Lumbosacral plexus neuropathy is a condition that begins with neuropathic pain involving the hip and the thigh. The pain is described as aching and stabbing and exhibits neuropathic qualities of electric-like shocks and burning with excessive tenderness to touch (allodynia). This anterior thigh and hip pain is followed by proximal lower limb muscle weakness and atrophy. The patient has particular difficulty rising from a squatting position. The knee jerk is usually absent, and sensory loss may be noted over the anterior thigh. Ankle jerks may be reduced, particularly if the patient has an underlying diabetic neuropathy. In diabetics, this condition is known by a variety of names, including diabetic lumbosacral radiculoplexus neuropathy, diabetic amyotrophy, proximal diabetic neuropathy, and Bruns-Garland syndrome. Diabetics and nondiabetics can present in a similar fashion. A significant historical detail is that recent weight loss of 10 to 40 lb is commonly reported predating the onset of symptoms.

Electrodiagnostic testing, including EMG and NCV, is helpful in supporting this diagnosis. The skill of the electromyographer is crucial. It also is important to consider MRI of the lumbar spine and pelvis to rule out an intraspinal process and MRI or CT of the pelvis to exclude malignant invasion of the lumbar plexus, a psoas abscess, or, in patients

who are on anticoagulation, a retroperitoneal hematoma. The average age of these patients is 65 to 70 years, and many unrelated asymptomatic findings on MRI of the lumbar spine can confuse the picture. The role of MRI neuronography in detecting signal abnormalities within the lumbosacral plexus is still under development.

This is a condition that presents a characteristic clinical picture requiring recognition. It can remain undiagnosed for months, and over time a substantial percentage of cases can show bilateral hip girdle involvement. Differential diagnosis includes iatrogenic causes of femoral neuropathy, including nerve trauma resulting from abdominal surgery, lithotomy positioning during delivery, or gynecologic procedures and urologic procedures in which sharp flexion of the hip can compress the inguinal ligament. Careful clinical examination, history, and appropriate electrodiagnostic studies can differentiate these conditions from lumbosacral plexus neuropathy.

Diabetic and nondiabetic lumbosacral plexus neuropathies are similar. Both neuropathies are associated with weight loss and often begin focally in the anterior thigh with severe neuropathic pain.[16] Biopsy suggests ischemic damage secondary to microvasculitis. Although unequivocal improvement occurs over time in most patients, total recovery is rare. The role of immunomodulating therapies is currently under evaluation. This diagnosis should be considered in middle-aged to elderly patients with severe anterior thigh pain and muscle weakness with or without diabetes. It is another condition sufficiently rare that misdiagnosis and delayed diagnosis is common. Although seen fairly commonly in neurologic practice, it may present a problem for an anesthesiology-based pain specialist.

■ TARSAL TUNNEL SYNDROME

Although tarsal tunnel syndrome is touted to be the lower extremity counterpart to carpal tunnel syndrome, this entity is far less common and of far less clinical significance as a common pain syndrome involving the lower extremity. Tarsal tunnel syndrome is caused by entrapment of the posterior tibial nerve and its tibial branches, the medial or lateral or calcaneal nerves, within the tarsal tunnel. This tunnel is located posterior and inferior to the medial malleolus and is formed by the flexor retinaculum. Causative factors include trauma with posttraumatic fibrosis, tenosynovitis, and ganglion formation affecting the nerves or tendons. The tarsal tunnel is different from the carpal tunnel in the hands in that the flexor retinaculum is thin compared with the thick volar carpal ligament. In addition, the tarsal tunnel is compartmentalized by several deep fibrotic septations that run between the tendons and the neurovascular bundle. In contrast to carpal tunnel syndrome, tarsal tunnel syndrome is less commonly associated with systemic diseases, such as diabetes, inflammatory arthritis, acromegaly, or hypothyroidism.[17]

The onset of tarsal tunnel syndrome is usually unilateral and insidious. The most common symptom is burning, tingling numbness over the territory of the plantar nerve. When symptoms are localized to the plantar surface of the medial two toes, the median plantar nerve is involved. When the lateral plantar nerve is involved, the numbness and paresthesias involve the surface of the lateral two toes. The calcaneal branch of the nerve supplies the plantar and medial surface of the heel. Symptoms classically are aggravated by activities such as prolonged standing or walking and are relieved by rest. In tarsal tunnel syndrome, the nocturnal aggravation of symptoms seen with carpal tunnel syndrome is far less common. Loss of strength in the intrinsic foot muscle has not been reported with tarsal tunnel syndrome. The most common reported objective findings are a positive Tinel sign at the tarsal tunnel and sensory impairment in the territory of any of the terminal branches.

MRI may be helpful in evaluating the tarsal tunnel for space-occupying or compressive lesions. The differential diagnosis includes lumbosacral radiculopathy, interdigital neuroma, plantar fasciitis, or posterior tibial tendonitis. MRI is helpful in evaluating rare cases, including neurilemoma, ganglion cysts, and posttraumatic neuroma.

NCV studies are the test of choice in confirming the diagnosis of tarsal tunnel syndrome. EMG is generally not helpful. With respect to NCV, distal motor latency has a low diagnostic sensitivity; sensory nerve conduction studies are far superior in confirming the diagnosis. There are technical difficulties in performing these studies, however, and the sophistication of the electromyographer is crucial. In most cases, the diagnosis rests on clinical grounds, and treatment should be conservative, including resting the ankle, use of a foot orthosis, nonsteroidal antiinflammatory agents, or local injection of corticosteroids. My overall impression is that this disorder is frequently considered, but rarely found in clinical neurologic practice. For every case of tarsal tunnel syndrome, we see hundreds of cases of carpal tunnel syndrome.

▮ CONCLUSION

Pain is the most common symptom that brings a patient to a physician. This pain is evaluated most effectively when an experienced physician spends ample time with the patient obtaining a targeted history and physical examination. The time and thoroughness of the physician's interview is in itself therapeutic in relieving patient anxiety. This is reflected in a euphoric response of relief and hope: "I finally found someone who is listening to me."

Society has currently devalued this essential interpersonal part of medicine. This devaluation is glaringly reflected in the inequities of the insurance system, in which imaging, dangerous invasive procedures, and novel, but unproven technologies are favorably reimbursed over basic cognitive consultative services. Self-preservation is inherent in human nature, and physicians have responded accordingly. Office visits are short and frequently conducted by physician "extenders" who often order multiple tests. Follow-up visits are rare, and the patient is ultimately informed of the test results over the telephone by a secretary. Patient and physician dissatisfaction is at an all-time high.

Most painful neuropathies are diagnoses that are almost exclusively made by this devalued history and physical examination. Some are common (Bell's palsy and carpal tunnel syndrome) and some are less common (trigeminal neuralgia and branchial neuritis). Often there are no specific treatments, and the basic therapeutic process is one of making a specific diagnosis, educating the patient, providing symptomatic treatment, and reassuring the patient that he or she will improve over time. Keep learning. We see and can recognize only what we know.

References

1. American Diabetes Association: Position statement: Diagnosis and classification of diabetes mellitus. Diabetes Care 28:537, 2005.
2. Boden SD, Davis DO, Dina TS, et al: Abnormal magnetic resonance scans of the lumbar spine in asymptomatic subjects. J Bone Joint Surg Am 72:402, 1990.
3. Weishaupt D, Zanetti M, Hodler J, Boos N: MR imaging of the lumbar spine. Radiology 209:661, 1998.
4. Kissel JT, Burde RM, Klingele TG, et al: Pupil sparing oculomotor palsies with internal carotid-posterior communicating artery aneurysm. Ann Neurol 13:149, 1983.
5. Keane JR: Multiple cranial nerve palsies: Analysis of 979 cases. Arch Neurol 62:1714, 2005.
6. Maxwell RE: Clinical diagnosis of trigeminal neuralgia and differential diagnosis of facial pain. In Rovit RL, Mutale R, Janetta P (eds): Trigeminal Neuralgia. Baltimore, Williams & Wilkins, 1990, p 53.
7. Gunsberg LE: MR imaging of peri neural tumor spread. Magn Reson Imaging Clin N Am 10:511, 2002.
8. Atroshi I, Gummeson C, Johnsson R, et al: Prevalence of carpal tunnel syndrome in general population. JAMA 282:153, 1999.
9. Stevens JC, Beard CM, O'Fallon WM, Kurland LT: Conditions associated with carpal tunnel syndrome. Mayo Clin Proc 67:541, 1992.
10. Jablecki CK, Andary MT, Floeter MK, et al: Practice parameter: Electrodiagnostic studies in carpal tunnel syndrome. Report of the American Association of Electrodiagnostic Medicine, American Academy of Neurology, and the American Academy of Physical Medicine and Rehabilitation. Neurology 58:1589, 2002.
11. Upton RM, McComas AJ: The double-crush in nerve entrapment syndromes. Lancet 11:359, 1973.
12. Wilbourn AJ, Gilliatt RW: Double-crush syndrome: a critical analysis. Neurology 49:21, 1997.
13. Parsonage MJ, Aldren Turner JW: Neuralgic amyotrophy: The shoulder girdle syndrome. Lancet 1:973, 1948.
14. Wilbourn AJ: Brachial plexus disorders. In: Peripheral Neuropathy. Philadelphia, WB Saunders, 1993, p 911.
15. van Slobbe AM, Bohner AM, Bernsen RM, et al: Incidence rates and determinants in neuralgia parasthetica in general practice. J Neurol 25:294, 2004.
16. Dyck PJB, Norvell JE, Dyck PJ: Non-diabetic lumbosacral radiculoplexus neuropathy. Brain 124:1197, 2001.
17. Pyasta RT, Panush RS: Common painful foot syndromes. Bull Rheum Dis 48:1-4, 1999.
18. Lee J-H, Lee H-K, Park J-K, et al: Cavernous sinus syndrome: Clinical features and differential diagnosis with MR imaging. AJR Am J Roentgenol 181:583, 2003.

chapter 39

Osteoarthritis and Related Disorders

Paul Dieppe, Philip Conaghan, Bruce Kidd, and Paul Creamer

■ HISTORICAL CONSIDERATIONS

Osteoarthritis (OA) is the most common form of disease of synovial joints, and a frequent cause of chronic pain in older people. It is characterized pathologically by focal areas of loss of articular cartilage with overgrowth of subchondral and marginal bone, and clinically by use-related pain and joint stiffness.

OA was first differentiated from other forms of arthritis at the beginning of the 20th century,[1] when pathologic and radiologic studies indicated that there were two major forms of joint disease: the *atrophic* form, occurring in younger people and characterized by synovial inflammation and bone erosion (this included rheumatoid arthritis and sepsis) and the *hypertrophic* form of arthritis, a condition of older people in which there was overgrowth of bone around affected joints. Hypertrophic arthritis subsequently became known as *osteoarthritis* (because of the prominent involvement of bone) or *degenerative arthritis* because of its relationship to age and the development of a belief that it was a consequence of wear and tear and tissue degeneration.

However, during a period of renewed interest in connective tissue research in the 1970s, along with the development of animal models of OA, it became apparent that there was increased turnover of matrix in both the articular cartilage and subchondral bone in hypertrophic arthritis, challenging the concept of degenerative joint disease. More contemporary studies have reemphasized the involvement of the bone, synovium and capsule in OA, which is now seen as an active disease process involving the whole joint organ and as the response of a synovial joint to injury or altered biomechanics.

Epidemiologic studies delineating the main risk factors for OA have aided the development of current concepts of the disease.[2] We know that, in addition to age, joint injury and certain forms of activity predispose joints to OA, and that obesity and genetic and hormonal factors are also associated with it. Figure 39–1 summarizes the contemporary view of the pathogenesis of OA.

■ THE CLINICAL SYNDROME

The science of OA has featured three different approaches to the disease:

1. Epidemiologists have studied the incidence, prevalence and associations of joint damage in the community, defining OA radiographically.
2. Clinical scientists have concentrated on a minority of those with joint damage or symptoms (i.e., those who present to doctors complaining of joint pain).
3. Basic science has been dominated by biochemical and biomechanical studies of the properties of articular cartilage.

Unfortunately, there is a paucity of common ground among these three groups.

Health scientists like to believe that they can unravel disease pathways that lead us from genetic and environmental causes of pathology or pathophysiology, directly to the symptoms and signs of a condition. OA does not fit comfortably into this paradigm. John Lawrence made a seminal observation in the 1960s—showing that the relation between radiographic evidence of OA in a joint and the amount of pain was poor, and that severely damaged joints were often asymptomatic.[3] This observation has been substantiated and enhanced by more recent work.[4] The "disconnect" between pathology and pain (the main symptom of OA) can be seen as a problem or an opportunity. It is a problem for the reductionist, who will offer the obvious explanation that we are simply looking at the wrong pathologic features when we take a radiograph of the joint; but it is an opportunity for the physician, who can then ask what the likely causes of pain are in any individual patient, without recourse of having to assess the degree of joint damage. The basic scientist can only sit on the sidelines and wonder if he or she has selected the right tissue to study (possibly not in our view: bone may be a better target than cartilage).

OA can affect any synovial joint in the body. The joints that most often cause clinical problems include the apophyseal joints of the spine (particularly in the midcervical and lower lumbar spine), the interphalangeal joints and first carpometacarpal joint (thumb base) in the hands, the knee (particularly the medial tibiofemoral and lateral patellofemoral compartments), the hip, and the first tarsometatarsal joint. One of the joints least likely to be affected is the ankle; shoulder disease is uncommon, whereas elbow OA is relatively common pathologically, but rarely symptomatic. The greatest burden of disease arises from knee disease, which affects some 25% of those over the age of 55, and from hip disease requiring joint replacement surgery.

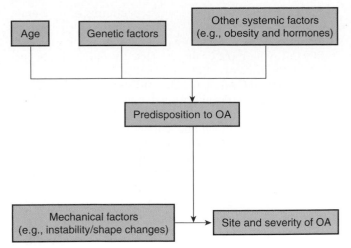

FIGURE 39–1 ■ A schematic representation of current views on the pathogenesis of osteoarthritis.

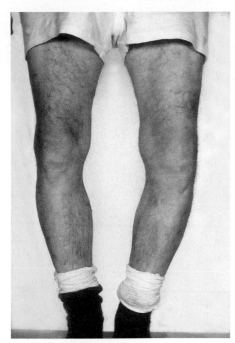

FIGURE 39–2 ■ Clinical photograph of a man with osteoarthritis of the knee joint who has the typical medial compartment involvement, resulting in a varus deformity (making him bowlegged); note the marked wasting of the quadriceps muscles but absence of any effusion in the joint.

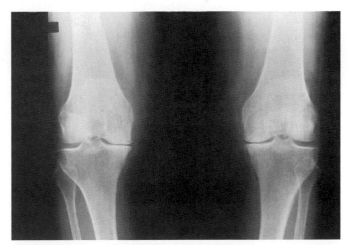

FIGURE 39–3 ■ A radiograph of patient with osteoarthritis of similar nature to that illustrated in Figure 39–2. Note the narrowing of the medial joint space in both knees, caused by loss of articular cartilage, and the early osteophyte formation.

The symptoms and signs of OA, as well as the disease associations, do vary somewhat between the different joint sites affected. However, there are a number of common features to all symptomatic OA joints. These include pain, usually use-related; short-lasting *gelling* of the joint after inactivity (difficulty initiating movement after rest); limitation of movement, with pain at the end of the range and often crepitus (creaking of the joint during movement); tenderness over the joint line and palpable bony swelling around it; and in some cases, signs of mild inflammation.

Spinal OA is a particularly difficult problem to investigate or understand because back pain is particularly poorly associated with any definable pathology. For this reason, and because back pain is dealt with elsewhere in this book (see Section 4, Part H), we will not deal with OA of spinal joints any further. Brief descriptions of the main features of OA of the most common peripheral joint sites are discussed subsequently. We then return to the subject of pain.

The Knee

There are two main groups of people who get knee OA: a younger male group, in whom there is often an antecedent history of joint trauma (such as cruciate ligament rupture or meniscal injury) or a work history that predisposes to the condition (bearing weight while in full-knee flexion); and an older female group in whom there is usually a family history of OA, often apparent from the presence of Heberden nodes on the fingers. Obesity is a strong predisposition in both groups. Overall, there are far more women than men with knee OA. The condition most often affects the medial tibiofemoral and lateral patellofemoral compartments, but as it progresses, more of the knee joint becomes involved.[5]

Knee OA manifests with pain and stiffness. Reduced flexion, as well as weakness of the quadriceps muscles, may contribute to disability. The predominant involvement of the medial tibiofemoral joint often results in varus deformity (Figs. 39–2 and 39–3). The natural history is one of slow progression, often punctuated by short-lasting *flares* of increased pain—although only a minority of the total number of people affected (some 25% of all people older than age 55) suffer enough to need a joint replacement, indicating that most cases stabilize at some stage.[5]

The Hip

Hip OA manifests over a wide age range (20s to 90s), but most often starts in the 50s or 60s. There is a roughly equal sex incidence. Several different anatomic types have been described, based on the direction of migration of the femoral head (superolateral or medial/concentric) or the degree of osteophyte formation (hypertrophic or atrophic), and these may be genetically distinct.[6] Predisposing factors include anatomic abnormalities of the hip such as dysplasia (the percent that can be attributed to such problems is disputed), certain occupations, particularly farming, a family history, and obesity (although this is much less important for hip OA than it is for knee disease).

The usual manifestation is pain on walking. The pain may be felt in the buttock, groin, thigh, or knee (hip disease manifesting with knee pain is a common source of diagnostic confusion). Stiffness and difficulty with selected activities are common complaints. The natural history is variable: some progress steadily, but others have relatively stable complaints for years, followed by a relatively sudden deterioration with the development of severe pain. A minority of instances resolve spontaneously.

The Hand

The principal joints affected are the interphalangeal joints (distal more than proximal) and the first carpometacarpal joint (thumb base). However, every other joint of the hand can, and often is, affected to some degree. Hand OA is extremely common in women (much less so in men) and strongly related to age, family history, and trauma. The classic features of hand OA are firm swellings of the distal (Heberden nodes) or proximal (Bouchard nodes) joints (Fig. 39–4). These swellings consist of chondrophyte or osteophyte and are sometimes associated with hyaluronan-filled cysts.

The presentation of interphalangeal joint OA may be an insidious one in older age, with the gradual and often largely painless development of swellings of the interphalangeal joints. However, in many cases it is more dramatic, with the sequential development of painful, hot, red swellings of these joints, most often in women in their 50s. This has led to the concept of *menopausal arthritis* and is strongly associated with the idea that there is a form of *generalized osteoarthritis* in which there is a strong genetic predisposition to the development of OA in multiple joint sites.[7] The exact process in this common condition is unclear; it is important to recog-

nize and differentiate OA from systemic forms of inflammatory joint disease, such as psoriatic arthritis. The natural history is one of resolution of pain but not swelling or joint stiffness, leaving most of those affected with knobby fingers that do not move as well as they once did.

Thumb-base OA is somewhat different. It is more clearly related to overuse or injury, and may be precipitated by damage to the ligaments that stabilize the joint in many cases. It causes use-related pain and can be a source of significant discomfort and disability to people who need fine movements of their fingers and the pinch grip in their daily activities (surgeons and those who do needlework for example).

Why Are Osteoarthritic Joints Sometimes Painful?

The question needs asking because of the poor correlation between structural evidence of joint damage and the presence and severity of joint pain. Creamer and Hochberg's data[4] suggest that OA joint damage predisposes to pain, but that there is little correlation between pain severity and the extent of joint damage thereafter—indicating that there might be a threshold point of predisposition to a painful condition.

There is surprisingly little research into pain in OA.[8,9] We know that use-related pain in OA is common, that rest pain and night pain sometimes occur, and that a variety of patterns of pain are described by different patients, varying from a dull ache to stabbing sharp pains. We also know that there are diurnal and other rhythms to pain severity, perhaps related to activity. However, attempts to discriminate between OA and other rheumatologic disorders, such as rheumatoid arthritis, through verbal descriptions of pain have generally proved unsuccessful, and we have not clearly defined the different experiences of pain in patients with OA. Similarly, we know precious little about the likely causes of OA pain.

The abandonment of the cartesian model of pain in the late 19th century, the recognition that the nervous system is not fixed or "hard wired," and the adoption of biopsychosocial models in the mid to latter part of the 20th century have radically changed our approach to pain. It is now appreciated that the perception of pain arises in response to a complex series of underlying neurophysiologic events involving transduction of stimuli, transmission of encoded information, and subsequent modulation of this activity at both peripheral and more central levels. In all but acute situations, the relation between tissue injury and resultant symptoms becomes less well-defined and more susceptible to extraneous influences originating both within and external to the individual. The relevance of this to chronic diseases such as OA are obvious and the model goes a long way toward explaining the heterogeneous symptoms described by individuals with this disorder.

In contrast to other sensory receptors, high-threshold receptors responding to tissue injury (nociceptors) are not stimulus specific and do not adapt, often becoming more responsive over time. Experimental studies have shown that sensitization of joint nociceptors following injury results in decreased response thresholds to mechanical stimuli such that hitherto innocuous events such as walking or simply weight bearing can then produce activity within nociceptive pathways. Parallel changes occur at more central levels with exaggerated responses to normal inputs and expansion of receptive

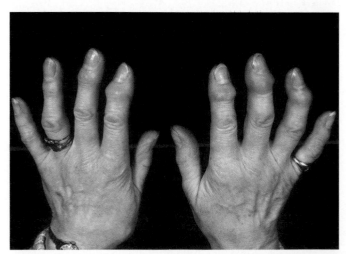

FIGURE 39–4 ■ Clinical photograph of someone with interphalangeal osteoarthritis. Note the large swellings of the distal interphalangeal joints (Heberden nodes) associated with some inflammation, and the earlier changes in the proximal interphalangeal joints resulting in Bouchard nodes.

field sizes producing tenderness and referred pain away from the initial site of injury (central sensitization). It seems highly likely that these central mechanisms are responsible for at least some of the clinical features of OA, including referred pain and the finding of tenderness over apparently normal tissues.

Given that many or possibly the majority of OA joints remain pain free, the pivotal question arises as to the underlying mechanism whereby an asymptomatic but diseased joint becomes symptomatic. Although a number of experimental models of OA have been developed, these are not accompanied by behavioral pain responses—consistent with the idea that OA is essentially a painless disorder rendered symptomatic by additional factors. Our hypothesis is that the tissue changes that accompany OA do not, in themselves, directly activate nociceptors and do not produce pain; rather they alter nociceptive mechanisms at both peripheral and central levels so that heretofore innocuous stimuli now cause symptoms.

Several lines of evidence point to the importance of mediators released from either synovium or bone. The presence of inflammation has been convincingly demonstrated in OA, and mediator-induced sensitization of articular nociceptors provides a convincing mechanism by which symptoms might occur. Consistent with this, the presence of knee pain has been shown to correlate with magnetic resonance imaging (MRI) findings of moderate or larger effusions as well as synovial thickening.

Periosteum, subchondral, and marrow bone are richly innervated with sensory fibers and are potential sources of OA pain. Bone marrow lesions detected on MRI are more prevalent in individuals with OA who have knee pain than in those who are symptom free. Raised intraosseous pressure arising from impaired venous drainage has long been linked with OA—probably explaining the immediate benefits of surgical procedures such as an osteotomy.[10]

Although there is good evidence that synovial and capsular problems as well as raised intraosseous pressure are all associated with pain in OA, it is also clear that periarticular problems, secondary to deformity and mechanical abnormalities, are common; for example, trochanteric bursitis around the hip and anserine bursitis around the knee are common accompaniments of OA of those joints.

An intervention study that we carried out a few years ago lends support to the variable contributions of altered peripheral and central nociceptive mechanisms to pain generation.[11] We studied pain in people with bilateral knee OA in response to an injection of local anesthetic or placebo into one knee. Pain was temporarily reduced to almost nothing in the injected knee in some, but not all patients; importantly, pain often got better in the contralateral knee.

In studies using quantitative sensory testing methodology, diffuse alteration of pain perception in response to various stimuli has been reported in subjects with symptomatic OA.[12] These subjects had increased pain intensity with significantly larger referred and radiating pain areas than matched controls. It is highly unlikely that local changes to nociceptive activity account for either set of results and point to the presence of enhanced central nociceptive mechanisms.

There is also good evidence that psychosocial factors affect pain perception, particularly anxiety, depression. and social isolation.[13,14] It seems likely that OA pain reflects altered nociceptive mechanisms such that everyday stimuli now

produce pain. These changes are likely to arise in response to a critical interaction with particular joint, bone, and periarticular factors that may well vary among individuals. The resultant sensitization of nociceptive pathways at both peripheral and central levels is then dependent on constitutional factors unique to an individual—such as gender, age and previous history, as well as environmental factors including culture and lifestyle. If this is true, then the unpredictability of pain responses to different interventions, which we experience in the management of OA, would not be surprising.

■ DIAGNOSIS AND INVESTIGATION

Diagnosis of OA may be considered in two ways. First, as a *clinical diagnosis* depending entirely on recognition of the patterns described above and differentiation of true OA joint pain from referred or periarticular problems. For example, the American College of Rheumatology (ACR) Classification Criteria for knee OA[15] include knee pain and age over 40 years with morning stiffness lasting less than 30 minutes and crepitus on motion. A reasonable working diagnostic approach to OA is to assume that knee pain in those older than age 50 is due to OA unless another cause can be found, especially if pain is worse on use and is associated with stiffness after inactivity and restricted movement. Table 39–1 indicates the typical features of OA and some of the alternative diagnoses that should be excluded at the hip and knee.

Second, OA can be defined by *pathologic changes*. Histopathology is, in general, unavailable and we rely on radiographs and other imaging modalities such as MRI as surrogates. No other investigations are of value, except perhaps use of synovial fluid analysis to differentiate simple OA from crystal-related disorders (discussed later)

Conventional Radiography

Plain radiographs are useful in confirming that established OA is present and in defining which joints (or parts of joints) are affected. Taken serially, they also allow assessment of the progression of anatomic changes, but care must be taken when comparing serial films to ensure appropriate patient repositioning (this is one of the major problems with clinical trials using radiographs as outcome measures).

They are also of value in excluding other causes of joint pain (e.g., fracture, avascular necrosis, or Paget disease of bone). Unfortunately radiographs do not accurately represent pathology because early changes (which may be confirmed by arthroscopy or MRI) are not seen on radiographs.[16] A normal radiograph does not exclude OA. Radiographs cannot indicate the impact of disease on the individual or allow a prognosis to be made. Possible indications for obtaining radiographs in a patient with knee pain might be

- Knee pain that suddenly gets worse
- Acute inflammation or other signs that suggest a diagnosis other than OA (Table 39–2)
- Possible referral of pain from spine to hip or hip to knee
- Investigation prior to surgery

Typical changes of OA on a plain radiograph include joint space narrowing (generally assumed to reflect articular cartilage loss) and osteophyte, sclerosis, and cyst formation

Table 39–1

Clinical and Differential Diagnosis of Knee and Hip Osteoarthritis

Typical features suggesting OA	Pain—deep, often poorly localized, worse on use Stiffness—localized to involved joints, rarely exceeds 30 minutes Crepitus on active motion Limited range of movement No systemic features	
Differential Diagnoses to Consider	**Knee**	**Hip**
Other arthritis	Rheumatoid arthritis, gout, CPPD	Rheumatoid arthritis, seronegative spondyloarthropathy
Bone disease	Avascular necrosis Paget disease	Avascular necrosis Paget disease
Soft tissue	Meniscal or ligament injuries, bursitis (anserine, prepatella)	Trochanteric bursitis, tendinopathy
Referred pain	From hip	From spine, SIJ

CPPD, calcium pyrophosphate dihydrate deposition.

Table 39–2

Some of the Potential Factors Influencing the Decision to Seek Medical Care by Individuals with Osteoarthritis

Disease severity (pain, disability)
Sudden worsening of symptoms
Socioeconomic or occupational factors
Comorbidity
Cultural expectations (such as influences of family or friends)
Coping strategies
Availability of services and ease of access to them

The Aims of Managing Osteoarthritis

Education and empowerment of patient and caregivers
Alleviating pain
Improving disabling effects by encouraging participation in activities
Reducing the risk of progression

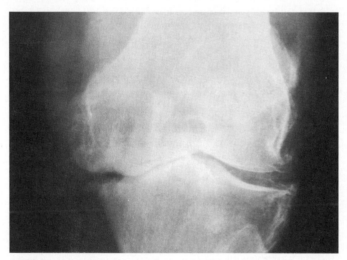

FIGURE 39–5 ■ Radiograph of a patient with severe knee joint osteoarthritis and associated chondrocalcinosis. The joint space has disappeared in the medial joint compartment, and there has been major remodeling of the subchondral bone with associated sclerosis and changes in contour. The chondrocalcinosis is seen in the lateral compartment, where there is still some cartilage. Fairly large osteophytes are also present.

(Fig. 39–5). These same features are seen at all sites affected by OA, although the correlation between radiographic features and symptoms may vary (e.g., osteophytes at the distal interphalangeal joint are often asymptomatic, whereas at the hip there is a closer correlation with pain).

In general, there is surprisingly little overlap between the clinical and radiographic diagnosis of OA. Community studies indicate that the risk of knee pain increases with radiographic severity of OA. In the NHANES-I study, for example, among subjects aged 65 to 74, knee pain was reported by 8.8% of subjects with normal radiographs, 20.4% with grade 1 OA, 36.9% with grade 2, and 60.4% with grade 3 or 4 [17]. However, about 10% of individuals with knee pain have completely normal radiographs, whereas up to 40% of subjects with severe radiographic changes apparently are pain free. If pain severity, rather than presence, is used as an outcome, there is even less association with radiographic change. Several studies now confirm that once an individual with knee pain becomes a patient seeking medical care there is virtually no relationship between radiographic severity and level of reported pain.[4,18] It may be that a certain level of structural change is required to produce symptoms but beyond that, other, nonstructural factors determine pain severity for an individual. A number of other imaging modalities can provide information about OA, although none are currently useful in routine clinical practice.

Isotope Bone Scans

Isotope bone scans appear to predict progression of radiographic OA and the need for surgery at the knee[19] and hand,[20] suggesting that bone responses may be a critical feature in the progression of OA.

Ultrasonography

Ultrasonography has many advantages over conventional radiography (e.g., it can image multiple joints in real time in the clinic and does not involve radiation exposure). In the hands of a trained ultrasonographer, it is a useful tool in both small and large joints. With respect to differential diagnosis of OA, in the small joints of the hands or feet, ultrasound may determine joint space narrowing, synovitis, periarticular erosions, and occasionally crystals.[21] Of course, both inflammatory arthritis and OA joints may have synovitis present. In the knee, ultrasound is able to distinguish both synovial hypertrophy and effusions, although care should be taken because there is little consensus on definitions for these abnormalities. A recent large study of 625 painful OA knees demonstrated that 34% had effusions and 17% had synovial hypertrophy (14% had both).[22] Although clinically detected effusions correlated modestly with ultrasonographic effusions, no other clinical symptom or sign was predictive of the presence of ultrasonographic synovitis or effusions.

If treating synovial inflammation is demonstrated to be critical in the management of OA, then ultrasound may well provide a simple and relatively cheap tool for monitoring patients. Ultrasound has the added benefit of providing a tool for guided injection therapy.[23]

Magnetic Resonance Imaging

MRI offers huge potential to the field of OA because it is able to image all the structural components involved in this whole-organ disease. Radiographs image calcified bone, whereas MRI presents a *proton map,* and the amount of information that MRI can provide is very much dependent on the particular sequences used. For example, the use of the intravenous contrast agent gadolinium allows optimal detection of synovitis, whereas fat-suppressed sequences allow for detection of bone marrow edema (Fig. 39–6). Unlike conventional radiographs, MRI also has the advantage, like computerized tomography, of being tomographic and, therefore, more sensitive in detecting abnormalities such as osteophytes (Fig. 39–7). Optimal sequence setting will depend on the information to be obtained because clinical trials may require different information from clinical practice.

Preliminary work from large MRI cohorts of OA subjects is just emerging; most of this work involves knee OA. Generally abnormalities of all tissues are present with increased frequency with increasing radiographic Killgren-Lawrence grade.[24] There is no consensus yet on the best ways to quantify or score these multi-abnormal features. However the ability of MRI to image joint pathology not seen on conventional radiographs has been highlighted. In a preliminary report of 445 knees with minimal radiographic abnormalities, MRI detected abnormal cartilage morphology in more than 75%, whereas abnormalities of bone marrow, menisci, ligaments, and synovium were seen in 30% to 60%.[25] The old belief that "there is no pathology because the radiograph is normal" is clearly wrong.

Such information throws important new light on our concepts of structure-pain relationships. Generally, more abnormal features correlate with pain. MRI is now providing us with ideas on candidates for structural associations of pain. One MRI study of 150 OA knees suggested that synovial hypertrophy and effusions were associated with pain.[26] Bone marrow edema, a feature described only with MRI and associated with histologic fibrosis and remodeled trabeculae, has

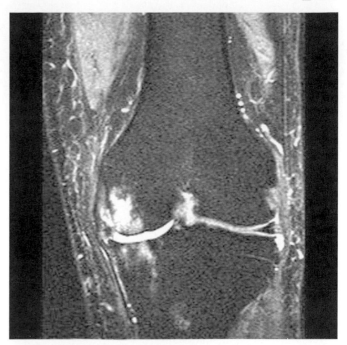

FIGURE 39–6 ■ MRI of an osteoarthritic knee: Coronal STIR sequence demonstrating high signal (*white area*) of both medial tibial and medial femoral bones. This is bone marrow edema. Note that the adjacent meniscus is severely degenerated.

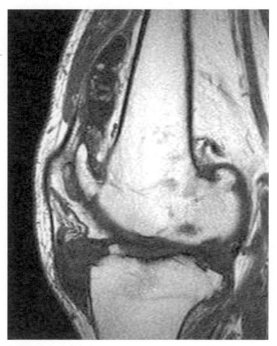

FIGURE 39–7 ■ MRI of an osteoarthritic knee: Sagittal T1-weighted image demonstrating large patellofemoral osteophyte. A posterior femoral condyle osteophyte is also visible.

also been associated with knee pain in another large cohort,[27] although this association is not universal and may relate to the size of the lesions. Bone marrow edema has been associated with compartment-specific progression of joint space loss; this risk for progression persisted even after correction for alignment, another known risk factor for structural progression.[28] MRI has also highlighted the relevance of extra-articular features (e.g., bursitis or iliotibial band syndrome) in causing knee pain.[29]

MRI holds the promise of creating subcategories of OA for targeted therapy, but much more work needs to be done to validate these abnormalities against relevant clinical outcomes and then provide methods that reliably quantify the abnormalities.

Differential Diagnosis

Four issues need to be thought about in the differential diagnosis of OA (1) the differentiation of OA from periarticular problems, referred pain, and generalized musculoskeletal pain (as in fibromyalgia); (2) crystal-associated arthropathies; (3) diffuse idiopathic skeletal hyperostosis (DISH); and (4) the development of complications.

Many aspects of the differentiation of OA *from periarticular disorders, referred pain, or generalized musculoskeletal pain* have just been discussed. However, it must be stressed that OA often occurs with periarticular or generalized musculoskeletal pain. Thus OA of the hip may be complicated by coexisting trochanteric bursitis, or knee OA by anserine bursitis, and anyone with OA may develop pain amplification, generalized pain, or fibromyalgia as well. The frequent coexistence of OA with other morbidity—including depression (its dominance in older people may complicate the situation, making it difficult for the clinician to be certain what the main causes of pain are) create uncertainty about the choice of interventions.

Calcium-containing *crystals* are often present in the tissues and synovial fluid of joints affected by OA. The two main categories are calcium pyrophosphate dihydrate (CPPD) and basic calcium phosphates (BCP), principally hydroxyapatite. The presence of CPPD crystals appears to be a marker of more hypertrophic forms of OA (extensive osteophyte formation and subchondral bone sclerosis) and BCP crystals of more atrophic forms (with destruction of bone). Whether these forms of OA should be regarded as distinct entities (such as pyrophosphate arthropathy or apatite-associated destructive arthropathy) or merely ends of the spectrum of OA changes in joints is contentious, although we favor the spectrum approach versus the distinct entity approach. In addition, these crystals, if released in sufficient quantity into the synovial space, can cause attacks of acute arthritis (pseudogout in the case of CPPD crystals). Pseudogout is the most common form of acute arthritis seen in older people and is particularly likely to occur after surgery for another condition or during an intercurrent illness. The synovial fluid may be blood stained; chondrocalcinosis is usually seen on the radiograph (see Fig. 39–5); and CPPD crystals can be seen in synovial fluid using polarized light microscopy. It is sometimes difficult to distinguish OA from chronic gout pain when the two arthritides coexist, commonly in the first metatarsophalangeal joint. The presence of early morning stiffness in the affected joint or other acutely inflamed joints may favor the diagnosis of gout, but sometimes

a pragmatic pharmacologic reduction of uric acid may be required to exclude ongoing gout.

Diffuse idiopathic skeletal hyperostosis (DISH) is a condition characterized by extensive enthesophyte ossification in the spine leading to bridging of vertebrae, and associated with peripheral enthesophyte ossification. It is a common age-related disorder, with a male-to-female preponderance of 2:1 associated with obesity, diabetes, gout, hypertension, and hyperinsulinemia. It leads to stiffening of the spine and of central peripheral joints such as the shoulder and hip, as well as, in some cases, peripheral joints. The development of peripheral bony enthesopathies may cause pain in some cases, but pain is not nearly as prominent a feature as in OA.

Severe *complications* of OA are rare, but exacerbations of pain are common, and physicians must be aware of the possibility of a serious complication, particularly if the nature of the pain is different, or if an exacerbation is persistent. The most common complication is acute crystal arthritis (see earlier). Acute increase in pain is associated with a warm effusion and crystals can be found in the synovial fluid. The main differential diagnosis is septic arthritis, which can coexist with an acute crystal-related synovitis. Trauma may also lead to rupture of a tendon or ligament, increasing joint instability. Finally, osteonecrosis can occur, particularly at the hip and knee, resulting in severe exacerbation of pain followed by accelerated joint destruction.

▮ THE MANAGEMENT OF OSTEOARTHRITIS

Currently there is no good evidence for disease-modifying therapy in OA: treatment is principally aimed at reducing the consequences of OA, of which pain is the most important. Important principles include the following: avoidance of iatrogenic complications (OA is rarely life threatening and risks of side effects are increased in the elderly, the group most at risk of OA); empowerment of patients to improve self efficacy over pain control and acknowledgment that pain in OA is, like most chronic pain, the result of an interaction between structural factors, host characteristics, and the environment. Implicit in this model is the concept of *individualization:* the development of a treatment strategy for each patient should be based on their particular needs and expectations as well as the evidence base. Management of OA requires a team approach involving healthcare professionals and the patient to develop a package of care tailored to the individual.

Most data on management of peripheral joint OA focus on the knee, although it seems likely that the general management principles will hold for the other common joint sites (hip, hand). There are good reasons for the knee to assume predominance because it is the joint site associated with most morbidity. In a population of 100,000 individuals, some 7500 will have knee pain and disability due to OA of whom about 2000 will have severe disability.[30] Clearly, the burden of such a prevalent condition falls mainly on primary care physicians, and management should be focused on the community rather than the hospital.

Not all individuals with knee pain seek medical attention, even those with severely painful and disabling symptoms. Why some individuals elect to seek care, whereas others do

Table 39–3

Therapeutic Options in the Management of Osteoarthritis

Education	Patient and spouse or family
Weight loss	For the overweight
Social support	Telephone, help lines, support groups, formal cognitive interventions
Exercise	Muscle strengthening, patellar strapping, aerobic exercise (walking, swimming, cycling)
Orthotics/footwear	Aides and appliances, joint protection, insoles
Dietary supplements	Glucosamine, vitamins C and D, ginger, avocado and soybean extracts, fish oils
Topical drugs	Topical nonsteroidal antiinflammatory drugs (NSAIDs), rubefacients, capsaicin
Oral drugs	Analgesics (paracetamol, codydramol, opiates) NSAIDs Cyclooxygenase-2 selective NSAIDs
Intra-articular treatment	Corticosteroids Hyaluronans
Surgical interventions	Tidal lavage and débridement Osteotomy Total joint arthroplasty
Other	Acupuncture, TENS and others

TENS, transcutaneous electrical nerve stimulation.

not is unclear but probably does not simply reflect disease severity (see Table 39–2). Physicians do not see people who are representative of all of those in the community with OA.

Treatments for OA are listed in Table 39–3. Several guidelines for the management of lower limb OA have been produced recently,[31-33] usually by consensus statements from expert panels. These provide a good summary of the evidence base underlying nonsurgical interventions but their use in daily practice is limited by a number of factors:

- Guidelines are designed to be applied to groups of patients, whereas an individualized approach to management is likely to be more effective. Clearly, the need for weight reduction, for example, is greater in some patients than in others.
- By definition, they can evaluate only available data, which for some (especially physical) interventions is sparse. Most published research has examined drugs (59%) or surgery (27%).[34] Most (94%) report positive results, suggesting a bias against publishing negative findings. The European League Against Rheumatism (EULAR) guidelines[33] reviewed 674 papers of which 564 concerned drug or surgical therapy (of which 365 were NSAIDs).
- Recommendations made in guidelines may not be practical due to local constraints or lack of resources.
- Guidelines do not distinguish between provision of primary and secondary care.
- In practice, treatments are rarely applied sequentially: rather, combinations of interventions are applied simultaneously. The effect of such "packages" of care is unknown.

Despite good evidence for many nonsurgical treatments in OA, most patients remain under-managed and significant improvement could be made simply by making better use of the therapies currently available.

Table 39–4

Issues to Be Considered When Planning Management of the Patient with Osteoarthritis

Age
Comorbidities
Risk factors
Impact of osteoarthritis
Individual preference
Availability of services

Table 39–4 indicates the issues that should be considered when planning treatment. The age of the patient is probably the least important but may affect the decision to consider surgery. Exactly how age affects this decision is not clear. Surgeons may prefer to operate on older people, reducing the chances of having to perform difficult revision surgery in the future; patients themselves may feel that younger, more active individuals should have the chance of total joint replacement (TJR). Comorbidity should be considered. Does the patient have contraindications to use of NSAIDs? Does the patient have cardiovascular disease limiting mobility more than the OA? Would the patient have a high operative risk if TJR were to be considered? Risk factors for OA should be assessed: is the patient obese or at risk of occupational overuse? Are there psychosocial factors that may confer a worse prognosis? The impact of OA should be assessed using the International Classification of Function (ICF) model, including pain severity, impairment of function, and the effect on the individual.

The patient's preference for treatment should be explored and attempts should be made to identify the issues that are of importance to that individual. The treatment plan should be developed through a dynamic partnership between patient and doctor. Finally, management is necessarily affected by local service provision such as length of waiting list, access to physiotherapy, and so on.

Given the variability introduced by the factors described, it is rarely practical to follow the standard sequential approach to managing patients advocated by guidelines. For all individuals with OA electing to seek medical care, a minimum care package should be offered including education, exercise, advice on weight reduction, correction of adverse mechanics, and advice on use of simple analgesics.

Education and Empowerment

Education is particularly important in OA. Much depends on the patient assuming control for his or her own care. It should aim to dispel myths such as the inevitability of OA or that "nothing will help" and provide information on the disease process, likely outcome, available treatments (and how to use them), and help with lifestyle adaptations to the disease. "Medicalization" should be avoided if possible: the concept of gradual joint failure with a variety of outcomes is preferable to a "disease" label. The effect of education by itself on important outcomes such as pain appears to be relatively weak, one study showing that only 38% of patients found education moderately or very helpful.[35] More remains to be learned about how and when to deliver education packages, but it may be that education allows a reduction in perceived helplessness, disability, and impact than on pain.

Exercise

Specific muscle-strengthening exercises (e.g., quadriceps for knee) can significantly reduce pain and disability and can be delivered at home.[36] Graded aerobic exercise programs have also been shown to be safe and effective for most individuals with knee OA and may be slightly more beneficial than isometric exercises. Importantly, compliance can be maintained at 60% to 70% with appropriate encouragement and support.[37] Participation in regular exercising can be encouraged by giving patients advice and backing this up with written instructions and literature; by making the exercises practical and enjoyable; and by regularly reinforcing the benefits of remaining active. The mechanism by which aerobic exercise reduces knee pain is unclear. As well as acting to strengthen local muscles (e.g., quadriceps) it may also reduce obesity and has documented psychological effects, including promoting independence, self-confidence, and self-esteem. Exercise is a good example of a treatment for OA that puts patients very much in control of their own management.

Weight Reduction

Obesity is an important risk factor for knee OA: subjects who lose weight are less likely to progress radiographically or to develop symptoms.[38] Proving that weight loss reduces pain levels is difficult—largely because of the problems in achieving significant weight reduction. Weight reduction is often combined with exercise, which itself has an effect on symptoms of OA. More remains to be learned about the best ways of encouraging weight loss: different approaches may be

effective in different individuals. *Weight reduction is a powerful, disease-modifying intervention that deserves intensive effort in all obese patients with lower limb OA.*

Biomechanical Approaches

OA is primarily a biomechanical condition and therapies directed at realignment, correction of deformity, and improved gait are effective and safe. Comfortable shoes with shock-absorbing insoles can reduce pain in OA. Heel wedges are a method of correcting the abnormal biomechanics seen in knee OA. A laterally elevated (valgus) insole may decrease lateral thrust and reduce pain in subjects with medial compartment OA (Fig. 39–8). Knee braces and Neoprene sleeves, combined with muscle-strengthening programs, can reduce pain—probably more by improving proprioception and patellar tracking than by physically realigning the tibiofemoral joint.[39] Provision of a cane or walking stick may reduce pain and improve function by "unloading" the joint. Taping of the patella (Fig. 39–9), designed to apply medial glide and medial tilt with unloading of the infrapatellar fat pad or pes anserinus, is an effective treatment that has been shown to improve pain by as much as 40%. This effect is greater than that seen with a control tape and persists for up to 3 weeks after stopping treatment.[40]

Medication

Patients should be informed about drug options but many may choose not to use drugs. It should be made clear to

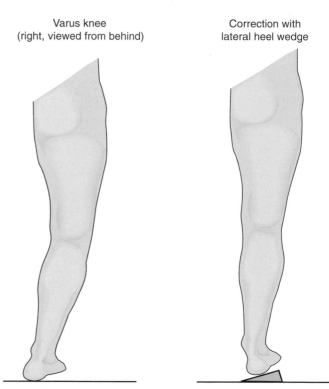

Varus knee
(right, viewed from behind)

Correction with
lateral heel wedge

FIGURE 39–8 ▪ A laterally elevated (valgus) insole within footwear can have the effect of correcting the varus deformity of the knee joint commonly seen in osteoarthritis and correcting much of the biomechanical abnormality. The shoe wedge should be combined with subtalar strapping to maintain the correction. (Adapted from Toda Y, Segal N: Usefulness of an insole with subtalar strapping for analgesia in patients with medial compartment osteoarthritis of the knee. Arthritis Rheum 47:468, 2002.)

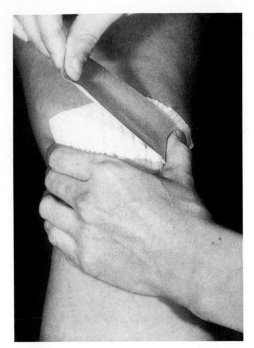

FIGURE 39–9 ■ A clinical photograph of someone undergoing taping for patellofemoral osteoarthritis. The operator is shifting the patella medially with her thumb while applying tape to keep it in that position, thus relieving pressure on the diseased lateral facet of the joint.

patients that drugs are purely for symptom relief and that it is entirely reasonable, if patients prefer, to put up with the pain rather than take medication. The main indication for drug therapy in OA is pain. Pharmacologic therapy should always be added to a program of nonpharmacologic modalities discussed earlier. This is particularly relevant in the elderly who are at high risk for adverse reactions to drugs. Reasons for this include altered drug metabolism associated with aging, increased likelihood of comorbidity and associated polypharmacy, including use of over-the-counter medications, and greater risk of errors in taking proper dosages of medications.

Analgesics

Non-opioid analgesics should probably remain the drug of first choice for symptomatic OA; paracetamol should be given at full dose, up to a maximum of 1 g four times a day, for a reasonable time before other drugs are considered. Paracetamol is superior to placebo and comparable in effectiveness to both ibuprofen and naproxen in patients with knee OA. Compound analgesics including co-proxamol and codydramol are more powerful. Some patients with severe end-stage OA of the hip or knee who are not candidates for total joint arthroplasty because of comorbid medical condition may require chronic treatment with opioid analgesics; in these patients, long-acting preparations of oxycodone or morphine may be used.

Concerns about patient addiction and vulnerability to legal action have led physicians to be reluctant to prescribe these drugs. In fact, addiction rates in otherwise psychologically stable individuals are very low. Reluctance to use powerful opiates is one example of the discrepancy that may exist between patient and doctor in analyzing the risk-benefit tradeoff of interventions: doctors perceive their patients to be suffering less than patients perceive themselves to be; as a result, patients are willing to accept greater risks to achieve pain reduction.

Topical Creams

Topical creams, either capsaicin or NSAIDs, can be helpful as either monotherapy or when added to oral analgesics, especially in patients with OA of the hand or knee if only one or a few joints are involved. In addition, they afford patients a measure of self-control over their therapy which may in itself be beneficial. Capsaicin cream needs to be applied three or four times per day and care must be taken to avoid getting the cream into the eyes or on mucous membranes because of severe burning. Most patients tolerate capsaicin cream, but some notice burning and rash that requires discontinuation.

Nonsteroidal Antiinflammatory Drugs

A variable proportion of patients will not respond to paracetamol, alone or in combination with a topical agent, and derive additional benefit from oral NSAIDs. It is reasonable to try NSAIDs in the elderly if, and only if, nonpharmacologic therapy and paracetamol have failed to provide adequate symptomatic relief. There is no clear evidence to suggest superiority of one NSAID over another; however, a recent meta-analysis found that piroxicam, ketoprofen, tolmetin, and azapropazone were associated with a greater risk of serious gastrointestinal complications, including perforation, ulcers, and bleeding, than other NSAIDs, especially low-dose ibuprofen. General principles of NSAID use in OA include the following: use of the minimum effective dose; avoidance of using more than one NSAID simultaneously; assessment of benefit after about a month (and cessation of a particular NSAID if no benefit is seen); and encouragement of "intelligent noncompliance" (i.e., patients should not feel obliged to take the NSAID if they do not have pain). The patient should be reassessed at 1 month and the additional benefit of NSAID, over and above that of analgesia, should be assessed.

The traditional NSAIDs carry a relatively high risk of adverse events, particularly in older people and especially to the gastrointestinal tract. A new class of NSAIDs, "coxibs," were introduced in the 1990s in the hope that their unique mode of action would avoid gastrointestinal toxicity. The first two agents to be introduced, celecoxib and rofecoxib, were both heavily promoted by the manufacturers for use in OA. It is clear that they can provide useful symptomatic relief in some people with OA and that they are less likely to cause gastrointestinal problems than traditional NSAIDs; however, they carry new risks of their own, to the cardiovascular system.[41] Rofecoxib has been withdrawn from the market, and the place of the other "coxibs" in the management of OA is unclear. Many people with OA have concomitant cardiovascular disease, limiting the use of coxibs.

Nutriceuticals

Many patients will seek alternative or complementary medications: this popular approach should be discussed and patients directed to those supplements for which some evidence of effectiveness exists (e.g., chondroitin, unsaturated oils). Glucosamine is widely used and appears to be relatively safe. Claims for a disease-modifying effect remain controversial but there may be a modest reduction in pain and stiffness by mechanisms that currently remain unclear.

Intra-articular Steroids

Intra-articular steroids are widely used in patients with OA, particularly knee or thumb base OA. Hip OA is also amenable to steroid injection although confirmation that the injection is correctly located—for example by ultrasound control—is recommended. There is good evidence supporting steroid efficacy, but only for up to 4 weeks.[42] This may contrast with clinical practice suggesting that some patients have a sustained response to intra-articular steroid. Triamcinolone hexacetonide at a dose of 40 mg with or without anesthetic is suitable for the knee, and post-injection rest of the injected joint may improve response. Efforts to identify clinical predictors of response have proved largely unsuccessful.

Intra-articular Hyaluronan

Intra-articular hyaluronan (previously *hyaluronic acid*) has also been shown to be effective in reducing pain in patients with mild-to-moderate knee OA confirmed by radiography; this therapy requires weekly injections for 3 to 5 weeks and at least one study has suggested greater efficacy than a single injection of intra-articular steroids. However, the magnitude of the effect is small and must be weighed against cost and the invasive nature of the intervention. Several preparations, which differ largely in molecular weight, are available and may be of value in those patients whose symptoms persist despite standard treatment and in whom surgery is contraindicated.

Surgery

What Operation?

Arthroscopic débridement and lavage is a less invasive option for milder disease, although doubts as to its efficacy have been raised by a recent randomized controlled trial.[43] If just one part of the joint is affected, for example the medial tibiofemoral part of the knee joint, then hemiarthroplasty can be performed. Osteotomy (division and realignment of the femur or tibia is effective at relieving pain and correcting biomechanics and does not preclude more extensive surgery at a later date. In general, however, surgery in OA means total joint replacement (TJR).

Who Currently Gets Total Joint Replacement?

OA is the main disease leading to total hip replacement (THR) or total knee replacement (TKR)—accounting for about 80% of such operations.[44,45] Current rates of joint replacement vary greatly between different countries, and within the United Kingdom there are large (threefold) variations in rates of THR between different regions. Rates of TJR are increasing rapidly—especially as revision surgery.

Women tend to have worse function at the time of surgery than do men. American data suggest that the elderly, obese, and African American populations are less likely to get a TJR than are middle-aged, middle class whites in spite of the fact that there is no evidence that older obese patients have worse outcomes. United Kingdom studies confirm that social deprivation reduces the chance of having a TJR.[46] Risk factors for TJR include pain, radiographic evidence of severe OA, obesity, and heavy manual work.[47]

Who Should Be Referred for Total Joint Replacement?

TJR is an effective but expensive intervention.[44] Although results from TJR in OA are generally excellent, outcomes do vary, with measurable perioperative death and morbidity rates and a small number of patients suffering continuing pain and disability in spite of a replacement.

There are currently no evidence-based indications for TJR in OA. Consensus-based criteria for who should get TJR have been produced in, for example, New Zealand.[48] In general TJR is recommended for moderate-to-severe persistent pain, disability, or both, that is not substantially relieved by an extended course of nonsurgical (medical) management.

Individuals undergoing TJR vary widely in preoperative severity of pain and disability.[44] Although all groups show improvement in terms of function at 3 months, greatest benefit is seen in those with lower baseline disability. There is, therefore, a potential trade-off between operating on more people who have less severe disability because those patients achieve greatest benefit and limiting surgery to those fewer patients with more severe disease, accepting that some of their disability may never improve, even with TJR. Geographic variations suggest that this determinant is already operating: patients in Australia having TJR have lower disability than those in the United States; those in the United Kingdom are most disabled at the time of surgery.

■ PREVENTION OF OSTEOARTHRITIS

The risk factors for large-joint OA are becoming well-understood. Although some (race, gender, age, genetic predisposition) are not possible to change, others are potentially modifiable, raising the possibility of primary prevention. Individuals at high risk for knee OA include those with obesity, a family history of "generalized OA as manifested by presence of nodal OA in the hands, a history of injury, and a high-risk occupation.

Obesity is a major risk factor for development and progression of knee OA and, to a lesser extent, hand and hip OA. Weight reduction has been shown to be disease modifying. Although weight reduction is part of all guidelines for the management of lower limb OA, strategies to reduce the community prevalence of obesity might also reduce the incidence of OA; conversely, the rapid rise in obesity in most Western countries has major implications for the community burden of OA in the future. Tackling obesity in the general population requires major public health initiatives and is likely to be achievable only by a combination of reducing intake (changing what we eat—particularly what our children eat) and increasing energy expenditure by promoting aerobic exercise. Again, exercise is beneficial in established OA but may also have a role in primary prevention: quadriceps weakness is a risk factor for development of OA.[49]

Repetitive adverse loading of the knee (during occupation or extreme competitive sports) is another potentially avoidable risk factor.[38] Occupations involving heavy physical work, especially prolonged kneeling and squatting have approximately twice the risk for knee OA. This risk interacts with that of obesity so that individuals with a body mass index (BMI) of ≥30 who also have occupational risk factors have a greatly increased odds ratio for developing knee OA of about 14.[50]

Not only is the risk of OA increased, but once an individual has OA, the combination of intense physical activity at work and a high BMI significantly increases the risk when undergoing TKR.[47] In this high-risk group, it would be possible to aggressively support weight reduction or discourage obese individuals from performing such jobs. Alterations in work practice by avoiding prolonged work in high-risk postures or using supporting knee pads may theoretically reduce OA.

Injury—for example meniscal damage at the knee—is a powerful, potentially preventable risk factor for later OA. The role of intervention for problems of alignment, joint laxity, and nutritional status is less clear.

Barriers to the Prevention and Management of Osteoarthritis

Some of the main problems encountered when attempting to make a difference in the huge health burden caused by OA include the following:

- The perception that OA is an inevitable consequence of aging for which little can be done. Something can be done for most people presenting with OA problems, and there is much to be offered for prevention.
- The belief that exercise may worsen the disease: although there may be a place for rest during acute flares of pain, there is a risk that rest will lead to a cycle of disuse, muscle atrophy, weakness, and increased pain. Therefore, appropriate exercise is important.
- The importance of nonpharmacologic therapies tends to be underestimated, even though at least two (weight reduction and quadriceps strengthening) are potentially both disease modifying and preventive).
- Therapies are not exclusive: for example intra-articular steroid injections may provide only short-term relief, but they can be used to reduce acute pain so that immediate exercise therapies can be instituted in the pain-free window.
- Packages of care, involving a large number of behavioral and other nonpharmacologic interventions are likely to be the way forward for both prevention and treatment. However, it is difficult to test this hypothesis because it is difficult to obtain funding for complex intervention trials or for the testing of nonpharmacologic treatments.
- There is a need for treatment to be individualized.

■ CONCLUSION

Although thought to be one of the major causes of chronic pain in older people, OA remains poorly understood and difficult to treat effectively. There is an urgent need for more research into the causes and treatment of pain in OA, using the biopsychosocial model, in addition to the reductionist research being undertaken on its pathogenesis.

References

1. Nichols EH, Richardson FL: Arthritis deformans. J Med Res 21:79, 1909.
2. Felson D, Lawrence R, Dieppe P, et al: Osteoarthritis: New insights: Part 1: The disease and its risk factors. Ann Intern Med 133:635, 2000.
3. Lawrence J, Bremner J, Bier F: Osteoarthrosis: Prevalence in the population and relationship between symptoms and x-ray changes. Ann Rheum Dis 25:1, 1966.
4. Creamer P, Lethbridge-Cejku M, Hochberg M: Determinants of pain severity in knee osteoarthritis. J Rheumatol 26:1785, 1999.
5. Dieppe P, Cushnaghan J, Shepstone L: The Bristol 'OA 500' study: Progression of osteoarthritis over 3 years and the relationship between clinical and radiographic changes at the knee joint. Osteoarthritis Cart 5:87,1997.
6. Lanyon P, Muir K, Doherty S, Doherty M: Influence of radiographic phenotype on the risk of hip osteoarthritis within families. Ann Rheum Dis 63:259, 2004.
7. Kellgren J, Moore R: Generalised osteoarthritis and Heberden's nodes. BMJ 1:181, 1952.
8. Dieppe P: What is the relationship between pain and osteoarthritis? Rheum Eur 27:55, 1998.
9. Creamer P, Hochberg M: Why is osteoarthritis painful—sometimes? Br J Rheum 37:726, 1997.
10. Arnoldi C: Vascular aspects of degenerative joint disorders. Acta Orthop Scand 65 (Suppl 261);1, 1994.
11. Creamer P, Hunt M, Dieppe PA: Pain mechanisms in osteoarthritis of the knee: Effect of intraarticular anesthetic. J Rheumatol 23:1031, 1996.
12. Bajaj P, Bajaj P, Graven-Nielsen T, Arendt-Nielsen L: Osteoarthritis and its association with muscle hyperalgesia: An experimental contolled study. Pain 93:107, 2001.
13. Summers MN, Haley WE, Reveille J, Alarcon G: Radiographic assessment and psychological variables as predictors of pain and functional impairment in osteoarthritis of the knee or hip. Arthritis Rheum 31:204, 1988.
14. Creamer P, Hochberg M: The relationship between psychosocial variables and pain reporting in osteoarthritis of the knee. Arthritis Care Res 11:60, 1998.
15. Altman R, Fries J, Bloch D, et al: Development of criteria for the classification and reporting of osteoarthritis of the knee. Arthritis Rheum 29:1039, 1986.
16. Fife RS, Brandt K, Braunstein E, et al: Relationship between arthroscopic evidence of cartilage damage and radiographic evidence of joint space narrowing in early osteoarthritis of the knee. Arthritis Rheum 34:377, 1991.
17. Davis M, Ettinger W, Neuhaus J, et al: Correlates of knee pain among U.S. adults with and without radiographic knee osteoarthritis. J Rheumatol 19:1943, 1992.
18. Bruyere O, Honore A, Rovati L, et al: Radiologic features poorly predict clinical outcomes in knee osteoarthritis. Scand J Rheum 31:1, 2002.
19. Dieppe P, Cushnaghan J, Young P, Kirwan J: Prediction of the progression of joint space narrowing in osteoarthritis of the knee by bone scintigraphy. Ann Rheum Dis 52:557, 1993.
20. McCarthy C, Cushnaghan J, Dieppe P: The predictive role of scintigraphy in radiographic osteoarthritis of the hand. Osteoarthr Cartil 2:25, 1994.
21. Tan AL, Wakefield RJ, Conaghan PG, et al: Imaging of the musculoskeletal system: Magnetic resonance imaging, ultrasonography and computed tomography. Clin Rheumatol 17:513, 2003.
22. D'Agostino MA, Le Bars M, Schmidely N, et al: Interest of ultrasonography to detect synovitis in painful knee osteoarthritis in daily practice. Arthritis Rheum 48(Suppl):S80, 2003.
23. Karim Z, Wakefield R, Conaghan PG, et al: The impact of ultrasonography on diagnosis and management of patients with musculoskeletal conditions. Arthritis Rheum 44:2932, 2001.
24. Link TM, Steinbach LS, Ghosh S, et al: Osteoarthritis: MR imaging findings in different stages of disease and correlation with clinical findings. Radiology 226:373, 2003.
25. Taouli B, Guermazi A, Zaim S, et al: Prevalence and correlates of knee cartilage defects, meniscal lesions and other abnormalities evaluated by MRI in a population sample of knees with normal x-rays. The Health ABC Study. Arthritis Rheum 46(Suppl):S148, 2002.
26. Hill CL, Gale DG, Chaisson CE, et al: Knee effusions, popliteal cysts, and synovial thickening: Association with knee pain in osteoarthritis. J Rheumatol 28:1330, 2001.
27. Felson DT, Chaisson CE, Hill CL, et al: The association of bone marrow lesions with pain in knee osteoarthritis. Ann Intern Med 134:541, 2001.
28. Felson DT, McLaughlin S, Goggins J, et al: Bone marrow edema and its relation to progression of knee osteoarthritis. Ann Intern Med 139:330, 2003.

29. Hill CL, Gale DR, Chaisson CE, et al: Periarticular lesions detected on magnetic resonance imaging: Prevalence in knees with and without symptoms. Arthritis Rheum 48:2836, 2003.
30. McAlindon T, Cooper C, Kirwan J, Dieppe PA: Determinants of disability in osteoarthritis of the knee. Ann Rheum Dis 52:258, 1993.
31. Scott DL: Guidelines for the diagnosis, investigation and management of OA of the hip and knee. J Roy Coll Phys 27:391, 1993.
32. Recommendations for the Medical Management of Osteoarthritis of the Hip and Knee: 2000 update. ACR Subcommittee on Osteoarthritis Guidelines. Arthritis Rheum 43:1905, 2000.
33. Jordan KM, Arden NK, Doherty M, et al: EULAR recommendations 2003: An evidence based approach to the management of knee osteoarthritis: Report of a Task Force of the Standing Committee for International Clinical Studies Including Therapeutic Trials (ESCISIT) Ann Rheum Dis 62:1145, 2003.
34. Chard JA, Tallon D, Dieppe PA: Epidemiology of research into interventions for the treatment of osteoarthritis of the knee joint. Ann Rheum Dis 59:414, 2000.
35. Chard JA, Dickson J, Tallon D, Dieppe PA: A comparison of the views of rheumatologists, general practitioners and patients on the treatment of osteoarthritis. Rheumatology 41:1208, 2002.
36. Thomas KS, Muir KR, Doherty M, et al: Home based exercise programme for knee pain and knee osteoarthritis: Randomised controlled trial. BMJ 325(7367):752, 2002.
37. Ettinger WH, Burns R, Messier SP, et al: A randomized trial comparing aerobic exercise and resistance exercise with a health education program in older adults with knee osteoarthritis. JAMA 277:25, 1997.
38. Felson DT, Zhang Y, Hannan M, et al: Risk factors for incident radiographic knee osteoarthritis in the elderly: The Framingham Study. Arthritis Rheum 40:728, 1997.
39. Kirkley A, Webster-Bogaert S, Litchfield R, et al: The effect of bracing on varus gonarthrosis. J Bone Joint Surg Am 81:539, 1999.
40. Hinman RS, Crossley KM, McConnell J, Bennell KL: Efficacy of knee tape in the management of osteoarthritis of the knee: Blinded randomised controlled trial. BMJ 327(7407):135, 2003.
41. Dieppe PA: Complicity Theory: An explanation of the coxib problem? JRSM 2006.
42. Creamer P: Intra-articular steroid injections in osteoarthritis: Do they work and if so how? Ann Rheum Dis 56:634, 1997.
43. Moseley JB, 'Malley K, Peterson NJ, Menke TJ, et al: A controlled trial of arthroscopic sugery for osteoarthritis of the knee. N Engl J Med 347:81, 2002.
44. Dieppe P, Basler HD, Chard J, et al: Knee replacement surgery for osteoarthritis: Effectiveness, practice variations, indications and possible determinants of utilization. Rheumatology 38:73, 1999.
45. Buckwalter JA, Lohmander S: Operative treatment of osteoarthrosis: Current practice and future development. J Bone Joint Surg 76(A):1405, 1994.
46. Dixon T, Shaw M, Ebrahim S, Dieppe P: Trends in hip and knee joint replacement: Socio-economic inequalities and projections of need. Ann Rheum Dis 63(7):825, 2004.
47. Flugsrud G, Nordsletten L, Espehaug B, et al: Risk factors for total hip replacement due to primary osteoarthritis. Arthritis Rheum 46:675, 2002.
48. Hadorn DC, Holmes AC: Education and debate: The New Zealand priority criteria project, part I: Overview. BMJ 314:131, 1997.
49. Slemenda C, Brandt KD, Heilman DK, et al: Quadriceps weakness and osteoarthritis of the knee. Ann Intern Med 127:97, 1997.
50. Coggon D, Croft P, Kellingray S, et al: Occupational physical activities and osteoarthritis of the knee. Arthritis Rheum 43:1443, 2000.

chapter 40

The Connective Tissue Diseases

Steven D. Waldman

The connective tissue diseases are a heterogeneous group of syndromes that have in common a number of features including (1) they are multisystem diseases; (2) there is significant overlap of the signs and symptoms associated with these diseases; (3) blood vessels and connective tissue are frequently affected; (4) there are significant abnormalities of the immune response that often account for the tissue damage associated with these diseases; (5) these diseases affect females more commonly than males; and (6) onset occurs more often in winter than in summer in the Northern Hemisphere (Table 40–1).[1] Common connective tissue diseases include rheumatoid arthritis, systemic lupus erythematosus, systemic sclerosis (also known as scleroderma), polymyositis and dermatomyositis, polymyalgia rheumatica, temporal arteritis, and polyarteritis nodosa (Table 40–2). Previously known as the collagen vascular diseases, the term connective tissue diseases is now preferred because it more accurately reflects the fact that collagen is just one type of connective tissue affected in patients suffering from this group of diseases.

■ RHEUMATOID ARTHRITIS

Rheumatoid arthritis (RA) is the most common of the connective tissue diseases with approximately 1.5% of the population affected. The cause of RA is unknown but there appears to be a genetic predisposition to the development of this disease. Environmental factors may trigger the activation of RA and initiate the autoimmune response that ultimately can lead to potentially devastating multisystem disease. The possibility of an infectious etiology has gained new credence as the pathophysiologic processes behind Lyme disease are being elucidated.

The disease can occur at any age with the juvenile variant termed *Still disease*. Patients between the ages of 22 and 55 are most often affected with increasing incidence with age.[2] Women are affected 2.5 times more often than men. Although the clinical diagnosis of RA is usually obvious in full-blown cases, the variability of presentation, severity, and progression can make the disease more difficult to diagnose. Because of the nonspecific nature of the signs and symptoms of RA, as well as the significant overlap of symptoms associated with other connective tissue diseases, the American College of Rheumatology has promulgated useful guidelines to assist the clinician in the its diagnosis. These guidelines are presented in Table 40–3.

Signs and Symptoms

The onset of the disease may be subtle with nonspecific early signs and symptoms. Easy fatigability, malaise, myalgias, anorexia, and generalized weakness are often the first symptoms the patient with RA may experience. Ill-defined morning stiffness most often will progress to symmetrical joint pain with color, tenosynovitis, and fusiform joint effusions (Fig. 40–1).[3] The rubor accompanying many of the other inflammatory arthritides (e.g., gout, septic arthritis, and so on) is not a predominant feature of RA. The wrists, knees, ankles, fingers, and bones of the feet are most often affected, although any joint can be affected. Untreated, the synovitis becomes worse and joint effusions are common (Fig. 40–2). Tendons may become inflamed and may spontaneously rupture.[4] Ultimately, the destruction of the cartilage and supportive bone will result in severe disability and pain. Deformities of the affected joints, including flexion contractures, ulnar drift of the fingers, and wrist as a result of slippage of the extensor tendons off the metacarpophalangeal joints, will ultimately occur with poorly treated or untreated disease (Fig. 40–1).

Extra-articular manifestations of RA are common. Carpal tunnel syndrome is frequently associated with RA and, in fact, may point to diagnosis if the clinician thinks about it.[5] Carpal tunnel syndrome and the other entrapment neuropathies such as tardy ulnar palsy are the result of proliferation and thickening of the affected connective tissue. Ruptured Baker cysts are not uncommonly seen in patients with RA and can mimic deep vein thrombosis leading to unnecessary anticoagulation therapy (Fig. 40–3).[6] Other extra-articular manifestations of RA include rheumatoid nodules, which are painless masses that appear under the skin and around the extensor tendons. These nodules can also occur in the lung. Ocular manifestations are common, and uveitis and iritis can be quite severe. Vasculitis and anemia can also occur and if undiagnosed can lead to life-threatening multisystem organ failure. Pericarditis and pleuritis herald significant extra-articular disease and must be treated aggressively.[7]

These signs and symptoms of RA are the result of the autoimmune response associated with the disease. Immunologic abnormalities associated with RA include inflammatory

Table 40–1

Common Features of the Connective Tissue Diseases

They are multisystem diseases

There is significant overlap of the signs and symptoms associated with these diseases

Blood vessels and connective tissue are frequently affected

There are significant abnormalities of the immune response which often accounts for the tissue damage associated with these diseases

These diseases affect females more commonly than males

Onset occurs more commonly in winter than in summer in the Northern Hemisphere

Table 40–2

The Connective Tissue Diseases

Rheumatoid arthritis (RA)
Systemic lupus erythematosus (SLE or lupus)
Polymyositis-dermatomyositis (PM-DM)
Systemic sclerosis (SSc or scleroderma)
Sjögren syndrome (SS)
Various forms of vasculitis.

Table 40–3

Clinical Classification Criteria for Rheumatoid Arthritis*

Using history, physical examination, laboratory and radiographic findings—four of the following symptoms must be present with the first four symptoms present a minimum of 6 weeks:

- Morning stiffness ≥1 hour
- Arthritis of three or more of the following joints: right or left PIP, MCP, wrist, elbow, knee, ankle, or MTP joints
- Arthritis of wrist, MCP, or PIP joint
- Symmetrical involvement of joints
- Rheumatoid nodules over bony prominences, or extensor surfaces, or in juxta-articular regions
- Positive serum rheumatoid factor
- Radiographic changes including erosions or bony decalcification localized in or adjacent to the involved joints

*From the American College of Rheumatology Subcommittee on Osteoarthritis Guidelines: Arthritis Rheum 43(9): 1905, 2000.

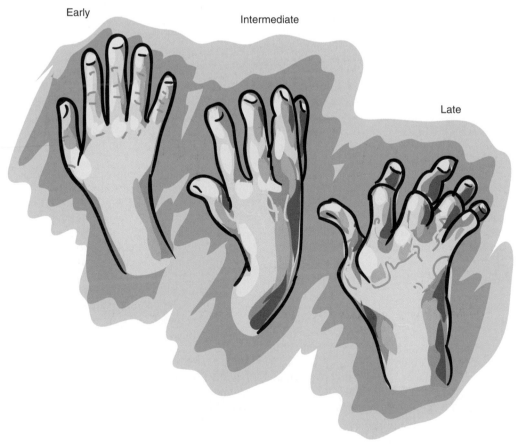

Early   Intermediate   Late

FIGURE 40–1 ▉ Stages of rheumatoid arthritis.

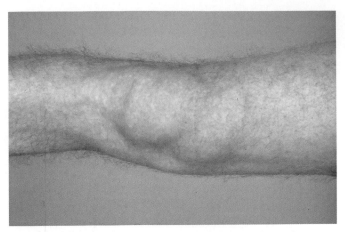

FIGURE 40–2 ■ Early rheumatoid arthritis of the knee showing extension of a small effusion into the suprapatellar pouch. (From Klippel JH, Dieppe PA [eds]: Rheumatology, 2nd ed. Philadelphia, Mosby, 1997, p 5.3.4, Figure 3.8.)

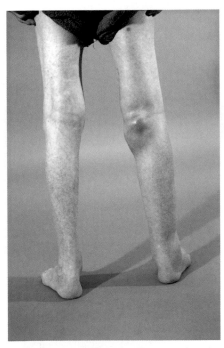

FIGURE 40–3 ■ Baker's popliteal cyst. Posterior view showing rheumatoid swelling behind the right knee. Swelling of the lower limb was related to venous compression by popliteal synovitis. (From Klippel JH, Dieppe PA [eds]: Rheumatology, 2nd ed. Philadelphia, Mosby, 1997, p 5.3.10 Figure 3.18.)

immune complexes in the synovial fluid as well as antibodies that are produced by the patient's own plasma cells. Among these antibodies is a substance called RF factor, which also serves as the basis of the serologic test used in the diagnosis of RA. As RA progresses, the patient's own T-helper cell lymphocytes infiltrate the synovial tissue of the joints. These T-helper cells produce cytokines that facilitate the inflammatory response and contribute to ongoing joint damage. Macrophages and their cytokines (e.g., tumor necrosis factor, granulocyte-macrophage colony-stimulating factor) are also abundant in diseased synovium. Increased adhesion mole-

cules contribute to inflammatory cell migration and retention in the synovial tissue. Increased macrophage-derived lining cells are prominent along with some lymphocytes and vascular changes in early disease.

Prominent immunologic abnormalities that may be important in pathogenesis of RA include immune complexes found in joint fluid cells and in vasculitis. Plasma cells produce antibodies (e.g., rheumatoid factor [RF]) that contribute to these complexes. Lymphocytes that infiltrate the synovial tissue are primarily T-helper cells, which can produce proinflammatory cytokines. Macrophages are also present in the diseased synovium of the patient suffering from RA and produce additional cytokines—which attract other cells involved in the inflammatory response—further perpetuating joint damage as well as setting the stage for vasculitis. These cells produce a variety of other substances that damage the joint, including fibrin, prostaglandins, collagenase, and interleukin-2. This ongoing inflammatory response leads to thickening of the synovium of the affected joints with pannus formation.

Laboratory Findings

A normochromic normocytic anemia is a common finding in patients suffering from RA with the patient's hemoglobin being mildly decreased with levels greater than 10g/dL usually seen unless there has been chronic bleeding from vasculitis of the stomach, kidneys, and so on. Neutropenia can occur in a small percentage of patients with RA and is usually associated with splenomegaly, which is termed *Felty syndrome*. Thrombocytosis and mild-to-moderate hypergammaglobulinemia may also be present. The erythrocyte sedimentation rate (ESR) is elevated in more than 90% of patients suffering from RA as is the C-reactive protein.

Antibodies to the aforementioned gamma globulins can be detected by a latex agglutination test and are called *rheumatoid factors* (RF).[8] Although not 100% diagnostic for RA, RF titers greater than 1:160 dilution are highly suggestive of the disease and their presence makes the diagnosis of RA one of exclusion. The RF titer is indicative of the severity of the disease with higher titers signaling more severe disease. These titers will drop and can be used as a rough measure of the success of the various treatments available for RA.

Synovial fluid analysis of patients suffering from active RA will reveal a leukocytosis consisting of predominately polymorphonuclear cells with lymphocytes and monocytes also present. The viscosity is decreased and the protein levels are increased. Unlike the crystal arthropathies, no crystals are present.

Radiographic Findings

Early in the course of the disease, the radiographic findings of RA are nonspecific and are often limited to soft tissue swelling and a suggestion of increased synovial fluid. As the disease progresses, osteochondral destruction and pannus formation become more evident. The earliest specific radiographic findings of RA are most often found in the second and third metacarpophalangeal joints and the third proximal interphalangeal joints.[9] Fusiform soft tissue swelling, concentric loss of the joint space, and periarticular loss of bone

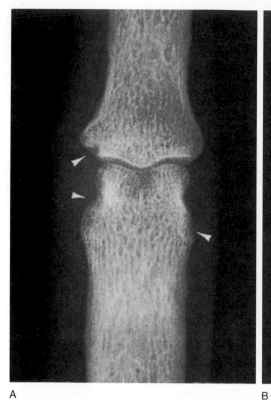 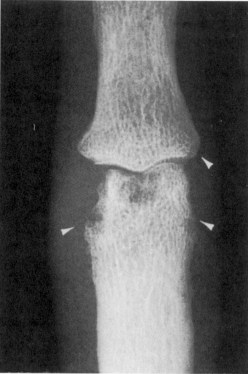

A   B

FIGURE 40–4 ■ Proximal interphalangeal joint abnormalities: Early changes. **A,** Initial radiographic changes include soft tissue swelling, joint space narrowing, and marginal erosions (*arrowheads*) **B,** Subsequently (in another digit), further loss of interosseous space and progressive erosions are evident (*arrowheads*). Note that the erosive changes are more extensive on the proximal phalanx than on the middle phalanx. (From Resnick D: Diagnosis of Bone and Joint Disorders, 4th ed. Philadelphia, Saunders, 2002, p 897, Fig. 21–4A and B.)

are also seen as are marginal erosions of the articular surfaces that have lost their protective articular cartilage (Fig 40–4). Superficial erosions beneath inflamed tendon sheaths may also occur. With further destruction of the joint, complete loss of the articular space can be seen and a variety of deformities and deviations of the joints and bones may occur (e.g., boutonnière and swan neck deformities of the digits; Fig 40–5). The characteristic ulnar drift or deviation of the metacarpophalangeal joints is pathognomonic of RA; this can be diagnosed by visual inspection of the affected joints and is vividly demonstrated on plain radiographs and magnetic resonance imaging (Fig. 40–6).

Differential Diagnosis

As mentioned earlier, the nonspecific nature of many of the signs and symptoms associated with RA, coupled with the significant overlap of symptoms associated with the other causes of arthritis and the connective tissue diseases, may make the diagnosis of RA challenging.[1] The American College of Rheumatology diagnostic guidelines presented in Table 40–3 may help decrease the confusion, but the clinician should be cautioned that more than one form of arthritis may coexist and synovial fluid analysis, which is often overlooked, may be the quickest way to sort things out.[10]

Osteoarthritis can be difficult to distinguish from early or mild RA because nontraumatic osteoarthritis is often symmetrical, with joint swelling and pain. Like RA, rubor is not a prominent feature of osteoarthritis when compared with the crystal and infectious arthropathies. Osteoarthritis preferentially affects the proximal and distal interphalangeal joints (as characterized by Heberden and Bouchard nodules), first carpometacarpal and first metatarsophalangeal joints, knee, shoulder joints, and spine early in the course of the disease,

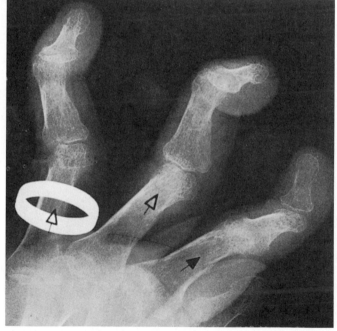

FIGURE 40–5 ■ Boutonnière and swan-neck deformities of the digits. A typical swan-neck deformity of the third and fourth digits (*open arrows*) and boutonnière deformity of the second digit (*closed arrow*) are evident in this patient with rheumatoid arthritis. (From Resnick D: Diagnosis of Bone and Joint Disorders, 4th ed. Philadelphia, Saunders, 2002, p 899, Fig. 21–7.)

whereas RA preferentially affects the second and third metacarpophalangeal joints and the third proximal interphalangeal joints (Figs. 40–7, 40–8). The absence of significantly elevated RF and ESR, rheumatoid nodules, and systemic symptomatology can also help distinguish RA from

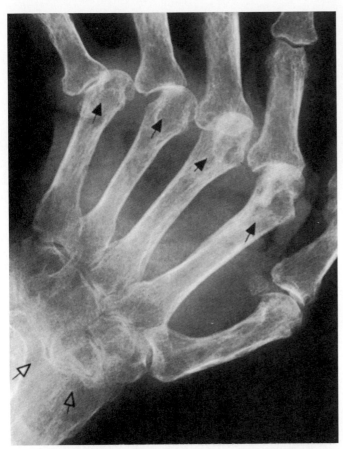

FIGURE 40–6 ■ Ulnar deviation of metacarpophalangeal joint. The simultaneous occurrence of ulnar deviation at the metacarpophalangeal joints (*solid arrows*) and radial deviation at the radiocarpal joint of the wrist (*open arrows*) is well shown in this patient. The resulting appearance is termed the zigzag deformity. (From Resnick D: Diagnosis of Bone and Joint Disorders, 4th ed. Philadelphia, Saunders, 2002, p 901, Fig. 21–8B.)

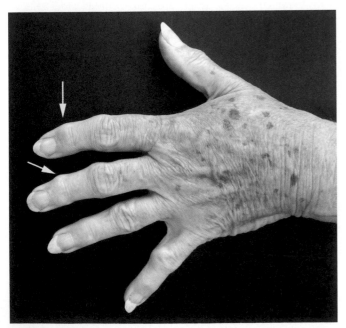

FIGURE 40–7 ■ The Heberden node sign for osteoarthritis of the distal interphalangeal joints. (From Waldman SD: Physical Diagnosis of Pain. Philadelphia, Saunders, 2005, p 197, Fig. 97-1.)

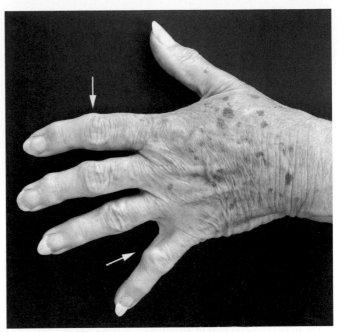

FIGURE 40–8 ■ The Bouchard node sign for osteoarthritis of the proximal interphalangeal joints. (From Waldman SD: Physical Diagnosis of Pain. Philadelphia, Saunders, 2005, p 198, Fig. 98-1.)

osteoarthritis. Evaluation of the synovial fluid in patients suffering form osteoarthritis will reveal white blood cell counts much lower than those seen in RA.

After osteoarthritis, systemic lupus erythematosus is probably the disease most commonly confused with active RA, although all of the other connective tissue diseases can, at times, be difficult to distinguish from RA. These diseases will be discussed in greater detail subsequently, and the diagnostic criteria presented should aid the clinician in the differential diagnosis of confusing clinical presentations of symmetrical arthritis.

In addition to the connective tissue diseases and crystal arthropathies—such as gout and pseudogout—amyloidosis, celiac disease, and sarcoidosis may also mimic RA as can acute rheumatic fever secondary to streptococcal infections. Infectious arthritis usually manifests as a monoarticular or asymmetrical arthritis—as does Lyme disease and Reiter's syndrome. Ankylosing spondylitis preferentially affects males and involves the sacroiliac joints and axial skeleton to a much greater extent than the peripheral joints.

Treatment

Although there is no cure for RA, most patients will experience good-to-excellent palliation of their symptoms and decrease the potential for severe disability with appropriate treatment of their disease.[11] In spite of optimal treatment, 8% to 10% of patients suffering from RA will experience serious disability that will interfere with the ability to provide self-care and carry out their activities of daily living.

The initial treatment of RA should focus on two factors (1) rest and protection of affected joints; and (2) aggressive treatment of the acute inflammatory process. The failure to rest and splint the joints acutely inflamed by RA can often lead to irreversible joint damage with attendant pain and disability. Splinting may also help slow the progression of hand and foot deformities that can be so distressing and disabling to the patient suffering from RA. Aggressive treatment of the inflammatory response associated with acute RA requires skillful use of the drugs discussed subsequently.

Pharmacologic Treatment with Anti-inflammatory Agents

Acute inflammation should be treated aggressively with the nonsteroidal antiinflammatory drugs (NSAIDs)—such as aspirin, ibuprofen, and the like. These drugs have significant renal, gastrointestinal, and hepatic side effects and must be used with caution. For patients with gastrointestinal side effects, enteric coated products or the nonacetylated salicylates, such as salsalate or choline magnesium salicylate, may be considered. The addition of cytoprotective drugs such as misoprostol or the proton pump inhibitors such as ranitidine may also help decrease the incidence of gastrointestinal side effects and allow the RA patient to continue to take these much needed drugs.[12] For patients who cannot tolerate the NSAIDs, the COX-2 inhibitors may be considered with an eye to their potential cardiac side effects. Fish oil supplementation may also help suppress intra-articular prostaglandins as well as promote cardiovascular health. Whether these drugs alter the ultimate course of the disease remains an area of intense debate.

Although NSAIDs are generally the first line of treatment for acute RA, it should be remembered that corticosteroids can provide dramatic relief of the pain and disability associated with acute exacerbations of the disease. Unfortunately, there are two major problems associated with the use of corticosteroids in the treatment of acute RA: (1) corticosteroids tend to become less effective in suppressing the acute inflammatory response over time; and (2) this class of drugs has significant side effects with chronic use. Like the NSAIDs, it is unclear whether treatment with corticosteroids will alter the ultimate course of RA in the individual patient, although the ability of this class of drugs to palliate the acute symptoms of RA is unsurpassed. In general, daily treatment of RA with corticosteroids should be limited to those patients who are unable to tolerate other treatment options or in those patients with life-threatening extra-articular manifestations of the disease, e.g., pericarditis, pleurisy, nephritis. Injection of acutely inflamed and painful joints with small amounts of antiinflammatory steroid may be useful to provide symptomatic relief, stop the inflammatory process, and allow the patient to avoid all of the side effects associated with the systemic administration of this class of drugs.

Pharmacologic Treatment with Disease-Modifying Drugs

As mentioned, it is unclear whether an NSAID or corticosteroid as a sole therapeutic agent can effectively modify the course of RA. For this reason, there is a move toward the use of disease-modifying drugs such as methotrexate, hydroxychloroquine, sulfasalazine, penicillamine, and gold salts earlier in the course of the disease. Methotrexate is an immunosuppressive drug that is reasonably well tolerated and is increasingly becoming a first-line drug in the treatment of RA (see later).[13] Gold is available as a parenteral solution that is usually administered via intramuscular injection on a

weekly basis; it is also available as an oral formulation. Although effective in the treatment of RA, gold salts are not without side effects. These side effects include significant renal and hepatic toxicity as well as potentially life-threatening skin and blood dyscrasias.

If gold therapy is ineffective or causes toxic side effects, oral penicillamine may be considered. Potentially serious side effects associated with penicillamine therapy include bone marrow suppression, renal damage, a lupus-like syndrome (Goodpasture syndrome), and myasthenia gravis. Careful monitoring for these potentially life-threatening side effects is mandatory and the drug should be used only by those familiar with its potential toxicity.

Hydroxychloroquine can also provide symptomatic relief for the patient suffering from mild to moderately active RA. Reasonably well tolerated, the major serious side effects of this drug include myopathy, which may be irreversible, and ophthalmologic side effects including reversible corneal opacities and potentially irreversible retinal degeneration. Both of these serious side effects require careful neurologic and ophthalmologic monitoring while the drug is being used.

Sulfasalazine, which is used primarily for treatment of ulcerative colitis, may also be used to treat RA. Less toxic than gold and penicillamine, it is slower acting but generally well tolerated. An enteric coated product has increased its tolerability. Monitoring of basic hematologic and blood chemistries to identify the relatively uncommon hematologic, renal, and hepatic side effects should be carried out in all patients treated with this drug

Pharmacologic Treatment with Immunosuppressive Drugs

In addition to the aforementioned disease-modifying drugs, the immunosuppressive drugs including methotrexate, azathioprine, and cyclosporine are increasingly being used relatively early in the course of RA. These drugs have in common their ability to suppress active inflammation in RA. Generally well tolerated, these drugs are not without side effects. Careful monitoring for bone marrow suppression, hepatic and renal dysfunction, and pneumonitis is mandatory. The potential of the immunosuppressive drugs to trigger malignancy is of real concern, especially with prolonged use of azathioprine.

As mentioned, the immunosuppressive drug methotrexate is now being used early in the course of active RA. It can be given orally as a once a week dose and is generally well tolerated. Side effects include interference with folic acid metabolism, which requires concomitant folic acid replacement. Methotrexate also has significant hepatotoxicity in some patients and any elevation of liver function tests and potentially fatal fibrosis of the liver requires immediate attention and liver biopsy. Although rare, fatal pneumonitis has been reported with the use of methotrexate in the treatment of RA.

Etanercept and infliximab are new disease-modifying drugs that have shown promise when given alone or in combination with methotrexate in the management of RA.[14] Both etanercept and infliximab block tumor necrosis factor alpha—a protein that the body produces during the inflammatory response.[15] The increased amounts of tumor necrosis factor alpha seen in patients with acute RA accelerate the inflammatory response and contribute to the pain, swelling, and stiffness associated with the disease. The mechanism of action for these drugs is thought to be via the binding of free tumor necrosis factor alpha, thereby decreasing the amounts available to promote the inflammatory response. Given via subcutaneous injection twice a week, etanercept is well tolerated with rare side effects including neurologic dysfunction, optic neuritis, and occasionally pancytopenia. Infliximab is given via intravenous infusion and these infusions are often accompanied by chills, fever, blood pressure abnormalities, and rash. These drugs should not be used in patients with active infections because even minor infections may become life threatening due to the drug's ability to suppress the inflammatory response. Reactivation of tuberculosis has also been reported following administration of these drugs when treating RA.

Treatment with Physical Modalities, Orthotics, and Physical and Occupational Therapy

As mentioned earlier, the pharmacologic treatment of the pain and disability of RA is only one part of a successful treatment strategy. Just as acute inflammation must be aggressively treated to avoid further joint destruction, the aggressive use of physical modalities, orthotics, and physical and occupational therapy is paramount to modify the relentless progression of inadequately treated RA.[16]

The use of local heat and cold can provide significant symptomatic relief for the pain, swelling, and stiffness of RA. Although conventional wisdom suggests that the application of heat should be avoided in the acutely inflamed joint, many patients suffering from RA find superficial moist heat to provide significant symptomatic relief. Other patients find the use of superficial cold more beneficial. Deep heating modalities such as ultrasound and diathermy should be avoided during the acute phases of RA, but may be useful as part of a comprehensive rehabilitation program for joints that are no longer acutely inflamed.

The use of orthotic devices to prevent joint deformity is an integral part of the treatment of the patient with RA. The use of night splints to slow the progression of ulnar drift should be considered early in the course of the disease. The use of shoe inserts and careful fitting of shoes can also help preserve function and ease pain. Protection of the elbows and Achilles tendons during periods of bedrest will also decrease the development of rheumatoid nodules at pressure areas. As the acute inflammation is brought under control, a gentle physical therapy program that focuses on reconditioning, joint protection, and restoration of range of motion and function should be undertaken.

Perhaps nowhere else in medicine is the role of patient education and the use of assistive devices more important than in the care of the patient suffering from RA. Instruction in proper lifting techniques and joint protection strategies as well as training in the use of assistive devices such as jar openers and button hooks are paramount if preservation of joint function is to be achieved.

Surgical Treatment Options

Surgical treatment should be limited to the repair of acute joint injuries (e.g., subluxated joints, torn cartilage, ruptured tendons, and so on) and the release of associated entrapment neuropathies. Total joint arthroplasty is indicated in those patients with severely damaged joints that are compromising the patient's ability to provide self-care and carry out their

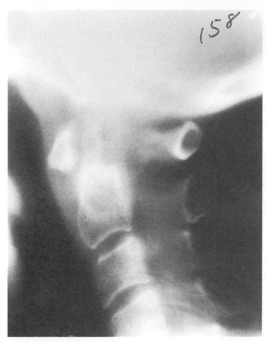

FIGURE 40–9 ■ CT scan of cervical spine showing erosion of the odontoid. (From Klippel JH, Dieppe PA [eds]: Rheumatology, 2nd ed. Philadelphia, Mosby, 1997, p 5.4.5, Fig. 4.10.)

activities of daily living. It should be remembered that patients suffering from RA are at particular risk for C1-C2 subluxations and that early surgical treatment may be required to avoid fatal spinal cord injury (Fig. 40–9). Any surgical interventions should include a concurrent plan of physical medicine and rehabilitation to avoid further loss of function in the postoperative period.

■ SYSTEMIC LUPUS ERYTHEMATOSUS

The second most common connective tissue disease encountered in clinical practice, systemic lupus erythematosus (SLE) is a disease of unknown etiology.[17] Ninety percent of patients suffering from SLE are women. There is an increased incidence of this disease among African Americans and Asians.[18] Affecting the joints, skin, blood vessels, and major organ systems, SLE has the potential to cause much suffering and disability—although a milder, less virulent variant of the disease is less problematic.

Signs and Symptoms

As mentioned, there is a wide spectrum of how SLE manifests. The clinical picture can range from a mild, nonprogressive disease to an aggressive syndrome affecting multiple organ systems and producing life-threatening sequelae.[19] SLE may manifest as an acute febrile illness with arthralgias and rash that are difficult to distinguish from the acute febrile exanthemas with involvement of the central nervous system and other major organ systems—or the onset may be much more subtle and insidious, leading to significant delays in diagnosis. Manifestations referable to any organ system may appear.[20] Either the cutaneous manifestations or the almost

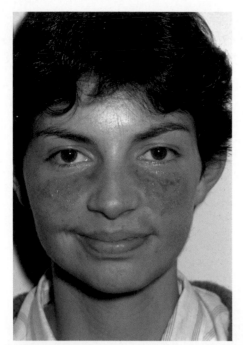

FIGURE 40–10 ■ Erythematous malar rash of systemic lupus erythematosus. Note that the rash does not cross the nasolabial fold. (From Klippel JH, Dieppe PA [eds]: Rheumatology, 2nd ed. Philadelphia, Mosby, 1997, p 7.1.3, Fig. 1.4.)

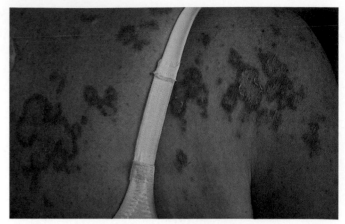

FIGURE 40–11 ■ Subacute cutaneous lupus lesions. (From Klippel JH, Dieppe PA [eds]: Rheumatology, 2nd ed: Philadelphia, Mosby, 1997, p 7.1.3, Fig. 1.5).

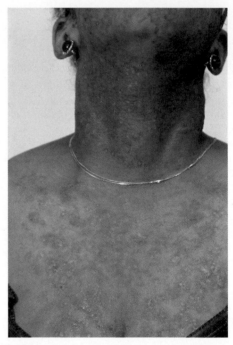

FIGURE 40–12 ■ Discoid lupus involving neck and upper chest. The lesions have characteristic central scarring. (From Klippel JH, Dieppe PA [eds]: Rheumatology, 2nd ed: Philadelphia, Mosby, 1997, p 7.1.3, Fig. 1.6.)

universal complaint of polyarthralgias usually lead the clinician to think about the diagnosis of SLE.[21]

Although polyarthritis is present in more than 90% of patients with SLE, in contradistinction to RA, the joint disease associated with SLE tends to be much less destructive and deforming.[22,23] This form of nonerosive arthritis called *Jaccoud arthritis* is usually seen in SLE patients who present acutely with a constellation of symptoms reminiscent of acute rheumatic fever. In rare patients, significant joint destruction and deformity resembling that seen in RA can be observed.[24]

The characteristic cutaneous lesion associated with SLE is the butterfly rash (Fig. 40–10).[21] A variant form of SLE, which is characterized by discoid cutaneous lesions, is known as discoid lupus erythematosus (Fig. 40–11). The discoid variant of the disease tends to be milder with less systemic involvement than SLE (Fig. 40–12). Recurrent mouth ulcers and focal areas of alopecia are reasonably common, as are purpuric lesions secondary to small vessel vasculitis (Figs. 40–13, 40–14). Photosensitivity is reported by more 40% of patients suffering from SLE.[25]

In addition to the joint and dermatologic manifestations of SLE, the clinician will do well to remember that this disease can affect virtually any organ system. Table 40–4 provides some of the common extra-articular manifestations of SLE. These include vasculitis, pleuritis, pneumonitis, myocarditis, endocarditis, pericarditis, glomerulonephritis, hepatitis, splenomegaly, and generalized adenopathy (Fig. 40–15).[21,26] Hematologic side effects including pancytopenia, thrombocytopenia, leukopenia, and a hypercoagulable state with secondary pulmonary and coronary artery embolic phenomenon and/or thrombosis can occur. Neurologic dysfunction including headaches, seizures, confusion, and occasionally frank psychosis can occur.[27]

Laboratory Findings

The antinuclear antibody (ANA) test is positive in more than 98% of patients suffering from SLE.[28] Occasional false positives occur in those patients with serology that is positive for syphilis, and positive ANA titers can occur from drug-induced lupus like states. If the clinical diagnosis is in doubt or if a patient's presentation is highly selective for SLE but the ANA is negative, more specific testing for the presence of anti–double-stranded DNA antibody can help clarify the situation because high titers of anti–double-stranded DNA antibody are highly specific for SLE.

The ESR is significantly elevated in most patients suffering from SLE. In contradistinction to RA with consistently

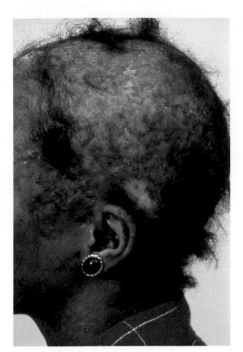

FIGURE 40–13 ■ Scarring discoid lupus of the scalp with permanent alopecia. (From Klippel JH, Dieppe PA [eds]: Rheumatology, 2nd ed: Philadelphia, Mosby, 1997, p 7.1.4, Fig.1.7.)

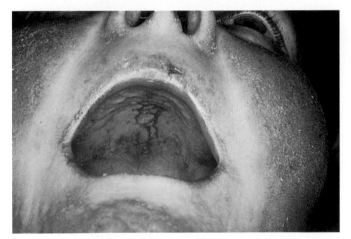

FIGURE 40–14 ■ Mouth ulcers in a patient with systemic lupus erythematosus. (From Klippel JH, Dieppe PA [eds]: Rheumatology, 2nd ed: Philadelphia, Mosby, 1997, p 7.1.4, Fig. 1.8.)

FIGURE 40–15 ■ Gangrene of the toe in a patient with systemic lupus erythematosus and vasculitis. (From Klippel JH, Dieppe PA [eds]: Rheumatology, 2nd ed. Philadelphia, Mosby, 1997, p 7.1.4, Fig. 1.11.)

Table 40–4

Extra-Articular Manifestations of Systemic Lupus Erythematosus

Dermatologic manifestations
  Butterfly rash
  Discoid lesions
  Focal alopecia
  Maculopapular lesions
Vascular manifestations
  Vasculitis
  Thrombosis
Pulmonary manifestations
  Pleuritis
  Pleural effusion
  Pleurisy
  Pulmonary embolus
Cardiac manifestations
  Myocarditis
  Endocarditis
  Pericarditis
Renal manifestations
  Proteinuria
  Glomerulonephritis
Hepatic manifestations
  Hepatitis
Hematologic manifestations
  Pancytopenia
  Leukopenia
  Thrombocytopenia
  Hypercoagulable state
Neurologic manifestations
  Headaches
  Seizures
  Peripheral neuropathy
  Stroke
  Confusion
  Psychosis
Generalized lymphadenopathy
Splenomegaly

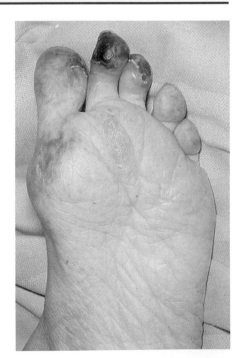

elevated C-reactive protein levels, C-reactive protein levels are surprisingly low, even in the face of active disease. As mentioned earlier, a wide range of hematologic abnormalities including pancytopenia, thrombocytopenia, leukopenia, and coagulopathy may be present. The presence of high levels of anticardiolipin antibodies should alert the clinician to the significantly increased possibility of hypercoagulability.

Differential Diagnosis

SLE is obvious when a patient (particularly a young woman) is febrile with an erythematous skin rash, polyarthritis, evidence of renal disease, intermittent pleuritic pain, leukopenia, and hyperglobulinemia with anti–double-stranded DNA antibodies. Early-stage SLE can be difficult to differentiate from other connective tissue disorders and may be mistaken for RA if arthritic symptoms predominate. Mixed connective tissue disease has the clinical features of SLE with overlapping features of systemic sclerosis, rheumatoid-like polyarthritis, and polymyositis or dermatomyositis (see later).[21,26]

As mentioned earlier, there are several drugs in current clinical use that can produce a clinical syndrome that resembles SLE and can also produce a positive ANA test. These drugs include hydralazine, procainamide, and several beta blockers. The lupus-like symptoms and positive ANA generally disappear after discontinuation of the offending drug.

Treatment

In general, if SLE is diagnosed early in the course of the disease and its affects on the joints and other organ systems are appropriately treated, the long-term prognosis of this disease is much better than for many of the other connective tissue diseases. The rational treatment of SLE is driven by the severity and extra-articular manifestations of the disease because long-term studies have shown that much of the morbidity and, in some cases mortality, associated with SLE are iatrogenically introduced complications of treatment. For purposes of treatment, SLE is divided into mild and severe disease classifications.

Mild SLE is manifested by fever, arthralgias, headache, rash, and mild pericarditis. Severe SLE is characterized by the symptoms of pleural effusions, severe pericarditis, myocarditis, renal dysfunction, thrombocytopenic purpura, vasculitis, hemolytic anemia, hypercoagulable state, and significant central nervous system involvement.[29-32] The patient with severe SLE must be viewed as suffering from a potentially life-threatening emergency and treated as such.

Mild SLE is treated symptomatically with an eye toward early identification of renal damage and the development of a hypercoagulable state. The NSAIDs and aspirin (especially if thrombosis is a concern) are an excellent starting point in the treatment of mild SLE. The antimalarial drugs such as chloroquine, hydroxychloroquine, or quinacrine can be added if dermatologic or joint manifestations are a problem. It should remembered that lupus is a disease that, like multiple sclerosis, is characterized by remissions and exacerbations and like multiple sclerosis, it has an extremely unpredictable course. Failure to recognize warning signs of increasing renal, cardiac, hematologic, or pulmonary dysfunction can have disastrous results.

The classification of a patient's lupus as severe represents a need for aggressive treatment with corticosteroids and close monitoring for occult system failure. Prednisone at a starting dose of 60 mg/day is indicated at the first sign of trouble although some experienced clinicians will utilize high-dose intravenous methylprednisolone at a dosage of 1000 mg for 3 to 4 days especially if florid central nervous system symptoms are present. The addition of immunosuppressive drugs such as azathioprine or cyclophosphamide is also useful if there is significant renal disease. The risk of thrombosis as heralded by high anticardiolipin antibodies may suggest a need for prophylactic anticoagulation.

As severe SLE is controlled, suppression of the autoimmune and inflammatory response is usually required. This is best accomplished with low-dose corticosteroids or low-dose immunosuppressive therapy. The effectiveness of suppressive therapy can be monitored by the subjective clinical response to the therapeutic regimen chosen and objectified by following titers of anti–double-stranded DNA antibody. The clinician should be vigilant for exacerbation of the inflammatory and autoimmune response as the corticosteroids are tapered and such exacerbations should be treated promptly to avoid sequelae. Intercurrent infections can be problematic for the patient suffering from SLE and should be treated aggressively. The clinician should also be aware that, even in the face of excellent disease control, pregnancy is associated with flaring of symptoms and spontaneous abortions and late-term fetal demise are quite common.

▮ SCLERODERMA AND SYSTEMIC SCLEROSIS

Scleroderma is a connective tissue disease of unknown etiology that is characterized by diffuse fibrosis of the skin and connective tissue, vascular damage, arthritis, and abnormalities of the esophagus, gastrointestinal tract, kidneys, heart, and lungs.[33] This fibrosis is the result of abnormal collagen deposition in the affected structures. The disease may be localized to the skin or a single organ system or may cause severe multisystem disease.[34] There is a trend to call the systemic variant of the disease *systemic sclerosis* to more accurately reflect the multisystem nature of the disease. Like SLE, the severity and course of the disease vary widely from patient to patient. Scleroderma is four times more common in women than in men and its onset is rare before the age of 30 or after the age of 50. Exposure to contaminated cooking oils, polyvinyl chloride, and silica have also been implicated as risk factors for the development of scleroderma.

Signs and Symptoms

Unlike RA, the onset of scleroderma can be very subtle and insidious. The initial complaints of patients suffering from scleroderma usually reflect the pain or deformity associated with swelling and loss of range of motion of the digits (sclerodactyly) and the associated Raynaud phenomenon.[35] Polyarthralgias and dysphagia can also be prominent initial features of the disease.

Most distressing to the patient are the cutaneous changes associated with scleroderma. Most often, the unsightly

FIGURE 40–16 ■ Digital and hand scleroderma. Advanced changes of scleroderma have caused digital contractions and limitation of finger movement. (From Klippel JH, Dieppe PA [eds]: Rheumatology, 2nd ed: Philadelphia, Mosby, 1997, p 7.9.3, Fig. 9.6)

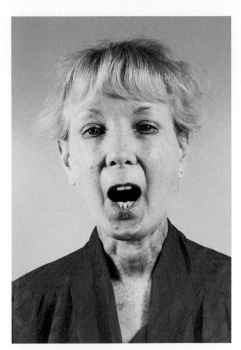

FIGURE 40–18 ■ Facial scleroderma. Taut, smooth skin over the face of a woman with long-standing disease. Oral aperture is reduced and radial furrowing is present around the lips. (From Klippel JH, Dieppe PA [eds]: Rheumatology, 2nd ed: Philadelphia, Mosby, 1997, p 7.9.6, Fig. 9.16.)

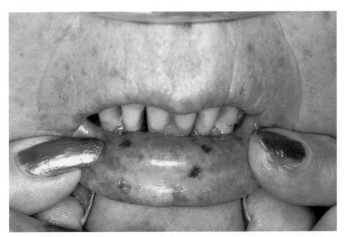

FIGURE 40–17 ■ Facial telangiectases. Punctate telangiectases are present on the lips and cheeks of this woman with long-standing limited scleroderma. (From Klippel JH, Dieppe PA [eds]: Rheumatology, 2nd ed. Philadelphia, Mosby, 1997, p 7.9.4, Fig. 9.9.)

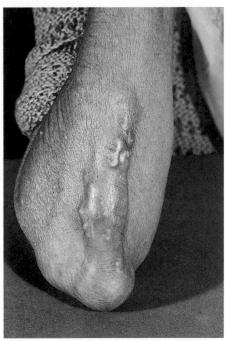

FIGURE 40–19 ■ Subcutaneous calcinosis. Extensive calcinosis is present on the exterior surface of forearm in a patient with limited scleroderma. (From Klippel JH, Dieppe PA [eds]: Rheumatology, 2nd ed. Philadelphia, Mosby, 1997, p 7.9.4, Fig.9.8.)

changes of sclerodactyly cause the patient to initially seek medical attention (Fig 40–16). The skin changes of scleroderma tend to be symmetrical—affecting the distal upper extremities first. Untreated, the skin will become shiny and atrophic looking with a swollen, taut appearance. Hyperpigmentation and telangiectases of the digits, face, chest, and lips may also occur (Fig. 40–17). A mask-like facies may appear, which can be quite distressing to the patient and family (Fig. 40–18). Subcutaneous calcifications of the fingers and over the elbows, ankles, and knees may cause further pain and deformity (Fig. 40–19). Ulcerations of the skin overlying these calcifications and the fingertips due to the trophic nature of the skin and vasculitis are common.[36]

Tendinitis and bursitis, especially of the large joints can contribute to pain and disability and can accelerate loss of range of motion of already compromised joints. Flexion contractures of the fingers, wrists, and elbows due to fibrosis of the synovium and overlying skin can be particularly problematic and very difficult to treat once they have occurred.

Complicating the cutaneous and musculoskeletal manifestations of the disease is the almost universal complaint of dysphagia due to impaired esophageal motility.[37] Fibrosis of the esophagus and lower esophageal sphincter can further exacerbate the problem of dysphagia as a result of acid reflux induced distal to esophageal strictures. Hypomotility of the small intestine can result in malabsorption, and diffuse fibrosis of the large intestine can further compromise gastrointestinal function.

Pulmonary fibrosis, pleurisy, and pleural effusions can compromise pulmonary function. Untreated, this fibrosis may affect the small vessels of the lung, and pulmonary hypertension with all of its attendant problems may develop. The fibrosis associated with scleroderma may also affect the muscle and conduction system of the heart. Cardiac arrhythmias may result, and compromised cardiac output secondary to myocardial fibrosis—combined with pulmonary hypertension—may result in treatment-refractory congestive heart failure. The onset of pulmonary and cardiac symptoms early in the course of the disease is a poor prognostic sign.

The kidneys are most often the most severely affected by scleroderma with fibrosis of the small arteries of the kidneys, resulting in the rapid deterioration of renal function and malignant hypertension. This deterioration of renal function may be exacerbated when concomitant heart failure is present. Untreated, it is the unremitting deterioration of renal function that is fatal in patients suffering from scleroderma.[32]

Laboratory Findings

Although the diagnosis of scleroderma is most often made on clinical grounds, confirmatory laboratory testing is sometimes useful when the diagnosis is in question or if a variant of scleroderma (e.g., CREST syndrome is being considered [see later]).[38] Antinuclear antibody (ANA) titers are elevated in more than 90% of patients suffering from scleroderma. Although not pathognomonic for the disease, the presence of high ANA titers at least points the clinician in the direction of connective tissue disease. If the diagnosis of scleroderma is still in question, the pattern of the ANA testing may be helpful. In patients with scleroderma, specific ANA testing will show an antinucleolar pattern, whereas patients with CREST syndrome will demonstrate an anticentromere pattern. Approximately one third of patients suffering from scleroderma will have a positive rheumatoid factor that may confuse the picture. The ESR will often be elevated in scleroderma, but frequently not to the extent seen in RA and SLE.

Differential Diagnosis

Due to the often subtle and insidious onset of scleroderma, the diagnosis is may be delayed or confused with other connective tissue diseases or other systemic diseases of the heart, lungs, joints, skin, and kidneys. Variants of scleroderma can manifest in myriad fashion and confuse the clinical picture. CREST syndrome is one such variant. Its constellation of systems include calcinosis, Raynaud phenomenon, esophageal dysfunction, sclerodactyly, and telangiectasia (Figs. 40–20 and 40–21A, B).[38] Also known as limited cutaneous scleroderma, this variant of scleroderma has a much more benign course and an infinitely better prognosis.[40] Scleroderma that is limited to the skin and adjacent connective tissue, but without multisystem involvement can also occasionally make the diagnosis of scleroderma more difficult.[39] Like CREST syndrome, the clinical course and prognosis of this localized variant of scleroderma is relatively benign. Mixed connective tissue disease(MCTD), which combines elements of polymyositis, SLE, and scleroderma can also

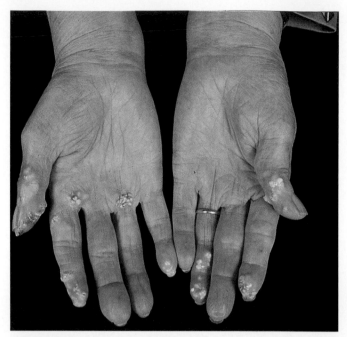

FIGURE 40–20 ▌ Calcific subcutaneous deposits in the fingers in a patient with limited scleroderma (CREST). (From Klippel JH, Dieppe PA [eds]: Rheumatology, 2nd ed. Philadelphia, Mosby, 1997, p 7.12.5, Fig. 12.8.)

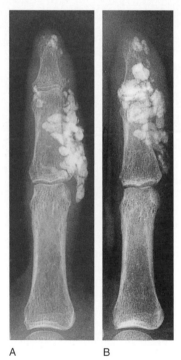

A   B

FIGURE 40–21 ▌ **A,** Calcifications in the soft tissue of the fingers in a patient with scleroderma. **B,** Following treatment with low-dose sodium warfarin for 18 months, there is redistribution of the calcifications without a decrease in extent. (From Klippel JH, Dieppe PA [eds]: Rheumatology, 2nd ed: Philadelphia, Mosby, 1997, p 7.12.5, Fig. 12.9 A and B.)

present a diagnostic dilemma.[41] If MCTD is being considered in the differential diagnosis of scleroderma, testing for the presence of antinuclear ribonucleoprotein antibody will prompt the clinician to suspect that MCTD is the culprit rather than classic scleroderma.

Treatment

The treatment of scleroderma has its basis in the treatment of specific organ system dysfunction related to the disease rather than any treatment that is specifically aimed at the underlying disease itself. Early treatment of organ system dysfunction is critical if the clinician hopes to improve the quality of life and prognosis for the patient suffering from scleroderma. Nowhere is this statement more valid than when dealing with renal dysfunction. The early use of angiotensin-converting enzyme inhibitors and vasodilators such as minoxidil is indicated to control hypertension and improve renal blood flow.[42]

The use of NSAIDs and corticosteroids in low doses to treat synovitis, arthritis, and myositis should be considered early in the course of the disease.[43] The calcium channel blockers may help ameliorate the symptomatology associated with Raynaud phenomenon, and there is anecdotal evidence that topical nitroglycerin ointment may also help provide symptomatic relief. Methotrexate and penicillamine may help slow the progression of fibrosis, especially of the skin and digits.[44] Immunosuppressive drugs may be of value in uncontrolled, rapidly progressive disease.[45,46]

Treatment of reflux with histamine blocking agents, bed blocks, and multiple small feedings may also provide symptomatic relief and help prevent lower esophageal erosions and stricture.[47] Oral antibiotics may also be used if malabsorption secondary to bacterial overgrowth in dilated small intestine and bowel is a problem. As with the other connective tissue diseases, the rational use of occupation and physical therapy can help decrease pain and preserve and improve function.

■ POLYMYOSITIS AND DERMATOMYOSITIS

Less common than RA, SLE, or scleroderma, polymyositis is a connective tissue disease of unknown etiology.[48] The disease is characterized by muscle inflammation that progresses to degenerative muscle disease and atrophy.[49] There are many variants of polymyositis, including dermatomyositis, which is from a clinical viewpoint simply polymyositis with significant cutaneous manifestations.[50] Affecting women twice as frequently as men, polymyositis can overlap with basically all of the connective tissue diseases, making diagnosis on purely clinical grounds somewhat more challenging.[51] Generally not occurring in adults before the age of 40 or after the age of 60, there is a childhood variant that carries a poor prognosis. The clinician should aware that there is a strong correlation with the presence of malignancy in patients that present with polymyositis, and a search for underlying malignancy must be an integral part of any diagnostic workup and treatment plan of patients suspected of having polymyositis.[48] Whether the malignancy serves as a trigger to the autoimmune response to muscle in this disease or is simply a trigger to an unknown cascade of events, has yet to be elucidated. There is a greater incidence of malignancy in those patients suffering from dermatomyositis relative to polymyositis. The type and location of tumor are not consistent, making the search for associated occult malignancy all the more difficult.

Signs and Symptoms

The onset of polymyositis is often preceded by an acute infection, often viral in nature. The onset of symptoms may be acute or may come on gradually with the patients thinking that they simply haven't shaken the initial febrile illness. Patients generally present with rash and muscle weakness as the initial symptoms with the proximal muscle groups affected initially more commonly than the distal muscle groups. Myalgias and polyarthralgias may be present as may constitutional symptoms resembling polymyalgia rheumatica (see later).[52] In some patients the onset of profound muscle weakness may be rapid with the patient presenting with the inability to rise from a sitting position or the complaint of the inability to raise the arms above the head to comb or curl the hair.

In rare patients, weakness of the muscles controlling the vocal cords may cause dysphagia, which may be mistaken for myasthenia gravis or a stroke. In severe cases, acute respiratory insufficiency may occur and the association of recent febrile illness may yield the mistaken diagnosis of Guillain Barré disease. Involvement of the gastrointestinal tract may lead to symptoms as described above in scleroderma. Cardiac arrhythmias and conduction defects are seen in many patients suffering from polymyositis as is renal failure due to acute myoglobulinemia from rhabdomyolysis in acute exacerbations of the disease. In general, the small muscles of the hands and feet are spared as are the muscles of facial expression.

When patients with polymyositis exhibit significant cutaneous manifestations, for clinical purposes the diseases is called dermatomyositis.[53] A heliotrope periorbital blush is pathognomonic for the disease (Fig. 40–22). There may be a

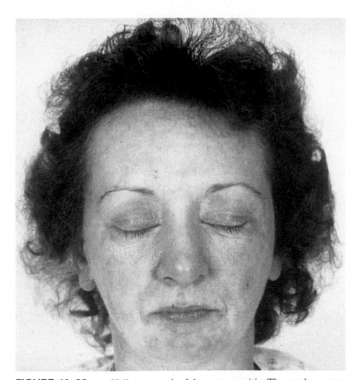

FIGURE 40–22 ■ Heliotrope rash of dermatomyositis. The erythematous and/or violaceous rash over the eyelids of this patient with dermatomyositis and breast cancer is a characteristic cutaneous feature. (From Klippel JH, Dieppe PA [eds]: Rheumatology, 2nd ed. Philadelphia, Mosby, 1997, p 7.13.5, Fig. 13.9.)

peeling or splitting of skin over the radial sides of the digits that is highly suggestive of dermatomyositis (Fig. 40–23). A generalized maculopapular rash may also appear (Fig. 40–24). Subcutaneous calcific nodules may be present in many patients with undiagnosed and untreated disease.

Laboratory Testing

There is no specific diagnostic test for polymyositis or der-matomyositis.[54] The ESR is usually elevated, as are the serum muscle enzyme determinations, especially in acute disease. The monitoring of creatine kinase (CK) levels may serve as a useful guide as to the efficacy of treatment. Approximately 60% of patients with polymyositis have antibodies to thymic nuclear antigen.

Differential Diagnosis

As with the other connective tissue diseases, the overlap of symptoms can make the diagnosis of a specific disease diffi-cult on purely clinical grounds. The findings of proximal

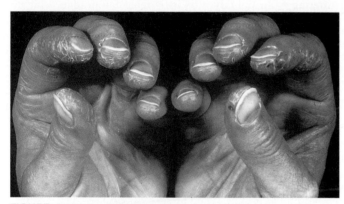

FIGURE 40–23 ■ "Machinist's hands." Note the cracking and fissuring of the distal digital skin of the finger pads in this patient wit dermatomyositis. (Courtesy of Dr. Frederick W. Miller. From Klippel JH, Dieppe PA [eds]: Rheumatology, 2nd ed: Philadelphia, Mosby, 1997, p 7.13.5, Fig.13.11.)

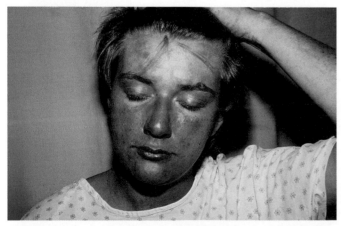

FIGURE 40–24 ■ The facial rash of dermatomyositis. Note the malar-like rash of dermatomyositis which involves the nasolabial area (an area often spared in systemic lupus erythematosus). Patchy involvement of the forehead and chin is also present in this patient. (From Klippel JH, Dieppe PA [eds]: Rheumatology, 2nd ed. Philadelphia, Mosby, 1997, p 7.13.4, Fig. 13.8.)

muscle weakness, characteristic skin rash (in the case of der-matomyositis), positive electromyography, and elevated serum muscle enzymes strongly support the diagnosis of polymyositis or dermatomyositis. If the diagnosis is still in doubt, muscle biopsy may help clarify the situation because in most cases it will be diagnostic.

Treatment

Corticosteroids are the first drug of choice for acute polymyositis.[55,56] A starting dose of 60 mg is usually adequate to control the acute inflammatory response and improve the clinical symptoms. The corticosteroids can be tapered based on both the clinical response to the drug and the decrease in elevated serum CK to normal. The minimum dose of corti-costeroid necessary to control symptoms and depress CK should be used to avoid steroid-induced myopathy, which may confuse the clinical management and exacerbate the patient's disability. A trial of immunosuppressive drugs including methotrexate, cyclosporine, azathioprine, and cyclophosphamide may be considered if corticosteroids fail to control the disease or the side effects associated with the drug preclude its use. It should be remembered that weakness unresponsive to the aforementioned therapies may be sec-ondary to associated malignancies (i.e., paraneoplastic syn-drome) and that treatment of the tumor may be required to ameliorate the patient's weakness. The use of physical and occupational therapy to optimize function and to help the patient learn to use assistive devices is indicated early in the course of the disease.

■ POLYMYALGIA RHEUMATICA

Polymyalgia rheumatica (PMR) is a connective tissue disease of unknown etiology that occurs primarily in patients older than 60 years of age.[57] It occurs in females twice as commonly as males and may be associated with temporal arteritis.[58] PMR is characterized by a constellation of musculoskeletal symp-toms that includes deep, aching pain of the cervical, pectoral, and pelvic regions; morning stiffness; arthralgias; and stiff-ness after inactivity.[59] Constitutional symptoms consisting of malaise, fever, anorexia, weight loss, and depression may be so severe as to mimic the cachexia and inanition of malig-nancy.[60] Unlike polymyositis, there is no significant proximal muscle weakness, but rather the feeling of more generalized weakness and lassitude. In contradistinction to polymyositis, muscle biopsies and electromyography are normal.

Signs and Symptoms

The onset of polymyalgia rheumatica is variable with some patients experiencing a rather acute, fulminant onset of symptoms and with other patients experiencing a more gradual onset of symptoms more like a flu syndrome that just won't go away. It is often the deep muscle aching and over-whelming feeling of fatigue that will lead the patient to seek medical attention. The astute physician may pick up on the gelling phenomenon (stiffness after periods of inactivity) which is very common with PMR and make the diagnosis on clinical grounds while awaiting confirmatory laboratory results (see next).

Laboratory and Radiographic Testing

The consistent finding in patients with PMR is the markedly elevated ESR.[59,61] Values are consistently over 100 mm/hour. The C reactive protein is also consistently elevated in patients with untreated PMR. As mentioned, objective tests for inflammatory muscle disease are negative in spite of the often dramatic muscle pain that patients report with this disease. In spite of the complaint of arthralgias, plain radiographs of the joints fail to reveal significant effusions or joint destruction that is often seen with RA and some of the other connective tissue diseases.

Differential Diagnosis

PMR is most often confused with other systemic diseases such as hypothyroidism, depression, or malignancy—such as multiple myeloma. It is often initially misdiagnosed as polymyositis, but can easily be distinguished from polymyositis by simple electromyography, which is negative in PMR and extremely positive in polymyositis. The relative absence of acutely inflamed joints and lack of evidence of destruction on plain radiographs of the small joints, coupled with the absence of rheumatoid nodules and a negative RF factor, should point the clinician away from the diagnosis of RA.

Treatment

The mainstay of treatment of PMR is the use of prednisone at a starting dose of 15 to 20 mg/day.[61] The symptoms of PMR will usually respond dramatically to the relatively low doses of steroids and the drug should be tapered as the clinical situation dictates. Unlike many of the other connective tissue diseases where the ESR serves as a useful marker as to the effectiveness of treatment, the ESR may remain significantly elevated in otherwise symptom-free patients.[61,62] It should be remembered that temporal arteritis is often seen concomitantly with PMR, and if temporal arteritis is suspected, a much higher dose of prednisone in the range of 60 to 100 mg should be used to decrease the risk of blindness (see later) until temporal artery biopsy can be obtained to confirm the diagnosis.

■ TEMPORAL ARTERITIS

Temporal arteritis(TA) is a collagen vascular disease of unknown etiology that occurs almost exclusively in the older patient.[63] It is also referred to in the literature as giant cell and/or cranial arteritis. TA occurs slightly more commonly in females than in males. Etiology and pathogenesis of temporal arteritis (TA) are unknown. Estimated prevalence is about 1/1000 in patients more than 50 years of age. There seems to be a slight female preponderance. TA is often seen concomitantly with polymyalgia rheumatica.[58]

TA is a disease that affects elastin-containing arteries.[64] It has a predilection for the cranial arteries, but the carotid arteries, coronary arteries, aorta, and occasionally peripheral arteries may be involved in the pathogenesis of the disease. The venous system is rarely involved in patients suffering from TA. Arteritis is the main feature of TA with the intima and inner layer of media of the artery being thickened by an inflammatory process (Fig. 40–25). The infiltration of lym-

phocytes and the presence of giant cells as a result of this inflammation are diagnostic for the disease (Fig. 40–26A,B). The arteritis may involve large segments of the affected artery or may manifest as multifocal areas with skin lesions.[65]

Signs and Symptoms

The patient with temporal arteritis is almost always over 50 years of age. As mentioned earlier, there is a slight female preponderance. The patient will often present with the complaint of severe temporal or occipital headache although in some patients the only symptoms are ophthalmologic (e.g., blurred vision, scotomata, amaurosis fugax, and so on).[63] Approximately 20% of patients with TA may present with the sudden onset of blindness due to ischemic optic neuritis, which is often permanent.[66] Scalp tenderness is common. In rare patients, involvement of the peripheral arteries may point the clinician in the direction of atherosclerosis and confuse the diagnosis.

Pain on chewing with jaw claudication is pathognomonic for TA.[67,68] Profound fatigue, lassitude, anorexia, weight loss, and deep muscle aching as seen in polymyalgia rheumatica are common and may initially be attributed to depression or other systemic diseases. Arthritis, fever, and carpal tunnel syndrome occur in many patients with TA. However, it is the finding of a swollen, tortuous, dilated, indurated temporal artery that frequently leads to the diagnosis of TA (Fig 40–27).

Laboratory Testing

As with polymyalgia rheumatica, extreme elevations of the ESR are invariably present in patients suffering from TA with levels frequently greater than 100 mm/hour. A normocytic normochromic anemia is present in the majority of patients with TA. Other serum markers for connective tissue disease (e.g., ANA, RF factor are rarely, if ever, present and there is no specific blood test available to diagnose TA).

Although the diagnosis of TA is usually made on clinical grounds, unfortunately sometimes after permanent blindness has occurred, it is the temporal artery biopsy that is needed to confirm the diagnosis. The clinician's tendency to delay or try

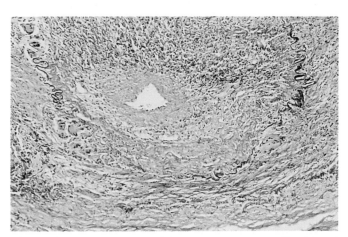

FIGURE 40–25 ■ Elastic stain of temporal artery showing disruption of elastic lamina in giant cell arteritis and narrowing of the lumen. (From Klippel JH, Dieppe PA [eds]: Rheumatology, 2nd ed. Philadelphia, Mosby, 1997, p 7.21.5, Fig. 21.7.)

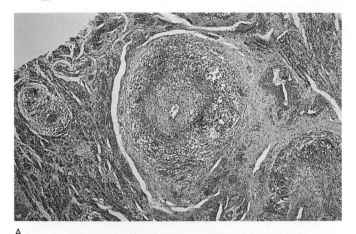

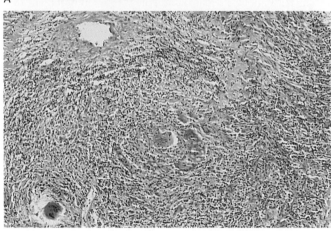

FIGURE 40–26 ■ Histology of giant-cell arteritis. **A,** Low-powered view of arterial wall showing infiltration by lymphocytes and plasma cells. **B,** High-powered view showing giant cells in close relationship to elastic lamina. (From Klippel JH, Dieppe PA [eds]: Rheumatology, 2nd ed. Philadelphia, Mosby, 1997, p 7.21.5, Fig. 21.8A and B.)

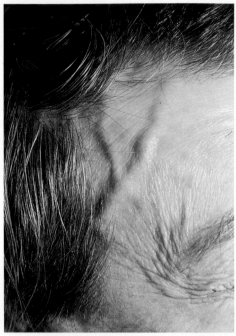

FIGURE 40–27 ■ Dilated temporal arteries in a patient with giant cell arteritis. (From Klippel JH, Dieppe PA [eds]: Rheumatology, 2nd ed: Philadelphia, Mosby, 1997, p 7.21.3, Fig. 21.2.)

to avoid temporal artery biopsy as the tendency to avoid initiation of treatment with high-dose steroids without a firm diagnosis should be assiduously avoided. If the diagnosis of temporal arteritis is being considered, treatment with at least 60 mg per day of prednisone should be started on an emergent basis while awaiting temporal artery biopsy. Failure to do so could result in permanent blindness. The clinician should remember that the physical examination of the temporal artery may be completely normal even in the presence of florid disease on biopsy, and a normal physical examination should never tempt the clinician to delay treatment. In general, biopsy should be obtained within 3 days of starting high-dose prednisone to avoid false-negative biopsy results.

Differential Diagnosis

The diagnosis of TA is generally straightforward if the clinician thinks about it. The headache associated with TA may be confused with migraine or tension-type headache and the symptom of jaw claudication may be attributed to a toothache given the prevalence of poor dentition in the elderly population. If eye symptoms are the primary presenting complaint, the patient may delay treatment, thinking that "they just need

new glasses." If there is predominant involvement of the peripheral arteries, the claudication symptoms may be attributed to the much more commonly occurring disease of atherosclerosis. Rarely, this peripheral involvement may lead to the erroneous diagnosis of Takayasu pulseless arteritis.

Treatment

As mentioned, if there is a clinical suspicion that a patient is suffering from temporal arteritis, treatment with high-dose prednisone at a dose of at least 60 mg per day should be instituted on an emergent basis to prevent blindness.[63,68] Temporal artery biopsy should be obtained as soon as possible with a goal of having a tissue diagnosis within 3 days of initiation of therapy to avoid treatment-induced false-negative biopsy results. If the patient continues to experience significant symptomatology on a starting dose of 60 mg of prednisone, hospitalization and administration of 1000 mg doses of methylprednisolone should be implemented immediately. Methotrexate, azathioprine, and dapsone have also been used in those patients who are unable to tolerate treatment with prednisone or experience flaring of ophthalmologic symptoms when high-dose prednisone is tapered.

■ CONCLUSION

The connective tissue diseases are a heterogeneous group of disorders that are commonly encountered in clinical practice. The overlap of symptoms associated with these diseases often leads to delayed diagnosis or misdiagnosis. The multisystem nature of these diseases allows the potential for not only much pain and functional disability, but life-threatening sequelae.

Early and accurate diagnosis is paramount if these potentially devastating diseases are to be successfully managed.

References

1. Alarcon GS, Williams GV, Singer JZ: Early undifferentiated connective tissue disease. I. Early clinical manifestation in a large cohort of patients with undifferentiated connective tissue diseases compared with cohorts of well established connective tissue disease. J Rheumatol 18(9):1332, 1991.
2. Emery P, Symmons DP: What is early rheumatoid arthritis?: Definition and diagnosis. Bailliere's Clin Rheumatol (1):13, 1997.
3. Barth WF: Office evaluation of the patient with musculoskeletal complaints. Am J Med 102(1A):3S, 1997.
4. Waldman SD: Achilles tendinitis. In Waldman SD: Common Pain Syndromes. Philadelphia, Saunders, 2002, p 291.
5. Waldman SD: Carpal tunnel syndrome. In Waldman SD: Common Pain Syndromes. Philadelphia, Saunders, 2002, p 118.
6. Waldman SD: Baker's cyst. In Waldman SD: Uncommon Pain Syndromes. Philadelphia, Saunders, 2003, p.266.
7. Alarcon GS: Predictive factors in rheumatoid arthritis. Am J Med 103(6A):19S, 1997.
8. Leeb BF, Weber K, Smolen JS: Rheumatoid Arthritis: Diagnosis and screening disease Management & Health Outcomes, 4:315, 1998.
9. Brown JH, Deluca SA: The radiology of rheumatoid arthritis. Am Fam Physician (5):1372, 1995.
10. Guidelines for the management of rheumatoid arthritis: Update. Arthritis Rheum 46(2):328, 2002.
11. Emery P: Therapeutic approaches for early rheumatoid arthritis. How early? How aggressive? Br J Rheumatol (Suppl) 2: 87, 1995.
12. Jain R, Lipsky PE: Treatment of rheumatoid arthritis. Med Clin North Am 81(1):57, 1997.
13. Furst DE: The rational use of methotrexate in rheumatoid arthritis and other rheumatic diseases. Br J Rheumatol 36(11):1196, 1997.
14. Fleischmann RM: Early diagnosis and treatment of rheumatoid arthritis for improved outcomes: Focus on etanercept, a new biologic response modifier. Clin Ther 21(9):1429, 1999.
15. Olsen NJ, Stein CM: New drugs for rheumatoid arthritis. N Engl J Med 350(21):2167, 2004.
16. Pincus T: Long-term outcomes in rheumatoid arthritis. Br J Rheumatol (Suppl) 2:59, 1995.
17. Hochberg MC: Systemic lupus erythematosus. Rheum Dis Clin North Am 16:617, 1990.
18. Hopkinson ND, Doherty M, Powell RJ: Clinical features and race-specific incidence/prevalence rates of systemic lupus erythematosus in a geographically complete cohort of patients. Ann Rheum Dis 153:675, 1994.
19. Ward MM, Studenski S: Clinical manifestations of systemic lupus erythematosus. Identification of racial and socioeconomic influence. Arch Intern Med 150:849, 1990.
20. Calvo-Alen J, Alarcon GS, Burgard SL: Systemic lupus erythematosus: Predictors of its occurrence among a cohort of patients with early undifferentiated connective tissue disease: Multivariate analyses and identification of risk factors. J Rheumatol 23(3):469, 1996.
21. Boumpas DR, Fessler BJ, Austin HA, et al: Systemic lupus erythematosus: Emerging concepts. Part 2: Dermatologic and joint disease, the antiphospholipid antibody syndrome, pregnancy and hormonal therapy, morbidity and mortality, and pathogenesis. Ann Int Med 123:42, 1995.
22. Cronin ME: Musculoskeletal manifestations of systemic lupus erythematosus. Rheum Dis Clin North Am 14:99, 1988.
23. Reilly PA, Evison G, McHugh NJ, Maddison PJ: Arthropathy of hands and feet in systemic lupus erythematosus. J Rheumatol 17:777, 1990.
24. Esdaile JM, Danoff D, Rosenthal L, Gutowsko A: Deforming arthritis in systemic lupus erythematosus. Ann Rheum Dis 40:124, 1981.
25. Emerit I, Michelson AM: Mechanism of photosensitivity in systemic lupus erythematosus patients. Proc Natl Acad Sci USA 78:2537, 1984.
26. Boumpas DT, Austin HA, Fessler BJ, et al: Systemic lupus erythematosus: Emerging concepts. Part 1: Renal, neuropsychiatric, cardiovascular, pulmonary and hematologic disease. Ann Int Med122:940, 1995.
27. Miguel EC, Rodriques Pereira RM, de Braganca Pereira CA, et al: Psychiatric manifestations of systemic lupus erythematosus: Clinical features, symptoms, and signs of central nervous system activity in 43 patients. Medicine 73:224, 1994.
28. Cervera R, Khamashta M, Font J, et al: Systemic lupus erythematosus: Clinical and immunologic patterns of disease expression in a cohort of 1000 patients. Medicine 72:113, 1993.
29. Segal AM, Calabrese LH, Ahmad M, et al: The pulmonary manifestations of systemic lupus erythematosus. Semin Arthritis Rheum14:202, 1985.
30. Orens JB, Martinez FJ, Lynch JP III: Pleuropulmonary manifestations of systemic lupus erythematosus. Rheum Dis Clin North Am 20:159, 1994.
31. Sturfelt G, Eskilsson J, Nived 0, et al: Cardiovascular disease in systemic lupus erythematosus. A study of 75 patients from a defined population. Medicine 71:216, 1992.
32. Austin HA, Muenz LR, Joyce KM, et al: Prognostic factors in lupus nephritis. Contribution of renal histologic data. Am J Med 75:382, 1983.
33. American Rheumatism Association: Preliminary criteria for the classification of systemic sclerosis (scleroderma). Subcommittee for scleroderma criteria of the American Rheumatism Association Diagnostic and Therapeutic Criteria Committee. Arthritis Rheum 23(5):581, 1980.
34. LeRoy EC, Black CM, Fleischmajer R, et al: Scleroderma (systemic sclerosis): Classification, subsets and pathogenesis. J Rheumatol 15:202, 1988.
35. Gerbracht DD, Steen VD, Ziegler GL: Evolution of primary Raynaud's phenomenon (Raynaud's disease) to connective tissue disease. Arthritis Rheum 28(1):87, 1985.
36. Prescott RJ, Freemont AJ, Jones CJP, et al: Sequential dermal microvascular and perivascular changes in the development of scleroderma. J Pathol 166:255, 1992.
37. Sjögren RW: Gastrointestinal motility disorders in scleroderma. Arthritis Rheum 37(9):1265, 1994.
38. Frayha RA, Scarola JA, Shulman LE: Calcinosis in scleroderma: A reevaluation of the CRST syndrome, abstracted. Arthritis Rheum16:542, 1973.
39. Velayos EE, Masi AT, Stevens MB, Shulman LE: The 'CREST' syndrome. Comparison with systemic sclerosis (scleroderma). Arch Intern Med 139(11):1240, 1979.
40. Akesson A, Wollheim FA: Organ manifestations in 100 patients with progressive systemic sclerosis: A comparison between the CREST syndrome and diffuse scleroderma. Br J Rheumatol 28(4):281, 1989.
41. Reichlin M: Undifferentiated connective tissue diseases, overlap syndromes, and mixed connective tissue diseases. In Koopman WJ (ed): Arthritis and Allied Conditions, 13th ed. Baltimore, Williams & Wilkins,1997, p 1309.
42. Steen VD: Systemic sclerosis—management. In: Klippel JH, Dieppe PA, eds: Rheumatology. London, Mosby, 1997, p 1.
43. Steen VD, Conte C, Medsger TA Jr: Case-control study of corticosteroid use prior to scleroderma renal crisis. Arthritis Rheum 37(Suppl):360A, 1994.
44. Jayson MIV, Lovell C, Black CM: Penicillamine therapy in systemic sclerosis. Proc Roy Soc Med 70:80, 1977.
45. Appleboon T, Itzkowitch D: Cyclosporin is successful control of rapidly progressive scleroderma. JAMA 82:886, 1986.
46. Silver RM, Warrick JH, Kinsella MB, et al: Cyclophosphamide and low-dose prednisone therapy in patients with systemic sclerosis (scleroderma) with interstitial lung disease. J Rheumatol 20:838, 1993.
47. Hendel L, Hage E, Hendel J, Stentoft P: Omeprazole in the long-term treatment of severe gastroesophageal reflux disease in patients with systemic sclerosis. Aliment Pharmacol Ther 6:565, 1992.
48. Bohan A, Peter JB: Polymyositis and dermatomyositis. N Engl J Med 292:344, 403, 1975.
49. Walton JN, Adams RD (eds): Polymyositis. Baltimore, Williams & Wilkins,1958.
50. DeVere R, Bradley WG: Polymyositis: Its presentation, morbidity and mortality. Brain 98:637, 1975.
51. Banker BQ, Engel AG: The polymyositis and dermatomyositis syndromes. In Engel AG, Banker BQ, eds: Myology, vol. 2. New York, McGraw-Hill, 1986, p 1385.
52. Kagen LJ: Polymyositis/dermatomyositis. In McCarty DJ (ed): Arthritis and Allied Conditions, 11th ed. Philadelphia, Lea & Febiger, 1989, p 1092.
53. Bezecny R: Dermatomyositis. Arch Dermat Syph 171:242, 1935.
54. Tanimoto K, Nakano K, Kano S, et al: Classification criteria for polymyositis and dermatomyositis. J Rheumatol 22:668, 1995.
55. Rose AL, Walton JN: Polymyositis. A survey of 89 cases with particular reference to treatment and prognosis. Brain 89:747, 1966.
56. Dalakas MC: Clinical, immunopathologic and therapeutic considerations of inflammatory myopathies. Clin Neuropharmacol 15:327, 1992.

57. Kyle V, Silverman B, Silman A, et al: Polymyalgia rheumatica/giant cell arteritis in general practice. BMJ 13:385, 1985.

58. Gonzalez-Gay MA: Giant cell arteritis and polymyalgia rheumatica: Two different but often overlapping conditions. Semin Arthritis Rheum 33(5):289, 2004.

59. Chuang TY, Hunder GG, Iistrup DM: Polymyalgia rheumatica: A 10-year epidemiologic and clinical study. Ann Intern Med 97:672, 1982.

60. Miller D, Allen SE, Walker SE: A primary care physician's guide to polymyalgia rheumatica. Primary Care Rep 4:91, 1998.

61. Kyle V, Hazleman BL: The clinical and laboratory course of polymyalgia rheumatica/giant cell arteritis after the first two months of treatment. Ann Rheum Dis 52(12):847, 1993.

62. Collier J: The management of polymyalgia rheumatica and giant cell arteritis. Drug Ther Bull 31:65, 1993.

63. Nordberg E, Bengtsson BA: Epidemiology of biopsy-proven giant cell arteritis. J Intern Med 227:233, 1990.

64. Wilkinson IMS, Russell RWR: Arteries of the head and neck in giant cell arteritis. A pathological study to show the pattern of arterial involvement. Arch Neurol 27:378, 1972.

65. Klein GE, Campbell RJ, Hunder GG, Carney JA: Skip lesions in temporal arteritis. Mayo Clin Proc 51:504, 1976.

66. Hayreh SS: Anterior ischaemic optic neuropathy. Differentiation of arteritis from non-arteritic type and its management. Eye 4:25, 1990.

67. Epperly TD, Moore KE, Harrover JD: Polymyalgia rheumatica and temporal arthritis. Am Fam Physician 62(4):789, 2000.

68. Waldman SD: Temporal arteritis. In Waldman SD: Uncommon Pain Syndromes. Philadelphia, Saunders, 2003, p 15.

chapter 41

Polymyalgia Rheumatica

Brian L. Hazleman

■ HISTORICAL CONSIDERATIONS

The first description of polymyalgia rheumatica (PMR) is believed to have been made in Scotland by Dr. William Bruce in 1884. In 1957, Barber suggested the present name.[1] In 1960, Paulley and Hughes reported on 67 patients, emphasizing the occurrence of "anarthritic rheumatism" in giant cell arteritis (GCA), providing more solid clinical evidence for the relation between PMR and GCA.[2] Histologic support came from the work of Alestig and Barr[3] and Hamrin and colleagues,[4] confirming the coexistence of the two conditions.

■ CLINICAL FEATURES

Patients usually locate the source of their pain and stiffness to the muscles. The onset is most common in the shoulder region and neck, with eventual involvement of the shoulder and pelvic girdles and the corresponding proximal muscle groups. Involvement of distal limb muscles is unusual. The symptoms are usually bilateral and symmetrical. Stiffness is usually the predominant feature, is particularly severe after rest, and may prevent the patient from getting out of bed in the morning. The muscular pain is often diffuse and movement accentuates the pain; pain at night is common. Muscle strength is usually unimpaired, although the pain makes interpretation of muscle testing difficult. There is tenderness of involved structures, including periarticular structures such as bursae, tendons, and joint capsules—although the muscle tenderness is generally not as severe as that in myositis. In late stages, muscle atrophy may develop, with restriction of shoulder movement. An improvement of shoulder range is rapid with corticosteroid therapy, unlike that seen in frozen shoulder. Occasionally the painful arc sign of subacromial bursitis is present; this is important to recognize because a local injection of corticosteroid will give relief and save the patient from an increase in systemic corticosteroid dosage.

PMR has traditionally been viewed as a condition affecting muscles and many reports have emphasized the rarity of joint involvement.[5] Recent emphasis has been given to a possible association between synovitis and the muscle symptoms in PMR.[6] It has also been suggested that both axial and peripheral synovitis often occur. Inflammatory synovitis and effusions have been noted by several authors—the reported incidence varying from 0% to 100% in various series.[7,8]

There are several essential features of PMR: (1) the musculoskeletal symptoms are usually bilateral and symmetrical, affecting the shoulder and pelvic girdles; (2) stiffness is usually the predominant feature; it is particularly severe after rest and may prevent the patient from getting out of bed in the morning; (3) muscle strength is unimpaired although the pain makes interpretation of muscle testing difficult; and (4) systemic features include low-grade fever, fatigue, weight loss, and an elevated erythrocyte sedimentation rate (ESR).

The variety of symptoms and lack of specificity of signs and symptoms make such studies difficult, and the epidemiology of PMR has been less well defined. One group, using a questionnaire in 656 patients over a period of 65 years, found a prevalence of arteritis/polymyalgia of 3300/100,000.[9] PMR has been found to account for 1.3% to 4.5% of the patients attending rheumatic disease clinics, but clearly these figures are influenced by the type of clinical load.

Familial aggregation of cases of PMR and GCA has been reported by several workers.[10-13] Clustering of cases in time and space suggests that, in addition to a genetic predisposition, environmental factors may be important. One author noted that 9 of 11 cases seen over 6 years in a practice of 3000 lived in one small part of the same village, and of these, 2 lived in the same house, 2 were neighbors and 2 others were close friends.[14]

Synovitis of the knees, wrists, and sternoclavicular joints is more common, but involvement is transient and mild. Erosive changes in joints and/or sclerosis of the sacroiliac joints have been reported, although they are difficult to demonstrate in the sternoclavicular joints except by tomography. Abnormal technetium pertechnetate scintigrams have shown widespread uptake over several joints—particularly shoulders, knees, wrists, and hands.[15] Abnormalities persisted after treatment, suggesting they are due to concurrent osteoarthritis.

■ DIFFERENTIAL DIAGNOSIS

Differential diagnosis of PMR is listed in Table 41–1.

■ TESTING

Table 41–2 lists baseline clinical investigations that are used to help make the diagnosis of PMR and exclude other condi-

Table 41–1

Differential Diagnosis of Polymyalgia Rheumatica

Neoplastic disease
Muscle disease
Joint disease
Polymyositis
Osteoarthritis, particularly cervical spine
Myopathy
Rheumatoid arthritis
Infections (e.g., bacterial endocarditis)
Connective tissue disease
Bone disease, particularly osteomalacia
Multiple myeloma
Hypothyroidism
Fibromyalgia
Parkinsonism
Lymphoma
Shoulder problems (e.g., capsulitis)

Table 41–2

Baseline Clinical Investigations Useful in Diagnosis of Polymyalgia Rheumatica

Full blood count
Biochemical profile
Protein electrophoresis
Urinary Bence Jones protein
Thyroid function test
Rheumatoid factor
Radiographs of chest and affected joint(s)
Erythrocyte sedimentation rate (ESR) measurement
Acute phase protein (e.g., C-reactive protein) measurement
Muscle enzymes (if indicated)
Specific investigations
Temporal artery biopsy: for suspected giant cell arteritis (GCA), not for polymyalgia rheumatica

tions. The diagnosis of PMR is initially one of exclusion. There is an extensive differential diagnosis in an elderly patient with muscle pain, stiffness, and an elevated ESR. There are no specific diagnostic tests and diagnosis depends on having a high index of suspicion supported by history, examination, and raised inflammatory markers. The differential diagnosis is large because the prodromal phases of several serious conditions can mimic PMR. In practice, nonspecific clinical features and the frequent absence of physical signs make diagnosis difficult.

Despite a typical pattern of musculoskeletal symptoms and the presence in many of significant systemic features, there is often a considerable delay of several months before diagnosis. Patients and physicians also tend to ascribe the symptoms to degenerative joint disease expected in an older population, or even to psychological illness. In others, the systemic features of the disease and the laboratory abnormalities can lead to diagnostic confusion and often extensive investigation.

A hidden malignancy can mimic the symptoms of PMR, but these patients do not usually respond to corticosteroids. Although there is no evidence to suggest that malignancy is more common in patients with PMR than in other people, deterioration in health or a poor initial response to corticosteroids must always be taken seriously and a search for an occult neoplasm should be undertaken.

The distinction between late-onset rheumatoid arthritis (RA) and PMR can be difficult, especially at onset. Polymyalgic symptoms may be the predominant clinical feature in elderly onset RA, whereas a transient symmetrical pauci- or polyarteritis is frequently found with PMR. Indeed, many studies of PMR have included patients who eventually were diagnosed with seropositive or seronegative RA.[16] Be aware of the possibility of rheumatoid arthritis if (1) there are peripheral joint signs such as synovitis; (2) there is failure to respond to an adequate dose of steroids; and (3) the initial dose of steroid cannot be reduced without exacerbating the symptoms.

There has been little evidence to support a concept of primary muscle disease in PMR. Serum aldolase and creatine phosphokinase levels are normal and there is no abnormality on electromyography. Muscle biopsy has shown type II atrophy alone and there is no evidence of inflammatory changes. Recently there have been reports of focal changes in muscle ultrastructure and abnormalities of mitochondrial form and function, similar to those associated with inherited mitochondrial myopathies (MM).[17,18] These abnormalities are not due to gene deletions or mutations associated with MM and persist even after successful treatment. The significance of these changes is unclear. Arteritis in skeletal muscle appears to be uncommon. Liver biopsy can show nonspecific inflammatory changes or focal liver cell necrosis. There are occasional reports of granulomata and hepatic arteritis. Synovial biopsy has shown nonspecific inflammatory changes with lymphocytic infiltration of knees, sternoclavicular joints, and shoulders.

Various authors have tried to set out diagnostic criteria for PMR, all of which include a combination of age, clinical features, and an elevated ESR. Bird and colleagues list six diagnostic criteria, three of which are required for the diagnosis of PMR (Table 41–3).[19] The presence of any three of these criteria has a 92% sensitivity and an 80% specificity for the diagnosis of PMR. If an additional criterion of a rapid response to oral steroid therapy is added, the specificity is increased to 99%.[20] Although ESR is usually significantly elevated in PMR, in some patients ESR is normal or only slightly elevated. In these patients and in those presenting with systemic features, other causes of illness should be excluded.

Table 41–3

Diagnostic Criteria for Polymyalgia Rheumatica

1. Age over 65
2. Erythrocyte sedimentation rate (ESR) >40 mm/h
3. Bilateral upper-arm tenderness
4. Morning stiffness of more than 1 h
5. Onset of illness less than 2 wk
6. Depression and/or weight loss

Table 41–4	

Treatment of Polymyalgia Rheumatica

Initial dose	Prednisolone 10-20 mg daily for 1 month
Reduce dose	By 2.5 mg every 2-4 weeks until dose is 10 mg, then by 1 mg every 4-6 weeks (or until symptoms return)
Maintenance dose	About 5 mg by 6 months after start of treatment. Most patients require treatment for 3-4 years, but withdrawal after 2 years is worth attempting.
Special points	In patients who cannot reduce prednisolone dosage because of recurring symptoms or who develop serious steroid-related side effects, azathioprine has been shown to have a modest steroid-sparing effect.
Main side effects	Weight gain, skin atrophy, edema, increased intraocular pressure, cataracts, gastrointestinal disturbances, diabetes, osteoporosis
Risk of side effects	Increased risk with high initial doses (>30 mg) of prednisolone, maintenance doses of 10 mg, and high cumulative doses. Maintenance doses of 5 mg are relatively safe.

■ TREATMENT

Unless there are any contraindications, patients should be started on 15 mg prednisolone per day. This dose should bring rapid relief of symptoms within days. Larger doses are rarely required. If there is no rapid response, reconsider the diagnosis. The dose of prednisolone should be titrated down slowly, according to symptoms rather than the ESR. The dose can often be reduced fairly rapidly to 10 mg per day and then reduced by 1 mg daily every 4 to 6 weeks. Then the dose should be reduced more slowly, aiming to have the patient off steroids by around 2 years, although some patients may require small doses of steroids for longer periods (Table 41–4).

As patients are weaned off steroid therapy, some patients may require a small dose of anti-inflammatory drugs to reduce the muscle pain. Relapses are common and should be diagnosed on clinical grounds. They are usually caused by a too rapid decrease in dose of corticosteroid and should be treated by increasing the dose again and then decreasing the dose more slowly. Relapses are more common in the first 6 to 12 months of treatment but can occur in the months after stopping corticosteroids. A few patients may need low-dose treatment indefinitely. It should be remembered that steroid therapy has risks and side effects, including the increased risk of osteoporosis. Bone loss is rapid in the early stages of steroid therapy and bone protection therapy should be considered at the time of starting steroid therapy, particularly in those patients 65 years or older or with a history of fragility fracture.

■ CONCLUSION

The cardinal symptoms of PMR—prolonged morning stiffness in the shoulder and pelvic girdles with an elevated ESR—are generally straightforward. However, PMR is essentially a diagnosis of exclusion. Because the differential diagnosis is extensive, it is important to exclude more sinister conditions at the outset with screening blood investigations. PMR is exceedingly rare in those younger than 50 years of age and occasionally the ESR is misleading, being normal or only slightly raised.

Of particular importance is the link between PMR and GCA. Many believe the two represent opposite ends of the spectrum of the same disease. In any patient who presents with PMR, it is mandatory to ask about headache, scalp tenderness, and jaw claudication because the catastrophic result of untreated GCA is irreversible blindness. In such cases, higher doses of steroids are required with possible referral for temporal artery biopsy.

Diagnosis of PMR can be difficult to make; however, when diagnosed correctly, treatment is highly effective. In prednisolone-resistant cases response to steroid-sparing agents has been disappointing. Patient education is paramount and patients should be warned that treatment is typically necessary for at least 2 years, with some patients requiring long-term maintenance therapy.

References

1. Barber HS: Myalgic syndrome with constitutional effects: Polymyalgia rheumatica. Ann Rheum Dis 16:230, 1957.
2. Paulley JW, Hughes JP: Giant cell arteritis, or arteritis of the aged. Br Med J 2:1562, 1960.
3. Alestig K, Barr J: Giant-cell arteritis: A biopsy study of polymyalgia rheumatica, including one case of Takayasu's disease. Lancet 1:1228, 1963.
4. Hamrin B, Jonsson N, Landberg T: Arteritis in "polymyalgia rheumatica." Lancet 41:397, 1964.
5. Kyle V, Tudor J, Wraight EP, et al: Rarity of synovitis in polymyalgia rheumatica. Ann Rheum Dis 49:155, 1990.
6. Frediani B, Falsetti P, Storri L, et al: Evidence for synovitis in active polymyalgia rheumatica: Sonographic study in a large series of patients. J Rheumatol 29:123, 2002.
7. Cantini F, Niccoli L, Nannini C, et al: Inflammatory changes of hip synovial structures in polymyalgia rheumatica. Clin Exp Rheumatol 23:462, 2005.
8. Malone CB, McCarthy GM: Polymyalgia rheumatica as an unusual cause of pleural and pericardial effusion. J Clin Rheumatol 11:59, 2005.
9. Kalke S, Mukerjee D, Dasgupta B: A study of the health assessment questionnaire to evaluate functional status in polymyalgia rheumatica. Rheumatology 39:883, 2000.
10. Liang GC, Simkin PA, Hunder GG, et al: Familial aggregation of polymyalgia rheumatica and giant cell arteritis. Arthritis Rheum 17:19, 1974.
11. Granato JE, Abben RP, May WS: Familial association of giant cell arteritis: A case report and brief review. Arch Intern Med 141:115, 1981.
12. Schwizer B, Pirovino M: Giant cell arteritis: A genetically determined disease? Schweiz Med Wochenschr 124:1959, 1994.
13. Bartolome MJ, Martinez-Taboda VM, Lopez-Hoyos M, et al: Familial aggregation of polymyalgia rheumatica and giant cell arteritis: Genetic and T cell repertoire analysis. Clin Exp Rheumatol 19:259, 2001.
14. Fietta P, Manganelli P, Zanetti A, Neri TM: Familial giant cell arteritis and polymyalgia rheumatica: Aggregation in two families. J Rheumatol 29:1551, 2002.

15. O'Duffy JD, Wahner HW, Hunder GG: Joint imaging in polymyalgia rheumatica. Mayo Clin Proc 51:519, 1976.

16. Pease CT, Haugeberg G, Morgan AW, et al: Diagnosing late onset rheumatoid arthritis, polymyalgia rheumatica, and temporal arteritis in patients presenting with polymyalgic symptoms: A prospective long-term evaluation. J Rheumatol 32:1043, 2005.

17. Miro O, Casademont J, Jarreta D, et al: Skeletal muscle mitochondrial function in polymyalgia rheumatica and in giant cell arteritis. Rheumatology 38:568, 1999.

18. Harle JR, Pellissier JF, Desnuelle C, et al: Polymyalgia rheumatica and mitochondrial myopathy: Clinicopathologic and biochemical studies in five cases. Am J Med 92:167, 1992.

19. Bird HA, Esselinckx W, Dixon AS, et al: An evaluation of criteria for polymyalgia rheumatica. Ann Rheum Dis 38:434, 1979.

20. Bird HA, Leeb BF, Montecucco CM, et al: A comparison of the sensitivity of diagnostic criteria for polymyalgia rheumatica. Ann Rheum Dis 64:626, 2005.

Regional Pain Syndromes

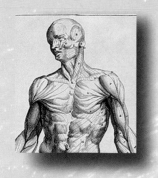

Part A

PAIN IN THE HEAD

chapter 42

Migraine Headache

Seymour Diamond

Historical Overview

Migraine has been identified, in some form, since ancient times. One of the first (and still questionable) citations about migraine is believed to be at least 6000 years old.[1] More detailed descriptions of headaches, including migraine, are traced to the time of Hippocrates who first identified headaches as a distinct disorder.[1] Also, Hippocrates first described a few of the well-known clinical features of migraine such as unilateral location of the pain, associated vomiting, and a possible visual aura that appeared as a shining light in one of the eyes followed by severe headache.

More citations about the clinical details have been traced to the first century AD (Greco-Roman period). Medical historians believe that the first accurate description of migraine was provided by Aretaeus of Cappadocia, a Greek physician[2,3] who wrote a book describing different neurologic disorders including epilepsy, headaches, and hysteria. Aretaeus also gained fame by proposing the very first classification of headache disorders, which has affected all future efforts at nomenclature. Aretaeus divided all headache types into three major categories: cephalalgia, cephalea, and heterocrania. This particular system provided the basis for the First International Classification of Headache Disorders.[4] Because Aretaeus was a migraine sufferer himself, he had a unique opportunity to study and describe his own headache, enabling him to detail his visual aura as well as a few associated symptoms, such as photophobia and phonophobia.

Later, in the second century AD, another Greek physician—Galen of Pergamon—added to the headache literature with more clinical and even pathophysiologic information.[5] He subscribed to a connection between the human brain and abdomen because nausea and vomiting were commonly associated with the headache attack. He thus explained the pathogenesis of migraine: yellow bile irritates brain meninges thus causing pain. He attributed the unilateral location of the headache by using information regarding anatomic structures of the human brain and head. He wrote that falx cerebri separates two halves of the brain and protects the unaffected side (side without headache pain) from being affected by the irritating yellow bile. Galen was the first to describe the throbbing pattern of the pain during an acute migraine. He also provided some pathophysiologic explanations of this phenomenon, asserting that the pain originates in blood vessels. Thus, he established some basis for the future vascular theories of migraine pathogenesis.

During the 16th century, the headache known as *heterocrania* (named by Aretaeus of Cappadocia) or *hemicrania* (named by Galen of Pergamon) was labeled migraine, a term derived form Galen's hemicrania which was first changed to the Latin *hemicranium.* The term was then transformed into *emigranea, migranea, megrim,* and finally, *migraine.*[1] In the second half of the 17th century, an English physician, Thomas Willis, wrote a textbook of neurophysiology in which he devoted two chapters to a discussion of different headache problems.[6] He expanded the vascular theory first proposed by Galen and identified two actions of the blood vessels during a migraine attack—vasoconstriction and vasodilatation. Thomas Willis was not only a remarkable scientist but also a very thorough physician. He attempted to treat migraine using various remedies. Willis was the first to discover the efficacy of *potus cophey*—coffee.

In the 18th century, it was discovered that the brain and nervous system, in addition to the blood vessels, are involved in migraine pathogenesis in which weather changes, peculiarities of diet, and stress can play a role as migraine triggers.[7] E. Sieveking, in the mid-19th century, attempted to find a relation between epilepsy and migraine, because about 60% of his patients with epilepsy were also diagnosed with migraine.[8] He also observed their common physiologic feature (which is actively discussed in our days)—paroxysmal activity of both epilepsy and migraine.[8,9] Later, the same correlation was applied to status migraine analogous to status epilepticus.[10] These similarities between migraine and epilepsy created the basis of a new migraine treatment with the use of anticonvulsants.[11]

The 20th century saw multiple achievements in determining the pathophysiology of migraine, as well as the beginning of a new era of specific, highly effective, antimigraine medications. In 1916, pure ergotamine was introduced and in 1928 it was compared to placebo.[11] The classic headache treatise, *Headache and Other Head Pain,* was written by Harold G. Wolff in 1948.[12] Dr. Wolff's book included all clinical and pathophysiologic data available at that time.

Pathogenesis

Further migraine studies identified the specific role serotonin plays in migraine pathogenesis, thus leading to the introduction of a totally new class of preventive medications—serotonin antagonists and abortive agents—serotonin agonists.[11] Also, toward the end of the 20th century, the first international classification and diagnostic criteria for headache disorders, cranial neuralgias, and facial pain were published.[4]

Although our understanding of migraine has expanded, we are opening new horizons in diagnostic and treatment options—helping us recognize the need for new, more accurate classifications and diagnostic criteria. These requirements were addressed in the second edition of the International Classification of Headache Disorders as proposed by the International Headache Society in September, 2003.[13] The study of migraine is still in process and continues to afford us important information that can lead to a better understanding

of this disorder and provide us with opportunities in diagnosis and treatment.

Recently, increasing attention has been devoted to the theory of central sensitization. Central sensitization is a collective term that reflects the tendency to decreased thresholds to nonpainful stimuli, clinically presented as hyperalgesia (decreased pain threshold) or cutaneous allodynia (pain response to a nonpainful stimuli). Central sensitization is primarily attributed to activation (sensitization) of peripheral C-fibers in the trigeminal system. These fibers could be activated by a variety of factors (mechanical, chemical, or thermal). Once activated, C-fibers start releasing multiple transmitters (calcitonin gene-related peptide [CGRP], substance P, glutamate) from their central terminals in the nucleus caudalis of the trigeminal system and from their peripheral terminals that produce the sterile neurogenic inflammation described earlier. These events will further activate the C-fibers by an increased level of histamine (5-HT) and prostaglandin E_2 elevated synthesis, which is observed in the area of the neurogenic inflammation. The release of C-fiber transmitters could be decreased by activation of m-opiate and 5-HT_{1D} receptors (by using their agonists) or increased by activation of *N*-methyl-D-aspartate (NMDA) receptors. The release of inflammatory peptides (prostaglandin E_2, and so on) could be diminished by using an NSAID. Another important feature of central sensitization is the increase of intracellular calcium in postsynaptic neurons that will activate protein kinase C and nitric oxide synthase (NOS). Activated protein kinase C will phosphorylate membrane-bound proteins changing the activity (activating) NMDA receptors so that these receptors could respond to glutamate—not only during depolarization but also at resting membrane potentials. NOS will cause synthesis of nitric oxide (NO) (vasodilator).

Thus, all these steps of reactions will cause the increased excitability of neurons in the trigeminal nuclei or central sensitization. As we can see, sensitization of the C-fibers occurs in the periphery (meningeal C-fibers)—peripheral sensitization and sensitization of the neurons of trigeminal nuclei occur in central sensitization. From that point of view, peripheral sensitization explains the intracranial hypersensitivity (aggravation of pain by bending over, coughing, walking, and so on), whereas central sensitization demonstrates the extracranial hypersensitivity (cutaneous allodynia).

Clinical Presentation

Migraine is one of the most common primary headache disorders. According to epidemiologic studies, migraine occurs in approximately 18% of females and 5% of males.[14] Migraine occurrence involves the most professionally active age group in the population with the highest prevalence between ages 25 and 55, with a female to male ratio of 3:1.[15] The World Health Organization ranked migraine 19th among all diseases that may cause disability.[13]

For diagnostic purposes, we use classification and diagnostic criteria proposed by the International Headache Society in 2003 (Table 42–1).[13] Criteria for migraine diagnosis are presented in Table 42–2.[13] Typically, patients with migraine will fulfill these criteria although there are some exceptions. First, the duration of an acute migraine attack may be briefer than 4 hours. We have observed in childhood migraine that an attack may last 1 or 2 hours.[16] In many cases of childhood

<table>
<tr><td>

Table 42-1

</td></tr>
</table>

Classification of Migraine

1.1. Migraine without aura
1.2. Migraine with aura
    1.2.1. Typical aura with migraine headache
    1.2.2. Typical aura with nonmigraine headache
    1.2.3. Typical aura without headache
    1.2.4. Familial hemiplegic migraine
    1.2.5. Sporadic hemiplegic migraine
    1.2.6. Basilar-type migraine
1.3. Retinal migraine
1.4. Complications of migraine
    1.4.1. Chronic migraine
    1.4.2. Status migrainosus
    1.4.3. Persistent aura without infarction
    1.4.4. Migrainosus infarction
    1.4.5. Migraine-triggered seizure
1.5. Probable migraine
    1.5.1. Probable migraine without aura
    1.5.2. Probable migraine with aura
    1.5.3. Probable chronic migraine

Table 42-2

Diagnostic Criteria of Migraine Without Aura

At least five headache attacks fulfilling criteria B-D:

A. Headache attack lasting 4-72 hours (untreated or unsuccessfully treated)
B. Headache has at least two of the following characteristics:
    1. Unilateral location of the pain (involves one half of the head)
    2. Throbbing or pulsating quality of the pain
    3. Moderate or severe pain intensity
    4. Aggravation by or causing avoidance of routine physical activity
C. During headache at least one of the following:
    1. Nausea and/or vomiting
    2. Phonophobia and photophobia
D. Not attributed to another disorder

migraine, the symptoms vary from the typical presentation because the headache may be located bilaterally or may involve the entire head.[17] Also, in adults with migraine, the attack may start as a typical unilateral headache but when it reaches its peak, the pain may radiate to the opposite side of the head thus becoming a generalized headache.

The pathophysiologic substrate of migraine consists of cerebral blood vessels, venous sinuses, trigeminal nerve, and upper cervical dorsal roots. The acute attack involves: activation of the pain-producing structures; release of CGRP, substance P (SP), NO; and, a sterile neurogenic inflammation. The trigeminocervical complex is stimulated by different triggers (neuronal and chemical: prostaglandins, serotonin, histamine) through which the series of reactions will cause the increase of concentrations of such vasoactive peptide as SP and CGRP.[18] Also, concentration of NO (another potent vasodilator) will be elevated.[19] These changes will result in vasodilatation followed by exudation of plasma in to the surrounding tissue—a phenomenon described as a sterile neurogenic inflammation.[20] All of these changes will produce a headache.

Clinical Example of Patient with Migraine

A female 24 years of age complains of severe, throbbing headache located more frequently (but not always) in the area of the left temple and forehead. The duration of the headache varies but usually lasts 24 hours. The headache is always associated with nausea, occasionally vomiting, and photophobia and phonophobia to the extent that the patient prefers to remain in a dark quiet room and, if possible, to sleep rather then do any physical activity that would exacerbate the headache. The patient's medical history as well as physical and neurologic examinations are normal.

The two major subgroups of migraine, migraine with aura and migraine without aura, are distinguished by a set of neurologic symptoms—the aura—which is typically visual in nature and precedes the headache by 30 to 60 minutes. Characteristically, the aura is focal, limited in time, and totally and completely reversible. The aura or prodrome manifests the initial vasoconstriction.[21] These neurologic symptoms have a gradual onset, developing over 5 to 20 minutes, and usually continue for less then 60 minutes. In order of frequency, the aura symptoms include scotoma (blind spots); teichopsia or fortification spectra; sensory symptoms (positive—pins and needles; negative—numbness); dysphasia; and, visual changes. Approximately 99% of the patients with migraine with aura describe visual symptoms.[22] The visual aura itself may consist of photopsia (flashing light) or scotoma (partial loss of sight). One of the most characteristic features of visual auras is the fortification spectrum (the arc of zigzag scintillating lights).[17] About 80% of patients with visual auras indicate that the aura usually precedes the headache itself.[23] Visual aura is rarely observed during or after the headache phase.[24]

The aura phenomenon has been attributed to the spreading depression of Leão, which represents the decrease of cerebral blood flow in cortex that starts posteriorly and spreads anteriorly without crossing the ischemic threshold.[24,25] A few hours later, areas that were exposed to the mentioned oligemia will become hyperemic.

Clinical Example of Patient with Migraine with Aura

Clinical presentation of headache pain itself might be the same as in the previous example. However, the patient will also mention that occasionally, or possibly with each acute migraine headache, an aura will occur. Approximately 40 to 60 minutes before the headache onset, the patient may start seeing flashing lights or zigzag lines or experience tunnel vision. These visual changes will last for a few minutes (10 to 40 minutes) and then will spontaneously disappear after the severe unilateral, throbbing headache has started.

In some cases, the typical aura may be followed by a headache that does not fulfill diagnostic criteria for migraine. In this case, we may suppose that the patient has typical aura with nonmigraine headache. In this case, other organic causes should be considered that may mimic typical aura (for example transient ischemic attack, multiple sclerosis).

In some elderly patients with a history of migraine with typical aura, the headache alters and the patient may finally lose the migraine headache although the aura persists. In those cases, patients will experience a typical aura that fulfills all of the previously cited criteria but will not suffer a headache during the aura or within the 60 minutes following those symptoms. We can describe this situation as typical aura without headache.[26,27]

Other types of migraine with aura may occur, although rarely. Hemiplegic migraine has motor weakness as part of the aura. The diagnostic criteria for hemiplegic aura are provided in Table 42–3.[13] Two types of hemiplegic aura have been identified. The first, familial hemiplegic migraine (FHM),[28] has a genetic substrate that has been identified. Patients with FHM type 1 have mutations in CACNA1A gene on chromosome 19,[13,29] and patients with FHN type 2 have mutations in ATP1A2 gene on chromosome 1. In addition to the diagnostic criteria listed in Table 42–3, we should note that patients with FHM should have at least one first- or second-degree relative with headache attacks that fulfill criteria A through D for hemiplegic migraine (see Table 42–3).[13,30] Also, patients with FHM1 may experience cerebellar symptoms (nystagmus and progressive ataxia), and are frequently diagnosed with chronic progressive cerebellar ataxia—the pathogenesis of which is also linked to the 19th chromosome.[31]

The other type of hemiplegic migraine is sporadic, and has the same occurrence and diagnostic criteria but without the genetic substrate described earlier. The patient with the sporadic form of hemiplegic migraine would not necessarily have a first- or second-degree relative with headache attacks fulfilling criteria A through D for hemiplegic migraine (see Table 42–3).[13,32,33] The diagnosis of hemiplegic migraine should be established only after a thorough physical and neu-

rologic examination and with the use of methods of neurovisualization (MRI, MRA).[34]

Clinical Example of Patient with Hemiplegic Migraine

A 36-year-old female complained about severe, throbbing unilateral headache, which is always associated with nausea, vomiting, photophobia, and phonophobia, and which has lasted up to 3 days. Occasionally, the patient has also experienced episodes of numbness and pronounced muscle weakness of the right side of the face and right arm and leg. She cannot drive the car or feed herself with the right hand. Her husband advised that during these episodes, her face is asymmetrical for up to 1 day. She has continued to experience some numbness and weakness (but not as severe) for another 1 or 2 days. Her medical history, physical, and neurologic examinations, as well as MRI and MRA, were negative.

Another form of migraine with neurologic symptoms is basilar artery migraine, which is rare. The nucleus of its clinical presentation are symptoms which originate from the brain stem or both hemispheres (posterior part of the brain that is supplied by the vertebrobasilar artery system). One of the characteristic features of basilar artery migraine is bilateral neurologic presentation of the aura signs. The diagnostic criteria are presented in Table 42–4.[13] During the acute basilar artery migraine attack, the headache itself may not manifest as bilateral pain or as a headache located in the occipital region. Basilar artery migraine is difficult to differentiate from migraine with typical sensory aura (paresthesias) in which the paresthesias are also a part of an aura. In the last case, the sensory phenomenon should be bilateral.[31]

Table 42–3

Diagnostic Criteria of Hemiplegic Migraine

I. At least two attacks fulfilling criteria B and C
  A. Aura consisting of fully reversible motor weakness and at least one of the following:
    1. Fully reversible visual symptoms (visual aura)
    2. Fully reversible sensory symptoms (sensory aura)
    3. Fully reversible dysphasic speech disturbance
  B. At least two of the following:
    1. At least one aura symptom develops gradually over ≥5 minutes and/or different aura symptoms occur in succession over ≥5 minutes
    2. Each aura symptom lasts more than 5 minutes but less than 24 hours
  C. Headache fulfilling criteria B to D for migraine without aura (Table 42–2) begins during the aura or follows onset of aura within 60 minutes
II. Not attributed to another disorder

Table 42–4

Diagnostic Criteria of Basilar-Type Migraine
At least two attacks fulfilling criteria B to D

A. Aura consists of at least two of the following fully reversible symptoms but no motor weakness:
  1. Dysarthria
  2. Vertigo
  3. Tinnitus
  4. Hypacusia
  5. Diplopia
  6. Visual symptoms simultaneously in both nasal and temporal fields of both eyes
  7. Ataxia
  8. Decreased level of consciousness
  9. Simultaneously bilateral paresthesias
B. At least one of the following:
  1. At least one aura symptom develops gradually over ≥5 minutes and or different aura symptoms occur in succession over ≥5 minutes
  2. Each aura symptom lasts more then 5 minutes but less than 24 hours
C. Headache fulfilling criteria B to D for migraine without aura (Table 42–2) begins during the aura or follows onset of aura within 60 minutes
D. Not attributed to another disorder

Clinical Example of Patient with Basilar-Type Migraine

The patient is a 17-year-old male complaining of severe, throbbing bilateral headache located in the occipital area, associated with severe nausea and vomiting, paresthesias of both legs and arms, which usually begins in the periphery and gradually radiates to the extremities. During these episodes, the patient also experiences dizziness and vertigo. The duration of these symptoms ranges between 20 and 40 minutes, and usually occur simultaneously with the headache. The history, physical, and neurologic examinations, as well as MRI and MRA, are negative.

Retinal migraine is associated with monocular visual loss which is usually preceded by scintillating scotoma. The migraine episode may continue for several hours and occasionally without close association with a headache. This type of migraine is usually a diagnosis of exclusion with other causes being ruled out.[35] The diagnostic criteria are presented in Table 42–5.[13]

Some patients may experience more frequent migraine episodes (with or without aura). If the migraine frequency is more then 15 days a month, and the patient experiences such frequency for more then 3 months, we may consider chronic migraine. Diagnostic criteria are presented in Table 42–6.[13] Also, it is important that the diagnosis should be established in the absence of medication-overuse.[13,36-38] The vast majority of the patients with chronic migraine will report the history of episodic migraine in the past.[38,39]

Another complication of migraine is status migrainosus. This condition is characterized by incapacitating severe migraine lasting more than 72 hours. During this episode, patients may experience continuous nausea and/or frequent copious vomiting which may cause severe dehydration of the patients which may require urgent hospitalization. During status migrainosus, the standard migraine abortive medications are not effective and the patient may need intravenous drug administration to resolve the headache status—another reason for patient's admission into the hospital. The diagnostic criteria for status migrainosus are presented in Table 42–7.[13]

Persistent aura without infarction should be considered when the migraine aura persists longer than 1 week without any radiographic evidence of infarction.[13] In those cases with prolonged aura associated with ischemic changes located in the areas consistent with aura presentation (considering that these changes had been proved by methods of neuroimaging), the diagnosis of migrainosus infarction can be established.[13]

Migraine-triggered seizure is a rare situation in which migraine aura is followed within 1 hour by a seizure.[13] In those cases when migraine-like headache does not fulfill at least one of the required diagnostic criteria and all other causes of the headache are ruled out, the diagnosis of probable migraine should be made.[13]

It is essential that the patient undergo a thorough examination. For many patients, completing the headache history is a difficult task, especially when little attention has been paid to such features as headache frequency, duration, location, and quality of the pain. Also, the associated symptoms should be evaluated and the physician should determine the type of aura the patient is experiencing because these two factors will affect treatment selections. We should also obtain information regarding previous treatment history and prior pitfalls in therapy. The history is probably the most important factor in establishing the diagnosis. To get more accurate information, we ask each of our patients to maintain a daily calendar to record any headache episodes, possible triggers, and medications used. The calendar details the following information: date of headache; time of onset and ending; severity (using 10-point visual analog scale in which 10 is the most severe); triggers (psychic, physical, emotional); and food and drink excesses. Patients should also indicate their treatment (which medications were taken and the dosage) as well as relief of headache (again using a 10-point visual analog scale in which 0 equals complete relief).[40] This calendar is easy to maintain and does not require a great deal of time to complete. It is also important to use the calendar for treatment evaluation purposes—determining the dynamics of the headache pattern, medication intake, possible triggers, and so on.

In addition to a thorough physical and neurologic examination, neuroimaging may be necessary. For all of our

---

Table 42–5

Diagnostic Criteria of Retinal Migraine

At least two attacks fulfilling criteria B and C

A. Fully reversible monocular positive and/or negative visual phenomena (scintillations, scotoma, or blindness) confirmed by examination during an attack or (after proper instructions) by the patient's drawing of a monocular field defect during an attack
B. Headache fulfilling criteria B to D for migraine without aura (Table 42–2) begins during the visual symptoms or follows them within 60 minutes
C. Normal ophthalmologic examination between attacks
D. Not attributed to another disorder

Table 42–6

Diagnostic Criteria of Chronic Migraine

A. Headache fulfilling criteria C and D for migraine without aura (Table 42–2) on more than 15 days a month for more than 3 months
B. Not attributed to another disorder

Table 42–7

Diagnostic Criteria for Status Migrainosus

A The present attack in a patient with migraine without aura is typical of previous attack except for its duration
B. Headache has both of the following features:
1. Unremitting for more than 72 hours
2. Severe intensity
C. Not attributed to another disorder

primary headache patients, we recommend an MRI of the brain, with and without contrast, if they have never undergone this test or if the last MRI was obtained more then 6 months earlier. Also, if the headache pattern had changed dramatically over the past few months, we also recommend repeating the study. An MRI and magnetic resonance angiography (MRA) of the head and neck should be undertaken in those patients complaining of severe, throbbing headaches associated with aura (especially hemiplegic, basilar, or retinal), or if the headache is exacerbated during or immediately after physical exercises, coughing, sneezing, or bending. The MRI and MRA are used to rule out other possible causes of the headache (brain tumor, aneurysm, intracranial hypertension, and so on). In acute subarachnoid hemorrhage, head trauma, or bone abnormalities, CT scanning should be ordered.[41] Lumbar puncture (LP) should be performed if a patient presents complaining of the worst headache ever or the first ever but very severe headache, if the headache is associated with fever or other signs of infection.[41] Also, we should be aware of a common complication of LP—low cerebral spinal fluid (CSF) pressure or post-lumbar puncture headache. This adverse effect from an LP may be reduced by using a smaller needle.[42]

▮ TREATMENT

Using the information we have obtained during the history and examinations and having established the diagnosis, we may select our treatment options. The goal of treatment is to reduce the patient's disability and improve quality of life. For that purpose, we use abortive, symptomatic, and preventive methods of treatment. At our clinic, we do not limit our treatment options to pharmacologic methods but also engage nonpharmacologic methods of treatment (biofeedback, relaxation techniques, physical therapy, and so on). It is important to educate patients regarding diagnosis and treatment—explaining possible side effects and benefits. We should also inform the patient that we are starting a treatment process that requires the patient's compliance, and if needed, will make corrections and changes in the treatment in the future.

We recommend the following basic rules:

1. Maintain regular sleep pattern (if possible, patients should awaken at the same time every day because oversleeping may trigger a migraine attack).
2. Maintain regular meal pattern (missing meals or fasting may trigger headache).
3. All patients should follow a low tyramine and low caffeine diet.[21]
4. Coping strategics (may help to handle stress more efficiently, thus decreasing its ability to trigger migraine).[21,38]

We have also established certain rules regarding abortive therapy:

1. Abortive agents should be taken as soon as possible at the beginning of a migraine attack.
2. Abortive agents should not be taken on a daily basis.

The most potent abortive agents are the triptans (5-HT agonists). Seven triptans are now available: sumatriptan, zolmitriptan, naratriptan, rizatriptan, almotriptan, frovatriptan, and eletriptan. These agents may be prescribed in a variety of administrative routes: oral tablets, nasal sprays, orally disintegrating tablets, and subcutaneous injections. The 5-HT agonists have variable affinity to the different 5-HT$_1$ receptors and inhibit release of 5-HT, norepinephrine, acetylcholine, and substance P. Thus, the triptans reduce the sterile neurogenic inflammation, described previously, and cause potent vasoconstriction in the cranial blood vessels.[43]

Because the triptans are potent vasoconstrictors, these medications should never be administered intravenously. The triptans should not be prescribed to patients with a history of ischemic heart disease, hypertension, myocardial infarction, or Prinzmetal angina.[44] Triptans should also be avoided in patients with hemiplegic and basilar-type migraine, and should never be used concomitantly with ergotamine-containing medications and monoamine oxidase inhibitors (MAOIs). The triptans differ in the time of action onset as well as in the duration of action—factors to be considered when deciding which triptan should be prescribed. If the patient experiences difficulties in identifying an impending migraine (for example, patient with chronic daily headache) or the headache attack develops within a very brief period of time (a few minutes), then we should consider triptans with a fast onset of action (rizatriptan[45]—for oral triptans or parenteral sumatriptan). In those patients experiencing prolonged migraine (longer than 24 hours), we recommend the use of triptans with a longer half-life, such as frovatriptan.

Generally, patients may take another triptan tablet 1 to 2 hours after the first dose if needed. However, triptan intake should be limited to only 2 days a week. We also recommend that a 4-day hiatus be maintained between days of use. The most common side effects are tingling sensation, chest pain, nausea and vomiting, and tightness of the throat.

Another highly effective group of antimigraine medications are the ergotamine-containing medications—ergotamine and dihydroergotamine (DHE). Because these agents are also potent vasoconstrictors, they should be avoided in patients with unstable hypertension, ischemic heart disease, history of myocardial infarction, impaired renal and hepatic function, infection, and pregnancy. DHE is available as a nasal spray and in parenteral preparation for subcutaneous, intramuscular, or intravenous administration. We also use DHE intravenously for treating patients with status migrainosus and other intractable forms of headaches. In this case, DHE 0.5 to 1.0 mg is administered intravenously over 2 to 3 minutes in combination with metoclopramide (10 mg) every 8 hours for 3 days. The most common side effects are nausea, vomiting, and chest pain.[46]

NSAIDs are also effective in migraine management due to their ability to inhibit inflammation. These agents are particularly effective in patients with mild-to-moderately severe migraine episodes. The most common side effects are nausea, abdominal distress, diarrhea, and dyspepsia. Recently, medications from the family of cyclooxygenase-2 (COX2) inhibitors (rofecoxib, celecoxib) are being widely used due to decreased effect on the gastrointestinal system. Phenothiazines (chlorpromazine, prochlorperazine) may also be beneficial owing to their dopaminergic and adrenergic effects as well as their sedative and antinausea actions.[47]

For those patients with contraindications for the afore-mentioned medications or for those in whom these medications were not effective, we may consider narcotic analgesics. In this case, patients should be advised about all possible side effects and complications of these agents, as well as possible addiction problems and rebound phenomenon. We should avoid prescribing narcotic analgesics for patients with chronic migraine due to the high risk of abuse.

For those patients who have been diagnosed with chronic migraine or who experience prolonged incapacitating migraines, we recommend prophylactic therapy. Preventive medications may be used singly or in combination with other prophylactic agents.

We recommend starting prophylactic treatment with beta (ß) blockers. The drug of choice from this group is the non-selective ß-blocker propranolol. Propranolol efficacy in migraine is attributed to its preventive effect due its ability to block ß-adrenergic receptors in the blood vessels, thus preventing their dilation and also possibly reducing platelet aggregation. Propranolol is effective in doses of 80 to 240 mg daily. The long-acting form of the drug enhances patient compliance with a once-daily dosage. The most common side effects are low blood pressure, decreased heart rate, fatigue, and depression.[48] These medications should be avoided in patients with asthma, chronic obstructive lung disease, congestive heart failure, or atrioventricular conduction disturbances. After long-term treatment, a slow tapering is recommended.[21] Other ß-blockers used in migraine prevention are timolol and metoprolol. For those patients with asthma, the use of a cardioselective ß-blocker such as metoprolol is indicated.

The calcium channel blockers, such as verapamil, have been used effectively in migraine prevention. These medications block calcium influx, which is essential for vasoconstriction, platelet aggregation, and the release of serotonin from the platelets. Verapamil is effective in doses of 120 to 360 mg daily. The most common side effects are constipation, flushing, low blood pressure, and nausea.[49] Gradual reduction of the dosage is also recommended.

The antidepressants are among the most potent preventive agents for chronic migraine and other forms of chronic daily headaches. These agents could be considered in patients with chronic migraine and concomitant depression. The tricyclic antidepressants (TCAs) are especially effective due to their ability to block serotonin reabsorption, and their anticholinergic and antihistaminic activity. All antidepressants require at least 2 to 3 weeks to elicit their effect, and the headache sufferer should be instructed to be patient and not abruptly terminate treatment. For those headache patients who also experience sleeping difficulties, the TCA of choice is amitriptyline (starting at 10 or 25 mg at bedtime slowly, increasing every 5 to 7 days, up to 100 mg if needed).[50] Other sedating TCAs include nortriptyline (starting from 10 mg or 25 mg at bedtime, increasing every 5 to 7 days up to 100 mg if needed) or doxepin (starting at 25 mg at bedtime slowly, increasing every 5 to 7 days up to 150 mg if needed). For patients who do not require a sedating TCA, protriptyline is indicated. In patients with prolonged chronic migraine and/or prominent psychological problems (depression, anxiety), a combination of these medications should be used.[21,44] The most common side effects are constipation, blurred vision, dry mouth, decreased libido, orthostatic hypotension, and weight gain. These medications should be avoided in patients with low-angle glaucoma or prostatic hypertrophy. To increase the efficacy of prophylactic treatment, antidepressant may be used in combination with ß-blockers or calcium channel blockers.

Another type of antidepressant used in patients with chronic migraine are the MAOIs (phenelzine, isocarboxazid).[51] These medications are not first-line drugs and should be considered only when patients fail all other standard prophylactic methods of treatment. These limitations are due to the extensive interactions between different groups of medications (most TCAs and all selective serotonin reuptake inhibitors [SSRIs]) are contraindicated with concomitant use of an MAOI.[51] Diet restrictions are essential for patients on MAOI therapy to avoid hypotensive problems. Generally, we prescribe this type of medication for patients admitted into our hospital unit (Diamond Inpatient Headache Unit). At that facility, we are able to instruct them on the intricacies of this medication, and the dietary and drug restrictions associated with MAOI therapy. We recommend starting phenelzine at 15 mg twice daily, and increasing it by 15 mg every 7 days up to 15 mg four times a day, if needed. Isocarboxazid should be started at 10 mg twice daily, and slowly increased by 10 mg every 7 days up to 10 mg four times a day, if needed. All patients on MAOI therapy should be instructed to wear medical identification to alert emergency personnel that the patient is on MAOI therapy and drug precautions must be followed.

Another class of preventive medications used in migraine prophylaxis are the anticonvulsants. Divalproex sodium may be efficiently used in combination with TCAs and ß-blockers. The most common side effects of divalproex therapy are nausea, hepatotoxicity, weight gain, and gastrointestinal distress. This medication should be avoided in patients with a history of hepatitis and abnormal liver function. Liver function tests should be performed before treatment and monitored at regular intervals during therapy.

Another anticonvulsant, topiramate, has demonstrated efficacy in different clinical studies.[52,53] Unlike other centrally acting drugs. topiramate is weight neutral and may be associated with weight loss—another benefit from this medication. We recommend starting treatment with 25 mg once a day, increasing the dose by 25-mg increments every week up to 100 to 200 mg per day if needed. The most common side effects are numbness in the hands and lightheadedness. This medication should not be used in patients with a history of kidney stones. Caution is advised in patients with glaucoma.

Recently, a few double-blind, placebo-controlled trials provided mixed results regarding botulinum toxin type A efficacy as a preventive agent in patients with frequent migraine attacks.[54,55] Until more data are available, we recommend using botulinum toxin type A for patients with intractable headache or in those who cannot tolerate other medications.[56]

For all forms of therapy, we should stress that the most common treatment mistake is its preliminary discontinuation (2 to 3 weeks after treatment was initiated). A brief treatment interval simply does not provide sufficient time to evaluate the efficacy of the preventive medication.

In addition to pharmacologic methods of treatment, we also highly recommend the use of nonpharmacologic interventions: biofeedback, physical therapy, stress management therapy, relaxation training, and psychologic and/or psychiatric consultations. According to our data, patients with chronic migraine and medication-overuse headaches have altered coping strategies that they use to cope with severe pain, chronic pain, and stress.[57] Biofeedback techniques, relaxation exercises, and psychotherapy may help modify the existing (and perhaps not efficient) coping strategies and modify the patient's attitude to the pain. These interventions may possibly teach new and more effective strategies to be used in the patient's daily life by reducing the severity and, in some cases, the frequency of the headaches. We believe that by using a multidisciplinary approach to the headache patients, we may achieve improvement in the treatment of patients with migraine.

References

1. Rose FC: The history of migraine from Mesopotamia to medieval times. Cephalalgia 15 (Suppl 15):1, 1995.
2. Adams F: The Extant Works of Aretaeus, the Cappadocian. London, New Sydenham Society, 1856.
3. Critchley M: Migraine: From Cappadocia to Queen Square. In Smith R (ed): Background to Migraine. London, Heinemann, 1967, p 16.
4. International Headache Society: Classification and diagnostic criteria for headache disorders, cranial neuralgias and facial pain. Cephalalgia 8 (Suppl 7):1, 1988.
5. Kuehn CG: Claudii Galeni opera omnia, vol. 12. Leipzig, Officina Car Cnoblochii, 1826.
6. Isler H: Thomas Willis' chapters on headache of 1672. Headache 26:95, 1986.
7. Whytt R: Observations on the nature, causes and cure of those diseases which are commonly called nervous, hypochondriac or hysteric; to which are prefixed some remarks on the sympathy of the nerves. London, Becket, Du Hondt, 1765.
8. Sieveking E: On Epilepsy and Epileptiform Seizures. London, John Churchill, 1858.
9. Vein A, Vorobeva O: Universal cerebral mechanisms in the pathogenesis of paroxysmal disorders. Zh Nevrol Psikhiatr Im SS Korsakova 12:8, 1999.
10. Mobius PJ: Die Migrane. Vienna, Alfred Holder, 1898.
11. Olesen J, Tfelt-Hansen P, Welch M: The Headaches, 2nd ed. Philadelphia, Lippincott Williams & Wilkins, 2000.
12. Wolff H: Headache and Other Head Pain. New York, Oxford University Press, 1948.
13. International Headache Society: The International Classification of Headache Disorders, 2nd ed. Cephalalgia 24 (Suppl 1):1, 2004.
14. Lipton R, Stewart W, Diamond S: Prevalence and burden of migraine in the United States: Data from the American Migraine Study II. Headache 41:646, 2001.
15. Scher A, Stewart W, Lipton R: Migraine and headache: A meta-analytic approach. In Crombie I (ed): Epidemiology of Pain. Seattle, IASP Press, 1999, p 159.
16. Diamond S, Diamond A: Headache and Your Child. The Complete Guide to Understanding and Treating Migraine and Other Headache in Children and Adolescents. New York, Simon and Schuster, 2001.
17. Wilkinson M: Clinical Features of Migraine. In Rose FC (ed): Handbook of Clinical Neurology. New York, Elsevier, 1986, p 117.
18. Goadsby P, Edvinsson L, Ekman R: Release of vasoactive peptides in the extracerebral circulation of man and the cat during activation of the trigeminovascular system. Ann Neurol 28:183, 1988.
19. Furchgott R: The requirement for endothelial cells in the relaxation of arteries by acetylcholine and some other vasodilators. Trends Pharmacol Sci 2:173, 1984.
20. Moskowitz M: Basic mechanisms in vascular headaches. Neurol Clin 8:801, 1990.
21. Diamond S: Migraine headache. In Diamond M, Solomon G (eds): The Practicing Physician's Approach to Headache, 6th ed. Philadelphia, WB Saunders, 1999, p 46.
22. Russell M, Olesen J: A nosographic analysis of the migraine aura in a general population. Brain 119:355, 1996.
23. Jensen K, Tfelt-Hansen P, Lauritzen M: Classic migraine, a prospective recording of symptoms. Acta Neurol Scand 73:359, 1986.
24. Olesen J, Edvinsson L: Basic Mechanisms of Headache. New York, Elsevier, 1988.
25. Woods R, Iacoboni M, Mazziotta J: Bilateral spreading cerebral hypoperfusion during spontaneous migraine headaches. N Engl J Med 331:1689, 1994.
26. Ziegler D, Hassanein R: Specific headache phenomena: Their frequency and coincidence. Headache 30:152, 1990.
27. Whitty C: Migraine without headache. Lancet ii:283, 1967.
28. Koeppen A: Familial hemiplegic migraine. Arch Neurol 60:663, 2003.
29. Wieser T, Mueller C, Evers S: Absence of known familial hemiplegic migraine (FHM) mutations in the CACNA1A gene in patients with common migraine: Implications for genetic testing. Clin Chem Lab Med 41:272, 2003.
30. Vanmolkot K, van den Maagdenberg A, Haan J, Ferrari M: New discoveries about the second gene for familial hemiplegic migraine, ATP1A2. Lancet Neurol 2:721, 2003.
31. Kunkel RS: Complicated and rare forms of migraine. In Diamond ML, Solomon GD (eds): Diamond and Dalessio's The Practicing Physician's Approach to Headache, 6th ed. Philadelphia, WB Saunders, 1999, p 95.
32. Tournier-Lasserve E: Hemiplegic migraine, episodic ataxia type 2, and the others. Neurology 53:3, 1999.
33. Thomsen L, Ostergaard E, Romer S, et al: Sporadic hemiplegic migraine is an aetiologically heterogeneous disorder. Cephalalgia 23:921, 2003.
34. Butteriss D, Ramesh V, Birchall D: Serial MRI in a case of familial hemiplegic migraine. Neuroradiology 45:300, 2003.
35. Corbett J: Neuro-ophthalmic complications of migraine and cluster headaches. Neurol Clin 1:973, 1983.
36. Warner J: Frequent migraine and migraine status without tension-type headaches: An unusual presentation of rebound headaches. Cephalalgia 23:309, 2003.
37. Feoktistov A, Filatova E, Vein A: Abuse headache. Zh Nevrol Psikhiatr Im S S Korsakova 12:58, 1999.
38. Feoktistov A, Filatova E, Vein A: Psychophysiological characteristic of groups of patients with analgesic rebound headache. Zh Nevrol Psikhiatr Im S S Korsakova 10:13, 2002.
39. Bussone G: Chronic migraine and chronic tension-type headache: Different aspects of the chronic daily headache spectrum. Clinical and pathogenetic considerations. Neurol Sci 24 (Suppl 2):90, 2003.
40. Diamond M, Solomon G: Taking a headache history. In Diamond ML, Solomon GD (eds): Diamond and Dalessio's The Practicing Physician's Approach to Headache, 6th ed. Philadelphia, WB Saunders, 1999, p 16.
41. Evans R, Rozen T, Adelman J: Neuroimaging and other diagnostic testing in headache. In Silberstein S, Lipton R, Dalessio D (eds): Wolff's Headache and Other Head Pain, 7th ed. New York, Oxford University Press, 2001, p 27.
42. Evans R, Armon C, Frohman E, et al: Assessment: Prevention of post-lumbar puncture headaches. Neurology 55:909-914, 2000.
43. Peroutka S: Developments in 5-hydroxytryptamine receptor pharmacology in migraine. Neurol Clin 8:829, 1990.
44. Diamond S: Diagnosing and Managing Headaches, 4th ed. Professional Communications, Caddo, Oklahoma, 2001.
45. Teall J, Tuchman M, Cutler N, et al: Rizatriptan (Maxalt) for the acute treatment of migraine and migraine recurrence. A placebo-controlled, outpatient study. Headache 38:281, 1998.
46. Raskin N: Repetitive intravenous dihydroergotamine as therapy for intractable migraine. Neurology 36:995, 1986.
47. Jones J, Pack S, Chun E: Intramuscular prochlorperazine versus metoclopramide as single agent therapy for the treatment of acute migraine. Am J Emerg Med 14:262, 1996.
48. Diamond S, Kudrow L, Stevens J, Shapiro D: Long-term study of propranolol in the treatment of migraine. Headache 22:268, 1982.
49. Solomon G, Diamond S, Freitag F: Verapamil in migraine prophylaxis: Comparison of dosages. Clin Pharmacol Ther 41:202, 1987.
50. Couch J, Ziegler D, Hassanein R: Amitriptyline in the prophylaxis of migraine. Neurology 26:121, 1976.
51. Anthony M, Lance J: Monoamine oxidase inhibition in the treatment of migraine. Arch Neurol 21:263, 1969.
52. Potter D, Hart D, Calder C, et al: A double-blind, randomized, placebo-controlled, parallel study to determine the efficacy of Topamax (topiramate) in the prophylactic treatment of migraine. Neurology 52(suppl 3):A115, 2000.

53. Edwards K, Glautz M, Shea P, et al: Topiramate for migraine prophylaxis: A double-blind, randomized, placebo controlled study. Headache 40:407, 2000.
54. Binder W, Brin M, Blitzer A, Pogoda J: Botulinum toxin type A (Botox) for treatment of migraine. Dis Mon 48:323, 2002.
55. Silberstein S, Mathew N, Saper J: Botox Migraine Clinical Research Group. Botulinum toxin type A as a migraine preventive treatment. Headache 40:445, 2000.
56. Loder E, Biondi D: Use of botulinum toxin for chronic headaches: A focused overview. Clin J Pain 18 (Suppl 6):S169, 2002.
57. Feoktistov A: Clinico-psychophysiological peculiarities of the patients with abuse headache. Monograph [dissertation for PhD], Ministry of Public Health of Russian Federation, Moscow Medical Academy, Moscow, p 1, 2001.

Tension-Type Headache

Frederick G. Freitag

■ HISTORICAL CONSIDERATIONS

Our concepts of what constitutes tension-type headache have been undergoing revision over the past several years. To a degree, this represents the continuing evolution of our understanding of this disorder. In past decades, tension-type headache was referred to as *muscle contraction* or *muscle tension headache, psychogenic headache, interval headache,* or *depressive headache.* Each of these terms describes components of the headache that individual clinicians thought were the cause of the headache or its association with other disease states. The term *muscle tension headache* was used to describe the musculoskeletal quality of the pain and its distribution in the head and neck area. Although association with musculoskeletal etiologies dates to the 19th century, it was Blumenthal[1] who made the direct association with the scalp and neck muscles. The vascular system was believed to contribute to the headache process; this was the reverse from that associated with migraine, and it was vasoconstrictive not vasodilatory. The term *psychogenic headache* and its variants were used by prominent headache physicians such as Ryan[2] and Wolff.[3] Diamond[4] used the term *depressive headache* to characterize headaches relieved by antidepressant medications. The term *interval headache*[5] was used to describe those headaches that patients with migraine headache might experience between their distinct migraine headache attacks. This process of describing tension-type headache began, in great part, with the work of Olesen[5] because, at that time, the potential associated symptoms and description of interval headache provided areas of overlap with migraine headache. Frequency of the headaches was the only differentiating element. Interval headache could occur with daily or near-daily frequency. Recently, work by Lipton and Cady[6] examining the treatment of migraine with sumatriptan[6] led to further differentiation of the true tension-type headache from those tension-type headaches occurring in patients with migraine—and possibly representing a mild or early form of migraine headache. Now, the most recent version of the International Headache Society diagnostic criteria provides a truly clear differentiation between migraine headache and tension-type headache.[7]

■ THE CLINICAL SYNDROME—SIGNS, SYMPTOMS, AND PHYSICAL FINDINGS

Tension-type headache is divided into several major groupings: episodic and chronic—and both of these with or without associated disorder of the pericranial muscles. The most common headache worldwide is episodic tension-type headache. It would seem that this is the headache that most everyone experiences when they have had a stressful day. However the actual prevalence of tension-type headache is much lower. A study by Schwatz[8] estimated the overall prevalence of episodic tension-type headache at 38.3% of the population. Increased prevalence was found in the age group 30 to 39 years old, reaching nearly 47% of the females in this age range. Those individuals of African American descent had a substantially lower overall prevalence rate of 22.8%. The prevalence rates also increased with increasing levels of education, being highest in those with graduate school level education where the rate approached half of the population. By contrast, chronic tension-type headache had a far lower prevalence of about 2%. Women were more likely than men to experience the chronic form of the disorder. The prevalence declined with increasing education compared to the increase seen with the episodic form. Although we expect episodic tension-type headache to have little impact on function, Schwartz found that 8.3% of individuals lost days from work and nearly half worked at decreased levels of effectiveness. Those with the chronic form were more highly affected with one fifth of patients missing work.

Tension headache is characterized by a number of clinical features (Table 43–1). The headache is a dull ache; it may be localized frontally or occipitally or may be more generalized—often in a band-like distribution about the head. The pain can extend into the neck where it may be associated with stiffness or limitation of motion. Chewing may be affected if there is involvement of the temporalis muscles or the muscles of mastication. Although the pain may be diffuse, it is not severe—except in those patients who have migraine headache that starts as a tension-type headache. It is devoid of other associated physical symptoms, such as nausea, that we traditionally associate with migraine headache. Although symptoms of photophobia and phonophobia are hallmarks of migraine, patients with tension-type headache may have one of these symptoms, but not both. The pain is self-limited and abates with the use of simple analgesics or removal of oneself from the stressful environment that may have contributed to the headache. As noted, this can be associated with involvement of the pericranial muscles. In most cases, this would be characterized by localized tenderness to palpation of the muscles. If there is involvement of an associated joint, such as in the neck or the temporomandibular joint, there may be limitation of motion. Patients rarely seek medical attention for episodic tension-type headache. Its presentation in the clinical setting should raise the suspicion for the migraine-like headache that fails to meet all of the criteria for migraine—such as migrainous headache.

The manifestation of chronic tension-type headache is very similar to that seen in the episodic versions. The most striking difference in presentation is the persistence of the headaches. Although, by definition, they occur at least 15 days in a month, it is rare to see a patient with the chronic form of headache where the headache is not daily (or near daily) over the course of months, years, and even decades. More variability may be present in the clinical presentation of chronic tension-type headache than in the episodic form. Although the pain is still most commonly described as a dull, aching sensation, there may be more notation of tightness and pulling sensation, especially with increased involvement of the pericranial muscles. Pain intensity may escalate in patients who have the headache on a long-standing basis. This is also more likely to be seen in patients whose headache is unassociated with the pericranial muscles. In the older terminology this increased pain intensity, which may be rated at maximal levels of severity, would have been associated with psychogenic or depressive headache. Typically when there is an element of depression present in these patients they may describe their pain as being worse in the morning on awakening, yet not waking them from sleep. In those with higher levels of chronic anxiety associated with these headaches, the pattern may be one of increasing severity throughout the day or of a spike in the headache pain in the later afternoon hours.

In patients with these chronic forms of tension-type headache there may also be the development of chronic alterations in their sleep patterns. Most typically, the patient has a concomitant problem with insomnia. Sometimes this is an initiating sleep disorder and occurs more frequently in patients with anxiety versus the frequent nighttime awakenings and difficulty falling back to sleep that occurs more commonly with depressive-type headache. More unusual than the insomnia problem is that of chronic fatigue with patients sleeping in excess of 10 hours per night and requiring a daytime nap as well.

Involvement of the pericranial muscles in these chronic tension-type headaches may be associated with pain or may be found with chronic spasticity of the muscles without associated palpatory tenderness. Diamond and Dalessio[9] postulated a multistep process contributing to the involvement of the pericranial and cervical muscles in tension-type headache. They suggested that local factors in the muscle tissue could provoke a local neural impulse, thereby initiating a reflex response at the spinal cord level, leading to muscle contraction but also to a polysynaptic relay (Fig. 43–1) of the stimulus to thalamic and cortical levels. Reflexively, the brain activates the reticulospinal system sending impulses through

---

Table 43–1

Clinical Characteristics of Tension-Type Headache

Symptoms of Tension-Type Headache
Less than 15 days per month: episodic
15 or more days per month: chronic
Band-like or localized unilateral or anterior or posterior pain
Mild to moderate typically may be severe in chronic
Dull aching pain, tightening, pulling
Increased headache with muscle activity (chewing)
With or without pericranial muscle tenderness
No exertional exacerbation
May have photophobia or phonophobia but not both
No nausea
No aura or premonitory symptoms
Coexisting issues and contributors: TMJ, minimal cervical dystonia, postural mechanical dysfunction of cervical spine, sleep disorder, anxiety, depression

TMJ, temporomandibular joint (disorder).

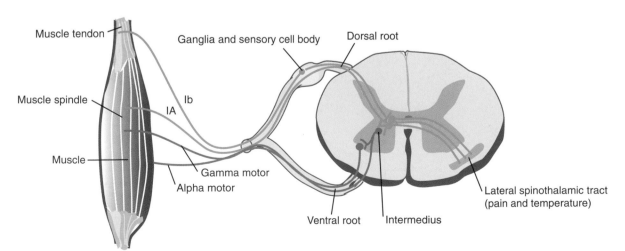

FIGURE 43–1 ■ Multisynaptic reflexes involved in regulation of muscle pain and spasm.

this efferent tract to the gamma efferent fibers at the spinal cord level causing activation of the muscle spindle. This would lead to a monosynaptic reflex through the ventral cord to efferent peripheral nerves augmenting the muscle contraction. In the absence of blocking factors, the increased muscle tone would lead to inhibition of the muscle spindle. If local factors continue to elicit activation of the afferent paths, or if changes in cortical activity promote reticulospinal efferent transmission, the muscle fibers would experience increasing muscle tone to the point of spasm and associated pain. There can be substantial overlap in the patient presenting with temporomandibular joint disorders and the patient presenting with chronic tension-type headache when the temporalis muscles are involved. Patients may have spasm and pain in these muscles with additional pain being generated from the joint because of compressive effects from the muscle spasm, yet not have a true TMJ syndrome. These patients, if they are experiencing substantial conflict in their life, may exhibit bruxism and clenching—creating muscle pain and joint tenderness as well but without having a temporomandibular joint syndrome.

Postural mechanical factors involving the cervical spine may also be present in patients with tension-type headache with pericranial muscle involvement. Underlying disk disease or degenerative joint disease of the apophyseal joints of the cervical spine may lead to increased localized muscle spasm and pain. Patterns of altered cervical mechanics may occur chronically, compounding the cervical contribution to the headache process. Although direct neural import from the cervical spine as a cause of headache would be limited to the upper two cervical segments and their interplay with the trigeminal nucleus caudalis, the structure of the neck musculature is such that even distant imitating factors may produce muscle spasm and pain referred to higher cervical levels. Elements of cervical dystonia may also be found in this group of patients with chronic tension-type headache. Typically, the amount of dystonia present is somewhat minimal and may be reflected by a slight tilt of the head toward the side of the dystonia. Involvement of muscles in the anterior and lateral neck is typically associated with this pattern of pericranial muscle involvement.

Physical examination findings are generally absent or minimal in the episodic varieties of tension-type headache. Transient tenderness on palpation or palpatory muscle spasm may be present if there is involvement of distinct muscle groups (Figs. 43–2, 43–3, and 43–4) in the head and neck region. In patients with chronic tension-type headache, where there is no involvement of the pericranial muscles, normal findings on examination is the rule. Despite the pain sometimes being of maximal intensity, there is a paucity of findings on examination. Pericranial muscle involvement patterns, as noted earlier, may be present—especially if the patient is examined in the headache phase.

Diagnostic testing must be considered in patients with tension-type headache (Table 43–2). In the primary headache disorder—such as migraine and tension-type headache—the incidence of abnormal radiologic findings in patients with a normal physical and neurologic examination is rare[10] or even

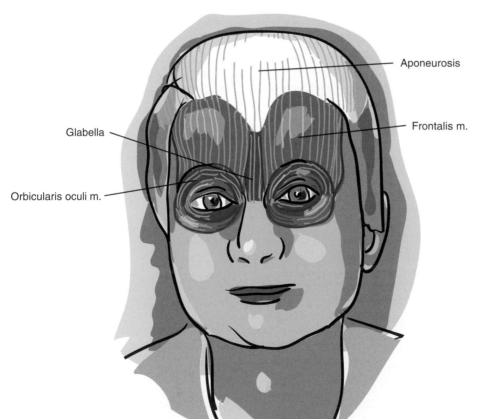

Aponeurosis

Frontalis m.

Glabella

Orbicularis oculi m.

FIGURE 43–2 ■ Areas of muscle pain in frontal region of head.

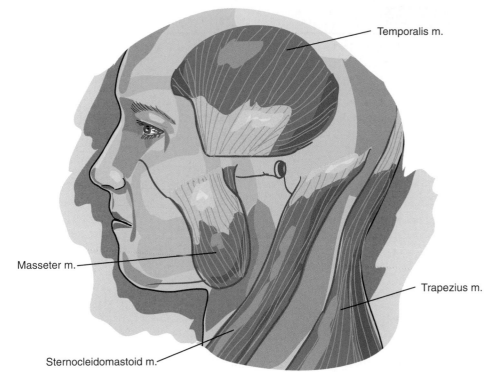

FIGURE 43–3 ■ Areas of muscle pain in lateral portion of head and neck.

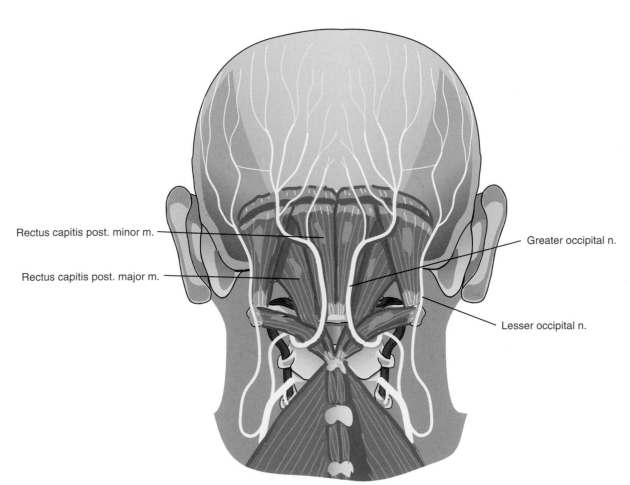

FIGURE 43–4 ■ Areas of muscle pain in posterior regions of head and neck.

Table 43–2

Diagnostic Testing in the Tension-Type Headache Patient

Neurologic and head and neck examination
CT scan of sinuses
MRI of brain with and without contrast
Cervical spine radiographs and or neurodiagnostic scan
Skull radiograph
Thyroid function tests
Baseline laboratory studies if using daily medications
Psychological testing (MMPI, Beck Inventory for Anxiety or Depression)

MMPI, Minnesota Multiphasic Personality Inventory.

Table 43–3

Diagnostic Concerns in Tension-Type Headache Differential Diagnosis

Migraine
Chronic migraine
Medication overuse headache
Hemicrania continua
New daily persistent headache
TMJ
Naso-sinus disease
Secondary tension-type headache related to coexisting medical disease, disorders of the eyes and musculoskeletal disorders (e.g., fibromyalgia, arthritis)

TMJ, temporomandibular joint (disorder).

nonexistent, as may be the case in tension-type headache. Despite this, neuroimaging (e.g., magnetic resonance imaging, computed tomography) should be strongly considered in the patient with a normal neurologic examination if (1) the headaches are rapidly increasing in frequency; (2) if the headaches are associated with dizziness or lack of coordination; (3) if there is a history of paresthesias associated with the headaches; or (4) if the headache awakens the patient from sleep. The choice of MRI versus CT scan is determined in part by the clinical suspicions of the physician. If an acute cerebral bleed is suspected or if nasal sinus disease is being investigated, then CT scan is most valuable. When other diseases entities are being considered, then an MRI with contrast enhancement is the test of choice. The resolution available with MRI, lack of interference with braces or fillings, and the ability to visualize the posterior fossa make MRI the preferred diagnostic test. Plain skull radiographs may be helpful in the elderly patient with a new onset of headache to examine for Paget disease. Plain radiographs of the cervical spine and or MRI of the cervical spine can be helpful in evaluating for concomitant conditions that might influence or cause tension-type headache.

Baseline chemistries and blood counts should be considered in the evaluation—especially if the patient will be taking daily preventive medications. This should include thyroid evaluation because hypothyroidism can manifest with a headache resembling tension-type headache.

In patients where psychiatric comorbidity[11] is present, the use of appropriate assessment by a psychologist and a screening psychological questionnaire should be considered. These might include the Minnesota Multiphasic Personality Inventory (MMPI). Beck's Inventory of Depression and Anxiety may provide helpful for comprehensive treatment of the patient with chronic tension-type headache. On the MMPI, patients with a significant physical response to stress have elevation of the first three scales. These are the Hy, D and Hs scales, short for hypochondriac, depression, and hysteria. Typically the Hy and Hs scales are higher than the D scale. If the D scale is the most elevated of the three, then further assessment for depression should be undertaken. Elevation of the scores on the Beck's Inventory of Depression and Anxiety may serve as guides to the intensity of behavioral intervention that may be required.

■ DIFFERENTIAL DIAGNOSIS

Perhaps the area that is most challenging in the tension-type headache patient may be differentiating tension-type headache (Table 43–3) from migraine headache. This becomes more problematic with daily and near-daily headache which is more likely to have similarities to chronic migraine.

Chronic migraine is a newer term for those patients who have a history of typical episodic migraine but have developed a now near-daily pattern of headache. In the past, this phenomenon has been known as *migraine with tension-type headache, mixed headache, combined headache, migraine with interval headache, transformed migraine* and *chronic daily headache.*

Migraine, by definition, is typically a moderate or severe headache attack that may be unilateral and may be exacerbated by physical activity, with the pain having a throbbing or pulsatile component. Normally the attacks have well-defined beginning and ending points with duration of headache between 4 and 72 hours. During the attack, patients have nausea and/or vomiting and/or photophobia and phonophobia. These symptoms will occur if the attack is permitted to go to maximal intensity of pain without successful treatment. Intervention by the patient even with medication that is not capable of fully alleviating the migraine may blunt the intensity of the associated symptoms and characteristics of the headache or alleviate entire components. This intervention and the failure to obtain this information in the headache history is perhaps the most common reason for migraine and tension-type headache to be misdiagnosed. The alleviation or blunting of the migraine symptoms can readily make the migraine attack appear to be a tension-type headache. Because migraine may associated with events that trigger the attacks, if these are of a psychological nature such as stress, then the physician may be even more likely to attribute the headache as a tension-type headache rather than migraine. Biologically, tension-type headache differs from migraine with factors such as biological peptides. Several studies have examined calcitonin gene-related peptide (CGRP),[12] substance P,[13] neuropeptide Y, and vasoactive intestinal peptide. These peptides do not change during pain versus pain-free times, nor do they differ from a control nonheadache population.

Migraine may evolve over time to a daily or near-daily headache. Although it may maintain the typical migraine characteristics for many of the headaches, patients may experience a blunting of the migraine characteristics as part of the evolutionary process. Chronic migraine terminology has been developed to aid in the clinical diagnosis of patients as part of the revised International Headache Society guidelines. The headache occurs on 15 or more days per month for at least 3 months, and has two of the following four characteristics as would occur for migraine without aura: (1) unilaterality; (2) throbbing or pulsatile pain; (3) moderate or severe intensity; or (4) exacerbation by physical activity. Additionally, the patient must still experience nausea and/or vomiting or photophobia and phonophobia with their headaches. Again the effects of acute treatment intervention are important to appreciate. In the patient with frequent use of acute medication, overuse headache may occur and further cloud the diagnosis.

The older, other terms for this type of headache should be briefly reviewed for understanding. In the previous version of the International Headache Society criteria, the term *chronic migraine* was not used; rather this type of headache pattern had to be classified as migraine headache and tension-type headache in one form or another based on the exact migraine and tension-type headache that was occurring and based on which headache was the more frequent. Combined headache and mixed headaches also reflected this dual diagnosis in abbreviated form. *Transformed migraine* was used to reflect the evolution of migraine from an episodic pattern with well-defined pain-free intervals to the daily or near-daily headache pattern. *Chronic daily headache* has been used to describe this type of headache and as a collective term for all of the daily or near-daily headaches—including *transformed migraine, chronic tension-type headache, chronic cluster headaches, new daily persistent headache,* and *hemicrania continua.*

Therefore, in the evaluation of the patient with possible tension-type headache, it is important to assess for several key factors. First, does the patient have a history of migraine headaches? If they have this in their history then tracking any changes in the migraine pattern may lead to a diagnosis of chronic migraine rather than chronic tension-type headache. Second, it is necessary to know if the attacks of headache that the patient is describing are treated or untreated headaches. If they are untreated and fail to meet criteria for migraine, then the diagnosis of tension-type headache is likely. If the attacks the patient describes are treated attacks, then it is best to obtain information on any attacks the patient may have had, but that went untreated. This second query is of importance in the patient whose headaches remain episodic because the partially treated episodic migraine without aura may appear to be a tension-type headache. A third factor to consider, more in differentiating episodic tension-type headache from the chronic variety, relates to the overuse of medications for acute treatment. Just as may occur in the migraine patient, so too in the tension-type headache, the overuse of acute medications may cloud the true diagnosis because only after the patient has been free of medication overuse for at least 3 months can the diagnosis be established with certainty.

Patients with chronic significant accommodation disorders of the eyes may develop headache that is referred to the forehead and vertex and may resemble tension-type headache. If accommodation disorders are suspected, a simple examination of the vision by an ophthalmologist or optometrist may provide needed information.

The nasal sinus regions may lead to headache with episodic infection as well as with chronic disorders of the sinuses. Overlap syndromes with migraine and tension-type headache may occur in these patients and require an appropriate examination of the nasal passages and, if necessary, a CT scan without contrast using coronal sections to establish the diagnosis. The absence of abnormal findings on examination or on scanning helps to eliminate the nasal sinus areas as a cause of the pain. On examination of the nasal passage, the patient with headache from this origin would be expected to have mucopurulent discharge and evidence of contact between the nasal septum and the turbinates. CT scan findings would reflect acute infection with significant air-fluid levels or complete obliteration of the sinus cavities by fluid. In an interesting experiment, Wolff[14] demonstrated that it required 200 mm Hg raised steadily over time to elicit pain from the maxillary sinuses and that sustained pressure over several hours of 50 to 80 mm Hg was needed to elicit even the sensation of pressure from the maxillary sinus cavity. Similarly, pain from engorgement of the nasal turbinates did not occur until these pressures had been achieved and maintained for several hours.

Pain in the temporalis muscle, which extends over the temporomandibular joint to attach to the mandible, may be a source of pain in tension-type headache. Because of the effects of sustained contraction of this muscle on the temporomandibular joint, there may be pain specifically elicited from this joint associated with tension-type headache. Differentiation from temporomandibular joint syndrome (TMJ) is necessary. In patients with TMJ, the jaw will have limitation in opening. This can be simply assessed in the office by having the patient insert the approximated first and second fingers jointly into the mouth. The ability to do so is a simple screening procedure for assessing the adequacy of the range of motion of this joint. Additionally there is an audible click or pop of the joint on opening. Not only must audible noise be elicited from the joint but also this should be associated with acute pain in the joint region. Oral examination should reveal malocclusion of the teeth. If this is not obvious to the medical practitioner, then appropriate referral to a dental professional should be made for the patient.

▮ TREATMENT CONSIDERATIONS

Treatment of tension-type headache may involve both pharmacotherapeutic agents as well as other approaches (Table 43–4). The pharmacotherapy of tension headache includes medications for acute treatment and medications for the chronic form of tension-type headache for preventative treatment. The other approaches to tension-type headache may include behavioral approaches—such as counseling and biofeedback; physical methods, including physical therapy, manipulative treatments, and injection treatments. The acute medications for tension-type headache are primarily directed for use as analgesic relief of the pain. The use of muscle relaxant agents is used both as episodic acute treatments and as part of preventive treatment.

Table 43–4

Treatment of Tension-Type Headache

Acute: simple and combination analgesics, skeletal
  muscle relaxants
Preventative medications: anxiolytics, SSRIs and
  novel antidepressants, tricyclic antidepressants,
  MAOIs, botulinum toxin type A
Behavioral approaches: biofeedback, cognitive
  behavioral treatment
Physical modalities: TENS, physical therapy, manual
  manipulative treatment, trigger point injection,
  neuroaxial and facet injection

MAOIs, monoamine oxidase inhibitor(s); SSRIs, selective
serotonin reuptake inhibitor(s); TENS, transcutaneous electrical nerve stimulation.

Because the pain of tension-type headache is mild to moderate in intensity for the majority of patients, the use of opioids should be avoided in this headache disorder, except for isolated headaches in patients who are well known to the treating clinician. Patients with chronic tension-type headache with daily or near-daily headaches are susceptible to becoming dependent on opioids if they are a primary pain medication.

Simple analgesics are the starting point for treating tension-type headache acutely. Acetaminophen, aspirin, and the over-the-counter nonsteroidal antiinflammatory drugs (NSAIDs) provide effective relief clinically. Because daily, excessive use of these agents may be linked to medication overuse headache, patients should be counseled in their appropriate use to avoid these sequelae. Combination analgesic agents with caffeine have been proven effective in clinical trials.[15,16] From our study,[16] caffeine may not serve as an adjunct in pain relief but may confer a portion of the analgesic activity.

The NSAIDs at both over-the-counter and at prescription strengths have been demonstrated to be useful in tension-type headache (Table 43–5). Diclofenac potassium at both the 12.5 and 25 mg strengths, ibuprofen at 400 mg[17] and ketorolac 60 at mg[18] by intramuscular administration have all been demonstrated to be effective. These results, along with clinical experience, suggest that the range of NSAIDs is effective in patients with tension-type headache. Similar results might also occur with the newer COX-2 inhibitors, which may offer improvement in gastrointestinal safety for patients. Which of these analgesic agents and the strength of the preparation are issues of individual patient response and clinician preference.

There are varieties of skeletal muscle relaxants and antispasticity agents that find their way into treatment of tension-type headache. Unfortunately, the use of these agents is merely anecdotal because there are no well-defined controlled trials relating to tension-type headache. There have been studies with tizanidine in the treatment of chronic daily headache, but most of these patients had medication overuse headache in addition to migraine.

For patients with chronic tension-type headache the use of episodic treatments may not be appropriate. The daily use of analgesics may have health consequences, potentiate the

occurrence of medication overuse headache, or lose efficacy over time. The same scenario commonly occurs with the muscle-relaxant agents. The relatively brief half-lives of many of these medications are likely responsible for the overuse phenomenon—as well as their diminished efficacy over time.

To minimize these issues and attempt to induce a remission of these headaches, the use of daily preventive medications may be in order. Although several of the long-duration antispasticity agents such as baclofen or tizanidine may be of benefit, the mainstay of preventive treatment in tension-type headache is the antidepressant medications.[19] Again there is a paucity of well-controlled trials with these agents to support their use; much of the literature is intermixed with chronic daily headache which includes patients with chronic migraine among other diagnoses. Practically, antidepressants are most likely to afford relief from the chronic recurrent headaches regardless of the etiologic issues underlying their cause. The antidepressants fall into three major groups: the tricyclic antidepressants (TCAs), the monoamine oxidase inhibitors (MAOIs), the selective serotonin reuptake inhibitors (SSRIs) and other novel antidepressants. The TCAs have the best clinical efficacy for tension-type headache, perhaps because of their breadth of pharmacologic activity, which may produce a direct analgesic effect.

The range of pharmacologic effects of TCAs (Table 43–6) needs to be appreciated for optimal selection of an agent based on the patient's tolerance of medications, coexisting illnesses, associated mood disorders, and sleep habits. Typically, it is wise to inquire whether a patient has a concomitant sleep disorder. Patients with insomnia usually fare best with a sedating TCA with or without a mild benzodiazepine to initiate sleep. Patients with chronic fatigue and daytime tiredness tolerate a TCA such as protriptyline quite well. The anticholinergic effects contribute to the dry mouth, constipation, and blurred vision that patients may experience as adverse events. The sedative effects are linked in part to the antihistaminic effects of these drugs. This antihistaminic effect may also contribute to carbohydrate cravings and weight gain as well as coupling with the anticholinergic activity to adversely affect cognitive issues.

The MAOIs are not commonly used outside of specialty clinics because of the issues related to drug interactions, dietary restrictions, and the potential for serious adverse events to occur with these interactions. However, in refractive patients who have failed to achieve benefit with more traditional therapies, they have proven efficacy.[20]

The newer antidepressants have been used in treating chronic daily headache but, again, much of this use has been in patients with chronic migraine or combination headache disorders. In general, in the absence of coexisting psychiatric disease, the efficacy of these compounds in headache tends to be limited. However, they possess comparatively exceptional tolerability compared to the TCAs. Novel agents that have activity at both norepinephrine and serotonin reuptake sites may have potentially better efficacy in the patient with headache without regard for coexisting psychiatric disease.

Of the nonpharmacologic techniques for tension-type headache, the preferred approach based on efficacy would be the combination of biofeedback along with cognitive behavioral counseling.[21] These techniques focus on not just the stress issues, which may contribute to the headaches, but with

Table 43–5

Guidelines for Use of Selected Abortive Therapies in the Treatment of Tension-Type Headache

Medication	Dose/Route/Clarification
NSAIDs (major side effects are GI-related)	
Acetylsalicylic acid	650 mg (2 regular-strength tablets) stat (PO)
Celecoxib	200-400 mg
Diclofenac	12.5-100 mg (PO)
Diflunisal	500 mg q 8-12 h
Etodolac	200-400 mg q 6-8 h
Fenoprofen	300-600 mg tid-qid
Flurbiprofen	100 mg stat, repeat in 1 h (PO)
Ibuprofen	400-600 mg q 6 h (PO)
Ketoprofen	100 mg stat, then 50 mg if needed in 1 h
Ketorolac	60 mg (IM). Limit use to one dose
Meclofenamate	200 mg stat, repeat 1× after 1 h (PO)
Mefenamic acid	50 mg q 4-6 h prn
Naproxen sodium	550 mg stat, then 275 mg in 1 h (PO)
Tolmetin	400-600 mg tid prn
Muscle Relaxants with/without Analgesics	
Baclofen	5-20 mg tid-qid (PO). Do not abruptly discontinue drug
Carisoprodol	350 mg tid (PO). Short-term use only—habit-forming. Subject to abuse by users of illicit drugs
Carisoprodol 200 mg and aspirin 325 mg	1 tablet tid (PO). Short-term use only—habit-forming. Subject to abuse by users of illicit drugs
Chlorzoxazone	500 mg qid
Cyclobenzaprine	10 mg tid (PO)
Metaxalone	800 mg (2 tablets) tid-qid (PO)
Methocarbamol	1000 mg qid (PO)
Orphenadrine citrate	100 mg bid (PO)
Orphenadrine citrate 50 mg, aspirin 770 mg, and caffeine 60 mg	1 tablet bid-tid (PO)
Tizanidine	2 mg qid
Other	
Isometheptene mucate 65 mg, Dichloralphenazone 100mg, and acetaminophen 325 mg	2 capsules stat, then 1 q h to maximum of 5 capsules/24 h OR 2 capsules stat, then repeat 2 capsules in 1 h (PO)

GI, gastrointestinal; IM, intramuscular(ly); PO, by mouth.

Table 43–6

Antidepressants and Receptor Affinity

Drug	Serotonin Inhibition	Norepinephrine Inhibition	Dopamine Inhibition	Sedative Effects	Anticholinergic Effects	Histamine Inhibitions
Amitriptyline	Moderate	Weak	Inactive	Strong	Strong	Moderate
Doxepin	Moderate	Moderate	Inactive	Strong	Strong	Strong
Nortriptyline	Weak	Fairly potent	Inactive	Mild	Moderate	Mild
Imipramine	Fairly potent	Moderate	Inactive	Moderate	Strong	Mild
Protriptyline	Weak	Fairly potent	Inactive	None	Strong	None
Desipramine	Weak	Potent	Inactive	Mild	Moderate	Mild or none
Trimipramine	Weak	Weak	Inactive	Moderate	Moderate	Moderate
Amoxapine	Weak	Potent	Moderate	Mild	Mild	Mild
Maprotiline	Weak	Moderate	Inactive	Moderate	Moderate	Moderate

the muscle relaxation training in biofeedback to offer a specific method to help reduce the pain of associated headaches. In the training for biofeedback, the patient has surface electrodes attached to the scalp, face, and/or neck region of pain to register the amount of muscle activity. Through guided exercises, patients learn to control the underlying muscle tension and help to alleviate the headache. The techniques require a combination of hands-on training with a therapist experienced in its use along with regular at-home practice sessions.

Massage and physical therapy have been examined in the treatment of tension-type headache. Although there may be specific patients who have postural mechanical factors at play in their headaches who benefit from these treatments, the techniques, in general, produce little in the way of positive benefits. Manual therapies performed by a chiropractor or osteopathic physician have also been studied in the treatment of tension-type headache. The results have been mixed. Some studies report significant benefit, others little if any. Many issues have clouded these results including diagnosis of the headaches being treated, the techniques used, and the choice of blinding or alternative active controls for assessment of outcome of these studies. Proper assessment of the patient for alterations in muscle tone, postural and mechanical effects—coupled with appropriate and comprehensive diagnosis—may lead to successful treatment with these techniques.

The use of injections such as trigger pointing, epidural, and cervical facet injection is covered elsewhere in this text. They remain useful adjuncts in the management of tension-type headache. For patients with localized areas of muscle pain and tenderness, injections may be useful as part of a comprehensive treatment program. Specific techniques to address tension-type headache have been examined with the use of botulinum toxin type A (BttA). The trials have been small and lacking in solid control groups but have suggested that there are some patients who will benefit from the injections.[22,23] The mechanism by which BttA exerts its effects in tension-type headache may be by direct effects at the neuromuscular junction as well as by potential central effects that may modulate the pain tracks centrally. The choice of injections sites (Table 43–7) is typically guided by the patient's areas of pain and associated muscle spasm. It is important to assess the mechanics that may contribute to the pain. For example, minimal cervical dystonia may occur involving the sternocleidomastoid muscle. The chronic shortening of the muscle may not be painful but the pull exerted on the posterior muscles on the opposite side of the neck may be the source of the pain. Inject-

ing into the area of pain fails to alleviate the problem and may intensify the situation in some patients, whereas injection into the affected sternocleidomastoid muscle produces relaxation of the spasticity and relief of the pain on the posterior opposite side of the neck. Repetitive injections with BttA may be required to demonstrate an adequate response. There may be a high rate of placebo response with the initial series of injections or the results may be minimal or brief. Repeating the injections will minimize placebo effects and may demonstrate more robust relief of the headaches, as well as expand the duration of relief from the headaches and neck pain. Side effects tend to be negligible for most patients beyond the initial discomfort of the injections. Cost may be prohibitive for many patients because its use in headache has not been approved by the Food and Drug Administration and many insurance companies have elected to consider the treatment experimental pending further studies and approval processes.

■ CONCLUSIONS

Although tension-type headache is ubiquitous, only a relatively small percentage of the population has these headaches occurring with sufficient frequency and severity to cause them to seek medical attention. This small group may experience substantial impact from their disease on productivity and quality of life. Assessment of the headaches includes assessment for other headache disorders, which may overlap it, such as a chronic migraine. Coexisting diseases that may contribute to the process, such as mood disorders and mechanical disorders of the spine and neck, require investigation.

Treatment is optimized by appropriate use of acute medications and preventive treatments that may include drugs in the antidepressant classes, along with nonpharmacologic modalities and other alternative treatments ranging from biofeedback to manual therapy to the use of botulinum toxin type A injections.

References

1. Blumenthal L, Fuchs M: Headache clinics; migraine headache. Am Pract Digest Treat 2:163, 1951.
2. Ryan RE: Psychogenic headache. In Ryan RE: Headache Diagnosis and Treatment. St. Louis, CV Mosby, 1954, p 117.
3. Wolff HG: Muscle of the head and neck as sources of headache and other pain. In Wolff HG: Headache and Other Head Pain. New York, Oxford University Press, 1948, p 496.
4. Diamond S: Depressive headaches. Headache 69:255, 1964.
5. Olesen J, Krabbe AA, Tfelt-Hansen P: Methodological aspects of prophylactic drug trials in migraine. Cephalalgia 1:127, 1981.
6. Lipton RB, Cady RK, Stewart WF, et al: Diagnostic lessons from the spectrum study. Neurology 58(9 Suppl 6):S27, 2002.
7. Headache Classification Subcommittee of The International Headache Society. The International Classification of Headache Disorders, 2nd ed. Cephalalgia 24:(Suppl 1), 2004.
8. Schwartz BS, Stewart WF, Simon D, Lipton RB: Epidemiology of tension type headache. JAMA 279:381, 1998.
9. Diamond S, Dalessio DJ: Muscle contraction headache. In Diamond D, Dalessio DJ: The Practicing Physician's Approach to Headache 4th ed. Baltimore, Williams & Wilkins, 1986, p 99.
10. Frishberg BM, Rosenberg JH, Matchar DB, et al: Evidence based guidelines in the primary care setting: Neuroimaging in the patient with non-acute headache. www.aan.com, April 2000.
11. London LH, Shulman B, Diamond S: The role of psychometric testing and psychological treatment in tension type headache. Curr Pain Headache Rep 5:467, 2001.

Table 43–7

Botulinum Toxin Type A Treatment for Tension-Type Headache

Botulinum Toxin Type A

Dose: 25 to 200 units

Injection locations: frontalis (bilateral even if unilateral headache), glabellar, temporalis, mastoid, sternocleidomastoid, rectus capitis, cervical paraspinal, trapezius.

Repeat treatment in 2 to 3 months based on headache pain recurrence

12. Ashina M, Bendtsen L, Jensen R, et al: Plasma levels of calcitonin-gene related peptide in chronic tension type headache. Neurology 55:1335, 2000.

13. Ashina M, Bendtsen L, Jensen R, et al: Plasma levels of Substance P, neuropeptides Y and vasoactive intestinal peptide in patients with chronic tension type headache. Pain 83:541, 1999.

14. Wolff HG: Muscle of the head and neck as sources of headache and other pain. In Wolff HG: Headache and Other Head Pain. New York, Oxford University Press, 1948, p 456.

15. Rabello GD, Forte LV, Galvao AC: Clinical evaluation of the efficacy of the paracetamol and caffeine combination in the treatment of tension headache. Arq Neuropsiquiatr 58:90, 2000.

16. Diamond S, Balm TK, Freitag FG: Ibuprofen plus caffeine in the treatment of tension-type headache. Clin Pharmacol Ther 68:312, 2000.

17. Kubitzek F, Ziegler G, Gold MS, et al: Low dose diclofenac potassium in the treatment of episodic tension-type headache. Eur J Pain 7:155, 2003.

18. Harden RN, Rogers D, Fink K, Gracely RH: Controlled trial of ketorolac in tension type headache. Neurology 50:507, 1998.

19. Holyroyd KA, O'Donnel FJ, Stensland M, et al: Management of chronic tension type headache with tricyclic antidepressants medication, stress management therapy, and their combination: A randomized controlled trial. JAMA 285:2208, 2001.

20. Freitag FG, Diamond S, Solomon GD: Antidepressants and the treatment of mixed headache: MAO inhibitors and combined use of MAO inhibitors and tricyclic antidepressants in the recidivist headache patient. Adv Headache Res 271, 1987.

21. Andrasik F: Behavioral treatment approaches to chronic headache. Neurol Sci 24 (Suppl 2):S80, 2003.

22. Freitag FG: Preventative treatment for migraine and tension-type headaches: Do drugs having effects on muscle spasm and tone have a role? CNS Drugs 17(6):373, 2003.

23. Gobel H, Heinze A, Heinze-Kuhn K, Jost WH: Evidenced-based medicine: Botulinum toxin A in migraine and tension type headache. J Neurol 248 (Suppl 1):34, 2001.

chapter 44

Cluster Headache

Seymour Diamond and George Urban

Cluster headache, a very distinctive and extremely painful primary headache disorder, is called by some sufferers a "killer" or "suicide" headache. The International Headache Society (IHS)[1] defines cluster headache as

> ... a severe unilateral, orbital, supraorbital, and/or temporal pain lasting 15 to 180 minutes untreated and associated with at least one of the several signs [Table 44–1] ipsilateral with the pain, occurring in frequency of attacks from one every other day to eight times a day.

■ HISTORY AND TERMINOLOGY

The earliest description of cluster headache occurred in the 18th century, when Gerhard van Swienten, a founder of the Vienna School of Medicine and the personal physician to the Empress Maria Theresa, presented an illustrative case of episodic cluster headache that was published (in Latin) in 1745 in his textbook of clinical medicine.[2] His description, which follows, actually fulfills the criteria established by the IHS in 1988 for episodic cluster headache[3]

> A healthy robust man of middle age [was suffering from] troublesome pain which came on every day at the same hour at the same spot above the orbit to the left eye, where the nerve emerges from the opening of frontal bone: after a short time the left eye began to redden, and to overflow with tears; then he felt as if his eye was slowly forced out of his orbit with so much pain, that he nearly went mad. After a few hours all these evils ceased, and nothing in the eye appeared at all changed.

Other incomplete accounts can be found in European medical literature in the 18th and 19th centuries. The first recorded account of cluster headache in the English medical literature has been traced to Wilfred Harris in 1926, in which he elaborated on the topic of *migrainous neuralgia*—a term used for cluster headache.[4] Harris identified differential features among migrainous neuralgia, trigeminal neuralgia, and migraine. He noted typical unilaterality in short duration of excruciating headache attacks, frequency, autonomic features,

and periodic occurrence of headaches and remission between cycles. His treatment recommendation consisted of barbiturate, ergotamine and, in intractable cases, an injection of alcohol into the gasserian ganglion.

Bayard Taylor Horton is considered the father of cluster headache treatment. His precise description of headache referred to "erythromelalgia of the head"[5] or "histaminic cephalalgia."[5] His devotion to the study of cluster headache forever linked his name to cluster headache— "Horton's headache." Horton introduced the use of histamine desensitization in the treatment of chronic cluster headaches following an observation that an injection of histamine would provoke a brief, unilateral, intense headache with symptoms similar to those of cluster headache in susceptible individuals.[6]

The term "cluster headache" was established in 1952 by Kunkle and his colleagues to describe[7] a typical periodic pain pattern. His term has been accepted worldwide under the English name or under a translated name in particular languages.

A variety of other titles are associated with cluster headache, although many refer to cluster-like headache. These other terms used in the past include: *histaminic cephalalgia; Horton's headache; migrainous neuralgia; sphenopalatine neuralgia; petrosal neuralgia; red migraine; Raeder's syndrome; erythromelalgia; Bing's erythroprosopalgia; Bing's headache; Bing's syndrome; Sluder's syndrome; periodic migrainous neuralgia; ciliary neuralgia; hemicrania intermittent;* and *neuralgia spasmodica.*

■ PREVALENCE AND EPIDEMIOLOGY

Cluster headache is a relatively uncommon headache disorder. A limited number of studies address the prevalence of cluster headache in the United States and worldwide. Results of these studies vary greatly in range and are inconclusive.

In Sweden, Ekbom and colleagues studied the prevalence of migraine and cluster headache in a homogeneous population of 9803 18-year-old men.[8] They found a prevalence of 0.09% for cluster headache, which is approximately 19 times less than the prevalence of migraine headache in the same age group of men. The flaw of the study is that the sample group is not representative across the population, not even for the mean age of the onset of this disorder.

Table 44–1

Signs Associated with Cluster Headache Attack

- Ipsilateral conjunctival injection and/or lacrimation
- Ipsilateral nasal congestion and/or rhinorrhea
- Ipsilateral eyelid edema
- Ipsilateral forehead and facial sweating
- Ipsilateral miosis and/or ptosis
- A sense of restlessness or agitation

A population-based study in Olmsted County, Minnesota[9] has drawn its results from the screening of 6476 patient records over a 3-year period. The overall age- and gender-adjusted incidence was 9.8 per 100,000 (0.01%) for males. In the same group, migraine occurrence was about 25 times higher. Included among the few weaknesses in this screening is that subjects were already experiencing headaches and did not represent the general population. Olmsted County is racially and socioeconomically homogeneous and the study is based on a small number of cluster cases.

Most recently, 1838 individuals from the Vågå study[10] were examined and 7 were found to fulfill the IHS criteria for cluster headache, corresponding to a prevalence of 381 per 100,000 (0.38%). In the small European country of San Marino with an entire population of 21,792, D'Alessandro and colleagues[11] derived a cluster headache prevalence of 0.13% for males and 0.009% for females. The overall prevalence was 69 per 100,000 (0.07%). Kudrow[12] estimated the prevalence of cluster headache at 0.24%. His higher estimate may be attributed to a larger cohort of cluster headache patients consulting him.

■ FAMILIAL OCCURRENCE AND GENETICS

The involvement of genetic factors in cluster headache is unclear and highly controversial. Some diseases with genetically determined predisposition have been associated with the presence of the HLA antigen. However, Cuypers and Altenkirch[13] have failed to find any significant deviations in HLA antigen frequencies in patients with episodic cluster headache. All of their five patients with chronic cluster headaches carried the HLA-A$_1$ antigen—a finding that is nonetheless inconclusive due to the small number of subjects. Similarly, the genetic importance of CACNAA1A gene mutation that has been found in some neurologic disorders, including familial hemiplegic migraine, is doubtful.[14]

Recently, some evidence has emerged suggesting familial occurrence and inheritance of cluster headache. El Amrani and coworkers[15] studied 186 probands (144 men and 42 women) with documented cluster headache diagnosis. A positive family history of cluster headache was found in 12 men and 8 women (a total of 10.75%), with 22 affected first-degree relatives (3.4%). No statistical difference was determined between probands with acute and chronic cluster headaches, although patients with the chronic type had a higher prevalence of familial occurrence. The authors could not demonstrate any mode of inheritance from this study. Likewise,

Kudrow[12] noted the occurrence of cluster headache in first-degree relatives in about 3% of patients.

In another study, Russell and colleagues[16] found a positive family history of cluster headache in 7% of 366 families—representing a 14-fold increased risk of cluster headache in first-degree relatives of probands and twofold in second-degree relatives. It has been suggested that the inheritance in some families may be through an autosomal dominant gene.

Clinical Picture

Cluster headache is characterized by recurrent bouts of extremely painful, unilateral headache attacks, of relatively short duration, and associated with symptoms and signs of autonomic dysfunction. The attacks are clustered over a period of several weeks and separated from another cycle by totally asymptomatic remission. Cluster headache is part of trigeminal autonomic cephalalgia and is divided into episodic and chronic types (Table 44–2).

Demographics

Traditionally, cluster headache has been considered a "male" headache disorder. The gender ratio varies from 3.5:1 to 6.7:1 in favor of males. A higher female occurrence has been reported by some investigators at larger, specialized headache clinics. This discrepancy can be explained by the tendency of headache clinics to attract patients with cluster headache and better recognition of the disease.

In a large case series, Horton[17] reported male-to-female ratio in 1176 patients to be 6.7:1 and Kudrow[12] found male-to-female preponderance among 425 patients to be 5:1. Manzoni[18] noted a decreasing trend of male-to-female ratio to 3.5:1 in the Italian population over several years. Similar findings were observed in the Swedish population[19] with a decline of male predominance comparing years before and after 1970. This study also showed a significant shift in proportion of females with respect to age at onset. The highest male-to-female ratio is in persons aged 40 to 49 and 30 to 39 years at onset (8.4:1 and 6.5:1, respectively), and lowest in the 40- to

Table 44–2

International Headache Society

Classification of Cluster Headache

3.1. Cluster headache
   3.1.1. Episodic cluster headache
   3.1.2. Chronic cluster headache
3.2. Paroxysmal hemicrania
   3.2.1. Episodic paroxysmal hemicrania
   3.2.2. Chronic paroxysmal hemicrania (CPH)
3.3. Short-lasting unilateral neuralgiform headache attacks with conjunctival injection and tearing (SUNCT)
3.4. Probable trigeminal autonomic cephalalgia
   3.4.1. Probable cluster headache
   3.4.2. Probable paroxysmal hemicrania
   3.4.3. Probable SUNCT

From The International Classification of Headache Disorders, 2nd ed: Cephalalgia 24 (Suppl 1), 2004.

69- and 10- to 19-year age groups, at onset (2.3 to 2.5:1 and 3.2:1, respectively). In a review of 225 charts of cluster patients, we reported 4:1 male preponderance.[20]

No racial or ethnic prevalence has been documented. In the study by Rozen and coworkers,[21] 25% of 32 women were African-American, and 17.4% of 69 male patients were African-American, which is consistent with Kudrow's findings.[22] These racial differences, however, should not be generalized.

Age of Onset

Cluster headache can begin at any age, including childhood and in the elderly. Onset at both extremes warrants detailed investigations to rule out secondary headache. The average mean age of onset in the various series is 31.5 years.[23] It is noteworthy that the diagnosis is commonly delayed by several years either because of unrecognized clinical symptoms or misdiagnosis as migraine, trigeminal neuralgia, or a sinus or dental problem. A slightly lower mean age of onset was noted in women (27.1%) as compared with 29.7% in men was found in several studies.[21-24]

Childhood onset is relatively rare and, therefore, not always recognizable. Three of nine cluster headache sufferers in a Swedish population of almost 10,000 18-year-old men,[8] had onset of symptoms before age 8 years. In the study by Maytal and associates,[25] 35 patients were identified with onset of cluster at or before 18 years of age. Seven of these subjects were 5 to 12 years old at the onset of the headaches. Other authors[11,19,25] also reported early onset before the age of 6 years. During childhood, the clinical features of cluster headaches are similar to those starting in adulthood. Treatment, however, is limited.

Periodicity

The main distinguishing feature of cluster headache is its periodicity. The term *cluster* derives from attacks tending to occur repeatedly within a relatively limited time span (called *period, cycle, bout,* or *cluster*). On average, a cluster period lasts 6 to 12 weeks and by definition cannot last longer than 12 months. The length of the cycle may vary considerably inter- and intra-individually. In the study by Manzoni and coworkers[28a] of 189 cluster headache patients, 78% of the cycles lasted 1 to 2 months. In another study of 225 patients with cluster headache, Urban and associates[20] reported 69% of patients reporting headache cycles with durations of up to 4 months. With treatment, the number of patients in this category increased to 75%. Frequency of cycle also varies, but more than one-half of patients' cycles occur one or fewer time per year.

Some investigators suggested that cluster cycles occur annually, and in spring and fall seem to be slightly more prevalent.[16,27,29,30] However, Kudrow[31] found an increased number of cluster cycles occur in February and June—coinciding with an increased number of daylight hours. It appears that cluster onset occurs 7 to 10 days before the longest and shortest days of the year. However, in some patients, the number of cycles decreases following the 1-hour resetting of clocks for daylight-saving and standard times in April and October, respectively. This observation with the fact that cycles start in most patients at the same time each year—circannual occurrence—suggests involvement of the biological clock located in the suprachiasmatic nucleus of the hypothalamus.

Another typical cluster headache feature is a circadian periodicity and predictability of acute cluster headache attacks. The majority of patients experience attacks almost exclusively nocturnally, awakening the individual usually 2 to 3 hours after falling asleep, between midnight and 2 AM. This timing corresponds with the REM phase of sleep when rapid fluctuation in autonomic functions occurs. The nocturnal episodes make patients anxious and apprehensive to fall asleep and many will remain awake to avoid an attack. Some patients report that daytime attacks are associated with napping or relaxation. Similarly, biofeedback relaxation during the cluster cycle may induce an acute episode in many patients. The clockwork regularity of daily attacks is also indicative of dysfunction of the modulatory role of the suprachiasmatic nucleus.

Attacks

The attacks are characterized by severe pain and associated symptoms. The pain is distinguishable by its localization, unilaterality, character, severity, and duration. The localization of pain is usually uniform. Typically, pain starts retro-orbitally, periorbitally, supraorbitally, or temporally. The pain area extends over a relatively small region that is easily identified by the patient with the finger or as the intersection of two lines in an area behind the eye. The ocular region is affected in 90% of cluster headache patients. When the pain is confined to the maxillary or mandibular region, it is described as lower-half syndrome.

In some patients, the pain may start in other parts of the head in extratrigeminal territory, including the occipital and cervical regions. The prevalence of neck pain and neck-related symptoms is not unusual. Solomon and colleagues[2] found that in 10% of their patients the neck was the initial site of pain in addition to the orbital distribution. In 37% of the subjects, the pain radiated to the nuchal area. Their patients also reported neck stiffness (40%) and tenderness (29%), and precipitation, aggravation, or amelioration by head movement. The nuchal symptoms in patients with cluster headache are probably related to the convergence of pain fibers from the first division of the trigeminal nerve and from upper cervical nerve roots.[32]

The pain is strictly unilateral and autonomic symptoms occur ipsilateral to the pain. In most cases, the attacks occur on the same side with every attack and every cycle. A slight predominance has been observed in right-sided headache attacks with 49% right side, 38% left side, and 13% that may shift sides or be bilateral.[22] It is atypical that the side of the pain would change during the attack, although some patients report a shift in sides between attacks or from cycle to cycle.

The pain may be preceded by prodromal symptoms heralding an oncoming attack of excruciating pain. This may manifest as a vague discomfort or poorly describable feeling in the region of one eye, temple, forehead, or neck. Fatigue, euphoria, depression or mood changes, apathy, irritability, and photo- and phonophobia may be experienced.

Symptoms that occur minutes or a few hours before the cluster attack are reported by up to 61%. In 8% of the patients, premonitory symptoms occur days or weeks before the cluster cycle.[33] Usually the patient does not spontaneously report this information because the prodrome may precede the attack by hours and the intensity of the pain may cause the patient to ignore warning signs. Therefore, the clinician should actively inquire about those symptoms. Although cluster patients do not typically describe an aura, some patients have identified its presence.[26,30,34] Silberstein and associates[35] described five patients with visual symptoms and one with olfactory aura, lasting 5 to 120 minutes, and always occurring before headache onset.

The character of the pain is also distinguishable from migraine and other headaches. Adjectives given to the degree of pain vary largely and the pain may change character during the attack. The pain is commonly described as boring, pressing, or burning, but also as piercing, stabbing, screwing, tearing, or sharp, knife-like, "a hot poker in the eye," and occasionally as pulsating, throbbing, tightening, squeezing, or aching. A lingering dull pain, the soreness may persist in the painful area for some time, perhaps for hours, and may resemble a tension-type headache or mild migraine attack. In some cases, the pain continues until the next attack. Cutaneous allodynia-hypersensitivity of the scalp in the affected area may also be present.

The severity of cluster attacks is notorious for its excruciating level of pain. Cluster headache is nicknamed as the "killer" or "suicide" headache, indicating the mental status of a sufferer during the unbearable attack. The headache has been described as the most severe form of pain a human can endure. It is not unusual for women who experience cluster headache to describe the pain as much worse than that associated with labor and delivery. The intensity of pain is the only feature of an attack that prompts a patient to visit a medical facility. The onset is usually sudden, with rapid crescendo, or peaks within a short time of 10 to 20 minutes. The intensity of pain is milder at the beginning and the end of the cluster period and more severe in the middle. Application of ice or heat may sometimes alleviate the pain.

The posturing and behavior during the painful attack are also typical and differ from an attack of migraine. Usually, patients cannot remain still and may rock back and forth while in a standing, kneeling, or sitting position. These patients hold their head in both hands, pace the floor, or leave the house for colder, outside air. They are restless and may even become violent during the attack. Facial expressions show grimacing and the horror of pain. In a futile attempt to alleviate the excruciating pain, the patient may vigorously rub the affected temple with the thumb, knuckles, fist, or a dull or sharp object such as a pen or screwdriver. The patient may bang the head against the wall or hit hard objects with their fists. Such violent and self-destructive behavior leads to injuries and sometimes to suicide.

Duration of the cluster attack averages between 40 and 90 minutes. Briefer and more prolonged attacks occur less frequently with the exception of the chronic form. At the onset and end of a cluster period, attacks are generally briefer. In the series by Manzoni and colleagues,[27] 73% reported attacks with durations ranging from 30 to 120 minutes. Some reports[11] have noted that females tend to experience longer attacks on average by 30 minutes. Also, nocturnal attacks seem to be more severe and longer.

Associated symptoms (Table 44–3) are another pathognomonic feature of cluster headache. These symptoms typically accompany the attack but on occasion may precede it. By definition, these symptoms are ipsilateral to the affected side. The most common accompanying sign is lacrimation which is reported by more than 80% of cluster headache

Table 44–3

Associated Symptoms (More Than 5%)

Ocular	Nasal
Lacrimation	Congestion/stuffiness
Conjunctival injection	Rhinorrhea
Partial Horner syndrome	**Gastrointestinal**
Photophobia	Nausea
Blurred vision	Vomiting
Vascular	**Cardiac**
Facial flushing	Tachycardia/bradycardia
Prominence and/or	Blood pressure fluctuation
tenderness of temporal	Arrhythmia
artery	
Eye puffiness	
Neurologic	
Cutaneous allodynia	
Visual aura	
Vertigo	
Neck muscle stiffness or	
tenderness	

patients. On occasion, lacrimation may manifest bilaterally. Conjunctival injection occurs slightly less frequently than lacrimation, described probably by 60% of these patients, is usually of a moderate degree, and may persist beyond the attack. Nasal congestion, with or without rhinorrhea, occurs in about 70% of cluster sufferers. Initially, the nasal mucosa swells to varying degrees causing stuffiness or congestion and may lead to nasal secretion of a clear and thin mucus. Nasal discharge often accompanies lacrimation, which may indicate that the discharge is indeed tears directed through the lacrimal duct to the nose. It is believed, though, that those two phenomena exist separately. The nasal stuffiness, lacrimation, and conjunctival injection are called the classic triad of cluster headache.

Photophobia also occurs frequently in around 60% to 70% of these patients. Some cluster headache sufferers may also experience phonophobia, nausea, and vomiting. Other symptoms and signs may include facial flushing, increased forehead or generalized sweating, prominence or bulging of the frontal or temporal blood vessels, and blurred vision. The term "partial" Horner syndrome accompanying cluster headache indicates that only two components of a Horner syndrome are present—miosis and ptosis, but without anhidrosis. This syndrome is observed on the ipsilateral side and occurs throughout the cluster period with a great variation—between 16% and 84%.[22] In some cases, these symptoms may persist indefinitely. The pathophysiology of the cluster headache-related Horner-like syndrome is unclear. It is speculated that patients with the partial Horner syndrome may represent a subgroup of cluster headache sufferers.

Other systemic findings may accompany the cluster attack. Cardiovascular changes are sometimes present in the form of blood pressure fluctuation, tachycardia during the onset of the attack, bradycardia after the attack, and occasional various types of arrhythmia (including transient episodes of atrial fibrillation, premature ventricular beats, and first degree A-V block or S-A block).[36] Cluster sufferers do not, for the most part, report autonomic symptoms—only 3% are affected.[37]

Trigger Factors

During the cluster cycle, acute attacks can be induced by alcohol, nitroglycerin, or histamine. The provoked attack occurs usually after the latency of 30 to 50 minutes. All three substances are vasodilators, which may suggest that vasodilatation is part of the mechanism of cluster headache. Alcohol has been known to provoke the cluster attack—but only during the cycle. Many patients will voluntarily abstain from alcohol during the cycle until the headaches are in remission. It is interesting that some patients report that alcohol in a large amount may postpone attacks by a few days. In the chronic form, alcohol consumption may reduce the number of attacks.

Nitroglycerin (1 to 3 mg) can induce an acute attack in a cluster sufferer that is identical to a spontaneous attack. This action—drug-induced headache—can occur only during an active period, and after a latency of 30 to 50 minutes. The provoked attack delays the next expected spontaneous attack. To provoke the bout, the patient should be outside of the refractory period—within 8 hours of a previous spontaneous attack.[23]

Histamine administration induces an acute cluster attack in 75% of patients.[38] Both cluster and noncluster headache patients respond within 5 minutes to histamine infusion with a bilateral, throbbing, moderate-to-severe headache of transitory nature that lasts for 5 to 10 minutes. This headache is not accompanied with typical cluster autonomic symptoms. Again, after the latency of 20 to 50 minutes, a unilateral headache similar to a spontaneous cluster attack will occur.[39]

The mechanism underlying the provocation of attacks by these vasodilatory agents is not entirely clear. Fanciullacci and colleagues[40] suggest that histamine and nitroglycerine activates the trigeminal vascular system. Calcitonin gene-related peptide (CGRP), one of the most potent endogenous vasodilators, is present in the trigeminal sensory neurons that supply the cephalic blood vessels. CGRP basal plasma levels were significantly higher during a cluster period than in remission, and an increase in CGRP was directly related to the peak of a nitroglycerin-induced attack and reversed after sumatriptan-induced alleviation. This activation is possible only during the phase of trigeminal vascular hyperactivity.

Kudrow and Kudrow[41] found that nitroglycerine causes oxygen desaturation at a larger magnitude and is longer in duration in active cluster patients. These researchers indicate that hypoxia may play a role in the mechanism of cluster attack as suggested by higher occurrence of attacks at night during sleep and at high altitudes.

Cluster Headache, Personality, and Psychological Factors

Traditionally, certain personality traits have been assigned to different headache sufferers. This situation has been supported by observations of clinicians, researchers, and/or patients' acquaintances as well as psychological profiling. More than 30 years ago, Graham observed and described the physical appearance of male cluster patients and ascribed to them particular behavioral characteristics.[34] He observed the preponderance of masculine or sometimes hypermasculine males with leonine facial features that were often associated with paradoxical gentle—even meek—personalities. Graham described the "leonine-mouse" syndrome depicting these patients as "mice living inside of lions." Such patients appear to be dependent and helpless, but also ambitious and diligent, heavy smoking, heavy drinking, executive-type men.

In many instances, in our own clinical experience and that of other headache specialists, this portrayal is fairly accurate. However, some researchers have not been able to document those discrepancies and their results are controversial. Cuypers and his coworkers[42] compared the personalities of 40 cluster headache patients to those of 49 migraineurs. This study revealed a slightly elevated score for nervousness and a slightly diminished score for masculinity—but no significant difference between migraine and cluster patients. Similarly, Kudrow and Sutkus[43] did not find a discrepancy in personality in those two headache groups. Levi and his coworkers[44] analyzed the results of a Swedish personality inventory and obtained outcomes indicating higher levels of anxiety, socializing difficulties, and more hostile attitudes toward others. The study of Pfaffenrath and his colleagues is more controversial,[45] as no statistically significant differences were noted between the various types of primary headaches. However, patients with cluster headache showed the highest number of abnormalities but also the highest percentage of completely normal results.

In classic works, cluster headache patients have been described as heavy drinkers and smokers. Kudrow[11] found that 78% of 280 cluster patients smoked an average of 33 cigarettes per day. A higher percentage (84%) of smokers were described by Manzoni and colleagues[27] in their study of 180 patients. The higher smoking rate is present in both male and female patients. Alcohol has been consumed in higher prevalence in cluster patients than in non-cluster headache controls. Manzoni and colleagues[27] reported alcohol drinking in more than 90% of 180 patients with cluster headache and significant proportions drank heavily. Similarly, Levi and colleagues[46] found heavy social drinking or alcoholism in 67%. However, 79% of their subjects decreased their alcohol consumption during the active cluster cycles.

The significance of tobacco and alcohol overuse is unclear. Smokers have been found to have low monoamine oxidase (MAO) activities in platelets—a factor which has also been documented in cluster patients who do not smoke.[47] Thus, smoking may increase the risk for cluster headache in predisposed individuals with reduced MAO activity.

Women and Cluster Headache

Cluster headache is predominantly a male headache disorder with a male-to-female ratio ranging from 3.5:1 up to 7:1. The gender ratio appears to be declining,[17] which can be attributed to new social and habitual activities of women, hormonal changes, or unknown causes. Many similarities and some peculiarities have been observed in the clinical presentation of women with cluster headache as compared to men. A higher coexistence of cluster and migraine headache in women has been recognized, and many female cluster headache sufferers are misdiagnosed with migraine. In women, cluster headache seems to start earlier in life, at the mean age of 27, as compared to 30 years of age in men.[19,20,23] Women may have bimodal distribution of the age of onset. Typically, the female sufferer will report the initial onset of cluster headaches at the age of 20 and the second peak around age 50 years of age or later.[20,48] Furthermore, females show a significantly higher mean age of onset of the primary chronic form as compared to the episodic type.[18] The frequency of attacks per day, character of pain, location, and duration of cycles and remission seem equivalent to those of male sufferers. Rozen and colleagues[21] noted a briefer duration of individual attacks in women that was approaching, but not reaching, statistical significance. Their finding was in contrast to Kudrow's study[21] that reported a longer duration of cluster attacks in women.

The associated symptoms are also similar in character and frequency in female and male cluster headache sufferers. However, women less commonly experience Horner syndrome, but complain of an equal frequency of lacrimation, rhinorrhea, and nasal congestion—suggesting less sympathetic dysfunction than found in men. However, the parasympathetic activation is similar to male cluster sufferers.[20] Women usually have more migrainous symptoms, such as nausea and vomiting.

It has been known that migraine in women is commonly influenced by hormonal changes. Migraine is affected by the natural fluctuations of female hormones at menarche, menstruation, pregnancy, perimenopause, or menopause. Also, the administration of hormone supplement therapy (oral contraceptives, hormone replacement therapy) has a direct or indirect role in migraine development and course. The role of hormonal factors in female cluster patients is less recognized. Ekbom and Waldenlind[49] analyzed 34 females with cluster headache. No relation between cluster headaches and menstruation was demonstrated in 25 of 26 women of childbearing age. Eight reported 13 pregnancies since the initial onset of cluster headache. During pregnancy, six women experienced remission of their cluster cycles. The researchers observed a significantly lower number of childbirths in cluster patients, when compared to a general population, as well as a lower parity rate. An infertility rate and premature menopause was noted in 11% of cases. Those results may be interpreted as possible hypofertility suggesting impairment in the hypothalamic-pituitary axis.

Chronic Form

The term chronic cluster headache describes attacks occurring for more than 1 year without remission or with a remission lasting less than 1 month.[1] Primary chronic cluster headache starts de novo, and secondary chronic cluster headache evolves from the episodic type. Some patients may alternate between chronic and episodic spontaneously or as a result of treatment.

About 4% to 26% of cluster headache patients experience the chronic form. In a series of 554 patients with cluster headache, Ekbom and colleagues[18] identified 12% of patients with the chronic form and male-to-female ratio of 4.5:1, which is approximately the same proportion as the episodic form. In some studies conducted by headache centers and larger neurologic groups,[28,29] the higher occurrence of the chronic form can be explained by the difficult or complex patient population at those centers. The chronic form usually starts between age 30 and 35 years, with greatly reduced occurrence of onset in men after age 50. Women show a significantly higher mean age of onset of the primary chronic form as compared to the episodic type.[18] Manzoni and col-

leagues[28a] found that, over a 10-year follow-up period, 80% of the patients maintained the primary episodic form and 12% evolved to a secondary chronic type. Only 53% maintained the primary chronic form de novo. A small percentage may acquire the combined forms. From this study, the encouraging observation is that almost one third of their patients who started with chronic cluster headaches transitioned into the episodic form. The clinical presentation is similar to the episodic form, although the attack frequency may be higher. However, the lower limit of the attacks can be as few as once weekly, and there may be a tendency toward higher rate of diurnal attacks.

Possible predictive factors in the evolution of chronic cluster headaches appear to be late onset, occurrence of more than one cluster cycle per year, brief remission periods, and possibly heavy smoking. Head injury, increased alcohol consumption, and perhaps, caffeine consumption of more than six servings per day, and prolonged duration of cluster periods (more than 8 weeks) may be additional risk factors.[50]

■ MECHANISM AND PATHOPHYSIOLOGY

The pathogenesis of cluster headache is unknown. Many methodological problems affect the study of cluster headache patients, including differences between active cycles and remission as well as during and between the attacks. All of these factors may play a decisive role in understanding the mechanism of cluster headache. The intensity, brevity, and behavior of patients during the cluster attack may be prohibitive to conducting investigational studies. To establish any unifying explanation for cluster headache, three major aspects of this disorder must be considered and include the following: (1) the trigeminal distribution of the pain; (2) the ipsilateral autonomic features; and (3) the periodicity of attacks.

The Source of the Pain

The location of pain is very consistent anatomically as well as laterality. Typically, the pain is located in trigeminal distribution, and in most cases, in the peri- or retro-ocular area. The fact that cluster headache developed in a patient following the ipsilateral orbital exenteration suggests the involvement of the retro-orbital structures.[51] The pain may emerge from pain fibers in the cranial nerves—anywhere along their course from the peripheral nerve endings to neurons of central endings in the brainstem or upper cervical cord. Anatomically, the intracavernous segment of the internal carotid artery and/or surrounding cavernous sinus was suggested as a likely site of involvement. Positron emission tomography (PET) studies, conducted during the induced cluster attacks, demonstrated activation in the region of the cavernous sinus.[52] On MRI, Sjaastad and Rinck,[53] however, did not find any definitive pathology in, or in the vicinity of, the cavernous sinus in 14 patients diagnosed with cluster headache. However, none of their patients were studied during the cluster attack; therefore, the negative study does not exclude any changes occurring during an acute attack of cluster headache.

The cavernous sinus region is packed with various structures that are implicated in the mechanism of a cluster attack. The cavernous sinus is occupied by the sympathetic fibers to the internal carotid artery, the dural sinuses and veins, and the eye, as well as the internal carotid artery itself and the branches of its nerves. This is the site where the trigeminal, parasympathetic, and sympathetic fibers converge. An inflammatory process in the cavernous sinus and branching veins (venous vasculitis) has been suggested as causing vascular congestion and damage to local sympathetic fibers.[54] An inflammatory process as a causative factor may explain why corticosteroids are effective in aborting the cluster cycle.

Vascular and Hemodynamic Changes

In cluster headache patients, studies of cerebral blood flow during and between cluster attacks have not demonstrated consistent results. Cluster headache is associated with the dilatation of proximal tributaries of the internal carotid artery but without consistent changes in cerebral blood flow. Transcranial Doppler and cerebral blood flow (CBF) studies have shown in both spontaneous as well as nitroglycerin-induced attacks, a bilateral decrease in middle cerebral artery blood flow velocities—with more pronounced decrease on the symptomatic side, suggesting vasodilatation during the cluster attack.[55]

Waldenlind and colleagues[56] were able to capture two spontaneous cluster attacks in one patient with magnetic resonance angiography (MRA). Imaging showed a markedly dilated, ipsilateral ophthalmic artery during both attacks with subsequent decrease of the vessel lumen after the attack. No other change in the internal carotid artery or other intracerebral arteries on either side was demonstrated. This patient had normal MRA findings during the clinical remission.

It is known that vasodilators such as alcohol, nitroglycerin, and histamine can induce an acute attack in individuals during the cluster cycle. The induced attack, however, starts after latency of at least 30 minutes. It is unclear if the vasodilatory effect of these drugs is responsible for the attack, or if it results from the activation of the trigeminal vascular system.[40]

Autonomic Changes

The autonomic symptoms that accompany cluster attack are an integral part of the cluster headache. These symptoms are described in not only an anatomic vicinity of cluster headache but also are more systemic as presented by cardiovascular changes. Clinical and experimental observation demonstrates dysfunction of the autonomic nervous system. Both parasympathetic and sympathetic nerves innervate cerebral blood vessels. The cranial parasympathetic innervation is provided via the seventh cranial nerve and supplies both lacrimal and nasal mucosal glands. The activation of the cranial parasympathetic system explains lacrimation, nasal congestion, and rhinorrhea as well as vasodilatation either directly or indirectly through vasoactive neuropeptides such as vasoactive intestinal polypeptide (VIP) and nitric oxide synthase.

Transient or incomplete paralysis—dysfunction of the ocular sympathetic nerve supply producing a partial Horner syndrome—is most likely localized in the cavernous sinus. The impairment of sympathetic activity during the cluster periods was corroborated by the pupillometric study done by Fanciullacci and colleagues.[57] The most likely explanation for autonomic symptoms is a combination of parasympathetic

hyperactivity and sympathetic hypofunction as the result of central dysregulation.

Biochemical and Hormonal Changes

Activation of the trigeminal vascular system occurring during attacks of migraine, cluster, or chronic paroxysmal hemicrania triggers the release of vasoactive neuropeptides such as substance P, CGRP, and neurokinin A. Histamine, a potent vasoactive substance, has been considered by Horton[58] to be a major "player" in cluster headache. Anthony and Lance[59] studied serum histamine levels from 20 patients with cluster headache during 22 attacks. They found histamine levels during the headache periods in 19 of 22 attacks to be significantly higher than during the preheadache phase by a mean increase of 20.5%. Appenzeller and colleagues,[60] from temporal skin biopsies in cluster headache patients, found evidence of mast cell degranulation and histamine release in proximity to cutaneous nerves. The clinical importance of histamine in cluster headache is still unclear because the H_1 and H_2 receptors antagonists fail to abort or reduce the cluster attack under controlled trial settings[61] as well as in real-life clinical conditions.

Because the majority of cluster headache patients are males, particular attention has been directed toward sex hormone level changes. Surprisingly, low plasma testosterone levels were found in a population with cluster headache suggesting hypothalamic-pituitary axis involvement. The reduced plasma levels of testosterone, however, have been found during the active cluster periods as well as in patients diagnosed with migraine with aura,[62] and those suffering from trigeminal neuralgia and radicular pain.[63] This finding indicates that a low plasma level of testosterone is a reaction to pain rather than a causative factor. Other alterations in secretion and responses in production of luteinizing hormone, cortisol, prolactin, growth hormone, follicle stimulating hormone, and thyroid stimulating hormone have been observed in cluster headache.

Recently, melatonin and its rhythmic secretion have received marked attention. Melatonin release from the pineal gland is regulated from the suprachiasmatic nucleus and is closely synchronized with the hours of sleep and wakefulness. Normally, melatonin levels are low during the day. The secretion is inhibited by light via retinal-hypophyseal pathway and increases during darkness and sleep. During cluster headache cycles, 24-hour production of melatonin is reduced and the nocturnal peak in melatonin concentration is blunted.[64] These observations prompted Leone and colleagues[65] to use melatonin in the prophylaxis of cluster headaches.

Chronobiological Changes

The cyclical occurrence of cluster headache periods and attacks and their circannual and circadian periodicity suggest pathology or dysfunction of the biological clock or pacemaker. In mammals, the biological clock is located in the suprachiasmatic nucleus and its lesion leads to abnormal circadian activities. The alterations in circadian secretion of testosterone, prolactin, melatonin, and cortisol occur simultaneously with cluster attacks. The hypothalamic activation in the area of the suprachiasmatic nucleus has been documented by positron emission tomography (PET) during both spontaneous and nitroglycerin-induced cluster attacks.[52] Voxel-based morphometric analysis of MRI has documented an increase in hypothalamic volume[66] in the inferior posterior hypothalamus which is almost identical to the area of activation seen on PET. This structural difference was seen only in cluster headache patients.

Carotid Chemoreceptor

Cluster headache attacks commonly occur at higher altitudes,[67] during sleep, and in association with sleep apnea.[68] Oxygen inhalation is highly effective in aborting attacks, which may suggest a role of hypoxemia in the pathogenesis of cluster headache. On the basis of these observations, Kudrow[67] proposed a hypothesis of a possible role of the carotid body in cluster headache. During the cluster headache attack, the disinhibition of the parasympathetic and inhibition of sympathetic systems affect the carotid body which is the most sensitive chemoreceptor, resulting in it reacting to hypoxemia by diminished activity.

Synthesis of Pathophysiology

Cluster headache has been well-defined clinically for several decades. However, its pathophysiology has been poorly understood. To understand and explain the mechanism of cluster headache, several unique features have to be considered. The following cannot be explained on the basis of only peripheral or central theory: circannual and circadian rhythm; male preponderance; strict unilaterality and the first division of trigeminal nerve distribution; extreme intensity of pain; and, characteristic autonomic symptoms. Traditionally, cluster headache and migraine headache have been described as vascular headache disorders. Recent studies of the trigeminal system, brain stem, and vascular changes in the cavernous sinus support the theory that cluster headache disorders are of neurovascular origin with both peripheral and central involvement.

Cluster headache has been attributed to a structural lesion in the cavernous sinus due to episodic local inflammation with resulting venous congestion and injury to the traversing sympathetic fibers of the intracranial internal carotid artery and its tributaries. This peripheral hypothesis is supported by findings of regional orbital vasodilatation on MRA[56] and activation in the region of the cavernous sinus by PET studies.[52] Studies of transcranial Doppler and cerebral blood flow (CBF) in both spontaneous, as well as nitroglycerin-induced attacks, suggest vasodilatation during the cluster attack.[55] Furthermore, peripheral vascular involvement is suggested by (1) induction of cluster attacks with vasodilators such as nitroglycerin, alcohol, and histamine; (2) finding of increased levels of vasoactive neuropeptides such as CGRP and VIP during the attacks; and (3) the therapeutic effect of vasoconstrictors including ergotamine and sumatriptan. The pain is transmitted by activation of the ophthalmic division of the trigeminal nerve and autonomic symptoms are mediated by parasympathetic activation of the seventh cranial nerve.

These peripheral changes, however, cannot explain rhythmicity, nocturnal occurrence, and hormonal irregularities in cluster patients. PET studies[52] demonstrated activation in the ipsilateral anteroventral hypothalamus which is the area involved in the control of circadian rhythm, sleep-wake cycling, and circadian secretion of hormones. It is also the area where morphometric analysis of MRI documented an increase in hypothalamic volume.[66] On the basis of localization of morphologic and functional changes, it has been suggested that the anatomic location for the central origin of cluster headache is the dysfunctional biological clock (pacemaker) in the hypothalamic gray area which is also known as the suprachiasmatic nucleus. Thus, vascular changes are secondary to activation of the trigeminal vascular system.

■ CLUSTER VARIANTS

Cluster variants are a group of uncommon headache disorders that differ from cluster headache in certain features of clinical presentation and treatment response. However, these disorders share the autonomic symptoms. The International Classification of Headache Disorders[1] divides the cluster variant group into paroxysmal hemicrania with its episodic and chronic variant, and the short-lasting unilateral neuralgiform headache attacks with conjunctival injection and tearing (SUNCT).

Paroxysmal Hemicrania

Paroxysmal hemicrania is defined as a headache with at least 20 attacks of severe unilateral orbital, supraorbital, or temporal pain lasting 2 to 30 minutes accompanied by at least one of the autonomic signs and symptoms typical of cluster headache. The attacks should have a frequency of no less than five per day for more than one-half of the time and are completely preventable by therapeutic doses of indomethacin. Episodic variants occur in periods with durations ranging from 7 days to 1 year, separated by pain-free periods lasting at least 1 month.

Chronic paroxysmal hemicrania (CPH) is defined as a series of attacks that occur for more than 1 year without remission or with remission lasting less than 1 month. CPH was first described in 1974 by Sjastaad and Dale.[69] CPH is a rare headache disorder and since 1974, approximately 120 cases have been described in the English-language literature. Compared to cluster headache, CPH is more prevalent in females, ranging from 62%[70] to 80% to 90%.[22] The mean age of onset is usually 30 to 40 years, with the range from 6 to 75 years of age.[70] Occasionally, head trauma may precede the onset of CPH.

The pain is strictly unilateral, mostly felt in the temporal, orbital, or maxillary regions. The quality of pain is usually described as sharp, throbbing, boring, piercing, or stabbing, and typically is rated as severe to excruciating. During the attacks, patients attempt to remain still in contrast to the erratic, sometimes bizarre, behavior of cluster patients. Alcohol or certain neck movements may precipitate attacks. Most patients experience a brief attack duration—between 10 and 15 minutes—with the maximum duration about 60 minutes. The mean attack frequency is between 3 to 13 in 24 hours, but there are reports of up to 40 attacks per day. No pronounced circadian or circannual periodicity has been observed.

By operational diagnostic criteria, the attacks should be accompanied by at least one of the following ipsilateral autonomic features: conjunctival injection; lacrimation; nasal congestion; or rhinorrhea. Other symptoms such as ptosis, photophobia, nausea, and facial flushing are not unusual. Seventy-five percent of patients do not report any coexisting primary headaches and there are no reports of familial occurrence of CPH.

The pathophysiology of CPH is unknown, but there are many similarities in biochemical, electrophysiologic, and blood flow studies with cluster headache. Increased levels of CGRP and VIP were observed in patients with CPH, with a return to normal levels after use of indomethacin.[71] Blood-flow studies and MRI studies demonstrated in some patients are identical to those with cluster headache. The autonomic symptoms are attributed to cranial parasympathetic activation. No distinct rhythmicity or hormonal changes have been observed, in contrast to cluster headache, and no findings show the activation of the hypothalamus. CPH appears to lack the central part of pathogenesis, but there is a definite peripheral neurovascular element present.

The responsiveness to indomethacin is a condition *sine qua non* for establishing the diagnosis. Some patients with a convincing clinical picture fail to respond to indomethacin but will be successful with other therapy. The standard treatment for CPH is indomethacin at doses of 25 to 50 mg, three times per day. Occasionally, a lower dose is sufficient for maintenance therapy. The beneficial effect usually occurs within 1 to 5 days after initiation of treatment. Anecdotal reports of successful treatment of CPH with other nonsteroidal antiinflammatory agents, such as naproxen,[72] have been published, as have reports of other drugs such as acetazolamide[73] and verapamil.[74] Oxygen was found to be beneficial in the acute treatment of some patients.[70] Combination treatment has been recommended with gastroprotective agents to reduce the risk of gastrointestinal side effects. It should be noted that indomethacin can cause a diffuse, low-grade headache. Another adverse reaction may include pseudotumor cerebri. Instances of symptomatic or secondary CPH have also been reported. Underlying causes include vascular pathologies such as aneurysm, intra- and extracranial space-occupying processes, inflammatory or infectious diseases, and other disorders.[75]

Short-Lasting Unilateral Neuralgiform Headache Attacks with Conjunctival Injection and Tearing

Described initially by Sjaastad and colleagues[76] in 1989, short-lasting unilateral neuralgiform headache attacks with conjunctival injection and tearing (SUNCT) is a very rare primary headache syndrome characterized by short-lasting attacks of unilateral headache often accompanied by prominent lacrimation and conjunctival injection of the ipsilateral eye. To fulfill the diagnostic criteria, at least 20 attacks of periorbital or temporal headache lasting 5 to 240 seconds must be reported. Attacks occur with a frequency from 3 to 200 per day and are not attributed to another disorder. This debilitating headache disorder is noteworthy for its resistance to treatment, including indomethacin. Originally, this disorder had been observed only in males. Recently, a few SUNCT cases have been described in females, with a ratio of 3:8.[77]

Characteristically, SUNCT is described as a short-lasting episode, typically lasting less than 120 seconds, with paroxysms with a rather abrupt onset and end. The pain is severe, stabbing or burning in quality, and is associated with ipsilateral massive conjunctival injection and lacrimation. The autonomic phenomena disappear on conclusion of the attack. Patients may experience up to 30 episodes per hour with a mean frequency of 28 attacks per day.[77]

The pathogenesis of this syndrome is unknown, but SUNCT has also been reported in a few patients with posterior structure lesions such as cerebellopontine angle arteriovenous malformations and a cavernous hemangioma of the brain stem which is demonstrated on MRI.[78,79] Therefore, all patients with SUNCT syndrome should undergo MRI investigation of the posterior fossa.

SUNCT syndrome is remarkably refractory to treatment. Most drugs that are effective in other short-lasting headaches are not useful. Two female patients responded to gabapentin[80,81] in doses of 800 mg to 900 mg per day. One male patient responded to topiramate,[82] and two other patients to lamotrigene.[83]

■ TESTING

As with other primary headache disorders, no biological marker or diagnostic procedure has been identified that could confirm the diagnosis of cluster headache. Diagnosis is established on the basis of a headache history. With the exception of a possible ipsilateral, partial Horner syndrome, the physical and neurologic examinations are essentially normal. In the majority of patients, the history of cluster headache is not ambiguous and once the temporal pattern has been identified, establishing the diagnosis should not be difficult.

MRI of the brain is essential in the investigation of cluster headache. An MRI should be ordered when the level of suspicion is increased as in any new case (especially when the temporal pattern is not as yet clearly defined) or in patients presenting with atypical features such as (1) atypical location; (2) prolonged duration of attacks; (3) age of onset above 50; (4) cluster headache in females; (5) migraine symptoms; (6) chronic form de novo; (7) atypical neurological signs; and (7) an abnormal neurologic examination. Established patients with a history of typical cluster headaches should undergo scanning when manifesting new symptoms or signs, unusual pattern, globalization of headache, new onset of coexisting headache, and new neurologic or mental changes.

Conventional electrophysiologic techniques, such as electroencephalography and evoked potentials, have demonstrated nonspecific changes. Some studies of trigeminal somatosensory evoked potentials have shown abnormalities of the trigeminal pathway present in patients with cluster headache—more on the symptomatic side and during the cluster period. Cerebrospinal fluid studies in cluster headache are nonrevealing; therefore, lumbar puncture is not essential in routine investigations of cluster headache.

■ DIFFERENTIAL DIAGNOSIS

The diagnosis of cluster headache is not difficult in its typical form. When a patient presents with the initial attack or a fairly new history (with the periodicity of attack still undetermined), the diagnosis may be more confusing. Similarly, the physician may be confronting a diagnostic dilemma with an elderly patient, a patient with an atypical presentation, or cluster headache in combination with migraine or rebound headache. Despite a typical clinical presentation, many patients are commonly misdiagnosed as atypical migraine, sinusitis, trigeminal neuralgia, or temporal arteritis.

The significant differences between cluster headache and migraine are presented in Table 44–4. Sinusitis is usually bilateral and follows rhinitis, common cold, or influenza. Pain is rarely as intense as during the cluster attack, and no periodicity or nocturnal occurrence is noted. The pain of sinusitis is rather continuous, dull, pressure-like, or pulsating and is accompanied by purulent nasal secretion. Sinusitis usually resolves with antibiotic treatment.

Trigeminal neuralgia is more common in middle-aged and elderly females, and is characterized by very brief attacks that last only seconds and are described as lancinating, shock-like, unilateral pain, mainly localized in the second and third divisions of the trigeminal nerve. The attacks occur several times a day without a nocturnal preponderance, and no autonomic symptoms accompany the pain. The acute attack of trigeminal neuralgia can be triggered by touching the face, brushing the teeth, or eating. However, the histamine or nitroglycerin-provocative tests are negative.

The diagnosis of temporal arteritis should be considered in any recent onset of unilateral headache in individuals older than age 50. In this disorder, a higher prevalence has been noted in females and the pain is less severe than in cluster attacks. The headache is accompanied by systemic symptoms such as night sweating, fever, malaise, polymyalgia, muscle stiffness and ache, anorexia and weight loss, and claudication pain on chewing. The diagnosis is confirmed by an elevated sedimentation rate by Westergren method and a biopsy of the temporal artery.

Tolosa-Hunt syndrome (recurrent painful ophthalmoplegia) is a rare disorder similar in certain features to cluster headache. The clinical presentation includes a headache that is (1) usually unilateral and periorbital; (2) of lesser intensity; intermittent, or more continuous; (3) does not cycle in clusters; and (4) has no associated autonomic symptoms. Tolosa-Hunt syndrome is caused by granulomatous infiltration of the superior ophthalmic vein and cavernous sinus.

Secondary Cluster Headaches

Primary cluster headache has no known cause. Occasionally, cluster headache results from an underlying intracranial or, less often, extracranial pathology. It may occur in 3% to 5% of cluster patients. Cluster-like or symptomatic cluster headaches should be suspected when the clinical presentation is atypical. A detailed neurologic examination and brain scanning, preferably MRI and MRA of both intra- and extracranial carotid arteries, is essential. The level of suspicion should be increased with any deviation from typical cluster symptomatology such as (1) an absence of typical periodicity or unexplained progression to a chronic stage despite adequate treatment; (2) new onset of cluster headache after age 50; (3) change in character or location of pain; (4) prolonged attacks; (5) unresponsiveness to abortive therapy; (6) background headache; (7) new symptoms; (8) presence of neurologic signs other than Horner syndrome; and (9) onset of a new type of headache during the cluster cycle.

The origin of secondary cluster headache can be divided into three categories:

1. Intracranial
   - Tumors and other mass lesions
   - Vascular abnormalities
   - Inflammatory
2. Extracranial
3. Posttraumatic cluster headaches

Several reports have been published of pituitary adenoma, meningioma, metastatic lesion, and other intracranial space-occupying lesions associated with onset of cluster headache or change in the pattern and clinical presentation. Milos and colleagues[84] described a 37-year-old male with a history of episodic cluster headache for 4 years when the frequency of attacks gradually increased and, incidentally, acromegaly was observed during evaluation. After resection

Table 44–4		
Characteristics of Cluster Headache versus Migraine		
	Cluster Headache	*Migraine*
Male to Female ratio	5:1	1:3
Onset of disease (mean)	25 to 30	10 to 15
Hereditary factors	Rarely	70%
Duration of cycle	2 to 3 months	No cycle
Seasonal occurrence	Spring and fall	No
Frequency of attack	1 to 2 a day and daily	Sporadic
Duration of attack	1 to 2 hours	Several hours
Onset of attack	Any time; typically 12 AM to 3 AM	Any time; typically AM or early PM
Localization of pain	Very localized, periorbital	Temporal, hemicranial, global
Rapidity of onset	Abrupt	Evolves over several hours
Unilateral headache	Almost 100%	70%
Character of pain	Boring, burning	Pulsating
Associated symptoms	Ipsilateral lacrimation, rhinorrhea, congestion, Horner syndrome	Nausea, vomiting, photo-/phonophobia
Aura	No	Yes
Affected by menstruation	No	Yes

of growth hormone-producing adenoma his cluster attacks abated. Similarly, other patients cited by Milos and colleagues experienced cluster headache associated with prolactinoma.[84] The site of an intracranial mass can be located anywhere in relation to the midline or cavernous sinus. Tentorial meningioma in the posterior fossa,[85] parasellar meningioma, trigeminal neurinoma, sphenoidal sinus aspergilloma, and brain metastasis of lung cancer have all been reported in association with cluster headache with subsequent remission after surgical treatment of the mass.

Similarly, A-V malformations, intracranial aneurysm or pseudoaneurysm, and carotid artery dissection or aneurysmal thrombosis at different locations may account for new onset or worsening of preexisting cluster headache. It is important to note that those patients usually have a normal neurologic examination.

Extracranial lesions, such as an upper cervical meningioma[86] and nasopharyngeal carcinoma without intracranial infiltration,[87] causing cluster symptoms cannot be explained by direct influence on the central factor of cluster headache mechanism. Disturbance in and around the cavernous portion of the carotid artery does not account for cluster headache in patients with vertebral artery aneurysm or cervical meningioma. Explanation for such phenomena remains to be suggested.

Posttraumatic headaches manifesting with typical or atypical cluster headaches have a relatively low incidence.[88] The onset of pain is usually rapid, with a relatively brief duration. The majority of those patients have incurred only minor head injury, with or without neck trauma.

■ THERAPY

As with management of other primary headaches, the right balance of value and risk should be found. The patient should understand the pathophysiology of cluster headache and that it is not a result of a catastrophic intracranial organic disorder. The treating physician must establish definable expectations of management with each patient, so they will understand the natural process and progress of the disease. The patient needs to responsibly participate in his or her own care. The treatment goal is relief of cluster attack and the shortening of cluster cycle. An established patient should be instructed to contact the physician's office as soon as possible at the start of the next cycle to initiate treatment within the first stage of the cluster period. Successful treatment requires symptomatic or abortive treatment and prophylactic medication (Tables 44–5 and 44–6). Lifestyle adjustment may help avoid precipitating attacks during the vulnerable periods. Alcohol consumption should be discouraged, although many patients will preemptively abstain due to fear of provoking the attacks. Daytime napping is not recommended. It is important to not discontinue prophylactic treatment prematurely.

Abortive Treatment

The rapid onset and brief duration of excruciating headache attacks limits the use of conventional analgesics. Therefore, oral narcotic-analgesics are inappropriate in the management of acute cluster attacks.

Table 44–5

Therapy of Acute Attack
- Oxygen
- Sumatriptan SQ or NS
- Zolmitriptan NS
- DHE IM/SQ/IV
- Ergotamine tartrate
- Ketorolac IM
- Chlorpromazine
- Lidocaine viscous solution—intranasal
- Cocaine—intranasal
- Capsaicin—intranasal

IM, intramuscularly; IV, intravenously; NS, nasal spray; SQ, subcutaneously.

Table 44–6

Prophylactic Therapy
- Corticosteroids
- Verapamil
- Lithium
- Ergotamine
- Topiramate
- Valproic acid
- Gabapentin
- Doxepin
- Indomethacin
- Clonidine
- Naratriptan
- Frovatriptan
- Methysergide
- Baclofen
- Melatonin
- Occipital nerve injection
- Histamine desensitization
- Civamide-intranasal

Oxygen

Oxygen was introduced as an effective treatment of acute cluster attacks by Horton[16] and has since been the standard of care for symptomatic relief. Inhaled 100% oxygen should be delivered via a nonrebreathing facial mask and inhaled slowly at a flow rate of 7 to 8 L/minute for 15 minutes, providing relief to about 70% of patients within 15 minutes.[89] The oxygen tank, reduction valve, and mask can be rented for home use and used at the beginning of an attack. The patient should be prohibited from smoking in proximity of the oxygen tank.

Sumatriptan

With the entry of the triptans to the migraine therapeutic armamentarium, new therapeutic options have been introduced in the abortive treatment of cluster attacks. In particular, subcutaneous sumatriptan with very short T_{max}, and rapid onset of action, has been effective in the symptomatic relief of cluster attacks. Complete relief within 15 minutes was achieved by 74% of patients in a placebo-controlled study and was well-tolerated as reported by the Sumatriptan Cluster Headache Study Group.[90] No evidence has been reported that repetitive daily use of sumatriptan for several weeks or months would cause tachyphylaxis or rebound phenomenon. Chronic cluster patients appear to respond to sumatriptan at a lower rate. Oral sumatriptan is not recommended because of the longer time to onset of action. Sumatriptan nasal spray 20 mg is less effective than the injectable form.

The common adverse reactions are local injection-site reaction, nausea and vomiting, chest and throat pressure sensation, and flushing. These side effects are usually temporary and short-lasting. Sumatriptan use should be limited to patients who suffer no more than one attack per day to avoid overuse. Another limiting factor to this therapy is the cost of the drug. Sumatriptan is contraindicated in patients with ischemic heart disease and uncontrolled hypertension.

Dihydroergotamine

Dihydroergotamine (DHE) is available in injectable and intranasal formulations. The intravenous administration of DHE 1 mg rapidly aborts cluster attack within 15 minutes, but it is not practicable because of difficulties in intravenous self-administration. In 54 hospitalized patients with cluster headache, intravenous DHE provided complete relief in all patients during treatment.[91] The intramuscular and subcutaneous administration is slower in obtaining relief because of the time to maximal concentration, but it remains an option. Intranasal formulation is a more convenient route of treatment in ambulatory patients. However, no efficacy data are available from larger studies. DHE is contraindicated in patients with coronary or peripheral ischemic disease.

Zolmitriptan

Zolmitriptan has been used as an effective agent for acute treatment of migraine attacks. In a double-blind study,[92] 124 patients with episodic and chronic cluster headaches required at least one dose of zolmitriptan 10 mg, 5 mg, or placebo. Mild or no pain at 30 minutes was reported by 60%, 57%, and 42%, respectively. It is important to note that these rates do not approach those of oxygen or injectable sumatriptan. No studies evaluating efficacy of intranasal zolmitriptan have been published to date.

Lidocaine

Anesthetic action of lidocaine on the sphenopalatine ganglion was studied by Kittrelle and colleagues,[93] and showed favorable responses in aborting cluster attacks. Lidocaine 4% viscous solution is instilled in the nostril ipsilateral to the pain in a carefully positioned patient with the body supine and the head extended over the head of a bed, inclined to the side of pain. The positioning is cumbersome, especially during a painful attack, but topical effect may be effective in some patients.

Cocaine

Barre[94] reported 80% or better reduction in intensity of cluster attacks induced by nitroglycerin within 2.5 minutes in 10 of 11 patients treated with cocaine 10% solution. Cocaine was instilled by nasal dropper to the sphenopalatine foramen region. Cocaine may be a valuable adjunctive abortive therapy in a cohort of patients who are refractory to oxygen or sumatriptan or patients with cardiac ischemic disease. The risk for addiction is slight when used for a limited interval of 4 to 12 weeks.

Other Agents

Anecdotal reports indicate marginal effectiveness of other drugs in aborting cluster attacks. Ketorolac IM/IV, chlorpromazine IM/IV, diphenhydramine HCl, and valproate sodium IV may help to reduce or abate the cluster attacks in some patients.

Prophylactic Treatment

The purpose of prophylactic therapy is to reduce the frequency, duration, and severity of attacks, and interrupt the cycle of cluster headache. The prophylactic treatment should be initiated at the onset of a new cycle simultaneously with symptomatic therapy. The patient should remain on the prophylactic regimen for at least 2 to 4 weeks after the last cluster attack to ensure that treatment is not discontinued prematurely within the cycle. Discontinuation of treatment should be gradual. Continuation of therapy beyond the cycle will not guarantee prevention of future cluster cycles. The next new cycle should be treated at the beginning, preferably within the first week.

Corticosteroids

Corticosteroids are effective inductive agents in suppressing attacks at the beginning of a cluster cycle during the interval when the standard prophylactic therapy is taking effect. This method of treatment was introduced by Horton[58] in 1952. The mechanism of action is not known. In appropriate doses, the corticosteroids usually provide relief within 1 to 2 days. Kudrow[11] reported significant relief in 77% of 77 patients with episodic cluster headache and partial relief in another 12% who initiated treatment with prednisone 40 mg, gradually tapering the dose over the course of 3 weeks. Treatment with prednisone is usually initiated with 60- to 80-mg doses per day for 2 to 3 days followed by 10-mg decrements every 2 to 3 days.

Dexamethasone 8 mg per day for 2 weeks, followed by 4 mg a day for 1 week may be used as an alternative. During the tapering of the corticosteroids, some cluster attacks may recur. Therefore, simultaneously with inductive therapy, other prophylactic agents should be initiated. Steroids are less effective in chronic cluster headache. Long-term use of these drugs should be avoided because of the potential for frequent, well-known adverse reactions.

Verapamil

The mechanism of action of the calcium channel blockers in preventing cluster headache is not clear. Verapamil is the most commonly used of these agents and is the most effective. However, at least 1 week of treatment is required before the drug demonstrates efficacy. Verapamil was first reported to be effective in cluster headaches in 1983.[95] The initial dose ranges from 240 to 360 mg, but some patients may require up to 600 mg a day. Up to 80% of patients with episodic cluster headache report a significant reduction in the number of the acute attacks as well as the consumption of analgesics within 2 weeks of treatment.[96] In a subsequent larger study involving 48 patients,[97] 69% of the patients improved by more than 75%. The average dose for episodic cluster was 354 mg/day and 572 mg/day for the chronic form.

Verapamil is usually well tolerated although constipation is a frequent and unpleasant side effect. A high dose of the agent may cause hypotension, bradycardia, or other cardiac abnormalities; therefore, patients should be monitored carefully. The prescribing physician should be aware of any potential drug-drug interaction.

Several other calcium channel blockers have been tried in cluster headache prophylaxis, including nifedipine and nimodipine. In small trials,[95] both nifedipine (at doses of 30 to 180 mg/day) and nimodipine (at doses of 120 mg/day) proved to be useful in the episodic as well as the chronic form of cluster headache.

Lithium Carbonate

The first line of treatment of chronic cluster headache is lithium carbonate. The reason for introducing lithium to cluster treatment during the 1970s was that cyclic features of cluster headache somewhat reminded an observer of manic-depressive disorder. Multiple trials have been undertaken that studied the effectiveness of lithium in both episodic and especially chronic forms of cluster headache.

In 1977, Kudrow reported a marked and sustained improvement in 27 of 28 patients with unresponsive chronic cluster headache.[98] The treatment was started at doses of 300 to 600 mg/day and increased by the end of the fourth week to 600 to 900 mg/day. A dramatic response was seen in many patients during the first week of treatment. Ekbom described immediate partial remission in eight patients with chronic cluster headache.[99] The average headache index improved within 2 weeks by 85.3%. In contrast, only 4 of 11 patients with episodic cluster responded with almost complete suppression of the cluster cycle.

A larger series evaluating 90 patients with episodic and chronic cluster headache (68 and 22, respectively) showed similar results.[100] One half of patients with the chronic type showed a definite, constant improvement both short- and long-term. Of the 68 patients with episodic cluster, 26 proved highly responsive, 26 were partially responsive, and 16 were refractory to treatment. However, a double-blind crossover study compared verapamil 360 mg/day with lithium 900 mg/day in 30 chronic cluster patients and failed to show a superiority for lithium.[101]

The mechanism of action of lithium in cluster headache is unknown. Lithium has no measurable effect on cerebral hemodynamics.[102] It is conceivable that lithium has a central neurogenic effect influencing the "biological clock" in the area of the suprachiasmatic nucleus.

The initial starting dose of lithium carbonate is 300 mg 3 times a day, or 450 mg of the sustained release form once or twice a day. Lithium has a narrow therapeutic window and the serum concentration ranges between 0.4 and 0.8 mEq/L which is effective for cluster headache and is usually lower than that required for treatment of bipolar disorder. The serum concentration should be measured at least 6 hours after the last dose and should not exceed 1.0 mEq/L.

Side effects include fatigue; tremor and other cerebellar symptoms; thirst; edema; weight gain; polyuria; and, abdom-

inal discomfort. Renal and thyroid function should be monitored on a regular basis. The concomitant use of diuretics and nonsteroidal antiinflammatory drugs (NSAIDs) is not recommended because it may increase the serum concentration of lithium to toxic levels.

Ergotamine Derivates

Ergotamine has lost its popularity with the introduction of sumatriptan. Ergotamine is useful in recurrent and predictable attacks, when it can be used as a targeted prophylaxis. Nocturnal attacks can be prevented by use of ergotamine tartrate 2 mg at bedtime. However, triptans as abortive therapy must be avoided. Ergotamine can be used in a combination preparation with caffeine or belladonna and phenobarbital. in approximately 80% of cluster headaches. Kudrow[11] documented benefit from ergotamine administered by various routes. Adding ergotamine to the regimen of lithium and/or verapamil increases the response to this combination. The vasoconstrictive effect of ergotamine is believed to be one of the mechanisms of action.

Adverse reactions are fairly common and include nausea and vomiting, numbness, itching, and pain in the extremities. Contraindications to ergotamine include peripheral vascular disease, coronary artery disease, uncontrolled hypertension, fever, sepsis, pregnancy, and within 24 hours of using triptans.

Methysergide

Methysergide, a semisynthetic ergot derivative, is no longer available in the United States. In the pre-triptan era, methysergide was a staple in the management of cluster headache. Methysergide is a serotonin antagonist with antihistaminic as well as anticholinergic actions. The efficacy of methysergide in cluster treatment has been reported in a larger series by Friedman and Elkind,[103] who treated 54 patients with cluster headache. The beneficial effect of 6 to 8 mg/day was ranging between 50% to 70%, comparable to that of verapamil or lithium.

Methysergide was used extensively after its introduction as a prophylactic agent until the discovery of its tendency to cause retroperitoneal fibrosis. We do not know if the fibrotic reaction is dose-related or idiosyncratic. Patients with lung or connective-tissue diseases are more likely to develop this complication. Other side effects include leg pain, nausea, peripheral edema, paresthesias, and chest pain. To reduce the incidence of fibrotic reaction, a therapeutic window for 2 or more months is recommended after 5 to 6 months of continuous therapy. Periodic imaging of the chest and abdominal cavity and monitoring renal function are recommended.

Valproic Acid

Valproic acid, a gamma aminobutyric acid (GABA) agonist successfully used in migraine headache, has been also proved to be efficacious in cluster headache prophylaxis. An open-label study in 15 patients confirmed a 73% favorable response rate to valproic acid at doses of 600 to 2000 mg/day.[104]

In another open-label trial,[105] 26 patients with episodic or chronic cluster headache were treated with divalproex sodium (equal proportions of valproic acid and valproate sodium) at a mean daily dose of 850 mg. The mean decrease of headache frequency in chronic cluster for a 28-day period was 53.9%, and 58.6% in the episodic type. Common side effects may include hand tremor, nausea, weight gain, and hair loss.

Topiramate

Anecdotal reports have described the effectiveness of topiramate in both episodic and chronic cluster headache.[106] Topiramate, an antiepileptic drug extensively used in migraine prophylaxis, at doses of 50 to 125 mg/day produced rapid improvement with remission occurring in 1 to 3 weeks into the treatment. A larger prospective trial involving 26 patients with episodic or chronic cluster headache confirmed the beneficial effect of topiramate in prophylactic treatment of cluster headache.[107] In 15 patients, the remission was induced at a mean time of 14 days, but in seven patients, remission was obtained within the first week of treatment.

The mechanism of action is not known, but may include enhancement of GABA antinociceptive property and blockage of voltage-dependent Na^+ channels. Adverse reactions of topiramate include appetite suppression, weight loss, cognitive impairment, paresthesias, taste distortion, and increased risk for renal calculi. These last three side effects are explained by the action of topiramate as a carbonic anhydrase inhibitor.

Gabapentin

In an open study,[108] eight patients with intractable cluster headache received gabapentin at the daily dose of 900 mg. All patients were headache-free at a maximum of 8 days after starting the treatment. Patients with the episodic type remained headache-free at 3 months after discontinuation of therapy. Patients with chronic cluster were headache-free during the 4 months after initiation of treatment while receiving this medication.

The mechanism of action of gabapentin, an anticonvulsant, is not known. However, it is speculated that gabapentin reduces pain messages by suppressing glutamate activity and enhancing GABA within the central nervous system. Side effects may include fatigue and lightheadedness.

Indomethacin

Although some trigeminal-autonomic headaches respond in an absolute manner to indomethacin, no large studies are available for evaluating this medication for prophylactic treatment of cluster headache. Only anecdotal evidence has been reported to suggest that indomethacin may reduce the frequency and intensity of cluster attacks.

Other Drugs

Clonidine

Clonidine, an alpha-2-adrenergic presynaptic agonist, regulates the sympathetic tone in the central nervous system. The efficacy of clonidine at doses of 5 to 7.5 mg delivered transdermally over 1 week was evaluated in a study involving 13 patients with both episodic and chronic forms of cluster headache.[109] The mean weekly frequency of attacks decreased from 17.7 to 8.7; the pain intensity measured on a visual scale (from 0 to 100) decreased from 98 to 41. The duration decreased from 59 to 34 minutes. In many patients, the beneficial effect of clonidine started during the first 24 hours of treatment. Possible explanation of action is central

sympathetic inhibition. High doses of clonidine may cause hypotension, dizziness, fatigue, drowsiness, dry mouth, and constipation.

Baclofen

Baclofen, a $GABA_B$ analog, has been shown to possess antinociceptive activity and is used primarily as an antispasmodic agent in multiple sclerosis, as well as in some cases of painful neuralgias and neuropathy. Hering-Hanit and Gadoth reported baclofen, at the daily dose of 15 to 30 mg in three divided doses, to be safe and effective in prevention of cluster headaches.[110] Within 1 week of treatment, 12 of 16 patients reported the cessation of attacks.

Tizanidine

Tizanidine, a central muscle relaxant, is structurally related to clonidine, and has a similar mechanism of action. D'Alessandro[111] used tizanidine as concomitant therapy in five patients refractory to treatment. The medication, administered daily at 12 to 24 mg in divided doses, proved to be effective in abating attacks in three patients. One patient reported marked improvement, and only one patient failed to respond. Tizanidine is generally well tolerated, but sleepiness, fatigue, vivid dreams, and dry mouth may be unpleasant side effects for some patients.

Chlorpromazine

Occasionally, use of chlorpromazine (a phenothiazine) has been tried to reduce and prevent cluster attacks. Caviness and O'Brien used chlorpromazine at doses ranging from 75 to 700 mg/day.[112] Twelve of 13 patients with cluster headache reported complete relief within 2 weeks of treatment. However, the authors suspected that some improved patients underwent spontaneous remission. Side effects may be common and include tiredness, drowsiness, stupor, restlessness, agitation, dystonia, tardive dyskinesia, and jaundice.

Doxepin

Doxepin, a tricyclic antidepressant with high affinity to H_1 receptors, has occasionally been used as adjunctive therapy in chronic cluster headache. The usual dose is 25 to 100 mg at night. Drowsiness, dry mouth, urinary retention, and weight gain may affect patient compliance.

Naratriptan

Naratriptan, a $5-HT_{1B,1D}$ agonist, is an effective and well-tolerated antimigraine agent with a relatively long half-life (6 hours). Several authors reported on the effectiveness of naratriptan in cluster headache prophylaxis.[113-115] Naratriptan was used as adjunctive treatment in 11 refractory cluster patients at doses of 2.5 mg at bedtime or twice a day. Complete cessation or marked improvement has been reported in seven of these patients. Patients tolerated daily use of naratriptan over longer intervals without clinically significant side effects. While a patient is on naratriptan, other triptan or ergotamine preparations including DHE are contraindicated.

Cyproheptadine

Anecdotally, cyproheptadine, an antihistamine, has been used in doses of 4 mg three times a day to prevent cluster headaches. Drowsiness, increased appetite, and weight gain are common side effects.

Greater Occipital Nerve Blockade

Injection of 1% lidocaine (3 mL) and triamcinolone 40 mg to the greater occipital nerve (GON) ipsilateral to the side of cluster headache in 14 patients, provided moderate-to-good response in nine patients, and five had no response.[116] GON blockade may offer an alternative in transitional cluster therapy for some patients.

Capsaicin

Capsaicin, a derivate of homovanillic acid found in hot peppers, has been shown to cause the release of substance P (SP) and other neuropeptides from primary sensory nociceptive neurons. The first exposure to capsaicin activates these neurons that antidromically generate neurogenic inflammation, clinically causing an intense burning-pain sensation, local flushing, and edema. Desensitization occurs after the first exposure, with the neurons becoming less sensitive to stimulation including capsaicin itself. Repeated application of capsaicin depletes the nerve terminals of SP. Capsaicin cream applied topically in the nostril ipsilateral to the pain twice daily for 7 days significantly reduces headache intensity.[117] A drawback to this treatment is the unpleasant, burning, and painful sensation produced at the beginning of the application. Not every patient is willing to endure the initial pain and, therefore, this agent has never gained widespread acceptance in the treatment of cluster headache.

Civamide

Civamide, a synthetic isomer of capsaicin, has been found to be significantly more potent at depleting SP and CGRP than capsaicin, and is less irritating. The release of CGRP and SP results in dilation of intracranial arteries and an increase of vascular permeability and perivascular inflammatory response. The effect of intranasal civamide has been examined in the double-blind study conducted by the Intranasal Civamide Study Group, in multiple centers in the United States[118] Eighteen cluster headache subjects who received civamide and 10 who received placebo over a 7-day treatment period and a 20-day post-treatment period showed a significantly greater percent decrease in the number of headaches from baseline to post-treatment during days 1 through 7.

Melatonin

Some authors[65,119] have found melatonin to be moderately effective as a preventive treatment in both episodic and chronic cluster headache. The treatment is based on circadian rhythmicity and observation of reduced serum melatonin levels in patients during a cluster period.[64] Another group did not find any benefit in adding melatonin as adjunctive therapy in patients with cluster headache who had incomplete relief of their headaches on standard therapy.[120]

Histamine Desensitization

Some patients with chronic cluster headaches do not respond to standard treatment and require a course of intravenous histamine desensitization. Histamine desensitization was introduced by Horton in 1941, who recommended it as the treatment of choice for chronic cluster headache.[5] He noted: "Histamine treatment is as specific for this syndrome as insulin is in treatment of diabetes mellitus."

The idea behind this treatment was a speculative pathogenesis of cluster symptoms, to be an "anaphylactoid reaction at the cellular level" toward histamine. To increase tolerance against endogenous histamine, Horton desensitized his patients by giving increasing doses of histamine subcutaneously. This suggestion was based on similar desensitization treatment for allergies. The intravenous route of histamine desensitization has also been found to be beneficial[121] in the treatment of intractable chronic cluster headache. However, enthusiasm for this treatment has gradually diminished. It requires hospitalization for several days and, in our current atmosphere of restricted use of inpatient resources, the treatment has been abandoned almost totally. At the Diamond Headache Clinic, the only center in the United States where this treatment is still provided, the report from 1986 indicates at least a 75% reduction in cluster attacks in 25 of 64 patients. All but nine patients demonstrated a partial reduction in their cluster attacks.[122] On the initial day of treatment, histamine is administered intravenously (2.75 mg histamine phosphate diluted in 250 mL of normal saline) followed by 5.5 mg of histamine phosphate in each consecutive dose. The infusion rate starts at 10 mL/hour and the rate is increased hourly up to 120 mL/hour. The rate of infusion is based on the patient's tolerability. Two to three doses are administered daily to a total dose of 110 mg. Side effects include flushing, nausea, cough, abdominal discomfort, and headache. These reactions can be limited by reducing the rate of infusion.

Surgical Management of Cluster Headache

A small percentage of patients with chronic cluster headache do not respond to pharmacologic therapy and may benefit from surgical treatment. This form of intervention should be reserved for patients refractory to outpatient as well as inpatient therapy, when a combination of different effective medications has failed, or in patients with a contraindication to pharmacologic treatment. Surgical management should be considered only in patients with chronic cluster headache who suffer from strictly unilateral headaches. This selection should be absolute to avoid recurrence on the contralateral side post-surgery in those whose attacks alternate sides. Patients with atypical cluster features should be excluded. Surgical candidates should have a stable psychological profile so as not to aggravate or trigger major depressive episodes with suicidal ideation in case of treatment failure.

Although a variety of surgical procedures have been used (Table 44–7) in the treatment of chronic cluster headache, these options have yielded only mixed results. Among neurosurgeons,[123] the consensus is that no one procedure provides consistent long-lasting relief; radiofrequency lesion and nerve avulsion are reasonable first-stage procedures. Procedures that carry the least risk should be implemented before more complicated surgeries. Most surgical techniques have been directed toward the sensory trigeminal system or parasympathetic fibers of the nervus intermedius, the greater superficial petrosal nerve, or the sphenopalatine ganglion.

The temporary benefit of lidocaine instillation anesthesia or cocainization of sphenopalatine ganglion has produced a more permanent procedure to provide long-lasting relief. However, sphenopalatine gangliectomy or chemical or physical destruction of the ganglion failed to have enduring results.

Table 44-7

Surgical Management of Chronic Cluster Headache

Involving Sensory Trigeminal Nerve
- Chemical denervation of the supraorbital and infraorbital nerves
- Avulsion of supraorbital, infraorbital, supratrochlear nerve
- Chemical denervation of the Gasserian ganglion
- Retrogasserian glycerol injection
- Radiofrequency ganglio-rhizolysis
- Trigeminal root section
- Gamma Knife radiosurgery

Involving the Autonomic Pathways
- Lesion of the greater superficial petrosal nerve
- Lesion of the nervus intermedius
- Sphenopalatine ganglion blockade

Because of their high unpredictability, these procedures are rarely performed.

Surgical intervention directly involving the trigeminal nerve such as nerve sectioning of the first branch, chemical denervation (using local anesthetic, alcohol, glycerol, or phenol), peripheral nerve avulsion, and trigeminal root section via the posterior fossa have not shown adequate and prolonged relief. Partial or complete retrogasserian sensory root lesion seems to be more effective. Nervus intermedius rhizotomy seems to be another approach that may benefit some cluster sufferers. The nervus intermedius relays parasympathetic impulses that mediate most of the autonomic features accompanying the cluster attack and the vasodilatation of the external carotid arterial tree.[124] Seven of Sachs'[125,126] nine patients obtained relief from resection of the nerve for several months to years. Complications related to this surgery include hearing and taste loss, vertigo, and facial palsy.

Resection of the greater superficial petrosal nerve on the symptomatic side, performed by Gardner[127] in 26 patients with unilateral headache, offered fair to excellent relief in 75%. However, only one half of these patients had cluster headaches. Watson[123] was unsuccessful in only 1 of 4 cases using this procedure. An effort to improve the rate of success in surgical intervention led to different combined procedures such as section of the greater superficial petrosal nerve or nervus intermedius and neurolysis of the sensory root of the trigeminal nerve.

Microvascular decompression of the trigeminal nerve, with or without section of the nervus intermedius, was reported to be effective in chronic cluster headache by Lovely and colleagues.[128] The purpose of the procedure is to remove a vascular loop that is compressing the nerve. In 50% of 30 initial procedures, greater than 90% pain relief was achieved and 50% or greater relief was reported in 73.3% of patients.

Gamma Knife is a noninvasive stereotactic radiosurgery that applies gamma radiation at the trigeminal root entry zone. The technique has been used somewhat anecdotally and has a low complication rate. The procedure appears to be effective initially but has a high recurrence rate.

More recent surgical methods seem to be more encouraging and safer. The radiofrequency wave thermocoagulation of the gasserian ganglion performed via percutaneous access to selectively destruct poorly myelinated pain fibers has low morbidity and mortality and can be repeated if pain returns. Onofrio and Campbell[129] reported excellent results using this technique in 54% of their 26 patients during a 10-month to 5-year follow-up period. Similar results were shown by Mathew and Hurt[130] over 6 to 63 months of observation in 27 patients. The procedure is relatively safe, has a low recurrence rate, and low mortality. A small percentage of patients undergoing percutaneous radiofrequency ganglio-rhizolysis may experience mild complications such as infection, damage to adjacent structures, temporary trigeminal motor weakness, anesthesia dolorosa, keratitis, and postoperative herpes simplex in the denervated area. However, these effects do not outweigh the benefit from the surgery. Corneal and cutaneous anesthesia within the first and second branch of the trigeminal nerve is essential if relief of the pain of cluster attack is to be achieved.

■ CONCLUSION

Cluster headache, although a relatively rare headache disorder, has a special place in headache pathophysiology and management. Establishing the diagnosis is facilitated if the physician is cognizant about the disorder. Most patients respond to treatment and if therapy is initiated within the first week of the cycle, the prognosis is excellent. Education, especially for a newly-diagnosed patient, is very important for the patient to understand the origin and natural course of the disorder. For the individual experiencing a first-ever cluster cycle, imaging provides significant reassurance. Appropriate management of patients with cluster headache should include flexible availability for a return visit in case of a new cycle. Treatment should be undertaken without waiting for more than a few days.

In the last decade, major steps have been reached in research and treatment of migraine headache, particularly with the introduction of triptans. Unfortunately, lack of interest and especially funding in cluster research—on both a basic level and within the pharmaceutical industry has impacted on the genesis of cluster headache treatment.

References

1. The International Classification of Headache Disorders, 2nd ed: Cephalalgia 24 (Suppl 1), 2004.
2. Isler H: Episodic cluster headache from a textbook of 1745: van Swienten's classic description. Cephalalgia 13:172, 1993.
3. International Headache Society: Classification and diagnostic criteria for headache disorders, cranial neuralgias and facial pain. Cephalalgia 8 (Suppl 7):35, 1988.
4. Harris W: Neuritis and Neuralgia. London: Oxford University Press, 1926.
5. Horton BT, MacLean AR, Craig WM: A new syndrome of vascular headache: Results of treatment with histamine: Preliminary report. Mayo Clin Proc 14:257, 1939.
6. Horton BT: The use of histamine in the treatment of specific types of headaches. JAMA 116:377, 1941.
7. Kunkle EC, Pfeifer JB, Wilhoit WM, et al: Recurrent brief headache in "cluster" pattern. Am Neurol Assoc Trans 77:240, 1952.
8. Ekbom K, Ahlborg B, Schele R: Prevalence of migraine and cluster headache in Swedish men of 18. Headache 18:9, 1978.

9. Swanson JW, Yanagihara T, Stang PE, et al: Incidence of cluster headaches: A population-based study in Olmsted County, Minnesota. Neurology 44:433, 1994.

10. Sjaastad O, Bakketeig LS: Cluster headache prevalence. Vågå study of headache epidemiology. Cephalalgia 23:528, 2003.

11. D'Alessandro R, Gamberini G, Benassi G, et al: Cluster headache in the Republic of San Marino. Cephalalgia 6:159, 1986.

12. Kudrow L: Cluster Headache: Mechanism and Management. Oxford: Oxford University Press, 1980.

13. Cuypers J, Altenkirch H: HLA antigen in cluster headache. Headache 19:226, 1979.

14. Sjöstrand C, Giedratis V, Ekbom K, et al: CACNA1A gene polymorphism in cluster headache. Cephalalgia 21:953, 2001.

15. El Amrani M, Ducros A, Boulan P, et al: Familial cluster headache: A series of 186 index patients. Headache 42:974, 2002.

16. Russell MB, Andersen PG, Thomsen LL: Familial occurrence of cluster headache. J Neurol Neurosurg Psychiatry 58:341, 1995.

17. Horton BT: Histaminic cephalalgia: Differential diagnosis and treatment. Mayo Clin Proc 31:325, 1956.

18. Manzoni GC: Male preponderance of cluster headache is progressively decreasing over the years. Headache 37:588, 1997.

19. Ekbom K, Svenson DA, Traff H, et al: Age at onset and sex ratio in cluster headache: Observations over three decades. Cephalalgia 22:94, 2002.

20. Urban GJ, Diamond S, Freitag FG, et al: Analysis of patients with cluster headache. Headache Q 5; 236,1994.

21. Rozen TD, Niknam RM, Schechter AL, et al: Cluster headache in women: Clinical characteristics and comparison with cluster headache in men. J Neurol Neurosurg Psychiatry 70:613, 2001.

22. Kudrow L: Cluster headache. In Goadsby P, Silberstein S (eds): Headache. Boston, Butterworth-Heinemann, 1997, p 227.

23. Sjaastad O: Cluster Headache Syndrome. London, WB Saunders, 1992.

24. Ekbom K: Studies on Cluster Headache. Stockholm, Solna Tryckeri, 1970.

25. Maytal J, Lipton RB, Solomon S, et al: Childhood onset cluster headaches. Headache 32:275, 1992.

26. Sutherland JM, Eadie MJ: Cluster headache. Res Clin Stud Headache 3:92, 1972.

27. Manzoni GC, Terzano MG, Bono G, et al: Cluster headache—Clinical findings in 180 patients. Cephalalgia 3:21, 1983.

28. Bahra A, May A, Goadsby PJ: Cluster headache. A prospective clinical study. with diagnostic implications. Neurology 58:354, 2002.

28a. Manzoni GC, Micieli G, Granella F, et al: Cluster headache—course over ten years in 189 patients. Cephalalgia 11:169, 1991.

29. Balla J, Walton JN: Periodic migrainous neuralgia. BMJ 1:219, 1964.

30. Ekbom K: A clinical comparison of cluster headache and migraine. Acta Neurol Scand 46 (Suppl 41):1, 1970.

31. Kudrow L: The cyclic relationship of natural illumination to cluster period frequency. Cephalalgia 7:76, 1987.

32. Solomon S, Lipton RB, Newman LC: Nuchal features of cluster headache. Headache 30:347, 1990.

33. Blau JN, Engel HO: Premonitory and prodromal symptoms in cluster headache. Cephalalgia 18:91, 1998.

34. Graham JR: Cluster headache. Headache 11:175, 1972.

35. Silberstein SD, Niknam R, Rozen TD, et al: Cluster headache with aura. Neurology 54:219, 2000.

36. Russell D, Storstein L: Cluster headache: A computerized analysis of 24 hours Holter ECG recordings and description of ECG rhythm disturbances. Cephalalgia 3:83, 1983.

37. Nappi G, Micieli G, Cavallini A, et al: Accompanying symptoms of cluster attacks: Their relevance to the diagnostic criteria. Cephalalgia 3:165, 1992.

38. Peters GA: Migraine: Diagnosis and treatment with emphasis on the migraine tension headache, provocative tests and use of rectal suppositories. Mayo Clin Proc 28:673, 1953.

39. Horton BT: Histaminic cephalalgia. JAMA 160:468, 1956.

40. Fanciullacci M, Alessandri M, Sicuteri R, et al: Responsiveness of the trigeminovascular system to nitroglycerine in cluster headache patients. Brain 120:283, 1997.

41. Kudrow L, Kudrow DB: Association of sustained oxyhemoglobin desaturation and onset of cluster headache attacks. Headache 30:474, 1990.

42. Cuypers J, Altenkirch H, Bunge S: Personality profiles in cluster headache and migraine. Headache 21:21, 1981.

43. Kudrow L, Sutkus BJ: MMPI pattern specificity in primary headache disorders. Headache 19:18, 1979.

44. Levi R, Edman GV, Ekbom K., et al: Episodic cluster headache I: Personality and some neuropsychological characteristics in male patients. Headache 32:119, 1992.

45. Pfaffenrath V, Hummelsberger J, Pollmann W, et al: MMPI personality profiles in patients with primary headache syndromes. Cephalalgia 11:263, 1991.

46. Levi R, Edman GV, Ekbom K, et al: Episodic cluster headache II: High tobacco and alcohol consumption in males. Headache 32:184, 1992.

47. Bussone G, Giovannini P, Boiardi A, Boeri R: A study of the activity of platelet monoamine oxidase in patients with migraine headaches or with "cluster headache." Eur Neurol 15:157, 1977.

48. Mosek A, Hering-Hanit R, Kuritzky A: New onset cluster headache in middle age and elderly women. Cephalalgia 21:198, 2001.

49. Ekbom K, Waldenlind E: Cluster headache in women: Evidence of hypofertility(?) Headache in relation to menstruation and pregnancy. Cephalalgia 1:167, 1981.

50. Torelli P, Cologno D, Cademartiri C, et al: Possible predictive factors in the evolution of episodic to chronic cluster headache. Headache 40: 798; 2000.

51. McKinney AS: Cluster headache developing following ipsilateral orbital exenteration. Headache 23:305, 1983.

52. May A, Bahra A, Buchel C, et al: Hypothalamic activation in cluster headache attacks. Lancet 352:275, 1998.

53. Sjaastad O, Rinck P: Cluster headache: MRI studies of the cavernous sinus and the base of the brain. Headache 30:350, 1990.

54. Hardebo JE: How cluster headache is explained as an intracavernous inflammatory process lesioning sympathetic fibers. Headache 34:125, 1994.

55. Dahl A., Russell D, Nyberg-Hansen R, et al: Cluster headache: Transcranial Doppler ultrasound and rCBF studies. Cephalalgia 10:87, 1990.

56. Waldenlind E, Ekbom K, Torhall J: MR-Angiography during spontaneous attacks of cluster headache: A case report. Headache 33:291, 1993.

57. Fancciullacci M, Pietrini U, Gatto G, et al: Latent dysautonomic pupillary lateralization in cluster headache: A pupillometric study. Cephalalgia 2:135,1982.

58. Horton BT: Histaminic cephalalgia. Lancet 2:92, 1952.

59. Anthony M, Lance JW: Histamine and serotonin in cluster headache. Arch Neurol 25:225, 1971.

60. Appenzeller O, Becker WJ, Ragaz A: Cluster headache. Ultrastructural aspects and pathogenetic mechanism. Arch Neurol 38:302, 1981.

61. Anthony M, Lord GDA, Lance JW: Control trials of cimetidine in migraine and cluster headache. Headache 18:261, 1978.

62. Nelson RF: Testosterone levels in cluster and non-cluster migrainous headache patients. Headache 18:265, 1978.

63. Klimek A: Plasma testosterone levels in patients with cluster headache. Headache 22:162, 1982.

64. Leone M, Lucini V, D'Amico D, et al: Twenty-four hour melatonin and cortisol plasma levels in relation to timing of cluster headache. Cephalalgia 15:224, 1995.

65. Leone M, D'Amico D, Moschiano D, et al: Melatonin versus placebo in the prophylaxis of cluster headache: A double-blind pilot study with parallel groups. Cephalalgia 16:494, 1996.

66. May A, Ashburner J, Bushel C, et al: Correlation between structural and functional changes in brain in idiopathic headache syndromes. Nat Med 5:732, 1999.

67. Kudrow L: A possible role of carotid body in the pathogenesis of cluster headache. Cephalalgia 3:241, 1983.

68. Nobre ME, Filho PFM, Dominici M: Cluster headache associated with sleep apnoea. Cephalalgia 23:276, 2003.

69. Sjaastad O, Dale I: Evidence for a new (?), treatable headache entity. Headache 14:105, 1974.

70. Boes CJ, Dodick DW: Refining the clinical spectrum of chronic paroxysmal hemicrania: A review of 74 patients. Headache 42:699, 2002.

71. Goadsby PJ, Edvinsson L: Neuropeptide changes in case of chronic paroxysmal hemicrania—evidence for trigemino-parasympathetic activation. Cephalalgia 16:448, 1966.

72. Hannerz J, Ericson K, Bergstrand G: Chronic paroxysmal hemicrania: Orbital phlebography and steroid treatment. A case report. Cephalalgia 7:189, 1987.

73. Warner JS, Wamil AW, McLean MJ: Acetazolamide for the treatment of chronic paroxysmal hemicrania. Headache 34:597, 1994.

74. Shabbir N, McAbee G: Adolescent chronic paroxysmal hemicrania responsive to verapamil monotherapy. Headache 34:209, 1994.

75. Trucco M, Mainardi F, Maggioni F, et al: Chronic paroxysmal hemicrania, hemicrania continua and SUNCT syndrome in association with other pathologies: A review. Cephalalgia 24:173, 2004.

76. Sjaastad O, Saunte C, Salvesen R, et al: Shortlasting unilateral neuralgiform headache attacks with conjunctival injection, tearing, sweating, and rhinorrhea. Cephalalgia 9:147, 1989.

77. Pareja JA, Shen JM, Kruszewski P, et al: SUNCT syndrome: Duration, frequency, and temporal distribution of attacks. Headache 36:161, 1996.

78. Bussone G, Leone M, Dalla Volta G, et al: Short-lasting unilateral neuralgiform headache attacks with tearing and conjunctival injection: The first "symptomatic" case? Cephalalgia 11:123, 1991.

79. Morales F, Mostacero E, Marta J, et al: Vascular malformation of the cerebellopontine angle associated with "SUNCT" syndrome. Cephalalgia 14:301, 1994.

80. Porta-Etessam J, Benito-Leon J, Martinez-Salio A, et al: Gabapentin in the treatment of SUNCT syndrome. Headache 42:523, 2002.

81. Hunt CH, Dodick DW, Bosch EP: SUNCT responsive to gabapentin. Headache 42:525, 2002.

82. Matharu MS, Boes CJ, Goadsby PJ: SUNCT syndrome: Prolonged attacks, refractoriness and response to topiramate. Neurology 58:1307; 2002.

83. Leone M, Rigamonti A, Usai S, et al: Two new SUNCT cases responsive to lamotrigene. Cephalalgia 20:845, 2000.

84. Milos P, Havelius U, Hindfelt B: Cluster like headache in patient with a pituitary adenoma. With a review of the literature. Headache 36:184, 1996.

85. Taub E, Argoff CE, Winterkorn JMS, et al: Resolution of chronic cluster headache after resection of a tentorial meningioma: Case report. Neurosurgery 37:319, 1995.

86. Kuritzky A: Cluster headache-like pain caused by an upper cervical meningioma. Cephalalgia 4:185, 1984.

87. Appelbaum J, Noronha A: Pericarotid cluster headache. J Neurol 236:430, 1989.

88. Packard RC, Ham LP: Incidence of cluster-like posttraumatic headache. Headache Q 7:139, 1996.

89. Kudrow L: Response of cluster headache attacks to oxygen inhalation. Headache 21:1, 1981.

90. Ekbom K: Treatment of acute cluster headache with sumatriptan. N Engl J Med 325:322, 1991.

91. Mather PJ, Silberstein SD, Schulman EA, et al: The treatment of cluster headache with repetitive intravenous dihydroergotamine. Headache 31:525, 1991.

92. Bahra A, Gawel MJ, Hardebo JE, et al: Oral zolmitriptan is effective in the acute treatment of cluster headache. Neurology 54:1832, 2000.

93. Kittrelle JP, Grouse DS, Seybold ME: Cluster headache. Local anesthetic abortive agents. Arch Neurol 42:496, 1985.

94. Barre F: Cocaine as an abortive agent in cluster headache. Headache 22:69, 1982.

95. Meyer JS, Hardenberg J: Clinical effectiveness of calcium entry blockers in prophylactic treatment of migraine and cluster headache. Headache 23:266, 1983.

96. Leone M, D'Amico D, Frediani F, et al: Verapamil in the prophylaxis of episodic cluster headache: A double blind study versus placebo. Neurology 54:1382, 2000.

97. Gabai IJ, Spierings ELH: Prophylactic treatment of cluster headache with verapamil. Headache 29:167, 1989.

98. Kudrow L: Lithium prophylaxis for chronic cluster headache. Headache 17:15, 1977.

99. Ekbom K: Lithium for cluster headache: Review of the literature and preliminary results of long-term treatment. Headache 21:132, 1981.

100. Manzoni GC, Bono G, Lanfranchi M, et al: Lithium carbonate in cluster headache: Assessment of its short- and long-term therapeutic efficacy. Cephalalgia 3:109, 1983.

101. Bussone G, Leone M, Peccarisi C, et al: Double blind comparison of lithium and verapamil in cluster headache prophylaxis. Headache 30:411, 1990.

102. Okayasu H, Meyer JS, Mathew NT, et al: Lithium carbonate has no measurable effect on cerebral hemodynamics in cluster headache, Headache 24:1, 1984.

103. Friedman AP, Elkind AH: Appraisal of methysergide in treatment of vascular headache of migraine-type. JAMA 184:125, 1963.

104. Hering R, Kuritzky A: Sodium valproate in the treatment of cluster headache: An open trial. Cephalalgia 9:195, 1989.

105. Freitag FG, Diamond S, Diamond ML, et al: Divalproex sodium in the preventive treatment of cluster headache. Headache 40:408; 2000.

106. Wheeler SD, Carrazana EJ: Topiramate-treated cluster headache. Neurology 53:234, 1999.

107. Lainez MJA, Pascual J, Pascual AM, et al: Topiramate in the prophylactic treatment of cluster headache. Headache 43:784, 2003.

108. Leandri M, Luzzani M, Cruccu G, et al: Drug-resistant cluster headache responding to gabapentin: A pilot study. Cephalalgia 21:744, 2001.

109. D'Andrea G, Perini F, Granella F, et al: Efficacy of transdermal clonidine in short-term treatment of cluster headache: A pilot study. Cephalalgia 15:430, 1995.

110. Hering-Hanit R, Gadoth N: The use of baclofen in cluster headache. Curr Pain Headache Rep 5:79, 2001.

111. D'Alesandro R: Tizanidine for chronic cluster headache. Arch Neurol 53:1093;1996.

112. Caviness VS Jr, O'Brien P: Cluster Headache: Response to chlorpromazine. Headache 20:128, 1980.

113. Eekers PJ, Koehler PJ: Naratriptan prophylactic treatment in cluster headache. Cephalalgia 21:75, 2001.

114. Loder E: Naratriptan in the prophylaxis of cluster headache. Headache 42:56:57, 2002.

115. Mulder LJ, Spierings ELH: Naratriptan in the preventive treatment of cluster headache. Cephalalgia 22:815, 2002.

116. Peres MFP, Stiles MA, Siow HC, et al: Greater occipital nerve blockade for cluster headache. Cephalalgia 22:520, 2002.

117. Marks DR, Rapoport A, Padla D, et al: A double-blind placebo-controlled trial of intranasal capsaicin for cluster headache. Cephalalgia 13:114, 1993.

118. Saper JR, Klapper J, Mathew NT, et al: Intranasal civamide for the treatment of episodic cluster headaches. Arch Neurol 59:990, 2002.

119. Peres MFP, Rozen TD: Melatonin in the preventive treatment of cluster headache. Cephalalgia 21:993, 2001.

120. Pringsheim T, Magnoux E, Dobson CG, et al: Melatonin as adjunctive therapy in the prophylaxis of cluster headache: A pilot study. Headache 42:787, 2002.

121. Blumethal LS: Current histamine therapy. Mod Med 18:51, 1950.

122. Diamond S, Freitag FG, Prager J, et al: Treatment of intractable cluster. Headache 26:42, 1986.

123. Watson CP, Morley TP, Richardson JC, et al: The surgical treatment of chronic cluster headache. Headache 23:289, 1983.

124. Solomon S: Cluster headache and the nervus intermedius. Headache 26:3, 1986.

125. Sachs E, Jr: The role of the nervus intermedius in facial neuralgia. Report of four cases with observations on the pathways for taste, lacrimation, and pain in the face. J Neurosurg 28:56, 1968.

126. Sachs E, Jr: Further observation on surgery of the nervus intermedius. Headache 9:159, 1970.

127. Gardner WJ, Stowell A, Dutlinger R: Resection of the greater superficial petrosal nerve in the treatment of unilateral headache. J. Neurosurg 4:105, 1947.

128. Lovely TJ, Kotsiakis X, Jannetta PJ: The surgical management of chronic cluster headache. Headache 38:590, 1998.

129. Onofrio BM, Cambpell JK: Surgical treatment of chronic cluster headache. Mayo Clin Proc 61:537, 1986.

130. Mathew NT, Hurt W: Percutaneous radio-frequency trigeminal gangliorhizolysis in intractable cluster headache. Headache 28:328, 1988.

45

Analgesic Rebound Headache

Roger Cady, Curtis Schreiber, and Kathleen Farmer

Most intriguing yet often frustrating are patients with daily or near daily headache who insist they need daily analgesic in order to function. The quantity of analgesic they require is often staggering and they frequently are seeking medical advice in hopes of being prescribed an even more potent analgesic medication. There is often a history spanning years to decades of increasingly frequent severe, disabling headaches and a concomitant history of escalating analgesic use. Confounding this clinical scenario is that patients assure the medical provider that they only seek medication in order to function effectively and that they have had experiences where the medication was unavailable and have endured severe, unrelenting headaches that often result in repeated visits to the emergency department. Reviewing these patients' histories, one frequently finds they have multiple medical providers.

The clinical dilemmas are obvious. Are these patients overtly seeking drugs? Are they accurately conveying to us that without their daily use of medications, headache would prevent them from functioning? Or, is the medication itself maintaining the headache? What are the therapeutic and management options for these chronic headache patients?

■ CLASSIFICATION OF CHRONIC HEADACHE

The 2004 edition of The International Classification of Headache Disorders of the International Headache Society (IHS) for the first time acknowledges a chronic form of each of the major primary headache disorders.[1] Commonly diagnosed chronic primary headache disorders are migraine, tension-type and cluster, with the latter being considerably more infrequent than the other two. Chronic migraine is defined as headaches fulfilling episodic migraine diagnostic criteria occurring more than 15 days per month over a period of at least 3 months and without evidence of medication overuse. Chronic tension-type headache is defined as headaches fulfilling criteria for tension-type headache occurring more than 15 days per month for greater than 3 months without evidence of analgesic overuse.

If medication overuse is suspected, a diagnosis of chronic migraine or chronic tension-type headache should not be made until medication has been withdrawn for at least 2 months. A diagnosis of probable migraine or probable tension-type headache is used in conjunction with probable medication-overuse headache until the withdrawal phase from medication is complete. Theoretically, a patient could have both chronic migraine and chronic tension-type headache but this is considered a rare occurrence by the IHS Classification Committee.[1] The most recent IHS diagnostic criteria acknowledge that chronic headaches likely evolve from the episodic form and thus a patient's history may be a valuable guide in differentiating chronic migraine and chronic tension-type headache. Chronic cluster headache is diagnosed when typical cluster attacks persist for greater than 1 year without a period of remission longer than 1 month. Medication overuse is not generally considered to be an etiologic factor for maintaining chronic cluster headache.

Arguably, the most significant advancement in the latest IHS revision is the inclusion of chronic migraine and medication-overuse headache in the diagnostic taxonomy (Table 45–1). In acknowledging chronic migraine, the IHS indirectly supported clinical observations that episodic migraine can evolve into chronic headache, thus supporting a potential transformational process for migraine. Further, symptomatic medications are considered a possible factor in maintaining chronic primary headache patterns. The IHS taxonomy expands the association of chronic headache and medication overuse by providing a diagnosis for each headache syndrome that is related to a specific medication that is being overused (Table 45–2). However, because many patients overuse multiple medications, it makes this aspect of the classification cumbersome in clinical practice. The revised IHS classification system also continues to recommend independent diagnosis of each episode of headache a patient experiences—thus necessitating the use of multiple diagnoses when more than one type of primary headache can be defined in an individual patient. Given that patients are the source of historical information and their belief (often fostered by past misunderstandings of primary headaches) in unique etiologies to different clinical presentations of primary headache, clearly influences symptom description provided to clinicians and consequently the diagnostic labels medical providers give to patients. This diagnostic confusion often makes clinical application of the IHS criteria cumbersome in clinical practice.

Table 45–1

International Headache Society Diagnostic Criteria for Chronic Migraine and Medication-Overuse Headache

Migraine
1. Migraine headache occurring on 15 or more days per month for more than 3 months in the absence of medication overuse and not attributable to other disorder
2. Headache has at least two of the following four characteristics:
   Unilateral location
   Pulsating quality
   Moderate-to-severe intensity
   Aggravated with activity
3. During the headache, at least one of the following:
   Nausea and/or vomiting
   Photophobia and phonophobia

Medication-Overuse Headache
1. Headache greater than 15 days per month that has developed or markedly worsened during medication overuse
2. Headache resolves or reverts to its previous pattern with 2 months of discontinuing the overused medication

Table 45–2

Quantities of Selected Medications Associated with Medication-Overuse Headaches

Ergotamine intake 10 or more days a month for >3 months

Triptan intake on 10 or more days a month for >3 months

Simple analgesic intake on 15 or greater days per month for >3 months

Opioid intake on 10 or more days a month for >3 months

Combination medications on 10 or more days a month for >3 months

Headache Classification Committee of the International Headache Society. The international classification of headache disorders. Cephalalgia 24(Suppl 1):8, 2004.

Further, the IHS taxonomy continues to state that clinicians should use the criteria to diagnose each attack of headache and not use the diagnostic labels provided by the IHS to define patients.

■ THE DEBATE OVER THE ROLE OF ANALGESICS IN PATIENTS WITH ANALGESIC OVERUSE

The idea that substances or withdrawal of substances may complicate or provoke headaches has been suggested for many years. In 1940, Dreisbach reported caffeine withdrawal headache[2]; in 1949, Graham reported ergotamine tolerance and withdrawal headache[3]; in 1951, Peters and Horton coined the term *rebound headache* referring to the severe headache that occurred when "vasoactive substances" were withdrawn from patients with underlying headache disorders.[4] However, it was not until 1982 that Kudrow[5] and concurrently Isler[6] published studies implicating overuse of commonly employed analgesics used in treating primary headache disorders as a factor in maintaining primary headache patterns. Further, withdrawal of the offending analgesic resulted in rebound headache and, with time, a reduction in headache frequency after the offending medications were discontinued.

In Kudrow's study, a population of 200 patients with daily headaches was divided into two groups. Group 1 was prescribed amitriptyline in addition to daily symptomatic medication; group 2 discontinued daily symptomatic medication prior to using amitriptyline for prophylaxis. The mean improvement of group 1 was 20% as compared with a mean improvement of 72% for group 2. This study noted that it could take up to 3 months for improvement to occur. Isler's study of 235 patients, many of whom were overusing ergotamine, reported that those using greater than 30 tablets a month suffered twice as many headaches as those using less than 30 tablets a month.

Mathew[7] in a retrospective analysis expanded the concept of chronic headache significantly by characterizing a clinical transformation or evolutive process by which patients with primary headaches transitioned from an episodic to a chronic headache condition. This landmark study noted the frequently associated analgesics overused by the chronic headache population and it described several important comorbid conditions observed to be associated with this patient population. In addition, the different medications and the quantities of use of these various analgesics were reported. Thus, an important paradigm shift occurred: from an IHS approach of clinical analysis of each episode of headache to an approach of making diagnoses based on the evolution of the headache pattern over time. This transition, although intuitive to many clinicians, remains an enigma to the academic community that was sought to provide to regulatory agencies worldwide a diagnostic classification system for use in clinical trials of medications.

Later, Mathew observed that patients with analgesic-dependent headache patterns were less responsive to both preventive medications and other abortive medications unless the offending medications were first discontinued. He used the terms *evolutive* and *transformational migraine* to describe the observed changes in the headache pattern in this patient population.[8]

In 1986, Rapoport and colleagues[9] published findings on 70 patients with daily headaches using 14 or more analgesics per week. He reported that with discontinuation of the offending analgesic, 66% had improved significantly within 1 month and that 81% had improved within 2 months. The use of either amitriptyline or cyproheptadine significantly added to the success reported in this patient population. These studies demonstrated that successful patient responses were attained by withdrawing frequently used analgesics. This research expanded the concept that symptomatic medications were mechanistically an important component in the etiology of chronic headaches.

Despite these important studies, the fact that few effective nonanalgesic options were available for treating migraine until the advent of the triptans in the early 1990s prevented the concept of analgesic rebound headache from being widely disseminated outside the headache community. With the advent of triptan medications, it was hoped that these migraine-specific medications would provide an option for reducing and perhaps preventing analgesic-maintained headaches. However, reports of triptan overuse headaches began to appear in the literature soon after the regulatory approval of sumatriptan, being formally reported in 1996 by Gobel.[10] Today, triptan rebound is considered a potential consequence of all triptans. Thus, it appears that a diverse group of symptomatic medications are implicated in maintaining chronic primary headache disorders. This prompted the IHS nomenclature committee to include the diagnosis of medication-overuse headache (MOH) and it cites analgesics, ergotamines, caffeine, and triptans as all being associated with this phenomenon.[1]

MEDICATION OVERUSE: CAUSE OR CONSEQUENCE OF HEADACHE?

Chronic primary headaches are common, affecting an estimated 2% to 4% of the American population.[11] Although several headache specialists report near epidemic proportions of analgesic-maintained headache patients in their specialty-based practices, not all patients with chronic headache appear to overuse symptomatic medications. Several large epidemiologic studies conducted outside the United States where OTC analgesics are not commonly available suggest that factors other than medication overuse may be involved in initiating and maintaining chronic headaches. Ravishankar reported less than 5% of a population of 1000 patients in India with chronic migraine had concomitant medication overuse.[12] Although many studies report that discontinuation of overused symptomatic medications resulted in the chronic headache reverting to an episodic headache pattern, rarely did any of these studies assess the discontinuation of symptomatic medication isolated from other interventions, such as education and the use of preventive medications. For example, Mathew's study of 200 patients found that 20% improved over 2 months by discontinuing overused symptomatic medications only. However, 80% improved over 2 months by discontinuing medication and utilizing preventive medications.[13] Further, the benefits of analgesic withdrawal appear in many studies to be short-lived. Pini reported that, after 4 years, only one third of treated patients still refrained from daily analgesics. In addition, those who returned to daily analgesic use had better quality-of-life scores than those who no longer used daily analgesics.[14]

Given the significant rate of analgesic relapse of nearly 60%, the debate has become whether analgesics are a cause or consequence of chronic daily headaches. Dodick has suggested that, whereas symptomatic medication can be associated with rebound headache, chronic migraine itself may be a progressive brain disorder that leads to overuse of symptomatic medication and that this may be a more common reason for chronic headache than overuse of medication.[15] This debate has crystallized given recent research by Welch and colleagues documenting iron deposition in the periaqueductal gray area (PAG) in migraineurs with histories of long-standing, frequent migraine. Welch hypothesized that this may reflect oxidative damage in this important pain inhibitory nucleus secondary to long-standing uncontrolled migraine. More recently Kruit and coworkers reported that subclinical cerebellar white matter lesions are noted on MRI scans of individuals with long-standing histories of frequent migraine.[16] These results suggest that for some patients, migraine may indeed be a progressive neurologic disease.[17]

PROPOSED MECHANISMS OF CHRONIC HEADACHE AND ANALGESIC REBOUND HEADACHE

Over the preceding 2 decades, the pathophysiology of migraine has changed significantly and has evolved from a stress to a vascular and now into a neurologic disorder. In addition, the notion that tension-type headache is a disorder of muscular etiology has been largely dispelled and a more unified model of primary headache appears to be emerging. The once-popular notion that migraine and tension-type headache are distinct pathophysiologic diseases has little scientific support—at least in the portion of the population capable of having migraine.[18] (The Spectrum Study found that migraine sufferers have various presentations of headaches that respond equally to migraine-specific medication.)

In 1980, Raskin and Appenzeller proposed a continuum model of migraine with *migraine with aura* on one end of the spectrum of headache activity and *chronic tension-type headache* on the other.[19] Between these two extremes fell the different clinical phenotypes of primary headache disorders observed in clinical practice. This model also suggested that, as migraine became more chronic, the threshold for the next migraine was lowered and that analgesics and ergotamine expedited this change in the threshold to migraine. Mathew observed that, when migraine was an episodic condition, patients complained of associated neurovascular and gastrointestinal symptoms but as it transformed into a more chronic condition, there was a greater association of myogenic and psychological symptoms.[20] This original observation may have found recent support in the American Migraine II study, with the population screening positive for migraine reporting the greatest frequency of primary headaches also reporting the greatest number of physician diagnoses of primary headaches.[21]

In 2001, Cady and associates expanded this concept by proposing the "convergence hypothesis," which suggested that primary headaches, at least in the migraine population, evolved from a single pathophysiologic mechanism. This model correlated the clinical phases of migraine with presumed underlying pathophysiologic mechanisms of the evolving process of migraine (Fig. 45–1). Different clinical diagnoses common to the migraine population were explained by the level of pathophysiologic disruption associated with a specific migraine attack.[22] Later, expanding this model to explain the evolution of episodic into chronic headache, it was suggested that the threshold to activating the migraine process was influenced by several factors beyond analgesics including genetics, biology, trauma (both physical and psychological), and uncontrolled headaches, and that uncontrolled migraine can become a progressive neurologic disease in a subset of primary headache sufferers (Fig. 45–2).[23]

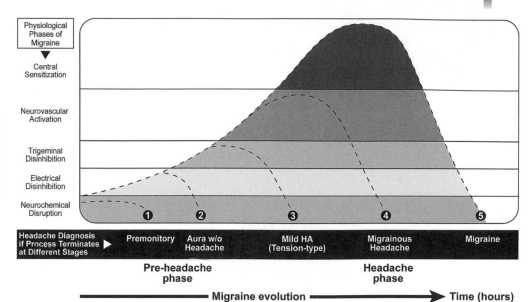

FIGURE 45–1 ■ Model of convergence hypothesis, which suggests that primary migraine headaches evolve from a single pathophysiologic mechanism. In this model, the clinical phases of migraine correlate with presumed underlying pathophysiologic mechanisms.

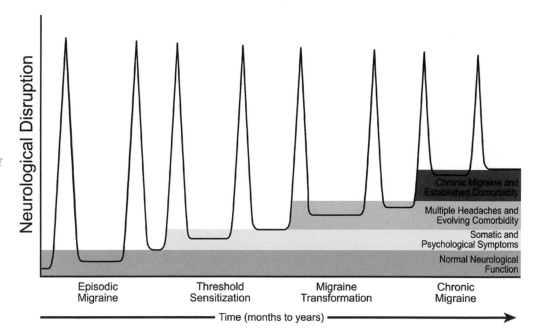

FIGURE 45–2 ■ Evolution of migraine from attacks to disease.

■ MECHANISMS OF MEDICATION-OVERUSE HEADACHE

The mechanism of analgesic-rebound or medication-overuse headache is unknown. However, there are data to suggest that this phenomenon is more common and perhaps unique to those individuals with migraine. Lance reported that analgesic overuse did not increase the frequency of headaches in those without a history of migraine.[24] Based on a study of individuals taking daily analgesics for arthritis, Lance postulated suppression or down-regulation of already suppressed nociceptive mechanisms caused by excessive use of symptomatic medications as a possible explanation for analgesic rebound headaches. Later Hering reported a reduction of serotonin in the blood of patients with chronic headaches and that these

levels increased significantly when the offending symptomatic medication was discontinued.[25]

Fields proposed increased nociception resulting in activation of "on cells" in the ventromedial medulla as a possible mechanism of analgesic rebound.[26] Mathew reported that stimulation of 5-HT-1 receptors was abortive for acute episodes of migraine but that activation of 5-HT-2 receptors increased pain transmission. Srikiatkochorn found an increase of 5-HT-2A receptors on platelets in patients with chronic migraine and analgesic overuse that decreased once the offending medication was withdrawn. Current theories suggest that, with medication overuse, there is a decrease in central serotonin and up-regulation of 5-HT-2A receptors leading to central hyperalgesia. Recent work by Ossipove and colleagues and Mao and associates has suggested that prolonged used of narcotics can produce a state of hyperalgesia.[27,28]

Consequently, the debate continues as to whether escalating headache attacks leads to more frequent medication use or whether escalating medication use leads to increases in headache frequency. Suffice it to say that once patients are caught in a web of chronic primary headaches and using acute medications frequently, they have significant treatment needs and will undoubtedly find greater benefit from discontinuing the offending medication than continuing a pattern of failure.

∎ CLINICAL FEATURES OF MEDICATION-OVERUSE HEADACHE

Medication-overuse headache or analgesic-rebound headache is characterized by a sustained pattern of headaches . . . medication . . . headaches . . . and more medication. Typically headaches occur on a daily or near-daily basis and the offending medication often appears to be the only medication capable of bringing relief, albeit temporary. The primary headache is low grade, waxing and waning, with pain varying in intensity, location, and severity. Superimposed on this headache pattern are periods of more intense headache activity. These headaches generally occur with characteristics suggestive of migraine. Often even mild physical and mental perturbations in daily activities trigger severe headaches.

Complicating this clinical scenario is the fact that this population of patients also exhibit psychological disruptions such as depression and symptoms such as irritability and memory difficulties. Commonly there is a complaint of sleep disturbance and predictable early morning headaches that often necessitate pharmacologic intervention. A detailed history often reveals the need for dose escalation of the medication(s) being overused. In addition, patients will frequently use medication in anticipation of headaches. Patients caught in the web of medication overuse generally believe that their medication is not as effective as it once was but also believe it is a lifeline for preventing severe disabling headaches. Further, they frequently have experienced severe withdrawal headaches when they have been without medication or medication use has been delayed. Consequently, the stage is set for a strong belief in their need for symptomatic medications.

∎ CLINICAL EVALUATION OF THE HEADACHE PATIENT WITH SUSPECTED MEDICATION OVERUSE

The suspicion of medication-overuse headache is first made on clinical grounds because the formal diagnosis is confirmed only after withdrawal of the offending medication and the patient's headache pattern reverting to its episodic form. The period of time required for chronic primary headache to become episodic may be 2 months or longer. Thus, it is paramount that clinicians have a high index of suspicion when evaluating chronic or transforming headache disorders associated with frequent use of symptomatic medications.

Several factors in a patient's history are suggestive of medication-overuse headache. Patients caught in this web

often begin treatment efforts early in the morning because presumably overnight the blood levels of the offending analgesic may have decreased to the point of causing a mini-withdrawal syndrome including the symptom of headache. Thus, a history of early morning headache is common. Further, the history of having stopped the potentially offending analgesics at some point for several days resulted in a severe "rebound" headache. Patient often interpret this as evidence they "need" their medication but in fact, it may be evidence that withdrawal of medication caused the headache and that medication overuse is maintaining the headache condition.

Several investigators have attempted to ascertain the threshold quantity of different analgesics that can result in chronic medication-induced headache patterns. Others have suggested that the time period of exposure is also critical. These studies, although interesting, are retrospective evaluations of patients from tertiary headache centers. Consequently, therapeutic efforts to manage these patients are frequently beyond simply discontinuing an offending medication. Given these limitations, the IHS has proposed a list of substances including several symptomatic medications that by consensus appear to relate to chronic headache disorders.

Recently, Limroth and colleagues looked at duration of exposure to various therapeutic acute agents and the development of chronic daily headache. In their study, they suggest that duration of triptan therapy of 1.7 years using 18 doses per month could result in medication-overuse headache. Using ergots for 2.7 years with an average of 37 doses per month or analgesics 4.8 years using 114 doses per month was also considered to result in medication-overuse headaches. Combination analgesics were not evaluated in this study. The limitations of this study reside in the different study populations in that those patients selected by medical providers for triptan therapy may have had more severe migraine or have been suffering migraine for a longer duration than those using analgesics.

∎ TAKING A HEADACHE HISTORY OF A PATIENT WITH MEDICATION OVERUSE

When patients have frequent headaches it is critical to determine the frequency and quantity of symptomatic medications the patient is using. Determining how many days a week the patient requires acute treatment is often challenging because patients often provide answers that are vague or reveal that the amount of medication being used is difficult to determine because its use varies depending on therapeutic need. It is critical that providers press for accurate quantifiable answers about all symptomatic medications being used by the patient including over-the-counter medications.

Medication-overuse headaches should be suspected when there is a daily or near daily pattern of headache and the patient uses any symptomatic medication on an average of more than 2 days a week. In addition, medication overuse should be suspected whenever patients report that their usual symptomatic medication is less effective than it had been in the past. Frequently, patients will convey the fact that medication controls their headache reasonably well unless there is a delay in administration. It is vital to determine the use of both prescription and nonprescription medications because many patients fail to realize that over-the-counter preparations are, in fact, medications.

The following questions may assist a provider in determining if medication overuse is a likely component of a chronic headache pattern:

1. Is the patient using analgesics to treat other types of pain or medical conditions?
2. How does the patient determine when to treat?
3. Is medication used in anticipation of headache?
4. Is there fear of developing a severe disabling headache if medications are not taken?
5. Are the medications used for headache treatment effective (i.e., do they get a pain-free response or only partial relief)?
6. What is the duration of effective relief that a dose of medication provides?
7. How long does a specific quantity of symptomatic medication typically last?

These questions provide a framework for assessing the role of medication as a contributing factor for chronic headache. In addition, they allow the patient and the provider to communicate about the relationship of chronic primary headaches and symptomatic medications. It is essential that these questions are explored in a nonjudgmental manner and that the provider is in alliance with the patient to solve this vexing clinical situation.

■ PSYCHOLOGICAL EVALUATION OF THE PATIENT WITH MEDICATION-OVERUSE HEADACHE

The evolution of episodic headaches into daily ones usually occurs over time, perhaps more than a decade.[29] During this evolutionary time period, individuals have maintained their ability to function through self-management and by following the advice of well-meaning friends, relatives, and medical providers. Today more than ever patients have access to a myriad of treatment ideas. They find advice on the Internet and from talk shows, books, and from many different health care practitioners. Often the message for headache sufferers is that their headaches should be something they are able to control on their own through lifestyle and adequate stress management.

Often, by the time headache sufferers seek medical consultation, they have failed with multiple self-treatment attempts. They are fearful that headaches will continue to worsen to the point of ultimately taking away their ability to function. Specifically, they may fear the loss of a scholarship, job, or marriage. At this juncture, patients often feel psychologically and physically vulnerable, worrying that headaches are an expression of physical and mental inadequacy. A recent study found that, before symptoms of depression or anxiety appear, there is an increase in somatic pain complaints. As the impact of headaches reaches severe (60+ on the Headache Impact Test [HIT-6] or 21+ on the Migraine Disability Assessment [MIDAS]), the number of somatic complaints increases to a significant degree, from an average of 5.0 at no or mild headache impact to 7.5 at severe headache impact. In fact, in this study of 93 individuals with disabling headaches, 71% complained of back pain and 54% were bothered by pain in arms, legs, joints, or lower abdomen.[30] From the patient's per-

spective, headache is but one of several medical conditions that is affecting their lives.

■ PSYCHOLOGICAL ASSESSMENT TOOLS

Several objective measurements have been devised to help clinicians to assess and define the headache sufferer with chronic primary headaches. These tools, although not specifically designed to define the population overusing medication, are valuable in defining the psychological and medical needs of this population. Headache impact tools are simple to use even in a busy clinical setting and should be considered an invaluable way to document therapeutic efficacy of management efforts in this population of patients:

1. Headache Impact Test (HIT-6)[31] or Migraine Disability Assessment (MIDAS)[32] to assess the impact of the headaches on the individual's life. These tests can also be used to follow the progress of patients over time.
2. Visual analog scale (VAS) of pain severity to measure pain levels before and after interventions. It is presented graphically with a 10-cm line and end point adjective descriptors ("the worst imaginable pain" on one end and "no pain" on the other). The patient is asked to place a mark along the line to indicate the current pain level. A difference of 13 mm between consecutive ratings of pain is the minimum change in a pain rating that is clinically significant.[33]
3. Symptom Index to record somatic symptoms associated with headaches. As mentioned, chronic daily headache is often one of several pain complaints.
4. Zung Depression Inventory[34,35] to measure the level of depression and suicide potential of the patient.
5. State Trait Anxiety Scale[36] to indicate the level of anxiety both at the present time and throughout the person's life. High anxiety generally implies that the individual is using medication to anticipate headaches and lessen the anxiety over not being able to perform in a certain setting due to headaches.
6. Minnesota Multiphasic Personality Inventory-2 (MMPI-2)[37] to appraise an individual's behavioral adaptation to the current life situation. It consists of 567 true/false statements, which usually takes a patient $1\frac{1}{2}$ to 2 hours to complete. It is an objective, valid, and reliable instrument that uncovers significant psychopathology that may complicate management and serve as a basis for referral.

Psychological testing of patients with chronic headache reflects a greater incidence of behavioral abnormalities. The MMPI-2 profile may be a 3-1 or 1-3, often called "Conversion V," that may also be interpreted as a call for help. After treatment, when headaches return to episodic, the MMPI-2 usually normalizes. Also elevation on Zung Depression Inventory is significant in terms of the psychological toll that headaches are having on the individual. Recently significant differences in HIT-6 and MIDAS scores are noted between patients with episodic and chronic headache conditions. In addition, a history of substance abuse, especially alcoholism, or physical and/or mental abuse appears higher in the chronic headache population, particularly among those who are refractory to treatment.

■ MANAGEMENT OF MEDICATION-OVERUSE HEADACHE

Perhaps the most critical aspect of managing a patient who is suffering from medication-overuse headache is for the clinician to avoid being overly judgmental. In many instances, medication overuse begins subtly and symptomatic medications are prescribed to the patient without knowledge of the risks. At times, patients may present for evaluation unsuspecting that medications are actually maintaining their headache pattern. Others may be aware of their reliance on medication but see no alternative. They fear discontinuing the medication instead of understanding the potential benefits of freeing themselves from medication dependency. Still other patients may view their reliance on medication as addiction and feel angry and guilty. Rarely, patients approach the clinician with the intent of using the complaint of headache to surreptitiously acquire specific medications. Thus, managing medication-maintained headache requires time, clinical skills, and clear communication between the medical provider and the patient. It is important to approach the patient with medication-overuse headache confidently and with compassion.

■ EDUCATION

Education is the cornerstone of effective management for patients caught in the trap of medication-overuse headache. From patients' perspective, it is often difficult to understand that discontinuing the only medication that provides relief, albeit temporary, will be beneficial. Clinicians are often met with considerable skepticism and fear when they recommend to their patients that the medication must be stopped. Likewise clinicians can offer no guarantee that discontinuing medication will improve the underlying headache pattern. However, they can convey that there is good evidence suggesting that most patients do, in fact, improve after stopping overused abortive migraine medications and that not stopping the medication will likely perpetuate and worsen the cycle of daily headaches.

The key component of education includes a clear explanation of medication-overuse headache and the spiral of ever escalating headache that occurs with this medical condition. It is also valuable to explain that uncontrolled migraine may evolve into a progressive neurologic disease that can impair the patient's ability to perform in all aspects of life.

■ DESIGNING A TREATMENT PLAN

Historically, analgesic withdrawal was often performed in the hospital setting. This is still a reasonable and preferred treatment approach for the more complicated spectrum of this patient population. However, in an era of managed care, most often patients will be managed in an outpatient setting. If patients agree to detoxification, it is critical to be frank and honest about the benefit of discontinuing an overused medication whether detoxification is done on an inpatient or outpatient basis. This education includes the fact that improvement might not be realized for 2 to 3 months and that

in all likelihood there will be a period of increased headache; a fact that many patients already know. Regardless, it is critical that clinicians establish a clear rationale for medication withdrawal and provide a plan for its implementation.

■ THE INITIAL VISIT

During the initial visit, many clinicians choose to provide education and do not discontinue the offending medication at that time. Instead the patient is instructed to change the use of the offending medication from symptom-based to time-based administration. This has the advantage of allaying a patient's fear and permits the patient to be open about the quantities of medication being consumed. During that same visit the patient is advised to withdraw from dietary caffeine and other potential dietary factors that may exacerbate the underlying headache pattern, such as tyramine and nitrates. The patient is given a date for discontinuing the medication which is generally not more than 2 weeks away from the first visit. This provides an opportunity for the patient to arrange a short leave of absence from work or family commitments when the withdrawal is commenced. A prophylactic medication can be provided, although it is unlikely to provide its full pharmacologic benefit until the acute medication withdrawal has been completed. Finally, the patient is provided a headache diary in which headaches and all medication usage are recorded. Many clinicians insist that the patient sign a medication contract with the "rules" clearly defined. Finally, whenever possible, behavioral therapy with a psychologist skilled in pain and headache management should be strongly recommended.

During the initial visit, a strategy for medication withdrawal should be improvised. Several factors should be considered in determining which approach is most appropriate for a specific patient. If patients are using significant quantities of narcotic or butalbital combination products, the risk of withdrawal seizure should be assessed. Phenobarbital with its longer half-life can be substituted for butalbital as a convenient and effective withdrawal strategy. Generally, patients are started on 90 mg and the dose is adjusted up or down based on the presence of agitation or sedation. Each week the phenobarbital dose can be reduced by 30 mg. A similar strategy can be employed with narcotics, as a short-acting medication is converted to a long-acting formulation and then slowly withdrawn over several weeks. When these strategies are employed, it is critical to communicate to the patient that this medication is not being used as an acute treatment for headache and that the patient is provided with an appropriate abortive for acute intervention. In addition, a clonidine patch can be prescribed to diminish the intensity of some of the withdrawal symptoms. Typically the 0.1-mg patch is used. Dose is patient dependent, but a typical regimen is to apply two patches for 1 week followed by one patch for 1 week, then discontinued.

In general, the authors recommend that withdrawal of overused symptomatic medications be done rapidly rather than using a slow taper. It is valuable to include the patient in these decisions and provide a realistic structure wherein both provider and patient have clear input into the decision-making process. Abrupt withdrawal may result in an intense rebound headache of shorter duration, whereas tapering may buffer withdrawal headache but may prolong the symptomatic time period. If withdrawal is done too slowly, undoubtedly migraine triggering events will ensue and a severe breakthrough headache will occur. This may result in a desperate patient's using more medication than the withdrawal schedule permits. Although a temporary worsening of headache often occurs with rapid withdrawal, there are many patients that are able to discontinue medications and have improvement in the headache pattern without an escalation in headaches. It is difficult to predict which patient will have a difficult time. Regardless of the method employed, patients need to be assured that they will not be abandoned and that several bridge therapies exist that can attenuate, although not necessarily prevent, all headaches.

■ BRIDGE OR TRANSITION THERAPIES

The concept of bridge therapy is to provide a short-term treatment that will attenuate the rebound headache and other symptoms of medication withdrawal through the time period when the nervous system is most vulnerable. Although commonly employed by headache specialists, these therapies have not been rigorously evaluated in large, placebo-controlled, randomized studies. The first of these was described by Tfelt-Hansen in 1981. Patients were hospitalized and treated with sedatives for an average of 9 days and three fourths were reported improved. In 1986, Raskin reported on the use of repetitive doses of intravenous dihydroergotamine (DHE) in hospitalized patients. Patients received nine doses of DHE 0.5 to 1 mg over a 5-day period in a tapering schedule. This protocol has been occasionally modified by several other headache specialists but still remains the standard for detoxification of patients in analgesic rebound. Generally, antidopaminergic medications such as metoclopramide are given with the DHE as an antiemetic agent. Subcutaneous sumatriptan has also been used in management of analgesic rebound with 6 mg given twice daily for 5 days.

More recently, oral triptans have been used as bridge therapies and are especially attractive in an outpatient setting. Triptans with longer half-lives, such as naratriptan and frovatriptan, appear particularly suited for this role. Typically, naratriptan 1 mg (or half of a 2.5-mg tablet) twice daily for 5 to 7 days with 2.5 mg as a rescue dose for breakthrough headaches with a total daily dose not to exceed 5 mg, is commonly used by headache specialists. Frovatriptan 2.5 mg daily with an additional 2.5 mg for breakthrough migraine with a daily dose not exceeding 5 mg, is an alternative. Many specialists also have recommended a burst of prednisone 60 to 80 mg tapered over 7 to 14 days as adjunctive therapy (Table 45–3).

■ ACUTE THERAPIES FOR INTRACTABLE HEADACHE

At times, patients may have a severe rebound headache that does not respond to outpatient treatment or bridge therapy. In principle, it is wise not to use rescue medication from the same pharmacologic class because that is the medication suspected of causing the rebound. Several rescue regimens may be employed in the outpatient setting.

Table 45–3

Bridge (Transition) Therapies for Medication-Withdrawal Headache

Dihydroergotamine (DHE): 0.5-1 mg IV, IM, or SC q8hr for 1 day, then q12hr for 2 days, then qd for 2 days. Metoclopramide 10 mg can be given 30 min before DHE for prevention of nausea. Common adverse events include nausea, vomiting, muscle cramps. Avoid in patient with coronary disease or significant risk factors, peripheral vascular disease, gastric ulcer, sepsis.

Naratriptan: 1-1.25 mg bid for 5 days with an additional 2.5 mg within any 24-hr time period provided for breakthrough headache. Adverse events are uncommon but may include triptan sensations. Avoid in patients with coronary heart disease or significant coronary risk factors, hypertension, hemiplegic or basilar migraine.

Diphenhydramine: 25-50 mg IM or IV tid

Various neuroleptics (e.g., chlorpromazine): 6.25-12.5 mg IV q 8-12 hr

Magnesium sulfate: 1-2 g IV qd for 3-5 days or 1 g bid for 3-5 days

Steroids: rapid tapering dose of oral or parenteral steroids such as prednisone 60 mg q AM for 3 days then 40 mg q AM for 2 days; 30 mg q AM for 2 days; 20 mg q AM for 2 days; 10 mg q AM for 2 days; 5 mg q AM for 2 days; then discontinue

Occipital nerve blocks with local anesthetics (such as 0.25% bupivacaine). Some physicians add long-acting steroids to the bupivacaine

bid, twice a day; IM, intramuscularly; IV, intravenously; qd, every day; SC, subcutaneously; tid, three times a day.

■ PSYCHOLOGICAL SUPPORT

In today's healthcare environment it is often difficult to convince third party payers or patients that effective management of chronic medical conditions requires more than a prescription and 10 minutes of time. However, successfully managing patients with chronic debilitating headaches and associated medication overuse is one clinical situation in which psychological support is critical. There are several levels of support to consider, including individual psychotherapy, biofeedback, group therapy, and patient support organizations. Integrating psychological therapy into a medical treatment plan early on improves treatment response and diminishes the patient's perception that chronic headache represents failure with medical therapy for which there is only psychological therapy.

This approach of integrating medical, physical, psychological, and spiritual therapy into the treatment plan is called the biopsychosocial treatment model (Fig. 45–3). In other words, analgesic rebound headache is more than an acute episode of headache that has become chronic. During this transformational process, it becomes a health problem that affects the patient's entire life and, likewise, factors other than analgesics may be affecting the patient's chronic headache, such as, biological, behavioral, and social factors. Physical problems, such as the diagnosis of a medical disease other

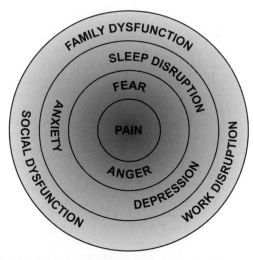

FIGURE 45–3 ■ Biopsychosocial model of chronic pain.

than headaches may short-circuit the system which is expressed by chronic headaches.

Trauma, whether psychological or physical, such as an automobile accident or a burglary of one's home, can be fodder for chronic headaches. Social factors, such as divorce, separation, loss of job, or relocation are high-impact events that affect the chronic headache condition as well as responsiveness to treatment.

These individuals are not seeking solutions. Instead, they desire the opportunity to discuss these issues in a supportive environment, either with a therapist or within a support group. Once they realize they are not alone, that others may be attempting to cope with as many problems as they are, they are encouraged to follow the treatment plan and venture into the realm of being a doer rather than a victim. For chronic problems, there is no linear relationship between cause and effect. By recognizing that the chronic headache has progressed over time, even years, patients see therapy as a process of healing the nervous system by several avenues, not just medication. This realization is at times essential for patients to respond to a treatment strategy.

WHAT IF MEDICATION WITHDRAWAL DOES NOT RESULT IN PATIENT IMPROVEMENT?

As previously discussed, withdrawal from medication does not always result in an improvement in the underlying daily headache pattern. If a patient persists in a debilitating chronic headache pattern, decisions about chronic maintenance with symptomatic medications should be discussed. Few data are available but in a study by Saper and colleagues, the clinical outcome of a population of patients with chronic headache using maintenance narcotics found that only 25% responded.[38] The obvious difficulty is predicting which patients will respond to a stable dose of narcotics without escalation and concomitant reduction in efficacy over time. If analgesic maintenance is recommended, it is critical that patients be followed regularly and that providers document objective improvement in functional status.

Far more difficult, is the patient frequently using non-narcotic abortive medications such as triptans and presumably controlling disabling headaches but requiring medication more than three times a week. In this scenario, clinicians are often triangulated between the needs of their patient and the restrictions of the payer of the pharmaceutical benefits. Managed care concerns often revert to tactics that imply clinicians are outside of normative prescription behavior standards, although the reality is that this patient population has never been studied by the stringent regulatory standards used to establish accepted evidence. Ironically, patients in this clinical scenario may have daily headaches but report that if they use a triptan early in the headache process, they can abort the impending headache and maintain normal function. For this reason, patients do not want to alter this management strategy. In truth, we do not know the long-term consequences of using abortive medications, such as triptans, on a chronic basis. But once the medications have been appropriately withdrawn without benefit and there has been documented deterioration in the patient's functional status, then the question becomes, should symptomatic medications be used on a chronic basis. Without scientific proof to guide decisions, one can decide this based only on individual assessment with risks and benefits fully discussed with the patient. Hopefully, over time, as more migraine sufferers develop the need for frequent abortive medication, pharmaceutical and regulatory agencies will see the need to evaluate this question more completely.

LONG-TERM CARE NEEDS

Patients in medication-overuse headache patterns almost always require long-term, ongoing headache management that will span decades of their lives. Through the lifetime of episodic migraine there is a significant chance that patients will, at some point, develop chronic headache. It is important for providers and patients to realize that, although it is convenient to blame medication overuse, there is a significant chance of developing chronic headache even after medication withdrawal has been successful.

The evolution from episodic to chronic primary headache is clearly about more than the headaches patients experience. Often, disruptions of sleep or mood are the first signal that a migraine patient is transitioning to a chronic daily headache pattern. Physiologic and neurologic function between headaches becomes abnormal in that symptoms such as irritability, fatigue, lethargy, and a sense of feeling "blue" or hypervigilant occur. These characteristics may become the basis for diagnosis of several disorders considered comorbid with migraine. Ironically, medication overuse can be a catalyst that signals the transformation of episodic migraine into a chronic headache pattern. Therefore, it is essential that patients understand the risks of migraine transformation which may become a progressive neurobiological disorder that leads to a chronic pain syndrome. Because overly zealous pharmacologic interventions can be a catalyst for this process, it is critical to set limits on the use of symptomatic medications early in the management of headache patients.

Maintaining medical care that optimizes treatment response can also potentially circumvent daily headache patterns associated with medication overuse. This often appears as a paradox because treatment failure or partial treatment responses often encourages use of additional medication. A treatment diary is invaluable in assessing response to treatment and medication use. The hallmark of quality headache care is to provide these tools for episodic headaches, thereby preventing the development of chronic headaches and the subsequent need to rescue patients from them.

■ SUMMARY

Medication-overuse headache can be a challenging clinical syndrome to manage. It is far easier to prevent than to treat. Clinicians should be mindful of medication-overuse headache in all headache patients they manage. Central to preventing this medical condition is to provide clear guidelines on frequencies and quantities of medication used as abortive. Further clear goals defining treatment success should be provided to all patients when prescribed migraine therapies. Patients should be advised to seek reevaluation whenever the goals of treatment are not being met, which includes reviewing the effectiveness of acute therapy as well as the institution of preventive measures.

Once patients are having chronic headaches associated with medication overuse it is paramount to discontinue the potentially offending medication for at least 2 months. Providing effective education, psychological support, preventive medications, and a bridge therapy for acute care are invaluable components of successful management of this condition. With a cogent approach to medication-overuse headache, most patients can be successfully managed and clinicians often find the condition of analgesic rebound headache rewarding to manage.

References

1. Headache Classification Committee of the International Headache Society: The international classification of headache disorders. Cephalalgia 24 (Suppl 1):8, 2004.
2. Dreisbach RH: Experimental caffeine withdrawal headache. J Pharmacol Exp Ther 69:283, 1940.
3. Wolfson WQ, Graham JR: Development of tolerance to ergot alkaloids in a patient with unusually severe migraine. N Engl J Med 241:296, 1949.
4. Peters GA, Horton BT: Headache: With special reference to the excessive use of ergotamine preparations and withdrawal effects. Mayo Clin Proc 26:153, 1951.
5. Kudrow L: Paradoxical effects of frequent analgesic use. In Critchley M, Friedman A, Gorini S, Sicuteri F (eds): Adv Neurol 33:335, 1982.
6. Isler H: Migraine treatment as a cause of chronic migraine. In Rose FC (ed): Advances in Migraine Research and Therapy. New York, Raven Press, 1982, p 159.
7. Mathew NT, Stubits E, Nigam MP: Transformation of episodic migraine into daily headache: Analysis of factors. Headache 22:66, 1982.
8. Mathew NT, Reuveni U, Perez F: Transformed or evolutive migraine. Headache 27:102, 1987.
9. Rapoport AM, Weeks RE, Sheftell FD, et al: Analgesic rebound headache: Theoretical and practical implications. Cephalalgia 5 (Suppl 3):448, 1985.
10. Gobel H, Stolze H, Heinze A, Dworschak M: Easy therapeutic management of sumatriptan-induced daily headache. Neurology 47:297, 1996.
11. Newman LC, Lipton RB, Solomon S, Stewart WF: Daily headache in a population sample: Results from the American Migraine Study. Headache 34(1):295, 1994.
12. Ravishankar K: Headache patterns in India—a headache clinic analysis of 1000 patients [abstract]. Cephalalgia 17:316, 1997.
13. Mathew NT, Kurman R, Perez F: Drug induced refractory headache: Clinical features and management. Headache 30:270, 1990.
14. Pini LA, Cicero AF, Sandrini M: Long-term follow up of patients treated for chronic headache with analgesic oveuse. Cephalalgia 21:878, 2001.
15. Dodick DW: Debate: Analgesic overuse is a cause, not consequence, of chronic daily headache. Headache 42:543, 2002.
16. Kruit MC, van Buchem MA, Hofman PA, et al: Migraine as a risk factor for subclinical brain lesions JAMA 291:427, 2004.
17. Lipton RB, Pan J: Is migraine a progressive brain disease? JAMA 291:493, 2004.
18. Lipton RB, Stewart W, Cady RK, et al: Lessons learned from the Spectrum study. Neurology 58:S57, 2002.
19. Raskin NH, Appenzellar O: Headache. Philadephia, Saunders, 1980, p 43.
20. Mathew NT: Migraine transformation and chronic daily headache. In Cady RK, Fox AW (eds): Treating the Headache Patient. Marcel Dekker, 1994, p 75.
21. Lipton RB, Diamond S, Reed ML, et al: Migraine diagnosis and treatment: Results of the American Migraine Study II. Headache 41:538, 2001.
22. Cady R, Schreiber C, Farmer K, Sheftell F: Primary headaches: A convergence hypothesis. Headache 42:204, 2002.
23. Cady RK, Schreiber CP, Farmer KU: Understanding the headache patient: The evolution from episodic to chronic migraine. A proposed classification of patients with headache. Headache 44(5):426, 2004.
24. Lance J, Parkes C, Wilkinson M: Does analgesic abuse cause headaches de novo? Headache 28:61, 1988.
25. Hering R, Catarci T, Glover V, et al: 5-HT in migraine patients with analgesic-induced headache. Ninth Migraine Trust International Symposium, London, Sept., 1992.
26. Fields HL, Heinricher MM: Brainstem modulation of nociceptor-driven withdrawal reflexes. Ann NY Acad Sci 563:34, 1989.
27. Ossipov MH, Lai J, Vanderah TW, Porreca F: Induction of pain facilitation by sustained opioid exposure: Relationship to opioid antinociceptive tolerance. American Headache Society Conference, Cancun, Mexico, January, 2004.
28. Mao J, Price DD, Mayer DJ: Mechanisms of hyperalgesia and morphine tolerance. A current view of their possible interactions. Pain 62(3):259, 1989.
29. Spierings EL, Ranke AH, Schroevers M, et al: Chronic daily headache: A time perspective. Headache 40(4):306, 2000.
30. Cady RK, Farmer KU, Schreiber CP: Evaluation of disease burden in subjects with migraine. Treating the difficult headache patient. February, 2004, Palm Springs, Calif.
31. Kosinski M, Bayliss MS, Bjorner JB, et al: A six-item short-form survey for measuring headache impact: The HIT-6. Qual Life Res 12(8):963, 2003.
32. Stewart WF, Lipton RB, Kolodner K, et al: Reliability of the migraine disability assessment scores in a population-based sample of headache sufferers. Cephalalgia 19:107, 1999.
33. Gallagher EJ, Liebman M, Bijur PE: Prospective validation of clinically important changes in pain severity measured on a visual analog scale. Ann Emerg Med 38:633, 2001.
34. Zung WK: A self-rating depression scale. Arch Gen Psychiatry 12:63, 1965.
35. Zung WK: From art to science: The diagnosis and treatment of depression. Arch Gen Psychiatry 29:328, 1973.
36. Spielberger CD, Gorsuch RL, Lushene R, et al: Manual for the State-Trait Anxiety Inventory (Form Y). Palo Alto, Calif., Consulting Psychologists Press, 1983.
37. Butch JN, Dahlstrom WG, Graham JR, et al: MMPI-2: Manual for administration and scoring. Minneapolis, University of Minnesota Press, 1989.
38. Saper JR, Hammel RL, Lake AE, et al: Long-term scheduled opioid treatment for refractory headache: Second interim outcome report. Headache 38:401, 1998.

46

Trigeminal Neuralgia

M. Alan Stiles and James Evans

■ HISTORICAL CONSIDERATIONS

Trigeminal neuralgia has been identified in the medical literature for centuries. Trigeminal neuralgia is the classic neuropathic pain syndrome and is thought first to have been described by Aretaeus in the first century AD. Many physicians have penned descriptions of this affliction; the first to comprehensively describe it was John Locke in 1677. He describes a patient as having

> . . . such violent and exquisite torment, that it forced her to such cries and shrieks as you would expect from one upon the rack, to which I believe hers was an equal torment, which extended itself all over the right side of her face and mouth. When the fit came there was, to My Lady's own expression of it, as it were a flash of fire all of a sudden shot into all of those parts, and at every one of those twitches which made her shriek out, her mouth was constantly drawn to the right side towards the right ear by repeated convulsive motions, which were constantly accompanied by her cries . . . These violent fits terminated of a sudden and then My Lady seemed to be perfectly well.[1,2]

John Hunter (1728-1793), an English physiologist and surgeon, describes trigeminal neuralgia in his *Treatise on the Natural History of the Human Teeth* in 1778 as follows:

> This pain is seated in some one part of the Jaws. As simple pain demonstrates nothing; a Tooth is often suspected, and is perhaps drawn out; but still the pain continues, with this difference however, that it now seems to be in the root of the next Tooth: it is then supposed either by the patient or the operator, that the wrong Tooth was extracted; wherefore, that in which the pain now seems to be, is drawn, but with as little benefit. I have known cases of this kind, where all the Teeth of the affected side of the Jaw, have been drawn out, and the pain has continued in the Jaw; in others, it has had a different effect, the sensation of pain has become more diffused, and has at last, attacked the corresponding side of the tongue. In the first case, I have known it recommended to cut down upon the Jaw, and even to perforate and cauterize it, but all without effect.

> Hence it should appear, that the pain in question, does not arise from any disease in the part, but entirely a nervous affection.

In 1912, Osler captured the essence of the clinical description of trigeminal neuralgia as it was understood in his time:

> In advanced cases the paroxysms follow one another rapidly and without assignable cause, and in the intervals the patient may never be quite free from pain. They are inaugurated by almost any form of external stimulus, by a draught of air, by movement of the facial muscles or of the tongue in speaking, by touching the skin, particularly over those points from which the pain seems to take its origin, by the act of swallowing, especially when the pain involves the mucous membrane field of distribution of the nerve. It is not a self-limited disease. In some instances the neuralgia reaches such a frightful intensity that it renders the patient's life insupportable. In former years suicide was not an uncommon consequence.[3]

■ THE CLINICAL SYNDROME

Trigeminal neuralgia is a severe, almost exclusively unilateral, neuropathic pain located within the distribution of the trigeminal nerve, manifesting as paroxysmal high-intensity stabbing pain lasting seconds. Each attack may be followed by a refractory period, a period of relief that lasts seconds, minutes, or even hours. The burst of pain can occur spontaneously and/or can be triggered by stimulating a specific area of the face known as a trigger zone. Trigger zones can be difficult to locate; they exist anywhere within the trigeminal distribution, including intraorally. The trigger zone is located in the same division of the trigeminal nerve as the pain. For this reason, patients characteristically avoid touching the face, washing, shaving, biting or chewing, or any other maneuver that stimulates the trigger zones and produces the pain.[4] This avoidance is an invaluable clue to the diagnosis. With almost every other facial pain syndrome, patients massage, abrade, or apply heat and cold to the painful area;

however, in trigeminal neuralgia, exactly the opposite occurs: patients avoid any stimulation of the face or mouth. The pain is often characterized as an "electric shock" and is typically accompanied by a unilateral grimace, hence the designation *tic douloureux*. The pain may occur daily for weeks or months and then cease, sometimes for years, before returning; these are known as periods of remission.

Although clinically described for centuries, the etiology of trigeminal neuralgia and the other cranial neuralgias is not fully understood. The integrity of the myelin sheath has been the focal point of investigation for years; however, the only agreement is that there is a dysfunction of the trigeminal sensory system.[5] Trigeminal neuralgia is classified as primary (idiopathic or type 1), or secondary (type 2), which is due to compression or irritation, tumor, or disease, such as multiple sclerosis.

Intermittent trigeminal neuralgia is uncommon in multiple sclerosis, with an incidence between 1% and 2%.[6,7] Conversely, the incidence of multiple sclerosis among patients with trigeminal neuralgia is approximately 3%. Patients with multiple sclerosis and trigeminal neuralgia typically have a classic trigeminal neuralgia history, except that the trigeminal neuralgia appears at a younger age when patients have multiple sclerosis than when the disease occurs in its idiopathic form. Some patients with multiple sclerosis manifest recurrent episodes of face pain that are generally long-lasting, not stabbing or lancinating, and without associated trigger zones. These patients are assumed to not have true trigeminal neuralgia, but a form of atypical facial pain.

Trigeminal neuralgia can occur as the first manifestation of multiple sclerosis, but this is rare. Most patients who have trigeminal neuralgia in association with multiple sclerosis have significant physical signs of multiple sclerosis for many years before the facial pain begins. Most, for example, have paraparesis or paraplegia, which are disorders of sensory function. Bilateral trigeminal neuralgia occurs more often than expected in patients with multiple sclerosis.

On rare occasions, trigeminal neuralgia may be a manifestation of brain stem disease and has been reported to result from pontine infarction.[8] Neoplasms involving the trigeminal nerve generally produce constant neuropathic pain associated with sensory loss. Animal models have not been able to reproduce the pain of trigeminal neuralgia, and this limits our ability to study the condition on a basic science level.

∎ TESTING

The diagnosis of trigeminal neuralgia is made from the clinical history. No medical testing is available to confirm the diagnosis; however, some have mentioned a response to carbamazepine as being diagnostic. When the condition is found, magnetic resonance imaging and evoked potential testing is strongly recommended to rule out secondary causes. Typically, the neurologic examination is normal. Clinically, the onset of trigeminal neuralgia is generally after the age of 50, although it can occur at any age. Women are affected twice as often as men. There is usually no sensory loss in idiopathic trigeminal neuralgia as measured by ordinary sensory testing, although some authors refer to occasional sensory findings.[9-12] In contrast, sensory disturbances in the distribution of the trigeminal nerve are relatively common when patients have

multiple sclerosis or a structural lesion involving the trigeminal nerve or roots. Such sensory loss may even involve the inside of the mouth. Some postulate that if left untreated, trigeminal neuralgia may become more atypical, accompanied by sensory disturbances and constant pain.[13]

Fromm and colleagues described 18 patients whose initial trigeminal pain was not characteristic of neuralgia, but suggested a toothache or sinus pain, and frequently lasted several hours.[14] Often this pain was set off by jaw movements or by drinking hot or cold liquids. Then, at some later time, ranging from several days to 12 years, more typical trigeminal neuralgia developed in the same general area as the initial pain. Six of these patients became pain free while taking carbamazepine or baclofen. The authors designated the problem pretrigeminal neuralgia. This neuralgia must be differentiated from trigeminal tumors, atypical facial pain, atypical odontalgia, and facial migraine, among other entities. A magnetic resonance imaging scan emphasizing the middle and posterior fossa is recommended as a diagnostic study in this situation.

In rare instances, trigeminal neuralgia is accompanied by hemifacial spasm. The combination has been designated *tic convulsif*.[15] Tic convulsif is characterized by periodic contractions of one side of the face, accompanied by great pain. It may be confused with the facial contortions on the involved side that can accompany the paroxysms of true trigeminal neuralgia.[15] Painful tic convulsif is reported to be more severe in women than in men. It may begin in or about the orbicularis oculi as fine intermittent myokymia, with some spread thereafter into the muscles of the lower part of the face. Occasionally, strong spasms involve all of the facial muscles on one side almost continuously. Rarely, the face becomes weak and some of the facial muscles atrophy. Tic convulsif is usually indicative of a tumor, ectatic dilation of the basilar artery, or a vascular malformation compressing the trigeminal and facial nerves.[16]

∎ DIFFERENTIAL DIAGNOSIS

Cluster-Tic

Trigeminal neuralgia in combination with cluster headache has been termed "cluster-tic syndrome."[17,18]

Glossopharyngeal Neuralgia

Glossopharyngeal neuralgia is an uncommon craniofacial pain syndrome characterized by severe, transient, stabbing or burning pain felt in the ear, base of the tongue, tonsillar fossa, or area beneath the angle of the jaw. Occasionally, pain spreads to other areas of the face, including the external auditory canal (otic variety) or neck (cervical variety). The distribution is in the sensory areas of the glossopharyngeal nerve, as well as the auricular and pharyngeal branches of the vagus nerve. It can be mistaken for trigeminal neuralgia with a mandibular nerve distribution.

The pain is frequently triggered by chewing, swallowing, talking, yawning, or coughing. Generally, the attacks of pain come in paroxysms and are lightning-like, but some patients have a more constant aching, burning, or pressure sensation. Glossopharyngeal neuralgia may be associated with severe bradycardia, hypotension, or transient asystole, resulting in syncope or convulsions.[19,20] The diagnosis can be confirmed if pain relief results from either topical anesthesia to the pharynx or glossopharyngeal block at the jugular foramen. As with trigeminal neuralgia, magnetic resonance imaging and evoked potential testing are strongly recommended to rule out secondary causes.

Geniculate Neuralgia

Geniculate neuralgia is an unusual condition caused by impairment of the sensory part of the seventh cranial nerve. In general, it is related to a herpes zoster infection of the geniculate ganglion. It is characterized by severe pain in the tympanic membrane, the walls of the auditory canal, the external auditory meatus, and the external structure of the ear. The pain is typically deep and may radiate toward other regions of the face. A herpetic rash in the auricle or in the external auditory canal may accompany the pain. The disease may be associated with peripheral facial palsy (Ramsay Hunt syndrome), difficulty with hearing, vertigo, and tinnitus. The pain may persist for more than 6 months, producing a chronic postherpetic neuralgia. The pain is usually constant and has a burning dysesthetic quality.

Tic-like Neuritides of the Fifth Cranial Nerve Associated with Tumors and Other Pathologic Processes

These relatively uncommon and painful states resemble trigeminal neuralgia, but can usually be differentiated because each painful paroxysm is commonly a sustained high-intensity ache of several minutes' duration, whereas the true trigeminal neuralgia is characterized by recurrent, brief, painful jabs lasting usually seconds. Cushing divided these neuralgias resulting from tumor involvement of the trigeminal sensory root, the trigeminal ganglion, or the fifth nerve into four groups on the basis of the site of the tumor.[15]

Herpetic and Postherpetic Neuralgia of the Trigeminal Nerve

Herpetic involvement of the trigeminal nerve is more common in elderly and immunosuppressed patients. These patients are also at higher risk to develop postherpetic neuralgia.[21] The pain of herpes zoster, in contrast to tic, is steady and sustained. Although the pain often spontaneously regresses within 2 or 3 weeks, it may persist for several months. When the pain occurs in persons past 70 years of age, as it frequently does, its duration may be a year or more. Rarely, it persists indefinitely. The pain is unilateral. The quality of the pain is usually both burning and aching (gnawing). It is nonthrobbing and relatively uniform, and it usually diminishes gradually in intensity. It may be accompanied by a paroxysmal shooting, jabbing pain or by sharp, radiating pain produced by light mechanical stimuli. It may be experienced in any part of the distribution of the fifth cranial nerve, although involvement of the forehead is most common. Examination soon after onset reveals erythema and the typical herpetiform lesions of the skin associated with

hyperalgesia and paresthesia. Examination later reveals hypesthesia and paresthesia of the involved areas, and sometimes scarring and pigmentation of the skin. There may be weakness of the masseter and pterygoid muscles on the ipsilateral side.

Herpetic and Postherpetic Neuralgia of Cervical Dorsal Root Ganglia

Steady pain in the face and ear, the back of the head, and the neck, associated with vertigo and palsy of the ipsilateral side of the face, results from widespread inflammation involving the gasserian and glossopharyngeal and the first two or three dorsal root ganglia, and the dorsal horns of the cervical portion of the cord. The pain has the qualities and duration described above. As with all herpes, there may be a slight or moderate palsy. There may or may not be herpetiform lesions.

Occipital Neuralgia

Occipital neuralgia remains a controversial subject, presumably because many physicians use the term broadly and nonspecifically for any pain in the occipital area. The term should be reserved for paroxysmal or continuous, unilateral, burning, jabbing, or stabbing occipital pain in the distribution of the greater occipital nerve.[22,23] The pain frequently radiates to the frontal region. It is usually accompanied by hypoalgesia, hyperalgesia, or dysesthesia in the affected area, and circumscribed tenderness over the nerve as it crosses the superior nuchal line.

Occipital neuralgia can be caused by trauma, injury, inflammation, or compression of the greater occipital nerve somewhere along its course from the C2 dorsal root to the periphery.[24] Although postherpetic occipital neuralgias have been described, most cases are caused by trauma or focal irritation of the nerve or its parent dorsal ramus.[25] In most cases, however, a clear-cut pathophysiologic relationship between the C2 root and the symptom complex is lacking. Myofascial trigger points in the suboccipital muscles (particularly the splenius capitis, splenius cervicis, multifidus, semispinalis capitis, and semispinalis cervicis) cause referred occipital pain that may prove difficult to distinguish from occipital neuralgia. Blockade of the occipital nerves with local anesthetic and steroid can be extremely effective in the management of the pain of occipital neuralgia.

Raeder Syndrome

Raeder paratrigeminal syndrome is a rare problem characterized by oculosympathetic paralysis, with ptosis, miosis, and the sudden onset of severe frontotemporal burning, aching pain, often in a periorbital or trigeminal distribution.[26-28] Normal sweating is present in the supraorbital area of the ipsilateral forehead. In essence, Raeder syndrome consists of ordinary Horner syndrome without the anhidrosis seen in the usual cases. This combination of signs may have many different causes, but the nature of the deficits points to a process involving the region of the carotid siphon.

Raeder's original cases all had evidence of involvement of one or more cranial nerves (e.g., optic, oculomotor, trochlear, trigeminal, abducens) caused by a variety of parasellar lesions (e.g., infiltrating tumors, head injury).[26] In most subsequent reports, cranial nerve involvement has not been a prominent feature. The eponym has become a source of confusion because it has been applied indiscriminately to all types of cases in which there is oculo-sympathetic paralysis associated with head pain.

Patients with Raeder syndrome may be divided into two groups: (1) patients with episodic pains that are clearly cluster headaches and (2) patients with more constant pain and definite lesions (aneurysms, tumors, trauma, infections, dissections) involving the internal carotid artery and impinging on the first division of the trigeminal nerve.[29]

Raeder syndrome has some value in localizing the site of pathology in cases of oculo-sympathetic paralysis and head pain, but has no value in distinguishing the cause of the process.

Atypical Facial Pain

Atypical facial pain or facial pain of unknown cause is characterized by a deep burning or aching pain that is continuous and poorly localized. The pain may be unilateral or bilateral and does not necessarily follow the distribution of the peripheral nerves. It may be accompanied by sensory changes, such as allodynia, dysesthesia, and paresthesia.[30] The usual sufferers are middle-aged women. Sleep and facial functions, such as eating and talking, are rarely affected, except when pain is located intraorally. Some patients have a history of trauma or a dental or surgical procedure prior to the onset of pain.

In 1993, Pfaffenrath and colleagues suggested modifying the International Headache Society diagnostic criteria for atypical facial pain[31] (Table 46–1). Since Pfaffenrath's crite-

ria could apply to pain symptoms of separate etiologies, clinicians further categorize these pains according to their specialty in hopes of a better understanding of the condition, as well as of directing treatment toward correcting the cause of the pain. Facial pain of unknown cause was also categorized by Graff-Radford, who proposed an outline to help clinicians compartmentalize their clinical findings and to create a more uniform approach to treating these disorders with limited knowledge of the etiology[32] (Table 46–2).

■ TREATMENT

Medical Management

Initial management of trigeminal neuralgia is medical, and surgical therapy should be considered if medical treatment fails or cannot be tolerated and if secondary causes are found during the initial work-up of the patient.[33,34] It is important to discuss all treatment options with the patient early in the treatment process. A neurosurgical consult early in the medical management of the patient allows the patient time to assimilate the multiple treatment options. It is impossible to predict which patients may become refractory to medications, so it is imperative that they understand treatment options before desperately seeking surgery after months of failed medication trials. Patient preference for either medical or surgical treatment as first-line therapy must be a part of the decision making as well, and this can be facilitated by having an early consultation with a neurosurgeon.

The medical treatment of trigeminal and other cranial neuralgias is based on the capacity of the drugs employed to decrease nerve hyperexcitability either peripherally or centrally. Clinically, pharmacologic therapies are aimed at providing rapid and sustainable pain relief with the least amount of side effects. Unfortunately, the clinical trials in trigeminal neuralgia are not adequate to enable us to fully understand each medication's impact on this disease. Each patient is evaluated individually, taking into account age, other systemic illnesses, and previous medications tried, and then medication choices can be made.

Generally, treatment is begun with an antiepileptic medication that has proven antineuralgic properties. Initial doses should be low and titrated up gradually, with close clinical

---

Table 46–1

Criteria for Atypical Facial Pain—Suggested Modifications

In 1993, Pfaffenrath and colleagues suggested modifying the International Headache Society diagnostic criteria for atypical facial pain.

- Pain is present daily and persists for most or all of the day, but may also appear attack-wise and with remissions.
- Pain is confined at onset to a limited area on one or both sides of the face. May spread to the upper and lower jaws or to a wider area of the face or neck. Can have different pain qualities and be perceived as superficial or deep, but is altogether poorly localized.
- Pain is not associated with sensory loss or other physical signs, but is often associated with dysesthesia.
- Laboratory investigations including radiographs of face and jaws do not demonstrate relevant abnormality.
- Comment: Pain may be initiated by operation or injury to the face, teeth, or gums but persists without any demonstrable cause.

Table 46–2

Facial Pain of Unknown Etiology (Atypical Facial Pain)

I. Neuropathic pain
   A. Intermittent
      1. Trigeminal neuralgia
      2. Glossopharyngeal neuralgia
      3. Occipital neuralgia
      4. Nervus intermedius neuralgia, etc.
   B. Continuous
      1. Trigeminal dysesthesia
      2. Trigeminal dysesthesia, sympathetically maintained
II. Myofascial pain

monitoring, until either the maximum tolerated dose or pain-free dose is attained. For years, the standard has been carbamazepine 100 mg to 200 mg two or three times daily, which provides benefit in more than 75% of patients. Today there are multiple medications from which to choose, but a response to carbamazepine has been described as being almost diagnostic.

If the initial medication is not tolerated due to side effects, then an alternative medication is employed. For example, if carbamazepine is not tolerated, other medications, including baclofen,[35-41] sodium valproate,[42] gabapentin,[43-47] lamotrigine,[44,45,48-52] oxcarbazepine,[53-57] topiramate,[53,58,59] felbamate,[60] zonisamide, vigabatrin, pregabalin, and clonazepam,[61,62] are sometimes effective, but adequate formal studies of the therapeutic efficacy of most of these agents have not been performed. There is a continuing need for new antineuralgic medications because of the limited tolerance and limited efficacy of those agents already available.[63] Blockade of the trigeminal nerve and its branches with local anesthetic and steroid can be extremely effective in the management of the acute pain of trigeminal neuralgia while waiting for pharmacologic interventions to become effective.

Those clinicians who have followed patients with trigeminal neuralgia for more than a few years realize that the disease often goes into remission; and a patient may enter remission during a treatment course. If the patient has been without an attack for several months, it can be beneficial to slowly taper the current medication, and if the patient has entered a remission period, no medication will be necessary until the remission period ends. Patient compliance with medication regimens is essential to determining what benefit if any is being achieved. Patients with trigeminal neuralgia will often taper the medication themselves as pain relief is sustained, only to have the pain start again. It is important to counsel patients to be extremely compliant in order to achieve maximum benefit from the medications.

If only limited benefit is realized with one medication and side effects prohibit additional dosing, a second medication may be used. Often a combination of antiepileptic medications is needed to achieve no pain. Surgical options may be considered after multiple medication failures, patient intolerance of side effects, or pain escalation. If the patient has consulted with a surgeon early in the treatment phase, this transition will be easier for both the patient and the treating physicians and will be achieved in a more timely manner, thereby limiting the patient's suffering.

Surgical Management

Surgical treatment of trigeminal neuralgia is considered for patients who have failed medical treatment or are unable to tolerate medical treatment due to side effects. *Failure* of medical therapy is a relative term that takes into account the number, duration, maximum dosage, and intolerable side-effects of medications used to attempt to control the pain of trigeminal neuralgia. On occasion, patients who are so significantly impaired by pain that they are rendered unable to chew or drink may be offered surgery before failing, or even beginning, medical treatment to avoid the prolonged time that may be associated with titrating medications to therapeutic doses.

Burchiel separated the diagnosis of idiopathic trigeminal neuralgia into type 1 and type 2.[64] Type 1 (or typical) trigeminal neuralgia is characterized by unilateral, lancinating, very brief attacks of pain in one or more of the trigeminal nerve distributions. Between attacks, there is no intervening pain. The neurologic exam is normal, and there is often a history of at least a temporary or prolonged initial good response to carbamazepine. Type 2 (or atypical) trigeminal neuralgia is similar to type 1, yet has a component of more constant, aching facial pain between the bouts of severe lancinating, paroxysmal pain. Also, type 2 trigeminal neuralgia patients may have some facial sensory loss and a history of poor response to medications. It is possible that type 2 trigeminal neuralgia represents an advanced stage of type 1.

Both type 1 and type 2 cases are believed to be caused by arterial and/or venous compression of the trigeminal nerve in the area of transition from central to peripheral myelin (Obersteiner-Redlich zone) near the root entry zone of the nerve to the brain stem. Operations such as microvascular decompression (MVD) directly address the underlying pathology. This procedure requires a general anesthetic and retrosigmoid craniotomy/craniectomy and, therefore, has historically been reserved for young, healthy patients. The remainder of surgical interventions for trigeminal neuralgia are directed at other areas along the course of the trigeminal pathway, such as the trigeminal tracts in the brain stem, the retrogasserian nerve root, the trigeminal (gasserian) ganglion, or the peripheral trigeminal nerve distributions (V1 to V3).

In addition to MVD, the most common surgical interventions for trigeminal neuralgia used today include percutaneous procedures directed at the gasserian ganglion or retrogasserian trigeminal nerve root and Gamma Knife radiosurgery (GKRS) treatment of the cisternal portion of the trigeminal nerve. The percutaneous techniques include glycerol (retro)gasserian rhizotomy, radiofrequency rhizotomy, and balloon compression of the trigeminal nerve. These percutaneous procedures produce a chemical, thermal, and physical injury, respectively, to the trigeminal nerve and ganglion. GKRS produces a radiation-induced injury of the trigeminal nerve. The percutaneous procedures, GKRS, and MVD will be addressed subsequently.

Percutaneous glycerol retrogasserian rhizotomy, otherwise known as a glycerol rhizotomy, is widely used for patients with type 1, type 2, or multiple sclerosis-related trigeminal neuralgia. Historically, this procedure was done with absolute alcohol[64,65] or phenol and subsequently with a phenol/glycerol mixture injected into the trigeminal cistern. Subsequently, Hakanson reported that glycerol alone (without phenol) could relieve facial pain with less facial sensory loss.[64,66]

Approximately 90% of patients achieved complete/immediate pain relief following glycerol injection, and 77% remain with good/excellent pain control over approximately a 10- year follow-up.[67,68] Facial sensory loss may occur following glycerol rhizotomy as follows: 32% to 48% mild, 13% moderate, 6% dense.[68,69] Facial dysesthesia has been reported in approximately 2% to 22% of patients[68] and anesthesia dolorosa in less than 1%.[69] Transient perioral herpes outbreak is seen in up to 3.8% to 37% of patients up to 1 week postoperatively.[68,69] Aseptic meningitis has been reported in 0.6% to 1.5% of patients.[68,69] Intraoperative vasovagal response can occur in 15% to 20% of cases and does not usually require aborting the procedure.[68,69]

Percutaneous balloon compression of the trigeminal nerve is based on the concept of squeezing, manipulating, or compressing the trigeminal nerve. Surgeons in the 1950s and 1960s reported that patients who had the trigeminal nerve traumatized during surgery seemed to have a better outcome with respect to pain relief. In 1983, Mullen reported a percutaneous technique for compression of the gasserian ganglion using a Fogarty catheter.[70] Currently, percutaneous balloon compression is mainly indicated for patients with type 1 or 2 (classic, idiopathic) trigeminal neuralgia and multiple sclerosis-related trigeminal neuralgia.

As with the other percutaneous techniques, pain relief following percutaneous balloon compression of the trigeminal nerve is usually immediate, but it can be delayed and occur as long as 1 week after the procedure. Numbness in the V2 and V3 distribution is the norm (occurring in approximately 80% of patients) but is typically mild and often improves with time to the point that it is not a major problem. Most patients have some degree of jaw/pterygoid weakness, which is usually mild and often resolves over weeks to months. In rare cases, the unilateral symptomatic jaw weakness is permanent. Because of the possibility of permanent jaw weakness, this procedure is contraindicated for patients with preexisting contralateral jaw weakness because "drop jaw" can result. Theoretically, this can also be a problem when performing this procedure bilaterally, such as for some multiple sclerosis patients. Other, more rare complications include diplopia from compression of the fourth or sixth cranial nerve.

Pain relief is immediate in 92% to 100% of patients and the recurrence rates are reported from 19% to 32% over 5 to 20 years.[71,72] Severe sensory loss or dysesthesia occurs in 3% to 20% of patients.[71,72] Three to 16% of patients develop masseter/jaw weakness, although most improve or resolve after 1 year.[71,72] Transient diplopia has been reported to occur in 1.6% of patients.[72] To our knowledge, corneal anesthesia and anesthesia dolorosa have not been reported.

Radiofrequency trigeminal (retrogasserian) rhizotomy is the third percutaneous procedure used to treat trigeminal neuralgia. The theory behind the use of radiofrequency (RF) to lesion the trigeminal nerve is that it may selectively injure/destroy the unmyelinated or poorly myelinated nociceptive nerve fibers and spares the (heavily) myelinated fibers that serve touch, proprioception, and motor function. The procedure consists of a low-current stimulation to determine the proper position of the electrode in the offending trigeminal nerve fibers followed by the creation of a permanent lesion using higher current to generate enough temperature to destroy the selected nerve fibers.

A mild paresthesia in the distribution of the facial pain is the goal of RF treatment of trigeminal neuralgia. Significant dysesthesia or sensory loss is reported in approximately 6% to 28% of patients and loss of the corneal reflex may occur in 3% to 8% of patients, depending on the technique employed.[73-75] Certainly, when treating ophthalmic distribution trigeminal neuralgia, the risk of corneal anesthesia and keratitis is greater. Trigeminal nerve motor weakness has been reported following RF treatment in up to 14% of patients; however, it is most often mild and transient.[73-75] Anesthesia dolorosa has been reported in 0.5% to 1.6% of patients.[73-75] Rare complications of carotid artery injury, stroke, diplopia, meningitis, seizures, and death have been reported.

It has been reported that 88% to 99% of patients obtain immediate pain relief following RF with 20% to 27% recurrence rates over a 9- to 14-year follow-up.[73,74] Patients with a more dense sensory loss from the RF lesion tend to have a lower rate of recurrence, but are subject to greater complications from dysesthesias and analgesia. One author reported that following recurrence of pain, 81% of patients obtained "good or excellent" pain relief with a second RF treatment.[73]

GKRS is the only noninvasive "surgical" treatment of trigeminal neuralgia. It is a same-day procedure that is performed in the outpatient radiosurgery center. Treatment delivery can take from 45 to 90 minutes, depending on the age of the cobalt sources in the Gamma Knife system being used. After the treatment is completed, the head frame is removed and bandages are placed over the pin sites. The patient is observed in the radiosurgery center to allow complete recovery from any residual intravenous sedation and discharged the same day.

Although GKRS can be done under general anesthesia, a particular advantage of this technique is that it can be done with minimal IV sedation. Drawbacks are the cost of purchasing and maintaining the radiosurgery device and the latency period between treatment and facial pain improvement. Pain relief typically occurs after a latency period of 4 to 12 weeks following treatment, with a range reported of 1 day to 13 months following treatment. The rates of pain control and recurrence of trigeminal neuralgia have been somewhat variable between reports. The variability is likely due to different pain scales used to report outcome, follow-up duration, number of patients lost to follow-up, prior surgical treatment, the size and placement of the radiation dosage, and the maximal radiation dose. An excellent (complete pain relief without medication) or good (50% to 90% improved pain with or without medication) response can be achieved in 57% to 86% of patients at 1 year following radiosurgery treatment.[76,77] As with most surgical treatments for trigeminal neuralgia, recurrence of facial pain following GKRS increases with time after treatment. Pain recurrence rates of 23%, 33%, 39%, and 44% have been reported 1, 2, 3, and 5 years following radiosurgery treatment.[78,79] Mild or tolerable facial numbness occurs in up to 25% to 29% of patients and significant numbness or dysesthesia can occur in 12% to 18% of patients.[76,80] Complications of facial weakness, trigeminal motor weakness, and anesthesia dolorosa have not been reported. Greater doses of radiation correlate with both higher rates of pain control and higher rates of complications, which mostly consist of facial numbness and bothersome facial dysesthesias. Patients who experience more facial numbness seem to have a better chance of pain control.[76] Repeat radiosurgery for patients with recurrent pain has also been reported, with approximately 50% excellent or good pain relief and an increased rate of facial sensory loss within a limited follow-up period.[81] Long-term follow-up studies of more than 10 to 20 years are needed. The ideal Gamma Knife dose and treatment strategy, as well as the role of other radiosurgery modalities, such as linear accelerator, remain to be determined.

Microvascular decompression (MVD) is the only medical or surgical intervention that directly addresses the presumed underlying pathology of classic trigeminal neuralgia: focal vascular compression of the trigeminal nerve near the brain stem root entry zone. The procedure requires a general anesthetic. Using the intraoperative microscope, the arachnoid membrane surrounding the trigeminal nerve is opened and the nerve is explored from the brain stem to the entrance of the nerve to Meckel's cave, where the trigeminal nerve ganglion (gasserian ganglion) is located. Under microscopic and endoscopic visualization, microdissection is performed to mobilize any arteries or veins compressing the trigeminal nerve. One or more Teflon sponges are then placed between the dissected blood vessels and the trigeminal nerve to prevent continued vascular compression of the trigeminal nerve. Veins compressing the trigeminal nerve can frequently be cauterized and divided. It is important to note that the compression is usually arterial, most commonly a branch of the superior cerebellar artery.[82] However, venous compression alone or a combination of arterial and venous compression may also occur.[83,84]

When offending vessels are identified and decompressed, most patients obtain immediate relief from their facial pain. Rates of immediate pain relief as high as 90% to 98% have been reported following MVD. Barker and colleagues reported Dr. Jannetta's large series of MVD procedures with up to 10-year follow-up and defined outcome as "excellent" if at least 98% pain relief was achieved without the need for medications and "good" if at least 75% pain relief was achieved with only intermittent need for pain medication.[85] In that series, excellent or good early postoperative outcome was achieved in 98% of patients. This number decreases to approximately 84% and 67% after 1- and 10-year follow-up, respectively. Tronnier and coworkers reported that 64% of their patients were pain free 20 years following MVD.[86] Whether or not there is continued recurrence of facial pain with time is debated. Some authors have reported the majority of recurrences early (within 2 years following MVD), whereas others have reported a more constant rate of recurrence at 3.5% annually in one series.[87,88]

Surgical complications associated with MVD have diminished since the regular use of brain stem and cranial nerve intraoperative neurophysiologic monitoring. Complications of MVD may include cerebellar injury (0.45%), transient facial numbness (15%), mild persistent facial numbness (12%), significant facial numbness (1.6%), facial dysesthesia (0% to 3.5%), hearing loss (<1%), transient or permanent facial weakness (<1%), cerebrospinal fluid leakage (1.5% to 2.5%), hematoma (0.5%), and mortality (0.3%).[82,89,90] Also, lower morbidity rates have been reported from high-volume centers and from high-volume surgeons.[90]

When no arterial or venous compression is identified, the trigeminal nerve may be "traumatized" by stroking or squeezing the nerve with micro-instruments, yet the resulting pain relief is only temporary and such manipulation can be associated with trigeminal dysesthesias. Some surgeons have advocated partial sectioning of the sensory portion of the trigeminal nerve for negative explorations or during repeat surgical exploration of the nerve for recurrent pain following MVD.[87,91,92]

For several decades, microvascular decompression has been the standard to which each of the other surgical treatments for classic trigeminal neuralgia has been compared. In an experienced surgeon's hands, however, any of the techniques outlined in this chapter may be used to successfully manage trigeminal neuralgia. Each procedure has its own attributes and limitations, and the procedure selected must be based on the patient's individual situation. Therefore, from a surgical perspective, trigeminal neuralgia patients are probably best managed at centers that are able to offer a variety of interventions, including one or more percutaneous techniques (i.e., GKRS, and MVD).

■ COMPLICATIONS AND PITFALLS

Diagnosis is extremely important when treating trigeminal neuralgia. A thorough history, clinical examination, and diagnostic imaging are the mainstays of diagnosing facial pain. When all information has been collected, a treatment plan can be formulated. Pharmacotherapy must be engaged in a systematic manner, testing each medication to its fullest potential. All cases should be evaluated from both a medical and surgical standpoint soon after the diagnosis is made to ensure the patient fully understands all available options before embarking toward his or her ultimate choice. Problems arise with one-sided approaches that may delay the ultimate goal of relieving the patient's pain. Multiple therapies have been discussed here and navigating these options has to be done on a case-by-case basis with the patient, medicine, and surgery all working together.

■ CONCLUSION

Although arriving at a clinical diagnosis is often flawed and results in multiple consultations, misguided treatments, and in some cases unnecessary procedures, once a diagnosis of trigeminal neuralgia is made, many therapeutic options become available. The initial treatment is medical management, and with newer agents becoming available there are many possibilities for monotherapy or even polypharmacy to greatly reduce the pain. Surgical interventions are available for patients who are intolerant of medication therapy or whose pain is extreme and unremitting. Secondary causes must be explored in all patients because, if discovered, surgical interventions may supersede medical options.

Each of the medications and each of the surgical procedures is associated with side effects and potential risks. These pitfalls must be weighed based on each individual's medical conditions, lifestyle, age, personal preference, and past therapies. The patient needs to be well-informed about both the medical and the surgical options as soon as the diagnosis is made. This allows time for the patient and the physicians to tailor the treatment plan to each individual. It is inappropriate to withhold surgical or medical options until one modality has failed. As part of the initial evaluation, the patient should be required to consult with both surgery and medicine. This allows for a planned therapeutic attack with all parties seeking timely and effective pain relief for the patient.

References

1. Locke J: The celebrated Locke as a physician. Lancet 2:367, 1829.
2. Locke J: Letters to Dr. Mapletoft: Letter VII, Paris, 9th August 1677; Letter IX X. Paris, 4th December, 1677. The European Magazine 85:185, 1789.
3. Osler W: The Principles and Practice of Medicine, 8th ed. New York, Appleton, 1912.
4. D'Alessio DJ: Trigeminal neuralgia. A practical approach to treatment. Drugs 24(3):248, 1982.

5. Fisher A, Zakrzewska JM, Patsalos PN: Trigeminal neuralgia: Current treatments and future developments. Expert Opin Emerg Drugs 8(1):123, 2003.
6. Harris W: Rare forms of paroxysmal trigeminal neuralgia and their relation to disseminated sclerosis. BMJ 2(4687):1015, 1950.
7. Hooge JP, Redekop WK: Trigeminal neuralgia in multiple sclerosis. Neurology 45(7):1294, 1995.
8. Kim JS, Kang JH, Lee MC: Trigeminal neuralgia after pontine infarction. Neurology 51(5):1511, 1998.
9. Dubner R, Sharav Y, Gracely RH, Price DD: Idiopathic trigeminal neuralgia: Sensory features and pain mechanisms. Pain 31(1):23, 1987.
10. Terrence CF: Differential diagnosis of trigeminal neuralgia. In Fromm GH (ed): The Medical and Surgical Management of Trigeminal Neuralgia. New York, Futura, 1987, p 43.
11. Nurmikko TJ: Altered cutaneous sensation in trigeminal neuralgia. Arch Neurol 48(5):523, 1991.
12. Sinay VJ, Bonamico LH, Dubrovsky A: Subclinical sensory abnormalities in trigeminal neuralgia. Cephalalgia 23(7):541, 2003.
13. Burchiel KJ, Slavin KV: On the natural history of trigeminal neuralgia. Neurosurgery 46(1):152, 2000.
14. Fromm GH, Graff-Radford SB, Terrence CF, Sweet WH: Pre-trigeminal neuralgia. Neurology 40(10):1493, 1990.
15. Cushing H: The major trigeminal neuralgias and their surgical treatment, based on experiences with 332 Gasserian operations. The varieties of facial neuralgia. Am J Med Sci 160:157, 1920.
16. Harsh GR, Wilson CB, Hieshima GB, Dillon WP: Magnetic resonance imaging of vertebrobasilar ectasia in tic convulsif. Case report. J Neurosurg 74(6):999, 1991.
17. Monzillo PH, Sanvito WL, Peres MF: Cluster-tic syndrome: Two case reports. Arq Neuropsiquatr 54(2):284, 1996.
18. Monzillo PH, Sanvito WL, Da Costa AR: Cluster-tic syndrome: Report of five new cases. Arq Neuropsiquatr 58(2B):518, 2000.
19. Ferrante L, Artico M, Nardacci B, et al: Glossopharyngeal neuralgia with cardiac syncope. Neurosurgery 36(1):58, 1995.
20. Ozenci M, Karaoguz R, Conkbayir C, et al: Glossopharyngeal neuralgia with cardiac syncope treated by glossopharyngeal rhizotomy and microvascular decompression. Europace 5(2):149, 2003.
21. Loeser JD: Herpes zoster and postherpetic neuralgia. Pain 25(2):149, 1986.
22. Bogduk N: The anatomy of occipital neuralgia. Clin Exp Neurol 17:167, 1981.
23. Hammond SR, Danta G: Occipital neuralgia. Clin Exp Neurol 15:258, 1978.
24. Kuhn WF, Kuhn SC, Gilberstadt H: Occipital neuralgias: Clinical recognition of a complicated headache. A case series and literature review. J Orofac Pain 11(2):158, 1997.
25. Weinberger LM: Cervico-occipital pain and its surgical treatment: The myth of the bony millstones. Am J Surg 135(2):243, 1978.
26. Raeder JG: Paratrigeminal paralysis of oculopupillary sympathetic. Brain 47:149, 1924.
27. Mokri B: Raeder's paratrigeminal syndrome. Original concept and subsequent deviations. Arch Neurol 39(7):395, 1982.
28. Grimson BS, Thompson HS: Raeder's syndrome. A clinical review. Surv Ophthalmol 24(4):199, 1980.
29. Selky AK, Pascuzzi R: Raeder's paratrigeminal syndrome due to spontaneous dissection of the cervical and petrous internal carotid artery. Headache 35(7):432, 1995.
30. Turp JC, Gobetti JP: Trigeminal neuralgia versus atypical facial pain. A review of the literature and case report. Oral Surg Oral Med Oral Pathol Oral Radiol Endod 81(4):424, 1996.
31. Pfaffenrath V, Rath M, Pollmann W, Keeser W: Atypical facial pain—application of the IHS criteria in a clinical sample. Cephalalgia 13 (Suppl 12):84, 1993.
32. Graff-Radford SB: Facial pain. Curr Opin Neurol 13(3):291, 2000.
33. Zakrzewska JM, Patsalos PN: Drugs used in the management of trigeminal neuralgia. Oral Surg Oral Med Oral Pathol 74(4):439, 1992.
34. Sidebottom A, Maxwell S: The medical and surgical management of trigeminal neuralgia. J Clin Pharm Ther 20(1):31, 1995.
35. Parmar BS, Shah KH, Gandhi IC: Baclofen in trigeminal neuralgia—a clinical trial. Indian J Dent Res 1(4):109, 1989.
36. Fromm GH, Terrence CF: Comparison of L-baclofen and racemic baclofen in trigeminal neuralgia. Neurology 37(11):1725, 1987.
37. Baker KA, Taylor JW, Lilly GE: Treatment of trigeminal neuralgia: Use of baclofen in combination with carbamazepine. Clin Pharm 4(1):93, 1985.
38. Hershey LA: Baclofen in the treatment of neuralgia. Ann Intern Med 100(6):905, 1984.
39. Fromm GH, Terrence CF, Chattha AS: Baclofen in the treatment of trigeminal neuralgia: Double-blind study and long-term follow-up. Ann Neurol 15(3):240, 1984.
40. Steardo L, Leo A, Marano E: Efficacy of baclofen in trigeminal neuralgia and some other painful conditions. A clinical trial. Eur Neurol 23(1):51, 1984.
41. Fromm GH, Terrence CF, Chattha AS, Glass JD: Baclofen in trigeminal neuralgia: Its effect on the spinal trigeminal nucleus: A pilot study. Arch Neurol 37(12):768, 1980.
42. Peiris JB, Perera GL, Devendra SV, Lionel ND: Sodium valproate in trigeminal neuralgia. Med J Aust 2(5):278, 1980.
43. Cheshire WP Jr: Defining the role for gabapentin in the treatment of trigeminal neuralgia: A retrospective study. J Pain 3(2):137, 2002.
44. Solaro C, Messmer UM, Uccelli A, et al: Low-dose gabapentin combined with either lamotrigine or carbamazepine can be useful therapies for trigeminal neuralgia in multiple sclerosis. Eur Neurol 44(1):45, 2000.
45. Carrazana EJ, Schachter SC: Alternative uses of lamotrigine and gabapentin in the treatment of trigeminal neuralgia. Neurology 50(4):1192, 1998.
46. Sist T, Filadora V, Miner M, Lema M: Gabapentin for idiopathic trigeminal neuralgia: Report of two cases. Neurology 48(5):1467, 1997.
47. Khan OA: Gabapentin relieves trigeminal neuralgia in multiple sclerosis patients. Neurology 51(2):611, 1998.
48. Leandri M, Lundardi G, Inglese M, et al: Lamotrigine in trigeminal neuralgia secondary to multiple sclerosis. J Neurol 247(7):556, 2000.
49. Canavero S, Bonicalzi V: Lamotrigine control of trigeminal neuralgia: An expanded study. J Neurol 244(8):527, 1997.
50. Lunardi G, Leandri M, Albano C, et al: Clinical effectiveness of lamotrigine and plasma levels in essential and symptomatic trigeminal neuralgia. Neurology 48(6):1714, 1997.
51. Canavero S, Bonicalzi V, Ferroli P, et al: Lamotrigine control of idiopathic trigeminal neuralgia. J Neurol Neurosurg Psychiatry 59(6):646, 1995.
52. Zakrzewska JM, Chaudhry Z, Nurmikko TJ, et al: Lamotrigine (lamictal) in refractory trigeminal neuralgia: Results from a double-blind placebo controlled crossover trial. Pain 73(2):223, 1997.
53. Solaro C, Uccelli MM, Brichetto G, et al: Topiramate relieves idiopathic and symptomatic trigeminal neuralgia. J Pain Symptom Manage 21(5):367, 2001.
54. Zakrzewska JM, Patsalos PN: Long-term cohort study comparing medical (oxcarbazepine) and surgical management of intractable trigeminal neuralgia. Pain 95(3):259, 2002.
55. Grant SM, Faulds D: Oxcarbazepine. A review of its pharmacology and therapeutic potential in epilepsy, trigeminal neuralgia and affective disorders. Drugs 43(6):873, 1992.
56. Patsalos PN, Elyas AA, Zakrzewska JM: Protein binding of oxcarbazepine and its primary active metabolite, 10-hydroxycarbazepine, in patients with trigeminal neuralgia. Eur J Clin Pharmacol 39(4):413, 1990.
57. Zakrzewska JM, Patsalos PN: Oxcarbazepine: A new drug in the management of intractable trigeminal neuralgia. J Neurol Neurosurg Psychiatry 52(4):472, 1989.
58. Gilron I, Booher SL, Rowan JS, Max MB: Topiramate in trigeminal neuralgia: A randomized, placebo-controlled multiple crossover pilot study. Clin Neuropharmacol 24(2):109, 2001.
59. Zvartau-Hind M, Din MU, Gilani A, et al:. Topiramate relieves refractory trigeminal neuralgia in MS patients. Neurology 55(10):1587, 2000.
60. Cheshire WP: Felbamate relieved trigeminal neuralgia. Clin J Pain 11(2):139, 1995.
61. Caccia MR: Clonazepam in facial neuralgia and cluster headache. Clinical and electrophysiological study. Eur Neurol 13(6):560, 1975.
62. de Negrotto OV, Dalmas JF, Negrotto A: [Trigeminal neuralgia. Treatment with clonazepam]. Acta Neurol Latinoam 20(1-4):139, 1974.
63. Fisher A, Zakrzewska JM, Patsalos PN: Trigeminal neuralgia: Current treatments and future developments. Expert Opin Emerg Drugs 8(1):123, 2003.
64. Burchiel KJ: A new classification for facial pain. Neurosurgery 53(5):1164, 2003.
65. Hartel F: Uber die intracranielle Injektionbehandlung der Trigeminusneuralgie. Med Klin 10:582, 1914.
66. Hakanson S: Trigeminal neuralgia treated by the injection of glycerol into the trigeminal cistern. Neurosurgery 9(6):638, 1981.
67. Young RF: Glycerol rhizolysis for treatment of trigeminal neuralgia. J Neurosurg 69(1):39, 1988.

68. Jho HD, Lunsford LD: Percutaneous retrogasserian glycerol rhizotomy. Current technique and results. Neurosurg Clin North Am 8(1):63, 1997.

69. Blomstedt PC, Bergenheim AT: Technical difficulties and perioperative complications of retrogasserian glycerol rhizotomy for trigeminal neuralgia. Stereotact Funct Neurosurg 79:168, 2002.

70. Mullan S, Lichtor T: Percutaneous microcompression of the trigeminal ganglion for trigeminal neuralgia. J Neurosurg 59(6):1007, 1983.

71. Brown JA, Gouda JJ: Percutaneous balloon compression of the trigeminal nerve. Neurosurg Clin North Am 8(1):53, 1997.

72. Skirving DJ, Dan NG: A 20-year review of percutaneous balloon compression of the trigeminal ganglion. J Neurosurg 94(6):913, 2001.

73. Nugent GR: Radiofrequency treatment of trigeminal neuralgia using a cordotomy-type electrode. A method. Neurosurg Clin North Am 8(1):41, 1997.

74. Taha JM, Tew JM, Jr: Treatment of trigeminal neuralgia by percutaneous radiofrequency rhizotomy. Neurosurg Clin North Am 8(1):31, 1997.

75. Kanpolat Y, Savas A, Bekar A, Berk C: Percutaneous controlled radiofrequency trigeminal rhizotomy for the treatment of idiopathic trigeminal neuralgia: 25-year experience with 1,600 patients. Neurosurgery 48(3):524, 2001.

76. Pollock BE, Phuong LK, Gorman DA, et al: Stereotactic radiosurgery for idiopathic trigeminal neuralgia. J Neurosurg 97(2):347, 2002.

77. Kondziolka D, Lunsford LD, Flickinger JC: Stereotactic radiosurgery for the treatment of trigeminal neuralgia. Clin J Pain 18(1):42, 2002.

78. Petit JH, Herman JM, Nagda S, et al: Radiosurgical treatment of trigeminal neuralgia: Evaluating quality of life and treatment outcomes. Int J Radiat Oncol Biol Phys 56(4):1147, 2003.

79. Maesawa S, Salame C, Flickinger JC, et al:. Clinical outcomes after stereotactic radiosurgery for idiopathic trigeminal neuralgia. J Neurosurg 94(1):14, 2001.

80. McNatt SA, Yu C, Giannotta SL, et al: Gamma knife radiosurgery for trigeminal neuralgia. Neurosurgery 56(6):1295, 2005.

81. Hasegawa T, Kondziolka D, Spiro R, et al: Repeat radiosurgery for refractory trigeminal neuralgia. Neurosurgery 50(3):494, 2002.

82. Lovely TJ, Jannetta PJ: Microvascular decompression for trigeminal neuralgia. Surgical technique and long-term results. Neurosurg Clin North Am 8(1):11, 1997.

83. Lee SH, Levy EI, Scarrow AM, et al: Recurrent trigeminal neuralgia attributable to veins after microvascular decompression. Neurosurgery 46(2):356, 2000.

84. Matsushima T, Huynh-Le P, Miyazono M: Trigeminal neuralgia caused by venous compression. Neurosurgery 55(2):334, 2004.

85. Barker FG, Jannetta PJ, Bissonette DJ, et al: The long-term outcome of microvascular decompression for trigeminal neuralgia. N Engl J Med 334(17):1077, 1996.

86. Tronnier VM, Rasche D, Hamer J, et al: Treatment of idiopathic trigeminal neuralgia: Comparison of long-term outcome after radiofrequency rhizotomy and microvascular decompression. Neurosurgery 48(6):1261, 2001.

87. Burchiel KJ, Clarke H, Haglund M, Loeser JD: Long-term efficacy of microvascular decompression in trigeminal neuralgia. J Neurosurg 69(1):35, 1988.

88. Elias WJ, Burchiel KJ: Trigeminal neuralgia and other neuropathic pain syndromes of the head and face. Curr Pain Headache Rep 6(2):115, 2002.

89. McLaughlin MR, Jannetta PJ, Clyde BL, et al: Microvascular decompression of cranial nerves: Lessons learned after 4400 operations. J Neurosurg 90(1):1, 1999.

90. Kalkanis SN, Eskandar EN, Carter BS, Barker FG: Microvascular decompression surgery in the United States, 1996 to 2000: Mortality rates, morbidity rates, and the effects of hospital and surgeon volumes. Neurosurgery 52(6):1251, 2003.

91. Klun B: Microvascular decompression and partial sensory rhizotomy in the treatment of trigeminal neuralgia: Personal experience with 220 patients. Neurosurgery 30(1):49, 1992.

92. Bederson JB, Wilson CB: Evaluation of microvascular decompression and partial sensory rhizotomy in 252 cases of trigeminal neuralgia. J Neurosurg 71(3):359, 1989.

47

Glossopharyngeal Neuralgia

Steven D. Waldman

Glossopharyngeal neuralgia is a rare condition characterized by paroxysms of pain in the sensory division of the ninth cranial nerve. Clinically, the pain of glossopharyngeal neuralgia resembles that of trigeminal neuralgia, but the incidence of this painful condition is significantly less. The pain of glossopharyngeal neuralgia is rarely complicated by associated cardiac dysrhythmias and asystole. This chapter will review the clinical features of glossopharyngeal neuralgia and discuss the current recommended treatment options for this uncommon pain syndrome.

■ HISTORICAL CONSIDERATIONS

Weisenburg first described pain in the distribution of the glossopharyngeal nerve in a patient with a cerebellopontine angle tumor in 1910.[1] In 1921, Harris reported the first idiopathic case and coined the term glossopharyngeal neuralgia.[2] Early attempts at treatment of glossopharyngeal neuralgia were primarily aimed at the extracranial surgical section of the glossopharyngeal nerve.[3] This approach met with limited success. Intracranial section of the glossopharyngeal nerve was first performed by Adson in 1925 and refined by Dandy. The intracranial approach appeared to yield better results but was a riskier procedure.[4]

■ CLINICAL SYNDROME

Demographic Considerations

The demographics of glossopharyngeal neuralgia are summarized in Table 47–1. Glossopharyngeal neuralgia is a rare disease with an incidence of 0.7 cases per 100,000 population.[5] Although the pain of glossopharyngeal neuralgia resembles that of trigeminal neuralgia, it occurs 100 times less frequently than trigeminal neuralgia.[6] Glossopharyngeal neuralgia occurs more commonly in patients older than 50 years but it can occur at any age. The quality of pain associated with glossopharyngeal neuralgia is often described as shooting, stabbing, or needle-like, occurring in paroxysms lasting from a few seconds to a minute. These paroxysms of pain are triggered by swallowing, chewing, coughing, or talking.

Location of the Pain

The localization of pain in the 217 patients suffering with glossopharyngeal neuralgia reviewed by the Mayo Clinic is summarized in Figure 47–1.[5] Otalgia was present in 155 patients, tonsillar pain in 147, laryngeal pain in 69, and tongue pain in 43. Sixty-eight patients had both ear and tonsillar pain—bilateral in approximately 2% of patients suffering from glossopharyngeal neuralgia. Investigators at the Mayo Clinic also noted the spread of pain beyond the usual sensory distribution of the glossopharyngeal nerve to areas innervated by the vagus and trigeminal nerves and upper cervical segments. This phenomenon is termed overflow pain. Overflow pain occurs in approximately 20% of patients suffering from glossopharyngeal neuralgia and was first noted by Keith in 1932.[7] It has been postulated that the overflow pain associated with glossopharyngeal neuralgia is related to the spillover of intense impulses from the glossopharyngeal nerve through the tractus solitarius of the medulla to the vagus.[8] Fibers of the glossopharyngeal nerve may also join the descending portion of the trigeminal nerve, thereby contributing to this phenomenon.

An alternative hypothesis to account for overflow pain holds that an artificial synapse exists between the glossopharyngeal and vagus nerves at the level of the proximal glossopharyngeal and vagus nerves.[9] The overflow of neural impulses to the vagus nerve is most likely responsible for the bradycardia and cardiac arrest observed in patients whose glossopharyngeal neuralgia is associated with syncopal episodes. The coexistence of glossopharyngeal pain and cardiovascular abnormalities is extremely rare; only 35 patients have been reported to suffer from this potentially lethal combination of symptoms.

Evaluation

As with most other head and facial pain syndromes, the diagnosis of glossopharyngeal neuralgia is made by performing a targeted history and physical examination.[10,11] Most cases of glossopharyngeal neuralgia are idiopathic; however, care must be taken to exclude tumors of the head and neck, especially those occurring at the cerebellopontine angle that may be the cause of the patient's symptoms (Fig. 47–2). Although exceedingly rare, a careful cardiac examination is indicated to rule out glossopharyngeal neuralgia with associated syncope.

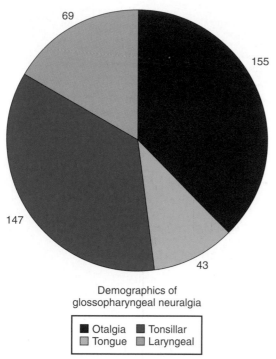

FIGURE 47–1 ■ Demographics of glossopharyngeal neuralgia.

Demographics of
glossopharyngeal neuralgia

Otalgia ■ Tonsillar
Tongue ■ Laryngeal

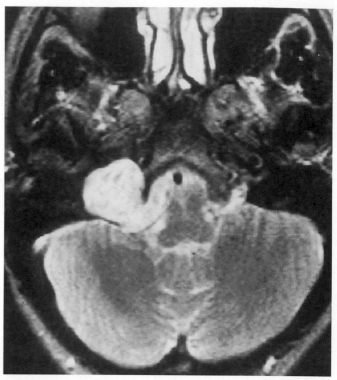

FIGURE 47–2 ■ Jugular fossa schwannoma in a 32-year-old woman. Axial T2-weighted magnetic resonance scan. The sharply defined tumor centered in the right jugular foramen is well seen. The tumor represents a benign schwannoma with smooth expansion of the skull base but no involvement of the right internal auditory canal. (From Stark DD, Bradley WG: Magnetic Resonance Imaging, 3rd ed. St. Louis, Mosby, 1999, p 1217.)

Table 47–1

Demographics of Glossopharyngeal Neuralgia

1. Incidence is 0.7 cases per 100,000 population.
2. Occurs 100 times less frequently than trigeminal neuralgia
3. Occurs more commonly in patients older than 50 years but can occur at any age
4. Quality of pain described as shooting, stabbing, or needle-like
5. Episodes of pain occur in paroxysms lasting from a few seconds to a minute.
6. Paroxysms of pain are often triggered by swallowing, chewing, coughing, or talking.

Testing

Clinical laboratory tests consisting of a complete blood count, erythrocyte sedimentation rate, antinuclear antibody, and automated serum chemistry are indicated to rule out occult systemic diseases including temporal arteritis, inflammatory conditions, infection, and malignancy that may mimic glossopharyngeal neuralgia.[13]

Magnetic resonance imaging of the head will help rule out intracranial tumor and demyelinating disease that may be responsible for the patient's symptomatology.[14] Imaging of the neck is also indicated, if tumor of the hypopharynx, larynx, or piriform sinus is being considered. And, differential neural blockade with local anesthetic will aid in establishing the diagnosis of glossopharyngeal neuralgia.

■ TREATMENT

In the vast majority of patients, the pain of glossopharyngeal neuralgia can be controlled. In the acute, uncontrolled attack of glossopharyngeal neuralgia, hospitalization is indicated to facilitate the relief of pain and to monitor for side effects from the treatments chosen.

Pharmacologic Treatment

Carbamazepine

Carbamazepine (Tegretol) represents the first line of treatment for glossopharyngeal neuralgia.[15] A rapid response to this drug

Idiopathic glossopharyngeal neuralgia has four major characteristics including (1) a history of shooting, stabbing, shock-like pain in the neck, throat and/or ear which occurs in paroxysms and is triggered by talking, chewing, drinking or coughing; (2) the neurologic examination is normal, and the ear, pharynx, hypopharynx, piriform sinuses, and larynx are free from objective disease; (3) the patient is relatively pain free between attacks and can carry out normal activities; (4) the pain is markedly improved or relieved by blockade of the glossopharyngeal nerve with local anesthetic.[13] Dull, aching, poorly localized pain that persists between paroxysms of tic-like pain is strongly suggestive of a space-occupying lesion and requires a thorough evaluation.[13]

helps confirm the clinical diagnosis of glossopharyngeal neuralgia. In spite of the efficacy and safety of this drug relative to other treatments for glossopharyngeal neuralgia, much confusion and unfounded anxiety surrounds the use of carbamazepine. Practical guidelines for the use of carbamazepine are summarized in Table 47–2.[16] Baseline clinical laboratory tests consisting of a complete blood count, blood chemistry, and urinalysis are obtained prior to initiation of carbamazepine. This pretreatment testing avoids having to discontinue carbamazepine because of an unsuspected laboratory abnormality that is erroneously attributed to the carbamazepine.

If the pain is not out of control, carbamazepine should be initiated slowly. Therapy begins with a 200 mg bedtime dose for 2 nights. The patient is cautioned regarding side effects including dizziness, sedation, confusion, and rash. The drug is increased in 200-mg increments (in equally divided doses) every 2 days, as side effects allow, until pain relief is obtained or a total dose of 1200 mg daily is reached. Careful monitoring of laboratory parameters is mandatory to avoid the (rare) possibility of life-threatening blood dyscrasias. At the first sign of blood count abnormality or rash, this drug should be discontinued. Failure to monitor patients started on carbamazepine can lead only to disaster. When pain relief is obtained, the patient should be maintained on this dose of carbamazepine for at least 6 months before tapering is considered. The patient should be informed that under no cir-

cumstances should the dosage of drug be changed or the drug refilled or discontinued without consultation with the pain management specialist. The patient should be aware that premature tapering or discontinuation of carbamazepine may lead to recurrence of pain with subsequent pain control being more difficult.

When treating a patient in whom the pain of glossopharyngeal neuralgia is unbearable, carbamazepine may be initiated in the inpatient setting at a dose of 200 mg three to four times a day with careful observation for central nervous system side effects.

Gabapentin

In the patient in whom carbamazepine does not adequately control the pain of glossopharyngeal neuralgia, gabapentin (Neurontin) is a reasonable next step.[13] Practical guidelines for the use of gabapentin are summarized in Table 47–3.[16] Baseline clinical laboratory tests consisting of a complete blood count, blood chemistry, and urinalysis are obtained prior to beginning treatment with gabapentin. Treatment is initiated with a 300 mg bedtime dose for 2 nights and is increased in 300-mg increments (in equally divided doses) every 2 days, as side effects allow, until pain relief is obtained or a total dose of 1800 mg daily is reached. At this point, if the patient has experienced partial relief of pain, the drug is carefully titrated upward in 100-mg doses. Rarely will more than 2400 mg be required. The patient is cautioned regarding side effects including dizziness, sedation, confusion, and rash.

Baclofen

Baclofen (Lioresal) has been reported to be of value in some patients suffering from glossopharyngeal neuralgia who fail to obtain relief from carbamazepine and gabapentin.[17] Practical guidelines for the use of baclofen are summarized in Table 47–4.[16] Baseline clinical laboratory tests consisting of a complete blood count, blood chemistry, and urinalysis are obtained prior to beginning treatment with baclofen. Treatment is initiated with a 10-mg bedtime dose for 2 nights. The drug is increased in 10-mg increments (in equally divided doses) every 5 days, as side effects allow, until pain relief is

---

Table 47–2

Guidelines for Use of Carbamazepine in Treatment of Glossopharyngeal Neuralgia

1. Order baseline complete blood count, blood chemistry, and urinalysis prior to initiation of therapy.
2. Start therapy slowly if the pain is not out of control.
3. Begin with a 200-mg bedtime dose for 2 nights.
4. Drug is increased in 200-mg increments in equally divided doses every 2 days, as side effects allow, until pain relief is obtained or a total dose of 1200 mg daily is reached.
5. Patient is cautioned regarding side effects including dizziness, sedation, confusion, and rash.
6. Carefully monitor laboratory data to avoid life-threatening blood dyscrasias.
7. Discontinue drug at the first sign of blood count abnormality or rash.
8. After pain relief is obtained, the patient should be left at this dose of carbamazepine for at least 6 months before tapering.
9. Patient should be informed that under no circumstances should the dose of drug be changed or the prescription refilled or discontinued without consultation with the pain management specialist.
10. Patient should be aware that premature tapering or discontinuation may lead to recurrence of pain with subsequent pain control being more difficult.
11. Hospitalize patients for pain emergencies.

Table 47–3

Guidelines for Use of Gabapentin in Treatment of Glossopharyngeal Neuralgia

1. Order baseline complete blood count, blood chemistry, and urinalysis.
2. Begin treatment with 300 mg bedtime dose for 2 nights.
3. Increase drug in 300-mg increments in equally divided doses every 2 days, as side effects allow, until pain relief is obtained or a total dose of 300 mg daily is reached.
4. If patient has experienced partial pain relief, blood level is drawn and the drug is carefully titrated upward using 100-mg tablets.
5. Rarely will more than 2400 mg be required to control pain.
6. Patient is cautioned regarding side effects including dizziness, sedation, confusion, and rash

obtained or a total dose of 80 mg daily is reached. The patient is cautioned regarding side effects including dizziness, sedation, confusion, and rash. Baclofen has significant central nervous system and hepatic side effects and is poorly tolerated by most patients. As with carbamazepine, careful monitoring of laboratory data is indicated during the initial use of this drug.

Neural Blockade

Glossopharyngeal Nerve Block

The use of glossopharyngeal nerve block with a local anesthetic and a steroid serves as an excellent adjunct to the phar-

macologic treatment of glossopharyngeal neuralgia.[11,12] The use of this technique allows rapid palliation of pain while oral medications are being titrated to effective levels.

Clinically Relevant Anatomy

The glossopharyngeal nerve exits from the jugular foramen in proximity to the vagus and accessory nerve and the internal jugular vein.[18] All three nerves lie in the groove between the internal jugular vein and internal carotid artery (Fig. 47–3). Inadvertent puncture of either vessel during glossopharyngeal nerve block can result in intravascular injection or hematoma formation. Even small amounts of local anesthetic injected into the carotid artery at this location can produce profound local anesthetic toxicity. The landmarks for glossopharyngeal nerve block involve locating the styloid process of the temporal bone. This osseous process represents the calcification of the cephalad end of the stylohyoid ligament. Although usually easy to identify, if ossification is limited it may be difficult to locate with the exploring needle.

Technique

The patient is placed in the supine position. An imaginary line is visualized running from the mastoid process to the angle of the mandible (Fig. 47–4). The styloid process should lie just below the midpoint of this line. The skin is prepped with antiseptic solution. A 22-gauge 1½-inch needle attached to a 10-mL syringe is advanced at this midpoint location in a plane perpendicular to the skin. The styloid process should be encountered within 3 cm (Fig. 47–5). After contact is made,

---

Table 47–4
Guidelines for Use of Baclofen for Treatment of Glossopharyngeal Neuralgia
1. Order baseline complete blood count, blood chemistry, and urinalysis
2. Begin treatment with 10 mg at bedtime for 2 nights
3. Increase drug in 10-mg increments in equally divided doses every 5 days, as side effects allow, until pain is controlled or a total dose of 80 mg daily is reached.
4. Patient is cautioned regarding side effects including dizziness, sedation, confusion, and rash.

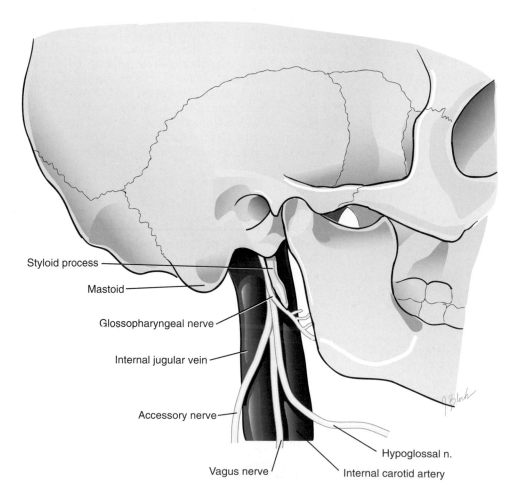

Styloid process
Mastoid
Glossopharyngeal nerve
Internal jugular vein
Accessory nerve
Vagus nerve
Hypoglossal n.
Internal carotid artery

FIGURE 47–3 ■ Clinically relevant anatomy for glossopharyngeal nerve block. (From Waldman SD: Atlas of Interventional Pain Management, 2nd ed. Philadelphia, Saunders, 2003, p 69.)

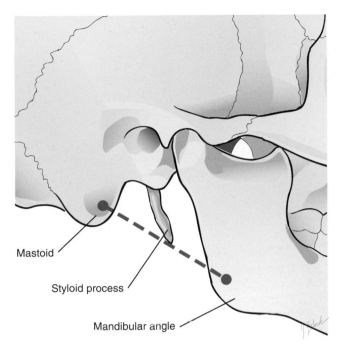

FIGURE 47–4 ■ In order to perform a glossopharyngeal nerve block, the patient is placed in the supine position and an imaginary line is visualized running from the mastoid process to the angle of the mandible. (From Waldman SD: Atlas of Interventional Pain Management, 2nd ed. Philadelphia, Saunders, 2003, p 71.)

Mastoid

Styloid process

Mandibular angle

the needle is withdrawn and walked-off the styloid process posteriorly. As soon as bony contact is lost and careful aspiration reveals no blood or cerebrospinal fluid, 7 mL of 0.5% preservative-free lidocaine combined with 80 mg of methylprednisolone is injected in incremental doses. Subsequent daily nerve blocks are carried out in a similar manner, substituting 40 mg of methylprednisolone for the initial 80-mg dose.[19] The nerve may also be blocked via an intraoral approach (Fig. 47–6). Either approach may be used for breakthrough pain in patients who previously experienced adequate pain control with oral medications.

Potential complications of glossopharyngeal nerve block are related to trauma of the internal jugular and carotid arteries.[19] Hematoma formation and intravascular injection of local anesthetic with subsequent toxicity can represent significant problems for the patient.

Neurodestructive Procedures

The injection of small quantities of alcohol, phenol, and glycerol into the area of the glossopharyngeal nerve has been shown to provide long-term relief for patients suffering from glossopharyngeal neuralgia who have not responded to optimal trials of the previously mentioned therapies.[18] Destruction of the glossopharyngeal nerve can also be carried out by creating a radiofrequency lesion, under biplanar fluoroscopic guidance.[20] This procedure is reserved for patients

FIGURE 47–5 ■ Glossopharyngeal nerve block technique. (From Waldman SD: Atlas of Interventional Pain Management, 2nd ed. Philadelphia, Saunders, 2003, p 71.)

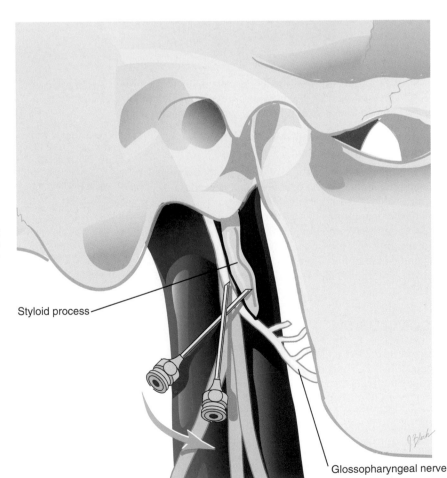

Styloid process

Glossopharyngeal nerve

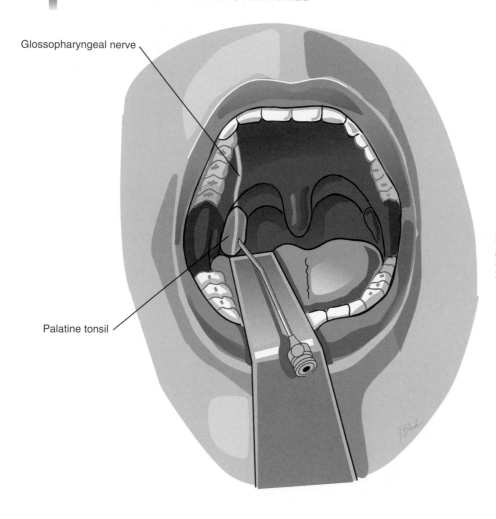

Glossopharyngeal nerve

Palatine tonsil

FIGURE 47–6 ■ Intraoral technique for glossopharyngeal nerve block. (From Waldman SD: Atlas of Interventional Pain Management, 2nd ed. Philadelphia, Saunders, 2003, p 74.)

who have failed all the treatments described for intractable glossopharyngeal neuralgia and whose physical status otherwise precludes more invasive neurosurgical treatments.

Microvascular Decompression of the Glossopharyngeal Root

Microvascular decompression of the glossopharyngeal root (Jannetta technique) is the neurosurgical procedure of choice for intractable glossopharyngeal neuralgia.[21] The theoretical basis of the operation is that glossopharyngeal neuralgia is, in fact, a compressive mononeuropathy. The operation consists of identifying the glossopharyngeal root close to the brain stem and isolating the offending compressing blood vessel. A sponge is interposed between the vessel and nerve, thereby effecting a cure.

■ CONCLUSION

The pain specialist should be aware of the severity of pain associated with glossopharyngeal neuralgia as well as the psychological effects of persistent, uncontrolled, severe pain. Correctly used, pharmacologic therapy combined with neural blockade should control the pain of glossopharyngeal neuralgia in the vast majority of cases. Surgical therapy should be considered if conservative therapy fails to provide long-lasting relief for patients suffering from glossopharyngeal neuralgia.

References

1. Weisenburg TH: Cerebellopontine tumor diagnosed for six years as tic doloureux. JAMA 54:1600, 1910.
2. Harris W: Persistent pain in lesions of the peripheral and central nervous system. Brain 44:557, 1921.
3. Doyle JB: A study of four cases of glossopharyngeal neuralgia. Arch Neurol Psychiatry 9:34, 1923.
4. Dandy WE: Glossopharyngeal neuralgia: Its diagnosis and treatment. Arch Surg 15:198, 1927.
5. Katusic S, Williams DB, Beard CM, et al: Incidence and clinical features of glossopharyngeal neuralgia, Rochester, Minn, 1945-1984. Neuroepidemiology 10:266, 1991.
6. Katusic S, Williams DB, Beard CM, et al: Epidemiology and clinical features of idiopathic trigeminal neuralgia and glossopharyngeal neuralgia: Similarities and differences, Rochester, Minn, 1945-1984. Neuroepidemiology 10:276, 1991.
7. Keith WS: Glossopharyngeal neuralgia. Brain 55:357, 1932.
8. Riley HA, German WJ, Words H: Glossopharyngeal neuralgia initiating or associated with cardiac arrest. Trans Am Neurol Assoc 68:28, 1942.
9. Chlamers AC, Olsen JL: Glossopharyngeal neuralgia with syncope and neck mass. Otolaryngol Head Neck Surg 100:252, 1989.
10. Rozen TD: Trigeminal neuralgia and glossopharyngeal neuralgia. Neurol Clin 22:185, 2004.
11. Donohoe CD, Waldman SD: The targeted physical examination. Intern Med 12:30, 1991.
12. Waldman SD: The role of nerve blocks in the management of headache and facial pain In Diamond S (ed): Practical Headache Management. Boston, Kluwer, 1993, p 99.
13. Ceylan S, Karakus A, Duru S, et al: Glossopharyngeal neuralgia: A study of 6 cases. Neurosurg Rev 20:196, 1997.
14. Donohoe CD, Waldman SD: Headache and facial pain conditions not detected by CT and MRI. Intern Med 12:37, 1991.

15. Saviolo S, Fiasconaro G: Treatment of glossopharyngeal neuralgia with carbamazepine. Br Heart J 58:291, 1987.
16. Waldman SD: Trigeminal neuralgia. Intern Med 13:48, 1992.
17. Waldman SD: The role of nerve blocks in pain management. In Wcincr R (ed): Comprehensive Guide to Pain Management. Orlando, PMD Press, 1990, p 10.1.
18. Bajaj P, Gemavat M, Singh DP: Ninth cranial nerve block in the management of malignant pain in its territory. Pain Clinic 6:153, 1993.
19. Waldman SD: Glossopharyngeal nerve block. In Waldman SD: Atlas of Interventional Pain Management. Philadelphia, Saunders, 2004, p 68.
20. Arbit E, Krol G: Percutaneous radiofrequency neurolysis guided by computerized tomography for the treatment of glossopharyngeal neuralgia. Neurosurgery 29:580, 1991.
21. Resnick DK, Jannetta PJ, Bissonnette D, et al: Microvascular decompression for glossopharyngeal neuralgia. Neurosurgery 36:64, 1995.

48

Giant Cell Arteritis

Brian L. Hazleman

■ HISTORICAL CONSIDERATIONS

The earliest description of giant cell arteritis (GCA) may have been in the 10th century in the Tadkwat of Ali Iba Isu, where removal of the temporal artery was recommended as the treatment. Jan Van Eyck's work depicting the Holy Virgin with Canon Van der Paele (1436) and Pieri di Cosimo's portrait of Fracesco Gamberti (1505) both show signs of prominent temporal arteries. Contemporary accounts document rheumatic pains and difficulty attending morning service with possible stiffness and general ill health. No further evidence for the existence of GCA exists until the late 19th century, when recognizable descriptions were documented in the British Isles. Jonathan Hutchinson in 1890 described "a peculiar form of thrombotic arteritis of the aged, which is sometimes productive of gangrene." For 40 years, there seem to be no published reports until Horton and colleagues (1932) described the typical histologic evidence of temporal artery biopsy.[1] In 1960, a report of 67 patients emphasized the occurrence of "anarthritic rheumatism" (an earlier title for polymyalgia rheumatica [PMR]) in GCA, providing clinical evidence for the relationship between PMR and GCA.[2]

■ THE CLINICAL SYNDROME

Key clinical features of GCA are the following:

1. There are a wide range of symptoms, but most patients have clinical findings related to involved arteries.
2. Frequent features include fatigue, headaches, jaw claudication, loss of vision, scalp tenderness, PMR, and aortic arch syndrome (decreased or absent peripheral pulses, discrepancies of blood pressure, arterial bruits).
3. Unlike other forms of vasculitis, GCA rarely involves the skin, kidneys, and lungs.
4. The ESR is usually highly elevated but may infrequently be normal.

The mean age of onset is approximately 70 years, and the condition is very rare in those younger than 50 years. Women are affected about three times as often as men. The onset can be dramatic but is usually insidious and the constitutional symptoms, including fever, anorexia, weight loss, and depression, are present in the majority of patients and may be an early or even an initial finding and can lead to a delay in diagnosis. Patients may present with a pyrexia of unknown origin and be subjected to many investigations. The condition causes a wide range of symptoms, but most patients have clinical features related to affected arteries. Common features include headache and tenderness of the scalp, particularly around the temporal and occipital arteries.

The most common symptom of GCA is headache, which is present in more than two thirds of patients. It usually begins early in the course of the disease and may be the presenting symptom. The pain is severe and localized to the temple. However, it may be occipital or be less defined and precipitated by brushing the hair. It can be severe even when the arteries are clinically normal and, conversely, may subside even though the disease remains active. The nature of the pain varies; some patients describe it as shooting and others as a more steady ache. Scalp tenderness is common, particularly around the temporal and occipital arteries, and may disturb sleep. Tender spots or nodules or even small skin infarcts may be present for several days. The vessels are thickened, tender, and nodular with absent or reduced pulsation. Occasionally they are red and clearly visible.

Visual disturbances have been described in 25% to 50% of cases, although the incidence of visual loss is now regarded as much lower, about 6% to 10% in most series, which is probably due to earlier recognition and treatment.[3] Visual symptoms are an ophthalmic emergency; if they are identified and treated urgently, blindness is almost entirely preventable. The variety of ocular lesions is essentially due to occlusion of the various orbital or ocular arteries. Blindness is the most serious and irreversible feature. The visual loss is usually sudden, painless, and permanent; it may vary from mistiness of vision, or involvement of a part of the visual field, to complete blindness. There is a risk of the second eye being involved if the patient is not treated aggressively. Involvement of the second eye can occur within 24 hours. Blindness may be the initial presentation in cases of GCA, but it tends to follow other symptoms by several weeks or months.

The incidence of various ocular manifestations given in the literature varies widely because the incidence depends on a number of factors—the most important of which is how early the diagnosis of GCA is established and the treatment started. It also depends on the rigor with which cases are diagnosed. The most common are optic nerve ischemic lesions. These are usually anterior and are associated with partial or more frequently complete visual loss. They can occasionally be posterior, which can lead to partial or complete loss. Extraocular mobility disorders are usually transient and not associated with visual loss. Pupillary abnormalities can be seen secondary to visual loss. Cerebral ischemic lesions producing visual loss are rare, as are anterior segment ischemic lesions and choroidal infarcts. Retinal ischemic lesions can affect the central retinal artery, and this is associated with severe visual loss. The cilioretinal artery can be occluded but is invariably associated with anterior ischemic optic neuropathy (AION).

Pain on chewing, due to claudication of the jaw muscles, occurs in up to two thirds of patients. Tingling in the tongue, loss of taste, and pain in the mouth and throat can also occur, presumably due to vascular insufficiency. The widespread nature of the vasculitis has been previously mentioned. Clinical evidence of large artery involvement is present in 10% to 15% of cases, and in some instances, aortic dissection and rupture occur.

Less common features of GCA include hemiparesis, peripheral neuropathy, deafness, depression, and confusion. Involvement of the coronary arteries may lead to myocardial infarction. Aortic regurgitation and congestive cardiac failure may also occur. Abnormalities of thyroid and liver function are well described. An association between carpal tunnel syndrome and PMR has been noted by several authors. Local corticosteroid injection and/or surgical decompression is sometimes necessary.

■ EPIDEMIOLOGY

GCA almost exclusively affects the white population. Most reports originate from northern Europe and parts of the northern United States; however, the diseases are recognizable worldwide. Both PMR and GCA affect elderly people and are seldom diagnosed before the age of 50 years (Table 48–1). A study of biopsy-proven GCA diagnosed from 1950 to 1985 in Olmsted County, Minnesota, demonstrated average annual incidence and prevalence of 17 and 223, respectively, per 100,000 inhabitants aged 50 years or more.[4] The age-adjusted incidence rates were approximately three times higher in women than in men.[4] In addition, the incidence increased with age in both sexes.[4] The incidence also increased significantly during the period 1950 to 1985 for females but decreased for

males over the same period.[4] The incidence rates reported from Olmsted County are similar to those in Göteborg, Sweden.[5] Between 1970 and 1975, the incidence rate was 16.8 per 100,000 inhabitants in Sweden versus 18.3 per 100,000 in Minnesota.[4,5]

The temporal arteries and aortas of all adults who died in Malmö throughout 1 year were examined, and although active GCA was not found, evidence of previous arteritis was found in 1.7% of the 889 cases.[6] It was found that in 75% of these subjects there had been either biopsy evidence or a clinical history suggestive of GCA.[6] This study certainly suggests that GCA may be underdiagnosed, but further studies are required.

■ RELATIONSHIP BETWEEN POLYMYALGIA RHEUMATICA AND GIANT CELL ARTERITIS

In recent years, GCA and PMR have increasingly been considered as closely related conditions.[7,8] The two syndromes form a spectrum of diseases and affect the same types of patients. The conditions may occur independently or may occur in the same patient, either together or separately.

In patients with PMR who have no symptoms or signs of GCA, positive temporal biopsies are found in 10% to 15%. Those wishing to preserve the identity of the two diseases base their argument on the latter figure and on the failure to find evidence of arteritis in many patients followed for many years with polymyalgia. Conversely, there are many similarities between the two conditions. The age and sex distributions are similar, the biopsy findings show an identical pattern, and the laboratory features are similar, even though many are nonspecific inflammatory changes. In addition, there is similarity in the myalgia, the associated systemic features, and in the response to corticosteroid therapy.

The onset of myalgic symptoms may precede, coincide with, or follow that of the arteritic symptoms. No difference has been found between the characteristics for those myalgia patients with a positive biopsy and those with no histologic evidence of arteritis. Mild aching and stiffness may persist for months after other features of GCA have remitted. There is little evidence to suggest that the musculoskeletal symptoms are related to vasculitis. Many patients with GCA do not have PMR, even when large vessels are involved. In addition, the finding of joint swelling in some patients and the production of pain by the injection of 5% saline solution into the acromioclavicular, sternoclavicular, and manubriosternal joints suggests that PMR in some patients may be a particular form of proximal synovitis.

■ CLINICAL TESTING

One of the most frequently performed diagnostic tests in suspected cases of GCA is temporal artery biopsy (Table 48–2). The choice of patients for biopsy depends on local circumstances, but a pragmatic policy would be to select only patients with suspected GCA (not those with obvious clinical features). Patients with PMR alone would need to be monitored carefully for development of clinical GCA would not need a biopsy.

Table 48–1

Epidemiologic Features of Giant Cell Arteritis

Peak incidence at ages 60-75 years
Sex distribution of three women to one man
Annual incidence and prevalence of biopsy-proven
  GCA are 17 and 223/100,000, respectively.
Mainly affects white people, but can occur worldwide
Familial aggregation has been reported suggesting a
  genetic association.

Table 48–2

Diagnostic Value of Temporal Artery Biopsy for Giant Cell Arteritis

Perform biopsy if diagnosis is in doubt, particularly if systemic symptoms predominate.

Biopsy is most useful within 24 hours of starting treatment, but do not delay treatment for sake of biopsy.

A negative biopsy result does not exclude GCA.

A positive result helps to prevent later doubts about diagnosis, particularly if treatment causes complications.

Table 48–3

Histologic Features of Giant Cell Arteritis

Histologically, there is a panarteritis with giant cell granuloma.

The involvement is patchy and skip lesions are often found.

Clinically, the artery is enlarged and nodular with a reduced or absent lumen.

The aorta and other arteries are involved.

One third of patients with signs and symptoms of cranial arteritis may have negative temporal artery biopsies, which may be due to the localized involvement of arteries in the head and neck. Temporal artery biopsy may show arteritis even after 14 days of corticosteroid treatment, so biopsy may be worthwhile for up to 2 weeks of treatment. However, the biopsy should be obtained as soon as possible and treatment for suspected GCA should not be delayed simply to allow a biopsy to be carried out.

Clinicians vary greatly in their approach to temporal artery biopsy. Some believe it emphasizes the value of a positive histologic diagnosis, especially months or years later when side effects of the steroid treatment have developed. Others feel that a high false-negative rate diminishes the value of the procedure. In most instances, the high false-negative rate can be attributed to the focal nature of involvement of the superficial temporal artery by the inflammatory process.

The histologic appearance of GCA is one of the most distinctive of vascular disorders (Table 48–3). The dense granulomatous inflammatory infiltrates that characterize the acute stages of the disease resemble those of Takayasu arteritis, but the clinicopathologic features in patients with positive temporal artery biopsies are diagnostic. The arteritis is histologically a panarteritis with giant cell granuloma formation, often in close proximity to a disrupted internal elastic lamina. Large and medium-sized arteries are affected; the involvement is patchy and skip lesions are often found. More patients with skip lesions have normal arteries to palpation but do not have a more benign disease.

The gross features are not characteristic. The vessels are enlarged and nodular and have little or no lumen. Thrombosis often develops at sites of active inflammation. Later, these areas may recanalize. The lumen is narrowed by intimal proliferation. This is a common finding in arteries and may result from advancing age, nearby chronic inflammation, or low blood flow. The adventitia is usually invaded by mononuclear and occasionally polymorphonuclear inflammatory cells, often cuffing the vasa vasorum; here fibrous proliferation is frequent. The changes in the media are dominated by the giant cells, which vary from small cells with two to three nuclei up to masses of 100 nm containing many nuclei. Here there is invasion by mononuclear cells resembling histiocytes. Fibrinoid necrosis is infrequent. Giant cells are not seen in all sections and, therefore, are not required for the diagnosis if other features are compatible. The more sections that are examined in the area of arteritis, the more likely it is that giant cells will be found. Fragments of elastic tissue can be demonstrated within giant cells, which are surrounded with plasma cell and lymphocytic infiltration.

Corticosteroids reduce the inflammatory cell infiltrate so temporal artery biopsy should, if possible, be carried out before treatment is started. Therapy should not be delayed until a biopsy has been performed. Involvement of the aorta and its branches, the abdominal vessels, and the coronary arteries have all been described. GCA as a cause of aortic dissection has been recorded rarely at autopsy, and most exceptionally during life. This probably reflects the relatively low incidence of aortic involvement in GCA. It is of note that most patients have a history of hypertension in life or features of hypertensive disease at autopsy.

The ESR is usually greatly elevated and provides a useful means of monitoring treatment, although it must be appreciated that some elevation of the ESR may occur in otherwise healthy elderly people. A normal ESR is occasionally found in patients with active biopsy-proven disease. Repeated measurements may show raised ESRs after an initial normal value.

Anemia, usually of a mild hypochromic type, is common and resolves without specific treatment, but more marked normochromic anemia occasionally occurs and may be a presenting symptom. Leukocyte and differential counts are generally normal; platelet counts are also usually normal but may be increased. Protein electrophoresis may show a nonspecific rise in α_2-globulin with less frequent elevation of α_1-globulin and γ-globulin. Quantification of acute-phase proteins and α_1-antitrypsin, orosomucoid, haptoglobin, and C-reactive protein (CRP) are no more helpful than the ESR in the assessment of disease activity.

Abnormalities of thyroid and liver function have also been well described. In a retrospective survey of 59 cases of GCA, five patients with hyperthyroidism were identified.[9] The arteritis followed the thyrotoxicosis by intervals of 4 to 15 years in three cases, and in two it occurred simultaneously. In 250 patients with autoimmune thyroid disease, seven cases of PMR or GCA were identified. All cases occurred in women older than age 60, giving a prevalence of 9.3% in this age group.[10]

Raised serum values for alkaline phosphatase were found in up to 70% of patients with PMR, and transaminases in some cases were mildly elevated. Liver biopsies have shown portal and intralobular inflammation with focal liver cell necrosis and small epithelioid cell granuloma. The pathologic significance of these abnormalities is unclear.

Table 48–4

Treatment of Giant Cell Arteritis

Initial dose: Prednisolone 20-40 mg daily for 8 weeks. Patients with ocular symptoms may need up to 80 mg daily.
Reduce dose by 5 mg every 3-4 weeks until dose is 10 mg daily; then as for PMR (see Table 41–4).
Maintenance dose: about 3 mg daily may be required.
Comment: Recurrence of symptoms requires an increase in the prescribed dose.

■ TREATMENT

Corticosteroids are mandatory in the treatment of GCA; they reduce the incidence of complications, such as blindness, and rapidly relieve symptoms (Table 48–4). Nonsteroidal antiinflammatory drugs (NSAIDs) will lessen the painful symptoms, but they do not prevent arteritic complications. The response to corticosteroids is usually dramatic and occurs within days. Corticosteroid treatment has improved the quality of life for patients, although there is no evidence that therapy reduces the duration of the disease. A fear of vascular complications in those patients with a positive biopsy often leads to the use of high doses of corticosteroids. Recent studies have emphasized the importance of adopting a cautious and individual treatment schedule, and have highlighted the efficacy of lower doses of prednisolone.

Initially, the corticosteroids should be given in a sufficient dosage to control the disease and then maintained at the lowest dose that will control the symptoms and lower the ESR. In patients with GCA, corticosteroids should preferably be given after the diagnosis has been confirmed histologically. However, when GCA is strongly suspected, there should be no delay in starting therapy because the artery biopsy will still show inflammatory changes for several days after corticosteroids have been started and the result is unlikely to alter therapeutic decisions. If the temporal artery (or other artery) biopsy shows no arteritis but the suspicion of disease is strong, corticosteroid treatment should be started. The great danger is delaying therapy because blindness may occur at any time.

There are few clinical trials to help decide the correct initial dose. Most clinicians have strong views on the dose required but some are based on tradition and anecdote. The recommended initial dose for PMR/GCA varies from 10 mg to 100 mg prednisolone daily. Intravenous corticosteroids are occasionally used if there are visual complications. In practice, most clinicians use 10 to 20 mg prednisolone daily to treat PMR and 40 to 60 mg for GCA because of the higher risk of arteritic complications in cases of GCA. Some ophthalmologists suggest an initial dose of at least 60 mg as they have seen blindness occur at a lower dose. However, this has to be balanced against the potential complication of high dosage in this older age group. Patients should be advised that although they are taking a maintenance dose of steroids, any sudden exacerbation of symptoms, particularly sudden visual deterioration, requires an immediate increase in dose.

■ PROGNOSIS

Rapid reduction or withdrawal of corticosteroids has been reported to contribute to deaths in patients with GCA. Fortunately, complications are rare and the activity of the disease seems to decline steadily. Relapses are more likely during the initial 18 months of treatment and within 1 year of withdrawal of corticosteroids. There is no reliable method of predicting those most at risk, but arteritic relapses in patients who presented with pure PMR are unusual. Temporal artery biopsy does not seem helpful in predicting outcome.

Controversy exists over the expected duration of the disease. Most European studies within the last 20 years report that between one third and one half of the patients are able to discontinue corticosteroids after 2 years of treatment. Studies from the Mayo Clinic in the United States have reported a shorter duration of disease for both PMR (11 months was the median duration of treatment and three quarters of patients had stopped taking corticosteroids by 2 years) and GCA (most patients had stopped taking corticosteroids within 2 years).[11] The consensus seems to be that stopping treatment is feasible from 2 years onward.

Patients who are unable to reduce the dosage of prednisolone because of recurring symptoms or who develop serious corticosteroid-related side effects pose particular problems. Drugs such as azathioprine and methotrexate have not been shown to exert a corticosteroid-sparing effect in "corticosteroid-resistant" cases of PMR/GCA.

Between one fifth and one half of patients may experience serious treatment-related side effects. Serious side effects are significantly related to high initial doses, maintenance doses, cumulative doses, and increased duration of treatment. Side effects can be minimized by using low doses of prednisolone whenever possible.

In elderly people corticosteroid treatment carries the risk of increasing osteoporosis. Glucocorticoids have more effect on the spine than on the femur. Bisphosphonates such as etidronate and alendronate have been shown to be useful in retarding bone loss in the setting of prolonged corticosteroid use.

■ CONCLUSIONS

GCA is the prime medical emergency in ophthalmology because it may result in loss of vision in one or both eyes. This is preventable if patients are diagnosed early and treated immediately with high doses of corticosteroids.

References

1. Horton BT, Magath TB, Brown GE: An undescribed form of arteritis of the temporal vessels. Mayo Clin Proc 7:700, 1932.
2. Paulley JW, Hughes JP: Giant cell arteritis, or arteritis of the aged. BMJ 2:1562, 1960.
3. Rahman W, Rahman FZ: Giant cell (temporal) arteritis: An overview and update. Surv Ophthalmol 50:415, 2005.
4. Salvarani C, Gabriel SE, O'Fallon WM, et al: Epidemiology of polymyalgia rheumatica in Olmsted County, Minnesota, 1970-1991. Arthritis Rheum 38:369, 1995.
5. Nordborg C, Johansson H, Petursdottir V, Nordborg E: The epidemiology of biopsy-positive giant cell arteritis: Special reference to changes in the age of the population. Rheumatology 42:549, 2003.

6. Ostberg G: An arteritis with special reference to polymyalgia arteritica. Acta Pathol Microbiol Scand 237(Suppl):1, 1973.

7. Cantini F, Niccoli L, Storri L, et al: Are polymyalgia rheumatica and giant cell arteritis the same disease? Semin Arthritis Rheum 33:294, 2004.

8. Gonzalez-Gay MA: Giant cell arteritis and polymyalgia rheumatica: Two different but often overlapping conditions. Semin Arthritis Rheum 33:289, 2004.

9. Thomas RD, Croft DN: Thyrotoxicosis and giant cell arteritis. BMJ 2:408, 1974.

10. Nicholson GC, Gutteridge DH, Carroll WM, Armstrong BK: Autoimmune thyroid disease and giant cell arteritis: A review, case report, and epidemiological study. Aust NZ J Med 14:487, 1984.

11. Proven A, Gabriel SE, Orces C, et al: Glucocorticoid therapy in giant cell arteritis: Duration and adverse outcomes. Arthritis Rheum 49:703, 2003.

chapter 49

Pain of Ocular and Periocular Origin

Steven D. Waldman

Pain of ocular and periocular origin represents a special challenge to the pain management physician. The reasons that pain in this anatomic region are unique include the fact (1) that most diseases of the eye and periocular regions that cause blindness are relatively painless yet the fear of blindness is ever present in any patient with eye pain; (2) that most painful conditions of the eye and periocular region do not cause blindness in spite of the aforementioned fear to the contrary; (3) that both lay persons and most healthcare professionals approach any problem involving the eye with great fear and trepidation because of the potential for disastrous consequences if a mistake in diagnosis and/or treatment is made; (4) that the rich innervation afforded the cornea, conjunctiva, and periocular region means that even minor problems such as a superficial corneal abrasion can result in severe pain that is completely out of proportion to the scope and risk of the injury; and (5) that if the pathologic process responsible for the patient's pain resides in the eye, an ophthalmologist is required and if it does not involve the eye the ophthalmologist has little to offer, thus leaving the pain management physician to sort out the cause and provide the treatment for the patient's pain. It has been my experience that an element of each of these factors is present in almost every patient presenting with the complaint of ocular and periocular pain. This makes the care of such patients more challenging to treat in comparison to less-threatening painful conditions such as low back pain. That being said, as a practical matter, the management of the vast majority of patients presenting with ocular and periocular pain is relatively straightforward. For the purposes of this chapter, we must accept the simple fact that primary diseases of the eye are best treated by an ophthalmologist and the pain management specialist's role in this setting is to attempt to identify those patients with primary eye disease and timely refer them to the ophthalmologist for definitive treatment of the ocular pathologic process responsible for the pain. For those patients suffering from ocular and periocular pain that is unrelated to primary eye disease, it usually becomes the responsibility of the pain management specialist to identify and treat the painful condition. In the following chapter, I provide an overview of primary eye diseases that require the treatment of an ophthalmologist and discuss those diseases that may cause ocular and periocular pain that do not find the nidus of their symptomatology in the eye and are best treated by the pain management specialist.

■ THE SENSORY INNERVATION OF THE EYE

The primary sensory innervation of the eye is mediated via the trigeminal ganglion.[1] The first division of the trigeminal nerve (V_1 ophthalmic division) carries the bulk of the pain impulses from the eye itself via the long ciliary branches of the nasociliary nerve (Fig. 49–1). The infratrochlear branch of the nasociliary nerve also provides sensory innervation to the medial portion of the eyelids, the adjacent nose, and the lacrimal sac. Trigeminal fibers intimately associated with the intraorbital parasympathetic ganglion and its parasympathetic fibers as well as the second cervical ganglion and its postganglionic sympathetic fibers may also subserve ocular and periocular pain. Other branches of the first division of the trigeminal nerve, the frontal and lacrimal nerves, provide sensory innervation to the upper eyelid, forehead, and the frontal sinus and the lacrimal gland and portions of the conjunctiva, respectively. Numerous fibers from the sphenopalatine ganglion also interact with trigeminal somatic fibers as well as the sympathetic and parasympathetic ganglia and fibers just mentioned and may serve an important role in some painful conditions involving the eye such as Sluder's neuralgia and cluster headache. The second division of the trigeminal nerve (V_2 maxillary) provides sensory innervation to the lower eyelid and conjunctiva via the infraorbital nerve.

Interestingly, the cornea receives the vast majority of the sensory innervation of the eye, with the density of sensory innervation of the cornea rivaled only by that of the anal mucosa.[2] Teleologically, this density of sensory innervation presumably serves to enhance the mechanisms to protect our most important sense organ by allowing the blink response and the convergence avoidance reflex to protect the eye.

In addition to the dense concentration of pain receptors to transmit the afferent sensation of pain via the trigeminal ganglion to higher centers, thermal receptors for cold and heat are also found throughout the eye. These mechanoreceptors are found in both the cornea and iris and may be responsible for afferent traffic carried via the trigeminal system that may be perceived by the patient as ocular pain even when no actual ocular tissue damage has occurred. Stretching of the extraocular muscles as well as the dural covering of the optic nerve by mass or tumor may also result in a sensation of ocular pain even in the absence of actual nerve damage.

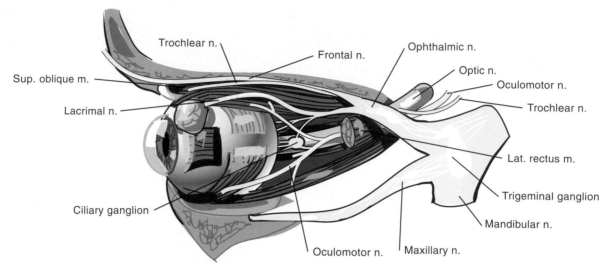

FIGURE 49–1 ■ The sensory innervation of the eye.

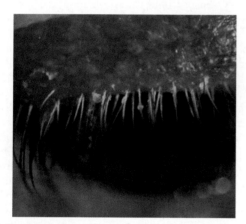

FIGURE 49–2 ■ Blepharitis. (From Swartz MH: Textbook of Physical Diagnosis, 4th ed. Philadelphia, WB Saunders, 2002, p 215.)

■ COMMON CAUSES OF OCULAR PAIN

The following section presents a brief description of the most common causes of eye pain encountered in clinical practice. The patient suffering from eye pain will often present in an anxious state armed with a detailed history of his or her symptoms. The pain management specialist should begin the evaluation of such patients first by offering reassurance and a calm demeanor and second by rapidly assessing whether the clinical condition presents immediate risk to the patient's vision so that immediate ophthalmologic referral can be undertaken.

Styes (Hordeolums)

Styes or hordeolums are probably the most common cause of eye pain encountered in clinical practice. Styes are the result of bacterial infection of the small oil-producing meibomian glands and/or the eyelash follicles at the margin of the eyelid (Fig. 49–2).[3] Over 98% of styes are caused by *Staphylococcus aureus*.[4] These pus-filled abscesses can appear quite suddenly and can run the gamut from small self-limited infections that produce little pain and resolve on their own to rapidly

growing, extremely painful abscesses that requires immediate surgical incision and drainage and systemic antibiotics for resolution. If identified early, the use of non–neomycin-containing antibiotic ointment such as gentamicin or polymyxin-B and bacitracin ophthalmic ointment combined with frequent applications of warm moist packs will usually resolve the problem.[4] If fever is present or the stye does not drain with conservative therapy, systemic antibiotics and immediate ophthalmologic referral for surgical incision and drainage is indicated.[5] If untreated, what begins as a simple localized folliculitis or meibomianitis can evolve into a vision- and life-threatening periorbital cellulitis that has the potential to spread to the adjacent central nervous system.

Corneal Abrasions

Corneal abrasions are another frequent cause of eye pain that prompt patients to seek urgent medical attention. The unique nature of the sensory innervation of the cornea results in the patient's perception of a foreign body in the eye any time the superficial corneal stroma is injured and the C-type polymodal nociceptors that richly innervate the cornea are stimulated. A foreign body sensation is usually felt by the patient as being located under the upper eyelid even when there is no foreign body present, and damage is limited to the corneal stroma. The continued firing of the polymodal receptors and recruitment of the corneal mechanoreceptors are probably responsible for this foreign body sensation, which occurs in almost all patients with corneal abrasion even in the absence of a foreign body.

Patients presenting with corneal abrasion will usually relate a history of grit or a foreign body being blowing into the eye or of minor mechanical trauma to the cornea during the insertion of contact lens or while playing sports.[6,7] Fluorescein staining will usually reveal the damage to the corneal stroma and rarely will a foreign body be seen.[8] The patient will bitterly complain of severe pain that is out of proportion to the apparent injury and will insist that there is something trapped under the upper eyelid even after repeated attempts to convince the patient to the contrary. Photophobia and excessive lacrimation as well as scleral and conjunctival

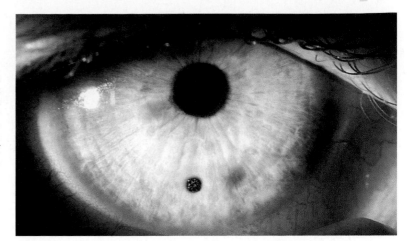

FIGURE 49–3 ■ An impacted metallic corneal foreign body is a common injury associated with drilling or grinding steel without protective goggles. These particles normally have insufficient energy to pass through the cornea and so lodge superficially. They become surrounded by a ring of rust within a few days and this should be lifted off with a sharp needle or dental burr under topical anesthesia to prevent delayed healing. (From Spalton DJ: Atlas of Clinical Ophthalmology, 3rd ed. Philadelphia, Mosby, 2005, p 170.)

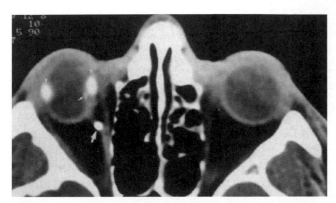

FIGURE 49–4 ■ CT scan shows intraconal, metallic foreign bodies just medial to the medial rectus *(large arrow)* and intraocular *(small arrow).* Scleral band is in place at the right *(arrowheads).* (From Haaga JR, Lanzieri C: CT and MR Imaging of the Whole Body, 4th ed. St. Louis, Mosby, 2003, vol 1, p 479.)

injection are often present, as is a significant substrate of anxiety.

In the presence of corneal abrasion, the clinician should evert the upper eyelid and rinse the eye with copious amounts of sterile saline solution to remove any residual foreign body that may not be readily apparent on initial investigation. If the corneal abrasion is the result of an accident that occurred during hammering or the use of power tools, a careful search for a metallic foreign body should be undertaken and a plain radiograph or CT scan of the orbit and orbital contents should be obtained to rule out occult intraocular metallic foreign body, which can present a significant risk to vision if undetected (Figs. 49–3 and 49–4). Treatment with non–neomycin-containing antibiotic ointment such as gentamicin or polymyxin-B and bacitracin ophthalmic ointment combined with patching of the eye and a large dose of reassurance will usually resolve the problem.[9]

Conjunctivitis

Infection of the conjunctiva is a common cause of eye pain. Caused by bacteria, fungus, or virus, conjunctivitis can range from a mild self-limited disease requiring no treatment to a purulent eye infection that can be quite painful and upsetting to the patient.[10] Bacterial and viral conjunctivitis, which is

also known as "pink eye," can be contagious; and all patients suffering from conjunctivitis should be instructed in good hand-washing techniques and informed of the need to sterilize fomites that they have in common with the family and coworkers (e.g., copy machines, faucets, telephones, computer keyboards). In addition to infectious causes, conjunctivitis can also be caused by environmental irritants, including pollen, dust, smog, and fumes.[11]

The patient with conjunctivitis will present with a red, irritated and painful eye that is often associated with excessive lacrimation and some degree of photophobia (Fig. 49–5). A purulent discharge is also often present. If the discharge is severe, the patient may awaken with the eyelids stuck together, resulting in extreme anxiety for the patient and often results in trips to the nearest emergency department for treatment. Treatment of acute conjunctivitis begins with reassurance and the use of a warm moist pack to the affected eye to afford symptomatic relief. Non–neomycin-containing antibiotic eye drops or ointment such as gentamicin or polymyxin-B and bacitracin should be used, with care being taken to avoid touching the affected eye with the dropper or the tip of the tube of antibiotic ointment to avoid reinfection.[12] If the possibility of sexually transmitted conjunctivitis is present, a culture should be taken and systemic antibiotics and ophthalmologic consultation on an urgent basis is indicated.[13]

Glaucoma

Glaucoma is the most common eye disease that results in blindness in the United States. It is not a single disease but a group of diseases that have in common dysfunction of the circulation and drainage of the aqueous humor inside the eyeball.[14] Glaucoma is rarely seen in the absence of trauma or a congenital abnormality of the globe before the age of 40. It occurs more commonly in blacks and those with a family history of glaucoma. Any severe trauma to the globe increases the risk of glaucoma.

For purposes of this discussion the pain management specialist must be aware that there are two types of glaucoma: (1) open-angle glaucoma and (2) angle-closure glaucoma.[15] A comparison of both types of this vision-threatening disease is provided in Table 49–1. Open-angle glaucoma has been called the "silent thief" in that the disease presents with little or no symptoms and gradually causes permanent eye damage due

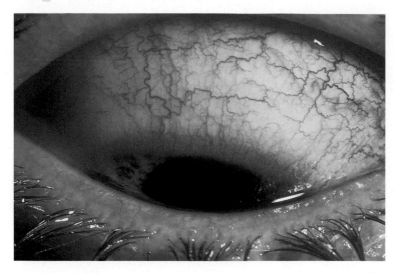

FIGURE 49–5 ■ Hyperemia of the conjunctiva may occur as part of any acute inflammatory process or in response to chronic irritative factors. There is an increase in the number, caliber, and tortuosity of the vessels, producing a characteristic bright red appearance. Hyperemia is often associated with increased vascular permeability and edema or cellular infiltration. (From Spalton DJ: Atlas of Clinical Ophthalmology, 3rd ed. Philadelphia, Mosby, 2005, p 65.)

Table 49–1

Comparison of Open-Angle and Angle-Closure Glaucoma

	Open-Angle Glaucoma	*Angle-Closure Glaucoma*
Occurrence	85% of all glaucoma	15% of all glaucoma
Cause	Unknown	Closed angle prevents aqueous drainage
Age at onset	Variable	Age 50 years or older
Anterior chamber	Usually normal	Shallow
Chamber angle	Normal	Narrow
Symptoms	Insidious loss of vision, no pain early in disease	Acute pain, halos around lights, vomiting, headache
Cupping of disc	Progressive if untreated	After untreated attacks
Visual fields	Peripheral visual fields affected early, central vision affected later	Loss occurs as disease progresses
Ocular pressure	Progressively higher as disease progresses	High as disease progresses
Other signs	None	Fixed, partially dilated pupil, red eye, steamy cornea
Treatment	Medical, laser surgery	Surgical
Prognosis	Good if diagnosed early, poor if treatment delayed	Good if treated early, poor if treatment delayed

Modified from Swartz MH: Textbook of Physical Diagnosis, 4th ed. Philadelphia, WB Saunders, 2002, p 235.

to increased intraocular pressure, which causes ischemic damage to the optic nerve. Open-angle glaucoma is caused by an inability of aqueous humor to drain from the anterior chamber of the eye even though the angle between the iris and cornea is opened (Fig. 49–6). Initially, only the peripheral vision is affected, but as the disease progresses the patient may present with painless vision loss and complain of tunnel vision. Fundoscopic examination will reveal disc cupping (Fig. 49–7). Because of the lack of pain associated with open-angle glaucoma, patients with this disease will rarely present to the pain management physician, although it should be remembered that all patients older than age 60 are at risk for glaucoma and thus an inquiry regarding visual loss should be part of every pain management assessment in this age group.

In contradistinction to open-angle glaucoma, the pain management physician will in all likelihood encounter patients with eye pain and visual loss that may be the result of angle-closure glaucoma. Angle-closure glaucoma occurs when the angle between the iris and the cornea becomes blocked, impeding the drainage of aqueous humor (Fig. 49–8). Angle-closure glaucoma represents a true ophthalmologic emergency, and failure to rapidly identify the disease and help the patient receive immediate ophthalmologic care will invariably result in permanent visual loss.[16] The patient with acute angle-closure glaucoma will present with the acute onset of severe eye pain, blurred vision, the complaint of a halo effect around lights, nausea and vomiting, and a red eye. The cornea may appear steamy, like looking though a steamy window. The pupil may be poorly reactive or fixed in mid position, and the iris may have a whorled appearance (Fig. 49–9). The patient will appear acutely ill in contradistinction to the chronically ill-appearing patient with temporal arteritis, which can also present in this age group. The onset of angle-closure glaucoma frequently occurs at night when the

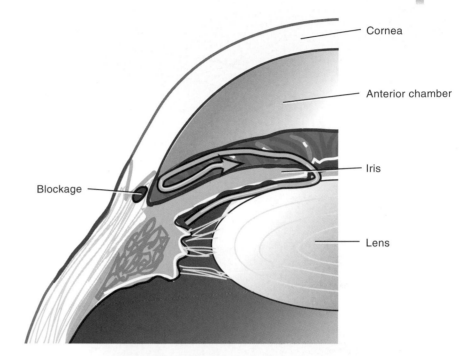

FIGURE 49–6 ■ Open-angle glaucoma.

Cornea

Anterior chamber

Iris

Lens

Blockage

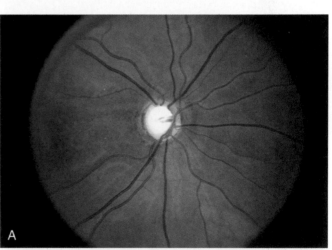

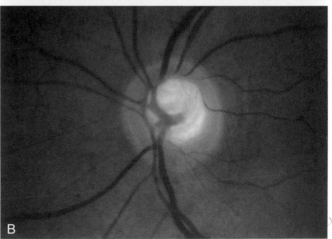

FIGURE 49–7 ■ **A** and **B,** Glaucomatous cupping of the optic nerve head. The cup-to-disc ratio is 50% to 60%. (From Swartz MH: Textbook of Physical Diagnosis, 4th ed. Philadelphia, WB Saunders, 2002, p 234.)

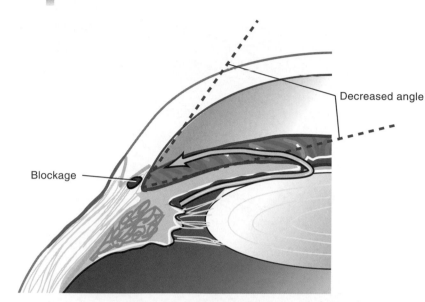

FIGURE 49–8 ■ Angle-closure glaucoma.

Decreased angle

Blockage

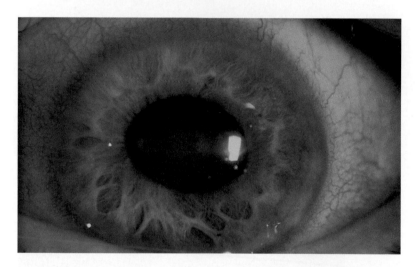

FIGURE 49–9 ■ After an episode of symptomatic angle closure the iris may have suffered a sectorial infarction of the sphincter muscle, causing distortion and recognized clinically by its whorled appearance. If this is severe, the eye is left with a poorly reactive ovoid pupil. (From Spalton DJ: Atlas of Clinical Ophthalmology, 3rd ed. Philadelphia, Mosby, 2005, p 210.)

pupil dilates, further impeding the flow of aqueous humor by further narrowing or closing the angle between the iris and the cornea.

The first step in the diagnosis of glaucoma is for the clinician to think of it. The diagnosis of both of the types of glaucoma can be made by simple measurements of intraocular pressure.[17] Although a rare low-pressure glaucoma exists, the vast majority of patients with glaucoma can be identified with simple ocular applanation or air-puff tonometry.

Uveitis

Uveitis is a term used to describe inflammation of the uvea that is not due to infection.[18] The uvea is divided into anterior and posterior parts. The anterior uvea consists of the ciliary body and iris, and the posterior uvea consists of the choroidal layer. Uveitis is a common cause of eye pain, and the pain is frequently associated with a red eye. Uveitis is frequently associated with the autoimmune diseases (e.g., rheumatoid arthritis, Behçet disease), although the causes of uveitis may defy specific diagnosis.[19] Patients with uveitis will present with eye pain, red eye, photophobia, blurred vision, and

"floaters" (Figs. 49–10 and 49–11).[20] The pain of uveitis can be exacerbated by shining a bright light into the eye, causing the inflamed iris to constrict. Uveitis is an ophthalmologic emergency, and immediate ophthalmologic evaluation and treatment with corticosteroids is mandatory if permanent visual loss is to be avoided.[21]

Optic Neuritis

Optic neuritis is another common cause of eye pain. Although pain is invariably present, it is the acute visual loss associated with the disease that usually prompts the patient to seek medical attention. The most common cause of optic neuritis is multiple sclerosis, with approximately 20% of patients suffering from multiple sclerosis having optic neuritis as their initial symptom.[22] Approximately 70% of patients with multiple sclerosis will suffer from optic neuritis at some point in their disease.[23]

Other causes of optic neuritis include temporal arteritis, tuberculosis, human immunodeficiency virus, hepatitis B, Lyme disease, and cytomegalovirus (Fig. 49–12).[24] Whether the optic neuritis is due to actual infection of the optic nerve

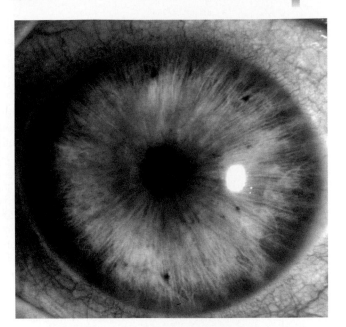

FIGURE 49–10 ■ Ciliary injection is seen here in its classical form as a dusky red circumlimbal vasodilatation in the area around the cornea where the ciliary and scleroconjunctival circulations anastomose. Its degree reflects the acuteness and severity of inflammation in the anterior uveal tract. With very severe inflammation the whole of the bulbar conjunctiva can be involved and the appearance may be difficult to distinguish from the diffuse appearance of conjunctival inflammation. (From Spalton DJ: Atlas of Clinical Ophthalmology, 3rd ed. Philadelphia, Mosby, 2005, p 290.)

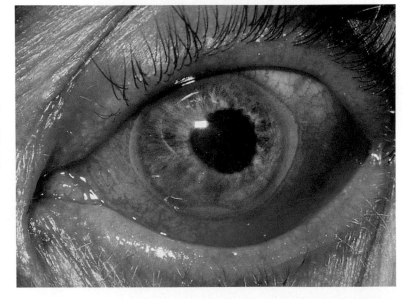

FIGURE 49–11 ■ The massive leukocytic response with an acute anterior uveitis can lead to cells precipitating as a hypopyon. This is typical of HLA-B27–positive anterior uveitis but is also seen with other causes of severe anterior uveitis such as Behçet disease. Hypopyon may also be the presenting sign of retinoblastoma in children, ocular lymphoma, and bacterial or fungal endophthalmitis. (From Spalton DJ: Atlas of Clinical Ophthalmology, 3rd ed. Philadelphia, Mosby, 2005, p 292.)

FIGURE 49–12 ■ The temporal arteries of this woman were tender, inflamed, thickened and nonpulsatile, although frequently the signs are more subtle. The diagnosis is suggested by finding a high erythrocyte sedimentation rate and C-reactive protein level and confirmed by temporal artery biopsy. Prompt treatment with corticosteroids is required because there is a grave risk of fellow eye involvement or stroke. (From Spalton DJ: Atlas of Clinical Ophthalmology, 3rd ed. Philadelphia, Mosby, 2005, p 591.)

or as part of a complex inflammatory response is the subject of debate. Optic neuritis is also seen as a sequela to sinus infection and occurs after radiation therapy.

The incidence of optic neuritis is approximately 7 cases per 100,000 patients. It occurs most commonly in whites of northern European ancestry. Blacks and Asians are rarely affected in the absence of an infectious cause. Optic neuritis occurs more often in females and usually presents between the ages of 20 and 50. In patients older than 50 with acute vision loss in one eye, ischemic optic neuritis is a more likely diagnosis.

Patients with optic neuritis present with a triad of symptoms, including (1) acute vision loss; (2) eye pain; and (3) dyschromatopsia, which is impairment of accurate color vision. Some patients with optic neuritis also complain of sound or sudden movement-induced flashing lights, which are known as phosgenes, as well as heat-induced visual loss. Approximately 70% of patients with optic neuritis have unilateral symptoms. On physical examination, the patient suffering from optic neuritis will exhibit a pale, swollen, optic disc (Fig. 49–13). MRI and visual evoked responses will confirm the clinical diagnosis (Fig. 49–14).[25] Urgent ophthalmologic referral for treatment with intravenous corticosteroids and/or α-interferon therapy is indicated in all patients suspected of having optic neurtis.[26,27]

■ REFERRED EYE PAIN

What all of the following disease entities have in common is their ability to cause eye pain. Given the broad range of anatomic structures that are either directly innervated by the first division of the trigeminal nerve (e.g., the orbit, the cavernous sinus) or that interact with the trigeminal ganglion via sympathetic or parasympathetic fibers (e.g., carotid artery, sphenopalatine ganglion), it is not surprising that many pathologic processes are perceived by the patient as ocular or periocular pain. As mentioned earlier, the patient's firm belief that the pathologic process resides within the eye makes the evaluation and treatment of ocular and periocular pain challenging. A discussion of diseases that can have eye pain as a prominent presenting feature follows.

Cluster Headache

Cluster headache is a common cause of referred ocular and periocular pain. It is presumed that interplay between the sphenopalatine ganglion and the trigeminal ganglion is responsible for the patient's perception of eye pain when suffering from cluster headache. Cluster headache derives its name from the pattern of its occurrence: namely, the headaches occur in clusters followed by headache-free remission periods.[28] Unlike other common headache disorders that affect primarily females, cluster headache occurs much more often in males by a ratio of 5:1. Much less common than tension-type headache or migraine headache, cluster headache is thought to affect approximately 0.5% of the male population.

The onset of cluster headache occurs in the late third or early fourth decade, in contradistinction to migraine, which almost always manifests itself by the early second decade. Unlike migraine, cluster headache does not appear to run in families and cluster headache sufferers do not experience aura. Attacks of cluster headache will generally occur approximately 90 minutes after the patient falls asleep. This association with sleep is reportedly maintained when a shift worker

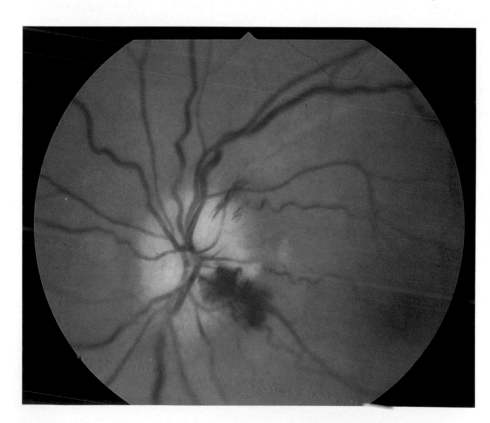

FIGURE 49–13 ■ Patients typically present with a chalky white, swollen disc with few hemorrhages. (From Spalton DJ: Atlas of Clinical Ophthalmology, 3rd ed. Philadelphia, Mosby, 2005, p 592.)

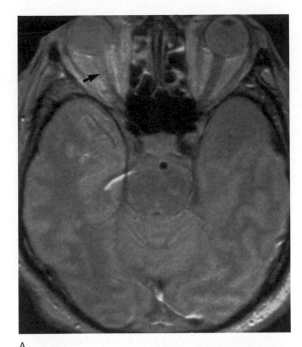

A

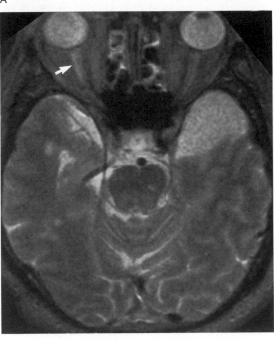

B

FIGURE 49–14 ■ High signal intensity is demonstrated in the right optic nerve in a patient with multiple sclerosis and optic neuritis *(arrow)*. When the classic spin-echo technique is used, the lesion is demonstrated on the spin-echo density-weighted image (**A**) but more clearly on the T2-weighted image (**B**) because of decreased signal from adjacent intraorbital fat. With modern fast imaging techniques, these lesions are better demonstrated with T2-weighted fast spin-echo imaging with fat suppression or fast STIR imaging. (From Stark DD, Bradley WG Jr: Magnetic Resonance Imaging, 3rd ed. St. Louis, Mosby, 1999, p 393.)

FIGURE 49–15 ■ Horner syndrome may be present during acute attacks of cluster headache. (From Waldman S: Atlas of Common Pain Syndromes. Philadelphia, WB Saunders, 2002, p 17.)

During a cluster headache period, attacks occur two to three times a day and last for 45 minutes to an hour. Cluster headache periods usually last for 8 to 12 weeks, interrupted by remission periods of less than 2 years. In rare patients, the remission periods become shorter and shorter and the frequency may increase up to 10-fold. This situation is termed *chronic cluster headache* and differs from the more common episodic cluster headache described previously.

Cluster headache is characterized as a unilateral headache that is ocular, retro-orbital, and temporal. The pain has a deep burning or boring quality. Physical findings during an attack of cluster headache may include Horner syndrome, consisting of ptosis, abnormal pupil constriction, facial flushing, and conjunctival injection (Fig. 49–15). Additionally, profuse lacrimation and rhinorrhea is often present. The ocular changes may become permanent with repeated attacks. Peau d'orange skin over the malar region, deeply furrowed and glabellar folds, and telangiectasia may be observed.

Attacks of cluster headache may be provoked by small amounts of alcohol, nitrates, histamines, and other vasoactive substances and occasionally by high altitude. When the attack is in progress, the patient may not be able to lie still and may pace or rock back and forth in a chair. This behavior contrasts to that in other headache syndromes, during which patients seeking relief will lie down in a dark, quiet, room.

The pain of cluster headache is said to be among the worst pain that mankind suffers from. Because of the severity of pain associated with cluster headaches, the clinician must watch closely for medication overuse or misuse.

changes to and from nighttime to daytime hours of sleep. Cluster headache also appears to follow a distinct chronobiologic pattern that coincides with the seasonal change in the length of daylight. This results in an increased frequency of cluster headaches in the spring and fall.

Suicides have been associated with prolonged, unrelieved attacks of cluster headaches.

There is no specific test for cluster headache. Testing is aimed primarily at identifying occult pathology or other diseases that may mimic cluster headache (see "Differential Diagnosis"). All patients with a recent onset of headache thought to be cluster headache should undergo MRI testing of the brain. If neurologic dysfunction accompanies the patient's headache symptomatology, the MRI should be performed with and without gadolinium contrast medium and MR angiography should also be considered. MRI testing should also be performed in those patients with previously stable cluster headache who are experiencing an inexplicable change in headache symptoms. Screening laboratory testing including a erythrocyte sedimentation rate, complete blood cell count, and automated blood chemistry should be performed if the diagnosis of cluster headache is in question. Ophthalmologic evaluation including measurement of intraocular pressures is indicated in those patients suffering with headache who experience significant ocular symptom.

In contradistinction to migraine headache, where most patients experience improvement with the implementation of therapy with β-adrenergic blockers, patients suffering from cluster headache will usually require more individualized therapy. A reasonable starting place in the treatment of cluster headache is to begin treatment with prednisone combined with daily sphenopalatine ganglion blocks with local anesthetic.[29] A reasonable starting dose of prednisone would be 80 mg given in divided doses tapered by 10 mg per dose per day. If headaches are not rapidly brought under control, the inhalation of 100% oxygen is added via a close-fitting mask.

If headaches persist and the diagnosis of cluster headache is not in question, a trial of lithium carbonate may be considered. It should be noted that the therapeutic window of lithium carbonate is small and thus this drug should be used with caution. A starting dose of 300 mg at bedtime may be increased after 48 hours to 300 mg twice a day. If no side effects are noted, after 48 hours the dose may again be increased to 300 mg three times a day. The patient should be continued at this dosage level for a total of 10 days, and the drug should then be tapered downward over a 1-week period. Other medications that can be considered if the just-mentioned treatments are ineffective include methysergide and sumatriptan and sumatriptan-like drugs.

Tolosa-Hunt Syndrome

Tolosa-Hunt syndrome is another disease whose primary presenting complaint is unilateral eye pain. The exact cause of Tolosa-Hunt syndrome is unknown, but the ocular and periocular symptoms are the result of nonspecific inflammation of the cavernous sinus or superior orbital fissure.[30] In addition to severe eye pain, which often heralds the onset of this disease, dysfunction of cranial nerves III, IV, and VI occurs as a result of granulomatous inflammatory damage to the nerves.[31] This results in ophthalmoparesis, which can be quite distressing to the patient. In some patients, the ophthalmoparesis may precede the pain, further confusing the diagnosis. Pupillary dysfunction due to inflammation of the sympathetic fibers and third cranial nerve may also be seen in patients suffering from Tolosa-Hunt syndrome. If the inflammation extends beyond the cavernous sinus and affects the optic nerve, blindness may result. Paresthesias into the forehead presumably via the supraorbital branch of the trigeminal nerve may also be present as part of the inflammatory response. Tolosa-Hunt syndrome rarely occurs before the second decade and affects males and females equally. The extent of physical findings is a direct function of which cranial nerves are affected by the inflammatory process. Although ophthalmopareses is a hallmark of Tolosa-Hunt syndrome, papillary abnormalities and ptosis may also be present. Fundoscopic examination may reveal edema of the optic disc.[32] The corneal reflex may be diminished or lost if there is significant trigeminal nerve involvement.

Because Tolosa-Hunt syndrome mimics many other diseases, laboratory testing including a complete blood cell count and determination of erythrocyte sedimentation rate, glucose level, Lyme disease titer, rapid plasma reagin, antinuclear antibody, HIV titer, and thyroid function are indicated.[33] MRI of the brain and orbit may reveal findings suggestive of a local inflammatory response but may be normal even in the presence of significant disease.[34] Biopsy of the region of inflammation may ultimately be required to confirm the diagnosis of Tolosa-Hunt syndrome. Tolosa-Hunt syndrome represents an ophthalmologic emergency and should be treated as such. Rapid treatment with high doses of intravenous corticosteroids may prevent loss of vision and cranial nerve function. Although spontaneous remissions have been reported, early treatment is key to avoiding disastrous results. Thirty to 40 percent of patients suffering from Tolosa-Hunt syndrome will experience a relapse of symptoms after successful treatment with corticosteroids.

The Cavernous Sinus Syndromes

The cavernous sinus syndromes are a heterogeneous groups of diseases that have in common their ability to produce ocular and periocular pain as well as a variety of neurologic symptoms, including ophthalmoplegia, pupillary abnormalities, orbital and conjunctival congestion, proptosis, and, if severe, visual loss.[35] Also known as the parasellar syndromes, the evaluation of all patients suffering from cavernous sinus syndrome should include including a complete blood cell count and determination of erythrocyte sedimentation rate, glucose level, Lyme disease titer, rapid plasma reagin, antinuclear antibody, HIV titer, and thyroid function. MRI of the brain, sinuses, cavernous sinus, and orbit is also indicated as is MR angiography of the carotid artery. Diseases comprising the cavernous sinus syndrome include cavernous sinus aneurysms, carotid-cavernous sinus fistulas, tumors, and cavernous sinus thrombosis, as well as the idiopathic inflammatory syndromes involving the cavernous sinus (e.g., Tolosa-Hunt syndrome).[36,37] Each is briefly discussed individually.

Cavernous Sinus Aneurysms

Aneurysms of the carotid artery as it passes through the cavernous sinus can cause all of the symptoms associated with cavernous sinus syndrome. Unlike intracranial aneurysms, which carry the risk of intracranial hemorrhage, unruptured carotid artery aneurysms in this region create symptoms by pressure on the various neural structures in proximity to the

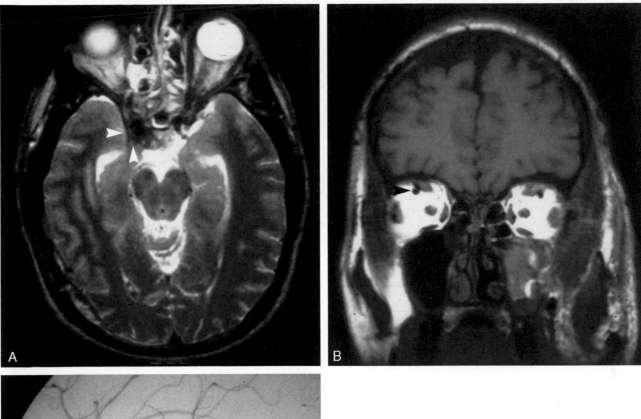

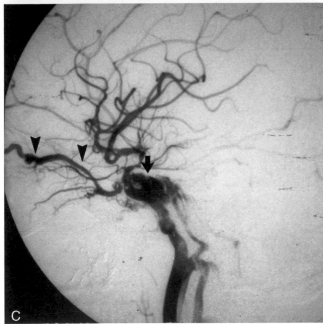

FIGURE 49–16 ■ **A,** Carotid cavernous fistula. Axial T2-weighted image (TR = 2500 ms, TE = 80 ms). Increased flow void is present in the region of the cavernous right internal carotid artery *(arrowheads).* **B,** Coronal T1-weighted image (TR = 500 ms, TE = 15 ms) reveals dilatation of the right superior ophthalmic vein *(arrowhead).* **C,** Lateral projection of right internal carotid artery arteriogram demonstrates opacification of the right cavernous sinus *(arrow)* with drainage into the right superior ophthalmic vein *(arrowheads). (*From Haaga JR, Lanzieri C: CT and MR Imaging of the Whole Body, 4th ed. St. Louis, Mosby, 2003, vol 1, p 343.)

aneurysm. When the aneurysm ruptures, a direct carotid artery-cavernous sinus fistula results (Fig. 49–16). Such fistulas can cause only limited symptoms or can result in massive neurologic dysfunction. A loud carotid and ocular bruit is often present. Treatment with endovascular occlusion has been attempted with some success.[38]

Cavernous Sinus Tumors

Tumors involving the cavernous sinus can be either primary or metastatic in origin. Primary tumors including meningiomas and neurofibromas are the most common primary

tumors seen involving the cavernous sinus.[39] Metastatic breast, prostate, lung, and craniopharyngeal tumors can also involve the cavernous sinus, often with disastrous results (Fig. 49–17).[40] Occasionally, large pituitary tumors may extend into the cavernous sinus (Fig. 49–18). Symptoms associated with tumors of this region will vary with the neurologic structures affected as the tumor grows and the onset of symptoms can be either acute or insidious. Treatment is primarily limited to palliative radiotherapy, and the results in most cases are poor at best, with the type of tumor the major determinant of outcome. The exception to this rule is endocrine-responsive

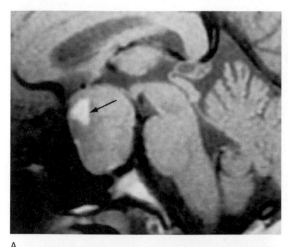

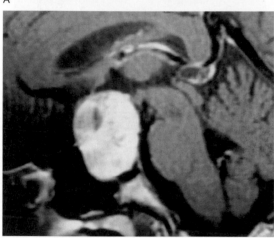

A

B

FIGURE 49–17 ■ Pituitary macroadenoma. **A,** Sagittal precontrast T1-weighted image shows oval mass with smooth border and sellar enlargement—typical MR features of macroadenoma. Hemorrhage-fluid level *(arrow)* is visible. **B,** Postcontrast T1-weighted image shows intense but heterogeneous enhancement of tumor. (From Stark DD, Bradley WG Jr: Magnetic Resonance Imaging, 3rd ed. St. Louis, Mosby, 1999, p 1226.)

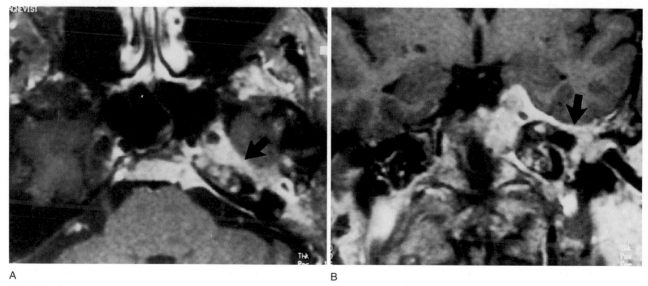

A   B

FIGURE 49–18 ■ Recurrent nasopharyngeal carcinoma with perineural spread into the left cavernous sinus and temporal bone. **A,** Axial enhanced image with fat saturation. There is a tumor surrounding the left trigeminal ganglion and extending from Meckel's cave into the left petrous apex *(arrow)*. **B,** Coronal enhanced image with fat saturation. The tumor extends laterally along the left greater superficial petrosal nerve and enters the temporal bone through the geniculate ganglion *(arrow)*. (From Stark DD, Bradley WG Jr: Magnetic Resonance Imaging, 3rd ed. St. Louis, Mosby, 1999, p 1223.)

pituitary tumors, which often respond to anti-endocrine drug therapy.

Carotid-Cavernous Fistulas

Fistulas between the carotid artery and the cavernous sinus can be the result of either a rupture of a preexisting carotid artery aneurysm or direct trauma to the carotid artery and cavernous sinus (Fig. 49–19).[41] Direct fistulas between the carotid artery and the cavernous sinus occur when a carotid artery aneurysm ruptures directly into the cavernous sinus or trauma to the region damages the artery. The onset of symptoms is immediate and often quite severe. Misdiagnosis is common, and prognosis if untreated is poor. A loud carotid and ocular bruit is often present. The patient may report hearing "water running" in the head. Indirect aneurysms between branches of the internal or external carotid arteries tend to be less symp-

tomatic. Both types of fistulas can be treated by endovascular occlusion techniques and carotid artery ligation.

Cavernous Sinus Thrombosis

A common sequela to periorbital or frontal and/or maxillary sinusitis in the preantibiotic era, cavernous sinus thrombosis is now primarily seen in patients who are immunocompromised (e.g., HIV-infected patients).[42] The patient with an infectious etiology to cavernous sinus thrombosis will appear septic, and the nidus of the infection may be clinically evident. Severe ocular and retro-ocular pain is often the first symptom, followed by diplopia and ptosis. Ophthalmoplegia and signs of meningeal irritation may also be present. Immediate treatment with antibiotics and corticosteroids combined with surgical drainage of any abscess formation is crucial to avoid blindness or, in some cases, death.

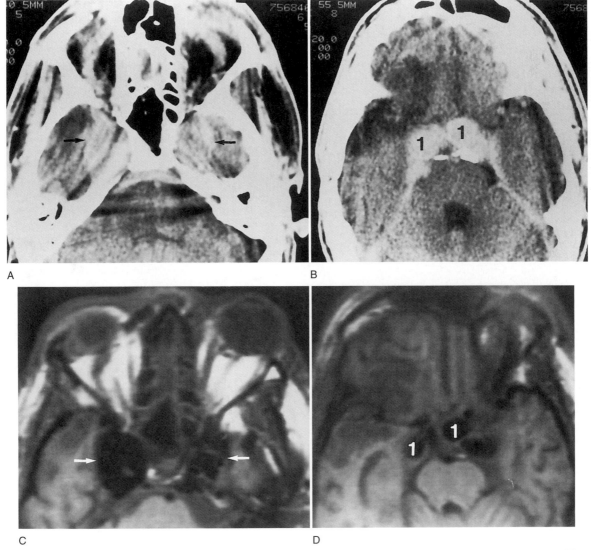

FIGURE 49–19 ■ Traumatic carotid cavernous fistula. **A,** Axial contrast medium–enhanced CT scan. **B,** Axial contrast medium–enhanced CT scan. **C,** Axial head surface-coil, short-TR, short-TE MR image. **D,** Axial head surface-coil, short-TR, short-TE MR image. Greatly distended superior ophthalmic veins and cavernous sinuses *(arrows)* are seen as enhancement in **A** and as signal void in **C.** Note that the enhancing suprasellar "masses" (1) in **B** are definitively diagnosed as massively dilated venous channels by MRI (**D**), obviating the need for intravenous contrast. (From Stark DD, Bradley WG Jr: Magnetic Resonance Imaging, 3rd ed. St. Louis, Mosby, 1999, p 1660.)

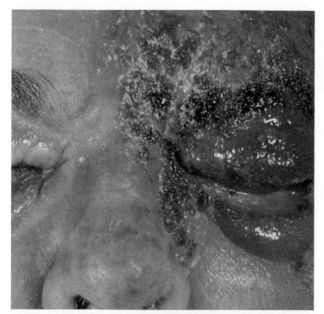

FIGURE 49–20 ■ Herpes zoster ophthalmicus. (From Swartz MH: Textbook of Physical Diagnosis, 4th ed. Philadelphia, WB Saunders, 2002, p 214.)

Other Inflammatory Conditions Associated with Cavernous Sinus Syndrome

Acute herpes zoster and sarcoidosis have both been implicated in the development of cavernous sinus syndrome (Fig. 49–20). The lesions of acute herpes zoster usually make the diagnosis a relatively straightforward endeavor, but the diagnosis of sarcoidosis can be much more subtle.[43] If uveitis is present as a component of ocular pain, sarcoidosis should always be included in the differential diagnosis.

■ CONCLUSION

Ocular and periocular pain represent a challenge in both diagnosis and treatment for the pain management physician. Familiarity with the more common pathologic processes that cause ocular and periocular pain will allow the pain management physician to more readily identify those diseases that present a risk to vision and allow more immediate ophthalmologic referral. More self-limited causes of ocular and periocular pain can often be managed with simple treatment and reassurance.

References

1. Waldman SD: Gasserian ganglion block. In Waldman SD: Atlas of Interventional Pain Management, 2nd ed. Philadelphia, WB Saunders, 2004, pp 27-28.
2. Muller LJ: Corneal nerves: Structure, contents, and function. Exp Eye Res 76:521, 2003.
3. Pavan-Langston D: Diagnosis and therapy of common eye infections: Bacterial, viral, fungal. Compr Ther 9:33, 1983.
4. Barza M, Baum J: Ocular infections. Med Clin North Am 407:131, 1983.
5. Briner AM et al: Surgical treatment of a chalazion or hordeolum internum. Aust Fam Physician 16:834, 1987.
6. Burke MJ, Sanitato JJ, Vinger PF, et al: Soccerball-induced eye injuries. JAMA 249:2682, 1983.
7. Stapleton F, Dart J, Minassian D: Nonulcerative complications of contact lens wear: Relative risks for different lens types. Arch Ophthalmol 110:1601, 1992.
8. Brunette DD, Ghezzi K, Renner GS, Rosen P (eds): Ophthalmologic disorders. In: Emergency Medicine: Concepts and Clinical Practice, 4th ed. St. Louis, CV Mosby, 1997, pp 2432-2440.
9. Patterson J, Fetzer D, Krall J, et al: Eye patch treatment for the pain of corneal abrasion. South Med J 89:227, 1996.
10. Bertolini J, Pelucio M: The red eye. Emerg Med Clin North Am 13:561, 1995.
11. Friedlaender MH: The current and future therapy of allergic conjunctivitis. Curr Opin Ophthalmol 9:54, 1998.
12. Steinert RF: Current therapy for bacterial keratitis and bacterial conjunctivitis. Am J Ophthalmol 112(4 Suppl):10S, 1991.
13. Bersudsky V, Rehany U, Tendler Y: Diagnosis of chlamydial infection by direct enzyme-linked immunoassay and polymerase chain reaction in patients with acute follicular conjunctivitis. Graefes Arch Clin Exp Ophthalmol 237:617, 1999.
14. Vaughn D, Riordan-Eva P, Asbury T (eds): Glaucoma. In General Ophthalmology, 13th ed. New York, McGraw-Hill, 1992, p 213.
15. Clark R: Ocular emergencies. In Emergency Medicine: A Comprehensive Study Guide, 3rd ed. New York, McGraw-Hill, 1992, p 834.
16. Choong YF, Irfan S, Menage MJ: Acute angle closure glaucoma: An evaluation of a protocol for acute treatment. Eye 13:613, 1999.
17. Campbell DG: A comparison of diagnostic techniques in angle-closure glaucoma. Am J Ophthalmol 88:197, 1979.
18. Nussenblatt R, Whitcup S, Palestine A: Uveitis: Fundamentals of Clinical Practice, 2nd ed. St. Louis, Mosby, 1996.
19. Pepose JS, Holland GN, Wilhelmus KR: Ocular Infection and Immunity. St. Louis, CV Mosby, 1996.
20. Tessler H: Classification and symptoms and signs of uveitis. In: Duane T (ed): Clinical Ophthalmology. New York: Harper & Row; 1987, pp 1-10.
21. Nishimoto JY: Iritis: How to recognize and manage a potentially sight-threatening disease. Postgrad Med 99:255, 1996.
22. Wray SH: Optic neuritis. In Albert DM, Jakobiec FA (eds): Principles and Practice of Ophthalmology. Philadelphia, WB Saunders, 1994, pp 2539-2568.
23. Noseworthy JH, Lucchinetti C, Rodriguez M, Weinshenker BG: Multiple sclerosis. N Engl J Med 343:938, 2000.
24. Ghezzi A, Martinelli V, Rodegher M, et al: The prognosis of idiopathic optic neuritis. Neurol Sci 21(4 Suppl 2):S865, 2000.
25. Miller DH, Newton MR, van der Poel JC, et al: Magnetic resonance imaging of the optic nerve in optic neuritis. Neurology 38:175, 1988.
26. Kaufman DI, Trobe JD, Eggenberger ER, Whitaker JN: Practice parameter: The role of corticosteroids in the management of acute monosymptomatic optic neuritis. Report of the Quality Standards Subcommittee of the American Academy of Neurology. Neurology 54:2039, 2000.
27. Jacobs LD, Beck RW, Simon JH, et al: Intramuscular interferon beta-1a therapy initiated during a first demyelinating event in multiple sclerosis. CHAMPS Study Group. N Engl J Med 343:898, 2000.
28. Waldman SD: Cluster headache. In Waldman SD: Common Pain Syndromes. Philadelphia, WB Saunders, 2002, pp 16-19.
29. Waldman SD: Sphenopalatine ganglion block. In Waldman SD: Atlas of Interventional Pain Management, 2nd ed. Philadelphia, WB Saunders, 2004, pp 11-14.
30. Cohn DF, Carasso R, Streifler M: Painful ophthalmoplegia: The Tolosa-Hunt syndrome. Eur Neurol 18:373, 1979.
31. Roca PD: Painful ophthalmoplegia: The Tolosa-Hunt syndrome. Ann Ophthalmol 7:828, 1975.
32. Hunt WE: Tolosa-Hunt syndrome: One cause of painful ophthalmoplegia. J Neurosurg 44:544, 1976.
33. Troost BT: In Miller NR, Newman NJ (eds): Walsh & Hoyt's Clinical Neuro-Ophthalmology. Philadelphia, Lippincott Williams & Wilkins, 1998, pp 1727-1729.
34. Yousem DM, Atlas SW, Grossman RI: MR imaging of Tolosa-Hunt syndrome. AJR Am J Roentgenol 154:167, 1990.
35. Thomas JE, Yoss RE: The parasellar syndrome: Problems in determining etiology. Mayo Clin Proc 45:617, 1970.
36. Hunt WE, Meagher JN, Lefever HE, et al: Painful ophthalmoplegia: Its relation to indolent inflammation of the cavernous sinus. Neurology 11:56, 1961.
37. Kline LB: The Tolosa-Hunt syndrome. Surv Ophthalmol 119:79, 1982.

38. Kupersmith MJ, Berenstein A, Choi IS, et al: Percutaneous transvascular treatment of giant carotid aneurysms: Neuro-ophthalmologic findings. Neurology 34:328, 1984.

39. Kattah JC, Silgals RM, Manz H, et al: Presentation and management of parasellar and suprasellar metastatic mass lesions. J Neurol Neurosurg Psychiatry 48:44, 1985.

40. Greenberg HS, Deck MD, Vikram B, et al: Metastasis to the base of the skull: Clinical findings in 43 patients. Neurology 31:530, 1981.

41. Debrun G, Lacour P, Vinuela F, et al: Treatment of 54 traumatic carotid-cavernous fistulas. J Neurosurg 55:678, 1981.

42. Hedges TR, Leung LS: Parasellar and orbital apex syndrome caused by aspergillosis. Neurology 26:117, 1976.

43. Belfer MH, Stevens RW: Sarcoidosis: A primary care review. Am Fam Physician 58:2041, 1998.

chapter 50

Pain of the Ear, Nose, Sinuses, and Throat

Steven D. Waldman

Pain originating from the ear, nose, sinuses, and throat accounts for a significant number of visits to primary care physicians and specialists each year. Although most of the painful conditions responsible for these visits are easy to diagnose and treat and, in general, will not harm the patient with proper treatment, there are a significant number of painful conditions of the ear, nose, and throat that have the potential to cause considerable morbidity and mortality (Table 50–1). The clinician should also remain vigilant for diseases of this anatomic region that do not cause pain but have the potential, if undiagnosed, to create significant problems for the patient, such as acoustic neuroma, thyroid carcinoma, and malignant melanoma. This chapter provides the clinician with a concise road map for the evaluation of painful conditions of the ear, nose, sinuses, and throat.

■ OTALGIA

Ear pain can result from local pathology, such as cellulitis or tumor, or can be referred from distant sites, most commonly the nasopharynx.[1,2] Because of the complex functions of the ear, local disease may cause disturbances in hearing and balance that can be quite distressing for the patient and may serve as a harbinger of serious diseases, such as acoustic neuroma. As mentioned, many of these conditions do not have pain as a predominant symptom.

Functional Anatomy of the Ear As It Relates to Pain

The ear and surrounding tissues are innervated by both cranial nerves and branches of nerves that have as their origin the spinal nerves (Fig. 50–1A and B). The auricle is innervated by the greater auricular nerve, as well as the lesser occipital nerve, the auricular branch of the vagus nerve, and the auriculotemporal branch of the mandibular nerve. The external auditory canal receives innervation from branches of the glossopharyngeal and facial nerves. The inferoposterior portion of the tympanic membrane receives its innervation from the auriculotemporal branch of the mandibular nerve, as well as the auricular branch of the vagus nerve and the tympanic branch of the glossopharyngeal nerve. The structures of the middle ear receive innervation from the tympanic branch of the glossopharyngeal nerve along with the caroticotympanic nerve and the superficial petrosal nerve. It is the overlap of these nerves, as well as their diverse origin, that can make localization of the pathology responsible for the patient's pain quite challenging.

Painful Diseases of the Ear

Auricular Pain

The skin of the auricle is richly innervated and is frequently the source of local ear pain. It should be noted that auricular cartilage is poorly innervated and diseases that are limited to cartilage may produce little or no pain until distention or inflammation of the overlying skin develops. Most painful conditions involving the auricle are due to infection, trauma, connective tissue disease, or tumor.

Superficial infections of the auricle include folliculitis, abscess, cellulitis, and infection by herpes simplex and zoster, including Ramsey Hunt syndrome[3] (Fig. 50–2). Deep infections involving the cartilage, once uncommon, are now occurring with much greater frequency because of the current increase in body piercing involving auricular cartilage.

Both superficial and deep infections of the auricle are quite painful. Early incision and drainage, débridement of nonviable cartilage, and aggressive use of antibiotics are necessary to avoid spread of infection to the middle ear, bone, and intracranial structures, including the central nervous system.

Trauma to the auricle can be quite painful and, if not appropriately treated, can result in loss of cartilage and disfigurement. Blunt trauma to the auricle can cause superficial ecchymosis or, if severe enough, perichondral hematoma or cauliflower ear[4] (Fig. 50–3). Lacerations of the lobule, tragus, and cartilage from body piercings that have been torn from the ear are increasingly common occurrences at local emergency rooms and urgent care centers. Prompt débridement and repair with careful observation for infection are crucial if disfiguring sequelae are to be avoided.

Thermal injuries from heat or cold are also common painful traumatic injuries to the ear that usually follow the use of heating pads or cold packs in patients who are also taking pain medications or self-medicating with alcohol, or both.

Table 50–1

Painful Conditions of the Ear, Nose, Sinuses, and Throat

Ear Pain

The Auricle
Superficial infections
  Folliculitis
  Cellulitis
  Herpes simplex
Ramsey Hunt syndrome
Deep infections involving cartilage
Trauma
  Ecchymosis of the auricle
  Perichondral hematoma
  Lacerations
Thermal injuries
  Heating pad burns
  Ice pack burns
  Frostbite
Chondritis- and perichondritis-associated connective tissue diseases
Primary tumors
Metastatic tumors

The External Auditory Canal
Otitis media
Cholesteatoma

The Tympanic Membrane and Middle Ear
Myringitis
Otitis media
Mastoiditis

Pain of the Nose and Sinuses
Superficial infection
  Folliculitis
  Vestibulitis
Intranasal foreign body
Acute sinusitis
Osteomyelitis
Primary tumors of the nose and sinuses
Metastatic tumors involving the nose and sinuses

Throat Pain
Superficial infection
  Acute pharyngitis
  Tonsillitis
Dental pain
  Deep infection
  Parapharyngeal abscess
Retropharyngeal abscess
Primary tumors of the throat and aerodigestive tract
Metastatic tumors involving the throat and aerodigestive tract
Carotidynia
Eagle syndrome
Hyoid syndrome

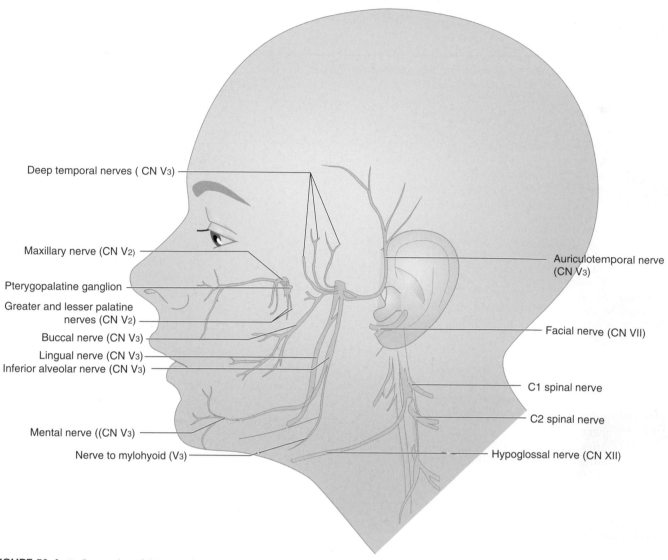

Deep temporal nerves (CN V₃)

Maxillary nerve (CN V₂)

Pterygopalatine ganglion

Greater and lesser palatine
nerves (CN V₂)

Buccal nerve (CN V₃)

Lingual nerve (CN V₃)
Inferior alveolar nerve (CN V₃)

Mental nerve ((CN V₃)

Nerve to mylohyoid (V₃)

Auriculotemporal nerve
(CN V₃)

Facial nerve (CN VII)

C1 spinal nerve

C2 spinal nerve

Hypoglossal nerve (CN XII)

FIGURE 50–1 ■ Innervation of the ear and surrounding tissues.

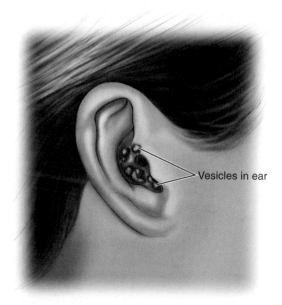

Vesicles in ear

FIGURE 50-2 ■ Ramsay Hunt syndrome is due to infection of the geniculate ganglion by varicella-zoster virus. (From Waldman SD: Atlas of
Uncommon Pain Syndromes. Philadelphia, WB Saunders, 2003.)

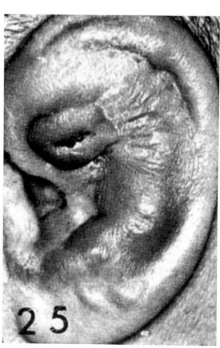

FIGURE 50–3 ■ Cauliflower ear. (Courtesy of Roy Sullivan, Ph.D.)

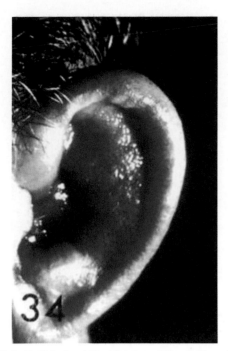

FIGURE 50–4 ■ Polychondritis. (Courtesy of Roy Sullivan, Ph.D.)

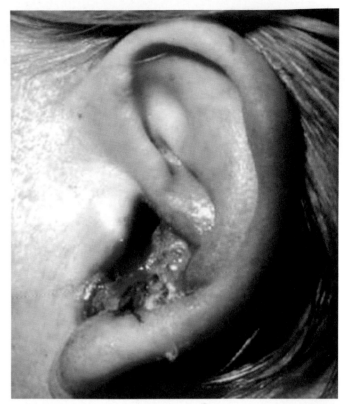

FIGURE 50–5 ■ Basal cell carcinoma. (Courtesy of Roy Sullivan, Ph.D.)

Frostbite injuries affecting the auricle are likewise common and are frequently related to alcohol or drug use (or both). Thermal injuries can initially appear less severe than they really are. Initial treatment with topical antibiotics such as silver sulfadiazine and sterile dressings should be followed by reevaluation and redressing of the affected area on a daily basis until the thermal injury is well on the way to healing.

Connective tissue diseases can cause inflammation of the auricular cartilage. Usually manifested as bilateral, acutely inflamed and painful swelling of the auricle, chondritis and perichondritis may initially be misdiagnosed as cellulitis (Fig. 50–4). The bilateral nature of the disease, as well as involvement of other cartilage, should alert the clinician to the possibility of a non-infectious cause of the pain, rubor, and swelling.[5] Because many of the connective tissue diseases affect other organ systems, prompt diagnosis and treatment are essential.

Primary tumors of the auricle are generally basal cell or squamous cell carcinoma caused by actinic damage of the skin (Fig. 50–5). Rarely, primary tumors of the cartilage can occur. Metastatic lesions to the auricle are uncommon, but not unheard of.

The External Auditory Canal

Far and away the most common painful condition of the external auditory meatus is otitis externa. Usually the result of swimming or digging in the ear with a fingernail, cotton swab, or hairpin, the initial symptom of otitis media is generally pruritus, followed by pain that is made worse by yawning or chewing. On physical examination, there is a reddened, wet-appearing, edematous canal that may reveal abraded areas from previous digging or itching as a result of the patient's attempt to relieve the symptoms[6] (Fig. 50–6). Pulling on the auricle posteriorly will usually exacerbate the pain of otitis media. The pain of this disease is often out of proportion to the findings on physical examination. Treatment

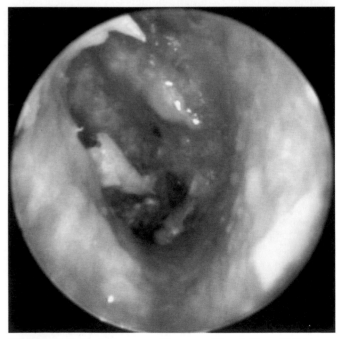

FIGURE 50–6 ■ Otitis externa. (Courtesy of Roy Sullivan, Ph.D.)

of otitis media consists of cleaning any debris from the acoustic auditory canal and instilling topical antibiotic drops or solution. If significant edema is present, the use of topical antibiotic drops or solution containing corticosteroid will speed recovery.

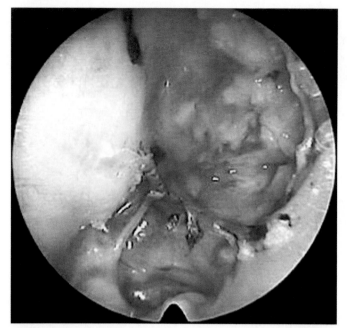

FIGURE 50–7 ▪ Cholesteatoma. (Courtesy of Roy Sullivan, Ph.D.)

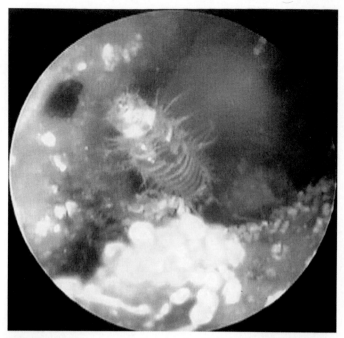

FIGURE 50–8 ▪ Insect in the external auditory canal. (Courtesy of Roy Sullivan, Ph.D.)

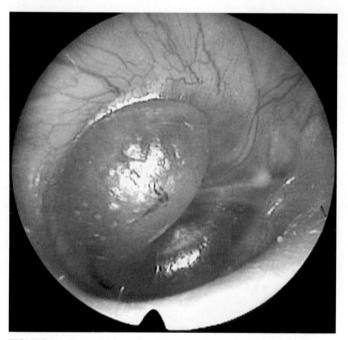

FIGURE 50–9 ▪ Otitis media. (Courtesy of Roy Sullivan, Ph.D.)

Another cause of external auditory canal pain is cholesteatoma, which most often occurs after trauma to the bone of the external auditory canal. Caused by invasion of the external auditory canal wall by exuberant tissue growth, cholesteatoma can become quite invasive if left untreated despite its benign tissue elements.[7] A patient with cholesteatoma will have a ball-like growth in the external auditory canal that has an onion skin–like appearance (Fig. 50–7). Unless infected, the pain will most often be dull and aching. Secondary infection may cause a foul-smelling purulent exudate to drain from the affected ear. CT scanning will help the clinician determine the amount of bone destruction and help guide microsurgical resection of this not uncommon cause of ear pain.

In younger patients and those with impaired mentation, foreign bodies are a frequently overlooked cause of ear pain originating from the external auditory meatus. Most problematic is vegetable matter such as dried peas and beans, which swell once inside the acoustic auditory canal and make removal quite difficult. If the foreign body remains in the external auditory canal for any period, secondary infection invariably occurs. Insects may also fly or crawl into the external auditory meatus and cause the patient much distress (Fig. 50–8). If the insect remains alive, instillation of lidocaine or mineral oil will stop the insect from moving around and make removal easier.[8]

The Tympanic Membrane and Middle Ear

Myringitis is a painful condition that may be caused by viral infection of the tympanic membrane. Vesicles or blebs of the tympanic membrane may be present on physical examination, or the tympanic membrane may appear normal. Antibiotic drops containing local anesthetic will usually provide symptomatic relief, although in the absence of physical findings, the diagnosis of idiopathic myringitis is one of exclusion and other diseases of the middle ear or referred pain remains an ever-present possibility.

Acute otitis media is perhaps the second most common cause of otalgia after otitis externa. Though more common in children, otitis media can occur at any age. The pain of otitis media is caused primarily by distention and inflammation of the tympanic membrane[9] (Fig. 50–9). Young children with otitis media may pull on their ear, whereas older patients will complain bitterly of a deep, severe, unremitting pain. Fever is also usually present. Untreated, the pain will become increasingly severe as the tympanic membrane becomes more distended until the tympanic membrane ruptures.

Although the pain may dramatically improve after spontaneous rupture, infection of the mastoid air cells can occur. Treatment of acute otitis media is based on the administration of oral antibiotics and decongestants. Topical local anesthetic drops administered via the external auditory canal may provide symptomatic relief while waiting for the antibiotics and decongestants to work. For otitis media that does not promptly resolve, therapeutic tympanocentesis with the placement of myringotomy tubes should be considered.

As mentioned earlier, acute mastoiditis is often the result of untreated or undertreated otitis media. Mastoiditis is characterized by pain, tenderness, and rubor in the posterior auricular region.[10] The condition is often misdiagnosed initially as recurrent otitis media because examination of the tympanic membrane will often reveal findings of the unresolved otitis media. Fever is invariably present, and the patient will generally appear more ill than with otitis media alone. Radiographic examination of the mastoid air cells reveals opacification of the normally aerated structure and, as the disease progresses, bony destruction. Untreated, mastoiditis can become life threatening as the infection spreads to the central nervous system (Fig. 50–10). The findings of headache, stiff neck, and visual disturbance are warning signs of central nervous system involvement and constitute a medical emergency. Surgical treatment combined with aggressive antibiotic therapy is required on an emergency basis for patients exhibiting signs of central nervous system infection.

A word of caution is in order whenever the clinician is unable to identify the cause of a patient's ear pain. Idiopathic otalgia, especially if unilateral, is a diagnosis of exclusion that should generally be resisted because it is invariably wrong.[11] Repeat physical examination and careful retaking of the history with special attention directed to areas where occult tumor might cause pain that is referred to the ear are essential if disaster is to be avoided. This is one clinical situation where serial MRI of the brain and soft tissues of the neck, as well as CT of these areas, will often yield results. All patients with unexplained ear pain should undergo careful endoscopic examination of the aerodigestive tract with special attention paid to the region of the piriform sinuses to identify any occult pathology responsible for the pain (see later).

■ PAIN OF THE NOSE AND SINUSES

Infection of the nose is the most common cause of nasal pain absent trauma. Superficial soft tissue infections can be quite painful and have the potential to spread to deep structures if left untreated. Folliculitis of the vestibule of the nose can also be very painful and, when secondary to *Staphylococcus*, can be quite difficult to treat.[12] It has been occurring more commonly as the use of intranasal steroid sprays to treat atrophic rhinitis increases, and the early use of topical intranasal antibiotics such as mupirocin at the first sign of intranasal tenderness can help prevent more severe disease. Persistent foul-smelling discharge from the nose should alert the physician to the possibility of an intranasal foreign body, especially in children or mentally impaired individuals.

Acute sinusitis is another painful condition of the midface that can be caused by all infectious agents. Blockage of the ostia of the sinus is usually the cause of acute sinusitis, with the pressure within the sinuses increasing because mucus from the affected sinuses cannot flow into the nose. The maxillary sinuses are most commonly affected, and the pain associated with this disease can be quite severe. The pain is usually localized to the area over the sinus and may be worse with recumbency.

The diagnosis of acute sinusitis is usually made on clinical grounds and then confirmed with plain radiographs or CT[13,14] (Fig. 50–11). Treatment with decongestant nasal sprays and antibiotics will resolve most cases of acute sinusitis. Untreated, osteomyelitis may occur. Surgery may ultimately be required for recurrent disease, disease that remains unresponsive to conservative therapy, or when radiographs reveal obstructive polyps or tumors.

Malignancies of the nose and sinuses can be notoriously difficult to diagnose. The most common tumors of the nose are basal cell and squamous cell carcinoma.[15] Usually not painful unless infection intervenes or a painful structure is invaded, these tumors can become quite large before being detected (Fig. 50–12). Squamous cell carcinoma of the sinuses is manifested in a manner identical to sinusitis, so the diagnosis is often delayed. Nasopharyngoma occurs most commonly in patients of Asian decent. Thought to be caused by Epstein-Barr virus, these tumors frequently cause referred pain to the face, neck, and retroauricular area. Other lesions known for their ability to cause referred nose and facial pain are tumors involving the parapharyngeal space.[16] Almost always causing unilateral symptoms such as facial paralysis and pain, parapharyngeal tumors are frequently of neural origin (Fig. 50–13). As previously mentioned, delay in diagnosis of these tumors can complicate treatment and worsen the prognosis.

■ THROAT PAIN

Pain emanating from this region is poorly localized because of mixed innervation of the anatomic structures by the trigeminal, glossopharyngeal, and vagus nerves, as well as rich innervation by the sympathetic nervous system. For this reason, referred pain from this region is not the exception, but the rule. Because of the patient's difficulty in accurately localizing the source of the pain when pathology affects this anatomic region, extra vigilance on the part of the clinician is required.

Both superficial and deep infections are a common source of throat pain. Acute pharyngitis and laryngotracheobronchitis are among the most common reasons that patients seek medical attention.[17] Dental infections are also common causes of pain in this anatomic region and often cause pain referred to the ear.[18] Generally self-limited, these infections can become problematic if they spread to the deep structures of the neck and aerodigestive tract or if they occur in immunocompromised patients. In particular, parapharyngeal and retropharyngeal space abscesses after acute pharyngitis and tonsillitis can become life threatening if not promptly diagnosed and treated.[19] Patients with these disorders will appear acutely ill and will talk with a characteristic muffled "hot potato voice." With the increased availability of MRI and CT, early diagnosis of parapharyngeal and retropharyngeal abscesses is much easier (Fig. 50–14).

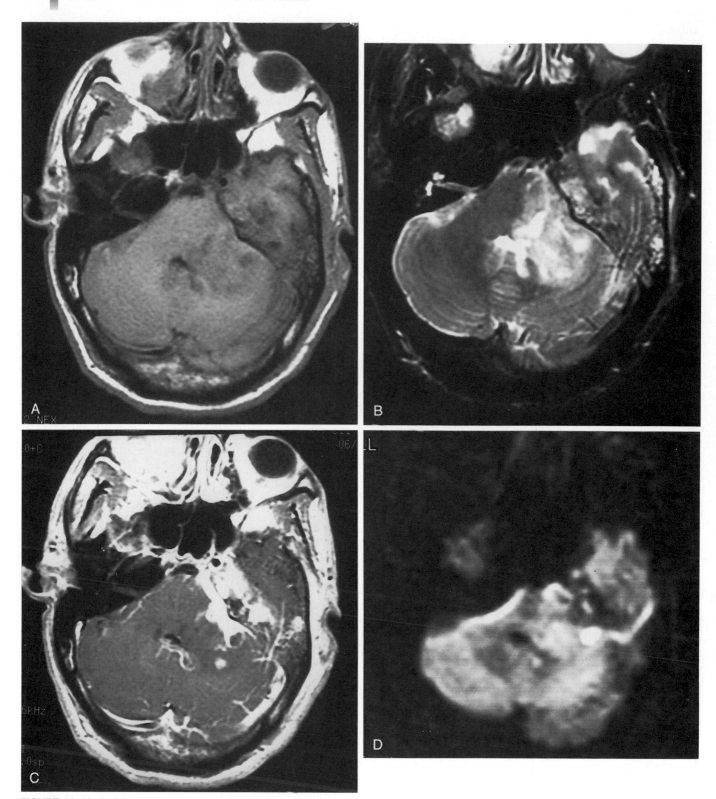

FIGURE 50–10 ■ Mastoiditis, cerebritis, and abscess formation. **A**, A T1-weighted MR image shows abnormal low signal intensity in the left temporal lobe, left brachium pontis, and left mastoid. **B**, A T2-weighted MR image shows heterogeneous high signal intensity involving the left temporal lobe, left brachium pontis, and left mastoid. **C**, A gadolinium-enhanced image demonstrates abnormal enhancement involving the left temporal lobe, left brachium pontis, and left mastoid. Note the presence of a small ring-like enhancement in the posterior aspect of the brachium pontis. **D**, A diffusion-weighted image reveals a focal area of increased signal intensity corresponding to the ring-like enhancement, consistent with restricted diffusion in an abscess. (From Haaga JR, Lanzieri CF, Gilkeson RC [eds]: CT & MR Imaging of the Whole Body, 4th ed. Philadelphia, CV Mosby, 2002.)

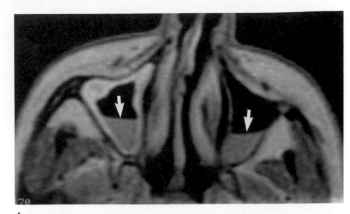

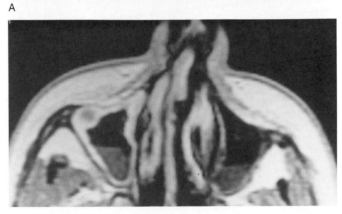

FIGURE 50–11 ■ Acute maxillary sinusitis on (**A**) T2-weighted (SE 2000/80) and (**B**) T1-weighted (SE 400/20) post–Gd-diethylenetriaminepentaacetic acid scans. Note the bilateral air-fluid levels (*arrows*) and mucosal thickening on the right. (From Grainger RG, Allison DJ: Grainger and Allison's Diagnostic Radiology: A Textbook of Medical Imaging, 3rd ed. New York, Churchill Livingstone, 1996.)

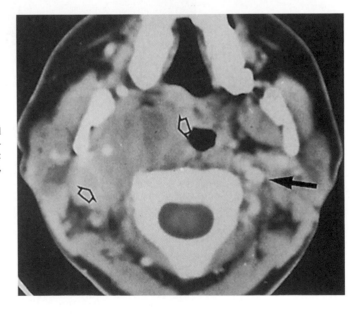

FIGURE 50–12 ■ Coronal CT scan showing a maxillary antral cholesterol granuloma (*black arrow*) (A). The antrum is expanded and occupied by material of soft tissue density (open arrows). (From Grainger RG, Allison DJ: Grainger and Allison's Diagnostic Radiology: A Textbook of Medical Imaging, 3rd ed. New York, Churchill Livingstone, 1996.)

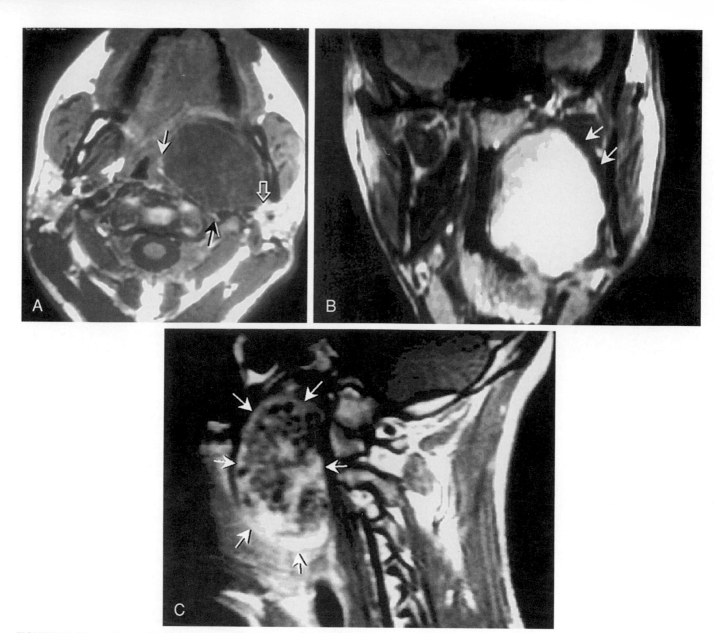

FIGURE 50–13 ■ Pleomorphic adenoma. **A**, A non-enhanced, T1-weighted axial MR image (TR = 500 msec, TE = 12 msec) demonstrates a well-defined mass of lower signal intensity than adjacent muscle that is replacing the prestyloid parapharyngeal fat; in addition, the minimal residual fat is displaced medially (*white arrow*) and the internal carotid artery is displaced posteriorly (*black arrow*). No intact fat plane can be demonstrated between the lesion and the deep lobe of the parotid gland (*open arrow*). **B**, An intermediate-weighted (TR = 2500 msec, TE = 30 msec) coronal MR image demonstrates the mass as relatively homogeneous, of increased signal intensity relative to adjacent muscles and lymphoid tissue, and well defined. The oropharyngeal mucosa is displaced medially. The left medial pterygoid muscle is compressed and displaced superolaterally (*arrows*). **C**, A contrast-enhanced, T1-weighted (TR = 500 msec, TE = 15 msec) sagittal MR image demonstrates marked heterogeneity of the mass, with multiple low–signal intensity regions that may represent areas of calcification or fibrosis. Both sagittal and coronal images are useful in revealing the craniocaudal extent of the lesion, which fills most of the prestyloid parapharyngeal space (*arrows*). The mass is inseparable from the deep lobe of the parotid gland and must be considered as arising from the deep lobe for surgical planning. However, the deep lobe of the parotid gland has been compressed and displaced laterally, with no visible connection to the mass at surgery. (From Haaga JR, Lanzieri CF, Gilkeson RC [eds]: CT & MR Imaging of the Whole Body, 4th ed. Philadelphia, CV Mosby, 2002.)

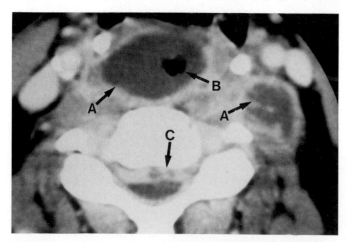

FIGURE 50–14 ■ Contrast-enhanced CT scan of a retropharyngeal abscess. There are two locules (A, A) shown in this section, along with a gas bubble (B). There is also an anterior epidural abscess (C). (From Grainger RG, Allison DJ: Grainger and Allison's Diagnostic Radiology: A Textbook of Medical Imaging, 3rd ed. New York, Churchill Livingstone, 1996.)

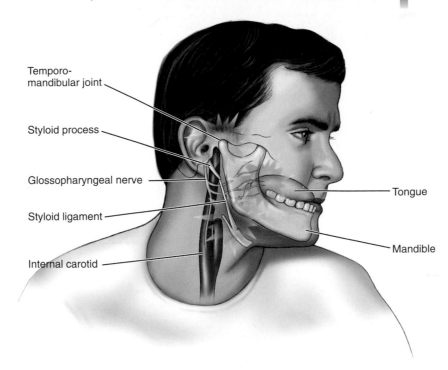

Temporo-
mandibular joint

Styloid process

Glossopharyngeal nerve

Styloid ligament

Internal carotid

Tongue

Mandible

FIGURE 50–15 ∎ The pain of Eagle syndrome is triggered by swallowing, movement of the mandible, or turning the neck. (From Waldman SD: Atlas of Uncommon Pain Syndromes. Philadelphia, WB Saunders, 2003.)

In addition to infections, tumors of this region can produce both local and referred pain.[20] These tumors are often hard to diagnose, and by the time that the pain is so severe that it causes the patient to seek medical attention, the tumors are already extremely problematic and in many cases have already metastasized. Most primary tumors in this region are squamous cell tumors, although primary tumors of the neural structures and craniopharyngiomas occur with sufficient frequency to be part of the differential diagnosis. Metastatic lesions can also cause local and referred pain in this anatomic area. Given the silent nature of this area insofar as symptoms are concerned, the clinician should make early and frequent use of MRI and CT to identify occult tumors and other pathology[21] (see Fig. 50–13). In particular, the clinician should never attribute pain in this region to an idiopathic or psychogenic etiology without serial physical examinations, laboratory evaluations, and imaging. In particular, unilateral otalgia in the absence of demonstrable ear pathology should be taken very seriously and considered to be referred pain from occult tumor until proved otherwise.

Other painful conditions unrelated to infection and tumor can also occur in this anatomic region, including Eagle syndrome, carotidynia, and hyoid syndrome.

Eagle syndrome is caused by calcification of the stylohyoid ligament and is characterized by paroxysms of pain with movement of the mandible during chewing, yawning, and talking[22] (Fig. 50–15). Carotidynia consists of deep neck pain in the region of the carotid that radiates to the ear and jaw. It is made worse with palpation of the area overlying the carotid artery. Hyoid syndrome is characterized by sharp paroxysms of pain with swallowing or head turning. The pain radiates to the ear and the angle of the jaw and can be reproduced with movement of the hyoid bone. In most cases, these unusual causes of ear, throat, and anterior neck pain are self-limited and will produce no long-lasting harm to the patient. However, before they are diagnosed, it is incumbent on the clinician to rule out other pathologic processes that may harm the patient because on a statistical basis they are much more common.

∎ CONCLUSION

Pain of the ear, nose, sinuses, and throat is commonly encountered in clinical practice. For the most part, the pathologic process responsible for the patient's pain symptomatology is easily identifiable after the physician performs a targeted history and physical examination. Unfortunately, the nature of this anatomic region makes it possible for the most thorough physician to miss pathology that may ultimately harm the patient. For this reason, the following rules for the treatment of ear, nose, sinus, and throat pain will serve both the patient and the clinician well: (1) take a targeted history; (2) perform a careful, targeted physical examination; (3) heed the warning signs of serious disease, such as fever, constitutional symptoms, or weight loss; (4) image early and frequently if the diagnosis remains elusive; (5) perform laboratory tests that will help identify "sick from well," such as the erythrocyte sedimentation rate, hematology, and blood tests; (6) avoid attributing the patient's pain to idiopathic or psychogenic causes; and (7) always assume that you have missed the diagnosis.

References

1. Olsen KD: The many causes of otalgia. Infection, trauma, cancer. Postgrad Med 80:50, 1986.
2. Al-Sheikhli AR: Pain in the ear—with special reference to referred pain. J Laryngol Otol 94:1433, 1980.
3. Waldman SD: Ramsey Hunt syndrome. In Waldman SD (ed): Uncommon Pain Syndromes. Philadelphia, WB Saunders, 2003, p 24.
4. Khalak R, Roberts JK: Images in medicine—cauliflower ear. N Engl J Med 335:399, 1996.

5. Khan AJ, Lynfield Y, Baldwin H: Relapsing polychondritis: Case report and review of the literature. Cutis 54:98, 1994.

6. Beers SL, Abramo TJ: Otitis externa review. Pediatr Emerg Care 20:250, 2004.

7. Kemppainen HO, Puhakka HJ, Laippala PJ, et al: Epidemiology and aetiology of middle ear cholesteatoma. Acta Otolaryngol 119:568, 1999.

8. Davies PH, Benger JR: Foreign bodies in the nose and ear: A review of techniques for removal in the emergency department. J Accid Emerg Med 17:91, 2000.

9. Bluestone CD: Clinical course, complications and sequelae of acute otitis media. Pediatr Infect Dis J 19(5 Suppl):S37, 2000.

10. Nadol JB Jr, Eavey RD: Acute and chronic mastoiditis: Clinical presentation, diagnosis, and management. Curr Clin Top Infect Dis 15:204, 1995.

11. Thaller SR, De Silva A: Otalgia with a normal ear. Am Fam Physician 36:129, 1987.

12. Eley CD, Gan VN: Picture of the month. Folliculitis, furunculosis, and carbuncles. Arch Pediatr Adolesc Med 151:625, 1997.

13. Kaliner MA, Osguthorpe JD, Fireman P: Sinusitis: Bench to bedside. Current findings, future directions. Otolaryngol Head Neck Surg 116(6 Pt 2):S1, 1997.

14. Laine K, Maatta T, Varonen H: Diagnosing acute maxillary sinusitis in primary care: A comparison of ultrasound, clinical examination and radiography. Rhinology 36:2, 1998.

15. Netscher DT, Spira M: Basal cell carcinoma: An overview of tumor biology and treatment. Plast Reconstr Surg 113(5):74E, 2004.

16. Pensak ML, Gluckman JL, Shumrick KA: Parapharyngeal space tumors: An algorithm for evaluation and management. Laryngoscope 104:1170, 1994.

17. Smith DS: Current concepts in the management of pharyngitis. Compr Ther 22:806, 1996.

18. Kreisberg MK, Turner J: Dental causes of referred otalgia. Ear Nose Throat J 66:398, 1987.

19. Beasley DJ, Amedee RG: Deep neck space infections. J La State Med Soc 147:181, 1995.

20. Yules RB: Differential diagnosis of referred otalgia. Eye Ear Nose Throat Mon 46:587, 1967.

21. Som PM, Curtin HD: Lesions of the parapharyngeal space. Role of MR imaging. Otolaryngol Clin North Am 28:515, 1995.

22. Waldman SD: Eagle's syndrome. In Waldman SD (ed): Uncommon Pain Syndromes. Philadelphia, WB Saunders, 2003, p 28.

51

Occipital Neuralgia

Steven D. Waldman

Perhaps one of the most over-diagnosed headache syndromes, occipital neuralgia represents a diagnostic and therapeutic challenge to the clinician. Further complicating any discussion of this painful condition is the contention by some headache specialists that the syndrome does not exist and represents a variant of cervicogenic headache emanating from the C1-C4 nerve roots.[1] Assuming that occipital neuralgia is a clinical entity distinct from cerviogenic headache, it is usually the result of blunt trauma to the greater and lesser occipital nerves.[2] Repetitive microtrauma from working with the neck hyperextended, e.g., painting ceilings, or working for prolonged periods with computer monitors whose focal point is too high causing extension of the cervical spine may also cause occipital neuralgia. The pain of occipital neuralgia is characterized as persistent pain at the base of the skull with occasional sudden shock-like paresthesias in the distribution of the greater and lesser occipital nerves. Tension-type headache which is much more common than occipital neuralgia will occasionally mimic the pain of occipital neuralgia.[3]

■ SIGNS AND SYMPTOMS

The greater occipital nerve arises from fibers of the dorsal primary ramus of the second cervical nerve and to a lesser extent fibers from the third cervical nerve. The greater occipital nerve pierces the fascia just below the superior nuchal ridge along with the occipital artery. It supplies the medial portion of the posterior scalp as far anterior as the vertex (Fig. 51–1).

The lesser occipital nerve arises from the ventral primary rami of the second and third cervical nerves. The lesser occipital nerve passes superiorly along the posterior border of the sternocleidomastoid muscle, dividing into cutaneous branches that innervate the lateral portion of the posterior scalp and the cranial surface of the pinna of the ear (see Fig. 51–1).

The patient suffering from occipital neuralgia will experience neuritic pain in the distribution of the greater and lesser occipital nerve when the nerves are palpated at the level of the nuchal ridge.[2] Some patients can elicit pain with rotation or lateral bending of the cervical spine.

■ TESTING

There is no specific test for occipital neuralgia. Testing is aimed primarily at identifying occult pathology or other diseases that may mimic occipital neuralgia (see Differential Diagnosis later). All patients with the recent onset of headache thought to be occipital neuralgia should undergo MRI testing of the brain and of the cervical spine. MRI testing should also be performed in those patients with previously stable occipital neuralgia who have experienced a recent change in headache symptomatology. Screening laboratory testing consisting of complete blood count, erythrocyte sedimentation rate, and automated blood chemistry testing should be performed if the diagnosis of occipital neuralgia is in question.

Neural blockade of the greater and lesser occipital nerves can serve as a diagnostic maneuver to help confirm the diagnosis and separate it from tension-type headache (see later). The greater and lesser occipital nerves can easily be blocked at the nuchal ridge (Fig. 51–2).

■ DIFFERENTIAL DIAGNOSIS

Occipital neuralgia is an infrequent cause of headaches and rarely occurs in the absence of blunt trauma to the greater and lesser occipital nerves. More often, the patient with headaches involving the occipital region, is in fact suffering from tension-type or cervicogenic headaches. Tension-type headaches will not respond to occipital nerve blocks, but are very amenable to treatment with antidepressant compounds such as amitriptyline in conjunction with cervical steroid epidural nerve blocks.[4] Therefore, the clinician should reconsider the diagnosis of occipital neuralgia in those patients whose symptoms are consistent with occipital neuralgia, but fail to respond to greater and lesser occipital nerve blocks.

■ TREATMENT

The treatment of occipital neuralgia consists primarily of neural blockade with local anesthetic and steroid combined with the judicious use of nonsteroidal antiinflammatories, muscle relaxants, tricyclic antidepressants, and physical therapy. Neural blockade of the greater and lesser occipital nerve is carried out using the following technique: The patient is placed in a sitting position with the cervical spine flexed

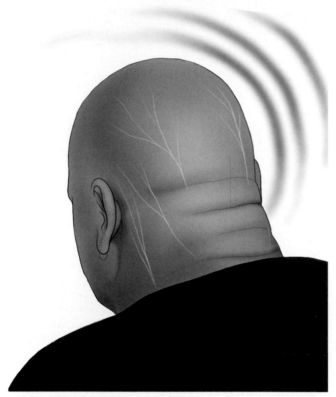

FIGURE 51–1 ■ Occipital neuralgia is caused by trauma to the greater and lesser occipital nerves. (From: Waldman SD: Atlas of Common Pain Syndromes. Philadelphia, WB Saunders, 2002, p 23, Fig 6–1.)

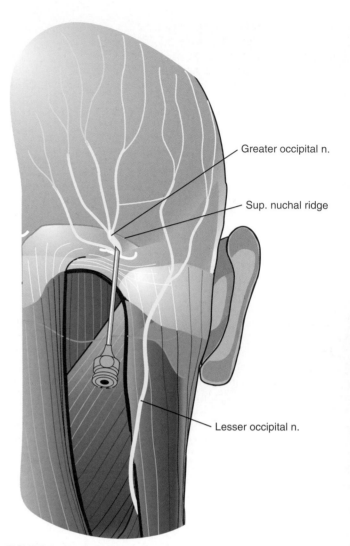

Greater occipital n.

Sup. nuchal ridge

Lesser occipital n.

FIGURE 51–2 ■ Technique for greater and lesser occipital nerve block.

and the forehead on a padded bedside table. A total of 8 mL of local anesthetic is drawn up in a 12-mL sterile syringe. When treating occipital neuralgia or other painful conditions involving the greater and lesser occipital nerve, a total of 80 mg of depot-steroid is added to the local anesthetic with the first block and 40 mg of depot-steroid is added with subsequent blocks.[5]

The occipital artery is then palpated at the level of the superior nuchal ridge. After preparation of the skin with antiseptic solution, a 22-gauge 1½-inch needle is inserted just medial to the artery and is advanced perpendicularly until the needle approaches the periosteum of the underlying occipital bone. A paresthesia may be elicited and the patient should be warned of such. The needle is then redirected superiorly and after gentle aspiration, 5 mL of solution is injected in a fanlike distribution with care being taken to avoid the foramen magnum which is located medially (see Fig 51–2).

The lesser occipital nerve and a number of superficial branches of the greater occipital nerve are then blocked by directing the needle laterally and slightly inferiorly. After gentle aspiration, an additional 3 to 4 mL of solution are injected (see Fig. 51–2).

■ COMPLICATIONS AND PITFALLS

The scalp is highly vascular and this—coupled with the fact that both the greater and lesser occipital nerves are in close proximity to arteries—means that the clinician should carefully calculate the total milligram dosage of local anesthetic

that may be safely given, especially if bilateral nerve blocks are being performed. This vascularity and proximity to the arterial supply gives rise to an increased incidence of postblock ecchymosis and hematoma formation. These complications can be decreased if manual pressure is applied to the area of the block immediately following injection. Application of cold packs for 20-minute periods following the block will also decrease the amount of postprocedure pain and bleeding the patient may experience. Care must be taken to avoid inadvertent needle placement into the foramen magnum, as the subarachnoid administration of local anesthetic in this region will result in an immediate total spinal anesthetic.

■ CONCLUSION

As with other headache syndromes, the clinician must be sure that the diagnosis is correct and that there is not coexisting intracranial pathology or diseases of the cervical spine that may be erroneously attributed to occipital neuralgia.

The most common reason that greater and lesser occipital nerve block will fail to relieve headache pain is that the headache syndrome being treated has been misdiagnosed as occipital neuralgia. Any patient with headaches bad enough to require neural blockade as part of their treatment plan should undergo an MRI scan of the head to rule out unsuspected intracranial pathology. Furthermore, cervical spine radiographs should be considered to rule out congenital abnormalities, such as Arnold-Chiari malformations, which may be the hidden cause of the patient's occipital headaches.

References

1. Edmeads J: Disorders of the neck: Cervicogenic headache. In Silberstein SD, Lipton RB, Dalessio D (eds): Wolff's Headache and Other Head Pain, 7th ed. New York, Oxford University Press, 2001, p 447.

2. Waldman SD: Occipital neuralgia. In Waldman SD: Atlas of Common Pain Syndromes. Philadelphia: WB Saunders, 2002, p 22.

3. Waldman SD: Tension-type headache. In Waldman SD: Atlas of Common Pain Syndromes. Philadelphia, WB Saunders, 2002, p 12.

4. Raj PP, Lou, L, Erdine, S, et al. Cervical epidural nerve block. In Raj PP, Lou L, Erdine S, et al (eds): Radiographic Imaging for Regional Anesthesia and Pain Management. Philadelphia, Churchill Livingstone, 2003, p 99.

5. Waldman SD: Cervical steroid epidural block. In Waldman SD: Atlas of Interventional Pain Management, 2nd ed. Philadelphia, Saunders, 2004, p 122.

chapter 52

Reflex Sympathetic Dystrophy of the Face

Kenneth D. Candido

Reflex sympathetic dystrophy (RSD) of the face is an unusual and rarely reported disease entity. Although the syndrome of RSD typically affects the distal upper or lower extremities, there are patients who present with facial pain of a nature reminiscent of that of extremity RSD, that is, pain not limited to the territory of a single peripheral nerve and pain that is spontaneous and associated with allodynia and hyperalgesia, edema, and abnormal skin blood flow. A recent review of the literature revealed that 13 cases had been described that loosely meet the International Association for the Study of Pain (IASP) criteria for complex regional pain syndrome type I (CRPS, RSD) (Table 52–1),[1] even though 8 of those case reports predate the 1994 IASP publication and the earliest is from 1947.[2] However, Behrman, in the commentary section of his single 1949 case report, stated that he had "encountered about ten cases" (of facial RSD), usually always after a difficult dental extraction.[3] If his description were even partially accurate, it may perhaps indicate that many cases of unusual or atypical facial pain have simply gone unrecognized as representing RSD or that they may have gone unreported.

■ CLINICAL PRESENTATION

The main features of RSD of the face are burning pain with allodynia, hyperalgesia, dysesthesia, hyperesthesia, and hyperpathia typically starting after some type of trauma to the craniofacial region, including dental extractions, vascular reconstructive surgery, gunshot wounds, and other insults. Physical signs are reported less often than the aforementioned symptoms (Table 52–2).[2] The pain of facial RSD appears to follow the topography of the sympathetically innervated vascular system rather than a radicular or dermatomal pattern. However, according to the actual case reports in the literature, facial RSD is infrequently associated with vasomotor and sudomotor changes and rarely progresses to a dystrophic or atrophic stage. The influence of the autonomic nervous system is considered separately from the type of CRPS (CRPS I [RSD] or CRPS II [causalgia]). Response to a sympatholytic procedure such as a stellate ganglion block (see Figs. 52–3 and 52–4) is used to differentiate between sympathetically mediated pain and sympathetically independent pain; this is

in addition to and independent of the diagnosis of CRPS types I or II.

The literature describes 13 cases of RSD of the face and neck from 1947 to 2000 (Table 52–3).[2-8,20,23-25] The male:female ratio of these cases was 8:5, and the mean age of patients at the time of presentation was 43.8 years.

Trauma was the inciting factor in 5 of the cases (38.5%), whereas it was secondary to surgery in 5 cases (38.5%) and to dental extraction in 3 cases (23%).

Traumatic injury or surgery of the face and neck may damage postganglionic sympathetic fibers distributed along the external carotid artery plexus. Sympathetic innervation to the facial skin, as well as the submandibular ganglion, is derived from the external carotid artery plexus (Figs. 52–1 and 52–2). Adventitial trauma or irritation at this location would be consistent with the clinical signs noted. Facial pain was consistently present, unlike the clinical reports of somatic RSD where pain is described about 75% of the time (see Table 52–2).[2] Pain was usually of a burning quality and was associated with hyperalgesia or hyperesthesia. Skin color changes, temperature changes, numbness, and hypoesthesia were reported less frequently. In rare cases, edema and trophic changes involving the skin of the face have been noted.[2] The profound bony, vascular, and trophic changes associated with advanced RSD of the extremities are not typical of facial RSD.[4] This lack of physical signs severely inhibits the assignation of the IASP criteria to confirm the diagnosis in all cases. However, this is typical of articles purporting to describe CRPS in general. Indeed, Reinders and colleagues, after performing a MEDLINE search, found 65 publications between January 1996 and July 2000 incorporating "complex regional pain syndrome," or "reflex sympathetic dystrophy" in their descriptions. IASP criteria were used scarcely in describing the syndrome in those 65 articles.[1] None of the articles reviewed fulfilled the strict IASP criteria for CRPS type I. Their conclusion was that the validity of the consensus diagnostic criteria is debatable.[1]

Although diagnostic tests may assist in confirming the diagnosis, the ultimate determination of whether CRPS is present lies with the clinical evaluation and with a high index of suspicion after eliminating other factors comprising the differential diagnosis. In the 13 cases reported, a successful analgesic response to sympathetic stellate ganglion block (SGB)

<table>
<tr><td colspan="2">

Table 52–1

</td></tr>
</table>

International Association for the Study of Pain (IASP) Classification of Complex Regional Pain Syndrome (CRPS), Type 1 (Reflex Sympathetic Dystrophy)

Diagnostic Criteria for CRPS I (RSD)

1. The presence of an inciting noxious event, or a cause of immobilization
2. Continuing pain, allodynia, or hyperalgesia with which the pain is disproportionate to any inciting event
3. Evidence at some time of edema, changes in skin blood flow, or abnormal sudomotor activity in the region of the pain
4. This diagnosis is excluded by the existence of conditions that would otherwise account for the degree of pain and dysfunction.

Note: Criteria 2-4 must be satisfied.

From Merskey H, Bogduk N (eds): Classification of Chronic Pain: Descriptions of Chronic Pain Syndromes and Definitions of Pain Terms, 2nd ed. Seattle, IASP Press, 1994.

Table 52–2

Comparison of the Signs and Symptoms of Facial RSD versus Those of Somatic RSD (CRPS Type I)

Signs/ Symptoms	Facial RSD	Somatic RSD
Pain	100%	75%
Hyperalgesia/ hyperesthesia	54%	70%-80%
Allodynia	38%	70%-80%
Dysesthesia	8%	70%
Edema	23%	50%
Sweating abnormalities	15%	50%
Skin color changes	46%	75%-98%
Skin temperature changes	46%	75%-98%

From Melis M, Zawawi K, Al-Badawi E, et al: Complex regional pain syndrome in the head and neck: A review of the literature. J Orofac Pain 16:93, 2002.

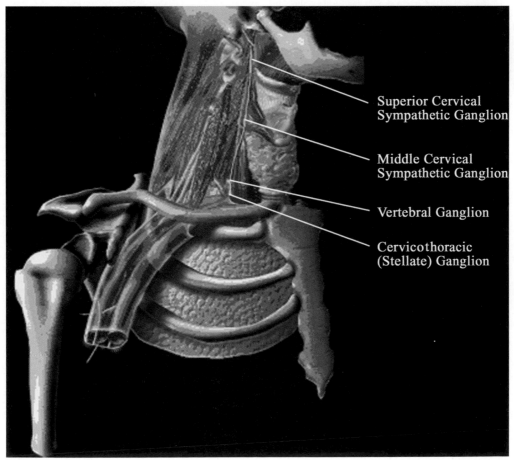

Superior Cervical Sympathetic Ganglion

Middle Cervical Sympathetic Ganglion

Vertebral Ganglion

Cervicothoracic (Stellate) Ganglion

FIGURE 52–1 ■ Sympathetic innervation to the facial skin.

Table 52–3

Summary of RSD Cases of the Face and Neck: 1947-2000

Author	Year	Age/ Sex	Etiology	Symptoms	Signs	Treatment	Outcomes	Ref. No.
Bingham	1947	28/M	Shell fragment in (R) cheek	Burning pain V1-V3 distribution	Hyperalgesia V1-V3	SGB, then cervical sympathectomy	Pain free at 3-mo follow-up	5
Bingham	1947	23/M	Mortar wounds (L) cheek	Burning pain V2	Hyperesthesia in cheek	SGB, then cervical sympathectomy	Symptoms resolved	3
Behrman	1949	?/F	Tooth extraction	Mandibular pain	Not reported	Stellate ganglion blocks	Not reported	3
Hanowell/ Kennedy	1979	59/M	Cancer of tongue; radical neck dissection	Phantom tongue pain; burning in cheeks and temples	Hyperemia on side of face; hyperesthesia; stabbing pain	Stellate ganglion blocks; aimtriptyline (Elavil)	Complete pain relief after 3 blocks	23
Khoury et al.	1980	60/M	Cancer: maxillectomy	Burning pain; eyelid, nose, face, lip	Skin edema, erythyema; coolness, side of face	Stellate ganglion blocks	75%-85% improved; still some lip sensitivity	24
Teeple et al.	1981	38/F	Trauma, side of face (sail boom)	Pain; left shoulder, arm	Papillary dilatation; face coolness	Stellate ganglion blocks; aspirin	Pain free at 6 mo; pupils equal	20
Jaeger et al.	1986	33/F	Tooth extraction	Facial pain; preauricular area to orbit, zygoma, mandible; photophobia	Facial swelling; trismus, temperature change	Stellate ganglion blocks	Pain free at 15-mo follow-up	4
Jaeger et al.	1986	31/M	Subtotal resection frontal sinus; reoperation	Burning in forehead radiating to orbits and maxilla	Tender scar; suprabrow; hyperesthesia	Stellate ganglion blocks with morphine	66% improved facial pain; scar pain persists	4
Veldman/ Jacobs	1994	47/F	Motor vehicle accident; zygomatic arch impaction; orbital floor fracture	Dull pain side of face and head	Hyperesthesia; facial paresis; swelling; erythema; warmth; hyperhidrosis	N-acetylcysteine, 600 mg tid	Partial decrease in face pain; decreased warmth, redness	7
Saxen/ Campbell	1995	32/F	Tooth extraction	Constant burning pain infraorbital area	Hyperesthesia on cheek; erythema	Stellate ganglion blocks; clonidine, 0.1 mg bid	Pain relief for 24 hr; long-term follow-up not specified	6
Arden et al.	1998	69/M	External carotid to distal vertebral artery transposition	Sharp cheek pain; excess salivation	Hyperesthesia lower part of face	Stellate ganglion blocks with LA and phenol	80%-85% relief at 3-yr follow-up	8
Arden et al.	1998	69/M	External carotid to distal vertebral artery transposition	Burning cheek pain; excess salivation; tongue claudication	Hyperesthesia lower part of face	Stellate ganglion blocks with LA	50%-70% relief at 2.5-yr follow-up	8
Figueroa et al.	2000	37/M	Motor vehicle accident; head and neck injury	Burning pain; hyperpathia; side of face	Increased skin temperature, pallor, side of face; allodynia	Steroids (methyl-prednisolone, 60 mg/kg/day)	100% pain relief at 6 days	25

LA, local anesthetics.
Summary:
Total cases: 13
Male/female: 8:5
Mean age: 43.8 years (12 cases)
Trauma: 5/13 (38.5%)
Surgery: 5/13 (38.5%)
Tooth extraction: 3/13 (23%)
Stellate ganglion blocks: 11/13 (85%)

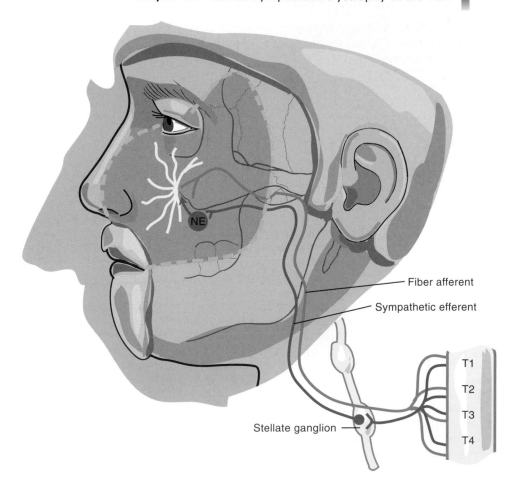

FIGURE 52–2 ■ Pharmacologic and physiologic pathways at the site of nerve injury. (From Khoury R, Kennedy SF, MacNamara TE: Facial causalgia: Report of a case. J Oral Surg 38:782, 1980.)

using local anesthetic was noted in 85% (11/13), and in one case each morphine SGB and phenol SGB were successfully used for treatment. One patient each was successfully treated with amitriptyline, oral clonidine, oral methylprednisolone, oral *N*-acetylcysteine, and intravenous guanethidine plus physical therapy. Two patients in the earliest report were successfully treated with cervical sympathectomies after analgesic stellate ganglion blocks were performed.[5] Ultimate pain relief after treatment ranged from 50% to 100% in all cases noted.[2]

Pain is the cardinal symptom of RSD, whether of the face or of the periphery (see Table 52–2). Pain is typically spontaneous, but it may be evoked by stimuli and may be episodic, paroxysmal, or continuous. The quality of pain may be burning, shooting, throbbing, pressing, or aching or some combination of these qualities. The intensity of the pain is typically out of proportion to the inciting event. Also noted are mechanical and thermal hyperalgesia, dysesthesia, hyperesthesia, allodynia, and hyperpathia. Signs of inflammation may or may not be present. Edema and abnormalities in sudomotor and vasomotor function experienced as increased (hyperhidrosis: warm, moist skin) or decreased (hypohidrosis: cool, dry skin) sweating secondary to autonomic dysfunction may be present. The skin may appear mottled and discolored (reddish, bluish, or purplish), or it may be pale. In the case report by Saxen and Campbell, the patient presented with noninflammatory atypical telangiectasia in the left infraorbital area and cheek.[6] The size and color of the skin lesion varied throughout the treatment period, although the burning

pain in that area remained unchanged for much of that time. The skin on the affected side may be warmer or colder than that of the nonaffected side. Facial hair may become coarser and thick or thin and sparse. Combing the hair on the scalp may be extremely painful.[4] There may be stiffness and ankylosing of the facet joints of the cervical spine or of the temporomandibular joint. Facial muscles may droop or become notably weaker on the affected side. In the case report of Veldman and Jacobs, the patient noted that the right side of her mouth and the right upper eyelid drooped, in a distribution that was unrelated to the anatomic innervation area of a peripheral nerve.[7] Hypersalivation may be present, as noted by Arden and associates.[8] Postganglionic fibers are distributed to approximately the same cutaneous areas as that supplied with sensory fibers by the corresponding radicular nerve (i.e., oral tongue–jaw–V_3 dermatome). Considering that 71% of resting salivation is provided by the submandibular glands, with the observation that copious secretions from this gland can be elicited in response to sympathetically stimulated alterations in vasomotor tone, it is plausible to presume a causal relationship between complaints of hypersalivation and heightened sympathetic activity in the submandibular ganglion.[8]

■ PATHOPHYSIOLOGY

The mechanism by which pain and other physical abnormalities develop in CRPS has not been clearly elucidated. Several theories have been devised to attempt to correlate the physical and biochemical findings with accepted mechanisms of peripheral and central nervous system functioning. Trauma usually precedes the syndrome, resulting in derangements in peripheral nerve functioning and inducing neurobiologic changes in both the peripheral and central nervous systems.[9] Simply stated, a deafferentation mechanism ensues that becomes self-perpetuating via the central sensitization syndrome involving activation of wide-dynamic range (WDR) or multireceptive neurons.[10] The initiation of this central sensitization is peripheral tissue injury that activates lightly myelinated A-delta or unmyelinated C-nociceptors, which in turn activate and sensitize WDR neurons in the dorsal horn whose axons ascend to higher centers. This sensitization persists, so that the WDR neurons now respond to mechanical activity in large-diameter, low threshold A-mechanoreceptor afferents, which are activated by brushing or light touch. A painful sensation results (allodynia), independent of and not proportional to any actual noxious stimulus applied to the nociceptors. Moreover, these sensitized WDR neurons respond to mechanoreceptive activity initiated by sympathetic efferent action on sensory receptors in the absence of cutaneous stimulation, thus producing spontaneous "sympathetically mediated pain." In this hypothetical model, the only abnormal neuronal state required is a persistent sensitization or increase gain of WDR neurons.

Although this hypothesis only focuses on central changes in sensitivity to afferent impulses, there is accumulating experimental evidence that the following changes take place: After peripheral nerve injury occurs, large-diameter myelinated axons sprout from their site of termination in lamina III or deeper into the upper laminae, a region normally only innervated by small-diameter, high-threshold afferents. Indeed, Woolf and colleagues described sprouting of A-fibers into lamina II of the dorsal horn of the spinal cord.[11] Thus, low-threshold afferents gain access to a pool of dorsal horn neurons involved in nociceptive processing that were originally accessed only by high-threshold afferent input. Some WDR neurons send their axons to the thalamus or to the reticular formation through the ventrolateral fasciculus in the company of axons from nociceptor-specific neurons.[10] This accounts, at least in part, for the development of allodynia after peripheral nerve injury.[9] One scenario postulated is that this neural rewiring alters lamina II recognition, so that this zone, which normally recognizes only nociceptive inputs, now receives non-nociceptive inputs that may be misinterpreted as noxious. Allodynia results when light touch or pressure is applied to the skin. Activation of second-order neurons in the dorsal horn might result from release of substance P and calcitonin gene–related peptide from normally non-nociceptive A-fibers after a phenotypic change occurs in those fibers after nerve injury.[2]

Additionally, after some types of nerve injury, primary afferent neurons undergo biologic changes that lead to abnormal sensitization and spontaneous ectopic discharge. This phenomenon resembles attempts of nerves to sprout after nerve injury and also resembles the formation of a neuroma on the cut end of a nerve.[9] It has been suggested that ephaptic (nonsynaptic) transmission, nerve collaterals, or nerve sprouting after injury may account for abnormal nerve functioning.[9] Total axonal disruption is not a prerequisite for a sprout to develop, but the nerve injury does result in a break-

down of the blood-nerve barrier (vaso-nervorum) and facilitates the entry of chemical mediators and/or blockers. These sprouts or "growth cones" seek to track down the original neural channels; however, such regrowth is often thwarted, leading to local collections of sprouts with chaotic organization, or "neuromas." A neuroma is not a true neoplasm but is a disorganized structure that includes axoplasmic elements, myelin, Schwann cells, and connective tissue elements.[2] Neuromas can produce spontaneous continuous pain or episodic pain triggered by external pressure or tension.[2] Many myelinated and unmyelinated afferents that innervate these neuromas can be excited by epinephrine and norepinephrine, thus raising the question whether damaged sensory fibers may express adrenergic receptors. Devor and Jänig demonstrated that afferent fibers from a neuroma are activated by sympathetic stimulation or by intravenous norepinephrine and that this activation can be blocked by the α-adrenergic antagonist phentolamine but not by the β-antagonist propranolol.[12] These findings have led to the hypothesis that nociceptors (A-delta and C fibers) develop sensitivity to norepinephrine through expression of α_1-adrenergic receptors on their terminals. Indirect mechanisms supporting this hypothesis include activation of α-adrenergic receptors on mast cells, leukocytes, and platelets by norepinephrine, which then release chemical mediators (histamine, bradykinin, prostaglandins), which in turn activate nociceptive afferents. Norepinephrine released by activity of sympathetic postganglionic axons excites primary afferent neurons by activating α-adrenergic receptors. According to the theory of Roberts, a vicious cycle develops when nociceptive input to the trigeminal ganglion stimulates sympathetic efferent responses as a result of tonic release of norepinephrine.[10] The combination of tonic norepinephrine release and sympathetic efferent responses results in further norepinephrine release, which perpetuates the pain.[6] Although compelling and theoretically plausible, the neuroma model is not relevant to those cases of sympathetically mediated pain in which the nerve is not injured. Furthermore, it cannot explain the efficacy of nerve blocks distal to the site of nerve injury or the immediate onset of RSD pain after nerve injury in some individuals.[12]

Another theory suggests that in sympathetically mediated pain, a short-circuiting phenomenon may develop in which collateral sympathetic efferents synapse with afferent sensory fibers at the site of peripheral injury. After peripheral nerve injury, sensory axons may express α- or β-adrenergic receptors on their membranes. These axons might subsequently become sensitized to circulating catecholamines. The same modification may be occurring at the dorsal root ganglion neurons.[9] The influence of the heightened sympathetic activity on peripheral afferent fibers may also occur secondary to norepinephrine-induced stimulation of prostaglandin synthesis, an effect reversible by the administration of antiinflammatory medications. Prostaglandins are known to sensitize sensory afferents, and this information led investigators to experiment with the use of intravenous regional blocks using ketorolac (a nonsteroidal antiinflammatory agent) for treatment of RSD of the extremity.[9] Ketorolac inhibits the enzyme cyclooxygenase and subsequently reduces prostaglandin synthesis, suggesting that because prostaglandins sensitize pain receptors to both chemical and mechanical stimuli, reduction of prostaglandin levels should reduce this sensitivity.[9] Nonsteroidal antiinflammatory agents may also interfere with the vasoconstriction produced by thromboxanes. Reduction in prostaglandin levels may lead to the inhibition of norepinephrine release and, in addition, may result in direct vasodilatation. At a cellular level, RSD is characterized, then, by cellular hypoxia, decreased oxygen extraction at the tissue level, and increased permeability for macromolecules, supporting a role for toxic oxygen radicals as a cause for the syndrome.[7] Sudek's theory of more than 60 years ago may indeed be true, that RSD is a pathologic course of a physiologic inflammatory response to an injury.[7,13]

In addition to pain, other abnormalities are seen in CRPS, some of which may be related to altered function of the sympathetic nervous system. Edema, abnormalities in skin blood flow, and abnormal sudomotor activity may all be blocked by sympathetic nervous system blockade. Vasculature in the vicinity of the insult may develop an increased sensitivity to local cold-temperature stimuli and catecholamines, demonstrated experimentally by testing the thermoregulatory response to skin cooling and warming, suggesting that both an inhibition and activation of sympathetic reflexes may be evident.[14] Trophic changes (not typically seen in facial RSD or CRPS) such as abnormal nail growth, increased hair growth, palmar and plantar fibrosis, thin glossy skin, and hyperkeratosis have been hypothesized to have an inflammatory pathogenesis. Scintigraphic investigations strongly support an inflammatory component in CRPS, hence the rationale for antiinflammatory medication use in treatment as described earlier.[2,9]

■ DIAGNOSTIC TESTS

The diagnosis of CRPS is a clinical one, based on careful analysis of signs, symptoms, and exclusion of other factors in the differential diagnosis. There are, however, objective tests described in the literature that, although not specific, tend to confirm the diagnostic impression of autonomic, sensory, and motor dysfunction, as follows:

- *Quantitative sensory tests (QST):* These tests measure subjective responses to superficial stimulation and provide information regarding peripheral nerve function of afferent fibers in response to tactile, pressure, thermal, and noxious stimuli.[14] QST can also test the functional status of large myelinated fibers with the dorsal columns by testing vibratory threshold activity.[15]
- *Laser Doppler flowmetry:* This test measures skin blood flow in the area tested; results may be compared with those from the contralateral side.[6,14]
- *Infrared thermography:* This modality records the distribution of skin temperature. Each area is subsequently compared with the contralateral side's equivalent area.[14]
- *Quantitative sudomotor axon reflex test (QSART):* This is a measure of evoked sweat response. It provides information on the function of the sudomotor reflex loops. Although it examines axon reflex response, it cannot be used to measure the effect of sympatholysis.[14]
- *Bone scintigraphy.* Changes in bone vascularity are noted using this test. Only an indication of changes occurring in the subacute period may be determined. A three-phase bone scan provides more discriminative scintigraphic description of the disease.[16]

- *Plain radiographs:* These may show the status of bone demineralization of the bones of the face, in contradistinction to those of the nonaffected side.[17]
- *Sympathetic nerve blocks:* A sympathetic nerve block (stellate ganglion block) may be used for diagnostic and therapeutic purposes for individuals suffering from CRPS of the face and neck (Figs. 52–3 and 52–4). A reduction of pain concomitant with signs of sympathetic block of the face (ipsilateral ptosis, miosis, anhidrosis, apparent enophthalmos—Horner syndrome) and an elevation of the temperature of the ipsilateral hand are sought. Care must be taken to interpret results of the block in light of underlying pathology, because Horner syndrome may be caused by interruption of the preganglionic fibers at any point between their origin in the intermediolateral cell column of C8-T1 spinal segments and the superior cervical ganglion or by interruption of the descending, uncrossed hypothalamospinal pathway in the tegmentum of the brain stem or cervical cord. Causes of Horner syndrome are tumorous or inflammatory involvement of cervical lymph nodes, surgical and other types of trauma to cervical structures, neoplastic invasion of the proximal part of the brachial plexus, basilar skull fractures, tumor, syringomyelia or traumatic lesions of the first and second thoracic spinal segments, and infarcts or other lesions of the lateral part of the medulla (Wallenberg syndrome). There is also an idiopathic variety that may be hereditary. A superior sulcus tumor of the lung may produce a chronic Horner syndrome as well. With preganglionic lesions, flushing may develop on the side of the sympathetic disorder; this effect may be brought on in some instances by exercise (harlequin effect).[18]

■ TREATMENT

The purpose of therapy is to relieve pain and improve function. Along with interventions, physical therapy is essential to help restore function and improve muscle strength. In the early stages of RSD, gentle controlled stimulation using heat, massage, pressure, cold, vibration, and movement may all help restore normal sensory processing. Appropriate counseling is essential to help deal with issues of depression, denial, anxiety, anger, and fear. A cognitive-behavioral approach is often helpful to overcome pain avoidance, overprotection, movement phobia, and bracing.[2]

Nonpharmacologic modalities attempted for pain relief have included the use of transcutaneous electrical nerve stimulation (TENS), peripheral nerve stimulation, or biofeedback. Biofeedback has been touted as a means of enabling the patient to alter sympathetic activity and increase blood flow to the affected area.

Medication management has included nonsteroidal antiinflammatory agents, corticosteroids, opioids, and membrane stabilizers acting on sodium channels, such as phenytoin, carbamazepine, mexiletine, and local anesthetics, with the purpose of reducing the normal and ectopic firing of neurons. Some success has been shown with phenytoin and carbamazepine in the treatment of painful diabetic polyneuropathy syndromes, and these agents have been tried in RSD cases as well.[15] Mexiletine, the oral congener of lidocaine hydrochloride, may have beneficial effects in chronic persistent neuropathic pain states and may be attempted in facial RSD if

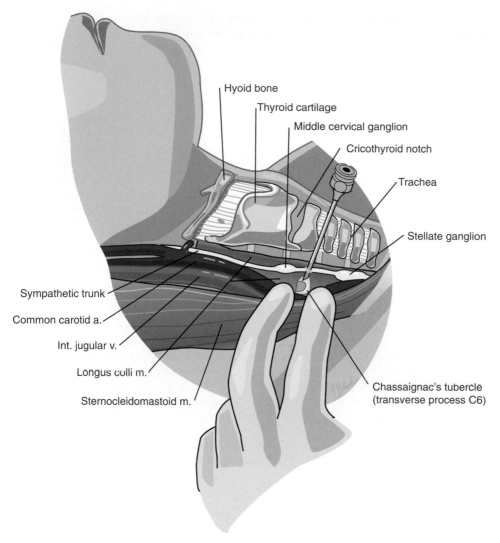

Hyoid bone

Thyroid cartilage

Middle cervical ganglion

Cricothyroid notch

Trachea

Stellate ganglion

Sympathetic trunk

Common carotid a.

Int. jugular v.

Longus colli m.

Sternocleidomastoid m.

Chassaignac's tubercle
(transverse process C6)

FIGURE 52–3 ■ Stellate ganglion block—anterior approach. (From Waldman SD [ed]: Atlas of Interventional Pain Management. Philadelphia, WB Saunders, 1998, p 103.)

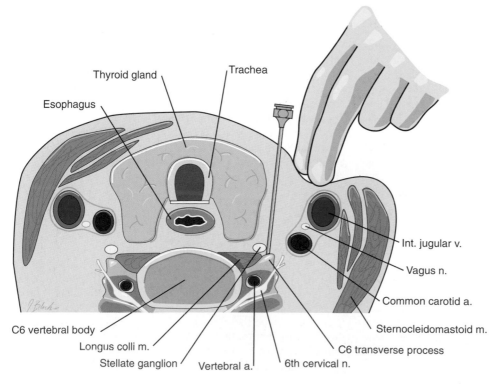

Thyroid gland

Trachea

Esophagus

Int. jugular v.

Vagus n.

Common carotid a.

Sternocleidomastoid m.

C6 vertebral body

Longus colli m.

Stellate ganglion

Vertebral a.

6th cervical n.

C6 transverse process

FIGURE 52–4 ■ Stellate ganglion block—transverse section of the anterior approach. (From Waldman SD [ed]: Atlas of Interventional Pain Management. Philadelphia, WB Saunders, 1998, p 103.)

patients have a positive response to an intravenous lidocaine test. Tricyclic antidepressants, particularly amitriptyline, have been used with some success in neuropathic pain.[15] The drugs of this class work at the CNS brain stem/dorsal horn nociceptive-modulating system, where they alter 5-hydroxytryptamine and norepinephrine activity.[15] They also bind to other receptor sites, including histaminergic, cholinergic, and adrenergic. Other types of antidepressants have not demonstrated the kind of success seen with amitriptyline for neuropathic pain states, but venlafaxine, a serotonin and norepinephrine reuptake inhibitor, has been suggested in the treatment paradigm.[15,19] Venlafaxine is a strong uptake inhibitor of both serotonin and norepinephrine with minimal muscarinic, histaminergic, and adrenergic activity.[15] Venlafaxine may produce analgesia similar to that of the tricyclic antidepressants without their frequent anticholinergic and histaminergic side effects. Gabapentin has been successfully used in the treatment of neuropathic pain states and has also been used in CRPS.[9,15] A major benefit of gabapentin use is its excellent safety profile, permitting repetitive escalating dose use without fear of catastrophic consequences. Clonidine, a peripheral α_2-receptor agonist with CNS activity, is available in an oral form, as a transdermal preparation, and for intrathecal use. Transdermal clonidine has been used successfully in the treatment of painful diabetic neuropathy and was successfully used in the facial RSD case report of Saxen and Campbell.[6] Capsaicin has been used topically in an effort to reduce peripheral inputs. The advantages of topical application of medications over oral administration include a directed activity at a mechanistic site of pain generation in the periphery with minimal risk of significant systemic side effects, no drug-drug interactions, and no need for dose titration.[15] In one case of facial RSD, *N*-acetylcysteine was used with significant reduction in allodynia.[7] Other modalities used have included scavengers of oxygen free radicals, deep brain stimulation in the sensory thalamus and medial lemniscus, and spinal cord stimulators.

Repeated stellate ganglion blocks (SGBs) have been used most frequently when a sympathetic component is present for RSD of the face and neck. SGB may be efficacious by removing sympathetic excitation of A-fiber mechanoreceptors. A reduction in tonic mechanoreceptor activity after sympathetic block should result in a disfacilitation of WDR neurons, and therefore a reduction in the allodynia and hyperpathia that accompanies sympathetically mediated pain if those symptoms are mediated by mechanoreceptors.[10] The sympathetic fibers that serve the orofacial structures arise from the upper thoracic (primarily the first and second) spinal segments (see Figs. 52–1 and 52–2). These fibers course upward through the stellate (fused inferior cervical and upper thoracic) and middle cervical ganglia to synapse in the superior cervical ganglion before leaving the chain to supply the face (see Figs. 52–1 and 52–2).[4] The cervicothoracic chain can be injected by anterior, posterior, or paravertebral approaches using local anesthetics or adjuvant medications (see Figs. 52–3 and 52–4). These medications tend to spread along the ganglia. Interruption of any of these levels can cause Horner syndrome. In the 13 case studies, SGB was used in 11 (85%). In 1, cervical plexus block was added to SGB to relieve muscle spasms in the neck.[20] Based on an atypical response to treatment, Arden and colleagues suggest implementing contralateral SGB when symptomatic improvement with ipsilateral blocks plateaus.[8]

Although the mechanism for this idiosyncratic response is unclear, observations of crossed lateral radiation responses (particularly of the hand) favorably influenced by ipsilateral injections have been documented.[1] Typically, local anesthetics such as bupivacaine or mepivacaine have been used. Mepivacaine, an amino-amide local anesthetic, may be the safest amide in terms of systemic toxicity and has a shorter duration of action at sodium channels than does bupivacaine. Because the actual duration of sympathetic block resulting from local anesthetic stellate ganglion block does not correlate with overall outcome,[9] it makes little sense to use long-acting agents. If a complication results from the misplacement of such agents in a blood vessel or in the central neuraxis during performance of the block, significantly greater morbidity may result from the longer-acting, highly protein bound, highly lipophilic action of such drugs.

Other agents used for stellate ganglion block have included neurolytics such as phenol or alcohol and opioids such as morphine and fentanyl. Other sympatholytics that act on the norepinephrine receptor may be used, including drugs such as guanethidine and reserpine. Guanethidine decreases the presynaptic release of norepinephrine at neuronal sites. Phentolamine reduces the action of norepinephrine on receptors by blocking both β_1 and β_2 receptors peripherally. The α_2-agonist clonidine, a centrally acting agent, decreases the release of norepinephrine from presynaptic neurons.

A somewhat more aggressive intervention, surgical cervical sympathectomy, may be reserved for refractory cases.[5]

■ CONCLUSION

RSD of the face is an uncommon and rarely reported clinical entity. Comparison between this and RSD (CRPS type I) in other parts of the body may not be valid because of the small number of reported cases of CRPS in the head and neck. Many of the older case summaries are notably brief, and the authors have probably not included the entire constellation of symptoms and signs. Indeed, in the report of Behrman from 1949, even the patient's age was not included.[3] In any event, only 13 cases have been reported between 1947 and 2000. It is entirely possible that facial RSD may be a variant or atypical presentation of a more common disorder such as myofascial pain with concomitant involvement of the autonomic nervous system.[2] An additional hypothesis is that the orofacial region, being overrepresented in a neurologic homunculus, may respond differently to trauma than other somatic areas. The rich collateral and anastomotic vascular supply of the face may minimize the development of the signs seen with extremity RSD.[4] This phenomenon of differential response to trauma between the head and other body areas has some support in nonhuman models.[21,22] In a rat model, peripheral nerve injury–induced sprouting of sympathetic nerve fibers occurred less frequently in the trigeminal ganglion than it did in spinal nerve regions, perhaps suggesting that the face is somewhat more resistant to developing RSD-related physiologic derangements than are the distal extremities.[21,22] A high index of suspicion, combined with a broad-based differential diagnosis, is essential to identifying and treating this group of patients. Ignoring or misdiagnosing them may ultimately result in their being overmedicated with opioids with the attendant addiction issues, potential for severe psychological disturbances, and possibly suicidal ideation. In that regard, it remains essential, when treating these patients, to not dismiss the important role that depression or anxiety plays in perpetuating the illness. Maladaptive coping skills need to be addressed, as well. Prompt initiation of physical therapy, once the acute stage has resolved, remains a mainstay of treatment.

References

1. Reinders MF, Geertzen JHB, Dijkstra PU: Complex regional pain syndrome type I: Use of the international association for the study of pain diagnostic criteria defined in 1994. Clin J Pain 18:207, 2002.
2. Melis M, Zawawi K, Al-Badawi E, et al: Complex regional pain syndrome in the head and neck: A review of the literature. J Orofac Pain 16:93, 2002.
3. Behrman S: Facial neuralgias. Br Dent J 86:197, 1949.
4. Jaeger B, Singer E, Kroening R: Reflex sympathetic dystrophy of the face: Report of two cases and a review of the literature. Arch Neurol 43:693, 1986.
5. Bingham JA: Causalgia of the face: Two cases successfully treated by sympathectomy. BMJ 1:804, 1947.
6. Saxen MA, Campbell RL: An unusual case of sympathetically maintained pain complicated by telangiectasia. Oral Surg Oral Med Oral Pathol Oral Radiol Endod 79:455, 1995.
7. Veldman PHJ, Dunkl Jacobs PB: Reflex sympathetic dystrophy of the head: Case report and discussion of diagnostic criteria. J Trauma 36:119, 1994.
8. Arden RL, Bahu SJ, Zuazu MA, Berguer R: Reflex sympathetic dystrophy of the face: Current treatment recommendations. Laryngoscope 108:437, 1998.
9. Winnie AP, Candido KD: Reflex sympathetic dystrophy, complex regional pain syndrome, and sympathetically-maintained pain. Prog Anesthesiol 15:55, 2001.
10. Roberts WJ: A hypothesis on the physiologic basis for causalgia and related pain. Pain 24:297, 1986.
11. Woolf CJ, Shortland P, Coggeshall RE: Peripheral nerve injury triggers central sprouting of myelinated afferents. Nature 355:75, 1992.
12. Devor M, Jänig W: Activation of myelinated afferents ending in a neuroma by stimulation of the sympathetic supply in the rat. Neurosci Lett 24:43, 1981.
13. Sudek P: Die Sog, acute Knochenatriphie als Entzündungsvorgang. Chirurgie 14:449, 1942.
14. Wasner G, Backonja MM, Baron R: Traumatic neuralgias: Complex regional pain syndromes (reflex sympathetic dystrophy and causalgia): Clinical characteristics, pathophysiological mechanisms and therapy. Neurol Clin 16:851, 1998.
15. Galer BS: Painful polyneuropathy. Neurol Clin 16:791, 1998.
16. Kozin F, Soin JS, Ryan LM, et al: Bone scintigraphy in the reflex sympathetic dystrophy syndrome. Radiology 138:437, 1981.
17. Kozin F, Genant HK, Bekerman C, McCarty DJ: The reflex sympathetic dystrophy syndrome: II. Roentgenographic and scintigraphic evidence of bilaterality and of periarticular accentuation. Am J Med 60:332, 1976.
18. Adams RD, Victor M (eds): Disorders of the autonomic nervous system. In Principles of Neurology, 5th ed. New York, McGraw-Hill, 1993, pp 470-471.
19. Woolf C, Mannion R: Neuropathic pain: Etiology, symptoms, mechanisms, and management. N Engl Pain Assoc Newsletter 5:4, 2000.
20. Teeple E, Ferrer EB, Ghia JN, Pallares V: Pourfour du petit syndrome: Hypersympathetic dysfunctional state following a direct non-penetrating injury to the cervical sympathetic chain and brachial plexus. Anesthesiology 55:591, 1981.
21. Bongenhielm U, Boissonade FM, Westermark A, et al: Sympathetic nerve sprouting fails to occur in the trigeminal ganglion after peripheral nerve injury in the rat. Pain 82:283, 1999.
22. Benoliel R, Eliav E, Tal M: No sympathetic sprouting in rat trigeminal ganglion following painful and non-painful infraorbital nerve neuropathy. Neurosci Lett 297:151, 2001.
23. Hanowell ST, Kennedy SF: Phantom tongue pain and causalgia: Case presentation and treatment. Anesth Analg 58:436, 1979.
24. Khoury R, Kennedy SF, MacNamara TE: Facial causalgia: Report of a case. J Oral Surg 38:782, 1980.
25. Figueroa M, Bruera O, Leston J: Reflex sympathetic dystrophy of the face: An unusual cause of facial pain. Headache Q 11:135, 2000.

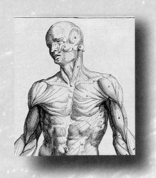

Part B

PAIN EMANATING FROM THE NECK AND BRACHIAL PLEXUS

53

Cervical Facet Syndrome

Khuram A. Sial, Thomas T. Simopoulos, Zahid H. Bajwa, and Carol A. Warfield

■ HISTORICAL CONSIDERATIONS

Cervical facet joints have gained considerable attention as a potential origin for head and neck pain. In 1911, lumbar facet joints were first identified as a source of back pain.[1] In 1977, Pawl[2] reported the reproduction of pain in patients with headache and neck pain after injections of hypertonic saline into the cervical facet joints. Similar findings were published by Hadden in 1940,[3] Raney and Raney in 1948,[4] Taren and Kahn in 1962,[5] Brain and Wilkinson in 1967,[6] and McNab[7] and Mehta in 1973.[8] Bogduk and Marsland[9] were pioneers in using diagnostic cervical medial branch blocks and facet joint injections to study the role of cervical facet joints in causation of idiopathic neck pain. Specific referral patterns of neck pain were mapped out by Dwyer and colleagues[10] by performing facet joint injections in normal volunteers. The accuracy of this pain chart by Dwyer and colleagues[10] was confirmed by anesthetizing the medial branches of the dorsal rami above and below the symptomatic joint. Similar results were obtained by Fukui and associates,[11] when they studied the referred pain distribution of cervical facet joints and cervical dorsal rami.

Windsor and coworkers[12] also studied cervical medial branch referral patterns using electrical stimulation.

■ CLINICAL SYNDROME

Ghormley[13] coined the term *facet syndrome* in 1933 to describe a constellation of symptoms associated with degenerative changes of the lumbar spine. Facet joint morphology varies with the regions of the cervical spine, gender, and location. Because of the lack of intervertebral disks in this region, variations in these geometric characteristics affect the biomechanical behaviors of the human spine secondary to external loads.[14] The term *cervical facet syndrome* (CFS) implies axial pain secondary to involvement of posterior spinal column elements. Degenerative changes in the cervical facet joints have been well documented in the literature using skeletal spinal column remains, with the C2-3 facet joints showing the highest rate of changes.[15,16]

The classic clinical presentation of CFS includes neck pain from the cervical facet joints with referred pain in the head and upper extremities. The facet joint is an important structure in resisting compression at higher loads, anterior shear, extension, lateral bending, and torsion.[17] Usually, no other cause is evident. Facet joints are extensively innervated, and the presence of neuropeptides, such as substance P and calcitonin gene–related peptide, lends credence to the cervical facet joint capsules as a key source of neck pain.[18] Patients may present with headaches and limited range of motion associated with classic neck pain. The quality of the pain is described as a dull ache in the posterior neck region, which sometimes radiates to the shoulder or the midback region or both areas. A previous history of whiplash injury always should be suspected and noted during history taking. Clinical features that may be present include tenderness to palpation over the facet joints or paraspinal muscles, accentuation of pain with cervical extension or rotation, and the absence of any neurologic deficits. CFS should be strongly considered in the differential diagnosis if these symptoms are present.

Degenerative changes, such as osteophytes, narrowing of the intervertebral foramina, and signs of cervical spondylosis, are equally prevalent in individuals with and without neck pain. Patients with CFS may fail to respond to conservative management, including physical therapy, heat, cryotherapy, ultrasound, transcutaneous electrical nerve stimulation, stretching and range-of-motion exercises, cervical traction, manual manipulation, chiropractic treatment, massage, phonophoresis, iontophoresis, acupuncture, muscle relaxants, nonsteroidal antiinflammatory medications, and other analgesics. Average pain level using the visual analog scale is usually greater than 5 on a scale of 0 to 10. The pain commonly may be severe enough to cause functional impairments as well. Referral pain patterns may resemble the patterns described in healthy volunteers via provocation/stimulation of facet joints. Radicular symptoms are not associated with CFS, although patients may present with coexisting upper extremity pain.

Imaging usually is not helpful and devoid of evidence of disk herniation or radiculitis, although it can help to rule out a fracture or tumors. Friedenberg and Miller[19] published an article in 1963 stating that signs of cervical spondylosis, narrowing of the intervertebral foramina, osteophytes, and other degenerative changes, are equally prevalent in individuals with and without neck pain. Neurophysiologic abnormalities are absent as well. Patients also may present with cervicogenic headache and upper back pain. The duration of pain is at least 3 months.

In compliance with the criteria established by the International Association for the Study of Pain,[20] the prevalence of CFS was determined by controlled diagnostic blocks of cervical facet joints and found to be 54% to 67% of patients with chronic neck pain.[21-24] Aprill and Bogduk[25] reviewed the records of 318 patients who had presented with neck pain for at least 6 months to estimate the prevalence of cervical facet joint pain. These studies indicate that the prevalence of cervical facet joint pain ranges from 26% to 65%. Because of the subjective nature of diagnostic blocks and the lack of specificity, there is a wide range in studies attempting to estimate the prevalence of CFS.

Cervical facet joint pain is a common sequela of whiplash injury. Numerous studies have been performed to estimate the prevalence of CFS as the cause of posttraumatic neck pain,

ranging from 63% to 100% with a mean of approximately 70%.[26-32] Using double-blind, controlled, diagnostic blocks of the facet joints of 38 patients with whiplash injury, Barnsley and associates[26] found that cervical facet joint pain had a prevalence of 54%, making cervical facet joint pain the most common cause of chronic neck pain after whiplash injury in this population. Lord and colleagues[27] studied a sample of 41 patients with neck pain of 3 months duration after a motor vehicle accident. These investigators used another double-blind, placebo-controlled protocol and found the prevalence of cervical facet joint pain after whiplash injury to be 60%; the most common levels were C2-3 and C5-6.

The referral patterns for cervical facet joint pain vary; however, particular radiation patterns have been identified for each facet joint level on painful stimulation. Even in asymptomatic subjects, provocation by capsular distention of the facet joints using contrast material produces neck pain in a specific pattern corresponding to a particular facet joint. Dwyer and coworkers[10] mapped out the referral patterns in five subjects (Fig. 53–1). The C2-3 facet joint refers pain to the posterior upper cervical region and head, whereas the C3-4 facet joint refers pain to the posterolateral cervical region, but does not radiate to the head or shoulder. The C5-6 joint refers pain to the posterolateral middle and primarily lower cervical spine and the top and lateral parts of the shoulder and caudally to the spine of the scapula. The C6-7 facet joint refers pain to the top and lateral parts of the shoulder and radiates caudally to the inferior border of the scapula. In patients with cervical pain, these pain referral maps may be powerful diagnostic tools. Fukui and associates[11] studied 61 patients with neck pain and employed two methods to stimulate their facet joints (Fig. 53–2). They compared pain referral maps constructed from injection of contrast medium into the joints with electrical stimulation of the medial branches and found that they correlated relatively well.

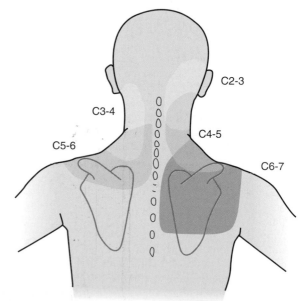

FIGURE 53–1 ■ Diagram of cervical zygapophyseal joint pain distribution in volunteers.

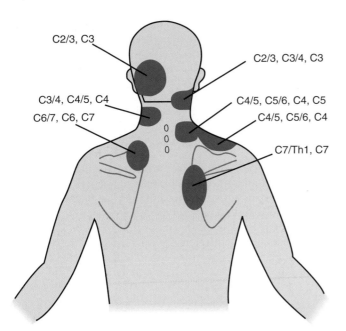

FIGURE 53–2 ■ Referred pain distributions for the zygapophyseal joints from C1 to T7-Th1 and the dorsal rami C3 to C7.

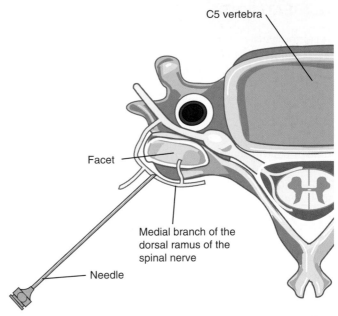

FIGURE 53–3 ■ Medial branch block technique employed for the diagnosis and treatment of cervical facet syndrome.

■ TESTING

The optimal method to diagnose CFS includes putting everything together, including a thorough history and physical examination, imaging techniques, and use of diagnostic blocks. Numerous attempts by investigators to correlate neurophysiologic findings, physical findings, radiologic findings, and other signs and symptoms with the diagnosis of facet joint syndrome have been unsuccessful.[28-30] Because there is no formal effective diagnostic study, the frequency of pain from CFS has been estimated by subjective relief in response to local anesthetic injections. Radiographs should be obtained in the neutral, flexed, and extended positions, and the range of motion should be documented. The angular displacement of one body on the next should be less than 11 degrees, and the horizontal movement of one vertebral body on the next should not exceed 3.5 mm. Cervical spine MRI may reveal degenerative changes consistent with cervical facet arthropathy. There is no way to tell by imaging alone that the facet joints are the true source of pain.

Cervical facet joint blocks can be performed to test the hypothesis that the target joint is the source of the patient's pain.[28,29,31] The cervical facet joints can be anesthetized by using local anesthetic injected directly into the intra-articular joint space or by anesthetizing the medial branches of the dorsal rami that innervate the corresponding joint (Fig. 53–3).[28,29] Below C2-3, each cervical facet joint is supplied by the medial branches above and below the joint, while the C2-3 joint is innervated primarily by the third occipital nerve (a small and variable contribution may derive from the greater occipital nerve). The joint may be considered the source of the pain if the pain is relieved.[28,29] The range of motion often improves, specifically rotation and extension. Controlled blocks are confirmed as true-positive responses in the form of placebo injections with normal saline or comparative local anesthetic blocks, in which the same joint is anesthetized using local anesthetics with differing durations of action on two separate occasions.[28,29] In practice, placebo injections are replaced by a series of local anesthetic blocks to confirm the pain generator and dissipate the placebo response.

■ DIFFERENTIAL DIAGNOSIS

The cervical spine includes many pain generators, including intervertebral disks, facet joints, ligaments, muscles, and nerve roots. Disk disease identified by diskography was present in 64% of patients with a positive cervical medial branch test for facet joint pain.[32] Degenerative changes to the facet joint include hypertrophic arthropathy, which may impinge on nerve roots and may irritate afferents on the posterolateral aspect of the disk. From the previous study population, a sample of 56 patients was selected to evaluate the contribution of the disk to neck pain. As part of the diagnostic process, this group had undergone diskography and facet joint nerve blocks at the same cervical segment.[32] Results revealed that 41% of the patients had a symptomatic disk and a symptomatic facet joint at the same segment, and an additional 23% had a painful facet joint, but not a painful disk at the same segment. In patients with incidental abnormalities of the facet joints, multiple other structures and pain generators could be the cause of pain, or at least may contribute to a condition more complex than a facet origin of pain. Blockade of medial branches denervates not only the joints they supply, but also the muscles, ligaments, and periosteum. Sources of pain in these alternative sites are relieved by medial branch block. Other painful conditions can overlap with signs and symptoms of CFS, including cervicodynia, cervical myofascial pain syndrome, cervical degenerative disk disease, ligamentous laxity, neck strain, compression fracture, cervical radiculopathy, and cervical stenosis.

■ TREATMENT

A comprehensive rehabilitation program is pertinent to a thorough and complete treatment program for patients with CFS. Three phases of rehabilitation are illustrated as defined by Cole and coworkers.[33] Reducing pain and inflammation and increasing the pain-free range of motion are the primary goals of the first phase. Application of ice during the acute phase decreases blood flow and subsequent hemorrhage into injured tissues, which ultimately reduces local edema. It also can relieve painful muscle spasms. Therapeutic modalities, such as ultrasound and electrical stimulation, also may be beneficial in terms of pain and muscle spasm. Manual therapy, joint mobilization, soft tissue massage, and muscle stretching often are helpful. Passive range of motion followed by active range of motion exercises in a pain-free range should be initiated in this phase. Finally, strengthening should begin with isometric exercises, progressing to isotonic exercises as tolerated. The recovery phase is entered as the patient is approaching pain relief. The goals of this second phase are improved range of motion, complete pain relief, and improved strength and neuromuscular control. The maintenance phase is the third and final phase, which entails balancing strength and flexibility while increasing endurance.

If a conservative approach does not suffice, more invasive procedures should be considered and employed. A significant role has been described for therapeutic facet joint injections, by intra-articular facet joint injections, medial branch blocks, or medial branch neurotomy (Fig. 53–4).[34] According to one randomized controlled trial, however, the evidence is poor for short-term and long-term relief of intra-articular injections of the cervical spine.[34] Manchikanti and associates[34] reviewed the literature extensively and concluded that except for one negative randomized control trial[35] for intra-articular injections, there were no other nonobservational trials qualifying to be included for evidence-based practice.

Barnsley and colleagues[35] studied the efficacy of intra-articular facet joint injections for the treatment of chronic cervical facet pain after whiplash injury and found a 50% reduction in pain compared with the preinjection level. The duration of pain relief from intra-articular facet joint injections varies among different investigators. Some studies of intra-articular joint injections report only minor pain relief lasting days to weeks,[35,36] whereas others report substantial relief for weeks to months.[37-39]

Medial branch blocks also have been employed for therapeutic purposes in the cervical spine (see Fig. 53–3). In one prospective, nonrandomized, and observational study,[40] significant effectiveness of medial branch blocks was shown in managing chronic neck pain. Barnsley and Bogduk[41] studied 16 patients with chronic neck pain who underwent repeated cervical medial branch blocks using 0.5 mL of local anesthetic in a double-blind, controlled protocol to obtain an esti-

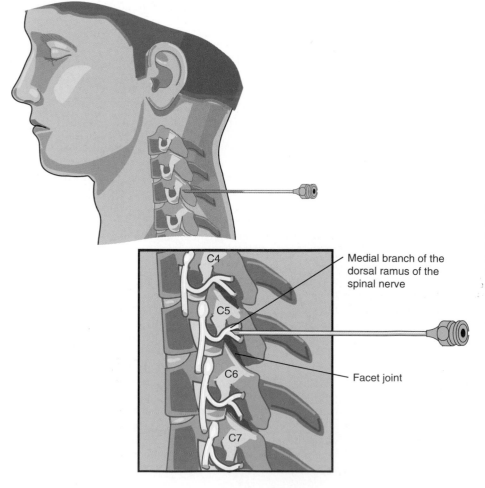

C4

C5

C6

C7

Medial branch of the dorsal ramus of the spinal nerve

Facet joint

FIGURE 53–4 ■ **A** and **B,** Radiofrequency ablation of the medial branch of the dorsal ramus of the spinal nerve. Radiofrequency energy is applied to the tip of the ablative probe to denature the medial branch nerve, preventing signals from entering the brain.

mated sensitivity and specificity of medial branch block in the diagnosis of CFS. The sensitivity of a single uncontrolled block was estimated to be 95% and the specificity 73%.[41] There is, however, a high false-positive rate (27%) for single, uncontrolled blocks.[42] Medial branch blocks also have been performed using comparative local anesthetics. In one study, 34 patients (77%) correctly identified the longer-acting agent when they received a series of injections using bupivacaine or lidocaine.[30]

In a related study, the sensitivity and specificity of comparative local blocks were evaluated.[43] These blocks were compared with placebo-controlled blocks in a randomized, double-blind trial. A low sensitivity of 54% indicated that there were many false-negative results (46%). The specificity was 88%, indicating that there were few false-positive results (12%). When surgical decisions are based on the results of the medial branch blocks, placebo-controlled triple blocks may be prudent.

Barnsley and Bogduk[41] used contrast material in another study to show that 0.5 mL of local anesthetic followed by 0.5 mL of contrast medium was an appropriate volume that does not spread far enough to affect structures other than the intended nerve. No spread of contrast material occurred above or below the intended level, no spread occurred anterior to the ventral ramus, and no spread occurred laterally beyond the semispinalis muscle. The anesthetic blocked only the facet joint and did not anesthetize any other structures that might be a source of chronic neck pain. Traditionally, therapeutic facet joint injections are performed only in patients in whom controlled diagnostic blocks establish a diagnosis of facet joint pain.

In suspected cases of CFS in our clinic, a diagnostic medial branch block technique is first employed. If there is a positive response, a series of three medial branch blocks is performed over 12 to 18 weeks to dissipate the placebo response and document length of time with good response. Patients with significant relief lasting 2 to 3 months may require a maintenance program of cervical medial branch blocks thereafter with a maximum of four to six repeat procedures per year. An evanescent response to diagnostic medial branch blocks may be an indication for radiofrequency ablation in hopes for longer-term relief with a maximum of four treatments per year.

Medial branch neurotomy also has been described with well-controlled trials (see Fig. 53–4). Their effectiveness has been described in systematic reviews, observational studies, randomized trials, and case reports, although inconclusive results were reported.[44-51] Most investigators have found that radiofrequency thermocoagulation of medial branches for facet arthropathy is a safe and efficacious modality with the potential for long-term benefit. Radiofrequency lesioning is performed using continuous or pulsed mode radiofrequency. Radiofrequency neurotomy denervates the facet joint by coagulating the medial branch of the dorsal ramus, which denatures the proteins in the nerve.[52] By doing so, nerve impulses sending electrical messages of pain to the dorsal root ganglion are inhibited. Because the dorsal root ganglion is preserved, however, the nerve is not destroyed, and the medial branch cell bodies are intact. Also, depending on the radiofrequency lesion site, the nerve may grow back to its target joint in 6 to 9 months, which could reproduce the facet joint pain. In this case, repeating the neurotomy is a viable option.

One should use caution when denervating multiple segments bilaterally because this can lead to an increased risk of cervical muscular fatigue with activities of daily living.[53]

A randomized double-blind trial with 24 patients was employed by Lord and colleagues[54] to evaluate the efficacy of radiofrequency neurotomy. After confirmation of painful facet joints using placebo-controlled, diagnostic blocks, the patients were randomized to treatment and control groups. The treatment group was subjected to heating of the medial branch to 80°C for 90 seconds, while in the control group, the temperature probe was maintained at 37°C. The 12 patients in the treatment group reported an average of 263 days before their pain level returned to 50% of their preoperative level. The 12 patients in the control group perceived this in just 8 days. At 27 weeks, 1 patient in the control group and 7 in the treatment group remained pain-free.[54]

Long-term efficacy of radiofrequency neurotomy was evaluated in 28 patients with neck pain secondary to motor vehicle accidents.[53] After the initial procedure, 71% of the patients reported complete relief of pain, and the mean duration was 422 days. The patients benefited from 219 days of relief when the procedure was repeated, and some patients maintained pain relief for years after multiple repeat procedures.

Cervical fusion should be considered only after aggressive nonsurgical care has failed. In patients with CFS, the outcome for surgical fusion is significantly less propitious than for radicular pain.[55,56] In a few medical centers, cervical pain without neurologic deficit with degenerative changes of the facet joints may represent a delicate indication for cervical fusion.[57] Spondylotic changes on plain films are not an indication for surgical fusion because these changes are evident in patients with and without symptoms and do not correspond to neck pain.[19] In some cases, cervical facet joint pain can occur even after anterior cervical fusion or may become increasingly more painful after surgery. Immobilization of specific levels renders the remaining joints responsible to take on the burden of the mechanical stresses. Cervicodynia also may be secondary to intrinsic mechanisms that are not motion dependent or may be related to small movements in the joints.[9] Nonsteroidal antiinflammatory drugs also can help to reduce pain and inflammation, although long-term use can lead to gastric irritation or ulceration in many individuals.

■ COMPLICATIONS AND PITFALLS

As with all invasive medical procedures, there are potential risks and complications associated with facet joint injections. In general, the risk is low, and complications are rare. Disastrous complications with cervical facet joint injections may occur, however, including complications related to technique with needle placement and those related to the administration of various drugs (Table 53–1). Patients who are taking anticoagulants (e.g., warfarin [Coumadin]) or have an active infection may not be able to have this procedure. These situations should be discussed with the treating physician.

Okada,[58] in a series of facet joint injections, showed a communicating pathway was found in 80% of subjects from the facet joint to the interlaminar portion, interspinous portion, contralateral facet joint, para-extradural space, and

Table 53–1

Risks Related to Cervical Facet Joint Injections

Potential Complications Resulting from Facet Joint Injection	Potential Side Effects of Steroid Medications
Allergic reaction—usually to x-ray contrast or steroid; rarely to local anesthetic. A history of allergies should be elicited before any procedure	Transient flushing with a feeling of warmth ("hot flashes")
Bleeding—a rare complication and typically occurs in patients with underlying bleeding disorders. Proximity to the vertebral artery makes the injection highly vulnerable. Intravascular injection into the veins also can occur	Fluid retention, weight gain, or increased appetite
Infection—minor infections occur in <1-2% of all injections; severe infections are rare and occur in 0.1-0.01% of injections. Infectious complications include epidural abscess and bacterial meningitis	Elevated blood pressure
Worsening of pain symptoms	Mood swings, irritability, anxiety, insomnia
Discomfort at the point of injection	High blood glucose—diabetic patients should inform their primary care physicians about the injection before their appointment
Nerve or spinal cord damage or paralysis—although rare, damage can occur from direct trauma from the needle or secondarily from infection, bleeding resulting in compression, or injection into an artery causing blockage	Transient decrease in immunity
Dural puncture, subdural injection, injection into the intervertebral foramen and intervertebral formation	Cataracts—a rare result of excessive or prolonged steroid usage
	Severe arthritis of the hips or shoulders (avascular necrosis)—a rare result of excessive or prolonged steroid usage
	Separation of pituitary-adrenal access
	Hypocorticism
	Cushing syndrome
	Osteoporosis
	Avascular necrosis of the bone
	Steroid myopathy
	Epidural lipomatosis

cervical extradural space. Dreyfuss and associates[59] showed that 7% of cases were found to have extra-articular leaks even with low volumes. Rare but potential complications include vertebral artery and ventral ramus damage and a risk of embolus resulting in serious neurologic sequelae with spinal cord damage and cerebral infarction. Other minor complications include headaches, pain at the injection site, syncope, hypotension, nausea, sweating, flushing, and lightheadedness.

Complications of radiofrequency thermoneurolysis are rare and include worsening of the usual pain and possible deafferentation pain, local pain (including myofascial, symptomatic hematoma, non-neuritic), neuritic pain, sensory or motor deficits, burning pain or dysesthesias, decreased sensation and allodynia in the paravertebral skin or the denervated facets, transient leg pain, and persistent leg weakness.[33,60,61] Spinal cord injury can lead to infarction, bowel and bladder dysfunction, proprioception and sensory loss, loss of motor function, Brown-Séquard syndrome, and paraplegia.

■ CONCLUSION

CFS occurs secondary to facet joint pain that manifests with neck pain and referral patterns in the head, shoulders, and upper extremities. The medial branches innervate these facet joints, transmitting pain signals via the spinal cord to higher central regions. Numerous studies have shown that blocks of cervical facet joints or medial branches using local anesthetics, steroids, or a combination of both can significantly relieve the pain of CFS. Although there is limited evidence for cervical intra-articular facet joint injections, there is a moderate amount of evidence for cervical medial branch blocks and even more evidence for radiofrequency thermoneurolysis. Multiple effective and therapeutic modalities are available to manage cervical facet joint pain. Although complications are rare, serious disastrous events are possible. Proper technique, adequate training and experience, meticulous observance of safety guidelines, and use of proper fluoroscopic imaging equipment are indispensable for safe and effective injection of cervical anatomy.

References

1. Goldthwait JE: The lumbosacral articulation: An explanation of many cases of lumbago, sciatica, and paraplegia. Boston Med Surg J 164:365, 1911.
2. Pawl RP: Headache, cervical spondylosis, and anterior cervical fusion. Surg Ann 9:391, 1977.

3. Hadden SB: Neurologic headache and facial pain. Arch Neurol 43:405, 1940.
4. Raney A, Raney RB: Headache: A common symptom of cervical disc lesions. Arch Neurol 59:603, 1948.
5. Taren JA, Kahn EA: Anatomic pathways related to pain in face and neck. J Neurosurg 19:116, 1962.
6. Brain L, Wilkinson M (eds): Cervical Spondylosis and Other Disorders of the Cervical Spine. London, Heinemann Medical, 1967.
7. McNab I: The whiplash syndrome. Clin Neurosurg 20:232, 1973.
8. Mehta M: Intractable Pain. Philadelphia, WB Saunders, 1973.
9. Bogduk N, Marsland A: The cervical zygapophyseal joints as a source of neck pain. Spine 13:610, 1988.
10. Dwyer A, Aprill C, Bogduk N: Cervical zygapophyseal joint pain patterns: A study in normal volunteers. Spine 6:453, 1990.
11. Fukui S, Ohseto K, Saiotam M, et al: Referred pain distribution of the cervical zygapophyseal joints and cervical dorsal rami. Pain 68:79, 1996.
12. Windsor RE, Nagula D, Storm S, et al: Electrical stimulation induced cervical medial branch referral patterns. Pain Physician 6:411, 2003.
13. Ghormley R: Low back pain with special reference to the articular facets, with presentation of an operative prodcedure. JAMA 101:1773, 1933.
14. Yoganandan N, Knowles SA, Maiman DJ, Pintar FA: Anatomic study of the morphology of human cervical facet joint. Spine 28:2317, 2003.
15. Weber J, Czarnetzki A, Spring A: Paleopathological features of the cervical spine in the early middle ages: natural history of degenerative diseases. Neurosurgery 53:1418, 2003.
16. Fukui S, Ohseto K, Shiotani M, et al: Referred pain distribution of the cervical zygapophyseal joints and cervical dorsal rami. Pain 68:79, 1996.
17. Ng HW, Teo EC, Lee KK, Qiu TX: Finite element analysis of cervical spinal instability under physiologic loading. J Spinal Disord Tech 16:55, 2003.
18. Kallakuri S, Singh A, Chen C, Cavanaugh JM: Demonstration of substance P, calcitonin gene-related peptide, and protein gene product 9.5 containing nerve fibers in human cervical facet joint capsules. Spine 29:1182, 2004.
19. Friedenberg Z, Miller W: Degenerative disc disease of the cervical spine. J Bone Joint Surg 45A:1171, 1963.
20. Merskey H, Bogduk N: Classification of Chronic Pain: Descriptions of Chronic Pain Syndromes and Definitions of Pain Terms, 2nd ed. Seattle, IASP Press, 1994, p 180.
21. Barnsley L, Lord SM, Wallis BJ, Bogduk N: The prevalence of chronic cervical zygapophyseal joint pain after whiplash. Spine 20:20, 1995.
22. Lord SM, Barnsley L, Wallis BJ, Bogduk N: Chronic cervical zygapophysial joint pain with whiplash: A placebo-controlled prevalence study. Spine 21:1737, 1996.
23. Manchikanti L, Siugh V, Rivera J, Pampati V: Prevalence of cervical facet joint pain in chronic neck pain. Pain Physician 5:243, 2002.
24. Manchikanti L, Singh V, Pampati V, et al: Is there correlation of facet joint pain in lumbar and cervical spine? Pain Physician 5:365, 2002.
25. Aprill C, Bogduk N: The prevalence of cervical zygapophyseal joint pain: A first approximation. Spine 17:744, 1992.
26. Barnsley L, Lord SM, Wallis BJ, Bogduk N: The prevalence of chronic cervical zygapophysial joint pain after whiplash. Spine 20:20, 1995.
27. Lord SM, Barnsley L, Wallis BJ, Bogduk N: Chronic cervical zygapophysial joint pain after whiplash: A placebo-controlled prevalence study. Spine 21:1737, 1996.
28. Bogduk N: International Spinal Injection Society guidelines for the performance of spinal injection procedures: Part 1. Zygapophyseal joint blocks. Clin J Pain 13:285, 1997.
29. Bogduk N, Lord S: Cervical zygapophysial joiut pain. Neurosurgery 8:107, 1998.
30. Lord SM, Barnsley L, Bogduk N: The utility of comparative local anesthetic blocks versus placebo-controlled blocks for the diagnosis of cervical zygapophysial joint pain. Clin J Pain 11:208, 1995.
31. Boswell M, Singh V, Staats PS, Hirsch JA: Accuracy of precision diagnostic blocks in the diagnosis of chronic spinal pain of facet or zygapophysial joint origin. Pain Physician 6:449, 2003.
32. Bogduk N, Aprill C: On the nature of neck pain, discography and cervical zygapophysial joint blocks. Pain 54:213, 1993.
33. Cole A, Farrell J, Stratton S: Functional rehabilitation of cervical spine athletic injuries. In Kibler B, Herring S, Press J (eds): Functional Rehabilitation of Sports and Musculoskeletal Injuries. Gaithersburg, MD, Aspen Publication, 1998, p 127.
34. Manchikanti L, Staats PS, Singh V, et al: Evidence-based practice guidelines for interventional techniques in the management of chronic spinal pain. Pain Physician 6:3, 2003.
35. Barnsley L, Lord SM, Wallis BJ, Bogduk N: Lack of effect of intra-articular corticosteroids for chronic pain in the cervical zygapophyseal joints. N Engl J Med 330:1047, 1994.
36. Moran R, O'Connell D, Walsh MG: The diagnostic value of facet joint injections. Spine 13:1407, 1988.
37. Dory MA: Arthrography of the cervical facet joints. Radiology 148:379, 1983.
38. Fairbank JC, Park WM, McCall IW, O'Brien JP: Apophyseal injection of local anesthetic as a diagnostic aid in primary low-back pain syndromes. Spine 6:598, 1981.
39. Roy DF, Fleury J, Fontaine SB, Dussault RG: Clinical evaluation of cervical facet joint infiltration. Can Assoc Radiol J 39:118, 1988.
40. Manchikanti L, Manchikanti KN, Damron KS, Pampati V: Effectiveness of cervical medial branch blocks in chronic neck pain: A prospective outcome study. Pain Physician 7:195, 2004.
41. Barnsley L, Bogduk N: Medial branch blocks are specific for the diagnosis of cervical zygapophyseal joint pain. Reg Anesth 18:343, 1993.
42. Barnsley L, Lord S, Wallis B, Bogduk N: False-positive rates of cervical zygapophysial joint blocks. Clin J Pain 9:124, 1993.
43. Barnsley L, Lord S, Bogduk N: Comparative local anaesthetic blocks in the diagnosis of cervical zygapophysial joint pain. Pain 55:99, 1993.
44. Lord SM, Barnsley L, Wallis BJ, et al: Percutaneous radiofrequency neurotomy for chronic cervical zygapophyseal-joint pain. N Engl J Med 335:1721, 1996.
45. Sapir D, Gorup JM: Radiofrequency medial branch neurotomy in litigant and nonlitigant patients with cervical whiplash. Spine 26:E268, 2001.
46. McDonald GJ, Lord SM, Bogduk N: Long-term follow-up of patients treated with cervical radiofrequency neurotomy for chronic neck pain. Neurosurgery 45:61, 1999.
47. Geurts JW, Van Wijk RM, Stolker RJ, Groen GJ: Efficacy of radio-frequency procedures for the treatment of spinal pain: A systematic review of randomized clinical trials. Reg Anesth Pain Med 26:394, 2001.
48. Manchikanti L, Singh V, Vilims B, et al: Medial branch neurotomy in management of chronic spinal pain: Systematic review of the evidence. Pain Physician 5:405, 2002.
49. Niemisto L, Kalso E, Malmivaara A, et al: Radiofrequency denervation for neck and back pain: A systematic review within the framework of the Cochrane Collaboration Back Review Group. Cochrane Collaboration Back Review Group. Spine 28:1877, 2003.
50. Mikeladze G, Espinal R, Finnegan R, et al: Pulsed radiofrequency application in treatment of chronic zygapophyseal joint pain. Spine J 3:360, 2003.
51. Royal M, Wienecke G, Movva V, et al: Retrospective study of efficacy of radiofrequency neurolysis for facet arthropathy. Pain Med 2:249, 2001.
52. Zervas NT, Kuwayama A: Pathological characteristics of experimental thermal lesions: Comparison of induction heating and radiofrequency electrocoagulation. J Neurosurg 37:418, 1972.
53. McDonald GJ, Lord SM, Bogduk N: Long-term follow-up of patients treated with cervical radiofrequency neurotomy for chronic neck pain. Neurosurgery 45:61, 1999.
54. Lord SM, Barnsley L, Wallis BJ, et al: Percutaneous radio-frequency neurotomy for chronic cervical zygapophyseal-joint pain. N Engl J Med 335:1721, 1996.
55. Wiberg J: [Cervical disk defects: Results of surgical treatment of cervical vertebral radiculopathy]. Tidsskr Nor Laegeforen 112:876, 1992.
56. Williams JL, Allen MB Jr, Harkess JW: Late results of cervical discectomy and interbody fusion: Some factors influencing the results. J Bone Joint Surg Am 50:277, 1968.
57. Grob D: Surgery in the degenerative cervical spine. Spine 23:2674, 1998.
58. Okada K: Studies on the cervical facet joints using arthrography of the cervical facet joint. J Jpn Orthop Assoc 55:563, 1981.
59. Dreyfuss P, Kaplan M, Dreyer SJ: Zygapophysealjoint injection techniques in the spinal axis. In Leonard (ed): Pain Procedures in Clinical Practice, 2nd ed. Philadelphia, Hanley & Belfus, 2000, p 276.
60. Curran MA: Lumbosacral facet joint radiofrequency. In Manchikanti L, Slipman CW, Fellows B (eds): International Pain Management: Low Back Pain—Diagnosis and Treatment. Paducah, KY, ASIPP Publishing, 2002, p 463.
61. Kornick CA, Kramarich SS, Sitzman BT: Complication rate associated with facet joint radiofrequency denervation procedures. Pain Med 3:175, 2002.

chapter 54

Cervical Radiculopathy

Laxmaiah Manchikanti, Vijay Singh, and Mark V. Boswell

■ HISTORICAL CONSIDERATIONS

Cervical radiculopathy is a term applied when a nerve root is irritated and inflamed, but it also implies that damage to the root has produced a clinically appreciable motor or sensory neurologic deficit in the distribution of the nerve root. In contrast, cervical radiculitis implies irritation and inflammation of a nerve root. Cervical radicular pain is a condition that poses several problems in clinical practice. Problems arise in recognizing the condition, how it should be investigated, and how best it should be treated. Failure to recognize the condition accurately can result not only in misdiagnosis but also in over-diagnosis, leading to unnecessary and ineffective treatment.

When the early clinicians wrote about the cervical spine, they were almost totally concerned with injuries rather than acquired nontraumatic disk disease.[1] Hippocrates[2,3] described cervical injuries in his book on the articulations. In general, he was pessimistic about the value of treatment. Hippocrates emphasized the importance of involvement of the cervical spine in head injuries. Early clinicians also appreciated the principle of traction to the cervical spine. The use of traction for neck injuries was reported as early as 1887 by Bontecou.[4] The Egyptians performed cervical laminectomies as part of the mummification process.[1] Paulus of Aegina[5] performed laminectomies for spinal cord compression. Around 1646, Fabricus Hildanus[6] of Padua described his attempt to replace a fractured disk by clamping of the spinous processes and manipulating the cervical spine. The first successful laminectomy in modern times was performed by Alban Smith of Danville, Kentucky (Fig. 54–1). By the 1930s, otolaryngologists were approaching the front of the cervical vertebra to remove osteophytes at about the C5 level, making swallowing difficult. However, little interest was evidenced by neurosurgeons or orthopedic surgeons until 1955, when Robinson and Smith[7] reported anterior disk removal and fusion. The official description of the cervical disk herniation with radiculopathy was by Semmes (Fig. 54–2) and Murphey (Fig. 54–3) in 1943[8]—9 years after Mixter (Fig. 54–4) and Barr described lumbar disk herniation with radiculopathy.[9] Subsequently, Spurling and Scoville[10] and Michelsen and Mixter[11] published additional reports of cervical disk herniation in 1944. In 1931, Elsberg[13] also described herniated cervical disks, even though he classified them as tumors. In 1953, Mair and Druckman[13]

provided a classic description of cervical spinal cord compression due to protruded disks in the neck, which they said caused clinical symptoms by compression of the anterior spinal artery.

Spinal stenosis of the cervical spine also has been recognized for about as long as stenosis of the lumbar spine. The earliest mention of what was certainly spinal stenosis in the cervical spine was by Stookey[12] in 1928. First attempts at treatment of cervical spinal stenosis in humans was with massive bony posterior decompression, opening the dura, and often cutting the dentate ligaments.[1] However, later treatments included anterior interbody fusion popularized by Robinson and Smith.[7] Whiplash injury was first described by Harold Crowe[14] of Los Angeles in 1928.

■ THE CLINICAL SYNDROME

Definition

Cervical radicular pain is a term applied to describe pain resulting from the stimulation of, or a disorder of, a cervical nerve root.[15] Thus, cervical radicular pain and cervical radiculitis appear to be synonymous because cervical radiculitis is a term applied when a nerve root is irritated and inflamed. In contrast, extension of both the terms is *cervical radiculopathy,* which implies that damage to the root has produced a clinically appreciable motor or sensory neurologic deficit in the distribution of the nerve root. Thus, *radiculopathy* is a disorder in which conduction along a nerve root is blocked, resulting in objective neurologic signs such as numbness or weakness; and/or in which the blood supply to a nerve root is compromised, resulting in paresthesia.[16] It has been generally believed that cervical radicular pain is perceived along the distribution of the affected nerve root in a dermatomal distribution.[17] However, cervical spinal nerves are distributed to deep structures, such as muscles, joints, and ligaments, as well as skin. Thus, radicular pain is felt in deep structures in areas remote from the expected dermatome. Combining all the experimental data, Bogduk[15] arrived at a workable definition of cervical radicular pain, which is consonant with the definition offered by the International Association for the Study of Pain (IASP).[16] Bogduk's definition incorporates these many various aspects as follows: "Cervical radicular pain is produced by the stimulation of cervical nerve roots; it may be

568

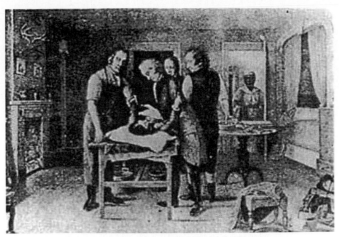

FIGURE 54–1 ■ Alban Smith, MD, of Danville, Kentucky, performed the first successful laminectomy after those of Paulus of Aegina in 1829. (© 2004 American Association of Neurological Surgeons.)

FIGURE 54–3 ■ Francis Murphey, MD, originating Member of the American Academy of Neurological Surgery.

FIGURE 54–2 ■ R. Eustace Semmes, MD, Professor of Neurosurgery in 1932 at the University of Tennessee.

FIGURE 54–4 ■ William Jason Mixter (1880-1958).

perceived in some or all of the tissues supplied by the affected nerve, both deep and cutaneous; radicular pain cannot be distinguished from somatic referred pain in either quality or distribution in the proximal upper limb; but pain in the forearm and or hand is far more likely to be of radicular origin; and pain that radiates into the upper limb, and is shooting or electric in quality, is bound to be radicular in origin."

Prevalence

The annual incidence has been described as approximately 85 per 100,000 population, and the most common causes are disk prolapse or spondylitic spurs at the corresponding level.[18,19] In a Swedish study, neck pain with transient radicular abnormalities was reported in almost 40% of the population at some time during their lives.[20,21] In a neuroepidemiologic study in 1997, pain in the neck and cervical radiculopathy were the most frequently occurring neurologic disorders in an indigenous tribe.[22] Even though degeneration of the cervical disk structures is a normal consequence of the aging process, it undoubtedly plays a significant role in the production of neck pain, nerve root pathology, and spinal cord compression.[23-43] However, herniated nucleus pulposus in the cervical region is much less common than in the lumbar region.[44-46] The most common areas of disk herniation are C5-C6 and C6-C7, with involvement of 6th and 7th cervical nerve roots.[17,23,47-51]

Etiology

The most common causes of cervical radicular pain and cervical radiculopathy are disk protrusion and cervical spondylosis. Other rare causes include facet joint pathology; vertebral body pathology; meningeal pathology; pathology secondary to the involvement of blood vessels, nerve sheath, and nerve.[52] Disk protrusions are described as soft and hard, with soft protrusions extruding into the vertebral canal.[53] Disk protrusions are also described as medial and lateral, with medial protrusions affecting primarily the spinal cord, and typically producing myelopathy, whereas lateral lesions protrude toward the intervertebral foramina and impinge on the spinal nerves and nerve roots causing radicular pain.[17,53] However, pain is an uncommon or inconspicuous feature of medial protrusions. In contrast to soft protrusions, hard protrusions are typically features of cervical spondylosis, accompanied by osteophytes from the facet joints, causing central or foraminal stenosis.

The present view is that clinical features of radiculopathy are produced by compression of the affected nerve. Compression accounts for numbness, paresthesia, weakness, and hyporeflexia by blocking conduction in nerves and causing ischemia. However, radicular pain may have additional explanations than compression. Lumbar disks and nerve roots have been studied extensively to explain lumbar radicular pain. Extensive studies have shown unique properties of spinal nerves and inflammatory mechanisms in the lumbar spine explaining various mechanisms other than mechanical compression and compression affecting dorsal root ganglion.[54] However, these mechanisms have not been confirmed in cervical radicular pain. Only one study[55] has demonstrated that herniated cervical intervertebral disks also produce met-

alloproteinases, nitric oxide, interleukin-6, and prostaglandin E_2. All these substances are considered as potential irritants of spinal nerves or marks of inflammation.

■ SIGNS AND SYMPTOMS

The symptoms and signs of cervical radiculopathy are related to pain and neurologic features. The typical patient has a history of intermittent neck pain with the sudden onset of radicular pain, which may follow a traumatic incident. Radicular pain is aggravated by coughing, sneezing, movement of the neck, especially extension, and the Spurling test. However, patients with radiculopathy may complain of pain in the neck, in the shoulder girdle, in the anterior chest wall, in the arm, forearm, or hand.[56] The reported prevalence of pain in various types of the neck and upper limb differs in different studies.[23,48,57-60]

Neurologic Features

The neurologic features of radiculopathy are numbness, weakness, paresthesia, and hyporeflexia.[23,48,57-60] It has been inferred that pain in the forearm associated with paresthesia is the cardinal feature of cervical radicular pain.[56,58] Table 54–1 summarizes various signs and symptoms of nerve root compression in the cervical region describing location of the lesion, referred pain, motor dysfunction, sensory dysfunction, and reflex changes. Cervical radiculopathy is suggested clinically by the presence of numbness and/or paresthesia in a dermatomal distribution, and/or weakness in a myotomal distribution. However, hyporeflexia alone is a not a diagnostic sign. Hyporeflexia is a feature that arises due to sensory block or motor block, and is, therefore, not independent of numbness or weakness as primary signs.[56] Finally, cervical radicular pain is most strongly suggested by pain in the forearm and hand, particularly if associated with paresthesia.[56] Although this distribution of pain is consistent with the classic notion of pain in a dermatomal distribution, pain radiating from the neck, through the shoulder region ,and into the upper limb, would also be consistent with the experimental evidence on radicular pain.[56] Neck pain alone, or pain in the shoulder girdle or proximal regions of the upper limb, is *not* diagnostic of radicular pain, and it suggests somatic referred pain.

Primary tumors of spinal nerves may present with radicular pain. However, this type of pain typically is characterized by profound sensory loss.[61] Thus, presentation dominated by neurologic signs, warrants a consideration of a primary neurologic disorder. Neurofibroma is usually associated with cutaneous phakomata.[61] Involvement of C8 or T1 spinal nerves may indicate apical tumors of the lung as these levels are involved very rarely by disk protrusion. The pulmonary masses are also associated with presence of Horner syndrome.[56]

Cervical radiculopathy secondary to intracranial tumor progresses rapidly.[62] For inflammatory disorders, systemic signs with fever and malaise are the hallmarks with elevated blood count and erythrocyte sedimentation rate.[63] Sarcoidosis also has been described with profound sensory and motor loss dominating the clinical presentation.[64]

Table 54–1

Signs and Symptoms of Nerve Root Compression of the Cervical Region

Root Involvement	Location of Lesion	Referred Pain	Motor Dysfunction	Sensory Dysfunction	Reflex Changes
C5	C4/5	Shoulder and upper arm	Shoulder muscles (deltoid-supraspinatus-infraspinatus) ↓ abduction and external rotation	↓ Upper and lateral aspect of the shoulder	↓ Biceps reflex
C6	C5/6	Radial aspect of forearm	Biceps and brachialis muscles ↓ flexion of the elbow andsupination ↓ wrist extensors	Radial aspect of forearm	↓ Thumb reflex and brachioradialis reflex
C7	C6/7	Dorsal aspect of forearm	Triceps muscle ↓ extension of the elbow	↓ Index and middle digits	↓ Triceps reflex
C8	C7/T1	Ulnar aspect of forearm	Intrinsics of the hand ↓ adduction and abduction	↓ Ring and little digits	No change

Physical Examination

For a patient with symptoms of neck pain with or without upper extremity pain, suspected disk herniation, or with radicular pain or radiculopathy, the neurologic examination should address the neck, trunk, upper extremities, and lower extremities. Lower extremity examination is required to determine presence or absence of long-tract signs evident with myelopathy. Further, in myelopathy, tests of proprioception, vibration, and two-point discrimination are also important. Additional tests including compression test, manual traction, abduction test, or a combination thereof, are also appropriate in evaluation of cervical spine.

Local neck pain has been described with an extremely high prevalence of more than 90%. **Numbness** in the upper limbs is a reasonably reliable sign.[65,66] However, it is not a universal feature in patients with radiculopathy. The prevalence has varied significantly from 24%,[58] 48%,[60] to as high as 86%.[23] Numbness is most often seen in C6 and C7 dermatomes, indicating the most frequent involvement of these nerve roots. The predictive validity of numbness was calculated to be 0.7 for C6 dermatome, whereas it was 4.4 for C7 dermatome.[65] Bogduk[65] described the likelihood of getting numbness in the C7 dermatome as diagnostic of 87% of the involvement of C7 nerve root, whereas it was 73% for C6 dermatomal involvement.

Weakness has been considered as a better and more reliable sign than numbness. Weakness has been reported in about 70% of the patients in older studies.[58,60] However, more recent studies have reported it in only one third of the patients.[23] Biceps weakness has been reported as very specific for C6 radiculopathy, however, its sensitivity was low.[65] In contrast, triceps weakness is very sensitive for C7 radiculopathy, even though it is not very specific. Bogduk[65] described that objective motor weakness provides a diagnostic confidence interval of 77% for C6 radiculopathy, whereas diagnostic confidence was 67% for C7 radiculopathy.

However, the weakness of wrist extensor and wrist flexors is not a discriminating sign[58] because it is seen with radiculopathy of C6, C7, or C8. Weakness of the hand muscles is seen only with C8 radiculopathy.[58]

Reflex abnormalities are seen in 70% of the patients.[23,58,60] However, this data is limited to biceps or triceps, whereas the data with brachioradialis is unconvincing. The strong correlation has been established between reflex inhibition of biceps and C6 and triceps and C7.[58,60,65]

Provocative Tests

Many specialized provocative tests have been described for physical examination of the neck and cervical spine. The majority of these relate to identification of radiculopathy, spinal cord pathology, or brachial plexus pathology. These include Spurling neck compression test, shoulder abduction test, neck distraction test, Lhermitte sign, Hoffman sign, and Adson test.[67] However, these tests are often performed routinely by many providers with variable methods and interpretations. The existing literature appears to indicate high specificity, low sensitivity, and good-to-fair interexaminer reliability for Spurling neck compression test, the neck distraction test, and shoulder abduction (relief) test when performed as described. For Hoffman sign, the existing literature does not address interexaminer reliability but appears to indicate fair sensitivity and fair-to-good specificity. For Lhermitte sign and Adson test, not even tentative statements can be made with regard to interexaminer reliability, sensitivity, and specificity, based on the existing literature.[67] In fact, Wainner and Gill[68] stated that with regard to cervical radiculopathy, many investigators believe that, "Given the paucity of evidence, the true value of the clinical examination . . . is unknown at this time." Malanga et al[67] examined the historical basis and scientific analysis of multiple provocative tests in cervical spine examination. Their summary, as shown in Table 54–2, includes multiple examination maneuvers, original descriptions, reliability analyses, and validity studies of each test.[69-72]

▆ DIAGNOSTIC TESTING

Diagnostic tests may be helpful in differentiating the causes of the neck and arm pain, along with localizing the level of the lesion. Among the multiple tests available, including imaging, electrodiagnostics and diskography, imaging is the most useful.

Imaging

Plain radiography is not of any significant use in radiculopathy. Myelography is an invasive and stressful investigation. However, this can show the deformations produced by intradural, dural, and some extradural lesions of the cervical vertebral canal. However, it does not demonstrate the lesion directly and it demonstrates poorly, if at all, lesions affecting the lateral reaches of the cervical spinal nerves.[72] Conventional computed tomography (CT) provides axial images, in which the lateral reaches of the intervertebral foramina can be seen. CT myelography is considered as an accurate and reliable test and has proven to be superior to myelography in the diagnosis of cervical disk protrusions. It is an expensive and invasive test, however.

Magnetic Resonance Imaging (MRI)

MRI is the choice of imaging in the modern era—replacing myelography, CT, and CT myelography.[73-75] MRI is considered to be as accurate as CT myelography for detection of cervical nerve root compression,[75,76] even though it may be slightly inferior for the detection of bony impingement of the nerve roots.[75-77] However, prevalence of numerous

---

Table 54–2

Examination Maneuvers for Cervical Radiculopathy

Test	Original Description	Reliability Studies	Validity Studies
Spurling/neck compression test	Passive lateral flexion and compression of head. Positive test is reproduction of radicular symptoms distant from neck.	Viikari-Juntura[66] 1987 Seated position. Kappa = 0.40-0.77 Proportion specific Agreement = 0.47-0.80	Viikari-Juntura, et al 1989[69] Seated position. Sensitivity: 40-60% Specificity: 92-100%
Shoulder abduction (relief) sign	Active abduction of symptomatic arm, placing patient's hand on head. Positive test is relief or reduction of ipsilateral cervical radicular symptoms	Viikari-Juntura[66] 1987 Seated position. Kappa = 0.21-0.40 Proportion specific Agreement = 0.57-0.67	Viikari-Juntura et al, 1989[69] Seated position. Sensitivity: 43-50% Specificity: 80-100%
Neck distraction test	Examiner grasps patient's head under occiput and chin and applies axial traction force. Positive test is relief or reduction of cervical radicular symptoms	Supine position. 10-15 kg traction force applied. Kappa = 0.50 Proportion specific Agreement =0.71	Viikari-Juntura et al, 1989[69] Supine position. 10-15 kg traction force applied. Sensitivity: 40-43% Specificity: 100%
Lhermitte sign	Passive anterior cervical flexion. Positive test is presence of "electric-like sensations" down spine or extremities.	Not reported	Uchihara et al, 1994[69a] Sensitivity: <28% Specificity: high
Hoffman sign	Passive snapping flexion of middle finger distal phalanx. Positive test is flexion-adduction of ipsilateral thumb and index finger	Not reported	Glaser et al, 2000[71] Sensitivity: 58% Specificity: 78% Positive predictive value: 62% Negative predictive value 75%
Adson test	Inspiration, chin elevation, and head rotation to affected side. Positive test is alteration or obliteration of radial pulse.	Not reported	Not reported

From Wainner RS, Gill H: Diagnosis and nonoperative management of cervical radiculopathy. J Orthoped Sports Phys Ther 30:728, 2000, reproduced with permission from authors and publisher.

abnormalities on MRI of the cervical spine in asymptomatic individuals has been a concern.[77-80]

Neurophysiologic Testing

Electromyography and nerve conduction studies offer no advantage in radiculopathy. However, they are of significant value in identifying and differentiating cervical radiculopathy with a peripheral lesion.

Diskography

Diskography is a diagnostic procedure designed to determine whether a disk is intrinsically painful. Even though originally introduced as a technique for the study of disk herniation, diskography is no longer used in this way. Thus, cervical diskography has no role in cervical radiculopathy; its usefulness is limited to diskogenic pain.

Differential Diagnosis

The most common causes of cervical nerve root compression are cervical spondylosis, disk degeneration, and disk herniation. However, there are numerous other causes. Radiculopathy is a shooting, radiating type of pain extending into the hand, accompanied by objective neurologic signs with sensory loss, objective motor weakness, or hyporeflexia.

Compression of the spinal cord in the neck may result in cervical myelopathy, which produces radicular symptoms in the upper extremities and long-tract signs in the lower extremities. Sensory impairment, muscle weakness, and loss of tendon reflexes may be found in the upper extremities. In the lower extremities, spastic weakness, hyporeflexia, clonus, extensor plantar reflexes, and impaired vibratory and position sense may be observed. Bowel and bladder function are usually intact. Pain associated with degenerative disk disease, facet joint arthropathy, or myofascial syndrome is somatic in nature with referred characteristics. Pain referred to the upper back, shoulders, and upper extremities with somatic characteristics without reflex changes and without radiation into distal upper extremities indicates causes other than radiculopathy. Myelopathy is characterized by symptoms and signs of long-tract impairment affecting the lower limbs and trunk. However, such features may be absent in the lower limbs and manifest only in the upper limbs. In that event, the distinction from radiculopathy is made by the nonradicular distribution of features, the absence of lower motor neuron signs, and the presence of upper motor neuron features.[80] Bilateral neurologic features that are present with myelopathy are most likely absent with radiculopathy.

Spinal cord lesions typically affect the lower extremities and trunk in a similar manner to cervical myelopathy. However, if the manifesting features are limited to the upper extremities, they are differentiated by their diffuse nature and bilateral presence for cord lesions.

Pancoast syndrome and thoracic outlet syndrome manifest with involvement of C8 or T1 radiculopathy that is rarely caused by disk herniation. Characteristic features of thoracic outlet syndrome and Pancoast syndrome are not diagnostic of cervical radiculopathy.

Peripheral neuropathies of the upper extremity are present with shooting pain, paresthesia, and numbness.

However, the distribution of this symptomatology is different from cervical radiculopathy without a dermatomal pattern. Nerve conduction studies, rather than imaging studies, are discriminating with peripheral neuropathies or a combination of cervical radiculopathy and peripheral neuropathy. Other conditions include brachial neuritis, multiple sclerosis, and postherpetic neuralgia.

Differential Diagnosis of a Symptomatic Level

For the purposes of differential diagnosis, indication of symptomatic level is also crucial. A symptomatic level may be identified by pain distribution, sensory loss, motor weakness, and reflex inhibition.

It has been shown that radicular pain alone is poorly predictive of the involved level. Nevertheless, pain in the lateral arm or the posterior arm is most likely to be encountered in patients with C7 radiculopathy, whereas pain and/or paresthesia in the medial or posterior forearm distinguishes C6 radiculopathy from C7. However, the pain in the medial or posterior forearm does not distinguish between C7 and C8. Pain or paresthesia in the lateral forearm distinguishes C6 and C7 radiculopathy from C5 and C8, but does not discriminate between C6 and C7.

Paresthesias are considered as more valid contributions in identifying the level of the lesion than dermatomal distribution. Bogduk[80] described that involvement of the C6 nerve root affects the thumb or index finger, C7 nerve root affects the middle finger, and C8 nerve root affects the little finger. Other fingers may also be involved, however, the cardinal features for the C8 dermatome are the little fingers, with or without involvement of the ring finger, whereas, the features for the C7 dermatome are the middle fingers, with or without involvement of the index finger. Motor dysfunction, sensory dysfunction, and reflex changes are shown in Table 54–1.

■ TREATMENT

Various modalities include conservative management with drug therapy or noninterventional modalities, interventional pain management, and surgical management.

Conservative Therapy

Conservative therapy includes drug therapy, physical therapy, traction, collar, bedrest, exercise, and TENS. Saal and colleagues[81] extensively described conservative management in cervical disk herniation. Although there are numerous reports of treatments in managing chronic neck pain, very few have studied cervical radiculopathy. During the past decades, there has been an increasing interest in summarizing and analyzing the available evidence on conservative management of neck pain. Hoving and coworkers[83] critically appraised review articles on the effectiveness of conservative treatment for neck pain. They evaluated 25 review articles, of which 12 were systematic reviews from more than 100 articles identified. They recommended that review articles should avoid bias in the selection of articles; explicitly describe the population and symptoms reviewed; detail the number of treatments and their specific characteristics; use accepted classifications if possible; and use systematic techniques in conducting the review. They also concluded that consumers should consider reports of reviews both carefully and critically, given the wide variety of review methodology, descriptive information, and conclusions. They considered the majority of the reviews to be of low quality.

van Tulder and associates[82] concluded that, because of methodologic problems, they believed it was not opportune to make any recommendations in favor of any type of treatment for chronic neck pain. The conservative modalities of treatments they included were drug therapy with muscle relaxants, manual therapy, physical therapy, behavioral therapy, acupuncture, traction, pillows, laser therapy, electromagnetic therapy, and proprioceptive exercises.

Interventional Pain Management

Interlaminar epidural steroid injections, as well as transforaminal epidural steroid injections have been used in managing cervical radicular pain. However, the data for cervical epidural steroids is lacking and mostly extrapolated from lumbar radiculopathy. There have been no systematic or pragmatic reviews of cervical epidural steroid injections. Literature search identified two randomized trials[84,85] evaluating cervical interlaminar epidural steroid injections and one nonrandomized trial[86] evaluating transforaminal epidural steroid injections. Other authors also have described management of cervical pain with epidural steroid injections.[87-93] However, the results are only modest in their effectiveness both for short-term (<3 months) and long-term (>3 months).[54] Retrospective analyses have demonstrated that the patients likely to obtain the best results are those with radicular pain[93] and those likely to obtain the worst results are patients with normal spine radiographs.[93] However, cervical interlaminar epidural steroid injections should be a part of conservative management before approaching surgical intervention. Transforaminal epidural steroid injections in the cervical spine have been associated with numerous complications in recent years.[94-102] Thus, cervical transforaminal epidural steroid injections are recommended only as a last resort and in highly experienced hands with the patient's understanding of potential complications.

Surgery

Surgery is always undertaken after the failure of the conservative management. Multiple reviews have claimed excellent or good results in 80% to 90% of patients treated by disk excision and anterior fusion, with comparable results for disk excision without fusion, and good-to-excellent results in 94% or more of patients treated by posterior foraminotomy.[103] Only one randomized controlled trial available in the literature by Persson and coworkers[104] showed that the surgical group reported significantly less pain, but this difference extinguished by 12 months. The results of this study showed that only 8% of the patients were 100% pain free, whereas, 19% were improved, 42% were unchanged, and 31% were worse.

COMPLICATIONS

Complications of disk herniation include nerve damage and spinal cord compression, apart from long lasting disability.

Cervical disk herniation may produce Brown-Séquard syndrome.[105] Conservative management, as well as surgical management, is associated with side effects. All types of analgesics, both narcotic and non-narcotic, have a multitude of side effects. Acetaminophen is associated with hepatic toxicity. NSAIDs can have serious side effects, particularly at high doses and in elderly patients. Opioids cause dizziness, respiratory depression, central nervous system dysfunction, and dependency and addiction. Muscle relaxants have significant adverse effects including drowsiness and carry a significant risk of habituation and dependency. Bedrest is associated with deconditioning, whereas traction also adds to other complications of immobilization including muscle wasting, loss of bone density, pressure sores, and thromboembolism. Although risks of manipulation are low, serious complications could occur in patients resulting in severe or progressive neurologic deficit. Manipulation under anesthesia is also associated with an increased risk of serious neurologic damage.

Interventional techniques are also associated with multiple complications. The most common and worrisome complications of interlaminar and transforaminal epidural injections are related to the needle placement and drug administration. Complications include dural puncture, spinal cord trauma, infection, hematoma formation, abscess formation, subdural injection, intracranial air injection, epidural lipomatosis, pneumothorax, nerve damage, headache, death, brain damage, increased intracranial pressure, intravascular injection, vascular injury, cerebrovascular pulmonary embolus, and effects of steroids.

Complications of surgical techniques include infection, nerve damage, spinal cord trauma, death, epidural fibrosis, and postlumbar laminectomy syndrome.

References

1. Wiltse LL: The history of spinal disorders. In Frymoyer JW, Ducker TB, Hadler NM, et al (eds): The Adult Spine. Principles and Practice, 2nd ed. Philadelphia, Lippincott-Raven, 1997, p 3.
2. Boucher HH: A method of spinal fusion. J Bone Joint Surg 41b:248, 1959.
3. Elsberg CA: Extradural spinal tumors. Primary, secondary, metastatic. Surg Gynecol Obstet 46:1, 1928.
4. Bontecou RB: Transactions of the New York Medical Association, vol. III, 1887, p 317.
5. Adams F: Paulus Aeginata, vol 2. London, Syndenham Society, 1816, pp 155, 193, 197.
6. Hildanus F: Opera. In Walker AE (ed): A History of Neurological Surgery. New York, Hatner, 1672, p 366.
7. Robinson RA, Smith GW: Anterolateral cervical disc removal and interbody fusion for cervical disc syndrome. Bull Johns Hopkins Hosp 96:223, 1955.
8. Semmes RE, Murphey MF: The syndrome of unilateral rupture of the sixth cervical intervertebral disc with compression of the seventh cervical nerve root. A report of four cases with symptoms simulating coronary disease. JAMA 121:1209, 1943.
9. Mixter WJ, Barr JS: Rupture of the intervertebral disc with involvement of the spinal canal. N Engl J Med 211:210, 1934.
10. Spurling RG, Scoville WB: Lateral rupture of the cervical intervertebral discs. A common cause of shoulder and arm pain. Surg Gynecol Obstet 78:350, 1944.
11. Michelsen JJ, Mixter WJ: Pain and disability of shoulder and arm due to herniation of the nucleus pulposus of cervical intervertebral discs. N Engl J Med 231:279, 1944.
12. Stookey B: Compression of the spinal cord due to ventral extradural cervical chondromas. Arch Neurol Psychiatr 20:275, 1928.

13. Mair WGP, Druckman R: The pathology of spinal cord lesions and their relation to the clinical features in protrusion of cervical intervertebral discs. Brain 76:70, 1953.
14. Crowe HE: Injuries to the cervical spine. In Proceedings of the Western Orthopaedic Association Meeting, San Francisco, 1928.
15. Bogduk N: Definition. In Medical Management of Acute Cervical Radicular Pain. An Evidence-Based Approach. University of Newcastle, Australia, Newcastle Bone and Joint Institute, 1999, p 5.
16. Merskey H, Bogduk N: Classification of Chronic Pain. Descriptions of Chronic Pain Syndromes and Definitions of Pain Terms, 2nd ed. Seattle, IASP Press, 1994.
17. Ahlgren BD, Garfin SR: Cervical radiculopathy. Orthop Clin North Am 27:253, 1996.
18. Van Gijn J: Management of cervical radiculopathy. Opinion 1. Eur Neurol 35:309, 1995.
19. Caplan LR: Management of cervical radiculopathy. Eur Neurol 35:309, 1995.
20. Horal J: The clinical appearance of low back disorders in the city of Gothenburg, Sweden. Comparisons of incapacitated probands with matched controls. Acta Orthop Scand 118:1, 1969.
21. Kelsey J, Githens P, Walter SD, et al: An epidemiological study of acute prolapsed cervical intervertebral disc. J Bone Joint Surg Am 66:907, 1984.
22. Heckmann JG, Duran JC, Galeoto J: Vorkommen neurologischer Erkrankungen im tropischen Südamerika: Erfahrungen aus Dem Tiefland Boliviens. Fortschr Neurol Psychiatr 65:291, 1997.
23. Heckmann JG, Lang CJG, Zöbelien I, et al: Herniated cervical intervertebral discs with radiculopathy: An outcome study of conservatively or surgically treated patients. J Spinal Disord 12:396, 1999.
24. Hirsch C, Schajowicz F, Galante J: Structural changes in the cervical spine. Acta Orthop Scand 109:68, 1967.
25. Buckwalter JA: Aging and degeneration of the human intervertebral disk. Spine 20:1307, 1995.
26. Brain WR, Northfield DW, Wilkinson M: The neurologic manifestations of cervical spondylosis. Brain 75:187, 1952.
27. Crandall PH, Batsdorf U: Cervical spondylotic myelopathy. J Neurosurg 25:57, 1966.
28. Hayashi H, Okada K, Hashimoto J: Cervical spondylotic myelopathy in the aged patient. Spine 13:618, 1988.
29. Lees F, Turner JWA: Natural history and prognosis of cervical spondylosis. Br Med J 2:1607, 1963.
30. Lestini WF, Wiesel SW: The pathogenesis of cervical spondylosis. Clin Orthop 239:69, 1989.
31. Ono K, Ota H, Tada K, et al: Cervical myelopathy secondary to multiple spondylotic protrusions: A clinicopathologic study. Spine 2:109, 1977.
32. Holt S, Yates P: Cervical spondylosis and nerve root lesions. J Bone Joint Surg (Br) 48:407, 1966.
33. Braakman R: Management of cervical radiculopathy: Opinion 3. Eur Neurol 35:317, 1995.
34. Grote W, Kalff R, Roosen K: Die operative Behandlung zervikaler Bandscheibenvorfälle. Zentralbl Neurochir 52:101, 1991.
35. Herkowitz HN, Kurz LT, Overholt DP: Surgical management of cervical soft disc herniation: A comparison between the anterior and posterior approach. Spine 15:1026, 1990.
36. Laumer R, Nissen U, Rissman M, et al: PMMA-Fusion nach ventraler Diskektomie unter besonderer Berücksichtigung von multisegmentalen Eingriffen. In Matzen KH (Hrsg): Die operative Behandlung der Halswirbelsäule. München, W. Zuckschwerdt, 1994, p 103.
37. Van den Bent MJ, Oosting J, Wouda EJ, et al: Anterior cervical discectomy with or without fusion with acrylate. A randomized trial. Spine 21:834, 1996.
38. Yamamoto I, Ikeda A, Shibuya N, et al: Clinical long-term results of anterior discectomy without interbody fusion for cervical disc disease. Spine 16:272, 1991.
39. Zdeblick TA, Cooke ME, Kunz DN, et al: Anterior cervical discectomy and fusion using a porous hydroxyapatite graft substitute. Spine 19:2348, 1994.
40. Zeidman SM, Ducker TB, Raycroft J: Trends and complications in cervical spine surgery: 1989-1993. J Spinal Disord 10:523, 1997.
41. Long DM: Lumbar and cervical spondylosis and spondylotic myelopathy. Curr Opin Neurol Neurosurg 6:576, 1993.
42. Maigne JY, Deligne L: Computed tomographic follow-up study of 21 cases of nonoperatively treated cervical intervertebral soft disc herniation. Spine 19:189, 1994.

43. Reiners KH, Toyka K: Management of cervical radiculopathy. Opinion 2. Eur Neurol 35:313, 1995.
44. Lawrence JS: Disc degeneration. Its frequency and relationship to symptoms. Ann Rheum Dis 28:121, 1969.
45. Hult L: The Munkfors investigation. Acta Orthop Scand 16:1, 1954.
46. Hult L: Cervical dorsal and lumbar spinal syndromes. Acta Orthop Scand 17:1, 1954.
47. Odom GL, Finney W, Woodhall B: Cervical disc lesions. JAMA 166:23, 1958.
48. Lunsford LD, Bissonette DJ, Janetta PJ, et al: Anterior surgery for cervical disc disease. Part 1: Treatment of lateral cervical disc herniation in 253 cases. J Neurosurg 53:1, 1980.
49. Raynor R: Cervical cord compression secondary to acute disc protrusion in trauma. Spine 2:39, 1977.
50. Rhoton AL, Henderson ED: Cervical disc disease with neural compression. Minn Med 55:998, 1972.
51. O'Laoire S, Thomas D: Spinal cord compression due to prolapse of cervical intervertebral disc. J Neurosurg 59:847, 1983.
52. Bogduk N: Pathology. In Medical Management of Acute Cervical Radicular Pain. An Evidence-Based Approach. University of Newcastle, Australia, Newcastle Bone and Joint Institute, 1999, p 5.
53. Yamano Y: Soft disc herniation of the cervical spine. Int Orthop 9:19, 1985.
54. Manchikanti L, Staats P, Singh V, et al: Evidence-based practice guidelines for interventional techniques in the management of chronic spinal pain. Pain Physician 6:3, 2003.
55. Kang JD, Georgescu HI, McIntyre-Larkin L, et al: Herniated cervical intervertebral discs spontaneously produce matrix metalloproteinases, nitric oxide, interleukin-6 and prostaglandin E$_2$. Spine 22:2373, 1995.
56. Bogduk N: Clinical Features. In Medical Management of Acute Cervical Radicular Pain. An Evidence-Based Approach. University of Newcastle, Australia, Newcastle Bone and Joint Institute, 1999, p 19.
57. Gregorius FK, Estrin T, Crandall PH: Cervical spondylotic radiculopathy and myelopathy: A long-term follow-up study. Arch Neurol 33:618, 1976.
58. Yoss RE, Corbin KB, MacCarthy CS, et al: Significance of symptoms and signs in localization of involved root in cervical disk protrusion. Neurology 7:673, 1957.
59. Honet JC, Puri K: Cervical radiculitis: Treatment and results in 82 patients. Arch Phys Med Rehabil 57:12, 1976.
60. Henderson CM, Hennessy RG, Shuey HM, et al: Posterior-lateral foraminotomy as an exclusive operative technique for cervical radiculopathy: A review of 846 consecutively operated cases. Neurosurgery 13:504, 1983.
61. Cusick JF: Differential diagnosis of neck and arm pain relative to symptoms caused by degenerative disorders of the cervical spine. In Cervical Spine Research Society Editorial Committee. The Cervical Spine, 2nd ed. Philadelphia, Lippincott, 1989, p 607.
62. Clar SA, Cianca JC: Intracranial tumor masquerading as cervical radiculopathy: A case study. Arch Phys Med Rehabil 79:1301, 1998.
63. Sanchez MC, Arenillas JIC, Gutierrez DA, et al: Cervical radiculopathy: A rare symptom of giant cell arteritis. Arth Rheum 26:207, 1983.
64. Atkinson R, Ghelman B, Tsairis P, et al: Sarcoidosis presenting as cervical radiculopathy: A case report and literature review. Spine 7:412, 1982.
65. Bogduk N: Physical Examination. In Medical Management of Acute Cervical Radicular Pain. An Evidence-Based Approach. University of Newcastle, Australia, Newcastle Bone and Joint Institute, 1999, p 35.
66. Viikari-Juntura E: Inter-examiner reliability of observations in physical examinations of the neck. Phys Ther 67:1526, 1987.
67. Malanga GA, Landes P, Nadler SF: Provocative tests in cervical spine examination: Historical basis and scientific analyses. Pain Physician 6:199, 2003.
68. Wainner RS, Gill H: Diagnosis and nonoperative management of cervical radiculopathy. J Orthop Sports Phys Ther 30:728, 2000.
69. Viikari-Juntura E, Porras M, Laasonen EM: Validity of clinical tests in the diagnosis of root compression in cervical disease. Spine 14:253, 1989.
69a. Uchihara T, Furukawa Jankagoshi: Compression of brachial plexus as a diagnostic test of cervical cord lesion. Spine, 19:2170, 1994.
70. Magee DJ: Cervical Spine. In Orthopedic Physical Assessment, 3rd ed. Philadelphia, Saunders Company, 1997.
71. Glaser JA, Curie JK, Bailey KL, et al: Cervical spinal cord compression and the Hoffman sign. Iowa Orthop J 21:49, 2001.

72. Bogduk N: Imaging. In Medical Management of Acute Cervical Radicular Pain. An Evidence-Based Approach. University of Newcastle, Australia, Newcastle Bone and Joint Institute, 1999, p 61.
73. Kaiser JA, Holland BA: Imaging of the cervical spine. Spine 23:2701, 1998.
74. Yousem DM, Atlas SW, Goldberg HI, et al: Degenerative narrowing of the cervical spine neural foraminal evaluation with high-resolution 3-DFT gradient echo MR imaging. Am J Roentgenol 156:1229, 1991.
75. Fortin JD: Precision diagnostic disc injections. Pain Physician 3:271, 2000.
76. Modic MT, Masaryk TJ, Mulopulos GP, et al: Cervical radiculopathy: Prospective evaluation with surface coil MR imaging, CT with metrizamide, and metrizamide myelography. Radiology 161:753, 1986.
77. Yousem DM, Atlas SW, Goldberg HI, et al: Degenerative narrowing of the cervical spine neural foraminal evaluation with high-resolution 3-DFT gradient echo MR imaging. Am J Roentgenol 156:1229, 1991.
78. Boden SD, McCowin PR, Davis DG, et al: Abnormal magnetic-resonance scans of the cervical spine in asymptomatic subjects: A prospective investigation. J Bone Joint Surg 72A:1178, 1990.
79. Teresi LM, Lufkin RB, Reicher MA, et al: Asymptomatic degenerative disk disease and spondylosis of the cervical spine: MR imaging. Radiology 164:83, 1987.
80. Bogduk N: Differential diagnosis. In Medical Management of Acute Cervical Radicular Pain. An Evidence-Based Approach. University of Newcastle, Australia, Newcastle Bone and Joint Institute, 1999, pp 51-54.
81. Saal JS, Saal JA, Yurth EF: Nonoperative management of herniated cervical intervertebral disc with radiculopathy. Spine 21:1877, 1996.
82. van Tulder MW, Goossens M, Hoving J: Nonsurgical treatment of chronic neck pain. In Nachemson AL, Jonsson E (eds): Neck and Back Pain. The Scientific Evidence of Causes, Diagnosis, and Treatment. Philadelphia, Lippincott Williams & Wilkins, 2000, p 339.
83. Hoving JL, Gross AR, Gasner D, et al: A critical appraisal of review articles on the effectiveness of conservative treatment for neck pain. Spine 26:196, 2001.
84. Castagnera L, Maurette P, Pointillart V, et al: Long-term results of cervical epidural steroid injection with and without morphine in chronic cervical radicular pain. Pain 58:239, 1994.
85. Stav A, Ovadia L, Sternberg A, et al: Cervical epidural steroid injection for cervicobrachialgia. Acta Anaesthesiol Scand 37:562, 1993.
86. Bush K, Hillier S: Outcome of cervical radiculopathy treated with periradicular/epidural corticosteroid injections: A prospective study with independent clinical review. Eur Spine J 5:319, 1996.
87. Rowlingson JC, Kirschenbaum LP: Epidural analgesic techniques in the management of cervical pain. Anesth Analg 65:938, 1986.
88. Pawl RP, Anderson W, Shulman M: Effect of epidural steroids in the cervical and lumbar region on surgical intervention for diskogenic spondylosis. In Fields HL, Dubner R, Cervero F (eds): Advances in Pain Research and Therapy, vol. 9. New York, Raven, 1985, p 791.
89. Shulman M: Treatment of neck pain with cervical epidural steroid injection. Reg Anesth 11:92, 1986.
90. Purkis IE: Cervical epidural steroids. Pain Clinic 1:3, 1986.
91. Cicala RS, Thoni K, Angel JJ: Long-term results of cervical epidural steroid injections. Clin J Pain 5:143, 1989.
92. Ferrante FM, Wilson SP, Iacabo C, et al: Clinical classification as a predictor of therapeutic outcome after cervical epidural steroid injection. Spine 18:730, 1993.
93. Mangar D, Thomas PB: Epidural steroid injections in the treatment of cervical and lumbar pain syndrome. Reg Anesth 16:246, 1991.
94. Helm II S, Jasper JF, Racz GB: Complications of transforaminal epidural injections. Pain Physician 6:389, 2003.
95. Schultz DM. Risk of transforaminal epidural injections. Pain Physician 6:390, 2003.
96. Kloth DS. Risk of cervical transforaminal epidural injections by anterior approach. Pain Physician 6:392, 2003.
97. Windsor RE, Storn S, Sugar R, et al: Cervical transforaminal injection: Review of the literature, complications, and a suggested technique. Pain Physician 6:457, 2003.
98. Baker R, Dreyfus P, Mercer S, et al: Cervical transforaminal injection of corticosteroids into a radicular artery: A possible mechanism for spinal cord injury. Pain 103:211, 2003.
99. Brouwers PJ, Kottnick EJ, Simon MA, et al: A cervical anterior spinal artery syndrome after diagnostic blockade of the right C6 nerve root. Pain 91:397, 2001.
100. McMillan MR, Crumpton C: Cortical blindness and neurologic injury complicating cervical transforaminal injection for cervical radiculopathy. Anesthesiology 99:509, 2003.
101. Rozin L, Rozin R, Koehler SA, et al: Death during transforaminal epidural steroid nerve root block (C7) due to perforation of the left vertebral artery. Am J Forensic Med Pathol 24:351, 2003.
102. Furman MB, Giovanniello MT, O'Brien EM: Incidence of intravascular penetration in transforaminal cervical epidural steroid injections. 28:21, 2003.
103. Chestnut RM, Abitbol JJ, Garfin SR: Surgical management of cervical radiculopathy. Orthop Clin North Am 23:461, 1992.
104. Persson LCG, Carlsson CA, Carlsson JY: Long-lasting cervical radicular pain managed with surgery, physiotherapy or a cervical collar: A prospective, randomized study. Spine 22:751, 1997.
105. Mastronardi L, Ruggeri A: Cervical disc herniation producing Brown-Séquard syndrome. Spine 29:E28, 2004.

chapter 55

Brachial Plexopathy

Divya Patel

■ HISTORY

Obstetrical brachial plexopathy was first described in 1779 by Smellie (Fig. 55–1). In the 1870s, Duchenne reported a series of infants with upper brachial plexus injury resulting in primary involvement of the proximal upper limb and leading to a characteristic upper limb posture. Around the same time Erb also reported on the upper brachial plexopathy. Since then neonatal upper brachial plexopathy is commonly known as Erb-Duchenne palsy. In the 1880s, Klumpke described lower brachial plexopathy affecting mainly the distal limb and pupil (Horner syndrome).

■ ANATOMY

The word *brachial* means "arm" and *plexus* means "network of nerves." The brachial plexus is one of the most complex structures in the peripheral nervous system. It is a triangular structure that extends anteroinferiorly from neck to axilla. It is usually 15 to 18 cm long in adults. It travels posterior to the anterior scalene muscle and anterior to the middle scalene muscle in the proximal portion. In the distal part it travels posterior to the clavicle and pectoralis minor muscle and anterior to the first rib (Fig. 55–2). It is subdivided into five components for better description and understanding: (1) anterior primary rami of C5-T1 spinal roots; (2) trunks: superior, middle, and inferior; (3) each trunk giving rise to anterior and posterior divisions; (4) cords: medial, lateral, and posterior; and (5) multiple peripheral nerves from rami, trunks, and cords (Fig. 55–3).

Multiple dorsal and ventral rootlets arise from each spinal cord segment. Rootlets join to form dorsal and ventral roots, respectively, which unite to become a spinal nerve. Each spinal nerve gives rise to anterior and posterior primary rami. Posterior rami innervate the paraspinal muscles.

Each spinal nerve from T1 to L2 gives rise to the white ramus communicans, which carries preganglionic sympathetic fibers, which in turn ends in sympathetic ganglia. Postganglionic fibers from ganglia enter the spinal nerve via the gray ramus communicans or travel along the blood vessels to reach the target organs (Fig. 55–4). Head and neck sympathetic supply emerges from the T1 spinal nerve to reach cervical sympathetic ganglia. Thus, lesions of the lower brachial plexus may result in Horner syndrome.

Usually, C5-C6 anterior rami join to form the upper trunk, the C7 anterior ramus forms the middle trunk, and the C8-T1 anterior rami unite to form the lower trunk. When the brachial plexus has more contribution from the C4 anterior ramus and very little from the T1 level it is called a prefixed plexus. In contrast, when the T2 rami contribute more with little or no contribution from the C5 level it is known as a post-fixed brachial plexus. The trunks are named for their relationship to each other. The lower trunk is adjacent to the subclavian artery and the apex of the lung.

Each trunk divides into anterior and posterior divisions. Anterior divisions of the upper and middle trunk unite to form the lateral cord. The anterior division of lower trunk continues as the medial cord, while the posterior divisions of all

FIGURE 55–1 ■ Mr. William Smellie.

Axilla (Dissection): Anterior View

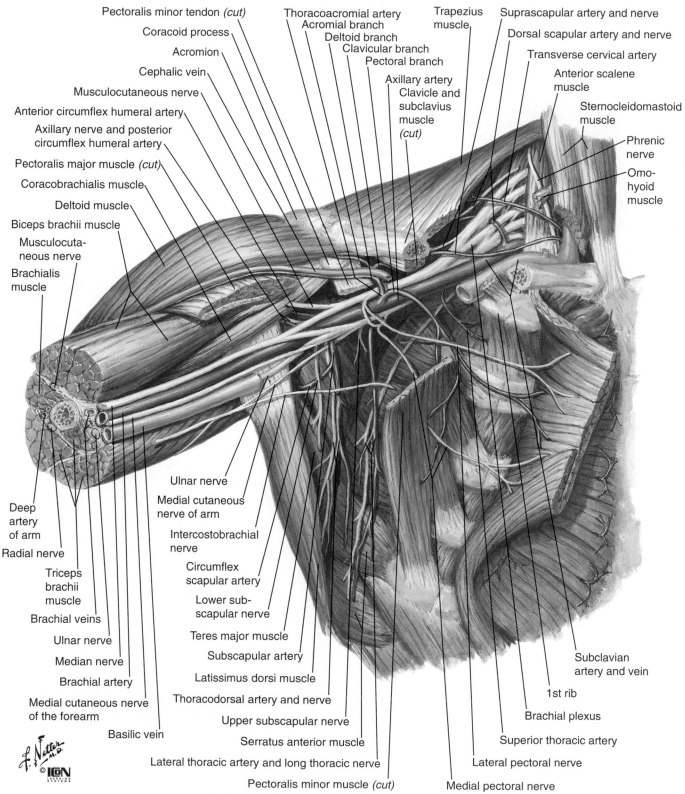

Pectoralis minor tendon *(cut)*
Coracoid process
Acromion
Cephalic vein
Musculocutaneous nerve
Anterior circumflex humeral artery
Axillary nerve and posterior
circumflex humeral artery
Pectoralis major muscle *(cut)*
Coracobrachialis muscle
Deltoid muscle
Biceps brachii muscle
Musculocuta-
neous nerve
Brachialis
muscle

Thoracoacromial artery
Acromial branch
Deltoid branch
Clavicular branch
Pectoral branch
Axillary artery
Clavicle and
subclavius
muscle
(cut)

Trapezius
muscle

Suprascapular artery and nerve
Dorsal scapular artery and nerve
Transverse cervical artery
Anterior scalene
muscle
Sternocleidomastoid
muscle
Phrenic
nerve
Omo-
hyoid
muscle

Deep
artery
of arm
Radial nerve
Triceps
brachii
muscle
Brachial veins
Ulnar nerve
Median nerve
Brachial artery
Medial cutaneous nerve
of the forearm
Basilic vein

Ulnar nerve
Medial cutaneous
nerve of arm
Intercostobrachial
nerve
Circumflex
scapular artery
Lower sub-
scapular nerve
Teres major muscle
Subscapular artery
Latissimus dorsi muscle
Thoracodorsal artery and nerve
Upper subscapular nerve
Serratus anterior muscle
Lateral thoracic artery and long thoracic nerve
Pectoralis minor muscle *(cut)*

Subclavian
artery and vein
1st rib
Brachial plexus
Superior thoracic artery
Lateral pectoral nerve
Medial pectoral nerve

FIGURE 55–2 ■ Position of the brachial plexus in relation to other structures in neck and upper chest. (From Netter F: Atlas of Human Anatomy, 2nd ed. Philadelphia, WB Saunders, 1997, plate 400.)

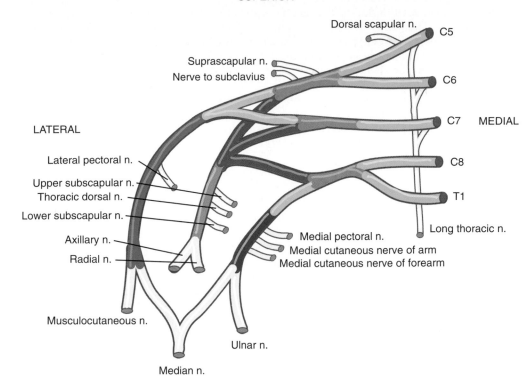

SUPERIOR

Dorsal scapular n.   C5

Suprascapular n.
Nerve to subclavius   C6

C7   MEDIAL

LATERAL

C8

Lateral pectoral n.

Upper subscapular n.
Thoracic dorsal n.   T1

Lower subscapular n.

Long thoracic n.

Axillary n.   Medial pectoral n.
Radial n.   Medial cutaneous nerve of arm
Medial cutaneous nerve of forearm

Musculocutaneous n.

Ulnar n.

Median n.

INFERIOR

FIGURE 55–3 ■ Brachial plexus.

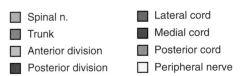

☐ Spinal n.   ☐ Lateral cord
☐ Trunk   ■ Medial cord
☐ Anterior division ☐ Posterior cord
■ Posterior division ☐ Peripheral nerve

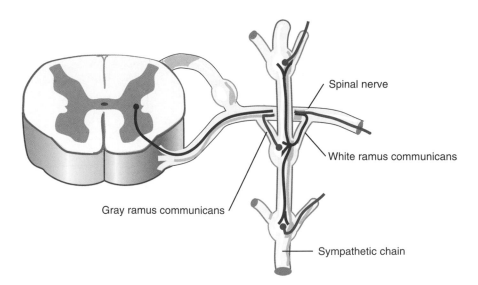

Spinal nerve

White ramus communicans

Gray ramus communicans

Sympathetic chain

FIGURE 55–4 ■ Cervical sympathetic chain.

■ Preganglionic neuron
■ Postganglionic neuron

three cords join to form posterior cord. The cords are named according to their relationship to the second segment of the axillary artery. The cords end by dividing into terminal branches. The medial and lateral cords innervate the pectoral region and flexors or anterior upper limb muscles. The posterior cord innervates the shoulder, posterior arm, and forearm muscles.

Branches are given at each subcomponent of the brachial plexus except at the level of divisions:

At the primary ramus level: *The dorsal scapular nerve* arises from the C5 anterior ramus to supply the levator scapulae and rhomboids major and minor. The C5 spinal segment also has some contribution to the *phrenic nerve* to supply the ipsilateral dome of the diaphragm. The *long thoracic nerve* is formed by union of branches from C5, C6, and C7 anterior rami and supplies the serratus anterior (see Fig. 55–3).

At the trunk level: The upper trunk gives rise to two branches. The *suprascapular nerve* innervates the supraspinatus and infraspinatus muscles. The nerve to the subclavius supplies the subclavius muscle (see Fig. 55–3).

At the cord level: Many preterminal nerves exit from all three cords. The medial cord gives rise to the *medial pectoral nerve,* which innervates the sternal part of the pectoralis major and minor muscles. The *medial brachial cutaneous nerve* and *medial antebrachial cutaneous nerve* innervate the skin of the medial arm and forearm, respectively. Then the medial cord ends by dividing into two main branches: *ulnar nerve* and

medial division of the median nerve. The ulnar nerve along with the median nerve supplies the anterior forearm and hand muscles as well as the cutaneous innervation to palm, digits, and medial half of the dorsal hand and one and a half digits. The lateral cord gives rise to the *lateral pectoral nerve,* which supplies the clavicular head of the pectoralis major muscle. Then the lateral cord ends by dividing into the *musculocutaneous nerve* and the *lateral division of the median nerve,* which joins the medial division to form the median nerve. The musculocutaneous nerve supplies the anterior arm muscles and lateral forearm skin. The posterior cord gives the *upper and lower subscapular nerves* that supply the subscapularis and teres major muscles. The *thoracodorsal nerve* innervates the latissimus dorsi muscle. Finally, the posterior cord divides into *axillary* and *radial nerves.* The axillary nerve innervates the deltoid and teres minor muscles as well as the skin over the upper lateral arm. The radial nerve supplies the posterior muscles of arm and forearm as well as skin over posterior arm, forearm, and lateral half of dorsal hand and three and a half digits.

The upper trunk has the most cutaneous sensory representation, followed by the lower and then by the middle trunk. The posterior cord has the most cutaneous sensory representation, followed by the lateral cord and the medial cord. The radial nerve has the most cutaneous sensory representation, and the least is in the ulnar nerve. The upper trunk and posterior cord have the most motor representation, and the least motor representation is in the middle trunk.

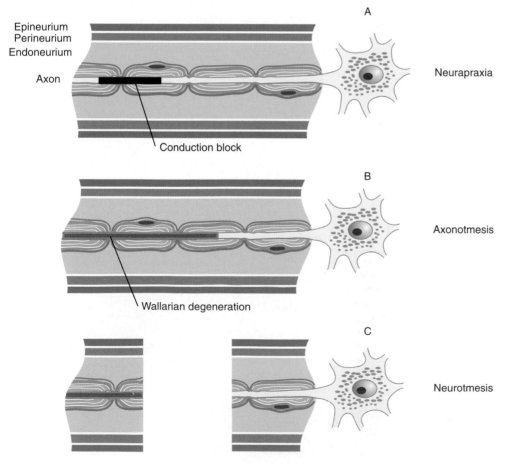

FIGURE 55–5 ■ Seddon classification of nerve injury. **A,** Neurapraxia: physiologic conduction block. **B,** Axonotmesis leading to wallerian degeneration of axon distal to the site of injury. Note, all three neural supporting structures are intact. **C,** Neurotmesis: axonotmesis with injury to one or more neural supporting structures.

■ PATHOPHYSIOLOGY

Nerve injury varies from mild to severe. Mild injury results in physiologic conduction block and is known as neurapraxia, in which only the myelin is damaged with no axon injury (Fig. 55–5). In such an injury symptoms are only of short duration and the prognosis for recovery of function is best. Examples of this type of an injury include burner or stinger and Saturday night palsy of the radial nerve. Moderate nerve injury at one or multiple places in the brachial plexus, in which individual axons are damaged with intact surrounding tissue, is called axonotmesis. This injury leads to degeneration (wallerian) of the axon distal to the site of insult. The axon regrows from the injury site in the endoneurium at a rate of 1 mm per day, thus, on average, 1 inch per month, to reach the end organ again. Examples of this type of injury include Erb-Duchenne palsy and Klumpke palsy due to fast progression of the birth. The most severe type of neural injury results in damage to the nerve axon as well as the surrounding connective tissue and is known as neurotmesis. Endoneurium may be blocked by scar tissue causing neuroma formation, or it may grow in multiple directions leading to aberrant pathways. Therefore, this injury has the worst prognosis. Examples of this type of injury include a gunshot wound or knife injuries to the area of the brachial plexus.

■ CLASSIFICATION

Brachial plexopathy can be classified according to etiology or site of lesion (Table 55–1).

■ CLINICAL PRESENTATION

Upper Brachial Plexopathy

In upper brachial plexopathy weakness is noted in the shoulder abductors, external rotators, elbow flexors, forearm supinators, and wrist extensor muscles. This pattern of weakness leads to the upper limb staying on the side of the body with the shoulder in adduction and internal rotation with the elbow hyperextended, forearm pronated, and wrist hyperflexed. This posture is well known as porter's tip or waiter's tip hand. Loss of muscle stretch reflexes is noted in the biceps,

Table 55–1

Classification of Brachial Plexopathy

Etiology	*Site of Lesion*

A. Traumatic
  1. Traction or stretch injury: fast progression: birth injury, motor vehicle accident, sports related (burner/stinger), fall, hanging from a height to prevent fall
  2. Penetrating injury: gunshot wound, knife cut, chainsaw injury, animal bites
  3. Slow progression: compression from muscle, fibrous band, cervical rib (thoracic outlet syndrome), enlarging aneurysm or hematoma, arteriovenous malformation, post-fracture callus of clavicle, rucksack paralysis
B. Infectious: herpes zoster
C. Neoplastic
  1. Primary
    a. Benign: schwannoma, neurofibroma, dermoids
    b. Malignant: neurofibrosarcoma, malignant schwannoma
  2. Secondary: metastasis from breast cancer, lung cancer, and lymphoma
D. Iatrogenic
  1. Radiation
  2. Surgical: shoulder area surgery, medial sternotomy
  3. Anesthesia: post narcosis paralysis or anesthesia paralysis
  4. Chiropractic manipulation
  5. Neuralgic amyotrophy also known as Parsonage-Turner syndrome, brachial plexitis, idiopathic brachial plexopathy, and brachial amyotrophy
	A. Supraclavicular (usually involves anterior rami and trunks)
	  1. Upper plexus
	    a. Erb-Duchenne palsy
	    b. Burner (stinger)
	    c. Rucksack (backpack) paralysis
	    d. Radiation plexopathy
	  2. Lower plexus
	    a. Klumpke palsy
	    b. Thoracic outlet syndrome
	    c. Neoplastic
	    d. Hanging from height to prevent fall
	B. Infraclavicular (usually involves cords and terminal branches)
	  1. Needle-induced plexopathy
	    a. Axillary angiography: medial brachial fascial compartment syndrome
	    b. Venous cannulation
	    c. Regional anesthesia
	C. Panplexopathy: trauma and neuralgic amyotrophy can involve any part of plexus

Modified from Dumitru D: Common Brachial Plexopathies: Findings and Prognosis. AAEM course C, 1994.

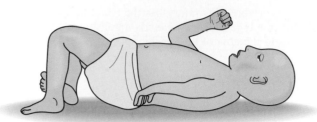

FIGURE 55–6 ■ Classic porter's tip hand in Erb palsy.

brachioradialis, triceps, and pronators. There is loss of sensation in the involved dermatomes and in the peripheral nerve distribution.

Lower Brachial Plexopathy

In lower brachial plexopathy weakness is noted in the distal limb and involves hand muscles and may mimic one or more of the distal nerve lesions. The hand position will typically include hyperextension of the metacarpophalangeal joints, flexion of the proximal and distal interphalangeal joints, and derotation of the thumb and is known as a simian or monkey hand. It may be accompanied by a stellate ganglion injury leading to Horner syndrome. The findings in Horner syndrome include ptosis (drooping of eyelid), miosis (pupil constriction), anhidrosis (loss of perspiration on ipsilateral face), and enophthalmos (retracted eyeball). Loss of muscle strength reflexes is noted mainly in the finger flexors. There will be loss of sensation in corresponding dermatomes and in the peripheral nerve distribution.

Traumatic Brachial Plexopathy

The basic mechanism of injury in traumatic brachial plexopathy varies from stretching to avulsion and from focal injury to pan-plexus involvement depending on the amount of force applied and the anatomy of the individual. Commonly, when the shoulder is adducted, contralateral cervical lateral hyperflexion will lead to upper plexus injury. An example of this is in a motorcycle accident when the rider falls and separates the head and the shoulder (Fig. 55–8). A fall on an abducted shoulder with the upper limb over the head separating the body and the upper limb will predominantly cause lower plexus injury. In patients with bilateral upper limb weakness involving the distal limb muscles it is important to rule out cervical spinal cord injury. Clinical features that strongly correlate with root avulsion include severe pain in an anesthetic limb and Horner syndrome.

The incidence of Erb-Duchenne palsy and Klumpke palsy is 4 per 1000 full-term deliveries. Many infants improve rapidly unless there is root avulsion. Permanent morbidity varies from 3% to 25%. Females are affected equally as males. Risk factors for these injuries include shoulder dystocia, weight more than 4 kg, breech presentation, prolonged second stage of delivery for more than 60 minutes, a previous child with obstetric brachial plexopathy, and multiparity (Fig. 55–6).[1] The right side is more frequently involved, and 4% of infants have bilateral symptoms. Infants with brachial plexopathy must be evaluated for associated injuries and pathologic processes such as clavicle or humerus fractures,

FIGURE 55–7 ■ Overstretching of the upper limb can lead to lower brachial plexus injury.

facial nerve or phrenic nerve palsy, cephalhematoma, and shoulder dystocia. The differential diagnosis includes hemiparesis and central hypotonia. An infant with hemiparesis has exaggerated muscle strength reflexes with the Moro reflex, and the electromyogram will be normal. In central hypotonia, muscle strength reflexes may not be present and the electromyogram is normal.

Stingers or burners are common in athletes, especially football players. They represent traction, compression, or a direct blow to the upper roots of the brachial plexus, causing abrupt intense burning dysesthesia, sometimes with weakness involving the entire limb. They are usually transient and usually resolve within minutes. Cervical canal stenosis with concurrent degenerative disk disease may predispose an athlete to persistent weakness and sensory changes. Return-to-play criteria are largely based on the number of previous episodes and the duration of symptoms. Appropriate counseling, including modification of tackling for a football player and addition of protective gear, in conjunction with complete rehabilitation, may be effective in preventing this condition or decreasing the rate of recurrence. The athlete, family, and coaches need to understand that recurrence remains unpredictable.[2]

Thoracic outlet syndromes (TOS) is an all-encompassing title for multiple entities including neurologic, vascular, and neurovascular entities, with true neurologic TOS, disputed

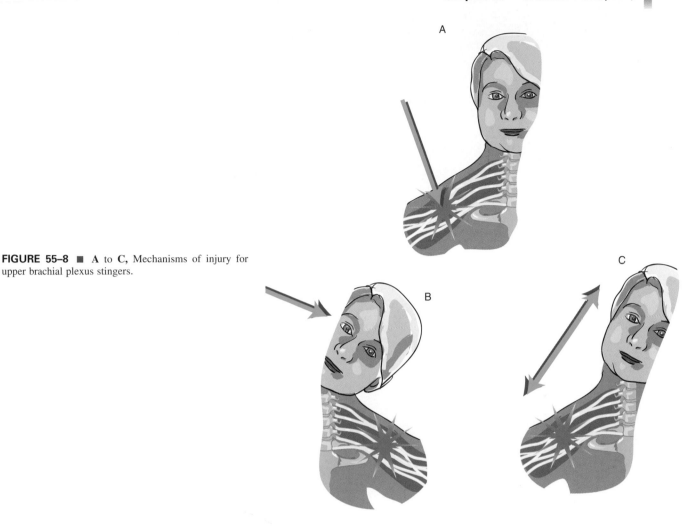

FIGURE 55–8 ■ **A** to **C,** Mechanisms of injury for upper brachial plexus stingers.

neurologic TOS, and traumatic TOS as subcomponents. The neurovascular bundle can get entrapped at different levels when entering the upper limb. The subclavian artery and trunks of the brachial plexus pass through a triangle called the scalene interval bounded by the anterior and middle scalene muscles and first rib. This interval can be narrowed by the cervical rib, anterior scalene spasm, or injury, which will encroach on artery and or plexus. TOS is also known as thoracic inlet syndrome, scalene interval syndrome, or anterior scalene syndrome (Fig. 55–9). Further down, the subclavian vessels and plexus can be compressed between the clavicle and first rib, and this is called the costoclavicular syndrome. Once the vessels and cords of the plexus cross the first rib they pass under the pectoralis minor and coracoid process. When the shoulder is fully abducted or flexed, this neurovascular bundle is tethered under these structures and produces paresthesias and other neurovascular symptoms. This is called pectoralis minor syndrome or coracopectoral syndrome.

Another entity that may occur is rucksack (backpack) paralysis. A rucksack is a cloth sack designed to carry 20 pounds on the shoulder. A backpack is bigger than a rucksack and has a metal frame that is supported by a waist belt. Waist belts prevent pack palsies because the weight is shifted to the hips, with shoulder straps used only to keep the pack in position. Soldiers, hikers, campers, and kids who carry books use these articles. Symptoms are gradual in onset and include weakness and numbness. Pain is usually rare.[3] The upper plexus is commonly involved. To prevent this condition, one should use wider and well-padded shoulder straps and secure the waist belt appropriately. Even then, frequent stops while hiking should be made to rest the shoulders and recover from any transient physiologic block.

Iatrogenic Brachial Plexopathy

Patients lose muscle tone during anesthesia and also lose the sensibility of stretch and any pain related to it. Patients who are positioned with their shoulders abducted 90 degrees or more and externally rotated in this setup will stretch the brachial plexus.[4] If the upper limb is extended at the same time (hanging from the table) or if the patient is put in the Trendelenburg position it will add to the trauma. Adding rotation and lateral flexion of the head to the opposite side of the arm being abducted may cause added trauma to the brachial plexus. Other positions that put the brachial plexus at risk are prone positioning with the shoulder in 90 degrees of abduction and external rotation.[5] When the patient is placed in the side-lying position with the upper limb in shoulder abduction and elbow extension with the arm suspended from a pole or overhead frame in the operating room for axillary or lateral chest wall skin grafting or in bed to decrease limb edema or to prevent axillary contracture, a traction injury to the brachial plexus can result. To prevent such an injury, with the patient

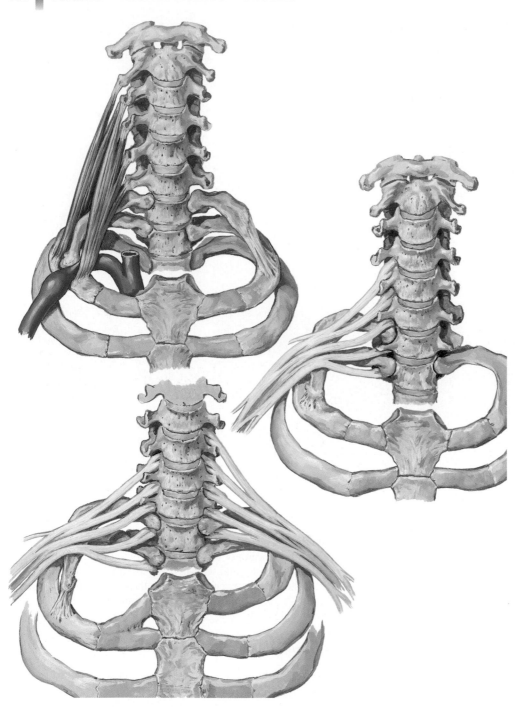

FIGURE 55–9 ■ Thoracic outlet syndrome. (From Netter F: Atlas of Human Anatomy, 2nd ed. Philadelphia, WB Saunders, 1997, plate 173.)

supine, adduction of the shoulder to 15 degrees can avoid traction. In a prone patient, placement of two pillows under the chest will avoid traction. In cardiothoracic surgery (median sternotomy), prolonged or substantial retraction of the sternum or hematomas from the internal jugular catheter may put stress on the lower trunk or medial cord of the brachial plexus and cause a neurapraxic-type injury.[6]

Radiation Plexopathy

Three types of syndromes are recognized after radiation treatment:

1. Transient plexus injury occurs in 1% of patients treated with 5000 cGy to the area. Symptoms usually start after 4 months.
2. Acute ischemic brachial neuropathy follows subclavian artery occlusion due to prior radiation. It is acute, is nonprogressive, and has painless weakness with sensory loss.
3. Symptoms of radiation fibrosis appear from months to years later. Risk factors include previous radiation, concomitant chemotherapy, and radiation of more than 5700 rad.

Symptoms of radiation plexopathy are chronic before the patient is diagnosed.[7] Radiation fibrosis is by far the most

Table 55–2	

Neoplastic vs. Radiation Plexopathy

Recurrent Neoplasm	*Post Radiation*
Severe pain predominant; Horner syndrome present.	Painless paresthesias; lymphedema present.
Lower plexus commonly involved.	Upper plexus commonly involved.
Myokymia usually absent.	Myokymia and fasciculation; motor conduction block on Erb's point stimulation.
Rapid onset of symptoms; less than 6 months post radiation.	Insidious onset of symptoms; symptom duration more than 4 years.
MRI with gadolinium will enhance the recurrent tumor.	May have chronic enhancement of the area on MRI.

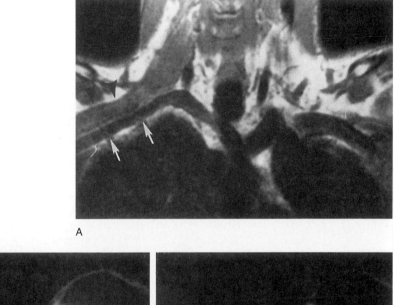

A

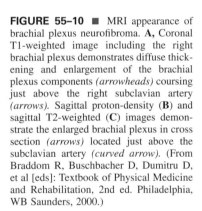

FIGURE 55–10 ■ MRI appearance of brachial plexus neurofibroma. **A,** Coronal T1-weighted image including the right brachial plexus demonstrates diffuse thickening and enlargement of the brachial plexus components *(arrowheads)* coursing just above the right subclavian artery *(arrows)*. Sagittal proton-density (**B**) and sagittal T2-weighted (**C**) images demonstrate the enlarged brachial plexus in cross section *(arrows)* located just above the subclavian artery *(curved arrow)*. (From Braddom R, Buschbacher D, Dumitru D, et al [eds]: Textbook of Physical Medicine and Rehabilitation, 2nd ed. Philadelphia, WB Saunders, 2000.)

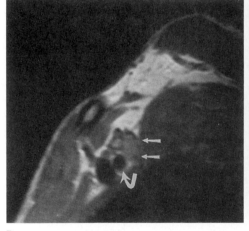

B

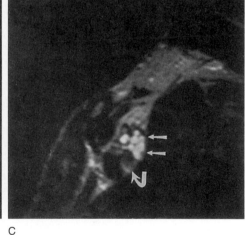

C

common type of radiation-induced brachial plexopathy. MRI will show postradiation changes in the soft tissue or bone. MRI with gadolinium will enhance the recurrent tumor. Postradiation patients may have chronic enhancement of the area on MRI (Table 55–2).[8]

Neoplastic Brachial Plexopathy

Primary tumors of the brachial plexus are less common than secondary neoplasms. Most of the primary tumors are benign. The most common primary tumor is neurofibroma, which is solitary, fusiform, and supraclavicular. Females are more often

affected than males. The second most common primary tumor is a benign schwannoma. Less common are primary malignant tumors of the neural sheath such as neurogenic sarcomas and fibrosarcomas. Secondary tumors are Pancoast tumor, lymphoma, small cell lung cancer, and breast cancer. MRI is the modality of choice for diagnosis (Fig. 55–10) (see Table 55–1).[9]

Parsonage-Turner Syndrome (Neuralgic Amyotrophy)

Viral illness, immunization, or surgery precedes this illness frequently but not all the time. The patient usually has a

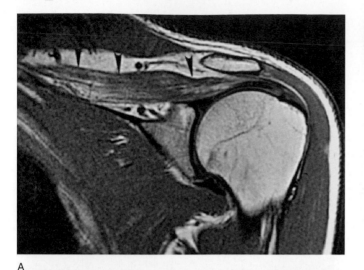

A

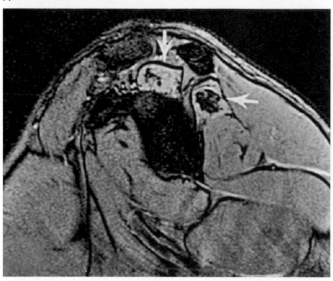

B

FIGURE 55–11 ■ Inflammatory neuritis. **A,** T1-weighted coronal image of shoulder. There is fatty infiltration of the supraspinatus muscle *(arrowheads)* without a tear of the rotator cuff, indicating a nerve abnormality. This patient had profound weakness and pain that was believed to be from a viral neuritis (Parsonage-Turner syndrome). **B,** T2-weighted sagittal image of shoulder. Higher signal intensity is present in both the supraspinatus and infraspinatus muscles *(white arrows),* rather than in the other musculature of the shoulder girdle, from muscle atrophy secondary to the brachial neuritis. (From Kaplan PA, Helms CA, Dussault R, et al [eds]: Musculoskeletal MRI. Philadelphia, WB Saunders, 2001, p 99.)

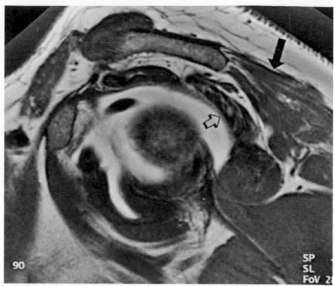

FIGURE 55–12. ■ Parsonage-Turner syndrome. Atrophy of deltoid and infraspinatus muscles. T1-weighted sagittal oblique MR arthrogram of shoulder. There is fat streaking in the deltoid *(solid arrow),* and the infraspinatus *(open arrow)* muscles. The patient had pain and weakness. The tendons were not torn. This was presumably from a viral brachial neuritis. (From Kaplan PA, Helms CA, Dussault R, et al [eds]: Musculoskeletal MRI. Philadelphia, WB Saunders, 2001, p 217.)

amyotrophy in patients with multiple episodes of painful brachial plexitis.

■ DIAGNOSIS

Electrodiagnosis

Electromyography/Nerve Conduction Studies (EMG/NCS)

Diagnosis of the exact site of the lesion in brachial plexopathy is a challenge for even an experienced physician (Table 55–3). Most of the EMG/NCS changes are more pronounced at 2 to 4 weeks after injury. The differential diagnosis of involvement of trunks versus cords is shown in Table 55–4.

C5-C6 root avulsion differs from upper trunk injury as follows: In root avulsion, on sensory nerve conduction study, the sensory nerve action potential (SNAP) from the median first or second digit, radial SNAP from the first digit, and lateral antebrachial cutaneous nerve SNAP will be normal (in a preganglionic lesion there is continuation of the cell body, that is in the dorsal root ganglion, to peripheral axon). On needle EMG there is involvement of the serratus anterior rhomboids and cervical paraspinals at the C5-6 area. Clinically there is involvement of these muscles in addition to those involved in the upper trunk lesion.

C7 root avulsion differs from middle trunk injury as follows: In root avulsion, on sensory nerve conduction study, SNAP from the median third digit and radial SNAP from the posterior antebrachial cutaneous nerve will be normal. On needle EMG there is involvement of the C7 area paraspinal muscles. Clinically they are identical.

C8-T1 root avulsion differs from lower trunk injury as follows: In root avulsion, on sensory nerve conduction study, SNAP from the ulnar fifth digit, the ulnar dorsal cutaneous

history of waking up at night from severe shoulder pain, which improves in 1 to 2 weeks. Once the pain is better, atrophy with weakness of shoulder and or upper limb becomes obvious. It can involve any nerve in the brachial plexus, but long thoracic, axillary, anterior interosseous, and suprascapular nerves are most commonly affected (Figs. 55–11 and 55–12). Sometimes nerve branches to the individual muscles may be affected (e.g., infraspinatus, pronator teres).[10] This pathology can be properly described as mononeuritis multiplex. It mostly occurs unilaterally, but needle electromyography may pick up involvement of the asymptomatic, contralateral side. One should rule out a rare dominantly inherited disorder known as hereditary neuralgic

Table 55–3

Diagnosis of Brachial Plexopathy

	Preganglionic Lesion as Seen in Root Avulsion or Radiculopathy	Postganglionic Lesion	Preganglionic + Postganglionic Lesion
Clinical Examination			
Sensation	Decreased or absent	Decreased or absent	Decreased or absent
Motor	Weakness	Weakness	Weakness
Nerve Conduction Studies			
SNAP amplitude	Normal	Decreased or absent	Decreased or absent
CMAP amplitude	Decreased or absent	Decreased or absent	Decreased or absent
Electromyography			
At rest: ↑insertional activity, PSW, fibrillation potentials	Present	Present	Present
Recruitment of motor unit potentials	Decreased or absent	Decreased or absent	Decreased or absent

SNAP, sensory nerve action potential; CMAP, compound motor nerve action potential; PSW, positive sharp waves.

Table 55–4

Differential Diagnosis of Nerve versus Muscle Involvement in Brachial Plexopathy

Abnormal Electrodiagnostic Study	Motor Nerve	Sensory Nerve	Involved Muscles on EMG
Upper trunk	Axillary Musculocutaneous Suprascapular	Lateral antebrachial cutaneous (terminal branch of musculocutaneous) Radial: thumb Median: first or second digit	Deltoid Biceps Brachioradialis Supraspinatus Infraspinatus Teres minor
Middle trunk	Radial	Radial: posterior antebrachial cutaneous Median: third digit	Triceps Pronator teres Flexor carpi radialis Extensor carpi radialis
Lower trunk	Median Ulnar Radial	Ulnar: fifth digit Ulnar: dorsal cutaneous nerve Medial antebrachial cutaneous	All muscles supplied by ulnar nerve; hand muscles supplied by median nerves Distal muscles supplied by radial nerve: extensor indicis, carpi ulnaris, and pollicis brevis
Lateral cord	Musculocutaneous	Lateral antebrachial cutaneous (terminal branch of musculocutaneous) Median: first, second, or third digit	Biceps Pronator teres Flexor carpi radialis
Posterior cord	Radial Axillary	Radial: posterior antebrachial cutaneous Radial: thumb	All muscles supplied by radial nerve in arm and forearm Latissimus dorsi Deltoid Teres major
Medial cord	Median Ulnar	Ulnar: fifth digit Ulnar: dorsal cutaneous nerve Medial antebrachial cutaneous	All hand muscles supplied by ulnar and median nerves All ulnar forearm muscles

nerve, and the medial antebrachial cutaneous nerve will be normal. There will be involvement of the C8-T1 paraspinal level in needle EMG. Clinically they are identical.

The presence of myokymia on EMG examination favors diagnosis of radiation plexopathy rather than recurrent neoplastic plexopathy. Fibrillations and positive sharp waves favor neoplastic plexopathy.

When brachial plexopathy is mild, motor and sensory conduction study may not reveal obvious abnormality at the same time and needle EMG may require a complete and detailed examination to record subtle abnormalities. Low limb temperature will increase SNAP amplitude, thus masking reduced amplitude from a postganglionic injury. Concomitant lesions such as carpal tunnel syndrome may make the sensory responses small, making diagnosis of root avulsion difficult.

Somatosensory Evoked Potentials (SSEP)

As the name suggests, this test evaluates somatic sensory fibers only. When terminal branches (median, ulnar, or radial nerves) of the brachial plexus are stimulated in the distal limb a response is recorded from the supraclavicular fossa at Erb's point (the negative wave obtained is called N9), at the C2 cervical spinous process over posterior column, (N13) and at the contralateral scalp over the parietal cortex (N19). When the N9 amplitude is reduced more than 30% as compared with a contralateral N9 with normal amplitude of N13, this is interpreted as a postganglionic lesion of the respective spinal nerve. That is, if the ulnar nerve was stimulated, the loss of N9 amplitude indicates a postganglionic lesion of the C8-T1, and for median nerve, a lesion at C5-6 (Table 55–5).

Lesion localization with SSEP correlated with surgical localization only in 50% of cases.[11] Because the SSEPs are more complex than the sensory NCSs and provide far less information about the status of the brachial plexus than a thorough electrodiagnostic examination they are of limited usefulness.[3]

Plain Radiography

Severe trauma that resulted in brachial plexopathy can also involve cervicobrachial bones, causing dislocation or fracture of the cervical vertebrae, clavicle, or upper humerus. C5-C7 anterior rami are closely related to transverse processes; therefore, a displaced fracture of cervical transverse process usually causes severe brachial plexus injury.[12]

Myelography

With root avulsion, dural covering of the root also gets pulled through the intervertebral foramen. After a few weeks this dural cover forms a diverticulum, which is easily seen on a cervical myelogram. This test is no longer in use for this purpose since MRI is available.

Computed Tomography

CT can be used to see a fracture that is not visible on plain radiography. CT myelography is better than conventional myelography but does not provide as good anatomic detail of brachial plexus and its branches as MRI. It is useful in detecting the fracture of the first rib as may happen with medial sternotomy that predominantly causes brachial plexopathy involving the C8 root or lower trunk.

Magnetic Resonance Imaging

MRI is noninvasive, and its soft tissue resolution is much better than that of previously mentioned studies. Therefore, MRI is the study of choice for evaluation of neural tissue. MRI can show signal intensity changes in denervated muscles a few days after injury. The findings are those of muscle edema with high signal intensity on T2-weighted images (see Figs. 55–10 and 55–11).[13] Three-dimensional MR myelography has a 92% diagnostic accuracy, 89% sensitivity, and 95% specificity.[14,15] MR neurography has been developed to evaluate peripheral nerves, but its accuracy has yet to be established.

■ TREATMENT

Rehabilitation

A comprehensive rehabilitation program includes joint range of motion (varying from passive, assisted, and active); strengthening exercises, exposure to various sensory modalities, proper positioning of the affected limb, a home exercise program, and use of various modalities such as transcutaneous electric nerve stimulation (TENS) to help in pain management and ultrasound for stretching contracted tendon. Use of appropriate orthoses to prevent contracture, maintain proper position, or improve functional gain is usually tailored to the patient's need. Therapy also addresses various activities of daily living with use of adaptive equipment and functional orthoses. Recreational therapy addresses compensatory techniques for arm use in various leisure activities.

Therapy for the child with neonatal brachial plexopathy begins in infancy. Gentle range of motion exercises are started in the first month. Parents are taught different exercises as well as how to give care without worsening the injury. A wrist extension splint is necessary to prevent contracture.

Table 55–5

Somatosensory Evoked Potentials in Brachial Plexopathy

	Amplitude of N9	Amplitude of N13
Preganglionic lesion	Normal or reduced < 30%	Reduced > 30% or absent
Postganglionic lesion	Reduced > 30%	Normal
Preganglionic + postganglionic lesion	Reduced > 30%	Absent or reduced > N9 amplitude reduction

Edema control with retrograde massage, compressive garments, elevation, and so on is important in postradiation plexopathy and some cases of recurrent neoplastic plexopathy.

Surgery

Surgical exploration and repair of brachial plexus lesions is technically feasible, and favorable outcomes can be achieved if patients are thoroughly evaluated and appropriately selected.[16] Surgery is indicated when the deficit does not improve with conservative treatment except in clean lacerating wounds with neural symptoms when immediate surgical exploration and repair may be indicated. For traumatic plexopathy, surgery gives better results when done by 3 months after the injury. If this fails, tendon transfer or osteotomy can improve function.[17] Common tendon transfers include triceps or pectoralis major or latissimus dorsi to biceps and may be good options for an encapsulated primary neoplasm.

Surgery varying from spinal cord stimulators, morphine pump, or dorsal root entry zone (DREZ) lesion may be used for pain control in brachial plexopathy.[18]

Pharmacologic Treatment

Nonsteroidal antiinflammatory agents, antiepileptics, tricyclic antidepressants, opiates, muscle relaxants, and antispasticity medications including botulinum A or B are used in various combinations to help reduce pain, paresthesias, muscle spasms, and spasticity.

■ COMPLICATIONS

Like any other peripheral nerve injury, brachial plexopathy of any origin can lead to complex regional pain syndrome type II or reflex sympathetic dystrophy. Myofascial pain syndromes, joint and muscle contracture, subluxation, and heterotopic ossification may complicate the recovery. Scoliosis from muscle imbalance is a possible complication in children. The sequelae that are commonly seen in children are due to muscle imbalance or contractures and may include osseous deformities of the shoulder and elbow, dislocation of both shoulder and elbow, and dislocation of both the humeral and radial heads. Patients with postradiation brachial plexopathy are at risk for lymphangiitis and cellulitis.

In general, prognosis for a lower trunk lesion is poor for two reasons: (1) C8-T1 roots have poor connective tissue support, making them more vulnerable to avulsion (preganglionic) injury compared with other roots; and (2) even in a postganglionic lesion, the target organs for motor and sensory nerves are farthest to reach. Muscle contracture, joint capsulitis, and fibrosis of the endoneural tube will go against the functional recovery. Prognosis in complete lesions is poor because the unaffected neural fibers are not available for collateral sprouting. Connective tissue disruption in the lesion site leads to fibrosis and impedes advancement of the axon that leads to a poor prognosis for recovery of function. Prognosis is best in upper trunk lesions.

■ CONCLUSION

Brachial plexus injury represents a complex clinical challenge from a diagnostic and treatment standpoint. Nerve grows 1

mm per day, thus, on average, 1 inch per month. Most postanesthetic and surgical brachial plexopathy improves rapidly. Supraclavicular brachial plexopathy are more common than infraclavicular plexopathy. Upper plexus lesions have a better prognosis than lower plexus lesions. Multiple specialties including physical medicine and rehabilitation, pain medicine, neurosurgery, orthopedics, plastic surgery, pediatrics, oncology, and radiation oncology should be consulted as appropriate. A list of organizations to consult for additional information is provided in Appendix 55–1.

References

1. Gherman RB, Ouzounian JG, Satin AJ, et al: A comparison of shoulder dystocia-associated transient and permanent brachial plexus palsies. Obstet Gynecol 102:544, 2003.
2. Weinberg J, Rokito S, Silber JS: Etiology, treatment, and prevention of athletic "stingers." Clin Sports Med 22:493, 2003.
3. Wilbourn AJ: Brachial plexus lesions. In Dyck PJ, Thomas PK (eds): Peripheral Polyneuropathy. Philadelphia, Elsevier, 2005, vol 2, pp 1339-1373.
4. Jackson L, Keats AS: Mechanism of brachial plexus palsy following anesthesia. Anesthesiology 26:190, 1965.
5. Dhuner KG: Nerve injuries following operations: A survey of cases occurring during a six-year period. Anesthesiology 11:289, 1950.
6. Graham JG, Pye IF, McQueen IN: Brachial plexus injury after median sternotomy. J Neurol Neurosurg Psychiatry 44:621, 1981.
7. Rowland LP: Merritt's Neurology, 10th ed. Philadelphia, Lippincott Williams & Wilkins, 2000.
8. Bowen BC, Verma A, Brandon AH, Fiedler JA: Radiation-induced brachial plexopathy: MR and clinical findings. Am J Neuroradiol 17:1932, 1996.
9. Kichari JR, Hussain SM, Den Hollander JC, Krestin GP: MR Imaging of the brachial plexus: Current imaging sequences, normal findings, and findings in a spectrum of focal lesions with MR-pathologic correlation. Curr Probl Diagn Radiol 32:88, 2003.
10. Ferrante MA: Brachial plexopathies: Classification, causes and consequences. Muscle Nerve 30:547, 2004.
11. Jones SJ: Diagnostic value of peripheral and spinal somatosensory evoked potentials in traction lesions of the brachial plexus. Clin Plast Surg 11:167, 1984.
12. Leffert RD: Brachial Plexus Injuries. New York, Churchill Livingstone, 1985.
13. West GA, Haynor DR, Goodkin R et al: Magnetic resonance imaging signal changes in denervated muscles after peripheral nerve injury. Neurosurgery 35:1077, 1994.
14. Gasparotti R, Ferrasesi S, Pinelli L, et al: Three-dimensional MR myelography of traumatic injuries of the brachial plexus. Am J Neuroradiol 18:1733, 1997.
15. Kufeld M, Claus B, Campi A, et al: Three-dimensional rotational myelography. Am J Neuroradiol 24:1290, 2003.
16. Kim DH, Cho YJ, Tiel RL, Kline DG: Outcomes of surgery in 1019 brachial plexus lesions treated at Louisiana State University Health Sciences Center: J Neurosurg 98:1005, 2003.
17. Ruhmann O, Gosse F, Schmolke S, et al: Osteotomy of the humerus to improve external rotation in nine patients with brachial plexus palsy. Scand J Plast Reconstr Surg Hand Surg 36:349, 2002.
18. Chen HJ, Lu K, Yeh MC: Combined dorsal root entry zone lesions and neural reconstruction for early rehabilitation of brachial plexus avulsion injury. Acta Neurochir Suppl 87:95, 2003.

Appendix 55–1

Organizations

Brachial Plexus Palsy Foundation: c/o 210 Springhaven Circle, Royersford, PA 19468. Email: *Brachial@aol.*

com; website: *http://membrane.com/bpp;* Tel: 610-792-4234

National Rehabilitation Information Center (NARIC): 4200 Forbes Boulevard, Suite 202, Lanham, MD 20706-4829. Email: *naricinfo@heitechservices.com;* website: *http://www.naric.com;* Tel: 301-562-2400 or 800-346-2742; Fax: 301-562-2401

National Organization for Rare Disorders (NORD): P.O. Box 1968 (55 Kenosia Avenue), Danbury, CT 06813-1968; email: *orphan@rarediseases.org;* website: *http://www.rarediseases.org;* Tel: 203-744-0100; Voice Mail 800-999-NORD (6673); Fax: 203-798-2291

United Brachial Plexus Network: 1610 Kent Street, Kent, OH 44240. Email: *info@ubpn.org;* website: *http://www.ubpn.org;* Tel: 866-877-7004

National Institute on Disability and Rehabilitation Research (NIDRR): 600 Independence Avenue, SW, Washington, DC 20013-1492. Website: *http://www.ed.gov/offices/OSERS/NIDRR;* Tel: 202-205-8134

chapter 56

Cervical Dystonia

Martin K. Childers and Chad Markert

■ HISTORICAL CONSIDERATIONS

Cervical dystonia (CD), one of the most common forms of primary torsion dystonia, is characterized by sustained involuntary contraction of the cervical muscles leading to twisting and repetitive head movements and abnormal postures.[1,2] Idiopathic CD (ICD) is the most common form of adult-onset focal dystonia.[3] The disorder is associated with a generalized abnormality of tone with coexisting hypotonia and hypertonia. Focal dystonias that affect the limbs were originally characterized by neurologists as cramps or occupational spasms. As early as 1836, J. H. Kopp reported a case of focal dystonia (writer's cramp) in a German medical monograph.[4] The term *dystonia* is attributed to the German neurologist Hermann Oppenheim who, in 1911, shortened the term *dystonia musculorum deformans* (reflecting the deforming nature of the syndrome). In his original article, Oppenheim (Fig. 56–1) described a childhood syndrome characterized by twisting of the torso, muscle spasms, jerky movements, and eventually progression of symptoms leading to fixed, contracted postures.[5] Today, *dystonia* is defined as a clinical syndrome characterized by sustained, involuntary muscular contractions that frequently lead to twisting and repetitive movements or abnormal postures.[2,6] Therefore, CD refers to focal dystonia of the neck muscles that often leads to twisting or turning of the head and is more commonly known by the name "torticollis" or "spasmodic torticollis."

■ CLINICAL PRESENTATION

Most CD patients present with a combination of neck rotation (torticollis), flexion (anterocollis), extension (retrocollis), side tilt (laterocollis), or a lateral shift.[7-9] These distinctive observable features of CD make the diagnosis fairly easy for the experienced clinician.[10] Neck posturing may be static, but more commonly the head moves in a rhythmic or continuous pattern. Over time, sustained abnormal postures can result in permanent and fixed contractures. The duration of the disease is variable, ranging from months to decades. Sensory tricks (geste antagonistique) may temporarily improve symptoms. Commonly used sensory tricks by patients with CD include touching the chin, back of the head, or top of the head (Fig. 56–2).[7] Symptoms of CD

stabilize over time, and remission rates are reported to occur 10% to 20% of the time, usually within the first few years. Symptoms of dystonia can spread to other parts of the body, most typically to the face, jaw, arms, or trunk.[3] For example, in a study of 72 British patients who were followed for 7 years, dystonia progressed to areas other than the neck (mainly the face and upper limbs in about one third of patients). Only 20% of patients experienced remission of symptoms.[11]

CD patients tend to be women in their fourth or fifth decades of life,[12] but few epidemiologic studies have been undertaken. One study in Europe[13] reported an annual prevalence for focal dystonia of 117 per million with CD representing 57 of the cases. The true prevalence in Europe and the United States is likely higher owing to underassessment of the disorder. Adolescents or children, particularly those patients with a sudden onset of symptoms, should be evaluated for other disorders (see Differential Diagnosis, later).

Patients with CD generally report insidious onset of symptoms that gradually worsen with time. Sleep helps relieve symptoms whereas tasks such as driving, reading, or working at the computer exacerbate the unwanted movement. Stressful situations such as meeting others in social gatherings, giving a presentation, or concentrating on a difficult task also tend to make the symptoms worse. Because the diagnosis of CD is dependent on clinical examination without confirmatory laboratory tests, one of the most difficult tasks for the clinician treating CD patients is to distinguish psychogenic CD from idiopathic CD. Those patients who present with sudden onset of symptoms or relentless progression of movement without abatement or changing suggest a psychogenic disorder. Fahn lists "situations" (Table 56–1) that may provide clues to identifying a patient with psychogenic CD.[6]

Pain attributed to CD differs from pain described by patients with diskogenic pain or fibromyalgia. CD patients do not attribute any particular head position to discomfort.[10] Myofascial trigger points are not present. Patients with CD describe unpleasant sensations accompanied by "pulling" or "tugging." Headaches are common[8] and may respond to local injections with botulinum toxin (BoNT). One theory[10] attributes CD pain to the "relentless contraction of neck muscles" and theorizes that one of the beneficial effects of BoNT is that it causes local muscle relaxation, thereby relieving pain. Undiagnosed CD patients often seek treatment for pain (rather

I. Originalmitteilungen.

1. Über eine eigenartige Krampfkrankheit
des kindlichen und jugendlichen Alters (Dysbasia lordotica
progressiva, Dystonia musculorum deformans).

Von H. Oppenheim.

Im Laufe der letzten 5 Jahre ist mir wiederholentlich ein Leiden entgegen-
getreten, dessen Deutung und Klassifizierung große Schwierigkeit bereitete. In

FIGURE 56–1 ■ German neurologist Hermann Oppenheim and the title page of his original article describing cervical dystonia. (From Goetz CG, Chmura TA, Lanska DJ: History of dystonia. Part 4 of the MDS-sponsored history of movement disorders exhibit, Barcelona, June, 2000. Mov Disord 16:339, 2001.)

FIGURE 56–2. ■ Touching the top or back of the head is one of the common "sensory tricks" in patients with cervical dystonia. (From Goetz CG, Chmura TA, Lanska DJ: History of dystonia. Part 4 of the MDS-sponsored history of movement disorders exhibit, Barcelona, June, 2000. Mov Disord 16:339, 2001.)

Table 56–1

Clues Suggesting Psychogenic Etiology of Cervical Dystonia

Movements
- Abrupt onset
- Inconsistent movements (changing characteristics over time)
- Incongruous movements and postures (movements do not fit with recognized patterns or with normal physiologic patterns)
- Presence of additional types of abnormal movements that are not consistent with the basic abnormal movement pattern or are not congruous with a known movement disorder, particularly rhythmical shaking, bizarre gait, deliberate slowness carrying out requested voluntary movement, bursts of verbal gibberish, and excessive startle (bizarre movements in response to sudden, unexpected noise or threatening movement)
- Spontaneous remissions
- Movements that disappear with distraction
- Response to placebo, suggestion, or psychotherapy
- Presence as a paroxysmal disorder
- Dystonia beginning as a fixed posture

Other Observations
- False weakness
- False sensory complaints
- Multiple somatizations or undiagnosed conditions
- Self-inflicted injuries
- Obvious psychiatric disturbances
- Employment in the health profession or in insurance claims
- Presence of secondary gain, including continuing care by a "devoted" spouse
- Litigation or compensation pending

Adapted from Fahn S: The varied clinical expressions of dystonia. Neurol Clin 2:541, 1984.

than for motor symptoms), with headache or neck pain as the presenting complaint. Therefore, it is advisable to examine new patients with neck pain or headache for physical findings consistent with CD.

PATHOGENESIS

CD was described by Meige as a disorder originating in "the mind itself." In the 1960s psychiatrists postulated that the disorder resulted from castration anxiety or a symbolic "turning away from the world." Thanks to modern imaging technology, electrophysiologic methods, and genetic analysis, the putative cause of CD has evolved from being considered a purely psychiatric disorder to a syndrome with links to a genetic etiology and objective features. The pathogenesis of CD is still unknown, although evidence suggests a role for genetic factors. In 2001, a polymorphism in the dopamine D5 receptor *(DRD5)* gene was associated with CD in a British population, suggesting that *DRD5* is a susceptibility gene for CD.[14] These findings were independently replicated by an Italian group who performed a large case-control study of the microsatellite DNA region containing a polymorphism (CT/GT/GA)(n) at the *DRD5* locus.[15] The frequency of allele 4 was higher in the CD patients compared with the controls, providing further evidence of an association between *DRD5* and cervical dystonia and supporting the involvement of the dopamine pathway in the pathogenesis of CD.

Several other lines of evidence point toward a relationship between dopamine and CD. For example, primary torsion dystonia (PTD), a genetically heterogeneous group of movement disorders that includes CD, is inherited in an autosomal dominant fashion and is reported to be caused by a protein encoded by the *DYT1* gene, torsion A, mutated in some forms of PTD. At least two other PTD gene loci have been mapped. The *DYT6* locus on chromosome 8 is associated with a mixed phenotype, whereas the *DYT7* locus on chromosome 18p is associated with adult-onset focal CD. A novel PTD locus *(DYT13)* was identified on chromosome 1 in a large Italian family with 11 affected members who displayed cervical, cranial, and upper limb dystonic symptoms.[16]

In another line of research, electrophysiologic tests were used to evaluate three patients with hereditary dopa-responsive dystonia, before and during treatment with levodopa.[17,18] Results were compared with those in a group of 48 healthy subjects. In the patients before levodopa treatment, the soleus H-reflex recovery curve showed increased late facilitation and depressed late inhibition, reflecting alterations in postsynaptic interneuronal activity. Of interest, the inhibition of the H-reflex caused by vibration (presumably reflecting presynaptic inhibition) was depressed. Normalization of these test results occurred during levodopa treatment, concurrent with a clear clinical response. Because the H-reflex tests are thought to reflect mechanisms operating at the spinal level, the authors concluded that spinal aminergic or dopaminergic systems are probably involved in dopa-responsive dystonia. Alternatively, patients with Parkinson's disease, when treated with levodopa, can develop dystonic symptoms (dyskinesias), and antipsychotic drugs that inhibit dopamine receptors are well known for their dystonic side effects.

TESTING

A family history of movement disorders may suggest a familial dystonia rather than idiopathic CD. Therefore, genetic tests based on DNA analysis for specific hereditary dystonias are available that use polymerase chain reaction (PCR) to detect and amplify DNA in blood samples. However, there is no simple test that confirms the diagnosis of CD or excludes a psychogenic component. Further research is needed before genetic testing is widely available in the clinic to identify patients at risk or to confirm a clinical diagnosis of idiopathic CD.

Cervical radiographs may identify structural changes of the spine caused by scoliosis or spondylosis secondary to long-standing CD. Similarly, magnetic resonance imaging (MRI) of the cervical cord is useful in determining the presence of spinal cord impingement secondary to bony changes from chronic CD. Contrast medium enhanced swallowing studies can be performed in consultation with a speech pathologist to evaluate and treat patients for swallowing disorders that accompany CD. Importantly, one treatment for CD, BoNT injections, may weaken muscles surrounding the larynx. Thus, patients at risk for aspiration should be evaluated by a speech pathologist and/or a swallowing study before treatment with BoNT. Brain imaging (by computed tomography [CT] or MRI) is indicated when the physical examination demonstrates findings consistent with an upper motor neuron syndrome, dementia, or pigmented corneal rings (e.g., Kayser-Fleischer rings seen in Wilson disease).

Electromyography (EMG) can help exclude the diagnosis in patients where the diagnosis is in question. For example, an EMG study of the sternocleidomastoid (SCM) and splenius capitis (SPL) muscles of eight patients with CD and eight age-matched controls demonstrated that all control subjects but one showed a peak in SPL EMG at 1 to 12 Hz, which was absent in all CD subjects.[19] Frequency analysis between CD patients and controls demonstrated differences suggesting that EMG may provide data to help distinguish CD from psychogenic torticollis. More commonly, EMG is used as a tool for mapping out injection patterns for patients treated with BoNT. Identifying muscles with EMG, particularly those deep to the surface that are contracting involuntarily, is useful before injection. The use of palpation alone to identify tight or contracting muscles may bias the examiner to only identify the most superficial muscles, whereas use of EMG can assist the clinician to identify deeper muscles that can contribute to dystonic postures.[10]

DIFFERENTIAL DIAGNOSIS

Torticollis is the observable feature of a twisted neck and may result from underlying causes other than CD.[3] Therefore, the differential diagnosis (Table 56–2) includes other disease states associated with abnormal postures, movement disorders, alterations in the dopaminergic system, and neurodegenerative processes. Rarely, CD with dystonic components occurs in the context of Parkinson disease. Head tremors may suggest the underlying cause to be essential tremor but should not occur with fixed abnormal postures as seen in CD. Patients with acquired (congenital) CD of

Table 56–2

Differential Diagnosis of Cervical Dystonia
- Idiopathic torsion dystonia
- Cerebral palsy
- Wilson disease
- Essential tremor
- Multiple sclerosis
- Myasthenia gravis
- Tardive dyskinesia
- Psychogenic torticollis
- Parkinson disease
- Congenital dystonia
- Side effects of psychogenic drugs

childhood should not display alternating hypertonia/hypotonia, and no palpable muscle hypertrophy or geste antagonistique should be present.

■ TREATMENT

In general, oral medications are not very effective for CD and only a few have been systematically evaluated in clinical trials.[20-22] Anticholinergic medications such as trihexyphenidyl or benztropine are worth a trial for CD patients, but these medications are more useful in generalized dystonias. Mexiletine was reported as helpful in the treatment of both CD and generalized dystonia.[23,24] Glutamate receptor blockers such as amantadine, or lamotrigine, and spasmolytic agents such as clonazepam and baclofen have all been reported to be useful in some patients with CD.[25] A subset of patients may respond to biofeedback training[26] and/or muscle relaxation training. A soft cervical collar can reproduce the sensory tricks that reduce head turning, but effects usually wane after a few hours of wear. In patients who are refractory to all other conservative treatments, including botulinum toxin injections, surgical resection of cervical muscles or deep brain stimulation is a treatment option.[27-35]

Because many CD patients find that specific postures, positions, or physical activities exacerbate symptoms, evaluation of the workplace or household ergonomics can be helpful. Occupational or physical therapists can assist in the evaluation and make strategic recommendations for ergonomic aids. Patients will often discover their own coping strategies to reduce physical stress, such as reducing the number of hours spent in front of a computer, working at a standing desk instead of a conventional desk, standing to the left or right of a person while carrying on a conversation, or making seat adjustments in the automobile.

The most effective therapy for patients with CD is local injections of BoNT, the treatment supported by evidence-based reviews and meta-analysis.[21,36-39] Indeed, chemodenervation via BoNT is generally considered the treatment of choice for patients with CD,[40-42] with 63% of patients reporting benefit at 5 years.[43] Success is determined by a number of clinical outcome measures: prevalence of complications, such as dysphagia[44]; score on the Tsui scale[45-47]; pain scores[46,48]; the Toronto Western Spasmodic Torticollis Rating Scale (TWSTRS)[37,49,50]; and relative cost of treatment.[51] However, because neurologic impairments may only have a small impact on the functional health of cervical dystonia patients, other outcome measures that include disability, handicap, and global disease scales may increase the relative response rate of CD patients treated with BoNT.[47]

The mechanism of action of BoNT is well studied. Three membrane proteins (collectively known as SNAREs), synaptobrevin (Sbr), synaptosome-associated protein of molecular weight 25,000 (SNAP-25), and syntaxin mediate the process of exocytosis of synaptic vesicles containing the neurotransmitter acetylcholine.[52] Vesicle membrane fusion at the neuromuscular junction transfers the contents of secretory proteins and transmitters. SNARE proteins provide the substrate for at least one of the seven serotypes (A to G) of BoNT or tetanus toxin (TeTx), which are bacterial proteases that act to block neurotransmitter release.[53] The family of BoNTs is also responsible for illness due to food contamination or wound infection. Botulinum neurotoxin type A (BoNT-A, Botox, Allergan, Inc., Dysport, Ipsen Pharmaceuticals) and type B (Myobloc, Solstice Neurosciences) are produced by the anaerobic bacteria *Clostridium botulinum,* an organism found in soil and water. Only BoNT-A and BoNT-B are clinically available for therapeutic use in the United States. BoNT-A and BoNT-E cleave the carboxyl terminus of SNAP-25,[54] whereas BoNT-B cleaves SBr. The time course of functional motor recovery after synaptic BoNT intoxication differs among serotypes.[54] Thus, the major assumption regarding the mechanism by which BoNTs decrease muscular contraction involves blocking acetylcholine release from presynaptic motor nerve terminal synapses. It is generally assumed that conditions such as dystonia and spasticity might be relieved subsequent to decreased muscular force in the areas injected, but this hypothesis has not been directly tested. Moreover, preclinical data may not necessarily apply to humans, because physiologic differences exist in the density, distribution, and morphology of the neuromuscular junction between species, age,[55] and disease states.[56,57]

There are no clear guidelines for the appropriate dose of BoNT for the treatment of CD. This is because the most appropriate dose depends on several clinical and logistical considerations. First, the dose of BoNT should be individualized. Koller and colleagues[58] noted that fixed-dose fixed-muscle controlled studies of BoNT for the clinical management of CD do not produce the same effects as studies (or case reports) in which the dosages and muscles are individualized according to the patient. Second, clinicians should strive to administer the lowest effective dosage of BoNT for treatment of CD to protect the patient from becoming immune to its therapeutic effect.[7,59] In general, patients should receive as few doses of toxin over their life span as possible, so long as their symptoms are manageable and until further studies of long-term effects of toxin therapy are completed.

EMG guidance may play a role in determining dosage, in that it may help with both effectively targeting affected muscles[60] and also with targeting motor endplates within those muscles,[61-63] thereby potentiating neurotoxin effects. However, when palpation alone is used to identify affected muscles, injection into either the mid belly or several sites of the muscle is generally recommended.

Table 56–3

Prospective Trials of Botulinum Neurotoxin in Cervical Dystonia

Serotype	Product	n	Dose	Injection Site(s)	Reference
A	Botox	55	30-250 U	SCM, trapezius, splenius capitis	Greene et al, 1990[69]
A	Oculinum	7	50-100 U	SCM, trapezius	Jankovic et al, 1987[70]
A	Botox	242	~222 U	Splenius capitis, SCM, trapezius, scalenus	Jankovic et al, 1991[44]
A	Botox	23	150 U	SCM, splenius capitis, trapezius	Lorentz et al, 1991[71]
A	Botox	20	500 U	Active muscles	Moore et al, 1991[72]
A	Botox	35	152 U (SD ± 45)	One or more clinically indicated muscles	Odergren et al, 1998[73]
A	Botox	54	NS	Individualized	Ranoux et al, 2002[74]
A	Dysport	32	262-292 U	Individualized	Brans et al, 1996[45]
A	Dysport	303	778 (SD ± 253)	SCM, trapezius, splenius capitis, levator scapulae	Kessler et al, 1999[75]
A	Dysport	38	477 U (SD ± 131)	One or more clinically indicated muscles	Odergren et al, 1998[73]
A	Dysport	75	500-1000 U	Splenius capitis and SCM	Poewe et al, 1998[76]
A	Dysport	54	NS	Individualized	Ranoux et al, 2002[74]
A	N/A	19	480 U	SCM, splenius capitis, trapezius	Blackie et al, 1989[77]
A	N/A	20	100-140 U	SCM, splenius capitis, trapezius	Gelb et al, 1989[78]
B	Myobloc	109	5,000-10,000 U	2-4 cervical muscles	Brashear et al, 1999[79]
B	Myobloc	76	10,000 U	2-4 cervical muscles	Brin et al, 1999[80]
B	Myobloc	122	2,500-10,000 U	2-4 cervical muscles	Lew et al, 1997[81]
F	BoNT-F*	5	520-780 MU	Affected neck muscles	Houser et al, 1998

*BoNT-F is not commercially available in the United States.
SCM, sternocleidomastoid muscle; NS, not specified; SD, standard deviation.

Finally, conversion of equivalent units between BoNT serotypes (or even different formulations of the same serotype) may not be a simple matter of mathematical calculation.[64] Two formulations of BoNT-A, marketed as Botox (Allergan, Inc.) and Dysport (Ipsen, Inc.), are available for clinical use. Although they are the same serotype, there is controversy regarding the conversion of units between available commercial formulations. Recent reviews[40-42] suggest that 200 units of Botox are roughly equivalent to 500 units of Dysport (i.e., a 2 : 5 ratio or a conversion factor of 2.5) as suggested by results of a comparison trial.[65] Only one formulation of BoNT-B, marketed as MyoBloc, is commercially available for the treatment of patients with CD.[37] Table 56–3 lists published dosages of BoNT-B for CD that range from 2,500 to10,000 units. Fewer data are available regarding efficacy, safety, and dosing for BoNT-B. The Cochrane Review suggests that uncontrolled comparisons of BoNT-A and BoNT-B should be regarded "with suspicion."[37] Therefore, dosing conversions between A and B serotypes may be speculative. Another serotype, BoNT-F, may be a future option for patients who are immunoresistant to serotypes A and B, although less literature exists for BoNT-F.[37a]

Effects of long-term treatment of CD with BoNT are not well studied. Three studies of long-term effects of BoNT-A in CD suggest that safety and efficacy persist over time. Brans and colleagues[66] reported improvements in disability, handicap, and perceived general health after 12 months of treatment; Kessler and colleagues[67] reported disease severity improvement over 5 years; Haussermann and colleagues[68] reported safety and efficacy data of BoNT treatment of 100 consecutive CD patients over 10 years. This line of evidence suggests that long-term treatment of CD with BoNT is both safe and effective, but further longitudinal studies will still be required.

■ COMPLICATIONS AND PITFALLS

Children or adults with fixed contractures of the neck caused by other problems (e.g., congenital torticollis) might be misdiagnosed with CD. Because a distinctive feature of CD is that the neck moves almost continually,[10] those with no active neck movement may not have true CD but rather a fixed contracture and will not respond to BoNT injections. Rarely, torticollis or torsion dystonia accompanies an upper motor neuron syndrome. In these cases when the neurologic examination reveals abnormalities, the patient should be referred to a neurologist or neurosurgeon for appropriate work-up to determine the underlying cause. Finally, for CD patients treated with BoNT injections, dysphagia can result from BoNT-induced weakening of the laryngeal muscles and place the patient at risk for aspiration. Any patient with an underlying swallowing disorder should be approached with caution when contemplating BoNT treatment. Swallowing studies are helpful in determining proper nutritional strategies for patients at risk or for those patients who develop dysphagia after injections.

■ CONCLUSION

CD causes involuntary head turning or tilting, may be painful, and most often affects women in the third or fourth decade of life. The diagnosis is made on clinical examination and the finding of abnormal head and neck position. A diagnosis of ICD is made in the presence of an otherwise normal physical examination, normal family history, and normal laboratory and imaging studies. Local injection of BoNT is the treatment of choice for CD. Dysphagia is a potential complication of the injections.

References

1. Fahn S: The varied clinical expressions of dystonia. Neurol Clin 2:541, 1984.
2. Markham CH: The dystonias. Curr Opin Neurol Neurosurg 5:301, 1992.
3. Dauer WT, Burke RE, Greene P, Fahn S: Current concepts on the clinical features, aetiology and management of idiopathic cervical dystonia. Brain 121:547,1998.
4. Kopp JH: Denkwurdigkeitenin der Arztlichen Praxis. Frankfurt, Hermann, 1836.
5. Goetz CG, Chmura TA, Lanska DJ: History of dystonia: Part 4 of the MDS-sponsored history of movement disorders exhibit, Barcelona, June, 2000. Mov Disord 16:339, 2001.
6. Fahn S: Dystonia. In Jankovic J, Hallett M (eds): Therapy with Botulinum Toxin. New York, Marcel Dekker, 1994, pp 173-190.
7. Velickovic M, Benabou R, Brin MF: Cervical dystonia pathophysiology and treatment options. Drugs 61:1921, 2001.
8. Galvez-Jimenez N, Lampuri C, Patino-Picirrillo R, et al: Dystonia and headaches: Clinical features and response to botulinum toxin therapy. Adv Neurol 94:321, 2004.
9. Kelleher JF, Mandell AJ: Dystonia musculorum deformans: A "critical phenomenon" model involving nigral dopaminergic and caudate pathways [Review]. Med Hypotheses 31:55, 1990.
10. Walker FO: Botulinum toxin therapy for cervical dystonia. Phys Med Rehabil Clin North Am 14:749, 2003.
11. Jahanshahi M, Marion MH, Marsden CD: Natural history of adult-onset idiopathic torticollis. Arch Neurol 47:548, 1990.
12. Claypool DW, Duane DD, Ilstrup DM, Melton LJ: Epidemiology and outcome of cervical dystonia (spasmodic torticollis) in Rochester, Minnesota. Mov Disord 10:608, 1995.
13. Epidemiological Study of Dystonia in Europe (ESDE) Collaborative Group: A prevalence study of primary dystonia in eight European countries. J Neurol 247:787, 2000.
14. Placzek MR, Misbahuddin A, Chaudhuri KR, et al: Cervical dystonia is associated with a polymorphism in the dopamine (D5) receptor gene. J Neurol Neurosurg Psychiatry 71:262, 2001.
15. Brancati F, Valente EM, Castori M, et al: Role of the dopamine D5 receptor (DRD5) as a susceptibility gene for cervical dystonia. J Neurol Neurosurg Psychiatry 74:665, 2003.
16. Valente EM, Bentivoglio AR, Cassetta E, et al: *DYT13*, a novel primary torsion dystonia locus, maps to chromosome 1p36.13-36.32 in an Italian family with cranial-cervical or upper limb onset. Ann Neurol 49:362, 2001.
17. Koelman JH, Speelman JD, Hilgevoord AA, et al: Dopa-responsive dystonia and normalization of soleus H-reflex test results with treatment. Neurology 45:281, 1995.
18. Koelman JH, Willemse RB, Bour LJ, et al: Soleus H-reflex tests in dystonia. Mov Disord 10:44, 1995.
19. Tijssen MA, Marsden JF, Brown P: Frequency analysis of EMG activity in patients with idiopathic torticollis. Brain 123:677, 2000.
20. Adler CH, Kumar R: Pharmacological and surgical options for the treatment of cervical dystonia. Neurology 55:S9, 2000.
21. Balash Y, Giladi N: Efficacy of pharmacological treatment of dystonia: Evidence-based review including meta-analysis of the effect of botulinum toxin and other cure options. Eur J Neurol 11:361, 2004.
22. Dauer WT, Burke RE, Greene P, Fahn S: Current concepts on the clinical features, aetiology and management of idiopathic cervical dystonia. Brain 121:547, 1998.
23. Ohara S, Hayashi R, Momoi H, et al: Mexiletine in the treatment of spasmodic torticollis. Mov Disord 13:934, 1998.
24. Lucetti C, Nuti A, Gambaccini G, et al: Mexiletine in the treatment of torticollis and generalized dystonia. Clin Neuropharmacol 23:186, 2000.
25. West HH: Treatment of spasmodic torticollis with amantadine: A double-blind study. Neurology 27:198, 1977.
26. Jahanshahi M, Sartory G, Marsden CD: EMG biofeedback treatment of torticollis: A controlled outcome study. Biofeedback Self Regul 16:413, 1991.
27. Braun V, Richter HP: Selective peripheral denervation for the treatment of spasmodic torticollis. Neurosurgery 35:58, 1994.
28. Bronte-Stewart H: Surgical therapy for dystonia. Curr Neurol Neurosci Rep 3:296, 2003.
29. Celayir AC: Congenital muscular torticollis: Early and intensive treatment is critical: A prospective study. Pediatr Int 42:504, 2000.
30. Goto S, Mita S, Ushio Y: Bilateral pallidal stimulation for cervical dystonia: An optimal paradigm from our experiences. Stereotact Funct Neurosurg 79:221, 2002.
31. Kiss ZH, Doig K, Eliasziw M, et al: The Canadian multicenter trial of pallidal deep brain stimulation for cervical dystonia: Preliminary results in three patients. Neurosurg Focus 17:E5, 2004.
32. Krauss JK: Deep brain stimulation for dystonia in adults: Overview and developments. Stereotact Funct Neurosurg 78:168, 2002.
33. Langlois M, Richer F, Chouinard S: New perspectives on dystonia. Can J Neurol Sci 30(Suppl 1):S34, 2003.
34. Lozano AM, Abosch A: Pallidal stimulation for dystonia. Adv Neurol 94:301, 2004.
35. Yu SW, Wang NH, Chin LS, Lo WH: Surgical correction of muscular torticollis in older children. Zhonghua Yi Xue Za Zhi (Taipei) 55:168, 1995.
36. Balash Y, Giladi N: Efficacy of pharmacological treatment of dystonia: Evidence-based review including meta-analysis of the effect of botulinum toxin and other cure options. Eur J Neurol 11:361, 2004.
37. Costa J, Espirito-Santo C, Borges A, et al: Botulinum toxin type B for cervical dystonia. Cochrane Database Syst Rev CD004315, 2005.
37a. Dressler D: Botulinum toxin mechanisms of action. Suppl Clin Neurophysiol 57:159, 2004.
38. Brefel-Courbon C, Simonetta-Moreau M, More C, et al: A pharmacoeconomic evaluation of botulinum toxin in the treatment of spasmodic torticollis. Clin Neuropharmacol 23:203, 2000.
39. Langlois M, Richer F, Chouinard S: New perspectives on dystonia. Can J Neurol Sci 30(Suppl 1):S34, 2003.
40. Jankovic J, Esquenazi A, Fehlings D, et al: Evidence-based review of patient-reported outcomes with botulinum toxin type A. Clin Neuropharmacol 27:234, 2004.
41. Jankovic J: Treatment of cervical dystonia with botulinum toxin. Mov Disord 19:S109, 2004.
42. Jankovic J: Botulinum toxin in clinical practice. J Neurol Neurosurg Psychiatry 75:951, 2004.
43. Hsiung GY, Das SK, Ranawaya R, et al: Long-term efficacy of botulinum toxin A in treatment of various movement disorders over a 10-year period. Mov Disord 17:1288, 2002.
44. Jankovic J, Schwartz KS: Clinical correlates of response to botulinum toxin injections. Arch Neurol 48:1253, 1991.
45. Brans JW, Lindeboom R, Snoek JW, et al: Botulinum toxin versus trihexyphenidyl in cervical dystonia: A prospective, randomized, double-blind controlled trial. Neurology 46:1066, 1996.
46. Poewe W, Deuschl G, Nebe A, et al: What is the optimal dose of botulinum toxin A in the treatment of cervical dystonia? Results of a double blind, placebo controlled, dose ranging study using Dysport. German Dystonia Study Group. J Neurol Neurosurg Psychiatry 64:13, 1998.
47. Lindeboom R, Brans JW, Aramideh M, et al: Treatment of cervical dystonia: A comparison of measures for outcome assessment. Mov Disord 13:706, 1998.
48. Lorentz IT, Subramaniam SS, Yiannikas C: Treatment of idiopathic spasmodic torticollis with botulinum-A toxin: A pilot study of 19 patients. Med J Aust 152:528, 1990.
49. Tarsy D: Comparison of clinical rating scales in treatment of cervical dystonia with botulinum toxin. Mov Disord 12:100, 1997.
50. Truong D, Duane DD, Jankovic J, et al: Efficacy and safety of botulinum type A toxin (Dysport) in cervical dystonia: Results of the first US randomized, double-blind, placebo-controlled study. Mov Disord 20:783, 2005.
51. Dodel RC, Kirchner A, Koehne-Volland R, et al: Costs of treating dystonias and hemifacial spasm with botulinum toxin A. Pharmacoeconomics 12:695, 1997.
52. Lawrence GW, Dolly JO: Multiple forms of SNARE complexes in exocytosis from chromaffin cells: Effects of Ca(2+), MgATP and botulinum toxin type A. J Cell Sci 115:667, 2002.
53. Lawrence GW, Dolly JO: Ca2+-induced changes in SNAREs and synaptotagmin I correlate with triggered exocytosis from chromaffin cells:

Insights gleaned into the signal transduction using trypsin and botulinum toxins. J Cell Sci 115:2791, 2002.

54. Eleopra R, Tugnoli V, Rossetto O, et al: Different time courses of recovery after poisoning with botulinum neurotoxin serotypes A and E in humans. Neurosci Lett 256:135, 1998.

55. Ma J, Smith BP, Smith TL, et al: Juvenile and adult rat neuromuscular junctions: Density, distribution, and morphology. Muscle Nerve 26:804, 2002.

56. Theroux MC, Akins RE, Barone C, et al: Neuromuscular junctions in cerebral palsy: Presence of extrajunctional acetylcholine receptors. Anesthesiology 96:330, 2002.

57. Jirmanova I, Thesleff S: Motor end-plates in regenerating rat skeletal muscle exposed to botulinum toxin. Neuroscience 1:345, 1976.

58. Koller W, Vetere-Overfield B, Gray C, Dubinsky R: Failure of fixed-dose, fixed muscle injection of botulinum toxin in torticollis. Clin Neuropharmacol 13:355, 1990.

59. Kessler KR, Benecke R: The EBD test—a clinical test for the detection of antibodies to botulinum toxin type A. Mov Disord 12:95, 1997.

60. Comella CL, Buchman AS, Tanner CM, et al: Botulinum toxin injection for spasmodic torticollis: Increased magnitude of benefit with electromyographic assistance. Neurology 42:878, 1992.

61. Childers MK: Targeting the neuromuscular junction in skeletal muscles. Am J Phys Med Rehabil 83(10 Suppl):S38, 2004.

62. Childers MK: The importance of electromyographic guidance and electrical stimulation for injection of botulinum toxin. Phys Med Rehabil Clin North Am 14:781, 2003.

63. Childers MK, Kornegay JN, Aoki R, et al: Evaluating motor end-plate-targeted injections of botulinum toxin type A in a canine model. Muscle Nerve 21:653, 1998.

64. Wohlfarth K, Kampe K, Bigalke H: Pharmacokinetic properties of different formulations of botulinum neurotoxin type A. Mov Disord 19(Suppl 8):S65, 2004.

65. Ranoux D, Gury C, Fondarai J, et al: Respective potencies of Botox and Dysport: A double blind, randomised, crossover study in cervical dystonia. J Neurol Neurosurg Psychiatry 72:459, 2002.

66. Brans JW, Lindeboom R, Aramideh M, Speelman JD: Long-term effect of botulinum toxin on impairment and functional health in cervical dystonia. Neurology 50:1461, 1998.

67. Kessler KR, Skutta M, Benecke R: Long-term treatment of cervical dystonia with botulinum toxin A: Efficacy, safety, and antibody frequency. German Dystonia Study Group. J Neurol 246:265, 1999.

68. Haussermann P, Marczoch S, Klinger C, et al: Long-term follow-up of cervical dystonia patients treated with botulinum toxin A. Mov Disord 19:303, 2004.

69. Greene P, Kang U, Fahn S, et al: Double-blind, placebo-controlled trial of botulinum toxin injections for the treatment of spasmodic torticollis. Neurology 40:1213, 1990.

70. Jankovic J, Orman J: Botulinum A toxin for cranial-cervical dystonia: A double-blind, placebo-controlled study. Neurology 37:616-623, 1987.

71. Lorentz IT, Subramaniam SS, Yiannikas C: Treatment of idiopathic spasmodic torticollis with botulinum toxin A: A double-blind study on twenty-three patients. Mov Disord 6:145, 1991.

72. Moore AP, Blumhardt LD: A double blind trial of botulinum toxin "A" in torticollis, with one year follow up. J Neurol Neurosurg Psychiatry 54:813, 1991.

73. Odergren T, Hjaltason H, Kaakkola S, et al: A double blind, randomised, parallel group study to investigate the dose equivalence of Dysport and Botox in the treatment of cervical dystonia. J Neurol Neurosurg Psychiatry 64:6, 1998.

74. Ranoux D, Gury C, Fondarai J, et al: Respective potencies of Botox and Dysport: A double blind, randomised, crossover study in cervical dystonia. J Neurol Neurosurg Psychiatry 72:459, 2002.

75. Kessler KR, Skutta M, Benecke R: Long-term treatment of cervical dystonia with botulinum toxin A: Efficacy, safety, and antibody frequency. German Dystonia Study Group. J Neurol 246:265, 1999.

76. Poewe W, Deuschl G, Nebe A, et al: What is the optimal dose of botulinum toxin A in the treatment of cervical dystonia? Results of a double blind, placebo controlled, dose ranging study using Dysport. German Dystonia Study Group. J Neurol Neurosurg Psychiatry 64:13, 1998.

77. Blackie JD, Lees AJ: Botulinum toxin treatment in spasmodic torticollis. J Neurol Neurosurg Psychiatry 53:640, 1990.

78. Gelb DJ, Lowenstein DH, Aminoff MJ: Controlled trial of botulinum toxin injections in the treatment of spasmodic torticollis. Neurology 39:80, 1998.

79. Brashear A, Lew MF, Dykstra DD, et al: Safety and efficacy of NeuroBloc (botulinum toxin type B) in type A-responsive cervical dystonia. Neurology 53:1439, 1999.

80. Brin MF, Lew MF, Adler CH, et al: Safety and efficacy of NeuroBloc (botulinum toxin type B) in type A-resistant cervical dystonia. Neurology 53:1431, 1999.

81. Lew MF, Adornato BT, Duane DD, et al: Botulinum toxin type B: A double-blind, placebo-controlled, safety and efficacy study in cervical dystonia. Neurology 49:701, 1997.

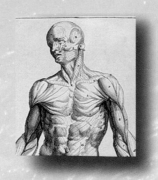

Part C

SHOULDER PAIN SYNDROMES

Degenerative Arthritis of the Shoulder

Steven D. Waldman

The shoulder joint is susceptible to the development of arthritis from a variety of conditions that have in common the ability to damage the joint cartilage.[1] Osteoarthritis is the most common cause of shoulder pain and functional disability.[2] It may occur following seemingly minor trauma or may be the result of repeated microtrauma. Pain around the shoulder and upper arm which is worse with activity will be present in most patients suffering from osteoarthritis of the shoulder. Difficulty in sleeping is also common as is progressive loss of motion (Fig. 57–1).

The majority of patients presenting with shoulder pain secondary to osteoarthritis, rotator cuff arthropathy, and post-traumatic arthritis pain will present with the complaint of pain that is localized around the shoulder and upper arm.[3] Activity makes the pain worse, whereas rest and heat provide some relief. The pain is constant and characterized as aching in nature. The pain may interfere with sleep. Some patients will complain of a grating or popping sensation with use of the joint and crepitus may be present on physical examination.

In addition to the aforementioned pain, patients suffering from arthritis of the shoulder joint will often experience a gradual decrease in functional ability with decreasing shoulder range of motion making simple, everyday tasks such as hair combing, fastening a brassiere, or reaching overhead quite difficult.[4] With continued disuse, muscle wasting may occur and a frozen shoulder may develop (Fig. 57–2).

■ TESTING

Plain radiographs are indicated in all patients who present with shoulder pain (Fig. 57–3).[5] Based on the patient's clinical presentation, additional testing, including complete blood count, erythrocyte sedimentation rate, and antinuclear antibody testing may be indicated. MRI scan of the shoulder is indicated if rotator cuff tear is suspected (Fig. 57–4).

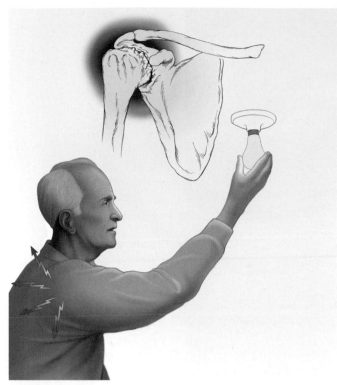

FIGURE 57–1 ■ Range of motion of the shoulder can precipitate the pain of osteoarthritis of the shoulder. (From Waldman SD: Atlas of Common Pain Syndromes. Philadelphia, Saunders, 2002, p 75, Fig 18–1.)

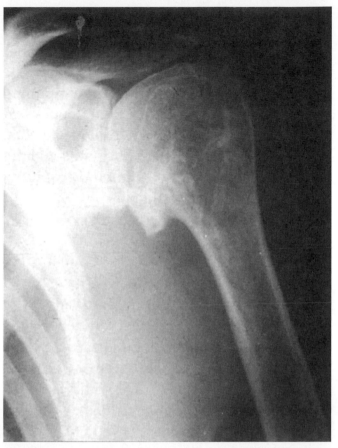

FIGURE 57–3 ■ Osteoarthritis of the shoulder. The radiograph shows all the features of a "hypertrophic" form of osteoarthritis of the glenohumeral joint, with joint-space narrowing, subchondral sclerosis, large cysts in the glenoid, and the massive inferior osteophytosis that is characteristic of this condition. (From Klippel JH, Dieppe PA: Rheumatology, 2nd ed. London, Mosby, 1998.)

FIGURE 57–2 ■ Arthrogram demonstrating adhesive capsulitis resulting in a frozen shoulder. (From Resnick D: Diagnosis of Bone and Joint Disorders, 4th ed. Philadelphia, Saunders, 2002, p 3108, Fig. 65–114A, B.)

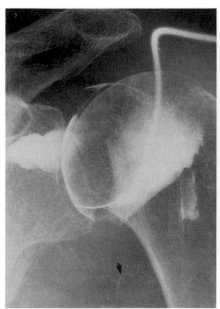
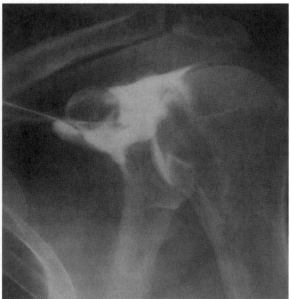

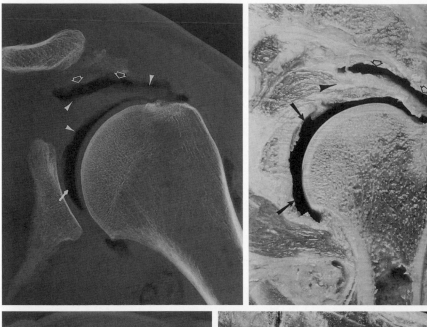

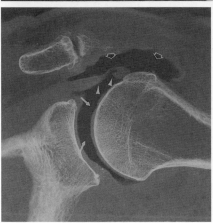

FIGURE 57-4 ■ (From Resnick: Diagnosis of Bone and Joint Disorders, 4th ed. Philadelphia, Saunders, 2002, p 3090, Fig 65–90A, B, C, D.)

Radionuclide bone scan is indicated if metastatic disease or primary tumor involving the shoulder is being considered.

■ DIFFERENTIAL DIAGNOSIS

Osteoarthritis of the joint is the most common form of arthritis that results in shoulder joint pain (Table 57–1).[6] However, rheumatoid arthritis, posttraumatic arthritis, and rotator cuff tear arthropathy are also common causes of shoulder pain secondary to arthritis. Less common causes of arthritis-induced shoulder pain include the collagen vascular diseases, infection, villonodular synovitis, and Lyme disease. Acute infectious arthritis will usually be accompanied by significant systemic symptoms including fever and malaise and should be easily recognized by the astute clinician and treated appropriately with culture and antibiotics, rather than injection therapy. The collagen vascular diseases will generally manifest as a polyarthropathy rather than a monoarthropathy limited to the shoulder joint, although shoulder pain secondary to collagen vascular disease responds exceedingly well to the intra-articular injection technique described below.

■ TREATMENT

Initial treatment of the pain and functional disability associated with osteoarthritis of the shoulder should include a combination of the nonsteroidal anti-inflammatory agents or COX-2 inhibitors and physical therapy. The local application of heat and cold may also be beneficial. For patients who do not respond to these treatment modalities, an intra-articular injection of local anesthetic and steroid may be a reasonable next step.[7]

Intra-articular injection of the shoulder is performed by placing the patient in the supine position and preparing with antiseptic solution the skin overlying the shoulder, subacromial region, and joint space. A sterile syringe containing the 2.0 mL of 0.25% preservative-free bupivacaine and 40 mg of methylprednisolone is attached to a 1½ inch 25-gauge needle using strict aseptic technique. With strict aseptic technique, the midpoint of the acromion is identified and at a point approximately 1 inch below the midpoint, the shoulder joint space is identified. The needle is then carefully advanced through the skin and subcutaneous tissues through the joint capsule into the joint (Fig. 57–5). If bone is encountered, the needle is withdrawn into the subcutaneous tissues and redi-

Table 57–1

Causes of Shoulder Pain

Localized Bony or Joint Space Pathology	Periarticular Pathology	Systemic Disease	Sympathetically Mediated Pain	Referred from Other Body Areas
Fracture	Bursitis	Rheumatoid arthritis	Causalgia	Brachial plexopathy
Primary bone tumor	Tendinitis	Collagen vascualr disease	Reflex sympathetic dystrophy	Cervical radiculopathy
Primary synovial tissue tumor	Rotator cuff tear	Reiter's syndrome	Shoulder/hand syndrome	Cervical spondylosis
Joint instability	Impingement syndromes	Gout	Dressler's syndrome	Fibromyalgia
Localized arthritis	Adhesive capsulitis	Other crystal arthropathies	Postmyocardial infarction adhesive capsulitis of the shoulder	Myofascial pain syndromes such as scapulocostal syndrome
Osteophyte formation	Joint instability	Charcot's neuropathic arthritis		Parsonage Turner syndrome (idiopathic brachial neuritis)
Joint space infection	Muscle strain			Thoracic outlet syndrome
Hemarthrosis	Muscle strain			Entrapment neuropathies
Villonodular synovitis intra-articular foreign body	Periarticular infection not involving joint space			Intrathoracic tumors
				Pneumothorax
				Subdiaphragmatic pathology such as subcapsular hematoma of the spleen with positive Kerr's sign

From Waldman SD: Physical Diagnosis of Pain. Philadelphia, Saunders, 2005, p. 55.

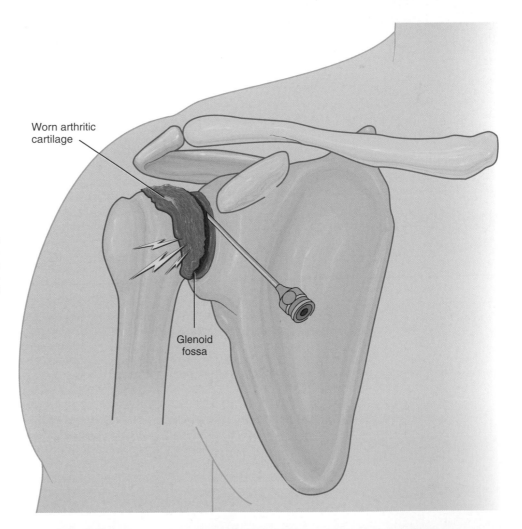

FIGURE 57–5 ■ Injection technique for intra-articular injection of the shoulder. (From Waldman SD: Atlas of Pain Management Injection Techniques. Philadelphia, Saunders 2000, p 39, Fig 10–1.)

rected superiorly and slightly more medial. After entering the joint space, the contents of the syringe is gently injected. There should be little resistance to injection. If resistance is encountered, the needle is probably in a ligament or tendon and should be advanced slightly into the joint space until the injection proceeds without significant resistance. The needle is then removed and a sterile pressure dressing and ice pack is placed at the injection site.

The major complication of intra-articular injection of the shoulder is infection. This complication should be exceedingly rare if strict aseptic technique is adhered to. Approximately, 25% of patients will complain of a transient increase in pain following intra-articular injection of the shoulder joint and should be warned of this.

■ CONCLUSION

Osteoarthritis of the shoulder is a common complaint encountered in clinical practice. It must be separated from other causes of shoulder pain including rotator cuff tears. Intra-articular injection of the shoulder is extremely effective in the treatment of pain secondary to the aforementioned causes of arthritis of the shoulder joint. Coexisting bursitis and tendinitis may also contribute to shoulder pain and may require additional treatment with more localized injection of local anesthetic and depot steroid. The above technique is a safe procedure if careful attention is paid to the clinically relevant anatomy in the areas to be injected. Care must be taken to use sterile technique to avoid infection and universal precautions to avoid risk to the operator. The incidence of ecchymosis and

hematoma formation can be decreased if pressure is placed on the injection site immediately following injection. The use of physical modalities, including local heat as well as gentle range-of-motion exercises should be introduced several days after the patient undergoes this injection technique for shoulder pain. Vigorous exercises should be avoided as they will exacerbate the patient's symptomatology. Simple analgesics and nonsteroidal anti-inflammatory agents or a COX-2 inhibitor may be used concurrently with this injection technique.

References

1. Gerber A, Lehtinen JT, Warner JJ: Glenohumeral osteoarthritis in active patients:Diagnostic tips and complete management options. Physician Sports Med 31:4, 2003.
2. Phillips WC, Jr, Kattapuram SV: Osteoarthritis: With emphasis on primary osteoarthritis of the shoulder. Del Med J 63(10):609, 1991.
3. Matsen FA, Rockwood CA, Wirth MA, et al: Glenohumeral arthritis and its management. In Rockwood CA, Matsen FA III, Wirth MA, et al (eds): The Shoulder, ed 2. Philadelphia, Saunders, 1998, p 840.
4. Kelly MJ, Ramsey ML: Osteoarthritis and traumatic arthritis of the shoulder. J Hand Ther 13(2):148, 2000.
5. Boenisch U, Lembcke O, Naumann T: Classification, clinical findings and operative treatment of degenerative and posttraumatic shoulder disease: What do we really need to know from an imaging report to establish a treatment strategy? Eur J Radiol 35(2):103, 2000.
6. Collins DN: Pathophysiology, classification, and pathoanatomy of glenohumeral arthritis and related disorders. In Iannotti JP, Williams GR Jr (eds): Disorders of the Shoulder: Diagnosis and Management. Philadelphia, Lippincott Williams & Wilkins, 1999, p 421.
7. Waldman SD: Intra-articular injection of the shoulder joint. In Waldman SD: Atlas of Pain Management Injection Techniques. Philadelphia, Saunders, 2000, p 37.

chapter 58

Disorders of the Rotator Cuff

D. Ross Henshaw and Edward V. Craig

Disorders of the rotator cuff, ranging from tendon inflammation to rupture, are a common source of anterior shoulder pain. The etiology of rotator cuff disease is a subject of debate between those who believe in extrinsic versus intrinsic causes for cuff injury. Although many extrinsic and intrinsic mechanisms have been described, the actual etiology for each patient is likely multifactorial. Whatever the etiology, cuff pathology from tendinosis to tearing has certain characteristic clinical and radiographic features that aid in diagnosis. Both operative and nonoperative treatments have their place in the definitive treatment of cuff pathology.

■ HISTORICAL CONSIDERATIONS

The rotator cuff is a composite of four tendons that insert circumferentially on the proximal humerus and is one of the largest tendinous structures in the body (Fig. 58–1). The unconstrained bony architecture of the glenohumeral joint allows for the highest range of motion of any joint, sacrificing stability to do so. Along with labroligamentous restraints, the rotator cuff contributes to maintaining a delicate balance between mobility and stability by providing crucial dynamic stability throughout the arch of motion. These demands make the rotator cuff susceptible to overload and failure.

The diagnosis and treatment of shoulder disorders was first described by Codman in his text *The Shoulder*, which represented 25 years of dedication to understanding and treating painful and stiff shoulders.[1] In 1941, Bosworth described the supraspinatus syndrome, and our understanding of this was amplified by McLaughlin in 1944.[2,3] Others focused on the biceps tendon as a source of shoulder pain.[4,5] However, until Neer introduced his concept of "impingement syndrome" in 1972, a clear understanding of the etiology and treatment of shoulder pain was poorly understood and often unsuccessfully treated.[6] His landmark articles clarified the source of rotator cuff injuries and how to treat them. He described the concept of primary impingement as an external source of mechanical injury to the rotator cuff, its pathologic stages, clinical diagnosis, and surgical treatment. Narrowing of the supraspinatus outlet is most frequently due to anterolateral subacromial spurring; however, hypertrophy of the coracoacromial ligament, acromioclavicular joint spurring, or greater tuberosity malunion can also lead to impingement with mechanical cuff abrasion.[7-9] Neer's concept of the acromion as a primary cause of cuff injury unified much of the thinking on rotator cuff surgery and led to anterior acromioplasty as the definitive surgical treatment. This operation has had success reported in the 80% to 90% range. However, disappointing results obtained with young athletes who throw overhand after acromioplasty and improved understanding of shoulder biomechanics have led several authors to offer alternative explanations to primary impingement as the cause of shoulder pain in athletes. Overuse syndromes are common in unconditioned athletes and occur when repetitive eccentric contractions lead to microtrauma within the tendon and inflammation.[10,11] Secondary impingement occurs in athletes who use their shoulders repetitively at the extremes of motion, which leads to gradual attenuation of static stabilizers and may result in instability. This "microinstability" causes the humeral head to sublux anteriorly and superiorly, creating secondary impingement as the cuff is compressed on the undersurface of the coracoacromial arch.[12,13] "Internal" impingement is another source of rotator cuff injury. This entity as described by Jobe and associates occurs when anterior subluxation leads to contact and abrasion of the undersurface of the supraspinatus tendon against the posterosuperior glenoid labrum, with impingement occurring "within" the joint rather than in the subacromial space.[14] Treatment of these injuries in throwers thus focuses on reducing inflammation and, if necessary, on correcting the instability through either strengthening of scapular stabilizers and rotator cuff or re-tensioning the capsuloligamentous complex.

In contrast to the theory of an extrinsic, mechanical cause for rotator cuff disease, Codman was the first to introduce the concept of an intrinsic tendon degeneration as a source of rotator cuff disorders.[1] From his anatomic dissections, he observed a "critical" zone near the insertion of the rotator cuff on the greater tuberosity of the proximal humerus that was both hypovascular and the common location where tears occurred. Further work by Rathbun and Macnab on the vascularity of the rotator cuff has supported this observation and has led some to emphasize primary anatomic pathology in the tendon itself that makes it prone to degeneration and tears.[15] This contrasted to the concept by Neer of mechanical impingement as the primary cause of rotator cuff injuries. However, changes within the cuff can occur without accompanying stenosis of the subacromial space. Uhtoff and asso-

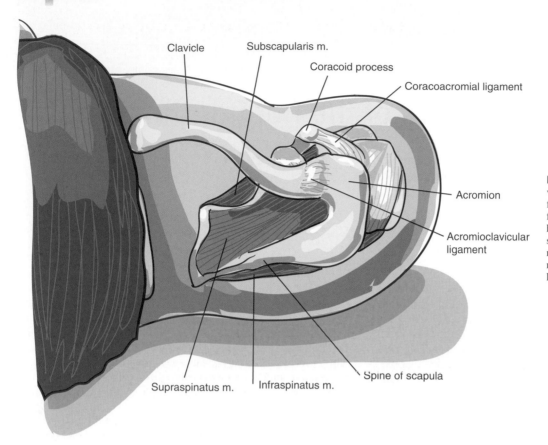

FIGURE 58–1 ■ A superior view of the rotator cuff shows the four cuff tendons inserting circumferentially around the proximal humerus: subscapularis, supraspinatus, infraspinatus, and teres minor. The coracoclavicular ligament and the acromion are also labeled.

ciates showed that most tears begin inside the joint on the articular surface rather than externally in the subacromial space.[16] Ozaki and colleagues looked at 200 anatomic shoulder specimens and correlated pathologic changes on the undersurface of the acromion with cuff tears.[17] Subacromial spurring was only present with cuff tears, and, with partial tears, the acromion was almost always nonpathologic. They concluded that primary cuff degeneration leads to tendon rupture. Nirschl and Pettrone call this degeneration angiofibroblastic hyperplasia and theorized that this leads to diminished tissue perfusion.[18] Recently, Yuan and associates showed apoptotic cells in areas of tendon degeneration implicating uncontrolled apoptosis may have a role in the pathogenesis of intrinsic rotator cuff degeneration.[19]

Although the primary etiology of rotator cuff disease may still be debated, it is likely that for each individual patient the cause is multifactorial and probably includes some component of extrinsic and intrinsic injury. If the etiology is multifactorial, then treatments should be tailored toward whichever etiology is thought to dominate the clinical picture.

■ CLINICAL PRESENTATION

Cuff disease usually presents as anterior shoulder pain. The signs and symptoms, however, can often be vague and difficult to interpret. Diagnosis of rotator cuff injury therefore requires a systematic approach, including history of presentation, physical examination, and diagnostic testing.

History

Patients with rotator cuff disorders most often present complaining of pain with an insidious onset and progressive course. There is often no history of trauma and patients frequently cannot clearly define when the pain started. Night pain, when present, is frequently associated with tendon tearing. Other symptoms include crepitus, catching, clunking, weakness, and loss of motion. Although weakness with loss of motion is characteristic of rotator cuff tears, this needs to be differentiated from strength deficiencies due to pain inhibition. The pain most commonly radiates to the anterolateral aspect of the shoulder to the deltoid insertion. However, there is significant overlap in this region with other shoulder conditions. Labral injury, biceps inflammation, glenohumeral arthritis, joint stiffness, and acromioclavicular arthropathy can also cause shoulder pain. Radicular pain with motion crossing the elbow to the hand and wrist may indicate lower cervical involvement. However, C5 root involvement may present as isolated shoulder pain. It is essential to have a high index of suspicion for cervical spine disease as a cause of the painful shoulder.

The age, occupation, and handedness of the patient and the onset, duration, timing, severity, quality, exacerbation, and relief of symptoms are important differentiating factors. Younger patients should be asked about their sports and activities and the relation of their symptoms to specific activities. A younger patient is more likely to have an underlying instability, whereas an older patient is more likely to have a mechanical or degenerative source of pain. Therapeutic history, whether with pain medication, physiotherapy, or corticosteroid injections, should also be elicited to determine if conservative therapy has been exhausted. Previous surgical treatment can also have an important impact on diagnosis and future management.

Physical Examination

The physical examination includes inspection, palpation, range of motion, and special provocative testing. The cervical spine, elbow, wrist, hand, and neurovascular status should also be thoroughly assessed as potential pathologic sources.

Cervical spine disease, particularly when it involves the C5 root, may present as shoulder pain. This is particularly true if neck pain with palpation, range of motion, and provocative maneuvers such as a Spurling test duplicates and reproduces the presenting symptoms of the patient. Unlike a patient who has a cuff tear, C5 root involvement may produce biceps weakness; and this may be a distinguishing feature.

The visual inspection of both shoulders should be performed on every patient. The shoulders are examined from the front and back in a search for previous scars, discoloration, swelling, deformity, asymmetry, muscle atrophy, acromioclavicular prominence, and biceps rupture (Fig. 58–2). Scapular winging may accompany an underlying scapulothoracic dysfunction and can be related to shoulder instability, muscle fatigue, muscle imbalance, scoliosis, kyphosis, and neurologic injury. The bony prominences of the neck, scapula, acromion, acromioclavicular joint, clavicle, and sternoclavicular joints are palpated. Acromioclavicular joint pain is an often overlooked but common source of anterior shoulder pain. Tenderness over the great tuberosity and in the bicipital groove can be helpful to differentiate between bicipital and cuff inflammation. Pain in the suprascapular notch or the

quadrilateral space may be associated with suprascapular and axillary nerve entrapment, respectively.

Range of motion should be performed in the standing and supine positions in all planes comparing the painful and nonpainful extremities. In the supine position compensatory movements of the scapula and torso are removed and give a more precise measurement of range of motion. Discrepancies between active and passive range of motion may be secondary to pain inhibition, cuff tears, glenohumeral arthritis, volitional factors, muscle disease, and neurogenic factors. Patients with rotator cuff tears will frequently have less range of motion actively than passively because of weakness. This differs from the loss of motion of arthritis and stiffness due to capsular contraction or inflammation, which frequently has both active and passive reduced mobility. Excessive passive external rotation may indicate subscapularis rupture. However, in throwing athletes excessive external rotation and decreased internal rotation are common and secondary to stretched anterior structures and a contracted posterior capsule.

Muscle strength testing of the deltoid, teres minor, infraspinatus, supraspinatus, subscapularis, and biceps should be determined. However, these may be unreliable in the presence of pain. Several tests exist to isolate the individual muscles of the rotator cuff to be tested and recorded separately.[20]

Because the subscapularis is less frequently torn then the supraspinatus tendon, diagnosis is often overlooked and may be delayed. There are two reliable clinical tests for subscapularis function. For the "liftoff" test described by Gerber and Krushell, the arm is internally rotated and the hand rests on the lower back or buttock. The patient then pushes the hand away in the horizontal plane, a maneuver that isolates the subscapularis.[21] This test can be inaccurate when the patient recruits the triceps to move the hand away. To avoid this, a modification of the test can be done in which the examiner holds the hand away from the small of the back and asks the patient to maintain the position. If the patient cannot do this, weakness or a tear of the subscapularis is suspected. Because for many patients the liftoff test is painful, the "belly-press" test as described by Tokish and associates may be used.[22] With this test, the patient places the hands on the abdomen and rotates the elbows forward with and without resistance. The subscapularis is responsible for the ability to press against the abdomen and push the elbows away from the body. Inability to do this is suggestive of tendon discontinuity.

Jobe and colleagues described a useful test to isolate supraspinatus strength.[23] Both arms are abducted to 90 degrees in the scapular plane and then fully pronated to point the thumbs toward the ground. Side-to-side comparison to resisted downward force gives an accurate indication of function. Pain and weakness are indicators of partial- or full-thickness tears.

The infraspinatus and teres minor are external rotators contributing about 90% and 10% rotational force, respectively. Their strength is best measured with the arm at the side in 0 degrees of abduction and the elbow flexed to 90 degrees. In this position, the patient externally rotates the hand and forearm against resistance. Weakness is suggestive of a tear and perhaps the best clinical test for cuff discontinuity. This test is particularly useful because both arms may be simultaneously tested and compared. The "hornblower's" or drop sign is an attempt to isolate the teres minor (Fig. 58–3). The patient's arm is placed in 90 degrees of abduction and 90

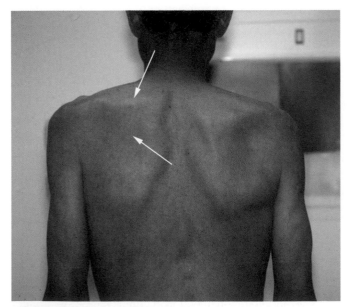

FIGURE 58–2 ■ Examination of both shoulders from behind the patient may reveal muscle asymmetry. In this patient there is atrophy of the supraspinatus and infraspinatus muscles, as evidenced by wasting in the infraspinatus and supraspinatus fossae *(arrows)* on the right as compared with the left side.

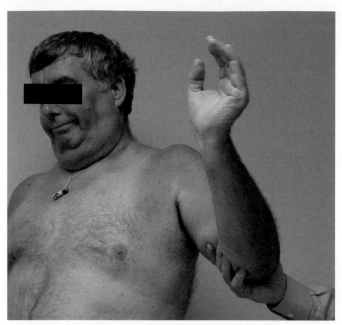

FIGURE 58–3 ■ Hornblower's sign. The inability to hold the forearm in 90 degrees of abduction indicates injury of the teres minor tendon.

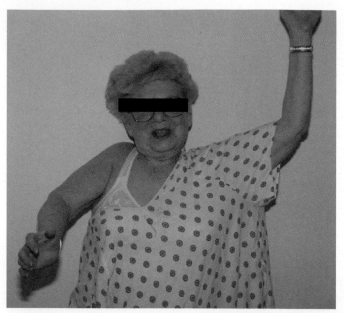

FIGURE 58–4 ■ Shrug sign. With massive cuff tears, patients will recruit accessory muscles when attempting forward elevation. When this patient tries to elevate her arm, her shoulder shrugs as her trapezium and deltoid fire to compensate for a massive cuff tear.

degrees of forward elevation in maximal external rotation, and the patient is asked to maintain the position of the arm.[24] Insufficient strength of the muscle or tendon is suggested if the patient cannot maintain this position.

Assessing each muscle individually enables the examiner to determine the size and location of a tear. Complete four tendon ruptures are rare. Most commonly, tears originate in the supraspinatus and enlarge to involve the tendons of the infraspinatus and teres minor. Small tears of the supraspinatus cause pain and weakness with the Jobe test, but external rotation usually remains strong. Large tears involving the supraspinatus and infraspinatus will have positive Jobe signs and weak external rotation, but an intact hornblower sign. Massive tears will have weakness in the supraspinatus and infraspinatus, and because the teres is involved the patient will not be able to hold the arm in the 90/90-degree position in maximal external rotation. Patients with massive cuff tears often use accessory muscles to elevate the arms. A common physical finding is the shrug sign in which the patient activates the trapezius and deltoid when attempting forward elevation (Fig. 58–4). Less common are isolated subscapularis tears, and patients will often report a history of prior surgery or trauma. These patients have intact supraspinatus, infraspinatus, and teres minor strength with isolated subscapularis weakness and excessive external rotation.

After assessing the shoulder musculature, a number of provocative tests can be used to identify specific disorders.[20] These tests include maneuvers that reproduce pain associated with impingement, instability, labral pathology, and bicipital involvement. Not all of these are applicable for each patient, and the history and physical findings guide the choice to use specific tests.

Impingement signs are not specific and only point to the etiology of pain within the subacromial space (subacromial spurs, bursitis, or cuff tear). In his description of impingement lesions, Neer described his classic impingement maneuver.

While stabilizing the scapula, the arm is elevated in the plane of the scapula. As the arm reaches the limit of forward elevation, the greater tuberosity is jammed underneath the acromion, producing pain. Hawkins described another test for subacromial inflammation. With the arm at 90 degrees of forward elevation, slight adduction, and with the elbow flexed at 90 degrees, the shoulder is internally rotated, which impales the greater tuberosity under the acromion.[25] In the presence of cuff pathology, this maneuver may elicit pain (Fig. 58–5). A simple adjunct used to confirm the location is the injection test. Local anesthetic is injected into the subacromial space, and the Neer and Hawkins tests are repeated. Significant reduction or elimination of pain within the subacromial space confirms that the etiology is in the subacromial space. If there is pain relief, range of motion and muscle testing should be repeated. Weakness due to pain inhibition is minimized and range of motion is improved. In this way this test is highly effective at both localizing the source of pain and differentiating between weakness that is from pain or secondary to rotator cuff tear. Internal impingement can be assessed with Jobe's "relocation test."[14] With the patient supine, the arm is placed in the abducted externally rotated position (the same as for testing anterior apprehension when instability is suspected). A positive test exists if the patient experiences pain or discomfort. This position puts the undersurface of the supraspinatus in contact with the posterosuperior labrum, the site of internal impingement. This pain can be relieved with gentle posterior pressure placed on the anterior aspect of the arm to minimize this contact. When the examiner's hand is withdrawn, the contact and pain return.

The most common direction of clinical instability is anterior. The anterior apprehension sign is performed by placing the patient's arm at 90 degrees of abduction and 90 degrees of external rotation. In this position the patient may feel the sensation of shoulder subluxation anteriorly. The examiner

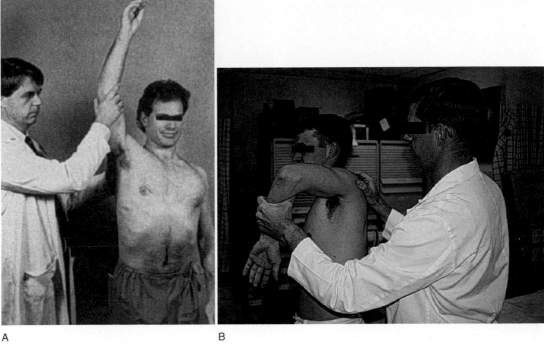

A   B

FIGURE 58–5 ■ Neer and Hawkins tests. For the Neer test (**A**) the scapula is stabilized and the arm is elevated in the plane of the scapula. As the arm reaches the limit of forward elevation the greater tuberosity is jammed underneath the acromion producing pain. The Hawkins test (**B**) is performed with the arm at 90 degrees of forward elevation, in slight adduction; with the elbow flexed at 90 degrees, the shoulder is internally rotated, which impales the greater tuberosity under the acromion.

should beware that the patient often will not let the arm be put in this compromising position and is thus "apprehensive" about this arm position (Fig. 58–6). Other assessments of instability are the load and shift and sulcus signs (Fig. 58–7). For the load and shift sign, axial pressure is place along the humerus with one hand to center the humeral head and with the other hand the humerus is translated anteriorly and posteriorly. Laxity is graded from 1 to 3. Grade 1 laxity is translation of the humeral head to the rim. For grade 2 laxity the humeral head translates over the rim but is reducible. Grade 3 laxity presents as translation over the rim and a humeral head that remains dislocated after pressure is removed. Inferior traction on the arm tests inferior translation and is noted by the presence of a sulcus under the lateral acromion: the sulcus sign. Anterior instability is called unidirectional if the instability is in one plane, and multidirectional laxity is increased translation in two or more directions when compared with the normal side. Generalized ligamentous laxity is not uncommon and should be assessed for every patient with multidirectional instability. Laxity should also be distinguished from instability. Many asymptomatic patients have loose or lax shoulders, but unless it causes pain or discomfort it is considered not to reflect clinical instability. Instability therefore is symptomatic laxity.

Involvement of the superior labrum and biceps anchor is best evaluated with the O'Brien active compression test.[26] The patient's arm is flexed, keeping the elbow straight and adducted to 15 degrees. In full pronation with the patient's palm facing down, an inferior force is applied to the arm. In the presence of superior labral pathology, this position will elicit pain; and when the arm is fully supinated palm upward, the pain with downward pressure is relieved. In internal rota-

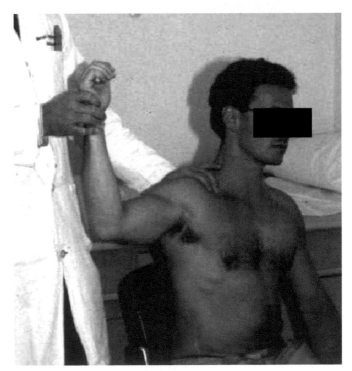

FIGURE 58–6 ■ Patients with anterior instability will often feel a sense of instability and apprehension with the arm placed in 90 degrees of abduction and 90 degrees of external rotation.

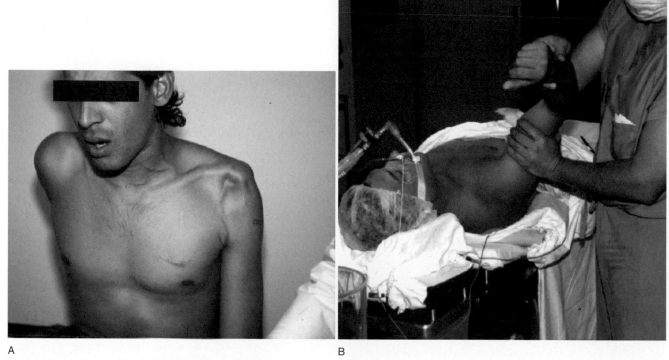

A   B

FIGURE 58–7 ■ In the load and shift maneuver, an axial load is placed along the humerus and the head is then shifted anteriorly and posteriorly (**A**). Inferior traction of the arm causing inferior subluxation will produce a sulcus under the acromion (**B**).

tion with arm adduction, the biceps anchor is impinged by the humeral head; and with supination, which externally rotates the humeral head, the biceps pressure is relieved.

Acromioclavicular pathology is often overlooked as a common cause of failed rotator cuff treatment. Clinical diagnosis is usually not difficult because patients are usually "point tender" over the joint. To test this source of pain the examiner palpates the joint with one finger and with the other hand adducts the shoulder. It is also useful to palpate both the involved and uninvolved acromioclavicular joints simultaneously to compare the degree of tenderness. The maneuver will often reproduce acromioclavicular symptoms.

■ DIAGNOSIS

Studies such as plain radiography, ultrasound, and magnetic resonance imaging can be extremely helpful to confirm the clinical diagnosis of rotator cuff disease and in some cases rule out other pathologic conditions. In some cases they can also help determine the severity of the disease, size of tears, and prognosis.

Plain Radiology

Five standard radiographs are recommended for every patient with shoulder pain. These include a "true" anteroposterior view to evaluate the integrity of the glenohumeral joint articulation and anteroposterior views with the arm in internal and external rotation to show Hill-Sachs lesions and greater tuberosity sclerosis, respectively. Hill-Sachs and reverse

Hill-Sachs lesions are indicative of anterior and posterior instability, respectively. With the arm in external rotation, the greater tuberosity is rotated orthogonal to the x-ray, allowing better evaluation of its bony contour and for the presence of sclerosis indicative of chronic injury from tendinosis or tear. The anteroposterior views will also show resting state glenohumeral articulation. In patients with chronic large cuff tears, the centering effect of the cuff is lost and the humeral head may migrate superiorly, decreasing the acromial humeral interval, which is normally 7 to 10 mm.[27] An "outlet" view that is a lateral one taken with 10 degrees of caudal tilt allows evaluation of acromial morphology (Fig. 58–8). In 1986, Bigliani described three types of acromial morphology: type 1 is smooth, type 2 is curved, and type 3 is hooked. Impingement and tears are more likely with curved and hooked acromions.[7] Also, the presence of acromial spurring and calcification of the coracoacromial ligament can also be seen and indicate impingement. Finally, axillary radiographs show articular congruity and integrity of the glenoid bony architecture.

Ultrasound

The potential use of ultrasound to evaluate rotator cuff disease has been recognized since the early 1980s.[28,29] Even though sonography of the rotator cuff is more difficult than for other large tendons, there has been a concerted effort to develop and refine shoulder sonography. This is primarily because the shoulder is a common site of symptomatology and clinical evaluation is difficult. Ultrasound is rapid, inexpensive, and comprehensive with comparison of the asymptomatic shoul-

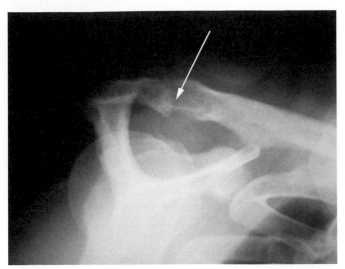

FIGURE 58–8 ■ Subacromial spur. The outlet view allows visualization of the anterior acromial bony shape. In this case a spur has formed that narrows the subacromial space and can cause impingement *(arrow).*

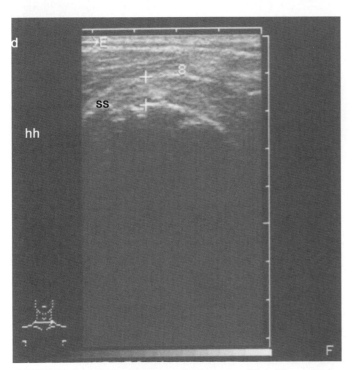

FIGURE 58–9 ■ Ultrasound has evolved into a useful tool for evaluating rotator cuff pathology. This image depicts a normal rotator cuff. Note deltoid (d), supraspinatus (ss), and humeral head (hh).

der possible. In the past 5 years there have been dramatic improvements in high-resolution transducers as well as advances in our understanding of the technique of shoulder sonography and more widespread agreement of the findings seen with rotator cuff tears. All of these factors have contributed to making the examination easier to perform and interpret (Fig. 58–9). Ultrasound has now evolved into a mature modality for evaluating rotator cuff tears and bicipital inflammation.[30,31] Teefy and associates reported their result of 100 shoulders evaluated preoperatively with ultrasound as

compared with their arthroscopic findings. They reported 100% sensitivity and 85% specificity with an overall accuracy of 96% for full-thickness rotator cuff tears. Ultrasound, however, was less sensitive in determining partial-thickness tears and biceps tendon ruptures. Although ultrasound has become a more sensitive and accurate diagnostic tool, its use is still not widespread and results depend on operator experience.

Magnetic Resonance Imaging

Magnetic resonance imaging is the modality of choice for assessing rotator cuff integrity. MRI is a noninvasive tool offering multiplanar analysis of not only the rotator cuff muscles and tendons but also the evaluation of cartilage, cortical and medullary bone, and labral and acromioclavicular pathology. Although sensitivities approach 100% and specificity 95% for detecting full-thickness tears, MRI is less reliable for diagnosing partial-thickness tears. The size, shape, and amount of retraction and muscle atrophy are characterized by MRI and determine repair potential (Fig. 58–10). The use of higher-resolution magnetic fields and improved pulse sequencing has made MRI arthrography with gadolinium less routine.[32] However, it may be useful in some instances for the identification of labral tears.

■ TREATMENT

The cause of rotator cuff disease is multifactorial and affects patients of variable age and activity level. Therefore, treatment should be individualized and tailored to meet the demands of each individual. Specifically, the physician should consider the patient's age, disability, and expectations and carefully review the risks and benefits of both nonsurgical and surgical treatment. For instance, the incidence of cuff tears in patients older than age 60 years has been reported as high as 40%, and not all of these patients are symptomatic.[30] For patients with asymptomatic tears, observation is prudent. In contrast, a physiologically young, active patient with acute rotator cuff tear may benefit from acute surgical repair to restore function and prevent retraction and secondary muscle atrophy, which can make repair more difficult and adversely affect prognosis. For most patients with symptomatic cuff injury, initial management is nonsurgical.

Nonoperative Management

The effectiveness of nonoperative management was recognized by Neer, who found that many patients with impingement responded to nonoperative management. Nonoperative management may also improve patients with symptomatic cuff tears.[33] The principles of rehabilitation are to allow healing of inflamed tissue, maintain motion, and restore function. Generally, the earlier a rehabilitation program is begun the more successful it is likely to be. A variety of nonoperative rotator cuff programs have been described and, in general, all emphasize phases of therapy and recovery. Wirth and associates described three phases of rotator cuff therapy: pain control, range of motion, and muscle strengthening, A fourth phase should also include modification of work or sport to avoid reinjury.[33]

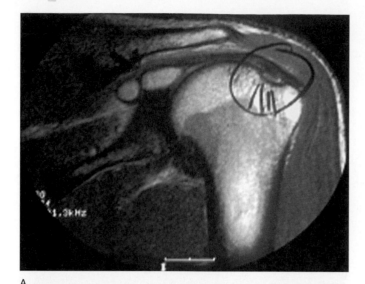

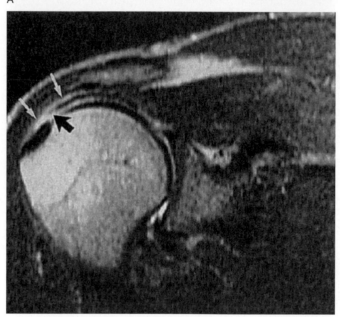

FIGURE 58–10 ■ MRI evaluation of rotator cuff tears. **A,** Partial-thickness tear is demonstrated by high signal intensity through the articular half of the supraspinatus tendon *(lines)*. The intact tendon has characteristic low signal intensity and is shown inserting onto the greater tuberosity. **B,** Full-thickness tear is demonstrated by the low-signal tendon that is detached from its insertion and retracted medially *(arrows)*.

Pain control and reducing inflammation are the primary goals of the first phase. This is accomplished through rest and working with the therapist to avoid aggravating activities. This may involve avoiding overhead activities, and for athletes it may involve changing throwing mechanics or technique. For the worker who must work over his or her head, it may involve changing the work environment or, if that is not possible, job retraining or vocational change. Pain modification techniques such as cryotherapy, infrared, ultrasound, transcutaneous electric nerve stimulation, and acupuncture can provide symptomatic relief. A course of nonsteroidal anti-inflammatory medication can be helpful but should be used with caution in older patients and those with peptic ulcer disease or hypertension. Subacromial corticosteroid injections can also be useful in refractory cases, but they should be limited to two to three injections spaced 2 to 3 months apart because of adverse effects that catabolic steroids may have on tendons.

After adequate control of the patient's pain has been achieved, the second phase begins with gentle stretching programs and restoration of range of motion to match that of the unaffected shoulder. The goal is to stretch out all area of tightness, with particular emphasis on the posterior capsule. Exercises progress variably from pendulum and wall walking to pulleys and often achieve capsular stretching.

When near-normal passive flexibility of the shoulder is restored, the third phase, focusing on muscle strengthening, is initiated. Scapular strengthening is an essential and often overlooked component of shoulder therapy and should be initiated early. Internal and external rotator strengthening exercises are carried out with the arm at the side to strengthen the anterior and posterior cuff muscles while avoiding the position of impingement, as can occur with flexion and abduction exercises. These exercises are most conveniently performed using rubber tubing anchored to a door knob. The resistance is increased as the patient's muscle strength improves. Deltoid and supraspinatus strengthening are added when they can be performed comfortably. The role of strength is in part to augment the resting tension of the humeral head "depressors" and, in effect, dynamically open the subacromial space.

Finally, in order to return the patient to the comfortable pursuit of normal activities, analysis and modification of working environment or recreational techniques should be made where necessary. These include simple aids such as the use of a stepstool for patients needing to reach for high items. For throwing athletes, modification of body mechanics may prevent relapse and return the athlete to the previous level of competition. In cases in which a patient's occupation requires vigorous or repeated use of the shoulder in provocative positions, job retraining may be required.

Operative Management

Surgical intervention is generally reserved for rotator cuff disease refractory to a 3- to 6-month period of conservative therapy. The precise technique of surgical intervention is dependent on etiology of cuff pathology and disease. Impingement and cuff tears caused by a narrowed subacromial space benefit from decompression or widening of the subacromial space via anterior acromial resection, whereas restoration of capsuloligamentous restraint is required for pathology secondary to instability.

Arthroscopic surgery has enabled more accurate diagnosis and treatment of shoulder injuries. The initial aim of surgery is to relieve pain and restore functional deficits. Traditional open procedures are gradually being enhanced or replaced by arthroscopic techniques, but the type of procedure chosen depends both on the nature and severity of the pathology and, to some extent, surgical experience and preference.

Classic impingement syndrome caused by a subacromial spur, thickened coracoacromial ligament, or other lesion is best treated with arthroscopic subacromial decompression. Decompression as described by Neer involved an open pro-

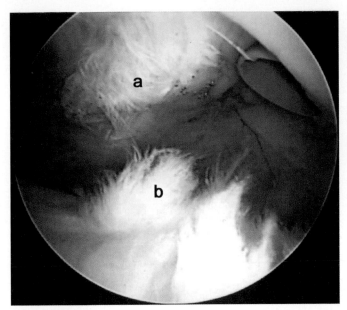

FIGURE 58–11 ■ Subacromial impingement. Arthroscopic evaluation of the subacromial space showing a subacromial spur (a) and fraying of the rotator cuff underneath (b).

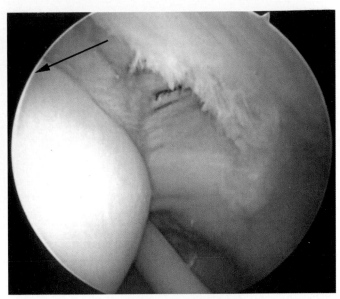

FIGURE 58–12 ■ Partial-thickness cuff tear of the undersurface of the supraspinatus tendon *(arrow)*. The frayed tendon was débrided but not repaired because it was less than 50% in thickness.

cedure with removal of up to 1 cm of anterolateral acromion. Modern arthroscopic techniques allow for accurate diagnosis of the source, location, and removal of the offending lesion (Fig. 58–11). Arthroscopic subacromial decompression has been shown to have equal success rates as open procedures with faster recovery time.[34] Another advantage of arthroscopic surgery is the ability to view both sides of the rotator cuff. In cases of impingement caused by subtle instability, capsular laxity or labral injury may be identified and treated.

For partial- and full-thickness rotator cuff tears the treatment is also based on treating both the cause of the injury and the tear itself. Decompression should be performed for impingement-associated tears, whereas a stabilization procedure may be necessary to treat tears associated with microinstability. The treatment of partial-thickness tears is controversial and no clear guidelines exist. In general tears, less than 50% thickness are treated with decompression and débridement and those greater than 50% are treated by resecting the damaged tendon and repairing the defect as if the tear was full thickness (Fig. 58–12).[35-38] Treatment of full-thickness tears is also moving progressively more toward all arthroscopic techniques (Fig. 58–13). Arthroscopically assisted, mini open procedures are also widely used as surgeons transition toward less invasive surgery (Fig. 58–14). As always, the choice of treatment is multifactorial depending on the size, location, chronicity, and quality of the muscle and tendon. Many authors have reported success with mini-open and arthroscopic repairs that are equal or superior to open repair.[39,40] The goal of surgery is to relieve pain. This can usually be achieved even in large tears; however, improved strength and function, although desirable and often achievable, are less predictable than pain relief. This is because tear size, quality of tissue, biologic healing potential, and irreversible muscle atrophy are not controllable.[41]

■ CONCLUSION

Disorders of the rotator cuff are a common cause of anterior shoulder pain. Although the primary etiology of rotator cuff disease may still be debated, it is likely that for each individual patient the cause is multifactorial and probably includes some components of extrinsic and intrinsic injury. If the etiology is multifactorial, then treatments should be tailored toward whichever etiology is thought to dominate the clinical picture. A careful history and physical examination are crucial for diagnosing the source of injury. The age, occupation, and handedness of the patient and the onset, duration, timing, severity, quality, exacerbation, and relief of symptoms are important differentiating factors. Night pain and weakness are associated with tendon tears. Younger patients should be asked about their sports and activities and the relation of their symptoms to specific activities. A younger patient is more likely to have an underlying instability, whereas an older patient is more likely to have a mechanical or degenerative source of pain. Physical examination can test for specific cuff muscle weakness and intraarticular pathology versus extraarticular sources of pain. Radicular pain from the cervical spine should always be considered as a source of shoulder symptoms. Adjunctive studies including plain radiographs and MRI are an integral part of the evaluation and help determine the source and extent of injury. Ultrasound is also becoming a useful, noninvasive method for diagnosing cuff pathology. Treatment is tailored to each individual patient's pathologic process. Although nonoperative modalities such as physical therapy, antiinflammatory agents, and corticosteroid injections are successful, some patients will require operative intervention. Both open and arthroscopic surgery are highly successful in treating rotator cuff disease. Arthroscopy has improved our ability to define the pathology and more precisely treat many lesions, but open techniques may be necessary in difficult cases.

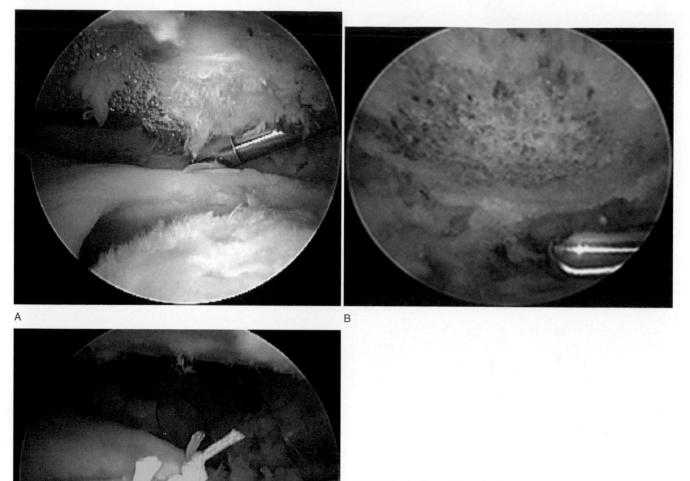

A

B

C

FIGURE 58–13 ■ Example of a full-thickness tear and a subacromial spur (**A**) treated with arthroscopic acromioplasty (**B**) and rotator cuff repair (**C**).

A   B

FIGURE 58–14 ■ **A** and **B,** Mini-open cuff repair. With arthroscopy-assisted rotator cuff repair, bursectomy, acromioplasty, and cuff mobilization can be achieved with arthroscopic techniques; and through a mini-open incision the cuff is repaired to the greater tuberosity.

References

1. Codman E: The Shoulder: Rupture of the Supraspinatus Tendon and Other Lesions In or About the Subacromial Bursa. Boston, Thomas Todd, 1934.
2. Bostworth B: The supraspinatus syndrome: Symptomatology, pathology, and repair. JAMA 111:422, 1941.
3. McLaughlin H: Lesions of the musculotendinous cuff of the shoulder: The exposure and treatment of tears with retraction. J Bone Joint Surg 26:31, 1944.
4. Bechtol CO: Biomechanics of the shoulder. Clin Orthop Rel Res 146:37, 1980.
5. Hitchcock HH: Painful shoulder: Observation on the role of the tendon of the long head of the biceps brachii in its causation. J Bone Joint Surg Am 30:263, 1948.
6. Neer C: Anterior acromioplasty for chronic impingement syndrome in the shoulder. J Bone Joint Surg Am 54:41, 1972.
7. Bigliani LU, April EW: The morphology of the acromion and the rotator cuff: Importance. Orthop Trans 10:228, 1986.
8. MacGillvray JD, Fealy S, Potter HG, O'Brien SJ: Multiplanar analysis of acromial morphology. Am J Sports Med 26:836, 1998.
9. Tytherleigh-Strong G, Hirahara A, Miniaci A: Rotator cuff disease. Curr Opin Rheumatol 13:135, 2001.
10. Herring SA, Nilson KL: Introduction to overuse injuries. Clin Sports Med 6:225, 1987.
11. Craig EV, Hsu KC: Shoulder problems in the weekend athlete. Orthop Rev 21:155, 1992.
12. Arroyo JS, Hershon SJ, Bigliani LU: Special considerations in the athletic throwing shoulder. Orthop Clin North Am 28:69, 1997.
13. Payne LZ, Deng XH, Craig EV, et al: The combined dynamic and static contributions to subacromial impingement: A biomechanical analysis. Am J Sports Med 25:801, 1997.
14. Jobe FW, Kvitne RS, Giangarra CE: Shoulder pain in the overhand or throwing athlete: The relationship of anterior instability and rotator cuff impingement. Orthop Rev 18:963, 1989.
15. Rathbun JB, Macnab I: The microvascular pattern in the rotator cuff. J Bone Joint Surg Br 52:540, 1970.
16. Uhtoff HK, et al: The pathogenesis of rotator cuff tears. In Takagishi N (ed): The Shoulder. Tokyo, Tokyo Professional Postgraduate Services, 1987, p 211.
17. Ozaki J, Fujimoto S, Nakagawa Y, et al: Tears of the rotator cuff associated with pathological changes in the acromion: A study in cadavers. J Bone Joint Surg Am 70:1224, 1988.
18. Nirschl RP, Pettrone FA: Tennis elbow: The surgical treatment of lateral epicondylitis. J Bone Joint Surg Am 70:832, 1979.
19. Yuan J, Murrell GA, Wei AQ, Wang MX: Apoptosis in rotator cuff tendonopathy. J Orthop Res 20:1372, 2002.
20. Tennent TD, Beach WR, Meyers JF: A review of the special tests associated with shoulder examination: I. The rotator cuff tests. Am J Sports Med 31:154, 2003.
21. Gerber C, Krushell RJ: Isolated rupture of the tendon of the subscapularis muscle: Clinical features in 16 cases. J Bone Joint Surg Br 73:389, 1991.
22. Tokish JM, Decker MJ, Ellis HB, et al: The belly-press test for the physical examination of the subscapularis muscle: Electromyographic validation and comparison to the lift-off test. J Shoulder Elbow Surg 12:427, 2003.
23. Jobe FW, Bradley JP: The diagnosis and nonoperative treatment of shoulder injuries in athletes. Clin Sports Med 8:149, 1989.

24. Walch G, Boulahia A, Calderone S, Robinson AH: The "dropping" and "hornblower's" signs in evaluation of rotator-cuff tears. J Bone Joint Surg Br 80:624, 1998.

25. Hawkins RJ, Hobeika PE: Impingement syndrome in the athletic shoulder. Clin Sports Med 2:391, 1983.

26. O'Brien SJ, Pagnani MJ, Fralye S, et al: The active compression test: A new and effective test for diagnosing labral tears and acromioclavicular joint abnormality. Am J Sports Med 26:610, 1998.

27. Flatow EL, Soslowsky LJ, Ticker JB, et al: Excursion of the rotator cuff under the acromion: Patterns of subacromial contact. Am J Sports Med 22:779, 1994.

28. Crass JR, Craig EV, Thompson RC, Feinberg SB: Ultrasonography of the rotator cuff: Surgical correlation. J Clin Ultrasound 12:487, 1984.

29. Crass JR, Craig EV, Feinberg SB: Ultrasonography of rotator cuff tears: A review of 500 diagnostic studies. J Clin Ultrasound 16:313, 1988.

30. Yamaguchi K, Tetro AM, Blam O, et al: Natural history of asymptomatic rotator cuff tears: A longitudinal analysis of asymptomatic tears detected sonographically. J Shoulder Elbow Surg 10:199, 2001.

31. Middleton WD, Teefey SA, Yamaguchi K: Sonography of the shoulder. Semin Musculoskel Radiol 2:211, 1998.

32. Potter HG, Schweitzer ME, Altchek DW: Advanced imaging in orthopaedics: Current pitfalls and new applications. Instr Course Lect 46:521, 1997.

33. Wirth MA, Basamania C, Rockwood CA Jr: Nonoperative management of full-thickness tears of the rotator cuff. Orthop Clin North Am 28:59, 1997.

34. Norlin R: Arthroscopic subacromial decompression versus open acromioplasty. Arthroscopy 5:321, 1989.

35. Fukuda H: The management of partial-thickness tears of the rotator cuff. J Bone Joint Surg Br 85:3, 2003.

36. McConville OR, Iannotti JP: Partial-thickness tears of the rotator cuff: Evaluation and management. J Am Acad Orthop Surg 7:32, 1999.

37. Breazeale NM, Craig EV: Partial-thickness rotator cuff tears: Pathogenesis and treatment. Orthop Clin North Am 28:145, 1997.

38. Cordasco FA, Backer M, Craig EV, et al: The partial-thickness rotator cuff tear: Is acromioplasty without repair sufficient? Am J Sports Med 30:257, 2002.

39. Murray TF Jr, Lajtai G, Mileski RM, Snyder SJ: Arthroscopic repair of medium to large full-thickness rotator cuff tears: Outcome at 2- to 6-year follow-up. J Shoulder Elbow Surg 11:19, 2002.

40. Lo IK, Burkhart SS: Current concepts in arthroscopic rotator cuff repair. Am J Sports Med 31:308, 2003.

41. Neer CS II: Shoulder Reconstruction. Philadelphia, Elsevier Science, 1990.

chapter 59

Acromioclavicular Joint Pain

Steven D. Waldman

The acromioclavicular joint is a common source of shoulder pain (Fig. 59–1).[1] The acromioclavicular joint is vulnerable to injury from acute trauma and repeated microtrauma. Acute injuries frequently take the form of falls directly onto the shoulder when playing sports or falling from bicycles. Repeated strain from throwing injuries or working with the arm raised across the body also may result in trauma to the joint. After trauma, the joint may become acutely inflamed, and if the condition becomes chronic, arthritis and osteolysis of the acromioclavicular joint may develop.[2]

■ SIGNS AND SYMPTOMS

A patient with acromioclavicular joint dysfunction frequently complains of pain when reaching across the chest (Fig. 59–2). Often the patient is unable to sleep on the affected shoulder and may complain of a grinding sensation in the joint, especially on first awakening. Physical examination may reveal enlargement or swelling of the joint with tenderness to palpation. Downward traction or passive adduction of the affected shoulder may cause increased pain (Fig. 59–3). If there is disruption of the ligaments of the acromioclavicular joint, these maneuvers may reveal joint instability.

■ TESTING

Plain radiographs of the joint may reveal narrowing or sclerosis of the joint consistent with osteoarthritis. MRI is indicated if disruption of the ligaments is suspected. The injection technique described subsequently serves as a diagnostic and a therapeutic maneuver. If polyarthritis is present, screening laboratory testing consisting of a complete blood count, erythrocyte sedimentation rate, and antinuclear antibody testing should be performed.

■ DIFFERENTIAL DIAGNOSIS

Osteoarthritis of the acromioclavicular joint is a frequent cause of shoulder pain. This condition is usually the result of trauma. Rheumatoid arthritis and rotator cuff tear arthropathy also are common causes of shoulder pain that may mimic the pain of acromioclavicular joint pain and confuse the diagnosis.[3] Less common causes of arthritis-induced shoulder pain include collagen vascular diseases, infection, and Lyme disease. Acute infectious arthritis usually is accompanied by significant systemic symptoms, including fever and malaise, and should be recognized easily by the astute clinician and treated appropriately with culture and antibiotics, rather than injection therapy. The collagen-vascular diseases generally manifest as a polyarthropathy, rather than a monarthropathy limited to the shoulder joint, although shoulder pain secondary to collagen-vascular disease responds well to the intra-articular injection technique described subsequently.

■ TREATMENT

Initial treatment of pain and functional disability associated with the acromioclavicular joint should include a combination of the nonsteroidal antiinflammatory agents or cyclooxygenase-2 inhibitors and physical therapy. The local application of heat and cold also may be beneficial. For patients who do not respond to these treatment modalities, an intra-articular injection of local anesthetic and steroid may be a reasonable next step.[4]

Intra-articular injection of the acromioclavicular joint is performed by placing the patient in the supine position and preparing with antiseptic solution of the skin overlying the superior shoulder and distal clavicle. A sterile syringe containing 1 mL of 0.25% preservative-free bupivacaine and 40 mg of methylprednisolone is attached to a 1½-inch 25-gauge needle using strict aseptic technique. With strict aseptic technique, the top of the acromion is identified, and at a point approximately 1 inch medially, the acromioclavicular joint space is identified. The needle is carefully advanced through the skin and subcutaneous tissues, through the joint capsule into the joint (Fig. 59–4). If bone is encountered, the needle is withdrawn into the subcutaneous tissues and redirected slightly more medially. After entering the joint space, the contents of the syringe are gently injected. There should be some resistance to injection because the joint space is small, and the joint capsule is dense. If significant resistance is encountered, the needle is probably in a ligament and should be advanced slightly into the joint space until the injection proceeds with only limited resistance. If no resistance is encountered on injection, the joint space is probably not intact, and MRI is recommended. The needle is removed, and a sterile pressure dressing and ice pack are placed at the injection site.

The major complication of intra-articular injection of the acromioclavicular joint is infection. This complication should

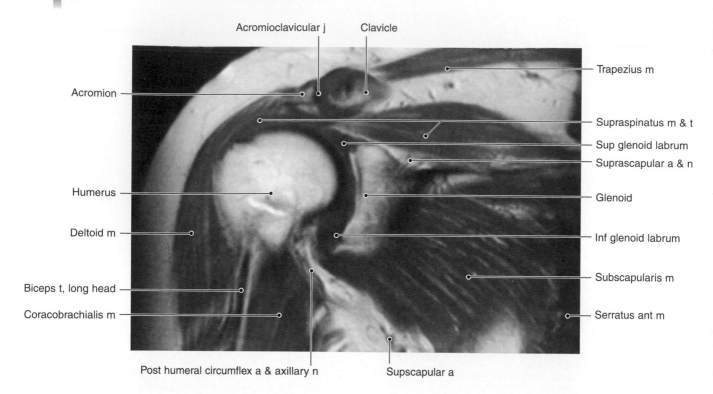

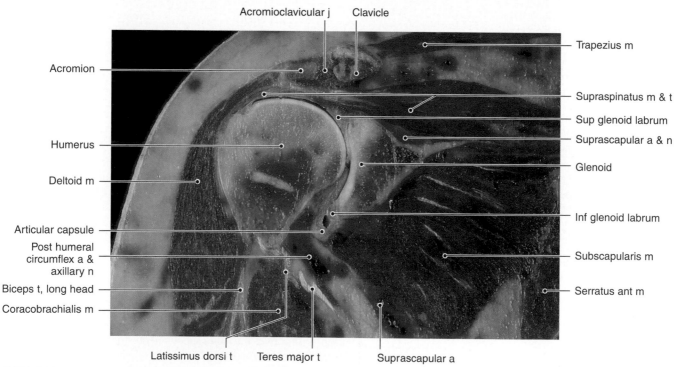

FIGURE 59–1 ■ Acromioclavicular joint. (From Kang HS, Ahn JM, Resnick D [eds]: MRI of the Extremities, 2nd ed. Philadelphia, WB Saunders, 2002, p 8.)

be exceedingly rare if strict aseptic technique is adhered to. Approximately 25% of patients complain of a transient increase in pain after intra-articular injection of the shoulder joint, and patients should be warned of this possibility.

This injection technique is extremely effective in the treatment of pain secondary to the above-mentioned causes of

arthritis of the acromioclavicular joint. Coexistent bursitis and tendinitis also may contribute to shoulder pain and may require additional treatment with more localized injection of local anesthetic and depot steroid.[2] This technique is a safe procedure if careful attention is paid to the clinically relevant anatomy in the areas to be injected. Care must be taken to use

FIGURE 59–2 ■ A patient with acromioclavicular joint dysfunction frequently complains of pain when reaching across the chest. (From Waldman SD: Acromioclavicular joint pain. In: Atlas of Common Pain Syndromes. Philadelphia, WB Saunders, 2002, p 77.)

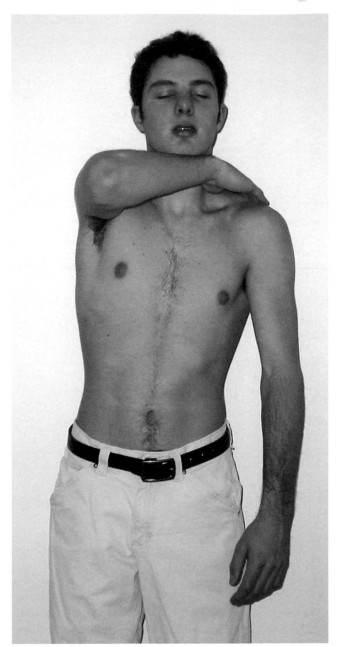

FIGURE 59–3 ■ The chin adduction test for acromioclavicular joint dysfunction. (From Waldman SD: Physical Diagnosis of Pain: An Atlas of Signs and Symptoms. Philadelphia, WB Saunders, 2006, p 105.)

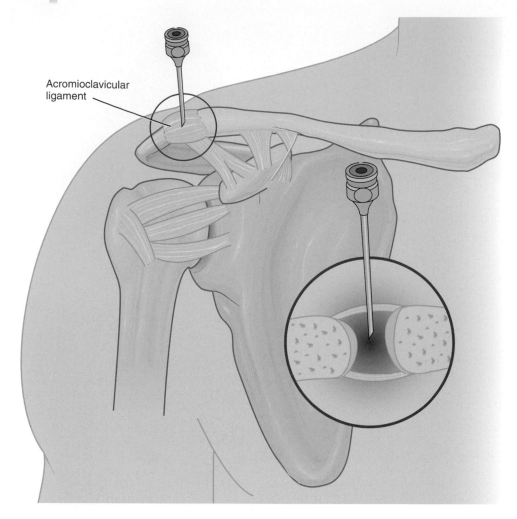

Acromioclavicular ligament

FIGURE 59–4 ■ Injection technique for acromioclavicular joint pain. (From Waldman SD: Acromioclavicular joint pain. In: Atlas of Pain Management Injection Techniques. Philadelphia, WB Saunders, 2000, p 41.)

sterile technique to avoid infection and universal precautions to avoid risk to the operator. The incidence of ecchymosis and hematoma formation can be decreased if pressure is placed on the injection site immediately after injection. The use of physical modalities, including local heat and gentle range of motion exercises, should be introduced several days after the patient undergoes this injection technique for shoulder pain. Vigorous exercises should be avoided because they exacerbate the patient's symptoms. Simple analgesics and nonsteroidal anti-inflammatory agents or cyclooxygenase-2 inhibitors may be used concurrently with this injection technique.

■ CONCLUSION

Acromioclavicular joint pain is commonly encountered in clinical practice. It may present as an independent diagnosis after trauma to the shoulder, but more frequently presents as a component of more complex shoulder dysfunction, including impingement syndromes and rotator cuff disease. Careful physical examination and confirmatory radiographic imaging usually confirm the diagnosis. If conservative treatment fails, injection of the acromioclavicular joint with local anesthetic and steroid is a reasonable next step.

References

1. Waldman SD: Acromioclavicular joint pain. In: Atlas of Common Pain Syndromes. Philadelphia, WB Saunders, 2002, p 76.
2. de la Puente R, Boutin RD, Theodorouw DJ, et al: Post-traumatic and stress-induced osteolysis of the distal clavicle: MR imaging findings in 17 patients. Skeletal Radiol 28:202, 1999.
3. Resnick D, Kransdorf J: Rheumatoid arthritis and related diseases. In Resnick D, Kransdorf J (eds): Bone and Joint Imaging, 3rd ed. Philadelphia, WB Saunders, 2005, p 234.
4. Waldman SD: Acromioclavicular joint pain. In: Atlas of Pain Management Injection Techniques. Philadelphia, WB Saunders, 2000, p 40.

chapter 60

Subdeltoid Bursitis

Steven D. Waldman

Inflammation of the subdeltoid bursa is a common cause of shoulder pain and functional disability.[1] The subdeltoid bursa is vulnerable to injury from both acute trauma and repeated microtrauma. Acute injuries frequently take the form of direct trauma to the shoulder when playing sports or falling from bicycles. Repeated strain from throwing injuries, bowling, carrying a heavy briefcase, working with the arm raised across the body, rotator cuff injuries, and/or repetitive motion associated with assembly line work may result in inflammation of the subdeltoid bursa. The subdeltoid bursa lies primarily under the acromion extending laterally between the deltoid muscle and joint capsule under the deltoid muscle. It may exist as a single bursal sac or in some patients may exist as a multisegmented series of sacs that may be loculated in nature (Fig. 60–1). If the inflammation of the subdeltoid bursa becomes chronic, calcification of the bursa may occur.

The patient suffering from subdeltoid bursitis will frequently complain of pain with any movement of the shoulder, but especially with abduction.[2] The pain is localized to the subdeltoid area with referred pain often noted at the insertion of the deltoid at the deltoid tuberosity on the upper third of the humerus (Fig. 60–2). Often the patient will be unable to sleep on the affected shoulder and may complain of a sharp, catching sensation when abducting the shoulder, especially on first awakening.

■ SIGNS AND SYMPTOMS

Physical examination may reveal point tenderness over the acromion and occasionally swelling of the bursa will give the affected deltoid muscle an edematous feel.[1] Passive elevation and medial rotation of the affected shoulder will reproduce the pain—as will resisted abduction and lateral rotation. Sudden release of resistance during this maneuver will markedly increase the pain. Rotator cuff tear may mimic or coexist with subdeltoid bursitis and may confuse the diagnosis (see Differential Diagnosis later)

■ TESTING

Plain radiographs of the shoulder may reveal calcification of the bursa and associated structures consistent with chronic inflammation (see Fig. 60–1). MRI scan is indicated if ten-dinitis, partial disruption of the ligaments, or rotator cuff tear is suspected. Based on the patient's clinical presentation, additional testing including complete blood count, erythrocyte sedimentation rate, and antinuclear antibody testing may be indicated. MRI scan of the shoulder is indicated if rotator cuff tear is suspected. Radionucleotide bone scan is indicated if metastatic disease or primary tumor involving the shoulder is being considered. The injection technique described later will serve as both a diagnostic and therapeutic maneuver.

■ DIFFERENTIAL DIAGNOSIS

Subdeltoid bursitis is one of the most common forms of arthritis that results in shoulder joint pain. However, osteoarthritis, rheumatoid arthritis, posttraumatic arthritis, and rotator cuff tear arthropathy are also common causes of shoulder pain secondary to arthritis. Less common causes of arthritis-induced shoulder pain include the connective tissue diseases, infection, villonodular synovitis, and Lyme disease.[3,4] Acute infectious arthritis will usually be accompanied by significant systemic symptoms including fever and malaise and should be easily recognized by the astute clinician and treated appropriately with culture and antibiotics, rather than injection therapy. The connective tissue diseases will generally manifest as a polyarthropathy rather than a mono-arthropathy limited to the shoulder joint, although shoulder pain secondary to connective tissue disease responds exceedingly well to the injection technique described subsequently.

■ TREATMENT

Initial treatment of the pain and functional disability associated with osteoarthritis of the shoulder should include a combination of the nonsteroidal antiinflammatory agents or COX-2 inhibitors and physical therapy. The local application of heat and cold may also be beneficial. For patients who do not respond to these treatment modalities, an intra-articular injection of local anesthetic and steroid may be a reasonable next step.[5]

Injection of the subdeltoid bursa is performed by placing the patient in the supine position; proper preparation with

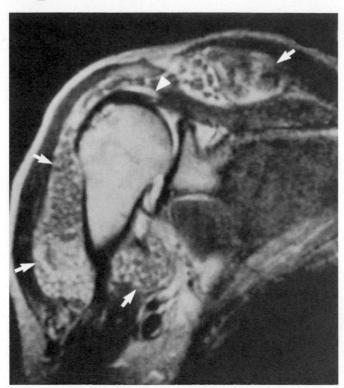

FIGURE 60–1 ■ Abnormalities of bursae in rheumatoid arthritis. Subdeltoid-subacromial bursitis. T2-weighted (TR/TE, 2000/80) coronal oblique spin echo MR image reveals a markedly distended bursa (*arrows*). Note the increase in signal intensity of fluid in the joint and in the bursa; however, regions of low signal density remain in the bursa. At surgery, these areas were found to be small fibrous nodules, or rice bodies. Also note the tear of the supraspinatus tendon (*arrowhead*), which may represent a complication of rheumatoid arthritis. (Courtesy of J Hodler, MD, Zurich, Switzerland. From Resnick D and Kransdorf MJ [eds]: Bone and Joint Imaging, 3rd ed. Philadelphia, Saunders, 2004, p 214, Fig 15–8)

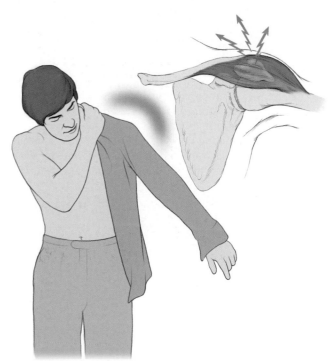

FIGURE 60–2 ■ Abduction of the shoulder will exacerbate the pain of subdeltoid bursitis. (From Waldman SD: Atlas of Common Pain Syndromes. Philadelphia, Saunders, 2002, p 81, Fig 20–1.)

antiseptic solution of the skin overlying the superior shoulder, acromion, and distal clavicle is carried out. A sterile syringe containing the 4.0 mL of 0.25% preservative-free bupivacaine and 40 mg of methylprednisolone is attached to a $1\frac{1}{2}$-inch 25-gauge needle using strict aseptic technique. With strict aseptic technique, the lateral edge of the acromion is identified and at the midpoint of the lateral edge, the injection site is identified. At this point, the needle is then carefully advanced in a slightly cephalad trajectory through the skin and subcutaneous tissues beneath the acromion capsule into the bursa (Fig. 60–3). If bone is encountered, the needle is withdrawn into the subcutaneous tissues and redirected slightly more inferiorly. After entering the bursa, the contents of the syringe is gently injected while slowly withdrawing the needle. There should be minimal resistance to injection unless calcification of the bursal sac is present. Calcification of the bursal sac will be identified as a resistance to needle advancement with an associated gritty feel. Significant calcific bursitis may ultimately require surgical excision to effect complete relief of symptoms. The needle is then removed and a sterile pressure dressing and ice pack are placed at the injection site.

The major complication of injection of the subdeltoid bursa is infection. This complication should be exceedingly rare if strict aseptic technique is adhered to. Approximately 25% of patients will complain of a transient increase in pain following injection of the subdeltoid bursa and should be warned of this.

This injection technique is extremely effective in the treatment of pain secondary to subdeltoid bursitis. Coexistent arthritis and tendinitis may also contribute to shoulder pain and may require additional treatment with more localized injection of local anesthetic and depot steroid. This technique is a safe procedure if careful attention is paid to the clinically relevant anatomy in the areas to be injected. Care must be taken to use sterile technique to avoid infection as well as the use of universal precautions to avoid risk to the operator. The incidence of ecchymosis and hematoma formation can be decreased if pressure is placed on the injection site immediately following injection. The use of physical modalities including local heat as well as gentle range-of-motion exercises should be introduced several days after the patient undergoes this injection technique for shoulder pain. Vigorous exercises should be avoided because they will exacerbate the patients symptomatology. Simple analgesics and nonsteroidal antiinflammatory agents may be used concurrently with this injection technique.

■ CONCLUSION

The pain of subdeltoid bursitis is commonly encountered in clinical practice. It may manifest as an independent diagnosis following trauma to the shoulder, but more frequently it occurs as a component of more complex shoulder dysfunction including arthritis, impingement syndromes, and rotator cuff disease. Careful physical examination combined with confirmatory radiographic imaging will usually confirm the diagnosis. If conservative treatment fails, injection of the subdeltoid bursa with local anesthetic and steroid is a reasonable next step.

FIGURE 60–3 ■ Technique for subdeltoid bursa injection. (From Waldman SD: Atlas of Pain Management Injection Techniques, Philadelphia, Saunders, 2000, p 61, Fig 17–1.)

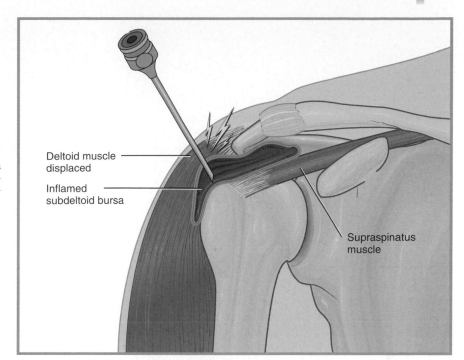

Deltoid muscle displaced

Inflamed subdeltoid bursa

Supraspinatus muscle

References

1. Waldman SD: Subdeltoid bursitis. In Waldman SD: Common Pain Syndromes. Philadelphia, WB Saunders, 2002, p 80.
2. Bland JH, Merrt JA, Boushey DR: The painful shoulder. Semin Arthritis Rheum 7:21, 1977.
3. Chartah EK, Good PK, Gould ES, et al: Septic subdeltoid bursitis: Semin Arthritis Rheum 22(1):25, 1992.
4. Salvarani EA: Proximal bursitis in active polymyalgia rheumatica. Ann Intern Med 127:27, 1997.
5. Waldman SD: Subdeltoid bursitis. In Waldman SD: Atlas of Pain Management Injection Techniques. Philadelphia, WB Saunders, 2000, p 60.

chapter 61

Biceps Tendinitis

Robert Trout

■ HISTORICAL CONSIDERATIONS

The role of the biceps tendon in shoulder pain has been controversial in the literature for most of the 20th century. The earliest descriptions of bicipital tendinitis as a clinical entity were a series of articles by Meyer in the 1920s,[1,2] in which he reported spontaneous subluxations and degeneration of the tendon. Many authors remained skeptical regarding the concept of the biceps tendon as a primary source of pain in the shoulder, and numerous articles were published that either supported or refuted the idea.[3,4] In hindsight, both groups may have been partly correct. In the 1970s, Neer was the first to describe biceps tendinitis as a secondary manifestation of impingement syndrome.[5] Thus, the biceps tendon does not usually act as a primary pain generator in the shoulder, but rather in association with other shoulder pathology, most notably rotator cuff disorders. A number of studies later supported this finding and eventually led to the classification of primary and secondary bicipital tendinitis.[6,7] Secondary tendinitis, occurring with other underlying shoulder problems is the most common type and may account for approximately 95% of cases.[8] Primary tendinitis, in which there is an isolated problem of the biceps tendon, is often seen in younger patients and may be related to abnormality of the bicipital groove, possibly from a previous trauma. These patients are at high risk for eventual rupture of the tendon.

Initially, articles focused on tenodesis of the tendon as definitive treatment of the problem.[9] However, this eventually fell out of favor due to a high failure rate.[10] More recently, arthroscopy has been combined with tenodesis and acromioplasty with better results; however, the main focus has been on early conservative treatment—with surgery being considered in selected cases only.

■ SIGNS AND SYMPTOMS

Although tendinitis implies an inflammatory condition, biceps tendinitis is usually a primarily degenerative problem as the tendon is subjected to wear and tear under the coracoacromial arch, similar to a process that can happen to the rotator cuff (Fig. 61–1).[5] The most common symptom that patients describe is pain in the anterior shoulder which may radiate to the biceps muscle and worsen with overhead activities. Patients often report significant nighttime pain. Usually there is no history of a specific traumatic event. Throwing athletes, in particular, will also develop an instability of the biceps tendon. They will experience an audible pop or snap while moving through their throwing motion.

On examination, the most common finding that patients will exhibit is point tenderness in the bicipital groove. The point of tenderness should move as the shoulder is passively internally and externally rotated. Other provocative tests that are specific for bicipital tendinitis include the Speed test and the Yergason test. In the Speed test, the patient holds the elbow in extension with the forearm supinated and then flexes the shoulder against resistance, reproducing the patient's pain (Fig. 61–2).[8] When performing the Yergason test, the patient supinates the forearm against resistance with the forearm flexed (Fig. 61–3). A positive test occurs when pain refers to the bicipital groove.[8] Instability should be evaluated by placing the arm in abduction and external rotation and then slowly bringing it down to the patient's side. A palpable snap will reflect a positive test as the tendon subluxes.

Because there is a high percentage of other common shoulder pathologies that occur with a bicipital tendinitis, a full shoulder examination should always be performed—including passive and active range of motion, subdeltoid bursal and acromioclavicular (AC) joint tenderness, and other provocative testing for impingement syndrome and rotator cuff tears.

■ TESTING

Initial testing consists of plain films of the shoulder, which are usually unremarkable, but they can detect glenohumeral arthritis, fracture, or articular abnormalities from an old trauma. A biceps groove view can also be performed to evaluate for spurring of the groove, which many predispose a patient to developing a primary tendinitis.

For patients with persistent symptoms or if a tendon rupture is suspected, MRI has become the most sensitive and specific test. Although expensive, it is the standard for imaging of the joint and surrounding tendons. It can elucidate both edema and full and partial tears of the biceps tendon while also identifying rotator cuff and labral pathology.

For patients unable to undergo an MRI, other possible alternatives include CT scan, ultrasound, and arthrography.

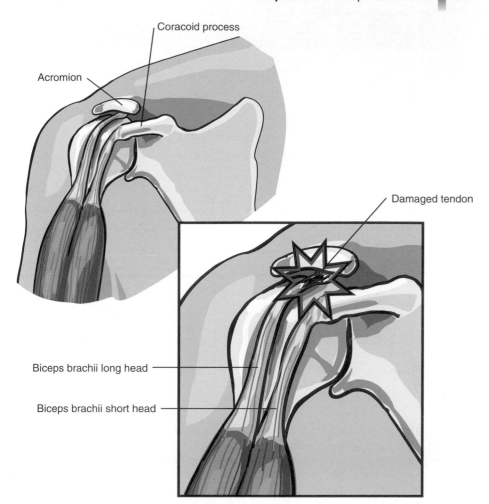

FIGURE 61-1 ■ The long head of the biceps may be subjected to wear and tear under the acromion arch.

Coracoid process

Acromion

Damaged tendon

Biceps brachii long head

Biceps brachii short head

FIGURE 61-2 ■ The Speed test for biceps tendon impingement.

FIGURE 61–3 ▮ The Yergason test for biceps tendon impingement.

CT is useful to evaluate for bony lesions when ruling out other possible causes of pain, such as humeral fractures or AC joint disease, but is unable to adequately assess for soft tissue damage. As a result, it has only limited use when attempting to make a definitive diagnosis. Arthrography and CT arthrography may detect full thickness tendon tears, but lack sensitivity for partial-thickness tears, particularly if the joint does not adequately fill with contrast. It is also invasive. Ultrasound is noninvasive and inexpensive and may have a role in initial testing. Ultrasound is able to reveal both rotator cuff and bicipital tendon tears. However, its sensitivity varies widely between institutions because it is highly operator dependent. It is also unable to reveal labral pathology.

Rarely, a primary tendinitis may occur secondary to a generalized inflammatory or autoimmune condition. If the patient's shoulder symptoms are accompanied by signs of synovitis or arthritis in other joints, routine laboratory tests should also be considered including erythrocyte sedimentation rate, antinuclear antibody, and rheumatoid factor.

▮ DIFFERENTIAL DIAGNOSIS

The temptation to rapidly diagnose a case of anterior shoulder pain as tendinitis should be resisted because of the often secondary nature of biceps tendinitis to other types of shoulder disorders such as impingement syndrome and rotator cuff pathology. Table 61–1 lists the differential diagnosis for bicipital tendinits. Patients with other neuropathic and neoplastic conditions may also exhibit radiating or referred pain to the anterior shoulder that may mimic a simple case of tendinitis. Fortunately, these problems can usually be identified with an adequate history and physical examination.

Impingement syndrome is typified by the "painful arc" of 60 to 120 degrees of active abduction. A helpful test is the

Table 61–1
Differential Diagnosis of Bicipital Tendinitis
Bicipital rupture
Impingement syndrome/rotator cuff tear
Glenohumeral arthritis
Adhesive capsulitis
Acromioclavicular joint arthritis
Cervical radiculopathy
Brachial plexitis
Autoimmune/systemic inflammatory disorders
Pancoast tumor/metastatic disease

Neer sign in which the patient's pronated arm is brought into full flexion, causing impingement under the acromion and reproducing the painful symptoms. Patients with adhesive capsulitis and glenohumeral osteoarthritis will exhibit decreased passive and active range of motion in all planes. Some patients with long-standing bicipital tendinitis may eventually progress to an adhesive capsulitis.

Clicking of the shoulder with overhead movements or a positive "clunk" sign may indicate labral pathology. Provocative tests, such as the Hawkins test may identify a rotator cuff disorder by eliciting pain when raising the arm to 90 degrees and then internally rotating the shoulder.

Pain that localizes more to the top of the shoulder may be an indication of AC joint arthritis and will often worsen with abduction greater than 120 degrees. It can be reproduced with the "cross-arm" test in which the patient raises the arm to 90 degrees and then actively adducts it.

Pain radiating distal to the elbow or other associated symptoms of numbness and paresthesias are typical of a radic-

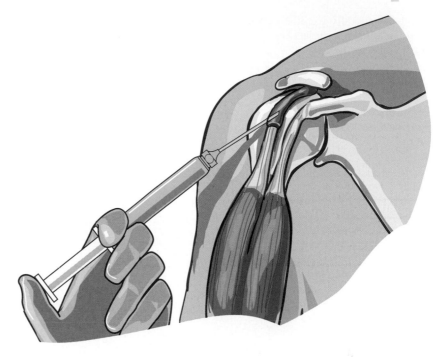

FIGURE 61–4 ■ Injection technique for relieving the pain of biceps tendinitis.

ular etiology or a brachial plexitis. Radicular pain is often exacerbated by coughing or sneezing, whereas a common presentation for brachial plexitis is acute pain followed within 2 weeks by weakness in the upper extremity. If these diagnoses are suspected, electro-diagnostic studies or cervical imaging may be considered.

■ TREATMENT

Initial treatment for both primary and secondary bicipital tendinitis is conservative with rest, icing, and antiinflammatory medications. Several studies have advocated the use of subacromial and glenohumeral steroid injections, which is logical given the high incidence of associated impingement syndrome and that the tendon of the long head is intra-articular.

For patients with primary tendinitis, injection into the biceps tendon sheath can be beneficial (Fig. 61–4). The technique for this injection is not difficult, but should be performed carefully to avoid direct injection into the tendon, which can increase the potential for tendon rupture. The patient is placed in the supine position with the shoulder externally rotated 45 degrees. A small volume of fluid is used with 1.0 mL of 0.25% bupivacaine and 40 mg methylprednisolone in a sterile syringe attached to a $1\frac{1}{2}$ inch 25-gauge needle. The insertion of the bicipital tendon is found by first identifying the coracoid process and then palpating the lesser tuberosity slightly lateral to it. The needle is slowly advanced until it hits bone, and then withdrawn 1 to 2 mm. The medication is injected and there should be a small amount of resistance. If there is no resistance, the needle is probably in the joint space. If there is significant resistance, the needle may be within the tendon itself and it should be withdrawn slightly.[11]

Once symptoms improve, physical therapy is initiated with range-of-motion exercises progressing to rotator cuff strengthening for patients with impingement syndrome. For patients with significant instability or with recalcitrant symptoms despite appropriate treatment, referral to an orthopedist may be needed for possible arthroscopy of the shoulder with or without tenodesis of the tendon.

■ COMPLICATIONS AND PITFALLS

The most likely pitfall that should be avoided is bicipital tendon rupture. The majority of tendon ruptures occur in previously degenerated and frayed tendons from prolonged wear and tear under the acromial arch. These patients are most often older and will give a history of chronic shoulder pain that improved after a sudden and brief episode of severe pain in the anterior shoulder. A large amount of bruising may be present, as well as a palpable lump in the biceps region. Tendon rupture purely secondary to acute trauma is rare.

Complications after injection, such as infection and hematoma, are rare if proper aseptic technique is used. The incidence of hematoma can be reduced by applying direct pressure immediately after the injection, and taking extra precaution with patients who are taking anticoagulants or who have clotting disorders.

■ SUMMARY

Bicipital tendinitis is a common cause of anterior shoulder pain that is seen mostly in individuals who have some other type of intra-articular pathology or abnormality. Patients will exhibit tenderness at the insertion of the tendon, and they report increased pain with active shoulder movements—most significantly flexion. Radiographs are most often unremarkable, although an MRI may demonstrate an inflamed or degenerated tendon and rule out other problems such as labral pathology or rotator cuff tear. Response to conservative treatment is generally excellent with anti-inflammatory medication, relative rest, injections, and gradual return to activity with physical therapy.

References

1. Meyer AW: Unrecognized occupational destruction of the tendon of the long head of the biceps brachii. Arch Surg 2:130, 1921.
2. Meyer AW: Spontaneous dislocation and destruction of the long head of the biceps brachii. Arch Surg 17:493, 1928.
3. Codman EA: The Shoulder. Boston, Thomas Todd, 1934.
4. Hitchcock HH, Bechtol CO: Painful shoulder: Observations on the role of the tendon of the long head of the biceps brachii in its causation. J Bone Joint Surg Am 30:263, 1948.
5. Neer CS II: Anterior acromioplasty for chronic impingement syndrome in the shoulder. J Bone Joint Surg 54:41, 1972.
6. Dines D, Warren RF, Inglis AE: Surgical treatment of lesions of the long head of the biceps. Clin Orthop 164:165, 1982.
7. Habermeyer P, Walch G: The biceps tendon and rotator cuff disease. In Burkhead WZ Jr (ed): Rotator Cuff Disorders. Philadelphia, Lippincott Williams & Wilkins, 1996, p 142.
8. Curtis AS, Snyder SJ: Evaluation and treatment of biceps tendon pathology. Orthop Clin North Am 24:33, 1993.
9. Depalma AF, Callery GE: Bicipital tenosynovitis. Clin Orthop 3:69, 1954.
10. Becker DA, Cofield RH: Tenodesis of the long head of the biceps brachii for chronic bicipital tendinitis: Long-term results. J Bone Joint Surg Am 71:376, 1989.
11. Waldman SD: Bicipital tendinitis. In Waldman SD: Atlas of Pain Management Injection Techniques. Philadelphia, Saunders, 2000, p 52.

chapter 62

Scapulocostal Syndrome

Bernard Abrams and Scott Goodman

The scapulocostal syndrome, also known as levator scapulae syndrome, is a common painful musculoskeletal syndrome that mainly affects the posterior shoulder area; however, because of the pattern of pain radiation, it can mimic numerous other conditions including cervical radicular pain, intrinsic shoulder joint disease, and even visceral pain. It can be diagnosed clinically with a careful history and physical examination. There are no related blood test abnormalities or neurophysiologic or imaging abnormalities in the syndrome, but these tests may be useful in eliminating other entities from diagnostic consideration.

■ HISTORICAL CONSIDERATIONS

This syndrome was first described by Michele and coworkers in 1950.[1] They pointed out that during the preceding 3 years, 30% of all middle-aged individuals presenting with shoulder complaints had this syndrome and the protean manifestations and radiation of this syndrome. The pain might radiate to the occiput or spinous processes of C3 and C4, or might appear to originate at the root of the neck and radiate into the shoulder joint, or radiate down the arm into the hand, usually located along the posteromedial aspect of the upper arm and along the ulnar distribution in the forearm and hand. They pointed out that the pain alternatively might radiate along the course of the fourth and fifth intercostal nerves, mimicking angina pectoris on the left, and cholecystitis on the right. Finally, the patient might present with any combination of the above symptoms and signs (Fig. 62–1). After some initial interest in this syndrome between 1956 and 1968,[2-5] interest languished until 1980s and early 1990s, when attention was turned to the anatomy of this region.

■ THE CLINICAL SYNDROME: SIGNS, SYMPTOMS, AND PHYSICAL FINDINGS

The hallmark of the scapulocostal syndrome is pain. The pain may be localized to the medial superior border of the scapula or it may radiate up into the neck, causing headache. It can also cause pain into the root of the shoulder, simulating rotator cuff syndrome or other shoulder disorders. It can radiate around the chest wall or down the arm, usually in an ulnar nerve distribution. The characteristic pattern is that of acute pain localized in the upper trunk. There may be complaints of radicular-type pain, with or without sensory features.[4,6] Although weakness of the arm and shoulder may be offered as complaints, these usually are a result of guarding, without atrophy or neurophysiologic evidence of denervation on EMG. The pain has been described variously as aching, burning, or gnawing, and rarely as a sharp or radicular pain. The symptoms may be intermittent, but a nagging, constant quality is not uncommon. Insomnia is a frequent complaint, due to inability to find a comfortable sleeping position.

The original paper of Michele and colleagues[1] cited an equal distribution between the sexes. Since that time, most observers have noted a female predominance, and also a predominance in the dominant shoulder. Clerical occupation, rounded shoulders, large pendulous breasts, and the carrying of personal items including handbags are often implicated.

Russek[7] classified the syndrome into three types: (1) primary, probably postural in origin; (2) secondary, a complication of preexisting neck or shoulder lesions; and (3) static, occurring in severely disabled patients who are unable to control the scapulothoracic relationship.

There are usually no muscular, reflex, or sympathetic, or sensory findings in the examination. The classic finding is a trigger point elicited by digital pressure at the medial scapular border in a line extending from the scapular spine. This trigger point (Fig. 62–2) may be missed (both diagnostically and therapeutically), unless the arm is adducted, with the palm of the affected hand flat on the opposite shoulder, crossing in front of the chest (Fig. 62–3). Alternatively, extension and internal rotation of the arm will also elicit the pain (Fig. 62–4) Secondary trigger points may be found in the trapezius and rhomboid (Fig. 62–5).[1] Diffuse tenderness over the chest wall is usually mild.

Consistent biochemical, rheumatologic, radiologic, or neurophysiologic (EMG) findings have not been reported. One study reported increased heat emission from the upper medial angle of the affected shoulder on thermography in more than 60% of patients.[8] Reproduction of the pain by palpation (and relief by local anesthetic infiltration) are the essential elements of this syndrome.

■ CLINICALLY RELEVANT ANATOMY

The constant location of the pain in the deep trigger point seems to indicate that the levator scapulae muscle is involved in this syndrome (Fig. 62–6). Considerable controversy exists

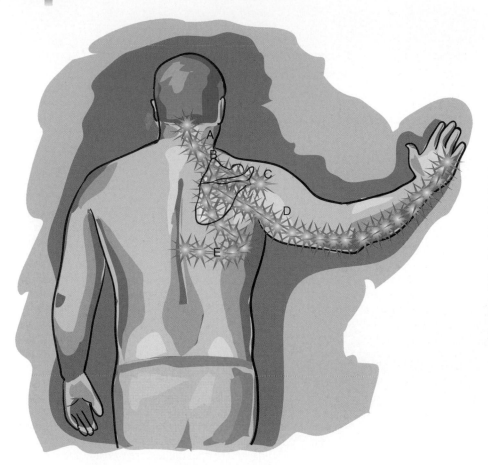

FIGURE 62–1 ■ Patterns of pain radiation. **A,** The pain radiates into the occiput. **B,** The pain is originating at the root of the neck and radiates into the shoulder joint. **C** and **D,** The pain radiates along the posteromedial aspect of the upper arm and the ulnar distribution of the forearm. Traction on the lower trunk of the brachial plexus as it passes over the first rib produces pain and numbness in the ulnar distribution of the hand and fingers. **E,** The pain may radiate into the fourth and fifth thoracic nerves due to the exaggerated lumbar lordosis. (Adapted from Michele AA, Davies JJ, Krueger FJ, Lichtor JM: Scapulocostal syndrome [fatigue-postural paradox]. New York J Med 50:1353, 1950.)

FIGURE 62–2 ■ The trigger point. (Adapted from Ormandy L: Scapulocostal syndrome. Va Med Q 121:105, 1994.)

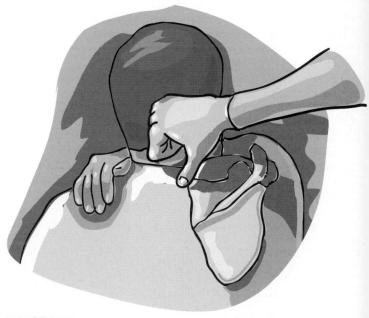

FIGURE 62–3 ■ Location of trigger point area of tenderness when the scapula has been retracted from the posterior chest wall. (Adapted from Michele AA, Davies JJ, Krueger FJ, Lichtor JM: Scapulocostal syndrome [fatigue-postural paradox]. New York J Med 50:1353, 1950.)

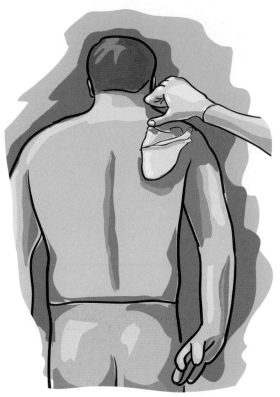

FIGURE 62–4 ■ Deep pressure over the superior medial angle of the scapula with compression of the posterior chest wall in conjunction with backward flexion of the internally rotated arm. (Adapted from Michele AA, Davies JJ, Krueger FJ, Lichtor JM: Scapulocostal syndrome [fatigue-postural paradox]. New York J Med 50:1353, 1950.)

FIGURE 62–5 ■ Digital pressure underneath midbelly of the descending fibers of the trapezius toward the anterior surface of the superior medial angle of the scapula. Reinforcement by internal rotation and backward flexion of the arm. (Adapted from Michele AA, Davies JJ, Krueger FJ, Lichtor JM: Scapulocostal syndrome [fatigue-postural paradox]. New York J Med 50:1353, 1950.)

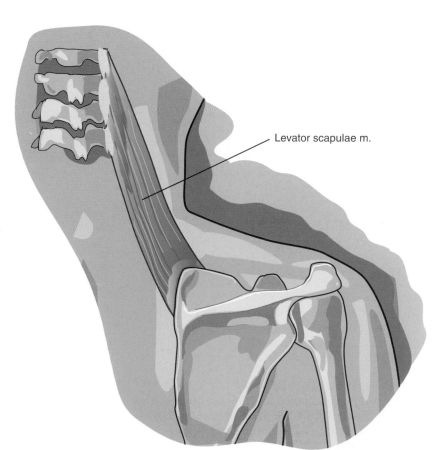

Levator scapulae m.

FIGURE 62–6 ■ Levator scapulae. Origin: Transverse process of C1-C4 vertebrae. Insertion: Vertebral border of scapula between medial angle and root of the spine. (Adapted from Quiring et al: The Extremities, 1944.)

Table 62–1

Three Layers of the Scapulothoracic Articulation

Structure	Superficial	Intermediate	Deep
Muscles	Latissimus dorsi Trapezius	Levator scapulae Rhomboid minor Rhomboid major	Subscapularis Serratus anterior
Bursae	Inferior angle (Number 1) 4 of 8 specimens	Superomedial angle (number 2) 8 of 8 specimens	Serratus space (number 3) 8 of 8 specimens Subscapularis space (number 4) 5 of 8 specimens
Nerves		Spinal accessory	

From Williams GR, Shakil M, Klimkiewicz J, Iannnoti J: Anatomy of the scapulothoracic articulation. Clin Orthop 359:237, 1999.

as to the constancy of a bursa in connection with the levator scapulae, which may be inserted in two layers enfolding the medial border of the scapula, and a second bursa found in the areolar tissue between the two layers.[8] Williams and coworkers[9] undertook a dissection of four frozen human cadavers, and noted that the surgical anatomy of the scapulothoracic region has been described infrequently. They pointed out that there were three layers of the scapulothoracic articulation (Table 62–1).[9] They described a superficial layer composed of the trapezius, latissimus dorsi, and an inconsistent bursa, which they found in four of eight specimens, between the inferior angle of the scapula and the superior fibers of the latissimus dorsi.

They then pointed out that the intermediate layer contains the rhomboid minor, rhomboid major, and levator scapulae muscles, along with the spinal accessory nerve, and a consistent bursa found in eight of eight specimens, between the superior medial scapula and the overlying trapezius. The deep layer consisted of the serratus anterior and subscapularis muscle in addition to two bursae. One of the two bursae was consistently located between the serratus anterior and the thoracic cage, whereas the other was inconsistently located between the serratus anterior and subscapularis. These relationships probably account for the clinical finding that turning the head opposite to the affected limb will reproduce the pain.

■ **DIFFERENTIAL DIAGNOSIS**

The differential diagnosis of pain in and about the scapula is extensive. Shoulder problems including rotator cuff disease, adhesive capsulitis, instability or arthritis of the glenohumeral joint, and vascular or neurogenic thoracic outlet syndrome, may be at play.[10] The pain in these individuals is generally exacerbated by scapulothoracic movement, and also by movements at the glenohumeral joint. Restriction of range of motion is frequent. Imaging of the shoulder with plain radiographs will generally show degenerative changes. MRI or CT arthrogram may be definitive.

An entity known as the "snapping scapula" has been used to describe the clinical scenario of tenderness at the superomedial angle of the scapula, painful scapulothoracic motion, and scapulothoracic crepitus.[10] Etiologies of "snap-

ping scapula" include scapular exostosis, malunion of scapula or rib fracture, and Sprengel deformity.[11,12]

Cervical radiculopathy can produce an aching pain into the scapula ("protopathic pain"), especially with C7 radiculopathy associated with sharp ("epicritic") pain down into the appropriate segment of the upper limb. In the case of the C7 radiculopathy, pain usually descends the posterior aspect of the upper arm (triceps muscle) into the middle finger and is associated with weakness of the triceps and wrist extensors, diminution of the triceps reflex, and hypesthesia in the C7 dermatome. Suprascapular nerve entrapment may produce deep, poorly circumscribed pain.[13] Because the suprascapular nerve is a motor nerve, the pain resulting from its irritation is deep and poorly circumscribed. It is roughly localized to the posterior and lateral aspects of the shoulder. When there is an appreciable traction stress element on the upper trunk, there will also be pain down the radial nerve axis. If the neuropathy has been present for a sufficient time, there will be visual and palpable atrophy of the supraspinatus and infraspinatus muscles. This weakness is confirmed when there is difficulty in initiating abduction and rotation at the glenohumeral joint. In most cases of suprascapular neuropathy, there is an earlier motion impediment at this joint. Deep pressure toward the region of the suprascapular notch will be painful. Motion of the scapula will cause pain. The cross-body adduction test, performed by adducting the extended arm passively across the midline, will be extremely painful because it lifts the scapular nerve away from the thoracic nerve and thereby tenses the suprascapular nerve. A suprascapular nerve block may be necessary for diagnosis. The region involved is somewhat lateral to the medial superior scapular border (at least 3 to 4 finger breadths in an average-sized person), so the tender area is clearly differentiated from the medial angle of the scapula where the levator scapulae muscle inserts in the scapulocostal syndrome (Fig. 62–7).

■ **TREATMENT**

Nonoperative treatment of patients sometimes is successful and is composed of activity modification, physical therapy, systemic antiinflammatory medications, and injection into the region of the medial superior scapular border. Mixtures of

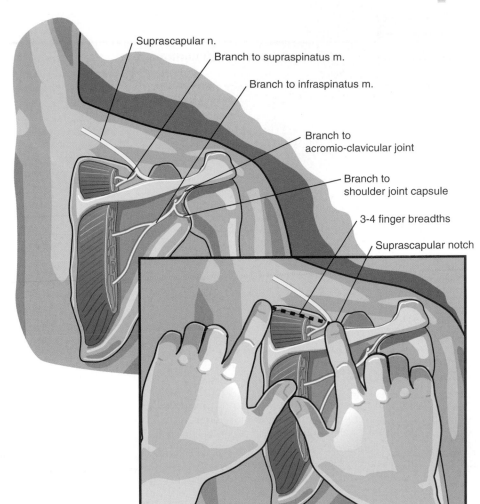

Suprascapular n.

Branch to supraspinatus m.

Branch to infraspinatus m.

Branch to acromio-clavicular joint

Branch to shoulder joint capsule

3-4 finger breadths

Suprascapular notch

FIGURE 62–7 ▮ Suprascapular nerve—motor and joint distribution. (Adapted from Kopell HP, Thomspon WAL: Surg Gynecol Obstet 109:92, 1959.)

2 to 8 mL of plain 1% lidocaine HCl, plus 1 mL of betamethasone followed by physical therapy exercises, have been advocated (Fig. 62–8).[14] Ormandy[14] treated 190 patients, 43% with one block, 40% with two blocks, and 17% with three blocks. On completion of treatment, approximately 98% of patients were relieved of pain and returned to their original occupation. Fourie[15] invoked the serratus posterior superior muscle, a member of the third muscle layer of the back. He used 1 mL of steroid and 1.8 mL of local anesthetic. In his report of 201 cases, conservative treatment was successful in 95.9% of patients. Very few writers on this subject mention that the arm needs to be cross-adducted or internally rotated and extended in order to get the scapula out of the way and expose the levator scapulae muscle at its insertion into the medial border of the scapula. If this is done, success is much more likely. We use a 25-gauge needle at a 90-degree angle to get underneath the scapula and to place it in the most lateral excursion of the scapula, and then infiltrate while withdrawing the needle toward the medial superior scapula border.

Surgical options for patients who did not respond to nonoperative management include scapulothoracic bursectomy, excision of the superior-medial angle of the scapula, and combined bursectomy and superior angle resection.[9,16,17] A recent report[18] concerned the operative treatment of scapulothoracic

bursitis in professional baseball pitchers, four of whom were operated on, and all returned to their pitching careers. Recently there has been treatment using endoscopic surgery in the scapulothoracic region.[19-21] Results of surgery have been reported infrequently and inconsistently.[9]

■ COMPLICATIONS AND PITFALLS

The major pitfall is a failure to diagnose this common and easily overlooked syndrome. Thorough history and a few simple physical diagnostic maneuvers involving the crossed adduction of the affected arm with palpation should be sufficient to make the diagnosis. The treatment can be unsuccessful if a similar posture for injection is not maintained, as one would be attempting to inject through the scapula itself, to reach the levator scapulae insertion or the putative bursa in this area. Once one attempts to inject in this area, the possibility of a pneumothorax should be kept in mind at all times and the patient warned of this possibility and its potential consequences, including traction pneumothorax. They should be instructed to go the emergency room with any pain on inspiration of the chest. Operative techniques have their own risks and morbidity. However, inconclusive results up to this point have clouded the issue.

FIGURE 62–8 ▪ Infiltration of the subscapular region. (Adapted from Ormandy L: Scapulocostal syndrome. Va Med Q 121:105, 1994.)

▪ CONCLUSION

Scapulocostal syndrome is a common occurrence, especially in posturally compromised, middle-aged individuals, usually women, especially with desk jobs or those vocations that force them to extend their arms in front of them for prolonged periods of time. There are no definitive biological markers for this syndrome. The differential diagnosis rests largely in ruling out cervical radiculopathy, intrinsic shoulder disease, osseus disease of the bony skeleton, and other afflictions of the scapula, including the snapping scapula syndrome and Sprengel deformity. It is easily diagnosed and may be treated with a relative degree of success by injection therapy, which should be combined with physical therapy and alteration of lifestyle. Surgical treatment may be considered in refractory cases, but its success remains largely controversial.

References

1. Michele AA, Davies,JJ, Krueger FJ, Lichtor JM: Scapulocostal syndrome (fatigue-postural paradox). New York J Med 50:1353, 1950.
2. McGovney RB: Scapulocostal syndrome. Clin Orthop 2:191, 1956.
3. Rose DL, Novak EJ: The painful shoulder: The scapulocostal syndrome in shoulder pain. J Kans Med Soc 67:112, 1966.
4. Shull JR: Scapulocostal syndrome: Clinical aspects. South Med J 62:956, 1969.
5. Michele AA, Eisenberg J: Scapulocostal syndrome. Arch Phys Med Rehabil 49:383, 1968.
6. Cohen CA: Scapulocostal syndrome: Diagnosis and treatment. South Med J 73:433, 1980.
7. Russek AS: Diagnosis and treatment of scapulocostal syndrome. JAMA 150:25, 1952.
8. Menachem A, Kaplan O, Dekel S: Levator scapulae syndrome: An anatomico-clinical study. Bull Hosp Jt Dis 53:21, 1993.
9. Williams GR, Shakil M, Klimkiewicz J, Iannoti J: Anatomy of the scapulothoracic articulation. Clin Orthop 359:237, 1999.
10. Butters KP: The scapula. In Rockwood CA, Matsen FA (eds): The Shoulder. Philadelphia, Saunders, 1990, p 335.
11. Milch H: Snapping scapula. Clin Orthop 20:139, 1961.
12. Parsons TA: The snapping scapula and subscapular exostoses. J Bone Joint Surg Br 55B:345, 1973.
13. Kopell HP, Thompson WAL: Suprascapular entrapment neuropathy. Surg Gynecol Obst 109:92, 1959.
14. Ormandy L: Scapulocostal syndrome. Va Med Q 121:105, 1994.
15. Fourie LJ: The scapulocostal syndrome. S Afr Med J 79:721,1991.
16. Milch H: Partial scapulectomy for snapping in the scapula. J Bone Joint Surg Am 32A:561, 1950.
17. Morse BJ, Ebraheim NA, Jackson WT: Partial scapulectomy for snapping scapula syndrome. Orthop Rev 22:1141, 1993.
18. Sisto DJ, Jobe FW: The operative treatment of scapulothoracic bursitis in professional pitchers. Am J Sports Med 14:192, 1986
19. Ciullo JV: Management of pain at the superiomedial angle of the scapula. J Shoulder Elbow Surg 5:589, 1996.
20. Ciullo JV, Jones E: Subscapular bursitis: Conservative and endoscopic treatment of "snapping scapula" or "washboard syndrome." Orthop Trans 16:740, 1992.

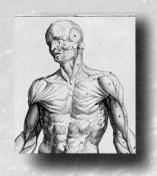

Part D

ELBOW PAIN SYNDROMES

chapter

63

Tennis Elbow

Steven D. Waldman

Tennis elbow (also known as lateral epicondylitis) is caused by repetitive microtrauma to the extensor tendons of the forearm.[1] The pathophysiology of tennis elbow is initially caused by micro-tearing at the origin of extensor carpi radialis and extensor carpi ulnaris (Fig. 63–1).[2] Secondary inflammation may occur that can become chronic as the result of continued overuse or misuse of the extensors of the forearm. Coexisting bursitis, arthritis, and gout may also perpetuate the pain and disability of tennis elbow.

Tennis elbow occurs in patients engaged in repetitive activities that include hand grasping (e.g., politicians shaking hands) or high-torque wrist turning (e.g., scooping ice cream at an ice cream parlor) (Fig. 63–2). Tennis players develop tennis elbow by two separate mechanisms: (1) increased pressure grip strain as a result of playing with too heavy a racquet; and (2) making backhand shots with a leading shoulder and elbow rather than keeping the shoulder and elbow parallel to the net (Fig. 63–3). Other racquet sport players are also susceptible to the development of tennis elbow.

■ SIGNS AND SYMPTOMS

The pain of tennis elbow is localized to the region of the lateral epicondyle. It is constant and is made worse with active contraction of the wrist. Patients will note the inability to hold a coffee cup or hammer. Sleep disturbance is common. On physical examination, there will be tenderness along the extensor tendons at, or just below, the lateral epicondyle.[1] Many patients with tennis elbow will exhibit a band-like thickening within the affected extensor tendons. Elbow range of motion will be normal. Grip strength on the affected side will be diminished. Patients with tennis elbow will demonstrate a positive tennis elbow test. The test is performed by stabilizing the patient's forearm and then having the patient clench his or her fist and actively extend the wrist. The examiner then attempts to force the wrist into flexion (Fig. 63–4). Sudden severe pain is highly suggestive of tennis elbow.

■ TESTING

Electromyography will help distinguish cervical radiculopathy and radial tunnel syndrome from tennis elbow. Plain

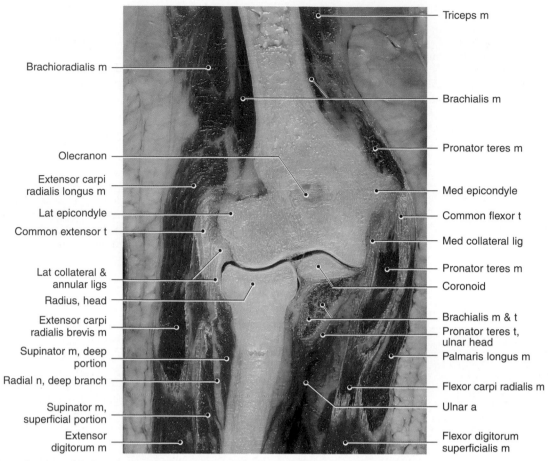

Brachioradialis m

Olecranon

Extensor carpi
radialis longus m

Lat epicondyle

Common extensor t

Lat collateral &
annular ligs

Radius, head

Extensor carpi
radialis brevis m

Supinator m, deep
portion

Radial n, deep branch

Supinator m,
superficial portion

Extensor
digitorum m

Triceps m

Brachialis m

Pronator teres m

Med epicondyle

Common flexor t

Med collateral lig

Pronator teres m

Coronoid

Brachialis m & t

Pronator teres t,
ulnar head

Palmaris longus m

Flexor carpi radialis m

Ulnar a

Flexor digitorum
superficialis m

FIGURE 63–1 ■ Anatomy of the lateral epicondyle. (From Kang SH, Ahn JM, Resnick D: MRI of the Extremities, 2nd ed. Philadelphia, Saunders, 2002, p 87.)

FIGURE 63–2 ■ The pain of tennis elbow is localized to the lateral epicondyle. (From Waldman SD: Atlas of Common Pain Syndromes. Philadelphia, Saunders, 2002, p 99.)

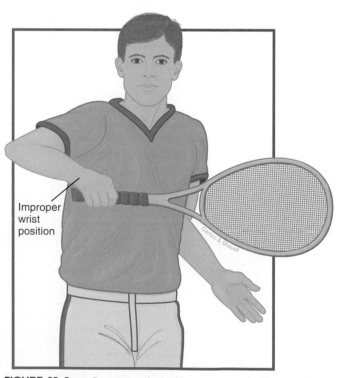

Improper
wrist
position

FIGURE 63–3 ■ Improper wrist position causes tennis elbow syndrome. (From Waldman SD: Atlas of Pain Management Injection Techniques, Philadelphia, Saunders, 2000, p 81.)

radiographs are indicated in all patients who present with tennis elbow to rule out joint mice and other occult bony pathology. Based on the patient's clinical presentation, additional testing including complete blood count, uric acid, sedimentation rate, and antinuclear antibody testing may be indicated. MRI scan of the elbow is indicated if joint instability is suspected. The injection technique described subsequently will serve as both a diagnostic and therapeutic maneuver.

■ DIFFERENTIAL DIAGNOSIS

Radial tunnel syndrome and occasionally C6-C7 radiculopathy can mimic tennis elbow. Radial tunnel syndrome is an entrapment neuropathy which is the result of entrapment of the radial nerve below the elbow. Radial tunnel syndrome can be distinguished from tennis elbow in that, with radial tunnel syndrome, the maximal tenderness to palpation is distal to the lateral epicondyle over the radial nerve, whereas with tennis

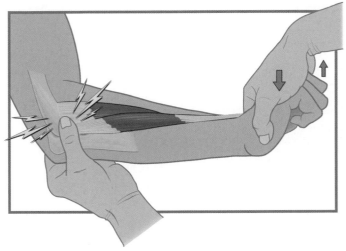

FIGURE 63–4 ■ Test for eliciting the pain due to tennis elbow. (From Waldman SD: Atlas of Pain Management Injection Techniques, Philadelphia, Saunders, 2000, p 83.)

elbow, the maximal tenderness to palpation is over the lateral epicondyle.[3]

The most common nidus of pain from tennis elbow is the bony origin of the extensor tendon of extensor carpi radialis brevis at the anterior facet of the lateral epicondyle. Less commonly, tennis elbow pain can originate from the extensor carpi radialis longus at the supracondylar crest, or rarely more distally at the point where the extensor carpi radialis brevis overlies the radial head. As mentioned earlier, bursitis may accompany tennis elbow. The olecranon bursa lies in the posterior aspect of the elbow joint and may also become inflamed as a result of direct trauma or overuse of the joint. Other bursae susceptible to the development of bursitis exist between the insertion of the biceps and the head of the radius as well as in the antecubital and cubital area.[4]

■ TREATMENT

Initial treatment of the pain and functional disability associated with tennis elbow should include a combination of the nonsteroidal antiinflammatory agents or COX-2 inhibitors and physical therapy. The local application of heat and cold may also be beneficial. Avoidance of any repetitive activity that may exacerbate the patient's symptomatology should be avoided. For patients who do not respond to these treatment modalities, the following injection technique may be a reasonable next step.[5]

Injection technique for tennis elbow is performed by placing the patient in a supine position with the arm fully adducted at the patient's side and the elbow flexed with the dorsum of the hand resting on a folded towel to relax the affected tendons. A total of 1 mL of local anesthetic and 40 mg of methylprednisolone is drawn up in a 5-mL sterile syringe.

After sterile preparation of skin overlying the posterolateral aspect of the joint, the lateral epicondyle is identified. Using strict aseptic technique, a 1-inch 25-gauge needle is inserted perpendicular to the lateral epicondyle through the skin and into the subcutaneous tissue overlying the affected tendon (Fig. 63–5). If bone is encountered, the needle is

FIGURE 63–5 ■ Injection technique for relieving the pain due to tennis elbow. (From Waldman SD: Atlas of Pain Management Injection Techniques, Philadelphia, Saunders, 2000, p 83.)

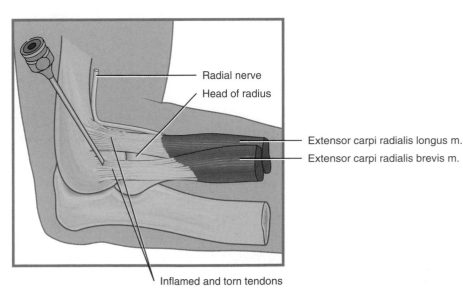

Radial nerve
Head of radius
Extensor carpi radialis longus m.
Extensor carpi radialis brevis m.
Inflamed and torn tendons

withdrawn into the subcutaneous tissue. The contents of the syringe is then gently injected. There should be little resistance to injection. If resistance is encountered, the needle is probably in the tendon and should be withdrawn until the injection proceeds without significant resistance. The needle is then removed and a sterile pressure dressing and ice pack are placed at the injection site.

The major complication associated with tennis elbow is the rupture of the affected inflamed tendons either from repetitive trauma or from injection directly into the tendon. Inflamed and previously damaged tendons may rupture if directly injected and needle position should be confirmed outside the tendon before injection to avoid this complication. Another complication of this injection technique is infection. This complication should be exceedingly rare if strict aseptic technique is followed. The ulnar nerve is especially susceptible to damage at the elbow and care must be taken to avoid this nerve when injecting the elbow. Approximately 25% of patients will complain of a transient increase in pain following this injection technique and should be warned of such.

This injection technique is extremely effective in the treatment of pain secondary to the tennis elbow. Coexistent bursitis and tendinitis may also contribute to elbow pain and may require additional treatment with more localized injection of local anesthetic and depot steroid. This technique is a safe procedure if careful attention is paid to the clinically relevant anatomy in the areas to be injected. The use of physical modalities including local heat, as well as gentle range-of-motion exercises should be introduced several days after the patient undergoes this injection technique for tennis elbow pain. A Velcro band placed around the extensor tendons may also help relieve the symptoms of tennis elbow. Vigorous exercises should be avoided because they will exacerbate the patients symptomatology. Simple analgesics and nonsteroidal antiinflammatory agents may be used concurrently with this injection technique. As mentioned earlier, cervical radiculopathy and radial tunnel syndrome may mimic tennis elbow and must be ruled out to effectively treat the underlying pathology.

References

1. Coonrad RW, Hooper WR: Tennis elbow: Course, natural history, conservative and surgical management. J Bone Joint Surg Am 55:1177, 1973.
2. Waldman SD: Tennis elbow. In Waldman SD: Atlas of Common Pain Syndromes. Philadelphia, Saunders, 2002, p 98.
3. Waldman SD: Radial tunnel syndrome. In Waldman SD: Atlas of Uncommon Pain Syndromes. Philadelphia, Saunders, 2003, p 83.
4. Waldman SD: Cubital bursitis. In Waldman SD: Atlas of Uncommon Pain Syndromes. Philadelphia, Saunders, 2003, p 80.
5. Waldman SD: Tennis elbow. In Waldman SD: Atlas of Pain Management Injection Techniques. Philadelphia, Saunders, 2000, p 80.

chapter 64

Golfer's Elbow

Steven D. Waldman

Although fifteen times less common than tennis elbow, golfer's elbow remains one of the most common causes of elbow and forearm pain.[1] Golfer's elbow (also known as medial epicondylitis) is caused by repetitive microtrauma to the flexor tendons of the forearm in a manner analogous to tennis elbow.[2] The pathophysiology of golfer's elbow is initially caused by micro-tearing at the origin of pronator teres, flexor carpi radialis, and flexor carpi ulnaris, and the palmaris longus. Secondary inflammation may occur that can become chronic as the result of continued overuse or misuse of the flexors of the forearm. The most common nidus of pain from golfer's elbow is the bony origin of the flexor tendon of flexor carpi radialis and the humeral heads of the flexor carpi ulnaris and pronator teres at the medial epicondyle of the humerus (Fig. 64–1). Less commonly, golfer's elbow pain can originate from the ulnar head of the flexor carpi ulnaris at the medial aspect of the olecranon process. Coexisting bursitis, arthritis, and gout may also perpetuate the pain and disability of golfer's elbow.[3]

Golfer's elbow occurs in patients engaged in repetitive flexion activities that include throwing baseballs, footballs, carrying heavy suitcases, and driving golf balls (Fig. 64–2). These activities have in common repetitive flexion of the wrist and strain on the flexor tendons due to excessive weight or sudden arrested motion. Interestingly, many of the activities that can cause tennis elbow can also cause golfer's elbow.[1]

■ SIGNS AND SYMPTOMS

The pain of golfer's elbow is localized to the region of the medial epicondyle (see Fig. 64–1). It is constant and is made worse with active contraction of the wrist. Patients will note the inability to hold a coffee cup or hammer. Sleep disturbance is common. On physical examination, there will be tenderness along the flexor tendons at or just below the medial epicondyle. Many patients with golfer's elbow will exhibit a band-like thickening within the affected flexor tendons. Elbow range of motion will be normal. Grip strength on the affected side will be diminished. Patients with golfer's elbow will demonstrate a positive golfer's elbow test.[2] The test is performed by stabilizing the patients forearm and then having the patient actively flex the wrist (Fig. 64–3). The examiner then attempts to force the wrist into extension. Sudden severe pain is highly suggestive of golfer's elbow.

■ TESTING

Plain radiographs are indicated in all patients who present with golfer's elbow to rule out joint mice and other occult bony pathology. Based on the patients clinical presentation, additional testing including complete blood count, uric acid, sedimentation rate, and antinuclear antibody testing may be indicated. MRI scan of the elbow is indicated if joint instability is suspected. Electromyography is indicated to diagnose entrapment neuropathy at the elbow and to help distinguish golfer's elbow from cervical radiculopathy. The injection technique described subsequently will serve as a diagnostic and a therapeutic maneuver.

■ DIFFERENTIAL DIAGNOSIS

Occasionally C6-C7 radiculopathy can mimic golfer's elbow. The patient suffering from cervical radiculopathy will usually have neck pain and proximal upper extremity pain in addition to symptoms below the elbow. Electromyography will help distinguish radiculopathy from golfer's elbow. Bursitis, arthritis, and gout may also mimic golfer's elbow and may confuse the diagnosis. The olecranon bursa lies in the posterior aspect of the elbow joint and may also become inflamed as a result of direct trauma or overuse of the joint. Other bursae susceptible to the development of bursitis exist between the insertion of the biceps and the head of the radius as well as in the antecubital and cubital area (Fig. 64–4).

■ TREATMENT

Initial treatment of the pain and functional disability associated with golfer's elbow should include a combination of the nonsteroidal antiinflammatory agents or COX-2 inhibitors and physical therapy. The local application of heat and cold may also be beneficial. Avoidance of any repetitive activity that may exacerbate the patient's symptomatology should be avoided. For patients who do not respond to these treatment modalities, the following injection technique may be a reasonable next step.[4]

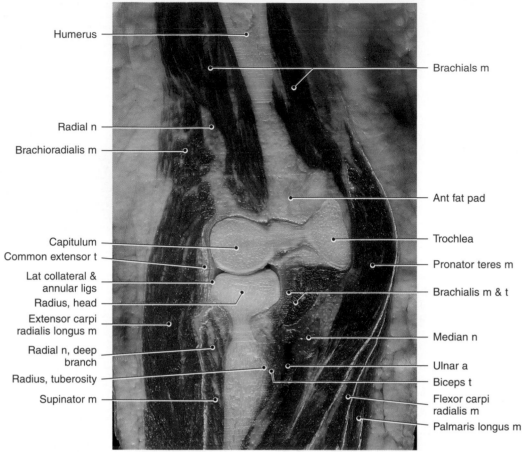

Humerus

Radial n

Brachioradialis m

Capitulum

Common extensor t

Lat collateral &
annular ligs

Radius, head

Extensor carpi
radialis longus m

Radial n, deep
branch

Radius, tuberosity

Supinator m

Brachials m

Ant fat pad

Trochlea

Pronator teres m

Brachialis m & t

Median n

Ulnar a

Biceps t

Flexor carpi
radialis m

Palmaris longus m

FIGURE 64–1 ■ Anatomy of the medial epicondyle. (From Kang SH, Ahn JM, Resnick D: MRI of the Extremities, 2nd ed. Philadelphia, Saunders, 2002, p 91.)

FIGURE 64–2 ■ The pain of golfer's elbow occurs at medial epicondyle. (From Waldman SD: Atlas of Common Pain Syndromes. Philadelphia, Saunders, 2002, p103.)

Injection for golfer's elbow is carried out by placing the patient in a supine position with the arm fully adducted at the patient's side and the elbow fully extended with the dorsum of the hand resting on a folded towel to relax the affected tendons. A total of 1 mL of local anesthetic and 40 mg of methylprednisolone is drawn up in a 5-mL sterile syringe.

After sterile preparation of skin overlying the medial aspect of the joint, the medial epicondyle is identified. Using strict aseptic technique, a 1-inch, 25-gauge needle is inserted perpendicular to the medial epicondyle through the skin and into the subcutaneous tissue overlying the affected tendon (Fig. 64–5). If bone is encountered, the needle is withdrawn into the subcutaneous tissue. The contents of the syringe is then gently injected. There should be little resistance to injection. If resistance is encountered, the needle is probably in the tendon and should be withdrawn until the injection proceeds without significant resistance. The needle is then removed and a sterile pressure dressing and ice pack are placed at the injection site.

■ SIDE EFFECTS AND COMPLICATIONS

The major complications associated with this injection technique are related to trauma to the inflamed and previously damaged tendons. Such tendons may rupture if directly injected and needle position should be confirmed outside the tendon prior to injection to avoid this complication. Another

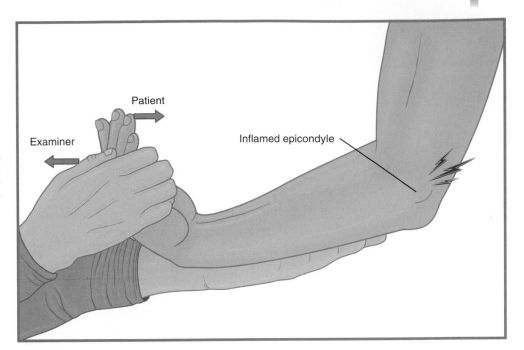

FIGURE 64–3 ■ Test for eliciting the pain of golfer's elbow. (From Waldman SD: Atlas of Pain Management Injection Techniques, Philadelphia, Saunders, 2000, p 89.)

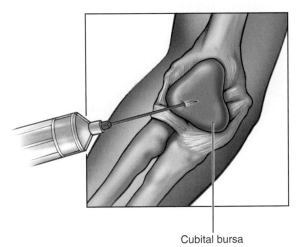

FIGURE 64–4 ■ Proper needle placement for injection for cubital bursitis. (From Waldman SD: Atlas of Uncommon Pain Syndromes. Philadelphia, Saunders, 2003, p 81.)

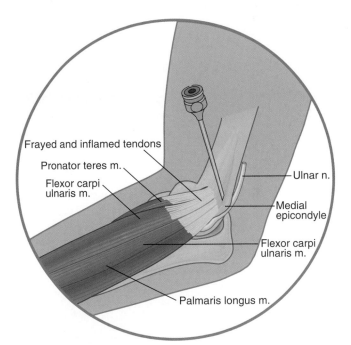

FIGURE 64–5 ■ Injection technique for relieving the pain due to golfer's elbow syndrome. (From Waldman SD: Atlas of Pain Management Injection Techniques, Philadelphia, Saunders, 2000, p 89.)

complication of this injection technique is infection. This complication should be exceedingly rare if strict aseptic technique is adhered to. The ulnar nerve is especially susceptible to damage at the elbow and care must be taken to avoid this nerve when injecting the elbow. Approximately 25% of patients will complain of a transient increase in pain following intra-articular injection of the elbow joint and should be warned of this.

This injection technique is extremely effective in the treatment of pain secondary to the golfer's elbow. Coexisting bursitis and tendinitis may also contribute to elbow pain and may require additional treatment with more localized injection of local anesthetic and depot steroid. This technique is a safe procedure if careful attention is paid to the clinically relevant anatomy in the areas to be injected. The use of physical modalities including local heat as well as gentle

range-of-motion exercises should be introduced several days after the patient undergoes this injection technique for elbow pain. A Velcro band placed around the flexor tendons may also help relieve the symptoms of golfer's elbow. Vigorous exercises should be avoided because they will exacerbate the patient's symptomatology. Simple analgesics and nonsteroidal antiinflammatory agents may be used concurrently with this injection technique. As mentioned earlier, cervical radiculopathy may mimic golfer's elbow and must be ruled out to effectively treat the underlying pathology.

■ CONCLUSION

Golfer's elbow is a common cause of elbow and forearm pain encountered in clinical practice. This painful condition frequently coexists with other elbow pathology including tendinitis, lateral epicondylitis, and bursitis. Entrapment neuropathy may also complicate the clinical picture. Identification of the activities responsible for the pathophysiology of golfer's elbow is paramount if rapid relief of pain and functional disability is to be achieved.

References

1. Coonrad RW, Hooper WR: Tennis elbow: Course, natural history, conservative and surgical management. J Bone Joint Surg Am 55:1177, 1973.
2. Waldman SD: Golfer's elbow. In Waldman SD: Atlas of Common Pain Syndromes. Philadelphia, Saunders, 2002, p 102.
3. Waldman SD: Cubital bursitis. In Waldman SD: Atlas of Uncommon Pain Syndromes. Philadelphia, Saunders, 2003, p 80.
4. Waldman SD: Golfer's elbow. In Waldman SD: Atlas of Pain Management Injection Techniques. Philadelphia, Saunders, 2000, p 87.

chapter 65

Olecranon and Cubital Bursitis

Steven D. Waldman

Olecranon and cubital bursitis are common causes of elbow pain encountered in clinical practice. Bursae are formed from synovial sacs whose purpose it is to allow easy sliding of muscles and tendons across one another at areas of repeated movement. These synovial sacs are lined with a synovial membrane which is invested with a network of blood vessels that secrete synovial fluid. Inflammation of the bursa will result in an increase in the production of synovial fluid with swelling of the bursal sac. With overuse or misuse, these bursae may become inflamed, enlarged, and, on rare occasions, infected. Although there is significant intrapatient variability as to the number, size, and location of bursae, anatomists have been able to identify a number of clinically relevant bursae including the olecranon and cubital bursae. The olecranon bursa lies in the posterior aspect of the elbow, whereas the cubital bursa lies in the anterior aspect. Both may exist as a single bursal sac or, in some patients, may exist as a multisegmented series of sacs that may be loculated.

■ OLECRANON BURSITIS

Olecranon bursitis may develop gradually due to repetitive irritation of the olecranon bursa or acutely due to trauma or infection.[1] The swelling associated with olecranon bursitis may, at times, be quite impressive and the patient may complain about difficulty in wearing a long-sleeved shirt (Fig. 65–1).

The olecranon bursa is vulnerable to injury from both acute trauma and repeated microtrauma. Acute injuries frequently take the form of direct trauma to the elbow when playing sports such as hockey or falling directly onto the olecranon process. Repeated pressure from leaning on the elbow to arise or from working long hours at a drafting table may result in inflammation and swelling of the olecranon bursa (Fig. 65–2). Gout or bacterial infection may rarely precipitate acute olecranon bursitis.[2] If the inflammation of the olecranon bursa becomes chronic, calcification of the bursa with residual nodules called *gravel* may occur.

Clinically Relevant Anatomy

The elbow joint is a synovial hinge-type joint that serves as the articulation between the humerus, radius, and ulna (Fig. 65–3). The joint's primary function is to position the wrist to optimize hand function. The joint allows flexion and

extension at the elbow as well as pronation and supination of the forearm. The joint is lined with synovium. The entire joint is covered by a dense capsule that thickens medially to form the ulnar collateral ligament and medially to form the radial collateral ligament (Fig. 65–4). These dense ligaments, coupled with the elbow joint's deep bony socket, makes this joint extremely stable and relatively resistant to subluxation and dislocation. The anterior and posterior joint capsule is less dense and may become distended if there is a joint effusion.

The elbow joint is innervated primarily by the musculocutaneous and radial nerves with the ulnar and median nerves providing varying degrees of innervation. At the middle of the upper arm, the ulnar nerve courses medially to pass between the olecranon process and medial epicondyle of the humerus. The nerve is susceptible to entrapment and trauma at this point. At the elbow, the median nerve lies just medial to the brachial artery and is occasionally damaged during brachial artery cannulation for blood gases.

Signs and Symptoms

The patient suffering from olecranon bursitis will frequently complain of pain and swelling with any movement of the elbow, but especially with extension. The pain is localized to the olecranon area with referred pain often noted above the elbow joint.[3] Often the patient will be more concerned about the swelling around the bursa than the pain. Physical examination will reveal point tenderness over the olecranon and swelling of the bursa which at times can be quite extensive (see Figs. 65–1 and 65–2).[4] Passive flexion and resisted extension of the elbow will reproduce the pain as will any pressure over the bursa. Fever and chills will usually accompany infection of the bursa. If infection is suspected, aspiration, Gram stain, and culture of the bursa followed by treatment with appropriate antibiotics is indicated on an emergent basis.

Testing

The diagnosis of olecranon bursitis is usually made on clinical grounds alone. Plain radiographs of the posterior elbow are indicated if there is a history of elbow trauma or if arthritis of the elbow is suspected. Plain radiographs may also reveal calcification of the bursa and associated structures

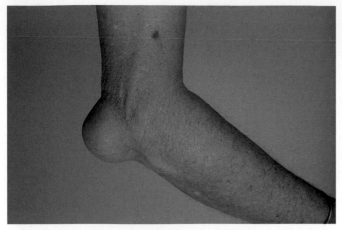

FIGURE 65–1 ■ Olecranon bursitis in early rheumatoid arthritis. (From Klippel JH, Dieppe PA [eds]: Rheumatology, 2nd ed. London, Mosby, 1998, p 4.14.3.)

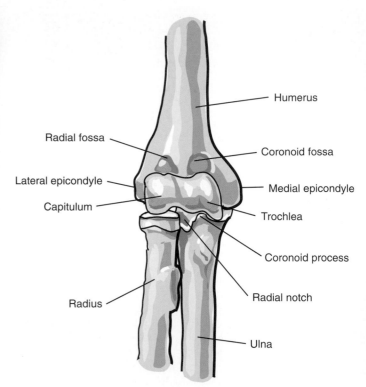

FIGURE 65–3 ■ Clinically relevant anatomy of the elbow. The elbow joint is a synovial hinge-type joint which serves as the articulation between the humerus, radius, and ulna.

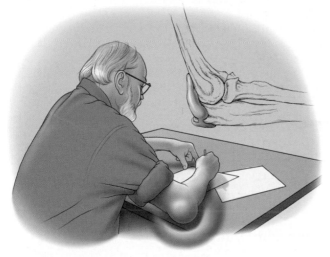

FIGURE 65–2 ■ Olecranon bursitis is often caused by repeated pressure on the elbow. (From Waldman SD: Atlas of Common Pain Syndromes. Philadelphia, Saunders, 2002, p 111.)

consistent with chronic inflammation (Fig. 65–5). MRI scan is indicated if infection or joint instability is suspected (Fig. 65–6). Complete blood count, automated chemistry profile including uric acid, sedimentation rate, and antinuclear antibody are indicated if collagen vascular disease is suspected. If infection is considered, aspiration, Gram stain, and culture of bursal fluid is indicated on an emergent basis.

Differential Diagnosis

Olecranon bursitis is usually a straightforward clinical diagnosis. Occasionally, rheumatoid nodules or gouty arthritis of the elbow may confuse the clinician. Synovial cysts of the elbow may also mimic olecranon bursitis. It should be remembered that coexisting tendinitis, (e.g., tennis elbow and golfer's elbow) may require additional treatment.

Treatment

A short course of conservative therapy consisting of simple analgesics, nonsteroidal antiinflammatory agents or COX-2 inhibitors, and an elbow protector to prevent further trauma is a reasonable first step in the treatment of patients suffering from olecranon bursitis. If the patient does not experience rapid improvement, the following injection technique is a reasonable next step.[5]

The patient is placed in a supine position with the arm fully adducted at the patient's side and the elbow flexed with the palm of the hand resting on the patient's abdomen. A total of 2 mL of local anesthetic and 40 mg of methylprednisolone is drawn up in a 5-mL sterile syringe. After sterile preparation of skin overlying the posterior aspect of the joint, the olecranon process and overlying bursa is identified. Using strict aseptic technique, a 1-inch, 25-gauge needle is inserted through the skin and subcutaneous tissues directly into the bursa in the midline (Fig. 65–7). If bone is encountered, the needle is withdrawn into the bursa. After entering the bursa, the contents of the syringe is gently injected. There should be little resistance to injection. The needle is then removed and a sterile pressure dressing and ice pack are placed at the injection site.

■ CUBITAL BURSITIS

The cubital bursa is vulnerable to injury from both acute trauma and repeated microtrauma. Acute injuries frequently take the form of direct trauma to the anterior aspect of the elbow. Repetitive movements of the elbow including throwing javelins and baseballs may result in inflammation and

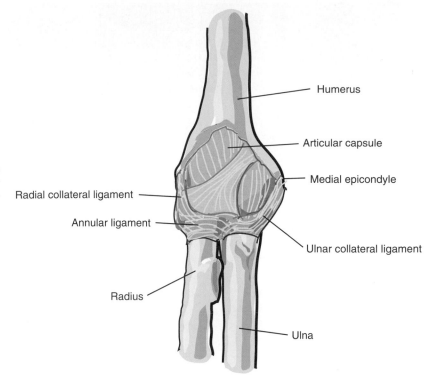

FIGURE 65–4 ■ The entire elbow joint is covered by a dense capsule that thickens medially to form the ulnar collateral ligament and medially to form the radial collateral ligament.

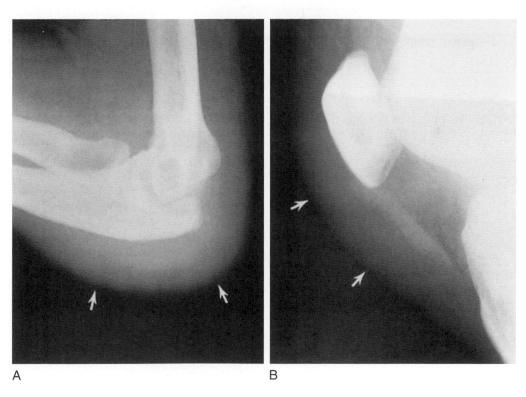

FIGURE 65–5 ■ Septic bursitis. **A,** Olecranon bursitis. Note olecranon swelling (*arrows*) and soft tissue edema due to *Staphylococcus aureus*. Previous surgery and trauma are the causes of the adjacent bony abnormalities. **B,** Prepatellar bursitis. This 28-year-old carpenter who had worked on his knees for prolonged periods of time developed tender swelling in front of the knee (*arrows*). Inflammatory fluid that was culture-positive for *Staphylococcus aureus* was recovered from the bursa. (From Resnick D [ed]: Diagnosis of Bone and Joint Disorders, 4th ed. Philadelphia, Saunders, 2002, p 2438.)

swelling of the cubital bursa. Gout or rheumatoid arthritis may rarely precipitate acute cubital bursitis. If the inflammation of the cubital bursa becomes chronic, calcification of the bursa may occur.

The patient suffering from cubital bursitis will frequently complain of pain and swelling with any movement of the

elbow (Fig. 65–8). The pain is localized to the cubital area with referred pain often noted in the forearm and hand. Physical examination will reveal point tenderness in the anterior aspect of the elbow over the cubital bursa and swelling of the bursa. Passive extension and resisted flexion of the shoulder will reproduce the pain—as will any pressure over the bursa.

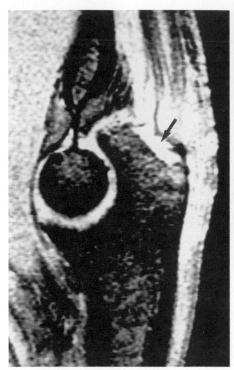

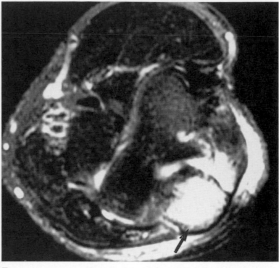

A

B

FIGURE 65–6 ■ Septic olecranon bursitis. A sagittal MPGR (TR/TE, 500/11; flip angle, 15 degrees) MR image (**A**) reveals abnormal high signal intensity in the region of the olecranon bursa with bone involvement (*arrow*), also of high signal intensity. A transaxial fat-suppressed fast spin echo (TR/TE, 5000/108) MR image (**B**) confirms bone involvement (*arrow*). (From Resnick D [ed]: Diagnosis of Bone and Joint Disorders, 4th ed. Philadelphia, Saunders, 2002, p 2439.)

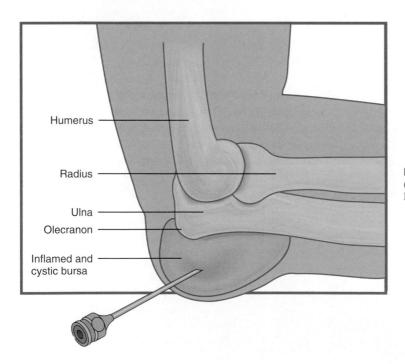

Humerus

Radius

Ulna

Olecranon

Inflamed and
cystic bursa

FIGURE 65–7 ■ Injection technique for olecranon bursitis pain. (From Waldman SD: Atlas of Pain Management Injection Techniques. Philadelphia, Saunders, 2000, p 91.)

Plain radiographs of the posterior elbow may reveal calcification of the bursa and associated structures consistent with chronic inflammation.

Clinically Relevant Anatomy

The elbow joint is a synovial hinge-type joint that serves as the articulation between the humerus, radius, and ulna (see Fig. 65–3). The joint's primary function is to position the wrist to optimize hand function. The joint allows flexion and extension at the elbow as well as pronation and supination of the forearm. The joint is lined with synovium. The entire joint is covered by a dense capsule that thickens medially to form the ulnar collateral ligament and medially to form the radial collateral ligaments (see Fig. 65–4). These dense ligaments coupled with the elbow joint's deep bony socket makes this joint extremely stable and relatively resistant to subluxation and dislocation. The anterior and posterior joint

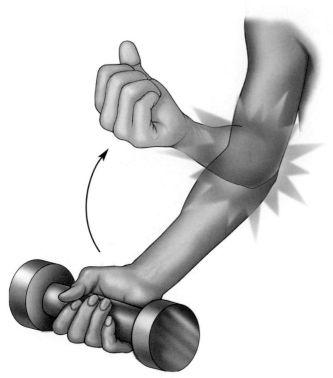

FIGURE 65–8 ■ A patient suffering from cubital bursitis complains of pain and swelling on movement of the elbow. (From Waldman SD: Atlas of Uncommon Pain Syndromes. Philadelphia, Saunders, 2003, p 81.)

capsule is less dense and may become distended if there is a joint effusion.

The cubital fossa lies in the anterior aspect of the elbow joint and is bounded laterally by the brachioradialis muscle, medially by the pronator teres, and contains the median nerve which is susceptible to irritation and compression from a swollen, inflamed cubital bursa. The elbow joint is innervated primarily by the musculocutaneous and radial nerves with the ulnar and median nerves providing varying degrees of innervation. At the middle of the upper arm, the ulnar nerve courses medially to pass between the olecranon process and medial epicondyle of the humerus. The nerve is susceptible to entrapment and trauma at this point. At the elbow, the median nerve lies just medial to the brachial artery and is occasionally damaged during brachial artery cannulation for blood gases. The median nerve may also be injured during injection of the cubital bursa.

Signs and Symptoms

The patient suffering from cubital bursitis will frequently complain of pain and swelling with any movement of the elbow, but especially with flexion. The pain is localized to the cubital fossa with referred pain often noted above the elbow joint.[6] Often the patient will be more concerned about the swelling around the bursa than the pain. Physical examination will reveal point tenderness over the cubital bursa and swelling of the bursa that, at times, can be quite extensive.[6] Passive extension and resisted flexion of the elbow will reproduce the pain as will any pressure over the bursa. Fever and chills will usually accompany infection of the bursa. If infection is suspected, aspiration, Gram stain, and culture of the bursa followed by treatment with appropriate antibiotics is indicated on an emergent basis.

Testing

The diagnosis of cubital bursitis is usually made on clinical grounds alone. Plain radiographs of the posterior elbow are indicated if there is a history of elbow trauma or arthritis of the elbow is suspected. Plain radiographs may also reveal calcification of the bursa and associated structures consistent with chronic inflammation. MRI scan is indicated if infection or joint instability is suspected. Complete blood count, automated chemistry profile including uric acid, sedimentation rate, and antinuclear antibody testing is indicated if collagen vascular disease is suspected. If infection is considered, aspiration, Gram stain, and culture of bursal fluid is indicated on an emergent basis

Differential Diagnosis

Cubital bursitis is usually a straightforward clinical diagnosis. Occasionally, rheumatoid nodules or gouty arthritis of the elbow may confuse the clinician. Occasionally, synovial cysts of the elbow may also mimic cubital bursitis. It should be remembered that coexistent tendinitis (e.g., tennis elbow and golfer's elbow) may require additional treatment.

Treatment

A short course of conservative therapy consisting of simple analgesics, nonsteroidal antiinflammatory agents or COX-2 inhibitors, and an elbow protector to prevent further trauma is a reasonable first step in the treatment of patients suffering from cubital bursitis. If the patient does not experience rapid improvement, the following injection technique is a reasonable next step.[7]

The patient is placed in a supine position with the arm fully adducted at the patient's side and the elbow extended with the dorsum of the hand resting on a folded towel. A total of 2 mL of local anesthetic and 40 mg of methylprednisolone is drawn up in a 5-mL sterile syringe. The clinician identifies the pulsations of the brachial artery at the crease of the elbow. After preparation of the skin with antiseptic solution, a 1-inch, 25-gauge needle is inserted just lateral to the brachial artery at the crease and slowly advanced in a slightly medial and cephalad trajectory through the skin and subcutaneous tissues (Fig. 65–9). If bone is encountered, the needle is withdrawn into the subcutaneous tissue. The contents of the syringe is then gently injected. There should be little resistance to injection. If resistance is encountered, the needle is probably in the tendon and should be withdrawn until the injection proceeds without significant resistance. The needle is then removed and a sterile pressure dressing and ice pack are placed at the injection site.

Injection of the cubital bursa at the elbow is a relatively safe block with the major complications being inadvertent intravascular injection and persistent paresthesia secondary to needle trauma to the median nerve. This technique can safely be performed in the presence of anticoagulation by using a 25- or 27-gauge needle, albeit at increased risk of hematoma, if the clinical situation dictates a favorable risk-to-benefit ratio. These complications can be decreased if manual pres-

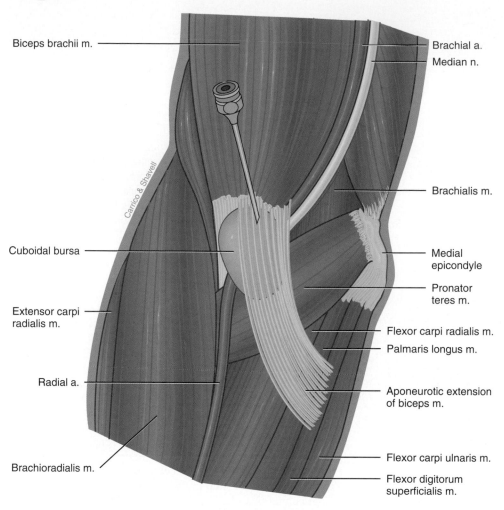

Biceps brachii m.

Brachial a.

Median n.

Brachialis m.

Cuboidal bursa

Medial
epicondyle

Pronator
teres m.

Extensor carpi
radialis m.

Flexor carpi radialis m.

Palmaris longus m.

Radial a.

Aponeurotic extension
of biceps m.

Flexor carpi ulnaris m.

Flexor digitorum
superficialis m.

Brachioradialis m.

Carrico & Shavell

FIGURE 65–9 ■ Injection technique
for cubital bursitis pain. (From Waldman
SD: Atlas of Pain Management Injection
Techniques. Philadelphia, Saunders, 2000,
p 95.)

sure is applied to the area of the block immediately following injection. Application of cold packs for 20-minute periods
following the block will also decrease the amount of post-procedure pain and bleeding the patient may experience.

■ CONCLUSION

Olecranon and cubital bursitis are common causes of elbow
pain encountered in clinical practice. Coexistent tendinitis and
epicondylitis often contribute to elbow pain and may require
additional treatment with more localized injection of local
anesthetic and depot steroid. Failure to adequately treat olecranon and cubital bursitis may result in the development of
chronic pain and loss of range of motion of the affected elbow.

References

1. Groff GD: Olecranon bursitis. In Klippel JH, Dieppe PA (eds): Rheumatology, 2nd ed. London, Mosby, 1998, p 4.14.3.
2. Raddazt DA, Hoffman GS, Frank WA: Septic bursitis: Presentation,
   treatment and prognosis. J Rheumatol 14:1160, 1987.
3. McAfee JH, Smith DL: Olecranon and prepatellar bursitis: Diagnosis and
   treatment. West J Med 149:607, 1988.
4. Waldman SD: Olecranon bursitis. In Waldman SD: Atlas of Common Pain
   Syndromes. Philadelphia, Saunders, 2002, p 109.
5. Waldman SD: Olecranon bursitis pain. In Waldman SD: Atlas of Pain
   Management Injection Techniques. Philadelphia, Saunders, 2000,
   p 90.
6. Waldman SD: Cubital bursitis. In Waldman SD: Atlas of Uncommon Pain
   Syndromes. Philadelphia, Saunders, 2003, p 80.
7. Waldman SD: Cubital bursitis pain. In Waldman SD: Atlas of Pain Management Injection Techniques. Philadelphia, Saunders, 2000, p 93.

Entrapment Neuropathies of the Elbow and Forearm

Steven D. Waldman

Entrapment neuropathies of the elbow and forearm provide significant diagnostic and therapeutic challenges to the clinician. Although reasonably common in clinical practice, they are frequently misdiagnosed and mistreated. This chapter will provide the clinician with a concise review of these clinical syndromes and present a step-by-step guide to treatment.

■ TARDY ULNAR PALSY

Ulnar nerve entrapment at the elbow is one of the most common entrapment neuropathies encountered in clinical practice.[1] The causes include compression of the ulnar nerve by an aponeurotic band that runs from the medial epicondyle of the humerus to the medial border of the olecranon, direct trauma to the ulnar nerve at the elbow, and repetitive elbow motion (Fig. 66–1). Ulnar nerve entrapment at the elbow is also called *tardy ulnar palsy, cubital tunnel syndrome,* and *ulnar nerve neuritis.* This entrapment neuropathy manifests as pain and associated paresthesias in the lateral forearm, which radiates to the wrist and ring and little finger (Fig. 66–2). Some patients suffering from ulnar nerve entrapment at the elbow may also notice pain referred to the medial aspect of the scapula on the affected side. Untreated, ulnar nerve entrapment at the elbow can result in a progressive motor deficit and ultimately flexion contracture of the affected fingers can result. The onset of symptoms is usually after repetitive elbow motion or from repeated pressure on the elbow, such as using the elbows to arise from bed. Direct trauma to the ulnar nerve as it enters the cubital tunnel may also result in a similar clinical presentation. Patients with vulnerable nerve syndrome (e.g., diabetics, alcoholics) are at greater risk for the development of ulnar nerve entrapment at the elbow (Fig. 66–3).

Signs and Symptoms

Physical findings include tenderness over the ulnar nerve at the elbow. A positive Tinel sign over the ulnar nerve as it passes beneath the aponeuroses is usually present. Weakness of the intrinsic muscles of the forearm and hand that are inner-vated by the ulnar nerve may be identified with careful manual muscle testing, although early in the course of the evolution of cubital tunnel syndrome, the only physical finding other than tenderness over the nerve may be the loss of sensation on the ulnar side of the little finger. Muscle wasting of the intrinsic muscles of the hand can best be identified by viewing the hand with the palm down. Tinel sign at the elbow is often present when the ulnar nerve is stimulated.

Testing

Electromyography with nerve conduction velocity testing is an extremely sensitive test and the skilled electromyographer can diagnose ulnar nerve entrapment at the elbow with a high degree of accuracy—as well as help sort out other neuropathic causes of pain that may mimic ulnar nerve entrapment at the elbow—including radiculopathy and plexopathy (see later). Plain radiographs are indicated in all patients who present with ulnar nerve entrapment at the elbow to rule out occult bony pathology. If surgery is contemplated, an MRI scan of the affected elbow may help further delineate that pathologic process responsible for the nerve entrapment (e.g., bone spur, tumor, or aponeurotic band thickening (Fig. 66–4). If Pancoast tumor or other tumors of the brachial plexus are suspected, chest radiographs with apical lordotic views may be helpful. Screening laboratory testing consisting of complete blood count, erythrocyte sedimentation rate, antinuclear antibody testing, and automated blood chemistry testing should be performed if the diagnosis of ulnar nerve entrapment at the elbow is in question to help rule out other causes of the patient's pain. The injection technique described subsequently will serve as a diagnostic and a therapeutic maneuver.[2]

Differential Diagnosis

Ulnar nerve entrapment at the elbow is often misdiagnosed as golfer's elbow and this fact accounts for the many patients whose "golfer's elbow" fails to respond to conservative measures.[3] Cubital tunnel syndrome can be distinguished from golfer's elbow in that in cubital tunnel syndrome, the

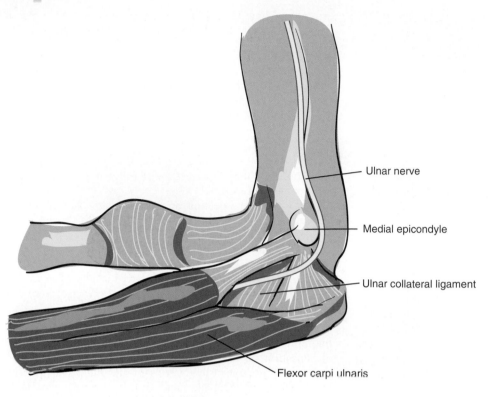

Ulnar nerve

Medial epicondyle

Ulnar collateral ligament

Flexor carpi ulnaris

FIGURE 66–1 ■ The causes of ulnar nerve entrapment at the elbow include compression of the ulnar nerve by an aponeurotic band that runs from the medial epicondyle of the humerus to the medial border of the olecranon, direct trauma to the ulnar nerve at the elbow, and repetitive elbow motion.

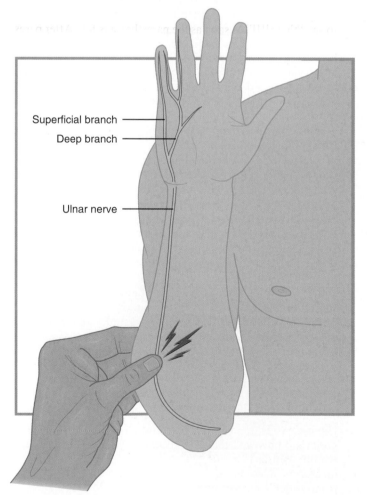

Superficial branch

Deep branch

Ulnar nerve

FIGURE 66–2 ■ Ulnar nerve entrapment at the elbow manifests as pain and associated paresthesias in the lateral forearm, which radiates to the wrist and ring and little finger. (From Waldman SD: Atlas of Pain Management Injection Techniques. Philadelphia, Saunders, 2000, p 105.)

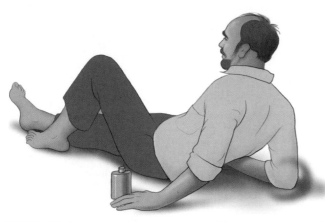

FIGURE 66–3 ■ The ulnar nerve is susceptible to compression at the elbow. (From Waldman SD: Atlas of Common Pain Syndromes. Philadelphia, Saunders, 2002, p 107.)

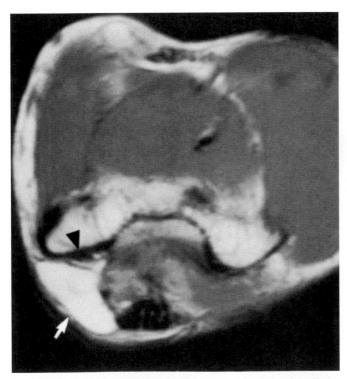

FIGURE 66–4 ■ Entrapment of the ulnar nerve: cubital tunnel syndrome. A lipoma (*arrow*) adjacent to the ulnar nerve (*arrowhead*) is well shown in these transverse intermediate-weighted (TR/TE 2000/20) spin echo MR images. The lipoma led to clinical findings of ulnar nerve entrapment in this 36-year-old man. (Courtesy of Z. Rosenberg, MD, New York.)

maximal tenderness to palpation is over the ulnar nerve 1 inch below the medial epicondyle, whereas with golfer's elbow, the maximal tenderness to palpation is directly over the medial epicondyle. Cubital tunnel syndrome should also be differentiated from cervical radiculopathy involving the C7 or C8 roots and golfer's elbow. It should be remembered that cervical radiculopathy and ulnar nerve entrapment may coexist as the so-called "double crush" syndrome. The double

crush syndrome is seen most commonly with median nerve entrapment at the wrist or carpal tunnel syndrome.[4]

Treatment

A short course of conservative therapy consisting of simple analgesics, nonsteroidal antiinflammatory agents or COX-2 inhibitors, and splinting to avoid elbow flexion is indicated in patients who present with ulnar nerve entrapment at the elbow. If the patient does not experience a marked improvement in symptoms within 1 week, careful injection of the ulnar nerve at the elbow using the following technique is a reasonable next step.[2]

Ulnar nerve injection at the elbow is carried out by placing the patient in the supine position with the arm fully adducted at the patient's side and the elbow slightly flexed with the dorsum of the hand resting on a folded towel. A total of 5 to 7 mL of local anesthetic is drawn up in a 12-mL sterile syringe. A total of 80 mg of depot steroid is added to the local anesthetic with the first block and 40 mg of depot steroid is added with subsequent blocks.

The clinician then identifies the olecranon process and the medial epicondyle of the humerus. The ulnar nerve sulcus between these two bony landmarks is then identified. After preparation of the skin with antiseptic solution, a 5/8-inch, 25-gauge needle is inserted just proximal to the sulcus and is slowly advanced in a slightly cephalad trajectory (Fig. 66–5). As the needle advances approximately $\frac{1}{2}$ inch, a strong paresthesia in the distribution of the ulnar nerve will be elicited. The patient should be warned that a paresthesia will occur and to say "there!!!!" as soon as the paresthesia is felt. After paresthesia is elicited and its distribution identified, gentle aspiration is carried out to identify blood. If the aspiration test is negative and no persistent paresthesia into the distribution of the ulnar nerve remains, 5 to 7 mL of solution is slowly injected, with the patient being monitored closely for signs of local anesthetic toxicity. If no paresthesia can be elicited, a similar amount of solution is slowly injected in a fan-like manner just proximal to the notch with care being taken to avoid intravascular injection.

If the patient does not respond to the aforementioned treatments or if the patient is experiencing progressive neurologic deficit, strong consideration to surgical decompression of the ulnar nerve is indicated. As mentioned earlier, MRI scanning of the affected elbow should help clarify the pathology responsible for compression of the ulnar nerve.

Complications and Pitfalls

Failure to promptly identify and treat ulnar nerve entrapment at the elbow can result in permanent neurologic deficit. It is also important to rule out other causes of pain and numbness that may mimic the symptoms of ulnar nerve entrapment at the elbow, such as Pancoast tumor, to avoid harm to the patient.

Ulnar nerve block at the elbow is a relatively safe block with the major complications being inadvertent intravascular injection into the ulnar artery and persistent paresthesia secondary to needle trauma to the nerve. Care should be taken to slowly inject just proximal to the sulcus to avoid additional compromise of the nerve because, as the nerve passes through the ulnar nerve sulcus, it is enclosed by a dense fibrous band.

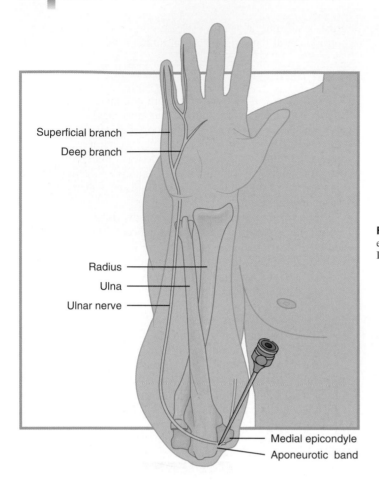

Superficial branch

Deep branch

Radius

Ulna

Ulnar nerve

Medial epicondyle

Aponeurotic band

FIGURE 66–5 ■ Injection technique for relieving pain due to ulnar nerve entrapment at the elbow. (From Waldman SD: Atlas of Pain Management Injection Techniques. Philadelphia, Saunders, 2000, p 105.)

■ THE PRONATOR SYNDROME

There are several sites of entrapment of the median nerve in the forearm. The median nerve may be entrapped at the lacertus fibrosus, at the lateral edge of the flexor digitorum superficialis, by fibrous bands of the superficial head of the pronator teres muscle, or most commonly, by the pronator teres muscle itself (Fig. 66–6). Compression of the median nerve by the pronator teres muscle is called *pronator syndrome*.[5] The onset of symptoms is usually after repetitive elbow motions such as chopping wood, sculling, or cleaning fish—although occasionally the onset is more insidious without apparent antecedent trauma (Fig. 66–7). Clinically, pronator syndrome manifests as a chronic aching sensation localized to the forearm with pain occasionally radiating into the elbow. Patients with pronator syndrome may complain about a tired or heavy sensation in the forearm with minimal activity as well as clumsiness of the affected extremity. The sensory symptoms of pronator syndrome are identical to those of carpal tunnel syndrome. However, in contradistinction to carpal tunnel syndrome, nighttime symptomatology is unusual with pronator syndrome.[5]

Signs and Symptoms

The physical findings of pronator syndrome include tenderness over the forearm in the region of the pronator teres muscle. Unilateral hypertrophy of the pronator teres muscle

may be identified. A positive Tinel sign over the median nerve as it passes beneath the pronator teres muscle may also be present. Weakness of the intrinsic muscles of the forearm and hand that are innervated by the median nerve may be identified with careful manual muscle testing. A positive pronator syndrome test, which is pain on forced pronation of the patient's fully supinated arm, is highly suggestive of compression of the median nerve by the pronator teres muscle (Fig. 66–8).

Testing

Electromyography will help distinguish cervical radiculopathy, thoracic outlet syndrome, and carpal tunnel syndrome from pronator syndrome. Plain radiographs are indicated in all patients who present with pronator syndrome to rule out occult bony pathology. Based on the patient's clinical presentation, additional testing including complete blood count, uric acid, sedimentation rate, and antinuclear antibody testing may be indicated. MRI scan of the forearm is indicated if primary elbow pathology or a space-occupying lesion is suspected (Fig. 66–9). The injection of the median nerve at the elbow will serve as a diagnostic and a therapeutic maneuver.

Differential Diagnosis

Median nerve entrapment by the ligament of Struthers manifests clinically as unexplained persistent forearm pain caused

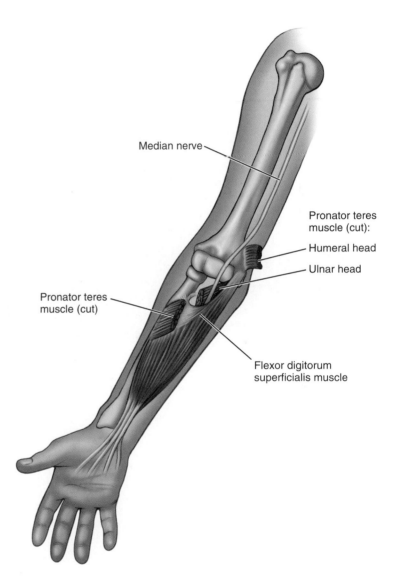

FIGURE 66–6 ■ The symptoms of pronator syndrome are due to compression of the median nerve by the pronator teres muscle. (From Waldman SD: Atlas of Uncommon Pain Syndromes. Philadelphia, Saunders, 2003, p 78.)

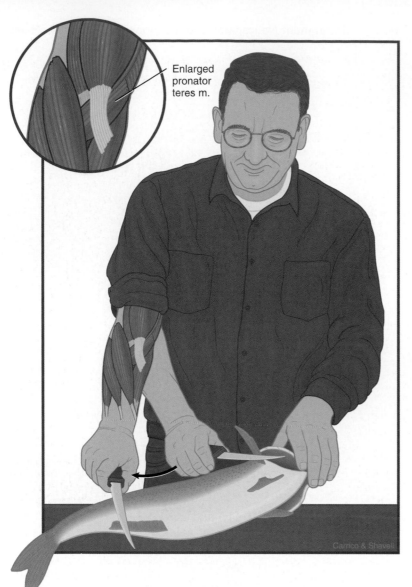

Enlarged pronator teres m.

FIGURE 66–7 ■ The onset of pronator syndrome is usually after repetitive elbow motions such as chopping wood, sculling, or cleaning fish, although occasionally the onset is more insidious without apparent antecedent trauma. (From Waldman SD: Atlas of Pain Management Injection Techniques. Philadelphia, Saunders, 2000, p 97.)

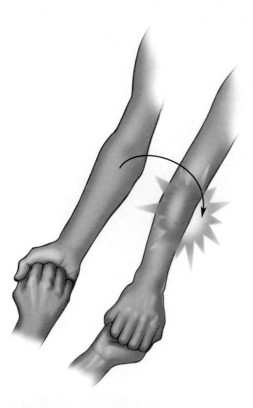

FIGURE 66–8 ■ A positive pronator syndrome test is highly indicative of pronator syndrome. (From Waldman SD: Atlas of Uncommon Pain Syndromes. Philadelphia, Saunders, 2003, p 79.)

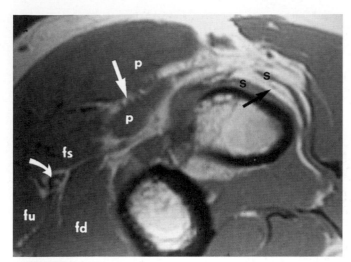

FIGURE 66–9 ∎ Median nerve anatomy. Transverse T1-weighted (TR/TE 500/20) spin echo MR image at the level of the proximal portion of the forearm of an extended elbow shows the median nerve (*straight white arrow*) located between the two heads of the pronator teres (*p*) muscles; the ulnar nerve (*curved white arrow*) between the flexor digitorum profundus (*fd*), flexor digitorum superficialis (*fs*), and flexor carpi ulnaris (*fu*) muscles; and the radial nerve (*black arrow*) between the two heads of the supinartor (*s*) muscle. (From Kim YS, Yeh LR, Trudell D, et al: Skeletal Radiol 27:419, 1998.)

by compression of the median nerve by an aberrant ligament that runs from a supracondylar process to the medial epicondyle. Clinically, it is difficult to distinguish from pronator syndrome. The diagnosis is made by electromyography and nerve conduction velocity testing, which demonstrate compression of the median nerve at the elbow, combined with the radiographic finding of a supracondylar process.

Both of these entrapment neuropathies can be differentiated from isolated compression of the anterior interosseous nerve that occurs some 6 to 8 cm below the elbow. These syndromes should also be differentiated from cervical radiculopathy involving the C6 or C7 roots that may, at times, mimic median nerve compression. It should be remembered that cervical radiculopathy and median nerve entrapment may coexist as the so-called "double crush" syndrome. The double crush syndrome is seen most commonly with median nerve entrapment at the wrist or carpal tunnel syndrome. Thoracic outlet syndrome may also cause forearm pain and be confused with pronator syndrome. However, the pain of thoracic outlet syndrome radiates into the ulnar rather than the median portion of the hand.

Treatment

The nonsteroidal antiinflammatory agents or COX-2 inhibitors represent a reasonable first step in the treatment of pronator syndrome. The use of the tricyclic antidepressants such as nortriptyline at a single bedtime dose of 25 mg titrating upward as side effects allow will be useful, especially if sleep disturbance is also present. Avoidance of repetitive trauma thought to be contributing to this entrapment neuropathy is also important. If these maneuvers fail to produce rapid symptomatic relief, injection of the median nerve at the elbow with local anesthetic and steroid is a reasonable next

step (Fig. 66–10).[6] If symptoms continue to persist, surgical exploration and release of the median nerve is indicated.

Complications and Pitfalls

Median nerve block at the elbow is a relatively safe block with the major complications being inadvertent intravascular injection and persistent paresthesia secondary to needle trauma to the nerve. This technique can safely be performed in the presence of anticoagulation by utilizing a 25- or 27-gauge needle, albeit at increased risk of hematoma if the clinical situation dictates a favorable risk-to-benefit ratio. These complications can be decreased if manual pressure is applied to the area of the block immediately following injection. Application of cold packs for 20-minute periods following the block will also decrease the amount of post-procedure pain and bleeding the patient may experience.

∎ ANTERIOR INTEROSSEOUS SYNDROME

Anterior interosseous syndrome is characterized by pain and muscle weakness secondary to median nerve compression syndrome below the elbow by the tendinous origins of the pronator teres muscle and flexor digitorum superficialis muscle of the long finger or by aberrant blood vessels (Fig. 66–11). The onset of symptoms is usually after acute trauma to the forearm or following repetitive forearm and elbow motions such as using an ice pick. An inflammatory etiology analogous to Parsonage-Turner syndrome has also been suggested as a cause of anterior interosseous syndrome.

Clinically, anterior interosseous syndrome manifests as an acute pain in the proximal forearm.[7] As the syndrome progresses, patients with anterior interosseous syndrome may complain about a tired or heavy sensation in the forearm with minimal activity as well as the inability to pinch items between the thumb and index fingers due to paralysis of the flexor pollicis longus and the flexor digitorum profundus (see Fig. 66–11).

Physical findings include the inability to flex the interphalangeal joint of the thumb and the distal interphalangeal joint of the index finger due to paralysis of the flexor pollicis longus and the flexor digitorum profundus.[8] Tenderness over the forearm in the region of the pronator teres muscle is seen in some patients suffering from anterior interosseous syndrome. A positive Tinel sign over the anterior interosseous branch of the median nerve approximately 6 to 8 cm below the elbow may also be present.

The anterior interosseous syndrome should also be differentiated from cervical radiculopathy involving the C6 or C7 roots that may at times mimic median nerve compression. Furthermore, it should be remembered that cervical radiculopathy and median nerve entrapment may coexist as the so-called "double crush" syndrome. The double crush syndrome is seen most commonly with median nerve entrapment at the wrist or carpal tunnel syndrome.

Clinically Relevant Anatomy

The median nerve is composed of fibers from C5-T1 spinal roots. The nerve lies anterior and superior to the axillary

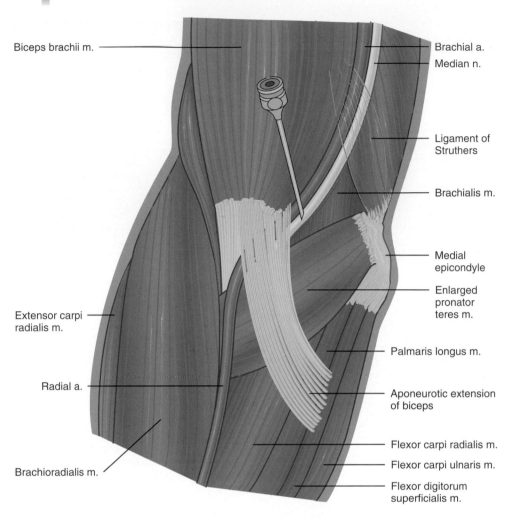

Biceps brachii m.

Brachial a.

Median n.

Ligament of Struthers

Brachialis m.

Medial epicondyle

Enlarged pronator teres m.

Extensor carpi radialis m.

Palmaris longus m.

Radial a.

Aponeurotic extension of biceps

Flexor carpi radialis m.

Flexor carpi ulnaris m.

Brachioradialis m.

Flexor digitorum superficialis m.

FIGURE 66–10 ■ Injection technique for relieving pain due to pronator syndrome. (From Waldman SD: Atlas of Pain Management Injection Techniques. Philadelphia, Saunders, 2000, p 99.)

artery. Exiting the axilla, the median nerve descends into the upper arm along with the brachial artery. At the level of the elbow, the brachial artery is just medial to the biceps muscle. At this level, the median nerve lies just medial to the brachial artery. As the median nerve proceeds downward into the forearm, it gives off numerous branches that provide motor innervation to the flexor muscles of the forearm including the anterior interosseous nerve. These branches are susceptible to nerve entrapment by aberrant ligaments, muscle hypertrophy, and direct trauma. The nerve approaches the wrist overlying the radius. It lies deep to and between the tendons of the palmaris longus muscle and the flexor carpi radialis muscle at the wrist. The terminal branches of the median nerve provide sensory innervation to a portion of the palmar surface of the hand as well as the palmar surface of the thumb, index, middle and the radial portion of the ring finger. The median nerve also provides sensory innervation to the distal dorsal surface of the index and middle finger and the radial portion of the ring finger.

Treatment

The nonsteroidal antiinflammatory agents or COX-2 inhibitors represent a reasonable first step in the treatment of

pronator syndrome. The use of a tricyclic antidepressant such as nortriptyline at a single bedtime dose of 25 mg titrating upward as side effects allow will also be useful, especially if sleep disturbance is also present. Avoidance of repetitive trauma thought to be contributing to this entrapment neuropathy is also important. If these maneuvers fail to produce rapid symptomatic relief, injection of the median nerve at the forearm with local anesthetic and steroid is a reasonable next step.[7] If symptoms continue to persist, surgical exploration and release of the median nerve is indicated.

The patient is placed in a supine position with the arm fully adducted at the patient's side and the elbow slightly flexed with the dorsum of the hand resting on a folded towel. A total of 5 to 7 mL of local anesthetic and 40 mg of methylprednisolone is drawn up in a 12 mL sterile syringe. The patient is then asked to flex his or her forearm against resistance to identify the biceps tendon at the crease of the elbow. A point 6 to 8 cm below the biceps tendon is then identified and marked with a sterile skin marker.

After preparation of the skin with antiseptic solution, an 1½-inch, 25-gauge needle is inserted at the previously marked point and slowly advanced in a slightly cephalad trajectory

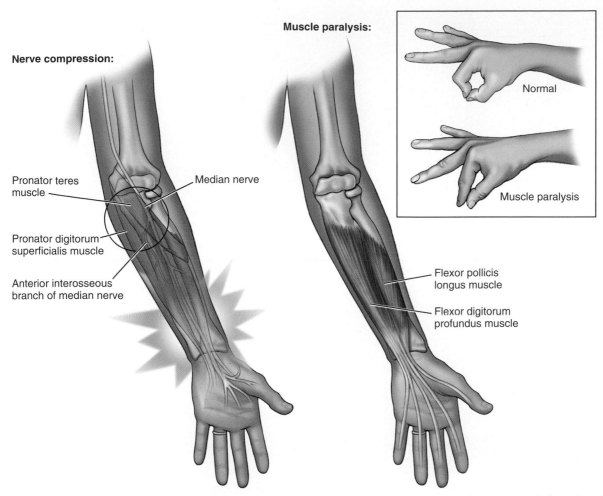

Nerve compression:

Muscle paralysis:

Pronator teres muscle

Median nerve

Pronator digitorum superficialis muscle

Anterior interosseous branch of median nerve

Normal

Muscle paralysis

Flexor pollicis longus muscle

Flexor digitorum profundus muscle

FIGURE 66–11 ■ Patients suffering from anterior interosseous syndrome exhibit acute forearm pain and progressive weakness of pinch. (From Waldman SD: Atlas of Uncommon Pain Syndromes. Philadelphia, Saunders, 2003, p 87.)

(Fig. 66–12). As the needle advances approximately ½ to ¾ inch, a strong paresthesia in the distribution of the median nerve will be elicited. If no paresthesia is elicited and the needle contacts bone, the needle is withdrawn and redirected slightly more medial until a paresthesia is elicited. The patient should be warned that a paresthesia will occur and to say "there!!!!" as soon as the paresthesia is felt. After a paresthesia is elicited and its distribution is identified, gentle aspiration is carried out to identify blood. If the aspiration test is negative and no persistent paresthesia into the distribution of the median nerve remains, 5 to 7 mL of solution is slowly injected, with the patient being monitored closely for signs of local anesthetic toxicity. If no paresthesia can be elicited, a similar amount of solution is injected in a fan-like manner with care being taken not to inadvertently inject into the anterior interosseous artery.

Complications and Pitfalls

Median nerve block below the elbow is a relatively safe block with the major complications being inadvertent intravascular injection and persistent paresthesia secondary to needle trauma to the nerve. This technique can safely be performed in the presence of anticoagulation by using a 25- or 27-gauge

needle, albeit at increased risk of hematoma, if the clinical situation dictates a favorable risk-to-benefit ratio. These complications can be decreased if manual pressure is applied to the area of the block immediately following injection. Application of cold packs for 20-minute periods following the block will also decrease the amount of post-procedure pain and bleeding that the patient may experience.

■ RADIAL TUNNEL SYNDROME

Radial tunnel syndrome is an entrapment neuropathy of the radial nerve that is often clinically misdiagnosed as resistant tennis elbow.[9,10] In radial tunnel syndrome, the posterior interosseous branch of the radial nerve is entrapped by a variety of mechanisms that have in common a similar clinical presentation. These mechanisms include aberrant fibrous bands in front of the radial head, anomalous blood vessels that compress the nerve, and/or a sharp tendinous margin of the extensor carpi radialis brevis (see Fig. 66–11). These entrapments may exist alone or in combination.

Regardless of the mechanism of entrapment of the radial nerve, the common clinical feature of radial tunnel syndrome is pain just below the lateral epicondyle of the humerus.[9] The

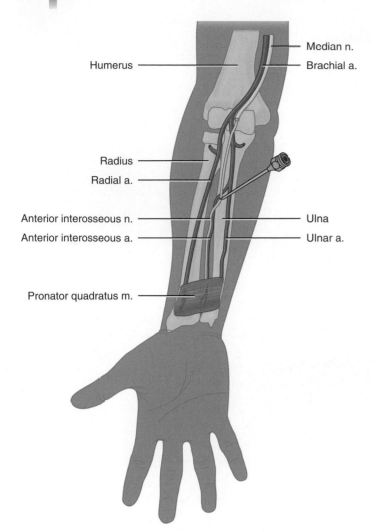

Humerus

Median n.

Brachial a.

Radius

Radial a.

Anterior interosseous n.

Anterior interosseous a.

Ulna

Ulnar a.

Pronator quadratus m.

FIGURE 66–12 ■ Injection technique for relieving pain due to anterior interosseous syndrome. (From Waldman SD: Atlas of Pain Management Injection Techniques. Philadelphia, Saunders, 2000, p 101.)

pain of radial tunnel syndrome may develop after an acute twisting injury or direct trauma to the soft tissues overlying the posterior interosseous branch of the radial nerve or the onset may be more insidious without obvious inciting factor (Fig. 66–13). The pain is constant and is made worse with active supination of the wrist. Patients will often note the inability to hold a coffee cup or hammer. Sleep disturbance is common. On physical examination, there will be tenderness to palpation of the posterior interosseous branch of the radial nerve just below the lateral epicondyle[11] (Fig. 66–14). Elbow range of motion will be normal. Grip strength on the affected side may be diminished. Patients with radial tunnel syndrome will exhibit pain on active resisted supination of the forearm.

Cervical radiculopathy and tennis elbow can mimic radial tunnel syndrome.[10] Radial tunnel syndrome can be distinguished from tennis elbow in that with radial tunnel syndrome, the maximal tenderness to palpation is distal to the lateral epicondyle over the posterior interosseous branch of the radial nerve, whereas with tennis elbow, the maximal tenderness to palpation is over the lateral epicondyle (see Fig. 66–12). Electromyography will help distinguish cervical radiculopathy and radial tunnel syndrome from tennis elbow. Plain radiographs are indicated to rule out occult bony pathology in all patients who present with radial tunnel syndrome.

Based on the patient's clinical presentation, additional testing including complete blood count, uric acid, sedimentation rate, and antinuclear antibody testing may be indicated. MRI scan of the elbow is indicated if joint instability is suspected. The injection technique described below will serve as a diagnostic and a therapeutic maneuver.[12]

Clinically Relevant Anatomy

The radial nerve is made up of fibers from C5-T1 spinal roots. The nerve lies posterior and inferior to the axillary artery. Exiting the axilla, the radial nerve passes between the medial and long heads of the triceps muscle. As the nerve curves across the posterior aspect of the humerus, it supplies a motor branch to the triceps. Continuing its downward path, it gives off a number of sensory branches to the upper arm. At a point between the lateral epicondyle of the humerus and the musculospiral groove, the radial nerve divides into its two terminal branches. The superficial branch continues down the arm along with the radial artery and provides sensory innervation to the dorsum of the wrist and the dorsal aspects of a portion of the thumb, index, and middle finger. The deep posterior interosseous branch provides the majority of the motor innervation to the extensors of the forearm.

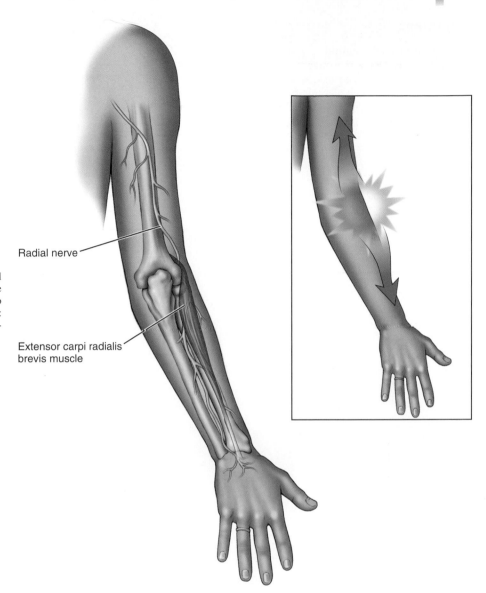

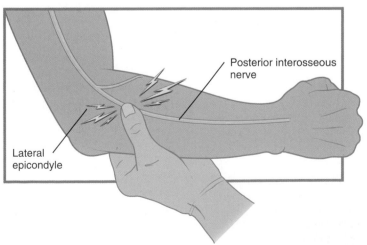

Radial nerve

Extensor carpi radialis
brevis muscle

FIGURE 66–13 ■ The pain of radial tunnel syndrome is localized to the deep exterior muscle mass and may radiate proximally and distally into the upper arm and forearm. (From Waldman SD: Atlas of Uncommon Pain Syndromes. Philadelphia, Saunders, 2003, p 84.)

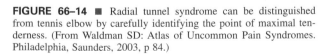

Posterior interosseous
nerve

Lateral
epicondyle

FIGURE 66–14 ■ Radial tunnel syndrome can be distinguished from tennis elbow by carefully identifying the point of maximal tenderness. (From Waldman SD: Atlas of Uncommon Pain Syndromes. Philadelphia, Saunders, 2003, p 84.)

Treatment

The nonsteroidal antiinflammatory agents or COX-2 inhibitors represent a reasonable first step in the treatment of pronator syndrome. The use of the tricyclic antidepressants such as nortriptyline, at a single bedtime dose of 25 mg titrating upward as side effects allow will also be useful, especially if sleep disturbance is also present. Avoidance of repetitive trauma thought to be contributing to this entrapment neuropathy is also important. If these maneuvers fail to produce rapid symptomatic relief, injection of the median nerve at the forearm with local anesthetic and steroid is a reasonable next step.[7] If symptoms continue to persist, surgical exploration and release of the radial nerve is indicated.

■ CONCLUSION

The myriad and overlapping clinical presentations of the entrapment neuropathies at the elbow and forearm present a diagnostic challenge to the clinician. To make the correct diagnosis, a targeted history and physical examination are mandatory. Electromyography and nerve conduction studies combined with judicious use of diagnostic imaging techniques will help confirm the diagnosis. Failure to timely diagnose and treat the entrapment neuropathies discussed herein can lead to significant suffering and disability for the patient.

References

1. Waldman SD: Ulnar nerve entrapment at the elbow. In Waldman SD: Atlas of Common Pain Syndromes. Philadelphia, Saunders, 2002, p 105.
2. Waldman SD: Cubital tunnel syndrome. In Waldman SD: Atlas of Pain Management Injection Techniques. Philadelphia, Saunders, 2000, p 103.
3. Waldman SD: Golfer's elbow. In Waldman SD: Atlas of Common Pain Syndromes. Philadelphia, Saunders, 2002, p 102.
4. Waldman SD: Carpal tunnel syndrome. In Waldman SD: Atlas of Common Pain Syndromes. Philadelphia, Saunders, 2002, p 118.
5. Waldman SD: Pronator syndrome. In Waldman SD: Atlas of Uncommon Pain Syndromes. Philadelphia, Saunders, 2003, p 77.
6. Waldman SD: Pronator syndrome. In Waldman SD: Atlas of Pain Management Injection Techniques. Philadelphia, Saunders, 2000, p 96.
7. Waldman SD: Anterior interosseous syndrome. In Waldman SD: Atlas of Uncommon Pain Syndromes. Philadelphia, Saunders, 2003, p 86.
8. Waldman SD: Anterior interosseous syndrome In Waldman SD: Atlas of Pain Management Injection Techniques. Philadelphia, Saunders, 2000, p 100.
9. Waldman SD: Radial tunnel syndrome. In Waldman SD: Atlas of Uncommon Pain Syndromes. Philadelphia, Saunders, 2003, p 83.
10. Waldman SD: Tennis elbow. In Waldman SD: Atlas of Common Pain Syndromes. Philadelphia, Saunders, 2002, p 98.
11. Waldman SD: Radial tunnel syndrome. In Waldman SD: Atlas of Pain Management Injection Techniques. Philadelphia, Saunders, 2000, p 84.

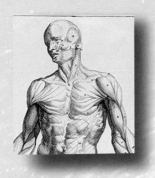

Part E

WRIST AND HAND PAIN SYNDROMES

chapter

67

Arthritis of the Wrist and Hand

Adel G. Fam

■ GENERAL CONSIDERATIONS

Pain in the wrist and hand is a relatively common symptom of diverse causes.[1] The pain may originate in the bones and joints of the wrist and hand, periarticular soft tissues (subcutaneous tissues, palmar fascia, tendon sheaths), nerve roots and peripheral nerves, or vascular structures, or be referred from the musculoskeletal structures of the cervical spine, thoracic outlet, shoulder, or elbow. Table 67–1 provides a classification of painful disorders of the wrist and hand based on the site of origin of pain and its predominant location. Precise diagnosis depends on a detailed history, a meticulous physical examination of the joints, tenosynovial sheaths and other periarticular structures, cervical spine, nerve and blood supplies to the hand, and a few rationally selected diagnostic studies.[1]

The onset of many painful hand disorders is often insidious. A history of unaccustomed, repetitive or excessive hand activity is particularly important in the diagnosis of wrist, thumb, or finger arthritis or tenosynovitis due to an overuse syndrome. A detailed occupational history is important for determining whether the hand tenosynovitis is work related,

either as a cumulative trauma disorder, or as an acute injury. Abnormal tensile stresses, exceeding the elastic limits of tendons, can lead to cumulative microfailure of the molecular links between tendon fibrils; a phenomenon referred to as *fibrillar creep*. With aging, tendons become less flexible and less elastic, rendering them more susceptible to injury. A shortened musculotendinous unit, from lack of regular stretching exercises, is more prone to cumulative trauma disorder.

A knowledge of applied anatomy of the wrist, metacarpophalangeal (MCP) proximal and distal interphalangeal (PIP and DIP) joints of the fingers and of the tendon sheaths (Figs. 67–1 and 67–2) is important for precise diagnosis. Initial diagnostic studies include a complete blood count, erythrocyte sedimentation rate, hand radiographs, synovial fluid analysis (when available), and, if indicated, serum urate, rheumatoid factor, and antinuclear antibody test. Additional studies are sometimes required and include skeletal scintigraphy, ultrasonography, nerve conduction studies, noninvasive vascular (Doppler) studies, arteriography, computed tomography (CT), magnetic resonance imaging (MRI), arthrography, and synovial biopsy.

Table 67–1

Differential Diagnosis of Wrist and Hand Pain

Articular	Arthritis of wrist, MCP, PIP and/or DIP
	Joint neoplasms
Periarticular	
Subcutaneous	RA nodules, gouty tophi, glomus tumor
Palmar fascia	Dupuytren contracture
Tendon sheath	de Quervain tenosynovitis
	Wrist volar flexor tenosynovitis (including carpal tunnel syndrome)
	Thumb or finger flexor tenosynovitis (trigger or snapping thumb or finger)
	Pigmented villonodular tenosynovitis (giant cell tumor of the tendon sheath)
Acute calcific periarthritis	Wrist, MCP, and rarely PIP and DIP
Ganglion	
Osseous	Fractures, neoplasms, infection
	Osteonecrosis including Kienböck disease (lunate) and Preiser disease (scaphoid)
Neurologic	
Nerve Entrapment Syndromes	
Median nerve	Carpal tunnel syndrome (at wrist)
	Pronator teres syndrome (at pronator teres)
	Anterior interosseous nerve syndrome
Ulnar nerve	Cubital tunnel syndrome (at elbow)
	Guyon canal (at wrist)
Posterior interosseous	Radial nerve palsy (spiral groove syndrome)
Lower brachial plexus	Thoracic outlet syndrome, Pancoast tumor
Cervical nerve roots	Herniated cervical disk, tumors
Spinal cord lesion	Spinal tumors, syringomyelia
Vascular	
Vasospastic disorders (Raynaud)	Scleroderma, occupational vibration syndrome
Vasculitis	With digital ischemia and ischemic ulcers, SLE, RA
Referred pain	
Cervical spine disorders	
Reflex sympathetic dystrophy syndrome (RSDS)	Shoulder–hand syndrome and causalgia
Cardiac	Angina pectoris

DIP, distal interphalangeal; MCP, metacarpophalangeal; PIP, proximal interphalangeal; SLE, systemic lupus erythematosus; RA, rheumatoid arthritis.

■ ARTHRITIS OF THE WRIST

Etiology

The radiocarpal (wrist) joint is a common site for inflammatory arthritides, such as rheumatoid arthritis (RA), systemic lupus erythematosus (SLE), psoriatic arthritis (PsA), ankylosing spondylitis (AS), reactive arthritis, and enteropathic arthritis.[1] Primary osteoarthritis (OA) of the wrist is rare but the joint can be affected in OA secondary to trauma, hemochromatosis, ochronosis, calcium pyrophosphate deposition (CPPD) disease, gout, osteonecrosis, or infection.

Clinical Features and Differential Diagnosis

Arthritis of the wrist is associated with pain, stiffness, diffuse, tender swelling just distal to the radius and ulna, reduced function, and sometimes deformity of the joint. Movements are often restricted and a crepitus may be palpable. The presence of fluctuance indicates a wrist effusion; pressure with one hand on one side of the joints produces a fluid wave transmitted to the second hand placed on the opposite side of the joint. Wrist deformities are common in RA and other chronic inflammatory arthritides. These include volar subluxation of the carpus with a visible step opposite the radiocarpal joint,

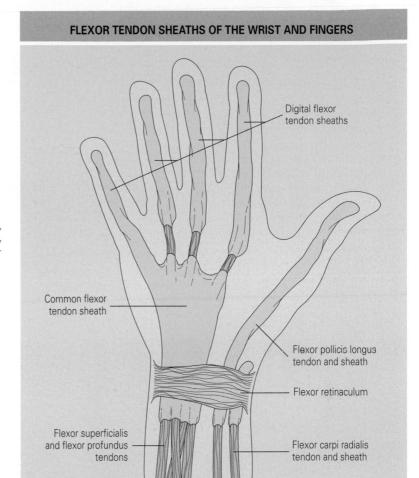

FLEXOR TENDON SHEATHS OF THE WRIST AND FINGERS

Digital flexor
tendon sheaths

Common flexor
tendon sheath

Flexor pollicis longus
tendon and sheath

Flexor retinaculum

Flexor superficialis
and flexor profundus
tendons

Flexor carpi radialis
tendon and sheath

FIGURE 67–1 ■ Flexor tendon sheaths of the wrist, fingers, and thumb. (From Hochberg M, Silman A [eds]: Rheumatology, 3rd ed. Philadelphia, Mosby, 2003, Figure 57.2, p 642, with permission.)

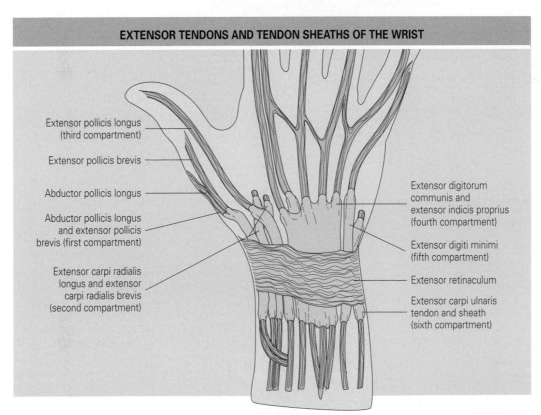

EXTENSOR TENDONS AND TENDON SHEATHS OF THE WRIST

Extensor pollicis longus
(third compartment)

Extensor pollicis brevis

Abductor pollicis longus

Abductor pollicis longus
and extensor pollicis
brevis (first compartment)

Extensor carpi radialis
longus and extensor
carpi radialis brevis
(second compartment)

Extensor digitorum
communis and
extensor indicis proprius
(fourth compartment)

Extensor digiti minimi
(fifth compartment)

Extensor retinaculum

Extensor carpi ulnaris
tendon and sheath
(sixth compartment)

FIGURE 67–2 ■ Extensor tendons and tendon sheaths of the wrist, fingers, and thumb. (From Hochberg M, Silman A [eds]: Rheumatology, 3rd ed. Philadelphia, Mosby, 2003, Figure 57.3, p 642, with permission.)

carpal collapse (loss of carpal height to less than half the length of the third metacarpal) and radial deviation of the carpus from the axis of the wrist and hand. Chronic inflammatory arthritis of the distal radioulnar joint is associated with local swelling, painful restriction of pronation and supination, and often instability with dorsal subluxation of the ulnar head and a "piano key" movement on downward pressure.

Extensor wrist tenosynovitis, by contrast, manifests as a superficial, linear or oval-shaped, dorsal, tender swelling localized to the distribution of the affected tendon sheath, and extending beyond the joint margins. When the fingers are actively extended, the distal margin of the swelling moves proximally and folds in, like a sheet being tucked under a mattress (tuck sign). Tenosynovitis of the common flexor

tendon sheath manifests as a swelling over the volar aspect of the wrist just proximal to the carpal tunnel (volar hot dog sign).[1]

■ ARTHRITIS OF THE METACARPOPHALANGEAL, PROXIMAL INTERPHALANGEAL, AND DISTAL INTERPHALANGEAL JOINTS

This occurs most commonly in RA, SLE, and PsA. MCP synovitis produces a diffuse, tender swelling of the joint that may obscure the valleys between the knuckles.[1] Swelling of a PIP joint produces a fusiform or spindle-shaped finger. To detect a PIP or DIP joint effusion, compression of the joint by one hand produces ballooning or a hydraulic lift sensed by the other hand (balloon sign). Unlike PIP synovitis, dorsal knuckle pads produce a nontender thickening of the skin localized to the dorsal surface of the PIP joints. Both the PIP and DIP joints are commonly affected in primary "nodal" OA, presenting as Bouchard and Heberden nodes, respectively. Digital flexor tenosynovitis, by contrast, produces a linear tender swelling over the volar aspect of the finger (sausage finger), often associated with thickening, nodules and a fine crepitus of the flexor tendon sheath.

Deformities of the MCP, PIP, and DIP joints are relatively common in inflammatory arthritis.[1] MCP joint deformities include ulnar drift, volar subluxation (often visible as a step), and a fixed flexion deformity. Boutonnière deformity describes a finger with flexion of the PIP joint and hyperextension of the DIP joint (Fig. 67–3). A swan-neck deformity describes the appearance of a finger in which there is hyperextension of the PIP joint and flexion of the DIP joint (Fig. 67–4). A Z-shaped deformity of the thumb consists of flexion of the MCP joint and hyperextension of the IP joint (see Fig. 67–4). Telescoped shortening of the digits, produced by partial resorption of the phalanges secondary to PsA, RA, or other destructive arthritis, is often associated with concentric wrinkling of the skin (opera-glass hand).

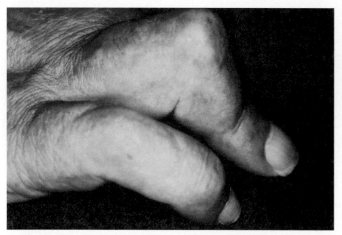

FIGURE 67–3 ■ Boutonnière deformity of right ring finger. (From Hochberg M, Silman A [eds]: Rheumatology, 3rd ed. Philadelphia, Mosby, 2003, Figure 57.6a, p 644, with permission.)

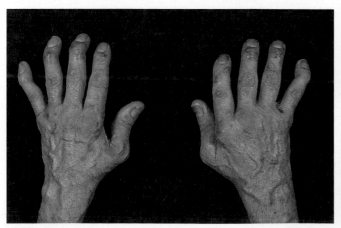
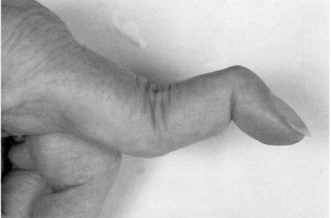

FIGURE 67–4 ■ Swan-neck deformities of the fingers and Z-shaped deformities of the thumbs. (From Hochberg M, Silman A [eds]: Rheumatology, 3rd ed. Philadelphia, Mosby, 2003, Figure 57.6b and c, p 644, with permission.)

Treatment

Treatment of arthritis of the wrist, MCP, PIP, or DIP joints depends primarily on the underlying cause. General measures include resting the affected joint by splinting, physical and occupational therapies, and symptomatic treatment with NSAIDs.[1]

For persistent inflammatory synovitis, intra-articular corticosteroids are often helpful. The radiocarpal (wrist) joint can be injected via a dorsoradial approach.[2] With the wrist slightly palmar flexed, the needle is inserted perpendicularly to a depth of 1 to 2 cm at a point distal to Lister tubercle of the distal radius and just ulnar to the extensor pollicis longus tendon. The MCP, PIP, and DIP joints can be readily entered via a dorsoradial or a dorsoulnar approach using a 28-gauge needle.[2] It is sometimes necessary to tease the needle tip into the joint space while a slight traction to the finger is applied to pull the articulating surfaces apart. A correctly placed intra-articular injection produces fluid distension of the joint on all sides.

References

1. Fam AG: The wrist and hand. In Hochberg H, Silman A (eds): Rheumatology, 3rd ed. Mosby, London, 2003, p 641.
2. Fam AG: Aspiration and injection of joints and periarticular tissues: The wrist and hand. In Klippel JH, Dieppe PA (eds): Practical Rheumatology. Mosby, London, 1995, p 117.

68

Carpal Tunnel Syndrome

Adel G. Fam

■ GENERAL CONSIDERATIONS

The first reported description of carpal tunnel syndrome (CTS) was made by James Paget in 1854.[1] Phalen, beginning in 1951 in a series of benchmark articles, further defined CTS and described " the Phalen sign."[1]Entrapment of the median nerve at the carpal tunnel of the wrist, or CTS, is the most common entrapment neuropathy. The tunnel is bound on its dorsal and lateral surfaces by the carpal bones and the intercarpal joints, and on the volar aspect by the transverse carpal ligament (flexor retinaculum).[2] The tendons of the flexor digitorum profundus and sublimus, and flexor pollicis longus and the median nerve pass through the tunnel. The flexor carpi radialis (FCR) has its own fibro-osseous canal, which is separated from the carpal tunnel by the deep portion of the transverse carpal ligament as it splits along its radial border encircling the FCR tendon to bridge the crest of the trapezium.[2]

■ ETIOLOGY

CTS results from swelling of the flexor tendons or from encroachment on the tunnel by amyloid, urate deposits, or other space-occupying lesions. CTS is associated with elevated intracarpal canal pressure (normal: 2 mm Hg in the neutral position, about 42 mm Hg in maximum wrist flexion and 33 mm Hg in maximum wrist extension) as measured by the use of a pressure-transducer catheter.[3] The pressure drops with surgical or endoscopic decompression of the carpal tunnel.[3]

The so-called *idiopathic* carpal tunnel syndrome is generally due to common flexor tenosynovitis from repetitive, occupational or recreational hand activities. Other causes include rheumatoid arthritis (RA), systemic lupus erythematosus (SLE), scleroderma, endocrine disorders (diabetes mellitus, hypothyroidism, obesity, acromegaly), hemodialysis, primary amyloidosis, infections (bacterial, mycobacterial, and fungal) and pregnancy. CTS is rarely caused by space-occupying lesions in the carpal tunnel, such as ganglion, lipoma, fracture callus, or urate tophus.

■ CLINICAL FEATURES

CTS is most common in women between 40 and 60 years of age.[4] Typical symptoms include burning pain, pins-and-needles sensations, numbness, tingling, and sometimes sensory loss in the distribution of the median nerve: the radial three digits and radial half of the ring finger. Patients are typically awakened at night by abnormal paresthesias. The pain is often relieved by shaking the hand or placing it under running warm water. The pain may radiate to the forearm, elbow, or shoulder. The pain and paresthesias are intensified by sustained or repetitive flexion and extension movements of the wrists (e.g., typing or grasping a steering wheel). Patients may also complain of weakness and clumsiness of the affected hand.

In the median nerve percussion test (Tinel sign), gently tapping the median nerve at the flexor retinaculum (just radial to the palmaris longus tendon at the distal wrist crease), with the wrist in slight extension, produces paresthesia in the median nerve distribution: thumb, index and middle fingers and the radial half of the ring finger.[4] Sustained palmar flexion of the wrist for 30 to 60 seconds may induce finger paresthesias (Phalen wrist flexion sign).[4] Wrist extension narrows the carpal tunnel, increases the pressure within the canal, and can exacerbate symptoms of CTS ("reverse Phalen maneuver"). If the wrist cannot be flexed because of arthritis, pressure over the median nerve for more than 30 seconds often produces the same effect (median nerve compression test or Durkan sign).[4] It is noteworthy that there is a wide variation in the sensitivity and specificity of these provocative tests among patients with CTS. Simple elevation of the affected hand for 1 to 2 minutes often reproduces the patient's symptoms.[4] Sensory testing may show impaired touch, pain, two-point discrimination and/or vibration sense in the median nerve distribution.[4] Atrophy of the thenar muscles is present in chronic cases, and there is often weakness of both the abductor pollicis brevis (weakness of resisted palmar abduction of the thumb) and opponens pollicis muscles (patient touches tip of thumb to tip of little finger, and the examiner attempts to break up the pinch).[4]

■ DIAGNOSIS

CTS is a clinical diagnosis, confirmed by electrodiagnostic studies. These typically show a slowed sensory median nerve conduction velocity across the carpal tunnel, often associated with prolonged distal motor latency. Ultrasonography and MRI can be useful in demonstrating swelling of the flexor tendons or any space-occupying lesion in the carpal tunnel. Median nerve entrapment at the elbow (pronator teres syndrome) can be distinguished from CTS by a positive Tinel sign at the elbow, negative provocative test for CTS at the wrist, frequent weakness of intrinsic muscles to the index and middle fingers with hyperextension of the MCP joints (papal sign), and by electrodiagnostic studies.

∎ TREATMENT

Conservative management of CTS consists of treatment of any underlying cause, modification of hand occupational and/or avocational activities, a volar wrist splint with the joint kept in the neutral or slightly extended position, and NSAIDs as required.[5,6] Local corticosteroid injections of the carpal tunnel may be useful for those with CTS of short duration (<1 year) in whom there is no significant weakness or atrophy of thenar muscles. The carpal tunnel and common flexor tendon sheath can be injected by a volar approach.[7] The median nerve lies radial and underneath the palmaris longus tendon and should be avoided. A 28-gauge needle is inserted tangentially, directed toward the palm, just ulnar to the palmaris tendon and proximal to the distal wrist crease. The needle is advanced to a depth of 2 to 4 mm until the sheath is entered, and 10 to 25 mg methylprednisolone acetate is injected.[7] Although most patients improve initially, recurrence of symptoms within 6 to 12 months occurs in about 50% of subjects. Potential complications include injury of the median nerve with worsening of symptoms, bleeding, and infection. Systemic corticosteroids, tendon-gliding exercises, ultrasound, and acupuncture are of limited long-term benefit.

Surgical treatment of CTS consists of release of the carpal tunnel by section of the transverse carpal ligament through a volar incision.[8] This is indicated in patients who do not respond to medical treatment and for those with persistent neurologic changes and progressive increase in distal motor latency times and atrophy of thenar muscles. In hemodialysis patients and in those with RA, decompression of the carpal tunnel is combined with flexor tenosynovectomy and lysis of any adhesions.[8] Closed, or endoscopic, carpal tunnel release, provides an equally effective and less invasive method for decompression of the medial nerve.[9] Recently, limited-incision carpal tunnel release has been shown to be as effective as open and endoscopic decompression of the median nerve but with fewer complications.[10] Most patients improve following open or endoscopic surgical decompression of the carpal tunnel. However, results are less favorable in those with long-standing CTS with neurologic deficit and atrophy of thenar muscles. Failures often result from incomplete release of the transverse carpal ligament.

References

1. Lo SL, Raskin K, Lester H, Lester B: Carpal tunnel syndrome: A historical perspective. Hand Clin 18:211, 2002.
2. Rotman MB, Donovan JP: Practical anatomy of the carpal tunnel. Hand Clin 18:219, 2002.
3. Schuind F: Canal pressures before, during, and after endoscopic release for idiopathic carpal tunnel syndrome. J Hand Surg 27A:1019, 2002.
4. Palumbo CF, Szabo RM: Examination of patients for carpal tunnel syndrome. Sensibility, provocative, and motor testing. Hand Clin 18:269, 2002.
5. Gerritsen AAM, de Krom MCTEM, Struijs MA, et al: Conservative treatment options for carpal tunnel syndrome: A systematic review of randomized controlled trials. J Neurol 249:272, 2002.
6. Osterman AL, Whitman M, Porta LD: Nonoperative carpal tunnel syndrome treatment. Hand Clin 18:279, 2002.
7. Fam AG: Aspiration and injection of joints and periarticular tissues: The wrist and hand. In Klippel JH, Dieppe PA (eds): Practical Rheumatology, Mosby, London, 1995, p 117.
8. Ting J, Weiland AJ: Role of ancillary procedures in surgical management of carpal tunnel syndrome: Epineurotomy, internal neurolysis, tenosynovectomy, and tendon transfers. Hand Clin 18: 315, 2002.
9. Nagle DJ: Endoscopic carpal tunnel release. Hand Clin 18: 307, 2002.
10. Higgins JP, Graham TJ: Carpal tunnel release via limited palmar incision. Hand Clin 18:299, 2002.

de Quervain's Tenosynovitis

Adel G. Fam

A total of 22 extrinsic tendons cross the wrist, providing a unique combination of power and dexterity to the hand. Each tendon passes through a narrow fibrous canal lined by a tubular synovial sheath.[1,2] The tendons are lined by an inner or visceral synovial layer that adheres closely to the tendon and by an outer or parietal synovium that covers the inside of the fibrous tendon sheath. The visceral and parietal synovial tubes arc united longitudinally by the mesotendon, a synovial fold that transmits vessels and nerves to the tendon.[1,2] The mesotendon may disappear partially in some tendon sheaths and be represented by threads or vincula. Excessive loads or repetitive movements of a tendon through its tendon sheath can cause chronic reactive or stenosing tenosynovitis with inflammation, fibrosis, and thickening of the sheath and "fibrillar creep" of the tendon with swelling, edema, and bunching of the fibers.[1,2] This tenosynovitis results in an impediment to the smooth gliding of the tendon through its sheath and ultimately "catching," "triggering," or "locking" on either side of the wrist retinacular ligament or finger annular pulleys. Less frequently, tenosynovitis may result from an isolated traumatic event.

Clinically, tenosynovitis is associated with local pain, swelling, and stiffness. There is linear tenderness, swelling, and crepitus over the affected tendon sheath, and the pain is worsened by placing the tendon under tension by muscular contraction or by passive stretching. de Quervain's stenosing tenosynovitis of the abductor pollicis longus and extensor pollicis brevis, trigger finger or thumb tenosynovitis, and wrist common flexor tenosynovitis are often due to "primary" tenosynovitis caused by occupation-related or avocation-related cumulative microtrauma. Primary "overuse" stenosing tenosynovitis affecting other wrist tendon sheaths is less frequent. Secondary causes of tenosynovitis are less common and include rheumatoid arthritis, systemic lupus erythematosus, psoriatic arthritis, infection (bacterial, mycobacterial, fungal, and viral), microcrystalline disorders (gouty, pyrophosphate, and hydroxyapatite or calcific tenosynovitis), amyloid deposition, sarcoidosis, and pigmented villonodular tenosynovitis.

In 1895, de Quervain described in detail fibrosing stenosing tenovaginitis of the first extensor compartment: abductor pollicis longus and extensor pollicis brevis.[1] de Quervain's stenosing tenosynovitis is most common in women 30 to 50 years old.[1-5] Repetitive activity, involving pinching with the thumb while moving the wrist in radial and ulnar directions,

results in frictional inflammation with thickening and stenosis of the fibrous tendon sheath as it passes over the distal radius beneath the extensor retinaculum. It also may occur in association with rheumatoid arthritis, psoriatic arthritis, direct trauma, pregnancy, and the postpartum period.[6] Most patients report several weeks of pain on the radial aspect of the wrist and at the thumb base during pinch grip, grasping, and other thumb and wrist movements. The affected tendon sheath is tender and often swollen 1 to 2 cm proximal to the radial styloid. A tendon crepitus is often palpable. Finkelstein's test is a useful diagnostic maneuver; passive ulnar deviation of the wrist with the fingers flexed over the thumb placed in the palm stretches the tendons and reproduces the pain over the distal radius and the radial side of the wrist.[1-7]

■ DIAGNOSIS

The diagnosis of de Quervain's tenosynovitis is often confused with osteoarthritis of the first carpometacarpal joint and with the intersection syndrome.[8] The latter is due to tenosynovitis of the second extensor compartment (extensor carpi radialis longus and brevis) at its intersection with the tendons of the first extensor compartment (abductor pollicis longus and extensor pollicis brevis). This syndrome, which results from frequent repetitive wrist movements, particularly in athletes (rowers, canoeists, weight lifters), is associated with pain, tenderness, swelling, and sometimes crepitus over the dorsoradial aspect of distal forearm, about 4 cm proximal to the wrist joint.[7] This differentiates the intersection syndrome from the more distal de Quervain's tenosynovitis.

■ TREATMENT

Treatment of de Quervain's tenosynovitis consists of local heat, nonsteroidal antiinflammatory drugs, and a wrist and thumb splint.[8] A radial gutter splint immobilizes the wrist in slight extension and radial deviation, the first carpometacarpal joint in slight abduction, and the first metacarpophalangeal joint in slight extension. The interphalangeal joint of the thumb is left unrestricted. Modification of hand activities, avoiding inciting tasks that require repetitive thumb movements or pinch grasping, is important.[8,9] These measures are usually effective in patients with mild to moderate symptoms and in women with pregnancy- or lactation-related de

Quervain's tenosynovitis. In patients with more severe or persistent pain interfering with activities of daily living, one or more local corticosteroid injections into the affected tendon sheath are often beneficial, giving complete and lasting relief in about 70% of patients. The injection can be done through a dorsoradial approach.[10] A 28-gauge needle is inserted tangentially into the distal end of the abductor pollicis longus and extensor pollicis brevis tendon sheath, 1 cm proximal to the radial styloid. If correctly placed, injection of a local anesthetic distends the sheath, producing a swelling proximal to the extensor retinaculum. Methylprednisolone acetate, 7.5 to 10 mg, is instilled into the sheath. Surgical decompression of the first extensor compartment, with or without tenosynovectomy and compartment reconstruction, is indicated in patients with persistent or recurrent symptoms for more than 6 months.[1] A septated tendon sheath, with separate compartments for the abductor pollicis longus and extensor pollicis brevis, can lead to recurrence owing to incomplete release of the tendon sheath.

References

1. Littler JW, Freedman DM, Malerich MM: Compartment reconstruction for de Quervain's disease. J Hand Surg 27B:242, 2002.
2. Fam AG: Bursitis and tendinitis: A practical approach to diagnosis. Geriatrics 8:35, 1992.
3. Thorson E, Szabo RM: Common tendinitis problems in the hand and forearm. Orthop Clin North Am 23:65, 1992.
4. Field JH: De Quervain's disease. Am Fam Physician 20:103, 1979.
5. Clarke MT, Lyall HA, Grant JW, Matthewson MH: The histopathology of de Quervain's disease. J Hand Surg 23B:732, 1998.
6. Nygaard IE, Saltzman CL, Whitehouse MB, Hankin FM: Hand problems in pregnancy. Am Fam Physician 39:123, 1989.
7. Grundberg AB, Keagan DS: Pathologic anatomy of the forearm: Intersection syndrome. J Hand Surg 10A:299, 1985.
8. Lane IB, Boretz RS, Stuchin SA: Treatment of de Quervain's disease: Role of conservative management. J Hand Surg 26B:258, 2001.
9. Avei S, Yilmaz C, Sayli U: Comparison of nonsurgical treatment measures for de Quervain's disease of pregnancy and lactation. J Hand Surg 27A:322, 2002.
10. Fam AG: Aspiration and injection of joints and periarticular tissues: The wrist and hand. In Klippel JH, Dieppe PA (eds): Practical Rheumatology. London, Mosby, 1995, p 117.

chapter 70

Dupuytren's Contracture

Adel G. Fam

HISTORICAL ASPECTS AND CLINICAL FEATURES

In 1834, Dupuytren first described the anatomic features of Dupuytren's contracture.[1] The disorder is relatively common and is characterized by nodular thickening and contraction of the palmar fascia drawing one or more fingers into flexion at the metacarpophalangeal joint (Fig. 70–1).[2-4] In most patients, it affects the ulnar side of both hands. The fourth finger is usually affected earliest, followed by the fifth, third, and second fingers in decreasing order of frequency.[2-4] The thumb is rarely involved.[5] Fibrous nodules, resulting from contraction of proliferating fibroblasts and myofibroblasts in the superficial layers of the palmar fascia, are the earliest abnormality. The dermis is invaded by fibroblastic cells, resulting in puckering, dimpling, and tethering of the overlying skin. There is usually little pain or tenderness initially, and if no further progression occurs, the hand function is preserved, and no treatment is required. After a variable period of months or years, however, the aponeurotic thickening may extend distally to involve the digits. The fingers become flexed at the metacarpophalangeal joints by taut fibrous bands or "cords" radiating from the palmar fascia, and the hand cannot be placed flat on a table top (positive table-top test).[2-4] Dupuytren's contracture has a variable course. Some patients show little change or incapacity over many years. In other patients, fascial contraction and aponeurotic thickening progress rapidly, with severe deformity and impairment of hand function.

ETIOLOGY

The mechanism of Dupuytren's contracture is poorly understood.[6-9] The disorder occurs most frequently in whites of Celtic or Scandinavian origin. It is rare in nonwhites. Its incidence increases with advancing age, and the sex ratio is predominantly male (7:1). Familial predisposition is frequent, suggesting an autosomal dominant pattern with variable penetrance. A pathogenetic role for local repetitive injury and occupational trauma is unproven. Dupuytren's contracture has been observed in association with idiopathic epilepsy, alcohol abuse, tobacco smoking, diabetes mellitus, chronic pulmonary disease, HIV infection, and reflex sympathetic dystrophy syndrome.

Pathologically, early lesions are characterized by marked fibroblastic proliferation; vascular hyperplasia; and clusters of macrophages, S100-positive epidermal dendritic (Langerhans) cells, and CD3+ and CD45+ T lymphocytes.[10] This is followed by dense, disorderly collagen deposition with thickening of the palmar fascia and nodule formation. The abnormal fascia shows elevated total amounts of collagen with increased content of reducible cross-links and hydroxylysine. About 25% of the collagen is type III, which is normally present in small amounts in the palmar fascia. Ultrastructurally, contractile, smooth muscle–like fibroblasts or myofibroblasts surrounded by bundles of disarrayed collagenous fibrils and completely or partially occluded capillaries are present in the fibrotic nodules and cords.[7-9] Although myofibroblasts are not specific to Dupuytren's contracture, they are believed to be responsible for contraction of the palmar fascia and finger deformities. The finding of isolated foci of fibroblasts positive for smooth muscle α-actin (an antibody marker for myofibroblasts) dispersed in the dermis, remote from the main Dupuytren's tissue, may explain the high recurrence rate after fasciectomy.[9,11]

Numerous cytokines and mediators are expressed in increased concentrations in Dupuytren's nodules and are thought to influence myofibroblast contractility and contribute to the formation of the contracture. These include interleukin-1α and interleukin-1β, tumor necrosis factor-α, the vasoactive prostaglandins PGE_2 and $PGF_{2\alpha}$, and fibronectin. Increased expression of growth factors, such as transforming growth factor-β, platelet-derived growth factor, basic fibroblast growth factor, and epidermal growth factor, in Dupuytren's fascial lesions suggests that these polypeptides may play a role in fibroblastic proliferation.[7,9,11] Adhesion molecules, including integrin VLA4 on macrophages and lymphocytes and vascular cell adhesion molecule-1 on endothelial cells, also are expressed in Dupuytren's lesions. These enhance transendothelial migration of inflammatory cells. More recently, increased expression of beta-catenin, a key signaling protein that coordinates cell adhesion and fibroblast mobility, has been shown in Dupuytren's nodules.[12] These observations suggest that Dupuytren's disease may represent a dendritic/T cell–mediated autoimmune disorder. In late stages of the disease, the lesions become less cellular and more fibrotic.

TREATMENT

Management depends on the rate of progression and severity of the lesions.[13] In patients with mild disease, local heat,

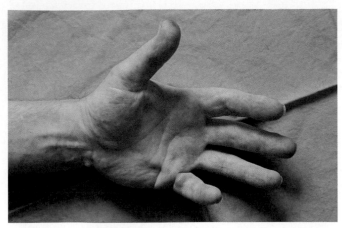

FIGURE 70-1 ■ Dupuytren's contracture of the palmar fascia. (From Hochberg M, Silman A [eds]: Rheumatology, 3rd ed. Philadelphia, Mosby, 2003, p 648.)

stretching exercises, and use of protective padded gloves during heavy manual grasping tasks are often helpful. Many patients learn the benign nature of the contracture and adapt to the disorder.[13] In more severe lesions, with pain and inability to straighten the fingers, intralesional corticosteroid injections are sometimes helpful. Steroids reduce the rate of fibroblastic and myofibroblastic proliferation, increase the rate of apoptosis of inflammatory cells, and reduce expression of transforming growth factor-β1 and proinflammatory fibronectin in Dupuytren's tissue.[14] Intralesional injections of clostridial collagenase, an enzyme that breaks collagen ("collagenase enzyme fasciotomy"),[15] and intralesional infiltrations of interferon-γ, a cytokine produced by T helper lymphocytes that inhibits fibroblastic proliferation and collagen formation,[13] are promising new treatments. In patients with advanced disease with progressive digital contracture of more than 30 degrees, a positive table-top test, and functional impairment, limited or total palmar fasciectomy with or without skin graft replacement is indicated.[16] The risk of recurrence is increased in young patients with active bilateral disease and cellular nodules and in patients with a strong family history or other ectopic fibrotic lesions or both.

References

1. McFarlane RM: On the origin and spread of Dupuytren's disease. J Hand Surg 27A:385, 2002.
2. Benson LS, Williams CS, Kahle M: Dupuytren's contracture. J Am Acad Orthop Surg 6:24, 1998.
3. Rayan GM: Clinical presentations and types of Dupuytren's disease. Hand Clin 15:87, 1999.
4. Saar JD, Grothaus PC: Dupuytren's disease: An overview. Plast Reconstr Surg 106:125, 2000.
5. Milner RH: Dupuytren's disease affecting the thumb and first web of the hand. J Hand Surg 28B:33, 2003.
6. Kloen P: New insights in the development of Dupuytren's contracture: A review. Br J Plast Surg 52:629, 1999.
7. Yi IS, Johnson G, Moneim MS: Etiology of Dupuytren's disease. Hand Clin 15:43, 1999.
8. Murrell GAC, Francis MJO, Howlett CR: Dupuytren's contracture: Fine structure in relation to aetiology. J Bone Joint Surg 71B:367, 1989.
9. Badalamente MA, Hurst LC: The biochemistry of Dupuytren's disease. Hand Clin 15:35, 1999.
10. Qureshi FI, Horngold R, Spencer JD, Hall SM: Langerhans cells in Dupuytren's contracture. J Hand Surg 26B:362, 2001.
11. Fam AG: The wrist and hand. In Hochberg H, Silman A, Smolen JS, Weinblatt ME, et al (eds): Rheumatology, 3rd ed. London, Mosby, 2003, p 641.
12. Varallo VM, Gan BS, Seney S, et al: Beta-catenin expression in Dupuytren's disease: Potential role for cell matrix interactions in modulating beta-catenin levels in vivo and in vitro. Oncogene 22:3680, 2003.
13. Hurst LC, Badalamente MA: Non-operative treatment of Dupuytren's disease. Hand Clin 15:97, 1999.
14. Meek RMD, McLellan S, Reilly J, Crossan JF: The effect of steroids on Dupuytren's disease: Role of programmed cell death. J Hand Surg 27B:270, 2002.
15. Badalamente MA, Hurst LC, Hentz VR: Collagen as a clinical target: Nonoperative treatment of Dupuytren's disease. J Hand Surg 27A:788, 2002.
16. Armstrong JR, Hurren JS, Logan AM: Dermofasciectomy in the management of Dupuytren's disease. J Bone Joint Surg 82B:90, 2000.

chapter 71

Trigger Finger and Trigger Thumb

Adel G. Fam

Trigger finger or thumb, also known as stenosing digital tenosynovitis or snapping finger or thumb, is the most common repetitive strain injury of the hand. It is more frequent in middle-aged women than men. The anatomic lesion is a tenosynovitis of the flexor tendons of the finger or thumb, which results in fibrosis, constriction, and occasionally fibrocartilaginous metaplasia localized to the first (A1) annular pulley that overlies the metacarpophalangeal joint.[1,2] A nodular thickening of the tendon often develops at the site of stenosis.

The most common cause of trigger finger or thumb is overuse trauma of the hands from repetitive gripping activities with increased pull and friction on the flexor tendons.[2] The disorder is often restricted to one digit, usually in the following order: thumb, ring, middle, little, or index finger. Secondary causes of flexor digital tenosynovitis include rheumatoid arthritis, psoriatic arthritis, diabetes mellitus, amyloidosis, hypothyroidism, sarcoidosis, pigmented villonodular tenosynovitis, and infections such as tuberculosis and sporotrichosis.[2]

■ CLINICAL FEATURES

Nodular thickening of the tendon or tendon sheath constriction interferes mechanically with normal tendon gliding, resulting in pain over the area of the A1 pulley and "snapping," "triggering," or "catching" with movement of the finger or thumb.[2] Pain along the course of the sheath with active or resisted flexion and pain on stretching the tendon passively in extension are common. Intermittent "locking" of the digit in flexion also may develop, particularly on arising in the morning. Passive extension of the proximal interphalangeal joint of the finger or interphalangeal joint of the thumb may produce crepitus and a popping sensation as the digit is straightened. Findings include tenderness over the area of the proximal A1 pulley, linear tenderness and swelling of the flexor tendon sheath, tendon crepitus, and limitation of digital flexion and extension.[2] A nodular tendon swelling often can be palpated in the palm just proximal to the metacarpophalangeal joint as it moves during finger or thumb flexion and extension. Over time, guarding on the part of the patient to avoid moving the digit through full range of motion can lead to a fixed flexion deformity of the proximal interphalangeal joint.[2]

■ TREATMENT

Management consists of modification of hand activities, local heat, gentle exercises, and nonsteroidal antiinflammatory drugs as required.[2] Splinting of the affected digit with the metacarpophalangeal joint in 10 to 15 degrees palmar flexed, but free movements at the proximal interphalangeal and distal interphalangeal joints, is sometimes helpful.[2] One or more corticosteroid injections of the affected flexor tendon sheath are often effective and curative in most patients. A 28-gauge needle is inserted tangentially into the flexor tendon sheath proximal to the A1 pulley, opposite the volar aspect of the metacarpal head.[5] The needle is advanced until gentle passive movements of the finger (or thumb) make a crepitant sensation, indicating that the needle tip is rubbing against the surface of the tendon.[5] The needle is withdrawn 0.5 to 1 mm before injecting 5 to 7.5 mg of methylprednisolone acetate into the sheath. Surgical release, with transection of the A1 pulley, is indicated for patients with chronic symptoms (>6 months) not responding to medical treatment.[3] Favorable results also have been reported with "closed" percutaneous trigger finger release, using the sharp edge of a hypodermic needle to section the A1 pulley.[4]

References

1. Bayat A, Shaaban H, Giakas G, Lees VC: The pulley system of the thumb: Anatomic and biomechanical study. J Hand Surg 27A:628, 2002.
2. Saldana MJ: Trigger digits: Diagnosis and treatment. J Am Acad Orthop Surg 9:246, 2001.
3. Patel MR, Bassini L: Trigger fingers and thumb: when to splint, inject or operate. J Hand Surg 17A:110, 1992.
4. Blumberg N, Arbel R, Dekel S: Percutaneous release of trigger digits. J Hand Surg 26B:256, 2001.
5. Fam AG: Aspiration and injection of joints and periarticular tissues: The wrist and hand. In Klippel JH, Dieppe PA (eds): Practical Rheumatology. London, Mosby, 1995, p 117.

chapter 72

Glomus Tumor of the Hand

Adel G. Fam

■ HISTORICAL ASPECTS AND PATHOLOGY

Wood, in 1812, was the first to describe glomus tumors.[1] In 1927, Masson fully characterized the tumor and recognized its origin from the neuromyoarterial glomus.[2] Glomus tumor or glomangioma is a rare, benign hamartoma, representing 1% to 5% of soft neoplasms of the hand.[1-3] These tumors are derived from the neuromyoarterial glomus body, a contractile, smooth muscle neuromyoarterial receptor that is sensitive to temperature changes, governing blood flow in the cutaneous microvasculature. The tumor consists of an arteriole, a venule, and an anastomotic vessel (Sucquet-Hoyer canal) surrounded by smooth muscle fibers, without an intervening capillary bed. Glomus tumors are usually solitary and occur most commonly beneath the nails (fingers more often than toes) and in the pulp space of the fingers and thumbs. The tumor is well encapsulated and consists of endothelial-lined vascular spaces (Sucquet-Hoyer canal), surrounded by polyhedral glomus cells, with round, darkly stained nuclei.[1-3] The cells stain with actin immunostain, which is diagnostic of glomus cells.[4]

■ CLINICAL FEATURES

Glomus tumors are most common in middle-aged women. The onset is often insidious, with pain, tenderness, and temperature sensitivity.[1-3] The pain is usually "burning," "bursting," "lancinating," and sometimes paroxysmal in nature. It often radiates proximally along the affected digit and typically is aggravated by cold caused by weather changes, holding a cold object, or contact with cold water. Mild warmth produces an alleviating effect. Severe tenderness in and around the lesion is the most striking finding. A reddish purple, small, nodular mass is rarely palpable. In subungual glomus tumors, the nail may be ridged and discolored. "Love's pin test" is useful in localizing the tumor by gently pressing the area of the pain in the digit with a pen tip or the round head of a metal pin. Severe pain at the site of the tumor and hand withdrawal indicate a positive test. In "Hildreth's test," the affected hand is exsanguinated by asking the patient to make a tight fist and elevate the affected arm while a sphygmomanometer cuff inflated to 250 mm Hg is applied to the upper arm.[5] Reduction of pain and tenderness at the site of the glomus tumor by this maneuver and its recurrence on releasing the cuff indicate a positive test.[5] The "cold sensitivity test" is performed by placing the affected hand in cold water. Severe pain and tenderness in and around the suspected lesion suggest an underlying glomus tumor.[1-3]

■ DIAGNOSTIC STUDIES

Glomus tumors can be difficult to diagnose and are often mistaken for a pigmented nevus, melanoma, neuroma, skin nodule, mucoid cyst, or angioma. Transillumination of the affected fingertip, using a penlight, may show an area of poor illumination indicating a glomus mass lesion. Radiographs of the affected digit may be normal, but smooth erosion of the cortex of the underlying distal phalanx may be seen in more advanced cases. On high-resolution ultrasound, glomus tumors manifest as a well-defined, hypoechoic oval or round mass in the fingertip.[6] The sensitivity of ultrasound is about 75%; small lesions <3 mm in diameter and flattened subungual glomus tumors are difficult to detect. MRI is more sensitive, detecting lesions 2 mm in diameter, allowing for accurate localization of the tumor before surgical exploration.[4,7] Arteriography, scintigraphy, and thermography are of limited diagnostic value.

■ TREATMENT

Treatment of glomus tumors is surgical. Complete excision of the lesion and its capsule is indicated to prevent recurrence.[1-3]

References

1. Carroll RE, Berman AT: Glomus tumors of the hand: Review of the literature and report on twenty-eight cases. J Bone Joint Surg 54A:691, 1972.
2. Heys SD, Brittenden J, Atkinson P, Eremin O: Glomus tumour: An analysis of 43 patients and review of the literature. Br J Surg 79:345, 1992.
3. Bhaskaranaud K, Navadgi BC: Glomus tumor of the hand. J Hand Surg 27B:229, 2002.
4. Sorene ED, Goodwin DR: Magnetic resonance imaging of a tiny glomus tumor of the fingertip: A case report. Scand J Plast Reconstr Hand Surg 35:429, 2001.
5. Giele H: Hildreth's test is a reliable clinical sign for the diagnosis of glomus tumours. J Hand Surg 27B:157, 2002.
6. Fornage BD: Glomus tumors in the fingers: Diagnosis with US. Radiology 167:183, 1988.
7. Drape JL, Idy-Peretti I, Goettmann S, et al: Standard and high resolution magnetic resonance imaging of glomus tumors of toes and fingertips. J Am Acad Dermatol 35:550, 1996.

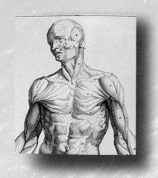

Part F

PAIN SYNDROMES OF THE CHEST WALL, THORACIC SPINE, AND RESPIRATORY SYSTEM

chapter

73

Chest Wall Pain Syndromes

Steven D. Waldman

Patients commonly seek medical attention for noncardiogenic chest pain syndromes. Often these calls for help take the form of middle of the night visits to the emergency department because of patients' fear that they are having a heart attack. Such emergent visits are increasing as a result of the increased marketing efforts by hospitals regarding their chest pain centers and cardiology services. Although these painful conditions are common, they are frequently misdiagnosed as cardiogenic pain, leading to unnecessary invasive cardiac catheterizations, expensive nuclear medicine studies, and much needless anxiety by patient and their families. This chapter provides the clinician with a clear roadmap of how to identify and treat most common musculoskeletal causes of noncardiac chest pain (Table 73–1). The ability to diagnose and treat these problems rapidly represents a very cost-effective endeavor and would help alleviate much anxiety and suffering.

■ COSTOSTERNAL SYNDROME

The costosternal joints can serve as a source of pain that often may mimic the pain of cardiac origin. These joints are sus-

ceptible to the development of arthritis, including osteoarthritis, rheumatoid arthritis, ankylosing spondylitis, Reiter syndrome, and psoriatic arthritis. The joints often are traumatized during acceleration/deceleration injuries and blunt trauma to the chest. With severe trauma, the joints may sublux or dislocate. Overuse or misuse also can result in acute inflammation of the costosternal joint, which can be quite debilitating for the patient. The joints also are subject to invasion by tumor from primary malignancies, including thymoma, and metastatic disease.

Functional Anatomy

The cartilage of the true ribs articulates with the sternum via the costosternal joints (Fig. 73–1). The cartilage of the first rib articulates directly with the manubrium of the sternum and is a synarthrodial joint, which allows a limited gliding movement. The cartilage of the second through sixth ribs articulates with the body of the sternum via true arthrodial joints. These joints are surrounded by a thin articular capsule. The costosternal joints are strengthened by ligaments, but can be subluxed or dislocated by blunt trauma to the anterior chest.

Table 73-1

Common Chest Wall Pain Syndromes
Costosternal syndrome
Tietze syndrome
Sternalis syndrome
Fractured ribs
Post-thoracotomy pain syndrome
Intercostal neuralgia
Xyphisternal syndrome
Sternoclavicular syndrome

Posterior to the costosternal joint are the structures of the mediastinum.

Signs and Symptoms

On physical examination of a patient with costosternal syndrome, the patient vigorously attempts to splint the joints by keeping the shoulders stiffly in neutral position (Fig. 73–2). Pain is reproduced with active protraction or retraction of the shoulder, deep inspiration, and full elevation of the arm. Shrugging of the shoulder also may reproduce the pain.[1] Coughing may be difficult, and this may lead to inadequate pulmonary toilet in patients who have sustained trauma to the anterior chest wall. The costosternal joints and adjacent intercostal muscles also may be tender to palpation. The patient

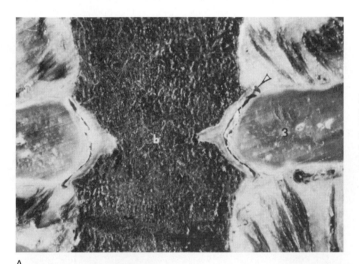

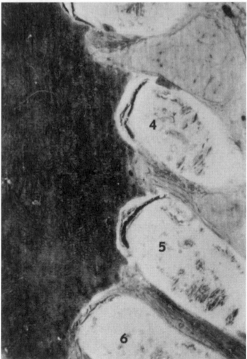

FIGURE 73–1 ■ Sternal, sternocostal, and intercostal joints: normal anatomy. **A,** Third sternocostal articulation (coronal section). Observe sternal body *(b)*, third costal cartilage *(3)*, and intervening synovial articulation *(arrowhead)*. **B** and **C,** Sternocostal articulations. Coronal section of a cadaveric sternum, showing second through seventh *(2-7)* sternocostal joints. (From Resnick D [ed]: Diagnosis of Bone and Joint Disorders, 4th ed. Philadelphia, WB Saunders, 2002, p 735.)

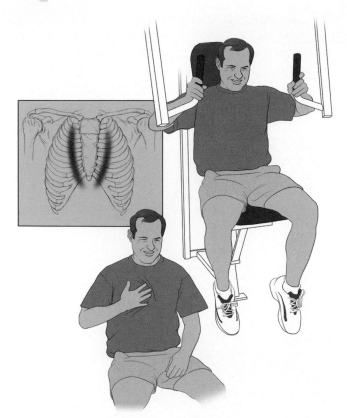

FIGURE 73–2 ■ Irritation of the costosternal joints from overuse of exercise equipment can cause costosternal syndrome. (From Waldman SD: Costosternal syndrome. In: Atlas of Common Pain Syndromes. Philadelphia, WB Saunders, 2002, p 146.)

also may complain of a clicking sensation with movement of the joint.

Testing

Plain radiographs are indicated in all patients who present with pain thought to be emanating from the costosternal joints to rule out occult bony pathology, including tumor. If trauma is present, radionucleotide bone scanning may be useful to rule out occult fractures of the ribs or sternum or both. Based on the patient's clinical presentation, additional testing, including complete blood count, prostate-specific antigen, sedimentation rate, and antinuclear antibody, may be indicated. MRI of the joints is indicated if joint instability or occult mass is suspected. The following injection technique serves as a diagnostic and a therapeutic maneuver.

Treatment

Initial treatment of the pain and functional disability associated with costosternal syndrome should include a combination of simple analgesics and nonsteroidal antiinflammatory drugs (NSAIDs) or cyclooxygenase-2 (COX-2) inhibitors. Local application of heat and cold also may be beneficial. The use of an elastic rib belt also may help provide symptomatic relief and help protect the costosternal joints from additional trauma. For patients who do not respond to these treatment modalities, the following injection technique using local anesthetic and steroid may be a reasonable next step.[2]

For intra-articular injection of the costosternal joint, the patient is placed in the supine position. Proper preparation with antiseptic solution of the skin overlying the affected costosternal joints is carried out. A sterile syringe containing 1 mL of 0.25% preservative-free bupivacaine for each joint to be injected and 40 mg of methylprednisolone is attached to a $1\frac{1}{2}$-inch 25-gauge needle using strict aseptic technique.

With strict aseptic technique, the costosternal joints are identified. The costosternal joints should be easily palpable as a slight bulging at the point where the rib attaches to the sternum. The needle is advanced carefully through the skin and subcutaneous tissues medially with a slight cephalad trajectory into proximity with the joint (Fig. 73–3). If bone is encountered, the needle is withdrawn out of the periosteum. After the needle is in proximity to the joint, 1 mL of solution is gently injected. There should be limited resistance to injection. If significant resistance is encountered, the needle should be withdrawn slightly until the injection proceeds with only limited resistance. This procedure is repeated for each affected joint. The needle is removed, and a sterile pressure dressing and ice pack are placed at the injection site.

■ TIETZE SYNDROME

Tietze syndrome is a common cause of chest wall pain encountered in clinical practice. Distinct from costosternal syndrome, Tietze syndrome was first described in 1921 and is characterized by acute painful swelling of the costal cartilages.[3] The second and third costal cartilages are most commonly involved. In contrast to costosternal syndrome, which usually occurs no earlier than 40 years of age. Tietze syndrome is a disease of 20- to 30-year-olds.[4] The onset is acute and is often associated with a concurrent viral respiratory tract infection (Fig. 73–4). It has been postulated that microtrauma to the costosternal joints from severe coughing or heavy labor may be the cause of Tietze syndrome. Painful swelling of the second and third costochondral joints is the sine qua non of Tietze syndrome. Such swelling is absent in costosternal syndrome, which occurs much more frequently than Tietze syndrome.

Functional Anatomy

The cartilage of the true ribs articulates with the sternum via the costosternal joints. The cartilage of the first rib articulates directly with the manubrium of the sternum and is a synarthrodial joint, which allows a limited gliding movement. The cartilage of the second through sixth ribs articulates with the body of the sternum via true arthrodial joints. These joints are surrounded by a thin articular capsule. The costosternal joints are strengthened by ligaments, but can be subluxed or dislocated by blunt trauma to the anterior chest. Posterior to the costosternal joint are the structures of the mediastinum.

Signs and Symptoms

On physical examination, a patient with Tietze syndrome vigorously attempts to splint the joints by keeping the shoulders stiffly in neutral position. Pain is reproduced with active protraction or retraction of the shoulder, deep inspiration, and full elevation of the arm. Shrugging of the shoulder also may

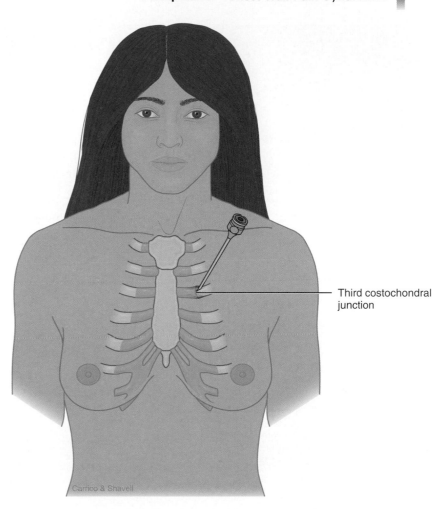

FIGURE 73–3 ■ Injection technique for relieving pain resulting from costosternal syndrome. (From Waldman SD: Costosternal syndrome. In: Atlas of Pain Management Injection Techniques. Philadelphia, WB Saunders, 2000, p 173.)

Third costochondral junction

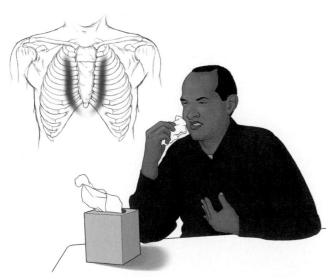

FIGURE 73–4 ■ Swelling of the second and third costochondral joints is the hallmark sign of Tietze syndrome. (From Waldman SD: Tietze's syndrome. In: Atlas of Common Pain Syndromes. Philadelphia, WB Saunders, 2002, p 159.)

reproduce the pain. Coughing may be difficult, and this may lead to inadequate pulmonary toilet in patients with Tietze syndrome. The costosternal joints, especially the second and third joints, are swollen and exquisitely tender to palpation. The adjacent intercostal muscles also may be tender to palpation. The patient may complain of a clicking sensation with movement of the joint.

Testing

Plain radiographs are indicated in all patients who present with pain thought to be emanating from the costosternal joints to rule out occult bony pathology, including tumor. If trauma is present, radionucleotide bone scanning should be considered to rule out occult fractures of the ribs or sternum or both. Based on the patient's clinical presentation, additional testing, including complete blood count, prostate-specific antigen, sedimentation rate, and antinuclear antibody, may be indicated. MRI of the joints shows costosternal joint inflammation on short tau inversion recovery sequences and is indicated if joint instability or an occult mass is suspected (Fig. 73–5). The following injection technique serves as a diagnostic and a therapeutic maneuver.[5]

Treatment

Initial treatment of the pain and functional disability associated with Tietze syndrome should include a combination of

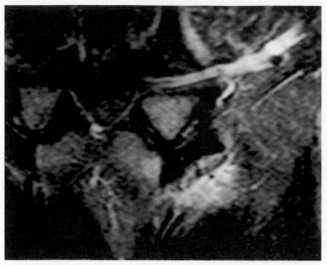

FIGURE 73–5 ■ Tietze syndrome. A coronal STIR mR image of the thorax, showing high-intensity signal at the costosternal joint. (From Resnick D [ed]: Diagnosis of Bone and Joint Disorders, 4th ed. Philadelphia, WB Saunders, 2002, p 2605.)

simple analgesics and NSAIDs or COX-2 inhibitors. Local application of heat and cold also may be beneficial. The use of an elastic rib belt may help provide symptomatic relief and help protect the costovertebral joints from additional trauma. For patients who do not respond to these treatment modalities, the following injection technique using local anesthetic and steroid may be a reasonable next step.

To perform injection for Tietze syndrome, the patient is placed in the supine position. Proper preparation with antiseptic solution of the skin overlying the affected costosternal joints is carried out. A sterile syringe containing 1 mL of 0.25% preservative-free bupivacaine for each joint to be injected and 40 mg of methylprednisolone is attached to a 1½-inch 25-gauge needle using strict aseptic technique.

With strict aseptic technique, the costosternal joints are identified. The costosternal joints should be easily palpable as a slight bulging at the point where the rib attaches to the sternum. The needle is advanced carefully through the skin and subcutaneous tissues medially with a slight cephalad trajectory into proximity with the joint (Fig. 73–6). If bone is encountered, the needle is withdrawn out of the periosteum. After the needle is in proximity to the joint, 1 mL of solution is gently injected. There should be limited resistance to injec-

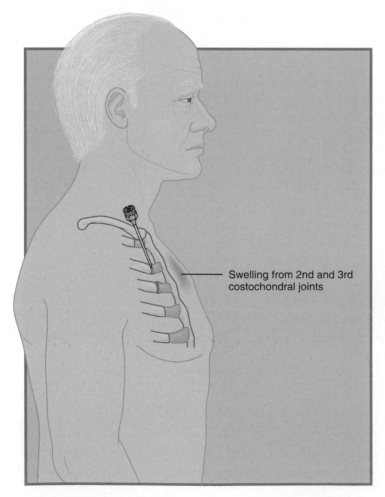

Swelling from 2nd and 3rd costochondral joints

FIGURE 73–6 ■ Injection technique for relieving pain resulting from Tietze syndrome. (From Waldman SD: Tietze syndrome. In: Atlas of Pain Management Injection Techniques. Philadelphia, WB Saunders, 2000, p 175.)

tion. If significant resistance is encountered, the needle should be withdrawn slightly until the injection proceeds with only limited resistance. This procedure is repeated for each affected joint. The needle is removed, and a sterile pressure dressing and ice pack are placed at the injection site.

■ STERNALIS SYNDROME

Chest wall pain syndromes are commonly encountered in clinical practice. Some syndromes occur with relatively greater frequency and are more readily identified by the clinician (e.g., costochondritis, Tietze syndrome). Others occur so infrequently that they are often misdiagnosed, resulting in less than optimal outcome. Sternalis syndrome is an infrequent cause of anterior chest wall pain. Sternalis is a constellation of symptoms consisting of midline anterior chest wall pain that can radiate to the retrosternal area and the medial aspect of the arm.[5]

Sternalis syndrome can mimic the pain of myocardial infarction and frequently is misdiagnosed as such. Sternalis syndrome is a myofascial pain syndrome and is characterized by trigger points in the midsternal area (Fig. 73–7). In contradistinction to costosternal syndrome, which also presents as midsternal pain, the pain of sternalis syndrome is not exacerbated by movement of the chest wall and shoulder. The intensity of the pain associated with sternalis syndrome is mild to moderate and described as having a deep, aching character. The pain of sternalis syndrome is intermittent.

Functional Anatomy

The sternalis muscle lies anterior to the sternal end of the pectoralis major muscle. The sternalis muscle runs parallel to the sternum and is not present in all individuals. Some anatomists believe that the sternalis muscle is a developmental abnormality and represents an aberrant portion of the pectoralis muscle. The sternalis muscle is innervated by the anterior thoracic nerves.

Signs and Symptoms

On physical examination, a patient with sternalis syndrome exhibits myofascial trigger points at the midline over the sternum. Occasionally, there is a coexistent trigger point in the pectoralis muscle or sternal head of the sternocleidomastoid muscle. Pain is reproduced with palpation of these trigger points, rather than movement of the chest wall and shoulders. A positive jump sign is present when these trigger points are stimulated. Trigger points at the lateral border of the scapula also may be present and amenable to injection therapy. As mentioned earlier, movement of the shoulders and chest wall does not exacerbate the pain.

Testing

Plain radiographs are indicated in all patients who present with suspected sternalis syndrome to rule out occult bony pathology, including metastatic lesions. Based on the patient's clinical presentation, additional testing, including complete blood count, prostate-specific antigen, sedimentation rate, and antinuclear antibody, may be indicated. MRI of the chest is indicated if a retrosternal mass, such as thymoma, is suspected. Electromyography is indicated in patients with sternalis syndrome to help rule out cervical radiculopathy or plexopathy, which may be considered because of the referred arm pain. Injection of the sternalis muscle with local anesthetic and steroid serves as a diagnostic and a therapeutic maneuver.

Treatment

Initial treatment of sternalis syndrome should include a combination of simple analgesics and NSAIDs or COX-2 inhibitors. Local application of heat and cold also may be beneficial to provide symptomatic relief of the pain of sternalis syndrome. The use of an elastic rib belt also may help provide symptomatic relief in some patients. For patients who do not respond to these treatment modalities, injection of the trigger areas located in the sternalis muscle using local anesthetic and steroid may be a reasonable next step.[6]

The goals of the injection technique are explained to the patient. The patient is placed in the supine position with the

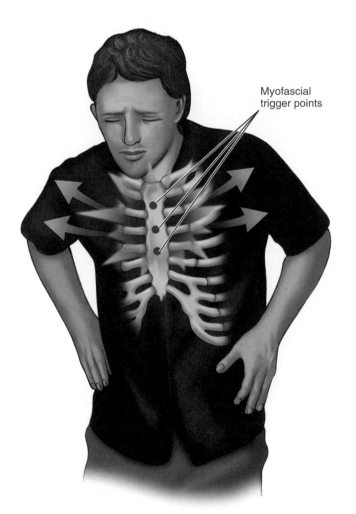

Myofascial trigger points

FIGURE 73–7 ■ Patients with sternalis syndrome exhibit myofascial trigger points at the midline over the sternum. (From Waldman SD: Sternalis syndrome. In: Atlas of Uncommon Pain Syndromes. Philadelphia, WB Saunders, 2003, p 124.)

arms resting comfortably at the patient's side. The midline of the sternum is identified and is palpated to identify myofascial trigger points in the sternalis muscle. A positive jump sign should be noted when a trigger point is identified. Each trigger point is marked with a sterile marker.

Proper preparation with antiseptic solution of the skin overlying the trigger points is carried out. A sterile syringe containing 1 mL of 0.25% preservative-free bupivacaine for each trigger point and 40 mg of methylprednisolone is attached to a 1½-inch 25-gauge needle using strict aseptic technique. With strict aseptic technique, each previously marked point is palpated, and the trigger point is identified again with the gloved finger. The needle is carefully advanced at this point through the skin and subcutaneous tissues into the trigger point in the underlying sternalis muscle (Fig. 73–8). The needle is fixed in place, and the contents of the syringe are gently injected. There should be minimal resistance to injection. The needle is removed, and a sterile pressure dressing and ice pack are placed at the injection site. Other trigger points at the lateral border of the sternum and pectoralis major are identified and injected in an analogous manner.

■ RIB FRACTURES

Rib factures are a common cause of chest wall pain. Fractures are associated most commonly with trauma to the chest wall. In osteoporotic patients or in patients with primary tumors or metastatic disease involving the ribs, fractures may occur with coughing (tussive fractures) or spontaneously.

The pain and functional disability associated with fractured ribs are determined in large part by the severity of injury (e.g., the number of ribs involved), the nature of the injury (e.g., partial or complete fractures), the presence of free-floating fragments, and the amount of damage to surrounding structures (e.g., the intercostal nerves and pleura).[7] The severity of pain associated with fractured ribs may range from a dull, deep ache with partial osteoporotic fractures to severe sharp, stabbing pain that limits the patient's ability to maintain adequate pulmonary toilet.

Signs and Symptoms

Rib fractures are aggravated by deep inspiration, coughing, and any movement of the chest wall. Palpation of the affected

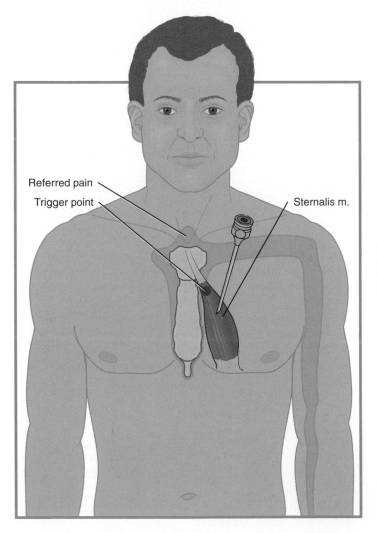

Referred pain

Trigger point

Sternalis m.

FIGURE 73–8 ■ Injection technique for relieving pain resulting from sternalis syndrome. (From Waldman SD: Sternalis syndrome. In: Atlas of Pain Management Injection Techniques. Philadelphia, WB Saunders, 2000, p 184.)

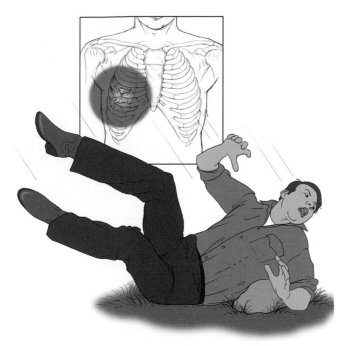

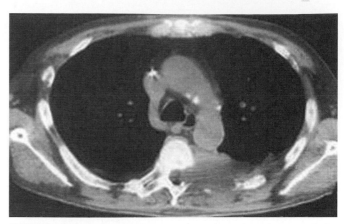

FIGURE 73–10 ■ Adenocarcinoma metastatic to rib and chest wall. CT shows the bone destruction and the soft tissue component inside and outside the rib and the invasion of the vertebra where tumor tissue reaches the spinal canal. (From Grainger R, Allison DJ (eds): Grainger and Allison's Diagnostic Radiology, 4th ed. Philadelphia, Churchill Livingstone, 2002, p 322.)

FIGURE 73–9 ■ The pain of fractured ribs is amenable to intercostal nerve block with local anesthetic and steroid. (From Waldman SD: Fractured ribs. In: Atlas of Common Pain Syndromes. Philadelphia, WB Saunders, 2002, p 163.)

ribs may elicit pain and reflex spasm of the musculature of the chest wall. Ecchymosis overlying the fractures may be present (Fig. 73–9). The clinician should be aware of the possibility of pneumothorax or hemopneumothorax. Damage to the intercostal nerves may produce severe pain and result in reflex splinting of the chest wall, further compromising the patient's pulmonary status. Failure to treat this pain and splinting aggressively may result in a negative cycle of hypoventilation, atelectasis, and ultimately pneumonia.

Testing

Plain radiographs of the ribs and chest are indicated in all patients who present with pain from fractured ribs to rule out occult fractures and other bony pathology, including tumor, and pneumothorax and hemopneumothorax (Fig. 73–10). If trauma is present, radionucleotide bone scanning may be useful to rule out occult fractures of the ribs or sternum or both. If no trauma is present, bone density testing to rule out osteoporosis is appropriate, as is serum protein electrophoresis and testing for hyperparathyroidism. Based on the patient's clinical presentation, additional testing, including complete blood count, prostate-specific antigen, sedimentation rate, and antinuclear antibody, may be indicated. CT of the thoracic contents is indicated if an occult mass or significant trauma to the thoracic contents is suspected. Electrocardiogram to rule out cardiac contusion is indicated in all patients with traumatic sternal fractures or significant anterior chest wall trauma. The following injection technique should be used early on to avoid the above-mentioned pulmonary complications.

Treatment

Initial treatment of rib fracture pain should include a combination of simple analgesics and NSAIDs or COX-2 inhibitors. If these medications do not control the patient's symptoms adequately, short-acting potent opioid analgesics, such as hydrocodone, represent a reasonable next step. Because opioid analgesics have the potential to suppress the cough reflex and respiration, the clinician must be careful to monitor the patient closely and to instruct the patient in adequate pulmonary toilet techniques. Local application of heat and cold also may be beneficial to provide symptomatic relief of the pain of rib fracture. The use of an elastic rib belt also may help provide symptomatic relief. For patients who do not respond to these treatment modalities, the following injection technique using local anesthetic and steroid should be implemented to avoid pulmonary complications.[8]

The patient is placed in the prone position with the patient's arms hanging loosely off the side of the cart. Alternatively, this block can be done with the patient in the sitting or lateral position. The rib to be blocked is identified by palpating its path at the posterior axillary line. The index and middle fingers are placed on the rib bracketing the site of needle insertion. The skin is prepared with antiseptic solution. A 1½-inch 22-gauge needle is attached to a 12-mL syringe and is advanced perpendicular to the skin aiming for the middle of the rib between the index and middle fingers (Fig. 73–11). The needle should impinge on bone after being advanced approximately ¾ inch. After bony contact is made, the needle is withdrawn into the subcutaneous tissues, and the skin and subcutaneous tissues are retracted with the palpating fingers inferiorly; this allows the needle to be walked off the inferior margin of the rib. As soon as bony contact is lost, the needle is slowly advanced approximately 2 mm deeper; this places the needle in proximity to the costal groove, which contains the intercostal nerve and the intercostal artery and vein. After careful aspiration reveals no blood or air, 3 to 5 mL of 1% preservative-free lidocaine is injected. If there is an inflammatory component to the pain, the local anesthetic is combined with 80 mg of methylprednisolone and is injected in incremental doses. Subsequent

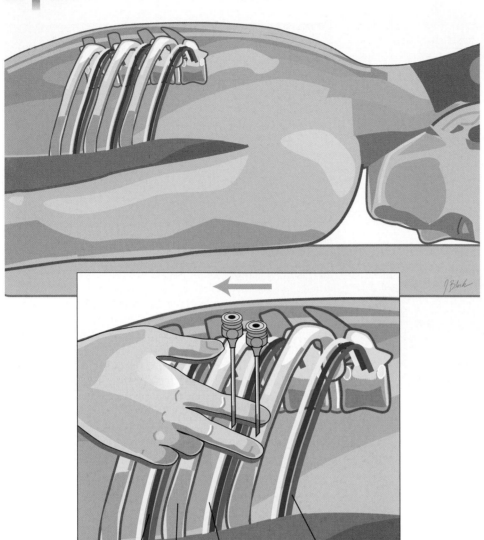

Intercostal a.

Rib

Intercostal n.

Intercostal v.

FIGURE 73–11 ■ Injection technique for relieving pain resulting from fractured ribs. (From Waldman SD: Intercostal nerve block. In: Atlas of Interventional Pain Management, 2nd ed. Philadelphia, WB Saunders, 2004, p 243.)

daily nerve blocks are carried out in a similar manner substituting 40 mg of methylprednisolone for the initial 80-mg dose. Because of the overlapping innervation of the chest and upper abdominal wall, the intercostal nerves above and below the nerve suspected of subserving the painful condition have to be blocked.

■ POST-THORACOTOMY PAIN

Essentially all patients who undergo thoracotomy have acute postoperative pain. This acute pain syndrome invariably responds to the rational use of systemic and spinal opioids and intercostal nerve block. A small percentage of patients who undergo thoracotomy have persistent pain beyond the usual course of postoperative pain. This pain syndrome is called post-thoracotomy pain syndrome and can be difficult to treat. The causes of post-thoracotomy pain (Table 73–2) include direct surgical trauma to the intercostal nerves, fractured ribs secondary to the rib spreader, compressive neuropathy of the

Table 73-2

Causes of Post-Thoracotomy Pain Syndrome

Direct surgical trauma to the intercostal nerves
Fractured ribs owing to the rib spreader
Compressive neuropathy of the intercostal nerves resulting from direct compression to the intercostal nerves by retractors
Cutaneous neuroma formation
Stretch injuries to the intercostal nerves at the costovertebral junction

intercostal nerves resulting from direct compression to the intercostal nerves, cutaneous neuroma formation, and stretch injuries to the intercostal nerves at the costovertebral junction.[9] With the exception of fractured ribs, which produce characteristic local pain that is worse with deep inspiration, coughing, or movement of the affected ribs, the other causes of post-thoracotomy pain result in moderate to severe pain that is constant in nature and follows the distribution of the affected intercostal nerves. The pain may be characterized as neuritic and occasionally may have a dysesthetic quality.

Signs and Symptoms

Physical examination of a patient with post-thoracotomy syndrome generally reveals tenderness along the healed thoracotomy incision. Occasionally, palpation of the scar elicits paresthesias suggestive of neuroma formation (Fig. 73–12). A patient with post-thoracotomy syndrome may attempt to splint or protect the affected area. Careful sensory examination of the affected dermatomes may reveal decreased sensation or allodynia. With significant motor involvement of the subcostal nerve, the patient may complain that the abdomen bulges out. Occasionally, patients with post-thoracotomy syndrome develop a reflex sympathetic dystrophy of the ipsilateral upper extremity. If the reflex sympathetic dystrophy is left untreated, frozen shoulder may develop.

Testing

Plain radiographs are indicated in all patients who present with pain thought to be emanating from the intercostal nerve to rule out occult bony pathology, including tumor. Radionucleotide bone scanning may be useful to rule out occult fractures of the ribs or sternum or both. Based on the patient's clinical presentation, additional testing, including complete blood count, prostate-specific antigen, sedimentation rate, and antinuclear antibody, may be indicated. CT of the thoracic contents is indicated if occult mass or pleural disease is suspected. The following injection technique serves as a diagnostic and a therapeutic maneuver. Electromyography is useful in distinguishing injury of the distal intercostal nerve from stretch injuries of the intercostal nerve at the costovertebral junction.

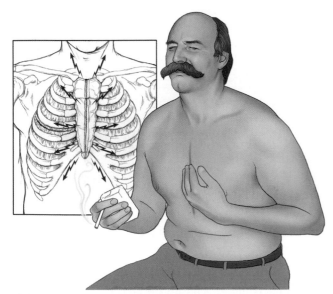

FIGURE 73–12 ■ The patient with post-thoracotomy syndrome exhibits tenderness to palpation of the scar. (From Waldman SD: Post-thoracotomy pain. In: Atlas of Common Pain Syndromes. Philadelphia, WB Saunders, 2002, p 164.)

Treatment

Initial treatment of post-thoracotomy syndrome should include a combination of simple analgesics and NSAIDs or COX-2 inhibitors. If these medications do not control the patient's symptoms adequately, a tricyclic antidepressant or gabapentin should be added.

Traditionally, tricyclic antidepressants have been a mainstay in the palliation of pain secondary to post-thoracotomy syndrome. Controlled studies have shown the efficacy of amitriptyline for this indication. Other tricyclic antidepressants, including nortriptyline and desipramine, also have been shown to be clinically useful. This class of drugs is associated with significant anticholinergic side effects, including dry mouth, constipation, sedation, and urinary retention. These drugs should be used with caution in patients with glaucoma, cardiac arrhythmia, and prostatism. To minimize side effects and encourage compliance, the primary care physician should start amitriptyline or nortriptyline at a 10-mg dose at bedtime. The dose can be titrated upward to 25 mg at bedtime as side effects allow. Upward titration of dosage in 25-mg increments can be carried out each week as side effects allow. Even at lower doses, patients generally report a rapid reduction in sleep disturbance and begin to experience some pain relief in 10 to 14 days. If the patient does not experience any improvement in pain as the dose is being titrated upward, the addition of gabapentin alone or in combination with nerve blocks with local anesthetics or steroid or both is recommended (see later). The selective serotonin reuptake inhibitors, such as fluoxetine, also have been used to treat the pain of diabetic neuropathy. Although better tolerated than the tricyclic antidepressants, selective serotonin reuptake inhibitors seem to be less efficacious.

If the antidepressant compounds are ineffective or contraindicated, gabapentin is a reasonable alternative. Gabapentin should be started with a 300-mg dose at bedtime for 2 nights. The patient should be cautioned about potential side effects, including dizziness, sedation, confusion, and rash. The drug is increased in 300-mg increments, given in equally divided doses over 2 days, as side effects allow until pain relief is obtained or a total dose of 2400 mg daily is reached. At this point, if the patient has experienced partial relief of pain, blood values are measured, and the drug is carefully titrated upward using 100-mg tablets. More than 3600 mg daily rarely is required.

Local application of heat and cold may be beneficial to provide symptomatic relief of the pain of post-thoracotomy syndrome. The use of an elastic rib belt also may help provide symptomatic relief. For patients who do not respond to these treatment modalities, the following injection technique using local anesthetic and steroid may be a reasonable next step.

The patient is placed in the prone position with the patient's arms hanging loosely off the side of the cart. Alternatively, this block can be done with the patient in the sitting or lateral position. The rib to be blocked is identified by palpating its path at the posterior axillary line. The index and middle fingers are placed on the rib bracketing the site of needle insertion. The skin is prepared with antiseptic solution. A 1½-inch 22-gauge needle is attached to a 12-mL syringe and is advanced perpendicular to the skin aiming for the middle of the rib between the index and middle fingers. The needle should impinge on bone after being advanced approximately ¾ inch. After bony contact is made, the needle is withdrawn into the subcutaneous tissues, and the skin and subcutaneous tissues are retracted with the palpating fingers inferiorly; this allows the needle to be walked off the inferior margin of the rib. As soon as bony contact is lost, the needle is slowly advanced approximately 2 mm deeper; this places the needle in proximity to the costal groove, which contains the intercostal nerve and the intercostal artery and vein. After careful aspiration reveals no blood or air, 3 to 5 mL of 1% preservative-free lidocaine is injected. If there is an inflammatory component to the pain, the local anesthetic is combined with 80 mg of methylprednisolone and is injected in incremental doses. Subsequent daily nerve blocks are carried out in a similar manner substituting 40 mg of methylprednisolone for the initial 80-mg dose. Because of the overlapping innervation of the chest and upper abdominal wall, the intercostal nerves above and below the nerve suspected of subserving the painful condition have to be blocked.

■ INTERCOSTAL NEURALGIA

In contradistinction to most other causes of pain involving the chest wall, which are musculoskeletal in nature, the pain of intercostal neuralgia is neuropathic.[12] Similar to costosternal joint pain, Tzietze syndrome, and rib fractures, many patients who have intercostal neuralgia first seek medical attention because they believe they are having a heart attack. If the subcostal nerve is involved, patients may believe they have gallbladder disease. The pain of intercostal neuralgia is due to damage or inflammation of the intercostal nerves. The pain is constant and burning in nature and may involve any of the intercostal nerves and the subcostal nerve of the 12th rib. The pain usually begins at the posterior axillary line and radiates anteriorly into the distribution of the affected intercostal and subcostal nerves (Fig. 73–13). Deep inspiration or movement of the chest wall may increase the pain of intercostal neuralgia slightly, but much less compared with the pain associated with the musculoskeletal causes of chest wall pain (e.g., costosternal joint pain, Tietze syndrome, or broken ribs).

Signs and Symptoms

Physical examination of a patient with intercostal neuralgia generally reveals minimal physical findings, unless there was a history of previous thoracic or subcostal surgery or cutaneous findings of herpes zoster involving the thoracic dermatomes. In contrast to the above-mentioned musculoskeletal causes of chest wall and subcostal pain, a patient with intercostal neuralgia does not attempt to splint or protect the affected area. Careful sensory examination of the affected dermatomes may reveal decreased sensation or allodynia. With significant motor involvement of the subcostal nerve, the patient may complain that the abdomen bulges out.

Testing

Plain radiographs are indicated in all patients who present with pain thought to be emanating from the intercostal nerve

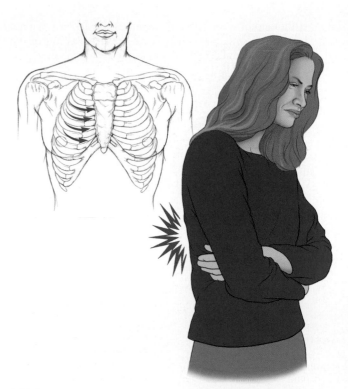

FIGURE 73–13 ■ The pain of intercostal neuralgia is neuropathic rather than musculoskeletal in origin. (From Waldman SD: Intercostal neuralgia. In: Atlas of Common Pain Syndromes. Philadelphia, WB Saunders, 2002, p 151.)

to rule out occult bony pathology, including tumor (Fig. 73–14). If trauma is present, radionucleotide bone scanning may be useful to rule out occult fractures of the ribs or sternum or both. Based on the patient's clinical presentation, additional testing, including complete blood count, prostate-specific antigen, sedimentation rate, and antinuclear antibody, may be indicated. CT of the thoracic contents is indicated if occult mass is suspected. The following injection technique serves as a diagnostic and therapeutic maneuver.

Initial treatment of intercostal neuralgia should include a combination of simple analgesics and NSAIDs or COX-2 inhibitors. If these medications do not control the patient's symptoms adequately, a tricyclic antidepressant or gabapentin should be added.

Traditionally, tricyclic antidepressants have been a mainstay in the palliation of pain secondary to intercostal neuralgia. Controlled studies have shown the efficacy of amitriptyline for this indication. Other tricyclic antidepressants, including nortriptyline and desipramine, also have been shown to be clinically useful. This class of drugs is associated with significant anticholinergic side effects, including dry mouth, constipation, sedation, and urinary retention. These drugs should be used with caution in patients with glaucoma, cardiac arrhythmia, and prostatism. To minimize side effects and encourage compliance, the primary care physician should start amitriptyline or nortriptyline as a 10-mg dose at bedtime. The dose can be titrated upward to 25 mg at bedtime as side effects allow. Upward titration of dosage in 25-mg increments can be carried out each week as side effects allow. Even at lower doses, patients generally report a rapid

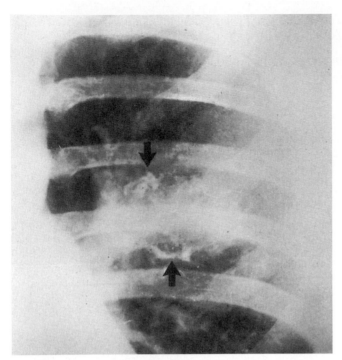

FIGURE 73–14 ■ A chondroma arising from the costochondral junction of the left third rib. This tumor commonly arises from the costochondral junction. It contains typical cartilaginous calcification *(arrows)*. (From Grainger R, et al [eds]: Grainger and Allison's Diagnostic Radiology, 4th ed. Philadelphia, Churchill Livingstone, 2002, p 322.)

reduction in sleep disturbance and begin to experience some pain relief in 10 to 14 days. If the patient does not experience any improvement in pain as the dose is being titrated upward, the addition of gabapentin alone or in combination with nerve blocks with local anesthetics or steroid or both is recommended (see later). The selective serotonin reuptake inhibitors, such as fluoxetine, also have been used to treat the pain of diabetic neuropathy. Although better tolerated than tricyclic antidepressants, selective serotonin reuptake inhibitors seem to be less efficacious.

If the antidepressant compounds are ineffective or contraindicated, gabapentin is a reasonable alternative. Gabapentin should be started with a 300-mg dose at bedtime for 2 nights. The patient should be cautioned about potential side effects, including dizziness, sedation, confusion, and rash. The drug is increased in 300-mg increments, given in equally divided doses over 2 days, as side effects allow until pain relief is obtained or a total dose of 2400 mg daily is reached. At this point, if the patient has experienced partial pain relief, blood values are measured, and the drug is carefully titrated upward using 100-mg tablets. More than 3600 mg daily is rarely required.

The local application of heat and cold also may be beneficial to provide symptomatic relief of the pain of intercostal neuralgia. The use of an elastic rib belt also may help provide symptomatic relief. For patients who do not respond to these treatment modalities, the following injection technique using local anesthetic and steroid may be a reasonable next step.[9]

The patient is placed in the prone position with the patient's arms hanging loosely off the side of the cart. Alternatively, this block can be done in the sitting or lateral posi-

tion. The rib to be blocked is identified by palpating its path at the posterior axillary line. The index and middle fingers are placed on the rib bracketing the site of needle insertion. The skin is prepared with antiseptic solution. A $1\frac{1}{2}$-inch 22-gauge needle is attached to a 12-mL syringe and is advanced perpendicular to the skin aiming for the middle of the rib between the index and middle finger. The needle should impinge on bone after being advanced approximately $\frac{3}{4}$ inch. After bony contact is made, the needle is withdrawn into the subcutaneous tissues, and the skin and subcutaneous tissues are retracted with the palpating fingers inferiorly; this allows the needle to be walked off the inferior margin of the rib. As soon as bony contact is lost, the needle is slowly advanced approximately 2 mm deeper; this places the needle in proximity to the costal groove, which contains the intercostal nerve and the intercostal artery and vein. After careful aspiration reveals no blood or air, 3 to 5 mL of 1% preservative-free lidocaine is injected. If there is an inflammatory component to the pain, the local anesthetic is combined with 80 mg of methylprednisolone and is injected in incremental doses. Subsequent daily nerve blocks are carried out in a similar manner substituting 40 mg of methylprednisolone for the initial 80-mg dose. Because of the overlapping innervation of the chest and upper abdominal wall, the intercostal nerves above and below the nerve suspected of subserving the painful condition have to be blocked.

■ XIPHISTERNAL SYNDROME

The xiphisternal joint can serve as a source of pain that often may mimic the pain of cardiac and upper abdominal origin. The xiphisternal joint is susceptible to the development of arthritis, including osteoarthritis, rheumatoid arthritis, ankylosing spondylitis, Reiter syndrome, and psoriatic arthritis. The joint is often traumatized during acceleration/deceleration injuries and blunt trauma to the chest. With severe trauma, the joint may sublux or dislocate. The joint also is subject to invasion by tumor from primary malignancies, including thymoma, and metastatic disease (Fig. 73–15). This joint seems to serve as the nidus of pain for xiphodynia syndrome. Xiphodynia syndrome, which is also known as xiphodynia, is a constellation of symptoms consisting of severe intermittent anterior chest wall pain in the region of the xiphoid process that is made worse with overeating, stooping, and bending. The patient may complain of a nauseated feeling associated with the pain of xiphodynia syndrome.

On physical examination, the pain of xiphodynia syndrome is reproduced with palpation or traction on the xiphoid.[11] The xiphisternal joint may feel swollen. Stooping or bending may reproduce the pain (Fig. 73–16). Coughing may be difficult, and this may lead to inadequate pulmonary toilet in patients who have sustained trauma to the anterior chest wall. The xiphisternal joint and adjacent intercostal muscles also may be tender to palpation. The patient may complain of a clicking sensation with movement of the joint.

Plain radiographs are indicated in all patients who present with pain thought to be emanating from the xiphisternal joint to rule out occult bony pathology, including tumor. Based on the patient's clinical presentation, additional testing, including complete blood count, prostate-specific antigen, sedimen-

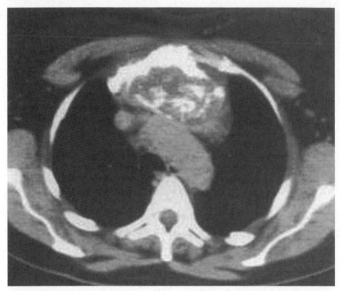

FIGURE 73–15 ■ Chondrosarcoma of sternum. CT shows manubrial irregularity and the preaortic soft tissue mass with its chondral calcification. Nearly all sternal tumors are malignant. (From Grainger R, et al [eds]: Grainger and Allison's Diagnostic Radiology, 4th ed. Philadelphia, Churchill Livingstone, 2002, p 323.)

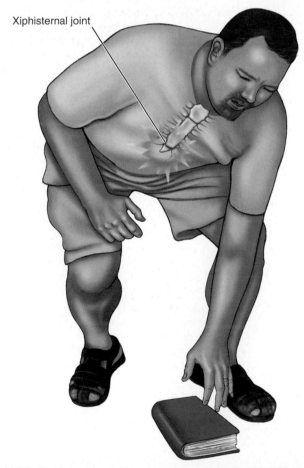

Xiphisternal joint

FIGURE 73–16 ■ The xiphisternal joint is swollen in patients with xiphodynia. (From Waldman SD: Xiphodynia. In: Atlas of Uncommon Pain Syndromes. Philadelphia, WB Saunders, 2003, p 129.)

tation rate, and antinuclear antibody, may be indicated. MRI of the joint is indicated if joint instability or occult mass is suspected. The following injection technique serves as a diagnostic and a therapeutic maneuver.

Functional Anatomy

The xiphoid process articulates with the sternum via the xiphisternal joint (Fig. 73–17). The xiphoid process is a plate of cartilaginous bone that becomes calcified in early adulthood. The xiphisternal joint is strengthened by ligaments, but can be subluxed or dislocated by blunt trauma to the anterior chest. The xiphisternal joint is innervated by the T4-7 intercostal nerves and the phrenic nerve. It is thought that this innervation by the phrenic nerve is responsible for the referred pain associated with xiphodynia syndrome. Posterior to the xiphisternal joint are the structures of the mediastinum. These structures are susceptible to needle-induced trauma during injections for xiphisternal syndrome if the needle is placed too deep. The pleural space may be entered if the needle is placed too deep and laterally, and pneumothorax may result.

Treatment

Initial treatment of the pain and functional disability associated with xiphisternal syndrome should include a combination of simple analgesics and NSAIDs or COX-2 inhibitors. The local application of heat and cold also may be beneficial. The use of an elastic rib belt also may help provide symptomatic relief and help protect the xiphisternal joint from additional trauma. For patients who do not respond to these treatment modalities, the following injection technique using local anesthetic and steroid may be a reasonable next step.[12]

The goals of this injection technique are explained to the patient. The patient is placed in the supine position, and proper preparation with antiseptic solution of the skin overlying the affected xiphisternal joint is carried out. A sterile syringe containing 1 mL of 0.25% preservative-free bupivacaine and 40 mg of methylprednisolone is attached to a 1½-inch 25-gauge needle using strict aseptic technique.

The xiphisternal joint is identified using strict aseptic technique. It should be easily palpable as a slight indentation at the point where the xiphoid process attaches to the body of the sternum. The needle is carefully advanced at the center of the xiphisternal joint through the skin and subcutaneous tissues with a slight cephalad trajectory into proximity with the joint (Fig. 73–18). If bone is encountered, the needle is withdrawn out of the perioistium. After the needle is in proximity to the joint, 1 mL of solution is gently injected. There should be limited resistance to injection. If significant resistance is encountered, the needle should be withdrawn slightly until the injection proceeds with only limited resistance. This procedure is repeated for each affected joint. The needle is removed, and a sterile pressure dressing and ice pack are placed at the injection site.

The major complication of this injection technique is pneumothorax if the needle is placed too laterally or too deep and invades the pleural space. Infection, although rare, can occur if strict aseptic technique is not adhered to. Trauma to the contents of the mediastinum remains an ever-present possibility. This complication can be greatly decreased if the clinician pays close attention to accurate needle placement.

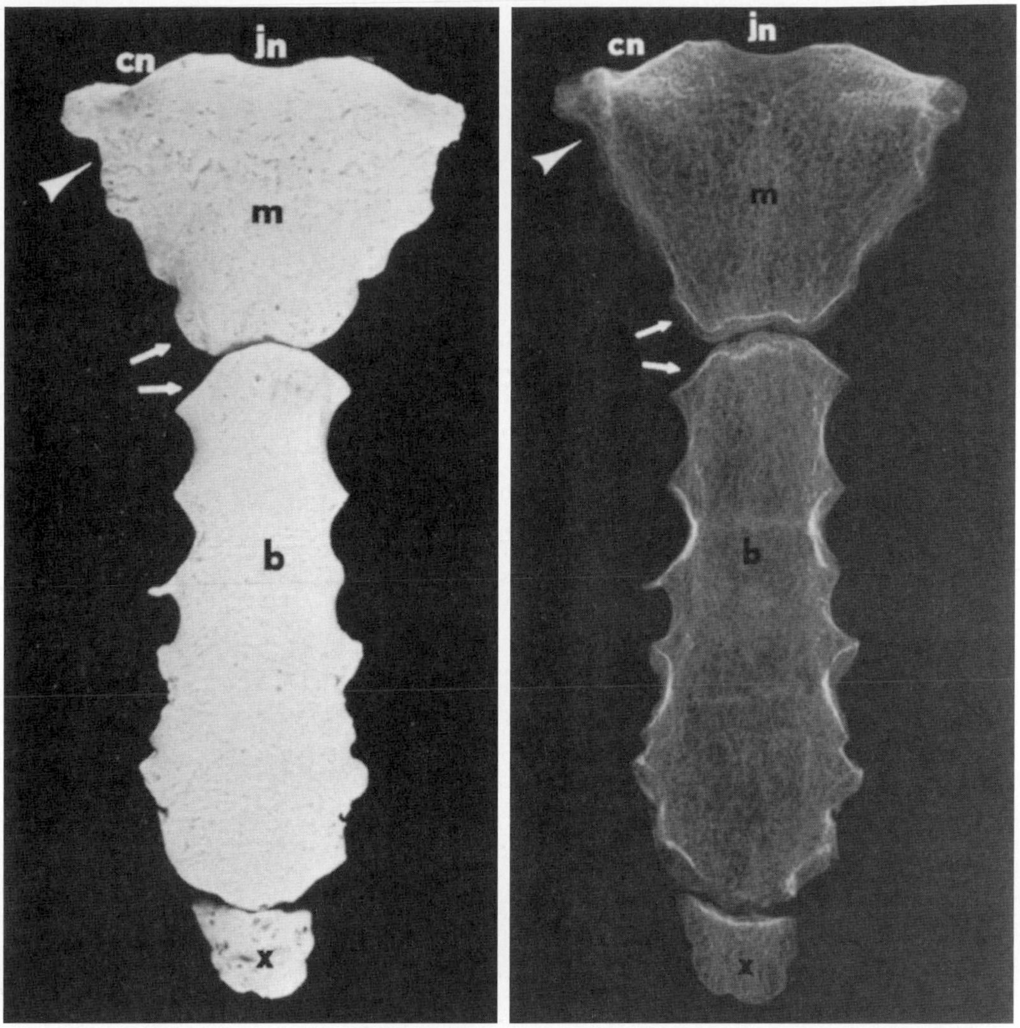

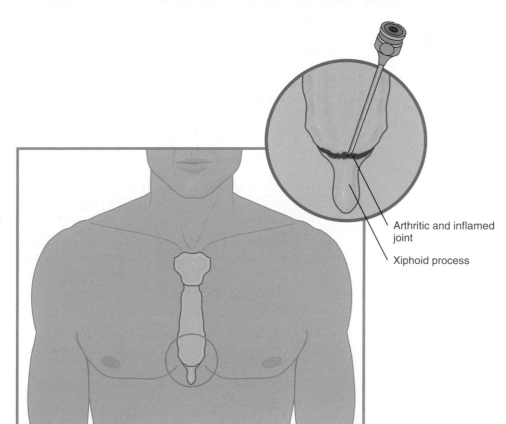

FIGURE 73–17 ■ Sternum: osseous anatomy. Anterior aspect. The three segments of the sternum are the manubrium *(m)*, body *(b)*, and xiphoid process *(x)*. Additional landmarks are the clavicular notch *(cn)* and jugular notch *(jn)*. A sternal facet for articulation with the first costal cartilage *(arrowheads)* and hemifacets for articulation with the second costal cartilage *(arrows)* are indicated. Other articular facets also are apparent on the body of the sternum. (From Resnick D [ed]: Diagnosis of Bone and Joint Disorders, 4th ed. Philadelphia, WB Saunders, 2002, p 731.)

FIGURE 73–18 ■ Injection technique for relieving pain resulting from xiphisternal syndrome. (From Waldman SD: Xiphodynia syndrome. In: Atlas of Pain Management Injection Techniques. Philadelphia, WB Saunders, 2000, p 187.)

Arthritic and inflamed joint

Xiphoid process

■ STERNOCLAVICULAR JOINT SYNDROME

The sternoclavicular joint can serve as a source of pain that often may mimic the pain of cardiac origin. The sternoclavicular joint is a true joint and is susceptible to the development of arthritis, including osteoarthritis, rheumatoid arthritis, ankylosing spondylitis, Reiter syndrome, and psoriatic arthritis. The joint is often traumatized during acceleration/deceleration injuries and blunt trauma to the chest. With severe trauma, the joint may sublux or dislocate. Overuse or misuse also can result in acute inflammation of the sternoclavicular joint, which can be quite debilitating for the patient. The joint also is subject to invasion by tumor from primary malignancies, including thymoma, and metastatic disease (Fig. 73–19).

On physical examination, the patient vigorously attempts to splint the joint by keeping the shoulders stiffly in neutral position. Pain is reproduced by active protraction or retraction of the shoulder and full elevation of the arm. Shrugging of the shoulder also may reproduce the pain. The sternoclavicular joint may be tender to palpation and feel hot and swollen if acutely inflamed.[13] The patient also may complain of a clicking sensation with movement of the joint.

Plain radiographs are indicated in all patients who present with pain thought to be emanating from the sternoclavicular joint to rule out occult bony pathology, including tumor. Based on the patient's clinical presentation, additional testing, including complete blood count, prostate-specific antigen, sedimentation rate, and antinuclear antibody, may be indicated. MRI of the joint is indicated if joint instability is suspected. The following injection technique serves as a diagnostic and a therapeutic maneuver.

Functional Anatomy

The sternoclavicular joint is a double gliding joint with an actual synovial cavity (Fig. 73–20). Articulation occurs between the sternal end of the clavicle, the sternal manubrium, and the cartilage of the first rib. The clavicle and sternal manubrium are separated by an articular disk. The joint is reinforced in front and back by the sternoclavicular ligaments. Additional support is provided by the costoclavicular ligament, which runs from the junction of the first rib and its costal cartilage to the inferior surface of the clavicle. The joint is dually innervated by the supraclavicular nerve and the nerve supplying the subclavius muscle. Posterior to the

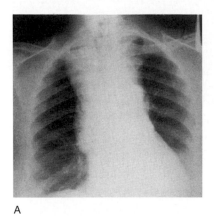
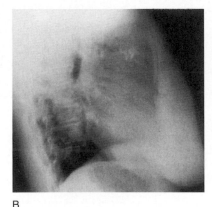
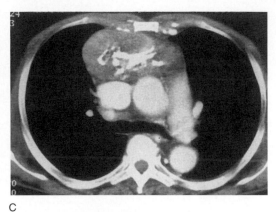

A   B   C

FIGURE 73–19 ■ Thymoma presenting on a chest radiograph obtained before orthopedic surgery in an otherwise asymptomatic elderly woman. **A-C,** There is a large anterior mediastinal mass (**A**) with coarse calcification visible on the lateral view (**B**) and the contrast-enhanced CT scan (**C**). (From Grainger R, et al [eds]: Grainger and Allison's Diagnostic Radiology, 4th ed. Philadelphia, Churchill Livingstone, 2002, p 357.)

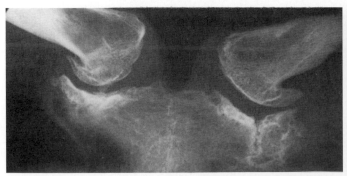
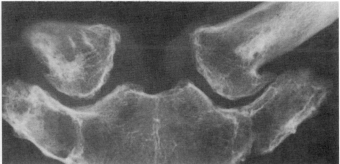

FIGURE 73–20 ■ Osteoarthritis of the sternoclavicular joint. Radiographs of coronal sections through the sternoclavicular joints in two different cadavers show the spectrum of osteoarthritis. Changes include subchondral osseous irregularity and osteophytosis of the medial ends of the clavicle and sternum. Note the large excrescences extending laterally from the inferior aspect of the clavicular heads. (From Resnick D [ed]: Diagnosis of Bone and Joint Disorders, 4th ed. Philadelphia, WB Saunders, 2002, p 1324.)

joint are numerous large arteries and veins, including the left common carotid and brachiocephalic vein and on the right the brachiocephalic artery. These vessels are susceptible to needle-induced trauma if the needle is placed too deep.

The serratus anterior muscle produces forward movement of the clavicle at the sternoclavicular joint with backward movement at the joint produced by the rhomboid and trapezius muscles. Elevation of the clavicle at the sternoclavicular joint is produced by the sternocleidomastoid, rhomboid, and levator scapulae. Depression of the clavicle at the joint is produced by the pectoralis minor and subclavius muscles.

Treatment

Initial treatment of sternoclavicular syndrome pain should include a combination of simple analgesics and NSAIDs or COX-2 inhibitors. If these medications do not control the patient's symptoms adequately, short-acting potent opioid analgesics, such as hydrocodone, represent a reasonable next step. Because opioid analgesics have the potential to suppress the cough reflex and respiration, the clinician must be careful to monitor the patient closely and to instruct the patient in adequate pulmonary toilet techniques. The local application of heat and cold also may be beneficial to provide symptomatic relief of the pain of sternoclavicular syndrome. For patients who do not respond to these treatment modalities, the following injection technique using local anesthetic and steroid should be implemented to avoid pulmonary complications.[14]

The goals of the injection technique are explained to the patient. The patient is placed in the supine position, and the skin overlying the root of the neck anteriorly and the skin overlying the proximal clavicle are prepared with antiseptic solution. A sterile syringe containing 1 mL of 0.25% preservative-free bupivacaine and 40 mg of methylprednisolone is attached to a 1½-inch 25-gauge needle using strict aseptic technique.

With strict aseptic technique, the sternal end of the clavicle is identified. The sternoclavicular joint should be easily palpable as a slight indentation at the point where the clavicle meets the sternal manubrium. The needle is advanced carefully through the skin and subcutaneous tissues medially at a 45-degree angle from the skin through the joint capsule into the joint (Fig. 73–21). If bone is encountered, the needle is withdrawn into the subcutaneous tissues and redirected slightly more medially. After entering the joint space, the contents of the syringe is gently injected. There should be some resistance to injection because the joint space is small, and the joint capsule is dense. If significant resistance is encountered, the needle is probably in a ligament and should be advanced or withdrawn slightly into the joint space until the injection proceeds with only limited resistance. The needle is removed, and a sterile pressure dressing and ice pack are placed at the injection site.

■ DIFFERENTIAL DIAGNOSIS OF CHEST WALL PAIN SYNDROMES

The pain associated with the above-mentioned chest wall pain syndromes is often mistaken for pain of cardiac origin and can lead to visits to the emergency department and unnecessary cardiac workups. If trauma has occurred, the above-mentioned chest wall pain syndromes may coexist with fractured ribs or fractures of the sternum itself, which can be missed on plain radiographs and may require radionucleotide bone scanning for proper identification. Because a patient with one of the above-mentioned chest wall pain syndromes

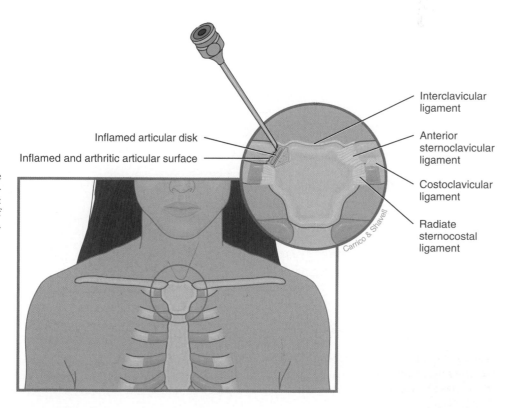

FIGURE 73–21 ■ Injection technique for relieving pain resulting from sternoclavicular joint syndrome. (From Waldman SD: Sternoclavicular syndrome. In: Atlas of Pain Management Injection Techniques. Philadelphia, WB Saunders, 2000, p 178.)

Interclavicular ligament

Anterior sternoclavicular ligament

Costoclavicular ligament

Radiate sternocostal ligament

Inflamed articular disk

Inflamed and arthritic articular surface

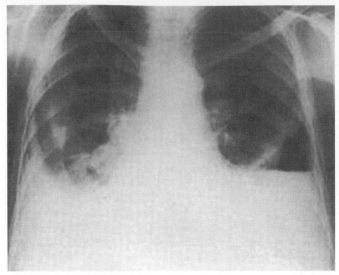

FIGURE 73–22 ■ Right pleural effusion and left hydropneumothorax. The pleural effusion obscures the hemidiaphragm and the right costophrenic angle. It has a curvilinear upper margin concave to lung and is higher laterally than medially. This contrasts with the straight horizontal upper border of the fluid in the left hydropneumothorax. The meniscus on the right has a second, faint medial component caused by intrusion of fluid into the oblique fissure. (From Grainger R, Allison DJ [eds]: Grainger and Allison's Diagnostic Radiology, 4th ed. Philadelphia, Churchill Livingstone, 2002, p 325.)

may be in acute pain and may be experiencing anxiety, careful physical examination is mandatory to help identify the exact chest wall pain syndrome and to allow reassurance that the pain is noncardiac in nature.

Neuropathic pain involving the chest wall also may be confused or coexist with the aforementioned musculoskeletal causes of chest wall pain. Examples of such neuropathic pain include diabetic polyneuropathies and acute herpes zoster involving the thoracic nerves. The possibility of diseases of the structures of the mediastinum is ever-present, and at times diagnosis can be difficult. Pathologic processes that inflame the pleura (e.g., pulmonary embolus, infection, Bornholm disease) also can confuse the clinical picture and make diagnosis more difficult (Fig. 73–22). Additionally, most of the joints of the chest wall are subject to the development of osteoarthritis and inflammation and destruction by the collagen-vascular diseases, including rheumatoid arthritis, ankylosing spondylitis, Reiter syndrome, and psoriatic arthritis (Fig. 73–23). The joints also are subject to invasion by tumor from primary malignancies, including thymoma, and metastatic disease.

■ COMPLICATIONS AND PITFALLS IN THE CARE OF PATIENTS WITH CHEST WALL PAIN SYNDROMES

The major problem in the care of patients thought to have chest wall pain syndromes is the failure to identify potentially serious pathology of the thorax or upper abdomen or occult cardiac conditions. Because of the proximity to the pleural space and mediastinum intercostal nerve and artery, the potential for iatrogenic complications from the above-mentioned nerve block techniques remains ever-present. Although

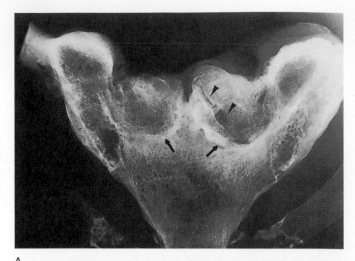

A

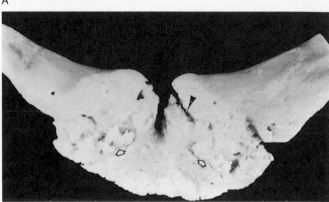

B

FIGURE 73–23 ■ Abnormalities of the sternoclavicular joint. **A,** Radiograph of a coronal section of the sternoclavicular joints indicates intra-articular osseous fusion *(arrows)* between the medial aspect of each clavicle and the sternum. A remnant of the articular space on one side can be identified *(arrowheads)*. **B,** Photograph of the anterior aspect of the coronal section in **A** shows the extent of intra-articular ankylosis. Note an identifiable segment of the articular space *(arrowhead)* and the irregular anterior bony excrescences *(open arrows)*. (From Resnick D [ed]: Diagnosis of Bone and Joint Disorders, 4th ed. Philadelphia, WB Saunders, 2002, p 1056.)

uncommon, infection after trauma or nerve block or both remains an ever-present possibility, especially in an immunocompromised cancer patient. Early detection of infection is crucial to avoid potentially life-threatening sequelae.

References

1. Waldman SD: Costosternal syndrome. In: Atlas of Common Pain Syndromes. Philadelphia, WB Saunders, 2002, p 145.
2. Waldman SD: Costosternal syndrome. In: Atlas of Pain Management Injection Techniques. Philadelphia, WB Saunders, 2000, p 171.
3. Epstein SE, Gerber LH, Borer JS: Chest wall syndrome: A common cause of unexplained cardiac pain. JAMA 241:2793, 1979.
4. Waldman SD: Tietze's syndrome. In: Atlas of Common Pain Syndromes. Philadelphia, WB Saunders, 2002, p 158.
5. Waldman SD: Sternalis syndrome. In: Atlas of Uncommon Pain Syndromes. Philadelphia, WB Saunders, 2003, p 123.
6. Waldman SD: Sternalis syndrome. In: Atlas of Pain Management Injection Techniques. Philadelphia, WB Saunders, 2000, p 183.
7. Waldman SD: Fractured ribs. In: Atlas of Common Pain Syndromes. Philadelphia, WB Saunders, 2002, p 161.
8. Waldman SD: Intercostal nerve block. In: Atlas of Interventional Pain Management, 2nd ed. Philadelphia, WB Saunders, 2004, p 241.

9. Waldman SD: Post-thoracotomy pain. In: Atlas of Common Pain Syndromes. Philadelphia, WB Saunders, 2002, p 164.

10. Waldman SD: Intercostal neuralgia. In: Atlas of Common Pain Syndromes. Philadelphia, WB Saunders, 2002, p 150.

11. Waldman SD: Xiphodynia. In: Atlas of Uncommon Pain Syndromes. Philadelphia, WB Saunders, 2003, p 128.

12. Waldman SD: Xiphodynia syndrome. In: Atlas of Pain Management Injection Techniques. Philadelphia, WB Saunders, 2000, p 186.

13. Waldman SD: Sternoclavicular syndrome. In: Atlas of Uncommon Pain Syndromes. Philadelphia, WB Saunders, 2003, p 117.

14. Waldman SD: Sternoclavicular syndrome. In: Atlas of Pain Management Injection Techniques. Philadelphia, WB Saunders, 2000, p 177.

chapter 74

Thoracic Radiculopathy

Steven D. Waldman

Thoracic radiculopathy is a common source of chest wall and upper abdominal pain that emanates from the thoracic nerve roots. In addition to the dorsal spine pain, which radiates in a thoracic dermatomal distribution, a patient with thoracic radiculopathy may experience associated paresthesias, numbness, weakness, and rarely loss of superficial abdominal reflexes. The causes of thoracic radiculopathy include herniated disk, foraminal stenosis, tumor, osteophyte formation, vertebral compression fractures, and rarely infection.[1]

■ SIGNS AND SYMPTOMS

A patient with thoracic radiculopathy complains of pain, numbness, tingling, and paresthesias in the distribution of the affected nerve root or roots.[2] Muscle spasms of the paraspinous musculature also are common. Decreased sensation, weakness, and rarely superficial abdominal reflex changes are shown on physical examination.[3] Patients with thoracic radiculopathy commonly experience a reflex shifting of the trunk to one side. This reflex shifting is called *list*. Occasionally, a patient with thoracic radiculopathy also experiences compression of the thoracic spinal nerve roots resulting in myelopathy. Thoracic myelopathy is most commonly due to midline herniated thoracic disk, spinal stenosis, demyelinating disease, tumor, or rarely infection.[4] Patients with thoracic myelopathy experience varying degrees of neurologic disturbance based on the level and extent of cord compression. Significant compression of the thoracic spinal cord results in Brown-Séquard syndrome with spastic paralysis of the ipsilateral muscles below the lesion and loss of sensation on the contralateral side (Fig.74–1). Thoracic myelopathy represents a neurosurgical emergency and should be treated as such.

■ TESTING

MRI of the thoracic spine provides the clinician with the best information regarding the thoracic spine and its contents. MRI is highly accurate and helps identify abnormalities that may put the patient at risk for the development of thoracic myelopathy (Figs. 74–2 and 74–3). In patients who cannot undergo MRI (e.g., pacemaker patients), CT or myelography followed by CT of the affected area is acceptable. Radionucleotide bone scanning and plain radiographs are indicated if fractures or bony abnormalities, such as metastatic disease, are being considered.

Although the aforementioned testing provides the clinician with useful neuroanatomic information, electromyography and nerve conduction velocity testing provide the clinician with neurophysiologic information that can delineate the actual status of each individual nerve root and the thoracic plexus. Screening laboratory testing, consisting of complete blood count, erythrocyte sedimentation rate, and automated blood chemistry, should be performed if the diagnosis of thoracic radiculopathy is in question.

■ DIFFERENTIAL DIAGNOSIS

Thoracic radiculopathy is a clinical diagnosis that is supported by a combination of clinical history, physical examination, radiographs, and MRI. Pain syndromes that may mimic thoracic radiculopathy include dorsal spine strain; thoracic bursitis; thoracic fibromyositis; inflammatory arthritis; mononeuritis multiplex; infectious lesions, such as epidural abscess; and disorders of the thoracic spinal cord, roots, plexus, and nerves (see Fig. 74–3).[5] MRI of the thoracic spine should be done on all patients suspected to have thoracic radiculopathy. Screening laboratory testing, consisting of complete blood count, erythrocyte sedimentation rate, antinuclear antibody testing, HLA-B27 antigen screening, and automated blood chemistry, should be performed if the diagnosis of thoracic radiculopathy is in question to help rule out other causes of the patient's pain.

■ TREATMENT

Thoracic radiculopathy is best treated with a multimodality approach. Physical therapy, including heat modalities and deep sedative massage, combined with nonsteroidal antiinflammatory drugs and skeletal muscle relaxants represents a reasonable starting point. The addition of thoracic steroid epidural nerve blocks is a reasonable next step. Thoracic epidural blocks with local anesthetic and steroid have been shown to be extremely effective in the treatment of thoracic radiculopathy. Underlying sleep disturbance and depression are best treated with a tricyclic antidepressant, such as nortriptyline, which can be started at a single bedtime dose of 25 mg.

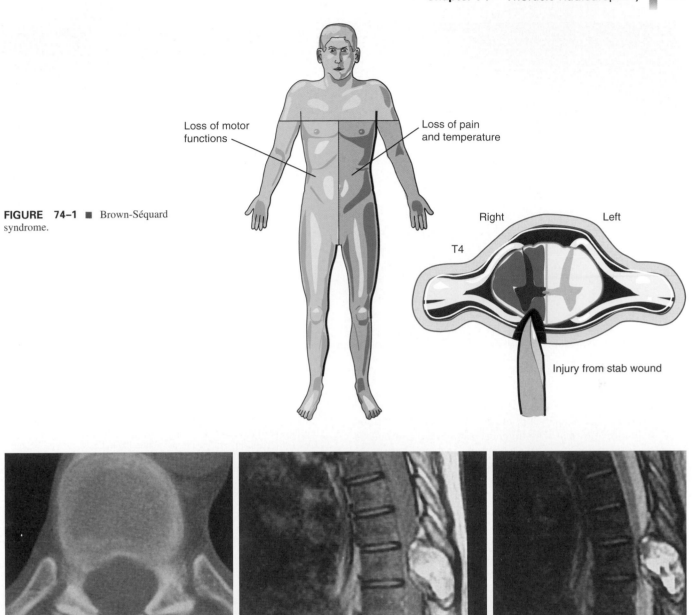

FIGURE 74–1 ■ Brown-Séquard syndrome.

Loss of motor functions

Loss of pain and temperature

Right

Left

T4

Injury from stab wound

A   B   C

FIGURE 74–2 ■ Aneurysmal bone cyst. CT and MRI abnormalities in the spine. **A,** In a 52-year-old man, transaxial CT shows an expansile lesion of the spinous process of the ninth thoracic vertebra. A calcified or ossified shell is evident about a portion of this lesion. **B** and **C,** Sagittal intermediate-weighted (TR/TE, 2000/30) (**B**) and T2-weighted (TR/TE, 2000/90) (**C**) spin echo MRI images show the lesion, which is inhomogeneous, but mainly of high signal intensity. Fluid levels are present in **A** and **C**. (From Resnick D [ed]: Diagnosis of Bone and Joint Disorders, 4th ed. Philadelphia, WB Saunders, 2002, p 4046.)

■ COMPLICATIONS AND PITFALLS

A failure to diagnose thoracic radiculopathy accurately may put the patient at risk for the development of thoracic myelopathy, which if untreated may progress to paraparesis or paraplegia. Electromyography helps sort out mononeuritis multiplex from radiculopathy, which can confuse the diagnosis because they may coexist in diabetic patients.

■ CONCLUSION

Thoracic radiculopathy is a common cause of chest and upper abdominal pain. It is often overlooked in the attempt to attribute the patient's pain complaints to intrathoracic or intra-abdominal pathology. Mononeuritis multiplex can mimic the signs and symptoms of thoracic radiculopathy, but both clinical syndromes may coexist, especially in patients with

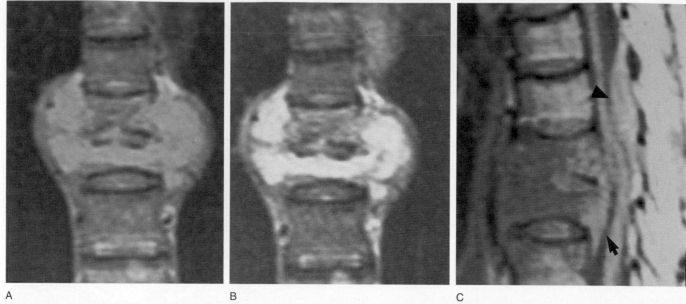

A   B   C

FIGURE 74–3 ■ Spinal infection. MRI of tuberculosis. **A** and **B,** Coronal intermediate-weighted (TR/TE, 1800/50) **(A)** and T2-weighted (TR/TE, 1800/100) **(B)** spin echo MRI images reveal spinal and paraspinal involvement in the midthoracic region. The infectious process is of higher signal intensity in **B.** **C,** Sagittal T1-weighted (TR/TE, 450/30) spin echo MRI image in the same patient reveals tuberculosis involvement of contiguous vertebral bodies with extension anteriorly. Also note the anterior *(arrow)* and posterior *(arrowhead)* extradural disease. (Courtesy of T. Mattsson, MD, Riyadh, Saudi Arabia. From Resnick D [ed]: Diagnosis of Bone and Joint Disorders, 4th ed. Philadelphia, WB Saunders, 2002, p 2497.)

diabetes. The clinician always must rule out causes of thoracic radiculopathy that if undiagnosed may result in neurologic disaster, including primary tumors, metastatic disease, infection, syringomyelia, multiple sclerosis, and spinal cord disease.

References

1. Ramamurthy S: Thoracic epidural block. In Waldman SD (ed): Interventional Pain Management, 2nd ed. Philadelphia, WB Saunders, 2001, p 391.

2. O'Connor RC, Andary MT, Russo RB, DeLano M: Thoracic radiculopathy. Phys Med Rehabil Clin North Am 13:623, 2002.

3. Dick JPR: The deep tendon and the abdominal reflexes. J Neurol Neurosurg Psychiatry 74:150, 2003.

4. Theodore N, Dickman CA: Current management of thoracic disc herniation. Contemp Neurosurg 18:1, 1996.

5. Waldman SD: Diabetic truncal neuropathy. In: Common Pain Syndromes. Philadelphia, WB Saunders, 2002, pp 153.

chapter 75

Painful Disorders of the Respiratory System

Jose L. Mendez and Douglas R. Gracey

This chapter reviews the most frequent causes of chest pain associated with pleuropulmonary diseases and options for management. A brief anatomic discussion of some facts about the sensory innervations of the lungs is followed by a clinically relevant approach to the differential diagnosis of chest pain syndromes arising from the respiratory system. The clinician must determine during the first encounter with the patient, most often in a primary care, urgent care, or emergency department setting, if the cause of the pain represents a life-threatening condition. The history and physical examination most often guide the clinician with respect to the next test to order and the immediate interventions that need to be taken.

The history is paramount in the diagnosis and management of most pulmonary disorders associated with chest pain. Pulmonary vascular disease, including acute or chronic thromboembolic disease and pulmonary hypertension, always should be considered and appropriately ruled out. Cardiac ischemia and major vascular catastrophes of the mediastinum, including aortic aneurysm and dissection or rupture, and gastroesophageal pathology also should be considered; these conditions are discussed in detail in other chapters.

■ SENSORY INNERVATION OF THE RESPIRATORY SYSTEM

The sensations originating from the respiratory system include those of pain and discomfort and nonpainful sensations such as dyspnea and chest tightness.[1,2] The irritation of the larynx, upper airway, and trachebronchial tree associated with inhaled irritants, endotracheal intubations, or mucosal inflammation induces a sensation of burning, rawness, and chest discomfort most often referred by patients to the retrosternal and midthoracic area.[3]

The lung parenchyma and the visceral pleura are considered insensitive.[3] The costal and the peripheral diaphragmatic parietal pleura have a rich innervation, however, supplied by the costal nerves. The stimulation of these areas causes pain referred to the adjacent chest wall. The central portion of the diaphragmatic pleura is innervated by the phrenic nerve, and the pain is referred to the ipsilateral shoulder.[4]

The visceral sensations from the respiratory system go through afferent fibers that travel within the vagus nerve to its nuclei located in the medulla oblongata. The fibers reach the lung via the thoracic branches of the vagus and the trachea in its upper portion via the recurrent laryngeal nerve.[3] The sensory pathway originates in close contact with the epithelium, submucosa, interstitium, smooth muscles, and pulmonary vessels, in three main groups of sensory receptors.[3,5-7]

The *slowly adapting stretch receptors,* mechanoreceptors connected to small myelinated afferent fibers, are thought to be located in the smooth muscle of the extrapulmonary and large intrapulmonary airways, respond to moderate lung inflation, and are responsible for the inflation and expiration Hering-Breuer reflexes. The inflation reflex consists of a reduction in the inspiratory time and prolongation of expiration with increased inflation; the expiration reflex is an increase in the respiratory rate associated with lung deflation.[1,6,8-12] The understanding of these concepts helps the clinician interpret the patient-ventilator synchrony and entrainment of respirations—resetting of the respiratory rhythm—in the ICU.[13]

The *rapidly adapting stretch receptors,* also known as "irritant receptors," are located in the lung parenchyma, bronchioles, and distal bronchi and are connected to small myelinated fibers.[11] The main stimuli for these receptors are rapidly adapting lung deflation, bronchial deformation, and mucosal irritation. They are involved in the cough reflex, bronchoconstriction, and mucus production.[1,6,8-10,12,14] There is general agreement that pain resulting from irritation of the airways is due to the activation of the rapidly adapting stretch receptors.[3]

The *C-fibers endings* associated with the *type J receptor,* a term coined by Paintal,[15] referring to the juxtapulmonary capillary location, reside close to the pulmonary capillaries and within the bronchi. They are chemosensitive, but also are activated by mechanical stimuli and are connected to unmyelinated afferent fibers. As described by Coleridge and Coleridge,[16] these receptors are involved in responses such as bronchoconstriction, secretion of mucus, bradycardia, and hypotension and can influence breathing rate.

■ CAUSES AND MANAGEMENT OF CHEST PAIN ASSOCIATED WITH PLEUROPULMONARY DISORDERS

The pain associated with pleuropulmonary disorders is usually described as "pleuritic" in nature and usually increases with forced maneuvers, respiratory movements, coughing, or sneezing; however, it must be separated from respirophasic chest pain of musculoskeletal origin.[17-19] Pleuritic chest pain is abrupt in onset, sharp and usually severe, unilaterally localized, and more intense in the lower lateral aspect of the chest. It usually is made worse by deep breathing and coughing and is ameliorated by splinting of the affected side.[17] Musculoskeletal pain also may vary with respiration, but is not as intense; is made worse by extension, abduction, or adduction of the arms and shoulders; and usually is accompanied by tenderness of the muscle group involved.[17] Most reviews state that potential musculoskeletal causes of chest pain represent 10% to 20% of the patients with chest pain of noncardiac origin.[20]

The sternum and its articulation with the ribs and clavicle are recognized as sites of involvement in some seronegative arthropathies, in particular those associated with pustular skin disease.[20] In addition, rheumatoid arthritis has been reported to affect the chest wall and cause chest pain, and pleuritic chest pain is the most common symptom in lupus pleuritis and occurs in 86% to 100% of cases of lupus pleurisy.[17,21] Tzietze syndrome is an uncommon but well-described chest wall syndrome.[21] Initially reported in 1921, Tzietze syndrome is defined as a benign, painful, nonsuppurative localized swelling of the costocondral, sternoclavicular, or costosternal joints in the area of the second and third ribs.[21,22]

The causes are numerous, and in general chest pain is a nonspecific pulmonary symptom. Characterizing the onset, course, and associated symptoms can guide the clinician, however, to construct a reasonable differential diagnosis. The chest pain associated with pneumothorax is usually sudden and sharp and manifests with significant shortness of breath, particularly in secondary spontaneous pneumothoraces. Fevers, chills, and sputum production usually accompany the classic description of pleuritic chest pain of sudden onset in lobar bacterial pneumonia. Sudden onset of chest pain, with a normal chest radiograph, usually raises the concern for pulmonary emboli.[23] Common causes of chest pain arising from the respiratory system are listed in Table 75–1.

■ GENERAL CONSIDERATIONS IN PAIN ASSOCIATED WITH LUNG CANCER

At presentation, lung cancer is symptomatic in more than 90% of the cases.[24] Chest pain is seen in 35% of cases at presentation. The pain may represent central tissue involvement or be related to a peripheral lesion affecting the pleura.[24] There are no randomized controlled trials to evaluate any aspects of lung cancer pain management. The American College of Chest Physicians published a series of evidence-based guidelines for the diagnosis and treatment of cancer-associated pain based on the recommendations by the Agency for Health Care Policy presented in 1994.[25-27]

In general, mild to moderate pain is treated initially with acetaminophen and nonsteroidal medications.[28] Opioids should be considered as a next step, always considering that they should be given orally; if possible, around-the-clock administration is preferred. Adjunctive medications, such as tricyclic antidepressants, anticonvulsants, and neuroleptic agents, usually augment the effect of the analgesic medica-

Table 75–1

Causes of Chest Pain Emanating from the Respiratory System

Nonmalignant Causes
Tracheobronchitis
Infectious bacterial, fungal, and tuberculous pneumonia
Lung abscess
Empyema
Pulmonary emboli
Pulmonary hypertension
Asbestos pleuropulmonary disease
Pleurisy
Pneumothorax
Chylothorax
Fibrothorax
Hemothorax
Sickle cell disease
Familial Mediterranean fever
Atelectasis ("lung migraine")
Shoulder pain associated with chronic bronchitis and emphysema
Traumatic chest pain
Postoperative thoracic pain

Malignant Causes
Lung cancer
Pancoast tumors
Mesothelioma and other primary tumors of the pleura
Tumors of the posterior mediastinum
Metastatic pleural disease

tion.[25,27] It is also important to recognize and treat promptly side effects such as constipation. As summarized in the American College of Chest Physicians recommendations, all patients should have a written management plan; activity and psychosocial support are important. Metastatic disease usually is treated with palliative radiation.[25,27]

■ SUPERIOR SULCUS TUMORS AND PANCOAST-TOBIAS SYNDROME

Superior sulcus tumors represent a variety of benign and malignant tumors with apical extension into the superior thoracic inlet.[29,30] The involvement of the first and second ribs and lower brachial plexus nerve roots T1, T2, and C8, cervical stellate ganglion, is associated with the Pancoast-Tobias syndrome, characterized by shoulder and arm pain radiating down to the inner aspect of the arm and forearm, weakness and atrophy of the hand muscles, and Horner syndrome.[29,30] Superior sulcus tumors include adenocarcinoma, large cell carcinoma, and squamous cell carcinoma of the lung.[30] Sarcomas, metastatic disease, bacterial and fungal pneumonia, parasitic infections, tuberculosis, hematologic malignancies, and amyloidosis also can be associated with this syndrome.[30,31]

The usual initial symptom is shoulder pain, radiating to the arm and neck. This pain is usually due to the involvement of the brachial plexus, endothoracic fascia, ribs, and parietal pleura.[30] The confusion of this syndrome with arthrosis or bursitis of the shoulder leads to common delays in the diagnosis of 10 months, as reported in the literature.[32-34] Horner syndrome, characterized by the presence of ipsilateral ptosis, miosis, and anhydrosis, is caused by the invasion of the paravertebral sympathetic chain (inferior cervical stellate ganglion) and has been reported in association with Pancoast syndrome in 14% to 45% of cases in various series.[32,35]

Other manifestations of this syndrome include involvement of the superior vena cava (superior vena cava syndrome) and involvement of the phrenic and recurrent laryngeal nerves. In later stages of the disease, compression of the spinal cord and paraplegia may occur.[33,36] Because of the peripheral locations of the superior sulcus tumors, cough hemoptysis and dyspnea are relatively uncommon in the initial stages of the disease.[30]

Diagnosis usually is made with percutaneous transthoracic needle biopsy or sampling of the supraclavicular nodes, if involved and easily accessible. It is important to recognize the value of MRI, in addition to the CT of the chest, to define better the thoracic wall, vessels, and brachial plexus involvement.[37-39] These tumors are usually T3 lesions owing to chest wall or mediastinal pleura involvement, but when the invasion includes the brachial plexus, mediastinal structures, and vertebral bodies, they become T4 lesions.[30,40] In the absence of distant metastasis, these tumors are usually either IIb or IIIa-b (Fig. 75-1).[30,40,41]

Standard treatment includes preoperative radiotherapy and extensive resection.[42,43] Anterior and posterior approaches have been described.[42,44,45] The former approach is preferred with anterior locations at the thoracic inlet and with vascular involvement.[44,45] Lobectomy is preferred for the lung resection.[46-48] Overall 5-year survival is poor and varies according to the series between 20% and 35%.[42,44,49] More recent series have reported an improved local control rate and outcome with aggressive combination therapy of chemoradiation and surgery.[50-52] The impact of local surgical control, age, and associated major illness on long-term survival has been emphasized.[53,54]

Surgery is contraindicated if there is extensive involvement of the brachial plexus and paraspinal region, venous obstruction, or involvement of the tissues of the base of the neck.[30,34,42,55] Vertebral invasion classically has been considered a contraindication to surgery with an ominous prognosis; 2-year survival of only 15% with radiation therapy has been reported.[50,56] This concept has been challenged in a report from the University of Texas, M.D. Anderson Cancer Center.[50] The study included 17 patients with superior sulcus tumors stage T4 owing to vertebral involvement and showed an overall actuarial survival of 54% at 2 years with an aggressive approach involving partial or total vertebrectomy and vertebral reconstruction plus preoperative or postoperative radiation therapy.[50]

■ ASBESTOS PLEUROPULMONARY DISEASE, MALIGNANT MESOTHELIOMA, AND OTHER PRIMARY TUMORS OF THE PLEURA

Asbestos exposure is mainly occupational in industrialized countries and occurs in mining, milling, and transporting of this substance.[57] Parenchymal pulmonary diseases or

pulmonary fibrosis is called *asbestosis*.[58] The disease tends to be more prominent in the lower lobes and in the subpleural areas.[58] Pathology shows honeycombing and in advanced forms is indistinguishable from end-stage fibrosis from any other cause except for the presence of asbestos bodies (Fig. 75-2).[58,59] In contrast to silicosis, it has been reported that asbestosis does not produce any changes in the tracheobronchial lymph nodes, and progressive massive fibrosis is unusual.[60,58] Patients present mainly with dyspnea.[57,58] Cough and sputum production also have been reported. Chest tightness and chest pain classically have been associated with the presence of pleural abnormalities.[58]

Irregular linear opacities are usually the main finding in the parenchyma in the chest radiograph.[57] These are more prominent in the lower lobes.[57] Changes in the parietal pleura—either thickening or plaques—seen in the plain radiograph provide evidence in favor of asbestos-related parenchymal disease and are a marker of prior exposure.[57,58,61] The pulmonary function test shows usually a restrictive pattern, but a mixed obstructive-restrictive pattern also may be seen.[59,62]

A study done in Wittenoom, Western Australia, which included 1280 subjects undergoing surveillance with chest radiographs because of prior asbestos exposure, found that 556 subjects (43%) had chest pain as the predominant symptom.[63] The study also showed that parenchymal and pleural disease in subjects exposed to asbestos was associated with chest pain particularly of the anginal type.[63]

The most common tumors involving the pleura are metastatic.[64] The primary tumors of the pleura include malignant mesothelioma, solitary fibrous tumor of the pleura, primary effusion lymphoma, and pyothorax-associated lymphoma.[65] Malignant mesothelioma (Fig. 75-3) has been associated with asbestos exposure,[65a] and the risk seems to be higher in manufacturing industries than in mining and milling.[66] Fibers of asbestos with a large length-to diameter ratio (crosidolite and amosite) are the most carcinogenic.[65,66] Patients with mesothelioma have a mean age of 60 years (range 40 to 70 years) with a history of exposure to asbestos 20 or more years in the past.[65,67] The most common presenting symptom is nonpleuritic chest pain, referred to the shoulder or upper abdomen owing to diaphragmatic involvement.[65] Cough, dyspnea, and weight loss are late manifestations.[65] The chest radiograph shows a large pleural effusion in 75% to 90% of the cases (Fig. 75-4).[68,69]

Pleural plaques are seen in the opposite hemithorax in about one third of patients.[64] CT shows the pleural involvement that is not visible in the plain radiograph because of the effusion.[64] The pleura is thickened with an irregular, nodular internal margin that is characteristic of this tumor (Fig. 75-5).[64]

At presentation, 40% of patients have dyspnea, and more than 50% have a large pleural effusion.[18,64] Patients presenting without large effusions are more likely to have chest pain as the predominant symptom.[64] Pleural fluid analysis reveals an exudate, serosanguineous in half of the patients; glucose and pH may be reduced, particularly in patients with large tumors.[70] Cytologic examination of the pleural fluid is diagnostic in approximately 25% of cases.[71] The diagnosis of malignant mesothelioma usually is made with thoracoscopy.[71]

Treatment with curative intention involves surgery, usually an extrapleural pneumonectomy followed by a

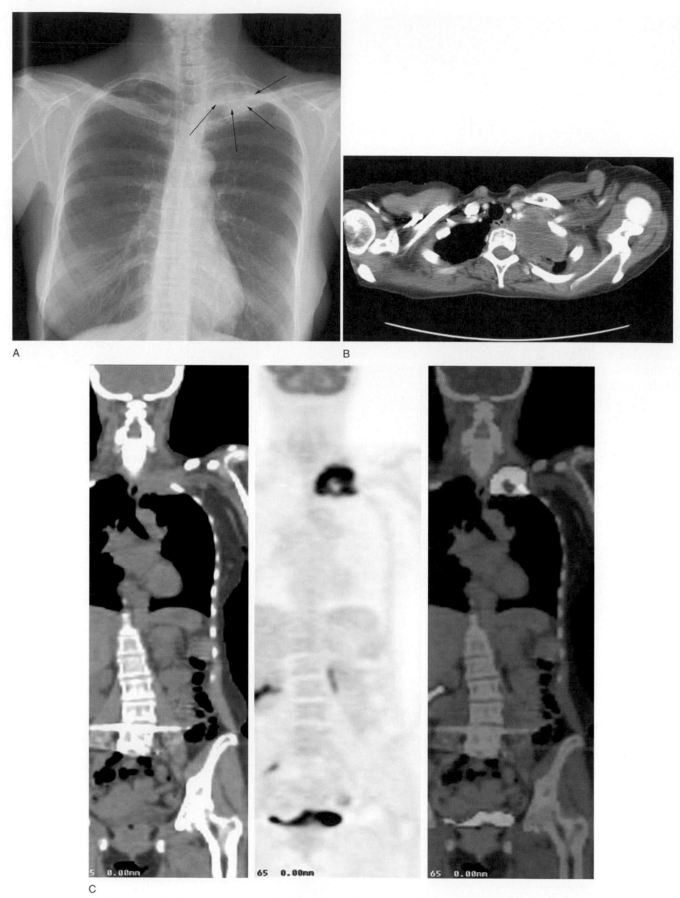

FIGURE 75–1 ■ Pancoast tumor. A 47-year-old woman presented with 5 months of shoulder pain that radiated to the left upper extremity and Horner syndrome. **A,** Chest radiograph shows a left upper lobe mass. **B,** CT shows a mass involving the subclavian vessels and structures of the superior sulcus. **C,** CT-positron emission tomography fusion images show increased left upper lobe uptake.

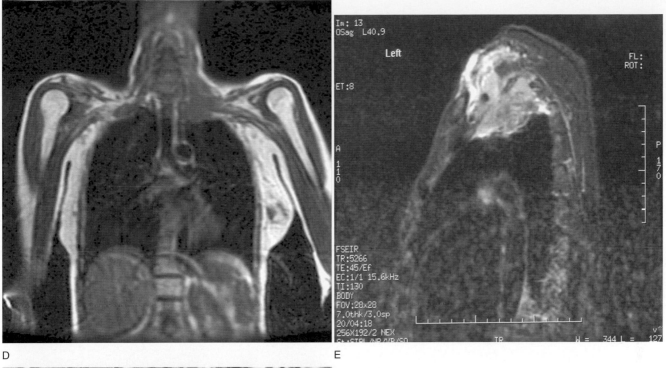

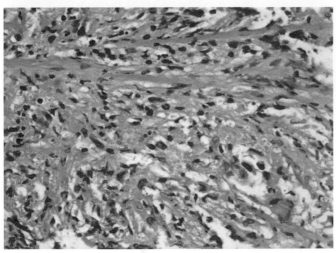

FIGURE 75–1 ■ **Cont'd. D** and **E,** MRI shows details of the soft tissue and bony involvement of the left upper thoracic area. **F,** Histology shows non–small cell carcinoma with spindle cell features.

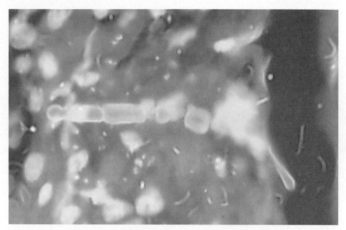

A

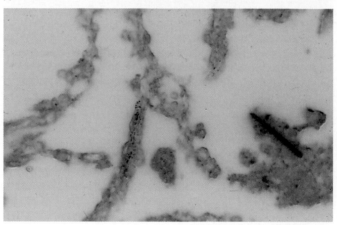

B

FIGURE 75–2 ■ Asbestos bodies. **A** and **B,** Asbestosis lung specimens, showing asbestos fibers. They are usually iron-coated and form ferruginous bodies present free in the alveoli or inside macrophages.

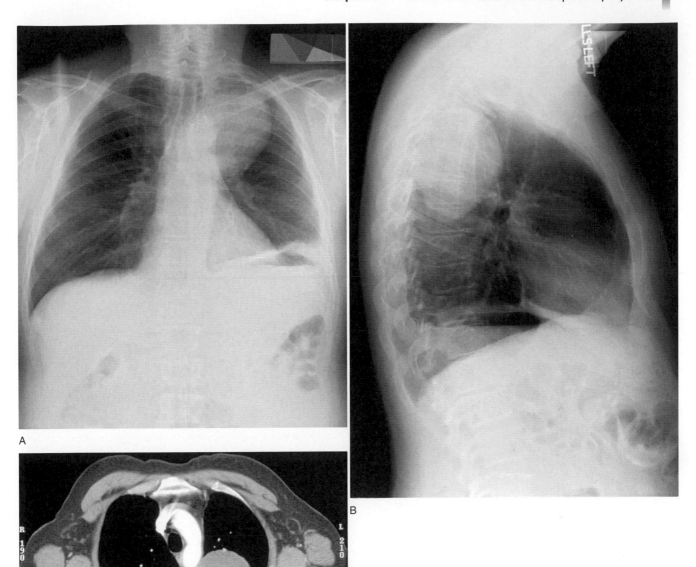

FIGURE 75–3 ■ Mesothelioma. A 63-year-old man presented with left pleuritic chest pain and a large mass. Posteroanterior (**A**) and lateral (**B**) chest radiographs show a large left pleural mass. **C,** CT confirms the mass.

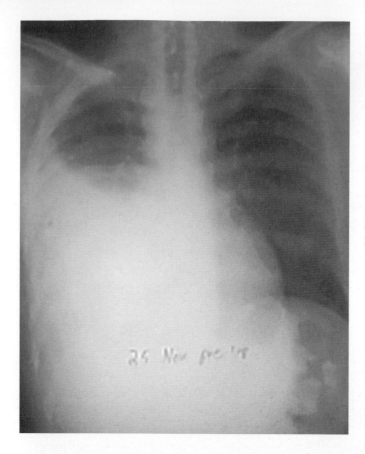

FIGURE 75–4 ■ Mesothelioma and pleural effusion. Large right pleural effusion in a patient with malignant mesothelioma presenting with right pleuritic chest pain and dyspnea.

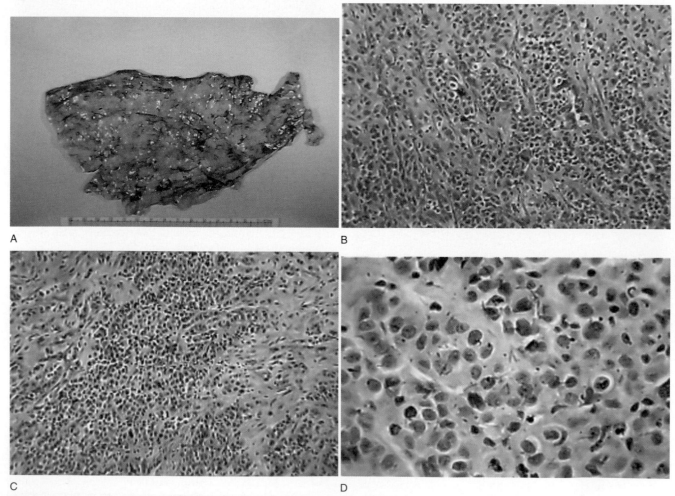

A

B

C

D

FIGURE 75–5 ■ Pathology of mesothelioma. **A,** Gross pathology shows a segment of a pleural tumor with nodular appearance. **B-D,** Microscopically, these tumors may have an epithelial, sarcomatous, or mixed appearance.

combination of chemotherapy and radiotherapy.[64] Pleurectomy/decortication has been suggested for patients who are not candidates for extrapleural pneumonectomy.[64,72] Palliative options for the management of dyspnea includes therapeutic thoracentesis, chemical pleurodesis, and pleuroperitoneal shunt pumps.[64,73] Chest pain is usually difficult to control, and radiotherapy has been reported to be of little help.[64,73]

Approximately 200,000 malignant pleural effusions are diagnosed annually in the United States.[18] The three main malignant etiologies representing about 75% of the diagnoses are lung (30%), breast (25%), and lymphomas (20%). Ovarian carcinoma is diagnosed in 6% of the cases and melanoma in 3% (Fig. 75–6).[64] The malignant pleural effusions are usually exudates.[74] Symptoms include dyspnea in more than 50% of cases and chest pain in about 25%. Chest pain has been described as dull rather than pleuritic.[64] The diagnosis is established by fluid cytology or thoracoscopic biopsy.[64] The cytology has a diagnostic yield of 60% to 90%.[75] Adenocarcinoma has the highest diagnostic yield for cytology. In contrast, the cytology is nondiagnostic in more than 80% of patients with squamous cell carcinoma, lymphoma, or mesothelioma.[64]

Because of the increased enthusiasm for thoracoscopic techniques, pleural biopsies are not recommended. In a series from the Mayo Clinic,[76] only 17% had a positive pleural biopsy after a nondiagnostic fluid cytology. The diagnosis currently is most often made thoracoscopically. In addition, the procedure has the advantage of being able to treat and control the effusion with pleurodesis (Fig. 75–7).[75]

Benign fibrous mesothelioma is a rare tumor that is unrelated to asbestos exposure.[77] Chest pain may occur in about 40% of patients.[64] Two paraneoplastic syndromes have been associated with benign fibrous mesotheliomas: hypertrophic pulmonary osteoarthropathy and hypoglycemia.[64] MRI may suggest the diagnosis because these tumors have a low intensity signal in all MRI sequences, whereas malignant mesotheliomas have a high intensity on T2-weighted images.[78] Treatment is surgical resection, and the disease may recur in about 10% of the cases.[64]

Primary effusion lymphomas are rare and may occur in HIV-positive patients with Kaposi's sarcoma–associated human herpesvirus-8, organ transplant recipients, and patients with Epstein-Barr virus.[64,79,80] The diagnosis is based on fluid cytology and prognosis is poor.[64] Pyothorax-associated lymphomas are mostly B cell–type lymphomas and occur in patients who several decades earlier had received an artificial pneumothorax as a treatment of pulmonary tuberculosis.[64] Presenting symptoms are dyspnea, chest pain, and masses without pleural effusions that are seen in CT scans.[64,81]

▮ TUMORS OF THE MEDIASTINUM

The mediastinum is the thoracic space bounded laterally by the pleural cavities, superiorly by the thoracic inlet, and inferiorly by the diaphragm.[82,83] It is classically divided into three compartments: anterior, middle, and posterior.[82,83] The anterior mediastinum, between the sternum and the pericardium, includes the thyroid, thymus, adipose tissue, aorta, brachiocephalic vessels, and lymph nodes.[82,83] The middle portion comprises the structures in the pericardial sac, all major vascular structures, trachea, main bronchi, and paratracheal and tracheobronchial lymph nodes.[83] The posterior mediastinum lies between the pericardium and the vertebral column and includes the descending aorta, esophagus, thoracic duct, vagus nerves, sympathetic nerve chains, azygos venous system, posterior mediastinal lymph nodes, and paravertebral tissues.[82,83]

Mediastinal tumors are symptomatic in 50% to 65% of the cases according to different series.[83-87] The most frequent complaints are chest pain, cough, dyspnea, dysphagia, and recurrent respiratory infections.[83] In addition, there are syndromes from the compression of the specific structures, such as Horner syndrome, superior vena cava syndrome, and spinal cord compression.[83]

Tumors that arise from the posterior mediastinum may have chest pain as the predominant symptom owing to nerve

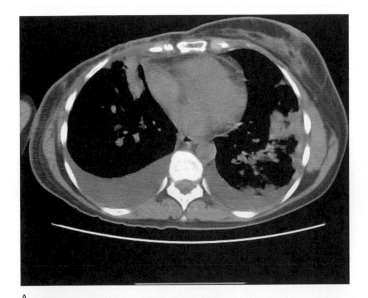

A

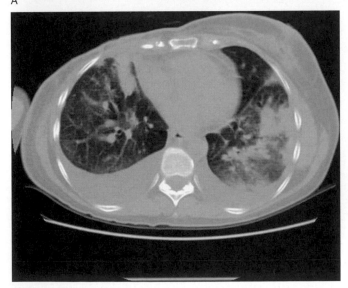

B

FIGURE 75–6 ▮ Metastatic pleuropulmonary disease. **A** and **B,** CT in a 46-year-old woman with metastatic breast cancer presenting with ulceration and cellulitis of the chest wall, believed to be locoregional invasion of the carcinoma. Pleural effusions, nodules, and infiltrates are manifestations of the disseminated malignancy.

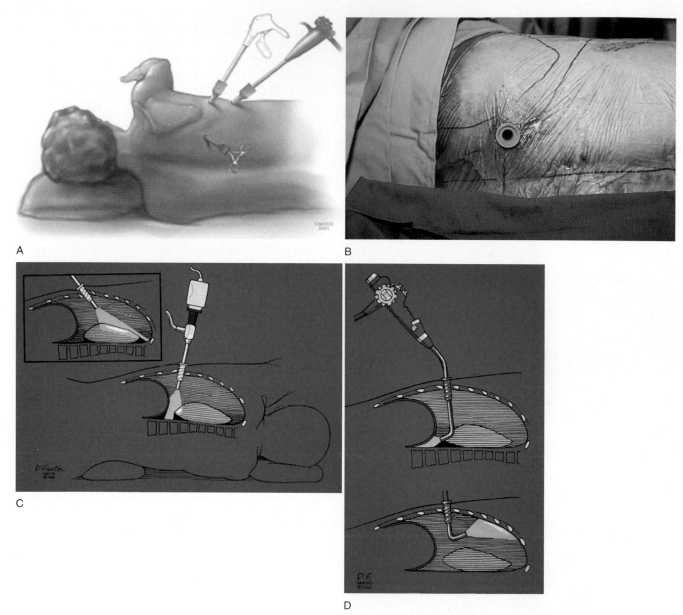

FIGURE 75–7 ■ Video-assisted thoracoscopy. **A,** Drawing of patient positioning and insertion sites for trocars and camera. **B,** Picture showing introducer in place. **C-D,** Representations of the different approaches used with the instrument to reach anterior and posterior intrathoracic areas.

or bone erosion. Between them, the neurogenic tumors, arising from the sympathetic ganglia, intercostal nerves, and chemoreceptor cells, are common and can be benign or malignant.[83,88] They usually appear on the chest radiograph as unilateral paravertebral masses.[88] Benign tumors should be surgically resected; neuroblastomas are usually unresectable.[88] A combined coordinated surgical effort including neurosurgeons, orthopedic surgeons, and thoracic surgeons is often necessary to approach some of these tumors, particularly when the spinal cord is involved.

■ PULMONARY MANIFESTATIONS OF SICKLE CELL DISEASE

Sickle cell disease is one of the most prevalent genetic disorders.[89] This hemoglobinopathy derives from a substitution of

glutamic acid by valine in the beta subunit of the hemoglobin molecule.[89] The deoxygenated hemoglobin S forms large polymers that aggregate leading to a change in the red blood cell shape, affecting its deformability and inducing vascular occlusion and hemolysis.[89]

The pulmonary manifestations of this disorder include acute chest syndrome and chronic restrictive pulmonary disease characterized mainly by pulmonary hypertension.[89] The Cooperative Study of Sickle Cell Disease followed the clinical course of sickle cell disease in 3751 patients at 23 centers from 1979 through 1988.[90] The incidence of acute chest syndrome in the Cooperative Study of Sickle Cell Disease population was reported to be higher for patients with homozygous sickle cell disease (SS; 12.8/100 patient-years) and in patients with sickle cell β-thalassemia (9.4/100 patient-years).[90,91] The incidence of acute chest syndrome was inversely related to age, being higher in children and lower in adults.[91]

Age has been found to have a striking effect on the mode of presentation, course, and outcome of acute chest syndrome.[92] Children have milder acute chest syndrome, more often secondary to infections, whereas adults have a more severe form often associated with pain and have a higher mortality.[92] In addition to young age, other risk factors associated with this condition are high hemoglobin levels, lower fetal hemoglobin levels, and high leukocyte counts.[91]

The syndrome is characterized by pleuritic chest pain, fevers, acute dyspnea, and the presence of new pulmonary infiltrates on a chest radiograph in a patient with bone pain known to have sickle cell disease.[89-93] Acute infection is always in the differential diagnosis of this presentation, which frequently is initially treated empirically as such. Pleural effusions may be present in 15% of cases.[89] The pathophysiology of acute chest syndrome is poorly understood but is believed to involve vascular injury, lung tissue infarction, and possibly infection. The proposed mechanisms for this phenomenon include intravascular red blood cell sickling, in situ thrombosis, and bone marrow embolism as suggested by the finding of fat globules sometimes reported in the sputum of these patients.[89-93] The infiltrates may remain localized or in some cases progress to respiratory failure and acute respiratory distress syndrome (ARDS).[89-93] The treatment includes intravenous fluids to reduce the hemoconcentration, empirical antibiotics, oxygen to reduce sickling, and incentive spirometry.[89-94] High doses of narcotics are sometimes necessary to control the pain.[89]

The chronic lung disease associated with sickle cell disease is characterized mainly by pulmonary hypertension. Pulmonary hypertension is responsible for the dyspnea and constitutes the dominant cause of mortality. Clinically it is characterized by progressive dyspnea and hypoxemia with restrictive physiology on pulmonary function testing. Small lung volumes and diffuse interstitial infiltrates usually are seen on the chest radiograph. The lungs of these patients histologically show a remarkable absence of interstitial fibrosis despite the radiologic appearance.[89]

It is believed that the repeated acute episodes are associated with lung function deterioration, vascular and tissue remodeling, increased restriction, loss of lung volume, and decreased lung diffusion capacity.[89] The chronic pulmonary complications may be the result of the repeated acute events impacting on the vasculature. Tissue infarction results from numerous proposed mechanisms, including plugging of the microvascular circulation by poorly deformed sickled cells, abnormal adherence of the red blood cells to the endothelial cells, in situ thrombosis, and embolic events from distant venous sites or bone marrow undergoing infarction.[89]

A similarity between this condition and ARDS has been mentioned by Weil and colleagues[89] because of the common vascular injury pathway leading to pulmonary edema. The interaction between the endothelial cells and the abnormal erythrocytes induces the activation of platelets, neutrophils, complement, and coagulation cascade that, as in the case of ARDS, leads to systemic multiple organ failure secondary to vascular injury. Alternatively, free fatty acids released from the bone marrow have been related to endothelial damage, as in the case of oleic acid–induced lung injury in experimental models.

■ PULMONARY EMBOLI AND PULMONARY HYPERTENSION

Approximately 250,000 patients are hospitalized annually in the United States because of venous thromboembolism.[95] Pleuritic chest pain with or without hemoptysis, dyspnea, and circulatory collapse have been classically associated with pulmonary thromboembolic disease.[96] In the Prospective Investigation of Pulmonary Embolism Diagnosis study, more than half of the patients with chest pain or hemoptysis (56%) had pleural effusions.[96-98] It has been reported that 75% of patients with pleural effusion associated with pulmonary emboli have pleuritic chest pain.[96,98] Dyspnea, when present, is usually out of proportion with the size of the pleural effusion.[96,99] Patients with pulmonary emboli and associated pleural effusions may or may not have an associated parenchymal infiltrate, and when present these are more common in the lower lobes, pleural based and convex toward the hilum (Hampton's hump) (Fig. 75–8).[100]

Pleural fluid analysis is nonspecific but can help, ruling out other causes, such as malignancy, tuberculosis, or pneumonia with a parapneumonic effusion.[100,101] The fluid may be transudative or exudative, sometimes bloody, and the white blood cell count usually ranges from 100 to more than 50,000 cells/mm^3 and may reveal large numbers of eosinophils and mesothelial cells.[100]

The clinical diagnosis of pulmonary embolism is inaccurate, and there is some controversy in the literature over the diagnostic value and sensitivity of certain signs and symptoms, such as dyspnea and pleuritic chest pain.[102-104] The diagnosis usually is based on the history and clinical suspicion plus finding of an unmatched ventilation-perfusion defect in a lung scan. There has been an increased interest in the use

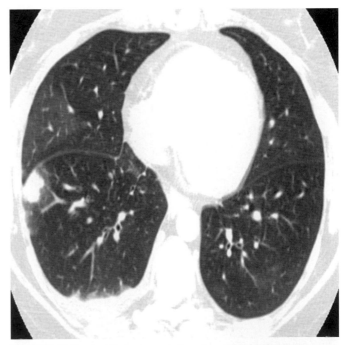

FIGURE 75–8 ■ Pulmonary embolism in a 45-year-old woman with chest pain and acute pulmonary emboli affecting the right lower lobe. Note Hampton's hump (pleural wedge-shaped density) and associated pleural effusion.

of CT angiography in the evaluation of patients with pulmonary embolism.[102,103]

Heparin is still the cornerstone of treatment for pulmonary emboli. As mentioned by Light,[100] pleural effusions rarely become bloody while the treatment with heparin is instituted, and the presence of a pleural effusion is not a contraindication for the use of heparin. If a pleural effusion has increased in size after heparin, and the hematocrit in the fluid is greater than 50% of the peripheral blood, the effusion should be drained with a chest tube and the anticoagulation stopped.[100]

Patients with pulmonary hypertension may present with significant chest pain radiating to the neck and arms.[105] This pain has been described in patients with acute and chronic conditions associated with pulmonary hypertension.[19] About half of patients who have primary pulmonary hypertension have chest pain.[106,107] The mechanism involved in this pain is unclear, but it has been postulated that acute dilation of the pulmonary artery and mechanoreceptors may be involved in acute pulmonary hypertension resulting from a massive pulmonary embolism.[19] Likewise for chronic primary pulmonary hypertension, it has been hypothesized that the pain may be induced over the right ventricle by the pressure overload, relative ischemia, or supply-demand imbalance and by compression of the coronary arteries by the dilated pulmonary artery.[19,107,108] Pulmonary artery aneurysms are dilations of more than 4 to 5 cm that can be congenital or acquired and present with or without pulmonary hypertension and chest pain (Fig. 75–9).[99,109]

■ ACUTE AND CHRONIC PLEUROPULMONARY INFECTIONS ASSOCIATED WITH CHEST PAIN

Pain of tracheal origin is usually felt in the midline anteriorly and is described as a raw or burning sensation, exaggerated by deep breathing.[19] Acute and chronic tracheobronchitis may be associated with this type of chest discomfort.

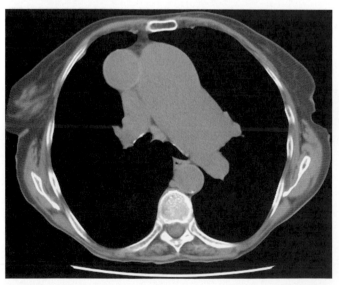

FIGURE 75–9 ■ Pulmonary artery aneurysm. Noncontrast CT in a 78-year-old woman shows a left pulmonary aneurysm.

Upper respiratory infections are the most common types of infectious diseases among adults.[110] Acute bronchitis refers to cases of acute respiratory disease with severe and prolonged cough that continues after other signs and symptoms of the acute infection have subsided.[111] Viral infections are mostly associated with this common condition, but *Mycoplasma pneumoniae* and *Chlamydia pneumoniae* also cause prolonged cough.[111] *Streptococcus pneumoniae* and *Haemophilus influenzae* play an unclear role in acute bronchitis, but their importance is well established in infectious exacerbations of chronic bronchitis.[111] Treatment in healthy individuals is directed toward suppression of the symptoms (cough suppressants and hydration). In selected cases with underlying lung disease, a short course of antibiotics, bronchodilators, and corticosteroids may be warranted. Management of secretions by the use of a flutter valve is usually beneficial to prevent further infections, particularly in cases of chronic bronchitis with production of large amounts of thick sputum.

Pneumonia has been ranked as the sixth cause of death in the United States.[110] Patients with community-acquired pneumonia caused by pyogenic organisms usually present with a clinical picture characterized by rigors, fevers and chills, productive cough, and pleuritic chest pain of sudden onset.[112] Because these symptoms are common to most respiratory infections, the identification of patients with pneumonia or at risk of a complication is paramount. Pneumonia still has a high mortality, and the reported figures range from 5% to more than 30% for patients with severe acquired pneumonia admitted to the ICU.[113] The etiologic agents associated with infectious pneumonia depend on the type of host, immunocompetent or immunodeficient; predisposing factors, such as chronic debilitating illness; and where the infection was acquired, the community or the hospital.[114] Underlying illnesses and other factors such as age, multilobar involvement, hypoxemia, bacteremia, and extrapulmonary involvement affect the mortality from pneumococcal pneumonia (Fig. 75–10).[114]

S. pneumoniae is the most frequent cause of community-acquired pneumonia among patients who require hospitalization.[114] *Staphylococcus aureus* accounts for 30% of nosocomial pneumonias.[114,115] Patients with pneumonia caused by hematogenous spread (endocarditis) may present with significant chest pain and hemoptysis, particularly when a pulmonary infarct develops.[114] *H. influenzae* and *Haemophilus parainfluenzae* may appear as patchy areas of consolidation.[114] Small areas of parapneumonic effusion are common, but cavitation is unusual, although we have seen this occurrence in our institution (Fig. 75–11).[114]

A parapneumonic effusion occurred in 90 of 203 patients (44%) with pneumonia studied prospectively by Light and coworkers[116]; the investigators reported 10 patients who had a complicated pleural effusion based on positive cultures, a pleural fluid pH of less than 7.00, or glucose lower than 40 mg/100 mL. Pleural fluid pH and glucose are definitive indications of chest tube drainage.[116] Lactate dehydrogenase greater than 1000 mg/100 mL and a pleural fluid pH between 7.00 and 7.20 are considered relative indications of chest tube drainage, and the procedure should be considered for each individual case.[116]

Most parapneumonic effusions resolve with antibiotic therapy, and there are no systematic prospective comparative

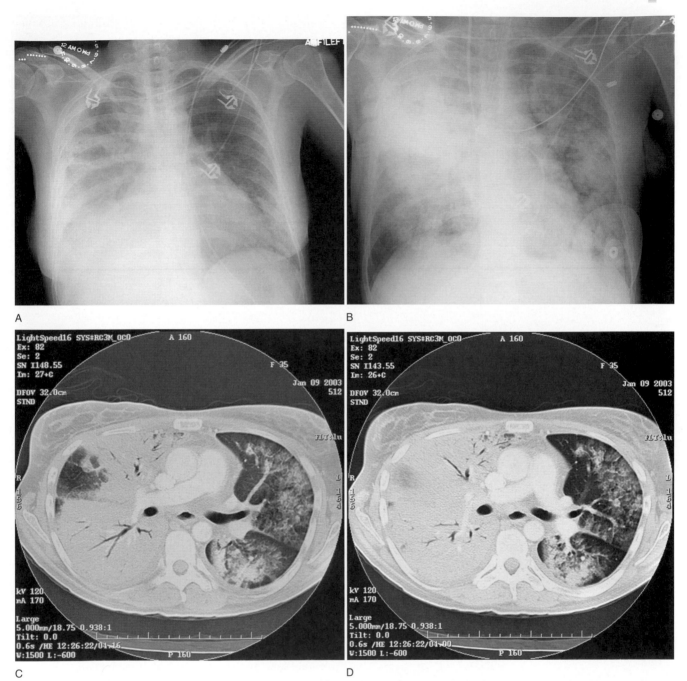

FIGURE 75–10 ■ Severe community-acquired pneumonia and lung abscess. A 35-year-old woman with diabetes type 1 presented with abrupt onset of chest pain, fevers, rapid development of respiratory failure, and ARDS, requiring mechanical ventilation. **A** and **B,** Presentation chest radiographs show a diffuse alveolar process involving the right hemithorax, with moderate-size pleural effusion and right upper lobe cavitation. **C** and **D,** CT shows bilateral diffuse infiltrates with a large area of dense consolidation in the right lung.

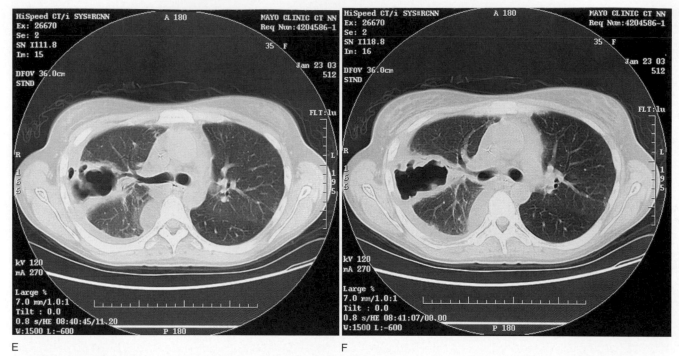

E

F

FIGURE 75–10 ■ **Cont'd**. **E** and **F**, Progressing to a consolidated area and associated cavitation opened to the airway and pleural space.

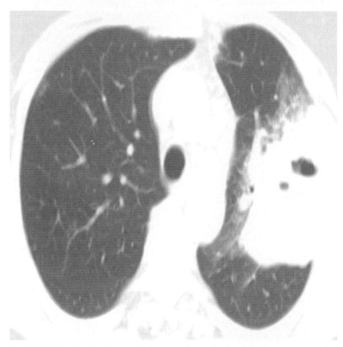

FIGURE 75–11 ■ *H. parainfluenzae* lung abscess. CT in a patient with fevers and chest pain who was diagnosed with *H. parainfluenzae* lung abscess.

studies looking at complications and outcome of parapneumonic pleural effusions. There is some controversy as to whether or not a thoracentesis should be performed in every free-flowing pleural effusion associated with pneumonia.[117] In the study by Light and coworkers,[116] patients who developed a parapneumonic pleural effusion were not clinically different from the patients who did not. Pleuritic chest pain was present in 64% of patients with pleural effusions and in 50% of patients without effusions.[116] Chest pain was not different between the patients in whom the pleural effusion was complicated versus the patients who did not require chest tube drainage.[116] In this study, anaerobic infections were more commonly associated with complicated parapneumonic pleural effusions.[116] Pleuritic chest pain also may be seen in pleurisy associated with viral infections from coxsackievirus B, coxsackievirus A, or echoviruses.[17]

Four pulmonary syndromes are associated with anaerobic bacterial infections: pneumonitis, necrotizing pneumonia, lung abscess, and empyema.[118] Actinomycosis of the lung follows aspiration of oropharyngeal material.[118] The clinical manifestations of this infection are insidious and include fatigue, weight loss, low-grade fever, productive cough, and pleuritic chest pain.[118] Patients look chronically ill, and in advanced stages the lung disease may progress to involve the pleural space and chest wall, with a fistulous opening to the exterior and drainage of the characteristic "sulfur granule" containing pus.[118]

Pulmonary nocardiosis presents with low-grade fever, weight loss, productive cough, and pleuritic chest pain.[114] Extension of the pulmonary infection to the pleural cavity occurs in about 10% of patients.[114] Fulminant pneumonia may occur in immunocompromised patients.[114] Hematogenous dissemination is the major hazard of this pulmonary infection (Fig. 75–12).[114,118]

Fungal infections commonly affect the lungs, and patients may present with chest pain. Histoplasmosis, caused by *Histoplasma capsulatum,* is endemic in the Ohio and Mississippi River Valleys.[119] Symptomatic disease is seen in less than 5% of infected individuals, and infection usually manifests in the normal host as a self-limited illness, with flulike symptoms, including fevers, chills, cough, and anorexia, in most cases and with pleuritic chest pain in 60%

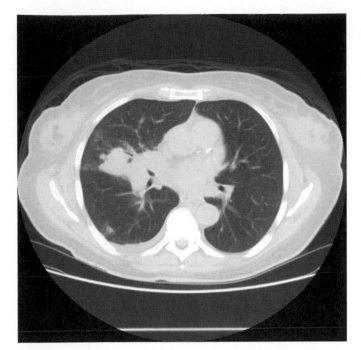

FIGURE 75–12 ■ *Nocardia nova.* Noncontrast CT shows a large right hilar mass in a 62-year-old woman with history of type 1 diabetes, status post pancreatic transplant on a triple-drug regimen for immunosuppression, presenting with cough. The patient underwent mediastinoscopy and right thoracotomy plus wedge resection. The path showed acute necrotizing pneumonia with microabscess formation and filamentous organisms; cultures from the tissue grew *N. nova.*

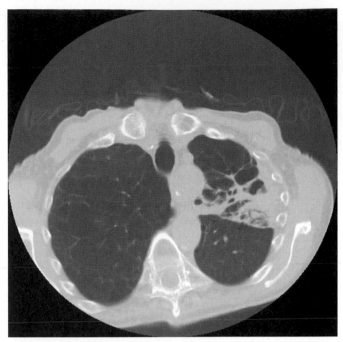

FIGURE 75–13 ■ Histoplasmosis. CT in a 73-year-old man with ankylosing spondylitis shows severe emphysema, a new left upper lobe infiltrate, and apparent mediastinal and pleural infiltration. Positive serology for histoplasmosis and negative cultures and biopsy specimens were obtained. The patient was treated with long-term antifungal therapy, for strong suspicion of histoplasmosis, with resolution of the symptoms (low-grade fevers, weight loss for a few weeks) and infiltrates.

to 85% of patients.[119-121] Other manifestations of the acute self-limited syndromes are pericarditis, arthritis, or arthralgias with erythema nodosum, seen in 5% to 10% of patients with histoplasmosis.[120,121] Acute pulmonary disease also can present as ARDS and rapidly progressive respiratory failure.[122]

Chronic pulmonary histoplasmosis is characterized by the presence of cough, dyspnea, chest pain, fatigue, fevers, sweats, and fibrotic apical infiltrates with cavitation (Fig. 75–13).[120] This form tends to be progressive, leading to cavity enlargement, new cavity formation, bronchopleural fistulae, and loss of pulmonary function.[119,120,123] Fibrosing mediastinitis is an uncommon manifestation that occurs as a result of an exaggerated inflammatory response to histoplasma.[119,120] Superior vena cava obstruction and tracheobronchial obstruction can be seen in this condition.[119,120,123] Antifungal therapy is recommended only for patients with severe illness, immunocompromised patients, or patients in whom moderate to severe symptoms persist for more than 2 to 4 weeks.[120]

Blastomycosis is concentrated along the Mississippi and Ohio River basin and the Great Lakes.[124] The acute pneumonia is often associated with abrupt onset of pleuritic chest pain, fevers, and constitutional symptoms.[120] The chronic involvement is characterized by the development of a masslike infiltrate often misdiagnosed as malignancy.[120] Most patients with mild to moderate disease are treated with oral azole therapy for at least 6 months.[120] Amphotericin B is used in life-threatening pulmonary and extrapulmonary disease or with central nervous system involvement.[120]

Coccidioidomycosis is endemic in the southwestern area of the United States, northern Mexico, and areas of Central and South America.[120] The clinical pulmonary manifestations vary between an acute flulike illness, with pneumonitis, chest pain, and fevers, and a micronodular or reticulonodular infiltrative type of disease with cavities in the more chronic forms of progressive disease. Thin-walled cavities are characteristic of this disease and may enlarge and progress toward the pleural space, leading to the formation of hydropneumothorax.[120]

Lung abscess is a pus-containing necrotic lesion of the lung, often with an air-fluid level.[114] A long list of pulmonary pathology, mainly infectious, but also noninfectious, may lead to the formation of an abscess.[114] Bacterial pneumonia and mycobacterial, fungal, and parasitic infections have been reported as causes of lung abscesses.[114] Pulmonary infarction after emboli, malignancy primary or metastatic to the lungs, and necrotic lesions of silicosis may appear as a lung abscess.[114]

Cough is the main symptom of pulmonary tuberculosis, but tissue necrosis and inflammation of the lung parenchyma adjacent to the pleura also may induce pleuritic chest pain.[125] In addition, spontaneous pneumothorax has been reported with this condition in 1% to 3% of patients, often associated with chest pain and dyspnea.[125] Pleural tuberculosis is considered as a form of extrapulmonary tuberculosis and has two modes of presentation: tuberculous pleuritis and tuberculous empyema (pseudochylous effusion).[125]

Chronic bronchitis has been defined as chronic productive cough for 3 months in each of 2 consecutive years in patients in whom other causes of chronic cough, such as carcinoma, chronic granulomatous diseases, and congestive heart failure, have been ruled out.[126] It is accepted that COPD is defined as a state of chronic airflow limitation secondary to chronic bronchitis or emphysema.[126] Secondary spontaneous pneumothorax is a serious complication associated with COPD that may occur with chest pain. COPD is the most common condition underlying secondary spontaneous pneumothorax, along with *Pneumocystis carinii* infection associated with HIV infection.[127] The rate of recurrence for patients with secondary spontaneous pneumothorax is appreciably higher compared with the average rate of recurrence of 30% in patients with primary spontaneous pneumothorax.[127] Some authors have recommended interventions to prevent recurrence of pneumothorax after the first episode of secondary spontaneous pneumothorax.[128]

Surgical management with mechanical pleurodesis, parietal pleurectomy, or talc insufflation seems to be more effective than instillation of a sclerosing agent through a chest tube.[128] This "aggressive treatment approach" has been suggested and outlined in the recommendations for management of secondary spontaneous pneumothorax published in the American College of Chest Physicians Delphi Consensus Statement.[128]

■ PLEURAL COMPLICATIONS OF PULMONARY LANGERHANS CELL HISTIOCYTOSIS AND LYMPHANGIOMYOMATOSIS: PNEUMOTHORAX AND CHYLOTHORAX

Pulmonary Langerhans cell histiocytosis (PLCH) is a rare interstitial lung disease that forms part of a spectrum of diseases characterized by the proliferation and infiltration of different organs by cells known as Langerhans cells.[129] Strongly associated with cigarette smoking, this disorder also has been previously referred to as *primary pulmonary histiocytosis X, pulmonary eosinophilic granuloma,* and *pulmonary Langerhans cell granulomatosis.*[129] It commonly affects young adults and has a variable and unpredictable course, ranging from asymptomatic to progressive disease with respiratory failure and death over months.[129-137] Secondary spontaneous pneumothorax, a complication with a reported mortality in the literature of 16%, occurs in 4% to 17% of patients with PLCH during the course of their disease.[132-138]

Patients with PLCH are predisposed to the development of pneumothorax based on destructive changes in the lung parenchyma resulting from the disease.[27,28] Thin-walled cysts, nodules (with or without cavitation), or a combination of these are present in the lungs of patients with PLCH (Fig. 75–14).[129]

Although dyspnea and cough are common presenting features, spontaneous pneumothorax and chest pain can be the initial manifestation of PLCH, as occurred in 11% of our cohort of 102 patients with PLCH examined over a 23-year period at the Mayo Clinic.[129-131,133-135,139,140] In a subgroup of 16 patients who experienced one or more pneumothoraces, we found that the recurrence rate was 58% to the ipsilateral side when the episode was managed by observation or chest tube without pleurodesis and 0% after surgical management with pleurodesis.[139] Surgical management in our cases was per-

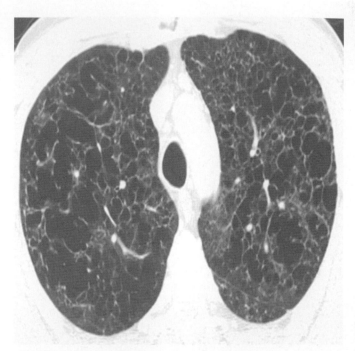

FIGURE 75–14 ■ PLCH in a 42-year-old man. High-resolution CT scan (in one to two collimations with use of a high spatial frequency reconstruction algorithm) was obtained. Irregularly shaped cystic changes with small peribronchiolar nodular opacities, predominantly in the middle and upper lobes, allows the clinician to make the diagnosis without a lung biopsy.[129]

formed through a thoracotomy because most of these patients were treated before thoracoscopic methods became popular. We currently perform many of these procedures thoracoscopically.[139] Promising results have been reported with video-assisted thoracoscopic surgery, which offers a shorter hospitalization and less morbidity for management of primary and secondary pneumothorax (see Fig. 75–7).[141,142]

Lymphangiomyomatosis is another rare disease that affects mainly premenopausal women and results from the proliferation of an atypical smooth muscle–like cell involving the small airway, pulmonary microvasculature, and intrathoracic and extrathoracic lymphatic systems.[143] The proliferation of these lymphangiomyomatosis cells produces airway obstruction, cystic changes, and pulmonary hemorrhage.[143] Lymphangiomyomatosis is associated with the development of pneumothorax and chylothorax, both pleural complications that usually present as chest pain and breathlessness (Fig. 75–15).

Patients with lymphangiomyomatosis most commonly present with dyspnea on exertion and nonproductive cough, but chest pain can be the initial symptom in 12% to 14% of the cases, according to different series.[144,145] In patients with lymphangiomyomatosis, the frequency of spontaneous pneumothorax ranges from 60% to 81%, with a recurrence rate of 64% without pleurodesis or surgery.[144-148]

A chylous pleural effusion or chylothorax is the accumulation of chyle within the pleural space usually caused by a disruption in the thoracic duct or in the lymphatic flow within the chest.[149] Pleural fluid triglyceride level of greater than 110 mg/dL or the presence of chylomicrons in the pleural fluid defines the presence of chylothorax.[149] Three mechanisms, described by Doerr and coworkers,[149] are associated

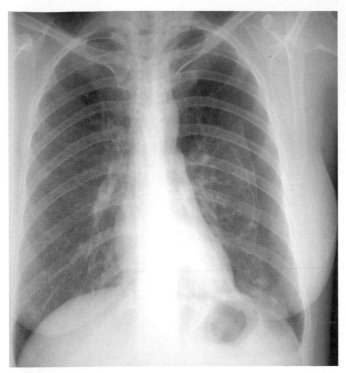

FIGURE 75–15 ■ Lymphangiomyomatosis. Pneumothorax in a 39-year-old woman with lymphangiomyomatosis presenting with acute left-sided chest pain.

with the accumulation of chyle in the pleural space: (1) a leak from the thoracic duct or its tributaries, (2) extravasation from pleural lymphatics, and (3) transdiaphragmatic flow of chylous ascites. The classic description of the chylous fluid as white, milky, and opalescent is seen in less than half of patients with a chylous effusion.[150] The fluid sometimes appears bloody or turbid with yellow or green discoloration and at other times serous or serosanguineous (Fig. 75–16).[149-151] The differential diagnosis includes pseudochylothorax (cholesterol-rich effusion) and empyema.[149] Chylothorax has been described in 0% to 14% of patients with lymphangiomyomatosis at presentation[144-147,152,153] and in 10% to 39% during the course of the disease.[144-146,148,151,152] Lymphangiomyomatosis-associated chylothorax represented 3.5% of the 229 patients with chylothorax seen over a 25-year period at Mayo Clinic.[151]

■ CHEST PAIN IN THE RECOVERY ROOM, INTENSIVE CARE UNIT, AND CHRONIC VENTILATOR UNIT: PULMONARY COMPLICATIONS

Uncontrolled pain is a major problem in the early postoperative period.[154] It has been reported that three fourths of patients who received parenteral opioids had uncontrolled moderate to severe pain with these drugs.[155] Poor control of postoperative chest pain is believed to contribute to the development of complications, owing to poor lung inflation, atelectasis, and hypoxemia.[156] Associated with the development of atelectasis and impaired cough and related to chest pain is the risk of development of pneumonia and with it, prolonged hos-

FIGURE 75–16 ■ Chylous pleural fluid. Chylous pleural effusion, with the classically described white, milky, opalescent appearance.

pitalization, and increased risk of chronic respiratory failure and need for mechanical ventilation. Death and mechanical ventilation dependence are rare, however, even in the case of severe COPD.[157,158] Optimal pain control to avoid splinting and atelectasis is paramount and may have a significant effect on postoperative events, such as earlier ambulation and discharge from the hospital.[154]

Decreased pulmonary complications[159,160] and improved lung function tests[161] have been shown in patients receiving epidural analgesia versus intramuscular or intravenous analgesia.[154] There is increasing evidence that newly available techniques in the management of postoperative pain, such as patient-controlled analgesia, epidural analgesia with use of local anesthetics, spinal opioids, intercostal nerve block, and interpleural analgesia, may provide superior analgesia, fewer fluctuations, improved pulmonary function tests, and fewer pulmonary complications than the administration of parenteral narcotics.[154,162-164]

Other investigators have found improved oxygenation, improved patient comfort, and faster recovery of intestinal function, but no difference in pulmonary complications in a group of patients who underwent abdominal surgery for cancer when parenteral opioids were compared with epidural analgesia with bupivacaine and opioids.[165] A more recent meta-analysis showed a significant decrease in the incidence of atelectasis when epidural opioids or local anesthetics were used instead of systemic opioids for postoperative analgesia.[154,166]

Estimates of the incidence of pulmonary complications in the postoperative period vary and are related to the type of surgery, prior lung pathology, and criteria used to define pulmonary complications.[156] Among the different series, it has been estimated that the overall incidence of pulmonary complications in the postoperative period is about 5% in the general population and less than 1% in patients undergoing major vascular, upper abdominal, and thoracic surgery.[167]

Thoracic and abdominal operations produce profound effects on the respiratory mechanics and function because of the action on the respiratory muscles.[154] Deep breathing and cough are profoundly affected.[154] Vital capacity and functional residual capacity are reduced by 60% and 20%.[161] The impaired cough and reduced clearance of the secretions can lead to atelectasis and pulmonary infections.[154] Other factors that have been implicated as risk factors for the development of pulmonary complications include smoking, age, obesity, COPD, malnutrition, prolonged operations, use of muscle relaxants, and emergency surgery.[156]

A combination of a catastrophic medical or surgical illness with prolonged bed rest, deconditioning, nutritional deficiency, and the use of sedatives, hypnotics, and analgesics frequently leads to prolonged mechanical ventilation and need for a chronic ventilator unit.[168,169] Mechanically ventilated tracheostomized patients have an extremely high incidence of swallowing disorders, which complicates greatly their already significant risk for aspiration pneumonia and other pulmonary complications.[168,169] Early ambulation with recognition of back pain and chest pain as a common problem that could affect the weaning process is important.[168,169] In our institution, as part of the rehabilitation of ventilator-dependent patients, the patients are taught proper body mechanics, and early ambulation is reinforced with the use of a Mayo podium walker that can fit a pressure-cycled ventilator and a portable gas source.[168,169]

Patients who undergo operations with the greatest effects on pulmonary function, such as thoracotomy and upper abdominal procedures, benefit the most from improved analgesia in the postoperative period.[159,161] In such patients, epidural administration of a narcotic, intercostal nerve block,[164] and interpleural analgesia should be used as the preferred method, if possible.[161]

■ TRAUMATIC CHEST PAIN

Chest trauma is present in 60% of patients with multisystem injuries.[156] On arrival in the emergency department, and after a brief history and vital signs evaluation, a brief physical examination should be done looking for additional posterior wounds and injuries.[170] If no breath sounds are heard on one side of the chest, and the patient is hemodynamically unstable, a thoracostomy tube should be inserted.[170] After intravenous access is secured, and an arterial catheter is inserted for blood pressure monitoring, a chest radiograph should be obtained.[170] The output from the chest tube is noted,

and the subsequent hours dictate whether or not a thoracotomy is needed. More than 100 mL of blood per hour of output usually indicates a lesion of a major pulmonary vessel or bronchial artery.[170] Interventional radiology procedures are now available for embolization of arteries and vessels in the pulmonary circulation in cases of significant posttraumatic pulmonary hemorrhage.[171]

The most serious injuries that need immediate attention are airway obstruction, tension pneumothorax, open pneumothorax, massive hemothorax, flail chest, and cardiac tamponade, as detailed by Owens and associates[156] (Fig. 75–17). When these have been ruled out, a second survey should consider the possibilities of simple pneumothorax, hemothorax, pulmonary contusion, traumatic aortic rupture, tracheobronchial disruption, esophageal disruption, traumatic diaphragmatic injury, and wounds penetrating to the mediastinum.[156]

The treatment of rib fractures is directed toward pain control, effective clearance of secretions, and preservation of lung function, to avoid complications.[156] Complications and greater severity of injury are seen when there are more than three ribs involved. Clearance of secretions and pain control are crucial.[156] Although oral or intravenous narcotics, patient-controlled analgesia, and intrapleural catheters are common methods for pain management in these cases, it has been suggested that epidural catheters may be superior in controlling the pain and maintaining lung function.[172,173]

Special consideration should be given to fractures of the first and second ribs because of the common association with lesions of the great vessels seen with these fractures.[156] Flail chest is the result of multiple rib fractures with chest wall instability that leads to abnormal or paradoxical movements with respiration (inward during inspiration and outward in expiration).[156] Patients with traumatic flail chest are usually in severe respiratory distress.[174]

For more than 4 decades, internal stabilization of flail chest has been advocated using mechanical ventilation, pain control, and muscle relaxants to prevent paradoxical motion of the chest wall.[156,170,174] Positive end-expiratory pressure is used to treat the underlying contusion.[174] There has been controversy over whether by using positive-pressure ventilation, and expanding the lung, the improvement is due to the pneumatic fixation of the chest wall or to improved gas exchange and protective effect of positive end-expiratory pressure over the lung parenchyma.[174] More recently, it has been shown that pain control and secretion management decrease complications and need for mechanical ventilatory support in flail chest cases.[175,176] Internal fixation is of value in patients with severe chest wall instability.

Numerous trials have shown the critical care and pulmonary community that ventilating patients with acute lung injury with large tidal volumes increases mortality.[177,178] Lung protective mechanical ventilation with small tidal volumes is now the standard of care for patients with acute lung injury.[179,180] Whether these concepts can be extrapolated to the traumatically injured lung is still controversial.

Three forms of traumatic pneumothorax have been described: simple, open, and tension penumothorax.[156] A chest tube is often needed. If conservative treatment of the pneumothorax was elected, owing to small size or stable clinical conditions, a close radiographic follow-up in 3 to 4 hours is advised.[156]

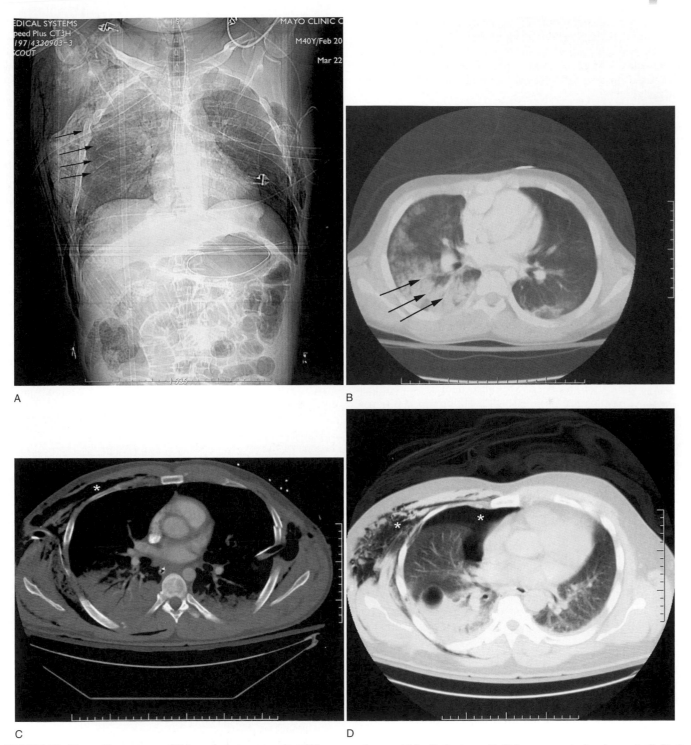

FIGURE 75–17 ■ Chest trauma. CT in a chest trauma patient (**A**); arrows show multiple rib fractures. **B,** Pulmonary contusion (*arrows*). **C, D,** *, Pneumothorax, and subcutaneous emphysema in a case of flail chest.

Hemothorax is defined as the presence of blood within the pleural space.[156] When greater than 250 mL, patients develop chest pain, dyspnea, tachycardia, and hypotension. The physical examination shows dullness to percussion and absent breath sounds in the affected lung.[156] Deviation of the trachea is present if there is mediastinal shift toward the unaffected side. Chest tube placement is usually the initial approach, and in 10% to 15% of the cases, surgery is

needed.[156] A few patients develop some complication of the hemothorax, including fibrosis, lung trapping, or infection progressing to an empyema.[156]

Pulmonary contusion and pulmonary hematoma are the ends of the spectrum of injury induced by trauma to the lungs. Conservative treatment is preferred and is centered in secretion toilette and pain control. These patients may deteriorate rapidly and should be monitored in an ICU. Oxygenation and

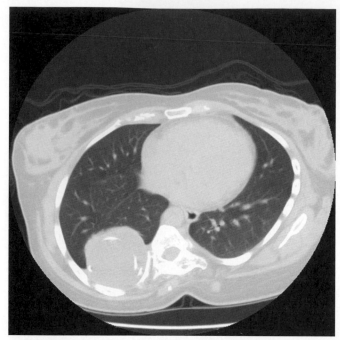

FIGURE 75–18 ■ Ventriculopleural catheter. CT in a 33-year-old woman with a ventriculopleural catheter placed, admitted to the hospital after minor chest trauma and development of headaches, nausea, and vomiting. A chest radiograph and CT scan showed a loculated fluid collection with the catheter coiled inside the collection. Observation for a few weeks showed that the fluid collection remained stable, and the symptoms disappeared. The catheter was not changed or removed and was believed to be functioning properly.

homodynamic support is warranted for these patients. The available resources in the ICU include the use of protective ventilatory strategies, appropriate fluid management, appropriate and early antibiotic use, and early recognition and treatment of relative adrenal insufficiency. Postural changes and aggressive and prompt use of respiratory therapy is helpful. Early changes of pneumonitis may not be apparent, and the patient should be followed closely by portable chest radiographs and when appropriate with CT.[156]

Traumatic injuries to the mediastinum may include life threatening and critical lesions, such as esophageal rupture, airway laceration, and diaphragmatic rupture.[156] These patients are critically ill and may present with enlargement of the mediastinum, hemothorax or pneumothorax, pneumomediastinum, and subcutaneous emphysema.[156] Treatment includes placement of a nasogastric tube, broad-spectrum antibiotics, and when necessary pleural drainage with a chest tube.[156]

References

1. Fillenz M, Widdicombe JG: Receptors of the lungs and airway. In Neil E (ed): Handbook of Sensory Physiology. Enteroceptors, vol III. Berlin, Springer-Verlag, 1971, p 81.
2. Guz A: Respiratory sensations in man. Br Med Bull 33:175, 1977.
3. Cervero F: Sensory innervation of the viscera: Peripheral basis of visceral pain. Physiol Rev 74:95, 1994.
4. Light RW: Anatomy of the pleura. In Light RW (ed): Pleural Diseases. Philadelphia, Lippincott Williams & Williams, 2001, p 1.
5. Coleridge HM, Coleridge JCG: Reflexes evoked for the tracheobronchial tree and lungs. In Fishman AP, Cherniack NS, Widdicombe JG (eds): Handbook of Physiology. The Respiratory System. Control of

Breathing, Sect 3, Vol 2, Chap 12. Washington, DC, American Physiological Society, 1986, pp 395-429.
6. Sant'Ambrogio G: Nervous receptors of the tracheobronchial tree. Annu Rev Physiol 49:611, 1987.
7. Coleridge JCG, Coleridge HM: Functional role of pulmonary rapidly adapting receptors and lung C fibers. In Lahiri S, Forster REII, Davies RO, et al (eds): Chemoreceptors and Reflexes in Breathing. New York, Oxford University Press, 1989, p 287.
8. Paintal AS: Effects of drugs on chemoreceptors, pulmonary and cardiovascular receptors. Pharmacol Ther [B] 3:41, 1977.
9. Paintal AS: Thoracic receptors connected with sensation. Br Med Bull 33:169, 1977.
10. Paintal AS: The visceral sensations—some basic mechanisms. Prog Brain Res 67:3, 1986.
11. Widdicombe JG: Sensory innervation of the lungs and airways. In Cervero F, Morrison JFB (eds): Visceral Sensation. Amsterdam, Elsevier, 1986, p 49.
12. Widdicombe JG: Enteroceptors. In Hubbard JI (ed): The Peripheral Nervous System. New York, Plenum, 1974, p 455-485.
13. Simon PM, Zurob AS, Wies WM, et al: Entrainment of respiration in humans by periodic lung inflations: Effect of state and CO_2. Am J Respir Crit Care Med 160:950, 1999.
14. Sant'Ambrogio G: Information arising from the tracheobronchial tree of mammals. Physiol Rev 62:531, 1982.
15. Paintal AS: Vagal sensory receptors and their reflex effects. Physiol Rev 53:159, 1973.
16. Coleridge JC, Coleridge HM: Afferent vagal C fibre innervation of the lungs and airways and its functional significance. Rev Physiol Biochem Pharmacol 99:1, 1984.
17. Donat WE: Chest pain: Cardiac and noncardiac causes. Clin Chest Med 8:241, 1987.
18. Light RW: Pleural Diseases, 3rd ed. Baltimore, Williams & Willkins, 1995.
19. Murray JF, Gebhart G: Chest pain. In Murray JF, Nadel JA (eds): Textbook of Respiratory Medicine, 3rd ed. Philadelphia, WB Saunders, 2000, p 567.
20. Wise CM: Chest wall syndromes. Curr Opin Rheumatol 6:197, 1994.
21. Dura PA, Daniel TM, Frierson HF Jr, Brunner CM: Chest wall mass in rheumatoid arthritis. J Rheumatol 20:910, 1993.
22. Tietze A: Ubber eine eigneartige Haufund zur Fallen mit Dystrophite der Rippenknorpel. Berlin Klin Wochenschr 58:829, 1921.
23. Manganelli D, Palla A, Donnamaria V, Giuntini C: Clinical features of pulmonary embolism: Doubts and certainties. Chest 107(1 suppl):25S, 1995.
24. Prager D: Bronchogenic carcinoma. In Murray JF, Nadel JA (eds): Textbook of Respiratory Medicine, 3rd ed. Philadelphia, WB Saunders, 2000, p 1415.
25. Kvale PA, Simoff M, Prakash UB: Lung cancer: Palliative care. Chest 123(1 suppl):284S, 2003.
26. Jacox A, Carr DB, Payne R: New clinical-practice guidelines for the management of pain in patients with cancer. N Engl J Med 330:651, 1994.
27. Jacox A, Carr DB, Payne R: Management of cancer pain. Clinical Practice Guideline No 9. AHCPR Publication No 94-0592. Rockville, MD, Agency for Health Care Policy and Research U.S. Department of Health and Human Services, Public Health Service, 1994.
28. Cancer Pain Relief and Palliative Care. Report of a WHO Expert Committee. World Health Organ Tech Rep Ser 804:1, 1990.
29. Tobias JW: Sindrome apico-costo-vertebral doloroso por tumor: Su valor diagnostico en el cancer primitivo pulmonar. Rev Med Latino Am 17:1522, 1932.
30. Arcasoy SM, Jett JR: Superior pulmonary sulcus tumors and Pancoast's syndrome. N Engl J Med 337:1370, 1997.
31. Mills PR, Han LY, Dick R, Clarke SW: Pancoast syndrome caused by a high grade B cell lymphoma. Thorax 49:92, 1994.
32. Hepper NG, Herskovic T, Witten DM, et al: Thoracic inlet tumors. Ann Intern Med 64:979, 1966.
33. Kanner RM, Martini N, Foley KM: Incidence of pain and other clinical manifestations of superior pulmonary (Pancoast) tumors. In Bonica JJ (ed): Management of Superior Sulcus Pulmonary Tumors. New York, Raven Press, 1982, p 27.
34. Anderson TM, Moy PM, Holmes EC: Factors affecting survival in superior sulcus tumors. J Clin Oncol 4:1598, 1986.
35. Sundaresan N, Hilaris BS, Martini N: The combined neurosurgical-thoracic management of superior sulcus tumors. J Clin Oncol 5:1739, 1987.

36. Attar S, Miller JE, Satterfield J, et al: Pancoast's tumor: Irradiation or surgery? Ann Thorac Surg 28:578, 1979.

37. Gefter WB: Magnetic resonance imaging in the evaluation of lung cancer. Semin Roentgenol 25:73, 1990.

38. Takasugi JE, Rapoport S, Shaw C: Superior sulcus tumors: The role of imaging. J Thorac Imaging 4:41, 1989.

39. Webb WR, Gatsonis C, Zerhouni EA, et al: CT and MR imaging in staging non-small cell bronchogenic carcinoma: Report of the Radiologic Diagnostic Oncology Group. Radiology 178:705, 1991.

40. Mountain CF: Revisions in the International System for Staging Lung Cancer. Chest 111:1710, 1997.

41. Wright CD, Moncure AC, Shepard JA, et al: Superior sulcus lung tumors: Results of combined treatment (irradiation and radical resection). J Thorac Cardiovasc Surg 94:69, 1987.

42. Paulson D: Technical considerations in stage III disease: The "superior sulcus lesion." In Delarue NC, Eschapasse H (eds): Lung Cancer, vol 1. Philadelphia, WB Saunders, 1985, p 121.

43. Detterbeck FC: Pancoast (superior sulcus) tumors. Ann Thorac Surg 63:1810, 1997.

44. Ginsberg RJ: Resection of a superior sulcus tumor. Chest Surg Clin North Am 5:315, 1995.

45. Dartevelle PG, Chapelier AR, Macchiarini P, et al: Anterior transcervical-thoracic approach for radical resection of lung tumors invading the thoracic inlet. J Thorac Cardiovasc Surg 105:1025, 1993.

46. Hilaris BS, Martini N, Wong GY, Nori D: Treatment of superior sulcus tumor (Pancoast tumor). Surg Clin North Am 67:965, 1987.

47. Ginsberg RJ, Martini N, Zaman M, et al: Influence of surgical resection and brachytherapy in the management of superior sulcus tumor. Ann Thorac Surg 57:1440, 1994.

48. Dartevelle P, Macchiarini P: Surgical management of superior sulcus tumors. Oncologist 4:398, 1999.

49. Maggi G, Casadio C, Pischedda F, et al: Combined radiosurgical treatment of Pancoast tumor. Ann Thorac Surg 57:198, 1994.

50. Gandhi S, Walsh GL, Komaki R, et al: A multidisciplinary surgical approach to superior sulcus tumors with vertebral invasion. Ann Thorac Surg 68:1778, 1999.

51. van Geel AN, Jansen PP, van Klaveren RJ, van der Sijp JR: High relapse-free survival after preoperative and intraoperative radiotherapy and resection for sulcus superior tumors. Chest 124:1841, 2003.

52. Attar S, Krasna MJ, Sonett JR, et al: Superior sulcus (Pancoast) tumor: Experience with 105 patients. Ann Thorac Surg 66:193, 1998.

53. Hagan MP, Choi NC, Mathisen DJ, et al: Superior sulcus lung tumors: Impact of local control on survival. J Thorac Cardiovasc Surg 117:1086, 1999.

54. Alifano M, D'Aiuto M, Magdeleinat P, et al: Surgical treatment of superior sulcus tumors: Results and prognostic factors. Chest 124:996, 2003.

55. Grover FL, Komaki R: Superior sulcus tumors. In Roth JA, Ruckdeschel JC, Weisenburger TH (eds): Thoracic Oncology. Philadelphia, WB Saunders, 1995, p 225.

56. Komaki R, Mountain CF, Holbert JM, et al: Superior sulcus tumors: treatment selection and results for 85 patients without metastasis (Mo) at presentation. Int J Radiat Oncol Biol Phys 19:31, 1990.

57. Selikoff IJ, Lee DHK: Asbestos and Disease. New York, Academic Press, 1978.

58. Becklake MR, Cowie RL: Pneumoconiosis. In Murray JF, Nadel JA (eds): Textbook of Respiratory Medicine, 3rd ed. Philadelphia, WB Saunders, 2000, p 1811.

59. Churg A, Green FHY: Pathology of Occupational Lung Disease, 3rd ed. Baltimore, Williams & Wilkins, 1998.

60. Craighead JE, Abraham JL, Churg A, et al: The pathology of asbestos-associated diseases of the lungs and pleural cavities: Diagnostic criteria and proposed grading schema. Report of the Pneumoconiosis Committee of the College of American Pathologists and the National Institute for Occupational Safety and Health. Arch Pathol Lab Med 106:544, 1982.

61. Miller WT Jr, Gefter WB, Miller WT Sr: Asbestos-related chest diseases: Plain radiographic findings. Semin Roentgenol 27:102, 1992.

62. Becklake MR: Asbestosis. In Liddell D, Miller K (eds): Mineral Fibers and Health. Boca Raton, CRC Press, 1991, p 103.

63. Mukherjee S, de Klerk N, Palmer LJ, et al: Chest pain in asbestos-exposed individuals with benign pleural and parenchymal disease. Am J Respir Crit Care Med 162:1807, 2000.

64. Light RW, Broaddus V: Tumors of the pleura. In Murray JF, Nadel JA (eds): Textbook of Respiratory Medicine, 3rd ed. Philadelphia, WB Saunders, 2000, p 2067.

65. Light RW: Primary tumors of the pleura. In Light RW (ed): Pleural Diseases, 4th ed. Baltimore, Williams & Wilkins, 2001, p 135.

65a. Wagner JC, Sleggs CA, Marchand P: Diffuse pleural mesothelioma and asbestos exposure in the North West Cape Provice. Br J Industr Med 17:260-271, 1960.

66. Pisani RJ, Colby TV, Williams DE: Malignant mesothelioma of the pleura. Mayo Clin Proc 63:1234, 1988.

67. Antman KH: Clinical presentation and natural history of benign and malignant mesothelioma. Semin Oncol 8:313, 1981.

68. Kawashima A, Libshitz HI: Malignant pleural mesothelioma: CT manifestations in 50 cases. AJR Am J Roentgenol 155:965, 1990.

69. Yilmaz UM, Utkaner G, Yalniz E, Kumcuoglu Z: Computed tomographic findings of environmental asbestos-related malignant pleural mesothelioma. Respirology 3:33, 1998.

70. Gottehrer A, Taryle DA, Reed CE, Sahn SA: Pleural fluid analysis in malignant mesothelioma: Prognostic implications. Chest 100:1003, 1991.

71. Boutin C, Rey F, Gouvernet J, et al: Thoracoscopy in pleural malignant mesothelioma: A prospective study of 188 consecutive patients. Part 2: Prognosis and staging. Cancer 72:394, 1993.

72. Rusch VW: Pleurectomy/decortication in the setting of multimodality treatment for diffuse malignant pleural mesothelioma. Semin Thorac Cardiovasc Surg 9:367, 1997.

73. Law MR, Hodson ME, Turner-Warwick M: Malignant mesothelioma of the pleura: Clinical aspects and symptomatic treatment. Eur J Respir Dis 65:162, 1984.

74. Light RW, Macgregor MI, Luchsinger PC, Ball WC Jr: Pleural effusions: The diagnostic separation of transudates and exudates. Ann Intern Med 77:507, 1972.

75. Sahn SA: Pleural diseases related to metastatic malignancies. Eur Respir J 10:1907, 1997.

76. Prakash UB, Reiman HM: Comparison of needle biopsy with cytologic analysis for the evaluation of pleural effusion: Analysis of 414 cases. Mayo Clin Proc 60:158, 1985.

77. Robinson LA, Reilly RB: Localized pleural mesothelioma: The clinical spectrum. Chest 106:1611, 1994.

78. Ferretti GR, Chiles C, Choplin RH, Coulomb M: Localized benign fibrous tumors of the pleura. AJR Am J Roentgenol 169:683, 1997.

79. Nador RG, Cesarman E, Chadburn A, et al: Primary effusion lymphoma: A distinct clinicopathologic entity associated with the Kaposi's sarcoma-associated herpes virus. Blood 88:645, 1996.

80. Jones D, Ballestas ME, Kaye KM, et al: Primary-effusion lymphoma and Kaposi's sarcoma in a cardiac-transplant recipient. N Engl J Med 339:444, 1998.

81. Kanno H, Ohsawa M, Iuchi K, et al: Appearance of a different clone of Epstein-Barr virus genome in recurrent tumor of pyothorax-associated lymphoma (PAL) and a mini-review of PAL. Leukemia 12:1288, 1998.

82. Prakash UBS: Mediastinum. In ACCP (ed): ACCP Pulmonary Board Review 2003. Northbrook, IL, ACCP, 2003, p 179.

83. Silverman NA, Sabiston DC Jr: Mediastinal masses. Surg Clin North Am 60:757, 1980.

84. Benjamin SP, McCormack LJ, Effler DB, Groves LK: Primary tumors of the mediastinum. Chest 62:297, 1972.

85. Burkell CC, Cross JM, Kent HP, Nanson EM: Mass lesions of the mediastinum. Curr Probl Surg 2, 1969.

86. Haller JA Jr, Mazur DO, Morgan WW Jr: Diagnosis and management of mediastinal masses in children. J Thorac Cardiovasc Surg 58:385-393, 1969.

87. Oldham HN Jr, Sabiston DC Jr: Primary tumors and cysts of the mediastinum. Monogr Surg Sci 4:243, 1967.

88. Gale AW, Jelihovsky T, Grant AF, et al: Neurogenic tumors of the mediastinum. Ann Thorac Surg 17:434, 1974.

89. Weil JV, Castro O, Malik AB, et al: NHLBI Workshop Summary. Pathogenesis of lung disease in sickle hemoglobinopathies. Am Rev Respir Dis 148:249, 1993.

90. Farber MD, Koshy M, Kinney TR: Cooperative Study of Sickle Cell Disease: Demographic and socioeconomic characteristics of patients and families with sickle cell disease. J Chronic Dis 38:495, 1985.

91. Castro O, Brambilla DJ, Thorington B, et al: The acute chest syndrome in sickle cell disease: Incidence and risk factors. The Cooperative Study of Sickle Cell Disease. Blood 84:643, 1994.

92. Vichinsky EP, Styles LA, Colangelo LH, et al: Acute chest syndrome in sickle cell disease: Clinical presentation and course. Cooperative Study of Sickle Cell Disease. Blood 89:1787, 1997.

93. Charache S, Scott JC, Charache P: "Acute chest syndrome" in adults with sickle cell anemia: Microbiology, treatment, and prevention. Arch Intern Med 139:67, 1979.

94. Bellet PS, Kalinyak KA, Shukla R, et al: Incentive spirometry to prevent acute pulmonary complications in sickle cell diseases. N Engl J Med 333:699, 1995.

95. Goldhaber SZ: Pulmonary embolism. N Engl J Med 339:93, 1998.

96. Stein PD, Terrin ML, Hales CA, et al: Clinical, laboratory, roentgeno-graphic, and electrocardiographic findings in patients with acute pulmonary embolism and no pre-existing cardiac or pulmonary disease. Chest 100:598, 1991.

97. Value of the ventilation/perfusion scan in acute pulmonary embolism: Results of the prospective investigation of pulmonary embolism diagnosis (PIOPED). The PIOPED Investigators. JAMA 263:2753, 1990.

98. Stein PD, Henry JW: Clinical characteristics of patients with acute pulmonary embolism stratified according to their presenting syndromes. Chest 112:974, 1997.

99. Bell WR, Simon TL, DeMets DL: The clinical features of submassive and massive pulmonary emboli. Obstet Gynecol Surv 32:598, 1977.

100. Light RW: Pleural effusions due to pulmonary embolism. In Light RW (ed): Pleural Disease. Philadelphia, Williams & Wilkins, 2001, p 219.

101. Dalen JE, Haffajee CI, Alpert JS 3rd, et al: Pulmonary embolism, pulmonary hemorrhage and pulmonary infarction. N Engl J Med 296:1431, 1977.

102. Ryu JH, Swensen SJ, Olson EJ, Pellikka PA: Diagnosis of pulmonary embolism with use of computed tomographic angiography. Mayo Clin Proc 76:59, 2001.

103. Ryu JH, Olson EJ, Pellikka PA: Clinical recognition of pulmonary embolism: Problem of unrecognized and asymptomatic cases. Mayo Clin Proc 73:873, 1998.

104. Stein PD, Saltzman HA, Weg JG: Clinical characteristics of patients with acute pulmonary embolism. Am J Cardiol 68:1723, 1991.

105. Viar WN, Harrison TR: Chest pain in association with pulmonary hypertension: Its similarity with the pain of coronary disease. Circulation 4:1, 1952.

106. Rich S, Dantzker DR, Ayres SM, et al: Primary pulmonary hypertension: A national prospective study. Ann Intern Med 107:216, 1987.

107. Rubin LJ: Pathology and pathophysiology of primary pulmonary hypertension. Am J Cardiol 75:51A, 1995.

108. Patrat JF, Jondeau G, Dubourg O, et al: Left main coronary artery compression during primary pulmonary hypertension. Chest 112:842, 1997.

109. Tami LF, McElderry MW: Pulmonary artery aneurysm due to severe congenital pulmonic stenosis: Case report and literature review. Angiology 45:383, 1994.

110. Garibaldi RA: Epidemiology of community-acquired respiratory tract infections in adults: Incidence, etiology, and impact. Am J Med 78:32, 1985.

111. Treanor JJ, Hayden FG: Viral infections. In Murray JF, Nadel JA (eds): Textbook of Respiratory Medicine, 3rd ed. Philadelphia, WB, Saunders, 2000, p 929.

112. Marrie TJ: Community-acquired pneumonia. Clin Infect Dis 18:501, 1994.

113. Fine MJ, Smith MA, Carson CA, et al: Prognosis and outcomes of patients with community-acquired pneumonia: A meta-analysis. JAMA 275:134, 1996.

114. Goetz MB, Finegold SM: Pyogenic bacterial pneumonia, lung abscess, and empyema. In Murray JF, Nadel JA (eds): Textbook of Respiratory Medicine. Philadelphia, WB Saunders, 2000, p 985.

115. Centers for Disease Control and Prevention: Guidelines for prevention of nosocomial pneumonia. MMWR Recomm Rep 46(RR-1):1, 1997.

116. Light RW, Girard WM, Jenkinson SG, George RB: Parapneumonic effusions. Am J Med 69:507, 1980.

117. Sahn SA, Light RW: The sun should never set on a parapneumonic effusion. Chest 95:945, 1989.

118. Bartlett JG, Finegold SM: Anaerobic infections of the lung and pleural space. Am Rev Respir Dis 110:56, 1974.

119. Goldman M, Johnson PC, Sarosi GA: Fungal pneumonias: The endemic mycoses. Clin Chest Med 20:507, 1999.

120. Wheat J: Histoplasmosis: Experience during outbreaks in Indianapolis and review of the literature. Medicine (Baltimore) 76:339, 1997.

121. Wheat LJ: Diagnosis and management of histoplasmosis. Eur J Clin Microbiol Infect Dis 8:480, 1989.

122. Kataria YP, Campbell PB, Burlingham BT: Acute pulmonary histoplasmosis presenting as adult respiratory distress syndrome: Effect of therapy on clinical and laboratory features. South Med J 74:534, 1981.

123. Goodwin RA, Nickell JA, Des Prez RM: Mediastinal fibrosis complicating healed primary histoplasmosis and tuberculosis. Medicine (Baltimore) 51:227, 1972.

124. Rippon JW: Blastomycosis. Medical Mycology: The Pathogenic Fungi and Pathogenic Actinomycetes. Philadelphia, WB Saunders, 1988, p 474.

125. Hopewell PC: Tuberculosis and other mycobacterial diseases. In Murray JF, Nadel JA (eds): Textbook of Respiratory Medicine. Philadelphia, WB Saunders, 2000, p 1043.

126. Petty TL, Weinmann GG: Building a national strategy for the prevention and management of and research in chronic obstructive pulmonary disease. National Heart, Lung, and Blood Institute Workshop Summary. Bethesda, MD, August 29-31, 1995. JAMA 277:246, 1997.

127. Sahn SA, Heffner JE: Spontaneous pneumothorax. N Engl J Med 342:868, 2000.

128. Baumann MH, Strange C, Heffner JE, et al: Management of spontaneous pneumothorax: An American College of Chest Physicians Delphi consensus statement. Chest 119:590, 2001.

129. Vassallo R, Ryu JH, Colby TV, et al: Pulmonary Langerhans'-cell histiocytosis. N Engl J Med 342:1969, 2000.

130. Ryu JH, Colby TV, Hartman TE, Vassallo R: Smoking-related interstitial lung diseases: A concise review. Eur Respir J 17:122, 2001.

131. Tazi A, Soler P, Hance AJ: Adult pulmonary Langerhans' cell histiocytosis. Thorax 55:405, 2000.

132. Vassallo R, Ryu JH, Schroeder DR, et al: Clinical outcomes of pulmonary Langerhans'-cell histiocytosis in adults. N Engl J Med 346:484, 2002.

133. Travis WD, Borok Z, Roum JH, et al: Pulmonary Langerhans cell granulomatosis (histiocytosis X): A clinicopathologic study of 48 cases. Am J Surg Pathol 17:971, 1993.

134. Friedman PJ, Liebow AA, Sokoloff J: Eosinophilic granuloma of lung: Clinical aspects of primary histiocytosis in the adult. Medicine (Baltimore) 60:385, 1981.

135. Crausman RS, Jennings CA, Tuder RM, et al: Pulmonary histiocytosis X: Pulmonary function and exercise pathophysiology. Am J Respir Crit Care Med 153:426, 1996.

136. Delobbe A, Durieu J, Duhamel A, Wallaert B: Determinants of survival in pulmonary Langerhans' cell granulomatosis (histiocytosis X). Groupe d'Etude en Pathologie Interstitielle de la Societe de Pathologie Thoracique du Nord. Eur Respir J 9:2002, 1996.

137. Schonfeld N, Frank W, Wenig S, et al: Clinical and radiologic features, lung function and therapeutic results in pulmonary histiocytosis X. Respiration 60:38, 1993.

138. Light RW: Pneumothorax. In Light RW (ed): Pleural Diseases, 4th ed. Philadelphia, Lippincott Williams & Wilkins, 2001, p 284.

139. Mendez JL, Nadrous HF, Vassallo R: Pneumothorax in pulmonary Langerhans' cell histiocytosis. Chest 125:1028-1032, 2004.

140. Basset F, Corrin B, Spencer H, et al: Pulmonary histiocytosis X. Am Rev Respir Dis 118:811, 1978.

141. Bertrand PC, Regnard JF, Spaggiari L, et al: Immediate and long-term results after surgical treatment of primary spontaneous pneumothorax by VATS. Ann Thorac Surg 61:1641, 1996.

142. Naunheim KS, Mack MJ, Hazelrigg SR, et al: Safety and efficacy of video-assisted thoracic surgical techniques for the treatment of spontaneous pneumothorax. J Thorac Cardiovasc Surg 109:1198, 1995.

143. Kalassian KG: Lymphangioleiomyomatosis. In Murray JF, Nadel JA (eds): Textbook of Respiratory Medicine, 3rd ed. Philadelphia, WB Saunders, 2000, p 1775.

144. Kitaichi M, Izumi T: Lymphangioleiomyomatosis. Curr Opin Pulm Med 1:417, 1995.

145. Taylor JR, Ryu J, Colby TV, Raffin TA: Lymphangioleiomyomatosis: Clinical course in 32 patients. N Engl J Med 323:1254, 1990.

146. Urban T, Lazor R, Lacronique J, et al: Pulmonary lymphangioleiomyomatosis: A study of 69 patients. Groupe d'Etudes et de Recherche sur les Maladies "Orphelines" Pulmonaires (GERM"O"P). Medicine (Baltimore) 78: 321, 1999.

147. Oh YM, Mo EK, Jang SH, et al: Pulmonary lymphangioleiomyomatosis in Korea. Thorax 54:618, 1999.

148. Johnson SR, Tattersfield AE: Clinical experience of lymphangioleiomyomatosis in the UK. Thorax 55:1052, 2000.

149. Doerr CH, Miller DL, Ryv JH: Chylothorax. Semin Respir Crit Care Med 22:617, 2001.

150. Staats BA, Ellefson RD, Budahn LL, et al: The lipoprotein profile of chylous and nonchylous pleural effusions. Mayo Clin Proc 55:700, 1980.

151. Ryu JH, Doerr CH, Fisher SD, et al: Chylothorax in lymphangioleiomyomatosis. Chest 123:623, 2003.

152. Chu SC, Horiba K, Usuki J, et al: Comprehensive evaluation of 35 patients with lymphangioleiomyomatosis. Chest 115:1041, 1999.

153. Maziak DE, Kesten S, Rappaport DC, Maurer J: Extrathoracic angiomyolipomas in lymphangioleiomyomatosis. Eur Respir J 9:402, 1996.

154. Lutz LJ, Lamer TJ: Management of postoperative pain: Review of current techniques and methods. Mayo Clin Proc 65:584, 1990.

155. Marks RM, Sachar EJ: Undertreatment of medical inpatients with narcotic analgesics. Ann Intern Med 78:173, 1973.

156. Owens MW, Chaudry MS, Eggerstedt JM: Thoracic trauma, surgery, and perioperative management. In George RB, Light RW, Matthay MA, et al (eds): Chest Medicine, Essentials of Pulmonary and Critical Care Medicine, 4th ed. Philadelphia, Lippincott Williams & Wilkins, 2000, p 593.

157. Kroenke K, Lawrence VA, Theroux JF, Tuley MR: Operative risk in patients with severe obstructive pulmonary disease. Arch Intern Med 152:967, 1992.

158. Wong DH, Weber EC, Schell MJ, et al: Factors associated with postoperative pulmonary complications in patients with severe chronic obstructive pulmonary disease. Anesth Analg 80:276, 1995.

159. Yeager MP, Glass DD, Neff RK, Brinck-Johnsen T: Epidural anesthesia and analgesia in high-risk surgical patients. Anesthesiology 66:729, 1987.

160. Rawal N, Sjostrand U, Christoffersson E, et al: Comparison of intramuscular and epidural morphine for postoperative analgesia in the grossly obese: Influence on postoperative ambulation and pulmonary function. Anesth Analg 63:583, 1984.

161. Muneyuki M, Ueda Y, Urabe N, et al: Postoperative pain relief and respiratory function in man: Comparison between intermittent intravenous injections of eperidine and continuous lumbar epidural analgesia. Anesthesiology 29:304, 1968.

162. Cuschieri RJ, Morran CG, Howie JC, McArdle CS: Postoperative pain and pulmonary complications: Comparison of three analgesic regimens. Br J Surg 72:495, 1985.

163. Hendolin H, Lahtinen J, Lansimies E, et al: The effect of thoracic epidural analgesia on respiratory function after cholecystectomy. Acta Anaesthesiol Scand 31:645, 1987.

164. Engberg G, Wiklund L: Pulmonary complications after upper abdominal surgery: Their prevention with intercostal blocks. Acta Anaesthesiol Scand 32:1, 1988.

165. Jayr C, Thomas H, Rey A, et al: Postoperative pulmonary complications: Epidural analgesia using bupivacaine and opioids versus parenteral opioids. Anesthesiology 78:666, 1993.

166. Ballantyne JC, Carr DB, deFerranti S, et al: The comparative effects of postoperative analgesic therapies on pulmonary outcome: Cumulative meta-analyses of randomized, controlled trials. Anesth Analg 86:598, 1998.

167. Pedersen T, Eliasen K, Henriksen E: A prospective study of risk factors and cardiopulmonary complications associated with anaesthesia and surgery: Risk indicators of cardiopulmonary morbidity. Acta Anaesthesiol Scand 34:144, 1990.

168. Gracey DR: Options for long-term ventilatory support. Clin Chest Med 18:563, 1997.

169. Gracey DR, Hardy DC, Naessens JM, et al: The Mayo Ventilator-Dependent Rehabilitation Unit: A 5-year experience. Mayo Clin Proc 72:13, 1997.

170. Avery EE, Benson DW, Morch ET: Critically crushed chests: A new method of treatment with continuous mechanical hyperventilation to produce alkalotic apnea and internal pneumatic stabilization. J Thorac Surg 32:291, 1956.

171. Jackson JE, Allison DJ: Vascular intervention techniques in the thorax. Section two: The respiratory system. In Grainger RG, Allison DJ, Adam A, Dixon AK (eds): Grainger & Allison's Diagnostic Radiology: A Textbook of Medical Imaging, 4th ed. London, Churchill Livingstone, 2001, p 607.

172. Luchette FA, Radafshar SM, Kaiser R, et al: Prospective evaluation of epidural versus intrapleural catheters for analgesia in chest wall trauma. J Trauma 36:865, 1994.

173. Mackersie RC, Karagianes TG, Hoyt DB, Davis JW: Prospective evaluation of epidural and intravenous administration of fentanyl for pain control and restoration of ventilatory function following multiple rib fractures. J Trauma 31:443, 1991.

174. Calhoon JH, Grover FL, Trinkle JK: Chest trauma: Approach and management. Clin Chest Med 13:55, 1992.

175. Richardson JD, Adams L, Flint LM: Selective management of flail chest and pulmonary contusion. Ann Surg 196:481, 1982.

176. Shackford SR, Virgilio RW, Peters RM: Selective use of ventilator therapy in flail chest injury. J Thorac Cardiovasc Surg 81:194, 1981.

177. Ventilation with lower tidal volumes as compared with traditional tidal volumes for acute lung injury and the acute respiratory distress syndrome. The Acute Respiratory Distress Syndrome Network. N Engl J Med 342:1301, 2000.

178. Amato MB, Barbas CS, Medeiros DM, et al: Effect of a protective-ventilation strategy on mortality in the acute respiratory distress syndrome. N Engl J Med 338:347, 1998.

179. Brower RG, Rubenfeld GD: Lung-protective ventilation strategies in acute lung injury. Crit Care Med 31(4 suppl):S312, 2003.

180. Tobin MJ: Culmination of an era in research on the acute respiratory distress syndrome. N Engl J Med 342:1360, 2000.

chapter 76

Postmastectomy Pain

Mirjana Lovrincevic and Mark J. Lema

■ HISTORICAL CONSIDERATIONS

Postmastectomy pain syndrome reportedly affects 27% of patients who underwent breast surgery.[1] Lumpectomy, mastectomy, and sentinel or complete lymph node dissection all can produce this chronic pain condition. The underlying mechanism seems to be damage to the intercostobrachial nerve,[2,3] a cutaneous, sensory branch of T1, T2, and T3, although the nerve damage may be difficult or impossible to document with conventional neurophysiologic methods. The symptoms are distressing and may be difficult to treat. The pain is usually felt in the region innervated by the damaged nerves, in the axilla, arm, or shoulder of the affected side, and is described as burning, stabbing, tingling, or electric shock–like.

Preoperative depression and anxiety were found to place a patient at risk for postmastectomy pain, although statistical significance was not achieved.[4,5] The increased frequency of postmastectomy pain seems to be influenced by marital status, employment status, housing conditions, and educational status of patients who report typical symptoms. Body weight and height also are associated with the frequency of postmastectomy pain syndrome.[6]

Intraoperative factors, such as the type of surgery, are probably the most important predictive factors. The large retrospective study by Tasmuth and colleagues showed that postmastectomy pain syndrome was more common in patients who had mastectomy combined with implantation of a breast prosthesis (53%) than in patients who had mastectomy alone (31%). Three months after axillary lymph node dissection, 61% of patients with preservation of the intercostobrachial nerve reported sensory deficits compared with 80% of patients in whom the nerve was divided.[7] It also was found that axillary dissection increased the likelihood of this syndrome and the greater extent of axillary dissection.[8,9] Postoperative factors thought to be the best predictors for the development of postmastectomy pain syndrome include the extent of immediate postoperative pain, the number of doses of postoperative analgesics received, and immediate adjuvant postoperative radiation therapy.[10]

■ CLINICAL SYNDROME—SIGNS, SYMPTOMS, AND PHYSICAL FINDINGS

Neuropathic pain refers to a chronic disorder of the central or peripheral nervous system (or both) poorly responsive to standard therapeutic approaches and standard doses of analgesics. In essence, the loss of normal somatosensory input and the increased input from sensitized peripheral nerve endings induce a central sensitization in the dorsal horn of the spinal cord. Ectopic impulses may be generated at sites other than the damaged nerve endings. When a peripheral nerve is damaged, a region near the dorsal root ganglion, which is distant from the site of injury, becomes capable of generating spontaneous impulses.[11]

The definition of postmastectomy pain syndrome is based on three criteria: (1) character of the pain, (2) location of the pain, and (2) timing of the pain. This definition was developed on the basis of numerous studies.[6,12,13] The pain usually is described as shooting, sharp, stabbing, pulling, tight, or burning, and it significantly interferes with daily activities. It is located in the axilla, arm, shoulder, or chest wall ipsilateral to the side of the surgery. The pain persists beyond the usual healing time of 3 months. Most studies have shown that straining, sudden movements, tiredness, clothes rubbing, cold weather, and coughing aggravate the pain, whereas resting and lying down relieve the pain. The most important risk factor according to the studies is younger age. It probably accounts for the differences in the other demographic characteristics, such as employment status, marital status, and household size. It also was observed that taller and heavier patients and patients with increased body mass index showed increased frequency of postmastectomy pain syndrome. Although most patients have undergone total mastectomy, only a few had excision of a pectoral muscle. It also was noted that complete lymph node dissection increases the incidence of postmastectomy pain syndrome as opposed to sentinel lymph node dissection, probably owing to a smaller incidence of nerve injury associated with the surgical procedure.[14] Numerous studies examined pain and sensory abnormalities in women after breast surgery. These studies showed an increased evoked pain intensity after repetitive pinprick and thermal stimulation and lower pressure pain threshold in patients who developed chronic neuropathic pain after breast surgery compared with patients who did not.[15,16]

There is a striking similarity between the pathophysiologic and biochemical mechanisms that are observed in neuropathic pain and in epilepsy: increased expression of sodium channels in the neural membrane and activation of NMDA receptors in wind-up phenomenon in chronic pain and hippocampal neurons kindling in epilepsy.[17] Antiepileptic medications are widely used to treat neuropathic pain. Increased monoamine activity (dopamine, norepinephrine, and serotonin) may inhibit nociception at the thalamic, brainstem, and spinal cord levels, which supports the use of tricyclic antidepressants and serotonin reuptake inhibitors in the treatment of neuropathic pain.

TESTING

The selection of an objective pain assessment tool should be based on the care setting, patient characteristics (e.g., age, cognitive ability, functional status), and other relevant considerations. Unidimensional pain scales (verbal descriptor scale, numerical rating scale, and visual analog scale) are useful in assessing pain intensity, whereas multidimensional pain scales (e.g., Brief Pain Inventory, Pain Disability Index) provide information on pain history, intensity, location, quality, and functional status.

Diagnostic studies and tests are often used to determine an etiology and to confirm a diagnosis suggested by the history and physical examination.[18] Chronic pain patients typically undergo many tests to determine a diagnosis. Very few patients have an alteration in their treatment, however. Because pain is a subjective experience, the final diagnosis of the etiology and a decision to pursue specific treatment is a clinical one and can be supported only by relevant data, including electromyographic findings.[19] In the case of postmastectomy pain syndrome, there is an obvious clue to a causative relationship between surgery and onset of pain. It might be important in selected cases, however, to determine the relevance of an established peripheral neuropathic lesion to the subjective complaint. These studies are best for separating neuropathy from myopathy and determining if a neuropathy is generalized axonal, demyelinating, mixed, or focal.

Psychological evaluation is often an important assessment strategy. When pain persists, psychosocial and behavioral factors affect the individual's personal and social relationships. The assessment determines the factors contributing to pain, suffering, and disability and helps to formulate treatment plans. The patient's social support, caregivers, family relationships, work history, cultural considerations, spirituality, and access to health care also are important contributors to the psychological response to persistent pain. The West Haven–Yale Multidimensional Pain Inventory, the Survey of Pain Attitudes, and the Barriers Questionnaire assess several dimensions related to patient beliefs about pain and pain treatment.

DIFFERENTIAL DIAGNOSIS

At the conclusion of the patient assessment, the clinician should be able to make a diagnosis of a pain syndrome on which to base treatments. Cancer patients often experience mixed pain syndromes, and often, in addition to what seems like a pure neuropathic postmastectomy pain syndrome, they may experience myofascial pain with distinctive trigger points, transient somatic pain at the site of the skin incision, or pain resulting from neuroma formation near the incision site. Because these other conditions all require different therapeutic modalities for successful treatment, it is important to take into consideration the typical "neuropathic" symptoms of the patient, such as allodynia (pain secondary to non-noxious stimuli when applied to the symptomatic cutaneous area), dysesthesia (spontaneous or evoked unpleasant sensation), hyperalgesia (an exaggerated pain response to a mildly noxious stimulus applied to the symptomatic area), hyperpathia (a delayed and explosive pain response to a noxious stimulus applied to the symptomatic area), and paresthesias (spontaneous intermittent painless abnormal sensations) (Table 76–1).

TREATMENT

Based on a comprehensive assessment, a multimodality approach can be devised for the treatment of postmastectomy pain syndrome. The most important treatments in most cases are pharmacologic. Some patients benefit from interventional strategies, however, which may involve neural blockade or sophisticated neuraxial stimulation or infusion.

Pharmacologic therapies for neuropathic pain include antiepileptics, antidepressants, local anesthetics, and other adjuvant analgesics. Opioid analgesics also have shown efficacy against neuropathic pain, although in higher doses than those usually necessary to treat nociceptive pain.

Antiepileptics

Antiepileptics have been used for many years to treat neuropathic pain, especially when it is lancinating, episodic, or burning. The exact mechanism by which these drugs prevent spread of abnormal activity is unknown but may involve posttetanic potentiation, reductions in movement of sodium or calcium ions, potentiation of presynaptic or postsynaptic inhibition, or reduction of responsiveness of various monosynaptic or polysynaptic pathways. Inhibition of postsynaptic neurons by some drugs may reflect binding to γ-aminobutyric acid receptors and may lead to greater chloride ion influx through chloride channels.

Table 76–1

Sensory Abnormalities Seen in Postmastectomy Pain Syndrome

Allodynia	Pain resulting from a touch or temperature stimulus that normally does not provoke pain
Dysesthesia	Unpleasant sensation that is spontaneous or evoked
Hyperalgesia	Excessive response to a painful stimulus
Hyperpathia	Increased reaction to a stimulus, especially a painful stimulus
Paresthesia	Abnormal sensation in the distribution of a nerve that is spontaneous or evoked

Neuropathic pain, whether of peripheral or central origin, is characterized by a neuronal hyperexcitability in damaged areas of the nervous system. In peripheral neuropathic pain, damaged nerve endings exhibit abnormal spontaneous and increased evoked activity, mainly as a result of an increased and novel expression of sodium channels.[20] Because the neuronal hyperexcitability and corresponding molecular changes are underlying mechanisms in certain forms of epilepsy, this fact has led to the use of anticonvulsant drugs for the treatment of neuropathic pain, including postmastectomy pain syndrome. Carbamazepine and phenytoin were the first anticonvulsants to be used for this purpose, although today gabapentin, oxcarbazepine, lamotrigine, and zonisamide are being used more often. Antiepileptics can produce adverse effects ranging from mild to serious. The most common side effects are drowsiness, dizziness, and gait disturbance. The side effects are usually dose dependent and can be minimized by a careful dose reduction. The most troublesome effects are hepatic toxicity and dermatologic effects ranging from rashes to life-threatening erythema, desquamation, and mucositis similar to Stevens-Johnson syndrome.

Tricyclic Antidepressants

Tricyclic antidepressants have been found to be useful in the treatment of a variety of painful syndromes, including postmastectomy pain. They exert their action by potentiation of the biogenic amines norepinephrine or serotonin or both in the central nervous system and by interfering with the reuptake of these amines into postganglionic sympathetic nerve endings.

Appropriate use of tricyclic antidepressants requires a good understanding of their pharmacologic features and actions,[21] careful selection of the drug to be used, slow adjustment of the dosage given, and close attention to the time of the day the medication is taken. Failure to consider these factors can make the difference between a successful response and failure. The evidence for analgesic efficacy is greatest for the tertiary amine tricyclic drugs, such as amitriptyline, doxepine, and imipramine. The secondary amine tricyclic antidepressants, such as desipramine and nortriptyline,[22] have fewer side effects and are preferred when concern about sedation, anticholinergic effects, or cardiovascular toxicity is high. The starting dose of a tricyclic antidepressant should be low, and doses can be increased every few days. Analgesia usually occurs within 1 week after achieving an effective dosing level (Table 76–2).

Opioids

The use of opioids to treat patients with chronic neuropathic pain is highly controversial. Although opioids traditionally have been avoided in treatment of patients with neuropathic pain, more recent trials and reports have led practitioners to reconsider this position.[23] The current thinking believes that not all persistent pain syndromes respond to opioid therapy, and opioid response needs to be assessed in a therapeutic titration trial. The titration is necessary because the initial prescribed dose may be too low or too high to achieve the optimal balance of analgesia and acceptable side effects.

Local Anesthetics

Topical lidocaine patch has proven efficacy and safety in the treatment of refractory neuropathic pain.[24] Several studies were performed on mexiletine, a class Ib antiarrhythmic agent that blocks sodium channels,[25] and it has been shown that it is effective in treating neuropathic pain mostly characterized by lancinating dysesthesias.[26] Because mexiletine is prone to many drug interactions, especially interactions resulting from the cytochrome P-450 2D6 system, it should be used with caution in patients already receiving tricyclic antidepressants and serotonin reuptake inhibitors. The most commonly encountered side effects are nausea and heartburn, but dizziness, tremor, nervousness, and headache might occur as well, although they tend to disappear with long-term use. The biggest concern is, however, propensity toward arrhythmias, and it should not be used in patients with second-degree or third-degree heart block.

Capsaicin

Many painful neuropathies involving small afferent fibers are resistant to the analgesic agents already mentioned. Capsaicin, the vanilloid compound derived from hot peppers, acutely and chronically depletes the neurotransmitter substance P from sensory nerves.[25] This effect suggests that long-term use of the drug could reduce central transmission of information about noxious stimuli. The choice to use a therapy must take into account the adverse event profile versus potential benefit: Degranulation of primary afferent

Table 76–2				
Commonly Used Tricyclic Antidepressants and Their Side Effects				
Drug	*Sedation*	*Anticholinergic Effects*	*Orthostatic Hypotension*	*Dysrhythmia Potential*
Doxepin	+++	++	++	++
Amitriptyline	+++	++++	+++	++
Imipramine	++	++	+++	++
Protriptyline	+	+++	+	++
Nortriptyline	+	+	+	++
Desipramine	+	+	+++	++

+ = low; ++ = moderate; +++ = high; ++++ = marked.

fibers can cause a burning sensation that can worsen the existing cutaneous hyperalgesia.[27]

Clonidine

Clonidine, an α-adrenergic agonist, exhibits analgesic efficacy when administered intrathecally or epidurally, probably by several different mechanisms, including reduction in peripheral norepinephrine release by stimulation of prejunctional inhibitory $α_2$-adrenoreceptors, inhibition of noxious neural transmission in the dorsal horn by presynaptic and postsynaptic mechanisms, and direct inhibition of spinal preganglionic sympathetic neurons.[28] Adverse reactions include hypotension, bradycardia, sedation, and dry mouth.

Neurostimulation

Transcutaneous electrical nerve stimulation (TENS) has been shown to give the best results when pain is due to deafferentation, in precisely localized pain, or when the treatment may be applied closely to the nervous structure supplying the painful area.[29] Nevertheless, a TENS trial needs to be conducted in patients to ensure that the pain is not aggravated by TENS, to ensure that the patient is responding to the treatment, and to determine the amount of time spent in stimulation needed to achieve pain relief. The few contraindications to TENS are pregnancy, presence of a pacemaker, and patient noncompliance.

Spinal cord stimulation generally is considered to be a treatment of last resort. It is usually reserved for cases when conservative measures have failed to control the patient's pain. It also is a modality of diminishing returns because the probability of reduced effectiveness increases with time; this can be attributed to several causes, including fibrosis around the stimulation arrays, disease progression in some cases, and lead migration, particularly in the cervical area. The mechanism of action is based on partial painful stimuli blockage and its ability to control the neuropathic component of a pain syndrome, while being relatively ineffective against the nociceptive component.[30] To improve success, several requirements need to be met, including localized pain, overlapping stimulation paresthesiae with painful area, positioning electrodes above pain segments, and absence of psychological disease in a patient.

Intraspinal Therapies

When pain control cannot be achieved with oral medications, the intraspinal route is considered.[31] Using opioids alone, profound analgesia can be achieved at a much lower dose, without the motor, sensory, or sympathetic block associated with intraspinal local anesthetic administration. In postmastectomy patients, addition of a local anesthetic, clonidine, or both is usually necessary to achieve adequate pain control. In the future, the use of adenosine, aspirin, and ziconotide may become a viable alternative for patients with intractable pain.[32,33]

Surgically implanted catheters with implanted infusion pumps at a fixed rate or constant flow pumps are made of titanium and silicone rubber and are available in different reservoir sizes. Changes in dosing are accomplished by modifying the concentration of the drugs placed in the pump.

∎ CONCLUSION

Although surgical incision at any location may result in chronic pain, only several syndromes are clearly recognized as sequelae of specific surgical procedures. Postmastectomy pain syndrome is one. Considering that one in eight women develops breast cancer, of which roughly 60% are treated with mastectomy, and the incidence of chronic pain after this procedure is 27%, it becomes clear that this problem warrants special attention. The underlying mechanism is believed to be neuropathic, related to damage to intercostobrachial nerve.

Treatment of postmastectomy pain syndrome requires a multidisciplinary approach in which each member of the team addresses a specific problem the patient faces. The team usually includes a pain physician, psychologist or psychiatrist, and physical therapist with the objectives to rationalize medications, teach coping skills, and help return to previous level of physical functioning. Strong consideration should be given to invasive approaches when conservative pharmacologic measures fail to provide pain control.

REFERENCES

1. Carpenter JS, Andrykowski MA, Sloan P, et al: Postmastectomy/postlumpectomy pain in breast cancer survivors. J Clin Epidemiol 51:1285, 1998.
2. Vecht CJ, Van de Brand HJ, Wajer OJ: Post-axillary dissection pain in breast cancer due to a lesion of the intercostobrachial nerve. Pain 38:171, 1989.
3. Wood KM: Intercostobrachial nerve entrapment syndrome. South Med J 71:662, 1978.
4. Tasmuth T, von Smitten K, Kalso E: Effect of present pain and mood on the memory of past postoperative pain in women treated surgically for breast cancer. Pain 68:343, 1996.
5. Tasmuth T, von Smitten K, Hietanen P, et al: Pain and other symptoms after different treatment modalities of breast cancer. Ann Oncol 6:453, 1995.
6. Smith WC, Bourne D, Squair J, et al: A retrospective cohort study of post-mastectomy pain syndrome. Pain 83:91, 1999.
7. Abdullah TI, Iddon J, Barr L, et al: Prospective randomized controlled trial of preservation of the intercostobrachial nerve during axillary node clearance for breast cancer. Br J Surg 85:1443, 1998.
8. Maunsell E, Brisson J, Deschenes L: Arm problems and psychological distress after surgery for breast cancer. Can J Surg 36:315, 1993.
9. Keramopoulos A, Tsionou C, Minaretzis D, et al: Arm morbidity following treatment of breast cancer with total axillary dissection: A multivariated approach. Oncology 50:445, 1993.
10. Tasmuth T, Kataja M, Blomqvist C, et al: Treatment-related factors predisposing to chronic pain in patients with breast cancer—a multivariate approach. Acta Oncol 36:625, 1997.
11. Cherny N, Portenoy R: Cancer pain: principles of assessment and syndromes. In: Textbook of Pain, 3rd ed. Churchill Livingstone, 1994.
12. Stevens PE, Dibble SL, Miaskowski C: Prevalence, characteristics, and impact of postmastectomy pain syndrome: An investigation of women's experience. Pain 61:61, 1995.
13. Wallace SW, Wallace AM, Lee J, Dobke MK: Pain after breast surgery: A survey of 282 women. Pain 66:195, 1996.
14. Miguel R, Kuhn AM, Shons AR, et al: The effect of sentinel node selective axillary lymphadenectomy on the incidence of postmastectomy pain syndrome. Cancer Control 8:427, 2001.
15. Gottrup H, Andersen J, Arendt-Nielsen L, Jensen TS: Psychophysical examination in patients with post-mastectomy pain. Pain 87:275, 2000.
16. Bolay H, Moskowitz MA: Mechanisms of pain modulation in chronic syndromes. Neurology 59:S2, 2002.

17. Jensen TS: Anticonvulsants in neuropathic pain: Rationale and clinical evidence. Eur J Pain 6:61, 2002.

18. Hansson P: Neuropathic pain: Clinical characteristics and diagnostic workup. Eur J Pain 6:47, 2002.

19. Abrams BM, Waldman HJ, Eckard VR, et al: Diagnostic tools available for pain management. In: Pain Medicine: A Comprehensive Review, 2nd ed. St. Louis, Mosby, 2003.

20. Backonja M: Use of anticonvulsants for treatment of neuropathic pain. Neurology 59:S14, 2002.

21. Godfrey RG: A guide to the understanding and use of tricyclic antidepressants in the overall management of fibromyalgia and other chronic pain syndromes. Arch Intern Med 156:1047, 1996.

22. Wallace MS, Barger D, Schulteis G: The effect of chronic oral desipramine on capsaicin-induced allodynia and hyperalgesia: A double blinded, placebo-controlled, crossover study. Anesth Analg 95:973, 2002.

23. Przewlocki R, Przewlocka B: Opioids in chronic pain. Eur J Pharmacol 429:79, 2001.

24. Devers A, Galer BS: Topical lidocaine patch relieves a variety of neuropathic pain conditions: An open-label study. Clin J Pain 16:205, 2000.

25. Sindrup SH, Jensen TS: Pharmacologic treatment of pain in polyneuropathy. Neurology 55:915, 2000.

26. Fassoulaki A, Konstantinos P, Sarantopoulos C, Hogan Q: The analgesic effect of gabapentin and mexiletine after breast surgery for cancer. Anesth Analg 95:985, 2002.

27. Watson CP, Evans RJ: The postmastectomy pain syndrome and topical capsaicin: A randomized trial. Pain 51:375, 1992.

28. Eisenach JC, De Kock M, Klimscha W: Alpha₂-adrenergic agonists for regional anesthesia: A clinical review of clonidine. Anesthesiology 85:655, 1996.

29. Sjolund BH: Transcutaneous electrical stimulation (TENS) in neuropathic pain. Pain Dig 3:23, 1993.

30. Magimbi AS, de Leon-Casasola OA: Spinal cord stimulation. Tech Regional Anesth Pain Manage 4:132, 2000.

31. Miguel R: Interventional treatment of cancer pain: The fourth step in the World Health Organization Analgesic Ladder? Cancer Control 7:149, 2000.

32. Bantel C, Li X, Eisenach J: Intraspinal adenosine induces spinal cord norepinephrine release in spinal nerve-ligated rats but not in normal or sham controls. Anesthesiology 98:1461, 2003.

33. Staats P, Yearwood T, Charpata S, et al: Intrathecal ziconotide in the treatment of refractory pain in patients with cancer or AIDS: A randomized controlled trial. JAMA 291:63, 2004.

chapter 77

Post-thoracotomy Pain

Debra A. DeAngelo and Vitaly Gordin

HISTORICAL CONSIDERATIONS

The most popular approach to the pleural cavity for lung resection has been through variations of the lateral thoracotomy. Important considerations regarding preservation of muscle function when employing these incisions have to do with making the incision no longer than necessary for adequate exposure and avoiding denervation of muscle as far as is practical.[1] Few authors believe acute post-thoracotomy pain can be sufficiently controlled with patient-controlled analgesia.[2] Most author believe that no matter the type of approach, post-thoracotomy pain is severe and debilitating. Many approaches have been tried over the years, including surgical excision or cryoablation of the intercostal nerves, placement of local anesthetic under direct visualization, and intravenous narcotic administration. The most superior treatment for acute post-thoracotomy pain is believed to be infusion of local anesthetic and narcotic into the thoracic epidural space. Not only are thoracic epidurals known to reduce acute postoperative pain, but also it is believed that they reduce the development of chronic post-thoracotomy pain and should be used as a preemptive treatment for chronic post-thoracotomy pain.[5]

When focusing on post-thoracotomy pain, whether it is acute or chronic, one must remember the trauma caused by the positioning and the destruction of tissue that occurs.

Chronic post-thoracotomy pain can be due to various etiologic mechanisms. It is believed to result from inadequate treatment of acute pain,[5] nerve entrapment of cutaneous branches or the intercostal nerves, myofascial pain, or nerve resection causing a neuroma formation.

CLINICAL SYNDROME

Post-thoracotomy pain is one of the most severe forms of pain after surgery, and it exacerbates ventilatory dysfunction. Because of the multiplicity of nociceptive inputs from the chest wall, thoracic viscera, diaphragm, and postoperative chest tubes, postoperative pain may be difficult to control with single modalities.[3] Inappropriate treatment of post-thoracotomy pain inhibits many normal bodily functions, such as adequate ventilation, coughing, movement, and ambulation. Use of large doses of systemic narcotics can worsen these problems by adding a sedative effect or by causing nausea and constipation. These problems can lead to potentially serious postoperative complications, such as atelectasis, pneumonia, hypoxemia, and even death. Adequate treatment of acute pain is imperative to prevent postoperative morbidity and mortality.

It has been shown that with appropriately placed thoracic epidurals, approximately 70% of patients had excellent pain relief (visual analog scalc 0-2) on postoperative day 1; 78%, on postoperative day 2; and 91%, on postoperative day 3. Additionally, early postoperative mobilization could be started in 63% of all patients.[4] The thoracic epidural must be placed at the dermatomal level associated with the surgery. Properly placed thoracic epidurals reduce the requirements of systemic opioids. By having improved pain control and respiratory function, patients are able to ambulate earlier in the recovery process.

In addition, thoracic epidurals instituted before thoracotomy are associated with a decreased incidence and intensity of pain in the perioperative period compared with epidurals placed after surgery or systemic analgesia. A decrease in pain also has been shown in the 6 months following surgery when a thoracic epidural is placed before surgery; it is the method of choice to prevent chronic post-thoracotomy pain.[5]

SIGNS, SYMPTOMS, AND PHYSICAL FINDINGS

Acute and chronic post-thoracotomy pain is a radicular pain over the area of intervention. Acute pain is usually sharp and tender to palpation and occasionally numb. Acute pain is severe, but eases over the first several days. Chronic pain can be burning, numb, aching, and hyperesthetic and even progress to allodynia. It is usually along the dermatome associated with the surgical incision. In contrast to postherpetic neuralgia, there are no skin lesions or discoloration. Trigger points may be elicited. Chronic post-thoracotomy pain may begin several months after surgery or may begin immediately after surgery with no improvement of the acute postoperative pain.

DIFFERENTIAL DIAGNOSIS

The differential diagnosis for acute and chronic post-thoracotomy pain is identical. Any problem causing thoracic radicular pain, such as postherpetic neuralgia, a thoracic herniated disk, or intercostal neuralgia from another source (i.e., rib fracture, vertebral compression fracture), should be considered. Other sources may be myofascial (i.e., muscle spasms).

One always must evaluate the type of pain (i.e., somatic versus neuropathic) when determining the cause.

■ TREATMENT

Therapeutic options other than thoracic epidurals for acute post-thoracotomy pain include the following:

- Lumbar epidurals—require larger volumes of infused medications and do not provide as adequate coverage of pain as thoracic epidurals, and the ability to ambulate is usually lost.
- Cryoanalgesia—has to be performed intraoperatively and does not provide complete pain relief, but is more efficient than internal (i.e., performed by the surgeon at the time of surgery) intercostal nerve blocks.[6]
- Intercostal or paravertebral catheters—have to be performed intraoperatively by a skilled surgeon under direct visualization, exit through the surgical site, and have been found to be inferior to epidural analgesia.[7,8]
- Interpleural catheters with infusion of local anesthetic—have to be placed by a skilled technician, exit through the surgical site, and have been found to be inferior to epidural analgesia.
- Intercostal nerve blocks—have to be performed perioperatively, last only the lifetime of the local anesthetic, and may not provide complete pain relief.[7]
- Systemic opioids (patient-controlled analgesia)—do not improve deep breathing, movement, or coughing; can cause sedation and constipation.

When choosing an approach to acute post-thoracotomy pain management, the thoracic surgeon and anesthesiologist must consider the following: (1) the physician's experience, familiarity, and personal complication rate with specific techniques; (2) the desired extent of local and systemic pain control; (3) the presence of contraindications to specific analgesic techniques and medications; and (4) availability of appropriate facilities for patient assessment and monitoring post-thoracotomy.[7]

The goal is to improve pain by selective and locally concentrated administration of drugs to the pain-causing anatomic region, rather than by systemic saturation with analgesics, which is associated with a higher incidence of side effects. Regional analgesia guarantees excellent pain control when administered through an epidural catheter. It has proved to be a gold standard method for pain control after thoracic operations.[8]

Treatment for chronic post-thoracotomy pain should be tailored to the type of pain. The pain can be somatic or neuropathic and may or may not have anatomic structures responsible for the pain (i.e., connective tissues, muscles, or nerves). Therapeutic options for chronic post-thoracotomy pain include the following:

- Medical management with antiepileptics, antidepressants, and nonsteroidal antiinflammatory drugs
- Symptomatic treatment with transcutaneous electrical nerve stimulation units
- Diagnostic, and possibly therapeutic, intercostal nerve blocks
- Trigger point injections of local anesthetic and steroid
- Local anesthetic patches (lidocaine [Lidoderm]) over the area of pain
- Thoracic paravertebral blocks
- Cryoablation of intercostal nerves
- Topical preparations, such as capsaicin cream, which is used as a substance P antagonist

■ CLINICALLY RELEVANT ANATOMY

The patient position—lateral or supine—depends on the surgical approach of the thoracotomy. The lateral position is the thoracotomy, which provides better overall exposure and accessibility to all portions of the pleural cavity, and the hilar structures can be approached from any direction. The two approaches differ as to the anatomy that they violate during entrance.

The lateral incision requires a skin incision followed by incising the subcutaneous tissue. The trapezius, rhomboid, latissimus dorsi, and serratus anterior muscles are divided. The ribs can be excised or more commonly divided with a retractor. The intercostal muscles are incised, and the parietal pleura is punctured. The supine incision requires a skin incision followed by division of the pectoralis major muscle and subcutaneous tissue. The intercostal muscles are divided, and the ribs are spread after the costal cartilage is divided. The parietal pleura is punctured. In both cases, the intercostal muscles are divided more closely to the rib below than to the rib above to avoid injury to the larger intercostal vessels and nerves, which course along the inferior rib margins.[9]

■ TECHNIQUES

Thoracic Epidural

Epidural needle and catheter insertion may be performed with the patient in the sitting or lateral position. Identification of the midline, a key to success in performing epidural anesthesia, is achieved more easily with the patient sitting, particularly in a stout subject.[10]

The skin is anesthetized after the bony landmarks have been identified. The epidural should be placed at the dermatome of the surgical incision, which usually lies between T5 and T9. The midline approach to the epidural space passes successively through the skin, subcutaneous tissue, and supraspinous and interspinous ligaments and into the ligamentum flavum. The steeply overlapping thoracic spinous processes require a comparable needle angle. The depth of the vertebral canal from the skin varies depending on the level in the vertebral column, amount of subcutaneous fat, body size, and needle angle so that no safe rule of thumb can be applied. Because the ligamenta flava are steeply arched, the vertebral canal is entered about 1 cm more superficially in the midline than laterally, adjacent to the facet joint.[10] The ligamentum flavum is 3 to 5 mm thick in the thoracic region versus 5 to 6 mm in the lumbar region. If needles are kept in the midline, the ligamentum flavum is perceived as a thicker ligament than when needles are allowed to be inserted off the midline and entered at the lateral extension of the ligamentum flavum.[11] The problem is that the spines of T5-8 tilt significantly downward, making a midline approach to the epidural space practically impossible.[12] This would necessitate a paramedian approach instead of a midline approach.

On passing anterior to the ligamentum flavum, injected air or saline readily passes into the plane between the nonadherent dorsal fat pad and canal wall. This is the "loss of resistance" noted when the syringe plunger suddenly yields to pressure exerted during needle advancement. Solution or air injected into the epidural space readily distributes between the surfaces of the various structures and encircles the dura, with only occasional impediment in the dorsal midline, where the dura may adhere to the lamina or fat. Less commonly, the needle might pass into the substance of the dorsal fat pad, making catheter passage difficult. If the needle enters the spinal canal lateral to the midline, it may encounter the dura with no further advancement because the dorsal epidural fat pad may be very thin at its lateral attenuations. For this reason, rotation of the needle should be avoided because it increases the chance of the point penetrating the dura.[10]

When the catheter is thought to be placed in the epidural space, a test dose of lidocaine plus epinephrine should be administered to ensure the catheter is not in the intrathecal space or intravascular. The test dose usually used consists of 3 to 5 mL of 1.5% lidocaine with 1:200,000 epinephrine. If no changes in the heart rate or spinal blockade are identified, the chest wall should be assessed to prove a sensory level. When this is done, the epidural can be dosed with approximately 5 to 8 mL of 0.125% bupivacaine and fentanyl, 4 µg/mL.

Intercostal Nerve Block

The intercostal nerves arise from the anterior rami of the 1st through 12th paired thoracic nerve roots. Fibers from the first thoracic nerve join with fibers of C8 to become the lowest trunk of the brachial plexus. The intercostal nerves pass at the inferior border of the corresponding rib between the external and internal intercostal muscles, which are superficial, and the innermost intercostal muscle. The nerve travels inferior to the intercostal artery and vein in the costal groove. At the midaxillary line, the intercostal nerve gives off the lateral cutaneous branch, which supplies cutaneous sensation to the lateral thorax and abdomen. The lateral cutaneous branch of the first intercostal nerve supplies sensation to the skin of the axilla. The lateral cutaneous branch of the second intercostal nerve is the intercostobrachial nerve, which supplies sensation to the skin of the medial aspect of the arm. Just before the midline, the intercostal nerve gives off the anterior cutaneous branch, which supplies cutaneous sensation to the anterior thorax and abdomen. Motor branches of the first six pairs of intercostal nerves supply the corresponding intercostal, subcostal, serratus posterior superior, and transverse thoracic muscles. The lower five pairs supply the intercostal, subcostal, serratus posterior inferior, transverse, oblique, and rectus abdominis muscles. The 12th thoracic nerve is not considered an intercostal nerve because it travels in a subcostal course. Fibers of the 12th thoracic nerve join with fibers from L1 to become the ilioinguinal and iliohypogastric nerves.

Lateral Technique

The patient is placed in the lateral recumbent position with the affected side up. The ipsilateral arm is raised above the head to assist in abducting the scapula, exposing the angles of the ribs. The corresponding rib is palpated and identified under fluoroscopic guidance. The skin over the rib is cleansed with povidone-iodine (Betadine), and a skin wheal is raised with local anesthetic.

A 3½-inch 22-gauge spinal needle is advanced through the skin wheal under fluoroscopic guidance and advanced toward the inferior border of the rib. The needle is "walked off" the inferior border of the rib and advanced 2 to 4 mm. After a negative aspiration, 1 to 2 mL of Omnipaque contrast material is injected to confirm proper needle placement. When proper placement has been confirmed, 3 to 5 mL of bupivacaine 0.25% is injected, and the needle is withdrawn.

Paravertebral Technique

The patient is placed in a sitting, prone, or lateral position, with the involved side up. The thoracic spinous processes are palpated. They are at an acute angle, and each tip lies adjacent to the transverse process of the vertebrae at one level inferior. The skin 3 cm lateral to the spinous process at the selected dermatome is retracted in a cephalad direction. The skin is cleansed with povidone-iodine, and a skin wheal is raised with local anesthetic. A 3½-inch, 22-gauge spinal needle is advanced at a 45 degree angle toward the junction of the transverse process and the adjoining rib, with a slight medial angle. After contact is made with the transverse process, the cephalad traction is slowly released, allowing the needle to be walked under the lateral processes at the same angle and advanced 2 mm. After careful aspiration for blood and CSF, 3 to 5 mL of 0.25% bupivacaine is injected.

The primary concern after this injection is a pneumothorax. These occur infrequently, but when they do occur, they may require placement of a chest tube for large or symptomatic pneumothoraces. Local anesthetic toxicity is another complication if multiple levels are performed owing to rapid absorption of local anesthetic after intercostal nerve blocks. When performing a paravertebral block, there is always a risk of a subarachnoid or epidural injection.[10]

References

1. Bloomer W: Thoracic incisions. In Glenn W, Baue AE, Geha AS, et al: Thoracic and Cardiovascular Surgery, 4th ed. East Norwalk, CT, Appleton & Lange, 1983, p 104.
2. Salzer G, Klingler P, Klingler A, et al: Pain treatment after thoracotomy: Is it a special problem? Ann Thorac Surg 63:1411, 1997.
3. Sandler AN: Post-thoracotomy analgesia and peri-operative outcome. Minerva Anestesiol 65:267, 1999.
4. Schultz AM, Werba A, Ulbingt S, et al: Peri-operative thoracic epidural analgesia for thoracotomy. Eur J Anaesthesiol 14:600, 1997.
5. Senturk M, Ozcan PE, Talu GK, et al: The effects of three different analgesia techniques on long-term postthoracotomy pain. Anesth Analg 94:11, 2002.
6. Joucken K, Michel L, Schoevaerdts JC, et al: Croanalgesia for post-thoracotomy pain relief. Acta Anaesthesiol Belg 38:179, 1987.
7. Savage C, McQuitty C, Wang D, et al: Post-thoracotomy pain management. Chest Surg Clin Am 12:251, 2002.
8. Kaiser A, Zollinger A, DeLorenzi D, et al: Prospective, randomized comparison of extrapleural versus epidural analgesia for postthoracotomy pain. Ann Thorac Surg 66:367, 1998.
9. Waldhausen J, Pierce WS, Johnson J: Incisions. In Johnson's Surgery of the Chest, 5th ed. Chicago, Year Book, 1985, p 42.
10. Hahn M: Intercostal nerve. In Hahn M, McQuillan P, Sherlock G: Regional Anesthesia. St Louis, Mosby, 1996, pp 241-246.
11. Brown D: Epidural block. In Atlas of Regional Anesthesia. Philadelphia, Saunders, 1996, p 286.
12. Ramamurthy S: Thoracic epidural nerve block. In Waldman S: Interventional Pain Management. Philadelphia, Saunders, 2001, p 392.

chapter 78

Mononeuritis Multiplex

Steven D. Waldman

Diabetic neuropathy is the name used by clinicians to describe a heterogeneous group of diseases that affect the autonomic and peripheral nervous systems of patients with diabetes mellitus. Diabetic neuropathy is now thought to be the most common form of peripheral neuropathy. An estimated 220 million people have diabetic neuropathy worldwide, for the first time outstripping leprosy as the leading cause of peripheral neuropathy.[1]

One of the most commonly encountered forms of diabetic neuropathy is mononeuritis multiplex.[2] The pain and motor dysfunction of mononeuritis multiplex are often attributed to intrathoracic or intra-abdominal pathology, leading to extensive work-ups for hernia, appendicitis, cholecystitis, and renal calculi.[3] The onset of symptoms frequently coincides with periods of extreme hypoglycemia or hyperglycemia or with weight loss or weight gain.[4] A patient with mononeuritis multiplex presents with severe dysesthetic pain with patchy sensory deficits in the distribution of the lower thoracic or upper thoracic dermatomes (or both). The pain often is worse at night, and significant sleep disturbance may result, further worsening the patient's pain symptoms.[5] The symptoms of mononeuritis multiplex often spontaneously resolve over 6 to 12 months. Because of the severity of symptoms associated with this condition, however, aggressive symptomatic relief with pharmacotherapy and neural blockade with local anesthetics and steroids is indicated.

■ SIGNS AND SYMPTOMS

Physical examination of a patient with mononeuritis multiplex generally reveals minimal physical findings, unless there was a history of previous thoracic or subcostal surgery or cutaneous findings of herpes zoster involving the thoracic dermatomes. In contrast to patients with the above-mentioned musculoskeletal causes of chest wall and subcostal pain, the patient with mononeuritis multiplex does not attempt to splint or protect the affected area. Careful sensory examination of the affected dermatomes may reveal decreased sensation or allodynia. With significant motor involvement of the subcostal nerve, the patient may complain that the abdomen bulges out.

■ TESTING

The presence of diabetes should raise a high index of suspicion that mononeuritis multiplex is present given the high incidence of this condition in patients with diabetes mellitus.[6] The targeted history and physical examination should allow the primary care physician to make the diagnosis of peripheral neuropathy in a large percentage of patients with diabetes.

If a diagnosis of mononeuritis multiplex is entertained on the basis of the targeted history and physical examination, screening laboratory testing, including a complete blood count, chemistry profile, sedimentation rate, thyroid function, antinuclear antibody, and urinalysis, should help rule out most peripheral neuropathies that may mimic mononeuritis multiplex and that are easily treatable. Electromyography and nerve conduction velocity testing are indicated in all patients with peripheral neuropathy to help identify treatable entrapment neuropathies and delineate further the type of peripheral neuropathy that is present. Electromyography and nerve conduction velocity also may help quantify the severity of peripheral or entrapment neuropathy. Additional laboratory testing is indicated as the clinical situation dictates (e.g., Lyme disease titers, heavy metal screens). MRI of the spinal canal and cord should be performed if myelopathy is suspected. Nerve or skin biopsy (or both) occasionally is indicated if no etiology for the peripheral neuropathy can be ascertained. Lack of response to the therapies discussed subsequently should cause the primary care physician to reconsider the working diagnosis and repeat testing as clinically indicated.

■ DIFFERENTIAL DIAGNOSIS

Diseases other than diabetic neuropathy may cause peripheral neuropathies in diabetic patients. These diseases may exist alone and may be clinically misdiagnosed as mononeuritis multiplex or may coexist with mononeuritis multiplex, making their identification and subsequent treatment more difficult.

Although uncommon in the United States, globally, Hansen disease is a common cause of peripheral neuropathy that may mimic or coexist with mononeuritis multiplex. Other infectious etiologies of peripheral neuropathies include Lyme disease and HIV. Substances that are toxic to nerves also may cause peripheral neuropathies that are indistinguishable from diabetic neuropathy on clinical grounds. Such substances include alcohol, heavy metals, chemotherapeutic agents, and hydrocarbons. Heritable disorders, such as Charcot-Marie-Tooth disease and other familial diseases of the peripheral nervous system, also must be considered, although treatment options are limited. Metabolic and endocrine causes of peripheral neuropathy that must be ruled out include vitamin deficiencies, pernicious anemia, hypothyroidism, uremia, and acute intermittent porphyria. Other causes of peripheral neuropathy that may confuse the clinical picture include Guillain-Barré syndrome, amyloidosis, entrapment neuropathies, carcinoid, paraneoplasitc syndromes, and sarcoidosis. Because many of these causes of peripheral neuropathy are treatable (e.g., pernicious anemia), it is imperative that the clinician rule out these treatable diagnoses before attributing a patient's symptoms solely to his or her diabetes.

Intercostal neuralgia and the musculoskeletal causes of chest wall and subcostal pain also may be confused with mononeuritis multiplex. As with these conditions, the patient's pain may be attributed erroneously to cardiac or upper abdominal pathology leading to unnecessary testing and treatment.

■ TREATMENT

Control of Blood Glucose

Current thinking suggests that the better the glycemic control, the less severe the symptoms of mononeuritis multiplex.[7] Significant swings in blood glucose values seem to predispose diabetic patients to the development of clinically significant mononeuritis multiplex. Some investigators believe that oral hypoglycemic agents, while controlling blood glucose, do not protect the patient from the development of mononeuritis multiplex as well as insulin. Some patients with mononeuritis multiplex who are on hypoglycemic agents experience improvement in symptoms when switched to insulin.

Pharmacologic Treatment

Antidepressant Compounds

Traditionally, tricyclic antidepressants have been a mainstay in the palliation of pain secondary to mononeuritis multiplex. Controlled studies have shown the efficacy of amitriptyline for this indication. Other tricyclic antidepressants, including nortriptyline and desipramine, also have shown to be clinically useful. This class of drugs is associated with significant anticholinergic side effects, including dry mouth, constipation, sedation, and urinary retention. These drugs should be used with caution in patients with glaucoma, cardiac arrhythmia, and prostatism. To minimize side effects and encourage compliance, the primary care physician should start amitriptyline or nortriptyline at a 10-mg dose at bedtime. The dose can be titrated up to 25 mg at bedtime as side effects allow. Upward titration of dosage in 25-mg increments can be done each week as side effects allow. Even at lower doses, patients generally report a rapid improvement in sleep disturbance and begin to experience some pain relief in 10 to 14 days. If the patient does not experience any improvement in pain as the dose is being titrated upward, the addition of gabapentin alone or in combination with nerve blocks with local anesthetics or steroid or both is recommended (see later). The selective serotonin reuptake inhibitors, such as fluoxetine, also have been used to treat the pain of mononeuritis multiplex, and although better tolerated than the tricyclic antidepressants, they seem to be less efficacious.

Anticonvulsants

The anticonvulsants have long been used to treat neuropathic pain, including mononeuritis multiplex. Phenytoin and carbamazepine have been used with varying degrees of success alone or in combination with the antidepressant compounds. The side effect profiles of these drugs have limited their clinical utility. More recently, the anticonvulsant gabapentin has been shown to be highly efficacious in the treatment of a variety of neuropathic painful conditions, including postherpetic neuralgia and mononeuritis multiplex. Used properly, gabapentin is extremely well tolerated compared with other drugs, including the aforementioned antidepressant compounds and anticonvulsants, which previously had been used routinely to treat mononeuritis multiplex. In most pain centers, gabapentin has become the adjuvant analgesic of choice when treating mononeuritis multiplex.

Gabapentin has a large therapeutic window, but the primary care physician is cautioned to start this medication at the lower end of the dosage spectrum and to titrate upward slowly to avoid central nervous system side effects, including sedation and fatigue. The following recommended dosage schedule minimizes side effects and encourages compliance. A single bedtime dose of 300 mg for two nights can be followed with a 300-mg dose twice daily for an additional 2 days. If the patient is tolerating this twice-daily dosage, the dosage may be increased to 300 mg three times a day. Most patients begin to experience pain relief at this dosage range. Additional titration upward can be done in 300-mg increments as side effects allow. Daily doses greater than 3600 mg in divided doses are not currently recommended. To simplify maintenance dosing after titration has been completed, 600-mg and 800-mg tablets have been made available. Clinical trials are currently under way with a gabapentin analog that may provide additional therapeutic options for patients with mononeuritis multiplex.

Antiarrhythmics

Mexiletine is an antiarrhythmic compound that has been shown to be possibly effective in the management of mononeuritis multiplex. Some pain specialists believe that mexiletine is especially useful in patients with mononeuritis multiplex whose pain manifests primarily as sharp lancinating or burning pain. This drug is poorly tolerated by most patients, however, and should be reserved for patients who have failed to respond to first-line pharmacologic treatments, such as gabapentin or nortriptyline alone or in combination with neural blockade.

Topical Agents

Some clinicians have reported success in the treatment of mononeuritis multiplex with topical application of capsaicin. An extract of chili peppers, capsaicin is thought to relieve neuropathic pain by depleting substance P. The side effects of capsaicin include significant burning and erythema and limit the use of this substance by many patients.

Topical lidocaine administered via transdermal patch or in a gel also has been shown to provide short-term relief of the pain of mononeuritis multiplex. This drug should be used with caution in patients who are taking mexiletine because there is the potential for cumulative local anesthetic toxicity. Whether topical lidocaine has a role in the long-term treatment of mononeuritis multiplex remains to be seen.

Analgesics

In general, neuropathic pain such as mononeuritis multiplex responds poorly to analgesic compounds. The simple analgesics, including acetaminophen and aspirin, can be used in combination with antidepressant and anticonvulsant compounds, but care must be taken not to exceed the recommended daily dose, or renal or hepatic side effects may occur. Nonsteroidal antiinflammatory drugs also may provide pain relief when used with antidepressants and anticonvulsant compounds, but given the nephrotoxicity of this class of drugs, they should be used with extreme caution in diabetic patients because of the high incidence of diabetic nephropathy, even early in the course of the disease. The role of cyclo-oxygenase-2 inhibitors in the palliation of the pain has not been adequately studied, and given the incidence of undiagnosed cardiac disease in diabetic patients, this class of drugs should be used with caution if at all.

Narcotic analgesics treat neuropathic pain such as mononeuritis multiplex poorly. Given the significant central nervous system and gastrointestinal side effects coupled with the problems of tolerance, dependence, and addiction, narcotic analgesics rarely, if ever, should be used as a primary treatment for the pain of mononeuritis multiplex. If a narcotic analgesic is being considered in this setting, consideration should be given to the analgesic tramadol, which binds weakly to the opioid receptors and may provide some symptomatic relief. Tramadol should be used with care in combination with antidepressant compounds to avoid the increased risk of seizures.

Neural Blockade

Neural blockade with local anesthetics alone or in combination with steroids has been shown to be useful in the management of acute and chronic pain associated with mononeuritis multiplex. For truncal neuropathic pain, thoracic epidural or intercostal nerve block with local anesthetic or steroid or both may be beneficial.[2] Occasionally, neuroaugmentation via spinal cord stimulation may provide sig-

nificant relief of the pain of mononeuritis multiplex in patients who have failed to respond to more conservative measures. Neurodestructive procedures rarely, if ever, are indicated to treat the pain of mononeuritis multiplex because they often worsen the patient's pain and cause functional disability.

■ CONCLUSION

The major problem in the care of patients thought to have mononeuritis multiplex is the failure to identify potentially serious pathology of the thorax or upper abdomen. Correct diagnosis is necessary to treat this painful condition properly and to avoid overlooking serious intrathoracic or intra-abdominal pathology. The use of pharmacologic agents discussed in this chapter, including gabapentin, allows the clinician to control the pain of mononeuritis multiplex adequately. Intercostal or epidural nerve blocks are simple techniques that can produce dramatic relief for patients with mononeuritis multiplex.

References

1. Dyck PJ, Kratz KM, Karnes JL, et al: The prevalence by staged severity of various types of diabetic neuropathy, retinopathy, and nephropathy in a population-based cohort. The Rochester Diabetic Neuropathy Study. Neurology 43:817, 1993.
2. Waldman SD: Mononeuritis multiplex. In: Common Pain Syndromes. Philadelphia, WB Saunders, 2002, p 153.
3. Parry GJ, Floberg J: Diabetic truncal neuropathy presenting as abdominal hernia. Neurology 39:1488, 1989.
4. Diabetes Control and Complications Trial Research Group: The effect of intensive treatment of diabetes on the development and progression of long-term complications in insulin-dependent diabetes mellitus. N Engl J Med 329:977, 1993.
5. Greene DA, Sima AF, Pfeifer MA, Albers JW: Diabetic neuropathy. Annu Rev Med 41:303, 1990.
6. Novella SP, Inzucchi SE, Goldstein JM: The frequency of undiagnosed diabetes and impaired glucose tolerance in patients with idiopathic sensory neuropathy. Muscle Nerve 24:1229, 2001.
7. UK Prospective Diabetes Study (UKPDS) Group: Intensive blood-glucose control with sulphonylureas or insulin compared with conventional treatment and risk of complications in patients with type 2 diabetes (UKPDS 33) [published correction appears in Lancet 1999;354:602]. Lancet 352: 837, 1998.

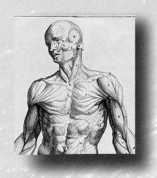

Part G

SYNDROMES OF THE ABDOMEN, RETROPERITONEUM, AND GROIN

chapter

79

Abdominal Wall Pain Syndromes

Steven D. Waldman

Abdominal wall pain syndromes are a common reason that patients seek medical attention. Often these calls for help take the form of middle of the night visits to the emergency room and the like because patients fear that they are suffering from appendicitis, a heart attack, an ulcer, or acute gallbladder disease. Unfortunately, although these painful conditions are common, they are frequently misdiagnosed, which can lead to unnecessary invasive cardiac and gastrointestinal studies and result in much needless anxiety for the patient and family. This chapter provides the clinician with a clear road map of how to identify and treat the more common musculoskeletal causes of abdominal wall pain. The ability to rapidly diagnose and treat these problems is a very cost-effective endeavor and will help alleviate much of the patient's anxiety and suffering.

■ ANTERIOR CUTANEOUS NERVE ENTRAPMENT SYNDROME

Anterior cutaneous nerve entrapment syndrome is a constellation of symptoms consisting of severe knife-like pain emanating from the anterior abdominal wall and associated point tenderness over the affected anterior cutaneous nerve.[1] The pain radiates medially to the linea alba but in almost all cases does not cross the midline. Anterior cutaneous nerve entrapment syndrome occurs most commonly in young females. The patient can often localize the source of pain quite accurately by pointing to the spot at which the anterior cutaneous branch of the affected intercostal nerve pierces the fascia of the abdominal wall at the lateral border of the rectus abdominis muscle. It is at this point that the anterior cutaneous branch of the intercostal nerve turns sharply in an anterior direction to provide innervation to the anterior wall (Fig. 79–1). The nerve passes through a firm fibrous ring as it pierces the fascia, and it is at this point that the nerve is subject to entrapment. The nerve is accompanied through the fascia by an epigastric artery and vein. There is the potential for small amounts of abdominal fat to herniate through this fascial ring and become incarcerated, which results in further entrapment of the nerve (Fig. 79–2). Contraction of the abdominal muscles or an increase in intraabdominal pressure will place additional traction on the nerve and may elicit sudden, sharp, lancinating pain in the distribution of the affected anterior cutaneous nerve (Fig 79–3).

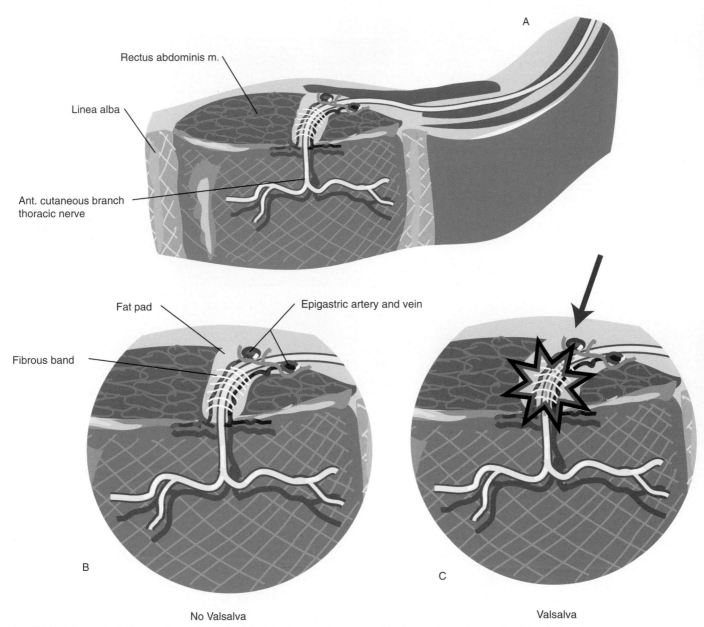

Rectus abdominis m.

Linea alba

Ant. cutaneous branch
thoracic nerve

A

Fat pad

Fibrous band

Epigastric artery and vein

B

No Valsalva

C

Valsalva

FIGURE 79–1 ■ **A-C,** The anterior cutaneous branch of the intercostal nerve provides innervation to the anterior abdominal wall.

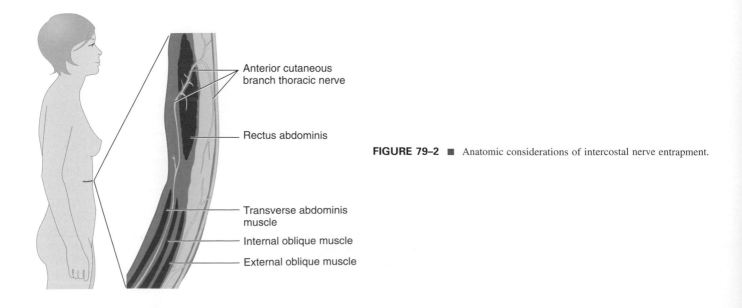

Anterior cutaneous
branch thoracic nerve

Rectus abdominis

Transverse abdominis
muscle

Internal oblique muscle

External oblique muscle

FIGURE 79–2 ■ Anatomic considerations of intercostal nerve entrapment.

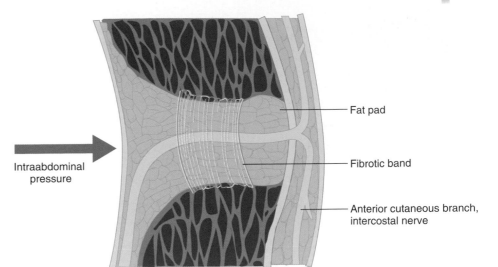

FIGURE 79–3 ■ Contraction of the abdominal muscles or an increase in intraabdominal pressure puts additional traction on the anterior cutaneous branch of the intercostal nerve and may elicit sudden, sharp, lancinating pain in the distribution of the affected anterior cutaneous nerve.

Intraabdominal pressure

Fat pad

Fibrotic band

Anterior cutaneous branch, intercostal nerve

Physical examination reveals that the patient will attempt to splint the affected nerve by keeping the thoracolumbar spine slightly flexed to avoid increasing tension on the abdominal musculature (Fig. 79–4). Pain is reproduced with pressure on the anterior cutaneous branch of the affected intercostal nerve at the point at which the nerve pierces the fascia of the abdominal wall at the lateral border of the abdominis rectus muscle. Having the patient do a sit-up will often reproduce the pain, as will the Valsalva maneuver.

Plain radiographs are indicated in all patients with pain thought to be emanating from the lower costal cartilage and ribs to rule out occult bony pathology, including rib fracture and tumor. Radiographic evaluation of the gallbladder is indicated if cholelithiasis is suspected. Based on the patient's clinical findings, additional testing, including a complete blood count, rectal examination with testing for the presence of occult blood, sedimentation rate, and antinuclear antibody testing, may be indicated. CT scan of the abdomen is indicated if intraabdominal pathology or an occult mass is suspected (Fig. 79–5). The injection technique discussed in the section on treatment serves as both a diagnostic and therapeutic maneuver.

Clinically Relevant Anatomy

The intercostal nerves arise from the anterior division of the thoracic paravertebral nerve. A typical intercostal nerve has four major branches. The first branch is the unmyelinated postganglionic fibers of the gray rami communicantes, which interface with the sympathetic chain. The second branch is the posterior cutaneous branch, which innervates the muscles and skin of the paraspinal area. The third branch is the lateral cutaneous division, which arises in the anterior axillary line. The lateral cutaneous division provides the majority of the cutaneous innervation of the chest and abdominal wall. The fourth branch is the anterior cutaneous branch supplying innervation to the midline of the chest and abdominal wall (see Figs. 79–1 and 79–2). The anterior cutaneous branch pierces the fascia of the abdominal wall at the lateral border of the rectus abdominis muscle. The nerve turns sharply in an anterior direction to provide innervation

to the anterior wall. The nerve passes through a firm fibrous ring as it pierces the fascia, and it is at this point that the nerve is subject to entrapment. The nerve is accompanied through the fascia by an epigastric artery and vein. Occasionally, the terminal branches of a given intercostal nerve may actually cross the midline to provide sensory innervation to the contralateral chest and abdominal wall. The 12th nerve is called the subcostal nerve and is unique in that it gives off a branch to the first lumbar nerve, thus contributing to the lumbar plexus.

Treatment

Initial treatment of the pain and functional disability associated with anterior cutaneous nerve entrapment syndrome should include a combination of nonsteroidal antiinflammatory agents or cyclooxygenase-2 (COX-2) inhibitors. Local application of heat and cold may likewise be beneficial. The use of an elastic rib belt may also help provide symptomatic relief and protect the affected nerves from additional irritation. For patients who do not respond to these treatment modalities, the following injection technique using local anesthetic and steroid may be a reasonable next step.[2]

Injection of the anterior cutaneous nerve is performed by placing the patient in the supine position, and proper preparation with the application of antiseptic solution to the skin overlying the affected nerves as they pierce the abdominal wall is carried out. A sterile syringe containing 1.0 mL of 0.25% preservative-free bupivacaine for each nerve to be injected and 40 mg of methylprednisolone is aseptically attached to a 1½-inch, 25-gauge needle.

The affected nerves are identified with strict aseptic technique and should be easily palpable; pressure on them should elicit a positive jump sign in most patients. The needle is then carefully advanced through the skin and into subcutaneous tissue through the anterior fascia of the rectus abdominis muscle (Fig. 79–6). The needle should be advanced just beyond the fascia, but no further, or damage to the abdominal viscera could result. After careful aspiration to ensure that the needle tip is not in a vein or artery, 1 mL of solution is gently injected. There should be limited resistance to

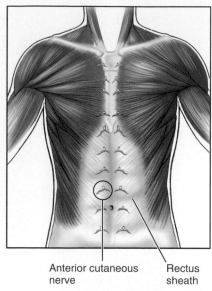

Anterior cutaneous
nerve

Rectus
sheath

FIGURE 79–4 ■ Patients often attempt to splint the affected nerve by keeping the thoracolumbar spine slightly flexed to avoid increasing tension on the abdominal musculature. (From Waldman SD [ed]: Atlas of Uncommon Pain Syndromes. Philadelphia, WB Saunders, 2003, p 136.)

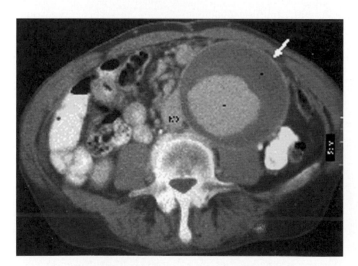

FIGURE 79–5 ■ CT scan of an abdominal aneurysm. (From Grainger RG, Allison DJ [eds]: Grainger and Allison's Diagnostic Radiology, 3rd ed. Philadelphia, Churchill Livingstone, 1999, p 2378.)

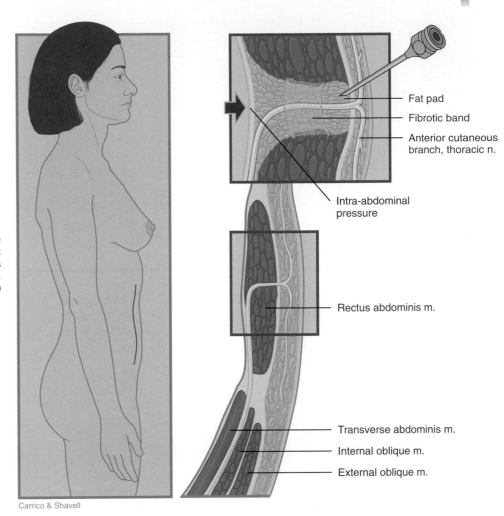

FIGURE 79–6 ■ Injection technique for anterior cutaneous nerve entrapment syndrome. (From Waldman SD [ed]: Atlas of Pain Management Injection Techniques. Philadelphia, WB Saunders, 2000, p 193.)

Fat pad

Fibrotic band

Anterior cutaneous branch, thoracic n.

Intra-abdominal pressure

Rectus abdominis m.

Transverse abdominis m.

Internal oblique m.

External oblique m.

Carrico & Shavell

injection, but the patient may experience paresthesia as the solution is injected. If significant resistance is encountered, the needle should be advanced slightly until the injection proceeds with only limited resistance. This procedure is repeated for each affected nerve. The needle is then removed and a sterile pressure dressing and ice pack are placed at the injection site.

The major complication of this injection technique is damage to the abdominal viscera and, rarely, pneumothorax if the needle is placed too deeply and invades the peritoneal cavity or pleural space. Infection, though rare, can occur if strict aseptic technique is not adhered to. These complications can be greatly decreased if the clinician pays close attention to accurate needle placement. Because this technique will block the anterior cutaneous nerve, the patient should be warned to expect some transient numbness of the abdominal wall, as well as bulging of the abdomen in the region injected secondary to blockade of the motor innervation to these muscles.

■ **SLIPPING RIB SYNDROME**

Slipping rib syndrome is a constellation of symptoms consisting of severe knife-like pain emanating from the lower costal cartilages associated with hypermobility of the anterior end of the lower costal cartilages.[3] The 10th rib is most commonly involved, but the 8th and 9th ribs can also be affected.[4] This syndrome is also known as rib-tip syndrome. Slipping rib syndrome is almost always associated with trauma to the costal cartilage of the lower ribs. This cartilage is often traumatized during acceleration/deceleration injuries and blunt trauma to the chest. With severe trauma the cartilage may subluxate or dislocate from the ribs. Patients with slipping rib syndrome may also complain of a clicking sensation with movement of the affected ribs and associated cartilage.

Physical examination reveals that the patient will vigorously attempt to splint the affected costal cartilage joints by keeping the thoracolumbar spine slightly flexed. Pain is reproduced with pressure on the affected costal cartilage. Patients with slipping rib syndrome exhibit a positive hooking maneuver test. The hooking maneuver test is performed by having the patient lie in the supine position with the abdominal muscles relaxed while the clinician hooks his fingers under the lower part of the rib cage and pulls gently outward (Fig. 79–7). Pain and a clicking or snapping sensation of the affected ribs and cartilage indicate a positive test.

Plain radiographs are indicated in all patients with pain thought to be emanating from the lower costal cartilage and

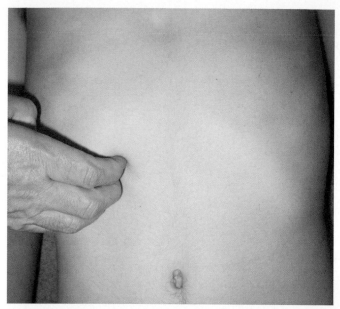

FIGURE 79–7 ■ The hooking maneuver test for slipping rib syndrome. (From Waldman SD [ed]: Physical Diagnosis in Pain: An Atlas of Signs and Symptoms. Philadelphia, WB Saunders, 2005, p 214.)

ribs to rule out occult bony pathology, including rib fracture and tumor. Based on the patient's clinical findings, additional testing, including a complete blood count, prostate-specific antigen, sedimentation rate, and antinuclear antibody testing, may be indicated. MRI of the affected ribs and cartilage is indicated if joint instability or an occult mass is suspected.

Clinically Relevant Anatomy

The cartilage of the true ribs articulates with the sternum via the costosternal joints. The cartilage of the first rib articulates directly with the manubrium of the sternum and is a synarthrodial joint that allows a limited gliding movement. The cartilage of the second through sixth ribs articulates with the body of the sternum via true arthrodial joints. These joints are surrounded by a thin articular capsule. The costosternal joints are strengthened by ligaments.

The 8th, 9th and 10th ribs attach to the costal cartilage of the rib directly above. The cartilages of the 11th and 12th ribs are called floating ribs because they end in the abdominal musculature. The pleural space and peritoneal cavity may be entered when performing the following injection technique if the needle is placed too deeply and laterally, and pneumothorax or damage to abdominal viscera may result.

Treatment

Initial treatment of the pain and functional disability associated with sleeping rib syndrome should include a combination of nonsteroidal antiinflammatory agents or COX-2 inhibitors. Local application of heat and cold may likewise be beneficial. The use of an elastic rib belt may also help provide symptomatic relief and protect the affected nerves from additional irritation. For patients who do not respond to these treatment modalities, the following injection technique with local anesthetic and steroid may be a reasonable next step.[5]

The goals of this injection technique are explained to the patient. The patient is placed in the supine position, and proper preparation with the application of antiseptic solution to the skin overlying the affected costal cartilage and rib is carried out. A sterile syringe containing 1.0 mL of 0.25% preservative-free bupivacaine for each joint to be injected and 40 mg of methylprednisolone is aseptically attached to a 1½-inch, 25-gauge needle.

The distal rib and costal cartilage are identified with strict aseptic technique. The lower margin of each affected distal rib is identified and marked with a sterile marker. The needle is then carefully advanced at the point marked through the skin and subcutaneous tissue until the needle tip impinges on the periosteum of the underlying rib (Fig. 79–8). The needle is then withdrawn back into subcutaneous tissue and walked inferiorly off the inferior rib margin. The needle should be advanced just beyond the inferior rib margin, but no further, or pneumothorax or damage to the abdominal viscera could result. After careful aspiration to ensure that the needle tip is not in an intercostal vein or artery, 1 mL of solution is gently injected. There should be limited resistance to injection. If significant resistance is encountered, the needle should be withdrawn slightly until the injection proceeds with only limited resistance. This procedure is repeated for each affected rib and associated cartilage. The needle is then removed and a sterile pressure dressing and ice pack are placed at the injection site.

The major complication of this injection technique is pneumothorax or damage to the abdominal viscera if the needle is placed too medially or deeply and invades the pleural space or peritoneal cavity. Infection, though rare, can occur if strict aseptic technique is not adhered to. These complications can be greatly decreased if the clinician pays close attention to accurate needle placement. Because this technique will block the intercostal nerve corresponding to the rib injected, the patient should be warned to expect some transient numbness of the chest and abdominal wall, as well as bulging of the abdomen in the subcostal region secondary to blockade of the motor innervation to these muscles.

■ LIVER PAIN

Liver pain is a common clinical occurrence, but it is often poorly diagnosed and treated. The liver can serve as a source of pain in and of itself via the sympathetic nervous system, as well as be a source of referred pain secondary to peritoneal irritation via the intercostal and subcostal nerves.[6] Pain emanating from the liver itself tends to be ill defined and may be referred primarily to the epigastrium. It is dull and aching in character and mild to moderate in severity. It can be related to swelling of the liver and concomitant stretching of the liver capsule or result from distention of the veins, as seen with portal obstruction. This pain is carried via sympathetic fibers from the celiac ganglion, which enter the liver along with the hepatic artery and vein. This type of liver pain responds poorly to adjuvant analgesics. Occasionally, hepatic enlargement causes diaphragmatic pain that is referred to the supra-

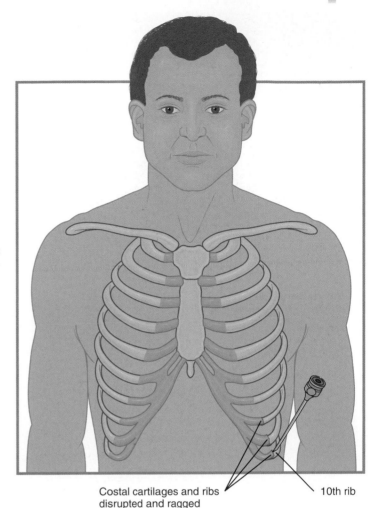

FIGURE 79–8 ■ Injection technique for slipping rib syndrome. (From Waldman SD [ed]: Atlas of Pain Management Injection Techniques. Philadelphia, WB Saunders, 2000, p 191.)

Costal cartilages and ribs
disrupted and ragged

10th rib

clavicular region (Fig. 79–9). This referred pain is transmitted via the phrenic nerve and is often misdiagnosed.

Referred liver pain is caused by mechanical irritation and inflammation of the inferior pleura and peritoneum. This pain is somatic in nature and is carried primarily via the lower intercostal and subcostal nerve. This somatic pain is sharp and pleuritic in nature and moderate to severe in intensity. This pain responds more favorably to nonsteroidal antiinflammatory agents and opioid analgesics than sympathetically mediated liver pain does.

Signs and Symptoms

The clinical manifestations of liver pain will be directly related to whether the pain is mediated via the sympathetic or somatic nervous system, or both. In patients with sympathetically mediated pain, the abdominal examination may reveal hepatomegaly with tenderness to palpation of the liver. Primary tumor or metastatic disease may also be identified. The remainder of the abdominal examination will be bland. Auscultation over the liver will fail to reveal a friction rub in most cases. As mentioned earlier, the patient may complain of ill-defined pain in the supraclavicular region.

Patients with somatically mediated liver pain will respond in an entirely different manner. The patient will often splint the right lower portion of the chest wall and abdomen

and take small short breaths to avoid exacerbating the pain. The patient may avoid coughing because the pain and accumulated upper airway secretions and atelectasis may be a problem. The abdominal examination may reveal signs of peritoneal irritation over the right upper quadrant. A friction rub is often present with auscultation over the liver. The liver may be extremely tender to palpation. Primary tumor or metastatic disease (or both) may be present.

Testing

Testing of patients with liver pain should be aimed at identifying the primary source of liver disease responsible for the pain, as well as ruling out other pathologic processes that may be responsible for the pain (Fig. 79–10). Plain radiographs of the chest and abdomen, including an upright abdominal film, are indicated in all patients with pain thought to be emanating from the liver. Radiographs of the ribs are indicated to rule out occult bony pathology, including tumor. Based on the patient's clinical findings, additional testing, including a complete blood count, automated chemistry panels, liver function test, sedimentation rate, and antinuclear antibody testing, may be indicated. CT scan of the lower thoracic contents and abdomen is indicated in most patients suffering from liver pain to rule out occult pulmonary and intraabdominal pathology, including cancer of the gallbladder and pancreas.

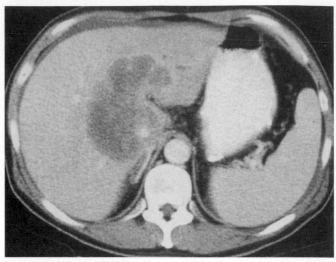

FIGURE 79–10 ■ Intrahepatic cholangiocarcinoma in a 45-year-old man. A contrast-enhanced CT scan demonstrates a large central, predominantly hypointense mass with peripheral enhancement. The lobulated mass encases the inferior vena cava, which remains patent. (From Haaga JR, Lanzieri CF, Gilkeson RC [eds]: CT & MR Imaging of the Whole Body, 4th ed. Philadelphia, CV Mosby, 2002, p 1290.)

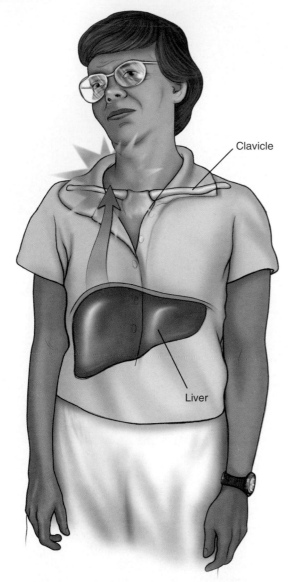

FIGURE 79–9 ■ Occasionally, hepatic enlargement causes diaphragmatic pain that is referred to the supraclavicular region. (From Waldman SD [ed]: Atlas of Uncommon Pain Syndromes. Philadelphia, WB Saunders, 2003, p 144.)

Differential neural blockade on an anatomic basis can serve as both a diagnostic and therapeutic maneuver (see "Treatment" later).

Differential Diagnosis

Pain of hepatic origin must be taken seriously. It is often the result of an underlying serious disease, such as biliary malignancy, portal hypertension, or hepatic metastatic disease. Pain emanating from the liver is often mistaken for pain of cardiac or gallbladder origin and can lead to visits to the emergency department and unnecessary cardiac and gastrointestinal work-ups. If trauma has occurred, liver pain may coexist with fractured ribs or fractures of the sternum itself, which can be missed on plain radiographs and may require radionuclide bone scanning for proper identification.

Neuropathic pain involving the chest wall may also be confused or coexist with liver pain. Examples of such neuropathic pain include diabetic polyneuropathies and acute herpes zoster involving the lower thoracic and upper lumbar nerves. The possibility of diseases of the structures of the inferior mediastinum and retroperitoneum remain ever present, and at times they can be difficult to diagnose. Pathologic processes that inflame the pleura, such as pulmonary embolism, infection, and Bornholm disease, may also mimic or coexist with pain of hepatic origin.

Treatment

Initial treatment of liver pain should include a combination of simple analgesics and nonsteroidal antiinflammatory agents or COX-2 inhibitors. If these medications do not adequately control the patient's symptomatology, an opioid analgesic may be added.

Local application of heat and cold may also be beneficial and provide symptomatic relief of liver pain. The use of an elastic rib belt over the liver may likewise help provide symptomatic relief. For patients who do not respond to these treatment modalities, an injection of local anesthetic and steroid may be a reasonable next step. If the pain is thought to be sympathetically mediated, a celiac plexus block is a reasonable next step (Fig. 79–11). This technique will provide both diagnostic and therapeutic benefit. If the pain is thought to be somatic in nature, intercostal nerve blocks should be the next step (Fig. 79–12). It should be remembered that pain of hepatic origin may be both somatic and sympathetic in nature and require both celiac plexus and intercostal nerve blocks for complete control.

The major problem in the care of patients thought to suffer from liver pain is failure to identify potentially serious pathology of the thorax or upper part of the abdomen. Given the proximity of the pleural space, pneumothorax is a distinct possibility after an intercostal nerve block. The incidence of

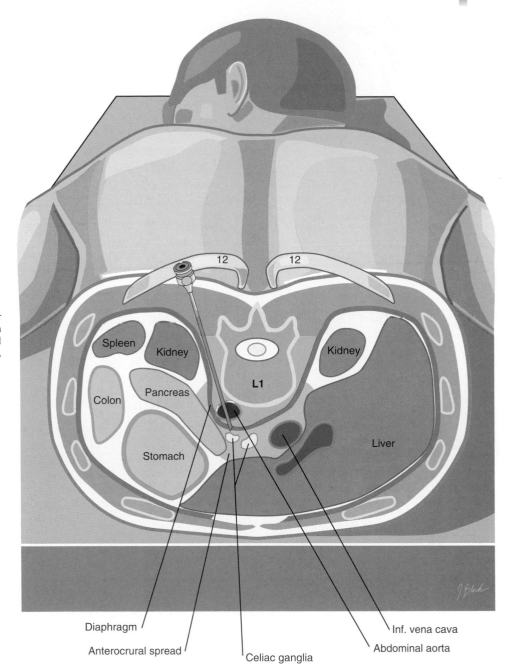

FIGURE 79–11 ■ Technique for transaortic celiac plexus block. (From Waldman SD [ed]: Atlas of Interventional Pain Management, 2nd ed. Philadelphia, WB Saunders, 2003, p 243.)

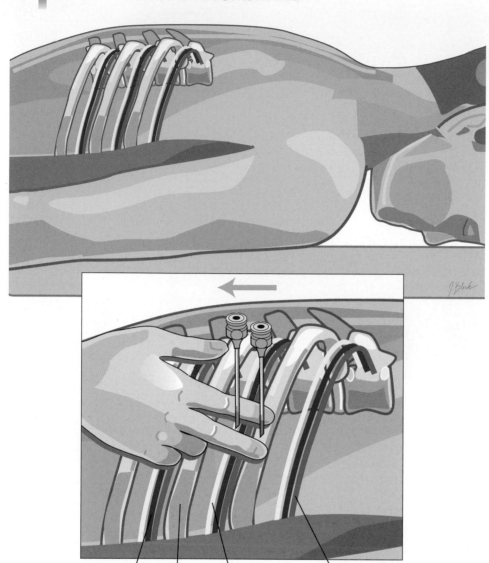

Intercostal a.

Rib

Intercostal n.

Intercostal v.

FIGURE 79–12 ■ Technique for intercostal nerve block. (From Waldman SD [ed]: Atlas of Interventional Pain Management, 2nd ed. Philadelphia, WB Saunders, 2003, p 286.)

the complication is less than 1%, but it occurs with greater frequency in patients with chronic obstructive pulmonary disease. Though uncommon, infection, including liver abscess, remains an ever-present possibility, especially in an immunocompromised cancer patient. Early detection of infection is crucial to avoid potentially life-threatening sequelae.

■ CONCLUSION

Patients suffering from the pain syndromes discussed in this chapter often attribute their pain symptomatology to appendicitis, a gallbladder attack, ulcer disease, or on occasion, a heart attack. Reassurance is required if the source of the pain is from the abdominal wall, although it should be remembered that musculoskeletal pain syndromes and intraabdominal pathology can coexist. Failure to diagnose occult pathology can lead to disastrous outcomes.

References

1. Waldman SD: Anterior cutaneous nerve entrapment syndrome. In Waldman SD (ed): Atlas of Uncommon Pain Syndromes. Philadelphia, WB Saunders, 2003, p 135.
2. Waldman SD: Anterior cutaneous nerve entrapment syndrome. In Waldman SD (ed): Atlas of Pain Management Injection Techniques. Philadelphia, WB Saunders, 2000, p 192.
3. Waldman SD: The hooking maneuver test for slipping rib syndrome. In Waldman SD (ed): Physical Diagnosis of Pain: An Atlas of Signs and Symptoms. Philadelphia, WB Saunders, 2006, p 214.
4. Waldman SD: Slipping rib syndrome. In Waldman SD (ed): Atlas of Common Pain Syndromes. Philadelphia, WB Saunders, 2002, p 122.
5. Waldman SD: Slipping rib syndrome. In Waldman SD (ed): Atlas of Pain Management Injection Techniques. Philadelphia, WB Saunders, 2000, p 189.
6. Waldman SD: Liver pain. In Waldman SD (ed): Atlas of Uncommon Pain Syndromes. Philadelphia, WB Saunders, 2003, p 143.

Evaluation and Treatment of Acute and Chronic Pancreatitis

Steven D. Waldman

It has been said that if one knows pancreatitis, one knows medicine. Anyone who has had experience in the care of a patient with acute or chronic pancreatitis is likely to agree. This chapter familiarizes the clinician with the broad scope of problems associated with pancreatitis and provides a concise roadmap for the management of associated pain.

■ ACUTE PANCREATITIS

Acute pancreatitis is one of the most common causes of abdominal pain. The incidence of acute pancreatitis is approximately 0.5% of the general population with a mortality rate of 1% to 1.5%.[1] In the United States, acute pancreatitis is most commonly caused by alcohol; gallstones are the most common cause in most European countries.[2,3] There are many causes of acute pancreatitis (Table 80–1). In addition to alcohol and gallstones, other common causes of acute pancreatitis include viral infections, tumor, and medications.

Abdominal pain is a common feature in acute pancreatitis.[4] It may range from mild to severe and is characterized by steady, boring epigastric pain that radiates to the flanks and chest. The pain is worse with the supine position, and a patient with acute pancreatitis often prefers sitting with the dorsal spine flexed and the knees drawn up to the abdomen (Fig. 80–1). Nausea, vomiting, and anorexia also are common features of acute pancreatitis.

Signs and Symptoms

A patient with acute pancreatitis appears ill and anxious. Tachycardia and hypotension resulting from hypovolemia are common, as is low-grade fever.[5] Saponification of subcutaneous fat is seen in approximately 15% of patients with acute pancreatitis, as are pulmonary complications, including pleural effusions and pleuritic pain that may compromise respiration. Diffuse abdominal tenderness with peritoneal signs is invariably present.[6] A pancreatic mass or pseudocyst owing to pancreatic edema may be palpable (Fig. 80–2). If hemorrhage occurs, periumbilical ecchymosis (Cullen sign) and flank ecchymosis (Turner sign) may be present (Figs. 80–3 and 80–4). Both of these findings suggest severe necrotizing pancreatitis and indicate a poor prognosis. If

hypocalcemia is present, Chvostek or Trousseau signs may be present.

Testing

Elevation of the serum amylase is the sine qua non of acute pancreatitis.[7] Levels tend to peak at 48 to 72 hours and then begin to drift toward normal. Serum lipase remains elevated and may correlate better with the actual severity of the disease. Because elevated serum amylase may be caused by other diseases (e.g., parotitis), amylase isoenzmes may be necessary to confirm a pancreatic basis for this laboratory finding. Plain radiographs of the chest are indicated in all patients who present with pain from acute pancreatitis to identify pulmonary complications, including pleural effusion, which result from the acute pancreatitis. Given the extrapancreatic manifestations of acute pancreatitis (e.g., acute renal or hepatic failure), serial complete blood count, serum calcium, serum glucose, liver function tests, and electrolytes are indicated in all patients with acute pancreatitis. CT scan of the abdomen helps identify pancreatic pseudocyst and may help the clinician gauge the severity and progress of the disease. Gallbladder evaluation with radionucleotides is indicated if gallstones are being considered as a cause of acute pancreatitis. Arterial blood gases help identify respiratory failure and metabolic acidosis.

The differential diagnosis should consider perforated peptic ulcer, acute cholecystitis, bowel obstruction, renal calculi, myocardial infarction, mesenteric infarction, diabetic ketoacidosis, and pneumonia. Rarely, connective tissue diseases, including systemic lupus erythematosus and polyarteritis nodosa, may mimic pancreatitis. Because the pain of acute herpes zoster may precede the rash by 24 to 72 hours, the pain may be attributed erroneously to acute pancreatitis.

Treatment

Most cases of acute pancreatitis are self-limited and resolve within 5 to 7 days. Initial treatment of acute pancreatitis is aimed primarily at putting the pancreas at rest. This is accomplished by keeping the patient NPO ("nothing per mouth") to decrease serum gastrin secretion and, if ileus is present, instituting nasogastric suction. Short-acting potent opioid

Table 80–1

Common Causes of Acute Pancreatitis

Alcohol abuse
Gallstones
Viral infections
Medications
Metabolic causes
Connective tissue diseases
Tumor obstruction of ampulla of Vater
Hereditary

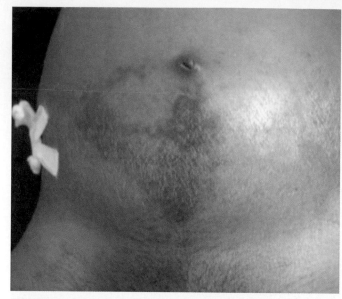

FIGURE 80–3 ■ Periumbilical ecchymosis (Cullen sign) in acute pancreatitis. (Courtesy of Vikram Kate, Jawaharlal Institute of Postgraduate Medical Education and Research, Pondicherry, India.)

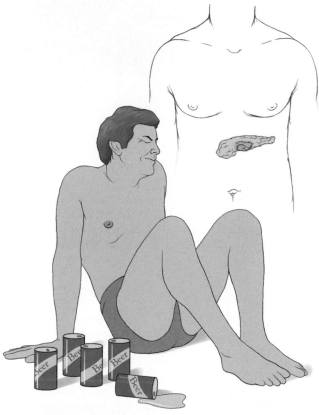

FIGURE 80–1 ■ Excessive consumption of alcohol is one of many causes of acute pancreatitis. (From Waldman SD: Acute pancreatitis. In: Atlas of Common Pain Syndromes. Philadelphia, WB Saunders, 2002, p 187.)

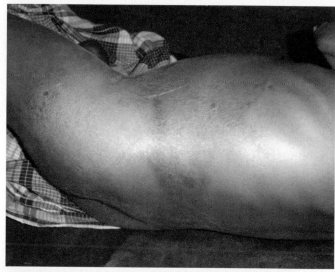

FIGURE 80–4 ■ Flank ecchymosis (Turner sign) in acute pancreatitis. (Courtesy of Vikram Kate, Jawaharlal Institute of Postgraduate Medical Education and Research, Pondicherry, India.)

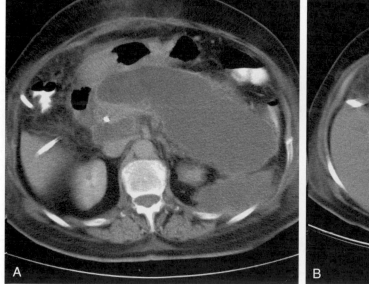

FIGURE 80–2 ■ **A** and **B,** In acute pancreatitis, a pancreatic mass or pseudocyst *(arrows)* owing to pancreatic edema may be present. (From Haaga JR, Lanzieri CF, Gilkeson RC: CT and MR Imaging of the Whole Body, 4th ed. Philadelphia, Mosby, 2003, p 1443.)

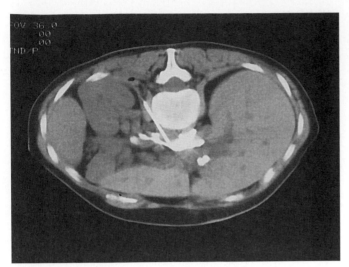

FIGURE 80–5 ■ CT-guided celiac plexus block for acute pancreatitis. (From Waldman SD: Neural blockade and neurolytic blocks. In: Interventional Pain Management, 2nd ed. Philadelphia, WB Saunders, 2001, p 500.)

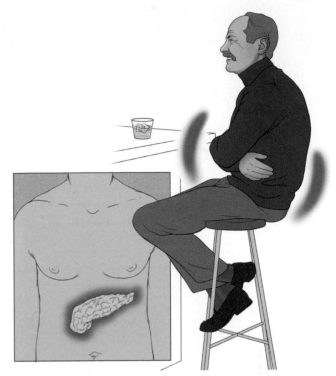

FIGURE 80–6 ■ Chronic pancreatitis may manifest in a manner analogous to the presentation of acute pancreatitis, but can be more challenging to treat. (From Waldman SD: Chronic pancreatitis. In: Atlas of Common Pain Syndromes. Philadelphia, WB Saunders, 2002, p 189.)

analgesics, such as hydrocodone, represent a reasonable next step if conservative measures do not control the patient's pain. If ileus is present, parenteral narcotics, such as meperidine, are a good alternative. Because the opioid analgesics have the potential to suppress the cough reflex and respiration, the clinician must be careful to monitor the patient closely and to instruct the patient in adequate pulmonary toilet techniques. If symptoms persist, CT-guided celiac plexus block with local anesthetic and steroid is indicated and may help decrease the mortality and morbidity associated with the disease (Fig. 80–5). As an alternative, continuous thoracic epidural block with local anesthetic or opioid or both may provide adequate pain control and allow the patient to avoid the respiratory depression associated with systemic opioid analgesics.

Hypovolemia should be treated aggressively with crystalloid and colloid infusions. For prolonged cases of acute pancreatitis, parenteral nutrition is indicated to avoid malnutrition. Surgical drainage and removal of necrotic tissue may be required in severe necrotizing pancreatitis that fails to respond to the above-mentioned treatment modalities.

Complications and Pitfalls

The major problem in the care of patients with acute pancreatitis is a failure of the clinician to recognize the severity of the patient's condition and to identify and treat aggressively the extrapancreatic manifestations of acute pancreatitis. Hypovolemia, hypocalcemia, renal failure, and respiratory failure occur with enough frequency that the clinician must look actively for these potentially fatal complications and manage them aggressively.[8]

■ CHRONIC PANCREATITIS

Chronic pancreatitis has numerous causes; alcohol abuse and gallstones account for approximately 85% of all cases (Table 80–2). Chronic pancreatitis may present as recurrent episodes of acute inflammation of the pancreas superimposed on chronic pancreatic dysfunction or as a more constant

Table 80–2

Common Causes of Chronic Pancreatitis

Alcohol abuse
Gallstones
Medications
Abdominal trauma
Hereditary diseases (e.g., cystic fibrosis and α_1-antitrypsin deficiency)
Post–endoscopic retrograde cholangiopancreatography
Viral infections (e.g., mumps)
Abnormalities of the pancreas or intestine (e.g., pancreatic divisum)
Hyperlipidemia

problem.[9] As the exocrine function of the pancreas deteriorates, malabsorption with steatorrhea develops. Abdominal pain is usually present, but it may be characterized by exacerbations and remissions. In the United States, chronic pancreatitis is caused most commonly by alcohol, followed by cystic fibrosis and pancreatic malignancies.[10] Hereditary causes, such as α_1-antitrypsin deficiency, also are common causes of chronic pancreatitis.[11] In the developing countries, the most common cause of chronic pancreatitis is severe protein calorie malnutrition.

Abdominal pain is a common feature in chronic pancreatitis.[12] It mimics the pain of acute pancreatitis; it may range from mild to severe; and it is characterized by steady, boring epigastric pain that radiates to the flanks and chest (Fig. 80–6). The pain is worse with alcohol and fatty meals.

Nausea, vomiting, and anorexia also are common features of chronic pancreatitis, but as mentioned, the clinical symptoms frequently encountered in chronic pancreatitis are characterized by exacerbations and remissions.

Signs and Symptoms

A patient with chronic pancreatitis presents similar to a patient with acute pancreatitis, but may appear more chronically ill than acutely ill. Tachycardia and hypotension resulting from hypovolemia are much less common in chronic pancreatitis and if present represent an extremely ominous prognostic indicator or suggest that another pathologic process, such as perforated peptic ulcer, is present.[13] Diffuse abdominal tenderness with peritoneal signs may be present if acute inflammation occurs. A pancreatic mass or pseudocyst secondary to pancreatic edema may be palpable.

Testing

Although elevation of serum amylase levels is the sine qua non of acute pancreatitis, amylase levels in chronic pancreatitis may be only mildly elevated or normal. Amylase levels tend to peak at 48 to 72 hours and then begin to drift toward normal.[12] Serum lipase levels also are attenuated in chronic pancreatitis compared with the findings seen in acute pancreatitis. Serum lipase may remain elevated longer than serum amylase in this setting and may correlate better with the actual severity of the disease. Because elevated serum amylase may be caused by other diseases, such as parotitis, amylase isozymes may be necessary to confirm a pancreatic basis for this laboratory finding. Plain radiographs of the chest are indicated for all patients who present with pain from chronic pancreatitis to identify pulmonary complications, including pleural effusion, that result from the chronic pancreatitis.

Given the extrapancreatic manifestations of chronic pancreatitis (e.g., acute renal or hepatic failure), serial complete blood count, serum calcium, serum glucose, liver function tests, and electrolytes are indicated in all patients with chronic pancreatitis. CT of the abdomen helps identify pancreatic pseudocysts, calcifications, or pancreatic tumor that may have been previously overlooked and may help the clinician gauge the severity and progression of the disease (Fig. 80–7). Gallbladder evaluation with radionucleotides is indicated if gallstones are being considered as a cause of chronic pancreatitis.[14] Arterial blood gases help identify respiratory failure and metabolic acidosis.

Differential Diagnosis

The differential diagnosis should include perforated peptic ulcer, acute cholecystitis, bowel obstruction, renal calculi, myocardial infarction, mesenteric infarction, diabetic ketoacidosis, and pneumonia. Rarely, collagen-vascular diseases, including systemic lupus erythematosus and polyarteritis nodosa, may mimic chronic pancreatitis. Because the pain of acute herpes zoster may precede the rash by 24 to 72 hours, the pain may be erroneously attributed to chronic pancreatitis in patients who have had previous bouts of the disease. The clinician always should consider the possibility of pancreatic malignancy in patients who are thought to have chronic pancreatitis (Fig. 80–8).

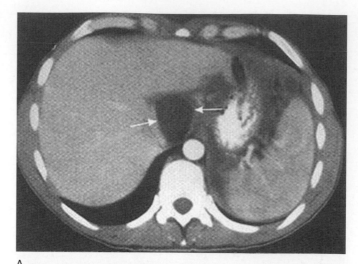

A

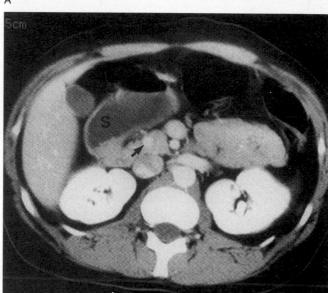

B

FIGURE 80–7 ■ **A,** Pancreatic pseudocyst. A well-defined fluid collection with a thin wall *(arrows)* lies superior to the pancreas. **B,** Pancreatic calcification. CT scan at the level of the head of the pancreas shows a dominant calcification site in the main pancreatic duct *(arrow).* (From Feeny PC: The pancreas. In Grainger RG, Allison DJ, Adam A, Dixon AK (eds): Grainger and Allison's Diagnostic Radiology, 4th ed. Philadelphia, Churchill Livingstone, 2002.)

Treatment

Initial management of patients with chronic pancreatitis should be focused on the treatment of the pain and malabsorption. Similar to acute pancreatitis, the treatment of chronic pancreatitis is aimed primarily at putting the pancreas at rest. This is accomplished by keeping the patient NPO to decrease serum gastrin secretion and, if ileus is present, instituting nasogastric suction. Short-acting potent opioid analgesics, such as hydrocodone, represent a reasonable next step if conservative measures do not control the patient's pain. If ileus is present, parenteral narcotics, such as meperidine, are a good alternative. Because opioid analgesics have the potential to suppress the cough reflex and respiration, the clinician must be careful to monitor the patient closely and to instruct the patient in adequate pulmonary toilet techniques. As with

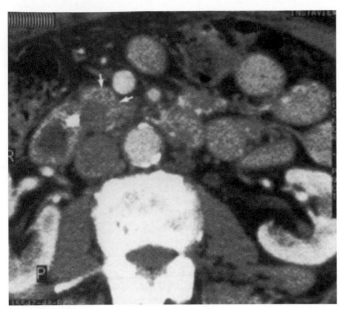

FIGURE 80–8 ▮ Small pancreatic carcinoma. CT shows a relatively poorly enhancing mass within normally enhancing pancreatic parenchyma *(arrows)*. (From Grainger RG, Allison DJ, Adam A, Dixon AK (eds): Grainger and Allison's Diagnostic Radiology, 4th ed. Philadelphia, Churchill Livingstone, 2002, p 1357.)

all chronic diseases, the use of opioid analgesics must be monitored carefully because the potential for misuse and dependence is high. If the symptoms persist, CT-guided celiac plexus block with local anesthetic and steroid is indicated and may help decrease the mortality and morbidity rates associated with the disease (see Fig. 80–5). If the relief from this technique is short-lived, neurolytic CT-guided celiac plexus block with alcohol or phenol is a reasonable next step. As an alternative, continuous thoracic epidural block with local anesthetic, opioid, or both may provide adequate pain control and allow the patient to avoid the respiratory depression associated with systemic opioid analgesics.

Hypovolemia should be treated aggressively with crystalloid and colloid infusions. For prolonged cases of chronic pancreatitis, parenteral nutrition is indicated to avoid malnutrition. Surgical drainage and removal of necrotic tissue may be required in patients with severe necrotizing pancreatitis that fails to respond to the above-mentioned treatment modalities.[15]

Complications and Pitfalls

Similar to patients with acute pancreatitis, the major problem in the care of patients with chronic pancreatitis is a failure of the clinician to recognize the severity of the patient's condition and to identify and treat aggressively the extrapancreatic manifestations of chronic pancreatitis. Hypovolemia, hypocalcemia, and renal and respiratory failure occur with sufficient frequency that the clinician must seek actively these potentially fatal complications and treat them aggressively. If opioids are used, the clinician must watch constantly for overuse and dependence, especially if the underlying cause of the chronic pancreatitis is alcohol abuse.

▮ CONCLUSION

Pancreatitis is a commonly encountered cause of abdominal pain. Correct diagnosis is necessary to treat this painful condition properly and to avoid overlooking serious extrapancreatic complications associated with this disease. The use of the above-mentioned treatment modalities, including the judicious use of opioid analgesics to treat the pain of acute exacerbations, allows the clinician to control the pain of chronic pancreatitis adequately. Celiac plexus block and thoracic epidural block are straightforward techniques that can produce dramatic relief for patients with chronic pancreatitis.

References

1. Steinberg W, Tenner S: Acute pancreatitis. N Engl J Med 1198:207, 1994.
2. Pitchumoni CS, Bordalo O: Evaluation of hypotheses on pathogenesis of alcoholic pancreatitis. Am J Gastroenterol 91:637, 1996.
3. Liu CL, Lo CM, Fan ST: Acute biliary pancreatitis: Diagnosis and management. World J Surg 21:149, 1997.
4. Waldman SD: Acute pancreatitis. In: Atlas of Common Pain Syndromes. Philadelphia, WB Saunders, 2002, p 185.
5. Baron TH, Morgan DE: Acute necrotizing pancreatitis. N Engl J Med 340:1412, 1999.
6. Dragonetti GC, Licht H, Rubin W: Pancreatitis: Evaluation and treatment. Prim Care 23:525, 1996.
7. Gamaste VV: Diagnostic tests for acute pancreatitis. Gastroenterologist 2:119, 1994.
8. Johnson CD: Severe acute pancreatitis: A continuing challenge for the intensive care team. Br J Intensive Med 8:130, 1998.
9. Gupta V, Toskes PP: Diagnosis and management of chronic pancreatitis. Postgrad Med J 81:491, 2005.
10. Cohn JA, Friedman KJ, Noone PG, et al: Relation between mutations of the cystic fibrosis gene and idiopathic pancreatitis. N Engl J Med 339:653, 1998.
11. Etemad B, Whitcomb DC: Chronic pancreatitis: Diagnosis, classification, and new genetic developments. Gastroenterology 120:682, 2001.
12. Waldman SD: Chronic pancreatitis. In: Atlas of Common Pain Syndromes. Philadelphia, WB Saunders, 2002, p 188.
13. Vlodov J, Tenner SM: Acute and chronic pancreatitis. Prim Care 28:607, 2001.
14. Elmas N: The role of diagnostic radiology in pancreatitis. Eur J Radiol 38:120, 2001.
15. Sakorafas GH, Farnell MB, Nagorney DM, Sarr MG: Surgical management of chronic pancreatitis at the Mayo Clinic. Surg Clin North Am 81:457, 2001.

chapter 81

Ilioinguinal, Iliohypogastric, and Genitofemoral Neuralgia

Steven D. Waldman

Ilioinguinal, iliohypogastric, and genitofemoral neuralgias are among the most common causes of lower abdominal and pelvic pain encountered in clinical practice. The anatomic variability of these nerves often leads to overlapping patterns of innervation, which can confuse the unsuspecting clinician. This chapter reviews the clinical presentation of ilioinguinal and genitofemoral neuralgia and provides the reader with a concise approach to the evaluation and treatment of these painful conditions.

■ ILIOINGUINAL NEURALGIA

Ilioinguinal neuralgia is caused by compression of the ilioinguinal nerve as it passes through the transverse abdominis muscle at the level of the anterior superior iliac spine.[1] The most common causes of compression of the ilioinguinal nerve at this anatomic location involve injury to the nerve induced by trauma, including direct blunt trauma to the nerve and damage during inguinal herniorrhaphy or pelvic surgery.[2,3] Rarely, ilioinguinal neuralgia occurs spontaneously.

Signs and Symptoms

Ilioinguinal neuralgia presents as paresthesias, burning pain, and occasionally numbness over the lower abdomen that radiates into the scrotum or labia and occasionally into the inner upper thigh.[2] The pain does not radiate below the knee. The pain of ilioinguinal neuralgia is made worse by extension of the lumbar spine, which puts traction on the nerve. Patients with ilioinguinal neuralgia often assume a bent-forward novice skier's position (Fig. 81–1). Untreated, progressive motor deficit consisting of bulging of the anterior abdominal wall muscles may occur. This bulging may be confused with inguinal hernia.

Physical findings include sensory deficit in the inner thigh, scrotum, or labia in the distribution of the ilioinguinal nerve (Fig. 81–2). Weakness of the anterior abdominal wall musculature may be present. A Tinel sign may be elicited by tapping over the ilioinguinal nerve at the point it pierces the transverse abdominis muscle.

Testing

Electromyography helps distinguish ilioinguinal nerve entrapment from lumbar plexopathy, lumbar radiculopathy, and diabetic polyneuropathy. Plain radiographs of the hip and pelvis are indicated in all patients who present with ilioinguinal neuralgia to rule out occult bony pathology. Based on the patient's clinical presentation, additional testing, including complete blood count, uric acid, sedimentation rate, and antinuclear antibody testing, may be indicated. MRI of the lumbar plexus is indicated if tumor or hematoma is suspected. The injection technique described subsequently serves as a diagnostic and therapeutic maneuver.

Differential Diagnosis

Lesions of the lumbar plexus resulting from trauma, hematoma, tumor, diabetic neuropathy, or inflammation can mimic the pain, numbness, and weakness of ilioinguinal neuralgia and must be included in the differential diagnosis. There is significant intrapatient variability in the anatomy of the ilioinguinal nerve, which can result in significant variation in patients' clinical presentation. The ilioinguinal nerve is a branch of the L1 nerve root with contribution from T12 in some patients. The nerve follows a curvilinear course, which takes it from its origin of the L1 and occasionally T12 somatic nerves to inside the concavity of the ilium. The ilioinguinal nerve continues anteriorly to perforate the transverse abdominis muscle at the level of the anterior superior iliac spine. The nerve may interconnect with the iliohypogastric nerve as it continues to pass along its course medially and inferiorly where it accompanies the spermatic cord through the inguinal ring and into the inguinal canal. The distribution of the sensory innervation of the ilioinguinal nerves varies among patients because there may be considerable overlap with the iliohypogastric nerve. In general, the ilioinguinal nerve provides sensory innervation to the upper portion of the skin of the inner thigh and the root of the penis and upper scrotum in men or the mons pubis and lateral labia in women.

Treatment

Pharmacologic management of ilioinguinal neuralgia is generally disappointing, and a general nerve block is required

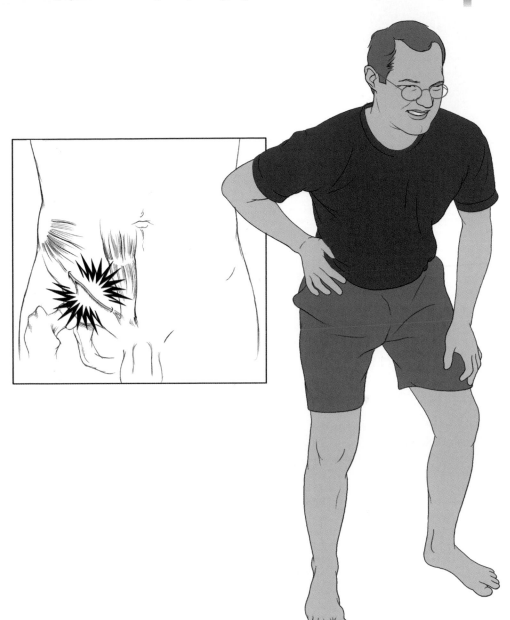

FIGURE 81–1 ■ A patient with ilioinguinal neuralgia often bends forward in the novice skier's position to relieve the pain. (From Waldman SD: Ilioinquinal neuralgia. In: Common Pain Syndromes. Philadelphia, WB Saunders 2002, p 193.)

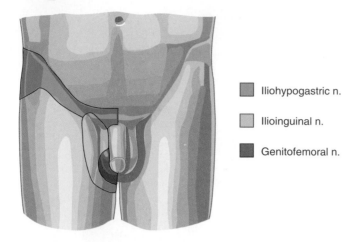

Iliohypogastric n.

Ilioinguinal n.

Genitofemoral n.

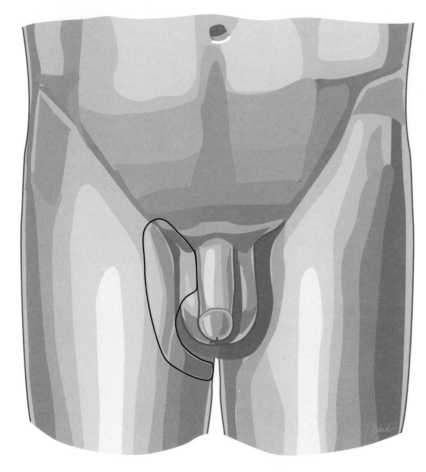

Ilioinguinal n.

FIGURE 81–2 ■ Sensory distribution of the ilioinguinal nerve. (From Waldman SD: Ilioinquinal nerve block. In: Atlas of Interventional Pain Management, 2nd ed. Philadelphia, WB Saunders, 2004, p 295.)

to provide pain relief. Initial management of ilioinguinal neuralgia should consist of treatment with simple analgesics, nonsteroidal antiinflammatory drugs (NSAIDs), or cyclooxygenase-2 (COX-2) inhibitors. Avoidance of repetitive activities thought to exacerbate the symptoms of ilioinguinal neuralgia (e.g., squatting or sitting for prolonged periods) also helps ameliorate the patient's symptoms. If the patient fails to respond to these conservative measures, a next reasonable step is ilioinguinal nerve block with local anesthetic and steroid.[4]

Ilioinguinal nerve block is performed by placing the patient in the supine position, with a pillow under the knees if lying with the legs extended increases the patient's pain owing to traction on the nerve. The anterior superior iliac spine is identified by palpation. A point 2 inches medial and 2 inches inferior to the anterior superior iliac spine is identified and prepared with antiseptic solution. A 1½-inch 25-gauge needle is advanced at an oblique angle toward the pubic symphysis (Fig. 81–3), and 5 to 7 mL of 1% preservative-free lidocaine in solution with 40 mg of methylprednisolone is

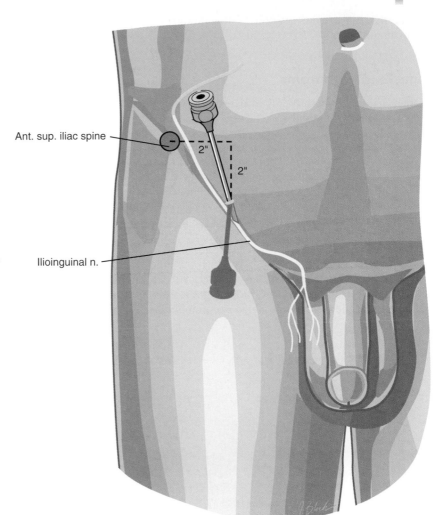

Ant. sup. iliac spine

Ilioinguinal n.

FIGURE 81–3 ■ Ilioinguinal nerve block technique. (From Waldman SD: Ilioinquinal nerve block. In: Atlas of Interventional Pain Management, 2nd ed. Philadelphia, WB Saunders, 2004, p 297.)

injected in a fanlike manner as the needle pierces the fascia of the external oblique muscle. Care must be taken not to place the needle too deep so as to enter the peritoneal cavity and perforate the abdominal viscera.

Because of overlapping innervation of the ilioinguinal and iliohypogastric nerves, it is not unusual to block branches of each nerve when performing ilioinguinal nerve block. After injection of the solution, pressure is applied to the injection site to decrease the incidence of post-block ecchymosis and hematoma formation, which can be quite dramatic, especially in an anticoagulated patient.

The clinician should be aware that because of the anatomy of the ilioinguinal nerve, damage or entrapment of the nerve anywhere along its course can produce a similar clinical syndrome. A careful search for pathology at the T12-L1 spinal segments and along the path of the nerve in the pelvis is mandatory in all patients who present with ilioinguinal neuralgia without a history of inguinal surgery or trauma to the region.

The major side effect of ilioinguinal nerve block is post-block ecchymosis and hematoma formation. If needle placement is too deep and enters the peritoneal cavity, perforation of the colon may result in the formation of intra-abdominal abscess and fistula. Early detection of infection is crucial to avoid potentially life-threatening sequelae.

■ ILIOHYPOGASTRIC NEURALGIA

Iliohypogastric neuralgia is caused by compression of the iliohypogastric nerve as it passes through the transverse abdominis muscle.[5] The iliohypogastric nerve is a branch of the L1 nerve root with a contribution from T12 in some patients. The nerve follows a curvilinear course that takes it from its origin of the L1 and occasionally T12 somatic nerves to inside the concavity of the ilium. The iliohypogastric nerve continues anteriorly to perforate the transverse abdominis muscle to lie between it and the external oblique muscle. At this point, the iliohypogastric nerve divides into an anterior and a lateral branch. The lateral branch provides cutaneous sensory innervation to the posterolateral gluteal region. The anterior branch pierces the external oblique muscle just beyond the anterior superior iliac spine to provide cutaneous sensory innervation to the abdominal skin above the pubis (see Fig. 81–2). The most common causes of compression of the iliohypogastric nerve at this anatomic location involve injury to the nerve induced by trauma, including direct blunt trauma to the nerve and damage during inguinal herniorrhaphy and pelvic surgery.[2,3] Rarely, iliohypogastric neuralgia occurs spontaneously. The nerve may interconnect with the ilioinguinal nerve along its course, resulting in variation of the distribution of the sensory innervation of the iliohypogastric and ilioinguinal nerves.

Signs and Symptoms

Ilioinguinal neuralgia presents as paresthesias, burning pain, and occasionally numbness of the abdominal skin above the pubis. The pain and paresthesia sometimes radiate into the posterior gluteal region.[5] The pain does not radiate below the knee. The pain of iliohypogastric neuralgia is worsened by extension of the lumbar spine, which puts traction on the nerve. Patients with iliohypogastric neuralgia often assume a bent-forward novice skier's position. Untreated, progressive motor deficit in the distribution of the nerve may occur.

Physical findings include sensory deficit of the abdominal skin above the pubis in the distribution of the iliohypogastric nerve (see Fig. 81–2). Weakness of the anterior abdominal wall musculature may be present. A Tinel sign may be elicited by tapping over the iliohypogastric nerve at the point where it pierces the transverse abdominis muscle.

Treatment

Pharmacologic management of iliohypogastric neuralgia is generally disappointing, and a general nerve block is required to provide pain relief. Initial treatment of iliohypogastric neuralgia should consist of treatment with simple analgesics, NSAIDs, or COX-2 inhibitors. Avoidance of repetitive activities thought to exacerbate the symptoms of iliohypogastric neuralgia (e.g., squatting or sitting for prolonged periods) also helps ameliorate the patient's symptoms. If the patient fails to respond to these conservative measures, a next reasonable step is iliohypogastric nerve block with local anesthetic and steroid.[6]

The patient is placed in the supine position, with a pillow under the knees if extending the legs increases the patient's pain because of traction on the nerve. The anterior superior iliac spine is identified by palpation. A point 1 inch medial and 1 inch inferior to the anterior superior iliac spine is identified and prepared with antiseptic solution. A 1½-inch 25-gauge needle is advanced at an oblique angle toward the pubic symphysis (Fig. 81–4), and 5 to 7 mL of 1% preservative-free

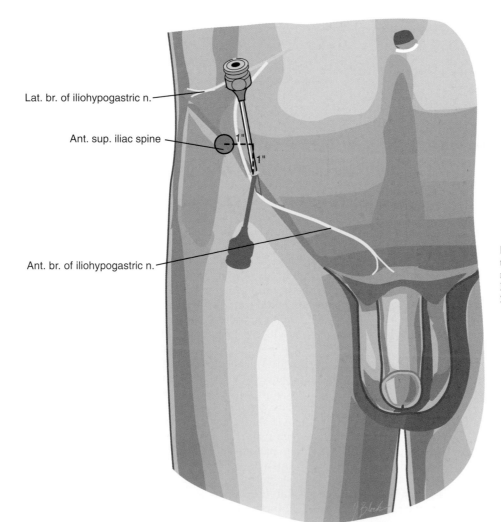

Lat. br. of iliohypogastric n.

Ant. sup. iliac spine

1"

1"

Ant. br. of iliohypogastric n.

FIGURE 81–4 ■ Iliohypogastric nerve block technique. (From Waldman SD: Iliohypogastric nerve block. In: Atlas of Interventional Pain Management, 2nd ed. Philadelphia, Saunders, 2004, p 301.)

lidocaine is injected in a fanlike manner as the needle pierces the fascia of the external oblique muscle. Care must be taken not to place the needle too deep to avoid entering the peritoneal cavity and perforating the abdominal viscera.

If the pain has an inflammatory component, the local anesthetic is combined with 80 mg of methylprednisolone and is injected in incremental doses. Subsequent daily nerve blocks are performed similarly, substituting 40 mg of methylprednisolone for the initial 80-mg dose. Because of overlapping innervation of the ilioinguinal and iliohypogastric nerves, it is not unusual to block branches of each nerve when performing iliohypogastric nerve block. After injection of the solution, pressure is applied to the injection site to decrease the incidence of post-block ecchymosis and hematoma formation, which can be dramatic, especially in a patient taking anticoagulants.

The main side effect of iliohypogastric nerve block is post-block ecchymosis and hematoma formation. If needle placement is too deep and enters the peritoneal cavity, perforation of the colon may result in intra-abdominal abscess and fistula formation. Early detection of infection is crucial to avoid potentially life-threatening sequelae.

■ GENITOFEMORAL NEURALGIA

Genitofemoral neuralgia is a common cause of lower abdominal and pelvic pain encountered in clinical practice.[7] Genitofemoral neuralgia may be caused by compression or damage to the genitofemoral nerve anywhere along its path. The genitofemoral nerve arises from fibers of the L1 and L2 nerve roots. The genitofemoral nerve passes through the substance of the psoas muscle, where it divides into a genital and a femoral branch. The femoral branch passes beneath the inguinal ligament along with the femoral artery and provides sensory innervation to a small area of skin on the inside of the thigh.[8] The genital branch passes through the inguinal canal to provide innervation to the round ligament of the uterus and labia majora in women. In men, the genital branch of the genitofemoral nerve passes with the spermatic cord to innervate the cremasteric muscles and provide sensory innervation to the bottom of the scrotum.

The most common causes of genitofemoral neuralgia involve injury to the nerve induced by trauma, including direct blunt trauma to the nerve and damage during inguinal herniorrhaphy and pelvic surgery. Rarely, genitofemoral neuralgia occurs spontaneously.

Signs and Symptoms

Genitofemoral neuralgia presents as paresthesias, burning pain, and occasionally numbness over the lower abdomen, which radiate into inner thigh in men and women and into the labia majora in women and the bottom of the scrotum and cremasteric muscles in men. The pain does not radiate below the knee. The pain of genitofemoral neuralgia is worsened by extension of the lumbar spine, which puts traction on the nerve. Patients with genitofemoral neuralgia often assume a bent-forward novice skier's position.

Physical findings include sensory deficit in the inner thigh and base of the scrotum or labia majora in the distribution of the genitofemoral nerve. Weakness of the anterior abdominal wall musculature occasionally may be present. A Tinel sign may be elicited by tapping over the genitofemoral nerve at the point it passes beneath the inguinal ligament.

Testing

Electromyography helps distinguish genitofemoral nerve entrapment from lumbar plexopathy, lumbar radiculopathy, and diabetic polyneuropathy. Plain radiographs of the hip and pelvis are indicated in all patients who present with genitofemoral neuralgia to rule out occult bony pathology. Based on the patient's clinical presentation, additional testing, including complete blood count, uric acid, sedimentation rate, and antinuclear antibody, may be indicated. MRI of the lumbar plexus is indicated if tumor or hematoma is suspected. The injection technique described subsequently serves as a diagnostic and a therapeutic maneuver.

Differential Diagnosis

Lesions of the lumbar plexus resulting from trauma, hematoma, tumor, diabetic neuropathy, or inflammation can mimic the pain, numbness, and weakness of genitofemoral neuralgia and must be included in the differential diagnosis. There is significant interpatient variability in the anatomy of the genitofemoral nerve, which can result in significant variation in patients' clinical presentation.

Treatment

Pharmacologic management of genitofemoral neuralgia is generally disappointing, and a general nerve block is required to provide pain relief. Initial management of genitofemoral neuralgia should consist of treatment with simple analgesics, NSAIDs, or COX-2 inhibitors. Avoidance of repetitive activities thought to exacerbate the symptoms of genitofemoral neuralgia (e.g., squatting or sitting for prolonged periods) also helps ameliorate the patient's symptoms. If the patient fails to respond to these conservative measures, a next reasonable step is genitofemoral nerve block with local anesthetic and steroid.[9]

Genitofemoral nerve block is performed by placing the patient in supine position with a pillow under the knees if lying with the legs extended increases the patient's pain owing to traction on the nerve. The genital branch of the genitofemoral nerve is blocked as follows. The pubic tubercle is identified by palpation. A point just lateral to the pubic tubercle is identified and prepared with antiseptic solution. A 1½-inch 25-gauge needle is advanced at an oblique angle toward the pubic symphysis (Fig. 81–5), and 3 to 5 mL of 1% preservative-free lidocaine and 80 mg of methylprednisolone is injected in a fanlike manner as the needle pierces the inguinal ligament. Care must be taken not to place the needle too deep to avoid entering the peritoneal cavity and perforating the abdominal viscera.

The femoral branch of the genitofemoral nerve is blocked by identifying the middle third of the inguinal ligament. After preparation of the skin with antiseptic solution, 3 to 5 mL of 1% lidocaine is infiltrated subcutaneously just below the ligament (see Fig. 81–5). Care must be taken not to enter the femoral artery of vein or inadvertently block the femoral nerve. The needle must be kept subcutaneous because too-deep placement may allow the needle to enter the peritoneal

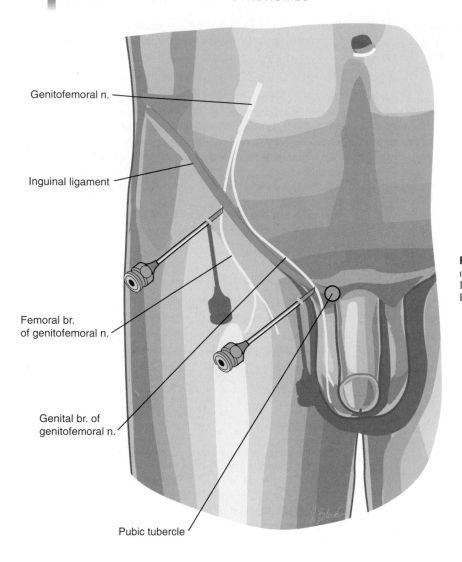

Genitofemoral n.

Inguinal ligament

Femoral br.
of genitofemoral n.

Genital br. of
genitofemoral n.

Pubic tubercle

FIGURE 81–5 ■ Genitofemoral nerve block technique. (From Waldman SD: Genitofemoral nerve block. In: Atlas of Interventional Pain Management, 2nd ed. Philadelphia, WB Saunders, 2004, p 305.)

cavity and perforate the abdominal viscera. If there is an inflammatory component to the pain, the local anesthetic is combined with 80 mg of methylprednisolone and is injected in incremental doses. Subsequent daily nerve blocks are carried out in a similar manner substituting 40 mg of methylprednisolone for the initial 80-mg dose.

Because of overlapping innervation of the ilioinguinal and iliohypogastric nerves, it is not unusual to block branches of each nerve when performing a genitofemoral nerve block. After injection of the solution, pressure is applied to the injection site to decrease the incidence of post-block ecchymosis and hematoma formation, which can be quite dramatic, especially in an anticoagulated patient.

■ CONCLUSION

Ilioinguinal, iliohypogastric, and genitofemoral neuralgia are common causes of lower abdominal and pelvic pain encountered in clinical practice. The anatomic variability of these nerves often leads to overlapping patterns of innervation, which can confuse an unsuspecting clinician. The clinician should be aware that because of the anatomy of the ilioinguinal, iliohypogastric, and genitofemoral nerves, damage or

entrapment of the nerves anywhere along their course can produce a similar clinical syndrome. A careful search for pathology at the T12-L2 spinal segments and along the path of the nerve in the pelvis is mandatory in all patients who present with neuralgia of the groin without a history of inguinal surgery or trauma to the region.

References

1. Waldman SD: Ilioinquinal neuralgia. In: Common Pain Syndromes. Philadelphia, WB Saunders 2002, p 192.
2. Cunningham J, Temple WJ, Mitchell PM: Postoperative hernia study: Pain in the postrepair patient. Ann Surg 224:598, 1996.
3. Smith SE, DeLee JC, Ramamurthy S: Ilioinguinal neuralgia following iliac bone-grafting. J Bone Joint Surg Am 66:1306, 1984.
4. Waldman SD: Ilioinquinal nerve block. In: Atlas of Interventional Pain Management, 2nd ed. Philadelphia, WB Saunders, 2004, p 294.
5. Bonica JJ: Iliohypogastric, ilioinguinal, and genitofemoral neuralgia. In: The Management of Pain. Philadelphia, Lea & Febiger, 1990, p 1388.
6. Waldman SD: Iliohypogastric nerve block. In: Atlas of Interventional Pain Management, 2nd ed. Philadelphia, Saunders, 2004, p 298.
7. Harms BA, DeHaas DH, Starling RK: Diagnosis and management of genitofemoral neuralgia. Arch Surg 119:1106, 1984.
8. Waldman SD: Genitofemoral neuralgia. In: Common Pain Syndromes. Philadelphia, WB Saunders, 2002, p 196.
9. Waldman SD: Genitofemoral nerve block. In: Atlas of Interventional Pain Management, 2nd ed. Philadelphia, WB Saunders, 2004, p 301.

Index

A

A fibers, 155, 156t
  alpha, 156t
  beta, 11-12, 12f, 12t, 13, 13f, 13t, 156t
  delta, 11-12, 12f, 12t, 13, 13f, 13t, 156t, 1081
  in acupuncture, 1095
Abdominal aortic aneurysm
  femoral neuropathy due to, 872
  imaging of, 730f, 755
  low back pain in, 755
  treatment of, 755
Abdominal exercises. *See also* Exercises.
  for low back pain, 1061-1062, 1062f
  for sacroiliac disorders, 815
Abdominal hysterectomy, femoral neuropathy after, 873
Abdominal pain. *See also* Abdominal wall pain.
  after celiac plexus block, 1278
  celiac plexus block for, 1265-1279
  cryoanalgesia for, 1469
  hypnosis for, 1022
  in acute pancreatitis, 737-739, 738f, 739f
  in chronic pancreatitis, 739-741, 739f, 740f
  in ilioinguinal neuralgia, 742-745
  in liver disease, 732-736, 734f-736f
  management of, limitations of, 1001, 1001t
  postoperative, ilioinguinal-iliohypogastric block for, 1322-1323
  relaxation techniques for, 1027
  transcutaneous electrical nerve stimulation for, 1053
Abdominal splinting
  in anterior cutaneous nerve entrapment, 729, 730f
  in liver pain, 733
Abdominal surgery, pulmonary complications in, 709-710
Abdominal viscera, innervation of, 1266-1268, 1266f-1268f
Abdominal wall pain, 727-736. *See also* Abdominal pain.
  in anterior cutaneous nerve entrapment, 727-731
  in liver disease, 732-736
  in slipping rib syndrome, 731-732, 732f, 733f
Abducens nerve
  anatomy of, 408f
  examination of, 42-43, 44t
Abducens nerve palsy, 407t, 409, 409t, 410
Abrasions, corneal, 524-525, 525f

Abscess
  brain
    headache in, 264-265
    in mastoiditis, 543, 544f
    treatment of, 266
  dental, 543
  epidural
    after cervical epidural block, 1218
    after implantable drug delivery device placement, 1391
    after lumbar epidural block, 1292
    after thoracic epidural block, 1247
    postoperative, 822
  iliac, femoral neuropathy due to, 872
  lung, 707
    bacterial, 704, 705f, 706, 706f
  pharyngeal space, 543, 546f
Abstinence syndrome. *See* Withdrawal.
Acetaminophen, 931-932. *See also* Nonsteroidal antiinflammatory drugs.
  adverse effects of, 932
  dosing guidelines for, 931
  drug interactions with, 932
  for cancer pain, 318-319, 319t
  for sickle cell pain, 259-260
  for tension-type headache, 470, 471t
  indications for, 932
  mechanism of action of, 931
  overdose of, 932
  pharmacokinetics of, 932
Acetazolamide
  for arachnoiditis, 796
  for pseudotumor cerebri, 267
Acetylaldehyde syndrome, celiac plexus block and, 1279
N-Acetylcysteine, 932
  for complex regional pain syndrome, 294t, 295
Acetylsalicylic acid. *See* Aspirin.
Achilles bursitis, 398-399, 916
Achilles tendinitis, 398, 399, 915
  prolotherapy for, 1116, 1116f, 1117f
Achilles tendinosis, prolotherapy for, 1116, 1116f, 1117f
Achilles tendon
  rupture of, 915-916
  stretching exercises for, for plantar fasciitis, 924
Acoustic nerve, examination of, 42-43, 44t
Acoustic neuroma, brain stem auditory evoked potentials from, 193, 193f
Acquired immunodeficiency syndrome. *See* Human immunodeficiency virus infection.
Acromial spurs, in rotator cuff disorders, 603, 608, 609f

Acromioclavicular joint
  anatomy of, 616f
  painful, 605, 608, 615-618
  subluxation of
    grading of, 79-80
    radiography of, 79-80
Actinomycosis, 706
Action-neuromatrix, 7, 9
Action potential
  conduction of, measurement of, 184-186
  generation of, 181, 182, 1087-1088
  in nerve conduction studies, 182
Active compression test, for rotator cuff tears, 607-608
Acupuncture, 991t, 994, 1093-1102. *See also* Complementary and alternative therapies.
  acupoints in, 1095-1096, 1096f
  adverse effects of, 1101-1102
  anatomic aspects of, 1095-1097
  auricular, 1098
  channels and collaterals in, 1096-1097
  complications and pitfalls in, 1101-1102
  credentialing for, 1102
  De Qi sensation in, 1095, 1097
  efficacy of, 1100-1101, 1100t
  electroacupuncture, 1097-1098
  for arachnoiditis, 796
  for cancer pain, 1100-1101
  for chronic pain, 220
  for connective tissue diseases, 1100, 1100t
  for dysmenorrhea, 1100, 1100t
  for low back pain, 1100, 1100t
  for lumbar radiculopathy, 765
  for neck pain, 1100, 1100t
  for oocyte aspiration, 1100, 1100t
  for osteoarthritis, 1100, 1100t
  for phantom pain, 311
  for pyriformis syndrome, 835
  for tennis elbow, 1100, 1100t
  history of, 1093-1094
  mechanisms of
    bioelectromagnetic, 1097
    neurohormonal, 1095
    viscerocutaneous, 1096
  morphogenetic singularity theory and, 1095
  moxibustion and, 1098-1099
  naloxone reversal of, 1095
  patient education about, 1102, 1102t
  principles of, 1094-1095
  scalp, 1098
  studies of, 1101
  techniques of, 1097-1098
  yin-yang theory and, 1094-1095, 1094f
Acupuncture points, anatomic aspects of, 1095-1096

Acute chest syndrome, in sickle cell disease, 257, 258t, 702-703
Acute lung injury, 710
Acute pain
  management of
    inadequate, reasons for, 225
    nerve blocks in, 229-237, 238t. *See also* Nerve blocks, for acute/postoperative pain.
    nonsteroidal antiinflammatory drugs in, 226-227
    opioids in, 227-229
    prevention of, 225
Acute pancreatitis, 71, 737-739, 738f, 739f
  celiac plexus block for, 1265
  diagnosis of, 71
  epidural nerve block for, 1244
Acute phase response, 66-68, 66f
  C-reactive protein in, 56-57
  erythrocyte sedimentation rate in, 56-57
Acute respiratory distress syndrome (ARDS), vs. acute chest syndrome, 703
Acyclovir, for herpes zoster, 281
Adamkiewicz's artery, inadvertent injection of, in celiac plexus block, 1278
Addiction. *See also* Drug abuse/dependency; Tolerance.
  dopamine in, 946-947, 947f
  to opioids, 946-947
  vs. dependency, 323
  withdrawal in. *See* Withdrawal.
Adductor origin, prolotherapeutic injection of, 1119, 1119f
Adductor spasticity, obturator nerve block for, 1331
Adductor tendinitis, 391-395, 393f-395f
Adhesions
  epidural
    endoscopic lysis of, 172
    lysis of, 1345-1349. *See also* Epidural adhesiolysis.
  failed back surgery syndrome and, 824-826, 825f, 826f
Adrenaline. *See* Epinephrine.
Adson test, in cervical radiculopathy, 571, 572t
Aerobic training, 1056, 1056t, 1058. *See also* Exercise.
Affective-motivational pain dimension, 17-18, 18f, 197, 198
Afferent line labeling, 17
Afferents. *See also* Pain processing system.
  activation of, 21, 22f
  dorsal horn projections of, 13, 13f, 13t
  in tissue injury, 21-22, 22f, 23f, 23t
  neurotransmitters in, 19-20, 19f, 19t
  primary, 11-12, 12f, 13, 13f
  secondary, 13-15, 13f, 13t, 14f
  sprouting of, in nerve injury, 26-28, 27f, 344, 556, 792, 792f, 1084
  supraspinal projections of, 15-16, 16f, 17f
Agranulocytosis, drug-induced, 58
AIDS. *See* Human immunodeficiency virus infection.
Alanine aminotransferase, 70
Alarms, for implantable drug delivery systems, 1398
Albumin, serum, 66
  in liver disease, 71
Alcohol
  for neurolytic blockade, 232-233, 344-345, 344t, 346, 347t. *See also* Neurolytic blockade.
    in glossopharyngeal neuralgia, 346, 347t
    subarachnoid, 1296-1299, 1297f-1298f

Alcohol *(Continued)*
    toxicity of, 73, 345, 347t
    vs. phenol, 346, 347t
    for pituitary neuroadenolysis, 1409, 1409f
Alcohol intoxication, from celiac plexus block, 1279
Alcohol neuropathy, 67t
Alcohol use/abuse
  acute pancreatitis and, 737-739, 738f
  chronic pancreatitis and, 739-741
  cluster headache and, 478, 480
  screening for, 73
    CAGE questionnaire in, 362
Aldehyde dehydrogenase deficiency, celiac plexus block and, 1279
Alendronate, for complex regional pain syndrome, 294, 294t
Alfentanil, 948t, 953f, 956. *See also* Opioid(s).
Allachesthesia, after cordotomy, 1512-1513
Allergy
  to contrast media
    in diskography, 124
    in epidurography, 147-148
  to local anesthetics, 986
  to prolotherapy solutions, 1110
Allesthesia, after cordotomy, 1512-1513
Allochira, 9
  after percutaneous cordotomy, 1512-1513
Allodynia
  definition of, 218
  pathophysiology of, 556
  tactile, 12, 26, 29
Almotriptan. *See also* Triptans.
  for migraine, 460
Alopecia, in discoid lupus erythematosus, 438, 439f
Alpha₂ adrenergic agonists, mechanism of action of, 31
Alpha antagonists, mechanism of action of, 28-29
Alpha globulins, 66, 66f
Alternative medicine. *See* Complementary and alternative therapies.
Ambrose, James, 93
American Association of Neuromuscular and Electrodiagnostic Medicine, 179, 190
American Osteopathic Foundation, 1075
Amines, in tissue injury, 23t
Amitriptyline, 967. *See also* Antidepressants.
  as prototypical tricyclic antidepressant, 965, 966f, 967
  for cancer pain, 323
  for chronic pain, 219
  for intercostal neuralgia, 683
  for medication-overuse headache, 493
  for migraine prophylaxis, 461
  for mononeuritis multiplex, 725
  for peripheral neuropathy, 277, 277t
  for phantom pain, 309
  for post-thoracotomy syndrome, 682
  for proctalgia fugax, 851-852
  for vulvodynia, 844
  side effects of, 718t
  structure of, 966
Ammonia, in hepatic encephalopathy, 71
Ammonium salts, for neurolytic blockade, 346
Amphetamines, screening for, 72
Amputation, phantom pain after, 304-312. *See also* Phantom pain/sensation.
Amygdala, projections into, 16, 17f
Amylase, serum
  in acute pancreatitis, 737
  in chronic pancreatitis, 740
Amyloidosis, 67t

Anal pain
  cryoanalgesia for, 1468
  in proctalgia fugax, 851-852, 852f
    vs. coccydynia, 848
Analgesic(s). *See also* specific indications and agents.
  advantages and disadvantages of, 998-999
  for cancer pain, 997, 998
  limitations of, 997-1001
  opioid. *See* Opioid(s).
  preemptive, 24
  risk-benefit ratio for, 997
  simple (over-the-counter), 927-932. *See also* Acetaminophen; Nonsteroidal antiinflammatory drugs; Simple analgesics.
  classification of, 928t
  overview of, 927-928
Analgesic diskography, 122, 138. *See also* Diskography.
Analgesic ladder (WHO), 349, 350f, 370, 371f
Analgesic rebound headache. *See* Medication-overuse headache.
Anaphylaxis. *See also* Allergy.
  in prolotherapy, 1110
Anemia
  diagnosis of, 57
  differential diagnosis of, 57
  in temporal arteritis, 62
  iron deficiency, diagnosis of, 57
  pernicious, diagnosis of, 64
  sickle cell. *See* Sickle cell disease.
Anesthesia
  general, brachial plexopathy during, 583-584
  local, 983-988. *See also* Local anesthetics.
  nerve blocks for. *See* Nerve blocks.
Anesthesia dolorosa, after trigeminal nerve block, 1160
Anesthesia/hypesthesia
  after alcohol neurolysis, 345
  corneal, after percutaneous therapy, for trigeminal neuralgia, 356
  facial, after percutaneous therapy, for trigeminal neuralgia, 356
  neuraxial, arachnoiditis due to, 791
Aneurysm(s)
  abdominal aortic. *See* Abdominal aortic aneurysm.
  carotid artery, of cavernous sinus, 532-533, 533f
  cavernous sinus, 410, 410f, 532-533, 533f
  cerebral
    magnetic resonance angiography of, 264
    rupture of
      headache in, 264
      treatment of, 266
  pulmonary artery, 704, 704f
Aneurysmal bone cyst, thoracic myelopathy due to, 690, 691f
Anger, in cancer, 369
Angina
  creatine kinase in, 71
  spinal cord stimulation for, 1379
  sympathectomy for, 358-359, 358f, 359f
  thoracic epidural nerve block for, 1244
Angiofibroblastic hyperplasia, in rotator cuff disorders, 604
Angiography, magnetic resonance. *See* Magnetic resonance angiography.
Angioplasty, percutaneous carotid, celiac plexus block for, 1189
Angle-closure glaucoma, 525-528, 526t, 528f

Ankle
    anatomy of, 911, 913f
    effusion in, 912
    radiography of, 83-84
Ankle pain
    anatomic aspects of, 911, 913f
    causes of, 912-913, 912t
    classification of, 912t
    cryoanalgesia for, 1469
    diagnosis of, 911
    in Achilles bursitis, 398-399, 399f, 400f
    in Achilles tendinitis, 398, 399, 915
    in Achilles tendon rupture, 915-916
    in arthritis, 84, 911-914
    in bursitis, 398-399, 400f, 911, 914, 916
    in deltoid ligament strain, 397-398, 398f
    nerve blocks for, 238t, 1367
Ankle sprains
    deltoid ligament, 397-398, 398f
    osteopathic manipulative treatment for,
        1078
    prolotherapy for, 1116-1117, 1117f
Ankylosing spondylitis, 753-755, 754f
    demographic factors in, 38t
Ankylosis, sternoclavicular, 689f
Annuloplasty, intradiskal electrothermal. See
    Intradiskal electrothermal annuloplasty.
Annulus fibrosus. See Intervertebral disk.
Anorectal pain
    cryoanalgesia for, 1468
    in proctalgia fugax, 851-852, 852f
    vs. coccydynia, 848
Anorexia, in cancer, 366
Anserine bursitis, prolotherapy for, 1115
Anterior apprehension test, for rotator cuff
    tears, 606-607, 607f
Anterior cingulate cortex, projections into, 16,
    17, 17f, 18f
Anterior cruciate ligament
    anatomy of, 884, 885f
    anterior drawer test for, 890-891, 891f
Anterior cutaneous nerve, anatomy of, 727,
    728f, 729
Anterior cutaneous nerve entrapment, 727-
    731
Anterior drawer test
    for anterior cruciate ligament tears, 890-891,
        891f
    for talofibular ligament tears, 912
Anterior horn cell disorders, electrodiagnosis
    of, 189
Anterior interosseous syndrome, 653-655, 654f,
    655f
    electrodiagnosis of, 188
Anterior sacroiliac ligament, anatomy of, 810,
    811f
Anterior scalene syndrome, 582-583, 584f
Anterior talofibular ligament, prolotherapeutic
    injection of, 1117, 1117f
Anterocollis, 591. See also Cervical dystonia.
Antianxiety agents
    for burn pain, 243t, 244, 246, 253
    for herpes zoster, 281
Antiarrhythmics
    for cancer pain, 324
    for chronic pain, 220
    for facial reflex sympathetic dystrophy, 557-
        559
    for mononeuritis multiplex, 725
    for neuropathic pain, 718
    for peripheral neuropathy, 277t
Antibiotics, prophylactic
    for diskography, 124
    for epidural adhesiolysis, 1346
Antibodies, 58

Anticoagulants
    aspirin and, 929-930
    for pulmonary embolism, 704
    international normalized ratio for, 59
    preoperative management of
        for cervical facet block, 1200
        for epidural adhesiolysis, 1346
        for implantable drug delivery devices, 1389
    prothrombin time and, 59
Anticonvulsants, 972-976
    category 1, 972-975, 973t
        mechanism of action of, 972
        types of, 972-975
    category 2, 972, 973t, 975-976
    classification of, 972, 973t
    for chronic pain, 219, 717-718
    for facial reflex sympathetic dystrophy, 559
    for glossopharyngeal neuralgia, 512-514,
        513t, 514t
    for herpes zoster, 281
    for medication overuse withdrawal, 499
    for migraine prophylaxis, 461
    for mononeuritis multiplex, 725
    for peripheral neuropathy, 277, 277t
    for phantom pain, 309
    for postmastectomy pain, 717-718
    for proctalgia fugax, 852
    for trigeminal neuralgia, 505-506
    for vulvodynia, 844
    side effects of, 718
    therapeutic monitoring of, 72
    toxicity of, 72
Antidepressants, 965-970. See also specific
    drugs and indications.
    classification of, 965, 966
    for anterior interosseous syndrome, 654
    for chronic pain, 219, 718, 718t
    for herpes zoster, 281
    for intercostal neuralgia, 683
    for migraine prophylaxis, 461
    for mononeuritis multiplex, 725
    for orchialgia, 840
    for peripheral neuropathy, 277, 277t
    for phantom pain, 309
    for post-thoracotomy syndrome, 682
    for postmastectomy pain, 718, 718t
    for proctalgia fugax, 851-852
    for pronator syndrome, 653
    for radial tunnel syndrome, 658
    for reflex sympathetic dystrophy, 294
        of face, 559
    for tension-type headaches, 470, 471t
    for thoracic radiculopathy, 690
    for vulvodynia, 844
    guidelines for, 970
    monoamine oxidase inhibitors, 969, 969t
        drug interactions with, 969, 970t
        food interactions with, 969, 969t
        for migraine prophylaxis, 461
        for tension-type headache, 470
    noradrenergic reuptake inhibitors, 969
    patient education for, 970
    selective serotonin reuptake inhibitors, 967-
        968
        abuse potential of, 968
        mechanism of action of, 967
        overdosage of, 968
        pharmacokinetics of, 967-968
        side effects of, 968
        types of, 968
        withdrawal symptoms with, 968
    serotonin and noradrenergic reuptake
        inhibitors, 968-969
    side effects of, 718t, 970
    tricyclic, 965-967

Antidepressants (Continued)
    abuse potential of, 966
    as prototype antidepressants, 965, 966f
    drug interactions with, 966
    mechanism of action of, 965
    overdosage of, 966-967
    pharmacokinetics of, 965-966
    prototypical, 965, 966f, 967
    side effects of, 966, 966f
    structure of, 965, 966f
    types of, 967
    withdrawal symptoms with, 966
Antidiuretic hormone, inappropriate secretion
    of, 60, 69
Antiemetics
    for cancer-related nausea, 364-365, 365f, 366
    for opioid-related nausea, 323
Antiepileptics. See Anticonvulsants.
Antihypertensives, for hypertensive headache,
    267
Antimalarial drugs, 981
    for systemic lupus erythematosus, 440
Anti–myelin-associated glycoprotein,
    neuropathy and, 64, 66
Antinuclear antibodies
    drugs affecting, 440
    in systemic lupus erythematosus, 438, 440
    tests for, 60-62
Antiseizure agents. See Anticonvulsants.
Antispasticity agents, for tension-type
    headaches, 470, 471t
Antiviral agents, for herpes zoster, 281
Anulus fibrosus
    anatomy of, 119-120, 119f, 120f
    tears of, 109
Anxiety, 198, 215, 217. See also Psychological
    factors.
    antidepressants for, 219
    biofeedback for, 1011. See also Biofeedback.
    drug therapy for. See Anxiolytics.
    in burn patients, 243t, 244-245, 246, 253
    in cancer, 367, 369
    in chronic pain, 1004, 1008
    in complex regional pain syndrome, 285-286
    in medication-overuse headache, 497, 499-
        500
    in vulvodynia, 845
    psychotherapy for, 1004-1008
    relaxation-induced, 1018, 1031
Anxiolytics
    for burn pain, 243t, 244, 246, 253
    for herpes zoster, 281
Aortic aneurysm, abdominal. See Abdominal
    aortic aneurysm.
Aortic dissection, in temporal arteritis, 520
Apnea, sleep, after cordotomy, 1501, 1513-1514
Appetite loss, in cancer, 366
Apprehension test, anterior, for rotator cuff
    tears, 606-607, 607f
Aquatic therapy, 1043. See also Hydrotherapy.
Arachnoidal cysts, in failed back surgery
    syndrome, 819-820, 820f
Arachnoiditis, 55, 791-798
    after intrathecal steroid injections, 339
    causes of, 791-792
    clinical features of, 794-795
    definition of, 791
    diagnosis of, 792-795, 792f
    electrodiagnostic studies in, 792-793
    epidural adhesiolysis and, 1345
    epiduroscopy in, 793
    failed back surgery syndrome and, 823-826,
        825f, 826f
    imaging studies in, 793-794, 793f-795f, 795
    laboratory findings in, 792

Arachnoiditis *(Continued)*
  lesion localization in, 795
  myeloscopy in, 793
  pain characteristics in, 794
  pain mechanisms in, 792
  prevention of, 795
  treatment of, 795-798
Arch sprains, prolotherapy for, 1117, 1117f
ARDS (acute respiratory distress syndrome), vs.
    acute chest syndrome, 703
Aretaeus, 455, 456
Arm. *See* Upper extremity.
Arrhythmias
  in cluster headache, 477-478
  opioid-induced, 945, 945f
Arsenic poisoning, 67t
Arteries, epidural vessels, 1212, 1212f
Arteritis, temporal. *See* Temporal arteritis.
Artery of Adamkiewicz, inadvertent injection
    of, in celiac plexus block, 1278
Arthritis
  biofeedback for, 1011. *See also* Biofeedback.
  cold application in. *See* Cold application.
  crystal, 70
    vs. osteoarthritis, 424
  degenerative. *See* Osteoarthritis.
  heat application in. *See* Heat application.
  hydrotherapy for, 1037, 1037f, 1040, 1046,
    1049-1050
  in systemic lupus erythematosus, 435, 438
  infectious, of shoulder, 615
  Jaccoud, 438
  menopausal, 420
  of hip, 419-420, 422t
    total joint replacement for, 86, 428
  of knee, 81-83, 83f, 419, 419f. *See also*
    Knee, osteoarthritis of.
  of sacrococcygeal joint, 848
  of sacroiliac joint, 810-815, 1358-1361
  of wrist, 660-662, 660t
  prolotherapy for, 1107-1108
  relaxation techniques for, 1026-1207
Arthritis Self-Management Program, 1026
Arthrography, magnetic resonance, 106-107
Arthroscopic débridement and lavage, for
    osteoarthritis, 428
Arthroscopic subacromial decompression, 610-
    611, 611f
Arthroscopic surgery, for rotator cuff tears, 610-
    611, 611f, 612f
Asbestos bodies, 697, 698f
Asbestos-related pleural disease, 695-701, 699f,
    700f
Asbestosis, 695, 698f
Ascending spinal tracts, 212-213, 1085-1086
  anatomy of, 15, 16f, 213f
  functions of, 17-18
  plasticity of, 18, 1085-1086, 1089
Asian medicine. *See* Chinese medicine.
Aspartate, 19t, 20
Aspartate aminotransferase, 70
Aspiration risk, with botulinum neurotoxin, 593,
    595
Aspirin, 928-930, 935. *See also* Nonsteroidal
    antiinflammatory drugs.
  advantages of, 928
  anticoagulants and, 929-930
  buffered, 935
  cervical facet block and, 1200
  contraindications to, 929, 930, 935
  dosing guidelines for, 929, 935
  drug interactions with, 929, 930, 935
  for cancer pain, 318-319, 319t
  for tension-type headache, 470, 471t
  indications for, 930

Aspirin *(Continued)*
  mechanism of action of, 928-929, 935
  pharmacokinetics of, 929-930, 935
  Reye syndrome and, 929, 930, 935
  side effects of, 930, 935
  structure of, 226f, 935f
Assistive devices, for rheumatoid arthritis, 437
Association for Applied Psychophysiology and
    Biofeedback (AAPB), 1011
Astrocytes
  in nerve injury, 28
  in tissue injury, 25-26
Atelectasis, postoperative, 709-710
Athletic injuries. *See* Sports injuries.
Atlanto-occipital nerve block, 1128-1131, 1130f,
    1131f
Atlantoaxial instability
  in rheumatoid arthritis, 437, 437f
  radiography of, 74-75
Atlantoaxial nerve block, 1131, 1132-1133
Auditory evoked potentials, brain stem, 193
Aura
  in cluster headache, 477
  in migraine headache, 457-458
    persistent, 459
Auricular acupuncture, 1098
Auriculotemporal nerve, 538, 540f, 1148, 1155
  cryoablation of, 1471
Auriculotemporal nerve block, 238t
Autogenic training, 1015, 1025-1031. *See also*
    Relaxation techniques.
  technique of, 1028-1029
Autoimmune disease. *See also* Connective
    tissue diseases.
  diagnosis of, 60-62, 67t
  neuropathy in, 64-66, 67t
Autonomic nervous system, anatomy of, 1266-
    1268, 1266f-1268f
Autonomic reflex testing, 276
Avascular necrosis. *See* Osteonecrosis.
Axillary artery, inadvertent injection of, in
    musculocutaneous nerve block, 1237
Axillary brachial plexus block, 1224-1226,
    1225f
Axillary nerve, 46t
  anatomy of, 578f, 579f, 580
Axillary node dissection, postmastectomy pain
    and, 716
Axillary plexus block, for cancer pain, 339
Axolemma, 343
Axon(s). *See also* Nerve fibers.
  A-alpha, 156t
  A-beta, 11-12, 12f, 12t, 13, 13f, 13t, 156t
  A-delta, 11-12, 12f, 12t, 13, 13f, 13t, 156t,
    1081
    in acupuncture, 1095
  conduction velocity of, 11
  diffuse injury of, imaging of, 107
  primary/secondary afferent, 11-13, 12t, 13f,
    13t. *See also* Afferents.
Axon reflex, 1083
Axon sprouting, 26-28, 27f, 344, 556, 792,
    792f, 1084, 1087-1088
Axonotmesis, 186, 580f, 581
Azotemia, diagnosis of, 68-69

B
B cells, 58
B fibers, 155, 156t
Babinski sign, 47
  in peripheral neuropathy, 272
Back brace. *See* Bracing.
Back exercises. *See* Exercises.

Back pain. *See also specific sites and disorders.*
  cauda equina syndrome and, 750-751
  cervical. *See* Neck pain.
  euphemistic, 780-781
  lumbar. *See* Low back pain.
  occupational, 777-790. *See also*
    Occupational back pain.
  persistent postoperative. *See* Failed back
    surgery syndrome.
  prolotherapy for, 1119-1120, 1119f-1121f
Back school, 764, 765
Backpack paralysis, 583
Baclofen, 980
  for chronic pain, 220
  for cluster headache, 487
  for complex regional pain syndrome, 294,
    294t
  for glossopharyngeal neuralgia, 513-514,
    514t
  for tension-type headache, 470, 471t
Bacterial infections, leukocytosis in, 58
Bacterial meningitis. *See also* Meningitis.
  cerebrospinal fluid findings in, 264
  headache in, 263t, 264, 266
  treatment of, 263t, 264, 266
Baker's cyst, 903-905, 904f
  in rheumatoid arthritis and, 431, 433f
Ball catcher's view, 80
Balloon compression, for trigeminal neuralgia,
    353-356, 354f, 355f, 506-507
Balloon kyphoplasty, 1477-1480, 1478f, 1479f,
    1481f
Balloon sign, in digital arthritis, 662
Ballottement test, 889-890, 889f
Bannwarth's syndrome, 64
Barbiturates, for seizure prophylaxis, in
    medication overuse withdrawal, 499
Barr, Joseph Seaton, 758, 759f
Barré-Liéou syndrome, prolotherapy for, 1121-
    1122, 1122f
Basal cell carcinoma, of ear, 541, 541f
Basic calcium phosphate arthropathy, vs.
    osteoarthritis, 424
Basilar-type migraine, 458-459, 458t. *See also*
    Migraine.
Bath(s). *See also* Hydrotherapy.
  contrast, 1041, 1041f, 1050
  whirlpool
    iced, 1040, 1049-1050
    warm/hot, 1037, 1037f, 1049-1050
Bathed length principle, 155
Beatles, 93
Beck's Inventory of Depression and Anxiety
  in medication-overuse headache, 497
  in tension-type headache, 468
Bed rest, 1055-1056
  for lumbar radiculopathy, 764
Behavioral therapy
  for chronic pain, 218, 1005
  for lumbar radiculopathy, 765
  for occupational back pain, 782
Bell's palsy, 409t, 412
Belly-press test, 605
Bence Jones proteins, 68
Benign fibrous mesothelioma, 701
Benign intracranial hypertension
  headache in, 265
  treatment of, 267
Benzodiazepines
  abuse potential of, 980
  for burn pain, 243t, 244, 246
  side effects of, 980
Beta blockers, for migraine prophylaxis,
    461
Beta globulins, 66, 66f

Betamethasone. *See also* Corticosteroids.
  for epidural adhesiolysis, 1347, 1348
  intralesional
      for scapulocostal syndrome, 631, 632f
      for trochanteric bursitis, 861
Biceps, Popeye, 381, 381f
Biceps tendinitis, 380-382, 381f, 382f, 622-626
  prolotherapy for, 1111, 1112f
Biceps tendon rupture, 381, 381f, 625
Biceps weakness, in cervical radiculopathy, 571
Bier's block, for complex regional pain
      syndrome, 295
Biliary disease, diagnosis of, 70-71
Biliary obstruction, 71
Bilirubin, elevated, 70-71
Bioelectromagnetic therapy, 991t, 994-995. *See
      also* Complementary and alternative
      therapies.
Biofeedback, 1010-1019
  adaptation phase of, 1015-1016
  applied, 1010
  autogenic, 1015
  baseline phase of, 1016
  biomedical engineering and, 1011
  cybernetics and, 1011
  definition of, 1010
  drug effects in, 1018
  duration of therapy with, 1018
  efficacy of, 1011-1013, 1012t
  electromyography-assisted, 1011, 1012,
      1013-1016, 1014f
  for anxiety, 1011
  for arthritis, 1011-1012
  for cystic fibrosis, 1012
  for depression, 1011
  for fibromyalgia, 1012
  for low back pain, 1011-1012
  for migraine, 461-462, 1012, 1015
  for phantom pain, 1013
  for Raynaud disease/phenomenon, 1012-
      1013
  for repetitive strain injuries, 1013
  for temporomandibular joint disorders, 1013
  for tension-type headache, 470-472, 1012
  historical perspective on, 1010-1011
  in muscle discrimination, 1016-1017
  in muscle relearning therapy, 1013
  in muscle scanning, 1016
  in psychophysiologic assessment, 1015-1017
  indications for, 1011-1013
  indirect approach in, 1017-1018
  patient education in, 1017-1018
  patient selection for, 1017-1018
  practitioner/patient considerations in, 1017-
      1018
  psychophysiology and, 1011
  reactivity phase of, 1016
  recovery phase of, 1016
  relaxation-induced anxiety in, 1018, 1031
  resources for, 1018-1019
  side effects and complications of, 1018
  skill learning and maintenance in, 1017-1018
  skin conductance–assisted, 1015
  skin temperature–assisted, 1015
  techniques of, 1013-1018
      general approach in, 1013-1015
      specific approaches in, 1015-1017
  Trojan horse aspect of, 1017
Biomedical engineering, biofeedback and, 1011
Biopsy, temporal artery, 519-520, 520t
Biopsychosocial treatment model, 499, 500f
Biostimulation techniques, 994
Birk, Lee, 1011
Bisphosphonate disodium clodronate, for
      trochanteric bursitis, 862

Bisphosphonates, for bone metastases, 332
Bites, tick, knee pain and, 888-889
Bladder catheterization, after spinal opioids,
      351, 352t
Blastomycosis, 707
Bleeding. *See also* Hemorrhage.
  from implantable drug delivery systems,
      1389-1390
  nasal, from sphenopalatine ganglion block,
      230
Blepharitis, 524, 524f
Blindness. *See also* Visual disturbances.
  in temporal arteritis, 518
Blood, in Chinese medicine, 1094, 1096-1097
Blood tests, 57-59
Blood urea nitrogen (BUN), 68
Body-self neuromatrix, 4-7, 5f, 9
Bodywork, Chinese, 1099
Bombesin, 19, 19t, 20
Bone contusions, magnetic resonance imaging
      of, 112
Bone cyst, aneurysmal, thoracic myelopathy due
      to, 690, 691f
Bone graft, iliac crest donor site pain after,
      cryoanalgesia for, 1465, 1465f, 1471-1473,
      1472t
Bone infarcts, in sickle cell disease, 257
Bone marrow
  characteristics of, 111
  edema-like lesions of, 111-112, 113f, 114f
  magnetic resonance imaging of, 111-112,
      113f, 114f
Bone marrow transplant, for sickle cell disease,
      260
Bone metastases. *See also* Cancer pain.
  bisphosphonates for, with radiation therapy,
      324
  imaging of, 86, 87f, 328-330, 329f
  radiation therapy for, 328-333. *See also*
      Radiation therapy, palliative.
  rib, 678, 680f
  vertebral, 751-753
Bone scintigraphy, 85, 86-91
  in cancer, 86
  in complex regional pain syndrome, 86, 88f-
      89f, 291, 292f
  of face, 557
  in joint prosthesis imaging, 86
  in osteoarthritis, 422-423
      of spine, 89-91, 91f
  in palliative radiation, 328-330, 329f
  in spondylolysis, 86-89, 90f-91f, 803-805,
      804t
  in vertebral metastasis, 751-752
Bone spurs
  in rotator cuff disorders, 603, 608, 609f
  in spinal osteoarthritis, 756, 756f
Bone tumors, imaging of
  CT in, 102
  FDG-PET in, 85-86
  radionuclide, 85
Borrelia burgdorferi, 64
Botulinum neurotoxin
  aspiration risk with, 593, 595
  dysphagia due to, 593, 595
  for cervical dystonia, 591, 593, 594-595,
      595t
  for fibromyalgia, 405
  for migraine prophylaxis, 461
  for tension-type headache, 472, 472t
  mechanism of action of, 594
Bouchard nodes, 80, 420, 420f, 434, 435f, 662
Boutonnière deformity, 434, 434f, 662, 662f
Brace. *See* Bracing.
Brachial neuritis, 407t, 414-415, 414f

Brachial plexopathy, 577-590
  anatomic aspects of, 577-580, 578f, 579f
  classification of, 581t
  clinical features of, 581-586
  complications of, 589
  diagnosis of, 586-588, 587t, 588t
  historical perspective on, 577
  iatrogenic, 582t, 583-585, 585t
  imaging studies in, 585, 585f, 588
  in coracopectoral syndrome, 583
  in costoclavicular syndrome, 583
  in Parsonage-Turner syndrome, 414-415,
      414f, 585-586, 586f
  in pectoralis minor syndrome, 593
  in thoracic outlet syndrome, 582-583, 584f
  information sources for, 589-590
  lesion sites in, 581t
      identification of, 586-588, 587t
  lower, 582
  neoplastic, 582t, 585, 586f
  nerve vs. muscle involvement in, 587t
  pathophysiology of, 580f, 581
  prognosis of, 589
  radiation, 584-585, 585t
  severity of, 581
  stingers in, 582, 583f
  support groups for, 589-590
  traumatic, 581t, 582-583
  treatment of, 588-589
  upper, 581-582
  with Horner syndrome, 582
  with superior sulcus tumors, radiation
      therapy for, 332-333
Brachial plexus
  anatomy of, 577-580, 578f, 579f, 1176f,
      1220, 1221f, 1223f, 1225f
  tumors of, 582t, 585, 586f
Brachial plexus block, 1220-1226
  anatomic aspects of, 1220, 1221f
  axillary, 1224-1226, 1225f
  differential, 160
  historical perspective on, 1220
  inadvertent, in stellate ganglion block, 1197
  indications for, 238t
  interscalene, 1220-1222
  supraclavicular, 1222-1224, 1223f
  with medial brachial cutaneous nerve block,
      1237, 1237f
Brachytherapy, vs. radiofrequency techniques,
      1412
Bracing. *See also* Orthotics; Splints.
  for low back pain, 1061
  for lumbar radiculopathy, 764
  for osteoarthritis, 426
  for sacroiliac joint disorders, 814
Bradycardia
  in sphenopalatine ganglion block, 1138
  opioid-induced, 945, 945f
Bradykinin, in tissue injury, 23t
Braid, James, 1021
Brain. *See also under* Cerebral.
  neuromatrix in, 5-7, 5f
Brain abscess
  headache in, 264-265
  in mastoiditis, 543, 544f
  treatment of, 266
Brain metastases, radiation therapy for, 333
Brain stem auditory evoked potentials, 193
Brain tumors
  diagnosis of, brain stem auditory evoked
      potentials in, 193
  headache and, 265
      cluster, 483-484
Breakthrough pain, 999-1000
  in burn patients, 242, 242f

Breast cancer
  pleural effusion in, 701, 701f
  postmastectomy pain in, 716-719
Breathing techniques, 1028. *See also* Relaxation
    techniques.
  for burn pain, 250
Bretylium, in intravenous regional
    sympatholysis, for complex regional pain
    syndrome, 295
Brief Pain Inventory, 203, 204f
Bronchitis
  acute, 704
  chronic, 707-708
Brown-Séquard syndrome, 690, 691f
Bruce, William, 449
Brudzinski sign, 264, 1391
Bruxism, prolotherapy for, 1111
Buccal nerve, 540f
Buccinator nerve, 1148, 1155
Bulbospinal systems, in tissue injury, 25
BUN (blood urea nitrogen), 68
Bunion, 920
  prolotherapy for, 1118
  tailor's, 921
Bunionectomy, 921
Bunionette, 921
Bupivacaine. *See also* Local anesthetics.
  for epidural adhesiolysis, 1347, 1348
  for epidural nerve block
    for phantom pain prevention, 308
    with methylprednisolone, 236
  for intercostal nerve block, 1257
  for interpleural analgesia, 1262-1263
  for intravenous regional sympatholysis, for
    complex regional pain syndrome, 295
  for lumbar epidural nerve block, 1291
  for peri/intraneural nerve block, for complex
    regional pain syndrome, 308-309
  for stellate ganglion block, 230
  for trigeminal nerve block, 236
  in continuous regional anesthesia, for cancer
    pain, 339
  in corticosteroid injections. *See*
    Corticosteroids, intra-articular;
    Corticosteroids, intralesional.
  intrathecal, for cancer pain, 339
  introduction of, 985f
  side effects of, 987
  structure of, 983, 984f
  with spinal opioids, 1394
Buprenorphine, 948t, 960, 960f. *See also*
    Opioid(s).
Burgdorfer, Willy, 64
Burn pain, 240-254
  assessment of, 242
  background, 242, 242f
    management of, 244
  breakthrough, 242, 242f
    management of, 245
  chronic, 242
  classification of, 242
  differential diagnosis of, 242
  duration of, 242
  from first-degree burns, 240-241, 241f
  from second-degree burns, 241, 241f
  from third-degree burns, 241, 241f
  historical perspective on, 240
  management of, 242-254
    anxiolytics in, 243t, 244, 246, 253
    avoidance in, 247-249
    cognitive restructuring in, 251
    complications in, 252-254
    consistency in, 253
    coping styles in, 247, 248f, 253
    deep breathing in, 250

Burn pain *(Continued)*
    distraction techniques in, 247-249
    drug/method selection for, 244
    environmental factors in, 254
    for background pain, 244
    for breakthrough pain, 245
    for postoperative pain, 245
    for procedural pain, 244-245
    future directions in, 254
    general philosophy of, 242-244
    hydrotherapy in, 1037, 1037f, 1040, 1049-
      1050
    hypnosis in, 248-249, 254, 1022, 1023
    imagery in, 247-248
    inadequate, 243
    institutional guidelines for, 242-244, 243t
    non-opioid analgesics in, 243t, 245-246
    nonpharmacologic, 247-252
    operant techniques in, 250-251
    opioids in, 243, 243t, 245, 250
    patient-controlled analgesia in, 245
    patient participation in, 252
    patient teaching in, 251
    pharmacologic, 243t, 244-247
      complications of, 252-253
    positive reinforcement in, 250-251
    progressive muscle relaxation in, 250
    quota system in, 250
    reframing in, 251
    regular medication scheduling in, 250
    relaxation techniques in, 248, 250-251,
      1027
    sample protocols for, 243t
    sedation in, 243t, 244
    staff changeover and, 253
    thought stopping in, 251
    virtual reality in, 249, 249f
  physical findings in, 240-421
  postoperative, 242, 242f
    management of, 245
  procedural, 242, 242f
    anticipatory anxiety in, 244-245
    management of, 244-245
  psychological aspects of
    patient-related, 242, 247, 248f, 253
    provider-related, 243
  severity of, 241-242, 242f
  sleep disturbance in, 253-254
  variability in, 241-242
Burners, 582, 583f. *See also* Brachial
    plexopathy.
Bursae
  of ankle and foot, 911, 913f, 914
  of knee, 885f, 886
Bursitis
  Achilles, 398-399, 916
  anserine, prolotherapy for, 1115
  bunionette, 921
  cubital, 642-646, 645f
    corticosteroid injection for, 637, 639f, 645-
      646, 646f
  gluteal, 853-855, 854f-856f
  medial epicondylitis and, 637
  of ankle and foot, 398-399, 911, 914, 916
    Achilles, 398-399, 916
    retroachilleal, 916
    retrocalcaneal, 916
    sub-Achilles, 916
    subcutaneous calcaneal, 916
    subtendinous, 916
  of hip, 398-399
    gluteal, 853-855, 854f-856f
    iliofemoral, 864-867
    iliopectineal, 864-867
    iliopsoas, 864-867

Bursitis *(Continued)*
    ischiogluteal, 855-858, 856f, 857f
    prolotherapy for, 1115, 1115f
    subgluteal, 859
    trochanteric, 81, 390-391, 392f, 393f, 859-
      862
    with rotator cuff tears, 379, 380
  of knee, 886, 886f, 893-902
    Baker's cyst and, 903-905, 904f
    complications and pitfalls in, 902
    infrapatellar, 886, 886f, 897-900, 898f,
      899f
    pes anserine, 900-902
    prepatellar, 396-397, 397f, 895-897, 895f-
      897f
    prolotherapy for, 1115
    suprapatellar, 893-894, 894f, 895f
  olecranon, 641-642, 642f-644f, 646
    lateral epicondylitis and, 384, 635
    medial epicondylitis and, 637
  retrocalcaneal, 916
  subacromial, prolotherapy for, 1112-1113,
    1113f
  subdeltoid, 619-621, 620f
    vs. Pancoast syndrome, 694-695
  subgluteal, in trochanteric bursitis, 859
  subtendinous, 916
  suprascapular, 627-632
  therapeutic ultrasound for, 1038
  trochanteric, 81
Butorphanol, 948t, 960. *See also* Opioid(s)
Butterfly rash, in systemic lupus erythematosus,
    438, 438f
Buttock pain, in gluteal bursitis, 853-855, 854f-
    856f

C
C-fibers, 155, 156t, 1081
  activation of, 1083
  anatomy of, 11-12, 12f, 12t, 13, 13f
  in acupuncture, 1095
  in migraine, 456
  in respiratory system, 693
  in tissue injury, 21-22
  in wind-up, 22-24
C-polymodal nociceptors, 11-12, 12f
C2 rami communicans, radiofrequency
    lesioning of, 1445-1446, 1446f
C-reactive protein
  in systemic lupus erythematosus, 440
  measurement of, 56-57
Cachexia, cancer
  management of, 366
  pain management and, 1001
Caffeine, for tension-type headaches, 470, 471t
CAGE questionnaire, 362, 369
Calcaneal bursitis, 916
Calcaneal jump sign, in plantar fasciitis, 401-
    402, 401f
Calcaneal stress fractures, plantar fasciitis and,
    922-924
Calcaneofibular ligament, prolotherapeutic
    injection of, 1116-1117, 1117f
Calcifications, digital, in scleroderma, 442,
    442f
Calcitonin
  for cancer pain, 324
  for complex regional pain syndrome, 294,
    294t
  for phantom pain
    for prevention, 309
    for treatment, 310
  spinal, 1394

Calcitonin gene–related peptide (CGRP), 19, 19t, 23t, 1083, 1084f
Calcium, in central facilitation, 24, 24f
Calcium channel blockers
  for cluster headache, 485-486
  for migraine prophylaxis, 461
Calcium imbalances, 69
Calcium ion channels, in nerve injury, 1085
Calcium pyrophosphate dihydrate deposition disease, 80
  vs. osteoarthritis, 424
Calculi
  biliary
    acute pancreatitis and, 737-739
    chronic pancreatitis and, 739-741
  renal, vs. orchialgia, 838
Calf squeeze test, for Achilles tendon rupture, 916
Canal of Guyon, ulnar nerve entrapment in, 1231, 1232f
  nerve block for, 1230-1233, 1232f
Cancer
  anger in, 369
  bone metastases in
    bisphosphonates for, 324
    imaging of, 86, 87f, 328-330, 329f
    radiation therapy for, 328-333. See also Radiation therapy, palliative.
    rib, 678, 680f
    vertebral, 751-753
  brain
    diagnosis of, brain stem auditory evoked potentials in, 193
    headache and, 265
      cluster, 483-484
  brain metastases in, radiation therapy for, 333
  breast
    pleural effusion in, 701, 701f
    postmastectomy pain in, 716-719
  depression in, 326, 361, 366-367
    anger and, 369
    sleep disturbances and, 366
  imaging in
    bone scintigraphy in, 85, 86, 87f
    FDG-PET in, 85-86
  lung
    chest pain in, 694-695
    Pancoast tumors in, 694-695, 696f-697f. See also Pancoast tumors.
    peripheral neuropathy in, 64, 67t
    referred pain in, 50
    superior sulcus tumors in, 694-695
  lymphoma
    pleural effusion in, 701
    pylothorax in, 701
  nasal/nasopharyngeal, 543, 545f, 546f
    cavernous sinus invasion by, 533, 534f
  neuropathy in, 64, 67t
  ovarian, pleural effusion in, 701
  palliative care in, 360-372
    assessment in, 361-369
      cognitive, 367-369, 367f
      for pain, 361-363. See also Cancer pain.
      for physical symptoms, 363-366
      for psychological distress, 366-367
      for quality of life, 367
      instruments for, 362-363, 363f
    communication in, 369-370
    definition of, 360
    family involvement in, 369-370
    for anorexia, 366
    for anxiety, 367
    for delirium, 367-370, 368f, 368t
    for depression, 361, 366-367, 369
    for drowsiness, 366

Cancer (Continued)
    for dyspnea, 365-366
    for fatigue, 363-364
    for general well-being, 367
    for nausea, 364-365, 364t, 365f, 366
    for pain, 360-372, 1000-1001. See also Cancer pain.
    for sleep disturbances, 366
    for vertebral fractures, 1475-1482. See also Vertebral fractures.
    goals of, 360, 361t
    psychological support in, 369-370
  pancreatic
    palliative radiation therapy for, 332-333, 333f
    vs. chronic pancreatitis, 740, 741f
  prostate, screening for, 62
  vertebral fractures in. See Vertebral fractures.
Cancer cachexia
  management of, 366
  pain management and, 1001
Cancer pain, 316-352
  acupuncture for, 1100-1101
  assessment of, 317-318, 361-363
    Edmonton Staging System in, 362, 363f, 998
    multidimensional, 362-367
  brachial plexus block for, 1220
  causes of, 317t
  cordotomy for, 356, 356f, 1501-1515
  drug therapy for, 318-324, 349-350, 370, 371f
    anticonvulsants in, 323-324
    antidepressants in, 323
    corticosteroids in, 324
    COX-2 inhibitors in, 318-319, 319t
    local anesthetics in, 324
    nonsteroidal antiinflammatory drugs in, 318-319, 319t
    opioids in, 319-323, 320t, 322t, 325, 349-350, 364-365, 997, 998
      side effects of, 364-365, 365f, 366
      spinal, 325, 350-351, 351t, 352t, 370, 372t
    WHO analgesic ladder for, 349, 350f, 370, 371f
  Edmonton Staging System for, 362, 363t
  epidemiology of, 360-361
  epidural nerve block for, 1210-1218
  epidural steroid injections for, 339-340
  etiology of, 328, 349
  hypnosis for, 1022, 1023
  intrapleural catheterization for, 324
  invasive procedures for, 998
  nerve blocks for, 324-325, 337-340, 350. See also specific nerve blocks.
    corticosteroids for, 339-340
    diagnostic, 337-338, 338t
    differential, 338, 338t
    epidural catheterization for, 339
    for continuous regional anesthesia, 339
    indications for, 338, 338t
    local anesthetics for, 337-339
    neurolytic, 325-326, 343-347
    peripheral nerve catheterization for, 339
    prognostic, 338
    somatic, 338, 338t
    sympathetic, 338, 338t
    therapeutic, 338-339
  neuropathic, 362. See also Neuropathic pain.
  neurosurgery for, 353-359
  palliative care for, 360-372, 1000-1001. See also Cancer, palliative care in.
    assessment in, 361-362, 363f
    definition of, 360

Cancer pain (Continued)
    goals of, 360, 361t
      therapeutic measures in, 370-371
  physiatric approaches in, 325, 370t
  pituitary neuroadenolysis for, 1405-1410
  psychological aspects of, 326, 361
  radiation therapy in, 328-334. See also Radiation therapy, palliative.
  relaxation techniques for, 1027
  somatic, 362
  subarachnoid neurolytic block for, 1294
  treatment of, 318-326, 349-350
    efficacy of, 370, 371f
    modalities in, 370t
    palliative, 370-371, 371f
    pharmacologic. See Cancer pain, drug therapy for.
  trigger point injections for, 338-339
  types of, 317t, 362
  under-treatment of, 360-361
  visceral, 362
Candidiasis, vulvovaginal, 843, 844
Cannabinoids, for cancer cachexia, 366
Capsaicin
  for cluster headache, 488
  for facial reflex sympathetic dystrophy, 559
  for mononeuritis multiplex, 725
  for neuropathic pain, 718
  for osteoarthritis, 427
  for phantom pain, 310
  for postmastectomy pain, 718
  in nociceptor studies, 1082
Carbamazepine, 974. See also Anticonvulsants.
  for glossopharyngeal neuralgia, 512-513, 513t
  for peripheral neuropathy, 277t
  for phantom pain, 309
  for trigeminal neuralgia, 505
  hyponatremia due to, 60
  structure of, 974f
  therapeutic monitoring of, 72, 974, 974t
Carbolic acid, for neurolytic blockade, 345-346, 345t, 347t
Carbon dioxide laser, 1489, 1490f, 1491. See also Laser therapy.
Cardiac arrhythmias
  in cluster headache, 477-478
  opioid-induced, 945, 945f
Cardiac enzymes, 71
Carisoprodol, 978, 978t. See also Muscle relaxants.
  for tension-type headache, 470, 471t
  meprobamate dependency and, 38
Caroticotympanic nerve, 538, 540f
Carotid angioplasty, percutaneous, celiac plexus block for, 1189
Carotid artery aneurysms, of cavernous sinus, 532-533, 533f
Carotid body, in cluster headache, 481
Carotid-cavernous fistula, 533, 533f, 535, 535f
Carotid endarterectomy, celiac plexus block for, 1173, 1189. See also Celiac plexus block.
Carotidynia, 547
Carpal tunnel syndrome, 385-388, 385f-387f, 412-414, 664-665. See also Entrapment neuropathies.
  anatomic aspects of, 385, 385f, 664
  corticosteroid injection for, 387-388, 387f, 665
  demographic factors in, 38t
  diagnosis of, 386, 412-414, 664-665
  differential diagnosis of, 386, 387f
  electrodiagnosis of, 64-65, 188, 413, 414
  etiology of, 664
  historical perspective on, 664

Carpal tunnel syndrome (*Continued*)
idiopathic, 664
imaging studies in, 115, 386, 414, 665
in double-crush syndrome, 386, 413-414, 413f, 653
intracarpal canal pressure in, 664
magnetic resonance imaging of, 115
nerve conduction studies in, 386, 412-413, 414
Phalen test in, 385, 385f, 412, 664
rheumatoid arthritis and, 431
signs and symptoms of, 385-386, 386f, 414, 664
surgical release for, 665
thenar atrophy in, 385-386, 386f
Tinel sign in, 385, 386f, 412, 664
transcutaneous electrical nerve stimulation for, 1053
treatment of, 386-387, 414, 665
median nerve block in, 1229, 1230f, 1234f
vs. carpometacarpal arthritis, 386, 387f
vs. pronator teres syndrome, 650, 665
Carpometacarpal joint, osteoarthritis of, 418, 420. *See also* Osteoarthritis.
vs. carpal tunnel syndrome, 386, 387f
Cartilage
growth factors for, 1109. *See also* Prolotherapy.
dextrose effects on, 1108t
magnetic resonance imaging of, 115
Catheter
percutaneous, 1385, 1385f. *See also* Implantable drug delivery systems.
subcutaneous tunneled, 1385, 1385f. *See also* Implantable drug delivery systems.
totally implantable reservoir/port, 1385, 1386f
Catheter infections, in spinal cord stimulation, 1377
Catheter-tip granuloma, 797
Catheterization
bladder, after spinal opioids, 351, 352t
epidural. *See also* Epidural nerve block.
for arachnoiditis, 797
for cancer pain, 339
for caudal epidural block, 1343
for spinal opioids, 719
interpleural, 324, 1259-1263, 1260t, 1261f, 1262f
intrathecal, for cancer pain, 339
lumbar intradiscal, 1426-1429, 1427f, 1428f
periaortic, in celiac plexus block, 1275
peripheral nerve, for cancer pain, 339
ventriculopleural, 712
Cauda equina, anatomy of, 173
Cauda equina syndrome, 750-751
Caudal epidural nerve block, 1335-1344. *See also* Epidural nerve block, caudal.
Cauliflower ear, 538, 540f
Causalgia. *See* Complex regional pain syndrome, type II.
Cavernous sinus
anatomy of, 407f, 479-480
aneurysms of, 410, 410f, 532-533
in cluster headache, 479-480, 481
inflammation of, 407t, 411f
thrombosis of, 535
tumors of, 533-535, 534f
Cavernous sinus syndrome, 532-536
Cavernous sinus–carotid artery fistula, 533, 533f, 535, 535f
CD antigens, 58
CD4 count, in HIV infection, 63
Cefazolin, prophylactic, for diskography, 124, 139

Ceftriaxone, for epidural adhesiolysis, 1346
Celecoxib, 937. *See also* COX-2 inhibitors.
for arachnoiditis, 796
for tension-type headache, 470, 471t
Celiac ganglia, anatomy of, 1266f, 1267
Celiac plexopathy, in pancreatic cancer, radiation therapy for, 332-333
Celiac plexus, anatomy of, 232, 232f, 1266-1268, 1266f-1268f
Celiac plexus block, 231-232
anatomic aspects of, 1266-1268, 1266f-1268f
complications of, 232, 1277-1279
contraindications to, 1266
diagnostic, 153-154, 231-232, 1265
differential, 161-162, 161t
drugs for, 1276-1277
for acute pancreatitis, 739, 739f
for acute/postoperative pain, 231-232
for chronic pancreatitis, 739f, 741
for liver pain, 734, 735f
historical perspective on, 1265
indications for, 231-232, 1265-1266
needles for, 1277
neurolytic, 231-232, 1266, 1270
for cancer pain, 325, 326
periaortic catheterization in, 1275
radiographic guidance in, 1277
technique of, 231f, 232, 735f, 1268-1275
anterior, 1270-1273, 1274f, 1275f, 1277
classic retrocrural, 1268-1270, 1268f-1270f
selection of, 1277
transaortic, 1270-1273, 1272f, 1277
transcrural, 1270, 1277
topographic landmarks for, 1268, 1268f
with intercostal nerve block, 1250
with splanchnic nerve block, 1275-1276, 1276f
Cellulitis, after back surgery, 822
Center of gravity, 811
Central canal neurons, 13f, 13t, 14, 14f
Central nervous system. *See also* Brain; Spinal cord.
reorganization of. *See also* Neuroplasticity.
in chronic pain, 214, 217
Central pain. *See also* Chronic pain.
diagnosis of, 157, 158t
Central sensitization, in migraine, 456
Central spinal stenosis, 763, 764
Cephalothin, prophylactic, for implantable drug delivery devices, 1390
Cerebral abscess
headache in, 264-265
in mastoiditis, 543, 544f
treatment of, 266
Cerebral aneurysms
magnetic resonance angiography of, 264
rupture of
headache in, 264
treatment of, 266
Cerebral metastases. *See* Brain metastases.
Cerebritis, mastoiditis and, 543, 544f
Cerebrospinal fluid examination
in bacterial meningitis, 264
in headache, 264, 265
in pseudotumor cerebri, 265
Cerebrospinal fluid leaks
after implantable drug delivery device placement, 1391
hygroma and, 1391
in pituitary neuroadenolysis, 1410
prevention of, 1405, 1409
Cerebrospinal fluid pressure, increased, from epidural injections, 172, 176
Cerebrovascular accident. *See* Stroke.

Cervical cordotomy. *See also* Cordotomy.
for cancer pain, 356, 356f
Cervical dorsal root ganglion, herpetic/postherpetic neuralgia of, vs. trigeminal neuralgia, 504
Cervical dorsal root ganglionotomy, 1441-1442, 1443f
Cervical dystonia, 591-596
clinical features of, 591-593, 592f
diagnosis of, 593
differential diagnosis of, 593-594, 594t, 595
epidemiology of, 591
genetic factors in, 593
imaging studies in, 593
pathogenesis of, 593
psychogenic, 591, 592t
remission in, 591
sensory tricks in, 591, 592f
spread of, 591
treatment of, 594-595
botulinum toxin type A in, 472, 591, 593, 594-595
Cervical epidural nerve block. *See* Epidural nerve block, cervical.
Cervical epidural space
age-related narrowing of, 1211
anatomy of, 145-146, 173, 234, 234f, 1211-1212, 1212f
contents of, 1211-1212
ligaments of, 1213, 1214f
size of, 1211
Cervical facet block, 1199-1208
anatomic aspects of, 1201-1202
anesthetics for, 1207
anticoagulation and, 1200
cervical medial branch, 1205-1207
blocked nerves in, 1205t
lateral approach in, 1206-1207, 1207f
posterior approach in, 1205, 1206f
complications of, 1207-1208
contraindications to, 1200, 1200t
diagnostic, 153, 1199-1200, 1200t
historical perspective on, 1199
indications for, 1199-1201, 1200t
intra-articular, 1202-1205
lateral approach in, 1202-1205, 1204f, 1205f
posterior approach in, 1202, 1203f
nonsteroidal antiinflammatory drugs and, 1200
therapeutic, 1200-1201
Cervical facet joint(s)
anatomy of, 118-119, 1201-1202, 1201f, 1436-1437, 1437f
as pain generators, 1436t
osteoarthritis of, imaging of, 89-91, 91f
Cervical facet joint injections, 564
complications of, 565-566, 566t
Cervical facet syndrome, 52, 52t, 561-566
causes of, 562
clinical features of, 561-562, 562f
diagnosis of, 562-563, 563f
differential diagnosis of, 563
historical perspective on, 561
imaging studies in, 562, 563
pain characteristics in, 562
pain distribution in, 562, 562f, 563f
pathophysiology of, 562
prevalence of, 562
treatment of, 564-566, 564f
complications and pitfalls of, 565-566, 566t
cryoanalgesia in, 1467-1468
radiofrequency techniques in, 1437-1440, 1438f-1441f

Cervical fusion, for cervical facet syndrome, 564f, 565

Cervical ganglia, anatomy of, 553f

Cervical myelopathy, vs. cervical radiculopathy, 573

Cervical pain. *See* Neck pain; Spinal pain.

Cervical plexus, anatomy of, 1174-1177
    deep, 1177, 1179f
    superficial, 1174-1177, 1174f-1179f

Cervical plexus block, 238t, 1173-1189
    anatomic aspects of, 1174-1177, 1174f-1180f
    anesthetic agents for, 1185-1187
    bilateral, indications for, 1173
    complications of, 1187-1189
    contraindications to, 1174
    deep
        Heidenhein's method of, 1181
        Labat's method of, 1181
        nerve stimulator in, 1184-1185, 1185f
        technique of, 182f-184f, 1181-1185
            single-injection, 1184-1185, 1184f
        Wertheim and Rovenstine's method of, 1185, 1186f
    failure of, 1187
    for carotid endarterectomy, 1173, 1189
    for percutaneous carotid angioplasty, 1189
    future directions for, 1189
    historical perspective on, 1173
    indications for, 1173-1174
    interscalene, 1184, 1184f
    lateral approach in, 1181-1185
    pitfalls in, 1187
    posterior approach in, 1173, 1185
    primary line in, 1181
    superficial, technique of, 1177-1181, 1180f-1182f

Cervical radiculopathy, 52t, 55, 55t, 568-574. *See also* Radiculopathy.
    case study of, 50
    clinical features of, 568-570, 571t
    definition of, 568
    diagnosis of, 571-573
    differential diagnosis in, 573
    etiology of, 570
    historical perspective on, 568
    imaging studies in, 572-573
    in double-crush syndrome
        with carpal tunnel syndrome, 413-414, 413f, 653
        with cubital tunnel syndrome, 649
    in whiplash, 568. *See also* Whiplash.
    intrathecal steroids for, 339-340
    physical examination in, 571
    prevalence of, 570
    provocative tests in, 571-572, 572t
    radiofrequency techniques for, 1435-1436, 1440-1444
    referred pain in, 570
    scapular pain in, 630
    shoulder pain in, 605
    treatment of, 573-574
        complications of, 574
    vs. anterior interosseous syndrome, 653
    vs. carpal tunnel syndrome, 386
    vs. cubital tunnel syndrome, 649
    vs. lateral epicondylitis, 635
    vs. medial epicondylitis, 637
    vs. median nerve entrapment, 650-653
    vs. radial tunnel syndrome, 655, 656
    vs. scapulocostal syndrome, 630

Cervical spinal fusion. *See* Spinal fusion.

Cervical spine. *See also under* Neck; Spinal; Spine.
    abnormalities of, tension-type headache and, 466
    atlantoaxial instability in
        in rheumatoid arthritis, 437, 437f
        radiography of, 74-75
    pain patterns in, 52, 52t. *See also* Neck pain.
    radiography of, 74-75, 75f

Cervical spondylosis, 52
    radiculopathy and, 570. *See also* Cervical radiculopathy.
    radiography of, 75, 75f

Cervical sympathetic chain, 577, 579f

Cervicalgia. *See* Neck pain.

Cervico-trigeminal interneuronal relay, 1141f

Cervicofacial complex regional pain syndrome, 552-560. *See also* Complex regional pain syndrome, type I, facial.

Cervicogenic headache
    atlanto-occipital nerve block for, 1128-1131, 1130f, 1131f
    occipital nerve block for, 1140-1144, 1143f
    occipital neuralgia and, 549, 1140
    radiofrequency techniques for, 1444-1445

Cervicothoracic ganglion. *See* Stellate ganglion.

CGRP (calcitonin gene-related peptide), 19, 19t, 23t, 1083, 1084f

Chance fracture, computed tomography of, 96f

Chaperone, for patient interview, 39

Charcot arthropathy, 59, 59t, 112, 272, 273f
    in diabetes mellitus, 59, 59t, 112
    magnetic resonance imaging of, 112
    vs. osteomyelitis, 112

Charged couple devices, 74

Cheiralgia paresthetica, 275, 275f, 390, 1233
    radial nerve block for, 1233-1235

Chemical packs
    cold, 1040, 1040f
    hot, 1035-1036

Chest, flail, 678-680, 710, 711f

Chest pain
    evaluation of, creatine kinase in, 71
    in pneumothorax, 708-709, 709f
    musculoskeletal, 694. *See also* Chest wall pain.
        traumatic, 710-712, 711f
    pleuropulmonary, 693-712
        asbestos-related, 695-701, 699f, 700f
        characteristics of, 693-694
        differential diagnosis of, 694
        from lung abscess, 704, 705f, 706, 706f, 707
        from Pancoast tumors, 694-695, 696f-697f
        from parapneumonic effusion, 704-706
        from pleural effusion
            malignant, 701, 701f
            parapneumonic, 704-706
        from pulmonary embolism, 703-704, 703f
        in actinomycosis, 706
        in acute chest syndrome, 702-703
        in asbestosis, 695
        in benign fibrous mesothelioma, 701
        in blastomycosis, 707
        in chronic obstructive pulmonary disease, 707-708
        in chylothorax, 708-709, 709f
        in coccidioidomycosis, 707
        in histoplasmosis, 706-707, 707f
        in laryngotracheobronchitis, 704
        in lung cancer, 694
        in lymphangiomyomatosis, 708, 709f
        in lymphoma, 701
        in malignant mesothelioma, 695-701, 699f, 700f

Chest pain (*Continued*)
    in mechanical ventilation, 710
    in mediastinal tumors, 701-702
    in nocardiosis, 706, 707f
    in pneumonia, 704-706, 705f-706f
    in pulmonary hypertension, 704
    in pulmonary Langerhans cell histiocytosis, 708, 708f
    in sickle cell disease, 702-703
    in tuberculosis, 707
    pleuritic, 693-694
    postoperative, 709-710
    respirophasic, 694
    traumatic, 710-712, 711f

Chest trauma, 710-712, 711f

Chest wall pain, 672-689, 673t, 694
    anatomic aspects of, 672-673, 673f
    complications and pitfalls in, 689
    differential diagnosis of, 688-689
    etiology of, 688-689
    in costosternal syndrome, 672-674, 673f, 674f
    in intercostal neuralgia, 682-684
    in rib fractures, 674-676, 675f-677f. *See also* Rib(s), fractures of.
    in sternalis syndrome, 676-678, 677f
    in sternoclavicular joint syndrome, 686-688, 687f, 688f
    in thoracic radiculopathy, 690-692
    in Tietze syndrome, 674-676, 675f-677f
    in xiphodynia syndrome, 684-686, 684f-686f
    intercostal nerve block for, 1251-1258
    post-thoracotomy, 680-682, 680t, 681f
    vs. liver pain, 734
    vs. pleuropulmonary chest pain, 694

Chewing, painful
    in Eagle syndrome, 547, 547f
    in temporal arteritis, 445, 446, 519

Childhood trauma, chronic pain in adults and, 217

Children
    cluster headache in, 476
    complex regional pain syndrome in, 296
    forced-choice technique for, 252
    hypnosis of, 1021, 1022, 1023, 1024
    knee pain in, 887, 888t
    pain assessment in, 203-208. *See also* Pain assessment, in children.
    positive reinforcement for, 250-251
    testicular torsion in, 839

Chin adduction test, for acromioclavicular pain, 615, 617f

Chinese bodywork, 1099

Chinese medicine, 1093-1102
    acupuncture in, 1093-1098
    blood in, 1094, 1096-1097
    cupping and scraping in, 1099
    diet in, 1099-1100
    herbal remedies in, 1099-1100
    history of, 1093-1094
    moxibustion in, 1098-1099
    qi gong in, 1099
    Qi in, 1094, 1095, 1097
    tai chi in, 1099
    tui na in, 1099

Chiropractic treatment, 993-994, 1081-1090
    clinical rationale for, 1088-1090
    for lumbar facet syndrome, 1088-1089
    for lumbar radiculopathy, 764, 765
    for neurogenic inflammation, 1089
    for sacroiliac disorders, 814
    nociception and, 1081-1088. *See also* Nociceptors.

Chloride imbalances, 60

Chlorofluoromethane spray, 1040

Chloroprocaine, 983
  in differential epidural block, 160
Chlorpromazine
  for cluster headache, 487
  in bridge therapy, for medication-overuse
    headache, 499, 499t
Chlorzoxazone, 978. See also Muscle relaxants.
  for tension-type headache, 470, 471t
Cholangiocarcinoma, computed tomography of,
    734f
Cholecystokinin, 19, 19t, 20
Cholelithiasis, acute pancreatitis and, 737-739
Cholestasis, 70
Cholesteatoma, 542, 542f
Cholesterol granuloma, maxillary antral, 543,
    545f
Cholestyramine, acetaminophen and, 932
Choline magnesium trisalicylate, 935. See also
    Nonsteroidal antiinflammatory drugs.
  for cancer pain, 318-319, 319t
Chondroblastoma, of proximal tibia, 902, 902f
Chondrocalcinosis, 80
Chondrosternal ligament, prolotherapeutic
    injection of, 1118, 1118f
Choy technique, modified, for laser diskectomy,
    1495-1496
Chronic bronchitis, 707-708
Chronic daily headache, 468-469
Chronic fatigue syndrome, fibromyalgia and,
    403
Chronic headache, 468-469, 492-493. See also
    Headache, chronic.
Chronic musculoskeletal pain syndrome,
    fibromyalgia and, 403
Chronic obstructive pulmonary disease, 707-708
Chronic pain, 212-221. See also Neuropathic
    pain.
  acupuncture for, 220
  ancillary studies in, 218
  anxiety in, 198, 215, 217
  back. See Low back pain.
  biofeedback for, 1011-1013, 1012t. See also
    Biofeedback.
  biopsychosocial model of, 499, 500f
  burn, 242
  childhood trauma and, 217
  comorbidity in, 215, 217
  cortical abnormalities in, 214
  depression in, 198, 215, 217
  diagnosis of, 217-218
  differential diagnosis of, 218
  drug abuse and, 1008
  genetic factors in, 214
  history in, 217-218
  in cancer. See Cancer pain.
  in central nervous system disorders, 217
  in elderly, 1000
  in sickle cell disease, 258, 258t
  insomnia in, 215, 1004
  invasive procedures for, 998
  legal issues in, 786, 1008
  malingering and, 1008
  management of, 218-221
    acupuncture in, 220
    anticonvulsants in, 717-718
    antidepressants in, 718, 718t
    capsaicin in, 718-719
    cordotomy in, 356, 356f
    cryoanalgesia in, 1463-1473
    deep brain stimulation in, 356-357, 357f
    diet in, 220-221
    dorsal root entry zone lesions in, 310, 357-
      358, 358f
    drug therapy in, 219-220, 717-719, 718t,
      997-1001

Chronic pain (Continued)
    intrathecal opioids in, 220
    intrathecal steroids in, 220, 339-340
    local anesthetics in, 718
    massage in, 221
    nerve blocks in, 220
    neurostimulation in, 719
    physical therapy in, 220
    psychotherapy in, 218-219
    spinal cord stimulation in, 220, 719
    spinal steroids for, 220
    sympathectomy in, 358-359, 359f, 360f
    transcutaneous electrical nerve stimulation
      in, 719
  neurogenic inflammation in, 1083-1084,
    1084f, 1089
  neuromatrix theory and, 4-7, 5f
  neuronal hyperactivity and, 8
  neuroplasticity in, 214, 1086, 1089
    vs. nociceptor activation, 1085-1086, 1089
  ongoing litigation and, 786, 1008
  pathophysiology of, 212-215
  patient teaching in, 217-218, 1005-1008
  personality disorders and, 1004
  physical examination in, 218
  post-traumatic stress disorder and, 215
  prevention of, 8
  processing and perception of, 212-215
  psychological aspects of, 198, 214, 215, 217,
    1003-1008
  psychotherapy for, 218-219, 1004-1008
    cognitive behavioral therapy in, 1005
    comprehensive multimodal treatment in,
      1005-1007
    effectiveness of, 1007
    obstacles in, 1007-1008
    operant conditioning in, 1005
  relaxation techniques for, 1025-1031. See
    also Relaxation techniques.
  secondary gain in, 1008
  types of, 215-217
  vs. acute pain, 212
Chronic pancreatitis, 71, 739-741, 739f, 740f
Chylothorax
  after celiac plexus block, 1279
  in lymphangiomyomatosis, 708, 709f
Cigarette smoking
  cluster headache and, 478
  failed back surgery syndrome and, 818, 819
Cinchonism, 981
Ciprofloxacin, prophylactic, for diskography,
    124
Circadian rhythms, in cluster headache, 480-481
Circulating water heating pads, 1035, 1035f
Civamide, for cluster headache, 488
Claudication, jaw, in temporal arteritis, 445,
    446, 519
Clavicle, distal, osteolysis of, 80
Claw toe, in peripheral neuropathy, 272, 273f
Clindamycin, prophylactic, for diskography,
    124
Clodronate, for complex regional pain
    syndrome, 294, 294t
Clonidine
  for chronic pain, 220, 719
  for cluster headache, 487
  for complex regional pain syndrome, 220
    of face, 559
  for medication-overuse headache, 499
  for postmastectomy pain, 719
  mechanism of action of, 28-29, 31
  spinal, 1393-1394
  topical, for complex regional pain syndrome,
    295
Clopidogrel, epidural adhesiolysis and, 1346

Clostridial collagenase, intralesional, for
    Dupuytren's contracture, 669
Clunk sign, in biceps tendinitis, 624
Cluster headache, 474-489, 530-532. See also
    Headache.
  age at onset of, 476
  associated symptoms in, 477-478, 477t
  autonomic changes in, 480
  biochemical and hormonal changes in, 480
  carotid body in, 481
  carotid chemoreceptor in, 481
  chronic, 479, 492, 531
    vs. medication-overuse headache, 492
  chronobiological changes in, 480-481
  classification of, 475t
  clinical features of, 475, 475t, 476-478
  demographic factors in, 38t, 474-476
  diagnosis of, 482, 532
  differential diagnosis of, 482-483
  during sleep, 476, 530-531
  epidemiology of, 38t, 474-476
  familial occurrence of, 475
  genetic factors in, 475
  historical perspective on, 474-489
  Horner syndrome in, 477, 480, 531, 531f
  in women, 478-479
  magnetic resonance imaging in, 482, 532
  ocular pain in, 530-532, 531f
  pain characteristics in, 37, 476-477, 479-480,
    531-532
  pain mechanisms in, 479-480
  partial Horner syndrome in, 477, 480
  pathogenesis and pathophysiology of, 479-
    480
  periodicity of, 476, 530-531
  personality factors in, 478
  posttraumatic, 484
  prevalence of, 474-475
  prodromal symptoms in, 476-477
  psychological aspects of, 478
  radiofrequency techniques for, 1444
  secondary, 483-484
  terminology of, 474
  treatment of, 484-489, 532
    abortive, 484-485, 484t
    drug therapy in, 484-488, 532
    gasserian ganglion block in, 1145-1151
    oxygen therapy in, 484
    prophylactic, 484t, 485-488
    radiofrequency techniques in, 1444
    sphenopalatine ganglion block in, 1134-
      1139
    surgery in, 488-489, 489t
    trigeminal nerve block in, 1152-1160,
      1153t
  triggering factors in, 478, 531
  variants of, 481-482
  vascular and hemodynamic changes in,
    480
  with trigeminal neuralgia, 503
Cluster-tic syndrome, 503
CO$_2$ laser, 1489, 1490f, 1491. See also Laser
    therapy.
Coagulation disorders
  drug-induced, 58
  laboratory tests in, 58-59
Cocaine, 983
  abuse of, screening for, 72
  for cluster headache, 485
Coccidioidomycosis, 707
Coccydynia, 848-850, 849f, 850f
  cryoanalgesia for, 1468
Coccyx
  anatomy of, 1337, 1337f
  localization of, 1339, 1339f, 1340f

Codeine, 944t, 948t, 952. *See also* Opioid(s).
for acute/postoperative pain, 228
for cancer pain, 320t, 321-323
structure of, 228f, 953f
Cognitive-behavioral therapy, for chronic pain, 218, 1005
Cognitive evoked potentials, 195
Cognitive function, assessment of, 42, 42t, 43t. *See also* Neurologic examination.
in cancer, 367-369, 368f
Cognitive restructuring, for burn pain, 251
Cold application, 1039-1041
contraindications to, 1040
for neurolytic blockade. *See* Cryoanalgesia.
for rheumatoid arthritis, 437
in contrast baths, 1041, 1041f, 1050
in hydrotherapy, 1040, 1049-1050
in RICE treatment, 1055
modalities of, 1039-1041
physiologic effects of, 1039
Cold packs, 1040, 1040f
Cold sensitivity test, for glomus tumor of hand, 671
Collagen vascular diseases. *See* Connective tissue diseases.
Collagenase, clostridial, for Dupuytren contracture, 669
Collateral ligaments
of elbow
anatomy of, 643f, 644
prolotherapeutic injection of, 1114, 1114f
of knee. *See* Lateral collateral ligament; Medial collateral ligament.
Comfort measures, 994
COMFORT scale, 203, 206f
Common peroneal nerve, anatomy of, 1365
Common peroneal nerve block, 1365-1366
Common peroneal nerve entrapment, electrodiagnosis of, 188
Complement, in autoimmune disease, 62
Complementary and alternative therapies, 989-995
acupuncture, 991t, 994, 1093-1102
biofeedback, 1010-1019
biostimulation techniques, 994
Chinese bodywork, 1099
Chinese medicine, 1093-1102
chiropractic treatment, 993-994, 1081-1090
classification of, 990, 991t
cold application, 1039-1041
comfort measures, 360-372, 994. *See also* Cancer, palliative care for.
definition of, 990
epidural adhesiolysis and, 1346
exercise and physical reconditioning, 1055-1066
for chronic pain, 220-221
for osteoarthritis, 427
guided imagery, 1025-1031
heat application, 1033-1039
hydrotherapy, 1043, 1050
hypnosis, 254, 993, 1021-1024. *See also* Hypnosis.
low-power laser therapy, 995
magnetic field therapy, 994-995
music therapy, 992
osteopathic manipulative treatment, 1069-1079
overview of, 989
popularity of, 989-990
prayer and spiritual healing, 992-993
regulation of, 990-991
relaxation techniques, 993, 1025-1031. *See also* Relaxation techniques.
scope of, 992

Complementary and alternative therapies *(Continued)*
transcutaneous electrical nerve stimulation, 326, 994, 1052-1054. *See also* Transcutaneous electrical nerve stimulation.
types of, 992-995
vs. holistic medicine, 990
Complete blood count, 57-59
Complex regional pain syndrome
definition of, 283
fludiotherapy for, 1037, 1037f
historical perspective on, 283-284
post-traumatic neuralgia and, 293
spinal cord stimulation for, 1378
type I, 216-217, 283-298
autonomic abnormalities in, 287
clinical presentation of, 284-286, 284f
clonidine for, 220
cold type, 287
definition of, 283
diagnosis of, 290-293
diagnostic criteria for, 553t
differential diagnosis of, 292-293
epidemiology of, 284
facial, 552-560
clinical presentation of, 552-555, 553t
clinical studies of, 554t
diagnosis of, 554-555, 557
pathophysiology of, 555-557, 555f
treatment of, 555, 557-559, 558f
vs. somatic, 552, 553t, 559
genetic factors in, 286
historical perspective on, 283-284
HLA antigens in, 286
hyperalgesia in, 286
hypoalgesia in, 286
hypoesthesia in, 286
imaging studies in, 86, 88f-89f, 112, 114f, 286-287, 286f, 291, 292f
in children, 296
motor abnormalities in, 288
neurogenic inflammation in, 287-288, 289f
occupational therapy for, 220
pain production in, 286-287
pathophysiology of, 286-290, 289f-291f, 555-557, 555f
physical therapy for, 220
precipitating event in, 284
prevention of, 296-298
prognosis of, 298
psychological aspects of, 217, 285-286, 296
in children, 296
psychotherapy for, 296
recurrence of, 298
signs and symptoms of, 284, 284f
skin temperature in, 291-292, 293f
somatosensory abnormalities in, 286-287
spatial distribution of, 284
spinal cord stimulation for, 295-296
stages of, 285
sympathectomy for, 295
sympathetic nerve blocks for, 295
sympathetically maintained pain in, 288-290, 290f
time course of, 284-285
transcutaneous electrical nerve stimulation for, 295
treatment of, 293-296, 294t, 297f
vasoconstriction in, 287
warm type, 287
type II, 283, 302-303
after laser diskectomy, 1497-1498
after spinal cord injury, 303

Complex regional pain syndrome *(Continued)*
after stroke, 303
clinical presentation of, 302
definition of, 283, 293, 302
diagnosis of, 302-303
differential diagnosis of, 293, 303
epidemiology of, 302
in children, 296
pathophysiology of, 302
post-thoracotomy, 680
prognosis of, 298, 303
sympathectomy for, 358-359
vs. post-traumatic neuralgia, 293, 303
Compression fractures, vertebral. *See* Vertebral fractures, compression.
Compression neuropathies. *See* Entrapment neuropathies.
Compression tests, in sacroiliac disorders, 813
Computed radiography, 74
Computed tomography, 93-105
advantages of, 99-102
artifacts in, 98
history of, 93
in brachial plexopathy, 588
in diskography, 98-99, 130, 130f, 131f
post-procedure, 138, 138f, 139f
in headache, 263
in orthopedic trauma, 95-98
in palliative radiation therapy, 328, 330f
in peripheral neuropathy, 276, 407
in tension-type headaches, 468
indications for, 99-102, 407
multi-detector row, 94-95
multiplanar reformation in, 95
myelographic, 99, 101f
of abdominal aneurysm, 755
of cholangiocarcinoma, 734f
of spine, 95, 98-102
in diskography, 98-99. *See also* Diskography.
in lumbar radiculopathy, 763
of vertebral metastases, 752
principles of, 93-95
scanner improvements for, 94
spiral/helical, 94
three-dimensional, 95, 96f
total-body trauma, 95
vs. magnetic resonance imaging, 99-102, 107
Conjunctival hyperemia, 525, 526f
Conjunctival injection
in cluster headache, 477
in short-lasting unilateral neuralgiform headache, 482
Conjunctivitis, 525, 526f
Connective tissue diseases, 431-447. *See also* *specific diseases.*
acupuncture for, 1100, 1100t
auricular involvement in, 541, 541f
common features of, 432t
demographic factors in, 38t
diagnosis of, 60-62, 67t
in CREST syndrome, 442, 442f
mixed connective tissue disease, 442
neuropathy in, 64-66, 67t
polymyalgia rheumatica, 444-445
polymyositis/dermatomyositis, 443-444, 443f, 444f
rheumatoid arthritis, 431-437
scleroderma/systemic sclerosis, 440-443
systemic lupus erythematosus, 437-440
types of, 432t
Conscious pain mapping, 1469
Consent, for cryoanalgesia, 1462

Constipation, opioid-induced, 322-323, 945
  with spinal administration, 1396-1397
Contract, physician-patient, for opioid therapy,
  219
Contracture, Dupuytren's, 668-669, 669f
Contrast baths, 1041, 1041f, 1050
Contrast media
  allergic reaction to
    in diskography, 124
    in epidurography, 148
  arachnoiditis due to, 791
  nephropathy due to, in epidurography, 148
Contusion
  bone, magnetic resonance imaging of, 112
  pulmonary, 711-712
Convergence hypothesis, for migraine, 494
Cooling sprays, 1040
Coping styles, in burn pain, 247, 248f, 253
Coracopectoral syndrome, 583
Cordotomy
  definition of, 1501
  history of, 1501
  open, 1501
    complications of, 1501
    for cancer pain, 356, 356f
    mortality from, 1501
    Ondine's curse and, 1501
  percutaneous
    anatomic aspects of, 1505-1508, 1505f-
      1508f
    complications of, 1513-1515
    contraindications to, 1503-1504
    dysesthesia after, 1512
    for cancer pain, 356, 356f
    history of, 1501-1502
    inadequate lesioning in, 1511
    indications for, 1502-1503
    mirror pain after, 1512-1513
    overview of, 1501-1502
    pain recurrence after, 1512
    pitfalls in, 1511-1513
    postoperative course in, 1511
    preoperative preparation for, 1508
    reference of sensation after, 1512-1513
    results of, 1504-1505
    technique of, 1508-1511, 1509f, 1510f,
      1510t
  ventrolateral, 15
Cormack, Allan McLeod, 93
Cornea
  abrasions of, 524-525, 525f
  foreign bodies in, 524-525, 525f
  innervation of, 523, 524f
Corneal anesthesia, after percutaneous therapy,
  for trigeminal neuralgia, 356
Corning, James Leonard, 149, 1281, 1282f
Cortical stimulation, 1380
Corticosteroids. See also Nerve blocks.
  after pituitary neuroadenolysis, 1409
  epidural, 339-340, 1282-1283. See also
    Epidural nerve block.
    complications of, 172, 176, 574, 765,
      1282t
    epidurography for, 145-148
    for cervical radiculopathy, 574
    for chronic pain, 220
    for intervertebral disk disease, 1244
    for lumbar radiculopathy, 765
    for thoracic radiculopathy, 765
    historical perspective on, 1281
    in adhesiolysis, 1347, 1348, 1349
    side effects of, 1291
    target site concentration of, 1282
  for cancer pain, 324, 339-340
  for cancer-related fatigue, 364

Corticosteroids (Continued)
  for chronic pain, 220
  for cluster headache, 485, 532
  for complex regional pain syndrome, 294,
    294t
  for glossopharyngeal nerve block, 514-515
  for herpes zoster, 281
  for occipital nerve block, 550
  for polymyalgia rheumatica, 445, 451, 451t
  for polymyositis/dermatomyositis, 444, 444f
  for rheumatoid arthritis, 436
  for systemic lupus erythematosus, 440
  for temporal arteritis, 266, 446, 521, 521t
  for trigeminal nerve block, 236
  in bridge therapy, for medication-overuse
    headache, 499, 499t
  intra-articular
    arachnoiditis due to, 791
    complications of, 172, 176, 862
    for ankle and foot arthritis, 914
    for cervical facet syndrome, 565-566, 566t
    for coccydynia, 848-850, 849f
    for costosternal syndrome, 674, 675f, 676,
      677f
    for golfer's elbow, 638-639, 639f
    for lumbar facet syndrome, 773
    for osteitis pubis, 832-833, 833f
    for osteoarthritis, 428
    for rotator cuff disorders, 610
    for sacroiliac disorders, 814-815, 815f,
      1358-1361, 1359f, 1360f
    for shoulder osteoarthritis, 600-602, 601f,
      615-618, 617f
    for sternalis syndrome, 678
    for sternoclavicular joint syndrome, 687-
      688, 688f
    for tennis elbow, 635-636, 635f
    for Tietze syndrome, 676, 677f
    for wrist and hand arthritis, 663
    for xiphodynia syndrome, 685-686, 686f
  intralesional
    complications of, 172, 176, 862
    for Achilles bursitis, 399, 399f, 400f
    for anterior interosseous syndrome, 654-
      655, 656f
    for Baker's cyst, 903-904, 904f
    for bicipital tendinitis, 382, 383f, 625, 625f
    for carpal tunnel syndrome, 387-388, 387f,
      665
    for cubital bursitis, 638, 639f, 645-646,
      646f
    for cubital tunnel syndrome, 649, 649f
    for de Quervain's tenosynovitis, 667
    for Dupuytren's contracture, 668
    for gluteal bursitis, 855, 856f
    for iliopsoas bursitis, 866-867, 866f
    for infrapatellar bursitis, 899-900, 899f
    for intercostal neuralgia, 684
    for ischiogluteal bursitis, 857-858, 857f
    for meralgia paresthetica, 868-869, 870f
    for olecranon bursitis, 642, 644f
    for orchialgia, 840
    for pes anserine bursitis, 901, 901f
    for post-thoracotomy syndrome, 682
    for prepatellar bursitis, 896-897, 897f
    for pronator syndrome, 653, 654f
    for pyriformis syndrome, 835-836, 836f
    for quadriceps expansion syndrome, 906-
      910, 909f
    for rib fractures, 680, 681f
    for scapulocostal syndrome, 631, 632f
    for slipping rib syndrome, 732, 733f
    for stenosing digital tenosynovitis, 670
    for subdeltoid bursitis, 619-620
    for suprapatellar bursitis, 894, 895f

Corticosteroids (Continued)
    for supraspinatus tendinitis, 378, 382,
      383f
    for trochanteric bursitis, 391, 393f, 861
  in diabetes, 862
  intravenous, for arachnoiditis, 796
  knee pain and, 888
  side effects of, 172, 176, 566t, 574, 765
  transforaminal
    disadvantages of, 1282, 1282t
    for chronic pain, 220
Costal cartilage. See also Rib(s).
  abnormalities of
    in costosternal syndrome, 672-674, 672f-
      674f
    in Tietze syndrome, 674-676, 676f-677f
  anatomy of, 732
  injection of, 732, 733f
Costoclavicular syndrome, 583
Costosternal joints
  anatomy of, 732
  corticosteroid injection of, 674, 675f, 676,
    677f
  pain in
    in costosternal syndrome, 672-674, 673f-
      675f
    in Tietze syndrome, 674-676, 675f-677f
Costotransverse ligament, prolotherapeutic
  injection of, 1119-1120, 1120f
Coughing, rib fracture from, 678
Coupling agents, in ultrasonography, 1038
COX-2 inhibitors, 937. See also Nonsteroidal
  antiinflammatory drugs.
  for arachnoiditis, 796
  for migraine, 460
  for osteoarthritis, 427
  for rheumatoid arthritis, 436
  for tension-type headache, 470, 471t
Cramps, leg, prolotherapy for, 1115
Craned neck posture, 1063, 1065f
Cranial nerve(s). See also specific nerves.
  anatomy of, 408f
  entrapment of, 407t. See also Entrapment
    neuropathies.
  examination of, 42-43, 44t
  inadvertent blockade of, in cervical plexus
    block, 1188
  injury of, in posterior fossa exploration for
    trigeminal neuralgia, 356
  paralysis of, 407-412, 407t, 409t
    multiple, 407t, 410-411, 411f
Craniofacial pain. See also Facial pain;
  Headache.
  cryoanalgesia for, 1470-1471, 1470f
Creatine kinase, 71
Creatine phosphokinase, after celiac plexus
  block, 1279
Creatinine clearance, 68
Cremation, implantable drug delivery devices
  and, 1398
Crescent sign, 81, 83f
CREST syndrome, scleroderma and, 442,
  442f
CRIES scale, 203, 207f
Cross-body adduction test, 627, 628f, 630
Crossed straight leg raising test, for lumbar
  radiculopathy, 761t, 762
Cryoanalgesia, 346, 1460-1473
  anatomic aspects of, 1462
  case report of, 1471-1473, 1472t
  cellular basis of, 1460-1462
  closed vs. open procedures in, 1462
  contraindications to, 1462
  cryoprobes for, 1460, 1461f
  duration of, 1462

Cryoanalgesia *(Continued)*
for cervical facet syndrome, 1467-1468
for chronic pain, 1463-1473
indications for, 1464-1473
technique of, 1463-1464
for coccydynia, 1468
for craniofacial pain, 1470-1471, 1470f
for genitofemoral neuropathy, 1469, 1469f
for iliac crest donor site pain, 1465, 1465f, 1471-1473, 1472t
for iliohypogastric neuropathy, 1469
for ilioinguinal neuropathy, 1469
for intercostal neuralgia, 1463, 1465f
for interspinous ligament pain, 1466f, 1468
for low back pain, 1465-1467, 1466f, 1467f, 1468
for lower extremity pain, 1469-1470
for lumbar facet syndrome, 1465-1467, 1466f, 1467f
for mechanical spine pain, 1468
for neurolytic blockade, 346
for neuromas, 1464-1465
for perineal pain, 1468
for postoperative pain, 1462-1463
future directions for, 1473
historical perspective on, 1460
indications for, 1462
informed consent for, 1462
mechanism of action of, 1473
physics of, 1460-1462
results of, 1473
vs. radiofrequency techniques, 1411
Cryoglobulins, 68
Crystal arthropathies, 70
vs. osteoarthritis, 424
Cubital bursitis, 642-646, 645f
corticosteroid injection for, 637, 639f, 645-646, 646f
Cubital tunnel syndrome, 115, 647-649, 648f-650f, 1231
magnetic resonance imaging in, 115, 647, 649f
ulnar nerve block for, 649, 650f, 1230-1233, 1233f
Cullen sign, in acute pancreatitis, 737, 738f
Cupping, 1099
Cybernetics, biofeedback and, 1011
Cyclic vulvitis, 843
Cyclobenzaprine, 978-979. *See also* Muscle relaxants.
for tension-type headache, 470, 471t
Cyclooxygenase inhibition
by acetaminophen, 931
by nonsteroidal antiinflammatory drugs, 929, 934, 935, 937. *See also* COX-2 inhibitors.
in tissue injury, 25
Cyproheptadine, for cluster headache, 487
Cyst(s)
aneurysmal bone, thoracic myelopathy due to, 690, 691f
arachnoidal, in failed back surgery syndrome, 819-820, 820f
Baker's, 903-905, 904f
in rheumatoid arthritis and, 431, 433f
subchondral, in osteoarthritis, 112, 115
Cystic fibrosis, biofeedback for, 1012. *See also* Biofeedback.
Cystitis, diagnosis of, 68
Cytokines
in complex regional pain syndrome, 288, 289f
in Dupuytren's contracture, 668
in tissue injury, 23t

D
δ (delta) receptor, 940-941, 941t
Dactylitis, in sickle cell disease, 258t
Dallas Discogram Description, 99, 130
Dantrolene sodium, 980-981
Dawbarn sign, 377
De Qi sensation, 1095, 1097
De Quervain's tenosynovitis, 80-81, 388-390, 389f, 390f, 666-667
prolotherapy for, 1114, 1114f
Deafness, diagnosis of, in brain stem auditory evoked potentials in, 193, 193f
Débridement
arthroscopic, for osteoarthritis, 428
of burns, hydrotherapy in, 1037, 1037f, 1040, 1049-1050
Decompression
arthroscopic subacromial, 610-611, 611f
for carpal tunnel syndrome, 665
for disk herniation. *See* Intervertebral disk disease.
glossopharyngeal nerve root, 1165
microvascular
for trigeminal neuralgia, 353-356, 355f
glossopharyngeal nerve root, 1165
pudendal nerve, for vulvodynia, 845
Decremental differential nerve blocks, 162-164, 163f
Decubitus ulcers, hydrotherapy for, 1037, 1037f, 1040, 1049-1050
Deep brain stimulation, 356-357, 357f, 1380
Deep breathing, 1028. *See also* Relaxation techniques.
for burn pain, 250
Deep peroneal nerve, cryoablation of, 1469-1470
Deep peroneal nerve block, 1367
Deep tendon reflexes. *See* Reflex(es).
Degenerative arthritis. *See* Osteoarthritis.
Degenerative disk disease. *See* Intervertebral disk disease.
Delirium, in cancer, 367-370, 367f, 368f, 368t
Deltoid ligament sprain, 397-398, 398f
Denervation hypersensitivity, pathogenesis of, 8
Dental extractions, facial reflex sympathetic dystrophy after, 552
Dental infections, 543
Department of Health and Human Services, Office of Alternative Medicine of, 990-991
Dependency, drug. *See* Drug abuse/dependency.
Depression. *See also* Psychological factors.
biofeedback for, 1011. *See also* Biofeedback.
in burn patients, 253
in cancer, 326, 361, 366-367, 369
sleep disturbances and, 366
in chronic pain, 198, 215, 217, 1003-1008
antidepressants for, 219
in complex regional pain syndrome, 285-286
in medication-overuse headache, 497, 499-500
in tension-type headache, 468
in vulvodynia, 843, 845
migraine and, 461
psychotherapy for, 1004-1008
relaxation techniques for, 1027
Dermatomes, 44, 45f, 1294, 1295f
Dermatomyositis. *See* Polymyositis/dermatomyositis.
Descartes, Rene, 149
Descending spinal tracts, 213, 214f, 1086
in tissue injury, 25

Desipramine, 967. *See also* Antidepressants.
for intercostal neuralgia, 683
for peripheral neuropathy, 277t
for post-thoracotomy syndrome, 682
side effects of, 718t, 967
Dexamethasone
for cancer pain, 324
for cancer-related nausea, 365, 365f
for cluster headache, 485
for epidural adhesiolysis, 1347
Dextroamphetamine, for opioid-induced sedation, 323
Dextromethorphan
for complex regional pain syndrome, 294
for phantom pain, 310
Dextrose
growth factors and, 1107, 1108t. *See also* Prolotherapy.
in prolotherapy, 1110. *See also* Prolotherapy.
Dezocine, 948t. *See also* Opioid(s).
Diabetes insipidus, 60
after pituitary neuroadenolysis, 1409, 1410
Diabetes mellitus
arthropathy in, 59, 59t
Charcot joint in, 59, 59t
vs. osteomyelitis, 112
corticosteroid injections in, complications of, 862
diagnosis of, 59, 59t, 406-407
foot problems in, 59, 59f, 112
mononeuritis multiplex in, 691-692
prediabetic state and, 406-407
Diabetic amyotrophy, 871, 881
Diabetic neuropathy, 67t, 216
femoral nerve, 871, 873
glucose testing in, 59, 59t, 406-407
lumbosacral plexus, 416-417
obturator nerve, 881
vs. carpal tunnel syndrome, 386
Diacetylmorphine. *See* Heroin.
Diagnosis. *See also* Differential diagnosis.
evoked potential testing in, 192-195
history in, 35-41
imaging studies in. *See* Imaging studies.
laboratory tests in, 56-73
nerve blocks in, 149-154. *See also* Nerve blocks, diagnostic.
physical examination in, 41-47
Diaphragmatic breathing, 1028
Diaphragmatic pain, referred to supraclavicular region, 732-733, 734f
Diaphragmatic paralysis
in cervical plexus block, 1188
in phrenic nerve block, 1170
Diathermy
microwave, 1039
slow-wave, 1039
Diazepine, 979-980
Dibucaine, 983
introduction of, 985f
Dichloralphenazone, for tension-type headache, 470, 471t
Diclofenac
for cancer pain, 318-319, 319t
for tension-type headache, 470, 471t
Diencephalon, projections into, 15, 16f
Diet, 991t
chronic pain and, 220-221
in cancer, 366
in Chinese medicine, 1099-1100
monoamine oxidase inhibitors and, 969, 969t
weight-loss, for osteoarthritis, 426
Differential block, 985

Differential diagnosis
case examples of, 50-51
generalized anatomic sites in, 51t
history in, 37
potential etiologies in, 51t
principles of, 50-51
Differential nerve blocks, 155-165. *See also*
Nerve blocks, diagnostic.
anatomic approach in, 160-162
brachial plexus, 160
celiac plexus, 161-162, 161t
controversies over, 162-165
conventional sequential spinal, 156-158,
156t-158t, 159
modified, 158-159, 158t
critical blocking length and, 162, 163f
decremental, 162-164, 163f
definition of, 155
diagnostic utility of, 164-165, 165t
epidural, 159-160
fiber size and, 155-156, 156t, 162-163, 163f,
164
for cancer pain, 338, 338t
frequency-dependent, 163, 163f
history of, 155
indications for, 165
internodal distance and, 162-163, 163f, 164
lumbar paravertebral sympathetic, 161-162,
161t
pharmacologic approach in, 155-160
stellate ganglion, 161-162, 161t
superior hypogastric plexus, 161-162, 161t
thoracic paravertebral sympathetic, 161-162,
161t
Diffuse axonal injury, imaging of, 107
Diffuse idiopathic skeletal hyperostosis
radiography of, 75, 75f, 76, 76f
vs. osteoarthritis, 424
Diflunisal, 935. *See also* Nonsteroidal
antiinflammatory drugs.
for cancer pain, 318-319, 319t
for tension-type headache, 470, 471t
Digital nerve block, for foot, 1368
Digits. *See* Finger(s); Toe(s).
Dihydroergotamine
for cluster headache, 485
for medication-overuse headache, 493t, 496
in bridge therapy, 499, 499t
for migraine, 460
Dimethylsulfoxide, for complex regional pain
syndrome, 294t, 295
Diphenhydramine
for pruritus, from spinal opioids, 351, 352t
in bridge therapy, for medication-overuse
headache, 499, 499t
Disability issues, 786, 1008
Discharge frequency, stimulus intensity and, 16
Discoid lupus erythematosus, 438, 438f, 439f
Disease-modifying drugs, for rheumatoid
arthritis, 436
Disk herniation. *See* Intervertebral disk disease,
herniation in.
Diskectomy
complications of, 765, 819-826. *See also*
Failed back surgery syndrome.
exercise program for, 1063
for cervical radiculopathy, 574
for lumbar radiculopathy, 765
historical perspective on, 817-818
percutaneous laser. *See* Laser diskectomy.
Diskitis
after back surgery, 822
after diskography, 139
prevention of, 124
radiography of, 77

Diskogenic pain. *See* Intervertebral disk disease;
Low back pain.
Diskography, 98-99, 118-140, 756, 756f
analgesic, 122, 138
cervical, technique of, 134-138, 136f-139f
complications of, 139-140
components of, 118
computed tomography in, 98-99, 130, 130f,
131f
post-procedure, 138, 138f, 139f
contraindications to, 123, 123t
contrast media for
allergy to, 124
selection of, 128
diagnostic utility of, 819
diskitis after, 139
prevention of, 124
equipment for, 124
history of, 120-122
in cervical radiculopathy, 573
indications for, 98, 99, 123, 123t
interpretation of findings in, 98-99, 100f
lumbar
interpretation of, 129-132, 130f, 131f
technique of, 124-129, 125f-129f
patient preparation for, 124
patient selection for, 123, 123t
post-procedure considerations in, 138-139
pre-/peri-procedure considerations in, 123-
124
provocative, 124
thoracic, technique of, 132-134, 132f-135f
validation of, 122-123
Dislocation. *See* Subluxation.
Distal dural sac ectasia, failed back surgery
syndrome and, 826, 826f
Distal interphalangeal joints. *See also* Finger(s);
Hand.
anatomy of, 661f
Distraction, for burn pain, 247
Distraction test, for sacroiliac disorders, 813
Divalproex, 976. *See also* Anticonvulsants.
for cluster headache prophylaxis, 486-487
for migraine prophylaxis, 461
Diving, scuba, with implantable drug delivery
systems, 1398
DMSO. *See* Dimethylsulfoxide.
Documentation, of occupational back pain, 789-
790
Donepezil
for cancer-related drowsiness, 366
for cancer-related fatigue, 364
Dopamine. *See also* Neurotransmitters.
cervical dystonia and, 593
in opioid addiction, 946-947, 947f
Dorsal column medial lemniscal system, 15
Dorsal column stimulation. *See also* Spinal
cord stimulation.
for phantom pain, 310-311
Dorsal funicular projection systems, 15
Dorsal horn
anatomy of, 12-13, 13f
neurons of, 13-15, 13f, 13t, 14f
anatomic localization of, 14
functional properties of, 14-15
in tissue injury, 22-24, 23f
in wind-up, 15, 22-24, 23f
neurotransmitters in, 19t, 20
nociceptive-specific, 14, 14f, 17, 18f
wide dynamic range, 14-15, 14f, 17,
18f
Dorsal raphe nucleus, 213, 214f
Dorsal root entry zone, 13
Dorsal root entry zone lesions, 357-358, 358f
for phantom pain, 310, 357-358, 358f

Dorsal root ganglion
cross-talk with neuroma, 27
herpetic/postherpetic neuralgia of, 504
in pain processing, 212, 213f
innervation of, in neuroma, 28-29, 29f
Dorsal root ganglionotomy, 1431-1435, 1431f-
1435f
cervical, 1441-1442, 1443f
indications for, 1435
lumbar, 1431, 1431f
sacral, 1431-1433, 1432f, 1433f
thoracic, 1433-1435, 1434f, 1435f
Dorsal sacroiliac ligament, anatomy of, 810,
811f
Dorsal scapular nerve, anatomy of, 578f, 579f,
580
Double-crush syndrome, 413-414, 413f
carpal tunnel syndrome and, 386, 413-414,
413f, 653
cubital tunnel syndrome and, 649
sciatic nerve entrapment and, 854
Doxepin
for cluster headache, 487
for migraine prophylaxis, 461
side effects of, 718t
Dronabinol, for cancer cachexia, 366
Drop arm test, for rotator cuff tears, 380, 380f
Drop sign, 605-606, 606f
Droperidol
for opioid-induced nausea, 351, 352t
spinal, 1394
Drowsiness
muscle relaxant–induced, 977
opioid-induced, methylphenidate for, 323,
364, 366, 1000
Drug abuse/dependency
addiction vs. dependence in, 323. *See also*
Addiction.
chronic pain and, 1008
commonly abused drugs in, 39, 40t
fear of, 947, 998
history taking in, 39, 40t
in cancer pain, 323
indicators of, 39, 40t
opioid, 39, 250, 323, 946-947, 947t
fear of, 947, 998
levo-alpha acetyl methadol for, 957-958
methadone for. *See* Methadone.
vs. addiction, 323
provider fear of, 947
red flags for, 39, 40t
screening for, 39, 40t, 71-72
tolerance and. *See* Tolerance.
vs. addiction, 323
withdrawal in. *See* Withdrawal.
Drug history, 38-39
Drug therapy. *See also specific drugs and drug
families.*
advantages and disadvantages of, 998-999
for cancer pain. *See* Cancer pain, drug
therapy for.
for chronic pain, 219-220. *See also* Chronic
pain.
for headache, medication-overuse headache
and. *See* Medication-overuse
headache.
risk-benefit ratio for, 997
therapeutic monitoring in, 71-72
Dupuytren's contracture, 668-669, 669f
Dura mater, anatomy of, 173
Dural puncture
headache after, 1302, 1391
in celiac plexus block, 1278
inadvertent, in cervical epidural block, 1217-
1218

Dural sac ectasia, failed back surgery syndrome and, 826, 826f
Durkan sign, in carpal tunnel syndrome, 664
Dynorphins, 939-940, 1085, 1086
  in nerve injury, 28
Dysesthetic vulvodynia, 843
Dysmenorrhea, acupuncture for, 1100, 1100t
Dyspareunia, prolotherapy for, 1118-1119, 1119f
Dysphagia
  from botulinum neurotoxin, 593, 595
  in scleroderma, 441-442
Dyspnea, in cancer, 365-366
Dysrhythmias
  in cluster headache, 477-478
  opioid-induced, 945, 945f
Dystonia
  cervical, 591-596. See also Cervical dystonia.
  definition of, 591
  hereditary, 593
  in complex regional pain syndrome, 284, 285t
  primary distortion, 593
Dysuria, diagnosis of, 68

E
Eagle syndrome, 547, 547f
Ear
  cauliflower, 538, 540f
  innervation of, 538, 540f
Ear pain, 538-543, 539t
  anatomic aspects of, 538, 540f
  auricular, 538-541, 541f
  diagnosis of, 543, 547
  from cholesteatoma, 542, 542f
  from foreign bodies, 542, 543f
  idiopathic, 543
  imaging studies in, 543
  in mastoiditis, 543, 544f
  in myringitis, 542, 543f
  in otitis externa, 541, 541f
  in otitis media, 542-543, 543f
  in Ramsay Hunt syndrome, 279, 538, 540f
Eccentric contractions, 1057
Ecchymosis
  flank, in acute pancreatitis, 737, 738f
  periumbilical, in acute pancreatitis, 737, 738f
Edema, bone marrow, 111-112, 113f, 114f
Edmonton Staging System, 362, 363f, 998
  for cancer pain, 362, 363t
Edmonton Symptom Assessment Scale, 362-363
Elbow
  anatomy of, 634f, 638f, 641, 642f, 644
  corticosteroid injection of
    for cubital tunnel syndrome, 649, 649f
    for golfer's elbow, 638-639, 639f
    for tennis elbow, 635-636, 635f
  cubital bursitis of, 642-646, 645f, 646f
    corticosteroid injection for, 637, 639f, 645-646, 646f
  entrapment neuropathies of, 647-658
    anterior interosseous syndrome, 653-655, 654f-656f
    pronator syndrome, 650-653, 651f-653f
    radial tunnel syndrome, 655-658, 657f
    tardy ulnar palsy, 647-649, 648f-650f
  golfer's, 637-640, 638f, 639f
    prolotherapy for, 1114, 1114f
    vs. cubital tunnel syndrome, 647-650
  olecranon bursitis of, 641-642, 642f-644f, 646
    lateral epicondylitis and, 384, 635
    medial epicondylitis and, 637
  osteoarthritis of, 80

Elbow (Continued)
  osteochondritis dissecans of, 80
  painful, 633-658
  radiography of, 80
  tennis, 382-385, 384f, 633-636, 634f, 635f
    acupuncture for, 1100, 1100t
    prolotherapy for, 1113, 1113f
    vs. radial tunnel syndrome, 635, 655, 656, 657f, 1233
Elderly
  chronic pain in, 1000
  drug therapy for, 1000
  knee pain in, 887, 888t
  pain assessment in, 208-209
Electrical nerve stimulation
  cortical, 1380
  deep brain, 356-357, 357f, 1380
  peripheral nerve, 1369-1371, 1380
  spinal cord, 1373-1380. See also Spinal cord stimulation.
Electroacupuncture, 1097-1098
Electrocoagulation, radiofrequency. See Radiofrequency techniques.
Electroconvulsive therapy, for phantom pain, 311
Electrodiagnostic procedures, 179-184
  advantages of, 180
  definition of, 179
  electroencephalography, 264
  electromyography, 179-184, 275
  equipment for, 180, 180f, 181f
  in anterior horn cell disorders, 189
  in arachnoiditis, 792-793
  in axonal neuropathy, 187
  in brachial plexopathy, 586-588, 587t
  in carpal tunnel syndrome, 64-65, 188, 413, 414
  in central nervous system disorders, 189
  in cervical dystonia, 593
  in cervical radiculopathy, 573
  in compression neuropathy, 187
  in demyelinating neuropathy, 187
  in entrapment neuropathy, 187-188, 407, 413, 414
  in femoral neuropathy, 874
  in lumbar radiculopathy, 763
  in mononeuropathy, 187
  in nontraumatic neuropathy, 187
  in peripheral neuropathy, 186-189, 274-276, 407
  in plexopathy, 189
  in polyneuropathy, 187
  in primary myopathy, 189, 189t
  in radiculopathy, 189
  in traumatic neuropathy, 186-187
  indications for, 186-189
  nerve conduction studies, 184-186, 275
  physiologic mechanisms of, 180-182
  quantitative sensory testing, 186, 275-276
  timing of, 190
Electroencephalography, in headache evaluation, 264
Electrolyte imbalances
  causes of, 69-70
  diagnosis of, 59-60, 69-70
  signs and symptoms of, 69-70
Electrolytic lesions
  direct current, 1412
  radiofrequency, 1412. See also Radiofrequency techniques.
Electromyography, 179-184, 275. See also Electrodiagnostic procedures.
  advantages of, 180
  definition of, 179
  equipment for, 180, 181f

Electromyography (Continued)
  history of, 179-180
  in brachial plexopathy, 586-588, 587t, 588t
  in cervical dystonia, 593
  in cervical radiculopathy, 573
  in femoral neuropathy, 874
  indications for, 179, 186-189, 275, 407
  interpretation of findings in, 182-184, 183f, 184f, 189-190, 190f
  physiologic mechanisms of, 180-182
  technique of, 182
  timing of, 190
  waveforms in, 183-184, 183f, 184f
  with biofeedback, 1011, 1012, 1013-1016, 1014f
Electronic security systems, implantable drug delivery devices and, 1397
Electrothermal annuloplasty, 1426-1431, 1484-1487. See also Intradiscal electrothermal annuloplasty.
Eletriptan. See also Triptans.
  for migraine, 460
Embolism, pulmonary, 703-704, 703f
EMLA, for burns, 246-247
Emphysema, 707-708
Empyema, 706
Encephalization, 158t
End-of-dose failure, 1000
Endocrine replacement therapy, after pituitary neuroadenolysis, 1409
Endocrine system, opioid effects on, 946
Endogenous opioids, 939-940, 1086
Endometriosis, low back pain in, 755
Endoneurium, 343
Endorphins, 939-940, 1086
Endoscopy, spinal canal, 167-177. See also Spinal canal endoscopy.
Endurance training, 1056, 1056t, 1058. See also Exercise.
Enkephalins, 939-940, 1085, 1086
Entrapment neuropathies, 406-417
  anterior cutaneous nerve, 727-731
  anterior interosseous syndrome, 653-655, 654f, 655f
  carpal tunnel syndrome, 385-388, 385f-387f, 412-414, 664-665. See also Carpal tunnel syndrome.
  central spinal stenosis, 763, 764
  cheiralgia paresthetica, 275, 275f, 390, 1233-1235
  clinical evaluation of, 406-407
  common peroneal nerve, electrodiagnosis of, 188
  cubital tunnel syndrome, 115, 647-649, 648f-650f, 1231
    magnetic resonance imaging of, 115, 647, 649f
    ulnar nerve block for, 649, 650f, 1230-1233, 1233f
  de Quervain's tenosynovitis, 80-81, 388-390, 389f, 390f, 666-667, 1114
  double-crush syndrome in, 413-414, 413f
    carpal tunnel syndrome and, 386, 413-414, 413f, 653
    cubital tunnel syndrome and, 649
    sciatic nerve entrapment and, 854
  electrodiagnosis of, 187-188
  femoral nerve, 871-874, 872f, 873t
  genitofemoral nerve, 747-748, 748f
  gluteal nerve, 855, 855f
  iliohypogastric nerve, 745-747, 746f
  ilioinguinal nerve, 742-745, 743f
  in intervertebral disk disease
    cervical, 52t, 55, 55t, 568-574. See also Cervical radiculopathy.

Entrapment neuropathies *(Continued)*
    lumbar, 758-766. *See also* Lumbar
        radiculopathy.
    thoracic, 690-692, 1429-1431, 1484-1487
    in meralgia paresthetica, 415-416, 868-870,
        869f, 1364
    in thoracic outlet syndrome, 582-583, 584f
    intercostal nerve, 727-731, 728f-731f
    lateral femoral cutaneous nerve, 36, 391,
        415-416, 415f, 868-870, 869f, 1328-
        1330, 1364
    lateral recess stenosis, 763, 764
    lumbar radicular, 760-761. *See also* Lumbar
        radiculopathy.
        differential diagnosis of, 763-764
    magnetic resonance imaging of, 115
    meralgia paresthetica, 36, 391, 415-416,
        415f, 868-870. *See also* Meralgia
        paresthetica.
    Morton neuroma, 918-919, 1118
    obturator nerve, 879-882, 881f, 882f, 882t
        diagnosis of, 1331
    of elbow and forearm, 647-658
    posterior tibial nerve, electrodiagnosis of,
        188
    pronator teres syndrome, 650-653, 651f-653f
        electrodiagnosis of, 188
        vs. carpal tunnel syndrome, 650, 665
    pudendal nerve, 845
    radial tunnel syndrome, 655-658, 657f, 1233-
        1235
        electrodiagnosis of, 188
        radial nerve block for, 1230f, 1233-1235
        vs. lateral epicondylitis, 384, 635, 1233
    rheumatoid arthritis and, 431
    sacroiliac and piriformis syndrome, 763, 834-
        836
    saphenous nerve, 874-876
    sciatic nerve, 188, 854
    spinal nerve root, 760-761
        cervical, 52t, 55, 55t, 568-574. *See also*
            Cervical radiculopathy.
        differential diagnosis of, 763-764
        lumbar, 758-766. *See also* Lumbar
            radiculopathy.
        thoracic, 690-692, 1429-1431, 1484-1487
    superior gluteal nerve, 855, 855f
        cryoanalgesia for, 1470
    suprascapular nerve, 630
    tarsal tunnel syndrome, 416-417
        vs. sesamoiditis, 400
    transcutaneous electrical nerve stimulation
        for, 1053
    ulnar tunnel syndrome, 1231, 1232f, 1234f
        ulnar nerve block for, 1231-1233, 1232f,
            1234f
Enzymes, pancreatic, in acute pancreatitis, 740
Eosinophilia, 58
Ephedrine, for opioid-induced hypotension,
    352t
Epicondylitis
    lateral, 382-385, 384f, 633-636, 634f, 635f
        prolotherapy for, 1113, 1113f
        vs. radial tunnel syndrome, 635, 655, 656,
            657f, 1233
    medial, 637-640, 638f, 639f
        prolotherapy for, 1114, 1114f
        vs. cubital tunnel syndrome, 647-649
Epidemiology, 38t
Epididymectomy, for orchialgia, 841
Epidural abscess
    after cervical epidural block, 1218
    after implantable drug delivery device
        placement, 1391
    after lumbar epidural block, 1292

Epidural abscess *(Continued)*
    after thoracic epidural block, 1247
    postoperative, 822
Epidural adhesiolysis, 172, 1345-1349
    anticoagulation management for, 1346
    complications of, 1348
    contraindications to, 1345
    drugs for, 1347
    imaging studies for, 1345, 1347f
    indications for, 1345
    laboratory studies for, 1346
    patient preparation for, 1345-1346
    results of, 1348-1349
    technique of, 1346-1348, 1347f
Epidural catheterization. *See also* Epidural
    nerve block.
    cervical
        complications of, 1218
        technique of, 1217
    for caudal epidural block, 1343
    in spinal cord stimulation, 1373-1374. *See*
        also Spinal cord stimulation.
        complications of, 1376
    thoracic
        catheter taping in, 1246, 1247f
        complications of, 1247
        technique of, 1246, 1246f
Epidural fat, 1211
Epidural fibrosis, in failed back surgery
    syndrome, 820, 820f
Epidural hematoma
    in caudal epidural block, 1343
    in cervical epidural block, 1218
    in lumbar epidural block, 1292
    in thoracic epidural block, 1247
Epidural infection, after cervical epidural
    block, 1218
Epidural injections
    complications of, 172, 176, 574, 765
    inadvertent
        in cervical epidural block, 1217-1218
        in stellate ganglion block, 1197-1198
    increased cerebrospinal fluid pressure and,
        172, 176
    of clonidine, for complex regional pain
        syndrome, 220
    of corticosteroids, 339-340, 1282-1283,
        1282t. *See also* Epidural nerve
        block.
        complications of, 172, 176, 574, 765,
            1282t
        disadvantages of, 1282, 1282t
        epidurography for, 145-148
        for cervical radiculopathy, 574
        for chronic pain, 220, 339-340
        for intervertebral disk disease, 1244
        for lumbar radiculopathy, 765
        for thoracic radiculopathy, 765, 1244
        historical perspective on, 1281
        in adhesiolysis, 1347, 1348, 1349
        side effects of, 1291
        target site concentration of, 1282
Epidural nerve block, 234-236, 234f, 235f
    arachnoiditis due to, 791
    caudal, 1335-1344
        anatomic aspects of, 1336-1337, 1337f
        catheterization in, 1343
        complications of, 1343-1344
        contraindications to, 1336
        disadvantages of, 1282, 1282t
        drug injection in, 1341
        drug selection in, 1341-1342
        historical perspective on, 1335
        increasing use of, 1335
        indications for, 1335-1336, 1336t

Epidural nerve block *(Continued)*
        needle placement in, 1340-1341, 1341f,
            1342-1343, 1343f
        needle selection for, 1339
        patient positioning for, 1337-1339, 1338f
        sacral hiatus localization in, 1339-1341,
            1339f, 1340f
        technique of, 1337-1343
        vs. lumbar epidural block, 1336
    cervical, 234-236, 234f, 235f, 1210-1218
        catheter placement in, 1217
        complications of, 1217-1218
        contraindications to, 1210-1213, 1213t
        drug injection in, 1216
        drug selection for, 1216
        epidural space identification in, 1215-
            1216
        for acute/postoperative pain, 234-236,
            234f, 235f, 238t
        for arachnoiditis, 797
        for cancer pain, 339, 797, 1210
        historical perspective on, 1210
        indications for, 1210, 1211t
        interspace identification in, 1215, 1215f
        lateral position for, 1213-1214
        needle insertion in
            pitfalls in, 1213
            structures encountered on, 1213,
                1214f
        needle selection for, 1215
        patient positioning for, 1213-1214
        patient preparation for, 1214-1215
        technique of, 1213-1217
            hanging-drop, 1215
            loss-of-resistance, 1215-1216, 1216f,
                1217f
    complications of, 325
    continuous, for cancer pain, 339
    corticosteroids in, 339-340, 1282-1283. *See*
        also Corticosteroids, epidural.
    differential, 159-160
        for cancer pain, 338, 338t
    for acute pancreatitis, 739
    for acute/postoperative pain, 234-236, 234f,
        235f, 709
    for arachnoiditis, 797
    for cancer pain, 324-325, 338, 338t, 339
    for chronic pancreatitis, 741
    for phantom pain prevention, 308
    for thoracic radiculopathy, 690
    inadvertent, in cervical plexus block, 1188
    lumbar, 234-236, 234f, 235f, 1281-1292
        anatomic aspects of, 1283
        complications of, 1291-1292
        contraindications to, 1283
        disadvantages of, 1282, 1282t
        drugs for, 1282-1283. *See also*
            Corticosteroids, epidural; Local
            anesthetics.
        for acute/postoperative pain, 234-236,
            234f, 235f
        historical perspective on, 1281
        indications for, 1281, 1283, 1283t
        interlaminar, 1282-1283, 1282t, 1288,
            1289f-1291f
        pitfalls in, 1282
        rationale for, 1282-1283
        technique of, 1283, 1284f-1287f
            fluoroscopic, 1283-1288, 1284f, 1285,
                1287f
        transforaminal, 1282-1283, 1282t
        vs. caudal epidural nerve block, 1336
    technique of
        blind, 1288-1291
        loss-of-resistance, 1286-1288

Epidural nerve block *(Continued)*
  thoracic, 234-236, 234f, 235f, 1243-1248
    anatomic aspects of, 1244-1245, 1245f
    cardiovascular effects of, 1245
    complications of, 1247-1248
    contraindications to, 1244
    drugs for, 1246-1247
    for acute pancreatitis, 1244
    for acute/postoperative pain, 234-236,
      234f, 235f
    for angina, 1244
    for cancer pain, 1244
    for herpes zoster, 1243-1244
    for post-thoracotomy pain, 722-723
    for postherpetic neuralgia, 1243-1244
    for rib fractures, 1244
    for vertebral fractures, 1244
    historical perspective on, 1243
    Horner syndrome and, 1245
    in spinal stimulation, 1244
    indications for, 1243-1244
    intraoperative use of, 1243
    laminar approach in, 1247
    midline approach in, 1246, 1246f
    paramedian lateral approach in, 1247
    pitfalls in, 1247
    postoperative use of, 1243
    pulmonary effects of, 1245
    technique of, 1245-1247, 1246f, 1247f
Epidural opioids. *See* Spinal opioids.
Epidural space
  anatomy of, 145-146, 173
    cervical, 145-146, 173, 234, 234f, 1211-
      1212, 1212f
    lumbar, 232, 233f, 1283
    thoracic, 1244-1245, 1245f
  cervical
    age-related narrowing of, 1211
    anatomy of, 145-146, 173, 234, 234f,
      1211-1212, 1212f
    contents of, 1211-1212
    ligaments of, 1213, 1214f
    size of, 1211
  lumbar, anatomy of, 232, 233f, 1283
  thoracic, anatomy of, 1244-1245, 1245f
Epidural venous plexus, anatomy of, 1337,
  1338f
Epidural vessels, 1211-1212, 1212f
Epidurography, 145-148
  implantable drug delivery devices and,
    1393
  in epidural adhesiolysis, 1346-1347, 1347f
Epiduroscopy. *See* Spinal canal endoscopy.
Epilepsy. *See also* Seizures.
  neuropathic pain and, 717
Epinephrine. *See also* Neurotransmitters.
  in complex regional pain syndrome, 556
  with local anesthetics, 986
Epineurium, 343
Epistaxis, from sphenopalatine ganglion block,
  230
Equianalgesic doses, of opioids, 322
Erb-Duchenne paralysis, 582. *See also* Brachial
  plexopathy.
Erectile dysfunction, after cordotomy, 1515
Ergotamine
  for cluster headache, 486
  for medication-overuse headache, 493, 496
    in bridge therapy, 499, 499t
  for migraine, 460
Er:YAG laser, 1489, 1491. *See also* Laser
  therapy.
Erythema migrans, 64, 65f, 66f, 889, 889f
Erythrocyte, sickled, 257, 258f
Erythrocyte distribution width, 57

Erythrocyte growth factor injections. *See*
  Prolotherapy.
Erythrocyte indices, 57
Erythrocyte sedimentation rate, 56-57
  in headache evaluation, 263
  in polymyalgia rheumatica, 444, 445, 450,
    450t
  in temporal arteritis, 263, 265, 445, 518,
    520
Erythrocyte sedimentation test, in systemic
  lupus erythematosus, 438-440
Esdaile, Jame, 1021
Eskimos, spondylolysis in, 800
Etanercept, for rheumatoid arthritis, 436-437
Ethyl alcohol. *See* Alcohol.
Ethyl chloride spray, 1040
Etidocaine, introduction of, 985f
Etodolac, for tension-type headache, 470, 471t
Euphemistic back pain, 780-781
Eutetic mixture of local anesthetics (EMLA),
  for burns, 246-247
Evaporative cooling sprays, 1040
Eversion test, for deltoid ligament sprain, 398,
  398f
Evoked potentials, 192-195
  brain stem auditory, 193
  cognitive, 195
  instrumentation for, 192
  somatosensory, 194-195, 194f
  visual, 192-193, 193f
Exercise
  contraindications to, 1056t, 1065
  endurance, 1056, 1056t, 1058
  goals of, 1059
  historical perspective on, 1055
  in fibromyalgia, 1060-1061, 1061f
  in hip arthritis, 1059-1060
  in knee arthritis, 1059-1060
  in low back pain, 1061-1062, 1062f, 1063f
  in spondylolisthesis, 1062-1063
  pain during, 1058
  patient education for, 1058-1059
  prescription writing for, 1059, 1059f
  rest and, 1055-1056
  treadmill test for, 1065
  well-being and, 1056-1058
Exercises. *See also* Physical therapy.
  after diskectomy, 1063
  for cervical facet syndrome, 564
  for low back pain, 1061-1062, 1062f,
    1063f
  for lumbar radiculopathy, 764, 1061-1062,
    1063, 1063f
  for neck pain, 1063
  for osteoporosis, 1063, 1064f
  for plantar fasciitis, 924
  for rotator cuff disorders, 610
  for sacroiliac disorders, 815, 815f
  for spondylolisthesis, 1062-1063
  for trochanteric bursitis, 862
  for vertebral compression fractures, 1063
  historical perspective on, 1055
  isokinetic, 1057
  isometric, 1057, 1057t
  isotonic, 1057, 1057t
  patient education for, 1058-1059
  quadriceps setting, 1059-1060, 1060f
  spinal, 1061-1063, 1062f
  strengthening, 1056-1058, 1056t
  stretching, 1056-1057, 1056t
  water-based, 1045-1049, 1047f, 1048f
Expiration reflex, 693
External pterygoid nerve, 1148, 1155
Extrapleural pneumonectomy, for malignant
  mesothelioma, 695-701

Eye
  abnormalities of. *See also* Visual
    disturbances.
    in temporal arteritis, 518-519
    painful. *See* Ocular/periocular pain.
  examination of, in peripheral neuropathy, 274
  herpes zoster of, cavernous sinus syndrome
    and, 536, 536f
  innervation of, 523, 524f
  pink, 525, 526f

F
F-wave, in nerve conduction studies, 185-186
Fabere maneuver, 813
Facet joints
  cervical
    anatomy of, 118-119, 1201-1202, 1201f
    pain in, 52, 52t, 561-566. *See also* Cervical
      facet syndrome.
  lumbar
    anatomy of, 118-119, 769-770, 770f
    pain in, 118, 769-774. *See also* Low back
      pain; Lumbar facet syndrome.
    referred pain from, 769-770, 770f
    osteoarthritis of, imaging of, 89-91, 91f
Facet ligament
  lumbar, prolotherapeutic injection of, 1123-
    1124, 1124f
  thoracic, prolotherapeutic injection of, 1120,
    1120f
Facet syndrome
  cervical, 52, 52t, 561-566. *See also* Cervical
    facet syndrome.
  lumbar, 55, 118, 769-774. *See also* Lumbar
    facet syndrome.
  thoracic, radiofrequency techniques for,
    1420-1421, 1422f
Facial nerve
  anatomy of, 408f
  examination of, 42-43, 44t
Facial nerve palsy, 407-409
  Bell's, 409t, 412
  differential diagnosis of, 409t
Facial numbness, after percutaneous therapy, for
  trigeminal neuralgia, 356
Facial pain
  atlantoaxial nerve block for, 1132-1133
  atypical, 411-412, 505, 505t
  cryoanalgesia for, 1470-1471, 1470f
  differential diagnosis of, 411-412, 1135t
  from tumors, 411, 412f
  glossopharyngeal nerve block for, 1161,
    1162t
  in Bell's palsy, 409t, 412
  in trigeminal neuralgia. *See* Trigeminal
    neuralgia.
  perineural spread of, 411, 412, 412f
  sphenopalatine ganglion block for, 1134-1139
  stellate ganglion block for, 1191
  trigeminal nerve block for, 1152-1160
  vagus nerve block for, 1166-1168
Facial paralysis, 407-409
  differential diagnosis of, 409t
  in Bell's palsy, 407-409, 409t
Facial skin, innervation of, 553f
Facial telangiectasia, in scleroderma, 441, 441f
Fade test, for sacroiliac disorders, 813
Failed back surgery syndrome, 817-828
  age and, 818
  arachnoiditis in, 823-826, 825f, 826f
  clinical manifestations of, 817
  deep brain stimulation for, 356-357, 357f
  definition of, 818

Failed back surgery syndrome *(Continued)*
  diagnosis of, 826-828, 827f
  distal dural sac ectasia in, 826, 826f
  epidemiology of, 818-819
  epidural adhesiolysis for, 1346
  epidural fibrosis in, 820, 820f
  historical perspective on, 817-818
  inadequate/improper surgery and, 819
  incidental durotomy in, 819
  incorrect diagnosis and, 818
  infections in, 822-823, 823f
  insufficient decompression in, 820-821
  intrathecal/peridural hematoma in, 819, 819f
  loose disk fragments in, 819
  mechanical instability in, 821
  nerve root cysts in, 819-820, 820f
  pathology in, 819-826
  predisposing factors for, 818-819, 828
  prevalence of, 818
  prognosis of, 828
  pseudoarthrosis in, 821-822, 822f
  pseudomeningocele in, 823, 824f
  residual/recurrent/adjacent herniated nucleus
      pulposus in, 821, 821f
  signs and symptoms of, 826-827, 827f
  spinal cord stimulation for, 1377-1378
  spinal stenosis in, 823, 823f
  spondylolisthesis in, 821, 822, 822f
  surgery at wrong level and, 823
  treatment of, 828
  unnecessary surgery and, 818
Famciclovir, for herpes zoster, 281
Fasciitis
  after back surgery, 822
  plantar, 400-402, 401f, 922-924, 923f
Fat, epidural, 1211
Fatigue
  in cancer, 363-364
    sleep disturbances and, 366
  in fibromyalgia, 403
FDG-PET, 85-86
Fecal incontinence, after alcohol neurolysis, 345
Feet. *See* Foot.
Felty syndrome, 433
Females
  cluster headache in, 478-479
  common pain syndromes in, 38t
  migraine in, 456, 479
Femoral herniorrhaphy, femoral neuropathy due
    to, 874
Femoral neck stress fracture, vs. iliopsoas
    bursitis, 866
Femoral nerve, 46t
  anatomy of, 871, 872f
Femoral nerve block, 238t, 1363-1364
Femoral nerve palsy, after ilioinguinal-
    iliohypogastric nerve block, 1326
Femoral neuropathy, 871-874, 872f, 873t
  vs. obturator neuropathy, 879
Femur
  chondroblastoma of, 902, 902f
  osteonecrosis, in sickle cell disease, 258t
Fenoprofen
  for cancer pain, 318-319, 319t
  for tension-type headache, 470, 471t
Fentanyl, 955-956. *See also* Opioid(s).
  for epidural adhesiolysis, 1348
  indications for, 956
  inhalational, 948-949
  oral transmucosal, 1000
  pharmacodynamics of, 956
  pharmacokinetics of, 948t, 956
  preparations of, 956
  routes of administration for, 949, 949f, 956
  side effects of, 956

Fentanyl *(Continued)*
  spinal administration of, 351t. *See also*
      Spinal opioids.
  structure of, 943f, 953f
  transdermal, 949, 949f, 956
Ferritin, serum, evaluation of, 57
Fever
  after implantable drug delivery device
      placement, 1391
  knee pain with, 887
Fiber dissociation theory, 280
Fibrillar creep, 659
Fibroblast growth factor injections. *See*
    Prolotherapy.
Fibromyalgia, 403-405, 404f
  biofeedback for, 1012. *See also* Biofeedback.
  exercise program for, 1060-1061, 1061f
  hypnosis for, 1022
  osteopathic manipulative treatment for, 1078
Fight-or-flight response, 1025
Finger(s). *See also* Hand; Thumb.
  anatomy of, 661f
  boutonnière deformity of, 434, 434f, 662,
      662f
  Dupuytren's contracture of, 668-669, 669f
  in dermatomyositis, 444, 444f
  osteoarthritis of, 418, 420, 420f
    prolotherapy for, 1108
  radiography of, 80-81
  rheumatoid arthritis of, 434, 434f, 435f
  scleroderma of, 441, 441f, 442, 442f
  stenosing digital tenosynovitis of, 670
  swan neck deformity of, 434, 434f, 662,
      662f
  trigger, 670
Fingernails
  abnormalities of, in complex regional pain
      syndrome, 284, 285t
  examination of, in peripheral neuropathy,
      274, 274t
Finkelstein test, for de Quervain's tenosynovitis,
    389, 389f, 666
First or worst syndrome, 36
Fish oil, for cancer cachexia, 366
Fistula, carotid-cavernous, 533, 533f, 535, 535f
Flabby back syndrome, 818
Flail chest, 678-680, 710, 711f
Flank ecchymosis, in acute pancreatitis, 737,
    738f
Flexor digitorum profundus, paralysis of, in
    anterior interosseous syndrome, 653, 655f
Flexor pollicis longus, paralysis of, in anterior
    interosseous syndrome, 653, 655f
Flick sign, in carpal tunnel syndrome, 412
Fluidotherapy, heat application with, 1037,
    1037f
Fluorescent treponemal antibody absorption test,
    63
Fluoroscopic prolotherapy, 1110-1111
Fluoxetine, 968, 968f. *See also* Antidepressants.
Flurbiprofen, for tension-type headache, 470,
    471t
Flushing, opioid-induced, 946
Focused ultrasound, vs. radiofrequency
    techniques, 1411
Folliculitis, nasal, 543
Folstein Mini Mental Status Examination, 42,
    43t
Food. *See also* Diet.
  monoamine oxidase inhibitors and, 969, 969t
Foot. *See also under* Heel; Toe(s).
  abnormalities of, in peripheral neuropathy,
      271, 272, 273f
  Charcot. *See* Charcot arthropathy.
  diabetic, 59, 59f, 112

Foot *(Continued)*
  radiography of, 83-84
  sprains of, prolotherapy for, 1117, 1117f,
      1118f
Foot pain
  anatomic aspects of, 911, 913f
  bunionette and, 921
  causes of, 912-913, 912t
  classification of, 912t
  cryoanalgesia for, 1469-1470
  diagnosis of, 911
  hallux rigidus and, 921-922
  hallux valgus and, 920-921
  in arthritis, 84, 911-914
  in bursitis, 911, 914, 916
  in metatarsalgia, 918-919
  in plantar fasciitis, 400-402, 401f, 922-924,
      923f
  in sesamoiditis, 399-400, 400f
  Morton neuroma and, 918-919
  nerve blocks for, 1368
  prolotherapy for, 1117-1118, 1117f, 1118f
Forearm pain
  in anterior interosseous syndrome, 653
  in cervical radiculopathy, 570
  in radial tunnel syndrome, 657f, 6565
Foreign bodies
  in ear, 542, 543f
  in eye, 524-525, 525f
  in nose, 543
Forst, J.J., 758, 759f
Fortification spectra, in migraine, 457
Fortin finger test, 813
Foundations of Osteopathic Medicine (Ward),
    1075, 1076
Fournier's gangrene, 839
Fractures
  bone marrow edema in, 111-112
  calcaneal, plantar fasciitis and, 922-924
  Chance, computed tomography of, 96f
  femoral neck, vs. iliopsoas bursitis, 866
  pars interarticularis, 800-806, 802f. *See also*
      Spondylolisthesis; Spondylolysis.
  rib, 678-680, 680f, 681f, 710
    epidural steroids for, 1244
    in flail chest, 678-680, 710, 711f
    intercostal nerve block for, 680, 681f,
        1250-1258
  sternal, 678
    parasternal block for, 1250, 1251f
  stress, 111-112. *See also* Stress fractures.
  vertebral. *See* Vertebral fractures.
Franklin, Benjamin, 1093
Free nerve endings, 11, 12, 1081
Free T₄ test, 62
Freezing agents, for neurolytic blockade, 346
Freiberg test, in piriformis syndrome, 834
Frequency-dependent differential nerve blocks,
    163-164, 163f
Frequency encoding, 16, 17
Frontal lobe, in nociception, 1087
Frontal nerve, anatomy of, 523, 524f
Frostbite, of ear, 541
Frovatriptan. *See also* Triptans.
  for medication-overuse headache, 499
  for migraine, 460
FTA-ABS test, 63
Functional Assessment of Cancer
    Therapy–Anemia Scale, 364
Functional magnetic resonance imaging. *See
    also* Magnetic resonance imaging.
  in acupuncture, 1095
Functional stereotaxy, in radiofrequency
    lesioning, 1419-1420
Furosemide, for pseudotumor cerebri, 267

G

GABA, in nerve injury, 28, 1086
Gabapentin, 975-976, 975f
　for arachnoiditis, 796
　for cluster headache, 487
　for complex regional pain syndrome, 294,
　　294t
　　of face, 559
　for glossopharyngeal neuralgia, 513, 513t
　for herpes zoster, 281
　for intercostal neuralgia, 683
　for mononeuritis multiplex, 725
　for peripheral neuropathy, 277, 277t
　for phantom pain, 309
　for post-thoracotomy syndrome, 682
　for proctalgia fugax, 852
　for short-lasting unilateral neuralgiform
　　headache with conjunctival injection and
　　tearing, 482
　for vulvodynia, 844
Gaenslen test, 813
Gait analysis, 47, 1074
Galanin, 19, 19t
Galen, 455-456
Gallstone pancreatitis
　acute, 737-739
　chronic, 739-741
Gamma-aminobutyric acid (GABA), in nerve
　injury, 28, 1086
Gamma globulin, 66, 66f, 68
Gamma glutamyltransferase, in liver disease, 70
Gamma Knife surgery
　for cluster headache, 489
　for trigeminal neuralgia, 334, 353-356, 507
Gangliorhizolysis, radiofrequency, for cluster
　headache, 489
Ganglion of Walker, anatomy of, 1354, 1354f
Ganglion of Walker block, 1354-1357, 1355f,
　1356f
Ganglionotomy
　dorsal root. See Dorsal root ganglionotomy.
　gasserian, 1447-1449
Gangrene, Fournier's, 839
Gasserian ganglion
　anatomy of, 1146, 1146f, 1153, 1153f
　radiofrequency thermocoagulation of, for
　　cluster headache, 489
Gasserian ganglion block, 1145-1151
　anatomic aspects of, 1146-1148, 1146f, 1147f
　complications of, 1148-1151
　contraindications to, 1145, 1146t
　historical perspective on, 1145
　indications for, 1145
　technique of, 1148-1151, 1148f-1150f
Gasserian ganglionotomy, 1447-1449
Gastrointestinal hypermotility, after celiac
　plexus block, 1278
Gastrointestinal toxicity, of nonsteroidal
　antiinflammatory drugs, 227, 930, 935, 937
Gastroparesis, in cancer, 364, 366
Gate control theory, 3-4, 4f, 1373
　vs. neuromatrix theory, 4-7, 5f
Gelling
　in osteoarthritis, 419
　in polymyalgia rheumatica, 444
Gemellar strain, prolotherapy for, 1126, 1126f
Gender differences
　in cluster headache, 478-479
　in common pain syndromes, 38t
　in migraine, 456, 479
General anesthesia, brachial plexopathy during,
　583-584
Genetic factors, in neuromatrix, 5, 5f, 7, 9
Geniculate neuralgia, vs. trigeminal neuralgia,
　504

Genital pain
　in orchialgia, 837-841
　in vulvodynia, 843-846
Genitofemoral nerve, anatomy of, 837, 838f
Genitofemoral nerve block, 238t, 747-748,
　748f
　for orchialgia, 840
　for vulvodynia, 844-845, 845f, 846f
Genitofemoral neuralgia, 747-748, 748f
　after alcohol neurolysis, 345
　in proctalgia fugax, 852f
　pain radiation in, 852f
Genitofemoral neuropathy, cryoanalgesia for,
　1469, 1469f
Gentamicin, prophylactic, for diskography,
　124
Geste antagonistique, in cervical dystonia, 591,
　592f
Giant cell arteritis. See Temporal arteritis.
Gilbert syndrome, 71
Gingival hyperplasia, phenytoin-induced, 974f
Glaucoma, 525-528, 526t, 527f, 528f
Gliocytes, peripheral, 343
Globulin, serum, 66
Glomus tumor, of hand, 671
Glossopharyngeal nerve
　anatomy of, 1161-1162, 1162f
　cryoablation of, 1471, 1471f
　examination of, 42-43, 44t
Glossopharyngeal nerve block, 238t, 514-515,
　514f-516f, 1161-1165
　anatomic aspects of, 1161-1162, 1162f
　complications of, 1164-1165
　contraindications to, 1161, 1162t
　extraoral approach in, 1162-1163, 1163f
　inadvertent, in cervical plexus block, 1188
　indications for, 1161, 1162t
　intraoral approach in, 1163, 1164f
　neurolytic, 1165
　technique of, 1162-1163
Glossopharyngeal nerve root, microvascular
　decompression of, 1165
Glossopharyngeal neuralgia, 511-516, 1161
　clinical features of, 511-512
　demographic factors in, 511, 512t
　diagnosis of, 511-512
　etiology of, 511
　historical considerations in, 511
　imaging studies in, 512
　laboratory findings in, 512
　overflow pain in, 511
　pain characteristics in, 511
　pain localization in, 511, 512f
　treatment of, 512-516
　　cryoanalgesia in, 1471, 1471f
　　drug therapy in, 512-514, 513t, 514t
　　Jannetta technique in, 516, 1165
　　nerve block in, 514-515, 514f-516f, 1161-
　　　1165. See also Glossopharyngeal
　　　nerve block.
　　neurodestructive procedures in, 515-516
　　vs. trigeminal neuralgia, 503-504
Glucose, growth factors and, 1107, 1108t. See
　also Prolotherapy.
Glucose testing, in diabetic neuropathy, 59, 59t,
　406-407
Glutamate, 19t, 20
Glutamate receptors, in tissue injury, 24, 25f
Gluteal bursitis, 853-855, 854f-856f
Gluteal nerve entrapment, 855, 855f
Gluteus tendinitis
　gluteal bursitis and, 853
　trochanteric bursitis and, 859, 861
Glycerol, for neurolytic blockade, 346. See also
　Neurolytic blockade.

Glycine, in nerve injury, 28, 1086
Gold salts, for rheumatoid arthritis, 436
Goldscheider's summation theory, 3, 4f
Golfer's elbow, 637-640, 638f, 639f
　prolotherapy for, 1114, 1114f
　vs. cubital tunnel syndrome, 647-650
Gonyalgia paresthetica, 875
Gout, 70
　vs. osteoarthritis, 424
Graft, bone, iliac crest donor site pain after,
　cryoanalgesia for, 1465, 1465f, 1471-1473,
　1472t
Granuloma
　catheter-tip, 797
　cholesterol, maxillary antral, 543, 545f
Gray matter, periaqueductal
　in pain processing, 213, 214f, 1086, 1087
　opioid action in, 29
Greater auricular nerve, 538, 540f
　anatomy of, 1174, 1174f, 1176f-1179f
Greater occipital nerve. See also Occipital
　nerve.
　anatomy of, 549, 1140, 1141f-1143f, 1143,
　　1174, 1176f, 1177f
Greater occipital nerve block, 1140-1144. See
　also Occipital nerve block.
　diagnostic, 153
　for cluster headache, 488
Greater palatine nerve, 540f
Greater splanchnic nerve
　anatomy of, 1267, 1267f
　radiofrequency lesioning of, 1454-1456,
　　1455f
Greater trochanteric pain syndrome. See
　Trochanteric bursitis.
Groin pain
　after alcohol neurolysis, 345
　cryoanalgesia for, 1469
　ilioinguinal-iliohypogastric block for, 1322-
　　1323
　in trochanteric bursitis, 859
　prolotherapy for, 1118-1119, 1118f, 1119f
Groin surgery, ilioinguinal-iliohypogastric block
　for, 1323
Group therapy, for chronic pain, 218
Growth factors
　ligament/tendon, dextrose effects on, 1107,
　　1108t. See also Prolotherapy.
　therapeutic injections of. See Prolotherapy.
Guanethidine, for complex regional pain
　　syndrome, 295
　in prevention, 298
Guided imagery, 1025-1031. See also
　　Relaxation techniques.
　for burn pain, 247-248
Guillain-Barré syndrome, 64
　areflexia in, 47

H

H-reflex, in nerve conduction studies, 186
Haemophilus influenzae pneumonia, 704,
　706f
Haglund's deformity, 916
Hair
　abnormalities of, in complex regional pain
　　syndrome, 284, 285t
　examination of, in peripheral neuropathy,
　　274, 274t
Hallux rigidus, 920-921
Hallux valgus, 920-921
　bunionette and, 921
　prolotherapy for, 1118
Haloperidol, for cancer-related nausea, 365

Hammer toe, 920
  in peripheral neuropathy, 272, 273f
Hampton's hump, 703, 703f
Hamstring strains, prolotherapy for, 1115,
  1116f, 1126, 1126f
Hand. *See also* Finger(s); Thumb; Wrist.
  anatomy of, 661f
  arthritis of, 418, 420, 420f, 659, 660t, 662-
    663. *See also* Osteoarthritis.
  Dupuytren's contracture of, 668-669, 669f
  glomus tumor of, 671
  machinist's, in dermatomyositis, 444, 444f
  opera glass, 662
  osteoarthritis of, 80, 418, 420, 420f, 659,
    660t, 662-663. *See also* Osteoarthritis.
    prolotherapy for, 1108, 1114
  pain in
    anatomic aspects of, 659, 661f
    differential diagnosis of, 659, 660t
    in cervical radiculopathy, 570
  radiation numbness of, prolotherapy for, 1119
  radiography of, 80-81
  scleroderma of, 441, 441f
  simian, 582
  tendons of, 661f
  tenosynovitis of, 659, 660
  waiter's tip, 581, 582f
Handcuff palsy, 275m275f
Hanging-drop technique, for epidural nerve
    block
  cervical, 1215
  thoracic, 1246
Hansen's disease, 64
Haptoglobin, serum, evaluation of, 57
Harris, Wilfred, 474
Harris-Beath view, 84
Hawkins impingement test, 606, 607f, 624
Head and neck tumors, facial pain from, 411-
  412, 412f
Headache, 262-267
  after cervical plexus block, 1189
  age and, 262
  cervicogenic
    atlanto-occipital nerve block for, 1128-
      1131, 1130f, 1131f
    occipital nerve block for, 1140-1144,
      1143f
    occipital neuralgia and, 549, 1140
    radiofrequency techniques for, 1444-1445
  chronic, 468-469, 492-493
    classification of, 492, 493t
  chronic daily, 468-469
  cluster, 474-489, 479, 492, 531. *See also*
    Cluster headache.
  differential diagnosis of, 264
  etiology of, 494
  from atlantoaxial nerve block, 1133
  from brain tumor, 265, 266-267
  history in, 262, 262t
  imaging studies in, 263-264
  in bacterial meningitis, 263t, 264, 266
  in brain abscess, 264-265
  in cervical dystonia, 591
  in hypertension, 265-266, 267
  in infectious disorders, 263t, 264-265
  in inflammatory disorders, 263t, 265
  in intracranial hypertension, 265, 267
  in occipital neuralgia, 504, 549-551, 550f
  in paroxysmal hemicrania, 481-482
  in sinus disorders, 469
  in stroke, 263t, 264, 266
  in subarachnoid hemorrhage, 263t, 264, 266
  in temporal arteritis, 265, 266
  in vasculitis, 264, 265
  interval, 464

Headache *(Continued)*
  location of, 262
  management of, 266-267
    biofeedback in, 1012, 1015. *See also*
      Biofeedback.
    cryoanalgesia in, 1470-1471, 1470f
    gasserian ganglion block in, 1145-1151
    hypnosis in, 1022, 1023
    prolotherapy in, 1122, 1122f, 1123f
    relaxation techniques in, 1027
    sphenopalatine ganglion block in, 1134-
      1139
    trigeminal nerve block in, 1152-1160,
      1153t
  medication-overuse, 469, 470, 492-501. *See
    also* Medication-overuse headache.
  migraine, 455-462, 459, 459t, 468-469, 492,
    493t. *See also* Migraine.
  neurologic examination in, 262-263
  occipital, 504, 549-551, 550f
    after cervical plexus block, 1189
  organic causes of, 263t, 264-266
  pathophysiology of, 494-496, 495f
  physical examination in, 262
  post–dural puncture
    after implantable drug delivery device
      placement, 1391
    in subarachnoid neurolysis, 1302
  pseudotumor cerebri and, 265, 267
  sentinel, 262
  short-lasting unilateral neuralgiform, with
    conjunctival injection and tearing, 482
  signs and symptoms of, 262
  tension-type, 464-472. *See also* Tension-type
    headache.
Headache Impact Test, for medication-overuse
    headache, 497
Hearing loss, diagnosis of, brain stem auditory
    evoked potentials in, 193, 193f
Heart rate, in endurance exercise, 1058
Heat application, 1033-1039
  contraindications to, 1034t
  for rheumatoid arthritis, 437
  for sacroiliac disorders, 814
  in contrast baths, 1041, 1041f, 1050
  indications for, 1034t
  modalities of
    deep, 1034t, 1038-1039
    selection of, 1034-1035
    superficial, 1034t, 1035-1038
  physiologic effects of, 1033, 1034t
  with chemical heating packs, 1035-1036
  with circulating water heating pads, 1035,
    1035f
  with fluidotherapy, 1037, 1037f
  with hydrocollator packs, 1035, 1035f
  with hydrotherapy, 1037, 1037f, 1043-1050
  with microwave diathermy, 1039
  with paraffin baths, 1036-1037, 1037f
  with reusable microwavable heating pads,
    1036, 1036f
  with short-wave diathermy, 1039, 1039f
  with ultrasound, 1034t, 1038
Hebb, D.O., 7
Heberden nodes, 80, 420, 420f, 434, 435f, 662
Heel pain. *See also* Ankle pain; Foot pain.
  causes of, 922
  differential diagnosis of, 922
  in plantar fasciitis, 400-402, 401f, 922-924,
    923f
  in retrocalcaneal bursitis, 916
Heel spurs, 922-924
Heel wedges, for osteoarthritis, 426, 426f
Heidenhein's method, for cervical plexus block,
  1181

Heliotrope rash, in dermatomyositis, 443-444,
  443f
Hematoma
  from implantable drug delivery systems,
    1390
  in brachial plexus block, 1221, 1224, 1226
  in caudal epidural block, 1343
  in cervical epidural block, 1218
  in lumbar epidural block, 1292
  in thoracic epidural block, 1247
  intrathecal/peridural, postoperative, 819
  pulmonary, 711-712
Hemiarthroplasty, for osteoarthritis, 428
Hemiplegic migraine, 458, 458t. *See also*
  Migraine.
Hemoglobin
  measurement of, 57
  normal values for, 57
Hemoglobin A1C, in diabetes, 59
Hemoglobin S, screening for, 57-58
Hemopneumothorax, rib fractures and, 678
Hemorrhage. *See also* Bleeding.
  macular, from epidural injections, 172,
    176
  retinal, from epidural injections, 172, 176
  retroperitoneal, femoral neuropathy due to,
    872, 873t
  subarachnoid
    cerebrospinal fluid findings in, 264
    headache in, 263t, 264
    treatment of, 266
Hemothorax, 711
Heparin. *See also* Anticoagulants.
  epidural adhesiolysis and, 1346
  for pulmonary embolism, 704
Hepatic disease. *See* Liver disease.
Hepatic encephalopathy, in liver disease, 71
Hepatocyte growth factor injections. *See*
  Prolotherapy.
Hepatomegaly, 732-736, 733f
  in peripheral neuropathy, 274
Hepatotoxicity, of acetaminophen, 932
Herbal remedies, 991t. *See also* Complementary
  and alternative therapies.
  Chinese, 1099-1100
  with anticoagulant action, epidural
    adhesiolysis and, 1346
Hernia, obturator, 879
Herniated disks. *See* Intervertebral disk disease,
  herniation in.
Herniorrhaphy
  femoral neuropathy due to, 874
  orchialgia after, 838, 839
  pain after, cryoanalgesia for, 1463
Heroin, 952. *See also* Opioid(s).
  abuse of, screening for, 72
  for cancer pain, 320t, 321-323
  structure of, 942f, 953f
Herpes zoster, 279-282, 281f
  complications of, 282. *See also* Postherpetic
    neuralgia.
  in Ramsay Hunt syndrome, 272, 538, 540f
  rash in, 279, 281f
  signs and symptoms of, 279, 281f
  treatment of, 280-282
    drug therapy in, 280-282
    nerve blocks in, 280
      stellate ganglion, 1152-1160
      thoracic epidural, 1243
      trigeminal nerve, 1152-1160
  trigeminal nerve involvement in, 280, 281f
    vs. trigeminal neuralgia, 504
Herpes zoster ophthalmicus, 536, 536f
  cavernous sinus syndrome and, 536, 536f
Herring-Breuer reflexes, 693

Hiccups
    causes of, 1169, 1170t
    celiac plexus block for, 1174
    complications of, 1170t
    drug therapy for, 1169, 1170t
    phrenic nerve block for, 1169-1172, 1170t
High altitude, implantable drug delivery devices
        at, 1397
Hildreth's test, for glomus tumor of hand, 671
Hill-Sachs lesions, radiography of, 608
Hinck needle, in pituitary neuroadenolysis,
        1406-1408, 1408f, 1409f
Hip
    avascular necrosis of
        imaging of, 99, 102f
        in sickle cell disease, 258t
    bursitis of, 398-399. See also Bursitis, of hip.
    imaging of
        computed tomographic, 99, 102f
        radiographic, 81, 82f, 83f
    osteoarthritis of, 81, 82f, 419-420. See also
        Osteoarthritis.
        differential diagnosis of, 422t
        exercise program for, 1059-1060
        imaging of, 81, 82f, 421-424
        prevention of, 428-429
        prolotherapy for, 1115, 1115f
        total joint arthroplasty for, 86, 428. See
            also Total joint arthroplasty.
            femoral neuropathy in, 873
            obturator neuropathy in, 879, 881
    osteonecrosis of, imaging of, 81, 83f, 99,
        102f
    radiography of, 81, 82f, 83f
    snapping, 862, 864-867
Hip abduction exercises, for sacroiliac
        disorders, 815
Hip adduction exercises, for sacroiliac
        disorders, 815
Hip extension exercises, for sacroiliac disorders,
        815
Hip pain
    in adductor tendinitis, 391-395, 393f-395f
    in gluteal bursitis, 853-855, 854f-856f
    in iliopsoas bursitis, 864-867
    in ischiogluteal bursitis, 855-858, 856f,
        857f
    in meralgia paresthetica, 36, 415-416, 868-
        870, 1328-1330, 1364
    in trochanteric bursitis, 81, 390-391, 392f,
        393f, 859-862
    lateral femoral cutaneous nerve block for,
        1328-1330, 1364
    obturator nerve block for, 238t, 1331-1334,
        1364-1365
Hip replacement. See Total joint arthroplasty.
Hippocrates, 455, 758, 759f
Histamine
    in cluster headache, 478, 480
    in tissue injury, 23t
Histamine desensitization, for cluster headache,
        488
Histoplasmosis, 706-707, 707f
History, 35-41
    associated factors in, 37
    character in, 37
    chief complaint in, 39, 41
    chronicity in, 36-37
    components of, 39-41
    drug dependency and, 39, 40t
    in differential diagnosis, 37
    interview in, 37, 39-41
    listening skills for, 35
    location in, 36
    medication, 38-39

History (Continued)
    mode of onset in, 36
    pain litany in, 35-37
    severity in, 37
    social, 41
    tempo in, 37
HIV infection. See Human immunodeficiency
        virus infection.
HLA antigens, in complex regional pain
        syndrome, 286
Hoffman reflex, in nerve conduction studies,
        186
Hoffman sign, in cervical radiculopathy, 571,
        572t
Holistic medicine, vs. alternative medicine, 990.
        See also Complementary and alternative
        therapies.
Hooking maneuver test, for slipping rib
        syndrome, 731, 732f
Hoppenfeld, S., 1074, 1074t
Hordeolum, 524, 524f
Hormones, opioids and, 946
Hornblower's sign, 605-606, 606f
Horner syndrome, 577
    after cordotomy, 1514-1515
    causes of, 557
    in cervical plexus block, 1189
    in cluster headache, 477, 480, 531, 531f
    in stellate ganglion block, 230, 557, 559,
        1197, 1198
    Pancoast syndrome and, 694, 695
    partial, in cluster headache, 477, 480
    Raeder syndrome and, 504
    stellate ganglion block and, 230
    with brachial plexopathy, 582
Horton, Bernard Taylor, 474
Hot tubs. See also Whirlpool baths.
    implantable drug delivery systems in, 1398
    miscarriage risk with, 1050
Hounsfield, Godfrey Newbold, 93
Housemaid's knee, 396-397, 397f, 895-897,
        895f-897f
Ho:YAG laser, 1489, 1490f. See also Laser
        therapy.
5-HT antagonists, for migraine, 460
5-HT receptors, in medication-overuse
        headaches, 495
Hubbard tank
    in cold therapy, 1040, 1049
    in heat therapy, 1037, 1037f, 1049
Human immunodeficiency virus infection
    diagnosis of, 62-63, 67t
    neuropathy in, 67t
    opportunistic infections in, 63
    pleural effusion in, 701
Human leukocyte antigens, in complex regional
        pain syndrome, 286
Hunter, John, 502
Hutchinson, Jonathan, 518
Hyaluronan, intra-articular, for osteoarthritis,
        428
Hyaluronidase
    for epidural adhesiolysis, 1347, 1348
    with local anesthetics, 986
Hydrocele, orchialgia and, 839, 840
Hydrocodone, 952-954, 953f. See also
        Opioid(s).
    for cancer pain, 320t, 321-323
    structure of, 942f, 953f
Hydrocollator packs, 1035, 1035f
Hydrogen ions, in tissue injury, 23t
Hydromorphone, 944t, 948t, 953f, 954. See also
        Opioid(s).
    for cancer pain, 320t, 321-323
    structure of, 942f

Hydropneumothorax, radiography of, 688f
Hydrotherapy, 1043-1050
    definition of, 1043
    heated whirlpool/Hubbard tank in, 1037,
        1037f, 1049-1050
    historical perspective on, 1043
    iced whirlpool/Hubbard tank in, 1049-
        1050
    physiologic effects of, 1044, 1044t
    principles of, 1043-1045
    techniques of, 1045-1050
    therapeutic effects of, 1044-1045, 1045t
    water-based exercises in, 1045-1049, 1047f,
        1048f
    with cold, 1040
    with heat, 1037, 1037f
Hydroxychloroquine, for rheumatoid arthritis,
        436
Hydroxyurea, for sickle cell pain, 260
Hydroxyzine, for cancer pain, 324
Hygroma, after implantable drug delivery
        device placement, 1391
Hyoid syndrome, 547
Hyperalgesia, 12
    definition of, 218
Hyperbaric subarachnoid neurolysis, 1299,
        1300f, 1301f. See also Subarachnoid
        neurolytic block.
Hyperbaric therapy, with implantable drug
        delivery systems, 1398
Hypercalcemia, 69
Hyperchloremia, 60
Hyperemia, conjunctival, 525, 526f
Hyperesthesia, secondary, 24
Hyperhidrosis, in complex regional pain
        syndrome, 284, 285t, 287
Hyperkalemia, 60
Hypernatremia, 60
Hyperparathyroidism, 69
Hyperpathia, definition of, 218
Hyperphosphatemia, 69
Hypersensitivity. See also Allergy.
    denervation, pathogenesis of, 8
Hypertension
    headache in, 265-266, 267
    intracranial
        benign, 265, 267
        headache in, 265, 267
        in pseudotumor cerebri, 265, 267
        treatment of, 267
    pulmonary, 704
        in sickle cell disease, 703
    treatment of, 267
Hyperthyroidism
    diagnosis of, 62
    in temporal arteritis, 62
Hypertonic solutions, for neurolytic blockade,
        346
Hyperuricemia, 70
Hypesthesia. See Anesthesia/hypesthesia.
Hypnosis, 993, 1021-1024
    anatomic aspects of, 1022
    for acute pain, 1022, 1023
    for burn pain, 248-249, 254, 1022, 1023
    for cancer pain, 1022, 1023
    for children, 1021, 1022, 1023, 1024
    for chronic pain, 1022, 1023
    for obstetric pain, 1022, 1023
    for perioperative pain, 1022-1023
    for phantom pain, 311
    historical perspective on, 1021
    indications for, 1021-1022
    side effects and complications of, 1023
    susceptibility assessment for, 254, 1024
    technique of, 1022-1023

Hypobaric subarachnoid neurolysis, 1296-1299, 1297f, 1298f. *See also* Subarachnoid neurolytic block.
Hypocalcemia, 69
Hypochloremia, 60
Hypogastric plexus, anatomy of, 837, 838f, 1350, 1351f
Hypogastric plexus block, 1350-1354
    anatomic aspects of, 1350, 1351f
    complications of, 1353-1354
    technique of, 1350-1353
        single-needle, 1350-1351, 1352f, 1353f
        two-needle, 1351-1353, 1354f
Hypoglossal nerve, 540f
    examination of, 42-43, 44t
Hypoglycemia, 59
Hypohidrosis, in complex regional pain syndrome, 284, 285t
Hypokalemia, 60
Hypomagnesemia, 69-70
Hyponatremia, 59-60
Hypoparathyroidism, 69
Hypophosphatemia, 69
Hypophysectomy, for cancer pain, 326
Hypopyon, 529f
Hyporeflexia, in cervical radiculopathy, 570, 571
Hypotension
    celiac plexus block and, 232, 1278
    intercostal nerve block and, 1257
    opioid-related, with spinal administration, 351, 352t
    thoracic epidural nerve block and, 1245
Hypothalamus, in cluster headache, 480-481
Hypothermia, for neurolytic blockade, 346
Hypothyroidism, diagnosis of, 62
Hypotonic solutions, for neurolytic blockade, 346
Hysterectomy, femoral neuropathy after, 873

I

Ibuprofen, 930-931. *See also* Nonsteroidal antiinflammatory drugs.
    for cancer pain, 318-319, 319t
    for tension-type headaches, 470, 471t
    structure of, 226f
Ice packs, 1040, 1040f
Ice rubs, 1040
Iced whirlpools, 1040, 1049-1050
IgA, 68
IgD, 68
IgE, 68
IgG, 68
IgM, 68
IgM monoclonal gammopathy, 67t, 68
Iliac abscess, femoral neuropathy due to, 872
Iliac crest donor site pain, cryoanalgesia for, 1465, 1465f, 1471-1473, 1472t
Iliac hemorrhage, femoral neuropathy due to, 872, 873t
Iliacus compartment, 871
Iliofemoral bursitis, 864-867
Iliohypogastric neuropathy, cryoanalgesia for, 1469, 1469f
Ilioinguinal-iliohypogastric nerve, anatomy of, 742, 744f, 745, 837, 838f
Ilioinguinal-iliohypogastric nerve block, 238t, 1322-1327
    analgesic, 1322-1323
        technique of, 1323-1326
    anatomic aspects of, 1323, 1324f, 1325f
    anesthetic, 1323
        technique of, 1323

Ilioinguinal-iliohypogastric nerve block (Continued)
    complications of, 1326-1327
    diagnostic, 1322
        technique of, 1323-1324
    for iliohypogastric neuralgia, 746-747, 746f
    for ilioinguinal neuralgia, 744-745, 745f
    for orchialgia, 840
    for vulvodynia, 844-845, 845f, 846f
    historical perspective on, 1322
    indications for, 1322-1323
    technique of, 1326f
    terminology of, 1322
Ilioinguinal-iliohypogastric neuralgia, 745-747, 746f
Ilioinguinal neuralgia, 742-745
    cryoanalgesia for, 1469
        after herniorrhaphy, 1463
Iliolumbar ligament
    anatomy of, 810, 811f, 812f
    prolotherapeutic injection of, 1124, 1124f
Iliopectineal bursitis, 864-867
Iliopsoas bursitis, 864-867
Iliotibial band syndrome, 862, 864-867
Imagery, 1025-1031
    for burn pain, 247-248
Imaging studies. *See also specific techniques and indications.*
    computed tomography, 93-105
    contrast media in, adverse reactions to, 124, 148, 791
    epidurography, 145-148
    magnetic resonance angiography, 106
    magnetic resonance arthrography, 106-107
    magnetic resonance imaging, 106-116
    nuclear medicine, 85-91
    radiography, 74-84
    with implantable drug delivery systems, 1398
Imipramine, side effects of, 718t
Immune system, opioid effects on, 946
Immunodeficiency. *See also* Human immunodeficiency virus infection.
    fulminant pneumonia in, 706
Immunoglobulins, 58
Immunosuppressive therapy
    for rheumatoid arthritis, 436-437
    for systemic lupus erythematosus, 440
Impar ganglion, anatomy of, 1355, 1355f
Impar ganglion block, 1354-1357, 1355f, 1356f
Impingement syndrome, 603, 606
    acromioclavicular joint pain and, 615-618
    biceps tendinitis and, 622, 624
    decompression surgery for, 610-611, 611f
    provocative tests for, 606, 607f, 624
    rotator cuff disorders and, 603, 606, 610-611, 611f
Implantable drug delivery systems, 1382-1386
    alarms for, 1398
    altitude and, 1397
    care of, 1392
    catheter care for, 1392
    classification of, 1384-1386, 1384t
    complications of, 1382, 1383t, 1388-1401
        bleeding, 1389-1390
        cerebrospinal fluid leak, 1391
        epidural abscess, 1391
        hygroma, 1391
        infection, 1390-1391
        intrathecal bolus administration, 1395
        meningitis, 1390-1391
        post–dural puncture headache, 1391
        postoperative fever, 1391
        published data on, 1400-1401

Implantable drug delivery systems (Continued)
        refilling problems, 1395-1396
        subcutaneous administration, 1395
        subcutaneous pocket malposition, 1392
        technical, 1392-1393
    costs of, 1384
    disease progression and, 1392
    failure of, 1392, 1399-1400
    history of, 1382
    hot tubs and, 1398
    hyperbaric therapy and, 1398
    imaging of, 1393
    implantation technique for, 1392
    infusion pump, 1385-1386, 1386f. *See also* Implantable infusion pump.
    mechanical failures in, 1393
    misinjections with, 1397
    patient selection for, 1382-1383, 1383t, 1384
    patient's support system for, 1383-1384
    percutaneous catheter, 1385, 1385f
    pre-cremation removal of, 1398
    preimplantation trials for, 1382, 1383t
    refilling problems with, 1395
    reservoir/port, 1385, 1386f
    scuba diving with, 1398
    security systems and, 1397
    subcutaneous tunneled catheter, 1385, 1385f
    technical aspects of, 1392-1396
    terminology of, 1388
    test doses with, 1393
    traveling with, 1397
    types of, 1384-1386, 1384t
Implantable infusion pump, 1385-1386, 1386f. *See* Infusion pump.
    care of, 1392
    complications of, published data on, 1400-1401
    for arachnoiditis, 797
    for cancer pain, 339
    programmable, 1386, 1386f
    reservoir contamination in, 1392
Implantable nerve stimulators, 1369-1371, 1370f, 1371f
Implantable reservoir/port, 1385, 1386f
Implanted pulse generator, for spinal cord stimulation, 1373, 1375f
Impotence, after cordotomy, 1515
Inappropriate antidiuretic hormone secretion, 60, 69
Incident pain, 1000
Incontinence
    fecal, after alcohol neurolysis, 345
    urinary
        after alcohol neurolysis, 345
        after caudal epidural block, 1344
        after cervical epidural block, 1218
        after cordotomy, 1514
Increased intracranial pressure
    benign, 265, 267
    headache in, 265, 267
    in pseudotumor cerebri, 265, 267
    treatment of, 267
Indomethacin
    for arachnoiditis, 796
    for cancer pain, 318-319, 319t
    for cluster headache, 487
    for paroxysmal hemicrania, 482
Induction heating, vs. radiofrequency techniques, 1411
Infectious arthritis. *See also* Arthritis.
    of shoulder, 615
Inferior alveolar nerve, 540f, 1155
Inferior hypogastric plexus, anatomy of, 837, 838f

Inflammation
    acute phase response in, 934-935
        indicators of, 56-57
    chronic, 935
    neurogenic, 1083-1084, 1084f, 1089
    nociceptors in, 1083-1084, 1084f
    physiology of, 934-935
Inflatable bone tamp, in kyphoplasty, 1479-
    1480, 1481f
Inflation reflex, 693
Infliximab, for rheumatoid arthritis, 436-437
Informed consent, for cryoanalgesia, 1462
Infraorbital nerve
    anatomy of, 1147, 1147f
    cryoablation of, 1470f, 1471
Infraorbital nerve block, 1157-1159, 1158f. See
    also Trigeminal nerve block.
Infrapatellar bursitis, 886, 886f, 897-900, 898f,
    899f
Infrapatellar nerve, cryoablation of, 1469
Infraspinatus tendinitis, 378-380
Infraspinatus tendon. See also Rotator cuff
    disorders.
    anatomy of, 603, 604f
    strength tests for, 605-606
Infusion pump, 1385-1386, 1386f
    care of, 1392
    complications of, published data on, 1400-
        1401
    for arachnoiditis, 797
    for cancer pain, 339
    programmable, 1386, 1386f
    reservoir contamination in, 1392
Inguinal herniorrhaphy
    femoral neuropathy due to, 874
    orchialgia after, 838, 839
    pain after, cryoanalgesia for, 1463
Injection therapy
    corticosteroid. See Corticosteroids, intra-
        articular; Corticosteroids, intralesional.
    prolotherapy, 1106-1126
Insects, in ear, 542, 543f
Insoles, for osteoarthritis, 426, 426f
Insomnia. See Sleep disturbances.
Intercostal nerve
    anatomy of, 727, 728f, 729, 1250-1251,
        1252f, 1253f, 1255f, 1463f
    cryoablation of, for post-thoracotomy pain,
        1462-1463, 1463f
    entrapment of, 727-731, 728f-731f
Intercostal nerve block, 236-237, 238f, 238t,
    1250-1257
    anatomic aspects of, 1250-1251, 1252f,
        1253f
    classic approach in, 1253, 1254f, 1255f
    complications of, 1257
    diagnostic, 153, 338, 1250
    efficacy of, 1257
    for acute/postoperative pain, 236-237, 238f
    for anterior cutaneous nerve entrapment, 729-
        731, 731f
    for cancer pain, 324, 338
    for intercostal neuralgia, 684
    for liver pain, 734, 736f
    for post-thoracotomy pain, 723
    for post-thoracotomy syndrome, 682
    for rib fractures, 680, 681f
    future directions for, 1257
    historical perspective on, 1250
    hypotension in, 1257
    indications for, 1250
    jet injectors for, 1257
    local anesthetics for, 1256, 1256t
        selection of, 1256, 1257
        systemic toxicity of, 1257

Intercostal nerve block (Continued)
    midaxillary approach in, 1253, 1255f
    parasternal, 1250, 1251f
    paravertebral approach in, 1253-1256
    pitfalls in, 1256-1257
    pneumothorax in, 1257
    respiratory effects of, 1257
    sedation for, 1256
    technique of, 736f, 1253-1256
    with celiac plexus block, 1250
Intercostal neuralgia, 682-684, 683f
    cryoanalgesia for, 1463, 1465f
Intercostobrachial nerve block, 1237, 1237f
Interdigital (Morton) neuroma, 918-919
    prolotherapy for, 1118
Interferon-gamma, intralesional, for
    Dupuytren's contracture, 669
Intermediate dorsal cutaneous nerve,
    cryoablation of, 1469
Intermetatarsophalangeal bursae, 914
Internal pterygoid nerve, 1148
Interosseous ligament, anatomy of, 810, 811f
Interphalangeal joints, of hand. See also
    Finger(s); Hand.
    anatomy of, 661f
    osteoarthritis of, 418, 420, 420f. See also
        Osteoarthritis.
    radiography of, 80-81
    rheumatoid arthritis of, 434, 434f, 435f. See
        also Rheumatoid arthritis.
Interpleural catheter analgesia, 324, 1259-1263,
    1260t, 1261f, 1262f
Interscalene cervical plexus block, 1184, 1184f
Intersection syndrome, 666
Intersegmental projection systems, 15
Interspinous ligament
    in cervical epidural block, 1213, 1214f
    pain in, cryoanalgesia for, 1468
    prolotherapeutic injection of, 1120, 1120f
Intertarsal arthritis, 914
Interval headache, 464
Intervertebral disk
    age-related changes in, 756
    anatomy of, 118-120, 119f, 120f, 1492-
        1493
    imaging of. See Diskography.
    infection of. See Diskitis.
Intervertebral disk disease
    anatomic aspects of, 118-120, 119f, 120f
    annular tears in, 109
        grading of, 99, 100f, 130-131, 130f, 131f
    cervical, 52, 52t, 53f, 54f, 55t, 568-574. See
        also Cervical radiculopathy.
    case study of, 50
    complications of, 574
    degenerative, 107
    grading of, 110-111
    herniation in, 107-109
        atypical presentation of, 764
        clinical features of, 761-762, 762f, 764,
            764t
        complications of, 765
        computed tomography of, 102, 103f, 104f,
            763
        diagnosis of, 762-763
        magnetic resonance imaging of, 107-109,
            763
        pain in. See Radicular pain; Radiculopathy.
        pathology of, 1492-1494
        percutaneous laser diskectomy for, 1489-
            1499
        predisposing factors in, 1493
        radiofrequency techniques for, 1425-1426,
            1426f
        recurrent postoperative, 821, 821f

Intervertebral disk disease (Continued)
    imaging in
        computed tomography in, 98-99, 102, 103f,
            104f, 763
        diskography in, 98-99, 118-140. See also
            Diskography.
        magnetic resonance imaging of, 107-111,
            108f-110f
        radiography in, 75-76, 76f
    inflammatory mediators in, 1492-1493
    lumbar, 52t, 53f, 54f, 55, 55t, 756, 756f. See
        also Lumbar radiculopathy.
        epidural nerve block for, 1281
    occupational. See Occupational back pain.
    pain in
        axial, 118
        axial vs. radicular, 118
        distribution of, 52-55, 52t, 53f, 54f
        production of, 120, 1087
        radicular, 118, 758-766
            vs. axial pain, 118
        percutaneous laser diskectomy for, 1489-
            1499
        radiculopathy in, 758-766. See also
            Radiculopathy.
        radiofrequency techniques for, 1425-1426,
            1426f
    spinal stenosis in, 111, 111f
    surgery for
        complications of, 765, 817-828. See also
            Failed back surgery syndrome.
        for cervical radiculopathy, 574
        for lumbar radiculopathy, 765
    thoracic, epidural steroids for, 1244
    vertebral end plate changes in, 109-110,
        110f
Intervertebral osteochondrosis, 107
Interview, in history taking, 37, 39-41. See also
    History.
Intra-articular injections. See Corticosteroids,
    intra-articular.
Intracranial hypertension
    benign, 265, 267
    headache in, 265, 267
    in pseudotumor cerebri, 265, 267
    treatment of, 267
Intracranial neurostimulation, for phantom pain,
    311
Intradiskal electrothermal annuloplasty, 1426-
    1431, 1484-1487
    alternatives to, 1484
    anatomic aspects of, 1485
    complications of, 1487
    contraindications to, 1484-1485, 1485t
    efficacy of, 1427, 1487
    history of, 1484
    indications for, 1484-1485, 1485t
    lumbar, 1427-1429, 1427f, 1428f
    mechanism of action of, 1426-1427
    technique of, 1485-1487, 1485f, 1486f
    thoracic, 1429-1431
Intrapleural catheterization, for cancer pain,
    324
Intrathecal catheterization. See also under
    Epidural; Spinal.
    for cancer pain, 339
Intrathecal corticosteroids, for chronic pain,
    220, 339-340
Intrathecal hematoma, postoperative, 819
Intrathecal injections. See also under Epidural;
    Spinal.
    inadvertent
        in lumbar epidural block, 1291
        in stellate ganglion block, 1197-1198
Intrathecal opioids. See Spinal opioids.

Intravascular injection
    in atlanto-occipital nerve block, 1130-1131
    in brachial plexus block, 1221
    in celiac plexus block, 1278
    in cervical epidural block, 1218
    in cervical plexus block, 1188
    in hypogastric plexus block, 1353-1354
    in lumbar sympathetic block, 1320
    in musculocutaneous nerve block, 1237
    in phrenic nerve block, 1170
    in radial nerve block, 1235
    in sphenopalatine ganglion block, 1138
    in stellate ganglion block, 1198
    of femoral nerve, 1364
    of suprascapular artery, 1242
Intravenous regional sympatholysis, for
        complex regional pain syndrome, 295
Intraventricular opioids, 949
Iohexol, for epidurography, 147
Ion channels, in nerve injury, 26, 1085
Ionizing radiation, vs. radiofrequency
        techniques, 1412
Iron, serum, evaluation of, 57
Iron deficiency anemia, diagnosis of, 5757
Ischiogluteal bursitis, 855-858, 856f, 857f
Isocarboxazid, 969. See also Antidepressants.
    for migraine prophylaxis, 461
Isokinetic exercises, 1057
Isometheptene mucate, for tension-type
        headache, 470, 471t
Isometric exercises, 1057, 1057t
    for sacroiliac disorders, 815
Isotonic exercises, 1057, 1057t
Itching, opioid-induced, 946
    with spinal administration, 351, 352t,
        1397
Ixodes scapularis, as Lyme disease vector, 63,
        63f

J
J receptor, 693
Jaccoud arthritis, 438
Jacobson, Edmund, 1025-1026
Jannetta technique, for glossopharyngeal
        neuralgia, 516, 1165
Jaundice, 71
Jaw claudication, in temporal arteritis, 445,
        446, 519
Jet injectors, for intercostal nerve block,
        1257
Jobe tests, for rotator cuff tears, 605, 606
Joint Commission on Accreditation of
        Healthcare Organizations (JCAHO), pain
        assessment standards of, 198-199, 199t
Joint laxity, prolotherapy of
    for knee, 1108, 1108f, 1116
    for shoulder, 1112-1113
Joint pain. See Arthritis *and specific joints and
        disorders.*
Jugular fossa schwannoma, glossopharyngeal
        neuralgia and, 512
Jump sign
    in fibromyalgia, 403, 404f
    in sternalis syndrome, 678

K
κ (kappa) receptor, 940-941, 941t
K-pads, 1035, 1035f
Keller procedure, for hallux valgus, 920
Kernig sign, 264, 1390
Kerr sign, 1169

Ketamine
    for burn pain, 243t, 244, 246
    for chronic pain, 220
    for phantom pain
        in prevention, 309
        in treatment, 310
    mechanism of action of, 31
Ketanserin, in intravenous regional
        sympatholysis, for complex regional pain
        syndrome, 295
Ketoprofen, 931. See also Nonsteroidal
        antiinflammatory drugs.
    for cancer pain, 318-319, 319t
    for tension-type headache, 470, 471t
Ketorolac
    for tension-type headache, 470, 471t
    structure of, 226f
Kidney. See under Renal.
Kinins, in tissue injury, 23t
Klumpke paralysis, 582. See also Brachial
        plexopathy.
Knee
    anatomy of, 883-892, 884f, 885f
    Baker's cyst of, 903-905, 904f
        in rheumatoid arthritis, 431, 433f
    bursitis of, 893-902. See also Bursitis, of
        knee.
    chondroblastoma of, 902, 902f
    housemaid's, 396-397, 397f, 895-897, 895f-
        897f
    instability of, prolotherapy for, 1115
    laxity in, prolotherapy for, 1108, 1108f, 1115,
        1116
    medial collateral ligament syndrome of, 395-
        396, 396f
    osteoarthritis of, 81-83, 83f, 419, 419f. See
        also Osteoarthritis.
        acupuncture for, 1100, 1100t
        differential diagnosis of, 422t, 424
        exercise program for, 1059-1060, 1060f,
            1065, 1065f, 1066f
        imaging of, 81-83, 83f, 112, 421-424, 422f,
            423f
        management of, 424-428
        prevention of, 428-429
        prolotherapy for, 1107-1108, 1116, 1116f
        total joint replacement for, 86, 428
    pseudorheumatism of, 888
Knee pain, 886-892
    age and, 887, 888t
    causes of, 886, 887t
    classification of, 887t
    common peroneal nerve block for, 1365-1366
    corticosteroid-related, 888
    cryoanalgesia for, 1469-1470
    differential diagnosis of, 886-889, 887t, 889t
    drug-related, 888
    femoral nerve block for, 238t, 1363-1364
    history in, 886-889
    imaging studies in, 892
    in Lyme disease, 888-889, 889f
    in quadriceps expansion syndrome, 906-910,
        909f
    physical examination in, 889-891
        anterior drawer test in, 890-891
        McMurray test in, 891-892, 891f
        palpation in, 889-890, 889f, 890f
        posterior drawer test in, 891, 891f
        valgus stress test in, 890, 890f
        varus stress test in, 890, 890f
    popliteal nerve block for, 1365
    posterior tibial nerve block for, 1365-1366
    prolotherapy for, 1115, 1116
    referred, 888t
    saphenous nerve block for, 1365-1366

Knee pain *(Continued)*
    traumatic, 887
    with constitutional symptoms, 888
    with effusion, ballottement test for, 889-890,
        889f
    with fever, 887
    with muscle weakness, 888
    with polyarthralgias, 887
    with weight changes, 888
Knee replacement. See Total joint arthroplasty.
Koller, Carl, 149
KTP laser, 1489, 1491. See also Laser therapy.
Kummel disease, 77, 78f
Kuntz nerves, 1198
Kyphoplasty, 1477-1480, 1478f, 1479f, 1481f
Kyphosis, Scheuermann, radiography of, 76

L
Labat's method, for cervical plexus block, 1181
Labor pains, hypnosis for, 1022, 1023
Laboratory tests, 56-73
    basic, 56-57, 57t
    C-reactive protein, 56-57
    cardiac enzymes, 71
    complete blood count, 57-59
    electrolytes, 59-60, 69-70
    erythrocyte sedimentation rate, 56-57
    for autoimmune disorders, 60-62, 61t
    for HIV infection, 62-63
    for Lyme disease, 63-64
    for syphilis, 63
    glucose, 59, 59t
    hematologic, 57-59
    liver function, 70-71
    osmolality, 68-69
    prostate-specific antigen, 62
    renal function, 68-69
    serum protein, 66-68
    thyroid function, 62
    uric acid, 70
Lacrimal nerve, anatomy of, 523, 524f
Lacrimation
    in cluster headache, 477
    in short-lasting unilateral neuralgiform
        headache, 482
Lactate dehydrogenase, 70
Lactulose, for opioid-induced constipation, 323
Laminae, Rexed, 13, 13f, 13t
Laminectomy. See also Diskectomy.
    arachnoiditis after, 791
    complications of, 819-826. See also Failed
        back surgery syndrome.
    historical perspective on, 817-818
    rationale for, 818
Lamotrigine, 974-975, 975f. See also
        Anticonvulsants.
Langerhans cell histiocytosis, pulmonary, 708,
        708f
Laparoscopy, femoral neuropathy after, 873
Lapidus procedure, for hallux valgus, 920
Laryngotracheobronchitis, 543
LASE system, for laser diskectomy, 1494-1495,
        1495f
Lasègue test, 758, 759f
Laser diskectomy, 1489-1499
    anatomic aspects of, 1492-1494
    animal studies of, 1492
    cervical, 1497
    complications of, 1497-1498, 1498t
    disadvantages of, 1498-1499
    history of, 1489-1490
    indications for, 1490-1491
    LASE system in, 1494-1495, 1495f

Laser diskectomy *(Continued)*
  laser-tissue interactions in, 1491-1492
  laser types in, 1489, 1490f, 1497
  lumbar, 1494-1497
  PercScope in, 1496-1497, 1496f
  results of, 1497
  safety of, 1491
  technical aspects of, 1491, 1491f
  techniques of, 1494-1497
    modified Choy technique, 1495-1496
    non-endoscopic laser fiber diskectomy, 1495-1496
    rigid-scope endoscopic laser diskectomy, 1496-1497
    stepwise laser disk decompression, 1494
  thoracic, 1497
  Wolf system in, 1496-1497
Laser therapy
  for intervertebral disk disease, 1489-1499. *See also* Laser diskectomy.
  laser types in, 1489, 1490f
  low-power, 995
  safety of, 1491
  technical aspects of, 1491, 1491f
  vs. radiofrequency techniques, 1412
Lateral collateral ligament
  anatomy of, 884, 885f
  varus stress test for, 890, 890f
Lateral epicondylitis, 382-385, 384f, 633-636, 634f, 635f
  acupuncture for, 1100, 1100t
  prolotherapy for, 1113, 1113f
  vs. radial tunnel syndrome, 635, 655, 656, 657f, 1233
Lateral femoral cutaneous nerve, anatomy of, 1328
Lateral femoral cutaneous nerve block, 1328-1330, 1364
Lateral femoral cutaneous nerve entrapment, 36, 391, 415-416, 415f, 868-870, 869f, 1328-1330, 1364
Lateral pectoral nerve, anatomy of, 578f, 579f, 580
Lateral recess stenosis, 763, 764
Lateral subcutaneous malleolar bursa, 911
Laterocollis, 591. *See also* Cervical dystonia.
Laxatives, for opioid-induced constipation, 323
Lead poisoning, 67t, 72-73
Least splanchnic nerve
  anatomy of, 1267, 1267f
  radiofrequency lesioning of, 1434-1456
Leg. *See also* Lower extremity.
Leg cramps, prolotherapy for, 1115
Leg-length inequality
  in sacroiliac joint disorders, 812, 814
  in trochanteric bursitis, 860, 861-862
Leg lengthening, for sacroiliac disorders, 814
Legal issues, in chronic pain, 786, 1008
Leprosy, 64, 67t
Lesser occipital nerve. *See also* Occipital nerve.
  anatomy of, 549, 1140, 1141f-1143f, 1143, 1174, 1174f, 1176f-1179f
Lesser occipital nerve block, 1140-1144. *See also* Occipital nerve block.
  diagnostic, 153
Lesser palatine nerve, 540f
Lesser splanchnic nerve
  anatomy of, 1267, 1267f
  radiofrequency lesioning of, 1434-1456
Leukemoid reaction, 58
Leukocyte count, 58
Leukocytosis, causes of, 58
Leukotrienes, 935
  in tissue injury, 23t

Levator scapulae
  anatomy of, 627, 629f
  prolotherapeutic injection of, 1120, 1121f
Levator scapulae syndrome. *See* Scapulocostal syndrome.
Levo-alpha acetyl methadol (LAAM), 957-958
Levobupivacaine, 985
  introduction of, 985f
Levofloxacin, for epidural adhesiolysis, 1346, 1348
Levorphanol, 944t, 948t, 954-955. *See also* Opioid(s).
  structure of, 943f, 953f
Levothyroxine, after pituitary neuroadenolysis, 1409
Lhermitte sign, in cervical radiculopathy, 571, 572t
Lidocaine. *See also* Local anesthetics.
  for celiac plexus block, 230
  for cluster headache, 485
  for complex regional pain syndrome, 294, 294t, 295
  for differential epidural block, 159
  for epidural adhesiolysis, 1348
  for epidural nerve block, 234, 235
  for intercostal nerve block, 680, 1256, 1256f
  for intravenous regional sympatholysis, for complex regional pain syndrome, 295
  for lumbar epidural nerve block, 1291
  for lumbar sympathetic block, 233
  for phantom pain, 309-310
  for spinal anesthesia, side effects of, 986
  in corticosteroid injections. *See* Corticosteroids, intra-articular; Corticosteroids, intralesional.
  side effects of, 986, 987
  structure of, 151f, 983, 984f
  topical, 988
    for burns, 246-247
    for chronic pain, 219-220
    for mononeuritis multiplex, 725-726
    for neuropathic pain, 718
Liftoff test, 605
Ligament(s). *See also* specific ligaments and joints.
  growth factors for. *See also* Prolotherapy.
    dextrose effects on, 1107, 1108t
    tissue response to, 1109
  injuries of. *See also* Sprains.
    magnetic resonance imaging of, 115
    osteopathic manipulative treatment for, 1078
    prolotherapy for, 1109, 1114-1118
    rest for, 1055
    RICE treatment for, 1055
  magnetic resonance imaging of, 115
Ligament of Struthers, median nerve entrapment by, 650-653
Ligamentous laxity, prolotherapy for
  for knee, 1108, 1108f
  for shoulder, 1112-1113
Ligamentum flavum, 1211, 1212f
  in cervical epidural block, 1213, 1214f
Ligamentum nuchae, in cervical epidural block, 1213, 1214f
Lignocaine, introduction of, 985f
Lingual nerve, 540f, 1155
Lipase, serum
  in acute pancreatitis, 737
  in chronic pancreatitis, 740
Lipidic acids, in tissue injury, 23t
Lipoidic acid, for arachnoiditis, 798
Lissauer's zone, 1084
Lithium, for cluster headache, 486, 532

Lithotomy position
  femoral neuropathy and, 874
  obturator neuropathy and, 879
  spinal anesthesia complications and, 986
Litigation, ongoing, chronic pain and, 786, 1008
Liver disease
  diagnosis of, 70-71
  hepatic encephalopathy in, 71
  in temporal arteritis, 520
  pain in, 732-736
Liver function tests, 70-71
Livingston's summation theory, 3, 4f
Load and shift test, for rotator cuff tears, 607, 608f
Local anesthetics, 983-988. *See also* specific agents and indications.
  alkalinization of, 985
  chemistry of, 983-985
  for epidural adhesiolysis, 1347, 1348
  for interpleural analgesia, 1262-1263
  for neuropathic pain, 718
  generic and trade names of, 987t
  historical perspective on, 983, 984f
  hyaluronidase with, 986
  in continuous regional anesthesia, for cancer pain, 339
  in corticosteroid injections. *See* Corticosteroids, intra-articular; Corticosteroids, intralesional.
  in nerve blocks. *See* Nerve blocks.
  in prolotherapy, 1110. *See also* Prolotherapy.
  intravenous, 31-32, 32f
  mechanism of action of, 31-32, 32f, 985
  myotoxicity of, 986-987
  pharmacodynamics of, 985
  pharmacokinetics of, 986, 986t
  preparations of, 987-988, 987t
  prototypical, 983
  sensitivity to, nerve fiber size and, 155-156, 156f
  side effects of, 986-987, 987f
  structure of, 983-985, 983f, 984f, 985f
  systemic toxicity of
    in intercostal nerve block, 1257
    in interpleural analgesia, 1257
    with spinal opioids, 1394
Locke, John, 502
Locus ceruleus, 213, 214f
Log roll swim, 1046-1048, 1048f
Long-term depression, 1085
Long-term potentiation, 1085
Long thoracic nerve, anatomy of, 578f, 579f, 580
Lorazepam, for burn pain, 243t, 244, 246
Loss-of-resistance technique
  in epidural nerve block
    cervical, 1215-1216, 1216f, 1217f
    lumbar, 1286-1288
    thoracic, 1246
  in lumbar sympathetic nerve block, 1316-1317, 1316f
Love's pin test, for glomus tumor of hand, 671
Low back pain, 215, 749-756. *See also* Back pain.
  axial vs. radicular, 118
  biofeedback for, 1011-1012
  bracing for, 1061
  cauda equina syndrome and, 750-751
  causes of, 118.1087, 749, 750t
    mechanical, 750t, 755-756
    nonmechanical, 750t, 751-755
  cryoanalgesia for, 1465-1467, 1466f, 1467f, 1468

Low back pain (Continued)
  definition of, 749
  epidural adhesiolysis for, 1345-1349
  epidural steroid injections for, 320, 339-340
  exercise program for, 1055-1056, 1061-1062, 1062f, 1063f. See also Exercise; Exercises.
  from abdominal aortic aneurysm, 755
  from lumbosacral strain, 755
  from vertebral metastases, 751-753, 753f
  imaging in
    bone scintigraphy in, 86-89, 90f-91f
    computed tomography in, 102, 103f, 104f
    diskography in, 98-99, 118-140. See also Diskography.
    radiography in, 76-78, 76f-79f
  in arachnoiditis, 791-798
  in coccydynia, 848-850, 849f, 850f
  in osteoporosis, 753
  in piriformis syndrome, 763, 764, 834-836
  in sacroiliac disorders, 810-815, 1358-1361
  in spondylolisthesis, 784, 785t, 800, 807-808
  in spondylolysis, 784, 785t, 800, 805
  in vertebral osteomyelitis, 77, 751, 752f
  initial evaluation in, 750
  local vertebral column, 753
  lumbar epidural block for, 1281
  lumbar facet block for, 1303-1310
  natural history of, 749
  occupational, 777-790. See also Occupational back pain.
  osteopathic manipulative treatment for, 1077-1078
  patient education in, 764, 765, 1061
  persistent postoperative. See Failed back surgery syndrome.
  physical examination in, 750
  prevalence of, 749
  prolotherapy for, 1107, 1123-1124, 1123f-1125f
  radicular, 758-766. See also Lumbar radiculopathy.
  radiofrequency techniques for, 1417-1420
  relaxation techniques for, 1207
  rest for, 1055-1056
  sacroiliac injection for, 814-815, 815f, 1358-1361, 1359f, 1360f
  sciatica in, 749-750
  signs and symptoms of, 749
  visceral, 755
  with fever, 751
  with prolonged morning stiffness, 753-755, 754f
  with recumbency, 751-753
  with weight loss, 751
Lower extremity. See also Leg and specific structures.
  cryoanalgesia for, 1469-1470
  peripheral nerve blocks for, 1362-1368
    femoral nerve, 238t, 1363-1364
    historical perspective on, 1362
    indications for, 1362
    lateral femoral cutaneous nerve, 238t, 1364
    sciatic nerve, 238t, 1362-1363
    root vs. nerve lesions in, 46t
Lower subscapular nerve, anatomy of, 578f, 579f, 580
Ludington test, for biceps tendinitis, 381, 381f
Lumbar epidural nerve block, 234-236, 235f, 238t, 1281-1292. See also Epidural nerve block, lumbar.

Lumbar epidural space, anatomy of, 145-146, 173, 232, 233f
Lumbar facet block, 1303-1311
  anatomic aspects of, 1305-1306
  complications of, 1310
  contraindications to, 1304, 1304t
  diagnostic, 1303-1304
  drugs for, 1310
  historical perspective on, 1303
  indications for, 1303, 1304t
  intra-articular, 1306, 1306f, 1307f
  medial branch, 1306-1310, 1308t, 1309f, 1311f
  therapeutic, 1304-1306
Lumbar facet joints
  anatomy of, 118-119, 769-770, 770f, 1305
  osteoarthritis of, imaging of, 89-91, 91f
  pain in, 118, 769-774. See also Low back pain; Lumbar facet syndrome.
  referred pain from, 769-770, 770f
Lumbar facet ligament, prolotherapeutic injection of, 1123-1124, 1124f
Lumbar facet rhizotomy, radiofrequency, 773-774, 774f, 1417-1420
Lumbar facet syndrome, 55, 118, 769-774, 1088-1089, 1417-1420
  anatomic features of, 769, 770f
  clinical presentation of, 772
  cryoanalgesia for, 1465-1467, 1466f, 1467f
  diagnosis of, 1089
  occupational, 783. See also Occupational back pain.
  orthopedic tests in, 1089
  pain characteristics in, 769-770, 770f
  pathophysiology of, 772, 1088-1089
  prevalence of, 772
  treatment of, 773-774, 774f
    intra-articular steroids for, 773
    lumbar facet block in, 1303-1310
    prolotherapy in, 1123-1124, 1124f
    radiofrequency techniques for, 773-774, 774f, 1417-1420
Lumbar ganglionotomy, 1431, 1431f
  indications for, 1435
Lumbar medial branch neurotomy, radiofrequency, for lumbar facet syndrome, 773-774, 774f
Lumbar neurolytic blockade. See Lumbar sympathetic nerve block.
Lumbar plexus block, 238t
Lumbar puncture
  in headache evaluation, 264, 265
    for migraine, 460
  in subarachnoid neurolysis, headache after, 1302
Lumbar radiculopathy, 52t, 55, 55t, 758-766. See also Low back pain.
  complications of, 765
  diagnosis of, 763
  differential diagnosis of, 763-764
  distribution of, 761
  epidural nerve block for, 1281
  etiology of, 758-761
  exercise program for, 1063, 1064f
  historical perspective on, 758, 759f, 760f
  imaging studies in, 763
  in spondylolisthesis, 807-808
  intrathecal steroids for, 339
  Lasègue test for, 758, 759f
  neurophysiologic studies in, 763
  numbness in, 762
  physical examination in, 762-763, 762f
  prolotherapy for, 1124-1126, 1125f, 1126f

Lumbar radiculopathy (Continued)
  radiofrequency techniques for, 1425-1429
    intradiskal electrothermal annuloplasty, 1426-1431, 1484-1487
    intradiskal lesioning, 1425-1426, 1426f
    ramus communicans nerve lesioning, 1425-1429, 1426f-1428f
  signs and symptoms of, 761-762, 761t, 762f
  treatment of, 764-765
  vs. gluteal bursitis, 854
  vs. iliopsoas bursitis, 866
  vs. meralgia paresthetica, 868
  vs. somatic pain, 761t
  with sciatic nerve entrapment, 854
Lumbar spinal stenosis, 55, 55t
Lumbar spine. See also under Spinal; Spine.
  pain patterns in, 52t, 55, 55t
  radiography of, 76-78, 76f-79f
Lumbar spondylosis, 756, 756f. See also Spine, osteoarthritis of.
Lumbar sympathetic ganglia
  anatomy of, 1315, 1451
  radiofrequency lesioning of, 1451-1452, 1452f
Lumbar sympathetic nerve block, 232-233, 233f, 1314-1320
  anatomic aspects of, 1315
  complications of, 1320
  contraindications to, 1315
  diagnostic, 232-233
  differential, 161-162, 161t
  drugs for, 1320
  for acute/postoperative pain, 232-233, 233f
  historical perspective on, 1314
  indications for, 1314
  loss-of-resistance determination in, 1316-1317, 1316f, 1319
  neurolytic, 232-233, 1314-1320
  results of, 1320
  technique of, 232-233, 233f, 1315-1320
    classic (traditional), 1315-1317, 1316f-1317f
    lateral, 1317-1319, 1318f, 1319f
Lumbosacral plexus neuropathy, 11, 407t
Lumbosacral strain, 755
Lung. See also under Pulmonary.
  contusion of, 711-712
Lung abscess, 704, 705f, 706, 706f, 707
Lung cancer
  chest pain in, 694
  neuropathy in, 67t
  Pancoast tumors in, 694-695, 696f-697f. See also Pancoast tumors.
  peripheral neuropathy in, 64
  referred pain in, 50
  superior sulcus tumors in, 694-695
Lupus erythematosus. See Discoid lupus erythematosus; Systemic lupus erythematosus.
Luthe, Wolfgang, 1026
Lyme disease, 67t
  case definition for, 65f
  diagnosis of, 63-64, 65f
  erythema migrans in, 64, 65f, 66f
  knee pain in, 888-889, 889f
Lymphangiomyomatosis
  chylothorax in, 709
  pneumothorax in, 708, 709f
Lymphocytes, 58
Lymphocytosis, 58
Lymphoma
  pleural effusion in, 701
  pyothorax in, 701

M

μ (mu) receptor, 940-941, 941t

Machinist's hands, in dermatomyositis, 444, 444f

Macular hemorrhages, from epidural injections, 172, 176

Magnesium block, 24

Magnesium imbalances, 69-70

Magnesium oxide, for arachnoiditis, 796

Magnesium sulfate, for medication-overuse headache, 499, 499t

Magnetic field therapy, 991t, 994-995

Magnetic gait, 47

Magnetic resonance angiography, 106
    in headache, 264
        cluster, 480
        migraine, 460
    of cerebral aneurysms, 264

Magnetic resonance arthrography, 106-107

Magnetic resonance imaging, 106-116
    advances in, 116, 117
    advantages of, 106
    contraindications to, 107
    functional, in acupuncture, 1095
    implantable drug delivery devices and, 1398
    in arachnoiditis, 793-794, 793f-795f
    in brachial plexopathy, 585, 585f, 588
    in cervical radiculopathy, 572-573
    in degenerative disk disease, 107-111, 108f-110f
    in headache, 263-264
        cluster, 482, 532
        migraine, 460
        tension-type, 468
    in lumbar radiculopathy, 763
    in occupational back pain, 783
    in osteoarthritis, 112, 115, 423-424, 423f
    in osteonecrosis, 112, 113f
    in peripheral neuropathy, 276, 407
    in pronator syndrome, 653, 653f
    in reflex sympathetic dystrophy, 112, 114f
    in spondylolysis, 805
    in subdeltoid bursitis, 619, 620f
    indications for, 99, 107-111, 407
    musculoskeletal, 106-115
    neurologic, 107-111, 115
    of abdominal aortic aneurysm, 730f
    of bone marrow, 111-112, 113f, 114f
    of brachial plexus tumors, 585, 585f, 588
    of cartilage, 115
    of ligaments, 115
    of muscle, 115
    of Pancoast tumors, 695, 696-697f
    of peripheral nerves, 115
    of rotator cuff disorders, 609, 610f
    of spine, 107-111, 108f-110f
    of stress fractures, 111-112
    of tendons, 112-115
    of vertebral compression fractures, 116
    principles of, 106-107
    T1/T2-weighted, 106
    vs. computed tomography, 99-102, 107
    vs. CT, 99-102

Magnetic resonance neurography, 115

Magnetic resonance spectroscopy, 106

Major histocompatibility complex antigens, in complex regional pain syndrome, 286

Malignant mesothelioma, 695-701, 699f, 700f

Malignant pleural effusion
    in breast cancer, 701, 701f
    in lymphoma, 701
    in mesothelioma, 695, 700f
    in ovarian cancer, 695, 700f, 701

Malingering, 1008
    diagnosis of, 158t
    in occupational back pain, 780, 786
    Waddell's signs of, 786

Malleolar bursa, 911

Mandibular nerve
    anatomy of, 1146-1147, 1146f, 1147f, 1148, 1154-1155, 1154f, 1155f
    cryoablation of, 1470f, 1471

Mandibular nerve block, 1155-1156, 1155f-1157f. See also Trigeminal nerve block.
    mental, 1159-1160, 1159f

Manual therapy, 991t. See also Osteopathic manipulative treatment.
    for lumbar radiculopathy, 764, 765
    for sacroiliac disorders, 814

MAOIs. See Monoamine oxidase inhibitors.

Marginal zone neurons, 13f, 13t, 14, 14f
    in tissue injury, 25, 26f

Marie-Strümpell disease, sacroiliac pain in, 813

Marijuana
    for cancer cachexia, 366
    screening for, 72

Massage therapy
    for chronic pain, 221
    for tension-type headache, 472

Masseteric nerve, 1148, 1155

Masticatory pain
    in Eagle syndrome, 547, 547f
    in temporal arteritis, 445, 446, 519

Mastoiditis, 543, 544f

Maxillary artery, inadvertent injection of, 1138

Maxillary nerve, anatomy of, 523, 524f, 1146-1147, 1146f, 1147f, 1153-1154, 1154f

Maxillary nerve block, 1155-1156, 1155f-1157f. See also Trigeminal nerve block.
    infraorbital, 1157-1159, 1158f

McGill Pain Questionnaire, 200-202, 201f
    short-form, 202, 202f

McMurray test, 891-892, 891f

Mean corpuscular hemoglobin, 57

Mean corpuscular hemoglobin concentration, 57

Mean corpuscular volume, 57

Mechanical lesioning, vs. radiofrequency techniques, 1412

Mechanical ventilation
    chest pain in, 710
    in flail chest, 710, 711f

Meckel's cave, 1146, 1146f, 1153, 1153f

Meclofenamate, for tension-type headache, 470, 471t

Meclofenamic acid, for cancer pain, 318-319, 319t

Medial antebrachial cutaneous nerve, anatomy of, 578f, 579f, 580

Medial brachial cutaneous nerve, anatomy of, 578f, 579f, 580

Medial brachial cutaneous nerve block, 1237, 1237f

Medial branch block
    diagnostic, in lumbar facet syndrome, 770-771, 771f
    for cervical facet syndrome
        in diagnosis, 563, 563f, 565
        in treatment, 564-565
    technique of, 563, 563f

Medial branch neurotomy
    for cervical facet syndrome, 564f, 565
    radiofrequency, for lumbar facet syndrome, 773-774, 774f

Medial collateral ligament
    anatomy of, 884, 885f
    prolotherapeutic injection of, 1115, 1116f
    valgus stress test for, 890, 890f

Medial collateral ligament syndrome, 395-396, 396f

Medial epicondylitis, 637-640, 638f, 639f
    prolotherapy for, 1114, 1114f
    vs. cubital tunnel syndrome, 647-649, 647-650

Medial lemniscal system, 15

Medial pectoral nerve, anatomy of, 578f, 579f, 580

Medial pectoralis, prolotherapeutic injection of, 1118, 1118f

Medial subcutaneous malleolar bursa, 911

Median nerve, 46t
    anatomy of, 653-654, 654f, 1227-1229, 1228f
    corticosteroid injection of, 387-388, 387f
    entrapment of. See Median nerve entrapment.
    lateral division of, anatomy of, 578f, 579f, 580
    medial division of, anatomy of, 578f, 579f, 580

Median nerve block, 238t, 1227-1230, 1228f-1231f
    at elbow, 1229, 1230f
    at wrist, 1229, 1230f, 1234f
    for anterior interosseous syndrome, 654-655, 656f
    for pronator syndrome, 653, 654f

Median nerve compression test, in carpal tunnel syndrome, 664

Median nerve entrapment
    by ligament of Struthers, 650-653
    electrodiagnosis of, 188
    in anterior interosseous syndrome, 653-655, 654f-656f, 655f
    in carpal tunnel syndrome, 385-388, 385f-387f, 664-665. See also Carpal tunnel syndrome.
    in pronator teres syndrome, 188, 650-653, 651f-653f
    types of, 660t

Median nerve percussion test. See Tinel sign.

Median sacral crest, 1336

Median sternotomy, parasternal block for, 1250, 1251f

Mediastinal tumors, 701-702

Medication history, 38-39

Medication-overuse headache, 469, 470, 492-501. See also Headache.
    associated drugs in, 493t
        dose and duration of therapy with, 496
        history-taking for, 496-497
    cause-and-effect debate about, 494-496
    clinical evaluation in, 496
    clinical features of, 496
    clinical studies of, 493-494
    diagnostic criteria for, 493t
    etiology of, 494
    historical perspective on, 493
    history in, 496-497
    management of, 498-501
        bridge/transition therapies in, 499
        initial visit in, 498-499
        long-term, 500-501
        maintenance therapy in, 500
        of withdrawal, 499-500
        patient education in, 498
        psychological support in, 499-500
        rescue therapy in, 499
        seizure prophylaxis in, 499
        treatment planning in, 498
    pathophysiology of, 494-496
    patient education in, 498
    persistent, 500
    psychological evaluation in, 497
    terminology of, 493

Medulla, projections into, 15, 16f, 25, 26f
Mefenamic acid
for cancer pain, 318-319, 319t
for tension-type headache, 470, 471t
Melatonin, cluster headache and, 480, 488
Melville, Herman, 304, 306f
Melzack, R., 3, 4
Melzack's neuromatrix theory, 4-7, 5f
Membrane potential
action
conduction of, measurement of, 184-186
generation of, 181, 182, 1087-1088
in nerve conduction studies, 182
resting, 181
Memorial Pain Assessment Card, 203, 205f
Mendell, Lorne, 22
Meniere syndrome, stellate ganglion block for, 1191-1198
Meningitis
after back surgery, 822
after lumbar facet block, 1310
bacterial
cerebrospinal fluid findings in, 264
headache in, 263t, 264, 266
treatment of, 266
Brudzinski sign in, 264, 1391
implantable drug delivery systems and, 1390-1391
Kernig sign in, 264, 1390
signs and symptoms of, 1390-1391
Meniscus
anatomy of, 883-884, 884f
tears of, McMurray test for, 891-892, 891f
Menopausal arthritis, 420
Mental nerve, 540f, 1148, 1155
cryoablation of, 1471
Mental nerve block, 1159-1160, 1159f. See also Trigeminal nerve block.
Mental status examination, 42, 42t, 43t. See also Neurologic examination.
Meperidine, 944t, 948t, 953f, 955. See also Opioid(s).
for cancer pain, 320t, 321-323
for sickle cell pain, 260
spinal administration of, 351t. See also Spinal opioids.
tachycardia due to, 945, 945f
toxicity of, 227
Mepivacaine. See also Local anesthetics.
for intercostal nerve block, 1256, 1256t. See also Nerve blocks.
introduction of, 985f
structure of, 983, 984f
Meprobamate, carisoprodol and, 38, 978
Meralgia paresthetica, 36, 391, 415-416, 415f, 868-870, 1328-1330, 1364
causes of, 1329t
differential diagnosis of, 1329t
lateral femoral cutaneous nerve block for, 1328-1330, 1329f, 1329t, 1364
vs. trochanteric bursitis, 391, 868
Meridians, in acupuncture, 1096-1097
Mesencephalic periaqueductal gray matter
in pain processing, 213, 214f, 1086, 1087
opioid action in, 29
Mesencephalon, projections into, 15-16, 16f
Mesmer, Anton, 1021
Mesmerism, 1021. See also Hypnosis.
Mesothelioma
benign fibrous, 701
malignant, 695-701, 699f, 700f

Metacarpophalangeal joints. See also Finger(s); Hand.
anatomy of, 661f
deviation of, in rheumatoid arthritis, 434, 435f
prolotherapeutic injection of, 1114, 1114f
Metallic foreign bodies, corneal, 524-525, 525f
Metastases
bone. See Bone metastases.
brain, radiation therapy for, 333
Metatarsal, fifth, bunionette of, 921
Metatarsal compression test, 914
Metatarsalgia, 918-919
prolotherapy for, 1118, 1118f
vs. sesamoiditis, 400
Metatarsophalangeal joints. See also Foot; Toe(s).
arthritis of, 914
first. See under Hallux.
pain in, 918-919, 919t. See also Foot pain.
prolotherapy for, 1118, 1118f
Metaxalone, 979. See also Muscle relaxants.
for tension-type headache, 470, 471t
Methadone, 944t, 948t, 957. See also Opioid(s).
for cancer pain, 320t, 321-323
half-life of, 321, 948t
pharmacodynamics of, 957
pharmacokinetics of, 948t, 957
toxicity of
delayed, 321
indications for, 957
preparations of, 957
Methamphetamine, screening for, 72
Methocarbamol, 979. See also Muscle relaxants.
for tension-type headache, 470, 471t
Methotrexate, for rheumatoid arthritis, 436
N-Methyl-D-aspartate. See NDMA.
Methylmalonic acid, in vitamin B$_{12}$ deficiency, 64
Methylphenidate
for cancer-related fatigue, 364
for opioid-induced sedation, 323, 364, 366, 1000
Methylprednisolone. See also Corticosteroids.
for cancer pain, 324
for epidural adhesiolysis, 1347, 1348
for epidural nerve block, 236
for glossopharyngeal nerve block, for glossopharyngeal neuralgia, 515
for systemic lupus erythematosus, 440
for trigeminal nerve block, 236
intra-articular. See Corticosteroids, intra-articular.
intralesional. See Corticosteroids, intralesional.
Methysergide, for cluster headache, 486
Metoclopramide, for cancer-related nausea, 365, 365f
Metoprolol, for migraine prophylaxis, 461
Mexiletine
for cancer pain, 324
for chronic pain, 220
for facial reflex sympathetic dystrophy, 557-559
for mononeuritis multiplex, 725
for neuropathic pain, 718
for peripheral neuropathy, 277t
MHC antigens, in complex regional pain syndrome, 286
Microdiskectomy, for lumbar radiculopathy, 765
Microglia
in nerve injury, 28
in tissue injury, 25-26

Microvascular decompression
for glossopharyngeal neuralgia, 516
for trigeminal neuralgia, 353-356, 355f, 506, 507-508
Microwavable heating pads, 1036, 1036f
Microwave diathermy, 1039
Midazolam, for diskography, 124
Midtarsal arthritis, 912-914
treatment of, 914
Migraine, 455-462. See also Headache.
assessment tools for, 497
aura in, 457-458
persistent, 459
basilar-type, 458-459, 458t
central sensitization in, 456
chronic, 459, 459t, 468-469, 492, 493t
diagnostic criteria for, 493t
evolution of, 469, 493, 494, 500
management of, 500-501
medication-overuse headache and, 492-501. See also Medication-overuse headache.
vs. tension-type headache, 468-469
classification of, 457t
clinical examples of, 457-459
clinical presentation of, 456-460
convergence hypothesis for, 494
demographic factors in, 38t
diagnosis of, 459-460
diagnostic criteria for, 456-457, 457t
epidemiology of, 456
evolutive, 493
frequency of, 459
hemiplegic, 458, 458t
historical perspective on, 455-456
history in, 459
imaging studies for, 459-460
in status migrainosus, 459
in women, 456, 479
pathogenesis and pathophysiology of, 456, 457, 468-469, 494, 495f
prevention of, 461
retinal, 459, 459t
seizures and, 459
transformation of, 469, 493, 494, 500
transformed, 469
treatment of, 460-462
biofeedback in, 1012, 1015
duration of, 461, 500
hypnosis in, 1022, 1023
medication-overuse headache and, 492-501. See also Medication-overuse headache.
osteopathic manipulative therapy in, 1078
radiofrequency techniques in, 1444
relaxation techniques in, 1027
sphenopalatine ganglion block in, 1134-1139
visual disturbances in, 457
vs. cluster headache, 483, 483t
vs. tension-type headache, 464
Migraine Disability Assessment, for medication-overuse headache, 497
Miller, Neal E., 1010
Mind/body control, 991t. See also Complementary and alternative therapies.
Mini Mental Status Examination, 42, 43t
in cancer, 362, 369
Minnesota Multiphasic Personality Inventory
for medication-overuse headache, 497
for tension-type headache, 468
Miosis, opioid-induced, 944
Mirror-image pain, 9
after percutaneous cordotomy, 1512-1513

Miscarriage, hot tub/whirlpool bath use and, 1050

Mitchell, Silas Weir, 26, 304, 305f

Mitochondrial myopathies, inherited, 450

Mixed connective tissue disease, 442

Mixter, William Jason, 568, 569f, 758, 759f

Modafinil, for cancer-related fatigue, 364

Modified Choy technique, for laser diskectomy, 1495-1496

Modified Dallas Diskogram Scale, 130

Modified Kappis approach, in celiac plexus block, 1270

Modified Lapidus procedure, for hallux valgus, 920

Modified superman exercise, 1046, 1047f

Monkey hand, 582

Monoamine oxidase inhibitors, 969. See also Antidepressants.
  drug interactions with, 969, 970t
  food interactions with, 969, 969t
  for migraine prophylaxis, 461
  for tension-type headache, 470

Monoclonal antibodies, for rheumatoid arthritis, 436-437

Monoclonal gammopathy, 68
  IgM, 67t, 68

Mononeuritis multiplex, 691-692, 724-726

Mononeuropathy, 187
  classification of, 269t
  multiple, 269t
  types of, 269t

Moore, James, 149

Morphine, 950-952. See also Opioid(s).
  abuse of, screening for, 72
  as prototype opioid, 950
  for cancer pain, 320t, 321-323
  for cancer-related dyspnea, 366
  for epidural nerve block, with methylprednisolone, 236
  for phantom pain, 309-310
  half-life of, 948t
  historical perspective on, 939
  in renal failure, 321
  indications for, 952
  mechanism of action of, 29-31
  pharmacodynamics of, 948t, 951-952
  pharmacokinetics of, 948t, 950-951, 951f
  preparations of, 952
  rescue dose of, 321-322
  routes of administration for, 952
  side effects of, 944-946
  sites of action of, 29
  spinal administration of, 351t, 949. See also Spinal opioids.
  structure of, 228f, 941, 941f-943f, 950, 951f

Morphogenetic singularity theory and, 1095

Mortise view, 83

Morton neuroma, 918-919
  prolotherapy for, 1118

Mosley test, for rotator cuff tears, 380

Motivational-affective pain dimension, 17-18, 18f, 197, 198

Motor conduction velocity. See Nerve conduction studies; Nerve conduction velocity.

Motor examination, 43-44, 44t

Motor points, acupoints and, 1095-1096

Motor unit, 181, 182f

Moxibustion, 1098-1099

Multi-detector row computed tomography, 94-95. See also Computed tomography.

Multidimensional Affect and Pain Survey, 203, 205f

Multiple myeloma, 67t, 68
  Bence Jones proteins in, 68
  diagnosis of, 68

Multiple sclerosis
  demographic factors in, 38t
  evoked potential testing in
    brain stem auditory, 193
    somatosensory, 194
    visual, 193
  optic neuritis in, 528-530
  primary, 503
  secondary, 503
  trigeminal neuralgia in, 503

Murphey, Francis, 568, 569f

Muscle(s)
  examination of, 43-44, 44t
  magnetic resonance imaging of, 115

Muscle contraction, 1057, 1057t

Muscle fibers, in motor unit, 181, 182f

Muscle injury, from local anesthetics, 986-987

Muscle pain
  electrodiagnosis of, 189t
  mechanisms of, 1087
  pathophysiology of, 465-466, 465f
  stretch injury in, 1087
  types of, 189t

Muscle potentials
  conduction of, 182
  in nerve conduction studies, 182
  production of, 180-181

Muscle relaxants, 977-979
  clinical efficacy of, 977
  contraindications to, 977-978
  drug interactions with, 978
  for arachnoiditis, 796
  for lumbar radiculopathy, 764
  for tension-type headaches, 470, 471t
  mechanism of action of, 977
  pharmacokinetics of, 977, 978t
  potential for abuse of, 978
  preparations of, 978-979, 978t
  side effects of, 977-978

Muscle relaxation. See Relaxation techniques.

Muscle relearning therapy, 1013

Muscle spasms
  adductor, obturator nerve block for, 1331
  from tumor invasion, trigger point injections for, 338-339
  in tension-type headache, 465-466, 465f
  pathophysiology of, 465-466, 465f
  treatment of, 977-981. See also Muscle relaxants.

Muscle strains. See Strains.

Muscle weakness
  in cervical radiculopathy, 570, 571
  in complex regional pain syndrome, 284, 285t
  in peripheral neuropathy, 272-274
  knee pain with, 888

Muscular rigidity
  of great toe, 920-921
  opioid-induced, 945

Musculocutaneous nerve, anatomy of, 578f, 579f, 580, 1236

Musculocutaneous nerve block, 1235-1237

Music therapy, 992

Myalgia
  causes of, 189t
  electrodiagnosis of, 189

Myelitis, arachnoiditis due to, 791

Myelography
  arachnoiditis due to, 791
  computed tomography, 99, 101f
  implantable drug delivery devices and, 1393
  in brachial plexopathy, 588

Myeloma, 67t, 68
  Bence Jones proteins in, 68
  diagnosis of, 68

Myelopathic syringomyelia, 793, 793f

Myelopathy
  cervical, vs. radiculopathy, 573
  thoracic, 690

Myeloscopy. See Spinal canal endoscopy.

Myocardial infarction
  angina in. See Angina.
  creatine kinase in, 71

Myofascial syndrome, prolotherapy for, 1109

Myofascial trigger points, 51, 1016. See also Trigger points.
  in fibromyalgia, 403-404, 404f

Myopathy, painful. See also Muscle pain.
  electrodiagnosis of, 189t
  types of, 189t

Myositis, electrodiagnosis of, 189t

Myotoxicity, of local anesthetics, 986-987

Myringitis, 542

N

Nails
  in complex regional pain syndrome, 284, 285t
  in peripheral neuropathy, 274, 274t

Nalbuphine, 944t, 948t, 959-960. See also Opioid(s).

Naloxone, 960-961
  acupuncture and, 1095
  for opioid-induced respiratory depression, 323
  for spinal opioids, 352t
  structure of, 960-961, 961f

Naproxen, 931. See also Nonsteroidal antiinflammatory drugs.
  for cancer pain, 318-319, 319t
  for tension-type headache, 470, 471t

Naratriptan. See also Triptans.
  for cluster headache, 487
  for medication-overuse headache, 499, 499t
  for migraine, 460

Nasal bleeding, from sphenopalatine ganglion block, 230

Nasal congestion, in cluster headache, 477

Nasal foreign bodies, 543

Nasal mucosa, perforation of, in sphenopalatine ganglion block, 1138

Nasal pain, 543, 547

Nasal tumors, 543, 545f, 546f

Nasopharyngeal cancer, cavernous sinus invasion by, 533, 534f

Nasopharyngeoma, 543, 545f

National Certification Committee for Acupuncture and Oriental Medicine, 1102

Natural killer cells, 58

Nausea and vomiting
  in cancer, 364-365, 364t, 365f, 366
  opioid-induced, 323, 944
  with spinal administration, 351, 352t, 1396-1397

Nd:YAG laser, 1489, 1490f. See also Laser therapy.

Neck. See also under Cervical.
  corticosteroid injection in, for cervical facet syndrome, 565-566, 566t

Neck distraction test, in cervical radiculopathy, 571, 572t

Neck pain
  atlanto-occipital nerve block for, 1128-1131, 1130f, 1131f
  atlantoaxial nerve block for, 1132-1133

Neck pain (Continued)
   axial vs. radicular, 118
   celiac plexus block for, 1173-1174
   differential diagnosis of, 563, 1135t
   diskogenic. See Cervical radiculopathy.
   epidural steroid injections for, 339-340
   exercise program for, 1063, 1065f, 1066f
   imaging studies in, 74-75, 75f
   in cervical dystonia, 591-596
   in cervical facet syndrome, 52, 52t, 561-566
   in cervical radiculopathy, 52t, 55, 55t, 568-574
   in cervical spondylosis, 52, 570
   in whiplash. See Whiplash.
   migraine-related, osteopathic manipulative treatment for, 1078
   prolotherapy for, 1121-1122, 1121f, 1122f
   radiofrequency techniques for, 1435-1446. See also Radiofrequency techniques, for cervical pain.
   referred, 52, 52t, 53f, 54f
   sphenopalatine ganglion block for, 1134-1139
   stellate ganglion block for, 1191
   structural generators of, 1436t
Needle electromyography. See Electromyography.
Needling
   in acupuncture. See Acupuncture.
   traumatic, 1108-1109
Neer impingement test, 606, 607f, 624
Nefazodone, for phantom pain, 309
Neonate, brachial plexopathy in, 582, 582f
Nephrolithiasis, vs. orchialgia, 838
Nerve(s)
   classification of, by fiber size, 155, 156t
   cranial. See Cranial nerve(s).
   degeneration of, 343-344
   peripheral. See under Peripheral nerve.
   regeneration of, 26-28, 27f, 343, 344
   sympathetic, anatomy of, 1315
Nerve blocks. See also specific types and indications.
   atlanto-occipital, 1128-1131, 1130f, 1131f
   atlantoaxial, 1131, 1132-1133
   brachial plexus, 1220-1226
   caudal epidural, 1335-1344. See also Caudal epidural nerve block.
   celiac plexus, 231-232, 1265-1279. See also Celiac plexus block.
      diagnostic, 153-154, 231-232
   common peroneal nerve, 1365-1366
   decremental, 162-163, 163f
   deep peroneal nerve, 1367
   diagnostic, 149-154
      celiac plexus, 153-154, 231-232
      cervical facet, 153
      clinical utility of, 151-152
      differential, 155-165. See also Differential nerve blocks.
      duration of relief in, 151-152
      for cancer pain, 337-338, 338t
      greater occipital nerve, 153
      guidelines for, 151, 151t
      history of, 149-150, 150f
      in lumbar facet syndrome, 770-772, 771f
      indications for, 151-152
      intercostal nerve, 153
      interpretation of results of, 151-152
      neuroaxial, 152-153
      occipital nerve, 153, 1140-1144
      selective nerve root, 154
      stellate ganglion, 153
      technical aspects of, 151-152
   digital nerve, 1368
   epidural nerve. See Epidural nerve block.

Nerve blocks (Continued)
   femoral nerve, 238t, 1363-1364
   fiber size and, 155-156, 156t, 162, 165
   for acute/postoperative pain, 229-237. See also specific indications.
      celiac plexus, 231-232, 231f
      epidural nerve, 234-236, 234f, 235f
      intercostal nerve, 236-237, 238f
      lumbar sympathetic, 232-233, 233f
      somatic, 233-237, 238t
      sphenopalatine ganglion, 229-230, 229f
      stellate ganglion, 230-231, 230f
      sympathetic, 229-231
      trigeminal nerve, 236, 237f
   for ankle pain, 1367
   for cancer pain, 324-325, 337-340, 350. See also Cancer pain, nerve blocks for.
   for chronic pain, 220
   for foot pain, 1368
   frequency-dependent, 163-164, 163f
   ganglion of Walker, 1354-1357, 1355f, 1356f
   gasserian ganglion, 1145-1151
   glossopharyngeal nerve, 1161-1165
   hypogastric plexus, 1350
   ilioinguinal-iliohypogastric nerve, 1322-1327
   intercostal nerve, 236-237, 238f, 1250-1257
      diagnostic, 153
   intercostobrachial nerve, 1237-1238, 1237f
   intravascular injection in. See Intravascular injection.
   lateral femoral cutaneous nerve, 1328-1330
   lumbar facet, 1303
   lumbar sympathetic, 232-233, 233f, 1314-1320
   medial brachial cutaneous nerve, 1237-1238, 1237f
   median nerve, 1227-1230, 1229f-1231f
   musculocutaneous nerve, 1235-1237
   neurolytic. See Neurolytic blockade.
   obturator nerve, 1331-1334
   occipital nerve, 1140-1144
      diagnostic, 153, 1140-1144
   phrenic nerve, 1169-1172
   plantar digital nerve, 1368
   posterior tibial nerve
      for ankle pain, 1367
      for knee pain, 1365-1366
   prognostic, for cancer pain, 338
   radial nerve, 238t, 1233-1235, 1235f, 1236f
   regional, for burn pain, 246
   saphenous nerve
      for ankle pain, 1367
      for knee pain, 1365-1366
   sciatic nerve, 238t, 1362-1364
   somatic, 233-237, 238t
   sphenopalatine nerve, 229-230, 229f, 1134-1139
   stellate ganglion, 230-231, 230f
      diagnostic, 153
   superficial peroneal nerve, 1367
   suprascapular nerve, 1239-1242
   sural nerve, 1367
   sympathetic
      definition of, 220
      for acute/postoperative pain, 229-231
      for cancer pain, 325, 338, 338t
      for chronic pain, 220
      lumbar, 232-233, 233f, 1314-1320
      mechanism of action of, 1314
   trigeminal nerve, 236, 237f, 1152-1160
   ulnar nerve, 238t, 649, 650f, 1230-1233, 1232f-1234f
   upper extremity peripheral nerve, 1227-1238
   vagus nerve, 1166-1168

Nerve conduction
   physiology of, 181-182, 343
   saltatory, 343
Nerve conduction studies, 184-186, 275. See also Electrodiagnostic procedures.
   advantages of, 180
   equipment for, 180
   in brachial plexopathy, 586-588, 587t, 588t
   in carpal tunnel syndrome, 412, 413
   in cervical radiculopathy, 573
   in tarsal tunnel syndrome, 417
   indications for, 186-189, 275, 407
   motor, 184-186, 275, 275f
   sensory, 275, 275f
Nerve conduction velocity
   factors affecting, 182
   fiber size and, 156t, 182
   formula for, 184
   measurement of, 184-186
Nerve entrapment syndromes. See Entrapment neuropathies.
Nerve fibers. See also Afferents; Axon(s).
   classification of, 11, 12t
      by size, 156t
   size of
      conduction velocity and, 156t, 182
      differential nerve blocks and, 155-156, 156t, 162-163, 163f, 164
      sensitivity to local anesthetics and, 155-156, 156t
   type A, 155, 156t
      alpha, 156t
      beta, 11-12, 12f, 12t, 13, 13f, 13t, 156t
      delta, 11-12, 12f, 12t, 13, 13f, 13t, 156t, 1081
         in acupuncture, 1095
   type B, 155, 156t
   type C, 12t, 155, 156t, 1081
      activation of, 1083
      anatomy of, 11-12, 12f, 12t, 13, 13f
      in acupuncture, 1095
      in migraine, 456
      in respiratory system, 693
      in tissue injury, 21-22
      in wind-up, 22-24
Nerve injury
   axonotmesis in, 186, 580f, 581
   magnetic resonance imaging of, 115
   neurapraxia in, 186, 580f, 581
   neurotmesis in, 186-187, 580f, 581
   pain in. See Neuropathic pain.
   Seddon classification of, 580, 580f
Nerve stimulator
   for cervical plexus block, 1184-1185, 1185f
   implanted peripheral nerve, 1369-1371, 1370f, 1371f
   implanted spinal cord, 1373-1374, 1374f
Nervus intermedius rhizotomy, for cluster headache, 489
Neural blockade. See Nerve blocks.
Neuralgia. See specific sites and types.
Neuralgic amyotrophy, 414-415, 414f
Neurapraxia, 186, 580f, 581
Neuraxial anesthesia, arachnoiditis due to, 791
Neurilemmoma. See Schwannoma.
Neuroadenolysis, of pituitary, 1405-1410. See also Pituitary neuroadenolysis.
Neuroaxial nerve blocks, diagnostic, 152-153
Neurofibroma, of brachial plexus, 582t, 585, 586f
Neurogenic inflammation, 1083-1084, 1084f, 1089
Neurography, magnetic resonance, 115
Neuroleptics, for medication-overuse headache, 499, 499t

Neurologic examination. *See also specific indications.*
  cranial nerve examination in, 42-43, 44t
  deep tendon reflexes in, 46-47, 47f, 47t
  gait in, 47
  in chronic pain, 218
  mental status examination in, 42, 42t
  motor examination in, 43-44
  sensory examination in, 44-46
Neurolytic blockade, 343-347. *See also* Nerve blocks *and specific nerves.*
  agents for, 344-346
    ammonium compounds, 346
    ethyl alcohol, 232-233, 344-345, 344t, 347t. *See also* Alcohol.
      toxicity of, 73, 345, 347t
      vs. phenol, 346, 347t
    glycerol, 346
    hyper/hypotonic solutions, 346
    phenol, 345-346, 345t, 347t
    selection of, 346, 347t
  celiac plexus, 1266
  cryoanalgesia for, 346
  for cancer pain, 325, 326
  for glossopharyngeal neuralgia, 515-516
  for trigeminal neuralgia, 353, 354f, 356, 506
  glossopharyngeal nerve, 515-516
  history of, 343, 344t, 345t
  hypophysectomy for, for cancer pain, 326
  hypothermia for, 346
  lumbar sympathetic, 232-233, 1314-1320. *See also* Lumbar sympathetic nerve block.
  obturator, 1333
  of celiac plexus, 231-232
    for cancer pain, 235, 236
  of gasserian ganglion, 1151
  of stellate ganglion, 1195-1196
    chemical, 1195-1196
    radiofrequency, 1196, 1196f
  of trigeminal nerve, 1152, 1160
  of vagus nerve, 1166, 1168
  physiology of, 343
  prognostic nerve blocks for, 338
  subarachnoid, 1294-1302. *See also* Subarachnoid neurolytic block.
  suprascapular nerve
    indications for, 1239
    technique of, 1241-1242
  vs. radiofrequency techniques, 1411. *See also* Radiofrequency techniques.
Neuroma. *See also* Pain processing system, in nerve injury.
  acoustic, brain stem auditory evoked potentials from, 193, 193f
  axon sprouting in, 26-28, 27f, 556, 792, 792f, 1084
  components of, 556
  cryoanalgesia for, 1464-1465
  dorsal root ganglion and, 27, 28-29, 29f
  innervation of, 28-29, 29f
  Morton (interdigital), 918-919
  prolotherapy for, 1118
  pain generation in, 556
Neuromatrix theory of pain, 4-7, 5f, 9
Neuronal hyperactivity, 8
Neurons
  dorsal horn, 13-15, 13f, 13t, 14f
    in tissue injury, 22-24, 23f, 25
    neurotransmitters in, 19t, 20
    peptides of, 19-20, 19t
  marginal zone, 13f, 13t, 14, 14f
    in tissue injury, 25, 26f
  nociceptive-specific, 14, 14f, 17, 18f, 1081. *See also* Nociceptors.

Neurons *(Continued)*
  sensory. *See also* Pain processing system.
    structure of, 1087, 1088f
    wide dynamic range, 14-15, 14f, 17-18, 18f, 1084f
      in complex regional pain syndrome, 556
      in tissue injury, 22-24
      in wind-up, 15, 22-24, 23f
Neuropathic pain. *See also* Chronic pain.
  anticonvulsants for, 717-718
  antidepressants for, 718, 718t
  clinical evaluation of, 406-407
  definition of, 215, 362, 716
  epilepsy and, 717
  etiology of, 406, 407t
  evaluation of, 64-66
  history in, 406
  in cancer, 362
  laboratory findings in, 406-407
  magnetic resonance imaging in, 115
  mechanisms of, 26-28, 27f, 344, 556, 792, 792f
  neuronal hyperactivity and, 8
  opioids for, 999
  processing of, 26-29. *See also* Pain processing system, in nerve injury.
  tactile allodynia and, 12, 26
  transcutaneous electrical nerve stimulation for, 1053
Neuropathy. *See also specific nerves and disorders.*
  alcohol, 67t
  causes of, 64-66
  diabetic. *See* Diabetic neuropathy.
  diagnosis of, 64-66
    evoked potentials in, 193-194
  immune-mediated, 64-66
  infectious, 67t
  inflammatory demyelinating, 64
  nonmalignant inflammatory sensory, 64-65
  of renal disease, 67t
  paraneoplastic, 64, 67t
  peripheral. *See* Peripheral neuropathy.
  small-fiber, 64
  vitamin B$_{12}$ deficiency, 64
Neurophysiologic testing. *See* Electrodiagnostic procedures.
Neuroplasticity, 7-8, 1085-1086, 1089
  in chronic pain, 214, 1085-1086, 1089
  of ascending projections, 18, 1085-1086, 1089
Neuropraxia, 186
Neurosignature, 6, 9
Neurostimulation. *See also* Spinal cord stimulation; Transcutaneous electrical nerve stimulation.
  for cancer pain, 326
  for complex regional pain syndrome, 295-296
  for phantom pain, 309, 310-311
  for postmastectomy pain, 326
Neurosurgery
  cordotomy in, 356, 356f
  deep brain stimulation in, 356-357, 357f
  dorsal root entry zone lesioning in, 310, 357-358, 357f
  for cancer pain, 311, 356
  for phantom pain, 310, 311, 357
  for trigeminal neuralgia, 353-356, 354f, 355f
  indications for, 353-359
  sympathectomy in, 358-359, 358f, 359f
Neurotmesis, 186-187, 580f, 581
Neurotomy, radiofrequency. *See* Radiofrequency techniques.

Neurotransmitters, 18-20, 213, 1086
  ascending projection system, 20
  in acupuncture, 1095
  in complex regional pain syndrome, 556
  in nociception, 556-557, 1086
  in tissue injury, 24, 24f
  primary afferent, 19-20, 19f, 19t
Neutropenia, 58
  causes of, 58
Neutrophil count, 58
Newborn, brachial plexopathy in, 582, 582f
Nifedipine, for cluster headache, 486
Night splints, for rheumatoid arthritis, 387
Nimodipine, for cluster headache, 486
Nitrates, in cluster headache, 478, 480
Nitric oxide, in tissue injury, 25
Nitrite test, 68
Nitroglycerine, in cluster headache, 478, 480
Nitrous oxide, for burn pain, 243t, 244, 246
Nixon, Richard, 1093
NMDA (*N*-methyl-D-aspartate), 20
NMDA receptor
  in nerve injury, 28, 1086
  in phantom pain, 25
  in tissue injury, 24, 25, 25f
  magnesium block in, 24
  phosphorylation of, 25
NMDA receptor antagonists
  for chronic pain, 220
  for complex regional pain syndrome, 294
  for phantom pain, 310
  mechanism of action of, 31
Nocardiosis, 706, 707f
Nociceptin, 939-940, 1086
Nociception. *See also* Pain processing system.
  vs. pain, 1090
Nociceptive-specific neurons, 14, 14f, 17, 18f
Nociceptors, 212, 1081-1084. *See also* Pain processing system.
  A-delta, 1081. *See also* A fibers.
  activation of, 1083, 1089
  C, 1081, 1083. *See also* C-fibers.
  C-polymodal, 11-12, 12f
  chemical stimuli for, 1083, 1083t
  deep vs. cutaneous, 1084
  definition of, 1081
  dorsal horn, 13-15, 13t
  free nerve endings (terminals) of, 11, 12, 1081
  functions of, 1083-1084
  in inflammation, 1083-1084, 1084f
  microenvironment of, 289f
  norepinephrine and, 556-557, 1086
  primary afferent, 1081-1082, 1082f
  spinal cord projections of, 1084-1085
  study of, 1082-1083
  tissue distribution of, 1082
Nocifensor system, 1083
Nodes of Ranvier, distance between, in differential nerve blocks, 162-163, 163f
Nodules
  Dupuytren's, 668
  rheumatoid, 80, 420, 420f, 431, 432t, 434, 435f, 662
Nonmalignant inflammatory sensory neuropathy, 64-65
Nonsteroidal antiinflammatory drugs, 928-931, 934-937. *See also specific indications and agents.*
  administration of, 227t
  antiinflammatory vs. antinociceptive effects of, 934
  aspirin, 928-930. *See also* Aspirin.
  cervical facet block and, 1200

Nonsteroidal antiinflammatory drugs (*Continued*)
  cyclooxygenase inhibition of, 929, 934, 935, 937. *See also* COX-2 inhibitors.
  dosing guidelines for, 226, 936
  for acute/postoperative pain, 226-227, 226t
  for arachnoiditis, 796
  for chronic pain, 220
  for cluster headache, 487
  for migraine, 460
  for mononeuritis multiplex, 726
  for osteoarthritis, 427
  for paroxysmal hemicrania, 482
  for rheumatoid arthritis, 436
  for tension-type headaches, 470, 471t
  for trochanteric bursitis, 862
  gastroprotection for, 436
  ibuprofen, 930-931
  indications for, 936
  ketoprofen, 930-931
  mechanism of action of, 31, 226, 934-935
  medication-overuse headache and, 493
  naproxen sodium, 930-931
  pharmacokinetics of, 936
  salicylates, 928-930, 935-936
  selection of, 226, 226t, 936, 936t
  side effects of, 227, 936-937
  sodium salicylate, 930
  structure of, 226f
  types of, 226
Norepinephrine. *See also* Neurotransmitters.
  in complex regional pain syndrome, 556
  in nociception, 556-557, 1086
  spinal, 1394
Norgaard view, 80
Normal pressure hydrocephalus, magnetic gait in, 47
Normeperidine, 948t. *See also* Opioid(s).
Norpropoxyphene, 948t. *See also* Opioid(s).
Nortriptyline, 967. *See also* Antidepressants.
  for anterior interosseous syndrome, 654
  for intercostal neuralgia, 683
  for migraine prophylaxis, 461
  for mononeuritis multiplex, 725
  for peripheral neuropathy, 277t
  for post-thoracotomy syndrome, 682
  for proctalgia fugax, 851-852
  for pronator syndrome, 653
  for radial tunnel syndrome, 658
  for thoracic radiculopathy, 690
  side effects of, 718t, 967
  structure of, 967f
Nose. *See under* Nasal.
Nosebleed, from sphenopalatine ganglion block, 230
Novice skier's position
  in genitofemoral neuralgia, 747
  in iliohypogastric neuralgia, 746
  in ilioinguinal neuralgia, 742, 743f
Nuclear medicine techniques, 85-91. *See also specific techniques and indications.*
  bone scintigraphy, 85, 86-91
  FDG-PET, 85-86
  SPECT, 85, 86, 89-91, 91f
  technetium-99m in, 85
Nucleus proprius neurons, 13f, 13t, 14-15, 14f
Nucleus pulposus. *See also* Intervertebral disk.
  anatomy of, 119-120, 119f, 120f
Numbness
  in cervical radiculopathy, 570, 571, 573
  radiating to hand, prolotherapy for, 1119
Numeric Intensity Rating Scale, 200, 200f
Nutriceuticals. *See* Complementary and alternative therapies.
Nutrition, in cancer, 366

Nutritional supplements, 991t. *See also* Complementary and alternative therapies.

O
Obesity
  meralgia paresthetica and, 868, 869f
  osteoarthritis and, 426, 428
  water-based exercises in, 1046
O'Brien active compression test, 607-608
Obstetric pain
  caudal epidural block for, 1343. *See also* Epidural nerve block, caudal.
  hypnosis for, 1022, 1023
Obstetric trauma, brachial plexopathy and, 582, 582f
Obturator hernia, 879
Obturator nerve, 46t
  anatomy of, 879, 880f, 1331, 1332f, 1364-1365
  sensory testing of, 879, 881f
Obturator nerve block, 238t, 1331-1334, 1364-1365
  anatomic aspects of, 1331, 1332f
  complications of, 1333-1334
  indications for, 1331-1332
  technique of, 1332-1333
    direct, 1332-1333, 1333f
    indirect, 1333-1334
Obturator nerve entrapment, 879-882, 881f, 882f, 882t
  diagnosis of, 1331
Obturator neuropathy, 879-882, 881f, 882f, 882t
Occipital artery, occipital nerve and, 1140, 1143, 1143f
Occipital headache, 504, 549-551, 550f
  after cervical plexus block, 1189
Occipital nerve, anatomy of, 549, 1140, 1141f-1143f, 1143
Occipital nerve block, 238t, 1140-1144
  anatomic factors in, 1140-1143, 1141f-1143f
  complications of, 1143-1144
  contraindications to, 1140
  diagnostic, 153, 549, 1140, 1143
  for medication-overuse headache, 238t
  for occipital neuralgia
    in diagnosis, 153, 549, 1140, 1143
    in treatment, 549-550, 550f
  future directions for, 1144
  historical considerations in, 1140
  indications for, 1140
  pitfalls in, 1143
  results of, 1143, 1143f
  technique of, 1143
Occipital neuralgia, 549-551, 550f
  causes of, 1141t
  diagnosis of, 153, 549, 1140, 1143
  historical perspective on, 1140
  nerve block for. *See* Occipital nerve block.
  radiofrequency techniques for, 1444-1445
  trigeminal neuralgia and, 504, 1140
  vs. tension-type headache, 549
  vs. trigeminal neuralgia, 504
Occipital back pain, 777-790. *See also* Back pain; Low back pain.
  acute, 777-781
  attribution of, 783-784
  certification for, 781-782
  chronic, 782-783
    diagnosis of, 783
    treatment of, 783
  compensation issues in, 784-786, 787
  confounding factors in, 787
    extraneous, 777, 778f

Occupational back pain (*Continued*)
  euphemistic, 780-781
  evaluation of, 777-778
  financial motives in, 786, 1008
  imaging studies in, 777-778, 783
  light duties in, 781
  malingering and, 786
  malingering in, 780
  medical report preparation for, 789-790
  modified duties in, 781-782
  overview of, 777
  preexisting abnormalities and, 784, 785t
  prevalence of, 777, 778f
  prevention of, 786-787
  psychosocial factors in
    in acute pain, 778
    in chronic pain, 782-783
    in euphemistic pain, 780-781
  red flags in, 777, 778f
  return to work in, 779-780, 781
  risk factors for, 784
  secondary gain in, 786
  spondylosis in, 784, 785t
  treatment of, 783
  workplace intervention in, 779-780, 781
Occupational therapy
  for cancer pain, 325-326
  for cervical dystonia, 594
  for complex regional pain syndrome, 220
  for rheumatoid arthritis, 437
Ocular/periocular pain, 523-536
  anatomic aspects of, 523
  causes of, 524-530
  from corneal abrasion, 524-525
  from stye, 524
  in conjunctivitis, 525, 526f
  in glaucoma, 525-528, 526t, 527f, 528f
  in uveitis, 528, 529f
  overview of, 523
  referred, 530-536
    in cavernous sinus syndromes, 532-536
    in cluster headache, 530-532, 531f
    in Tolosa-Hunt syndrome, 532
Oculocardiac reflexes, in sphenopalatine ganglion block, 1138
Oculomotor nerve, examination of, 42-43, 44t
Oculomotor nerve palsy, 407t, 409-410
Office of Alternative Medicine, 990
Oldendorf, William, 758, 760f
Older adults. *See* Elderly.
Olecranon bursitis, 641-642, 642f-644f, 646
  lateral epicondylitis and, 384, 635
  medial epicondylitis and, 637
Olfactory nerve
  anatomy of, 408f
  examination of, 42-43, 44t
Ondansetron, for cancer-related nausea, 364, 365
Ondine's curse, cordotomy and, 1501
One-legged stork test, 813-814
Oocyte aspiration, acupuncture for, 1100, 1100t
Open-angle glaucoma, 525-528, 526t, 527f
Opera glass hand, 662
Operant techniques
  for burn pain, 250-251
  for chronic pain, 1005
Ophthalmic nerve, anatomy of, 523, 524f, 1146, 1146f, 1147f, 1153, 1154f
Ophthalmic nerve block, 1156-1157, 1158f. *See also* Trigeminal nerve block.
Ophthalmologic examination, in peripheral neuropathy, 274
Ophthalmoplegia, in Tolosa-Hunt syndrome, 407t, 411f, 532

Opioid(s), 939-961. *See also specific types.*
 absorption of, 947-950
 abuse of
  fear of, 947, 998
  screening for, 72
 addiction to, vs. dependence, 323
 administration of, 228-229
  routes of, 228, 322t
  scheduled vs. prn, 250
 agonist, 227, 321
 agonist-antagonist, 227, 321, 958-960
 breakthrough pain with, 999-1000
 caudal epidural catheterization for, 1342
 classification of, 227, 321, 941, 942t
 constipation due to, 322-323
  with spinal administration, 1396-1397
 cross-tolerance to, 1394
 dependence on, 39, 250, 323, 946-947, 947t.
   See also Drug abuse/dependency.
  fear of, 947, 998
  levo-alpha acetyl methadol for, 957-958
  methadone for. *See* Methadone.
  vs. addiction, 323
 distribution of, 950
 dosage of, 227-228, 321
  equianalgesic, 322
  inadequate, 947
 dose-limiting effects of, 999
 drowsiness due to, methylphenidate for, 323,
   364, 366, 1000
 duration of effect of, 227-228, 321
 end-of-dose failure with, 1000
 endogenous, 939-940, 1086
 epidural. *See* Spinal opioids.
 equianalgesic doses of, 944
 excretion of, 950
 for acute pancreatitis, 737-739
 for acute/postoperative pain, 227-229
 for breakthrough pain, 999-1000
 for burn pain, 243, 243t, 245
 for cancer pain, 319-323, 320t, 322t, 325,
   349-350, 364-365, 997, 998
  advantages and disadvantages of, 998
  side effects of, 364-365, 366f
  spinal administration of, 325, 350-351,
    351t, 352t
 for cancer-related delirium, 367-369, 368f
 for cancer-related dyspnea, 366
 for chronic pain, 39, 219, 718, 997, 998-999
 for chronic pancreatitis, 740-741
 for complex regional pain syndrome, 293-
   294, 294t
 for herpes zoster, 280-281
 for incident pain, 1000
 for migraine, 461
 for mononeuritis multiplex, 726
 for movement-related pain, 999-1000
 for neuropathic pain, 999
 for osteoarthritis, 427
 for phantom pain, 309-310
 for postmastectomy pain, 718
 for rib fractures, 678-680
 for sickle cell pain, 260
 for sternoclavicular joint syndrome, 687
 for substance abusers, 39, 250
 half-life of, 948t
 historical perspective on, 939
 implantable infusion pump for. *See also*
   Spinal opioids.
  for arachnoiditis, 797
  for cancer pain, 339
 in medication-overuse headache, 493
 in patient-controlled analgesia, 228-229
 incident pain with, 999-1000
 intrathecal. *See* Spinal opioids.

Opioid(s) *(Continued)*
 intraventricular, 949
 mechanism of action of, 29-31, 943
  peripheral, 30-31
  spinal, 30, 30f
  supraspinal, 29, 30f, 31
 metabolism of, 950
 nausea due to, 944
 overdose of, naloxone for, 323, 352t, 960-
   961, 961f
 patient-physician contract for, 219
 pharmacodynamics of, 944-946
 pharmacokinetics of, 947-950
 phenanthrene, 941, 942t, 943f, 950-952
 physiologic effects of
  analgesic, 944
  antitussive, 944
  cardiovascular, 945, 945f
  central nervous system, 944-945
  cutaneous, 946
  gastrointestinal, 944, 945
  genitourinary, 946
  immunologic, 946
  miotic, 944
  mood-altering, 944
  neuroendocrine, 946
  respiratory
  rewarding, 944
  uterine, 946
 potency of, 227
 preparations of, 950-960
 prototype, morphine as, 950
 pseudoaddiction to, 947
 relative potencies of, 944, 944t
 rescue dose of, 321-322
 respiratory depression due to, 323, 945
  naloxone for, 352t
  with spinal administration, 351, 352t
 risk-benefit ratio for, 997
 routes of administration for, 947-950
  inhalational, 948-949
  intramuscular, 948
  intravenous, 948
  neuraxial, 949. *See also* Spinal opioids.
  oral, 947
  rectal, 948
  subcutaneous, 947-948
  transdermal, 949, 949f
  transnasal, 948
 sedative effects of, methylphenidate for, 323,
   364, 366, 1000
 seizures due to, 944-945
 semisynthetic, 941, 942t, 943f, 952-954
 side effects of, 227, 322-323, 364-365, 366,
   944-946
  in cancer patients, 364-365, 366
  management of, 999, 999t
  with spinal administration, 351, 352t
 sites of action of, 29
 spinal. *See* Spinal opioids.
 structure of, 228f, 941, 941f-943f
 synthetic, 941, 942t, 943f, 954-960
 tolerance to, 244, 323, 946
 weak vs. strong, 320
 withdrawal from, 947
  with spinal administration, 1397
Opioid agonists, 943, 943f
Opioid antagonists, 960-961, 961f
 for respiratory depression, 323
 for spinal opioids, 352t
Opioid motif, 939
Opioid receptors, 940-941, 941t, 1086
Opiophobia, 947, 998
Opium, 940, 950
Oppenheim, Hermann, 591, 592f

Opportunistic infections, in HIV infection, 63
Optic disc
 cupping of, in glaucoma, 526, 527f
 edema of, in optic neuritis, 530, 530f
Optic nerve
 anatomy of, 408f
 examination of, 42-43, 44t
 ischemia of, in temporal arteritis, 519
Optic neuritis, 528-530
Oral ulcers, in discoid lupus erythematosus,
  438, 439f
Orchialgia, 837-841
 anatomic aspects of, 837-838, 838f
 causes of, 839, 839t
 cryoanalgesia for, 1468
 diagnosis of, 839-840, 839t
 differential diagnosis of, 838-839, 839t
 ilioinguinal-iliohypogastric block for, 1322-
   1323
 referred pain in, 838, 839t
 treatment of, 840-841, 841t
Orchidectomy, for orchialgia, 841
Orchitis, self-palpation, 839
Organ convergence, 15, 15f
Oriental medicine. *See* Chinese medicine.
Orphanin FQ, 939-940
Orphenadrine, 979. *See also* Muscle relaxants.
 for tension-type headache, 470, 471t
Orthostatic hypotension. *See* Hypotension.
Orthotics
 for Morton neuroma, 918
 for osteoarthritis, 426, 426f
 for plantar fasciitis, 924
 for rheumatoid arthritis, 437
 for trochanteric bursitis, 861-862
Osler, William, 1093-1094
Osmol gap, 69
Osmolality, 69
Osteitis pubis, 81, 831-833, 832f, 833f
 prolotherapy for, 1118-1119, 1118f, 1119f
 vs. iliopsoas bursitis, 866
Osteoarthritis, 418-429. *See also* Arthritis.
 bone marrow lesions in, 112
 Bouchard nodes in, 80, 420, 420f, 434, 435f,
   662
 carpometacarpal, 418, 420
  vs. carpal tunnel syndrome, 386, 387f
 comorbidities in, 424
 diagnosis of, 421-424, 422t
 differential diagnosis of, 422t
 facet, imaging of, 89-91, 91f
 generalized, 420
 Heberden nodes in, 80, 420, 420f, 434, 435f,
   662
 historical perspective on, 418
 imaging in, 421-424
  bone scintigraphy in, 89-91, 91f, 422-423
  magnetic resonance imaging in, 112, 115,
    423-424, 423f
  plain radiography in, 421-422, 423f
  SPECT in, 89-91, 91f
 involved joints in, 418-421, 434
 management of, 422t, 424-428
  barriers to, 429
  complementary therapies in, 427
  drug therapy in, 427-428
  education in, 426
  exercise in, 426
  goals of, 422t
  guidelines for, 425
  orthoses in, 426, 426f
  patellar taping in, 426, 427f
  reasons for seeking care and, 422t, 424-
    425
  surgery in, 426, 428

Osteoarthritis *(Continued)*
  therapeutic options in, 425t, 426-428
  weight reduction in, 426
 menopausal, 420
 obesity and, 426, 428
 occupational factors in, 428-429
 of ankle and foot, 84, 911-914
 of elbow, 80
 of hip, 81, 82f, 419-420
  differential diagnosis of, 422t
  exercise program for, 1059-1060
  imaging of, 81, 82f, 421-424
  prevention of, 428-429
  prolotherapy for, 1115, 1115f
  total joint arthroplasty for, 86, 428. *See also* Total joint arthroplasty.
  femoral neuropathy in, 873
  obturator neuropathy in, 879, 881
 of knee, 81-83, 83f, 419, 419f
  acupuncture for, 1100, 1100t
  differential diagnosis of, 422t, 424
  exercise program for, 1059-1060, 1060f, 1065, 1065f, 1066f
  imaging of, 81-83, 83f, 112, 421-424, 422f, 423f
  management of, 424-428
  prevention of, 428-429
  prolotherapy for, 1116, 1116f
  total joint arthroplasty for, 86, 428. *See also* Total joint arthroplasty.
 of sacrococcygeal joint, 848
 of sacroiliac joint, 810-815, 1358-1361
 of shoulder, 79, 598-602
  acromioclavicular, 605, 608, 615-618, 617f
  clinical features of, 598, 599t
  diagnosis of, 598-600, 599f, 600f
  differential diagnosis of, 600, 601t
  imaging studies of, 598-600, 599f, 600f
  prolotherapy for, 1111, 1111f
  treatment of, 600-602, 601f, 615-618, 617f
 of spine, 756
  imaging of, 89-91, 91f, 756f
  involved joints in, 107
 of sternoclavicular joint, 686-688, 687f
 of wrist and hand, 80, 418, 420, 420f, 659, 660-663, 660t
  prolotherapy for, 1114
 pain in
  exacerbations of, 424
  pathophysiology of, 420-421
  radiographic findings and, 418, 422
  structural correlates of, 423-424
 pathogenesis of, 418, 419f
 prevention of, 428-429
 prolotherapy for. *See* Prolotherapy, for arthritis.
 relaxation techniques for, 1026-1207
 signs and symptoms of, 419-420, 419f, 420f
 subchondral cysts in, 112, 115
 vs. crystal arthropathies, 424
 vs. diffuse idiopathic skeletal hyperostosis, 424
 vs. gout, 424
 vs. pseudogout, 424
 vs. rheumatoid arthritis, 434-435
Osteochondritis dissecans, of elbow, 80
Osteochondromatosis, synovial, 83, 84f
Osteochondrosis, intervertebral, 107
Osteoid osteoma
 computed tomography of, 102
 of spine, 751
Osteolysis, of distal clavicle, 80

Osteomyelitis
 magnetic resonance imaging of, 112
 vertebral, 751, 752f
  radiography of, 77
  vs. Charcot joint, 112
Osteonecrosis
 aseptic vertebral, 77, 78f
 magnetic resonance imaging of, 112, 113f
 of femur, in sickle cell disease, 258t
 of hip
  imaging of, 81, 83f, 99, 102f
  in sickle cell disease, 258t
Osteopathic manipulative treatment, 1069-1079
 clinical applications of, 1077-1078
 drug therapy and, 1077
 facilitated segment concept in, 1070
 for ankle sprains, 1078
 for fibromyalgia, 1078
 for low back pain, 1077-1078
 for lumbar radiculopathy, 764, 765
 for migraine cephalgia, 1078
 for sacroiliac disorders, 814
 for scoliosis, 1078
 for structural vs. functional pathology, 1075-1076
 for whiplash, 1078
 gait analysis in, 1074
 history of, 1069
 history taking in, 1071
 motion pattern grading in, 1071-1074, 1073f
 nociceptive model and, 1070-1071
 overview of, 1069
 pain processing and, 1070-1071
 patient education in, 1076-1077
 patient selection for, 1075-1076
 physical examination in, 1070, 1070t
 postural evaluation in, 1071, 1071t, 1072f
 principles of, 1069, 1070t
 prone evaluation in, 1075, 1075t
 repeat treatments in, 1078
 seated evaluation in, 1074
 somatic dysfunction and, 1070-1071
 standing evaluation in, 1074
 structural examination in, 1071-1075
 supine evaluation in, 1074-1075, 1075t
 TART examination in, 1070, 1070t
 therapeutic modalities in
  arthrodial, 1076
  complications of, 1076
  myofascial, 1076
  selection of, 1076
Osteophytes
 in rotator cuff disorders, 603, 608, 609f
 traction, in spinal osteoarthritis, 756, 756f
Osteoporosis
 exercise program for, 1063, 1064f
 low back pain in, 753
 rib fractures in, 678
 vertebral compression fractures in, 77
  magnetic resonance imaging of, 116, 116f
 vertebral microfractures in, 753, 754f
Osteotomy
 for hallux valgus, 920
 for osteoarthritis, 428
Otalgia, 538-543. *See also* Ear pain.
Otitis media, 542-543, 543f
Oucher Scale, 208, 209f
Outlet view, of rotator cuff, 608, 609f
Ovarian cancer, pleural effusion in, 701
Over-the-counter analgesics, 927-932. *See also* Acetaminophen; Nonsteroidal antiinflammatory drugs; Simple analgesics.
 classification of, 928t
 indications for, 927-928
 overview of, 927-928

Overflow pain, in glossopharyngeal neuralgia, 511
Overuse injuries, 376, 377t. *See also* Sports injuries *and specific injuries.*
 biofeedback for, 1013. *See also* Biofeedback.
 muscle relearning therapy for, 1013
Oxycodone, 944t, 948t, 954. *See also* Opioid(s).
 for acute/postoperative pain, 228
 for burns, 243t, 245
 for cancer pain, 321-323
 structure of, 228f, 942f, 954f
Oxygen therapy
 for cancer-related dyspnea, 366
 for cluster headache, 484
Oxymorphone, 948t, 954. *See also* Opioid(s).
 for cancer pain, 321-323
 structure of, 942f, 953f

P
P38 mitogen activated protein kinase C, in tissue injury, 25
Pace test, in piriformis syndrome, 834
Paced respiration, 1028
Paget, James, 664
Pain
 acute, 212
 affective-motivational dimension of, 17-18, 18f, 197, 198
 breakthrough, 999-1000
  in burn patients, 242, 242f
 cancer. *See* Cancer pain.
 central, diagnosis of, 157, 158t
 chronic. *See* Chronic pain.
 clinical trials for, 1138
 cognitive-evaluative dimension of, 197
 definition of, 212
 encephalization of, 158t
 gate control theory of, 3-4, 4f, 1373
  vs. neuromatrix theory, 4-7, 5f
 historical perspective on, 3-4, 149-150, 150f
 incident, 1000
 mirror-image, 9
  after percutaneous cordotomy, 1512-1513
 muscle, pathophysiology of, 465-466, 465f
 neuromatrix theory and, 4-7, 5f
 neuromatrix theory of, vs. gate control theory of, 4-7, 5f
 neuronal hyperactivity and, 8
 neuropathic. *See* Neuropathic pain.
 phantom, 304-312
 prevention of, 8
 psychogenic
  diagnosis of, 38, 157
  differential nerve blocks in, 155-165. *See also* Differential nerve blocks.
  labeling and, 38
 psychophysics of, 21-32. *See also* Pain processing system.
 radiation of, mechanisms of, 1087-1088
 radicular, 118
 referred. *See* Referred pain.
 sensation of vs. unpleasantness of, 197
 sensory-discriminative dimension of, 17, 18f, 197
 somatic, 362
 subjectivity of, 4-7, 5f, 197-198
 sympathetically maintained, 288-290, 290f
 theories of, 3-4, 4f, 280
 visceral, 362
 vs. nociception, 1090

Pain assessment
    Brief Pain Inventory in, 203, 204f
    Edmondton Staging System for, 362, 363f
    for cancer pain, 362-369
    in children, 203-208
        COMFORT scale in, 203, 206f
        CRIES scale in, 203, 207f
        Faces Pain Scale in, 208, 208f
        FLACC scale in, 203, 208f
        Oucher Scale in, 208, 209f
        Wong-Baker Faces Scale in, 203-208, 208f
    in elderly, 208-209
    JCAHO standards for, 198-199, 199t
    McGill Pain Questionnaire in, 200-202, 201f
        short-form, 202, 202f
    Memorial Pain Assessment Card in, 203, 205f
    Multidimensional Affect and Pain Survey in, 203, 205f
    multidimensional scales in, 200-203
        patient selection for, 203
    numerical rating scales in, 200, 200f
    objective, 198
    single-dimension scales in, 199-200
        patient selection for, 199-200
    standardized measures for, 198
    verbal descriptor scales in, 200, 200f
    verbal numeric scales in, 200
    visual analog scales in, 199-200, 200f
Pain history. See History.
Pain mapping, conscious, 1469
Pain patterns
    case examples of, 50-51
    diagnostic approach to, 50-51, 51t
    referred. See Referred pain.
    spatial, 50, 51t
    spinal, 52-55
    temporal, 49-50
Pain processing system
    activation of, 21
    afferent line labeling in, 17
    afferents in. See also Afferents.
        primary, 11-12, 12f, 13, 13f, 13t
        secondary, 13-15, 13t
    anatomy of, 11-20
    ascending pathways in, 15, 16f, 17-18, 212-213, 213f
    components of, 22f
    cortical mechanisms in, 1086-1087
    descending pathways in, 25, 213, 214f, 1086
    differential block in, 985
    dynamics of, 21-32
    endogenous opioids in, 939-940, 1086
    frequency encoding in, 15-16, 16, 16f, 17, 17f
    functional overview of, 16-18
    in chronic pain, 214-215
    in nerve injury, 26-29
        afferent sprouting in, 26-28, 27f, 344, 556, 792, 792f, 1084
        astrocytes in, 28
        central sensitization in, 26-27
        dorsal horn reorganization in, 28
        dorsal root ganglion cell cross-talk in, 27
        dynorphin in, 28
        evoked hyperpathia in, 27-29
        glutamate in, 28
        loss of GABAergic/glycemic control in, 28
        microglia in, 28
        morphologic correlates in, 26
        peripheral sensitization in, 26-27
        psychophysics of, 26
        sympathetic innervation in, 28-29, 29f

Pain processing system (Continued)
    in tissue injury, 21-26, 1087
        afferent response in, 21-22, 22f, 23f, 23t
        algogenic agents in, 22, 23t
        astrocytes in, 25-26
        bulbospinal systems in, 25, 26f
        central sensitization in, 22-24
        lipid mediators in, 24-25, 25f
        microglia in, 25-26
        nitric oxide in, 25
        NMDA receptor in, 24, 24f, 25
        peripheral sensitization in, 21-22, 23t
        phosphorylation in, 25
        psychophysics of, 21
        secondary hyperesthesia in, 24
        spinal facilitation in, 24-26, 24f
        wind-up in, 15, 22-24, 23f, 25
    inhibitory mechanisms in, 213, 214f, 939-940, 1086
    neuroplasticity in, 7-8, 18, 214, 1085-1086
    neurotransmitters in, 18-20, 213, 556-557, 1086
    nociceptive-specific pathway in, 17-18, 18f
    nociceptors in, 11-15, 212, 1081-1085. See also Nociceptors.
    osteopathic view of, 1070-1071
    psychological aspects of, 1086-1087
    somatosensory cortex in, 213
    spinal dorsal horn in, 12-15
    supraspinal projections in, 15-16, 16f, 17f, 1084
    wide dynamic range system in, 17-18, 18f, 212
Painful arc sign, 915
Palatine nerves, 540f
Palliative care. See Cancer, palliative care in.
Pancoast-Tobias syndrome, 694-695
Pancoast tumors, 694-695, 696f-697f
    radiation therapy for, 332-333, 333f
    vs. cervical radiculopathy, 573
    vs. cubital tunnel syndrome, 649
    vs. shoulder bursitis, 694-695
Pancreatic cancer
    palliative radiation therapy for, 332-333, 333f
    vs. chronic pancreatitis, 740, 741f
Pancreatic enzymes
    after celiac plexus block, 1279
    in acute pancreatitis, 740
    in chronic pancreatitis, 740
Pancreatic pseudocyst
    in acute pancreatitis, 737, 738f
    in chronic pancreatitis, 740, 740f
Pancreatitis
    acute, 71, 737-739, 738f, 739f
        celiac plexus block for, 1265
        epidural nerve block for, 1244
    chronic, 71, 739-741, 740f
    diagnosis of, 71
Panner disease, 80
Paracetamol
    for osteoarthritis, 427
    for trochanteric bursitis, 862
Paraffin baths, 1036-1037, 1037f
Paraneoplastic neuropathy, 64, 67t
Parapharyngeal abscess, 543, 546f
Parapharyngeal tumors, 543, 546f, 547
Parapneumonic effusion, 704-706
Parasternal block, 1250, 1251f
Paravertebral nerve block, 1253-1256, 1256f. See also Intercostal nerve block.
Paravertebral space, anatomy of, 1251, 1252f
Paré, Ambrose, 304, 305f

Paresis, after percutaneous cordotomy, 1514
Paresthesias, in cervical radiculopathy, 570, 571, 573
Paroxetine, 968. See also Antidepressants.
Paroxysmal hemicrania, 481-482
Pars interarticularis
    anatomy of, 800, 801f
    defects in, 800-802, 802f, 803f. See also Spondylolisthesis; Spondylolysis.
Parsonage-Turner syndrome, 414-415, 414f, 585-586, 586f
Patella, anatomy of, 884, 884f
Patellar taping, for osteoarthritis, 426, 427f
Patellofemoral osteoarthritis, 81-83
Pathologic fractures, vertebral. See Vertebral fractures, compression.
Pathologic pain. See Pain.
Patient-controlled analgesia, 228-229
    for burns, 245
Patient-physician contract, for opioid therapy, 219
Pattern theories, 3, 4, 4f
    body-self neuromatrix and, 4-7, 5f
Pavementing, 935
Pectoralis minor syndrome, 593
Pelvic floor, prolotherapeutic injection of, 1119, 1119f
Pelvic pain
    ganglion of Walker block for, 1353-1357
    hypnosis for, 1022
    hypogastric plexus block for, 1350-1354
    impar ganglion block for, 1354-1357
    in coccydynia, 848-850, 849f, 850f
    in ilioinguinal neuralgia, 742-745
    in osteitis pubis, 831-833, 832f, 833f
    in piriformis syndrome, 834-836
    in proctalgia fugax, 851-852
    in sacroiliac joint disorders, 812, 813f. See also Sacroiliac joint disorders.
    management of, limitations of, 1001, 1001t
Pelvic plexus, anatomy of, 837, 838f
Pelvic plexus block, for orchialgia, 840
Pelvic rock test, 1358, 1359f
Pelvic tilt exercises, 1061, 1062f
    for sacroiliac disorders, 815
Pelvic traction, for sacroiliac disorders, 814
Pelvis
    anatomy of, 810, 811f, 812f
    center of gravity in, 811
    movement of, 811-812
    radiography of, 81
Penicillamine
    for arachnoiditis, 798
    for rheumatoid arthritis, 436
Pentazocine, 944t, 948t, 958-959, 959f. See also Opioid(s).
    structure of, 943f, 959f
Peptic ulcers, relaxation techniques for, 1027
PercScope, 1496-1497, 1496f
Percutaneous balloon compression, for trigeminal neuralgia, 353-356, 354f, 355f, 506-507
Percutaneous carotid angioplasty, celiac plexus block for, 1189
Percutaneous catheter, 1385, 1385f. See also Implantable drug delivery systems.
Percutaneous cordotomy, 1501-1515. See also Cordotomy, percutaneous.
Percutaneous laser diskectomy, 1489-1499. See also Laser diskectomy.
Periaqueductal gray matter
    in pain processing, 213, 214f, 1086, 1087
    opioid action in, 29
Perichondritis, auricular, 541, 541f
Peridural hematoma, postoperative, 819

Perineal pain, cryoanalgesia for, 1468
Perineurium, 343
Periocular pain. *See* Ocular/periocular pain.
Peripheral blood smear, 57
Peripheral gliocytes, 343
Peripheral ischemia, spinal cord stimulation for, 1379
Peripheral nerve blocks
  for lower extremity, 1362-1368. *See also* Lower extremity, peripheral nerve blocks for.
  for upper extremity, 1227-1238. *See also* Upper extremity, peripheral nerve blocks for.
Peripheral nerve catheterization, for cancer pain, 339
Peripheral nerve injury
  cryoanalgesia for, 1464-1471. *See also* Cryoanalgesia.
  neuronal hyperactivity and, 8
Peripheral nerve stimulation, 1369-1371, 1380
Peripheral nerves, anatomy of, 343
Peripheral neuropathy. *See also* Neuropathic pain; Neuropathy *and specific neuropathies.*
  autonomic dysfunction in, 274
  autonomic reflex testing in, 276
  causes of, 64-66
  classification of
    anatomic, 268, 269t
    temporal, 269, 270t
  clinical manifestations of, 272-274, 272t, 273f, 274t
  computed tomography in, 276
  cranial nerve dysfunction in, 274
  diagnosis of, 186-189, 269-276, 269t
  drug-related, 271, 271t
  electrodiagnostic testing in, 186-189, 274-276
  electromyography in, 179-184, 275. *See also* Electromyography.
  foot examination in, 272, 273f
  generalized
    electrodiagnosis of, 187
    types of, 187t
  heritable, 271, 272
  history in, 268, 269-271
    family, 271
    medication, 271, 271t
    occupational, 271, 271t
    past medical and surgical, 269-271, 270t
    social, 271, 271t
  magnetic resonance imaging in, 276
  neurologic examination in, 272-274
  neurophysiologic testing in, 274-276
  ocular involvement in, 274
  organomegaly in, 274
  patient's verbal description of, 269, 269t
  physical examination in, 272-274, 272t, 273f, 274t
  quantitative sensory testing in, 186-189, 275-276
  review of systems in, 271-272
  skin/hair/nail abnormalities in, 274, 274t
  treatment of, 276-277, 276t
    analgesic, 277, 277t
    deep brain stimulation in, 356-357, 357f
  vitamin B$_{12}$ deficiency, 64
  vs. cervical radiculopathy, 573
  weakness in, 272-274
Peripheral vascular disease, transcutaneous electrical nerve stimulation for, 1053
Periumbilical ecchymosis, in acute pancreatitis, 737, 738f
Pernicious anemia, diagnosis of, 64

Peroneal nerve, 46t
  cryoablation of, 1469-1470
Peroneal nerve block
  deep, 1367
  superficial, 1367
Personality factors. *See also* Psychological factors.
  in chronic pain, 1004
  in cluster headache, 478
  in tension-type headache, 468
Perspiration, abnormal, in complex regional pain syndrome, 284, 285t
Pes anserine bursitis, 900-902
Pes cavus, in peripheral neuropathy, 272, 273f
Pes planus, in peripheral neuropathy, 272, 273f
PET. *See* FDG-PET; Positron emission tomography.
Phalen test, in carpal tunnel syndrome, 385, 385f, 412, 664
Phantom pain/sensation, 304-312
  amputation site and, 304
  biofeedback for, 1013
  course of, 305, 307
  definition of, 304
  differential diagnosis of, 307-308
  disability from, 305
  duration of, 304
  epidemiology of, 304
  epidural anesthesia for, 308
  historical perspective on, 304
  incidence and prevalence of, 304
  mechanisms of, 8, 305-307, 1088
  neuromatrix and, 4-7, 5f, 306
  neuronal hyperactivity and, 8, 306
  physical examination in, 307
  prevention of, 8, 308-309, 1210
  psychological aspects of, 306, 311
  regional anesthesia for, 308-309
  risk factors for, 304-305
  signs and symptoms of, 307
  telescoping in, 307, 307f
  time of onset of, 304
  treatment of, 308-311
    dorsal root entry zone lesioning in, 310, 357-358, 358f
    drug therapy in, 309-310
    electroconvulsive therapy in, 311
    hypnosis for, 311
    nerve blocks in, 310
    neurostimulation in, 310-311
    neurosurgery in, 311
    physical therapy in, 311
    psychotherapy for, 311
    relaxation techniques for, 311
    side effects and complications of, 311
    stump revision in, 311
Pharyngeal pain, 543-547
Pharyngeal tumors, 546f, 547
Pharyngitis, 543
Phenelzine, 969, 970f
  for migraine prophylaxis, 461
Phenobarbital
  for seizure prophylaxis, in medication overuse withdrawal, 499
  therapeutic monitoring of, 72
Phenol
  in neurolytic blockade, 345-346, 345t, 347t. *See also* Neurolytic blockade.
  in prolotherapy, 1110. *See also* Prolotherapy.
Phenothiazines, for migraine, 460
Phentolamine, mechanism of action of, 28-29
Phenylbutazone, for cancer pain, 318-319, 319t

Phenytoin, 972-974. *See also* Anticonvulsants.
  dosing guidelines for, 972-974
  for herpes zoster, 281
  for peripheral neuropathy, 277t
  side effects of, 972, 973t
  structure of, 973f
  therapeutic monitoring of, 72
  toxicity of, 72
Phosphohexoisomerase, 19
Phospholipase A$_2$, epidural steroids and, 340
Phosphorus imbalances, 69
Photophobia, in cluster headache, 477
Phrenic nerve
  anatomy of, 578f, 579f, 580, 1169, 1171f, 1179f
  cervical plexus and, 1179f, 1188
  inadvertent blockade of, in cervical plexus block, 1188
Phrenic nerve block, 238t, 1169-1172
  anatomic aspects of, 1169, 1171f
  inadvertent
    in interscalene brachial plexus block, 1221
    in stellate ganglion block, 1197
    in supraclavicular brachial plexus block, 1224
  indications for, 1169, 1170t
  technique of, 1169-1170
Physical examination, 41-47
  cranial nerve examination in, 42-43, 44t
  deep tendon reflexes in, 46-47, 47f, 47t
  general survey in, 41
  mental status examination in, 42, 42t, 43t
  motor examination in, 43-44, 44t
  sensory examination in, 44-46
  spinal, 41
Physical Examination of the Spine and Extremities (Hoppenfeld), 1074, 1074t
Physical therapy, 1055-1066. *See also* Exercise; Exercises.
  for brachial plexopathy, 588-589
  for cancer pain, 325-326
  for cervical dystonia, 594
  for cervical facet syndrome, 564
  for chronic pain, 220
  for complex regional pain syndrome, 220
  for phantom pain, 311
  for pyriformis syndrome, 835
  for rheumatoid arthritis, 437
  for sacroiliac disorders, 814
  for tension-type headache, 472
  historical perspective on, 1055
Physician-patient contract, for opioid therapy, 219
Piedallu test, 814
Pilocarpine, for complex regional pain syndrome, 295
Pin test, for glomus tumor of hand, 671
Pinch, impaired
  in anterior interosseous syndrome, 653, 655f
  in carpal tunnel syndrome, 664
  in de Quervain's tenosynovitis, 666
Pink eye, 525, 526f
Piper Fatigue Self-Report Scale, 364
Piriformis syndrome, 763, 764, 834-836
  prolotherapy for, 1125-1126, 1125f
  vs. gluteal bursitis, 854
Piroxicam
  for cancer pain, 318-319, 319t
  structure of, 226f
Pituitary neuroadenolysis, 1405-1410
  anatomic aspects of, 1405
  cerebrospinal fluid leakage after, prevention of, 1405, 1409
  complications of, 1410
  contraindications to, 1405

Pituitary neuroadenolysis (Continued)
history of, 1405
indications for, 1405
mechanism of action of, 1409
patient preparation for, 1406
postoperative care in, 1409
results of, 1409-1410
technique of, 1405, 1406-1409, 1406f-
1409f
Pituitary tumors, cavernous sinus invasion by,
533, 534f
Placebo effect, 198
ethical aspects of, 198
in conventional sequential differential spinal
block, 157
Plantar digital nerve block, 1368
Plantar fascia, anatomy of, 922, 923f
Plantar fasciitis, 400-402, 401f, 922-924
Plantar ligament sprains, prolotherapy for, 1117,
1117f
Plantar reflex, assessment of, 47
Plasticity. See Neuroplasticity.
Platelet count, 58
Pleomorphic adenoma, parapharyngeal, 546f,
547
Pleural effusion
after celiac plexus block, 1279
chylous, 708-709, 709f
in acute chest syndrome, 703
malignant
in breast cancer, 701, 701f
in lymphoma, 701
in mesothelioma, 695, 700f
in ovarian cancer, 701
parapneumonic, 704-706
pulmonary embolism and, 703, 703f
radiography of, 688f
Pleural puncture, inadvertent, in thoracic
epidural nerve block, 1248
Pleural tuberculosis, 707
Pleural tumors, 695-701, 699f-701f
metastatic, 695
Pleuropulmonary chest pain, 693-712. See also
Chest pain, pleuropulmonary.
Plexopathy, 189
definition of, 189
electrodiagnosis of, 189
Pneumococcal pneumonia, 704
Pneumonectomy, extrapleural, for malignant
mesothelioma, 695-701
Pneumonia, 704-706, 705f-706f
bacterial, 704-706
fulminant, 706
fungal, 706-707
Pneumothorax, 708-709, 709f
in brachial plexus block, 1222, 1223,
1224
in celiac plexus block, 1279
in diskography, 124
in intercostal nerve block, 1257
in interpleural analgesia, 1263
in lymphangiomyomatosis, 708, 709f
in pulmonary Langerhans cell histiocytosis,
708, 708f
in stellate ganglion block, 1197, 1198
in suprascapular injection, 631
rib fractures and, 678
tension, 710, 711f
traumatic, 710-711
Polyarteritis nodosa, diagnosis of, 62
Polychondritis, auricular, 541, 541f
Polymodal nociceptors, 11-12, 12f
Polymyalgia rheumatica, 265, 444-445, 449-
451
temporal arteritis and, 265, 445, 451, 519

Polymyositis/dermatomyositis, 443-444, 443f,
444f
electrodiagnosis of, 189t
vs. polymyalgia rheumatica, 445
Polyneuropathy. See also Peripheral neuropathy.
electrodiagnosis of, 187
types of, 187t, 269t
Pools, for water-based exercises, 1046
Popeye biceps, 381, 381f
Poppy plant, 940, 941f, 950
Porter's tip hand, 581, 582f
Ports, totally implantable, 1385, 1386f
Positive ulnar variance, 80
Positron emission tomography (PET), 85-86
Post-thoracotomy pain, 680-682, 682f, 721-723
cryoanalgesia for, 1462-1463
persistent, 680-682, 682f
Post-traumatic neuralgia, vs. complex regional
pain syndrome, 293, 303
Post-traumatic stress disorder, 215
Postdural puncture headache
after implantable drug delivery device
placement, 1391
in subarachnoid neurolysis, 1302
Posterior cervical sympathetic syndrome,
prolotherapy for, 1121-1122, 1122f
Posterior cruciate ligament
anatomy of, 884, 885f
posterior drawer test for, 891, 891f
Posterior fossa exploration, complications of,
356
Posterior inferior cerebellar artery occlusion,
557, 1188
Posterior interosseous syndrome,
electrodiagnosis of, 188
Posterior longitudinal ligament, ossification of,
radiography of, 75, 75f, 77
Posterior superior trapezius, prolotherapeutic
injection of, 1120, 1121f
Posterior tibial nerve, anatomy of, 1365
Posterior tibial nerve block
for ankle pain, 1367
for knee pain, 1365-1366
Posterior tibial nerve entrapment,
electrodiagnosis of, 188
Posterior tibialis strain, prolotherapy for, 1117,
1117f
Postganglionic sympathetic terminals, in
neuroma, 28-29, 29f
Postherpetic neuralgia, 215-216, 279-280. See
also Herpes zoster.
age and, 279, 280f
fiber dissociation theory of, 280
pathogenesis of, 280
prevention of, 280-282
stellate ganglion block for, 1191-1198
thoracic epidural nerve block for, 1243-1244
vs. trigeminal neuralgia, 504. See also
Trigeminal neuralgia.
Postmastectomy pain, 716-719
Postoperative pain
chest, 709-710
in mastectomy, 716-719
management of
hypnosis in, 1022-1023
inadequate, reasons for, 225
nerve blocks in, 229-237, 238t. See also
Nerve blocks, for acute/postoperative
pain.
nonsteroidal antiinflammatory drugs in,
226-227
opioids in, 227-229
relaxation techniques for, 1027
prevention of, 225
Postrenal azotemia, diagnosis of, 69

Posture, osteopathic evaluation of, 1071, 1071t,
1072f
Potassium imbalances, 60
Potassium ions, in tissue injury, 23t
Prayer, 992-993
Prednisolone. See also Corticosteroids.
for polymyalgia rheumatica, 451, 451t
for temporal arteritis, 521, 521t
Prednisone. See also Corticosteroids.
after pituitary neuroadenolysis, 1409
for cancer-related fatigue, 364
for cluster headache, 485, 532
for complex regional pain syndrome, 294,
294t
for medication-overuse headache, 499, 499t
for polymyalgia rheumatica, 445
for systemic lupus erythematosus, 440
for temporal arteritis, 266, 446
Preemptive analgesics, 24
Pregnancy
de Quervain's tenosynovitis in, 666-667, 667
femoral neuropathy in, 873
hot tub/whirlpool bath use during, 1050
hypnosis in, 1022
obturator neuropathy in, 879
prolotherapy in, 1110
Prepatellar bursitis, 396-397, 397f, 895-897,
895f-897f
Prerenal azotemia, diagnosis of, 68-69
Press-ups, 1061, 1062f
Pressure ulcers, hydrotherapy for, 1037, 1037f,
1040, 1049-1050
Priapism, in sickle cell disease, 258, 258t
Prilocaine
introduction of, 985f
structure of, 983
Primary afferents. See Afferents.
Primary distortion dystonia, 593
Primidone, therapeutic monitoring of, 72
Principle of orderly recruitment, 183, 183f
Probenecid, for arachnoiditis, 797-798
Procaine, 983
as prototypical local anesthetic, 983
historical perspective on, 983, 984f
in differential spinal block, 156t, 157, 157t
structure of, 983, 984f
Proctalgia fugax, 851-852
vs. coccydynia, 848
Proenkephalins, 940
Prognostic nerve blocks, for cancer pain, 338
Progressive muscle relaxation, 1025-1031. See
also Relaxation techniques.
for burn pain, 250
technique of, 1029, 1029t
Proliferant injections, in sacroiliac joint
disorders, 812
Prolotherapy, 1106-1126
anaphylaxis in, 1110
cartilage growth and, 1107
collagen fiber diameter and, 1106
complications of, 1110-1111
definition of, 1106
fluoroscopic guidance for, 1110-1111
for arthritis, 1107-1108
of Achilles tendinitis, 1116, 1116f, 1117f
of finger, 1114-1115, 1114f
of hip, 1115, 1115f
of knee, 1116, 1116f
of shoulder, 1109-1110, 1111, 1111f
of toe, 1118
for biceps tendinitis, 1111, 1112f
for bursitis
of hip, 1115, 1115f
of shoulder, 1112-1113, 1113f
for dyspareunia, 1119, 1119f

Prolotherapy (Continued)
for foot pain, 1117-1118, 1117f, 1118f
for golfer's elbow, 1114, 1114f
for groin pain, 1118, 1118f
for hallux valgus, 1118
for headaches, 1122, 1122f, 1123f
for knee instability, 1108, 1108f, 1115
for knee pain, 1115-1116, 1116f
for leg cramps, 1115, 1116f
for ligament tightening, 1108, 1108f
for low back pain, 1107, 1123-1124, 1123f-1125f
for metatarsalgia, 1118, 1118f
for Morton neuroma, 1118
for myofascial syndrome, 1109
for neck pain, 1121-1122, 1121f, 1122f
for osteitis pubis, 1118-1119, 1118f
for pseudo-costochondritis, 1118, 1118f
for pseudo de Quervain's stenosing
tenosynovitis, 1114, 1114f
for pseudo-radiculopathy, 1119
for pseudo–reflex sympathetic dystrophy,
1119
for rotator cuff injuries, 1111, 1112f
for shoulder instability, 1112-1113
for sports injuries, 1108
for sprains, 1109
of ankle, 1116-1117, 1117f
of finger, 1114-1115, 1114f, 1115f
of foot, 1117, 1117f
of plantar ligament, 1117, 1117f
of wrist, 1114, 1114f
for strains, 1109
of hamstring, 1115, 1116f, 1126, 1126f
of posterior tibialis, 1117, 1118f
for temporomandibular joint syndrome, 1111,
1111f
for tennis elbow, 1113, 1113f
for upper back pain, 1119-1120, 1119f-
1121f
in pregnancy, 1110
indications for, 1109-1110
ligament strength and, 1107
ligament thickness/mass and, 1106
musculoskeletal, 1106-1108
animal research in, 1106-1107
human research in, 1107-1108, 1108t
non-musculoskeletal, 1106
patient selection for, 1110
solutions for, preparation of, 1110
tendon strength and, 1107
tendon thickness/mass and, 1106
Pronator teres syndrome, 650-653, 651f-653f
electrodiagnosis of, 188
vs. carpal tunnel syndrome, 650, 665
Proopiomelanocortin, 939
Propofol
for burn pain, 243t, 244, 246
for diskography, 124
Propoxyphene, 948t, 953f, 958
for cancer pain, 320t, 321-323
Propranolol
for arachnoiditis, 796
for migraine prophylaxis, 461
Prostaglandins, in tissue injury, 24-25, 25f
Prostanoids, in tissue injury, 23t
Prostate-specific antigen, 62
Prostheses, in total joint replacement. See also
Total joint arthroplasty.
imaging of, 86
Protein kinase C, in tissue injury, 25
Proteinases, in tissue injury, 23t
Proteins, serum, assays for, 66-68
Prothrombin time, 59
in liver disease, 71

Protriptyline
for migraine prophylaxis, 461
side effects of, 718t
Proximal interphalangeal joints. See also
Finger(s); Hand.
anatomy of, 661f
prolotherapeutic injection of, 1114, 1115f
Pruritus, opioid-induced, 946
with spinal administration, 351, 352t, 1397
Pseudarthrosis, failed back surgery syndrome
and, 821-822, 822f
Pseudo-costochondritis, prolotherapy for, 1118,
1118f
Pseudo de Quervain's stenosing tenosynovitis,
prolotherapy for, 1114, 1114f
Pseudo-radiculopathy, prolotherapy for, 1119
Pseudoaddiction, to opioids, 947
Pseudo–carpal tunnel syndrome, prolotherapy
for, 1119
Pseudocyst, pancreatic
in acute pancreatitis, 737, 738f
in chronic pancreatitis, 740, 740f
Pseudogout, vs. osteoarthritis, 424
Pseudomeningocele, failed back surgery
syndrome and, 823, 824f
Pseudo–reflex sympathetic dystrophy,
prolotherapy for, 1119
Pseudorheumatism, of knee, 888
Pseudotumor cerebri
headache and, 265
treatment of, 267
Psoas muscle, bleeding in, femoral neuropathy
due to, 872
Psoriatic arthritis. See also Arthritis.
of ankle and foot, 912-914
of hand and wrist, 659 663
of sternoclavicular joint, 686-688
Psychogenic pain. See also Psychological
factors.
diagnosis of, 38
differential nerve blocks in, 155-165. See
also Differential nerve blocks.
labeling and, 38
Psychological factors, 8-9. See also Anxiety;
Depression.
in arachnoiditis, 794-795, 796
in biopsychosocial model, 499, 500f
in burn pain, 242, 253
in cancer pain, 326, 361, 366-367, 369
in cervical dystonia, 591, 592t
in chronic pain, 198, 215, 217, 1003-1008
in cluster headache, 478
in complex regional pain syndrome, 217,
285-286, 296
in children, 296
in fibromyalgia, 403, 404, 405
in medication-overuse headache, 497, 499-
500
in occupational back pain, 778, 780-783
in orchialgia, 837, 839
in pain perception, 1086-1087
in phantom pain, 306, 311
in postmastectomy pain, 717
in tension-type headaches, 468
in vulvodynia, 843, 845
psychotherapy and, 218-219, 1004-1008
Psychophysiologic assessment, biofeedback in,
1015-1017
Psychophysiology, 1011
Psychosis. See also Psychological factors.
chronic pain and, 1008
Psychostimulants
for cancer-related fatigue, 364
for opioid-related sedation, 323, 364, 366,
1000

Psychotherapy, 1004-1008
for arachnoiditis, 796
for cancer pain, 326
for chronic pain, 218-219, 1004-1008
cognitive behavioral therapy in, 1005
comprehensive multimodal treatment in,
1005-1007
effectiveness of, 1007
obstacles in, 1007-1008
operant conditioning in, 1005
for complex regional pain syndrome, 296
for phantom pain, 311
Pterygoid nerve, 1148, 1155
Pterygopalatine fossa, anatomy of, 1136
Pterygopalatine ganglion, 540f
Pubic symphysis, anatomy of, 810, 811, 811f,
812f
Pubic symphysis test, 813
Pudendal canal syndrome, 845
Pudendal nerve decompression, for vulvodynia,
845
Pulmonary artery aneurysm, 704, 704f
Pulmonary contusion, 711-712
Pulmonary embolism, 703-704, 703f
Pulmonary hematoma, 711-712
Pulmonary hypertension, 704
in sickle cell disease, 703
Pulmonary infarction, in sickle cell disease,
703
Pulmonary Langerhans cell histiocytosis, 708,
708f
Pulmonary nocardiosis, 706
Pulsed electromagnetic flowmeter, in
suprascapular nerve block, 1242
Pulsed radiofrequency ablation. See also
Radiofrequency techniques.
of sphenopalatine ganglion, 1138
Pump, implantable infusion. See Implantable
infusion pump.
Pump bumps, 916
Pursed-lip breathing, 1028
Pyelonephritis, diagnosis of, 68
Pylothorax, in lymphoma, 701

Q
Qi, 1094, 1095, 1097
circulation of, 1096-1097
Qi gong, 1099
Quadriceps expansion syndrome, 906-910,
909f
Quadriceps setting exercises, 1059-1060,
1060f
Quadriceps tendinitis, 397, 899
in quadriceps expansion syndrome, 906-910
Quadriceps tendon
anatomy of, 906, 907f
tears of, quadriceps expansion syndrome and,
906-910, 909f
Quality of life, in cancer, 367-368
Quantitative sensory testing. See also
Electrodiagnostic procedures.
in complex regional pain syndrome, 291
indications for, 186-189, 275-276
Quantitative sudomotor axon reflex test, 186
in complex regional pain syndrome, 291
of face, 557
Quinine sulfate, 981

R
Racz technique, for epidural adhesion lysis,
1345-1349. See also Epidural adhesiolysis.

Radial artery, inadvertent injection of, in radial nerve block, 1235
Radial collateral ligament
  anatomy of, 643f, 644
  prolotherapeutic injection of, 1114, 1114f
Radial nerve, 46t
  anatomy of, 578f, 579f, 580, 656, 657f, 1228f, 1229f, 1234
Radial nerve block, 238t, 1233-1235, 1235f, 1236f
  at distal humerus, 1234-1235, 1235f
  at elbow, 1230f, 1233, 1235
  at wrist, 1235, 1236f
Radial nerve palsy, 275, 275f
Radial tunnel syndrome, 655-658, 657f, 1233-1235
  electrodiagnosis of, 188
  radial nerve block for, 1230f, 1233-1235
  vs. lateral epicondylitis, 384, 635, 1233
Radiation therapy
  brachial plexopathy due to, 584-585, 585t
  palliative, 328-334
    bisphosphonates with, 332
    clinical trials of, 330, 331t
    cost effectiveness of, 334
    dosing in, 330, 331t
    for bone pain, 328-332
    for brachial plexus involvement, 332-333, 333f
    for brain metastases, 333
    for celiac plexus involvement, 332-333
    for neuropathic pain, 332
    for pancreatic cancer, 332-333, 333f
    for spinal cord compression, 332
    for superior sulcus tumors, 332-333, 333f
    for trigeminal neuralgia, 333-334
    for vertebral fractures, 1475
    for visceral pain, 333
    hemibody, 330
    history of, 328
    imaging studies for, 328-330, 329f, 330f
    indications for, 328-334
    radiopharmaceuticals for, 330-332
    response to, 330, 331t
    side effects of, 331t
    technique of, 330
Radicular artery, inadvertent injection of, in cervical facet block, 1207
Radicular pain
  cervical, 52t, 55, 55t, 568-574
  characteristics of, 761t
  definition of, 758
  lumbar, 758-766
  pathophysiology of, 758-761
  signs and symptoms of, 761-762, 762f
  thoracic, 690-692
  vs. radiculopathy, 758. See also Radiculopathy.
  vs. somatic referred pain, 761, 761t
Radiculopathy, 118, 189
  cervical, 52t, 55, 55t, 568-574. See also Cervical radiculopathy.
  definition of, 189, 568
  diagnosis of, somatosensory evoked potentials in, 194
  electrodiagnosis of, 189
  epidural/intrathecal steroids for, 339-340
  lumbar, 52t, 55, 55t, 758-766. See also Lumbar radiculopathy.
  pathogenesis of, 758-761
  thoracic, 690-692
    epidural steroids for, 1244
  vs. radicular pain, 758. See also Radicular pain.

Radiofrequency techniques, 1411-1456
  advantages of, 1412-1413
  bone effects in, 1413f, 1415
  C2 rami communicans lesioning, 1445-1446, 1446f
  cervical dorsal root ganglionotomy, 1441-1442, 1443f
  clinical applications of, 1416-1449
  dorsal root ganglionotomy, 1431-1435
    indications for, 1435
    lumbar, 1431, 1431f, 1435
    sacral, 1431-1433, 1432f, 1433f, 1435
    thoracic, 1433-1435, 1434f, 1435f
  equipment for, 1416
  for cervical facet syndrome, 1437-1440, 1438f-1441f
    oblique approach in, 1437-1439, 1438f
    parasagittal approach in, 1439-1440, 1439f, 1440f
  for cervical pain, 1435-1446
  for cervical radiculopathy, 1440-1444
  for cervicogenic headache, 1444-1445
  for cluster headache, 489, 1444
  for glossopharyngeal neuralgia, 515-516
  for lumbar facet syndrome, 773-774, 774f, 1417-1420
  for lumbar radiculopathy, 1425-1429, 1427f, 1428f
  for occipital neuralgia, 1444-1445
  for sphenopalatine neuralgia, 1137-1138, 1446-1447
  for thoracic facet syndrome, 1420-1421, 1422f
  for thoracic radiculopathy, 1429-1431, 1429f, 1430f
  for trigeminal neuralgia, 353-356, 354f, 507, 1447-1449, 1448f
  functional stereotactic guidance in, 1419-1420
  Gasserian ganglionotomy, 1447-1449
  glossopharyngeal nerve lesioning, 515-516
  golden rules for, 1414-1415
  history of, 1412
  in cordotomy, 356, 356f
  intradiscal electrothermal annuloplasty, 1426-1431, 1484-1487
    lumbar, 1427-1429
    thoracic, 1429-1431
  lesion reversibility in, in brain, 1414, 1414f
  lesion size in, 1413-1414, 1413f
    consistency for, 1415
    empirical data on, 1414f, 1415-1416
  lesioning circuit in, 1413, 1413f
  lumbar intradiscal lesioning, 1425-1426, 1426f
  medial branch lesioning, for cervical facet syndrome, 564f, 565
  nonhomogeneous tissue effects in, 1415, 1415f
  percutaneous cordotomy, 1501-1515
  physical principles of, 1413-1416, 1413f-1415f
  practical aspects of, 1416
  ramus communicans nerve lesioning, 1425
  recording parameters for, 1416
  sphenopalatine ganglion lesioning, 1137-1138, 1446-1447
  spinal cord stimulation, 1373, 1375f. See also Spinal cord stimulation.
  stellate ganglion lesioning, 1196, 1196f, 1442-1444, 1444f
  sympathectomy
    lumbar, 1449-1452, 1452f
    thoracic, 1452-1456, 1453f-1456f

Radiofrequency techniques (Continued)
  temperature in
    as fundamental lesion parameter, 1413-1414, 1414f
    control of, 1416
    monitoring of, 1414-1415
    tip characteristics in, 1414-1415
    tissue heating mechanisms in, 1413-1414, 1413f, 1414f
  unpredictable factors in, 1415, 1415f
  vs. brachytherapy, 1412
  vs. chemical destruction, 1411
  vs. cryogenic surgery, 1411
  vs. focused ultrasound, 1411
  vs. induction heating, 1411
  vs. ionizing radiation, 1412
  vs. laser therapy, 1412
  vs. mechanical methods, 1412
  vs. neurolytic blockade, 1411
Radiography, 74-84
  computed, 74
  film-screen, 74
  in osteoarthritis, 421-422, 423f
  in rheumatoid arthritis, 433-434, 434f, 435f
  indications for, 99. See also specific indications.
  of ankle and foot, 83-84
  of elbow, 80
  of knee, 81-83, 83f, 84f
  of pelvis and hip, 81, 82f, 83f
  of rotator cuff disorders, 608, 609f
  of shoulder, 78-80, 79f, 608, 609f
  of spine, 74-78, 75f-79f
    cervical, 74-75, 75f
    lumbar, 76-78, 76f-78f
    thoracic, 75-76, 76f
  of wrist and hand, 80-81
  plain-film, 74
  principles of, 74
Radioisotope scanning, 85-91. See also Nuclear medicine techniques.
Radiosurgery, stereotactic
  for cluster headache, 489
  for trigeminal neuralgia, 334, 353-356, 507
Raeder syndrome, 504-505
Ramsay-Hunt syndrome, 279, 538, 540f
Ramus communicans nerve, radiofrequency lesioning of, 1425, 1426, 1426f
Range of motion, grading of, 1071-1074, 1073f
Rapid plasma reagin (RPR) test, for syphilis, 63
Rapidly adapting stretch receptors, 693
Rash
  butterfly, in systemic lupus erythematosus, 438, 438f
  in dermatomyositis, 443-444, 443f
  in herpes zoster, 279, 281f
  in Lyme disease, 64, 65f, 66f, 888-889, 889f
  knee pain with, 887-888
Raynaud disease/phenomenon
  biofeedback for, 1012-1013
  in scleroderma, 440, 442, 443
  sympathectomy for, 358-359, 358f, 359f
Rebound headache. See Medication-overuse headache.
Reboxetine, 969, 969f. See also Antidepressants.
Rectal examination, in sacroiliac disorders, 814
Rectal pain, in proctalgia fugax, 851-852, 852f
  vs. coccydynia, 848
Recurrent laryngeal nerve, inadvertent blockade of
  in interscalene brachial plexus block, 1222
  in stellate ganglion block, 1197
  in supraclavicular brachial plexus block, 1224

Red blood cells. *See under* Erythrocyte.
Referred pain, 51, 1088
  diagnostic nerve blocks in, 770-772, 771f
  from facet joints, 769-770, 770f
  in fibromyalgia, 403-404
  Kerr sign and, 1169
  organ convergence and, 15, 15f
  to eye, 530-536. *See also* Ocular/periocular
    pain, referred.
  to hand and wrist, 660t
  to knee, 888t
  to liver, 733
  to spine, 52-55, 52t, 53f, 54f
  to throat, 547
  trigger points for, 51
Reflex(es)
  axon, 1083
  Babinski, 47
    in peripheral neuropathy, 272
  deep tendon
    grading of, 46-47, 47f, 47t
    in peripheral neuropathy, 272
  expiration, 693
  H (Hoffman), in nerve conduction studies,
    186
  Herring-Breuer, 693
  inflation, 693
  oculocardiac, in sphenopalatine ganglion
    block, 1138
  somatovisceral, 1069
  viscerosomatic, 1069
Reflex sympathetic dystrophy. *See* Complex
  regional pain syndrome.
Reframing, 251
Regional anesthesia. *See* Nerve blocks.
Rehabilitation. *See also* Exercise;
  Exercises.
  aquatic, 1043. *See also* Hydrotherapy.
  for rotator cuff disorders, 609-610
  in brachial plexopathy, 588-589
  physical reconditioning in, 1055-1066
Relaxation-induced anxiety, 1018, 1031
Relaxation response, 1025
Relaxation techniques, 993, 1025-1031
  anxiety in, 1018, 1031
  autogenic training, 1025-1031
  biofeedback, 1013-1015. *See also*
    Biofeedback.
  for burn pain, 248, 250-251
  for migraine, 461-462
  for phantom pain, 311
  guided imagery, 1025-1031
  historical perspective on, 1025-1026
  hypnosis, 1013-1015, 1022-1024. *See also*
    Hypnosis.
  indications for, 1026-1027
  patient response to, 1031
  progressive muscle relaxation, 1025-1031
  R-states and, 1031
  regimen for, 1029-1031
  relaxed breathing, 250, 1028
  side effects of, 1031
  techniques of, 1028-1031
Relaxed breathing, 1028
  for burn pain, 250
Relocation test, for rotator cuff tears, 606
Remifentanil, 953f, 957
  for burn pain, 243t, 244, 246
Renal calculi, vs. orchialgia, 838
Renal disease
  in sickle cell disease, 257
  neuropathy in, 67t
Renal failure, morphine use in, 321
Renal function tests, 68-69
Renal puncture, in celiac plexus block, 1278

Renal toxicity, of nonsteroidal antiinflammatory
  drugs, 227, 936
Renal transplantation, femoral neuropathy after,
  873-874
Repetitive strain injuries. *See* Overuse injuries.
Reservoir, implantable, 1385, 1386f
Resisted abduction release test, for trochanteric
  bursitis, 391, 392f
Resisted hip adduction test, for iliopsoas
  bursitis, 864, 865f
Respiratory dysfunction
  after cordotomy, 1501, 1513-1514
  chest pain in, 693-712. *See also* Chest pain,
    pleuropulmonary.
  in intercostal nerve block, 1257
  in thoracic epidural nerve block, 1245
  opioid-induced, 323, 945
    naloxone for, 352t
    with spinal administration, 351, 352t, 1396
Respiratory infections, 704-708
Respiratory system, sensory innervation of, 693
Rest, 1055-1056
  for lumbar radiculopathy, 764
Resting potential, 181
Restless legs syndrome, prolotherapy for, 1115
Reticulocyte count, 57
Retinal hemorrhages, from epidural injections,
  172, 176
Retinal migraine, 459, 459t
Retroachilleal bursae, 911
Retroachilleal bursitis, 916
Retrocalcaneal bursa, 911
Retrocollis, 591. *See also* Cervical dystonia.
Retroperitoneal hemorrhage, femoral
  neuropathy due to, 872, 873t
Retropharyngeal abscess, 543, 546f
Retropharyngeal tumors, 546f, 547
Return to work, in occupational back pain, 779-
  780
Reusable microwavable heating pads, 1036,
  1036f
Reverse Hill-Sachs lesions, radiography of, 608
Reverse Phalen maneuver, 664
Rexed laminae, 13, 13f, 13t
Reye syndrome, aspirin and, 929, 930, 935
RF factor, in rheumatoid arthritis, 433
Rheumatoid arthritis, 431-437. *See also*
  Arthritis.
  atlantoaxial subluxation in, 437, 437f
  Baker's cyst in, 431, 433f, 903-905
  demographic factors in, 38t
  diagnosis of, 62
  diagnostic criteria for, 432t
  differential diagnosis of, 434-435
  epidemiology of, 431
  etiology of, 431
  extra-articular manifestations of, 431
  immunologic abnormalities in, 432-433
  laboratory findings in, 433
  of ankle and foot, 912-914
  of hand, 659, 660t, 662-663
  of shoulder, 615
  of sternoclavicular joint, 686-688
  of wrist, 660-662, 660t
  radiographic findings in, 433-434, 434f, 435f
  relaxation techniques for, 1026-1207
  signs and symptoms of, 431-432, 432f, 432t,
    433f
  treatment of, 435-437
    anti-inflammatory agents in, 436
    cold/heat application in, 436-437
    disease-modifying agents in, 436
    immunosuppression in, 436-437
    orthotics in, 437
    physical/occupational therapy in, 437

Rheumatoid arthritis *(Continued)*
  splinting in, 436
  surgery in, 437
  vs. osteoarthritis, 434-435
  vs. polymyalgia rheumatica, 450
Rheumatoid disorders. *See* Connective tissue
  diseases.
Rheumatoid factors, 62, 433
Rheumatoid nodules, 80, 420, 420f, 431, 432t,
  434, 435f, 662
Rheumatoid spondylitis, sacroiliac pain in, 813
Rhinorrhea, in cluster headache, 477
Rhizotomy. *See also* Neurolytic blockade.
  glycerol, for trigeminal neuralgia, 353, 354f,
    356, 506
  nervus intermedius, for cluster headache, 489
  radiofrequency, 1411-1456. *See also*
    Radiofrequency techniques.
Rhomboid insertion, prolotherapeutic injection
  of, 1120, 1121f
Rib(s)
  anatomy of, 672-673, 673f, 732
  cartilage abnormalities of
    in costosternal syndrome, 672-674, 672f-
      674f
    in Tietze syndrome, 674-676, 676f-677f
  fractures of, 678-680, 680f, 681f, 710
    epidural steroids for, 1244
    in flail chest, 678-680, 710, 711f
    intercostal nerve block for, 680, 681f,
      1250-1258
  metastases to, 678, 680f
  slipping, 731-732, 732f, 733f
Rib-tip syndrome, 731-732, 732f, 733f
RICE treatment, 1055
Rigidity
  of great toe, 920-921
  opioid-induced, 945
Rizatriptan. *See also* Triptans.
  for migraine, 460
Roentgen, William Conrad, 758, 760f
Rofecoxib, 934
  for tension-type headache, 470, 471t
Rollo, John, 871
Romberg sign, 47
Röntgen, Frederic, 328
Ropivacaine, 985. *See also* Local anesthetics.
  for epidural adhesiolysis, 1347, 1348
  for nerve blocks. *See* Nerve blocks.
  introduction of, 985f
  structure of, 983, 984f
Rotator cuff disorders, 378-380, 379f, 380f,
  603-613
  anatomic aspects of, 603, 604f
  angiofibroblastic hyperplasia in, 604
  as overuse syndromes, 603
  biceps tendinitis and, 622-626
  clinical presentation of, 604-608
  diagnosis of, 605-609
  extrinsic vs. intrinsic mechanisms of, 603-
    604
  historical perspective on, 603-604
  history in, 604-608
  imaging studies in, 79, 608-609, 609f
  impingement syndrome and, 603, 606, 610-
    611, 611f
  pathophysiology of, 603-604
  physical examination in, 605-608, 605f-608f
  radiography of, 79
  signs and symptoms of, 604-605
  treatment of, 609-611
    indications for, 609
    nonoperative, 609-610
    operative, 610-611, 611f, 612f
    prolotherapy in, 1111, 1112f

Royal London Hospital test, 915
RPR test, for syphilis, 63
Rucksack paralysis, 583
Rynd, F., 149

S
Σ (sigma) receptor, 940-941, 941t
Sacral canal, anatomy of, 1337, 1338f
Sacral cornua, 1336
Sacral dorsal root ganglionotomy, 1431-1433,
        1432f, 1433f
    indications for, 1435
Sacral hiatus
    anatomy of, 1337, 1338f
    localization of, 1339, 1339f, 1340f
Sacrococcygeal joint, osteoarthritis of, 848
Sacrococcygeal joint injection, for coccydynia,
        848-850, 849f
Sacrococcygeal tumors, 848, 849f
Sacroiliac and piriformis syndrome, 763, 834-
        836
Sacroiliac belt, 814
Sacroiliac joint
    anatomy of, 810-812, 811f, 812f
    movement of, 811-812
Sacroiliac joint disorders, 810-815, 1358-1361
    anatomic aspects of, 810-812, 811f, 812f
    etiology of, 812
    evaluation of, 813-814
    imaging studies in, 813
    injection technique for, 814-815, 815f, 1358-
        1361, 1359f, 1360f
    pain characteristics in, 812, 813f
    pelvic rock test for, 1358, 1359f
    provocative testing in, 813
    radiofrequency techniques for, 1422-1425,
        1423f, 1424f
Sacroiliac ligament, prolotherapeutic injection
        of, 1124, 1125, 1125f
Sacroiliitis, radiography of, 77-78, 79f
Sacrospinous ligament
    anatomy of, 810, 811f
    prolotherapeutic injection of, 1125, 1125f
Sacrotuberous ligament
    anatomy of, 811, 811f, 812f
    prolotherapeutic injection of, 1125, 1125f
Sacrum, anatomy of, 810, 811f, 812f, 1336-
        1337, 1337f
Salicylates, 928-930, 935-936. See also Aspirin;
        Nonsteroidal antiinflammatory drugs.
    nonacetylated, 930, 935-936
        for cancer pain, 318-319, 319t
Salsalate, 935. See also Nonsteroidal
        antiinflammatory drugs.
    for cancer pain, 318-319, 319t
Saltatory conduction, 343
Saphenous nerve, anatomy of, 874, 875f, 1365
Saphenous nerve block, 1365-1366
    for ankle pain, 1367
    for knee pain, 1365-1366
Saphenous neuropathy, 874-876
Sarcoidosis, cervical radiculopathy in, 570
Scalene insertion, prolotherapeutic injection of,
        1121, 1122f
Scalene interval syndrome, 582-583, 584f
Scalp acupuncture, 1098
Scapula, snapping, 630
Scapular pain, differential diagnosis of, 630
Scapulocostal syndrome, 627-632
    anatomic aspects of, 627-630, 629f, 630f
    causes of, 627
    clinical features of, 627, 628f
    differential diagnosis of, 630

Scapulocostal syndrome (Continued)
    epidemiology of, 627
    historical perspective on, 627
    pain characteristics in, 627, 628f, 629f
    treatment of, 630-631
    trigger points in, 627, 628f, 629f
Scar, thoracotomy, pain in, 680-682, 682f
Scheuermann disease, radiography in, 76
Schmorl's nodes, 76
Schultz, Johann, 1026
Schwann cells, 343
Schwannoma
    brachial plexus, 585
    jugular fossa, glossopharyngeal neuralgia
        and, 512
Sciatic nerve, 46t
    anatomy of, 1362-1363
Sciatic nerve block, 238t, 1362-1364
Sciatic nerve entrapment
    electrodiagnosis of, 188
    with lumbar radiculopathy, 854
Sciatica. See Lumbar radiculopathy.
Scleroderma, 440-443, 441f, 442f
Sclerotomes, 1295f, 1296
Scoliosis
    failed back surgery syndrome and, 821
    osteopathic manipulative treatment for,
        1078
Scotoma, in migraine, 457
Scotty dog sign
    in lumbar facet block, 1308, 1308f
    in lumbar facet cryoablation, 1466, 1467f
    in spondylolysis, 803, 804f
Scraping, 1099
Screening
    for sickle cell disease, 57-58, 258-259
    for substance abuse, 71-72, 73, 362
    toxicologic, 72
Scrotal pain. See Orchialgia.
Scrotitis, 839
Scuba diving, with implantable drug delivery
        systems, 1398
Seated flexion test, 814
Secondary afferents, 13-15, 13f, 13t, 14f. See
        also Afferents.
Security systems, implantable drug delivery
        devices and, 1397
Sedation
    for burn pain, 244, 246
    for diskography, 124
    for intercostal nerve block, 1256
    muscle relaxant–induced, 977
    opioid-induced, 323, 364, 366, 1000
Seddon classification, of nerve injuries, 580
Seizures
    in atlanto-occipital nerve block, 1131
    in drug withdrawal, 499-500
    in sphenopalatine ganglion block, 1138
    migraine-triggered, 459
    neuropathic pain and, 717
    opioid-induced, 944-945
Selective nerve root block, diagnostic, 154
Selective serotonin reuptake inhibitors (SSRIs),
        967-968. See also Antidepressants.
    abuse potential of, 968
    mechanism of action of, 967
    overdosage of, 968
    pharmacokinetics of, 967-968
    side effects of, 968
    types of, 968
    withdrawal symptoms with, 968
Semmes, R. Eustace, 568, 569f
Sensation, neuromatrix in, 4-7, 5f
Sensory-discriminative pain dimension, 17, 18f
Sensory examination, 44-46

Sensory neurons. See also Pain processing
        system.
    afferents of, 11-13, 12f, 13, 13f, 14f. See also
        Afferents.
    structure of, 1087, 1088f
Sensory stereotaxy, in radiofrequency lesioning,
        1419-1420
Sentient neural hub, 6
Sentinel headache, 262
Serotonin, in nociception, 23t, 1086
Serotonin antagonists, for migraine, 460
Sertraline, 968. See also Antidepressants.
Serum osmolality, 69
Sesamoiditis, 399-400, 400f
Sevoflurane, for burn pain, 246
Sex hormones
    in cluster headache, 479, 480
    in migraine, 479
Sexual dysfunction
    after cordotomy, 1515
    in arachnoiditis, 794
Sexual intercourse, painful, prolotherapy for,
        1119, 1119f
Shapiro, David, 1011
Shingles. See Herpes zoster.
Shoe(s)
    ill-fitting
        hallux valgus and, 920-921
        Morton neuroma and, 918-919
        plantar fasciitis and, 922
    modified
        for bunionette, 921
        for hallux rigidus, 920
Shoe inserts
    for Morton neuroma, 918
    for osteoarthritis, 426, 426f
    for plantar fasciitis, 924
    for rheumatoid arthritis, 437
    for trochanteric bursitis, 861-862
Short-lasting unilateral neuralgiform headache
        with conjunctival injection and tearing, 482
Shoulder
    acromioclavicular joint disorders of, 615-618
    arthritis of, differential diagnosis of, 600,
        601t
    biceps tendinitis of, 380-382, 381f, 382f,
        622-626
    corticosteroid injection in
        for osteoarthritis, 600-602, 601f, 615-618,
            617f
        for rotator cuff disorders, 610
    osteoarthritis of, 79, 598-602
        acromioclavicular, 605, 608, 615-618,
            617f
        clinical features of, 598, 599t
        diagnosis of, 598-600, 599f, 600f
        differential diagnosis of, 600, 601t
        imaging studies of, 598-600, 599f, 600f
        prolotherapy for, 1111, 1111f
        treatment of, 600-602, 601f, 615-618, 617f
    painful, 598-632
        arthritis-related, 615-618
        causes of, 600, 601t
        differential diagnosis of, 600, 601t, 615,
            619, 624-625
        in cervical radiculopathy, 605
        Pancoast tumors and, 694-695, 696f-697f
        suprascapular nerve block for, 1239-1242
    radiography of, 78-80, 608-609, 609f
    rotator cuff disorders of. See Rotator cuff
        disorders.
    scapulocostal syndrome of, 627-632
    stiff, in polymyalgia rheumatica, 449

Shoulder *(Continued)*
  subacromial bursitis of, prolotherapy for, 1112-1113, 1113f
  subdeltoid bursitis of, 619-621, 620f
    vs. Pancoast syndrome, 694-695
  supraspinatus tendinitis of, 376-378
    with rotator cuff tears, 378, 379-381
  weakness of
    in brachial plexopathy, 577-590
    in rotator cuff disorders, 605-606
Shoulder abduction (relief) test, in cervical radiculopathy, 571, 572t
Shoulder dystocia. *See also* Brachial plexopathy.
  Erb-Duchenne paralysis and, 582, 582f
  Klumpke paralysis and, 582
Shoulder pain
  in biceps tendinitis, 380-382
  in rotator cuff tears, 379-380
  in supraspinatus tendinitis, 376-378
Shrug sign, 606, 606f
Sicard, Jean-Anthanase, 1281
Sickle cell disease
  chest pain in, 702-703
  clinical presentation of, 257-258, 257-260
  diagnosis of, 258-259
  differential diagnosis of, 259, 259t
  historical perspective on, 257
  hypnosis for, 1022
  pain in
    assessment of, 259, 259f
    chest, 702-703
    types and characteristics of, 258, 258t
  pathophysiology of, 257, 258f
  pulmonary hypertension in, 703
  screening for, 57-58, 258-259
Side effects
  definition of, 1388
  vs. complications, 1388
Sieveking, E., 456
Simian hand, 582
Simple analgesics, 927-932. *See also* Acetaminophen; Nonsteroidal antiinflammatory drugs.
  classification of, 928t
  indications for, 927-928
  overview of, 927-928
Simvastatin, for arachnoiditis, 798
Single-photon emission computed tomography (SPECT), 85
  of facet osteoarthritis, 89-91, 91f
  of spondylolisthesis, 89
  of tumors, 86
Singulus. *See* Hiccups.
Sinonasal tumors, 543, 545f, 546f
Sinus disorders, 543, 545f, 546f, 547
  headache in, 469
  vs. cluster headache, 483
Sinusitis, 543, 545f
  arachnoiditis due to, 792
  cavernous sinus thrombosis and, 535
Sit-ups, 1061, 1062f
Skeletal metastases. *See* Bone metastases.
Skeletal muscle relaxants. *See* Muscle relaxants.
Skeletal traction
  for lumbar radiculopathy, 765
  for sacroiliac disorders, 814
Skier's view, 84
Skin
  abnormalities of, in complex regional pain syndrome, 284, 285t
  examination of, in peripheral neuropathy, 274, 274t
  opioid effects on, 946
Skin cancer, of ear, 541, 541f

Skin conductance–assisted biofeedback, 1015
Skin temperature–assisted biofeedback, 1015
Sleep, cluster headaches during, 476, 530-531
Sleep apnea, after cordotomy, 1501, 1513-1514
Sleep disturbances
  in burn pain, 253-254
  in cancer, 366
  in chronic pain, 215, 1004
  in fibromyalgia, 404, 405, 406
  in peripheral neuropathy, 277, 277t
  pathogenesis of, 465-466, 465f
  with tension-type headache, 465
Slipping rib syndrome, 731-732, 732f, 733f
Slow-wave diathermy, 1039
Slowly adapting stretch receptors, 693
Smellie, William, 577, 577f
Smith, Alban, 568, 569f
Smoking
  cluster headache and, 478
  failed back surgery syndrome and, 818, 819
Snapping hip, 862, 864-867
Snapping scapula, 630
SNARE proteins, botulinum neurotoxin and, 594
Snow World virtual environment, for burn pain, 249, 249f
Social history, 41
Sodium channel blockers
  for neuropathic pain, 718
  intravenous, mechanism of action of, 31-32, 32f
Sodium imbalances, 59-60
Sodium ion channels, in nerve injury, 26, 1085
Sodium morrhuate, in prolotherapy solutions, 1111
Sodium salicylate, 930. *See also* Nonsteroidal antiinflammatory drugs.
Soleus origin, prolotherapeutic injection of, 1115, 1116f
Solutions
  for differential spinal nerve blocks, 156-157, 156t, 158t
  for prolotherapy, 1110
  hyper/hypotonic, for neurolytic blockade, 346
Somatic nerve blocks, 233-237
  for cancer pain, 338, 338t
  indications for, 238t
Somatic pain, 362
Somatosensory cortex, activation of, 213
Somatosensory evoked potentials, 194-195, 194f
  in brachial plexopathy, 588, 588t
Somatostatin, 19, 19t
  spinal, 1394
Somatovisceral reflexes, 1069
Spasmodic torticollis. *See* Cervical dystonia.
Spasticity
  adductor, obturator nerve block for, 1331
  from tumor invasion, trigger point injections for, 338-339
  in tension-type headache, 465-466, 465f
  pathophysiology of, 465-466, 465f
  treatment of, 977-981. *See also* Muscle relaxants.
Specificity theory, 3, 4f
  vs. neuromatrix theory, 6
SPECT. *See* Single-photon emission computed tomography (SPECT).
Spectator posture, 1063, 1065f
Speed test, for biceps tendinitis, 622, 623f
Spermatic cord block, for orchialgia, 840
Spermatic plexus, anatomy of, 837, 838f
Spermatocele, orchialgia and, 839
Sphenopalatine gangliectomy, for cluster headache, 488-489

Sphenopalatine ganglion
  anatomy of, 523, 524f, 1135-1136
  Gasserian ganglionotomy for, 1447-1449
  radiofrequency lesioning of, 1446-1447
Sphenopalatine ganglion block, 229-230, 229f, 1134-1139
  anatomic aspects of, 1135-1136
  anesthesia for, 1136
  complications and pitfalls in, 1138
  diagnostic studies and, 1134-1135, 1135t
  for acute and postoperative pain, 229-230, 229f
  for cluster headache, 532
  historical perspective on, 1134
  indications for, 1134, 1135t
  infrazygomatic approach in, 1137, 1137f
  radiofrequency ablation in, 1137-1138
    pulsed, 1138
  results of, 1138-1139
  technique of, 1136-1138
  transnasal approach in, 1136-1137
Sphenopalatine neuralgia, sphenopalatine ganglion block for, 1134-1139
Spinal accessory nerve, examination of, 42-43, 44t
Spinal anesthesia
  with lidocaine, side effects of, 986
  with opioids. *See* Spinal opioids.
Spinal canal, anatomy of, 172-173
Spinal canal endoscopy, 167-177
  anatomic aspects of, 172-173
  caudal approach in, 171-172
  complications of, 172, 176
  consensus paper on, 170-171
  contraindications to, 171, 171t
  definition of, 171
  development of, 167-170
  epidural adhesion lysis in, 172
  epidural images in, 176
  in arachnoiditis, 793
  indications for, 171, 171t
  paramedian approach in, 171, 173
  post-procedure management in, 176
  pre-procedure considerations in, 173
  technique of, 173-176, 174f-175f
  terminology for, 170
  with fluoroscopy, 176
Spinal catheterization, for cancer pain, 339. *See also* Spinal catheterization; Spinal opioids.
Spinal cord
  anatomy of, 13, 13f, 13t
  laminae of, 13, 13f, 13t
  nociceptor projections into, 1084
Spinal cord compression
  after diskography, 124
  after epidurography, 147
  malignant, radiation therapy for, 332
Spinal cord injury
  complex regional pain syndrome after, 302
  in lumbar epidural block, 1291
Spinal cord stimulation, 1373-1382. *See also* Neurostimulation.
  amplitude in, 1377
  complications of, 1376, 1398-1401
    dural puncture, 1399
    lead migration, 1399
    neurologic, 1399
    pain at connector/transmitter site, 1400
    published data on, 1400-1401
    surgical, 1398
  cost effectiveness of, 1379
  electrodes for
    infection of, 1376
    lead failure in, 1376

Spinal cord stimulation *(Continued)*
  selection of, 1377
  types of, 1373, 1374f
  equipment for, 1373-1374, 1374f-1376f, 1374t
    failure of, 1399-1340
    preoperative check of, 1398
  failure of, 1398
  for angina, 1244
  for arachnoiditis, 797
  for chronic pain, 220, 719
  for complex regional pain syndrome, 295-296, 1378
  for failed back surgery syndrome, 1377-1378
  for phantom pain, 310
  historical perspective on, 1373
  implanted lead trial in, 1373-1374
  implanted pulse generator for, 1373, 1375f
  lead placement in, 1373-1374, 1392, 1398-1399
    difficulties in, 1398-1399
    migration after, 1399
    spinal levels for, 1399t
    subarachnoid, 1399
  mechanism of action of, 1373
  pacemakers and, 1400
  patient selection for, 1374-1376
  positional stimulation in, 1399
  principles of, 1379t
  programming in, 1377
  pulse width in, 1377
  rate of, 1377
  results of, 1377-1379, 1380
  security systems and, 1400
  technique of, 1373-1374, 1392, 1398-1399
    pitfalls in, 1398-1399
  thoracic, 1244
  trial period for, 1376
  truncal stimulation in, 1399
Spinal dorsal horn
  anatomy of, 12-13, 13f
  neurons of, 13-15, 13f, 13t, 14f
Spinal exercises, 1061-1063, 1062f
  after diskectomy, 1063
  for low back pain, 1061-1062, 1062f
  for lumbar radiculopathy, 1063
  for neck pain, 1063
  for osteoporosis, 1063, 1064f
  for spondylolisthesis, 1062-1063
  for vertebral compression fractures, 1063
Spinal facilitation, in tissue injury, 24-26, 24f
Spinal fusion
  arachnoiditis after, 791
  complications of, 817. *See also* Failed back surgery syndrome.
  computed tomography after, 97f, 101f
  for cervical facet syndrome, 564f, 565
  for cervical radiculopathy, 574
  for failed back surgery syndrome, 828
  historical perspective on, 818
  indications for, 828
Spinal manipulation
  chiropractic, 993-994, 1081-1090. *See also* Chiropractic treatment.
  for lumbar radiculopathy, 764, 765
  osteopathic, 1075-1077. *See also* Osteopathic manipulative treatment.
Spinal metastases, 751-753, 753f
Spinal nerve block, differential
  conventional sequential, 156-158, 156t-158t, 159
  for cancer pain, 338, 338t
  modified, 158-159, 158t
  solutions for, 156t, 158t

Spinal nerve root entrapment. *See also* Radicular pain; Radiculopathy.
  cervical, 52t, 55, 55t, 568-574
  in lumbar radiculopathy, 758-766, 760
  thoracic, 690-692
Spinal nerve roots
  alignment with vertebrae, 1296f
  cysts of, in failed back surgery syndrome, 819-820, 820f
Spinal nerve tumors, cervical radiculopathy and, 570
Spinal nerves, 46t
  anatomy of, 1315
Spinal opioids, 220, 719, 949
  arachnoiditis due to, 791
  catheter-tip granuloma and, 797
  costs of, 1384
  cross-tolerance to, 1394
  delivery systems for, 325, 719, 1382-1386. *See also* Implantable drug delivery systems.
  disease progression and, 1392
  dosage of, 351, 351t
  duration of action of, 351
  failure of, 1392
  fentanyl, 351t
  for arachnoiditis, 797
  for cancer pain, 325, 339, 350-351, 350t, 351t
  for chronic pain, 220
  for postmastectomy pain, 719
  for postoperative pain, 709
  meperidine, 351t
  morphine, 351t
  non-opioid alternatives to, 1393-1394
  patient selection for, 1382-1383, 1383t, 1384
  patient's support system for, 1383-1384
  post-procedure care for, 351, 352t
  preimplantation trials for, 1382, 1383t
    pain assessment in, 1383, 1383t
  routes of administration for, 350-351
  side effects of, 325, 351, 352t, 1382-1383, 1396-1398
  technical aspects of, 1392-1396
  test doses of, 1393
  tolerance to, 1392-1395
    prevention of, 1393
    titration-resistant, 1393
    treatment of, 1393
  with local anesthetics, 1394
Spinal pain, 52-55
  characteristics of, 52
  distribution of, 53f, 54f
  patterns of, 52-55, 52t, 53f, 54f, 55t
Spinal radiculopathies, 52, 52t, 55, 55t
Spinal stenosis, 55, 55t
  central, 763, 764
  cervical radiculopathy in, 568. *See also* Cervical radiculopathy.
  failed back surgery syndrome and, 821, 823, 823f
  imaging of
    CT in, 102
    radiography in, 77
  in degenerative disk disease, 111, 111f
Spinal surgery. *See also* Diskectomy; Laminectomy; Spinal fusion.
  arachnoiditis after, 791
  complications of, 819-826. *See also* Failed back surgery syndrome.
  for failed back surgery syndrome, 828
  frequency of, factors affecting, 818
  historical perspective on, 817-818

Spinal tracts
  ascending, 212-213, 1085-1086
    anatomy of, 15, 16f, 213f
    functions of, 17-18
    plasticity of, 18, 1085-1086, 1089
  descending, 213, 214f, 1086
  in tissue injury, 25
Spinascope, 167
Spine. *See also under* Spinal; Vertebrae.
  cervical. *See under* Cervical; Neck.
  examination of, 41
  facet osteoarthritis of, 89-91, 91f
  imaging of
    computed tomography in, 95, 96f, 97-102, 97f, 100f, 101f, 105f
    diskography in, 98-99, 118-140. *See also* Diskography.
    magnetic resonance imaging in, 107-111, 108f-110f
    myelography in, 99, 101f
    radiography in, 74-78, 75f-79f
    radionuclide, 89-91, 91f
    SPECT in, 89-91, 91f
  metastasis to, 751-753, 753f
  osteoarthritis of, 756. *See also* Osteoarthritis.
    facet joint, 89-91, 91f
    imaging of, 89-91, 91f, 756, 756f
    involved joints in, 107
  osteoid osteoma of, 751
  rheumatoid arthritis of, atlantoaxial subluxation in, 437, 437f
  tuberculosis of, 692
  tumors of, 750t, 751-753, 753f
SpineCath. *See* Intradiscal electrothermal annuloplasty.
Spinofugal projection systems, 15-16
Spinomesencephalic projections, 15-16, 16f
Spinoparabrachial projections, 16, 17f
Spinoreticulothalamic projections, 15, 16f
Spinothalamic projections, 16, 17f
Spiral/helical computed tomography, 94. *See also* Computed tomography.
Spiritual healing, 992-993
Spirochetal disease, diagnosis of, 62-64
Splanchnectomy, chemical, 1454-1455
Splanchnic nerve block, 1265, 1275-1276, 1276f. *See also* Celiac plexus block.
  definition of, 1267
Splanchnic nerves, anatomy of, 1267, 1267f
Splenic sequestration, in sickle cell disease, 257
Splenomegaly, in peripheral neuropathy, 274
Splinting, abdominal
  in anterior cutaneous nerve entrapment, 729, 730f
  in liver pain, 733
Splints. *See also* Bracing; Orthotics.
  for carpal tunnel syndrome, 387
  for de Quervain's tenosynovitis, 666
  for rheumatoid arthritis, 387, 437
  for stenosing digital tenosynovitis, 670
Spondylitis, rheumatoid, sacroiliac pain in, 813
Spondyloarthropathy, 753-755, 754f
Spondylolisthesis, 55, 806-808
  anatomic aspects of, 800, 801f
  biomechanics of, 803f
  bone graft for, donor site pain after, cryoanalgesia for, 1471-1473, 1472t
  classification of, 806, 806t
  definition of, 806
  etiology of, 806, 806t
  exercise program for, 1062-1063
  failed back surgery syndrome and, 821, 822, 822f
  grading of, 806, 807f

Spondylolisthesis *(Continued)*
　imaging of
　　bone scintigraphy with SPECT in, 89
　　computed tomography in, 102, 105f
　　radiography in, 77, 78f
　pain in, 784, 785t, 800, 807-808
　pathology of, 803f
　prevalence of, 802
　slippage in, 806-807
　treatment of, 807
Spondylolysis, 800-806
　anatomic aspects of, 800, 801f, 802f
　biomechanics of, 800-802
　diagnosis of, 802-805
　genetic factors in, 800
　imaging of
　　bone scintigraphy in, 86-89, 90f-91f, 803,
　　　804t
　　radiography in, 76, 77f, 802-805, 804f,
　　　804t, 805t
　pain in, 784, 785t, 800, 805
　pathology and pathogenesis of, 800-802,
　　801f, 802f
　treatment of, 806
Spondylosis, 107. *See also* Intervertebral disk
　disease.
　cervical, 52
　　radiculopathy and, 570. *See also* Cervical
　　　radiculopathy.
　　radiography of, 75, 75f
　occupational back pain due to, 784, 785t
Sports injuries, 376-402
　Achilles bursitis, 398-400, 399f, 400f
　Achilles tendinitis, 398, 399, 915
　acromioclavicular, 615-618
　adductor tendinitis, 391-395, 393f-395f
　biceps tendinitis, 380-382, 381f, 382f, 622-
　　626
　carpal tunnel syndrome, 38t, 115, 385-388,
　　385f-387f
　de Quervain's tenosynovitis, 388-390, 389f,
　　390f
　deltoid ligament sprain, 397-398, 398f
　golfer's elbow, 637-640, 638f, 639f
　iliopsoas bursitis, 864-867
　medial collateral ligament syndrome, 395-
　　396, 396f
　overuse, 376, 377t, 603
　pars interarticularis fractures, 800-806, 802f,
　　803f
　plantar fasciitis, 400-402, 401f
　prepatellar bursitis, 396-397, 397f
　prolotherapy for, 1108
　quadriceps tendinitis, 397
　rotator cuff disorders, 378-380, 379f, 380f,
　　603-613
　sesamoiditis, 399-400, 400f
　spondylolysis, 800-806, 802t
　stingers (burners), 582, 583f
　subdeltoid bursitis, 619-621, 620f
　supraspinatus tendinitis, 376-378, 377f
　tennis elbow, 382-385, 384f, 633-636, 634f,
　　635f
　traumatic, 376, 377t
　trochanteric bursitis, 390-391, 392f,
　　393f
Sprains
　ankle, 397-398, 398f
　　deltoid ligament, 397-398, 398f
　　osteopathic manipulative treatment for,
　　　1078
　　prolotherapy for, 1116-1117, 1117f
　finger, prolotherapy for, 1114-1115, 1114f,
　　1115f
　foot, prolotherapy for, 1117, 1117f, 1118f

Sprains *(Continued)*
　hamstring, prolotherapy for, 1115, 1116f,
　　1126, 1126f
　magnetic resonance imaging of, 115
　osteopathic manipulative treatment for, 1078
　plantar ligament, prolotherapy for, 1117,
　　1117f
　prolotherapy for, 1109, 1114-1118
　rest for, 1055
　RICE treatment for, 1055
　wrist, prolotherapy for, 1114, 1114f
Spreading depression of Leão, in migraine, 457
Spring ligament, prolotherapeutic injection of,
　1117, 1117f
Spurling test, in cervical radiculopathy, 571,
　572t, 605
Stanford Hypnotic Clinical Scale, 254
Staphylococcal pneumonia, 704
State Trait Anxiety Scale, for medication-
　overuse headache, 497
Status migrainosus, 459
Stellate ganglion
　anatomy of, 230, 230f, 553f, 1191-1192,
　　1193f
　injury of, in Horner syndrome. *See* Horner
　　syndrome.
　radiofrequency lesioning of, 1442-1444,
　　1444f
Stellate ganglion block, 230-231, 1191-1198
　agents for, 559
　anatomic aspects of, 1191-1192, 1193f
　anesthetics for, 1191
　bilateral, 1197
　C7 anterior approach in, 1195
　complications of, 231, 1196-1198, 1197f
　contraindications to, 1191
　diagnostic, 153
　　in facial reflex sympathetic dystrophy, 554-
　　　555, 558f
　differential, 161-162, 161t
　efficacy of, 1198
　equipment for, 1191
　final injection in, 1194-1195
　for acute/postoperative pain, 230-231
　for complex regional pain syndrome, 295
　　in prevention, 298
　for facial reflex sympathetic dystrophy
　　diagnostic, 554-555
　　therapeutic, 557, 558f
　Horner syndrome and, 557, 559
　indications for, 230, 1191
　neurolytic, 1195-1196
　　chemical, 1195-1196, 1195f
　　radiofrequency, 1196, 1196f
　paratracheal approach in, 1192-1194
　patient preparation for, 1191, 1192
　technique of, 230, 230f, 558f, 1192-1198,
　　1194f, 1195f
Stereotactic radiosurgery
　for cluster headache, 489
　for trigeminal neuralgia, 334, 353-356, 507
Sternal fractures, 678
　parasternal block for, 1250, 1251f
Sternal pain. *See also* Chest wall pain.
　in xiphodynia syndrome, 685, 685f
Sternalis muscle, anatomy of, 676
Sternalis syndrome, 676-678, 677f
Sternoclavicular joint, ankylosis of, 689f
Sternoclavicular joint syndrome, 686-688, 687f,
　688f
Sternocleidomastoid muscle, botulinum toxin
　injection in, 472
Sternotomy, parasternal block for, 1250, 1251f
Sternum, anatomy of, 685, 685f
Steroids. *See* Corticosteroids.

Stiffness, spinal
　in spondyloarthropathy, 75f, 753-755
　prolonged morning, 753-755
Still, Andrew Taylor, 1069, 1070f
Still's disease, 431. *See also* Rheumatoid
　arthritis.
Stimulants, for opioid-induced sedation, 323,
　364, 366, 1000
Stimulus intensity, discharge frequency and,
　16
Stingers, 582, 583f. *See also* Brachial
　plexopathy.
Stomatitis, in discoid lupus erythematosus, 438,
　439f
Straight leg raising test
　for lumbar radiculopathy, 761t, 762
　for sacroiliac disorders, 813
Strains
　gemellar, prolotherapy for, 1126, 1126f
　hamstring, prolotherapy for, 1115, 1116f,
　　1126, 1126f
　lumbosacral, 755
　posterior tibialis, prolotherapy for, 1117,
　　1117f
　prolotherapy for, 1109
　RICE treatment for, 1055
Strength assessment, 43-44, 44t
Strength training, 1056-1058, 1056t, 1058t. *See
　also* Exercise.
Stress fractures. *See also* Fractures.
　bone marrow edema in, 111-112
　calcaneal, plantar fasciitis and, 922-924
　femoral neck, vs. iliopsoas bursitis, 866
　of pars interarticularis, 800-806, 802f. *See
　　also* Spondylolysis.
Stretch injuries, muscle pain in, 1087
Stretch receptors
　rapidly adapting, 693
　slowly adapting, 693
Stretching, 1056-1057, 1056t
　in low back pain, 1061
Stroke
　complex regional pain syndrome after, 302
　headache in, 263t, 264, 266
　in sickle cell disease, 257
　treatment of, 266
　water-based exercises for, 1046, 1047f,
　　1048f, 1407f
Strontium-89, in palliative radiation therapy,
　330-332
Stump pain. *See also* Phantom pain/sensation.
　characteristics of, 307
　definition of, 304
　etiology of, 307
Stump revision, for phantom pain, 311
Styes, 524, 524f
Sub-Achilles bursitis, 398-399, 916
Subacromial bursitis, prolotherapy for, 1112-
　1113, 1113f
Subacromial spurs, in rotator cuff disorders,
　603, 608, 609f
Subarachnoid hemorrhage
　cerebrospinal fluid findings in, 264
　headache in, 263t, 264
　treatment of, 266
Subarachnoid neurolytic block, 1294-1302
　complications of, 1300f-1301f, 1301-1302
　efficacy of, 1299-1302
　informed consent for, 1294
　level of, determination of, 1296, 1296f
　patient positioning for, 1299, 1300f-1301f
　patient selection for, 1294
　technique of, 1294-1296
　with alcohol, 1296-1299, 1297f-1298f
　with phenol, 1299, 1300f-1301f

Subarachnoid opioids. *See* Spinal opioids.
Subcalcaneal bursae, 911
Subchondral cysts, in osteoarthritis, 112, 115
Subclavian artery, inadvertent injection of, in brachial plexus block, 1221
Subcutaneous calcaneal bursitis, 916
Subcutaneous malleolar bursa, 911
Subcutaneous tunneled catheter, 1385, 1385f. *See also* Implantable drug delivery systems.
Subdeltoid bursitis, 619-621, 620f
    vs. Pancoast syndrome, 694-695
Subdural injection, inadvertent, in lumbar epidural block, 1291
Subdural puncture, inadvertent, in cervical epidural block, 1218
Subgluteus bursitis, in trochanteric bursitis, 859
Subjectivity, of pain, 4-7, 5f, 197-198
Subluxation
    acromioclavicular, 79-80
    atlantoaxial, in rheumatoid arthritis, 437, 437f
Suboccipital nerve, anatomy of, 1174, 1174f, 1176f
Subscapularis tendon, in rotator cuff disorders, 603, 604f, 605. *See also* Rotator cuff disorders.
    anatomy of, 603, 604f
    strength tests for, 605
Subspinatus tendon, strength tests for, 605
Substance abuse. *See* Alcohol use/abuse; Drug abuse/dependency.
Substance P, 19, 19t, 20, 1083
    in complex regional pain syndrome, 288, 290f
    in tissue injury, 23t
Substance P antagonists, 19
Substantia gelatinosa neurons, 13f, 13t, 14, 14f
Subtalar arthritis, 912
    treatment of, 914
Subtendinous bursitis, 916
Sudeck atrophy, sympathectomy for, 358-359, 358f, 359f
Sufentanil, 948t, 953f, 956. *See also* Opioid(s).
Sulcus sign, in rotator cuff tears, 607, 608f.
Sulfasalazine, for rheumatoid arthritis, 436
Sulindac, for cancer pain, 318-319, 319t
Sumatriptan. *See also* Triptans.
    for cluster headache, 484-485
    for medication-overuse headache, 499
    for migraine, 460
Summation theory, 3, 4f
Superficial peroneal nerve, cryoablation of, 1469-1470
Superficial peroneal nerve block, 1367
Superior gluteal nerve, cryoablation of, 1470
Superior gluteal nerve entrapment, 855, 855f
    cryoanalgesia for, 1470
Superior hypogastric plexus, anatomy of, 837, 838f
Superior hypogastric plexus block, differential, 161-162, 161t
Superior sulcus tumors. *See* Pancoast tumors.
Superior vena cava syndrome, Pancoast tumors and, 695
Supine sculling, 1046, 1048f
Supraclavicular brachial plexus block, 1222-1224, 1223f. *See also* Brachial plexus block.
Supraclavicular nerve, anatomy of, 1174, 1174f, 1176f-1179f
Supraclavicular pain, from hepatomegaly, 732-733, 734f

Supraorbital nerve
    anatomy of, 1153
    cryoablation of, 1470-1471, 1470f
Supraorbital nerve block, 1156-1157, 1158f. *See also* Trigeminal nerve block.
Suprapatellar bursitis, 893-894, 894f, 895f
Suprascapular artery, inadvertent injection of, 1242
Suprascapular nerve
    anatomy of, 578f, 579f, 580, 630, 631f, 1239, 1240f
    entrapment of, 630
Suprascapular nerve block, 1239-1242
    anatomic aspects of, 1239, 1240f
    complications of, 1242
    contraindications to, 1239
    drugs for, 1239
    efficacy of, 1242
    equipment for, 1239
    historical perspective on, 1239
    indications for, 1239
    neurolytic
        indications for, 1239
        technique of, 1241-1242
    patient positioning for, 1239
    patient preparation for, 1239
    technique of, 1240-1241
        blind, 1240, 1240f
        radiographic, 1240-1241, 1240f
        with pulsed electromagnetic flowmeter, 1242
Supraspinal projections, 15-16, 16f, 17f
Supraspinatus tendinitis, 376-378, 377f
    with rotator cuff tears, 378-380, 379-381
Supraspinatus tendon
    anatomy of, 603, 604f
    in rotator cuff disorders, 378-380, 603, 604f, 605, 606. *See also* Rotator cuff disorders.
Supratrochlear nerve, anatomy of, 1153
Supratrochlear nerve block, 1156-1157, 1158f. *See also* Trigeminal nerve block.
Sural nerve block, 1367
Surgical procedures, nerve blocks for. *See* Nerve blocks.
Swallowing problems
    from botulinum neurotoxin, 593, 595
    in scleroderma, 441-442
Swan neck deformity, 434, 434f, 662, 662f
Sweating, abnormal, in complex regional pain syndrome, 284, 285t, 287
Sympathectomy, 358-359, 359f, 360f
    for complex regional pain syndrome, 295
    radiofrequency
        lumbar, 1449-1452, 1452f
        thoracic, 1452-1456, 1453f-1456f
Sympathetic nerve blocks
    definition of, 220
    for acute/postoperative pain, 229-231
    for cancer pain, 325, 338, 338t
    for chronic pain, 220
    lumbar, 232-233, 233f
    mechanism of action of, 1314
Sympathetic nervous system, anatomy of, 1315
Sympathetically maintained pain, in complex regional pain syndrome, 288-290, 290f
Symphysis pubis
    pain in, 831-833, 832f, 833f
    prolotherapeutic injection of, 1118-1119, 1118f
Symptom Index, for medication-overuse headache, 497
Syndrome of inappropriate antidiuretic hormone secretion, 60, 69

Synovial osteochondromatosis, 83, 84f
Synovitis, in polymyalgia rheumatica, 449
Syphilis, diagnosis of, 63
Syringomyelia, myelopathic, 793, 793f
Systemic lupus erythematosus, 437-440
    course of, 440
    diagnosis of, 60-62, 61t, 67t
    differential diagnosis of, 440
    epidemiology of, 437
    hand and wrist involvement in, 660-662
    laboratory findings in, 438-440
    signs and symptoms of, 437-438, 438f, 439f, 439t
    treatment of, 440
    vs. rheumatoid arthritis, 435
Systemic sclerosis, 440-443, 441f, 442f

T

T cells, 58
Table top test, for Dupuytren's contracture, 668
Tachycardia, opioid-induced, 945, 945f
Tactile allodynia, 12, 26, 29
Tai chi, 1099
Tailor's bunion, 921
Talofibular ligament
    prolotherapeutic injection of, 1117, 1117f
    tears of, 912
Taping
    of epidural catheter, 1246, 1247f
    patellar, for osteoarthritis, 426, 427f
Tardy ulnar palsy, 647-650, 648f-650f
    magnetic resonance imaging of, 115, 647, 649f
Targeted pain history. *See* History.
Tarsal coalition, 84
Tarsal tunnel syndrome, 416-417
    vs. sesamoiditis, 400
TART examination, 1070, 1070t
Tearing
    in cluster headache, 477
    in short-lasting unilateral neuralgiform headache, 482
Technetium 99m diphosphonates, 85. *See also* Nuclear medicine techniques.
Teeth. *See under* Dental.
Teichopsia, in migraine, 457
Telangiectasia, in scleroderma, 441, 441f
Temporal arteritis, 518-521
    arterial biopsy in, 519-520, 520t
    clinical features of, 518-519
    corticosteroids for, 521, 521t
    demographic factors in, 38t
    diagnosis of, 519-520
    epidemiology of, 519, 519t
    erythrocyte sedimentation rate in, 263, 265, 445, 518, 520
    extracranial manifestations of, 520
    headache in, 265, 518
    histologic features of, 520, 520t
    historical considerations in, 518
    jaw claudication in, 445, 446, 519
    ocular involvement in, 518-519
    optic neuritis in, 528-530, 529f
    polymyalgia rheumatica and, 265, 445, 451, 519
    prognosis of, 521
    treatment of, 266, 521
        complications of, 521
    vs. cluster headache, 483
Temporal artery, biopsy of, 519-520, 520t
Temporal nerves, deep, 1148, 1155
Temporalis muscles, in tension-type headache, 465

Temporomandibular joint disorders
  biofeedback for, 1013
  pain characteristics in, 37
  prolotherapy for, 1111
  vs. tension-type headache, 466, 469
Tendinitis. *See also* Tenosynovitis.
  Achilles, 398, 399, 915
    prolotherapy for, 1116, 1116f, 1117f
  adductor, 391-395, 393f-395f
  biceps, 380-382, 381f, 382f, 622-626
    prolotherapy for, 1111, 1112f
  extensor, of wrist, 662
  gluteus, 853, 859
    gluteal bursitis and, 853
    trochanteric bursitis and, 859, 861
  infraspinatus, with rotator cuff tears, 378-380
  quadriceps, 397, 899
    in quadriceps expansion syndrome, 906-910
  rotator cuff. *See* Rotator cuff disorders.
  supraspinatus, 376-378, 377f
    with rotator cuff tears, 378, 379-381
  therapeutic ultrasound for, 1038
Tendons. *See also specific tendons.*
  age-related changes in, 659
  fibrillar creep in, 659
  growth factors for. *See also* Prolotherapy.
    dextrose effects on, 1107, 1108t
    tissue response to, 1109
  magnetic resonance imaging of, 112-115
Tennis elbow, 382-385, 384f, 633-636, 634f, 635f
  acupuncture for, 1100, 1100t
  prolotherapy for, 1113, 1113f
  vs. radial tunnel syndrome, 635, 655, 656, 657f, 1233
Tenosynovitis. *See also* Tendinitis.
  de Quervain's, 80-81, 388-390, 389f, 390f, 666-667
    prolotherapy for, 1114, 1114f
  extensor, of wrist, 662
  in intersection syndrome, 666
  magnetic resonance imaging of, 115
  of ankle, 912
  of hand, 659, 660
  stenosing digital, 670
Tension pneumothorax, 710, 711f
Tension-type headache, 464-472. *See also* Headache.
  chronic, 464-465, 492
    differential diagnosis of, 469
    vs. medication-overuse headache, 492
  clinical features of, 464-466, 465t
  diagnosis of, 466-468, 468t
  differential diagnosis of, 468-469, 468t
  epidemiology of, 464
  episodic, 464-465
  historical perspective on, 464
  imaging studies in, 467-468
  muscle involvement in, 464-465, 464f-467f
  prevalence of, 464
  prevention of, 470, 471t
  psychological factors in, 468
  terminology for, 464
  treatment of, 469-472, 470t
    behavioral methods in, 470-472
    biofeedback in, 1012
    drug therapy in, 470-472, 471t
    hypnosis in, 1022, 1023
    prolotherapy in, 1122, 1122f, 1123f
    relaxation techniques in, 1027
    trigger point injections in, 472

Tension-type headache *(Continued)*
  vs. migraine, 464
  vs. occipital neuralgia, 549
  vs. temporomandibular joint syndrome, 466, 469
Teres minor tendon
  in rotator cuff disorders, 603, 604f, 605-606, 606f. *See also* Rotator cuff disorders.
  strength tests for, 605-606, 606f
Testicular denervation, 841
Testicular pain, 837-841. *See also* Orchialgia.
Testicular torsion, 839
Testosterone, in cluster headache, 480
Tetracaine, 983
  structure of, 983, 984f
Thalamic stimulation, for phantom pain, 311
Thalamus
  in complex regional pain syndrome, 286-287, 286f
  in pain processing, 15, 16, 16f, 17, 17f, 18f, 212, 213f
  in phantom pain, 25
Thalidomide, for cancer-related fatigue, 364
Thebaine, 952
Thenar muscle atrophy, in carpal tunnel syndrome, 385-386, 386f
Therapeutic drug monitoring, 71-72
Thomas test, for iliopsoas bursitis, 864
Thompson test, for Achilles tendon rupture, 916
Thoracic epidural nerve block, 234-236, 235f, 1243-1248. *See also* Epidural nerve block.
Thoracic extension exercises, 1064f
Thoracic facet ligament, prolotherapeutic injection of, 1120, 1120f
Thoracic facet syndrome, radiofrequency techniques for, 1420-1421, 1422f
Thoracic ganglionotomy, 1433-1435, 1434f, 1435f
  indications for, 1435
Thoracic myelopathy, 690-692
Thoracic outlet syndrome, 582-583, 584f
  vs. pronator syndrome, 653
Thoracic paravertebral sympathetic block, differential, 161-162, 161t
Thoracic radiculopathy, 690-692. *See also* Radiculopathy.
  intradiscal electrothermal annuloplasty for, 1429-1431, 1484-1487
Thoracic spine. *See under* Spinal; Spine.
Thoracic splanchnic denervation, radiofrequency, 1454-1456, 1455f, 1456f
Thoracic sympathetic chain/ganglion, radiofrequency lesioning of, 1452-1456, 1453f-1456f
  posterior parasagittal approach in, 1452-1454, 1454f, 1455f
  thoracic splanchnic denervation in, 1454-1456, 1455f, 1456f
Thoracodorsal nerve, anatomy of, 578f, 579f, 580
Thoracoscopy, video-assisted, 701, 702f
  for pulmonary Langerhans cell histiocytosis, 708
Thoracotomy
  pain after, 721-723
    cryoanalgesia for, 1462-1463
    persistent, 680-682, 682f
  pulmonary complications in, 709-710
Thought stopping, 251
Three-dimensional computed tomography, 95, 96f. *See also* Computed tomography.
Throat pain, 543-547
Thromboangiitis obliterans, demographic factors in, 38t

Thrombocytopenia, 58
Thrombocytosis, 58
Thrombosis
  cavernous sinus, 535
  vs. Baker cyst, 903
Throwing athletes. *See also* Sports injuries.
  biceps tendinitis in, 380-382, 622
  rotator cuff disorders in, 378-380, 603-613
  subdeltoid bursitis in, 619-621, 620f
Thumb. *See also* Finger(s); Hand.
  arthritis of, prolotherapy for, 1114-1115, 1115f
  trigger, 670
  Z-shaped deformity of, 662, 662f
Thumb base, osteoarthritis of, 418, 420. *See also* Osteoarthritis.
  vs. carpal tunnel syndrome, 386, 387f
Thymoma, sternoclavicular invasion by, 686, 687f, 689
Thyroid disease
  diagnosis of, 62
  in temporal arteritis, 62
Thyroid-stimulating hormone, assay for, 62
Thyroidectomy, celiac plexus block for, 1173. *See also* Celiac plexus block.
Thyroxine, assay for, 62
Tiagabine, 976, 976f. *See also* Anticonvulsants.
Tibial chondroblastoma, 902, 902f
Tibial nerve, 46t
Tibial nerve compression, in tarsal tunnel syndrome, 416-417
Tic convulsif, 503. *See also* Trigeminal neuralgia.
Tic douloureux, 503. *See also* Trigeminal neuralgia.
Tic-like neuritides of fifth cranial nerve, vs. trigeminal neuralgia, 504
Tick bites
  knee pain and, 888-889
  Lyme disease and, 63, 63f
Ticlopidine, epidural adhesiolysis and, 1346
Tietze syndrome, 674-676, 675f-677f, 694
Timolol, for migraine prophylaxis, 461
Tinel sign
  in anterior interosseous syndrome, 653
  in carpal tunnel syndrome, 385, 386f, 412, 664
  in cubital tunnel syndrome, 647
  in iliohypogastric neuralgia, 746
  in ilioinguinal neuralgia, 742
  in meralgia paresthetica, 868
  in pronator syndrome, 650
Tinnitus, aspirin-related, 930
Tissue injury, nociception in, 21-26. *See also* Pain processing system, in tissue injury.
Tizanidine, 979. *See also* Muscle relaxants.
  for chronic pain, 220
  for cluster headache, 487
  for tension-type headache, 470, 471t
Toe(s). *See also* Foot.
  arthritis of, 914
    prolotherapy for, 1118
  claw, in peripheral neuropathy, 272, 273f
  fifth, bunionette of, 921
  great. *See under* Hallux.
  hammer, 920
    in peripheral neuropathy, 272, 273f
  pain in, 918-919, 919t
    prolotherapy for, 1118, 1118f
Toenails
  in complex regional pain syndrome, 284, 285t
  in peripheral neuropathy, 274, 274t
Tolerance, to opioids, 244, 323, 946

Tolmetin
  for cancer pain, 318-319, 319t
  for tension-type headache, 470, 471t
Tolosa-Hunt syndrome, 407t, 411f, 532
  vs. cluster headache, 483
Tonsillitis, 543
Tooth. See under Dental.
Topical anesthetics, 983-988. See also specific
    agents.
  for chronic pain, 219-220
  generic and trade names of, 987t
  historical perspective on, 983, 984f
  mechanism of action of, 985
  pharmacodynamics of, 985
  pharmacokinetics of, 986, 986t
  preparations of, 987-988, 987t
  side effects of, 986-987
  structure of, 983-985, 984f, 985f
Topiramate, 975, 975f. See also
    Anticonvulsants.
  for cluster headache prophylaxis, 487
  for migraine prophylaxis, 461
  for peripheral neuropathy, 277t
Torticollis
  causes of, 593-594, 594t
  differential diagnosis of, 595
  in cervical dystonia, 591-596, 592f. See also
    Cervical dystonia.
Total iron-binding capacity, 57
Total joint arthroplasty
  for osteoarthritis, 86, 428
  for rheumatoid arthritis, 437
  of hip, 86, 428
    femoral neuropathy in, 873
    obturator neuropathy in, 879, 881
    prosthesis imaging in, 86
Totally implantable infusion pump, 1385-1386,
    1386f. See also Implantable drug delivery
    systems.
  care of, 1392
  complications of, published data on, 1400-
    1401
  for arachnoiditis, 797
  programmable, 1386, 1386f
  reservoir contamination in, 1392
Totally implantable reservoir/port, 1385, 1386f.
    See also Implantable drug delivery
    systems.
Touhy needle, 339
Toxicology, 69t, 72-73
Toxicology screening, 72
Toxoplasmosis, HIV-related, 63
Tracheobronchitis, 704
Traction
  for lumbar radiculopathy, 765
  for sacroiliac disorders, 814
Traction osteophytes, in spinal osteoarthritis,
    756, 756f
Training. See also Exercise.
  endurance, 1056, 1056t, 1058
  strength, 1056-1058, 1056t
Tramadol, 958
  for chronic pain, 219
Transcutaneous electrical nerve stimulation,
    326, 994, 1052-1054. See also
    Neurostimulation.
  contraindications to, 1054
  development of, 1052
  equipment for, 1053, 1053f
  for abdominal and visceral pain, 1053
  for acute pain, 1052-1053
  for behavioral pain, 1053
  for cancer pain, 326
  for complex regional pain syndrome, 295
  for lumbar radiculopathy, 764, 765

Transcutaneous electrical nerve stimulation
    (Continued)
  for musculoskeletal pain, 1053
  for neuropathic pain, 1053
  for orchialgia, 840
  for peripheral vascular insufficiency, 1053
  for phantom pain
    in prevention, 309
    in treatment, 310
  for postmastectomy pain, 326
  for sacroiliac disorders, 814
  indications for, 1052-1053
  scientific basis of, 1052
  technique of, 1054
Transcutaneous nerve stimulation, local
    anesthetic–related, 986
Transfer lesion, in hallux valgus, 920
Transferrin, evaluation of, 57
Transforaminal corticosteroid injections
  disadvantages of, 1282, 1282t
  for chronic pain, 220
Transformed migraine, 469
Transient ischemic attacks, headache in, 264
Transient nerve root irritation syndrome, 793
Transplantation
  bone marrow, for sickle cell disease, 260
  renal, femoral neuropathy after, 873-874
Transverse cervical nerve. See also Cervical
    plexus.
  anatomy of, 1174-1177, 1174f, 1176f-1179f
Tranylcypromine, 969. See also Antidepressants.
Trapeziometacarpal joint, arthritis of,
    prolotherapy for, 1114-1115, 1115f
Trapezius, posterior superior, prolotherapeutic
    injection of, 1120, 1121f
Traumatic needling, 1108-1109
Travel, with implantable drug delivery devices,
    1397
Trazodone, 967. See also Antidepressants.
  for peripheral neuropathy, 277t
Treadmill test, 1065
Tremor, in complex regional pain syndrome,
    284, 285t
Trendelenburg sign, in trochanteric bursitis, 860
Treponemal tests, 63
Triamcinolone. See also Corticosteroids.
  for epidural adhesiolysis, 1347
  in greater occipital nerve block, for cluster
    headache, 488
  intra-articular, for osteoarthritis, 428
  intralesional, for trochanteric bursitis, 861
Tricyclic antidepressants, 965-967. See also
    Antidepressants.
  abuse potential of, 966
  as prototype antidepressants, 965, 966f
  drug interactions with, 966
  mechanism of action of, 965
  overdosage of, 966-967
  pharmacokinetics of, 965-966
  prototype of, 965, 966f, 967
  side effects of, 966, 966f
  structure of, 965, 966f
  types of, 967
  withdrawal symptoms with, 966
Trigeminal cistern, 1146, 1153
Trigeminal nerve
  anatomy of, 408f, 523, 524f, 1146-1148,
    1146f, 1147f, 1152-1155, 1153f, 1154f,
    1470f
  cryoablation of, 1470-1471, 1470f
  distribution of, 36, 36f
  examination of, 42-43, 44t
  herpes zoster of, 280, 281f. See also Herpes
    zoster.
    vs. trigeminal neuralgia, 504

Trigeminal nerve (Continued)
  microvascular decompression of, for cluster
    headache, 489
  somatosensory evoked potentials from, 194
  tic-like neuritides of, 504
Trigeminal nerve block, 236, 237f, 1152-1160
  anatomic aspects of, 1152-1155, 1153f,
    1154f
  complications of, 1160
  contraindications to, 1152
  coranoid approach in, 1155-1156, 1155f-
    1157f
  for acute/postoperative pain, 236, 237f
  future directions for, 1160
  indications for, 1152, 1153t
  nonselective, 1155-1156, 1155f, 1156f
  selective
    mandibular nerve, 1156, 1157f, 1159-1160,
      1159f
    maxillary nerve, 1156, 1157-1159, 1157f,
      1158f
    ophthalmic nerve, 1156-1157, 1158f
  technique of, 1155-1160, 1155f-1159f
Trigeminal neuralgia, 407t, 411, 502-508
  atypical presentation of, 503
  classification of, 506
  clinical features of, 502-503
  demographic factors in, 38t, 503
  diagnosis of, 503
  differential diagnosis of, 503-505
  etiology of, 503
  historical perspective on, 502
  in multiple sclerosis, 503
  occipital neuralgia and, 504, 1140
  pain characteristics in, 37
  pain location in, 36, 36f
  referred from occipital nerve, 1140
  remission in, 506
  tic convulsif in, 503
  tic douloureux in, 503
  treatment of, 505-508
    complications and pitfalls in, 508
    deep brain stimulation in, 356-357, 357f
    gasserian ganglion block in, 1145-1151
    glycerol rhizotomy in, 353, 354f, 356,
      506
    microvascular decompression in, 353-356,
      355f, 506, 507-508
    percutaneous balloon compression in, 353-
      356, 354f, 355f, 506-507
    percutaneous techniques in, 353-356, 354f,
      506-508
    radiation therapy in, 333-334
    radiofrequency techniques in, 353-356,
      354f, 507, 1447-1449, 1448f
    sphenopalatine ganglion block in, 1134-
      1139
    stereotactic radiosurgery in, 334, 353-356,
      507
    surgical, 353-356, 506-508
    trigeminal nerve block in, 1152-1160
  trigger zones in, 502
  vs. atypical facial pain, 505, 505t
  vs. cluster headache, 483
  vs. geniculate neuralgia, 504
  vs. glossopharyngeal neuralgia, 503-504
  vs. herpetic/postherpetic neuralgia, 504
  vs. occipital neuralgia, 504, 1140
  vs. Raeder syndrome, 504-505
  vs. tic-like neuritides, 504
  vs. trigeminal neuropathy, 411
  with cluster headache, 503
Trigeminal neuropathy, vs. trigeminal neuralgia,
  411
Trigger finger, 670

Trigger point injections
 for cancer pain, 338-339
 for fibromyalgia, 405
 for sternalis syndrome, 678, 679f
 for tension-type headache, 472
Trigger points, 1016
 acupoints and, 1095-1096
 for myofascial pain, 51
 for referred pain, 51
 in fibromyalgia, 403-404, 404f
 in scapulocostal syndrome, 627, 628f, 629f
 in sternalis syndrome, 676-678, 677f
Triptans
 for cluster headache, 484-485, 487
 for medication-overuse headache, 493, 494,
  496, 499
 for migraine, 460
Trochanteric bursitis, 81, 390-391, 392f, 393f,
  859-862
 vs. meralgia paresthetica, 391, 868
Trochlear nerve
 anatomy of, 408f
 disorders of, 407t, 409
 examination of, 42-43, 44t
Troponin I, 71
Tuberculosis, 707
 pleural, 707
 spinal, 692
 trochanteric bursitis and, 860-861
Tuck sign, in wrist tenosynovitis, 662
Tui na, 1099
Tumor necrosis factor-α
 in disk herniation, 1493
 in nerve injury, 26-28, 27f, 1083
Tunneled catheters. See Implantable drug
  delivery systems.
Turner sign, in acute pancreatitis, 737, 738f
Tursky, Bernard, 1011
Tussive rib fractures, 678
Tympanic membrane, infection of, 542
Tympanic nerve, 538, 540f
Type J receptor, 693

U
Ulcer(s)
 oral, in discoid lupus erythematosus, 438,
  439f
 peptic, relaxation techniques for, 1027
 pressure, hydrotherapy for, 1037, 1037f,
  1040, 1049-1050
Ulcerative colitis, relaxation techniques for,
 1027
Ulnar collateral ligament, anatomy of, 643f, 644
Ulnar nerve, 46t
 anatomy of, 578f, 579f, 580, 1228f, 1229f
 corticosteroid injection of, 649, 650f
Ulnar nerve block, 238t, 1230-1233, 1232f-
  1234f
 at elbow, 1232-1233, 1233f
 at wrist, 1233, 1234f
 for cubital tunnel syndrome, 649, 650f, 1230-
  1233, 1233f
Ulnar nerve entrapment
 at elbow, 115, 647-649, 648f-650f, 1231
  magnetic resonance imaging in, 115, 647,
   648, 649f
  ulnar nerve block for, 649, 650f, 1230-
   1233, 1233f
 at wrist, 1231, 1232f, 1234f
  ulnar nerve block for, 1230-1233, 1232f,
   1234f
 electrodiagnosis of, 188
 signs and symptoms of, 270f

Ulnar tunnel syndrome, 1231, 1232f, 1234f
 ulnar nerve block for, 1231-1233, 1232f,
  1234f
Ulnar variance, positive, 80
Ultrasonography
 coupling agents in, 1038
 focused, vs. radiofrequency techniques, 1411
 in osteoarthritis, 423
 in rotator cuff disorders, 608-609, 609f
 of abdominal aneurysm, 755
 therapeutic
  heat production in, 1038
  indications for, 1034t, 1038
  technique of, 1038
U.S. Department of Health and Human
 Services, Office of Alternative Medicine
 of, 990-991
Upper extremity. See also specific structures.
 peripheral nerve blocks for, 1227-1238
  intercostobrachial nerve, 1237, 1237f
  medial brachial cutaneous nerve, 1237,
   1237f
  median nerve, 1227-1230, 1228f-1231f
  musculocutaneous nerve, 1235-1237
  radial nerve, 1233-1235, 1235f, 1236f
  ulnar nerve, 1230-1233, 1232f-1234f
 root vs. nerve lesions in, 46t
Upper respiratory infections, 704
Upper subscapular nerve, anatomy of, 578f,
 579f, 580
Uric acid, elevated serum, 70
Urinalysis, 68
Urinary catheterization, after spinal opioids,
 351, 352t
Urinary incontinence
 after alcohol neurolysis, 345
 after caudal epidural block, 1344
 after cervical epidural block, 1218
 after cordotomy, 1514
Urinary retention
 after caudal epidural block, 1344
 after cervical epidural block, 1218
 after cordotomy, 1514
 opioid-induced, 946
  with spinal administration, 351, 352t,
   1396-1397
Urinary tract infections, diagnosis of, 68-69
Urine osmolality, 69
Uterine contractions, opioid effects on, 946
Uveitis, 528, 529f

V
Vagal neuralgia, nerve block for, 1166-1168,
 1167f
Vaginal candidiasis, 843, 844
Vaginitis, diagnosis of, 68
Vagus nerve
 anatomy of, 1166, 1167f
 examination of, 42-43, 44t
Vagus nerve block, 1166-1168, 1167f
 inadvertent, in cervical plexus block, 1188
Valdecoxib, for tension-type headache, 470,
 471t
Valgus stress test, for medial collateral ligament
 syndrome, 395, 396f, 890f
Valproic acid, 976. See also Anticonvulsants.
 for cluster headache prophylaxis, 486-487
 for migraine prophylaxis, 461
 therapeutic monitoring of, 72
Van Durson standing flexion test, 814
Van Swienten, Gerhard, 474
Vancomycin, prophylactic, for implantable drug
 delivery devices, 1390

Varicella zoster virus, 279
Varicocele, orchialgia and, 839, 840
Varus stress test, for lateral collateral ligament
 tears, 890, 890f
Vasculitis, 60
 diagnosis of, 60-62, 67t
 headache in, 264, 265
 in discoid lupus erythematosus, 438, 439f
 pathogenesis of, 61f
 types of, 60t
Vasectomy, orchialgia after, 839
Vasoactive intestinal peptide, 19, 19t, 20
Vasoactive neuropeptides, in cluster headache,
 480, 481
Vasoconstrictors, with local anesthetics, 986
VDRL test, 63
Veins, epidural, 1212, 1212f
Venereal Disease Research Laboratory (VDRL)
 test, 63
Venlafaxine, 968-969, 969f. See also
 Antidepressants.
 for facial reflex sympathetic dystrophy, 559
Ventilatory support
 chest pain in, 710
 in flail chest, 710, 711f
Ventral funicular projection systems, 15-16, 16f,
 17f
Ventral medial nucleus projections, 16, 17f
Ventral root afferents, 13
Ventriculopleural catheterization, 712
Ventrolateral cordotomy, 15
Verapamil
 for cluster headache, 485-486
 for migraine prophylaxis, 461
Verbal descriptor scale, 200, 200f
Verbal numeric scale, 200
Vertebrae. See also under Spinal; Spine.
 anatomy of, 119, 1244-1245, 1245f
 inferior articular processes of, 800, 801f
 spinal nerve root alignment with, 1296f
Vertebral artery
 inadvertent injection of
  in atlanto-occipital nerve block, 1130-
   1131
  in cervical facet block, 1207
  in cervical plexus block, 1188
  in stellate ganglion block, 1198
 tortuosity of, 1131
Vertebral fractures
 Chance, 96f
 compression, 753, 754f
  biomechanical effects of, 1475
  computed tomography of, 95, 96f
  epidural steroids for, 1244
  exercise program for, 1063
  in cancer, 1475
  in osteoporosis, 753, 754f, 1475
  incidence of, 1475
  kyphoplasty for, 1477-1480, 1478f, 1479f,
   1481f
  magnetic resonance imaging of, 116,
   116f
  mortality and, 1475
  pars interarticularis, 805
  pathophysiology of, 1475
  radiography of, 77
  thoracic, epidural steroids for, 1244
  vertebroplasty for, 1475-1477, 1476f
Vertebral ganglion, anatomy of, 553f
Vertebral metastases, 751-753, 753f
Vertebral osteomyelitis, 77, 751, 752f
Vertebral osteonecrosis, aseptic, 77, 78f
Vertebral pain, 52-55, 52t. See also Back pain;
 Cervical pain; Low back pain.
 distribution of, 53f, 54f

Vertebroplasty, 1475-1477, 1480
  contraindications to, 1475
  disadvantages of, 1476
  efficacy of, 1476
  indications for, 1475
  technique of, 1476
Vesalius, Andreas, 758
Vestibulitis, vulvar, 843
Video-assisted thoracoscopy, 701, 702f
  for pulmonary Langerhans cell histiocytosis, 708
Viral infections, lymphocytosis in, 58
Virtual environment, for burn pain, 249, 249f
Visceral pain, 362
Viscerosomatic reflexes, 1069
Vision impairment
  after epidural injections, 172, 176
  from pituitary neuroadenolysis, 1410
  headache in, 469
Visual analog scale, 199-200, 200f
  for medication-overuse headache, 497
Visual disturbances
  from epidural injections, 172, 176
  headache in, 469
  in glaucoma, 526, 526t
  in migraine, 457-458
  in optic neuritis, 530
  in temporal arteritis, 518-519
  in Tolosa-Hunt syndrome, 532
  in uveitis, 528, 529f
Visual evoked potentials, 192-193, 193f
Vitamin B$_{12}$ deficiency, diagnosis of, 64, 67t
Vitamin C, for complex regional pain syndrome prophylaxis, 296
Vitamin K deficiency, in liver disease, 71
VMpo, projections from, 16, 17f
Vogt, Oskar, 1026
Volar hot dog sign, 662
Vomiting. See Nausea and vomiting.
Vulvar vestibulitis, 843
Vulvitis, cyclic, 843
Vulvodynia, 843-846
Vulvovaginal candidiasis, 843, 844

W
Waddell's signs
  in failed back syndrome, 827-828
  in occupational back pain, 786
Waiter's tip hand, 581, 582f
Waldenström's macroglobulinemia, 68
Waldman test, for adductor tendinitis, 394, 394f, 395f
Walking, gait examination for, 47
Walking forward/backward exercises, in hydrotherapy, 1046, 1047f
Wall, P.D., 3, 4

Wall crunch, 1046, 1048f
Wall sit, 1046, 1047f
Wallenberg syndrome, 557, 1188
Wallerian degeneration, 343-344
Warfarin. See also Anticoagulants.
  epidural adhesiolysis and, 1346
  international normalized ratio for, 59
Wartenberg syndrome. See Cheiralgia paresthetica.
Water-based exercises, 1045-1049, 1047f, 1048f. See also Hydrotherapy.
Water walking forward/backward exercises, 1046, 1047f
Watson test, for carpometacarpal arthritis, 386, 387f
Weakness
  in cervical radiculopathy, 570, 571
  in complex regional pain syndrome, 284, 285t
  in peripheral neuropathy, 272-274
  knee pain with, 888
Weaver's bottom, 853-855, 854f-856f
Wegener's granulomatosis, 64, 67t
Weight loss, for osteoarthritis, 426
Weight training, 1056-1058, 1056t, 1058t
Wertheim and Rovenstine's method, for cervical plexus block, 1185, 1186f
Westergren method, for erythrocyte sedimentation rate, 57
Whiplash
  cervical facet joint injections for, 564
  complications of, 565-566, 566t
  cervical facet syndrome and, 562
  cervical radiculopathy in, 568. See also Cervical radiculopathy.
  osteopathic manipulative treatment for, 1078
Whirlpool baths
  iced, 1040, 1049-1050
  warm/hot, 1037, 1037f, 1049-1050
White blood cell count, 58
Wide dynamic range neurons, 14-15, 14f, 17, 18f, 212, 1082f
  in complex regional pain syndrome, 556
  in tissue injury, 22-24
  in wind-up, 15, 22-24, 23f
Willis, Thomas, 456
Wind-up, 15, 22-24, 23f, 1085
Winnie, A.P., 152
Wintrobe method, for erythrocyte sedimentation rate, 57
Withdrawal, 947, 947t
  in medication-overuse headache, 499-500
  opioid, with spinal administration, 1397
  seizures and, 499-500
  selective serotonin reuptake inhibitor, 968
  tricyclic antidepressant, 966
Wolf system, for laser diskectomy, 1496-1497
Wolff, Harold G., 456

Wolpe, Joseph, 1026
Women
  cluster headache in, 478-479
  common pain syndromes in, 38t
  migraine in, 456, 479
Wong-Baker Faces Scale, 203-208, 208f
World Health Organization (WHO)
  analgesic ladder of, 349, 350f, 370, 371f
  palliative care definition of, 360
Wrist
  arthritis of, 80, 660-662, 660t
  corticosteroid injection for, 663
  median nerve entrapment in, 385-388, 385f-387f, 664-665. See also Carpal tunnel syndrome.
  pain in
    anatomic aspects of, 659, 661f
    differential diagnosis of, 659, 660t
  radiography of, 80-81
  tendons of, 661f, 666
  tenosynovitis of
    de Quervain's, 80-81, 388-390, 666-667, 1114, 1114f
    extensor, 662
    flexor, 662

X
Xanthochromia, in subarachnoid hemorrhage, 264
Xiphisternal syndrome, 684-686, 684f-686f
Xiphodynia syndrome, 684-686, 684f-686f
Xiphoid process, anatomy of, 685, 685f
Xylocaine, in prolotherapy, 1110. See also Prolotherapy.

Y
Yergason test, for biceps tendinitis, 381, 382f, 622, 624f
Yin-yang theory, 1094-1095, 1094f
Yoga, for sleep disturbances, 366

Z
Z-shaped deformity, of thumb, 662, 662f
Zinc, toxicity of, 72
Zolmitriptan. See also Triptans.
  for cluster headache, 485
  for migraine, 460
Zoster sine herpete, 279
Zung Depression Inventory, for medication-overuse headache, 497
Zygapophyseal joints. See Facet joints.
Zygomatic nerve, anatomy of, 1147